AGE, WEIGHT &

For use with 7

Distance	Age	Mar.	Apr.	May					
5f	4	10–0	10–0	10–0			10–0	10–0	10–0
	3	9–0	9–2	9–4	9–6	9–8	9–10	9–11	9–12	9–13
	2	6–8	6–13	7–3	7–7	7–11	8–1	8–5	8–8	8–11
6f	4	9–13	10–0	10–0	10–0	10–0	10–0	10–0	10–0	10–0
	3	8–11	9–0	9–2	9–4	9–6	9–8	9–10	9–11	9–12
	2			6–13	7–3	7–7	7–11	8–1	8–5	8–8
7f	4	9–12	9–13	10–0	10–0	10–0	10–0	10–0	10–0	10–0
	3	8–8	8–11	9–0	9–2	9–4	9–6	9–8	9–10	9–11
	2					7–4	7–8	7–12	8–2	8–5
1m	4	9–11	9–12	9–13	10–0	10–0	10–0	10–0	10–0	10–0
	3	8–6	8–9	8–12	9–1	9–3	9–5	9–7	9–9	9–10
	2							7–9	7–13	8–2
9f	4	9–11	9–12	9–13	9–13	10–0	10–0	10–0	10–0	10–0
	3	8–4	8–7	8–10	8–13	9–2	9–4	9–6	9–8	9–9
1¼m	4	9–10	9–11	9–12	9–13	10–0	10–0	10–0	10–0	10–0
	3	8–2	8–5	8–8	8–11	9–0	9–3	9–5	9–7	9–8
11f	4	9–9	9–11	9–12	9–13	9–13	10–0	10–0	10–0	10–0
	3	8–0	8–4	8–7	8–10	8–13	9–2	9–4	9–6	9–7
1½m	4	9–9	9–10	9–11	9–12	9–13	10–0	10–0	10–0	10–0
	3	7–12	8–2	8–5	8–8	8–11	9–0	9–3	9–5	9–7
13f	4	9–8	9–10	9–11	9–12	9–13	9–13	10–0	10–0	10–0
	3	7–11	8–1	8–4	8–7	8–10	8–13	9–2	9–4	9–6
1¾m	4	9–7	9–9	9–10	9–12	9–13	9–13	10–0	10–0	10–0
	3	7–9	7–13	8–3	8–6	8–9	8–12	9–1	9–3	9–5
15f	4	9–6	9–8	9–10	9–11	9–12	9–13	10–0	10–0	10–0
	3	7–8	7–12	8–2	8–5	8–8	8–11	9–0	9–2	9–4
2m	4	9–6	9–8	9–10	9–11	9–12	9–13	10–0	10–0	10–0
	3	7–7	7–11	8–1	8–5	8–8	8–11	9–0	9–2	9–4
2¼m	4	9–6	9–8	9–9	9–11	9–12	9–13	10–0	10–0	10–0
	3	7–6	7–10	8–0	8–4	8–7	8–10	8–13	9–1	9–3
2½m	4	9–5	9–7	9–9	9–10	9–11	9–12	9–13	10–0	10–0
	3	7–5	7–9	7–13	8–3	8–6	8–9	8–12	9–1	9–3

For 5-y-o's and older, use **10-0** in all cases.

3

SAVE MONEY MAKE MONEY

THAT'S just what you can do with the Sporting Chronicle. You save because the Chronicle is the cheapest daily racing paper . . . and you can make punting pay by following our top tipping team. From BEAT THE BOOK, easily the country's best tipster, to FRANCIS KELLY, our phenomenally successful Fixed Odds expert, our service is a real winner. Add our comprehensive form guide and racecards, reports, results, comments and feature articles, plus a lively Postbag, and you just cannot afford to be without your daily Chronicle.

●●●●●●●●●●●●●●●●●●●●●●●●●●●●●

POWER
TO THE PUNTER!

FORM, TIME, SYSTEMS, BETTING . . . we've got the racing scene covered from all angles.

In-depth articles by our team of racing experts, weekly index-linked returns, programmes for seven days, plus special pages for Pools and greyhound fans.

Add to this informative lot our readers letter-page, "Sports Forum", and "Arena", a wide-angle look at the racing scene, and you will see why the HANDICAP BOOK is the nationwide hot favourite in betting circles.

"WILL I GET THE CREDIT I NEED FROM PTS?"

YOU BET.

PTS **CREDIT CARD**

Commissions may be placed at any of our offices
(Leatherhead 9am–7pm, other offices 9.30am–6pm)

	Leatherhead 0372-3 74466	(London Area 537 44661
Birmingham	021-356 6977	Manchester 061-969 3636
Bristol	0272 26011	*Newcastle 0632 26051
Leeds	0532 440244	Nottingham 0602 45591
Liverpool	051-236 9242	*Wardless & Pallister

Just fill in the coupon below stating the credit you require. We will be pleased to open an account for you for amounts from £50 upwards, subject to satisfactory references.

The PTS credit card showing your personal account number enables you to 'phone any of our offices at Leatherhead (London Area), Birmingham, Bristol, Leeds, Liverpool, Manchester, Newcastle and Nottingham.

PTS accept every type of bet at S.P. or Tote with stakes as low as 10p, plus a host of unique money making multiple bets. Ante-post and board prices and race by race results are always available.

POST THIS COUPON NOW TO OPEN A CREDIT ACCOUNT

Full name _____

Address _____ (I am over 18)

Credit Required if over £50 [____] A bookmakers reference

ensures the speedy opening of an account _____

YOU BET
PTS
NATIONWIDE
BOOKMAKERS

Deposit Accounts welcomed (Minimum £25). Send Cash today, start betting tomorrow. *Cheques accepted subject to clearance.*
If you prefer send cash with your bet. (Minimum total stake £3). *Subject to rules.*
Registered office: PO Box 40, Leatherhead, Surrey. Regd. No. 1007700 (England)

TF 81

Established 1890

HEATHORNS

BOOKMAKERS

OVERSBY HOUSE
ONSLOW STREET
GUILDFORD
SURREY GU1 4SR
Telephone: (0483) 31233

14

Airlie .... *for the best selection of stallions in Europe and the best care that money can buy*

The studs under the control of Captain A. D. D. Rogers comprise over 1,500 acres of fenced and watered lands. Each of the four main studs have a completely separate staff and are run independently. Of the two smaller studs one is used completely for isolation and the other for the resident yearlings. There are three private veterinary surgeons and a private laboratory staffed seven days a week during the covering season.

For the convenience of overseas patrons we can offer accommodation for mares prior to the start of the covering season. This enables mares visiting the stallions **ACAMAS, ARTAIUS, BALLAD ROCK, CUT ABOVE, DOUBLE FORM, ELA-MANA-MOU, HABITAT, HENBIT, STRADAVINSKY** and **TUMBLE WIND** to settle in their new surroundings.

Under the management of Captain A. D. D. Rogers

Airlie Stud
Lucan, Co. Dublin

Grangewilliam Stud
Maynooth, Co. Kildare

Loughmore Stud
Killeen, Dunsany, Co. Meath

Loughtown Stud
Donadea, Co. Kildare

Simmonstown Stud
Celbridge, Co. Kildare

Williamstown Stud
Clonsilla, Co. Dublin

16

RACEHORSES
OF
1981

A Timeform Publication   Price £38.00

A Timeform Publication

Compiled and Produced under the direction of
Phil Bull, B.Sc., and Reg Griffin

by members of the Timeform Organisation
G. Greetham, B.A. (Deputy Managing Director),
J. G. Clarke (Director), G. F. Walton, Dip.A.D.
(Director), J. D. Newton, B.A. (Editor), D. P.
Adams, A. M. Caulfield, G. C. J. Dench, B.A.,
J. P. Early, B.A., A. Elves, B.A., R. M. Gibson,
B.A., J. C. McGrath and C. S. Williams.

Published by Portway Press Limited, Timeform House,
Halifax, Yorkshire, and Printed by Walter Pearce & Co.,
Brentford, Middlesex.

Registered at Stationers' Hall

© **Portway Press Limited 1982**

ISBN 0 900599 33 2

CONTENTS

Foreword

"Racehorses of 1981" deals individually, in alphabetical sequence, with every horse that ran under Jockey Club Rules in 1981, plus a number of foreign-trained horses that did not race here. For each of these horses is given (1) its age, colour and sex, (2) its breeding, (3) a form summary giving details of all its performances during the past two seasons, (4) a rating of its merit, (5) a commentary upon its racing or general characteristics as a racehorse, with some suggestions, perhaps, regarding its potentialities in 1982, and (6) the name of the trainer in whose charge it was on the last occasion it ran.

The book is published with a twofold purpose. Firstly, it is designed to provide the betting man with data for practical use in analysing the racing programmes from day to day, and instructions as to its use in this capacity will be found in the Explanatory Notes which follow this Foreword; and secondly, the book is intended to have some permanent value as a review of the exploits and achievements of the more notable of our thoroughbreds in 1981. Thus, while the commentaries upon the vast majority of the horses are, of necessity, in note form, the best horses are more critically examined, and the short essays upon them are illustrated by half-tone portraits and photographs of the finishes of some of the races in which they were successful.

The attention of foreign buyers of British bloodstock, and others who are concerned with Timeform Ratings as a measure of absolute racing class in terms of a standard scale, is drawn to the section headed "The Level of the Ratings" in the Explanatory Notes on page 37.

February, 1982.

THE BROWNSTOWN STUD

CURRAGH, CO. KILDARE

One of the World's Great Breeding Establishments

BROWNSTOWN mares have produced many top horses including 16 individual Group 1 winners:

Levmoss
(8 races, £143,483, including Prix de l'Arc de Triomphe, Prix du Cadran and Ascot Gold Cup)

Sweet Mimosa
(Prix de Diane, 1970, £76,407)

Arctic Prince
(Derby Stakes; leading broodmare sire)

Panastrid
(Irish 1000 Guineas)

Panaslipper
(Irish Derby; a leading sire)

Lucero
(Irish 2000 Guineas)

Solar Slipper
(Champion Stakes, broodmare sire of Royal Palace)

Royal Danseuse
(Irish 1000 Guineas)

Allangrange
(Irish St Leger)

Mart Lane
(St Simon Stakes 1976)

Ballad Rock
(Champion Irish sprinter)

Le Moss
(Ascot Gold Cup twice, Goodwood Cup twice, Doncaster Cup twice and 2nd St Leger)

Captain James
(Waterford Crystal Mile)

Sutton Place
(Coronation Stakes)

Weavers' Hall
(Irish Sweeps Derby and £67,757)

Silken Glider
(Irish Oaks, 2nd Epsom Oaks)

Feevagh
(Yorkshire Oaks; dam of Feemoss; grandam of LEVMOSS, LE MOSS and SWEET MIMOSA)

Sixpence
(leading two-year-old; dam of Four-and-Twenty, won Santa Anita and Hollywood Derbys)

Arctic Sun
(leading two-year-old; dam of Arctic Prince)

Le Levanstell
(Queen Elizabeth II Stakes; a leading sire and grandsire)

Nikoli
(Irish 2000 Guineas)

Discipliner
(dam of Skymaster, Martial and El Gallo)

Bog Road
(Gallinule Stakes, Ballymoss Stakes and £37,419)

Silk Buds
(Silken Glider Stakes)

Poacher's Moon
(Tetrarch Stakes, Irish Cambridgeshire)

El Badr
(Prix du Cadran)

Spence Bay
(Century Handicap USA)

All enquiries to Joseph McGrath, Brownstown Stud, Curragh, Co. Kildare. Tel. Curragh 41303

INDEX TO PHOTOGRAPHS

PORTRAITS & SNAPSHOTS

25

26

27

28

Watties Rock ..	2 ch.c.	Record Token–Camerons Counsel (Jolly Jet)	*Jacqueline O'Brien* 932
Wind and Wuthering ..	2 br.c.	No Robbery–J. A's Joy (Johns Joy)	*W. W. Rouch & Co.* 946
Zilos	2 b.c.	Grundy–Sandarey (Darius)	*W. W. Rouch & Co.* 960
Zinzara	2 b.f.	Stage Door Johnny–Old Gypsy (Olden Times)	*J. Crofts* 963

RACE PHOTOGRAPHS

Prix du Jockey-Club (Chantilly)	.. .. ..	*P. Bertrand*	129
Prix du Moulin de Longchamp	.. .. ..	*P. Bertrand*	601
Prix Eclipse (Saint-Cloud)	.. .. ..	*P. Bertrand*	629
Prix Eugene Adam (Saint-Cloud)	.. .. ..	*P. Bertrand*	120
Prix Fille de l'Air (Saint-Cloud)	.. .. ..	*P. Bertrand*	811
Prix Foy (Longchamp) ..	.. .. ..	*P. Bertrand*	261
Prix Ganay (Longchamp)	.. .. ..	*P. Bertrand*	89
Prix Hocquart (Longchamp) ..	.. ..	*P. Bertrand*	693
Prix Jacques le Marois (Deauville) ..	.. ..	*P. Bertrand*	599
Prix Jean de Chaudenay (Saint-Cloud)	.. ..	*P. Bertrand*	918
Prix Jean Prat (Longchamp) ..	.. ..	*P. Bertrand*	346
Prix Kergorlay (Deauville) ..	.. ..	*P. Bertrand*	882
Prix Lupin (Longchamp)	.. .. ..	*P. Bertrand*	594
Prix Marcel Boussac (Longchamp) ..	.. ..	*P. Bertrand*	655
Prix Maurice de Gheest (Deauville) ..	.. ..	*P. Bertrand*	559
Prix Morny (Deauville) ..	.. .. ..	*P. Bertrand*	361
Prix Niel (Longchamp)	.. .. ..	*P. Bertrand*	53
Prix Perth (Saint-Cloud)	.. .. ..	*P. Bertrand*	672
Prix Quincey (Deauville)	.. .. ..	*P. Bertrand*	647
Prix Robert Papin (Maisons-Laffitte)	.. ..	*P. Bertrand*	509
Prix Royal-Oak (Longchamp)	.. .. ..	*P. Bertrand*	87
Prix Saint-Alary (Longchamp)	.. .. ..	*P. Bertrand*	893
Prix Vermeille (Longchamp) ..	.. ..	*P. Bertrand*	77
Queen Anne Stakes (Ascot) ..	.. ..	*Sport and General*	121
Queen Elizabeth II Stakes (Ascot)	.. ..	*W. Everitt*	887
Queen Mary Stakes (Ascot) ..	.. ..	*Sport and General*	313
Queen's Vase (Ascot) ..	.. .. ..	*W. Everitt*	616
Railway Stakes (The Curragh)	.. ..	*M. Ansell*	68
Regent Diamond Stakes (**Ladies Race**) (Ascot)	..	*Sport and General*	227
Ribblesdale Stakes (Ascot)	.. .. ..	*W. Everitt*	840
Richmond Stakes (Goodwood)	.. ..	*George Selwyn*	867
Rockfel Stakes (Newmarket) ..	.. ..	*A. Russell*	894
Rockingham Handicap (Doncaster) ..	.. ..	*A. Russell*	185
Ronaldshay Cup (Redcar) ..	.. ..	*A. Russell*	97
Rowley Mile Nursery Handicap (Newmarket)	..	*A. Russell*	591
Royal Hunt Cup Handicap (Ascot)	.. ..	*A. Russell*	862
Royal Lodge Stakes (Ascot) ..	.. ..	*W. Everitt*	604
Royal Yorkshire Stakes (York)	.. ..	*A. Russell*	266
Sancton Stakes (York)	.. .. ..	*A. Russell*	162
September Stakes (Kempton)	.. ..	*Sport and General*	445
Sirenia Stakes (Kempton)	.. .. ..	*George Selwyn*	750
Somerville Tattersall Stakes (Newmarket)..	..	*Sport and General*	944
Sporting Chronicle Spring Handicap (Doncaster)		*A. Russell*	146
Star Stakes (Sandown)	.. .. ..	*Press Association Photos*	576
St James's Palace Stakes (Ascot)	.. ..	*W. Everitt*	885
St Leger Stakes (Doncaster) ..	.. ..	*A. Russell*	241
Stockholm Cup (Taby, Sweden)	.. ..	*Stefan Uppstrom*	739
Strensall Stakes (York)	.. .. ..	*A. Russell*	663
St Simon Stakes (Newbury) ..	.. ..	*George Selwyn*	488
Sun Chariot Stakes (Newmarket)	.. ..	*A. Russell*	400
Sussex Stakes (Goodwood) ..	.. ..	*E. G. Byrne*	450
Timeform Derby Special Offer Stakes (Thirsk)	..	*A. Russell*	712
Timeform Race Card Stakes (Redcar)	.. ..	*A. Russell*	179
Tote Cesarewitch Handicap (Newmarket) ..	..	*A. Russell*	370
Tote-Ebor Handicap (York) ..	.. ..	*A. Russell*	677
Tote European Free Handicap (Newmarket)	..	*Sport and General*	565
Tote Lockinge Stakes (Newbury)	.. ..	*W. Everitt*	121
Tote Stewards' Cup (Goodwood)	.. ..	*Press Association Photos*	230
Turf Classic (Aqueduct)	.. .. ..	*Bob Coglianaso*	78
Two Thousand Guineas Stakes (Newmarket)	..	*A. Russell*	884
U.B.M. Merchants International Fillies' Stakes			
(Kempton)	..	*W. Everitt*	583

33

Sales Programme 1982
Bloodstock Sales

March Sale	March 30th
Derby Sale of top class potential hurdlers & chasers	June 26th
September Yearling Sale	September 13th
October Horses in training	October 19th
November National Hunt Sale	October 31st
December Flat bred Sale of Horses In Training Yearlings, Mares & Foals	December 6th/9th

Ballsbridge Tattersalls Ltd.

Anglesea House, Anglesea Road,
Royal Dublin Society, Ballsbridge, Dublin 4,
Telephone: 605544. Telex 30854 BIBS EI

Brindley

36

EXPLANATORY NOTES

TO assess the prospects of any horse in a race it is necessary to
know two things about him: first, how good he is; and
second, what sort of horse he is. In this book the merit of each
horse is expressed in the form of a *rating* (printed on the right);
and the *racing character* of the horse given in the commentary.

TIMEFORM RATINGS

The Timeform Rating of a horse is simply the merit of the horse
expressed in pounds. More precisely, it is *the number of pounds
which, in our opinion, the horse would be entitled to receive in an
average Free Handicap*. Thus, a horse which we regard as worth
9 st 7 lb in an average Free Handicap, i.e., 133 lb, would receive a
rating of 133: and one regarded as worth 8 st (112 lb) would
receive a rating of 112; and so on.

This explains what the ratings are; but of course individual
ratings are not actually allocated in this way, merely by "inspection." The rating of any horse is a result of careful examination
of its running against other horses. We maintain a "running"
handicap of all horses in training throughout the season, or, to
be strictly accurate, two handicaps, one for horses aged three
years and over, and one for two-year-olds.

THE LEVEL OF THE RATINGS

At the close of each season all the horses that have raced are
re-handicapped from scratch, and each horse's rating is revised.
It is also necessary to adjust the general level of the handicap, so
that the mean of all the ratings is kept at the same standard level
from year to year. Left to itself, the general level of the ratings,
in each succeeding issue of Timeform, tends to rise steadily.
For technical reasons it is desirable to allow it to do so during the
season: but, in the winter, when the complete re-handicap is done,
the ratings, must, of course, be put back on their proper level again.

This explains why, in this book, the ratings are, in general,
different from those in the final issue of the 1981 Timeform series.

RATINGS AND WEIGHT-FOR-AGE

These matters, however, are by the way. What concerns the
reader is that he has, in the ratings in this book, a universal handicap embracing all the horses in training it is possible to weigh up,
ranging from tip-top classic performers, with ratings from 130 to
145, down to the meanest selling platers, rated around the 40 or
50 mark. And what we now have to explain is the practical use
of these ratings in the business of weighing up a race.

Before doing so, it is important to mention that all ratings are at weight-for-age, so that equal ratings mean horses of equal merit: perhaps it would be clearer if we said that the universal rating handicap is really not a single handicap, but four handicaps side by side: one for 2-y-o's, one for 3-y-o's, one for 4-y-o's and one for older horses. Thus, a 3-y-o rated, for argument's sake, at 117 is deemed to be identical in point of "merit" with a 4-y-o also rated at 117: but for them to have equal chances in, say, a mile race in June, the 3-y-o would need to be receiving 13 lb from the 4-y-o, which is the weight difference specified in the Age, Weight and Distance Table on the page facing the front cover. However, let us to cases!

USING THE RATINGS

In using Timeform Ratings with a view to discovering which horses in any race have the best chances at the weights, we have two distinct cases, according to whether the horses taking part are of the same age or of different ages. Here is the procedure in each case:—

A. Horses of the Same Age

If the horses all carry the same weight there are no adjustments to be made, and the horses with the highest ratings have the best chances. If the horses carry different weights, jot down their ratings, and to the rating of each horse add one point for every pound the horse is set to carry less than 10 st, or subtract one point for every pound he has to carry more than 10 st. When the ratings have been adjusted in this way the highest resultant figure indicates the horse with the best chance at the weights.

Example (any distance: any month of the season)

2 Good Girl (9-6)	.. Rating 119	.... add 8	 127
2 Paulinus (9-4)	.. Rating 113	.... add 10	 123
2 Abilene (8-11)	.. Rating 107	.... add 17	 124
2 Bob's Joy (8-7)	.. Rating 108	.... add 21	 129
2 Time Warp (8-2)	.. Rating 100	.... add 26	 126
2 Eagle Eye (7-7)	.. Rating 92	.... add 35	 127

Bob's Joy (129) has the best chance; Good Girl (127) and Eagle Eye (127) are next best.

B. Horses of Different Ages

Take no notice of the weight any horse receives from any other. Instead, consult the Age, Weight and Distance Table on the page facing the front cover. Treat each horse separately, and compare the weight it has to carry with the weight prescribed for it in the table, according to the age of the horse, the distance of the race and the month of the year. Then, add one point to the rating for each pound the horse has to carry less than the weight given in the table: or, subtract one point from the rating for every pound he has to carry more than the weight prescribed by the table. The highest resultant figure indicates the horse most favoured by the weights.

38

Example (1½ miles in July)

(Table Weights: 5-y-o 10-0; 4-y-o 9-13; 3-y-o 8-11)

6 Nimitz (9-12)	.. Rating 115	.... add	2	....	117
4 Red Devil (9-9)	.. Rating 114	.... add	4	....	118
6 Sweet Cindy (9-5)	.. Rating 115	.... add	9	....	124
3 Jailhouse (8-12)	.. Rating 120	subtract	1	....	119
4 Haakon (8-11)	.. Rating 101	.... add	16	....	117
3 Fine Strike (8-7)	.. Rating 112	.... add	4	....	116

Sweet Cindy (124) has the best chance at the weights, with 5 lb in hand of Jailhouse.

JOCKEYSHIP AND APPRENTICE ALLOWANCES

There is just one further point that arises in evaluating the chances of the horses on the basis of their ratings: the question of jockeyship in general, and apprentice allowances in particular. The allowance which may be claimed by an apprentice is given to enable apprentices to obtain race-riding experience against experienced jockeys. For the purposes of rating calculations it should, in general, be assumed that the allowance the apprentice is able to claim (3 lb, 5 lb, or 7 lb) is nullified by the boy's inexperience. Therefore, the *weight adjustments to the ratings should be calculated on the weight allotted by the handicapper, or determined by the conditions of the race*, and no extra addition should be made to a rating because the horse's rider claims an apprentice allowance.

The above is the general routine procedure. But of course there is no reason why the quality of jockeyship should not be taken into account in assessing the chances of horses in a race. Quite the contrary. Nobody would question that the jockeyship of a first-class rider is worth a pound or two, and occasionally an apprentice comes along who is riding quite as well as the average jockey long before he loses the right to claim. There is no reason whatever why, after the age and weight adjustments have been made to the ratings, small additional allowances should not be made for these matters of jockeyship. This, however, is a matter which must be left to the discretion of the reader.

WEIGHING UP A RACE

It having been discovered, by means of the ratings, which horses in a particular race are most favoured by the weights, complete analysis demands that the racing character of each horse, as set out in the commentary upon it, shall be checked to see if there is any reason why the horse might be expected not to run up to his rating. It counts for little that a horse is thrown in at the weights if he has no pretensions whatever to staying the distance, or is unable to act on the prevailing going.

These two matters, suitability of distance and going, are, no doubt, the most important points to be considered. But there are others. For example, the ability of a horse to accommodate himself to the conformation of the track. Then there is the matter of pace versus stamina: as between two stayers of equal merit, racing over a distance suitable to both, firm going, or a small field with the prospect of a slowly-run race, would favour the one with the better pace and acceleration, whereas dead or soft going, or a big field with the prospect of a strong gallop throughout the race, would favour the sounder stayer. There is also the matter of temperament and behaviour at the start: nobody would be in a hurry to take a short price about a horse with whom it is always an even chance whether he will consent to race or not.

A few minutes spent checking up on these matters in the commentaries upon the horses concerned will sometimes put a very different complexion on a race from that which is put upon it by the ratings alone. We repeat, therefore, that the correct way to use Timeform, or this annual volume, in the analysis of individual races is, first to use the ratings to discover which horses are most favoured by the weights, and second, to check through the comments on the horse to discover what factors other than weight might also affect the outcome of the race.

Incidentally, in setting out the various characteristics, requirements and peculiarities of each horse in the commentary upon him, we have always expressed ourselves in as critical a manner as possible, endeavouring to say just as much, and no whit more than the facts seem to warrant. Where there are clear indications, and definite conclusions can be drawn with fair certainty, we have drawn them: if it is a matter of probability or possibility we have put it that way, being careful not to say the one when we mean the other; and where real conclusions are not to be drawn, we have been content to state the facts. Furthermore, when we say that a horse *may not* be suited by hard going, we do not expect the reader to treat it as though we had said that the horse is *not* suited by hard going. In short, both in our thinking and in the setting out of our views we have aimed at precision.

THE FORM SUMMARIES

The form summary enclosed in the round brackets shows for each individual horse the distance, the state of the going and where the horse finished in each of its races on the flat during the previous two seasons. Performances are in chronological sequence, the earliest being given first.

The distance of each race is given in furlongs, fractional distances being expressed in the decimal notation to the nearest tenth of a furlong.

The going is symbolised as follows: h=hard or very firm; f=firm; fg=fairly good, or on the firm side of good; g=good; d=dead, or on the soft side of good; s=soft, sticky or holding; v=heavy, very heavy or very holding.

Placings are indicated, up to fourth place, by the use of superior figures, an asterisk being used to denote a win.

Thus, 1981 10s* 12f³ 11.7g signifies that the horse ran three times in 1981, winning over ten furlongs on soft going first time out, finishing third over twelve furlongs on firm going next time out, and then unplaced, not in the first four, over 11.7 furlongs on good going. NR means that the horse did not race.

Included in the pedigree details are the highest Timeform Annual ratings during their racing careers of the sires, dams and sires of dams of all horses, where the information is available.

Where sale prices are given F denotes the price in guineas sold as a foal, Y the price in guineas sold as a yearling. The prefix IR denotes Irish guineas.

THE RATING SYMBOLS

The following symbols, attached to the ratings, are to be interpreted as stated:—

p   the horse is likely to make more than normal progress and to improve on his rating.

P   there is convincing evidence, or, to say the least, a very strong presumption that the horse is capable of form much better than he has so far displayed.

+   the horse may be rather better than we have rated him.

d   the horse appears to have deteriorated, and might no longer be capable of running to the rating given.

§   a horse who is somewhat ungenerous, faint-hearted or a bit of a coward; one who may give his running on occasions, but cannot be relied upon to do so.

§§   an arrant rogue or a thorough jade; so temperamentally unsatisfactory as to be not worth a rating.

?   if used in conjunction with a rating this symbol implies that the rating is based upon inadequate or unsatisfactory data, upon form which it is impossible to assess with confidence. The use of a query without a rating implies that although the horse has form, his merit cannot be assessed on the data at present available.

Goffs Ireland

Kildare Paddocks,
Kill,
Co. Kildare,
Ireland.

February 8th

August 15th-16th
National Hunt Sale

October 5th-8th
Yearling Sales.

October 18th
Autumn Horse in Training Sales

November 8th-10th
November Sales Part 1

November 21st-23rd
November Sales Part 2.

Goffs France

73, Rue du Faubourg St, Honore,
75008 Paris France.

June 17th
Horses in Training Sale

October 2nd
Arc De Triomphe Sale

October 4th
International Arc Yearling Sale

November 8th
Horses in Training Sale

November 13th
Breeding Stock Sale

Tel:Kildare 9211
Telex:24227

SALES DATES

FOR 1982

Tel. 742-6660
Telex:660156

RACEHORSES OF 1981

AABORUN 2 gr.c. Run The Gantlet–Aabora (Don II 123) (1981 8d) Mar 21;   —
third foal; half-brother to 2 winners by Balidar, including English and French
5f and 7f winner Powder 'n Patch; dam well beaten all outings; 8/1 when well-
beaten eighth of 18 to Sugar and Mint in maiden race Leicester in November.
J. Dunlop.

ABALIGHT 3 gr.g. Abwah 118–Moonlight 101 (Djebe) (1980 5s 5d² 5fg   —
6fg 7fg² 7g³ 1981 7d 8d³ 7f 7f⁴ 7g 7f³ 8fg 8.2s⁴) small gelding; plater; stays
1m; usually blinkered nowadays; bandaged fifth outing. *W. Wharton.*

ABERCORN FLYER 3 b.f. Silly Season 127–Miss Casanova 84 (Galivanter   —
131) (1980 5f² 5f⁴ 5d 6fg 6fg 5g 8g 1981 8.2g 8f 8.2fg) lightly-made filly;
probably stays 1m (ran respectably over trip first outing); acts on firm going.
W. Musson.

ABERFIELD 4 ch.c. Northfields–Abergara (Abernant 142) (1980 8fg 10f²   **62**
10d³ 12fg³ 12g³ 14d⁴ 1981 15.8s 13d* 12.5g 12g² 12g* 12.3fg³ 12f⁴ 12fg 10f³
12f²) leggy, narrow colt; won poor maiden race at Hamilton in April and
ladies event at Ripon in June; stays 13f (seemed to find 2m too far first start);
probably acts on any going; blinkered once in 1980; good mount for an inexperienced rider; sold to P. Kelleway 4,000 gns Newmarket Autumn Sales. *C.
Brittain.*

ABEROYALE 3 b.f. Nos Royalistes 119–Phyl's Pet (Aberdeen 109) (1980   —
NR 1981 12g 10.1fg) first foal; dam of little account; behind in maiden race
at Lingfield (tailed-off last) and minor event at Windsor, both in June. *M.
Bolton.*

ABINGTON 4 b.c. Jukebox 120–Silky 112 (Nijinsky 138) (1980 8f 6fg 7g   **78**
8fg 8f 7s 1981 8d 6g 6g³ 5fg) strong, good-bodied, most attractive colt;
very good mover; fairly useful at his best but is none too consistent; stays
1m; acts on firm going; blinkered third and fourth outings; sometimes sweats
up; ran badly second start; not one to rely on; sold 16,000 gns Newmarket
December Sales. *H. Wragg.*

ABLA 3 ch.f. English Prince 129–Humble Portion (Mossborough 126 or   **76**
Major Portion 129) (1980 NR 1981 10s* 12d 12g 12d) lengthy filly; third
foal; half-sister to Spare A Bit (by Track Spare), winner of a 1m seller as a
2-y-o; dam placed over 5f at 2 yrs; beat Jo-Jo San by 1½ lengths in maiden
race at Salisbury in April; didn't reproduce that form; stays 1¼m; acts on soft
going. *R. Price.*

ABLE KATE 3 b.f. Malacate 131–Amicable 73 (Bold Ruler) (1980 NR 1981   —
10fg 8.2s) third foal; half-sister to fair middle-distance handicapper Mickey
Tim (by Gay Fandango); dam, placed over 1⅛m, is half-sister to Sir Wimborne
and Lady Capulet; in mid-division in maiden races at Salisbury and Nottingham
in September; sold 10,500 gns Newmarket December Sales. *J. Dunlop.*

ABO ACE 3 ch.g. Hotfoot 126–Linum 81 (Takawalk II 125) (1980 5fg 6fg   **71**
7d 7g 6fg 7f 8d 1981 10.1d 11.5f 10f 10f⁴ 14fg* 16g² 13d 12d² 16s) good
walker; mainly poor form, including in a seller, before making all in poor maiden
race at Yarmouth in August; good second at Yarmouth and Wolverhampton
subsequently; stays well; acts on a firm and a soft surface; sometimes blinkered
but is better without. *M. Ryan.*

ABOARD 2 gr.g. Abwah 118–Fair Marina 93 (Hethersett 134) (1981 5s 5d   **67**
5fg³ 5f*) May 18; small gelding; third foal; half-brother to 7f seller winner Swift Marina
and a winning jumper (both by Birdbrook); dam 2-y-o 6f winner; attracted
no bid after making all to win 7-runner seller at Folkestone in July by 3 lengths
from Inch High but was sold privately afterwards and is a winner in Belgium;
will stay 6f. *R. Smyth.*

ABROVIAN ROSE 3 br.f. Blue Cashmere 129–Saucy Jane 82 (Hard Sauce   —
131) (1980 5v 6g 5fg 5f* 5f 8s 1981 5g 6s 5f 5f 8f) lengthy filly; good walker;
won seller at York as a 2-y-o; little worthwhile form in 1981; should stay 6f,
but is unlikely to stay 1m; acts well on firm going. *M. W. Easterby.*

ABSOLUTE (FR) 2 ch.f. Luthier 126–Artistically (Ribot 142) (1981 5.5g **105**
6g* 7s² 8s²) half-sister to French 3-y-o 9f winner Artful (by Forli) and a winner
in Germany; dam, winner over 6f at 2 yrs in USA, is sister to St Leger winner
Boucher; won minor event at Evry in July, dead-heating with Gay Spring;
subsequently second in more valuable races, going down by 2 lengths to Talaja
in Prix de l'Obelisque at Longchamp in September and by a head to Ilenia
in Group 2 Premio Dormello at Milan in October; will stay at least 1¼m. *F.
Boutin, France.*

ABSTAINER 2 b.g. Abwah 118–Nae Bird 78 (Birdbrook 110) (1981 5d 6d —
5g 7fg) robust gelding; second foal; half-brother to a winner in Belgium;
dam won over 1m; behind in maiden races. *R. Smyth.*

ABU TORKEY 4 gr.g. Majority Blue 126–Nantgarw (Abernant 142) (1980 **56**
7f 1981 8v² 12g³ 8g² 8d 8g² 8f 8s 8.2f⁴ 8g 7g 9f* 8f³ 11d⁴ 10.5s) big, strong,
good-topped gelding; won apprentice race at Ripon in August; stays 9f; acts
on any going; suitable mount for an apprentice; blinkered ninth start (went
very freely to post); sold 2,800 gns Doncaster November Sales. *Denys Smith.*

ABWACADABWA 3 br.f. Abwah 118–Jetwitch 56 (Lear Jet 123) (1980 **59**
7f³ 7f⁴ 6d² 7d 8f⁴ 7s³ 8d⁴ 1981 8g 7fg 9fg* 8fg⁴ 12d) neat filly; returned to
form when beating Unique Lady by 1½ lengths in selling handicap at Newcastle in June (no bid); stays 9f; acts on any going; trained by R. D. Peacock first
4 outings. *J. Blundell.*

ABWAY 3 ch.c. Abwah 118–Teresa Way 66 (Great White Way) (1980 NR —
1981 8f 6v 8s 5s) small, strong colt; first foal; dam second over 5f at 2 yrs;
behind in maiden and minor events, 3 times finishing last. *R. Hollinshead.*

ACADEMIC (USA) 2 b.c. King Pellinore 127–Faneuil Hall (Bolinas Boy) **104**
(1981 5.5d⁴ 5.5g* 7f² 8s) Apr 4; $165,000Y; half-brother to several winners,
including 3-y-o middle-distance winner Ecube (by Youth), Hall of Reason
(by Bold Reason), a smart stakes winner up to 1m, and very useful 1m to 11f
winner Celebrated (by Native Charger); dam smart stakes winner at up to 1m;
won minor race at Evry in July by a nose from newcomer Zino; beaten in better
races after, finishing 5 lengths second of 6 to Zino in Criterium de Bernay at
Deauville in August and distant seventh of 8 to Bon Sang in Prix des Chenes
at Longchamp the following month; should stay 1¼m; acts on firm going. *J.
Fellows, France.*

ACAPULCO GOLD 5 ch.h. Gulf Pearl 117–Capsville (Cyane) (1980 12d **63**
10g 10f 11f³ 10fg 8fg³ 10d⁴ 10.6d 12g 10g* 10f³ 10g³ 1981 10f³ 10fg² 10fg²
10fg⁴ 10f⁴ 10g) strong, well-made horse; good mover; stays 1½m; seems to
act on any going; blinkered twice at 4 yrs. *A. Pitt.*

ACCESSION 3 b.c. Crowned Prince 128–Sapphire Spray (Floribunda 136) **90 d**
(1980 7s³ 1981 8s* 7g 10s² 8g 10d 7fg³ 11g) Irish colt; confirmed the promise
of his only outing as a 2-y-o when beating Republican by ¾ length in 17-runner
maiden race at the Curragh in April; placed in £2,100 race on same course
later in month and minor event at Galway in September; last but one in 2,000
Guineas won by To-Agori-Mou at Newmarket and in rear in Nijinsky Stakes
at Leopardstown in between; stays 1¼m; probably better on soft going than
firm. *M. O'Toole, Ireland.*

ACCLAIMED 3 b.f. Luthier 126–Acoma 121 (Rheffic 129) (1980 7.3d 7g³ **67**
1981 8s 10d³ 14f*) tall filly; stayed on strongly and beat stable-companion
Gauleiter by 1½ lengths in maiden race at Yarmouth in August; suited by
1¾m; probably acts on any going; sold 70,000 gns Newmarket December Sales.
H. Cecil.

ACCOUNTABILITY 3 br.g. Jukebox 120–Fiji Express (Exbury 138) (1980 —
5d 5f 5f 5fg⁴ 5g 7s 8g 8.2g 8d 7d 1981 10s 7v 12.2g) useful-looking gelding;
only poor form, including in sellers; stays 1m; sold 750 gns Doncaster May Sales.
R. Hollinshead.

ACHIEVED 2 ch.c. Thatch 136–Last Call 74 (Klairon 131) (1981 5fg* 5fg* **124**
7fg*)
The maxim 'if you can't beat 'em, join 'em' must have flashed through the
minds of the O'Brien/Sangster team as they watched a yearling son of Thatch
and Last Call walk round the ring at the Houghton Sales in 1980. The colt was
a full brother to Final Straw, the conqueror of the team's number-one hope for
the 1980 classics, Monteverdi, in the Clerical, Medical Greenham Stakes earlier
in the year. They outbid Henry Candy to take the colt for 162,000 guineas;

they subsequently gave him the name Achieved and now own a very valuable prospect, unbeaten in three races.

Easily Achieved's best performance came in the Laurent Perrier Champagne Stakes at Doncaster in September, another race won by Final Straw. Favourite ahead of Achieved was the Gimcrack winner Full Extent, aiming to extend his winning sequence to five, and also in the field of eight were the promising Cecil-trained Padalco, the beaten favourite for the Richmond Stakes Hays, those useful colts Ashenden and Chulia Street, and Red Sunset who had disappointed in both his races since his Coventry Stakes victory. Full Extent and Chulia Street stopped as if shot after disputing the lead for four and a half furlongs, leaving Achieved in front. Although seeming to be travelling very smoothly Achieved soon came under pressure as Hays produced a splendid turn of foot and drew alongside. For the next furlong the race could have gone either way but Achieved started to edge clear in the closing stages and was well on top by the line. Hays was beaten a length and a half with Ashenden running on to take third place a further two and a half lengths behind. The first two came a bit close together at one stage but the result rightly stood after a stewards inquiry and an objection. Achieved's time supported the view that he had put up the best performance by a two-year-old up to that stage of the season, and the form certainly looked no worse after Hays ran out a three-length winner of the Mill Reef Stakes ten days later. Achieved's next target was said to be the Royal Lodge Stakes but he reportedly suffered a minor setback and wasn't seen out again.

Although the seven furlongs of the Champagne Stakes suited Achieved extremely well he had been sufficiently effective over five furlongs the previous month to win Ireland's only Group 1 race for two-year-olds, the Gallaghouse Phoenix Stakes at Phoenix Park, in 1981 an extremely weakly-contested affair for a Group 1 event. Achieved, an easy course and distance winner of a minor race the previous month, started at 6/4 on to beat The Primate, who had proved no match for Jester on his one trip to England; Watties Rock, beaten six and a half lengths by Peterhof on his previous excursion into pattern-race company; Dance Empress, a newcomer; Lorn Goddess, beaten in seven of her eight previous races; and two animals who had each won only once from four starts, Shir Khan and Zanskar. Achieved landed the odds only narrowly and in controversial style. He took some time to hit his stride, and coming from behind Eddery forced him through a narrow gap one and a half furlongs out, hampering Lorn Goddess. Once clear Achieved quickened like a very good colt, getting up on the line to beat The Primate a short head. At the subsequent inquiry the stewards cautioned Eddery 'concerning the necessity of keeping a straight course' before leaving the placings unaltered. The connections of both Lorn Goddess and The Primate decided to appeal against the decision but Lorn Goddess' appeal was withdrawn to prevent her carrying a penalty in her next race; the Stewards of the Turf Club let the result stand.

Achieved is the sixth winner from his dam's first eight foals. He and Final Straw are easily the best of them but the Britannia Stakes winner Final Chord (by Tudor Melody) and the mile-and-a-half filly Curtains (by Busted) were also well above average. Incidentally Curtains' second foal, Heighten, won his last

Laurent Perrier Champagne Stakes, Doncaster—Achieved wins decisively from Hays

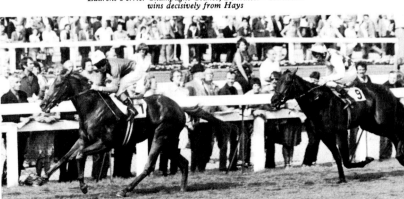

Mr R. E. Sangster's "Achieved"

five races in 1981 and another good winner from the family was the high-class middle-distance colt Pelerin, like Achieved a great-grandson of Bashful. Achieved's sire didn't have so good a year as usual, with only Achieved of his juveniles winning a race in England and Ireland compared to nine two-year-old winners in 1980.

	⎰ Thatch	⎰ Forli	⎰ Aristophanes	
Achieved	⎱ (b 1970)	⎱ (ch 1963)	⎱ Trevisa	
		Thong	⎰ Nantallah	
(ch.c. May 13, 1979)		(b 1964)	⎱ Rough Shod	
	⎰ Last Call	⎰ Klairon	⎰ Clarion III	
	⎱ (b 1964)	⎱ (b 1952)	⎱ Kalmia	
		Stage Fright	⎰ Big Game	
		(ch 1954)	⎱ Bashful	

Readers who have a copy of *Racehorses of 1979* will be able to compare Final Straw's portrait as a two-year-old with Achieved's. The photographs show the two to be very similar types, but in the flesh Achieved seems to lack just a little of his brother's strength and scope. Nevertheless Achieved is a good-looking colt and a high-class one who is likely to develop into a leading fancy for the Two Thousand Guineas, the distance of which will suit him. As yet he has raced only on a firm surface but his brother acted on any going and the chances are that Achieved will, too. *V. O'Brien, Ireland*

ACKERMANN (USA) 3 br.c. Cornish Prince–Had My Way (Summer Tan) **111** (1980 NR 1981 7fg* 6g* 7g² 6fg) $110,000Y; lengthy colt; brother to very smart 1975 2-y-o stakes winner Imacornishprince, successful at up to 6f, and half-brother to several winners, including stakes winners Camp Whip (by Seaneen) and Doing It My Way (by Exclusive Native); dam unraced half-sister to Gimcrack winner Eudaemon; favourite when winning first 2 races, 20-runner maiden event at Newmarket in April (clear going into Dip and coasted in 1½ lengths ahead of Icen) and Northumberland Sprint Trophy (Handicap) at Newcastle in August (short-priced favourite, beat Princess Gayle a neck with a bit in hand); suffered a variety of problems in between, including a pulled muscle in his quarters; came up against another improving colt when going down by 5 lengths to Indian King in Battle of Britain Handicap at Doncaster in September, but finished clear of remainder despite being eased slightly; had stiff task and weakened in last 2f when seventh of 10 behind Moorestyle in Diadem Stakes at Ascot later in September; bred to stay 1m; very useful; sent to USA. *H. Cecil.*

ACKSTATIC (USA) 2 br.c. Ack Ack–Space Happy (Never Say Die 137) (1981 7d* 7d) Apr 8; $50,000Y; half-brother to numerous winners, including useful Irish 1¼m winner March Hywell (by Pretense) and Vacation Lady (by Tatan), a smart stakes winner at up to 1m; dam stakes-placed daughter of 1,000 Guineas third Solar Myth; made virtually all and had only to be pushed out to beat Northleigh 1½ lengths in 14-runner minor event at Brighton in September; second favourite for similar race at Chepstow the following month but was beaten about 8 lengths into eighth-of-22 place behind Starbells; will stay 1½m. *M. Stoute.* **89**

ACTION 2 br.c. Tower Walk 130–Delayed Action 113 (Jolly Jet 111) (1981 6f 6f 7f) July 3; workmanlike colt; second foal; half-brother to fairly useful sprinter Force of Action (by Galivanter); dam won seven 5f races, six of them at 2 yrs; 20/1 and blinkered, ran on when fairly close-up seventh of 18 to Connaught River in maiden race at Redcar in September, third outing and easily best effort; evidently suited by 7f. *G. Toft.* **62**

Mr C. A. B. St George's "Ackermann"

ACTON WOOD LAUREL 3 b.f. Sassafras 135–Moana (Zucchero 133§) — (1980 5d 6d 7d 1981 8.2fg 12d 12f 13.8g) leggy, unfurnished filly; poor plater; pulled very hard third start; sold 300 gns Doncaster November Sales. *D. Francis.*

ACUITY 3 ch.f. Sharp Edge 123–Mismillari (Double Jump 131) (1980 NR — 1981 9d 8fg 10fg) neat filly; first foal; dam of little account; behind in maiden events and a seller. *D. Ringer.*

ACUSHLA MACREE 4 ch.f. Mansingh 120–Cannie Cassie 70 (Canisbay 120) **51** (1980 7s 8f 10f 10.2fg³ 10g 11fg 10.1g 10fg⁴ 10g 9d 10s 10g 1981 10f 10.8fg³ 8.2g⁴ 10f 8.3g* 8g 8d* 8s 10.2g) neat filly; plater nowadays; apprentice ridden when winning at Windsor in August (no bid) and Brighton in September (bought in 1,350 gns); stays 1¼m well; acts on a firm and a soft surface; blinkered nowadays and also wore a hood last 4 starts; sometimes bandaged behind. *F. J. Houghton.*

ADAM CRAIG 3 b.c. Connaught 130–Karenina 95 (Silver Shark 129) (1980 **63** 8.2s 7d³ 1981 12f 10.2fg 10d² 11d³ 12.2g 12s²) strong, good sort; placed in minor events at Ayr and Hamilton in September and Redcar in October; stays 1½m; sweating second outing; trained most of season by J. Hanson. *M. Naughton.*

ADAMSON 3 b. or br.c. Blakeney 126–Set Free 90 (Worden II 129) (1980 — 7g 1981 12d 10s 16f) 175,000Y; compact, attractive colt; good mover; brother to 4 winners, including Oaks and Irish Guinness Oaks winner Juliette Marny, St Leger winner Julio Mariner and very smart 11f winner Saviour, and half-brother to 2 winners, including Oaks winner Scintillate (by Sparkler); dam won at 1m; an extremely well-bred colt but hasn't shown much form (usually runs against stiff opposition); made much of running and wouldn't settle when ninth of 13 behind Ore in Queen's Vase at Royal Ascot in June on final start, should stay well. *M. O'Toole, Ireland.*

ADDERYBURY LAD 2 ch.c. Tachypous 128–Pretty Mall 80 (Pall Mall 132) — (1981 5s 5g 7fg 7f 7d) Mar 25; 560Y; strong colt; half-brother to useful 1973 2-y-o Rupert Bear (by Runnymede) and a winner in Brazil; dam placed over 6f; no sign of ability, including in auction events; blinkered fifth outing. *J. Townson.*

ADDISON'S JUBILEE 2 b.f. Sparkler 130–Red Sunset III 105 (High Hat — 131) (1981 6fg 6g) June 6; 16,000Y; compact, rather lightly-made filly; half-sister to 2 winners, notably smart 7f to 1m winner Kashmir Love (by Kashmir II); dam stayed 1½m; 20/1 and in need of race, wasn't knocked about once chance had gone in minor events at Newmarket in August (seventh of 14 to Aegean Beauty) and Redcar the following month; will stay 1m. *G. Pritchard-Gordon.*

ADJUSTED 2 ch.c. Busted 134–Angel Row 96 (Prince Regent 129) (1981 — 6fg 8d 8.2d 8s 8s 10.2g) May 16; 7,000Y; big colt; second foal; half-brother to fair 1979 2-y-o 5f performer Welcombe (by Mountain Call); dam, winner over 1m, is daughter of Irish 1,000 Guineas winner Front Row; just under 10 lengths fifth of 11 to subsequently-disqualified Rajhaan in nursery at Newbury in October, fifth outing and only form; should be suited by 1¼m+. *R. Hobson.*

ADMINISTRATOR 4 b.g. Gay Fandango 132–Maureen's Slipper (Gratitude **50** 130) (1980 6fg* 6fg 6v 1981 6g 6g³ 8h³ 7g* 8d⁴ 7g) lengthy, useful-looking, ex-Irish gelding; plater; bought in 1,500 gns after winning at Yarmouth in September; stays 1m; seems to act on any going; sweated up badly third start; used to be none too reliable; has been taken down early. *H. O'Neill.*

ADMIRAL GRENVILLE 5 b.g. Sweet Revenge 129–Soverena 98 (Sovereign — Lord 120) (1980 8d 8s 10f 11.7fg 10d 12s* 10g⁴ 12f² 12f⁴ 12g* 12f* 12fg* 12f* 1981 8s 12d 12g) big, rangy gelding; won 5 handicaps in 1980; ran moderately at 5 yrs; suited by 1½m; acts on any going; has been tried in blinkers; suitable mount for an apprentice. *J. Jenkins.*

ADMIRAL'S BARGE 4 ch.c. Brigadier Gerard 144–Pirogue 99 (Reliance — II 137) (1980 8d 8s 10fg³ 10g 10.1f 11.7h³ 14d* 12fg 1981 16s 12g 13.1g 17.1h 14fg 12fg 10.2g 11s) neat, lightly-made colt; quite moderate at his best; well beaten in handicaps at 4 yrs; suited by 1¾m; probably acts on any going; sometimes sweats up; has run creditably for an apprentice; sold 620 gns Newmarket Autumn Sales. *W. Wightman.*

ADMIRAL'S HEIR (USA) 3 b.c. Crafty Khale–Triggs'z (Successor) (1980 **107** 6fg 6fg⁴ 6g* 7g* 7d* 7f* 7g 7.6g* 8d 1981 12.3g 10.1s² 10.6s³ 12f² 12f⁴) quite attractive, compact colt; good mover; won 5 times as a 2-y-o; didn't win in 1981 but confirmed himself a very useful colt; ran particularly well when about 3 lengths third to Bustomi in King Edward VII Stakes at Royal Ascot in June and was moved up a place on disqualification of second; unsuited by slow pace when last of 4 behind Six Mile Bottom in Welsh Derby at Chepstow on only subsequent start, following month; placed earlier in minor event at Windsor and valuable handicap at Haydock, having stiff task when 3½ lengths third to Feltwell in latter; stays 1½m; acts on any going; genuine and consistent; operated on for a wind infirmity in July. *P. Cole.*

ADMIRAL'S PRINCESS (USA) 2 b.f. Groton–Triggs'z (Successor) (1981 **108** 5s³ 5d* 5fg² 5f* 6fg³ 6c³ 7g⁴) Apr 1; $27,000Y; small, workmanlike filly; half-sister to 3 winners, including very useful 1980 2-y-o 6f to 7.6f winner Admiral's Heir (by Crafty Khale); dam won over 6f; won 8-runner maiden race at Brighton in May (made all) and Erroll Stakes at Ascot the following month (beat Corley Moor 2 lengths); not seen out again until September when third in 2 good races, finishing 6 lengths behind Sandhurst Prince in 6-runner Sirenia Stakes at Kempton and 3 lengths behind Woodstream in 13-runner William Hill Cheveley Park Stakes at Newmarket; far from disgraced when tried over 7f, finishing 2¾ lengths fourth of 8 to Top Hope after having every chance 1f out, in Rockfel Stakes at Newmarket in October; stays 7f; probably acts on any going but has shown best form on a sound surface; sweated up third and fifth outings; game and consistent. *P. Cole.*

ADMIRING GLANCE 2 ro.f. Northern Flash–Che Bella (Beau Sabreur 125) — (1981 7f 7f) May 20; heavy-topped filly; poor walker; half-sister to several winners, including useful 7f to 1¼m winner Pabella (by Pardao) and sprinter Twixt' Tween (by The Go-Between); dam won Irish Cambridgeshire; apprentice ridden when well behind in maiden races at Yarmouth in August. *H. T. Jones.*

ADONIS REX (USA) 2 gr.c. One For All–Scottish Lass (Scotland) (1981 **89** 7g³ 7fg³ 7g* 7d³) Feb 10; $55,000F, 62,000 gns Y; well-made colt; half-brother to several winners, including smart 1974 staying 2-y-o Silverbatim (by Verbatim); dam ran 8 times unplaced; landed the odds in 16-runner maiden race at Leicester in September by ½ length from Sir Blessed, the pair clear; third all other starts, running moderately behind Ackstatic in minor race at Brighton in September on final appearance when blinkered; will be suited by middle distances; to race in U.S.A. *H. Cecil.*

ADVERTRACK 3 ch.f. Arch Sculptor 123–St Pet (St Chad 120) (1980 5fg **66** 5fg 5d 5g* 5d⁴ 1981 5s⁴ 5fg 5s⁴ 5fg² 5g) useful-looking, good-quartered filly; sprint handicapper; probably acted on any going; destroyed after breaking down at Nottingham in August. *G. Hunter.*

AEGEAN BEAUTY 2 ch.f. Sharpen Up 127–Camina Bay 109 (Whistling Wind **89** 123) (1981 6fg* 6g) Apr 7; short-backed, rather leggy filly; half-sister to 3 winners, including very smart 6f to 8.5f winner Foveros (by Averof); dam useful sprinting 2-y-o; took a clear advantage 1½f out in minor event at Newmarket in August and held on by a neck from Dish Dash; never dangerous when 25/1 for William Hill Cheveley Park Stakes, again at Newmarket, the following month but wasn't disgraced in finishing 9 lengths eighth of 13 to Woodstream; will probably stay 7f. *C. Brittain.*

AEROLITE (USA) 2 gr.c. Al Hattab–Francie T (Grey Dawn II 132) (1981 — p 7fg) Apr 4; $85,000Y; second foal; brother to 1980 2-y-o American 1m winner Al Jr; dam unraced granddaughter of champion handicap mare Mar-Kell; led for nearly 5f when second favourite for 15-runner maiden race at Yarmouth in August but dropped back to finish 14 lengths fifth of 15 to Skytrick; not seen out afterwards. *H. Cecil.*

AFDAL 2 b.c. Realm 129–Golden Gorse (Crepello 136) (1981 7g) Apr 28; **70** p 11,500Y; strong colt; half-brother to winning Irish stayer Quarter Bridge (by Thatch); dam, winner over 1¼m in Ireland, is half-sister to Derby fourth Royal Sword; 20/1, led for over 5f before finishing 11 lengths fifth of 23 to Simply Great in maiden race at Newmarket in October. *W. O'Gorman.*

AFFILIATION ORDER (USA) 2 b.c. Intrepid Hero–Lovers Lane (Raise **89** A Native) (1981 6g³ 7fg 7fg⁴ 7fg³ 8g) May 12; $47,000Y; tall, rangy colt; excellent mover; half-brother to 2 minor winners in USA and one in Puerto Rico; dam never ran; sire, son of Forli, was high-class winner from 1m to 1½m; prominent in maiden races, staying on strongly when 5¾ lengths sixth of 30 to Farioffa in 1m event at Newmarket in October; will stay 1¼m+; sure to win in ordinary maiden company. *P. Cole.*

AFGHAN (USA) 2 b.c. The Minstrel 135–Quilly (Bagdad) (1981 5d 7f2 **107**
6fg* 7d 7.5d 6g*) half-brother to Irish 5f winner Rooftree (by Thatch); dam
unraced half-sister to outstanding American filly Revidere; landed the odds
by a length from Bar Bender in maiden race at Phoenix Park in July and put
up a fine effort under 9-7 in valuable Birdcatcher Nursery at Naas in October,
disputing lead throughout and winning a shade comfortably by ½ length from
Rathvinden; wore blinkers in between, disputing lead 5f before fading to finish
7¾ lengths sixth of 11 to Day Is Done in National Stakes at the Curragh and
same distance seventh of 13 to Furry Berg in Waterford Glass Nursery at
Gowran Park; better at 6f than 7f at 2 yrs but is bred to stay 1m. *V. O'Brien,
Ireland.*

AFLOAT 2 ch.f. Targowice 130–Creperie (Dapper Dan) (1981 5d 6f) May 18; —
1,250Y; narrow filly; fifth foal; dam once-raced half-sister to smart animals
Pithiviers and Blinis; blinkered when distant seventh of 17 to Singing Sailor
in maiden auction event at Salisbury in May and when tailed-off last of 12 in
maiden race won by Woodcutter at Haydock in July (started slowly). *C.
James.*

AFRICAN BERRY 2 b.f. African Sky 124–Cotoneaster (Never Say Die 137) **84**
(1981 5fg 5v2 6f2 6f2 6fg 5fg* 5f3 5g 5g3) Apr 5; IR 4,200F, IR 4,800Y; compact filly; half-sister to 3 winners, including Irish 1½m and 1¾m winner Nolnocan
(by Colum); dam once-raced twin; kept on strongly to beat Golden Spray
by 3 lengths in 16-runner maiden race at Catterick in August; placed in most
of her other races, running well when third subsequently in small race and a
nursery at Beverley; stays 6f and is bred to get further but is evidently considered
a 5f performer; acts on any going; wears blinkers. *H. T. Jones.*

AFRICANOS 4 b.g. African Sky 124–Welshpool 75 (Henry the Seventh 125) **85**
(1980 5fg 5f 6g 8d* 8.2s2 9.4g4 8.2g* 7d* 8fg* 8g2 8s2 8f 8fg3 8s4 1981 8.2d
7d3 8g3 7.2s4 8g 7g2 7g4 8g* 8fg* 7g* 8g 8g2 8g2 8fg4 8d3 10fg) strong gelding;
fair handicapper, in magnificent form in June and picked up 3 valuable races,
namely Long John Scotch Whisky Handicap at Ayr and Dobson Peacock
Handicap and Journal Good Morning Handicap, both at Newcastle; best at
up to 1m; probably acts on any going; blinkered once in 1980; sometimes
sweats up; sometimes wears a tongue strap; goes well for apprentice N. Carlisle;
does best when held up; most tough and genuine. *H. Bell.*

AFRICAN PEARL 3 b.c. African Sky 124–Stickpin 74 (Gulf Pearl 117) (1980 **79**
5fg 5f3 6d* 6g 1981 7g 7d3 8g 8g 8.3fg) quite attractive colt; gamely won
maiden race at Newmarket as a 2-y-o; had stiff task when staying-on third
behind easy winner Beeleigh in £4,000 handicap at Chester in May, best effort
of 1981; promises to stay 1m; sometimes sweats up; trained until after fourth
start by G. Pritchard-Gordon. *R. Simpson.*

AFTER SHAVE 5 b.h. Sallust 134–Blue Fragrance (Blue Prince 123) (1980 —
10.2d 7v 7f 8f 10f 10fg 10g 1981 8s 8g) strong horse; not a good mover;
plater nowadays; stays 1m; probably acts on any going; often wears blinkers.
K. Stone.

AGE OF REASON 3 b.g. Red Alert 127–Pampered Belle (Pampered King **81**
121) (1980 5f 5fg2 6d* 7s4 7f 6s 1981 10v4 11fg 8g 8g* 8f4 7fg*) strong,
well-made gelding; won handicaps at Ayr in June and Redcar in July; stays
1m; seems to act on any going; wears blinkers; exported to Hong Kong. *Denys
Smith.*

AGE QUOD AGIS (USA) 3 gr.c. Al Hattab–Alps (Pavot) (1980 5fg 6f* **116**
6g* 6s* 5.5g3 6g 1981 7d2 6s2) quite an attractive colt; has rather a round
action; half-brother to several winners in USA, including stakes-placed To the
Top (by Bold Hour); dam very useful stakes winner at up to 1m; successful
at Yarmouth, Doncaster and Newmarket (in July Stakes) as a 2-y-o; did well
over the winter and made a satisfactory reappearance in 6-runner Clerical,
Medical Greenham Stakes at Newbury in April, running on quite well under
pressure to finish 3 lengths second to Another Realm; stuck on quite well again
when 1½ lengths second of 6 behind top-class 3-y-o filly Marwell in Gus Demmy
Memorial Stakes at Haydock the following month; will stay 1m; appears to
act on any going; didn't stride out at all well going to start at Newbury; reportedly collided with a car and injured himself when getting loose on gallops in June.
H. Cecil.

AGRELOUI 2 ch.f. Tower Walk 130–Greenhill Lass (Upper Case) (1981 6g —
6g) Apr 4; 4,000F; small, lightly-made filly; first produce; dam, from same

family as Sing Sing and Burglar, never ran; unquoted when in rear in end-of-season maiden races at Newmarket. *R. Armstrong.*

AHONAJLA 2 gr. or ro.c. Godswalk 130–Denaneer 78 (Green God 128) (1981 — 5s 5g) May 22; quite attractive, rather leggy colt; good mover; second foal; half-brother to 3-y-o 1m winner Banoco (by Nonoalco); dam 1¼m winner; well beaten in 2 early-season outings but showed good speed for a long way against fairly useful company on second occasion. *R. Price.*

AHWAZ 3 b.f. Manado 130–Meli (Acropolis 132) (1980 NR 1981 14d) — 8,000Y; tall, lengthy filly; half-sister to 2 winners, including fairly useful 1973 2-y-o 5f winner Big String (by King's Leap), subsequently a prolific winner in Italy; dam half-sister to very smart African Sky; unquoted when ninth of 13 behind Thahul in maiden race at Sandown in June; sold 3,000 gns Newmarket December Sales. *C. Nelson.*

AIGLON (HOL) 2 b.f. Shamaraan–Anzeige (Soderini 123) (1981 7fg 7g **66** 7f) Jan 10; compact filly; half-sister to top Dutch filly Libelle (by Arratos); dam German; about 6 lengths sixth of 16 to Hostess in maiden race at Brighton in August, third outing and best effort; likely to stay 1¼m+. *G. Harwood.*

AIRBORNE DEAL 2 ch.c. Sandford Lad 133–Acropolita Mia 75 (Acropolis — 132) (1981 7fg) May 11; 14,000Y; brother to Mia Saint, 4 times a winner over 5f at 2 yrs in 1976, and half-brother to 3-y-o 1¼m winner Royal Vulcan (by Royal Match) and a winner in Austria; dam won over 11.7f; 16/1, started slowly when remote sixth of 8 to Ashenden in £4,200 event at Newmarket in July. *N. Callaghan.*

AIR COUPON 2 ch.f. Air Trooper 115–Gift Coupon 64 (Gift Card 124) (1981 — 8fg 7.6s) May 6; 1,200F; first produce; dam ran only at 2 yrs; unquoted when behind in maiden races at Leicester in September and Lingfield in October. *J. Bethell.*

AIREDALE BOY 2 b.g. Decoy Boy 129–Consula 88 (Privy Councillor 125) **61** (1981 5g 5fg⁴ 6g 7g 7d³ 6fg³ 8.2fg³ 6fg 8fg) Mar 2; strong gelding; plater; stays 1m but showed best form at shorter distances; blinkered fifth, eighth and ninth outings. *M. W. Easterby.*

AIREDALE JUNCTION 3 b.g. Karabas 132–Dinant 114 (Abernant 142) — (1980 NR 1981 12.2fg 10fg 9s) 2,300Y, resold 3,100Y; tall, leggy gelding; brother to 2 winners in Ireland, including 7f to 13f winner Karant, and half-brother to 2 winners; dam winning sister to 1,000 Guineas winner Abermaid; little worthwhile form in Northern maiden races; unseated rider on way to start on second outing. *G. Toft.*

AIR POWER 4 gr.g. Supreme Sovereign 119–Queen Of The Winds (Borealis) — (1980 9v 1981 8g 8g 9.4g 8s 10.1fg 12g) small, fair sort; no sign of ability in varied company; has worn a bandage on his near-hind; blinkered final outing; sold out of Mrs A. Cousins' stable 680 gns Doncaster June Sales after fourth start. *M. Chapman.*

AIRSHIP 3 br.c. Manado 130–High Sphere (St Paddy 133) (1980 5f* 5f² 5f **73** 6fg* 6fg² 7g 1981 7fg 8.2fg 7d 7g 7.2s³ 7f³ 8f³ 7.2f 7g⁴) rather lightly-made colt; third in handicaps at Haydock, Leicester and Doncaster in June; suited by 1m; acts on any going; started slowly seventh outing. *R. Hollinshead.*

AIRSLEE 3 gr.c. Town Crier 119–Tavaro (Gustav 121) (1980 5fg 6g 6fg 5fg⁴ — 8.2g 6g 6f³ 7s⁴ 6d⁴ 1981 8s 8fg 10fg 11.7fg) useful sort; good walker; in frame in varied company at 2 yrs, including selling; well beaten in 1981; best form at 6f; acts on firm going; often blinkered; trained by Mrs R. Lomax first 2 starts; sold 1,500 gns Newmarket Autumn Sales. *G. Pritchard-Gordon.*

AIRSPIN 2 gr.c. Jukebox 120–Whispering Breeze (Caliban 123) (1981 6fg³ 7g* **93** 7s 7v 7g²) Jan 30; IR 5,000F, 10,000Y; compact colt; second living foal; half-brother to Credit Centre (by Tudor Music), a fairly useful winner at 1½m; dam poor plater; favourite when winning going away by 2 lengths from World Record in 16-runner maiden race at Leicester in September; kept on well when 3 lengths second of 14 to Hello Sunshine in well-contested nursery at Doncaster in November; will stay 1m; acts on a sound surface and ran poorly on very soft ground third and fourth starts. *R. Price.*

AIRSTREAM 3 br.g. Saritamer 130–Midsummertime (Midsummer Night II — 117) (1980 6d 1981 8fg 8d 10.1d 11.7g⁴ 13.3d 11g 12fg 8h) compact gelding; slow maiden; often blinkered. *F. J. Houghton.*

AIRWAIR 2 br.g. Godswalk 130–Haunting Melody 96 (Sing Sing 134) (1981 7f⁴ **76** p 7g*) Mar 23; 17,500Y; good mover; half-brother to 4 winners, 3 of them useful,

51

including 1979 2-y-o 5f performer Northern Eclipse (by Derring-Do); dam miler; swept through in final furlong when winning 16-runner maiden race at Leicester in September cleverly by ½ length from Hintonado; runs as though he'll stay 1m; tenderly handled at Leicester and probably still has improvement in him. *A. Hide.*

AJIMURA (USA)   3 b.c. Wajima–Clover Princess 110 (Right Tack 131)   (1980   —
6d⁴   1981 7g⁸ 7d)   lightly-built colt; not the best of movers; nearest at finish when 3 lengths fourth of 19 to stable-companion Barwin in minor event at Newmarket in May, better effort; will stay 1¼m; hasn't a lot of scope; sent to USA.   *H. Cecil.*

AKARAD (FR)   3 b. or br.c. Labus–Licata (Abdos 134)   (1980 NR   1981 10.5g* **130**
12d* 12g² 12.5g* 12f* 12d)

Akarad, in the same ownership as the absent Shergar, started 2/1 favourite for the Prix de l'Arc de Triomphe at Longchamp in October thanks to the strength of local opinion behind him.   Ardross had been favourite in the English ante-post books all the preceding week.   Whether Akarad, who had run only five times, deserved to start favourite was debatable but he certainly had a fine record.   His second place in the Prix du Jockey-Club at Chantilly in June had been his only defeat and he had subsequently turned the tables on the Jockey-Club winner Bikala in the Grand Prix de Saint-Cloud, a race in which the best-placed of the older horses had finished third.   At the time of the Arc he could be regarded as the leading French three-year-old middle-distance colt.   In the event Akarad ran respectably, better than his half-brother Acamas did against Alleged three years earlier, and finished a clear seventh of twenty-four behind Gold River.   He came strongly on the outside round the last turn and made his challenge to Bikala, Ardross and Perrault early in the straight; he was soon beaten off, though, and he finished about seven lengths behind the winner and over six behind Bikala.

Akarad didn't race as a two-year-old.   He was very short of experience, the least-experienced in the twelve-horse field, when he ran in the Prix du Jockey-Club.   He hadn't even taken part in a pattern race before.   He had won an event for newcomers at Longchamp in May in cracking style, and then the Prix de l'Avre on the same course three weeks later by a length and a half from his stable-companion Vayrann.   There were only four runners in the Prix de l'Avre, a race whose conditions of entry effectively excluded horses already proven in high-class company.   Possibly Akarad's lack of experience told against him in the Prix du Jockey-Club.   Saint-Martin would surely have hoped for a more forward position as the field turned for home with Bikala in a clear lead; Akarad had been among the backmarkers for much of the way, and still had a lot to do to catch a horse whom we now know to be a very powerful front runner.   To make matters worse Akarad had difficulty obtaining a run early in the straight.   When he got through he made ground steadily to show a clear second approximately a furlong out, and he chased the winner all the way home without making much impression.   Bikala beat him by four lengths.

Flying in the face of the Chantilly result, and despite the presence in the field of both the Coronation Cup second Prince Bee (who had top-class form in France the previous autumn) and the Prix du Cadran winner Gold River, Akarad started favourite for the Grand Prix de Saint-Cloud, a race run three weeks before the King George VI and Queen Elizabeth Diamond Stakes and one which is nearly always the first to bring together the best of different generations at a mile and a half.   The 1980 running had seen the defeat of the Prix du Jockey-

Grand Prix de Saint-Cloud—Akarad wins from
Bikala, Lancastrian and April Run

*Prix Niel, Longchamp—the long odds-on Akarad is
pushed out to beat Rahotep*

Club winner Policeman (another front-runner) by the dead-heaters Dunette
(a four-year-old filly) and Shakapour (second in the Jockey-Club), with Lancastrian fourth. In 1981 Lancastrian was to finish a good third, just ahead of
the three-year-old filly April Run with Gold River, Prince Bee and Argument
next, the last three clearly below their best and Prince Bee returning without
front shoes. Akarad won really well, by two lengths from Bikala. Significantly,
Akarad stuck closer to Bikala this time, and when Bikala, who was always up
there, hit the front early in the straight April Run, Akarad and, to a lesser
degree, Lancastrian, were in an attacking position. On this occasion, unlike in
the Arc, Akarad showed better pace than April Run: he produced much the best
turn of foot in the closing stages and put the two lengths between himself and
Bikala over the last furlong or so.

After the Grand Prix de Saint-Cloud Akarad was given a special preparation
for the Prix de l'Arc de Triomphe; most years, it seems, a good number of French
horses enjoy the benefit of such a preparation whereas desperately few English-
trained ones do. He didn't run again until September, nine weeks later, when
he took part in the Prix Niel over the Arc course; the Prix Niel is framed to
attract leading three-year-olds, and in 1980 was won by Prince Bee with Policeman unplaced. Many good horses have run in it over the years, some a fair bit
better than Prince Bee or Akarad. The latest field for the race wasn't up to
the usual standard and Akarad along with his pacemaker Vanann started at long
odds on. Akarad duly won, pushed out by half a length from the Prix du
Jockey-Club fourth Rahotep to whom he gave 2 lb. Making due allowance for all
the circumstances, including Akarad's looking a shade burly after his short
break, the winner didn't run a particularly impressive trial—nowhere near so
impressive as, for instance, Ardross' at Newbury three weeks earlier—and it was
a surprise that he started so short for the Arc.

Akarad (Fr) (b. or br.c. 1978)	Labus (br 1971)	Busted (b 1963)	Crepello
			Sans le Sou
		Cordovilla (b 1957)	Pharis
			Cordova
	Licata (b 1969)	Abdos (br 1959)	Arbar
			Pretty Lady
		Gaia (br 1962)	Shantung
			Gloriana

Akarad has an interesting pedigree, and a slightly unusual one for a top
horse. For a start he's not from one of the Aga Khan's long-established
families, as Shergar is. In the last few years the Aga Khan has acquired many
of the animals formerly belonging to two other leading French owner-breeders,
Mme Dupre and M Boussac; Vayrann comes from one of the Dupre families,
Akarad from one of Boussac's. Among the Boussac string at the time of its
dispersal were two stallions, Labus and Faunus, whom the Aga Khan subsequently presented to the French National Stud. Labus, sire of Akarad, stood
at a fee of approximately £50 at the beginning of the year. He made only three
starts as a three-year-old—winning a maiden race at Chantilly, and finishing
second to Kamaraan in the Prix du Conseil de Paris at Longchamp and third to
Card King in the Grand Prix de Marseille, each race run at a distance of around
a mile and a half; to say the least he must have been very useful. He has sired
other winners, among them Akarad's sister Akiyda who won a two-year-old race
over a mile and a quarter at Saint-Cloud in November and Sharsha who won a
mile nursery at Nottingham in 1980, but Akarad is easily his best so far. The

H.H. Aga Khan's "Akarad"

dam Licata was sent to the resident stallion Labus at a time when Boussac's textile business was in serious financial difficulties. She had been one of the better French middle-distance fillies of her generation, the winner of two pattern races, and was covered by top-class stallions in the early part of her stud career. She produced two winners by Mill Reef (Acamas and Eupalinos) and one by Caro (Licara) before Akarad. Acamas, of course, won the Prix du Jockey-Club and Prix Lupin and was a disqualified second to Ile de Bourbon in the King George VI and Queen Elizabeth Diamond Stakes. Licara was a very useful filly who finished second to Detroit in the Prix Chloe at Evry and a creditable sixth to Mrs Penny in the French Oaks; Eupalinos was a minor winner over thirteen and a half furlongs at Dundalk. Neither Licata's dam Gaia nor her grandam Gloriana managed to win, but Gloriana's full sister Corejada won the French One Thousand Guineas and Irish Oaks, and produced the Gold Cup winner Macip, the Derby runner-up Arcor and the French Oaks winner Apollonia. One could write on this family at considerably greater length if it were necessary, the fifth dam Djezima being one of the mainstays of Boussac's stud.

Akarad, a strong colt, has been retired to stud. He was well suited by a mile and a half. He never raced on really soft ground but he seemed to act on any other. *F. Mathet, France.*

AKIYDA 2 br.f. Labus–Licata (Abdos 134) (1981 10s*) April 21; sister to top-class French middle-distance 3-y-o Akarad, and half-sister to 3 winners, notably Prix Lupin and Prix du Jockey-Club winner Acamas (by Mill Reef); dam good winner at up to 1¼m in France; a very promising filly who won 14-runner maiden race at Saint-Cloud in November by 5 lengths from Miss Mat; sure to win good middle-distance races at 3yrs. *F. Mathet, France.* **113** p

AKRAM 3 ch.c. Sandford Lad 133–La Marne (Nashua) (1980 5s 5f* 5f⁴ 6g³ 7.2d² 7g³ 7fg 8d* 7v 1981 7g 7g 8f 7fg* 8g 8g⁴) sturdy colt; good mover; won handicap at Yarmouth in June easing up by 1½ lengths from Goldliner Game; had run creditably in well-contested handicaps earlier; stays 1m; seems to act on any going except perhaps heavy; sometimes sweats up but is genuine and consistent: sold to S. Pattemore 6,200 gns Newmarket Autumn Sales. *W. O'Gorman.* **86**

ALABAMA 3 gr.f. Warpath 113–Montana (Mossborough 126) (1980 8fg — 10d* 10.2s 1981 10d 10fg 10d 11.7d 12s⁴ 15.8g 18g 12d) strong, deep-girthed, sturdy filly; trotted up in seller at Leicester as a 2-y-o; no worthwhile form in 1981; should stay at least 1½m; suited by a soft surface; retained 1,000 guineas Doncaster November Sales. *D. Wilson.*

ALADYAT 4 b. or br.f. Home Guard 129–Moon Cake (Red God 128§) (1980 — 10.2fg 10.1g 10.1s 11.5g 8.2s 8d 1981 10f 15.8g) light-framed filly; only plating class; not certain to stay 1½m. *J. Blundell.*

ALAHLI (USA) 2 b.c. What A Pleasure–Jovial Josie (Sea-Bird II 145) (1981 — 5g) Feb 11; $90,000Y; strong, attractive colt; half-brother to 2 minor winners; dam poor sister to high-class filly Kittywake; 25/1 and distinctly burly, started very slowly when eighth of 10 to Prowess Prince in maiden race at Doncaster in May, only outing. *F. Durr.*

AL-ALLAM 3 ch.c. Sun Prince 128–Ladys View 109 (Tin Whistle 128) (1980 82 5fg 6g 5g 7v 1981 7g 7.3g 8f* 10f² 8g* 8d* 8fg) sturdy, well-made colt; good mover and a particularly good walker; won maiden race and handicap at Pontefract and a handicap at Beverley; stays 1¼m; probably acts on any going, except possibly very soft; rather disappointing final start (August). *B. Hills.*

AL AMEEN (USA) 2 b.c. Lyphard 132–Priceless Gem (Hail to Reason) — p (1981 7g) May 23; $375,000Y; well-grown, good sort; half-brother to several winners, notably outstanding filly Allez France (by Sea-Bird II); dam second best 2-y-o of her year, winning at up to 1m, and half-sister to champion American filly Affectionately; unquoted, led to halfway when last of 15 to Ivano in Houghton Stakes at Newmarket in October; should do better over further at 3yrs. *H. T. Jones.*

ALANGROVE SOUND (CAN) 3 gr.c. Champagne Charlie–De Soto Queen 58 (Fleet Nasrullah) (1980 6g³ 8fg³ 8g³ 10s 1981 12g 12g² 12.5f 14f³ 16f* 14fg³ 16.5f) neat colt; won poor maiden race at Beverley in June narrowly; stays 2m; acts on firm going; wears a tongue strap. *B. Hanbury.*

ALASIA 2 b.f. Thatch 136–Topling 85 (High Top 131) (1981 6g⁴) Mar 22; 81 p 17,000Y; compact filly; first foal; dam, half-sister to very useful sprinter Meiwa King, won over 7f and 1¼m; unquoted, didn't find her stride until last 2f in maiden race at Newmarket in October but then ran on very nicely to finish 3¼ lengths fourth of 22 to Ash Ridge, without jockey resorting to whip; will be suited by 7f and 1m; a useful filly in the making. *G. Pritchard-Gordon.*

ALASTOR O MAVROS (USA) 2 gr.c. Tentam–Carte Noire (Native Charger) 74 p (1981 7d 7fg 7g) May 7; $47,000Y; rangy, good sort; third foal; half-brother to a winner by Minnesota Mac; dam ran only twice; about 9 lengths seventh of 21 finishers behind Count Pahlen in maiden race at Newmarket in October, third outing and best effort; will stay 1¼m; the type to do better at 3yrs. *G. Harwood.*

ALAYHOM 2 br.g. Home Guard 129–Terramar Lass (Tom Rolfe) (1981 5d⁴ 5fg³ 60 5g 6g³ 6fg 6f⁴ 6fg) May 25; 6,600Y; brother to a plating-class animal, and half-brother to 2 winners, including fairly useful sprinter St Terramar (by St Alphage); dam ran once; poor maiden; will be suited by 7f; has given impression of being none too genuine and wore blinkers fifth and sixth outings; sold to Newmarket BA 720 gns Newmarket Autumn Sales. *W. O'Gorman.*

AL BINNS 3 br.g. So Blessed 130–Levandale 102 (Le Levanstell 122) (1980 NR — 1981 8g) second reported foal; half-brother to quite useful 1m to 1¼m winner Jondale (by Le Johnstan); dam prolific winner from 5f to 1¼m; unquoted when in rear in 25-runner minor event won by Park Place at Doncaster in November. *A. Smith.*

ALBION PRINCE 7 b.g. Prince Regent 129–Albionia 85 (Faberge II 121) 59 (1980 NR 1981 12.2d 9g 12s 10.6s³) fair stayer at his best; lightly raced on flat nowadays; not seen out after finishing third in seller at Haydock in May; suited by long distances; probably acts on any going; trained part of year by F. Rimell. *D. Leslie.*

ALBOSAGGIA (ITY) 3 b.f. Swing Easy 126–Acireale (Veronese) (1980 5f — 6d 8.2g 1981 7f 8f 10f) small, lightly-made filly; behind in maiden races and sellers. *E. Incisa.*

ALBUQUERQUE 3 ch.c. Hotfoot 126–Dancing Fire (Crepello 136) (1980 — NR 1981 8.3fg 7f 8.3g 8fg² 10fg 9d) smallish, sturdy colt; first foal; dam, sister to smart staying filly Pink Gem, started slowly only outing; stayed on well when second in seller at Salisbury in September; should be suited by 1¼m; sold 1,900 gns Ascot December Sales. *P. Cole.*

ALC

ALCOCK 8 b.g. Alcide 136–Bird 80 (Firestreak 125) (1980 NR 1981 14.6f **37** 19g³ 16f 15.8fg⁴ 16f) poor staying handicapper; acted on firm going; broke down final start; dead. *W. Elsey.*

ALCONBURY HILL 2 br.g. Pals Passage 115–Varamette (Varano) (1981 — 5g 6fg 7fg 7fg) Mar 15; IR 1,050F, 2,800Y; quite a useful sort; good mover; well behind in maiden races at Newmarket (3) and Catterick. *A. Jarvis.*

ALDEBURGH FESTIVAL 5 ch.h. Club House 110–Minor Chord 88 (Major **70 §** Portion 129) (1980 8fg 7.6f⁴ 8.5f² 8g 8fg³ 10f* 8fg³ 10g 8s 1981 10s 10fg 10g 8.5g 8g 7.6fg² 8fg² 8f 8.3g³ 8fg⁴ 8fg) good-looking, well-made horse; stays 1¼m; best on a firm surface; suitable mount for an apprentice; didn't look too genuine on occasions in 1981; sold 4,100 gns Newmarket Autumn Sales. *D. Whelan.*

ALDENHAM (USA) 3 ch.g. His Majesty–Mama's Silver (Silver King 119) **76** (1980 7g² 7d 6fg³ 7g 1981 10fg* 12g 10g³ 8f 10fg 10g⁴ 12fg 10fg 11.7g² 10.1fg³ 10f⁴ 11.7d 10d) smallish, fair sort; excellent mover; beat Ridgefield by a length in handicap at Kempton in April; in frame several times subsequently; stays 1½m; best form on a sound surface; blinkered eighth start. *G. Balding.*

ALDERSHAWE HALL 2 b.c. Wollow 132–Hatha 78 (Bold Reason) (1981 — 6s 6fg 6fg 6g) Apr 29; smallish, fair sort; poor walker; first foal; dam useful winner over 7f in France at 2 yrs but rather disappointing at 3 yrs; well behind in minor and maiden events, 3 of them at Newmarket. *R. Hollinshead.*

ALDINGTON BOY 3 b.c. Redundant 120–Golden Amaryllis 69 (Klondyke — Bill 125) (1980 NR 1981 8g 8fg) fair sort; second foal; dam stayed 6f; behind in minor event at Salisbury in June and maiden race on same course in August; still needed race in latter. *Mrs J. Reavey.*

ALDINGTON HONEY 2 b.f. Cawston's Clown 113–Dear Catalpa (Dear — Gazelle 113) (1981 8fg) May 12; fifth foal; dam won over hurdles; unquoted when behind in 17-runner maiden race won by Napa Valley at Leicester in September. *Mrs J. Reavey.*

ALEDA ROSE 4 b.f. Charlottown 127–Urugano 101 (Buisson Ardent 129) **42** (1980 11fg 8fg 7.2fg⁴ 7fg 7d* 7g⁴ 8fg* 9g 8s 12f 8f 8.2s 1981 8g 8g 7g 10f 9fg 10g* 9g) leggy, unfurnished filly; plater; won at Ayr in July (no bid); stayed 1¼m; acted on a firm and a soft surface; sold 3,000 gns, covered by Billion, Newmarket December Sales. *J. Wilson.*

ALEOS (FR) 4 b.g. Faunus–Aphytis (Crepello 136) (1980 12f⁴ 10f* 10fg* — 10.1g 10fg³ 10g³ 10fg*) 1981 12s) workmanlike gelding; fairly useful in 1980; well beaten in amateur riders handicap at Ascot in October on only start at 4 yrs; stays 1¼m; acts on firm going; sweated up, misbehaved in paddock and looked ungenuine when blinkered once in 1980. *J. Old.*

ALETHE 3 br.f. Derring-Do 131–Argitone (Aureole 132) (1980 6d 1981 **55** 8g 8d 9.4g³ 9f 7d⁴ 8s 8s) quite a well-made filly; in frame in maiden races at Carlisle and Ayr; stays 9f; sold to BBA 2,000 gns Newmarket December Sales. *J. Douglas-Home.*

ALEV 2 ch.c. Hot Spark 126–St Citrus 108 (Relic) (1981 5s 5g⁴ 5f 5d³ 5g⁴) **84** Apr 15; 12,000Y; useful-looking colt; brother to fairly useful 1979 2-y-o 5f performer Lucy Limelight, and half-brother to several winners, including smart sprinter Florestan (by Petingo) and very useful French 9f to 1¼m winner Schoeller (by Nashua); dam miler; in frame at Newbury twice, running well when 1¼ lengths third of 20 to Path To Glory in maiden race in September, and at Ascot (6½ lengths fourth of 12 to Hampton Bay in £3,200 event) later in month; will stay 6f; ran poorly at Folkestone third start and is possibly not at his best on firm going. *M. Masson.*

ALEXANDER NEVSKY 3 b.c. Furry Glen 121–Levanstell Queen (Le Levanstell — 122) (1980 6g 6s 1981 10s 11.7g 8fg 10.8fg) rangy, useful-looking colt; behind in varied company, including selling; sold 1,400 gns Ascot August Sales. *M. Blanshard.*

ALEX CHOICE 2 ch.g. Gay Fandango 132–Eileen's Choice 106 (Tin Whistle — 128) (1981 7fg) Mar 22; IR 13,500F, IR 17,000Y; strong gelding; half-brother to a winner in Italy by Green God; dam won all her 5 starts, each over 5f at 2 yrs; 14/1, well there 5f when ninth of 15 to Jiretta in minor event at Doncaster in July, only outing. *B. Hanbury.*

ALEY 3 ch.f. Mount Hagen 127–Alsaga 86 (Alcide 136) (1980 6fg 6fg⁴ 7d³ **76** 1981 8d 10g³ 10.4d⁴ 10fg 9s*) deep-girthed, useful-looking filly; beat Masquerader by 6 lengths in maiden race at Wolverhampton in October; stays 1¼m; got rather upset before third start; sold 9,800 gns Newmarket December Sales. *J. Dunlop.*

ALFANZINA 2 ch.f. Gay Fandango 132–Schloss 87 (Busted 134) (1981 6g) —
Mar 24; 7,000Y; robust filly; second foal; dam, 1¼m performer, is sister to dam
of Gimcrack winner Stanford; 33/1 and backward, moved short to post when last
of 17 to Merlin's Charm in maiden race at Newmarket in October. *G. Pritchard-Gordon.*

ALFIE DICKINS 3 ro.c. Spanish Gold 101–Vila Real 76 (Town Crier 119) **53**
(1980 7d 6g 1981 7s 8d 8fg 7s 8.2g³ 8fg 8.2f⁴ 8fg 9.4g⁴ 7.6s 9g 8d⁴ 9s) robust
colt; plating-class maiden; stays 1m; ran respectably in blinkers twelfth start.
R. Hollinshead.

ALFRED MILNER 4 gr.c. Roan Rocket 128–French Music (French Beige 127) **41**
(1980 8fg³ 8fg 10f 8.2f³ 8fg 8g 10f* 10s² 1981 10g 10f 10fg⁴ 10f 10f 10.6f 11fg
10f³ 10g⁴ 10g 10f² 10g 10fg 10f 10.6s) small colt; not a good mover in his
slower paces; plater; suited by 1¼m; acts on any going; best in blinkers; twice
looked sour in 1981. *W. Stubbs.*

ALGARDI (USA) 2 ch.c. Avatar–Abergwaun 128 (Bounteous 125) (1981 **91**
including 5g* 5g³ 6d* 6f²) well-made, attractive colt; good mover; half-
brother to 3-y-o Henrietta Maria (by Forli); dam top-class and courageous
sprinter; convincing winner of minor event at Newmarket in May and 7-runner
Staff Ingham Stakes at Epsom (by 2½ lengths from Little Robert) the following
month; odds on when 5 lengths second of 6 to My Dad Tom in minor event at
Pontefract later in June; subsequently raced in USA; will probably stay 1m;
best form with some give in the ground. *H. Cecil.*

AL HASA (USA) 2 gr.g. Al Hattab–Rosey Rolfe (Tom Rolfe) (1981 5d **88**
5f² 6fg 6f 6g* 6f²) Mar 29; $35,000Y; attractive gelding; good mover; third
foal; half-brother to winners by Executioner and Youth; dam, half-sister to
very successful broodmare Peace, won over 1¼m; showed much improved form
when making all to beat Prince Gleam by 3 lengths in 26-runner maiden race at
Nottingham in August; no match for odds-on Wattlefield in small race at Yarmouth later in month; will be suited by 7f and 1m; blinkered last 2 outings;
racing in Hong Kong. *H. Cecil.*

ALICE TOWN (USA) 3 b.f. Prince Dantan–South Bimini (Sir Ribot) (1980 **56**
8g 7s 7g 1981 11.7f 8f³ 12.2g 10d⁴ 8fg 10s 10s) lengthy, useful-looking filly;
ridden by 7-lb claimer when third in poor maiden race at Pontefract in July;
little other worthwhile form, including in sellers; best run at 1m on firm going
though should stay further; sold 1,050 gns Newmarket December Sales. *R. Sheather.*

ALIK (FR) 3 br.f. Targowice 130–Kaliope (Klairon 131) (1980 6g⁴ 8g² 8g² **113**
8g² 8v⁴ 1981 8g* 8s* 10s 8g) French filly; half-sister to 4 winners, including
useful French middle-distance winner Princesse Kay (by Roi Lear); dam, very
useful 7½f and 10½f winner, is sister to dam of Irish River; won maiden race at
Maisons-Laffitte in April and Group 3 Prix de Sandringham at Chantilly in
June, beating by a length from Attirance after getting loose at start; in rear in
Prix de Malleret at Longchamp and Prix d'Astarte at Deauville subsequently;
stays 1m; acts on soft going. *A. Head, France.*

AL KHASHAB 4 ch.g. Habat 127–Parlais 101 (Pardao 120) (1980 8v 8h 9g³ **58**
8g³ 8f 9s² 8d 10d 1981 10g 8d 8d 10.6s 9f 10.6f² 8f⁴ 11.5d 10g 10fg² 10g⁴ 12d
10.2g 12s 10.2g⁴) workmanlike gelding; poor maiden; fourth in valuable seller
final start; stays 1¼m; acts on any going. *R. Hollinshead.*

AL KUWAIT 5 br.h. Blakeney 126–Camenae 72 (Vimy 132) (1980 12d² 12fg² **86**
14g² 16.1d* 12f⁴ 18d 1981 13s* 16fg 14fg² 18.4d 16s⁴ 16fg* 14d 14fg 16s² 13s³
14g²) strong, good-bodied horse; fair handicapper; awarded race at Nottingham in April and beat Dragon Palace a neck at Newbury in July; stays well;
acts on any going, but is suited by some give in the ground; doesn't always look
too enthusiastic, has shown a tendency to hang and is not an easy ride; blinkered
last 3 starts in 1980; trained part of season by J. Sutcliffe. *G. Harwood.*

ALLANSTOWN 5 b.g. Charlottown 127–Saucy Kate 85 (March Past 124) —
(1980 NR 1981 8d 8f 7g 12f) of little account on flat though has won a selling
hurdle; usually wears blinkers. *H. O'Neill.*

ALLAN WELLS 2 ch.g. Queen's Hussar 124–Baggage 86 (Zeus Boy 121) **80**
(1981 5v 5g 5g 5d 5fg 7fg 7g* 7fg⁴ 7g 8fg 8.2d 7d 8d) Mar 15; compact gelding;
half-brother to fair sprinter Bunny Boy (by Right Boy); dam stayed 1m; 33/1,
improved enormously on previous efforts when making all to win 9-runner
maiden race at Ayr in July by a length from odds-on Ishkomann; respectable

fourth to Chulia Street in minor event at Redcar later in month; should stay
1m; blinkered tenth and eleventh outings (last of 15 when faced with stiff task
in nursery on eleventh). *T. Craig.*

ALLA TURCA 2 ch.g. Steel Heart 128–Icaza (Go Marching) (1981 6fg 7f
8.2d 5g) Feb 10; IR 9,000F, IR 15,500Y; compact gelding; in rear in maiden
race and sellers; blinkered third outing. *P. Haslam.*

ALLEGRETTA 3 ch.f. Lombard 126–Anatevka (Espresso 122) (1980 8fg* **97**
9d* 10g² 1981 12g² 12g 14.6g) tall, lightly-made filly; won at Leicester and
Wolverhampton as a 2-y-o; in need of race, kept on when 3 lengths second of 7
to Leap Lively in Johnnie Walker Oaks Trial at Lingfield in May; tailed off in
Oaks at Epsom the following month and in Park Hill Stakes at Doncaster in
September; sweating and unimpressive in paddock when blinkered in last-
named race; stays 1½m; sold 24,000 gns Newmarket December Sales. *M.
Stoute.*

ALLEGRO STAR 2 ch.c. Sir Albert 72–Orbenita (Orbit 106) (1981 6g 10g) —
May 24; plain colt; of little account. *J. Mulhall.*

ALL FOR YOU 2 b.f. Martinmas 128–Blue Draco (Majority Blue 126) (1981 **69**
5g 5fg 6f⁴ 5fg³ 6g 7f 5h) Feb 26; 5,400Y; leggy filly; first foal; dam unraced
half-sister to very useful French miler Welsh Game; quite moderate form in
varied company; stays 7f; yet to race on a soft surface; not disgraced in blinkers
fifth outing; consistent. *W. O'Gorman.*

ALLIED BEAUMEL 3 ch.f. Jimmy Reppin 131–Tarmandy (Black Tarquin —
136) (1980 5s 6fg 6s 7d 6d 1981 8fg 8s 8g 8d 7fg⁴ 7f) compact filly; has shown
a little ability; stays 1m. *S. Harris.*

ALLIED CARDIFF 3 b.f. Import 127–Monday Morning (Royal Record II) **44**
(1980 5f 5fg 5f 6f² 6g 6fg 6fg³ 6f 6s* 6fg 8d 1981 6g 6g 7g³ 8f 8f 8f⁴ 7s 8s⁴ 8.2s²)
compact filly; plater; stays 1m; has run respectably on firm going, but goes
well on soft; wears blinkers; retained 720 gns Newmarket Autumn Sales. *G.
Blum.*

ALLIED LONDON 2 ch.c. Jimmy Reppin 131–Yofi (Articulate 121) (1981 —
5d 5s 5f 6g) June 12; strong colt; second foal; dam poor novice hurdler; no
worthwhile form in maiden and minor events; off course 4 months before final
start (dwelt). *S. Harris.*

ALL IN 3 ch.c. Lauso–Summer Rain (Palestine 133) (1980 7f 8d⁴ 10s 1981 **59**
7fg* 8g 10d 8f 10.1fg²) small, narrow colt; bought in 2,250 gns after beating
Venja gamely by 1½ lengths in seller at Kempton in April; ran best subsequent
race on final start (June); stays 1¼m. *D. Sasse.*

ALL IN ORDER 2 b.c. Tudor Melody 129 or Riboboy 124–Set Right (Never ?
Bend) (1981 7s*) May 28; first live foal; dam, winner over 6f in Ireland, is
sister to very smart stakes winner Triple Bend; won 8-runner newcomers event
at Saint-Cloud in October by a length from Lysippos; a late foal who will make
a useful 3-y-o over 1¼m+. *J. Cunnington, jnr, France.*

ALL MOSS 3 b.f. Prince Tenderfoot 126–All Beige (Ballyciptic 122) (1980 **66**
7d 7g 1981 8fg 11.7s⁴ 12d² 11.7f² 11.7fg 10.2f³ 10.8fg* 12g) neat, strong
filly; beat Oratavo a neck in apprentice handicap at Warwick in July; gives
impression she'll stay beyond 1½m; acts on any going; usually apprentice
ridden nowadays. *P. Cole.*

ALLOCATED (USA) 2 ch.c. Nodouble–Necie's Pride (Sky High II) (1981 **90**
6fg* 8g) Mar 13; $145,000Y; smallish, strong, quite attractive colt; quite
closely inbred to outstanding Australian stallion Star Kingdom; first foal;
dam, winner of 6 sprint races, is half-sister to very useful stakes winners He's
Dewan and Don't Be Late Jim; looked decidedly in need of race on debut in
10-runner Clarence House Stakes at Ascot in September but put up a very
pleasing effort to win by ¾ length from Snow Forecast, making steady progress
at halfway and then running on well under sympathetic handling to lead inside
final furlong; beaten a fair way when sixth of 11 to Maria Stuarda in Premio
Tevere at Rome in November; should stay 1m. *W. Hastings-Bass.*

ALLO CHERIE (FR) 3 ch.f. Sanctus II 132–Nobla (Dicta Drake 126) (1980 **51**
NR 1981 10g 10fg 16.5f 14.6f 12fg 13.8g²) 12,000 francs Y (approx £1,270);
neat, lightly-made filly; third foal; sister to modest stayer Noblissimo; dam
won twice at around 1¼m in France; second in seller at Catterick in September;
suited by a test of stamina; sold 460 gns Newmarket Autumn Sales. *D. Morley.*

ALL RISKS 2 b.f. Pitcairn 126–Willow Bird 74 (Weepers Boy 124) (1981 **90**
8fg 8d* 8g) Apr 15; IR 10,000Y; lengthy, attractive filly; half-sister to 3-y-o
First Contact (by Simbir) and 2 winners, including Willow Red (by Red Alert),

successful at up to 1m; dam stayed 1m; stayed on bravely when winning 11-runner maiden race at Wolverhampton in October by 1½ lengths from Sunny Look; not disgraced next time out; will stay 1¼m; acts on a soft surface. *P. Cole.*

ALL SUMMER 3 ch.f. Sun Prince 128–Right Now 100 (Right Royal V 135)   **56**
(1980 7.2s 1981 12.2g² 12fg 12f) lightly-made filly; head second of 15 to Quickbeam in maiden event at Catterick in June, easily best effort; stays 1½m; possibly needs some give in the ground. *M. Jarvis.*

ALLTEN UNLIMITED 2 b.g. Scottish Rifle 127–Habilite 94 (Habitat 134)   **71**
(1981 6g* 6f 6g³ 6g²) Apr 24; IR 4,000F, 1,800Y, 1,000 2-y-o; small, lightly-made gelding; third produce; half-brother to 1979 2-y-o 5f winner Primula Girl (by Mount Hagen); dam best at up to 6f; sold out of M. Naughton's stable 5,400 gns after winning £1,700 seller at Newcastle in June; not disgraced subsequently; will be suited by 7f; racing in Hong Kong. *B. Hanbury.*

ALL THERE (USA) 2 gr.g. Al Hattab–Luring Dora (Lurullah) (1981 5s   **—**
5d 6g 6d) Feb 22; $40,000Y; stocky, short-legged gelding; half-brother to 5 winners by Mito, including 2 stakes-placed animals; dam never ran; no worthwhile form; off course 3 months before fourth outing (prominent over 4f). *B. Swift.*

ALLYA (USA) 2 gr.f. Little Current–Harrapan Seal 117 (Habitat 134) (1981   **74**
7g 7f 7fg 7g*) Apr 21; $140,000Y; neat filly; second foal; dam, smart at 2 yrs when winner over 7f, is sister to Steel Heart and Smokey Lady; kept on when 1½ lengths third of 19 to My Destiny in maiden event at Yarmouth in September, easily best effort; ran moderately at Catterick next time out; will stay 1m. *H. T. Jones.*

ALMA ATA 3 b.f. Bustino 136–Armandia 61 (Alcide 136) (1980 NR 1981   **113**
10fg 12d* 10.2g² 12.2fg* 12.2fg³ 12fg² 14d* 12fg³ 14fg² 14.6g* 16g* 15.5v)
    The fields for the Park Hill Stakes, which used to be known as the fillies' St Leger, have varied in standard in recent seasons. The race sometimes clashes with the more prestigious Prix Vermeille, as it did in 1981 when the Park Hill lost the English and French Oaks thirds, Leap Lively and April Run, to the greater attraction of the Longchamp race. Favourite at Doncaster was the Irish-trained Condessa, who had won the Yorkshire Oaks by a neck from Leap Lively; the best of the other twelve runners seemed to be Ma Femme, Rollrights and Canton Lightning, the first three in the Galtres Stakes at York, and Rhein Bridge and Royal Realm who had fought out a close finish to the Lancashire Oaks. Truth to tell, the leading three-year-old staying fillies trained in England weren't a particularly bright lot and the Park Hill field was more notable for its quantity—it was the largest field assembled for the race since 1954—than for its quality. Victory went to the 25/1-chance Alma Ata who was having her eleventh outing of the season and was running for the first time in a pattern race. Alma Ata's victories before Doncaster had been gained in minor events

Park Hill Stakes, Doncaster—Alma Ata (second from left) wins in a driving finish from Salora Lady (breastgirth), Ma Femme (right) and Royal Realm (far left)

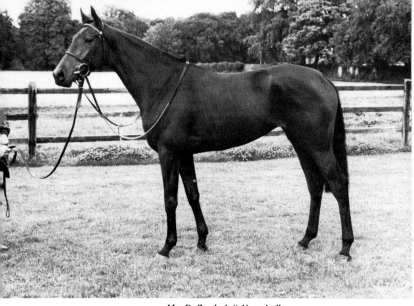

Mrs D. Zurcher's "Alma Ata"

at Salisbury and Folkestone in May and Catterick in June and in a handicap at Yarmouth in July; she had shown herself to be a most genuine and consistent performer, well suited by a test of stamina, but she looked no better than fairly useful. Alma Ata stayed on very well to get up close to the line in the Park Hill after looking likely to finish only third or fourth with less than two furlongs to go. One of the 50/1 rank outsiders Salora Lady came second, three quarters of a length behind Alma Ata and half a length in front of Ma Femme with the strong-finishing Royal Realm, who would probably have won with a clear run, a close fourth. Both Alma Ata and Salora Lady showed much improved form at Doncaster and both won handicaps before they could be re-assessed—Alma Ata won a £4,000 event at Newmarket by five lengths, carrying a 5-lb penalty, and Salora Lady won the more valuable Bogside Cup at Ayr. Alma Ata also performed with credit in the Prix Royal-Oak at Longchamp at the end of October, finishing a ten-length fifth of seven to Ardross.

Alma Ata (b.f. 1978)	Bustino (b 1971)	Busted (b 1963)	Crepello / Sans le Sou
		Ship Yard (ch 1963)	Doutelle / Paving Stone
	Armandia (b 1965)	Alcide (b 1955)	Alycidon / Chenille
		Success (br 1955)	Arctic Prince / Lake Success

We shall not be concerned with Alma Ata in the next season; she has been retired to the paddocks and is to be covered by Final Straw. A good-topped filly, Alma Ata cost 26,000 guineas as a yearling and did not race as a two-year-old. Her dam Armandia, a lightly-raced sister to the Observer Gold Cup (now the William Hill Futurity) winner Approval, has bred two other winners: Levandia (by Le Levanstell), a moderate filly who won twice at a mile and a half as a three-year-old, and the five-year-old Carlingford Lough (by Thatch) who has won on the flat in Ireland at up to a mile and a half and is also a winner over hurdles. Alma Ata probably acted on any going. She had

60

a very busy season, being kept on the go from the end of April to the end of October, and she proved herself a thoroughly tough and sound individual. *L. Cumani.*

ALMIGHTY ZEUS 4 ch.g. High Line 125–Zeus Girl 75 (Zeus Boy 121) (1980 —
11fg⁴ 16f 12g 16g 1981 18fg) staying maiden. *D. Gandolfo.*

ALMOND VALLEY 4 ch.f. Jimmy Reppin 131–Videmanette (High Perch 85
126) (1980 11fg² 12.2d* 12fg* 14g³ 1981 16.1fg² 18.4d³ 20fg 16g 16g³ 17.4g³
18g) useful sort; good walker; fair staying handicapper; placed 4 times,
running well on final occasion when a length third to subsequently-disqualified
Beechwood Seeker in Eglinton and Winton Memorial Handicap at Ayr in
September; probably suited by some give in the ground; sold 14,500 gns Newmarket December Sales. *J. W. Watts.*

ALMUNICAR 4 b.f. Sharpen Up 127–Zorelia (Chingacgook 128) (1980 8f 72
6g 6g 1981 6g⁴ 7g 7fg) leggy, unfurnished filly; best form at 6f though is
bred to stay further; acts well on firm going; blinkered third start. *R. Boss.*

AL NASR 3 b.c. Green Dancer 132–Padrona 103 (St Paddy 133) (1980 8g 1981 80 §
10.2f 14g²(dis) 14g² 14fg* 18.8fg³ 14fg² 16g³ 14s² 16s) rangy, good-looking
colt; long odds on when winning 3-runner maiden event at Yarmouth in August;
moved down a place after beating Court Cavalier 2 lengths in similar race at
Sandown on previous start (swerved violently left) and after beating Splendidly
Gay a head in £3,200 event at York in September on penultimate outing (looked
most unwilling to struggle and bumped runner-up twice); stays very well;
probably acts on any going; has a fair amount of ability but is ungenuine and
not to be relied upon. *J. Dunlop.*

AL NASR (FR) 3 b.c. Lyphard 132–Caretta (Caro 133) (1980 8g* 1981 11g* 121
10v* 12d 10g² 10f*) 550,000 francs Y (approx £58,000); strong, good sort;
first foal; dam, minor winner over 9.5f and 11f in France, is half-sister to Klaizia,
herself dam of smart miler Lypheor (by Lyphard); won Prix de Suresnes and
Group 3 Prix la Force, both at Longchamp in May, and Group 3 Prix de la
Cote Normande at Deauville in August; beat Brustolon easily by 2½ lengths
in last-named race; went down by only a neck to Bellman in 10-runner Prix
Eugene Adam at Saint-Cloud on fourth start (had Church Parade and Kirtling
behind in third and fourth), but was never going and ran unaccountably badly
when last but one behind Shergar in Derby on his only other outing; will stay
1½m; acts on any going; very smart; reportedly injured a fore-joint on the gallops
after final start, and subsequently had a quarter share in him sold to Spendthrift Farm, but remains in training in 1982. *A. Fabre, France.*

ALOA (USA) 2 b.c. Hawaii–C'mon Up (on-and-On) (1981 7g 8g 8.2s) June —
2; $26,000Y; lengthy, plain colt; half-brother to 6 minor winners; dam won
over 6f at 2 yrs; behind in large fields of maidens prior to finishing about 7
lengths sixth of 14 to Sovereign's Image in seller at Nottingham in October
(blinkered); will be suited by middle distances. *G. Harwood.*

ALOE (USA) 2 b.f. Silent Screen–Turning Bold (Turn-to) (1981 7d 6d*) Apr 93 p
25; $275,000Y; third foal; half-sister to Explosivo (by Delta Judge), a very useful
stakes winner at up to 1m; dam, stakes-placed winner at up to 7f, is out of half-
sister to Red God; bumped at start when 5/4 favourite for Group 3 Park Stakes
at the Curragh in October on debut and failed to recover, coming home sixteenth
of 18 behind More Heather; left that form well behind when odds on for 22-
runner maiden race on same course later in month, winning impressively by
4 lengths from Red Realm; sure to make a smart filly at around 1m. *V. O'Brien,
Ireland.*

ALPHA-EL-GRECO 2 gr.c. Abwah 118–Eurolink (Current Coin 118) (1981 51
5g 5f 7fg 7fg 8.2fg 6fg 6s) Feb 3; small, strong colt; only poor form, including
in sellers; blinkered final start. *R. Whitaker.*

ALPHA OMEGA 2 b.g. Auction Ring 123–Hey Dolly (Saint Crespin III 132) 70
(1981 5s 5s³ 5s³ 5fg⁴ 6s² 7fg 7f 8d 8s) May 18; 6,400Y; well-grown, workmanlike
gelding; good mover; fifth foal; dam, half-sister to smart sprinter Royal Captive,
was third twice in USA; only quite moderate; will probably stay 1¼m; seems to
act on any going; very coltish and unruly in paddock when blinkered on seventh
outing and was subsequently gelded. *R. Williams.*

ALPINE ROCKET 4 ch.g. Shiny Tenth 120–Dusty Bluebell (Sky Gipsy 117) 86
(1980 6s 7d·6fg* 6f* 6fg* 6g* 5.8fg 6d³ 6g² 6g 6g 6fg 6gf 6d 1981 6s 6fg² 6g 6s
6g 6fg 6g³ 6f 6fg 6fg 6f 6fg 6fg 6gf 6fg* 6g 6s* 6s) lengthy, useful sort; sprint
handicapper; won at Leicester in September and Folkestone (apprentices) in
October; best at 6f; acts on any going but is ideally suited by top-of-the-ground;

61

wears blinkers; suitable mount for a boy; sold to D. H. Jones 5,000 gns Doncaster November Sales. *G. Balding.*

AL ROS 2 b.c. Comedy Star 121–Soldier Girl (Queen's Hussar 124) (1981 5f 6f 6fg³ 6d 6fg 8g 8s) Feb 27; 350Y, 4,000 2-y-o; small, heavy-topped colt; poor plater; blinkered fifth start. *J. Czerpak.* —

AL ROSINA 2 br.f. Cawston's Clown 113–Wayside Dancer 57 (Road House II) (1981 5fg 5f) Apr 22; 1,600 2-y-o; fair sort; second foal; dam won 1m seller; well behind in maiden races at Warwick and Wolverhampton (still needed race) in June. *J. Czerpak.* —

AL SANDRO 2 ch.g. Jimmy Reppin 131–Runaway (St Paddy 133) (1981 5f 7fg 6d³ 5f) May 8; workmanlike gelding; no sign of ability, including in a seller. *J. Czerpak.* —

ALTAGHADERRY RUN 6 b.m. Deep Run 119–Curry Lass (Light Thrust 114) (1980 N R 1981 12s) ex-Irish mare; winning hurdler; remote fifth in minor event won by Ilmaz at Folkestone in March, first outing on flat. *J. Yardley.*

ALTALENA (USA) 2 b.f. Torsion–Penelope Who (Researching) (1981 5g 7f) Apr 30; $13,000F; leggy, quite attractive filly; first produce; dam won 5f claiming race at 2 yrs; having first race for over 2 months, faded quickly after leading to 2f out when 11 lengths fifth of 10 to Fol Hardi in maiden race at Yarmouth in August. *L. Cumani.* —

ALUWHITE HABIT 2 b.c. Hittite Glory 125–Tritonia 69 (Tyrant) (1981 6g) May 31; strong, well-made colt; first foal; dam placed from 6f to 1m here and in Ireland; unquoted when behind in 22-runner maiden race won by Ash Ridge at Newmarket in October (showed a round action on way to start). *W. Holden.* —

ALUWHITE VENTURE 4 ch.c. Reliance II 137–Fierte (Relic) (1980 10g 14.6d 1981 10s) leggy colt; in rear in varied company, including selling. *W. Holden.* —

ALVOR (GER) 2 b.c. Lombard 126–Agora (Pantheon) (1981 7g* 7s² 7g) lengthy, rather lightly-made colt; half-brother to German 1,000 Guineas winner Aviatik (by My Swallow); dam, half-sister to German Derby winner Alpenkonig, was second best German 2-y-o filly in 1971 and won at up to 9f; didn't have a great deal to beat when favourite for 17-runner maiden race at Leicester in September but did so in great style, scoring by 5 lengths from Change Habit; far from disgraced when 7 lengths second of 11 to Paradis Terrestre in Hyperion Stakes at Ascot the following month but could finish only sixth of 18, 6 lengths behind Straeker, when well-backed favourite for £4,500 nursery at Newmarket later in October; will stay 1½m; acts on soft going. *M. Stoute.* **101**

ALWAYS ALERT 2 b.f. Red Alert 127–Lancette (Double Jump 131) (1981 6d 7fg) Apr 14; big, well-made filly; third foal; closely related to fairly useful 1979 Irish 2-y-o 7f winner Lagolette (by Green God), and half-sister to smart 3-y-o 7f winner Rasa Penang (by Gay Fandango); dam, half-sister to Gimcrack winner Golden Horus, placed at up to 1½m in France; far from fully wound up when in rear in Woodcote Stakes at Epsom in June and £3,800 event at Sandown (last of 12) in July; sold to Curragh BA 9,000 gns Newmarket Autumn Sales. *R. Simpson.* —

ALWAYS A VALENTINE 2 ch.f. Moulton 128–Ice Ballet 87 (Ballymoss 136) (1981 5s 8g) Feb 13; 18,000Y; good-bodied filly; half-sister to several winners, including fairly useful 1½m winner Tanara (by Romulus), herself the dam of Count Pahlen; dam stayer; behind in maiden races at Windsor in May and Newmarket in October (decidedly burly); bred to stay at least 1½m. *G. Huffer.* —

ALWAYS EIRLYS 3 ch.f. Toujours Pret 121–Eirlys 90 (Elopement 125) (1980 7g 5d 1981 7g 8g 8s² 8s* 10.6s* 10.2d 8f 10f³ 12.3s 12fg) rangy filly; good walker; improved and won handicaps at Wolverhampton and Haydock (slowly-run 3-horse race by 10 lengths from Dawn Redwood), both in May; stays 1½m; acts on any going, but is well suited by soft; often apprentice ridden; sometimes starts slowly. *N. Callaghan.* **58**

ALYEM 2 br.f. Lear Jet 123–Hethersent 71 (Hethersett 134) (1981 5s) May 9; 1,400Y; small filly; half-sister to 2 winning platers and a winner in Sweden; dam won at 1½m; unquoted and apprentice ridden, swerved at start and always tailed off in 16-runner auction event at Leicester in March, only start. *R. Smyth.* —

AMALFI BAY 4 b.f. Lauso–Sweet Alcide 52 (Alcide 136) (1980 N R 1981 12s 12d 14f 16d) beaten a long way in maiden and minor events. *M. Bolton.* —

AMAL NAJI 3 b.c. Rheingold 137–Nothing On (St Chad 120) (1980 7f 7d 8g³ 10.2s 1981 12g³ 10d 12g* 12fg* 14g 12fg⁴ 12fg 14g) tall, leggy, narrow colt; stayed on very strongly when winning maiden race at York (by 7 lengths from Northern Supremo, who was eased) and handicap at Newmarket (beat Jamshid **96**

1½ lengths), both in July; also in frame twice at Newmarket, making running and staying on when about 2½ lengths fourth to Grain Race in handicap in August; stays 1½m well; possibly needs a sound surface; blinkered last 2 outings in 1980; reportedly broke a blood vessel second outing; had stiff task seventh start. *W. O'Gorman.*

AMANDALEX 2 ch.f. Roi Soleil 125–South Georgia 80 (Ballymoss 136) (1981 — 5d) May 20; first reported foal; dam well suited by long distances; tailed-off eleventh of 13 to Floral Elegance in maiden race at Newbury in April, only start; sold 300 gns Ascot September Sales. *P. Cole.*

AMANDA MARY 3 b.f. Wishing Star 117–Marchpane (Parthia 132) (1980 46 5v 5v 5g³ 5d 5g 5f⁴ 5g 5g³ 5g 5f 5d 5g⁴ 5d 1981 6g 8fg 8f 6f⁴ 6g³ 7fg³ 6d² 7s⁴ 6v 6g 6d) lengthy filly; in frame in maiden and minor events and sellers; stays 7f; usually wears blinkers; none too genuine. *W. Stubbs.*

AMBER AFFAIR 2 ch.f. Amboise 113–Dawn Affair 77 (Entanglement 118) — (1981 5d 5d 6f 6g 5fg 7f) Mar 15; second foal; dam ran 49 times on flat and over hurdles but failed to win; no worthwhile form, including in sellers. *P. K. Mitchell.*

AMBERDAMUS 2 b.c. Mandamus 120–Amber Moon (Amber Rama 133) (1981 57 5d 5fg 5f³ 5f* 6f 5f) Apr 9; 1,900F, 3,000Y; small, sturdy colt; good walker; first produce; dam, half-sister to Sharpen Up, was tailed off both starts; bought in 1,200 gns after making all to win 5-runner seller at Hamilton in June; should stay 6f; blinkered third outing. *H. Wharton.*

AMBER PALACE 3 ch.f. Sallust 134–Breide's Wood (Le Levanstell 122) — (1980 5f 5fg⁴ 5.8fg⁴ 5g⁴ 1981 5fg 6s⁴ 6g) attractive filly; only plating class; runs as though 5f is her trip; sold 1,050 gns Newmarket July Sales. *G. Hunter.*

AMBERUSH 4 ch.f. No Rush–Amberdonna 52 (Amber Rama 133) (1980 41 NR 1981 7fg 10d 12f⁴ 12g 12g) plater; stays 1½m. *P. Ashworth.*

AMBER VALE 4 gr.f. Warpath 113–Jackies Joy (Skymaster 126) (1980 82 10.5f 11fg* 11d* 9.4g* 12g 11s² 10.6s 11fg² 10.2d* 10g 12v 1981 10.6d 12d 11g 9g 12s 12g) tall filly; fairly useful at her best; below form most starts in 1981 though wasn't disgraced in £7,600 handicap at Ayr in September on third outing; should stay 1½m; probably acts on any going; sold 6,300 gns Doncaster November Sales. *J. Hanson.*

AMBER WAVES 2 b.f. Run The Gantlet–Oatlands (Secretariat) (1981 8d — 7g) June 3; small, narrow, short-backed filly; first foal; dam winner over 9.5f in Ireland, is out of half-sister to high-class American horse State Dinner; always behind in maiden races at Wolverhampton and Leicester in October; bred to stay middle distances; lacks scope. *F. J. Houghton.*

AMBIANCE 2 gr.c. Three Legs 128–Ambient 68 (Amber Rama 133) (1981 82 7g 7d⁴) Apr 3; 10,000Y; compact, useful-looking colt; third foal; half-brother to useful sprinter Westacombe (by Huntercombe); dam lightly raced; noted staying on nicely when about 13 lengths seventh of 23 to Simply Great in maiden race at Newmarket in October and about 4½ lengths fourth to Parthia's Picture in minor event at Chepstow later in month; runs as though he'll stay 1m. *M. Jarvis.*

AMBLER 5 b.h. Simbir 130–Am Stretchin (Ambiorix 130) (1980 12d 12g² 83 16.1f⁴ 14g⁴ 12g² 12g* 16.1d 11.7d 12fg 12g 12fg⁴ 12g* 12g³ 1981 12g 12fg⁴ 12s 11d 12fg 12d 12g 12g 14d 12fg* 12fg⁴ 13.3d 12d⁴ 10d⁴) attractive, well-made horse; fair handicapper; raced alone up centre of course when winning at Epsom (scored by a length from Path of Peace in Northern Dancer Stakes) and Brighton in June and at Epsom again in August; best form at up to 1½m and appears not to stay 2m; acts on any going; usually wears blinkers; suitable mount for an inexperienced rider; doesn't always look too enthusiastic and is inconsistent; goes well on a switchback track. *G. Balding.*

AMELVA 2 b.f. Royal Palace 131–Secret Song 83 (Tudor Melody 129) (1981 69 5g 6g 7fg³ 8g⁴) Mar 23; quite well-made, attractive filly; fourth foal; half-sister to 3-y-o 1½m winner Humming (by Bustino), very useful but temperamental 1977 2-y-o 6f winner Royal Harmony (by Sun Prince) and a winner in Jersey; dam won at up to 6f; in frame in maiden races at Catterick in August and Edinburgh in September; will probably stay 1¼m.; sold to M. Ryan 8,400 gns Newmarket December Sales. *B. Hobbs.*

AMERICAN DANCER 3 gr.f. No Mercy 126–Quickmatch 89 (Match III 135) — (1980 7s 7g 1981 8.5fg 7g 10.1fg 12f) useful-looking filly; behind in maiden and minor races and sellers; blinkered last 2 starts. *P. Ashworth.*

AMERICAN GIRL   2 b. or br.f. Yankee Gold 115–Grannys Whistle (Whistling   —
Wind 123) (1981 7f) Feb 12; IR 1,250F; leggy, lengthy, shallow-girthed filly;
first produce; dam Irish 2-y-o 6f winner; unquoted and in need of race, ran on
without being knocked about when 10 lengths sixth of 16 to Imagination in
maiden race at Yarmouth in August, only outing. *W. Marshall.*

AMERICUS   2 ch.c. Sallust 134–Cat O'Mountaine (Ragusa 137) (1981 6f* **110**
6.3fg² 6.3fg 7d 5g* 5d*}
        By the middle of September the 182,000 guineas paid for Americus at the
1980 Goffs Premier Yearling Sales didn't look money well spent. Although
Americus had made all to win a maiden race at Phoenix Park at the beginning
of August he had then been beaten in three pattern races at the Curragh: at
15/8 on he'd gone down by a length and a half to the 66/1-shot Dara Monarch
in the Ballsbridge-Tattersalls Anglesey Stakes; in the Railway Stakes he'd
trailed in over twelve lengths behind Anfield after making little show; and in
the National Stakes over seven furlongs he'd started at 33/1 and finished only
fifth, nearly six lengths behind Day Is Done. Were there any reasons for
Americus' defeats other than that he simply wasn't good enough? We couldn't
see any for the first two, though there was the possibility that the softish ground
hadn't suited him in the National Stakes. As to the distance of the National
Stakes, in theory he should have been able to get the seven furlongs—his sire
was a miler, his dam won at up to a mile and a half and his full brother Tap On
Wood himself won the National Stakes in 1978 prior to taking the following
year's Two Thousand Guineas.
        Subsequent events went to show that theory was some way removed from
reality. Americus' trainer decided to try him over five furlongs, no doubt
swayed by Eddery's assertion that he had run too freely in the Anglesey Stakes
and by the way he dropped out in the National Stakes after leading inside the
final quarter mile We saw a much improved Americus in his last two starts,
both at the Curragh. In the Goffs Two-Year-Old Stakes at the end of September
The Primate justifiably started favourite on the strength of his efforts in the
Curragh Stakes and the Gallaghouse Phoenix Stakes in which he had gone down
narrowly to those good colts Peterhof and Achieved. The Primate was to meet
his third consecutive defeat at the hands of an O'Brien-trained colt. Americus
moved up smoothly to deprive him of the lead at the distance and went on to
beat him comfortably by a length with the others, including five previous winners, at least four lengths further back. Americus put up another good effort
the following month when winning the nine-runner Waterford Testimonial
Stakes under top weight. The only horse backed to beat him was the filly
Celestial Path, unbeaten previously in three races, but she ran badly and Americus was left to win easily after disputing the lead from the start. The second,
third and fourth horses all went on to frank the form: Conversion, beaten two
lengths in receipt of 7 lb, won a twenty-two-runner race at the Curragh; Toast
of the Town, beaten seven lengths in receipt of 10 lb, won her next start; and
the eight-length fourth Tinnycross, who also received 10 lb, went on to win an
eighteen-runner maiden race and a fifteen-runner minor event. Incidentally
Americus showed here that far from being unsuited by a soft surface he is very
much at home on easy ground.

			Pall Mall	Palestine
			(ch 1955)	Malapert
	Sallust		Bandarilla	Matador
	(ch 1969)		(ch 1960)	Interval
Americus		Ragusa	Ribot
(ch.c. Feb 20, 1979)		(b 1960)	Fantan II
	Cat O'Mountaine		Marie Elizabeth	Mazarin
	(ch 1967)		(ch 1948)	Miss Honor

        It's still hard to visualise any son of Cat O'Mountaine as a sprinter. Cat
O'Mountaine, a daughter of the St Leger winner Ragusa and the useful middle-
distance winner Marie Elizabeth, stayed quite well and she is a half-sister to a
high-class stayer in Bounteous. Tap On Wood is her best winner but when
mated to the sprinter Tudor Music she produced the useful Piping Rock, a
winner at up to nine furlongs in Ireland before meeting with a lot of success in
Malaya. Americus must have inherited his speed from his sire who is out of a
speedy daughter of the sprinter Matador. Sallust made his name as a top-class
miler but as a two-year-old he was a headstrong individual who wore blinkers
in three of his five races and frequently sweated up. Interestingly up to the

Mr D. Schwartz's "Americus"

end of 1980 Sallust's stock, other than two-year-olds, had won forty-five races at up to a mile and only fourteen over longer distances.

Perhaps a more-relaxed Americus will stay beyond sprint distances as a three-year-old. It's far more likely though that his owner and trainer will be trying to do the same with him as with another of their horses, Solinus, who swept the board in the 1978 sprints. With such as Marwell, Moorestyle, Rabdan, Runnett and King of Spain now retired, the chances are that Americus won't need to be nearly so good as Solinus to win one or two of the sprint pattern races. *V. O'Brien, Ireland.*

AME TO KILL 3 b.c. Gay Fandango 132–Towards 69 (Worden II 129) (1980 5.1g³ 1981 6g 6g⁴ 6g* 6d² 6f 6g⁴ 7g² 7.2v² 7d* 7s⁴) neat, attractive colt; won maiden event at Redcar in May and minor event on same course in October; will probably stay 1m; acts on heavy going; started slowly fifth start (first outing for nearly 3 months); sold 4,800 gns Newmarket Autumn Sales. *L. Cumani.* **83**

AMINA 3 b.f. Brigadier Gerard 144–Nedda 113 (Alcide 136) (1980 7fg³ 1981 10.5s³ 10d² 12g² 10fg* 10g⁴) smallish, attractive filly; having first race for 2 months when landing the odds by 2 lengths from Taj El Moulouk in maiden race at Epsom in September; second in similar events won by Western Knight at Sandown and Fair of Face at Lingfield earlier; stays 1¼m; probably acts on any going. *B. Hobbs.* **78**

AMINTA 3 b. or br.f. Silly Season 127–Blue Book 101 (Majority Blue 126) (1980 6g 1981 8s 8s³ 8g 8s 10.2d 12.2g 9s³ 11g³ 12.2fg 10d 10.4d 10.6fg³ 10d⁴ 10.6v 12d 10s) neat filly; third in maiden races and handicaps; stays 11f; wears blinkers; inconsistent. *W. Elsey.* **54**

AMIRAH 2 ch.f. Grundy 137–Shelby (Pall Mall 132) (1981 8fg) Apr 25; leggy, rather unfurnished filly; good mover; half-sister to 2 winners, including fairly **—**

65

AMO

useful 1m and 1½m winner Beirut (by Northfields); dam won at up to 1¾m in Ireland; 20/1, always towards rear in 16-runner maiden race won by Gin at Beverley in September. *W. O'Gorman.*

AMOA   2 b.c. Rustingo 94–Tamoa (Tamerlane 128)   (1981 6fg)   Apr 9; second reported foal by a thoroughbred stallion; dam last on only start; unquoted when behind in 17-runner seller won by Miss Posy at Warwick in June.   *G. Price.* —

AMOROUS   3 b.g. Mummy's Pet 125–Maxim's 88 (Major Portion 129)   (1980 5f* 5fg³ 5f² 5.1fg³ 5g³ 5fg 6f² 6g* 6g   1981 7g 7g 6f 6fg 6f 6g)   lightly-made, leggy gelding; genuine and consistent as a 2-y-o, when winning maiden race and well-contested nursery at Newmarket; didn't recover his form; suited by 6f; acts well on firm going and has yet to race on a soft surface; blinkered final start; sold to M. McCourt 2,000 gns Newmarket Autumn Sales.   *J. Hindley.* —

AMPERE   2 b.f. Pitskelly 122–Coulomb 108 (Crepello 136)   (1981 6g 7fg 7h 8.2s)   Mar 6; useful sort; half-sister to 9.4f winner Concern (by Brigadier Gerard) and a winner in Belgium; dam miler; blinkered when fair seventh of 12 to Knightsbridge Game in seller at Nottingham in October on final start, best effort; stays 1m; acts on soft going; sold 2,800 gns Newmarket December Sales. *Sir Mark Prescott.* —

AMSAM   3 b. or br.f. Prince de Galles 125–Lovage (Linacre 133)   (1980 5fg 5fg 5fg* 6fg 5g³ 7g 7g² 6g   1981 8s 8s³ 7v)   narrow, light-framed filly; plater; will probably stay 1¼m.   *A. Smith.* —

AMYNDAS   3 b.c. Sparkler 130–Gem of Gems 106 (Grey Sovereign 128§)   (1980 NR   1981 12g* 12g² 10.5s* 10.5g* 12fg⁴ 10d⁴ 10g³)   **125**

Without exception, by the time the Champion Stakes is run at Newmarket in mid-October some of the race's participants or would-be participants are past their prime, their training usually having been geared to the classics, Royal Ascot and such prestigious midsummer races as the King George VI and Queen Elizabeth Diamond Stakes.   This wasn't the case though with Amyndas who hadn't raced at all as a two-year-old, hadn't run in any of the classics and had been kept mainly in lesser company.   He came to the Champion Stakes fresher than most, having been brought back steadily with just one race since a break of almost two months through August and September, and he looked particularly well.   A strong, compact, attractive colt he had clearly thrived and was carrying considerably more condition than he had earlier in the year.   He ran a race to match his appearance too, belying his starting price of 66/1 with a much improved performance.   He raced in the first half-dozen or so all of the way and kept on really strongly up the hill when switched to the outside for a run to finish third of sixteen, beaten two lengths and the same by the impressive French-trained winner Vayrann and the 1980 victress Cairn Rouge.   He had some very well-known horses behind, better known than he, including two classic winners.   At the time of writing an inquiry concerning Vayrann, which could affect the placings, was pending.

Amyndas had won three of his six races before the Champion Stakes.   He had made a successful debut when beating Protection Racket in the April Maiden Stakes at Newmarket—a race his trainer was winning for the fourth successive time—and had subsequently scored two good wins at York.   In the Glasgow Stakes in May he had romped home eight lengths clear of Brigadier Hawk and in the John Smith's Magnet Cup in July he had accounted for a field of seasoned handicappers, beating Galveston by two and a half lengths after travelling well throughout.   There were plausible explanations for each of his defeats, the most important with regard to his prospects as a four-year-old being that he failed to act on the firmish going in the Gordon Stakes at Goodwood.   There he sweated up quite badly, went to post as if feeling the ground, and trailed home a soundly-beaten fourth of five behind Bustomi, never having been a serious factor.   On at least one other occasion he was withdrawn from a race because of firm ground and there seems little doubt that he needs some give underfoot.

		Sparkler	Hard Tack	Hard Sauce
Amyndas		(b 1968)	(b 1955)	Cowes
(b.c. 1978)			Diamond Spur	Preciptic
			(ch 1961)	Diamond Princess
		Gem of Gems	Grey Sovereign	Nasrullah
		(b 1963)	(gr 1948)	Kong
			Twice Blessed	Tulyar
			(b 1956)	Phase

Amyndas' sire Sparkler, the sire also of the classic winners Enstone Spark and Scintillate, proved a good friend to the Hobbs's stable in 1981, for Scintil-

66

John Smith's Magnet Cup, York—comfortable win for Amyndas

lating Air is by him too. Amyndas, a half-brother to four winners the best of them the miler Cacique (by Derring-Do), was purchased for 28,000 guineas as a yearling, 17,000 guineas above his sale price as a foal. The dam Gem of Gems is the granddaughter of a famous broodmare, Phase, who produced a string of high-class racehorses and broodmares, including the Oaks winner Neasham Belle and Champion Stakes winner Narrator. Gem of Gems, by the sprinter Grey Sovereign, won at up to a mile and a half but gave the impression she was better at shorter distances. Amyndas has done just the same thing, and is probably best at a mile and a quarter. We should anticipate his doing better as a four-year-old in races such as the Westbury Stakes and the Brigadier Gerard Stakes than in the Hardwicke Stakes, for example. *B. Hobbs.*

ANATOLIA 2 b.f. Hittite Glory 125–Slip Stitch 120 (Parthia 132) (1981 **71** 6d 7g*) Apr 4; half-sister to several winners, including 3-y-o Emblazon (by Wolver Hollow), successful at up to 1½m, and fairly useful 1974 2-y-o 6f and 7f winner Moss Stitch (by Star Moss); dam good staying 2-y-o; 8/1, stayed on well to beat Cough by 1½ lengths in 13-runner seller at Edinburgh in October (bought in 820 gns); likely to stay 1¼m at 3 yrs; sold to CBA 2,300 gns Newmarket Autumn Sales. *Sir Mark Prescott.*

ANATOLIAN ELF 2 b.f. Hittite Glory 125–La Mome 109 (Princely Gift **—** 137) (1981 6fg) Apr 28; 4,700Y; tall, close-coupled filly; half-sister to fairly useful 5f to 10.2f winner La Lutine (by My Swallow) and a winner in Italy; dam stayed 1¼m; unquoted when behind in 17-runner maiden race won by Cricket Field at Newbury in August. *R. Hannon.*

ANCIENT REGIME (USA) 3 gr.f. Olden Times–Caterina 124 (Princely **120** Gift 137) (1980 5.5g* 5g⁴ 5.5g² 6fg* 7g 1981 8fg 8g⁴ 5fg² 6g 6.5fg⁴ 6fg 6d² 5d⁴ 5v³ 6v*) rather a leggy filly; sister to very useful sprint stakes winner Olden, and half-sister to French middle-distance winner Firing Squad (by Pronto) and to Mug Punter (by Warfare), a stakes winner at up to 9f; dam won Nunthorpe Stakes; best of her sex in France as a 2-y-o, when winning Prix Morny at Deauville; didn't gain her first success of 1981 until October, when landing the odds by a length from Tassmoun in 15-runner minor event at Evry; in frame most previous starts, notably when 3 lengths second in both Prix du Gros Chene at Chantilly (to Sonoma) and Prix de Seine-et-Oise at Maisons-Laffitte (behind Rabdan), 3¼ lengths fourth to Marwell in Prix de l'Abbaye de Longchamp (dwelt and was hopelessly outpaced early on) and 2 lengths third to Park Romeo in Prix du Petit Couvert at Longchamp again; dropped right out to finish last of 14 after chasing leaders to past halfway in William Hill July Cup won by Marwell at Newmarket on fourth start; finds 5f on sharp side in top company and seems to stay 1m; seems to act on any going. *J. Fellows, France.*

ANDREA'S PET 3 ch.f. Sharp Edge 123–Warm Slipper (King's Company **60** 124) (1980 5f 5g 7f 7g 7f³ 8fg³ 8d* 8s² 7d 1981 12.5f 8f 8f 10s 10s*) lengthy, fair sort; plater; wandered badly under pressure but held on by 2½ lengths from Red Petal at Nottingham in October, only form of 1981 (attracted no bid); suited by 1¼m; acts on any going, but has shown her best form on soft; suitable mount for an apprentice; trained first 3 outings by P. Wigham; sold to J. Yardley 1,000 gns Newmarket Autumn Sales. *C. Spares.*

ANDY LOU 3 b.g. Be Friendly 130–Ribara (Barbare II 128) (1980 5v² **69** d
5d* 5h² 5fg 5g⁴ 5g 5d 5fg 1981 6g⁴ 5g* 5d³ 5f³ 6s³ 5f³ 8g 7fg 7fg 5f³ 5fg 6d
6s 5d 6g) good-topped gelding; poor mover in his slower paces; short-head
winner from Be Sharp in handicap at Redcar in May; stays 6f (not disgraced
over 1m); acts on any going; blinkered final outing. *G. Toft.*

ANFIELD 2 b.c. Be My Guest 126–Mother 88 (Whistler 129) (1981 7fg* **115**
6.3fg* 8g* 8s⁴)
Few young men can have started their training careers in so privileged a
position as Vincent O'Brien's son David in 1981. Among his string of around
fifty horses were two-year-olds out of such good fillies as Calahorra, Hurry
Harriet, Merry Madcap and Miss Toshiba, and three-year-old colts who had
cost $1,400,000, $445,000, $350,000, $300,000 and $260,000 as yearlings;
his impressive list of owners included such names as Binet, Fluor, Sangster,
Schwartz, St George and Wildenstein; and to ride for the stable he had Christy
Roche, who had won the Irish jockeys' championship the previous season.
By the end of the season though the younger O'Brien had proved himself
thoroughly worthy of the tremendous support he'd received, picking up three
of Ireland's eleven pattern races for two-year-olds (matching his father's total)
plus the Group 3 Prix Eclipse with Pas de Seul in France.
Anfield credited O'Brien with his first pattern-race victory in the Railway
Stakes at the Curragh in August. Although the horse had done well to win
a maiden race at Leopardstown earlier in the month, after having plenty to
do at halfway, Anfield appeared to need to improve if he was to beat Day Is
Done, winner of the Norfolk Stakes at Royal Ascot, or the first two in the
Anglesey Stakes, Dara Monarch and Americus. Improve he did, leading at
around halfway and keeping on extremely well to win by a length and a half
from Day Is Done who was meeting defeat for the first time in four races.
Whereas Anfield was in receipt of 7 lb from Day Is Done here it was he who was
conceding 7 lb to the National Stakes fourth Sun Worship in the Ashford Castle
Stakes at the Curragh a month later. The pair started co-favourites and had
the race to themselves. Again Anfield was in the lead by the halfway mark
but he couldn't shake off Sun Worship in the final two furlongs and scraped
home by only a short head, with the rest at least eight lengths further behind.
Of the stable's wins this must have been one of the sweetest—Sun Worship
is trained by O'Brien senior who was trying to gain his seventh successive victory
in the Ashford Castle Stakes.
Although Anfield stayed the mile well on good ground at the Curragh he
seemed to find the combination of a mile and very soft going too much for him

Railway Stakes, the Curragh—Anfield gives David O'Brien
his first pattern-race win

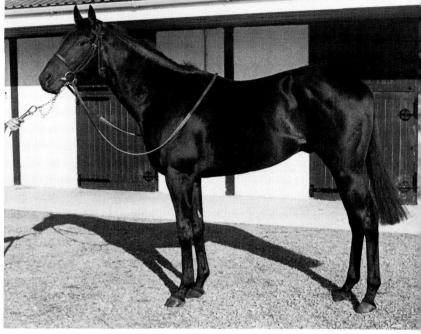

M J. P. Binet's "Anfield"

when sent to Longchamp for the Grand Criterium fifteen days later. Going well early in the straight, he was still on the heels of Green Forest and Norwick with three hundred metres to run but then weakened very rapidly and at the line was nearly ten lengths behind Green Forest in fourth place.

Anfield (b.c. Apr 13, 1979)	Be My Guest (ch 1974)	Northern Dancer (b 1961)	Nearctic Natalma
		What a Treat (b 1962)	Tudor Minstrel Rare Treat
	Mother (b 1963)	Whistler (ch 1950)	Panorama Farthing Damages
		Esmeralda (br 1956)	Tulyar Mahallat

It wasn't entirely surprising a mile in testing conditions found Anfield out at two. Although he shares the same dam and paternal grandsire as that top-class middle-distance colt North Stoke he isn't stoutly bred; his sire Be My Guest didn't show his best form until brought back to a mile from longer distances and his dam, a daughter of the very fast Whistler, was kept to five furlongs in her only season to race, winning one of her five starts. North Stoke and Anfield are easily the best of Mother's five winners and also easily the best winners to come from the family for a long time, although their third dam Mahallat was a useful sister to the Oaks and Irish Oaks winner Masaka. Mahallat in turn was out of Majideh, winner of both the One Thousand Guineas and Oaks in Ireland in 1942.

Unfortunately North Stoke died after only one season at stud. His yearlings were quite well received at the 1981 sales, fetching up to 45,000 guineas, and Anfield has only to win another pattern race or two to become an attractive replacement at stud for his close relative. An attractive, medium-sized colt, Anfield cost 53,000 Irish guineas as a yearling. *D. O'Brien, Ireland.*

*Doncaster Town Plate Handicap—Angelo Salvini makes all to win
from Donegal Prince and Russian
George (almost hidden)*

ANFIELD LADY 3 b. or br.f. Averof 123–Graceful Scot (Aberdeen 109)
(1980 5v 5f 1981 6v) leggy filly; poor mover; temperamental plater; one
to leave alone. *W. H. H. Williams.* —

ANGELA EDELSON 2 b.f. Owen Dudley 121–Mauritania 74 (The Brianstan
128) (1981 5s 6g 5d) May 11; 1,400F, resold 1,700Y; lightly-made filly;
first foal; dam placed at up to 1m; little worthwhile form in maiden and minor
events, including one at Hamilton. *N. Guest.* —

ANGELO SALVINI 5 br.g. Relko 136–Sweet Sauce (Fr) (Hard Sauce 131)
(1980 12h2 13.8fg* 12.1fg* 12g* 18.4g3 13d* 14.7g 16d3 16f4 17.4s* 18d 1981
18s* 18.4d 16g 15g4 14.7d* 14d 17.4g 16.1s3 14s3) narrow, rather sparely-
made gelding; fairly useful handicapper; made all when accounting for Donegal
Prince by a length in £8,200 Doncaster Town Plate in March and when beating
Feelings 2 lengths at Redcar in August; ran respectably in valuable races third
and fourth starts; suited by a test of stamina; acts on any going but is very
well suited by soft; most game and genuine; good mount for an inexperienced
race-rider. *M. H. Easterby.* **93**

ANGEL SONG (USA) 3 ch.f. Graustark–Primonetta (Swaps) (1980 6s
1981 12d* 12f3) big, rangy filly; said to have been hobdayed; short-priced
favourite and looking fit and well when making all and beating Goldyke decisively
by 3 lengths in maiden race at Haydock in August; had stiffer task when 4½
lengths third of 4 behind Bedford in minor event at York the following month,
only other start; would have stayed beyond 1⅜m; possibly better suited by
a soft surface than a firm one; retired to stud. *R. Hern.* **82**

ANGELUS CHIMES 2 b.f. Northfields–Twelve O'Clock (Hardicanute 130)
(1981 5f 6fg4(dis) 7fg 6fg 6g3 7g2) Feb 18; 62,000Y; quite attractive, lightly-
made, lengthy filly; second foal; dam, very useful French 2-y-o 6f winner, is
half-sister to Irish Sweeps Derby runner-up Lombardo; prominent most starts;
went down by only a short head to Positron in maiden event at Leicester in
October on final outing; likely to stay 1¼m; should win a little race at 3 yrs.
D. Whelan. **80**

ANGEVIN 3 b.f. English Prince 129–Paddyflower 88 (St Paddy 133) (1980
7.3d 1981 9s3 10fg 12d 12g 14g 8d) big, well-made filly; ran best race when
staying-on third in maiden event at Wolverhampton in April; should be suited
by middle distances; blinkered fourth start; sold out of P. Walwyn's stable
4,700 gns Newmarket July Sales afterwards. *D. Ringer.* **61**

ANGLE FIRE (USA) 3 b.c. Angle Light–Mary Biz (T. V. Lark) (1980 6fg2
7g3 7d 6fg3 8.2s2 1981 8s* 8g* 8d4 9fg* 10.6s4 9fg 8f3 9f2 8f 8.2f4) strong,
lengthy colt; carries plenty of condition; half-brother to Gimcrack winner
Full Extent (by Full Out); won maiden race at Redcar and minor event at **78**

70

Hamilton in May; also awarded maiden race at Beverley in April when original winner Regal Touch was found to have traces of illegal substance in his system; ran creditably on other occasions; stays 1¼m; acts on any going; didn't look an ideal mount for an inexperienced apprentice on seventh start; blinkered eighth and ninth starts; sent to race in USA. *S. Norton.*

ANGLEPOISE (USA) 4 b.c. Angle Light–Burns' Babe (Fleet Nasrullah) **85** (1980 8f³ 8f 8.2g 8s³ 8s* 8g* 10g 1981 8v³ 9g 10.2g 9d⁴ 8g 8g³ 8g 8g 11d) compact colt; fair handicapper; best at up to 9f; suited by some give in the ground; blinkered when successful once in 1980; suited by front-running tactics; genuine; retained 5,800 gns Newmarket Autumn Sales. *S. Norton.*

ANGLO GREEK 4 b.g. English Prince 129–Orange Sensation 69 (Floribunda — 136) (1980 6f⁴ 6f* 6fg 5d 1981 7g 8g 7.2v) attractive, well-made gelding; well beaten in 1981; should stay beyond 6f; acts on firm going. *L. Barratt.*

ANGOSTURA 5 ch.g. Tudor Music 131–Angels Hair (Le Haar 126) (1980 — 12f³ 17f* 12f 16f* 16.5g 16g³ 1981 12f² 13g³) big ex-Irish gelding; won handicaps at Limerick and Clonmel in 1980; beaten easily when placed in small races at Pontefract and Ayr in September; stays well; acts on firm going. *R. Fisher.*

ANGUS SPRITE 2 b.f. Saulingo 122–Saratoga Springs 92 (Worden II 129) **78** (1981 5fg 5fg 6g 6fg 6g 7f² 7.2v* 7g 7d⁴ 7g) Feb 25; IR 1,150Y; unfurnished filly; half-sister to a winner in Ireland and one in Italy; dam 2-y-o 6f winner; won 16-runner seller at Haydock in October (no bid); ran very well in minor event at Catterick and nursery at Leicester (apprentice ridden) on next 2 starts but didn't impress in paddock and was below her best final appearance; suited by 7f; acts on any going; trained first 3 starts by F. Durr. *K. Ivory.*

ANIECE 3 br.c. Ballymoss 136–Gay Maria (Tacitus 124) (1980 7fg 10s² 10.2s **81** 1981 10g 8d² 11.5f³ 10.1fg³ 12d* 16fg² 12f 16s* 18g) well-made colt; won maiden race at Redcar in August and handicap at Warwick in October, putting up a good effort in latter when beating Sarah Bernhardt 1½ lengths (pair clear); ran easily better race in between when good 4 lengths second to Bulldozer in handicap at Kempton; very well suited by a test of stamina; probably acts on any going; sometimes coltish in paddock. *F. Durr.*

ANIKONERI 6 br.m. Yukon Eric–Sayarani 96 (Hard Tack 111§) (1980 **35** 5f⁴ 5fg⁴ 5fg 6f⁴ 6g 6d 6g⁴ 5g 6f 8g 7fg 8.2s 6fg 1981 7g⁴ 11g 8fg⁴ 8.2d) poor handicapper nowadays; seems to stay 1m; well suited by fast ground; suitable mount for an apprentice. *W. H. H. Williams.*

ANITRA'S DANCE (FR) 3 b.f. Green Dancer 132–Azurella (High Hat 131) **118** (1980 8g³ 9d² 8d⁴ 1981 10s* 12v³ 12d* 13.5f² 12.5s) French filly; third foal; dam, smart middle-distance performer, won Prix de Malleret and Prix de Royaumont; won minor event at Saint-Cloud in May and Group 3 Prix de Minerve at Evry in July, latter by ½ length and ¾ length from Landresse and Sass-Go after being held up; finished well when 5 lengths second to April Run in Group 3 Prix de Pomone at Deauville in August, better subsequent effort; stays 13.5f; acts on any going. *A. Head, France.*

ANNADANT 2 b.f. Ascendant 96–Anasayra (Sayajirao 132) (1981 7fg 5f) — June 17; small filly; probably of little account. *G. Toft.*

ANNESLEY 2 b.c. Relkino 131–My Candy 81 (Lorenzaccio 130) (1981 6g* **86** 7fg³ 7g² 7h³ 8fg) Apr 22; well-made, attractive colt; good walker and mover; second foal; half-brother to 3-y-o 1½m winner Bunduq (by Scottish Rifle); dam placed over 7f at 2 yrs; beat Macmillion a shade cleverly by ¾ length in 15-runner maiden event at Salisbury in June; placed in most of his subsequent races but is only moderate; will be suited by middle distances; blinkered fifth outing. *R. Hern.*

ANNIE HILL 3 gr.f. Dragonara Palace 115–Tudor Velvet (Tudor Music 131) — § (1980 5g 5f³ 5s 1981 6s 6s 6g² 6g 7f) leggy filly; temperamental sprint plater; trained part of season by C. Crossley; sold 500 gns Doncaster September Sales. *J. Berry.*

ANNIVERSARY WALTZ 2 b.f. Random Dancer 113–Duresme 76 (Starry Halo **55** 122) (1981 6f³ 5fg* 6f 5.8f² 5f) May 11; 250Y; has a high knee action; fourth foal; half-sister to winning hurdler Palmero (by Palm Track); dam third twice over 7f at 2 yrs; bought in for 2,100 gns after winning 8-runner seller at Wolverhampton in July; will probably stay 7f; yet to race on a soft surface; sold 600 gns Newmarket Autumn Sales. *D. H. Jones.*

ANNSOME BOY 2 br.c. Saulingo 122–Ruby Rose 93 (Tudor Treasure 119) **89**
(1981 5s⁴ 5d³ 5fg* 5g* 5s² 5f³ 5g 6fg 5fg² 5fg⁴ 5d) May 4; IR 4,100Y; fair
sort; half-brother to 2 winners in Ireland, including 1977 2-y-o 5f winner
Fleetwood Express (by Sallust), and a winner abroad; dam won from 5f to 7f at 2
yrs in England and also over hurdles in Ireland; made all to win 16-runner
maiden race at Warwick in April and 5-runner minor event at Brighton in
May; excellent second to Haverhill Lass in nursery at Warwick in August on
ninth outing; gives impression 5f is his trip; seems to act on any going; blinkered
eighth start; sent to Hong Kong. *M. McCourt.*

ANOINTED 5 b.h. Crowned Prince 128–Saint Agata (Wild Risk) (1980 15.8d **63**
1981 15.8s* 18fg 15.8g) big, strong horse; staying handicapper; won at
Catterick in April; acts on any going; sold out of G. Richards' stable 10,000 gns
Doncaster March Sales. *Mrs J. Pitman.*

ANOTHER CITY 2 ch.f. Scallywag 127–Must Improve 47 (Lucky Brief 128) —
(1981 8g 8d) Apr 17; half-sister to 3-y-o 6f and 7f seller winner City's Sister
(by Maystreak) and a winning jumper; dam won over hurdles; in rear in maiden
races at Edinburgh in September (carried very wide on bend) and October. *G.
Richards.*

ANOTHER FIDDLER 10 ch.g. Burglar 128–Izeste (Lavandin 128) (1980 —
6g 5fg 7g 8.3f 7f 7g 1981 7f 5fg 8.3g 6f 5h) dipped-backed gelding; plater;
stays 7f; acts on any going; used to wear blinkers; good mount for an apprentice.
G. Balding.

ANOTHER MEMORY 2 br.c. Free State 125–Saxelby Melody 88 (Highland —
Melody 112) (1981 6fg 6f 6f 7f 7.2g 8.2s 8d) Mar 31; neat colt; first live foal;
dam won over 5f at 2 yrs; poor plater; blinkered sixth and seventh starts. *K.
Stone.*

ANOTHER MOVE 5 ch.m. Farm Walk 111–Darling Do (Derring-Do 131) **45**
(1980 10v 12d 12fg* 11g 12f² 12.22fg 12gfg³ 12g* 12v⁴ 15d 1981 12.3d 12g 12d
12g² 12g 11d⁴ 12t 12t 12t 11tg 12d 13.8g) neat, lightly-made mare; poor
handicapper; suited by 1½m (well beaten over further); acts on any going,
except possibly heavy; has raced with her tongue tied down; sometimes inclined
to hang under pressure. *J. Calvert.*

ANOTHER REALM 3 gr.c. Realm 129–Tiara III (Persian Gulf) (1980 5f² **118**
5fg² 5fg* 5f* 6d⁴ 6d* 5g³ 6g* 6fg 1981 7d* 8g 8fg 6g 8fg³ 8f 8s)
Another Realm's three-year-old career showed him to be a fair way behind
the very best milers, but a very useful performer all the same. This seemed
the likely outcome on his form the previous season, when he won the Group
2 Richmond Stakes at Goodwood but was beaten on three other ventures in
pattern-race company. Nevertheless, Another Realm's connections must have
taken heart from his decisive victory in the Group 3 Clerical, Medical Greenham
Stakes at Newbury in April, in which he accounted for some of the previous
season's leading two-year-olds—Age Quod Agis, Beldale Flutter, Cut Throat
and Sheer Grit; although excuses were made for some of the losers, Another
Realm's three-length victory from Age Quod Agis looked a very smart performance. In recent years the Greenham Stakes has been contested by a number of horses who subsequently went on to enhance their reputations in high-
class company, among them Known Fact, Hello Gorgeous, Posse, Kris, Young

*Clerical, Medical Greenham Stakes, Newbury—Another Realm wins
this valuable Guineas trial from Age Quod Agis and Beldale Flutter*

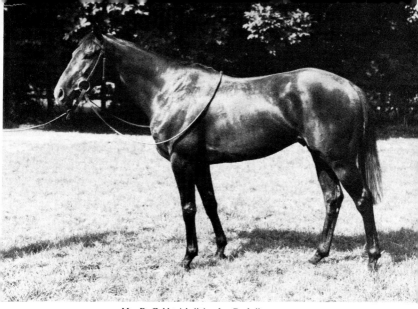

Mrs D. Goldstein's "Another Realm"

Generation, He Loves Me, Tachypous, Wollow, Grundy and the sprinters Double Form and Gentilhombre. The latest field did contain one who subsequently showed high-class form in Beldale Flutter, but Another Realm was not to win again. He was campaigned in the highest class, running in Group 1 or Group 2 pattern races on all but his final start and acquitting himself with credit on a number of occasions. He put up his best performances after the Greenham Stakes when fifth in the Two Thousand Guineas in May and third in the Waterford Crystal Mile at Goodwood in August, in both races finishing under six lengths behind To-Agori-Mou, and when sixth to Northjet, again beaten under six lengths, in the Prix du Moulin de Longchamp in September.

		Realm (b 1967)	Princely Gift (b 1951)	Nasrullah
Another Realm (gr.c. 1978)				Blue Gem
			Quita II (b 1962)	Lavandin
				Eos
		Tiara III (gr 1964)	Persian Gulf (b 1940)	Bahram
				Double Life
			Parure (gr 1956)	Abernant
				Diamantina II

Another Realm was bought for 12,500 guineas at the Newmarket Houghton Yearling Sales. He is one of three pattern-race winners in 1981 by Realm, and is the best produce to date of his dam, who ran only once, unplaced, as a two-year-old before being retired to stud after an accident. Of Tiara III's previous seven foals, five have been successful. They include the fair seven-furlong winner Crown Major (by Majority Blue), the fairly useful sprinter Linda Jill (by Native Prince) and Another Realm's sister Landed Lady, who showed fair form at five and six furlongs at two years. Tiara III's ninth produce, the two-year-old Probabilist (by Mount Hagen), ran twice in 1981 without reaching the frame.

Another Realm, a strong, well-made colt, showed himself a genuine performer throughout his fairly hard season. He is suited by a mile, and ran below his best although staying on at the finish when sixth behind Marwell in the six-furlong July Cup at Newmarket. He probably acts on any going, although he

73

ANO

seemed not to run up to his best on his final outing, when encountering very
soft ground for the first time. Another Realm is now racing in the USA with
Charlie Whittingham. *F. Durr.*

ANOTHER RUMBO 3 ch.g. Royben 125–Fiord (Mountain Call 125) (1980 —
5fg* 5f² 5h* 5f* 6fg² 5fg 5s² 5g² 5d 1981 5s 5d 6g 5f 5.8f 7f 8g 6g) workmanlike
gelding; mainly disappointing in 1981, best effort when about 4 lengths fifth of
12 behind Sanu in James Lane Handicap at Ascot in June on fourth start; stays
6f; acts on any going; sometimes blinkered nowadays; retained 3,100 gns
Newmarket Autumn Sales. *G. Hunter.*

ANOTHER SAM 4 b. or br.c. Comedy Star 121–Balandra Star 92 (Blast 125) 93
(1980 7fg 8fg 11f 10f 16g* 16fg⁴ 14fg 16.5fg* 16f² 16.1g⁴ 16fg⁴ 16d* 14g 1981
13s 16fg 14fg* 14s² 16f 16g² 18.4fg² 14d 14d² 14.6fg² 13.3d 17.1d* 16s) leggy,
narrow colt; fairly useful handicapper; won at Sandown in April and Bath in
October; also ran creditably when second in Northumberland Plate at Newcastle
(2 lengths behind Dawn Johnny), Tote-Ebor at York (hung left when beaten 1½
lengths by Protection Racket) and Rockingham Handicap at Doncaster (went
down by 1½ lengths to Centroline); suited by a test of stamina; acts on any
going; tends to drop himself out in early stages and is not an easy ride. *R.
Hannon.*

ANOTHER THRILL 2 b.c. Morston 125–Another Treat 92 (Derring-Do 131) 80
(1981 7fg 7g⁴) Apr 13; 13,000F, 13,500Y; attractive colt; first foal; dam,
daughter of smart Fab, won over 1¼m and 1½m; 33/1 and in need of race, shaped
well when 2½ lengths sixth of 29 to Hayakaze in maiden race at Newmarket in
August; looked to have run up light when just over 5 lengths fourth of 16 to
Airspin in similar event at Leicester the following month; an immature colt who
will do better over middle distances in 1982. *M. Stoute.*

ANOTHER VENTURE 4 b.g. Roan Rocket 128–Myna Tyna 85 (Blast 125) 50
(1980 5d 6y 6fg 5 8g³ 6g 6g 6g⁴ 0g² 1981 6tg 6g 7d 7s³ 8d 8g 10f 8fg) strong
gelding; poor handicapper; third in seller at Kempton in May; stayed 7f; acted
on soft going; occasionally wore blinkers; sometimes gave trouble at start; dead.
R. Atkins.

ANOTHER WAY 2 b.f. Wolverlife 115–Free and Easy (Liberator III) (1981 68
5.8f 6fg 5f² 5.8h 5fg) Apr 12; 2,000Y; smallish, useful sort; half-sister to
numerous winners, including smart 5f sprinter Bold and Free (by Bold Lad, Ire)
and good miler Watergate (by Sovereign Path); dam useful Irish miler; went
down by a length to Red Ellette in 9-runner maiden auction event at Folkestone
in August, easily best effort; evidently best at 5f; yet to race on an easy surface;
blinkered third and fourth outings. *N. Vigors.*

ANSTRUTHER 2 b. or br.c. Oats 126–St Tropez 99 (Princely Gift 137) (1981 97
6d 6fg* 7.3d) Mar 28; IR 27,000Y; big colt; excellent mover; half-brother to
useful sprinter Tre Fontane (by Windjammer, USA) and numerous other
winners, including Madrid Free Handicap winner Market Square and useful 5f
to 7f winner Parbleu (both by Pardao); dam ran only at 2 yrs when successful
over 5f; made all to win 20-runner maiden event at Newmarket in August by
1½ lengths from Knave of Trumps; led for over 5f when second favourite for
nursery at Newbury the following month but faded to finish about 8 lengths sixth
to Candide; should stay 7f; acts on a firm surface. *D. Ringer.*

ANTERES 3 b.f. Andrea Mantegna–The Lady Brianstan (Signa Infesta 114) —
(1980 9d 1981 12d 14f 16f 13f) well-grown filly; slow maiden; sold to Mrs E.
Kennard 1,000 gns Newmarket Autumn Sales. *H. Collingridge.*

ANTILLA 2 b.f. Averof 123–Anegada 79 (Welsh Pageant 132) (1981 5g* 5s 87
5f⁴ 5g³ 5g² 5fg 6s) Feb 13; quite attractive, useful-looking filly; first foal; dam,
half-sister to smart Derrylin, showed some ability at 2 yrs; made all to win 11-
runner maiden race at Kempton in April; put up best subsequent efforts in
nurseries in August on fourth and fifth starts, finishing just over length third of
12 to Chellaston Park at Goodwood and 2 lengths second of 9 to Pass No Remarks
at Nottingham; should be suited by 6f (reared up in stalls and dwelt when tried
at trip); form only on good ground so far. *P. Cole.*

ANVIL INN 3 b.g. Roi Soleil 125–Floor Show 78 (Galivanter 131) (1980 8.2s 70 d
8.2s 1981 11v 8g 7g² 7fg 8fg 9d³ 10f* 8g 8.2f 9d³ 11d 12g) compact gelding;
won seller at Redcar in August by a neck from Lady Ever-So-Sure, showing
much improved form; bought in 2,200 gns afterwards; evidently well suited by
1¼m and firm going. *T. Craig.*

ANYWHICHWAYYOUCAN 2 ch.c. Town Crier 119–Golden Herb 80 (Goldhill 57
125) (1981 5s 5d 5d 5fg² 6g* 7g) Apr 4; 1,250Y; leggy colt; half-brother to

74

two 2-y-o winners by Tycoon II; bought in 3,500 gns after leading close home to beat Easy Maud a short head in 7-runner seller at Lingfield in June (well-backed favourite); dead. *G. Kindersley.*

APACHEE LOVE 3 ch.f. Apalachee 137–Collatteral (Jim J) (1980 5f 5g 1981 **67** 7g 10.2f 12fg 11.7h* 13fg 11.7d 12v) attractive filly; beat More Oats by ½ length in maiden race at Bath in August, easily best effort; suited by 1¼m; acts on hard going; blinkered last 2 outings (sweated up on second occasion); sold to M. Ryan 25,000 gns Newmarket December Sales. *B. Hills.*

APAPA PORT 3 ch.f. My Swanee 122–Cotton Town (Takawalk II 125) (1980 **71** 5d⁴ 5v⁴ 5v 5g 5fg³ 5fg⁴ 5fg 5f 5f 5f 5d³ 5d 5d⁴ 5s² 5d* 1981 5g 5d* 6s 5fg 5g) strong, leggy filly; beat Noble Whin 2 lengths in handicap at Thirsk in May; should stay 6f; revels in the mud; effective with or without blinkers. *K. Stone.*

APERITIVO 3 ro.c. Sharp Edge 123–Feasting (Sayajirao 132) (1980 5f 6d⁴ 7g **97** 7.6f 8g* 1981 8s* 10d* 10fg 10fg 12d 10g⁴ 10g 10s 12g) lengthy colt; produced with a strong late run when comfortably winning handicaps at Goodwood in May (by ½ length from Park Place) and Sandown in June (by 4 lengths from Commonty), in latter going clear in good style in last furlong after being confidently ridden; not disgraced in similar events at Ascot on sixth and eighth starts; stays 1½m; possibly needs some give in the ground; can produce a useful turn of foot on his day. *R. Armstrong.*

APHRA BEHN 2 b.f. Malinowski 123–Masina (Current Coin 118) (1981 7g³) **67 p** Apr 4; 20,000Y; first live foal; dam, half-sister to Champion Stakes winner Giacometti, won over 9f in Ireland; second favourite but looking as though run would do her good, ran on to finish 9 lengths third of 16 to Tants in maiden race at Leicester in October; will stay 1¼m; likely to do better. *R. Price.*

APOLLO DANCER 2 b.c. Runnymede 123–Treasure Flower 67 (Donore 119) **—** (1981 6fg 7g 6g 5s) Mar 9; 3,200F, 6,400Y; short-coupled colt; has a rather round action; half-brother to numerous winners, including fairly useful 1980 2-y-o 6f winner Moores Miracle (by Manacle); dam stayed 1m; only a plater; dwelt when blinkered final outing. *P. Haslam.*

APPALOOSA 3 b.c. Bay Express 132–Fivepenny Piece 78 (Fortino II 120) **—** (1980 5fg² 5g* 6g* 6fg 1981 6g 6d 8fg 8s³ 10.8s) attractive colt; good mover; quite a useful performer as a 2-y-o; didn't recover his form and was beaten 17 lengths when staying-on third to Sir Tristan in apprentice race at Ascot in October; stays 1m; sold 4,000 gns Newmarket Autumn Sales. *R. Price.*

APPELLE 3 b.f. Relko 136–Appellanda 92 (Reform 132) (1980 6d 6g 7f 7g 8d **—** 1981 10s 12fg 15.5f 12d 11.7g) small filly; plating-class maiden; stays 1½m; blinkered third start. *R. Smyth.*

APPLE BLOSSOM 2 ch.f. Orange Bay 131–Appleshaw (St Alphage 119) **81** (1981 6fg 6f 6g² 7g 8fg 7s) May 9; 2,300Y; tall, leggy filly; has a round action; third foal; half-sister to 3-y-o Cider Man (by Manacle), a winner over 5f and 6f at 2 yrs; dam unraced half-sister to Grand Prix de Paris winner Pleben; 1½ lengths second of 14 to Jump Jar in Chesters Stakes at Newcastle in June; 33/1 when most creditable 5¼ lengths fifth of 11 to Spanish Pool in valuable nursery at Lingfield in October on sixth outing; will stay 1¼m; seems well suited by some give in the ground. *G. Beeson.*

APPLEMINT (USA) 3 b.f. Sir Ivor 135–Eltisley 82 (Grey Sovereign 128§) **100** (1980 6g³ 1981 8.5fg² 8s 7g*) quite an attractive, compact filly; second foal; half-sister to useful sprinter Dare Me (by Derring-Do); dam 2-y-o 5f winner; needed run and ran an excellent race when ½-length second to Petroleuse in Princess Elizabeth Stakes at Epsom in April on reappearance, leading 2f out until caught close home; not seen out after easily landing the odds from Seven Seas in 19-runner maiden event at Salisbury in June; probably unsuited by the soft going when fifth of 6 behind impressive winner Nasseem in UBM Merchants International Fillies Stakes at Kempton in between; stays 1m well. *R. Hern.*

APPLES OF GOLD 2 ro.f. Godswalk 130–Apple Peel 109 (Pall Mall 132) **93** (1981 6fg² 6f² 6d²) Feb 7; 40,000Y; strong, quite attractive filly; first foal; dam won 5 times over 1m and 1¼m; second in 3 good races, accounting for 5 previous winners when beaten 10 lengths by Circus Ring in Princess Margaret Stakes at Ascot in July, going down by ½ length to On The House in Crathorne Stakes at York in September and by 1¼ lengths to Warm Hearted in Firth of Clyde Stakes at Ayr later same month; will be suited by 7f and 1m; a taking filly who seems sure to win a race or two at 3 yrs. *R. Hern.*

APPLE WINE 4 ch.g. Ribston 104–Ruffino 99 (Como 120) (1980 8v* 9g⁴ **64** 8f 8f 9g 8fg² 7f 8g 9g 8.2d 8s* 1981 10.2s* 9g) workmanlike gelding; gamely held on to win amateur riders race at Doncaster in March; suited by 1¼m; probably acts on any going but revels in the mud; blinkered twice at 2 yrs; sweated up badly once in 1980; suitable mount for an inexperienced rider. *M. W. Easterby.*

APRICOT ROSE 2 ch.f. Mill Reef 141–Jolie Fleur 111 (Exbury 138) (1981 7g) Apr 25; fourth foal; half-sister to 2 winners, including useful 1980 2-y-o 7f winner The Thatcher (by Thatch); dam, half-sister to Connaught, was very useful at 1m to 1¼m: 20/1 when behind in 29-runner maiden race won by stable-companion Chalon at Newmarket in October; will do better over middle distances. *H. Cecil.* — p

APRIL BOUQUET 4 ch.g. Silly Season 127–Floral Gift 84 (Princely Gift 137) (1980 8f 8fg2 8.2fg 8fg* 8d2 8fg 1981 8s 9d 10s 8v 10.2g) strong, well-made, good-looking gelding; slaughtered his field in Britannia Stakes (Handicap) at Royal Ascot in 1980; ran badly at 4 yrs, including in a valuable seller; stays 1m; acts on a firm and a soft surface; bolted on way down first start and was taken to post early afterwards; one to be wary of; trained first 3 starts by J. Sutcliffe. *D. Kent.* —

APRIL LUCKY 8 b.g. St Alphage 119–Susceptible 86 (Supreme Court 135) (1980 6g 6d2 6f 6h3 6f 6g* 6d3 6g* 7fg3 6g4 7f 6s 1981 6s 6g2 6d* 6g4 6f2 6f3 6fg 6f4 7f 6f4 6d) leggy gelding; narrowly won handicap at Pontefract in May; stays 7f; acts on any going; blinkered twice at 3 yrs; sometimes sweats up; good mount for an inexperienced rider; needs to be held up; goes well at Hamilton (has won 7 times there); broke blood vessel seventh start and ran poorly final outing. *C. Crossley.* 64

APRIL MEMORIES 2 b.f. Rolfe 77–Sweet Memories 58 (Runnymede 123) (1981 6fg 5d) Apr 27; first foal; dam poor sprint maiden; showed ability in maiden races, finishing eighth of 19 to Enthralment at Salisbury in September and seventh of 16 to Kash-In at Bath in October; will be suited by a return to 6f+. *N. Vigors.* 70

APRIL RUN 3 b.f. Run The Gantlet–April Fancy (No Argument) 107) (1980 NR 1981 10s2 12d* 10.5s* 10.5fg3 12.5g4 13.5f* 12g* 12d3 12g* 12fg2) 131

April Run is the latest in the line of superb French fillies which has so enriched middle-distance racing in that country over the last few years. She is well up to her predecessors' standards. A good filly in the summer, third in the French Oaks and fourth in the Grand Prix de Saint-Cloud, she, like most of the others, was even better in the autumn when in strong contention in all four starts in the highest class. She won the Prix Vermeille and the Turf Classic and she finished third, after a slightly unlucky run, in the Prix de l'Arc de Triomphe and second in the Washington International.

Winning the Prix Vermeille at Longchamp in September was the highlight of April Run's career up to then. The race is nearly always the most strongly contested in France over a mile and a half confined to three-year-old fillies, and is often the hottest of its type in Europe too—requiring more winning than an Oaks. The latest Prix Vermeille attracted a field of genuine quality, and afforded April Run the opportunity of turning the tables on the two in front of her in the French Oaks (the Prix de Diane de Revlon), Madam Gay and Val d'Erica. Following very decisive victories at Saint-Cloud in the spring in a maiden race and the Prix Cleopatre April Run had started second favourite

Prix Cleopatre, Saint-Cloud—April Run wins her first pattern race

Prix Vermeille, Longchamp—April Run wins from Leandra (No. 10) and Madam Gay

for the French Oaks; she had gone well at Chantilly, beating the Guineas winner Ukraine Girl and the favourite Tootens among others, and had lost second place by a very narrow margin behind the four-length winner Madam Gay. Tootens took the field once again in the Vermeille, along with another four French pattern-race winners, Last Love, Leandra, Sangue and Snow Day, plus Landresse, who had finished second in the Cleopatre, and a second English challenger Leap Lively.

With such a good field the outcome was much more difficult to forecast than the betting on the race, which saw Madam Gay favourite from Val d'Erica and April Run. Val d'Erica, who was considered by some not to have been well ridden in the French Oaks, Madam Gay and April Run had all added to their standing since Chantilly. April Run for her part had finished less than three lengths behind Akarad in the Grand Prix de Saint-Cloud, and on her only other outing had routed the opposition in the Prix de Pomone at Deauville, a Group 3 race for fillies and mares run over a distance of almost a mile and three quarters. When we saw April Run in the paddock before the Vermeille she impressed tremendously: big, good-quartered, very well in herself, she definitely looked the part. She won the race in the style of a very good filly, going to the front early in the straight and never appearing in any danger of being caught. Leandra came past the others in the straight to take second place, a length and a half down, just in front of Madam Gay who beat the rest easily enough.

April Run's owner held a strong hand in the Prix de l'Arc de Triomphe, for she also started the dual Oaks winner Blue Wind and the two were paired in the betting at 13/2. The race showed the fillies' careers moving in opposite directions: Blue Wind was well past her best, whereas April Run was still improving. April Run put up a fine performance, finer even than some people may realise, for her rider had the bad luck to track Akarad into the straight. When Akarad weakened surprisingly quickly almost two furlongs from home April Run couldn't get through on the inside because Argument stood in the way, and she had to be switched wide. She made more ground on the leader Bikala from that point than anything else in the race, showing top-class acceleration, but it was noticeable that she gained very little on Gold River in the last half-furlong; she also hung in slightly towards the running rail halfway through that last furlong. In the end she went down by three parts of a length and a nose, clear of the remainder; Blue Wind finished fifteenth of twenty-four. April Run was the fourteenth French-trained filly to be placed third or higher in the Arc since 1970; in that period, of course, San San, Allez France, Ivanjica, Three Troikas, Detroit and Gold River managed the highest placing, and both Allez France and Comtesse de Loir finished in the first three on two occasions.

In this modern age the connections of a top-class, in-form middle-distance performer needn't be frustrated by the limitations of the European Calendar as autumn slips by. There are plenty of opportunities in North America (one can race through the winter in Florida or California if one so chooses), and not even Australia is too far to travel nowadays (Ardross may challenge for the Melbourne Cup in the first week in November in 1982 on completing another season here). Just twenty days after the Arc, April Run, Detroit and another French horse, Nemr, were in New York on the tight, left-handed Aqueduct course, challenging for the 300,000-dollar Turf Classic against worthy local opposition. The previous season the Prix Gladiateur winner Anifa had surprised the locals by winning at odds of more than 40/1; this time April Run (26/10) caused much less surprise by winning, though she did beat the favourite, the ex-English five-year-old Galaxy Libra. Shrewdly ridden by Paquet, April Run adapted well to the track and fast early pace, responding to her jockey's pushing to secure a place close to the front. She was very impressive indeed in moving strongly into the lead half a mile out and shooting clear off the last bend for a three- or four-length advantage; in the end she held on by three quarters of a length from the fast-finishing Galaxy Libra. The mare The Very One, second to Argument in the 1980 Washington International and winner of over a million dollars, was three lengths further back.

April Run looked a very live candidate for the latest Washington International once officialdom consented to overlook the letter of United States' quarantine regulations. At one time there was talk of her being compelled to make the return journey to France before she could go on to Laurel Park. She ran very well at Laurel, only to be beaten a length by the ex-French outsider Providential, a stable-companion of Galaxy Libra whom April Run this time beat by three and a half lengths despite Paquet's dropping his whip a furlong out.

April Run (b.f. 1978)	Run The Gantlet (b 1968)	Tom Rolfe (b 1962)	Ribot
			Pocahontas II
		First Feather (ch 1963)	First Landing
			Quill
	April Fancy (b 1967)	No Argument (b 1960)	Narrator
			Persuader
		April Slipper (ch 1962)	Panaslipper
			April View

The stallion Run The Gantlet has hit the headlines here with his offspring Ardross and April Run since his return to the United States from Ireland; strange to relate, Providential is also by him. Run The Gantlet wasn't very fashionable when April Run came up at Goffs as a yearling and she, out of a mare by the six-furlong to one-mile handicapper No Argument, fetched a bargain-price 11,500 guineas. The mare April Fancy had produced two winners from three foals—the useful Northern View (by Northfields) who finished fourth

Turf Classic, Aqueduct—April Run holds on from Galaxy Libra

in the Irish Two Thousand Guineas in 1976 and Aherlow Boy (by Tudor Music), successful in a mile-and-a-half maiden at Roscommon and over hurdles. April Fancy was quite a useful winner at up to nine and a half furlongs in Ireland and was allowed to take her chance in the Irish One Thousand. She finished well down the field on that occasion behind Black Satin who, coincidentally, is a fairly close relative. Black Satin is out of that outstanding broodmare Panaview, a full sister to April Fancy's dam April Slipper. The last named was no mean broodmare either: among her winners are the 1977 Gladness Stakes winner Rare April and the 1974 Prix du Lys runner-up Hard April.

The decision whether or not to keep a good filly in training is probably all the harder to arrive at if one is an owner-breeder, as April Run's owner is; whether to go for the prize money or the foal. If she kept her form April Run would take an enormous amount of beating in the top European races at a mile and a half; she could even be fast enough for the top race in France in the spring for older horses, the Prix Ganay at just over a mile and a quarter, though her chance, like that of the Arc second Bikala, would be improved by soft ground to make for a stiffer test of stamina. In the ordinary way, the state of the ground isn't important to April Run; she acts on any going. She's altogether a fine filly, genuine and outstandingly reliable, and we hope we shall see her racing again. *F. Boutin, France.*

AQUA BLUE 4 ch.f. Blue Cashmere 129–Aquanimba (Acropolis 132) (1980 **43** 8fg 8f 7d⁴ 7.2d 6g* 6g 6d 6f 7d 7g⁴ 7s 1981 7s 6g 7g 8g 8.2fg 7f 7f 6fg* 6fg 6fg) lightly-made filly; inconsistent plater; attracted no bid after winning at Ayr in July; stays 7f; acts on a firm surface; has been tried in blinkers; sold 760 gns Doncaster August Sales. *P. Asquith.*

AQUARIAN STAR 2 b.f. Cavo Doro 124–Noddy Time 97 (Gratitude 130) **§§** (1981 5s⁴ 5fg² 6fg 6d 5fg 5f 6g 6fg) Mar 23; 3,200Y; leggy filly; sister to 1980 2-y-o 5f winner Snoozy Time and half-sister to 2 winners, including smart 1¼m performer The Dunce (by High Hat); dam stayed 1m; in frame in minor events, looking unlucky not to win when failing by only a neck to catch Golfer's Dream at Hamilton in May; showed more temperament than ability in most of her subsequent races, on final outing finishing last of 13 in a seller; should be suited by 7f; blinkered fifth outing; slipped up on seventh; one to leave alone. *T. Fairhurst.*

AQUA VERDE 2 b.g. Auction Ring 123–Regal Guard (Realm 129) (1981 **71 p** 5g*) Mar 15; IR 5,000Y, 1,550 2-y-o; first produce; dam unplaced 5 times in Ireland; favourite and blinkered, won 14-runner seller at Catterick in October by 1½ lengths from Etoile d'Or despite being slowly into stride; sold 1,400 gns afterwards; will stay 6f; should have improvement in him. *G. Huffer.*

ARAB ART 2 b.f. Artaius 129–Limbara (Espresso 122) (1981 7f) May 16; — 25,000Y; second foal; dam, half-sister to very useful animals Saraceno and Caprera, was placed in several small races over 11f in France; 50/1 when twelfth of 16 to Hostess in maiden race at Brighton in August, only start. *B. Swift.*

ARANDAR 3 gr.c. Royal and Regal–Sister Supreme 64 (Runnymede 123) — (1980 5fg 6d 6g 6g³ 5d 8g 5s² 8.2s 6v 1981 6v 6s 8g 10fg² 9f 11f 11d) leggy, unfurnished colt; second to Pick A Straw in maiden race at Ayr in August; well beaten in a seller at Hamilton final start; stays 1¼m; probably acts on any going; inconsistent. *W. H. H. Williams.*

ARAX 3 b.g. Auction Ring 123–Inner Guard (King's Bench 132) (1980 6g — 7g 1981 6s 8.5fg⁴ 8d 7f 8h) tall, rather lightly-made gelding; good mover; plating-class maiden; stays 1m; blinkered final start; sold 1,600 gns Ascot September Sales. *G. Hunter.*

ARC D'OR (USA) 3 b.c. Ack Ack–Arme d'Or (Armistice 131) (1980 6.5d² **116** 7.5g* 8g⁴ 9fg² 10s 1981 11fg² 9s² 10.5v) half-brother to several winners, including smart French middle-distance colts Caron (by Caro) and Oreste (by Luthier) and good North American stakes winner Morold (by Sir Gaylord); dam smart at around 1½m; smart performer at 2 yrs; 2½ lengths third of 12 behind subsequently-disqualified Explorer King in Group 2 Prix Noailles at Longchamp in April and length second of 5 to Mourtazam in Prix Matchem at Evry in May; not seen out again until December (ran poorly); stays 11f; probably acts on any going. *J. Cunnington, jnr, France.*

ARCHIMBOLDO 3 b.c. Midsummer Night II 117–Quenilda 101 (Fair Copy) **89** (1980 5fg² 6d³ 5fg² 5g⁴ 5g 1981 5fg 6d 6d* 6g² 6g* 6d 6g) lightly-built, useful-looking colt; showed improved form when winning handicaps at Brighton in April and May; good length second to Marking Time in £4,100 handicap at

Lingfield in between; should stay 7f; acts on a firm and a soft surface; sweated up badly final start; sold 4,400 gns Doncaster November Sales. *M. Masson.*

ARCH MELODY 3 b.c. Arch Sculptor 123–Prophetic Melody (Tudor Melody 129) (1980 5v 5f*(dis) 5fg*(dis) 5d 5g² 5g* 5g² 5d 1981 6g 6g 6fg 5g² 5.3f² 5fg 5fg 5g 5d⁴ 5s 5d 5s² 5s⁴) neat, strong colt; fourth foal; half-brother to Irish 6f and 7f winner Michael's Tower (by Tower Walk) and a winner in Holland; dam placed over 5f at 2 yrs in Ireland; won maiden race at Leopardstown at 2 yrs; also first past post in races at Naas and Leopardstown but was disqualified after failing dope tests; runner-up in 1981 in handicaps at Lingfield in June (to Belfort), Brighton in July (behind Miss Worth) and Warwick in October (went down by 5 lengths to Crosby Triangle); had stiff tasks first 3 starts; speedy and isn't sure to stay 6f; acts on any going; effective with blinkers and without; formerly trained by K. Kerr. *G. Harwood.* **87**

ARCH SCULPTRESS 3 b.f. Arch Sculptor 123–Effervescence II (Charlottesville 135) (1980 5fg 6s² 5d* 5fg 6fg 6g 1981 5d 6fg 5fg 6g³ 6s) strong, sturdy filly; mainly disappointing in 1981, best effort when 5 lengths third behind Marking Time in £4,100 handicap at Lingfield in May; stays 6f; acts well on soft ground. *J. Holt.* **64**

ARCTIC DUET 5 b.m. Comedy Star 121–Arctic Well (Arctic Slave 116) (1980 NR 1981 12g 12s⁴ 15.5d 12g 10f 10f) poor maiden; well beaten in seller final start; has worn blinkers. *J. Scallan.* **—**

ARCTIC RUNNER (USA) 2 gr.f. Northern Fling–Fleet of Foot (Native Dancer) (1981 5g³ 5d* 6f 5g⁴ 5s) Mar 1; $15,500F; tall, lightly-made, leggy filly; half-sister to several minor winners; dam, second once at 3 yrs, is sister to fairly successful sire Iron Warrior; ran on well to beat Lavender Gray by 2¼ lengths in 8-runner maiden race at Lingfield in August; not disgraced subsequently, including when fourth of 10 to Bright View in £7,600 nursery at Redcar in September; stays 6f but is possibly better at 5f; probably acts on any going. *L. Cumani.* **81**

ARCTIC SPARK 3 ch.c. Hot Spark 126–Blue Wings (Majority Blue 126) (1980 7f 1981 6g 8.2s⁴ 8.2f³ 8fg) lengthy, quite attractive colt; in frame in maiden events at Haydock and Hamilton (apprentice event) in June; stays 1m; sold 920 gns Newmarket Autumn Sales. *R. Hills.* **60**

ARCTIC TRIBUNE 7 ch.g. Sallust 134–Arctrullah (Great Captain) (1980 7v² 8f 8f 7f³ 8s 7f 8fg² 8f⁴ 8g³ 7fg³ 8g 8.2s² 7d⁴ 8s 1981 8s 8v⁴ 8d⁴ 9g 8fg 10g 9f³ 8fg³ 8f 9g⁴ 8g) poor handicapper; beaten in sellers on occasions; stays 9f; acts on any going; often sweats up; has been tried in blinkers; suitable mount for an apprentice; none too reliable; sold 1,100 gns Doncaster October Sales. *Miss S. Hall.* **53**

ARCTIQUE ROYALE 3 b.f. Royal and Regal–Arctic Melody 113 (Arctic Slave 116) (1980 5fg* 6s* 1981 7s⁴ 8v* 10fg² 12fg 10g 9.2d) **114**

Paris-based owner J. P. Binet had an eventful fortnight in May. On the sixteenth of the month Kings Lake became his first classic winner when narrowly beating To-Agori-Mou in the Airlie/Coolmore Irish Two Thousand Guineas at the Curragh, but Binet's joy was short-lived as Kings Lake was subsequently disqualified. The following Saturday Binet gained compensation when Arctique Royale got up in another thrilling finish to beat Blue Wind in the Goffs Irish One Thousand Guineas. And before the month was over the Curragh stewards' decision to disqualify Kings Lake was quashed on appeal and he was reinstated. Thus Binet, who had come desperately close to having a classic winner in 1978 when Acamas touched off his Frere Basile in the last strides of the Prix du Jockey-Club, and whose wife owned the 1979 Irish Two Thousand winner Dickens Hill, achieved the notable distinction of having the winners of both Irish Guineas in the same year.

Arctique Royale was acquired from the executors of the estate of Paddy Prendergast after winning both of her races as a two-year-old, including the Moyglare Stud Stakes at the Curragh. She was already established amongst the leading fillies of her age when her trainer announced before the end of August that she was unlikely to run again as she needed more time. Following a fourth place behind Martinova in the Athasi Stakes at the end of April on her reappearance Arctique Royale started joint-third favourite with Star Pastures in a field of fifteen for the Irish Guineas, behind Martinova and Blue Wind. She and Blue Wind dominated the last two furlongs of the race and under very strong riding Arctique Royale got the better of a fierce duel by a short head. Martinova ran on into third place, a length behind them.

Possibly Arctique Royale's hard race left its mark for she was rather disappointing after the Guineas and managed only one place from four starts, in the mile-and-a-quarter Pretty Polly Stakes at the Curragh again, late in June. Even then she ran some way below her best, merely keeping on without threatening the winner Happy Bride and finishing a three-length second. She gave the strong impression that she was ill at ease on the firmish going, and although she had won on a similar surface on her first outing as a two-year-old there is no doubt that she was much better suited by plenty of give underfoot. It was also reported afterwards that she had come into season. Arctique Royale never held out much hope in the straight when sixth behind Blue Wind in the Irish Guinness Oaks on the same course in July and was subsequently off the course for two months. On her return she finished sixth again behind Kings Lake in the Joe McGrath Memorial Stakes at Leopardstown in September, beaten by Blue Wind, and finally finished in the rear in the Prix de l'Opera at Longchamp on Arc day. We were struck on the last-named course by how light she looked.

Arctique Royale (b.f. 1978)	Royal and Regal (b 1970)	Vaguely Noble (b 1965)	Vienna
			Noble Lassie
		Native Street (gr 1963)	Native Dancer
			Beaver Street
	Arctic Melody (b 1962)	Arctic Slave (b 1950)	Arctic Star
			Roman Galley
		Bell Bird (ch 1954)	Mustang
			Belpatrick

Arctique Royale at her best is a rather lightly-made, good-quartered filly; she impressed as a particularly good mover when we watched her go to post at Leopardstown. She is the first classic winner sired by the Florida Derby winner Royal and Regal, who has been returned to the States and is to stand at the Cashel Stud in Florida in 1982. The dam Arctic Melody, who beat Aunt Edith in the 1965 Musidora Stakes, has produced five other winners; remarkably, all of them are fillies. They include the very smart Racquette (by Ballymore), placed in the Irish Guinness Oaks in 1980, and the useful performers Le Melody (by Levmoss) and Nilie (by Relko). Le Melody and Nilie have already made their mark as broodmares, the former as the dam of Ardross and the latter as the dam of Pollerton, and connections have every reason to feel hopeful that Arctique Royale will maintain the family tradition. She visits Kings Lake in 1982. *K. Prendergast, Ireland.*

Goffs Irish One Thousand Guineas, the Curragh—Arctique Royale (rails) keeps on gamely to beat Blue Wind (centre) and Martinova

ARDAR 3 b.c. Relko 136–Adayra (Le Haar 126) (1980 6d³ 1981 11s* 11d **87** 10fg² 8fg⁴ 8fg 15.8g³ 14fg³) tall, attractive colt; ran very green and seemed to be beaten on merit when ½-length second of 16 to Northern Supremo in maiden race at Newbury in May, but didn't have smoothest of passages and was subsequently awarded race; in frame in handicaps at Newmarket (2), Chester and Salisbury, over a wide range of distances, subsequently, on last-named course rather spoiling his chance by hanging (blinkered); suited by further than 1m and evidently stays 2m; probably acts on any going; sometimes sweats up; sold 15,000 guineas Newmarket December Sales. *F. J. Houghton.*

ARDENT LADY 2 ch.f. Status Seeker–Hello Amy 70 (Forlorn River 124) (1981 **65** 6g 5fg³ 5g⁴ 5fg 6s⁴) Jan 30; 5,200Y; strong filly; fourth foal; half-sister to useful sprinter Touch Boy (by Touch Paper); dam placed over 5f at 2 yrs; in frame in maiden races at Catterick and Chester in August and nursery at Nottingham in October (had stiffish task); stays 6f; probably acts on any going. *D. Morley.*

ARDENT WARRIOR 2 b.g. Roman Warrior 132–Ardent Belle (Buisson Ardent **53** 129) (1981 5s³ 5g 5f) May 28; 2,200Y; big gelding; half-brother to several winners here and abroad; dam won over 5f at 2 yrs in Ireland; 8½ lengths third of 6 to Take the Floor in maiden race at Haydock in May; in rear both subsequent outings (off course 3 months before final start). *A. W. Jones.*

ARDGOUR 3 b.c. Nonoalco 131–Hecla 117 (Henry the Seventh 125) (1980 **—** 5fg³ 7s 1981 7fg 8d 8s⁴ 8.3fg 8fg 8fg 8g) attractive, well-made colt; ran best race when 6 lengths fourth behind Aperitivo in handicap at Goodwood in May; ran moderately in sellers last 2 outings; stay 1m; gives impression he needs strong handling; sometimes blinkered; sold to A. Ingham 1,000 gns Newmarket Autumn Sales. *P. Walwyn.*

ARDMAY 3 ro.f. Roan Rocket 128–Nettlebed 84 (Hethersett 134) (1980 NR **57** 1981 7v³ 7d 12d 10s 10g) rangy, useful-looking filly; sister to 3 winners, notably very smart 7f to 1¼m winner Gairloch and smart miler Whistlefield; dam won over 7f; most disappointing after finishing promising 4 lengths third of 9 to Singwara in maiden race at Goodwood in May; should be suited by 1m+; blinkered final start. *R. Price.*

ARDOONY 3 b.c. Ardoon 124–Linbel (Linacre 133) (1980 5f⁴ 5g 6fg 5g³ 5d* **78** 6g² 6a 1981 7d* 7g 8g² 8.2s 8f 8f* 8g 8fg 8fg 8d 8.2v 8d⁴) neat colt; won Northern Free Handicap at Newcastle in April (by 2½ lengths from Sovereign Landing) and Welbred Handicap at Beverley in July (by 1½ lengths from Montclair); often disappointing however; stays 1m; acts on any going; suitable mount for an apprentice; sometimes sweats up; started slowly and ran miserably eighth outing. *R. Hollinshead.*

ARDROSS 5 b.h. Run The Gantlet–Le Melody 102 (Levmoss 133) (1980 10v **131** 16fg* 20g² 21fg² 18g² 16f* 15.5v³ 1981 14d* 20f* 21fg* 13.3fg* 12d 15.5v*) The parish pump was given some heavy-handed cranking in the British media after the most recent running of Europe's richest race, the Prix de l'Arc de Triomphe. The failure of any of the six British-trained challengers to reach a place—fifth-placed Ardross did easily the best—ranked very high among the numerous humiliations British stables have suffered in what is widely acknowledged as Europe's supreme test for middle-distance horses. Ardross, Prince Bee, Cut Above, Pelerin and Beldale Flutter (supplemented by the British-based New Zealand champion Ring The Bell) looked a very strong team, probably as strong, taken all round, as any recently sent for the Arc. Their poor collective showing seemed too much for some critics to stomach. Excuses abounded: it was said that the dead going was against most of the British runners; it was said that some, including Ardross, were beaten by a 'bad' draw; and it was also said that the British jockeys were out-manoeuvred by their counterparts on the best home-trained runners. Finding excuses for British-trained Prix de l'Arc runners should be second nature to some of our Press correspondents. They have had plenty of practice. Mill Reef and Rheingold are the only British-trained winners of the Prix de l'Arc in the period since 1949 when the value of the race was raised sharply to make it a race of world-wide importance; and British stables have provided nineteen of the sixty-six starters in the last three runnings of the Arc—among them three winners of the King George VI and Queen Elizabeth Diamond Stakes, Ile de Bourbon, Troy and Ela-Mana-Mou—with only the third places of Troy and Ela-Mana-Mou to show for it.

In our view the reasons for the apparently disappointing showing of the British-trained Prix de l'Arc challengers in 1981 can quickly be reduced to one:

they weren't good enough on the day. None of the excuses holds water: with the possible exception of Pelerin who is probably at his best on a sound surface, the major British-trained challengers were proven on soft going; and we shouldn't dream of laying any of the blame for a horse's defeat in a race over a mile and a half on the draw; as for the British jockeys, we thought them blameless—Piggott and Murray in particular rode copybook races on the two leading British challengers Ardross and Beldale Flutter, taking up forward positions and being well placed at the start of the long, sweeping turn to the home straight. The Prix de l'Arc de Triomphe provides a stringent test of a horse's ability and very few horses win it without showing ability well above classic standard. The overwhelming majority of its winners have to give the best performance of their careers to earn victory. The Prix de l'Arc is a magnificent race. But it is not without its drawbacks: it is run late in the season, a shade too late perhaps; the going is apt to be soft; and there is almost always a big field which increases the risk of some of the runners meeting with interference in the course of the race. Britain's greatest post-war trainer Noel Murless is on record as saying: 'The Prix de l'Arc is just three weeks too late for a horse which has undergone a proper classic preparation, working up to the Guineas in the spring, followed by Epsom and Ascot. The St Leger is just about the last time that such a horse can be kept at his peak'. Mill Reef finished second in the Two Thousand Guineas and went on to win the Derby, the Eclipse, the King George and the Prix de l'Arc in the same season, but he is one of the few recent examples of a three-year-old's winning the Prix de l'Arc after showing top-class form in the spring and going through a full programme of big races in the summer. Indeed, it happens more frequently nowadays that a three-year-old wins the Arc after showing himself, or herself, to be a top-class performer for the first time in the late-summer or the autumn—San San, Alleged and Detroit are recent examples.

The Prix de l'Arc is woven into the fabric of European racing but its timing is geared to the French Calendar. In their classic programme the French place less emphasis on very early development—the French Guineas, for example, are not held in such high esteem as their British equivalents—and the best of the French classic generation with pretensions to staying middle distances are rarely at their peak before the Prix du Jockey-Club and the Prix de Diane in June. By contrast, the British programme of top middle-distance events ends before the season has entered the home straight. After the King George VI and Queen Elizabeth Diamond Stakes in July there isn't another Group 1 pattern race at a mile and a half or more open to top-class horses from different generations. The Yorkshire Oaks and the St Leger are restricted to three-year-olds; the Sussex Stakes, the Benson and Hedges Gold Cup and the Champion Stakes, the only Group 1 races open to four-year-olds and upwards after the King George, are at a mile or a mile and a quarter. France has two open-aged international Group 1 races after July at a mile and a half or more: the Prix de l'Arc and the Prix Royal-Oak, formerly the French St Leger which was opened to older horses in 1979. Germany has two: the Grosser Preis von Baden and the Preis von Europa. And Italy has two: the Gran Premio del Jockey Club and the Premio

Gold Cup, Ascot—Ardross coasts home from Shoot A Line

Roma. Why none in Britain? Surely the racing public should have an opportunity to see the best middle-distance stayers competing on British tracks in the second part of the season. Like any other spectator sport, racing should strive to put on the best entertainment for its customers. As we see it, it is quite a simple matter for the Jockey Club to do something about this disturbing omission from the British Calendar.

The case for opening up the St Leger to four-year-olds and upwards is one that we have argued so often that there is a grave danger of our becoming tiresome on the subject. But we can't see why our best older middle-distance performers and stayers should have to go to France, Germany or Italy to find suitable opportunities in the second part of the season. The vast majority of top-class horses on the flat make few enough appearances as it is. As we have said before, the St Leger has lost prestige and is no longer an automatic target for the best of the classic generation bred to stay: Shergar was the first Derby winner to go on to Doncaster since Nijinsky eleven years earlier. As a stepping stone to the following year's Cup races, now very much less important than they were up to thirty years ago, the Leger has largely outlived its usefulness. Most St Leger winners that remain in training nowadays are put back to a mile and a half, the conventionally-accepted classic distance at which it often pays better dividends to race them. Open the St Leger to four-year-olds and upwards and increase its prize-money to the value of the Prix de l'Arc—sponsorship would not be hard to find—and it would make a magnificent race, the European championship at a mile and three quarters. The St Leger course is one of the fairest in Europe, perfectly flat except for a slight hill about a mile and a quarter from home with a run-in of five furlongs and an exceedingly wide straight. There are always fewer 'after-the-race' stories of interference and bad luck after a St Leger than after an Arc. The timing of the St Leger is arguably better than that for the Prix de l'Arc, coming three weeks earlier in the season, and the going on Leger day is usually good.

We are strongly opposed to any reduction in the distance of the St Leger. There are already enough—arguably more than enough—really big stakes races in Europe at a mile and a half; and a reduction to a mile and a quarter would favour a group already catered for in the second part of the British season by the Benson and Hedges Gold Cup and the Champion Stakes. Generally speaking, a horse capable of staying a mile and a half at Epsom in the Derby in June should be better served by a race over the Leger distance in September than

84

by one over a mile and a quarter. There have been Derby winners who have failed at Doncaster for want of stamina but of the twelve post-war Derby winners that have contested the St Leger there have been only two, Parthia and Shergar, who possibly failed through lack of stamina. An open St Leger would also provide a much-needed worthwhile target later in the season for four-year-old and older stayers of the highest class, of whom Sagaro, Buckskin, Le Moss and Ardross are notable recent examples. The authorities have belatedly begun to take action to restore some prestige to the Gold Cup—its first prize has risen steadily from £17,837 to £39,013 over the past five seasons—but there is no other Group 1 race in Europe for long-distance horses above the age of three until the Prix Royal-Oak (worth £33,461 to the winner in 1981) at Longchamp at the end of October. The opening of the St Leger would help to provide a more balanced domestic and European programme of big races. And, with its prize boosted to match that of the Arc, it would provide a fitting climax to the British season. The French, it seems, are the dominating influence when it comes to questions involving the pattern of racing in Europe and they would probably feel that the St Leger in its changed form would be a threat to the supremacy of the Prix de l'Arc de Triomphe. So it would be, although as a mile-and-three-quarter race it would not be in direct competition. The French, however, could hardly oppose the opening of the St Leger so soon after doing the same to the Prix Royal-Oak and, in any case, the Leger and the Arc would still be three weeks apart, time enough for the best middle-distance stayers to take part in both.

The benefits of opening the St Leger should also be seen in a wider context. The career of a top-class horse on the flat in Europe is usually very short. The programme of racing as it stands offers the greatest rewards to horses bred and trained to be successful at two and three years. A hundred years ago another great trainer Matt Dawson warned that 'horses for years have had too great a strain put on them in their two- and three-year-old days, consequently every succeeding generation becomes less robust, and you will find that as time goes on horses will less and less be able to stand the work that their more hardy ancestors did.' Since Dawson's day the emphasis on two- and three-year-old racing has become very much greater—the sharp decline in the relative rewards offered for stayers and in the demand for their services at stud is proof of that. Is it desirable for the career of a racehorse to begin when he is still a baby barely two years of age, to continue while he is still growing and developing, and to terminate before he has reached maturity? Wouldn't it be better for breeders to find out which are the best horses when they have arrived at maturity, not while they are still in the process of developing? The remedy is to place the emphasis upon racing merit at three and four years, instead of at two and three—to lower the number and value of first-class races for two-year-olds (four of the six Group 1 pattern races in Britain after the end of August are for two-year-olds) and to create or elevate in their place three or four open-aged races with added money to put them on a par with the best races. These additional 'glamour' events should be of such value and prestige that it must seem as necessary for a good horse to take part in them as it is now for him to take part in races such as the Two Thousand Guineas and the Derby. The financial

Goodwood Cup—another effortless win for Ardross

pressure on an owner to retire a top-class colt at the end of his three-year-old days is very strong indeed and any change in the racing programme that might persuade owners of good horses to keep them on the racecourse for another season must be worth considering.

If Ardross had not stayed in training after his three-year-old career what would his achievements have amounted to? He would have gone down in history as no better than a useful performer, the 50/1-winner of the Gallinule Stakes, a Group 2 pattern race for three-year-olds run at the Curragh in the spring. Like many a true stayer, Ardross was slow to mature but as a four-year-old he took part in three magnificent and memorable races with Le Moss which lifted the series of Cup races to a prominence as great as they have enjoyed in any season since the 'forties. Ardross came out of his races against Le Moss with enormous credit, going down narrowly on each occasion, and he was bought after the end of the season from the executors of the late Paddy Prendergast for an undisclosed sum. Ardross was sent to Henry Cecil who had saddled Le Moss to win the Gold Cup, the Goodwood Cup and the Doncaster Cup—the so-called stayers' triple crown—in 1979 and 1980. A similar programme was announced for Ardross and he made his first appearance for his new connections in the Yorkshire Cup over a mile and three quarters at York in the middle of May. His principal rivals Nicholas Bill and Shining Finish had the benefit of a previous outing but Ardross, looking a shade in need of the race, won comfortably by three lengths from Nicholas Bill, showing the best turn of foot at the end of a fairly-run race. Ardross had demonstrated when winning the two-mile Jockey Club Cup as a four-year-old that his excellent stamina was supplemented by a useful turn of finishing speed.

The fillies Shoot A Line and Gold River looked the only serious dangers to Ardross in the Gold Cup and the late decision by Gold River's connections to reserve her for the much more valuable Grand Prix de Saint-Cloud, run over a mile and a half at the beginning of July, must have been a great disappointment to the Ascot executive. Compared to some recent Gold Cups the latest was a tame affair. There were only four runners, the smallest Gold Cup field for more than sixty years, and Ardross started at 100/30 on with Shoot A Line at 7/2, Pragmatic at 20/1 and the modest handicapper Ayyabaan, who opened at 200/1, at 50/1. Ayyabaan set only a fair pace and turning into the final straight the runners were tightly bunched. Ardross had held a slight lead from about half a mile out and was challenged only by Shoot A Line in the last two furlongs; the winning margin was a length but there was no mistaking Ardross' great superiority. Ardross gave Piggott his tenth winning ride in the Gold Cup. For the record, Ayyabaan came home third, ten lengths behind Shoot A Line, rewarding the enterprise of his connections with £7,013. The heavily-bandaged Pragmatic, making his only appearance of the season, earned for his owner £3,054. Not for the first time the question was asked: 'What do owners want?'

Geoffrey Freer Stakes, Newbury—Ardross puts up a superb performance to beat Castle Keep

Prix Royal-Oak, Longchamp—Ardross becomes the first older horse to win the French St Leger since it became an open-aged event in 1979

The majority are prepared to spend thousands on untried yearlings, yet they often show cavalier indifference to golden opportunities for getting some of their money back. It was apparent some time in advance that there would be a very small field for the Gold Cup. It seems that the racing world in general puts overwhelming emphasis on winning, as opposed to finishing second, third or fourth and, if that is so, perhaps the Jockey Club should revise its rules governing the distribution of prize money in flat pattern races in which, at present, the placed horses receive a larger share of the total prize money than in races of lower status.

There was a field of six for the Goodwood Cup including the geldings Donegal Prince, Popsi's Joy and Mon's Beau, who had been barred from the Gold Cup. Almost everyone, except those with the authority to do something about it, acknowledges that the top races should be open to the best horses, whether they be entires or not. The prohibition on geldings in Group 1 races is absurd. The front-running Donegal Prince, winner of the Ladbroke Chester Cup and the Queen Alexandra Stakes, made the Goodwood Cup, which is a Group 2 pattern race, much more of a spectacle than the Gold Cup. The pace was a good one from the start but, as at Royal Ascot, Piggott gave Ardross as easy a race as possible: passing Donegal Prince on the bridle with two furlongs to go, Ardross beat him cheekily by a length with the three-year-old Halsbury three lengths away third. At 9/2 on, Ardross was the shortest-priced favourite for the Goodwood Cup since Tiberius won at the same odds in 1935.

After the Goodwood Cup, Ardross had his sights set on the Prix de l'Arc de Triomphe, a race at which Gold River, who had won the Prix du Cadran (French Gold Cup) in May, was also being aimed. Until he ran in the Geoffrey Freer Stakes at Newbury in August we had always entertained serious doubts about Ardross' proving as effective at a mile and a half as he was at longer distances. There was no doubting that Ardross was a fine stayer but it seemed to us that a really good middle-distance horse would always have the edge on him at a mile and a half; his turn of foot was very effective when measured against that of most stayers but, unlike Gold River, whose turn of finishing speed was even more formidable, Ardross had no high-class performances to his credit at a mile and a half and had always given the impression of being a thorough stayer. We weren't so sure of ourselves after Ardross won the one-mile-five-furlong Geoffrey Freer Stakes. The pace was very slow until Ardross increased it markedly after about half a mile. Piggott was pressing Ardross to his top pace soon after the field turned into the straight and approaching the two-furlong marker the four-year-old Castle Keep, in receipt of 8 lb from Ardross, seemed to be going very much better. But Ardross, urged on vigorously by Piggott, lengthened his stride in fine style and drew away to beat Castle Keep by five lengths with the subsequent St Leger winner Cut Above a length and a half further behind in third place. Ardross was to have run in the Doncaster Cup before being sent to Longchamp but he by-passed Doncaster because his trainer considered the going too firm. Nevertheless, after the defeat of Shergar in the St Leger, Ardross became favourite in the ante-post market on the Prix de l'Arc.

At 11/2 third favourite on the French Tote, Ardross was the shortest-priced of the British Prix de l'Arc challengers. The very early pace wasn't quite so

Mr C. A. B. St George's "Ardross"

cut-throat as usual and Piggott didn't have to set Ardross alight to take up a position among the leaders from his outside draw. Ardross settled down close behind the front-running Bikala after tacking over towards the inside when the runners 'broke' after running straight for a furlong or so, as they are required to do in France. Approaching the home turn it was apparent from our vantage point that Ardross was in difficulties; he was finding the pace set by Bikala too hot. Backers of Ardross knew their fate very early in the straight and although he kept on gamely he couldn't match Gold River, Bikala, April Run and Perrault for finishing speed. Ardross came home just under five lengths behind the winner Gold River. Ardross took his revenge on Gold River three weeks later in the Prix Royal-Oak, in which Gold River had beaten him into third place the previous year. Gold River didn't reproduce her best form in the latest Prix Royal-Oak but Ardross certainly seemed to appreciate the return to a longer trip. Slipping through into the lead on the inside rounding the home turn, Ardross strode out magnificently under strong riding to win by four lengths and two and a half lengths from Proustille and Gold River. Ardross was particularly impressive in the last furlong, running on with great resolution and showing unmistakeable enthusiasm for his job.

It is good news that Ardross is to remain in training. He is to be aimed again at the Gold Cup but will then be returned to middle distances with a view to tackling both the King George VI and Queen Elizabeth Diamond Stakes and the Prix de l'Arc de Triomphe. It is not easy at this stage to think of a stayer that could be backed with confidence to beat him at Royal Ascot in 1982, provided he remains in good form. However, judged on his performance in the most recent Prix de l'Arc, we have to say that we're not sanguine about Ardross' prospects of winning a King George or an Arc. He is extremely difficult to beat at distances upwards of a mile and five furlongs—he'd have a good chance in an open-aged St Leger—but the latest Prix de l'Arc showed that he lacks that dash of top-class finishing pace that is so often a hallmark of the outstanding mile-and-a-half performer. Not that Ardross' chance in the King George and the Prix de l'Arc is a remote one. Clearly he is a high-class performer at a mile and a half and there are circumstances—soft ground and a searching end-to-end gallop, both of which would put a premium on stamina—in which we could envisage Ardross' improving on the form he has shown at the trip. He acts on any going and is very game and genuine.

Ardross (b.h. 1976)	Run The Gantlet (b 1968)	Tom Rolfe (b 1962)	Ribot Pocahontas II
		First Feather (ch 1963)	First Landing Quill
	Le Melody (ch 1971)	Levmoss (b 1965)	Le Levanstell Feemoss
		Arctic Melody (b 1962)	Arctic Slave Bell Bird

Ardross is an attractive horse by the same sire as the Prix de l'Arc third April Run; Run The Gantlet won the Man o'War Stakes and the Washington International as a three-year-old. Ardross is the first foal of Le Melody, a very well bred mare by the Gold Cup, Prix du Cadran and Prix de l'Arc winner Levmoss out of the Musidora Stakes winner Arctic Melody. Le Melody won at seven furlongs as a two-year-old and at a mile and a quarter at three on her only starts. She was also represented on the racecourse in the most recent season by the D. O'Brien-trained three-year-old Karol (by Kalamoun), winner of a maiden race over a mile at Leopardstown in October on his only start. Le Melody's two-year-old of 1981 is the unraced Thistlewood, a sister to Karol who is also trained by O'Brien. *H. Cecil.*

A REJECT 3 b.c. The Brianstan 128–Aurelia 68 (Aureole 132) (1980 NR — 1981 7fg 6fg 9g 9d⁴) 12,500Y; quite an attractive colt; half-brother to a winning plater, a winner in Brazil and a winning hurdler; dam stayer; ran better than finishing position suggests when fourth behind easy winner Keshoon in seller at Wolverhampton in October; trained by F. Durr first 2 outings. *D. Leslie.*

ARGUMENT (FR) 4 b.c. Kautokeino–Arantelle (Tapioca 123) (1980 8s* 8g³ **129** 10.5fg² 12fg 11s* 10d² 12g 12f² 12f* 1981 10d* 10.5g* 12d 12.5g 10s 12d 13s⁴ 12f)
'Have horses, will travel' would have been an appropriate motto for Maurice Zilber who announced in October that his training activities in France were to cease at the end of the season. During the 'seventies a string of top-class horses passed through his hands and most were raced in a very enterprising fashion, with Zilber never being afraid to challenge for the best races wherever they were run. While in his care Dahlia won in five countries, Exceller and Youth in three and Nobiliary in two, with each of the four gaining important successes in North America. The Washington International fell to horses trained by him four times, the Canadian International Championship three and in an era of increasingly international racing Zilber was a master of the art.

Argument, who had smoothly won the 1980 Washington International not long after Zilber took over from J. Cunnington, jnr, as his trainer, was the best of his age in Europe over middle distances at three. Before his Laurel win he had finished a splendid second to Detroit in the Prix de l'Arc de Triomphe and he looked sure to take a lot of beating in the top races of 1981. Predictably enough for a French four-year-old of his ability, Argument ran in the Prix d'Harcourt and Prix Ganay at Longchamp early in the year and in both he

Prix Ganay, Longchamp—Argument sprints clear to beat Armistice Day

Mr B. McNall's "Argument" (A. Lequeux)

exacted revenge on Detroit for his Arc defeat, though the filly admittedly wasn't at her best on either occasion. In the Harcourt Argument came with a strong run to catch Katowice close home, winning by a head, and in the Ganay he justified short-priced favouritism impressively, leading over a furlong out and sprinting clear to account for Armistice Day by three lengths with In Fijar a length away third.

Argument (Fr) (b.c. 1977)	Kautokeino (b 1967)	Relko (b 1960)	Tanerko
			Relance III
		Cranberry (b 1957)	Aureole
			Big Berry
	Arantelle (ch 1966)	Tapioca (b 1953)	Vandale
			Semoule d'Or
		Neptune's Doll (ch 1960)	Neptune II
			Dzena

After this good start Argument surprisingly failed to win another race and his campaign disappointingly tapered off into something approaching anti-climax. Next time out he was demoted from third behind Vayrann in the Prix Jean de Chaudenay at Saint-Cloud, where he was the victim as well as the instigator of some barging that took place early in the straight; and in the Grand Prix de Saint-Cloud his fortunes reached a nadir, with his sweating up and never threatening to take a hand when seventh to Akarad. Argument ran once more in Europe, in the Prix de l'Arc de Triomphe in October, and went some way towards redeeming himself, staying on well to be sixth to Gold River, beaten just over six lengths. In the best traditions of his stable, Argument's other starts were in North America where he ran respectably in the Arlington Million at Chicago, the Rothmans International at Woodbine and the Hollywood Turf Cup at Hollywood Park.

Argument has been retired to Gainesway Farm, Kentucky. By the lightly-raced but smart Kautokeino out of a Tapioca mare who won twice at around a mile and a quarter in France, his breeding is unremarkable compared with that of many of the Gainesway stallions, and it is to be hoped he will be given the chance at stud that his excellent form at three entitles him to. Arantelle, who has been purchased by Argument's owners, is the dam of several winners in addition to Argument, two of them, the one-mile and nine-furlong winner Akena and the three-year-old Arad, successful over nine and ten and a half furlongs, also by Kautokeino. The grandam, Neptune's Doll, was smart at her best and came from the family of Doria II, second in the French Oaks, and Tahiti II, who won the French Oaks. Argument, a genuine sort, stayed a mile and a half. He acted on any going, but went particularly well on firm. His fee is 30,000 dollars. *M. Zilber, France.*

ARIADNE 2 b.f. Bustino 136–Zerbinetta 96 (Henry the Seventh 125) (1981 8fg — 8g) Feb 11; good-bodied, attractive filly; good walker and mover; half-sister to 2 winners, including quite useful sprinter General Wade (by Bold Lad, Ire); dam sprinter; showed a little ability when about 11 lengths ninth of 15 to Rockfest in £3,600 race at Goodwood in September; unquoted when behind in·30-runner maiden event won by Farioffa at Newmarket the following month. *J. Dunlop.*

ARIDJE 3 b.f. Mummy's Pet 125–Derrede (Derring-Do 131) (1980 5fg* 5g 6g 5g3 — 1981 6g) lightly-made filly; won maiden race at Kempton as a 2-y-o when trained by R. Boss; had stiff task and was badly drawn when in rear on only outing of 1981 (May); form only at 5f; sold 3,000 gns Newmarket December Sales. *M. Stoute.*

ARIOS 3 b.g. Manacle 123–Blue Bird 84 (Majority Blue 126) (1980 8s 1981 8g 65 8g 8fg4 8f 10fg4 12.2g 12s*) big, strong gelding; second favourite, hung quite sharply left when beating Adam Craig by a length in 20-runner maiden event at Redcar in October, best effort; suited by 1½m; acts well on soft going. *M. Camacho.*

ARKAN 3 b.c. Prince Tenderfoot 126–Adamantos 92 (Yellow God 129) (1980 7f 78 8d4 10g 1981 8.2fg3 12g3 11g2 10f* 10.1f3 10g4 10fg3 10g* 10fg 10f* 10d* 9s4 10g) strong, good sort; not a good walker; successful in handicaps at Yarmouth, Newcastle, Ripon and Ayr, beating Royal Vulcan by ½ length in slowly-run event on last-named course in September; stays 1½m, but seems best at 1¼m; acts on a soft surface but is well suited by firm going; reportedly suffering from a minor injury when below his best ninth start. *J. Hindley.*

ARKENGARTHDALE 7 b.m. Sweet Story 122–Fortzeno 78 (Fortino II 120) — (1980 NR 1981 16.5g 18g) small mare; lightly raced and no sign of ability on flat though has won over hurdles. *N. Bycroft.*

ARLINGTON GIRL 2 b.f. Rarity 129–Santa Nan (Santa Claus 133) (1981 60 7f4 7g 7d 10d 8.2s3 8d) Mar 20; 6,000Y, 5,200Y; narrow, light-framed filly; sister to 1978 Irish 2-y-o 7f winner Santa Brigida, and half-sister to a winner in Italy; dam half-sister to Chester Vase winner Gulf Pearl; plater; 3¼ lengths third of 14 to Sovereigns Image at Nottingham in October; should stay 1¼m; acts on soft going. *Mrs J. Reavey.*

ARMALOU 2 gr.f. Ardoon 124–Sweet Rocket (Roan Rocket 128) (1981 5g 5fg — 5g4 6fg 6g 7g 6d) May 9; IR 2,000Y; robust filly; half-sister to 6f and 7f winner Astral Suite (by On Your Mark); dam lightly-raced half-sister to very smart sprint winner Harem; plating-class maiden. *D. Sasse.*

ARMATEX 4 b. or br.g. Kambalda 108–Marina (Supreme Court 135) (1980 9f — 12s4 10.1s3 15.5s 10.1g 12f3 1981 12s 15.5d 10.1d) strong gelding; poor form, including in a seller; stays 1½m; acts well on soft going; has worn blinkers. *M. Bolton.*

ARMENISTIS 2 b.c. Relkino 131–Persian Market 105 (Taj Dewan 128) (1981 65 7fg 7f3 8g 8g) May 14; 15,500Y; compact, quite useful sort; second live produce; dam awarded 1975 Princess Elizabeth Stakes; seems little better than a plater; should be suited by 1m; sold 2,000 gns Newmarket Autumn Sales. *C. Brittain.*

ARMINIUS 4 b.g. River Beauty 105–Armenia (Buisson Ardent 129) (1980 63 11.5g2 11.5d2 12s 1981 22.2f4 12g4) ex-Irish gelding; respectable fourth to Donegal Prince in Queen Alexandra Stakes at Royal Ascot in June on first start; evidently suited by long distances; probably acts on any going. *G. Balding.*

ARMIS 2 b.c. Guillaume Tell 121–Time Tell's (Le Levanstell 122) (1981 7fg 8s) —
May 6; IR 5,800F, 5,200Y; half-brother to Irish middle-distance winners Break
of Dawn (by Ballymoss) and Weaver's Shed (by Weavers' Hall); dam 7f winner
at 2 yrs in Ireland; behind in sizeable fields of maidens at Newmarket in August
and Warwick in October. *A. Jarvis.*

ARMISTICE DAY 5 b. or br.h. Rheingold 137–Peace 113 (Klairon 131) (1980 **121**
12g² 12g³ 11g* 12.5g² 11.5g* 13.5g* 12g 10s* 11g³ 10g* 1981 10.5v⁴ 10s* 10d³
10.5g² 9.7s) smart performer; won Prix Exbury at Saint-Cloud in March by
1½ lengths from Perrault; ran well in races won by Argument at Longchamp on
next 2 starts, finishing just over 3 lengths third in Prix d'Harcourt and 3 lengths
second in Prix Ganay; didn't run up to his best in Prix Dollar at Longchamp
again in May and was subsequently sent to race in USA; effective from 1¼m to
1¾m; acted well on soft going; stud in USA. *C. de Watrigant, France.*

ARM THE LAW 4 b.f. Royal Palace 131–Escape 93 (Gilles de Retz 132) (1980
7.2d 12.2g 1981 9f 5g) small filly; of little account; sold 440 gns Doncaster
November Sales. *K. Stapleton.*

ARMY COUNCIL 2 b.g. Brigadier Gerard 144–Roman Meeting (Quorum 126) **67**
(1981 6g 8g³) Mar 20; fair sort; fifth foal; dam unraced half-sister to high-class
chaser Spanish Steps; 16/1, began to run on on meeting rising ground when 7
lengths third of 14 to Arrowood Dream in maiden race at Beverley in September;
will be suited by 1½m. *W. Hastings-Bass.*

ARNALDO 3 b.g. Upper Case–Flower Petals (Busted 134) (1980 6g 6s 7d 8fg⁴ **75**
1981 10fg* 12fg² 11.7fg* 12f² 10.4s) neat gelding; favourite when trotting up
in 19-runner seller at Windsor in June (bought in 3,200 gns) and when beating
Carved Opal 2 lengths in 18-runner handicap on same course in July; stays 1½m;
acts on firm going (ran moderately in a ladies race on soft final start); usually
front runner. *N. Callaghan.*

AROVING 2 br.f. Rapid River 127–Kumon Lass 92 (King's Coup 108) (1981 5g) —
May 16; 500Y; half-sister to 1m winner Most Jubilant (by Most Secret); dam won
twice over 5f at 2 yrs; 16/1 when about 9 lengths sixth of 7 to Lucky Season in
seller at Carlisle in May, only outing. *W. A. Stephenson.*

ARRABIDA 2 b.f. Bold Lad (Ire) 133–Chippings (Busted 134) (1981 6d² 6f*) **108**
Mar 22; IR 62,000Y; second foal; half-sister to useful Irish 7.5f to 1½m winner
Red Chip (by Red God); dam unraced half-sister to smart 5f performer Silver
God; led inside final furlong to win 8-runner maiden race at Deauville in August
by a length from Mac Rhefna; looked promising at this time but wasn't seen out
again; will stay 1m. *F. Boutin, France.*

ARRAS GIRL 2 br.f. Rapid River 127–Arras Gem 82 (Three Wishes 114) **46**
(1981 5s⁴ 5g² 5d³ 5f 5f 6g 5f 5f) neat filly; first foal; dam won twice over 1m
and also won over hurdles; plater; no worthwhile form after third outing; should
stay 6f. *A. Smith.*

ARROWHEAD 3 b.c. Steel Heart 128–First Round 97 (Primera 131) (1980 **93**
5g² 5g³ 1981 8.2s³ 7f 7fg* 8f² 6fg⁴ 7g 5s) well-made, attractive colt; had stiff
task and ran very well when about 8 lengths fifth of 20 behind Rasa Penang in
Jersey Stakes at Royal Ascot in June on second start; needed to be kept up to
his work when landing the odds by 1½ lengths from Casa Esquillina (pair 10
lengths clear) in maiden race at Newcastle later in month; head second to
Ramannolie in minor event at Bath in July; stays 1m, but is possibly best at up
to 7f; acts well on fast ground; had stiff tasks last 2 outings; sold to J. Gosden
21,000 gns Newmarket December Sales. *R. Price.*

ARROWOOD DREAM (USA) 2 b.c. Far North 120–Dear Annie (Impressive) **98**
(1981 7g² 7fg³ 8g* 8s*) Mar 28; $42,000Y; rather lightly-made colt; fourth
foal; half-brother to a minor winner; dam won 8 times at up to 9f; successful in
maiden event at Beverley in September (beat Tancred Walk by 6 lengths) and
29-runner minor race at Redcar the following month (by 2½ lengths from Twist
Home); would probably also have won on debut had his fairly inexperienced rider
not eased him up well inside final furlong; will stay middle distances; possibly
needs some give in the ground and acts well on soft going; should make a useful
handicapper at 3 yrs. *J. Dunlop.*

ARSENAL (HUN) 6 b.g. Nagyvezer–Ara (Balto 127) (1981 10fg 16d 11.7fg) —
Hungarian-bred gelding; has won 8 times in Hungary from 1m to 2m; well
beaten in amateur riders races and a minor event in the South. *K. Brassey.*

ARTIPIAR 4 ch.f. Tyrant–Persian Coach (Parthia 132) (1980 8fg 5f 5f 5g³(dis) **91**
5g³ 6fg 5d³ 6g 5f³ 5.6g 5fg² 5s² 1981 6g 5g² 6v) fair sort; good mover; useful
performer at 3 yrs; put up best effort in 1981 when ½-length second to Walter

Osborne in minor event at Edinburgh in September; finds 5f on sharp side and should stay 7f; acts on any going; usually blinkered nowadays; often starts slowly. *W. O'Gorman.*

ARTISTRY 3 gr. or ro.f. Gold Form 108–Palmural 111 (Palestine 133) (1980 5g 5d* 5fg² 5g 1981 5s 5d 5.8d 5fg) compact filly; not a good mover in her slower paces; won maiden race at Newbury as a 2-y-o; well beaten in 1981 (had stiffish tasks first 2 starts); not sure to stay 6f; acts on a firm and a soft surface; sold to Horse France 9,600 gns Newmarket Autumn Sales. *Mrs R. Lomax.* —

ARTRACIN 3 ch.f. High Line 125–Silleys Maid 100 (Continuation 120) (1980 NR 1981 9d) sparely-made filly; third foal; half-sister to fairly useful 6f to 1m winner Silley's Knight (by Derring-Do); dam sprinter; dwelt and was always struggling when ninth of 11 behind Mistress Gay in maiden race at Wolverhampton in May, only outing; sold 720 gns Newmarket Autumn Sales. *M. Stoute.* —

ARUSE 3 ch.f. Sharpen Up 127–Wind Break 81 (Borealis) (1980 5f 5f³ 6s² 6g 7d² 6g 1981 8g⁴ 8d 8g 10s 10g) very lightly-made filly; good mover; in frame in maiden races; stays 1m; off course 4 months before third start; trained early in season by F. Durr. *A. Hide.* —

ASANIA (FR) 3 b.f. Ace of Aces 126–Aurinette (Sheshoon 132) (1980 6.5g 7.5d³ 8v* 1981 9.6fg³ 10v 10.5fg 9d³ 8g 8f) 360,000 francs Y (approx £38,000); compact filly; second foal; dam smart French winner at around 1¼m; third in Group 3 Prix Vanteaux at Longchamp in April (narrowly beaten behind Bernica) and Group 3 Prix Chloe at Evry in July (2¾ lengths behind Kilmona); also ran creditably when 4¼ lengths fifth to Tootens in Prix Saint-Alary at Longchamp on second start; well beaten on her other starts, including in Prix de Diane de Revlon at Chantilly; will stay 1½m; seems to act on any going; blinkered fifth start. *J. Cunnington, jnr, France.* **112**

ASCENMOOR 2 b.c. Ascendant 96–Honeymoor 64 (Pardao 120) (1981 5s 5g⁴ 7g 8.2fg 8fg 8.2d) Mar 1; leggy colt; bad plater; sold out of F. Dever's stable 1,900 gns Doncaster August Sales after third start. *R. Hobson.* —

ASCOT AGAIN 5 gr.g. Track Spare 125–Petite Path 106 (Sovereign Path 125) (1980 12.2s 12fg 12fg 12fg⁴ 10.6fg 10s 12g² 12d² 11fg² 11d⁴ 12fg 10.4d 10.6s 10.8d² 12d 1981 12d⁴ 12f⁴ 13.4fg 13g² 12g 12g 18g) workmanlike gelding; poor handicapper; behind in sellers on occasions; stays 1½m; acts on any going; inconsistent. *R. Mason.* **50**

ASCOT BLUE 8 b.g. Majority Blue 126–Pebble Ridge 107 (Big Game) (1980 5s³ 5g* 6g 5f 5f 5.8fg 5g 5fg 5d⁴ 5g 5g³ 5fg² 5d⁴ 5f³ 6g 5.8g 5d* 5d⁴ 5d 6s 1981 5d 5d 5s³ 5.8g 5fg⁴ 5.8d 5fg 5.8f 5.8g 5s³ 5d² 5s 6d³) sprint handicapper; suited by some given in the ground nowadays; suitable mount for an inexperienced rider; has twice worn blinkers. *M. Bradley.* **69**

ASHBRITTLE 3 ch.f. Great Nephew 126–Solar 120 (Hotfoot 126) (1980 5fg⁴ 5fg* 5f* 5g 5fg⁴ 5fg* 6fg 1981 7s 8.5fg 6g⁴ 5fg 6g 5f 5d) good-bodied, workmanlike filly; very good mover; useful performer at 2 yrs; had stiff tasks in 1981, best efforts when fourth of 9 behind Chemin in minor event at Lingfield in June, about 6 lengths sixth of 8 behind King of Spain in King George Stakes at Goodwood in July and about 5 lengths fifth of 10 behind Ackermann in Northumberland Sprint Trophy at Newcastle in August; best at sprint distances; acts well on firm going; blinkered sixth outing. *W. Wightman.* **94**

ASHBUD 2 br.f. Ashmore 125–Love-In-The-Mist 78 (Aureole 132) (1981 6g) May 15; 25,000Y; light-framed filly; half-sister to several winners, including smart French middle-distance winner Lodovico (by Prince Regent) and smart 1972 2-y-o Perdu (by Linacre); dam, daughter of 1,000 Guineas winner Belle of All, won at 7f; 25/1 when behind in 22-runner maiden race won by Ash Ridge at Newmarket in October. *G. Hunter.* —

ASHENDEN 2 b.c. Blakeney 126–Ravenshead (Charlottown 127) (1981 7f² 7fg* 7g² 7fg³ 8d) Apr 1; 11,000Y; lengthy, attractive colt; third foal; dam poor half-sister to smart sprinter Nevermore; landed the odds by 2½ lengths from Firsyjabs in Limekilns Stakes at Newmarket in July but wasn't impressive in doing so, having hung very badly left for much of the last 2 furlongs; left that form behind, going down by only ¾ length to Height of Fashion when giving weight all round in Acomb Stakes at York in August (again showed tendency to hang when challenging) and staying on without looking dangerous to finish 4 lengths third of 8 to Achieved in Laurent Perrier Champagne Stakes at Doncaster the following month; not disgraced when about 6 lengths sixth of 13 to Count Pahlen in William Hill Futurity Stakes at Doncaster in October; **114**

will be suited by middle distances; a smart colt who should win a decent race at 3 yrs. *B. Hills.*

ASHFORD (USA) 2 br.c. Torsion–Tenfore (Bupers) (1981 6g 7f) Mar 27; $23,000Y; rather leggy colt; half-brother to a stakes-placed winner by Flip Sal; dam, half-sister to 2 stakes winners, won at up to 1m; unquoted and in need of race, not disgraced in finishing ninth of 18 to Bravado after being slowly away in maiden race at Newcastle in July; towards rear in similar event at Redcar in September; should stay 7f. *G. Richards.*   —

ASH KING 2 b.c. Ashmore 125–Four Queens (Quorum 126) (1981 5d² 5d 6fg³ 8.2s 8d) Mar 31; IR 3,000F, 4,000Y; half-brother to useful stayer Candy Royal and a winner in France (both by Candy Cane); dam placed at up to 1¼m in Ireland; only plating class; will be suited by middle distances. *W. Musson.*   64

ASHLEIGH BOY 4 gr.g. Habat 127–Vimy Line (Vimy 132) (1980 7f 10.8g 7fg 10fg 8.2s 8.3g³ 8fg 1981 12s 7d 8s 8f) small gelding; poor handicapper; beaten in a seller second start; stays 1m; suited by some give in the ground; blinkered once at 2 yrs. *R. Hoad.*   —

ASHMO 3 b.f. Ashmore 125–Brown Lavender (Le Levanstell 122) (1980 NR 1981 12.2g 16.5f) 600Y; half-sister to a winner over jumps; dam lightly raced; tailed off in maiden races at Catterick in July (backward) and Redcar in August; sold 470 gns Doncaster September Sales. *H. Wharton.*   —

ASHORE 3 ch.g. Ashmore 125–Ornella (Princely Gift 137) (1980 5fg 6s 7g 7fg 1981 10s 12fg⁴ 12g) fair sort; finished well when 4 lengths fourth to Sulzano in apprentice handicap at Newmarket in April; not disgraced only subsequent start (June); will probably stay 1¾m. *H. Candy.*   —

ASH RIDGE (USA) 2 b.f. Bold Reason–Favoletta 115 (Baldric II 131) (1981 6g 6g*) Apr 8; good-bodied, attractive filly; half-sister to 3 y-o 1¼m winner Pipina (by Sir Gaylord) and 3 other winners, including smart 5f performer Amaranda (by Bold Lad, Ire); dam won Irish 1,000 Guineas; produced an   89 p

Lord Ranfurly's "Ashenden" (S. Cauthen)

Beresford Stakes, the Curragh—Assert wins from Longleat

electrifying turn of foot when winning 22-runner maiden race at Newmarket in October with impressive ease by 1½ lengths from Beldale Lustre; will be suited by 7f and 1m; likely to develop into a very useful filly at 3 yrs. *H. Wragg.*

AS I WISH 5 b.m. Red Alert 127–Ballydust (Bally Joy 112) (1980 10v 10fg —
10h 12fg 1981 10v 6g 10g) of little account. *R. Ward.*

ASSERT 2 b.c. Be My Guest 126–Irish Bird (Sea-Bird II 145) (1981 8g2 8d* **113**
8d)

Although no winner of the Curragh's Beresford Stakes has gone on to classic success since Boucher won the 1972 St Leger, the race remains one of Ireland's most competitive juvenile races. Saritamer, Mark Anthony, Orchestra, Icelandic, Huguenot and the champion American filly Just A Game have all won the race in recent years, while Artaius and Sandy Creek both filled the runner-up position. The 1981 race also looks to have fallen to a smart colt in Assert. Furry Berg, winner of the valuable Waterford Glass Nursery, Mistral Man, who had upset the odds laid on Raconteur by five lengths on his previous start, and the three-times successful Gold Exchanged were all left trailing as Assert and the odds-on Longleat drew away in the final quarter mile. Assert quickly showed he was no longer the very green youngster who had proved no match for the impressive Golden Fleece in a Leopardstown maiden race three weeks earlier. This time he responded in fine style to his rider's urgings, had Longleat in trouble a furlong out and then galloped on strongly to win by four lengths. Furry Berg took third place, six lengths behind Longleat.

Longleat had convinced us he was a good colt in the making on the second of his two previous outings when he came from last place at halfway to win the valuable Coolmore Try My Best Stakes. In beating him four lengths Assert stamped himself as a dangerous challenger for the William Hill Futurity later in October. However, after starting third favourite in a field of thirteen, he

95

came home about seven lengths behind Count Pahlen in eighth place. Admittedly he was hampered two furlongs out but was already struggling at the time.

		Northern Dancer	Nearctic
	Be My Guest	(b 1961)	Natalma
	(ch 1974)	What a Treat	Tudor Minstrel
Assert		(b 1962)	Rare Treat
(b.c. Apr 17, 1979)		Sea-Bird II	Dan Cupid
	Irish Bird	(ch 1962)	Sicalade
	(b or br 1970)	Irish Lass	Sayajirao
		(b 1962)	Scollata

Assert's recent family history shows some of the ups and downs of racehorse breeding. His grandam Irish Lass was the height of fashion in the early 'seventies. A very useful middle-distance winner herself and a full sister to an even better one in the Irish Oaks and Irish St Leger winner Lynchris, she made a splendid start to her stud career. Her first foal, the very useful French colt Exbury Lad, was followed by the Irish Sweeps Derby winner Irish Ball and the top-priced French yearlings of 1970 and 1971, Sanctus Lass and Irish Bird, both of whom won over eleven furlongs in France. Since then however Irish Lass has produced only two more winners. Her daughter Irish Bird also had a disappointing time at stud in the mid-'seventies. Her first foal, the Run The Gantlet gelding Irish Gantlet, never raced on the flat but won twice over hurdles as a five-year-old; her second, the Dancer's Image colt Shadowbrook failed to win both in Ireland and the USA; and her third, a colt by Kalamoun, fetched only 6,000 guineas when sold as a yearling. Presumably Irish Bird had by then tried her owner's patience to the limit and the Moyglare Stud sold her in October, 1979. The filly who had once set a new French record yearling price of 700,000 francs was sold in foal for a mere 200,000 francs. How her owners must regret having sold her so cheaply. The Kalamoun colt, none other than Bikala, won the Prix du Jockey-Club and all but won the Prix de l'Arc;

Mr R. E. Sangster's "Assert"

her foal of 1979, sold for a meagre 160,000 francs (approximately £16,000) is Assert; and the foal she was carrying at the time of her sale, a colt by Bold Lad (Ire), fetched 170,000 Irish guineas in 1981!

Assert is likely to enhance Irish Bird's reputation even further. A medium-sized, attractive, long-striding colt, he strikes us as the type to show to better advantage at three. Obviously he needs to improve if he's to beat the top English colts but it will surprise us if he fails to win a decent race or two in Ireland at distances up to a mile and a quarter, possibly even further. He has yet to race on a firm surface. *D. O'Brien, Ireland.*

ASSERTER (USA) 2 b.c. Go Go Roger–Laura Dora (Pleiades 115) (1981 — p 7f) $3,300F, $5,700Y; leggy, fair sort; fourth produce; half-brother to 2 minor winners in USA; dam unplaced in 7 starts; sire raced until he was 7, winning 15 races at up to 9f; made a promising first appearance when about 4½ lengths ninth of 18 behind Connaught River in maiden race at Redcar in September, running on really well over last 2f after missing break and getting a long way behind (not knocked about); will stay 1¼m; likely to improve at 3 yrs. *S. Norton.*

ATHENS STAR 6 ch.g. Athens Wood 126–Maushe Joan 78§ (Major Portion — 129) (1980 NR 1981 17.1d 16f) of little account on flat though has won a selling hurdle. *M. Bradley.*

ATHERSMITH 2 ch.f. Goldhill 125–Tunbridge Lane 77 (Privy Councillor 125) — (1981 6s 5g) May 18; sturdy filly; second foal; dam second once over 1m; 7½ lengths fifth of 7 to Bolivar Baby in 5f maiden race at Wolverhampton in September, better effort; should stay 6f. *J. Tierney.*

ATHFORD 5 b.g. High Line 125–Centro 86 (Vienna 127) (1980 16fg² 14fg⁴ **72** 16fg⁴ 16fg 20d 16s* 19g² 16d² 16g 19g* 18d³ 1981 17.1g⁴ 18d 20fg 16.1g² 16fg⁴ 19fg 16.1fg² 16s² 18g) tall, rather narrow gelding; staying handicapper; acts on any going but seems suited by some give in the ground nowadays; genuine; one paced; sold 11,500 gns Newmarket Autumn Sales. *H. Candy.*

ATKINSON GRIMSHAW 3 b.c. Martinmas 128–Melba Sauce (Sing Sing 134) — (1980 6g 6fg 7d 1981 7s 8fg 5v 6f 6f) compact colt; little worthwhile form in maiden and minor events and a seller; sometimes bandaged in front; blinkered final start; retained 500 gns Newmarket May Sales but sold 430 gns Ascot August Sales. *W. Wightman.*

ATLANTA LADY 3 b.f. Run The Gantlet–Roman Twilight (Romulus 129) — (1980 7g 1981 10s 12d 8g 7f 8f) quite attractive filly; soundly beaten in maiden and minor races; blinkered fourth start. *J. Bethell.*

ATLANTIC BOY 4 b.c. Busted 134–Coming About 99 (Right Tack 131) (1980 **105** 8f* 8.2fg 7g⁴ 8g* 8fg* 8g³ 8d* 8fg 9f 1981 8fg 8f 8fg* 8fg³ 8fg 10d* 9g) compact

Ronaldshay Cup, Redcar—Atlantic Boy is pushed clear to beat Norfolk Realm

colt; useful handicapper; won Ronaldshay Cup at Redcar in June by 2½ lengths from Norfolk Realm and Peter Hastings Stakes at Newbury in September by a neck from Morality Stone; stays 1¼m; probably acts on any going; genuine; sold 27,000 guineas Newmarket December Sales. *M. Stoute.*

ATLANTIC LINK 2 gr.f. The Go-Between 129–Atlantica (Tulyar 134) (1981 6fg) Apr 5; half-sister to a winning plater and a winner in Austria; dam never ran; 50/1 when last of 22 in maiden race won by Bless The Match at Lingfield in June. *P. Mitchell.* —

ATLANTIC TRAVELLER (USA) 4 b.c. Noholme II–Mlle Quille (On-and-On) (1980 12f 12.3f³ 12fg³ 16g* 16.9d³ 16f² 18f³ 16.1s 1981 16s 16g³ 18d² 20fg* 20.4fg* 19fg² 18f³ 17.4g 18g) useful-looking colt; out-and-out staying handicapper; battled on well to beat Dawn Johnny by 1¼ lengths in Ascot Stakes at Royal Ascot in June and accounted for Splendid Again by 2 lengths at Ayr in July; well suited by top-of-the-ground; seems suited by strong handling; game. *J. W. Watts.* **82**

ATOSSA 2 ch.f. Artaius 129–Living Free 81 (Never Say Die 137) (1981 6f* 6g* 6fg 5fg) Mar 29; neat, strong filly; good walker and mover; half-sister to 2 minor winners; dam, half-sister to Free State, stayed 1½m; successful in maiden race at Doncaster in June and 7-runner John Courage Stakes at York the following month, in latter making all to win by 3 lengths from Cheap Seats; towards rear subsequently in Princess Margaret Stakes at Ascot in July and well-contested race at Salisbury in September (7½ lengths fifth of 7 to Fairy Tern); bred to stay middle distances; hasn't much scope. *F. J. Houghton.* **97**

A.T.S. PRINCE 2 b.g. He Loves Me 120–Miss Holborn (Pall Mall 132) (1981 5g 6d 6fg 7g⁴ 7d 8f 8f* 8.2s 8d* 8.2s) Feb 20; 5,000Y; rather lightly-made, quite attractive gelding; half-brother to several winners, including 3-y-o Ring Bidder (by Auction Ring), successful at up to 1m, and useful 1m to 1¼m winner Saffron Hill (by Gulf Pearl); dam sister to very smart sprinter Holborn; led close home to win nurseries at Pontefract in September and October, scoring by a short head from Idle Warrior and by a neck from Storton respectively; sweated up when running moderately in between; had earlier finished fourth of 19 to Starter's Image in valuable seller at Newmarket in July; runs as though he'll stay 1¼m; acts on any going except perhaps very soft; none too consistent. *P. Rohan.* **80**

ATTACHED 3 b.c. Thatch 136–Veruschka 101 (Lorenzaccio 130) (1980 NR 1981 8g 8d 9s 8d³ 8.2s³ 9s) 11,000Y; workmanlike colt; first foal; dam, half-sister to high-class sprinter Abergwaun, won over 6f at 2 yrs; third in maiden races at Bath in June (to Elegant Dancer) and Haydock in October (to Turn Back The Time); stays 1m; sold 5,000 gns Newmarket Autumn Sales. *I. Balding.* —

A TUNEFUL SONG 5 b.g. Silly Season 127–Tuneful 81 (Reliance II 137) (1980 10fg 8g 10d 8h 7fg³ 8d 6d 1981 8d) small ex-Irish gelding; needs further than 6f and stays 9f; acts on firm going; has run respectably for a boy; sold to S. Pattemore 675 gns Ascot October Sales. *J. Dodd.* —

AUCTION BRIDGE 3 b.f. Auction Ring 123–Brig O'Doon (Shantung 132) (1980 NR 1981 8g 8fg² 8g* 8g⁴ 9f) 71,000Y; raging filly; not the best of movers; half-sister to several winners, notably high-class miler Young Generation (by Balidar) and useful stayer Another Generation (by Fine Blade); dam poor maiden; ran on strongly to beat Lichen Green in good style by 4 lengths in 12-runner maiden race at Ayr in July (well-backed favourite); had earlier been in rear in 1,000 Guineas at Newmarket and gone down by a neck to Chrome Mag in minor race at Ayr again; stayed 1m; gave impression she would always be suited by an easy surface; stud. *B. Hills.* **76**

AUDIT 3 ch.c. Henry the Seventh 125–Red Again (Red God 128§) (1980 5h 5fg 5d⁴ 6g 6fg 7g 8.2d² 8fg² 8.2s* 1981 10v 8.2s² 10g³ 9.4g 12g² 12g⁴ 13.8fg 12f³ 12.2fg⁴ 10g 10f 10f² 13.8g* 11g) small, stocky colt; attracted no bid after winning seller at Catterick in September; stays 1¾m; seems to act on any going; effective with blinkers and without; sold out of G. Richards' stable 2,000 gns Doncaster September Sales after thirteenth outing. *D. Yeoman.* **56**

AUDLEY END (USA) 4 b.c. Nijinsky 138–Favoletta 115 (Baldric II 131) (1980 12fg 11f 10.2fg 12g 10s³ 12d* 10g* 11d 11.1g⁴ 1981 10.2d 10s 10g³ 12s 10g⁴ 11g* 10fg* 9fg) strong, lengthy colt; carries plenty of condition; good mover; hasn't always been too consistent or reliable but did nothing wrong when winning handicaps at Ayr and Yarmouth in June; stays 1½m; acts on a firm and a soft surface; sent to South Africa. *H. Wragg.* **74**

AVE

AUGUSTA'S PET 2 b.f. Mummy's Pet 125–Aunt Augusta 80 (Counsel 118) **67**
(1981 5s 5f 5d³ 5s 6g) big, strong filly; first foal; dam won over 1¼m and 1¾m;
having first race for 4 months when 3½ lengths third of 9 to Spanish Fury in
maiden race at Hamilton in October; should be suited by 6f (weakened quickly
in closing stages when tried at trip). *G. Huffer.*

AULD MUNG 3 gr.g. Scallywag 127–Linton Spring 84 (Khalkis 127) (1980 **43**
5fg 7fg 8d 1981 11v³ 12s⁴ 16g* 15.8g 12.3fg) rangy gelding; won poor maiden
race at Thirsk in April when apprentice ridden; had very stiff tasks when tailed
off in handicaps last 2 outings; stays well. *Denys Smith.*

AUNT JOBISKA (USA) 3 br.f. What Luck–Aunt Aurilla (Tinsley) (1980 —
6f 1981 5f 5fg 6f) strong, compact filly; ran best race when never-dangerous
fifth of 10 behind Josephina Bin in maiden race in July on second
start; sold 5,000 guineas Newmarket December Sales. *W. Hastings-Bass.*

AUNT THEA 7 gr.m. Capistrano 120–Tuned-In (Tamerlane 128) (1980 NR —
1981 11.7f) poor plater; has been tried in blinkers. *R. Keenor.*

AURMEL 2 b.f. Meldrum 112–Auregirl 57 (Aureole 132) (1981 5g) Apr 8; —
neat filly; first reported foal; dam middle-distance plater; 20/1 and backward
when tailed-off seventh of 8 to Lady Stittenham in seller at Stockton in April;
only start; has very little scope. *I. Vickers.*

AUTOWAY 8 ch.g. Astec 128–Sam's Daisy 81 (Super Sam 124) (1980 NR —
1981 14d 10f 12f 17.1h) sturdy gelding; poor handicapper nowadays;
stays 1½m; acts on any going; has worn blinkers. *G. Cottrell.*

AUTUMN BALLET 2 b.f. Averof 123–Autumn Ballad 75 (Tudor Melody 129) —
(1981 5g 5.1f⁴ 5f 8d 7g 8g) Mar 16; big, workmanlike filly; third foal; half-
sister to 3-y-o 13f winner Karminski (by Pitskelly); dam second twice over 6f;
only poor form though raced prominently for a long way last 3 starts; should
stay 1m. *W. Marshall.*

AUTUMN BOY 3 b.g. Bigivor–Nynon Princess 91 (Kalydon 122) (1980 —
NR 1981 9.4g 12d) 980Y, resold 2,000 as a 3-y-o; second foal; dam stayed
1½m; tailed-off last in maiden race at Carlisle in July; brought down at Redcar
only subsequent start. *G. Richards.*

AUTUMN DAZE 2 gr.c. Sallust 134–Red Roan (Roan Rocket 128) (1981 5d³ **67**
5g⁴ 6fg 7fg 6fg 6f³ 8.2d 6d⁴) Apr 12; IR 10,500Y; sturdy, compact colt; second
foal; brother to 1979 2-y-o 6f winner Grey Mask; dam never ran; in frame in
maiden and minor events and a nursery; stays 1m; seems to act on any going;
blinkered fifth outing (had stiffish task). *W. Elsey.*

AUTUMN SUN 4 ch.g. Amber Rama 133–Rainswept (Charlottesville 135) **58**
(1980 7f 7f 10g 10s³ 10g 12fg 15.5g 1981 16d 11.7d 14s 12d 14fg 16fg² 17.1h³)
fair sort; poor handicapper; stays well; probably acts on any going; sometimes
wears blinkers. *D. Elsworth.*

AVANOTHER 3 b.f. Averof 123–Another Princess 83 (King Emperor) (1980 —
NR 1981 7g 10fg 10f 8fg) rather a lightly-made filly; second foal; half-sister
to 7.6f and 1m winner Molon Lave (by Welsh Pageant); dam won over 1m; still
needed race when about 8 lengths sixth of 10 behind Flighting in minor event at
Salisbury in August on second outing, best effort. *C. Brittain.*

AVANT COURIER 3 b.g. Averof 123–Treasure Boat 54 (Hook Money 124) —
(1980 NR 1981 8g 12g 8s) 300F; workmanlike gelding; in rear in sellers.
P. Asquith.

AVEC L'AMOUR 3 ch.f. Realm 129–Hasta (Skymaster 126) (1980 5fg⁴ —
1981 5g 5f 6v) compact filly; disappointing maiden; should stay 6f; bandaged
in front on first outing (subsequently off course 4 months). *Sir Mark Prescott.*

AVENGE 5 b.h. Mummy's Pet 125–B.S.R. 68 (March Past 124) (1980 7fg —
7fg⁴ 6g 7g 6d 7.6d 8fg 8h* 8g³ 1981 8.2g) neat horse; plater; stays 1m; seems
to act on any going; often wears blinkers; sold 2,500 gns Ascot July Sales. *J.
Cann.*

AVENTURA 3 gr.c. No Mercy 126–Queens To Open 75 (Darius 129) (1980 **68**
5fg 1981 8d 8fg² 10s 8d 8fg³ 8.3g 8fg² 10.2g*) lengthy, useful-looking colt;
won handicap at Bath in September by 1½ lengths from Blakenor; stayed 1¼m;
seemed best on a sound surface; blinkered second and fourth outings; dead.
H. Candy.

99

AVERNUS 2 b.g. Averof 123–Lacemaker (Astec 128) (1981 7fg 8g 10g) Mar — 30; 2,500Y; well-grown gelding; second foal; dam twice-raced half-sister to good 1964 2-y-o Leonardo; well beaten in maiden races and £6,500 event at Newmarket in second half of season. *I. Walker.*

AVERSUN 5 b.g. Averof 123–Pirate Queen 77 (Pirate King 129) (1980 12.2fg⁴ — 16g⁴ 1981 16s) plating-class staying maiden; has worn blinkers. *W. Haigh.*

AVONDALE PRINCESS 3 b.f. The Brianstan 128–Roseanne 68 (St Paddy **53** 133) (1980 5fg⁴ 5fg 5fg 6s 5d 7g 7f 7g³ 6s 6s³ 6d 1981 5d 7g 7f 6fg 5.3fg 5g³ 6f 5fg 5g 6g 5s 6d) sturdy filly; third in handicap at Nottingham in August; not totally disgraced in varied company previous 3 starts, including selling; will probably stay 1m; blinkered nowadays. *M. McCourt.*

AVONMORE WIND 2 b.c. Tumble Wind–Gay Friend (Be Friendly 130) **86** (1981 5d³ 5s³ 5d*) May 26; IR 2,900Y; quite attractive, useful-looking colt; second foal; dam third over 5f and 7f at 2 yrs in Ireland; favourite, confirmed promise of first 2 races when quickening clear to beat Sea Havoc by 3 lengths in 15-runner maiden event at Wolverhampton in October; will be suited by 6f; yet to race on a sound surface. *S. Mellor.*

AVRAEAS (USA) 2 b.c. Key To The Mint–Rosewater (Sir Ivor 135) (1981 — 6s 7g) neat colt; third foal; half-brother to fair 1979 2-y-o 7f winner Quai Hais (by Arts and Letters); dam won twice at up to 1m; soundly beaten in Duke of Edinburgh Stakes at Ascot (last of 11 to Slightly Dangerous) and 18-runner maiden race at Doncaster (behind Leg Glance) in October. *H. T. Jones.*

AVVI 2 ch.f. Vitiges 132–Best Offer 96 (Crepello 136) (1981 6d) Apr 21; — 950Y; first foal; dam won over 7f and 1m; 25/1 and burly when behind in 22-runner maiden race by Late Hour at Leicester in November. *A. Jarvis.*

AWAASIF (CAN) 2 b.f. Snow Knight 125–Royal Statute (Northern Dancer) **78** P (1981 6fg⁴ 7g*) Apr 27; $325,000Y; good-looking filly; half-sister to several winners, including 1,000 Guineas second Konafa (by Damascus) and very smart American 3-y-o Akureyri (by Buckpasser), a winner at up to 9f; dam winning sister to leading Canadian middle-distance performer Dance Act; favourite when winning 15-runner maiden race at Ayr in September by 2 lengths from French Scribe; had previously finished promising fifth of 12 to Bless The Match in St Catherine's Stakes at Newbury in July (moved up a place on fourth's disqualification on a technicality); will be suited by middle distances; a fine individual who should improve considerably on her 2-y-o form. *J. Dunlop.*

AYYABAAN 4 b.c. Sun Prince 128–Adayra (Le Haar 126) (1980 10.6d³ 12f⁴ **84** 12f² 10.1g 12f 12g⁴ 12fg 1981 16g 20f³ 12g 16fg*) well-made, attractive colt; excellent mover; fair handicapper; battled on exceptionally gamely to beat Crispin by a short head in Brown Jack Stakes at Ascot in July; had earlier run creditably in Gold Cup on same course when 11 lengths third of 4 to Ardross; stays well; acts on firm going; blinkered once in 1979. *J. Jenkins.*

AZAAM 3 b.c. Mummy's Pet 125–Emperor Star (King Emperor) (1980 5d* **81** 6g³ 1981 5s⁴ 5d⁴ 7d* 8g 7fg³ 6fg² 7f* 7g⁴ 7f 7f 7fg⁴ 7g² 6g) useful-looking colt; won handicaps at Warwick in May and Catterick (didn't handle track well) in July; didn't have a clear run when ½-length second to Sharp Celeste in similar event at Newmarket in October; stays 7f; probably acts on any going; has twice run well below his form in blinkers; sold 5,600 gns Newmarket Autumn Sales. *W. O'Gorman.*

AZD 5 ch.g. Be Friendly 130–Portden (Worden II 129) (1980 12g 1981 12s* **68** 12d² 12d³ 12g³ 12g² 12d* 15.5d* 12g³ 12f 12d 12f 12d* 12d³ 12s 13s) moody handicapper; successful at Folkestone (twice) and Brighton (twice); stays well; acts on any going but seems suited by some give in the ground nowadays; used to wear blinkers; suitable mount for an inexperienced rider; refused to race final start. *M. Masson.*

B

BAAS 3 b.c. Dancer's Image–Snobby Kate (Snob 130) (1980 7d 7d² 7fg³ 8.2g* **77** 8g* 10g 1981 10fg 10g 8fg 8fg³ 10d 10f) lengthy, useful sort; disappointing in 1981 and is possibly no longer completely genuine; should stay 1¼m; blinkered last 4 starts; sold 1,450 gns Newmarket Autumn Sales. *J. Hindley.*

BABAS BALLY 3 gr.c. Ballynockan 112–Clare Blue 83 (Blue Streak 106) **55** (1980 5f 5fg³ 5fg² 5g 5f 5s³ 5d* 6fg 5fg 6s 1981 5d 6g³(dis) 6d 6fg³ 6f 6fg 7.6s) workmanlike colt; not disgraced on occasions, but is little better than a plater; stays 6f but best form at 5f; acts on a firm surface but is best on an easy one; blinkered fourth outing in 1980 *Peter Taylor.*

BABBINGTON 3 b.g. Gay Fandango 132–Skipton (Breton 130) (1980 6d 7d — 6g 1981 7g 7fg 8g⁴ 7fg 10fg) small, strong gelding; only a glimmer of ability; last in seller final outing; has raced with a tongue strap; trained by R. Armstrong until after fourth start. *D. Leslie.*

BABUSINGH 2 br.c. Mansingh 120–Queen of Time (Roi Dagobert 128) (1981 — 6g 8s 7d) Mar 16; third foal; brother to 3-y-o 6f winner Time-Table; dam poor maiden; well beaten in large fields for maiden event at Newmarket in July and minor races at Redcar and Leicester at the back-end. *M. Jarvis.*

BABY POWER 2 ch.f. Ashmore 125–Power Girl 77 (Tyrant) (1981 6s) Apr — 24; leggy filly; first foal; dam won over 5f and 6f; unquoted and badly in need of race when behind in 20-runner seller won by Pair-of-Deuces at Goodwood in September; sold 300 gns Ascot November Sales. *C. Nelson.*

BACCHANTINA 3 ch.f. Gulf Pearl 117–Miss Maverick 76 (Vilmorin) (1980 5f — 7g 6g 6fg 7g 7g 8fg 1981 8fg 15.5d 12d 16d 16.9fg 10f) small, useful-looking filly; poor plater; blinkered last 2 outings in 1980; bandaged final start; sold out of S. Harris' stable 1,000 gns Ascot July Sales after fifth start. *D. Garraton.*

BACK STAGE 2 b.c. Busted 134–Bold Words (Bold Ruler) (1981 8d) Feb — 26; 21,000Y; second living foal; half-brother to 3-y-o 1m winner Essam (by Sallust); dam, winner twice at up to 9f in USA, is out of half-sister to very good American horses Malicious and The Axe; 20/1 when behind in 23-runner maiden race at Leicester in November won by Roanoke River. *M. Albina.*

BADINAGE 2 br.f. Brigadier Gerard 144–Adina (Neckar) (1981 6fg 7d⁴) Apr **73** 19; rangy filly; good mover; sister to 2 maidens and half-sister to fairly useful 5f and 6f winner Edna (by Shiny Tenth); dam German; stayed on at one pace when 6¾ lengths fourth of 18 to Sans Blague in maiden race at Newbury in September; will stay 1¼m. *W. Hastings-Bass.*

BAD LOVE 7 gr.h. Town Crier 119–Tiger Doll 85 (Tiger 125) (1980 NR 1981 — 12.2fg 11.7fg) poor middle-distance handicapper; acts on hard going; suited by a strong gallop. *W. Charles.*

BADSWORTH GIRL 3 b.f. Arch Sculptor 123–Falcade (Falcon 131) (1980 — 5g³ 5d 8fg 6g³ 6fg² 6d 1981 7fg 7fg 5f⁴ 7f) big, rangy filly; race easily best race of 1981 when less than 2 lengths fourth to Sami in maiden race at Nottingham in July (gambled on); not bred to stay 1m. *G. Toft.*

BAFFIN 3 b.c. Busted 134–Ocean 112 (Petition 130) (1980 7d⁴ 1981 10g* **116** 8g³ 12s² 10g) strong, useful-looking colt; half-brother to 2 winners, including useful 1½m winner Baltic (by Ribero); dam won Coronation Stakes; looked particularly well but slightly in need of race when beating Le Gran Brun decisively by 4 lengths on reappearance in minor event at Goodwood in September; ran an excellent race when neck second to stable-companion Little Wolf in 7-runner St Simon Stakes at Newbury the following month, staying on extremely well in a driving finish and finishing clear of remainder; found trip too sharp and in circumstances ran well when 3¾ lengths third of 5 to Motavato in £3,800 event at Newmarket in between, but was a disappointing favourite when sixth of 12 behind King's Glory in Tia Maria Autumn Handicap on same course later in October on final start; suited by 1½m and will stay further; yet to race on a firm surface; should win more races. *R. Hern.*

BAG OF GOLD 2 b.f. Tudor Rhythm 112–Heart of Gold 72 (Infatuation 129) — (1981 5s 5d) Mar 27; rather leggy filly; half-sister to several minor winners; dam stayed 2m; in rear in maiden race at Leicester and seller at Warwick early in season. *R. Smyth.*

BAHAMAS PRINCESS 2 b.f. Sharpen Up 127–Coal Face 61 (Kalydon 122) **89** (1981 5g* 6f) May 13; 36,000Y; good-quartered, quite attractive filly; half-sister to 2 winners by High Top, including smart 1m and 9f winner Miner's Lamp, and to Irish 3-y-o Eusebio (by Hotfoot); dam, placed at up to 1¾m, is sister to very useful stayers Shaft and Bunker; led 2f out to beat Pleasant Dream a short head (pair 6 lengths clear) under a very sympathetic ride in 19-runner maiden race at Salisbury in June; third favourite for Cherry Hinton Stakes at Newmarket the following month but never got in a blow, finishing 4½ lengths sixth of 10 to Travel On, only subsequent start; will be suited by 7f and 1m. *F. J. Houghton.*

BAK

BAKLAWA 2 b.f. Orange Bay 131–Colonial Cousin (Tom Rolfe) (1981 7fg 6fg **75**
8fg) Apr 18; big filly; second foal; half-sister to 3-y-o 1¼m winner Soukab (by
Good Counsel); dam never ran; showed first sign of ability when 6¾ lengths
seventh of 15 to Rockfest in £3,600 race at Goodwood in September on third
outing (backed from 50/1 to 9/1); will stay middle distances. *G. Lewis.*

BAKST (USA) 2 b.c. Native Royalty–Erin O'Connell (Dondeen 123) (1981 6fg) — p
Mar 13; $127,000Y; third foal; brother to useful 3-y-o Irish sprinter Severiano;
dam won claiming races at up to 1m at 3 yrs; weak 8/1-shot, showed up 4f when
12½ lengths sixth of 15 to Rosier in minor event at Windsor in August, only
outing. *J. Tree.*

BALAFALLAY 2 b.f. Priamos 123–Friedrichsruh (Dschingis Khan) (1981 6fg⁴ **77**
7d) Apr 29; leggy, lightly-made, quite attractive filly; first foal; dam won
German Oaks over 11f after finishing head second in German 1,000 Guineas, and
is daughter of 10.5f Prix de Flore winner Friedensbotschaft; well-backed second
favourite, kept on well without quickening when 1¼ lengths fourth of 14 in
minor race won by Aegean Beauty at Newmarket in August; 11 lengths sixth of
19 behind My Destiny in maiden event at Yarmouth the following month; bred
to stay middle distances; possibly unsuited by a soft surface. *M. Stoute.*

BALAINE (GER) 3 b.f. Balidar 133–Donine (Soleil II 133) (1980 5fg 5g 6fg 5g —
1981 5d 6d 7v 10s 12g 12f 7f) lightly-made filly; no better than plating class;
blinkered final outing; sweated up badly once in 1980. *S. Woodman.*

BALANCE (USA) 2 b.f. Youth 135–Hippodamia 130 (Hail to Reason) (1981 **101**
6g⁴ 6f³ 7f* 7s³ 7v*) Apr 13; $160,000Y; third foal; dam won Criterium des
Pouliches by 6 lengths; successful in maiden race at Clairefontaine in August
and Prix de Martinvast at Longchamp in October, latter by ½ length from Gay
Spring; not disgraced in between when 3½ lengths third of 10 to Talaja in
80,000 france race at Longchamp, will stay 1¼m; a well-bred filly who should
make a very useful 3-y-o. *J. Cunnington, jnr, France.*

BALANCHINE 2 b.c. Ballymore 123–Ambuscade 77 (Relko 136) (1981 6f² **88**
6fg² 6s* 7g*) May 3; IR 23,000Y; well-made, attractive colt; good mover; half-
brother to 1m winner Hornet's Nest (by Realm) and a winner in Italy; dam,
winner over 1½m, is half-sister to Smuggler; won minor events at Chester in
August and Brighton in September, giving weight all round when beating
Charbonnel ¾ length in 13-runner race on latter; will stay 1½m; could well
develop into a useful handicapper in 1982. *M. Stoute.*

BALARUM 2 b.f. Goldhill 125–Balquhidder (Pardao 120) (1981 6d 5f 6g 7.2v) —
May 16; leggy filly; third foal; dam half-sister to very smart sprinter Ampney
Princess; well beaten in varied races in the North, including a seller. *P. Rohan.*

BALATINA 3 ch.f. Balidar 133–Toccatina 79 (Bleep-Bleep 134) (1980 6s 6g —
5fg 5f² 5fg³ 5.3g⁴ 5d* 6d⁴ 1981 5f 5fg 5g 6g) fair sort; in rear all starts in 1981
(needed race and dwelt on first occasion); best form at 5f; probably acts on any
going; apprentice ridden when successful; often bandaged. *A. Dalton.*

BALAUSTIN 2 b.f. Balidar 133–Princess Log 78 (King Log 115) (1981 5f —
7fg 8s) Feb 24; close-coupled filly; fourth foal; half-sister to very useful French
middle-distance winner Ragnel (by Ragstone); dam miler and half-sister to Roi
Soleil; in rear in good company; not certain to stay 1m. *R. Price.*

BALAYER 2 ch.f. Balidar 133–Feather Duster 80 (Tickler 106) (1981 5g 5.8f **59**
6fg³ 7d 6fg 7d 5s) June 3; 900Y; rather lightly-made filly; half-sister to 1978
2-y-o 6f seller winner Dusty Brown (by Golden Mallard); dam won twice over
1m; prominent in maiden auction events at Bath and Kempton in July, in latter
finishing 4 lengths third of 20 to Walter Mitty; should be suited by 7f; possibly
unsuited by soft ground; blinkered final start. *S. Woodman.*

BALCANOONA 2 b.f. Cawston's Clown 113–Duns Tew 70 (Mandamus 120) **87**
(1981 5d³ 5fg 5d* 5s³ 6fg² 6fg 6fg 5d² 7s 6v 6g) Mar 22; lightly-made filly;
good mover; first known foal; dam won over 5f at 2 yrs; won maiden event at
Leicester in April easily by 4 lengths from Ash King; second afterwards in
nursery at Windsor in August and 4-runner minor event at Goodwood in September, being eased a length close home when beaten 3 lengths by To The Point
in latter; suited by 6f but isn't sure to stay 7f; seems to act on any going. *R.
Hannon.*

BALDA 3 br.f. Relko 136–Basilia Dea (Habitat 134) (1980 8g 8g 1981 10fg **57**
12fg 12d⁴ 12fg² 12f*) tall, leggy filly; beaten a length by Kenny O'Reilly in
seller at Thirsk in September but was denied a clear run by the winner and

102

placings were subsequently reversed; sold 4,000 gns afterwards; stays 1½m; acts on firm going; sweated up fourth start. *W. Hastings-Bass.*

BALDINGSTONE BOY 3 b.c. Seaepic 100–Vivyiki (Kirtonian 88) (1980 **54**
5fg 5fg 5fg 5.1f 5fg 5f 6g 7.2s 10.2s 1981 8s 8g 12f* 12f 12g* 13.8fg* 12f 13d)
compact, narrow colt; bought in after winning sellers at Pontefract in July
(1,350 gns) and August (1,450 gns) and at Catterick later in August (2,600 gns);
little other form; suited by 1½m and more; acts on firm going; often apprentice
ridden; inconsistent. *A. Balding.*

BALI DANCER 2 ch.c. Habitat 134–Miss Bali 95 (Crepello 136) (1981 6fg³ **90**
6g²) Mar 9; strong, attractive colt; fourth foal; half-brother to Miss Waterloo
(by Brigadier Gerard), successful in Italy; dam won over 1½m and is half-sister
to smart Welsh Harmony; ran green to halfway in 20-runner maiden race at
Newmarket in August but then kept on nicely to finish 2½ lengths third to Anstruther; favourite, put in a renewed challenge in closing stages when head second of
11 to Master Cawston in Ribero Stakes at Doncaster the following month; will
be suited by 7f and 1m; sure to win a race at 3 yrs. *M. Stoute.*

BALIDILEMMA 2 ch.f. Balidar 133–Charybdis (Chanteur II 135) (1981 —
6fg 6g 7g) Mar 21; strong filly; half-sister to several winners, notably high-class
6f to 1m horse Joshua (by Welsh Rake); dam slow maiden; unquoted when in
rear in maiden races. *P. Makin.*

BALI GEORGE 3 b.g. Balidar 133–Ballyarctic (Arcticeelagh 119) (1980 7fg **64**
6g³ 6g 7fg 7.6f⁴ 7f² 8.2s 8d 1981 8fg 16s 10fg³ 12f 10f*) workmanlike gelding;
apprentice ridden when winning claiming race at Brighton in August; stays
1¼m (tailed off over further); acts on firm going and is probably unsuited by soft
ground; often wears a tongue strap. *A. Jarvis.*

BALI HYATT 3 b.c. Steel Heart 128–Maid of Iron (Crozier USA) (1980 6fg **70**
1981 12g 16s⁴ 14f 14fg² 16fg⁴ 14g 12f* 11.7fg 16g³) useful-looking colt; won
poor maiden race at Ripon in August; tailed off next time, but had stiff task;
stays well; acts on firm going; wears blinkers; sold 7,400 gns Newmarket Autumn
Sales. *C. Brittain.*

BALILYCA 3 b.f. Balidar 133–Polycarpa (Polyfoto 124) (1980 5f 5g 5g 5fg 5g —
1981 6f 5d 5fg 5fg 10fg 5s) neat filly; only plating class; trained until after first
outing by M. Francis. *D. Ancil.*

BALIMAR 3 ch.f. Balidar 133–Sea-Hit 85 (Bleep-Bleep 134) (1980 5g 5d 5s 5d —
1981 5fg) quite a useful sort; plating-class maiden at 2 yrs; last in a seller on
only outing of 1981; sold 550 gns Ascot July Sales. *C. Booth.*

BALLINFOILE 2 ch.c. Shiny Tenth 120–Bernina (Prudent II 133) (1981 **79**
5s³ 5.8d⁴ 6g 7f³ 7f 7s 7s 8d) Mar 5; leggy, rather unfurnished colt; brother
to a winner in Belgium, and half-brother to 3 winners, including very useful 6f
and 7f winner Asa Yolson (by Luthier); dam won over 5f at 2 yrs in France;
ran on when in frame in maiden races and a nursery; beaten 1¼ lengths when
third of 4 to Diamond Shoal in latter at Brighton in August; soundly beaten
afterwards, once sweating up; stays 7f but isn't certain to get 1m; seems to act
on any going; has run well for an apprentice; sold 1,600 gns Ascot December
Sales. *D. Marks.*

BALLNACARN 2 ch.c. Firestreak 125–Deer Forest (Huntercombe 133) (1981 **62**
5g 5d 5g 5.8f⁴ 5f) Mar 29; 2,100Y; leggy colt; first foal; dam showed no form
in 3 outings; beaten less than 5 lengths in maiden races at Catterick in June
and Bath (auction event) in July on third and fourth starts; will stay 7f. *J.
Toller.*

BALLY-GO 4 b.g. Ballymoss 136–Cloudy (Nyrcos 130) (1980 NR 1981 **44**
12.5s³) winning hurdler; odds on when 6½ lengths third to Pomposity in 15-
runner maiden race at Stockton in April, first outing on flat; will stay 1¾m.
M. W. Easterby.

BALLYLINGO 3 b.f. Saulingo 122–Bally Keys 72 (Bally Russe 113) (1980 **69**
5fg 5fg* 5g³ 5g 5f⁴ 5fg² 5g³ 5fg⁴ 5d 1981 6fg⁴ 6d 6d 5fg³ 5h⁴ 5f 5s 5s) workmanlike filly; sprint handicapper; best form on a sound surface; blinkered sixth
start; sold 2,100 gns Newmarket Autumn Sales. *G. Lewis.*

BALLYSEEDY HERO 3 gr.g. Supreme Sovereign 119–Knocknagrena (Worden **63**
II 129) (1980 6fg 6g 7fg 1981 7fg 8g 6fg 6f² 7f³ 6fg 8g 8d 10d) tall, lengthy
gelding; plating-class maiden; stays 7f; blinkered final start. *D. Whelan.*

BALLYTOP 4 b.c. High Top 131–Ballydowa 90 (Ballymoss 136) (1980 8s² **97**
8fg⁴ 10.1s* 10d² 10.1g* 12g² 12g* 13s² 1981 14g² 12g* 12g* 12g⁴ 12f 12g²)
rangy colt; good mover; fairly useful performer; performed creditably most

starts and won minor event at Pontefract in April and amateur riders race at Thirsk in May; stays 1¾m; acts well on soft ground and is possibly not at his best on firm; suitable mount for an inexperienced rider; genuine and consistent. *I. Balding.*

BALLYWACKMACROO 4 b.c. Ballymore 123–Mountain Lark (Chamier 128) **82** (1980 9g² 8fg⁴ 9f* 9fg* 9g 9fg* 9g* 12fg 11s 12s 1981 12g 10g 12d* 12f 12fg² 16f 12f* 12fg 12f 12f² 12fg) compact, well-made ex-Irish colt; won modest minor event at Pontefract in May and handicap at Beverley in July; stays 1½m but not 2m; best form on a sound surface. *G. Pritchard-Gordon.*

BALTIC LOVE 9 b.g. Current Coin 118–Arctic Villa (Arctic Star) (1980 10d³ — 16s 18fg 1981 16s) poor staying handicapper; acts on soft going. *G. Blum.*

BALTIMORE BELLE (Ire) 2 ch.f. Bold Lad (Ire) 133–Wichuraiana (Worden II **95** 129) (1981 6fg² 6f* 7d* 7fg³) Apr 18; neat, good-bodied filly; good mover; half-sister to French 3-y-o Wolverwich (by Wolver Hollow) and 3 winners, notably top-class 6f to 10.5f winner Wollow (also by Wolver Hollow); dam half-sister to good stayer Exar; won 23-runner maiden race at Nottingham in July (beat Loup de Mer by 2½ lengths) and 8-runner Sweet Solera Stakes at Newmarket in August (came to challenge leaders 2f out and battled on gamely under hard driving to beat Tickletimes by ½ length); held up when creditable 3½ lengths third of 6 to Stratospheric in Waterford Candelabra Stakes at Goodwood later in August; will stay 1m; yet to race on very soft ground but acts on any other; genuine; sent to France. *H. Cecil.*

BALVIMA 5 b.h. Balidar 133–Sevima 59 (Sovereign Lord 120) (1980 5d 5s² **75** 5g³ 5f* 5f² 5s 5g* 5g² 5fg 1981 5s 5d 5g 5d³ 5g 6f 5fg 5fg 5.6fg 5s) compact horse; sprint handicapper; ran creditably fourth start but disappointed on a number of occasions; best at 5f; acts on any going; sometimes blinkered; good mount for a boy and goes well for B. Crossley; sometimes wears a small bandage on near-fore; looked unsuited by Epsom track fifth outing. *A. Dalton.*

BAM EXPRESS 3 b.c. Bay Express 132–Beguiling 66 (Tower Walk 130) — (1980 5g 1981 12.2fg 7fg) of no account. *T. Barnes.*

BAMP 5 ro.g. Supreme Sovereign 119–Light Jumper 100 (Red God 128§) (1980 — 7f 8s 8.2s² 8.2s 1981 8s) fairly useful handicapper in 1979; lightly raced subsequently; best at around 1m; acted on any going but revelled in the mud; sometimes blinkered at 3 yrs; dead. *M. H. Easterby.*

BANBURY CROSS 3 b.c. Tower Walk 130–Hark Hark 75 (Sing Sing 134) **61** (1980 5d 5s 5f 5g 5d⁴ 5g 7fg⁴ 6g⁴ 7fg³ 6d³ 6s* 1981 6fg 6g⁴ 6d 6g 5.3f 5h² 7f 7g 7d) useful sort; ran respectably in handicaps on occasions; stays 7f; acts on any going; blinkered fourth start; dwelt fifth outing. *W. Wightman.*

BANCARIO 2 ch.c. Owen Dudley 121–Brescianina (Hugh Lupus 132) (1981 **106** 6g* 7fg² 7d² 7fg² 8.2fg* 8d* 8s*) Apr 13; rather sparely-made colt; half-brother to several winners in Italy, including fairly useful Bettina Falcini (by Viani); dam, from same family as Botticelli, showed useful form at up to 11.5f in Italy; ridden by apprentice N. Day when successful in maiden race at Newcastle, £4,000 event at Haydock, 5-runner nursery at Yarmouth and minor event again at Newcastle; put up useful efforts under top weight when leading virtually throughout for last 3 wins, scoring respectively by 10 lengths from Outlaw, 3 lengths from Sanches and by 4 lengths from The Red Duke after being eased several lengths; will be very well suited by middle distances; probably acts on any going; a tough and resolute galloper who looks sure to win more races at 3 yrs. *H. Cecil.*

BANCHORY BRIDGE 2 ch.c. Bay Express 132–Renoir Picture 90 (Relko 136) — (1981 7d 7d) Apr 12; 11,500F, 5,800Y; half-brother to useful 3-y-o 1m to 1¼m winner Say Primula (by Hotfoot) and 2 minor winners; dam stayed 1¼m; unquoted when in rear in minor events at Brighton in September and Chepstow the following month. *J. Bethell.*

BANCO 6 b.h. Shoolerville 121–Coup 106 (Hook Money 124) (1980 7fg 7fg **83** 7.6f⁴ 7d 7d 6g² 7fg 6d 1981 6s⁴ 7d) close-coupled, useful-looking horse; fair handicapper; effective at 6f but is ideally suited by 7f; appears to act on any going. *F. J. Houghton.*

B AND K EMPEROR 4 ro.g. Young Emperor 133–Fiery Clare (Firestreak — 125) (1980 9.4d 8g 8fg 10g 10fg 1981 10.2d) leggy gelding; plating-class maiden on flat though has won over hurdles; stays 1m; probably needs some give in the ground; sometimes blinkered. *M. W. Easterby.*

BANFF SPRINGS 4 gr.f. Sir Albert 72–Valli 81 (Vigo 130) (1980 NR 1981 —
10.6d 12f 10f³ 10s) leggy filly; fifth reported living foal; dam showed ability at
2 yrs; plater; sweated up when third at Pontefract in September; seems to stay
1¼m. *Miss L. Siddall.*

BANKNOTE 3 b.c. Lombard 126–Polychord (Tudor Melody 129) (1980 NR **58**
1981 8d 12g 10.1fg³ 10fg² 9f 10.1g 8fg 9s) 4,000Y; quite attractive, lengthy
colt; half-brother to a winner in Denmark; dam ran twice unplaced; placed in
minor event at Windsor and maiden race at Lingfield in summer; will probably
stay 1½m; never going very well when apprentice ridden fifth start; sold to Miss
S. Morris 3,200 gns Newmarket Autumn Sales. *P. Walwyn.*

BANK RUN 6 br.g. Gilded Leader 75–Seminole Squaw 66 (Seminole II) (1980 —
12f* 12fg² 8fg 12g* 16d 1981 12f) strong gelding; won minor event and
handicap at Pontefract in 1980; needed run only start at 6 yrs in June; stays
1½m; acts on any going; has worn blinkers. *B. McMahon.*

BANNONWARD 5 b.m. Forlorn River 124–Double Bank 80 (Double Jump 131) —
(1980 6f 5g³ 5g² 5fg 5fg 5fg 1981 5g 5f 5g) neat mare; short-running plater;
acts on hard going; tried in blinkers at 2 yrs; has worn bandages; sold 520 gns
Doncaster October Sales. *T. Taylor.*

BANOCO 3 b.c. Nonoalco 131–Denaneer 78 (Green God 128) (1980 5g² 5d **84**
1981 7s 6d 8g* 7g 8s³ 8g) useful-looking colt; good mover; having first race
for over 3 months when making all to beat Ring Bidder by ¾ length in handicap
at Brighton in September; ran best subsequent race when third behind Bronzamer
in handicap at Redcar in October; suited by 1m; yet to race on a firm surface;
sold out of R. Price's stable 3,700 gns Doncaster September Sales after fourth
start. *T. Craig.*

B. A. POUNDSTRETCHER 2 b.f. Laser Light 118–Grecian Flame (Sound **82**
Track 132) (1981 5s* 5d* 5v² 6fg² 6fg 6fg 6fg 6s) June 4; IR 600F, 2,500Y;
lengthy, workmanlike filly; half-sister to quite useful sprinter Greek Street (by
Road House II) and fairly useful 5f to 1m winner Flambeau (by Pall Mall); dam
ran only twice; successful in maiden race at Wolverhampton in April (beat
Chellaston Park ¾ length) and minor event at Windsor in May (by 2 lengths from
Leixlip); second twice at Windsor subsequently, running well when short-headed
by Paul's Ivory in 6f race in June; last of 5 in Group 3 event won by Landsgirl at
Baden-Baden in September on seventh appearance; stays 6f; seems to act on any
going; has worn bandages behind; moved badly to start and ran below form fifth
outing. *R. Hannon.*

BARBARA ALLEN 3 b.f. Song 132–Brave Ballard (Derring-Do 131) (1980 —
5f 5.8h² 1981 6s 5.8g 6g 5g 7g³ 7fg 7f 7f 7d) neat filly; poor maiden; unplaced
in sellers on occasions; suited by 7f; wears blinkers; sold 600 gns Newmarket
Autumn Sales. *J. Bethell.*

BARBAROSSA 2 ch.g. Queen's Hussar 124–Glencora (Ribero 126) (1981 7g) —
Mar 25; 920Y; small gelding; second foal; dam unraced twin; 20/1 and burly,
always behind in 18-runner maiden race won by Leg Glance at Doncaster in
October. *J. Winter.*

BAR BENDER 2 b.c. Artaius 129–Chivas Regal 70 (Sword Dancer) (1981 **85**
6fg² 6f²) Mar 31; IR 30,000Y; third foal; dam, half-sister to numerous winners,
including smart Open Season and smart stakes winner Tilt Up, was placed at
up to 1¼m; put up a pleasing first effort in 8-runner maiden race at Phoenix
Park in July, going down by only a length to odds-on Afghan after disputing lead
throughout; clear of 5 others when running odds-on Americus to 1½ lengths in
another Phoenix Park maiden event in August; not seen out again; will stay
1¼m; sure to win at 3 yrs. *A. Maxwell, Ireland.*

BARB'S BEAU 4 b.g. Festino 105–Beauatire 86 (Beau Sabreur 125) (1980 **60**
NR 1981 10g 12d⁴ 14d² 16d⁴ 16g 19s) lengthy, useful-looking gelding; in
frame in maiden races; should stay well; yet to race on a firm surface. *M.
Masson.*

BARB'S BOLD (USA) 3 b.f. Bold Forbes–Goofed (Court Martial) (1980 **112**
NR 1981 10g² 10s 10s* 10.5g² 8s 8v) $1,450,000Y, resold 6,100,000 francs
2-y-o (approx £645,000); half-sister to several winners, notably top-class French
7f to 1¼m colt Lyphard (by Northern Dancer) and top-class 1m to 1½m filly
Nobiliary (by Vaguely Noble); dam stakes winner at up to 1¼m; put up a smart
effort on fourth start when 2 lengths second of 7 to Snow Day in Group 3 Prix
Fille de l'Air at Saint-Cloud in June; didn't reproduce that form; had earlier
been second in newcomers race at Longchamp and beaten Golden Moony by

4 lengths in minor event at Saint-Cloud; suited by 1¼m; yet to race on a firm surface. *O. Douieb, France.*

BARE ESSENTIALS 2 b.c. Streak 119–Gardenia (Cagire II 122) (1981 6fg **60** 6f 7f² 7g 7f³ 7f 8f) Apr 26; leggy colt; closely related to fair 1978 2-y-o 7f winner James Ward (by Runnymede); placed in seller at Beverley and nursery at Thirsk in July; suited by 7f but didn't run up to his best over 1m; blinkered fourth outing; trained by T. Marshall first 3 starts. *R. Whitaker.*

BARFOOT 2 b.f. Hotfoot 126–Barchessa 67 (Prince Chevalier) (1981 7fg 7g 8s*) **82** Apr 29; quite attractive filly; half-sister to winners here, in USA and in France; dam won at 1¼m; showed improved form when winning 17-runner maiden race at Warwick in October by 1½ lengths from Hippo Disco, despite hanging badly left at distance; will be suited by 1¼m; acts on soft going. *B. Hobbs.*

BARLEY BIRCH 3 b.g. Crooner 119–Bella Sandra 88 (Botticelli 129) (1980 **—** NR 1981 10.1fg 8fg 11.5g) compact, short-legged gelding; sixth foal; brother to fair middle-distance performer Bella Canto and half-brother to a winner in Norway; dam won over 13f; behind in minor event at Windsor and maiden races at Newbury and Yarmouth. *M. Tompkins.*

BARNABY SAM 2 br.c. Comedy Star 121–Balandra Star 92 (Blast 125) (1981 **78** 5g 6g³ 7fg 6fg 8fg) Apr 16; useful sort; good walker; brother to useful stayer Another Sam and useful sprinter Middleton Sam, and half-brother to a winner; dam won over 5f at 2 yrs; showed ability in good-class races, on fourth outing finishing about 7 lengths last of 6 to Custer at Newbury in August; stays 7f (had very stiff task in nursery when tried over 1m). *R. Hannon.*

BARNET HEIR 3 ch.c. Great Nephew 126–Right as Rain 96 (King's Bench **81** 132) (1980 5d 5s* 5g* 5f⁴ 5g 5fg* 5f⁴ 5fg 1981 5s 5fg⁴ 5f 5fg⁴ 5.3f³ 6g 5fg⁴ 5.6fg 6g⁴ 6g) small, sturdy, very attractive colt; good mover; in frame 5 times, running particularly well when 2 lengths third to Pontin Lad in minor event at Brighton in August and when 4½ lengths fourth to Steel Charger (after being badly hampered when moving up nicely) in handicap at Epsom in September; very speedy and best at 5f, acts on any going; has run creditably for an apprentice; ran miserably final start. *B. Swift.*

BARNEY KEMPINSKI 3 br.f. Karabas 132–Bristol Milk 88 (Raise You Ten **—** 125) (1980 NR 1981 9d 10d 10d) 2,600Y; fourth living foal; half-sister to Majestic Nurse (by On Your Mark), successful several times at up to 1½m; dam stayed 1½m; well behind in newcomers event at Wolverhampton and maiden races at Salisbury and Brighton in the spring, finishing last on 2 occasions; sold 2,900 gns Goffs November Sales. *C. Nelson.*

BARNLOUGH 3 br.f. Blue Cashmere 129–Stick 'Em Up (Burglar 128) (1980 **53** 5fg 1981 6g 5f 6f 7f⁴ 6fg² 5h 5g) compact filly; made running when in frame in maiden race at Folkestone and handicap at Yarmouth in August; stays 7f. *M. Haynes.*

BARON ARTHUR 2 b.c. Furry Glen 121–Myastrid 108 (Le Levanstell 122) **67** p (1981 7fg 8g⁴) Mar 24; IR 20,000Y; leggy colt; has a rather round action; half-brother to French 3-y-o Odov and useful Irish 7f and 9f winner Protectorate (both by Home Guard) and to a minor winner; dam third in Oaks; ran on well when 4½ lengths fourth of 14 to Outlaw in maiden event at Ayr in September; will stay 1¼m; the type to improve with racing. *Denys Smith.*

BARON BLAKENEY 4 gr.c. Blakeney 126–Teleflora 89 (Princely Gift 137) **77** (1980 12s* 12g³ 12f 12fg 13s 14fg³ 16f 14g 16fg 14g⁴ 16s 1981 16fg⁴ 18fg* 18.4d) neat colt; beat Tweel 2½ lengths easing up in Great Metropolitan Handicap at Epsom in April; tailed off in Ladbroke Chester Cup in May on only subsequent start; suited by a test of stamina; probably acts on any going; suited by strong handling; ran badly in blinkers final start at 3 yrs; won Triumph Hurdle in March. *M. Pipe.*

BARONET 9 b.g. Huntercombe 133–Chagrin Falls 101 (Polic 126) (1980 **110** 10s* 10f 8f 8g⁴ 8g 8d 8g⁴ 10.2g 8fg* 9f* 1981 8s 10fg 8g 8s* 8f 10fg³ 8fg 8fg⁴ 8fg⁴ 8fg² 9g² 10g)
  In the early years of this century a grand handicapper named Dean Swift ran eight times in the City and Suburban Handicap, winning it twice and being placed on four occasions. Baronet's record in the Cambridgeshire doesn't yet match that one but in 1981 he finished an excellent second to Braughing on his fifth start in the race following successes in 1978 and 1980, a second in 1977 and a sixth in 1979. How long he can go on we don't know—Dean Swift ended up being called 'Been Swift' by bookmakers—but to date there is no sign of Baronet's deteriorating with age and he remains one of a handful of equine characters on the flat.

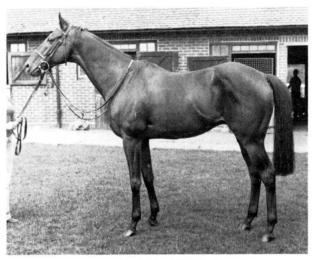

Mrs F. Harris' "Baronet"

Trainer Benstead always ensures that the old fellow reaches his peak for the big Newmarket event, which is sponsored by the William Hill Organisation these days. Baronet's form beforehand had seen his winning once, in the valuable Hambleton Stakes (Limited Handicap) at York in May, when he battled on with great gusto to beat Seven Hearts by a short head. He had also originally been pronounced the short-head winner of the Swinley Forest Stakes at Ascot in September from Herons Hollow but the judge had subsequently reversed his decision after examining a revised print. Baronet ran his customary game race at Headquarters. Moving through to challenge two furlongs out, he couldn't quite get to the 50/1-shot Braughing and had to settle for the runner-up position, two and a half lengths off the winner. He will no doubt be back to try and go one better in 1982.

			Derring-Do	Darius
	Huntercombe		(br 1961)	Sipsey Bridge
	(b 1967)	Ergina	Fair Trial
Baronet			(br 1957)	Ballechin
(b.g. 1972)		Polic	Relic
	Chagrin Falls		(br 1953)	Polaire
	(br 1967)	Brabantia	Honeyway
			(br 1953)	Porthaven

Chagrin Falls, a sister to Polyfoto, won over five furlongs at two and produced several winners in the USA after foaling Baronet. The latter, a lengthy, attractive gelding who often sweats up, stays a mile and a quarter and acts on any going. Usually held up, he has a good turn of foot and goes well in strongly-run races. He is a credit to his trainer who kept another splendid campaigner, Operatic Society, going until the age of eleven in the 'sixties. *J. Benstead.*

BARON HOPKINS 7 ch.g. Frankincense 120–Jolie 64 (Jolly Jet 111) (1980 — NR 1981 8g) plater; stays 1m; probably acts on any going. *A. W. Jones.*

BAROOQ (USA) 2 br.c. Turn And Count–Ballet Pleasure (What A Pleasure) **94** (1981 5f 6fg² 6fg² 7g² 6fg* 8g 7g) May 10; $37,000Y; well-made colt; good

Sheikh Mohammed's "Barooq"

mover; second foal; dam won 4 times at up to 1m; stayed on well when winning 11-runner Philip Cornes Nickel Alloys Stakes Final (nursery) at Newmarket in August by 1½ lengths from Lamlash; wasn't disgraced when seventh in 2 more nurseries at Newmarket afterwards; will stay 1¼m; fairly useful. *F. Durr.*

BAROWIN 2 br.c. Owen Dudley 121–Garnette Rose 74 (Floribunda 136) (1981 — 7fg) Apr 27; 5,600Y; quite well-made colt; half-brother to 1977 2-y-o 5f winner Superior Class (by Decoy Boy); dam seemed to stay 1m; unquoted, made no show when out of first 9 of 24 to Busaco in maiden race at Newbury in August. *C. Nelson.*

BARRIE'S LAND 2 b.g. Royben 125–The Doyle (Faberge II 121) (1981 5g **44** 5g⁴ 6fg) Apr 28; compact gelding; bad plater; sold 670 gns Doncaster September Sales. *P. Haslam.*

BARRYPHILIPS DISCO 4 br.g. Firestreak 125–Appollo Fourteen 78 (Space — King 115) (1980 NR 1981 16.5g) 2,600 3-y-o; strong gelding; winning hurdler; behind in poor minor race at Redcar in September, first outing on flat. *R. Whitaker.*

BARTRA 3 b.g. Mandamus 120–Pandomyne 71 (Pandofell 132) (1980 5fg* 5fg **60** 6s 6g³ 6d 6g 8fg 8.2g⁴ 8.2s² 1981 7g* 8g* 6f³ 7.6g 5.3f⁴ 7.6fg 8g) compact gelding; successful in selling handicaps at Redcar (no bid) and Brighton (sold out of W. Wharton's stable 4,700 gns) in May; subsequently ran creditably in non-selling handicaps on occasions; stays 1m and is bred to get further; acts on any going; sometimes dwells at start. *M. Masson.*

BARWIN (USA) 3 ch.g. Barachois–Winning Rosy (Winning Hit) (1980 6d³ **95** 1981 6fg* 7g* 7g* 7.2s² 7f* 8g 7fg⁴ 7fg* 7g) robust gelding; had a successful season and was gaining his fifth win when beating Traditional Miss by a length in handicap at Salisbury in September; had earlier won maiden race at Nottingham, minor events at Redcar and Newmarket and handicap at Wolverhampton; suited by 7f (ran below form over 1m); acts on any going; goes well for apprentice N. Day; refused to race final start; sold to BBA (Italia) 6,000 gns Newmarket Autumn Sales. *H. Cecil.*

BAY

BARZINI 2 br.g. Baragoi 115–Primeapple (Primera 131) (1981 8d) May 8; brother to winning stayer Our Bara Boy and half-brother to a winning plater; dam of little account; 33/1 when behind in end-of-season maiden race at Leicester. *C. Williams.* — —

BASIL BOY 2 b.c. Jimsun 121–Slick Chick 89 (Shiny Tenth 120) (1981 5s* **88** 5fg² 5d⁴ 5g³ 6fg 6fg 6fg* 7.3d 6g 7g 8.2s) Mar 10; sturdy colt; first foal; dam stayed 13f; successful in maiden race at Nottingham in April and in nursery at Doncaster in September, running best race for some time when wearing down Come On The Blues to win latter by ¾ length; beaten only 4 lengths when eighth of 17 to Vaigly Star in valuable nursery at Newmarket in October on ninth outing; yet to show he stays 7f; has won on soft ground but has shown better form on firm. *R. Hannon.*

BASTA 2 b.f. Busted 134–The Woodbird (Tudor Melody 129) (1981 7g) Apr — 13; 5,400Y; rangy, attractive filly; second foal; half-sister to 3-y-o Papagena (by Lyphard); dam won small 7f race at 2 yrs in France; 33/1 and very backward, dwelt and was always struggling in 29-runner maiden race at Newmarket in October won by Chalon. *G. Pritchard-Gordon.*

BATIK 3 ch.f. On Your Mark 125–Taffeta 72 (Shantung 132) (1980 5fg 6fg 6fg — 6g 1981 6g 8.5d 8fg 6fg 6g) lengthy filly; poor plater; should stay 1m+; wears blinkers. *D. Sasse.*

BATONI 2 b.c. Realm 129–Martha Meynet (Welsh Pageant 132) (1981 5g* **83** 5g* (dis)) Apr 22; neat, rather leggy colt; good mover; first foal; dam never ran; put in best work in last furlong to win minor events at Pontefract in April (by 4 lengths) and Doncaster in May (beat Chellaston Park ½ length, the pair clear); disqualified from his Doncaster win over 2 months later after failing a dope test; bred to stay 6f+; presumably had a setback after Doncaster. *M. H. Easterby.*

BATTALION 3 br.c. Bustino 136–True Love 89 (Princely Gift 137) (1980 NR **77** 1981 6g² 8f⁴ 8d² 9s* 8g* 10d²) rather a hollow-backed colt; brother to fairly useful 7f winner Peek-A-Boo, and half-brother to 1m winner Love Story (by Aureole) and 1¼m to 2m winner Wedded Bliss (by Relko); dam 2-y-o 5f winner; in frame on all starts and won maiden event at Hamilton and minor event at Edinburgh in October, beating Fearless Flight by 4 lengths in latter; stays 1¼m; acts on soft going and was a shade disappointing on firm second outing; sold out of C. Thornton's stable 11,500 gns Newmarket Autumn Sales before final start. *D. Chapman.*

BATTLE DANCER 2 ch.g. Music Boy 124–Wellington Girl 62 (Tribal Chief 125) — (1981 5f 5s 5d 6s) Feb 28; strong gelding; first foal; dam plating class at 2 yrs; emulating his dam; wears blinkers. *W. C. Watts.*

BATTLE SPLENDID 5 b.h. Royal Splendid 116–Rechauffe (Firestreak 125) — (1980 NR 1981 10fg 8d 12.2g) poor maiden. *J. Yardley.*

BAUHINIA 2 ch.f. Sagaro 133–Boswellia 109 (Frankincense 120) (1981 8s⁴) **70 p** Mar 7; small, unimpressive-looking filly; third foal; half-sister to 2 winners, including 1m winner Cape Chestnut (by Bustino); dam won William Hill Gold Cup; 9/1, shaped quite well when staying on strongly to finish 5¼ lengths fourth of 14 to Florida Son in maiden race at York in October; doesn't possess a great deal of scope but may improve over middle distances at 3 yrs. *W. Hastings-Bass.*

BAVAL (FR) 4 b.g. Baroque 128–Valse des Coeurs (Homere) (1980 8g⁴ 8g² — 8d³ 9g 8d 10d 8d 8g³ 8d* 8v 1981 7d 10g 16.1s 8.2d⁴) tall ex-French gelding; not a particularly good walker or mover; won handicap at Saint-Cloud in 1980; showed only poor form over here at 4 yrs; promises to stay 1¼m (tailed off over 2m); yet to race on a firm surface. *A. Jarvis.*

BAWDSEY 4 ch.g. Red Alert 127–Tribal Lass (Tribal Chief 125) (1980 6v⁴ 6f — 5.8f 5h 1981 8f 7fg 7fg) good sort; ran badly in 1981; has worn blinkers. *W. Wharton.*

BAY FOULARD 3 b.f. Shantung 132–Vardo 92 (Crepello 136) (1980 6g 7g — 7fg 8d 1981 8.2s) quite well-made filly; well behind in varied company, including in a selling nursery as a 2-y-o. *R. Hollinshead.*

BAY OF MIST 3 b.f. Ragstone 128–Tashkin 103 (Red God 128§) (1980 NR **74** 1981 12d 14f* 12f² 14.6g 16g) lengthy, useful sort; fourth foal; sister to 1¼m winner Rags and Bags; dam sprinter; beat Alangrove Sound by a short head in maiden race at Yarmouth in June; stays 2m (had stiff task and wasn't disgraced over trip final start). *J. Winter.*

109

BAZ BOMBATI 3 ch.c Sun Prince 128–Salsafy 81 (Tudor Melody 129) (1980 **105**
7fg* 7.2d² 7fg* 7g 8g² 1981 8g 12g* 12fg³ 12fg 12v³ 12d 12g) well-made,
useful-looking colt; good walker and mover; won maiden race at Yarmouth and
Fitzroy House Stakes at Newmarket as a 2-y-o; led entering final furlong and
battled on gamely to beat Bonol ½ length in minor event at Beverley in June;
kept on quite well and was moved up a place when about 4 lengths fourth to
Bustomi in King Edward VII Stakes at Royal Ascot later in month; behind in
Irish Sweeps Derby at the Curragh, Great Voltigeur Stakes at York and Stockholm Cup at Taby subsequently, and didn't run up to his best when 10 lengths
third of 7 to Index in Bayerisches Zuchtrennen at Munich; suited by 1½m;
best form on a sound surface; sold privately and is hurdling with S. Mellor.
G. Pritchard-Gordon.

B. B. OIL 3 b.g. Netherkelly 122–Blue Mountain (Mountain Call 125) (1980 —
5fg 5s 6s 8.2s 1981 12.2g 8g 8f) small, lightly-made gelding; poor plater.
B. Richmond.

BEACON HEIGHTS 4 b.g. Guillaume Tell 121–Moana (Zucchero 133§) —
(1980 10fg 1981 14g) tall, lengthy gelding; well beaten in minor and maiden
events; blinkered once at 2 yrs; sold 1,150 gns Ascot December Sales. *J. Cann.*

BEACON HILL 3 ch.f. Bustino 136–Highclere 129 (Queen's Hussar 124) **81**
(1980 NR 1981 10fg² 12g 10g) attractive, lengthy filly; good walker and
mover; third foal; sister to good staying 2-y-o Height of Fashion, closely related
to useful stayer Burghclere (by Busted) and half-sister to smart middle-distance
winner Milford (by Mill Reef); dam won 1,000 Guineas and Prix de Diane;
favourite, led 3f out and kept on well under pressure when going down by a neck
to Home On The Range (pair clear) in 16-runner maiden event at Sandown in
April; didn't reproduce that form in similar events at Goodwood in September
(odds on) and Newmarket in October; looks very short of pace. *R. Hern.*

BEACON RAMBLER 7 br g New Member 119–Infidelity (Doubtless II 111) —
(1980 NR 1981 10.1fg) of little account over fences; behind in minor event at
Windsor in June, first outing on flat; sold 2,000 gns Ascot 2nd June Sales.
M. Scudamore.

BEAMING LASS 2 b. or br.f. Silly Season 127–Oh Well 61 (Sahib 114) (1981 **52**
5g 5fg 5g 5g⁴ 5f³ 6fg⁴ 5g 6f* 5d 8.2d) Mar 23; 1,700F; plain filly; second produce;
dam stayed 1m; attracted no bid after winning seller at Hamilton in August by ¾
length from Palos Heights; better suited by 6f than 5f, and should stay 1m; acts
on firm going; ran poorly in blinkers seventh outing. *J. S. Wilson.*

BEAMOF 2 b. or br.g. Averof 123–Beamless 73 (Hornbeam 130) (1981 5g 6g —
7fg 7.2fg) May 15; 3,000F, 4,600Y; strong gelding; closely related to 3 winners
by Song, including quite useful sprinter Bill's Song, and half-brother to a winner
in Norway; dam stayed 1½m; behind in minor and maiden events. *G. Toft.*

BEAMWAM 3 br.g. Bing II–Canute Lady 66 (Hardicanute 130) (1980 NR —
1981 12g⁴) fourth foal; dam won a 11f seller; unquoted when remote fourth of
7 behind Elizabeth Howard in minor event at Edinburgh in September. *H. Bell.*

BEAN BOY 3 ch.g. Some Hand 119–Battling 75 (Pinza 137) (1980 NR 1981 **57**
8s 7v 12.2g² 12g* 9g 12fg) workmanlike gelding; apprentice ridden when
winning 18-runner seller at Thirsk in May in good style by 5 lengths from Audit
(sold out of M. McCormack's stable 3,200 gns); towards rear in non-sellers afterwards; stays 1½m; blinkered last 3 outings. *Denys Smith.*

BEARWOOD BELLE 3 ch.f. Shiny Tenth 120–Flight Feathers (Ribocco 129) —
(1980 5d 5d 1981 6v 7g 7f 8fg) small, light-framed filly; poor plater. *D.
Marks.*

BEAUCOUP D'ARGENT 3 b.g. Streak 119–Mona's Own (Entanglement 118) —
(1980 8g 8g 1981 7.6g) small, lengthy gelding; lightly raced and well beaten in
maiden and minor races. *E. Eldin.*

BEAU JANGLES (FR) 2 gr.c. Dancer's Image–Kate's Intent (Intentionally) **67**
(1981 5d 5g⁴ 6g) Apr 24; 60,000Y; well-made, quite attractive colt; brother to
2 winners, including top-class sprinter Godswalk, closely related to another and
half-brother to 2 more; dam very useful stakes winner at up to 7f in USA;
having first race for nearly 3 months when 7½ lengths sixth of 15 to Celestial
Dancer in maiden race at Yarmouth in September (ridden along after having
plenty to do at halfway); will probably stay 1m. *J. Sutcliffe.*

BEAULAH 5 ch.g. Track Spare 125–Rippling Water 80 (Star Moss 122) (1980 **41**
NR 1981 7s 10fg² 16f) runner-up in apprentice seller at Beverley in June;
stays 1¼m. *W. C. Watts.*

BEAUMAINS (USA) 3 b.g. Advocator–Firstboam (First Landing) (1980 6f **61**
7fg 1981 8.2s 10f³ 10fg² 10fg) quite a moderate maiden; always behind final
start; stays 1¼m; sold 3,900 gns Ascot September Sales. *J. Sutcliffe.*

BEAU PRETENDER (FR) 2 ch.c. Anne's Pretender 124–Belle de Reux **115**
(Diatome 132) (1981 7.5fg 7.5fg⁴ 8d* 10v*) May 15; 30,000 francs Y (approx
£3,000); first foal; dam, minor middle-distance winner, is daughter of smart
1962 French 2-y-o Chesa; won maiden race at Chantilly in September by 2½
lengths and bettered that effort in Group 3 Prix de Conde at Longchamp the
following month, getting up in last 100 yards to win by ½ length from Dear
Patrick; stays very well; acts on heavy going; trained by B. Margueritte first 2
outings. *R. Touflan, France.*

BEAUSOLEIL 2 b.c. Nonoalco 131–Miss Monaco 107 (Crepello 136) (1981 6g³ **80**
8g³) Apr 17; third foal; half-brother to 3-y-o Miss Menton (by Brigadier
Gerard), a winner over 6f at 2 yrs, and to a winner in Italy by Reform; dam, a
sprinter, at her best at 2 yrs; third in maiden races at Yarmouth in September
(unlucky, being badly squeezed out at start before staying on very well to be 2½
lengths behind Celestial Dancer) and Edinburgh in October (odds on when 4½
lengths behind Brigado); stays 1m; sold to German International BA 8,000 gns
Newmarket Autumn Sales. *W. Hastings-Bass.*

BEAUX ARTS 3 br.c. Music Boy 124–Blessed Beauty 97 (Rustam 127) (1980 —
NR 1981 6f) 6,000Y; strong, stocky colt; half-brother to 2 winners, including
1979 2-y-o 7f winner Burnside (by Roan Rocket); dam winner at up to 7f; backward and soon struggling when in rear in maiden event won by Mrs Leadbetter
at Nottingham in July; withdrawn after giving trouble at stalls on same course
later in month; sold 2,000 gns Doncaster August Sales. *G. Huffer.*

BEAUX ARTS (FR) 3 ch.c. Luthier 126–Bon Appetit 107 (Major Portion 129) **85**
(1980 8g² 1981 10fg² 12d² 10fg³ 10fg*) tall colt; trotted up by 6 lengths from
Star Fleet in 17-runner amateur riders race at Newmarket in July; will stay
beyond 1½m (needs a strong gallop to be effective at 1¼m); acts on a firm and a
soft surface; hurdling in France and has done very well there. *H. Cecil.*

BE BE OF KUWAIT 2 br.g. Prince Tenderfoot 126–Spinning Jenny (Timmy **97**
My Boy 125) (1981 5g 5s² 6fg* 6fg² 6fg* 7fg⁴) Apr 10; 13,000Y; strong, well-
made gelding; second living foal; half-brother to Irish 8.5f and 1½m winner
Synarria (by Guillaume Tell); dam never ran; won minor event at Windsor in
July and landed odds in 10-runner nursery at Salisbury in August (beat Lively
Rose 3 lengths); ran very well in between when short-head second of 6 to El
Mansour in New Ham Stakes at Goodwood; should stay 7f (sweated up badly
and took a strong hold when short-priced favourite for £5,900 event at Newmarket on first attempt at trip, coming home 4½ lengths fourth to Chulia Street
after seeming to be going very well 2f out); subsequently gelded; has run
respectably on soft going but has shown best form on a firm surface. *J. Sutcliffe.*

BECKY SHARP 3 ch.f. Sharpen Up 127–Paddy's Darling 73 (St Paddy 133) **66**
(1980 NR 1981 9d 8fg 8fg² 8s* 8fg 10fg³ 8f 8g) 3,800F, 9,800Y; tall, quite
attractive filly; first foal; dam won over 1½m; beat Prince Reviewer a neck in
18-runner maiden race at Yarmouth in July; tended to hang when creditable
third to Flighting in minor event at Salisbury the following month; finds 1m on
firm ground on sharp side and stays 1¼m; seems to act on any going but has a
round action and is possibly ideally suited by some give in the ground; bandaged
near-hind first outing. *F. Durr.*

BE CONTENT 3 ch.g. Manado 130–Clytemnestra 81 (Bullrush 106) (1980 NR —
1981 7d) 6,400F, 7,400Y; lengthy gelding; half-brother to 3 winners, notably
very useful sprinter King of Troy (by King's Troop); dam sprinter; backward
when last of 10 behind Nureddin in newcomers race at Doncaster in March. *W.
Marshall.*

BEDFORD (USA) 3 b.c. Nijinsky 138–Drumtop (Round Table) (1980 7f 7d² **109**
1981 10d 12d 10fg 10fg² 11fg* 12f* 13.1g* 14d³ 14s) quite an attractive, well-
made colt; good mover; took a while to confirm his 2-y-o promise, but won maiden
event at Kempton (made all), 4-runner minor event at York (idled a bit in front
and got home by only 1½ lengths from Judd), and minor event at Bath (won
by 4 lengths from White Saint), all in late summer; had much stiffer tasks
afterwards, and ran another good race when 8 lengths third of 7 behind Protection

Racket in Irish St Leger at the Curraghi n October; stays 1¾m; acts on firm going and a soft surface; blinkered in Ireland. *I. Balding.*

BEE ALIVE (USA) 2 gr.c. Drone–Whirled 116 (Globemaster) (1981 7g 6s) **75 p** rangy, useful-looking colt; half-brother to several winners, including fairly useful 1m to 1¼m winner Wind (by Tom Rolfe); dam smart miler; soundly beaten in good-class events at Ascot in the autumn but showed speed for over 4f when 13½ lengths seventh of 11 to Slightly Dangerous on second outing; should stay 7f. *P. Walwyn.*

BEECH DALE 3 b.f. The Go-Between 129–Wasdale 97 (Psidium 130) (1980 — 5fg 5fg 5g 1981 8s 10f 10f 13.8f) light-framed filly; behind in varied company, including selling. *F. Dever.*

BEECHWOOD CON 5 ch.g. Siliconn 121–Look Out 84 (Vimy 132) (1980 8.2s — 1981 8f) plater; stays 1m; acts well on firm going; has worn bandages. *R. F. Peacock.*

BEECHWOOD SEEKER 3 b.g. Status Seeker–Julie's Gi-Gi (Brave Invader) **78** (1980 6s 6s 7g 7fg* 7d 8.2s² 8g² 8.2v³ 8s 1981 10s 12g 12d* 12g 12.5f² 13fg 12.3fg 12.3g⁴ 16f³ 16g* 18f* 17.4g²) workmanlike gelding; good walker; improved and won handicaps at Ripon in May, Newcastle in August and Ripon again in September; beat Wild Rosie by a length in Eglinton and Winton Memorial Handicap at Ayr later in September but hampered runner-up just inside last furlong and placings were subsequently reversed; very well suited by a test of stamina; acts on any going; has run well in blinkers. *K. Stone.*

BEE IMPERIAL 3 b.f. Connaught 130–Barbarina (Molvedo 137) (1980 NR — 1981 7g 10g 10.2g) half-sister to 5 winners in Italy, including prolific scorer Be Regal (by Viceregal); dam unraced daughter of Italian St Leger winner Barbara Sirani; behind in maiden race and Playboy Pretty Polly Stakes at Newmarket and minor event at Doncaster (seventh of 13), sweating and hanging under pressure on latter course in May on final start (still didn't look ready). *H. Wragg.*

Mr J. B. Moseley's "Bedford"

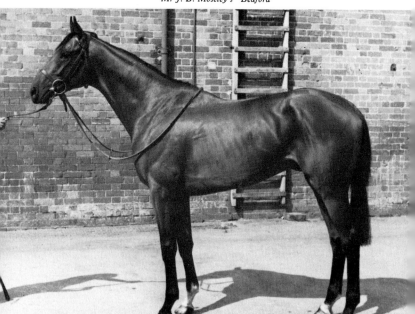

BEL

BEELEIGH 3 b.g. Sallust 134–Mythical Lady 86 (Track Spare 125) (1980 6d **92**
7fg 7g² 6fg² 1981 7s* 8.2fg* 8fg* 7d* 8.2s 8f 8g 9d 8fg²) leggy, useful sort of
gelding; in very good form early in year and was winning his fourth successive
race when beating Melon Patch very easily by 2½ lengths in Laskys Video
Handicap at Chester in May; had earlier won maiden event at Leicester, Valspar
Paints Handicap at Haydock and Esher Cup at Sandown; put up several
moderate performances afterwards, but ran well final start; stays 1m; probably
acts on any going; has won for an apprentice but has a tendency to hang; sometimes sweats up and often fails to impress in paddock. *N. Callaghan.*

BEE SIDE 2 br.c. Record Token 128–Pure Honey 94 (Don II 123) (1981 5g —
5f 5fg) Apr 15; 4,000Y; neat colt; second foal; dam 5f performer; no sign of
ability; blinkered third outing; sold 3,800 gns Ascot August Sales. *Mrs J.
Reavey.*

BE FRIENDLY TOO 4 ch.f. Be Friendly 130–Cann Track 90 (Sound Track 132) —
(1980 8.2g 12.2f 7g 12.5s² 1981 12g) sharp sort; poor performer; stays 1½m;
acts on soft going; sometimes wears blinkers. *R. Fisher.*

BEGGAR'S BRIDGE 6 br.h. Linacre 133–Monsel (Hook Money 124) (1980 **98**
10s 10s³ 12f 10.4f 12g 10g* 10.5g 12f* 10.5g* 12s² 10g 12d⁴ 10g 1981 10fg⁴
10.2g 10fg 12d² 12d 11.1f 10d 10.8s² 10.2g) strong, good-looking horse; useful
performer; second in minor events at Lingfield in August (head behind Rheinsteel)
and Leicester in October (beaten 3 lengths by Show-A-Leg); stays 1½m; acts on
any going but is well suited by some give in the ground; blinkered sixth outing;
sometimes bandaged in front; sold 8,200 gns Newmarket Autumn Sales. *R.
Laing.*

BEGGAR'S BUSH (USA) 3 gr.g. Al Hattab–Sailly Le Sec (Yorky) (1980 —
5f 5d² 6d² 5.8f² 7d² 7h⁴ 8d³ 8d² 1981 8d 12d 11.7s 10s 8d² 8fg) small, lightly-
made gelding; disappointing maiden; should stay beyond 1m; seems to act on
any going; pulled up second outing and wore blinkers afterwards; one to be
wary of. *H. Candy.*

BEGHAM BAY 2 b.f. Bay Express 132–Beseech 84 (Petition 130) (1981 **81**
5f⁴ 5fg² 5fg² 5fg² 5f* 5g* 6g 6s) June 5; fair sort; good walker; half-sister to
several winners, including quite useful middle-distance performer Cream Wave
(by Espresso) and fairly useful 1978 2-y-o Man of the Sea (by Mansingh); dam
won over 11f; favourite when winning maiden race at Hamilton in August and
21-runner event at Catterick in September, latter by 1½ lengths from My Fancy;
best form at 5f but wasn't disgraced on first attempt at 6f; acts on firm going.
M. Stoute.

BE IN TOUCH 3 b.f. Windjammer (USA)–Claddie (Karabas 132) (1980 —
6s 1981 8s 8s 8g) little sign of ability, including in sellers; usually apprentice
ridden; sometimes starts slowly; sold 2,400 gns Newmarket July Sales. *P.
Rohan.*

BEL BOLIDE (USA) 3 ch.c. Bold Bidder–Lady Graustark (Graustark) (1980 **121**
5fg* 6d³ 6g* 6g² 6g* 6f² 1981 7g⁴ 8g³ 8s 8fg³ 7.3fg)
Bel Bolide surprisingly went through his second season without a win.
One of the most consistent two-year-olds of 1980, winner of the Gimcrack Stakes
and second to Mattaboy in the Middle Park Stakes, he raced only five more
times and after two good runs at Newmarket in the spring failed, like so many
from his stable, to do himself full justice.
When Bel Bolide reappeared in the Tote European Free Handicap at Newmarket in April we were immediately struck by how little he had changed physically over the winter. An early-maturing type, he looked fit but hadn't made
anything like so much progress as some of the others, notably Motavato. However he ran with great credit, joining issue two furlongs out and keeping on well
to finish fourth less than two lengths behind Motavato. The following month,
in the Two Thousand Guineas, his rider employed more forceful tactics, similar
to those which had served so well in 1980, and Bel Bolide ran really well. He
was a clear leader towards the far rails with three furlongs or so to go and battled
on really gamely to finish third behind To-Agori-Mou and Mattaboy, beaten a
neck and a length and a half, giving best only in the last half furlong.
Little went right for Bel Bolide during the remainder of the year. Very
soft going proved all against him in the Tote Lockinge Stakes a fortnight after
the Guineas and he trailed in fifth of six behind Belmont Bay. We weren't
too surprised that he didn't act on the ground for he's a fluent, easy mover with
a long stride, the type that tends to be particularly well suited by top-of-the-
ground; his connections had reportedly considered withdrawing him. He

113

fared better in the St James's Palace Stakes at Royal Ascot, but after setting a good gallop he was completely outpointed when To-Agori-Mou and Kings Lake quickened and was beaten about six lengths into third. It seemed possible that he might benefit from a return to a shorter trip, but he disappointed when tried over an extended seven furlongs in the Hungerford Stakes at Newbury in August, dropping out rather quickly in the last furlong or so and finishing only seventh to Dalsaan. It was subsequently intended to run Bel Bolide in the newly-instituted Arlington Million over a mile and a quarter at Chicago but after making the long journey to the States he had to miss the race owing to a pricked foot. He was later engaged in the Petition Stakes at Newmarket but was withdrawn on race-day after heavy rain.

Bel Bolide (USA) (ch.c. 1978)	Bold Bidder (b 1962)	Bold Ruler (b 1954)	Nasrullah / Miss Disco
		High Bid (b 1956)	To Market / Stepping Stone
	Lady Graustark (ch 1969)	Graustark (ch 1963)	Ribot / Flower Bowl
		Invala (ch 1963)	My Babu / Roman Ronda

Bel Bolide is an attractive colt by Bold Bidder, sire of Spectacular Bid, out of Lady Graustark who won twice at up to six furlongs as a two-year-old. All of Lady Graustark's previous foals are winners, two of them in the USA and one in Holland, easily the best of them being the Nijinsky filly Excitable who was very useful at around a mile at three and was stakes-placed as a four-year-old. Bel Bolide remains in training and will possibly add to his reputation. However he fares, he will probably always need a galloping track and a sound surface to be seen to advantage. *J. Tree.*

BELDALE BID (USA) 2 ch.c. Raise A Bid–Starlet O'Hara (Silent Screen) **104** (1981 5s² 6s³ 7fg² 7fg* 7f* 7fg* 7s) Apr 5; $42,000 2-y-o; strong attractive colt, good mover; second foal; dam, placed 3 times from 13 starts, is half-sister to Kentucky Oaks winner Blue Norther; sire, stakes-winning son of Raise A Native, won at up to 9f; picked up a valuable prize when winning 5-runner Grand Criterium International d'Ostende in August by a length from Red Sunset; had previously won a maiden race at Ayr and 5-runner nursery at Redcar, latter by a length from Bustello; came under whip early in straight and dropped out to finish 11 lengths last of 5 to Green Forest in Prix de la Salamandre at Longchamp in September; will stay 1¼m; acts well on top-of-the-ground. *M. Jarvis.*

BELDALE DYNASTY (USA) 2 b.c. Dynastic–Saureole Joy (Johns Joy) **81** (1981 6g 7g²) Feb 27; $36,000 2-y-o; compact, good sort; brother to Joyfull Ruler, a stakes winner at up to 1m, and half-brother to 3 winners, including sprint stakes winner Lt's Joy (by Lt Stevens); dam won 5f claiming race at 2 yrs; weak in market when 1½ lengths second of 17 to Northleigh in maiden race at Leicester in September, giving impression he'd have given winner more to do if he hadn't had to be switched a couple of times in last 3f; will be well suited by 1m. *M. Jarvis.*

BELDALE FLEET (USA) 2 b.c. Fleet Nasrullah–Adjudicate Miss (Traffic **91** Judge) (1981 7fg² 7g⁴ 7f) Apr 14; $50,000Y, $150,000 2-y-o; big colt; has a round action; half-brother to 4 winners, including smart 1977 2-y-o sprinting filly Lov Tov (by Kfar Tov) and smart stakes winner Score Twenty Four (by Golden Eagle), successful at up to 9f; dam never ran; ran on strongly to go down by only a short head to Oxslip in 22-runner maiden race at Newmarket in July; again showed promise when favourite for 8-runner Acomb Stakes at York the following month, finishing 3 lengths fourth to Height of Fashion after coming to lead 2f out, but ran badly in valuable race won by Marquessa d'Howfen on same course in September; will stay 1¼m; immature at 2 yrs and could show considerable improvement in 1982. *M. Jarvis.*

BELDALE FLUTTER (USA) 3 b.c. Accipiter–Flitter Flutter (Cohoes) (1980 **130** 6fg⁴ 7.2d* 7f* 8fg⁴ 8d* 1981 7d³ 8g 10.5s* 10.5g* 12d 12fg)
Beldale Flutter experienced mixed fortunes in his second season. On the credit side he picked up the two most valuable races staged at York, the Mecca-Dante Stakes and the Benson and Hedges Gold Cup; on the debit he was well beaten in the.Two Thousand Guineas, Prix de l'Arc de Triomphe and Washington International. He also had the wretched luck to be involved in a training accident the week before the Derby which not only forced him to pass up what

114

Mecca-Dante Stakes, York—Beldale Flutter wins Britain's most valuable Derby trial from Shotgun

seemed at the time a first-rate opportunity in that race but also kept him off the course until late-August, through a period which can be very important in the racing career of a classic horse.

Beldale Flutter stood at 7/1 second favourite when withdrawn from the Derby, following his win in the Mecca-Dante Stakes in May and reports of an outstanding recent home gallop. He was already being referred to as the only horse to have beaten Shergar. On his final outing in 1980 Beldale Flutter had come up against Shergar and several other leading staying two-year-olds in the William Hill Futurity over a testing mile at Doncaster and had won the race on merit by two and a half lengths from Shergar, with Sheer Grit third. The Mecca-Dante Stakes thoroughly re-established him in the public favour, after his modest fifteenth in the Guineas had taken the shine off his promising third, when backward, to Another Realm in the Clerical, Medical Greenham Stakes at Newbury on his seasonal reappearance. He was allowed to start at 11/1 for the Mecca-Dante, opposing Kalaglow (11/10), Robellino (7/2), Centurius (9/2), Shotgun (9/1) and Scintillating Air (18/1). Ridden by Eddery, who got on with him particularly well, Beldale Flutter turned the Derby market into some confusion by a smooth success, while the three best-fancied horses ran moderately. Sweating a shade (he had sweated up more at Newmarket), Beldale Flutter was always travelling easily in a race run at a slow pace which led to there still being a fairly tight bunch remaining with only three furlongs left. Asked for his effort approaching the final furlong, he quickened up nicely, soon got on top, ran on strongly and, in the end, won a shade comfortably by three quarters of a length from Shotgun, who at around that time was regarded as the best Derby hope produced in the North for a while. The Mecca-Dante Stakes form doesn't look so hot now as it did then, and Beldale Flutter improved considerably on it over the same course in the Benson and Hedges Gold Cup when he at last became fit enough to race again. Beldale Flutter's accident could have been even worse than it turned out. He ran loose on the Heath one morning, collided with Moorestyle, and eventually came down on the road, cutting his off-fore knee so badly that it was left permanently enlarged. He had to be confined to his box for over three weeks after the incident, suffering also from badly bruised ribs. Fortunately both he and Moorestyle lived to fight another day.

Shotgun reopposed Beldale Flutter in the Benson and Hedges Gold Cup but his chance looked slim after his disappointing performance in the Scottish Derby. Even though the field was not so strong a one as we have come to expect there were better horses than he in the race, including the previous year's winner Master Willie, the improved Hard Fought and another four-year-old Fingal's Cave, third to Shergar in the King George VI and Queen Elizabeth Diamond Stakes at Ascot. Also present were Centurius and two other three-year-olds, Kirtling and the French-trained Ecube, the latter well beaten

115

Benson and Hedges Gold Cup, York—Beldale Flutter beats Kirtling and Master Willie after a 14-week absence through injury

behind Akarad in the Grand Prix de Saint-Cloud. Looking at Beldale Flutter in the paddock we got the impression he might just be better for the race. However he gave the performance of his all-too-short racing life; it was a very fine training feat to bring him back in such good shape after three months off. The race turned out to be an interesting battle of tactics, and Kirtling was given a particularly shrewd ride by Piggott. Kirtling made the running, not at a particularly strong gallop to start with but stepping up the pace when his jockey thought necessary, which led to some of the runners getting in each other's way, and some struggling to quicken. The ones who were up there early on were also those fighting out the finish. Beldale Flutter was kept in the first two from the start and along with Kirtling and Master Willie quickened away from the rest early in the straight. These three had slipped their rivals two furlongs out. Beldale Flutter seemed to be going best; he got on top approaching the final furlong and ran on well for a three-quarter-length win from the hard-ridden Kirtling. Master Willie finished the same distance down in third, clear of Centurius.

Beldale Flutter wasn't raced again until he went for his main objective of the autumn, the Prix de l'Arc de Triomphe. His prospects in that race were difficult to weigh up, as difficult as almost any of those engaged. Where did he stand among Europe's leading middle-distance horses? The possibility existed that he was, or could improve sufficiently after his injury to be, good enough to win that most prestigious contest, but it had to be borne in mind that he was unproven over the distance and on breeding wasn't likely to show any better form at a mile and a half. The dead ground, as was perfectly plain to see from his record, was decidedly in his favour. He started at 12/1. In the event he ran a poor race, already showing signs of beating a retreat from a striking position when badly jostled at the bottom of the hill before the home turn; he dropped back to last but one of the twenty-four runners by the finish. He had little chance in the Washington International on this performance, and

116

although it was thought that the sharp track there would suit him he was again well beaten, fading quickly into seventh-of-ten place behind Providential after running well enough to secure a good place going into the final turn. The firmish ground would have been against him.

Beldale Flutter won't be racing again, so he leaves us still with a difficult problem in assessing him. The task would probably have been made easier had he remained in training as a four-year-old. Judged on the evidence of his sadly-disrupted season as a three-year-old he was a horse just short of top classic standard, a horse who on his best form would definitely have been in the frame in the Derby he so unfortunately had to miss. On the limited evidence he was best at distances short of a mile and a half, ideally suited by a mile and a quarter. He did need some give in the ground to show to best advantage although he twice ran creditably on firmish going as a two-year-old.

Beldale Flutter (USA) (b.c. 1978)	Accipiter (b 1971)	Damascus (b 1964)	Sword Dancer / Kerala
		Kingsland (b or br 1965)	Bold Ruler / Landmark
	Flitter Flutter (br 1966)	Cohoes (b 1954)	Mahmoud / Belle of Troy
		Ellerslie (br 1954)	Nasrullah / Effie B.

A shapely colt, Beldale Flutter was picked up at the Florida Two-Year-Olds in Training Sales for a mere 20,000 dollars, perhaps first attracting the attention of his purchaser by the fact that he was a half-brother to a smart English two-year-old of 1976 Our Jimmy (by Tom Rolfe). All the dam's foals before Beldale Flutter were winners. Besides Our Jimmy in England there was the quite useful Chappelle Blanche (by Olden Times) who won over six furlongs at Goodwood for Guy Harwood's stable; in France there was one called Good Ad (by Advocator) and in the United States there were Star Fortune (by Pia Star) and Extravagation (by King's Bishop); the last three were all minor winners. Beldale Flutter's sire ran no less than twenty-six times as a three-year-old for seven wins, including stakes wins in the one-mile Withers and one-mile Saranac. He is siring stakes winners, too, in the United States. The dam Flitter Flutter won two small races in the States as a two-year-old. She is out of a mare who bred eight starters, all

Mr A. J. Kelly's "Beldale Flutter"

winners, from ten foals. Among them were Flitter Flutter's half-brother Low
Son, winner of the World's Playground Stakes as a two-year-old, and the Beverley
Handicap winner Short Fall. One of the unraced pair, Candy's Best, became
the dam of an outstanding filly over there called Candy Eclair. Beldale Flutter
was syndicated at £60,000 a share, and is standing at Banstead Manor Stud,
Newmarket. *M. Jarvis.*

BELDALE LEADER (USA) 3 b.c. Mr Leader–Aptobe Fleet (Fleet Nasrullah) **63**
(1980 7g 7g 8.2s 1981 10.2g 10.5f 12.3g 12g 13.8g² 11d) good-looking colt;
very good mover; claimed for £1,500 out of J. Hanson's stable after finishing
second to Hassi R'mel in selling handicap at Catterick in October; claimed by V.
Thompson £3,000 at Hamilton 2 days later; stays 1¾m; blinkered fourth outing.
G. Lockerbie.

BELDALE LUSTRE (USA) 2 br.c. Explodent–Added Lustre (Clandestine) **90**
(1981 6g³ 6g³ 6g² 6g²) Apr 10; $26,000Y, $38,000 2-y-o; big, strong, good sort,
with plenty of scope; fourth foal; half-brother to 3 minor winners in USA; dam,
out of half-sister to Kentucky Derby winner Foolish Pleasure, won 5f claiming
race at 4 yrs; placed in 2 good-class maiden races, coming out best of newcomers
when 1¾ lengths third to Rebollino in Convivial Stakes at York in August, and
finishing 1½ lengths third of 21 to Mirabeau at Doncaster the following month;
well-backed favourite for maiden events at Newmarket in October subsequently
but on both occasions found little off bridle after seeming to be hacking going into
Dip and possibly lacks resolution; gives us impression he's far from certain to
stay much beyond 6f; has the ability to win races. *M. Jarvis.*

BELDALE RULER (USA) 2 ch.c. Orbit Ruler–Togotobattle (Nevada Battler) **84**
(1981 6g² 5g 6fg⁴ 8s³) Feb 10; $45,000 2-y-o; strong colt; brother to 2 winners,
including minor 1980 2-y-o stakes winner Super Strut, and half-brother to a
winner; dam never ran; sire won 9f Del Mar Derby; in frame in maiden races
and a nursery, running best race when short-head second of 20 to Linda Beard at
Newmarket in August on debut; should stay 1m; possibly unsuited by soft ground,
sold to BBA (Italia) 9,200 gns Newmarket Autumn Sales. *M. Jarvis.*

BEL EMIR (FR) 2 gr.c. Targowice 130–Nativka (Caro 133) (1981 8g* 8v*) **108**
Mar 30; first foal; dam placed several times over jumps in France; won maiden
race at Fontainebleau in September and accounted for 3 useful colts, after being
held up, in 60,000 francs event at Maisons-Laffitte the following month, scoring
by a neck from Riverhill; will probably stay 1¼m. *A. Fabre, France.*

BEL ESPRIT 2 b.f. Sagaro 133–Esprit d'Or 86 (Jolly Jet 111) (1981 6f 5.8f) **—**
Mar 16; 1,200F, 1,800Y; second foal; dam, half-sister to high-class miler Gold
Rod, won 1m amateur riders race; last in minor event at Chepstow and maiden
auction race at Bath in the summer. *G. Cottrell.*

BELFE 2 ch.f. Tachypous 128–Appian Way 89 (Romulus 129) (1981 8d⁴ 8g 8g⁴) **90**
Mar 31; 5,000Y; small filly; half-sister to useful 3-y-o stayer Valentinian (by
Morston) and to winners here and in Hungary; dam won over middle distances;
prominent in end-of-season maiden and minor races (last 2 at Newmarket),
running particularly well on final outing to finish 3½ lengths fourth of 27 to
Dudley Wood; will be suited by middle distances. *R. Hollinshead.*

BELFORT (FR) 4 gr.c. Tyrant–Belle de Retz 104 (Gilles de Retz 132) (1980 **89**
5s 6g* 7g 5g 5.8g²(dis) 5g 5d² 5d 5v 1981 6s³ 5s 5fg* 6g* 6s 6s⁴ 5g⁴ 5g* 6fg²
5d² 6f* 6d 5g⁴ 6v) quite well-made ex-French colt; sprint handicapper; successful at Warwick, Kempton, Lingfield and Ripon; made all to win quite valuable
races on last 3 courses, beating Crofthall 2 lengths in Great St Wilfrid Handicap
on last-named in August; appears not to stay 6f in testing conditions; probably
acts on any going; blinkered once in 1980; has run creditably for an apprentice;
usually wears a tongue strap; consistent. *M. McCourt.*

BELFRY BOY 2 ch.c. Import 127–Elbeam (Hornbeam 130) (1981 6f 6fg 6g) **—**
Apr 18; 3,200F, 5,000Y; compact, sturdy colt; half-brother to Irish 3-y-o Star
Stroller (by Tower Walk), successful at up to 7f, and to a winner in Italy; dam
won in Sweden; beaten long way in maiden races at Newcastle in August and
Doncaster in September; pulled up after 2f on debut; sold to H. Wharton 700
gns Doncaster October Sales. *J. Hanson.*

BEL HARBOUR 2 ch.g. Northfields–Rose of Tralee 114 (Buisson Ardent 129) **76**
(1981 5g 5g 6fg³ 7fg 5d 8f 8fg) Apr 16; IR 10,500F, 12,500Y; small, quite well-
made gelding; good mover; brother to 5f winner Seafields, and half-brother
to several winners; dam very speedy at 2 yrs; put up best effort when staying-on
5½ lengths third of 10 to Winter Words in maiden race at York in July; not

entirely disgraced after running a bit freely when tried over 7f but finished well beaten over 1m; usually wears blinkers. *P. Kelleway.*

BELIEVER 2 b.f. Blakeney 126–Seein Is Believin (Native Charger) (1981 7d²) Feb 24; well-made, attractive filly; sister to French 3-y-o 1¼m winner Prince Blakeney and closely related to fairly useful 13f winner No Evil (by Morston); dam daughter of Prix Morny winner Princeline; 10/1 and in need of race, ran on very well without being knocked about when ¾-length second of 18 to Melting Snows in maiden race at Newbury in September; promising and looks sure to win races over middle distances in 1982. *J. Dunlop.* **86 p**

BELLA TRAVAILLE 3 b.f. Workboy 123–Thorganby Bella (Porto Bello 118) (1980 5g* 5f 5f³ 5fg² 5f 5g 5fg² 5g* 5f 5g 5f 5f 5d 1981 5d 5s 5fg 5f 5fg 5f 5g 5fg 5fg 5g³ 5fg⁴ 5g) lengthy filly; ran creditably in handicaps in autumn; speedy and is unlikely to stay 6f; acts on firm going; occasionally blinkered and wore a hood on eighth start; dwelt fourth outing. *R. Hobson.* **46**

BELLBROOK 2 ch.c. Porto Bello 118–Miss Bubbly 78 (Track Spare 125) (1981 6g 7fg 5g 7.6s) May 16; 2,200Y; brother to 3-y-o 8.2f winner Bertida, and half-brother to a winning plater; dam 1¼m winner; unquoted when behind in maiden and minor events. *W. Wightman.* **—**

BELLCO 3 b.f. Comedy Star 121–Vectis 75 (Quorum 126) (1980 6d 1981 10s 12d 12d) behind in maiden and minor races; ridden by 7-lb claimer. *A. Pitt.* **—**

BELLEAIR DREAM 3 b.f. Tower Walk 130–Dowerless (Busted 134) (1980 5fg⁴ 1981 8g 6g 7.6g) wiry filly; ran with promise on only outing as a 2-y-o but showed no form in 1981 (way out of her depth in 1,000 Guineas on first outing); sold 500 gns Newmarket Autumn Sales. *F. Durr.* **—**

BELLE SOUK 3 ch.f. Native Bazaar 122–Belle Bergere 104 (Faberge II 121) (1980 8fg 8d 10d⁴ 1981 11.7f 13.1f 12fg 8h⁴) leggy, lightly-made filly; plater; probably stays 1¼m; sold 390 gns Ascot September Sales. *P. Cole.* **—**

BELLE VUE 8 b.g. Track Spare 125–Royal Camp 91 (Sovereign Path 125) (1980 8s 7g 8fg 8s 9g 8fg⁴ 8.2g* 8fg⁴ 8s⁴ 8f 8g* 9g 8d³ 8.2s³ 1981 8fg) neat gelding; poor performer; stays 9f; acts on any going; used to wear blinkers; occasionally sweats up; suitable mount for an inexperienced rider. *R. Mason.* **—**

BELL GREEN 2 b.g. Dragonara Palace 115–Anna Boleyna 84 (Right Royal V 135) (1981 7d 7fg) Mar 30; well-made gelding; half-brother to 2 winners, including very useful French middle-distance filly La Route Millard (by Busted); dam won over 1¼m; unquoted when behind in minor event at Lingfield in August and maiden race at Salisbury in September. *D. Kent.* **—**

BELLICOSA 3 ch.f. Porto Bello 118–Tavira (Prince Tenderfoot 126) (1980 5fg* 5f³ 5fg³ 5fg 6fg³ 5g 5f² 6fg 6fg² 5d 6d 6g 7v 1981 5d 7fg 6d 6g) leggy filly; won maiden auction event at Salisbury in 1980; ran moderately in 1981; suited by 6f; probably needs a sound surface; blinkered third outing and usually was at 2 yrs; sent to USA. *M. Haynes.* **—**

BELLINA BENEDETTA 2 b.f. Pablond 93–Benedetta da Castello (St Paddy 133) (1981 7g 8s 10.2g) June 21; smallish filly; half-sister to middle-distance winner Glazepta Rework (by Caliban) and to winners in Italy and Brazil; dam never ran; unquoted and apprentice ridden at overweight, stayed on well to finish eighth of 26 to Yard Bird in minor event at Doncaster in November, third outing; beaten some way here but may well improve when given a thorough test of stamina at 3 yrs. *K. Stone.* **—**

BELLINO 4 b.f. Andrea Mantegna–Idle Spell 83 (Galivanter 131) (1980 8s 11fg⁴ 12fg 13s 16g⁴ 16.1d 10s 16s 16fg 16d 16s 1981 16s) plating-class maiden; suited by a test of stamina. *W. Musson.* **—**

BELLMAN (FR) 3 b.c. Riverman 131–Belga (Le Fabuleux 133) (1980 NR 1981 10d² 10s* 12fg* 10g* 10s 12s³) half-brother to 2 winners, notably top-class miler Bellypha (by Lyphard); dam, a winner over 9f at 3 yrs, is half-sister to smart 1969 French 2-y-o Belmont; developed into a very smart colt and put up a fine performance on fifth outing when winning Group 2 Prix Eugene Adam at Saint-Cloud in July, scoring with more authority from Al Nasr (Fr) and Church Parade than the margin of a neck and a short neck would suggest; successful earlier in 2 races at Longchamp and in Group 3 Prix du Lys at Chantilly, beating Ecube a neck on latter course; never better than mid-division when fifth of 9 behind Vayrann in Prix du Prince d'Orange at Longchamp in September, first outing for 2 months; 7½ lengths third of 7 to Konigsstuhl in Gran Premio del Jockey Club at Milan in October on final start; stayed 1½m; probably acted on **123**

Prix Eugene Adam, Saint-Cloud—Bellman wins from Al Nasr (Fr) and the British challengers Church Parade (rails) and Kirtling

any going, but best form on a sound surface; to stand at Haras D'Etreham. *Mme C. Head, France.*

BELLOC 3 b.c. Wollow 132–Fly For Home 78 (Habitat 134) (1980 7g⁴ 7f* **98** 8d² 7d* 1981 8s* 12fg² 12.3g 10.1s 11f² 12fg) lengthy, lightly-made colt; always going well when landing the odds by 4 lengths from Grain Race in minor event at Leicester in March; second in Warren Stakes at Epsom the following month (beaten 1½ lengths by Glint of Gold) and in Grand Prix de Bruxelles at Groenendael in June (went down by 3 lengths to Junta); ran too freely and didn't find a great deal off bridle when fifth behind very impressive winner Shergar in Chester Vase on third start and finished last in minor event at Windsor and handicap at Newbury on his other outings; stays 1½m; acts on any going; sold 8,200 gns Newmarket Autumn Sales. *R. Price.*

BELL RAMMER (USA) 3 ch.c. Nijinsky 138–Shellshock 110 (Salvo 129) **80** (1980 NR 1981 10.5s⁴ 12s 13.4fg* 12f² 12g 14f 12g) robust, sturdy colt; very good mover; third foal; half-brother to 1¼m to 13.8f winner Sir Billy (by Sir Ivor) and 7f winner Love Divine (by Droll Role); dam, half-sister to top-class Dibidale, was third in 1,000 Guineas and stayed 13f; overcame difficulties in running when winning 15-runner maiden race at Chester in July in very good style by 3 lengths from Pegasse, easing up; didn't seem to go through with his effort when neck second to Fair of Face in minor event at Ripon later in month, and was largely disappointing afterwards; stays 1¾m; probably needs a firm surface. *B. Hills.*

BELL-TENT 10 b.g. Bivouac 114–Chilcombe Belle 75 (Robert Barker 125) **55** (1980 10fg 10h³ 10fg 10fg² 10g 10g 8f 10f² 10f 10d 1981 10g⁴ 10v² 10.8fg 10f 10f) one-time useful handicapper but has deteriorated; best at 1¼m; acts on any going but is suited by top-of-the-ground; usually held up; a difficult ride who needs strong handling and goes well for P. Eddery; ran poorly final start. *W. Wightman.*

BELMONT BAY 4 b.c. Auction Ring 123–Royal Escape 94 (King's Bench 132) **125** (1980 7f³ 8fg 8d* 8d* 8g 10d 1981 8s* 7d* 8s* 8fg* 8fg 8f 7s* 7v⁴)

After Belmont Bay's battling half-length success from Saher under 10-0 in the Playboy Bookmakers' Newbury Spring Cup in April his trainer remarked that the colt had been purchased privately out of Walker's stable at the end of 1980 to give his new owner, M Wildenstein, a bit of fun. It is safe to assume that Belmont Bay achieved that objective. A very useful handicapper at three, he improved even more than those other established horses Lucky Wednesday and Gunner B had when transferred to Cecil's care, winning five times and developing into a high-class miler whose consistency and fighting qualities in a hard season were second to none.

Belmont Bay followed up his Spring Cup win with a ready defeat of Captain Nick and some lesser opponents in the Philip Cornes Trophy at Leicester prior to returning to Newbury in May for a much stiffer assignment in the Group 2 Tote Lockinge Stakes. The most dangerous of his five opponents in the Lockinge appeared to be the Two Thousand Guineas third Bel Bolide, not certain to be suited by the testing conditions, the lightly-raced but very smart Dalsaan and the

*Tote Lockinge Stakes, Newbury—Belmont Bay battles on gamely to get
the better of French-trained Hilal*

French challenger Hilal, a smooth winner of the Prix de Ris-Orangis at Evry on
his previous start. After making the running at a steady gallop Belmont Bay was
challenged over a furlong from home by Dalsaan and Hilal, the latter still on the
bridle. While Dalsaan, slightly squeezed between his rivals, ran out of steam a
hundred yards out Hilal moved perhaps half a length ahead of the strongly-
ridden Belmont Bay, and looked an almost certain winner. Probably a number
of those that had backed Belmont Bay and Piggott down to 11/10 favouritism felt

*Queen Anne Stakes, Ascot—another brave performance by Belmont Bay
who holds off Last Fandango*

resigned to their fate at this point, but such pessimism reckoned without the determination of the partnership and the failure of Hilal to find a great deal when fully let down. Sensing that Hilal was producing less than his easy progress to the front suggested he would, Piggott redoubled his efforts, and with Belmont Bay running his heart out they got up again in the last few strides to win an exciting race by a head. Dalsaan was two lengths further away with the remainder well beaten off. On the crest of a wave now, Belmont Bay continued his excellent run in the Queen Anne Stakes at Royal Ascot. Giving weight all round, he again made the running and this time stayed in the lead throughout, holding off the strong-finishing Last Fandango, who didn't have an entirely trouble-free passage, by a neck in a driving finish.

Belmont Bay (b.c. 1977)	Auction Ring (b 1972)	Bold Bidder (b 1962)	Bold Ruler High Bid
		Hooplah (b 1965)	Hillary Beadah
	Royal Escape (br 1961)	King's Bench (br 1949)	Court Martial King's Cross
		Pope's Oak (b 1948)	King Legend Chincapin

Success proved harder to find afterwards and Belmont Bay won just one of his remaining races, the Harroways Stakes at Goodwood in September where he ran on well once shaken up two furlongs out to beat Recitation by a couple of lengths. The Sussex Stakes at Goodwood and the Prix du Moulin and Prix de la Foret, both at Longchamp, proved that he wasn't up to beating top-notchers but in each race he fought hard and ran up to his best, finishing respectively fifth to Kings Lake, fifth to Northjet and fourth to Moorestyle, twice being run out of a place only in the final furlong. After the Prix de la Foret his owner revealed that Belmont Bay would be syndicated to stand at the Hamilton Stud, Newmarket in 1982.

M D. Wildenstein's "Belmont Bay"

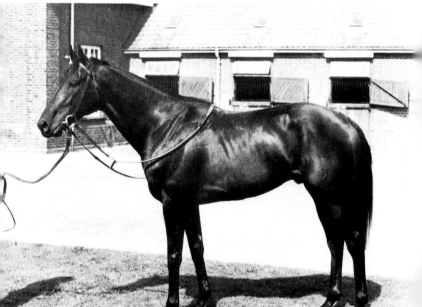

Belmont Bay's sire, the sprinter Auction Ring, was champion first-season sire in 1979 and he has continued to do well at stud with Luck Of The Draw, Maelstrom Lake, Lone Bidder and The Quiet Bidder also winning pattern races in the past two years. The dam, Royal Escape, has produced four winners besides Belmont Bay, notably the very useful mile handicapper Mendi (by Gratitude) and that tough old campaigner Prince of Light (by Laser Light) whose tally of wins in eight seasons' racing reached fifteen in 1981. Royal Escape ran only at two, winning a seven-furlong nursery at Newmarket when tried in blinkers. She is a half-sister to four winners here and one in Belgium out of Pope's Oak, who won over five furlongs as a two-year-old and stayed a mile and a half at three when she finished third in the Lingfield Oaks Trial. Belmont Bay cost 15,500 guineas as a yearling at the Houghton Sales. An attractive colt who impressed us greatly in appearance in 1981, he stayed a mile well and acted on any going, though he was ideally suited by some give in the gound. *H. Cecil.*

BELMONT BLUE 4 br.f. Kashmir II 125–Joie de France (Reliance II 137)   —
(1980 8f 12fg 10s 8f 10s 10s* 1981 12.2d 10g 11d 10d) tall filly; showed no form at 4 yrs; stays 1¼m; acts on soft going; has twice worn blinkers, including when successful at 3 yrs; trained by M. Tate first outing. *W. Wharton.*

BELMONT VIEW 3 ch.f. Roan Rocket 128–Deed 86 (Derring-Do 131) (1980   —
NR 1981 8fg 7f 8s) 11,500Y; compact filly; half-sister to 1978 2-y-o 6f winner Super Jack (by Blakeney); dam won over 5f at 2 yrs; soundly beaten in maiden races; sold 3,100 gns Newmarket Autumn Sales. *I. Walker.*

BELROSE 2 ch.f. Music Boy 124–Red Form (Reform 132) (1981 5g) May   —
27; fifth living foal; dam of no account; 14/1 when behind in 21-runner minor event won by Begham Bay at Catterick in September. *S. Norton.*

BELTED EARL (USA) 3 ch.c. Damascus–Moccasin (Nantallah) (1980 NR **122**
1981 6f* 7fg* 8g*)
When we interviewed Vincent O'Brien at Ballydoyle about his horses in the spring he spoke highly of the unraced three-year-old Belted Earl. We had to wait until August, when he started at odds on for a maiden race at Phoenix Park, to see Belted Earl on a racecourse, but the manner of his first victory went some way towards confirming his trainer's high opinion. Having been slowly into his stride, Belted Earl made up the lost ground with the minimum of fuss and then showed a tremendous turn of foot to come home six lengths clear of Zillionairess.

Belted Earl also started at odds on for his second race, the seven-furlong Counters Gate Stakes for three-year-olds at Goodwood at the end of August, but this time he didn't have things all his own way. Waited with, he came under pressure after the two-furlong marker and only after very strong driving from Eddery did he wear down Indian King, whom he beat by half a length. All the same, that looked a useful performance. The runner-up had landed a gamble in good style when making a belated reappearance in another minor event at Goodwood earlier in the month and went on to win a valuable and very competitive handicap at the Doncaster St Leger meeting by five lengths. The third horse, Melodrama, had also won on her previous appearance and went on to land a £3,000 event at Newbury the following month.

	Damascus	Sword Dancer	Sunglow
	(b 1964)	(ch 1956)	Highland Fling
Belted Earl (USA)		Kerala	My Babu
(ch.c. 1978)		(b 1958)	Blade of Time
	Moccasin	Nantallah	Nasrullah
	(ch 1963)	(b 1953)	Shimmer
		Rough Shod	Gold Bridge
		(b 1944)	Dalmary

Belted Earl confirmed himself a good and improving colt when successfully stepping up to pattern-race company on his third and final start, beating Cairn Rouge by a short head in the Desmond Stakes over a mile at the Curragh in September. He carried the same weight as the year-older Cairn Rouge, thus meeting her on terms 7 lb worse than weight-for-age, and it wasn't particularly surprising, notwithstanding her absence since Royal Ascot, that Cairn Rouge was made favourite. Belted Earl put up a really game and gritty performance to hold off her powerful late challenge, and these two drew six lengths clear of Slaney Maid, who headed the remaining sixteen runners. Cairn Rouge subsequently made Belted Earl's effort look even better when she ran so well in the Champion Stakes.

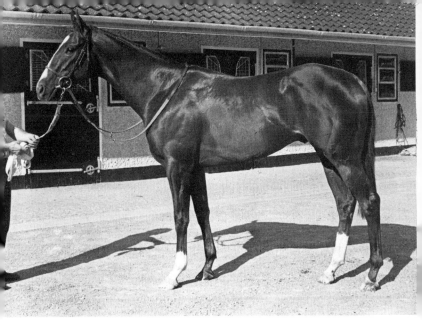

Mr R. E. Sangster's "Belted Earl"

It is not surprising Robert Sangster had to pay 650,000 dollars for Belted Earl at the Keeneland Summer Yearling Sale. One could write a book about this colt's pedigree. His sire, Damascus, won twenty-one races including the Preakness Stakes, the Belmont Stakes and the two-mile Jockey Club Gold Cup, and was Horse of the Year at three years. Moccasin, Belted Earl's dam, was the leading two-year-old filly of her year in the United States, winning all eight of her starts from five and a half to eight and a half furlongs. Incidentally, she was rated a pound superior in the Experimental Handicap to Priceless Gem, the dam of Allez France. As a broodmare Moccasin has also proved outstanding, Belted Earl being her fifth pattern- or stakes-race winner from her first six foals to race. Of the first four, three—Indian, Apalachee and Brahms—were by Round Table and the other, Nantequos, by Tom Rolfe. Outstanding among this quartet is Apalachee, who looked destined for great things after his victory in the Observer Gold Cup of 1973, but who didn't race again after finishing third in the Two Thousand Guineas. Brahms also had a short racing career, winning both his starts at two before injury enforced his retirement, but Indian was a six-year-old when winning a minor stakes race over a mile and Nantequos became a stakes winner in the United States at five, having won the nine-furlong Group 3 Whitehall Stakes at Phoenix Park two years earlier. Apalachee, Nantequos and Brahms were all, like Belted Earl, trained in Ireland by O'Brien.

Belted Earl's second dam, Rough Shod, has an even better record as a broodmare than Moccasin: of eight foals to race, seven won, including two champion two-year-olds in Ridan and Moccasin. She also produced Lt Stevens, a winner of almost a quarter of a million dollars and now a successful sire, and two more excellent broodmares in Gambetta and Thong. Gambetta produced Zonah, the dam of Take Your Place, and Gamely, a half-million-dollar earner who herself produced Cellini. Thong's produce include Thatch, King Pellinore, Lisadell, Marinsky and Nureyev's dam, Special.

Belted Earl, an attractive, lengthy colt, remains in training as a four-year-old, when he could go on to even better things. He stays a mile and will in all probability get further; should he stay a mile and a quarter, that will increase his opportunities. He has yet to encounter a soft surface. *V. O'Brien, Ireland.*

124

BELVOIR VALE 3 b.c. Ribero 126–Plumtree Plain (Primera 131) (1980 —
6fg 1981 12s 16fg 16fg) strong, compact colt; soundly beaten in Southern
maiden races; blinkered final start; sold 1,250 gns Ascot August Sales. *B.
Hills.*

BE MY NATIVE (USA) 2 b. or br.c. Our Native–Witchy Woman (Strate **115**
Stuff) (1981 6g⁴ 7g² 6g⁴ 7s* 7g²)
    Robert Armstrong has to start the 1982 season without his two leading
money winners now that Moorestyle and Rabdan have gone to stud. It's
expecting a great deal of any of his latest two-year-olds to reach the same heights
as that wonderfully tough pair but it may be worth remembering that neither
revealed his true ability at two—Moorestyle ended his first season weighted 19 lb
below Monteverdi in the Free Handicap while Rabdan received a rating of 66
in *Racehorses* for his efforts—and it's not beyond the bounds of possibility that
Be My Native, the best of the Armstrong juveniles, will develop into a very
good three-year-old.
    Be My Native was certainly a progressive two-year-old. Although he
ran well enough on his first three outings, finishing fourth of twenty-six to Tin
Boy at Newmarket, second to Lyphmas on the same course and fourth of twenty-
one to Mirabeau at Doncaster, he left that form far behind next time out in the
Tankerville Nursery at Ascot in October. There, giving weight to all but two
of his thirteen opponents, he quickened impressively through a narrow gap on
the rails inside the final furlong to win by two lengths from Dageegah. The
rest were well strung out. An obvious explanation for Be My Native's improved
showing was that he was tackling much softer ground than previously. However,
he improved even on this performance when back on good going in the William
Hill Dewhurst Stakes at Newmarket a week later. Even though he started at
50/1 he didn't look out of place in a good-looking field—he's a neat individual
of some quality who both walks and moves well. In the race nothing looked
likely to trouble the front-running Wind and Wuthering from well over two
furlongs out but Be My Native stayed on so well up the final hill that he got up
to deprive Tender King of second place by a neck, seven lengths behind the
winner.

Be My Native (USA) (b. or br.c. Feb 16, 1979)	Our Native (b or br 1970)	Exclusive Native (ch 1965)	Raise A Native
			Exclusive
		Our Jackie (gr 1964)	Crafty Admiral
			Rakahanga
	Witchy Woman (ch 1972)	Strate Stuff (ch 1965)	Noholme II
			Lady Vale
		Witchy Norma (ch 1967)	Crimson Satan
			Tomratta

    Both Moorestyle and Rabdan were cheap yearlings and Be My Native was
by no means expensive by American standards at 45,000 dollars. Naturally
his pedigree isn't one that would attract undue attention from the buyers. He's
the second foal and first winner bred by Witchy Woman, a winner at two, three
and four years of five minor sprint races. She is a daughter of the comparatively
unknown stallion Strate Stuff, who did all his winning at two years when very
useful at up to a mile, and the unraced Witchy Norma who bred two winners
from only four foals. The next dam Tomratta was also unraced but she was a
sister to the very tough Chompion, successful in numerous good races at up to
thirteen furlongs. Be My Native's sire Our Native isn't well known on this side
of the Atlantic—indeed Be My Native is only his second winner in Britain or
Ireland. He was a high-class colt though, the winner of fourteen of his thirty-
seven races as well as finishing third in the Kentucky Derby and the Preakness
Stakes. The champion two-year-old of 1979, Rockhill Native, is also a son of
Our Native.
    Although Be My Native's dam was a sprinter he gives the strong impression
he'll be very well suited by a mile or more as a three-year-old. He ran respectably
in blinkers on his third outing but subsequently did much better without them.
R. Armstrong.

BENFEN 2 b. or gr.g. Lochnager 132–Ensign Steel 57 (Majority Blue 126) **74**
(1981 5v² 5d 5g* 5d 5fg⁴) Mar 16; sturdy gelding; second foal; brother to
3-y-o 1m winner Gray Loch; dam, placed over 6f, is half-sister to very useful
sprinters Red Track, Sovereign Set and Burwell; made all to land the odds by
2¼ lengths from Record Review in 4-runner minor event at Redcar in May; 2¼
lengths fourth of 10 to Golfer's Dream when giving at least 10 lb all round in

small race at Hamilton later in month; will stay 6f; well suited by a sound surface; gelded after fifth start. *M. H. Easterby.*

BENGIAMIGO 2 ch.c. Wollow 132–Howrytuar 90 (Sound Track 132) (1981 — 7f 7g) Mar 20; 10,000Y; close-coupled colt; good mover; half-brother to useful 5f and 1m winner My Therape (by Jimmy Reppin); dam won at 5f to 7f; well-beaten eighth of 13 to Balanchine in minor event at Brighton in September, second outing; looks immature at present; sold 1,600 gns Newmarket Autumn Sales. *C. Brittain.*

BENIFORM 3 ch.f. Gold Form 108–Benign 67 (King's Bench 132) (1980 5f — 5s 1981 8v⁴ 8g 8.2fg) bad walker; well beaten in varied company, including selling. *Mrs A. Bell.*

BEN JARROW 2 ch.c. Roman Warrior 132–Shady Desire 88 (Meldrum 112) **65** (1981 7f 5d⁴ 5s 7g 5d⁴) May 3; big, workmanlike colt; good walker; first foal; dam won from 5f to 1m; quite a moderate maiden; will probably stay 6f but has yet to show he gets 7f. *T. Fairhurst.*

BENS BOOKS 2 b.c. Lonsdale Boy–River Gem (Arctic Judge 94) (1981 — 8s 8d) Mar 14; second foal; dam never ran; well behind in end-of-season maiden events in the Midlands. *G. Balding.*

BE PATIENT 3 b.g. Dubassoff–Fighting Winnie (Fighting Charlie 127) (1980 **50** 6fg 8.2s 8g 1981 7s⁴ 8g⁴ 7fg² 8.2g 9fg 8fg 7g*) leggy gelding; attracted no bid after winning seller at Edinburgh in September (ridden by 7-lb claimer); stays 1m; started slowly twice in 1980; blinkered sixth start. *Denys Smith.*

BE QUIET 2 ch.f. Continuation 120–Quiet Colleen (Be Friendly 130) (1981 **56** 6f 7g 6g 6d⁴ 5d) Mar 25; 640Y; compact filly; second foal; dam placed over 6f at 3 yrs in Ireland; length fourth of 12 to Profit Warrant in seller at Lingfield in August, best effort; sold 400 gns Newmarket Autumn Sales. *N. Guest.*

BE RESOLUTE 2 ch.c. Relko 136–All Hail 112 (Alcide 136) (1981 8d 10s³) **84** Apr 13; quite a well-made colt; good mover; half-brother to several winners, including middle-distance winners Geminiani (by Lorenzaccio) and Bunce Boy (by King Emperor), dam staying daughter of St Leger second None Nicer; 12/1, stuck on well when 1¾ lengths third of 22 to Luxury in maiden race at Nottingham in October; a stoutly-bred colt who looks one paced and will be very well suited by a good test of stamina as a 3-y-o. *M. Stoute.*

BERMONDO 10 gr.g. Cumshaw 111–Amber Mona (Amber Light 114) (1980 — NR 1981 8d 7.6fg 8d 10s) poor handicapper; well beaten in seller third start; stays 1¼m; suitable mount for a boy. *J. Benstead.*

BERNARD SUNLEY (USA) 2 ch.c. Rainy Lake–Charling (Charabanc) **84** (1981 5s 6g 5g³ 5f² 6g² 6s³ 6g) Apr 5; $6,000Y; lengthy, deep-girthed colt; fourth foal; dam placed in 8 of her 27 starts; second in maiden races at Folkestone and Lingfield in September, failing by only a short head to catch Tardous in 22-runner event on latter; suited by 6f and will probably stay 7f; acts on firm going and is probably not at his best on soft. *G. Hunter.*

BERNICA (FR) 3 gr.f. Caro 133–Bernicia 81 (Native Prince) (1980 6d* 7g* **114** 8f⁴ 1981 9.5fg* 10v 10.5fg 8g 9.2d) attractive, good-bodied filly; third foal; half-sister to French 1m and 1¼m winner Berfan (by Gay Fandango); dam won over 5f at 2 yrs and is granddaughter of Oaks winner Masaka; made a successful reappearance in Group 3 Prix Vanteaux at Longchamp in April, leading inside final furlong and holding off Derly by a neck in a driving finish; sixth on next 3 starts, behind Tootens in Prix Saint-Alary at Longchamp again (given plenty to do), behind Madam Gay (beaten 5 lengths) in Prix de Diane de Revlon at Chantilly and behind Epsiba in Prix d'Astarte at Deauville, last-named in August; not certain to stay beyond 1¼m; possibly unsuited by very soft going but seems to act on any other. *F. Boutin, France.*

BERNINI 3 b.c. Balliol 125–Night Fire (Night and Day II) (1980 5g 8d 8d 10d **45** 1981 8f 10.8fg 10h 9d⁴ 8s² 11s⁴) plater; probably stays 11f. *D. Wintle.*

BERTHON BROOK 2 ch.f. Scallywag 127–Romany Girl 103 (Worden II 129) **51** (1981 5s 6fg 5.8f⁴ 6g) Apr 6; 520Y; leggy filly; half-sister to 7f winner Remainder Imp (by Jimmy Reppin) and a winner in Brazil; dam won at up to 13f in Ireland; only quite a moderate plater; bred to stay well. *M. Bradley.*

BERTIDA 3 b.f. Porto Bello 118–Miss Bubbly 78 (Track Spare 125) (1980 5d **64** 7g⁴ 6g 7d 1981 8.2g* 7.2v³ 8d³ 8d) useful mare; plater at 2 yrs when trained by P. Cole; 50/1 and apprentice ridden when beating Hot Press by ¾ length in 20-runner handicap at Nottingham in August on reappearance; third in similar events at Haydock and Redcar in October; suited by 1m; acts on heavy going. *E. Eldin.*

126

BERTIE ME BOY 6 b.g. Philip of Spain 126–Well Scored 104 (Final Score 113)   **84**
(1980 8d 8d 8.2s 8.2s 1981 12v* 12s) fairly useful handicapper at his best;
made all and trotted up at Beverley in April; didn't run up to that form on only
subsequent start in May; suited by 1½m; seems to act on any going but goes well
on soft; usually ridden up with pace; usually blinkered in 1980. *M. H. Easterby.*

BERTIE'S WISH 2 ch.f. Mr Bigmore 123–Jamaya 71 (Double-U-Jay 120)   **—**
(1981 8s 8d) Apr 15; first foal; dam won 11f seller and also won over hurdles;
behind in maiden races at Warwick (apprentice ridden, started slowly) and
Leicester late in season. *R. Laing.*

BERTRAM PERSONNEL 4 ch.c. Saintly Song 128–Lady in Trouble 112 (High   **68**
Treason 126) (1980 10f⁴ 12.5fg* 12f* 12g² 11g³ 12.3fg* 16f³ 11d 12d 13.8d³
12.5s³ 12v 1981 12v 12.3d³ 12d⁴ 12d 12g 12f 12f⁴ 14f 12d) leggy, quite useful
sort; stays 1¾m; acts on any going; sold 3,700 gns Newmarket Autumn Sales.
J. Etherington.

BERYL'S GIFT 4 b.f. Sayfar 116–Flying Nun 66 (Welsh Abbot 131) (1980 8f   **—**
7fg² 7fg 7g⁴ 6g 10g 12d 15.8fg³ 12.2d⁴ 15s 1981 12.2fg⁴ 12fg 12f⁴ 12fg) plain,
workmanlike filly; plating-class maiden; seems to stay 15.8f; probably acts on
any going; trained by J. Calvert first start. *N. Tinkler.*

BE SAUCY 2 br.f. Scottish Rifle 127–Birthday Present 80 (Bleep-Bleep 134)   **—**
(1981 5d 5fg⁴ 5d 6f) Apr 3; 420Y; small filly; sister to a poor filly and is only a
bad plater herself; has worn blinkers. *Peter Taylor.*

BE SHARP 3 b.f. Sharpen Up 127–Natasha 87 (Native Prince) (1980 5fg 5fg*   **74**
5f 5f 5d 5fg 5f³ 5d² 5f 6d 1981 5s 5g² 5d 5f 5f 5fg² 5fg 5g 5fg 5s) rather leggy,
fair sort; scored in handicaps at Redcar in May and Chester in July; probably
doesn't stay 6f; has run creditably on a soft surface but is probably better on a
firm one; blinkered fourth outing in 1980. *J. Berry.*

BESIEGED (USA) 3 b.c. Cannonade–Regal Royal (Swoon's Son) (1980 7d   **82**
1981 10fg 11g 12fg³ 14fg* 13.1g³ 14g⁴) strong, attractive, deep-girthed colt;
beat Scheming by 4 lengths in maiden race at Haydock in September; looks
slow and will be suited by 2m; acts on a firm surface; usually wears blinkers;
sold to P. Cundell 12,500 gns Newmarket Autumn Sales. *R. Hern.*

BEST ALWAYS (USA) 4 ch.c. Vaguely Noble 140–Big Mistake (Barbizon)   **42**
(1980 8g 8d⁴ 1981 12s 12s 12g⁴ 12g 15.5d⁴ 18.8fg) quite attractive, well-made
colt; poor walker and mover; plating-class maiden; stays well. *M. Ryan.*

BEST BOLD (USA) 2 ch.c. Bold Hour–Couldn't Be Better (Better Bee)   **82**
(1981 5g 5d⁴ 5d* 6g² 5fg⁴ 6g 6d) Apr 17; $30,000Y; strong colt; good mover;
third foal; half-brother to 2 winners, including Better's Delight (by Barb's
Delight), a stakes-placed winner of over $100,000; dam never ran; made all to
win 16-runner maiden race at Folkestone in June by ¾ length from Cause For
Applause; ran well when head second to My Dad Tom in small race at Catterick
later same week; finds 5f on sharp side and will be suited by 7f and 1m; acts on a
firm and a soft surface; had stiff tasks in nurseries last 3 outings. *M. Jarvis.*

BEST TRADITION 4 b.g. Laser Light 118–Glorious Light 53 (Alcide 136)   **34**
(1980 8fg 7fg³ 8.3g 7f 7f 7g 1981 8s 7s³ 8.2s 8g 7g 8g 6fg 6fg) good-topped
gelding; plater; stays 7f; probably acts on any going; has been tried in blinkers.
M. Naughton.

BETHNAL GREEN 3 ch.c. Grundy 137–Photo Flash 119 (Match III 135)   **57**
(1980 NR 1981 10fg 10.1fg⁴ 12fg 12f 16g⁴ 12.2s) 520 2-y-o; strong, good-
topped colt; half-brother to very useful stayer Golden River (by Rheingold)
and fairly useful Lucky Shot (by Reform), a winner at up to 1¾m; dam second in
1,000 Guineas and half-sister to Welsh Pageant; has shown a little ability in
maiden and minor events; had stiffish task when behind in handicap final start;
stays well; sometimes bandaged behind. *V. Soane.*

BETTABET GERAGHTY 3 b.g. Blue Cashmere 129–Piccadilly Etta 76   **84§**
(Floribunda 136) (1980 NR 1981 7s 7fg 6g* 6g² 7.3g 6s 6f 7fg) 5,500F,
7,400Y; neat, strong gelding; second produce; half-brother to fairly useful 5f
winner Jose Collins (by Singing Bede); dam won from 1½m to 2m; won maiden
race at Pontefract in April in good style by 5 lengths from Thai King; ½-length
second to Praetorian Guard (pair well clear) in minor event at Thirsk later in
month, easily best subsequent effort; best form at 6f; found little under pressure
fifth and sixth starts; well beaten in blinkers seventh outing; sometimes very
coltish in paddock, but was gelded after final start; one to treat with caution.
G. Huffer.

BETTER PORTION   2 ch.c. Music Boy 124–Shirwani 77 (Major Portion 129) **103**
(1981 5d 5fg² 5g* 5g² 5d⁴ 5d 5s² 6s* 6g³) Apr 1; 4,000Y; quite a well-made
colt; third foal: dam 2-y-o 5f winner; made all to win by ½ length from Tender
King in 5-runner minor event at Lingfield in May; ran well in nurseries later in
season, quickening up well to defeat Open The Box 4 lengths in 14-runner event
at Newbury in October; suited by 6f nowadays; yet to race on very firm going
but seems to act on any other; sometimes taken early to start. *P. Ashworth.*

BETTYKNOWES   3 b.g. Satingo 129–Djimbaran Bay (Le Levanstell 122) **94**
(1980 6g 8d⁴ 1981 11s 10s* 11d² 10fg² 10fg* 10fg⁴ 12fg) lengthy, workmanlike
gelding; successful in 24-runner maiden race at Kempton in May (cantered up by
4 lengths from Nepentha) and in small handicap on same course in July (landed
the odds by ½ length from Rekal, but wasn't particularly impressive); second in
handicaps at Newbury and Sandown (beaten 3 lengths by impressive winner
Galveston in valuable race) in between; finds 1¼m on fast ground on sharp side
and should stay 1½m (beaten some way out when disappointing over trip on
final start in August); probably acts on any going, but is well suited by soft;
game. *J. Tree.*

BETTY'S BID   3 b.f. Auction Ring 123–Galway Gate (Laser Light 118) (1980 **—**
5f 6d 7g 5fg 5d 1981 5g 6g) small filly; poor maiden; blinkered fourth outing
in 1980. *S. Norton.*

BEWERLEY   8 b.m. John Splendid 116–Ardent Worker 88 (Buisson Ardent 129) **—**
(1980 NR 1981 12.3g 12.2fg 11fg 12.2g 12f 8s) of little account nowadays;
has worn blinkers. *M. Reddan.*

BEWICK   6 b.g. Blakeney 126–Eringa 101 (Saint Crespin III 132) (1980 12d* **§§**
12d 12fg² 1981 16fg 16d 16.9s) small, compact gelding; fairly useful handicapper at his best; appears to have gone the wrong way temperamentally and
ran poorly in 1981, giving trouble going down and at start on second outing;
should stay beyond 1½m; acts on any going except perhaps very soft; best left
alone; sold 775 gns Ascot 2nd June Sales. *D. Ancil.*

BEWITCHED   4 br.f. African Sky 124–Pavlova (Fidalgo 129) (1980 7d⁴ 8g⁴ **—**
12d 8g 9s 8s 10g 1981 7fg 7f 8f 10f 8s 8s 8g) light-framed filly; plating-class
maiden; not certain to stay 1½m. *W. Wightman.*

BEZIQUE   4 ch.f. Simbir 130–Tell The Bees (Narrator 127) (1980 6s³ 6d 8f* **—**
8.5f³ 8fg 10g² 10g 10g* 8g 10s 1981 8d 8fg 10g) tall, useful sort; finished well
clear of those racing on disadvantageous stand side when creditable ninth to
Saher in William Hill Lincoln Handicap at Doncaster in March; well beaten both
subsequent starts; suited by 1¼m; probably acts on any going; sold to B.
Hanbury 6,600 gns Newmarket Autumn Sales. *M. Smyly.*

BHAIBUNDI CHEWUNJA   2 b.g. Spanish Gold 101–Pensong 84 (Pendragon) **67**
(1981 5fg 6s 6f 5fg 7.2v³ 10d* 8s) Mar 22; lightly-made, narrow gelding;
brother to a useless filly and half-brother to 6f and 1⅛m winner Streets Ahead
(by Ovid); dam stayed 1m; plater; won at Pontefract in October (bought in
1,000 gns); will stay 1½m; goes well in the mud. *J. Wilson.*

BIBOROS (HUN)   8 b.g. Imperial–Balaklava (Nostradamus) (1981 5d) big
ex-Hungarian gelding; has won in Hungary; 66/1, blinkered and unfit, started
slowly and was soon tailed off when last of 8 to Welshwyn in £4,500 event at
Sandown in June. *M. McCormack.*

BIDDABLE   2 b.c. Auction Ring 123–Imperial Levee (Levmoss 133) (1981 5f **68**
5g³ 5f⁴ 5g 5d) Apr 15; 12,500F, 6,600Y; rather lightly-made colt; second foal;
half-brother to French 3-y-o Darial (by Targowice); dam never ran; kept on
well when 1¼ lengths equal third of 11 to Thunderbridge in maiden race at
Newcastle in August, best effort; probably needs further. *W. Elsey.*

BIG BLONDE   2 ch.f. Ballymore 123–Lunar Star (Star Gazer 123) (1981 6g **75**
6g³) May 10; 3,300Y; leggy, narrow filly; half-sister to 3 winners, including
fairly useful 1978 2-y-o 5f winner Moving Star (by Windjammer); dam won over
9.5f in Ireland; stayed on to finish 2 lengths third of 19 to One Degree in maiden
. race at Newmarket in October; will be suited by 1m; bandaged near-hind both
starts. *N. Guest.*

BIG-ED   2 ch.c. Sparkler 130–Ours 76 (Yours 125) (1981 7g 7g) Mar 26; **—**
9,000Y; big, tall colt; half-brother to fair 1977 2-y-o 5f winner Working Girl (by
Workboy) and a winner in Holland; dam stayed middle distances; backward,
didn't trouble leaders when ninth of 18 behind General Anders in £4,100 race at
Ascot in September; unquoted when out of first 9 in 22-runner maiden race won
by Count Pahlen at Newmarket the following month. *P. Kelleway.*

BIG JOHN (FR) 3 br.c. Gift Card 124–Trelex (Exbury 138) (1980 7d* 8d³ **119**
7.5g* 1981 8v* 8g 9g³ 9s² 10g 8f) French colt; third foal; dam half-sister to
very smart Dandy Lute; one of the best 2-y-o's in France in 1980, winner of
Prix Thomas Bryon at Saint-Cloud; made a successful reappearance in 90,000
francs event at Saint-Cloud in March, beating Valgo by ½ length; finished 6½
lengths sixth of 10 behind Recitation in Poule d'Essai des Poulains at Longchamp the following month and was placed subsequently in Prix Jean Prat at
Chantilly in June (2½ lengths third to Cresta Rider) and Prix Daphnis at Longchamp again in July (½-length second to Dunphy); stays 9f; acts on heavy
going; has raced with his tongue tied down. *E. Chevalier du Fau, France.*

BIG LAND 2 ch.c. Habitat 134–Bay Triumph (Canisbay 120) (1981 6f 6g)   —
Apr 14; 15,000Y; neat colt; first foal; dam, sister to top-class Orange Bay, was
placed in Italian 1,000 Guineas and Oaks; unquoted, made little show in
maiden races at York in June and Newmarket (looked fit) in July; sold to
National Horse Belgium 1,850 gns Newmarket Autumn Sales. *F. Durr.*

BIG OIL (USA) 4 b. or br.f. Permian–Little Amazon (Intentionally) (1980   —
10f 8d 8s 12s³ 1981 12d 18.8fg 17.1d 10g 10.8s) bad mover; plating-class
maiden; best run at 1½m on soft going; has worn blinkers. *M. McCourt.*

BIG PAL 6 gr.g. Pals Passage 115–Queen's Honey (Tudor Treasure 119) (1980 **85**
10g 12g² 10d³ 12d* 1981 10.2d³ 12d 12fg⁴ 12g 12f³ 12f 12fg² 12f⁴ 10f* 10fg 9g
10s² 10.2g 10g⁴) big gelding; front-running handicapper; won at Folkestone
in July; twice ran creditably afterwards; stays 1½m; acts on any going. *G.
Harwood.*

BIG TROUBLE 2 b.g. Reform 132–Estructura 102 (Gulf Pearl 117) (1981 6d **100**
6fg² 7g* 7g³ 7fg³ 8g² 10g⁴) Jan 13; rangy gelding; has a round action; second
foal; dam useful staying 2-y-o; 13/8 on when winning 11-runner maiden race at
Yarmouth in July by 5 lengths from Torsion Prince; in frame all subsequent
starts, on fifth staying on really well to finish 1¼ lengths behind Chulia Street in
£5,900 event at Newmarket; put up another good effort when ½-length second to
Meeka Gold in nursery at Ayr in September; lacks pace and should be well suited
by 1¼m+ (a little below his best when fourth to Paternoster Row in £6,500
event at Newmarket when tried at 1¼m); game and genuine. *G. Pritchard-
Gordon.*

BIHAS BOUNTY 5 br.g. Sahib 114–Unclaimed Treasure 61 (Nice Guy 123)   —
(1980 7fg* 7h⁴ 7fg 7g 7.6d 7fg 1981 6s 7d 10d) good-bodied gelding; plater;
stays 7f; suited by top-of-the-ground; usually blinkered. *A. Pitt.*

BIKALA 3 b.c. Kalamoun 129–Irish Bird (Sea-Bird II 145) (1980 9d 7v⁴ **134**
1981 10v² 9.2fg* 10.5s⁴ 12g² 12.5g² 10s² 12d²)
    It has been said with a certain amount of justification that when buying
yearlings at auction you get what you pay for: no-one should reasonably expect
a good horse for a plater's price. Yet money can't guarantee success. Each
season provides its fund of cautionary tales, of huge sums poured down the
drain on worthless animals; and always some genuine bargains from the opposite
end of the market come to light. One of the best yearling buys of 1979 must
surely have been Bikala at 6,000 guineas. There were many around in Europe
in 1981 who cost a lot more but very few who could hold a candle to him, and
his last four runs brought his owner winning prize money in the French Derby
(£90,827) and second-place money in the Grand Prix de Saint-Cloud (£29,038),
the Prix du Prince d'Orange (£6,524) and the Prix de l'Arc de Triomphe (£77,369).
What must he be worth now?
    How Bikala, a big, strong individual as a three-year-old, came to be bought
for a song by the bloodstock agents Horse France at Goffs September Yearling
Sales has never been explained. He must have been worth more on his pedigree,
by the top-class French miler Kalamoun out of a winning mare from a good, well-

*Prix du Jockey-Club, Chantilly—an admirable performance by Bikala who
is never in any danger in the straight*

known family. Possibly prospective purchasers were put off him by the fact that the first of the dam's only two previous foals, the four-year-old Irish Gantlet (by Run The Gantlet), hadn't at that time raced and the other, the three-year-old Shadowbrook (by Dancer's Image), seemed only moderate. The dam Irish Bird won a newcomers race over eleven furlongs at Longchamp. She is by Sea-Bird II out of a very useful sister to the top-class Irish staying filly Lynchris, and in her day had been the highest-priced yearling sold at a French auction. However, all this is water under the bridge now; one bidder's loss was another's gain.

Bikala began his career in France under the guidance of R. Collet, running once for that trainer before his transfer to his present one and becoming the ride of the latest apprentice discovery in France Serge Gorli. Bikala showed considerable promise as a two-year-old in the hock-deep ground of the late-autumn but needed time to develop. He ran three times in 1981 before the French Derby, the Prix du Jockey-Club, at Chantilly in June, and his form put him among the longer-priced in the twelve-runner field. He won a handicap at Longchamp in April by half a length; prior to that he was beaten a head by No Lute in a small race at Saint-Cloud and subsequently he finished fourth to No Lute, The Wonder and Dunphy, coming from behind, in the Prix Lupin at Longchamp. No Lute and The Wonder re-opposed him over the longer distance at Chantilly, and they, the first and second also in the Prix Greffulhe, seemed to have the best form of the French runners. Five of the other home-based horses had taken part in another classic trial, the Prix Hocquart, which Rahotep had won from Mbaiki, Mariacho and Nijinsky's Secret, with Bikala's stable-companion Gap of Dunloe last of seven. Redoutable had finished second to Recitation in the French Two Thousand Guineas; Akarad had won his two races, neither of them pattern events; the other French runner Magnum was in to make the pace for the favourite No Lute. Recitation was the only foreign challenger.

The race for the Prix du Jockey-Club turned out little different in the way it unfolded from the previous season's won by the outsider Policoman, very enterprisingly ridden by Carson. The eighteen-year-old Gorli rode Bikala as though in no doubt whatever of his mount's stamina, having him second to Magnum until deciding to press on going into the home turn. Bikala straightened up with a two-length advantage over the pack, quite quickly increased it by another couple of lengths and galloped on extremely powerfully over the last two and a half furlongs. Gorli, who's not averse to using the whip, drove him hard running towards the distance and kept him up to his work until near the finish but never faced a serious challenge. At the distance Gap of Dunloe, on the rails, Rahotep, Nijinsky's Secret and Akarad were almost in line abreast at least four lengths down, and only Akarad of the four, coming from a poor position, had any speed left in him. In the end the impressive Bikala had four lengths in hand of Akarad; Gap of Dunloe finished two and a half lengths further back in third.

While Bikala did not manage to win again he succeeded in adding considerably to his stature, and by the end of the season he had earned a reputation as a very tough, front-running horse. His finest hour came in the Prix de l'Arc de Triomphe on his final outing, when he led nearly all the way in Europe's most strongly-contested middle-distance race—twenty-four runners and, on this rare occasion, not a pacemaker among them. It says a good deal for Bikala that he could stay out in front for so long and that so few in the field proved capable of having a cut at him. After setting what appeared a reasonable gallop he quickened sufficiently to stretch almost all his opponents descending the hill towards the last turn; hardly anything made ground on him in the straight, and of those who did he shook off all except Gold River, who got past him well inside the final furlong to win by three quarters of a length. A really genuine performance!

One who did show up in the straight at Longchamp, albeit fleetingly, was the favourite Akarad. Eventually he weakened into seventh place. In the Grand Prix de Saint-Cloud in July Akarad had fared better against Bikala; in fact, he'd turned the Jockey-Club tables just four weeks after Chantilly, beating him by two lengths and showing the better finishing speed on that occasion. Bikala lost nothing in defeat in what is one of France's most important races open to three-year-olds and upwards, though it was said that the track didn't suit him so well as Chantilly. After racing close up to the pacemakers Sir Raleigh and Choucri, Bikala went on early in the straight chased by April Run; Akarad had given him less rope this time though, and was able to overtake with about two furlongs to go. Bikala once again battled on, holding on

M J. Ouaki's "Bikala"

to second place by half a length from Lancastrian, the fourth in the previous year's race. Bikala's only other start came in a Prix de l'Arc preparatory race, the Prix du Prince d'Orange at Longchamp in September in which Storm Bird made his long-awaited reappearance. The distance of a mile and a quarter probably suited the winner Vayrann better than it suited Bikala. Once again Bikala put up a splendid performance. First or second from the off he took up the running from Storm Bird soon after the turn, was immediately pressed by Vayrann and fought it out with that horse to the finish, remaining in front until well inside the last furlong. Vayrann, receiving 2 lb, beat him only half a length.

Bikala (b.c. 1978)	Kalamoun (gr 1970)	Zeddaan (gr 1965)	Grey Sovereign
			Vareta
		Khairunissa (gr 1960)	Prince Bio
			Palariva
	Irish Bird (b or br 1970)	Sea-Bird II (ch 1962)	Dan Cupid
			Sicalade
		Irish Lass II (b 1962)	Sayajirao
			Scollata

Kalamoun died prematurely and his last crop reached the racecourse in 1981; the most promising of that crop appear to be in France where Persepolis, Pomme d'Ebene and Talaja have won decent races. The pick of Kalamoun's runners in England in 1981 were the more senior Kalaglow and Castle Keep. Bikala's dam had another important winner representing her in the latest season, the Irish two-year-old Assert (by Be My Guest), bought for approximately £16,000 at the Deauville Yearling Sales. Bikala, as we have implied, is a robust colt, one who has thrived on racing, and it is no surprise to learn that he is to remain in training for a crack at the King George VI and Queen Elizabeth Diamond Stakes and another tilt at the Arc. He is well suited by the distance of those races and by the strong pace at which they are usually run, but he couldn't be discounted on the score of distance from another of his main objectives, the Prix Ganay run at Longchamp in the spring, certainly not if the ground is soft enough to make for a reasonable test of stamina. Bikala acts

BIL

well on soft going; his only race on firmish ground was in the Longchamp handicap, which he won without showing, or needing to show, anything like his best form. Although Bikala tends to race with his head high, especially when fully extended, he is a really genuine sort. *P. Biancone, France.*

BILA SHAKA 3 ch.g. No Mercy 126–Powderhall 81 (Murrayfield 119) (1980 6g 6g 1981 7s 7fg 7fg* 8d² 6g 7g) lightly-made gelding; bought in 1,850 gns after narrowly winning quite valuable seller at Brighton in July; stays 1m; acts on a firm and a soft surface; apprentice ridden. *W. Hastings-Bass.* **61**

BILDARA 2 br.f. Balidar 133–Dido's Grandaughter (By Thunder! 122) (1981 6fg 7fg 8s 10s) Feb 15; well-grown, quite attractive filly; half-sister to several winners, including fairly useful sprinter Heartbeat (by Burglar); dam never ran; little better than plating class on form at 2 yrs. *H. T. Jones.* **—**

BILLBROKER 5 br.g. Lombard 126–Eastern Blue 84 (Majority Blue 126) (1980 12fg⁴ 14f⁴ 16g 16d 1981 13.4d² 10s⁴(dis)) big, strong gelding; useful performer; ran very well in Ormonde Stakes at Chester in May, being collared only close home by 1½-length winner Pelerin (pair well clear); veered right when 4 lengths fourth to Triomphe in Clive Graham Stakes at Goodwood following month and was disqualified; not seen out again; stays 2m, but is probably better over shorter distances; acts on any going; sometimes sweats up before his races but is genuine and consistent; suited by front-running tactics; ridden by 5-lb claimer unable to draw his allowance both starts in 1981. *R. Simpson.* **102**

BILL GIBB 4 ch.c. Cavo Doro 124–Fair Helen (Hopeful Venture 125) (1980 12s 12d 12d 12.2d 11d³ 1981 12s 12g 18.8fg) neat colt; poor form, including in a seller; should stay 1½m; has worn blinkers. *R. Morris.* **—**

BILLIE GIBB 3 ch.f. Cavo Doro 124–Fair Helen (Hopeful Venture 125) (1980 7f 7g 7g 8.2g² 10d² 10s³ 10.2s 1981 12d 10s⁴ 12d 16.9s 12f 13.8f² 13.8fg³) small, lightly-made filly; plater; suited by 1¾m; acts on any going; wears blinkers. *Mrs J. Reavey.* **43**

DILLIE JEAN 4 ch.f. Sweet Revenge 129 Volley (Ratification 129) (1980 8s² 7s² 8.5f 7d 7fg⁴ 8fg 1981 8.2g) tall, sparely-made filly; plater nowadays; stays 1m; suited by soft going; doesn't always impress in paddock. *C. Wildman.* **—**

BILLSBAY 4 b.g. Bilsborrow 85–Maggie Malloy (Goldhill 125) (1980 NR 1981 16f) tailed-off last in poor maiden event at Beverley in June. *J. Jefferson.* **—**

BILLY KIP 4 b.g. Shoolerville 121–Shall Do (Passenger 122 or Derring-Do 131) (1980 9.4g 8f 8f 5g 1981 8.2s 6g 8g) plater; not certain to stay 9f; acts on firm going; has been tried in blinkers. *R. Fisher.* **—**

BINCLEAVES 3 ch.c. Tumble Wind–Pink Doll (Palestine 133) (1980 5fg 5fg* 6g³ 1981 6.5s 5s) close-coupled, quite attractive colt; not a good mover in his slower paces; won maiden race at Newmarket as a 2-y-o; towards rear at Cagnes-sur-Mer and Salisbury early in 1981; stays 6f. *M. McCormack.* **—**

BINFIELD 2 b.f. Rheingold 137–White Meadow (Bold Bidder) (1981 7fg 7h) Apr 9; 7,200F; third produce; sister to American 3-y-o Speed Delight; dam, from same family as Meadow Court, was third over 5f and 9f in Ireland; 50/1 and ridden by 7-lb claimer when 12½ lengths fifth of 16 to Top Hope in maiden race at Yarmouth in August, first start and better effort; bred to stay 1¼m+. *R. Sheather.* **—**

BIONIC BILL 6 b.g. Sovereign Bill 105–Soldier Girl (Queen's Hussar 124) (1980 NR 1981 8f* 8f³ 8fg) winner of apprentice race at Brighton in June; best form at 1m on firm going; good mount for a boy. *J. Old.* **44**

BIRTHDAY FROLIC (USA) 2 br.c. Drone–Sailor Frolic (Cap Size) (1981 6g 6fg 6fg 6fg⁴ 6g 8d) Apr 3; $25,000Y; workmanlike colt; third foal; brother to a minor winner in USA; dam, minor stakes winner, won over 4f and 6f; modest fourth of 9 to Manchesterskytrain in maiden race at Epsom in September, probably best effort; stays 6f; blinkered fourth and fifth outings. *N. Vigors.* **63**

BISHENPUR 2 gr. or ro.c. No Mercy 126–Bashara (Royal Orbit) (1981 7g 7d 7f) Feb 25; lengthy colt; first foal; dam ran at 2 yrs when only plating class; in rear in minor and maiden events; blinkered third outing; sold to T. Hallett 500 gns Doncaster September Sales. *C. Spares.* **—**

BISHOPS RIDE 2 ch.g. Hot Spark 126–Montcall (Mountain Call 125) (1981 5.8d 6g 6fg 6f 5f) Feb 6; 8,400F, 5,000Y; stocky gelding; third foal; dam unraced half-sister to French Champion Hurdle winner Hardatit; no worthwhile form in varied company. *R. Baker.* **—**

132

BISKERYL 4 b. or br.f. Biskrah 121–Keryl 106 (Infatuation 129) (1980 11.7fg —
12g 16.9d* 16fg² 1981 18d 15g) staying handicapper; acts on a firm and a
soft surface. *G. Lockerbie.*

BIT BENT 7 b.g. Foggy Bell 108–Lady Honey 75 (Taste of Honey 92) (1980 —
NR 1981 8fg) of little account. *K. Bridgwater.*

BITING WIT (USA) 3 b.f. Vitriolic–Lakewoods 83 (Hyperion) (1980 6f **69**
1981 7g³ 10g 7g 7.6s³ 5fg* 6f³ 6g 5fg) quite an attractive filly; won maiden
event at Warwick in August; bred to stay at least 1m (had stiff task over 1¼m).
J. Hindley.

BITTE SCHON (USA) 3 b.f. Bold Bidder–Santa Paula II (Santa Claus **83**
133) (1980 NR 1981 8f 8fg 10f* 10.1g² 12fg² 10fg² 10g 10s) tall, attractive
filly; half-sister to several winners, notably very smart 11f to 1¾m winner Noble
Saint (by Vaguely Noble); dam unraced half-sister to leading American performers Tom Rolfe and Chieftain; 20/1 when beating Johnnie Hussar in very
good style by 4 lengths in maiden race at Nottingham in July; second the
following month in minor event at Windsor and handicaps at Kempton and
Newmarket (apprentices); stays 1½m; acts on firm going (well beaten only
outing on soft); hampered at start seventh outing. *R. Armstrong.*

B JASKI 2 ch.c. Malinowski 123–Fair Halo (Nimbus 132) (1981 8g) Apr 6; —
useful sort; half-brother to several winners here and abroad, including fairly
useful middle-distance stayer Rowland (by Le Levanstell); dam ran only twice;
50/1 when behind in 27-runner minor event won by Dudley Wood at Newmarket
in October. *M. Jarvis.*

BLACKBOOSH 2 b.c. Tarboosh–Riberina (Ribero 126) (1981 5d³ 5g 5fg **51**
7f 6f 5g) Mar 17; leggy colt; poor plater: should be suited by 7f; form only
on a soft surface; sold 350 gns Ascot September Sales. *M. W. Easterby.*

BLACKBROOK MELODY 4 ch.f. Jukebox 120–Naranja 81 (Roan Rocket **58**
128) (1980 8v 8.5g³ 8fg 6fg 5.8g 5.8f⁴ 6fg* 6fg 5.8g² 6fg 1981 6g³ 7f 6f* 5.8f
6f) small, lightly-made filly; won handicap at Brighton in July; stays 6f and
wasn't disgraced over 7f second start; acts on firm going. *M. Francis.*

BLACK EARL 4 br.c. So Blessed 130–La Presidente (Primera 131) (1980 —
7d³ 8.2d³ 8f³ 8g 10s 1981 10.8fg 8d 8f 12f 11.7fg) leggy colt; stays 1m but
probably not 1¼m; seems to act on any going; blinkered once at 3 yrs. *T.
Hallett.*

BLACKER 3 b.c. Arch Sculptor 123–Party Love (Parthia 132) (1980 5g 6g **75**
1981 6fg² 6g* 6d³ 6g 6fg) deep-girthed, useful-looking colt; won maiden race
at Pontefract in May in quite good style; will stay 7f; didn't run up to his best
last 2 starts; sold 1,300 gns Newmarket Autumn Sales, probably for export to
Scandinavia. *G. Hunter.*

BLACK FLAME 2 b. or br.c. Blakeney 126–Flamethrower 77 (Forli) (1981 **80**
7fg 7g⁴ 10s 10.2g) June 8; 11,500Y; neat colt; first foal; dam, winner over
1m, is half-sister to smart animals Lighted Glory and Torus; prominent in
maiden races at Leicester in September (2 lengths fourth of 16 to Airwair) and
Nottingham the following month (under 4 lengths fifth of 22 to Luxury); will
be suited by 1½m+. *F. Durr.*

BLACKFOOT (USA) 3 bl.c. Charles Elliott–Augusta J (Lenso) (1980 7g **90**
7f* 7d³ 7.5g 1981 7s 8.5fg 10fg⁴ 12fg² 10.2fg 12d) well-made, good sort; ran
best races of year when 4½ lengths fourth to Sticky Habit in handicap at Kempton and head second to Grain Race in similar race at Newmarket, both in August;
well beaten on his other starts, including classic trials on his first 2; suited
by middle distances; acts on any going; never going particularly well when
blinkered final outing; sent to France. *R. Sheather.*

BLACK MIKE 6 b.h. Hardicanute 130–Sariette (Barbare II 128) (1980 7f² **81**
12f 11.7g⁴ 8fg 7.2d 7d² 1981 8s 7s⁴ 7d⁴ 8d 9fg* 10d* 8.5g 8g* 9fg² 10g²) smallish, strong sort; moderate handicapper; won at Hamilton and Brighton in May
and at Beverley in June; stays 1¼m; seems to act on any going; has run creditably
for a boy. *P. Haslam.*

BLACK MINSTREL 7 b.h. Luthier 126–Innocent Air 75 (Court Martial) —
(1980 8d⁴ 7s* 6fg 7g 8d 7.2d 7s* 8s³ 7s 1981 8v 8d 7d² 7d 7g 7v 7d 7.3d 7s 7s 7s)
fair handicapper at his best; ran respectably first 3 starts but moderately most
outings afterwards; best at up to 1m; revels in the mud; has been tried in
blinkers; suitable mount for an apprentice; often bandaged in front. *D. Sasse.*

BLACK PENNY 3 b.f. West Partisan 101–Penny Miss (Songedor 116) (1980 —
NR 1981 11s 12d 16.9s 11d 11.7d) sturdy filly; fourth foal; sister to a poor

animal; dam well beaten in maiden races; soundly beaten in maiden and minor events and handicaps. *J. Old.*

BLACK PIRATE 4 bl.g. Barbary Pirate 91–Fire Fairy 70 (Firestreak 125) — (1980 10s³ 10fg* 9fg 11fg³ 9g 12g² 12fg 11d 11s 1981 10d 8g⁴ 10d 12fg 10f 10fg² 8.2s³ 10s 10.2g) neat, lightly-built gelding; plater; stays 1¼m; probably acts on any going; has worn blinkers; has run respectably for a boy. *A. W. Jones.*

BLACK SUNSET (FR) 3 b. or br.f. Scottish Rifle 127–Rosie Bacardi (Bally- **46** moss 136) (1980 6d 1981 10s 9d 9.4g 8d 10fg 8f² 9d³ 10s 10s) small, lightly-made filly; plater; should stay 1¼m; retained 540 gns Newmarket July Sales. *M. Ryan.*

BLADNOCH BOY 3 ch.g. Ellkar 87–Bonnie Bladnoch (Lord of Verona 120) — (1980 8g 8.2s 1981 12d 12.2fg) small, sturdy gelding; well behind in maiden and minor events. *G. Richards.*

BLAKENEY POINT 3 b.c. Blakeney 126–Lichen Lady 70 (Pardao 120) **69** (1980 7g 7d 7fg 7fg 1981 12.5s 12s⁴ 12g 10g 9.4g³ 12fg³ 12f⁴ 13f⁴ 12g³ 12.2fg³ 16fg³ 14.7fg* 14g³ 13.8fg³ 13d 16s) neat, attractive colt; quite moderate form in varied company, and eventually got off mark when beating Consenting by 2½ lengths in maiden race at Redcar in July; one paced and stays well; often apprentice ridden (wasn't at Redcar). *R. Hollinshead.*

BLAKENOR 3 b.c. Blakeney 126–Mary Connor 99 (Royal Avenue 123) (1980 **77** NR 1981 8d 8d⁴ 9s* 10fg 10fg 10.2g² 12v 13.3s⁴) neat colt; third living foal; half-brother to a winner in Trinidad by Reliance II; dam won 4 times over 1m; confirmed earlier promise when beating Ramannolie a neck in 17-runner maiden race at Wolverhampton in May; ran best subsequent race when 1½ lengths second to Aventura in handicap at Bath in September; seems to stay 13¼; seems to need some give in the ground, but has run badly on heavy ground; sold 7,800 gns Newmarket Autumn Sales and is to be trained in 1982 by A. Klimscha in France. *M. Smyly.*

BLAKES BEACON 4 b.c. Blakeney 126–Lighted Lamp (Sir Gaylord) (1980 **94** 12fg² 14f 13.3fg* 16g 14g* 13.3d 13s* 14g 1981 14g³ 14fg³ 16d² 16.1s³ 22.2f³ 12s 18g) neat, strong colt; fairly useful performer; placed in varied company, on fifth start finishing third to Donegal Prince in Queen Alexandra Stakes at Royal Ascot in June; stays well; probably acts on any going; used to wear blinkers; one paced. *P. Walwyn.*

BLAKESWARE 2 b.f. Home Guard 129–Barbarina (Molvedo 137) (1981 6g 7g) Mar 9; 9,000Y; quite attractive, well-made filly; half-sister to 5 winners in Italy, including prolific scorer Be Regal (by Viceregal); dam unraced daughter of Italian St Leger winner Barbara Sirani; well behind in end-of-season maiden races at Newmarket. *L. Cumani.*

BLAKESWARE COUNTY 2 b.f. Wolverlife 115–Dream County 78 (Sing Sing **86** 134 or Breeders Dream 116) (1981 6fg⁴ 5fg² 6fg² 7f² 7g 7g²) Feb 2; IR 10,000Y; rangy filly; second foal; half-sister to Italian 3-y-o Red Dream (by Red Alert), successful several times; dam won twice over 1½m; second 4 times, to Cojean in maiden race at Sandown, to Cheri Berry in minor race at Epsom (didn't act too well on course), to Tropical Blaze in £4,600 race at Chepstow (dead-heated with Top Hope) and to Chalon in 29-runner maiden race at Newmarket in October; beaten less than 2 lengths each time; will probably stay 1m. *M. Jarvis.*

BLAKESWARE SAINT 2 b.f. Welsh Saint 126–Regency Girl 89 (Right Boy **68** 137) (1981 5g 5s 5g³ 5d⁴) Feb 7; IR 2,400F, 7,200Y; lengthy filly; half-sister to a minor 2-y-o winner by Jukebox; dam stayed 6f; showed speed on all outings, putting up probably best effort when 1½ lengths third of 15 to Bold Saracen in maiden race at Bath in September (first race for nearly 4 months); not sure to stay 6f. *M. Tompkins.*

BLAKEY BANK 2 b.g. Blakeney 126–Be Tuneful 130 (Be Friendly 130) (1981 — 8g 8g) Apr 17; neat gelding; not the best of walkers; first foal; dam top-class filly at up to 7f; unquoted when well beaten in large fields for maiden and minor events at Newmarket in October. *J. Hindley.*

BLA-MARKIE'S DREAM 5 gr.m. The Go-Between 129–Lords Lady (Lord — of Verona 120) (1980 NR 1981 10s 8g 8f 8f 9g 12f) little sign of ability in varied company. *S. Nesbitt.*

BLANDOR 2 b.f. Le Coq d'Or 101–Blandford Lady (Blandford Lad 96) (1981 **79**
6g 6f* 6f⁴ 8f² 8.2d* 8.2s³) Mar 15; leggy non-thoroughbred filly; good mover;
fifth reported foal; dam ran over hurdles in Ireland; winner of seller at Thirsk
in July (bought in 1,700 gns) and nursery at Hamilton in September, holding
on by a short head from Perplex in latter despite hanging left; will stay middle
distances; acts on any going; consistent; sold to Mrs G. Forbes 4,000 gns
Newmarket Autumn Sales. *J. W. Watts.*

BLARE 3 b.c. Bustino 136–Swift Harmony 107 (Elopement 125) (1980 7d² **96**
1981 11s² 12g 12f* 12fg 12f* 11.1fg* 12fg 11.7d) big, strong, good-looking colt;
won 4-runner minor event at Leicester in July (took time to warm up); rather
disappointing next time but returned to form after a soft palate operation
and subsequently made nearly all in handicaps at Ripon in August and Kempton
in September, on latter course staying on really well and holding on by 1½ lengths
from Prince Bless; disappointed again last 2 starts however; will be suited by
further than 1½m; acts on any going, but clearly goes well on firm; sold 8,000 gns
Newmarket Autumn Sales. *R. Hern.*

BLAZE OF HONOUR 2 ch.f. Quiet Fling 124–Streak of Honour 102 (Fire- —
streak 125) (1981 5g) May 16; 1,400F, 1,000Y; fifth produce; dam won three
5f races at 2 yrs; unquoted when in rear in 14-runner maiden race won by Gold
Key at Carlisle in May. *Mrs A. Bell.*

BLEACH 4 ch.f. Sun Prince 128–Brilliantine 109 (Stage Door Johnny) (1980 —
12g 12s 1981 10.2s 10.8d) rangy filly; well beaten in varied company; covered
by Music Boy. *R. Boss.*

BLESSED GOSSIP 2 b.c. So Blessed 130–Gossip Column 94 (Tamerlane 128) **64**
(1981 6fg 5f 5.1f³ 5f 5s) May 17; 400Y; small colt; poor walker; a twin; half-
brother to two winners in Ireland; dam 9f to 1¼m winner; plater; should stay
6f; acts on any going. *N. Guest.*

BLESSED MITE 2 b.f. Beatic–Fredas Hope (Fighting Don) (1981 5fg 5f —
7f 6s) Mar 4; compact filly; half-sister to a winning plater; dam of little account;
well beaten in maiden race and sellers; blinkered final start. *S. Norton.*

BLESSED SILENCE 3 b.c. So Blessed 130–Cease Fire 112 (Martial 131) —
(1980 NR 1981 6fg⁴ 6f 8f) 4,400F; fair sort; half-brother to several winners,
including useful 1976 2-y-o 6f winner Truce of Oman (by Gulf Pearl); dam 6f
sprinter; showed a little ability in maiden and minor events on first 2 starts;
not certain to stay 1m. *P. Asquith.*

BLESSED SON 5 br.g. Averof 123–Blessed Queen 91 (So Blessed 130) (1980 —
NR 1981 8fg 8g) plater; stays 7f; sometimes blinkered. *A. W. Jones.*

BLESS'EM ALL 2 b.c. So Blessed 130–Misnomer 85 (Milesian 125) (1981 7f **85**
8s² 7g) Mar 18; strong, lengthy colt; fourth foal; closely related to 1m winner
Snow Chief (by Tribal Chief) and half-brother to fairly useful 1½m winner York
Cottage (by Royal Palace); dam, winner at up to 1½m, is daughter of St Leger
third Cold Storage; stayed on gamely under strong pressure when 2 lengths
second of 14 to Florida Son in maiden race at York in October; prominent for
long way when in rear behind Ivano in 15-runner Houghton Stakes at Newmarket
later in month; will probably stay 1¼m; sure to win a race or two if not tried
too highly. *W. Elsey.*

BLESS THE MATCH 2 b.f. So Blessed 130–Matloch 70 (Matador 131) (1981 **101**
5g³ 6fg* 6fg³ 6f 6fg* 6g) Apr 15; quite a useful-looking filly; good mover; closely
related to smart 1973 2-y-o 5f performer Eveneca and useful sprinter Elegante
(both by Frankincense) and half-sister to a winner; dam sister to useful sprinter
Spanish Sail; successful in 22-runner maiden race at Lingfield in June and 12-
runner St Catherine's Stakes at Newbury the following month, scoring a little
cleverly by a length from Silojoka in latter after disputing lead throughout;
good 4¾ lengths fifth of 13 to Woodstream in William Hill Cheveley Park Stakes
at Newmarket in September only subsequent start; stays 6f well and may get a
little further at 3 yrs; yet to race on a soft surface; suited by forcing tactics.
G. Pritchard-Gordon.

BLOAK MOSS 3 b.g. Cavo Doro 124–Tabasheer (Indian Chief) (1980 6fg 6d **50**
6g 7fg 1981 12d 11fg 12.3g 12fg² 12fg) neat, good-topped gelding; second
in seller at Newmarket in July; stays 1½m; blinkered second start; sold 2,400 gns
Ascot September Sales. *Sir Mark Prescott.*

BLOCHAIRN SKOLAR 3 ch.f. Most Secret 119–Olibanum 61 (Frankincense **47**
120) (1980 5d 5f 5fg 5g 1981 5g 5f 5f 5fg³ 5f² 6f 5f 5fg 5s 6d) compact filly;
placed in handicap at Carlisle and apprentice race at Edinburgh in July. *V.
Mitchell.*

BLO

BLOEMFONTEIN 2 ch.c. Free State 125–Belligerent 74 (Roan Rocket 128) —
(1981 5g 5g 5fg 7fg 8s) Apr 22; neat, strong colt; half-brother to 2 winners,
including useful sprinter Goldhills Pride (by Goldhill); dam half-sister to very
good French miler Kenmare; plating-class maiden. *F. Durr.*

BLONDE BOMBSHELL 3 ch.f. Warpath 113–Poncho 80 (Ragusa 137) —
(1980 NR 1981 10.2g 12.2g) strong filly; third foal; sister to 1978 2-y-o 1m
winner Sombrero; dam stayed 1½m; unplaced in minor event at Haydock in
May (backward and apprentice ridden, had tongue tied down) and Catterick in
June (not beaten very far when eighth of 15 to Quickbeam); sold to T. Hallett
900 gns Doncaster November Sales. *C. Thornton.*

BLOOD ORANGE 6 ch.g. Warpath 113–Sunflower 96 (Paveh 126) (1980 18d
13.8f 1981 12s 12g) poor maiden; stays 1¾m; sometimes has his tongue tied
down; inconsistent. *W. Stubbs.*

BLOW MY TOP 2 gr.f. Some Hand 119–Tempered Wind (Fleece 114) (1981 **59**
6s 8d 8s³) Apr 5; third foal; dam never ran; apprentice ridden when third of 17
to 10-length winner Whenyourtrainsgone in seller at Warwick in October, best
effort; evidently needs at least 1m. *P. Cundell.*

BLUE BABY 3 br.f. The Brianstan 128–Le Brillante (Eudaemon 129) (1980 —
NR 1981 8.2f 5f 5d) 900F; small, sturdy filly; seventh reported living foal;
dam showed little worthwhile form; behind in varied company, including selling;
sweating final start. *D. Francis.*

BLUEBIRDINO 2 ch.c. Bustino 136–Blue Bird 84 (Majority Blue 126) (1981 — p
8s) June 14; half-brother to 4 winners, including middle-distance stayer
Sockburn (by My Swallow); dam stayed 1¼m; unquoted and decidedly backward, tired early in straight when eighth of 15 to Twist Home in maiden
race at York in October; has scope and should do better over 1½m+ in 1982.
M. Camacho.

BLUE CLOUD 2 ch.f. Blue Cashmere 129–Hill Cloud 60 (El Gallo 122) (1981 **82**
5d 5d 5s³ 5g⁴) May 20; compact filly; third foal; half-sister to Morning Line
(by Owen Anthony), winner of a 1½m match; dam stayed 7f; showed ability most
starts, including in a nursery on final outing when 1¼ lengths fourth of 21 to
Preparation at Newmarket in October; not sure to stay beyond 5f (weakened
quickly closing stages second and third starts); yet to race in a firm surface.
Mrs R. Lomax.

BLUE DO 2 b.g. Swing Easy 126–Nylon Pirate (Derring-Do 131) (1981 5v **80**
5d 7fg 7fg 8g² 8.2d⁴) Feb 7; 4,600F, 8,000Y; workmanlike gelding; half-brother
to 2 minor winners; dam of little account; put up easily best efforts when
in frame in sizeable fields of maidens at Edinburgh (2½ lengths second to
Spring Lane) and Hamilton (3¼ lengths fourth behind Trickshot) in the autumn;
evidently better at 1m than shorter distances; blinkered third outing (coltish
in paddock). *T. Craig.*

BLUE EMMANUELLE 2 b.c. Lochnager 132–Julie Be Quick (Selari) (1981 **89**
6g³ 7fg 5fg² 5d³ 5g² 6g²) Apr 25; 23,000Y; big, rangy colt; good mover;
third foal; half-brother to fairly useful 1980 2-y-o 5f performer Queen of Prussia
(by Bay Express); dam won at up to 1m in USA; placed in maiden races and
valuable nurseries; looked unlucky when beaten ½ length by Bright View at
Redcar in September on fifth outing (received a hefty bump early on and then
hung in closing stages) but had every chance when 1½ lengths second of 17 to
Vaigly Star at Newmarket in October; stays 6f well but isn't sure to stay 7f;
acts on a firm and a soft surface; well capable of winning a race. *N. Callaghan.*

BLUE EMPRESS 3 b.f. Blue Cashmere 129–Emperor's Treasure (King —
Emperor) (1980 5f 5fg 1981 6v 5d 5.8g 6fg) light-framed filly; in rear in
varied company; sometimes bandaged; blinkered third start. *M. Francis.*

BLUE EROTICA 3 b.g. Sharpen Up 127–Turf 116 (Ballymoss 136) (1980 —
NR 1981 10f 10fg 12f 11g 8g 12g) 5,800F, 4,000Y; big, workmanlike gelding;
brother to a poor animal and half-brother to 2 minor winners; dam a sprinter;
plating-class maiden; was tried in blinkers; usually ridden by an apprentice
or amateur; swerved and unseated rider second start; killed after winning 3
early-season juvenile hurdles. *D. Wilson.*

BLUE FANDANGO 2 b.f. Gay Fandango 132–Bluets 74 (Hitting Away) —
(1981 6fg 7g) Jan 13; quite well-made filly; fourth foal; dam won over 1¼m;
behind in sizeable fields for maiden races at Newbury in August and Newmarket
in October; sent to France. *M. Smyly.*

BLUE FIRE LADY 2 b. or br.f. Pitcairn 126–Bold Aroon (Bold Lad, Ire 133) —
(1981 5fg 5.3f 6fg 6f 7f 5g 5s) Mar 7; IR 4,200F, 13,000Y; compact filly;

136

second produce; half-sister to 1980 2-y-o 6f seller winner Spanish Tormenta (by Furry Glen); dam never ran; well beaten, including under 7-7 in a Warwick nursery; blinkered sixth outing. *J. Benstead.*

BLUE FOX 4 ch.g. Apollo Eight–Lady Blue (Majority Blue 126) (1980 NR 1981 12f 16.5g 10s) 300Y; compact gelding; probably of little account. *J. Doyle.* —

BLUE GARTER 3 ch.f. Targowice 130–Blue Rag 70 (Ragusa 137) (1980 5s 6s 7fg 7g 8fg* 8fg² 6g³ 8d* 8d³ 7g 1981 10g 10.1f 8f 12d 11.7g³ 13.3s³ 12d) compact filly; fairly useful in selling company at 2 yrs; not entirely disgraced in handicaps on occasions in 1981; stays 13f; yet to show she acts on extremes of going; often wears blinkers but is effective without. *P. Mitchell.* 54

BLUE GULF 3 ch.f. Gay Fandango 132–Gulf Bird 71 (Gulf Pearl 117) (1980 NR 1981 7d 8d 8f 12g 10.2h* 11.1fg 10.2g) strong filly; second foal; half-sister to very useful 5f performer Blue Persian (by Majority Blue); dam 1½m winner; 40/1 and apprentice ridden when beating Crimson Royale by 2 lengths in maiden race at Bath in July (made all); had stiff tasks in handicaps subsequently; stays 1¼m; evidently acts on hard going. *B. Hanbury.* 68

BLUE JANE 4 b.f. Blue Cashmere 129–Westmorland Jane 76 (Vimy 132) (1980 7d 7v 6fg³ 6fg 11.7s 8f² 10g 8g³ 5d 7g 1981 8s 7d 7d) quite attractive, compact, good-quartered filly; well beaten in 1981; stays 1m; acts on firm going; sometimes blinkered; has run respectably for inexperienced riders. *D. H. Jones.* —

BLUE RAIN 2 b.f. Blue Cashmere 129–Aquanimba (Acropolis 132) (1981 5fg 5g 5f²) Apr 19; leggy filly; sister to 6f seller winner Aqua Blue and half-sister to fair 1978 2-y-o miler Top Stream (by Highland Melody); dam poor sister to smart stayer Acrania; claimed after finishing 1½ lengths second to Trust Sally on only outing in selling company at Ripon in August. *P. Asquith.* 56

BLUE REALM 2 b.f. Realm 129–Honey Tower 70 (Tower Walk 130) (1981 5g) Mar 22; 2,900F; first produce; dam 2m winner; 20/1, stayed on to finish eighth of 21 to Begham Bay in minor event at Catterick in September, only outing; will be suited by 6f. *G. Richards.* —

BLUE RHAPSODY 3 ch.c. Sandford Lad 133–Sovereign Court 87 (Sovereign Path 125) (1980 5f 5fg 6s* 6fg 7g 8.2g 7fg 7.2s 1981 6s 5fg 6s 7fg 6g) strong, useful sort; has run moderately since winning a maiden auction event at Nottingham as a 2-y-o, including in sellers; should stay 7f; acts on soft going; blinkered last 3 outings; one to be wary of; sold 410 gns Ascot August Sales. *R. Williams.* —

BLUES 4 b.c. Song 132–Lyrical 100 (Gratitude 130) (1980 6s 6d 7g 6g 7g³ 6g 6g² 7fg 6d 6g³ 5fg 5d 6d 5s² 1981 5s 5s² 6s 5d 6fg 5fg 5g 5.3f 6g⁴ 6f) strong, compact colt; poor handicapper; stays 7f; probably acts on any going but goes well on soft; blinkered sixth start; suitable mount for a boy; sold 620 gns Newmarket Autumn Sales, probably for export to Scandinavia. *N. Guest.* 58

BLUE SAPPHIRE 2 br.c. Blue Cashmere 129–The Maid (Milesian 125) (1981 5s 5v 5g⁴ 5s 5fg 5fg 6f⁴ 5f 5g² 5g 5f) May 10; 4,100F, 3,800Y; leggy colt; good mover; half-brother to minor winners here and abroad; dam won over 6f at 2 yrs in Ireland; in frame in maiden auction event and sellers; best form at 5f; evidently needs a sound surface; ran poorly in blinkers eleventh outing; trained by R. Hollinshead and W. Stubbs for part of season. *T. Taylor.* 54

BLUE SINGH 3 ch.f. Mansingh 120–Great Blue White 73 (Great Nephew 126) (1980 5f 6fg* 6d 6g 7fg 8g 6g³ 1981 6fg³ 6g 5s 6d³ 5d 5f³ 5f* 6fg 5fg 5g³ 5f³ 5.6fg 5g 5s 5s* 5g) leggy, fair sort; successful in handicaps at Doncaster in June and Newbury in October, responding well to hard pressure to beat Sir Samuel by ½ length on latter course; best form at up to 6f but wasn't disgraced over 7f as a 2-y-o (not certain to stay further); probably acts on any going; had stiff task fifth start. *R. Boss.* 89

BLUETHROAT 2 b.f. Ballymore 123–Sabrewing 105 (Petingo 135) (1981 5d⁴ 6fg 6g* 7f³ 7g³ 8.2s² 8d 8.2s*) Apr 6; quite attractive filly; third foal; half-sister to Borisgudunov (by Home Guard), successful at up to 1¼m in Ireland; dam won over 6f at 2 yrs; favourite when winning 8-runner maiden race at Hamilton in July by 3 lengths from Towering; ran well in nurseries afterwards, on final outing beating Trickshot decisively by 4 lengths at Nottingham in October; suited by 1m and will stay further; acts on any going. *B. Hobbs.* 95

BLUE WIND 3 ch.f. Lord Gayle 124–Azurine 108 (Chamossaire) (1980 6s 7g² 7.5s* 8g* 8f 1981 8g* 8v² 12g* 12fg* 10g⁴ 12d) 127
Blue Wind was one of the most decisive Oaks winners ever. The finish

of the race bore some resemblance to that of a three-mile steeplechase, sixth-placed Fruition thirty-two lengths down on the winner, Go Leasing twenty-nine, Ivory Wings twenty-two, Leap Lively seventeen and Madam Gay, the runner-up, seven. We have been treated to a number of dazzling performances in the race's comparatively recent history but not even Pawneese, Juliette Marny, Mysterious, Lupe or La Lagune won by so great a distance, and nearly twenty years have passed since Noblesse's crushing ten-length victory. Blue Wind progressed to complete the double in the Irish Guinness Oaks by two and a half lengths from the Musidora Stakes winner Condessa and around that time she seemed to be the best three-year-old middle-distance filly in training, especially as Madam Gay had by then won the French Oaks and finished second to Shergar at Ascot. There was even speculation, unreal though it now sounds, that Blue Wind might be capable of beating Shergar. Her reappearance in the autumn was eagerly anticipated but when she came out again she proved rather disappointing and had only two races, being retired to stud after finishing fifteenth in the Prix de l'Arc de Triomphe, while her owner's April Run was selected to carry the colours in the United States.

Blue Wind, on whom Piggott replaced stable-jockey Swinburn senior for the occasion, started 3/1 co-favourite with Leap Lively for the Oaks. In the end the race attracted a below average-sized field of twelve, but the outcome had been thrown wide open by the Musidora Stakes defeat and subsequent withdrawal of the One Thousand Guineas winner Fairy Footsteps. Neither co-favourite ran in the Guineas. Leap Lively, the winner of the previous autumn's Hoover Fillies Mile, had run in the Johnnie Walker Oaks Trial at Lingfield (which she won from Allegretta, Condessa and Fruition); Blue Wind stayed at home for the Goffs Irish One Thousand Guineas. Like Leap Lively, Blue Wind had been a very useful staying two-year-old. She won the Silken Glider Stakes at Leopardstown and finished a fairly close sixth in the Prix Marcel Boussac at Longchamp for Paddy Prendergast junior's stable. Sold for 180,000 guineas at Goffs towards the end of 1980, she gave every encouragement to her new connections in the spring by defeating the colt Cimon in the Edenderry Stakes at Phoenix Park and, much more importantly, by running Arctique Royale to a short head in very testing conditions at the Curragh in the Irish One Thousand Guineas; on the latter occasion she battled for the lead through the last three furlongs, and by the way she ran would clearly be well suited by a longer trip. Two of the Oaks field had run behind Fairy Footsteps in the Guineas—Go Leasing, a close and strong-finishing third, and Madam Gay, a close and strong-finishing fifth. Madam Gay in the meantime had finished four lengths behind Condessa at York. Of the others in the Oaks Tropicaro possessed the best form. She had won the Prix Marcel Boussac and two of her six other races, including the Prix de la Grotte; she had also been fifth in the French Guineas and second to Tootens in the Prix Saint-Alary. The other French challenger Ivory Wings, a lightly-raced filly by Sir Ivor, had won at Longchamp on her last two starts, the second time over a mile and a half.

The Oaks shared three points of similarity with the Derby which very few who had witnessed Shergar's stunning performance could possibly have antici-pated. Most of the runners were beaten entering the straight and the winner, who won by an astonishing margin in a classic, could be named a long way from the line. Leap Lively set a pace too strong for the comfort of any of her opponents or their riders: some in the field, such as Rhein Bridge and Fiesta Fun, simply couldn't keep up, while four or five of the others were backpedalling coming down the hill; at the latter stage Tropicaro had lost touch completely, as though something serious had befallen her. Turning for home Leap Lively led by about four lengths from Madam Gay, Ivory Wings, Canton Lightning and Blue Wind who were quite well bunched and detached from the remainder. Very soon the five with a chance became four and then three, as first Canton Lightning then Ivory Wings dropped back, nothing behind them managing to stage the semblance of a rally. Leap Lively couldn't maintain her gallop the full distance. She was very tired three furlongs out and before the two-furlong pole both Madam Gay and Blue Wind caught up with her, all three principals being hard ridden at the latter point. Blue Wind, whose progress up the straight had been unremitting, quickly got on top on the outside and she was

Irish Guinness Oaks, the Curragh—Blue Wind readily accounts for
Condessa (partially obscured) and Stracomer Queen

driven clear for her overwhelmingly decisive victory.

Leap Lively's effort on ground no softer than good didn't result in a particularly fast time for the Oaks. Nevertheless one of the main impressions left by the race was of the strain the gallop had imposed on her and her rivals; each of the runners seemed subjected to an abnormally rigorous test, even the seven-length winner. This was the second hard race Blue Wind had had in two weeks. She had another, not so severe but severe enough, six weeks later in the Irish Guinness Oaks at the Curragh. They weren't a great lot for a classic against her that day, Condessa and Arctique Royale easily the pick, and the latter ran a long way below her form. Blue Wind was always close to the front in a ten-runner field and took the lead entering the straight under four furlongs out; she was ridden clear of the previous leader Waffles, Arctique Royale and the Mulcahy Stakes winner My Sister passing the two-furlong marker and needed to be kept up to her work to beat Condessa, who stayed on well, decisively.

Blue Wind's strenuous spring and summer is, we think, the key to understanding her performances in the autumn: she's not very big. She was given a well-earned rest in preparation for the Arc, missing the Yorkshire Oaks and the Prix Vermeille, returning for the Joe McGrath Memorial Stakes over a mile and a quarter at Leopardstown in the third week in September. In that race she finished fourth of twelve behind Kings Lake, Erins Isle and Kind of Hush, beaten six and a half lengths, an unimpressive fourth to our eyes although some thought she ran promisingly all things considered. She looked fit, but showed little sparkle in the race; she was never going particularly well, was being niggled at four furlongs from home and was well held at the line. Unfortunately, she ran even worse in the Arc, being pushed along virtually all the way without ever raising a hope. She finished alongside Cut Above, beaten by five of her sex—Gold River, April Run, Tootens, Leandra and Snow Day. The majority of fillies sent for the Arc nowadays are those fast approaching their best. Blue Wind was demonstrably not in that category; the more's the pity because one can't judge her fairly on her running in Paris. However, we should be very

140

surprised if at her best she could have beaten her owner's other filly April Run over a mile and a half.

Blue Wind (ch.f. 1978)	Lord Gayle (b 1965)	Sir Gaylord (b 1959)	Turn-to / Somethingroyal
		Sticky Case (ch 1958)	Court Martial / Run Honey
	Azurine (b 1957)	Chamossaire (ch 1942)	Precipitation / Snowberry
		Blue Dun (b 1950)	Blue Train / Dunure

Blue Wind's dam died in 1979. She enjoyed a long and highly fruitful career at stud, and has now produced a total of eight winners here and abroad. None of her other winners was in the same class as Blue Wind but two were placed in pattern races, the Italian-based Tora Tora (by Majority Blue), winner of at least eighteen races, and Madelon (by Saint Crespin III), second in the Silken Glider Stakes at Leopardstown. Blue Wind's full brother Callernish won at nine and a half furlongs and a mile and a half in Ireland in 1980. At least three of the dam's foals are dams of winners themselves, the most significant of them so far the unsuccessful racemare Azurn who bred the Stewards' Cup winner Touch Paper. Azurine, the dam of Blue Wind, was very useful on the track at distances up to thirteen furlongs. She was beaten only half a length into third place in the Irish One Thousand Guineas, she finished second in the Ormonde Stakes, fourth in the Irish Oaks and she won the Royal Whip at the Curragh. The second dam Blue Dun, one of the very few mares by Blue Train to appear in the pedigree of recent prominent horses, was a winning half-sister to the Irish Derby winner Dark Warrior; she won as a two-year-old and went on to take fourth place in the Irish St Leger. The sire of Blue Wind stands at the Irish National Stud. He has been a great asset to the Stud, what might usefully be described as 'a trainer's stallion', the sire of many excellent runners even though Blue Wind is his first classic winner. A fair number of Lord Gayle's

Mrs B. Firestone's "Blue Wind"

stock have been dual-purpose horses: Pollardstown is probably the best-known of these.

A neat filly, extremely shrewdly bought in the first instance for 5,600 guineas as a yearling, Blue Wind was very well suited by a distance of a mile and a half. Possibly by the time of the Joe McGrath Memorial she found a mile and a quarter altogether too sharp. Genuine, as she well illustrated in three successive classics, she acted on any going. *D. Weld, Ireland.*

BLUEWITCH 2 b.f. Blue Cashmere 129–Jetwitch 56 (Lear Jet 123) (1981 5g **65** 6f 6g⁴ 7g 7v) Apr 24; unfurnished filly; second foal; half-sister to 3-y-o 9f seller winner Abwacadabwa (by Abwah); dam, plater, stayed at least 1m; 6¾ lengths fourth of 18 to Bravado in maiden race at Newcastle in July; had plenty to do at weights when last in nursery at Catterick in September and was out of depth when tailed off final start; should stay 7f. *W. Haigh.*

BLUNT 3 ch.g. Bold Lad (Ire) 133–Treechka (Reform 132) (1980 6g 6s 5s — 1981 6s 6fg 8s) 1,000Y; workmanlike ex-Irish gelding; first foal; dam Irish 1½m winner; little worthwhile form, including in a seller at Haydock in April on second start (blinkered) and an amateur riders event at Goodwood in September; trained until after second outing by M. Kauntze. *J. Bridger.*

BLUSHING GOD 5 gr.g. Red God 128§–Bella Nicole (Bounteous 125) (1980 — NR 1981 8f 7fg 11.7f) no sign of ability in varied company. *R. Akehurst.*

B.M.C. SPECIAL 6 br.h. Supreme Sovereign 119–Agapimou (Great White **56** Way) (1980 9fg 7fg 8fg 8s 8d 9d 8fg* 7fg 8g⁴ 1981 8s 8.2fg 8fg* 8d⁴ 12d 8fg 8g 8.2f 8f 8fg² 10.4s³ 10f 8g 8d 8fg 9s) plater; won at Warwick in April; suited by 1m; seems to act on any going; blinkered once at 3 yrs; bandaged nowadays; suitable mount for a boy; retained 1,550 gns Ascot March Sales. *J. Gilbert.*

BOARDMANS BEAUTY 2 b.g. Lauso–Torbay (Hill Prince) (1981 7fg 8s⁴ **76** 10s⁴) Mar 15; quite a useful sort; half-brother to winning jumper St Torbay (by St Paddy); dam winning Irish sprinter; ridden by 5-lb claimer when fourth in maiden races at Warwick (6¾ lengths behind Port Garry) and Nottingham (beaten 4¼ lengths by Sunny Look) in October; suited by 1¼m and will stay 1½m+ at 3 yrs; acts on soft going. *A. Jarvis.*

BOARDMANS CROWN 2 b.g. Lauso–Taj Girl 68 (Taj Dewan 128) (1981 — 8g) Apr 29; first foal; dam won 1½m seller; unquoted and backward when behind in 27-runner minor event won by Dudley Wood at Newmarket in October. *A. Jarvis.*

BOARDMANS STAR 2 ch.f. Cawston's Clown 113–Weewanda 94 (Cagire II **63** 122) (1981 5fg³ 5d² 5s⁴ 6s 5.3f 6fg) Mar 26; 1,200F; small, lightly-made filly; good mover; half-sister to quite useful sprinter Little Poacher (by Poaching) and a winner in Germany; dam won at 5f and 1m; in frame in maiden races at Haydock, Salisbury and Windsor in the spring but subsequently disappointed, final outing a valuable seller at Goodwood in July; form only at 5f. *R. Hannon.*

BOARHUNT 2 ch.c. Queen's Hussar 124–Muninga 108 (St Alphage 119) — (1981 5s 6fg 6g 5s) Feb 27; tall, good sort; second foal; dam 5f sprinter; behind in sizeable fields of maidens *J. Winter.*

BOATHOUSE 3 b.f. Habitat 134–Ripeck 90 (Ribot 142) (1980 7.3d* 1981 **116** 8fg* 10d 10g3) rangy filly; half-sister to several winners, including Oaks winner Bireme (by Grundy), very good middle-distance stayer Buoy (by Aureole), smart sprinter Fluke (by Grey Sovereign) and very useful stayer Balinger (by Welsh Pageant); dam stayed 1½m; put up a most pleasing first effort when winning Radley Stakes at Newbury as a 2-y-o; didn't impress in coat when making a belated reappearance in September, but led 3f out and steadily strode clear to beat Cut Throat 7 lengths in 5-runner £3,100 event at Goodwood; ran deplorably when last of 8 behind Atlantic Boy in Peter Hastings Stakes (Handicap) at Newbury later in month but put up a much better effort in Sun Chariot Stakes at Newmarket in October, sticking on well and finishing 2¾ lengths third to Home On The Range; stayed 1¼m; acted on a firm and a soft surface; visits Known Fact in 1982. *R. Hern.*

BOATROCKER 2 b.c. African Sky 124–Cheap and Sweet (Rising Market) **70** p (1981 5v 5d*) May 14; 4,000Y; quite useful-looking colt; second foal; half-brother to Irish 3-y-o 1½m winner Cheap Display (by Daring Display); dam ran twice in France; improved greatly on first effort when winning 13-runner maiden race at Redcar in October by ½ length from 3-y-o Congo Express, finishing strongly; will be suited by 6f; reportedly unsuited by heavy going. *S. Norton.*

BODA 3 b.c. Bustino 136–Roller Bird 69 (Ribocco 129) (1980 NR 1981 8f — 10fg) big, rangy colt; fifth foal; half-brother to a winner in Jersey; dam disappointing daughter of Park Hill Stakes winner Cursorial; needed race and moved poorly to start when about 15 lengths sixth of 9 behind Al-Allam in maiden race at Pontefract in June (apprentice ridden and 33/1); in rear in similar race at Newmarket the following month. *H. Wragg.*

BODHAM 3 b.f. Bustino 136–Cley 85 (Exbury 138) (1980 NR 1981 10fg⁴ **88** 12d* 11.7fg⁴ 12d³ 13.3s* 12g⁴) lightly-made filly; third foal; half-sister to 1¼m winner Creake (by Derring-Do) and French 12.5f winner Habey (by Habat); dam 1½m winner and half-sister to Blakeney and Morston; put up an extraordinary display when slaughtering 10 rivals in handicap at Newbury in October, winning by 15 lengths from Regal Heiress despite being eased; had earlier won maiden race at Lingfield in August; will stay 1¾m; best with plenty of give in the ground. *J. Dunlop.*

BODNANT 3 b.f. Welsh Pageant 132–Pot Pourri 97 (Busted 134) (1980 7.3d — 1981 10fg 12d) small, robust filly; soundly beaten in £5,000 event at Newbury as a 2-y-o, maiden event at Sandown in April and minor race at Salisbury in May; sold 3,700 gns Newmarket July Sales. *P. Walwyn.*

BOHEMIAN RHAPSODY 3 b.f. On Your Mark 125–Schull (Yorick II 127) **67** (1980 5d² 5v* 5f² 5h* 5f 6s⁴ 6g⁴ 5f² 5d² 5g 1981 6f 6g 5fg⁴) compact filly; fair performer at 2 yrs; not seen out until September in 1981, but ran respectably; seems best at 5f; probably acts on any going; usually blinkered. *P. Haslam.*

BOIS DE GRACE (FR) 2 b.c. Luthier 126–Tafarette (Ballymoss 136) (1981 **112** 8d* 10v³) Mar 7; half-brother to 2 winners in France, including 3-y-o middle-distance winner Helisara (by Brigadier Gerard); dam, daughter of smart 1962 2-y-o French winner Chesa, was very useful over 1¼m; created a favourable impression when winning 14-runner newcomers event at Maisons-Laffitte in September by 3 lengths; also ran very well to be 1½ lengths third of 12 to Beau Pretender, after showing up throughout, in Group 3 Prix de Conde at Longchamp the following month; will stay 1½m; likely to make a smart 3-y-o. *F. Mathet, France.*

BOKARAH IN SHALLAH 4 b.g. Forlorn River 124–My Worry 72 (March **60** Past 124) (1980 5s⁴ 6s 6g* 7fg 5fg³ 6d 6d 1981 6s² 6d 6f 6f 6fg 6g 6s 6g) sprint handicapper; stays 6f; probably acts on any going; suitable mount for a boy. *Peter Taylor.*

BOLD DESIGN 2 b.f. Bold Lad (Ire) 133–Polycarpa (Polyfoto 124) (1981 6f — 6g) Mar 5; IR 25,000Y; strong, well-made, attractive filly; second foal; dam, unraced twin, is half-sister to very useful Claddagh (by Bold Lad, Ire); behind in large fields of maidens in July (swerved badly at flag start) and Newmarket in August (50/1). *J. Hindley.*

BOLD EAGLE 3 b.g. Legal Eagle 126–Vacation 102 (Remainder 106) (1980 — 6d 6g 7f 1981 10s 8g 8.2f 5fg 6fg 7f 8g 9g 7f 8f) lengthy, sparely-made gelding; only poor form, including in sellers; blinkered nowadays; sold 600 gns Doncaster September Sales. *T. Fairhurst.*

BOLD FLAWLESS (USA) 3 b.f. Bold Bidder–Hardliner (Buckpasser) **73** (1980 5f³ 5fg² 5g⁴ 5fg 1981 11.7fg 14.7fg⁴ 12.2fg⁴ 10f² 12f* 10d) compact filly; good mover; beat Elizabeth Howard by 5 lengths in maiden race at Folkestone in September; stays 1½m; acts on firm going (ran badly on softish ground final start); ran badly in blinkers final start as a 2-y-o; tends to sweat up; sold 90,000 gns Newmarket December Sales. *B. Hills.*

BOLD FORT 2 b.c. Auction Ring 123–Via Mala 81 (Pall Mall 132) (1981 **100** 5s² 5g³ 5d² 5d* 5f 6fg* 6f² 5d 6f 7s 6g* 6g 7g) Apr 15; 6,200Y; neat, sharp sort; good mover; second living foal; winner of small race at Catterick in May, quite well-contested event at Chester in July and £4,500 nursery at Newmarket in October, showing improved form when making all to win last-named event by ½ length from Mummy's Game, starting at 25/1; better suited by 6f than 5f but has yet to show he stays 7f; probably acts on any going; tough and genuine but lacks scope and may not train on. *R. Hollinshead.*

BOLD HAWK 2 br.c. Bold Lad (Ire) 133–Slavissima (Sea Hawk II 131) (1981 **79** p 6g⁴) Apr 10; IR 10,000Y; attractive colt; third foal; half-brother to Irish 3-y-o 1¼m to 2m winner Rommels Star (by Arratos) and a winner in Germany by Pentathlon; dam never ran; 33/1, although looked pretty fit and very well, shaped pleasingly on his debut to finish fourth, beaten just over 3½ lengths, to Perang Tejam in 26-runner maiden race at Doncaster in November, running on strongly in latter stages and not being knocked about; will be suited by 7f and 1m; sure to win a maiden race at least in 1982. *G. Harwood.*

BOLDIE 2 b.f. Bold Lad (Ire) 133–Amadina 96 (Great Nephew 126) (1981 **71** 5fg² 6g⁴) Apr 22; first foal; dam, half-sister to very useful 1972 2-y-o Claudius, won from 6f to 8.5f; in frame in maiden races at Warwick (started slowly) and Lingfield in June; favourite when 4 lengths fourth of 13 to Wink on latter; should be suited by 6f. *F. J. Houghton.*

BOLD IKE 3 b.c. The Brianstan 128–Carina 98 (Tamerlane 128) (1980 5d 6fg 7g 8fg 1981 6d 10d) small colt; bad plater; has worn blinkers. *J. Edmunds.* —

BOLD ILLUSION 3 ch.g. Grey Mirage 128–Savette (Frigid Aire) (1980 5fg 5f⁴ 5f 5f⁴ 6g 7fg 7d 7fg⁴ 8.2s 7.2s 8d 1981 8s 8s 8f 8fg) sturdy gelding; only poor form, including in sellers; should stay 1m; blinkered final start. *A. W. Jones.* —

BOLD IMAGE 4 b. or br.c. Balidar 133–Darinda (Darius 129) (1980 7f 6fg* 5f 5f 6fg 1981 6s 6f 6f 7fg 8f² 8fg 8fg 8d 8d⁴) useful-looking colt; shows quite a bit of knee action; fair handicapper nowadays; suited by 1m; seems to act on any going; unseated rider leaving stalls second and fourth starts; inconsistent; sold 4,000 gns Newmarket Autumn Sales and is to be trained by W. Hastings-Bass. *J. Winter.* **80**

BOLD JACK 7 ch.g. Bold Lad (Ire) 133–Gallissa (El Gallo 122) (1980 NR 1981 17.1d 8fg 10fg) poor performer nowadays; stays 1½m; best form on a sound surface; has worn blinkers. *D. Elsworth.* —

BOLDLY GO 3 b.c. Realm 129–Kilcarn Lass 74 (Bold Lad, Ire 133) (1980 5d 6d 1981 5d³ 5.8g 5.8f³ 6f⁴ 6f⁴ 5fg 5g 6g) workmanlike colt; in frame in maiden races and a handicap; stays 6f; swerved leaving stalls seventh start. *R. Akehurst.* **61**

BOLDON LADY 2 b.f. Broxted 120–Dane Valley (Simbir 130) (1981 5s 6d) May 18; first foal; dam ran only once; unquoted when well behind in end-of-season maiden events at Lingfield and Leicester. *D. Wilson.* —

BOLD POLLY 4 b.f. Bold Lad (Ire) 133–Pipeline 85 (Gulf Pearl 117) (1980 8f 8fg⁴ 8.2g 8f 8g 5d³ 5d 5d² 6d 1981 5fg² 5d* 5s 5g 5fg² 5f³ 5f 5d³ 5f 6g 5f 6fg² 6fg 5d* 5s 5g 5g) neat filly; sprint handicapper; won at Wolverhampton in May and October; stays 6f; probably acts on any going; suitable mount for a claimer. *J. Spearing.* **67**

BOLD PRINT 2 ch.c. High Line 125–Star Story 117 (Red God 128§) (1981 6d 6fg) Feb 19; attractive, lightly-made colt; half-brother to 1980 2-y-o 5f winner Hot Press (by Hotfoot) and several other winners; dam prolific winner at 5f and 6f; 50/1, always outpaced but showed ability when 5½ lengths fifth of 6 to Custer in Washington Singer Stakes at Newbury in August, first race for 2 months; will stay 1¼m. *F. J. Houghton.* **82**

BOLD RAIDER (FR) 3 ch.c. Bold Lad (USA)–Kalise 107 (Kashmir II 125) (1980 6fg 7d⁴ 7g² 1981 7g 8fg 10g 8g* 10d 10.2g) big, rangy, quite attractive colt; showed very useful form in good company as a 2-y-o; rather disappointing in 1981, but just got up to win by short head from Naif in 9-runner maiden race at Sandown in July (short-priced favourite); had stiff task and wasn't disgraced when fifth of 7 behind Oratavo in handicap at Lingfield next time; stays 1¼m; sold 3,000 gns Newmarket Autumn Sales. *R. Hern.* **94**

BOLD SARACEN (USA) 2 b. or br.c. Forli–Mohmond (Jaipur) (1981 5s 5.8d² 5.3f³ 5f² 7h 5g* 5s²) Mar 28; $130,000Y; small, lengthy, quite attractive colt; good mover; half-brother to several winners, notably Deerslayer (by Tom Rolfe), a smart winner at up to 1¼m; dam never ran; favourite when winning 15-runner maiden race at Bath in September by ½ length from High Poppa; ran well in a nursery at Folkestone next time out; stays 5.8f (swerved at start when always behind over 7f); best form with some give in the ground. *P. Walwyn.* **85**

BOLD SCUFFLE 3 b.c. Bold Lad (Ire) 133–Cloe (Shantung 132) (1980 5f 5s² 6g⁴ 6g 6d⁴ 5g* 1981 5s 6s* 6fg⁴ 6g 6g 6s* 6fg* 6f² 6g 6d³ 5f 5s 5g*(dis)) useful-looking colt; successful in handicaps at Stockton in April, Haydock in May, and Newmarket in June, making all and holding on gamely by a short head from Steel Pass on last-named course; also won at Doncaster in November from Northern Eclipse, but edged quite badly to his left and was disqualified; ran some moderate races too; suited by 6f; acts on any going. *R. Hollinshead.* **92**

BOLD SELECTION (USA) 5 b.g. Raja Baba–Slogan (Lurullah) (1980 NR 1981 12fg 18g) big gelding; poor performer nowadays; stays 1½m; good mount for an inexperienced rider. *J. Wilson.* —

BOLD TREATY 4 b.f. Welsh Saint 126–Treatise (Bold Lad, Ire 133) (1980 NR 1981 12g 8g 13.4fg) ex-Irish filly; little worthwhile form, including in a seller; unlikely to stay 1½m. *R. Morris.* —

BOLD TYPE 3 ch.g. Grundy 137–Thalassa 94 (Appiani II 128) (1980 NR —
1981 10s 11.7g 16.9s 16g 16g 12g)   big, strong gelding; first foal; dam won over
middle distances in England and France; poor maiden; stays 1½m; blinkered
fifth start; trained first 3 outings by P. Walwyn. *C. Austin.*

BOLDWIN 3 ch.g. Song 132–Final Game 83 (Pardao 120)   (1980 5s 5d 6s 7d⁴   **52** d
5.3fg 6s 8fg 5d   1981 5s 5d* 5f 5fg 5fg 5fg 6g 6g 6fg 5g 7s 6g)   neat, strong gelding; turns his front feet in; won poor maiden event at Wolverhampton in April;
in rear in varied company afterwards, including sellers; stays 7f; often blinkered
(didn't wear them when successful); gives impression he's not an ideal mount
for an apprentice. *R. Ward.*

BOLIVAR BABY 2 b.f. Gay Fandango 132–Readies (Red God 128§)   (1981   **95**
6d² 5g² 5fg³ 5g* 5g³ 5.3d* 6v*)   Apr 11; 12,000Y; quite attractive filly; good
walker; fourth foal; dam ran once; successful in maiden and minor events at
Wolverhampton and Brighton in September and in nursery at Kempton in
October; put up a game effort under top weight at Kempton, staying on really
well to catch Lingreta close home; will probably stay 1m; acts well on heavy
going; apprentice ridden to 2 of her wins; consistent. *P. Cole.*

BOMBIL 2 b.g. The Brianstan 128–Bombay Duck 65 (Ballyciptic 122)   (1981   **83**
5d 5s⁴ 6fg 7fg² 6g 6g³ 7f* 8f⁴ 7fg)   Feb 19; neat gelding; first foal; dam won
over 13f; looked to have good chance at weights in nursery at Wolverhampton
in August and stayed on under hard driving to win going away by 4 lengths
from Robout; ran well in similar race next time out; suited by 7f and 1m, and
will probably stay further; acts on firm going. *P. Rohan.*

BOMBSHELL (FR) 2 b.f. Ashmore 125–Broadway Dancer 131 (Northern   — p
Dancer)   (1981 6d)   second foal; half-sister to fairly useful maiden Behave
(by Brigadier Gerard); dam won Prix Morny by 6 lengths; easy favourite,
kept on after starting none too well when about 7 lengths eighth of 25 to Dev
in maiden event at Doncaster in October; lacks scope but may do better over
further in 1982. *H. Cecil.*

BON CHAT 3 br.c. Dubassoff–Kitten 102 (Pardal 130)   (1980 NR   1981 12g   —
13.3d 16fg 15.5f)   big, useful-looking colt; half-brother to useful middle-distance
stayer Grand Chat (by Grand Roi) and fairly useful middle-distance winner
Mon Chat (by Great Nephew); dam best at up to 7f; soundly beaten in maiden
races; pulled up lame on final start; trained part of season by G. Lewis. *N.
Callaghan.*

BOND DEALER 4 gr.g. Habat 127–Sounion 69 (Vimy 132)   (1980 8d³ 8.2s*   **61**
10d⁴ 10f³ 10fg 10f 8.3d 11.7g   1981 10d 8d 8v 8s⁴ 7g³ 7.6fg* 7fg³ 8g² 8fg* 10fg
8h³ 10f 10g)   good-looking gelding; made all in apprentice handicaps at Lingfield
in July and Salisbury in August; stays 1¼m; acts on any going; suitable mount
for an apprentice; best in blinkers. *B. Swift.*

BOND HOUSE 2 ch.c. Tumble Wind–Rold Gold (Bold Combatant)   (1981   —
5s 5fg 8s 7d 6g)   Feb 2; IR 4,300Y; big colt; second foal; half-brother to 1980
2-y-o 5f winner Love For Money (by Be Friendly); dam won over 9f at 2 yrs
in France; poor form in maiden races; should stay 1m. *D. H. Jones.*

BONFIRE NIGHT 2 ch.f. Jimmy Reppin 131–Firework Party 115 (Roan   —
Rocket 128)   (1981 5g 8s)   Mar 29; first foal; dam, very useful at up to 1m,
is half-sister to good fillies Example, Amphora and Expansive; 10/1 when
distant sixth of 17 to Barfoot in maiden race at Warwick in October, second
outing; sold 5,000 gns Newmarket Autumn Sales. *I. Balding.*

BONITO 4 ch.g. Bonne Noel 115–Meadow Rhapsody (Ragusa 137)   (1980 10f   **45**
10s 8fg 8g⁴ 6s 8d 8d   1981 12.2fg 11.7d 8fg 10fg 10f³ 11.5d⁴ 8d 10f)   leggy,
close-coupled gelding; plating-class maiden; will stay well; seems to act on any
going; sold 1,200 gns Ascot November Sales. *G. Thorner.*

BONNE BAISER 2 ch.f. Most Secret 119–Condonna 92 (Constable 119)   **88**
(1981 5s* 5g* 5d³ 5d 5fg 5d² 5s* 5g²)   Apr 23; 1,000Y; half-sister to 1m and
15f winner Paratus (by Firestreak); dam 5f winner at 2 yrs; successful in maiden
auction event at Hamilton and minor event at Edinburgh in April; also ran well
in nurseries in the autumn and dead-heated with Four Marks after making nearly
all in 13-runner event at Warwick; will stay 6f; acts on soft going; suitable
mount for an apprentice. *A. Jarvis.*

BONNIE CHARLIE 3 br.c. Mummy's Pet 125–Aberdonia 71 (Alycidon 138)   **95**
(1980 5fg³ 6fg² 6d* 6g³   1981 7s 8f 7.2f 8fg 7fg 8fg 8d 8d 8v³)   good-bodied
colt; not a good walker; had stiff task under top weight and ran well when

about 7 lengths sixth of 18 behind stable-companion Olympic Glory in Britannia Stakes (Handicap) at Royal Ascot in June on second start; 9 lengths third to Princes Gate in handicap at Kempton in October; disappointing in between; stays 1m; acts on any going; dwelt and was always struggling when apparently intended as a pacemaker for To-Agori-Mou on sixth start; sold to BBA (Italia) 6,200 gns Newmarket Autumn Sales. *G Harwood.*

BONNIE'S DELIGHT   2 br.f. Idiot's Delight 115–Bonnie Bladnoch (Lord of   —
Verona 120)   (1981 5fg 5d 7g 6d)   Apr 27; half-sister to very useful staying hurdler Garliestown and leading point-to-pointer Glasserton (both by Sea Wolf); seemingly of little account herself. *T. Taylor.*

BONNY BASSETT   2 b.f. Gold Form 108–Lady Cortina 80 (Cortachy 107)   54
(1981 5g* 5f 6d 5fg)   May 3; 420F; narrow filly; sister to 1980 2-y-o 5f winner Ruswarp, and half-sister to a winner; dam won at up to 1m; plater; attracted no bid after winning 6-runner race at Redcar in May by ½ length from Calsong; creditable sixth to Erroll's Boy in nursery at Redcar in September on fourth start, best subsequent effort; form only at 5f; has worn bandages. *D. Garraton.*

BONNY BLINK   3 gr.f. Jimsun 121–Patel 101 (Constable 119)   (1980 5f 8fg 5s   —
1981 7g 12g 12.2g 10f 13.8f)   poor mover; soundly beaten in maiden races and sellers; sometimes blinkered. *Hbt Jones.*

BONNYBRIDGE   3 br.f. Home Guard 129–Marypark 93 (Charlottown 127)   61
(1980 6fg 7d⁴   1981 10s⁴ 7fg 8.2g³ 8.2f 8.2s)   quite a useful sort; in frame in maiden race and handicap at Nottingham; will be suited by a return to middle distances; ran poorly final start; sold 3,700 gns Newmarket December Sales. *B. Hobbs.*

BONNY GOLD   3 br.c. Goldhill 125–Politely 55 (Polic 126)   (1980 5f 6g 6s³   62
7g 7f 7fg* 7g 8f⁴ 8.2g 8d* 8.2s⁴ 7v   1981 10s⁴ 8g 8g² 9s 8fg 9g⁴ 10f 10fg 8g 8d³ 11d 8s)   strong colt who carries plenty of condition; good walker; ran best race for some time when third to Winart in handicap at Pontefract in October; ran moderately afterwards; stays 1m well; acts on any going. *K. Stone.*

BONOL   4 b.c. Ridan–Lynda's Own (Schapiro 99)   (1980 7d* 7d* 8f⁴   1981 8s²   114
8d⁴ 9g 10.2g* 12g² 10fg 10fg² 11g)   strong, good-bodied colt; good walker; very useful performer; cracked a bone in hind leg after winning 2 of his 3 races in 1980, including Northern Free Handicap; showed himself better than ever at 4 yrs, putting up a splendid performance to beat Running Rocket by 2½ lengths in £9,300 Sporting Chronicle Spring Handicap at Doncaster in May; ran well most other starts, including when second to Cracaval in £7,200 race at Doncaster, fourth to Saher under 10-0 in William Hill Lincoln Handicap on same course, second to Baz Bombati in well-contested minor event at Beverley and length second of 4 to Magesterial in Land of Burns Stakes at Ayr; evidently stays 1½m; suited by some give in the ground; best on a galloping track; tailed off final start. *M. H. Easterby.*

Sporting Chronicle Spring Handicap, Doncaster—Bonol puts up a splendid performance to beat the grey Running Rocket and Rhyme Royal

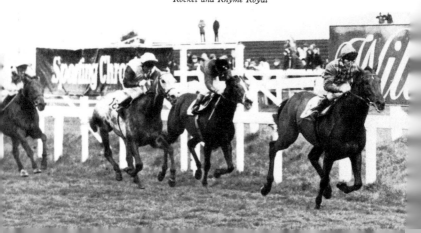

Criterium de Saint-Cloud—Bon Sang wins from Marcao

BON SANG (FR) 2 ch.c. Gyr 131–La Caldera (Mourne 126) (1981 7d* 8s* **121** 10v 10s*)

The French rarely send their very best for the Derby because of its clash with the Prix du Jockey-Club. Since Sea-Bird II's year only one French-trained horse, Empery, has won the Derby, and he was sent to Epsom to avoid a clash with his superior stable-companion Youth who took the Prix du Jockey-Club four days after Empery's Derby win. Some French trainers have an aversion to running horses abroad but Bon Sang's trainer is not among them and it is possible that Bon Sang, one of the best staying two-year-olds in France in 1981, will be in the Derby line-up. His presence would be more than wel-come: he looks a high-class racehorse in the making. Bon Sang won three of his four races, including the Prix des Chenes at Longchamp over a mile in Septem-ber and the Criterium de Saint-Cloud over a mile and a quarter in November. Both events enjoy pattern-race status, the former Group 3 and the latter Group 2. With a small race at Chantilly under his belt, Bon Sang ran out a comfortable winner at Longchamp, winning by two lengths and the same from Tampero and Ypsilon; he had a stiffer task and put up a better performance at Saint-Cloud, taking the lead with about a furlong and a half to go, after being close to the leaders from the start, and holding off Marcao and the filly Coussika by a length and a half and three lengths.

		Sea-Bird II	Dan Cupid
	Gyr	(ch 1962)	Sicalade
	(ch 1967)	Feria	Toulouse Lautrec
Bon Sang (Fr)		(b 1956)	Feira de Rio
(ch.c. Apr 27, 1979)		Mourne	Vieux Manoir
	La Caldera	(ch 1954)	Ballynash
	(ch 1965)	Love's Way	Honeyway
		(ch 1960)	Careless Love

Bon Sang's sire, the best son of the mighty Sea-Bird, was a top-class middle-distance performer, runner-up to Nijinsky in the Derby, but he was an awkward customer to handle in his races and frequently worked himself up into a nervous state beforehand. Bon Sang has also shown a tendency to become excitable; his only poor run, in the Prix de Conde at Longchamp in October, came after he got very stirred up in the preliminaries. If Bon Sang is saddled for the Derby, there is sure to be speculation about his ability to handle the so-called Epsom 'ordeal'—the mobbing in the crowded paddock, the lengthy parade and the long trail in Indian file across the course to the start—but Gyr himself survived it, as have other notably temperamental types, and it's our view that the importance of placid temperament in a Derby horse is generally much over-stated. Gyr's stud career has been a fiasco: his problem has been one of very poor fertility and, after standing in England and France, he is now in Australia; the Dante Stakes winner Hobnob and the Chester Cup winner Arapahos are probably his best-known runners in Britain. Bon Sang's dam, who ran once as a two-year-old, had bred two other winners in France, the useful Dernier

Tango (by Tapalque), a winner three times at around two miles as a three-year-old, and the modest Coudray (by Sherluck), successful in a seven-furlong seller as a two-year-old and afterwards a winner in Sweden. The second dam Love's Way didn't race but the third dam Careless Love, a half-sister to Vareta the dam of Zeddaan, was a useful middle-distance performer and is the dam of six minor winners in Britain and Ireland. Bon Sang, a rangy colt, should be suited by a mile and a half; he has so far raced only on soft ground but Gyr, as well as Hobnob and Arapahos, acted on any going. *M. Saliba, France.*

BONZOLENA 2 ch.f. Air Trooper 115–Aberdeen Lassie 102 (Aberdeen 109) — (1981 6fg 5g 7d 7g) May 19; 4,000Y; stocky filly; second foal; dam won from 5f to 7f at 2 yrs; behind in maiden and minor events in the South; should be suited by 7f. *Mrs R. Lomax.*

BOODLEBIRD (USA) 2 b.f. Plenty Old–Curtain Raiser (Duel) (1981 5g 58 5d 5g 5fg 5fg) Mar 14; 7,400Y; big, rangy filly; dam won 12 races at up to 1m in USA; plating-class maiden; should be suited by 6f +; sweated up final start. *D. Whelan.*

BORDER BROOK 4 b.g. Forlorn River 124–Kelso Girl (Royal Palm 131) 66 (1980 7v* 10s² 10g 8fg³ 8f* 8g² 8fg⁴ 1981 8v 8fg⁴) plain, workmanlike gelding; burly both starts in 1981 and wasn't seen out after May; stays 1¼m; acts on any going; game. *W. C. Watts.*

BORDER GIRL 2 b. or br.f. Mummy's Pet 125–Kelso Girl (Royal Palm 131) — (1981 6f 8fg) Apr 29; small filly; half-sister to several winners, including 7f and 1m winner Border Brook (by Forlorn River); dam never ran; unquoted when behind in maiden races at Thirsk in July and Beverley in September. *W. C. Watts.*

BORDER KNIGHT 6 br.g. Targowice 130–Bruntlaw 94 (Bounteous 125) — (1980 12f² 10.5f⁴ 10fg² 11g* 12fg* 10fg² 12g 12.2fg 12g 11fg⁴ 1981 10fg 12.2g 11d) middle-distance handicapper; well beaten in 1981; acts on any going; often wears blinkers; sometimes sweats up; good mount for an apprentice. *J. Haldane.*

BOREAS 6 br.g. Boreen (Fr) 123–Great Aunt 74 (Great Nephew 126) (1980 34 12d 12h 12fg 16fg 12g 13.8f³ 16g 15.8g⁴ 15.8d 15d 1981 15.8g 9g 10.6s 10.6s³ 12f 15fg 13.8fg) poor plater; stays 1¾m; acts on any going; usually wears blinkers. *S. Nesbitt.*

BOREHAM DOWN 2 b.g. High Top 131–Woodwind 103 (Whistling Wind 123) 78 (1981 5g 7g 7fg 7fg) Feb 20; 9,000Y; big, rangy gelding; second foal; half-brother to 3-y-o 1¼m to 2m winner Bulldozer (by Busted); dam, half-sister to very smart sprinter Le Johnstan, won twice over 6f at 2 yrs; prominent 3 times in maiden and minor events; will be suited by 1m; the type to do better at 3 yrs. *W. Hastings-Bass.*

BORIOLI 3 ch.g. Bustino 136–Stardom 75 (Hornbeam 130) (1980 NR 1981 — 12g 14f) 21,000F, 36,000Y; robust gelding; half-brother to 4 winners, including fairly useful middle-distance performer Tolstoy (by Reform); dam, half-sister to Irish Oaks winner Discorea, won over 13f; showed signs of ability in maiden races at Yarmouth in June, on second start finishing 9 lengths fifth to Bay of Mist (probably still in need of race); gelded subsequently. *L. Cumani.*

BORN HERO 2 br.c. Blakeney 126–Regal Lady 93 (Relko 136) (1981 8g*) 98 p Feb 22; robust, attractive colt; brother to Oaks third Britannia's Rule; dam won at up to 13f and is half-sister to Vaguely Noble; 15/2, won 29-runner maiden race at Newmarket in October rather impressively, always travelling smoothly and needing to be pushed out only with hands and heels to win by ¾ length from Pedometer (who raced on opposite side of course); will stay 1½m +; looks certain to develop into a very useful 3-y-o. *W. Stoute.*

BOSSALL 5 br.g. Warpath 118–Miss Barbara 87 (Le Dieu d'Or 119) (1980 — 10f 10fg 11g⁴ 12d* 11fg 14.6fg³ 16g* 16.1s 18d 1981 18fg) lengthy, useful sort; good walker; staying handicapper; acts on a firm and a soft surface; wears blinkers. *Mrs J. Pitman.*

BOSSANOVA BOY 2 b.c. Rhodomantade 110–Samba 69 (Sammy Davis 129) — (1981 7d) May 10; third foal; half-brother to successful 3-y-o 5f performer Sammy Bear (by Rupert Bear); dam won over 5f; unquoted when not in first 10 in 22-runner minor event won by Starbells at Chepstow in October. *P. Makin.*

BOTTISHAM 3 ch.c. Moulton 128–Relkalim 102 (Relko 136) (1980 6d 7.6g 54 8d 1981 10.5s 8.2s⁴ 7d 8f³ 8fg³ 8fg 8d 8d) robust, short-legged colt; ran best races when third in maiden race at Pontefract in June and handicap at Kempton (apprentice ridden) in July; should stay at least 1¼m; seems suited by a sound surface; sold to W. Marshall 3,900 gns Newmarket Autumn Sales. *H. Wragg.*

BOTTLE TOP 3 b.c. High Top 131–Bananaquit 103 (Prove It) (1980 7f 6d **64** 1981 6g³ 6g* 7g 7f⁴ 8fg 8g 6d) lengthy colt; had to be really hard ridden to hold Josephina Bin by a neck in maiden race at Ayr in May; stays 7f; blinkered last 2 starts; sold 4,600 gns Newmarket Autumn Sales. *H. T. Jones.*

BOUILLONNANTE (FR) 2 b.f. Lithiot–Elyade (Chimistgris) (1981 6fg³ **108** 7g* 7f⁴ 8d² 8d 8v²) second foal; dam ran once in France; ran well in several pattern races after winning maiden race at Saint-Cloud in July, finishing 1½ lengths fourth to Exclusive Order in Prix du Calvados at Deauville, 4 lengths second of 8 to Play It Safe in Prix d'Aumale at Chantilly, 6 lengths sixth to Play It Safe in Prix Marcel Boussac at Longchamp and 2 lengths second of 9 to Coussika in Prix des Reservoirs, again at Longchamp; will stay 1¼m; acts on any going. *J. Laumain, France.*

BOUKAYR 2 b.c. Kouban–Busarella (Busted 134) (1981 6fg 6g 7fg⁴ 8d²) **74** Mar 31; leggy colt; first foal; dam, from excellent family, ran only once; left his previous form behind when tried over 1m in 15-runner maiden race at Bath in October, going down by 3 lengths to The Nub; will be well suited by middle distances. *F. J. Houghton.*

BOUNDARY BAY 3 b.c. Jukebox 120–Class Poet (Arts and Letters) (1980 **94** 6g 6s 6d 7.9s³ 6s 6s* 6d³ 6.3v⁴ 1981 7s 6d³ 7s 7g³ 8s 7v⁴ 6f 5fg* 5f⁴ 6fg) strong Irish colt; led 1½f out and was driven out to beat Roman Consul by 2½ lengths in handicap at the Curragh in June; raced in top company on several occasions, including in Airlie/Coolmore Irish 2,000 Guineas at the Curragh (eighth of 13 to Kings Lake), and Cork and Orrery Stakes at Royal Ascot (in rear behind The Quiet Bidder); not seen out after July; effective at 5f and stays 1m; acts on any going; blinkered last 3 outings. *M. O'Toole, Ireland.*

BOUNTY BAY 2 b.f. Pitcairn 126–Hark Hark 75 (Sing Sing 134) (1981 5d³ **74** 6s) Apr 4; 27,000Y; strong, quite attractive filly; half-sister to 2 winners, including 1980 2-y-o 6f winner Banbury Cross (by Tower Walk); dam disappointing; 8/1, going on well at finish when 2½ lengths third of 16 to Kash-In in maiden race at Bath in October; had stiffer task and was bit slowly into stride when remote sixth of 15 over 6f (should be suited by trip). *I. Balding.*

BOUNTY SEEKER 4 br.f. Pitcairn 126–Miss Lomond 74 (Preciptic 122) **—** (1980 8fg 1981 12s 12g 8d 10fg 10s 10s) leggy filly; poor form, including in a seller; seems to stay 1¼m; has sweated up. *R. Carter.*

BOURGEONETTE 2 b.f. Mummy's Pet 125–Enlighten (Twilight Alley 133) **78** (1981 7fg² 7g 7f² 7fg³) Apr 20; 8,200Y; strong, good-bodied filly; half-sister to fairly useful 1¼m winner Godoliero (by Green God); dam poor maiden; second twice, going down by 1½ lengths to Clare Island after getting well behind in £3,800 event at Sandown in July and running Fol Hardi to 2½ lengths in 10-runner maiden race at Yarmouth the following month; seems to have inherited a fair amount of stamina from her maternal grandsire and will be suited by 1m; below her best final outing. *G. Pritchard-Gordon.*

BOURIENNE 3 b.f. Bolkonski 134–Blanche Hardy (Ribot 142) (1980 5d **55** 5g 5.8f³ 6s 7g³ 8d³ 8d⁴ 1981 8s 9s 8g² 8g 8f 9fg² 10h⁴ 9g* 10s⁴ 8s* 7g) small, lightly-made filly; plater; attracted no bid after winning at Wolverhampton in September (awarded race on disqualification of My Bluette) and Warwick in October; stays 1¼m; acts on any going. *D. H. Jones.*

BOUZY ROSE 3 b.f. Roi Soleil 125–Scoop (Bleep-Bleep 134) (1980 5g 8g 6d **—** 1981 12g 11.7fg 16.5fg) fair sort; well behind in maiden and minor events and a handicap. *B. Hills.*

BOVEY BELLS 3 b.f. Supreme Sovereign 119–Canteen Katie (King's Troop 118) **50** (1980 5.8fg 5.8f 1981 5d 7s³ 8f 10.1g) fair sort; third to S. D. Demo in seller at Kempton in May, first form; dwelt final start. *B. Wise.*

BOWDEN 3 b.g. St Paddy 133–Signora (Botticelli 129) (1980 NR 1981 12s) **—** big, useful-looking gelding; half-brother to winners abroad; dam never ran; 33/1 when last of 10 behind Only A Shanty in moderately-contested maiden race at Newbury in October (never going well). *I. Dudgeon.*

BOWSCAR 2 ch.f. Gallo Gallante 96–Judy Barton (Mummy's Pet 125) (1981 5g* **60** 5d*) Mar 4; strong filly; first foal; dam of little account; attracted no bid after winning sellers at Catterick in July (from Sallwah) and Haydock in August (by a head from Orp Baltic); stays 6f; sold 1,500 gns Doncaster October Sales. *W. Haigh.*

BOWTHATCH 2 br.c. Thatch 136–Sally Bowles 87 (Blakeney 126) (1981 —
7g 7g 8s) May 6; compact colt; first foal; dam, half-sister to smart sprinter
Nevermore, ran twice at 2 yrs; unquoted when behind in sizeable fields of
maidens. *D. Dale.*

BOXBERGER BEAUTY (HOL) 2 ch.f. Filandre–Cook (Hail to All) (1981 ?
7g 6.5g⁴ 9fg) Apr 9; fair sort; half-sister to Dutch Derby winner Boxberger
Cook (by Mummy's Pet) and Dutch St Leger winner Boxberger Bloem (by
Track Spare), both no better than modest performers in this country; dam won
at up to 6f in USA, including a claiming event; 40/1 and burly, wasn't given a
hard time once chance had gone when distant sixth of 11 to Big Trouble in
maiden race at Yarmouth in July; very close fourth of 9 to stable-companion
Boxberger Dream at Duindigt, Holland, the following month; should stay 1m+.
M. Ryan.

BOXBERGER BOY 3 b.g. The Brianstan 128–Dolphinetta 88 (Gulf Pearl ?
117) (1980 NR 1981 9d 11.5f 10fg 12g² 10d 14fg⁴) strong gelding; fourth
foal; half-brother to successful jumper Sea Image (by Our Mirage); dam 1m
winner; 2¼ lengths second to Ishamo in Dutch Derby at Duindigt in July,
possibly best effort; stays 1¾m. *M. Ryan.*

BOXBERGER CADKO (HOL) 3 ch.c. Cadmus 124–Cook (Hail to All) (1980 —
NR 1981 10fg 8g 9g 12fg 12g 14.5g 15.5s 10g) sturdy colt; half-brother to Dutch
Derby winner Boxberger Cook (by Mummy's Pet) and Dutch St Leger winner
Boxberger Bloem (by Track Spare), both no better than modest performers
in this country; dam won at up to 6f in USA, including a claiming event; well
beaten in maiden and minor races (including an apprentice event) here and
Dutch 2,000 Guineas, Dutch Derby and Dutch St Leger at Duindigt; has worn
blinkers. *M. Ryan.*

BOXBERGER CAPRI (HOL) 3 ch.f. Cadmus 124–Crepella (Crepello 136) ?
(1980 7fg 7fg 6.5g 9g 6.5g² 9g² 1981 9s 9g³ 12g 12g³ 14.5g³) workmanlike filly;
half-sister to middle-distance winners in France by Charlottown and Blue
Tom; dam unraced daughter of smart Toscanella; third behind Marmorera
in Dutch 1,000 Guineas and Dutch Oaks and behind Ishamo in Dutch St Leger,
all at Duindigt; stays 1¾m. *M. Ryan.*

BOXBERGER CLIO (HOL) 2 b. or br.c. Filandre–Clio (Riboprince 118) (1981 ?
5d 6fg 7g 6.5fg 9g 6.5v 9v²) Feb 21; compact Dutch-bred colt; in rear in maiden
races here but finished second in a nursery in Holland; stays 9f; trained by M.
Ryan first four starts. *P. van Bloemen Waanders, Holland.*

BOXBERGER DREAM (HOL) 2 ch.f. My Swanee 122–Dolphinetta 88 ?
(Gulf Pearl 117) (1981 6fg 6.5g* 9fg⁴) Mar 21; lengthy, workmanlike filly;
half-sister to useful jumper Sea Image (by Our Mirage); dam 1m winner; unquoted and backward when tailed off in 15-runner maiden race won by Pomegranate at Yarmouth; came out best in tight finish to Clingendaal-ren at Duindigt,
Holland, in August, getting home by a nose from Boxberger Speed, but was
beaten 8 lengths by same horse when fourth to him in Dutch Criterium the
following month; probably stays 9f. *M. Ryan.*

BOXBERGER PRINS 6 b.g. The Brianstan 128–Queen's Ring (Royal Record —
II) (1980 11.7s 11.5g 11.7f 10s 10fg 10f 10g³ 10fg³ 10g 12g⁴ 12g⁴ 11d 8s 1981
8g⁴ 10.5d) strong, compact gelding; won 8 races in 1979; mainly disappointing
since; suited by middle-distances; acts on any going but is well suited by fast
ground; has often worn blinkers; used to have a good turn of foot; pulled up
lame final start. *P. Rohan.*

BOXBERGER RELKO (HOL) 3 br.c. Filandre–Head High 92 (Star Gazer ?
123) (1980 7g 6.5g 9g⁴ 1981 10fg 9g² 10f 14.5g 14g 10.7d²) Dutch-bred colt;
fair sort; has shown little sign of ability in this country but has been in frame
in Holland, including when 3 lengths second to Ishamo in Dutch 2,000 Guineas
at Duindigt in May; stays 11f. *M. Ryan.*

BOXBERGER RIVER 2 b.c. Ercolano 118–Montespan 83 (Roi Soleil 125) —
(1981 6g 5g 5.1d) compact colt; first foal; dam stayed 1m; in rear in maiden
races at Newmarket in July (very coltish in paddock) and Yarmouth in September (eighth of 9 to stable-companion Worlingworth); 8 lengths seventh of 9 to
stable-companion Boxberger Speed in Holland in between; bred to stay at least
1m. *M. Ryan.*

BOXBERGER SPEED 2 b.c. Lombard 126–Alison's My Girl 77 (Appiani II ?
128) (1981 6g 5g* 6.5g² 9fg*) Apr 14; second foal; dam won 1¼m seller at
2 yrs; unquoted, always struggling when behind in 26-runner maiden race

won by Tin Boy at Newmarket in July; subsequently ran well in Holland, winning Van Brienens Memoriaal by a neck from Season Raaphorst in July and Dutch Criterium by 5½ lengths from same horse in September; will be suited by 1½m. *M. Ryan.*

BOXLAW 3 b.g. Jukebox 120–April Twelfth (King's Leap 111) (1980 5fg 6s 6s 7fg 8d 7d 1981 8.3fg 8.2f) tall, leggy gelding; no sign of ability, including in a seller; has been tried in blinkers. *H. O'Neill.* —

BOY LEIGH 2 ch.c. Music Boy 124–Playbird (My Swallow 134) (1981 5d 5g 5fg) Mar 20; 2,000F, 1,300Y; first foal; dam never ran; in rear all outings, including in a seller. *P. K. Mitchell.* —

BOYNE HILL 5 b. or br.m. Baroque 128–Swing On (Sheshoon 132) (1980 9g 12fg 10fg 8g³ 10d 1981 12s) small mare; plater; stays 1m. *O. O'Neill.* —

BOY PIPER 2 br.c. Bold Lad (Ire) 133–Pipeline 85 (Gulf Pearl 117) (1981 6g) Apr 4; 6,600Y; half-brother to 3 winners, including fairly useful Messenger of Peace (by Simbir), successful at around 1m; dam won over 6f at 2 yrs; 16/1 when ninth of 18 behind Music Lover in maiden event at Newmarket in October. *F. J. Houghton.* —

BOY SANDFORD 2 br.c. Sandford Lad 133–Perldia (Diatome 132) (1981 5v² 5g 6g 6g 5f 7fg 6fg) Feb 17; 4,500F, 2,200Y; first foal; dam won over 4.5f at 2 yrs in a minor event at Ayr in March but was last of 5 in seller at Hamilton in July on seventh outing. *H. Bell.* **53**

BOZ 2 gr.c. Pitcairn 126–Soft Ware (Right Royal V 135) (1981 6fg 5f) Mar 25; 7,200F, 2,400Y; fair sort; first foal; dam placed over 1¼m in French Provinces; in rear in £4,200 event at Kempton in August (speed 4f) and maiden race at Folkestone in September; sold 650 gns Doncaster November Sales. *M. Masson.* —

BRACADALE 3 b.g. The Brianstan 128–Can't Wait (Eudaemon 129) (1980 6g 6s 6fg² 6g 5.1g⁴ 1981 6fg 6f⁴ 6fg* 6fg* 6g* 5g⁴ 6f) neat, good-quartered gelding; good mover; returned to form with blinkers, winning handicaps at Kempton (impressively) and Newmarket in July and apprentice event at Nottingham in August; best form at 6f on a sound surface; ran miserably final start and had possibly had enough for time being; usually held up. *R. Armstrong.* **93**

BRACKEN GILL 3 gr.c. Ribston 104–Gill Breeze (Farm Walk 111) (1980 5f 5f³ 5f* 6fg 5fg⁴ 5d³ 5f² 5d 1981 6g 5fg) quite moderate form as a 2-y-o; well beaten in 1981; should stay 6f; best form on a sound surface and goes well on firm going. *Mrs A. Bell.* —

BRADAMANTE 5 ch.h. Royal Prerogative 119–Cracker 103 (Court Harwell 130) (1980 8d² 10g 10.4f² 8f² 10f 8d⁴ 8d 8d* 8g 8f³ 8g 8.2s 1981 7d 10.4g 8g 10fg* 10fg 11g) tall, leggy horse; won handicap at Redcar in July; stays 1¼m; possibly not at his best on really soft going; inconsistent. *Denys Smith.* **80**

BRADETTE 4 b.f. Great Nephew 126–Dashing Diana (Silver Shark 129) (1980 11fg 7f* 7fg 7f 8.3g 11.7d 12s 1981 5fg 8f 8.3g 8h) good sort; well beaten in 1981; not certain to stay 1½m; acts on any going; usually blinkered in 1980. *J. Hill.* —

BRADY 2 gr.g. Pitcairn 126–Brenda (Sovereign Path 125) (1981 8g 6g) Feb 25; 15,000F, 14,000Y; good-bodied gelding; first produce; dam unplaced 5 times in Ireland; burly when behind in large fields for maiden races at Newmarket in October and Doncaster the following month. *M. Ryan.* —

BRAE TOP 2 ch.g. Import 127–Taj Jahan 77 (Hornbeam 130) (1981 6g 6fg 6g 8g) June 9; 680F, 400 2-y-o; strong gelding; first reported living foal; dam placed over 7f at 2 yrs; unquoted when in rear in maiden races. *N. Bycroft.* —

BRAHMS AND LISZT 5 b.g. Will Somers 114§–Fancy Pants 80 (Galivanter 131) (1980 7f 7fg 1981 11d⁴ 8fg 8f) poor plater; probably doesn't stay 11f; has been tried in blinkers and a hood; trained by A. Balding first 2 starts. *W. Charles.* —

BRANCASTER 7 b.h. Huntercombe 133–Cigarette Case 89 (Faberge II 121) (1980 17.1f 12s 1981 14g) poor handicapper; stays 2m; acts on firm going; used to wear blinkers; bandaged only start in 1981. *J. Cann.* —

BRANDO 4 ch.c. Busted 134–Cafe au Lait 97 (Espresso 122) (1980 12s 12fg 16f* 16f² 16g⁴ 14d³ 14g 16d 1981 16s) leggy, lightly-made colt; fairly useful stayer at 3 yrs; tailed-off last only start in 1981 in October; probably acts on any going. *G. Thorner.* —

BRANDON CREEK 2 b.f. Be My Guest 126–La Creperie 70 (Crepello 136) **79**
(1981 7g² 7g) Apr 7; neat filly; first foal; dam stayed well; clear of remainder
when 4 lengths second of 16 to odds-on Tants in maiden race at Leicester in
October; 12/1 for 29-runner event at Newmarket later in month but dropped
right out in final 2f to finish well beaten behind Chalon; will stay 1m. *P. Cole.*

BRASS CHANGE 3 gr.g. Town Crier 119–Brass Finisher 93 (Cash and Courage —
116) (1980 6d 1981 7s 7s 8d 6fg⁴ 8g 11.7fg) neat, rather lightly-made gelding;
blinkered and dropped in class when running respectably in sellers on fourth and
fifth outings; stays 1m; sold out of A. Bailey's stable 1,750 gns Newmarket May
Sales after fifth start. *I. Dudgeon.*

BRASSY 3 b.f. Bold Lad (Ire) 133–Monaco Melody 103 (Tudor Melody 129) **79**
(1980 5fg² 5f³ 5f⁴ 6g⁴ 6g 1981 5f* 6fg 5.3fg* 5f³(dis) 5fg² 5f* 5fg² 5d) lengthy
filly; successful in minor event at Chepstow in June and handicaps at Brighton in
August and Chepstow again in September; apprentice ridden on first 2 occasions;
stays 6f, but is probably better at 5f; acts well on firm going; wears blinkers.
H. T. Jones.

BRAUGHING 4 b.c. Martinmas 128–Lucasta (High Hat 131) (1980 7f 8.5f⁴ **105**
8fg 12f 8d 8s 8f² 10g 8d* 1981 8s³(dis) 9g 8g 8s 8.5d⁴ 8f 8f² 8fg³ 8fg 9d 8fg 9g*)
strong, round-barrelled colt; useful handicapper; returned to form in William
Hill Cambridgeshire at Newmarket in October, leading 2f out and staying on well
to beat Baronet by 2¼ lengths; stays 9f well; acts on any going; sometimes
sweats up; blinkered once at 3 yrs; inconsistent; racing in USA. *C. Brittain.*

BRAUN 3 ch.c. Joshua 129–Bun (Never Say Die 137) (1980 NR 1981 10g **51**
16fg³ 12.2fg 14.6f) big colt; second foal; dam never ran; had anything but a
clear run and looked unlucky when third behind Minsden's Image in poor maiden
race at Newcastle in June; well beaten both subsequent outings; suited by 2m;
probably needs a galloping track. *Miss S. Hall.*

BRAVADO (GER) 2 b.c. Alpenkonig–Babylon (Priamos 123) (1981 6fg⁴ **94**
6g* 6f² 7g*) compact, workmanlike colt; half-brother to German winner
Blau-Rot (by Dancer's Image); dam won 9f Nereide-Rennen and was second in
1975 German Oaks; won 18-runner maiden race at Newcastle in July by 4
lengths and got home by a neck from Crackhill in minor event at Catterick in
October; the type to make a useful handicapper over middle distances. *M.
Stoute.*

BRAVE BRIDGE 2 b.g. Jolly Me 114–Spaniard's Darling (Darling Boy 124) —
(1981 8g) May 2; 700F; 1,000Y; brother to a winner in Malaya and half-brother
to winners here and abroad; dam of little account; unquoted when never-
dangerous 7¼ lengths fifth of 15 to Spring Lane in maiden race at Edinburgh in
September; probably stays 1m. *Miss L. Siddall.*

BRAVE FELLOW 7 b.g. Giolla Mear 113–Mirastar (Miralgo 130) (1980 —
12.3s* 12.3f² 12f 16d 13g³ 1981 12s) won maiden race at Newcastle at 6 yrs;
didn't impress in paddock and ran moderately only start in 1981 in March;
stays 13f well; acts on any going. *J. Fitzgerald.*

BRAVE GEM 3 b.c. Sparkler 130–Fearless 77 (Derring-Do 131) (1980 6d —
1981 7s 9s 6g⁴ 7g 6s) lengthy colt; ran best race when fourth behind Dawn's
Delight in handicap at Newbury in June (nearest finish); best form at 6f but is
bred to stay at least 1m; sold to M. Chapman 760 gns Newmarket Autumn
Sales. *P. Cundell.*

*William Hill Cambridgeshire Handicap, Newmarket—the season's most
valuable handicap is won by 50/1-shot Braughing who foils Baronet's
attempt to win a third Cambridgeshire*

BRAVE HUSSAR 3 ch.g. Brigadier Gerard 144–Tirana 101 (Ragusa 137) **90**
(1980 8g 1981 11s* 12g* 10.5s 12fg) lightly-made, quite attractive gelding;
successful in maiden race at Newbury in April (beat Blare 2½ lengths) and minor
event at Kempton in May (won by ¾ length from Sass-Go), on latter course
making all and staying on really well; twice disappointed at York subsequently,
in £4,000 event won by Amyndas in May and in handicap won by Keelby
Kavalier in July; will stay 1¾m; gelded after final start. *H. Cecil.*

BRAVE KNIGHT 3 b.c. Busted 134–King's Gem 88 (King's Troop 118) **—**
(1980 NR 1981 11fg) workmanlike colt; half-brother to fairly useful 1972
2-y-o African God (by Runnymede) and 2 winners in France; dam sprinter;
always towards rear when last of 6 behind Bedford in maiden race at Kempton in
August; dead. *J. Winter.*

BRAVE MAIDEN 2 gr.f. Three Legs 128–Julie's Gi-Gi (Brave Invader) (1981 **63**
5g³ 5s 5d 6f⁴ 7g³ 8.2fg² (dis) 8d) May 1; IR 400F, resold IR 1,850Y; neat filly;
half-sister to 2 winners by Status Seeker, including 3-y-o Beechwood Seeker,
successful at up to 2½m; dam poor Irish maiden; in
frame in large fields of platers at Windsor, Newmarket and Haydock; went
down by only ½ length to Helshaw Grange on last-named in September but
hampered several of her rivals by hanging badly left and was disqualified; will
probably stay 1¼m; acts on firm going; wears blinkers. *J. Bethell.*

BRAVE SONG 2 b.c. Busted 134–Net Call 108 (Song 132) (1981 7fg 7g 7d) **—**
Apr 11; attractive colt with scope; first foal; dam seemed best at 6f; noted
running on in large fields at Salisbury (10 lengths sixth of 18 to Tulsa Flyer in
£2,600 event) in August and Leicester (seventh of 16 to Airspin in maiden race)
in September on first 2 starts; immature at 2 yrs and may do better in 1982.
J. Bethell.

BRAVE THE REEF (USA) 4 ch.c. Mill Reef 141–Gallina 120 (Raise A Native) **75**
(1980 12s² 12f² 16f 12.3s⁴ 12.3d* 12g⁴ 11.7d* 1981 13s 13s 13.1g 12g³ 12g²
13.1f² 14fg⁴ 15.8g² 16.1fg* 16.1s 18g) small, lengthy, attractive colt; beat
Athford a length in handicap at Haydock in September; stays 2m; acts on any
going; suitable mount for an inexperienced rider; genuine; sold 13,000 gns
Newmarket Autumn Sales. *I. Balding.*

BRAVO ROMEO (USA) 2 b.c. Gallant Romeo–In Succession (Bold Ruler) **—**
(1981 6fg 7g 6g) IR 36,000Y; attractive colt; half brother to American 1¼m
winner Hereditary (by Le Fabuleux); dam, who ran only twice, is from an
outstanding family and is sister to champion American 2-y-o's Bold Lad and
Successor; behind in minor and maiden events at Newmarket. *R. Armstrong.*

BRAZEN BID 2 b.f. Auction Ring 123–Parmassia (Pampered King 121) **57**
(1981 6s⁴ 5fg 6g) May 22; IR 7,400Y; small filly; fourth foal; half-sister to
middle-distance winner Bucklow Hill (by Rheingold); dam French 2-y-o 1m
winner; ran on without being knocked about when 6½ lengths fourth of 13 to
Westonbirt in maiden race at Haydock in June, first outing and only sign of
ability; will be suited by 7f and 1m; possibly needs soft going. *B. Hanbury.*

BREATHING EXERCISE 8 ch.g. Pall Mall 132–Karen Chase 82 (Will Somers **—**
114§) (1980 7d 7fg 6fg 7fg 6s 6d 6g 7.3fg 6fg 6d 7d 1981 6s 7d 8d 7g 8v 7fg 7.6g)
well-made gelding; moderate handicapper at his best but has deteriorated
markedly; stays 7f; acts on any going; has been tried in blinkers; occasionally
sweats up. *J. O'Donoghue.*

BRECQHOU BELLE 3 b.f. Roi Soleil 125–Barn Owl 73 (Space King 115) **—**
(1980 NR 1981 8.2s 8d) small filly; first reported foal; dam second over 5f
and 1½m; behind in maiden races at Nottingham in September (moved badly
to start) and Edinburgh in October. *J. Toller.*

BRECQHOU CHIEF 3 b.c. Roi Soleil 125–Miss Vanadium (Helmar) (1980 **43**
5fg 6g 8.2s 8d 1981 6g 8fg⁴ 10fg 8g² 8d 7g 8s) plater; stays 1m; has raced
with his tongue tied down. *J. Toller.*

BREEZE HILL 2 b.c. Swing Easy 126–Jester's Girl 71 (Will Somers 114§) **81**
(1981 7fg⁴ 7fg³ 7g³ 7d) Apr 11; rangy colt; very good mover; second foal;
half-brother to 5f and 6f winner Jester's Boy (by John Splendid); dam stayed
1½m; prominent all outings, finishing 6 lengths fifth of 22 to Starbells in minor
event at Chepstow in October on final appearance; will probably stay 1m.
P. Cole.

BRENAN'S GLEN 6 gr.g. Petingo 135–Clear Path (Sovereign Path 125) **—**
(1980 8s² 10fg* 8.5fg² 7s* 13g 1981 9v 8s 9d 8fg) moderate handicapper;

seventh of 24 to Dellersbeck in Irish Lincolnshire Handicap at the Curragh in April, second start and best effort in 1981; had stiffish tasks at Wolverhampton and Kempton third and fourth starts; stays 1¼m; acts on any going except very firm. *M. Kauntze, Ireland.*

BRENDAN 6 br.g. Saintly Song 128–Tigerlee 57 (Tiger 125) (1980 5v⁴ 5s 5g 5f 6fg 5fg 6g 1981 5g 7f) small gelding; plater; best at 5f; suited by some give in the ground; sometimes wears blinkers but does better without; often wears a tongue strap; suitable mount for a boy; inconsistent. *S. Nesbitt.* —

BRENHINES 2 b.f. Mount Hagen 127–Gay Surrender 70 (Sir Gaylord) (1981 5g 6f 8fg) Apr 25; short-backed filly; first foal; dam, half-sister to very smart Double-U-Jay, won over 1¼m; only plating class; looked to have run up very light on third outing (mid-September). *F. J. Houghton.* —

BRENTEX 3 gr.c. Birdbrook 110–Black Mink 83 (Gratitude 130) (1980 5g⁴ 5fg³ 5s³ 6fg 5.8f⁴ 5d³ 5f⁴ 5fg² 5f² 5d* 5g⁴ 1981 6g 5.8g 5.8g 5f 5g) neat colt; lightly raced and rather disappointing in 1981, best effort on second start when seventh to Dungeon Ghyl in handicap at Bath in May; best form at 5f; appears to act on any going; blinkered sixth and seventh starts in 1980; suited by waiting tactics; missed break fourth outing. *N. Vigors.* —

BRETON BANQUET 3 gr.g. Brittany–Nosh (Court Martial) (1980 5fg 5fg 6f 7d 7fg 6s 6g 5.1fg 6d⁴ 6fg 6g³ 8fg 8.2g 8d 1981 7s 8s 8g 7g 8.3s 6g³ 8fg 6g*) compact gelding; poor mover; plater; 33/1-winner of claiming handicap at Newmarket in August; best form at 6f; often blinkered. *W. Marshall.* **54**

BRETTON PARK 3 b.c. Mummy's Pet 125–Trickster 92 (Major Portion 129) (1980 5s⁴ 6fg⁴ 6g 5g² 5d² 6v* 6d² 1981 6g 7.2s 6s* 6f 6f* 7g 7g) strong, fair sort; has a round action; won handicaps at Carlisle and Hamilton in June; always struggling in between and never got into race either subsequent race; stays 6f well; evidently acts on and goes particularly well on soft; often blinkered (has worn them when successful). *S. Norton.* **83**

BREVET 2 b.c. Busted 134–Major Barbara 90 (Tambourine II 133) (1981 7g) Apr 26; well-made colt; good walker and quite a good mover; half-brother to several winners, notably very smart 1975 2-y-o Dame Foolish (by Silly Season); dam was at up to 7f as a 2-y-o; 16/1, showed up all the way without being unnecessarily knocked about when 8 lengths sixth of 18 to General Anders in £4,100 event at Ascot in September; could make up into a useful colt over middle distances in 1982. *P. Walwyn.* **82 p**

BREWMASTER 8 br.h. John Splendid 116–Ronelda (Tyrone 130) (1980 8.2d 9d 10fg 1981 10g) short-backed horse; poor plater; stays 1¼m; acts on any going; blinkered once; often apprentice ridden. *J. Mulhall.* —

BRIANKA 4 b.f. The Brianstan 128–Slightly Saucy 74 (Galivanter 131) (1980 7d 8v 8f 7fg 8fg 10.1g³ 10g² 12.2g³ 12g 10s 10g 1981 13.1g 11.7f) fair sort; poor maiden; suited by middle distances; blinkered once at 3 yrs; has worn bandages; sometimes has her tongue tied down. *M. McCormack.* —

BRIANS BRIDGE 2 b.f. The Brianstan 128–Villa Vera (Gilles de Retz 132) (1981 5g 5s) Apr 2; 3,000Y; sister to 1980 2-y-o 5f winner The Barons Lodge; dam won 3 times over 1½m in Ireland; in rear in Northern sellers in October; unruly in paddock second start. *Miss L. Siddall.* —

BRIAN'S STAR 6 br.h. The Brianstan 128–Claral Star 71 (Top Star 96) (1980 5s 5fg 5f² 5g 5.1f³ 5fg 5fg 5g⁴ 5g³ 5f 5d 5d 1981 5s 5s 5g*(dis) 5fg⁴ 5g⁴ 5g* 5fg 5fg 5g⁴ 5d² 5fg³ 5f 5g²) workmanlike horse; sprint handicapper; bought in 950 gns after winning apprentice seller at Carlisle in May but was subsequently disqualified when illegal substances were found in his system; landed odds in non-seller at Edinburgh in June; best form at 5f on a sound surface; wears blinkers; good mount for an apprentice. *A. Balding.* **52**

BRIANSTANWAY 4 br.c. The Brianstan 128–Carina 98 (Tamerlane 128) (1980 6s* 6fg² 6fg 6fg* 6g 6g 6s* 5g³ 6d 6s 6d⁴ 1981 8s 6s³ 6s 6g 6s 6g 6f 6g 6g³ 6fg 6s) small, compact sort; sprint handicapper; best at 6f; seems to act on any going, but goes well in the mud; has run creditably for an apprentice. *D. Nicholson.* **71**

BRIAR 3 b.f. Brigadier Gerard 144–Conciliation 98 (St Paddy 133) (1980 5f 7f⁴ 8d 1981 8.5g 8h²) strong, good-quartered filly; fair performer at 2 yrs; not seen out in 1981 after finishing ¾-length second to Steel City in apprentice event at Bath in July (short-priced favourite); stays 1m; acts on firm going. *R. Hern.* **86**

BRIDGE O'GOLD 3 b.g. Chantro 104–Auto-Speed 69 (Faberge II 121) — (1980 NR 1981 12f 8g) compact gelding; first foal; dam second over 7f at 2 yrs; in rear in maiden races at Beverley and Ayr in July. *W. Stubbs.*

BRIDSTOW 8 br.g. Breeders Dream 116–Nancy 106 (Tamerlane 128) (1980 — NR 1981 8h) plater; stays 1m; acts on firm going; has worn blinkers; has worn bandages. *G. Balding.*

BRI-EDEN 7 b.h. The Brianstan 128–Dainty Eden 53 (Orbit 106) (1980 **76** 5f² 5fg² 5fg* 5g³ 6d 5fg* 5g³ 5fg* 5d 5f 5d⁴ 1981 5fg³ 5g 5g 5g 5s 5g) sprint handicapper; has reportedly been operated on for a soft palate; best at 5f; acts on any going; has won for an amateur rider; wears bandages nowadays. *J. Berry.*

BRIGADIER GREEN 4 b.g. Brigadier Gerard 144–Queen's Parole (Worden — II 129) (1980 10.2d* 9g 12g 14f² 12f 12g 16g³ 16s⁴ 14.6fg 13g⁴ 13.8d 1981 10v 11s 9fg 13d⁴ 12s 13d) neat gelding; poor handicapper; stays well; probably acts on any going; ran badly in blinkers once in 1980; sold 720 gns Newmarket Autumn Sales. *W. H. H. Williams.*

BRIGADIER HAWK 3 b.c. Brigadier Gerard 144–Flibbertigibbet 97 (Klairon **81** 131) (1980 6g 7fg 1981 11s 10d³ 10.5s² 12f 14fg* 11g 14.6g 12g² 16s) compact, good-bodied colt; beat Sass a short head in 15-runner maiden race at Sandown in July, getting up in last stride after his rider had been hard at work from halfway; ran best subsequent race when ½-length second to King's Ride in £4,000 event at Lingfield in September; usually had stiff tasks on his other outings, including in St Leger on seventh start; will be suited by 2m; probably acts on any going. *C. Brittain.*

BRIGADIER VICTOR 3 br.c. Brigadier Gerard 144–Humming Top 92 (Tudor — Melody 129) (1980 NR 1981 10.5f 13.4g⁴ 10.2fg 15d³ 14s 12s 10.2g) 4,600Y; strong, quite attractive colt; has a very round action; second foal; dam won twice over 1¼m; still didn't look ready and wasn't knocked about when his chance had gone when about 5 lengths fourth of 15 behind Bell Rammer in maiden race at Chester in July; mainly disappointing subsequently, but ran respectably in a valuable seller on final start; suited by 13f; started slowly first outing. *J. Hanson.*

BRIGADO 2 ch.f. Brigadier Gerard 144–Selham 71 (Derring-Do 131) (1981 **87** 5g 6fg 8g*) Mar 24; 1,600Y; tall filly; first foal; dam, winner over 1m, is daughter of half-sister to So Blessed and Lucasland; apprentice ridden, showed much improved form when keeping on well to beat Ginger Tart by ½ length in 13-runner maiden race at Edinburgh in October; will stay 1¼m. *Denys Smith.*

BRIGHT EDGE 3 b.g. Sharp Edge 123–Gold Of The Day 72 (Bing II) (1980 — 5d 7d 1981 10fg 6d) lightly raced and no worthwhile form in varied company. *Mrs N. Kennedy.*

BRIGHT IMP 2 ch.f. Import 127–Star of Light 85 (Counsel 118) (1981 **64** 5f 6d 5d³) Apr 9; fair sort; half-sister to Starlight Lad (by Willipeg), a winner at up to 1¼m and quite a useful chaser; dam won at 9f and over hurdles; stayed on when 3¼ lengths third of 13 to Hazim in maiden race at Redcar in October, best effort; should be suited by 6f+. *P. Calver.*

BRIGHT MORNING 3 b. or br.g. Duc d'Orleans 76–Top of The Morning — (Bush Fire 108) (1980 NR 1981 16g 14fg) big gelding; first foal; dam, of no account on flat, won a point-to-point; tailed off in maiden races at Nottingham (ran wide on turn) and Yarmouth, both in August. *R. Thompson.*

BRIGHTON ROAD 2 ch.c. Gulf Pearl 117–Gossamer Wings 73 (The Phoenix) — (1981 7g 8g 8g) Mar 21; IR 6,600Y; strong colt; half-brother to several winners, including useful miler Floating Melody (by Tudor Melody); dam ran only at 2 yrs; unquoted and burly when behind in large fields for maiden races and a minor event at Newmarket at the back-end; the type to do better at 3 yrs. *R. Armstrong.*

BRIGHT PROMISE 3 gr.f. Balidar 133–Aabora (Don II 123) (1980 5d — 5g 6fg⁴ 6g* 6g 6d 7s 1981 6g) won maiden race at Folkestone as a 2-y-o; soundly beaten in a seller only outing of 1981 (sweating); should stay 7f; none too reliable. *D. Ringer.*

BRIGHT VIEW 2 ch.f. Hot Spark 126–Gilliflower 90 (Great Nephew 126) **110** (1981 5d 5g² 5g* 6g² 5fg* 5f³ 6f² 6f² 5g*) Apr 20; 7,400F, 5,000Y; leggy, well-grown filly; second foal; dam lightly-raced winner over 1m; made all to win maiden race at Carlisle in May and easily bettered that effort when staying on strongly to score by 2 lengths from Admiral's Princess in £2,600 event at York the following month and when ½-length winner from Blue Emmanuelle of £7,600 Whelmar Nursery at Redcar in September (ridden by 7-lb claimer); also put up useful efforts when game 1½-length second of 10 to Travel On in Group 3 Cherry Hinton Stakes at Newmarket and when ½-length second to Mydrone in £2,700 race at Thirsk on seventh and eighth outings; not sure to stay beyond 6f; acts well on firm ground; most genuine and consistent, and very useful. *T. Fairhurst.*

BRIGHT WIRE 2 ch.c. Condorcet–Fairy Tree (Varano) (1981 6g 6f 6f*) **64**
Mar 24; IR 3,900F, 2,500Y; lengthy, useful sort; half-brother to Irish 1m winner Forest Park (by Bluerullah); dam 9f winner in Ireland; well-backed favourite, showed improved form when keeping on under strong pressure to win 11-runner maiden auction event at Nottingham in June by a short head from Idle Market; will stay 1¼m. *A. Jarvis.*

BRI-GYLL 4 b.g. The Brianstan 128–Aequanimitas (Infatuation 129) (1980 —
10fg 7s 1981 5s 8g) plater nowadays; best form at 5f on soft ground; blinkered once at 2 yrs. *J. Berry.*

BRISBANE 3 ch.g. Welsh Pageant 132–Pavello 94 (Crepello 136) (1980 7f —
8g 10s 1981 12s 12fg 12d) compact, good-bodied gelding; good mover; showed ability in maiden races as a 2-y-o; had stiff tasks in handicaps in 1981 and didn't show much promise; blinkered last 2 starts; sold 1,300 gns Ascot June Sales. *J. Hindley.*

BRIT 2 b.f. Pardigras 91–Brighty (Connaught 130) (1981 8d 8s 10s) Mar 23; —
first foal; dam poor maiden; in rear in maiden races in the Midlands in October. *W. Turner.*

BRITANNIA TRAILER 2 br.f. Dawn Review 105–Senna (Sica Boy 132) **60**
(1981 5fg² 5d³ 5g³ 6fg 5fg* 6g 6g) Mar 21; 800Y; half-sister to several winners, including 3-y-o sprinter My Jem (by My Swallow); dam won over 11f in France; having first race for over 2 months when winning 5-runner seller at Windsor in August by 1½ lengths from Lady Auctioneer (no bid); well beaten when tried over 6f; blinkered nowadays; sold 660 gns Newmarket Autumn Sales. *D. H. Jones.*

BRITAVIGO 3 gr.c. Britanny–Vigoa (Vigo 130) (1980 NR 1981 8f 6f 8g) —
lengthy colt; seventh foal; dam ran only twice; behind in maiden races; sold 360 gns Ascot October Sales. *D. Dale.*

BRITISH CROWN 5 ch.g. English Prince 129–Chapeau Bleue (High Hat 131) —
(1980 10g 10.2g² 1981 12f 12g) strong gelding; only plating class; stays 1¼m; possibly unsuited by heavy going; bandaged in front both starts in 1981. *D. Elsworth.*

BRITWELL LAD (USA) 3 b.c. Son Ange–Hurricane Helen (Etonian) (1980 **63**
7fg 8g⁴ 1981 11s 10d³ 10s 12fg⁴ 11.7h 11.7fg) small, sturdy colt; good walker; in frame in maiden races; probably stays 1¼m. *P. Cole.*

BRIZLEE 5 ch.g. Take a Reef 127–Hills of Honey (Zucchero 133§) (1980 NR —
1981 14g 12f) fairly useful handicapper in 1979; well beaten both starts at 5 yrs; stays 2m; acts on any going; bandaged first outing. *B. Hobbs.*

BROADMEAD 2 br.f. Malinowski 123–Flying Spice (Charlottown 127) (1981 —
7g 6d 8.2s) Apr 1; IR 2,100 F, 3,900Y; small filly; seems of little account. *P. Butler.*

BROAD PRINCIPLE 4 b.g. Bustino 136–Hazy Idea 118 (Hethersett 134) **81**
(1980 10d* 12f³ 10.6fg 10s 13g 11.5fg⁴ 1981 10fg 12.3d* 12g 14d* 16fg³ 14.7fg 16fg 12d) strong, close-coupled gelding; excellent mover; fair handicapper; won at Chester in May and Sandown in June; seventh in valuable selling handicap at Doncaster on final start; stays well; probably acts on any going; sold 7,400 gns Newmarket Autumn Sales. *M. Stoute.*

BROADSWORD (USA) 4 b.c. Ack Ack–Cutting (Bold Ruler) (1980 12f —
12fg 14fg* 12s³ 16fg² 14g² 16g² 1981 14d) big, strong colt; useful performer at his best on flat and a good young hurdler; last of 6 to Ardross in Yorkshire Cup at York in May on only start of 1981; suited by a test of stamina; seems to act on any going; genuine. *D. Nicholson.*

BROADWAY LODGE 2 b.f. Go the Go-Between 129–Canteen Katie (King's **85**
Troop 118) (1981 5s³ 5d* 5g⁴ 5d* 5g 6d⁴ 6d² 6g 6f 6fg 6fg 6s 6s⁴) Apr 6; 600F, 300Y; leggy, lightly-made filly; half-sister to 3 winners in Italy; dam never ran;

finished strongly to win maiden race at Warwick in April and was awarded £3,400
event at Salisbury the following month because length-winner Crimson Court
carried 3 lb less than he should have done; also ran well several times over 6f,
particularly when failing by only a short head to hold off Mosso in Kingsclere
Stakes at Newbury in June; suited by 6f; seems to act on any going; game.
C. Wildman.

BROCKIE LAW 3 br.g. Bing II–Scots Pearl (Combat 123) (1980 NR 1981 —
12.3g 11f 8fg 15fg) workmanlike gelding; third foal; dam temperamental
plater; little worthwhile form in maiden races. *H. Bell.*

BROCKLEY BELLE 2 ch.f. Track Spare 125–Just Jolly 80 (Jolly Jet 111) **73**
(1981 5g 5fg 6g 6fg²) Mar 18; tall, light-framed filly; not a good mover; first foal;
dam won over 1½m and 2m on flat and up to 3m over hurdles; ran easily best race
when backed from 20/1 to 9/1 in £4,000 seller at Kempton in August, going down
by only a neck to Sweet Ecstasy after disputing lead throughout; will stay at
least 1m; sure to win if kept to selling company. *T. Marshall.*

BROCKLEY WOOD 3 ch.f. Sharp Edge 123–Hot Number 75 (Firestreak 125) —
(1980 6fg 6d 7g 6g 6s 1981 7s 8g 7fg) neat, strong filly; bad plater; sometimes
blinkered. *R. Ward.*

BRODI CRYSTAL (FR) 2 gr.c. Crystal Palace 132–Brodie (Bryan G) (1981 —
7g 8g) Feb 18; 210,000 francs Y (approx £21,000); small, rather narrow colt;
half-brother to French 3-y-o Brodie Dancer (by Dancer's Image) and to 3 winners
in France and USA; dam, from same family as Riva Ridge, won 6f claiming race
in USA at 2 yrs; unquoted when in mid-division in 29-runner maiden race won by
Born Hero at Newmarket in October, second outing; lacks scope. *L. Cumani.*

BROKEN LACE 3 ch.g. Redundant 120–Brocette (Brocade Slipper 116) —
(1980 5.8fg 1981 10.1fg 8d) strong gelding; little worthwhile form in maiden
and minor races. *Mrs N. Kennedy.*

BROKEN RAIL 2 b.c. Busted 134–First Huntress 64 (Primera 131) (1981 8s²) **77 p**
Mar 31; half-brother to several winners, notably very smart middle-distance
horse Town and Country (by Town Crier); dam of little account; third favourite,
failed by only a short head to catch Mrs Currie in 17-runner maiden race at
Warwick in October; will be well suited by middle distances; sure to win a
maiden race in 1982. *R. Hern.*

BROKEN SEAL 2 br.f. Privy Seal 108–Histoun (Behistoun 131) (1981 5g³ —
5fg 5f 8.2d 8g) Apr 26; 300Y; leggy, narrow filly; has a round action; bad plater.
C. Gray.

BRONOWSKI (USA) 2 b.c. Raja Baba–Dance Across (Sword Dancer) (1981 **93**
5g² 6fg³ 6g 5g) May 31; $125,000Y; well-made, attractive colt; good mover;
half-brother to several winners, including smart French 1m to 10.7f winner
Silver Bells (by Tambourine II); dam from same family as 2,000 Guineas winner
Baldric II; favourite on 3 of his 4 outings, putting up easily best effort when 3½
lengths third of 16 to Red Sunset in Coventry Stakes at Royal Ascot; disappointed
afterwards and was off course 3 months before final outing; ran at Ascot as
though 7f would suit him; to race in USA. *H. Cecil.*

BRONTOLINO 4 ch.g. Sandford Lad 133–Living Free 81 (Never Say Die 137) —
(1980 6s 7f 8h³ 8f 10.2g 16fg² 16s³ 16f² 15.8fg⁴ 17.1d 16d³ 14.6d 1981 17.1d 16d
16fg) small, strong gelding; good mover; staying maiden; acts on any going;
normally blinkered nowadays; usually sweats up. *G. Thorner.*

BRONZAMER 4 gr.f. Saritamer 130–Palmitin 68 (Crepello 136) (1980 7v³ **70**
7d³ 6fg³ 8f 8f² 8fg 8fg 9g 8.2g 8f 8f 8fg 1981 8f 8f 8fg 9fg 8f 7g 8.2f 8f 8s*)
small, lightly-made filly; returned to form when trotting up in handicap at
Redcar in October; stays 1m; acts on any going but is evidently ideally suited by
soft nowadays; blinkered last 2 starts. *P. Asquith.*

BRONZE MEDAL 3 ch.g. Jimmy Reppin 131–Maroon 92 (Roan Rocket 128) **82**
(1980 6d 1981 10.1f² 10.4fg³ 12fg*) rangy, quite attractive gelding; took a
while to warm up when beating More Oats by 1½ lengths in rather slowly-run
maiden race at Newbury in August; in frame earlier at Windsor and Chester
(didn't handle track at all well); stays 1½m; acts on firm going; sold 11,000 gns
Newmarket Autumn Sales. *R. Hern.*

BROOK GREEN 3 b.g. Run The Gantlet–Fortezza 106 (Botticelli 129) (1980 —
NR 1981 8g 8g 10s 10d 12.3g) good sort; half-brother to 4 winners, including
very useful 1m to 2m winner Hurrah (by Exbury) and useful 6f to 1m winner
Royal Emblem (by Reform); dam miler; well beaten in a newcomers and 4
maiden events; blinkered fourth outing. *H. Wragg.*

BROOKLINE 2 ch.c. Hotfoot 126–La Lidia 78 (Matador 131) (1981 5g* 5d 7d* **76**
7.6g² 7s 7g³) Mar 26; 13,000Y; leggy colt; half-brother to numerous winners,
including 3-y-o 1¼m winner Kings Parade (by Realm) and 5f to 1m winner
Laodamia (by So Blessed); dam, half-sister to Irish Derby winner Your Highness,
won at up to 13f; won 8-runner minor event at Ripon in May and 9-runner
nursery at Newmarket in August, making up 6 lengths in last 2f to lead close home
and beat Bancario a neck in latter; creditable third of 18 to Straeker in another
Newmarket nursery in October; will stay middle distances; didn't run up to
his best on only outing on very soft ground and has yet to race on a firm surface.
R. Sheather.

BROON'S SECRET 7 b.g. Most Secret 119–Vaudaville 77 (Vigo 130) (1980 6f **73**
5fg 5g 6d 6f 5d² 6d² 5v 1981 5g³ 6g 6g* 5fg 6g 5.1f 6f 5g* 5fg⁴ 5h² 6fg*) strong
gelding; sprint handicapper; successful at Thirsk in May, Ayr in July and Nottingham (apprentices) in September; stays 6f; acts on any going; has twice worn
blinkers; suitable mount for a claimer. *A. Jarvis.*

BROONS SURPRISE 3 ch.f. Most Secret 119–Kinegar (Attractive 72) (1980 —
5fg 7f 1981 8f) workmanlike filly; well beaten in maiden races; sweated
badly and threw her rider before start only outing of 1981. *T. Barnes.*

BROTHER KEMPINSKI 6 b.g. Right Tack 131–Tuna 63 (Silver Shark 129) —
(1980 NR 1981 8f 8d) strong gelding; good walker; useful handicapper at
his best but has shown no form for a long time; stays 1¼m; revels in the mud;
has worn blinkers. *J. Spearing.*

BROUGH'S BOY 2 b.c. Lucky Wednesday 124–Ruffino 99 (Como 120) —
(1981 6f 7.2d 6f) May 15; big, strong colt; half-brother to numerous winners,
4 at least useful, including smart sprinter Bream (by Hornbeam); dam a sprinter;
well beaten in maiden and minor events; troublesome at start first outing.
M. W. Easterby.

BROUGH SCOTT 2 ch.c. Steel Heart 128–Parthian Song (Parthia 132) — p
(1981 6fg) Apr 13; 16,000Y; small, useful-looking colt; half-brother to 3-y-o
Piperhill (by Red God), a useful winner at up to 7f, and a winner abroad; dam
unraced half-sister to Porto Bello; 20/1, showed up 4f and wasn't persevered with
once he began to weaken when distant ninth of 13 to Sandhurst Prince in £4,200
event at Kempton in August; will stay 7f; should improve at 3 yrs. *R. Price.*

BROWFOLD 2 ch.c. Realm 129–Trusian (Milesian 125) (1981 5d 5g 6g 6g 6s 5s) **66**
May 18; 4,500Y; smallish, lightly-made colt; closely related to a winner by
Divine Gift, and half-brother to several winners, including successful sprinter
Oh Simmie (by African Sky); only a plater himself; stays 6f. *P. Rohan.*

BROWN DIAMOND 5 ch.g. Native Bazaar 122–Crystal Clear 113 (Chamossaire) —
(1980 NR 1981 12fg) distant sixth of 8 to Karadar in maiden race at Brighton
in August, first outing on flat. *S. Mellor.*

BROWNE ECLIPSE 4 b.c. Tudor Music 131–Mary Bold (Hard Ridden 131) —
(1980 12g⁴ 10fg 8d 14fg 12d 8.4v 7.5s 10s 1981 10s⁴ 12f⁴ 12g² 16f) big ex-Irish
colt; poor handicapper; stays 1½m; suited by some give in the ground; trained
first start by L. Browne. *H. Collingridge.*

BROWN GOLD 2 b.f. Cavo Doro 124–Minna 59 (Pirate King 129) (1981 6f **87**
7fg⁴ 7g 7g² 7f 8fg 8d⁴) Mar 13; 6,200F, 8,400Y; plain filly; third foal; dam poor
half-sister to 2,000 Guineas winner Only for Life; ran best race in 1m nursery
at Pontefract in October, leading 3f out and keeping on to finish 1¾ lengths
fourth of 20 to A.T.S. Prince; will stay 1¼m; possibly needs some give in the
ground; best on a galloping track. *M. H. Easterby.*

BROWN'S BABU 4 b.f. Top Rush 106–Irish Pearl (Gulf Pearl 117) (1980 9.4fg —
1981 10s²) lean filly; poor maiden; will stay 1½m; acts on soft going; has run
respectably for an apprentice. *Denys Smith.*

BRUMMENDELLE 2 gr.f. Bruni 132–Make Amends 74 (Tutankhamen) —
(1981 7fg) Mar 27; rather unfurnished filly; half-sister to 2 winners by The
Brianstan, including useful 1977 2-y-o 6f winner Reparation; dam won over
5f at 2 yrs and stayed well; 50/1, ran out after 2f in £5,900 event won by Chulia
Street at Newmarket in August. *D. Wintle.*

BRUMMER (USA) 3 b.c. Bold Hour–Rainwater (Rainy Lake) (1980 7g 6g* —
1981 8fg 7.6d⁴) rangy colt; won £3,200 event at Doncaster as a 2-y-o; looked
very well but ran as if needing race when eighth of 9 behind Noalto in Easter
Stakes at Kempton in April; ran rather a sour race in blinkers when fourth of 5
behind Mushref in minor event at Chester the following month; should stay 1m;
sent to USA. *R. Price.*

BRUSH STROKE 2 b. or br.c. Thatch 136–Kiyofuji 98 (Grey Sovereign 128§) **70**
(1981 6s⁴ 7.2fg 7f 8d) Feb 17; IR 7,200Y; big, good sort; fourth foal; dam won
twice over 5f at 2 yrs; 5 lengths fifth of 19 to Wibis Range in maiden race at
Redcar in September, third outing and only worthwhile form; stays 7f; bandaged
off-fore on debut. *W. Elsey.*

BRUSTOLON 3 ch.c. Sharpen Up 127–Berthe Manet (Crepello 136) (1980 **117**
9d³ 10d* 1981 10.5fg² 10v 8fg* 10fg* 10f² 10f⁴) French colt; half-brother
to winners in Italy; dam daughter of Italian St Leger winner Barbara Sirani;
won 7-runner Prix de Pontarme at Chantilly in June by 3 lengths from Valgo
and put up a very useful performance when making all to beat Redoutable
(rec 7lb) by ½ length in Prix de la Ville de Trouville at Deauville in August;
also ran well in pattern races, including when 2½ lengths second to Al Nasr (Fr)
in 6-runner Prix de la Cote Normande at Deauville again later in August and
when 3½ lengths third of 6 to No Lute in Prix Greffulhe at Longchamp in April
(moved up a place on disqualification of winner for having traces of nandrolone in
his system); stays 1¼m; seems to act on any going, but goes well on firm; didn't
run up to his best final start. *F. Boutin, France.*

BUCHANAN (USA) 6 gr.g. Dancer's Image–Fiery Diplomat 120 (Diplomat —
Way) (1980 14g 1981 10.2s 5f) of little account on flat nowadays; has
been tried in blinkers; wears a tongue strap. *M. Chapman.*

BUCKLAND 5 b.g. Busted 134–Queensferry 81 (Pindari 124) (1980 NR **66**
1981 12.2d 12.2fg 12g 12d*) big gelding; good mover; middle-distance handicapper; won at Leicester in May (ridden by 5-lb claimer); probably acts on
any going; bandaged in front nowadays. *B. Palling.*

BUCKLOW HILL 4 b.g. Rheingold 137–Parmassia (Pampered King 121) **82**
(1980 10fg² 12.2d³ 10.2d 12v 1981 12f* 12f* 13.8fg* 12f* 12g² 18g 12g) tall
gelding; had a good year, winning minor events at Pontefract and Catterick
and handicaps at Ripon and Beverley; stays 1¾m (behind in Tote Cesarewitch
over further); acts well on firm ground. *J. Fitzgerald.*

BUCKTON 2 ch.f. Double-U-Jay 120–Remana (Remainder 106) (1981 5.1f —
6fg 6d 6g 8g 8g) Apr 29; plain filly; half-sister to a winning plater; plater; stays
1m; co-favourite on third outing at Yarmouth but was still wearing a blindfold
when stalls opened and took no part. *W. Holden.*

BUD'S GIFT 2 ch.g. Tudor Music 131–Recapped (Sallust 134) (1981 5.8g 6fg **63**
6fg⁴ 6s⁴) Mar 16; neat gelding; first foal; dam unplaced 3 times in Ireland;
fair form in sellers; will stay 1m; seems to act on any going; should win a seller.
G. Balding.

BUFFAVENTO 3 b.c. Connaught 130–Duke Street (Lorenzaccio 130) (1980 **103**
5f⁴ 6g 6g* 7g² 6g² 6fg² 1981 8.2fg³ 10g⁴ 8g* 8fg 8fg⁴ 8f⁴ 8d⁴ 8g) neat, strong
colt; held up when beating Mushref ½ length in 6-runner Balmoral Castle Stakes
at Ayr in May; in frame in valuable handicap at Haydock and Heathorn Stakes
at Newmarket (close fourth to Shotgun) earlier and in good handicaps at
Newcastle, Kempton and Ayr afterwards; stays 1¼m, but is possibly best at
1m; yet to race on very soft going, but acts on any other; had stiff task fourth
outing; ran moderately final start. *G. Pritchard-Gordon.*

BUFFOON 6 ch.g. Silly Season 127–Paphos 99 (Vilmorin) (1980 11.7g 10g **50**
10f² 8d² 12.3g⁴ 11.7d² 11.7g 16.9f³ 1981 11.7v 12f 20fg 11.7fg 13.1f³) poor
handicapper; suited by middle distances and seems to stay 2m; acts on any
going; carries head on one side and is no great battler. *D. Elsworth.*

BUGATTI 3 ch.g. Arch Sculptor 123–Mandetta (Mandamus 120) (1980 5fg⁴ —
6g 6s* 6s 6g 6g 1981 7s 8s 7.2s 8.2g 8.2s 11s 10s 10d) strong, good sort;
plater; stays 6f well; acts on soft going; blinkered third start; sold out of M.
Jarvis' stable 2,300 gns Doncaster June Sales after third outing. *S. Holland.*

BUGLE 3 gr. or ro.f. Warpath 113–Golden Jewel (Aureole 132) (1980 8d —
1981 14g 12d 10.1g) leggy, lightly-made filly; tailed off in maiden and minor
races; blinkered final start; sold 1,000 gns Ascot September Sales. *G. Balding.*

BUILD CARTWRIGHT (USA) 2 ch.c. Try Sheep–Maid of Arc (Knight in —
Armor) (1981 7fg) Feb 25; $3,000Y; strong colt; first foal; dam, from good
Argentinian family, never ran; sire won 1¼m San Luis Rey Handicap; 50/1
and in need of race when behind in 22-runner maiden event won by Oxslip
at Newmarket in July. *B. Hanbury.*

BUKARA 2 ch.c. Red Alert 127–Solar Jinks (Immortality or Delirium 126) —
(1981 6fg 7f 7g) Mar 19; 9,000Y; plain colt; poor walker; half-brother to 2

winners by Irish Love, including useful Irish 5f and 1¼m winner Jinkitis; dam
ran once; in mid-division in maiden races at Yarmouth in August and Leicester
in September on last 2 outings. *J. Winter.*

BULLDOZER 3 b.c. Busted 134–Woodwind 103 (Whistling Wind 123) (1980 **93**
8d 1981 11s 12g 11.7g* 12s² 13.3g 16f² 16fg* 15.5f* 17.4g⁴ 16g) well-made,
attractive, long-striding colt; improved and won maiden race at Bath in May
(made all), handicap at Kempton in August and amateur riders event at
Folkestone in September; quickened really well when given the office and
won very comfortably by 4 lengths from Aniece at Kempton; second in minor
event at Wolverhampton and handicap at Thirsk; suited by a test of stamina;
acts on any going; finished lame final start. *P. Walwyn.*

BULLRING 2 gr.g. Warpath 113–Loop The Loop 81 (Hopeful Venture 125) **78**
(1981 7f 10s² 10.2g) Mar 23; well-grown gelding with scope; good walker;
second foal; dam won at 9.4f and is half-sister to smart Aviator and to Derby
fourth Shotgun (by Warpath); 16/1, stayed on very strongly in last 3f to finish
1½ lengths second of 20 to Sunny Look in maiden event at Nottingham in October;
well-beaten sixth of 26 to Yard Bird in minor event at Doncaster the following
month; will stay 1½m+; possibly needs the mud; should win a maiden race
in the North at 3 yrs. *C. Thornton.*

BUNCE BOY 5 b.g. King Emperor–All Hail 112 (Alcide 136) (1980 11.7f² **75**
12fg* 12d² 11.7s 12fg² 12f³ 12fg* 12fg³ 12fg 14g 1981 11.7d 12f⁴ 12fg* 12.3fg⁴
12f* 12f² 12f* 12fg⁴ 12d³ 12v) useful sort; middle-distance handicapper;
goes well at Brighton and won three times there in the summer; ideally suited by
top-of-the-ground conditions; suited by forcing tactics; blinkered once at 3 yrs;
suitable mount for an apprentice. *A. Hide.*

BUNDLE OF KISSES (USA) 2 b.c. Nijinsky 138–Bundler (Raise A Native) **77 p**
(1981 8d³) second foal; half-brother to 3-y-o Veloche (by Olden Times), a
very useful sprint stakes winner at 2 yrs in USA; dam, one of best American
2-y-o fillies of 1973, won 11 races at up to 1m; third favourite, clear of remainder
when 2½ lengths third of 23 to Roanoke River in maiden race at Leicester in
November; should do better over further in 1982. *G. Harwood.*

BUNDU (FR) 2 b.f. Habitat 134–No Relation 94 (Klairon 131) (1981 6fg² **77**
7v³) smallish, close-coupled filly; half-sister to several winners, including
fairly useful middle-distance handicapper Warbeck (by Royal Palace); dam
stayed 1m; never far from leaders when neck second of 19 to Enthralment in
maiden race at Salisbury in September; not disgraced when 7 lengths third of
15 to My Destiny in £3,400 event at York the following month, doing just
enough to hold on to third place once first 2 had her measure; will stay 1m.
H. Wragg.

BUNDUQ 3 ch.f. Scottish Rifle 127–My Candy 81 (Lorenzaccio 130) (1980 **67**
NR 1981 12f³ 13f 12f³ 12f* 10d) fair sort; first foal; dam placed over 7f at
2 yrs; beat Sir Domino by a length despite hanging badly left in closing stages
in maiden race at Redcar in September; stays 1½m; acts on firm going. *N.
Gaselee.*

BUNTER 3 b.c. Prince de Galles 125–New Flag (Royal Serenade 131) (1980 **99**
NR 1981 8g 8g* 10.6s 8fg 8fg 8fg* 8g* 9g) quite an attractive, good sort;
half-brother to 2 winners in North America; dam stakes winner at up to 7f in
Canada; beaten a length by Silver Season in maiden event at Kempton in May
but was subsequently awarded race; returned to form with impressive wins
in Northern Goldsmiths Handicap at Newcastle in August (beat Silver Season
by 3 lengths) and Kyle and Carrick Handicap at Ayr in September (quickened
clear 2f out and won by 4 lengths from Doogali), in both races travelling well
throughout; started clear favourite for William Hill Cambridgeshire won by
Braughing at Newmarket in October but faded in last 2f after having every
chance and finished towards rear; best at 1m; acts on a firm surface. *R. Price.*

BURFORD BELLE 3 b.f. Roman Warrior 132–Motionless 109 (Midsummer **—**
Night II 117) (1980 NR 1981 6g 7g 8fg 8.2s 10s) big, strong, lengthy filly;
half-sister to 1m winner Speedy Tack (by Right Tack); dam third in English
and Irish 1,000 Guineas; plating-class maiden. *W. Wightman.*

BURGLARS BOY 7 ch.g. Burglar 128–Tilt Guard 75 (Crepello 136) (1980 **46**
5d 5g 5f 5f 6fg 5g⁴ 5fg³ 5d 6f 1981 5s 5d 5g 5g 6fg 5f⁴ 5fg 5f 5f 5f 5h) poor
sprint handicapper; best at 5f; acts on any going; sometimes wears blinkers;
sometimes sweats up; has a tendency to hang left; has given trouble at start.
L. Barratt.

Mr R. E. Sangster's "Bulldozer"

BURGLARS GOLD 2 br.f. Bronze Hill 96–Lardana 65 (Burglar 128) (1981   —
6g 6fg) Mar 27; 260Y; first foal; dam 9f winner; last but one in maiden and
minor events at Ayr in June and July. *T. Craig.*

BURGLAR'S MINK 4 ch.f. Burglar 128–Minkala (Master Rocky 106) (1980   —
10s 8fg 6f 6fg³ 8g⁴ 8fg 6g⁴ 7f 1981 8s 5g 6s 6g) small filly; poor plater; not
certain to stay 1¼m; acts on a firm surface; blinkered final start. *T. Taylor.*

BURGUNDY 2 b.c. Bustino 136–Land of Fire 99 (Buisson Ardent 129) (1981   **83**
7g 7s) May 6; 9,200Y; tall, fair sort; half-brother to 3 winners, including useful
1¼m to 2m winner No Bombs (by St Paddy); dam genuine performer at up to
1m; disputed lead 5f when 13 lengths sixth of 11 to Paradis Terrestre in Hyperion
Stakes at Ascot in October, second outing; should win races over middle
distances at 3 yrs. *P. Walwyn.*

BURKE'S FOLLY 4 ch.g. Shiny Tenth 120–Miss Sousa (March Past 124)   **33**
(1980 8f 7fg 7s³ 8s* 10.8fg² 8fg 9f 8d 8d 10d 1981 8fg 8d 10s³ 7f 9fg) lightly-
made gelding; poor mover; plater; stays 1¼m; suited by soft going; has worn
blinkers; suitable mount for a boy; races with head in air. *K. Bridgwater.*

BURLEIGH 9 ch.g. Charlottown 127–Running Blue 115 (Blue Peter) (1980   **57**
10fg 13.1fg² 10g² 12d⁴ 12g 10g⁴ 14g² 10d 1981 12d 12g 10fg³ 14fg³ 12g 10.2d²
10g) one-time fairly useful handicapper; was used by stable for educating its
apprentices; gave impression he needed at least 1½m and stayed 1¾m; acted on
any going; sometimes started slowly; sometimes wore blinkers; sometimes
sweated up; dead. *R. Hern.*

BURLINGTON LAD 2 ch.c. Sweet Revenge 129–Allegretto (Preciptic 122)   **62**
(1981 5d 5d⁴ 5f³ 6g 6s) Mar 21; 4,000F, 4,900Y; small colt; half-brother to
several minor winners; dam of little account; ran creditably when in frame in

maiden race at Leicester in May and valuable seller at York in June; subsequently off course until September and was well beaten on return; should stay 6f; seems to act on any going. *C. James.*

BURMA PINK 8 gr.g. Gulf Pearl 117–Magna 107 (Runnymede 123) (1980 — 8d 1981 8v) one-time useful handicapper; no longer seems of much account; used to wear blinkers; needs strong handling. *A. Smith.*

BURNBECK 2 b.c. Music Boy 124–Festival Night 115 (Midsummer Night II 85 117) (1981 5d³ 5g* 5fg²) Mar 20; good-quartered, quite attractive colt; second foal; half-brother to winning hurdler Falkland Palace (by Royal Palace); dam won from 6f to 1½m; odds on when easily winning 15-runner maiden race by 2 lengths from Diamond King at Salisbury in June; again odds on when 2 lengths second of 10 to Prairie Dunes in minor event at Windsor the following month, only subsequent start; will by suited by 6f. *P. Cole.*

BURN'S MONUMENT 3 b. or br.c. Tower Walk 130–Corsuedei (King's — Troop 118) (1980 NR 1981 8v 7g 5fg⁴ 6d) 6,000Y; third foal; half-brother to 1978 2-y-o 5f winner First Class Mail and a winner in Italy (both by Windjammer); dam ran 4 times unplaced at 2 yrs in Ireland; fourth in apprentice race at Edinburgh in July; well beaten in a seller only subsequent outing; sold 950 gns Doncaster October Sales. *W. H. H. Williams.*

BURN UP 2 b.f. Blue Cashmere 129–Stick 'Em Up (Burglar 128) (1981 5g³ 67 5g³ 5g⁴ 5fg* 5g⁴ 5fg 6d² 6fg* 6fg 7g 8d) Apr 27; neat, sharp sort; third foal; dam never ran; won 14-runner maiden race at Catterick in June by a neck from Chrisdee and 10-runner nursery on same course in August by ½ length from Chere Jane; suited by 6f and wasn't disgraced over 7f; acts on a firm and soft surface; suitable mount for an apprentice. *P. Asquith.*

BUSACO 2 b.g. Bustino 136–Deed 86 (Derring-Do 131) (1981 6d² 6g⁴ 7fg* 114 7f* 7.6g³ 7.3s²) Feb 17; strong, compact gelding; half-brother to 1978 2-y-o 6f winner Super Jack (by Blakeney); dam won over 5f at 2 yrs; ran on strongly when successful in 24-runner maiden race at Newbury in August and 8-runner Sancton Stakes at York the following month (won going away by 1½ lengths from Rebollino); continued to improve, finishing length third of 7 to Triple Axel in £7,100 event at Lingfield in September and putting up a very useful effort when strong-finishing 1½-length second of 8 to easy winner Montekin in Horris Hill Stakes at Newbury the following month (dwelt at start); disappointed on second outing after becoming upset by repeated false starts from a flag; will stay middle distances; acts on any going; the type to train on and looks sure to win more races. *R. Hern.*

Sancton Stakes, York—Busaco wins from Rebollino

BUS

BUSHY BAY 7 b.g. Polyfoto 124–Latest Bird 81 (Pardal 130) (1980 NR 1981 — 10f) useful performer at up to 1¼m in Ireland in 1979, winner of Irish Lincolnshire; well beaten in minor event at Brighton in July, only outing on flat since. *M. Chapman.*

BUSIRIS 7 b.g. Busted 134–Tudor Gal 106 (Henry the Seventh 125) (1980 — 17.1f² 17.1fg* 1981 13.1f) attractive gelding; tailed off only start in 1981; stayed well; acted on any going; one paced; dead. *L. Kennard.*

BUSTEDAWAY 5 b.g. Busted 134–Kissing 98 (Sing Sing 134) (1980 NR — 1981 10v 11s) well-made gelding; poor performer nowadays; stays 1½m; seems to act on any going. *G. Richards.*

BUSTED DATE 2 b.f. Decoy Boy 129–Spoilt Date (Busted 134) (1981 5fg⁴ **63** 5g² 5d²) Jan 25; 1,500Y; lengthy, useful sort; good walker; first foal; dam never ran; second in maiden auction events at Kempton and Brighton in May, failing by only a neck to hold off Sam-Bam in latter; dead. *M. Hinchliffe.*

BUSTELLA 3 b.f. Bustino 136–Be Merry 104 (Charlottown 127) (1980 NR **67** 1981 8g 10.1fg 12f² 11.7h 14fg 12g² 12d⁴) quite a well-made filly; half-sister to Norwegian 1,000 Guineas winner Just Married (by Habitat); dam, half-sister to very smart May Hill, stayed at least 13f; second in maiden races at Folkestone in July and Brighton (didn't seem to run on) in September; suited by 1½m (well beaten over further); blinkered last 2 outings; sold 10,000 gns Newmarket December Sales. *J. Dunlop.*

BUSTELLINA 3 b.f. Busted 134–Naughty Party (Parthia 132) (1980 7.2s⁴ 6f **61** 8s 6s² 1981 10.6g 8g* 8s 8g³ 9g³ 9.4fg² 11g 12.3g 8.2f 11d) tall, leggy filly; won maiden event at Carlisle in May; stays 9f. *R. Hollinshead.*

BUSTELLO (GER) 2 b. or br.c. Experte–Ballista (Dike) (1981 6fg 6f* 7fg* **81** 7f² 7fg³ 7g) strong colt; first foal; dam officially rated third-best 2-y-o filly in Germany in 1976; sire top German 2-y-o of 1971 and second in German Derby and St Leger; successful twice in minor events in July, making all to win 23-runner event at Nottingham and staying on to win 5-runner race at Catterick by 1½ lengths from Mosswern; ran creditably in nurseries on next 2 outings but finished last of 9 in Ratiborrennen at Krefeld when sent to Germany in September; will stay middle distances. *Sir Mark Prescott.*

BUSTING 7 b.h. Busted 134–Yasseen (Charlottesville 135) (1980 13s² 12fg* **70** 1981 12d 14d³) staying handicapper; acts on any going; good mount for a claimer; genuine. *R. Turnell.*

BUSTLE 3 b.f. Busted 134–Arrival 102 (Henry the Seventh 125) (1980 NR — 1981 7g 10.2h 10.1fg) attractive filly; sister to Broken Date, placed over sprint distances here and a winner in Austria, and half-sister to several winners; dam, a sprinter, at her best at 2 yrs; in rear in maiden and minor races. *J. Douglas-Home.*

BUSTOMI 3 b.c. Bustino 136–Mineown 85 (Roan Rocket 128) (1980 6g 7g² **123** 7f* 7fg² 1981 12f* 12fg* 14.6g³)
Bustomi was in the region of two stone behind the very best of his age as a two-year-old, when his sole success from four starts was in the Sancton Stakes at York, but he made such progress from two to three that he went to the St Leger with excellent credentials and started third favourite in one of the strongest fields for years. He had looked every inch a Leger prospect when winning the King Edward VII Stakes at Royal Ascot and the Gordon Stakes at Goodwood on his only two previous starts, but in the race itself he was a shade disappointing and finished third behind his much longer-priced stable-companion Cut Above, beaten six and a half lengths.
Bustomi found Centurius his toughest opponent at both Royal Ascot and Goodwood. Centurius had beaten him by a length in the Mornington Stakes at Ascot on Bustomi's final outing as a two-year-old and looked long odds on to do so again in the King Edward VII Stakes as he cruised through to make his challenge, but he spoilt his chance by hanging left towards Bustomi throughout the last furlong. Bustomi, dashed into the lead early in the straight after being held up, was driven out for all he was worth with typical Carson assistance and battled on really gamely to beat Centurius by a neck, the pair finishing three lengths clear of Admiral's Heir. Centurius was subsequently disqualified and his rider suspended. In the Gordon Stakes Bustomi again showed by far the greater resolution and beat Centurius by a length and a half. The form of the race looked good, the pair finishing a long way clear of the improving handicappers Taher and Amyndas and the decent Irish colt Erins Isle. Bustomi was clearly going very much the right way and the St Leger was immediately confirmed as his main

163

objective. His stable had an extremely strong entry and at that time was quoted as low as 6/4 for the race in the anticipated absence of Shergar. It was expected that Carson would choose to ride Bustomi again, but following his unfortunate injury at York the mount went to Piggott.

In the eventual line-up for the Leger Bustomi was joined by stable-companions Cut Above and the pacemaking Magikin in a field of seven. Magikin, in the same ownership as Bustomi, and Bustomi himself, were ridden in a manner designed thoroughly to test Shergar's stamina, but such tactics probably benefited Cut Above far more than they did Bustomi, for Cut Above looked much the stouter stayer on the day. Bustomi tracked Magikin in second for over a mile and went on fully five furlongs from home but it was clear that Piggott was growing anxious with three furlongs still to run. The pair forfeited their lead to Glint of Gold two out and Bustomi could keep on only at one pace. Carson said afterwards that, knowing Bustomi as he did, he would have held him up for longer. Certainly a great deal more use was made of Bustomi than in either previous race and it is possible that we didn't quite see the best of him. The plan to run Bustomi in the Irish St Leger, in which we would have had another chance to assess him as a stayer, was dropped when it became apparent that the going would be on the soft side; Bustomi has yet to race on ground softer than good and clearly goes well on firm going.

Bustomi (b.c. 1978)	Bustino (b 1971)	Busted (b 1963)	Crepello
			Sans le Sou
		Ship Yard (ch 1963)	Doutelle
			Paving Stone
	Mineown (ro 1970)	Roan Rocket (ro 1961)	Buisson Ardent
			Farandole
		Whoopee (ro 1958)	Anwar
			Sea Gipsy

Bustomi was bred by his owner Lady Beaverbrook, for whom both his sire and dam also raced. His sire Bustino won the 1974 St Leger but is perhaps even better remembered for his gallant second to Grundy in the following year's King George VI and Queen Elizabeth Diamond Stakes. The dam Mineown was placed over five and six furlongs. Mineown is a half-sister to the good

King Edward VII Stakes, Ascot—Bustomi holds on well to beat the subsequently-disqualified Centurius

Lady Beaverbrook's "Bustomi"

Italian colt Weimar and from the same family as Counsel but the family has produced little of note in recent years besides Bustomi. Neither of Mineown's two foals prior to Bustomi was of much account: Le Chaleur (by Biskrah) died as a two-year-old after showing no worthwhile form while Filepso (by Royalty) is a hurdler. Mineown has since produced a filly by Relkino named Relkown, which is as yet unraced, and two others by Bustomi's sire.

Bustomi stays in training and could well pick up another good prize or two, for he is lightly raced and just the sort one would expect to continue to train on. A lengthy, attractive colt who walks and moves well, he's a very smart performer and an admirably genuine one too. *R. Hern.*

BUSY BEE (USA) 2 b.f. Drone–Solid Booking (Boldnesian) (1981 7g) — Apr 29; $55,000Y; lengthy filly; second foal; half-sister to 1980 American 2-y-o 7f winner Swing Time Miss (by Ack Ack); dam won twice over 6f; unquoted when ninth of 16 to Positron in maiden race at Leicester in October. *W. Hastings-Bass.*

BUSY BUBBLE 2 b.f. Red Alert 127–Chanson (Tudor Melody 129) (1981 — 5g 5fg 5fg 7fg) May 13; IR 1,400F, 3,300Y; neat, strong filly; half-sister to a winner in Ireland by Apalachee; dam never ran; no worthwhile form in varied company but still didn't look fit on final start. *D. Thom.*

BUT BEAUTIFUL 3 b.f. Moulton 128–Alisarda (Aureole 132) (1980 6g 6fg — 8fg 7d 1981 10s 10.1d 12f 12fg 16.5f 12fg 10.2g) rather unfurnished filly; in rear in varied company, including selling. *G. Fletcher.*

BUTLERS PET 2 b.g. Mummy's Pet 125–Reluctant Maid 94 (Relko 136) — (1981 5d 5d 6f 6fg) Mar 29; 2,300Y; tall, fair sort; seemingly of little account. *M. Blanshard.*

165

BUTOSKY 4 b.f. Busted 134–Patosky 94 (Skymaster 126) (1980 10fg 7d **70**
10.1f 12f 10.1g⁴ 11.7h 12f 13g² 12g³ 12d 1981 10.8d³ 12g 11.7v³ 10.8fg* 12.2fg²
11.7fg* 11.7fg³ 11.7d*) moderate handicapper; successful at Warwick and
Windsor (twice) in the summer; stays 13f; probably acts on any going; blinkered
twice in 1980; possibly needs strong handling; sold 32,000 gns Newmarket
December Sales. *J. Benstead.*

BUTTON TOP 3 b.f. Jimmy Reppin 131–Red Lupus (Red God 128§) (1980 **92**
7g 6f 6d³ 7d* 7g* 7v⁴ 1981 7g* 7fg³ 7g* 6g 7g³ 8f) rangy filly; good walker;
won handicaps at Newmarket in April (by neck from Olympic Glory) and May
(comfortably, by 3 lengths from Lord Wimpy); badly hampered and possibly
unlucky in between; finds 6f too sharp and should stay 1m (had stiff task when
tried at trip); probably acts on any going; suitable mount for an apprentice;
not seen out after Royal Ascot. *N. Callaghan.*

BUZZARDS BAY 3 b.c. Joshua 129–Grande Merci 82 (Gratitude 130) (1980 **88**
6g 7g 7fg 7.2d² 7g 1981 10s³ 10f³ 8f* 8g³ 8g* 8fg* 8.2f* 8d* 9g 8s²) strong-
topped, good sort; improved and had an excellent season; won maiden event
at Beverley and handicaps at Yarmouth, Goodwood, Hamilton and Ayr, gaining
clever wins in quite valuable races at Goodwood and Ayr; ran an extraordinary
race when eighth of 28 behind Braughing in William Hill Cambridgeshire at
Newmarket in October, making up a deal of ground after being reluctant
to take part and tailed-off last for much of way (mulish on way to post too);
behaved himself far better when 8 lengths second to Princes Gate in handicap
at Ascot later in month; stays 1¼m; acts on any going; has a useful turn of foot.
H. Collingridge.

BYBLOS 3 br.c. No Mercy 126–Aberside (Abernant 142) (1980 NR 1981 5d **52**
5f 5f 6g³ 5fg⁴ 5fg) 2,200F, 6,400Y; tall, leggy colt; has been tubed; half-
brother to 2 winners, including 5f performer Setmark (by Sharpen Up); dam
never ran; in claiming handicap at Newmarket (tired in last furlong) and
maiden race at Warwick, both in August; possibly best at 5f. *W. O'Gorman.*

BYCLOUGH BOY 4 br.g. The Brianstan 128–Corcyra Beach 60 (Behistoun 131) **—**
(1980 5f 8f 7f 5h 7f 6fg 5g 8d 1981 8s 5g 7g 6fg 6g 5d) compact gelding; poor
plater; sometimes wears blinkers; sold to R. Allan 1,000 gns Doncaster October
Sales. *A. Gillam.*

BYCLOUGH PRIDE 3 ch.g. Native Bazaar 122–High Moor 104 (Sayajirao 132) **—**
(1980 5f 1981 8g 12.3g) leggy gelding; well behind in maiden auction event
and maiden races; sold 800 gns Ascot July Sales. *R. Whitaker.*

BYE APPEAL 5 ch.g. Busted 134–One Extra 85 (Abernant 142) (1980 15f³ **57**
14g 16g 16.5g* 16.5fg³ 14fg 1981 15.5d 16g* 16g 16.5f⁴ 16.5f) rangy gelding;
staying handicapper; won at Lingfield in June; suited by top-of-the-ground;
often makes the running; wears bandages. *J. Winter.*

BYE-LAW 2 ch.c. Legal Eagle 126–Kimolina (Ki Myth 96) (1981 5g 5f **52 §**
6f²(dis) 6f 6f² 6f 7g 6s 5s 5s) Apr 4; compact colt; good walker; neck second
in sellers at Doncaster in June (hung badly away from whip and was disqualified)
and Pontefract in July (had his ground taken by Royal Question and seemed
unlucky not to be awarded race); should stay 7f; seems best in blinkers;
inconsistent and isn't genuine; sold out of M. H. Easterby's stable 675 gns
Ascot August Sales after seventh outing. *M. James.*

BY HEAVEN 2 b.f. Royal Hotel–Venetian (Hill Gail) (1981 8d) Feb 9; **—**
sister to a poor animal; dam of no account; unquoted and on backward side
when tailed off behind Misty Halo in 11-runner maiden event at Wolverhampton
in October. *W. Turner.*

BYLON 2 ch.c. No Loiterer 90–Pinzamber (Pinicola 113) (1981 5g 5s 5.1fg **56**
5.1f 6g² 6g) May 10; workmanlike colt; half-brother to Zamber Boy (by Weepers
Boy), winner of a 6f seller and in Hong Kong; dam winning hurdler; plater;
5 lengths second of 11 to Keep Silent at Yarmouth in September, easily best effort;
will be suited by 1m. *A. Dalton.*

BYROC BOY 4 b.g. Runnymede 123–Royal Pat 80 (King's Troop 118) **47**
(1980 7d 7fg 5f 5fg² 7f 6d 5s 1981 7d 8g 6d 5.3f⁴ 6f 5fg³ 5.3f 5fg⁴ 5fg⁴ 6g)
plater; best at sprint distances; probably acts on any going; sometimes blinkered.
D. Jermy.

BYRON'S DAUGHTER 2 ch.f. Hot Spark 126–Blak-en-Bloo 72 (Blakeney 126) **71** d
(1981 5fg 5fg³ 5f 7fg 5g) Apr 13; small filly; second foal; dam stayed 1½m;
2¼ lengths third of 13 to Vanity Fair in maiden race at Warwick in June; in
rear when blinkered in seller at Catterick in October on fifth outing and seemed
not to train on; should stay 7f; trained by C. Nelson first 2 starts. *W. O'Gorman.*

BY THE LAKE 3 b.f. Tyrant–Holiday Inn (Le Haar 126) (1980 NR 1981 12fg **48**
12g 16.5g2) 31,000Y; big, lengthy filly; second foal; dam unraced half-sister to
smart French miler Gracious Knight and very useful 9f to 1½m winner Christmas
Box; blinkered first time when 2 lengths second to Young Robin in poor minor
event at Redcar in September; suited by 2m; sold 1,500 gns Newmarket December
Sales. *B. Hills.*

C

CAAMORA (USA) 2 b. or br.f. Jacinto–Flame Burgoo (Bernburgoo) (1981 —
6fg 7fg 6d) lightly-made, lengthy filly; half-sister to 2 minor winners in USA;
dam, very useful at 2 yrs, won 13 sprint races; no sign of ability in maiden and
minor events; sent to France. *R. Sheather.*

CABBAGE MAN 3 b.c. Song 132–Star Trophy 63 (Umberto 118) (1980 6fg **66**
6d2 6g2 8fg 1981 7fg 7.6g2 7f 7fg2 10fg4 9g4) small, useful-looking colt;
second in maiden and minor races; gives impression he'll stay 1½m; often blinkered. *H. Candy.*

CABLE LAYER 2 b.g. Swing Easy 126–Mehir 71 (King's Company 124) **55**
(1981 5g 5g 6f 7g 8.2fg) May 5; 3,200F, 3,200Y (privately); rangy gelding;
third foal; dam poor maiden; beaten about 7 lengths when seventh of 19 to
Starter's Image in valuable 7f seller at Newmarket in July, best effort; not
sure to stay 1m. *P. Rohan.*

CADEAU D'ELISE 3 b.g. Le Coq d'Or 101–Katie Little (Nulli Secundus 89) —
(1980 NR 1981 7g 7g 8f 16f) lightly-made gelding; first known foal; dam never
ran; ran best race on third start, when eighth of 14 to dead-heaters Quite Ducky
and Queensway Rose in minor event at Stockton in June; trained by A. Scott
until after second outing; withdrawn after taking charge of his apprentice rider
on last intended appearance. *J. Mason.*

CADEM'S LAW 2 b.g. Legal Eagle 126–Alcadem 75 (Alcide 136) (1981 8s —
10.2g) May 2; 1,700Y; big, workmanlike gelding; seventh foal; half-brother
to a winning jumper; dam, half-sister to very smart American horse Tyrant,
won over 1¼m and 1½m; unquoted when behind in large fields for minor events
at Redcar (bandaged behind) and Doncaster at the back-end. *J. Wilson.*

CADI HA 2 b.f. Welsh Pageant 132–Super Dancer 72 (Taj Dewan 128) (1981 **97** p
7fg 7f*) May 4; good sort; excellent mover; first foal; dam lightly-raced
daughter of half-sister to Blakeney and Morston; had plenty to do after 2f
in 14-runner minor event at Leicester in August but gradually wore down
leaders under vigorous driving to win by ½ length from Chulia Street; will be
suited by middle distances; the type to improve further at 3 yrs. *B. Hobbs.*

CAERNARVON BAY 5 b.g. Right Tack 131–Ever Swinging 104 (Immor- —
tality) (1980 8g 7d3 1981 8v4 10.6s 8g) plater; stays 1m; acts on any going;
has worn bandages; trained part of season by W. Stubbs. *Mrs A. Cousins.*

CAERNARVON LAD 2 ch.g. Jimmy Reppin 131–Goldbell (Sovereign Path —
125) (1981 5g 6fg 7f 6d) Apr 19; 1,900Y; leggy, workmanlike gelding; unquoted when in rear in varied company, including selling; withdrawn at start
(lame) at Haydock in September on intended fifth appearance. *R. Hollinshead.*

CAESAR'S GHOST 2 gr.g. Young Emperor 133–Xanthoria (Levmoss 133) —
(1981 5g 6fg) May 25; 5,800Y; first foal; dam, poor maiden, is half-sister to
very useful animals Gerard Street and Ghazwan; in rear in maiden and minor
events at Windsor in August. *R. Baker.*

CAESAR'S WARNING 3 b.g. Red Alert 127–March the First 90 (Martial —
131) (1980 NR 1981 6f 6g 5fg) 8,600Y; workmanlike gelding; brother to
a plating-class filly and half-brother to 3 winners, including middle-distance
performer Regalus (by Dike); dam placed over 5f at 2 yrs; showed good speed
3f when sixth of 14 behind Bracadale in apprentice event at Nottingham in
August on second outing, best effort (still bit burly). *D. Underwood.*

CAIRN ROUGE 4 b.f. Pitcairn 126–Little Hills (Candy Cane 125) (1980 **126**
7v 7s* 8fg* 8g* 10.5d2 12f 10d* 1981 10fg 8g2 10g2 12fg4 9s)
        After a triumphant 1980 when she won four races, including the Goffs Irish
One Thousand Guineas, the Coronation Stakes and the Champion Stakes,
Cairn Rouge followed another recent Champion Stakes winner of her sex, Swiss
Maid, by failing to pass the post first as a four-year-old. She did, though, have

only five starts; moreover, at the time of writing, an inquiry is pending concerning Vayrann's performance in the Champion Stakes which could affect the placings in that race in which Cairn Rouge fiinished second.

Cairn Rouge took time to come to hand and wasn't seen out until the Prince of Wales's Stakes at Royal Ascot where, despite the fact that it was her first run of the year, she started favourite to account for such as Hard Fought and Vielle. The confidence proved misplaced, for after travelling well for most of the way she failed to quicken when put under pressure in the last two furlongs and finished fifth to Hard Fought. Trainer Cunningham at first put her defeat down to lack of fitness but he subsequently discovered that the filly had hurt herself in the race and she was off the course until September. On her return Cairn Rouge had a tremendous battle with Belted Earl, meeting him on favourable terms, in the Desmond Stakes at the Curragh, going down by a short head with the pair six lengths clear of a very useful field.

Though not yet back to her very best Cairn Rouge was evidently well in herself and her chances of winning the Champion Stakes for the second year in a row couldn't be entirely discounted. At Newmarket (as at Royal Ascot) she failed to impress in the paddock, having the lean and hungry look that Shakespeare endowed Cassius with in *Julius Caesar*, but she ran a cracking race. Held up, Cairn Rouge made strong progress on the bridle from halfway, followed Vayrann through coming into the Dip and kept on well without being able to match the French colt's pace to go down by two lengths. Those behind Cairn Rouge included a number of the best middle-distance performers in training and we believe her performance in running second to Vayrann was just about as good as her defeat of Master Willie in 1980. Both Cairn Rouge's other runs were in America, the better being in the Washington International at Laurel, in which she ran respectably to be fourth to the ex-French Providential, beaten over five lengths, fading after being just behind the leaders turning into the final straight.

Cairn Rouge (b.f. 1977)	Pitcairn (b 1971)	Petingo (b 1965)	Petition
			Alcazar
		Border Bounty (b 1965)	Bounteous
			B Flat
	Little Hills (b or br 1971)	Candy Cane (b 1965)	Crepello
			Candy Gift
		Ballyogan Queen (br 1956)	Ballyogan
			Stone Crop

Cairn Rouge is the first foal of Little Hills who revelled in the muddy conditions when trotting up in a Galway maiden race over a mile and a half and a Navan hurdle event over two furlongs further. In 1978 Little Hills foaled Tumbledownhill (by Tumble Wind), successful over six furlongs at two, and after being barren to Patch she produced a Wolverlife colt that sold for 72,000 guineas as a yearling at Goffs in 1981. Little Hills's dam, Ballyogan Queen, a half-sister to the good hurdler Normandy from the family of Zarathustra and Althrey Don, stayed a mile and finished second in the Irish Cambridgeshire. She produced four winners besides Little Hills, notably the Dewhurst Stakes third and Liverpool Spring Cup winner Countermarch (by Hard Ridden).

Cairn Rouge was retained for 3,000 guineas as a yearling; before the 1981 season started she was sold to the American Craig Singer (who also bought Condessa during the year) for an undisclosed sum which no doubt saw her original owner showing a good profit. A lightly-built filly who has a round action and doesn't impress in her slower paces, Cairn Rouge was best at around a mile and a quarter and seemed to act on any going. Genuine and consistent, she has been retired and visits Northern Dancer. *M. Cunningham, Ireland.*

CAJOLERY 5 br.h. Pall Mall 132–Do Please (I Say 125) (1980 7f 7.2fg⁴ 7fg* **89** 7g 7fg* 7fg 7g 7g 7d* 1981 7.2fg* 7fg⁴ 7.6fg* 7g 7f⁴ 8fg 7g 7d) lightly-made horse; fairly useful handicapper; won at Haydock in April and beat Optimate 2½ lengths in valuable Queen Elizabeth Stakes at Lingfield in June; ran easily best race afterwards when fourth to Captain Nick in Ward Hill Bunbury Cup at Newmarket in July; best at around 7f; seems to act on any going. *I. Walker.*

CAJUN 2 ch.c. Red Regent 123–Ermyn Lass 64 (Ennis 128) (1981 5s⁴ 6f* 6fg **120** 6fg² 7g³ 6fg² 6g*)

At the start of the 1981 season no trainer looked to have a stronger team of two-year-olds than Henry Cecil: according to *Horses in Training* he had no fewer than eighty-nine juveniles, nearly all of excellent parentage. Nevertheless

Chesham Stakes, Ascot—Cajun wins from Treboro and Mubhedj (hidden)

by the end of the season Cecil had won only one of the twenty-five English pattern races open to two-year-olds, compared to four in 1980 and 1978 and three in 1979. And his 1981 win, with Cajun in the William Hill Middle Park Stakes at Newmarket, was such a surprise that Cajun, at 20/1, became the longest-priced winner of the race since the war.

The Middle Park in October was Cajun's seventh race, and he had the remarkable record of having started favourite for five of the previous six and of having won only once. His win came in the Chesham Stakes at Royal Ascot where he held off the fast-finishing Treboro by three quarters of a length after looking likely to win in fine style a furlong out. Perhaps Cajun's connections thought he was running out of stamina in the Chesham because he was held up longer in the Anglia Television July Stakes at Newmarket on his next start. If anything he was given too much to do and in the circumstances he ran creditably to get into fifth place at the post, only two and a half lengths behind End of the Line. Nor was he at all disgraced in finishing a close second to Tender King, ahead of End of the Line, in the Richmond Stakes at Goodwood three weeks later.

Cajun's next two performances weren't so pleasing. His form entitled him to start favourite for the Seaton Delaval Stakes at Newcastle in August, even though the distance of seven furlongs wasn't sure to suit him. Defeat looked out of the question as Cajun cruised up to the leaders with a quarter of a mile to run but, unhappily for his supporters, Cajun's response was very limited once he came off the bridle and he finished no better than third, half a length and a head behind Zilos and Telephone Man. Although lack of stamina seemed a made-ready excuse for this display, worse was to follow in a small race over six furlongs at Windsor in September. Day, the stable apprentice, quickly sent him into the lead but even in this company Cajun started to make heavy weather of it in the final furlong and Epithet got up by a neck. The newcomer She's Incredible was only a neck further behind.

Epithet could finish only third in a nursery at Ascot later in the month, receiving 12 lb from the second-placed El Mansour, so it isn't surprising that neither Cecil nor Piggott was keen to run Cajun in the Middle Park. In addition to his old rivals Tender King and End of the Line he was faced with two other pattern-race winners in Hays and Peterhof, impressive winners respectively of the Mill Reef Stakes and the Flying Childers Stakes on their latest appearances. Also at a shorter price than Cajun was Wattlefield, the disappointing favourite in the Mill Reef. It was becoming apparent that Cajun doesn't find a great

169

deal in front and Piggott immediately dropped him out towards the rear as Lucky Hunter made the running. The pace wasn't particularly strong and the field, which had originally split into two, was still closely grouped at half-way. With two furlongs to run only End of the Line was definitely behind Cajun but Cajun then started to make smooth headway. By the distance he'd reached the heels of Lucky Hunter and Peterhof and, far from hanging fire, he maintained his effort to the line, getting on top well inside the final furlong to beat Lucky Hunter three quarters of a length. Wattlefield, keeping on well to be third, was only a neck further behind and little more than seven lengths covered the entire field of thirteen. Not a vintage Middle Park by any means! Besides providing his trainer with his only two-year-old pattern-race success of the season, Cajun landed him in front of the stewards. They asked Cecil to explain Cajun's improved showing compared to Windsor and accepted the explanation that 'the colt was difficult, had hesitated when making his run at Windsor, and ran on much better up the hill than he expected on this occasion'.

		Red Regent (b 1972)	Prince Regent (br 1966)	Right Royal V Noduleuse
Cajun (ch.c. Apr 3, 1979)			Redowa (ch 1964)	Red God Sally Deans
		Ermyn Lass (ch 1963)	Ennis (b 1954)	Golden Cloud First House
			Rye Girl (ch 1949)	Blue Water Brosna

In an interview for the *Timeform Black Book* Henry Cecil provided us with an interesting story about how he acquired Cajun. 'This colt was bought for me by "Tote" Cherry-Downes in Ireland. I had glandular fever at the time so he was acting on my behalf. He kept ringing me up and saying what a lovely colt he was, I must buy him, so in the end I said 'for God's sake get on with it then'—I got rather fed up with his persistency. I couldn't wait to criticise the horse when he got back but found it very difficult. He's a lovely colt by Red Regent out of Ermyn Lass. We paid 33,000 guineas for him, which seems a lot.' Cajun certainly doesn't look expensive any more—he's already won over £60,000, with promise of more to come—but 33,000 guineas had seemed a high price to pay for a colt by Red Regent, even a well-made, attractive, easy-moving one like Cajun. Although standing at a fee of only 750 guineas, Red Regent had attracted only twenty-one mares in his first season at stud in 1978, including Ermyn Lass, and the number dropped to only fifteen the following year. The next-highest price paid for a Red Regent yearling in 1980 was a mere 5,000 guineas. Red Regent saw more of the world than most racehorses. He reached his peak as a four-year-old when as well as winning the Ladbroke City and Suburban Handicap he won a Group 3 event over a mile and a quarter in Germany and finished second in a good race in Spain. The next year he won one of his five starts in the USA before being retired to stud in his native land, Ireland.

Red Regent gained most of his nine wins over middle distances but it's unlikely that Cajun will stay anything like so well. Ermyn Lass, a daughter of the very speedy Ennis, gained her sole success in a five-furlong seller as a four-year-old and has previously bred four winners of fifteen races in Britain, none of which was over further than six furlongs. Easily best of the four are Ubedizzy

William Hill Middle Park Stakes, Newmarket—20/1-shot Cajun finishes strongly to win from Lucky Hunter and Wattlefield

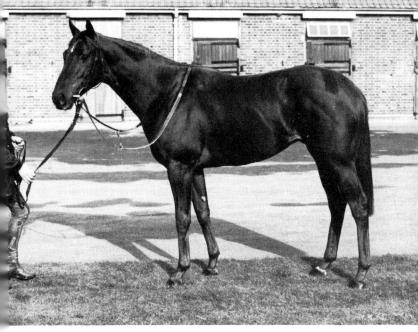

Mr J. Stone's "Cajun"

(by Carnival Dancer) and the useful three-year-old Princess Gayle (by Lord Gayle). Ubedizzy became so savage as a five-year-old that his trainer had to give an assurance not to race him again in England but in his younger days he was a smart, tough sprinter. Another good winner from the family is Red Alert, the product of a mating between Ermyn Lass's close relative Ashton Jane and Red God who is also maternal grandsire of Red Regent. Although Red Alert stayed a mile well enough to finish fourth in the Irish Two Thousand Guineas he was decidedly better at shorter distances, winning the Jersey Stakes and the Spillers Stewards' Cup. Cajun could well prove a similar type of three-year-old. There's no denying that his best form was over six furlongs at two but he came close enough to victory over Newcastle's stiff seven furlongs, giving weight to those that beat him, to suggest he'll stay the trip at three, especially if, as seems certain, he is held up for a late run. Even though he can't be spoken of in the same breath as many previous winners of the Middle Park, Cajun is among the best of his age and should win more races. It's possibly a bit premature to say he needs a sound surface—he's encountered soft ground only once and that was on his debut—but his very smooth, daisy-cutting action suggests strongly that he does. *H. Cecil.*

CALEDONIAN 5 b.h. Philip of Spain 126–Blasllyn 88 (Blast 125) (1980 7f⁴ **63** 6f³ 6h* 5f² 5fg 6d 6fg 5d² 5f 6g 5s 5d 5d⁴ 1981 5s 6g 6g 6g³ 5g* 5g* 5f* 5fg 5f⁴ 5f 5f 5fg 5g 5d) tall horse; sprint handicapper; successful at Thirsk in May and Beverley and Stockton in June; acts on any going; wears blinkers; suitable mount for a boy. *J. Calvert.*

CALIBUNDA 6 b.g. Caliban 123–Fairabunda 59 (Floribunda 136) (1980 10v — 11d* 8f 14.7f 9f 11g 9fg 15s 1981 12fg 14d) poor handicapper; stays 13f; suited by a soft surface. *S. Holland.*

CALIDORE 3 br.f. Scottish Rifle 127–Callidice 77 (Worden II 129) (1980 6g —
1981 10s 8d) workmanlike filly; behind in maiden races at Leicester as a 2-y-o
and at Salisbury and Warwick (last of 14) in April. *T. Marshall.*

CALISOLON 7 b.g. Caliban 123–Solensister 100 (Ennis 128) (1980 NR 1981 **53**
8s 12f 10s 10s* 14g) plater; successful in better company (apprentices) at
Lingfield in October; effective from 1m to 2m; acts on any going; has worn
blinkers and bandages. *P. K. Mitchell.*

CALL BEC 4 ch.g. Upper Case–Mountain Of Mourne 87 (Mountain Call 125) —
(1980 7s 8fg 10.1fg 10f 7g 8.3s² 8fg 10f⁴ 10d 1981 7d 8g 8.3s) compact
gelding; plater; stayed 1¼m; acted on soft going; was tried in blinkers; had
worn bandages; dead. *A. Pitt.*

CALL BIRD 4 ch.f. Le Johnstan 123–Shrubbery 86 (Ballymoss 136) (1980 —
5fg³ 5.8g 5fg 5fg 5.8f 6g 5g 6g 1981 12s 16d) poor plater. *M. Haynes.*

CALL ME CANDY 3 ch.f. Roman Warrior 132–Tit-Bit 61 (Hornbeam 130) —
(1980 5g 5g 5g 5g 5g 5d 1981 8s) useful-looking filly; plating-class maiden
at 2 yrs; last of 16 in handicap at Newbury in October on only outing of 1981.
G. Kindersley.

CALMACUTTER 4 br.g. Murrayfield 119–Snow Leap 66 (King's Leap 111) —
(1980 6v 6fg 6f 7f 8fg 8f 8.2s 1981 11s) poor maiden; sometimes wears
blinkers. *A. W. Jones.*

CALSONG 2 b.c. Song 132–Calspea 81 (Calpurnius 122) (1981 5s 5g² 6s 5g) **54**
Apr 20; 2,800Y; leggy colt; first foal; dam won at up to 13.8f; favourite when
½-length second of 6 to Bonny Bassett in seller at Redcar in May; having first
race for 5 months when tried over 6f and gave impression on next outing that
he would be suited by trip; sold 310 gns Doncaster October Sales. *J. Hardy.*

CALVANIST (FR) 4 b.g. Reform 132–Calve 117 (Bold Ruler) (1980 8g —
1981 12f) strong, compact gelding; winner over hurdles but has shown no
form on flat; sold 2,000 gns Newmarket July Sales. *M. Chapman.*

CALVOCORESSI (USA) 4 br.g. Cornish Prince–Wire Chief (Gallant Man) —
(1980 8g 10d⁴ 1981 12s) lengthy gelding; won maiden race at Newmarket
at 2 yrs; lightly raced and well beaten since; should stay middle distances;
acts on a firm surface. *F. Winter.*

CALYPSO BAY 2 b. or br.c. Blue Cashmere 129–Lobster Pot 64 (Silver Shark **80** p
129) (1981 7g) Apr 27; lightly-made colt; second foal; dam, poor handicapper,
stayed 1½m; 20/1, always prominent on outside when 4¾ lengths fifth of 22 to
Rocamadour in maiden race at Newmarket in October; promises to stay 1m;
should improve. *E. Eldin.*

CALYPSO JOE 5 ch.g. Sovereign Gleam 117–Sarah Gee (Goldhill 125) (1980 —
18d 16s 16s 14g 1981 12s) big, strong gelding; stays well; seems to act on
any going; sold 5,000 gns Ascot October Sales. *N. Gaselee.*

CAMACHO (USA) 6 b.g. Mickey McGuire–To My Lady (Amber Morn) **72**
(1980 6g 8g² 8fg 8f³ 8g 8h³ 10g* 10.2g 10.2d* 10d² 11d 1981 10d 10g 12f* 11.7fg
10fg² 12h² 10f³ 12s⁴ 10.2d⁴) quite a modest handicapper; won at Chepstow
in July; stays 1½m; acts on any going but goes well on top-of-the-ground;
suitable mount for a boy; does best when ridden up with pace; game. *G. Cottrell.*

CAMALOO 3 b.f. Take a Reef 127–Evening Storm (Arctic Storm 134) (1980 NR —
1981 5fg⁴ 5f 6f 6fg 5g 6s 6fg 6d) 600Y; compact filly; third live foal; half-sister
to 1978 2-y-o 5f winner Nadwa (by Tyrant); dam won over 7f in Ireland; poor
form, including in selling and claiming handicaps. *D. Wilson.*

CAMBRIDGE GOLD 7 b.g. Sassafras 135–Greyia (Grey Sovereign 128§) —
(1980 NR 1981 12d) lightly raced on flat nowadays; stays 1¾m well; acts
on firm going; suitable mount for an inexperienced rider. *M. Tate.*

CAMBRO BOY 5 b.g. Mandamus 120–Palmette 103 (Premonition 130) —
(1980 18d 1981 16s⁴ 12s 18d) workmanlike gelding; plater; suited by a test
of stamina; acts on soft going; has been tried in blinkers. *R. Hobson.*

CAMERATA (USA) 2 b.c. Stage Director–Foxy Pam (Tudorich 115) (1981 **63**
5g⁴ 5g² 5fg³ 6g 6fg 7fg 8f 7d) Apr 16; $16,000Y, resold $25,000Y; compact
colt; half-brother to 2 minor winners; dam won over 5f at 3 yrs; in frame in
maiden races in the spring but isn't much better than a plater; stays 7f; blinkered
fifth and final outings. *S. Norton.*

CAMISITE 3 ch.c. Hittite Glory 125–Camisole 94 (Psidium 130) (1980 6g **88**
5d² 6d* 6d³ 1981 5s³ 5s² 6g 6s² 6d) leggy colt; ran on strongly when in
frame in handicaps at Doncaster and Nottingham in the spring and at Lingfield
in October; unlucky in running third start; suited by 6f and will probably stay
further; yet to race on a firm surface. *W. O'Gorman.*

CAMPTON 3 b.g. Sharp Edge 123–Gretel (Grey Sovereign 128§) (1980 5s **67**
7g² 7f² 7fg 8d 8s³ 8.2s 8d 1981 10s² 12g 12g* 13fg 16.5f) workmanlike
gelding; has looked ungenuine on occasions, but did nothing wrong when beating
Monevette in good style by 2½ lengths in seller at Thirsk in May; sold out of
J. Sutcliffe's stable 4,100 gns afterwards; well beaten when next seen out in
September; stays 1½m (not certain to get 2m); acts on any going; has been tried
in blinkers. *M. W. Easterby.*

CANADIAN CHARISMA 3 b.f. Supreme Sovereign 119–Howrytuar 90 **—**
(Sound Track 132) (1980 NR 1981 7f 7g) neat filly; half-sister to useful 5f
to 1m winner My Therape (by Jimmy Reppin); dam won at 5f to 7f; no show
in minor event at Leicester and maiden race at Salisbury in June. *R. Laing.*

CANAILLE 3 b.f. African Sky 124–Canning Place (Never Say Die 137) (1980 **101**
6s 7g 7g* 1981 8s* 8s³ 8f* 7g³ 8.2v) quite attractive, rangy filly; neck winner
of handicaps at Wolverhampton in April (from Majorian) and Pontefract in June
(from Rio Deva), on latter course being eased right up after quickening clear;
sweating when third in similar events at Wolverhampton in between and Newmarket in July; off course 3 months afterwards and soundly beaten on return;
will stay 1¼m; acts on any going; suitable mount for an apprentice. *H. Cecil.*

CANDAULES 3 b.c. Supreme Sovereign 119–Sweet and Naughty 76 (Connaught **70**
130) (1980 5.8fg² 5.8g² 7g⁴ 6fg 7h³ 7g* 1981 7d³ 5.8d 10f 10f) strong, quite
attractive colt; not disgraced in handicaps first 2 outings, but wasn't seen out
after July; not certain to stay 1¼m; acts on hard going; sometimes blinkered;
dwelt third start. *C. James.*

CANDESCENCE 2 ch.f. Roan Rocket 128–Miss Candine 66 (King Emperor) **65**
(1981 5d 5fg² 5g⁴ 5g³ 5d³ 5fg 7g) Mar 7; 5,000Y; compact filly; first foal; dam,
half-sister to very useful sprinters Canteen and Staincross, was placed over 1¼m
and 2m; in frame in maiden and minor events in the spring; should be suited by
6f or more. *R. Hannon.*

CANDIDE 2 gr.f. Bustino 136–Matinee 119 (Zeddaan 130) (1981 7.2d* 7.3d* **109**
7g) Feb 22; tall, rangy filly; third foal; closely related to 3 y-o 6f and 1m
winner Melodrama (by Busted) and half-sister to 1978 2-y-o 5f winner Safety
Curtain (by Roan Rocket); dam won Portland Handicap and is half-sister to
smart Kittyhawk (by Bustino); successful in maiden race at Haydock in August
and 11-runner nursery at Newbury the following month, putting up an excellent
effort under top weight when winning latter very comfortably by 4 lengths
from Man Overboard; last of 8 to Top Hope after leading for over 5f in Rockfel
Stakes at Newmarket in October (wore bandages behind and looked to have gone
over the top); will stay at least 1m; much better than her Newmarket running
suggests and should make a very useful 3-y-o. *R. Hern.*

CANDLE POWER 3 br.f. Dynastic 105–Shine Bright 72 (Scintillant) (1980 **—**
NR 1981 12fg⁴ 15fg 11f 11d) third live foal; dam stayed 1m and also won over
hurdles; showed signs of a little ability at Hamilton on first and last starts.
Mrs A. Cousins.

CAN-DO-MORE 4 gr.c. Dancer's Image–Macha's Jewel (Majestic Prince) **64**
(1980 8d 7f² 7fg 7f 7.2g 1981 8v 8g 8g 7d 8f 8.3fg* 8g) useful-looking colt; has
stringhalt; dropped in class when easily winning selling handicap at Windsor in
July (bought in 3,100 gns); stays 1m well; acts on firm going; usually blinkered;
seemed to shirk the issue fourth start; sold 4,100 gns Doncaster September
Sales, resold 1,450 gns Ascot December Sales. *N. Callaghan.*

CANDY CASTLE 2 b.f. Habitat 134–Jujube 102 (Ribero 126) (1981 6s³) **82** p
Apr 19; tall, rangy filly; third foal; half-sister to fairly useful 1m and 1¼m winner
Maintop (by High Top); dam, a stayer, won 5 of her 6 races; 14/1-shot, moved well
to start and stayed on nicely without being knocked about to be 4 lengths third of
12 to Dancing Rocks in Blue Seal Stakes at Ascot in September; will stay at
least 1m; sure to improve and win races in 1982. *P. Walwyn.*

CANDY STREET 3 b.f. Streetfighter 120–Sweet Boronia 96 (Mandamus 120) **—**
(1980 5g 5fg 5d 5s 5fg 5g 6g 6fg 1981 7d 10d 8.3s 8d 10d 8f 7fg) sturdy filly;
useless; has been tried in blinkers. *R. Hoad.*

CANIO 4 b.g. Welsh Pageant 132–Nedda 113 (Alcide 136)   (1980 8f 10.4f 10g 8g   —
8d 8f⁴ 1981 10g 12d³ 10g 12g 14fg)   lightly-made gelding; fairly useful handicapper; stayed on very gamely when close third to Morality Stone in Newbury
Summer Cup in June, easily best effort in 1981; suited by 1½m; acts on a firm and
a soft surface; blinkered once at 3 yrs; sold to J. Old 5,800 gns Ascot September
Sales. *H. Candy.*

CANNON FLYER 2 gr.f. Imperial Crown 96–Sovereign Jewel (Pirate King 129)   —
(1981 5.8f 6g)   Mar 3; 400Y; second reported foal; dam of no account; in rear in
sellers at Bath in July and Nottingham in August. *J. Bosley.*

CANNON KING 5 b.h. Owen Anthony 102–Primmy 56 (Primera 131)   (1980   —
8d 8fg 8fg* 8d 10g³ 10fg³ 10g² 9fg* 9f 8.2s 10g³ 1981 10g)   smallish horse;
quite a useful handicapper in 1980; soundly beaten only start at 5 yrs in May;
stays 1¼m; acts on any going; good mount for an apprentice. *J. Dunlop.*

CANNON SHELL (USA) 2 ch.c. Torsion–Promise Us (Promise)   (1981 6g³   **86** P
5s*)   Apr 7; $65,000Y; good-topped, useful sort; good mover; first foal; dam
won 13 races, including claiming events, and $112,000 at up to 1m; stormed
clear 1½f out when winning £3,300 event at York in October in great style
by 5 lengths from odds-on Path To Glory; will stay 6f+ (very green when tried
over 6f); acts on soft going; a likeable individual who should improve considerably
on his 2-y-o form in 1982. *M. Albina.*

CANNON SHOT 3 ro.g. Ragstone 128–Kinharvie 63 (Abernant 142)   (1980   **59**
NR   1981 10fg 11.7f² 12s)   3,500Y; small gelding; third living foal; brother to
useful 1¼m performer Lanarkland; dam placed over 1m; clear of remainder
when 2 lengths second to Java Lights in maiden race at Bath in July, best
effort; stays 1½m. *J. Dunlop.*

CANOODLE 3 ch.f. Warpath 113–Turtle Dove (Gyr 131)   (1980 7d 8s 1981 8g   **66**
12.5f* 12fg* 12.5f² 13fg 12.2g 13d³ 16s² 16s³ 18g)   small, lightly-made filly;
successful in June in handicaps at Stockton (beat Beechwood Seeker very
narrowly after running green) and Beverley (won by 1½ lengths from The Small
Miracle); placed in similar events afterwards; stays 2m (didn't seem to get 2¼m
on final start); acts on any going. *C. Thornton.*

CANTABILE 2 b.f. Bustino 136–Penumbra 99 (Wolver Hollow 126)   (1981 5g   —
6g)   Mar 30; sparely-made filly; fourth foal; dam sprinter; unquoted when in
rear in sizeable fields of maidens at Lingfield in September (last) and Newmarket
in October. *P. Mitchell.*

CANTELUPE 6 ch.m. Brioche 108–Robbi Tobbi (Rapace 130)   (1980 12d³ 13d   —
12h 12d 1981 10.2s 12s 16d)   poor maiden; stays well; has worn blinkers;
suitable mount for an amateur rider. *J. Priday.*

CANTENAC BROWN (USA) 2 b.g. Sham–Swingster (Bold Ruler)   (1981   **74**
6g 7g 7fg)   Apr 24; $60,000Y; neat, attractive gelding; half-brother to very
useful French 1m winner Clodion (by Prove Out); dam, stakes-placed winner at up
to 7f, comes from very good family; nearest at finish when about 7 lengths fifth
of 8 to Triple Axel in minor event at Epsom in September, third outing and best
effort; will stay at least 1m. *B. Swift.*

CANTON LIGHTNING 3 ro.f. Rheingold 137–Canton Silk 108 (Runnymede   **102**
123)   (1980 7g² 8f² 1981 12.3d⁴ 10.2g* 12g 12fg² 12d² 12d³ 14.6g 15g²)   tall
filly; third foal; half-sister to very useful 5f to 8.5f winner Royal Pinnacle (by
High Top); dam 5f performer; made all and kept on gamely when beating Alma
Ata by 1½ lengths in minor event at Doncaster in May; also in frame in Cheshire
Oaks, quite valuable handicaps at Goodwood (close second to Grain Race)
and Newmarket, Galtres Stakes at York (about 7 lengths third to Ma Femme),
and amateur riders event at Ayr; best form at up to 1½m; yet to race on very soft
going but acts on any other; wore blinkers in 1980 and again on last 2 outings;
sold 50,000 gns Newmarket December Sales. *B. Hills.*

CAN'T SWIM 2 b.f. Bruni 132–Out of Depth 65 (Deep Diver 134)   (1981 7g   **59**
7g 7fg 6fg 8.2fg 8g)   May 8; compact, strong-quartered filly; first foal; dam 5f
winner; plater; best run at 6f; blinkered last 3 outings; sweated up badly on third
and fourth starts. *P. Cundell.*

CAPELLI 3 bl.g. Lord Nelson 107–Lady Courageous (Cash and Courage 116)   —
(1980 7s 1981 10s 11.5f 8f 8.2f 7f 9d)   lightly-made gelding; no worthwhile
form in varied company, including selling; springer in market final start; trained
most of season by Miss A. Hill-Wood. *W. Charles.*

174

CAPRICORN LINE   3 ch.c. High Line 125–Floradora Do 85 (Derring-Do 131) **102**
(1980 7fg² 7fg³ 1981 7fg 10s* 10g² 10d* 10.6s² 13.3g² 12fg² 12g² 14g*) lightly-
made colt; won maiden race at Nottingham and handicap at Leicester in the
spring and £3,900 handicap at Newmarket in October, all in smooth fashion;
stayed on strongly to beat Keelby Kavalier by 2½ lengths in last-named; runner-
up in well-contested handicaps at Haydock, Newbury (to very cheeky winner
Taher in Morland Brewery Trophy and to Karadar in A.T.S. Trophy) and at
Newmarket in between his last 2 wins; suited by 1¾m; yet to race on very firm
going but acts on any other; sometimes tends to sweat up and is not the easiest of
rides, but is nevertheless most genuine and consistent. *L. Cumani.*

CAPRILI (FR)   3 gr.f. Caro 133–Vivarella (Cambremont 121) (1980 6fg 6g   —
1981 7g 10f 8fg 8.2s 8s 10v) close-coupled filly; showed some ability at 2 yrs but
didn't find her form in 1981; blinkered final outing. *G. Balding.*

CAPSTAN   3 b.c. Welsh Pageant 132–Packet 96 (Royal Palace 131) (1980 6g² **115**
1981 10fg 12f⁴ 12fg* 12d³ 14fg* 12fg⁴ 16g²) strong, compact, good sort; second
foal; dam, half-sister to smart stayer Mariner, won at up to 1¾m; ran an extraordinary race when about 6½ lengths fourth to Light Cavalry in Princess of Wales's
Stakes at Newmarket in July, making up an astonishing amount of ground in
closing stages after looking at one stage as if he might be pulled up; confirmed
that promise with all-the-way wins in 5-runner Alycidon Stakes at Goodwood
later in month (beat Castle Keep gamely by ¾ length) and 3-runner March Stakes
on same course in August (responded really well when ridden 3f out and came
home 8 lengths clear of On A Cloud), breaking course record in both events;
shade disappointing when 10 lengths third to Glint of Gold in Great Voltigeur
Stakes at York in between, but wasn't disgraced when 8 lengths fourth to
Critique in Cumberland Lodge Stakes at Ascot in September (blinkered, made
running at a tremendous gallop) or when 5 lengths second to Centroline in
Jockey Club Cup at Newmarket in October (tended to hang before delivering
his challenge); suited by a test of stamina; possibly needs a sound surface. *R.
Hern.*

CAPTAIN BRASSBOUND   4 b.g. Brigadier Gerard 144–Hardware 86 (Hard **41**
Sauce 131) (1980 10s 8g* 7f⁴ 8fg 11g 12.3fg⁴ 10s 8s⁴ 8d 1981 7g⁴ 8.2d 12g²)
fair sort; poor handicapper; stays 1½m; seems to act on any going. *R.
McDonald.*

CAPTAIN HENRY   2 ch.c. Bay Express 132–Astraline 97 (Skymaster 126) **85**
(1981 5s 5f³ 6g 6d 6fg* 6d³ 6g) May 4; 10,000F, 6,200Y; well-made colt;
good mover; third foal; half-brother to minor 9f winner Fast Green (by Cavo
Doro); dam sprinter; returned to form when winning 11-runner maiden race
at Yarmouth in August by 2½ lengths from Sandwalker; far from disgraced
when 8 lengths third of 16 to Hollywood Party in nursery at Nottingham the
following month but was quickly beaten and finished last of 17 when gambled
on in similar race at Newmarket in October; stays 6f; probably acts on any
going. *R. Armstrong.*

CAPTAIN NICK   5 b.h. Sharpen Up 127–Centime 82 (Double Jump 131) **112**
(1980 6f 6f³ 6fg* 6fg 6fg 6fg⁴ 7g* 6s 7g² 7g³ 7fg³ 7g 1981 6g 7d² 8s 7g 8f 7fg
7f* 8fg 8d² 7fg⁴ 7g 7s) strong horse; very useful performer; returned to form
in Ward Hill Bunbury Cup (Handicap) at Newmarket in July, coming with a
strong run to lead inside final furlong and beat Tower Joy by 1½ lengths; fine
1½ lengths second to Silver Season in Rose of York Handicap at York in August;
stays 1m; acts very well on firm ground and is unsuited by very soft; has twice
worn blinkers; suitable mount for an apprentice; best on a galloping track;
sent to America. *J. Hindley.*

CAPTAIN OATES   2 b.c. Oats 126–Gay Signal (Lord Gayle 124) (1981 **64**
5g 6fg) Apr 18; IR 3,200Y; first foal; dam won over 1m in Ireland; 50/1
and having first race for 4 months when 9 lengths sixth of 11 to Epithet in
minor event at Windsor in September, better effort; bred to stay middle distances.
N. Vigors.

CAPTAIN SYD   2 ch.c. Import 127–Rumstar 59 (Rum) (1981 6fg 6fg 8d   —
8s) Apr 6; 3,000Y; strong, big-barrelled colt; first foal; dam won 7f seller;
in rear in varied company, including selling. *S. Matthews.*

CAPTIVE MAIDEN   3 b.f. Manacle 123–Sally Ann III (Port Corsair 98)   —
(1980 5g 5d⁴ 5fg 5g 5g 7d 1981 8d 9s 8d) workmanlike non-thoroughbred filly;
poor maiden; sometimes sweats up. *M. Bradley.*

CAPVISTA 6 b.g. Captain's Gig–Alta-Vista (Skymaster 126) (1980 8g 1981 —
10.2d) winning hurdler; well beaten both starts on flat. *J. Spearing.*

CARALIA 3 b.f. Caracolero 131–Mortefontaine (Polic 126) (1980 7g 7.2d³ —
8fg³ 1981 9s 12d⁴ 12d⁴ 11.7h⁴ 15.5s) big, well-made filly; fourth in minor
event at Salisbury in May and maiden races at Lingfield and Bath in August;
suited by 1¼m; wears blinkers; sold 3,500 gns Newmarket December Sales. *R.
Hern.*

CARAN D'ACHE 2 ch.g. Huntercombe 133–Alfambra (Nashua) (1981 5s —
6s 6g) May 29; 5,400Y; quite well-made gelding; first foal; dam, second over
11f in France, is half-sister to smart American 2-y-o Silver Spook; behind in
maiden races at Warwick, Newbury and Newmarket in October. *G. Balding.*

CARDIE GIRL 3 ch.f. Sharpen Up 127–Gold Cypher 76 (Pardao 120) (1980 —
6f² 7g² 1981 8f³) leggy, lightly-made filly; good walker and mover; second to
Star Pastures and to Golden Bowl at York as a 2-y-o; looked fit but didn't
run up to her best when close third of 20 behind Reedmace in maiden race at
Doncaster in July on only outing of 1981 (tenderly ridden); possibly only just
stays 1m; sent to race in USA. *W. Hastings-Bass.*

CARDIFF 4 ch.c. Appiani II 128–Christiana 106 (Double Jump 131) (1980 **73**
10d* 12f 9.6f 9fg³ 11.7s³ 10fg⁴ 1981 12s² 12d 14d* 14s 16s 16fg) lightly-made
colt; narrowly won handicap at Salisbury in May; possibly stays 2m; suited
by some give in the ground; bandaged in front final start. *R. Hoad.*

CARDINAL FLOWER 4 ch.c. Sharpen Up 127–Ixia 91 (I Say 125) (1980 **90**
8fg² 8fg* 10.5d² 10s 10g* 9fg⁴ 9f 1981 10fg 10.2g 8g² 9fg 8fg² 8g² 8fg* 8fg³
8fg²) good sort; good mover; fairly useful handicapper; beat Prince Diligence
in quite good style by a length at Ayr in August; stays 1¼m; acts on a firm
and a soft surface; has run respectably for an amateur rider; ran poorly second
start. *G. Pritchard-Gordon.*

CARDINAL PALACE 3 ch.f. Royal Palace 131–Early Rose 61 (Will Somers **85**
114§) (1980 NR 1981 9.4g 8g² 9.4fg² 9.4g* 10f 11fg 11d² 11d⁴ 12g*) 3,500Y;
tall, lightly-made filly; half-sister to 3 winners, including 1m and 1¼m winner
Secateurs (by Sharp Edge); dam of little account; successful in maiden race
at Carlisle in July and handicap at Newmarket in October, showing much
improved form when beating The Small Miracle by 4 lengths in latter; suited
by 1½m; acts on a firm and a soft surface. *R. D. Peacock.*

CARDINALS WALK 3 ch.g. Red Alert 127–Stay Nice 85 (Nice Guy 123) —
(1980 6fg 6d 8fg 8d⁴ 1981 10d 12g 8.3fg 10.1fg³ 12fg) attractive, shapely
gelding; has shown only a little ability; promises to stay 1½m (tailed off in a
seller over 1½m); sweated up second and third starts. *R. Hannon.*

CARD PALMER 5 ch.h. Malicious–Pardilly 71 (Pardao 120) (1980 16f* —
16f 15h³ 12f⁴ 15f 14.6g 1981 12f 12.2fg 12f) poor handicapper; suited by a test
of stamina; acts on any going; sold 850 gns Doncaster October Sales. *R.
Fisher.*

CARELESS TALK (FR) 3 ch.g. Swing Easy 126–War Talk 90 (Assagai) —
(1980 NR 1981 10s 10.1v 12g 10h 9g) big, lengthy gelding; no sign of ability,
including in sellers. *C. Wildman.*

CAREY'S CHOICE 6 b.g. Reliance II 137–Piave (Alcide 136) (1980 10g **58**
10g 11.7s 10g* 10g 10.2g 10g 1981 10s 10.6g 12g² 10.5d 12g 10g 10f 12.3fg
10g) strong gelding; poor handicapper nowadays; stays 1½m; acts on firm
going; suitable mount for an apprentice; usually wears blinkers; sold 2,800
gns Doncaster September Sales. *W. Elsey.*

CARFLAX (USA) 3 ch.g. Prove Out–Sewing Circle (Round Table) (1980 —
5s 5f 6d 7s 1981 12s 8fg 12s 12f) neat gelding; behind in varied company;
backward and proved difficult to steer on reappearance (apprentice ridden);
quite stoutly bred; sweating third start; sold 660 gns Ascot 2nd June Sales.
D. Ancil.

CARIBBEAN BLUE 3 b. or br.f. Blue Cashmere 129–Dido's Granddaughter —
(By Thunder! 122) (1980 6s 1981 8g 7.6g 11.5g³ 8.2s⁴ 10s) fair sort; quite
a moderate maiden; probably stays 11.5f. *J. Winter.*

CARIBBEAN DREAM 2 b.g. Saucy Kit 76–Lady Lake (Tennyson 119) **60**
(1981 5g 5d 6g 5fg 6fg³ 5g 7g² 7fg 8f 8.2d) May 25; small, non-thoroughbred
gelding; half-brother to successful chaser Lakeside (by Waterfall); dam placed
over hurdles; plater; proved well suited by 7f when length second of 11 to

Idle Warrior at Newcastle in July, best effort; should stay 1m; possibly unsuited by a soft surface. *T. Barnes.*

CARIBBEAN SUN 3 ch.g. Midsummer Night II 117–Sleepy (Hereward the Wake 75) (1980 10d 1981 10s) plater; tailed off on only start at both 2 yrs and 3 yrs, but needed race each time. *T. Kersey.* —

CARLTON HALL 4 b.g. Club House 119–Donna Lollo 102 (Donatello II) (1980 10f⁴ 8f² 8f 8fg 9.4g³ 8fg 8d* 9g 10s 10.6s 1981 11s 12d 7g 8fg* 9g* 8fg⁴ 10.5s⁴) workmanlike gelding; won ladies race at Redcar in June and apprentice handicap at Newcastle in July; stays 9f; acts on any going and on any track; good mount for an inexperienced rider. *Denys Smith.* **59**

CARLTON LADY 3 b.f. Redundant 120–Gala Honey 66 (Honeyway 125) (1980 5fg 5g 1981 8s 13.8f) useless. *D. Yeoman.* —

CARMEN MARIA 2 b.f. Bold Lad (Ire) 133–Eulalie 85 (Queen's Hussar 124) (1981 7g) Apr 5; compact, rather lightly-made filly; first foal; dam, half-sister to very useful animals Honorius and Suni, won at up to 10.8f; 12/1, dropped right out after halfway when behind in 16-runner maiden race won by Tants at Leicester in October. *P. Walwyn.* —

CARNATION 3 ch.f. Runnymede 123–Natural Flora (Floribunda 136) (1980 5fg 5fg³ 5g² 5g³ 5g 5f 5g 5s⁴ 6s 1981 5g 5fg) fair sort; well beaten in 1981, including in seller; best form at 5f; blinkered fifth outing as a 2-y-o. *E. Weymes.* —

CARNIVAL DAN 2 b.c. Carnival Dancer 113–Alegria (Right Boy 137) (1981 5g) May 2; first reported foal; dam of little account; unquoted when last of 14 in seller won by Aqua Verde at Catterick in October. *D. Yeoman.* —

CAROLINE FISHER 2 b.f. English Prince 129–Travelling Fair 95 (Vienna 127) (1981 6fg 6s 6d) May 6; 2,600F, 1,950Y; unfurnished filly; half-sister to 3 winners, including fairly useful 1m and 1¼m winner Dibbinsdale Lad (by Sandford Lad); dam best at around 1m; in rear in maiden auction event at Kempton in July (moved badly to start) and maiden races at Hamilton and Leicester at the back-end. *A. Jarvis.* —

CAROUSER 4 b.g. Warpath 113–Brandy (Busted 134) (1980 12.3f 12fg³ 11fg⁴ 8g 9.4g² 10d³ 9s 12g* 12g³ 12.2d² 12d² 12d² 1981 12g 12g⁴ 12fg 12g 12.2fg 12f⁴) lightly-made, lean gelding; plater; suited by 1½m; acts on a firm and a soft surface; has run creditably for a boy; has worn bandages; sold to D. Chapman 2,100 gns Doncaster October Sales. *C. Thornton.* **42**

CARPENTER'S BOY 3 b.g. Steel Heart 128–Grandee Ann (Cyane) (1980 6g 1981 6s 6g 7g 6d 6d 5f) neat, strong gelding; soundly beaten in maiden and minor races and a seller. *Denys Smith.* —

CARPET GENERAL 5 b.g. Sallust 134–Red Val 110 (Red God 128§) (1980 6s² 7.2d* 7f* 8f* 7fg 8g* 1981 8d 12d 8f 8g³ 8fg 8g) strong gelding; poor mover nowadays; much improved in 1980 and developed into a useful handicapper; didn't run up to his best at 5 yrs; stays 1m well but doesn't stay 1¼m; acts on any going but is possibly suited by some give in the ground; suitable mount for an apprentice; genuine. *Sir Mark Prescott.* —

CARREG CENNEN 2 ch.c. Native Bazaar 122–Cennen-Olive (Wolver Hollow 126) (1981 5g 5s⁴ 5.8g² 5f 5g) Apr 28; tall, leggy colt; third foal; brother to a winner in Trinidad; dam of no account; in frame in maiden races at Wolverhampton in May and Bath in June; seen out infrequently afterwards; suited by 6f; ran badly only outing on firm going. *Dr A. Jones.* **68**

CARRIAGE WAY 7 br.h. Track Spare 125–Polyandrist 92 (Polic 126) (1980 8g 7.5g² 8g 8g 8d³ 8fg* 8f⁴ 8f 8fg* 8d³ 7d 8g 8g 8fg 8d 8d² 1981 8s* 8v² 7d 8g 8fg 8fg 8d* 8d 8s 8v 8g) modest handicapper; won apprentice events at Doncaster in March and Yarmouth in September; best form at around 1m; acts on any going; blinkered once in 1979; good mount for a boy; not particularly consistent. *W. Stubbs.* **86** d

CARROLLS 2 b.f. Yankee Gold 115–Artist's Model (Pampered King 121) (1981 5g 5fg 5f 5g 5s) small filly; worthless plater; blinkered final start; sold 310 gns Doncaster November Sales. *W. Stubbs.* —

CARRY ON AGAIN 3 ch.g. Swing Easy 126–Hi-Conkers 86 (Sica Boy 132) (1980 5s⁴ 5f⁴ 5f* 5fg² 5f³ 6f 6g 6fg 7fg 1981 6fg 6g 8g) rangy gelding; won maiden race at Sandown as a 2-y-o; lightly raced and no form in 1981 (off

course nearly 6 months after second outing); not sure to stay 7f; looked temperamental when blinkered fourth outing in 1980; trained until after second start
by R. Armstrong. *G. Fletcher.*

CARRY OVER 3 b.g. Some Hand 119–Hardella 60 (Hard Ridden 131) (1980   **61**
6g 7fg 6g 1981 8d 8fg 8fg³ 7f³ 8fg 8f² 8g 7d) lengthy, workmanlike gelding;
placed in 2 handicaps and a maiden race; unplaced in sellers on other occasions;
stays 1m; acts on firm going; moved badly to start and pulled hard seventh
outing. *G. Balding.*

CARTRON 3 b.g. Military 112–Belle Tack (Hard Tack 111§) (1980 NR 1981   —
10.6d 5fg) half-brother to 2 minor sprint winners; dam unraced; in rear in
maiden races at Haydock and Warwick (last of 11) in August. *J. Tierney.*

CARVED OPAL 3 gr.c. Arch Sculptor 123–Pale Maid 93 (Rise 'N Shine II)   **88**
(1980 NR 1981 7d² 8d³ 7g² 10s² 11d 10fg* 12fg³ 10.1fg² 11.7fg² 10d* 10g³)
3,000Y; useful sort; half-brother to a winner in Belgium and to a winning
hurdler; dam won over 6f at 2 yrs and stayed 1½m; successful in maiden race
at Folkestone in June (made most to beat Justiniani 4 lengths) and handicap
at Newbury in September (stayed on really well under strong pressure to beat
Seven Seas 1½ lengths); placed most other outings; stays 1½m; probably acts
on any going; sold privately to be trained by F. Winter after final outing.
B. Hills.

CARVERS CORAH 7 br.m. Easter Island 101–Marieran (Pappatea 114)   **50**
(1980 12.2v 10.8f³ 12fg 12f³ 12f³ 12fg 12.2s⁴ 12fg 12d³ 11.5g 12g* 12.2g² 12g²
13.1h 12g 12g² 18d 12d 1981 13s 16fg² 12g 12d³ 15.8g 14f 12f⁴ 12.2fg 12fg³ 12f
12f 12f⁴ 13fg 12g⁴ 12g 12g) poor handicapper; stays 2m; acts on any going
except heavy; good mount for an inexperienced rider; needs to be held up
and doesn't find much off bridle. *D. Leslie.*

CASA ESQUILLINA (USA) 3 b.c. Key To The Kingdom–Missile Miss   **82**
(Cyclotron) (1980 6d 7fg² 6d² 1981 8g 7g³ 7fg² 6f* 8g 6g² 6g 6d) workmanlike, slightly hollow-backed colt with a round action; beat Pykestaff 1½ lengths
in 20-runner maiden race at Brighton in July; second to Arrowhead in similar
event at Newcastle the previous month and to Think Ahead in handicap at
Yarmouth in September; should stay at least 1m; yet to race on very soft going,
but acts on any other. *P. Cole.*

CASE HISTORY 3 gr.c. Track Spare 125–Petite Path 106 (Sovereign Path 125)   **72 d**
(1980 5fg 5g 5f 6f 5d² 1981 5d* 6d⁴ 6g 6fg 6fg 5s 6s) lightly-made, fair sort;
won handicap at Warwick in April by a length from Royal Blood, finishing
strongly; ran best subsequent race third start; bred to get further than 6f;
possibly needs a soft surface; often wears a bandage on his off-fore. *R. Hannon.*

CASE THE JOINT 3 b.f. Upper Case–Ribo Pride 77 (Ribero 126) (1980 7g   —
1981 10s 10fg 10fg 8.2s) useful-looking filly; no sign of ability in maiden and
minor races; sold 450 gns Ascot October Sales. *D. Elsworth.*

CASH CACHE 2 ch.f. Continuation 120–Mia Chiloe (Royal Palm 131) (1981   **44**
5d⁴ 6f³ 7fg⁴ 8g) June 13; well-grown, leggy filly; first foal; dam ran twice;
plater; stays 7f (tailed off over 1m); sold 300 gns Doncaster October Sales.
J. Hardy.

CASHEL BAY 2 ch.c. Riboboy 124–Beech Tree 67 (Fighting Ship 121) (1981   **69**
5s³ 5d 5d³ 6d 5d 6g 7g 8g 7g 8s 10s) Mar 18; 6,000F, 5,200Y; workmanlike
colt; good mover; half-brother to 2 winners, including 7f winner Swing The
Axe (by No Mercy); dam a stayer; showed a fair amount of ability in varied
company but could finish only fifth when favourite for 17-runner seller at
Warwick in October on tenth outing; stays well; sweated up fourth outing;
wore blinkers on seventh and final starts. *G. Beeson.*

CASHMOOR 3 b.c. Ashmore 125–Go Friendly (Be Friendly 130) (1980 7d³   —
8g 1981 8g 8fg 10f 11.7h 10fg³ 12g 12f) strong, close-coupled colt; has shown
signs of ability in maiden races, on last occasion when running-on third to
Amina at Epsom in September; should stay 1½m; didn't move well final start.
R. Baker.

CASHWELL 4 b. or br.g. Blue Cashmere 129–Well Matched 79 (Niccolo Dell'   —
Arca) (1980 12g 10g 1981 8g 10fg 16.5fg) lengthy gelding; probably of
little account and looks temperamental; has worn blinkers; sold to S. Cole
510 gns Doncaster August Sales. *Hbt Jones.*

*Timeform Race Card Stakes, Redcar—Cassley River lands the odds
from First Tee*

CASS ARTE 4 ch.c. Bay Express 132–Last Report 86 (Democratic 124) (1980 —
7f 7.6f 8d 11d 8g 8.2g 8g 1981 9g 10g 8f) well beaten in varied company;
sometimes blinkered. *A. Jarvis.*

CASSIO LIL 2 b. or br.f. Scottish Rifle 127–Solway Bay 86 (Tamerlane 128) —
(1981 5d 5fg 5g 6f 7g 6d⁴) Feb 21; 3,000Y; leggy, lightly-made filly; half-
sister to several winners here and abroad, including Norsk St Leger winner
Halcyon Bay (by Henry the Seventh); dam 1¼m winner; poor plater; bred to
stay much further than 6f; usually blinkered; has worn bandages. *K. Ivory.*

CASSLEY RIVER 2 b.f. Relkino 131–Strathoykel 94 (Aberdeen 109) (1981 **94**
6f³ 7fg* 7d* 7fg* 8g⁴ 7g) Feb 25; leggy, rather narrow filly; good mover;
first foal; dam best at sprint distances; successful in maiden race at Warwick,
Timeform Race Card Stakes at Redcar and nursery at Wolverhampton; stayed
on well to beat Pinxton by 2 lengths on last-named course in August; again
ran well when 4½ lengths fourth of 13 to Nioulargo in nursery at Newmarket
in September; suited by 7f and 1m; acts on a firm and a soft surface; consistent
until running moderately final start. *Sir Mark Prescott.*

CASTAWAY (FR) 2 ch.f. Filiberto 123–Castania (Orsini 124) (1981 6fg —
6s 6d) workmanlike filly; fifth living foal; half-sister to French middle-distance
winner Stanaure (by Aureole) and very speedy Standaan (by Zeddaan); dam
never ran; behind in maiden races at Salisbury and Leicester and in Blue Seal
Stakes at Ascot. *C. Austin.*

CASTELNAU (USA) 3 b.c. Irish Castle–Bay of Lundy (Portsmouth) (1980 **98**
7fg² 8g² 10g³ 1981 12fg² 12s 16d² 16.9fg* 16f² 19fg* 18g) strong, good-
looking colt; has a good, long stride; won handicap at Wolverhampton and
Goodwood Stakes (Handicap) in very good style in July; sent to front 1½m
out and set a really good pace in latter event, and galloped on in tremendous
style up straight to win by 5 lengths from Atlantic Traveller; off course nearly
3 months before running in Tote Cesarewitch at Newmarket in October and
weakened very quickly to finish in rear behind Halsbury after striding along
very well in front for a long way (carried a lot of condition); stays extremely

179

Mr Richard Barber's "Castelnau"

well; has run creditably on a soft surface but is very well suited by top-of-the-ground. *P. Cole.*

CASTLE KEEP 4 b.c. Kalamoun 129–Fotheringay 101 (Right Royal V 135) **121**
1980 10fg* 12f3 13.3d* 12fg* 14.6g* 13.3fg* 1981 12g 12f4 12f2 12fg2 13.3fg2 13.5f2 11g* 10g)

Ragstone, Castle Keep's half-brother, won a maiden race, two minor events and a handicap from four starts at three years, improving steadily and giving every indication of developing into a good stayer. The following year he went on to win the Henry II Stakes and the Gold Cup. Castle Keep's record at three was also one of great improvement: racing exclusively in handicaps, he won five of his six races, finishing up with excellent victories against older horses in the Rockingham Handicap over the St Leger course and in the Coral Autumn Cup at Newbury. We reckoned he would have gone close in the Irish St Leger had he run. Castle Keep ran well enough as a four-year-old without reaching Ragstone's standards, and proved much better than a handicapper. Aimed principally at pattern races, he finished second in three Group 2 events; his one victory came in a listed race, the Doonside Cup at Ayr.

Three of Castle Keep's wins in 1980 were gained at distances in excess of a mile and a half, and it seemed reasonable to assume that a mile and three quarters or perhaps two miles would suit him ideally at four. In fact it wasn't until August, when he contested the Geoffrey Freer Stakes over an extended thirteen furlongs at Newbury, that he was given the opportunity of racing beyond a mile and a half as a four-year-old. He had previously run four times at a mile and a half, performing dismally in the Jockey Club Stakes at Newmarket in May, more encouragingly in the Hardwicke Stakes at Royal Ascot and creditably when second twice in July, being denied by Light Cavalry's rally in the Princess of Wales's Stakes at Newmarket and by Capstan's in the

Alycidon Stakes at Goodwood. In the Geoffrey Freer Stakes, as in his previous race, Castle Keep looked to be going really well as he ranged up two furlongs from home, but he was unable to cope with the Gold Cup winner Ardross, who left him surprisingly easily and beat him five lengths. In his next start, the Grand Prix de Deauville, Castle Keep came closest to winning a pattern race. Running him here seemed a shrewd piece of placing, for he received weight from the best horses. Unfortunately he came up against the improving Perrault, who was conceding 5 lb, and was beaten a short head by the subsequent Arc fourth. The Grand Prix distance, thirteen and a half furlongs, was the longest Castle Keep tackled in 1981. On his penultimate outing he picked up fairly valuable compensation, not being troubled to hold Shoot A Line by a length in the four-runner, eleven-furlong Doonside Cup, and he then finished a creditable eighth of sixteen to Vayrann in the mile-and-a-quarter Champion Stakes at Newmarket the following month, showing prominently until being outpaced in the last furlong.

Castle Keep (b.c. 1977)	Kalamoun (gr 1970)	Zeddaan (gr 1965)	Grey Sovereign
			Vareta
		Khairunissa (gr 1960)	Prince Bio
			Palariva
	Fotheringay (b 1964)	Right Royal V (br 1958)	Owen Tudor
			Bastia
		La Fresnes (ch 1953)	Court Martial
			Pin Stripe

Kalamoun, who died in 1979, had his first English pattern-race winners in 1980 with Kampala and Kalaglow. With Kalaglow and Castle Keep to represent him in 1981 he seemed sure to have similar success, if not greater, but neither managed to win a pattern race in the end. Castle Keep is one of four winners out of his dam, the two not so far mentioned being Castle Keep's full sister Castle Moon, who stayed two miles, and another modest filly Forsaken (by Bold Lad, Ire), successful at a mile and having form up to a mile and a half. The dam was a miler out of the very smart sprinter La Fresnes. Castle Keep stays in training. He is not an easy horse to assess. It is a pity that we were denied in 1981 the opportunity of seeing him race at a mile and three quarters or two miles, for that sort of distance might have shown him to better advantage. On the other hand he wasn't troubled to win at eleven furlongs and he ran well enough in the Champion Stakes. What is certain is that he is some way below the very best, for he was receiving weight when finishing second to Light Cavalry

Doonside Cup, Ayr—Castle Keep wins this listed race from Shoot A Line and Shotgun (grey)

CAS

and Ardross as well as when second to Perrault. Castle Keep, a neat, strong, good sort of colt, has yet to race on really soft going and is reported not to be suited by it, but he acts on any other. He isn't the easiest of rides. *J. Dunlop.*

CASTLEMAINE 3 ch.f. Lord Gayle 124–Mettle 107 (Pretendre 126) (1980 NR **96** 1981 8d³ 7g* 7s³ 8v 10f 8fg³ 9f* 12fg 8d 8d³) 8,400F, 31,000Y; sister to Melody, a fairly useful winner from 7f to 1½m in Ireland, and half-sister to a winner in USA; dam won twice over 5f at 2 yrs and stayed 1¼m; went down by a head to River Prince in maiden race at Phoenix Park in April but placings were reversed after a stewards enquiry; beat Northern Wings by a length in minor event at Gowran Park in August; usually had stiff tasks on her other starts, but finished third in Athasi Stakes at the Curragh, Cornelscourt Stakes at Leopardstown and handicap at Leopardstown again; stays 9f; acts on any going. *A. Maxwell, Ireland.*

CASTLESIZE 3 ch g. Status Seeker–Unharmed (Breakspear II) (1980 6g 6s — 6g 5d 6s⁴ 1981 7d 8g) workmanlike gelding; no worthwhile form in a variety of races. *J. Leigh.*

CASWELL ROAD 3 b.g. Tycoon II–Cherry Brandy (Tenerani 135) (1980 NR — 1981 9d) half-brother to several winners, including very useful miler Ndabibi (by Primera); dam never ran; 20/1 when seventh of 9 behind easy winner Nob in seller at Hamilton in September. *T. Taylor.*

CATISFIELD FLYER 2 gr.g. Dragonara Palace 115–Villarrica (Dan Cupid 132) — (1981 8s) May 25; useful-looking gelding; good walker; half-brother to 2 winners, including good French stayer Ribecourt (by Ribero); dam stayed 1½m; 50/1, didn't show a great deal when tenth of 12 to Jalmood in £3,300 event at Goodwood in September; gave trouble at start and was withdrawn at Newmarket the following month. *A. Ingham.*

CAUSE FOR APPLAUSE (USA) 2 b.c. Quack–Knowing Smile (Ruken) **81** (1981 5d² 6f²) Apr 19; $32,000F, $45,000Y; useful-looking colt; second foal; dam unraced sister to stakes winner and half-sister to high-class stayer Quicken Tree; second in maiden race at Folkestone in June and Fenwolf Stakes at Ascot (running on well when beaten a length by Norwick) later in month; looked a fair staying 2-y-o in the making but wasn't seen out again; will stay 1¼m. *G. Huffer.*

CAUTIOUS 2 ch.g. Malicious–Summer Rain (Palestine 133) (1981 5s 5g 5g **61** 6f² 6f² 6fg 6fg 7f³ 7.2v⁴(dis)) Mar 31; compact gelding; placed in sellers at Ripon (2) and Redcar; stays 7f; acts on any going; hung most of way on sixth outing and was blinkered next 3 starts. *M. W. Easterby.*

CAVA ALTA 3 b.g. Upper Case–Spring Exploit (Exploitation 108) (1980 NR — 1981 9.4g 12d 15.5g) fair sort; half-brother to useful stayer Mark Hush (by Lauso) and fair stayer The Froddler (by Philemon); dam unraced half-sister to top-class chaser Domacorn; never in race but showed signs of a little ability when about 15 lengths fifth of 6 finishers behind Aniece in maiden race at Redcar in August on second start. *N. Crump.*

CAVALIER 4 b.g. Moulton 128–Reload 119 (Reiko 136) (1980 10.1g 10g 14d — 14g 14.6d 1981 15.8g) strong gelding; well beaten in varied company; blinkered once in 1980; looks slow. *M. McCormack.*

CAVALIER SERVENTE 3 gr.c. Barbaro–Quoro Star (Quorum 126) (1980 **63** 6fg 7g 6f 7d⁴ 6d 1981 10s 10v 10fg 10fg³ 11d 8g 10d² 8g) strong colt; placed in maiden event at Beverley in September and minor race at Leicester in November; stays 1¼m; has worn bandages. *P. Wigham.*

CAVALLERIZZO (USA) 2 ch.c. Little Current–Lucky Traveler (Derring-Do **86** 131) (1981 5g* 5g²) Apr 30; $32,000Y; neat, attractive colt; excellent mover; fourth foal; half-brother to Irish 3-y-o 11.5f and 1¾m winner Airbus (by Best Turn) and a winner in Holland; dam, daughter of Oaks winner Homeward Bound, was very useful stakes winner at up to 7f; put up a remarkable display in 12-runner maiden race at Epsom in June, missing the break so badly he was tailed off after 1f but then finding his stride to such purpose that he got up to win going away by ¾ length from Cheap Seats; 11/4 on for minor event at San-down later in month but went down by ½ length to Plagal after disputing lead all way, only subsequent start; bred to stay middle distances; reportedly to race in California. *R. Price.*

CAVE DIVER 3 b.f. Cavo Doro 124–Jenny Diver 86 (Jimmy Reppin 131) **82** (1980 NR 1981 9d³ 12d 11.5g* 12f² 12g*) 2,000Y; big, strong filly; second living foal; half-sister to 5f winner Elmanoak (by Sharp Edge); dam sprinter; slowly away when 3 lengths third of 12 to Halsbury in newcomers event at

182

Wolverhampton in April; soundly beaten next time but did well when sent to Ireland; won maiden race at Down Royal in September and minor event at Dundalk in October, on former course beating Music Tree by 20 lengths when backed from 5/1 to evens; stays 1½m; formerly trained by G. Beeson. *P. Russell, Ireland.*

CAVENDISH 3 b.f. Kalamoun 129–Golden Gorse (Crepello 136) (1980 5fg 8d **64** 8d 1981 10s² 10s⁴ 10s³ 11.7s³ 14fg 16g² 12fg² 14fg) small filly; in frame in maiden races, a handicap, and an amateur riders event; stays well. *P. Bailey.*

CAVORT 3 b.f. Cavo Doro 124–Astraline 97 (Skymaster 126) (1980 6d 6g 7fg **58** 7g 8fg⁴ 1981 11.7s 10s 11.7f³ 13.4fg³ 12g 12.2fg 14fg) well-made filly; third in handicap at Windsor and maiden race at Chester in summer; stays 13f; well beaten last 3 starts, wearing blinkers on last occasion; sold 2,500 gns Ascot September Sales. *G. Pritchard-Gordon.*

CAVOTINA 3 b.g. Cavo Doro 124–Sweet Flight 81 (Falcon 131) (1980 NR — 1981 12d 15.5s) fifth foal; dam won at 1¼m and 13f; tailed off in gentleman riders race at Brighton (started slowly) and maiden event at Folkestone, both in October. *G. Balding.*

CAVO VARKA 4 ch.f. Cavo Doro 124–Treasure Boat 54 (Hook Money 124) — (1980 9f 10d 8d² 10g⁴ 8fg* 8fg 8.2g³ 8.2d 1981 8v 8g 8fg 8.2f 9fg 8fg 10.4s) quite attractive, well-made filly; ran moderately at 4 yrs; stays 1m well; acts on a firm and a soft surface; sometimes wears bandages; suited by enterprising riding tactics. *R. E. Peacock.*

CAWSTONELLA 2 b.f. Cawston's Clown 113–Lantao Lady 63 (King's Troop **54** 118) (1981 5d 5fg 6f² 6f³) Mar 22; 820Y; first foal; dam ran only twice; plater; runs as though she'll stay 7f. *J. Wilson.*

CAWSTON STAR 2 br.f. Comedy Star 121–Telouet 90 (Sing Sing 134) (1981 **66** 5.1f 5.1fg 6g 5f³ 5f² 5fg⁴ 5fg 5g 5g) smallish, fair sort; excellent mover; sister to a seemingly poor animal and half-sister to 3 winners, including useful 1977 2-y-o 5f performer Edna's Choice (by So Blessed); dam ran only 4 times; placed in maiden company at Folkestone and Beverley in August but is little better than plating class; promises to stay 6f; hung and nearly unseated rider on seventh outing, and didn't break too well on eighth. *H. Collingridge.*

CECCHETTI 2 gr c. Kalamoun 129–Kinharvie 63 (Abernant 142) (1981 8g) — Jan 26; 6,200F; half-brother to useful 1¼m winner Lanarkland (by Ragstone); dam placed twice over 1m; 16/1 shot in mid-division behind Dudley Wood in 27-runner minor event at Newmarket in October (not knocked about once chance had gone). *R. Price.*

CECCONI 4 b.g. High Top 131–Stardom 75 (Hornbeam 130) (1980 8f 12.3f — 12fg⁴ 13d² 13.4g² 16.9d* 16f⁴ 16f* 15.5f² 17.1d² 15.8d*12.5s* 1981 12.2d) workmanlike gelding; good walker; won 4 races in 1980; well beaten only start at 4 yrs in April; stays well; acts on any going; blinkered once at 3 yrs; good mount for an inexperienced rider. *S. Mellor.*

CEDRELLA 2 b.f. Averof 123–Maria Da Gloria (St Chad 120) (1981 6f 5f³ 6fg³ **73** 5g² 5fg² 5f* 5g³ 5d) May 2; lightly-made filly; not a good mover; third foal; half-sister to Italian winner Marfisa (by Green God); dam never ran; had excellent chance at weights in 4-runner nursery at Hamilton in September and made all to win by a length from Mummy's Delight; will be suited by a return to 6f; best form on a sound surface. *E. Weymes.*

CELESTIAL CHARMER 2 b.c. Star Appeal 133–Gloria Maremmana (King **72** p Emperor) (1981 5s³ 6f) Jan 26; neat, strong, attractive colt; good mover; first foal; dam won at 2 yrs in Italy and is daughter of useful Italian 5f and 1m winner Gloria Romana; second favourite but looking far from fully tuned up, when promising 5¼ lengths third of 16 to End of the Line in maiden race at Haydock in May; still looked as though run would do him good when about same distance sixth of 13 to Sangalkan in £5,600 maiden race at York the following month, only subsequent start; bred to stay at least 1m; probably still has improvement in him. *F. J. Houghton.*

CELESTIAL CITY 2 gr.f. Godswalk 130–Nibbler 66 (Primera 131) (1981 **97** 5g* 5g* 5g* 5f) Apr 16; IR 18,000Y; lengthy, attractive filly; half-sister to 3 winners here and abroad, including fairly useful 1977 Italian 2-y-o filly Shirleen (by Daring Display); dam granddaughter of celebrated broodmare Horama; put up a good performance to win 8-runner Uplands Park Acorn Stakes at Epsom in June, smoothly by 2½ lengths from To The Point; had previously run out a ¾-length winner of maiden race at Newmarket and Wilkinson Memorial

Stakes at York, beating Super Act and Hello Cuddles respectively; looked to be running up a bit light when odds on for Queen Mary Stakes at Royal Ascot and ran poorly, finishing ninth of 11 to Fly Baby after being in trouble some way from home; possibly unsuited by firm going; showed a distinct tendency to hang left both at York and Epsom. *H. Cecil.*

CELESTIAL DANCER 2 b.c. Godswalk 130–Oulanova (Nijinsky 138) (1981 **97**
7d 6fg 6g* 6g³ 6s³ 7g) Mar 4; lengthy, quite useful sort; carries plenty of condition; third foal; dam won over 12.5f in France; very hard ridden to beat Professors Choice a short head in maiden race at Yarmouth in September, after looking to be going easily at halfway; subsequently ran well in nurseries, notably on final start when fifth of 14 to Hello Sunshine at Doncaster; will stay 1m; consistent. *A. Hide.*

CELESTIAL PATH 2 br. or gr.f. Godswalk 130–Princess Hattab (Al Hattab) **98**
(1981 5g* 6f* 6f* 5d) May 11; IR 3,200Y; second foal; dam never ran; proved a bargain, winning 15-runner maiden race at Tralee in June by 5 lengths, auction event at Punchestown in September by a neck from Exhilarate and minor race at Navan later in September by 2½ lengths from Sougoli; ran poorly when second favourite for Waterford Testimonial Stakes at the Curragh in October, finishing last of 9 to Americus after weakening quickly at halfway; stays 6f well; suited by firm going. *C. Magnier, Ireland.*

CELIA'S HALO 4 b.f. Mountain Call 125–Aurelia 68 (Aureole 132) (1980 8.2d **43**
10.8f 10.2fg 10.6fg 10d² 10g 1981 10d 10d 10.6s⁴ 10f³ 10f* 10f³ 10fg) strong, compact, well-made filly; plater; won at Nottingham in July (bought in 1,250 gns); stays 1¼m; acts on any going; has worn blinkers (did when successful). *W. Holden.*

CELLINE 3 ch.f. London Company–Like For Like (What A Pleasure) (1980 **37**
5.8h 5g 6d 1981 8s² 9g² 10s 9fg⁴ 8g³ 8d 8f³ 8.2f⁴) lightly-made filly; plater; should stay 1¼m; blinkered last 2 starts (hung left and found very little on first occasion); sold 1,050 gns Ascot December Sales. *W. Musson.*

CELTIC GEM 2 b.f. Connaught 130–Opalina (Tudor Melody 129) (1981 5g **—**
5d 8fg 6g 10s 10.2g) Apr 12; 4,200Y; lengthy filly; seventh foal; half-sister to a winner in USA; dam, unplaced twice in Ireland, is daughter of very useful 1m to 1½m winner Green Opal; behind in maiden races and a minor event and looks a plater; blinkered final start; sold 900 gns Newmarket December Sales. *D. Dale.*

CELTIC HALO 5 b.h. Welsh Saint 126–Levanswood 74 (Le Levanstell 122) **91**
(1980 7.2fg 7g³ 6fg 6d 6fg 6g³ 6s 7fg* 6d³ 8g³ 6fg 7g 6d* 6s 1981 6g³ 6d 6g² 6s² 6f 6fg 7f 6fg 8g²(dis) 10.8s 8v 7s) neat horse; fairly useful handicapper; ran creditably several times without managing to win; effective from 6f to 1m but doesn't stay 1¼m; acts on any going but is ideally suited by some give in the ground; suited by strong handling; successful with blinkers and without; game; to be trained by S. Norton. *A. Jarvis.*

CELTIC LEGEND 2 ch.f. Whistling Top 107–Wacoty (Typhoon 125) (1981 5g **—**
5f) Apr 11; IR 2,000F, IR 450Y; sixth produce; sister to Irish 9f winner Oak Park Lady; dam placed twice over 6f at 2 yrs in Ireland; backward when in rear in maiden races at Chester and Beverley (tailed off) in August. *Mrs C. Lloyd-Jones.*

CELTIC PRIDE 3 ch.f. Celtic Cone 116–Second Glance (Prince Hansel 118) **—**
(1980 5f 6s 6g 6s 5d 1981 8d 14f) small, lightly-made filly; probably of no account; sold 440 gns Doncaster September Sales. *J. Harris.*

CELTIC TARA 5 b.m. Welsh Saint 126–La Sarmate (Hard Sauce 131) (1980 **44**
13g 1981 12d² 18d³ 12g 16f³) neat mare; plating-class maiden; stays well; probably acts on any going. *C. Booth.*

CENTRAL CARPETS 2 b.f. Garda's Revenge 119–Homecomings (Primera **70**
131) (1981 5d³ 5s³ 5fg 5g³ 5fg³ 5fg 6fg³ 7.2fg 6f 6d⁴ 6g 5d² 5g) Apr 16; lightly-made filly; fourth foal; half-sister to a winning plater and a winner in Austria; dam poor maiden; in frame in varied races, including when 2¾ lengths fourth of 9 to Wink in £4,200 nursery at Ayr in September; probably stays 7f; has run well for a 7-lb claimer; sold out of N. Guest's stable 3,000 gns Doncaster June Sales. *W. Stubbs.*

CENTROLINE 3 b.c. High Line 125–Centro 86 (Vienna 127) (1980 NR 1981 **122**
8d⁴ 12g³ 13.3d* 15.5f* 14fg² 14g* 14.6g* 16g*)
As a brother to Nicholas Bill, the Lancashire Oaks winner Centrocon and the staying handicapper Athford, Centroline had some family tradition to live up to

Rockingham Handicap, Doncaster—Centroline stays on strongly from Another Sam (hoops)

on the racecourse. Events in his first season proved him well up to the task; so much so that he could very well turn out to be the best of the lot. He still has a little way to go to equal Nicholas Bill at his best, but it's interesting to note that Centroline, in our opinion, is already significantly better than was Nicholas Bill at the same stage in his career.

Centroline improved with virtually every race (again a family tradition) and crowned a fine season with an impressive win in the Jockey Club Cup at New-

Jockey Club Cup, Newmarket—Centroline ends his season in fine style with a pattern-race win

market in October, a race won by his sire High Line in 1969, 1970 and 1971 and by Nicholas Bill as a four-year-old in 1979. That Centroline started clear favourite, even though it was his first venture outside handicap company, shows what strides he had made since being beaten in maiden and minor races at Newbury and Kempton in the spring. The opposition wasn't so tough as it might have been—the 1980 winner Ardross was being saved for the following day's Arc and Protection Racket was taken out at the overnight stage to be aimed instead for the Irish St Leger—but Centroline's task was still no easy one. He looked to be struggling a bit six furlongs out but gradually came good and took up the running at around the two-furlong marker. He quickly went clear and came right away to win in really good style by five lengths from Capstan. Coincidentally his sire High Line had won by the same margin as a three-year-old.

Centroline had already won four times and had been in the frame in his other three races. After getting off the mark in a maiden event at Newbury he trotted up in a small race at Folkestone and won the Melrose Handicap at York's Ebor meeting, another race which Nicholas Bill had won, and the Rockingham Handicap at Doncaster's Leger meeting. At York he was off the bridle before the straight but got a good run up the rails to dispute the lead at the three-furlong pole. He soon had his race sewn up and he came clean away to win by six lengths from Dragon Palace. At Doncaster, against such good older handicappers as Shaftesbury and Popsi's Joy, he was always handily placed and was on top throughout the last two furlongs, coming home two and a half lengths in front of Another Sam.

We had a good deal to say about High Line's success as a sire in *Racehorses of 1980* and he did well again in 1981. Besides Centroline he was represented successfully by Nicholas Bill, who won the Sagaro Stakes, by Master Willie whose three excellent wins included the Coronation Cup and the Coral Eclipse, and by

Mr R. Barnett's "Centroline"

the useful handicapper Capricorn Line. Centroline's dam, the seven-furlong winner Centro, had another representative on the racecourse in 1981, the two-year-old Sarajill (also by High Line). Sarajill didn't make much show at Newbury on her only outing, but it would take a brave man to deny that she'll do much better in time.

Centroline (b.c. 1978)	High Line (ch 1966)	High Hat (ch 1957)	Hyperion
			Madonna
		Time Call (b 1955)	Chanteur II
			Aleria
	Centro (b 1966)	Vienna (ch 1957)	Aureole
			Turkish Blood
		Ocean Sailing (br 1950)	Big Game
			Kyanos

It will be interesting to see how Centroline and Protection Racket fare against Ardross in the Gold Cup should they meet. Both are some way behind Ardross at present but neither looks as if he has finished improving. It has been reported that Ardross will revert to middle-distance races after Royal Ascot; if he does, so much the better for the others. Centroline's brother Nicholas Bill appeared not to stay the extreme distance of the 1979 Goodwood Cup, when third to Le Moss, but Centroline looks a stouter stayer and in any case Cup races are rarely run at such a searching gallop as Le Moss used to set. A small, lightly-made colt bearing much more physical similarity to Athford than Nicholas Bill, he races in the manner of a colt who will stay beyond two miles; he's ideally suited by a good gallop and he responds really well to hard driving. A thoroughly genuine sort who probably acts on any going, Centroline seems certain to win more good races. *H. Candy.*

CENTURION PRINCE 2 b.c. Martinmas 128–Cobblers Daughter 84 (Right Boy 137) (1981 5s) Apr 2; 3,200Y; fair sort; half-brother to several minor winners, including 1980 2-y-o 7f winner Toe Tapper (by Record Run); dam stayed 1m; 6/1, never went pace when last of 9 to Haycombe Barn in maiden race at Nottingham in September. *B. Hills.* —

CENTURIUS 3 ch.c. Great Nephew 126–Word from Lundy 93 (Worden II 129) **119 §** (1980 7g² 7fg* 7s 1981 8.5g* 10.5s 12f²(dis) 12f³ 12fg² 10.5g⁴ 12fg)
Grundy's brother Centurius has a justifiable reputation for not doing on the racecourse what he is capable of at home. Regarded at one time by his trainer as classic material, Centurius won only one of his seven races as a three-year-old. There is little room to doubt that Centurius is somewhat ungenerous; he races genuinely until he finds himself near the front whereupon he gives up. At Royal Ascot, for example, he threw away the King Edward VII Stakes, signalling his unwillingness by hanging towards his main rival Bustomi throughout the last furlong after appearing to be cantering over him two furlongs out. Centurius' antics at Royal Ascot—he was disqualified after passing the post a neck behind Bustomi—resulted in his rider's receiving a six-day suspension which cost him the mount on Shergar in the Irish Sweeps Derby. Centurius met Bustomi on terms 3 lb better in the Gordon Stakes at Goodwood in July but again the fire went out of him after he closed on Bustomi in seemingly effortless fashion in the straight; Centurius went down by a length and a half. It was a similar story in the Princess of Wales's Stakes at Newmarket earlier in July, Light Cavalry and Castle Keep running Centurius out of it close home after he had taken the lead inside the final furlong.

Centurius (ch.c. 1978)	Great Nephew (b 1963)	Honeyway (br 1941)	Fairway
			Honey Buzzard
		Sybil's Niece (ch 1951)	Admiral's Walk
			Sybil's Sister
	Word from Lundy (b 1966)	Worden II (ch 1949)	Wild Risk
			Sans Tares
		Lundy Princess (b 1960)	Princely Gift
			Lundy Parrot

Centurius will race in the colours of Captain Tim Rogers as a four-year-old; Rogers, who is believed to have offered £375,000 for a half-share in Centurius in the summer, bought him for an undisclosed sum at the end of the season. A rangy, attractive colt and a good walker, Centurius has the looks, as well as the pedigree, of a potential stallion; and there's no doubt he has the ability to win good races. Epsom is a course on which chicken-hearted horses are

Ladbroke Blue Riband Trial Stakes, Epsom—the exasperating Centurius scrapes home from Robellino (noseband)

sometimes to be seen running with more than their accustomed zest—Centurius won the Ladbroke Blue Riband Trial at Epsom in April, scraping home by a neck from Robellino after idling in front—and we shouldn't be at all surprised to see him in the line-up for the Coronation Cup. He will probably need at least a mile and a half at four and has shown his best form on a sound surface. We have formed the impression that Centurius requires very strong handling—he did nothing wrong when ridden by Starkey in the Benson and Hedges Gold Cup, in which he finished a creditable fourth over a trip on the sharp side for him. This should not be taken as criticism of Swinburn who has had the unenviable task of partnering Centurius in most of his races; at this early stage of his career Swinburn may lack the strength of a Starkey or a Piggott but he showed enough sound qualities in his first season as stable jockey at Beech Hurst to suggest that he could be champion one day. *M. Stoute.*

CENTURY CITY 2 b.c. High Top 131–Pearl Wedding 83 (Gulf Pearl 117) **89** p
(1981 7g²) May 21; 10,000Y; workmanlike colt; second foal; dam won over 1¼m and 1½m; 10/1, had no chance with 3-length winner Simply Great but nonetheless put up a creditable first effort when second of 23 in maiden race at Newmarket in October; will stay 1¼m+; sure to improve. *L. Cumani.*

CENTURY TOWER 2 b.c. Pitskelly 122–Hybrid (Floribunda 136) (1981 5s **57**
5d² 5v⁴ 5g³ 6g 6f 5f) May 2; 4,000Y; rather leggy colt; disappointing plater; blinkered on a couple of occasions; sold 1,600 gns Newmarket Autumn Sales. *P. Haslam.*

CERAMIC 4 b.g. Cavo Doro 124–Nimble Gate 84 (Nimbus 130) (1980 8d **46**
10fg* 10fg⁴ 12f⁴ 10fg 11.7s 10fg 10f² 10g 16d 1981 10d 10g 10.8fg² 10f 10f⁴ 11.7fg* 10f 12f) compact gelding; good mover; poor handicapper; won at Windsor in July; not certain to stay 2m; acts on firm going and is probably unsuited by soft; blinkered second start. *T. M. Jones.*

CEREMONIOUS 3 ch.f. Queen's Hussar 124–Queen's Keys 84 (Right Royal V **42**
135) (1980 5d 5s 5g 5d 6g³ 7g 7f⁴ 6g⁴ 8g 8g 8g 1981 12.2s 8d 12.2g* 12g³ 12g 12fg 12.5f 15.8g 12fg 12g⁴ 13.8g³ 16.5f 13.8g⁴ 11s³ 10d) small, unfurnished filly; plater; attracted no bid after winning at Catterick in April; stays at least 1¾m; often apprentice ridden; blinkered thirteenth start. *R. Whitaker.*

CEROLANE 11 b.m. Romancero 100–Crystalane 67 (Premonition 130) (1980 **—**
NR 1981 10f) poor maiden. *J Long.*

188

CESARIO (FR) 4 gr.c. Caro 133–Illyria 100 (Reform 132) (1980 10g² 10g² **110** 10fg* 9d 8d² 8d 10g 9.5f* 1981 10fg 8fg 10g* 10d³ 10v) quite attractive, robust colt; made all and was in no danger in straight when beating Dragon by 1½ lengths in 70,000 francs race at Longchamp in September; third to Bobiffic in handicap on same course in October; soundly beaten in Westbury Stakes at Sandown and Prix Quincey at Deauville first 2 starts; stays 1¼m; probably acts on any going; spent early part of season with R. Hern. *J. Cunnington, jnr, France.*

CHABRIAS (FR) 6 b.h. Bold Lad (Ire) 133–Almerilla (Abdos 134) (1980 9f **45** 12fg 8fg 11fg³ 19fg² 11.7d 9fg 10.6s 8.2f 7f³ 7f 8.2g) fair sort; ex-French horse; poor handicapper; well beaten in seller final start; stays 11f; acts on any going; wears blinkers. *A. Jarvis.*

CHADS GAMBLE 6 ch.g. St Chad 120–Another Flutter 75 (Credo 123) **72** (1980 7fg 7f 7h² 8fg² 7d 7f² 8g³ 7f² 7fg* 7f 1981 8g² 7g 7g 7f 7f² 8h⁴ 7f² 7h* 6f³) quite a moderate handicapper; won at Chepstow in September; stays 1m; appears to act on any going but is suited by a sound surface; sometimes blinkered; has run creditably for an apprentice. *J. Bethell.*

CHALKEY ROAD 2 b.f. Relko 136–Feather Bed 111 (Gratitude 130) (1981 7d **77** p 6g 7g⁴) Mar 12; rangy, attractive filly; half-sister to several winners, including useful stayer Popaway (by Run The Gantlet) and smart middle-distance filly Cheveley Princess (by Busted); dam second in Irish 1,000 Guineas; about 3½ lengths fourth of 16 to Clymene in maiden race at Leicester in October, best effort; has scope and should do better over much further at 3 yrs. *H. Wragg.*

CHALON 2 ch.f. Habitat 134–Areola 114 (Kythnos 126) (1981 7g³ 7g*) **90** p May 5; IR 46,000Y; big, strong filly; half-sister to 2 winners in USA; dam won Phoenix Stakes; well-backed favourite, confirmed promise of her debut when winning 29-runner maiden race at Newmarket in October by 1½ lengths from Blakesware County, staying on really well up hill; will stay at least 1m; has plenty of scope and should train on well. *H. Cecil.*

CHAMBESY 2 br.g. Moulton 128–Verdun 82 (Relic) (1981 6f 7g 8d) Apr 15; — 2,000Y; rather leggy gelding; half-brother to a minor winner and a winner in Malaya; dam half-sister to good stayer Rally; in rear in maiden auction event at Folkestone in July and maiden races at Leicester in the autumn. *D. Morley.*

CHAMPAGNE CHARLIE 4 br.c. Charlottown 127–The Guzzler 69 (Behistoun **69** 131) (1980 10.8s² 11.7fg² 11.7f² 12g⁴ 11fg² 12g 13.1g 14g* 13.3d 14g 16f* 14fg 16fg⁴ 16g 13.3d 1981 14fg 14d 14s⁴ 14d³ 16f³ 16fg* 16fg 19fg 14d 16h⁴ 16fg 16s 18g) compact colt; staying handicapper; made all at Sandown in July; appears to act on any going; suitable mount for an inexperienced rider; not particularly consistent. *P. M. Taylor.*

CHAMPAGNE DOLLY 2 b.f. Grey Mirage 128–Santa Marta 51 (Lavandin 128) **52** (1981 5s 5fg 5fg 5.8f 8.2s 8s) May 14; 1,500Y; lengthy filly; sister to 6f winner W. G. Greys and half-sister to a winning plater; dam won over 6f at 4 yrs; poor form in maiden company and in nurseries; should be suited by 6f+. *P. M. Taylor.*

CHAMPAGNE GLORY 2 b.c. Hittite Glory 125–Tilt Guard 75 (Crepello 136) **59** (1981 7fg 7fg 7g 7g 8s) Mar 23; 3,200Y; short-backed colt; half-brother to 3 winners, including 3-y-o 7f and 1m winner Minibank (by Saritamer); in mid-division in maiden races on first 2 outings but was well beaten in 2 sellers subsequently; sold 260 gns Ascot November Sales. *T. Marshall.*

CHAMPAGNE PRINCESS 2 b.f. Welsh Pageant 132–Campagna (Romulus **64** 129) (1981 6fg 7fg⁴ 8fg) Feb 3; 28,000Y; strong, attractive filly; half-sister to 3 winners, including miler Druimfada (by No Mercy); dam won over 1¼m in France; 25/1 when 11½ lengths fourth of 16 to Top Hope in maiden race at Yarmouth in August, best effort; should stay at least 1m. *M. Jarvis.*

CHAMP D'AVRIL 4 b.f. Northfields–April Twelfth (King's Leap 111) (1980 — 5s* 5f² 5f⁴ 6s 6fg² 6g 5d³ 6s 1981 8s 7g 7d⁴ 5d⁴ 6f 11.7fg 7fg 6g 10fg) lightly-made filly; seems to stay 7f (unlikely to stay 1¼m); acts on any going; suitable mount for a claimer. *D. Whelan.*

CHAMPERELLE 3 ch.f. On Your Mark 125–Pretty Asset 100 (Galivanter 131) — (1980 5f 6g 5fg 5g³ 5fg 6d 5d 1981 6d 7g 5.3f) poor maiden; sold privately out of R. Hollinshead's stable 550 gns Ascot January Sales. *J. Jenkins.*

CHAMPERS CLUB 4 ch.f. Run The Gantlet—Vein (Kalydon 122) (1980 8f — 10.1s 10.1d² 12g 10d 10d 1981 15.5d) fair sort; plater; stays 1¼m; acts on a soft surface. *D. Weeden.*

CHANDHEER 5 b.g. Swing Easy 126–Babucon 90 (My Babu 136) (1980 12d **66** 18f⁴ 14.7f² 12.2fg⁴ 12g 12d 10s 10f² 10fg² 15.5f⁴ 8g³ 1981 8f³ 9g³ 12fg⁴ 10f* 12fg 16d) fair sort; won amateur riders handicap at Folkestone in July; effective at 1m and stays well; acts on firm going; used to wear blinkers; suitable mount for an inexperienced rider; trained part of season by P. Rohan. *R. Smyth.*

CHANEY 3 b.g. Sparkler 130–Anippe 102 (Aggressor 130) (1980 6d 1981 7g **—** 7d 7d 7fg 6fg 8d) strong, compact gelding; bad mover; poor form in varied company, including selling; sold 1,550 gns Newmarket Autumn Sales. *R. Armstrong.*

CHANGATU 2 b.g. Touch Paper 113–Good Reliance (Good Bond 122) (1981 **96** 5d² 5s 5f* 6fg 6f³ 6f* 6f³ 7g) Apr 12; 8,400Y; neat gelding; good mover; third foal; brother to fairly useful 5f to 1m winner Changabang; dam never ran; successful in maiden race at Leicester in June and minor events at Pontefract in July and August; had only odds-on Bravado to beat when gaining final victory and did so with a little more in hand than head verdict suggests; will probably stay 1m (had stiffish task under top weight in Newmarket nursery when tried over 7f); acts well on firm going and is probably unsuited by really soft; gelded at end of season; sent to Hong Kong. *R. Hollinshead.*

CHANGE HABIT 2 b.g. Reform 132–Eminence Grise 85 (Grey Sovereign 128§) **94** (1981 6g 6fg³ 5.8f 7g² 7.6s* 8s* 7d²) Apr 26; 50,000Y; well-grown, quite attractive gelding; good mover; half-brother to 3 winners, including smart French middle-distance stayer El Mina (by Reliance II); dam, half-sister to Bounteous, won over 6f; very coltish early on but settled down well and won twice in October, beating Dawn Raid a length in maiden race at Lingfield and Mister Pitt a head under 9-13 in nursery at Wolverhampton; suited by 1m; acts well on soft going and has run respectably on a firm surface; sold to BBA, reportedly to race in Hong Kong, 18,000 gns Newmarket Autumn Sales (gelded before export). *G. Harwood.*

CHANNING GIRL 2 b.f. Song 132–Maternal 93 (High Top 131) (1981 6fg **73** 6f³ 6f 7f 8.2fg³ 7.6g³ 8d 7g) Apr 1; 6,400Y; first foal; dam won over 5f and 6f at 2 yrs; quite moderate form in varied company; stays 1m; acts on firm going; blinkered sixth and seventh starts. *C. Brittain.*

CHANTAGE 2 b.f. Sweet Revenge 129–Wedding March (March Past 124) **—** (1981 7g) Mar 16; 2,500Y; big filly; half-sister to 2 minor winners; dam ran twice; 25/1 and backward when behind in 17-runner maiden race won by Loup de Mer at Leicester in October. *Sir Mark Prescott.*

CHANTILLY GIRL 2 br.f. Royal Smoke 113–Little Charter 65 (Runnymede **57** 123) (1981 5d² 5d 5g² 6fg 6fg² 6f² 6f*) Feb 19; unfurnished filly; good mover; second reported foal; dam won 1m seller; plater; sold 2,300 gns after winning 8-runner race at Leicester in July by 2½ lengths from Manns Brown; will be suited by 7f; seems to act on any going; blinkered last 3 starts. *D. Gandolfo.*

CHANTRY BRIDGE 3 ch.c Porto Bello 118–Prime Thought 69 (Primera 131) **105** (1980 5fg 6d² 6fg* 1981 6g* 7g⁴ 6f³ 6fg 6fg 6d⁴ 6g² 6g) strong, useful-looking colt; useful handicapper; beat Composer by 3 lengths in £4,000 race at York in May; placed subsequently at York again (½-length third to Marking Time in William Hill Trophy) and Newmarket (1½ lengths second to Kathred); stays 6f; acts on firm going and a soft surface; blinkered fifth, seventh and final starts; inconsistent; sold to BBA 10,000 gns Newmarket December Sales. *J. W. Watts.*

CHAPEL ASH 3 b.c. Derring-Do 131–Angel Beam 115 (Hornbeam 130) (1980 **—** 6fg⁴ 6fg 5d 5d³ 5s 1981 7d 8g 8f 8.2g 8g 10s) well-made colt; good walker and mover; plater; should be suited by 1¼m. *W. Holden.*

CHAPERON 5 b.m. Sit In The Corner–Kissing Grove (Midsummer Night II 117) **—** (1980 8s² 12.5s 1981 13fg) plater; stays 1m; acts on soft going; sometimes wears blinkers. *J. Harris.*

CHARADE (USA) 2 ch.f. Exclusive Native–Clairvoyance (Round Table) **76** (1981 6fg 6fg 7.3s) Apr 6; $195,000Y; well-made, attractive filly; third foal; dam, placed at 4 yrs, is daughter of smart French and Italian middle-distance mare Psyche; 14/1, weakened from distance when 2¾ lengths sixth of 17 to Cricket Field in maiden race at Newbury in August, second outing and best effort; should be suited by 7f+. *J. Tree.*

CHARBONNEL (USA) 2 b.c. Roberto 131–Chocolate Beau (Beau Max) **82** (1981 6h* 7g² 6g) May 8; $45,000Y; leggy colt; half-brother to several winners here and in USA, including useful miler Fawn (by Tom Rolfe) and 2 stakes winners; dam stakes winner at 2 yrs; had his 6 opponents well strung out when winning newcomers event at Chepstow in September by 5 lengths from Gaiters; ran well behind Balanchine in minor event at Brighton next time and wasn't disgraced when having stiffish task in well-contested nursery at Newmarket on final appearance; will stay at least 1m. *P. Walwyn.*

CHARJIM 3 ch.g. Scottish Rifle 127–Legal Love 105 (King's Bench 132) (1980 NR 1981 10d 15.5s) half-brother to several winners, including useful 1977 2-y-o 5f and 6f winner Bondi (by Good Bond); dam, a sprinter, at her best at 2 yrs; behind in minor event at Brighton in September and maiden race at Folkestone in October. *A. Moore.* —

CHARLCOMBE 2 b. or br.f. Crooner 119–Shell Fish 54 (Hard Ridden 131) (1981 7f) Mar 24; 390Y; fifth living foal; dam of little account; 33/1, when 4½ lengths fifth of 18 to Zostera Marina in seller at Chepstow in September, only outing. *J. Bethell.* **53**

CHARLES BOOT 2 ch.g. Sun Prince 128–Tudor Gal 106 (Henry the Seventh 125) (1981 6g 6fg 6f4 8.2s 6s 8g 8d) May 24; 3,200F, 3,200Y; compact gelding; half-brother to 3 winners, including stayer Linkenholt (by Reliance II); dam won at up to 1¼m; 2 lengths fourth of 15 to Panatella in maiden auction event at Folkestone in July, only sign of ability; should stay 1m; blinkered fifth and sixth outings; well beaten in sellers last 3 starts. *M. Tompkins.* **64**

CHARLES STREET 4 ch.g. Huntercombe 133–Limerick Queen (Whistling Wind 123) (1980 5d 6f3 5fg 6f 7f 5f 5s2 6g 6g 5s 5g 5d 1981 7fg) neat gelding; not a good mover in his slower paces; stays 6f; acts on any going but is well suited by some give in the ground; often blinkered. *Miss A. Sinclair.* —

CHARLES STUART (FR) 2 b.c. Anne's Pretender 124–Kerline (Spy Well 126) (1981 7.6s 7d) Apr 26; 12,500F; half-brother to 2 winners in France, including 3-y-o middle-distance winner Carapace (by Caracolero); dam won over 7.5f in France; unquoted when soundly beaten in maiden event at Lingfield and minor race at Chepstow in October. *R. Baker.* —

CHARLIE DAN 3 ch.c. Sandford Lad 133–Sensitive Touch (Sensitivo) (1980 7d 1981 8fg 10fg3 12fg2 14f 15.5s 12s2) big, rangy colt; placed in maiden and minor races at Ascot, Salisbury and Newbury; stays 1½m; blinkered final start; usually a good mover, but didn't move well at Ascot; looked decidedly unwilling fourth start and is one to treat with caution; sold to A. Moore 3,300 gns Newmarket Autumn Sales. *G. Harwood.* **69**

CHARLIE KILGOUR 2 b.g. Pitskelly 122–Nuageuse (Prince Regent 129) (1981 7fg 8d 7d) Mar 9; IR 15,000Y; third foal; half-brother to fair 3-y-o sprinter Cumulus (by Relko); dam won 4 times over 5f at 3 yrs in Ireland; beaten some way in maiden and minor events in September and October. *H. Candy.* —

CHARLIE'S PROSPECT (USA) 2 ch.c. Prove Out–Chill (Nearctic) (1981 6f 8g) Apr 17; $40,000Y; smallish colt, first foal; dam won over 1m; 25/1 and backward, showed good speed until lack of fitness told in final 2f when tenth of 17 to Kamal in maiden race at Yarmouth in June; again in need of race when next seen out in October and finished well down the field in 27-runner minor event at Newmarket won by Dudley Wood; should stay 1m. *G. Pritchard-Gordon.* —

CHARLIE'S SONG 3 b.f. Song 132–Sound Venture (Hopeful Venture 125) (1980 5g4 5d 5s 5fg4 6fg2 1981 6s 6fg 5fg2 6g 6fg 6fg 5fg3 5g* 6v4) workman-like filly; won maiden race at Lingfield in September; will stay beyond 6f; sold 2,900 gns Newmarket Autumn Sales. *J. Holt.* **63**

CHARLIE'S SUNSHINE 4 b.f. Jimsun 121–Dracaena 62 (Double Jump 131) (1980 7g3 7.6d* 7s 8fg 8s 10.2v 1981 11s4 12g 12g) small filly; poor performer; stays 11f; acts on soft going; has sweated up; sold to J. Townson 3,000 gns Ascot June Sales. *R. Fisher.* **57**

CHARLIE THEODORE 4 ch.g. Sheshoon 132–Theodora Courage (Cash and Courage 116) (1980 8f 12.5h 16d 12.2g 16f 12s 12.5s 1981 12g) neat gelding; poor maiden; has twice worn blinkers; sold 620 gns Doncaster June Sales; resold 370 gns same venue in September. *J. Calvert.* —

CHARLOTTE'S CHOICE 6 b.g. Blakeney 126–Queendom 109 (Quorum 126) (1980 NR 1981 12s 12fg 12g 16s 13.3g* 12g 16fg 12g3 12d3 12.3s* 14f* 13.3d) neat, attractive gelding; won handicaps at Newbury in June, Chester in August and York in September; came with a well-timed run to beat Tomaschek by a length on last-named; stays well; acts on any going; has been tried in blinkers; bandaged in front several starts in 1981. *W. Wightman.* **75**

CHA

CHARMER (FR) 2 ch.f. Crystal Palace 132–Glena (Riverman 131) (1981   ?
8.5s*) Mar 12; 240,000 francs Y (approx £24,000); first foal; dam, sister to
Gold River, won twice over 7f at 3 yrs; favourite, finished strongly to win 9-
runner newcomers event at Longchamp in October by ½ length from Seleucie;
a well-related filly who should win decent middle-distance races at 3 yrs. *F.
Mathet, France.*

CHARMING CHARLES 2 ch.c. Welsh Pageant 132–Orapa 88 (Aureole 132)   —
(1981 8g 10g) Mar 26; 10,000Y; attractive colt; good walker; half-brother to
2 winners, including middle-distance filly Khaki Kate (by Brigadier Gerard);
dam won at up to 1m and is half-sister to smart African Dancer; unquoted, got
the hang of things in closing stages and ran on to finish in first dozen in 30-
runner maiden race won by Farioffa at Newmarket in October; soon struggling
in £6,500 event on same course later in month; bred to stay middle distances.
P. Kelleway.

CHARM TO SPARE (USA) 3 b.g. Gallant Romeo–Fabled (Illustrious) (1980   —
6fg4 6f2 7f4 1981 7fg 8f) neat, quite attractive gelding; in frame in maiden
and minor races in 1980; behind in maiden events in 1981; should stay 1m.
M. Jarvis.

CHARTER PLEA 3 gr.g. Runnymede 123–Impassioned Plea 91 (Counsel 118)   —
(1980 8d 1981 12g 12g 12.2g) fair sort; well behind in varied company,
including selling; not certain to stay 1½m. *R. Hobson.*

CHART TOPPER 2 b.c. Music Boy 124–Tzi-Tzi Girl 85 (Sovereign Path 125)   **80**
(1981 5f 6fg 5f4 5v2 6g 6d3 6g 6g3) Mar 25; 17,000Y; compact colt; first foal;
dam won from 7f to 1¼m at 5 yrs; quite moderate form in maiden races; not
sure to stay beyond 6f; dwelt last 2 starts; hung left under pressure sixth outing.
F. Durr.

CHASE THE WIND (USA) 2 ch.c. King's Bishop–Tempest Flower (Crafty   **97**
Admiral) (1981 6fg4 7fg* 7fg 7g) Apr 7; $36,000Y; strong, good-bodied, quite
attractive colt; half-brother to 5 minor winners in USA; dam won twice at up
to 6f; had only Steelstock to beat when 7/2 on for £4,200 event at Newcastle in
August and won pulling up by 2½ lengths; 12/1, wasn't disgraced when never-
dangerous 10½ lengths fifth of 8 to Achieved in Laurent Perrier Champagne
Stakes at Doncaster the following month, but finished well beaten behind
General Anders in £4,100 race at Ascot later in September; will stay 1m+;
useful. *G. Hunter.*

CHASTE LADY 2 ch.f. Sandford Lad 133–King's Chase (King's Leap 111)   **67**
(1981 5s 6g 7f2 6g3 7h 7fg 8.2d4) Mar 7; 7,200Y; fair sort; good mover; third
foal; dam ran only twice; quite a moderate maiden; head second of 8 to Razor
Sun in maiden race at Brighton in July; suited by 7f and 1m; yet to show she
acts on very soft ground but acts on any other. *C. Nelson.*

CHASTITY BELT 4 b.g. So Blessed 130–Queen's Keys 84 (Right Royal V   —
135) (1980 11v 12d 12d 1981 15g) workmanlike gelding; poor maiden.
R. Allan.

CHATEAU DANCER (USA) 3 ch.f. Giacometti 130–Delray Dancer (Chate-   —
augay) (1980 5f2 5g2 6fg* 6d4 6g* 8g3 1981 7.3s4 8.5f3) rangy, attractive filly;
half-sister to winners here and in USA, including very useful 1¼m winner Stanis-
lavsky (by Sir Ivor); won at Newbury and York (John Courage Stakes) as a
2-y-o; outpaced in final 2f when 7½ lengths last of 4 behind Marwell in Fred
Darling Stakes at Newbury in April on only outing over here in 1981 (looked
fairly fit); finds 7f too sharp nowadays and will be suited by middle distances;
probably acts on any going; has been stakes placed in USA. *R. Price.*

CHATRU 3 b.g. Realm 129–Kaiserin (Carapalida) (1980 5s 5d 7f4 8g 7g   —
1981 8fg 5f 6g3 5f 11d) workmanlike gelding; third in seller at Hamilton in
July; stays 7f and wasn't completely disgraced over 11f; trained by D. Thom
until fourth outing. *N. Callaghan.*

CHATTY DOLLY 3 gr.f. The Go-Between 129–Cloister Rose 70 (Track Spare   —
125) (1980 5g 1981 5d 6g 6g 5v 5fg) small, useful-looking filly; behind in
maiden and minor races in a seller; blinkered last 2 starts. *G. Lewis.*

CHEAP SEATS (USA) 2 b.f. Stage Director–Fair Bargain (No Robbery)   **94**
(1981 5s3 5g2 5fg2 5g* 6fg* 6g2 6fg* 5d) May 7; $40,000Y; strong, close-
coupled, attractive filly; half-sister to 2 winners, including One Lucky Devil
(by Governor's Party), a stakes winner at up to 9f; dam won over 4f at 2 yrs;
sire stakes-placed brother to high-class animals Queen of the Stage and Reviewer;

192

ridden by apprentice K. Willey when justifying favouritism in minor events at Ayr in June and Carlisle in July and in nursery at Ayr in August; gave impression 6f is her limit when gaining last success, holding on by only ½ length from La Tourelle after seeming to be going smoothly for most of race; acts on a firm surface; consistent. *B. Hills.*

CHEEKO   2 gr.c. No Mercy 126–Socialite 96 (Sica Boy 132) (1981 5g) Mar   —
28; 1,700F; strong colt; has scope; half-brother to 4-y-o 1¼m winner Dance Little Lady (by Moulton) and 3 other minor winners here and abroad; dam won twice over 5f at 2 yrs; unquoted, none too well away and never went pace when in rear in 15-runner maiden race won by Red Sunset at Newmarket in May; not raced subsequently. *M. Ryan.*

CHEEKY MONKEY   2 ch.f. Shiny Tenth 120–Evvoia 53 (Khalkis 127) (1981   **61**
5fg 5g⁴ 5d³ 6g 6fg 6f³ 6g) Mar 13; 1,200Y; neat filly; half-sister to fairly useful 1976 2-y-o 6f winner Firemaiden (by Firestreak) and 2 winners in Sweden; dam of no account; third in maiden auction event at Salisbury in May and nursery at Folkestone in August, running best race in latter when beaten 1¼ lengths by Little Smasher; will stay 7f; seems to act on any going. *G. Blum.*

CHEF MARCEL (USA)   3 b.c. Personality–Raise A Big Peach (Raise A   **79**
Native) (1980 7f 1981 11s³ 16s* 13fg 19fg 18.1d) lengthy colt; favourite when staying on strongly to beat Fitzgayle 15 lengths in modest maiden event at York in May; in rear in handicaps subsequently, wearing blinkers on last occasion; stays well; shows a lot of knee action and probably needs some give in the ground; sold to N. Bycroft 2,600 gns Newmarket Autumn Sales. *J. Hindley.*

CHEKA (USA)   5 b.g. Russian Bank 110–Sweet Seventeen (County Delight)   **76**
(1980 13g* 16f⁴ 14fg 16.1s 1981 17.1g* 16.1 17.1g* 18d* 20fg 17.1d 18g) strong gelding; staying handicapper; won at Bath and Doncaster in May; seems to act on any going; genuine. *I. Balding.*

CHELLASTON PARK   2 b.f. Record Token 128–Acquire 105 (Burglar 128)   **109**
(1981 5s² 5s* 5g* 5g* 5f² 5fg* 5g* 5d² 5fg²) Apr 24; 2,200F, 3,500Y; small, well-made filly; good mover; second produce; half-sister to 1980 2-y-o 5f winner Lady Acquiesce (by Galivanter); dam won twice over 5f at 2 yrs; successful in maiden race at Nottingham in April, minor event at Pontefract in May and in nurseries at Leicester in July and Goodwood in August; just held on by a head from Lucky Hunter when gaining final win; went down by ½ length to Batoni in minor race at Doncaster in May on third outing but was awarded race over 2 months later after winner failed dope test; also second of 5 in good-class races on eighth and ninth outings, going down by a head to Jester in Prince of Wales's Stakes at York in August and by 2¼ lengths to Glancing in Prix d'Arenberg at Chantilly in September; acts on any going but has distinct stamina limitations and probably isn't best served by very soft ground; thoroughly genuine and consistent. *B. Hobbs.*

CHELSEA MAID   2 b.f. So Blessed 130–De Nada 79 (Ragusa 137) (1981   —
5v 6fg 6fg 7d 5s 6d) May 9; 3,000Y; fair sort; half-sister to 2 winners, including Irish and French 1½m winner Carlos Place (by Connaught); dam stayed 1½m; in rear in maiden races, including one at Folkestone; should stay 7f; sold 500 gns Ascot November Sales. *M. Blanshard.*

CHEMIN   3 ch.f. Steel Heart 128–Supreme Lady 86 (Grey Sovereign 128§)   **107**
(1980 6g* 6d³ 7g 1981 7fg⁴ 6g 6g* 7fg 6fg 6g) workmanlike filly; half-sister to several winners, notably Irish St Leger winner M-Lolshan (by Levmoss); dam 2-y-o 5f performer; won £4,400 event at Newmarket as a 2-y-o; creditable fourth to Fairy Footsteps in Ladbrokes Nell Gwyn Stakes at Newmarket in April on reappearance; beat Sweet Monday in good style by 4 lengths in 9-runner minor event at Lingfield in June, best subsequent effort; stayed 7f; retired to stud. *J. Hindley.*

CHEMIN DE GUERRE   4 gr. or ro.f. Warpath 113–Flying Florrie 74 (I Say   **78**
125) (1980 9s 14.6d² 12s 1981 12f 12.2fg³ 19g* 12f* 16f² 16s⁴ 18g*) rangy, workmanlike filly; good walker; successful in handicaps at Beverley in July and Ripon in August and minor event at Doncaster in October (made all); finds 1½m on sharp side and stays very well; seems to act on any going; game; cracked a cannon bone in November. *M. H. Easterby.*

CHENNEL LANE   7 b.h. Caerdeon 98–Glebe 83 (Tacitus 124) (1980 11fg 12fg⁴   —
13f⁴ 1981 12.5g 12g 10g 10fg) poor middle-distance handicapper; acts on any going but goes well in the mud; suitable mount for an apprentice; sold 1,400 gns Doncaster June Sales. *T. Barron.*

CHENSTONE 3 ch.g. Royben 125–On Remand 83 (Reform 132) (1980 5v **54**
5f 5fg 5.8f² 6g 6fg 7g² 8d² 7.2s* 8d 1981 7d 10.2f⁴ 8d 8h² 6fg 8g) compact
gelding; second in seller at Bath in August; stays 1m; acts on any going;
blinkered fourth and fifth outings. *J. Hill.*

CHERCHEZ LA FEMME 5 b.m. Mon Fils 124–Angele 98 (Match III 135) **49**
(1980 14d 12g 8d³ 8d 10s 1981 8d³ 10f 8f) poor handicapper; best at 1m
on a soft surface. *M. Pipe.*

CHERE JANE 2 br.f. Auction Ring 123–Jane Merryn (Above Suspicion 127) **88**
(1981 5f 5fg* 6fg² 5f² 5g 6g 5g⁴) May 5; 9,000Y; strong, compact filly; half-
sister to several winners here and abroad; dam never ran; stayed on strongly
when winning 15-runner maiden race at Catterick in May by 2 lengths from Begham Bay; creditable second in nursery on same course and in small race at
Beverley (beaten a length by Fimi) afterwards; stays 6f; yet to race on a soft
surface; sold 12,000 gns Newmarket Autumn Sales. *Sir Mark Prescott.*

CHERI BERRY 2 b.f. Air Trooper 115–Diorina 91 (Manacle 123) (1981 **87**
5fg 5d³ 5.8h* 6fg* 7s) May 4; small, lengthy filly; first foal; dam at her best
at 2 yrs when winner over 5.3f; showed improved form in August, winning maiden
race at Bath and landing a gamble in minor event at Epsom by a length from
Blakesware County; last of 11 in valuable nursery won by Spanish Pool at Lingfield in October (had stiffish task); should stay 7f; best form on a firm surface.
W. Wightman.

CHERRY CORNER 3 br.g. Sit In The Corner–Tudor Gus 64 (Gustav 121) **70**
(1980 5fg* 8.2d 7f 8fg* 8s 1981 8g² 6fg* 8fg*) leggy gelding; useful plater;
bought in after winning in good style at Redcar in August (3,200 gns) and
September (1,600 gns); effective at 6f and stays 1m; suited by a sound surface;
usually blinkered (wasn't on reappearance); probably capable of winning outside
plating company. *M. W. Easterby.*

CHESTER COUNTY 2 ch.f. Realm 129–Some Thing (Will Somers 114§) **69**
(1981 5d 6s 5.3f³ 5f*) Feb 9; 30,000Y; neat filly; second foal; sister to smart
1979 French 2-y-o 6.5f and 1m winner Light of Realm; dam sister to 4 winners,
notably very smart 1m to 1¼m filly La Troublerie; improved steadily, and ran
on gamely under hard riding to win 13-runner minor event at Beverley in
July by ¾ length from Starlust; not seen out subsequently; should be suited
by 6f; form only on firm ground. *H. T. Jones.*

CHESTNUT PALE 2 ch.f. Record Token 128–Whitestake 74 (Compensation **62**
127) (1981 5fg 5fg 5f⁴ 7g 6f³ 6fg 7f 6s 5g⁴) Apr 18; 4,000Y; stocky filly;
half-sister to winners here and abroad, including useful sprinter Palmvinnia
(by Royal Palm); dam won 5f seller at 2 yrs; in frame in a seller and maiden
races; probably stays 7f; wears blinkers. *Hbt Jones.*

CHETINKAYA 5 b.h. Ragstone 128–Satina 83 (Pall Mall 132) (1980 12fg³ 14g* **?**
14.6f 12g 12g 1981 17.1h 13.1f) sturdy, lengthy horse; stays 1¾m well (well
beaten over further); acts on any going; has worn blinkers; suitable mount
for an apprentice; sold 400 gns Ascot October Sales. *G. Balding.*

CHEVELEY STAR 2 b.c. Roman Warrior 132–Tipsy Rider 60 (Hard Ridden **?**
131) (1981 7g 6s³) Apr 14; 1,700Y; sturdy colt; half-brother to 1980 Irish
2-y-o 8.5f winner Rapidity (by Rapid River); dam won 1¼m seller; 33/1, appeared
to put up a fairly useful effort, but may have been flattered by proximity,
when length third of 8 to Risk Taker in slowly-run minor event at Redcar in
October; should stay 7f. *C. Spares.*

CHICANERY 2 ro.c. Abwah 118–Chiana (Compensation 127) (1981 5d 5fg **61**
6fg² 6f⁴ 6d³ 6f² 8fg 7.2v⁴ 6s) June 4; 1,850F; small colt; poor walker; plater;
stays 7f but isn't sure to get 1m; acts on any going. *T. Marshall.*

CHICHESTER BIRD 7 gr.g. Birdbrook 110–Fair Marina 93 (Hethersett 134) **?**
(1980 NR 1981 8.3g) plating-class maiden on flat though has won over
jumps; usually blinkered. *R. Smyth.*

CHICKEN AGAIN 4 b.g. Royalty 130–Dust Sheet (Silly Season 127) (1980 **62**
8.2d 10.6f 9g 8.2d 7d² 7fg⁴ 6f 6s 6g* 6s* 7s 6d 1981 7.2g 7.2s 6fg³ 7fg³ 7g 7d
6s³ 6s) tall gelding; best at up to 7f; probably acts on any going; sometimes
sweats up; often blinkered but is effective without; suitable mount for an
apprentice. *C. Crossley.*

CHIEF ADMIRAL (USA) 3 b. or br.c. Chieftain–Robadan (Prince John) **86**
(1980 5d² 5fg² 6g* 6s² 7f 6f 1981 6s 7d 8.2d* 8g 8.2s 8f 10.6f³ 10f 11d) tall,
well-made, attractive colt; got up close home and beat Mr Marshall ½ length in

amateur riders race at Haydock in May; rather disappointing subsequently; should be suited by 1¼m; possibly not at his best on very firm going; often starts slowly; blinkered sixth and seventh starts (hung under pressure on latter); sold 6,200 gns Newmarket Autumn Sales. *S. Norton.*

CHIEF MOORE 3 b.c. Bold Lad (Ire) 133–Nadjina 76 (Petition 130) (1980 5d — 1981 6g 5fg 6g 5f 5g) neat colt; behind in maiden races and a handicap; blinkered fourth start; sold 1,150 gns Ascot July Sales. *S. Woodman.*

CHIEF SPEAKER 3 b.c. Nonoalco 131–Anice (Crepello 136) (1980 6g 7.2d³ **89** 8fg² 7.3d 1981 9fg 12.3g³ 12fg⁴ 10d² 9s* 8d*) tall colt; won minor events at Newcastle (by 3 lengths from Icen) and Redcar (beat Christmas Cottage 1½ lengths) in October; best at distances short of 1½m (faded in closing stages in both races at that distance); probably acts on any going. *R. Sheather.*

CHILCOMBE 2 b.f. Morston 125–Parvati 82 (Paveh 126) (1981 8d) Apr 7; 14,000F; half-sister to Irish 3-y-o Castle Howard (by Lochnager) and 2 winners, including 1978 2-y-o sprinter Tantra (by Song); dam stayed very well; 33/1 when behind in 23-runner maiden race won by Roanoke River at Leicester in November. *G. Balding.*

CHILDOWN BLUE 2 ch.g. Blue Cashmere 129–Gay Donna (Tudor Jinks 121) **95** (1981 5.1f³ 5.3f* 5fg³ 5fg* 5d² 5fg* 6fg 5g) Apr 24; neat, robust gelding; excellent mover; brother to 7f and 1m winner Kashmir Blue and fairly useful 1980 2-y-o 5f winner Blue Lass, and half-brother to two 2-y-o 5f winners; dam of little account; winner of maiden race at Brighton in June, minor event at Hamilton the following month and nursery at Kempton in August, making up several lengths in final furlong when scoring convincingly by ¾ length from Red Rosie at Kempton; stays 6f (had very stiff task when 8¾ lengths fifth to 6 of Sandhurst Prince in Sirenia Stakes at Kempton in September); seems to act on any going; genuine; gelded late in season and sent to Hong Kong. *M. Stoute.*

CHILD'S HOPE 2 ch.c. Owen Dudley 121–Bally's Mil 98 (Ballymoss 136) — (1981 6g 6g 7fg) May 5; medium-sized, workmanlike colt; half-brother to several winners, notably very smart 1¼m to 1¾m filly Mil's Bomb and Cheshire Oaks winner Milly Moss (both by Crepello); dam won twice at 1¼m; poor maiden; bred to stay 1¼m+; sold 1,100 gns Newmarket Autumn Sales. *P. Walwyn.*

CHILSTON 3 b.g. Tower Walk 130–Formula 72 (Reform 132) (1980 5g 5s 5d³ **44** 6d 6s 1981 7fg 5v* 6fg 6fg 6fg 6fg) narrow gelding; attracted no bid after winning seller at Chepstow in May; should be suited by 6f; well suited by plenty of give in the ground; sold 380 gns Ascot October Sales. *T. Marshall.*

CHIMANGO 3 b.c. African Sky 124–Cockatoo (Indiana 129) (1980 7d⁴ 7d 6s — 1981 7s 7fg³ 8fg 6f) lightly-made gelding; half-brother to several winners, including Irish 7f winner Cockakelly (by Pitskelly); dam poor half-sister to very smart Chil the Kite; favourite, though unimpressive in paddock, when third to All In in seller at Kempton in April; should stay 1m; blinkered final outing in 1980; trained by M. Kauntze in Ireland until after second outing. *G. Balding.*

CHINA ROYAL 4 ch.c. Sovereign Path 125–King's Mate 91 (King's Bench 132) **80** (1980 8fg* 8g³ 11g* 8.2g 10.2g* 12d 12s⁴ 1981 8fg 10.4g² 9fg 10g³ 10fg 10g 10d) lightly-made, quite attractive colt; good mover; stays 1½m; probably acts on any going; possibly needs strong handling; sold 4,000 gns Newmarket Autumn Sales. *B. Hills.*

CHINA RUN 3 ch.g. Chingnu 99–Gay Runner (Clear Run 109) (1980 7d 5f 5d — 1981 5f 9d 10s) small gelding; only poor form, including in sellers; stays 1¼m. *J. Yardley.*

CHINESE KUNG FU 5 ch.h. Roan Rocket 128–Gerfalcon 105 (Falcon 131) — (1980 6d 6g 6g 7.6d 1981 7f 7fg) really powerful horse; has shown no form for a long time; stays 6f; acts on any going; has worn blinkers; unreliable. *Mrs A. Finch.*

CHINESE QUEEN 3 b.f. Tarim–Chinese Melody (Salvo 129) (1980 NR — 1981 14g 12d) lengthy filly; half-sister to German winner Cressin (by Lorenzaccio); dam won in Germany as a 3-y-o; 50/1 when well beaten in maiden races at Newmarket in May (needed race) and Folkestone in June. *G. Huffer.*

CHINOOK 2 b.f. Tumble Wind–Papoosette (Raise You Ten 125) (1981 5s 5d³) — Apr 4; 8,000Y; small filly; first living foal; dam ran only twice; tailed-off last in minor event at Catterick and 3-runner maiden race at Hamilton in April. *N. Guest.*

Woodcote Stakes, Epsom—Chris's Lad (breastgirth) battles on well to wear down Crimson Court (rails)

CHIPPENHAM 4 b.g. Brigadier Gerard 144–Fardo 86 (Tudor Melody 129) **68**
(1980 8fg 9f⁴ 1981 10d 7g 7g³ 8f 8f 8f 12d 8fg) attractive gelding; disappointing
maiden; stayed 9f but not 1½m; blinkered fifth start; carried head a bit high;
broke a leg in seller at Kempton in September and was destroyed. *H. Wragg.*

CHIPTOWN BOY 2 gr.c. Town Crier 119–Sparkation (Communication 119) **—**
(1981 6f 5v 5s) neat colt; first foal; dam won 9f seller; poor maiden; should
stay 6f; blinkered final start (had stiffish task). *S. Norton.*

CHIVALRY (USA) 2 b.c. Nijinsky 138–Cloonlara 130 (Sir Ivor 135) (1981 **88**
6fg* 7g⁴) attractive colt; first foal; dam, 6-length winner of Phoenix Stakes
and fourth in 1,000 Guineas, is half-sister to top-class Kings Lake (by Nijinsky);
5/4 favourite, in front rank throughout when winning 17-runner maiden race
at the Curragh in August by ½ length from Exhilarate; again prominent all
the way and wasn't given too hard a time once his measure had been taken
when just under 7 lengths fourth of 18 to General Anders in £4,100 race at
Ascot in September; will be suited by 1m. *V. O'Brien, Ireland.*

CHOW 4 gr.f. Warpath 113–Full of Flavour (Romulus 129) (1980 8v 10f **—**
8f⁴ 10fg 10.6d 1981 8f 10f 12fg 12g 12d) neat filly; poor form, including in
a valuable seller; possibly stays 1¼m; sometimes blinkered; sold 4,000 gns
Doncaster November Sales. *C. Thornton.*

CHRISDEE 2 b.f. Le Johnstan 123–Little Bo Bleep 71 (Bleep-Bleep 134) **61**
(1981 5s² 5v² 5g 5fg² 5f 5fg² 5f³ 5fg⁴) May 19; 1,000F; lengthy, unfurnished
filly; poor walker; sister to 2 winners, including sprinter Quistador; dam placed
over 5f at 2 yrs; plater; may stay beyond 5f; well suited by a firm surface;
sent to Belgium and is a winner there. *K. Ivory.*

CHRIS'S LAD 2 ch.c. Sandford Lad 133–Perfect Bid (Baldric II 131) (1981 **106**
5s² 5g² 5g* 5g* 6d* 6fg² 6fg 6f² 6d 6g) Feb 25; 6,000Y; strong, good sort;
first foal; dam, poor staying maiden, is daughter of smart middle-distance filly
Pretty Puffin; won maiden and minor events at Newmarket in the spring and
9-runner Woodcote Stakes at Epsom in June, battling on really well to wear
down Crimson Court by ¾ length in last-named; subsequently ran well in 3
important races, going down by ¾ length to Red Sunset in 16-runner Coventry
Stakes at Royal Ascot in June, finishing 8 lengths fifth of 8 to Hays in Mill
Reef Stakes at Newbury in September on ninth start and being beaten only
5½ lengths when tenth of 13 to Cajun in William Hill Middle Park Stakes at
Newmarket in October; will stay 1m; seems to act on any going; sometimes
sweats up; thoroughly consistent except for a moderate run on seventh start.
A. Goodwill.

CHRISTINES FOLLY 3 b.f. Communication 119–Road Star (Road House **48**
II) (1980 5fg 6s 5g 5d 5g 5d 5f³ 5fg 5f 5g² 5d³ 5s⁴ 1981 5g 5fg 5f 5fg 6f 6fg
5f 6d 5g² 5d 5d) leggy, unfurnished filly; sprint handicapper; 3 lengths second
to Courageous Buzby in seller at Beverley in September; form only at 5f; best
form on a sound surface; inconsistent; sold 320 gns Doncaster October Sales.
S. Nesbitt.

CHRISTMAS COTTAGE 3 br.g. Lochnager 132–Nelski 83 (Skymaster **83**
126) (1980 5g 5g⁴ 5s 1981 7s 8s² 8s² 7g³ 7g² 6fg 8f² 8d² 7g² 8d* 8d²) workmanlike gelding; landed the odds by 2½ lengths from Battalion in maiden race
at Edinburgh in October; second in handicaps on previous 3 starts and in minor
event on final outing, when giving impression he might be suited by a return
to 7f; acts on any going; blinkered fourth and fifth outings. *J. Mason.*

CHRISTMAS GREETING 3 ch.g. Bonne Noel 115–Princess Mea (Meadow **82**
Court 129) (1980 7g 7fg 7f 8fg 8.2s 1981 12.2fg³ 16f* 16.5f³ 16s 15.8g*)
strong, well-grown gelding; successful in maiden event at Beverley in August
and handicap at Catterick in October; will be suited by extreme distances;
acts on firm going; possibly ran a bit too freely when blinkered fourth start.
M. H. Easterby.

CHROME MAG 3 br.f. Prince de Galles 125–Pat 98 (Ennis 128) (1980 6g **63**
6fg 1981 7v⁴ 8g 7g⁴ 7d⁴ 8.2f 8f² 8fg* 9f⁴ 8.2g 8f² 8f³ 8g) leggy, rather sparely-
made filly; in frame in varied company, including selling, before beating Auction
Bridge by a neck in minor event at Ayr in July; ran well when placed in 2 handicaps won by Paterno at Ripon the following month; stays 1m; probably acts
on any going, but is well suited by firm; had stiff task final start. *W. Bentley.*

CHRONICLE 2 b.c. Blakeney 126–Word from Lundy 93 (Worden II 129) **85** p
(1981 7g*) Feb 21; 122,000Y; half-brother to several winners, notably Derby
winner Grundy and smart 3-y-o Centurius (both by Great Nephew); dam
stayed 2m; weak in market, stayed on well to lead inside final furlong when
winning 15-runner minor event at Naas in October by ¾ length from Saints 'n'
Scholars; a stoutly-bred colt who will leave this form well behind over 1¼m
or more. *V. O'Brien, Ireland.*

CHRYSIPPOS (USA) 4 ch.g. Damascus–Better Begin (Buckpasser) (1980 **—**
6fg⁴ 7g 6g 7d 8g 8f³ 8g 6d 1981 8fg 11.7fg 10.4s) big, rangy, attractive gelding;
fairly useful at his best; behind all starts at 4 yrs; stays 1m; probably acts
on any going; often sweats up. *J. Priday.*

CHUKAROO 9 b.h. Kibenka 119–Wild Words 76 (Galivanter 131) (1980 **84**
8fg² 8f⁴ 10h* 10fg⁴ 10fg 1981 8d² 10f² 9fg⁴ 8g 8f* 8d 10g⁴ 8d) fairly useful
handicapper; beat Bold Image by 1½ lengths at Brighton in August; stays 1¼m;
acts on a soft surface but is best suited by top-of-the-ground; suitable mount
for an apprentice; sometimes sweats up; blinkered twice in 1979; sometimes
bandaged in front. *R. Laing.*

*Monasterevin Race, Naas—Grundy's half-brother Chronicle makes a
winning debut*

CHULIA STREET 2 gr.c. Dragonara Palace 115–Ribble Girl 96 (Trouville **111** 125) (1981 5fg³ 5g* 5g² 5f⁴ 7fg* 7f² 7fg* 7fg) Apr 24; 6,000Y; leggy, close-coupled, rather lightly-made colt; good mover; half-brother to 3 winners, including 5f to 7f winner Kings Offering (by Frankincense); dam won twice over 5f at 2 yrs; successful in minor events at Thirsk and Redcar prior to picking up quite a valuable prize in 9-runner Fitzroy House Stakes at Newmarket in August; made all when gaining his second and third victories, putting up a particularly gritty display at Newmarket when holding off newcomer Lyphard's Pride by a neck; distant sixth of 8 to Achieved when 10/1 for Laurent Perrier Champagne Stakes at Doncaster in September; well suited by 7f; a thoroughly genuine colt. *W. O'Gorman.*

CHUMMY'S BEST 3 b.g. Tower Walk 130–Bright Diadem (Pall Mall 132) — (1980 6fg 6d 6d 1981 6d 8f 8fg 10f 14fg) sturdy, useful-looking gelding; good mover; poor form in maiden and minor races; blinkered last 2 starts; trained first outing by R. Smyth. *R. Williams.*

CHUMMY'S SPECIAL 3 b.c. Mummy's Pet 125–Go Too 78 (Goldhill 125) **93** (1980 5f* 5fg² 5g* 6g 5g 1981 6d³ 5g 7.2s 6f) shapely, attractive colt; won at Haydock and Royal Ascot (Norfolk Stakes) in 1980; didn't run up to his best when 1½ lengths third to Swan Princess in minor event at Folkestone in April; had stiff tasks afterwards and wasn't seen out after June; best form at 5f; sold 3,500 gns Newmarket Autumn Sales. *G. Hunter.*

CHUMWAR 3 b.c. So Blessed 130–Lynwood Sovereign 102 (Connaught 130) — (1980 5fg 6d 6f 6fg 5fg* 5fg* 1981 5s 5s 7g) sturdy colt; won at Newcastle and Thirsk as a 2-y-o; had a very unlucky run and was eased right up when his chance had gone when seventh of 9 behind Prison Payment in handicap at Salisbury in April on second start; runs as if 5f is too sharp for him nowadays and is bred to stay at least 7f; acts on a firm surface; sent to USA. *D. Thom.*

CHURCHES GREEN 2 b.g. Sassafras 135–Alice Johnston (Majetta 115) — (1981 7g 10s) May 28; 2,800F, 7,400Y; good sort; half-brother to Irish 5f winner An Cailin Deas (by St Alphage); dam Irish 2-y-o 5f winner; sixth in maiden races at Leicester and Nottingham, staying on fairly well after dwelling when beaten just under 10 lengths by Sunny Look on latter course in October; seems suited by 1¼m. *S. Mellor.*

CHURCH MOUNTAIN 3 b.f. Furry Glen 121–Milly Whiteway 112 (Great — White Way) (1980 6s² 6s* 7d 7v 1981 8g 8.2f) lengthy, unfurnished filly; won maiden race at Hamilton as a 2-y-o; last both starts in 1981 (June); should be suited by 7f; acts on soft going. *W. H. H. Williams.*

CHURCH PARADE 3 b.c. Queen's Hussar 124–Christchurch 88 (So Blessed 130) **116** (1980 6d* 7fg* 7g³ 1981 8g 12d 10g³ 10.5g* 11.1f²) well-made, handsome colt; has an enlarged near-hind hock; first foal; dam, 1½m winner, is half-sister to 1,000 Guineas and French Oaks winner Highclere (by Queen's Hussar); won maiden race at Newmarket and Lanson Champagne Stakes at Goodwood as a 2-y-o; odds on, made all and kept on well to hold Robellino by 1½ lengths in 3-runner High Line Stakes at York in August; tried to make all but had no answer to winner's pace when 3 lengths second to Kind of Hush in September Stakes at Kempton on only subsequent outing; had run creditably on second and third starts, when 18 lengths fifth of 18 to runaway winner Shergar in Derby (possibly found trip too far) and very close third to Bellman in Group 2 Prix Eugene Adam at Saint-Cloud (pulled quite hard and battled on gamely once headed inside distance); blinkered when behind in 2,000 Guineas at Newmarket on other start; stays 11f; acts on a firm and a soft surface. *R. Hern.*

CHURRA 2 b.f. Realm 129–Venus of Stretham 107 (Tower Walk 130) (1981 **74** 5s² 5s⁴ 6d) Apr 3; 14,000Y; first foal; dam won 10 races at up to 1¼m, 7 of them at 2 yrs; quite moderate form in maiden races at the back-end; stays 6f. *F. J. Houghton.*

CIDER MAN 3 b.g. Manacle 123–Appleshaw (St Alphage 119) (1980 5fg 5fg — 5f* 6fg 6d* 8f 8fg 6g 1981 6g 7g 7.2s 8s) good sort; poor form in sellers in 1981; stays at least 6f (not disgraced over 1m); seems to act on any going; often blinkered nowadays; sold 1,150 gns Ascot 2nd June Sales. *B. Hanbury.*

High Line Stakes, York—Church Parade gives Carson his last winner of season; the 1980 champion jockey was badly injured later in afternoon and did not ride a

CIDER QUEEN 2 b.f. Oats 126–Damascus Sky (Skymaster 126) (1981 6fg 7d 7.6s) Mar 31; IR 4,100Y; strong, rangy filly; good walker; half-sister to 2 winners, including 6f to 7.5f winner Sky Jump (by Double Jump); dam unplaced 4 times; unquoted when well beaten in maiden and minor races but is the type to do better in time. *R. Smyth.* —

CIMA 3 br.g. High Top 131–Lemon Blossom 83 (Acropolis 132) (1980 5f 5f 6fg⁴ 7d⁴ 7g² 8g 8g⁴ 1981 12s* 12d* 10d 12g* 12d* 12f³ 12fg 16s) quite well-made gelding; good mover; an improved sort who had a fine season; got on top in last furlong and was ridden out to beat Royal Vulcan a length in £4,600 handicap at Epsom in June; successful earlier at Leicester (twice) and Brighton, winning by 5 lengths each time; didn't have best of runs when excellent third behind Feltwell in King George V Stakes (Handicap) at Royal Ascot; suited by 1½m; acts on any going; genuine; off course 3 months after sixth start. *J. Old.* 98

CIMARRON 3 ch.f. Carnival Dancer 113–Duresme 76 (Starry Halo 122) (1980 5s 5s 8d 1981 8fg³ 8g 10g³ 10.2f 10f 10g) leggy filly; third in maiden race at Warwick and minor event at Ripon; stays 1¼m. *J. Harris.* 65

CIMON 3 br.c. Sallust 134–Fortlin 95 (Fortino II 120) (1980 8g 8s* 1981 7s² 10s 8g² 7d 7g² 8fg) leggy, short-backed colt; brother to top-class French and American filly Sanedtki, successful at up to 9f, and half-brother to 2 winners; won maiden race at the Curragh impressively in 1980; didn't win as a 3-y-o but was runner-up in Gladness Stakes at the Curragh in April (went down by only a short head to Prince Echo), Edenderry Stakes at Phoenix Park in May (beaten 1¼ lengths by Blue Wind) and minor event at Tralee in June; stays 1m well; acts on soft going; ran moderately in blinkers; sent to USA. *A. Maxwell, Ireland.* 95

CINCO MILL 2 b.f. Jimmy Reppin 131–Six Wives 80 (Royal Record II) (1981 7fg) Mar 22; 600F; sixth foal; dam at her best at 2 yrs; tailed-off last of 12 to Cassley River in maiden race at Warwick in July. *W. Wharton.* —

CINDERWENCH 3 b.f. Crooner 119–Burning Deck 56 (Fighting Ship 121) (1980 7f 8f* 9d* 1981 12g⁴ 12.2fg² 13.3g 12fg⁴ 10.8s 12d*) leggy filly; very much flattered by her proximity but nevertheless ran well when neck second to Home On The Range in Warwick Oaks in June; beat Great Light by 2½ lengths in apprentice event at Chepstow in October; suited by 1½m; seemed to act on any going; ridden by apprentice M. Malham each time when successful; retired to stud. *P. Cole.* 95

CINDRUM 3 ch.g. Meldrum 112–Jacine Tudor (Henry the Seventh 125) (1980 7f 1981 8s) small, compact gelding; tailed off in sellers. *D. Yeoman.* —

CIRCUS RING 2 b.f. High Top 131–Bell Song 101 (Tudor Melody 129) (1981 6fg* 6fg* 6g*) 122

It's high praise indeed when a journalist of Peter Willett's vast experience ventures the opinion 'I doubt whether those flying fillies of the past, Pretty Polly, Mumtaz Mahal and Myrobella, more profoundly impressed onlookers by their brilliant performances as two-year-olds than Circus Ring has done by her victories'. A resume of these fillies' two-year-old careers will be enlightening: Pretty Polly won all her nine starts in 1903, including the National Breeders', the Champagne, the Cheveley Park and the Middle Park Stakes; Mumtaz Mahal's five victories in six outings in 1923 included a ten-length win in the Queen Mary, a four-length win in the National Breeders' Stakes and a three-length success in the Champagne; and Myrobella took the last five of her six races in 1932, among them the National Breeders' Stakes by five lengths and the Champagne by six. To underline further the compliment being paid to Circus Ring it must be added

Princess Margaret Stakes, Ascot—a most impressive performance by Circus Ring

Lowther Stakes, York—Circus Ring is never off the bit to beat Travel On

that Pretty Polly was one of the greatest fillies in English racing history and that both Mumtaz Mahal and Myrobella topped the Free Handicap, ahead of the colts, by 2 lb and 3 lb respectively. However, we haven't been able to rate Circus Ring within 9 lb of the best colts of her generation. Without doubt she was the best of the two-year-old fillies, potentially a brilliant one, but a bout of lameness in mid-September prevented her from taking her chance in the Cheveley Park Stakes. All that she can be judged on are three cantering victories against unexceptional opposition and these, in our view, aren't enough to rate her a champion. Let's hope she has more opportunities at three to show whether or not she deserves to be spoken of as one of the all-time greats.

Circus Ring's first two starts came in July, in the Princess Maiden Stakes at Newmarket and the Princess Margaret Stakes at Ascot, both of which had been won the previous year by one of the season's top fillies, Tolmi. Tolmi had won the races in highly impressive fashion but even her performances were over-shadowed by Circus Ring's. At Newmarket Circus Ring was always going nicely and she left the seventeen other runners for dead when asked for an effort two furlongs out, responding so magnificently that she had put seven lengths between herself and her nearest rival, Wintergrace, by the line. To reinforce the promise of her display, Circus Ring's time in the second division of the Princess Maiden Stakes was 1.16 seconds faster than that recorded by Corsky in the first division. An even better display was to follow at Ascot. Her eight opponents included Fairy Tern, a beautifully-bred filly who had made a winning debut at Newbury the previous week, Atossa, unbeaten in two starts, and Silojoka, in the frame in both the Queen Mary Stakes and the St Catherine's Stakes, but Circus Ring started at 6/4 on. She put up one of the most breath-taking displays by a two-year-old filly that we have seen in a long time. Even though still in the rear at halfway, as she'd been from the start, it was clear Circus Ring was travelling very strongly on the bridle. It was equally clear she would win once she started her run and, after sweeping through into the lead below the distance, she shot clear to score by ten lengths from the newcomer Apples of Gold.

The manner of Circus Ring's Ascot victory made us doubt whether any of the colts that had been seen out was capable of beating her at this stage of the season. However she was kept to her own sex in her remaining race of the season, the Lowther Stakes at York's August meeting. Only Travel On of the seven other runners looked capable of posing a threat but as the winner of the

Group 3 Cherry Hinton Stakes at Newmarket she had to give 5 lb to Circus
Ring who started at 4/1 on. Circus Ring produced the anticipated impressive
performance. Never off the bridle, she cruised into the lead with a quarter of
a mile to race and her jockey spent the last hundred yards looking round as
Travel On struggled gamely to stay in contention. Circus Ring's winning
margin of two lengths bore no relation to the ease of her victory.

Circus Ring (b.f. Feb 8, 1979)	High Top (br 1969)	Derring-Do (br 1961)	Darius / Sipsey Bridge
		Camenae (b 1961)	Vimy / Madrilene
	Bell Song (b 1966)	Tudor Melody (br 1956)	Tudor Minstrel / Matelda
		Campanette (b 1948)	Fair Trial / Calluna

Circus Ring won her races with such overwhelming authority that she
dominated the early betting on the One Thousand Guineas, with the Tote going
4/1 Circus Ring, 14/1 bar. Will she follow in Pretty Polly's footsteps and win
the Guineas or will she fail, through lack of stamina as Mumtaz Mahal and Myrobella,
or even because she's not good enough? There seems to be no reason why
she shouldn't stay a mile; she races in an extremely relaxed manner and both her
sire High Top and her dam Bell Song won over a mile. High Top often gave the
impression he would have stayed further had he been given the chance and it's
noticeable that many of his offspring stay reasonably well. Indeed his best-
known winners apart from Circus Ring are the St Leger winner Cut Above, the
Prix du Jockey-Club winner Top Ville and the tough Stoute-trained filly Triple
First, winner of the Musidora, Nassau and Sun Chariot Stakes. Incidentally,
while on the subject of High Top, John Gaines reportedly tried to buy the
horse for America in the autumn, offering 120,000 dollars a share, but the bid was
turned down.

Bell Song seemed to stay a mile and a quarter, even though by Tudor Melody,

The Snailwell Stud Company Limited's "Circus Ring"

and she's related to numerous horses who stayed quite well; Lucky Finish, her half-brother by the sprinter Milesian, won the Dante Stakes from Ribero and stayed a mile and three quarters; Priddy Fair, a half-sister, won at up to eleven furlongs and became the grandam of the Irish Guinness Oaks winner Dibidale as well as Shellshock and Cracaval; and Belle of Athens, another half-sister, bred the Leger winner Athens Wood and the good middle-distance filly Sleat. Circus Ring's grandam Campanette was herself a granddaughter of the 1934 One Thousand Guineas winner Campanula.

The next question to be answered is will Circus Ring make normal progress? The question arises largely because the two previous winning fillies out of Bell Song appeared not to train on. The first of the two, both daughters of Great Nephew, was the smart 1974 two-year-old Great Paul who, like Circus Ring, was unbeaten in three races over six furlongs. Since she stood only 14.2 hands there was always a chance Great Paul wouldn't progress, but there was no obvious reason why the fairly useful 1978 six-furlong winner Great Tom should fail to do so. Bell Song's other winners weren't so good but Night Porter (by Connaught) won over nine furlongs at three and Wimsey (by Run The Gantlet) won a two-mile private sweepstakes at four. Bell Song's next foal, a yearling colt by Sassafras, was sold under the name Your Song to Guy Harwood for 1,050,000 francs at the 1981 Deauville Sales. Michael Stoute believes Circus Ring will train on and we think she will too. Although by no means an imposing filly she's attractive enough and once she starts to move she really takes the eye with her action. She's capable of producing a prodigious burst of speed and must have a first-rate chance of compensating her trainer for his near misses with Marwell, Our Home and Fair Salinia in three of the last four runnings of the One Thousand Guineas. Circus Ring has yet to race on a soft surface. *M. Stoute.*

CISTO (FR) 6 b.h. Presto–Cypris (Devon III 125) (1980 14f 14.7f*(dis) 12fg⁴ **64**
22.2fg 14g 15s 1981 16g³ 14g³ 18.8fg 14d² 16f 16.1g 14d⁴) big, strong ex-French horse; has a round action; staying handicapper; possibly unsuited by very soft going but acts on any other; sweated up badly once in 1980; suitable mount for an inexperienced rider. *A. Goodwill.*

CITADEL ROC 6 ro.g. Cratloe Rocket 95–Rocita (Roc du Diable 125) (1980 —
NR 1981 12f 16.1f 12f) poor maiden; has worn blinkers. *M. Bradley.*

CITISSIMA 3 ch.f. Simbir 130–Airgead Beo (Hook Money 124) (1980 8g 9d* **96**
8s³ 1981 7s 10g* 8v 12s 12fg 10g* 10d 10d) Irish filly; won 10-runner Azalea Stakes at Phoenix Park in May (by a neck from Diamond Land) and apprentice handicap on same course in August (by ¾ length from The Centaur); soundly beaten in between, including in Goffs Irish 1,000 Guineas and Irish Guinness Oaks (acted as pacemaker for stable-companion Blue Wind), both at the Curragh; should stay 1½m; acts on soft going. *D. Weld, Ireland.*

CITRUS 2 ch.c. Orange Bay 131–Lady Lowndes 97 (Tamerlane 128) (1981 — p
7fg) May 8; 15,500Y; well-made, good sort; good walker; half-brother to a winner in Cyprus; dam won from 1¼m to 13.8f; 5/1, couldn't find any extra after leading 2f out when 9½ lengths fifth of 16 to Rajhaan in maiden race at Salisbury in September (eased once chance had gone); may do better over middle distances in 1982. *P. Walwyn.*

CITY LINK EXPRESS 4 ch.g. Dubassoff–Chaddy (St Chad 120) (1980 10s **42**
7f 7f 10.1s 8.3s³ 7g³ 8.3g⁴ 8.3f³ 8g 8g⁴ 10fg 10f 10g 1981 7.6g 8.3fg⁴ 8.3g 8.3g) leggy gelding; plater; best at around 1m; acts on any going; sometimes wears blinkers; has run creditably for a boy. *D. Wilson.*

CITY LINK LAD 5 ch.g. Jimmy Reppin 131–Aleta 71 (Montaval 129) (1980 —
7.6f 10fg 13.3g 8g 8f 8g 7f 8fg* 8g 10d 8s 1981 8fg 8g 8f 7fg 8fg 10g 10fg 8fg 8s) big, strong gelding; poor handicapper; stays 1m; acts on a firm surface; suitable mount for an apprentice; sometimes blinkered; trained by P. Ashworth first 3 starts. *D. Wilson.*

CITY LINK STAR 3 ch.g. My Swallow 134–Come On Girl (Sheshoon 132) —
(1980 7g 7d⁴ 7fg 1981 8s 12fg 10.2d 8g 10fg) rangy gelding; little worthwhile form in varied company; trained by P. Ashworth until after second outing. *D. Wilson.*

CITY LIVING 3 ch.g. Scallywag 127–Clear View (Supreme Sovereign 119) —
(1980 NR 1981 12d) 1,000F; second produce; half-brother to 1m winner I'll See You Again (by Saintly Song); dam never ran; tailed-off last of 11 behind Luz Bay in claiming race at Newmarket in August; sold 650 gns Ascot Sales later in month. *A. Bailey.*

CITY'S SISTER 3 ch.f. Maystreak 118–Must Improve 47 (Lucky Brief 128)   **72**
(1980 NR   1981 8s 9s 8g 6g* 7.2s* 8g⁴ 7fg 8g² 9.4fg³ 10f 10.6fg 7g 8.2v³ 8d 11d²)
lengthy, rather lightly-made filly; sister to fair jumper New City; dam won
over hurdles; won sellers at Thirsk (no bid) and Haydock (bought in 3,600 gns)
in May, on latter course making all and trotting up by 12 lengths; ran respectably
in non-sellers afterwards; stays 11f; acts on a firm surface but is well suited by
soft going; sometimes sweats up. *G. Richards.*

CLAIRE'S LEGEND 3 b.f. Imperial Crown 96–Laura Lou (Lauso)   (1980 NR   **—**
1981 10.1fg 8fg 10.1fg 6f)   small filly; poor maiden; sold 450 gns Ascot
September Sales. *R. Atkins.*

CLANDESTIN (FR) 2 b.c. Quiet Fling 124–Saucy Kate 85 (March Past 124)   **?**
(1981 6fg 5fg 8fg 6.5d 8g 8g⁴ 7g³ 8d)   fourth foal; dam won three 5f races at 2
yrs; no worthwhile form in this country when trained by C. Austin; in frame in
maiden race at Compiegne and minor event at Fontainebleau late in season;
stays 1m. *F. Doumen, France.*

CLANDESTINA (USA) 3 b.f. Secretariat–My Charmer (Poker) (1980 5g²   **98**
1981 10fg 10fg* 8d³ 12s) $750,000Y; strong, well-made, attractive filly; good
mover; fourth foal; half-sister to 2 winners, including brilliant American triple
crown winner Seattle Slew (by Bold Reasoning); dam minor stakes winner at up to
1m; 3/1 on when beating Tante Yvonne by 5 lengths in maiden race at Phoenix
Park in July; ran creditably in better company at the Curragh on 2 of her other
starts, when staying-on 6 lengths fifth of 13 to Happy Bride in Pretty Polly
Stakes in June and ¾-length third of 12 to Tumblella in Gilltown Stud Stakes in
September; lost her place soon after halfway when disappointing tenth of 11
behind easy winner Flighting in Princess Royal Stakes at Ascot in October;
should stay 1½m; acts on a firm and a soft surface. *V. O'Brien, Ireland.*

CLARE ISLAND 2 b.f. Connaught 130–Island Lore 100 (Court Martial) (1981 **107**
7fg* 8g² 8fg) Mar 13; rangy, attractive filly; half-sister to several winners,
notably very smart 1½m horse Caliban (by Ragusa); dam 2-y-o 5f winner; put
up a very pleasing first effort when short-priced favourite for £3,800 event at
Sandown in July, leading 2f out and running on under very tender handling to

The Snailwell Stud Company Limited's "Clare Island"

win by 1½ lengths from Bourgeonette; beaten subsequently in good races won by Height of Fashion in September, putting up a very useful effort when running her to ¾ length in May Hill Stakes at Doncaster (rec 3 lb) but finishing only 5½ lengths fifth of 8, after looking to be going as well as anything early in straight, in Hoover Fillies Mile at Ascot; stays 1m; possibly past her best for year at Ascot. *H. Cecil.*

CLARENDON 4 gr.g. Brigadier Gerard 144–France (Milesian 125) (1980 8d² 8g* 8fg 8.3g 1981 12s 16s 12d 15.8g) compact, deep-girthed gelding; well beaten in 1981; should stay middle distances; possibly needs some give in the gound. *J. Yardley.* —

CLARES LOCH 2 br.f. Lochnager 132–Aberklair 72 (Klairon 131) (1981 5d 5g 6fg 6f 5s⁴ 5s) Mar 22; 2,500Y; first foal; dam, half-sister to very useful Blue Courtier, won over 5f and 1m; plater; should stay 6f; formerly trained by Mrs R. Lomax. *R. Baker.* **54**

CLARISTA (USA) 3 b.f. Riva Ridge–Furioso 116 (Ballymoss 136) (1980 7d 1981 7g 10g 8fg⁴ 10f⁴ 10d 10f³ 10fg 9s² 10g) lengthy filly; in frame in maiden races; one paced and will stay 1½m; has been tried in blinkers and looks none too enthusiastic; sold 96,000 gns Newmarket December Sales. *H. Wragg.* **67**

CLASSICAL DANCER 2 gr.c. Godswalk 130–Classical Music 85 (Santa Claus 133) (1981 6f 6g 6d*) Mar 29; 16,000F, 6,000Y; half-brother to useful Italian winner Lot of Class (by Home Guard); dam half-sister to high-class miler Saintly Song; put up easily best effort when winning 17-runner maiden race at the Curragh in October by a short head from odds-on Solar Wind; will stay 7f; acts on a soft surface. *D. Hughes, Ireland.* **82**

CLASSY DEB 3 b.f. Abwah 118–Near The Line 88 (Nearula 132) (1980 NR 1981 7.2f 8f 8g) half-sister to several winners, including useful 1½m performer Borderline (by Silly Season); dam half-sister to Derby second Alcaeus; well behind in maiden races at Haydock (on burly side) and Thirsk in July and in minor event at Edinburgh in October. *Miss S. Hall.* —

CLAUDIUS CROZET (USA) 2 b.c. Halo–Ima Roan (Determine) (1981 5fg 6fg 6g 6fg⁴ 6g² 8s 7g) neat colt; blind in near eye; half-brother to 2 winners, including stakes-placed Ravidus (by Vitriolic); dam very useful stakes winner at up to 9f; showed ability in varied company, running very well on final start when 6½ lengths sixth of 11 to Not For Show in £4,300 race in December in November; should stay 1m; possibly unsuited by soft ground. *G. Huffer.* **86**

CLAUDIUS SECUNDUS 4 b.g. Idiot's Delight 115–Versailles 93 (Never Say Die 137) (1980 9fg* 10g 10g 8.3f 8.2d 8d* 7g² 1981 10s 10g* 10s* 12f 10d*) big gelding; fair handicapper; successful at Kempton (twice) in the spring and at Newmarket in August; well-backed favourite when winning in good style from Lusitanica on latter track; stays 1¼m but found 1½m too far fourth outing; probably acts on any going but seems suited by some give in the ground; game. *M. Jarvis.* **87**

CLAVALINO 2 b.c. On Your Mark 125–Pulcinella 95 (Shantung 132) (1981 5s 5s 5fg⁴ 5f 5.3f 5.3f) Mar 4; 4,000F, 7,000Y; neat colt; first foal; dam won over 1m; ran best race when 3 lengths fourth of 16 to Annsome Boy in maiden race at Warwick in April; off course 2 months afterwards; evidently suited by a firm surface; blinkered last 2 starts; sold 2,500 gns Newmarket Autumn Sales. *N. Vigors.* **61**

CLAVERHAM MANOR 2 br.c. Saulingo 122–Edissa 66 (Honeyway 125) (1981 5fg 6fg 8d 7.6s) May 18; 6,200Y; lightly-made colt; closely related to a minor winner by African Sky and half-brother to several other winners, including very smart French 1¼m performer Odisea (by Majority Blue); dam 1½m winner; soundly beaten in maiden and minor events. *R. Hannon.* —

CLAVERTON 3 b.f. Gold Form 108–Sea Baby (Babur 126) (1980 5f 5f³ 5fg³ 5d 5g 1981 8s 7d 6d 7f³ 8h 7fg 6fg) very lightly-made filly; poor maiden; soundly beaten in a seller final start; seems to stay 1m; trained by C. Wildman until after third outing. *J. Bethell.* **42**

CLEAR VERDICT (USA) 3 b.c. Judger–Ideal Day (Buckpasser) (1980 7g² 7fg* 8g* 1981 9fg² 12g 12f) attractive, well-made colt; good walker and mover; a progressive individual as a 2-y-o who won at Newmarket and Goodwood (by neck from Recitation); looked as if he'd be better for the race when 4 lengths second to Kalaglow in Heath Stakes at Newmarket in April (completely outpaced by winner over last 2f); put up a lack-lustre display when 4¾ lengths fifth to Riberetto in Ladbrokes Derby Trial Stakes at Lingfield following month **98**

(odds on) and weakened in straight when seventh of 10 behind Bustomi in King Edward VII Stakes at Royal Ascot in June; not seen out again; should be suited by middle distances; yet to race on soft going. *H. Cecil.*

CLERE LIGHT 3 b.f. Idiot's Delight 115–Mistress Clare 95 (Prince de Galles 125) —
(1980 7.3d 1981 6g 10s 12d) lengthy filly; in rear in maiden and minor races; sold 400 gns Newmarket Autumn Sales. *I. Balding.*

CLEWISTON 5 b.g. Manacle 123–Blue Bird 94 (Majority Blue 126) (1980 8f **56**
8fg 6fg 7d 1981 7g* 7g³ 8fg 7.2v 7g³) leggy gelding; backed from 14/1 to 4/1, returned to form when winning apprentice handicap at Doncaster in May; twice ran respectably afterwards; stays 1m; suited by top-of-the-ground; sometimes sweats up. *M. Camacho.*

CLICKHAM LAD 3 ch.g. Keren 100–Native Queen (Native Prince) (1980 —
6f³ 7g 7g 6g 1981 8g 9.4g 10g 8fg 16fg) sturdy gelding; well behind in varied company, and has shown signs of temperament; has been tried in blinkers. *N. Chamberlain.*

CLIFF BANK 3 b.c. Take a Reef 127–Villa Marina 96 (Tudor Melody 129) **81**
(1980 5fg 5f 5s³ 6g³ 6fg* 6g⁴ 6g 6g³ 6g² 6d* 1981 8f 7g 8g) useful-looking colt; said by trainer to have a very poor mouth; developed into a useful colt as a 2-y-o; lightly raced in 1981, best effort on final start when sixth of 22 behind Gallea in handicap at Leicester in September; stays 1m; probably acts on any any going but seems well suited by some give in the ground; blinkered first outing as a 2-y-o; missed break second outing; sold 660 gns Newmarket Autumn Sales. *B. Hobbs.*

CLIPHOME 3 gr.g. Sandford Lad 133–Seamyside (Sea Hawk II 131) (1980 **79**
5f 6g 7fg 8g³ 8fg* 7s⁴ 1981 10fg³ 10.6d² 10g 10g 9.4fg* 8g) useful-looking gelding; beat Bustellina by 1½ lengths in small handicap at Carlisle in July; probably needs further than 1m and stays 1¼m; probably acts on any going; sold to a patron of M. H. Easterby's stable 7,400 gns Ascot August Sales and subsequently gelded. *G. Pritchard-Gordon.*

CLOCK TOWER 2 b.c. Tower Walk 130–Cappucilli 111 (Lorenzaccio 130) —
(1981 8g 8d 8s) Mar 26; 4,200Y; sturdy colt; second foal; half-brother to 1¼m seller winner Truper Gee (by Rheingold); dam very useful staying 2-y-o but failed to train on; well beaten in maiden and minor events in the autumn. *S. Wiles.*

CLONEASH EMPEROR 5 gr.g. Young Emperor 133–Gambling Queen 80 —
(Pretendre 126) (1980 NR 1981 8fg 12f) ex-Irish gelding; successful 3 times from 9f to 1½m in Ireland; well beaten in amateur riders races at Warwick in June and Beverley in July; appears very well suited by a sound surface; has won for an apprentice; sold 1,150 gns Ascot October Sales. *R. Cambidge.*

CLONEY BOY 3 gr.c. Sovereign Path 125–Moorland Chant (Double Jump 131) **67**
(1980 6f⁴ 6s 6fg 1981 6v* 8.2d 8g 6g 6fg) strong, useful sort; apprentice ridden, beat Java Tiger by ¾ length in minor event at Ayr in March; had stiff task and wasn't disgraced in amateur riders event next start; probably stays 1m; acts on heavy going; blinkered fourth start; sold 1,500 gns Newmarket Autumn Sales. *Denys Smith.*

CLOUDED VISION 2 b.f. So Blessed 130–Bundling (Petingo 135) (1981 **74**
5.8g 7d 7v) Apr 16; rangy filly; blind in near eye; half-sister to 2 winners, including 1m and 10.6f winner Boltingo (by Bold Lad, Ire); dam, half-sister to dam of Enstone Spark, won over 5f in Ireland; prominent most of way when 6¼ lengths fifth of 18 to Melting Snows in maiden race at Newbury in September, second outing and best effort; not sure to stay beyond 7f. *I. Balding.*

CLOUDS HEAVEN 2 ch.f. Import 127–Fragrant Cloud 69 (Balidar 133) —
(1981 6fg 6s 6d 6d) Apr 28; 2,300Y; strong filly; first foal; dam best at 5f and 6f; little sign of ability in maiden races; fell first start. *W. Elsey.*

CLOUDWALKER 3 gr.c. Dragonara Palace 115–Misfired 101 (Blast 125) **73**
(1980 5d 6d4 6s³ 1981 7g 7d 7s* 7g 8fg 7f 7fg 8g* 7g 8d) rangy colt; successful in handicaps at Wolverhampton in May (tended to hang) and September (gambled on), beating Dr Steve ¾ length on latter course; stays 1m; seems to need some give in the ground; often blinkered (has worn them when successful); suitable mount for an apprentice. *G. Balding.*

CLOWNISH 2 b. or br.c. Idiot's Delight 115–Mistress Clare 95 (Prince de **73**
Galles 125) (1981 5f 7g 7fg² 7fg³ 8s⁴) Mar 9; second foal; dam won from 7f to 2m; in frame in maiden events and a nursery; will be suited by middle

COC

distances; probably acts on any going; blinkered third outing; sold to Newmarket BA 4,500 gns Newmarket Autumn Sales. *I. Balding.*

CLUB CLASS (USA) 2 b.f. Roberto 131–Queen of the Sky (Bold Ruler) **82 p** (1981 7g 10g) Apr 3; $185,000Y; medium-sized, quite well-made filly; closely related to 2 winners by Hail to Reason, including stakes-placed Halcyon Queen, and half-sister to 4 winners, including 3-y-o stayer Consenting (by Judger); dam unraced sister to champion 2-y-o's Bold Lad (USA) and Successor; 25/1, going on in fine style without being knocked about when most promising 6¼ lengths seventh of 15 to Ivano in Houghton Stakes at Newmarket in October; looked over the top and was never really in the hunt in well-contested £6,500 event on same course later in month; should be well suited by middle distances; must be given another chance to confirm the very favourable impression she created on her debut. *J. Hindley.*

CLWYD 7 ch.h. Crepello 136–Caerphilly 129 (Abernant 142) (1980 8d 8.2g³ **54** 8fg³ 8g 8s* 9g⁴ 8.2g 10.4d⁴ 8fg 8.2s³ 1981 7s³ 8d² 8g 7g) poor handicapper nowadays; stays 11f; probably acts on any going but is well suited by some give in the ground; has been tried in blinkers; suitable mount for an inexperienced rider. *Denys Smith.*

CLYMENE 2 b.f. Vitiges 132–Siraf 85 (Alcide 136) (1981 7g*) Mar 24; **86 p** half-sister to several winners here and in France, including useful 6f and 7f winner Saluzzo (by Sallust); dam staying half-sister to smart Harmony Hall; 6/1, always in command when winning 16-runner maiden race at Leicester in October by 2½ lengths from Tequilla Sunrise; will be suited by middle distances; likely to do better things. *H. Cecil.*

COAL BUNKER 3 ch.c. On Your Mark 125–Powder Box (Faberge II 121) **67** (1980 5s³ 5s 5s 5f 5h³ 6f³ 6s 6d³ 6d 6f³ 7h² 7g² 8fg* 8d 1981 8d 8g 8.3fg 8fg 7f 8.3fg⁴ 10fg 10f* 10f 11.7d⁴ 10d) small, compact colt; shows a lot of knee action; returned to form steadily and at Folkestone in September beat Private Audience by 2 lengths in a handicap; probably stays 11.7f; has run respectably on soft ground, but best form on a sound surface; blinkered third outing in 1980. *R. Hannon.*

COASTING BREEZE 3 br.g. Windjammer (USA)—Etoile Freda (Florescence — 120) (1980 5fg 1981 6fg 6g 5fg 5g) little sign of ability in varied company. *J. Bosley.*

COASTLINE 2 b.c. So Blessed 130–Coaster 61 (Right Tack 131) (1981 5g 6g **62** 5g 6g 6g 8d) Apr 17; robust colt; third foal; half-brother to 1m and 1¼m winner We'll Meet Again (by Song) and fairly useful 1980 2-y-o Gandoorah (by Record Token); dam, half-sister to top-class sprinter Roman Warrior, won over 1m; only poor form in maiden and minor events and a nursery. *J. Benstead.*

COBBLER'S INN 2 ch.c. Spanish Gold 101–Toccatina 79 (Bleep-Bleep 134) **63** (1981 5g 5g 6g 5f 6d 5f 5f 7f 6s³) May 15; neat, strong colt; half-brother to 1980 5f winner Balatina (by Balidar) and a winning plater; dam sprinter; kept on when 4½ lengths third of 15 to Purnima in £2,800 seller at York in October; stays 6f; suited by soft going; blinkered fifth and sixth outings. *M. W. Easterby.*

COBBLER SMITH 3 b.c. Crowned Prince 128–Galloping Nell 68 (Worden — II 129) (1980 6d 6fg 6g 5fg³ 6s 6s³ 7d³ 1981 10v 10f 9f) big, strong colt; showed fair form as a 2-y-o but was well beaten in 1981; should be suited by middle distances; probably acts on any going; moved badly to start final outing. *T. Fairhurst.*

COCAINE 3 ch.g. High Line 125–Golden Thoughts 86 (Golden Cloud) (1980 **102** 7d* 8fg 1981 12fg³ 12g³ 16f 12fg⁴ 12fg) small, leggy, lightly-made gelding; ran creditably in Warren Stakes at Epsom in April (3 lengths third to Glint of Gold) and Ladbrokes Derby Trial at Lingfield in May (2½ lengths third behind Riberetto), on each occasion battling on well; also ran respectably when fourth to Grain Race in quite valuable handicap at Goodwood in July; should stay 2m (didn't run up to his best over trip but was unsuited by very firm going); has a very free and round action which suggests he'll always be ideally suited by some give in the ground; game; sold to S. Pattemore 12,500 gns Newmarket Autumn Sales. *J. Hindley.*

COCKFOSTERS 2 b.c. Music Boy 124–Sunny Bloom 71 (Forlorn River 124) — (1981 5s 5s) Feb 20; second foal; brother to 3-y-o 5f winner Fairgreen; dam sprint maiden; behind in maiden races in October at Warwick (33/1) and Wolverhampton (16/1). *H. Westbrook.*

207

COCOBAN 2 b.f. Targowice 130–Be Best (Santa Claus 133) (1981 6f) Apr —
17; fifth foal; half-sister to minor French 1½m winner Be A Lady (by
Roi Dagobert); dam, daughter of Gimcrack and Champagne Stakes winner Be
Careful, won small 9f race in France; 11/1, weakened inside final 2f when seventh
of 10 to Tropical Blaze in minor event at Ripon in August; sold to BBA (Italia)
5,600 gns Newmarket Autumn Sales. *M. Stoute.*

CODRINGTON 2 b.c. Malinowski 123–Manfilia 95 (Mandamus 120) (1981 **111**
6fg* 6fg² 7d² 7g⁴) Feb 2; IR 115,000Y; good-looking colt; half-brother to 3
winners by African Sky, notably high-class 5f to 1⅛m performer Kilijaro and
smart French 9f to 13f winner African Hope; dam won at up to 1¼m; won 14-
runner Granville Stakes at Ascot in July without being given a hard time, scoring by a neck from Montekin; in frame in good races afterwards, notably when
failing by a neck to catch Day Is Done in 11-runner National Stakes over 7f at
the Curragh in September and when never-dangerous 8¾ lengths fourth of 9 to
Wind and Wuthering in William Hill Dewhurst Stakes at Newmarket the following month; will stay middle distances; a splendid type who will win more races.
B. Hills.

COEUR VALLIANT 3 b.c. Grundy 137–Petalca 81 (Dewan) (1980 NR **67**
1981 8g 8g 10d 12.3g⁴ 12g³ 9s) 22,000Y; very big colt; first foal; dam, half-
sister to Petingo, won at up to 10.6f; in frame in maiden races at Newcastle in
August and Goodwood in September; stays 1½m; coltish in paddock third outing.
C. Brittain.

COFFEE DAY 3 b.f. Broxted 120–Palmette 103 (Premonition 130) (1980 —
5v 5f⁴ 5fg 6fg 8.2d 8fg 6s 5s 1981 8s 8fg) plain filly; poor plater; will stay
middle distances; blinkered eighth start at 2 yrs; sold 480 gns Doncaster May
Sales. *J. Berry.*

COJ 3 b.g. Copte–Warm Spring 67§ (Mid-day Sun) (1980 5fg 6s 1981 10s —
10d 10s) small gelding; well beaten in varied company, including selling. *D.
Leslie.*

COJEAN (USA) 2 b.f. Prince John–Cornish Pet (Cornish Prince) (1981 5fg* **86**
6fg 5fg⁴ 6s⁴) Apr 5; $195,000Y; neat, attractive filly; second foal; dam, winner
over 6f at 3 yrs, is half-sister to 3 USA stakes winners; ran on very gamely to
win 11-runner maiden race at Sandown in July by a neck from Blakesware
County; creditable fourth in nurseries at Goodwood the following month (to
Ghawar) and Ascot in September (behind Ten-Traco); will stay at least 1m;
probably acts on any going. *P. Walwyn.*

COLADA 3 ch.f. Manado 130–Yellow Temptress (Yellow God 129) (1980 —
6g 6fg 5d 1981 6s) lightly-made filly; in rear in maiden and minor events in
1980 and in a handicap (last of 18) in April; sold 400 gns Newmarket May Sales.
A. Bailey.

*Granville Maiden Stakes, Ascot—Codrington (diamonds) wins
from Montekin (left)*

COLARO 3 b.f. Tennyson 124–Montcall (Mountain Call 125) (1980 6g 7d 7g —
7fg 7fg 1981 12.2s) leggy, plain, unfurnished filly; poor maiden; blinkered
only outing of 1981; sold 420 gns Newmarket May Sales. *A. Bailey.*

COLD FOURPENNY 2 ch.g. Scallywag 127–Raver 71 (Runnymede 123) —
(1981 8g) Apr 24; first foal; dam, a plater, placed numerous times over sprint
distances; unquoted and apprentice ridden, dwelt and was always behind in
13-runner maiden race won by Brigado at Edinburgh in October. *T. Craig.*

COLD JUSTICE 8 br.g. Arctic Judge 94–Rimelo (Richard Louis 116) (1980 —
NR 1981 10g 16d 16g⁴) quite a moderate hurdler; very lightly raced on flat
nowadays; stays well. *J. Benstead.*

COLEBROOK FOLLY 2 b. or br.c. Hittite Glory 125–Pahlavi Line 65 (Young —
Emperor 133) (1981 7fg 6g 7.6s 10.2g) May 29; 5,600F, 4,400Y; third foal;
half-brother to 1980 2-y-o 7f winner Schiller (by Lorenzaccio); dam placed at
1¼m; unquoted when behind in maiden races and a minor event at Doncaster.
T. Gosling.

COLEY 2 b.c. Morston 125–Consistent 90 (Connaught 130) (1981 5s 5d⁴ 6g **73**
6g 6f 6d 7d³) Jan 27; 5,000Y; neat colt; second foal; half-brother to 3-y-o 1m
seller winner Consistent Queen (by Queen's Hussar); dam won over 5f on first
outing; 16/1, showed easily best form when 2½ lengths third of 14 to Danish
Express in nursery at Edinburgh in October; will stay 1¼m; acts on a soft surface; ran very freely in blinkers sixth outing. *Denys Smith.*

COLONEL MAD 2 gr.c. Town Crier 119–Golden Thoughts 86 (Golden Cloud) **60**
(1981 5s³ 6fg⁴ 6fg 6fg 7.3d 6g) Apr 5; 3,600Y; leggy, narrow colt; good walker;
brother to fairly useful miler Dream Town, and half-brother to several winners,
including useful 1980 2-y-o 7f winner Cocaine (by High Line); dam won over 5f
at 2 yrs; in frame in maiden auction events, running well when ½-length third
to Steel Stockholder at Haydock in June, but was twice well beaten in valuable
sellers afterwards; should stay 6f; possibly needs soft ground; blinkered third
start. *J. Bethell.*

COLONEL SANDERS 3 ch.c. On Your Mark 125–Purple Heron (Great Heron **89**
127) (1980 5f 5f* 5g 6.3v 1981 10g* 11g 10s² 9d³ 10f* 9fg 11.5f² 11.5f 12fg
10d 11.5d) 10,500Y; second foal; brother to 1978 2-y-o 5f winner Purple
Mark; dam never ran; won handicaps at Navan in May and Phoenix Park in
July, latter by ½ length from Speedy Dance; also ran well when ¾-length second to
Dance Bid (gave 7 lb) in Ulster Harp Derby at Down Royal later in July; suited
by middle distances; acts on any going; had stiff task ninth outing. *T. Curtin,
Ireland.*

COLONIAL LINE (USA) 3 ch.f. Plenty Old–Es Cabalistica (Eslavo) (1980 **57**
6g 6g³ 5s 5d 1981 6v⁴ 5g² 5s*) lengthy filly; made virtually all and held off
Diamond Horseshoe by ½ length in 17-runner maiden race at Nottingham in
October; bred to stay 1m; acts on soft going. *P. Cole.*

COLORADO FALLS 2 b.c. Rapid River 127–Long Drop 78 (Tower Walk 130) **50**
(1981 5d 5d⁴ 5g 6f⁴ 7f) Feb 12; 1,050Y; small, good-bodied colt; first foal; dam
probably stayed 1m; 2½ lengths fourth of 9 to Eightpence in seller at Warwick
in May, second outing and best effort; not sure to stay 7f. *T. Marshall.*

COLORWOOD SILK (USA) 2 b. or br.f. Charles Elliott–Color Me Blonde **70**
(Craigwood) (1981 5s 5fg 5d³ 6f 6fg 6g⁴ 8fg* 8.2s) Mar 14; workmanlike filly;
good mover; sister to fair 1980 2-y-o 6f winner Nello and to a winner at up to 9f
in USA; bought in 1,700 gns after winning 16-runner selling nursery at Beverley
in September by 2 lengths from Golden Lisle under co-top weight (always going
well); will stay 1¼m; possibly not at her best on very soft ground; sold to National
Horse Belgium 4,400 gns Doncaster November Sales. *G. Balding.*

COLUMBOOLA 2 b.f. Rapid River 127–Heckley Royal (Lord of Verona 120) —
(1981 5fg 6g 6g 6fg 7fg) May 23; fair sort; seventh foal; half-sister to a winning
hurdler by Hamood; dam never ran; behind in maiden and minor events in the
North. *T. Craig.*

COLUMNIST 4 b.c. Swing Easy 126–Namecaller 83 (Malicious) (1980 6s 6fg³ **119**
6d 6g² 6g³ 1981 6g³ 7d* 6g² 7s 6f 8fg 6d⁴ 7s) lengthy colt; good mover; smart
performer; beat Rabdan by 5 lengths under 9-13 in Autobar Victoria Cup
(Handicap) at Ascot in April; ran creditably on a number of other occasions,
beaten by no more than 2 lengths when third to Rabdan in Ladbrokes Abernant
Stakes at Newmarket (started slowly and didn't get the best of runs), second to
King of Spain in Duke of York Stakes, sixth to The Quiet Bidder in 4f Cork and
Orrery Stakes at Royal Ascot and fourth to First Movement under top weight
in Ladbrokes (Ayr) Gold Cup in September; suited by 7f (well beaten over 1m);

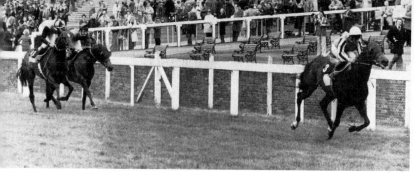

Autobar Victoria Cup (Handicap), Ascot—Columnist comes right away from Rabdan and Murillo (rails)

probably not at his best on very soft ground; wears blinkers; not the most consistent of colts. *J. Tree.*

COLWAY BOY 7 b.g. Faraway Son 130–Crassula (Canisbay 120) (1980 18.8g² 14g 16.5fg 1981 15.5d 18.8fg³ 15.5fg⁴ 16fg) staying handicapper; appears to act on any going. *R. Akehurst.* **42**

COMEDIAN 3 b.g. Comedy Star 121–Ruetina 74 (Rugantino 97) (1980 6g 6d 7fg² 1981 10g 12fg* 12fg* 11.5d² 12d³) small, quite attractive gelding; good mover; showed improved form when winning handicaps at Doncaster (apprentice event from Alma Ata) in June and Lingfield (readily from Needs Supporting) in July; suited by 1½m; acts on a firm and a soft surface. *J. Dunlop.* **80**

COMEDY CROFT 4 b.g. Comedy Star 121–Twyford Ridge (Schapiro 99) (1980 8f 10fg 10f² 12f 11fg⁴ 11.7g 10fg³ 11.5g² 12g* 14fg 16fg 12fg* 12g 1981 12fg 13s 12g 12g) compact, good sort; quite a moderate handicapper at his best; twice ran badly in 1981; doesn't stay 2m; probably acts on any going; sometimes wears blinkers, but didn't when successful; sold 4,500 gns Newmarket July Sales. *R. Hannon.* **—**

COMEDY LADY 3 b.f. Comedy Star 121–Sayida 65 (Kalydon 122) (1980 NR 1981 7g 10.1fg 10fg 8fg 8fg 6g) compact, useful-looking filly; first known foal; dam temperamental middle-distance performer; poor form, including in a seller and a claimer. *R. Hannon.* **—**

COME ON SONNY 2 gr. or ro.g. Funny Man 107–Milton Maid (Pannier 106) (1981 7g 5d) small, lengthy non-thoroughbred gelding; third reported foal; dam never ran; tailed off in maiden events. *M. James.* **—**

COME ON TAFFY 4 ch.c. Welsh Pageant 132–Come On Honey 94 (Never Say Die 137) (1980 10s 14g* 13.8g* 12.3d 1981 14d 14s) robust, deep-girthed colt; odds on when winning maiden race at Yarmouth and minor event at Catterick in 1980; well beaten in handicaps at 4 yrs; suited by 1¾m and will stay further. *I. Wardle.* **—**

COME ON THE BLUES 2 b.c. Blue Cashmere 129–Floral Gift 84 (Princely Gift 137) (1981 5s 5.1f² 5f 6fg* 6fg³ 6g⁴ 6f² 6f² 6g 6s²) Apr 24; 12,000Y; quite attractive, lengthy colt; good walker; half-brother to 3 winners, including fairly useful miler April Bouquet (by Silly Season); dam 2-y-o 5f winner; won maiden race at Brighton by a neck from Ghawar in July; second afterwards in Champion Two Yrs Old Trophy at Ripon in August (went down by only a neck to Glancing), nursery at Doncaster the following month (beaten ¾ length by Basil Boy after seeming to have race sewn up) and Marston Moor Stakes at York in October (beaten 5 lengths by Mirabeau); stays 6f; acts on any going; has shown a tendency to hang and is suited by strong handling; consistent. *C. Brittain.* **103**

COME PLAY WITH ME 6 b.g. Jukebox 120–Compatriot (Pindari 124) (1980 10fg 10g 7fg 7d 8g 1981 14d 7g 12fg 11.7fg) poor handicapper; suitable mount for a boy; has been tried in blinkers. *R. Atkins.* **—**

COMMANDER GENERAL (AUS) 9 gr.g. Warwick 110–Queen Willis (Bucks King 98) (1980 NR 1981 10g 8fg 10g 12f) successful several times on flat in Australia but has shown no ability over here, including in a seller. *T. Marshall.* **—**

COMMELINA 3 ch.f. Amber Rama 133–Coulisse 85 (Right Royal V 135) (1980 —
NR 1981 10fg) strong filly; third foal; dam, daughter of very speedy Couloir,
won over 6f at 2 yrs and stayed 1m; dwelt and was soon well behind when
eleventh of 12 behind Jill Buck in maiden race at Beverley in September. *G.
Pritchard-Gordon.*

COMMISSAR 2 ch.g. Mandrake Major 122–Siouxsie 90 (Warpath 113) (1981 **75**
5f 5v⁴ 6g*) Apr 12; rangy gelding; first foal; dam ran only at 2 yrs, when 6f
winner; well-backed favourite when driven out to beat Golden Spray a length
in valuable 21-runner seller at Newmarket in October; sold 5,700 gns afterwards,
probably to race abroad; runs as though 7f and 1m will suit him. *C. Thornton.*

COMMODORE BLAKE 4 br.c. Blakeney 126–Ribamba 82 (Ribocco 129) **107**
(1980 12s⁴ 1981 10g* 12f 10.5g⁴ 10g* 8fg* 8d⁴ 10.2g* 9g) neat, quite attractive
colt; landed odds readily in maiden race at Stockton in April; showed himself a
useful handicapper afterwards, winning Chesterfield Cup at Goodwood (virtually
unchallenged by 5 lengths from Easter Sun), £7,400 race at Newbury (confidently
ridden to beat Seven Hearts by 2 lengths) and Holsten Pils Handicap at Doncaster (accounted for Easter Sun by 1½ lengths); bred to stay at least 1½m but is
evidently best at up to 1¼m; acts on a firm surface; below form sixth start and
ran badly in William Hill Cambridgeshire on final outing. *M. Stoute.*

COMMONTY (USA) 3 b.c. Empery 128–Duke's Little Gal (Duke of Dublin) **74**
(1980 8d² 1981 11s 10d* 12s⁴ 10d² 10fg⁴ 10fg⁴ 10d 10g 10.6s* 12s² 11s²)
well-made, quite attractive colt; won maiden race at Salisbury in May and
£3,900 amateur riders handicap at Haydock in October in good style, beating
Priestcroft Boy 4 lengths in latter; ran moderately on occasions though; stays
1½m; probably acts on any going but is suited by some give. *J. Bethell.*

COMMUNITY STAR 3 b.c. Manado 130–Destinee (Roan Rocket 128) **56**
6fg 1981 6g 7fg 6g² 6s 7g 6f⁴ 6f 7f⁴ 7f⁴ 6fg² 8g) strong, attractive colt; quite
a moderate maiden; stays 7f. *B. Swift.*

COMPACTOR 2 br.c. Silly Season 127–Rubbish (Major Portion 129) (1981 **64**
7fg 7.2fg 8g 8g 10.2g) May 6; 2,300F; half-brother to 1978 2-y-o 5f winner
Ratan Boy (by Workboy) and a winner in Sweden; dam ran only twice; showed
ability in maiden races on first 2 starts but finished in rear in £2,500 seller at
Newmarket in October on fourth; should stay 1m. *R. Hobson.*

*Holsten Pils Handicap, Doncaster—Commodore Blake runs on well to beat
Easter Sun*

COMPANIONSHIP 4 br.g. Kalamoun 129–Cupid's Delight 82 (St Paddy 133) **44**
(1980 7f 8fg 10fg   1981 12g 10.6s 12f 12f 15.5f⁴ 10g 10fg² 8h 10h² 10f³ 12g 12g)
strong, shapely gelding; plater; stayed 1¼m; acted on hard going; had been tried
in blinkers; dead. *G. Balding.*

COMPOSER 3 ch.c. Music Boy 124–Contadina (Memling) (1980 6d² 6g*   **82**
1981 6g² 6s³ 7.2f⁴ 6f⁴ 6g 6g 6s²) big, lengthy, useful-looking colt; turns his
front feet in; placed in handicaps at York and Kempton in May and at Nottingham in October, but was rather disappointing; should stay 7f; acts on soft
going; blinkered sixth start; sold to W. Marshall 6,000 gns Newmarket Autumn
Sales. *W. Hastings-Bass.*

COMPOUND 7 b.g. Siliconn 121–Compose 94 (Compensation 127) (1980   **49**
6f 6h³ 8f² 6g³ 8fg 7f² 7g⁴ 7f 6g⁴ 6fg 6fg   1981 8d 7g² 6f 7f 8.3g 6fg⁴ 8fg 8d³
6d) unreliable plater; stays 1m; seems to act on any going; suitable mount
for a boy; sometimes starts slowly; has run respectably in blinkers. *Mrs
N. Kennedy.*

COMRA 2 b.g. Moulton 128–Armelle 87 (Tribal Chief 125) (1981 7fg 8d 8s) Apr   **—**
17; 9,000Y; lengthy gelding; first living foal; dam 2-y-o 5f winner; little worthwhile form in varied company. *H. Candy.*

COMTEC 7 b.g. Communication 119–Tecllyn 97 (Technion 96) (1980 6s   **—**
5d 5d 6d 6g 5d 5d 6s   1981 5s 6s) poor sprint handicapper; acts on any going;
usually wears a hood and blinkers. *K. Bridgwater.*

COMTEC PRINCESS 2 ch.f. Gulf Pearl 117–Miss Hart 75 (Track Spare   **73**
125) (1981 5g 5f 6g 8d*) Apr 2; IR 4,000Y (privately); leggy, lengthy filly;
third produce; sister to Irish 6f winner Pearl Locket, and half-sister to a winner
in Holland; dam stayed 1m; backed at long odds, stayed on strongly and led
close home when winning 17-runner seller at Leicester in November by ½ length
from Sir John Falstaff; retained 1,900 gns subsequently; suited by 1m; possibly
needs some give in the ground. *P. Rohan.*

CONA 3 br.g. Connaught 130–Lowna 120 (Princely Gift 137) (1980 7fg 7d⁴   **—**
6g   1981 7fg 10.2f 12g 11g 11d⁴ 12d) well-grown, useful sort; has shown
some ability in varied company; stays 11f; has a tendency to hang; ran freely
in blinkers fourth start; trained most of season by Denys Smith. *D. Francis.*

CONACRE 5 b.g. Connaught 130–Mrs Pankhurst 78 (Reform 132) (1980   **35**
8v 6v 6f 7f   1981 6g³ 5g 8fg) plater; stays 6f. *A. W. Jones.*

CONCERT PITCH 2 ch.g. Royal Match 117–Ballychord (Ballymoss 136)   **81**
(1981 7fg 8g 7g²) Feb 4; IR 6,000F, 6,000Y; strong, dipped-backed gelding;
half-brother to 3 winners, including prolific Italian winner Brilli Peri (by Windjammer); dam reportedly won in Denmark; flattered by proximity to ½-length
winner Cordite Spear in small race at Catterick in October but had 7 others
well beaten off; should improve and win a race over middle distances at 3 yrs.
Miss S. Hall.

CONDELL 2 ch.c. Condorcet–Liberty Nell (Weavers' Hall 122) (1981 6.3fg   **88**
8g⁴ 9g² 8d² 8s*) Apr 9; first foal; dam, an unraced twin, is half-sister to top-
class mare Park Top; ran well in big fields of maidens in the autumn, going
down by a head to Duke of Dollis at Mallow, by 2½ lengths to Lords at Leopardstown and winning 28-runner event at the Curragh by ¾ length from Skylane;
will be suited by 1¼m+. *J. Bolger, Ireland.*

*Musidora Stakes, York—Condessa causes a shock with her defeat of
Madam Gay and the odds-on Fairy Footsteps*

Yorkshire Oaks, York—Condessa (far left) finishes very strongly to catch Leap Lively with Fiesta Fun (right) third and Home On The Range fourth

CONDESSA 3 ch.f. Condorcet–Varinessa (Varano) (1980 5f 5g³ 6.3d⁴ 7g² **121** 7d* 8g 7.5d* 7d³ 1981 12g* 12g³ 10.5s* 12fg 12fg² 12fg⁴ 12g* 12fg³ 14.6g 12d 13s 12f 13fg)

Where to begin is a problem with Condessa. She has had a very busy, eventful career, being raced particularly hard for a good-class filly as a three-year-old, and has met some of the best, with varying results, in five different countries. Three performances stand well above the others—her wins in the Yorkshire Oaks and Musidora Stakes and her second in the Irish Guinness Oaks—but instead of going straight to them it may be better to take things in chronological sequence and begin at the beginning as long as we are concise. Condessa had already run eight times by the end of her two-year-old season. There were few signs of classic potential in her form though she had won two races, both at Gowran Park, including the Waterford Glass Nursery; she was only fifth behind Blue Wind in the Silken Glider Stakes at Leopardstown and received 7-8 in the Irish Classification, 27 lb less than Storm Bird. Staying would obviously be her game. Condessa began her second season tackling a mile and a half, in a small handicap at Clonmel in April. She ran out a cheeky head winner, then stepped up considerably in class and soon created one of the biggest upsets of the season. In the space of four days Condessa took part in two important Oaks trials, the Johnnie Walker-sponsored event at Lingfield and the Musidora Stakes at York. She never threatened at Lingfield but ran creditably for third place behind a winner (Leap Lively) who had been one of the leading English staying two-year-olds, and she probably improved on her own useful form. Any improvement she had made still left her a long way behind the best fillies' classic form, represented at the time by the Oaks favourite Fairy Footsteps, and as Fairy Footsteps was in the Musidora along with the One Thousand Guineas fifth Madam Gay and the Ladbrokes Nell Gwyn Stakes third Miss Markey there seemed no reason to doubt that England would also keep this race at home. Condessa put the cat among the pigeons by winning in most decisive fashion. She came from behind, last of five into the straight after finding the early pace a sharp one, made relentless progress from the three-furlong pole to lead well over a furlong out, and drew four lengths clear of Madam Gay despite edging left; she made Fairy Footsteps appear a non-stayer, the way she left her.

Quite a few theories were propounded to explain the Musidora result, one of the most sensible being that the soft going had had a big influence on the outcome. Frankly, after Condessa had run a very disappointing eighth of nine to Strigida next time out on firmish ground at Royal Ascot when favourite for the Ribblesdale Stakes, we never expected to see her reproduce her York form on anything other than soft. However, she proceeded to finish an excellent second to Blue Wind in the Irish Guinness Oaks, beaten two and a

213

half lengths, on ground very similar to that at Ascot, and then won the Yorkshire Oaks on good. So why she should have run as she did at Ascot we don't know. Truth to tell she isn't the most consistent of fillies, and in between the Irish Oaks and the Yorkshire Oaks, only three days before the Yorkshire Oaks, she never looked better than fourth best in the Blandford Stakes won by Magesterial, failing to show her best form.

Condessa ran a remarkable race in the Yorkshire Oaks. She was already last, having been outpaced, when Silken Knot fell towards the head of affairs and hampered most of the field; in taking avoiding action Condessa had to run wide round the prostrate Carson and started up the straight facing an apparently hopeless task. She made some headway on the wide outside but came to the furlong marker under pressure with Leap Lively, Fiesta Fun and Home On The Range at least three lengths up, Overplay also in front of her and three more level. From this point she began to eat into the others' lead, and fairly breezed to the front fifty yards out; in the end she won going away by a neck from the Lingfield Trial winner Leap Lively.

	Condorcet (b 1972)	Luthier (br 1965)	Klairon
Condessa (ch.f. 1978)			Flute Enchantee
		Pan American (ch 1962)	Pan II
			Visibility Good
	Varinessa (b 1970)	Varano (b 1962)	Darius
			Varna II
		Silken Princess (ch 1956)	Arctic Prince
			Silken Slipper

It was a pity that such a fine performance proved the last one of its kind we saw from Condessa. She subsequently finished a modest third in the Brownstown Stakes at the Curragh, a very disappointing sixth to Alma Ata in the Park Hill Stakes at Doncaster (when favourite over a trip that her York running suggested would suit her well), then tackled company which would almost certainly have been far too strong for her at her best. Once an intended runner for the St Leger, she eventually got her chance against Cut Above and the other colts in the Prix de l'Arc de Triomphe but muffed it by walking

Mr Craig B. Singer's "Condessa"

214

reluctantly out of the stalls and trailing round at the back, wearing blinkers. Subsequently she ran for her American owner, who had bought her for a sum reportedly in excess of half a million dollars following the Musidora Stakes, at Woodbine in Ontario and Aqueduct in New York, putting up easily her best performance when a respectable seventh of fourteen in the Rothmans International on the former course. Incidentally, Condessa would have run in the St Leger had she recovered from her exertions in the Park Hill the previous day. In 1982 the Park Hill will be run on Wednesday instead of Friday, giving the fillies a fairer chance of emulating Cantelo.

Condessa is of the first crop of the Brownstown Stud-based Condorcet. Condorcet ran twenty-two times for five wins at up to twelve and a half furlongs in France. He won the Prix Maurice de Nieuil and finished second in the French Two Thousand Guineas but wasn't quite in the top flight, and stood at 700 guineas in his first season. The family is one of the best of Brownstown's, though the dam didn't win and the next two dams didn't race. Silken Slipper is a half-sister to two classic winners, Godiva and Windsor Slipper; Silken Princess is a half-sister to another, Silken Glider; and Varinessa is a half-sister to another, Allangrange. Varinessa produced one previous foal, the minor Irish six-furlong to one-mile winner Sagosha (by Irish Love); her next foal, a filly by Saulingo, was purchased as a yearling for IR 47,000 guineas by Steve Norton.

Condessa herself cost 13,000 guineas as a yearling. She is a small, rather lightly-made filly, not one who often catches the eye but she looked particularly well before the Yorkshire Oaks, as well as any in the paddock we thought. Her action betokens one very well suited by soft ground, and connections reportedly regarded her as such. Still, her fine showing in the Irish Oaks can't be overlooked, much as it would simplify matters. Condessa stayed a mile and a half so well that she should have managed further. She has been retired to stud in the United States and will visit Spectacular Bid. *J. Bolger, Ireland.*

CONDOMINIUM 3 b.g. Roan Rocket 128–Without Reproach 102 (Above Suspicion 127) (1980 5fg 5f 6d 7d⁴ 8f 8s 1981 11g 16fg⁴ 16.5fg) rangy gelding; fourth in maiden race at Beverley in June; stays well. *G. Lockerbie.* — —

CONEY 3 bl.f. Healaugh Fox–Queen's Lace (Marshal Pil 108) (1980 NR 1981 10s 8fg 12d 10.8fg 10.1fg 8.3fg) lightly-made filly; sister to a winning hurdler; dam half-sister to Cesarewitch winner and high-class hurdler Flash Imp; behind in varied company, including selling; sold 925 gns Ascot September Sales. *C. Wildman.* — —

CONEY DELL 2 ch.f. Ercolano 118–Shot Gold (Vimy 132) (1981 5d 7fg 7f² 8fg⁴ 7g⁴) Apr 23; 13,000F; leggy, fair sort; half-sister to numerous winners, including fairly useful 6f and 7.3f winner Conan Doyle (by Derring-Do); dam Irish 9f winner; in frame in sizeable fields for maiden and minor events at Brighton, Beverley and Catterick; will stay 1¼m; blinkered third and fourth outings; sold to London Thoroughbred Services 10,000 gns Newmarket Autumn Sales and exported to USA. *I. Balding.* 77

CONFESSION 2 b.g. So Blessed 130–Compulsion 56 (Aggressor 130) (1981 6g 6s* 6fg² 7g* 7fg³ 8.2fg⁴) Apr 11; leggy gelding; excellent mover; brother to fairly useful 6f to 9f winner Confessor; dam poor sister to very useful 1m to 1¼m winner Activator; came from behind when winning maiden race at Carlisle in June but made all and showed improved form when running on strongly to beat Sangalkan 5 lengths in 10-runner minor event at York the following month; respectable 4¼ lengths third of 7 to Full Extent in Heronslea Stakes at Ayr in August; suited by 7f but was soundly-beaten fourth of 6 to Bancario at Haydock when tried over 1m (should stay trip); possibly best with some give in the ground; sold 6,000 gns Newmarket Autumn Sales. *J. W. Watts.* 96

CONFLICT 5 ch.h. Tyrant–Make A Pass (Prominer 125) (1980 10s⁴ 8.2s* 8fg 8g 8.2s³ 8.2g 8s 1981 10.2d 8.2d* 8d 9fg 8g 10s 8.2d 8.2s²) workmanlike horse; won handicap at Hamilton in April; stays 1¼m; acts on soft going; usually wears blinkers; ran badly sixth start; sold 2,100 gns Newmarket Autumn Sales. *I. Walker.* 60

CONFORM 3 b.f. Reform 132–Peace and Concorde 112 (Jolly Jet 111) (1980 NR 1981 12d 12s 8fg 10fg*) 10,000Y; rangy filly; second foal; half-sister to French 1½m winner Kashmir Prince (by Kashmir II); dam won over 5.5f and 1m at 2 yrs and stayed 1½m; not seen out after beating Beaumains by 3 lengths in maiden race at Folkestone in June; suited by 1¼m and should stay further; sold to S. Leadbetter 12,000 gns Newmarket December Sales. *G. Harwood.* 64

215

CONGO EXPRESS 3 b.c. Bay Express 132–Congola (Bold Lad, Ire 133) **92** (1980 NR 1981 8g 5d² 6g⁴) 12,000Y; tall, quite attractive colt; third foal; half-brother to a winner in Italy; dam never won but showed very useful form over 5f on only start at 2 yrs; had a poor run and looked unlucky when beaten ½ length by 2-y-o Boatrocker in maiden event at Redcar in October; had stiff task and ran very well indeed when 3½ lengths fourth of 15 behind Great Eastern in £5,000 event at Doncaster in November; stays 6f (on backward side when tried at 1m); sure to win a race. *C. Brittain.*

CONNAUGHT KING 4 b.c. Connaught 130–Ruling Class 92 (King Emperor) — (1980 NR 1981 12f 10s 10.6s) of little account; has worn bandages. *M. Eckley.*

CONNAUGHT NYMPH 3 b.f. Connaught 130–Constant Nymph 85 (Venture — VII 129) (1980 5fg⁴ 7g⁴ 6s³ 8d 8s⁴ 1981 10v 12fg 8g 12f⁴ 8f 11f 12fg 10s) compact filly; poor maiden; should stay beyond 1m. *R. Hollinshead.*

CONNAUGHT RIVER 2 b.c. Connaught 130–Ebb and Flo 82 (Forlorn River **95** 124) (1981 7g⁴ 7f³ 7f*) Apr 23; lengthy, useful sort; second foal; half-brother to 3-y-o 7f winner Rivers Edge (by Sharpen Up); dam 2-y-o 6f winner and stayed 1¼m; under pressure before halfway and hung away from the rails when odds on for 18-runner maiden event at Redcar in September, but managed to scramble home by a short head from Done Good; had finished in frame in much better company in minor events at Newmarket and Leicester earlier; will probably stay beyond 1m. *M. Stoute.*

CONNAUGHT SKY 4 b.f. Connaught 130–Mura 68 (Romulus 129) (1980 NR — 1981 8d 12.2g) 1,000 3-y-o; fourth foal; dam won at 6f and stayed 1m; no sign of ability in maiden race and minor event. *Denys Smith.*

CONNECTOR 2 ch.c. Red Alert 127–Polana 68 (Silver Shark 129) (1981 5fg **69** 5d² 5d 6fg 6fg 6fg 6g) Mar 31; small colt; half-brother to 2 minor winners; dam temperamental maiden; runner-up in early-season maiden race but finished out of first 6 in nurseries on last 4 starts; acts on a soft surface; sold to W. Marshall 1,100 gns Newmarket Autumn Sales. *J. Holt.*

CON O'MORA 2 ch.f. Morston 125–Sweet and Naughty 76 (Connaught 130) **65** (1981 6f³ 7fg³ 8fg 8s 8s) Mar 11; sturdy filly; second foal; half-sister to 1980 2-y-o 7f winner Candaules (by Supreme Sovereign); dam ran only at 2 yrs when winner at 5f; third in maiden races at Yarmouth in June and Wolverhampton in July, sweating up prior to going down by 2 necks to Lucky Joker in latter; off course some time afterwards and ran poorly on her return; should stay 1m; sold 540 gns Ascot November Sales. *B. Hobbs.*

CONSENT 3 br.f. Connaught 130–Truly Yours 93 (So Blessed 130) (1980 5fg² **46** 5g 5g³ 6d* 5d 6s 8fg⁴ 8.2v² 1981 8v 8.2s⁴ 8g³ 8g 7g³ 6fg³ 6fg 7f⁴ 8.2f³ 6d) lightly-made filly; plater; will stay 1¼m; probably acts on any going; had stiffish task when blinkered final start. *J. S. Wilson.*

CONSENTING (USA) 3 b. or br.c. Judger–Queen of the Sky (Bold Ruler) **66** (1980 8g 8g⁴ 1981 12fg 12g 12d 13g² 14.7fg² 16.5g* 18.8fg⁴ 16g) lengthy, quite attractive colt; won small maiden race at Redcar in August; stays well; blinkered last 2 outings, running creditably on first occasion; sold to J. Baker 5,800 gns Newmarket Autumn Sales. *J. Hindley.*

CONSISTENT QUEEN 3 b.f. Queen's Hussar 124–Consistent 90 (Connaught **40** 130) (1980 5fg 5fg³ 6g 5d 5fg 5d⁴ 5s 1981 7g 6g 7f⁴ 6fg 8fg³ 8g* 10s 9d 10s 12d) small, compact filly; plater; sold out of E. Weymes's stable 1,000 gns after winning at Carlisle in July; stays 1m; blinkered last 2 starts at 2 yrs; sold 1,500 gns Newmarket December Sales. *J. Douglas-Home.*

CONSORTIUM 4 b.c. Targowice 130–Annerbelle 108 (Aureole 132) (1980 **42** d 8v⁴ 6fg 10fg 10s⁴ 10.2g² 10.8fg⁴ 12g⁴ 12d⁴ 10.2d⁴ 8d 1981 7d 8.3s³ 6f 5f 8g 7v 8s) strong colt; good walker; poor performer nowadays; remote third in seller at Windsor in May; stays 1¼m; suited by some give in the ground; has twice worn blinkers; suitable mount for a boy; claimed out of G. Kindersley's stable after second start. *K. Ivory.*

CONS PAL 3 b.f. Connaught 130–Palotra 86 (Palestine 133) (1980 NR 1981 **74** 8s 12g⁴ 10f 12f² 14fg 12f 10.6v* 12.2g⁴ 10.2d²) 3,000 2-y-o; plain filly; has a round action; third foal; sister to 1m seller winner Queen of the Hills and half-sister to Lydiate (by Tower Walk), successful over 1¼m; dam 2-y-o 6f winner; beat Mills High 2½ lengths in minor event at Haydock in October; had stiff task and showed improved form when staying-on 3 lengths second to all-the-way winner Rollrights in £6,400 event at Doncaster later in month; possibly doesn't stay 1¾m; has run respectably on firm going, but is much better with some give in the ground; refused to enter stalls once. *R. D. Peacock.*

CONSTANT ROSE 5 br.m. Confusion 118–Maizenrose 89 (Rustam 127) — (1980 10fg³ 10fg* 10f 10.6g 10g* 10g* 10g* 10fg 10g 10fg² 1981 10s 10g 10f 10f 10f 10d⁴ 8.2s) leggy, rather sparely-made mare; didn't find her form in 1981; ran as though an extended 1¼m was too far for her at 4 yrs; acts well on firm ground; usually held up. *J. Harris.*

CONTINUAL 2 b.c. Crooner 119–Tamerlante (Tiger 125) (1981 5g 8.2d 8s) — Jan 19; 2,500 F, 2,300Y; compact colt; poor plater; sold to A. Neaves 400 gns Newmarket Autumn Sales. *J. Hardy.*

CONTOSA 3 ch.f. Condorcet–La Casita (Ballyciptic 122) (1980 7d 8d 1981 — 10s 7fg 7d 8d 10d⁴ 10f 8f) tall, lengthy filly; plater; stays 1¼m. *P. K. Mitchell.*

CONTRARIA 3 ch.f. Song 132–Oh Mary (Matador 131) (1980 NR 1981 6g⁴ **65** 5f 6f³ 5fg³ 6s⁴ 8fg 7d² 8g) 13,000Y; well-grown filly; half-sister to several winners here and abroad; dam unraced half-sister to Bolkonski and very useful sprinter Golden Plume; placed in apprentice races at Pontefract and Edinburgh and in maiden race at Ayr; stays 7f (running on and not entirely disgraced first attempt at 1m). *N. Callaghan.*

CONVERSION 2 b.c. Saulingo 122–Satire (St Paddy 133) (1981 5s 5g 5d² 5s*) **97** May 18; IR 12,000Y; second foal; dam, placed in a bumpers race, is half-sister to extremely speedy Sigy and smart sprinter Sonoma; improved in the autumn, finishing 2 lengths second of 9 to comfortable winner Americus in Waterford Testimonial Stakes at the Curragh and looking a very useful sprinter in the making when winning 22-runner apprentice race on same course by 2 lengths from Exhilarate; will stay 6f; yet to race on firm ground. *M. O'Toole, Ireland.*

COODEN 5 b.m. Northfields–Nonstopnell 92 (Arctic Time 127) (1980 NR — 1981 14fg 14g 16d) poor maiden; has worn blinkers; sold 775 gns Ascot December Sales. *R. Atkins.*

COOL DECISION 4 b.g. Furry Glen 121–Aran Jacket (Le Levanstell 122) **88** (1980 9s 12f 1981 10g³ 12g² 11.5fg* 10f² 12.3fg² 12g⁴ 10g² 10.2g) lengthy ex-Irish gelding; landed odds very easily from Star Fleet in ladies race at Yarmouth in August; runner-up in varied company on 4 other occasions; stays 1½m; acts on firm going; suitable mount for an inexperienced rider; sold to Miss S. Hall 12,000 gns Newmarket Autumn Sales. *M. Stoute.*

COOLEEN JACK 3 b.c. Targowice 130–Polyxo (Polyfoto 124) (1980 6d 5g **113** 5g* 5g 5g* 5g* 5s⁴ 1981 6d³ 6s 5s* 5f⁴ 6fg 5g 5d) Irish colt; second produce; dam won over 5f and 7f in Ireland; finished very close third behind Prince Echo and Jasmine Star in Ballyogan Stakes at Leopardstown in June and was awarded race after a stewards' inquiry; ran on well and showed improved form when 3¾ lengths fourth of 12 behind Marwell in King's Stand Stakes at Royal Ascot later in month; didn't reproduce that form however in 2 pattern races and a handicap; stays 6f; acts on any going; sold 540,000 francs (approx £54,000) Arc de Triomphe Sale on evening prior to final race. *E. O'Grady, Ireland.*

COOLIDGE 2 b.f. Northern Flash–Miss Twights (Hopeful Venture 125) (1981 **60** 7g³ 7f 8fg 8g) Mar 17; small, workmanlike filly; third foal; half-sister to a winner in Trinidad; dam twice-raced half-sister to smart miler Miracle; just over 5 lengths third of 11 to Big Trouble in maiden race at Yarmouth in July, best effort; well beaten when favourite for 18-runner seller at Newmarket in October on fourth outing; should stay 1m. *M. Jarvis.*

COOLINEY PRINCE 3 gr.c. Tumble Wind–Aquaria (Double-U-Jay 120) **103** (1980 5f 5f* 6fg* 5g* 5fg* 6f 1981 7g* 8g 6d 7f 8fg 7f²) 2,750Y (privately); strong colt; half-brother to fairly useful 1¼m winner Killer Shark (by Tyrant) and a winner abroad; dam ran once; proved a very shrewd purchase as a 2-y-o, winning at Phoenix Park, the Curragh and at Royal Ascot (Windsor Castle Stakes); won Group 3 McCairns Trial Stakes at Phoenix Park on reappearance in April, leading inside final furlong to beat Light Here (rec 3 lb) by a head; ran best subsequent race on final start when 4 lengths second to Star Bound in handicap at Down Royal in July; in rear all other outings, including 2 000 Guineas at Newmarket and Jersey Stakes at Royal Ascot; should stay 1m; form only on a sound surface; successful with blinkers and without; moved badly to post at Ascot. *P. Prendergast, Ireland.*

COOLINEY PRINCESS 2 ch.f. Bruni 132–Windfield Lily (Hard Tack 111§) **91** p (1981 7s*) Feb 6; IR 61,000Y; half-sister to 3 winners, including Irish St Leger winner Conor Pass (by Tiepolo II) and useful 1975 Irish 2-y-o Lace Curtain Lil (by Whistling Wind); dam prolific winning Irish sprinter; put up an encouraging first effort when winning 15-runner maiden race at the Curragh in November by ¾ length from Red Realm; likely to stay middle distances. *P. Prendergast, Ireland.*

COOLNALIRA 5 b.g. Ballymore 123–Celtic Oak 70 (Celtic Ash) (1980 NR — 1981 12d) ex-Irish gelding; lightly raced on flat nowadays; stays 1½m; acts on soft going. *M. Tate.*

COOL WIND 2 ch.f. Windjammer (USA)–Cool Mistress 59 (Skymaster 126) **59** (1981 5d 5g² 5fg* 6g 6fg* 6d 5fg 5d³ 5d) May 24; IR 2,000Y; neat filly; sister to 3-y-o Crosby Triangle, a prolific winner at up to 6f, and to a winner in Italy, and half-sister to a winner; dam poor maiden; made all when clear-cut winner of sellers at Newcastle in June (no bid) and Hamilton in July (bought in 1,900 gns after scoring by 4 lengths from Chicanery); stays 6f; acts on a firm and a soft surface; sweated up ninth and ninth outings. *J. Berry.*

COPPER BEECHES 4 b.g. Owen Anthony 102–Primmy 56 (Primera 131) **74** (1980 5fg² 5fg 6g 5s² 6fg³ 7d 7g 1981 6f 6g 6g⁴ 6fg* 6fg² 6fg⁴ 6g³ 6fg 5s) quite attractive, lightly-made gelding; sprint handicapper; well-backed favourite when winning by 1½ lengths from Gabitat at Goodwood in July; stays 6f; acts on any going; best in blinkers. *J. Holt.*

COPPER PRINCE 3 ch.g. Ampney Prince 96–Wandering Rose (Tudor Minstrel — 144) (1980 6fg 6fg 5fg 8d 7s 1981 7d 11.7g 10s) rangy gelding; plating-class maiden; unlikely to stay 1½m. *S. Mellor.*

COPT AGAIN 3 ch.f. Copte—Annie 65 (Damremont 121) (1980 6fg 7s 7g 8d **36** 8d 1981 9s 16g 12d 10.6s 8f 12f² 13.8f* 15.8fg 12fg 12f 13.8g 12d) compact filly; plater; bought in 1,700 gns after winning at Catterick in July; stays 1¾m; acts well on firm going; blinkered last 3 outings (ran creditably first occasion). *R. Hollinshead.*

COPT HALL PRINCESS 3 b.f. Crowned Prince 128–Gwendolyn (Bagdad) **70** (1980 6g 6f 1981 7.6d³ 7v⁴ 8fg 7f* 8.2f² 7fg² 8f³ 7fg 7g 7g 7g³) quite attractive filly; beat Musical Minx decisively by 4 lengths in handicap at Folkestone in July and was placed in similar events afterwards; stays 1m but is a free-running sort who is possibly better at 7f; seems to act on any going, but clearly goes well on firm. *J. Winter.*

COPT HALL REALM 3 ch.f. Realm 129–Darinda (Darius 129) (1980 6g³ **77** 5g* 1981 6fg 7g 6fg 6f) smallish, well-made filly; won maiden event at Lingfield as a 2-y-o; about 3½ lengths sixth to Bracadale in handicap at Newmarket in July on third start, best effort of 1981; rather slowly away on only subsequent start; stays 6f (not certain to get 7f). *J. Winter.*

COPT HALL ROYALE 4 b.f. Right Tack 131–Sauce Royale (Royal Palace **77** 131) (1980 8fg* 12f⁴ 8.5f 8fg 10fg 8s 11d 1981 10fg 12v 12f³ 12fg 10d⁴ 10fg* 10f 8g* 10d⁴ 8s) tall, lightly-made filly; won handicaps at Folkestone in August and Yarmouth in September; ran moderately in between; best at up to 1½m; acts on a soft surface but is well suited by top-of-the-ground; sweated up badly third start. *J. Winter.*

CORAL CAVE 2 b.f. Ashmore 125–Princess Cecilia 109 (Princely Gift 137) **79** (1981 6f 5fg* 5fg) Apr 17; neat filly; half-sister to several winners, including high-class miler Saintly Song (by St Paddy) and Limuru (by Alcide), the dam of Cavo Doro; dam very useful at 2 yrs; made all and held on gamely under pressure to win 6-runner maiden race at Ayr in August by short head from Begham Bay; last of 15 in nursery at Windsor the following month, only subsequent start; should stay at least 6f. *W. Hastings-Bass.*

CORAL LEISURE 4 b.g. Welsh Saint 126–Bessborough (Mossborough 126) — (1980 7s 8fg² 8fg* 10f 10g⁴ 8d³ 8g² 8g* 1981 8g) lengthy, good sort; won handicap at Redcar and amateur riders race at Goodwood in 1980; well beaten only start at 4 yrs in May; best form at 1m; acts on a firm and a soft surface; blinkered nowadays. *Mrs R. Lomax.*

CORALLIE REEF 2 ch.f. Sandford Lad 133–French Oyster (Gulf Pearl 117) **61** (1981 5g 5g 5fg 7g 6d 8.2d) Feb 10; 3,700Y; compact, lightly-made filly; third living foal; dam second over 7f and 9f from 3 starts in Ireland; showed only worthwhile form when tried over 7f, finishing just over 7 lengths seventh of 15 to Awaasif in maiden race at Ayr in September. *G. Richards.*

CORBIE 3 b.g. Supreme Sovereign 119–Sarum Lady 97 (Floribunda 136) — (1980 7f 1981 8.2s 9.4g 8.2s 9fg 9d² 11d 8d) good-topped gelding; remote second to Nob in seller at Hamilton in September; stays 9f; has been tried in blinkers; trained most of season by J. Etherington. *G. Richards.*

CORDITE SPEAR (USA) 2 br.c. Explodent–Lovely Lance (Assagai) (1981 **89**
7g 6g³ 7.2fg² 7g⁴ 7.6s* 7g* 7d³) May 11; $17,000Y, resold $28,000Y; strong, well-
made colt; very good mover; half-brother to 3 minor winners; dam won at
up to 1m; won 15-runner maiden race at Lingfield in October comfortably by
2½ lengths from Lantic Bay and had plenty in hand when winning small race
at Catterick later in month by ½ length from Concert Pitch; also placed in
varied company, including Rous Memorial Stakes (3¼ lengths third to The
Dinmont) at Goodwood in August; will stay middle distances; seems to act
on any going; ran moderately at Brighton fourth start. *G. Harwood.*

CORDUROY 5 ch.h. Hotfoot 126–Twill 89 (Crocket 130) (1980 8.2g⁴ 8fg **70**
10g² 8d³ 10g³ 10g* 11g* 10d 11s* 1981 12s² 10.5d* 12fg* 12fg⁴ 12fg) rangy
horse; middle-distance handicapper; won at York in May and June; stays 1½m;
acts on any going; needs strong handling. *D. Morley.*

CORINNE'S GOLD 3 b.f. Gold Rod 129–Beaute Royale (Duc de Gueldre 129) **—**
(1980 5fg 5d 5g 5f 1981 5f 6g) small filly; little worthwhile form, including
in a valuable seller; bred to stay 1¼m. *P. Butler.*

CORKED 2 b.c. Tumble Wind–Bristol Milk 88 (Raise You Ten 125) (1981 7fg² **96**
7f 8s³ 8g²) May 18; 10,500Y; well-made, quite attractive colt; half-brother
to Majestic Nurse (by On Your Mark), a winner at up to 1½m; dam stayed
1½m; acquitted himself extremely well in £3,100 event at Kempton in August,
coming through strongly to finish 2 lengths second of 9 to more experienced
Montekin; shade disappointing against good-class rivals next 2 starts but ran
well on final appearance when 2 lengths second of 27 to Dudley Wood in minor
event at Newmarket in October; will stay 1¼m +; sure to win a race at 3 yrs.
B. Hobbs.

CORKER (USA) 5 b.g. Rheingold 137–Lets Hope (One Count) (1980 NR **—**
1981 16g) small gelding; lightly raced on flat nowadays; bandaged near-hind and
sweating only start at 4 yrs in May; stays 2m; acts on any going; changed
hands 1,950 gns Ascot June Sales. *W. A. Stephenson.*

CORLEY MOOR 2 b.f. Habitat 134–Regal Twin 77 (Majestic Prince) (1981 **97**
6d 5f² 5fg* 5f* 6g³ 5fg² 5g⁴ 6g 5s⁴) Mar 8; 85,000F; compact, quite attractive
filly; none too good a mover in her slower paces; second foal; dam won over
8.2f; successful twice in the summer, making all to win 4-runner maiden race
at Chester, despite looking unsuited by course, and quickening well to beat
Gavo 2 lengths in 5-runner Horn Blower Stakes at Ripon; ran well under 9-7
in nursery at Goodwood in August, going down by only a short head to Ghawar,
and also showed up in Lowther Stakes at York (6 lengths third to Circus Ring),
Flying Childers Stakes at Doncaster, William Hill Cheveley Park Stakes at
Newmarket (6 lengths sixth of 13 to Woodstream) and Cornwallis Stakes
at Ascot (4 lengths fourth of 7 behind My Lover); stays 6f; acts on any going;
consistent. *W. Hastings-Bass.*

CORN BELLE 5 b.m. Cornuto 111–Ballabeg 61 (Typhoon 125) (1980 NR **—**
1981 12.2g) no worthwhile form on flat though has won selling hurdles. *N.
Tinkler.*

CORNERING 5 b.g. Sit In The Corner–Lingcroft (Tutankhamen) (1980 NR **65** d
1981 10g² 16f⁴ 12f 12.2g) tall gelding; staying maiden; possibly not at his
best on very firm ground. *M. H. Easterby.*

CORNISH BLUE 3 b.c. Blue Cashmere 129–Donzella 82 (Fidalgo 129) (1980 **—**
6g 7fg 1981 8g 8.5d 10f) lengthy colt; little worthwhile form, including
in a seller. *T. Marshall.*

CORNISH ECHO 2 ch.g. Oats 126–Blue Echoes 105 (Mountain Call 125) **73**
(1981 7g⁴ 7fg 7fg) May 2; IR 34,000Y; compact, well-made, attractive gelding;
very good mover; third foal; half-brother to very smart middle-distance colt
Fingal's Cave (by Ragstone); dam 2-y-o 5f winner; only quite moderate form
so far but looks capable of better; will stay 1m; gelded after third start. *J.
Sutcliffe.*

CORNISH EXPRESS 3 b.f. Sweet Revenge 129–Luckhurst (Busted 134) **—**
(1980 6fg 6fg 6d 1981 6fg) small, lengthy filly; towards rear in maiden
company, including in an apprentice event; moved badly to start third outing
as a 2-y-o. *Mrs R. Lomax.*

CORNISH GEM 2 br.c. Cornish Prince–Jeanie Duff 83 (Majestic Prince) **—**
(1981 6g) Mar 27; 42,000Y; compact colt; half-brother to Sharp Arthur
(by Sharpen Up), winner at up to 6f in USA; dam, daughter of smart stayer

Turf, won over 1¼m and 1½m; unquoted, never placed to challenge when behind in 22-runner maiden race won by Ash Ridge at Newmarket in October. *P. Haslam.*

CORNISH GRANITE 3 gr.c. Ragstone 128–Pasty 122 (Raffingora 130) **73**
(1980 6g 1981 8d² 8d³ 8s² 8d* 8g³ 10.2f 8h 8.2g 8g) small colt; beat Olderfleet by 3 lengths in maiden race at Bath in June; stays 1m; best form with some give in the ground; ran poorly last 4 starts, including in blinkers once; sold to M. Pipe 3,800 gns Newmarket Autumn Sales. *P. Walwyn.*

CORNISH HEROINE (USA) 2 b.f. Cornish Prince–Pomade (Prince John) **81 p**
(1981 7f 8fg*) Feb 18; $150,000Y; lengthy filly; good mover; third foal; closely related to Beauty Hour (by Bold Hour), a very useful stakes winner over 1m at 2 yrs, and half-sister to a winner; dam 2-y-o 1m winner; favourite, won 17-runner maiden race at Leicester in September comfortably by 1½ lengths from Grand Palace; will stay 1¼m; should improve further. *M. Stoute.*

CORNISH LULLABY 3 ch.f. Crooner 119–Long Valley 71 (Ribero 126) **—**
(1980 6fg 6d 6d 1981 8g 12g) neat filly; showed a little ability as a 2-y-o but well beaten both outings in 1981; should stay at least 1m; sold 500 gns Newmarket Autumn Sales. *F. Durr.*

CORNISHMAN 3 ch.c. Connaught 130–Alley Cat 100 (Alycidon 138) (1980 **88 d**
8.2s 7d 1981 12d³ 12g² 12g* 12.3d⁴ 12d 16f 12fg 14s 14g 12g) big, strong, long-striding colt; staged a tremendous late rally after looking to have no chance 2f out when beating Amyndas a neck in maiden race at Newmarket in May; placed at Doncaster and Haydock earlier but subsequently lost his form; should stay well (had stiffish task and was first off bridle when tried at 2m); very much above himself seventh start. *R. Hollinshead.*

CORNISH MINER 2 ch.c. Jimmy Reppin 131–Wheal Harmony (Song 132) **—**
(1981 7g) Mar 5; 2,700Y; plain colt; second foal; half-brother to 3-y-o 1½m and 13f winner Eastern Air (by Levanter); dam never ran; 50/1 and burly when remote ninth of 16 to Adonis Rex in maiden race at Leicester in September. *C. James.*

CORN STREET 3 ch.c. Decoy Boy 129–Diamond Talk (Counsel 118) (1980 **87**
5g 5g 5d⁴ 5d* 7v 1981 6g² 6s² 6g² 6f² 7f⁴ 6fg 7g³ 6s⁴ 8s* 8s² 7d²) workmanlike colt; gained a well-deserved success when beating Rollin Hand in good style by 6 lengths in 22-runner minor event at Warwick in October; in frame on all but one of his other starts; evidently suited by 1m; acts on any going. *J. Bosley.*

CORNY STORY 2 b.f. Oats 126–Twaddle II (Tim Tam) (1981 7d 8s) **73 p**
Feb 28; well-made, attractive filly; half-sister to several winners, including smart sprinter Petipa (by Habitat) and useful 5f and 7f winner Swagger (by Prominer); dam placed at 1¼m in France; 25/1, close up for 5f when seventh of 18 to Sans Blague in maiden race at Newbury in September; 6/1, made a little late headway, without being knocked about, when just over 7 lengths sixth behind Twist Home in 15-runner maiden event at York the following month; likely to do better over 1¼m+ at 3 yrs; trained first outing by J. Dunlop. *R. Baker.*

CORRIB 8 b.g. Polyfoto 124–Lucky Seven 79 (King's Bench 132) (1980 NR **46**
1981 8f² 10f) very useful at his best but had deteriorated; ran respectably first start but poorly on second in 1981; stayed 1¼m; acted on firm going; was tried in blinkers; dead. *G. Balding.*

CORSKY 2 b.f. Pitskelly 122–Corsuedei (King's Troop 118) (1981 6fg* 8fg) **81 p**
Feb 5; IR 7,200Y; well-made filly; fourth foal; half-sister to 1978 2-y-o 5f winner First Class Mail and a winner in Italy, both by Windjammer (USA); dam unplaced 4 times at 2 yrs in Ireland; led approaching final furlong when winning 18-runner maiden race at Newmarket in July a shade comfortably by 1½ lengths from Dame de Fer; didn't race again until late-September and didn't impress in her coat before finishing last of 8 to Height of Fashion in Hoover Fillies Mile at Ascot (10/1, in touch for 6f); will probably stay 1m at 3 yrs. *G. Harwood.*

CORVEN 4 b. or br.g. Owen Anthony 102–Cameo 114 (Como 120) (1980 7s 7f **43**
5fg 5g 5g⁴ 1981 8s³ 8fg 7d* 8d 6f 11.7fg) plater; won at Brighton in April (sold out of W. Wightman's stable 1,250 gns); stays 1m; acts on any going; sometimes blinkered (was at Brighton); inconsistent. *A. Pitt.*

CORVILLA 3 b.f. Forlorn River 124–Irresistable (Siliconn 121) (1980 5s 1981 **—**
10.1fg 12d) little worthwhile form in maiden and minor races. *M. Bolton.*

Mr J. H. Richmond-Watson's "Corsky"

COTTAGERS LANE 5 b.m. Farm Walk 111–La Sirene (Pinturischio 116)
(1980 NR 1981 12.5s) third foal; half-sister to fair hurdler/chaser River
Sirene (by Another River); dam, of no account on flat, was placed over hurdles;
well beaten in poor maiden race at Stockton in April, first outing on flat. *T.
Barron.* —

COTTAM EXPRESS 2 b.f. Runnymede 123–Royal Bit (King's Troop 118)
(1981 5s 5s³ 5d* 5g 6f 5f 6f)   Mar 21; 500Y; leggy filly; half-sister to Royal John
(by John Splendid), winner on flat in Norway and over hurdles here; dam never
ran; won 5-runner seller at Newcastle in April by a length from odds-on Epona's
Grey; bought in 2,000 gns afterwards; well beaten subsequently and is best left
alone until showing a return to form; should stay 6f; possibly needs a soft
surface; changed hands 1,500 gns Doncaster August Sales after fifth start. *M.W.
Easterby.*   58

COUCHETTE 2 b.f. Bay Express 132–Maxim's 88 (Major Portion 129)   (1981
5g 5fg 5f 7d 6d)   May 7; 12,000Y; lengthy, rather lightly-made filly; half-sister to
numerous winners, including very useful 1980 2-y-o sprinter Amorous (by
Mummy's Pet); dam 2-y-o 5f winner; only plating class; ran best race over 6f;
sweated up when tried in blinkers third outing; sold to National Horse Belgium
1,400 gns Newmarket Autumn Sales. *J. Hindley.*   64

COUGH 2 ch.g. Most Secret 119–Outburst 57 (Articulate 121)   (1981 5fg 6fg
6f⁴ 8g 8.2d⁴ 8d 7g² 8d)   Apr 25; first foal; dam won over 11f; plater; not disgraced over 1m but ran best race over 7f. *T. Craig.*   71

COUNTACH 2 br.g. Balidar 133–Fiji Express (Exbury 138)   (1981 6fg 6f 6fg*
5d 5s)   Mar 6; 7,000Y; sturdy gelding; second foal; dam won over 7f and 1¼m in
Ireland; clear from 2f out when scoring by 3 lengths from Tender Trader in
valuable seller at Doncaster in September (bought in 5,000 gns); had unseated
rider and galloped up course beforehand; well beaten in nurseries afterwards;
finds 5f too sharp and will stay 7f+. *G. Huffer.*   75

221

COUNT DI LUNA 2 br.g. Young Emperor 133–Grangemore (Prominer 125) — (1981 7fg 7g) Mar 24; IR 2,400F; neat, quite well-made gelding; finished last in maiden races at Salisbury and Leicester in September, wearing blinkers in latter; sold 320 gns Ascot November Sales. *P. Makin.*

COUNT DU BARRY 2 b.c. Wolver Hollow 126–Rose Dubarry 127 (Klairon ? 131) (1981 6f 6f 6g² 7fg⁴) Mar 28; leggy colt; third foal; half-brother to 1976 2-y-o 5f winner Scented Air (by Derring-Do); dam fastest 2-y-o filly of 1971; dropped in class and favourite when 4 lengths second to 13 to Hearty Hunter in seller at Nottingham in August, subsequently claimed out of H. Cecil's stable and raced in Belgium, finishing just over 9 lengths fourth of 5 to Beldale Bid in Grand Criterium International d'Ostende in August; evidently suited by 7f. *J. Dore, Belgium.*

COUNTESS OLIVIA 3 b.f. Prince Tenderfoot 126–Coralivia (Le Levanstell **77** 122) (1980 6fg³ 7s* 1981 7d 8fg² 10g⁴ 9f² 10f* 10g² 8s²) lengthy filly; led early in straight and held off Jo-Jo-San under pressure by ½ length (pair clear) in handicap at Yarmouth in August; second on 4 other occasions, easily best effort when going down by a neck to Slaney Maid in Marlborough House Stakes at Ascot in October (stayed on very gamely under quite strong driving); ran badly third start but reportedly finished slightly distressed and a little lame; stays 1¼m; acts on any going; sold 15,000 gns Newmarket December Sales. *G. Pritchard-Gordon.*

COUNTESS TULLY 3 b.f. Hotfoot 126–Zoomie 78 (Pinza 137) (1980 8.5d **112** 7d 8.5v* 7d³ 8s⁴ 1981 10g³ 10d* 12fg 12fg² 10g 10g⁴ 12s² 12d) 9,000Y; strong, attractive filly; half-sister to 3 winners, including 1m and 9f winner Zepha (by Great Nephew); dam, winner over 1m and 9f, is half-sister to smart animals Pithiviers and Blinis; beat Stracomer Queen by 2 lengths in minor event for fillies at Phoenix Park in May; in frame subsequently in Brownstown Stakes at the Curragh (5 lengths second to Gilded Vanity), Sun Chariot Stakes at Newmarket (about 5 lengths fourth to Home On The Range) and Princess Royal Stakes at Ascot (staying-on 4 lengths second to easy winner Flighting); dropped out after chasing leader until straight when last of 9 behind Strigida in Ribblesdale Stakes at Royal Ascot; stays 1½m; probably acts on any going; sold 84,000 gns Newmarket December Sales. *L. Browne, Ireland.*

COUNTESS VIRGINIA 6 ch.m. Virginia Boy 106–La Casita (Ballyciptic 122) **81** (1980 7g 8fg⁴ 8fg⁴ 7f 8g* 7g³ 7g² 7d 7fg 7g 8.3fg 1981 8d 7f 8.2f 7.6fg³ 8.3fg² 8fg³ 7f* 8d*) leggy mare; won apprentice handicap at Folkestone and ladies race at Newmarket in August; stayed 1m; appeared to act on any going; blinkered once in 1980; sometimes sweated up; good mount for an inexperienced rider; not particularly consistent; has been covered by John de Coombe. *R. Hannon.*

COUNT FERNANDO 4 b.g. Connaught 130–Ankole 85 (Crepello 136) (1980 — 8h 10.5f 12g² 12.2d 11g* 10g 1981 10d 10.6f 10.5g 10f 12f) smallish, leggy gelding; stayed on strongly to win handicap at Ayr in 1980; in rear all subsequent starts; stays 1½m; possibly unsuited by soft ground; sometimes sweats up; blinkered fourth outing. *J. Hanson.*

COUNT OF SICILY 2 b.c. Dubassoff–Sicilia (Die Hard 127) (1981 8s 8s) — Apr 20; 900F, 2,100Y; half-brother to 3 minor winners here and abroad; dam half-sister to French St Leger winner Sicilian Prince; in rear in maiden event at York and minor race at Redcar in October. *P. Calver.*

COUNT ON ME 5 gr.m. No Mercy 126–Rose Blanche 89 (French Beige 127) — (1980 14fg 15f 11.7s 13s 1981 17.1d 15.5fg) rather lightly-made mare; poor performer nowadays; stays well; acts on a firm and a soft surface. *S. Harris.*

COUNT PAHLEN 2 gr.c. Hotfoot 126–Tanara 93 (Romulus 129) (1981 **127** 7fg³ 7g³ 8d 7g* 8d*)
  Everyone trying to make sense of the form of the juvenile colts must have hoped that the last and most valuable two-year-old pattern race of the 1981 season, the William Hill Futurity, would throw new light on the matter. The previous fifteen pattern races for two-year-old colts had produced no less than fifteen different winners, and of the dozen English-trained winners Red Sunset, End of the Line, Prowess Prince, Tender King, Zilos, Full Extent, Hays and Norwick had all been beaten in their subsequent races. Two of these colts— End of the Line, winner of the Anglia Television July Stakes, and the much-improved Norwick, winner of the Royal Lodge and a good second in the Grand Criterium—were in the thirteen-strong field for the Futurity at Doncaster. Also present were the highly-impressive Hyperion Stakes winner Paradis Ter-

William Hill Futurity, Doncaster—Count Pahlen stays on well to win from Paradis Terrestre (nearest camera), Jalmood and Norwick (rails)

restre, who started a short-priced favourite ahead of Norwick; the potentially high-class Irish colt Assert, a four-length winner of the Beresford Stakes; two rapidly-improving young stayers in Jalmood and Super Sunrise, winners between them of their last five starts; and Ashenden, a creditable four-length third to Achieved in the Laurent Perrier Champagne Stakes. Instead of clarifying the situation the Futurity complicated matters further, with the race going to the virtually-unconsidered Count Pahlen, a 25/1-shot who had won only one of his four previous starts. To confuse things still more the favourite was considered a most unlucky loser by many people.

The sprint-bred End of the Line prevented Norwick from employing the front-running tactics he'd used to such effect in the Royal Lodge, quickly pulling his way to the front. Close up behind came General Anders, who'd made all to win his last race by five lengths, followed by Count Pahlen, Super Sunrise and Assert, but the then-prominent Paradis Terrestre was chopped off after covering little more than two furlongs, twice stumbled badly and entered the straight with only one behind him. End of the Line was done with by halfway, leaving General Anders the leader until both Norwick and Count Pahlen went past soon afterwards. Although Count Pahlen came to take the lead with nearly three furlongs left to run it wasn't until inside the final furlong that he finally shook off the persistent Norwick, by which time Jalmood and Paradis Terrestre were in full flight towards the centre of the course. Count Pahlen ran on most genuinely though and held off the favourite by half a length with Jalmood just a head further behind.

It has to be said that Paradis Terrestre looked unlucky not to win, but he would have had to have won by quite a margin to justify his being made a 10/1-chance for the Two Thousand Guineas, as he was. Count Pahlen was quoted at no less than 25/1 for the Guineas. Perhaps it's worth pointing out that onlookers weren't generally impressed by the Futurity result the previous year either, when Beldale Flutter beat a horse called Shergar! In our opinion Count Pahlen put up a high-class performance. His timefigure of 0·94 fast was one of the fastest of the year by a two-year-old; he beat Norwick by only a little less than Green Forest had done in the Grand Criterium and Ashenden by two lengths more than Achieved had done in the Champagne; and Assert, one of the best two-year-olds in Ireland, never managed to get into the race.

Whereas Count Pahlen benefited from Paradis Terrestre's luckless run in the Futurity, he himself had been none too fortunate in most of his earlier races. On his debut at Yarmouth in July, when clearly in need of the race, he ran into all sorts of difficulties before finishing third to Vin St Benet. In the Acomb Stakes at York the following month he was quite badly hampered below the distance and in the circumstances did well to finish third behind Height of Fashion and Ashenden. And when fifth of twenty-two in a £4,200 race at Newbury in September he came out best of the far-side group, giving the impression he would have given the winner Super Sunrise much more to do with a better draw. Finally everything went right for Count Pahlen in the second division of the Westley Stakes, a twenty-two runner maiden race at Newmarket early in October. There he ran on too strongly for the newcomer Noble Gift whom he beat half a length.

Although Count Pahlen put up easily his best performance over a mile it was a little surprising to hear that his trainer regards him as much more a Derby horse than a Guineas candidate. Since Bruce Hobbs also trained Count Pahlen's sire, dam and maternal grandam, his opinion has to be doubly respected but it was noticeable in the Futurity that the colt hadn't the slightest difficulty lying up with the pace from the start. We don't see why he shouldn't be effective over a mile in the spring of his three-year-old days. Perhaps there was another reason why Count Pahlen took so long to show his true worth—lack of peak fitness. He's a strong, good sort of colt who carries plenty of condition, altogether a rather stuffy individual.

Count Pahlen (gr.c. Feb 12, 1979)	Hotfoot (br 1966)	Firestreak (br 1956)	Pardal / Hot Spell
		Pitter Patter (br 1953)	Kingstone / Rain
	Tanara (gr 1968)	Romulus (b 1959)	Ribot / Arietta
		Ice Ballet (gr 1963)	Ballymoss / Snow Shower

Count Pahlen's pedigree suggests he will stay the Derby distance but it isn't that of a horse crying out for a mile and a half. Neither his sire Hotfoot nor his paternal grandsire Firestreak attempted a longer distance than a mile and a quarter and his dam Tanara, a daughter of the miler Romulus, gained all her four successes over a mile and a quarter. To previous matings with Hotfoot Tanara produced the useful two-year-old mile winner Schumann who never fulfilled his promise, and the moderate filly Espadrille, who was placed at up to a mile and a quarter. She has also produced an unnamed colt by Hotfoot and her only other previous foal, conceived while she was still in training, was the selling hurdle winner Sils Maria (by Midsummer Night II). Count Pahlen's

Mrs A. Villar's "Count Pahlen"

grandam Ice Ballet stayed well, winning small races over thirteen furlongs and two miles just a year before foaling Tanara. Herself a half-sister to nine winners, including the smart stayer Oakville, the Lincolnshire winner John's Court and the successful American broodmare Pat's Irish, Ice Ballet has bred four winners from her first ten foals. None has been anything out of the ordinary but another of her daughters, the once-raced Fallen Star, has made her mark at stud, producing that smart and versatile performer Uncle Pokey.

Hotfoot had easily his best season for some time in 1981, siring the healthy total of twenty-four winners of forty-five races. He hasn't yet sired a classic winner but one of his sons, Tachypous, came within a length of winning the Two Thousand Guineas and another, Hot Grove, failed by only a neck to win the Derby. Perhaps Count Pahlen will get him off the mark in 1982. *B. Hobbs.*

COUNTRYCLASS LAD 2 b.c. Track Spare 125–Ring True 80 (Gulf Pearl 117) **69**
(1981 7fg 8.2d) Mar 9; 7,000Y; brother to winning miler Track Belle; dam stayed 1m; sixth in large fields of maidens at Warwick in August (5¾ lengths behind Return To Power) and Hamilton in September (nearly 9 lengths behind Trickshot when favourite); should be well suited by 1m. *Sir Mark Prescott.*

COUNTRY MARKET 2 ch.f. Native Bazaar 122–Easy Swinger (Swing Easy **—**
126) (1981 5d³ 5d 5g⁴) May 9; fair sort; second reported foal; dam never ran; only poor form in sellers in first half of season; sold 400 gns Ascot July Sales. *P. Cole.*

COUNT VINDALOO 4 b.g. Hotfoot 126–Saucy Smokey (Kibenka 119) (1980 **33**
NR 1981 15.5f 8.3fg 10f 8.3g⁴ 10f 12g) poor plater. *A. Neaves.*

COUPOLE (USA) 3 ch.f. Vaguely Noble 140–Silana (Silnet 131) (1980 NR **71**
1981 9d 14f⁴ 12fg* 12f⁴ 10g 12fg² 13d 12g) $43,000Y; fair sort; good walker; half-sister to several winners in USA and France, including useful 1979 French 2-y-o 6f winner Boulad (by Roberto); dam very useful French 1¼m to 13f winner; beat Karminski a neck in maiden race at Carlisle in July; sweated up when staying-on second of 4 to Royal Baize in apprentice handicap at Salisbury in September; finds 1¼m on sharp side and stays 1¾m; acts on a firm surface but didn't move well on very firm ground on fourth start. *L. Cumani.*

COURAGEOUS BUZBY 5 b.g. Communication 119–Courageous Chic 75 **67**
(Cash and Courage 116) (1980 5fg 8g⁴ 6g³ 8fg 7g 6f 6fg 5d 5d 1981 6f 5g* 7.2v 6s* 5g³) workmanlike gelding; won seller at Beverley in September (no bid) and handicap at Nottingham in October (made all); stays 6f; acts on soft going; has sweated up on occasions. *B. McMahon.*

COURCHEVEL 3 ch.c. Reliance II 137–Christiana 106 (Double Jump 131) **89**
(1980 7g⁴ 8g 1981 12fg³ 12f* 14d* 14g) attractive, robust colt; won maiden race at Brighton in July (made all) and valuable Tia Maria Handicap (amateur riders) at Haydock in August; showed much improved form when beating Wiveton by 6 lengths in latter, leading 3f out and coming home unchallenged; finished rather disappointing eighth of 14 behind Centroline in Melrose Handicap at York later in August; suited by 1¾m; probably acts on any going. *B. Hills.*

COURREGES 3 b.f. Manado 130–Silk and Satin 108 (Charlottown 127) **—**
(1980 5fg⁴ 6g⁴ 5g 5g² 5f² 6f² 6d 1981 8g⁴) lengthy, lightly-made filly; second in maiden and minor events in 1980; below her best in maiden race at Edinburgh on only outing of 1981; should stay 1m; possibly unsuited by a soft surface; sold 4,400 gns Newmarket December Sales. *J. W. Watts.*

COURT CAVALIER 4 ch.g. Simbir 130–Rosenkavalier 88 (Vienna 127) **69**
(1980 12f⁴ 1981 12g³ 14g*) good-topped gelding; second to Al Nasr in maiden event at Sandown in July, but was awarded race at subsequent inquiry; stays 1¾m; sold 2,100 gns Newmarket Autumn Sales. *D. Kent.*

COUSIN SARAH 3 b.f. Farm Walk 111–Ritratto (Pinturischio 116) (1980 **—**
NR 1981 11g 11s 12s) small, strong filly; third foal; half-sister to fair 1979 2-y-o 7f winner Italian Master (by Workboy); dam never ran; looked backward when withdrawn at start (apparently lame) on intended first appearance at Beverley in August; well beaten afterwards, including in sellers. *D. Garraton.*

COUSSIKA (FR) 2 br.f. Sanctus II 132–Lisguile (Native Guile) (1981 7g² **112**
8g² 6.5d* 6.5s⁴ 8v* 10s³) Mar 9; half-sister to Ichkeul (by Beau Garcon), successful at up to 9f in France, and to a winner over jumps; dam minor 9f winner; 20/1-winner of Group 3 Prix des Reservoirs at Longchamp in October, heading front-running Bouillonnante inside final furlong to win by 2 lengths; had earlier won 50,000 francs event at Craon in September, after finishing second in maiden

225

races at Dieppe and Deauville; also in frame in 2 other pattern races, notably Criterium de Saint-Cloud in November (4½ lengths third of 14 to Bon Sang); will stay 1½m; acts well on heavy going. *F. Boutin, France.*

COVENT GARDEN (USA) 3 ch.g. Stage Door Johnny–Rock Garden 86 **68** (Roan Rocket 128) (1980 8d³ 8d 1981 11.7g² 16.9s² 14d) strong, well-made gelding; excellent mover; runner-up in maiden races at Bath and Wolverhampton; stays well; yet to race on a firm surface; one paced; didn't look particularly willing in blinkers final start (June). *J. Tree.*

COVERGIRLS CHOICE 4 b.c. Red Alert 127–Singe (Tudor Music 131) **74** (1980 5fg 5g³ 6g 5d 6s³ 5v* 1981 5s* 6s⁴ 5fg 5g² 5g² 6g² 6g* 6g 6f 6f³ 7fg 6g 6fg³ 6s 6s 6d) slightly hollow-backed colt; poor mover; sprint handicapper; won at Doncaster in March and Ayr in May; good second in between at Doncaster (twice in valuable races) and Lingfield; not disgraced several other starts; stays 6f; best with some give in the ground and revels in the mud; good mount for a boy; has run respectably in blinkers. *N. Callaghan.*

COWDENBEATH (USA) 4 b.c. Buffalo Lark–Intervene (Prince John) **81** (1980 10fg 10g³ 12fg 12s⁴ 11d 10.1f³ 12d* 12fg³ 12.2d² 12g² 1981 10.2s 14g 12g 12d 12.3fg* 12f* 12fg* 12f² 12d 12f³ 14f⁴ 14.6fg 12.2g 16g*) good-bodied, attractive colt; good mover; modest handicapper; had a good year, winning at Newcastle, Haydock, Leicester (awarded race by stewards) and Beverley; stays 2m; probably acts on any going but goes well on a sound surface; ran well in blinkers once in 1980. *R. Hollinshead.*

CRACAVAL 5 ch.h. Mount Hagen 127–Priddy Maid 111 (Acropolis 132) **119** (1980 9f³ 12fg³ 10fg³ 10g 12f² 10.5d³ 12g 10g 10d 1981 8s* 12s² 9.7s³ 10fg⁴ 9.2s⁴ 12fg 12g² 8s³ 13s) good mover; smart performer; quickened well after being held up to beat Bonol going away by 2 lengths in £7,200 race at Doncaster in March; in frame in good company most subsequent starts, finishing head second to Pelerin in John Porter Stakes at Newbury, length third of 11 to P'tite Tete in Prix Dollar at Longchamp, 1½ lengths fourth to Hard Fought in Prince of Wales's Stakes at Royal Ascot, 3¼ lengths fourth to The Wonder in Prix d'Ispahan at Longchamp, short-neck second to Lord Jack in Grand Prix de Vichy (looked unlucky since another runner swerved across him when he was about to begin his run) and length second to To-Agori-Mou in Queen Elizabeth II Stakes at Ascot; moved down to third after hanging badly left and causing interference in last-named; stays 1½m; acts on any going but seems suited by some give in the ground nowadays; blinkered 3 times in 1980 and on eighth start; tends to drop himself out; has hung under pressure and isn't an easy ride; ran in Canada final outing. *R. Hills.*

Doncaster Mile—Cracaval wins the inaugural running of this valuable event at the March meeting

Regent Diamond Stakes (Ladies Race), Ascot—Cracking Form and Franca
Vittadini win for the second year running

CRACKAWAY 3 b.c. Auction Ring 123–Milonia (Tambourine II 133) (1980 **70**
6g 6g 7fg² 8fg² 8.2s) 1981 10s⁴ 12d⁴ 10s⁴ 10f² 10.2f³ 10f³ 10f 10f² 10f² 10f 12f)
neat, strong colt; second in handicap at Leicester in June and maiden races
at Ripon in August (found little off bridle) and September (had none too clear a
run); stays 1½m; probably acts on any going but goes well on firm; blinkered
seventh and eighth outings; sold to S. Wright 4,200 gns Ascot November
Sales. *W. Wharton.*

CRACKHILL 2 b.g. Legal Eagle 126–Mexican Music 71 (Astec 128) (1981 6f **86**
6fg 7.2fg⁴ 8.2d² 7g² 7g) May 19; 3,000F; lengthy, good sort; third produce;
dam, half-sister to dam of Pitcairn, was placed over 10.8f; second twice in the
autumn, going down by 2 lengths to Trickshot in maiden race at Hamilton
and by a neck to Bravado, after hanging right in final furlong, in minor event
at Catterick; not disgraced in nursery final start; suited by 1m and will probably
stay further; capable of winning a maiden race in the North. *J. Hanson.*

CRACKING FORM 4 b.c. Habitat 134–Miss Petard 113 (Petingo 135) (1980 **101**
8fg* 9fg* 10d 8g² 8g* 7g³ 1981 8d² 9d³ 8.5d 10g² 8fg* 8d 10.2fg² 9g 8v* 8s)
big, strong, rangy colt; useful performer; won ladies race at Ascot in July by 1½
lengths from Madison Style and made most to beat Lombardi 3 lengths in
4-runner £3,000 race at York in October; stays 1¼m; acts on any going; not
particularly consistent; sold 37,000 gns Newmarket December Sales; to race in
California. *P. Walwyn.*

CRAGADOR 4 b.c. Hoist the Flag–Croda Rossa (Grey Sovereign 128§) **110**
(1980 8.2fg⁴ 8d 7fg 1981 8s 7d* 7fg³ 7s) neat, attractive colt; excellent
mover; only lightly raced but is very useful; beat Vaslav a shade comfortably
by ¾ length in City of York Stakes in August; creditable 3 lengths third of 6
to Kittyhawk in Kiveton Park Steel Stakes at Doncaster in September; ran
below his best in valuable handicap at Ascot later in month and wasn't seen
out again; will stay beyond 1m; acts on a firm and a soft surface; blinkered
once at 3 yrs. *H. Wragg.*

CRAIGOUR 3 br.c. Mill Reef 141–Sudden Glory 98 (Luthier 126) (1980 6g 7fg³ **78** d
7.2d* 8fg 1981 8s⁴ 10fg⁴ 10d³ 12fg 11f³ 10.1fg 8g 18g 10d) small, attractive
colt; good mover; in frame in handicaps at Salisbury (2), Epsom and Wolverhampton; stays 1¼m; blinkered fifth and sixth starts; trained by P. Walwyn
until after seventh outing. *C. Austin.*

227

CRA

CRANLEIGH FLYER 2 b.c. Bay Express 132–Rosey's Ragusa (Ragusa 137) — (1981 5fg 5.3fg 5f) Feb 15; 300Y; small, sharp sort; of little account; sold 460 gns Ascot September Sales. *T. M. Jones.*

CRATHIE 3 b.f. Lochnager 132–Safety Walk 77 (Sovereign Path 125) (1980 **66** NR 1981 8fg³ 8fg 8s 7d) 26,000Y; rather a leggy filly; first foal; dam, daughter of Irish Guinness Oaks winner Celina, won over 1¼m; ran best race when staying-on third behind comfortable winner Lady Be Mine in maiden event at Yarmouth in June; stays 1m; usually wears bandages in front; moved badly to start second outing. *B. Hanbury.*

CRAZYFOOT 4 b.f. Luthier 126–Great Guns 109 (Busted 134) (1980 10fg **66** 11.7fg² 12.2fg² 14g³ 1981 11s 12g 12fg² 12f 11.7fg*) useful sort; has rather a round action; won minor event at Windsor in September; should stay 1¾m; acts on a firm surface; sometimes sweats up; has run creditably for an apprentice; sold 35,000 gns Newmarket December Sales. *P. Walwyn.*

CREAMY 3 ch.g. Double-U-Jay 120–Pot de Creme 68 (Candy Spots) (1980 **56** 5g* 5h³ 6g 5f 7f* 6d³ 6g² 8d 1981 10s 10g 9s 8fg³ 10f) lengthy gelding; won seller at Beverley and nursery at Thirsk in 1980; third in handicap at Beverley in June; may not stay 1¼m; seems suited by top-of-the-ground; blinkered last 3 starts; exported to Hong Kong. *Hbt Jones.*

CREATIVE STAR 3 b.g. Wishing Star 117–Rag Flowers (Tarqogan 125) **51** (1980 5f 5f 6g 8g⁴ 8d 1981 8.2s 10s* 12d 16.5f 16s 16s) big gelding; poor walker; quite moderate form in varied races, including seller as a 2-y-o; just lasted out when beating Winart a length in handicap at Newcastle in April; suited by 1½m (sometimes pulls hard and has yet to show he stays further); seems suited by plenty of give in the ground; saddle slipped fourth start. *J. Fitzgerald.*

CREE BAY 2 b.c. Bay Express 132–Porsanger (Zeddaan 130) (1981 5d 5fg² **62** 5g² 5d 6d 6g) May 15; useful-looking colt; third foal; brother to 1980 2-y-o 5f winner Royal Blood; dam from family of Grey Dawn II; favourite when second in maiden races at Nottingham in April and Catterick in June; a free-running colt who seems to find 5f his limit; ran moderately fourth start (got loose on way to racecourse stables and bolted); blinkered sixth outing; disappointing; sold 420 gns Ascot November Sales. *C. Nelson.*

CREE BREEZE 3 b. or br.g. Persian Breeze 121–Kalyanda 77 (Kalydon 122) — (1980 5d 7d 5d 1981 6s) well beaten in varied company in Scotland. *G. Richards.*

CREEPIN SUZIE 3 ch.f. Red Alert 127–Perceptive (Ballyciptic 122) (1980 **53** 5f³ 6f 5fg⁴ 5g² 5g 5g 5g 1981 6g² 7g⁴ 6f 8h³ 8.2s) quite a moderate maiden; probably stays 1m; possibly needs a sound surface. *C. Nelson.*

CREE SONG 5 b.h. Song 132–Gentle Gael 97 (Celtic Ash) (1980 5fg⁴ 5f³ 6fg³ **83** 5g* 6fg³ 5d³ 5g 5.6g 6s 6d 5v 1981 6v² 5g 6d 5g 6fg 5g⁴ 5g⁴ 5g 6d 6g) strong, sprint type; poor mover in his slower paces; sprint handicapper; stays 6f; acts on firm going but is particularly well suited by some give in the ground; sometimes blinkered and isn't one to rely on. *W. H. H. Williams.*

CREEZAR 3 b.c. Noble Decree 127–Zaratella (Le Levanstell 122) (1980 NR — 1981 8d 10.1d 7g) small, lengthy colt; in rear in varied company, including selling; dead. *D. Ringer.*

CRELLISTOVI (USA) 2 ch.c. Sir Ivor 135–Cellist (Bagdad) (1981 5.8g **84** 6fg² 6f⁴ 7g³ 7fg* 7fg 7.3d 8g) Mar 11; $80,000Y; small, lengthy, quite attractive colt; third foal; half-brother to Irish 3-y-o 6f winner Rostropovich and 9f winner Wild Fandango (both by Forli); dam, smart stakes winner at up to 1m, is half-sister to top-class Gay Fandango; only moderate himself; won 18-runner maiden race at Ayr in August a shade comfortably by 1½ lengths from Luxury; suited by 7f and should stay 1m; didn't run up to his best when ridden by 7-lb claimer on sixth start and had stiff tasks on seventh and eighth. *B. Hills.*

CREME DE LA CREME 3 gr.f. Saritamer 130–Dairy Queen 76 (Queen's — Hussar 124) (1980 5fg 5g³ 1981 6s) well-made filly; lightly raced and no worthwhile form. *R. Smyth.*

CRESTA RIDER (USA) 3 br.c. Northern Dancer–Thoroly Blue (Blue Prince **123** 123) (1980 6d* 7g* 8d⁴ 1981 8d* 8g³ 9g* 9.2s³ 8f 7v) $475,000Y; strong, powerful, good-bodied colt; good mover; fourth foal; half-brother to a winner by T.V. Lark; dam very smart stakes winner at up to 9f; won newcomers event at Deauville and Criterium de Maisons-Laffitte and was a close fourth to Recitation in Grand Criterium at Longchamp as a 2-y-o; successful as a 3-y-o in Prix de

228

Fontainebleau at Longchamp in April (beat Redoutable ½ length) and in Prix
Jean Prat at Chantilly in June (won by a length from Dunphy), leading well
inside last furlong on first occasion but making all on second; third on 2 other
occasions, both at Longchamp, finishing 3½ lengths behind Recitation in Poule
d'Essai des Poulains in May (tended to hang but was reportedly struck into) and
2¾ lengths behind The Wonder in Prix d'Ispahan in July (again tried to make all
and kept on gamely once headed); looked to be going really well 2f out but
produced little under the whip when seventh of 11 behind Northjet in Prix
Jacques le Marois at Deauville in August; finished tailed-off eighth of 9 behind
Moorestyle in Prix de la Foret at Longchamp in October on only other start;
stayed 9f; unsuited by heavy going; occasionally wore a pricker on his off side;
standing at Gainesway Farm, Lexington at $50,000 n.f.n.f. *F. Boutin, France.*

CRESTBOY 2 ch.g. Scottish Rifle 127–Ginger Puss (Worden II 129) (1981 —
5.8g 6g 7f 8s) Apr 7; smallish, plain gelding; half-brother to 2 minor winners;
blinkered when distant seventh of 17 to Whenyourtrainsgone in 1m seller at
Warwick in October final start; bred to stay middle distances. *K. Cunningham-
Brown.*

CRESTED GREBE 6 b.g. Blakeney 126–Palmavista 120 (Royal Palm 131) —
(1980 10s 1981 12.2fg 12f 12.2fg 11.7fg) well-made gelding; useful handicapper
at his best but has shown no form for a long time; stays 1½m; acts well on soft
going; has worn blinkers. *D. Gandolfo.*

CRESTED LARK 5 ch.h. Crowned Prince 128–Bird of Dawning (Sea-Bird II 72
145) (1980 8fg 8g 10.1f 10g³ 8g 10g 12g* 11d 1981 12d* 12g² 14s 12g*
12g* 12d² 12g 12g) big, rangy ex-Irish horse; won handicaps at Folkestone
in April, Lingfield in June and Salisbury in July; suited by 1½m (pulled hard
when well beaten over 1¾m); acts on a soft surface. *M. Smyly.*

CREST WINDOWS 6 ch.g. Levanter 121–Midsummer Magic (Midsummer —
Night II 117) (1980 NR 1981 12s 13fg 8d 6f 7f) probably of little account.
T. Gosling.

CREVER 6 b.h. Crepello 136–Forever 68 (Never Say Die 137) (1980 8fg⁴ 7f —
6fg 7g 7fg⁴ 1981 12d 8d) well-made horse; poor plater nowadays; occasionally
blinkered. *G. Beeson.*

CREWS HILL 5 b.g. High Top 131–Patosky 94 (Skymaster 126) (1980 7v 122
5g⁴ 5f* 5fg* 5f* 5f* 5g 5g 5g 5f² 6g 5.6g 5g³ 1981 5g 5g 5fg³ 6f² 5fg* 6fg* 5d⁴
6fg* 6fg⁴ 6fg2)
The four great sprint handicaps—the Wokingham Stakes, Stewards' Cup,
Portland Handicap and Ayr Gold Cup—are as much a part of the British racing
scene as the best weight-for-age events and are, as a group, unparalleled in
Europe. They are always well contested and nearly always closely fought, and
their popularity, which would be unthinkable for similar races on the Continent,
hasn't diminished appreciably over the years. Indeed, a late-Victorian
journalist's explanation of the appeal of the Stewards' Cup at Goodwood
still holds good in its essentials—'When the bugle note announces that the
contest has begun, and the long line of horses, topped by many-coloured
jackets, comes streaming towards the junction of the two courses, a deep buzz
of admiration always arises among the crowd.'
The 1981 Stewards' Cup, sponsored by the Tote, was worth over £25,000
to the winner and it saw a fine weight-carrying performance by Crews Hill who,
at the age of five, improved dramatically to become one of the best sprinters in
training. Prior to Goodwood Crews Hill had taken three runs to get fully fit,
had then finished an excellent half-length second to The Quiet Bidder in the
Cork and Orrery Stakes at Royal Ascot, going on very strongly in the last two
furlongs, and had just managed to hold on when dead-heating with Ponchielli in
a controversial photo-finish to a handicap at Sandown in July. In the Tote
Stewards' Cup later in the month Crews Hill wasn't top weight—that honour
went to Rabdan—but in carrying 9-9 he was giving upwards of a stone to most
of the other twenty-eight runners. Held up as first Tinjar, then Ferryman,
took them along, Crews Hill was brought with a perfectly-timed challenge to
cut down Ferryman well inside the last furlong, winning going away by three
quarters of a length. His performance was a record for the race—the previous
highest weight carried to success was Epirus' 9-7 in 1840 when the range was
admittedly much broader. Incidentally, in the essay on Home Guard in *Racehorses of 1973* we stated that Longbow won with 9-9 in 1853; further research
has revealed that he in fact carried 9-4.
Crews Hill ran in one more handicap, the Top Rank Club Handicap at

Mr C. Henry's "Crews Hill"

Newcastle in August, and he put up a most impressive display. Top weight with 10·0, he was always travelling sweetly, cruised through from halfway and sprinted past Crofthall in great style when shaken up to win by a comfortable two lengths. His three other starts were in pattern races, and each time he performed creditably. In the William Hill Sprint Championship at York, where the trip and the ground were not ideal for him, Crews Hill stayed on when the race was over to be five lengths fourth to Sharpo, and in the Vernons Sprint Cup at Haydock he never managed to land a blow but was still beaten less than three lengths into fourth behind Runnett. His final race in England, the Diadem Stakes at Ascot in September, saw Crews Hill put up the best performance of his career so far. Held up as usual, he was the only one to look the slightest danger

Tote Stewards' Cup, Goodwood—Crews Hill (dark cap) comes with a well-timed run to beat Ferryman (fourth left), Sparkling Boy (far right) and Gamblers Dream (stripes)

to the front-running Moorestyle in the last two furlongs, but though running
on with his customary enthusiasm he went down by a length and a half. The
rest of the field, headed by Dalsaan and including King of Spain and Sayyaf,
were well strung out, and there is no doubt that this was a high-class display
by Crews Hill who has now been sent to America for a campaign in the care of
John Gosden.

Crews Hill (b.g. 1976)	High Top (br 1969)	Derring-Do (br 1961)	Darius
			Sipsey Bridge
		Camenae (b 1961)	Vimy
			Madrilene
	Patosky (b 1969)	Skymaster (ch 1958)	Golden Cloud
			Discipliner
		Los Patos (b 1963)	Ballymoss
			Patagonia

   A 10,000-guinea yearling, Crews Hill is the second living foal and first
winner out of Patosky, who was a most genuine and consistent performer at up
to a mile, finishing in the frame in sixteen of her twenty-one starts. She was
also represented on the track in 1981 by Butosky (by Busted), successful in
three middle-distance handicaps. The grandam, Los Patos, won over a mile
and a half and two miles and was a half-sister to numerous winners, notably
Tierra del Fuego, winner of the 1962 Woodcote Stakes.
   When fit Crews Hill invariably impresses in appearance, for he is a big,
strong, good-topped gelding who carries a tremendous amount of condition.
One fault to be found with him is that he is not a good mover in his slower paces,
but that has never hampered him in the least. Though capable of running with
credit over five furlongs on soft ground, as he showed at York, Crews Hill is
ideally suited by six furlongs on a firm surface, and by waiting tactics. He is
a genuine and consistent performer. *F. Durr.*

CRICKETERS CLUB 4 gr.c. Touch Paper 113–Mairi's Love (His Highness) —
(1980 5fg 7f 6g 6g 5g 5g 1981 5g 6f 6g 5d³ 5fg 5g) small colt; poor handicapper; best run at 5f on a soft surface. *M. Haynes.*

CRICKET FIELD 2 b.f. Northfields–Emma Canute 93 (Hardicanute 130) 86
(1981 6d⁴ 6fg 6fg* 6f) Apr 21; 62,000Y; attractive, shapely filly; excellent
mover; half-sister to 2 winners by Sovereign Path, including very useful 5f
to 10.5f winner Everything Nice, and to 3-y-o 1½m winner Well Appraised (by
Wolver Hollow); dam stayed 1¾m; always close up when winning 17-runner
maiden race at Newbury in August by a neck from Rosananti; 12 lengths fifth
of 9 to Circus Ring in Princess Margaret Stakes at Ascot on previous outing and
creditable fifth of 8, 3¾ lengths behind On The House, in Crathorne Stakes
at York in September; will stay 1¼m. *B. Hobbs.*

CRIMOND 2 b.g. Music Boy 124–Midnight Prayer 67 (Meldrum 112) (1981 76
7g 6d 6g) Mar 26, 2,500F; good-topped gelding; third foal; dam won over 5f
at 2 yrs; showed a little ability in end-of-season maiden races; not sure to stay
beyond 6f; sold 4,500 gns Newmarket Autumn Sales. *W. O'Gorman.*

CRIMSON COURT 2 b.g. Garda's Revenge 119–Crimson Velvet 89 (Above 89
Suspicion 127) (1981 5s* 5fg² 5d* 5d*(dis) 6d² 5f 6fg 5d) Apr 24; IR 3,500F,
5,200Y; compact, sturdy gelding; half-brother to several winners, including useful
middle-distance 3-y-o Grain Race (by Windjammer); dam stayer; won 5-runner
Garter Stakes at Ascot in April by a length from Royal Revenge, also awarded
maiden race won by El Pato at Doncaster in March after winner failed dope
test, but was himself disqualified for carrying 3 lb too little after winning £3,400
event at Salisbury in May by a length from Broadway Lodge; gave Chris's
Lad a tremendous battle before going down by ¾ length in 9-runner Woodcote
Stakes at Epsom in June but ran moderately afterwards; (sweated up and
didn't stride out on way to start final outing); will probably stay 7f; evidently
needs some give in the ground; sent to Hong Kong. *R. Hannon.*

CRIMSON FLASH (USA) 3 ch g. Crimson Streak–Anthesis (Big Game) 44
(1980 7fg 7g 8d 8fg 1981 12g 12g 12g 12.2g* 10.6s 12f 13.8f³ 12fg 13.8fg 12f 13.8g⁴)
small, stocky gelding; plater; bought in 625 gns after winning at Catterick in
May; ran moderately in his last few races; stays 1¾m; usually blinkered; front
runner. *S. Norton.*

CRIMSON KNIGHT 2 b.c. Blushing Groom 131–Sirnelta (Sir Tor) (1981 93
6fg 7d* 7.6g) Mar 9; rather lightly-made colt; excellent mover; second reported

foal; dam, winner from 1m to 1¼m in France, is daughter of sister to Sanctus II; came from behind to win 14-runner maiden race at Chester in August by 2½ lengths from Saenredam; also ran well next start, finishing sixth of 7, beaten less than 3 lengths, to Triple Axel in £7,100 event at Lingfield the following month; will stay 1¼m. *F. J. Houghton.*

CRIMSON ROYALE 3 ch f. High Line 125–Crimson Belle 80 (Red God 128§) **84** (1980 NR 1981 10fg 9d³ 8f⁴ 10.1fg² 10.2h² 10fg* 12f⁴ 10.1g* 12g 11.7d*) small, fair sort; sister to very smart 1¼m horse Crimson Beau and to a winner in Belgium, and half-sister to several winners; dam won at 7f; won valuable maiden race at Ascot in July (by 2½ lengths from Bedford), minor event at Windsor in August (by 2 lengths from Green Memory, whose rider mistook winning post) and handicap at Bath in October (made all); stays 11.7f; yet to race on really soft going, but acts on any other; sweated up and was mounted on course seventh outing. *P. Cole.*

CRIMSON SATIN 5 ch.m. Porto Bello 118–La Muleta (Matador 131) (1980 — 8.2fg 7fg 5g 6s 8g 8g 8g 8.2s 8d 10d 1981 8fg 7g 8d 8f 8s) unfurnished mare; plater; stays 1m; sometimes blinkered; trained part of season by R. Mason; sold 650 gns Ascot September Sales. *J. Webber.*

CRIMSON SILK 7 ch.g. Counsel 118–La Muleta (Matador 131) (1980 **61** 6d 6fg 6f 6fg 6fg 6d⁴ 6fg 8d 6d 6g 5.6g 6d 7d 6s 7d 1981 7.2fg 6g² 7fg² 7fg 7.6fg 8g⁴ 7gf⁴ 6g 7s) poor handicapper nowadays; possibly stays 7f; appears to act on any going; has run creditably for an apprentice; used to wear blinkers; trained most of season by R. Mason. *M. Chapman.*

CRINGLEFORD 4 b.c. Sterling Bay–Paludamentum (Royal Palm 131) (1980 **58** 7f 7.6f⁴ 8g 8g* 8d 7d 1981 10d 8v 8g³ 8f³ 8fg 8g* 10fg 8.3g² 8g³ 8s³) workman-like colt; won apprentice handicap at Carlisle in July; stays 1m; suited by some give in the ground; sold out of D. Weeden's stable 4,300 gns Doncaster January (81) Sales. *C. Spares.*

CRISP AND KEEN 3 ch.f. Crisp and Even 116–Anxious Coin (Prince Silver 98) **66** (1980 NR 1981 7f 12d 8.2s 9d²) leggy, compact filly; second foal; half-sister to winning chaser Saucy Coin (by Saucy Kit); dam a hurdler; ran well when 3 lengths second of 22 behind easy winner Park Place in handicap at Chepstow in October; bred to stay middle distances; has worn bandages. *M. Eckley.*

CRISPIN 4 b.c. Welsh Pageant 132–Syrona 113 (Salvo 129) (1980 12f 11fg 12d⁴ **87** 12s² 13g 12g* 12.3d² 11.7g*(dis) 12g² 14.7f² 16g* 14s³ 1981 12d* 12g² 20fg 16.1g³ 16fg² 16d² 16fg³ 14fg⁴ 16fg* 18g) attractive colt; fairly useful handicapper; won apprentice event at Ascot in April and £4,000 race on same course in September; beat Heighlin by 1½ lengths in latter; stays very well; acts on any going; suitable mount for an inexperienced rider nowadays (used to hang under pressure on occasions). *J. Dunlop.*

CRISTINA TIMES 3 b. or br.f. Will Somers 114§–Reina Cristina 84 (Tamerlane — 128) (1980 5f 5fg 5g 5fg 7g 7fg⁴ 7f² 7fg 7g⁴ 6g 8.2d 7f 8.2s 1981 8d 6d) lightly-made filly; poor plater; stays 7f; acts on firm going; usually blinkered in 1980. *B. McMahon.*

CRITERION 2 b.c. Royal Palace 131–Climbing Rose 81 (Pirate King 129) **85 p** (1981 7fg²) Mar 27; 13,000Y; well-grown, short-backed, quite attractive colt; half-brother to several winners, including smart 1m to 1½m performer Saint Jonathon (by Welsh Saint) and useful 6f to 1m winner Rocket Symphony (by Roan Rocket); dam 2-y-o 5f winner; ran very green after taking lead inside final 2f and failed by ½ length to hold off Dageegah when well-backed favourite for 20-runner maiden race at Salisbury in September; would certainly have won with more experience at Salisbury and will gain compensation over middle distances at 3 yrs. *G. Harwood.*

CRITICAL PATH 2 ch.g. Shiny Tenth 120–Tamaqua 69 (Tamerlane 128) — (1981 6fg 5d 6g) Apr 28; big, strong gelding; fifth foal; dam poor maiden; unquoted when behind in varied company, including selling. *G. Balding.*

CRITIQUE (USA) 3 br.c. Roberto 131–Cambrienne 95 (Sicambre 135) (1980 **125** 6s 8g* 8d² 1981 8d⁴ 10s⁴ 10d 8fg* 10fg* 12fg* 10g)
    Critique's three-year-old career turned out very differently from that envisaged for him at the beginning of the season. He was a Derby hope during the winter, justifiably on his form and pedigree and the record of his trainer Vincent O'Brien, but by the time the Derby came to be run he had failed in three starts in Ireland and had been sold as a potential stallion. Salvaging

Cumberland Lodge Stakes, Ascot—Critique is given a superb ride by Piggott to win from Fingal's Cave

Critique's reputation was a priority thereafter. This operation was successful to the extent that all concerned with him could feel well satisfied with their progress; complete success eluded them when on his final outing of the season Critique finished seventh to Vayrann in the Champion Stakes.

Critique's short-head second to Recitation in the Grand Criterium placed him well up among the best of his age at two years. However, he was beaten three times in a short period in the following spring—into fifth place, subsequently promoted to fourth, in the The Minstrel Stakes (5/2 on), fourth place in the Sean Graham Ballymoss Stakes (5/4 favourite) and seventh in the Nijinsky Stakes (5/2 favourite). Soon after, he was purchased by the owners of the Derisley Wood Stud at Newmarket and transferred to the nearby stables of Henry Cecil. He began his rehabilitation programme on the racecourse much lower down the ladder in a £1,600 event at Kempton late in August. He won that, and a less-well contested race at Nottingham two weeks later, without convincing everyone that he was ready for good horses once again. Towards the end of September he clearly returned to something approaching his best form in the Cumberland Lodge Stakes at Ascot, improving his stud prospects by winning this pattern race by two and a half lengths from Fingal's Cave. For a long, long time Critique seemed most unlikely to figure in the shake-up: he was very slow to warm up and didn't start running until half a mile out. Once he left last place behind and got into the thick of the fray he looked a different animal, staying on purposefully under pressure in a quite rough race in the straight and shaking off Fingal's Cave to win going away and, in the end, impressively.

Critique's performance in the Cumberland Lodge Stakes was that of a staying type, one who needs at least a mile and a half in top company; his overall record is, by and large, the record of that sort of horse, too. So far as distance is concerned he would have been better off in the Prix de l'Arc de Triomphe than the Champion Stakes. In the circumstances he was far from disgraced at Newmarket. He

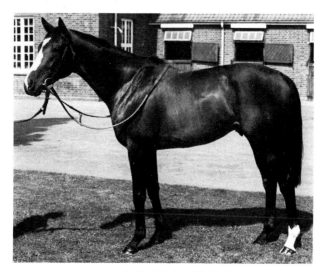

Mr Garo Vanian's "Critique"

came from the back of the field under driving to go sixth or seventh alongside To-Agori-Mou two furlongs out, but hadn't the pace to challenge; he was beaten seven and a half lengths by the winner.

	┌ Roberto	┌ Hail to Reason	┌ Turn-to
	│ (b 1969)	│ (br 1958)	└ Nothirdchance
Critique (USA)	│	└ Bramalea	┌ Nashua
(br.c. 1978)	┤	(b 1959)	└ Rarelea
	│	┌ Sicambre	┌ Prince Bio
	└ Cambrienne	│ (br 1948)	└ Sif
	(br 1969)	└ Torbella III	┌ Tornado
		(br 1955)	└ Djebellica

Had Critique won the Champion Stakes he would almost certainly have been retired there and then. Instead he will remain in training for another year, setting his trainer the task of keeping his interest going and finding the right races. Occasionally Critique has seemed to lack concentration, and he was equipped with blinkers on his second outing at two and on his second and third outings at three. When the time comes for Critique to be retired his pedigree should stand him in good stead. His dam, who won over seven furlongs as a two-year-old, is from a top-class family. Her grandam Djebellica won the Irish Oaks and produced three important foals—the French Two Thousand Guineas winner Cambremont; Djebel Idra, the dam of the Prix de l'Arc de Triomphe winner Bon Mot III; and Torbella III who finished second in the Irish Oaks and bred the Sussex Stakes winner Carlemont and the good French one-mile to mile-and-a-quarter horse Avaray. The last two winners are half-brothers to Critique's dam. Critique is a neat, attractive colt. He hasn't yet shown his form on extremes, but has run well on good to firm and good to soft. *H. Cecil.*

CROCKATTEER 3 b.g. Brittany–Hazelwood 71 (Lucky Brief 128) (1980 NR — 1981 12.2fg 10f 12.3g) 6,400Y; lengthy gelding; third living foal; half-brother to winning jumper Tuffnut Prince (by Prince Consort); dam placed over 5f and

7f at 2 yrs; showed signs of ability when seventh of 14 behind Mr Freshness in maiden race at Ripon in August on second outing; blinkered last 2 starts. *M. W. Easterby.*

CROCKFORDS GREEN 3 gr.f. Roan Rocket 128–Consister 89 (Burglar 128) **71**
(1980 5fg 5fg³ 6fg 5g⁴ 5g⁴ 6g² 6d⁴ 6g 6fg⁴ 7f 1981 6f 8f 8f² 8fg* 8f³ 7d³ 7.2v 8d) lengthy filly; won maiden race at Warwick in August; stays 1m; below form on very soft going, but probably acts on any other; usually blinkered at 2 yrs and wore them again on fifth start. *J. Etherington.*

CROFT FARM 4 ch.g. Silent Spring 102–Lady Morello (Ballylinan 118) —
(1980 NR 1981 11.7f 10.1fg 15.5f 12s) seemed of little account; dead. *R. Armytage.*

CROFTHALL 4 ch.c. Native Bazaar 122–Woodland Promise 76 (Philemon 119) **83**
(1980 6d* 7fg* 7.2g⁴ 7f² 7g³ 6s 7d⁴ 7fg* 7g⁴ 7g⁴ 7.2d 1981 6s 7d 6fg* 6g³ 6g* 6fg⁴ 6fg² 5d* 5g* 6f² 6fg² 7g 5g³ 6s² 6d³) compact colt; fairly useful handicapper; successful at Nottingham in April (made all), Doncaster in May and Haydock and York in August; beat Belfort a length in Better Bet Coral Handicap at Haydock and just got up to account for Tobermory Boy by short head in Harewood Handicap at York; stays 7f; seems to act on any going; suitable mount for a boy; genuine and most consistent; trained by A. Balding first 6 starts. *R. Whitaker.*

CROFT RISE 2 br.c. Sit In The Corner–Como Queen (Como 120) (1981 5f —
5g 8g 6s) Mar 10; compact, fair sort; brother to a winner in Malaysia and half-brother to a winner in Spain; dam of little account; no better than his dam. *Hbt Jones.*

CROGHAN HILL 6 b.h. Lord Gayle 124–Good Report (Golden Cloud) (1980 **95** d
9v 10v*(dis) 10g² 16fg² 13g³ 22.2fg³ 12s 12d² 1981 10d* 16d* 12v 12g 12g 12d) Irish horse; useful performer; successful in 2 valuable races at Leopardstown, beating Triomphe decisively by 1½ lengths in Mooresbridge Stakes in April and Diomedes by a neck in Saval Beg Stakes in May; effective from 1¼m to 2m but doesn't stay extreme distances; acts on any going. *D. Weld, Ireland.*

CROPLEY GROVE 3 ch.f. Moulton 128–Whitefoot 108 (Relko 136) (1980 NR —
1981 11.5f 10f) big filly; sister to ungenuine 1¼m winner Barrow, and half-sister to several winners, including useful 1979 2-y-o 6f winner Neenah (by Bold Lad, Ire); dam stayed at least 1½m; never-dangerous ninth of 14 behind Lakenheath in maiden race at Yarmouth in June (looked fairly straight); saddle slipped only subsequent start; apprentice ridden; sold 15,000 gns Newmarket December Sales. *H. Wragg.*

CROSBY EMPEROR 2 gr.g. Young Emperor 133–Lady Whistler (Whistling —
Wind 123) (1981 5d 5g 6fg 7f 8s) Mar 17; IR 1,800F, 1,300Y; lightly-made gelding; second produce; dam never ran; in rear in varied company in the North; blinkered fourth start. *J. Calvert.*

CROSBY TRIANGLE 3 b.f. Windjammer (USA)–Cool Mistress 59 (Skymaster **72**
126) (1980 5s 5g* 5f* 5s* 5f³ 6g* 5fg 1981 5s⁴ 6fg³ 6g² 6fg 5fg 6g 5fg 5s*) strong, compact filly; comfortably beat Arch Melody by 5 lengths in handicap at Warwick in October; twice placed in similar events earlier, on one occasion spoiling her chance by hanging; stays 6f; acts on any going; blinkered seventh start; suitable mount for an apprentice. *P. Haslam.*

CROSSWAYS 2 b.c. Habitat 134–Silky 112 (Nijinsky 138) (1981 5g 6s 7g) **73** p
Mar 30; well-grown, strong, good-bodied, good-looking colt; third foal; half-brother to very smart middle-distance 3-y-o Kirtling (by Grundy) and fairly useful Abington (by Jukebox), successful over 6f; dam Irish 1,000 Guineas second and half-sister to Moulton and Freefoot; an excellent type of colt but showed only a modicum of ability in good-class races at Ascot (2) and Newmarket; looks capable of much better in time. *H. Wragg.*

CROUTON 5 ch.g. Cornuto 111–Golden Stork 93 (Golden Cloud) (1980 12g⁴ —
12fg 1981 13s) strong gelding; won twice in 1979; lightly raced since; stays 1½m; acts on any going. *R. Price.*

CROWDOWN 3 ch.c. Morston 125–Barlassina (Taine 131) (1980 8g 7g 8d —
1981 10d 10.1f 16f) big, rangy colt; showed a little ability at 2 yrs; will stay 1½m; sold 925 gns Ascot July Sales. *D. Sasse.*

CROWEBRASS 3 ch.f. Crowned Prince 128–Sapientia (Prudent II 133) —
(1980 5fg 5fg 8d   1981 9s 8g 9.4fg 7f 9g) leggy filly; in rear in maiden and minor
races. *R. Hollinshead.*

CROWEBRONZE 3 ch.f. Huntercombe 133–Frances Louise 88 (Saint Crespin   56
III 132) (1980 5d 5f 5f   1981 5d⁴ 6g 6s 5d 5s 5f* 6f 5fg² 5f³ 5fg⁴ 6f 5g 5fg³
5g 5s 6g 5s 6d) compact filly; apprentice ridden when winning handicap at
Ripon in June narrowly; bred to stay 1m but is speedy and seems best at 5f;
acts on firm going and is possibly not at her best on very soft; sometimes starts
slowly. *R. Hollinshead.*

CROWN 2 b.c. Realm 129–Moneycashen 72 (Hook Money 124) (1981 5s² 5fg²   68
5g 6g 5s⁴ 5g) Apr 8; IR 7,400F, IR 8,200Y; sturdy, compact colt; brother to a
modest animal and half-brother to 3-y-o 6f and 7f winner Ring Moylan (by
Auction Ring); dam stayed 1m; second in minor and maiden races in the spring;
didn't fulfil the promise of first 2 starts and finished well beaten under a low
weight in nursery at Newmarket on final outing (blinkered); should stay 6f;
acts on soft going. *C. Booth.*

CROWNED HARE 3 ch.c. Crowned Prince 128–Virna (Coursing) (1980 8g 7s   80
1981 12d 10s* 10.5f⁴ 12fg 11.5f 12fg 10fg³ 11.5fg 10d 14s) 10,000Y; good-bodied
colt; second foal; half-brother to 1979 Irish 2-y-o 1m winner Laide the Floor
(by Dancer's Image); dam won from 6f to 9f in France; 33/1 when beating Eusebio
a length in minor event at the Curragh in May; had stiffish task and was off bridle
virtually all way when about 9 lengths fourth of 8 behind Dogberry in £4,900 event
at York the following month; stays 1½m; probably acts on any going; usually
apprentice ridden (sometimes unable to claim); blinkered last 2 outings, running
creditably in a valuable handicap on first occasion. *J. Murphy, Ireland.*

CROWNING MOMENT 6 br.g. Royalty 130–Moment Supreme 102 (Supreme   56
Court 135) (1980 12.3s³ 12fg³ 11.7f⁴ 11.1fg² 10s 12.2s 12g 10fg 10g* 10g⁴ 12d
1981 12s 11.1s 10.8fg 10f³ 12.2fg³ 11.7fg) poor handicapper; stays 1½m;
seems to act on any going; suitable mount for an apprentice. *J. Bethell.*

CROWN JULES 3 gr.f. Abwah 118–Charville 73 (Town Crier 119) (1980 6g   —
7g 6g 1981 8f 10.1fg 8.3fg 12fg 10f 12g) neat filly; poor plater; sometimes
blinkered. *P. Cundell.*

CROWN PAGEANT 5 b.g. Welsh Pageant 132–High Rise (Ballymoss 136)   —
(1980 16f² 16fg³ 1981 16f) poor maiden; stays 2m; seems to act on any
going; blinkered once; sold 1,160 gns Ascot July Sales. *P. Cundell.*

CRUISE PORT 2 b.f. Homeric 133–Easy Landing 110 (Swing Easy 126)   73
(1981 5s³ 6fg⁴ 5.3f⁴ 5g) Mar 13; small, lightly-made, quite attractive filly;
has a beautifully smooth action; first foal; dam very useful sprinting 2-y-o;
in frame in maiden and minor events; probably needs further than 5f; had
stiffish task in nursery final outing; sent to France. *J. Tree.*

CRUSADER CASTLE (USA) 2 ch.c. The Minstrel 135–Mille Fleurs 100   99 p
(Jacinto) (1981 7s 10g³) Mar 15; big, handsome colt; third foal; half-brother
to 3-y-o Buckwheat Cake (by Buckpasser) and a winner in USA by Damascus;
dam, winner over 7.6f, is a half-sister to Mill Reef; still looked very green when
starting at 14/1 for £6,500 event at Newmarket in October on final outing but
began to get the hang of things by halfway and stayed on very strongly throughout last ½m to finish 2¾ lengths third of 13 to Paternoster Row (first 3 well clear of
remainder); a grand individual who is likely to do a lot better over 1¼m+ at 3 yrs.
I. Balding.

CRUSOE (USA) 2 b.c. The Minstrel 135–Gay Meeting (Sir Gaylord) (1981   88 p
6g*) Apr 11; $160,000Y; closely related to fairly useful Irish 1¼m winner
French Canadian and very smart 1m stakes winner Gay Jitterbug (both by
Northern Dancer) and to French middle-distance winner Nijinskaia (by
Nijinsky), and also half-brother to 3 winners; dam very useful 2-y-o 5f stakes
winner; evens favourite, made much of running when winning 13-runner maiden
race at Punchestown in October by 2 lengths from Kentucky Kid; will stay at
least 1m; sure to make a useful performer. *V. O'Brien, Ireland.*

CRUSTY PIE 3 b.f. Wishing Star 117–Cap A Pie 69 (High Hat 131) (1980   —
7fg 7.2d 8f 10d 8d   1981 12d 14f 12f 13.8fg) neat filly; plater; bred to stay well;
sometimes blinkered and wore a hood final start. *I. Walker.*

CRYSTAL BRIGHT 2 br.f. Bold Lad (Ire) 133–Brilliant Reay 74 (Ribero   75
126) (1981 5g 5d⁴ 5.8h 5f³ 5d) Apr 16; 10,000Y; smallish, lightly-made filly;
good mover; second foal; half-sister to fair 1979 2-y-o sprinter Braconda (by

So Blessed); dam won over 10.6f; quite a moderate maiden; should be suited by 6f; has run well for an apprentice; blinkered third outing. *H. Candy.*

CRYSTAL GAEL 3 b.f. Sparkler 130–Gentle Gael 97 (Celtic Ash) (1980 6s 6g 7g 7g 8fg* 1981 11.7f 12d⁴ 12f⁴) quite attractive filly; improved in 1980 and won maiden race at Beverley; had stiff tasks and little worthwhile form in 1981; suited by 1m as a 2-y-o and should stay further; acts on a firm surface. *J. Dunlop.*   —

'C' TOP 4 b.f. Swing Easy 126–Comotose 75 (Como 120) (1980 8d* 8f³ 9f 12fg 8d* 10g* 8g 10g* 9s³ 10fg³ 11s³ 1981 12v 12.3d 10g⁴ 12g 12s 10.6s) leggy, lightly-made filly; plater; seems to stay 11f; suited by some give in the ground; sometimes sweats up and doesn't always impress in paddock. *G. Lockerbie.*   —

CUDGEL 8 br.g. The Brianstan 128–Pelta (Border Chief 101) (1980 5d 5g² 6g⁴ 6f² 7.2fg 6d 6g 6fg* 6fg 7f 6f* 7g* 1981 6g 5f 6fg 6fg 5g 6g² 6fg 6fg² 6v*) fairly useful handicapper at his best; gamely held on by ¾ length from Fast Friend at Kempton in October; stays 1m but has done all his winning at shorter distances; acts on any going; ideal mount for an inexperienced rider; goes well at Redcar. *P. Rohan.*   **94**

CUEVAS (USA) 2 b.c. Caro 133–Strip Poker (Bold Bidder) (1981 6g⁴ 6g⁴) Apr 8; $300,000Y; lengthy, lightly-made, quite attractive colt; half-brother to 2 winners by Indian Chief, including Clout, a smart winner at up to 9f; dam half-sister to Arc de Triomphe winner Prince Royal II; fourth in 2 good-class events in August, finishing 4¾ lengths behind The Dinmont in Rous Memorial Stakes at Goodwood and 6¾ lengths behind Rebollino in Convivial Maiden Stakes at York; looked fairly promising but wasn't seen out again; will be suited by 1m+. *P. Walwyn.*   **80**

CUILLIN GAEL 2 ch.f. Scottish Rifle 127–Gentle Gael 97 (Celtic Ash) (1981 6g) Apr 6; well-made filly; half-sister to several winners here and abroad,

Chivas Regal Sprint, Kempton—Eddery's win on Cudgel (right) clinches the Chivas Regal Trophy for Britain in a three-race competition against a team of American jockeys

including 3-y-o Crystal Gael (by Sparkler), successful over 1m as a 2-y-o, and useful sprinter Cree Song (by Song); dam, sister to high-class Italian colt Hoche, won from 5f to 1m; 16/1, started none too well when behind in 21-runner maiden race won by Not For Show at Newmarket in October. *J. Dunlop.*

CUMULUS 3 br.c. Relko 136–Nuageuse (Prince Regent 129) (1980 6f 7g² 7s 5g⁴ 6fg² 6g² 6g 1981 5s 5g* 6v³ 6d* 6f* 6fg 6fg 6g) strong, good-topped colt; successful in minor events at Thirsk and Folkestone and in handicap at Brighton, beating Dead Strait ¾ length in last-named in June; stays 7f (bred to stay further); acts on any going; has run creditably for an apprentice; ran moderately sixth and seventh starts. *H. T. Jones.*   **82**

CURALE 4 ch.g. Le Johnstan 123–Last Sensation (Compensation 127) (1980 5fg 5s 1981 5g 7f 6fg 6g 5f 5g 10s) hollow-backed gelding; bad plater; has worn blinkers and bandages. *R. Ward.*   **—**

CURLEEN 3 bl.f. Mansingh 120–Top Of The Tree 66 (Lorenzaccio 130) (1980 5g 5g 1981 6g 7g) small, lightly-made filly; soundly beaten in varied company, including selling; sold 620 gns Doncaster May Sales. *J. Winter.*   **—**

CURLYLAND 6 ch.h. Sterling Bay–Morning Glow (Grey Dawn II 132) (1980 NR 1981 10f) ex-Irish horse; no sign of ability in varied company. *H. O'Neill.*   **—**

CURRENT CHARGE (USA) 4 b.c. Little Current–Midway Island (Turn-to) (1980 6f 7g* 8f 12s 7g 1981 8d³ 6v* 8fg 6.3fg⁴ 8f 6.3fg*) strong, well-made colt; successful in handicaps at the Curragh in May (beat Chads Supreme by ½ length) and July (accounted for Tilden by 3 lengths); had stiff task when well beaten in Queen Anne Stakes at Royal Ascot on third start; best at 6f and 7f; acts on heavy going; racing in USA. *C. Grassick, Ireland.*   **103**

CURRENT ISSUE 4 ch.g. Raisin–Hard Hearted (Hard Sauce 131) (1980 NR 1981 10g) behind in apprentice event at Brighton in May, first outing on flat; sold 360 gns Ascot November Sales. *G. Beeson.*   **—**

CURRENT PATTIE (USA) 2 ch.f. Little Current–Proud Pattie (Noble Commander) (1981 6g 6g⁴) Apr 19; $97,000Y; attractive filly; good mover; first foal; dam, half-sister to dam of Nonoalco, won 6 times at up to 7f; 25/1,   **102 p**

Washington Singer Stakes, Newbury—Custer (right) holds on very gamely from Codrington

kept on well to finish about 4 lengths fourth of 13 to Woodstream in William
Hill Cheveley Park Stakes at Newmarket in September; had been gambled
on when seventh of 12 to Rebollino in Convivial Maiden Stakes at York the
previous month; bred to stay middle distances; highly regarded, has scope and
looks sure to make a very useful 3-y-o. *B. Hills.*

CURTSEY 3 b.f. Royal and Regal–Time To Be Careful (Olden Times) (1980 —
7g 1981 11s 12d 11s 12fg 14g 11.7f³ 12d 10fg) neat filly; poor maiden; stays
1½m. *W. Wightman.*

CURVE THE WIND 2 b.c. Windjammer (USA)–Caught In The Rye 97 **77**
(Manacle 123) (1981 5fg³ 5g 5g) Apr 6; 12,000Y; tall colt; second foal; half-
brother to 3-y-o 5f winner Sanjarida (by Sandford Lad); dam won 3 times over
sprint distances at 2 yrs; showed plenty of speed until lack of experience told
in final furlong when about 3 lengths third of 8 to House Pitch in maiden race
at Kempton in April; soundly beaten in good company in September on both
subsequent outings but ruined his chance by swerving at start on second
occasion. *P. Haslam.*

CURZON HOUSE 4 ch.f. Green God 128–Laburnum Grove 70 (Pall Mall —
132) (1980 6fg⁴ 6fg 8s 5g 6fg 5f 5d 1981 5s 5s⁴ 6s 5d 7fg 5f 6g 7f) short-
coupled filly; poor sprint handicapper; behind in seller final start; stays 6f;
probably acts on any going; used to wear blinkers. *J. Perrett.*

CUSTER (USA) 2 b.c. Chieftain–La Chunga (Bolero) (1981 6f* 5f* 5.1d* **107**
6d* 6fg* 6fg⁴) Apr 20; $75,000Y; strong, good-bodied, attractive colt;
brother to American 6f winner Chungero, closely related to a stakes-placed
winner by Vitriolic and to 2 winners by Amazing, and half-brother to 3 other
winners; dam won 5 times at up to 6f; unbeaten in his first 5 races, gaining his
most important successes in Chesterfield Stakes at Newmarket in July on second
start (made all to win by 2½ lengths from Torrey) and in 6-runner Washington
Singer Stakes at Newbury the following month on fifth (quickened to lead inside
final furlong and won gamely to beat Codrington a neck); picked up
his other wins at Leicester, Yarmouth and Windsor; had his limitations exposed
in Sirenia Stakes at Kempton in September, finishing 8 lengths fourth of 6 to
Sandhurst Prince after having every chance; stays 6f; seems to act on any going.
H. Cecil.

CUT ABOVE 3 b.c. High Top 131–Cutle 86 (Saint Crespin III 132) (1980 7g³ **130**
7.3d² 1981 10d* 12fg² 13.3fg³ 14.6g* 12d)
There have been one or two disappointing fields for the St Leger of late
but the presence among the runners for the 1981 St Leger of the exceptional
Derby winner Shergar ensured that the final classic was one of the most eagerly-
anticipated races of the season. In the eyes of the majority Shergar looked
invincible and he started at 9/4 on, the shortest-priced St Leger favourite since
Nijinsky eleven years earlier. Among Shergar's six opponents at Doncaster
were the Derby runner-up Glint of Gold and Cut Above who had been beaten
four lengths by Shergar in the Irish Sweeps Derby. Cut Above was one of three
runners saddled by his trainer whose main hope was the Piggott-ridden Bustomi,
winner of the King Edward VII Stakes at Royal Ascot and the Gordon Stakes
at Goodwood on his only appearances as a three-year-old. Glint of Gold, who
had won the Grand Prix de Paris and the Great Voltigeur Stakes since Epsom,
started second favourite at 4/1, with Bustomi at 13/2 and Cut Above next at
28/1.
Cut Above's stable gears itself largely to producing top second- and third-
season horses and Cut Above ran only twice as a two-year-old, impressing us with
his determination when runner-up to Kalaglow in the Horris Hill Stakes at
Newbury on his final outing. The official handicapper didn't include Cut
Above in the Tote European Free Handicap which was published in December,
but we thought Cut Above one of the most promising of the season's two-year-
olds and he looked, to us at any rate, sure to make the grade at three. He
reappeared, looking to have done well over the winter, in the White Rose Stakes
at Ascot in April and gave a sound performance to beat Ridgefield by three
lengths, quickening to take the lead about a furlong and a half out and running
on strongly. Cut Above seemed sure to improve—he looked distinctly in need
of the run—but he wasn't seen out again for two months during which time
the West Ilsley stables were hit by a virus which reduced the number of runners
to a trickle. Cut Above was one of those affected but he recovered in time to
take his place in the line-up for the Irish Sweeps Derby which had been his
objective since the start of the season. Cut Above was greatly flattered by

White Rose Stakes, Ascot—Cut Above makes a successful reappearance

his proximity to Shergar at the Curragh but he kept on very gamely to be clear second-best on the day after making most of the running. Cut Above seemed very well suited by a mile and a half and looked certain to stay the St Leger trip. His only race between the Sweeps Derby and the Leger was the valuable Geoffrey Freer Stakes, over one mile five furlongs at Newbury in August. The race attracted only four runners including the Gold Cup winner Ardross whom Cut Above met on terms 5 lb better than weight-for-age. The pace in the first half mile was very slow which turned out to be much more of a handicap to Cut Above than to Ardross; while Ardross lengthened his stride in fine style in the straight, Cut Above gave the impression of being very one paced, finishing only third, six and a half lengths behind Ardross and a length and a half behind the four-year-old Castle Keep.

		⎧ Derring-Do	⎧ Darius
	⎧ High Top	⎨ (br 1961)	⎨ Sipsey Bridge
	⎨ (br 1969)	⎩ Camenae	⎩ Vimy
Cut Above	⎨	(b 1961)	⎧ Madrilene
(b.c. 1978)	⎨	⎧ Saint Crespin III	⎨ Aureole
	⎩ Cutle	⎨ (ch 1956)	⎩ Neocracy
	(ch 1963)	⎩ Cutter	⎧ Donatello II
		(b 1955)	⎩ Felucca

In a St Leger horse the possession of first-class pace is usually nowhere near so important as the possession of sound stamina and it was a very different Cut Above that the public saw at Doncaster four weeks after the Geoffrey Freer Stakes. The fairly useful handicapper Magikin, in the same ownership as Bustomi, led the field at a true gallop for about a mile before Bustomi took up the running. The St Leger developed into a four-horse race very soon after the field straightened up for home. Bustomi, Glint of Gold, Shergar and Cut Above were clear with half a mile to go, at which point Mercer was already getting down to brass tacks on Cut Above. As Shergar faltered inside the three-furlong marker Glint of Gold moved up to challenge Bustomi and went into the lead entering the final quarter of a mile, looking all over a winner. But this was reckoning without the redoubtable Cut Above who showed great resolution under the strongest pressure to collar Glint of Gold just inside the final furlong; Cut Above went away to beat Glint of Gold most decisively by two and a half lengths with Bustomi four lengths away third and Shergar another five lengths further behind in fourth. Cut Above was his trainer's fifth St Leger winner, following Hethersett, Provoke, Bustino and Dunfermline. Mercer, who rode Provoke and Bustino, also partnered the 1980 winner Light Cavalry. Incidentally, Provoke pulled off a major surprise in the Astor colours when he won the 1965 St Leger by ten lengths from Meadow Court who started at 11/4 on.

Cut Above took his chance in the Prix de l'Arc de Triomphe in October but, broken in his coat, he never showed with a chance and came home fourteenth of twenty-four, one place behind his better-fancied stable-companion Prince Bee. Soon afterwards Cut Above was bought by Captain Tim Rogers for a sum in the region of £600,000; he will stand at Rogers' Airlie Stud complex in Ireland at a fee of IR £4,000 (IR £1,000 plus IR £3,000 if the mare is in foal on October 1st). Rogers controls one of the largest and most successful stallion operations in Europe, an operation centred on Ireland where the Airlie Stud, the Grangewilliam Stud and the Simmonstown Stud, his principal studs, will house eight stallions in 1982 including Habitat, Ela-Mana-Mou, Artaius, Double Form and another new arrival, Henbit. One of the hallmarks of the Airlie operation in the last ten years or so has been its large turnover of stallions. Rogers is never slow to replace with young horses those stallions that do not fulfil his expectations—'It's no good waiting until a horse is an abject failure before selling'—and the most recent season saw the departure of Nonoalco to Japan. Ashmore, sire of the Italian One Thousand Guineas and Oaks winner Val d'Erica, has been moved to Italy where he will be on lease, and Manado has been moved to England. Northern Baby, who stood his first season at Grangewilliam in 1981, has gone to the United States—'All the Airlie stallions can be bought at the right price, except Habitat whom I would never sell, and the shareholders have made a good profit on Northern Baby who has been sold for 12,000,000 dollars'. Rogers also says he would never have sold Petingo who enjoyed a very successful stud career until his premature death in 1976. Earlier Airlie notables included Vienna (sire of Vaguely Noble), Atan (sire of Sharpen Up) and High Hat (sire of High Line). Cut Above is a neat colt by the Two Thousand Guineas winner High Top,

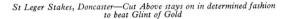

St Leger Stakes, Doncaster—Cut Above stays on in determined fashion to beat Glint of Gold

Sir John Astor's "Cut Above"

a fashionable sire who was also represented on the racecourse in the most recent season by the leading English two-year-old filly Circus Ring and the high-class sprinter Crews Hill.   On the distaff side Cut Above comes from a family noted for stamina.   His dam Cutle was a winner at up to thirteen furlongs and would have stayed further; and his grandam Cutter won the Park Hill Stakes and the Yorkshire Cup and was a half-sister to the Park Hill winners Ark Royal and Kyak, the latter the grandam of the Oaks winner Bireme and the Coronation Cup winner and St Leger runner-up Buoy, and the great-grandam of that very good out-and-out stayer Sea Anchor.   Cut Above is a half-brother to three other winners on the flat: the Irish Two Thousand Guineas winner Sharp Edge (by Silver Shark), the useful mile-and-a-quarter winner So Sharp (by So Blessed) and the Brigadier Gerard colt Murat who was a useful winner at seven furlongs as a two-year-old.   Another of Cut Above's half-brothers Scar (by Relic) made a name for himself over hurdles and in the point-to-point field.   Cutle's two-year-old of 1981 Cut Loose, a sister to Cut Above, showed promise on her only outing and there will be a brother to Cut Above, named Cutting Edge, in training in 1982.   Cut Above stayed very well and was a most game and genuine racehorse; he would have been first-class Cup material had he remained in training.   In an all-too-short career, he never encountered extremes of going.   *R. Hern.*

CUT A DASH   2 b.c. Bold Lad (Ire) 133–Rosalie II 66 (Molvedo 137) (1981   — p
6s)   Apr 13; quite attractive, well-made colt; half-brother to several winners, notably very smart 6f to 1¼m winner Cistus (by Sun Prince) and smart 1½m performer Lancastrian (by Reform); dam won at 1¼m; weak 11/1-shot, made little show but wasn't knocked about at all when about 14 lengths eighth of 11 to Slightly Dangerous in Duke of Edinburgh Stakes at Ascot in October; will be suited by 1m; will do better if looks are anything to go by.   *R. Hern.*

CUT AND RUN 7 b.g. Run The Gantlet–Waterford Glass 97 (St Paddy 133) — (1980 NR 1981 14.6fg 16f) slow maiden; dead. *K. Morgan.*

CUTLER HEIGHTS 4 ch.f. Galivanter 131–Lucky Deal 93 (Floribunda 136) — (1980 6d 6f 8f³ 8f³ 8.2fg 8fg³ 9g 10g⁴ 12d* 13.8g* 12g 11s 1981 10f) sturdy filly; plater; pulled up lame only start at 4 yrs in July; stays 1¾m; probably acts on any going; sold 400 gns Doncaster November Sales. *J. Doyle.*

CUT LOOSE 2 b.f High Top 131–Cutle 86 (Saint Crespin III 132) (1981 7fg) **77** p May 2; compact, good-bodied filly; sister to St Leger winner and Irish Sweeps Derby second Cut Above, and half-sister to 3 winners, all at least useful, including Irish 2,000 Guineas winner Sharp Edge (by Silver Shark); dam, winner at up to 13f, is daughter of Park Hill Stakes and Yorkshire Cup winner Cutter; 10/1 and very fit, chased leaders and kept on nicely when promising 2¼ lengths fifth of 29 to Hayakaze in maiden race at Newmarket in August; looks sure to improve and win a race or two over middle distances in 1982. *R. Hern.*

CUT THROAT 3 br.c. Sharpen Up 127–Zantedeschia 91 (Zimone) (1980 **115** d 5f² 5fg* 5fg* 5g* 6d 6fg* 6f² 6fg* 1981 7d 8g⁴ 7f⁴ 7fg² 6g 7.3fg 8fg²) lightly-made, quite attractive colt; good mover; half-brother to 2 winners; dam miler; a smart 2-y-o, winner 5 times; ran extremely well when about 4 lengths fourth to To-Agori-Mou in 2,000 Guineas at Newmarket in May, particularly considering he had a poorish run in early stages; ran best subsequent race when ½-length second to Dalsaan in Van Geest Stakes, also at Newmarket, in June, running on gamely; hung under pressure when 8 lengths fourth of 20 behind Rasa Penang in Jersey Stakes at Royal Ascot in between (reportedly struck into himself), and on last 3 outings failed to show a great deal of sparkle in William Hill July Cup at Newmarket (fifth to Marwell), Hungerford Stakes at Newbury and £3,100 event at Goodwood (7 lengths second of 4 finishers to Boathouse); stays

Captain M. M. C. Clark's "Cut Throat"

1m; possibly needs a sound surface; ran poorly when blinkered once as a 2-y-o; bandaged near-hind fourth start. *H. Candy.*

CUTTING COMMENT 6 b.g. Sharpen Up 127–Mrs Hauksbee 102 (Pindari — §
124) (1980 10g 7.6g 8.2g 11g² 11g⁴ 12fg 15.8d 1981 10.4g) disappointing
and ungenuine handicapper; stays 11f; probably acts on any going; usually
wears blinkers. *M. James.*

CWMYREITHIN 5 b.m. Roxy–Whitney (Venture VII 129) (1980 9.4g 53
16.9d 11.7f⁴ 14.6fg* 16fg³ 15.8d 16g* 17.1d 18s 1981 16fg⁴ 18fg 12f 12f 17.1h²
14.6f 16h 12g) staying handicapper; acts on hard going; suitable mount for
an apprentice. *M. Tate.*

CYBRANDIAN 3 b.g. Prince Regent 129–Lavenham Rose 85 (Floribunda 62
136) (1980 6g 7g 8.2s 1981 12f 12f⁴ 12.3g 16.5f² 14.6f³ 16.5g³ 12d²) big
gelding; second in maiden races at Redcar in August and Hamilton in October;
stays well. *M. H. Easterby.*

CYPRUS GARDEN 3 ch.f. Wishing Star 117–French Furze (Hard Tack 111§) 47
(1980 6s 6.3d 7g 6v⁴ 9.5s 1981 7fg 7g 6v 7s² 7f 8f⁴) ex-Irish filly; blinkered
when in frame in seller at Kempton in May and claiming race at Brighton in June;
stays 1m; sold to M. Chapman 400 gns Newmarket Autumn Sales. *D. Elsworth.*

CYPRUS SKY 4 ch.g. Redundant 120–Palestra 92 (Palestine 133) (1980 90
7v² 7f 12f 10f⁴ 12fg 8g³ 8g³ 8.5fg 8g² 8g⁴ 10d 1981 8d 9g* 10g⁴ 8fg² 8fg* 10fg⁴
12f² 15.5f² 8s³ 12s*) tall, close-coupled gelding; fairly useful performer;
won amateur riders races at Ripon in May, Warwick in June and Ascot in
October; beat Commonty by 2½ lengths on last-named; stays 1½m; acts on any
going; suitable mount for an inexperienced rider; trained part of season by
F. Durr. *R. Smyth.*

CYPRUS SUN 4 b.c. My Swallow 134–Shirwani 77 (Major Portion 129) (1980 46
10fg 12fg 14fg 12g 12g³ 12fg⁴ 14fg 14fg⁴ 12fg² 1981 10g² 12s 12g 10.1fg 10f
10.8fg) fair sort; plater; stays 1½m; seems to act on any going; has been tried
in blinkers; sold 650 gns Ascot August Sales; resold 350 gns Doncaster November
Sales. *W. Musson.*

CYRIL 2 ch.c. Cawston's Clown 113–Trixie Dean (Drumbeg 94) (1981 5fg 5g 5d —
5g) Apr 13; 300Y; fair sort; in rear in maiden races and a seller. *J. Spearing.*

CYRIL'S CHOICE 2 b.c. Malicious–Saran (Le Levanstell 122) (1981 5f 87
5fg* 5f⁴ 5g* 7g* 6f³ 7f³ 7.2fg 6d³) May 29; 1,000Y; neat colt; second foal;
dam ran only twice; quickened in good style when successful in maiden auction
event at Carlisle and small race at Ayr in July, but had to struggle to win
nursery at Beverley by 1½ lengths from Mosswern later in month; third in
nurseries subsequently, on final occasion finishing well when beaten 2¼ lengths
by Wink at Ayr in September; finds 6f on sharp side nowadays and will stay at
least 1m; seems to act on any going; genuine and consistent. *S. Mellor.*

CZAR'S BRIDE (USA) 2 b.f. Northern Dancer–American Legacy (Hail 78
to Reason) (1980 5.8h⁴ 8fg 7g²) Apr 23; $430,000Y; first foal; dam, unplaced
5 times, is half-sister to top-class filly and broodmare Fanfreluche and good
Canadian colt Barachois (both by Northern Dancer); prominent in maiden races,
on third occasion going down by 2 lengths to Loup de Mer in 17-runner event
at Leicester in October; will stay middle distances. *P. Walwyn.*

CZERNIN 4 b.g. Forli–Nonsensical 99 (Silly Season 127) (1980 9f 7h² 7.2g —
7g 9s 7fg 8g 1981 7s 7g) narrow, quite attractive gelding; poor performer;
beaten in sellers on occasions; should stay 9f; suited by top-of-the-ground;
blinkered once in 1980; inconsistent. *R. Johnson.*

CZUBARYK (POL) 5 b.h. Erotyk–Czeczma (Deer Leap 125) (1980 including ?
20g* 1981 12g 12fg 11g⁴ 10fg 12s 12f 14g* 12v² 12g 14s³) strong Polish-bred
horse; dam one of best 2-y-o's in Poland in 1971; sire top Polish 3-y-o of 1968,
winner of Polish Derby; one of top Polish colts in 1979, when placed in Polish
2,000 Guineas, Derby and St Leger and good ½-length second to Nebos (gave 4 lb)
in Preis von Europa at Cologne; confirmed his status in 1980 when winning
5 of his 9 races in Poland, including a 2½m race at Warsaw in October; put up
best effort at 5 yrs when 3½ lengths second to Glint of Gold in Preis von Europa
at Cologne in October; had earlier won Preis der Stadtsparkasse at Hanover;
also ran respectably when about 7 lengths fourth of 9 to Konigsstuhl in Grosser
Preis von Dusseldorf, 7¼ lengths fifth to Pelerin in Grosser Preis von Baden at
Baden-Baden and just over 3 lengths third to Dentz in Premio Roma; tailed-off
last to Master Willie in Coral-Eclipse Stakes at Sandown in July on fourth
outing; stays well; acts on heavy going. *H. Bollow, Germany.*

D

DADDY'S DAUGHTER 5 b.m. Charlottown 127–Shot (I Say 125) (1980 — NR 1981 12f 16.5f) poor plater. *J. Bridger.*

DAELTOWN (FR) 4 b. or br.f. Dictus 126–Hagerstown (Ruysdael II 122) **117** (1980 8g² 9.5g* 8g* 11g² 12g⁴ 9.5g³ 8g* 9.5f 8s 9v² 8v³ 1981 9d* 8fg* 10.5d* 10v 10.5g³ 8g² 10f 8fg 8s* 9.2d³ 8s) small filly; first foal; dam won over 5.5f and 7f in France; won 3 races at Bordeaux in 1980; raced in much better company at 4 yrs and developed into a smart performer, winning 90,000 francs race at Maisons-Laffitte in March, 80,000 francs event at Longchamp and Prix Corrida at Saint-Cloud (by nose from Liki Liki) in April and Prix du Rond-Point at Longchamp again in September; beat Diamond Prospect by ½ length in last-named; also placed in Prix Fille de l'Air at Saint-Cloud (2½ lengths third to Snow Day), Prix Messidor at Maisons-Laffitte (2 lengths second behind Ya Zaman) and Prix de l'Opera at Longchamp (just over length third to Kilmona); stays 1¼m well; seems to act on any going; genuine; sold 2,200,000 francs Prix de l'Arc de Triomphe Sale before tenth start. *D. Smaga, France.*

DAFFODIL DAY 3 b.f. Welsh Pageant 132–Nagaika 117 (Goyama 127) (1980 — § NR 1981 7f 8fg) quite a well-made filly; half-sister to numerous winners, including top-class middle-distance horse Connaught (by St Paddy); dam stayer; favourite for maiden races at Leicester in July and Warwick in August, but gave trouble at start both times and ran disappointingly; visits Blakeney. *H. Cecil.*

DAFYDD 5 b.h. Welsh Saint 126–Fire Bell 93 (Firestreak 125) (1980 5f* **90** 5fg⁴ 5d³ 5fg* 5fg⁴ 5d 5f* 5g 5d 1981 5g* 5g 5d 5g* 5g 5fg² 6fg 5fg² 5.6fg 5g³ 5g) small horse; good walker and mover; has been hobdayed and has had a soft palate operation; sprint handicapper; scored by 3 lengths at Edinburgh in April (apprentices) and Epsom in June (showed improved form to beat Sandra's Secret); best at 5f on a sharp track; suited by top-of-the-ground; good mount for an apprentice; racing in USA. *S. Norton.*

DAGEEGAH (USA) 2 b.c. Timeless Moment–Pia's Lady (Pia Star) (1981 **99** 5g 5g⁴ 7fg⁴ 6fg² 7fg* 7.3d³ 8.2s* 7s² 8.2s⁴) Mar 8; $77,000Y; strong, attractive colt who carries plenty of condition; good mover; fourth foal; half-brother to 2 winners in USA; dam ran twice unplaced; won 19-runner maiden race at Salisbury and 18-runner nursery at Nottingham in September, latter by 1½ lengths from Bluethroat; runs as though he'll stay 1¼m; probably acts on any going but seems particularly well suited by soft ground; best with strong handling. *F. Durr.*

DALBREAC 2 br.f. Bustino 136–Corriefeol 102 (Jaipur) (1981 6fg 8fg⁴ 8d **73** 6d) Apr 15; rather leggy, lightly-made filly; second foal; dam useful sprinting 2-y-o; quite a moderate maiden; stays 1m and finds 6f on sharp side. *J. Dunlop.*

DALBY LODGE 3 b.g. Workboy 123–Dutch May 109 (Maystreak 118) (1980 — 5f⁴ 5g 5f 6fg 1981 6g 7f) light-framed gelding; useless plater. *M. W. Easterby.*

DALBY MUSTANG 3 b.c. Welsh Saint 126–Princess Tam (Prince Regent **108** 129 (1980 5g* 5g* 6g* 6g* 7v* 1981 7s³ 8g³ 8g 7s 8g² 5g 6g* 6g³ 7v) 2,900F; small colt; first foal; dam placed once from 8 starts in Ireland; unbeaten in 4 races in Sweden and one in Norway as a 2-y-o; third in Salisbury 2,000 Guineas Trial won by Recitation and Ladbrokes Craven Stakes at Newmarket won by Kind of Hush in April, in latter keeping on extremely well when headed and finishing less than 4 lengths behind the winner; also ran well when returned to Scandinavia, finishing 5½ lengths second to Dalby Jaguar in Norwegian 2,000 Guineas at Ovrevoll in June, beating Hillability a length in a minor event at Taby in September and finishing length third to Music Streak in Taby International Sprinters Stakes later in September; tailed-off last of 9 behind Moorestyle in Prix de la Foret at Longchamp in October; stays 1m; acts on heavy going; evidently very useful; trained early in season by T. Dahl. *J. Tandari, Sweden.*

DALEELAH 2 b.f. Pitcairn 126–Rocketina 57 (Roan Rocket 128) (1981 5d **65** 5f³ 5fg⁴ 6g 7fg) Mar 7; 11,500F; 11,000Y; rather unfurnished filly; first foal; dam won 1m seller; in frame in maiden races at Wolverhampton and Warwick in June; should be suited by 7f. *F. Durr.*

DALEGARTH 3 ch.g. Laser Light 118–Inkflash (Hul a Hul 124) (1980 5d² 5s **94** 5g* 5f⁴ 5g³ 5g 5s 5.1g³ 5fg 5g³ 5.1fg² 5g* 5f⁴ 5fg 1981 5d* 5g³ 5fg³ 5d 5d 5f⁴ 5fg 5fg 5d³ 5g) compact, sturdy gelding; good mover; beat Little Starchy by 3 lengths in handicap at Newbury on reappearance in April; also in frame at Haydock, Epsom, Ascot and Newbury; very speedy and unlikely to stay beyond 5f; possibly not at his best on very soft ground; blinkered ninth outing in 1980; often bandaged; consistent; slow into stride fifth start; hung and hampered several other runners eighth outing. *K. Ivory.*

DALES FLYER 2 b.g. Starch Reduced 112–Elixir 99 (Hard Tack 111§) (1981 6s 6f³) Apr 12; 400F; workmanlike gelding; second produce; dam sprinter; didn't find a lot off bridle but wasn't knocked about when 2½ lengths third of 14 finishers behind Straeker in maiden race at Pontefract in July; stays 6f. *G. Lockerbie.* **78**

DALHAM 5 ch.g. Moulton 128–Feather Bed 111 (Gratitude 130) (1980 NR 1981 9g 9d 12.3g) 1,000 2-y-o; big gelding; well bred but looks slow. *J. Wilson.* **—**

DALKEITH 3 b.g. Rapid River 127–Swallow Princess (My Swallow 134) (1980 NR 1981 6g 8fg) strong gelding; first foal; dam never ran; unplaced in maiden races at Redcar in May (needed race and dwelt) and Warwick in June. *M. Cousins.* **—**

DALLAS EXPRESS (USA) 3 b. or br.c. Key to the Mint–Rokeby Venus (Quadrangle) (1980 6d 6d² 6.5g² 1981 8d* 8g 10f³ 10.5s 9s*) $130,000Y; third foal; half-brother to fair 7f to 1m winner Plum Run (by Run The Gantlet) and Rokeby Rose (by Tom Rolfe), a smart middle-distance stakes winner; dam, half-sister to top American horse Arts and Letters, won 3 races at up to 1m in USA; won maiden race at Maisons-Laffitte in March and handicap on same course in November; 5 lengths third of 6 behind Al Nasr (Fr) in Prix de la Cote Normande at Deauville in August; stays 1¼m; acts on any going. *M. Saliba, France.* **110**

DALLIAN 2 ch.c. Dance In Time–Herbary (Herbager 136) (1981 5g 5.1f) Mar 14; small, deep-girthed colt; good mover; second foal; well beaten in maiden races at Newmarket (speed 3f) in April and Yarmouth (blinkered and had to be ridden along down to start) in June. *J. Winter.* **—**

DALMALLY 2 ch.f. Sharpen Up 127–Victa 79 (Northfields) (1981 6d*) Mar 25; big, strong, good sort; good mover; first foal; dam won twice over 1m and seemed to stay 1½m; favourite for 23-runner maiden race at Leicester in November and ran on well to win by half a length from Zaynala after chasing leaders from start (flashed her tail when hit with whip); will stay 1m; likely to improve further at 3 yrs. *R. Price.* **89 p**

DALSAAN 4 b.c. Habitat 134–Dumka 117 (Kashmir II 125) (1980 7fg* 8d⁴ 1981 7.2d* 8s³ 8fg⁴ 7fg* 8fg⁴ 7.3fg* 6fg³ 7g²) **125**

As a four-year-old Dalsaan at last enjoyed a complete season's racing and fully realised the potential which had been hinted at in his restricted opportunities at two and three when, from just four starts, he had won the Marston Moor Stakes at York by five lengths, hacked up in a £3,200 event at Kempton and finished in the frame in the Ribero Stakes at Doncaster and the St James's Palace Stakes at Royal Ascot. He wasn't the world-beater his scintillating win at Kempton suggested he might develop into but he was a high-class colt, and a consistent one.

Sore shins and a pulled muscle prevented Dalsaan's racing after Royal Ascot until the four-runner Cold Shield Windows Trophy at Haydock in May, where with Known Fact's running dismally he had little to beat and won smoothly by a

Van Geest Stakes, Newmarket—Dalsaan (left) leads close home to beat Cut Throat

Hungerford Stakes, Newbury—Dalsaan quickens splendidly to account for Star Pastures with Noalto third

length and a half from the useful handicapper Jebb Lane. This race proved little more than that Dalsaan was in good heart but his performance in the Tote Lockinge Stakes over a mile at Newbury later in the month was more revealing. Produced with a well-timed effort over a furlong from home, he was squeezed between Belmont Bay and Hilal one hundred yards out but was already weakening at this stage and came in just over two lengths third to Belmont Bay. It struck us that Dalsaan's failure to go through with his effort was quite possibly due to a lack of stamina—in the St James's Palace Stakes his challenge had also petered out in the closing stages—and his two other runs at a mile, in the Queen Anne Stakes at Royal Ascot and the Sussex Stakes at Goodwood, lent further support to this idea. In each race he looked dangerous at the distance before fading to finish fourth to Belmont Bay at Royal Ascot and to Kings Lake, beaten one and three quarter lengths, at Goodwood.

At around seven furlongs Dalsaan was a much tougher nut to crack and it took a horse of the calibre of Moorestyle to lower his colours. The Van Geest Stakes at Newmarket in June provided Dalsaan with a good opportunity to pick up another valuable sponsored prize and he duly did so—starting favourite, he came with a strong, steady run to lead near the finish and beat the Two Thousand Guineas fourth Cut Throat by half a length. The Hungerford Stakes at Newbury in August presented him with an altogether stiffer task. The nine other runners included Cut Throat again, Noalto, a strong-finishing third in the Sussex Stakes, the good filly Star Pastures and Bel Bolide, third in the Two Thousand Guineas. Dalsaan excelled himself. Settled in behind the leading group and obviously going well as Rasa Penang took them along, he quickened splendidly when an opening appeared approaching the final furlong and stormed clear to beat Star Pastures, whose saddle slipped in the dying moments, and Noalto by two and a half lengths and two lengths.

Dalsaan finished behind Moorestyle in both his subsequent races. The six furlongs of the Diadem Stakes at Ascot proved too sharp for him and after struggling to go the pace for most of the way he passed the post in third, over five lengths off the winner. Back to seven furlongs in the Bisquit Cognac Challenge Stakes at Newmarket in October, Dalsaan tried hard to get on terms with the front-running Moorestyle in the last two furlongs but never looked like troubling him, going down by a length and a half with Motavato and Kittyhawk among those further back. Dalsaan was taken out of another race won by Moorestyle, the Prix de la Foret, because of the state of the ground and has been syndicated at the reasonable sum of IR £20,000 per share to stand at the Castle Hyde Stud in Ireland; his fee is IR 6,500 gns (Oct 1st).

Dalsaan has an impressive pedigree. His sire, Habitat, boasts a superb record as a stallion and his dam, Dumka, showed very useful form at two before

247

H. H. Aga Khan's "Dalsaan"

winning the Poule d'Essai des Pouliches the following year at 30/1. Subsequently unplaced in three hotly-contested races at around a mile and a quarter, Dumka was bought by the Aga Khan for 60,000 guineas at the 1974 Newmarket December Sales. Dalsaan is her second foal and winner—the first, Dayzaan

Dalsaan (b.c. 1977)	Habitat (b 1966)	Sir Gaylord (b 1959)	Turn-to Somethingroyal
		Little Hut (b 1952)	Occupy Savage Beauty
	Dumka (br 1971)	Kashmir II (br 1962)	Tudor Melody Queen of Speed
		Faizebad (br 1962)	Prince Taj Floralie

(by Riverman), won over a mile and ten and a half furlongs in France—but since foaling him she has not had the best of luck, being barren to Mill Reef, Wollow and Jaazeiro before foaling a filly by Northfields in 1981. Dumka's dam Faize-bad, a half-sister to the shock 1969 Champion Stakes winner Flossy from the celebrated Lost Soul family of the late Major Holliday's, produced two other winners at around a mile in France by Mincio and Bon Mot III.

An attractive, well-made colt who didn't always stride out too well and twice wore a bandage on his near-hind, Dalsaan was ideally suited by seven furlongs and seemed to act on any going. He wore blinkers on his fifth, sixth and final starts but didn't lack courage. *M. Stoute.*

DALTRA 3 ch.g. Majority Blue 126–Pretty Breezy (Signal Light) (1980 NR 1981 8.2s) brother to useful miler Votecatcher and half-brother to several other winners; dam never ran; unquoted when about 7 lengths sixth of 12 behind Turn Back The Time in maiden race at Haydock in October. *J. Toller.*

DALYTAT 2 b.c. Habitat 134–Lady Phoebe (Northern Dancer) (1981 7fg — 8.2d) Mar 16; 10,000Y; strong, deep-girthed, short-legged colt; second foal; dam won 3 times from 9.5f to 1¼m in Ireland and French Provinces; behind in maiden races at Salisbury and Hamilton in September, starting at 33/1 and 16/1 respectively. *C. Nelson.*

DAME DE FER 2 b.f. Nonoalco 131–Hardware 86 (Hard Sauce 131) (1981 **76** 6f² 6fg² 7f³ 7d²) Feb 25; rather leggy, lightly-made filly; half-sister to 2 winners, including useful 1977 2-y-o 5f and 6f winner Sarissa (by Reform); dam won at up to 1m; placed in maiden races at Doncaster in June (1½ lengths second to Atossa), Newmarket in July (beaten 1½ lengths by Corsky) and at Yarmouth in August and September (beaten a length by My Destiny); favourite on 3 occasions; will stay 1m; probably acts on any going; lacks scope. *H. Cecil.*

DAME SUE 5 b.m. Mandamus 120–Catherine Rose 59 (Floribunda 136) (1980 **52** 8f³ 10fg⁴ 8g⁴ 10d 8fg³ 8g³ 12f³ 12s² 12.5s 1981 12f 12.2fg² 12g* 16f⁴ 12h³ 14fg) strong mare; won handicap at Carlisle in July; stays 2m; acts on any going. *S. Mellor.*

DAMPIER (ITY) 4 b.c. Prince Regent 129–Dorothy Sil (Silnet 131) (1980 — 11d 10.1f 12s⁴ 1981 12fg 16g 17h 18.8fg) strong, good sort; winning hurdler but is only plating class on flat; stays well. *J. Baker.*

DANCE BID (USA) 3 b.c. Northern Dancer–Highest Trump 112 (Bold Bidder) **114** (1980 7g 7d* 1981 8d³ 7s* 8s 12fg³ 11.5f* 12fg³ 9f² 11v² 13s) strong, shapely colt; reportedly syndicated for $600,000 as a foal; first produce; dam won Queen Mary Stakes and stayed 1m; won Tetrarch Stakes at the Curragh in April (by short head from Swallanga) and Ulster Harp Derby at Down Royal in July (by ¾ length from Colonel Sanders); ran well in between when 3½ lengths fifth to Kings Lake in Airlie/Coolmore Irish 2,000 Guineas at the Curragh and when 5½ lengths third to easy winner Shergar in Irish Sweeps Derby on same course, in latter event quickening up nicely to challenge for second 2f out but staying on at one pace; placed behind Magesterial in Blandford Stakes at the Curragh again in August (very close third) and in Whitehall Stakes at Phoenix Park in September (1½ lengths second) and finished 4 lengths second of 5 to Nemr in Group 2 Premio Federico Tesio at Milan later in September; twelfth of 14 behind Open Call in Rothmans International at Woodbine, Canada, the following month; stayed 1½m; acted on any going; standing at Pillar Stud, Lexington, at $30,000 live foal. *D. Weld, Ireland.*

DANCE IN ROME 2 b.f. Dance In Time–Romella (Romulus 129) (1981 **79** 6fg³ 6g* 6g² 7fg) Jan 18; rangy, attractive filly; good walker; half-sister to 2 winners, including 1m winner Pulcinella (by Shantung); dam never ran; quickened up well after not having best of runs when beating Karkana by a neck in 14-runner maiden race at Nottingham in August; went down by 4 lengths to Mubhedj in 12-runner minor event at Windsor later in month; bred to stay at least 1m (had stiff task under top weight in nursery when tried at 7f) and may well get 1¼m. *J. Tree.*

DANCE LITTLE LADY 4 b.f. Moulton 128–Socialite 96 (Sica Boy 132) **52** (1980 8s⁴ 7.2d⁴ 12d 10.4d⁴ 9.4fg 10.6d³ 10.2d 1981 10s* 11s² 10.5d) lengthy filly; trotted up in poor maiden race at Stockton in April; stays 11f; suited by some give in the ground; blinkered once at 3 yrs; has run creditably for an apprentice; sold 900 gns Newmarket December Sales. *J. Fitzgerald.*

DANCE OF LIFE 2 b.c. Green Dancer 132–Petrovna (Reliance II 137) (1981 **81** 5.8d 5.8f* 7s 7g) Apr 6; 51,000Y; half-brother to 3 winners in France, including useful 3-y-o sprinter Peymour (by Habitat); dam won over 1m in France and is daughter of French 1,000 Guineas winner Pola Bella; won 12-runner maiden race at Bath in July by ¾ length from Erotas; in rear in nurseries afterwards; should be well suited by 7f; acts on firm going; sold 5,200 gns Newmarket Autumn Sales. *I. Balding.*

DANCE TILL DAWN 2 gr.f. No Mercy 126–Sonseeahray 67 (March Past 124) — (1981 5.3f 6fg 5f 5s) Apr 14; third foal; dam seemed best at sprint distances; unquoted when behind in maiden races, including 2 at Folkestone. *M. Masson.*

DANCING DEVIL (DEN) 5 gr.h. Dancing Lad–Prascovia (Welsh Saint 126) **?** (1980 7g³ 6d 8g 10d 1981 9s² 8d⁴ 10s 8g 9g 7g² 5g 6f 6d 6g*) big, strong ex-French horse; won race at Taby, Sweden, in September; placed at Evry and Klampenborg earlier; well beaten in 2 valuable handicaps in this country on eighth and ninth starts; stays 9f; acts on any going; has won for an apprentice; trained part of season by A. Paus and A. Klimscha. *G. Fletcher.*

Sir Philip Oppenheimer's "Dancing Rocks"

DANCING FEVER 2 br.f. Sweet Revenge 129–Great Emerald 75 (Great — Nephew 126) (1981 5s 5g⁴ 5g 6s 6f 6f 7fg 7d) Mar 2; poor plater; blinkered seventh and eighth outings; bandaged near-fore final start. *J. Mason.*

DANCING KATE 6 ch.m. Jukebox 120–Epee (Cranach) (1980 12.5v 9g 9fg 8fg — 12f² 8fg 10g 14.6fg² 10.6d² 12f⁴ 12d 12s 12d 1981 12g 13.4fg 10f 10.6d⁴ 12g) poor maiden; stays well; probably acts on any going; used to wear blinkers; suitable mount for an apprentice. *A. Arnold.*

DANCING NYMPH 2 ch.f. Dance In Time–Constant Nymph 85 (Venture — VII 129) (1981 6d 6g 6g) Mar 9; 6,400Y; strong filly; half-sister to winners in Belgium and Austria; dam stayed at least 7f; unquoted when soundly beaten in large fields for maiden and minor races. *A. Gillam.*

DANCING ROCKS 2 b.f. Green Dancer 132–Croda Rossa (Grey Sovereign **100** p 128§) (1981 5fg* 6s*) May 22; good-bodied, attractive filly; good mover; half-sister to Cragador (by Hoist the Flag), a useful winner at up to 7f; dam won 3 of her 4 starts in Italy, including 1¼m Premio Lydia Tesio, and is half-sister to Italian Derby winner Cerreto and good Italian filly Croda Alta; favourite when winning £3,100 event at Goodwood in September (by 2 lengths from Gravina) and 12-runner Blue Seal Stakes at Ascot later in month; made most of the running and beat Jade Ring 1½ lengths on latter course, being shaken up approaching last furlong but not being asked to do more than necessary; will stay 1m; probably acts on any going; useful and is sure to win more races. *H. Wragg.*

DANCING SALLY 3 ch f. Sallust 134–Dance All Night 106 (Double-U-Jay 120) **100** (1980 6g* 6g 7.3d 1981 8.5fg³ 7g* 8fg³ 7.2g* 7fg² 7fg* 7.3d 8g) quite attractive filly; ran consistently well and won handicaps at Salisbury in June and at Haydock (by 6 lengths) and Epsom in August; made nearly all and held off Myra's

250

Pet by ¾ length in 4-runner race on last-named course; gives impression she'll stay further than 1m; best form on a firm surface; genuine. *J. Dunlop.*

DANCING SOVEREIGN 2 b.c. Dance In Time–Golden Treasure 106 (Crepello 136) (1981 7fg 7fg 7fg³) May 6; 7,000Y; quite well-made colt; has a rather round action; fourth foal; half-brother to fairly useful 3-y-o 1½m winner Fair of Face (by Grundy); dam, unbeaten in 3 races over 5f and 6f at 2 yrs, stayed 1¼m; improved steadily and finished 4 lengths third of 16 to Nunsruler when 14/1 for minor event at Warwick in August; will stay 1¼m+. *J. Dunlop.* **78**

DANCING SPRING 3 b.g. Carnival Dancer 113–Cathro (Appiani II 128) (1980 8.2d 6s 1981 7v 6fg 12s 8g 7g 11f 13.8f) bad plater. *T. Barnes.* **—**

DANDY GUY 6 ch.g. Continuation 120-Martita 99 (Tacitus 124) (1980 8fg* 6g 5g* 7g* 6d 6fg 7d 6g² 1981 5g 12g 9g 7g 8g 6d⁴ 7g) leggy ex-Irish gelding; won 3 handicaps at Phoenix Park in 1980; showed only poor form over here in 1981 and was well beaten in valuable seller fifth start; stays 1m (unlikely to stay 1½m); acts on a firm and a soft surface; blinkered once at 5 yrs. *J. Fitzgerald.* **—**

DANGEROUS MOONLITE 2 gr.f. Warpath 113–Midsummer Madness 66 (Silly Season 127) (1981 6f 7g 8d⁴) Mar 13; strong, attractive filly; good walker; second foal; half-sister to 1980 2-y-o 6f winner Moonlight Sonata (by So Blessed); dam won over 1½m; 6 lengths fourth of 14 to Sent For You in maiden event at Edinburgh in October, best effort; will be suited by middle distances; dwelt first outing. *C. Thornton.* **65**

DANISH EXPRESS 2 ch.c. Music Boy 124–Ptarmigan 75 (Hill Clown) (1981 5s 6g 6fg³ 6fg⁴ 6fg⁴ 6f 7d* 6s 7d³) May 7; powerful, deep-girthed colt; first foal; dam stayed 1½m; won 14-runner nursery at Edinburgh in October by short head from Scottish Boy, rallying to regain lead on line; also ran well in nursery on final start; suited by 7f and may well get 1m at 3 yrs; acts on a firm and a soft surface. *W. Hastings-Bass.* **84**

DANLIFAR (FR) 3 b.c. Lyphard 132–Lady Dan (Dan Cupid 132) (1980 7g 7fg 7d² 1981 10.1d² 11.7g* 10.1f* 10.1fg² 10g³ 10fg 10.1fg²) neat colt; good mover; won maiden race at Bath (beat Isanemos cleverly by a neck) and minor event at Windsor (by 1½ lengths from Bronze Medal), both in June; good second subsequently in minor event at Windsor (to Fiesta Fun) and handicap at Windsor; will probably stay beyond 1¼m; probably acts on any going. *J. Tree.* **80**

DANNY LA RUE 4 ch.g. Sharpen Up 127–Oceania (Aureole 132) (1980 7d 5d 8f 1981 8g 6g 6g 6f 8g 6fg³ 5fg³ 6f 5f 5d) plater; stays 6f; blinkered nowadays; changed hands 700 gns Doncaster September Sales. *J. Berry.* **37**

DANNY PARK 3 b.c. Double-U-Jay 120–Plain Chant (Song 132) (1980 5fg* 5fg 5d 7d 1981 7g 10fg 8g 8s 8f 8fg 6fg³ 6d² 6fg⁴ 6f* 7g) rangy colt; beat Think Ahead by a length in handicap at Ripon in August; ran moderately only subsequent start; seems best at sprint distances; yet to race on very soft going but acts on any other; has run well in blinkers. *R. Armstrong.* **78**

DANSACHA (USA) 3 ch.c. What Luck–Bellywhopper (First Landing) (1980 5d 5s³ 1981 5fg³ 5g² 5f* 5f² 5.3f 5.6fg) well-made colt; made virtually all on stand side when beating Josephina Bin in really good style by 5 lengths in maiden race at York in June; length second to Brassy in minor event at Chepstow later in month, best subsequent effort; bred to stay 1m but is speedy and will probably prove best at 5f; well suited by firm going. *L. Cumani.* **84**

DAN'S PET 3 b.f. Cavo Doro 124–Double Mint 82 (Double-U-Jay 120) (1980 NR 1981 11.5g 8.2s³ 12d 12s) fair sort; second foal; dam won at 1½m and was also successful over hurdles; staying-on 8½ lengths third to Gray Loch in poor maiden race at Nottingham in September; should stay middle distances. *E. Eldin.* **—**

Basil Samuel Plate, York—Dansacha is clear and wins in good style

DANZIG 4 b.g. Wolver Hollow 126–None-So-Pretty (Never Say Die 137) — (1980 8d 8.2s 12g⁴ 11.7f⁴ 11.7f³ 8.3fg 8g 10g 1981 12g 10.5d 8g 12f) compact gelding; poor performer nowadays; stays 1½m; acts on firm going. *J. Fitzgerald.*

DARA MONARCH 2 b.c. Realm 129–Sardara 106 (Alcide 136) (1981 6f **108** 7g² 6.3fg* 6.3fg³ 8g) Mar 11; 6,400F, 5,000Y; fourth produce; dam staying half-sister to St Leger winner Intermezzo; 66/1 when finishing strongly to win 6-runner Ballsbridge-Tattersalls Anglesey Stakes at the Curragh in August by 1½ lengths from odds-on Americus; excellent third of 9 to Anfield, beaten 1¾ lengths, in Railway Stakes on same course later in month; last of 11 behind Anfield again in Ashford Castle Stakes at the Curragh in September; stays 7f; twice ridden by apprentice unable to claim his 5-lb allowance. *L. Browne, Ireland.*

DARINE 3 b.f. Nonoalco 131–Be Noble (Vaguely Noble 140) (1980 NR **78** 1981 9.4g² 12fg³ 10g* 13.3d³ 11.7d² 10.8s³) 66,000Y; strong, good sort; third foal; half-sister to a winner in Italy by So Blessed; dam, pulled up through injury on only outing, is daughter of high-class 1958 2-y-o Be Careful; beat White Saint a short head in 17-runner maiden event at Nottingham in August; placed subsequently in handicaps at Ayr (Bogside Cup) and Bath and in minor event at Warwick; will possibly prove best at around 1¼m. *F. Durr.*

DARING DAME 3 b.f. Derring-Do 131–Noble Countess (Mossborough 126) **66** (1980 NR 1981 8s* 8d 10d) rangy filly; half-sister to several minor winners; dam closely related to Oaks winner Noblesse; beaten 1½ lengths on merit by On Song in maiden event at Leicester in March but placings were reversed after a stewards inquiry; apprentice ridden when soundly beaten afterwards; should be suited by 1¼m. *P. Cole.*

DARING KNIGHT 4 ch.g. Daring Display 129–Sabotage 96 (High Treason — 126) (1980 16f 12s⁴ 10d 10g 10g 1981 16g) compact gelding; poor form in varied company, including selling; unreliable and virtually refused to race once in 1980; probably stays 1½m; sometimes wears blinkers. *M. Tompkins.*

Mrs Liam Browne's "Dara Monarch"

252

DAW

DARK HOPE 4 gr. or br.g. Meldrum 112–Coy Lady (Damremont 120) (1980 — 12g 12f 12.3f 11.7g 12.2d 12d 1981 9s 12g 12s) plater; stays 1½m; has worn blinkers; changed hands 1,450 gns Doncaster June Sales. *B. Richmond.*

DARK INGOT 2 b.f. Perdu 121–Noble Nugget (Klondyke Bill 125) (1981 5g) — May 4; 600Y; fifth living foal; sister to plating-class filly; dam won at up to 10.7f at 4 yrs in French Provinces; unquoted when thirteenth of 14 to Gold Key in maiden race at Carlisle in May. *Mrs A. Bell.*

DARK MONARCH 3 b.c. Scottish Rifle 127–Outward Bound 79 (Sing Sing **93** 134) (1980 6fg³ 7g³ 7g² 7fg⁴ 1981 8f² 10f* 10.1fg* 10g) neat colt; favourite, landed the odds in minor events at Brighton (by 8 lengths) and Windsor, on latter course in September beating Habitor by 4 lengths after being held up; stayed 1¼m well; acted on firm going; destroyed after breaking a leg at Goodwood in September. *J. Dunlop.*

DARK MYSTIQUE (USA) 2 b. or br.f. Fleet Allied–Zerosa (Silky Sullivan) — (1981 6f 6d) Feb 4; $28,000Y, $34,000 2-y-o; fourth foal; half-sister to 2 minor winners in USA; dam won 3 times at up to 1m; soundly beaten in minor event at Pontefract (33/1) and maiden race at Hamilton (4/1) in September. *P. Haslam.*

DARK PROPOSAL (USA) 3 b.c. Blood Royal 129–Lady Gertrude (Mr **76** Leader) (1980 7v⁴ 1981 16s 10.2f 10fg 13f* 12.3g² 13fg³ 16.5f) rather leggy, quite useful sort; rather disappointing until winning maiden event at Nottingham in July by 6 lengths from Prince Lightning; suited by 13f (ran moderately over 2m); suited by firm ground. *B. Hanbury.*

DASMAN 6 ch.g. Tower Walk 130–A Deux 80 (Crepello 136) (1980 7fg 10f² **76** 10g³ 10g 10fg² 12g* 12fg 12v 1981 12s³) fair handicapper; burly when creditable staying-on third to Glasgow Central at Ascot in September on only start at 6 yrs; may stay beyond 1½m; acts on any going; usually wears blinkers nowadays; suitable mount for an apprentice; usually held up. *F. Winter.*

DATE PALM (USA) 2 br.f. Damascus–Oraza (Zank) (1981 7v) well- — made filly; half-sister to 2 winners, including fairly useful 1m and 1½m winner Countess Palotta (by Brigadier Gerard); dam won German 1,000 Guineas and Oaks; 20/1 and on backward side when virtually last throughout in 8-runner minor event won by Rocamadour at Kempton in October. *H. Candy.*

DAVENPORT BOY 5 br.h. Workboy 123–Sea Tycoon 80 (Tycoon II) (1980 **?** 6g* 6f³ 6f* 6fg 6fg 1981 6g 6fg 6g 6s 6g 6g 6s²) strong fore; fair handi- capper; ran best race at 5 yrs on final start; best form at 6f but has run creditably over 7f; acts on any going; sweated up seventh start; genuine. *A. Pitt.*

DAVIDGALAXY AFFAIR 4 b.c. Tower Walk 130–Lady's Walk (Pall Mall **66** 132) (1980 6fg 6d 5g 7d 7fg 7.2d³ 6s 7d³ 8s 1981 8s³ 10s 8s 7.2d³ 12.3d 5fg 6f³ 8f 6f) strong, good sort; best at up to 1m; acts on any going; sometimes blinkered; suitable mount for a boy; ran moderately final start. *J. Yardley.*

DAVID'S ISOPON 2 b.f. Saulingo 122–Better Than None (Compensation 127) — (1981 5fg 6fg 6fg 6g) May 1; IR 460Y; strong, lengthy, dipped-backed filly; third foal; half-sister to a winner here and in Jersey; dam unplaced 6 times in Ireland; behind in varied races, including a valuable seller. *H. O'Neill.*

DAWNBALLET (USA) 2 ch.c. Nijinsky 138–Dauntu (Grey Dawn II 132) **76** (1981 7fg⁴ 8s) Apr 8; 57,000Y; big, somewhat unfurnished colt; half-brother to several winners, including very smart 1975 American 2-y-o Eustace (by Delta Judge); dam unraced half-sister to high-class filly Double Delta; stayed on strongly in final 2f when 9 lengths fourth of 19 to Dageegah in maiden race at Salisbury in September; co-favourite, proven along early in straight when 7 lengths fifth of 15 in similar event won by Twist Home at York the following month; gives impression he won't reach his best until given a test of stamina at 3 yrs. *H. Candy.*

DAWN DITTY 2 ch.f. Song 132–Chick 106 (My Swanee 122) (1981 5d 6fg⁴ **100** 6fg* 6d³ 7g) Apr 21; 12,500Y; rangy filly; second foal; half-sister to fairly useful 1979 sprinting 2-y-o Wren Rocket (by Roan Rocket); dam won over 6f and 7f at 2 yrs; had her 18 opponents quite well strung out when winning maiden race at Salisbury in September by 3 lengths from Ecstatica; creditable 2 lengths third of 6 to Warm Hearted in Firth of Clyde Stakes at Ayr later in month and wasn't disgraced when 6¼ lengths seventh of 8 to Top Hope in slowly-run Rockfel Stakes over 7f at Newmarket in October; acts on a firm and a soft surface. *H. T. Jones.*

253

Northumberland Plate, Newcastle—Dawn Johnny's nearest pursuers are Another Sam and Higham Grey

DAWN JOHNNY (USA) 4 gr.c. Grey Dawn II 132–Door Star (Stage Door **88** Johnny) (1980 10fg 8d 8g* 9g² 10f³ 10fg² 14g* 16g² 14g 1981 16fg² 18.4d 16s 20fg² 16g* 16.1g 19fg⁴ 14d 16.1fg³ 16fg³) well-made colt; fairly useful handicapper; always going well when beating Another Sam by 2 lengths in Northumberland Plate at Newcastle in June; runner-up previously in Queen's Prize at Kempton (behind Russian George) and Ascot Stakes at Royal Ascot (to Atlantic Traveller); stays well; needs top-of-the-ground; best in blinkers (ran poorly without them sixth start); looked rather half-hearted ninth outing. *M. Sioute.*

DAWN RAID (USA) 2 ch.c. Hail The Pirates 126–Shy Dawn (Grey Dawn II **77** p 132) (1981 7.6s²) May 17; $75,000Y; first living foal; dam smart winner of 19 races from 2 yrs to 6 yrs, scoring at up to 9f; well-backed second favourite, ran green when length second of 14 to Change Habit in maiden event at Lingfield in October; will stay 1¼m; a fair first effort. *P. Cole.*

DAWN REDWOOD 3 b.f. Mummy's Pet 125–Brazilian Beauty (Busted 134) **62** (1980 5g 5g⁴ 5d 5g 5fg 1981 7v² 8s* 8s² 8s⁴ 10.6s² 10f 8g⁴ 8f 8f³ 9f 7.2fg 8g⁴ 7g 8v 8d 7g 6d⁴) big filly; none too good a mover; beat Susanna (USA) ½ length in slowly-run maiden race at Newcastle in April; yet to prove she stays 1¼m; has run respectably on firm going but has run most of her best races when there is plenty of give in the ground; blinkered last 2 starts; finds little off bridle and is none too genuine. *T. Fairhurst.*

DAWN'S DELIGHT 3 b.g. Dawn Review 105–Bird of Passage (Falcon 131) **81** (1980 5fg⁴ 5fg³ 6f⁴ 7fg 8s 1981 6s* 7v³ 6g* 6d* 6s* 6s⁴ 6g* 6fg⁴ 6g² 6f² 6fg³ 6d 5g 6g) leggy, lightly-made gelding; ran consistently well after winning selling handicap at Folkestone (bought in 720 gns) and gained further successes in apprentice handicaps at Stockton and Salisbury and handicaps at Windsor and Newbury (£4,200 event, narrowly from Steel Pass); best form at 6f; acts on any going; blinkered once at 2 yrs; usually apprentice ridden when successful; sometimes bandaged; very tough and genuine. *K. Ivory.*

DAY AFTER 5 b.g. High Top 131–Bisley (Polic 126 or Punchinello 97) (1980 **90** 12g 16g⁴ 12g² 16.5g 1981 10.6s⁴ 12g² 10f* 12g 12f³ 11.7fg² 12fg² 12f* 10.4s* 12fg⁴) good-looking gelding; won handicap at Chepstow in June and amateur

254

riders race at Redcar and ladies race at Chester in August; best form at up to 1¼m; acts on any going; usually wears blinkers; suitable mount for an inexperienced rider; consistent. *S. Mellor.*

DAYARA (USA) 2 ch.f. Empery 128–Diriyya (Riboccare 118) (1981 7fg*) **84 p**
Mar 24; first foal; dam won over 7f and 1m in France; 8/1, won 12-runner maiden race at Warwick in July by 3 lengths from Nunsruler; will stay 1¼m; likely to improve considerably on her 2-y-o form. *M. Stoute.*

DAY DREAM BELIEVER 3 ch.f. Wishing Star 117–Tackienne (Hard Tack **66**
111§) (1980 5f⁴ 5h² 6g⁴ 5.8f⁴ 5d 5fg³ 7g 5g⁴ 5d 1981 5g 5.8d⁴ 5.5fg* 5.5fg*
5g 5.8g) sturdy filly; showed improved form, despite hanging, when close fourth behind Khedive in handicap at Bath in June; subsequently won twice in Jersey; stays 6f; acts on hard going and a soft surface. *K. Lewis.*

DAY IS DONE 2 ch.c. Artaius 129–Headin' Home 105 (Habitat 134) (1981 **112**
5s* 5s* 5f* 6.3fg² 7d*)
 Artaius finished only sixth on the 1981 list of first-season sires but the competition, which included such as The Minstrel, Godswalk and Be My Guest, was the stiffest for years and Artaius can be said to have made a thoroughly satisfactory start to his stud career. In addition to the useful winners Atossa, Final Strike, Honest Broker, Present Arms and Royal Rendevouz he sired the Italian winner Delices, the French winner Malakya and one of the most consistent of the leading colts in England and Ireland, Day Is Done. No wonder Artaius' yearlings were much sought after at the 1981 sales, with fillies fetching 400,000 guineas and 100,000 guineas at Goffs and a colt selling for 148,000 guineas at Newmarket.
 Day Is Done made only one trip to England, when second favourite to the unbeaten Fool's Dance in the Norfolk Stakes at Royal Ascot. Fool's Dance had comfortably accounted for the subsequent Coventry Stakes winner Red Sunset in his second race and Day Is Done had also shown himself a potentially smart colt. Early in April he'd been tenderly handled when narrowly winning a nineteen-runner race at the Curragh and six weeks later, on the same course, he started a short-priced favourite to account for five other previous winners in the Marble Hill Stakes. Despite having to give weight to four of them he beat them all well, being ridden right out to score by two and a half lengths from Red Jersey. With Fool's Dance running disappointingly at Royal Ascot it was the 20/1-shot Prowess Prince who proved Day Is Done's principal rival. The pair started to draw away with a furlong to run but Prowess Prince, after

National Stakes, the Curragh—Day Is Done wins one of Ireland's most prestigious two-year-old events from British opponent Codrington (right)

Mr B. R. Firestone's "Day Is Done"

challenging towards the outside, started to veer badly left. To his credit, when Day Is Done found himself with little room on the rails he refused to give in, battling on to win by a neck even though he looked ill at ease on the firm going.

In the post-race interviews Day Is Done's target was said to be the Gimcrack Stakes. The Gimcrack went by without him though and shortly afterwards he was withdrawn from the Prix Morny because the ground was too firm. Day Is Done finally reappeared in the Railway Stakes at the Curragh late in August. His ten-week absence from the course didn't stop his being made a short-priced favourite to beat eight others, including Dara Monarch and Americus, the first and second in the Anglesey Stakes, and the promising Anfield. Day Is Done didn't win but he took some of the honours in finishing second, only a length and a half behind Anfield who was receiving 7 lb. Surprisingly, in the National Stakes at the Curragh in September punters preferred the Leopardstown maiden race winner Sun Worship to Day Is Done, presumably swayed more by the reputation of Sun Worship's trainer, Vincent O'Brien, than by the colt's achievements in his two races. More danger seemed likely to come from the good-looking English challenger Codrington, winner of the Granville Stakes, and so it proved. As Americus began to fade out entering the final quarter-mile Day Is Done was pushed into a decisive lead, getting first run on Codrington. Once Codrington got clear he relentlessly cut back the deficit but Day Is Done, who's nothing if not game, held on to his advantage by a neck. A length further back the 66/1-shot Philip Martin took third place by half a length from Sun Worship.

The subsequent classic winners Roberto, Pampapaul and Tap On Wood all won the National Stakes in the previous ten years but it's doubtful whether Day Is Done's performance, courageous though it was, was that of a potential classic winner. Codrington was subsequently beaten nearly nine lengths in the Dewhurst Stakes, Philip Martin could finish only eighth to Cajun in the Middle Park, albeit beaten little more than four lengths, and Sun Worship received a 7-lb beating from Anfield and a four-length beating from Sharp Singer in his last two races. Day Is Done isn't without scope though—he's a strong, good sort of colt—so it's possible that he'll make more than normal improvement. Also in his favour as a Guineas candidate is the fact that he was able to show his form very early in the year as a two-year-old, and his determination alone will always make him a colt to be reckoned with.

Day Is Done (ch.c. May 9, 1979)	Artaius (b 1974)	Round Table (b 1954)	Princequillo
			Knight's Daughter
		Stylish Pattern (b 1961)	My Babu
			Sunset Gun
	Headin' Home (b 1971)	Habitat (b 1966)	Sir Gaylord
			Little Hut
		Miss Doree (ch 1957)	Aureole
			Review

Day Is Done also possesses a very attractive pedigree with Artaius as his sire, Habitat as his maternal grandsire and that wonderful broodmare Review as his great-grandam. Review's name was rarely out of the headlines in the time she was at stud. After her first foal, Spithead, topped the Irish Free Handicap for two-year-olds, she produced four top-class fillies in Display, winner of the Cheveley Park and second in the One Thousand Guineas, Pourparler and Fleet, both winners of the Guineas, and Democratie, winner of the Prix de la Forêt. Two more of her foals, La Hague and Princely Review, set new European record prices when sold as yearlings. Review's second foal, Miss Doree, wasn't anything like so good as many of the others but she did win over five furlongs as a two-year-old and has bred some useful winners, including Day Is Done's dam Headin' Home, who was successful once over seven furlongs and twice over a mile at three. Of Headin Home's three previous foals only one, the Run The Gantlet colt Victoria Station, has won a race and that was in Belgium.

Artaius was a marvellously versatile colt, who put up prodigious exhibitions of front running to win both the Eclipse and the Sussex Stakes after finishing a close second in the Prix du Jockey-Club. It will be most interesting to see how much stamina he imparts to his offspring. Day Is Done showed both speed and a fair measure of stamina at two and he will be suited by a mile at three. It's worth reiterating that although he has won on firm he gives the impression he's better suited by easier going. *D. Weld, Ireland.*

DAYLAY QUEEN 3 ch.f. Cili Smoker–Conkers Princess (Autre Prince 125) —
(1980 5fg 6g 6g 7g 1981 8fg 12d) sturdy filly; little worthwhile form in maiden and minor races. *B. Palling.*

DAYTON LEGACY 2 b.c. Auction Ring 123–Mansi (Pardao 120) (1981 6fg) —
Mar 23; IR 5,200F, 7,800Y; rangy colt; third foal; half-brother to fair 1976 2-y-o maiden Swinging Girl (by Swing Easy); dam won over 7f at 2 yrs in France; 16/1 fairly fit, soon struggling when tenth of 11 to Tropical Blaze in maiden race at Doncaster in July. *I. Walker.*

DEADLY SMILE 4 gr.g. Deadly Nightshade 107–Sunny Spell 74 (Vigo 130) —
(1980 NR 1981 9s) 3,800Y; lengthy gelding; in need of race when tailed-off last in minor event at Ripon in April. *G. Fletcher.*

DEAD STRAIT 3 b.c. Welsh Saint 126–Shade 87 (Gratitude 130) (1980 **75**
6fg 7g 6g* 6fg 5fg 6d 1981 5s 6fg 6d 5d² 6f² 6f² 6fg 6fg 7f² 8.3fg 7f 6s 6s) robust, good-quartered colt; second in handicaps at Brighton (3) and Windsor; stays 7f; seems to act on any going; often apprentice ridden but seems suited by stronger handling. *R. Smyth.*

DEAL ON 2 b.g. Quiet Fling 124–Remould 83 (Reform 132) (1981 7f 7fg **77**
7fg² 7f 8f⁴ 8d³) June 1; 5,000Y; useful sort; first foal; dam won over 5f at 2 yrs; in frame in minor event at Doncaster in July (went down by short head to Jiretta) and in nurseries at York and Yarmouth in September; looks short of pace and will be suited by 1¼m+. *W. Hastings-Bass.*

DEAR ALICIA 3 gr.f. Runnymede 123–Dibby's Cousin (Be Friendly 130) —
(1980 5d 5fg 5g³ 6fg 1981 6f 6f 6fg 5fg) lightly-made filly; quite a moderate maiden; yet to show she stays 6f; blinkered final start. *J. Bosley.*

DEAREST DOROTHY 4 gr.f. Sun Prince 128–Ivory Gull 70 (Sea Hawk II —
131) (1980 7f 8fg 9f 8d⁴ 12d³ 10d 10g 12f 15.5g 1981 16d 13.1h 12fg 16g) rangy filly; plating-class maiden; stays 1½m; suited by some give in the ground; ran badly in blinkers once at 3 yrs. *R. Akehurst.*

DEAR JEM 3 b. or br.f. Dragonara Palace 115–Czar's Diamond 66 (Queen's **56**
Hussar 124) (1980 5s 5fg² 5f 5fg* 7.2g 6g 6fg² 6g 6g 5fg 5d 5d⁴ 1981 5d 5g 5.8g 5s² 6f 5g 5g 6f 6s) lightly-made filly; quite a moderate performer; stays

6f; probably acts on any going; usually apprentice ridden; inconsistent; blinkered final start. *A. Bailey.*

DEAR OCTOPUS 5 br.g. Pieces of Eight 128–Larkspur's Love (Larkspur 128) — (1980 12.2v 16s 18f 12.3f 1981 18d 15.8g 12g 13fg 15.8g⁴) small gelding; poor performer; acts on any going; wears blinkers; sold 2,000 gns Ascot November Sales. *G. Lockerbie.*

DEAR PATRICK (FR) 2 b.c. Gyr 131–Alderney Inn 72 (Road House II) **114** (1981 6fg* 6g⁵ 6.5s³ 10v²) fifth foal; brother to minor French 5f winner Gyralderna and half-brother to 2 other winners in France: dam at her best at 2 yrs; won 13-runner newcomers event at Chantilly in June by 2½ lengths from Rollins; also ran well in 2 pattern races in the autumn, finishing 2½ lengths third of 10 to Pas de Seul in Prix Eclipse at Saint-Cloud and going down by only ½ length to Beau Pretender in Prix de Conde at Longchamp; suited by 1¼m and will probably stay further. *P-L. Biancone, France.*

DEBACH RIVER 2 b.c. Forlorn River 124–Debach Game 69 (Darius 129) — (1981 7.6s 6g) Apr 22; well-made colt; half-brother to 3 winners, including fair 1978 2-y-o 6f winner Jenny's Rocket (by Roan Rocket); dam stayed 1¼m; behind in maiden races at Lingfield (last of 14) and Newmarket in October. *P. K. Mitchell.*

DEBIAN 2 ch.f. Relko 136–Brightelmstone 105 (Prince Regent 129) (1981 **71** 5g 5d* 6fg 6fg³ 5g³ 5s³ 6s) Apr 7; 20,000Y; fair sort; first foal; dam raced up to 7f; made all to win 16-runner maiden race at Warwick in May by 4 lengths from Minuetto; off course 3 months afterwards and finished third in nurseries at Catterick, Newmarket and Warwick on her return; bred to stay at least 7f but pulls hard and isn't certain to do so; seems to act on any going. *D. Ringer.*

DEBSBOY 6 b.h. Malicious–Double Justice (Double Jump 131) (1980 NR **46** 1981 9d 12d) poor performer nowadays; acts on 1½m on an easy surface; has worn blinkers and bandages. *K. Cunningham-Brown.*

DECORATIVE 4 b.c. Martinmas 128–War Ribbon (Anwar 120) (1980 8fg **90** 8fg³ 8.2s* 8d 10d* 1981 10.6g* 10.2g 11s² 11.1s* 10.5g 12fg 10fg 10d) compact, attractive colt; won handicaps at Haydock in April (beat Side Track by 7 lengths) and Kempton in May (easily landed odds by 4 lengths from Tolstoy); also ran creditably third start; stays 11f; ideally suited by an easy surface; blinkered nowadays; sweated up final start. *D. Kent.*

DECOY DANCER 4 b.f. Decoy Boy 129–Second String 95 (Tudor Minstrel 144) **36** (1980 7f 5f 6s 6d² 6d 8d 1981 8g 8g³ 7g) fair sort; plater; stays 1m; acts on soft going. *R. Allan.*

DECOY LAD 3 gr.g. Decoy Boy 129–Tiffany Case 72 (Never Say Die 137) **45** (1980 NR 1981 10fg 10s 11s² 10s³) 2,400Y, 400 2-y-o; half-brother to several winners here and abroad, including successful Italian performers Tersiva (by Song) and Rissoso (by Manacle); dam a twin; plater; stays 11f; sold to M. Pipe 500 gns Newmarket Autumn Sales. *M. Tompkins.*

DEEANDEMMTIP 3 b.f. Gulf Pearl 117–Long Shadow 77 (Royal Palm 131) — (1980 5s 6s 6s 7g 9d 10s 10.2s 1981 13f 14.7fg 13.8fg) of little account. *R. Hobson.*

DEEP RIVER 9 b.h. Tudor Melody 129–Lucky Stream 99 (Persian Gulf) (1980 — 12f 11s 12d 12v 1981 12d 12g) useful handicapper at his best; stayed 1½m; acted on any going; had been tried in blinkers; retired to Stockwood Stud, Worcestershire. *I. Walker.*

DELTA DIGGER (USA) 5 bl.g. Delta Judge–Sucha Snob (Dedicate) (1980 **53** 8fg 12fg 8d³ 10s 1981 8s³ 10d³ 8fg 12g 10d*) rangy gelding; plater; attracted no bid after winning at Folkestone in May; stays 1½m; acts on soft going; usually blinkered; inconsistent; has run respectably for an apprentice; sold 1,000 gns Newmarket July Sales. *G. Lewis.*

DELTA'S PRIDE 5 b.g. Mummy's Pet 125–Alexandria 71 (Primera 131) **64** (1980 5d 5v* 5fg 5f⁴ 5fg 5s 6d 5fg³ 5fg 5d 6g 6g 6g 5fg 1981 5s 5s* 5s 5d 6d 5s* 6d 5.1f² 5f 5.1fg 5d 5g 5d 5g) leggy gelding; inconsistent sprint handicapper; won at Folkestone in March and Wolverhampton in May; twice ran poorly in between; stays 6f; acts on any going; sometimes wears blinkers but is effective without; suitable mount for a boy; sold 940 gns Newmarket Autumn Sales. *K. Ivory.*

DEM AN DOZE 2 b.c. Malacate 131–Cinquapace 61 (Tudor Melody 129) **75** (1981 7g 6fg 5g 5fg 5d 5.3d⁴ 5s) Apr 12; 4,300Y; stocky colt; first produce; dam won twice over 7f at 4 yrs; quite a moderate maiden; not bred to be a 5f performer and should be suited by 7f+. *R. Hannon.*

DEMI FEU 5 b.g. Firestreak 125–Moiety Bird (Falcon 131) (1980 10s 8d 10s 10g §§
10d 12.3g 11.7fg 1981 10d) lengthy, quite attractive gelding; one-time
modest middle-distance handicapper but is thoroughly unreliable nowadays;
has been tried in blinkers; one to leave severely alone. *N. Callaghan.*

DEMMY MANCHESTER 2 gr.g. Red Alert 127–Noaxe To Grind (The Axe 115) —
(1981 5s 5f 5f 7.2fg 7.2v 5s 8d) Apr 17; 3,000Y; workmanlike gelding; third foal;
dam plating-class novice hurdler; well beaten, including in sellers; blinkered
last 2 starts; sold 260 gns Ascot November Sales. *R. Hollinshead.*

DEMO'S LADY 3 ch.f. Status Seeker–Milesian Lady 85 (Milesian 125) (1980 5s —
5.8h 5d 1981 6s 5d⁴ 5v 8.5d 5fg 6f) useful-looking filly; good mover; quite
moderate form in maiden races and sellers; blinkered fifth start; sold 560 gns
Newmarket July Sales. *R. Hannon.*

DENIM JEAN 3 br.c. Lord Nelson 107–Talgita 72 (Talgo 130) (1980 6s —
1981 10.8fg) seemingly useless. *J. Czerpak.*

DENMORE 5 ch.h. Moulton 128–Dugo 90 (Dumbarnie 125) (1980 8fg 7fg² 86
7f² 6fg* 6g* 6d³ 6fg 6fg² 6g² 6g* 6s 1981 6s 6fg* 6g 7g³ 6f 6fg³ 6fg 6f 6fg⁴)
sturdy, good-bodied horse; fair handicapper; beat Alpine Rocket a length in
£4,400 race at Epsom in April; creditable 2½ lengths third to Enchantment in
Tote Sprint Trophy at Ayr in July on sixth start; best form at 6f and 7f; acts
on any going; sometimes blinkered but not when successful; genuine and consistent. *C. Nelson.*

DEPUTY 4 b.g. Deep Diver 134–Lindera 71 (Linacre 133) (1980 6v* 5f³ 8fg 6d 52
7f 10.6d 7fg 7g 7d² 7s³ 6d² 1981 6v 6s⁴ 6g 6fg³ 6fg 8g 8.2s) tall gelding; good
walker; plater; stays 7f; suited by some give in the ground; trained first 4 starts
by J. Fitzgerald (claimed). *N. Tinkler.*

DERGRET 4 b.g. Great Nephew 126–Dereta 92 (Aggressor 130) (1980 12fg 12fg 46
12.3s 1981 12.5s 12s² 13.8fg 13d² 15.8fg² 16d²) strong gelding; poor staying
handicapper; seems to act on any going; sometimes blinkered. *M. Camacho.*

DERLY (FR) 3 b.f. Lyphard 132–Derna II (Sunny Boy III) (1980 8g⁴ 8s* 113
1981 9.5fg² 10.5fg 10f 9g³ 8v* 10.5v) sister to top 1976 2-y-o filly Durtal, successful at up to 7.3f, and half-sister to several winners, notably Prix de l'Arc de
Triomphe winner Detroit (by Riverman); dam placed from 1¼m to 13f in France;
stayed on well when neck second to Bernica in Group 3 Prix Vanteaux at Longchamp in April; ran best subsequent race when blinkered in minor event at Evry
in November, beating Reine Gold by 2 lengths; finished in rear behind Madam
Gay in Prix de Diane de Revlon at Chantilly and behind Sangue in Prix de Psyche
at Deauville and could manage only third in a small race at Compiegne in
between; will stay 1½m; probably acts on any going. *Mme C. Head, France.*

DERRING PRINCE 3 b. or br.g. Derring-Do 131–Native Fleet (Fleet Nasrullah) —
(1980 NR 1981 7fg 6d 6g 6fg 6f 7f 7fg) 21,000Y; first foal; dam won twice
in Italy; poor maiden; ran best race on fifth start; sold to P. Mitchell 2,100 gns
Ascot September Sales. *B. Swift.*

DERRING ROSE 6 b.h. Derring-Do 131–Bandi Rosa (Relko 136) (1980 NR 97
1981 16d³ 13.3s* 13.3d³ 16g 18g) compact ex-French horse; a top-class if unreliable staying hurdler and a fairly useful performer on the flat; battled on well
to beat Mirror Boy a length (pair clear) in Aston Park Stakes at Newbury in
May; ran creditably most other starts, notably when strong-finishing third to
Telsmoss in Coral Autumn Cup at Newbury again in September and just over
3 lengths fifth to Halsbury in Tote Cesarewitch at Newmarket in October on
final start; stays well; acts well on soft going; wore blinkers at 4 yrs. *F. Winter.*

DERRY DOE 3 b.f. Derring-Do 131–Salmorin 91 (Salvo 129) (1980 5d 8.2s 8d 52
1981 12.2s 10v 8g 8g 8g⁴ 7fg 7g 10f 8f 8.2f 11g⁴ 9d* 12d) lightly-made filly;
bought in 2,500 gns after beating Price of Peace comfortably by 2 lengths in seller
at Wolverhampton in October: stays 9f; acts on a soft surface; fell fourth
outing; trained until after ninth outing by D. Garraton. *S. Norton.*

DERWENT RIVER 2 b.f Another River 89–Aldy (Varano) (1981 5g 5d² 58
5fg⁴ 5g 6fg 6g⁴ 6d 8.2fg 8g 8.2d²) May 29; narrow, lightly-made filly; second
living foal; half-sister to a bad plater; dam of no account; in frame in a variety
of races, including a seller; stays 1m; acts on a firm and a soft surface; has
little scope. *T. Barnes.*

DESERT COMMAND 5 ch.g. Sandford Lad 133–High Command (High Hat — 131) (1980 NR 1981 10d) well-made gelding; plater; stays 1m but has been well beaten over further; acts on a firm surface and seems unsuited by a soft one; has worn blinkers. *R. Hannon.*

DESERT STAR 4 ch.c. Hot Spark 126–Ice Ballet 87 (Ballymoss 136) (1980 **67** 8fg 10fg 11g* 10s 10fg 10fg 1981 13fg^2 12d 12g^3 10f^2 12g 12d 12g) attractive, well-made colt; stays 13f; possibly unsuited by soft ground; blinkered and bandaged once in 1980; good mount for an inexperienced rider. *R. Akehurst.*

DESROSE 2 bl.f. Godswalk 130–Rose Noir (Floribunda 136) (1981 5g^4 5f 7g) **74** May 30; IR 20,000Y; leggy, light-framed filly; half-sister to 3 winners, including Irish 1,000 Guineas runner-up Clover Princess (by Right Tack); dam lightly-raced sister to Florescence; quite close up in maiden and minor events; gives impression she'll stay 1m; lacks scope; sold to BBA 5,600 gns Newmarket Autumn Sales. *M. Stoute.*

DESTINY HILL (USA) 10 b.g. Power of Destiny–Scotts Hill (Colonel O'F) — (1980 16fg 1981 16g) strong gelding; probably no longer of any account. *S. Holland.*

DETROIT (FR) 4 br.f. Riverman 131–Derna II (Sunny Boy III) (1980 10.5s* **126** 10.5d* 9d* 10g* 12f3 12f* 1981 10d^4 10.5g 11f* 10f* 12g* 12d 12g)
It wasn't until the second half of the season that the genuine Detroit found something resembling the form which had enabled her to win five races, notably the Prix de l'Arc de Triomphe from Argument and Ela-Mana-Mou, at three. In fact her first two starts, in the Prix d'Harcourt and Prix Ganay, both at Longchamp, might well have made her connections wonder whether the decision to keep her in training had been a wise one. Both times she physically looked a shadow of the grand stamp of filly seen at the end of 1980 and faded out of contention in the closing stages, finishing fourth of six to Argument in the Harcourt and fifth of nine to him, beaten also by Armistice Day, In Fijar and Ruscelli, in the Ganay. Detroit was off the course for sixteen weeks afterwards, during which period she improved markedly in appearance, putting on a lot of condition, and on her return she ran up a sequence of three successes, the first two of which saw her wearing bandages. Against five modest opponents in a 40,000 francs event at Clairefontaine in August she did no more than was necessary to win, and four days later she experienced little difficulty in accounting for Ruscelli by one and a half lengths in the Prix Ridgway at Deauville with some very useful performers well beaten.

	Riverman (b 1969)	Never Bend (b 1960)	Nasrullah / Lalun
Detroit (Fr)		River Lady (b 1963)	Prince John / Nile Lily
(br.f. 1977)	Derna II (b 1961)	Sunny Boy III (b 1944)	Jock II / Fille de Soleil
		Miss Barberie (b 1950)	Norseman / Vaneuse

Detroit was obviously coming to herself, and in the four-runner Prix Foy at Longchamp in September she put up an impressive display, albeit in a slowly-run race. Looking very well, she started at odds on to beat Gold River, Lancastrian and Lord Jack, all of whom were conceding her weight. The almost-funereal pace was of little assistance to her rivals and once Detroit strolled up to the leader Lord Jack soon after turning into the straight the race was to all intents and purposes over. She drew well clear as Lancastrian and Gold River, the latter of which had, as usual, been held up, struggled to get on terms and though both made ground Detroit, eased down close home, was value for twice her winning margin of two lengths over Lancastrian. Results of slowly-run events frequently need to be taken with a pinch of salt, but even so Detroit still appeared to have a reasonable chance of gaining a second win in the Arc, and with Head riding her in preference to Gold River, trained by his father, she started second favourite at Longchamp, coupled with Kings Lake and Snow Day. The result must have had a nightmarish quality for Head. The filly he rejected, Gold River, won while Detroit, in a good position for much of the way, dropped right out in the last two furlongs to finish a most disappointing twentieth. She ran once more before being retired to stud, finishing a soundly-beaten fifth to the Arc third April Run in the Turf Classic at Aqueduct. On balance it has to be concluded that despite her very easy win in the Prix Foy Detroit, though still a good filly, was less of a force in 1981 than the previous year.

Prix Foy, Longchamp—Detroit is a comfortable winner from Lancastrian, Gold River and Lord Jack

Derna II, Detroit's dam, has bred six other winners, notably the useful middle-distance fillies Darcounette (by Dapper Dan) and Valderna (by Val de Loir), and Durtal (by Lyphard) who won the 1976 William Hill Cheveley Park Stakes. Covered by Caro, Derna II was sold to the Comte de Chambure for 100,000 francs in 1972 and is beginning to repay the investment handsomely— Detroit was sold privately as a foal for a reported £100,000 and the 1979 foal, an as-yet unraced Green Dancer colt called Dilligham, cost Detroit's trainer, acting on behalf of Serge Fradkoff, 530,000 guineas as a yearling at the 1980 Houghton Sales. There is also a yearling colt by Arctic Tern named Dorchester. Derna II, who was placed at ten to thirteen furlongs in France, comes from quite a stout family. Her dam, a daughter of a middle-distance winner, won at up to eleven and a half furlongs and bred two minor winners, one of whom stayed long distances. With this breeding on her dam's side and with a sire, Riverman, who stayed one and a half miles, it was no surprise that Detroit stayed a mile and a half well. An attractive filly with a good turn of foot, she acted on any going but went especially well on firm. She visits Kings Lake. *O Douieb, France.*

DEUTZIA 3 br.f. Derring-Do 131–Peach Blossom (Blakeney 126) (1980 5.8h 6fg 1981 8d 8d³ 7g⁴ 8fg 8fg 10.1g 10fg) small, lightly-made filly; in frame in maiden races; should be suited by middle distances; sold 15,000 gns Newmarket December Sales. *I. Balding.*   —

DEV 2 b.c. Free State 125–Meadow's Alley (St Paddy 133) (1981 7d 7fg 7fg 6d* 6g) Mar 14; 8,800Y; well-made colt; half-brother to several winners, including quite useful 1m to 1¼m handicapper Loudoun Bah (by Pall Mall); dam never ran; 20/1, showed first worthwhile form when leading close home to beat Lady Cox a neck in 25-runner maiden race at Doncaster in October; had stiff task in nursery next time out; should stay 7f. *G. Harwood.*   **81**

DEVIL MAY CARE 4 b.g. Galivanter 131–Taffimai (Never Say Die 137) (1980 8fg 8fg 10fg³ 8.2s² 8s⁴ 7g³ 1981 7.5g² 8.5d² 7.5g² 8s 7g² 7fg³ 8d³ 8fg 8g 8s³ 10.2g) strong, good sort; stays 1m well (beaten in valuable seller over 1¼m final start); seems to act on any going; has run respectably for an apprentice. *W. Hastings-Bass.*   **66**

DEVIL ROCK 3 br.c. Arch Sculptor 123–Charity Concert 80 (Vimy 132) (1980 6g 6s 1981 8g 8fg 9f⁴ 10.1g² 12fg* 12d²) good-bodied, attractive colt; beat Cavendish by 2 lengths in gentleman riders event at Kempton in September; stays 1½m; acts on a firm and a soft surface. *J. Dunlop.*

DEVILS ALTERNATIVE 2 br.f. Hotfoot 126–Heaven Knows 113 (Yellow God 129) (1981 5d 6fg) Mar 8; first foal; dam won Lingfield Oaks Trial but was best at up to 9f; unquoted and apprentice ridden when behind in large fields of maidens at Folkestone and Lingfield in June. *R. Smyth.*   —

DEVISDALE 2 b.c. Swing Easy 126–Miss By Miles 91 (Milesian 125) (1981 5d 5g² 6fg 5d 6d) Mar 9; 63,000Y; most attractive colt; good walker; fourth foal; half-brother to smart 6f and 1m winner Missed Blessing (by So Blessed) and to a winner over hurdles; dam genuine miler; nowhere near so good as he looks and, after finishing length second to Spanish Pool in 4-runner maiden race at Ayr in May and ninth of 16 to Red Sunset in Coventry Stakes at Royal Ascot the following month, disappointed twice, including in moderate maiden company at Doncaster on final start; will probably stay 7f; to be trained by J. Fitzgerald. *P. Rohan.*   **73**

DEV

DEVON AIR 2 b.f. Sparkler 130–Vicomtesse 97 (Relko 136) (1981 6fg 7fg² **101**
8fg⁴) Apr 24; big, rangy, deep-girthed filly; half-sister to useful stayer Vicomte
(by Firestreak) and winning hurdler Royal Beacon (by Manacle); dam won over
1½m; improved with each race and ran extremely well when 33/1 for 8-runner
Hoover Fillies Mile at Ascot in September, staying on so strongly she was beaten
only 2½ lengths into fourth place behind Height of Fashion (gave 9 lb); will
probably stay 1½m; useful and will win races if not tried too highly. *J. Cann.*

DEWANADANCE (USA) 2 b.f. Dewan–Right Hop (Right Combination) (1981 **84**
7f² 6d* 7g⁴) Mar 22; $70,000Y; big, strong, well-made filly; third foal; sister
to 1980 American 2-y-o 6f winner She's Dewan and half-sister to a winner by
Kamaraan; dam won at up to 1m, including claiming events; 7/2 on, won 10-
runner maiden race at Nottingham in September unimpressively by a length from
La Pirouette after hanging under strong pressure; 3 lengths fourth to Bravado in
small race at Catterick the following month; will stay 1¼m. *H. Cecil.*

DEWBERRY 3 b.f. Bay Express 132–Rosaberry 94 (Rockefella) (1980 6d 6g **68**
5d 6s⁴ 1981 6fg² 6s² 6g² 5f⁴ 6f* 6fg 7fg 6fg³ 5.8g) compact, well-made filly;
good mover; beat Persian Pact in quite good style by 2 lengths in apprentice
maiden race at Pontefract in June; stays 6f; acts on any going. *C. Nelson.*

DHANTERAS 3 b.g. Nonoalco 131–Classic Tune (Ribero 126) (1980 NR 1981 **—**
8d 8.5fg⁴ 9s⁴ 7g) 16,000Y; rangy gelding; second foal; half-brother to a
moderate filly; dam, daughter of Irish Guinness Oaks winner Aurabella, placed
over 7f at 2 yrs; didn't come down hill well but was far from disgraced when
about 9 lengths fourth of 6 to Centurius in Ladbroke Blue Riband Trial at
Epsom in April; rather disappointing afterwards, but didn't have at all a smooth
run on third outing and ran a bit too freely on fourth start; best form on a firm
surface; gelded after final outing. *G. Lewis.*

DHUARD 4 br.c. Perdu 121–High Fidelyty (Hautain 128) (1980 6f 5g⁴ 6s 5g² **64**
5fg 5d 6g 5s 1981 6s² 5s* 6g* 5s 5d 6d 7g) good-topped colt; won handicaps
at Wolverhampton and Catterick in April; blinkered when sixth in fairly
valuable selling handicap on final start; seems to stay 7f; acts on soft going; has
run respectably when sweating up; doesn't always look too keen; ran poorly
sixth outing. *D. Hanley.*

DIAL A DISC 3 b.f. Record Token 128–Clear Song 67 (Saintly Song 128) **39**
(1980 NR 1981 7d 5d 7fg 6fg⁴ 5g⁴ 5fg 6fg) 3,700Y; small, lightly-made filly;
first foal; dam, half-sister to very useful middle-distance colt Dieu Soleil, won over
5f at 2 yrs; fourth in selling handicaps at Catterick (didn't have best of runs)
and Edinburgh in June; stays 6f; sold 520 gns Newmarket Autumn Sales. *A.
Bailey.*

DIAMOND CHARM 2 b.f. Sparkler 130–Molly Morgan 91 (Pirate King 129) **—**
(1981 5d 5fg 6fg) Feb 24; 2,200Y; compact filly; seventh living foal; dam 6f
2-y-o winner; behind in maiden races. *R. Smyth.*

DIAMOND CUTTER 2 b.c. Song 132–Lucinda Anne (Abernant 142) (1981 **84**
5g* 5d 7g 7g) Feb 25; 10,000Y; big, rangy colt; half-brother to 3 winners,
including sprinter Wynburry (by No Mercy); dam apparently poor maiden;
kept on strongly to get on top close home when winning 10-runner maiden race
at Newmarket in May by a neck from dead-heaters Bronowski and Prowess
Prince; ran as though something was wrong with him at York later in May
and wasn't seen out again until October when last of 9 to Wind and Wuthering in
William Hill Dewhurst Stakes at Newmarket and second last to Not For Show in
£5,000 race at Doncaster in November; not sure to stay beyond 5f; has given
trouble at start. *R. Williams.*

DIAMOND GALLERY 3 ch.f. Record Token 128–Stroppy Lou (Shantung **—**
132) (1980 6s 7fg 1981 10f 8.2s 8s) unfurnished filly; poor form in maiden
and minor races. *R. Boss.*

DIAMOND HORSESHOE 3 b.g. Some Hand 119–Hammerwood (Combat **56**
123) (1980 5f 6f 6s² 6fg 6g 6fg 6d 5g 1981 5s 5d 6fg 5v 5fg 6g 5s² 6d) lengthy
gelding; quite a moderate maiden; behind in sellers on occasions; stays 6f; well
suited by soft going; seems best in blinkers. *R. Akehurst.*

DIAMOND KING 2 ch.c. Music Boy 124–Long Valley 71 (Ribero 126) (1981 **79**
5s 6d 5g² 5fg 5fg 5d 6g) May 8; 11,000Y; sturdy, short-legged colt; third foal;
half-brother to 3-y-o Cornish Lullaby (by Crooner) and a winning plater by
Perdu; dam showed a little ability at 2 yrs; quite a moderate colt; stays 6f;
seems to need some give in the ground. *J. Benstead.*

DIAMOND PROSPECT (USA) 3 b.c. Mr Prospector–Sociable Angel (Social **126**
Climber) (1980 5g² 5s² 5.5g 6d* 7g² 1981 7d* 7s² 7s⁴ 6.5fg² 8fg² 10s³ 8s² 7v³
8s²) $120,000 2-y-o; half-brother to several winners, including 2 minor stakes
winners by Stevward; dam stakes-placed winner at 2 yrs; won Prix Djebel at
Maisons-Laffitte in April by ½ length from Spoleto; didn't manage to win again
but ran consistently well in top company; second in 5 pattern races, in Prix
du Palais Royal at Longchamp in May (beaten 2 lengths by Prince Mab), Prix
Maurice de Gheest at Deauville in August (flattered by proximity to length
winner Moorestyle but ran very well nonetheless), Prix Quincey on same course
later in month (beaten a neck by Phydilla), Prix du Rond-Point at Longchamp
in September (beaten ½ length by Daeltown) and Prix Perth at Saint-Cloud in
November (beaten ½ length by Princes Gate); third in Prix du Prince d'Orange
at Longchamp in September (stayed on extremely well from rear and was beaten
only ½ length by Vayrann) and Prix de la Foret on same course in October
(about 4 lengths behind Moorestyle); stayed 1½m well, but was effective at much
shorter distances; seemed to act on any going; standing at Hyllview Stud,
Florida. *M. Saliba, France.*

DIAMOND SHOAL 2 b.c. Mill Reef 141–Crown Treasure (Graustark) (1981 **101**
5.8d* 7g² 7f* 7g⁴ 7s 8s) May 6; small, quite attractive colt; good mover; second
foal; brother to 3-y-o Glint of Gold, runner-up in Derby and St Leger and winner
of Italian Derby and Grand Prix de Paris; dam very useful at 2 yrs in USA
when winner over 5f, and is half-sister to smart filly Diomedia; successful in
maiden race at Bath in June and Duke of Norfolk Memorial Nursery at Brighton
in August, giving plenty of weight to his 3 opponents when winning latter by
a length from Idle Market; also ran creditably when keeping on strongly to be
length second of 8 to Treboro in Donnington Castle Stakes at Newbury and
when about 3 lengths fourth of 7 to Zilos in Seaton Delaval Stakes at Newcastle;
well beaten under large weights in nurseries last 2 starts; should be well suited
by middle distances; appears to act on any going except very soft. *I. Balding.*

Mr Paul Mellon's "Diamond Shoal"

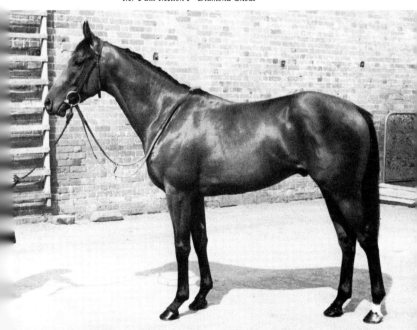

DIBBINSDALE LAD 5 ch g. Sandford Lad 133–Travelling Fair 95 (Vienna — 127) (1980 10.4f 1981 13s 12d) fair sort; quite useful handicapper at his best; lightly raced nowadays; stays 1½m; acts on any going; used to wear blinkers; tends to hang but has run well for an apprentice. *C. Crossley.*

DIBBINSDALE LASS 3 ch.f. Amber Rama 133–Bella Canto 82 (Crooner 119) **66** (1980 6s 7d 7s 6s 1981 6g 7.6d 5g³ 6d* 7f 6f 7.2fg 6g 6d) leggy, unfurnished filly; beat Song Minstrel by 1½ lengths in handicap at Hamilton in July; stays 6f; acts on any going, but best form with some give in the ground. *C. Crossley.*

DICK'S FOLLY 2 b.c. Martinmas 128–No Princess (Prince Regent 129) (1981 **81** 5g 6g² 6fg2 6s) May 23; IR 4,100F, IR 14,500Y; lightly-made colt; first produce; dam won over 1¼m in Ireland; second in maiden race at Newcastle in June (beaten 3 lengths by Bancario) and minor event at Redcar in July (dead-heated with Rapid Knot, 1½ lengths behind Mummy's Game); will stay at least 1m; possibly unsuited by soft ground. *W. Elsey.*

DIJLA 2 ch.f. Hittite Glory 125–La Meme 90 (Pall Mall 132) (1981 6fg 7fg³ **82** 7fg³ 7h* 7.3d 8.2d) Mar 26; close-coupled filly; second foal; closely related to winning 3-y-o stayer Le Beau (by Hot Spark); dam won 3 times over 2m and also won over hurdles; favourite when beating Spring Lane by 2 lengths in 13-runner maiden race at Chepstow in August; not disgraced in nurseries afterwards; will probably stay 1¼m; seems to act on any going. *H. T. Jones.*

DIMITRI 2 ch.c. Sharpen Up 127–Doushiska 78 (Hornbeam 130) (1981 7g) — p Mar 10; well-made, attractive colt; half-brother to several winners, including very useful 7f and 10.5f winner Bozovici (by Queen's Hussar) and very useful 1m to 13f winner Serge Lifar (by Lyphard); dam won at 1½m; 20/1, well there 5f when tenth of 18 behind General Anders in £4,100 race at Ascot in September; will stay 1m; certainly looks capable of better. *C. Nelson.*

DINKUM CHIEF 7 gr.g. Tribal Chief 125–Sara Lady 81 (Roan Rocket 128) — (1980 7fg 6h 8g 6s 5d³ 6d³ 5g 6g 6f³ 5d 1981 6g 5g 6g 6g) small gelding; poor handicapper; stays 7f; probably acts on any going; good mount for an inexperienced rider; sold 800 gns Doncaster June Sales; resold 900 gns Ascot August Sales. *T. Barron.*

DIOKLIS 3 ch.c. Busted 134–Honeysuckle Rose 105 (Honeyway 125) (1980 — 6s 1981 11s 12d 10fg 8g) big, deep-girthed colt; little worthwhile form in maiden races; blinkered final start; sold 2,700 gns Newmarket Autumn Sales. *H. T. Jones.*

DIONE 2 gr.f. Mill Reef 141–La Speroana 68 (Roan Rocket 128) (1981 7g³) **77 p** Mar 20; small, well-made filly; sister to smart middle-distance stayer Beau Reef and 4-y-o middle-distance winner Madigan Mill; dam 1m winner; promising 3 lengths third of 16 to Hula Ruler in maiden race at Sandown in July, despite being hampered inside final furlong; will stay 1½m; presumably met with a setback after Sandown. *J. Dunlop.*

DIONYSUS 2 ch.c. Red God 128§–Queen's Keys 84 (Right Royal V 135) **74** (1981 5d 8s³ 8d) Apr 21; big, well-made, attractive colt; eighth foal; half-brother to a winning plater and a winner over hurdles; dam won over 1¼m; 1½ lengths third of 17 to Mrs Currie in maiden race at Warwick in October, easily best effort; will probably stay 1¼m. *P. Walwyn.*

DIOR PRINCESS 3 b. or br.f. Manacle 123–Dior 80 (Dionisio 126) (1980 — 9d 7d 1981 8s 8fg 8g) leggy, unfurnished filly; in rear in varied company, including selling; blinkered final start; sold 400 gns Newmarket Autumn Sales. *J. Tierney.*

DIRECTORATE 3 ch.c. Gay Fandango 132–Gentle Way 74 (Gentle Art 121) **82** (1980 5s 5.1g* 5s 1981 5fg⁴ 6g⁴ 6fg 6s² 6f³ 6f³ 8.5fg³ 8f⁴ 8d⁴ 8d) strong colt; in frame in handicaps most starts in 1981 but finds little off bridle and is no battler; stays 1m; usually taken down early; sold 4,400 gns Newmarket Autumn Sales. *M. Stoute.*

DISCO 3 ch.g. Jukebox 120–Only A Game (Whistling Wind 123) (1980 6d 6g³ **71** 1981 6s* 6s⁴ 7d³ 7s 7fg 7g) neat, strong gelding; beat Thai King by a length in maiden event at Leicester in March; usually faced stiffer tasks afterwards, but finished in frame in minor event at Nottingham in April and handicap (apprentice ridden) at Warwick in May; ran poorly fourth outing; stays 7f; acts on soft going; blinkered first 2 outings and again on fourth; sold to L. Kennard 2,800 gns Newmarket Autumn Sales. *P. Walwyn.*

DISCO FEVER 3 br.f. Workboy 123–Gin A Go Go 72 (Cash and Courage 116) **50** (1980 5g 5f 5d* 5s 5fg 5s³ 1981 5s 6g 5d 6g 5f 5f 5fg³ 7fg 6f 5d²) strong, compact filly; placed in sellers; best form at 5f; blinkered final start. *J. Mason.*

DISCO LASS 3 b.f. Record Token 128–Pladda (Reliance II 137) (1980 5d 7g — 1981 10s 7fg 7d 12d) tall, close-coupled filly; poor plater; blinkered first outing as a 2-y-o. *S. Matthews.*

DISH DASH 2 b.f. Bustino 136–Loose Cover 106 (Venture VII 129) (1981 **80** 6fg² 7d² 6d*) Apr 14; lengthy filly; excellent walker; half-sister to several winners, including 3-y-o 1m winner The Friend (by Run The Gantlet) and Smoggy (also by Run The Gantlet), a smart winner at up to 9f in France and USA; dam miler; had difficulty going early pace but ran on strongly to win 7-runner maiden race at Nottingham in September by a length from Falaka; had run well when second previously in minor event at Newmarket (finished fast when beaten neck by Aegean Beauty) and maiden race at Newbury (not so well drawn as 4-length winner Sans Blague); will stay 1¼m. *R. Armstrong.*

DISMANTLER 5 ch.g. Laser Light 118–Ballydell (Pall Mall 132) (1980 11fg **§§** 8f 12.2fg 10g 8fg 1981 12f 13.8fg) short-coupled, good-bodied gelding; modest middle-distance handicapper at his best but has become thoroughly unreliable and refused to race both starts in 1981 with result that trainer has undertaken not to run him again. *P. Wigham.*

DISTINCTION 2 br.c. Star Appeal 133–Love Resolved (Dan Cupid 132) — (1981 7g 7g 7.6s 10s) Apr 17; 5,000Y; strong, compact colt; good mover; half-brother to 3 winners, including Lingfield Derby Trial winner Riberetto (by Ribero) and fairly useful 5f and 7f winner Tribal Warrior (by Tribal Chief); dam placed over 13f in France; a good type of colt but showed little ability in maiden and minor races; bred to stay middle-distances; very coltish and gave a lot of trouble at start when withdrawn at Leicester on intended second start; trained first 3 starts by B. Hobbs; sold 1,800 gns Doncaster November Sales. *R. Boss.*

DITTON WOOD 4 b.c. Moulton 128–Fortezza 108 (Botticelli 129) (1980 **91** 12fg 13.3fg³ 12g* 13.3d 12fg² 12d² 1981 10s 12v 8g* 8fg* 9fg³ 8g² 9d³ 8v) big, strong colt; fairly useful handicapper; won at Newmarket (by short head from State Trooper in apprentice event) and Redcar (from Smackover) in May; stays 1¼m but is better at shorter distances; acts on a firm and a soft surface; suitable mount for a boy. *H. Wragg.*

DIVERS WORLD 2 b.f. Deep Diver 134–Worldling (Linacre 133) (1981 5s 5s) — May 13; IR 200F, 1,000Y; first produce; dam placed over 1¼m in Ireland; last in maiden races at Lingfield and Folkestone in October. *D. Wilson.*

DIVINE MADNESS 2 ro.c. Godswalk 130–Crash Helmet 77 (Crocket 130) **75** (1981 5s 6f 6fg 6fg³) Apr 18; IR 4,000Y; half-brother to winning sprinter Una Yappa and a winner in Italy (both by Realm); dam best at up to 1¼m; quite moderate form in minor and maiden events; may well stay 7f. *R. Armstrong.*

DIVINE TRUTH 2 b.c. So Blessed 130–False Evidence 53 (Counsel 118) — (1981 5g 6g 6g) May 9; 20,000Y; good-looking colt; good mover; brother to Irish 9f winner Truly Blest, and half-brother to numerous winners, notably very smart sprinter Melchbourne (by Forlorn River) and top-class 1974 2-y-o Cry of Truth (by Town Crier); dam placed over 1½m; favourite and pick of paddock, showed excellent speed until weakening in final furlong when 6½ lengths sixth of 11 to Prima Voce in maiden race at Sandown in July; not seen out again until October when out of first 9 in 2 maiden races at Newmarket (prominent in market both times); evidently thought better than he's shown so far. *G. Harwood.*

DIWALI 3 b.c. Great Nephew 126–Upanishad 85 (Amber Rama 133) (1980 **79** 6fg 7g 1981 8d 8.5fg³ 10d* 10.1s⁴ 10g* 12d* 12g4 12f² 12fg 10fg) well-made colt; did well in first half of season and won handicaps at Salisbury (by 5 lengths), Epsom (rallied to beat Prince Diamond a head) and Lingfield (made all and beat Navajo Brave 1½ lengths); ran moderately last 2 starts; stays 1½m; probably acts on any going; a lazy individual who needs a lot of driving. *G. Lewis.*

DIXIELANDER 3 ch.c. Son of Silver 123–Warmspun 86 (Specific 103) (1980 — 5g 7f³ 8.2g 8.2s 10d 1981 8fg 12f) leggy, narrow colt; bad plater; blinkered final start. *P. Rohan.*

D.I.Y. MOTOR STORE 5 b. or br.m. Brave Invader–Welcome Home — (Kythnos 126) (1980 NR 1981 10g 12d 10g 12fg) behind in varied company. *H. O'Neill.*

DIZZY HEIGHTS 3 b.f. Daring Display 129–Balholm 61 (Le Levanstell 122) **52** (1980 5g 5g4 5f²(dis) 7d 5.1fg 5.1fg³ 5.1fg 6fg 8fg* 10d 8.2s* 1981 7v 8g* 8f 9f 10fg³ 10f* 8d 10f 10fg 7s 10s³ 10.2g) small, lengthy filly; plater; apprentice

DLO

ridden when winning at Doncaster in May (no bid) and Nottingham in July (bought in 2,100 gns); stays 1¼m; acts on any going; blinkered twice at 2 yrs. *H. Fleming.*

D'LO 3 b.g. Sovereign Path 125–Blaskette 99 (Blast 125) (1980 7.2d 8d 1981 10s 10.1f 11g* 10f* 12fg 10f 10d) rangy, quite attractive gelding; won handicaps at Ayr and Pontefract in summer; stays 11f; acts on firm going; best in blinkers; ran moderately last 3 starts and is one to treat with caution. *J. Bethell.* **77**

DOBSON'S CHOICE 3 gr.c. Birdbrook 110–Dualvi 91 (Dual 117) (1980 7f 1981 8g⁴ 10fg 10g 8fg) tall, narrow colt; fourth behind Sally Rose in minor event at Salisbury in June, only form; stays 1m; blinkered final outing; sold 3,900 gns Newmarket Autumn Sales. *H. T. Jones.* **—**

DOCKLANDS 4 gr.f. On Your Mark 125–Persuader 118 (Petition 130) (1980 8fg 8.5f 8g 8.2g 9s⁴ 10g 1981 7s² 7d 8g* 7g 8.5g* 8.2f² 8fg* 8fg³ 10fg³ 8.2fg² 8fg³ 10g) fair sort; successful in maiden race at Thirsk in May (made most) and handicaps at Epsom in June (from Havon Cool) and Kempton in July (beat Cardinal Flower by 1½ lengths); best at up to 1m; acts on any going. *C. Brittain.* **69**

DOC MARTEN 3 b.c. Hotfoot 126–Rockney 84 (Roan Rocket 128) (1980 6g³ 5d² 6g* 5g⁴ 6fg* 7f² 5s* 7v³ 1981 7g 6g) quite useful sort; useful performer as a 2-y-o and a notably genuine and consistent one too; took the eye in paddock and ran very creditably when seventh of 13 behind Motavato in Tote European Free Handicap at Newmarket in April; struggling at halfway when seventh of 12 behind Sharp Venita in £7,900 handicap on same course in May, only subsequent start; stays 7f; acts on any going except perhaps heavy; often bandaged behind; to be trained by A. Hide in 1982. *W. O'Gorman.* **—**

DOCTOR FAUSTUS 3 gr.g. Martinmas 128–Pampatamy 75 (Immortality) (1980 5f³ 5fg 6fg 8s 1981 6fg* 7d* 6d² 8g⁴ 8f 7g 8fg 7fg) small, sturdy gelding; apprentice ridden when winning handicaps at Kempton and Warwick (in quite good style) in April; didn't run well last 4 outings (blinkered once); probably stays 1m; has won on a firm surface but has a round action and seems well suited by some give in the ground; sold 3,600 gns Newmarket Autumn Sales. *P. Cole.* **82 d**

DOCTOR PANGLOSS 2 ch.c. Sheshoon 132–Palouci 59 (Palestine 133) (1981 8d 7g) Apr 28; 13,000Y; well-made, attractive colt; good mover; brother to very useful French 1¼m winner Aberdeen Park and half-brother to a winner here and a winner abroad; dam plater; showed signs of ability in well-contested minor event at Newbury (staying-on eighth of 22 to Super Sunrise) and maiden **76 p**

Royal Yorkshire Stakes, York—Dogberry makes all and bravely holds off Fandango Time

*Old Newton Cup, Haydock—an impressive front-running
performance by Dogberry*

race at Newmarket (prominent 5f before finishing eleventh of 23 to Simply
Great) in second half of season; a good sort who will probably improve a fair bit
over 1¼m+ in 1982. *M. Stoute.*

DOCTOR SORBET 3 ch.f. Sweet Revenge 129–Beau Fleece (Fleece 114) —
(1980 6d 5s 5g 6fg 7fg 1981 10.1d 8f 8.3fg 10f) bad plater. *R. Hoad.*

DOCUMENTARY 6 b.g. Pontifex–All England 93 (St Paddy 133) (1980 NR **49**
1981 8d³ 10g 8g 8f 8f 7fg 8fg 8fg 10f 8s) slightly hollow-backed ex-Irish gelding;
poor performer; needs further than 7f and stays 13f; acts on a soft surface; ran
freely in blinkers final start. *S. Woodman.*

DOGBERRY 3 ch.c. Sassafras 135–Ombra Del Sol (Ballymoss 136) (1980 6fg **101**
6g 1981 12d² 12g⁴ 12g³ 12s* 10.5f* 12f* 13.3g 10.5f²) tall, quite well-made colt;
good walker; gave a most impressive front-running performance when beating
Lafontaine by 5 lengths in Old Newton Cup (Handicap) at Haydock in July
when apprentice ridden, going well clear 3f out and being in no danger thereafter;
had made all and responded well to strong driving when winning maiden race at
Goodwood and £4,900 event at York earlier, holding off Fandango Time by a
neck in latter; disappointed on seventh start but did nothing wrong when ½-
length second of 4 behind Kings General in Garrowby Stakes (Limited Handicap)
at York in September, making running and keeping on well; will stay 1¾m; acts
on any going but is well suited by firm; genuine. *H. Wragg.*

DOIKAS 3 b.g. Condorcet–Rullabelle (Bluerullah 115) (1980 6d 7d 7fg³ 7fg 6s **64**
1981 7d⁴ 9fg² 9g² 12.2fg⁴ 10f 8fg³ 8.2s⁴ 8g³) smallish, lengthy, rather lightly-
made gelding; quite a moderate maiden; possibly doesn't stay 1½m; wears
blinkers; ran moderately fifth start; sold 2,600 gns Newmarket Autumn Sales.
I. Walker.

DO IT NOW 2 b.g. Deep Diver 134–Pim-Pam (Acropolis 132) (1981 5v² **58**
5s⁴ 5g 5fg 6g) May 13; 3,000Y; well-grown gelding; half-brother to a winner in
Italy and a winning hurdler; in frame in early-season maiden events but is
little better than a plater. *J. Berry.*

267

Ladbroke Chester Cup—Donegal Prince wins in good style from Nation Wide

DOJUMOLA   5 b.m. Double Jump 131–Lady Molly (King's Troop 118)   (1980   —
NR   1981 16fg 12fg)   poor maiden.   *W. Storey.*

DOLLARERINA   3 b. or br.f. Sit In The Corner–Goldwis 94 (Golden Cloud)   —
(1980 5fg 6fg 6s 6fg² 7f 6g   1981 8f 7g 6fg 7g)   neat filly; poor mover; plater;
seems to stay 7f; ran poorly in blinkers final outing.   *W. Atkinson.*

DOLLAR POCKET (USA)   3 ch.g. Full Pocket–Stew Zoo (Sunrise Flight)   —
(1980 5s 5fg⁴ 5fg⁴ 5f 7d 5f 5fg³ 5fg*(dis) 6f 5d   1981 6d 6fg 6d 5g 8s 5.1fg 6fg 6g)
sturdy, compact gelding; disappointing in 1981 and showed little worthwhile
form; best at 5f on top-of-the-ground; blinkered occasionally in 1980; has run
well for an apprentice; bandaged behind fifth start; sold 1,200 gns Newmarket
Autumn Sales.   *R. Simpson.*

DOLLYFUL   3 b. or br.f. Track Spare 125–Ever Joyful (Aureole 132)   (1980 6fg   —
5fg   1981 6g 7f 8.2g 8f)   poor maiden; blinkered final start; sold 1,500 gns
Ballsbridge December Sales.   *R. Armstrong.*

DOLLYMIXTURE BOY   3 b.g. Connaught 130–Country Niece (Great Nephew   **68**
126)   (1980 6d 7g 7fg 8g 8g   1981 8d 10g² 10d 10f 10f 8fg² 8.3fg³ 8.2f⁴ 10fg
8fg³ 9f² 8.2s 7g)   small, stocky gelding; good walker and mover; second in
minor event at Brighton in May, handicap at Kempton in July and maiden race
at York in September; stays 1¼m; often blinkered, and has also worn a hood,
but has run creditably without either.   *R. Armstrong.*

DOM DONIZETTI   2 b.c. Lightning 129–Blue Sash (Baldric II 131)   (1981 8g*   **113**
8.5v* 10s)   May 5; fourth foal; half-brother to 3 minor French winners, including 1m to 1¼m winner Dom Eudes de Crepy (by Amber Rama); dam, winner of
small 1¼m race, is daughter of 1,000 Guineas and Oaks winner Never Too Late II;
trotted up by 6 lengths from Irkoust when favourite for 8-runner newcomers
race at Evry in September and landed the odds in good style by 2 lengths from
Alfred's Choice in 4-runner Prix Herbager at Maisons-Laffitte the following
month; 5/4 favourite when 7 lengths eighth of 14 to Bon Sang in Criterium de
Saint-Cloud in November; should stay 1¼m.   *F. Mathet, France.*

DONALLAN   3 gr.f. No Mercy 126–Wait Now 90 (Vimy 132)   (1980 6d 6s 8g   **42**
8.2s   1981 12s 8f 12fg 12g 9g 8fg 8fg² 7g 6fg 7f 8.2f² 7g⁴ 9d 8d³ 8d)   dipped-
backed filly; plater; stays 1m; behind in blinkers ninth start.   *T. Craig.*

268

DONATELLA 3 b.f. Arch Sculptor 123–Raglin (Ragusa 137) (1980 5f* 5fg **51**
6f² 5f* 1981 5s 5s 5g 5f 5f 7f 7fg 6fg⁴ 6f 7g) compact, rather plain filly;
didn't run up to her best in 1981 but finished fourth in handicap at Yarmouth in
August; stays 6f; acts on firm going; goes well for an apprentice; blinkered
ninth outing; sold 1,000 gns Newmarket Autumn Sales. *W. Wharton.*

DONEGAL PRINCE 5 b.g. Prince de Galles 125–Serena Rose 76 (Hethersett **109**
134) (1980 16.1d³ 8fg 12f⁴ 12fg⁴ 22.2fg² 18.4g⁴ 21fg⁴ 14.7g 14g 1981 18s²
16.1fg* 16d⁴ 18.4d* 14d⁴ 20fg³ 22.2f* 16g⁴ 21fg² 16d* 18fg³ 20s⁴ 16g³ 18g⁴)
quite attractive gelding; useful handicapper; a tough performer who won at
Haydock in April, Chester in May (beat Nation Wide by 5 lengths in Chester Cup),
Royal Ascot in June (held off Good Thyne by a head in Queen Alexandra Stakes)
and York in August (made all to beat Russian George easily); ran creditably on
most other starts, notably when length second to easy winner Ardross in Goodwood Cup in July and 3 lengths fourth to Halsbury under 10-0 in Tote Cesarewitch at Newmarket in October on final outing; needs a thorough test of stamina;
acts on any going; effective with or without blinkers; suited by a strong gallop;
suitable mount for an apprentice. *P. Kelleway.*

DONE GOOD 2 gr.g. Jolly Good 122–Donna Julia 79 (Don II 123) (1981 6g **70**
7fg 7fg 7g 7f² 7d 7d³) May 20; 1,500 2-y-o; big, lengthy gelding; good walker;
third foal; dam won over 6f at 2 yrs; short-head second of 18 behind Connaught
River in maiden race at Redcar in September, fifth start and easily best effort;
will stay 1m; best form on firm going; blinkered last 3 outings. *R. Whitaker.*

DON GIOVANNI 2 b.c. Dance In Time–Magic Flute 124 (Tudor Melody 129) **87** p
(1981 6g 7g*) Apr 29; attractive colt; half-brother to 3 winners, including very
useful middle-distance performer Lost Chord (by Busted) and very useful 7f and
1m winner Pamina (by Brigadier Gerard); dam won Cheveley Park Stakes and

Mr J. McGonagle's "Donegal Prince"

was very smart at up to 1m; 16/1, made all and ran on well to beat Northleigh by a length in 11-runner maiden race at Leicester in November; ruined chance by swerving start on debut; will be suited by 1m. *H. Cecil.*

DONNA LUISA 2 b.f. Native Bazaar 122–Imperial Miss 75 (Philip of Spain 126)   **63**
(1981 5d³ 5g³ 5v 5fg*) Jan 25; small, useful-looking filly; first foal; dam 2-y-o
5f winner; plater; sold 3,700 gns after winning 8-runner event by 2½ lengths from
Parabems at Lingfield in July (first race for 7 weeks); best form on a firm surface
and is probably unsuited by heavy going; ran poorly in blinkers third outing.
P. Cole.

DONNA'S ROSE (HOL) 3 br.f. Cadmus 124–Donna Maria (Don Carlos) (1980   —
6s 7g 8fg 9d 1981 10fg 8fg 10.8fg 10g 9g) lightly-made Dutch-bred filly; little
worthwhile form, including in sellers; should be suited by 1m. *K. Bridgwater.*

DON'T SULK (USA) 3 b.f. Graustark–Dinner Partner (Tom Fool) (1980 8d **115**
10d 7.5g 1981 12s 12s* 12f* 12.5s* 14s4) $390,000Y; French filly; sister to 2
winners, including Jim French, winner of Santa Anita Derby and second in
Kentucky Derby and Belmont Stakes, and half sister to numerous other winners,
including smart middle-distance colt Triomphe (by Hoist the Flag); dam very
useful stakes winner over 6f and 1m; won 3 of her 5 races and developed into a
smart filly; got on top in last furlong and was ridden out to beat Give Off by 2½
lengths in Group 3 Prix de Royallieu at Longchamp in October on her penultimate
start; had earlier won handicap at Chantilly and minor event at Longchamp,
latter by a nose from stable-companion Maiden's Blush who subsequently acted
as a pacemaker in the Royallieu; best form at 1½m; acts on any going; blinkered
final outing at 2 yrs. *F. Boutin, France.*

DOOBIE DO 3 b.f. Derring-Do 131–Tortola§ (Narrator 127) (1980 5g* 6g² **94**
6d² 6g 7g³ 8fg⁴ 1981 8.5fg⁴ 8.5g⁴ 7g⁴ 8fg³ 8g⁴) small, well-made filly; won
maiden event at Sandown and was second in Cherry Hinton Stakes as a 2-y-o;
rather disappointing in 1981, although was fourth in Princess Elizabeth Stakes
and NMT Ebbisham Stakes (Handicap) at Epsom, in quite valuable handicap at
Newmarket and in minor event at Doncaster; 1½ lengths last of 3 behind Vocalist
in Atalanta Stakes at Kempton on her only other start; stays 1m, but would
possibly benefit from a return to a shorter trip; acts well on a soft surface. *M.
Stoute.*

DOOGALI 7 ch.m. Doon 124–Rogali 80 (Royal Avenue 123) (1980 8d* 10g 8f **69**
11fg 11d² 11s 11fg 10.2d 1981 8.2d³ 10fg 10.2g 8g 11fg 10g⁴ 10fg³ 10f³ 8g² 11d
8.2d 8g) lengthy mare; doesn't often impress in paddock; best form at up to
11f; acts on any going; good mount for an apprentice; sometimes sweats up.
W. H. H. Williams.

DOONALLY 5 b.g. Gold Rod 129–Bust 93 (Tenerani 135) (1980 15.5fg⁴ 15.5fg⁴   —
16f³ 1981 10.6s 12g 10f) small, stocky gelding; poor maiden on flat though
has won over hurdles; has been tried in blinkers. *C. James.*

DO OR DIE 4 b.g. Warpath 113–Shenandoah 88 (Mossborough 126) (1980 12g **57**
12g 14.6fg 12s 15s 1981 12s 13d 16g*) strong, good sort; good walker; showed
improved form to win handicap at Beverley in June; not seen out again; suited
by a test of stamina. *C. Thornton.*

DORISIMO 6 b.g. Cavo Doro 124–Blessed Queen 91 (So Blessed 130) (1980   —
NR 1981 15g 13d⁴ 12d) poor middle-distance handicapper; refused to race
once in 1979. *G. Richards.*

D'ORLEANS 4 b.f. Duc D'Orleans 76–What A Performance (Gala Performance)   —
(1980 8s 8s 1981 7g) of little account. *B. Richmond.*

DOROTHY BREWIS 2 ch.f. Gulf Pearl 117–Dubarry (Quisling 117) (1981 6g)   —
Apr 8; 2,200Y; leggy, sparely-made filly; third living foal; dam won over 7f at
2 yrs in Ireland; unquoted, always struggling when 8¼ lengths ninth of 12 to
Marilena in auction event at Newcastle in July. *G. Richards.*

DOROTHY JANE 2 b.f. He Loves Me 120–Merette 63 (Runnymede 123) (1981 **47**
5g 5fg 6s 5fg⁴ 6g 6fg⁴ 7fg) Apr 13; 600Y; 1,200 2-y-o; neat filly; half-sister to
3-y-o middle-distance winner French Knot (by Take a Reef); poor plater; sold
260 gns Doncaster September Sales. *W. Storey.*

DOROTHY KATE 4 ch.f. Pee Mai 107–Aderf (Pendragon) (1980 16.1s 1981   —
12.2g) strong filly; poor maiden. *S. Norton.*

DORTIA 2 b.f. Martinmas 128–Mulattin (Henry the Seventh 125) (1981 6fg)   —
Mar 26; 40,000Y; fair sort; sister to middle-distance winner Cooks Corner and

half-sister to very smart and tough 1979 2-y-o Sonnen Gold (by Home Guard); dam never ran; unquoted, moved badly to start but showed up well for 4f before finishing last of 10 to Allocated in £4,500 race at Ascot in September. *C. Nelson.*

DOTY 4 b.c. High Top 131–Luscinia 73 (Sing Sing 134) (1980 8g² 8g 9d 10s   —
1981 9d 10f) strong, attractive colt; good walker; quite a moderate maiden at his best but has shown no form for a long time; stays 1m. *M. Bradley.*

DOUBLE ACEPOT 2 ch.c. Double Jump 131–Helen Claire (Fine Blade 121)   **68**
(1981 5fg⁴ 7f 6d⁴ 7g 8.2s³) Apr 15; 4,500Y; narrow colt; first foal; dam never ran; plater; suited by 1m; acts on soft going; has run respectably for an apprentice; sold for export to Belgium, 1,600 gns Newmarket Autumn Sales. *P. Rohan.*

DOUBLE ACTION 10 br.g. Dual 117–Irish Harp (Owenstown) (1980 NR   —
1981 16d) successful chaser; well beaten only start on flat (amateur riders). *P. K. Mitchell.*

DOUBLE BIRTHDAY 3 ch.f. Cavo Doro 124–Vision Splendid (Aureole 132)   —
(1980 NR 1981 10.2h) 2,600F, 4,000Y; half-sister to several winners, including useful stayer Gospel Truth (by Above Suspicion); dam never ran; unquoted and blinkered when behind in 16-runner maiden race won by Blue Gulf at Bath in July. *J. Hill.*

DOUBLE DISCOUNT 3 b. or br.c. Double-U-Jay 120–Quick Sort (Henry the   **68**
Seventh 125) (1980 NR 1981 7d 11.5f 8s 10d 10f⁴ 8fg 10d* 10d³) leggy, lightly-made colt; third foal; dam unraced half-sister to very smart 1¼m performer Jimsun; made much of running and rallied well when beating Embustera a head in minor event at Yarmouth in September; stays 1¼m; probably acts on any going; tends to pull hard; sold 4,700 gns Newmarket Autumn Sales. *J. Winter.*

DOUBLE FLORIN (USA) 4 b.g. His Majesty–Stamp and Cash (Roi Rouge)   **95 d**
(1980 9fg 12fg* 11.7f* 14f* 12fg² 12s 14g 16.5fg² 16f 14g 16fg² 1981 16f* 16fg⁴ 21fg 16.1d 16fg 17.4g) small gelding; good mover; fairly useful handicapper; beat Mountain Monarch by 3 lengths at Ascot in June; not disgraced in Goodwood Cup on third start; stays well; needs a sound surface; needs strong handling; ran badly towards end of season. *J. Dunlop.*

DOUBLE JET 2 ch.g. Double Jump 131–Aleta 71 (Montaval 129) (1981 5s 5g   —
7g 8s) Apr 27; workmanlike gelding; brother to a poor animal and half-brother to minor winners here and in Scandinavia; dam placed at up to 7f at 2 yrs; in rear in maiden and minor events. *Miss A. Hill-Wood.*

DOUBLE MEANING 5 gr.g. High Top 131–Pseudonym 110 (Acropolis 132)   **71**
(1980 8d 8d 8f 10fg 8g 7d 8g 8h⁴ 9f⁴ 8g* 8d 1981 8s 8g 8g 8h⁴ 9fg³ 8g) useful sort; good mover; has reportedly been pin-fired; fairly useful handicapper at his best; below form in 1981 and was well beaten in valuable seller final start; should stay beyond 9f; acts well on a sound surface; has won for an apprentice; ran appallingly third start. *A. Bailey.*

DOUBLE REVENGE 3 ch.f. Sweet Revenge 129–Dyna Bell 62 (Double Jump   —
131) (1980 NR 1981 8.2s 9d) fourth foal; half-sister to a winner in Malaya; dam won 1¼m seller; in rear in poor maiden race at Nottingham and seller at Wolverhampton. *J. Spearing.*

DOUBLE SHARP 3 gr.g. Sharp Edge 123–Florintina 104 (Floribunda 136)   —
(1980 8d² 1981 8s³ 8d 10s) tall, useful-looking gelding; not the best of movers; had stiff task and was by no means disgraced when 4½ lengths third of 6 to all-the-way winner Belloc in minor event at Leicester in March, best effort; stays 1m; blinkered final outing; sold to E. Eldin 5,800 gns Newmarket July Sales. *P. Cole.*

DOUBLE SHUFFLE 2 b.f. Tachypous 128–Ali Drake (Dicta Drake 126)   **78 p**
(1981 8g) Apr 17; 8,400Y; rangy filly; half-sister to several winners, including very useful 5f to 1m winner Crown Bowler (by Supreme Sovereign); dam lightly raced; unquoted, looked decidedly backward and green in preliminaries for 30-runner maiden race at Newmarket in October but performed pretty well, running on strongly in last 3f to finish about 10 lengths seventh to Farioffa; will stay middle distances; has scope and is the type to improve at 3 yrs. *G. Pritchard-Gordon.*

DOUBLE TOPS 3 ch.f. Paddy's Progress 113–Peg Top 93 (Star Moss 122)   —
(1980 5s 5fg 7g 8d 10s 1981 10s 10v 10s 12f) strong filly; only poor form; sold 440 gns Ascot August Sales. *D. Dale.*

271

DOUBLE VIE (FR) 2 br.f. Brigadier Gerard 144–Blondinette (Zeddaan 130) **86**
(1981 5f* 5fg³ 6fg³ 7d) May 26; 240,000 francs Y (approx £24,000); lightly-built
filly; first foal; dam third in Group 3 Prix du Gros-Chene but failed to win in
10 starts; got first run on odds-on Pleasant Dream in 7-runner maiden race at
Pontefract in July and held her off to win by a length; third afterwards in small
race at Hamilton and 11-runner nursery at Haydock, showing improved form
when beaten 2 lengths by Glossy Ibis in latter; better at 6f than 5f, and promises
to stay 7f. *Sir Mark Prescott.*

DOUBTFUL 2 br.c. Pitskelly 122–Mistrust (Rustam 127) (1981 5fg 6d 7d)
Apr 17; 14,000Y; half-brother to several winners, including useful 1971 2-y-o
5f winner Pollster (by Majority Blue); dam raced only at 2 yrs; evidently no
better than plating class; should stay 7f. *Sir Mark Prescott.*

DOUBTFUL PORTION 3 gr.g. Grey Mirage 128–Uproar 62 (Major Portion —
129) (1980 6fg⁴ 6g 6fg 1981 8d 8f) neat gelding; little worthwhile form,
including in a seller. *J. Hill.*

DOUBTWASH GIRL 3 b.f. Hot Spark 126–Arodstown Alice (Sahib 114) **69**
(1980 5f⁴ 5g 5f³ 5g 5g² 5fg* 5g³ 1981 6g 5g 6f⁴ 5fg 5f 5g* 5g) small filly; 25/1
when beating subsequently-disqualified Waresley a head in 21-runner handicap
at Catterick in October; speedy and is best at 5f. *M. W. Easterby.*

DOUKO 2 b.c. Dragonara Palace 115–Silkwood 95 (Shantung 132) (1981
6f 6fg 6fg 7g) Apr 21; 2,000F, 3,000Y; workmanlike colt; poor walker; half-
brother to several minor winners here and abroad; dam won over 5f at 2 yrs;
in rear in maiden auction event and sellers, once starting co-favourite; sold to
M. Tate 340 gns Ascot November Sales. *C. Nelson.*

DOUMAYNA 2 b.f. Kouban–Delsy (Abdos 134) (1981 5fg 6f³ 6fg) Mar 31; **79**
well-made, quite attractive filly; good walker and excellent mover; third foal;
half-sister to useful French 3-y-o middle-distance winner Dalal (by Labus);
dam useful middle-distance filly; 2½ lengths third of 15 to Swift Wing in maiden
race at Nottingham in July; beaten only 1¾ lengths when fifth of 17 to Cricket
Field in maiden event at Newbury the following month; will stay middle
distances. *F. J. Houghton.*

DOUSCHKINA 3 b.f. Dubassoff–Marbella II 64 (Match III 135) (1980 6fg* —
1981 12d 8g 11.7fg 8.2f) compact, quite useful sort; has been tubed; won minor
event at Newmarket as a 2-y-o; no worthwhile form in 1981; should be suited
by 1¼m; sold 3,600 gns Newmarket December Sales. *B. Hobbs.*

DOVER FORT 2 br.g. High Top 131–Idover 95 (Fortino II 120) (1981 7g³ **78**
7g) Feb 10; 12,000F, 10,000Y; lengthy, useful sort; half-brother to several
winners, including 5f to 7f winner Hamdani (by Welsh Pageant); dam sprinter;
33/1, prominent throughout when 1¾ lengths third of 17 to Northleigh in maiden
race at Leicester in September; made no show when 16/1 for 23-runner maiden
event won by Simply Great at Newmarket the following month (out of first 11);
will probably stay 1m. *J. Sutcliffe.*

DOVETAIL 3 br.f. Brigadier Gerard 144–Duboff 120 (So Blessed 130) (1980 **80**
7g 1981 10fg² 12fg 10fg³ 10.6v 10s*) lightly-made, quite attractive filly;
first foal; dam won 11 races, including Sun Chariot Stakes and Child Stakes;
beat Norfolk Queen in good style by 10 lengths in maiden race at Nottingham
in October; suited by 1¼m (ran badly over 1½m); probably acts on any going.
P. Walwyn.

DOWNBEAT 4 b.f. Busted 134–Land of Song 82 (Sing Sing 134) (1980 8s⁴ **61**
8g³ 8.2g³ 1981 7g³ 8g 8f 8g³ 10.1g*) unfurnished filly; narrowly won maiden
race at Windsor in August; suited by 1¼m; sweated up badly second start;
suitable mount for a boy. *W. Hastings-Bass.*

DOWN EAST 5 b.h. Tumble Wind–Finishing Touch 81 (Candy Cane 125) —
(1980 NR 1981 10.6s 10f) little sign of ability in varied company, including
selling; used 825 gns Ascot 2nd June Sales. *J. Edwards.*

DOWN THE HATCH 3 b.c. Relko 136–Swallow (Forli) (1980 6g 6fg* 7.6g **65**
1981 8.2d 10g 12fg 16.5f 16f) tall, quite attractive colt; won maiden race at
Salisbury as a 2-y-o; had stiffer tasks in 1981 and wasn't disgraced on occasions,
including in an amateur riders event; takes a strong hold and isn't certain to
stay middle distances; blinkered final start. *F. Durr.*

DOWN TO DARKIE 6 ch.g. Shantung 132–Nutting Grove 95 (Crepello 136) **61**
(1980 16fg* 16f 15f² 14f 12g 16.5g 16.1fg 1981 16s² 18fg³ 14d 14s 16g 16f 16g*
18.4fg* 16fg 16fg 14fg⁴ 12fg³ 16g 18g) staying handicapper; won at Lingfield
in June and Chester in July; acts on any going; suitable mount for a lady rider.
M. Haynes.

DOWNTOWN AGENT 4 b.f. Rheingold 137–Bundling Board (Pretense) —
(1980 10v* 10f 12d 11.7s 8fg 8fg 1981 9d 10d) big, well-made filly; in rear all
starts since winning maiden race at Salisbury early in 1980; should stay 1½m + ;
acts on heavy going. *C. Brittain.*

DOYLE'S FOLLY 2 b.f. Rheingold 137–Belida (Prince Taj 123) (1981 5g
7g 8g) Mar 23; 1,000Y; rather lightly-made filly; half-sister to a winner in
France by Ridan; dam, half-sister to Prix de l'Arc de Triomphe winner Bon
Mot III, won over 1¼m in France; beaten some way in maiden events, one of
them an auction race. *G. Fletcher.*

DRAGO 2 b.g. Dragonara Palace 115–Wax Fruit 91 (John Splendid 116) (1981   **88**
5v² 5g³ 5fg² 5g⁴ 5f* 5f* 5d² 5f* 5d⁴ 5f) May 22; 1,800F, 3,600Y; compact gelding;
first living foal; dam won twice over 6f at 2 yrs; developed into a fair performer in
the summer, winning maiden race at Catterick by 4 lengths from Bold Saracen
and auction event at Thirsk by ½ length from Pass No Remarks; will be suited by
6f; seems to act on any going; consistent; sent to Hong Kong. *W. Haigh.*

DRAGON FIRE 2 b.f. Dragonara Palace 115–Firella 56 (Firestreak 125)   **67**
(1981 5s 6f² 7f³ 6g 7g⁴ 6d) Mar 24; lightly-made filly; fourth foal; dam fourth
twice over 1m; placed in maiden race at Yarmouth in June and minor event
at Beverley in July but was subsequently well beaten in nurseries; probably
stays 7f. *H. T. Jones.*

DRAGONIGHT 4 b.g. Dragonara Palace 115–Justerina (Aureole 132) (1980   —
10v 10.8s 7fg 7f 8g 1981 8g 10.2f 7.6fg 5g) workmanlike gelding; little
worthwhile form in varied company, including selling; blinkered last 3 starts;
sold out of J. Hardy's stable 1,050 gns Doncaster January Sales (81). *R. Ward.*

DRAGONIST 3 b.f. Dragonara Palace 115–Tzu-Hsi 66 (Songedor 116) (1980   **73**
5g⁴ 5fg² 5s* 5g⁴ 5d* 6d⁴ 5fg⁴ 5s⁴ 1981 6g² 5g² 6s 6fg 6fg 6fg 5.8g* 5s 5d) tall,
quite well-made filly; sprint handicapper; beat Roger Bacon a neck at Bath in
September; probably acts on any going but is ideally suited by some give
in the ground. *J. Bethell.*

DRAGON PALACE (USA) 3 ch.c. Le Fabuleux 133–Barbara Longhi (Ribot   **96**
142) (1980 7f 8g* 10.2s 1981 10.6d 12s 11.7f 16fg* 16fg² 14fg* 14g² 14.6fg³
16g³) compact colt; won handicaps at Lingfield (trotted up) and Goodwood
(well-contested event) in July, on latter course quickening really well to challenge
at distance and beat Centroline by ¾ length; placed behind Centroline in Melrose
Handicap at York in August and Rockingham Handicap at Doncaster in
September, in latter finishing well into third after being held up and having a
poorish run; sweating and never really in contention when 7 lengths third to
Alma Ata in handicap at Newmarket later in September on final outing; suited
by a test of stamina; probably needs a sound surface. *M. Jarvis.*

DRAGON STEED 3 gr.c. Northfields–Etoile Grise 77 (Sea Hawk II 131)   **90**
(1980 NR 1981 10d⁴ 10.5s 10fg² 12fg*) 74,000Y; strong colt; first foal;
dam, placed over 13f, is half-sister to Irish 2,000 Guineas winner Northern Treasure
(by Northfields); not seen out after beating Regain a neck (pair 8 lengths clear)
in maiden race at Lingfield in July; in frame earlier in White Rose Stakes at
Ascot and minor event at Nottingham; suited by 1½m; acts on a firm surface;
burst out of stalls on intended first appearance; sent to Australia. *M. Jarvis.*

DRAGUNN 2 ch.g. Dragonara Palace 115–Maria Bicknell (Jolly Jet 111)   **83**
(1981 5fg* 5d⁴ 5g⁴ 5f³ 5f 5d 6s) May 2; 3,800Y; rather sparely-made gelding;
first foal; dam poor sister to very useful sprinter Jolly Me; won 9-runner maiden
race at Haydock in April by a head from Crown, the pair 5 lengths clear; in
frame in well-contested events in the North subsequently; should be well suited
by 6f; off course nearly 3 months after fourth outing and had stiff tasks in
nurseries on his return. *R. Hollinshead.*

DRAKE'S LADY 3 b.f. Pieces of Eight 128–Bally Tudor 75 (Henry the Seventh   —
125) (1980 NR 1981 8f 12fg 10.6v 12.2g) fair sort; first foal; dam won
3 times over 1¼m; well beaten in maiden and minor events in the North; refused
to enter stalls twice earlier; sold to W. Clay 460 gns Doncaster October Sales.
M. Camacho.

DRAMA (USA) 3 ch.f. Sir Ivor 135–Drury Nell (Bold Lad, Ire 133) (1980   **84**
NR 1981 7fg 6s* 8v 6fg) $130,000Y; tall, attractive, full-quartered filly;
closely related to 1981 2-y-o stakes winner Taylor Park (by Sir Gaylord); dam
half-sister to Typhoon and outstanding broodmare Moment of Truth; none too
well away when beating Gods Mark by ¾ length in 7-runner Greenlands Stakes

at the Curragh in May; behind in Goffs Irish 1,000 Guineas on same course later in month (last of 15) and Matt Gallagher Sprint Stakes at Phoenix Park in July; should stay 1m. *V. O'Brien, Ireland.*

DRAS LASS 5 bl.m. Don Carlos–Lantern (Relic) (1980 8fg 8s² 8.2d 8g 10.6s 8s 8s 1981 8.2f 8.2d 12f) lightly-made mare; has shown no form for a long time; stays 1¼m; seems to act on any going; blinkered once in 1980; sold privately 1,300 gns Doncaster November Sales. *D. Yeoman.*

DRAW THE LINE 2 b.g. High Line 125–Minibus 77 (John Splendid 116) — (1981 5g 6g 7g) Apr 6; 3,200F, 8,000Y; leggy, close-coupled gelding; first foal; dam won over 6f at 3 yrs; plating-class maiden; will stay 1¼m. *G. Richards.*

DREAMING AWAY (USA) 2 ch.f. Sir Ivor 135–Northern Gem 121 (Northern 92 Dancer) (1981 6fg 7d³ 8fg² 8fg) strong, well-made, attractive filly; very good mover; third foal; half-sister to fairly useful 3-y-o 9f and 1¼m winner Government Program and useful miler World Affair (both by Secretariat); dam won Fred Darling Stakes and was second in Champion Stakes; ran well in good-class races, including when ½-length second of 15 to Rockfest in £3,600 event at Goodwood in September and when 6¼ lengths sixth of 8 to Height of Fashion (gave 9 lb) in Hoover Fillies Mile at Ascot later in month; will stay 1¼m+; a most taking individual who is sure to win a race at 3 yrs. *I. Balding.*

DRED SCOTT (USA) 9 b.g. Tom Rolfe–Free Model (Phideas) (1980 18d — 12.2v 16s 8g 12g 12g 1981 13fg 8fg 10fg 8fg 12fg 16d 11.5fg 10f⁴ 12f) poor handicapper nowadays; stays 1¾m; acts on any going; usually wears blinkers; trained part of season by Mrs A. Finch. *C. Wildman.*

DRESSEDTOKILL 3 b.f. Sharpen Up 127–Boudoir 95 (Klairon 131) (1980 68 5fg³ 5fg* 1981 7d 5.1f 6fg) leggy, narrow filly; won maiden race at Leicester in 1980; didn't recapture her form, but wasn't disgraced under a stiffish weight on second outing; didn't impress in paddock final start (July). *B. Hobbs.*

DRILL 4 gr.f. No Mercy 126–Geology 74 (Rockavon 120) (1980 7f⁴ 7f 8s 6g 6s⁴ — 1981 7d 8.3s 10d) lengthy filly; plater nowadays; probably stays 7f; best form on a sound surface; has worn blinkers; sold 490 gns Ascot October Sales. *J. Jenkins.*

DRINK DEEP 3 ch.g. Record Run 127–Penny Wise (Hook Money 124) — (1980 5d 5s 7g 6fg 1981 10fg) leggy, lengthy gelding; little sign of ability, including in sellers. *W. Wharton.*

DRIVE YOU HOME (USA) 2 gr.c. Hempen–Swerving Mammy (Swerve) 76 (1981 6fg³ 5g³) $32,000Y; plain, workmanlike colt; excellent mover; brother to 2 minor winners in USA; dam, winner over 5f and 6f, is sister to very smart Rushing Man; managed to lead 2f out in maiden race at Newmarket in June, despite having lost ground by swerving at start, but found his exertions telling in closing stages and faded to finish third of 20, 3½ lengths behind Pamperdale; odds on when 6 lengths third of 7 in small race won by Cyril's Choice at Ayr the following month, only subsequent start; possibly needs 6f. *J. Hindley.*

DROMOLAND CASTLE 2 b.c. Joshua 129–Westmead Lady 60 (King's Troop 68 118) (1981 5s 5.8g 7fg 8g 8s³ 8.2s² 8d) May 1; lightly-made colt; second reported foal; dam plater; plater; evidently suited by 1m and soft going. *J. Spearing.*

DROPSHOT 6 br.g. Town Crier 119–Lunawood 71 (Blast 125) (1980 12f — 1981 16g³ 16.1f 19fg 16.5f²) inconsistent plater; suited by a test of stamina; acts on firm going; has been tried in blinkers. *G. Balding.*

DR STEVE 3 ch.c. Wishing Star 117–Tabankula (Selko) (1980 5fg 6fg 6g 84 6g 6g³ 7fg³ 1981 7fg 8g³ 8g* 8g* 10.2g³ 10g 8d² 9f³ 8g² 8s² 10.6s) workmanlike colt; won maiden race at Stockton and handicap at Pontefract, beating Ring of Quality 4 lengths on latter course in May; placed in varied company subsequently, on last occasion in an amateur riders event; stays 1¼m; acts on any going; sold to Mrs N. Smith 6,000 gns Newmarket Autumn Sales. *R. Sheather.*

DRUMCROON 2 br.c. Crooner 119–Cuddly Toy (Sovereign Lord 120) (1981 — 5g 5f 6g 7.6s 6g) Apr 4; neat colt; has a sharp action; half-brother to 5f to 11f winner Keira (by Keren); dam of little account; in rear in maiden races but showed up for 2f penultimate start. *P. K. Mitchell.*

DRUMMER JESS 3 b.f. Rapid River 127–Jet Princess (Jolly Jet 111) (1980 54 5g 5.8fg 5g⁴ 5s 5g 5f 5f 5d 1981 7f 5fg 6fg* 6g*) leggy, lengthy, lightly-made filly; not a good mover; won apprentice seller at Windsor (sold out of J. Bosley's stable, 1,750 gns) and seller at Yarmouth (bought in 1,600 gns) in July; stays 6f; acts on a firm surface. *B. Hanbury.*

DRUMMOND STREET 2 ch.c. Ragstone 128–Scottish Lullaby 92 (Aberdeen —
109) (1981 8.2d 8s 8.2d) Mar 17; 6,200Y; lengthy colt; half-brother to a
minor winner; dam won at up to 7f; little worthwhile form. *A. Jarvis.*

DUBASSOFF MAID 2 br.f. Dubassoff–Fahal Saya (Stupendous) (1981 6g 6d) —
May 3; first foal; dam of little account; unquoted when behind in maiden race at
Lingfield in September and minor event at Brighton (last of 15) in October.
M. Masson.

DUBJO 2 br.c. Steel Heart 128–Fairly Flattered 73 (Pall Mall 132) (1981 6d   **84** p
6g*) Feb 8; 45,000Y; half-brother to fairly useful 1980 Irish 2-y-o Personal
Guard (by Home Guard) and 3 winners, including quite useful 1974 Irish 2-y-o
Kogiku (by Lord Gayle), successful at up to 7.5f; dam won at up to 1¼m; kept
on when winning 17-runner maiden race at Navan in September by 2 lengths from
Truculent Scholar; will be suited by 7f and 1m; probably still has improvement
in him. *D. Weld, Ireland.*

DUCHESS OF HOWFEN 3 b. or br.f. Steel Heart 128–Ballymaglasson —
(Ballyciptic 122) (1980 5f 7g 8fg 7d⁴ 1981 12.2fg 12.2fg 11f 12.3fg 10fg 12d 12d)
small filly; plater; stays 11f; sold 4,400 gns Newmarket December Sales. *K.
Stapleton.*

DUCK SOUP 3 b.f. Decoy Boy 129–Coup 106 (Hook Money 124) (1980 NR   **55**
1981 7.2f* 8fg 8fg) 6,800Y; compact filly; sister to 6f winner Quiet Touch,
and half-sister to 2 winners, including useful 7f performer Banco (by Shoolerville);
dam middle-distance stayer; battled on well when beating My Louise ½ length in
maiden race at Haydock Park in July; had stiffish tasks in handicaps afterwards;
stays 7f; acts on firm going; sold 1,100 gns Newmarket Autumn Sales. *J. Toller.*

DUDLEY WOOD (USA) 2 ro.g. One For All–Aglimmer (Grey Dawn II 132)   **100** p
(1981 7g 8g 8g*) Apr 15; $25,000F, 20,000 gns Y; attractive gelding; fourth foal;
brother to Arctic Service, a winner up to 9f in USA; dam very smart winner of
13 races up to 9 furlongs in USA; 33/1, showed much improved form when blinkered for 27-runner minor event at Newmarket in October, quickening up well,
after being held up, to beat Corked a shade comfortably by 2 lengths; will stay
middle distances; a taking individual who should make a useful 3-y-o. *J.
Hindley.*

DUGALD 4 b.g. Six O'Clock–Toys (Sammy Davis 129) (1980 12.2g 12.2g —
10f² 10fg 12.5s⁴ 1981 12s) useful sort; poor maiden; best run at 1¼m on
firm going. *J. Fitzgerald.*

DUKEDOM 4 ch.c. Connaught 130–Albany 120 (Pall Mall 132) (1980 8f³   **105** d
10fg* 10.5f 12g 12fg² 12v 1981 10d 10fg 10fg 10g 12d 12g) strong, deep-bodied
colt; has been hobdayed and has had a soft palate operation; smart performer at
3 yrs; put up best efforts in 1981 on second and third starts when 7 lengths sixth
to Hard Fought in Prince of Wales's Stakes at Royal Ascot and just under 7
lengths fifth to Galveston in valuable handicap at Sandown in July; stays 1½m;
acts well on firm ground and is probably unsuited by soft; disappointing. *I.
Balding.*

DUKE OF BRITTANY 3 gr.c. Saritamer 130–Belle Bretonne 90 (Celtic Ash) —
(1980 5.8fg 6fg 5.8g 7d 8g 8d⁴ 7d 10s⁴ 1981 12s 12s 12d 12g³) compact colt;
quite a moderate maiden; will stay beyond 1½m; probably needs some give in
the ground. *S. Woodman.*

DUKES GOLD 4 b.g. Goldhill 125–Tuwin (Tudor Treasure 119) (1980 9.4fg —
8.2s 1981 12.5s) poor maiden. *G. Richards.*

DUKE'S HEIR 2 gr.g. Saritamer 130–La Pitore (Will Somers 114§) (1981   **68**
6f³ 6d 6fg⁴ 7g 7g) May 27; 2,600F, 400Y; useful-looking gelding; turns hind
feet in; half-brother to 3 winners, including fairly useful 1973 2-y-o 6f winner
Lapis (by Bold Lad, Ire); dam, half-sister to very smart Tacitus, won over 1m
and 9f in Ireland; in frame in sellers at Ripon and Kempton in August; should
be suited by 7f; acts on a firm surface. *W. Musson.*

DULLINGHAM LAD 3 gr.g. Saulingo 122–Ambient 68 (Amber Rama 133)   **65**
(1980 5d⁴ 6s⁴ 1981 6fg³ 6g 7.6g 7f 6f) lengthy, dipped-backed gelding; soundly
beaten in maiden events and handicaps after finishing 2½ lengths third to Barwin
in maiden race at Nottingham in April; stays 6f; started slowly and ran wide
second outing at 2 yrs. *H. Collingridge.*

DUMPLING 3 ch.g. Warpath 113–Pie (So Blessed 130) (1980 NR 1981 10.2g —
10fg) rangy gelding; second foal; dam, a twin, never ran; needed race when
behind in minor event at Doncaster in May; pulled up lame at Nottingham the
following month and was reported dead shortly afterwards; raced with his tongue
tied down. *C. Thornton.*

DUNGEON GHYL 3 ch.f. Roman Warrior 132–Birdcage 78 (Manacle 123) **73** (1980 5d 5g⁴ 6f 1981 5.8g* 6d 5fg² 5.8f³ 5fg*) big, well-made filly; won handicaps at Bath in May and Salisbury in September, latter in good style from Quae Supra; needs a strongly-run race at 5f and will probably stay 7f; acts well on fast ground. *D. Gandolfo.*

DUNHAM PARK 4 b.g. Manacle 123–Sweet Reproach 94 (Relic) (1980 7d **71** 8fg² 8.2s⁴ 8s 10.2v 1981 8g² 8g⁴ 8fg⁴ 8f² 8g² 8f⁴ 8g² 8f 8.2fg⁴ 7.2v* 7s) tall, useful sort; won handicap at Haydock in August; stays 1m; acts on any going; blinkered twice at 2 yrs; sometimes sweats up; doesn't always look too keen; to be trained by J. Fitzgerald. *P. Rohan.*

DUNNO THEN 3 b.g. Coronash 74–Hot Curry (Sayajirao 132) (1980 NR **—** 1981 12fg) compact gelding; half-brother to 1973 2-y-o 6f winner Indian Captive (by Manacle) and 1¼m winner Dunno (by Dionisio); dam unraced daughter of winner of 3 Indian classics; tailed off in gentleman riders event won by Devil Rock at Kempton in September. *N. Mitchell.*

DUNPHY 3 b.c. Riverman 131–Dourdan (Prudent II 133) (1980 8fg* 8d* **120** 8d³ 1981 9.7fg² 10.5s³ 9g² 9s* 10f⁴) French colt; fifth foal; half-brother to 4 winners, including very useful middle-distance performer Doux Lord (by Sir Gaylord); dam a useful performer, winner of 10.5f Prix Cleopatre, is daughter of top-class Denisy; one of the best colts of his age in France in 1980, winner of a newcomers event at Evry and Prix des Chenes at Longchamp; gained sole success of 1981 when beating Big John by ½ length in Group 3 Prix Daphnis at Longchamp in July; didn't run up to his best when 6¼ lengths fourth of 6 behind Al Nasr (Fr) in Prix de la Cote Normande at Deauville the following month on only subsequent outing; placed earlier in year in Prix de Guiche at Longchamp (short-head second to Silky Baby), Prix Lupin on same course (blinkered when 4½ lengths third to No Lute) and Prix Jean Prat at Chantilly (length second to Cresta Rider); would probably have stayed 1½m; possibly not at his best on very firm going, but acted on any other; syndicated at IR £28,000 and is to stand at Ballykisteen Stud, Co. Tipperary. *Mme C. Head, France.*

DUNSYRE 3 b. or br.f. Lorenzaccio 130–Black Fire 92 (Firestreak 125) (1980 **53** NR 1981 8g 12.2g⁴ 10d³ 12d 12g) small filly; second foal; dam middle-distance handicapper; in frame in maiden race at Catterick and moderately-contested minor event at Ayr; stays 1½m; sold 1,050 gns Newmarket Autumn Sales. *J. W. Watts.*

DURANDAL 4 br.c. Bay Express 132–High Ransom 88 (High Treason 126) **91 d** (1980 5fg³ 5f 6fg⁴ 6g 6d 5fg 1981 6fg 5g 6d⁴ 6g 5f 5fg 5g 5fg² 5fg 5.3f 5f 5g 5s 6d) strong, good sort; excellent mover; sprint handicapper; creditable 1¼ lengths second to Sayyaf in 4-runner Rous Memorial Stakes at Ascot in July; suited by 6f; acts on a firm and a soft surface; sometimes blinkered; trained part of season by D. Marks. *W. Haigh.*

DUREL 3 b.c. Reliance II 137–Dugo 90 (Dumbarnie 125) (1980 NR 1981 **—** 8f 5f 6v) compact, workmanlike colt; half-brother to numerous winners, including high-class sprinter Abergwaun (by Bounteous); dam best at around 7f; in rear in minor events at Thirsk, Redcar and York. *P. Calver.*

DURUN 2 b.f. Run The Gantlet–Duboff 120 (So Blessed 130) (1981 5f 7fg 7h³ **67** 8s⁴) May 11; small, well-made, quite attractive filly; good mover; second foal; half-sister to 3-y-o 1¼m winner Dovetail (by Brigadier Gerard); dam won 11 races, including Sun Chariot Stakes and Child Stakes; beaten at least 6 lengths when in frame in maiden race at Chepstow and nursery at Wolverhampton; bred to stay 1¼m+. *H. Candy.*

DUSTY FARLOW 2 b.g. Jukebox 120–Reelin Bridge (New Day) (1981 5s **78** 5s 6d 6g) Feb 8; IR 9,000F, 9,200Y; brother to 3 winners, including very useful Irish sprinter Reelin Jig; dam Irish 1½m winner; finished first on far side of course when fifth, beaten about 4 lengths, to Perang Tejam in 26-runner maiden race at Doncaster in November; stays 6f; blinkered third start; sold only 1,050 gns Ascot December Sales. *R. Boss.*

DUSTY ISLES 3 gr.g. Saritamer 130–Scilly Isles 54 (Silly Season 127) (1980 **66** NR 1981 9d² 8g 7g³ 9.4g² 10 2d 8fg 8f² 8d 12s) 1,550Y; leggy gelding; half-brother to 2 winning jumpers; dam half-sister to smart miler Murrayfield; placed in newcomers race at Wolverhampton and maiden races at Lingfield, Carlisle and Thirsk; stays 9f; ran moderately fifth and last 2 starts; blinkered eighth outing. *M. McCormack.*

DUSTY PATH 3 gr.g. Warpath 113–The Squeeze 85 (Bing II) (1980 7f 7fg **61** 7g 8s⁴ 7f 8s 1981 8d 12.5fg 12.2fg 13g² 12f² 10fg 12.2fg 12.3g 15.5g 16s 13.8g

12s) workmanlike gelding; placed in maiden events at Ayr and Beverley in summer but was beaten in a selling handicap once afterwards; stays 13f; often wears blinkers (didn't at Beverley). *W. Bentley.*

DUTCH GIRL 4 b.f. Workboy 123–Dutch Gold 117 (Goldhill 125) (1980 8f **78**
5f* 6f 5h3 5f4 5fg* 5fg2 5fg2 5.6fg2 5d4 5fg 5d 1981 6g4 5fg 6f4 5fg* 5f* 5g2
5f3 5d 5f 5fg* 5g 5g4) compact filly; sprint handicapper; successful at Wolverhampton, Ripon and Redcar; beat Zoilo by ½ length on last-named in September;
best at 5f; ideally suited by fast ground; suitable mount for a boy. *M. W.
Easterby.*

DUTCH PRINCESS 3 b.f. Royalty 130–Miss Wilhemina 84 (Quorum 126) **70**
(1980 NR 1981 10s4 10fg 12g 12s2 15.5s2) workmanlike filly; second foal;
dam won over 1m; second in £2,000 race at Lingfield and maiden event at
Folkestone in October; stays 2m; seems suited by some give in the ground.
Miss A. Sinclair.

DUTCH ROMANTIC 2 ch.c. Tachypous 128–Top Line 99 (Saint Crespin III —
132) (1981 6g 7g 6s4 7g) Feb 4; 10,000Y; well-made colt; quite a good mover;
half-brother to 1½m seller winner Fealar (by Silly Season) and a winning hurdler;
dam won at 1m and 1½m and is daughter of smart Reel In; showed a little ability
when fourth of 15 to Risk Taker in maiden race at Newbury in October; should
stay 7f+. *W. Wightman.*

DUTCH TREAT 8 b.h. Le Levanstell 122–Northern Beauty (Borealis) (1980 **72**
12d 12s 12g3 12f 12fg3 12g* 1981 12g4 14s 11.1s 12g) middle-distance
handicapper; acts on any going but has done nearly all his winning on an easy
surface. *R. Price.*

DUTY WATCH 2 ch.f. Import 127–Radar Girl 75 (Bleep-Bleep 134) (1981 —
5fg 5f 5fg 6g 5f 5d) Apr 22; sturdy filly; first foal; dam won over hurdles;
plating-class sprint maiden. *W. C. Watts.*

DWIGHT 2 b.c. Reform 132–Limerick Queen (Whistling Wind 123) (1981 5d) —
May 22; rangy, fair sort; fourth foal; half-brother to 3-y-o 1m winner Irish
Sparkle (by Sparkler) and fairly useful 1979 2-y-o 5f performer Charles Street
(by Huntercombe); dam never ran; 14/1 and on burly side, moved poorly to
start and finished tailed off in 15-runner maiden race won by Avonmore Wind at
Wolverhampton in October. *R. Akehurst.*

DYK-A-TAK 6 ch.g. Dike–Takawin 109 (Takawalk II 125) (1980 12f2 12fg2 **43**
10.7g2 10s3 10d* 10s 12fg 10g3 10fg2 10g 10d 10fg 1981 12.2fg2 12d 10fg 10f4)
middle-distance handicapper; acts on any going; wears blinkers; good mount for
an inexperienced rider; sold 4,300 gns Ascot 2nd June Sales. *J. Benstead.*

DYNABOY 3 b.c. Jukebox 120–Wood Grouse 56 (Celtic Ash) (1980 6g2 6s 1981 —
8fg 8d) lengthy colt; second to Composer in maiden race at Newmarket as
a 2-y-o; not disgraced when fifth of 16 behind Sharp End in similar race at
Salisbury in September on reappearance but seemed to drop himself out when
remote fifth of 6 behind Melodrama in £3,000 event at Newbury later in month;
probably stays 1m; bandaged near-fore both starts at 2 yrs; sold to W. Wharton
1,150 gns Ascot October Sales. *J. Dunlop.*

E

EAGLE BOY 5 ch.g. Huntercombe 133–Island Princess (Raise A Native) —
(1980 7f 6fg3 6fg3 7g 6fg 6fg4 7f* 6fg2 6s 6g4 6g* 6s3 7s 6d 1981 5d 6g) compact,
rather lightly-made gelding; fairly useful handicapper at his best; needed run both
starts in 1981; stays 7f; acts on any going; suitable mount for an apprentice;
sometimes sweats up. *W. Bentley.*

EAGLE ISLAND 6 b. or br.g. Tower Walk 130–Musaka (Guard's Tie 131) **65**
(1980 NR 1981 9g 9d 6g 10.2fg 10f 10f 10fg2 10g4 10f4 11fg* 12d 11d4) strong,
compact ex-Irish gelding; has been fired; middle-distance handicapper; won
at Redcar in September; stays 11f; seems to act on any going; usually bandaged
near-fore. *P. Calver.*

EAGLES DAUGHTER 2 b.f. Legal Eagle 126–Doonella (Doon 124) (1981 —
5d 5fg 5g 6g 7g) Apr 4; small filly; first foal; dam of no account; well behind
in maiden and minor events; sold 350 gns Ascot December Sales. *W. Charles.*

EAGLESFIELD 4 ch.c. Mountain Call 125–Rubella (Buisson Ardent 129) **80**
(1980 5fg 5d3 6g 5g2 5s* 5.3fg* 5fg4 5f 6s 1981 6fg4 6g 6g* 6fg3 6fg 6fg) good
mover; sprint handicapper; beat Mott The Hoople by 5 lengths at Hamilton
in June; stays 6f; probably acts on any going; blinkered second start. *C. Nelson.*

EAGLE'S QUEST 3 b.f. Legal Eagle 126–My Cervantes (Hill Clown or Nulli   **62**
Secundus 89) (1980 5g 5g 1981 6fg 6g 5g² 5f 5fg² 5f² 6f⁴ 5fg* 6f⁴) leggy,
unfurnished filly; good second 3 times before winning maiden race at Warwick
in August; stays 6f; unseated her apprentice rider after start on reappearance;
dwelt on fourth start. *J. Holt.*

EARL'S COURT 5 ch.h. Lord Gayle 124–Paddy's Rose 81 (St Chad 120)   **62**
(1980 10fg³ 9g 10.6d 9f 10fg⁴ 12.3d² 12d* 13.8d 12d 1981 12f 12f² 12.3fg 11d
10.6d³ 12.3s² 16.1fg 12v³ 13s* 12d³) small horse; poor handicapper; made all
at Nottingham in October; stays 13f; acts on any going but goes well on soft;
suitable mount for a boy; suited by front-running tactics; genuine. *C. Crossley.*

EARLY TUDOR 6 b.m. Royalty 130–Early Rose 61 (Will Somers 114§)   **—**
(1980 NR 1981 8fg⁴) poor performer; suited by 1m; acts on hard going;
good mount for an apprentice. *T. Hallett.*

EASILY 2 br.f. Swing Easy 126–Fearless 77 (Derring-Do 131) (1981 5.8h³)   **— p**
Mar 5; sister to 7f and 1m winner Gibbon; dam, winner at 7f, is half-sister to
More Light and Shoot A Line; eased from 11/10 to 5/2 prior to finishing 8¼
lengths third of 7 to Wish 'n' Time in weakly-contested maiden race at Bath in
July, only outing. *R. Hern.*

EAST COAST GIRL 2 ch.f. Relko 136–Starboard Belle 85 (Right Tack 131)   **—**
(1981 5v 5fg 5s 6f 8fg 7.2f 7f 7fg 7d 7f 10d) Apr 10; 1,000Y; lightly-made
filly; sister to a poor animal; dam won over 6f and 7f at 2 yrs; poor plater;
blinkered final start. *J. Gilbert.*

EASTER CANDLE 5 b. or br.m. So Blessed 130–Palmitin 68 (Crepello 136)   **—**
(1980 8s 10fg 10fg 8fg 11.7f 13.1h 1981 12.2fg 15.8g 18.8fg) quite well-made
mare; winning hurdler but is only poor handicapper on flat; has worn blinkers
and bandages. *J. Edmunds.*

EASTERLY WIND 3 b.f. Windjammer (USA)–Lucky Plum (Lucky Guy 121)   **86**
(1980 5g³ 7s³ 6g* 6fg* 6f 1981 6g* 6g³ 6g⁴ 7g 6f 6s) lengthy, good sort; won
handicap at Haydock in April in good style by 4 lengths from Kathred; ran
moderately last 3 starts; stays 7f; probably unsuited by very firm going but seems
to act on any other; sweated up fifth start. *C. Nelson.*

EASTERN AIR 3 ch.f. Levanter 121–Wheal Harmony (Song 132) (1980   **82**
5.8g⁴ 6g 7fg 6g 1981 10.2g² 10d² 12f* 12f² 13.1h* 12d² 13.1h) useful sort;
walks well; made all in maiden race at Brighton in June (apprentice ridden) and
handicap at Bath in July (beat Brave The Reef 2 lengths); second on 4 other
starts, but ran moderately final start; will stay at least 1¾m; probably acts on any
going. *H. Candy.*

EASTERN PALACE 7 gr.g. Habitat 154–Al Burak 103 (Silver Shark 129)   **—**
(1980 8fg 10fg 10fg 10.6g 12d 8fg 8g 10g⁴ 12f 1981 8g 10d 17.1d) lengthy
gelding; has shown no form for a long time; stays 1¼m; needs top-of-the-ground;
best in blinkers; suitable mount for an apprentice; often starts slowly nowadays.
G. Beeson.

EASTERN SHORE 2 ch.f. Sun Prince 128–Land Ho (Primera 131) (1981 7g)   **— p**
Apr 1; attractive filly; sister to French 3-y-o 1m to 10.5f winner Bright Landing,
and half-sister to 3 winners, including very useful 1976 2-y-o 5f winner Easy
Landing (by Swing Easy); dam daughter of very smart sprinter Lucasland;
33/1, wasn't punished unduly when ninth of 29 to Chalon in maiden race at
Newmarket in October; will be suited by 1m; wore a brush-pricker on near-side
of her bridle at Newmarket. *J. Tree.*

EASTERN VALLEY 2 b.c. Mansingh 120–Wolver Valley 72 (Wolver Hollow   **—**
126) (1981 6g 7f) Feb 16; fair sort; second foal; dam won 5 middle-distance
races; in need of the outing when behind in maiden events at Doncaster and
Redcar in September. *Miss S. Hall.*

EASTER SUN 4 b.c. Bustino 136–Magical 95 (Aggressor 130) (1980 10fg   **106**
10f* 10fg² 10g² 10g³ 9f 8s⁴ 1981 10g* 10d* 10.5g 10g² 9d² 10.2g² 9g⁴) compact,
useful sort; very useful handicapper; successful at Newmarket in May (by 4
lengths from Funny Spring) and Epsom in June; held off One Fleet Street
by a head in Daily Mirror Handicap on latter; in frame afterwards in valuable
races at Goodwood, York, Doncaster and Newmarket; about 4 lengths fourth to
Braughing in William Hill Cambridgeshire on last-named in October; stays 1¼m;
appears to act on any going but goes well on fast ground; consistent. *M. Jarvis.*

EAST MEON 2 b.g. Gulf Pearl 117–Palgal (Le Prince 98) (1981 6g 7fg 7fg 7g   **—**
8d) Apr 29; IR 1,600Y, 5,200Y; quite attractive gelding; brother to a winner
in Italy and half-brother to 3 other winners here and abroad, including 1980

2-y-o 5f winner Royal Bid (by Auction Ring); dam won at up to 1½m in Ireland; seems little better than plating class but may need a thorough test of stamina; blinkered fourth and fifth outings. *J. Douglas-Home.*

EAST PLAISTOW 7 b.g. Manacle 123–Silver Comb (Silver Cloud 121) (1980 — raced abroad 1981 12.5s 12g 12g) won 2 races in Sweden and one in Belgium in 1980; soundly beaten in handicaps in 1981; suited by 1m and 9f and forcing tactics; best form on a soft surface; used to be blinkered; dead. *G. Lockerbie.*

EASY MAUD 2 ch.f. Swing Easy 126–Maud 87 (Vilmorin) (1981 6fg³ 6fg² 6g²) **54** May 7; lengthy, lightly-made filly; half-sister to 2 minor winners; dam won over 6f, and is sister to smart sprinter Scandale; runner-up in sellers at Nottingham and Lingfield in June; claimed £3,000 after being beaten short head by Anywhichwayyoucan on latter; stays 6f. *Mrs J. Reavey.*

EASY PITCH 2 b. or br.f. Wollow 132–Misalliance 87 (Royal Palace 131) — (1981 7g) Apr 4; small filly; first foal; dam suited by a test of stamina; 8/1, always struggling after starting none too well when behind in 16-runner maiden race won by Clymene at Leicester in October; sold 500 gns Newmarket Autumn Sales. *J. Tree.*

EBONY GUARD 2 bl.f. Home Guard 129–Bouboulina (Hornbeam 130) (1981 — 6s 7d) May 12; 550Y; big, rangy filly; half-sister to 1¼m seller winner Andalucia (by Rheingold) and a winner in Malaya; dam reportedly won in Greece; unquoted when well beaten in maiden events at Haydock in June (far from fully wound up) and Yarmouth in September. *A. Jarvis.*

EBONY HILL 3 br.f. Bronze Hill 96–Sweet Electra (Straight Cut 103) (1980 — NR 1981 8f 11f) first foal; dam never ran; tailed off in minor event at Stockton (last of 14) and maiden race at Hamilton (sixteenth of 17) in summer; trained by Mrs S. Chesmore first outing. *R. Allan.*

EBORACUM 3 ch.g. Sheshoon 132–Swift Fire 85 (Firestreak 125) (1980 NR — 1981 7fg 8fg 12f 12f 15.5h 16.5g 13.8g 16s) 520Y; resold 1,200Y; plain gelding; second living foal; dam won over 5f at 2 yrs; poor form in varied company, including selling; trained part of season by Hbt Jones. *W. Bentley.*

ECCHINSWELL OAK 4 gr.c. Sharp Edge 123–Lutescens (Skymaster 126) **53 d** (1980 6fg 6fg⁴ 7g 6g* 7f³ 8d² 7fg 8.2d² 8f⁴ 8.2s⁴ 8g³ 1981 8s 8.2s* 8g 9g³ 8d 8fg) neat colt; plater; bought in 3,800 gns after winning at Hamilton in April; stays 9f; acts on any going; good mount for an inexperienced rider. *N. Guest.*

ECONOMY PEP 5 ch.m. Jimmy Reppin 131–Pepperita 79 (Nelcius 133) — (1980 10g 14.6fg 16s 12f 16fg 1981 16g) big, strong mare; poor stayer nowadays; seems to act on any going; sometimes sweats up badly. *P. Felgate.*

ECSTATICA (USA) 2 b.f. Damascus–Fantastic Review (Reviewer) (1981 **81 p** 6fg²) Apr 9; $110,000Y; well-made, quite attractive filly; good mover; second foal; half-sister to very useful 1980 American 2-y-o Bit of Coral (by Buffalo Lark); dam, half-sister to King's Stand winner Flirting Around, won 6f maiden race; heavily-backed favourite, put up a pleasing first effort when 3 lengths second of 19 to more-experienced Dawn Ditty in maiden race at Salisbury in September; will be suited by 7f and 1m; clearly well thought of. *F. J. Houghton.*

ECUBE (USA) 3 b.c. Youth 135–Faneuil Hall (Bolinas Boy) (1980 NR 1981 **114** 10.5s* 12fg² 12.5g 10.5g) $130,000Y; big, leggy colt; half-brother to several winners, including Hall of Reason (by Bold Reason), a smart stakes winner at up to 1m, and very useful 1m to 11f winner Celebrated (by Native Charger); dam smart stakes winner at up to 1m; 6-length winner of 22-runner newcomers race at Saint-Cloud in May; ran really well when neck second to Bellman in Prix du Lys at Chantilly the following month but was well beaten afterwards in Grand Prix de Saint-Cloud in July (eighth of 10 behind Akarad) and Benson and Hedges Gold Cup at York in August (scratched down to start and finished last of 9 to Beldale Flutter); stays 1½m; probably acts on any going. *M. Zilber, France.*

EDGEDALE 3 gr. or ro.c. Sharp Edge 123–Queen's Penny (Queen's Hussar 124) **64 d** (1980 5fg 5g³ 5d 6d 1981 6g 7d* 8g 8s⁴ 7d 8.2g 10d 10s⁴ 13.3s) lightly-made colt; apprentice ridden when beating Lord Wimpy by a short head in handicap at Salisbury in May; ran best subsequent race on eighth start; stays 1¼m; acts on soft going; sold to T. Marshall 5,400 gns Newmarket Autumn Sales. *P. Cole.*

EDSNEWHIP 2 b. or br.c. Saulingo 122–Pampered Belle (Pampered King 121) — (1981 6f) Feb 24; IR 600Y; brother to winners in Belgium and France and half-brother to other winners, including 3-y-o Age of Reason (by Red Alert), successful from 6f to 1m; dam won at up to 13f in Ireland; unquoted, coltish in paddock and moved badly to start prior to finishing tailed off in 15-runner maiden race won by Swift Wing at Nottingham in July. *W. Stubbs.*

EDWARD LADELL 3 ch.g. Sweet Revenge 129–Princess Lorna 63 (Royal Palm — 131) (1980 7f 7d 6d 1981 8f) strong gelding; plating-class maiden; sold 3,000 gns Doncaster October Sales. *Miss S. Hall.*

EFFECT 5 b.g. Martinmas 128–Sweet Sharlie 77 (Fighting Charlie 127) (1980 **77** 6g 6fg 6h 7g 8.3fg 6g 6fg⁴ 6g 1981 5d² 6d* 6g² 6d* 7g³ 7fg³ 6g⁴ 6d³ 6f 6g*(dis) 6fg² 6fg² 6fg 6g 5s* 5g) well-made gelding; has rather a round action; won handicaps at Folkestone (apprentices) and Ripon in May and York in October; beat Westacombe a shade comfortably by 3 lengths in £5,100 race on last-named; also first past post at Chester in August but was disqualified; stays 7f; acts on any going; racing in USA. *N. Callaghan.*

EFFIE MAY 2 b.f. Tudor Rhythm 112–Sand Valley 61 (Arabian) (1981 6d) — Apr 10; 580F; fifth living foal; half-sister to a minor winner in USA; dam won 3 sellers at around 1¼m; unquoted when in rear in 15-runner maiden race won by Welsh Partner at Windsor in August. *M. Hinchliffe.*

EGGINGTON 3 ch.g. Baragoi 115–Primeapple (Primera 131) (1980 5f 5f⁴ — 5fg 6s 7g 7f 7d 1981 16g 16.9s 12g 16f) fair sort; poor maiden; sometimes blinkered. *S. Mellor.*

EGGNCHIPS 3 b.c. My Swallow 134–La Mariposa (T.V. Lark) (1980 7d 7fg³ — 8fg 10d 1981 15.5s) plain colt; poor plater; should stay beyond 7f; has worn bandages. *A. Davison.*

EGNOUSSA 2 b.f. Swing Easy 126–Devon Night 100 (Midsummer Night II 117) **63** (1981 5g 6g 5f 5s 5s⁴) June 6; 18,500Y; fair sort; half-sister to several winners, notably very smart Devon Ditty (by Song), a winner here and in USA at up to 9f; dam won at up to 7f at 2 yrs; 6¼ lengths fourth of 9 to Cannon Shell in minor event at York in October; best effort; blinkered third and fifth outings and raced alone on fourth. *C. Brittain.*

EIGHT BALL 4 ch.g. Jukebox 120–Hillberry Corner 70 (Atan) (1980 6d 1981 — 10d 8d 7fg 10f) light-framed gelding; plater; stays 7f; has worn blinkers; sometimes sweats up; sold 675 gns Ascot July Sales. *G. Richards.*

EIGHTPENCE 2 ch.f. Pieces of Eight 128–Canisburn 77 (Canisbay 120) (1981 **65** 5d² 5d* 5g 6f* 7g⁴ 7f 6fg⁴) Apr 21; small filly; good mover; second live foal; dam won over 11f; retained after winning sellers at Warwick in May (cost 1,650 gns) and Yarmouth the following month (cost 2,400 gns after winning by 1½ lengths from Next Decade); will stay 1¼m; seems to act on any going, but is particularly well suited by firm. *M. Tompkins.*

EIGHT ROSES 4 ch.f. Pieces of Eight 128–Miss Rosy (Quorum 126) (1980 **53** 11.7fg 8fg³ 8fg³ 10fg 12fg* 10f 12d⁴ 1981 16.9s 15.5d 17.1d³ 15.5fg 17.1h 16.5f³ 12g* 12g² 12.2s² 12d) small, narrow filly; plater; attracted no bid after winning at Lingfield in September; stays well; seems to act on any going; often sweats up. *P. Cole.*

ELARIM 2 br.c. Meldrum 112–Souriciere 73 (Count Albany 99) (1981 6fg 6f **68** 7g³ 6g³ 6f 6fg 6d 7f 7s) May 3; workmanlike colt; fourth reported foal; dam sprinter; beaten about 2½ lengths when third in maiden races won by Allan Wells and Sign Dancer within space of 3 days at Ayr in July; stays 7f; rider lost irons on sixth outing; pulled hard final start. *J. Carr.*

ELA ZINA MOU 2 b. or br.f. Prince de Galles 125–Reine d'Etat 53 (High Hat **58** 131) (1981 6g 5g) Apr 3; 3,200Y; fair sort; sister to 3 winners here and abroad, including 1980 2-y-o 5f winner Fleur de Galles; dam placed over 1½m; 6¾ lengths sixth of 20 to Welwyn in maiden race at Lingfield in September, second outing; should be suited by 6f+. *D. Ringer.*

EL CITO 4 b.c. Ridan–Airgead Beo (Hook Money 124) (1980 8g² 9.5f³ 11fg² — 12d 8g 16g 14s³ 12s 1981 10.4s 15.5f 10fg 10d) lengthy, rather lightly-made ex-Irish colt; placed in various company in 1980; soundly beaten at 4 yrs; stays 1¾m; acts on any going; good mount for an apprentice; has worn blinkers, including when successful on only outing at 2 yrs. *G. Balding.*

EL CUBANO 3 b.c. Pitskelly 122–Aurorian (Rise 'N Shine II) (1980 6fg 6fg — 8g 8g 8g 1981 8g 12.2g³ 12d) workmanlike colt; poor form, including in a valuable seller; suited by 1½m; blinkered final start at 2 yrs; sold to M. Hinchliffe 740 gns Newmarket Autumn Sales. *E. Eldin.*

ELDERBERRY 5 b.h. Shoolerville 121–Caprice 90 (King's Leap 111) (1980 6h **53** 5f 5fg 5fg 5g 6g 6d 1981 5g³ 5f 5g) workmanlike horse; sprint handicapper; best form at 5f; acts on firm going; suitable mount for an apprentice; ran badly in blinkers once in 1980. *W. Haigh.*

ELP

EL DJEM   2 br.g. Mansingh 120–Mumtaz (Sheshoon 132)   (1981 5s 6g 7fg⁴ 6f   **70**
7f 7s)   Apr 21 ; 3,100Y ; neat gelding ; half-brother to numerous winners in France ;
dam, French 1¼m winner, is daughter of half-sister to Petite Etoile ; 8 lengths
fourth of 15 to Super Sunrise in minor event at Newcastle in August, easily best
effort ; evidently suited by 7f.   *P. Wigham.*

ELECTRIC   2 b.c. Blakeney 126–Christiana 106 (Double Jump 131)   (1981 7fg²   **85 ?**
7.2fg)   Feb 19 ; 32,000Y ; well-made, quite attractive colt ; good walker ; half-
brother to several winners, including 3-y-o 1½m and 1¾m winner Courchevel (by
Reliance II) and smart 7f and 1m winner Chalet (by Luthier) ; dam, half-sister to
very smart 1m and 1¼m performer Calpurnius, won over 5f at 2 yrs ; put up a
pleasing first effort when 2 lengths second of 24 to Busaco in maiden race at
Newbury in August, keeping on well after showing signs of inexperience ; most
disappointing when 2/1 on for similar race at Haydock the following month,
finishing tenth of 13 behind Scoutsmistake after being beaten over 2f out ; will
stay middle distances ; must be given another chance to confirm the favourable
impression he created at Newbury.   *M. Stoute.*

ELEGANT DANCER   3 ch.f. Wollow 132–Omentello 91 (Elopement 125)   **73**
(1980 7fg 6f 7d⁴ 1981 8fg 10d 8d* 8f 8fg⁴ 8.3g 8d³ 8g 8g)   leggy, lightly-made
filly ; beat Place Concorde by 5 lengths in maiden race at Bath in June ; also ran
creditably last 3 outings ; should stay middle distances ; well suited by some give
in the ground.   *R. Laing.*

ELITE PETITE   3 b.f. Welsh Saint 126–Super Amber (Yellow God 129)   (1980   **65**
6g 1981 5d 6g 7v 7d 7f 8.3f 10f* 10f² 8.3g 10s 10s*)   light-framed filly ; plater ;
bought in when successful at Folkestone in August (1,100 gns) and October
(880 gns), on latter occasion after winning by 10 lengths ; suited by 1¼m ; acts on
any going.   *M. Haynes.*

ELIZABETH HOWARD   3 ch.f. Sharpen Up 127–Molly Flo (Paveh 126)   **68**
(1980 6g 7d 7fg 7.2d⁴ 7fg 8d³ 1981 7g 12d 14f 14.6fg³ 11f² 12f² 11.5g* 12g* 10.6v
12g)   strong, fair sort ; decisively won modest maiden race at Yarmouth and
minor event at Edinburgh in September ; gives impression she doesn't stay
1¾m ; blinkered second start in 1980 ; slipped up third outing : sold 4,700 gns
Newmarket Autumn Sales.   *I. Walker.*

ELIZA DE RICH   4 b.f. Spanish Gold 101–Dumb Kathy (Dumbarnie 125)   **54**
(1980 6d 7fg 6fg³ 8.2f 6g² 7d 8g 8d 7d 6d 1981 8g 8g⁴ 7f* 7fg² 8fg 6fg² 8.2g
8f² 8fg⁴ 8.2s 7s 7g)   lightly-made filly ; plater ; bought in 780 gns after winning
at Stockton in June ; stays 1m ; suited by top-of-the-ground ; has sweated up on
occasions.   *R. Hollinshead.*

EL JACKO (USA)   3 ch.g. Bold Commander–Latin Fling (Around Two Turns)   —
(1980 6d 1981 8d 8fg 7f 8fg 8fg 6g)   big, strong gelding ; has been hobdayed ;
poor form in varied company, including selling.   *G. Harwood.*

EL KABIR   4 b.g. Green God 128–Sweet Serenade 93 (High Perch 126)   (1980   **74**
8d 10g³ 10.6f² 12fg* 12.2fg 12d 1981 12s*(dis) 13s 16.1fg 12s)   big gelding ;
made virtually all to win handicap at Doncaster in March (subsequently
disqualified for having caffeine and theobromine in system) ; well beaten afterwards ; suited by 1½m ; acts on any going.   *J. Hardy.*

ELLERENE   2 b.c. Hot Spark 126–My Cecilia 83 (Prevailing)   (1981 5g 5d² 6s*)   **85**
May 28 ; 2,100 2-y-o ; small, close-coupled, quite attractive colt ; first foal ; dam
6f winner ; quickened well to win 15-runner maiden race at Newbury in October
a shade cleverly by 2 lengths from Top Lad ; runs as though he'll stay 7f ;
acts on soft going ; bandaged behind when successful.   *P. Mitchell.*

EL MANSOUR   2 b.c. Tower Walk 130–Gay Amanda 75 (Counsel 118)   (1981 **105**
5s⁴ 6d⁴ 6f* 6fg* 6f² 6fg* 6f 6s²)   30 ; leggy colt ; half-brother to 1980 2-y-o
6f seller winner La Fedhala (by Swing Easy) and a winner in Malaya ; dam stayed
1¼m ; picked up quite a valuable prize when coming out best in tight finish
with Be Be of Kuwait and Plagal in 6-runner New Ham Stakes at Goodwood
in July ; had previously shown progressive form, winning minor events at
Chepstow and Lingfield ; pulled very hard early on but wasn't disgraced when
giving weight all round in Champion Two Yrs Old Trophy at Ripon in August,
finishing 6½ lengths sixth of 8 to Glancing ; good ¾-length second to Ten-Traco
in £4,500 nursery at Ascot the following month ; will probably stay 7f ; acts
on any going but put up best effort on soft ; admirably tough, genuine and
consistent.   *N. Gaselee.*

EL PATO   2 br.f. Moulton 128–Black Mink 83 (Gratitude 130)   (1981 5s*(dis) 5s   **68**
5g 5fg 6fg 5s 5s)   Apr 21 ; 3,000F ; small filly ; poor walker ; half-sister to 2

281

ELP

fairly useful 2-y-o winners, including 1980 5f winner Brentex (by Birdbrook), and a winner abroad; dam won twice over 5f at 2 yrs; short-head winner from Crimson Court in 11-runner maiden race at Doncaster in March but traces of caffeine and theobromine were found in her system and she was disqualified in July; only plating class on subsequent efforts; should stay 6f. *W. Wharton.*

EL-PEZ-ESPADA 3 b.f. Windjammer (USA)–Miss Peseta 95 (Sovereign Path 125) (1980 5d 6d 1981 5g 5g² 5f 5fg) plating-class maiden; will be suited by a return to 6f or more; sold 250 gns Newmarket Autumn Sales. *R. Morris.* **54**

EL PRESIDENTE 3 b.g. Bold Lad (Ire) 133–Inquisitive Girl 97 (Crepello 136) (1980 5fg* 5f³ 6g 5g 5d 6d 5g 1981 5s² 5s 5s² 5d³ 7d 6g⁴ 6s⁴ 6g⁴ 6f 5g³ 6fg 6f² 6g 6g 5s) strong, good sort; not a good mover in his slower paces; placed in several handicaps; stays 6f (not disgraced over 7f); acts on any going; sometimes blinkered but is better without; looks a difficult ride, although has run creditably for an apprentice; trained most of season by A. Bailey. *K. Ivory.* **69**

ELSELL 6 ch.m. Grey Mirage 128–Mary's Twiggy (Queen's Hussar 124) (1980 NR 1981 12s³ 13s²) narrow, lightly-made mare; plater; placed twice in better company early in year; stays 13f; acts on soft going. *M. Eckley.* **41**

ELWORTH 4 ch.c. Elvis 96–Fairworth 74§ (Fair Seller 126) (1980 10fg 9f 10g 13.8f* 1981 10fg) leggy colt; plater; tailed off only start at 4 yrs in September; suited by 1¾m; acts on firm going. *T. Kersey.* —

ELYSEE PALACE 5 br.g. Royal Palace 131–Kentucky Robin 73 (Falcon 131) (1980 NR 1981 10s 9d 8fg 6fg 8f) rangy gelding; poor handicapper nowadays; stays 1½m; acts on any going; takes a very strong hold. *B. Palling.* —

EMBARRASSED (USA) 2 b.f. Blushing Groom 131–My Bupers (Bupers) (1981 5.5g* 7f³ 8d⁴) Mar 3; $47,000Y; half-sister to several winners in USA, notably champion sprinter My Juliet (by Gallant Romeo), successful in 24 of her 36 starts; dam placed several times; in frame in 2 good races after winning minor event at Evry in July, finishing length third of 8 to Exclusive Order in Prix du Calvados at Deauville and 8 lengths fourth of 8 to Play It Safe in Prix d'Aumale at Chantilly; stays 7f well and should get 1m; acts on firm going; wears blinkers; entered in 1,000 Guineas. *O. Douieb, France.* **109**

EMBLAZON 3 br.f. Wolver Hollow 126–Slip Stitch 120 (Parthia 132) (1980 8d* 8.2s* 8s 1981 12g 12.2fg⁴ 14d 12d*) useful sort; good walker; modest fourth to Home On The Range in Warwick Oaks in June; beat Jolliffe's Double gamely by a neck in gentleman riders race at Brighton in October; stays 1½m; acts well on soft going. *Sir Mark Prescott.* **77**

EMBROIDER 2 b.f. Royalty 130–Petitpoint 77 (Petition 130) (1981 6fg 7.6s 10s) May 26; 3,800Y; tall, leggy, lightly-made filly; half-sister to useful French miler Pachiza (by Habitat) and a winner in Belgium; dam won at 1½m and is half-sister to smart stayers Ovaltine and Guillotina; behind in maiden races at Yarmouth in August and Lingfield and Nottingham (sweating badly) in October; sold to Mrs G. Forbes 2,000 gns Newmarket Autumn Sales. *D. Morley.* —

EMBUSTERA 3 ch.f. Sparkler 130–Mecca II 90 (Exbury 138) (1980 6d 6d 1981 8s³ 8g² 7f⁴ 8g³ 10.4fg² 8d² 10.4d* 10g³ 10d² 10g) lightly-made filly; beat Mountain High by 2 lengths in maiden race at Chester in August; in frame nearly all her other starts, including in a lady riders race; stays 1¼m; probably acts on any going; tends to swish her tail; sold 16,000 gns Newmarket December Sales. *G. Pritchard-Gordon.* **73**

EMERALD EMPEROR 7 b.g. Ribero 126–Frangipani 77 (Crepello 136) (1980 12fg² 16f 12f⁴ 12g 12g² 15fg³ 13.8f 1981 16s) poor handicapper; stays well; best form on a sound surface; looked none too keen once in 1980 and has worn blinkers. *M. Naughton.* —

EMERGLEN 3 b.f. Furry Glen 121–Grass Emerald (Alcide 136) (1980 7g 6fg 7g 1981 12fg 10.2h 10fg) lengthy filly; little worthwhile form in maiden and minor races; started slowly when blinkered final start. *N. Vigors.* —

EMILY ETHEL 3 b.f. Impecunious–Edith 90 (French Beige 127) (1980 NR 1981 13.1g) sister to winning hurdler Mellie, and half-sister to another winning hurdler; dam disappointing stayer; unquoted when remote sixth of 10 finishers behind Bedford in minor event at Bath in September. *R. Blakeney.* —

EMMA LA DOUCE 2 b.f. Shiny Tenth 120–Four Lawns 77 (Forlorn River 124) (1981 5s 5s³ 6d) May 25; first foal; dam 5f winner; 16/1 when 3 lengths third of 11 to Sonseri in maiden race at Wolverhampton in October; not sure to stay 6f. *D. Marks.* **68**

282

EMMA ROYALE 2 b.f. Royal and Regal–Moment To Remember (Assagai) —
(1981 7f 8.2fg) Mar 9; 700F; fair sort; first produce; dam second over 5f and
1½m in Ireland; 33/1 and in need of race when behind in 22-runner maiden event
won by Treboro at Newmarket in July; distant last of 6 to Bancario in £4,000
event at Haydock in September. *R. Hollinshead.*

EMMYLIZ 2 b.f. Windjammer (USA)–Playtime (Primera 131) (1981 5g 6fg **61**
6f* 6f 5.1fg3) May 4; IR 7,800Y; neat, quite attractive filly; half-sister to
several winners here and abroad; dam poor half-sister to good 1½m horse Auroy;
put up easily best effort when winning 13-runner seller at Ripon in July by
2½ lengths from Cautious; attracted no bid; will stay at least 1m; acts on firm
going; sold, probably for export, 1,000 gns Newmarket Autumn Sales. *P.
Haslam.*

EMO 2 b.c. Red Alert 127–Voronto 59 (Derring-Do 131) (1981 6g 5s) Mar 30; —
2,500Y; plain colt; first foal; dam, placed over 5f, ran only at 2 yrs; burly when
behind in maiden races at Yarmouth and Nottingham in September. *H.
Collingridge.*

EMPEROR MARK 3 br.g. Young Emperor 133–Chinchilla II (Sicambre 135) —
(1980 5v 5f 6f 1981 8fg) leggy gelding; poor plater. *I. Vickers.*

EMPEROR'S COURT 2 b.c. Young Emperor 133–Lea Landing 81 (Meadow **72**
Court 129) (1981 5d 5.8g2 5d) Apr 10; IR 8,600Y; rather leggy, useful sort;
excellent mover; half-brother to 3 winners, including fairly useful 1979 Irish
2-y-o 7.5f winner Tilbury (by Realm); dam placed from 5f to 7f; ½-length second
of 15 to clever winner Norwick in maiden race at Bath in June; didn't reproduce
that form when blinkered in £3,400 event won by Janndar on same course later
in month; suited by 6f; sent to race in Italy. *I. Balding.*

EMPERY CARD (USA) 2 b.c. Empery 128–My Card (My Babu 136) (1981 **110**
7g* 9d2 10v) May 8; 230,000 francs Y (approx £23,000); neat, attractive colt;
half-brother to several minor winners in USA; dam, half-sister to Belmont
Stakes winner One Count, was a very useful winner at up to 1m; evens favourite
when winning 10-runner newcomers event at Maisons-Laffitte in September by 1½
lengths; stayed on well when short-neck second of 9 to Trigonome in Group 3
Prix Saint-Roman at Longchamp the following month but could finish only
seventh of 12, about 7 lengths behind Beau Pretender, in Group 3 Prix de Conde
on same course later in October; should stay 1¼m. *F. Boutin, France.*

EMPHASIS 3 ch.c. On Your Mark 125–Grey Mink 86 (Double Jump 131) **64**
(1980 6s2 6g 6f 7g2 7d3 1981 7d 7fg3 8fg 7f) compact colt; didn't recover his
2-y-o form and was beaten 9 lengths when third to Sheer Delight in minor event
at Folkestone in June; should stay 1m; best form with some give in the ground;
ran badly in blinkers final start, and is possibly none too genuine. *J. Dunlop.*

EMPRESS JEANNIE 4 b.f. Young Emperor 133–Jean Armour 88 (Delirium —
126) (1980 6f 10.1d 11.5g3 11fg3 10g 1981 10s 10.8d4 12f 12f 10f 10.1g 10s 10g)
compact filly; stays 11f; acts on a firm and a soft surface. *H. Collingridge.*

ENBY ARCO 6 b.g. Streetfighter 120–Altarnum (Alcide 136) (1980 NR —
1981 10.2s) poor handicapper; has been blinkered. *Miss S. Hall.*

ENCHANTED EVENING 5 br.m. Warpath 113–Enchanting 83 (Behistoun 131) —
(1980 NR 1981 17.1d 16.1f 15.5f) poor form in varied company; has worn
blinkers. *M. Hinchliffe.*

ENCHANTMENT 4 b.c. Habitat 134–Lady of Chalon (Young Emperor 133) **115**
(1980 6s 8f3 7.2f2 7f* 6g3 6g* 6g 6g2 6g* 6fg3 6d* 1981 6fg 6s3 6f2 6fg* 6fg2)
strong, good sort; good mover; very useful handicapper; beat Sanu a length in
Tote Sprint Trophy at Ayr in July; had probably lost race by hanging right when
short-headed by Great Eastern in 29-runner Wokingham Stakes (Handicap) at
Royal Ascot on previous start; excellent 2 lengths second to Rabdan in Prix
de Meautry at Deauville on final outing in August; best at 6f; acts on any going;
wears blinkers; needs to be held up; sent to USA. *J. Tree.*

END OF THE LINE 2 b.c. Saulingo 122–Harbrook 95 (Le Haar 126) (1981 **109**
5s* 5.8g2 5g* 6fg* 6fg3 6g 8d)
Had Barry Hills forecast after End of the Line's impressive victory in a
maiden race at Haydock in May that his colt would go on and take Newmarket's
Anglia Television July Stakes, he would have caused little surprise. Yet
End of the Line's victory in that race came as something of a shock, and he
started at 16/1. He had run twice in between, going down by half a length to the
filly Wicked Wave, to whom he was conceding 10 lb, at Bath in June and then by-
passing Royal Ascot to account for five previous winners in a £3,000 event at

Ayr later in the month. Useful though End of the Line's form was, it looked well below the standard required to win the July Stakes, sponsored for the first time by Anglia Television. The field of eleven included Cajun, Chris's Lad, Prowess Prince, Red Sunset and Tender King, all of whom had run well at Royal Ascot; also prominent in the betting were Solaboy, The Minstrel's first English winner, and Zilos, both winners on their debuts. The race is easily described: having broken smartly, End of the Line led almost from the outset. He was clear at the two-furlong marker but was tackled and headed by Tender King a furlong out. Rallying splendidly under quite a powerful ride from Cauthen, End of the Line got home by a short head from Tender King, who was conceding 3 lb, with Prowess Prince a further two lengths away in third. End of the Line had been waited with in his previous race and had put his head in the air when taking the lead, so different tactics were tried at Newmarket.

End of the Line didn't win again; he ran respectably in his next two races, finishing third to Tender King and Cajun in the Richmond Stakes at Goodwood and sixth of thirteen behind Cajun in the William Hill Middle Park Stakes at Newmarket. At Goodwood he again showed a tendency to carry his head high in the closing stages, but this probably had little bearing on the result. In his final race, the William Hill Futurity Stakes at Doncaster, End of the Line again bowled along in front but had little chance of keeping it up for a mile and he dropped out at halfway to finish last behind Count Pahlen.

End of the Line (b.c. Feb 18, 1979)	Saulingo (br 1970)	Sing Sing (b 1957)	Tudor Minstrel
			Agin the Law
		Saulisa (br 1963)	Hard Sauce
			L-S-D
	Harbrook (ch 1970)	Le Haar (ch 1954)	Vieux Manoir
			Mince Pie
		Caronbrook (b 1962)	Gilles de Retz
			Shandrim Queen

End of the Line's trainer went to 33,000 guineas at Goffs Premier Yearling Sales to secure him, and also paid 31,000 guineas for the still-unraced Go Sandicliffe at the Newmarket October Yearling Sales. These were easily the highest prices paid for Saulingo yearlings at public auction in 1980. End of the Line is the second foal of his dam, Harbrook, who won over seven furlongs at two and was placed at up to a mile and a half at three. The second dam stayed well, winning three races at up to a mile and three quarters. However, Saulingo was very speedy, and End of the Line is almost certainly going to be a sprinter. End of the Line is a good-topped, attractive colt with an excellent, easy action.

Anglia Television July Stakes, Newmarket—End of the Line (rails) rallies splendidly to beat TenderKing; Prowess Prince is third and Match Master fourth

Mr R. A. N. Bonnycastle's "End of the Line"

He raced fairly consistently throughout the season, his below-par performance at Bath being ascribed to a very high white blood cell count. He has put up his best performances on a sound surface. *B. Hills.*

END OF WAR (USA) 4 b. or br.c. Bustino 136–Peace 113 (Klairon 131) **96**
(1980 12g 11d* 12g² 11d³ 10g   1981 10fg 10.5d⁴ 12d⁴ 12f 12g* 14d 12g 12g² 12g* 12g) well-made colt; fairly useful handicapper; won at Goodwood in August (beat Le Soleil by 2 lengths) and Newmarket in October (accounted for Lusitanica by a neck); stays 1½m well (behind in Tote-Ebor over further); acts on a firm and a soft surface; ran moderately fourth start; sold out of J. Tree's stable 24,000 gns Newmarket Autumn Sales after ninth outing; sent to North America. *B. Hanbury.*

ENDONADA 3 br.f. Manado 130–Cherry Bird 68 (Abernant 142) (1980 NR   —
1981 8g 6g 6fg) 7,000Y, 1,800 2-y-o; lengthy filly; half-sister to numerous winners; dam ran only at 2 yrs; tailed off in maiden races and a seller; dwelt second outing. *J. Etherington.*

ENERGY PLUS 6 b.h. Tyrant–Reformed Maid (Reform 132) (1980 6g 6g 6f **57**
6fg 6fg² 6f 6g 6d⁴ 6g 6d⁴ 7g 5f 6fg   1981 6g⁴ 6g³ 6g* 6d 5fg 6fg 6fg⁴ 6f 6s 6d 6d) neat, strong horse; poor mover; poor handicapper; won at Redcar in May; fourth in seller at Pontefract earlier; stays 6f; acts on any going; has been tried in blinkers; often bandaged nowadays. *W. Wharton.*

ENGLISH MAID 3 b.f. English Prince 129–Naval Artiste (Captain's Gig) —
(1980 5fg 5d 7d 6s 7fg 6f 7.2s   1981 8fg 7g⁴ 9.4g 8f 10fg) plain filly; poor form, including in sellers; should stay 1¼m; best form on a firm surface; blinkered fourth start. *A. Jarvis.*

ENGLISH PRINCESS 3 ch.f. English Prince 129–Shenkel (Vertex) (1980 —
NR   1981 8s⁴ 9s 7f 12g 13f 16fg) 8,400F, 5,000Y; leggy, narrow filly; sister

285

to useful performer Sir Chris, successful over 5f and 7f at 2 yrs, and to a winner in USA; dam won over 6f at 3 yrs in USA; has shown a little ability in maiden and minor races; needs further than 7f and probably stays 1½m (well beaten over 2m). *H. Westbrook.*

ENGLISH REEL 3 b.g. Party Mink–Pink Foot 97 (Wilwyn 129) (1980 7d 1981 6v 6d 7d 7.5g² 8f³ 8.5f⁴ 9f³ 9f⁴ 8.5g* 9.5f*) sparely-made gelding; half-brother to several winners, including fairly useful miler Cissbury Boy (by Galivanter); dam stayed 1¼m; seventh of 11 behind King of Spain in £8,100 event at Doncaster in March on second outing; relegated to third after winning maiden race at Killarney in July on fifth start, but gained compensation in September when making virtually all in similar event at Galway and handicap at Dundalk; stays 9f well; acts on firm going; usually apprentice ridden. *J. Murphy, Ireland.* **76**

ENGULF 3 b.g. Gulf Pearl 117–Primrose 86 (Primera 131) (1980 5fg³ 6g³ 7d* 7s* 7g 1981 10.6fg⁴ 12.3g) strong, compact, deep-girthed gelding; good walker and mover; won twice at Ayr as a 2-y-o, and was a useful performer (rated 108); brought down final start however and gave impression in 1981 that he hadn't recovered from the experience; was gelded after being well beaten in minor event at Haydock in April and in Chester Vase (blinkered, finished last) in May; should stay at least 1¼m; revels in the mud; one to treat with caution until showing signs of recovering his form. *J. W. Watts.* **—**

ENMAR 3 b.g. Acrania 110–Tamblast (Tamerlane 128) (1980 NR 1981 12s 10v) lengthy gelding; half-brother to 6f winner Bluehill (by Blue Streak); dam lightly-raced plater; well beaten in minor event at Lingfield and maiden race at Kempton in October; still backward in latter. *G. Balding.* **—**

ENSIGN'S KIT 6 b.m. Saucy Kit 76–Ensign's Last (Dumbarnie 125) (1980 NR 1981 6fg 8fg 10.6d) winning hurdler; well beaten in varied company on flat. *M. James.* **—**

ENTEBBE 6 b.g. Derring-Do 131–Argitone (Aureole 132) (1980 7v 12f 16fg 16.1s⁴ 12.5s² 12d 1981 12s⁴ 12g 16s 13s) fair sort; good walker; stays 2m; acts on any going; used to wear blinkers. *J. Yardley.* **—**

ENTERPRISE EXPRESS 3 br.g. New Chairman–Smart Shoes (Langton Heath 97) (1980 7d 1981 11.7g) last in maiden races on his only outing at both 2 yrs and 3 yrs. *G. Beeson.* **—**

ENTHRALMENT (USA) 2 b. or br.f. Sir Ivor 135–Trevisana (Aristophanes 116) (1981 6fg* 6s) Feb 14; $275,000Y; lengthy, attractive filly; excellent mover; fourth foal; half-sister to 2 winners, including very useful French and Italian middle-distance winner Sifounas (by Secretariat); dam, winner in Argentina, is sister to Forli; second favourite, took a long time to realise what was required of her in 19-runner maiden race at Salisbury in September but made steady headway from halfway to win by a neck from Bundu, without jockey resorting to whip; dropped right out and finished ninth of 12 to Dancing Rocks in Blue Seal Stakes at Ascot later in month; bred to stay at least 1¼m. *J. Tree.* **78**

ENTHUSIASM 3 b.f. Abwah 118–Arodstown Girl (Lucero 124) (1980 NR 1981 7g 9d 10g 10fg 8.2s 7s) leggy, unfurnished filly; behind in minor and maiden events and a seller. *R. Thompson.* **—**

EPITHET 2 b.f. Mill Reef 141–Namecaller 83 (Malicious) (1981 6fg 5g* 6fg* 6s³) Feb 28; small, quite attractive, lightly-made filly; good mover; third foal; half-sister to smart 6f and 7f performer Columnist (by Swing Easy); dam won over 1m; narrow winner of maiden race at Chester in August (beat Bolivar Baby ½ length) and minor event at Windsor the following month (led in final furlong to beat odds-on Cajun a neck); never going well but kept on most gamely to be 1½ lengths third of 11 to Ten-Traco in £4,500 nursery at Ascot later in September; will stay 1¼m. *J. Tree.* **91**

EPONA'S GREY 2 gr.f. Pals Passage 115–Kindle (Firestreak 125) (1981 5s⁴ 5s* 5d² 5g² 5fg 6fg³ 5f² 5g) Apr 25; 1,850Y; neat filly; second foal; dam placed twice over 1½m in Ireland; awarded race after finishing head second of 18 to She's My Girl in auction event at Ripon in April and made all to win 6-runner seller at Redcar the following month (bought in 4,700 gns); subsequently ran well in nurseries; stays 6f but is evidently considered a 5f performer; acts on any going; wears blinkers; has run well for an apprentice; sweated up and ran badly final outing. *P. Haslam.* **66**

EPSIBA 4 b.f. Sharpen Up 127–Kaolin 98 (Kalydon 122) (1980 including **114**
10g* 12g* 11s 11g* 15g* 1981 9d⁴ 11fg 8g* 8fg 10s 9.2d) 5,600F; fourth living
foal; dam won over 9f and 1¼m; outstanding performer in Belgium at 2 yrs and
3 yrs, winning 8 races worth over £97,000 including Grand Criterium Belge,
Belgian Triple Crown and Grande Handicap International d'Ostende; raced
mainly in France in 1981 and showed herself a smart performer, winning Prix
d'Astarte at Deauville in August by 2 lengths from Phydilla; also ran well on
fourth and final starts when about 3 lengths sixth to Phydilla in the Prix Quincey
at Deauville in August and 1½ lengths fifth to Kilmona in Prix de l'Opera at Longchamp;
effective at 1m and stays 15f; acts on a firm and a soft surface. *H. van de Poele,
France.*

EPSOM IMP 8 br.g. St Alphage 119–Sarah Jane 80 (Pardao 120) (1980 **101**
5fg² 5fg 5f³ 5g 6fg 5f 5g³ 5fg 1981 5g 5fg 5.3f² 6f³ 5g² 5s 5s) useful sprinter
on his day though hasn't won since 1979; best at 5f; acts on any going; blinkered
once at 2 yrs; good mount for an apprentice. *J. Holt.*

ERINS ISLE 3 b.c. Busted 134–Chemise 75 (Shantung 132) (1980 10v 8g⁴ 7d² **121**
9d² 9v⁴ 1981 10d* 10s* 10d² 12v* 12d 12fg² 12fg 10g² 14d²) big, rangy,
good-looking colt; fourth foal; half-brother to a winner in Malaya; dam won
over 1¼m; developed into a very smart performer and ran race of his life when
length second to Kings Lake in Joe McGrath Memorial Stakes at Leopardstown
in September, staying on very well and finishing clear of remainder; no match
for Protection Racket in Irish St Leger at the Curragh the following month but
kept on to finish 3 lengths second; had earlier won minor event at Leopardstown,
Group 2 Sean Graham Ballymoss Stakes at the Curragh (decisively by 2½ lengths
from Magesterial) and Group 2 Gallinule Stakes, also at the Curragh, accounting
for Young Kildare by a length in last-named in May; also ran creditably when
½-length second to Last Light (rec 7 lb) in Group 3 Royal Whip Stakes at the
Curragh on fifth outing, but found going too firm when last of 5 behind Bustomi
in Gordon Stakes at Goodwood next time; stays 1¾m; acts well on soft ground;
consistent; sent to race in California. *J. Bolger, Ireland.*

*Gallinule Stakes, the Curragh—Erins Isle (right) has the
measure of Young Kildare*

ERMAC 3 br.g. Balidar 133–Sateen 63 (High Treason 126) (1980 5h 6fg 6d² — 6d 6g* 7s* 7d 7g² 8g 8g⁴ 7v 1981 8s³ 7d⁴ 8.2fg 7g) tall, useful-looking gelding; had stiff tasks when in frame in slowly-run Roseberry Stakes at Stockton (5¾ lengths third of 4 to Kirtling) and Clerical, Medical Greenham Stakes at Newbury (50/1 when about 5 lengths fourth of 6 to Another Realm), both in April; soundly beaten in handicaps subsequently, and wasn't seen out after May; best form at 7f; acts very well on soft going. *E. Weymes.*

ERNEL 7 ch.g. Sassafras 135–Belaying Pin (Iron Peg **§§**) (1980 17.1fg 12d — 17.1fg³ 16.5g 17.1d 1981 15.5d 16g 18.8fg 12g 15.5fg 10fg 17.1h) poor staying handicapper; suited by top-of-the-ground conditions; suitable mount for an amateur. *J. Benstead.*

EROTAS 2 b.c. He Loves Me 120–Whistling Chimes (Whistling Wind 123) **82** (1981 6d 6g 5.8f² 6f² 6fg³ 6fg 6g 6d³) May 4; 10,500Y; tall, lengthy, quite attractive colt; second foal; half-brother to Irish 3-y-o 1m and 9f winner Memories Call (by Martinmas); dam ran only once; placed in maiden and minor events; will stay 7f; probably acts on any going; has shown a tendency to hang left and wore blinkers seventh outing; sold 6,200 gns Newmarket Autumn Sales. *G. Harwood.*

ERRANTRY 6 br.g. Sterling Bay–Burletta (Derring-Do 131) (1980 12d 13d — 12fg 8g 10fg 10g 8g³ 10fg 12d 1981 10g) compact gelding; poor performer; seems to stay 1½m but not 1½m; suited by a sound surface; blinkered once at 2 yrs; has run respectably for a lady rider. *D. Jermy.*

ERROLL'S BOY 2 b.c. Bay Express 132–Brave Sally (Sallymount 125) (1981 **80** 5g 5g* 5g³ 5f 5fg 5fg* 5g) Mar 4; strong, well-made colt; brother to 1979 5f winner Errollston and half-brother to 1978 2-y-o 5f winner Brave Connection (by Manacle); dam of no account; winner of maiden race at Thirsk in May and nursery at Redcar in September, making most to beat Witch's Point by 1½ lengths in latter; evidently thought best at 5f; yet to race on a soft surface. *M. W. Easterby.*

ERROLL'S ELITE 3 b.f. Saulingo 122–Silly Sue 55 (Great Nephew 126) (1980 — 5f 5fg 6s 5s 6g 5f 6d 1981 5g 5g 6g) leggy filly; not a good mover; plater; blinkered sixth outing in 1980; sweated up second start. *M. W. Easterby.*

ERROLL'S WAY 3 ch.g. Sandford Lad 133–Picnic Dancer 71 (Hul a Hul 124) — (1980 6g 5g 6fg 6g 6d 1981 8f 7f) strong gelding; behind in maiden and minor events; has been tried in blinkers. *M. W. Easterby.*

ESAL BOY 4 ch.g. Lorenzaccio 130–Idiot's Delight (USA) (Bold Ruler) (1980 **30** 8f 8fg 8fg 1981 13s 12s³) small, strong gelding; well-backed favourite when third in seller at Wolverhampton in May (sweated up); seems to stay 1½m; acts on soft going. *D. Kent.*

ESCAPE CLAUSE 2 gr.f. Godswalk 130–Bethlehem (Santa Claus 133) (1981 **70** 5v 5s²) May 9; IR 6,200F; half-sister to fairly useful 6f to 1m winner Serigma (by Jukebox); dam never ran; 2½ lengths second of 11 to Sonseri in maiden race at Wolverhampton in October; will stay 6f. *W. Wharton.*

ESCAPE FROM HELL 2 b.c. Nonoalco 131–Border Bounty 113 (Bounteous **75** 125) (1981 7g 5s 6s) Jan 13; 52,000Y; strong, good-bodied colt; half-brother to 4 winners, including high-class miler Pitcairn and very smart middle-distance stayer Valley Forge (both by Petingo); dam runner-up in Yorkshire Oaks and Park Hill Stakes; 4 lengths fifth of 13 to Puesdown in maiden race at Hamilton in October, third outing and best effort; will stay 1¼m. *N. Callaghan.*

ESCAPISM (USA) 2 b.c. Native Royalty–Dont Wanta Hear It (Dead Ahead) **88** (1981 7fg³ 7fg² 7fg²(dis) 8d 7.6s² 6d² 8g) Feb 26; $50,000Y; strong, good-looking colt; excellent mover; half-brother to a winner in USA by Nashua; dam 6f winner; prominent on all outings, notably when second in maiden races at Goodwood (to Paperetto), Salisbury (disqualified after going down by short head to Tender Venture), Lingfield (to Sandwalker) and Redcar (beaten ¼ length by Professor's Choice); will probably stay 1¼m; probably acts on any going; genuine and consistent. *G. Harwood.*

ESCAPIST 2 b.c. Run The Gantlet–Chappelle Blanche 96 (Olden Times) (1981 **67** 7.2fg 8g) Apr 10; 12,000Y; well-grown, attractive colt; first foal; dam, half-sister to Beldale Flutter, won over 6f and stayed 1m; off bridle a long way out but stayed on to be nearest at finish when 4½ lengths fifth of 14 to Outlaw in maiden event at Ayr in September on second outing; gives impression he will be suited by a stiff test of stamina; played up in paddock on debut. *J. W. Watts.*

ESCARLA 3 b.f. Averof 123–O'Shaunessy (Charlottesville 135)   (1980 5s 5g 5g⁴   —
5fg³ 5fg 8g 8fg 10d⁴ 8d   1981 13.8g)   quite a useful-looking filly; bad plater;
stays 1¼m; blinkered fourth start in 1980; sold out of J. Calvert's stable 410 gns
Doncaster August Sales.   *D. Yeoman.*

ESCOVITCH 5 ch.g. Shiny Tenth 120–Shusheta (Martial 131)   (1980 6v 6f*   **111**
6fg* 6fg 6d 6fg 6s 6g³ 6s 7g 6d   1981 6g 6g² 5d² 6s 6f 6fg 5d 6fg² 6d)   big,
good sort; useful handicapper; runner-up at Kempton, York (3 lengths behind
Walter Osborne in David Dixon Sprint Trophy) and Goodwood; beaten ½ length
by Gamblers Dream on last-named in August; suited by 6f; probably acts on
any going but is suited by top-of-the-ground; good mount for an apprentice;
trained by G. Balding first 5 starts.   *W. Musson.*

ESCULTURA 3 br.f. Home Guard 129–Final Bridge (Welsh Abbot 131)   (1980   —
6s 6f   1981 9s 7fg 8f)   strong, sturdy filly; quite moderate form in varied
company; dead.   *B. Hanbury.*

ESKVIEW LAD 3 br.g. Abwah 118–Safe Anchorage 63 (Quayside 124)   (1980   —
5g 6d 6g 5g³ 6g³ 7s³ 8d 8.2s 7g² 7.2s² 8.2v   1981 7v³ 9.4g 8g)   small gelding;
plater; stays 1m; yet to race on a firm surface.   *T. Craig.*

ESSAM 3 b.g. Sallust 134–Bold Words (Bold Ruler)   (1980 7.9v 6s   1981 8.2s   **69**
10fg 8g 8g² 8.2g² 7fg 8.2f⁴ 8g⁴ 8f² 8f* 8f 8g 8d)   strong, compact ex-Irish
gelding; not a good mover; won maiden event at Beverley in August (sweated up)
and handicap at Ripon in September; awarded latter when Yorkshire Dancer, who
beat him 1½ lengths, was disqualified for causing interference at start; stays 1m;
acts on firm going; usually blinkered; has sometimes given impression he's not
entirely genuine and disappointed in his later races; retained 5,600 gns Newmarket Autumn Sales.   *A. Hide.*

ESSEX 6 b.g. Tudor Melody 129–Fashion Model 100 (Road House II)   (1980   —
12d   1981 12v)   lightly raced on flat nowadays; stays 1¼m; acts on any going.
D. McCain.

ESTHERS FOLLY 2 b.c. Royal Captive 116–Ardria 76 (Major Portion 129)   **44**
(1981 6fg 5fg⁴ 6g³ 7g 6f)   Apr 23; IR 1,650F, 2,800Y; small colt; bad mover;
poor plater; not disgraced when tried over 7f; sold 650 gns Doncaster September
Sales.   *P. Haslam.*

ESTIMA 2 b.f. Lucky Wednesday 124–Safe Anchorage 63 (Quayside 124)   (1981   —
7g 8.2d 8g)   Mar 16; second foal; dam, plater, placed from 7f to 1¼m; soundly
beaten in 3 maiden races in Scotland.   *T. Craig.*

ESTREMADURA 3 b.f. Comedy Star 121–Miss Merida 64 (Midsummer Night II   —
117)   (1980 NR   1981 7f)   2,000Y; second foal; dam seemed to stay 1¼m;
needed race and didn't move well to start when last of 20 behind Rose Music in
minor event at Leicester in June.   *J. Douglas-Home.*

ETERNAL PLEASURE 3 b.g. Manado 130–Come Back 106 (Bold Lad USA)   **68**
(1980 NR   1981 11s 10s 16.9s³ 16fg³ 15.5f* 18.8fg)   29,000Y; lengthy, lightly-
made gelding; half-brother to Irish 1m winner Homing Pigeon (by Habitat);
dam won at up to 12.5f in France and is daughter of Oaks winner Long Look;
third at Wolverhampton and Beverley (hung right under pressure) before
winning small maiden race at Folkestone in August; suited by a test of stamina;
acts on any going; ran moderately final start.   *M. Jarvis.*

ETESIAN 3 b.f. Tumble Wind–Mansfield (Star Gazer 123)   (1980 5f³ 5fg*   **67**
5fg²(dis) 5f* 5h³   1981 6s 6fg 7g³ 7d 8.2f³ 6g² 7f 6fg)   strong, attractive filly;
good walker; placed in handicaps in Scotland; probably stays 7f.   *C. Nelson.*

ETOILE-DE-MANOIRE 2 b.f. Comedy Star 121–Polly Buckle 97 (Polic 126)   —
(1981 5f 6fg 5d)   last in maiden and minor events and is of no account.   *G.
Cottrell.*

ETOILE D'OR 2 b. or br.c. Comedy Star 121–Burdigala (Tudor Music 131)   **67**
(1981 6f 5fg 6f 6fg 5f 5g 5g² 5s⁴)   Apr 20; 480Y; resold 500Y; fair sort; poor
mover; plater; best at 5f; wears blinkers.   *R. Hobson.*

ETOILE LEADER 5 b.g. Gilded Leader 75–Etoile Bleu (Lord of Verona 120)   —
(1980 NR   1981 12d 8f 8f 10f⁴ 15.5fg 12h⁴)   compact gelding; well backed
when fourth in 1¼m seller at Pontefract in August, only sign of ability; stays
1¼m.   *B. McMahon.*

ETONIAN 6 ch.h. Majority Blue 126–Gilded Egg (Faberge II 121)   (1980   **67**
5fg 7f 6fg 6s   1981 7g⁴ 7fg* 6fg)   quite a modest handicapper; decisively beat
Helexian by 4 lengths at Lingfield in June; stays 7f; probably acts on any
going; suitable mount for an apprentice; sold 1,200 gns Newmarket Autumn Sales.
M. Smyly.

ETTY 3 b.f. Relko 136–Ma Griffe (Indian Ruler 89) (1980 NR 1981 10.2h **81**
10.6d³ 10.4d³ 12g 10g*) 14,000F; small, lightly-made filly; half-sister to 6
winners, notably very smart English and German winner Whip It Quick (by
Philemon); dam never ran; 33/1 when beating Fruition by ¾ length in maiden
race at Newmarket in October; should be suited by 1½m. *F. J. Houghton.*

EUCLID 3 b. or br.c. Lyphard 132–Lucky For Me 116 (Appiani II 128) (1980 **97**
7d² 6s* 8s* 1981 7g⁴ 10.4d³) smallish, well-made colt; second foal; dam
smart winner at up to 1½m and is half-sister to smart middle-distance performer
Nor; odds-on winner of 2 races at the Curragh as a 2-y-o, on second occasion
getting home by a short head from Lord Never in Group 2 Beresford Stakes;
ran only twice in 1981, finishing less than 3 lengths fourth of 7 behind Cooliney
Prince in McCairns Trial Stakes at Phoenix Park in April and 8½ lengths third
to Kirtling in Dee Stakes at Chester in May, in latter event staying on without
ever looking dangerous; would have stayed 1½m; acted on soft going and didn't
race on a firm surface (gave impression one might have suited him); standing
at Pillar Stud, Lexington, at a fee of $10,000 (live foal). *V. O'Brien, Ireland.*

EURODANCER (USA) 2 b.c. Caucasus 127–Tumbling Dancer (Dancer's Image) **89**
(1981 6fg⁴ 7g³ 7f³) Mar 29; $61,000F; good-topped colt; second produce;
dam won over 6f in USA; third in maiden race at Chester in August (went down
by only a neck and a head to Rockfest) and in 8-runner Sancton Stakes at York
the following month (made much of running when beaten 3 lengths by Busaco);
will stay middle distances; sure to win an ordinary maiden race. *B. Hills.*

EVA ANNIE 3 ch.f. Galivanter 131–Amba Princess (Amber Rama 133) **—**
(1980 6fg 5d 1981 8fg 12.2g) sturdy filly; in rear in maiden races and a seller;
sold 825 gns Ascot September Sales. *V. Soane.*

EVADNE 3 b.f. Bold Lad (Ire) 133–War Lass 100 (Whistler 129) (1980 5fg **—**
1981 5d) neat, strong filly; no show in maiden race at Goodwood as a 2-y-o;
well-backed favourite when sixth of 8 to Boldwin in poor maiden event at
Wolverhampton in April, only outing of 1981; will be suited by 6f+. *R. Price.*

EVEN BANKER 2 ch.c. Lombard 126–Eventura 87 (Huntercombe 133) **77**
(1981 5g 5d⁴ 5f 6fg 7g 8g 8d⁴ 8s* 7d) Apr 24; 3,300Y; workmanlike colt;
second foal; dam won over 7f; probably second best on merit when going down
by a length to Rajhaan in 11-runner nursery at Newbury in October (pair 6
lengths clear), but was clearly hampered by winner and was awarded race;
will stay 1¼m; probably acts on any going but ran best race on soft; consistent.
R. Hannon.

EVEN WONDER 4 ch.f. Crisp and Even 116–I Wonder (Perhapsburg 112) **—**
(1980 NR 1981 10g 12f 12f 11.5d 16d 15.5f) compact filly; of little account.
W. Charles.

EVER GREAT 2 b.c. Grundy 137–Forever 68 (Never Say Die 137) (1981 8g) **—**
May 24; unfurnished colt; half-brother to 3 winners, including Dante Stakes
winner Hobnob (by Gyr); dam, half-sister to 2,000 Guineas third Balustrade,
stayed 1m; unquoted, chased leaders for 4f when out of first 10 of 29 in maiden
race won by Born Hero at Newmarket in October (unseated rider and galloped
loose to start beforehand) *P. Walwyn.*

EVER-SO-SURE 3 ch.g. No Mercy 126–Monet Royal 79 (Monet 127) (1980 **—**
7fg 7f 1981 10g 7fg 7f 8.2g 8f 8f 10f⁴ 8f 10fg 7s 8d) rangy gelding; plater;
stays 1¼m; wears blinkers; sold 1,400 gns Doncaster October Sales to W. Clay.
J. Etherington.

EVERYBODYS FRIEND 3 b.g. So Blessed 130–Attitude 116 (Gratitude 130) **66**
(1980 5fg³ 5f 5fg 5.3d⁴ 6s 1981 5fg 6g* 6d⁴ 6fg* 6s² 6f⁴ 6fg³) neat gelding;
won handicap at Carlisle and 3-runner minor event (apprentice ridden) at
Hamilton, both in May; stays 6f; probably acts on any going; ran creditably
in blinkers third start; exported to Hong Kong. *N. Callaghan.*

EVERYMAN 2 ch.g. Porto Bello 118–Fiery Comet 82 (Star Moss 122) (1981 **59**
6g 5f 6f 5g³) Apr 16; 2,100F; half-brother to 3 winners, including 1978 2-y-o
5f winner Rapid Fellow (by Club House); dam, placed at up to 7f, is half-sister
to brilliantly speedy Sica Dan; dropped in class and well backed when 4½ lengths
third of 14 to Pandora's Gold in seller at Catterick in October; not sure to stay
6f. *G. Richards.*

EVITA OF RUSHALL 2 ch.f. Master Sing 109–Pantala (Psidium 130) **—**
(1981 5.8g 5g 5fg) May 23; leggy filly; fourth known foal; dam of little account;
behind in maiden races in the South. *R. Turnell.*

EVZON 3 ch.c. English Prince 129–Spanish Empress 64 (Don II 123) (1980 NR **92**
1981 10s 12g* 12fg) 4,500F, 10,000Y; useful sort; second foal; dam placed over
1¼m; beat Ma Femme comfortably by 5 lengths in maiden race at Lingfield
in June; rather coltish in paddock when fifth to Lulav in minor event at
Newmarket the following month, only subsequent outing; will stay beyond
1½m C. Brittain.

EXCAVATOR LADY 2 b.f. Most Secret 119–Forgets Image 87 (Florescence 120) **65**
(1981 5fg 5f³ 5g⁴ 5f 5d 6d 6s) Apr 21; 7,400Y; compact filly; first foal; dam,
half-sister to Millingdale Lillie, won 3 times over 1m; in frame twice at Beverley
in July, beaten 1½ lengths by Chester County in minor event and just over 5
lengths by Russeting in maiden race; in rear in valuable seller at York on fourth
outing; should be suited by 6f; seems to act on any going. S. Nesbitt.

EXCITEMENT 2 ro.c. Sagaro 133–Belinda Mede 86 (Runnymede 123) (1981 **69**
5g 5s³ 6d² 7fg 5d) Mar 20; 8,600Y; small colt; first foal; dam fair sprint maiden
at 2 yrs; close-up third of 11 to Major Irish in maiden race at Wolverhampton in
May; not seen out again until August when 4 lengths second of 3 to easy winner
Custer in small race at Windsor; last of 24 after holding every chance 2f out when
tried over 7f; acts on soft going. R. Laing.

EXCLUSIVE AIR (USA) 2 ch.c. Avatar–Alyne Que (Raise A Native) (1981 **91**
7f² 8d) Apr 24; $67,000Y; tall, useful-looking colt; third foal; half-brother to
useful Irish 6f to 9f winner Muscovite (by Nijinsky); dam, winner over 6f at 2 yrs,
is sister to very useful sprinter L'Natural and closely related to champion sire
Exclusive Native; 5/1, led inside last furlong but then wandered left and was
collared in last strides and beaten a neck by Wibis Range in 19-runner maiden
event at Redcar in September; out of depth in William Hill Futurity Stakes at
Doncaster next time out; will stay 1¼m; clearly capable of winning in maiden
company. G. Richards.

EXCLUSIVE FOX (USA) 4 ch.c. Exclusive Native–Indian Lassie (Indian —
Chief) (1980 NR 1981 10s³ 10g⁴ 10s) big colt; ran creditably in Houghton
Stakes at Newmarket only start at 2 yrs; showed only poor form in 1981; possibly
stays 1¼m; pulled hard second outing; sold 2,400 gns Newmarket Autumn Sales.
M. Stoute.

EXCLUSIVELY RAISED (USA) 3 gr.f. Exclusive Native–The Rarest 105 **101**
(Rarity 129) (1980 6s² 7g* 7g⁴ 8g* 8fg² 1981 7fg 12g 8f⁴ 8fg 7fg⁴ 7f 6s)
$100,000Y; lengthy, quite attractive filly; first foal; dam, second in 7f National
Stakes on only start at 2 yrs, won over 5f in Ireland at 3 yrs; developed into one
of the best fillies of her age at 2 yrs and won May Hill Stakes at Doncaster;
rather disappointing in 1981, best efforts when 3½ lengths fifth to Fairy Footsteps
in Ladbrokes Nell Gwyn Stakes at Newmarket in April, 5½ lengths fourth to Tolmi
in Coronation Stakes at Royal Ascot in June and 4¾ lengths fourth of 6 behind Star
Pastures in American Express Royal Wedding Day Stakes at Goodwood in July;
reportedly injured herself in stalls when tailed-off last in Johnnie Walker Oaks
Trial at Lingfield; not sure to stay beyond 1m; blinkered final start (had stiff
task in handicap). M. Stoute.

EXCLUSIVE ORDER (USA) 2 ch.f. Exclusive Native–Bonavista (Dead **111**
Ahead) (1981 6f* 7f* 7s⁴) May 13; most attractive, strong, good-bodied filly;
sister to Teddy's Courage, a smart winner at up to 9f in USA, closely related to 2
stakes-placed winners by Raise A Native, and half-sister to 3 minor winners; dam
won 3 times at up to 4f, and is half-sister to 2 minor stakes winners; successful in
maiden race and Group 3 Prix du Calvados at Deauville in August, finishing very
strongly to win latter by ½ length from Play It Safe; stayed on after being held up
when 5 lengths fourth of 5 to Green Forest in Prix de la Salamandre at Longchamp
the following month; will stay 1¼m; acts well on firm going; an extremely taking
filly who should make a good 3-y-o. J. Cunnington, jnr, France.

EXPEDIER 3 b.g. Sharpen Up 127–Be Serious (Laugh Aloud) (1980 6fg 7fg **47**
1981 8d 8f 10.1fg³ 10f 10g* 12f) rangy gelding; plater; sold out of R. Akehurst's
stable 1,200 gns after winning at Nottingham in August; bandaged when always
behind only subsequent start; stays 1¼m; often blinkered, but didn't wear
them at Nottingham; sold 460 gns Newmarket Autumn Sales. D. Leslie.

EXPLORER KING (FR) 3 b. or br.c. Roi Dagobert 128–Explorelka (Relko 136) **121 ?**
(1980 7.5g³ 10d 10d⁴ 1981 10d*(dis) 11fg*(dis) 10.5s 9g 11fg* 12g² 10.5g*)
38,000 francs Y (approx £4,000); second foal; dam once-raced daughter of sister
to Bold Ruler; won minor event and Group 2 Prix Noailles at Longchamp in
April, latter by a length from Lydian, but was disqualified from both when
traces of nandrolone were found in his system; subsequently won at Clairefontaine

and Saint-Cloud, beating Chaud et Froid by ½ length on latter course in September; stays 1½m; acts on a firm and a soft surface; trained part of season by A. Paus and M. Blackshaw. *D. Becquemin, France.*

EXPRESS FINISH 2 ch.f. Bay Express 132–Whip Finish 77 (Be Friendly 130) — (1981 5fg) Apr 29; first foal; dam won twice over 5f at 2 yrs; unquoted when twelfth of 14 to Burn Up in maiden race at Catterick in June; sold 500 gns Doncaster November Sales. *R. D. Peacock.*

EXPRESSIONIST (USA) 2 b.c. Exclusive Native–Lady's Prerogative (Nashua) — p (1981 6s) Apr 18; $225,000Y; good-looking, rangy colt; half-brother to a winner by Judgable; dam unraced half-sister to top Canadian filly Royal Tara; unquoted but looking very well, dropped out from halfway when about 14 lengths ninth of 11 to Slightly Dangerous in Duke of Edinburgh Stakes at Ascot in October; looks the sort to do better over middle distances at 3 yrs. *P. Walwyn.*

EXPRESSLY YOURS 2 ch.f. Bay Express 132–Never Part (Never Say Die 137) **74** (1981 5g 5g 6fg⁴ 6g³ 6g 6fg 5f⁴ 5d) Feb 5; 4,100Y; lengthy filly; third foal; half-sister to quite useful 1978 2-y-o 5f winner Tribal Princess (by Tribal Chief); dam never ran; in frame at York (maiden race) and Redcar (similar event and a nursery); stays 6f; well out of her depth fifth appearance and probably ruined her chance on next outing by taking part in false start. *P. Asquith.*

EXTRA STEEP 3 ch.f. Exbury 138–Directissima (Devon III 125) (1980 5g — 5fg 6g² 7f³ 7g 1981 9s 12d 12fg 15.5f² 15.5fg) lightly-made filly; placed in maiden races; stays well; sometimes sweats up; ran badly third start; sold 1,000 gns Newmarket Autumn Sales. *G. Lewis.*

EXTRAVAGANT NATIVE (USA) 3 br.f. Full Pocket–Native Glow (Exclusive — Native) (1980 5g 6g 7g 7fg 7fg 7g 8fg 1981 9.4g 12.5f 12fg⁴ 8g) narrow, lengthy filly; good mover; poor form, including in a seller; blinkered fifth outing in 1980. *P. Calver.*

EYELIGHT 4 gr.g. Roan Rocket 128–Pie Eye 88 (Exbury 138) (1980 7.6f **60** 8fg⁴ 10fg² 8fg 12g 10d 8fg 8d⁴ 8g⁴ 9f³ 9d 8.2s 1981 8fg 7.2s 6fg 7.6fg 8fg⁴ 9fg³ 8g³ 8f² 8f 8g* 8d² 8fg⁴ 8.2s 7g) robust, short-legged gelding; plater; attracted no bid after winning valuable event at Doncaster in September; stays 1¼m; seems to act on any going; effective with or without blinkers; a front runner; suitable mount for an inexperienced rider; has shown signs of being none too keen on occasions. *R. Hollinshead.*

F

FABRO 2 br.c. Busted 134–Caprera 112 (Abernant 142) (1981 8f² 9d*) May 7; **101** p brother to high-class middle-distance colt Pevero, and half-brother to several winners, including Irish 3-y-o 1¼m winner Cervo (by Habitat); dam fourth in 1,000 Guineas; evens favourite, came with a strong late run but failed by a neck to catch Abraje in newcomers race at Longchamp in September; odds on for 11-runner maiden race at Evry the following month and won by 1½ lengths from Duc d'Aubry; will stay 1½m; likely to leave this form well behind at 3 yrs. *F. Boutin, France.*

FABULOUS DUNCE (USA) 3 b.c. Le Fabuleux 133–Dulia (Dunce) (1980 7f **69** 1981 10d⁴ 10fg* 12f²) rangy colt; beat Kyoto a length in maiden event at Yarmouth in August; ran disappointingly only subsequent outing; should be suited by 1½m; sweated up first outing; sold to A. Pitt 3,300 gns Ascot November Sales. *M. Stoute.*

FABULOUS PRINCE (USA) 4 b.c. Le Fabuleux 133–Call The Queen (Hail **109** to Reason) (1980 10s* 12d² 12fg 12g⁴ 10d³ 10d 1981 10s⁴ 11s³ 10.5g 11v* 10.5d 12g² 12d³ 12g) ex-French colt; beat Tuxedo Junction by 2 lengths in 70,000 francs event at Longchamp in May; about 1¼ lengths third to 5 to Rheinsteel in minor event at Lingfield in August, only run in this country; stays 1½m; acts well on soft ground; trained part of season by A. Paus and A. Klimscha. *G. Balding.*

FABULOUS SALT (USA) 3 ch.f. Le Fabuleux 133–Morgaise (Round Table) **98** (1980 NR 1981 8fg* 10g³ 10g 12fg) $95,000Y; fine, big, well-made filly; half-sister to 2 winners, including Ballare (by Nijinsky), winner of 1m Senorita Stakes; dam smart winner at 2, 3 and 4 yrs, scoring at up to 1m; ran green in early stages and had plenty to do turning for home when second favourite for 10-runner Masaka Stakes at Kempton in April, but accelerated in splendid style when an opening appeared in last furlong and beat Wilderness by a neck;

rather disappointing afterwards; best effort when 3½ lengths third to Humming in Playboy Pretty Polly Stakes at Newmarket in May; not seen out after Royal Ascot; should stay 1½m. *M. Stoute.*

FACING 2 b.f. Quiet Fling 124–Facade 99 (Double Jump 131) (1981 7g 8g) — Apr 26; 1,500Y; lengthy, slightly hollow-backed filly; half-sister to a winning hurdler by My Swanee; dam stayed 6f; unquoted when behind in big fields of maidens at Newmarket in October. *D. Dale.*

FAI LA BELLA (USA) 2 b.f. Fifth Marine–No Need Askin (Reflected Glory) — (1981 7f 7d 7.6s) May 8; $27,000Y, resold 21,000 gns Y; quite attractive filly; excellent mover; half-sister to a winner by Lt Stevens; dam unraced half-sister to smart filly Kootenai; seemingly only plating class. *L. Cumani.*

FAIR AND FREE 3 b.f. Reliance II 137–Matala 65 (Misti IV 132) (1980 7g — 8d 8d 8d 1981 10.2g 11.7s) light-framed filly; little worthwhile form; probably needs at least 1½m; blinkered final outing. *Mrs R. Lomax.*

FAIR ARTIST 3 ch.f. Fair Decision 93§–Melpo 73 (Hook Money 124) (1980 — 5fg 5.3g 1981 8d 7f 6g 6fg) little worthwhile form, including in sellers; sold 410 gns Ascot December Sales. *B. Wise.*

FAIR CITY 4 b.g. Charlottown 127–Fair Amanda 105§ (Firestreak 125) (1980 **55** 10v³ 10.6f 9g 11d² 13g³ 1981 13v 12g 18.4d 13fg 12g 12fg³ 12g 15g 12.2g) leggy gelding; poor performer; stays 13f; suited by some give in the ground; has run creditably for a boy; blinkered last 2 starts; sold 1,700 gns Doncaster October Sales. *W. H. H. Williams.*

FAIR COLUMBINE 2 b.f. Comedy Star 121–Equal Chance 95 (Hitting Away) — (1981 5fg 5.8g 5f) Feb 27; neat filly; half-sister to several winners here and abroad, including useful 1979 Irish 2-y-o 5f performer Jay Bird (by Hot Spark); dam sprinter; evidently of little account herself. *M. Hinchliffe.*

FAIRDALE 3 gr. or ro.g. Roan Rocket 128–Catalonia 97 (Abernant 142) (1980 **50** 5d 5d 1981 5d 5fg 5.8g⁴ 5g 6f³ 5.8f⁴ 6fg 6fg³ 8h 8fg) small, stocky gelding; in frame in handicaps at Bath (2) and Chepstow and in apprentice maiden race at Newbury, best efforts; stays 6f. *G. Cottrell.*

FAIR DUEL 4 b.g. Status Seeker–Double Irish (Dual 117) (1980 6s 10.1fg **44** 11.7s 10s⁴ 10.1f² 10.1f⁴ 10.1g 10fg 10f 8s 1981 10d 10s³ 10v 8f 10f) strong, well-made gelding; stays 1¼m; acts on any going; sometimes wears blinkers. *P. Makin.*

FAIRFIELD LADY (USA) 2 b.f. North Sea–Kitten Too (Tamao) (1981 — 5g 5v 5f 5g 5.3d 5s) Mar 29; $11,000F, $15,000Y; third foal; half-sister to 2 minor winners; dam won claiming races at up to 1m; sire smart winner from 6f to 9f; in rear in maiden and nursery events; blinkered last 2 starts. *G. Lewis.*

FAIR FIGHT 3 br.f. Fine Blade 121–Nortia 123 (Narrator 127) (1980 6fg **84** 7g 8f⁴ 1981 10fg 10.2g³ 14s³ 16f* 16f³ 16f* 15.8g 17.4g 16g) close-coupled, good sort; made all in maiden race at Nottingham in June and handicap at Thirsk in July, in latter winning virtually unchallenged by 3 lengths from Bulldozer; didn't run particularly well afterwards; suited by a test of stamina; acts on any going but best form on firm; suited by front-running tactics. *H. Candy.*

FAIRGREEN 3 b.g. Music Boy 124–Sunny Bloom 71 (Forlorn River 124) **78 d** (1980 6g 5fg 6f 6g⁴ 5d* 5g³ 1981 5s* 6fg 6g 5fg 5fg 8f) big, strong gelding; bad walker; won handicap at Leicester in March; didn't reproduce that form, but didn't have conditions in his favour; possibly better suited by 5f than 6f; acts on soft going. *H. Westbrook.*

FAIRMAN 8 ch.h. Manacle 123–Fairabunda 59 (Floribunda 136) (1980 8g — 10g 1981 18fg) poor handicapper; stayed 13f; acted on any going; sometimes wore blinkers; dead. *D. Jermy.*

FAIR MOUNT LAD 2 ch.c. Mount Hagen 127–Jabula 99 (Sheshoon 132) **74** (1981 5fg 5d* 6fg 6fg 6fg 7s² 8fg 7s) Mar 27; 3,400Y; small, close-coupled colt; half-brother to 2 winners, including fairly useful 1976 2-y-o 5f and 7f winner The Bowler (by Bold Lad, Ire); dam winner at up to 1m; 33/1, won 20-runner maiden race at Salisbury in May by 1½ lengths from Nunsruler; returned to form when head second of 13 to Legs of Man in £4,400 nursery at Chester in August (might have won had jockey not dropped reins in final furlong); should be well suited by 1m; evidently needs a soft surface; started slowly third outing and wore blinkers on fourth. *S. Matthews.*

FAIR OF FACE 3 ch.f. Grundy 137–Golden Treasure 106 (Crepello 136) **91** (1980 6g 1981 7s⁴ 8fg² 12.2g 12g* 12f* 10.1fg² 12f* 12fg 12fg) lightly-made, useful-looking filly; in good form in summer and won maiden race at Lingfield, minor event at Ripon and handicap at Leicester; steadily drew clear from 2f out when beating Bunce Boy by 3 lengths on last-named course; sweated up badly but ran creditably next start; suited by 1½m; acts on firm going and wasn't disgraced on soft on reappearance; usually wears bandages or boots in front; game and genuine; sold 62,000 gns Newmarket December Sales. *H. Candy.*

FAIR ROSALIND 3 b.f. Mummy's Pet 125–Sweet Success 81 (Privy Councillor 125) (1980 5d 5f² 5g³ 5fg 6g² 5.8h² 6g* 6fg 1981 7d 7g 6fg 6f) lengthy filly: didn't recover her 2-y-o form, best effort on first outing; stays 7f; acts on hard going and on a soft surface. *N. Vigors.* —

FAIR SARA 3 br.f. McIndoe 97–Fairstar 86 (Star Moss 122) (1980 6d 6fg 6g 7fg 8.2d² 8fg⁴ 9d⁴ 7.2s⁴ 1981 8s 9s 8g 8g⁴ 11.7f 8.3fg⁴ 10fg⁴ 8.3fg² 8d* 10fg⁴ 8fg 8d 7d) unfurnished filly; bought in 2,000 gns after winning selling handicap at Newmarket in August; should stay 1¼m; seems to act on any going; has worn bandages in front; sold 1,000 gns Ascot November Sales. *K. Ivory.* **46**

FAIRSTEAD (USA) 3 b.c. Plenty Old–Bayadera (Venerador) (1980 6g 1981 10d 12s 15.5s) rangy colt; soundly beaten in varied company. *R. Sheather.* —

FAIR SUE 4 b.f. Workboy 123–Dialice 61 (King's Troop 118) (1980 5s 5f 5f³ 5h 6g 1981 7s 5g 6g 6fg 7f 8g 10g 8f) small, unfurnished filly; poor plater; not sure to stay 7f; acts on any going; often looks most unimpressive in paddock. *C. Gray.* —

FAIR TRACK 3 ch.f. Track Spare 125–Fair Samela 108 (Constable 119) (1980 6s 6f⁴ 6fg 5f 1981 5f 7fg⁴ 7f* 8fg) lightly-made filly; attracted no bid after winning seller at Beverley in August; seems suited by 7f; acts on firm going; blinkered fourth outing in 1980; sent to Barbados. *P. Rohan.* **52**

FAIRY FOOTSTEPS 3 b.f. Mill Reef 141–Glass Slipper 100 (Relko 136) (1980 7g⁴ 7g² 7g* 1981 7fg* 8g* 10.5s³) **123**
Fairy Footsteps' retirement to the paddocks following a poor run in the Musidora Stakes and a baffling trial gallop for the Oaks was one of the disappointments of the season. Up to the York spring meeting she had seemed to have the Oaks at her mercy. A beautifully-bred filly, bred to be much better suited by a mile and a half than a mile, she had been one of the leading staying two-year-olds of 1980 and had begun her second season in tremendously encouraging fashion, winning the seven-furlong Ladbrokes Nell Gwyn Stakes at Newmarket barely off the bridle and then the One Thousand Guineas narrowly but very gamely from a field consisting, in the main, of less stoutly-bred fillies. Fairy Footsteps' defeat by Condessa and Madam Gay at York provided one of

One Thousand Guineas Stakes, Newmarket—Fairy Footsteps (left)
is an all-the-way winner from Tolmi (spots), Go Leasing
(second left) and Marwell

the season's biggest surprises but for a while she remained an Oaks probable. However, two weeks before Epsom her trainer announced: 'I worked Fairy Footsteps this morning and although she worked well the fact is that she does not stay. She moved smoothly but simply had nothing left after a mile. There is no point in running her in the Oaks'. Shortly afterwards it became known that Fairy Footsteps had run her last race.

Now there are precedents in racing, however rare, for a horse's stamina to fall as far short of expectations as Fairy Footsteps' trainer evidently believed his filly's did, and it's true that she gave the distinct impression she didn't stay in the Musidora: she failed to respond when ridden along after appearing to be going well, close up, three furlongs out, and eventually finished five lengths down on Condessa. Nevertheless any consideration of Fairy Footsteps' pedigree does drive one to seek more plausible explanations for her defeat. She is by one of the best middle-distance horses of our time, a proven influence for stamina, out of a mare who stayed at least a mile and three quarters; the mare's only previous foals were Crystal Coach (by Exbury) who showed no form at less than a mile and three quarters and won at up to two miles, and the St Leger winner Light Cavalry (by Brigadier Gerard). Deeper examination of the pedigree only serves to confirm first impressions. Much more likely she didn't act on the soft ground; more likely still, especially since she was so quickly taken out of training, her hard race in the Guineas finished her.

Enough of Fairy Footsteps in defeat. What of her in victory? Well, she was one of the most convincing Nell Gwyn winners anyone is likely to see, value for considerably more than the two and a half lengths she beat Shark Song, and while she couldn't by any stretch of the imagination be said to compare with the best One Thousand Guineas winners she distinguished herself in that race by making all, a feat in any classic and all the more meritorious in one run over the Rowley Mile. Altesse Royale in 1971 was the last One Thousand Guineas winner to lead throughout. Fairy Footsteps' performance in the Nell Gwyn Stakes halfway through April established her a hot favourite for the Guineas and on the day she started at 6/4 in a field of fourteen; she had been promoted past Marwell and Tolmi to the head of the ante-post lists at the beginning of the month. Both Marwell and Tolmi got to the start for the Guineas. Marwell, the best two-year-old filly of 1980, about whom there were serious stamina doubts, had had an outing during the current season: she had won a weakly-contested Fred Darling Stakes at Newbury. On the other hand Tolmi hadn't run since winning the Princess Margaret Stakes at Ascot the previous July; another bred in the purple, she too had outstanding form as a two-year-old but jarred herself in the autumn and then had a slight setback in the spring which interrupted her preparation for the Guineas. These three—Fairy Footsteps, Marwell and Tolmi—dominated the betting on the Guineas, with only Kittyhawk, second to Tolmi at Ascot, and the Salisbury Trial winner Go Leasing quoted at less than 33/1 among the rest. There was no overseas challenge nor, surprisingly for these days, was there an American-bred in the field.

In the race Piggott jumped Fairy Footsteps quickly ahead on the far side (to make her stamina count, naturally!) and she strode out powerfully and keenly, a length or so in front of the pack setting a reasonable pace. For a long time she seemed to be moving well within herself but she never threatened to run away with the contest, and at the bushes there were at least half a dozen at her heels with a chance: Tolmi was there, so was Marwell, the 100/1-shots Vocalist and What Heaven, Kittyhawk on the outside and her stable-companion Grecian Sea. Fairy Footsteps came under the whip a furlong and a half out as things really hotted up, and for a while it seemed that Tolmi, who'd been moving a shade more comfortably than the leader most of the journey, might edge in front. Under continuing pressure Fairy Footsteps stuck on exceptionally well up the hill, so well that even though in the end she had only a neck to spare over Tolmi she had, or so we thought, more in hand than the winning margin. Go Leasing finished strongest of all, really tearing along, to snatch third place from Marwell; Madam Gay also finished strongly for fifth place ahead of Vocalist. Less than a length and a half covered the first six home, and What Heaven was only another length down. The obvious conclusion to be drawn with so many of the principals in a heap is, in this instance, the right one: the latest One Thousand Guineas was non-vintage. For the winning rider, only just returned to the saddle after receiving severe ear injuries in a starting-stall accident at Epsom the previous week, the race marked a notable milestone in his career—his twenty-fourth classic victory. Subsequently Blue Wind in the Oaks put him a clear second in the record books and only two behind Frank Buckle. Piggott eventually became champion jockey for the

Mr H. J. Joel's "Fairy Footsteps"

first time since 1971. His total of 179 was his second-highest in ten championship victories and placed him well ahead of his rivals, one of whom, Carson, was in the lead on 114 when a very bad fall in the Yorkshire Oaks ended his season. For the winning trainer Fairy Footsteps' victory marked a second success in the race following that of One In A Million in 1979; for the winning owner it was also a second, following that of Fairy Footsteps' fourth dam Picture Play in 1944.

Fairy Footsteps (b.f. 1978)	Mill Reef (b 1968)	Never Bend (b 1960)	Nasrullah / Lalun
		Milan Mill (b 1962)	Princequillo / Virginia Water
	Glass Slipper (br 1969)	Relko (b 1960)	Tanerko / Relance III
		Crystal Palace (b 1956)	Solar Slipper / Queen of Light

The sires of the first three fillies all stand at Newmarket, Mill Reef at the National Stud. As we pointed out in *Racehorses of 1980* the National Stud's production in 1978 was drastically reduced because of the metritis outbreak; Mill Reef had only nine reported foals. There's no mistaking Mill Reef's place in British and European racing though: even with so few representing him, through no fault of his own, he had another top-class three-year-old Glint of Gold. Fairy Footsteps' dam Glass Slipper is similarly well established, having bred two classic winners in successive years. Her first foal, by the way, the quite useful handicapper Crystal Coach, was put down after breaking a cannon bone in New Zealand in April; he had been retired to stud there at the end of his three-year-old days. Glass Slipper is maintaining a family tradition established over the preceding three generations. Picture Play produced seven winners, among them Queen of Light and Red Shoes (the dam of West Side Story, placed in the One Thousand Guineas and Oaks in 1962); Queen of Light produced six winners, including the excellent broodmares Crystal Palace, Picture

Light, Chandelier and Lovely Light; Crystal Palace produced eight winners, the pick of them the top colts Royal Palace, Prince Consort and Selhurst.

Of Crystal Palace's winners we know for certain seven stayed a fair bit further than a mile; the other, the unsound Owen Jones, never had the opportunity of racing further. Crystal Palace herself, a very useful filly, was effective at seven furlongs to a mile and a quarter. If one looks hard enough there are horses to be found in the family that showed much more speed than stamina. Those people who accept, or would find it convenient to accept, that Fairy Footsteps didn't stay, will gain comfort and support from the commentary in *Racehorses of 1952* on her great-grandam Queen of Light, a mare by Borealis: 'It would seem that a mile is her best distance, though one would have thought she would have stayed well enough considering her breeding'. To see how Fairy Footsteps' foals turn out will be one of the future's pleasures.

Fairy Footsteps is a well-made, robust filly, a good walker with a very light action. She was extremely well suited by a sound surface. She visits Bustino. *H. Cecil.*

FAIRY KING 8 br.g. Prefairy–Miss Pindado (Pinza 137) (1980 NR 1981 **77** 12f² 16f²) big gelding; smart chaser; not without ability on flat and finished second to Jamestino and Weavers' Pin in amateur riders races at Beverley in July and August; stays well. *J. Fitzgerald.*

FAIRY TERN 2 b.f. Mill Reef 141–Elegant Tern 102 (Sea-Bird II 145) (1981 **99** 5g* 6fg 5d³ 5fg* 5g³) May 23; quite attractive, rather lightly-made filly; third foal; sister to a moderate filly; dam won 3 times at around 1m and stayed 1½m; came through very late when winning maiden race at Newbury in July and well-contested race at Salisbury in September, beating Haditos 1½ lengths in latter; also third of 5 in 2 good races won by Jester, beaten a length in Prince of Wales's Stakes at York and 3½ lengths in Harry Rosebery Challenge Trophy at Ayr (looked a bit light and didn't move well to start at Ayr); bred to stay at least 1¼m but ran badly on only attempt at a distance beyond 5f; acts on a firm and a soft surface. *I. Balding.*

Mr Paul Mellon's "Fairy Tern"

FAITHFUL DON (USA) 2 br.c. Dawn Flight–Always Faithful 103 (Super — Sam 124) (1981 7fg 7d 7fg 7g 7d) Apr 10; $11,500Y; first foal; dam won 4 times at 1m; sire, son of Grey Dawn II, won seven times at up to 9f; a useful-looking colt but showed no worthwhile form at 2 yrs. *G. Balding.*

FAIZ 3 b.c. Prince Tenderfoot 126–Grazia 90 (Aureole 132) (1980 5d² 5f² 6g* **109** 6d² 5fg³ 6d* 1981 7fg* 7fg* 7fg* 7d* 7g) well-made, quite attractive colt; good mover; had a poorish run when strong-finishing length second to Lord Wimpy in handicap at Epsom in April on reappearance and was subsequently awarded race; went from strength to strength afterwards and won handicaps at Goodwood in July (gamely by ¾ length from Lucky Man), Kempton in August (beat Porto-gon a length after hanging quite badly) and Ayr in September (responded well to strong driving and held off Hurricane Hill by a head in Holsten Diat Pils Handi-cap); didn't have clearest of runs final start; will stay 1m; seems to act on any going; genuine and consistent; sent to race in USA. *J. Dunlop.*

FALAKA 2 ch.f. Sparkler 130–Falassa (Relko 136) (1981 5g² 5fg² 6fg⁴ 5g³ 6d² **77** 5d²) Mar 10; small, quite attractive filly; third foal; half-sister to 1½m winner Falnama (by Queen's Hussar); dam, placed at up to 1¼m in France, is half-sister to top-class Silver Shark; second in maiden races at Newbury in June (beaten a neck), Goodwood in July (went down by ½ length), Nottingham in September (ran on strongly when beaten a length by odds-on Dish Dash) and Bath in October; will be suited by 7f; acts on a firm and a soft surface; consistent; sold to CBA 16,500 gns Newmarket Autumn Sales. *F. J. Houghton.*

FALCON'S HEIR (USA) 2 b.c. Accipiter–Famous Princess (Diplomat Way) **75** (1981 6d 6g⁴ 5fg⁴) Mar 19; $17,000Y; lengthy, quite attractive colt; first foal; dam, placed at 3 yrs, is half-sister to very useful Famed Princess; fourth in maiden races at Salisbury in June and Windsor in July; beaten 3½ lengths by Annesley and 4 lengths by Warm Hearted respectively, better effort on former course; should be suited by 7f+. *P. Cole.*

FALDOR 4 ch.g. Falaise–Little Dora (Bounteous 125) (1980 12g 12g² 13.8f 10g — 12g 13.8fg³ 13.8d 11s* 8d 1981 12g 8g 10fg 15fg 13.8fg 12f 12.2g) plain gelding; plater; probably stays 13.8f; acts on soft going; sometimes blinkered; suitable mount for a claimer. *J. Calvert.*

FALKLAND PALACE 4 b.g. Royal Palace 131–Festival Night 115 (Midsum- **47** mer Night II 117) (1980 9fg² 11.7fg 13.3fg 16d⁴ 1981 12.5s²) big, leggy, un-furnished gelding; only plating class; appears not to stay 2m; probably acts on any going. *D. Morley.*

FALLEN ANGEL 2 b.f. Quiet Fling 124–Alangia 101 (Shantung 132) (1981 **81** 7fg 6fg 7fg 8fg² 8d) Mar 25; lightly-made filly; third foal; dam won from 7f to 1½m; neck second of 17 to Napa Valley in maiden race at Leicester in September, easily best effort; will be suited by 1½m; possibly needs a sound surface. *H. Candy.*

FALLIG SCHNELL 5 ch.g. King's Leap 111–Sea Melody 79 (Tudor Minstrel 144) — (1980 6f 9fg 7f 7d 1981 10.6s 8g 7fg) workmanlike gelding; poor plater; has worn bandages. *S. Wiles.*

FALSETTA 3 b.f. Song 132–Deceptive (Great Nephew 126) (1980 NR 1981 — 7d 8f 6f 6fg) strong, well-made filly; first foal; dam lightly-raced half-sister to good broodmare Calvine; behind in maiden races and sellers; sold 460 gns Ascot September Sales. *T. M. Jones.*

FAMOUS STAR 2 ch.c. Sharpen Up 127–Hecla 117 (Henry the Seventh 125) **97** (1981 5f 6s²) Apr 29; 25,000Y; close-coupled colt; half-brother to 3 winners, including useful miler Be Better (by Busted); dam, smart over 6f at 2 yrs, is half-sister to very speedy fillies Mange Tout and Rose Dubarry; having first race for over 3 months, led until inside final furlong when length second of 15 to Risk Taker in maiden race at Newbury in October; not sure to stay beyond 6f; acts on soft going; sure to win a maiden race. *M. Albina.*

FANDANCE 2 ch.f. Gay Fandango 132–Clariden 82 (Hook Money 124) (1981 **64** 5d³ 6f 5fg³ 5g 6d 6s) Apr 1; IR 10,000Y; sturdy filly; half-sister to several winners, including useful 5f to 7f performer Yonge St Clare (by Queen's Hussar) and fairly useful 1978 2-y-o 5f performer St Claire Tourier (by Dike); dam moderate over 5f at 2 yrs; poor form in 5f maiden and minor events (well beaten over 6f). *W. Wharton.*

FANDANGLE 3 ch.c. Gay Fandango 132–Sandra II (Le Haar 126) (1980 6g⁴ **79** 8g² 1981 7fg 6g* 6g 6fg 7fg³ 7fg³ 7.3d² 8s⁴) medium-sized, quite attractive colt; has been hobdayed; won maiden event at Brighton in May; ran creditably most subsequent starts, on last 2 finishing in frame in handicaps at Newbury; effective at 6f and stays 1m; probably acts on any going; didn't move to post well fifth start. *J. Tree.*

FANDANGO TIME 3 ch.c. Gay Fandango 132–Sapho 59 (Raeburn II) (1980 **104** 7f⁴ 1981 8d² 10d* 10.5f² 8g² 8g* 8fg* 8d) lengthy, rather lightly-made colt; developed into a useful colt and beat Teamwork most convincingly in handicap at Goodwood in July, having his field stone cold when taking up running 2f out and coming home 3 lengths clear despite swerving to left; had earlier passed post first in maiden event at Epsom, minor race at Salisbury and handicap at Newcastle, but at Salisbury gave runner-up Ramannolie a hefty bump when diving left under the whip and placings were reversed; second twice at York, on second occasion going down by a neck to Dogberry in £4,900 race; stays 1¼m; seems to act on any going; not always the easiest of rides; looked rather hard trained and ran disappointingly final start (August). *B. Hills.*

FANFARE MAID 2 b.f. Swing Easy 126–Just Jenny 88 (Ennis 128) (1981 5g — 6g) May 4; useful-looking filly; good walker; half-sister to several winners, including 5f sprinter Just Fred (by Town Crier); dam sprinter; little worthwhile form in end-of-season minor events in the North. *R. Hollinshead.*

FARASI 2 b.c. Shiny Tenth 120–Cecilia Gallerani (Pinturischio 116) (1981 7g **78** 7.6s⁴ 7g³) Apr 29; 5,600Y; compact colt; fourth living foal; half-brother to 3 winners, including useful 5f to 1m winner Tudor Maid (by Henry the Seventh); dam poor maiden; 6¾ lengths fourth of 13 to Sandwalker in maiden race at Lingfield in October, easily best effort; will probably stay 1m. *G. Huffer.*

FARIDELLA 3 gr.f. Silly Season 127–Fair Fabiola 94 (Acropolis 132) (1980 5f **65** 6fg⁴ 6g⁴ 7g³ 7s⁴ 8g³ 8d² 8d⁴ 1981 12d 12.2g 16f 12.2g² 12.2fg* 12f³ 11g² 10s* 12d³ 10.2g³) leggy, rather unfurnished filly; won maiden race at Catterick in August and seller at Lingfield in October; bought in 2,500 gns after winning latter by 5 lengths from Hannonball; stays 1½m; acts on any going; effective with or without blinkers; not the easiest of rides. *I. Walker.*

FARIOFFA 2 gr.c. Hotfoot 126–Lapis Lazuli 84 (Zeddaan 130) (1981 8g*) **102 p** May 6; 7,000Y; tall, lengthy colt; poor walker; half-brother to a winner in Malaya; dam won over 5f at 2 yrs, and is half-sister to smart Bas Bleu; unquoted and decidedly backward, put up a splendid first effort when winning 30-runner maiden race at Newmarket in October by 1½ lengths from Gouverno, making up ground hand over fist in final 2f to win going away; will probably stay 1¼m; looks a very useful colt in the making. *L. Cumani.*

FARLEIGH 3 b.f. Sandford Lad 133–Get Ready 91 (On Your Mark 125) (1980 — 5fg 5d 6g 8d 1981 7fg 9g) neat filly; bad mover; useless plater; has worn blinkers. *S. Matthews.*

FARM LANE 2 b.f. Moulton 128–Country Path 101 (Mossborough 126) (1981 — p 6g) Mar 7; smallish, rather lightly-made, quite attractive filly; half-sister to several winners, including very useful 9f and 1¼m winner Old Kate and very smart soft-ground stayer Old Bill (both by Busted); dam won at 1¼m and 13f; 4/1, chased leaders for some way before finishing nearly 12 lengths fifth of 14 behind Knave of Trumps in maiden event at Yarmouth in September; will probably improve when tackling 1¼m+ in 1982. *H. Wragg.*

FAROLITO (USA) 2 b.c. Foolish Pleasure–Dotty Jay Jay (Lurullah) (1981 **82** 6g⁴ 6fg⁴) May 7; $90,000Y; big, strong, lengthy colt; good walker; half-brother to several winners, including minor stakes winner Casarulla (by Cast Loose) and good Puerto Rican horse Charles McGreevy (by Selari); dam unraced; fourth in 2 quite valuable events in September, beaten 4 lengths by Master Cawston after leading to distance in Ribero Stakes at Doncaster and 4¾ lengths by Allocated after having every chance 2f out in Clarence House Stakes at Ascot; has plenty of scope and should be seen to better advantage over longer distances at 3 yrs. *R. Hern.*

FAR SAHARA (USA) 2 b.c. Far North 120–Rare Relish (Johns Joy) (1981 **76** 5fg 7fg 7f 8g) May 29; $150,000Y; small, rather leggy colt; half-brother to numerous winners, including very smart French sprinter Black Sulphur (by Drone) and a stakes winner by Grey Dawn II; dam placed at 3 yrs; showed ability in maiden and minor events, notably when 6 lengths fifth of 17 to Queen's Home at Goodwood in September on final outing; will stay 1¼m. *R. Smyth.*

FARSEEING 2 b.f. High Top 131–Montania 68 (Mourne 126) (1981 7g) Feb — 12; lengthy filly; third living foal; closely related to middle-distance winner Base Camp (by Derring-Do); dam won over 7f and half-sister to very useful Look Sharp; 33/1 when behind in 29-runner maiden race at Newmarket in October won by Chalon; has some scope and may do better over middle distances in 1982; wore a boot on her off-fore at Newmarket. *W. Hastings-Bass.*

FARSOUND 3 b.f. Wolver Hollow 126–Farfisa 86 (Sassafras 135) (1980 7g **79** 1981 11.5f 13f³ 13g⁴ 16g* 16s* 16s²) leggy filly; decisively won maiden race at Nottingham in August and handicap on same course in September, in latter staying on gamely to beat Athford by 5 lengths; stays very well; seems to act on any going; sold 13,000 gns Newmarket December Sales. *M. Stoute.*

FAR TOO MUCH 2 b.g. Windjammer (USA)–Sweet Princess (Prince Regent **81 p** 129) (1981 8g) Mar 24; IR 4,600Y; second foal; dam unraced sister to useful filly Brightelmstone; unquoted and looking as though race would do him good, led running into the Dip when about 8 lengths seventh of 29 to Born Hero in maiden race at Newmarket in October; probably stays 1m; a fair first effort. *M. Smyly.*

FASCADALE 7 br.g. Frankincense 120–Straight Off 88 (Straight Deal) (1980 **91** 10v* 10.6fg 12fg* 12f* 12g⁴ 12g³ 12d* 11s 10.5s⁴ 12v 1981 10v³ 12fg 12s² 12g 12f* 11fg² 12f³ 12d³ 11g* 11d³ 12g) fairly useful handicapper; won at Ripon in June and Ayr in September; beat Fine Sun by ¾ length in Ladbrokes' Ayrshire Handicap on latter; stays 1½m; acts on any going; suitable mount for a boy; sometimes sweats up; needs to be held up and is suited by a strong gallop. *J. W. Watts.*

FASHION BOY 3 b.g. Go Marching–Telstop (Fine Top 125) (1980 7g 8g — 1981 10d 11s 16d) attractive, well-made gelding; in rear in maiden and minor races, finishing last twice; sold 725 gns Ascot October Sales. *G. Lewis.*

FAST AND SURE (USA) 2 gr.g. Tudor Grey 119–Miss Adorable (Ramsinga — 115) (1981 7g) second foal; dam won sprint claiming races at 3 yrs; 14/1 and fairly fit when behind in 18-runner maiden race won by Leg Glance at Doncaster in October. *G. Pritchard-Gordon.*

FAST FRIEND 3 ch.f. Be Friendly 130–Hastily 99 (Hornbeam 130) (1980 5f **91** 5g² 5fg 6s³ 6d* 6g 6fg 7d 1981 6d 7.3s³ 7fg 7g⁴ 6g 7s 7s 6v² 5g) rather leggy filly; usually had stiff tasks but ran creditably on occasions, including when 3½ lengths third of 4 behind Marwell in Fred Darling Stakes at Newbury in April; also in frame in handicaps at Newcastle in July (first outing for over 3 months, didn't have much of a run) and Kempton in October (good ¾-length second to Cudgel); stays 7f; possibly needs some give in the ground and acts on heavy going; missed break fifth start. *P. Kelleway.*

FAST LAD 2 b.c. No Loiterer 90–Young Rowette 99 (Delirium 126) (1981 5g³ **79** 5fg² 6f 6g³ 6d 5s* 6d) Mar 6; 2,800Y; small, sturdy colt; half-brother to several winners here and abroad, including 1974 2-y-o 7f winner King Solomon (by Mandamus); dam, sprinter, is sister to smart miler Young Christopher; apprentice ridden, led close home to win 17-runner maiden race at Warwick in October by a neck from Godstruth; in rear under a penalty when favourite in nursery at Hamilton later in month; will stay 7f; probably acts on any going. *A. Jarvis.*

FASTNET ISLAND 4 b.g. Young Emperor 133–Long Shadow 77 (Royal Palm **53** 131) (1980 8f 9f 12s 12d 1981 10s 15.5d 14s³ 14d 12.3g 12f) lengthy gelding; staying handicapper; acts on soft going; usually blinkered nowadays. *P. Kelleway.*

FAST SERVICE 2 ch.c. Sharpen Up 127–Ginnies Pet 106 (Compensation 127) **75** (1981 5.8f 5fg³ 5fg 5g) May 28; small, close-coupled colt; second foal; dam game sprinter; quite a moderate maiden; blinkered first and fourth outings, and sweated up on third; lacks scope. *P. Cundell.*

FAST TRICK 3 b.f. Northfields–Fascinating Trick (Buckpasser) (1980 NR **76** 1981 8fg* 9f* 10.1g) leggy, fair sort; third foal; dam twice-raced sister to best 1971 American 2-y-o filly Numbered Account and smart middle-distance colt Cunning Trick; apprentice ridden when winning minor events at Newmarket in July and Wolverhampton in August, on latter course making all and staying on very well to beat Leonidas by a length; odds on when disappointing on only subsequent outing; should be suited by 1¼m; acts on firm going; sold 70,000 gns Newmarket December Sales. *H. Cecil.*

FATA MORGANA 6 gr.g. Grey Mirage 128–Monica Rose (Forlorn River 124) — (1980 18d² 16s 16f 1981 15.8s) poor staying handicapper; acts on any going; suitable mount for an apprentice. *D. Weeden.*

FATHER ROONEY (USA) 2 b.c. Val de l'Orne 130–Royal Honoree (Round **91** Table) (1981 7g² 7g) Apr 6; $70,000Y; attractive, tall, rangy colt; first foal; dam, winner 3 times at up to 6f, is sister to top 1972 French 2-y-o Targowice; took a while to get going but made excellent late progress when 5 lengths second of 18 to General Anders in £4,100 race at Ascot in September (wore small bandage on near-hind); second favourite when never-dangerous 4 lengths fifth of 15 to Ivano in Houghton Stakes at Newmarket the following month; will stay 1¼m; the type to make a better 3-y-o. *B. Hills.*

FAVOLOSO 2 b.c. Sun Prince 128–Lovely Clare (Sing Sing 134) (1981 6fg 7fg 8s² 8d) Feb 8; 12,500Y; rangy, quite attractive colt; half-brother to 2 winners by Prince Tenderfoot, including fairly useful 1980 2-y-o 6f winner Lord Clarence; dam 2-y-o 5f and 6f winner; made much of running and kept on well after being headed when ½-length second of 15 to Twist Home in maiden race at York in October; out of depth in William Hill Futurity Stakes at Doncaster later in month; stays 1m well; should win in ordinary maiden company. *R. Boss.* **90**

FAVOURED LADY 2 b.f. Mummy's Pet 125–Tender Courtesan 90 (Primera 131) (1981 5fg 5fg² 6g⁴ 5f 5d) Mar 8; small filly; good walker; sister to very useful 1977 2-y-o 6f performer Lambkin, and half-sister to 2 winners, including very useful sprinter Overtown (by Raffingora); dam won twice over 7f at 2 yrs; in frame in maiden races at Redcar in July (failed by ¾ length to overhaul Queen of the Blues) and August (appeared not to stay 6f); ruined chance by starting slowly when favourite fourth outing; sold 7,400 gns Newmarket Autumn Sales. *J. W. Watts.* **72**

FEARLESS FLIGHT 4 ch.c. Golden Mallard 103–Fear Not 106 (Faubourg II 127) (1980 8fg 8.2f 10f 11fg 10.5d 10.2g 6g² 6g⁴ 7fg 1981 6s³ 6g 6g³ 6g³ 7g 7g⁴ 6f 7.6s 7g 9d² 8d 9s 8g² 8g) big, strong colt; stays 9f; suited by some give in the ground; sold 1,500 gns Doncaster November Sales. *W. Elsey.* **52**

FEARLESS LAD 2 ch.c. Import 127–No Fear 91 (Quayside 124) (1981 6g 5f* 6d² 5g*) Mar 10; big, strong colt; first foal; dam 1¼m winner; improved with his races and on final start put up a very useful performance when giving weight to 8 rivals in Doncaster Stakes in October, leading inside last to beat Special Pleasure by ½ length; had won 7-runner Highflyer Stakes at Thirsk the previous month by 2 lengths from Lavender Dance; stays 6f; seems to act on any going; looks the sort to train on well. *R. D. Peacock.* **112**

FEAR NO MORE 4 b.f. Morston 125–Fearless 77 (Derring-Do 131) (1980 10.1f 1981 9g 8g 9fg⁴ 7fg 7fg) plating-class maiden; should stay 1¼m+; sometimes sweats up. *C. Nelson.* **53**

FEAST (NZ) 7 gr.g. Coeur Volant II–Whence (The Summit) (1980 8fg 1981 8d) wiry gelding; lightly raced and little worthwhile form. *R. Atkins.* **—**

FEAST-RITE 3 b.f. Reform 132–Tribal Feast 100 (Tribal Chief 125) (1980 5fg 1981 6f) small, lightly-made filly; behind in minor event at Catterick as a 2-y-o and in maiden race at Nottingham in July. *K. Stone.* **—**

FEATHERED (USA) 2 b.c. Al Hattab–Miss Plumage (Bold Legend) (1981 7g 8s³ 10s) Mar 13; $70,000Y; close-coupled, useful-looking colt; half-brother to 3 winners, 2 of them stakes placed; dam stakes winner at up to 7f; staying on when beaten over 7 lengths in maiden races in October, finishing third to Fort Garry at Warwick and sixth behind Luxury at Nottingham; suited by a test of stamina; didn't stride out on way to start on debut. *P. Walwyn.* **75**

FEATHER SOUND 2 ch.g. Be My Guest 126–Muffet 75 (Matador 131) (1981 5fg 5g 5fg³ 6fg 7.3d⁴ 7s 7g 7d 6g⁴) Apr 24; 19,000Y; quite attractive, well-made gelding; half-brother to Irish 3-y-o Lasater (by Lochnager), winning sprinter Hanovia Gold (by Yellow River) and a winner in Trinidad; dam (known as Matty) won over 5f; in frame 3 times, notably on fifth and ninth starts when fourth in nurseries at Newbury and Newmarket; stays 7f; possibly unsuited by very soft ground; blinkered fifth to eighth outings; takes a good hold. *R. Armstrong.* **88**

FEE 3 gr.f. Mandamus 120–Currency (Crepello 136) (1980 5d 5d⁴ 6s² 6g* 6fg³ 6d² 7g* 1981 10g* 10d⁴ 10g* 10g* 10fg² 10.6d* 10g*) leggy filly; good walker and mover; first foal; dam never ran; developed into a very useful filly and had a most successful season; won handicaps at Pontefract in April, Lingfield (two) in June, Haydock in August (by 6 lengths from Sally Rose) and Newmarket in October; quickened well and ran on strongly to beat Government Program by 1½ lengths after being held up on last-named course; looked unlucky when neck second to Sally Rose in similar event at Newbury (rider of winner got first run); would have stayed 1½m; seemed to act on any going; thoroughly genuine and consistent and clearly thrived on her racing; retired to stud. *B. Hobbs.* **111**

FEELINGS (FR) 4 b.c. Green Dancer 132–Fast Iron (Iron Peg §§) (1980 12d 12fg⁴ 12fg³ 10.2g 10.2g 10s* 12g⁴ 14.7d² 15d 1981 12g* 12g* 13g 12.3fg² 12fg² **81**

15g 14.7d² 14d 13d) well-made, quite attractive ex-French colt; fair handi-capper; made all to win at Pontefract (from Gleaming Wave) and Doncaster (beat Jamshid 2½ lengths) in May; stays well; seems to act on any going; blinkered nowadays. *J. Hanson.*

FELIPA 7 b.m. Philip of Spain 126–City Carriage 88 (Counsel 118) (1980 NR 1981 8fg 7f 7g 8s) of little account; has been to stud and produced a colt by Bay Express. *J. O'Donoghue.*

FELIXSTOWE LAD 2 br.g. Pongee 106–The Squeeze 85 (Bing II) (1981 7fg 6fg 8d) May 14; fourth foal; dam won 8 times from 5f to 1½m; beaten less than 2 lengths when sixth of 13 to Royal Carnival in seller at Newcastle in August, second outing; not disgraced when 100/1 in better race on same course in October; will stay 1¼m. *R. Johnson.* **64 ?**

FELTHORPE MARINER 2 b.c. Be My Guest 126–Sea Horse 98 (Sea-Bird II 145) (1981 6f 5f⁴ 7fg⁴ 7fg* 7d⁴ 7fg 7g³ 6d) May 18; IR 20,000F; neat, good sort; fourth foal; half-brother to 2 winners in Italy, including useful African Horse (by African Sky); dam won over 7f and 1¼m; beat odds-on Bancario a neck in 4-runner minor event at Chester in July; ran best subsequent race when third to clever winner Nioulargo in nursery at Yarmouth in September; probably finds 6f on sharp side nowadays and will stay 1m. *C. Brittain.* **87**

FELTWELL (USA) 3 b.c. Habitat 134–Reload 119 (Relko 136) (1980 8g 7d 8g 1981 10s 10v² 10.6d* 10g⁴ 12g2² 10.6s* 12f* 12fg 11g) good-bodied colt; apprentice ridden when winning Stones Best Bitter Handicap at Haydock (held on by ½ length from strong-finishing Capricorn Line) and King George V Stakes Handicap at Royal Ascot (produced with a well-timed run and beat Grain Race by a similar margin), both in June; had earlier made all in another handicap at Haydock; off course 2 months after seventh start and didn't recover his form; suited by 1½m; acts on any going; genuine. *H. Wragg.* **89**

FENKIN 3 b. or br.c. Swing Easy 126–Path of Pride (Sovereign Path 125) (1980 NR 1981 10s 10fg 10s 12d) 3,800F, 6,400Y; rangy colt; second foal; half-brother to useful 1978 2-y-o 1m winner Spring With Pride (by Scottish Rifle); dam never ran; soundly beaten in maiden and minor events; dwelt first outing. *M. Ryan.* **—**

FENNEY MILL 4 b.f. Levmoss 133–Pidget 120 (Fortino II 120) (1980 10fg* 12d³ 1981 12g³ 16f) very attractive ex-Irish filly; lightly raced but is fairly useful at her best; won small race at Phoenix Park and finished third in Ribblesdale Stakes at Royal Ascot at 3 yrs; remote third of 6 to Master Willie in Jockey Club Stakes at Newmarket in May; wasn't entirely disgraced when eighth of 13 to Ore in Queen's Vase at Royal Ascot 6 weeks later; subsequently sent to race in USA; should stay well; acts on a firm and a soft surface. *J. Dunlop.* **—**

FERINGGI 2 b. or br.c. Sweet Revenge 129–Home Waters 83 (Gulf Pearl 117) (1981 6g 6fg 7f 7g 8g) Apr 28; 4,200Y; neat, good-bodied colt; bad mover; second foal; dam stayed 1¼m; 12½ lengths sixth of 16 to Adonis Rex in maiden race at Leicester in September, fourth outing and only sign of ability; sold 820 gns Doncaster November Sales. *R. Armstrong.* **—**

King George V Stakes Handicap, Ascot—Feltwell is brought with a well-timed run on the outside to beat Grain Race

FERNARO 4 ch.g. Sharpen Up 127–Sea Fern (Klondyke Bill 125) (1980 8v **64**
8fg 7fg* 8h* 8f 7g³ 7d³ 8g 7g³ 7d⁴ 7g* 10.2g 8fg 8g 1981 6s 8s 7d 8f⁴ 7.6g⁴ 8f
8g 7fg³ 8f³ 7fg 8fg) useful-looking gelding; best at up to 1m; acts on any going;
blinkered once at 3 yrs and on last 3 starts; genuine. *R. Hannon.*

FEROCIOUS KNIGHT (USA) 2 b.g. Fearless Knight–Fallaha's Love **70**
(Our Love 97) (1981 6fg 7fg 10s) Feb 3; $4,200F; tall, close-coupled gelding;
first living foal; dam won 10 times at up to 9f in USA, including claiming events;
sire stakes-placed son of Round Table; only poor form in maiden races but looks
the type to do better at 3 yrs; gelded at end of season. *P. Cole.*

FERRIBY FLYER 2 b.c. Vitiges 132–Lily Langtry 102 (Prince de Galles 125) —
(1981 6g 7f) May 8; 4,600Y; fair sort; has a round action; first foal; dam, half-
sister to very smart stayer Mr Bigmore, won from 1¼m to 1½m; not fully fit
when in rear in seller at Newcastle in June (last of 10) and minor event at Beverley
in July. *A. Smith.*

FERRIBY HALL 4 b.g. Malicious–Gallic Law 91 (Galivanter 131) (1980 5d² **92**
5g 6fg* 6fg² 6f³ 6f 6g³ 6g 5f 6s 6d² 7s 5s³ 6d³ 1981 6g 5d 6g 7fg³ 6f³ 5fg* 6fg
6g 5.6fg 6d 6s 5d) strong gelding; quite a useful handicapper; ran on gamely to
beat Sanu a neck in valuable Gosforth Park Cup at Newcastle in June; had run
very well previous start when third, beaten 2 short heads, to Great Eastern in
Wokingham Stakes at Royal Ascot; stays 6f; acts on any going; used to wear
blinkers; sometimes sweats up; has run well for an apprentice; trained part of
season by T. Fairhurst; retained 3,700 gns Newmarket Autumn Sales. *A. Smith.*

FERRYMAN 5 b.g. Forlorn River 124–La Miranda 80 (Miralgo 130) (1980 **94**
5g² 6fg² 5.8fg 5fg* 5d² 5f 5g² 5d² 5g* 5d 1981 5fg² 5d 5g³ 6fg² 5d⁴ 5fg³ 5g 5s²
6v³) small gelding; fair handicapper; runner-up at Epsom in April, Goodwood
in July (excellent ¾ length behind Crews Hill in Tote Stewards' Cup) and Ascot
in October; spoiled his chance by hanging right in £6,300 race on last-named and
went down by a short head to Maryland Cookie; best at sprint distances; probably
acts on any going; blinkered sixth start; sometimes sweats up. *D. Elsworth.*

FESTAL SPIRIT 2 b.f. Jimmy Reppin 131–Celebrate 85 (Rockavon 120) — p
(1981 7g) May 8; big, strong filly; sister to Beldale Rep, successful over 7f at 2
yrs in this country before winning Norwegian Derby; dam half-sister to Peleid
and Coup de Feu; 25/1 and in need of race, stayed on nicely when promising
6¼ lengths fifth of 15 to Awaasif in maiden event at Ayr in September; has plenty
of scope and should improve sufficiently to win in maiden company in the
North over middle distances in 1982. *W. Elsey.*

FESTIVE LADY 3 ch.f. Ragstone 128–Lavington 64 (Ratification 129) (1980 **66**
NR 1981 10fg 12d² 14d³) long-backed filly; fifth foal; half-sister to 3 winners,
including 1976 2-y-o 7f winner Bushy Pieces (by Ribero); dam, placed twice at
1m, is half-sister to top sprinters So Blessed and Lucasland; placed in minor event
at Salisbury in May and maiden race at Sandown in June; looks slow and will
be suited by 2m; sold 4,100 gns Newmarket December Sales. *P. Cole.*

FETTERED 7 b.g. Manacle 123–Anatevka (Privy Councillor 125) (1980 8fg* **43**
7f 8f² 8fg 7.6d 8g² 8g⁴ 8fg 1981 7d 8fg³ 8g 7g² 8s³ 8d 7f) lengthy gelding;
poor handicapper; stayed 1m; acted on any going except hard; often wore
blinkers; dead. *N. Vigors.*

FETTER LANE 5 b.h. Manacle 123–La Colline 97 (Acropolis 132) (1980 11.7fg³ **59**
12f² 12f 12g⁴ 12.2s² 12d 16.9d² 1981 15.5d 12s* 15.5d) unfurnished horse;
won apprentice handicap at Leicester in May; seemed to stay 2m; acted on any
going; sometimes wore blinkers; dead. *B. Palling.*

FICKLE FIGHTER 3 br.g. Mummy's Pet 125–Breathalyser (Alcide 136)
(1980 5f 7f 6d 1981 8g 8g) no worthwhile form, including in a seller (last).
W. Bentley.

FICKLE FORTUNE 2 ch.f. Mount Hagen 127–Coumfea (Gulf Pearl 117)
(1981 5g) Apr 1; IR 13,000Y; first foal; dam ran only once; 10/1, started slowly
when tenth of 11 behind Four Marks in maiden event at Edinburgh in June.
C. Nelson.

FIDALCO (FR) 2 br.c. Nonoalco 131–High Fidelyty (Hautain 128) (1981 6g)
half-brother to several winners, including useful French middle-distance winner
Moulin (by Mill Reef); dam won in Italy; unquoted and in need of race when
in rear in 13-runner minor event won by Knave of Trumps at Leicester in
October. *C. Austin.*

303

FID

FIDDLER 4 b.g. Song 132–Silent Swindler 59 (Tacitus 124) (1980 5v* 5fg* — 5f* 5fg4 5fg3 5d 5g 5.8f 5d4 5d 5d* 6d 1981 5s 5.8g 5g 5f 5g 5s) sturdy gelding; has an enlarged near-hind hock; sprint handicapper; well beaten most starts at 4 yrs; best at 5f; acts on any going; blinkered twice at 2 yrs. *C. Austin.*

FIDDLERS FERRY 2 br.c. Jolly Good 122–Shifty (Shantung 132) (1981 6fg — 7fg) May 4; 1,050Y; lengthy, lightly-made colt; half-brother to 3-y-o King's Spy (by Queen's Hussar); dam never ran; in rear in sellers at Nottingham in June (swerved at start) and Redcar in July. *K. Stone.*

FIDURI 2 b.f. Wolver Hollow 126–Sans Blague (Above Suspicion 127) (1981 — 5d 7f) Jan 11; third foal; dam won over 1½m and 1¾m in Ireland; unquoted when in rear in maiden races at Lingfield and Brighton in August. *C. James.*

FIELD LADY 2 ch.f. Habitat 134–Meadow Pipit 103 (Worden II 129) (1981 6g) — p Feb 23; 100,000Y; strong, well-made filly; half-sister to several winners, notably St Leger and Irish Sweeps Derby second Meadowville (by Charlottesville) and good middle-distance stayer Nuthatch (by Levmoss); dam won both her starts; 20/1 and distinctly burly, wasn't given an unnecessarily hard time when ninth of 17 to stable-companion Merlin's Charm in maiden race at Newmarket in October; will stay at least 1¼m; a nice individual who's sure to do better. *B. Hills.*

FIERY AMBER 2 ch.f. Streak 119–Crop (Acropolis 132) (1981 5s 5fg 5fg 6f 5f4 **56** 6g) Feb 17; 3,200Y; neat filly; half-sister to 2 winners, including fair sprinter Spanish Issue (by Philip of Spain); dam of little account; 5 lengths fourth of 9 to Red Ellette in 5f maiden auction event at Folkestone in August, best effort. *C. James.*

FIESTA FUN 3 br.f. Welsh Pageant 132–Antigua 100 (Hyperion) (1980 6f **105** 7g 7g2 8fg3 1981 10g 10d* 12g 10f* 10.1fg* 10g 12g3 12s) workmanlike filly; half-sister to several winners, including smart 6f and 7f winner Derrylin (by Derring-Do); dam won at 1½m; successful in maiden and minor events at Brighton and minor event at Windsor, beating Danlifar by 2½ lengths with remainder well strung out in 17-runner race on latter course in June; had much stiffer tasks on her other starts, easily best effort when about ¾-length third to Condessa in Yorkshire Oaks in August, making running and sticking on most gamely; suited by 1½m; probably acts on any going; genuine. *P. Cole.*

FIGHETTA (FR) 2 b.f. Free Round 127–Lean On (Turn-to) (1981 7f) Apr — 19; 140,000 francs Y (approx £14,000); tall, leggy, close-coupled filly; excellent mover; second foal; half-sister to a winner over jumps in France; dam, half-sister to Nonoalco's dam, won 6f claiming race; 50/1 and in need of race, showed good speed 4f when behind in 16-runner maiden race won by Imagination at Yarmouth in August; sold 1,800 gns Newmarket Autumn Sales. *R. Sheather.*

FIGHTING FIDDLER 6 b.g. Derring-Do 131–Zither 72 (Vienna 127) (1980 — NR 1981 16s) poor maiden; suited by a test of stamina in the mud; used to wear blinkers. *W. Charles.*

FIGHT THE FIRE 2 b.c. Firestreak 125–Fighting Winnie (Fighting Charlie — 127) (1981 5s 5s 5s3) May 18; plain, rather lightly-made colt, no worthwhile form in early-season races, one of them a seller. *W. Holden.*

FILAO (USA) 2 ch.g. Fleet Allied–Space Odyssey (Promised Land) (1981 — 6fg 6g) Apr 26; $130,000Y; big, handsome gelding; fourth foal; dam, sister to dam of Spectacular Bid, won at up to 1m, including a minor stakes race; sire, son of Fleet Nasrullah, won 6f stakes events; favourite, showed excellent speed until lack of fitness told in final 2f when tenth of 14 to Codrington in Granville Stakes at Ascot in July; blinkered when only ninth of 12 to Rebollino in Convivial Maiden Stakes at York the following month (coltish in preliminaries); gelded subsequently. *R. Hern.*

FILARIO (FR) 2 b.c. Filiberto 123–Escaria (Right Royal V 135) (1981 6h) — third foal; half-brother to minor French 7f and 1¼m winner Caranos (by Auriban) and to a winner in Italy; dam never ran; 11/1 when tailed-off last of 7 to Charbonnel in newcomers race at Chepstow in September. *A. Jarvis.*

FILLETTS FARM 7 b.g. Stephen George 102–Markeeba (March Past 124) **58** (1980 NR 1981 12.3g 12f 12f 16g* 15.8fg* 18.8fg2 16.1fg) strong gelding; staying handicapper; won at Nottingham and Catterick within space of 3 days in August; yet to race on a soft surface. *J. Etherington.*

FIMI 2 br.f. Tachypous 128–Chequered Flag 70 (King's Troop 118) (1981 5g3 **95** 5fg2 5s* 5f2 6d* 5f* 6f*) Mar 16; 7,200Y; good-quartered, well-made filly; good mover; half-sister to three 2-y-o winners, including 1979 5f winner Saintly

304

Simon (by Saintly Song); dam won over 5f at 2 yrs; made most of running when winning maiden race at Leicester and minor events at Hamilton, Beverley and Pontefract; rallied gamely when gaining last 2 victories scoring respectively by a length from Chere Jane in August and by ½ length from Chris's Lad in September; stays 6f well; acts on any going; a thoroughly genuine and consistent filly who thrived physically. *B. Hobbs.*

FINAL STRIKE 2 b.c. Artaius 129–Cape Race 88 (Northern Dancer) (1981 **102** 5g 5d* 5s³ 5g³ 6fg⁴ 6f³ 7f⁴ 8fg² 7s³ 7g* 7g) May 8; 40,000Y; compact colt; first foal; dam, half-sister to very smart colts Lord Gayle and Never Return, won over 1m; won maiden race at Folkestone in May and all-aged event at Newmarket in October, in latter beating Parthia's Picture 4 lengths; also ran extremely well in competitive nurseries in between, finishing neck second of 16 to Lobkowiez at Doncaster in September, and 3½ lengths third of 11 to Spanish Pool at Lingfield the following month; will be suited by middle distances; seems to act on any going. *F. Durr.*

FIND THE SUN 4 ch.g. Galivanter 131–Sunshine Holyday 96 (Three Wishes **47** 114) (1980 10f 10f 13.8fg² 12d 13.8f 13.8g 10fg 12s³ 12d 1981 15.8s 16s² 15.8g 16g 13d³ 15.8g³) leggy gelding; staying handicapper; probably acts on any going; ran badly fourth start. *C. Gray.*

FINE ASSET 2 b.f. Hot Spark 126–Omentello 91 (Elopement 125) (1981 6s 6s) — June 7; 18,000Y; good-bodied, useful-looking filly; half-sister to numerous winners, including useful Lyric Dance (by Lyphard), successful over 6f and 7f, and smart 7f performer Tudor Mill (by Derring-Do); dam won over 13f; in rear in Blue Seal Stakes at Ascot in September and in maiden race at Newbury in October. *R. Laing.*

FINE HONEY (USA) 3 b.f. Drone–She's Sofine (Bold Hour) (1980 5d² 5fg* — 6fg³ 1981 8.5fg 8g) lengthy, attractive filly; won maiden race at Goodwood as a 2-y-o; disappointing in 1981 in handicaps at Epsom in April and Leicester (blinkered) in September; should stay 1m. *J. Tree.*

FINE POINT 4 b.c. Sharpen Up 127–Kalyanda 77 (Kalydon 122) (1980 5d **56** 5v⁴ 8f* 9f² 9fg* 8d 8f 8d 10s 8f 1981 10v 8.2g 7d 9fg² 7g⁴ 7g 9fg 8g³ 8.2g 8fg 10g³ 12f* 10f 13d 11d 13.8g) neat, strong colt; front-running handicapper; won at Hamilton in August; stays 1½m; best served by a sound surface; hasn't looked too genuine on occasions. *Denys Smith.*

FINE SUN 4 ch.g. Fine Blade 121–All Sunshine (Miralgo 130) (1980 12f³ **110** 10f* 10.6fg 10g² 10g³ 10.5g* 14g 11s³ 12fg* 10g² 12v 1981 10.2g 9d* 10d³ 12f 10.5g 12f⁴ 10.2g³ 11g² 8g 9s*(dis) 10g²) fair sort; useful handicapper; stayed on well to beat Milk of the Barley by ¾ length in well-contested minor event at Ripon in May; beat Seven Hearts 1½ lengths in valuable apprentice handicap at York in October but was disqualified for hampering second; good head second to King's Glory in Tia Maria Autumn Handicap at Newmarket later in month; stays 11f; probably acts on any going; often sweats up; has twice won for 5-lb claimer N. Howe; game; to be trained by M. Lambert. *Miss S. Hall.*

FINE TOUCH 2 ch.f. Touch Paper 113–Fine Mesh (Match III 135) (1981 5s **49** 5d* 5d* 5d² 5d² 6fg² 6fg³) Mar 1; 1,500Y; compact filly; half-sister to useful 1976 Irish 2-y-o 5f and 6f winner Jeremy Fisher (by Prevailing) and a winning hurdler; dam ran only 3 times; bought in 1,000 gns. after making all to beat Chantilly Girl ¾ length in seller at Warwick in April; placed in 5 more sellers afterwards and was awarded race won by Houghton Weaver at Hamilton in April after winner failed dope test; will stay 7f; acts on a firm and a soft surface. *P. Haslam.*

FINGAL'S CAVE 4 b.c. Ragstone 128–Blue Echoes 105 (Mountain Call 125) **123** (1980 9f² 12fg* 12s 12fg² 10.5g² 10d³ 12fg* 10d 1981 10fg³ 12fg³ 10.5g 10s 12fg²)
In 1980 Fingal's Cave showed that when everything went right for him he was capable of good form. The Churchill Stakes and Cumberland Lodge Stakes, both at Ascot, saw him producing a fine turn of foot to win decisively after being held up, yet some of his other runs were less satisfactory, largely because he seemed to need very precise conditions to give of his best. As a four-year-old he again ran well on occasions and was better than ever, but he failed to win during the year, becoming only the sixth horse placed in the King George VI and Queen Elizabeth Stakes to whom this has happened since the race started in 1951, the others being Tarqogan, Felicio, Topyo, Hogarth and Crepellana.
Because of a damaged hock Fingal's Cave missed his engagements, including the Hardwicke Stakes at Royal Ascot, in the first part of the season and had his

initial outing in the Coral Eclipse Stakes at Sandown in July. He found the pace a bit hot early on and was some way back turning into the straight, but ran on very strongly in the closing stages to be a creditable fourth to Master Willie, giving the impression a return to a longer trip would suit him. On the disqualification of Hard Fought Fingal's Cave was moved up to third. Later in the month he got the chance to run over a mile and a half again when returning to the scene of his best previous performance, Ascot, for the King George VI and Queen Elizabeth Diamond Stakes. Significantly Fingal's Cave surpassed himself. Held up as usual, he followed Shergar through on the rails over two furlongs out and though unable to match the latter's acceleration he kept on well, losing second place to Madam Gay by only a short head, four lengths off the winner. With Master Willie, Pelerin, Cracaval and Light Cavalry behind him this was unquestionably Fingal's Cave's finest hour so far.

In only one of his three subsequent starts, the Cumberland Lodge Stakes at Ascot, did Fingal's Cave run up to form. In that race he looked to have a good opportunity of getting off the mark for the year and started favourite. Making ground from the rear half a mile out, he had to be switched off the rails to obtain a clear run one and half furlongs from home and became involved in a slight barging match with Critique, who had come from even further back. Rather surprisingly Critique proved to have the stronger finish and he drew clear to win by two and a half lengths from Fingal's Cave who was well held at the end. Fingal's Cave's two other outings saw his finishing in the rear in the Benson and Hedges Gold Cup at York, where he was badly hampered when commencing a run halfway up the straight, and in the Arlington Million at Chicago, where the trip and the very soft ground were against him.

		Ragusa (b 1960)	Ribot
	Ragstone (b 1970)		Fantan II
		Fotheringay (b 1964)	Right Royal V
Fingal's Cave (b.c. 1977)			La Fresnes
		Mountain Call (ch 1965)	Whistler
	Blue Echoes (b 1972)		Cloudy Walk
		Red Favourite (b 1964)	Floribunda
			Maiden Speech

By a Gold Cup winner out of a sprinter, Fingal's Cave is the product of extremes. Ragstone, the 1974 Gold Cup winner, had only four years at stud before he died after an accident; Fingal's Cave is the best horse he sired although Rollrights also showed very useful form in 1981. Fingal's Cave is the first foal of Blue Echoes who ran just four times, showing useful form over five furlongs at two years. The grandam, a speedy two-year-old that didn't train on, is a half-sister to the smart middle-distance handicapper New Member and to the 1969 Acomb Stakes winner Dubrava.

A neat colt and a good walker and mover, Fingal's Cave is ideally suited by a mile and a half on a firm surface and a right-handed track. He has been sent to race with Charlie Whittingham in California. Whittingham has done well with ex-European horses in the past decade and in 1981 Galaxy Libra, Kilijaro, Providential and Queen To Conquer all won big races for the stable. It will be interesting to see if Fingal's Cave, who will hardly be favoured by the left-handed tracks in the USA, manages to add to his modest total of two wins. *J. Dunlop.*

FINWOOD 3 b.f. Ashmore 125–Souza Rose 80 (Songedor 116) (1980 NR 1981 16fg 16f 10.6v 12.2g 12d) 5,000F; tall, leggy filly; fourth produce; half-sister to 5f to 7.6f winner Roman Scribe (by Sallust) and fairly useful middle-distance performer Meadow Monarch (by Meadow Mint); dam, 2-y-o 5f winner, is half-sister to high-class sprinter Abergwaun; well beaten in maiden and minor events and a claiming handicap. *W. Wharton.*   —

FIONA (HOL) 3 gr.f. Vesins–Lovely (Royal Unity 126) (1980 6s 6.5fg4 9g 6.5g2 6.5d4 9s* 1981 8s4 9g2 10g* 12g4 12g2 12d 10.4s3 14.5g2 12.5fg4 11.3d) unfurnished Dutch-bred filly; beat Mistress Gay in quite good style by 4 lengths in ladies race at Lingfield in June; in frame on most other starts, including in Dutch 1,000 Guineas, Dutch Derby, Dutch Oaks and Dutch St Leger, all at Duindigt; stays 1¾m; pulled up lame final start. *M. Ryan.*   **81**

FIONAS PRIDE 2 gr. or ro.f. Runnymede 123–Crowberry (Crozier 117) (1981 7f 7f 7g) Mar 4; 2,200Y; compact filly; poor mover; temperamental plater. *G. Toft.*   **—§**

FIRBECK 5 ch.m. Veiled Wonder–Highview Jill 73 (Proud Chieftain 122) (1980 5s 6f 5f4 5fg 5d* 5g2 5fg 5fg3 5d2 5s 5g 5s 1981 5g3 5s 5f 5f 5.6f 5f 5f 5fg)   **70**

strong mare; sprint handicapper; yet to show she stays 6f; acts on any going except perhaps very soft; usually wears blinkers. *A. Balding.*

FIRDALE FLYER 2 gr.f. The Go-Between 129–Cullen 80 (Quorum 126) — (1981 5s 5fg 5fg 5g 5f) Apr 6; compact, rather narrow filly; half-sister to several winners, including fairly useful middle-distance stayer Lorelene (by Lorenzaccio); dam stayer; poor maiden; not raced after August. *W. Wharton.*

FIRDALE PASS 2 b.f. Malicious–Pretty Pass (Alcide 136) (1981 8d) Apr 13; — third foal; dam, poor novice hurdler, is sister to very useful stayer Predicament; 33/1 when behind in end-of-season maiden race at Leicester. *W. Wharton.*

FIRDALE ROSIE 2 gr.f. Town Crier 119–Hethabella 62 (Hethersett 134) **78** (1981 5s* 6f 7g 7g 6s 7d) May 12; lightly-made filly; sixth foal; sister to winning hurdler The Pukaar Bell; dam won over 1½m; won 12-runner maiden race at Wolverhampton in May by 2½ lengths from Miss Trilli; ran creditably on 3 occasions subsequently; will stay 1¼m; acts on any going. *W. Wharton.*

FIRE CHIEFTAIN 3 b.g. Owen Anthony 102–Fire Hawk 70 (Firestreak 125) — (1980 6g 1981 7.6g 8fg 8.3g 8fg⁴ 7d) compact gelding; plater; stays 1m; started slowly third outing. *J. Holt.*

FIRE IN THE WIRE (USA) 2 br.c. Big Burn–Thespianess (Parthia 132) — (1981 6fg 6g) half-brother to 2 winners in USA; dam, winner at up to 1m in USA, is half-sister to very successful broodmare Money For Nothing; sire, unplaced in 3 starts, has sired several American stakes winners; behind in large fields of maidens at Newmarket in August and Lingfield in September (ridden by 7-lb claimer). *J. Sutcliffe.*

FIREMASTER 2 b.g. Gracious Melody 117–Tudor Blossom 66 (Tudor Cliff) **57** (1981 5v 5fg 6f 8.2fg 8g 8.2d² 10d) Apr 4; 800Y (privately); lightly-made gelding; plater; stays 1m (well beaten over 1¼m); seems suited by some give in the ground; sold 480 gns Doncaster October Sales. *S. Nesbitt.*

FIRE MOUNTAIN 3 gr.f. Dragonara Palace 115–Rosalina 71 (Porto Bello 118) — (1980 5fg 5fg⁴ 5fg⁴ 6g⁴ 5g* 5d³ 5d³ 5d 5g* 1981 5fg 6s 6g 6s) tall, useful sort; fair performer at 2 yrs; no form in 1981 (blinkered final start), but had to be withdrawn at start after being found to have cracked a bone in her near-fore at Lingfield in May before intended second start; stays 6f; best form on an easy surface; good mount for an apprentice. *R. Hannon.*

FIRESPARK 2 ch.f. Hot Spark 126–Kari Simbi 63 (Galivanter 131) (1981 6g — 6g 5v 6d) May 9; IR 3,100F; strong, compact filly; fourth foal; half-sister to a winning plater; dam ran best race at 5f; no worthwhile form in maiden and minor events. *M. Camacho.*

FIRE TRACK 2 ch.c. Track Spare 125–Rosy Glow 60 (Hotfoot 126) (1981 5g — 5fg) May 24; first foal; dam, moderate plater at 2 yrs in England, subsequently won 6 times in Norway; in rear in maiden races at Epsom and Warwick in June. *D. Whelan.*

FIRM CONVICTION 4 gr.f. Scottish Rifle 127–Kinharvie 63 (Abernant 142) — (1980 10.1d 10.1g 1981 12f 10.1fg) unfurnished filly; no sign of ability in maiden and minor events; blinkered second start. *T. Hallett.*

FIRM EVALUATION (USA) 2 ch.c. Vaguely Noble 140–Valmara 104 **81** (Fleet Nasrullah) (1981 8g 10s) Mar 22; $105,000Y; big, rangy colt; fifth foal; half-brother to French 9f and 1¼m winner Rominetto (by Busted); dam, useful 5f and 1¼m winner, is half-sister to very smart 1972 American 2-y-o Vaguely Familiar (by Vaguely Noble); good 7¾ lengths fifth of 29 to Born Hero in maiden event at Newmarket in October (decidedly backward); favourite, finished only seventh of 22, beaten over 8 lengths by Luxury, in similar event at Nottingham later in month; should be well suited by 1¼m. *J. Hindley.*

FIRM FOUNDATION 4 br.g. Pieces of Eight 128–Streetcar 87 (Crocket 130) **48** (1980 8fg 11fg 8d³ 10g 13.8f⁴ 12g* 12fg* 12g⁴ 1981 15.5d³ 16g) leggy gelding; plater; third in better company at Folkestone in April; stays well; acts on a firm and a soft surface; blinkered both starts at 4 yrs. *M. Hinchliffe.*

FIRST AWARD 3 ch.f. New Member 119–Cash Award (Cash and Courage 116) — (1980 5f 5h 8fg 7d 10s 1981 8d 10.2f 13f) compact filly; in rear in minor and maiden events. *H. Fleming.*

FIRST CHILD 3 br.f. Keren 100–Only Child 68 (Foggy Bell 108) (1980 5fg — 6s 5f 5f 6f⁴ 6d² 6s 1981 8s 8d 12g 12.2g 8g) neat filly; well beaten in 1981, including in sellers; should stay at least 1m; probably acts on any going; has run well for an apprentice; blinkered last 2 starts; sold 600 gns Doncaster June Sales and resold 380 gns Newmarket July Sales. *Denys Smith.*

FIRST CLASS MAIL 5 b. or br.h. Windjammer (USA)–Corsuedei (King's Troop 118) (1980 NR 1981 9.4g 8f 6f) poor handicapper; stays 1m; has worn blinkers; sometimes starts slowly; inconsistent. *Mrs S. Chesmore.* —

FIRST CONNECTION 2 br.g. Bay Express 132–Gamlingay (Daring Display 129) (1981 5g 5g⁴ 5fg* 6f* 6fg 5d 5d⁴) Apr 23; 5,600Y; short-backed gelding; good mover; first foal; dam unraced daughter of useful 6f to 1¼m winner Gambola; speedy in plating company and made all to win sellers at Lingfield and Windsor in June, costing 5,000 gns to retain after scoring by 2½ lengths from Sweet For Days in 20-runner race on latter; 2¼ lengths fourth to Haditos in nursery at Lingfield in August (apprentice ridden); stays 6f; best form on a sound surface; wears blinkers; sent to Hong Kong. *P. Haslam.* 74

FIRST CONTACT 3 ch.f. Simbir 130–Willow Bird 74 (Weepers Boy 124) (1980 6d⁴ 1981 8g³ 8fg 8fg 10.4d 8fg 8.2s) leggy filly; about 2 lengths fourth of 20 behind subsequently-disqualified Silver Season in maiden event at Kempton in May, running on; didn't reproduce that form; should stay 1¼m; blinkered third and fifth starts; sold 2,600 gns Ascot December Sales. *M. Smyly.* 79 d

FIRST DEGREE 3 b.g. Balliol 125–Barbara Bryce (Yellow God 129) (1980 NR 1981 8fg 9s 8d 7g) 6,900Y; strong, lengthy gelding; second foal; brother to 1979 2-y-o 5f winner Willing To Learn; dam never ran; gave signs of a little ability in minor events on last 2 outings. *C. Booth.* —

FIRST KNIGHT (USA) 2 ch.c. Roberto 131–Showyourself (Sir Gaylord) (1981 6fg⁴ 7g 7s) Feb 6; $120,000Y; tall, lengthy colt; fourth foal; half-brother to 2 minor winners in USA; dam placed at 2 yrs in USA; ran on nicely without being given a hard time when 11 lengths fourth of 13 to Sandhurst Prince in £4,200 race at Kempton in August; well behind subsequently in races won by very promising colts at Newmarket and Ascot (last of 11); should be well suited by 7f+. *R. Armstrong.* 71

FIRST MINT (NZ) 2 gr.c. Sovereign Edition 109–La Douce (Le Filou 110) (1981 8g³) Mar 4; New Zealand-bred colt; good walker; half-brother to at least 2 winners in Australasia; dam, winner in Australia, is sister to 2 good Australian performers, including Melbourne Cup winner Light Fingers; 33/1, shaped promisingly when 2 lengths third of 27 to Dudley Wood in minor event at Newmarket in October, racing up with leaders throughout and not being knocked about unnecessarily; will benefit from this experience and looks sure to win a maiden race at least over middle distances in 1982. *M. Stoute.* 96 p

FIRST MOVEMENT 3 b.c. Music Boy 124–Lunar Princess 109 (King's Bench 132) (1980 6g 6fg* 5g² 6s⁴ 1981 6g 6g 6g 6f* 6d*) strong, good sort; 50/1 when returning to form in handicap at Yarmouth in August, producing a tremendous turn of speed after having difficulty getting a run and winning a shade comfortably by ¾ length from El Presidente; looked magnificent when winning Ladbrokes (Ayr) Gold Cup by a head from stable-companion Tina's Pet the following month, producing a strong run in final furlong to lead close home; stays 6f; acts on any going; bandaged near-hind fourth start as a 2-y-o. *G. Huffer.* 96

Ladbrokes (Ayr) Gold Cup Handicap—first and second, the stable-companions First Movement and Tina's Pet, head the stand-side group

FIRST NIGHT FLIGHT 3 b.g. Tumble Wind–Aracara (Prince Tenderfoot 126) — (1980 5g⁴ 5fg 5s 6fg 6d 7d 1981 8.2s 8d 11.5d 12fg) compact gelding; soundly beaten in varied company, including selling; trained part of season by D. Whelan. *K. Ivory.*

FIRST PHASE (USA) 2 b.c. Cannonade–Precious Elaine (Advocator) (1981 **75** 6fg 7g³ 8s) May 2; $24,000Y; first foal; dam stakes-placed winner at up to 1m; 1¾ lengths third of 13 to Balancheine in minor event at Brighton in September, best effort; bred to stay middle distances. *G. Hunter.*

FIRST ROW 2 b.f. Kalamoun 129–Single Line (Rash Prince) (1981 5fg⁴) — May 14; leggy, lightly-made filly; fifth living foal; half-sister to Ski Lift (by Mount Hagen), successful at around 1¼m; dam, closely related to CCA Oaks winner Magazine, won at up to 6f in USA; third favourite and very fit, faded in final furlong when 5¾ lengths fourth of 13 to Pleasant Dream in maiden race at Wolverhampton in July, only outing; bred to stay at least 1m; sold 8,500 gns Goffs November Sales. *B. Hills.*

FIRST TEE 2 gr.f. Ballymore 123–Shek-O (Forward Pass) (1981 6fg 7fg **83** 7d² 8fg 8.2s³ 8.2s) Apr 13; robust, well-made filly; second living produce; dam 2-y-o 6f winner; placed in £3,100 race at Redcar in August and 18-runner nursery at Nottingham the following month; stays 1m well; seems to need some give in the ground. *R. Armstrong.*

FIRSYJABS 2 b.f. Saritamer 130–Miss Osprey 93 (Sea Hawk II 131) (1981 **85 ?** 6g 7fg 7fg² 7d⁴) Apr 18; 7,000Y; lengthy, well-made filly; second foal; dam suited by extreme distances; went down by 2½ lengths to odds-on Ashenden in £4,200 event at Newmarket in July; staying-on 4¾ lengths fourth of 18 in maiden race won by Melting Snows at Newbury 2 months later; runs as though middle distances will suit her. *B. Hobbs.*

FIT FOR A KING 2 b.f. Royalty 130–Confidante (Gulf Pearl 117) (1981 5g — 6fg 6fg 7d) June 6; unfurnished filly; first foal; dam behind in 3 maiden and minor events; little sign of ability in maiden and minor events. *J. Winter.*

FITZGAYLE 3 br.c. Lord Gayle 124–Puka (Parthia 132) (1980 NR 1981 **82** 10s³ 12g⁴ 16s² 12d* 12fg 12fg 12d⁴ 12d 13.8g² 13.3s) well-made, quite attractive colt; third foal; half-brother to fair Irish stayer Nitucket (by Yellow God) and a good winner in Japan by Northfields; dam unraced; beat Le Beau ½ length in maiden race at Brighton in May; second to Pittencrieff in handicap at Catterick in October; probably stays 2m; best form with some give in the ground; sold to D. Barons 12,500 gns Newmarket Autumn Sales. *G. Harwood.*

FITZPATRICK 2 b.c. Oats 126–Shannon Prince (Connaught 130) (1981 7g 7g) — Apr 19; close-coupled, robust colt; first live foal; dam won over 1m and 1¼m in Ireland; unquoted when behind in maiden race and Houghton Stakes at Newmarket in October, in latter finishing ninth of 15 to Ivano; will stay 1½m; may do better at 3 yrs. *P. Walwyn.*

FITZROY 3 b.g. Furry Glen 121–Miss Wittington (Red God 128§) (1980 NR **67** 1981 8g³ 8fg 10d 12g) 2,900F, 12,000Y; lengthy, hollow-backed gelding; half-brother to 3 winners abroad, and to very useful 2-y-o 5f performer My Lover (by Pitskelly); dam fourth once from 5 starts at 3 yrs in Ireland; 33/1 when 1¾ lengths third of 18 behind Magikin in Wood Ditton Stakes at Newmarket in April, keeping on well; off course afterwards until September, and ran best race on his return when 12½ lengths fifth to Sextant in 1¼m minor event at Nottingham later that month. *M. Smyly.*

FITZWARREN 2 ch.c. Busted 134–Dove 92 (Sea Hawk II 131) (1981 8d 7s 8g) **88** May 16; 26,000Y; strong, good sort; second foal; half-brother to useful 1980 2-y-o 5f winner Palumba (by Derring-Do); dam 2-y-o 6f winner; showed ability when eighth of 11 to Paradis Terrestre in 7f Hyperion Stakes at Ascot in October and when ninth of 27 behind Dudley Wood in minor event at Newmarket later in month; will be suited by 1¼m and 1½m; the type to win races at 3 yrs. *G. Balding.*

FIZZIE LIZZIE 3 br.f. Persian Breeze 121–Counteswells (Behistoun 131) — (1980 6d 5g³ 7f⁴ 7fg 6g 7g 7f 10d 1981 7fg 7f 5fg 7g 7f 8fg) leggy filly; plater; stays 7f; apprentice ridden; has worn blinkers; sold 320 gns Doncaster October Sales. *S. Nesbitt.*

FJORD LADY 3 ch.f. Busted 134–Macha's Jewel (Majestic Prince) (1980 NR — 1981 10f 10.6v 18g) 12,000Y; rather lightly-made filly; second foal; half-sister to 7f and 8.3f winner Can-Do-More (by Dancer's Image); dam second over 7.5f at 2 yrs in Ireland; well beaten in maiden and minor events; sold 2,000 gns Newmarket December Sales. *M. Jarvis.*

FLA

FLAIRS BOY 6 gr.g. Lord Gayle 124–Magic Maid (Majetta 115) (1980 NR —
1981 13.4fg 14g 16f 12f) poor plater; has worn blinkers and bandages; not an
easy ride. *S. Holland.*

FLAMEGUARD 3 ch.f. Hot Spark 126–Street Vendor 60 (High Perch 126) —
(1980 5fg 5fg 5s 6g 6f 7g 1981 8s 6g 8d 12s) small filly; behind in varied
company in 1981, including selling; stays 7f; has worn blinkers; trained part of
season by R. Armstrong. *S. Matthews.*

FLASH CONNECTION 4 b.c. Hot Spark 126–Carcosa 103 (Sovereign Lord 120) —
(1980 5g* 5g* 6s 6fg 1981 6v) strong, useful sort; decisive winner of 2 races at
Cagnes-sur-Mer in 1980; last in handicap only start at 4 yrs in March; stayed 6f;
probably unsuited by soft going; dead. *Mrs A. Cousins.*

FLASH EMMA 2 b.f. Queen's Hussar 124–Brightly 95 (Aureole 132) (1981 **51**
6g 7fg 6g 7f 10d) Apr 24; 2,700Y; small filly; first foal; dam won Cheshire Oaks;
plater; should stay 1¼m. *J. Fitzgerald.*

FLASH GORDON 3 ch.c. Streak 119–Pibroch III (Specific 103) (1980 5fg*
5fg4 6g 6s4 5s4 5f4 5fg4 5g 6fg 8s 1981 7d 6s 5.3f 5.8f) compact non-thoroughbred colt; won at Salisbury as a 2-y-o; behind in handicaps in 1981; best form
at 5f and is unlikely to stay 1m (always behind in valuable seller when tried at
trip at 2 yrs); seems to act on any going; blinkered last 3 starts. *T. Marshall.*

FLASHING GAZE 3 br.f. Ashmore 125–Gazelle (Tudor Music 131) (1980 NR —
1981 12g4 14fg 16fg 16g) workmanlike filly; third foal; dam placed over 7f and
1m in Ireland; showed some ability in maiden races on first 2 starts. *F. J.
Houghton.*

FLASH LAMP 2 b.g. Maystreak 118–Alumia (Great Nephew 126) (1981 5d **57**
6fg 6fg 5s) Mar 2; fair sort; first foal; dam unplaced 3 times at 2 yrs; poor
sprint maiden; twice beaten in sellers; sometimes sweats up. *D. Leslie.*

FLASH MINT 2 ch.c. Streak 119–Treasury (Henry the Seventh 125) (1981 7d) —
Apr 20; fifth foal; dam of little account; 50/1 when last of 11 in minor event
at Leicester in November won by Don Giovanni. *V. Soane.*

FLASH 'N' FIRE (USA) 3 ch.f. Charles Elliott–Thundering Streak (Craigwood) (1980 6f* 6fg2 7.3d4 1981 7s 8fg 10f) workmanlike filly; showed
fair form as a 2-y-o and won minor event at Redcar; well beaten in 1981 when
facing stiff tasks in Salisbury 1,000 Guineas Trial and Masaka Stakes at Kempton
in April and in handicap at Pontefract (apprentice ridden, finished last) in July;
should stay 1m; appears to act on any going; sent to France. *R. Sheather.*

FLASHRAY 3 ch.c. Flashback 102–Dumette 89 (Dumbarnie 125) (1980 5d 7d —
1981 10s 8g 6d 8.3s 6v 6g) well beaten in varied company, including selling;
blinkered fifth start. *A. Davison.*

FLAUTIST 9 b.g. Whistling Wind 123–Lovely Colleen (Rise 'N Shine II) —
(1980 NR 1981 12s) of little account. *G. Harman.*

FLAVELLS RECORD 2 b. or br.c. Record Token 128–Hascombe Lady 70 —
(Galivanter 131) (1981 5s 5g 5g 6g 7g 5s 10.2g) May 25; 2,400F, 2,200Y;
rather leggy colt; no sign of ability, including in a valuable seller; sweated up
fifth outing; blinkered last 2 outings. *G. Fletcher.*

FLAYOSC (FR) 2 b.c. Go Marching–Munda (Traffic) (1981 5g* 5.5g* 5.5s* **103**
6g3 7g4 7d2 8d2 8v* 10s*) Mar 28; 32,000 francs Y (approx £3,200); half-brother
to 3 winners in France, including 3-y-o middle-distance winner Shala (by Dictus);
dam won 7 small races from 1¼m to 1¾m in France; had a remarkable season,
winning maiden race at Le Croise-Laroche, small race at Marseilles and minor
event at Evry in the spring in addition to nursery under top weight at Saint-
Cloud in October and 70,000 francs Prix Isonomy at Evry in November; got
home by a neck from Famoso in last-named; also ran well in Prix Fast Fox
at Saint-Cloud (beaten neck and a head by Tompkins, giving 11 lb all round),
Prix la Fleche at Evry (1½ lengths fourth to Setkatdeu) and minor event also at
Evry (beaten neck by Trigonome), but was surprisingly raced in claiming event at
Longchamp in October on seventh outing (claimed out of C. Bartholomew's
stable after finishing 2 lengths second of 21); suited by 1¼m and will stay further;
acts on heavy going. *G. Philippeau, France.*

FLEET STEED (USA) 4 b.c. Gummo–Mark-ye-Maid (Mark-Ye-Well) (1980 **?**
including 8.5fg* 8fg* 1981 6fg2 6fg3 8fg3 11.1f 8fg4 10.8s) quite attractive,
compact ex-American colt; won 2 of his 13 starts in USA in 1980, maiden race and
allowance race at Bay Meadows; placed in 2 allowance races at Golden Gate
in May; well beaten in varied company over here; stays 1m; blinkered final
start; wears a bandage on his off-fore. *P. Cole.*

310

FLICKER TO A FLAME (USA) 2 ch.f. Empery 128–Lovelight 112 (Bleep-   **85** P
Bleep 134) (1981 6g³) rangy filly; good walker; fourth foal; half-sister to
3-y-o Motavato (by Apalachee), a very smart winner at up to 1m; dam very
game sprinter; second favourite, put up an eye-catching display in 17-runner
maiden race at Newmarket in October, staying on very well through beaten
horses to finish 4 lengths third to I'm Hot; will be suited by 7f and 1m; has
plenty of scope and should improve considerably in 1982. *B. Hills.*

FLIGHTING 3 b.f. Pitcairn 126–Ruddy Duck 84 (Dicta Drake 126) (1980 **119**
6f⁴ 7fg* 8g² 1981 8.5fg 12fg⁴ 11g³ 10g 10fg* 10h* 12s*)

Flighting put up easily her best
performance when winning the
Princess Royal Stakes in very good
style at Ascot in October. Much
earlier in the year her trainer had
expressed doubts that Flighting was
as good as her sister Bonnie Isle, who
was second to Scintillate in the 1979
Oaks, but this one performance marked
Flighting down as a really smart filly,
in our estimation slightly better
than Bonnie Isle. She was travelling
well throughout the race, and although
she didn't take the lead until inside
the last furlong she could be named the
winner before the field had turned
into the straight, so strongly was she
going. Once given her head Flighting was quickly clear and her rider
Rouse was able to spend the last half
furlong easing her down. She passed
the post four lengths clear of the
favourite Countess Tully—a margin
that could well have been doubled—
and the remaining nine fillies were
well strung out behind. Probably
the most important factor which
contributed to her improved form was
the soft ground: the Princess Royal
was the first race she had contested on

*Princess Royal Stakes, Ascot—a
pattern-race success for Flighting*

going softer than good and clearly she handled it extremely well, far better than
anything else in the field seemed to. It's also worth noting, though, that
reportedly she had done extremely well in the preceding four weeks and her
improved showing was by no means unexpected.

We should have liked to have seen Flighting confirm her improvement but
plans to run her either in Italy or in the William Hill November Handicap at Doncaster were dropped. Her weight in the latter race rose to 9-11 at the four-day
stage and she was withdrawn overnight. Flighting had looked nothing like so
good a filly in her earlier races, although in fairness to her she didn't once run badly.
She had won a minor event at Salisbury in August and a two-runner race at
Chepstow in September on her two outings before the Princess Royal, and had
earlier finished in the frame twice from four outings in much better company.
In the Ribblesdale Stakes at Royal Ascot in June she had finished fourth behind
Strigida and her stable-companion Rollrights, beaten almost six lengths, and in
the five-runner Mecca Bookmakers Scottish Derby at Ayr in July she had finished
third behind Little Wolf and Six Mile Bottom, beaten around two lengths.

		Petingo	Petition
	Pitcairn	(b 1965)	Alcazar
	(b 1971)	Border Bounty	Bounteous
Flighting		(b 1965)	B Flat
(b.f. 1978)		Dicta Drake	Phil Drake
	Ruddy Duck	(b 1958)	Dictature
	(b 1964)	Cheongsam	Tantieme
		(b 1957)	Eastern Glamour

Flighting is by Pitcairn out of Ruddy Duck, a sister to the very useful stayer
Chinatown. Ruddy Duck won at up to a mile and a half in modest company
on the flat and was also successful several times over hurdles before beginning

FLI

a highly productive career at stud. Flighting is Ruddy Duck's ninth foal and ninth winner. Easily the best before Flighting were Bonnie Isle and the useful middle-distance handicapper Falls of Lora (by Scottish Rifle); the remainder gained their wins in a variety of races including sellers, chases, hurdles and races abroad. Ruddy Duck has since produced another filly by Scottish Rifle, unraced as yet, and a colt by Hittite Glory.

The decision to keep Bonnie Isle in training for a third season didn't really pay off—although placed several times in good company she managed to win only a modest race at Brighton—but Flighting has been sold privately and will be racing in the United States. A well-made filly and a good mover, she is suited by a mile and a half and might well stay a bit further. She acts on any going but has shown much her best form on soft. *J. Dunlop.*

FLIGHTY FRANCIS 2 b.f. Workboy 123–Painter's Bay 75 (Monet 127) (1981 **49**
5v 5g² 5g 5f 5fg 5d² 5f 6f) May 8; 1,500Y; compact filly; half-sister to a winner abroad by Manacle; dam, placed over 1m here, won in Scandinavia; length second in maiden auction event won by Welsh Cloud at Catterick in April and in seller won by Star Cove at Hamilton in July; should stay 6f; well beaten when blinkered seventh start. *K. Stone.*

FLIGHTY FRIEND 3 ch.g. Be Friendly 130–Glimmer of Light (Only for Life **69**
126) (1980 NR 1981 10fg 9s³ 8g 8g) 660 2-y-o; workmanlike gelding; half-brother to very useful 1977 2-y-o 5f performer Negative Response (by Polyfoto) and a winner in Belgium; dam well beaten only start; 8 lengths third of 7 to Chief Speaker in minor event at Newcastle in October, disputing lead for a long way; finished last at Edinburgh next time but wasn't disgraced final outing. *R. Woodhouse.*

FLOATING CHARGE 3 ch.g. Hotfoot 126–Loweswater 74 (Saint Crespin III —
132) (1980 7g³ 7g 1981 12fg 12g 11.7d) big, tall gelding; no form in 1981 but was still on backward side second start and was subsequently off course 5 months; should stay middle distances; trained by N. Vigors until after second outing. *M. McCourt.*

FLOGERA 2 b.f. Owen Dudley 121–Argentina 115 (Nearco) (1981 6fg 7f 8g) —
Feb 11; smallish, rather unfurnished filly; half-sister to very smart Averof (by Sing Sing), a winner at up to 1¼m, to good stayer Falkland (by Right Royal V) and to very useful 1½m winner Tierra Fuego (by Shantung); dam stayed 1½m; in mid-division in maiden races at Newmarket and Leicester on first and third outings. *C. Brittain.*

FLO-MERCY 2 ch.f. No Mercy 126–Flora Leigh 94 (Floribunda 136) (1981 6f —
6g 5g) Apr 26; narrow, lightly-made filly; probably of little account. *W. Holden.*

FLORAL DANCE 3 br.f. Record Token 128–Floral 82 (Floribunda 136) (1980 **69**
6d 1981 6fg* 6g³ 6s 7fg 7g 8.2g³ 8g) lengthy filly; good walker; apprentice ridden when winning minor event at Warwick in April; ran creditably on several subsequent occasions; stays 1m; best form on a sound surface. *H. Candy.*

FLORAL ELEGANCE 2 b.f. Martinmas 128–Our Duck (The Go-Between 129) **64**
(1981 5s⁴ 5d* 5fg 5g 6fg 6fg 6fg 5g 5d 6v 6s) Apr 12; small, lightly-made filly; good mover; first foal; dam never ran; made all in maiden race at Newbury in April; well beaten subsequently and seemed not to train on; yet to show she stays 6f; acts on a soft surface; blinkered final outing. *Mrs J. Reavey.*

FLORENCIA 2 b.f. Moulton 128–Spanish Sail 113 (Matador 131) (1981 6g⁴) **70** p
May 10; half-sister to 3-y-o 1m winner Spanish Bay (by Roan Rocket) and fairly useful 1977 2-y-o 5f winner Artiste Management (by Some Hand); dam sprinter; 16/1, unable to quicken after having every chance when 4 lengths fourth of 19 behind One Degree in maiden race at Newmarket in October; will probably stay 1m. *G. Pritchard-Gordon.*

FLORIDA DANCER 2 b.f. Realm 129–Cambus O'May 100 (Sing Sing 134) —
(1981 5fg) Feb 7; 1,800Y; fourth foal; half-sister to fairly useful 1977 2-y-o 5f winner Gruinard (by Amber Rama); dam useful 6f winner; unquoted when seventh of 11 to dead-heaters Town Special and Sussex Queen in maiden race at Lingfield in July. *Peter Taylor.*

FLORIDA GIRL 2 b.f. Owen Dudley 121–Natural Flora (Floribunda 136) —
(1981 5d 6fg 5f) May 5; 3,800F, resold 7,000Y; neat, strong, attractive filly; half-sister to 3 winners here and abroad, including quite useful 1976 Irish 2-y-o

6f winner Fairhaven Lady (by Runnymede); beat only one horse home in 3 starts in maiden and minor events; sold 675 gns Ascot August Sales. *B. Swift.*

FLORIDA SON 2 b.c. Busted 134–Peach Stone (Mourne 126) (1981 6g 8g 8s*) 89
Apr 5; 9,800Y; big, strong colt; brother to Irish 1½m winner Fauchee and half-brother to 2 winners; dam won at around 9f in France; 25/1 but fully fit for first time, made much of running and kept on to win 14-runner maiden race at York in October by 2 lengths from Bless'em All; will stay well; acts on soft going. *J. Hanson.*

FLOWER 4 br.f. So Blessed 130–Sunflower 96 (Paveh 126) (1980 6fg 5g 6s* —
5f 6s 7s 6d³ 6d³ 6d 1981 6g 6f 6d 7s) quite a useful-looking filly; fairly useful handicapper at 3 yrs; didn't run up to her best in 1981 and performed atrociously in blinkers final start; suited by 6f and should stay further; acts well on soft going; sold 8,200 gns Newmarket December Sales. *C. Thornton.*

FLUELLEN 8 b.g. Welsh Pageant 132–Ya Ya 84 (Primera 131) (1980 10fg 10d §§
11.1fg 12fg 12d 10g 1981 10g 10s 10d 10g 10d) tall, useful-looking gelding; one-time very useful performer but has deteriorated, is completely unreliable and none too generous in a finish; stays 1½m; acts on any going; often wears blinkers. *H. Wragg.*

FLY BABY 2 b.f. African Sky 124–Gay Bird 111 (Birdbrook 110) (1981 5d 94
5g* 5d³ 5f* 6fg 5g³) Apr 5; IR 2,000Y; workmanlike filly; half-sister to useful 1980 2-y-o 7f winner Principal Dancer (by Prince Tenderfoot); dam best at up to 1¼m; 40/1-winner of substandard Queen Mary Stakes at Royal Ascot in June, leading well below distance and keeping on gamely to resist Princess Seal's strong challenge by a short head; had previously made all to win 18-runner maiden auction event at Kempton by 8 lengths; having first race for 2 months when 9 lengths third of 7 to Peterhof in Flying Childers Stakes at Doncaster in September (showed excellent speed 3f); form only at 5f; acts well on firm going; genuine. *R. Hannon.*

FLYING BID 4 b.f. Auction Ring 123–Skyway 76 (Skymaster 126) (1980 8s 71
10h² 10f 14g³ 11fg² 14fg 1981 14d 12fg 16g 12.8f³ 16f³ 14f² 10g* 12g² 12g 10d) well-made ex-English filly; good mover; sister to 1981 Prix Robert Papin winner Maelstrom Lake; won handicap at Listowel in September; stays 1¾m; acts on any going; trained by S. Woodman first 2 starts. *H. de Bromhead, Ireland.*

FLYING DORA 3 b.f. Cavo Doro 124–Flying Bridge 71 (Bleep-Bleep 134) —
(1980 NR 1981 10fg 8.2s) small filly; first foal; dam won sellers at 7f and 1m; tailed-off last in maiden races at Redcar and Nottingham in September; sold 290 gns Doncaster November Sales. *S. Nesbitt.*

FLYING DREAMER 3 b.g. My Swallow 134–Forgotten Dreams 82 (Shoemaker —
121) (1980 5fg⁴ 5.8fg⁴ 7s 8.2g 8d* 1981 8d 12d 12d 11.7fg⁴ 10f 11.7fg 16g 13.1h 10.1fg 10.2g) leggy gelding; good walker; ran best races in handicaps at Windsor on fourth and ninth starts (blinkered first time in latter); stays 1½m; acts on a firm and a soft surface; inconsistent. *M. Blanshard.*

Queen Mary Stakes, Ascot—40/1-shot Fly Baby (No. 5) keeps on gamely to resist Princess Seal and Quest (far side)

FLYING GOLD 5 ch.h. Shiny Tenth 120–Quick Aim (Pardal 130) (1980 10.2g 10fg² 10fg³ 1981 10fg) big, strong horse; very good mover; stays 1¼m; possibly not at his best on soft ground. *G. Fletcher.*

FLYING MAIL 2 b.f. Pretty Form 97–Miss Little 78 (Dunoon Star 110) (1981 **58** 5d² 5g³ 5d 6d 5f) Mar 1; leggy filly; third reported foal; dam stayed 1½m; in frame in early-season maiden and minor events in Scotland; last on next 2 starts and could finish only 7 lengths fifth of 16 to Rounstan in seller at Ripon in September; should be suited by 6f. *A. W. Jones.*

FLYING OCTOPUS 4 b.c. Welsh Saint 126–Gang Plank 84 (Tower Walk 130) — (1980 6f 5f 6fg 5fg 8.5f 7s 6fg 7g 1981 7f) small, close-coupled colt; poor plater; not sure to stay 1m; sold 400 gns Ascot November Sales. *M. Bradley.*

FLYING OFFICER 4 b.g. Warpath 113–Rosie Wings 102 (Telegram II 120) — (1980 10.2g 12fg 12f 15.8fg* 14.7f* 16g* 14.7d* 16s 1981 12s 14f² 16g 12g 14s⁴ 15.8g) neat, rather lightly-made gelding; good walker; showed improved form once given a test of stamina at 3 yrs, winning 4 times; mainly disappointing in 1981; stays well; probably unsuited by very soft going. *C. Thornton.*

FLYING OPTICIAN 6 ch.h. Divine Gift 127–Game Coach (Big Game) (1980 — 10.2g 12d 8.2s 7d 1981 8d 7v 8f) quite a moderate handicapper at his best but has deteriorated; stays 1m; best form on a sound surface; has worn blinkers. *M. Bradley.*

FLYING RAGS 5 b.m. Ragstone 128–Sybilla (Relic) (1980 8.3f 10fg 9.6f — 6g 8.3s 8.3f 8d 1981 8fg) poor plater; has worn blinkers; sold 380 gns Ascot 2nd June Sales. *H. O'Neill.*

FLYING SAPPORO 5 gr.m. Mummy's Pet 125–Pall Nan 86 (Pall Mall 132) — (1980 5g 5fg 5f 8d 1981 6s 6d) lengthy, lightly-made mare; poor sprint maiden; acts on firm going; has been tried in blinkers. *A. Hide.*

FLYING SISTER 3 b.f. St Paddy 133–Quick Aim (Pardal 130) (1980 7s — 1981 12d 12fg 8fg 8fg 10d 12g⁴) tall, lightly-made filly; plating-class maiden; will stay beyond 1½m. *G. Fletcher.*

FLYING TYKE 6 ch.h. Huntercombe 133–Maid of Iron (Crozier USA) (1980 **72** d NR 1981 6s 5s² 5d* 6s 6d 5fg 5fg 5g³ 5d 5g 6s 5g) useful sort; not a good mover; sprint handicapper; beat Walter Osborne 1½ lengths at Newcastle in April; stays 6f; suited by some give in the ground nowadays; sometimes blinkered; sometimes bandaged in front. *A. Smith.*

FLYNN 2 ch.c. Malacate 131–Army Court (Court Martial) (1981 6fg 8s 8s) — Mar 6; 11,000Y; rangy, rather plain colt; half-brother to 2 winners in France, including 1980 2-y-o 5f winner Nonoalcourt (by Nonoalco); dam, out of sister to Bold Ruler, was very smart winner at up to 1¼m in France; behind in minor and maiden races in the North; may improve over middle distances. *J. Fitzgerald.*

FLY START 2 b.f. Run The Gantlet–Free French (Northern Dancer) (1981 **101** 7f* 7fg* 6.3fg³ 8d) May 3; first foal; dam unraced daughter of Forward Gal, the best 2-y-o filly in USA in 1970 and a high-class winner at up to 9f at 3 yrs; won maiden race at Phoenix Park in July (by 2 lengths from Afghan) and 7-runner Ardenode Stud Stakes at Leopardstown the following month (ran on to beat Prince's Polly ¾ length); not disgraced when 1½ lengths third of 6 to Dara Monarch in Group 3 Ballsbridge-Tattersalls Anglesey Stakes at the Curragh later in August but could finish only sixth of 15, nearly 8 lengths behind Prince's Polly, when second favourite for Silken Glider Stakes at Leopardstown the following month (soon off the bit); should stay middle distances. *D. O'Brien, Ireland.*

FOAM BATH 2 b.c. Wollow 132–Lemon Blossom 83 (Acropolis 132) (1981 **111** 6g* 6fg* 6fg²) Mar 17; medium-sized, well-made, attractive colt; good mover; fifth foal; half-brother to useful 3-y-o 1½m winner Cima (by High Top) and to a winner in Austria; dam won over 11f; won 2 races at Salisbury in impressive fashion, beating Martialis comfortably by 3 lengths in 14-runner minor event in July and quickening clear inside distance to account for Manchesterskytrain by 5 lengths (value 8) in 11-runner £3,300 race in August; came up against a very smart colt in Sandhurst Prince in 6-runner Sirenia Stakes at Kempton in September and wasn't disgraced in finishing 3 lengths second to him; will stay 1¼m; very useful. *D. Elsworth.*

FODEN WARRIOR 2 ch.c. Roman Warrior 132–Fodens Eve 80 (Dike) (1981 **65** 5d 5g³ 5.8g 5fg 5h) Apr 16; tall, workmanlike colt; first foal; dam 2-y-o 5f winner; stayed on fairly well when 3 lengths third of 15 to Red Sunset in maiden race at Newmarket in May; well beaten afterwards, running badly third outing, swerving violently at start on fourth and having stiff task when blinkered on final start; sold 1,200 gns Newmarket Autumn Sales. *R. Hannon.*

FOL HARDI 2 b.f. Brigadier Gerard 144–Sans Gene 77 (Songedor 116) (1981 **92**
6fg 7f* 7fg²) Mar 22; rather leggy filly; third foal; half-sister to 1m winner Wise Man (by Frankincense); dam won over 1m; put up quite a useful effort when winning 10-runner maiden race at Yarmouth in August by 2½ lengths from Bourgeonette; caught near line after being clear most of way when neck second of 8 to Triple Axel in minor event at Epsom the following month; will stay at least 1m; ridden by apprentice D. McKeown last 2 outings; sold to BBA 16,000 gns Newmarket December Sales. *W. Hastings-Bass.*

FOLK HERO 5 b. or br.g. Levanter 121–Faerie Rose 59 (March Past 124) —
(1980 9v³ 8g* 8f 7s² 7f 8g 7d* 8s 8g 6s 1981 9v³ 8d) small Irish gelding; creditable third to Dellersbeck in Burmah Lincolnshire Trial Handicap at Phoenix Park in March; reportedly finished lame when favourite for William Hill Lincoln Handicap at Doncaster later in month (subsequently found to have traces of caffeine and theobromine in his system); not seen out again; stays 9f; acts on any going but revels in the mud; usually wears blinkers. *R. McCormick, Ireland.*

FOLKLAW 3 ch.g. Song 132–Judiciary 74 (Above Suspicion 127) (1980 6d —
6s 8fg 1981 8g 8d 10f 8g 8f) big gelding; towards rear in maiden and minor events and handicaps; not sure to stay 1m; blinkered last 2 outings; sold to T. Barnes 5,000 gns Doncaster October Sales. *Miss S. Hall.*

FOLLOW ME HOME 3 b.f. Welsh Saint 126–Redolence (Red God 128§) —
(1980 5g 7g 7d 1981 11.7g 16fg 12d) no worthwhile form in maiden races; dead. *J. Douglas-Home.*

FOLLY LANE 4 b.f. Pompous 118–Amber Anne (Amber X 133) (1980 8s —
8f 8fg 7f 8g 10g 10.6d 1981 8fg 5g) poor plater; stays 1m; has worn bandages; sold 400 gns Doncaster October Sales. *R. E. Peacock.*

FOODBROKER BOY 2 b.g. Averof 123–Villa Tenata 73 (Vienna 127) (1981 —
5d 5.3f 6fg 8.2s) May 25; 900Y; plain gelding; half-brother to quite useful 1976 2-y-o 5f winner Aeras (by So Blessed); dam stayed well; no sign of ability in varied company, including selling; sweated up fourth start. *D. Whelan.*

FOOLISH PET 4 ch.f. Silly Season 127–Petecracy 102 (Petingo 135) (1980 **53**
8d³ 10s² 8fg³ 8fg³ 10fg 8s³ 10s 1981 8d³ 8fg) workmanlike filly; suited by 1¼m; probably acts on any going; blinkered once at 3 yrs. *F. J. Houghton.*

FOOLISH WAYS 2 b.c. Comedy Star 121–Susie Hall (Gold Rod 129) (1981 **62**
6g 5fg 6g⁴ 7f 8s 8d) Jan 10; deep-girthed colt who carries plenty of condition; first foal; dam unraced half-sister to top 1970 2-y-o filly Cawston's Pride, the dam of top sprinter Solinus (by Comedy Star); showed some ability in maiden races; weakened closing stages when 10 lengths fourth of 14 to Knave of Trumps at Yarmouth in September; not sure to stay 1m; dwelt fifth start. *F. Durr.*

FOOL'S DANCE 2 br.c. Gay Fandango 132–Libonia (Le Haar 126) (1981 **103**
5d* 5s* 5f⁴) Mar 22; IR 16,000Y; neat, quite attractive colt; good mover; third foal; half-brother to 1979 2-y-o 5f winner Bional Scramble (by Red Alert); dam never ran; successful in maiden race at Windsor and £2,700 event at Kempton in May, putting up a useful effort when accounting for Red Sunset by 2 lengths with 3 other previous winners well beaten off in latter (had an advantageous draw); short-priced favourite, broke well and had every chance 2f out but was unable to maintain his position and came home 6½ lengths fourth of 8 to Day Is Done in Group 3 Norfolk Stakes at Royal Ascot (eased inside distance); bred to stay at least 1m; possibly needs some give in the ground; presumably had setback after Ascot. *J. Tree.*

FOOL'S TESTIMONY 4 ch.g. High Line 125–Lady Advocate 116 (King's —
Bench 132) (1980 10fg 7fg 8d 1981 10.1fg² 12f³ 12fg⁴(dis)) well-made, good sort; poor maiden; stays 1½m. *N. Vigors.*

FOOTBALL 3 br.g. Hotfoot 126–Born Free 106 (Alycidon 138) (1980 6g⁴ 6fg **79**
1981 8.5fg² 10d² 8f* 10.1fg* 10.1fg*) strong, attractive gelding; won maiden race at Pontefract in June and 2 minor events at Windsor in July, last of them by 1½ lengths from Wise Owl; suited by 1¼m; probably acts on any going; troublesome at start early in year and was subsequently gelded; sent to Hong Kong. *P. Walwyn.*

FOOTHOLD 2 gr.f. Hotfoot 126–Path of Fortune (Sovereign Path 125) (1981 —
6fg 6fg) Apr 27; quite well-made, good sort; second live produce; dam won

over 10.7f in French Provinces; behind in sizeable fields of maidens at Newbury in August (25/1) and Salisbury in September (11/1); sold 620 gns Newmarket Autumn Sales. *R. Hern.*

FOOTREST 3 b.f. Hotfoot 126–Restive 96 (Relic) (1980 5fg 5g 1981 6fg³ 8g 8g³ 7f 10.1fg) rather lightly-made filly; third in minor event at Warwick and maiden race at Thirsk in spring; stays 1m. *B. Hobbs.* **59**

FORCE OF ACTION 3 ch.f. Galivanter 131–Delayed Action 113 (Jolly Jet 111) (1980 5g* 5f 5f² 5f² 5fg² 5f 5d³ 5g 5fg* 6d² 6g* 5d 5f 6s³ 1981 7d 6f* 6d³ 6f 6fg 5d² 6f³ 6f 5f 5g) lengthy filly; beat Geary's For Steel by ¾ length in handicap at Pontefract in June, making virtually all; placed in similar races afterwards; suited by 6f; acts on any going; genuine and consistent; usually apprentice ridden; bandaged near-hind on last outing; ran poorly eighth start. *G. Toft.* **84**

FORDIGAYLE 3 ch.f. Lord Gayle 124–Ragusalina 84 (Ragusa 137) (1980 6d 7d 1981 14f 14g) neat filly; behind in maiden races; should be suited by middle distances; saddle slipped on first outing; looks a difficult ride; sold 420 gns Newmarket Autumn Sales. *I. Walker.* **—**

FORESTERS BOY 4 br.g. Swinging Junior 118–Wilden (Will Somers 114§) (1980 7v 7d 10f⁴ 8fg³ 8fg 9g 7f 8d 8.2d 8fg 1981 7g 7f) leggy, lop-eared gelding; only plating class; not certain to stay 1¼m; probably acts on any going; blinkered twice in 1980. *W. Haigh.* **—**

FORESTERS LAD 3 gr.c. Porto Bello 118–Raffinata (Raffingora 130) (1980 5fg⁴ 5fg 6d* 6d⁴ 6d 6d³ 6g 1981 6g 7d 7g 7.2s⁴ 6g⁴ 6d 7.2g 6g 7.2v) leggy colt; not disgraced on occasions in handicaps; best at 6f; acts well on a soft surface. *W. Haigh.* **72**

FOREST LODGE (USA) 6 b.g. Executioner–Forest Friend (Linacre 133) (1980 NR 1981 10.2d 9d 8fg 8.3g) strong ex-Irish gelding; poor performer nowadays; stays 1¼m; acts on any going; wears blinkers; suitable mount for an inexperienced rider. *D. Gandolfo.* **—**

FOREST RIDE (USA) 2 gr.c. Al Hattab–Papamiento (Blade) (1981 5g³ 6g² 6fg) Apr 16; $100,000Y; neat, short-backed colt; good mover; second foal; dam, half-sister to high-class Twice Worthy, a stakes winner at up to 1¼m, and to Grand Prix de Paris winner Armistice, was placed at 2 and 3 yrs in USA; placed in maiden races at Salisbury in June and Newmarket in July, soon getting badly outpaced in latter but making up ground hand over fist under pressure in final 2f to get within ¾ length of Tin Boy; second favourite for New Ham Stakes at Goodwood later in July but finished only 7 lengths fifth of 6 to El Mansour after being pushed along throughout; finds 6f much too sharp and is bred to stay 1¼m. *R. Hern.* **90**

FORLITO 3 b.c. Home Guard 129–Sweet Mimosa 122 (Le Levanstell 122) (1980 NR 1981 11s 12g 8g 8fg) 31,000Y; lengthy, shallow-girthed colt; brother to 1979 Irish 2-y-o 7.9f winner Yellow Plume and half-brother to another winner; dam won Prix de Diane and is sister to Levmoss and Le Moss; behind in maiden races and an apprentice event; moved poorly to post first outing; swerved start when blinkered final start. *N. Callaghan.* **—**

FORLORN BEAUTY 5 b.m. Forlorn River 124–Blessed Beauty 97 (Rustam 127) (1980 NR 1981 10f 6fg) poor plater. *M. Bradley.* **—**

FORLORN RAIDER 2 gr.g. Forlorn River 124–Vicki Ann (Floribunda 136) (1981 5d 5d 6f) Mar 28; 360Y; leggy, narrow gelding; half-brother to fair 1976 2-y-o 5f winner Rushley Bay (by Crooner); in rear all outings, one of them a seller; took charge of rider on way to start on second appearance. *W. Holden.* **—**

FORM SETT 6 b.g. Pretty Form 97–Miss Atalanta 83 (Hethersett 134) (1980 6fg 5g³ 5d 5g 6g 8d 1981 6g 5fg 8.2g) plater; best form at 5f; probably acts on any going; sometimes wears blinkers; bandaged nowadays. *L. Barratt.* **—**

FORT GARRY 2 b.c. Relkino 131–Partridge Brook 109 (Birdbrook 110) (1981 5g 6d⁴ 6g² 7g 7h² 8s* 8s) Mar 18; small, quite attractive colt; first foal; dam won from 5f to 1¼m; close-up second in minor event and a nursery prior to winning 17-runner maiden race at Warwick in October by 4 lengths from Mycenaen; never going particularly well when having stiff task final outing; will be suited by middle distances; acts on any going. *B. Hills.* **89**

FOR THE FLAG (USA) 3 b.f. Forli–In The Offing (Hoist the Flag) (1980 7.3d 7g 1981 9s² 10g 8g² 8g 10.2d) leggy, unfurnished filly; runner-up in maiden races at Wolverhampton and Thirsk; soundly beaten afterwards; stays 9f; blinkered final start (June). *I. Balding.* **66**

FOR THE RECORD 2 ch.c. Record Token 128–Pirana (High Hat 131) (1981 — p
7fg 7g) Apr 7; 41,000Y; medium-sized, attractive colt; excellent mover;
half-brother to several winners here and abroad, including Royal Hunt Cup winner
Tender Heart (by Prince Tenderfoot); dam never ran; beaten 16 lengths when
tenth of 19 to Dageegah in maiden race at Salisbury in September but ran much
better than final placing suggests, moving into a prominent position 2½f out
and then being eased right up once leader clearly had his measure; behind in
similar event won by Simply Great at Newmarket the following month; unquoted
both times; will stay 1m; the type to do better in time. *B. Swift.*

FORT LAMY 2 b.c. African Sky 124–Mayfield Girl (Le Prince 98) (1981 6fg 80
5g 7d⁴) Feb 5; IR 5,200Y; sturdy, well-made colt; second foal; dam useful
Irish 2-y-o; showed ability first 2 outings, finishing 7½ lengths fifth of 12 to
Hampton Bay in £3,200 event at Ascot in September on second start; should stay
7f; may do better in time. *B. Hills.*

FORTUNE'S FANCY 4 b.f. Workboy 123–Polly Peachum 123 (Singing 48
Strand) (1980 5d 6g 5f 8g 5f 5f 1981 8.3fg 9f 8.3g 6fg 6g³ 6s) strong filly; poor
maiden; best at 6f on a sound surface; has worn blinkers. *Mrs J. Pitman.*

FORWARD (USA) 2 b.c. Caro 133–Tipping Time (Commanding II) (1981 7d 80
7fg 8.2fg³ 8g²) Apr 20; $135,000Y; well-made colt; good walker; half-brother to
winners in USA, France and Italy, including Fast (by Bold Bidder), a smart
winner at up to 9f; dam very smart stakes winner at up to 9f; placed in £4,000
event at Haydock and maiden race at Beverley in September, on latter course
having little luck in running and spoiling his chance by hanging when 2 lengths
second of 15 to Sagamore; will be suited by 1¼m; should win a race. *J. Dunlop.*

FOUNDRYMAN 4 b.c. Silly Season 127–Game Girl 85 (Abernant 142) (1980 50
5h 6fg 5d 5fg* 6s 5f⁴ 7d 1981 6g 5g 5g³ 6fg² 6fg 6g* 6f 5fg) robust colt; plater
nowadays; won at Newcastle in August (no bid); stays 6f; probably acts on
any going; suitable mount for an apprentice. *W. Haigh.*

FOUNTAIN VALLEY 2 ch.c. Red Regent 123–Lovely Season (Silly Season —
127) (1981 6f 7g 7g 8g) Mar 1; 5,000Y; smallish, workmanlike colt; half-
brother to fairly useful 1980 Irish 2-y-o sprint winner Likely Sort (by Red Alert)
and a winning hurdler; dam never ran; poor form, including under a low weight
in a selling nursery; blinkered third start; sold 360 gns Doncaster November
Sales. *G. Hunter.*

FOUR FATHOMS 7 ch.g. Gulf Pearl 117–Capule (Middleground) (1980 72
NR 1981 12.2d* 16d² 12d³ 12g 14f 18.1d) robust gelding; not the best of
movers; won handicap at Warwick in April; effective at 1½m and stays well;
acts on any going; has worn bandages. *A. Goodwill.*

FOUR FOR MUSIC 2 ch.c. Music Boy 124–Visitation 84 (Tarqogan 125) 76
(1981 5s 5f 5.3f 5fg⁴ 6g² 7d 6fg³ 6fg 5d² 5g²) Mar 31; 9,200Y; compact, fair
sort; brother to 1980 2-y-o 5f winner Merely Mozart, and half-brother to a
winner; dam stayed 1½m; got home by a neck from Miss Prudent when heavily-
backed favourite for valuable 18-runner seller at York in July but drifted badly
left in final furlong and was demoted to second; blinkered when running well
subsequently to be placed in another valuable seller at Kempton and nurseries
at Ayr (apprentice event) and Newmarket (finished well when 3 lengths second
of 10 to My Lover); effective at 5f and 6f but doesn't stay 7f; acts on a firm and
a soft surface; consistent. *P. Haslam.*

FOUR MARKS 2 b.c. Song 132–Petite Path 106 (Sovereign Path 125) (1981 91
5g 5g* 5f 5fg 5fg⁴ 5g 5d 5s 5s* 5g* 5g) Feb 25; 10,000Y; big, useful sort with
plenty of scope; half-brother to 3 winners by Track Spare, including fair 1m to
1¼m winner Ascot Royale; dam won Queen Mary Stakes and Ayr Gold Cup;
successful in maiden race at Edinburgh in June and nurseries at Warwick and
Edinburgh again in October, beating Bonne Baiser ½ length in last-named event;
disappointing most other starts; will probably stay 6f; acts well on soft going.
N. Callaghan.

FOX 2 ch.c. Free State 125–Red Velvet 114 (Red God 128§) (1981 6fg 6g) — p
Mar 26; big, rangy colt; good walker; half-brother to 4 winners, including 3-y-o
6f winner Velvet Habit (by Habitat), very useful 1974 2-y-o Red Cross (by
Crepello) and useful 1¼m winner Red Rufus (by Busted); dam at her best at 2
yrs; looked very green and distinctly backward when 33/1 for £4,500 event at
Ascot in September but showed a bit of promise, making steady late progress
to finish 8¾ lengths eighth of 10 to Allocated; still green and was pushed along
throughout when ninth in 22-runner maiden race won by Ash Ridge at Newmarket the following month; the type to do much better over 1m+ at 3 yrs.
P. Walwyn.

FOX

FOXY FELLOW 3 ch.c. Porto Bello 118–Phlox 101 (Floriana 106) (1980   **37**
5s 5.8fg³ 5.8f³ 6g 6g 1981 7s 8fg³ 8g 7.6g 8f 8fg 7f 8fg 6fg³) small colt; plater;
stays 1m; best form on a firm surface; ran moderately in blinkers sixth start;
sold 1,000 gns Newmarket Autumn Sales. *C. Nelson.*

FRAASH 8 ch.g. Frankincense 120–Desert Ash (Celtic Ash) (1980 12s 13s³   —
1981 12s 12.5s 12.3d) poor handicapper nowadays; stays well; well suited by
some give in the ground; has been tried in blinkers; usually wears bandages;
suitable mount for an apprentice. *B. Lunness.*

FRABWAH 3 b.f. Abwah 118–Frau 60 (Frankincense 120) (1980 5fg 6d 6d   —
1981 5fg 5fg 7fg 6fg 6g 7f 7g) small, lengthy filly; little worthwhile form in
varied company, including selling; has been tried in blinkers; sold 480 gns
Doncaster September Sales. *B. Lunness.*

FRANCESCO 5 b.h. Royal and Regal–Rising Lark (Ballymoss 136) (1980   **93**
14f⁴ 16fg 12fg 12fg² 14.7g² 14fg* 14g³ 14g³ 1981 14f² 12f* 12f³ 14fg* 12g*)
strong, deep-girthed, round-barrelled horse; fairly useful handicapper; successful at Beverley in July and Goodwood in September (apprentice race); also won
slowly-run 3-horse minor event at Beverley again later in September; stays well;
acts on any going; sometimes sweats up; good mount for an inexperienced
rider; has won 3 times at Yarmouth. *H. Cecil.*

FRANCISCUS 4 br.c. Lord Gayle 124–Frances Jordan 102 (Prince Regent 129)
(1980 12g* 12g 12f⁴ 11.7g³ 11.1g² 12g* 13.3d³ 1981 16s 18fg 14g 13fg 12g 14f
14g³) neat ex-Irish colt; fair at 3 yrs; didn't find his form in 1981; stays 1¾m
but found 2¼m too far second outing; suited by some give in the ground; blinkered
sixth start. *A. Jarvis.*

FRANK BERRY 3 ch.c. Lorenzaccio 130–Bora Bora 91 (Hethersett 134) (1980   **70** d
6g 7f 6g 7d⁴ 7g 8d 1981 7s 7fg 7d 11.7s 7fg³ 8g* 8.2d² 7f³ 7g 8s 7g⁴) lengthy,
attractive colt; good walker; beat Hyjill a neck in seller at Ayr in July (bought
in 3,500 gns); in frame in varied company afterwards, including in non-sellers;
bred to stay at least 1¼m; acts on any going, except possibly very soft; best in
blinkers. *G. Lewis.*

FRANKLY SPEAKING 9 br.g. Frankincense 120–Luscinia 73 (Sing Sing 134)   —
(1980 NR 1981 8fg) of little account; has been tried in blinkers. *S. Kernick.*

FRANKNESS 5 br.g. Frankincense 120–Twice Shy (Lord of Verona 120) (1980   **35**
12.3d 10g⁴ 15d 12g⁴ 12d 1981 15.8s 11g³) fair sort; plater nowadays; seems
to stay 2m; probably acts on any going; sometimes races with his tongue tied
down; sold to J. Harris 1,800 gns Doncaster May Sales. *G. Richards.*

FRANK STEWART 4 ch.g. Grey Mirage 128–Bontet (Bounteous 125) (1980   —
8v* 10fg 8d 13.8fg 1981 7s 11d 6g) compact gelding; poor plater; should stay
1¼m; suited by some give in the ground; has worn blinkers and bandages;
changed hands 360 gns Doncaster January (81) Sales. *R. Ward.*

FRASASS 4 b.g. Sassafras 135–Desert Flame 96 (Baldric II 131) (1980 12fg   **79**
12f 12d³ 10d³ 12fg* 14d² 15.8d* 16g 16.1s 1981 16.1fg⁴ 16g² 13s) strong,
compact gelding; temperamental staying handicapper; acts on a firm and a soft
surface; one to be wary of. *M. H. Easterby.*

FREDA FLOCKTON 3 br.f. Arch Sculptor 123–Nearumba 73 (Quorum 126)   —
(1980 5s 6d 1981 6g 9d 8.2s) sturdy filly; probably of little account. *S.
Wiles.*

FREE NEWS 3 ch.f. Tickled Pink 114–Friendly Gift (Be Friendly 130) (1980   —
NR 1981 7g 6f 5f 8fg) small filly; first foal; dam unraced sister to successful
sprinter Friendly Fun; last to finish in 4 maiden races in the summer. *R. Laing.*

FREE PRESS 2 b.g. Free State 125–Miss McWorden 75 (Worden II 129) (1981   **75**
6g 7fg⁴ 7fg³ 8d) Mar 30; 41,000Y; compact gelding; half-brother to 5 winners,
including very useful 1980 2-y-o sprinter Parkdale (by Swing Easy); dam stayer;
quite moderate form in maiden races; will stay 1¼m. *I. Balding.*

FREE RANGE 2 gr.f. Birdbrook 110–Micky Goleah (Quorum 126) (1981   **61**
5d 5fg 5.3f 5fg⁴ 6g 6g³) Apr 7; leggy, lengthy, lightly-made filly; first living
foal; dam well beaten all starts; third of 16 under a low weight in selling nursery
won by Typecast at Brighton in September; will stay 1m. *R. Smyth.*

FREEWAY FOLLY (USA) 2 ch.f. One For All–Forliane (Forli) (1981 8d)   —
Apr 27; $75,000Y; sixth foal; half-sister to 2 winners in USA; dam, unplaced
6 times, is daughter of Irish 1,000 Guineas third Banri An Oir; 10/1 when ninth
of 16 to Portette in maiden race at Bath in October. *B. Hills.*

318

FREEZE FRAME 4 b.f. Averof 123–Snowfield 69 (Meadow Court 129) (1980 —
  10f 12g 12d 12s 12.5s 10d 1981 10f 12g 8h 10.1fg) well beaten in varied
  company; sometimes sweats up. *M. Stephens.*

FRENCH ART 9 gr.g. Articulate 121–Moselle Mist (Sovereign Path 125) —
  (1980 NR 1981 16f 16.5g) winning hurdler; of little account on flat. *N.
  Bycroft.*

FRENCH COOKING 5 b.m. Royal and Regal–Costmary 108 (Grey Sovereign —
  128§) (1980 12f 1981 16.1f 13f) well-made mare; poor performer nowadays;
  stays well; yet to race on soft ground; has worn blinkers. *W. Clay.*

FRENCH CURRENT (AUS) 2 b.c. Without Fear 128–Cap D'Antibes (Better — p
  Boy 91) (1981 6fg) Feb 27; 8,000Y; strong, rangy, attractive colt; second
  foal; dam won 2 of Australia's most important sprints, the 5f Lightning Stakes
  and 6f Newmarket Handicap, after finishing ½-length second in 12.5f VRC
  Oaks; 20/1 and on backward side, ran on steadily without being knocked about
  when eighth of 12 to Torrey in maiden race at Goodwood in July; looked fairly
  promising here but wasn't seen out again. *B. Hills.*

FRENCH GENT 2 b.c. Sassafras 135–Nom de Plume 70 (Aureole 132) (1981 **104**
  5d* 6g* 6f 7g 7s*) Apr 24; 1,500Y; compact colt; third foal; half-brother to
  1980 2-y-o 6f and 7f winner Monevette (by Sweet Revenge); dam ran only
  at 2 yrs when winner over 7f; successful in Tattersalls' Yorkshire Stakes at
  York and minor event at Ripon in first half of season, putting up a remarkable
  display to win going away by a length from Royal Revenge after losing several
  lengths at start at York; sixth subsequently in Chesham Stakes at Royal
  Ascot and Seaton Delaval Stakes at Newcastle, beaten 6½ lengths by Zilos in
  latter, but returned to winning form in 13-runner nursery at York in October,
  putting up a splendid performance to beat Miss Prudent a length; will stay 1½m;
  acts well on soft going and possibly isn't suited by firm; ridden by apprentice
  K. Hodgson to 2 successes; doesn't always impress in paddock. *M. H. Easterby.*

Mr Colin Webster's "French Gent"

FRENCH KNOT 3 b.g. Take a Reef 127–Merette 63 (Runnymede 123) (1980 **71**
6fg 6g 7f 7g 8.2s⁴ 8d³ 1981 10v* 10s* 9.4g³ 11fg² 10g⁴ 11g 10.5s 11d* 12d)
neat gelding; won handicaps at Ayr in March, Beverley in April and Redcar in
October; stays 11f; acts on a firm surface but is well suited by plenty of give
in the ground; wears blinkers. *J. W. Watts.*

FRENCH SCRIBE (USA) 2 ch.f. Arts and Letters–Chez Elle (Mongo) (1981 **73**
7fg 7g² 7v) Mar 18; $140,000Y; lengthy filly; excellent mover; half-sister to
several winners, including stakes-winning fillies In Our Time (by Timeless
Moment) and Place Dauphine (by Quadrangle); dam, placed at 2 yrs, is daughter
of very useful Mlle Dianne; always in touch when 2 lengths second of 15 to
Awaasif in maiden race at Ayr in September; well beaten in £3,400 event won
by My Destiny at York the following month; will stay 1¼m. *J. Hindley.*

FRENCH TOUCH 4 ch.f. Dieu Soleil 111–Fabric 77 (Sheshoon 132) (1980 5f **53**
7fg 5f* 6fg 5fg 5fg³ 5g 5g 6d 6g 5g³ 5d 1981 5s 6g 6g 6fg 5g 6fg 5fg 5f 5d* 5g)
neat filly; plater; bought in 680 gns after winning at Edinburgh in October;
stays 6f; acts on any going. *A. Balding.*

FRESA 4 gr.f. Lorenzaccio 130–Chokeberry (Crepello 136) (1980 8f⁴ 8fg 7g —
10fg 10g 8s 1981 10g 7fg 6f) small filly; poor maiden. *A. Moore.*

FRESH FORD 2 b.f. Pampapaul 121–Independence 64 (Runnymede 123) —
(1981 7fg 7f 8fg 7g) Apr 28; IR 7,800F, 4,000Y, 12,000 2-y-o; lightly-made
filly; half-sister to 3 winners, including useful sprinter Swing Alone (by Swinging
Junior); dam poor sprinter; in rear in maiden and minor events. *K. Stone.*

FRIDAY STREET 2 ch.g. Town Crier 119–Honey Palm 86 (Honeyway 125) **86**
(1981 5fg⁴ 5s 6g³ 7g 6f³ 6g 7fg⁴ 5.3d³ 6d*) Apr 27; 4,300F; quite attractive
gelding; half-brother to 2 winners, including fair 1m and 1¼m winner Honegger
(by King's Troop); dam, a sprinter, at her best at 2 yrs; in frame in most of
his races prior to winning 15-runner minor event at Brighton in October by
1½ lengths from Town Flier; will stay 1m; gelded at end of season. *R. Smyth.*

FRIENDLY ECHO 3 ch f. Reliance II 137–Misty Echo 58 (Mountain Call 125) —
(1980 5.3d⁴ 5s 5g 6fg 7fg 1981 7g 8s 7d 7fg 7fg 7f) small filly; poor walker;
no form in 1981, including in a quite valuable seller; bred to stay beyond
sprint distances; saddle slipped first outing. *Mrs J. Reavey.*

FRIENDLY FUN 6 ro.g. Be Friendly 130–Primerva (Primera 131) (1980 5d **81**
5s² 5fg 5f³ 5f 5s 5g 5fg 5fg 5d 5d² 5.6g 6s 5g³ 5s³ 5v² 1981 5s 5d 5d³ 5d 6d
5g 5fg 5f³ 6fg⁴ 5f³ 5g 5g 5g 6s* 5d 6d 5g) sprint handicapper; made all and
ran on well to beat Crofthall by 3 lengths in £8,100 race at Haydock in October;
stays 6f; acts on any going, but is well suited by some give in the ground;
effective with and without blinkers (usually wears them nowadays). *N. Crump.*

FRIENDLY SOVEREIGN 3 b.g. Hard Fact 74–Friendly Queen 73 (Be Friendly —
130) (1980 6fg 8d 7s 1981 11.7g 16.9s 11.7g) plain gelding; plating-class
maiden. *A. Andrews.*

FRIENDLY SPARKLE 2 ch.c. Sparkler 130–Northern Queen (Northfields) **74**
(1981 6g⁴ 7f 7fg³ 7f.¸ 7g) May 5; rather lightly-made colt; first foal; dam Irish
1½m winner; in frame in maiden races at Salisbury and Warwick; second favourite
for 29-runner seller at Newmarket in September on final outing but finished out
of first 11 to Perchance; will stay 1¼m. *J. Sutcliffe.*

FRIESLAND LASS 4 b.f. Warpath 113–Elche 107 (Flush Royal 127) (1980 —
8d 8v 10s 12fg 12d 1981 18.4fg⁴ 10.8fg) lightly-made filly; useless plater; has
worn blinkers. *J. H. Peacock.*

FRITHS FOLLY 4 ch.f. Good Bond 122–Drinka Pinta 101 (Court Feathers 120) —
(1980 6v 5f 7f 9g⁴ 12g³ 10d 12f³ 12fg 12fg 12g 10d 1981 8.2s 8g) not a good
mover in her slower paces; plater; stays 1½m; probably needs a sound surface;
often blinkered; has worn bandages; sometimes sweats up; ran badly second start;
sold 500 gns Doncaster June Sales; resold 800 gns same venue in October.
R. Hobson.

FRIVOLOUS RELATION (USA) 3 b. or br.f. Buckpasser–Aunt Edith 128 **59**
(Primera 131) (1980 7d 1981 10f 10f 12.3g²) attractive filly; not the best
of movers; stuck on at one pace when 3 lengths second behind Hot Fire in
maiden race at Newcastle in August, only form; suited by 1½m and an easy
surface. *J. Dunlop.*

FROGTOWN (USA) 3 b.g. One For All–Ave Valeque (Bold Ruler) (1980 5fg **67**
8g 1981 8g 10fg 10d 8fg⁴ 8fg⁴ 8.2s² 9s² 8g²) well-made, attractive gelding;

runner-up in maiden races at Haydock and Hamilton and in minor event at Doncaster in autumn; should stay 1¼m. *G. Harwood.*

FROME (USA) 3 ch.c. Gentleman's Game–Happy Donna (Prince Blessed) **73**
(1980 5f 6fg 6d² 7fg³ 7d³ 1981 7fg⁴ 7g 10d⁴ 11.7f 10fg⁴ 8.3fg* 8.3g 10fg 10.1fg*
11.7d 12s 10d) strong, lengthy colt; successful in 2 handicaps at Windsor,
beating Danlifar by 3 lengths on second occasion in September; not disgraced
over 1½m on eleventh start; acts on a firm and a soft surface; best in blinkers;
sold to BBA (Italia) 8,000 gns Newmarket Autumn Sales. *R. Smyth.*

FRUITION 3 b.f. Rheingold 137–Welsh Flame 106 (Welsh Pageant 132) (1980 **89**
8g⁴ 1981 8fg 12g⁴ 12v² 12g 10g 10g²) lengthy filly; first foal; dam won 4
times over 1m; had stiff tasks on most outings and was far from disgraced when
about 4 lengths fourth of 7 behind Leap Lively in Johnnie Walker Oaks Trial at
Lingfield and when 3 lengths second of 4 behind impressive winner Golden Bowl
in Lupe Stakes at Goodwood, both in May; didn't run up to her best when ¾-
length second to Etty in maiden event at Newmarket in October; suited by 1½m.
P. Kelleway.

FUDDLED 2 br.f. Malacate 131–Egualita 111 (Democratic 124) (1981 7g 8s 7g) **74**
Apr 22; IR 21,000Y; neat, attractive filly; half-sister to numerous winners here
and abroad, including quite useful sprinter Equal Chance (by Hitting Away); dam
won Ayr Gold Cup; fifth in maiden races at Warwick and Newmarket in October
on last 2 starts, on latter finishing 6¾ lengths behind Chalon in 29-runner event;
probably stays 1m. *B. Hills.*

FUEGO 2 b.g. High Line 125–Manche 82 (Palestine 133) (1981 5g 5d 6g) May **—**
18; 1,050F; neat gelding; dam second in three 5f races at 2 yrs; well beaten all
outings, including in a seller; retained 600 gns Doncaster June Sales and 300 gns
Doncaster October Sales. *G. Richards.*

FUEGO DIABLO 4 gr.g. Sparkler 130–Black Fire 92 (Firestreak 125) (1980 **—**
NR 1981 10s⁴ 10s 10g 16.1f 12f 12g 16.5g 13.8g) strong gelding; only plating
class; sold out of J. W. Watts's stable 2,300 gns Ascot June Sales after third
outing. *P. Bevan.*

FUGACIOUS 3 ch.c. Sallust 134–Phantasmagoria 65 (Le Haar 126) (1980 6g **—**
6fg³ 8d 6v² 7d 1981 6fg 7d 6g 5v 7fg 5g 6f 9g) small, stocky colt; poor form
in 1981, including in a seller; stays 6f; seems to act on any going; sometimes
blinkered; sold to M. Hinchliffe 2,000 gns Ascot 2nd June Sales. *D. Sasse.*

FULL EXTENT (USA) 2 b.c. Full Out–Mary Biz (T.V. Lark) (1981 5g⁴ 6fg* **113**
6fg* 7fg* 6d* 7fg)
It is no exaggeration to say that a horse's career is often greatly conditioned
by what happens to him on his first appearance on a racecourse. Most newcomers are apprehensive to some degree, and any unpleasant experience can
have damaging consequences. An experience first time out such as that
suffered by Full Extent at Ayr in May would have been the undoing of many a
promising two-year-old. He had a most unfortunate introduction, getting so
worked up in the stalls that his rider was said to have been calling to the handlers
to take the horse out as the starter let the runners go. It is to Lowe's credit

Gimcrack Stakes, York—Full Extent makes all to beat
Take The Floor and Mydrone

Mr Martin Korn's "Full Extent"

that he didn't make Full Extent race seriously, allowing him to come home at a canter, a long way last of four; Full Extent came back very distressed, his hind legs gashed. When he reappeared three weeks later at Redcar permission was given for him to be put into the stalls last. He gave no trouble and was well away but he had to overcome difficulties in running. Full Extent was carried badly to the left and bumped several times in the final two furlongs by the subsequently-disqualified Killingholme Clay but even so he reached the post first, showing great resolution. After Redcar, Full Extent won two fairly important juvenile events in the North, the Black Duck Stakes at York in July and the Heronslea Stakes at Ayr in August, showing improved form on each occasion. By the time he lined up for the Gimcrack Stakes at York's August meeting Full Extent had shown himself to be a useful juvenile, among the best around at that stage of the season.

Northern-trained colts had won three of the previous nine runnings of the Gimcrack, one of Britain's oldest and most prestigious two-year-old races, and Full Extent started joint-second favourite with the Molecomb winner Prowess Prince behind the odds-on Irish challenger Peterhof. Full Extent led the Gimcrack field from start to finish; he appeared to be going a little better than the speedy Peterhof from halfway and ran on strongly under pressure to win decisively by two and half a lengths and half a length from Take The Floor and Mydrone with Lucky Hunter and Peterhof close behind. What seemed a good-class performance by Full Extent at the time didn't look so good at the end of the season: Take The Floor failed to finish in the first six in either the Mill Reef Stakes or the William Hill Middle Park Stakes and Mydrone was beaten three times in the North after the Gimcrack and finished last in the Middle Park. Full Extent ran only once after York, and started favourite for the Laurent Perrier Champagne Stakes at Doncaster in September. He finished a well-beaten seventh of eight but we don't attach too much significance to his defeat—he was beaten a long way from home and plainly did not show his form. His connections, who now suspect that Full Extent struck into himself at Doncaster, evidently felt that further racing might damage his prospects as a three-year-old and he was let down after Doncaster. His main objective is the Two

322

Thousand Guineas and plans are that he will reappear in the Timeform Race Card Stakes at Thirsk in April, a race won in 1979 by the subsequent Two Thousand Guineas winner Tap On Wood. On what he has achieved so far Full Extent is not up to classic standard but it is in his favour that he was retired for the season after his display at Doncaster. He will have had plenty of time to recover from his two-year-old campaign and, if looks are anything to go by, he should train on; he's a strong, sturdy type with scope. There doesn't seem much doubt about his staying a mile and although his best performance came on dead ground in the Gimcrack he is an excellent mover, with a long, raking stride, and has won three times on a firm surface.

		Never Bend	Nasrullah
	Full Out	(b 1960)	Lalun
	(b 1973)	Running Juliet	Round Table
Full Extent (USA)		(b 1966)	Juliets Nurse
(b.c. May 2, 1979)		T.V. Lark	Indian Hemp
	Mary Biz	(b 1957)	Miss Larksfly
	(b 1972)	Proprietress	Your Host
		(br 1959)	Omelet Souffle

Full Extent's sire, a son of Mill Reef's sire Never Bend, showed high-class form at two and was rated 124, the second-best sprinter of that year, in the *Daily Racing Form* Free Handicap as a four-year-old; Full Out won over a mile but was evidently best at shorter distances. Full Extent was Full Out's first winner. Full Extent's dam Mary Biz, who was unplaced four times as a two-year-old, is a half-sister to a smart North American performer called Terrible Tiger. Full Extent is the third foal of Mary Biz, following the filly Chuckle (by Shecky Greene), a winner in the States, and the modest three-year-old Angle Fire (by Angle Light) who won twice at a mile and once at nine furlongs in Britain in 1981. Full Extent's trainer bought 325,000 dollars (Full Extent cost 67,000 dollars) at the latest Keeneland Fall Sale for a yearling half-brother to Full Extent by The Minstrel's brother Far North. *S. Norton.*

FULL OF FORTUNE 2 b.f. Full of Hope 125–Alisma II (Alizier 131) (1981 — 8s 10s) half-sister to 2 winners in France, including Alicall (by Mountain Call), successful in three 5f claiming races at 2 yrs; dam placed at up to 1¼m in France; unquoted when behind in large fields of maidens at Warwick and Nottingham in October; sold 400 gns Newmarket Autumn Sales. *C. James.*

FULL OF GRACE 2 ch.f. Full of Hope 125–Flaming Peace 104 (Queen's 58 Hussar 124) (1981 5g 5d 5s³ 6fg 7d 7h 7fg 7f⁴ 8fg) Apr 30; 1,000Y; small, lightly-made filly; second foal; half-sister to 1980 2-y-o 6f winner Sovereign Flame (by Supreme Sovereign); dam won twice over 7f at 2 yrs; quite a moderate plater; should stay 1m (ran very wide into straight at Beverley on first attempt at trip). *Mrs J. Reavey.*

FULL OF LOVE 2 br.f. Full of Hope 125–Lovage (Linacre 133) (1981 7g 6d) — Apr 24; big filly; half-sister to 2 winners, including speedy filly Chain Lady (by Manacle); dam of little account; well beaten in maiden races at Leicester in October (dwelt and finished last) and November. *D. Elsworth.*

FULL OF REASON (USA) 3 br.f. Bold Reason–Tasteful (Ribot 142) (1980 105 7g* 1981 8.5fg³ 10.2d² 10f² 10fg³ 12fg⁴ 11.5d* 12d⁴ 12g² 12s⁴) neat, lightly-made filly; half-sister to winners in USA by Viceregal and Personality; dam unraced sister to Kentucky Derby second Dapper Dan; made virtually all and beat Comedian in pretty good style by a length (pair 10 lengths clear) in handicap at Yarmouth in July; ran creditably when neck second to Karadar in £4,700 handicap at Goodwood in September and when about 5½ lengths fourth to easy winner Flighting in Princess Royal Stakes at Ascot in October, keeping on well both times; stays 1½m; acts on any going. *L. Cumani.*

FULL VALUE 10 br.g. Relko 136–How Far 107 (Hethersett 134) (1980 8f — 1981 8fg 8f) fair hurdler; does little racing on flat; has worn bandages. *D. Ringer.*

FUNNY SPRING 6 b.g. Rheingold 137–Lotus 79 (Aureole 132) (1980 10s 76 10fg⁴ 9g 10g 10g 10g* 1981 10g² 10g³ 11s 10s 10g) stocky gelding; carries a lot of condition; fair handicapper; best form at up to 1¼m; acts on any going; genuine but needs strong handling and seems to do best for W. Carson. *L. Cumani.*

FURRY BERG 2 b.c. Furry Glen 121–Lauch Berg (Faberge II 121) (1981 92 6.3fg 7fg 6fg² 6.3fg 7g⁴ 7.5d* 8d³) Mar 30; third foal; dam Irish middle-distance winner; in first 2 throughout when winning valuable Waterford Glass Nursery at Gowran Park in October by 1½ lengths from Remanded; also in frame behind Longleat in maiden race at the Curragh (beaten ¾ length) and Coolmore Try My Best Stakes at Leopardstown (4¾ lengths fourth of 10) and wasn't disgraced when 10 lengths third of 10 to Assert in Beresford Stakes at the Curragh; will stay 1¼m; acts on a firm and a soft surface. *A. Keane, Ireland.*

FUTAN 5 b.g. St Chad 120–Andara (Hugh Lupus 132) (1980 12s 11.7d 14.6fg 16.5fg 12fg 12d² 12d 12d 1981 18.8fg) quite moderate at his best but has deteriorated; suited by 1½m; probably acts on any going; often wears blinkers; suitable mount for an apprentice; sold 3,800 gns Ascot September Sales. *D. Gandolfo.* —

FUTURE FOREST 8 ch.h. Continuation 120–Sylvan Wood (Red God 128§) (1980 6v 5fg 6f 6fg 5g 5s 5v 1981 6s 6fg) smart sprinter in his prime; no longer seems of any account; sweated up badly once in 1980; has worn bandages; sold 1,200 gns Doncaster November Sales. *D. Leslie.* —

FUTURE SPA 2 b.c. Ballymore 123–Breakage (Breakspear II) (1981 8s 8.5s*) Mar 18; 10,000Y; brother to Irish 7f and 1¼m winner Bennaunmore and half-brother to a winner; dam won over 6f at 2 yrs in Ireland; 5/4 favourite, won 14-runner maiden race at Galway in October by a length from Gainsay, the pair 6 lengths clear; will stay at least 1¼m; sure to win more races. *P. Prendergast, Ireland.* **82**

FUTURE UNSEEN 3 b. or br.f. Prince de Galles 125–Fulfilment (David Jack 125) (1980 6g 7g 7fg 6g 1981 10s 10d 11.7fg 10f⁴ 10f) sparely-made filly; plater; stays 1¼m; sold 440 gns Doncaster October Sales. *W. Holden.* —

G

GABITAT 3 ch.c. Arch Sculptor 123–Golden Hostess (Kythnos 126) (1980 5s 5.8f 6g³ 6g 6d* 6d³ 7v 1981 6d 6v* 6s 6f 6fg³ 6f³ 6fg* 7g³ 6fg² 6g 6d 6g 8s 6g) useful-looking colt; has been hobdayed; won handicaps at Windsor in May and Lingfield in July, putting up a good performance when beating Sleepline Princess a length in latter; ran very well indeed when about 2 lengths fifth of 16 behind The Quiet Bidder in Cork and Orrery Stakes at Royal Ascot on fourth outing; best at 6f; acts on any going; blinkered nowadays; not particularly consistent. *B. Gubby.* **101**

GABLES STAR 2 gr.f. Tack On 114–Gables Grey 66 (Colonist II 126) (1981 5s 5d* 5v³ 6f) Mar 11; compact filly; second reported foal; dam, moderate winning hurdler, is sister to useful chaser French Colonist; placed in sellers at Leicester in April (beaten ½ length by Ten-Traco) and Goodwood in May; awarded the Leicester race because winner failed dope test; subsequently sold to race in Belgium and won at least twice there; should be well suited by 6f; possibly unsuited by firm going. *R. Smyth.* **56**

GAELIC HARP 6 ch.g. Paddy's Birthday 110–Condicote Lane (Sunny Way 120) (1980 NR 1981 16f 16fg 16.5fg) workmanlike gelding; winner over fences; behind in poor maiden races in the North. *G. Lockerbie.* —

GAITERS 2 br.c. Godswalk 130–Tenderly (Prince Tenderfoot 126) (1981 6h² 6f²) May 11; 20,000Y; third foal; half-brother to 2 winners in Ireland, including fairly useful 5f to 7f winner Lord Trendy (by Lord Gayle); dam fairly useful from 5f to 9f in Ireland; favourite when 5 lengths second to Charbonnel in newcomers race at Chepstow and to Miguelini in maiden event at Hamilton, both in September; may well stay 7f. *Sir Mark Prescott.* **69**

GALA LAD 7 ch.g. Gala Performance–Land 62 (Baldric II 131) (1980 NR 1981 12g 12s 12s 12v 12d) poor middle-distance handicapper; blind in right eye; acts on any going; suitable mount for a boy. *N. Bycroft.* —

GALE AGENCY 2 ch.c. Hittite Glory 125–Tale of Two Cities (Charlottesville 135) (1981 5fg 7fg⁴ 7fg 7h⁴ 8f 8g 8g) Apr 21; 5,200F, 7,600Y; small, compact colt; half-brother to a winner in France by St Alphage; dam poor Irish maiden; modest fourth of 6 in maiden race at Sandown in July and nursery at Bath in August; stays 7f; quickly tailed off when equipped with hood and blinkers in seller at Newmarket in October on seventh start. *C. Williams.* **64**

GALIBIER (USA) 3 b.c. Marshua's Dancer–Bojon (Beau Max) (1980 8g 1981 10d 9s 8f⁴ 8fg 8f 8d⁴ 8fg* 8fg 8s) strong, compact colt; ran best race when winning apprentice race at Yarmouth in August; well beaten afterwards; stays 1m; best form on a sound surface. *L. Cumani.* **55**

GALIVEAR 2 b. or br.c. Galivanter 131–Earall (Khalkis 127) (1981 6g) Mar —
23; half-brother to 2 winners, including fairly useful middle-distance stayer
Lochranza (by Highland Melody); dam tailed off both outings; 50/1 and backward when tailed-off last of 21 to Mirabeau in maiden race at Doncaster in
September. *J. Blundell.*

GALLEA 3 b.g. Prince de Galles 125–Russellia (Red God 128§) (1980 7fg **71**
1981 10s 10s 10s 10.8fg 10fg 8.3fg 8f* 8d³ 7f* 8fg* 8f 8g* 7g 8d⁴ 8.2s) leggy,
narrow gelding; bought in after winning sellers at Yarmouth (2,000 gns) and
Leicester (3,800 gns) in August; ran well in non-sellers afterwards and won
handicaps at Yarmouth and Leicester; stays 1m; ideally suited by a sound
surface; genuine front runner; sold to N. Guest 3,100 gns Newmarket Autumn
Sales. *M. Ryan.*

GALLIC PRIDE (USA) 3 b.f. Key To The Kingdom–Gallina 120 (Raise A —
Native) (1980 7d 7g 1981 10s 10v 11.7g 12d) well-made, quite attractive
filly; second foal; half-sister to modest stayer Brave The Reef (by Mill Reef);
dam won Ribblesdale Stakes; quite moderate form in maiden and minor races;
will stay beyond 1½m; blinkered final outing; ran badly second start. *I. Balding.*

GALLOWAY FLAME 5 gr.m. Dike–Porsanger (Zeddaan 130) (1980 NR —
1981 16f) poor maiden; stays 1½m; has run badly in blinkers; sold 550 gns
Ascot October Sales. *P. Bevan.*

GALLY 3 b.g. Comedy Star 121–Galliphanto (Galivanter 131) (1980 5fg⁴ —
5fg 5.8fg 6g 7g 6d 1981 8fg 7f 7f) compact gelding; soundly beaten in varied
company, including selling; unseated rider at start second outing of 1980;
blinkered final start. *J. Spearing.*

GALVESTON 4 b.c. Sir Ivor 135–Happy Music 84 (Hethersett 134) (1980 **114**
7g 10.5g 10g* 10g* 11s* 12fg* 10g⁴ 12v 1981 8g² 12d³ 10fg* 10fg* 10.2g 9g²
10fg* 10.5g² 9g) big, strong colt; very useful handicapper; had a good year,
winning Rosebery Stakes at Kempton (by 7 lengths from Rhyme Royal) and
Sandown Cup and Queen Mother's Cup at Sandown; well-backed favourite,
beat Bettyknowes impressively by 3 lengths in last-named in July; also ran well
when second to Strong Gale in Grosser Preis von Dortmund and to Amyndas,
beaten 2½ lengths under 10-1, in John Smith's Magnet Cup at York; stayed
1½m; well suited by a sound surface; had a good turn of foot; stud in Australia.
W. Hastings-Bass.

GAMBLERS DREAM 4 b. or br.g. Prince Regent 129–Red Laser 95 (Red God **95**
128§) (1980 6s* 6f² 6f 6g 7d⁴ 6fg 7g 6s 6fg 5g 6d² 5s² 1981 6fg 6g 6s⁴ 6f 6f²
6fg 6fg⁴ 6fg* 6fg* 6d 6g 5s 6v) strong, attractive gelding; good mover; fairly
useful handicapper; won Brighton Sprint Handicap (from Copper Beeches)
and £5,700 race at Goodwood (beat Escovitch) in August; also ran well on
seventh start when fourth to Crews Hill in Tote Stewards' Cup at Goodwood;
well beaten last 4 starts; stays 7f; acts on any going; effective with or without
blinkers. *D. Wilson.*

GAMBLING WREN 5 br.m. Knave To Play 79–Parade 97 (March Past 124) —
(1980 13.8fg 16g 16d 16.9d 14.6fg 12g 12fg* 12.2fg⁴ 14.7f² 12.2d 13s 12d 1981
12f 12fg) poor handicapper; stays well; best form on a sound surface; has won
for an apprentice. *W. Clay.*

GAME FOX 2 gr.c. Relkino 131–Game All 109 (Alcide 136) (1981 8s⁴ 8s) **72**
June 2; 8,200Y; rather leggy colt; hasn't much scope; half-brother to several
winners, including 3-y-o 6f winner Pavilion (by Habitat) and very smart French
1m and 1½m winner Bally Game (by Ballymoss); dam, half-sister to Birdbrook,
was game performer at up to 11f; favourite when 2¾ lengths fourth of 17 to Mrs
Currie in maiden race at Warwick in October; well beaten in 29-runner minor
event won by Arrowood Dream at Redcar later in month; bred to stay middle
distances; sold to German International BA 4,200 gns Newmarket Autumn
Sales. *M. Stoute.*

GAMMA 3 b.g. Dragonara Palace 115–Aspiration 53 (Roan Rocket 128) (1980 —
5d* 5f* 5f⁴ 5fg 5g⁴ 6g² 7d 7.2g 6g 1981 6s 6d 8.5d) tall, leggy, useful-looking
gelding; soundly beaten as a 3-y-o, on final occasion in a seller; stayed 6f; dead.
A. Pitt.

GANIMEDE 3 ch.c. Red God 128§–Gone Gay 86 (Crepello 136) (1980 7fg* **108 §**
7fg 1981 6s² 8d* 7g² 6s⁴ 7f 7g³ 7.3fg 8fg³ 7fg 8d²) well-made, most attractive
colt; good mover; beat Cracking Form quite smoothly by 1½ lengths in £3,100
event at Brighton in April; ran best subsequent races when in frame in valuable
handicap at York, Gus Demmy Memorial Stakes at Haydock, and Beeswing
Stakes and Northern Goldsmiths Handicap at Newcastle, on last-named course

finishing third respectively to Milk of the Barley and Bunter; showed no resolution whatsoever after looking sure to win when beginning his challenge in £3,000 event at Newbury in September, and finished 2 lengths second to Melodrama; disappointing on other occasions too; finds 6f on sharp side and stays 1m; probably acts on any going; sometimes troublesome at start; racing in Florida. *L. Cumani.*

GAP OF DUNLOE (FR) 3 b.c. Sassafras 135–Absaretch (Dancer's Image) **117** (1980 8d 8g 1981 12fg* 12s 12g³ 12fg 11fg² 12d 12v) 20,000Y; well-made, attractive ex-English colt; half-brother to Mossy Plume (by Levmoss), successful over 1m in France and also a winner in USA, and to a winner in USA by Targowice; dam won 7f maiden race at 2 yrs in USA; showed a little promise in maiden and minor events as a 2-y-o when trained by J. Dunlop; made a successful reappearance in maiden race at Longchamp in April, beating Roi Guillaume by 1½ lengths; showed much improved form and ran a fine race when 6½ lengths third of 12 behind stable-companion Bikala in Prix du Jockey-Club at Chantilly in June and also ran creditably when 6 lengths second to Strong Gale in Grand Prix Prince Rose at Ostend in July; not disgraced when about 11 lengths sixth of 12 behind easy winner Shergar in Irish Sweeps Derby at the Curragh in between, but on last 2 starts finished in rear behind Gold River in Prix de l'Arc de Triomphe and Rahotep in Prix du Conseil de Paris, both at Longchamp in October; stays 1½m; best form on a sound surface; wears blinkers. *P.-L. Biancone, France.*

GARDIENNE 2 b.f. Home Guard 129–Erics Girl (Skymaster 126) (1981 6g⁴ 8fg) **69** Mar 30; first foal; dam won over 1m in France; 25/1 and decidedly backward, came out best of newcomers when 4 lengths fourth of 14 to Dance in Rome in maiden race at Nottingham in August; 11/2 when behind in similar event won by Cornish Heroine at Leicester the following month; not sure to have stayed 1m as a 2-y-o. *F. Durr.*

GARFUNKEL 2 b.c. Music Boy 124–First Court 82 (Primera 131) (1981 **81** 6g 6fg⁴ 6f² 7f* 7f 8g 7d²) Mar 2; 3,000Y; big, good-topped, quite attractive colt; good mover; brother to a plating-class animal; dam 1½m winner; favourite when running on strongly to win 14-runner maiden auction event at Doncaster in July by 1½ lengths from Gold Rifle; creditable 4 lengths second to Neighboring in £2,100 nursery at Doncaster in October; suited by 7f and wasn't disgraced over 1m; seems to act on any going; sweated up fifth and sixth starts. *P. Mitchell.*

GARNISH ISLAND 3 gr.f. Ardoon 124–Tarpon Springs (Grey Sovereign 128§) — (1980 5.1fg* 5g 1981 7f) compact filly; good mover; won maiden race at Yarmouth as a 2-y-o; had stiffish task and needed race when making no show in apprentice handicap on same course in June, only outing of 1981; should be suited by 6f+; sold 2,500 gns Newmarket July Sales. *G. Pritchard-Gordon.*

GARTER STAR 3 b.c. Star Appeal 133–Visite Royale (Dapper Dan) (1980 7s **69** 1981 9.5g* 12f 9.4fg⁴ 11.5g³ 10f* 12.2g⁴ 11.7d) smallish, quite attractive colt; won maiden race at Carlisle in May and ladies race at Brighton in August; stays 1½m; acts on firm going (not disgraced on a soft surface final start); sold to B. Forsey 4,000 gns Ascot November Sales. *Sir Mark Prescott.*

GARTHLAND ARMS 2 br.g. Lucky Wednesday 124–Katebird 89 (Birdbrook **61** 110) (1981 5g³ 6g 7fg² 6fg* 6f 6fg) Mar 23; second foal; dam, best at sprint distances on flat, won over hurdles; bought in for 1,700 gns after winning 6-runner seller at Ayr in August by 4 lengths from Starproof; will stay 1m; acts on a firm surface; wears blinkers. *M. H. Easterby.*

GASKINS NITESPOT 2 b.f. Quayside 124–Frensham 67 (Floribunda 136) — (1981 5d 5g) Apr 29; small filly; soundly beaten in sellers at Ripon and Thirsk in May; dead. *S. Nesbitt.*

GATHER NO MOSS 4 ch.c. Ballymoss 136–Swoop (Pandofell 132) (1980 **46** NR 1981 12s 12d 14g 10.1g 16g 19s³ 18g) lengthy colt; staying maiden; best run on soft going. *G. Beeson.*

GAULEITER (USA) 3 gr.c. Vaguely Noble 140–Gray Dove (T.V. Lark) (1980 **68** NR 1981 14f² 14g*) fair sort; half-brother to 2 winners in France, notably top-class miler Gravelines (by Cadmus), subsequently a good winner in USA and Canada; dam unraced sister to very smart American middle-distance performer Pink Pigeon; needed outing when 1½ lengths second to stable-companion Acclaimed in maiden race at Yarmouth in August; scrambled home by a short head from Royal and Loyal when odds on for similar event on same course in September; stays well; sent to France. *H. Cecil.*

GAVO 2 b.c. Windjammer (USA)–Eleanor Clare 89 (Petingo 135) (1981 6f⁴ **98** 6g⁴ 5f² 6f 7g 10v) Apr 19; 10,000Y; neat, strong, good-bodied colt; has an excellent, smooth action; second foal; brother to a plater in France; dam disappointing maiden; off the bridle from start to finish but ran well when 2 lengths second of 5 to Corley Moor in £3,800 race at Ripon in August; appeared to run best race when 7 lengths last of 5 to Green Forest after leading for 4f, in Prix Morny at Deauville later in month on next outing; not disgraced when tried over 1¼m in Prix de Conde at Longchamp in October, finishing about 10 lengths tenth to Beau Pretender. *P. Kelleway.*

GAWNMYSUN 3 br.c. Furry Glen 121–Fair Colleen (King Emperor) (1980 **60** 5d³ 6d 7g 1981 6fg 6d 6g 6v² 6f 6s) neat colt; usually had stiff tasks but ran creditably when second in small handicap at Windsor in May; should stay 7f; suited by some give in the ground; changed hands 1,700 gns Ascot August Sales. *A. Pitt.*

GAY BELLO 3 b.f. Porto Bello 118–Bonsella 68 (Carlemont 132) (1980 5g **—** 5f 6f 5s 1981 6fg 5g 8.2d 8.2g 8fg 7g 7g) compact, good-bodied filly; no worthwhile form in maiden races and handicaps; blinkered final start; trained until after second outing by R. Hollinshead. *J. Spearing.*

GAY GEORGE 5 br.h. Prince Regent 129–Kazanlik 116 (Ommeyad 120) **93** (1980 11.7g² 12fg³ 1981 11.7fg² 12fg²) nice, compact horse; fair performer on flat and a very smart hurdler; runner-up in minor event at Windsor and Moet and Chandon Silver Magnum (gentlemen riders) at Epsom in August; caught close home and beaten a neck by No Bombs in latter; probably stays 1⅜m; seems to act on any going; usually ridden up with the pace. *F. Walwyn.*

GAY GEORGIA 3 ch.f. Gay Fandango 132–Georgina (Never Say Die 137) **62** (1980 NR 1981 7d² 7d⁴ 8fg² 7fg³ 9.5f 7f 8g³ 7d 9s 12d³ 12s*) 6,400Y; lengthy, lightly-made filly; half-sister to 1⅛m winner Lough Iron (by African Sky) and fairly useful 1977 Irish 2-y-o 1m winner Regal Anna (by Royal and Regal); dam from same family as Fleet; in frame in varied company before winning maiden event at Thurles in November; suited by 1½m; probably acts on any going; blinkered eighth outing; sold out of F. J. Houghton's stable 11,500 gns Newmarket July Sales after fourth start. *E. O'Grady, Ireland.*

GAY HERALD 6 ch.h. Dike–Daisy June (Epaulette 125) (1980 NR 1981 12d) **—** modest (rated 80) in 1979; backward, bandaged and tailed off only start of 1981 in October; stays 1½m; acts on any going; blinkered twice at 3 yrs; suitable mount for an apprentice. *D. Ringer.*

GAY IVOR 3 b.g. Bigivor–Pin Drop (Pinhurst 94) (1980 NR 1981 10fg) **—** leggy, light-framed gelding; first known foal; dam unraced; backward when last of 17 finishers behind More Harmony in minor event at Nottingham in June. *L. Barratt.*

GAYLES BAMBINA 4 b.f. Lord Gayle 124–Hasten Slowly (Mark-Ye-Well) **62** (1980 6fg³ 8fg² 10.1fg⁴ 11.7g 10fg* 1981 10f³ 11.7fg⁴ 10g 10fg² 10.2g 10s² 10d*) strong filly; middle-distance handicapper; won at Chepstow in October; acts on any going; suitable mount for an apprentice; sold 10,000 gns Newmarket December Sales. *G. Harwood.*

GAY MEADOW 2 b.c. Goldhill 125–Dumb Kathy (Dumbarnie 125) (1981 6fg) **—** June 8; strong colt; half-brother to 3 winners, including fair 1⅛m winner Moon Dance (by Doudance); dam never ran; unquoted when twelfth of 14 to Codrington in Granville Stakes at Ascot in July. *R. Hollinshead.*

GAY MILANO (USA) 2 b.c. Giacometti 130–Yale Girl (Quadrangle) (1981 8g) **—** Apr 2; $22,000Y; tall, quite attractive colt; has scope; third known foal; half-brother to a winner in USA and one in Spain; dam, unraced half-sister to very smart stakes winner Navajo, has been at stud in Spain; 33/1, always in rear in 27-runner minor event won by Dudley Wood at Newmarket in October. *E. Eldin.*

GAY MINSTREL 3 br.g. Tudor Music 131–Belen (Milesian 125) (1980 5f 6f **65** 1981 5fg 8g 7f 7fg⁴ 8fg* 8g³ 8g) good-topped gelding; dropped in class when winning seller at Salisbury in September in quite good style (bought in 2,000 gns); ran creditably in non-seller next time; stays 1m; acts on a firm surface. *G. Lewis.*

GAYONARA 2 ch.f. Dragonara Palace 115–Gay Nipper 70 (Aggressor 130) **76** (1981 6s 6f* 6fg² 6fg) May 11; 4,400Y; rather lightly-made filly; good mover; second live foal; dam won over 9f and is half-sister to 2 good Italian winners; wore down African Berry to win 17-runner maiden race at Stockton in June by 1½ lengths; blinkered when going down by 4 lengths to odds-on Time Charter in 3-runner event at Leicester the following month; will stay 1m; well beaten final start. *B. Hanbury.*

GAY PATRICIA 2 b.f. Gay Fandango 132–Moon Cake (Red God 128§) — (1981 6fg 7d) Mar 17; 6,200Y; well-made filly; sixth foal; dam twice-raced half-sister to Hardicanute; unquoted when behind in large fields of maidens at Salisbury and Newbury in September. *A. Pitt.*

GAYTHORN 3 b.f. Laser Light 118–Olivia Stapleton 88 (Road House II) — (1980 5s 5g 6g2 6g 5g 1981 7g 8g 7s 6g 5g) plain sort; plater; should stay 1m; slowly away second start. *A. Davison.*

GAY TROUBADOUR 2 b.c. Song 132–First Delight 80 (Primera 131) (1981 — 5g 5.8f 7g) Mar 15; 5,400Y; good sort; half-brother to 2 winners, including useful 9f to 1¼m winner Celtic Pleasure (by Irish Ball); dam won at 9f and 1¼m; poor form in maiden races at Bath in July and Leicester in September, last 2 outings; moved badly to start at Leicester. *J. Bethell.*

GAY TWENTIES 7 b.m. Lord Gayle 124–Schull (Yorick II 127) (1980 NR — 1981 16s) poor maiden on flat but has won over hurdles; has worn blinkers; suitable mount for an amateur rider. *R. Carter.*

GAY WALK 5 ch.m. Farm Walk 111–Gay Breeze (Con Brio 121) (1980 12fg — 16g 12d3 12g 12fg 12.2fg 12f 1981 15.8s) smallish mare; plater; stays 1½m; acts on soft going. *D. Yeoman.*

GAY WHISTLER 3 b.c. Gay Fandango 132–Tin Saint 99 (Tin Whistle 128) **47** (1980 6g 5g 7fg 1981 9d 8g 7g4 8fg 6g 7f) smallish, lengthy colt; fourth in seller at Newmarket in May, best effort; stays 7f; sometimes blinkered; sold to H. Fleming 600 gns Doncaster September Sales. *A. Jarvis.*

GAY WONDER 3 b.f. Gay Fandango 132–March Wonder 99 (March Past 124) — (1980 NR 1981 7d4 8d 7g 8fg 10.2h 6f) 3,600F, 13,500Y; big, well-made filly; half-sister to several winners, including useful Yunkel (by Amber Rama), successful at up to 7.6f, and fairly useful sprinter Watawonder (by Deep Diver); dam won 5 races at 1¼m; disappointing after finishing respectable 9 lengths fourth of 11 behind Wilderness in newcomers race at Newbury in April; should stay 1m. *C. Brittain.*

GAZAAN 3 ch.g. Margouillat 133–Goldena (Relko 136) (1980 7f4 8d 1981 12g2 **56** 12f3 15.5f4 16g) lengthy, quite useful sort; plating-class maiden; tailed off final start; stays well; sold out of M. Stoute's stable 5,600 gns Newmarket July Sales after second outing. *M. Hinchliffe.*

GEARY'S FOR STEEL 3 ch.c. Realm 129–Vita (Roan Rocket 128) (1980 **62** 5f 5f* 5g3 5fg 5s 5fg 1981 5g 8g 5g 5f 6f2 6fg* 6f 6fg4 6f 6f) compact colt; made nearly all when winning handicap at Carlisle in July; stays 6f; well suited by firm going; blinkered nowadays; none too consistent; moved poorly and ran badly ninth start. *Denys Smith.*

GEARY'S FOR STRIP 5 b.h. Mansingh 120–Sociable (Be Friendly 130) **79 d** (1980 5d 5v2 5s 5f* 5fg 5f 6fg 5g 5d 5fg 5f 5d 5.6g 1981 5d2 5d* 5fg 5g2 5fg2 6f 5fg 6fg 5f 5g 5s) big, strong, good-looking horse; sprint handicapper; won at Chester in May; ran well fifth start but moderately on several subsequent occasions; stays 6f; acts on any going; has worn blinkers but seems better without. *Denys Smith.*

GEARY'S STEEL STOCK 3 gr.c. Sovereign Path 125–Beautician (Barron's **62** Court) (1980 5d 5f* 6g 5fg 1981 7d 8g 7d4 8g3 7.2s 7g 6g 7g) quite a useful-looking colt; ran well when in frame in quite valuable handicaps at Chester and Thirsk in May; suited by 1m and may stay further; well beaten last 4 starts, wearing blinkers on one occasion; sold to D. Hanley 3,200 gns Newmarket Autumn Sales. *Denys Smith.*

GEMA ROSS 4 gr.f. Town Crier 119–Popover (Dumbarnie 125) (1980 8fg — 7g 6fg 7g 9.4g 9fg 8fg 8fg4 6g 6d 1981 10.1fg 8f 6fg 7f 8h) leggy, unfurnished filly; poor plater nowadays; sometimes sweats up; has worn blinkers. *M. McCourt.*

GEMSBOK 3 br.g. Redundant 120–Duiker 81 (Sovereign Lord 120) (1980 5s3 — 5v2 5s2 1981 6s 5d 5fg) leggy gelding; quite a moderate sprint maiden; well beaten in blinkers final start. *C. V. Miller.*

GENERAL ANDERS 2 ch.c. Habat 127–Camenae 72 (Vimy 132) (1981 7fg2 **100** 6g2 7f3 7g* 8d) Jan 28; big, rangy, quite attractive colt; carries plenty of condition; good mover; half-brother to several winners, notably 2,000 Guineas winner High Top and very smart miler Camden Town (both by Derring-Do); dam won at 1¾m, and is half-sister to dams of Paulista and Tudor Music; placed in good-class races before putting up a useful display to beat Father Rooney 5 lengths in 18-runner Mornington Stakes at Ascot in September, being in front

rank throughout, going clear 1½f out and staying on really strongly; not disgraced
when having much stiffer task next outing; runs as though middle distances will
suit him. *R. Hern.*

GENERAL BREYFAX 3 ch.g. Sweet Revenge 129–Perbury 88 (Grisaille 115) —
(1980 5fg 5g 6d³ 6s* 7.3fg 8d 1981 8s 7d 11.7s 12s 10fg) strong, workmanlike
gelding; little worthwhile form in 1981, but usually had stiffish tasks; not sure to
stay beyond sprint distances but wasn't completely disgraced over 1½m on third
start; acts on soft going. *M. McCourt.*

GENERAL CARL 6 ch.g. Brigadier Gerard 144–Alcarelle 86 (Alcide 136) (1980 —
NR 1981 16s) workmanlike gelding; useful performer at his best; lightly
raced on flat nowadays; stays 1¾m; acts an any going. *B. Forsey.*

GENERAL WADE 6 b.h. Bold Lad (Ire) 133–Zerbinetta 96 (Henry the Seventh 84
125) (1980 5g⁴ 5.3d² 5d 5g⁴ 5d 5v 1981 5s 6g⁴ 6fg* 6f 6f⁴ 6fg 6g 5h* 6f⁴ 5.8g³
6d³) strong, good sort; fair handicapper; won at Nottingham in June (sweated
up) and Chepstow in September (beat Broon's Secret a head); stays 6f; acts
on any going; wears blinkers. *P. Makin.*

GENEROSO 3 ch.g. Gay Fandango 132–Magnanimous 65 (Runnymede 123) 73
(1980 7f 1981 6s 7fg³ 8fg* 8s) rather a lightly-made gelding; beat Johnnie
Hussar a length in maiden race at Redcar in June; behind in amateur riders
event at Goodwood in September on only subsequent start; suited by 1m;
seems suited by a firm surface; sold out of J. W. Watts's stable 4,500 gns Newmarket July Sales. *L. Cumani.*

GENOVESE 8 b.g. Ribero 126–Gold Frame (Royal Serenade 131) (1980 NR —
1981 12d) lightly raced on flat nowadays; stays 1¾m. *D. Grissell.*

GENTLE STAR 2 b. or br.f. Comedy Star 121–Super Princess 85 (Falcon 131) 77
(1981 5d⁴ 6fg 6fg 5f 6d² 6v 6d⁴) Apr 23; lightly-made filly; first foal; dam won
over 7f at 2 yrs and also over hurdles; quite moderate form in maiden races at
the back-end; will stay 7f; blinkered fifth and sixth starts; hung badly fourth
outing. *K. Ivory.*

GENTLE TOUCH 2 b.f. Some Hand 119–Tacoma 89 (Hard Tack 111§) (1981 —
5g 5f 6f) Feb 28; 1,650F, 1,000Y; half-sister to fair 1978 2-y-o 5f winner
Tigertamer (by Saritamer); dam won twice over 5f at 2 yrs; no sign of ability,
including in a seller; sold 520 gns Ascot August Sales. *D. Thom.*

GENTLE WARRIOR 2 b.f. Warpath 113–Gentle Spring 118 (Gentle Art 121) —
(1981 5.1f) Apr 28; 1,000Y; small, lightly-made filly; a rabbit on looks; half-
sister to a minor winner; dam, a sprinter, at her best at 2 yrs; 100/1, tailed off
after 100 yards and was virtually pulled up in 12-runner maiden race won by
Lavender Dance at Yarmouth in June; probably useless and has no scope
whatsover. *J. Gilbert.*

GENTLY DOES IT 9 b.g. Le Levanstell 122–Soft Fall 85 (Chamossaire) —
(1980 NR 1981 17.1h) poor handicapper. *L. Kennard.*

GEOMANCER 2 gr.c. Shiny Tenth 120–Future Chance 86 (Hopeful Venture 68
125) (1981 5fg 5s³ 5d) Mar 2; fair sort; third foal; brother to a bad plater;
dam, daughter of top-class sprinter Abelia, won over 10.6f; 6 lengths third of
18 to Town Flier in maiden race at Nottingham in October, best effort; will be
suited by 6f+; possibly needs the mud. *P. Makin.*

GEORDIE LAD 3 b.g. Track Spare 125–Silesca (Silent Screen) (1980 NR —
1981 8g 9d 12fg³ 12g⁴ 16fg 16s) 2,100Y; workmanlike gelding; first foal; dam
won over 7.5f at 2 yrs in France; in frame in maiden races in Scotland; looks
slow. *Denys Smith.*

GERALD MARTIN 5 b.h. Martinmas 128–Willowy (Mourne 126) (1980 —
8f 1981 8d⁴ 7g 7.3d) lengthy, useful-looking ex-Irish horse; has been pin-fired;
useful performer at 3 yrs, winner of 4 of his 5 starts; lightly raced and well beaten
subsequently; possibly stayed 1m; revelled in the mud; sold out of Sir Mark
Prescott's stable 11,500 gns Newmarket July Sales after second start; stud
in Turkey. *R. Smyly.*

GERARDINA'S BOY 2 ch.c. Music Boy 124–Solace (Floribunda 136) (1981 71
5d³ 5d* 5g 5f 5d) May 15; 3,800F, 7,000Y; well-grown colt; half-brother to 3
winners, including fairly useful 1974 2-y-o 6f winner Richmond Castle (by Royal
Palm); dam never ran; placed in small races at Warwick and Thirsk in the
spring, going down by 2 lengths to Mydrone in latter, but was awarded the race
at Thirsk when winner was disqualified 2 months later for failing dope test;
well beaten subsequently, finishing last of 15 in nursery after a 16-week absence
on final outing; acts on a soft surface; one to leave alone until he shows a return
to form. *A. Goodwill.*

GERARD'S DAUGHTER 3 ch.f. Brigadier Gerard 144–Neptune's Daughter —
76 (Neptunus 132) (1980 NR 1981 12fg 10d 10g) 5,200Y; big, somewhat
unfurnished filly; half-sister to several winners, including fair stayer and smart
juvenile hurdler Rodman (by Relko); dam won over 9f and is half-sister to very
smart 1966 French 2-y-o Tiepolo II; just over 4 lengths fifth of 14 behind Noblanna in apprentice maiden race at Newmarket in June, first and best effort
(off course 3 months afterwards); will probably stay beyond 1½m. *C. Brittain.*

GETAWAY GIRL 7 gr.m. Capistrano 120–Battling Bessie (Typhoon 125) —
(1980 10.2d* 10s 10.6fg⁴ 10h⁴ 12f³ 9f⁴ 13g³ 10g 1981 10f 10g 10.5s) middle-
distance handicapper; well beaten in 1981; stays 13f; probably acts on any going;
sometimes bandaged off-hind. *W. Stubbs.*

GET STONED 5 ch.h. Home Guard 129–Romp Home 89 (Chanteur II 135) **94**
(1980 10fg⁴ 12g² 12s³ 14g⁴ 12g* 18d 12v 1981 12fg³ 12s 12g³ 12f⁴ 12fg³ 12d 14d
12fg³) big, leggy horse; fairly useful handicapper at his best; in frame several
times in 1981; stayed 1¾m; acted on any going; usually sweated up; broke a leg
passing post at Epsom in August and was destroyed. *L. Cumani.*

GETTING PLENTY 2 b.f. Oats 126–Allander Girl (Miralgo 130) (1981 **72**
6d 8fg 8s² 10g*) Apr 15; IR 7,400F; half-sister to 2 winners, including fair
sprinter Gaelic Affair (by Irish Love); dam unplaced 5 times in Ireland; bought
in 1,200 gns after beating Rizla Red by 2¼ lengths in 14-runner seller at Leicester
in October; will be suited by 1½m; acts on soft going. *G. Hunter.*

GHADEER (FR) 3 b.c. Lyphard 132–Swanilda (Habitat 134) (1980 6g³ **107**
1981 10.5s 8f* 7d⁴ 8fg³ 8d³ 8v² 10s* 8s²) 625,000Y; strong, good-bodied, attractive colt; third foal; dam won over 1m in France and is half-sister to Super Dan,
a very useful winner at up to 13f; successful in minor event at Brighton in
August (beat Dark Monarch ¾ length after making virtually all) and in Group
3 Premio Carlo Porta at Milan in October (won by ½ length from Bold Brigadier);
placed in 3 other pattern races abroad, in Oettingen-Rennen at Baden-Baden,
Grosser Kaufhof Preis at Cologne (neck second to Aspros) and in Premio Ribot
at Rome (length second to Vargas Llosa); stays 1¼m; acts on any going; has
raced with his tongue tied down. *H. T. Jones.*

GHAWAR 2 b.c. Malacate 131–Gulf Bird 71 (Gulf Pearl 117) (1981 5g⁴ 5fg² 5s **89**
5.3f² 6fg² 5f* 5fg* 5d 6s) Apr 28; 14,000Y; quite attractive, good sort; good
mover; third foal; half-brother to very useful 5f performer Blue Persian (by
Majority Blue) and 3-y-o 1¼m winner Blue Gulf (by Gay Fandango); dam 1½m
winner; second in 3 maiden races, twice going down by only a neck, prior to
winning maiden race at Folkestone and nursery at Goodwood in August; sweated
up at Goodwood but kept on extremely well under strong driving to get the
better of Corley Moor and Hiding in tight finish; again ran well next start; bred
to be suited by 7f+ but is evidently considered a sprinter; yet to show his form
on very soft ground but acts on any other; consistent. *R. Smyth.*

GHENTING 2 gr.g. On Your Mark 125–Miss Vickie 94 (Roan Rocket 128) **65**
(1981 5g 5d³ 7f 6d) Apr 20; small gelding; good mover; brother to moderate
1978 2-y-o 5f winner Pointillist, and half-brother to 2 winners; dam won twice
over 5f at 2 yrs; favourite when about 4 lengths third of 8 to Balcanoona in
maiden race at Leicester in April; gelded subsequently and was soundly beaten
both subsequent starts; lacks scope; sold to Susan Piggott Bloodstock 1,050 gns
Doncaster November Sales. *R. Armstrong.*

GHIDALGO 3 b.c. Music Boy 124–First Court 82 (Primera 131) (1980 5fg —
5fg 5.1g³ 6g 6fg 5f 5d 5d 1981 8d 7fg 8s 7fg 6g) big colt; poor walker and bad
mover; only plating class; possibly doesn't stay 6f. *G. Blum.*

GIANNUTRI 3 b.f. Wolver Hollow 126–Cesarea 108 (Raeburn II) (1980 6f **64**
7fg* 1981 7g 8d 8g⁴(dis) 7f 7.2fg) lengthy, quite attractive filly; good walker;
won minor event at Newbury as a 2-y-o; rather disappointing in 1981, although
was running on strongly at finish when fifth to Ring Moylan in handicap at
Haydock in September on final start (blinkered first time); will stay 1¼m; sold
17,000 gns Newmarket December Sales. *P. Walwyn.*

GIBBON 5 br.g. Swing Easy 126–Fearless 77 (Derring-Do 131) (1980 8d **61**
7.2d 7f 8s 8d 9f² 9fg 10.2g 1981 10.6g 8g* 10.5d 8fg 8d 9f 9fg 8.2d* 10g 8g 8.2d)
strong, good-bodied gelding; won handicaps at Thirsk in April (apprentices) and
Hamilton in July; behind in valuable seller tenth start; stays 9f but isn't sure
to stay further; acts on any going except perhaps soft; blinkered once at 3 yrs;
faint-hearted; sold privately to N. Bycroft. *P. Rohan.*

GIBRALTAR 5 b.h. Philip of Spain 126–Nasira 94 (Persian Gulf) (1980 7d —
6v* 6g 8.2s 1981 8fg 7g) neat horse; poor performer; best form at 6f; seems to
need some give in the ground; occasionally blinkered. *S. Wiles.*

GIDDY ANN 2 br.f. Dubassoff-Giddy Lyn (Relko 136) (1981 5g 5s 6fg 7g) —
Feb 13; 2,300F, 900Y; neat filly; half-sister to Irish 1¼m winner Mr Skin (by
High Top) and winners in Belgium and Norway; dam won in USA, including a
6f claiming race at 4 yrs; behind in sizeable fields of maidens and in a valuable
seller. *G. Blum.*

GIFFORD 3 b.g. Joshua 129-Mayfell 107 (Rockefella) (1980 6d 7g 8g 8fg* 7g² **95**
7s 8g 1981 10g 12d 10f³ 10g² 10f* 12.2fg* 12f² 12.2fg* 12fg* 11.5fg⁴ 11fg)
compact gelding; had a successful time and won handicaps at Beverley and
Catterick in July and at Catterick again and Folkestone in August; beat Ripcorn
by 3 lengths on last-named course; stays 1½m well; suited by top-of-the-ground;
best in blinkers; suited by forcing tactics; thoroughly genuine, although ran
moderately final start; sold 11,000 gns Newmarket Autumn Sales, reportedly to
race in Malaysia. *D. Morley.*

GIGGLE 2 gr.f. Sagaro 133-Joking 81 (Ribero 126) (1981 6fg 8fg) Mar 10; —
second foal; dam, winner over 1½m, is half-sister to Queen's Hussar; behind in
sizeable fields of maidens at Newbury in August and Leicester in September;
stoutly bred and may improve when given a test of stamina. *R. Hern.*

GIGONDAS 2 b.f. Brigadier Gerard 144-Gingerale (Golden Horus 123) (1981 **71 p**
6g) Feb 13; smallish filly; sister to 1m winner Countess Walewski and American
winner Byrrh; dam useful at up to 9.5f in France; third favourite, faded after
holding every chance over 1f out when 4 lengths sixth of 20 to Linda Beard in
maiden race at Newmarket in August, only outing; will stay 1m. *H. Cecil.*

GILDED VANITY 4 b.f. Run The Gantlet-Sunset Temple 104 (Golden Horus **113**
123) (1980 9f³ 10.2fg* 8fg⁴ 11.1fg 12fg* 1981 10s* 12s 11s 12fg* 10g 12d)
lengthy ex-English filly; beat Saint Jonathon 2½ lengths in small race at Cagnes-
sur-Mer early in year and put up a much improved performance to account for
Countess Tully by 5 lengths in Brownstown Stakes at the Curragh in August
(backed from 66/1 to 10/1); also ran creditably when under seven lengths fifth
of 12 to Kings Lake in 1¼m Joe McGrath Memorial Stakes at Leopardstown the
following month (sweated up); stays 1½m; seems to act on any going but goes well
on a firm surface; wears a bandage on off-hind; trained by G. Beeson first 3 starts;
sold 90,000 gns Newmarket December Sales. *P. Russell, Ireland.*

GILLIES PRINCE 2 b. or br.c. Furry Glen 1?1-Rosy O'Leary (Majetta 115) **60**
(1981 5f 6f 7f 6fg⁴ 6fg 7.2v⁴ 8g) May 11; IR 1,150F, IR 1,000Y; leggy, lightly-
made colt; quite a moderate plater; stays 1m; probably acts on any going; sold
1,600 gns Newmarket Autumn Sales. *P. Rohan.*

GIMITA 2 b.f. Blue Cashmere 129-Gimima 54 (Narrator 127) (1981 6fg 6fg **70**
5g⁴ 7fg 5g) Apr 9; lengthy, lightly-made filly; half-sister to winners here and
abroad, including 1978 2-y-o 5f winner Galleypot Girl (by Philip of Spain);
dam won 1m seller; plating-class maiden; by no means sure to stay 7f. *E. Eldin.*

GIMRI 8 ch.g. Quayside 124-Conita 94 (Constable 119) (1980 7v 7fg 7g 7g **65**
7fg 7fg³ 8fg² 7g 7g* 7.6d* 7d* 8g⁴ 8g 7fg 7.3fg 7g 8d 1981 7d³ 8g 7d² 7g 7v⁴
7fg 7.6g 7fg 7fg 7fg 7g 7s* 7s 7d) workmanlike gelding; beat Secret Gill decisively
by ¾ length in £4,400 handicap at York in October; stays 1m; acts on any going,
but is particularly well suited by some give in the ground; excellent mount for
an apprentice. *J. Benstead.*

GIN 2 ch.f. Warpath 113-Brandy (Busted 134) (1981 7g 8fg*) Apr 27; leggy, **84 p**
sparely-made filly; sister to 1½m seller winner Carouser; dam poor daughter of
half-sister to top sprinters Lucasland and So Blessed; always going well and led
in final furlong when winning 16-runner maiden race at Beverley in September by
a length from Luxury; will stay at least 1½m; still has improvement in her and
looks sure to win again in the North at 3 yrs. *C. Thornton.*

GIN GAME 4 b.g. Red Alert 127-Watermark 83 (Henry the Seventh 125) **79**
(1980 6g 7d⁴ 6s* 6g 6g² 6g* 6s 6d 6d 1981 6s 7d 7g² 7v 6f³ 6f 6g² 7fg⁴ 7fg 6fg
6f² 5.8g 6s³ 6d*) neat, strong, attractive gelding; fair handicapper at his best;
beat Jeckel by ¾ length at Chepstow in October; stays 7f; acts on any going;
blinkered once at 3 yrs; sold 2,700 gns Newmarket Autumn Sales. *P. Walwyn.*

GINGER PUDDING 4 ch.f. Shiny Tenth 120-Shusheta (Martial 131) (1980 —
6f 5fg 5g 6s 1981 5s 5d 6g) compact, lightly-made filly; poor form, including
in a seller; stays 6f; sold 440 gns Ascot October Sales. *D. Marks.*

GINGER TART 2 br.f. Swing Easy 126-Santa Anita 78 (Pardao 120) (1981 **87**
5g⁴ 8g²) Mar 19; 3,000F, 1,550Y; small, light-framed filly; half-sister to
winning stayer Bright Comet (by Derring-Do); dam won over 1¼m; apprentice
ridden, tended to hang when ½-length second of 13 to Brigado in maiden race at
Edinburgh in October; will probably stay 1¼m. *A. Jarvis.*

GIN

GIN N' LIME 7 ch.g. Divine Gift 127–Fruit Cup 72 (Silver Shark 129) (1980 —
  14g 1981 11.7f⁴) poor maiden on flat; has been tried in blinkers. *C. V. Miller.*

GINNY GO-GO 2 gr.f. Grey Mirage 128–My Nan 65 (Pampered King 121) —
  (1981 5fg 6fg 5fg 7f 8s) bad plater. *R. Morris.*

GINOSA 3 b.f. Kalamoun 129–Taranto 90 (Major Portion 129) (1980 NR **62**
  1981 7g 10fg 10.1fg⁴ 12d⁴ 12fg² 12f³ 12s) neat filly; half-sister to 1½m winners
  Bombardier (by Sing Sing or King's Troop) and Naval Victory (by Hopeful
  Venture); dam middle-distance handicapper; in frame in maiden and minor races;
  stays 1½m; possibly needs a sound surface; blinkered last 3 outings; sold 2,600 gns
  Newmarket December Sales. *J. Dunlop.*

GIORSAL 2 b.f. Tudor Rhythm 112–Mary Newall 69 (Coronation Year 124) —
  (1981 5s) May 5; sister to juvenile hurdles winner The Polchar and closely
  related to 2 winners by Highland Melody, including very useful sprinter Hei'land
  Jamie; dam won sellers over 6f and 1m; 50/1 when ninth of 10 to Sharokee in
  maiden race at Lingfield in October. *G. Pritchard-Gordon.*

GIPSY PRINCE 6 ch.g. Sky Gipsy 117–Orseniga 97 (Privy Councillor 125) — §
  (1980 10.2d 10v 8f² 8d 8fg 9f 11.5fg 1981 9d 10.6s 10f) fair sort; poor maiden;
  well beaten in seller third start; stays 1m but probably not 1¼m; acts on firm
  going; has given us the impression he is none too genuine. *J. Tierney.*

GIPSY SINGER 6 ch.m. Sky Gipsy 117–Wall Street 82 (Cash and Courage 116) —
  (1980 NR 1981 6f 8f 10.1fg) poor maiden; has worn blinkers. *J. Bridger.*

GLACIER BAY 3 b.c. Decoy Boy 129–Polar Cloud (Crisp and Even 116) (1980 —
  5g 7fg 5d 5d 1981 8g 8d 7s⁴ 8f 8f) plater; stays 7f. *R. Hannon.*

GLAD TIDINGS (FR) 2 b.f. Pharly 130–Gaily 121 (Sir Gaylord) (1981 7d³ **74** p
  7v) attractive, well-made filly; closely related to 3-y-o Hard To Say (by Lyphard) and half-sister to 1m winner Gay Milly (by Mill Reef); dam won Irish
  1,000 Guineas and was third in Prix Vermeille; 20/1, came out best of newcomers when 6½ lengths third of 18 to stable-companion Sans Blague in maiden
  race at Newbury in September; favourite for £3,400 event at York the following
  month but seemed unsuited by the heavy going and finished remote seventh of
  15 to My Destiny after being eased; will stay 1¼m; a taking individual who
  must be given another chance on better ground to confirm the favourable
  impression she created at Newbury. *R. Hern.*

GLADYS ELLEN 3 b.f. Shantung 132–Santa Marta 51 (Lavandin 128) (1980 —
  NR 1981 10.1fg 11.7f 13.1g) half-sister to 2 minor winners; dam won over 6f
  at 4 yrs; in rear in maiden and minor events. *P. Bailey.*

GLAMOUR SHOW 5 b.g. Welsh Pageant 132–Maladie d'Amour 98 (Fidalgo —
  129) (1980 16fg 1981 18fg 16s) staying maiden. *J. Gifford.*

GLANCEAWAY (USA) 3 b.c. Key To The Kingdom–Popaway (Cyclotron) **79**
  (1980 NR 1981 8fg) $40,000Y; attractive, lengthy colt; half-brother to
  numerous winners in USA, including minor stakes winner Stop The Rain (by
  Rainy Lake); dam unraced; 8 lengths fifth of 13 behind Home Coming in minor
  event at Sandown in April, but wasn't seen out again. *J. Dunlop.*

GLANCING 2 b.f. Grundy 137–Splashing 123 (Petingo 135) (1981 6fg³ 5g* **113**
  6f* 5fg*)
      Glancing's smooth two-and-a-half-length win from her compatriot Chellaston
  Park in the Prix d'Arenberg at Chantilly in September confirmed that
  she's a very useful filly; it also confirmed the desperate shortage of sprinting
  talent in France. The home side could muster only three runners, two of them
  maidens, to defend the £15,000 prize, an extraordinary situation when there
  are so few worthwhile opportunities for sprint-bred two-year-olds in France.
  Whereas England has fourteen two-year-old pattern races over five and six
  furlongs, France has only four run over less than seven furlongs—the d'Arenberg,
  the Papin, Morny and Éclipse. The last three fell respectively to the Irish-bred
  Maelstrom Lake, the American-bred Green Forest and the English-bred, Irish-
  trained Pas de Seul in 1981. Presumably the lack of opportunities for two-
  year-old sprinters in France lessens the demand for sprint-bred yearlings at the
  sales which in turn dissuades breeders from producing that type of animal: a
  vicious circle. And, of course, if there are no juvenile sprinters in France, where
  are the older sprinters to come from? The answer to that question in 1981 was
  from England and Germany! Only one of the seven pattern sprints fell to a
  French-trained animal, and when Marwell took the Prix de l'Abbaye de Longchamp she became the thirteenth foreign winner in the last fifteen years. Surely

*Prix d'Arenberg, Chantilly—British raiders Glancing and
Chellaston Park finish first and second*

the time has come for the Societe d'Encouragement to review the whole pattern
of two-year-old racing in France.

To return to Glancing, she had to miss the Cheveley Park Stakes because of a
slight blood disorder and the d'Arenberg proved to be her last race. Previously
she had had three races in England, losing only on her debut when third to
Johara in the Virginia Water Stakes at Ascot in July. She quickly confirmed
the promise of that run, making all to land the odds easily by four lengths in a
Windsor maiden race, and then collected quite a valuable prize in the Champion
Two Yrs Old Trophy at Ripon in late-August. Glancing was receiving weight
from several useful colts at Ripon, including the recent Gimcrack Stakes third
Mydrone, the speedy Never Talk and the New Ham Stakes winner El Mansour,
but her apprentice rider was unable to claim his 5-lb allowance because of the
value of the race. She showed excellent speed from the start, took over from
the weakening El Mansour below the distance and then kept on strongly to hold
off the fast-finishing Come On The Blues by a neck. Glancing didn't stride out
very well on the firm going on the way to the start at Ripon but she showed in
the race that she's perfectly at ease on fast ground; indeed she has yet to race
on a soft surface.

		Great Nephew	Honeyway
	Grundy	(b 1963)	Sybil's Niece
	(ch 1972)	Word from Lundy	Worden II
Glancing		(b 1966)	Lundy Princess
(b.f. Feb 6, 1979)		Petingo	Petition
	Splashing	(b 1965)	Alcazar
	(b 1971)	Pelting	Vilmorin
		(ro 1958)	Firmament

Glancing is quite an attractive filly, compact and short-legged, and a well-
bred one too. A cursory look at her pedigree—she's by Grundy out of a Petingo
mare—suggests she will stay at least a mile. However she comes from a very
speedy female line and there must be some doubts whether she will unless she
learns to settle. Her grandam Pelting was a five-furlong sprinter who bred
numerous winners, none of which won over further than a mile even though one
was by Pinza and another by Aggressor; and her dam, the very smart Splashing,
seemed best at distances short of seven furlongs, gaining her most important
win in the Cornwallis Stakes. It's encouraging though that Splashing's previous
winner Adams, by the sprinter/miler Thatch, won at up to a mile and when
Splashing's half-sister Gliding was mated to Grundy she produced Bay Street,
winner of the Princess Elizabeth Stakes over eight and a half furlongs. Glancing
must therefore have reasonable prospects of staying a mile, provided she races
less freely than she did at two, and she could put up a bold show in the Guineas.
W. Hastings-Bass.

GLASGOW CENTRAL 4 b.c. Roan Rocket 128–Nettlebed 84 (Hettersett 134) **91**
(1980 8fg 10s* 10.1s² 12d⁴ 10.1s* 10f³ 1981 8d 10fg⁴ 10g 10s³ 10d² 12g* 10fg²
12fg³ 12.3fg* 12f⁴ 13.3d² 12s* 12g) short-backed colt; good mover; fair
handicapper; won amateur riders race at Salisbury in June, ladies race at Newcastle
in August and handicap at Ascot in September; suited by 1½m or more; suited by

some give in the ground; possibly best on galloping track; genuine; ran poorly third start; changed hands 17,500 gns Newmarket Autumn Sales. *R. Price.*

GLAZEPTA AGAIN 2 gr.c. Gay Fandango 132–Grande Promesse (Sea Hawk **73** II 131) (1981 6fg 6f 6g² 6d² 7f 7fg 7f³ 8.2d 6g 7g³) May 13; IR 2,000F, resold 2,000Y; dipped-backed colt; second reported foal; dam won over 10.5f in France; twice narrowly beaten within a week in Scotland in July and was beaten less than a length when third to Connaught River in 18-runner maiden event at Redcar in September; subsequently descended to selling company on 2 occasions without being able to win; suited by 7f and should stay 1m; probably acts on any going; blinkered final start; usually apprentice ridden. *A. Jarvis.*

GLEAMING WAVE 7 b.h. Sovereign Gleam 117–Sapphire Spray (Floribunda **61** 136) (1980 12d 11.7fg 12f³ 12f* 12g 11.7g⁴ 11.7fg 12f 12.2fg 11s³ 12d 12d 1981 13s 12.2fg⁴ 13s³ 12g² 12g³ 12f⁴ 15.5fg 13f 12f⁴ 12f⁴ 13fg 12fg) middle-distance handicapper; acts on any going; suitable mount for a boy. *G. Huffer.*

GLEEMAN 2 ch.c. The Minstrel 135–Isobelline (Pronto) (1981 6fg 7fg²) **84** May 3; 350,000Y; small, quite attractive colt; third foal; half-brother to high-class 1980 staying 2-y-o Robellino (by Roberto); dam Irish 7f winner; promoted to second by stewards after finishing 1½ lengths third of 17 to Tender Venture in maiden race at Salisbury in September (hampered close home but was only third best on merit); will be suited by 1¼m. *J. Tree.*

GLEN AFFRIC 2 b.f. Mount Hagen 127–Albionia 85 (Faberge II 121) (1981 **64** 5d 5v* 6fg 6g³ 6g 6g 7g) May 1; 2,000Y; small, sharp sort; good mover; half-sister to winning stayer Albion Prince (by Prince Regent) and to a winner in Belgium; dam won at up to 1m; won 10-runner seller at Goodwood in May (no bid); 2¾ lengths third of 7 to Walter Mitty in nursery at Windsor in August, best subsequent effort; should be suited by 7f+ ; acts well on heavy ground. *R. Hannon.*

GLEN AIR 3 b.g. Furry Glen 121–Mountain Air 74 (Tudor Melody 129) **64 d** (1980 6s 7fg 8fg 8d 8s³ 1981 10fg³ 10.1d³ 10g 10f 10g 11.5g 8d 10d) neat, lightly-made gelding; disappointing maiden; stays 1¼m; acts on soft going; blinkered final outing; trained for first 4 starts by G. Pritchard-Gordon; sold 1,450 gns Ascot December Sales. *R. Carter.*

GLENBANK LASS 3 ch.f. Patch 129–Pamaloo 93 (Pall Mall 132) (1980 5g **—** 6fg* 8g* 1981 10.2d 8f⁴ 11fg 10f) workmanlike filly; rather disappointing in 1981, best effort on second outing; not seen out after July; should be suited by middle distances; sold 2,500 gns Newmarket December Sales. *H. Wharton.*

GLENORUM (CAN) 4 b.c. Prove Out–Cailey Jane (Right Combination) **124** (1980 8v* 8s² 9.2fg* 8.5d⁴ 10fg³ 10d* 13.5g* 12f 1981 12s 10g* 12.5f² 13.5f³ 10s* 13s) smart performer; won apprentice race at Chantilly in July and La Coupe de Maisons-Laffitte in September; smoothly landed the odds by a length from Val de Mougins in latter; placed in between in 2 races at Deauville, on second occasion finishing creditable ¾-length third to Perrault in Grand Prix; soundly-beaten fifth of 14 to Open Call in Rothmans International at Woodbine, Canada, in October; effective at 1¼m and stays 1¾m; seems to act on any going. *D. Smaga, France.*

GLENRIEFFE 3 b. or br.g. Scottish Rifle 127–Jendean 68 (Florescence 120) **—** (1980 NR 1981 8fg 8fg 8.2s 8s 8d) small gelding; second foal; dam placed over 5f at 2 yrs; little worthwhile form, although wasn't entirely disgraced in a handicap final start (apprentice ridden); blinkered fourth outing. *R. Baker.*

GLENSIDE LADY 2 b.f. So Blessed 130–Croomedale (Alcide 136) (1981 5fg **79** 8d³ 7g³ 8g) Apr 16; 9,200Y; half-sister to several winners here and in France, including 9f winner Louise Moulton (by Moulton); dam, winner over 11f in France, is daughter of smart Mirnaya; third in maiden and minor events in October, beaten 5½ lengths by Suez at Bath and ¾ length by Spring Lane at Catterick; will stay 1¼m. *F. Durr.*

GLENTANAR 3 b.f. Lochnager 132–Pink Standard 81 (Tudor Melody 129) **—** (1980 5fg 6s 5f 1981 8d 12s) seemingly useless. *M. W. Easterby.*

GLENVARA 4 b.g. Furry Glen 121–Varamette (Varano) (1980 12.3f 10fg **—** 12fg 10g⁴ 13d* 12.3fg² 13.8g³ 15s 16g³ 15.8d² 15d 1981 13v 16g 13.8fg) useful-looking gelding; staying handicapper; possibly unsuited by very soft ground; has run creditably for a boy; sold to T. Craig 6,800 gns Doncaster August Sales. *R. D. Peacock.*

GLIDEAGAIN 2 ch.g. Gay Fandango 132–Buttermilk Sky (Midsummer Night **—** II 117) (1981 7fg) Feb 23; 2,300F, 4,600Y; fourth produce; brother to

Glideaway, successful at up to 1¾m in Ireland; dam only ran twice; 50/1, burly and apprentice ridden when behind in 29-runner maiden race won by Hayakaze at Newmarket in August; sold 260 gns Ascot November Sales. *I. Walker.*

GLIDE PATH 3 b.f. Sovereign Path 125–Falcon Bess (Falcon 131) (1980 7g **81** 1981 9d 8fg 7f 10f* 9f³ 10.1g³ 10g* 10s 11d 12g³) sparely-made filly; successful in maiden race and handicap at Yarmouth, making all and showing much improved form when beating Countess Olivia comfortably by 6 lengths in latter in September; suited by 1¼m; acts on firm going (well beaten on soft); sweated up first 2 outings. *J. Winter.*

GLIDER PILOT 2 gr.c. Red Alert 127–Gliding Gay (Hill Gail) (1981 5g) — neat, strong colt; good walker; half-brother to 2 winners; dam, daughter of Irish Oaks winner Silken Glider, won over 11f in Ireland; unquoted and looking as though race would do him good, always outpaced when last of 12 to Jester in maiden race at Newmarket in April; sold 460 gns Newmarket Autumn Sales. *B. Hanbury.*

GLIDING HOME 3 ch.c. Home Guard 129–Gliding Gay (Hill Gail) (1980 NR — 1981 8d 11.7g 13f) 4,100F, 10,500Y; quite an attractive, well-made colt; brother to US winner Erica Kelly and half-brother to a winner; dam, daughter of Irish Oaks winner Silken Glider, won over 11f in Ireland; in rear in maiden races; finished last when blinkered on final outing; sold 480 gns Doncaster August Sales. *G. Hunter.*

GLIMMER 3 ch.f. Hot Spark 126–Nasira 94 (Persian Gulf) (1980 NR **58** 1981 5d² 5fg 6g) quite an attractive filly; half-sister to several winners, including very smart 5f to 7f performer Glen Strae (by Reform); dam won at up to 1m; ran easily best race when second in maiden race at Wolverhampton in April; should stay 6f. *R. Price.*

GLINT OF GOLD 3 b.c. Mill Reef 141–Crown Treasure (Graustark) (1980 **128** 7f* 7d² 8s* 1981 12fg* 12g* 12d² 15s* 12d* 14.6g² 12v*)

'I was flat to the boards the whole way. In the straight I just kept pushing and when I came between them I thought I'd won . . . Shergar had gone so far clear I didn't see him.' Matthias' description of his Derby ride on Glint of Gold was one of the season's memorable quotes. A good quote is like a good photograph: it sums up, without much ado, a situation or a personality. Matthias' quote certainly sums up the most recent Derby. Very early in the straight the race was over, or rather that for first place was, as Shergar set up an unassailable lead. Although beaten ten lengths by Shergar, Glint of Gold came out of the Derby with great credit. Horses drawn low who don't take up a position with the leaders sometimes find themselves cut off or squeezed out after about two and a half furlongs when the field comes back to the left-

Derby Italiano, Rome—Glint of Gold wins with Matthias looking round

Grand Prix de Paris, Longchamp—another impressive foreign
victory for Glint of Gold

hand rail after negotiating the right-hand bend soon after the start. Glint of Gold, who wasn't well away from the number-three draw, was almost stopped in his tracks during scrimmaging that took place around this point and although he managed to keep clear of further trouble he was only eighth, still some way behind the leading group, rounding Tattenham Corner. Much of the Derby course is on the turn and the three-and-a-half-furlong run-in is downhill until approaching the final furlong; prospects of recovering lost ground are much worse at Epsom than on flat, galloping courses such as York and Doncaster. Glint of Gold stayed on very strongly in the final quarter of a mile to finish two lengths in front of third-placed Scintillating Air and four in front of fourth-placed Shotgun, both of whom had been better positioned at Tattenham Corner.

The Derby was the second defeat suffered by Glint of Gold in six races. He showed useful form as a two-year-old, winning the Sandwich Stakes at Ascot and Italy's most important two-year-old race the Gran Criterium at Milan—he finished second when even money for the Acomb Stakes at York in between. His stable-companion the Royal Lodge Stakes winner Robellino seemed the better classic prospect as the most recent season opened. Both reappeared on the first day of Epsom's spring meeting, Glint of Gold winning the Warren Stakes decisively over the Derby course and distance and Robellino finishing a close second to Centurius in the more important Ladbroke Blue Riband Trial Stakes. Hills offered 33/1 against Glint of Gold's winning the Derby after his performance in the Warren Stakes; Robellino stood at 16/1. Glint of Gold went first for the Derby Italiano at Rome, an event confined in earlier years to horses born and bred in Italy. With a first prize of £37,768 in 1981, the Derby Italiano seems sure to attract good-class foreign opposition in future, especially as Glint of Gold, the only British-trained challenger, started at odds on and ran out a comfortable winner. Glint of Gold took the lead about half a mile out and won with Matthias looking round by two lengths from My Franky with the Gran Criterium runner-up Bold Brigadier another five lengths away third in a field of thirteen.

Glint of Gold's performance in the Derby made him appear to us a sound St Leger prospect and it came as no surprise when he by-passed further clashes with Shergar in the Irish Sweeps Derby and the King George VI and Queen Elizabeth Diamond Stakes. Glint of Gold's programme was mapped out with one eye on Doncaster. A Grand Prix de Paris challenge was almost foiled by a strike of Pari-Mutuel workers whose action led to Longchamp's programme on June 28th being called off. At first no plans were announced to stage the Grand Prix de Paris or the Prix d'Ispahan, another Group 1 event on the day's programme, but Glint of Gold (and Britain's challengers for the Prix d'Ispahan, Robellino, Cracaval and Recitation) remained in Paris in case of a change. When the strike was settled, Longchamp took over Evry's fixture on July 4th, retaining some of Evry's races including the Group 3 Prix Daphnis to which Robellino was transferred. Glint of Gold became the first British-trained winner of the Grand Prix since Lemonora in 1921, winning by three lengths from Tipperary Fixer who subsequently defeated the British six-year-old Nicholas Bill by half a length in the Prix Kergorlay at Deauville. The Grand Prix, run over fifteen furlongs, is a searching test for a three-year-old even though it is not quite so well contested as it used to be, having become a victim of the turf authorities' progressive destruction of long-distance racing in Europe—its prize money has fallen dramatically in recent years, Glint of Gold earning £40,614 compared to the £124,924 first prize in 1975. If Glint of Gold's performances at Epsom and Longchamp failed to convince everyone that he was a first-rate St Leger contender, his impressive victory in the Great Voltigeur Stakes at York's August meeting was a magnificent advertisement for his chance. The Great Voltigeur, run over a mile and a half, is the most important of the recognised St Leger trials: twelve St Leger winners have run in the race since it was founded as the Voltigeur Stakes in 1950 and eight have won it, including Athens Wood and Bustino in the 'seventies. Glint of Gold looked magnificent at York, taking the eye in the paddock and on the way to post as he did before most of his races as a three-year-old. Conceding 7 lb to each of his five rivals, Glint of Gold gave a striking performance, showing the best finishing pace after being waited with until well into the straight, to win a truly-run contest by three lengths and seven lengths from Little Wolf and Capstan, stable-companions of the St Leger contenders Bustomi and Cut Above. The way the Voltigeur runners were strung out at the finish illustrates what a blistering gallop it was throughout and Glint of Gold recorded a timefigure of 1.38 fast, the fastest at a mile and a half during the season. He deposed Bustomi as second favourite to Shergar on St Leger day—he was again the pick of the paddock—but, although he beat Shergar and Bustomi, he could not hold the challenge of Cut Above after looking likely to win when taking the lead entering the last two furlongs. Glint of Gold was beaten two and a half lengths by Cut Above; Bustomi finished four lengths behind Glint of Gold in third place with Shergar another five lengths away fourth.

In an age of high-speed transport, the leaders of the training profession in Britain, particularly the younger ones, are quick to identify outstanding opportunities for winning races abroad. Glint of Gold's trainer is a master of the craft; he sends his horses far and wide, with excellent results. Balding won more first-prize money abroad than any other British trainer in 1980, and he achieved the feat again in 1981. Balding became the first winner of a trophy put up by the International Racing Bureau for the most successful trainer on foreign soil; in total prize money, he led the field from Kelleway, Stoute, Harwood, Armstrong and Wragg. Having already won Group 1 races in Italy and France during the season with Glint of Gold, Balding sent him in October to challenge for Germany's most valuable event, the Preis von Europa at Cologne. Taking advantage of the absence of Europe's leading middle-distance performers, most of whom had contested the Prix de l'Arc de Triomphe seven days earlier, Glint of Gold won the Preis von Europa in good style. Taking command under pressure early in the straight he won going away by three and a half lengths from the German-trained five-year-old Czubaryk, maintaining his unbeaten record overseas and lifting his total first-prize earnings to £204,189. Glint of Gold has won seven of his ten races so far and has finished second in the others. He is a very hardy, genuine and courageous racehorse and we were delighted by the news that he remains in training. He made physical progress throughout the season and should he go on developing over the winter he will make a magnificent-looking four-year-old; he is a strong, well-made, attractive colt and an excellent mover, and some observers have commented that he reminds them greatly in appearance and fluency of action of his sire Mill Reef, although Glint of Gold is bigger than Mill Reef. Balding describes Glint of Gold as the nicest Mill Reef he has trained so far—'a big horse with the most lovely temperament'—

Great Voltigeur Stakes, York—Glint of Gold wins from Little Wolf

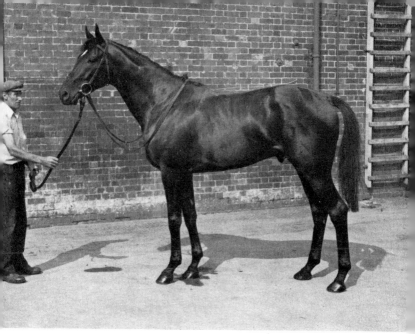

Mr Paul Mellon's "Glint of Gold"

and we shall be most surprised if Glint of Gold fails to add to his fine record.
Glint of Gold stays very well but he is almost certain to be campaigned mainly
at a mile and a half as a four-year-old. In conditions such as those which
obtained in the Great Voltigeur Stakes—a soft surface and a pillar-to-post
gallop—Glint of Gold could prove a tough nut to crack. A wet summer would
help his cause considerably; Glint of Gold acts on any going but is very much at
home with some give in the ground. Whatever the underfoot conditions,
Glint of Gold's connections clearly intend that any race he contests in 1982 will
be truly run. Balding paid 34,000 guineas at the Newmarket Autumn Sales for
the useful and genuine mile-and-a-quarter performer Show-A-Leg who will act
as pacemaker for Glint of Gold.

Glint of Gold (b.c. 1978)	Mill Reef (b 1968)	Never Bend (b 1960)	Nasrullah
			Lalun
		Milan Mill (b 1962)	Princequillo
			Virginia Water
	Crown Treasure (b 1973)	Graustark (ch 1963)	Ribot
			Flower Bowl
		Treasure Chest (b 1962)	Rough 'n Tumble
			Iltis

Glint of Gold is the first foal of Crown Treasure who showed very useful
form as a two-year-old in the United States where she was a winner over five
furlongs. Crown Treasure is a half-sister to a smart filly by Sea-Bird II called
Diomedia, a stakes winner at a mile and at nine furlongs. Their dam Treasure
Chest was a stakes winner at up to a mile. Crown Treasure was sent to England
to be covered by Mill Reef in 1977 and the import restrictions imposed by the
North Americans later that year, and only recently relaxed, prevented her return.
She was covered again by Mill Reef in 1978 and 1979 and produced a colt (the
useful two-year-old Diamond Shoal) and a filly; Crown Treasure had a filly foal
by Troy in 1981 and is due to Shirley Heights in 1982. *I. Balding.*

338

GLORIAMA 3 br.f. Targowice 130–Maria da Gloria (St Chad 120) (1980 5fg —
6s⁴ 5f² 5d² 1981 7.2fg 7d 6v) leggy, narrow filly; no form in 1981 (not seen out
until September and had stiff task on first outing); should stay 7f; sold 700 gns
Newmarket December Sales. *E. Weymes.*

GLORINO 3 b.f. Bustino 136–Gloria Romana (Galivanter 131) (1980 6s 6fg⁴ —
6d 5d 1981 6g 7fg 7f 10fg) small, quite well-made filly; disappointing maiden;
possibly stays 1¼m; sold 4,200 gns Newmarket December Sales. *W. Hastings-
Bass.*

GLORIOUS 3 ch.g. Hittite Glory 125–Cathays Park (Reliance II 137) (1980 **59**
6fg 6d 5g 5d 6d 6g⁴ 6s 1981 6s 6g 6s 5g⁴ 7fg* 7g) strong gelding; showed
distinct promise in non-seller before justifying heavy support in selling handicap
at Redcar in May, breaking smartly and beating Be Patient ½ length; bought in
4,300 gns afterwards; will stay 1m. *M. W. Easterby.*

GLORY BIRD 2 ch.c. Hittite Glory 125–Partridge 65 (Mossborough 126) **68**
(1981 5d 5s 6fg 6d 7d 7g 8d⁴) Feb 25; 3,200Y; useful-looking colt; half-brother
to 1¼m winner Ascot Weather (by Silly Season); dam suited by distance of ground;
second favourite and blinkered when 4 lengths fourth of 17 to Milanion in seller
at Leicester in November, final start; stays 1m; acts on a soft surface. *P. Rohan.*

GLOSSY IBIS 2 b. or br.f. Queen's Hussar 124–Lily Trotter 75 (Blakeney 126) **90**
(1981 5f² 5fg² 6g* 6fg* 7g² 7s) Mar 14; neat filly; first foal; dam stayed 1¼m;
short-head winner of 17-runner maiden race at Redcar in August (from Shining
Start) and of nursery at Haydock the following month (beat Roman Quest);
failed by a head to catch Robout when short-priced favourite for 16-runner nursery at Catterick later in September; will stay at least 1¼m; ran disappointingly
on soft going in valuable nursery at Lingfield in October, and probably needs a
sound surface; sold 26,000 gns to BBA Newmarket December Sales. *W.
Hastings-Bass.*

GLOWING HALO 2 ch.f. Grundy 137–Blessed Again 90 (Ballymoss 136) — p
(1981 7g) Apr 13; useful-looking filly; half-sister to 3 winners by Kashmir II,
notably high-class 5f to 7f performer Blue Cashmere; dam daughter of good
stayer No Saint; unquoted and in need of race when never-dangerous 7½ lengths
sixth of 16 to Positron in maiden event at Leicester in October; may do better
over 1¼m+ in 1982. *H. Candy.*

GLOWING TAN (USA) 4 b.c. Plenty Old–Serving Wench (Mister Black) **86 d**
(1980 7d⁴ 10.4f³ 8fg² 8fg² 12d² 10g² 10g² 10g⁴ 11f 8g² 8fg* 1981 10fg 8g² 8v 8f 8fg
11fg) workmanlike colt; good mover; made much of running and kept on very
well when neck second to Greenwood Star in Jubilee Stakes at Kempton in
May; well beaten afterwards; best at up to 1¼m; possibly unsuited by heavy
going; ran a bit freely in blinkers once at 3 yrs. *R. Sheather.*

GLYNDEBOURNE (USA) 3 ch.c. Annihilate 'Em–Worthy Charm (Boldnesian) **91**
(1980 5fg 5f³ 6d² 6g* 1981 7s 7g 6g 6d 8g) robust, useful sort; not extended
when winning £2,700 event at Leicester as a 2-y-o; had stiffish tasks in 1981 but
ran respectably on occasions, including when about 8 lengths fifth behind
Recitation in Salisbury 2,000 Guineas Trial on reappearance in April and when
fairly close up in handicaps at Newmarket and Doncaster in October on third and
fourth starts; off course over 6 months after second outing; probably stays 7f.
G. Balding.

GNOS 7 b.g. Song 132–No Recall 85 (Tutankhamen) (1980 6g 5f 7fg 6f 8s **51**
1981 7f³ 6f 8fg 8.2d) strong gelding; moody and inconsistent handicapper;
stays 1m; acts on any going; usually wears blinkers; suitable mount for an
apprentice; sometimes sweats up; has worn a tongue strap; wears bandages;
sold privately to R. Thompson 2,000 gns Doncaster October Sales. *P. Wigham.*

GOBLIN 6 ch.h. Sun Prince 128–Rocelle 101 (Sodium 128) (1980 12f 1981 12f **75**
12f⁴ 12f) big, strong, workmanlike horse; good mover; useful handicapper at
his best but has deteriorated; suited by 1½m; needs a sound surface. *M. Bradley.*

GOD BLESS 2 b.f. So Blessed 130–Lady Gaylord (Double Jump 131) (1981 —
6g) May 9; 7,800Y, 10,500Y; strong filly; half-sister to 2 winners, including
3-y-o Sage King (by Shantung), successful at up to 13f; dam unraced half-sister
to smart colt Romper; 33/1 and burly when in mid-division in 26-runner maiden
race at Doncaster in November won by Perang Tejam. *H. Collingridge.*

GODLY 2 ro.c. Godswalk 130–Desert Pet 77 (Petingo 135) (1981 6g) May 29; — p
1R 7,200Y, 2,000Y; smallish, useful sort; first foal; half-sister to very useful
animals New Jerusalem and Empty Jest, won over 1½m; chased leaders and
kept on quite well without being knocked about when eighth of 26 to Perang

Tejam in 26-runner maiden race at Doncaster in November; will probably stay 1m; should improve. *W. Elsey.*

GODS MARK (USA) 5 ch.h. Little Current–Director (Swaps) (1980 8g 10g **98** 8fg* 7.2fg2 6fg* 8fg 7v 1981 6d 6s2 6f 7fg2 6fg 6g 8d4 8g) well-made, quite attractive horse; useful performer; runner-up in Greenlands Stakes at the Curragh in May (¾ length behind Drama) and Ballycorus Stakes at Leopardstown in July (beaten 2 lengths by Tellurano); never-dangerous tenth of 16 to The Quiet Bidder in Cork and Orrery Stakes at Royal Ascot in between; creditable 3¼ lengths fourth under top weight to Majestic Nurse in Irish Cambridgeshire Handicap at the Curragh in September; stays 1m; acts on any going; consistent. *C. Grassick, Ireland.*

GODSTRUTH 2 gr. or ro.c. Godswalk 130–Light Opera 101 (Vienna 127) **78** (1981 5g 5g 5f2 5f3 5fg2 5.1d2 5g 5s2) Mar 28; IR 15,000Y; neat, strong colt; good walker and mover; half-brother to several winners, including useful 1980 2-y-o 5f winner Vienna Miss (by Thatch); dam, closely related to smart sprinter Laser Light, stayed 7f; runner-up in maiden races at Folkestone, Wolverhampton, Yarmouth and Warwick, coming closest to success at Warwick in October when beaten a neck by Fast Lad; evidently thought best at 5f; acts on any going; blinkered last 2 outings. *H. T. Jones.*

GO-GEM 3 gr.c. The Go-Between 129–Moon Gem (Moontrip) (1980 NR **—** 1981 10.1fg 8fg) 780Y; second foal; dam, well beaten all outings, is half-sister to 3 American stakes winners; last in sellers at Windsor in June and Leicester in July. *D. Wintle.*

GOING STRAIT 4 b.g. Manacle 123–Miss Atalanta 83 (Hethersett 134) **—** (1980 7v 8s 5f3 6f* 6g 5fg 6g 7g4 7g4 7g 10d4 12g 1981 7g 7fg 7g 8f 7fg 7g) good-bodied gelding; didn't find his form at 4 yrs; stays 1¼m; acts well on firm going; blinkered once in 1980; sold 4,300 gns Newmarket Autumn Sales. *R. Smyth.*

Mr Paul Mellon's "Golden Bowl"

GOING WELL 2 b.f. Dance In Time–Little Firefly (Bold Ruler) (1981 5s —
5g 5d 5g 6f) May 21; 5,000Y; leggy, rather lightly-made filly; sixth foal; dam
Irish 5f winner; 11 lengths sixth of 14 to stable-companion Gold Key in maiden
race at Carlisle in May, second outing and only glimmer of ability; in rear in
seller final start; blinkered fourth outing. *M. W. Easterby.*

GOLDBORN DAVID 3 b.g. Wabash 99–Panyana 88 (Pandemonium 118) —
(1980 6g 8.2s 1981 8g 10d 12.2g) lightly-made non-thoroughbred gelding;
well behind in sellers in North; blinkered at 2 yrs; slipped up final start. *C.
Crossley.*

GOLD BREEZE 3 b. or br.f. Persian Breeze 121–Gold Poulet 84 (Goldhill 125) **42**
(1980 5f 5fg* 5d³ 5fg 5d 5d 5f 1981 6v 5d 5g³ 5g 6g) strong filly; poor handicapper; well beaten in a seller on reappearance; unlikely to stay 6f; has run badly
when tried in blinkers. *W. H. H. Williams.*

GOLDEN ALRAY 3 br.f. Ballynockan 112–Mollie (I Say 125) (1980 6d 6g **54**
7d³ 1981 10f 12g 10s³ 11d* 12d) leggy filly; bought in 1,200 gns after winning
seller at Hamilton in October; stays 11f. *B. McMahon.*

GOLDEN BABY 3 ch.f. Sharpen Up 127–Obedience (Reliance II 137) (1980 —
5f 6fg 5d⁴ 5d 5fg 6g 5d 6s 1981 6s 6fg) small, compact filly; poor plater;
will stay 1m; sold 270 gns Doncaster November Sales. *A. W. Jones.*

GOLDEN BOWL (USA) 3 b.f. Vaguely Noble 140–Rose Bowl 133 (Habitat 134) **100**
(1980 6fg² 7g 6fg² 7g* 7g* 1981 8fg 12.3d² 12v* 12fg 12d 12d 14.6g) attractive,
lightly-made filly; first foal; dam, outstanding performer from 1m to 1½m and
winner of Queen Elizabeth II Stakes twice and Champion Stakes, is half-sister to
top-class Ile de Bourbon; very useful performer at 2 yrs, winner at Salisbury
and York; just failed to get up after having to be switched to outside entering
straight when beaten a head by Hunston in Cheshire Oaks in May; gained
compensation in impressive fashion in 4-runner Lupe Stakes at Goodwood later
in month, travelling easily behind leaders most of the way and quickening
smoothly to win by 3 lengths from Fruition; didn't run up to her best afterwards;
suited by 1½m and should stay further (beaten a long way out when tailed off in
Park Hill Stakes over 1¾m); has run respectably on a firm surface but is better
with some give in the ground and acts on heavy. *I. Balding.*

GOLDEN BRIGADIER 3 b.c. Brigadier Gerard 144–Golden Fez (Aureole 132) **96 §**
(1980 7s² 7f 7g³ 7g* 7.6f 1981 8s* 10fg² 12.3g 12g² 12d 12f 12f³ 10g 12fg
10.5g³ 12g 10d 10d 12v 12g 12g) strong, good sort; beat Soukab a shade
cleverly by ½ length in handicap at Salisbury in April; often had stiffish tasks
afterwards but was placed on several occasions, including in £3,700 event at
Thirsk (put head in air and was beaten 1¼ lengths by Rhein Bridge) and slowly-
run Welsh Derby at Chepstow (2¼ lengths third of 4 behind Six Mile Bottom);
stays 1½m; seems to act on any going, but is probably ideally suited by some
give in the ground; occasionally blinkered, and has won in them; sometimes
bandaged behind; often apprentice ridden (unable to claim allowance 3 times,
including in Derby); inconsistent and not one to trust implicitly. *C. Brittain.*

GOLDEN DESTINY 2 b.c. Gold Rod 129–Caradoc Queen (Dumbarnie 125) —
(1981 7g) Apr 11; 400F; third produce; dam never ran; 50/1, very backward
and green when tailed-off last of 17 to Alvor in maiden race at Leicester in
September. *J. Harris.*

GOLDEN ELDER 6 gr.h. High Top 131–Silver Birch 122 (Silver Shark 129) **91**
(1980 8d 7fg 7.6f* 7.6f 8g 7d⁴ 8fg* 8f 8g³ 7fg⁴ 8d* 1981 8s 7d 8g 7.6g⁴ 8f 8fg
8h* 8fg 8h² 8fg³ 8fg) big, lengthy horse; fairly useful handicapper; made all
to beat Traditional Miss by 2½ lengths at Bath in July; very well suited by 1m
nowadays and stays 1¼m; acts on any going but goes particularly well on
top-of-the-ground; a hard puller who needs strong handling and has won only
for J. Mercer since his 2-y-o days. *P. Walwyn.*

GOLDEN EMPRESS 3 b.f. Cavo Doro 124–Rosaura 105 (Court Martial) —
(1980 NR 1981 7g 9s 10s 10g) strong, compact filly; half-sister to several
winners, including useful 1m and 11.7f winner Roses (by Ribero); dam a sprinter
and a daughter of 1,000 Guineas winner Belle of All; apprentice ridden, unquoted
and on backward side when about 4 lengths sixth of 19 to Barwin in minor event
at Newmarket in May; not seen out again until autumn and was soundly
beaten all starts; should stay beyond 7f; bandaged near-fore final start; sold
7,600 gns Newmarket December Sales. *R. Sheather.*

GOLDEN END 10 ch.g. Remainder 106–Golden Reed 65 (Cabalistic II 81) —
(1980 NR 1981 15fg 12.2fg) poor handicapper; stays well; has worn blinkers.
R. Cross.

GOLDEN FLAK (USA) 3 b.c. Ack Ack–Faith in Gold (Nashua) (1980 6g **110** 6fg 6fg⁴ 7.6f* 8fg³ 8d* 8d⁴ 1981 8fg⁴ 8fg⁴ 8.2s 8f³ 8g² 8fg* 10fg²) neat, strong colt; developed into a very useful handicapper; quickened clear inside distance to beat Spark of Life decisively by 2 lengths in Food Brokers Trophy at Newmarket in July; came with a good run to lead in last furlong but was caught near post when beaten a head by Indian Trail under stiff penalty in Extel Stakes (Handicap) at Goodwood later in month; placed earlier in Britannia Stakes at Royal Ascot (heavily-backed favourite when third to Olympic Glory) and £8,200 handicap at Newmarket (¾-length second to Master Golfer); stays 1¼m; seems to act on any going; sent to race in USA. *M. Jarvis.*

GOLDEN FLEECE (USA) 2 b.c. Nijinsky 138—Exotic Treat (Vaguely **99]** Noble 140) (1981 8g*)

Although only Achieved of Vincent O'Brien's juveniles succeeded in winning one of the major races for staying two-year-olds, it seems unlikely that O'Brien will be short of good three-year-olds in 1982. Many of the choicest lots from the 1980 yearling sales are now in his stable, and who would like to risk much against there being amongst them a Kings Lake, an Artaius or even an Alleged still waiting to show his worth? Grundy's half-brother Chronicle, the expensive Hoist the Flag colt Lords, Gay Fandango's three-parts brother Punctilio and The Minstrel's brother Pilgrim all won their only starts in splendid style. Even more impressive than these though was Be My Guest's close relative Golden Fleece in winning a maiden race at Leopardstown in September. Our race-reader summed up Golden Fleece's performance like this:

'Golden Fleece took a furlong or so to warm up but he was pretty quickly up with the pace and on the bridle, racing in third or fourth place towards the outside. It was obvious from the time the runners swung into the straight that he was going to win. Rounding the turn Eddery asked him to quicken and the horse immediately lengthened his stride, cruised into the lead and was going on in great style at the finish, despite the fact that he was eased down considerably in the closing stages. I would say he was value for four lengths here.'

The colt he beat so easily was Assert who, only three weeks later, won the Group 2 Beresford Stakes by four lengths. No doubt Assert improved a great deal between the two races but the third and fourth horses at Leopardstown also went on to win; Duke of Dollis, beaten eight and a half lengths by Golden Fleece, won a maiden race next time out and Condell, a head further back at Leopardstown, later won a twenty-eight-runner event at the Curragh. Unfortunately Golden Fleece himself didn't race again although the Larkspur Stakes had been spoken of as a likely target.

Golden Fleece (USA) (b.c. Apr 1, 1979)	Nijinsky (b 1967)	Northern Dancer (b 1961)	Nearctic
			Natalma
		Flaming Page (b 1959)	Bull Page
			Flaring Top
	Exotic Treat (ch 1971)	Vaguely Noble (b 1965)	Vienna
			Noble Lassie
		Rare Treat (ch 1952)	Stymie
			Rare Perfume

As can be seen from our photograph Golden Fleece is an excellent type of colt. Like many of Nijinsky's offspring he has plenty of size and scope and it's no wonder he cost 775,000 dollars as a yearling, a sum which placed him among the ten highest-priced yearling colts of the year in the States along with Lords and Pilgrim. He's the second winner from the first three foals of Exotic Treat, an unraced mare who was bred to be a champion. Her grandam Rare Perfume bred Jaipur, a top-class winner at up to a mile and a half, and the fine racemare Rare Treat, who numbered the mile-and-a-half Ladies Handicap among her sixteen victories. Rare Treat's hundred-and-one races didn't stop her making her mark at stud. Her son Ring Twice was a very smart middle-distance performer, winner of the 100,000-dollar Widener Handicap, and even better was her daughter What A Treat, the champion three-year-old filly of 1965 when a winner from six furlongs to a mile and a quarter. What A Treat set a new record price for a broodmare of 450,000 dollars when sold in 1972 and later produced the high-class miler Be My Guest to a mating with Golden Fleece's grandsire Northern Dancer. Although Be My Guest was better at a mile than longer trips Golden Fleece gives the impression he'll be suited by middle distances. If he's as good as we think he is, you'll be hearing a lot of him! *V. O'Brien, Ireland.*

M J. P. Binet's "Golden Fleece"

GOLDEN GREEN 2 gr.c. Godswalk 130–Kentucky Green 100 (One For All) **97**
(1981 5f³ 5s) Feb 8; IR 30,000Y; well-made, good sort; first foal; dam won
over 6f and 7f in Ireland and is half-sister to very smart sprinter Sarasota Star;
promising 3 lengths third of 8 to Admiral's Princess in £4,000 race at Ascot in
June; not seen out again until October when 5 lengths fifth of 7 to My Lover
in Cornwallis Stakes on same course (close up for long way and was eased once
chance had gone); may well stay 6f; fairly useful and is certainly capable of
winning a maiden race. *J. Bethell.*

GOLDEN HOLLY 3 ch.g. Golden Mallard 103–Holly Doon (Doon 124) (1980 6f **54**
1981 8s⁴ 8s⁴ 7g 9g³ 12d 8d 8s 5fg* 6fg 5g 6g 6g 6g⁴) leggy gelding; bought in
1,750 gns after winning selling handicap at Redcar in June (apprentice ridden);
seems best at sprint distances; occasionally blinkered. *G. Harman.*

GOLDEN HORSESHOE 4 b.g. Tarboosh–Christmas Gift (Princely Gift 137) **—**
(1980 10.8v 10fg 12f 16g 12fg 1981 12f 12g) close-coupled gelding; poor
plater. *R. Akehurst.*

GOLDEN KNOLL 2 ch.g. Ardoon 124–Red Petticoat (Red God 128§) (1981 **69**
5d 5s 6g 7g³ 6g 7g 8g 7fg 8d) Apr 16; IR 4,000F, 3,600Y; strong gelding;
carries plenty of condition; third foal; half-brother to Irish 12.8f winner Slip
a Disc (by Jukebox); dam ran once; 3½ lengths third of 18 in maiden race won
by Warri at Salisbury in July, best effort; should be suited by 1m. *S. Mellor.*

GOLDEN LADDIE 2 ch.c. Northern Flash–Annalie (Crepello 136) (1981 **64**
5fg 5g 7d 7fg 7fg) compact, short-legged colt; second foal; dam unraced daughter of half-sister to Giacometti; beaten about 6 lengths when fifth of 14 to Loyal
Toast in minor event at Lingfield in August, third outing and best effort; will
stay 1¼m; possibly needs a soft surface. *M. Haynes.*

GOLDEN LEICESTER 5 br.g. Workboy 123–Snow Rum (Quorum 126) **58**
(1980 6f 8f 7f⁴ 7g⁴ 8f 10d 7f 8d 1981 7s 12d 8fg³ 10f 10fg⁴) strong gelding;
stays 1¼m; acts on any going; blinkered twice in 1980; sometimes sweats up;
has worn bandages; sold 1,900 gns Doncaster November Sales. *P. Wigham.*

GOLDEN LISLE 2 br.c. Pieces of Eight 128–Lisle's Filly (Burglar 128) (1981 **66**
5fg 5f 6g 7g* 6f 8.2fg 8fg² 7d 8g⁴) Mar 13; 2,200F, 3,000Y; strong, compact
colt; second reported foal; dam well beaten, including in a seller; fair plater;
winner at Beverley in July (no bid); stays 1m; acts on a firm surface; wears
blinkers nowadays. *J. Etherington.*

GOLDEN MATCH 3 ch.g. Royal Match 117–Hunea (Hornbeam 130) (1980 —
6g³ 7fg 1981 10fg 10f) lightly-raced maiden; showed only worthwhile form
on first outing at 2 yrs; should be suited by middle distances; sold to M. Hinchliffe
2,000 gns Doncaster August Sales. *G. Pritchard-Gordon.*

GOLDEN PIN 2 b.f. Golden Dipper 119–Pin Hole 83 (Parthia 132) (1981 —
6d 5d) Apr 5; 1,600F, 1,900Y, 1,300 2-y-o; third reported foal; half-sister
to a winner in Trinidad; dam 1¼m winner; in rear in October in minor event at
Pontefract (dwelt) and maiden race at Redcar (speed 3f). *E. Carter.*

GOLDEN REEF 4 b.g. Mill Reef 141–Photo Flash 119 (Match III 135) (1980 **58**
10g² 14f⁴ 1981 9s² 10g 12fg) well-made, attractive sort; plating-class maiden;
will stay well; acts on soft going. *W. Hastings-Bass.*

GOLDEN RIVER 5 b.g. Rheingold 137–Photo Flash 119 (Match III 135) —
(1980 13.3f³ 16.1fg⁴ 12fg² 12g* 1981 10s 8fg) lengthy gelding; useful performer at his best; well beaten in Clive Graham Stakes at Goodwood and valuable
handicap at Newbury in 1981; stays well; acts on any going; ran moderately in
blinkers once in 1979; retained 7,200 gns Ascot June Sales. *R. Turnell.*

GOLDEN ROMANY 3 ch.f. Le Coq d'Or 101–Border Gypsy (Bishop's Move —
92) (1980 NR 1981 12.3g 11f) lengthy filly; second foal; dam ran only twice;
tailed off in maiden races at Newcastle and Hamilton in August. *T. Craig.*

GOLDEN ROYALTY 4 b.f. Royalty 130–Golden Wonder (Golden Cloud) —
(1980 10f 12g 12.2f² 13.8g 14.6d⁴ 15.8fg 12.2d 1981 10g 12s 12f) unfurnished
filly; poor performer; best run at 1½m on firm going; has worn blinkers; sometimes sweats up. *J. Calvert.*

GOLDEN SHERRY 2 b.f. Golden Sammy–Sherry Bird (Sherry Netherland —
113) (1981 7g 8d) lightly-made, plain filly; first reported foal; dam of little
account on flat but won a point-to-point; unquoted when behind in maiden races
at Leicester at the back-end. *J. Scallan.*

GOLDEN SPRAY 2 ch.f. Hot Spark 126–Moeru Bara 107 (Firestreak 125) **76**
(1981 5f³ 5fg² 5f⁴ 5f 5d 6g²) Mar 21; 3,700Y; neat filly; half-sister to several
winners, including very useful middle-distance stayer Fire Red (by Salvo);
dam 5f sprinter; showed ability in varied company, on final start going down
by a length to Commissar in valuable 21-runner seller at Newmarket in October;
stays 6f; probably acts on any going; has run creditably for an apprentice;
sold 5,400 gns Newmarket Autumn Sales. *W. Hastings-Bass.*

GOLDEN VENTURE 2 b.f. Golden Tack 102–Sovereign Venture 67 (Lucky —
Sovereign) (1981 5s 5f 5fg) May 11; plain filly; useless plater. *M. Bradley.*

GOLDEN VIRGINIAN 6 ch.g. Virginia Boy 106–Golden Hostess (Kythnos —
126) (1980 8.2fg 1981 10f) poor plater; dead. *J. Mulhall.*

GOLDEN VOW 7 b.g. Good Bond 122–Sunsaly 75 (Sallymount 125) (1980 —
12g 10fg 1981 12d) lightly raced on flat nowadays; stays 1¼m; acts on any
going; suitable mount for an inexperienced rider. *R. Hartop.*

GOLDEN WILKIE 2 b. or br.c. Averof 123–Royal Handful (Some Hand 119) **60**
(1981 5d* 5f⁴ 6f 6f 5f 5f 7f) Apr 18; 1,000F, 900Y, 1,100 2-y-o; leggy colt;
good mover; first foal; dam never ran; hard ridden most of way when winning
by 2 lengths from Miss Prudent in 10-runner seller at Ripon in May (bought in
2,100 gns); ran best subsequent race on final start; stays 7f; probably acts on
any going; blinkered fifth start; suitable mount for an apprentice. *B. Wilkinson.*

GOLD EXCHANGED (USA) 2 b.c. Blushing Groom 131–Gaite (Tom Rolfe) **87**
(1981 6d 7f 7g* 7g* 10f* 8d) June 5; first foal; dam, winner 3 times at up to
1m in USA, is daughter of top-class filly Gay Matelda; in good form in the
summer, winning at Sligo (beat Dara Monarch 1½ lengths), Down Royal and
Tralee (beat subsequently-disqualified Chammsky ½ length); 12/1 when moderate
sixth of 10 to Assert in Beresford Stakes at the Curragh in October; stays 1¼m
well; acts on firm going. *D. Weld, Ireland.*

GOLD GROUND 3 ch.c. Grundy 137–Paltrasse 84 (Palestine 133) (1980 **63**
NR 1981 11.7g* 12s³ 12s) 23,000Y; strong, good-looking colt; fourth live foal;
half-brother to 2 winners, notably 1976 Mill Reef Stakes winner Anax (by Right
Tack); dam, 1m winner, is sister to Bay Express' dam Pal Sinna; won maiden
event at Bath in May very narrowly; lacks pace and will stay well; sold out of
J. Tree's stable 3,100 gns Ascot August Sales and was tailed off on only outing
for new connections. *M. Masson.*

GOLD KEY 2 b.f. Lochnager 132–Gold Cheb 88 (Chebs Lad 120) (1981 5s³ **66**
5g* 6fg 5g 6d 6s⁴) Apr 27; strong-quartered filly; first reported foal; dam won
three 7f races; won 14-runner maiden race at Carlisle in May by ½ length from
Trade High; in rear in nurseries next 3 outings and was beaten 9½ lengths when
fourth in valuable seller at York, final start; best form at 5f. *M. W. Easterby.*

GOLDLINER ABBEY 3 b. or br.g. Abwah 118–Bright and Early (Rise 'N **45**
Shine II) (1980 5v 5d³ 5f 7g* 7fg² 7g 1981 10s⁴ 12d 12.5f 10f* 12.2g 12d)
fair sort; always going well when winning selling handicap at Beverley in July
(no bid); stays 1¼m; acts on firm going; wears blinkers. *J. Hardy.*

GOLDLINER COUNTESS 2 ch.f. Touch Paper 113–Narita 86 (Narrator —
127) (1981 5v 5fg 6f 5g) Mar 10; IR 2,000F, 3,600Y; sturdy filly; half-sister to
2 winners; dam won over 7f and 1m at 2 yrs; well behind in maiden and minor
events; off course 4 months before third outing; sold 520 gns Newmarket Autumn
Sales. *J. Hardy.*

GOLDLINER GAME 4 ch.g. King's Leap 111–Hasten Up (Galivanter 131) **75**
(1980 7d 7d 7f 7fg² 7f⁴ 7fg³ 7.2g 8fg² 8.2d⁴ 7g 1981 8fg 7g⁴ 7fg³ 7fg² 8f*) big,
rangy gelding; made all to beat Prince by ½ length in handicap at Pontefract in
July; stays 1m; suited by firm ground; suitable mount for an apprentice. *J.
Hardy.*

GOLDLINER IMP 3 b.c. Import 127–Strathclair (Klairon 131) (1980 5g **49**
5fg 5g 6g⁴ 6d⁴ 7f² 7g 1981 8.2s 8fg 7g³ 7fg³ 7g 5fg 6f) strong, useful sort;
plater; suited by 6f and 7f (well beaten over 1m); sometimes blinkered; sold
500 gns Newmarket Autumn Sales. *J. Hardy.*

GOLD MARKET 2 br.f. Hotfoot 126–Gold Rupee 86 (Native Prince) (1981 —
6fg) May 1; plain, lengthy filly; first foal; dam won twice over 5f; 50/1 and
in need of race, tailed off at halfway when in rear in 18-runner maiden race won
by Corsky at Newmarket in July. *J. Winter.*

GOLD MEASURE 4 br.c. Goldhill 125–Fair Measure (Quorum 126) (1980 **46**
11fg 8fg 10.1fg 8fg 8s 9.4fg 1981 16f 17.1m 14g⁴ 16f* 16g 15.8g) lengthy colt;
stayed on well to win apprentice handicap at Thirsk in July; suited by a test of
stamina; acts on firm going. *J. Spearing.*

GOLDORATION 6 b.g. Gold Rod 129–Fair Jinks 65 (Tudor Jinks 121) (1980 **39**
NR 1981 6s³ 8fg² 8f 7g) plater; needs further than 6f and stays 1¼m; probably
acts on any going. *H. O'Neill.*

GOLD RIFLE 2 br.c. Scottish Rifle 127–Bar Gold 80 (Lucky Brief 128) (1981 **70**
5g 6g 6fg⁴ 7f² 7f⁴ 8f³ 8.2d³ 8.2s) Apr 5; 1,150Y; neat colt; brother to a poor
plater and half-brother to a winning plater; dam won twice at around 1¼m; in
frame in maiden auction events and nurseries; will stay 1¼m; probably acts on
any going; blinkered final outing. *J. Etherington.*

GOLD RIVER (FR) 4 ch.f. Riverman 131–Glaneuse 118 (Snob 130) (1980 **132**
10g* 10d* 10.5d² 12d³ 13.5g* 12f⁴ 12.5d² 15.5v* 1981 15.5g* 20v* 12.5g 12g³
12d* 15.5v³)
  Of all the windmills at which our sometimes-quixotic pen has tilted none
has remained so unmoved as the turf authorities' policy of progressively contracting the pattern of European racing around a mile and a quarter to a mile
and a half centre. The authorities' excessive preoccupation with endowing
races such as the Derby and the King George VI and Queen Elizabeth Stakes,
their French counterparts the Prix du Jockey-Club and the Prix de l'Arc de
Triomphe, and the Irish Sweeps Derby with comparatively massive prizes has
brought the status of these races to a point where the majority of racing's
followers probably believe that the middle-distance champions are *ipso facto*
better than their counterparts in other spheres. Ask any racegoer which was
the best horse to race in Europe at a mile and a half or more in 1980 and it's
odds on he'll select one who made his or her name in the big mile-and-a-half
events—and yet our answer would be Le Moss, a horse who never ran at a distance shorter than two and a quarter miles during the season. Le Moss's

victories in the Gold Cup, the Goodwood Cup and the Doncaster Cup, in each of which he defeated Ardross, earned for his owner a total of £66,748; the Derby, the King George, the Irish Sweeps Derby and the Prix de l'Arc de Triomphe, all run over a mile and a half, were each worth more than £100,000 to the winner.

Few horses are capable of winning in top company at a mile and a half *and* at two miles and a half—the different trips call for different qualities in a horse—and any example of such versatility is to be celebrated. Gold River's triumphs in the Prix du Cadran, France's equivalent of the Gold Cup, and the Prix de l'Arc de Triomphe in 1981 will take their place alongside the achievement of Le Moss's brother Levmoss, the only other horse in the post-war era to win both races in the same year. The top stayers' races had already lost much of their former prestige by the time Levmoss took part in them in 1969— he also won the Gold Cup—and their status has continued to be eroded. The Prix du Cadran was worth £25,769 to the winner when Levmoss won it; Gold River earned £30,541. By contrast the first prize for the Prix de l'Arc de Triomphe has more than doubled: Levmoss earned £89,589; Gold River £193,424. The situation is similar in Britain: the Gold Cup (£39,013 to the winner in 1981) lags well behind the most valuable middle-distance event, the Derby (£149,900). What's the justification for so wide a disparity between the prizes offered for the big mile-and-a-half races and those offered for the best staying races—or the top sprints and mile races for that matter? On none of the occasions that this situation has been highlighted have we heard the turf authorities defend this disproportionate allocation of prize money. Why should the European racing programme for three-year-olds and upwards greatly favour horses whose best distance is a mile and a quarter to a mile and a half? Why have the Cup races been downgraded in the post-war era? Can the authorities offer no better defence than silence?

Gold River's connections were faced at the start of the most recent season with the choice of aiming her at races such as the Gold Cup and the Prix du Cadran—she was a most impressive winner of the Prix Royal-Oak over fifteen furlongs on her final outing at three—or putting her back to shorter distances at which there was much more prize money and prestige to be earned. Gold River improved steadily as a three-year-old, her first season on the racecourse, and showed high-class form at a mile and a half, including when fourth in the Prix Vermeille beaten less than two lengths by the winner Mrs Penny. Her performances at a mile and a half were plenty good enough to suggest that she could continue to do well at middle distances provided she made normal progress from three to four. However, the Prix du Cadran, run at Longchamp in May, was chosen as her first major objective. She had a preliminary outing in the Prix Jean Prat over the Prix Royal-Oak distance at Longchamp in April. Conceding weight to her eight rivals, each of whom had the benefit of an outing, Gold River was ridden with enormous confidence by Head who brought her from last to first in the straight—she was at least ten lengths behind the leader on the turn—to win by a neck from the only other filly in the field Proustille. Gold River showed exceptional finishing speed for a horse racing at long distances and we shouldn't have been surprised to learn after this performance that the plan to go for the Cadran had been abandoned in favour of a more valuable mile-and-a-half event such as the Coronation Cup.

In the absence of the English-trained Ardross, the Prix du Cadran proved easy pickings for Gold River. Her five rivals, who included a former Cadran winner El Badr and a St Leger winner Son Of Love, had finished behind her in the Prix Jean Prat and she met them all on more favourable terms. The only question seemed to be whether she would stay the trip. In a truly-run race Gold River gave a spectacular performance, winning in the manner of an outstanding stayer. Gold River's rider again employed extravagant waiting

Prix Jean Prat, Longchamp—the confidently-ridden Gold River beats Proustille by a neck

*Prix du Cadran, Longchamp—Gold River confirms her status as a
stayer of the highest class*

tactics and running down towards the final straight Gold River was about
twelve lengths behind the leader Hereas. She made up a little ground before the
home turn but did not begin her challenge in earnest until well into the straight.
Switched to the outside Gold River produced a dazzling turn of foot and, ridden
only with hands and heels, came home a very easy three-length winner from
Hereas, her jockey looking round twice after taking the lead and easing her
near the finish. A race between Gold River and Ardross at Royal Ascot presented an exciting prospect, but Gold River's performance at Longchamp
convinced her connections that she was far too good a filly to be running for
relatively paltry prizes in the Cup races. It was announced that she would go
for the Grand Prix de Saint-Cloud, a race almost twice as valuable as the Gold
Cup.

Gold River didn't show her best form in the Grand Prix de Saint-Cloud,
finishing fifth of ten, a little over five lengths behind the winner Akarad. She
was off the course for ten weeks afterwards before being returned to Longchamp
in September for the Prix Foy, an established warm-up race for some of the top
older horses aimed at the Prix de l'Arc de Triomphe. We thought Gold River
ran a fine trial: conceding 7 lb to the 1980 Prix de l'Arc winner Detroit, Gold
River finished only two and a half lengths behind her in third place, going on
best of all at the finish after being waited with in a very slowly-run race. We
went on record as saying that Gold River looked a lively outsider for the Prix
de l'Arc but her connections apparently considered running her instead in the
two-and-a-half-mile Prix Gladiateur which takes place a week before the Arc.
In the event Gold River went to post for the Arc deserted by Freddie Head in
favour of Detroit. The mount on Gold River went to the Hong Kong-based
Australian Gary Moore, whose father won the Prix de l'Arc on Saint Crespin

*Prix de l'Arc de Triomphe, Longchamp—Gold River wins Europe's
richest race from Bikala (rails) and April Run with Perrault fourth*

III for Gold River's trainer; Gary Moore had ridden winners for the stable including Ivanjica in the 1975 Prix Vermeille.

The Prix de l'Arc de Triomphe brought together a typically strong and representative field, although it was the poorer for the loss of Shergar who had well and truly dominated middle-distance racing up to the end of July. Among the twenty-four runners were the cream of the French middle-distance performers including: the first four in the Prix du Jockey-Club, Bikala, Akarad, Gap of Dunloe and Rahotep; the highest-placed home-trained filly in the Prix de Diane de Revlon April Run, who had turned the tables on Madam Gay and Val d'Erica in the Prix Vermeille; the first two in the 1980 Prix de l'Arc Detroit, winner of her last three races, and Argument, winner of the Prix Ganay in May; and Perrault, winner on his last two starts of the Prix Maurice de Nieuil and the Grand Prix de Deauville, both Group 2 pattern races. There were eleven foreign-trained challengers including Ardross (Gold Cup), Blue Wind (Oaks and Irish Guinness Oaks), Beldale Flutter (Benson and Hedges Gold Cup), Cut Above (St Leger), Kings Lake (Irish Two Thousand Guineas), Condessa (Yorkshire Oaks) and the high-class English-trained four-year-olds Pelerin and Prince Bee.

It has become fashionable for jockeys on fancied horses in the Prix de l'Arc to take up a forward position from the start, one of the reasons being that horses towards the head of the field are thought to have a better chance of keeping clear of the trouble that frequently attends the running of the race. But the Prix de l'Arc is almost always run at a cut-throat pace and San San, Star Appeal, Ivanjica and Three Troikas all succeeded in winning it in the 'seventies after being waited with, exploding the myth that a horse has to be in the first half dozen all the way to have any chance of winning. Although the very early pace wasn't quite so strong as usual, Gold River won the Arc after being among the backmarkers at the end of the first furlong and in the middle of the field for most of the race. With the exception of Condessa, who dwelt at the start, Gold River was one of the last away, her rider tacking over from the number-fourteen draw to take up a position near the inside rail behind the main bunch. Gold River was about seven or eight lengths behind the clear leader Bikala rounding the turn at the far corner of the track. She made ground very smoothly on the long, sweeping descent to the home straight, enjoying an uninterrupted run along the rails. As the field reached the straight, with about three furlongs to run, Bikala led from Ardross, Perrault and Detroit with Akarad, Gold River, April Run and Argument next. Ardross had been struggling before the home turn and both Detroit and the favourite Akarad were beaten early in the straight. Bikala, strongly challenged by Perrault and then by Gold River, kept on very gamely and it was well inside the final furlong when Gold River's powerful finishing run took her to the front. She won by three quarters of a length and a nose from Bikala and April Run, who unleashed a fine burst in the last two furlongs, with Perrault two lengths further back in fourth place ahead of Ardross, Argument and Akarad. With such a large field there were bound to be hard-luck stories, the most valid of which concerned April Run who had to be switched round Akarad to make her challenge and then spoiled her chance by hanging. But Gold River looked a worthy winner on the day. The French Tote paid a winning dividend equivalent to odds of 53/1.

Gold River further improved the Head family's very fine record in the Prix de l'Arc. Her trainer had previously saddled Nuccio (1952), Saint Crespin III (1959) and Ivanjica (1976) to win the race while the father of Gold River's trainer sent out the 1947 winner Le Paillon and the 1966 winner Bon Mot III. Three Troikas, victress in 1979, was trained by Christiane Head, daughter of Gold River's trainer. No-one rides Longchamp better than Freddie Head who is retained by Gold River's owner. Head has ridden four Prix de l'Arc winners, Bon Mot III, San San, Ivanjica and Three Troikas, and Gold River's victory must have been a bitter-sweet occasion for him. 'Freddie made a big mistake', said Alec Head afterwards. 'But that's life. You've got to stick to your people and I hope this will give him a bit of a lesson.' One of George Lambton's most memorable sayings was that 'retainers are like marriage lines—for better or worse'. Unfortunately, the spirit is not always observed, although the boot is more often on the other foot, a retained rider finding himself replaced by a top-flight jockey in a big race.

One other point before we leave the Arc. Gold River was the sixth filly to win the race in its last ten runnings. As we said in our essay on Detroit in *Racehorses of 1980*, there have been three or four vintage crops of middle-distance fillies recently and some of them coincided with crops of colts which were moderate by comparison with those of most other years. We have done a little

M J. Wertheimer's "Gold River"

more research; there are some interesting facts forthcoming from a comparison of the Prix de l'Arc results over the last ten years with those of the previous twenty-six years (1946-1971). In the last ten years fifty-seven fillies have run, an average of 5.7 per race; but in the previous twenty-six years the total number of fillies running was ninety-one, an average of 3.5 per race. The average number of colts participating has remained almost constant (16.2 per race from 1946-1971 and 16.3 per race from 1972-1981). Another factor, therefore, in the apparently better showing of fillies in the last ten years is that more of them run in the race nowadays—in 1981 there were nine fillies in the field, a number not exceeded in the post-war era. Thirteen of the fifty-seven fillies that ran between 1972 and 1981 were placed (22.8%) compared to sixteen of the ninety-one between 1946 and 1971 (17.6%). Although the proportion of fillies-placed to fillies-running has increased, the proportion is not statistically significant. If only four more fillies had been placed between 1946 and 1971—and this might easily have happened—the percentages would have been about the same. The difference is of no more real significance than the turning up of twelve 'heads' or 'tails' in the tossing of twenty coins. A third factor, as we see it, is that some owners with high-class fillies like Gold River are more prepared, in these days of relatively high prize money for the top middle-distance races, to keep them in training and give them a crack at the top colts (Allez France and Ivanjica were also four when they won the Arc). And with good reason, they have something to gain and stand to lose at most the value of one foal. The old idea that a strenuous racing career was damaging to a filly's future as a broodmare is also now recognised for what it always was—a myth. There seems no need for further explanation of the success of fillies in the Arc in recent years. Outstanding fillies pop up now and then and sometimes the 'fillies years' bunch together. It's pure chance. There's nothing more to it than that.

On her only outing after the Prix de l'Arc, Gold River was a disappointing third to Ardross in the Prix Royal-Oak, beaten also by Proustille. Gold River's retirement was announced after the Prix Royal-Oak and she is to visit Northern Dancer. Gold River was bred in France by her owner; her sire Riverman and her dam Glaneuse raced in the Wertheimer colours. Riverman, a strong, very attractive, deep-bodied colt by Mill Reef's sire Never Bend, was a top-class racehorse with a very fine turn of finishing speed. He had much to recommend him as a stallion and it's no surprise that he has turned out to be a successful sire. Gold River provided him with his second successive winner of the Prix de l'Arc de Triomphe and his second successive season as leading sire in France. Riverman is now in the United States, having been syndicated for eighteen

Gold River (Fr) (ch.f. 1977)	Riverman (b 1969)	Never Bend (b 1960)	Nasrullah
			Lalun
		River Lady (b 1963)	Prince John
			Nile Lily
	Glaneuse (b 1966)	Snob (b 1959)	Mourne
			Senones
		Glamour (br 1960)	Djebe
			Tudor Gleam

million dollars in 1980. Gold River's dam was a very successful racemare, winner of the Gran Premio del Jockey Club at Milan and two fairly important races in France, the Prix Chloe and the Prix de Malleret; she also finished third in the Prix de Diane and fourth in the Prix Vermeille. A half-sister to the One Thousand Guineas runner-up Gleam, she produced three minor winners from three foals before Gold River. Gold River's half-sister Gracious (by Habitat) and her full sister Glena have bred winners—Gracious is the dam of the smart French sprinter Greenway. Gold River, a strong, attractive filly, acted on any going although she seemed particularly well suited by some give in the ground. Her seven victories earned for her owner £298,481, a sum exceeded by only three European-based fillies, Dahlia, Allez France and Three Troikas. *A. Head, France.*

GOLD SHOVELER 6 b.g. Workboy 123–March Poulet (March Past 124) **45**
(1980 NR 1981 12.5fg³ 13fg 16.5g) big, strong gelding; poor maiden; stays 1½m; blinkered first 2 starts. *K. Stone.*

GOLD T.V. (USA) 7 ch.h. T.V. Lark–Faith in Gold (Nashua) (1980 12.2fg **—**
16.1d 1981 16.5fg) of little account on flat; sold 400 gns Doncaster September Sales. *H. Wharton.*

GOLDWIG 8 gr.m. Sovereign Spitfire 81–Wigmore Street 80§ (Aureole 132) **—**
(1980 NR 1981 13fg³ 13.8fg⁴ 8.2f) poor performer; races mainly over hurdles nowadays; hooded last 2 starts. *T. Cuthbert.*

GOLDYKE 3 ch.f. Bustino 136–Hilldyke Flower 79 (Klondyke Bill 125) **63**
(1980 NR 1981 8g 8.5g 10fg 12d² 14f³ 12f) 26,000Y; lengthy filly; half-sister to 2 winners, including middle-distance winner Duberly (by Queen's Hussar); dam stayed 7f; in frame in maiden races at Haydock and Yarmouth in August; suited by 1½m; didn't have best of runs second outing; ran poorly final start; sold 9,800 gns Newmarket December Sales. *L. Cumani.*

GO LEASING 3 ch.f. Star Appeal 133–Grand Velvet 83 (Grand Roi 118) **121**
(1980 6fg* 6g⁴ 6d 7g 7d 7g 7s* 7d* 1981 7s* 8g³ 12g 8fg 10g* 12g 10g 10g)
Go Leasing is a smart filly on her day though her consistency leaves something to be desired. A nursery winner at two years she fulfilled her trainer's first objective for her in the spring by winning the Salisbury One Thousand Guineas Trial, went on to give a splendid account of herself in the Guineas itself and later in the year picked up one of the big prizes for fillies, the Nassau Stakes at Goodwood; she failed to reach the frame in five other starts.

Go Leasing isn't quite so inconsistent as she might seem: the state of the going is a critical factor with her, and apparently the distance of her race is, too. As her two-year-old form foreshadowed she needs some give in the ground to be seen to best advantage. Conditions were against her, therefore, when Star Pastures, Tolmi, Seasurf and Viendra beat her in the Child Stakes at Newmarket fourth time out. On the other hand they were right up her street when she stormed four lengths clear of Welshwyn in the last furlong at Salisbury, and they were favourable when she finished third to Fairy Footsteps and Tolmi in the Guineas. Go Leasing really caught the eye in the Guineas; she finished fastest of all after none too clear a run, tearing up the hill, and would have won the race with a bit further to travel. As it was she went down by only a neck and the same. She did not repeat that form in similar conditions on the same course in the autumn, in the Sun Chariot Stakes (she hung very badly when pulled out to challenge two furlongs out) and in the Champion Stakes (admittedly she had

Nassau Stakes, Goodwood—Go Leasing stays on strongly to win from
Vielle (stripes) and Strigida (far left)

little chance here against the top colts). Go Leasing's other races apart from
the Nassau Stakes were at a mile and a half. There were extenuating circumstances for her substantial defeats on both occasions—she got stirred up in the
preliminaries to the Oaks and was hampered by the faller Silken Knot in the
Yorkshire Oaks—yet there was more than a suggestion in her performances
that she didn't get the trip. She is a strong-pulling sort, and despite her stayer's

Mr W. E. Norton's "Go Leasing"

pedigree we should say that she is undoubtedly best at up to a mile and a quarter.

The Nassau Stakes is run over a mile and a quarter, and was run on good ground in 1981 thanks to heavy overnight rain. Go Leasing was well backed to improve on her Child Stakes form though Nasseem, the previous season's winner Vielle, Strigida, Silken Knot and Viendra were at shorter odds in a very open market. Go Leasing won well. She was held up in a truly-run race which was led by Majieda and then, when Majieda slipped very nearly five furlongs from the finish, by Nasseem. Nasseem wasn't able to keep up the gallop for much more than another three furlongs. Viendra took over and then Vielle, but Go Leasing, who'd obtained a very good opening a furlong and a half out, quickened in excellent style up the stand rail to take the lead well inside the final furlong and she ran on strongly to beat Vielle, who was conceding 3 lb more than weight-for-age, by a length.

		Appiani II	Herbager
	Star Appeal	(b 1963)	Angela Rucellai
	(b 1970)	Sterna	Neckar
Go Leasing		(br 1960)	Stammesart
(ch.f. 1978)		Grand Roi	Charlottesville
	Grand Velvet	(ch 1962)	Ginetta
	(b 1968)	Spanish Velvet	Alcide
		(ch 1962)	Fluorescent

Go Leasing's sire won the Prix de l'Arc de Triomphe, her dam won over fifteen furlongs and her grandam Spanish Velvet, a middle-distance maiden, is a half-sister by Alcide to the staying Triumph Hurdle winner Blarney Beacon; so there is plenty of stamina in the pedigree. The next dam Fluorescent, by Blue Peter out of the One Thousand Guineas second Ariostar, was no stayer, though—she made all the running in a five-furlong handicap at Newmarket as a three-year-old. The dam of Go Leasing (that genetic impossibility, a bay from chestnut parents!) produced three previous foals—the platers Amanda Blue (by Mummy's Pet) and Arrowsmith (by Sky Gipsy), the latter a winner in Belgium, and a filly by Town Crier who was exported to Hungary. Go Leasing is a compact, sharp sort of filly, one that doesn't always impress in the paddock. She was very well bought for 5,000 guineas as a foal, and she realized 175,000 guineas at the 1981 December Sales, purchased to race in the USA. *G. Harwood.*

GOLFERS DREAM 2 b.f. Carnoustie 132–Dream (Hornbeam 130) (1981 5d² 5fg* 7fg 7fg⁴ 7f) Apr 6; 3,000Y; small, workmanlike filly; third foal; dam won in Sweden and was placed in Swedish and Danish 1,000 Guineas; got home by a neck from unlucky-in-running Aquarian Star in small race at Hamilton in May; 3½ lengths fourth of 5 to Bustello in minor event at Catterick in July, best subsequent effort; will stay at least 1¼m. *A. Jarvis.* — 70

GOLIAD 3 b.c. Nonoalco 131–Queen of the South 98 (Gallant Man) (1980 9v 1981 8d 10s 8d 8g 8fg 8f 11.7h³ 10.1fg⁴ 10fg⁴ 10v⁴) 72,000Y; robust, well-made ex-Irish colt; second foal; dam won four 1m races; in frame in maiden and minor races; stays 1¼m; wears blinkers; sold 5,000 gns Newmarket Autumn Sales. *J. Bethell.* — 60

GO LIGHTLY 4 b.f. Galivanter 131–Rosia Steps 98 (Red Pins 114) (1980 6d 5fg 6fg 7fg 8d 8fg 1981 6s 9s³ 12g⁴ 10.5d 10g 12s⁴ 11g 9g⁴ 8f 10f 10fg 8d) leggy filly; only plating class; stays 1½m; acts on soft going; has worn blinkers; sometimes sweats up. *N. Crump.* — —

GO LISSAVA 3 gr. or ro.g. The Go-Between 129–Lissava Queen (Our Babu 131) (1980 5f 5h 5fg⁴ 6fg⁴ 5d³ 6fg³ 6g 5d 5fg 1981 6v 8s⁴ 6g 7g 8g 5fg 8fg 6fg 6g) small gelding; in frame in sellers; has run respectably at 1m but is better at shorter distances; blinkered second outing at 2 yrs. *D. Chapman.* — —

GOLLYNO 4 b.g. Giolla Mear 115–Nonnie (Dumbarnie 125) (1980 8v⁴ 10s 11.2g² 12f 10f² 9g* 9.5f⁴ 11g² 12s* 12f⁴ 12g² 16s 1981 8d 13.3s 10g) tall, narrow, short-backed ex-Irish gelding; won maiden race at Limerick Junction and small race at Tramore in 1980; soundly beaten in varied company at 4 yrs; stays 1½m; acts on any going. *I. Wardle.* — —

GO MARTELL 4 b.g. Golden Mallard 103–Ruritania (Pampered King 121) (1980 10g 10f 10s* 11g 1981 16d 12s 10g 12d 10.2g) compact gelding; poor handicapper; well beaten in valuable seller final start; stays 1¼m; revels in soft going; has been tried in blinkers but seems better without; sometimes bandaged in front. *J. Doyle.* — —

GO METRO 2 ro.c. Roan Rocket 128–Exquisite 80 (Exbury 138) (1981 5d 6s³ 6fg 6d⁴ 7s 6fg⁴ 6fg 8g 8d² 10g³ 8d) May 8; 4,200Y; lengthy, workmanlike colt; — 68 second foal; dam suited by a test of stamina; in frame in maiden race, nurseries and sellers; will be suited by 1½m; seems to act on any going; possibly needs a stiff course (ran badly at Chester fifth start); wears blinkers. *S. Mellor.*

GONE SAILING 2 b.f. Malacate 131–Go Surfing (Go Marching) (1981 7fg)   — p
Jan 19; big, lengthy, unfurnished filly; excellent mover; second foal; half-sister to Italian winner Go Gold (by Gold Rod); dam ran twice at 3 yrs; 33/1, ruined chance by starting very slowly in 29-runner maiden race at Newmarket in August and in circumstances did well to finish 9 lengths thirteenth to Hayakaze; not seen out again. *L. Cumani.*

GOODBYE STARTER 3 ch.c. Owen Dudley 121–Curfew 76 (Midsummer **102**
Night II 117) (1980 5f* 6f 1981 7g 7.6d² 8g) smallish colt; won maiden race at Newmarket and finished fifth to Mattaboy in William Hill Middle Park Stakes on same course as a 2-y-o; not disgraced in Tote European Free Handicap, again at Newmarket, in April, making much of running and keeping on to finish 2½ lengths fifth to Motavato; didn't have best of luck in running and was eased when his chance had gone when 6 lengths second to Mushref in minor event at Chester the following month (odds on); off course 5 months afterwards and was well beaten in handicap at Newmarket on his return; should be suited by 1m; sold 9,000 gns Newmarket Autumn Sales. *H. Cecil.*

GOOD HABIT 3 ch.g. Habat 127–Parlais 101 (Pardao 120) (1980 5f 5f 6d 6g   —
8g 8d 1981 10d 10s 12g) small, fair sort; poor maiden. *G. Beeson.*

GOOD HAND 2 gr.g. Some Hand 119–Aberside (Abernant 142) (1981 5g³ 6f³ **57**
5f⁴) Mar 28; leggy gelding; half-brother to 2 winners, including 5f performer Setmark (by Sharpen Up); dam never ran; third in sellers at Catterick in July (well-backed favourite but gave away too much ground by rearing as stalls opened) and Thirsk later in month; claimed by J. Calvert at Ripon the following month (favourite, again unruly at start); gave impression at Thirsk he may be better suited by 5f than 6f. *N. Tinkler.*

GOOD MAN FRIDAY (USA) 2 b.g. Noble Commander–Tinker Jet (Hi-Hasty) **75**
(1981 6fg 7g³ 5d³ 8g 7d) Apr 13; $9,700 2-y-o; short-backed gelding; second foal; dam stakes-placed winner of 8 small races; third in maiden race at Leicester in September and Wolverhampton the following month; ran moderately last 2 starts, although had fairly stiff task over 1m. *D. Thom.*

GOOD OFFICES 3 br.g. Murrayfield 119–Sun Queen 76 (Lucky Sovereign)   —
(1980 6g 6fg³ 6fg⁴ 6s 6g² 6g 1981 6g 6f 7fg) compact, attractive gelding; well beaten in 1981; should stay 7f; acts on a firm surface; sometimes blinkered; sold 1,300 gns Newmarket Autumn Sales. *F. Durr.*

GOOD ON YOU 4 br.f. Virginia Boy 106–Mini Skirt (Bald Eagle 119) (1980 **48**
8s 8fg 8g* 10.2g 9g* 12d 8.2s 1981 8.2d² 9fg⁴ 7g 8f* 7fg 8.2d 8s 8.2s*) small filly; poor mover; plater; won at Pontefract in June (bought in 2,200 gns) and Hamilton in October (bought in 820 gns); stays 9f; acts on any going. *R. Johnson.*

GOOD PERFORMER 2 b.c. Sun Prince 128–Haymaking 115 (Galivanter 131) **81**
(1981 6d 6fg³ 7g⁴ 8s³ 7d) Apr 10; IR 21,000Y; strong, attractive colt; half-brother to several winners, including very useful 1975 2-y-o 5f winner Hayloft (by Tudor Melody); dam won Coronation and Nassau Stakes; in frame in £4,000 event at York and in large fields of maidens at Newmarket and Warwick, at Warwick finishing 3 lengths third of 17 to Barfoot in October when co-favourite; suited by 1m and will probably stay 1¼m. *N. Callaghan.*

GOOD THYNE (USA) 4 b.c. Herbager 136–Foreseer (Round Table) (1980 **98**
10fg 10fg⁴ 12fg² 16g² 15s 12g* 15s* 14s² 1981 10d³ 14d* 20fg 22.2f²) big, well-made colt; useful performer; favourite when beating Keppols by 2 lengths under top weight in handicap at Leopardstown in May; not beaten far in 2 long-distance races at Royal Ascot in June, but didn't look resolute when going down by a head to Donegal Prince in Queen Alexandra Stakes; subsequently sent to race in USA; stays well; acts on any going; seems best in blinkers. *D. Weld, Ireland.*

GOODY GOODY 3 b.f Mummy's Pet 125–Righteous Girl 93 (Right Boy 137)   —
(1980 5g* 5fg 1981 5fg 7fg 6f) workmanlike filly; very good walker and extravagant mover; won minor event at Goodwood as a 2-y-o; unplaced in handicaps in 1981; yet to prove she stays beyond 5f; sold 6,000 gns Newmarket December Sales. *F. J. Houghton.*

GO ON GREEN 2 br.g. On Your Mark 125–Catilina (Sallust 134) (1981 5s 5s **69**
5g² 5g³ 5g 6g 6fg 5fg 5f² 5g) Apr 21; IR 2,000F, 3,500Y; fair sort; first foal; dam, half-sister to smart juvenile hurdler Batista, ran only 3 times; led 4f when

GOO

placed in minor events at Pontefract and Catterick and in nursery at Redcar (length second to Will George in September); speedy and will probably prove best at 5f; evidently needs a sound surface. *Denys Smith.*

GOOSALLEY 2 b.f. Run The Gantlet–Indian Maid 117 (Astec 128) (1981 8v²) Mar 20; third living foal; half-sister to 2 winners, including French Gold Cup winner El Badr (by Weavers' Hall); dam won at up to 1m; promising short-neck second of 14 to Vidor in newcomers race at Maisons-Laffitte in October; sure to win races over 1¼m+; entered in Oaks. *C. Bartholomew, France.* **?**

GORGEOUS GIRL 3 ch.f. Dragonara Palace 115–Daughter of Song 73 (Song 132) (1980 5f* 5fg³ 5f² 6g 6g³ 5f 6g 6d 5fg 6d 1981 6d 5.8g 5fg* 5h 5fg⁴ 5f⁴ 5d 5s) neat, well-made filly; ran best race for a long time and landed a gamble when beating Star of Enzo by 1½ lengths in 15-runner handicap at Warwick in June; probably stays 6f; acts on firm going; sometimes troublesome at start; trained first 2 starts by R. Baker. *P. Cole.* **71**

GORSKY 5 b.g. Dubassoff–Artistically (Ribot 142) (1980 12fg² 12f² 12f 14f 11g 16d³ 15fg² 20.4g 16fg⁴ 16.1s 1981 13d² 16d 12g) small gelding; good mover; inconsistent maiden; stays 2m; seems to act on any going; used to wear blinkers; not resolute. *B. Richmond.* **— §**

GOSPORT 5 bl.h. Tudor Melody 129–Greek Gift (Acropolis 132) (1980 8g 8v⁴ 10s 9.7g³ 9.2d² 9fg 8d³ 8s³ 6.5d 8d 8d 9g² 1981 9s* 8d³ 8v* 8d* 7s* 8f 8f) French horse; showed improved form in 1981 and won 40,000 francs race at Evry in March, 45,000 francs event at Saint-Cloud in May, Prix du Chemin de Fer du Nord at Chantilly in June (beat Moon Ingraver by ½ length) and Prix de la Porte Maillot at Longchamp in July (accounted for Mistra by a short neck); also ran respectably when third to Hilal in Prix de Ris-Orangis at Evry but was well beaten behind Northjet in Prix Jacques le Marois at Deauville and Prix du Moulin de Longchamp on last 2 starts; stayed 9f; ideally suited by some give in the ground; standing at Haras de Sai, Orne. *J. C. Cunnington, France.* **117**

GO TOTAL 5 br.h. Philip of Spain 126–Lazy Time (Linacre 133) (1980 5f 6fg 5s² 5g² 5g⁴ 5fg 5.3g³ 5f⁴ 5d* 5fg 5g 5d² 5v 1981 6g 5d 5fg 5g⁴ 5f 5fg 5g 6g⁴ 5g³ 6g² 5g 5s 5d 5s) robust, short-coupled horse; sprint handicapper; stays 6f; acts on any going; blinkered occasionally at 3 yrs; has run respectably for an apprentice; trained part of season by A. Hide; sold to P. Makin 3,200 gns Newmarket Autumn Sales. *P. Cundell.* **85**

GOUMI 2 b.c. Grundy 137–Gay Trinket 72 (Grey Sovereign 128§) (1981 7g) Apr 13; 62,000Y; well-made, quite attractive colt; half-brother to useful sprinter Nusantara (by Lorenzaccio) and useful Italian winner Gaudi (by Saritamer); dam headstrong half-sister to French Derby second Patch; 9/1 and bit backward, never dangerous and dropped out to finish last of 8 to Height of Fashion in Acomb Stakes at York in August, only outing. *M. Stoute.* **— p**

GOUVERNO 2 b.c. Star Appeal 133–Gundula (Mercurius) (1981 6g 6fg 8d² 8s 8g² 8d) Feb 19; well-grown, attractive colt; good mover with a long stride; brother to German 6f to 1m winner Grandola; second twice in big fields, going down by 2½ lengths to Super Sunrise in £4,200 event at Newbury in September and by 1½ lengths to Farioffa in maiden race at Newmarket the following month (finished very strongly to come out best of far-side group); put up far and away his best effort on final outing when seventh of 13 to Count Pahlen in William Hill Futurity at Doncaster in late October, beaten just over 7 lengths; will stay 1¼m; will take a deal of beating in any maiden race judged on his final effort. *F. Durr.* **112**

GOVERNMENT PROGRAM (USA) 3 ch.c. Secretariat–Northern Gem 121 (Northern Dancer) (1980 6g 6g 6g 7g 8.3fg² 1981 8.2s³ 9d* 10.4g 12g³ 12d⁴ 10f* 10d² 10f* 10fg* 10g⁴ 10g² 10s 10g³) strong ex-American colt; second foal; brother to useful miler World Affair; dam won Fred Darling Stakes and was second in Champion Stakes; placed once from 5 starts in USA as a 2-y-o; did well in 1981 and won minor event at Newcastle and handicaps at Nottingham, Leicester and Epsom, beating No-U-Turn on last 2 courses; also in frame in varied company, on final start finishing less then a length third to King's Glory in Tia Maria Autumn Handicap at Newmarket in October; stays 1½m; probably acts on any going; game and genuine; successful with blinkers and without (wore them in his later races). *H. T. Jones.* **99**

GRACEFUL BOY 6 b.g. Prince de Galles 125–Only By Chance (Golden Cloud) (1980 7fg 6g* 6fg 6g 6s 6g³ 1981 6fg⁴ 6g 7g 6d⁴) poor handicapper; has been fired; stays 6f; used to wear blinkers; wears bandages. *D. H. Jones.* **49**

GRACE HARWAR 2 b.f. Windjammer (USA)–Stand Off 61 (Murrayfield 119) **46**
(1981 5d 5d 5v 6f 6f⁴ 7f⁴ 8.2fg 8.2d 8g) neat filly; poor plater; usually wears blinkers; sold 720 gns Newmarket Autumn Sales. *G. Balding.*

GRADE WELL 6 b.m. Derring-Do 131–Authors Correction 69 (Narrator 127) **53**
(1980 11fg 12fg 10f³ 11.7s³ 12d* 11.7d 11.7fg 10g 12d² 12.2d⁴ 12d 12d⁴ 1981 12s 10.8d* 11.7d³ 12d² 10.8fg) middle-distance handicapper; won at Warwick in April; acted on any going; genuine; sold 8,000 gns Newmarket December Sales, covered by Manor Farm Boy. *G. Blum.*

GRADWOOD STAR 4 br.f. Comedy Star 121–Miss Taurus 79 (Bullrush 106) —
(1980 NR 1981 10g 8g) strong filly; poor maiden; was tried in blinkers; dead. *R. Hollinshead.*

GRAF METTERNICH 6 b.h. High Top 131–All Shy 64 (Alcide 136) (1980 **62**
10s 11fg* 10.7fg⁴ 10f 11f⁴ 10h³ 10.7g 10s 12fg 9f* 11.7fg 12d 12.2d 13s 12d 1981 11fg 13.8g 12g* 12d) shapely horse; won handicap at Edinburgh in October; stays 1¼m; acts on any going; has worn blinkers; has run respectably for a boy; needs to be held up. *Miss S. Hall.*

GRAF TRAUN 3 b.g. Huntercombe 133–Golden Lania 78 (Sea Hawk II 131) **67**
(1980 6g 7fg 7fg 7fg 8d 1981 12d 12g 8s² 10.2d 8fg 16fg² 12fg⁴ 14.6f² 14f⁴) strong gelding; second in trainers race at Kempton and maiden events at Warwick and Ripon; stays 2m; blinkered fifth outing. *C. Brittain.*

GRAFTY GREEN 6 ch.g. Traditionalist–Crusheen (Typhoon 125) (1980 —
10g² 10g 8fg 11.7fg 10fg² 10fg³ 8g 10fg 12d* 8d 10s 12d 1981 10f 10f⁴ 12f 12fg 10fg 10f) poor handicapper; stays 1½m; probably acts on any going; has worn blinkers; sometimes sweats up; suitable mount for a boy. *D. Dale.*

GRAIN RACE 3 br.c. Windjammer (USA)–Crimson Velvet 89 (Above Sus- **105**
picion 127) (1980 5fg* 5fg* 5f* 6s³ 6fg⁴ 7s 8fg² 8.2s³ 1981 8s² 9fg⁴ 10d 12f² 10fg⁴ 10.5g³ 12fg* 12fg³ 12fg* 12fg) well-made, useful-looking colt; good mover; useful handicapper; won at Goodwood in July (beat Canton Lightning a neck in William Hill Southern Handicap) and Newmarket in August (gamely by a head from Blackfoot); in frame on most other outings, including when

Mrs B. H. Fyfe-Jamieson's "Grain Race"

½-length second to Feltwell under top weight in King George V Stakes at Royal Ascot on fourth outing and 4 lengths third behind stable-companion Amyndas in John Smith's Magnet Cup at York on sixth start; suited by 1½m; has run well on soft going but is better on a sound surface; sweated up badly fifth start; took a long time to get going eighth start; genuine and consistent. *B. Hobbs.*

GRANADOS BEAUTY 3 b.f. Levanter 121–Twigelle (Tenterhooks 128) —
(1980 NR 1981 7s 10d) fourth foal; dam ran twice; well beaten in sellers at Kempton in May and Folkestone in June. *W. Turner.*

GRANADOS QUEEN 5 b.m. Supreme Red 93–Twigelle (Tenterhooks 128) —
(1980 NR 1981 8fg 8fg 8d) poor plater; stays 1m. *W. Turner.*

GRAND ALLIANCE 4 b.g. Sweet Revenge 129–Lima 105 (Abernant 142) 37
(1980 10v 9g 7g 8f 7g 8g 1981 8s 6g 7g 7f² 8f 10f 8f 7v) strong gelding; has had a soft palate operation; plater; stays 7f; acts on firm going; sometimes sweats up; has had his tongue tied down. *M. Camacho.*

GRANDIOSE 4 ch.c. Grundy 137–Secret Session 108 (Court Martial) (1980 9f 12fg³ 12g 12d* 13.1g* 12fg⁴ 14g* 13.3fg 14g 1981 14s) strong, rangy colt; developed into a fairly useful handicapper at 3 yrs; didn't impress in paddock and ran as though something was wrong with him only start in 1981 (May); suited by 1¾m; suited by some give in the ground; genuine; standing at Semley Stud, Dorset. *D. Elsworth.*

GRAND LEGACY 3 ch.f. Relko 136–Grandpa's Legacy 102 (Zeus Boy 121) 56
(1980 8d 1981 11s 11.7g³ 8.3s 11.7d 10s⁴) smallish, useful-looking filly; third in maiden race at Bath in May, best effort; suited by 1½m and may stay further; trained by H. Candy until after second outing (off course afterwards over 4 months). *P. M. Taylor.*

GRAND MANOR 3 b.c. Great Nephew 126–Town House 91 (Pall Mall 132) —
(1980 7g 1981 12g 12s 14f 12fg 12.2fg) compact, well-made, attractive colt; soundly beaten in varied company; bandaged in front third outing; blinkered fourth start; sold 440 gns Newmarket Autumn Sales. *F. Durr.*

GRAND PALACE 2 b.f. Royal Palace 131–Grand Central 79 (Grand Roi 118) 77
(1981 6fg 8fg 8fg² 7g³) May 5; big, rangy filly; second foal; half-sister to winning stayer Lady Mantegna (by Andrea Mantegna); dam won twice over 1m; placed in sizeable fields of maidens at Leicester in the autumn; will be suited by 1½m. *R. Laing.*

GRAND UNIT 3 b.c. Home Guard 129–Silken Topper (High Hat 131) (1980 NR 1981 8g² 8.2s² 8fg) 19,000Y; strong colt; third foal; half-brother to a winner in Norway; dam won over 1½m in Ireland; stayed on when second in Wood Ditton Stakes at Newmarket in April (beaten 1½ lengths by Magikin) and maiden race at Haydock in June; found very little when let down and ran disappointingly only subsequent start; will be suited by 1¼m; possibly needs some give in the ground; bandaged at Newmarket. *E. Eldin.* 68

GRANGE SPRING 5 b.g. Dubassoff–Praga (Sigebert 131) (1980 NR 1981 12g) strong gelding; lightly raced on flat nowadays; stays well. *M. W. Easterby.* —

GRANNY SUE 2 b.f. Owen Anthony 102–Chumba (Cambremer 132) (1981 5v 5fg 5d 6f 5f⁴ 7d) poor plater; sold 400 gns Newmarket Autumn Sales. *D. Thom.* 40

GRANOBLE 2 br.c. Perdu 121–Grand Slam 65 (Fidalgo 129) (1981 6g 7.6s 8s 10g 7g) May 4; well-grown, rather leggy colt; half-brother to several winners here and in France, including fairly useful 1m winner Noble Venture (by Hopeful Venture); dam disappointing; plater; seems to stay 1m; blinkered second start. *C. Austin.* 48

GRANPARK 3 b.g. Huntercombe 133–Solandri (Resurgent) (1980 6fg³ 5d³ 6s 5s 5d 5s³ 6s 1981 6v² 5g⁴ 5g 6g 8.2fg 6g 5g⁴ 6g 10fg⁴ 11g³ 10g 9d) plater; races mainly at sprint distances but wasn't disgraced over 1¼m on ninth start; acts on soft going; sometimes blinkered, but is better without; sold 1,000 gns Ascot August Sales. *J. S. Wilson.* —

GRAPHICS ESKA 4 ch.f. Jimmy Reppin 131–Tina Fort (Fortina) (1980 NR 1981 10d 10s) 6,000Y; tall, narrow filly; half-sister to a winner over jumps; dam staying chaser; beaten a long way in minor event and apprentice race at Nottingham in the autumn. *B. McMahon.* —

GRAPHICS SOLAR   3 b.c. Royal Palace 131–Tina Fort (Fortina)   (1980 8d 7d   —
1981 10s 12s 12g 13fg 12f 14g⁴ 16f 14fg)   leggy colt; poor form in varied company;
stays well; sweating seventh start.   *B. McMahon.*

GRASMERE GIRL   3 b.f. Jimsun 121–Firebeat 94 (Firestreak 125)   (1980   —
NR   1981 13.8fg 15.5g)   1,250Y; half-sister to fair 1970 2-y-o 7f winner Rifle
(by Con Brio); dam sprinter; tailed off in maiden and minor events at Catterick.
I. Jordon.

GRAVEL PIT   2 b.f. Reform 132–Abertywi 87 (Bounteous 125)   (1981 5s 5s)   —
Mar 31; 1,000Y; neat filly; third living foal; dam, winner at up to 1m, is sister
to high-class sprinter Abergwaun; backward when tailed off in maiden auction
event and a seller in the spring.   *M. W. Easterby.*

GRAVINA   2 gr.f. Godswalk 130–Gradiva 110 (Lorenzaccio 130)   (1981 5fg²)   **89 p**
Feb 22; small, strong, lengthy filly; first foal; dam, half-sister to top sprinter
Double Form, won from 5f to 1m; 7/1, did well to finish 2 lengths second of 8
to Dancing Rocks in £3,100 event at Goodwood in September, having missed
break completely and then having to be switched when beginning to improve;
will stay 6f; should win a maiden race.   *F. J. Houghton.*

GRAY LOCH   3 b.f. Lochnager 132–Ensign Steel 57 (Majority Blue 126)   **59**
(1980 5fg 6d 5s³ 5d 5f   1981 6g 5f 6g 6g 5f⁴ 6d 6g 6fg 5fg 8.2s* 8d 8g 10d)   big,
strong filly; won poor maiden race at Nottingham in September; had been soundly
beaten in a seller eighth start; suited by 1m; seems well suited by some give
in the ground; often blinkered (wasn't when successful).   *T. Fairhurst.*

GRAY PORT   2 gr. or ro.f. Boco 87–Port Relic 90 (Relic)   (1981 6fg 7f 7f 8g)   —
May 7; 280Y; fair sort; half-sister to 3 winners, including successful 6f performer
Oyston Estates (by Goldhill); dam 1m and 1¼m handicapper; no sign of ability,
including in sellers.   *D. H. Jones.*

GREASE   2 b.f. Filiberto 123–Greedy of Gain (Habitat 134)   (1981 5v* 5g* 5g*   **114+**
6g* 5.5d³ 6v* 8s*)

Her name may lack the elegance of a Marguerite Vernaut, Tadolina, La
Zanzara, Orsa Maggiore, Carnauba or Val d'Erica but Grease has plenty in
common with those Italian fillies before her; like them, she's up to taking on
top international company.   She won her six races in her home country by the
highly impressive total of thirty-seven lengths and on her single venture outside
Italy acquitted herself most creditably in the Prix Robert Papin at Maisons-
Laffitte in July.

What Grease's form amounted to before the Papin was anyone's guess.
She'd had four races, all at Milan's San Siro track, in a six-week spell in May
and June, taking the Premio Poncia by four lengths, the Premio dell'Avvenire
by six, the Premio Bimbi by four and the Group 3 Premio Primi Passi by ten.
In the Primi Passi she slaughtered Beivars, a colt who had previously finished
second in three of his four races in France, and the French punters were
sufficiently impressed to make Grease second favourite in the ten-strong Papin
field, behind the Prix du Bois winner Maelstrom Lake.   Receiving only 2 lb
from the colts Grease put up a bold show, disputing the lead from the start; and
after Maelstrom Lake took her measure at the distance she kept on so well that
he beat her no more than a length, with Green Forest getting up only close
home to deprive her of second place.   The quality of Grease's performance was
emphasised a month later when one of the best French fillies, River Lady, tried
her hand in the Prix Morny against the first two in the Papin.   She fared no
better than Grease had done, finishing third to Green Forest and Maelstrom
Lake, beaten three quarters of a length and a head.

Grease was given plenty of time to recover from her arduous trip to France and
didn't race again until the Group 3 Criterium Nazionale at Milan eight weeks
later.   Her ten-length win over Ormeggio suggested that she had Italy's top
two-year-old race, the Gran Criterium at San Siro in October, at her mercy.   So
it proved.   The fair English maiden Man Overboard and the once-raced French
colt Nijinsky Model were among the opposition; more danger was to come from
the home-trained runners which included Pardolero, unbeaten in four previous
races, and the admirably tough filly Dark Angel who had five wins to her credit,
one of them in the Group 3 Premio Toscana, as well as five seconds from eleven
starts.   So effective over shorter distances, once covering five furlongs in less
than a minute, Grease stayed the very testing mile well, proving too good for
Dark Angel by three lengths.   The Bruni colt How to Go took third place a

further five lengths behind, and her old rival Ormeggio, in fourth place, was again beaten ten lengths.

In winning the Gran Criterium Grease followed in the footsteps of some very good animals. The Prix de l'Arc de Triomphe winners Ribot and Molvedo both won the race, as did the Champion Stakes winner Marguerite Vernaut, and of the more recent winners New Model, Sirlad and Glint of Gold all went on to meet with considerable success outside Italy. It looks as though one way or another Grease, too, has been lost to Italian racing. One story has it that her owner is sending her to race in the USA while another version says that Grease has been sold to the Pin Oak Farm, Kentucky, and is to be trained by Boutin in France as a three-year-old. The latter story seems to be the likelier as Grease has been entered for the One Thousand Guineas and Oaks in the name of the owner of Pin Oak Farm. If Grease comes over for the Guineas she looks sure to run very well and should prove one of the major threats to Circus Ring.

			Ribot		Tenerani
		Filiberto	(b 1952)		Romanella
		(b 1970)	Fast Line		Mr Busher
Grease			(b 1958)		Throttle Wide
(b.f. Apr 27, 1979)			Habitat		Sir Gaylord
		Greedy of Gain	(b 1966)		Little Hut
		(b 1971)	Gently		Grey Sovereign
			(gr 1962)		Be Careful

It's unlikely that Grease will stay well enough for the Oaks—there isn't much stamina to be found on the distaff side of her pedigree. Her third dam Be Careful was a high-class two-year-old, winner of the Gimcrack Stakes and the Champagne Stakes in the days when both were over six furlongs, and her grandam, Gently, gained her wins over six and seven furlongs, one of her successes coming in a substandard Nell Gwyn Stakes. The best of Gently's five winners was Godzilla, a very useful two-year-old in Italy in 1974 who subsequently bred the smart French filly Phydilla. Greedy of Gain also had quite a lot of ability, winning four times in Italy including the five-furlong Premio Cordusio. All of Greedy of Gain's three previous foals are winners in Italy, including Grease's sister Great Race and the Canisbay colt Godot. Godot was rated the fifth-best two-year-old of 1979, when he too won the Criterium Nazionale, and trained on well enough to win the Group 3 Premio Umbria the following year. No wonder Greedy of Gain's next foal, the Godswalk colt Gotama, proved one of the star attractions at the 1981 Deauville yearling sales, fetching 1,650,000 francs. He is now in training with David O'Brien and is surely one to watch out for in 1982.

Grease was sold as a yearling in Italy for 38,000,000 lire or approximately £17,700. Appropriately she's a granddaughter of Ribot, arguably the best Italian horse of all time, but her male line is not exclusively Italian. Her sire is the American-bred Filiberto who was sent to stud in France after his very promising career was cut short by an injury in the Grand Criterium. After his first three crops met with only modest success Filiberto was dispatched to the Newmarket December Sales in 1978, fetching 65,000 guineas. He then spent 1979 at Newmarket and is now standing in Canada. Interestingly, all three pattern race winners by him are fillies, namely Grease, the Prix de Royallieu winner Sealy and the Oaks d'Italia and Gran Premio d'Italia winner Maria Waleska. *G. Benetti, Italy.*

GREAT BRIANNA 2 b.f. The Brianstan 128–Great Freda 94 (Great Nephew 126) (1981 6fg 5g 8d) May 7; plain filly; first foal; dam won over 1¼m and 1½m, and also won several hurdle races; behind in maiden races at Salisbury and Bath (2) in the autumn. *M. Bradley.*   —

GREAT DEVELOPER 4 br.g. Royalty 130–Spring Music (Silly Season 127) (1980 12.5v* 12.3f² 14fg⁴ 12g² 12d 15s³ 16d⁴ 1981 16s* 16.1fg 16g⁴) lengthy gelding; good walker; staying handicapper; beat Down To Darkie quite comfortably by 2½ lengths at Newbury in April; acts on any going but is particularly well suited by the mud. *D. Nicholson.*   **75**

GREAT EASTERN 4 br.c. Jukebox 120–Miss Bangkok (Sovereign Path 125) (1980 6f* 6g* 6fg 1981 6g 5d³ 6f* 6fg 6fg³ 6d 6g*) leggy colt; good mover; very useful performer; got up in final stride to beat Enchantment a short head in Wokingham Stakes at Royal Ascot in June and Lightning Label by same margin in £5,000 race at Doncaster in November; needs further than 5f and will stay 7f; probably acts on any going; sweated up once in 1980. *J. Dunlop.*   **116**

GREATEST HITS 4 b.c. Derring-Do 131–Vallota 85 (Klairon 131) (1980 8fg   **63**
8d 8g 8g 8g 8s* 8.2s² 1981 10s⁴ 9d 10d 10v* 10f² 10g 10g) attractive, well-made
colt; won handicap at Chepstow in May; stays 1¼m; acts on any going; best in
blinkers; has run creditably for an apprentice. *R. Laing.*

GREAT GUNNER 2 ch.g. Ercolano 118–Joan of Arc 94 (Never Say Die 137)   **—**
(1981 6f 8.2fg) Mar 8; 4,000Y; compact gelding; half-brother to 3 winners
abroad; dam won over 1½m; looked very green and was always struggling when
eighth of 9 to Cajun in Chesham Stakes at Royal Ascot; not seen out again until
September when never-dangerous fifth of 6 to 10-length winner Bancario in
£4,000 race at Haydock; subsequently gelded. *P. Kelleway.*

GREATHAM HOUSE 5 b.g. Run The Gantlet–Nyeri 104 (Saint Crespin III   **—**
132) (1980 12d 12d 11.7d 1981 16g 22.2f 16g 19fg) poor mover; useful performer at 3 yrs; has shown little form since on flat though has won over hurdles;
stays well; acts on a firm surface; blinkered once in 1980. *J. Jenkins.*

GREAT LIGHT 3 ch.g. Great Nephew 126–Failing Light 70 (Ballymoss 136)   **81**
(1980 7fg 1981 10s³ 10s* 9d⁴ 12g 12g 10.2d⁴ 10.2d 12d* 13.3s 12d²) rangy
gelding; won maiden race at Nottingham in April (made all) and apprentice
handicap at Pontefract in October, on latter course beating Ruby Red Dress
rather comfortably by ½ length; suited by 1¼m; acts well on soft going; ran below
form ninth start; sold 15,000 gns Newmarket Autumn Sales. *R. Williams.*

GREAT LUCK 2 ch.c. Great Nephew 126–Lucky Girl (Lucky Brief 128) (1981   **84**
6g 7f 8s³ 8.2d 10.2g⁴) Mar 18; workmanlike colt; third foal; dam, slowly away
both outings, is half-sister to 1,000 Guineas winner Mrs McArdy; in frame in
sizeable fields for minor events at York and Doncaster in second half of season;
kept on well when fourth, beaten just over 4 lengths, to Yard Bird on latter;
one paced and gives impression 1½m will suit him very well; acts on soft going.
M. H. Easterby.

GREAT MAN 4 ch.c. Grundy 137–Gwen 114 (Abernant 142) (1980 NR 1981   **—**
8d 10f 10d) stocky colt; soundly beaten in minor events; sold 660 gns
Newmarket Autumn Sales. *P. Walwyn.*

GREAT MOVE 3 ch.f. Great Nephew 126–Manoeuvre 105 (Mountain Call 125)   **—**
(1980 7g 6fg 1981 7g 7.2f⁴ 7f 8fg 8.2s³) well-made, quite attractive filly; poor
maiden; stays 1m. *P. Walwyn.*

GREAT MYTH 4 ch.f. Sharpen Up 127–Leonora's Legend 83 (Rockefella)   **—**
(1980 8f 9.4d 10s 1981 10f 10f 10f 10s 8.2s⁴) leggy filly; poor plater; has worn
bandages. *J. Fitzgerald.*

GREAT RANGER 4 b.g. Private Walk 108–Sham Alarm (Chamier 128) (1980   **—**
7fg⁴ 8g 8g 7.3fg 8d 1981 8d⁴ 10v 8f) small, plain ex-Irish gelding; poor
handicapper; seems to stay 1m; sold 390 gns Ascot October Sales. *J. Dodd.*

GREAT RELIEF 3 br.f. Great Nephew 126–No Surtax 112 (Never Say Die 137)   **52**
(1980 NR 1981 7fg⁴ 7f 10f 8fg 5fg³ 5g) 13,500Y; leggy filly; second live foal;
dam, half-sister to Busted, won twice over 1½m; has shown a little ability in
maiden races; evidently effective at 5f, but is bred to stay much further. *G.
Huffer.*

*Wokingham Stakes, Ascot—Great Eastern (nearest camera) gets up
in the last strides to short head Enchantment (blinkers) with Ferriby
Hall (far side) third and Over The Rainbow fourth*

GREAT SUBSTENCE (USA) 3 br.c. Pretense–Gay Northerner (Northern 112
Dancer) (1980 8g* 8d 1981 8d⁴ 10.5s 8fg 10.5s 10.5v*) $25,000Y; neat,
attractive colt; half-brother to 3 minor winners; dam won 6f stakes race at 2 yrs
in Canada; won Prix de Villebon at Longchamp and finished fifth of 11 to
Recitation in Grand Criterium on same course as a 2-y-o; reportedly bruised
himself extensively on leaving stalls when 2¾ lengths fourth of 10 to impressive
winner Cresta Rider in Group 3 Prix de Fontainebleau at Longchamp in April;
beat Ivor's Date by 2 lengths in Prix Phil Drake at Maisons-Laffitte in November; sixth behind No Lute in Prix Lupin in May and behind To-Agori-Mou
in St James's Palace Stakes at Royal Ascot in June, being left toiling from the
turn in latter; stays 1¼m; acts on heavy going. *M. Saliba, France.*

GREAT TRIUMPH 2 b.c. Grundy 137–Orange Triumph (Molvedo 137) (1981 66
6fg 8d 10s) Feb 21; quite well-made colt; half-brother to several winners here
and in Italy, notably top-class middle-distance performer Orange Bay (by
Canisbay); dam ran once at 2 yrs; about 8 lengths sixth of 16 to Portette in 1m
maiden race at Bath in October; gave trouble at start and ran moderately when
blinkered next time; should be well suited by 1¼m. *P. Walwyn.*

GRECIAN FIGHTER 9 ch.g. Fighting Ship 121–Arethusa 94 (Acropolis 132) —
(1980 18d 1981 15g) winning hurdler but seems of little account on flat. *B.
Richmond.*

GRECIAN PIECE 4 gr.f. Precipice Wood 123–Miss Helen (Only for Life 126) —
(1980 NR 1981 16.5fg 13.8fg) leggy filly; well beaten in maiden company;
pulled up lame final start; dead. *G. Lockerbie.*

GRECIAN SEA (FR) 3 ch.f. Homeric 133–Sea Venture 98 (Diatome 132) 107
(1980 5g³ 6d* 7g⁴ 1981 8g 7fg³ 7d³ 10f 9.2d) well-made, deep-girthed ex-
French filly; first foal; dam, from same family as Reform, won over 6f at 2 yrs
and stayed 1¼m; won maiden event at Saint-Cloud as a 2-y-o; prominent for
much of way and was by no means disgraced when fairly close-up tenth of 14
behind Fairy Footsteps in 1,000 Guineas at Newmarket in April; third behind
Star Pastures in American Express Royal Wedding Day Stakes at Goodwood in
July (possibly needed race and ran well) and behind Cragador in City of York
Stakes at York in August; should have been suited by 1¼m; pulled hard final
outing; retired to stud. *R. Hern.*

GREEK PRINCE 4 b.g. English Prince 129–Kaniz (Darius 129) (1980 8d² 12f —
10f 10s³ 10fg 10fg 1981 10s) deep-girthed gelding; poor maiden; stays 1¼m;
probably acts on any going; blinkered twice in 1980; sold 1,100 gns Ascot May
Sales. *J. Old.*

GREEN DAWN (USA) 3 ch.c. Grey Dawn II 132–Boheme (Exbury 138) 81
(1980 5.8f 7.2d 1981 7s⁴ 10.1fg⁴ 12.2fg* 13fg* 13.8fg³ 13.1h² 17.4g 16g)
neat, good sort; good mover; showed much improved form and outclassed his
rivals when winning maiden race at Catterick in July (by 12 lengths) and small
race at Ayr in August (very easily); placed in handicaps at Catterick and Bath
later in August; best at around 1½m (doesn't seem to stay long distances); acts
well on top-of-the-ground; sometimes sweats up (did so at Bath). *B. Hills.*

GREEN FOREST (USA) 2 ch.c. Shecky Greene–Tell Meno Lies (The Axe 115) 130
(1981 4s* 5s⁴ 5.5d² 6f* 7s* 8s*)
    According to an article in *The Thoroughbred Record* Mahmoud Fustok
hopes one day to dominate the world racing scene. He still has some way to go,
and a lot of money to spend, if he's to overtake the likes of Robert Sangster and
the Aga Khan but he's already made spectacular progress up the list of leading
owners in France—after finishing in forty-first position in 1977, the year he
first had runners there, he rose to take second place behind the Aga Khan in
1980 and third place in 1981. As well as having more than sixty horses in
training in France he now races a stable in the USA under the name Buckram
Oak Farm and in 1981 had horses trained in England for the first time, by
Michael Albina at Newmarket. Clearly Fustok is still expanding his interests
and, who knows, he may achieve his objective. He certainly possesses one
talent needed to reach the top—he's a good judge of a young horse. Fustok
personally selects many of his yearling purchases and for relatively small sums
he has bought numerous good winners. He bought the Turf Classic winner
Anifa for 62,000 dollars, the Prix du Cadran winner El Badr for 17,000 guineas,
the Poule d'Essai des Poulains winner In Fijar for 36,000 dollars, the top miler
Hilal for 9,000 guineas, the smart colts Ya Zaman and Moulouki for 20,000
dollars and 20,000 guineas respectively and the triple pattern-race winner
Nemr for 84,000 guineas. He also bought Dragon for about £65,000 shortly

Prix Morny, Deauville—Green Forest reverses Prix Robert Papin
placings with Maelstrom Lake (No. 2); River Lady is third
and British-trained Tender King fourth

before the colt won the 1979 Grand Criterium but surely his best buy so far has been Green Forest, the top French two-year-old of 1981 who cost no more than 100,000 dollars at the Fasig-Tipton Kentucky Selected Summer Yearling Sales.

It's not unusual for a French two-year-old to win two of the four Group 1 juvenile events for which colts are eligible, the Prix Robert Papin, the Prix Morny, the Prix de la Salamandre and the Grand Criterium. Indeed no fewer than fifteen have achieved the feat since 1950. However, to win more than two of the four legs calls not only for outstanding merit but also for a high degree of versatility; the races range in distance from five and a half furlongs to a mile; two are run on a straight course, the other two round a bend; and the series frequently demands an ability to act on any going, since the first two races take place in the summer and the other two in the autumn. Only My Swallow and Blushing Groom have ever succeeded in sweeping the board and until Green Forest came along in 1981 the only other colts to win as many as three of the four in the last thirty years were Grey Dawn and Irish River.

It was only by half a length that Green Forest failed to win all four. The race he lost was the Robert Papin at Maisons-Laffitte in July which marked his third meeting in as many races with the Irish-bred Maelstrom Lake. The pair had made their first appearance early in May on the same course in the aptly-named Prix de Debut, a four-furlong dash which is the first non-claiming race for two-year-olds on the Paris tracks. The pair outclassed their nine opponents, with victory going narrowly to Green Forest. It was a different story when the pair met again two months later in the Prix du Bois at Longchamp, the race going to Maelstrom Lake by a length and a half with Green Forest only fourth, beaten just over four lengths. Green Forest dropped out quickly from the distance and his disappointing display was attributed to his having run far too freely in the early stages. Fresh tactics were employed in the Papin. Gibert held Green Forest up, as the unbeaten Italian filly Grease disputed the lead with the Prix du Bois third Pampabird. Maelstrom Lake was also ridden more patiently than previously but whereas he started to challenge fully two and a half furlongs from home, Green Forest didn't appear on the scene until the closing stages. So strongly did Green Forest finish that he managed to snatch second place from Grease by half a length, giving some the impression he would have won had he started his challenge earlier.

If Green Forest was slightly unlucky at Maisons-Laffitte fortune certainly

Prix de la Salamandre, Longchamp—Green Forest wins from Zino

smiled on him when he took his revenge in the Prix Morny at the Deauville meeting in August. None of the eight other runners in the Papin took on Maelstrom Lake and Green Forest again, leaving the French filly River Lady and two challengers from England, the Richmond Stakes winner Tender King and the maiden Gavo, to make up the field of five. River Lady had been so impressive in her first two races, trotting up in a newcomers event at Chantilly and then cantering over five colts in Deauville's Prix de Cabourg, that she was made odds on for the Morny; Tender King was also preferred to the French colts. Unfortunately the race became rather rough despite there being only five runners. The first to suffer was Tender King, hampered by Maelstrom Lake soon after the start, but he had plenty of time to recover since the early pace set by Gavo was slow. Soon after halfway Green Forest moved through into the lead with River Lady looking very dangerous. While Green Forest was fighting off River Lady, Maelstrom Lake was running into all sorts of trouble, first of all trying to challenge between the two leaders and then finding his way blocked when switched to the rails. It was only inside the final furlong that Maelstrom Lake managed to find an opening and by then it was too late. Green Forest held him off by three quarters of a length with River Lady only a head away third and Tender King a further length behind in fourth place.

It was hoped that a re-match of the colts in the Prix de la Salamandre at Longchamp in September would show whether Green Forest had indeed been a lucky winner of the Morny, but unfortunately Maelstrom Lake was withdrawn shortly before the race because of the soft going. Even then Green Forest didn't start favourite. Preferred to him was Zino, a stable-companion of River Lady who had won his last two races by five lengths. Also well fancied was the most attractive filly Exclusive Order who had shown a bright turn of foot to win the Prix du Calvados, a Group 3 event, on her latest start. Making up the field were the English-trained Beldale Bid, recent winner of the valuable Grand Criterium International d'Ostende, and the dual winner Star Princess who looked rather out of her depth. Zino quickly went into the lead, setting a fast pace, while Green Forest threatened to repeat his Prix du Bois performance, proving very hard to settle and throwing his head about until tucked in behind another horse. With Zino still apparently coasting on the bridle early in the straight Green Forest looked to have a hard battle on his hands, especially as his struggle with his jockey must, one would have thought, have taken something out of him. However, he moved up impressively to challenge below the distance and maintained his effort to the line to beat Zino going away by a length and a half. Zino subsequently won the valuable Criterium de Maisons-Laffitte.

The French punters had evidently learnt their lesson, and when Green Forest met a strong foreign challenge in the Grand Criterium at Longchamp three weeks later they at last made him favourite. Second choice was the three-length Royal Lodge winner Norwick, a much-improved colt from the same stable as the last Grand Criterium winner Recitation. Also at less than 10/1 were the Group 3 Prix La Rochette winner Persepolis, coupled with his pacemaker Pushkin; the second English-trained colt, Triple Axel, who had beaten both Wind and Wuthering and Busaco last time out; the Prix Eclipse runner-up Rollins; and the unbeaten Irish challenger Anfield, with two pattern-race wins already to his name. Norwick, who had made all in the Royal Lodge, this time allowed the pacemaker to do the donkey work until moving ahead a furlong before the turn into the straight. Also well placed at this stage were Green Forest,

362

Anfield and Triple Axel; but Triple Axel was done with soon afterwards and it was clear fully two furlongs out that Anfield was also in trouble. It was equally clear that Green Forest was still full of running. He quickly took Norwick's measure at the distance, despite hanging to his right for a moment, and only one crack of the whip was needed to make him stride away in excellent style. He won by two and a half lengths from Norwick, showing great enthusiasm and determination. The others were all soundly beaten off, with Rollins running on to take third place, beaten six and a half lengths. It takes a top-class colt to beat Norwick so easily on soft ground and, as the winner's trainer said after the race, Green Forest is 'vraiment un crack'.

	Shecky Greene (b 1970)	Noholme II (ch 1956)	Star Kingdom
			Oceana
		Lester's Pride (b 1957)	Model Cadet
Green Forest (USA)			Meadow Flower
(ch.c. Feb 18, 1979)	Tell Meno Lies (gr 1971)	The Axe (gr 1958)	Mahmoud
			Blackball
		Filatonga (b 1960)	Count of Honor
			Blarney Castle

Some observers were surprised that Green Forest improved each time he tackled a longer distance. No doubt their surprise stems from the fact that his sire Shecky Greene is usually referred to as the champion sprinter of 1973, but it must be remembered that the Americans' idea of a sprinter doesn't entirely coincide with the European definition. Dr Patches, the co-champion American sprinter of 1976, ended that season winning a stakes race over a mile and a quarter. Although primarily a very fast horse Shecky Greene wasn't without a degree of stamina. All the eleven victories he gained after his two-year-old days were over six furlongs or more and besides winning the Fountain of Youth Stakes over eight and a half furlongs he equalled the Gulfstream Park track record for seven furlongs when beating Forego in the Hutcheson Stakes. He is now proving a prolific sire of two-year-old winners, with no fewer than fourteen representing him in 1981. Incidentally both Shecky Greene and Nodouble, the leading American sire of 1981, are sons of the top Australian horse Noholme II.

Green Forest is the second foal of Tell Meno Lies, a winner over five furlongs and a mile in the States. Her previous foal Honest and True (by Mr Leader) was also a very smart animal at around a mile, winning the Fair Ground Oaks as well as finishing third in the Kentucky Oaks, so the purchaser of Tell Meno Lies' third foal, a yearling colt by Full Pocket, seems to have secured a bargain at only 55,000 dollars. Filatonga, the grandam, won only one of her fifty-four starts but bred five winners in all, including the minor stakes winners Emerald Landing and Energy Boy. Filatonga's grandam, Bold Irish, is also the grandam of the brilliant American filly Ruffian and the high-class animals Castle Forbes, Icecapade and Buckfinder.

Green Forest stayed a mile extremely well at two, but it's doubtful whether he'll stay beyond a mile and a quarter, if he stays as far as that. His best chance of classic success therefore lies in either the Poule d'Essai des Poulains or the Two Thousand Guineas. Although the former race was initially said to be his target, preceded by a warm-up race in the Prix de Fontainebleau, later reports suggested that the Guineas hadn't been completely ruled out. Much as we would love to see a clash between the front-running Wind and Wuthering and the strong-finishing Green Forest at Newmarket, we don't really expect it: the Poulains is at Green Forest's mercy, and there's his temperament to consider. He has a reputation

Grand Criterium, Longchamp—Green Forest gains his third Group 1 victory, defeating British challenger Norwick

Mr M. Fustok's "Green Forest" (A. Gibert)

for being nervous. Apart from pulling hard in both the Prix du Bois and the Salamandre Green Forest gave little indication in his races of being highly strung but his connections went to great lengths to keep him calm before his last three races. He never appeared in the paddock at Deauville, being led around near the stables instead, and he was taken directly onto the track after being mounted at the last minute; before the Salamandre he came into the paddock with a lad leading him on either side, after being mounted in the stables; and spectators hardly had a chance to see him before the Grand Criterium when the latter routine was followed. Apart from this Green Forest has everything one hopes to see in a top-class colt. He races most genuinely, acts on any going and in addition to being a very attractive individual he's an excellent mover. He looks certain to make a formidable three-year-old. *M. Saliba, France.*

GREEN KASH 2 ch.c. Kashiwa 115–Kelly Green (Kelly 122) (1981 5fg) — Mar 18; 8,600Y; half-brother to several winners, including very useful 5f to 1m winner Super Kelly (by Supreme Sovereign); dam won over 5f at 2 yrs in Ireland; unquoted when last of 11 in maiden race won by dead-heaters Town Special and Sussex Queen at Lingfield in July. *P. Haslam.*

GREEN MEADOWS INN 2 b.c. Saulingo 122–Just Alice (Worden II 129) — (1981 5v 5g 5f) of no account. *Mrs A. Bell.*

GREEN MEMORY (USA) 3 ch.f. Forli–Memory Lane 100 (Never Bend) **71** (1980 6f 9d⁴ 7d² 1981 10s³ 9s 10s² 10.2g 10.2d³ 10.2d² 12f³ 10.2f² 12.2g* 12f² 10.1g² 10fg³ 10.2d³ 12.2g*) rather lightly-made, useful-looking filly; won maiden race at Catterick in July and apprentice race on same course in October (trotted up from Kenny O' Reilly); placed in varied company on most other starts and would have beaten Crimson Royale in minor event at Windsor in August on eleventh start if her apprentice rider hadn't mistaken the winning post; stays 1½m; acts on any going; blinkered fifth start (tended to hang); sometimes starts slowly; one paced; tough and consistent. *I. Balding.*

GREENSWARD BLAZE 2 ch.f. Sagaro 133–Urugano 101 (Buisson Ardent — 129) (1981 6fg 6g 6fg 7.6s) Apr 5; half-sister to 1¼m to 13f winner Stormy Princess (by Ballymoss) and a winning plater; dam middle-distance winner;

behind in maiden and minor events; likely to need 1½m+ to show what ability she may possess. *M. Blanshard.*

GREENWOOD BOY 2 b.g. Immortal Love–Parky (Delaunay 100) (1981 — 5d 5d⁴ 6fg 8g) Apr 20; small gelding; bad plater. *D. Leslie.*

GREENWOOD LADY 2 ch.f. Malinowski 123–Chantry Pearl (Gulf Pearl 117) **75** (1981 5d* 5s* 5fg³ 5d³ 5g² 6g³ 6g 5s) Feb 18; IR 6,200Y; well-made filly; half-sister to fairly useful 5f and 7f winner Jewelled Turban (by Mansingh); dam of little account; won maiden race at Nottingham in April by 1½ lengths from Martini Time; had previously finished second to Hello Cuddles in minor event at Doncaster but was awarded race 3 months later after winner failed her dope test; placed in minor events on 4 of her next 5 starts but was off course over 2 months before finishing last of 13 in nursery on final appearance; suited by 6f; seems to act on any going; sometimes wears a tongue-strap. *G. Hunter.*

GREENWOOD STAR 4 gr.c. No Mercy 126–Golden Palermo 70 (Dumbarnie **100** 125) (1980 8fg 8.2f* 7f² 8.2fg* 10.5g 8d 1981 8d 8g* 8s 8f² 7fg 7f) strong, robust colt; useful handicapper; ran on gamely to beat Glowing Tan a neck in Jubilee Stakes at Kempton in May; caught close home when neck second of 20 to Teamwork in Royal Hunt Cup at Royal Ascot; not certain to stay 1¼m; needs a sound surface; is sometimes rather slow into his stride; finished lame final start (July). *G. Hunter.*

GRENADIER 2 b.g. Queen's Hussar 124–Carrigeen 94 (Royalty 130) (1981 — 5d 5.8g) Apr 11; robust, useful-looking gelding; first foal; dam won 4 times from 1¼m to 1¾m; in rear in maiden races at Newbury in April and Bath (16/1, still not fully wound up) in June; gelded subsequently. *W. Wightman.*

GRESTEXPORT 4 ch.f. Porto Bello 118–Philanderess (Philemon 119) (1980 — 8g 8d² 7fg 8f 10fg 9s* 8.2s 8.2v 1981 10f 10f 9d) strong filly; plater; probably stays 1¼m; acts on soft going; inconsistent. *K. Morgan.*

GREY ACE 2 ro.g. Grey Ghost 98–Mary McQuaker 82 (Acer 123) (1981 5g — § 6f 7fg) Apr 4; leggy, light-framed gelding; temperamental plater; wears blinkers; started slowly first 2 outings; had tongue tied down third start. *H. Bell.*

Jubilee Stakes, Kempton—the grey Greenwood Star runs on gamely to beat Glowing Tan

GREY AT LAST 3 gr.f. Copte–Marie Denise 68 (Dual 117) (1980 5f 6fg 6d — 1981 10g) compact filly; unquoted when in rear in maiden and minor events; will need a test of stamina. *C. Spares.*

GREY EAGLE 5 gr.g. Warpath 113–Whisky Lima 82 (Midsummer Night II — 117) (1980 13.8fg 16d 20.4g 14.7d⁴ 1981 15g 15fg) big, strong gelding; poor staying maiden. *T. Craig.*

GREY GATE 4 gr.g. Grey Mirage 128–Contentment (Nulli Secundus 89) — (1980 NR 1981 14d 8s) good sort; second in private sweepstakes at Plumpton in May; well beaten both starts on flat. *D. Underwood.*

GREY GEM 2 gr.f. Zeddaan 130–Ming Vase 84 (Princely Gift 137) (1981 **57** 5s² 5g 5g⁴ 5f) Mar 26; 5,400F; lengthy, unfurnished filly; half-sister to minor winners here and abroad; dam 2-y-o 5f winner; plating-class sprint maiden; best form on a sound surface. *T. Fairhurst.*

GREY GREEN 2 b. or br.c. Sit In The Corner–Bollin Charlotte 79 (Immortality) **63** (1981 6f 7fg 7.2fg 7f 7.2v³ 8d) May 7; smallish, lightly-made, short-backed colt; half-brother to 2 winners, including Immortal Knight (by Midsummer Night II), useful winner at up to 9f; dam a miler; plater; should stay 1m; suited by heavy going; blinkered last 2 outings; sold 500 gns Doncaster October Sales. *M. H. Easterby.*

GREY HUNTER 3 gr. or ro.c. Warpath 113–Janabelle 101 (Gentle Art 121) **66** (1980 5h 5fg 7s³ 7d³ 7g 7fg 6g 8d 1981 12g 12d 12.5f 13fg³ 16.1f² 14d³ 16.5g) tall, rather leggy, narrow colt; placed in handicaps, at Haydock in July being outbattled and beaten a neck by Thahul; stays well; acts on any going; blinkered second outing in 1980; ran poorly final start. *E. Eldin.*

GREY LINE 2 ch.g. Run The Gantlet–Grey Shoes 104 (Grey Sovereign 128§) — (1981 8g 10s) May 4; 8,800Y; tall, rangy gelding; has been hobdayed; third foal; half-brother to Irish 1½m winner Shoemender (by Busted); dam sprinter; unquoted when out of first 10 in large fields of maidens at Newmarket (green) and Nottingham (dwelt) in October; retained 660 gns Newmarket Autumn Sales. *A. Hide.*

GREY MERCY 2 gr.c. No Mercy 126–Queens To Open 75 (Darius 129) (1981 **86** 5d³ 5s 5g* 6g⁴ 6f⁴ 7.2f² 7fg² 6d² 7f 7fg⁴ 8.2s 7s) Apr 30; 2,100Y; leggy, long-striding colt; good walker; brother to 2 winners, including useful 5f to 1m winner No Cards, and half-brother to 3 winners: dam won at 1m; won 10-runner maiden race at Thirsk in May by a head from Run Like Mad; creditable second 3 times afterwards, final occasion when going down by a neck to Knight Security under top weight in nursery at Haydock in August; seemed to find 1m just too far for him at 2 yrs; acts on any going; tough and consistent. *S. Mellor.*

GREY MOUNTAIN 8 gr.g. Town Crier 119–Abernette 102 (Abernant 142) **70** (1980 12d⁴ 12s* 13s* 12d 13.3fg 12d⁴ 12s 13s⁴ 12v 1981 12s² 12s 12fg 12d* 12g⁴ 12d 12f³ 12s 10.6s 12d) moderate handicapper; won at Brighton in April; stays 13f; acts on any going, but revels in the mud; usually held up; good mount for an apprentice. *P. Kelleway.*

GREY RIVER 2 gr.c. Rapid River 127–Titre 74 (Vigo 130) (1981 6f 7.2v **57** 7g⁴) May 22; ninth produce; dam won over 6f; poor plater; sold 360 gns Doncaster November Sales. *A. Gillam.*

GREY WATTY 3 gr.c. Runnymede 123–Lucy Jane (Palestine 133) (1980 — 6g 5d 1981 7fg 10.1fg 8.3fg) workmanlike colt; poor plater; blinkered final start; sold 480 gns Ascot November Sales. *S. Matthews.*

GRID 5 b. or br.g. Track Spare 125–Jacine 72 (Owen Tudor) (1980 12f 18fg — 12d 1981 16s) neat gelding; has shown no form on flat for a long time, including in a valuable seller; stays 1½m; acts on any going; has worn blinkers; sold 5,000 gns Ascot June Sales. *M. H. Easterby.*

GRIMA 4 b. or br.c. Rheingold 137–Ravie (Relko 136) (1980 10fg 10.5d⁴ 12g — 10fg³ 12g 1981 11s⁴) strong, lengthy colt; quite a moderate maiden; will be suited by 1¾m. *I. Dudgeon.*

GRINALDA 3 b.f. Brigadier Gerard 144–Cranberry Sauce 119 (Crepello 136) — (1980 NR 1981 10fg 8fg) tall, lengthy, unfurnished filly; half-sister to 5 winners, including very smart 1m to 1¼m filly Sauceboat (by Connaught); dam best 1¼m filly of 1967; showed signs of ability in maiden races at Sandown in April and Warwick in June; dead. *P. Cole.*

GRINGA 3 b.f. Morston 125–Teesdale 97 (Aggressor 130) (1980 7g 1981 10d **71** 12f 10fg* 10fg 10d⁴ 10fg 10f³ 10d² 10d) lightly-made filly; beat Banknote by

6 lengths in maiden event at Lingfield in July; well beaten in an amateur riders race next time out but ran creditably afterwards; should stay 1½m; yet to race on very soft going but acts on any other; sold 2,100 gns Newmarket Autumn Sales. *G. Harwood.*

GROAT 3 b.c. Connaught 130–Grisbi 96 (Grey Sovereign 128§) (1980 NR 1981 12fg³ 12.3fg*) big, good-topped colt; brother to fairly useful 1½m winner Bagshot, and half-brother to quite useful 1½m winner Greats (by Great Nephew); dam, winner over 1m, is half-sister to smart middle-distance stayer Rouser; showed signs of inexperience and didn't have clearest of runs when 4½ lengths third to Bronze Medal in 14-runner maiden race at Newbury in August (short-priced favourite, despite not looking fully wound up); landed the odds by ¾ length from Imperial Amber without coming off a tight rein in 3-runner minor event at Newcastle later in month on only subsequent start; will stay beyond 1½m; acts on a firm surface, but has a rather high knee action and may prove suited by some give underfoot. *B. Hobbs.* **73**

GROOVY GIRL 4 b.f. Averof 123–Brass Finisher 93 (Cash and Courage 116) (1980 10s 7fg² 7g 8fg 7g 10s 10.2v* 1981 10.2d 12v⁴ 12g 11.7v 10f 11s 8g) strong filly; showed improved form to win handicap at Doncaster in 1980; soundly beaten in similar events at 4 yrs; appears not to stay 1½m; probably needs some give in the ground and acts well on heavy going; blinkered fourth start. *R. Boss.* —

GROUCHO 4 ch.g On Your Mark 125–Helen Maire (Queen's Hussar 124) (1980 NR 1981 8g 8g 8g* 10f 10fg² 11.7fg 12g⁴ 10g) 5,000 3-y-o; lightly-made gelding; plater; favourite when winning at Edinburgh in June (bought in 2,500 gns); stays 1¼m; yet to race on a soft surface; sold to T. Craig 2,000 gns Doncaster November Sales. *N. Callaghan.* **53**

GROWING WILD 2 b. or br.f. Free State 125–Crab Apple (Nelcius 133) (1981 7d 7.6s) Apr 5; lengthy, workmanlike filly; third foal; dam unraced daughter of very useful 1962 2-y-o Tzigane; not disgraced in maiden races, running on to be sixth of 18 to Sans Blague at Newbury in September and finishing 7 lengths fifth of 13 to Sandwalker at Lingfield the following month; will stay 1¼m. *R. Baker.* **74**

GRYLOS 3 b.g. Dubassoff–Nevilles Cross 67 (Nodouble) (1980 6d 6g 10.2s 1981 7g 14g 16g 15.5fg 6f 10f 7f) useful sort; good walker; behind in varied company, including selling; last in an amateur riders handicap when blinkered sixth start. *O. Jorgensen.* —

GRYSBOK 2 b.f. Legal Eagle 126–Duiker 81 (Sovereign Lord 120) (1981 5f 5fg 5fg 5.8f) May 14; third foal; half-sister to modest 1980 2-y-o Gemsbok (by Redundant); dam won over 5f at 2 yrs; behind in maiden races; sold 380 gns Ascot August Sales. *C. V. Miller.* —

GUARDIAN 4 ch.g. Home Guard 129–Orina 84 (Amber Rama 133) (1980 NR 1981 6d) 1,600 2-y-o; 25/1, always behind when last of 10 to King of Spain in £4,900 event at Thirsk in May; sold 420 gns Newmarket Autumn Sales. *R. Sheather.* —

GUARDIAN (USA) 2 ch.c. Tom Rolfe–Duchess of Malfi (Prince John) (1981 8s⁴) Apr 10; $155,000F; $300,000Y; third produce; half-brother to 1½m winner Musketeer's Motto (by One For All) and a winner in USA; dam, winner over 9f at 4 yrs, is sister to Alleged's dam Princess Pout; 6/4 favourite for 28-runner maiden race at the Curragh in November but faded a little in closing stages to finish 4 lengths fourth to Condell; will stay 1½m; sure to do better. *V. O'Brien, Ireland.* **80** p

GUERRIER (USA) 2 b.c. Forli–Brown Hare (Coursing) (1981 6s) well-made colt; half-brother to French 1¼m winner La Chaize (by Graustark) and a winner in USA; dam unraced half-sister to high-class colts Unconscious, Avatar and Monseigneur; 11/1 and rather backward, never dangerous when remote sixth of 15 to Ellerne in maiden race at Newbury in October; quite a nice sort who should improve over further in 1982. *F. J. Houghton.* — p

GUEST SPEAKER 2 ch.c. Honoured Guest 113–Spring Gipsy 75 (Sky Gipsy 117) (1981 7fg 7g) Apr 25; 7,000Y; well-grown, attractive colt; good mover; half-brother to 1976 2-y-o 5f winner Gipsy Maramick and good Brazilian winner Miss Welsh (both by Mummy's Pet) and to another winner abroad; dam placed over 6f at 2 yrs; showed a little ability when sixth in sizeable fields of maidens at Salisbury and Newmarket in second half of season; will stay 1m; has scope and may improve at 3 yrs. *G. Harwood.* —

GULF PALM 3 ch.c. Gulf Pearl 117–Oriental Palm (Royal Palm 131) (1980 — 5d 6g⁴ 7d 8g 7fg 8d 1981 5s 10d⁴ 12g 12g 12d) neat colt; only poor form in 1981; running on when tried at 1¼m and wasn't disgraced; blinkered fifth start in 1980. *R. Smyth.*

GUN 4 b.c. Ribero 126–Mafia (Milesian 125) (1980 12g 10f³ 12f 14v 12s 1981 — 9s 13d 8f 7fg³ 8.2f 8d 7g) ex-Irish colt; poor maiden on flat though has won over hurdles; stays 1¼m; suited by a sound surface; blinkered final start. *R. Fisher.*

GUSTY'S GIFT 7 ch.g. Divine Gift 127–Gusty Girl 71 (Darling Boy 124) **73** (1980 5s 6g² 6fg 7fg⁴ 7h 5.8fg³ 7d⁴ 6g 6g³ 6fg 7g* 7f³ 6g 7g 1981 7d* 7g 7d³ 8f 6f 7f 7f³ 7h 7g⁴ 6fg 7s²) lengthy, good-topped gelding; good mover; made all to beat Gimri 2 lengths in handicap at Salisbury in May; suited by 7f; acts on any going but is well suited by top-of-the-ground; sometimes blinkered but is effective without; goes well for an apprentice. *P. Cole.*

GUSTY SOMERS 10 b.g. Will Somers 114§–Gusty Girl 71 (Darling Boy 124) — (1980 NR 1981 12f) of little account. *B. Richmond.*

GUYWOOD 3 b.g. Tudor Rhythm 112–Smokey Dawn 68 (March Past 124) — (1980 5g 8fg 7s 1981 8fg 8.3fg 8fg) lengthy gelding; behind in varied company, including selling. *P. M. Taylor.*

GWYNFI NI 5 b.h. Joshua 129–March Fairy (March Past 124) (1980 8s 10fg — 12.2s 16.1d 10d 12fg 16f 1981 13fg 18.8fg 12f 11.5d 12g) useless. *K. Bridgwater.*

GYMER 3 ch.g. Crowned Prince 128–Anadyomene 101 (Sea Hawk II 131) — (1980 6d 6g 6g 1981 12g) strong, workmanlike gelding; well beaten, including when badly drawn in a valuable seller as a 2-y-o; sold 1,750 gns Newmarket Autumn Sales. *A. Bailey.*

GYPSY CASTLE 7 ch.h. Habitat 134–Romany 87 (King's Bench 132) (1980 **68** 8fg² 8d* 8d³ 8g³ 8g 1981 8fg 8d⁴ 8g 8fg⁴ 8d⁴ 8fg 8.3g 8fg) moderate handicapper; stays 1¼m; acts on any going; gives impression that he needs strong handling nowadays; tends to get behind in early stages and is suited by an uphill finish. *J. Winter.*

GYPSY DANCER (FR) 6 gr.g. Dancer's Image–La Tzigane (Barbare II 128) **112** (1980 6f* 6f² 5f* 6g 5fg³ 6s³ 6d 6v 1981 5g² 5g² 6d 6g⁴ 5fg* 6fg) strong, useful-looking gelding; not a good mover in his slower paces; very useful performer; held on by ½ length from Geary's For Strip in £2,300 race at Beverley in June; runner-up earlier in Field Marshal Stakes at Haydock (2 lengths behind King of Spain) and Palace House Stakes at Newmarket (came with a strong run in final furlong when beaten 3 lengths by Standaan); stays 7f but is best at sprint distances; acts on any going; game and genuine; winner in USA. *W. O'Gorman.*

GYPSY WOMAN 2 ch.f. Gay Fandango 132–Milosun 79 (Milesian 125) (1981 — 7.2d 7.2fg 8fg) Jan 14; 4,500Y; sturdy filly; half-sister to very useful 1973 Irish 2-y-o 5f and 6f winner Milly Whiteway (by Great White Way); dam ran only at 2 yrs; backward when in rear in maiden races. *N. Tinkler.*

GYVELD 3 ch.c. Manacle 123–Mow Meadow (Acropolis 132) (1980 5g 6fg³ 7fg — 1981 10d 11.7g 10f) workmanlike colt; no form in 1981, including in a seller on final start (blinkered). *T. Marshall.*

H

HABALOOK 4 gr.c. Habat 127–Private View 74 (Derring-Do 131) (1980 6s³ — 6d 5f⁴ 7fg 6g 5g³ 5fg* 6s* 6s 1981 6s 5d⁴ 5g 6g 6g 6d 8g 8g 8f 8fg 7g 6g) big, strong colt; has been hobdayed and tubed; plater; best at sprint distances; acts on any going; suitable mount for a boy; wears blinkers. *H. Bell.*

HABATASHIE 3 gr.f. Habat 127–Shenachie 79 (Sheshoon 132) (1980 5fg³ — 5g 6d 6d 1981 7s 6g 6g⁴ 6g 7fg 8fg 7f) strong filly; plating-class maiden; has run creditably in blinkers. *W. Wharton.*

HAB DANCER 3 b.c. Habitat 134–Come Dancing 91 (Northern Dancer) **75** (1980 7d 7d 8g 1981 5g³ 6.5g 8d 5s 5s 6fg 6g⁴ 6d³ 7d 6f* 7f² 7f* 5fg⁴ 6f 6fg) strong, heavy-bodied colt; won handicaps at Ripon in June and Leicester in July despite looking ungenuine and a far from easy ride; superbly ridden when getting home by a short head from Hanham Road on latter course; seems to need further than 5f and stays 7f; acts on firm going; sometimes blinkered (wasn't when successful); well beaten last 2 starts (lost chance by rearing in stalls on first occasion). *R. Armstrong.*

HABELLA 3 b.f. Habitat 134-Galana (Reform 132) (1980 NR 1981 6fg 8g⁴ **82** 8fg 6f² 6g³ 6fg 6v* 6d 7d*) 106,000Y; smallish, quite attractive filly; good walker; first foal; dam, half-sister to Derby runner-up Cavo Doro, won over 1¼m and 1½m in Ireland; won minor event at York in October (easily, revelling in the testing conditions) and handicap at Leicester in November (by ¾ length from Corn Street when ridden by 7-lb claimer); ran moderately in between; stays 1m; ran rather disappointingly in blinkers third start; sold 41,000 guineas Newmarket December Sales. *M. Stoute.*

HABILLE 3 ch.f. On Your Mark 125-Lake Constance 85 (Star Gazer 123) — (1980 6s 5fg 1981 5d 5fg 5.3f 5g) lightly-made filly; poor maiden; well beaten in blinkers final start; sold 400 gns Ascot October Sales. *M. Masson.*

HABITOR 3 ch.c. Habitat 134-Daphne 106 (Acropolis 132) (1980 5f 5f² 7g³ 8g **85** 1981 7fg⁴ 8g² 8f⁴ 8fg 10fg 10.6d* 10.1fg² 10g³) strong, well-made, quite attractive colt; eventually got off mark in maiden event at Haydock in August, beating Wise Owl in nice style by 3 lengths; in frame most other outings, running particularly well when strong-finishing fourth of 18 behind impressive winner Olympic Glory in Britannia Stakes (Handicap) at Royal Ascot on third start and third to Liberated in handicap at Leicester in September; suited by 1¼m; hasn't always looked entirely genuine; blinkered nowadays; sold 11,500 gns Newmarket Autumn Sales. *R. Hern.*

HABOOB (USA) 2 b.c. Graustark-Angenora (Two Relics) (1981 7f 7g 7g) — May 3; $190,000Y; smallish, strong, quite attractive colt; second foal; dam stakes winner of 16 races at up to 1m from 2 yrs to 5 yrs; showed a little ability on first outing but was subsequently well beaten in large fields for maiden events at Leicester and Newmarket; bred to stay 1¼m+. *F. J. Houghton.*

HABUS 3 b.c. Habitat 134-Rebus 97 (Busted 134) (1980 NR 1981 10s 10d⁴ **73** 10.2f* 12f³ 14fg³ 14g) 70,000Y; compact colt; fourth foal; brother to very useful Irish 7f and 1m winner Habitus; dam stayed well; won maiden race at Doncaster in June by 1½ lengths from Majieda; third behind Fair of Face in minor event at Ripon and behind Dragon Palace in handicap at Goodwood, both in July, staying on well from back of field and showing improved form in latter; stays 1¾m; acts on firm going; apprentice ridden when successful; ran poorly final start, dropping out quickly in straight. *C. Brittain.*

HACKBRIDGE 6 gr.h. Levanter 121-Signal Melody 70 (Bleep-Bleep 134) — (1980 7fg 7.6f 8d 7g 7.6d 8.3s 8g 10g³ 10g 8d 1981 8.3g) only plating class nowadays; stays 1m. *T. Gosling.*

HADAJAR 6 b.g. Royalty 130-Sea Gal (Sea Hawk II 131) (1980 12d 12d² 12d **48** 1981 16.9s⁴ 18.8fg² 12.2s 12d⁴) strong gelding; suited by a test of stamina; acts on a firm and a soft surface. *M. Tate.*

HADDFAN 6 ch.g. Lorenzaccio 130-Golden Windlass 79 (Princely Gift 137) **66** (1980 7g³ 7.6f² 8f* 8d⁴ 8d* 8g² 8g 8g 10f⁴ 8.3fg 8fg 1981 8g 8f 8fg 8f* 8fg³ 8f⁴ 8.3g⁴) quite a moderate handicapper; returned to form when beating Monte Acuto by 1½ lengths at Brighton in July; stays 1¼m; acts on any going; suitable mount for an apprentice. *J. Dunlop.*

HADERA 6 ch.m. Northfields-Flat Impulse 75 (Meadow Court 129) (1980 8fg **58** 8fg 7fg 8g⁴ 8d 9f 8.3fg² 8.3f* 8.3fg 8d* 8.2s 1981 8fg 8.3fg 8h³ 8.3g 8.3g 8.3g² 10.8s 8g) quite a moderate handicapper; stays 1m; possibly not at her best on very soft ground but acts on any other; suitable mount for an apprentice. *B. Gubby.*

HADITOS 2 b.f. Averof 123-Peta's Bay 67 (I Say 125) (1981 5s 5fg³ 5.8g 6fg² **102** 5fg* 5g⁴ 5d* 5d⁴ 5fg²) Feb 22; 4,100Y; big, workmanlike filly; half-sister to 2 winners, including 1979 2-y-o 5f winner Repeat Performance (by Targowice); dam, half-sister to high-class Gold Rod, won over 7f; held off La Tourelle by a neck in 12-runner maiden event at Newcastle in June and made virtually all to beat Childown Blue by 2 lengths in nursery at Lingfield in August; also ran well when in frame in Star Stakes at Sandown on sixth start, Prince of Wales's Stakes at York on eighth and well-contested race at Salisbury on ninth, going down by 1½ lengths to Fairy Tern in last-named; stays 6f but has shown better form at 5f; acts on a firm and a soft surface; tough, genuine and consistent. *G. Beeson.*

HADLEY ROCKET 4 ro.g. Roan Rocket 128-Mockbridge 106 (Bleep-Bleep 134) — (1980 8g 8s 1981 8f 7g 5f) lengthy gelding; poor maiden; sold 560 gns Ascot September Sales. *R. Turnell.*

HAEMAVITE 2 b.c. Swing Easy 126–Katira 83 (Paveh 126) (1981 6d 6fg³ **73** 5s 6g) Apr 10; 2,000Y; workmanlike gelding; fourth foal; half-brother to a winner in Belgium; dam, half-sister to high-class sprinter Royben, won over 2m; quite moderate form in large fields for a maiden auction event and maiden races; will stay 1m; blinkered last 3 outings. *A. Jarvis.*

HAGEN QUEEN 2 b.f. Mount Hagen 127–Fenland Queen (King's Troop 118) **—** (1981 7v 7g) Mar 17; 6,400Y; fair sort; fourth foal; half-sister to 3 winners, including fairly useful 1977 2-y-o 7f winner Fosterfridge (by St Chad); dam never ran: 20/1 when remote sixth of 15 to My Destiny in £3,400 event at York in October; in rear in maiden race at Leicester later in month. *C. Crossley.*

HALE LANE 2 br.f. Comedy Star 121–King's Fillet (King's Bench 132) (1981 **59** 5s 6g³ 6fg 6fg 6fg 8.2fg 6g 7g) Feb 23; 1,000Y; compact, well-made filly; sister to a poor animal and half-sister to winning sprinter My Raff (by Raffingora); 1¼ lengths third of 15 to Sylvan Barbarosa in maiden auction event at Epsom in June; didn't reproduce that form, including in sellers; should stay beyond 6f. *T. M. Jones.*

HALLEL (USA) 2 b.c. Shecky Greene–Escondidas (Better Self) (1981 6fg 7g) **—** Mar 30; $30,000 2-y-o; lengthy colt; brother to a minor winner in USA, and half-brother to several other winners; dam 6f winner; well beaten in fairly useful maiden company at Goodwood in July and Newmarket (led 4f) in October. *R. Hannon.*

HALLO CHEEKY 5 ch.m. Flatbush 95–Artlight (Articulate 121) (1980 **42** 10.6fg 10f 10g 10g 10d² 1981 8v² 8.2g 10.6s 10f) plater; been tried in blinkers; acts on heavy going; has been tried in blinkers; has run respectably for an apprentice. *J. Fitzgerald.*

HALL'S TREASURE 7 b.g. Quisling 117–Aggyus 86 (Aggressor 130) (1980 **—** 12d 1981 12g) lightly raced and little worthwhile form since 1977. *W. Marshall.*

HALSBURY 3 b.c. Exbury 138–Wig and Gown (Mandamus 120) (1980 NR **102** 1981 9d* 10d² 12g* 12s³ 16f 16f* 15g² 21fg³ 15d* 18g*) big, well-made colt; half-brother to useful Freight Forwarder (by Calpurnius), a winner on flat and over hurdles, useful 1m winner Star Chamber (by Tower Walk) and to a winner in Austria; dam never ran; confirmed himself a useful young stayer when winning Tote Cesarewitch at Newmarket in October, getting up inside last to beat Heighlin by 1¼ lengths despite not having had the best of runs; had earlier won newcomers race at Wolverhampton in April and minor events at Thirsk in May, Chepstow in June and Ayr in September; also ran well on other occasions, including in Tennent Trophy at Ayr (short-head second to Jondi) and Goodwood Cup (4 lengths third to easy winner Ardross), both in July; stays very well; acts on any going; usually blinkered nowadays (wasn't at Chepstow); suited by strong handling. *P. Walwyn.*

Tote Cesarewitch Handicap, Newmarket—Halsbury wins the second leg of the 'autumn double' from Heighlin with the favourite Military Band third

Mr A. D. G. Oldrey's "Halsbury"

HAL'S JOY (USA) 2 b.c. L'Heureux–Majestic Flight (Majestic Prince) (1981 —
7fg 8d) Apr 28; $23,500Y; good-bodied colt; third foal; dam unraced half-
sister to 3 stakes winners; well beaten in maiden race at Newmarket in August
and minor event at Newbury the following month. *M. Jarvis.*

HALSTON 3 ch.g. Simbir 130–Yorkist (Crepello 136) (1980 7g 8d 1981 8f —
11g 11.7d 13.3s) tall, workmanlike gelding; soundly beaten in varied company;
should stay at least 11f. *P. Cundell.*

HAMMERTON PRIDE 5 b.g. Lineage 99–Claral Star 71 (Top Star 96) (1980 —
7d 7f 7f 8g 7s⁴ 6d 6g 7f 7f 6g 6s 8f 7d 1981 8fg) leggy gelding; plater; should
stay 1m; appears to act on any going; sometimes wears blinkers. *J. Harris.*

HAMPTON BAY 2 b.f. Habitat 134–Petocracy 102 (Petingo 135) (1981 **101**
5fg³ 5g* 7g) Mar 10; 26,000Y; big, powerful, deep-girthed filly; second foal;
dam, daughter of Italian Oaks winner Anticlea, stayed 1¼m; 13/8 favourite,
responded very genuinely to strong pressure to get up on line and beat Path
To Glory a head in £3,200 event at Ascot in September; 20/1, wasn't disgraced
when about 6 lengths sixth of 8 to Top Hope in Rockfel Stakes at Newmarket
the following month; will be suited by 1m; has a lot of scope and could well
make a useful 3-y-o. *R. Armstrong.*

HAMTRAMCH 2 gr.c. Saritamer 130–Pearl Haven 93 (Raffingora 130) (1981 **62**
5.1f 6fg 5d 5g) Apr 13; 1,750; leggy colt; first foal; dam 6f 2-y-o winner; about
7½ lengths fifth of 15 to Avonmore Wind in maiden event at Wolverhampton
in October on third outing, best effort; had stiff task in nursery next time;
sweated up second start. *G. Fletcher.*

HANABI 2 b.g. Hittite Glory 125–Derry Willow (Sunny Way 120) (1981 —
6h 7fg 6g 6g) Apr 16; 7,400F, 8,800Y; neat gelding; half-brother to 2 winning
platers and a winner in Belgium; dam middle-distance maiden; little sign of
ability in maiden races. *W. Wightman.*

371

HANAVA 3 b. or br.f. Some Hand 119–Ava (Aggressor 130) (1980 NR 1981 —
7g 6d 6d 5fg) plain filly; second foal; dam twice-raced half-sister to smart
middle-distance colt Arthur; towards rear in varied company, including selling.
R. Akehurst.

HAND OF GOD 5 ch.g. Green God 128–Man's Hand 65 (Golden Cloud) (1980 **41**
12fg 17.1fg 12fg² 15.8g* 12f 12f 16fg 1981 14s 15.5fg 15.8g³ 14.6f³ 15.8fg³
18.8fg) poor performer; had been fired; suited by a test of stamina; acted on
firm going; had worn blinkers; sometimes sweated up; had worn bandages; dead.
J. Yardley.

HAND-ROLLED 2 b.f. Sagaro 133–Self Satisfied 100 (Great Nephew 126) — p
(1981 6d) Mar 23; useful sort; good mover; second foal; dam a sprinter; 33/1
for maiden race at Leicester but showed a little promise in finishing seventh
of 22 to Late Hour, breaking smartly and disputing lead until lack of fitness
and experience told in closing stages; has scope and may do better in 1982.
W. Wightman.

HANDSOME BLAZE 6 b.g. Some Hand 119–Court Whisper 83 (Queen's **65**
Hussar 124) (1980 NR 1981 8.2g* 8g* 8f⁴ 8g 8.2g*) plater; bought in after
winning at Haydock in April (2,600 gns) and August (2,200 gns); won non-
selling handicap at Ayr in May; stays 1m; acts on any going but is suited by some
give in the ground; sweated up badly but ran respectably third start; taken
down early final outing. *C. Booth.*

HANDSOME HAZE 3 b.g. Some Hand 119–Noon Mist (Barbary Pirate 91) —
(1980 8d 7s 1981 10.1d 8fg) plain gelding; probably of little account. *R.
Blakeney.*

HANDSOME KID 5 b.g. Polyfoto 124–Helen Maire (Queen's Hussar 124) —
(1980 8d 10s 8g 7s 8.2s³ 8.2s 1981 10½g 8.3g 10g 10.2g) quite attractive gelding; modest handicapper at his best; well beaten in 1981; stays 1m; acts on
soft going; suitable mount for an apprentice; blinkered twice in 1980; usually
held up. *S. Harris.*

HANDSOME TRAILBOSS 3 ch.c. Some Hand 119–Cedez Cela (Bleep-Bleep **48**
134) (1980 5f³ 6d 7s 1981 7fg⁴ 7g 7g 8d² 7g 7f 8f 10f 9d 8f 10s⁴ 10d) workmanlike colt; plater; stays 1¼m; blinkered fifth start. *J. Douglas-Home.*

HANDYCUFF 9 b.g. Manacle 123–Black Rage 91 (My Babu 136) (1980 8d 8d **51**
10d³ 8f 8.2d 10.2g 8g³ 8.2s 8d³ 8s³ 1981 8d 9d 8g³ 9.4g 8fg 8g) tall gelding;
poor performer nowadays; stays 1¼m; acts on any going but is ideally suited by
an easy surface; has worn blinkers. *A. Scott.*

HANDY GRAY 3 gr.g. Grey Mirage 128–Ishka 58 (Tribal Chief 125) (1980 —
NR 1981 6fg 6s 6d 7fg 8fg 9d 8s 6d) 550Y; big, rangy gelding; second foal;
dam best at 5f; ran best race in a seller on third start; dwelt first outing. *R.
Cambidge.*

HANDYLAD 2 b.g. Mandamus 120–Rosie Crucian (Polkemmet 91) (1981 **76**
7fg 7d 7fg⁴ 7fg 8d) Apr 15; robust, good sort; brother to useful 1m and 1¼m
winner Mandrian and half-brother to a winner abroad; dam novice hurdler;
put up best effort when running on to finish 6¾ lengths fourth of 8 in minor event
won by Triple Axel at Epsom in September; should be well suited by 1m. *P.
Ashworth.*

HANG-ON ELVIS 6 br.g. Right Tack 131–Prairie Princess (Sayajirao 132) —
(1980 12g 10fg 11f 10f 11.7d 12g 11.7f⁴ 10f 10g 12g³ 12v³ 15d⁴ 1981 8s) disappointing handicapper nowadays; stays 15f; acts on any going; best in blinkers;
suited by strong handling; very slowly away only outing in 1981. *F. Durr.*

HANGSENG 9 b.g. Sing Sing 134–Miss Charisma 104 (Ragusa 137) (1980 —
8d 13g 15h² 15f* 13.3g² 17.1fg 13.1h 1981 12s 13s 15.5d 15.5d 10.8fg) poor
staying handicapper; refused to race most starts in 1981 and must be left alone;
has worn blinkers; trained part of season by W. Musson. *G. Fletcher.*

HANHAM ROAD 3 b.c. Shiny Tenth 120–Prompt Delivery (Catullus) (1980 **57**
5f²(dis) 5.8fg 6d 5d 1981 8.2s 7fg 7d 7d² 7s³ 8g² 8g⁴ 7fg 7f 7f² 10.8s 6d) lengthy
colt; placed in several handicaps; will be suited by a return to 1m; often blinkered,
but has run well without; dwelt but ran creditably in apprentice event final
start. *D. Marks.*

HANNONBALL 3 ch.g. Patch 129–Tudorella 104 (Tudor Minstrel 144) (1980 **58**
6g 1981 11s 10s² 11.7g 8.5d⁴ 10.1f 10f 10s²) big, strong gelding; second in
maiden race at Nottingham in April and seller at Lingfield in October; finds 1m

HAR

too short and should stay 1½m; possibly needs some give in the ground. *R. Hannon.*

HANOVER LAD 3 b.c. Continuation 120–Amber Anne (Amber X 133) (1980 5fg 5s 5f 8fg 6g 5d 1981 7v 12.2g 8g 7f) leggy, fair sort; bad plater; blinkered third outing at 2 yrs; unseated rider leaving stalls on final start; sold 410 gns Doncaster June Sales. *J. Hardy.* —

HANOVIA HAUT GIRL 3 b.f. Roman Warrior 132–Last Report 96 (Democratic 124) (1980 6g 5fg 7g 7g 5d 1981 6g 8fg) tall filly; showed some ability as a 2-y-o; evidently stays 7f. *M. Haynes.* —

HANS BRINKER 6 ch.g. Dike–Final Orders (Prince John) (1980 12s 12v 1981 18s 16s 18fg 16.1s 13.3g 17.1h) poor handicapper nowadays; stays well; probably acts on any going; blinkered second and third starts; trained part of season by G. Harwood. *I. Wardle.* —

HANS CRESCENT 3 ch.g. Dragonara Palace 115–Hi Tess 65 (Supreme Court 135) (1980 5.8fg³ 6s⁴ 6fg 6fg 7d 8g³ 8.2s 8d 8s 1981 7fg³ 6d 8.3d³ 10f³ 8g) leggy, lightly-made gelding; plater; best form at up to 1m; unsuited by really soft going; well beaten in blinkers. *J. Toller.* **54**

HANUMAN (FR) 3 ch.c. Giacometti 130–Stereo (Ribero 126) (1980 NR 1981 10.1fg 10.1g) first foal; dam won over 1¼m in France; in rear in minor events at Windsor in July and August. *C. Austin.* —

HA'PENNY CATCH 3 b.g. Ampney Prince 96–Moon Ray 62 (Halation 82) (1980 NR 1981 8fg) small, short-backed gelding; third foal; dam plater; unquoted, started slowly and was always behind when last of 21 behind Taken For Granted in maiden race at Newbury in July; sold 575 gns Ascot August Sales. *R. Armytage.* —

HA'PENNY NAP 3 br.g. Simbir 130–Strip Poker 70 (Raise You Ten 125) (1980 NR 1981 13fg⁴ 12f⁴) 1,900Y, resold 1,600Y and 2,400Y; plain gelding; second foal; dam plater; beaten a long way in small fields for minor events at Ayr in August and Hamilton in September. *H. Bell.* —

HAPPY BRIDE 3 b.f. Royal Match 117–Topping Girl (Sea Hawk II 131) (1980 6fg 6f⁴ 6g* 7g⁴ 7fg* 1981 7v³ 7s* 7g⁴ 8v 9g 8f² 10fg*) rangy, deep-bodied filly; second foal; half-sister to Irish 1979 2-y-o 7.5f winner Thread of Gold (by Huntercombe); dam never ran; successful in a £4,400 event at the Curragh in April and Pretty Polly Stakes on same course in June, in latter event being in no danger in last 2f and winning in good style by 3 lengths from Arctique Royale; also ran well when 4½ lengths fifth of 15 to Arctique Royale in Goffs Irish 1,000 Guineas at the Curragh in May and ½-length second to Tolmi in Coronation Stakes at Royal Ascot, particularly in latter (although flattered by her proximity); suited by 1¼m; acts on any going; reportedly sold privately for £1m and was sent to USA to be trained by L. Barrera. *J. Bolger, Ireland.* **116**

HAPPY WORKER 6 b.g. Workboy 123–Gypsy Refrain 86 (Romany Air 118) (1980 12fg 16f³ 14.7f* 15.8fg 16g 13.8f 15.8f 12d 12fg 12.2fg 16fg 1981 13.8g) big gelding; poor performer; suited by a test of stamina on a sound surface; does best when ridden up with the pace. *M. W. Easterby.* —

HAPPY YAPPY 4 b.g. Pieces of Eight 128–Junipero Serra 85 (Sing Sing 134) (1980 5v² 6s 8f 7f 5d 5fg 12g 1981 6s 6g 5g) strong, good-bodied gelding; has shown no form since first start at 3 yrs; unlikely to stay 1½m; acts on any going; has worn blinkers. *R. Carter.* —

HARBOUR (FR) 2 ch.f. Arctic Tern 126–Heres to You (Molvedo 137) (1981 8.5s³ 8s*) May 14; third reported foal: half-sister to successful French miler Heresty (by Tyrant); dam, French middle-distance winner, is granddaughter of Nasrina, the joint-top American 2-y-o filly of 1955; drew clear from distance to win 11-runner maiden race at Maisons-Laffitte in November by 4 lengths from Kazatska; the type to make a very useful middle-distance 3-y-o. *Mme C. Head, France.* **111**

HARD BOILED 2 gr.c. No Mercy 126–Bird in the Hand 82 (Major Portion 129) (1981 5s 6g 6g) Apr 30; 3,600F; lengthy colt; half-brother to 2 winners, including fairly useful stayer and hurdler Taffy (by Prince de Galles); dam won over 7f; seems of no account himself. *W. Holden.* —

HARDBRIDGE 3 b.c. So Blessed 130–Mockbridge 106 (Bleep-Bleep 134) (1980 5d⁴ 1981 6fg 10s 6f) attractive, well-made colt; creditable sixth to Barwin in maiden event at Nottingham in April and to Havon Cool in 25-runner handicap at Windsor in June; not certain to stay 1¼m. *R. Armstrong.* —

373

Prince of Wales's Stakes, Ascot—Hard Fought runs on strongly to beat Vielle with Magesterial third and Cracaval (far side) fourth

HARD FOUGHT 4 ch.c. Habitat 134–Ambrosia 102 (Alcide 136) (1980 7f³ **125** 7.2fg* 7g* 6d 7.3d³ 8g² 8fg⁴ 1981 9g* 10fg* 10fg* 10fg²(dis) 10.5g)

In 1980 Hard Fought had sufficient speed to win the seven-furlong Jersey Stakes at Royal Ascot but towards the end of the season he gave the impression that middle distances wouldn't be beyond him at four. So it proved. Campaigned at around a mile and a quarter Hard Fought improved and won three important races in the first half of the year before being found out in his sternest tests, the Coral Eclipse Stakes and the Benson and Hedges Gold Cup.

In none of his three successes did Hard Fought score by a wide margin but each time he won with authority, showing a turn of foot. The Earl of Sefton Stakes at Newmarket in April saw his always having the measure of Morayshire as they drew clear in the closing stages, eventually getting the verdict by half a length, while in the Westbury Stakes at Sandown later in the month he came with a steady run to cut Rankin down in the final furlong, winning by a length and a half with a backward Vielle the same distance away third. The Prince of Wales's Stakes at Royal Ascot has been won by some tip-top horses in recent years, notably Royal Palace, Connaught, Brigadier Gerard, Admetus and Ela-Mana-Mou. Hard Fought wasn't quite in the same league as they were but he still put up a good display to beat a field containing Cairn Rouge, favourite though having her first run for eight months, the consistent but rather exasperating Cracaval, the lightly-raced O'Brien colt Magesterial and Vielle. Always travelling comfortably, Hard Fought moved up to lead over a furlong out and ran on much too strongly for Vielle and Magesterial who were beaten three quarters of a length and the same. Cairn Rouge dropped out to be fifth after looking dangerous halfway up the straight.

A run in the Prince of Wales's Stakes is frequently used as a prelude to one in the Eclipse two and a half weeks later and Hard Fought duly went to Sandown to take on seven rivals including Master Willie, Vielle again and Madam Gay. It was not a happy race for him or his jockey, Swinburn. Sweating and coltish in the paddock, Hard Fought was held up in fourth as Master Willie took them along and he began to launch a serious challenge soon after they came round the final turn. At three he had shown a tendency to hang on occasions and unfortunately the Coral Eclipse saw his reverting to old habits with the result that he ended up on the far rail, Master Willie ahead of him and Vielle outside him. Swinburn was in a considerable dilemma during most of the last two furlongs as he attempted to get a run, for with Master Willie battling on resolutely and Vielle keeping on well despite edging in towards the rails Hard Fought was completely boxed in. Swinburn, whose riding of Centurius at Royal Ascot had earned him a suspension, threw caution to the winds about a hundred yards out, became involved in a barging match with Vielle and forced his way into second at the line, three quarters of a length behind Master Willie. At the inevitable stewards inquiry Hard Fought was disqualified and Swinburn's performance referred to the Stewards of the Jockey Club who suspended him for ten days. With a clear run Hard Fought would have been second

374

and it was bad luck for his owner and trainer that he was demoted. Hard Fought ran once more before being retired to the Baroda Stud in Ireland but he put up a below-par effort in the Benson and Hedges Gold Cup at York, finishing seventh to Beldale Flutter after hanging badly again, putting paid to the chances of Fingal's Cave in the process.

Hard Fought (ch.c. 1977)	Habitat (b 1966)	Sir Gaylord (b 1959)	Turn-to / Somethingroyal
		Little Hut (b 1952)	Occupy / Savage Beauty
	Ambrosia (ch 1965)	Alcide (b 1955)	Alycidon / Chenille
		Bride Elect (br 1952)	Big Game / Netherton Maid

Hard Fought in the Prince of Wales's Stakes was the first of four winners for the admirable Habitat at the Royal meeting, the others being Strigida, Feltwell and Marwell; another, Olympic Glory, is by Habitat's son Hittite Glory. Habitat's reputation and the popularity of his progeny at the Sales have never been greater. His exceptional record along with the impeccable distaff side of Hard Fought's pedigree explains why the latter was sold for some £2,000,000 in the autumn and will stand at IR £7,500 plus IR £7,500, almost twice the fee of Moorestyle, a far better racehorse. Ambrosia, successful over a mile at three, produced three winners before Hard Fought—the stayer Lotus Eater (by Le Levanstell) and the useful middle-distance handicappers London God (by Pall Mall) and St Briavels (by Sovereign Path)—and was a daughter of the second-best two-year-old filly of 1954, Bride Elect. This family keeps producing good horses—the 1981 Washington International winner Providential is out of a half-sister to Ambrosia—and also produces stallions, for Bride Elect's offspring included the St Leger winner Hethersett (sire of Blakeney, Highest Hopes and Rarity), Never Beat (champion sire in Japan) and the miler Royal

Mr L. B. Holliday's "Hard Fought" (W. Swinburn)

Prerogative (a top sire in South Africa). Bride Elect was a half-sister, out of the Oaks second Netherton Maid, to Pampered King, also a successful sire, and the high-class Chatsworth and Pirate King. With this pedigree Hard Fought has a head start in his new career and he ought to do well. A strong, good sort who carried a lot of condition, he had a nice easy action as a three-year-old but went down moderately more than once in 1981. Hard Fought was suited by a mile and a quarter and seemed to act on any going; though genuine and consistent he was rather a nervous sort who sweated up on occasions and needed strong handling. *M. Stoute.*

HARD TO SAY (FR) 3 b.c. Lyphard 132–Gaily 121 (Sir Gaylord) (1980 NR **74** 1981 8fg 10d 10d³) neat, attractive colt; third foal; half-brother to 1m winner Gay Milly (by Mill Reef); dam won Irish 1,000 Guineas and was third in Prix Vermeille; ran as though needing further when seventh of 9 behind stablecompanion Cut Above in White Rose Stakes at Ascot in April and when about 2½ lengths third of 14 to Morice in maiden event at Salisbury the following month on last 2 outings; will be suited by 1½m. *R. Hern.*

HARDWICK SUN 3 ch.f. Dieu Soleil 111–Hyper Rose 62 (Pinza 137) (1980 5f 5f 5f 1981 12.2s 9s) narrow, leggy filly; little better than plating class; should stay 9f; saddle slipped on reappearance. *G. Richards.*

HARESCEUGH 3 b.g. Andrea Mantegna–Mertola (Tribal Chief 125) (1980 **79** 8d 1981 10s³ 10fg² 10d³ 12d* 12s* 12g* 12f 13.3g 12g 12fg 12d) strong, workmanlike gelding; improved and won handicap and minor event at Wolverhampton in May and another minor event at Carlisle in June, in last-named quickening well to beat Rodeo by 3 lengths; had stiffish tasks in handicaps afterwards, but wasn't disgraced on tenth start; suited by 1½m; probably acts on any going, but best form with some give in the ground. *N. Vigors.*

HARLESTON LASS 2 ch.f. Bold Lad (Ire) 133–Court Sensation 73 (Appiani **50** II 128) (1981 5g 5v³ 5.1f 6f 6fg 6g) Apr 22; 1,600Y; leggy, fair sort; half-sister to middle-distance winner Haverhill Lad (by Queen's Hussar); dam 1m winner; only plating class; blinkered fifth outing (moved badly to start). *G. Blum.*

HARLEW 3 b.f. Fine Blade 121–Jillaroo 79 (Javelot 124) (1980 5f 6g 6fg 6fg **58** 7g⁴ 8.2s 8d² 7d³ 1981 8.2s 10g 12d* 12d 11fg 10.8fg 12d 12g) small filly; sweated up and showed best form of year when beating Right Regent easily by 2 lengths in handicap at Warwick in May; stays 1½m; acts on a soft surface; trained by N. Guest until after sixth start (subsequently off course 4 months). *A. W. Jones.*

HARMONY BAY 3 b.f. Jimmy Reppin 131–Even Song (Falcon 131) (1980 6g — 1981 8s 8s) small filly; little sign of ability, including in a seller; apprentice ridden. *C. Spares.*

HARPERS BAZAAR 2 ch.g. Native Bazaar 122–French Salute (Salvo 129) **86** (1981 6f 6fg³ 5f*) Apr 30; fourth reported foal; dam never ran; favourite when winning 14-runner maiden race at Folkestone in September by 2 lengths from Bernard Sunley; stays 6f. *R. Smyth.*

HARPERS FERRY (USA) 3 b.g. Angle Light–Flower Vase (Round Table) — (1980 7g 7d 1981 8s 7d) strong, good-bodied gelding; little sign of ability in maiden and minor events; sold to P. Mitchell 900 gns Newmarket May Sales. *J. Bethell.*

HARP STRINGS (FR) 3 br.f. Luthier 126–Gilding 103 (Kauai King) (1980 **109** 5f³ 6g 6g* 7g⁴ 7d² 1981 8.5fg* 7fg 8f* 9.2d 10.2d) lengthy filly; first foal; dam won Ascot 1,000 Guineas Trial; put up good performances when winning handicap at Epsom in April under top weight (quickened clear below distance to beat Polisteppin by 2 lengths) and Geoffrey Hamlyn Stakes (Limited Handicap) at Kempton in September (led close home to beat Praetorian Guard by ½ length); took the eye before Group 2 Prix de l'Opera at Longchamp in October, but lost her position after 2f and finished about 5 lengths ninth of 18 to Kilmona (noted running on in closing stages); probably stayed 9f (didn't get 1¼m though on final start); probably acted on any going; stud. *I. Balding.*

HARRIS TWEED 2 b.c. Red Alert 127–Grey Fleck (Sing Sing 134) (1981 5s **77** d 5g² 6f 6f² 7fg 6g 7f 6fg² 7g) Feb 22; IR 6,200Y; neat, quite attractive colt; closely related to winners here and in France by Green God, and half-brother to a winner abroad; dam never ran; second in maiden races at Doncaster in May and Haydock in July and in seller at Doncaster again in September (went down by neck to Super Sunset); well beaten in all races over 7f; acts on firm going; usually wears blinkers; sweated up last 3 outings; sold 4,000 gns Newmarket Autumn Sales. *G. Pritchard-Gordon.*

HARROW CROSS 3 b.f. Master Sing 109–Highland Night (Night Thought 83) — (1980 6fg 6g 5d 1981 8.2s 10s) useless plater. *J. Scallan.*

HARRY HASTINGS (USA) 2 b.c. Vaguely Noble 140–Country Dream (Ribot — 142) (1981 7g) Apr 1; $200,000Y; big, rangy colt; half-brother to minor winners by Damascus and Canonero II; dam, unplaced 4 times, is closely related to high-class middle-distance stayer Prove Out; weak 14/1-shot and decidedly backward, disputed lead before weakening quickly at halfway and dropping right out to finish last of 13 behind Final Strike in £2,900 event at Newmarket in October; will stay 1½m+; has lots of scope and should improve in time. *G. Harwood.*

HARRY LAWRENCE 3 b.c. Murrayfield 119–Hard to Catch 59 (Hardicanute 130) (1980 5fg 6g 6fg 5fg 1981 11d 8fg 10h) small colt; poor plater; bred to stay 1m; blinkered first outing in 1980. *L. Barratt.*

HARRY SIPPERS 4 b.g. Galivanter 131–Linloskin (Hard Sauce 131) (1980 NR 1981 10.1fg 8f 8s) no sign of ability in varied company; broke blood vessel second start. *D. Underwood.*

HARTFIELD LAD 2 br.g. Jimsun 121–Julita 87 (Rockavon 120) (1981 5g **70** 5d 6d 8g 8d 10g 8d³) Apr 30; 2,300Y; neat gelding; half-brother to 3 winners, including prolific sprint winner Magnolia Lad (by Mummy's Pet); dam stayed 13f; plater; suited by 1m but was well beaten over 1¼m; out of depth when blinkered fifth outing. *A. Pitt.*

HARTNELL'S IN LOVE 2 ch.f. Joshua 129–Sahibs Daughter 88 (Sahib 114) **63** (1981 5g 5f² 6g 6fg 5g 6s 8.2s 8d) Apr 2; sturdy filly; first foal; dam won 5 times at up to 7f; 3 lengths second of 12 to Starlust in maiden race at Leicester in June; beaten in sellers afterwards, including when blinkered on final start; should stay beyond 5f. *P. Makin.*

HARTSFIELD 4 ch.c. Grundy 137–Omentello 91 (Elopement 125) (1980 **74** 11fg 12f* 12fg* 11fg³ 12fg 12d³ 12fg 1981 12fg 12g 12s³ 12fg⁴ 11.7d⁴ 12f³ 12f 12s) big, strong, slightly hollow-backed colt with a very long stride; will stay 1¾m; acts on any going; seems to need strong handling; ran poorly seventh start. *R. Laing.*

HARVESTER GLORY 3 b.g. Warpath 113–Pasdeux 107 (Ballyogan) (1980 **63** 8.2s 8g 1981 12g 12s 12fg 14fg 16.9fg 16.5f*) medium-sized, quite attractive gelding; won maiden race at Redcar in August; needs a test of stamina; acts well on firm going. *M. Jarvis.*

HARVEYSFIELD 3 ch.g. Northfields–Dancing Rib 87 (Sir Ribot) (1980 **73** 6d³ 7fg 7.9g² 8g² 1981 10d³ 9d² 16f 12.8f 9f) 10,000Y; lightly-made gelding; closely related to 7f winner Dancing Robe (by Habitat) and half-brother to a winner; dam 2-y-o 1m winner; made running when placed in maiden races at Leopardstown and Gowran Park in May; had stiff task when last in Queen's Vase at Royal Ascot in June on third start (sweating and looked hard trained); should be suited by 1½m+; ran poorly last 2 starts. *M. Kauntze, Ireland.*

HASHOFET 6 gr.g. George Spelvin–Grandpa's Gift (Celtic Ash) (1980 NR — 1981 12fg 10f) poor front-running handicapper nowadays; stays 11f; seems to act on any going but goes well on firm; has worn blinkers; suitable mount for a boy; sold to M. Pipe 1,800 gns Ascot August Sales. *A. Ingham*

HASSI R'MEL 3 ch.g. Clear Run 109–Nuchiru (Chingnu 99) (1980 5fg 7d **48** 7g 7g 8fg 1981 7f⁴ 8f 16.9fg 12.2fg 12g 12g 13.8g* 16s) plater; bought in 825 gns after winning at Catterick in October; stays 1¾m. *J. Yardley.*

HASSY PERFECTION 3 gr.f. Town Crier 119–Beamless 73 (Hornbeam 130) — (1980 NR 1981 7d 7f 7fg) 1,300F; leggy, lightly-made filly; half-sister to 4 winners here and abroad, including quite useful sprinter Bill's Song and fair sprinter Song Beam (both by Song); dam stayed 1½m; little worthwhile form, including in a seller on final start (last of 19, wearing blinkers); retained 560 gns Newmarket July Sales. *G. Blum.*

HASTY DALE 2 ch.f. Hasty Word 84–Severndale (Bounteous 125) (1981 **59** 6fg 6fg 5f 5fg² 5fg 5.8f 5f 5g⁴ 5s) Mar 22; 280F; neat filly; bad mover; plater; should stay at least 6f; acts on firm going. *K. Bridgwater.*

HASTY GODDESS 2 ch.f. Nebbiolo 125–No Delay 72 (Never Say Die 137) — (1981 5d) Apr 26; IR 11,000Y; half-sister to French middle-distance winner

HAS

Sandina (by Sovereign Path) and to Sandford Lass, a fair performer up to 1m, and 3-y-o 1½m winner Sandalay (both by Sandford Lad); dam, suited by a distance of ground, is daughter of Nassau Stakes winner Cracker; 20/1 when behind in 16-runner maiden race won by Kash-In at Bath in October, only outing; bred to need 1m+. *T. Robson.*

HASTY IMPORT 2 ch.g. Import 127–Isis Rapide (I Say 125) (1981 5d 6g) — May 21; 580F, 4,000Y; leggy gelding; half-brother to a winner in Austria; dam ran only once; in rear in minor events at Pontefract in May and Catterick (last of 8) in June; gelded afterwards. *J. Mason.*

HASTY KATE 2 ch.f. Hasty Word 84–Salvo's Grace (Salvo 129) (1981 6f 7d — 8fg 8s 7g) Apr 17; neat filly; second foal; dam won twice over hurdles after birth of first foal; in rear in maiden and minor events. *R. Hollinshead.*

HASTY'S GOLD 3 b.g. Gold Rod 129–Carina Janie 88 (Silver Cloud 121) — (1980 5.8fg 7fg 6fg 8fg 8d³ 10d 1981 12s 11.7g 8d 10.1fg 8fg) plater; suited by 1m but possibly doesn't stay middle distances; best run on a soft surface; bandaged near-hind final start. *J. Cann.*

HATTAN 3 b.c. Rheingold 137–Bally's Gift 83 (So Blessed 130) (1980 7g 8fg — 8d³ 7d 1981 12fg 11.5d 12g 12g) good-looking colt; showed a little ability at 2 yrs; promises to stay 1½m; trained part of season by P. M. Taylor and K. Brassey. *P. Mitchell.*

HAUGHTY MANNER 3 b. or br.f. High Top 131–Pugnacity 117 (Pampered **63** King 121) (1980 NR 1981 7d 8.5g³ 7g⁴ 6f) small, light-framed filly; half-sister to numerous winners, most of them at least useful, including top-class 1m to 1½m horse Relkino (by Relko); dam smart from 5f to 1m; moved up a place after finishing fourth to Sea Miss in maiden race at Epsom in June; well beaten next outing; stays 1m; doesn't have much scope. *H. Candy.*

HAVANEZA 3 b.f. Simbir 130–Lucindale (Ballyciptic 122) (1980 5fg 7d 7fg — 8fg 7g 1981 8fg) leggy, workmanlike filly; showed a little ability at 2 yrs; behind on only outing of 1981; probably needs a stiff test of stamina. *E. Eldin.*

HAVEN CENTURION (USA) 2 ch.c. Giacometti 130–Indialucie (Sir Ivor 135) **74** (1981 7f 8d 10s) Apr 2; $26,000Y; fair sort; good mover; first foal; dam, grand-daughter of excellent broodmare Levee, won over 1½m in France; little sign of ability in maiden races; should be suited by 1¼m. *P. Cole.*

HAVEN'S PRIDE (USA) 2 b.c. Dewan-Victoire (Crafty Admiral) (1981 5f **81** 6fg⁴ 7g 7d⁴ 7h 7fg 8d³ 8s⁴ 8d²) Feb 12; $32,000Y; lightly-made colt; half-brother to numerous minor winners in USA; dam won 1m claiming race; prominent in 4 nurseries and in a maiden race; ½-length second of 23 to Roanoke River in latter at Leicester in November on final start; (blinkered) will stay 1¼m; acts on soft going; ran very wide and crashed through rails on fifth start. *P. Cole.*

HAVENWOOD 2 br.c. Relko 136–Pepin (Midsummer Night II 117) (1981 5fg — 6f 7fg 7g 8s) Apr 27; 6,000Y; leggy colt; fourth foal; half-brother to 2 winners, including fairly useful 6f winner Shayboob (by The Go-Between); dam poor maiden; little worthwhile form in maiden and minor events. *P. Felgate.*

HAVERHILL LAD 5 ch.g. Queen's Hussar 124–Court Sensation 73 (Appiani II **59** 128) (1980 8fg³ 10f³ 10fg* 10fg 10d* 10g⁴ 11.7s 8g 10g* 11g² 10fg² 10.5s³ 10s³ 1981 8g 10g² 10d³ 10f 10fg³ 10d³ 10fg 10fg² 12g) quite a modest handicapper; stays 11f; acts on any going; has worn blinkers but does better without; consistent. *G. Blum.*

HAVERHILL LASS 2 b.f. Music Boy 124–March Queen 88 (March Past 124) **67** (1981 5s* 5s 5g³ 5d 5fg 6g 5fg* 5g² 5g² 5f 5s 5g) June 7; 2,000Y; sturdy filly; half-sister to 1m winner King-Ki (by Kibenka), to a winner in Austria and to a winning jumper; dam 6f sprinter; winner of maiden auction event at Catterick in April and of nursery at Warwick in August, making all under 7-7 in latter; not disgraced when tried over 6f but is clearly considered best at minimum distance; seems to act on any going; usually blinkered nowadays. *G. Blum.*

HAVERING HILL 3 b.c. So Blessed 130–Heaven and Earth (Midsummer Night **68** II 117) (1980 7d⁴ 1981 7fg 8g³ 9s 8fg³ 10fg² 9s⁴) fair sort; placed in maiden races at Stockton, Salisbury and Beverley; stays 1¼m; sold 3,700 gns Newmarket Autumn Sales. *P. Walwyn.*

HAVOC 3 br.c. Swing Easy 126–Bobelle 62 (Pirate King 129) (1980 6g 1981 **96** 8d 8fg² 8g* 7g* 7.6g 7.6fg⁴ 7g 7g 7g) big, rangy colt; successful twice at Don-caster in May, making heavy weather of beating Round Dance in a maiden event

378

on first occasion but winning in good style by 4 lengths from Sea Aura in quite valuable Impel Handicap on second; didn't run up to his best afterwards; stays 1m; a front runner who possibly needs things his own way. *C. Brittain.*

HAVON AIR 3 ch.f. Celtic Cone 116–Mary's Date 60 (The Phoenix) (1980 7g 7g 8d 1981 6fg 8fg 9g 10.2d 13.8g 10s) lightly-built filly; little worthwhile form; will be suited by long distances. *J. Spearing.* —

HAVON COOL 5 b.h. Celtic Cone 116–Lucky Affair 83 (Stephen George 102) (1980 8fg³ 10h 10.6g 8g³ 8fg 7.5g* 8fg* 8.3fg³ 8g² 7.6d⁴ 7.2d 8d 1981 7.6g³ 8d³ 7.2s³ 8.5g² 6f* 6fg* 7fg 6g 6s 7s 6d 7d) neat, strong horse; poor mover; fair handicapper; beat Dead Strait 1½ lengths at Windsor in June and Belfort going away by a length at Chester in July; best at up to 1m; acts on any going; wears blinkers; suitable mount for a boy. *Mrs M. Rimell.* 81

HAWAIIAN HEIR (USA) 2 b.c. Hawaii–Madam Fox (Rising Market) (1981 7fg 10s²) May 15; small, quite attractive, useful-looking colt; first foal; dam, daughter of CCA Oaks winner A Glitter, ran 4 times unplaced; showed some promise both outings, on second start keeping on well to be 1½ lengths second of 22 to Luxury in maiden event at Nottingham in October (first race for over 2 months); will be suited by 1½m. *P. Cole.* 84

HAWAIIAN SUNSET 2 ch.f. Streak 119–Dorothy Darling 76 (Red God 128§) (1981 5g 5g 6f 5fg) Feb 17; light-framed filly; closely related to a modest animal by Runnymede and half-sister to 3 winners; dam placed over 5f at 2 yrs; soundly beaten in claiming race and sellers; blinkered fourth outing. *P. Cundell.* —

HAWALI 4 b.f. Gay Fandango 132–Gentle Way 74 (Gentle Art 121) (1980 7v 6fg* 6f⁴ 7.3f⁴ 7g 8g 1981 7fg² 7fg* 7fg⁴) quite attractive filly; ridden with great confidence when beating Lucky Man a head in handicap at Salisbury in August (sweated up badly); should stay 1m (ran moderately when tried at trip); acts on firm going; sold 12,500 gns Newmarket Autumn Sales. *J. Sutcliffe.* 70

HAWKBARROW 3 br.g. Appiani II 128–Glistening 84 (Aureole 132) (1980 NR 1981 12g 10.1fg) half-brother to 11f winner Glitter (by Reliance II) and a winner in Italy; dam winning stayer and half-sister to high-class long-distance horse Proverb; beaten some way in maiden race at Haydock in April and minor event at Windsor in July. *D. Gandolfo.* —

HAWKS NEST 2 b.f. Moulton 128–Good Try 92 (Good Bond 122) (1981 5fg 5fg²) Mar 1; neat filly; first foal; dam 2-y-o 5f winner; prominent in maiden races at Sandown and Wolverhampton in July, going down by 4 lengths to Pleasant Dream when favourite on latter course; not seen out again. *H. Candy.* 66

HAYAKAZE 2 ch.c. Hotfoot 126–Sugar Cookie 71 (Crepello 136) (1981 7fg 7fg* 8d) Apr 4; 7,400Y; well-made colt; first foal; dam placed 3 times at up to 13f; 20/1, stayed on strongly to catch Rare Gift on line when winning 29-runner maiden race at Newmarket in August by a short head; 12/1 when tenth of 22 to Super Sunrise in £4,200 event at Newbury the following month; will stay middle distances. *G. Pritchard-Gordon.* 86

HAYATO 3 ch.c. Music Boy 124–Linden Lea 91§ (Hornbeam 130) (1980 6fg 5.1g² 5d² 1981 5d³ 5fg⁴ 6fg⁴ 5fg 5f 5fg) small, lengthy colt; good walker and mover; below form in 1981, although was in frame in maiden events; should stay 6f; sweated third start; blinkered sixth outing. *J. Winter.* —

HAYCOMBE BARN 2 ch.c. Hittite Glory 125–Jolisu 110 (Welsh Abbot 131) (1981 6fg 6g 5s*) Apr 10; 11,500F, 9,200Y; good-bodied, fair sort; good mover; half-brother to fairly useful 1½m to 2¼m winner Jolimo (by Fortissimo) and successful stayer Kansu (by Caliban); dam miler; led well inside final furlong to win 9-runner maiden race at Nottingham in September a shade cleverly by ½ length from Kenson Venture, best effort; should be suited by 6f; clearly well suited by soft going. *W. Hastings-Bass.* 77

HAY GUINNESS 3 b.f. Birdbrook 110–Molvitesse 75 (Molvedo 137) (1980 NR 1981 8fg 9s 8.2fg 8.2d) sister to a poor animal and half-sister to 2 winners by Caliban, including 6f to 1¼m winner Calaburn; dam won over 1m; behind in maiden and minor events. *T. Craig.* —

HAY HABIT 2 ch.c. Habitat 134–Hayrake 98 (Galivanter 131) (1981 6s³ 6d* 7g² 8g 7d) May 4; 21,000Y; strong, compact, attractive colt; half-brother to very useful 1977 Irish 2-y-o Thunor (by Green God); dam stayed 1¼m; won 17-runner minor event at Naas in June by 1½ lengths from Roselita; ran well when next seen out 3 months later, finishing ¾-length second of 10 to Longleat 94

HAY

in Coolmore Try My Best Stakes at Leopardstown, but disappointed subsequently: should stay 1m; yet to race on a firm surface. *S. Murless, Ireland.*

HAY RIDE 8 br.h. Galivanter 131–Haytime (Alycidon 138) (1980 12f² 12d* — 12g² 12f² 13s* 10fg 1981 11s 12f 12fg 12g 10.4s 12f 12d) fair middle-distance performer at his best; well beaten in 1981; acts on any going; has been tried in blinkers; excellent mount for an inexperienced rider. *N. Guest.*

HAYS 2 b.c. Wolver Hollow 126–Sing a Song 115 (Sing Sing 134) (1981 5fg* **120** 6f* 6fg 7fg² 6d* 6g)

'This is a top two-year-old and may even be my best' said Guy Harwood after Hays's victory in the Mill Reef Stakes at Newbury in September. Considering that Harwood also trains Sandhurst Prince, the winter favourite for the Two Thousand Guineas, and Norwick, the three-length Royal Lodge Stakes winner, this is high praise. We too have a high opinion of Hays but unfortunately, like his stable-companion Recitation the previous year, Hays took some of the shine off his best performances by throwing in a couple of poor ones. However, Hays's disappointing efforts are the easier to explain; there's one obvious reason for both of Hays's below-par displays—too many races in, for him, too short a time.

Hays's first three races came in a spell of twenty-seven days in July. Although palpably green on his debut in the Year of the Cockerel Stakes at Sandown Hays showed plenty of potential; after racing close behind the leaders he kept on strongly under really hard driving to lead close home, winning by a length from the 25/1-shot Sylvan Barbarosa. Thanks largely to the tremendous early pace set by that very nippy filly Mumruffin, Hays recorded a time-figure of 0.46 fast, an excellent effort for a debutant, and he started odds on for his next race, the Willow Stakes at Kempton. Though a little noisy on first entering the paddock he wasn't nearly so coltish as he'd been at Sandown and quickly showed he'd suffered no ill effects from his very hard race there. Clearly in control of his field with two furlongs still to run, he won easing up by half a length from El Mansour. Then came the first anti-climax. After starting favourite to beat Tender King, Cajun and End of the Line, respectively second, fifth and first in the July Stakes on their latest appearance, Hays finished only fifth of seven in the Richmond Stakes at Goodwood. In his trainer's words he 'boiled over at the start'. Certainly he broke very fast, led or disputed the lead for nearly five furlongs and then dropped back quickly to be beaten over six lengths by Tender King.

Hays came back a much better colt six weeks later in the Laurent Perrier Champagne Stakes at Doncaster's St Leger meeting when he started at 8/1 behind the Gimcrack winner Full Extent, the Phoenix Stakes winner Achieved and Padalco. The front-running Full Extent began to fade over two furlongs out, as did Padalco, leaving Achieved in the lead. It was at this stage of the race that Hays was at his most impressive: he quickened in tremendous style to draw alongside the Irish colt, seemingly travelling the better, and for the next furlong the pair were locked together. Only entering the final furlong did Hays start to crack and, although he eventually went down by a length and a half

Mill Reef Stakes, Newbury—Hays quickens well to beat Macmillion

H. H. Prince Yazid Saud's "Hays"

to Achieved, this was a very smart effort. Another followed only ten days later in the Mill Reef Stakes at Newbury. Favourite was Wattlefield, a most impressive winner in unexceptional company on his last two starts, but Hays, who looked magnificent in the paddock, started second favourite ahead of the Selsey Stakes winner Torrey, the Gimcrack second Take The Floor, the Woodcote winner Chris's Lad, the July Stakes fourth Match Master and two others. As at Doncaster Hays settled well. He could be seen going easily on the rails just behind the leaders while the 20/1-shot Macmillion made the running. Although for a moment he looked as if he might have trouble finding an opening, Hays again produced his excellent turn of foot to lead coming to the final furlong. Drawing away in style, he won by three lengths from Macmillion with the third horse Match Master beaten a total of five and a half lengths.

Punters were sufficiently impressed by Hays's performance to make him favourite for the William Hill Middle Park Stakes at Newmarket, ahead of two other pattern race winners Peterhof and Tender King. Once more he impressed in the paddock but again disappointed when having his third race in less than four weeks. After looking to be travelling strongly on the bridle over two furlongs out Hays was soon struggling and dropped back to finish only twelfth of the thirteen runners. Admittedly he was beaten less than six lengths by the winner Cajun but Wattlefield, Take The Floor, Chris's Lad and Match Master all managed to beat him this time.

It's hard to say with any degree of certainty how good Hays is; it's also hard to say what his optimum trip will be at three. No doubt he'll be aimed at the Two Thousand Guineas either here or in France or Ireland but, even if he has the ability to win one of those races, it's a brave man who will say at this stage he'll stay the trip. The average winning distance of the Eclipse Stakes winner Wolver Hollow's progeny is nearly ten furlongs and, of his best offspring, Wollow, Furry Glen, Galaxy Libra, Charlie Bubbles, Wolverton,

My Hollow and Gift Wrapped all won over further than a mile. However, to a previous mating with a Sing Sing mare Wolver Hollow sired the fairly useful sprinter Penumbra. Not only is Hays out of a Sing Sing mare, he comes from an extremely speedy female line: his dam Sing a Song was a smart two-year-old who never raced beyond five furlongs, and one of her two previous winners from five other foals is the fairly useful five-furlong winner Red Shield, a son of So Blessed; his grandam, the useful Soltera, was also a five-furlong performer, and the better of her two other winners in England was the very fast Song of Songs, a close relative of Sing a Song; his third dam, No Appeal, was summed up in her day as 'a smart 5f handicapper; requires a sharp track and a firm surface to be seen to best advantage'. Another of No Appeal's daughters, the Hill Gail filly No Ball, was exported to South Africa carrying a foal by Hays's grandsire Sovereign Path. The resultant offspring, named Lords, became a performer of note and is now one of South Africa's most promising stallions. Incidentally No Ball was the Broodmare of the Year in South Africa in 1981 and Soltera too was sent to that country in 1974.

Hays (b.c. Feb 16, 1979)	Wolver Hollow (b 1964)	Sovereign Path (gr 1956)	Grey Sovereign
			Mountain Path
		Cygnet (b 1950)	Caracalla II
			Mrs Swan Song
	Sing a Song (b 1968)	Sing Sing (b 1957)	Tudor Minstrel
			Agin the Law
		Soltera (ch 1962)	Matador
			No Appeal

But what of Hays himself? Although he put up an excellent effort when tried over seven furlongs he seemed not to stay the trip so well as the winner and Harwood himself said he wasn't quite sure whether Hays got the seven furlongs. The only thing that can tell us for sure is further evidence on the racecourse. What can safely be said of Hays, a 15,000-guinea yearling, is that he's an eye-catching individual with plenty of quality, even if a little on the leg at two; that he acts on any going with the possible exception of very soft which he has yet to encounter; and that, whatever his trip turns out to be, he'll make a high-class three-year-old. *G. Harwood.*

HAYSTACK (USA) 2 ch.f. Farewell Party–Firecracker Love (Crackpot) **74** (1981 8fg 8fg 8d²) Apr 14; sturdy filly; half-sister to hurdler July the Fourth (by Goose Creek); dam placed 3 times in USA; ran best race when 2¼ lengths second of 16 to Portette in maiden race at Bath in October; will probably stay well. *I. Balding.*

HAZIM 2 b.c. Mill Reef 141–Angel Chile (Herbager 136) (1981 6f 5fg² 6d 5d **100** 5d*) May 29; IR 55,000Y; neat, attractive colt; good mover; brother to French middle-distance winner Wild Surf, subsequently a stakes winner over 1¼m in USA, and half-brother to 3 winners, including fairly useful 1980 2-y-o 6f winner Beulah Land (by Targowice); dam half-sister to high-class 1971 American 2-y-o Tarboosh; got home by only a neck from Shamrock Nail when short-priced favourite for 13-runner maiden race at Redcar in October (disputed lead throughout); had earlier shown up in 2 pattern races, finishing 1½ lengths second to Prowess Prince in Molecomb Stakes at Goodwood in July and 7½ lengths sixth of 8 to Full Extent in 6f Gimcrack Stakes at York in August; bred to stay middle distances and is unlikely to fulfil his potential until he's taught to settle and tried over a trip more in keeping with his pedigree. *H. T. Jones.*

HEAD IN THE CLOUDS 3 b.g. Habat 127–All Hail 112 (Alcide 136) (1980 — NR 1981 10.2g 14s) strong gelding; half-brother to several winners, including middle-distance winners Geminiani (by Lorenzaccio) and Bunce Boy (by King Emperor); dam staying daughter of St Leger second None Nicer; needed race and wasn't disgraced when sixth of 13 behind Canton Lightning in minor event at Doncaster in May; tailed off at York in October on only other start; trained by M. Stoute first outing. *J. Blundell.*

HEAD OF STATE (FR) 3 b.g. Crowned Prince 128–Sweet and Gay (Sir — Gaylord) (1980 8d 1981 7fg 8d 8f 10.1fg) tailed off in varied company, including selling and claiming. *P. Cole.*

HEAD WAITER 2 ch.g. Habat 127–Header 78 (High Hat 131) (1981 5s 7d) — May 21; rather leggy, quite attractive gelding; half-brother to 2 winners, including useful 1976 2-y-o 6f winner Rockery (Fr) (by Roan Rocket); dam half-sister to good stayer Charlton; well beaten in maiden race at Wolverhampton in May and minor event at Chepstow in October (blinkered); sold 980 gns New-market Autumn Sales. *I. Balding.*

HEADWAY 2 b.f. Pieces of Eight 128–Horns Dilemma (Quadriga 97) (1981 — 6fg 7fg 6s 7fg 6g) Feb 20; small, lightly-made filly; second foal; half-sister to 9f winner Tudor's Dilemma (by Tudor Rhythm); dam of little account; emulating her dam. *J. Gilbert.*

HEARTBREAKER 3 gr.f. Steel Heart 128–Tetrazzini 70 (Sovereign Path 125) **55** (1980 6g⁴ 1981 5g 6fg² 6s 5s) strong, compact filly; beaten a neck by Every-body's Friend in 3-runner minor event at Hamilton in May; in rear both subse-quent starts (October); not sure to stay beyond 6f. *Sir Mark Prescott.*

HEARTH 4 b.f. Home Guard 129–Fair Path (Javelot 124) (1980 11fg* 12fg* **83** 12h* 11.1f³ 11.5fg* 12g 11.7fg³ 12g³ 12fg³ 1981 12g* 12f 12g⁴ 12fg⁴ 12s 12v*) tall, leggy filly; fairly useful performer; successful at Taby in Sweden in May and in handicap at Kempton in October; beat Le Soleil by 2 lengths on latter; stays 1½m well; acts on any going; suitable mount for a boy; trained by B. Olsson in Sweden part of season. *M. Stoute.*

HEART OF STEEL 2 ch.c. Steel Heart 128–Tetrazzini 70 (Sovereign Path 125) — p (1981 6g) Mar 20; 56,000Y; third foal; half-brother to useful 1979 2-y-o 5f to 7f winner Lady Downsview (by Prince Regent); dam placed over 6f; 11/1 and reasonably straight, soon outpaced and wasn't knocked about unduly when seventh of 18 to Music Lover in maiden event at Newmarket in October; should benefit from the experience. *M. Albina.*

HEARTS ARE TRUMPS 7 b.m. Knave To Play 79–Bilton Belle 88 (Star — Gazer 123) (1980 14.7f 12.2fg 12g 16.1s 1981 9g) of no account. *A. Watson.*

HEART'S CONTENT 2 ch.c. Some Hand 119–Can't Wait (Eudaemon 129) — (1981 8s 7d) Apr 13; brother to 6f and 7f winner Steady Hand, and half-brother to 3 winners, including fairly useful 3-y-o 6f winner Bracadale (by The Brianstan); dam of little account; well beaten both races (October), first of them a Warwick seller. *C. Williams.*

HEARTY HUNTER 2 gr.g. Huntercombe 133–Quantity 77 (Quorum 126) **71** (1981 5d 5d 5v 5g 6fg* 6fg 6g*) Apr 18; quite well-made gelding; half-brother to 2 winners, including miler Loudly (by Crooner); gambled on when successful in sellers at Nottingham in June (from Easy Maud) and August (beat Count Du Barry by 4 lengths); bought in 4,800 gns on first occasion and 4,400 gns on second; may stay 7f; best form on a sound surface; best in blinkers. *J. Sutcliffe.*

HEATED DEBATE 3 br.g. Politico 124–Lady Phoenix (Lorenzaccio 130) — (1980 6g 6fg 1981 16.9fg 16.5fg) big gelding; behind in minor and maiden events. *J. Gilbert.*

HEATHEN PRINCE 3 ch.g. Sun Prince 128–Heather Grove (Hethersett 134) — (1980 5d 6d 6f 6fg 5g 6d 6s 1981 5d 7d 6d) small, strong gelding; good walker; quite a moderate maiden; form only at 5f but is bred to stay at least 7f; blinkered sixth start in 1980. *J. Benstead.*

HEATHER'S REEF 2 b.f. Mill Reef 141–Heatherside 80 (Hethersett 134) **76 p** (1981 8g) Feb 14; 58,000Y; rangy filly; half-sister to a winner in Italy; dam, half-sister to several very useful animals, won over 1¾m; unquoted, had plenty to do at halfway in 29-runner maiden race at Newmarket in October but made rapid headway in closing stages to finish 8½ lengths tenth to Born Hero; a pleasing first effort by a stoutly-bred filly who has the scope to do better at 3 yrs. *G. Huffer.*

HEAVENLY CHORD 3 b.f. Hittite Glory 125–Dulcimer (Double Jump 131) — (1980 5fg² 6fg 6d* 7.2s² 7f³ 7.2g² 7s 1981 6g 8s 8g 8g) well-grown filly; well beaten in 1981 (had stiffish tasks first 2 starts); should stay 1m; acts on any going. *A. Gillam.*

HEAVENLY CHORUS 5 b.m. Green God 128–Lingay 99 (Sing Sing 134) **57** (1980 7fg 7fg³ 7g 6g⁴ 7fg² 7g³ 7g 1981 7g 7fg 7g 7fg 7fg 7f⁴) big, strong, good-bodied mare; front-running handicapper; stays 7f; acts well on firm going and is not at her best on soft; suitable mount for an apprentice; blinkered fourth start. *P. Cundell.*

HEAVENLY RULER (CAN) 4 b.c. Riva Ridge–Heavenly Power (Bold Ruler) **40** (1980 8f 10f 1981 7s² 8v 12.5g 10.6s 12g 10s 8.2s) good-bodied colt; bad mover; plater nowadays; not certain to stay 1½m; has worn bandages in front. *A. Smith.*

HEAVENLY SCENT 2 b.f. Wishing Star 117–Brown Lavender (Le Levanstell **45** 122) (1981 5s⁴ 5d 5d³ 6f 5.1fg² 5fg) May 12; 550Y; small filly; half-sister to winning jumper Tamdhu (by Hardicanute); plater; should be well suited by 6f; blinkered last 2 outings; moved very badly to start final appearance; sold 760 gns Newmarket July Sales. *G. Blum.*

HEAVENS 3 gr. or ro.f. Sovereign Path 125–Kals Angel 68 (Kalydon 122) **81** (1980 5f³ 5d 7g 1981 8s* 8s³ 8g 8g) leggy, good-topped filly; heavily backed when beating Always Eirlys by 1½ lengths in handicap at York in May; having first outing for almost 4 months when creditable sixth to Bunter in £5,000 handicap at Ayr in September; gives impression she'll be suited by further than 1m; probably acts on any going; ran moderately in blinkers final start; sold 10,000 gns Newmarket December Sales. *B. Hills.*

HEAVY WEAPON 3 b.g. Bay Express 132–Autumn Double 72 (Double Jump **75** 131) (1980 5f³ 6d 5d 1981 5g 5s⁴ 5s 5g* 5s* 5g⁴ 5s⁴ 5fg² 5fg 5g² 5f² 5g 5s 5d) lightly-made gelding; won minor event at Cagnes-sur-Mer and handicap at Doncaster in March, in latter making all and holding on by ¾ length from subsequently-disqualified Voting Day; runner-up 3 times afterwards; form only at 5f; acts on any going; blinkered nowadays. *W. Hastings-Bass.*

HEDINGHAM BOY 6 br.h. Amber Rama 133–Aberangell 96 (Abernant 142) — (1980 8f 6f* 7f 6fg 7fg 6s² 6g 6d² 6g 7g* 7fg 6fg 6g 7g 7d 7s 1981 8s 7d 7fg 7g 7fg 6fg) former plater; well beaten in 1981; stays 7f; acts on any going; has twice worn blinkers; often wears bandages; has worn a tongue strap. *G. Blum.*

HEGO'S HERO 3 b.c. L'Homme Arme 111–Shopping Centre (Miralgo 130) **59** (1980 5f 5fg* 5g* 6fg⁴ 7f⁴ 8.2g⁴ 8f² 8.2s³ 7g 1981 9.4g 10.6s 8g* 12fg⁴ 11fg⁴ 12fg³ 12f² 9g 12.2g 11g³ 12d⁴ 13.8g³) neat colt; good walker and mover; apprentice ridden when winning handicap at Hamilton in June; placed several times afterwards, including in sellers; probably stayed 1¾m; best form on a sound surface; blinkered last 3 starts; dead. *G. Richards.*

HEIGHLIN 5 b.g. High Line 125–Filiform 76 (Reform 132) (1980 16s² 18f* **109** 18.4f 16fg² 18.8fg* 20d* 16.1d² 16g* 19g* 16.1fg 16d* 16.1g* 16fg* 16g³ 18d 1981 18fg² 16fg² 18g²) lightly-made gelding; very smart hurdler and very tough horse to beat in handicaps on flat; good 1½ lengths second all 3 starts at 5 yrs, going down to Protection Racket in Doncaster Cup in September, to Crispin at Ascot later in month and to Halsbury in Tote Cesarewitch at Newmarket in October; stays extremely well; acts on any going; best held up for a late run; very tough and genuine. *D. Elsworth.*

HEIGHTEN 3 b. or br.c. High Top 131–Curtains 113 (Busted 134) (1980 6fg² **104** 8d 1981 8d 11d 11.7f* 10.1g* 10.1fg* 10f* 10.2fg*) well-made, good sort; developed into a useful colt and won maiden race at Bath and minor events at Windsor (2), Ripon and Doncaster; adopted his usual front-running tactics and beat Cracking Form decisively by 2½ lengths in Fitzwilliam Stakes on last-named course in September; stays 1½m; acts well on firm going, but wasn't disgraced on a soft surface on reappearance; possibly has further improvement in him and should win more races. *R. Hern.*

HEIGHT OF FASHION (FR) 2 b.f. Bustino 136–Highclere 129 (Queen's **115** Hussar 124) (1981 7g* 8g* 8fg*)

The Queen is still waiting for her first Derby winner nearly thirty years after Aureole finished second in the race in her Coronation Year, but the Derby is the only English classic to elude her. Pall Mall won the 1958 Two Thousand Guineas; Highclere the 1974 One Thousand Guineas plus the Prix de Diane, the French Oaks, for good measure; Carrozza won the Oaks in 1957 and Dunfermline took both the Oaks and the St Leger in 1977. Now, with Highclere's daughter Height of Fashion, the Queen must have a first-rate chance of winning the Oaks yet again.

Height of Fashion's career has so far run on similar lines to Dunfermline's. Both ran only three times in their first season, starting with an outing over seven furlongs before tackling a mile in the May Hill Stakes at Doncaster and the Hoover Fillies Mile at Ascot (known as the Argos Star Fillies' Mile when Dunfermline ran in it). There the similarity ends though—Dunfermline finished only third on her debut and was beaten half a length in the other races whereas Height of Fashion went through the season unbeaten, ending up unquestionably the best of the staying two-year-old fillies in England.

Coincidentally Height of Fashion made her debut in the same race as her

May Hill Stakes, Doncaster—The Queen's filly Height of Fashion wins from Clare Island

sire, Bustino, had done eight years previously, the Acomb Stakes at York's Ebor meeting. Although at first we thought her too immature to make much show—she looked a big, rangy, raw-boned baby—we had to revise our opinion drastically when we saw her move to the start with a magnificent, long-striding action. She went down better than any of her seven rivals, quickly showing why she was a well-backed 7/2 shot. In the race, soon close up and travelling smoothly, she ran a little green and needed to be given a couple of reminders to take the lead inside the final two furlongs. In the end though she didn't have to be hard ridden to hold off the Newmarket winner Ashenden by three quarters of a length, with the unlucky-in-running Count Pahlen coming out best of the others, two lengths further behind.

Only the well-regarded Clare Island of Height of Fashion's three rivals proved capable of giving her a race in the May Hill Stakes on St Leger day. Although both fillies looked to be going well as the odds-on Height of Fashion moved into the lead with three furlongs to run, Clare Island was under strong pressure by the time they reached the distance. For a moment it looked as though Height of Fashion would win decisively but Clare Island rallied bravely. In the end Height of Fashion held on by less than a length—a very pleasing effort considering she was giving the second 3 lb and never had to be troubled with the whip. When the pair met again in the Hoover Fillies Mile twelve days later the betting suggested that more danger to Height of Fashion was likely to come from Stratospheric than from Clare Island. The betting was on the mark. Stratospheric, so impressive when making all to win the Waterford Candelabra Stakes on her latest appearance, was held up at the rear this time as Height of Fashion quickly went to the front. Record Answer and Clare Island, Height of Fashion's nearest pursuers as the field entered the straight, both found the pace too hot before long and it was Zinzara, a smooth winner of a newcomers race on her only start, who looked the biggest threat at the distance. Height of Fashion, sticking to her task splendidly, gradually fought her off and then had to contend with another challenge as Stratospheric crept up on the rails. Although Height of Fashion didn't keep a straight course she proved the stronger and held on by half a length with Zinzara, who received 4 lb from the first two, the same distance away third. Interestingly Height of Fashion still showed signs of greenness on this her third outing, particularly in the closing stages when she raced with one ear cocked forward towards the noise from the stands while the other was tilted back towards Stratospheric! What will she be capable of when she matures both mentally and physically?

Height of Fashion (Fr) (b.f. Apr 14, 1979)	Bustino (b 1971)	Busted (b 1963)	Crepello / Sans le Sou
		Ship Yard (ch 1963)	Doutelle / Paving Stone
	Highclere (b 1971)	Queen's Hussar (b 1960)	March Past / Jojo
		Highlight (b 1958)	Borealis / Hypericum

There were signs at Ascot that Height of Fashion was beginning to thrive—she appeared to have put on weight and developed more muscle on her quarters. She has only to continue to do so over the winter to develop into the top-class middle-distance filly she's bred to be. Bustino, a late-developer himself, is steadily proving one of the most promising sires in England and apart from Height of Fashion he was represented in 1981 by numerous good winners, including Bustomi, Alma Ata, Ma Femme, Kittyhawk, Humming, Candide, Overplay, Easter Sun and Busaco.

Height of Fashion comes from a family that has served the royal family admirably over the years. Her third dam Hypericum won the One Thousand Guineas and among her six winners were the King Edward VII Stakes winner Restoration and the mile-and-a-half winner Highlight. Although not so good a racehorse as her dam, Highlight excelled her at stud, producing no fewer than nine winners including Highclere and the smart colt Gloss. In addition to Highclere she had three other winning fillies by Queen's Hussar, two of whom, the Ribblesdale Stakes and Yorkshire Oaks second Light Duty and the fairly useful stayer Blaze of Glory, have been retained. Also retained are two more of Highlight's winning daughters, the Blue Seal Stakes winner Circlet and Christchurch, so Highlight is likely to prove a major influence on the future success of the Royal Studs. Already Light Duty, Christchurch and Highclere have bred at least one notable winner, their respective first foals being Paradise Bay, Church Parade and Milford. Incidentally Milford is now reportedly doing well at stud in Herefordshire after returning a fertility figure of only 33.3% in his first season at stud in Ireland. In between Milford and Height of Fashion Highclere produced two other fillies, the winning stayer Burghclere (by Busted), who sold for 460,000 guineas at the 1981 Newmarket December Sales, and Beacon Hill, a lightly-raced sister to Height of Fashion. Highclere was barren to Riverman in 1980 and her Sharpen Up foal of 1981 died.

Hoover Fillies Mile, Ascot—Height of Fashion (second right) makes virtually all the running and holds on bravely from Stratospheric (spots on cap) and Zinzara

Height of Fashion will need at least a mile and a quarter at three and consequently it is planned to run her in the Musidora Stakes and then the Oaks, following the course taken by her trainer's last Oaks winner Bireme. She must have an excellent chance in both races, provided she's able to adapt her long, flowing stride to Epsom's gradients. Her trainer can't have many doubts about her acting on the course though; in the past he's had no qualms about sending a filly for the Prix de Diane if he thought she'd be better suited by Chantilly than Epsom. *R. Hern.*

HEIRLINE 3 ch.f. Great Nephew 126–Cropfall 79 (Acropolis 132) (1980 7g³ 8g 8fg 5g 6d 1981 10fg 8.2s) quite a well-made filly; good walker and mover; third in £3,000 maiden event at Sandown as a 2-y-o, only sign of ability; not seen out until September in 1981; should be suited by 1m. *P. Cole.* —

HELANDY 4 br.g. Downstream 105–Steak House 68 (Road House II) (1980 8f³ 8h* 9fg 8fg² 8fg 8fg 8.2g 8fg 1981 9g 9fg⁴ 8g³ 8s* 10f 8.2g⁴ 8g 8fg) neat, strong gelding; not a particularly good mover; won handicap at Carlisle in June; stays 1m; acts on any going but is ideally suited by some give in the ground; suitable mount for a boy. *J. Berry.* 63

HELEXIAN 4 b.c. Song 132–Permutation 79 (Pinza 137) (1980 6s* 6fg³ 6fg³ 6f⁴ 6fg³ 6f³ 6fg 5.8fg 6g* 7d 7s⁴ 6fg 6fg⁴ 7fg⁴ 7g 8.3fg 8fg 1981 7d* 7fg 7g 7v* 7d² 7fg² 8f 7.3d 6s) compact, good sort; good mover; won handicaps at Warwick in April (from Sky Jump) and Chepstow in May (beat Prince of Spain 3 lengths); best at up to 7f; acts on any going but goes well in the mud; has worn blinkers but does at least as well without; suitable mount for a boy; genuine. *A. Ingham.* 78

HELLO CUDDLES 2 b.f. He Loves Me 120–Royal Sensation 103 (Prince Regent 129) (1981 5d*(dis) 5s 5g² 5g³ 5g² 5f 6f 5fg 5fg* 5fg³ 5s³) Feb 22; 4,000Y; quite a well-made filly; third foal; dam stayed 1¼m; 33/1, put up remarkable performance against 3 older horses in Scarbrough Stakes at Doncaster in September, having race sewn up a long way out and keeping on strongly to win by 2 lengths from Sayyaf; had previously been disqualified from her win in minor event on same course in March because theobromine was found in her system; also placed several times, notably finishing 3¼ lengths third of 7 to My Lover in Cornwallis Stakes at Ascot in October on eleventh outing; should stay 6f; acts on any going; said to have finished distressed when last on seventh and eighth starts and is none too consistent. *R. Hollinshead.* 99

HELLO SOLDIER 4 b.g. Military 112–Hey There (I Say 125) (1980 NR 1981 8f 8.3g) poor maiden. *A. W. Jones.* —

HELLO SUNSHINE 2 b.c. Song 132–Tropical Fruit (Tropique 128) (1981 6f 6fg 5d 6s* 6g* 7g*) Apr 10; small, well-made colt; half-brother to several winners here and abroad; dam of little account; bought in 3,200 gns after running on strongly to win valuable 17-runner seller at York in October by 1¼ lengths from Relkilia; subsequently showed himself a fairly useful handicapper, winning well-contested nurseries at Newmarket and Doncaster towards the back-end, at Doncaster coming home 3 lengths clear of Airspin; stays 7f; well suited by some give in the ground and acts on soft going; ridden by 7-lb claimer S. Dawson last 2 starts. *J. Holt.* 90

HELLO SUSIE GREENE 3 ch.f. Shecky Greene–Speranza 89 (Hopeful Venture 125) (1980 5d² 5h⁴ 5g* 6d³ 5fg 5s² 5g* 5fg² 1981 5fg) neat filly; won twice at Chester as a 2-y-o; stayed 6f, but showed best form at 5f; seemed to act on any going except hard; dead. *R. Simpson.* —

HELSENA 3 b.f. Ellkar 86–Porec (I Say 125) (1980 5fg 6f 5fg 5.8fg 6d 1981 8g 12d 10s 8.2s 8f 8fg 10.8fg 8f 10g 8fg 10h 9g 16g 12s) compact, good-topped filly; plater; had stiff task and ran quite well in non-seller when tried at 2m; sometimes blinkered; swerved badly at start and refused to race once as a 2-y-o. *K. Bridgwater.* —

HELSHAW GRANGE 2 b. or br.g. Tycoon II–Douraine (Doubtless II 111) (1981 6d 5f 6s 8.2fg* 6fg 7.2v) May 3; small gelding; third foal; dam reportedly won 8 times at up to 2m on flat and 10 times over hurdles in Channel Islands, as well as 4 point-to-points; 33/1, came with a long, steady run to win 18-runner seller at Haydock in September by ½ length from subsequently-disqualified Brave Maiden; attracted no bid; soundly beaten afterwards; will stay 1¼m; acts on a firm surface; blinkered last 3 outings. *J. Wilson.* 67

HELVIC (USA) 3 b. or br.c. Angle Light–Red River (Diatome 132) (1980 6d 7fg⁴ 7g 7f 1981 7g² 6g 9.4g⁴ 8g 9s⁴ 8.2f 8fg* 8.2g 8f* 8.2f⁴ 8f 7g) small, 55 useful sort; won maiden race at Edinburgh in July and apprentice handicap at Pontefract in August; will stay 1¼m; best on a sound surface; successful with blinkers and without; has worn a tongue strap; sold to M. Haynes 580 gns Newmarket Autumn Sales.   *G. Richards.*

HENBIT (USA)   4 b.c. Hawaii–Chateaucreek (Chateaugay)   (1980 10f* 12.3f*   — 12f*   1981 12g 12fg)

The fact that the first four home in the previous year's Derby stayed in training for the first time since 1975 promised to add considerable interest to the best middle-distance races in 1981.   Unfortunately history repeated itself to a large extent.   Six years ago Snow Knight (in North America) and Bustino added to their reputation while Imperial Prince and Giacometti failed to; in 1981 Master Willie (second at Epsom) and Pelerin (fourth) enjoyed a successful season whereas the winner, Henbit, and third, Rankin, achieved little.

The decision to keep Henbit in training was a brave one given the singular circumstances attending his career.   He won all his races at three, the Classic Trial at Sandown, the Chester Vase and the Derby, winning in workmanlike but very courageous fashion by three quarters of a length from Master Willie at Epsom despite cracking his off-fore cannon bone about one furlong out.   After being confined to his box in a light plaster for several months Henbit appeared to make a full recovery and his owners (Mrs Plesch having sold an interest in him to Lord Weinstock, Simon Weinstock and Tim Rogers) pressed ahead with the plan to run him again.   Their enterprise was not rewarded.   In the Jockey Club Stakes at Newmarket in May Henbit led for nine furlongs before dropping right out and being allowed to come home in his own time, eventually trailing in a remote last of six to Master Willie; in the Royal Whip Stakes at the Curragh in July, his warm-up for a possible tilt at the King George VI and Queen Elizabeth Diamond Stakes, Henbit again disappointed, leading two furlongs out but fading rapidly thereafter to finish a modest fifth to Last Light.   It was immediately announced that Henbit had run his last race, Hern expressing the

Mrs Arpad Plesch's "Henbit" (W. Carson)

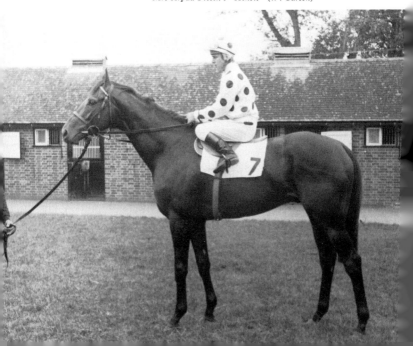

view that his charge never got over the injury sustained at Epsom. Henbit will be at the Airlie Stud in 1982 at a fee of IR £5,000 plus IR £5,000 if the mare is tested in foal by October 1st.

Henbit (USA) (b.c. 1977)	Hawaii (b 1964)	Utrillo II (ch 1958)	Toulouse Lautrec Urbinella
		Ethane (br 1947)	Mehrali Ethyl
	Chateaucreek (ch 1970)	Chateaugay (ch 1960)	Swaps Banquet Bell
		Mooncreek (ch 1963)	Sailor Ouija

Hawaii, Henbit's sire, was bred in South Africa and showed excellent form over middle distances there and in America where he was voted the top turf horse in 1969. The dam, Chateaucreek, a half-sister to three winners in America and one in Puerto Rico, won six times over sprint distances at three years. One of those successes came in a minor stakes event but Chateaucreek ended up being claimed for 25,000 dollars in 1974 before injury curtailed her career later that season. The second dam, Mooncreek, who was sent to Venezuela in 1976, is an unraced daughter of a stakes winner and a half-sister to the smart 1959 two-year-old Ouija Board. Chateaucreek's only foal prior to Henbit was the French jumping winner Lead Creek (by Mr Leader); since Henbit she has produced the colt Airgator (by Dewan) and a filly by Stop the Music. The latter cost 260,000 dollars as a yearling at Saratoga compared with the 24,000 dollars paid for Henbit at the Keeneland yearling sales two years before.

What made Henbit's inability to show his true form on either start at four all the more regrettable was the evident physical improvement he had made over the winter; he had developed into one of the best-looking four-year-olds in training, a strong, good-bodied, handsome individual. He stayed a mile and a half well and acted on firm going, never having raced on soft. *R. Hern.*

HENRIETTA MARIA (USA) 3 b.f. Forli–Abergwaun 128 (Bounteous 125) **55**
(1980 N.R. 1981 6d 5f⁴ 7f² 6f² 5g³ 5s³ 6g) quite a well-made filly; dam topclass and courageous sprinter; in frame in varied company; stays 7f; acts on any going. *R. Price.*

HENRY BOOT 3 gr.g. Abwah 118–Double Bank 80 (Double Jump 131) —
(1980 5h 5f 5fg 6fg 7s 5.1fg 7f 1981 6g) poor maiden; last in a seller only outing of 1981; sometimes blinkered. *M. Tompkins.*

HENRY'S WENCH 2 b.f. Tudor Rhythm 112–Pretty Asset 100 (Galivanter 131) —
(1981 6fg 5g 8d) June 10; small, lengthy filly; half-sister to 3 winners, including 1¼m winner Nosebob (by Reform); dam miler; in rear in maiden events. *G. Cottrell.*

HENRY'S WISH 3 b.g. Wishing Star 117–Tudor Story 96 (Henry the Seventh —
125) (1980 6g⁴ 6g 1981 7s 7fg 8g 8.5d) strong, good sort; didn't have the best of runs when about 3 lengths fifth of 12 behind All In in seller at Kempton in April on second start; soundly beaten afterwards, but on final start was given a lot to do and may have been unsuited by softish ground; bred to stay middle distances. *N. Callaghan.*

HERACLES 8 b.h. Breeders Dream 116–Papillon Rouge 60 (Klairon 131) —
(1980 7h 6h⁴ 7f 7.2d 7g 1981 7fg 6d 7g) dipped-backed horse; has shown no form for some time; stays 1m; appears to act on any going but goes extremely well on a sound surface; ran badly when tried in blinkers; good mount for an apprentice; sold 330 gns Ascot September Sales. *I. Walker.*

HERBIE QUAYLE 3 b.c. Thatch 136–Bella Carlotta (Charlottesville 135) **96**
(1980 7f 1981 7s⁴ 10.4d⁴ 8.2s* 8g² 8g⁴ 12fg 9d 8fg³ 7.3d⁴ 8g) big, strong colt; really took the eye and strode out tremendously well before landing the odds most impressively by 6 lengths from Round Dance in 8-runner minor event at Haydock in May; placed behind Tugoflove in £3,100 event at Newbury in June (½-length second) and in £6,100 handicap at Doncaster in September (less than a length third) and finished fourth behind Silca Star Key in another handicap at Newbury in September, in last 2 races being noted going on well in closing stages; stays 1¼m (always towards rear when tried at 1½m); probably acts on any going; possibly needs strong handling. *B. Hills.*

HEREAS (FR) 4 b.c. Hard to Beat 132–Sarila (Snob 130) (1980 10.8s* 12d² **114**
12fg* 12d² 12g³ 12g 11g* 15d* 1981 10g³ 12s 15.5d³ 15.5g 20v² 15.5d 15f⁴
14g*) workmanlike ex-English colt; won minor event at Vichy in August;

ran well in better company earlier, finishing length third to Kelbomec in Prix de Barbeville at Longchamp on third start, 3 lengths second to easy winner Gold River in Prix du Cadran on same course and 3 lengths fourth to Tipperary Fixer in Prix Kergorlay at Deauville; suited by a test of stamina; acts on any going. *C. de Watrigant, France.*

HERE'S ANDREW 2 ch.c. Guillaume Tell 121–Kitty O'Shea (Sky Gipsy 117) — (1981 6f) Apr 27; IR 3,200F, IR300Y; lengthy colt; second produce; dam Irish 1¾m winner; 33/1 and in need of race when behind in 17-runner maiden event won by Kamal at Yarmouth in June; sold to E. Owen 450 gns Doncaster October Sales. *A. Jarvis.*

HERE'S SUE 2 b.f. Three Legs 128–Gaino (Chaparral 128) (1981 5fg* 5d* **76** 5g3) Mar 14; IR 2,500F, 6,000Y; rather lightly-made filly; first foal; dam poor French maiden; made all to win maiden race at Warwick in April and 10-runner minor event at Ripon the following month; had limitations exposed when 5 lengths third of 10 to Major's Affair in similar race on latter course in June; will stay 6f; acts on a firm and a soft surface; well-backed favourite and ridden by 5-lb claimer all starts; sold 1,750 gns Newmarket Autumn Sales. *A. Jarvis.*

HER EXCELLENCY 4 b.f. Dragonara Palace 115–My Paddy 83 (St Paddy 133) — (1980 6f3 5h4 6g3 1981 5s 5fg 6g 7f 6fg 7fg4 8fg 7f 7f) plater; stays 7f; acts on firm going; has run respectably for a boy; blinkered final start. *J. Bridger.*

HER GRACE 3 ch.f. Great Nephew 126–Front Row 111 (Epaulette 125) **94** (1980 6g* 6d4 6g3 1981 8f) lightly-made filly; won maiden race at Doncaster by 10 lengths and was in frame in Cherry Hinton Stakes at Newmarket and Princess Margaret Stakes at Ascot as a 2-y-o; having first race for nearly a year but well backed when seventh of 10 behind Tolmi in Coronation Stakes at Royal Ascot in June, only outing of 1981, should have been suited by 1m; visits Godswalk. *H. Cecil.*

HERIOT 9 b.g. Mandamus 120–Henry's Daughter 95 (Tudor Jinks 121) (1980 — NR 1981 11.7fg 12d) probably of little account on flat nowadays. *J. Priday.*

HERMIA 4 ch.f. Midsummer Night II 117–Cecilia Gallerani (Pinturischio — 116) (1980 8s4 7f 8fg 10f 7d* 1981 7d 8d) small, lengthy filly; won maiden race at Salisbury at 3 yrs; well beaten both starts in 1981; stays 1m; needs some give in the ground; sold 6,800 gns Newmarket Autumn Sales. *J. Winter.*

HEROIC JAMES 2 b.c. Bold Lad (Ire) 133–Elm 88 (Realm 129) (1981 **76** 7f 7fg4 7fg 7d) Feb 24; 9,000Y; strong colt; first foal; dam won over 5f on her first 2 starts; ran creditably on second and third starts, both in July, finishing 9 lengths fourth of 8 to Ashenden in £4,200 event at Newmarket and about 1½ lengths fifth of 15 to Jiretta in minor event at Doncaster; gave impression on only subsequent start the following month that 7f was beyond him. *R. Williams.*

HEROIC SAGA 3 ch.c. Hittite Glory 125–Who Can Tell 109 (Worden II — 129) (1980 NR 1981 8d) half-brother to numerous winners, notably high-class 1¼m horse Rarity (by Hethersett); dam won Fred Darling Stakes; 20/1 when eighth of 12 behind Cornish Granite in maiden race at Bath in June; sold 1,200 gns Newmarket July Sales and resold 625 gns Ascot October Sales. *M. Stoute.*

HERONS HOLLOW 4 gr.c. Wolver Hollow 126–Sunbittern 112 (Sea Hawk **103** II 131) (1980 8d* 8g* 10d3 8fg 8d 8g* 8d3 8d* 10g 1981 8d2 8s3 7.6g3 7f3 8fg4 8fg* 8v3 8g) neat, strong colt; has a round action; useful handicapper; beat Baronet a short head in Swinley Forest Stakes at Ascot in September; placed in William Hill Lincoln at Doncaster (½-length second to Saher), Play-boy Bookmakers' Newbury Spring Cup, Queen Elizabeth Stakes at Lingfield and Ward Hill Bunbury Cup at Newmarket earlier; best at up to 1m; acts on any going but goes well on soft; hung badly right at Ascot and ran moderately last 2 starts. *G. Harwood.*

HERON'S ROSE 2 ch.f. Leander 119–Heron's Strike (Combat 123) (1981 — 5s 7fg 7fg) May 6; leggy filly; fourth living foal; dam quite moderate hurdler; in rear in maiden races in the Midlands. *J. Peacock.*

HERO'S PARADE 2 br.c. Queen's Hussar 124–Changing Tides (Swaps) **70** (1981 7g 7.6s 6s) Feb 16; 7,000F; useful-looking colt; second reported foal; dam won over 9f in France; showed signs of ability in maiden races; should stay 1m. *C. James.*

HETHERMAI 4 b.f. Pee Mai 107–Hethersent 71 (Hethersett 134) (1980 **54** 10h 12g 16g 16d 12s 1981 8f* 8h 10.2g 10.2d) small filly; attracted no bid after winning seller at Bath in July (apprentice ridden); stays 1m; acts on firm going; has sweated up on occasions; sometimes wears blinkers. *S. Kernick.*

HEVER 6 br.g. Tudor Melody 129–Queen's Castle 98 (Sovereign Path 125) **58**
(1980 NR 1981 8fg4 8h 8f4) one-mile handicapper; acts on firm going; often blinkered. *M. Pipe.*

HEXAMERON (USA) 2 b.c. Halo–Mountain Legend (Jacinto) (1981 8s4 8s*) **?**
Feb 19; $60,000Y; attractive colt; second foal; dam, winner of 6f maiden race at 3 yrs, is half-sister to smart 1962 American 2-y-o Catullus and smart middle-distance performer No Turning; led early in straight when winning 6-runner maiden race at Longchamp in October comfortably by 1½ lengths from Masmak; will make a very useful middle-distance colt. *F. Boutin, France.*

HEXGREAVE 4 ch.f. Mount Hagen 127–Granville Lady (High Hat 131) **—**
(1980 11f4 12.2f 1981 13.4fg 8g 12fg 12.2fg 8f 10fg3 8d 9d 12s 10.2g) smallish, well-made filly; poor performer nowadays; well beaten in valuable seller final start; stays 1¼m; acts on a firm surface; wears blinkers. *R. Hobson.*

HEXGREAVE STAR 3 b. or br.g. Comedy Star 121–Double Grand (Coronation **78**
Year 124) (1980 5v2 5v* 5f2 5v2 5fg3 6d 6g 6g*(dis) 6d 6g 6fg 6f3 1981 8s4 8v 7d 6g3 6g 6f 5fg) strong, compact gelding; ran best races of year in handicaps on fourth and seventh starts, when third to Chantry Bridge at York in May and sixth of 15 behind Ferriby Hall in Gosforth Park Cup at Newcastle in June; best at sprint distances; acts on any going; has worn bandages; blinkered nowadays. *M. W. Easterby.*

HI-DE-HI 2 b.c. Ardoon 124–Best Exhibit (Kalydon 122) (1981 5g 5d 8s) **—**
Feb 20; IR 500Y; half-brother to fairly useful 1976 2-y-o 7f winner Exploiteur (by Sharpen Up); dam never ran; poor maiden; well beaten in seller final start; should stay 1m. *S. Mellor.*

HIDING 2 br.f. So Blessed 130–Bolting 108 (King's Bench 132) (1981 5g* 5f **84**
5fg3) Mar 8; 11,500Y; neat, well-made filly; half-sister to 2 winners, including very smart sprinter Turnkey (by Tudor Melody); dam sprinting half-sister to numerous winners; did well to get up and win 8-runner maiden race at Pontefract in August by ½ length from Cedrella after having to be switched below distance; disappointed when 11/4 on for small race next time out but was beaten only a short head and a head by Ghawar after having none too clear a run in nursery at Goodwood later in August; not sure to stay beyond 5f; possibly not at her best on very firm going. *M. Stoute.*

HIGH ACCLAIM 3 b.c. High Top 131–Love and Care 96 (Ballymoss 136) **—**
(1980 NR 1981 8g 8f 7.6s4) 15,000Y; small colt; second living foal; half-brother to a winner in Italy; dam, daughter of Gimcrack Stakes winner Be Careful, won over 5f at 2 yrs; showed a little ability in minor event at Bath in July and maiden race at Chester in August on last 2 starts; stays 1m; ridden by 7-lb claimer first 2 starts; sold 700 gns Ascot September Sales. *J. Tree.*

HIGHAM GREY 5 gr.g. Warpath 113–Jackies Joy (Skymaster 126) (1980 **76**
10.2d 12fg 10h 7f 12f 12f* 12fg* 12f2 12d* 12g3 10g2 12g 8g 8fg2 8g* 7s 15d 1981 8g* 10.5d 8g2 10f2 12f2 16g3 10f* 11fg* 10g* 10g 13fg3 12f 11g 8s 18g) useful-looking gelding; used to be none too reliable; reformed nowadays and is a fair handicapper; awarded race at Redcar in May on a technicality and won at Pontefract and Ayr (twice) in July; also ran very well sixth start when 3 lengths third to Dawn Johnny in Northumberland Plate at Newcastle; effective at 1m to 2m; seems to act on any going; effective with or without blinkers; ran moderately last 4 starts, unseating rider beforehand on first occasion. *D. Chapman.*

HIGH AUTHORITY 2 b.f. High Award 119–Elia (Narrator 127) (1981 **80**
5s2 5fg 5d 5d 5g* 6g4 5f 6f 7fg 5g3 5d2 5g* 5g 6s) May 5; workmanlike filly; good mover; half-sister to a winner in Belgium; dam of little account; won seller at Doncaster in May (no bid) and ran out a clear-cut winner of 12-runner nursery at Wolverhampton in September; effective at 5f and 6f (out of depth over 7f); best form with some give in the ground; used to be troublesome at start, unseating rider leaving stalls on fourth outing and ruining her chance by starting slowly on seventh; sweated up final appearance. *D. Leslie.*

HIGH BUTTON BOOTS 2 b.f. Tower Walk 130–Sincerity 91 (Soderini 123) **—**
(1981 5.8h 6g 5s) Mar 2; half-sister to quite useful The Sergeant (by King's Troop), a winner over 6f and 7f, and fair 1979 2-y-o 6f winner Come What May (by Derring-Do); dam best at up to 7f; little worthwhile form; sold 620 gns Newmarket Autumn Sales. *B. Swift.*

391

HIGH CIRCLES 3 b.g. High Line 125–Misnomer 85 (Milesian 125) (1980 **54**
10.2s 1981 10s² 12g 12s 10f 14.6f 16f) big, leggy gelding; second in maiden
race at Newcastle in April, best effort; should be suited by 1½m+; has a round
action and almost certainly needs give in the ground; sold 4,100 gns Newmarket
Autumn Sales. *W. Elsey.*

HIGH CLASS BUILDER 3 ch.f. Flair Path 122–Holly (Chamossaire) (1980 —
6s* 7g³ 6g³ 7fg⁴ 7g 7g* 7g³ 8d 1981 10s 9g⁴ 8d 10f 9d⁴ 8g 10g 9g 13.8g) compact
filly; plater; will stay 1½m; seems to act on any going; occasionally blinkered;
sold privately 380 gns Doncaster September Sales. *K. Stone.*

HIGHCROFT 3 b.f. Welsh Saint 126–Maryfield (Hul a Hul 124) (1980 5f —
5fg³ 5g 6fg 6d 5fg 6g³ 5f* 5f² 5fg 5g 1981 5s 5d 5d 5.3f) well-made, attractive
filly; towards rear in handicaps; best form at 5f; acts well on firm going; sometimes blinkered; sold 700 gns Newmarket Autumn Sales. *G. Lewis.*

HIGHDALGO 4 ch.c. Most Secret 119–Waltham Lady 78 (Highland Melody —
112) (1980 8fg 8fg 9s 8f 1981 8f) compact colt; bad plater. *Miss L. Siddall.*

HIGHER AND HIGHER 2 b.f. High Award 119–Tide And Time (Easter —
Island 101) (1981 6f) May 23; compact filly; half-sister to 5f winner Tampa
Bay (by Ickford); dam never ran; unquoted and in need of race when beaten
long way in seller at Yarmouth in June. *D. Leslie.*

HIGHFIELD 4 b.g. Blue and Grey 93–Whistlewych 40 (Whistler 129) (1980 —
6fg 9g 7fg 6s 8f 7g 1981 8f) neat, strong gelding; poor plater; suited by 1m; has
worn blinkers. *J. Carr.*

HIGHFIELD JET 6 b.h. High Top 131–Cloudbreaker 95 (Nimbus 130) (1980 **48**
10.2d 12f 8g 1981 8s* 8.2g² 10.6s² 9.4g⁴) plater; well-backed favourite when
winning at Ripon in April (no bid); effective from 1m to 1½m; probably acts on
any going; has run well in blinkers; sold 3,600 gns Newmarket Autumn Sales.
A. Smith.

HIGH FORM 2 ch.f. Gold Form 108–Highview Jill 73 (Proud Chieftain 122) —
(1981 5d 6g) Feb 14; 750F, 2,200Y; well-grown filly; half-sister to winning
sprinter Firbeck (by Veiled Wonder) and a winner in Italy; dam won over 1¼m;
eased once chance had gone in final 2f when behind in valuable seller at York
in July, second outing; sold 400 gns Doncaster August Sales. *M. W. Easterby.*

HIGH HEAVEN 3 br.c. High Top 131–Arics (Acropolis 132) (1980 NR 1981 —
8g) 10,000Y; attractive colt; half-brother to 3 winners, including fairly useful
stayer Rainfall (by Relko) and smart 1m to 1¼m performer Air Trooper (by
King's Troop); dam, from excellent family, never ran; badly needed race and
dropped back in last 2f when out of first 9 of 16 behind St Pedro in maiden race
at Newmarket in April; sold to A. Moore 2,400 gns Ascot October Sales. *J.
Dunlop.*

HIGH HILLS 7 gr.g. High Top 131–Charity Walk (Sovereign Path 125) (1980 **63**
13v³ 11d 12f 13fg² 12f⁴ 12d² 12g⁴ 12g² 12d 13s⁴ 13s 1981 13v² 14s) middle-
distance handicapper; acts on any going; often blinkered; suitable mount for an
apprentice; goes well at Hamilton. *T. Craig.*

HIGH HOPE 2 ch.c. Mount Hagen 127–Sazan (Weimar) (1981 5d 5fg 5d 5.8g —
7fg) Mar 15; 11,000F, 8,000Y; neat colt; first produce; dam, half-sister to
Italian Derby winner Suffolk, was placed in Italy at 3 yrs; pushed along throughout when 4¾ lengths sixth of 20 to Fair Mount Lad in maiden race at Salisbury
in May, third outing and best effort; should be suited by 6f+; trained by P. M.
Taylor first 4 outings. *G. Huffer.*

HIGHLAND BEAUTY 2 ch.f. High Line 125–Fire Queen (Prince Hansel 118) —
(1981 8d 10s) Mar 30; 3,500Y; short-backed, quite attractive filly; first foal;
dam never ran; well beaten in maiden races at Wolverhampton (badly needed
race) and Nottingham in October. *A. Goodwill.*

HIGHLAND BERRY 2 br.f. Scottish Rifle 127–Spice Berry 63 (Tutankhamen) — p
(1981 6g) Mar 18; 4,600Y; workmanlike filly; sister to 1m winner Scotsezo;
dam half-sister to smart animals Red Berry and Big Bead; unquoted, stayed
on without being knocked about when over 10 lengths ninth of 17 to I'm Hot
in maiden race at Newmarket in October; will be suited by 1m; will probably
do better. *P. Walwyn.*

HIGHLAND LINNET 4 b.g. Highland Melody 112–Golden Linnet 96 (Sing —
Sing 134) (1980 12f⁴ 16d 12g 1981 10fg 9s) leggy gelding; little worthwhile
form in maiden and minor events; not certain to stay middle distances. *B.
Richmond.*

HIGHLAND RANGE 3 ch.g. Crowned Prince 128–Caramel 93 (Crepello 136) **75** (1980 7g 7g 7f* 1981 10fg 12d 12g* 12d 16f 10g⁴ 14fg) tall, useful-looking gelding; excellent mover; stayed on really well when beating Tender Angus a head in handicap at Newbury in May; rather disappointing at Epsom on next outing; promises to stay further than 1½m (had stiff tasks when tried over 1¾m and 2m); best form on a sound surface. *G. Lewis.*

HIGHLAND SPICE 7 br.g. Highland Melody 112–Sugar Sweet 87 (Zucchero — 133§) (1980 10d 1981 12s 16f) poor plater; sometimes wears blinkers; has worn bandages; retained 750 gns Ascot June Sales. *K. Morgan.*

HIGH PITCHED 2 ch.g. Crooner 119–Lucky Run 101 (Runnymede 123) **77** (1981 7f 7d² 8g³) May 25; second living foal; half-brother to 1979 2-y-o 5f winner One Off The Edge (by Master Sing); dam won over 5.9f at 2 yrs; neck second to odds-on Loyal Toast in 14-runner maiden event at Lingfield in August; 5½ lengths third of 17 to Queen's Home in maiden race at Goodwood the following month; seems to stay 1m; ridden by apprentice G. Dickie last 2 starts. *R. Smyth.*

HIGH POPPA 2 b.c. Mummy's Pet 125–Two For Joy (Double-U-Jay 120) **74** (1981 7fg 6g 5g² 5s⁴) May 9; lengthy, lightly-made colt; second foal; dam, 2-y-o 7f seller winner, also won over hurdles and fences; in frame in the autumn in maiden events at Bath (½-length second to Bold Saracen) and Warwick (2¾ lengths fourth of 17 to Fast Lad); promises to stay 6f. *P. Cundell.*

HIGH PORT 2 b.c. Import 127–High Walk (Tower Walk 130) (1981 5g **78** 6s 6f 6f 6fg⁴ 6g³ 8f* 6d² 7d 7g) Mar 24; leggy, quite useful sort; good mover; first foal; dam bad plater; showed improved form when enterprisingly ridden in 1m nursery at Thirsk in September, making all and holding on by ½ length from Blandor; 1½ lengths second of 9 in nursery won by Nagalia at Hamilton later in month; ran moderately next outing and bolted a full circuit of course before final start; effective at 6f to 1m; seems to act on any going. *G. Toft.*

HIGH RAINBOW 4 b.g. High Line 125–Darwin Tulip (Campaign 106 or **76** Pirate King 129) (1980 12fg 12g³ 12.2d³ 12g 12.2f² 12g* 12.2g* 12g³(dis) 12f 1981 12g 10.6s² 11g³ 11d² 13fg* 12d) useful-looking gelding; won handicap at Ayr in August; eighth in valuable selling handicap at Doncaster in October; will be suited by 1¾m; acts on any going; sometimes sweats up; carried head high and didn't look easiest of rides in amateur riders event second start. *J. Etherington.*

HIGH REALM 2 b. or br.c. Realm 129–Melodramatic 112 (Tudor Melody 129) **79** (1981 5d⁴ 5s) Mar 24; 23,000Y; lengthy colt; good mover; half-brother to 3 winners, all at least fairly useful, including miler Crown Witness (by Crowned Prince) and useful Irish 3-y-o Overplay (by Bustino); dam very useful winner over 7f and 9f; 16/1, came out easily best of low-drawn horses when 3¼ lengths fourth of 20 to Path To Glory in maiden race at Newbury in September; evens favourite for 18-runner maiden event at Nottingham later in month but ruined chance by rearing as stalls opened and then colliding with a rival, eventually finishing out of first 9 behind Town Flier (performance best ignored); will be suited by 6f. *M. Albina.*

HIGH RIDGE 2 b.g. High Top 131–Naughty Party (Parthia 132) (1981 7fg) — Apr 1; 8,000Y; well-made gelding; fourth foal; half-brother to 3-y-o 1m winner Bustellina (by Busted); dam, 7f winner in Ireland, is half-sister to Whistling Wind; 14/1 when last of 18 to Macmillion in maiden race at Newbury in July. *G. Hunter.*

HIGH RISER 2 b.f. Connaught 130–Absent 66 (Abernant 142) (1981 6f — 6g 6d 8s) Apr 27; leggy filly; fourth foal; dam won half-sister to Gimcrack winner Wishing Star; towards rear in varied company; sweated up second start. *M. Camacho.*

HIGH STEWARD 8 b.g. Taj Dewan 128–Fervent (French Beige 127) (1980 — NR 1981 18g 18g) staying handicapper; has a round action; acts on a soft surface; has worn blinkers and bandages. *F. Dever.*

HIJAZIAH 2 ch.f. High Line 125–Keadby Bridge (Petition 130) (1981 8d) — p May 25; 4,300F; fair sort; half-brother to fair 1¼m winner Queensferry (by Pindari); dam unraced half-sister to Gloria Nicky, Edmundo and Libra; unquoted and in need of the outing, couldn't quicken and wasn't unduly knocked about when 10 lengths fifth of 11 to Misty Halo in maiden race at Wolverhampton in October; will stay middle distances. *A. Hide.*

Mr M. Fustok's "Hilal"

HILAL 5 ch.h. Royal and Regal–Whistling Rex (Whistling Wind 123) (1980 **125**
8v³ 8g⁴ 8d² 8g² 7s² 8g³ 10s² 8g 8g⁴ 8d* 8d* 1981 8d* 8s² 9.2s 8f⁴ 8f² 8s 7v)
Horses that need to be held up certainly make for exciting racing but they
often present their jockeys with considerable problems. If the field is small
covering up a runner can be difficult; with a lot of contestants there is no guarantee of a clear run at the right time; in a slowly-run race it is possible to be left
with too much to do once the pace quickens; and in a strongly-run race there's
a chance of hitting the front too soon should the leaders weaken earlier than
expected. It follows that horses suited by waiting tactics sometimes need
uncommon luck on their side as well as sound tacticians on their backs.
Hilal is such a horse. He has a good turn of foot but tends not to find
much in front and given his style of racing the criticism which some levelled
at his regular pilot Gibert after the Tote Lockinge Stakes in May was far from
justified. Hilal came to Newbury with three successive pattern-race wins to
his name. A decisive winner of the Prix du Rond-Point and Prix Perth at
the end of 1980, he had started the current season in good style with a smooth
length-and-a-half success from Joberan in the Prix de Ris-Orangis at Evry
a month before the Lockinge. At Newbury Gibert and he were unlucky to
come up against so redoubtable a combination as Piggott and Belmont Bay.
Covered up at the rear as Belmont Bay set the pace, Hilal moved through two
furlongs out, challenged on a tight rein at about the distance and cruised into
a lead of perhaps half a length from the strongly-ridden Belmont Bay. It
looked odds on Hilal here but the picture changed rapidly, for rather than
quickening clear when asked to by his jockey he found very little, put his head
in the air when the by-now uneasy Gibert subjected him to full pressure and
was caught in the dying strides and beaten a head by Belmont Bay on whom
Piggott staged a storming finish. No blame attaches to Gibert—had Hilal
been a little more enthusiastic and had Belmont Bay been ridden by a lesser
jockey the spoils would definitely have been taken back to France.
Hilal was seen once more in England but due to an abscess in his mouth
he ran well below form in the Queen Elizabeth II Stakes won by To-Agori-
Mou at Ascot in September, finishing fifth. At his best he would probably

have made a race of it with the Guineas winner. In France he twice ran well behind Northjet over a mile. In the Prix Jacques le Marois at Deauville he came to challenge up the centre of the course two furlongs out but, like everything else, was completely outpaced in the closing stages and came in fourth, only losing out narrowly to To-Agori-Mou and Kings Lake in a desperate struggle for the minor placings. In the Prix du Moulin de Longchamp Hilal ran on strongly in the straight and was closing on Northjet at the end where he was beaten one and a half lengths into second, ahead of The Wonder, Phydilla and Belmont Bay. Hilal's other starts saw his failing to reach the frame at Longchamp in the Prix d'Ispahan, in which the extended nine furlongs seemed too far for him and he finished fifth to The Wonder, and the Prix de la Foret, in which he never reached a challenging position behind Moorestyle.

Hilal (ch.h. 1976)	Royal and Regal (b 1970)	Vaguely Noble (b 1965)	Vienna
			Noble Lassie
		Native Street (gr 1963)	Native Dancer
			Beaver Street
	Whistling Rex (b 1969)	Whistling Wind (ch 1960)	Whistler
			Good as Gold
		Gallop On (gr 1960)	Grey Sovereign
			Tinted Venus

Hilal was bred in Ireland and fetched 9,000 guineas as a yearling at the Newmarket Houghton Sales. He is the third foal out of the unraced Whistling Wind mare Whistling Rex; the first, Ballinavail (by Rarity), won over a mile in Ireland. The grandam, Gallop On, was a useful two-year-old, winning the Acorn Stakes and finishing third in the Cherry Hinton Stakes, out of the prolific winner-producing mare Tinted Venus, dam of the very fast Fortune's Darling. Hilal, a strong horse with a look of quality about him, is best at a mile and acts on any going though he sometimes wears bandages in front and didn't look entirely happy going down on the very firm ground at Deauville. Though consistent he is evidently not an easy ride. *M. Saliba, France.*

HILAL SOVEREIGN 2 b.f. Grisaille 115–Impetuous Miss (Don Carlos) (1981 — 5fg 6d 6fg) of no account. *Mrs R. Lomax.*

HILARIO 2 b.c. Tower Walk 130–Taffimai (Never Say Die 137) (1981 6fg **54** 7fg 6g³ 8g) Mar 30; neat, good sort; very good walker; half-brother to quite moderate Devil May Care (by Galivanter) and fairly useful 1978 2-y-o Taffalla (by Royalty); dam never ran; weak favourite in sellers at Yarmouth (chased along throughout and finished 5¾ lengths of 11 to Keep Silent) and Leicester in September (claimed £2,400); should be suited by 1m. *W. Hastings-Bass.*

HILL OF BARRA 3 ch.g. Pieces of Eight 128–Red Sea 70 (Zimone) (1980 — 5d 5v 5f 7f 7d 6s 1981 6fg 8g) leggy gelding; in rear in varied company, including selling; blinkered final outing. *N. Vigors.*

HILL OF SLANE 5 b.g. The Parson 119–Polenka (First Landing) (1980 **73** NR 1981 18.1d² 16s 18g 18g) strong, useful-looking gelding; suited by a test of stamina; acts on any going; blinkered once at 3 yrs; needs strong handling nowadays; fairly useful hurdler. *A. Jarvis.*

HILLSDOWN GOLD 4 b.c. Goldhill 125–Dumana 96 (Dumbarnie 125) (1980 **90** 8g³ 8f⁴ 8fg* 8fg² 8.2g³ 1981 10s 10.6g 10.2fg 10f 8fg* 10g³ 8fg 8fg² 9g 8.2s 8g) neat colt; modest handicapper; 50/1 when beating Tugoflove decisively by 2½ lengths at Ascot in July; best at around 1m; probably acts on any going; has run creditably in blinkers and when sweating up. *G. Huffer.*

HILLSDOWN LAD 3 b.c. Forlorn River 124–Alchorus 78 (Alcide 136) (1980 **76** d 6d³ 1981 8.2s² 8g⁴ 8d 6g) rangy colt; good mover; looked in need of run when in frame in maiden races at Nottingham in April and at Yarmouth when next seen out in September; stays 1m; blinkered last 2 starts (found little under pressure on first occasion and never going on second); possibly one to be wary of. *G. Huffer.*

HILL'S GUARD 2 br.c. Home Guard 129–Ballinkillen (Levmoss 133) (1981 **68** p 7d) Mar 27; 11,000F, 26,000Y; first foal; dam, daughter of smart Windy Gay, won over 1¼m in Ireland; drifted from 6/1 to 14/1 for 11-runner minor event at Leicester in November and was beaten about 8½ lengths into fifth place behind Don Giovanni; will stay 1m; should improve. *M. Stoute.*

HILL'S NORTHERN 4 ch.c. Northfields–Sovereign Court 87 (Sovereign Path 125) (1980 8.2s² 8fg* 8f* 8fg* 8g 8g 8h 8d 1981 7.6g 8f) neat colt; fair performer at his best; well beaten at 4 yrs; will stay 1¼m; probably acts on any going; blinkered twice at 3 yrs; often hangs badly and isn't an easy ride; sold out of R. Turnell's stable 7,400 gns Ascot June Sales after first outing; resold 3,200 gns same venue in December. *J. Harris.* —

HILL'S PAGEANT 2 b.c. Welsh Pageant 132–Reita 87 (Gilles de Retz 132) **80** (1981 7fg 7.2fg³ 7g) Apr 10; 18,500Y; good-looking colt; half-brother to several winners, including very useful Homeboy (by King's Troop); dam miler; ran on well without being knocked about unnecessarily when 2½ lengths third of 14 to Jalmood in maiden race at Haydock in September; not disgraced when ninth of 16 to Wind and Wuthering in Somerville Tattersall Stakes at Newmarket the following month; will stay 1¼m; looks the type to train on well. *P. Walwyn.*

HILL'S PRINCE 3 b.c. Prince Tenderfoot 126–Peta 93 (Petingo 135) (1980 **67** NR 1981 8g 8fg 10.1f 10fg 8fg² 8h 8s) 25,000Y; big colt; first foal; dam, 2-y-o 6f winner, comes from a prolific winning family; looked really well and showed improved form when ½-length second to Mianach Oir in maiden race at Salisbury in August; ran poorly afterwards; will be suited by a return to 1¼m; sold 3,400 gns Newmarket Autumn Sales. *P. Walwyn.*

HILL'S REALM (USA) 3 br.f. Key To The Kingdom–Princess Dare (Impressive) (1980 5f⁴ 5.1f⁴ 6g⁴ 1981 5d 6fg 6d 6f 6f 6fg 7f 10f) neat filly; plating-class maiden; stays 6f; has been tried in blinkers. *B. Swift.* —

HILL VIXEN 2 b.f. Goldhill 125–Foxy Fanny 66 (Space King 115) (1981 **69** 6f⁴ 6g 7d) May 3; neat filly; first foal; dam won over 1½m and also won 2 selling hurdles; unquoted when running on 3½ lengths fourth of 23 to Bustello in minor event at Nottingham in July; well beaten in maiden races at Redcar and Newbury subsequently; should stay 7f. *P. Rohan.*

HIMORRE 2 b.c. Song 132–Monagram 77 (Mon Fetiche 120) (1981 6g² 7g³ **88** 7.6s³) Apr 3; 5,400F, 7,500Y; lengthy, good-quartered, attractive colt; good walker; half-brother to useful 1976 2-y-o 5f winner Japora (by Raffingora) and a winner abroad; dam won at 1m; placed on all outings, putting up best effort when strong-finishing 5 lengths third to General Anders in £4,100 race at Ascot in September on second outing; didn't reproduce that form next time out and possibly finds an extended 7f too far. *R. Price.*

HINDI 3 b.f. Mummy's Pet 125–Sarong 97 (Taj Dewan 128) (1980 6f 5d* 5g **100** 1981 6fg 6g³ 6s³ 7f² 7g² 8g² 7fg⁴ 8g* 8s⁴) quite attractive filly; came with a very good late run and just got up to beat Melodrama a short head in Taylor Woodrow Diamond Jubilee Charity Handicap Stakes at Ascot in September (pair clear); 4 lengths fourth of 8 to Noda in Group 3 Premio Bagutta at Milan the following month; very close second at Wolverhampton, Newmarket and Yarmouth earlier; stays 1m; acts on any going; looked ungenuine on third start and ran poorly seventh start; sent to USA. *M. Jarvis.*

HINND 3 b.f. Comedy Star 121–Verbally 79 (Ballymoss 136) (1980 NR 1981 — 8.2f 10.1g 12g) 4,000Y; half-sister to several winners here and abroad; dam half-sister to smart stayer By Thunder!; little worthwhile form in maiden races; sold 460 gns Newmarket Autumn Sales. *C. Nelson.*

HINTONADO 2 b.c. Manado 130–Sea Dog (Sea Hawk II 131) (1981 6fg 6fg **76** 7g² 8d³ 10s) Feb 14; 13,000F, 9,200Y; neat, compact colt; rather lacking in scope; third living foal; half-brother to 1m and 1¼m winner Seaway (by Kalamoun); dam useful Irish middle-distance performer; looked promising on debut but proved only moderate, gaining his places in maiden races at Leicester (½-length second to Airwair in September) and Bath; should stay 1¼m. *P. Cole.*

HINTSBROOK 3 b.c. Upper Case–Leisure Hour (Persian Gulf) (1980 8d — 1981 8d 8.2s 10fg 8f) useful sort; well beaten in maiden and minor races; has twice started slowly. *B. McMahon.*

HIPPO DISCO 2 b.c. Wollow 132–Yell Aloud (Laugh Aloud) (1981 7g 8s² 8d) **82** May 17; well-made colt; half-brother to several winners, including useful 1976 2-y-o 5f winner Shush (by Diplomat Way); dam won at up to 6f in USA; 1½ lengths second of 17 to Barfoot in maiden race at Warwick in October; well-beaten favourite in similar race at Leicester the following month; stays 1m.   *M. Stoute.*

HIRSUTE   4 ch.g. Blue Cashmere 129–Queen Flush (Twilight Alley 133)   (1980   **39**
10s 10f 8f 8g 8g³ 8g² 8d² 9g   1981 8.2s³ 10g)   lengthy gelding; one-paced plater;
stays 1m; probably acts on any going; has been tried in blinkers; sometimes
bandaged; sold 540 gns Doncaster August Sales.   *P. Asquith.*

HISLAND   3 ch.g. Roi Soleil 125–Parterre (Tudor Treasure 119)   (1980 5f   —
6s 6fg   1981 8.2s)   leggy gelding; well beaten in maiden and maiden auction
events.   *L. Barratt.*

HIS MASTER'S VOICE   3 ch.g. Brigadier Gerard 144–Heavenly Sound   **68**
115 (Sound Track 132)   (1980 6fg 7f   1981 8f 8.2f* 8f* 8fg² 8f² 8fg)   strong,
useful sort; improved and won handicaps at Hamilton in June and Ripon
in July, on latter course staying on much the best and beating Monza Lady
by 3 lengths; second twice afterwards, including in an apprentice handicap;
will probably stay 1¼m; acts on firm going; gives impression he's suited by strong
handling; ran moderately final start.   *Sir Mark Prescott.*

HISSING SID   3 gr. or ro.g. Royal Match 117–Serissa (Supreme Sovereign   **81**
119)   (1980 6g 6s 6d³ 8.2s 7.2d*   1981 8s* 8s 7fg³ 8g³ 8d* 8s 8g* 10f 8f³ 9f* 8f
8f 10g 8.2d)   robust gelding; good mover; did well and won seller at Doncaster
in March (bought in 4,200 gns) and handicaps at Ripon in May, June and August,
making all twice; stays 9f; acts on any going; good mount for an apprentice;
seems well suited by a turning track.   *R. Hollinshead.*

HISSY MISSY   2 b.f. Bold Lad (Ire) 133–Sassanian (Sassafras 135)   (1981   **70**
7fg⁴ 7f 7fg³ 8.2d 7g)   Feb 20; neat, deep-girthed filly; not the best of walkers
and has a round action; first reported foal; dam won 5 races in Spain; in frame
in maiden races at Newmarket in July (length fourth of 22 to Oxslip) and Ayr
in September (stayed on when 3½ lengths third of 15 behind Awaasif); soundly
beaten on her other outings; should stay 1m.   *H. T. Jones.*

HIT BITS   2 b.f. Hittite Glory 125–Tickled To Bits (Sweet Revenge 129)   —
(1981 6fg 6d 5g)   Apr 20; 11,500Y; small, dipped-backed filly; first foal; dam
poor maiden; behind in maiden races at Newmarket in July and Windsor (2)
in August.   *R. Armstrong.*

HI THERE   3 b.f. High Top 131–Thereby 99 (Star Moss 122)   (1980 5fg 5f*   —
5f⁴ 5g 6g   1981 6s 6d 5d)   small, useful-looking filly; fair performer at 2 yrs;
not disgraced in 1981; bred to stay 1m; best form on a sound surface.   *H. Candy.*

HITHERMOOR LASS   2 b.f. Red Alert 127–Splosh (Silly Season 127)   (1981   **75**
5g³ 5fg³ 6fg 5.8f⁴ 6fg² 6g³ 6fg 6d 6g)   Mar 22; 6,000Y; quite well-made filly;
first foal; dam poor sister to smart handicapper Idiot's Delight; placed in maiden
races and a nursery; will stay 7f; blinkered when running poorly on eighth
and ninth starts and is not particularly consistent.   *Mrs J. Reavey.*

HIT ME AGAIN   3 ch.c. Quayside 124–Nell 76 (Gilles de Retz 132)   (1980   —
5fg 5.8fg 6g 8s 6g   1981 6s 8fg 10d 8f)   leggy, close-coupled colt; bad plater;
blinkered fifth start in 1980.   *C. Mackenzie.*

HI-TOPSY   2 b.f. High Top 131–Noble Countess (Mossborough 126)   (1981   **67**
7f 7.6s⁴)   Mar 16; closely related to 3-y-o 1m winner Daring Dame (by Derring-
Do) and half-sister to several minor winners; dam closely related to Oaks
winner Noblesse; fairly prominent in maiden races at Brighton in August (5¾
lengths fifth of 16 to Hostess) and Lingfield in October (12½ lengths fourth of
15 behind Sabutai); will stay at least 1¼m.   *P. Cole.*

HITRAVELSCENE   2 b.f. Mansingh 120–Kassiope 54 (Sir Gaylord)   (1981   —
5d 5g 5s)   May 11; lightly-made filly; first foal; dam in frame over 1¼m once
from 5 starts; well beaten in maiden and minor events; off course 4 months
before third outing.   *N. Callaghan.*

HIT RECORD   3 ch.c. Record Token 128–Silk Willoughby (Pirate King 129)   **82**
(1980 5fg⁴ 7d³ 6g⁴ 5f 6d² 6d²   1981 6g⁴ 7d* 7g 7d² 7f⁴ 7g² 6g³ 8d 7g 7s* 7d 8g³)
quite an attractive, well-made colt; successful in maiden race at Leicester in April
and handicap at Redcar in October; stays 1m; acts on any going, but is well
suited by some give underfoot.   *F. Durr.*

HIT THE HAMMER 4 b.c. Blakeney 126–Guessing Game 87 (Doutelle 128) **68**
(1980 11f 10.2fg⁴ 16g² 14g³ 14d 12d² 1981 12d 12f³ 16s³) strong, quite attractive colt; staying maiden; suited by some give in the ground; bandaged in front last 2 starts; sold to D. Elsworth 1,300 gns Newmarket Autumn Sales. *C. Brittain.*

HIT THE LINE 2 br.f. Saulingo 122–Speed Easy (On Your Mark 125) (1981 **71**
5fg 6fg² 6d³) Mar 3; lengthy filly; first foal; dam ran twice unplaced in Ireland; placed in maiden races at Folkestone in August and Nottingham the following month; suited by 6f; sweated up at Nottingham. *C. Nelson.*

HIT THE ROAD (FR) 3 b.g. Sovereign Path 125–Hit It Off (Hardicanute **78**
130) (1980 7.2d 8d² 10s² 8d 1981 14g 16.9s 9s² 9g³ 12f* 11g* 12g² 12.3s) strong, compact gelding; won maiden race at Beverley (tended to hang right) and small race at Hamilton in July; suited by 1½m (well beaten over further); acts on any going; blinkered first 2 outings; ran very badly and was eventually pulled up at Chester on final start; sold to S. Pattemore 9,000 gns Newmarket Autumn Sales. *B. Hanbury.*

HITTITE CONQUERER 2 ch.c. Hittite Glory 125–Paravant (Parthia 132) —
(1981 5d) May 6; 7,600F; half-brother to 2 winners, including useful 1979 French 2-y-o Plisetskaja (by Sir Gaylord); 6/4 favourite when last of 6 to Ten-Traco in seller at Leicester in April; sold 860 gns Newmarket July Sales. *G. Richards.*

HITTITE PRINCE 2 b.g. Hittite Glory 125–Lady R. B. (Gun Shot) (1981 **65**
5g 5d³ 5g 5f² 6g⁴ 6g² 7g 7f* 6fg) May 10; compact gelding; half-brother to several winners here and in USA, including 1m and 1¾m winner Rifle Brigade (by High Top); dam poor sister to top-class American horse Gun Bow; won 14-runner seller at Thirsk in July by ¾ length from Sierra Morena; bought in 4,000 gns; suited by 7f; seems to act on any going; ran well in blinkers on fourth outing but didn't wear them subsequently. *B. Hanbury.*

HIYA JUDGE 3 b.c. Ashmore 125–Grey Home 110 (Habitat 134) (1980 **62**
NR 1981 7g 7fg 8g* 8.3g 8f 7g 8s 7v² 8d) 420 2-y-o; compact, rather plain colt; first foal; dam very useful 2-y-o 5f winner from only 3 starts; bought in 1,500 gns after beating Cherry Corner a shade comfortably by 1½ lengths in seller at Redcar in August; ran in better company afterwards, best effort when 2 lengths second to Quarry Bank in apprentice handicap at York in October; suited by 1m; acts on heavy going; sweated up sixth start. *A. Bailey.*

HIZ 3 gr.c. Persian Plan–Miss Swift 79 (Canisbay 120) (1980 6s 7fg⁴ 6g 6s* **86**
7d 1981 8s³ 8d 10d² 10g⁴ 10d⁴ 10d*) big, strong colt; in frame most starts, and beat Battalion decisively by 1½ lengths in minor event at Leicester in November; stays 1¼m; acts on a firm surface, but is well suited by soft ground. *R. Price.*

HLA TUN 2 b.g. High Top 131–Clippie 99 (Nimbus 130) (1981 5d 7g 7fg²) **86**
Apr 6; 12,000Y; strong gelding; half-brother to several winners, including quite useful stayer Harridan (by Fighting Charlie) and quite useful 2-y-o 6f winners Crowdie (by Crepello) and Erebus (by Sammy Davis); dam won at up to 1m; put up easily best effort when 1½ lengths second of 16 to Nunsruler in minor event at Warwick in August; will stay 1¼m. *P. Cundell.*

HOBA SUPREME 3 br.g. Sit In The Corner–Open Arms 77 (Dignitary 121) **45** d
(1980 5f 5d 6d 1981 5d² 5g 5s 6f 5fg 6fg 8fg 7g) compact gelding; second in poor maiden race at Wolverhampton in April, best effort; behind in sellers last 2 outings; should stay 6f; possibly needs some give in the ground; trained by R. E. Peacock until after fourth outing. *Mrs A. Cousins.*

HOBA TARA 3 b.f. Workboy 123–Scorton Gold 101 (Reverse Charge 115) —
(1980 NR 1981 8g 8f) half-sister to several minor winners; dam won at up to 17f; unquoted when behind in maiden race at Thirsk in May and minor event at Stockton in June. *J. Mason.*

HOBOURNES LAD 2 ch.c. Palm Track 122–Magic Garden (Florescence 120) **56**
(1981 5d 5f 6g 7.2v 5g) Feb 19; neat colt; poor plater. *R. Hollinshead.*

HOLDALL 3 ch.f. Manacle 123–Berostina 88 (Ribero 126) (1980 5g³ 5f³ 5f 5f —
6g 6fg⁴ 6fg 6g* 6f⁴ 7fg 1981 6f 6f 6fg 6f 7g 6d 7g 7s⁴ 7g 7g) compact filly; ran respectably on occasions, including in a seller; stays 6f but is by no means sure to stay 7f; probably acts on any going; sometimes blinkered; has often hung badly. *P. Asquith.*

HOLD FIRE 3 br.g. Rheingold 137–Little Firefly (Bold Ruler) (1980 8g 8fg —
1981 11.7f 12g) lightly-made gelding; probably of little account; sold 460 gns
Ascot November Sales. *P. Ransom.*

HOLD TIGHT 2 b.c. Reform 132–Silk Rein 107 (Shantung 132) (1981 8d 7g⁴ **92 p**
8g³) Apr 29; big, handsome colt; third foal; dam, half-sister to Troy and
Admetus, won over 1½m; in frame in large fields of maidens at Newmarket in
October, finishing 6 lengths fourth to Count Pahlen and 4½ lengths third to
Farioffa; a progressive colt who still has improvement in him and is certainly
capable of winning a race or 2 over middle distances at 3 yrs. *R. Hern.*

HOLIDAY CLUB 3 b.c. So Blessed 130–Gay Shadow 99 (Northfields) (1980 —
6g 6fg² 7d 1981 7d 6g⁴ 7fg 6f 8fg) strong colt; quite a moderate maiden;
probably stays 7f; sold 2,200 gns Newmarket Autumn Sales. *H. T. Jones.*

HOLLOW HEART 2 b.f. Wolver Hollow 126–Shortwood 90 (Skymaster 126) **89**
(1981 5fg 5fg* 6g) Mar 13; 21,000Y; big, rangy filly; good mover; closely
related to smart middle-distance handicapper Royal Match (by Sovereign Path)
and half-sister to 3 winners, including very useful Tranos (by Caliban); dam
sprinter; with leaders from start and kept on well to win 13-runner minor event
at Goodwood in August by a length from Path To Glory; third favourite for
William Hill Cheveley Park Stakes at Newmarket the following month but
dropped out to finish last of 13 to Woodstream after showing early speed; should
be well suited by 6f. *G. Lewis.*

HOLLOW LAUGH 3 b.c. Wolver Hollow 126–Catherine's Sister 96 (Petition **68**
130) (1980 6g 6g² 7g 1981 8.2d 10d 12fg⁴ 12s³) rangy, good sort; quite a
moderate maiden; stays 1½m; sold to M. Banks 7,400 gns Newmarket Autumn
Sales. *F. J. Houghton.*

HOLLYWOOD PARTY 2 ch.g. Be My Guest 126–Western Goddess 95 (Red **108**
God 128§) (1981 5s* 5fg* 5d³ 5g³ 6fg 6f* 7fg 7g 6d*) Feb 23; 28,000Y;
smallish, well-made, quite attractive gelding; good mover; second foal; dam,
successful Irish sprinter, is half-sister to very smart 1975 2-y-o Western Jewel;
won Brocklesby Stakes at Doncaster in March, 5-runner event at Newmarket
in April, small race at Catterick in July and 16-runner nursery at Nottingham in
September; left his previous form behind when beating Tough Critic 4 lengths
on last-named course (apprentice ridden); suited by 6f but isn't sure to stay 7f
(hampered when tried at trip for second time); acts on any going but put up
best effort on a soft surface; blinkered fourth outing. *B. Hills.*

HOLMBURY LAD (USA) 3 gr.g. Al Hattab–Fairly Faithful 87 (Prove It) —
(1980 6g 5fg*(dis) 5d³ 1981 7s 6fg 6g 6d 6d 10g 8s 8d 12.2g) useful-looking
gelding; disqualified after winning maiden race at Newbury as a 2-y-o; disappointing in 1981; not certain to stay 7f, let alone 1¼m; blinkered sixth start; trained most
of season by B. Swift. *K. Ivory.*

HOLYWELL BAY 2 ch.g. The Go-Between 129–Highly Paid (Compensation **62**
127) (1981 5d 5d 5g 7fg 7fg 7g) Apr 12; 5,000Y; quite a useful sort; fourth
foal; half-brother to a winner in Hong Kong; dam ran once; plating-class maiden.
R. Hannon.

HOME COMING 3 gr.c. Habitat 134–Zeddera (Zeddaan 130) (1980 NR **111**
1981 6g* 8fg* 7fg³ 7s* 8g⁴) 20,000Y; strong, well-made colt; good walker and
mover; third foal; half-brother to 2 winners, including 6f winner Daring Era (by
Derring-Do); dam French 1m winner; won maiden event at Newmarket (despite
swerving badly left at start) and minor event at Sandown (slowly away again),
both in April; scored in promising style both times and at Sandown won quite
comfortably by ¾ length from Havoc despite being all of 15 lengths behind on
home turn; reportedly jarred himself in latter and wasn't seen out again until
August, but came right back to his best and beat Lucky Man going away by 3
lengths in Cavendish Cape South African Sherry Stakes (Handicap) at Ascot
the following month; also ran well when fourth of 25 behind Swift Palm in
handicap at Doncaster in November; stays 1m well; probably acts on any going,
but is well suited by some give underfoot; a very useful colt who must be kept
on the right side. *G. Harwood.*

HOME DAN 2 b.g. Homeric 133–Dance All Night 106 (Double-U-Jay 120) **72**
(1981 7.6s 8d) Apr 16; IR 6,400Y; third foal; half-brother to 2 winners, including
3-y-o Dancing Sally (by Sallust), a useful winner at up to 7f; dam won from 5f
to 9f; 6¾ lengths fifth of 15 to Cordite Spear in maiden race at Lingfield in
October; well beaten behind Roanoke River in similar race at Leicester the
following month; bred to stay 1¼m+. *M. Smyly.*

HOME ON THE RANGE   3 br.f. Habitat 134–Great Guns 109 (Busted 134) **124**
(1980 6s 7fg⁴ 7g² 1981 10fg* 10.5s⁴ 10g* 12.2fg* 12g⁴ 10f* 10g*)

Warren Place, which passed the hundred-winner mark for the third season in the last four and again managed to give the impression it housed a horse for almost every occasion, wasn't so actively engaged as usual in the classics: its only runner in 1981 was Fairy Footsteps in the One Thousand Guineas.   The three-year-old colts didn't come up to the standards of some of their predecessors, and after Fairy Footsteps' shock defeat in the Musidora Stakes the stable had nothing left to run in the Oaks—neither Strigida nor Home On The Range held the engagement.   Strigida and Home On The Range were the pick of Cecil's three-year-old fillies once Fairy Footsteps was retired.   Of the pair Strigida would have been the stronger Oaks candidate, for she stayed better and was in much better form at the time; Home On The Range was ideally suited by a mile and a quarter, showing her best form when winning the Sun Chariot Stakes over the distance at Newmarket in the autumn.

Home On The Range began the season seeking her first win after three runs in maiden company as a two-year-old; she began by winning the April Maiden Stakes at Sandown and was not allowed to contest a top race until the Yorkshire Oaks in August.   On the way she lost only once, running poorly on soft ground at York in May; she won a four-runner event at Newbury fairly comfortably from Sextant and the somewhat grandiosely-titled Warwick Oaks, seven runners, with plenty in hand from Cinderwench.   When she took on much stronger company in the Yorkshire Oaks Home On The Range, co-favourite with Go Leasing, seemed not to stay the mile and a half so well as the three who eventually beat her, Condessa, Leap Lively and Fiesta Fun.   Condessa, in fact, went by with a wet sail inside the final furlong.   Second to Fiesta Fun into the straight Home On The Range looked as though she had the race within her grasp at that stage but she took a long time to pass Fiesta Fun and couldn't hold on from two furlongs out; she tended to hang under pressure, and weakened slightly to go down by around a length and a half to the winner.

The possibility existed that Home On The Range was no better than her Yorkshire Oaks form; she had, after all, run a fine race and improved 10 lb on any previous effort.   However, following another win over Sextant, this time an even easier one in the £7,765, three-runner Sean Graham Stakes over a mile and a quarter at Kempton (Oraston completed the field), she clearly ran the race of her life in the Sun Chariot Stakes.   The Sun Chariot took every bit as much winning as the Yorkshire Oaks; in winning it Home On The Range put up an extremely game performance, one reminiscent of Fairy Footsteps' in the Guineas.   She helped force the pace from the start, pressing the outsider Docklands, and took a definite advantage three furlongs out, closely followed by Boathouse, Countess Tully, Star Pastures and Vielle.   Nothing beats Star

Sun Chariot Stakes, Newmarket—Home On The Range gains her most important victory of the season; Star Pastures presses her closely

Mr Louis Freedman's "Home On The Range"

Pastures without a fight, and the two fillies, Home On The Range and Star Pastures, gave marvellous value all the way to the line, Home On The Range holding on in front up the hill under hard riding to win by a neck, a further two and a half lengths clear of Boathouse.

Home On The Range (br.f. 1978)	Habitat (b 1966)	Sir Gaylord (b 1959)	Turn-to
			Somethingroyal
		Little Hut (b 1952)	Occupy
			Savage Beauty
	Great Guns (b 1971)	Busted (b 1963)	Crepello
			Sans le Sou
		Byblis (b 1961)	Grey Sovereign
			Niobe

Home On The Range's dam Great Guns was also a very genuine, likeable racemare, one who showed form over much longer distances. She had a tremendous season as a three-year-old in minor and handicap company, winning six times in ten starts at up to two miles; she also finished a fair fourth in the Galtres Stakes at York. Home On The Range is her second foal, following Crazyfoot (by Luthier) who finally managed to break her duck over a mile and a half at Windsor in September. The grandam and great grandam were half-sisters to the dams of well-known horses. Byblis, a winner at up to a mile herself, was a half-sister to the dams of Prince de Galles and Crisp and Even; Niobe was a half-sister to the dam of Aggressor and High Perch.

Home On The Range is an attractive, well-made filly. Summing her up it would be fair to say that she stayed a mile and a half but was better suited by a mile and a quarter; she seemed to need a sound surface and acted well on firm going. She is to be covered by High Top. *H. Cecil.*

HOME RIDE 2 b.f. Homeric 133–Maride (Ridan) (1981 5s 5.1f 6f 5.1fg⁴ 8s) — bad plater. *W. Marshall.*

HOME WIN 7 b.g. Habitat 134–Triumphantly (Bold Ruler) (1980 8d 10.4d —
12g 9s 12.5s 1981 10.6s 12fg 8fg 12fg) bad plater; sometimes wears blinkers;
wears bandages. *M. James.*

HONEST BROKER 2 b.c. Artaius 129–Nakomis (Sky High) (1981 7f*) May   **86 p**
9; IR 56,000Y; half-brother to fairly useful 6f and 7f winner Sipapu (by Targowice); dam won at up to 9f in USA, and is out of half-sister to Sham; 6/4 favourite,
missed break but came through to lead inside final furlong when winning 19-
runner maiden race at Naas in September by a neck from Kentucky Kid; will
stay 1¼m; should go on to better things. *D. O'Brien, Ireland.*

HONEST OPINION 2 b.f. Free State 125–Misfield 99 (Sahib 114) (1981   **68**
5d⁴ 5fg* 5d 5d 5d) Mar 9; 6,800F, 4,800Y; small, attractive filly; first foal; dam
a sprinter; favourite for 9-runner maiden race at Epsom in April and ran on so
strongly she got up to win by a length from Candescence; soundly beaten afterwards, finishing eighth of 9 in nursery at Lingfield on final start in August; will
be suited by 6f. *G. Hunter.*

HONEST RECORD 3 b.f. Record Token 128–Be Honest 95 (Klairon 131)   **75**
(1980 NR 1981 9d³ 10s 9g* 9.4fg* 9fg² 10fg³ 10g) 1,200 2-y-o; lengthy, useful
sort; good walker; half-sister to 1½m seller winner Wealthy (by Gold Rod); dam
won over 1m; successful in maiden race at Hamilton in June and minor event at
Carlisle in July; edged left under pressure when 1½ lengths second to Reside in
slowly-run handicap at York later in July; stays 9f well; possibly not at her
best on very soft going; sold 9,600 gns Newmarket December Sales. *G. Pritchard-
Gordon.*

HONEST TOKEN 2 b. or br.c. Record Token 128–Be Honest 95 (Klairon 131)   **68**
(1981 6g 6g 6s) May 25; compact colt; brother to 3-y-o 9f winner Honest
Record, and half-brother to a winning plater; dam won over 1m; showed ability
in maiden races at Doncaster and Hamilton on last 2 starts; will stay 1m. *C.
Thornton.*

HONEY BARRON 4 b.c. Pitcairn 126–Rogan Honey (Abernant 142) (1980   **82**
7fg 8.2fg 8g 7d² 7g* 7d 7g² 7g 7.2fg³ 7.2d⁴ 7d² 1981 8fg³ 7.6g* 8d³ 7.6g³ 7fg
7g 7fg 7f⁴ 7g 8d) neat, attractive colt; good mover; fair handicapper; beat
Rabdan a neck in £4,300 race at Lingfield in May (hung quite badly left); stays
1m; seems suited by some give in the ground (moved badly to start on a firm
surface seventh outing); blinkered twice in 1980; has run creditably for an
apprentice; sold 4,500 gns Newmarket Autumn Sales. *J. Dunlop.*

HONEY HARFAT 6 b.m. Right Tack 131–Regal Winnie 88 (Royal Avenue —
123) (1980 NR 1981 17.1d) poor maiden; has worn blinkers; retained 625
gns Ascot September Sales. *M. Bradley.*

HONEYLAND (USA) 2 ch.c. Stop the Music–Honey Pot (Drone) (1981 **112**
5fg³ 8fg² 7.5g³ 7v* 7v³) Apr 2; $75,000F; second foal; dam, stakes-placed
winner over 5f at 2 yrs, is out of half-sister to top-class broodmare Alanesian;
made nearly all when winning 10-runner maiden race at Maisons-Laffitte in
October by 1½ lengths; bettered that effort when 3 lengths third of 10 to Zino
in Group 2 Criterium de Maisons-Laffitte later in month; stays 1m. *A. Head,
France.*

HONRIETTE 2 ch.f. Henry the Seventh 125–My Own II 96 (El Relicario 124)   **80**
(1981 7v² 7g) Mar 16; tall, lengthy filly; half-sister to very smart middle-distance performer Haul Knight (by Firestreak) and a winner in Belgium; dam won
from 1m to 11f in France; 10/1, soon nicely placed and really well when
promising ½-length second of 8 to Rocamadour in minor event at Kempton in
October; second favourite for 29-runner maiden race at Newmarket later in
month, but was never going well and finished well beaten behind Chalon; will
stay 1¼m; possibly needs the mud. *G. Harwood.*

HOOD HILL 5 ch.g. Silly Season 127–Whatawind (Typhoon 125) (1980 6fg —
7g 10g 12f 8d 10d³ 10s 6g 1981 8d 8f) plater; stays 1¼m; best in blinkers.
G. Fletcher.

HOODWINK 3 br.g. No Mercy 126–Rose Blanche 89 (French Beige 127) (1980   **60**
5fg 5fg 5.8fg 7fg³ 7fg² 8d 1981 7fg² 7d 8g 7f 8f³ 7fg² 8.3fg 10f² 9g³ 8f³ 8fg²)
quite a well-made gelding; beat Hyjill a short head in selling handicap at
Kempton in September on final start, but placings were reversed after a
stewards inquiry; stays 1¼m; acts on firm going; often blinkered and probably
isn't entirely genuine. *N. Vigors.*

HOPE COVE 2 b.f. High Top 131–Greek Gift (Acropolis 132) (1981 6fg 7f)
Jan 6; lengthy filly; half-sister to 3 winners, including Gosport (by Tudor Melody),

a smart winner at around 1m in France; dam twice-raced half-sister to very smart Rocky Royale; last in newcomers race at Ascot in July and in 16-runner maiden event at Brighton in August. *D. Whelan.*

HOPEFUL ANN 2 b.f. Abwah 118–Hopeful Subject 82 (Mandamus 120) **63** (1981 5f 6fg 6g 7f) Apr 9; workmanlike filly; second live foal; half-sister to fairly useful 3-y-o Paulager (by Lochnager), a winner at up to 7.6f; dam won over 1m at 2 yrs; about 7 lengths fifth of 10 to Indigine in maiden race at Ayr in July, second start; well out of her depth next 2 outings; should stay 7f; dwelt final appearance. *G. Lockerbie.*

HORKEY 4 ch.f. Shoolerville 121–Omnia Opera 83 (Major Portion 129) (1980 **38** 8.2s 8g 8fg 8f 8fg 13.8fg 10s 1981 10.1d 10d³ 12.2fg 12f 10fg⁴ 10f 10f² 11.5d) leggy filly; plater; stays 1¼m; seems to act on any going. *J. Harris.*

HOROS (USA) 5 ch.h. Head of the River–Sound of Success (Successor) (1980 9fg 10.6f 12f 12d 8fg⁴ 12fg 10.6s 1981 12g 8fg 8g 8.2d 11d) lengthy horse; quite a moderate handicapper at his best but has deteriorated and was behind in valuable seller third start; best form at up to 1m; acts on any going. *W. H. H. Williams.*

HOSTESS 2 b.f. Be My Guest 126–Ginger 90 (Red God 128§) (1981 6f 7f* **81** 7fg) Mar 5; neat, good sort with an excellent, smooth action; second foal; dam, granddaughter of 2,000 Guineas winner Garden Path, won over 5f at 2 yrs; won 16-runner maiden race at Brighton in August by 1½ lengths from Coney Dell; favourite for 20-runner nursery at Leicester the following month but was beaten some way out and finished only ninth to Towering; suited by 7f and may stay further. *H. Cecil.*

HOT ANNA 2 ch.f. Hotfoot 126–Lantana 74 (St Paddy 133) (1981 5g⁴ 5g **66** 6g 6fg² 6g 7f 8.2fg) Feb 16; 4,000Y; useful-looking filly; good mover; third foal; half-sister to 1½m winner Nepotism (by Great Nephew); dam won over 1¼m; quite a moderate maiden; quite stoutly bred but has yet to show she stays beyond 6f. *P. Feilden.*

HOTBELOO 3 ch.f. Roi Soleil 125–Bleue Horizon II (Mourne 126) (1980 6g **—** 5.8h 6f 1981 10s 8d 8fg 10.1d 10d 10d 10.1fg 8d 10f 10s) small filly; only poor form, including in sellers; stays 1¼m; has worn bandages behind; blinkered last 2 starts. *A. Bailey.*

HOT CAPTAIN 2 b. or br.g. Roi Soleil 125–Telling 91 (High Treason 126) **—** (1981 5g 6g 7fg 8.2d) Apr 27; 8,200Y; neat gelding; half-brother to 2 winners, including useful 7f to 1½m winner Len Ashurst (by Prince Regent); dam, daughter of Oaks winner Steady Aim, stayed 6f; in rear in minor and maiden events. *G. Richards.*

HOT EMBER 3 b.f. Hot Spark 126–Royal Rosette 66 (Pardao 120) (1980 **72** 5g 6fg⁴ 6fg 1981 6g* 7d³ 7d³ 10g 11.7d) close-coupled filly; poor walker; won 18-runner minor event at Kempton in May on reappearance; third to Minmax in similar race at Leicester later in month and to Montclair in handicap at Sandown in June; possibly stays 1½m (had stiff task and wasn't entirely disgraced final start). *R. Price.*

HOT FIRE 3 b.c. Hotfoot 126–Mischief 76 (Sassafras 135) (1980 7f² 8g³ **75** 1981 8g³ 10.5s³ 14s 12.3g⁴ 12fg 12.3g* 14g 12fg² 12v² 12v²) rangy, good sort; successful in maiden race at Newcastle in August (made most) and handicap at Beverley in September, in latter staying on well to beat Ski's Double a length; suited by a strongly-run 1½m; acts on any going. *J. Fitzgerald.*

HOT GLOSS 2 b.c. Fine Blade 121–Green Marvedo (Green God 128) (1981 **—** 5s) May 1; 1,750F, 2,000Y; short-backed colt; first produce; dam second once over 7f in Ireland; started slowly when last of 10 to Hollywood Party in Brocklesby Stakes at Doncaster in March; sold 320 gns Doncaster May Sales. *W. Stubbs.*

HOT HEART 3 ch.c. Hot Spark 126–Laxmi 108 (Palestine 133) (1980 6s) **—** 1981 6g 5fg 8s) small, sturdy colt; good walker; behind in maiden events and a handicap; showed early speed first 2 outings; dwelt final start; sold 300 gns Goffs October Sales. *R. Armstrong.*

HOT JACKIE 2 b.f. Hot Spark 126–Miss Jack 97 (Pampered King 121) (1981 **—** 5s) Mar 9; half-sister to 2 winners, including useful stayer Nopac (by King's Leap); dam, sister to very smart David Jack, won at up to 2¼m; unquoted when distant ninth of 10 to Fimi in maiden race at Leicester in May. *M. Ryan.*

HOTMANTLE   2 b.c. Hotfoot 126–Dismantle 77 (Aureole 132)   (1981 5fg 5g³ 7d   **68** 6d 6g 8s)   Apr 7; 6,200Y; sturdy colt; second living foal; half-brother to 7f winner Triple Bar (by Jimmy Reppin); dam, winner over 7f at 2 yrs, is half-sister to very smart Joking Apart; 3½ lengths third of 11 to Prima Voce in maiden race at Sandown in July, best effort; should be well suited by 6f+. *J. Benstead.*

HOT PRESS   3 ch.f. Hotfoot 126–Star Story 117 (Red God 128§)   (1980   **65** 5g* 6g 6g   1981 6s 7g² 7fg² 8.3fg 8.2g² 10.2g 8d 8s 12d 8g)   smallish, stocky filly; ran creditably in handicaps in the summer and was second at Salisbury, Kempton (apprentice event) and Nottingham, running on at finish each time; stays 1m; occasionally blinkered (has run respectably in them). *F. J. Houghton.*

HOT PRETENCE (USA)   4 b.g. Sham–Donut's Bunnie (Donut King)   (1980   — 8g 14f   1981 10g 12s 14s 12d² 16f 14g³ 16f 12f³ 15g 12.2g)   big ex-Irish gelding; poor performer on balance of form; stays 1¾m (well beaten over further); acts on a soft surface; has worn blinkers; ran out second start in 1980; trained part of season by M. O'Toole. *J. S. Wilson.*

HOT PROPERTY   2 br.f. Hot Spark 126–Klairette (Klairon 131)   (1981   — 5fg 6fg 7d)   Feb 12; 9,400F, 14,000Y; quite attractive, well-made filly; half-sister to a winning plater; dam unraced daughter of smart filly Vhairi; behind in sizeable fields of maidens at Windsor in July and Newbury in August and September. *J. Sutcliffe.*

HOT STONE   3 br.f. Hotfoot 126–Quarry Wood 89 (Super Sam 124)   (1980   — NR   1981 11f 13.4fg 12d³ 14.7fg)   big, rangy filly; turns her front feet in; first reported foal; dam won at up to 1¾m; poor third in maiden race at Hamilton in July; possibly stays 1½m; usually apprentice ridden. *D. Francis.*

HOT TRAMP   7 b.m. Country Retreat 91–Sara Must (Mustang)   (1980 NR   — 1981 16d)   winner over hurdles but seems of little account on flat; pulled up only outing in 1981. *J. Bridger.*

HOTWAVE   3 ch.f. Hotfoot 126–Pinwave 82 (Pinza 137)   (1980 6f 7s 7g   **61** 1981 7f 10f⁴ 9f 8d 9s⁴)   compact, fair sort; good mover; quite moderate form in varied company; stays 1¼m; tends to sweat up; bridle broke on reappearance. *Miss S. Hall.*

HOT WIND   3 ch.g. Hotfoot 126–Wind Goddess (Whistling Wind 123)   (1980   **69** 5fg⁴ 5f 6d 6d³ 7g 7fg² 7fg⁴ 7d⁴   1981 7g 10s 8fg 8fg² 8g³ 8fg² 8.2fg⁴)   strong, good-looking gelding; placed in maiden race at Kempton and in a handicap and an apprentice race at Yarmouth in the summer; stays 1m. *B. Hobbs.*

HOUGHTON WEAVER   2 b.c. Warpath 113–Broughton Flyer (Hunter-   **84** combe 133)   (1981 5d*(dis) 5fg* 6f³ 5d* 6g* 7s³ 6fg⁴ 6d³)   May 4; leggy, rather narrow colt; second foal; dam never ran; bought in after winning sellers at Hamilton, costing 2,200 gns after scoring by 8 lengths in April and 3,800 gns after beating Miss Prudent ½ length in May; disqualified in July from his first success, having failed dope test; subsequently showed improved form in better company, winning nurseries at Hamilton and Redcar; will stay 1m; probably acts on any going; genuine and consistent. *J. Berry.*

HOUND SONG   3 b.f. Jukebox 120–Artemis 91 (King Emperor)   (1980   **65** 5s 5g⁴ 5fg³ 5f⁴ 5fg³ 5.3d 6g* 6fg* 6fg 6s   1981 6g 6g 6f 6fg³ 6f² 6f³ 5.8g)   lightly-made filly; placed in handicaps in the summer; stays 6f; acts on firm going and is probably unsuited by a soft surface; used to wear blinkers. *C. Nelson.*

HOUSEGO   2 gr.c. Habat 127–Sweet Reproach 94 (Relic)   (1981 6g 7fg)   — May 15; 5,200Y; lengthy colt; half-brother to 7f winner Dunham Park (by Manacle) and middle-distance winner Cee Beauty (by Ribero); dam 2-y-o 6f and 1m winner; on burly side when behind in maiden races at Salisbury in June (20/1) and September (33/1). *N. Vigors.*

HOUSE PITCH   2 br.g. Most Secret 119–Pamora (Blast 125)   (1981 5d 5fg*   **83** 5g² 5d³)   Feb 1; 5,400Y; compact gelding; half-brother to fairly useful 1977 2-y-o 6f winner Selobore (by Maystreak); dam twice-raced sister to smart Irish sprinter Sandy Row; won maiden race at Kempton in April by a head from Better Portion; 1½ lengths second to Algardi in £2,600 event at Newmarket in May but wore blinkers when disappointing last of 3 behind Petite Realm in £2,300 race at Folkestone later in month; will be well suited by 6f; best form on a sound surface; sent to Hong Kong. *R. Hannon.*

HOUT BAY 2 b.c. Mandrake Major 122–Arrangement 72 (Floribunda 136) **78**
(1981 5g 6f⁴ 6fg³ 5.1d³ 6s) May 10; 2,500Y; workmanlike colt; half-brother
to fair 5f winner Strictly Swing (by Swing Easy), to 1980 2-y-o 6f winner Sweet
Pleasure (by Sweet Revenge), and to a winner over hurdles; dam stayed 7f;
quite a moderate maiden; gives impression 6f is his limit; ran poorly in blinkers
fifth outing; sold 820 gns Doncaster October Sales. *A. Jarvis.*

HOWTH 3 ch.f. Roman Warrior 132–Blakey (Blakeney 126) (1980 NR 1981   **—**
8g) 1,500Y; first foal; dam slow maiden; unquoted when behind in maiden
race at Thirsk in May. *M. Camacho.*

HOYDEN 2 b.f. English Prince 129–Kelfresco 59 (Kelly 122) (1981 5f⁴ 6g   **—**
6d) Feb 11; IR 4,600F, 4,200Y; stocky filly; third reported produce; dam
poor half-sister to top-class German sprinter Pentathlon; 16/1, ran respectably
for a newcomer when 4 lengths fourth of 12 to Starlust in maiden race at Leicester
in June; soundly beaten in similar races at Nottingham afterwards; should
stay 6f. *A. Jarvis.*

H. R. MICRO 3 br.f. High Award 119–Crusheen (Typhoon 125) (1980 5fg   **60**
6g⁴ 6g 6s 5fg³ 6g 5fg³ 5g 5f 5d 5fg⁴ 5g⁴ 6d⁴ 5s⁴ 6d² 1981 6s 6fg 6g 6f 5f* 6fg
5.3fg³ 6fg 5f 5f 5f 7d 6s 6g⁴) small, lengthy filly; won handicap at Beverley
in July; stays 6f; probably acts on any going; occasionally blinkered; suitable
mount for an apprentice. *D. Dale.*

HULA RULER (USA) 2 b.f. Chieftain–Native Go-Go (Raise A Native) (1981   **97**
6fg³ 7g* 7f*) Mar 19; $80,000Y; big, rangy filly; very good walker and good
mover; fourth foal; dam, minor stakes winner, won at up to 1m; justified favouritism in 16-runner maiden race at Sandown in July and in 6-runner minor event
at Yarmouth the following month, making most of running to score by ½ length
from Rockfest and by ¾ length from Two Minutes respectively; said to have
met with a minor setback afterwards; will be suited by 1m; has plenty of scope
and could well improve further at 3 yrs. *L. Cumani.*

HUMBILLIE 3 ch.f. Silly Season 127–Chumba (Cambremer 132) (1980 6d 7f   **—**
1981 8.5fg) small, narrow filly; well beaten in minor events, twice finishing
last; sold 520 gns Ascot 2nd June Sales. *D. Whelan.*

HUMBLE BLUE 3 ch.c. Some Hand 119–Papillon Rouge 80 (Klairon 131)   **71**
(1980 5fg 5fg 5.1g⁴ 5s 1981 5s² 5s* 5g* 6d 5f⁴ 5fg² 5g* 5fg 6fg 5d⁴ 5g) useful
sort; improved and won handicaps at Nottingham in April, Chester in May and
Beverley (by 6 lengths) in July, making all on first 2 occasions; unlucky in
running eleventh start; best at 5f; probably acts on any going, but is well suited
by soft; has run creditably in blinkers; bandaged near-hind ninth start. *G.
Fletcher.*

HUMBOLDT 5 b.g. Levmoss 133–Bonne Femme (Bold Lad, Ire 133) (1980   **43**
NR 1981 12s* 16.1f) awarded poor maiden race at Beverley in April when
winner failed dope test; finished lame only subsequent start; should stay well;
wears bandages. *M. McCormack.*

HUMMING 3 b.f. Bustino 136–Secret Song 83 (Tudor Melody 129) (1980   **94**
NR 1981 7d³ 10g* 12g) 37,000Y; smallish, lengthy filly; good walker; third
foal; half-sister to very useful but temperamental 1977 2-y-o 6f winner Royal
Harmony (by Sun Prince) and a winner in Jersey; dam won at up to 6f; co-
favourite though on backward side when promising 3 lengths third of 11 to
Wilderness in newcomers race at Newbury in April; looked really well in herself
when beating Rollrights by 1½ lengths in Playboy Pretty Polly Stakes at Newmarket the following month; behind from halfway when tailed-off tenth of 12
behind Blue Wind in Oaks at Epsom in June on only subsequent start; stayed
1¼m; stud in USA. *R. Hern.*

HUNNY NEL 2 b.f. Auction Ring 123–Yellow Mel (Yellow God 129) (1981   **39**
5fg 6fg 5.1fg³ 5fg⁴) Apr 29; 1,450Y; small filly; poor plater; blinkered second
outing; sold 660 gns Newmarket July Sales. *M. Tompkins.*

HUNSTON 3 b.f. Blakeney 126–Catherine Wheel 116 (Roan Rocket 128) **105**
(1980 5f 5f³ 6fg² 7g* 7.6g³ 10g⁴ 1981 12.3d* 12v³ 12f⁴ 12fg² 10g⁴ 14f³ 12f 11g³
8.5g* 9fg) small, well-made filly; half-sister to 1977 2-y-o 6f winner Azucena (by
Queen's Hussar); dam, smart and tough, stayed at least 1¼m; made a successful
reappearance in Cheshire Oaks in May, holding on by a head from
unlucky-in-running Golden Bowl; in frame all her subsequent outings over
here, in Lupe Stakes at Goodwood, Lancashire Oaks at Haydock and handicaps
at Ascot, Goodwood again, and York; wouldn't settle early on and didn't get
the trip when about a length third to Charlotte's Choice on last-named course
in September; subsequently sent to USA and won an allowance race at Aqueduct

Cheshire Oaks, Chester—front-running Hunston wins from unlucky-in-running Golden Bowl with Rhein Bridge third

in November; stays 1½m; not at her best on heavy going, but acts on any other; game. *B. Hobbs.*

HUNTER HAWK 2 ch.c. Huntercombe 133–White Legs (Preciptic 122) (1981 6fg 6fg 6d 6g 5f⁴ 5v 5s 6d) May 3; 16,000Y; strong colt; half-brother to numerous winners, 3 of them very useful, but showed only poor form himself at 2 yrs; blinkered last 2 outings, swerving badly left at start on first occasion. *A. Balding.* **60**

HUNTER'S DELIGHT 2 ch.c. Huntercombe 133–Light Grey 115 (Grey Sovereign 128§) (1981 7g 7d⁴ 7.5d² 6d³ 7g) May 24; big, good-topped colt; brother to a winner in Austria, and half-brother to 3 winners, including very useful 6f and 7f winner Miss Scotland (by Henry the Seventh) and good German performer Lemon Hart (by Acropolis); dam smart top-of-the-ground sprinter; placed in maiden races in October at Gowran Park (¾-length second to Fantastique) and the Curragh (2½ lengths third of 17 to Classical Dancer); always struggling when eighth of 11 in £4,300 event won by Not For Show at Doncaster the following month; stays 7f. *P. Canty, Ireland.* **76**

HUNTING HEIR 4 b.g. Huntercombe 133–Reddish Radish (Red God 128§) (1980 8fg 10d 1981 10s 7d² 8g 7s 7f) leggy gelding; plater; stays 7f; has worn blinkers. *Mrs J. Pitman.* **49**

HUNTING LAD 2 b.c. Huntercombe 133–Pot de Creme 68 (Candy Spots) (1981 7d 6d 6s) June 18; 3,100Y; tall, narrow, rather unfurnished colt; half-brother to 2 winners, including 1980 2-y-o 5f and 7f winner Creamy (by Double-U-Jay); dam stayed well; little sign of ability in maiden and minor events. *S. Matthews.* **—**

HUNT THE THIMBLE (USA) 2 b.f. Turn And Count–Esprit Belle (Ack Ack) (1981 6f⁴ 6fg³ 6fg³) Apr 1; $26,000Y; rather unfurnished filly; second foal; dam once-raced daughter of smart 1969 American 2-y-o Belle Noire; sire smart performer at around 9f; in frame in large fields of maidens at Yarmouth and Newmarket prior to finishing 11½ lengths third of 9 to Circus Ring in Princess Margaret Stakes at Ascot in July; will stay 1¼m; reared as stalls opened on debut and sweated up at Ascot. *L. Cumani.* **86**

HUPPEL 3 ch.f. Huntercombe 133–Polonaise (Takawalk II 125) (1980 NR 1981 7g 8d⁴ 8d* 7fg* 8f² 8fg² 8g* 8g² 7g) 7,400Y; stocky filly; fourth foal; **83**

Mr T. F. Blackwell's "Hunston"

half-sister to useful middle-distance colt Prince of Padua (by Wolver Hollow) and to a winner over jumps in France; dam won over 9f at 2 yrs in Ireland; won maiden race at Pontefract in May and handicap at Newmarket in August, gaining upper hand 2f out and running on strongly to beat Train of Thought by 2 lengths in latter; second on 4 other occasions, including to Petite Hester in minor event at Catterick in between (placings were subsequently reversed); will be suited by 1¼m; probably acts on any going; a grand sort of filly; sold 20,000 gns Newmarket December Sales. *G. Pritchard-Gordon.*

HURRICANE HILL 4 b.g. Golden Dipper 119–High Corries (Soleil II 133) **75** (1980 5fg 6s³ 5fg⁴ 5g³ 6fg 6fg* 6s 1981 8d³ 8s 8fg 8g 8f 8d⁴ 7fg 7f 7d² 7.2v) workmanlike gelding; good mover; suited by 1m; suited by some give in the ground; sometimes wears blinkers but is effective without; possibly best on a galloping track; sold to F. Muggeridge 7,200 gns Ascot November Sales. *W. Musson.*

HURTWOOD LASS 3 ch.f. Realm 129–Abroad (Takawalk II 125) (1980 **54** 6s⁴ 6g 7g 5d 6g* 5fg 7g⁴ 6s 1981 5s 6g 5d 5fg 5f⁴ 6g 5.6f 5fg² 6f 5g 5fg 7g 7g 6g²) leggy, rather lightly-made filly; won valuable seller at Doncaster as a 2-y-o; second in trainers race at Catterick and claiming handicap at Newmarket in 1981; best form at up to 6f; blinkered last 2 starts; trained first 4 outings by A. Balding; sold 950 gns Doncaster November Sales, reportedly to race in Sweden. *R. Whitaker.*

HURWORTH HOUSE 5 ch.g. Habitat 134–Light Opera 101 (Vienna 127) **77** (1980 6d* 6fg² 6fg 6d* 6fg 6g 6s 6d⁴ 6s⁴ 1981 6fg 6g³ 6d² 6s 6s 6s) smallish, sturdy gelding; sprint handicapper; acts on a firm surface but is particularly well suited by some give in the ground; best in blinkers; suitable mount for an apprentice. *H. T. Jones.*

HYALINE 3 ch.f. High Line 125–Goldilocks II (Pinza 137) (1980 NR 1981 **—** 9.4g 10f) non-thoroughbred filly; sister to 2m winner Young Robin; dam ran twice; unquoted when soundly beaten in maiden races at Carlisle in July and Ripon in August. *N. Crump.*

407

HYJILL 4 br.f. No Mercy 126–Politesse 65 (Polic 126)   (1980 6d 7.6g 6g 7.2d   **55**
8f² 7d 8d   1981 8.2fg⁴ 7fg* 8g² 8f* 8fg* 8g² 8g 7g)   neat, strong filly; plater
nowadays; won at Edinburgh in July (bought in 1,150 gns), Beverley in August
(bought in 975 gns) and Kempton in September (attracted no bid after being
awarded race); stays 1m; acts on any going; has worn blinkers but is better
without; consistent; sold 2,000 gns Newmarket Autumn Sales. *J. Fitzgerald.*

HYMNOS (FR) 4 ch.c. Luthier 126–Hairbrush (Sir Gaylord)   (1980 8v*(dis)   **72**
9f² 12g* 10fg³ 12d 12g 12g* 12v³ 10s   1981 12s³ 12g³ 9g⁴ 10d 12f* 10fg* 13g²
12fg² 11.7d 12f² 12g)   workmanlike ex-Irish colt; won handicaps at Leicester
and Nottingham in June; stays 13f; acts on any going; best in blinkers; has run
respectably for an amateur rider. *J. Bethell.*

HYPERION CHIEF 5 ch h. Mansingh 120–Hyperion Lass (Punchinello 97)   —
(1980 7d 6d 5f 6f 5f* 6s 6d 5fg² 5d 5d 6d 5.8g 6s   1981 5s 6s 8d 8fg)   fair sort;
modest at his best; showed no form in 1981; stayed 6f; acted on any going;
dead. *W. Wharton.*

HYPERION PRINCESS 2 gr.f. Dragonara Palace 115–Hyperion Girl 59   —
(Royal Palm 131)   (1981 8fg)   Apr 13; first foal; dam placed over 6f at 2
yrs; unquoted when well behind in 17-runner maiden race won by Cornish
Heroine at Leicester in September. *W. Wharton.*

HYPNOSIS (USA) 2 ch.c. Unconscious–Puzzesca (Law and Order) (1981   —
5d 7g 7fg)   Apr 7; $20,000Y; strong, lengthy colt; half-brother to 6 winners,
including Mighty Mouse (by Shecky Greene), a stakes winner at up to 1m in
USA; dam won over 1m in USA, and is half-sister to high-class Buffle, a stakes
winner at up to 1¼m; little sign of ability in minor and maiden races, final start
in July. *D. Elsworth.*

HYPNOTHERAPIST 4 b.g. Forlorn River 124–Molly Flo (Paveh 126)   (1980   **43**
7d³ 0f³ 7f 8g 8g 8d 7s 7s   1981 5d 0g 7d 8g 8f 8f⁴ 7fg⁴ 7f² 6fg 10f)   leggy gelding;
plater; stays 1m; seems to act on any going; has worn blinkers; sold 520 gns
Doncaster September Sales. *J. Calvert.*

HYPOL-ADI 4 b.g. Andrea Mantegna–Cuzco (Obermaat)   (1980 NR 1981   —
14d)   fair sort; unquoted when tailed-off last of 13 in maiden race at Sandown
in June. *J. Bosley.*

I

IBOLYAN SOUND 2 ch.c. Music Boy 124–Ibolya Princess 87 (Crowned   —
Prince 128)   (1981 6g 6d)   Apr 5; 4,500Y; strong colt; first foal; dam won
over 7f and 9f; beaten a fair way in useful maiden and minor company in the
North. *B. Lunness.*

IBTIHAJ (USA) 2 b.f. Raja Baba–Pas de Nom (Admiral's Voyage)   (1981   **97**
5f 6fg⁴ 5fg* 5g³ 5f)   Feb 13; $330,000Y; neat, well-made filly; third foal;
half-sister to Danzig (by Northern Dancer), a very promising but hard-to-
train winner in USA; dam very useful sprinter; never headed when winning
8-runner maiden race at Goodwood in July by ½ length from Falaka; close-up
third of 4 to clever winner Lavender Dance in £2,800 event at Windsor the
following month; stays 6f; ran poorly both outings on very firm ground;
did well physically. *H. T. Jones.*

I. C. DOLLAR (USA) 4 b.f. Iceecapade–In Prosperity (Crimson Satan)   (1980   **69**
6f 7d 10s⁴ 10f 10.6d³ 10fg² 10fg* 9g* 10s⁴   1981 11s 10.8d 9.4g² 10fg 10g)
strong, good-bodied filly; middle-distance handicapper; probably acts on any
going; blinkered third and fourth outings and doesn't look too genuine. *G.
Pritchard-Gordon.*

ICE 3 b.g. Northfields–Carmine City 104 (Charlottesville 135)   (1980 6g 8d²   **66**
8g   1981 12s 12d 12d³ 10g² 10v)   well-made, attractive gelding; placed in
maiden race at Brighton in May and handicap at Lingfield in June; will probably
stay further than 1½m. *I. Balding.*

ICE HARBOUR (USA) 3 b. or br.c. Iceecapade–Harbour Queen (Young   **86**
Emperor 133)   (1980 7fg 7g* 7g⁴   1981 8fg 12g 8g* 8f⁴ 7g* 7f 7f⁴ 7g² 8g⁴ 7g)
tall, rather leggy colt; won apprentice race at Carlisle in June (made all) and
handicap at Ayr in July; beat Tumbledownhill by a length in latter; best at
up to 1m; sweated up second start; blinkered nowadays; possibly needs a
galloping track; ran moderately when held up sixth outing; sold 4,600 gns
Newmarket Autumn Sales. *J. Hindley.*

ICEN 3 b.c. Tycoon II–Pepstep 66 (Polic 126)   (1980 6fg⁴ 7fg³ 1981 7fg²   **82**
8g⁴ 8fg² 8f² 8fg² 8fg* 9s²)   well-made, quite attractive colt; short-priced

favourite, in no danger in last 3f when beating Johns Present by 4 lengths in 16-runner maiden race at Salisbury in September; runner-up on 5 other occasions; gives impression he'll be suited by 1¼m; suited by a sound surface (tended to hang and ran below form on soft going final start). *M. Smyly.*

I-CHING 3 gr.f. No Mercy 126–China Girl 76 (Shantung 132) (1980 5fg 6s **58** 5.8f 5.8h 8fg* 7g 8d 8g⁴ 1981 8s 8f 10.1fg 10.8fg² 10f 10fg* 10d) unfurnished filly; plater; ridden by 7-lb claimer when winning at Leicester in September; sold out of R. Laing's stable 1,300 gns afterwards; suited by 1¼m+; acts on a firm surface; sometimes wears blinkers or a hood; has worn a tongue strap; tends to dwell at start. *B. Richmond.*

IDLE DAYS 2 b.f. Hittite Glory 125–Paresseuse 114 (Relko 136) (1981 5g²) **80 p** Mar 7; compact, sturdy filly; half-sister to 3 winners in France, including useful Stand Hill (by Mountain Call); dam middle-distance stayer; went down by ¾ length to Senorita Querida when favourite for 13-runner minor event at Newmarket in May, taking some time to find her stride but running on strongly up hill; off course afterwards with split pasterns; will stay at least 1m. *W. Hastings-Bass.*

IDLE MARKET 2 b.c. Native Bazaar 122–Young Frances (Rockavon 120) **67** (1981 5s 5d³ 5fg⁴ 5d³ 6g 6fg² 5.8f² 7f² 7fg) Feb 1; 880F, 2,700Y; small, useful-looking colt; fourth foal; dam ran 4 times; second in maiden auction events and a nursery, making most of running each time; stays 7f; wears blinkers. *R. Hannon.*

IDLE WARRIOR 2 b.c. Sandford Lad 133–Mink Fur (Victoria Park) (1981 **72** 5v 5g 6f 7g* 7fg 8f² 8d²) Mar 9; IR 2,100F, IR 3,000Y; neat, strong colt; very good mover; second foal; half-brother to Reliance News (by English Prince), winner of sellers over 1¼m; dam unplaced once in France; sold out of J. Fitzgerald's stable 3,100 gns after winning 11-runner seller at Newcastle in July by a length from Caribbean Dream; second subsequently in nurseries at Pontefract and Redcar (seller); suited by 7f and 1m; seems to act on any going; sold to German International BA 4,100 gns Newmarket Autumn Sales. *G. Pritchard-Gordon.*

IDYLLIC GLEN 2 br.f. Furry Glen 121–Idylle (Dan Cupid 132) (1981 10.2g) — Apr 14; IR 1,600F; half-sister to 2 winners, including fairly useful 1½m winner Bellium (by Bon Mot III); dam won small 9f race in France; 20/1 and backward when behind in 26-runner minor event won by Yard Bird at Doncaster in November. *C. Spares.*

IF AND WHEN 6 b.m. Balliol 125–Juries Act 88 (Marsolve 125) (1980 NR — 1981 10.2s) poor handicapper; stays 7f; suited by some give in the ground; has worn blinkers. *J. Priday.*

ILAKAN 3 b.f. Forlorn River 124–Nikali 89 (Siliconn 121) (1980 5f 5fg⁴ — 5fg 6g 8g 7fg 6s 1981 8g 8d) plating-class maiden; unlikely to stay 1m. *M. Bradley.*

ILKLEY 2 ch.f. Import 127–Tin Pan 58 (Tin Whistle 128) (1981 5fg 5fg 5f — 7.2v 5g) May 21; 700F, 600 2-y-o; sturdy filly; useless plater; has worn blinkers. *N. Bycroft.*

ILLICIT 2 b.g. He Loves Me 120–Princess Parthia (Parthia 132) (1981 6fg **85** 6g 5s² 5s*) Feb 17; IR 38,000Y; well-grown, quite attractive gelding; closely related to French Hollow (by Wolver Hollow), a very useful winner at up to 1¼m in France, and half-brother to several other winners, including 1979 2-y-o 5f winner Gay Parthia (by Gay Fandango); dam ran only once; finished well to win 20-runner maiden race at Warwick in October by 3 lengths from The Cairnwell; best form at 5f; acts on soft going; gelded at end of season. *J. Hindley.*

ILLINI 3 b.c. Prince Tenderfoot 126–Ashling 98 (Nashua) (1980 NR 1981 **83** 9d 11.5f 8g* 8fg 8g 8.2g* 8fg⁴ 10fg* 9f 10.6fg² 10d) 26,000Y; strong, good sort; half-brother to several winners, including very useful 7f winner Ashleigh (by Ragusa); dam won over 7f; reportedly split a pastern as a 2-y-o and didn't race; did well in 1981 and was gaining his third win when beating Lady of Cornwall decisively by 3 lengths in small handicap at Ayr in August; had earlier won a maiden event on same course and a handicap at Hamilton; ran well on other occasions too, including in a ladies race; suited by 1¼m; acts on a firm surface; well beaten when tried in blinkers; didn't have best of runs ninth start. *B. Hanbury.*

ILL

I'LL SEE YOU 3 b.c. Averof 123–Keeps (Roan Rocket 128) (1980 5f2 5fg2 **80**
6d 5.1g* 6g 1981 8fg2 8fg 8fg2 8d4) rangy colt; good mover; second to Jim's
Tricks in 4-runner minor event at York in July and to Critique in 6-runner
minor event at Kempton in August, in latter making running and keeping on
well although no match for winner; blinkered, found nothing under pressure when
15 lengths fourth of 6 behind Melodrama in £3,000 event at Newbury in
September; stays 1m; acts on firm going. *C. Brittain.*

ILMAZ 5 ch.h. Morston 125–Merisette (Phil Drake 132) (1980 13v4 14s 12fg **74**
13d 14g2 15.5fg* 12d 16fg4 15.8d 1981 12s* 16s 12d) compact ex-French
horse; trotted up in minor event at Folkestone in March; stays well; seems to
act on any going; has been tried in blinkers; sold 1,000 gns Newmarket Autumn
Sales. *D. Morley.*

ILSA KEMPINSKI 4 b.f. Right Tack 131–Allegretto (Preciptic 122) (1980 7d **—**
7v 6d 10.2fg 10.6fg 7g 6s* 6g 1981 5s 6fg 5d 7g 6f 5fg 6s) unfurnished filly;
inconsistent handicapper; behind in sellers on occasions; best at 6f on soft going;
sometimes blinkered; occasionally sweats up; has won for an apprentice; sold
to C. Nelson 2,800 gns Goffs November Sales. *J. Spearing.*

IMAGINATION 2 b.f. Relko 136–Romancing 82 (Romulus 129) (1981 7f* 7g **91**
7g2) Mar 17; 9,200Y; small filly; half-sister to numerous winners here and
abroad, including fairly useful 1975 2-y-o Stormy Affair (by Prevailing); dam
won over 6f at 2 yrs; put in a storming late run to win going away by 1½ lengths
from odds-on Dewanadance when 33/1 and apprentice ridden in 16-runner
maiden race at Yarmouth in August; also ran well in 2 races at Newmarket in
October, finishing 7 lengths fifth of 16 to Wind and Wuthering in Somerville
Tattersall Stakes and staying on strongly to be 3 lengths second of 18 to Straeker
in £4,500 nursery; will stay middle distances; lacks scope. *L. Cumani.*

I'M HOT (USA) 2 ch.f. Dike–Royal Hula (Raise A Native) (1981 6g* 7.3s3) **95**
Mar 20; $60,000 2-y-o; quite well-made filly; half-sister to 3 winners in USA,
including stakes-placed Yoka (by Triple Bend), a winner at up to 1m; dam
won 4 times at up to 1m; easy third favourite but pretty fit, ran on strongly
to beat Rose Du Soir by 2½ lengths in 17-runner maiden race at Newmarket in
October; kept on without quickening when 10 lengths third of 8 to Last Feather
in £6,300 event at Newbury later in month; will stay 1¼m. *M. Albina.*

IMMORAL 3 b.g. Silly Season 127–Impertinent (King's Troop 118) (1980 NR **59**
1981 10f 15.5g* 16.5g3) 1,750F; strong gelding; third produce; dam never ran;
beat Snooze by 4 lengths in maiden event at Catterick in September; ran too
freely next time; stays well. *M. Camacho.*

IMPECCABLE LADY 2 br.f. Silly Season 127–Gorse Bush (Hallez 131) (1981 **—**
6fg 5.8h 7.6s 7g) Mar 24; 1,400F, 1,500Y; leggy, rather lightly-made filly;
second foal; half-sister to 1980 2-y-o 6f winner Fath-El-Keir (by Record Token);
dam won twice over 1¼m in Ireland; little worthwhile form in maiden and minor
events. *C. Williams.*

IMPERIAL ACE 5 bh. Derring-Do 131–Buss 102 (Busted 134) (1980 8f* 10f **88**
1981 8g4 8f 8fg 10g2 10d) strong, attractive horse; fair handicapper; stays 1¼m;
acts on any going; often sweats up; ran atrociously final start; sold 3,300 gns
Newmarket Autumn Sales. *M. Stoute.*

IMPERIAL AMBER 5 br.g. Amber Rama 133–Pampered Angel 97 (Pampered **—**
King 121) (1980 8g 9g4 12f 12.2fg 1981 10f4 12.3fg2 16f3 16.5g4 12v) strong,
fair sort; poor handicapper; stays 1½m; blinkered once at 3 yrs. *M. Naughton.*

IMPERIAL MEASURE 3 b.c. Derring-Do 131–Buss 102 (Busted 134) (1980 **82**
5f4 6d* 7d2 7g2 1981 8d3 8d2 10d 10fg 10d 10d) small, sturdy colt; very good
walker; ran creditably when placed in handicaps at Newbury and Salisbury,
finishing length second to Santellas in latter in May; probably stays 1¼m; acts
on a soft surface; well beaten in blinkers final start; sold 5,000 gns Newmarket
Autumn Sales. *H. Candy.*

IMPERIAL ROSE 2 b.f. Imperial Crown 96–Rosie Glow (Royben 125) (1981 **—**
5fg 5f 6g) Mar 19; first foal; dam never ran; well behind in sellers. *R. Hoad.*

IMPERIUM 4 ch.g. Mount Hagen 127–Idea (Ragusa 137) (1980 10fg2 10g 10.2g **—**
7g2 6fg 7f 1981 14fg 12g) well-made gelding; stays 1¼m (well beaten over
further at 4 yrs); yet to race on a soft surface; blinkered once in 1980. *J. Old.*

IMPISH EARS 3 ch.f. Import 127–Golden Ears 94 (Gratitude 131) (1980 5g **—**
5g 7.2d 7s4 8g 1981 7f 9.4g 10fg) compact filly; poor maiden; stays 7f;
evidently suited by soft going. *E. Weymes.*

410

IMPISH SIOUX 3 ch.f. Import 127–Sioux 95 (Nimbus 130) (1980 5g 5fg 5fg —
8d 1981 6f) neat filly; no sign of ability, including in sellers. *W. Stubbs.*

IMPLICATION (USA) 2 b.c. Tentam–Caught in the Act (Nijinsky 138) (1981 —
7g) May 9; $90,000Y; second foal; dam, closely related to very smart filly
Northern Gem, won small race over 1m; unquoted when in rear behind Ivano
in 15-runner Houghton Stakes at Newmarket in October. *G. Harwood.*

IMPLICATOR 3 b.f. Imperial Crown 96–Sutania (Supreme Sovereign 119) —
(1980 8.2s 1981 10.1fg 8.3fg 7f) small, lightly-made filly; little sign of ability
in varied company, including selling. *R. Hoad.*

IMPORTANT 3 gr.g. Import 127–Donrae 106 (Don II 123) (1980 5f 5f 1981 —
8f 8f 8f 10fg) compact gelding; little worthwhile form in maiden races; blinkered
final outing at 2 yrs; pulled hard third start. *W. Wharton.*

IMPORT EXPORT (FR) 3 b.c. Import 127–Lucy 83 (Sheshoon 132) (1980 **56**
8fg 8.2s 7.2d⁴ 1981 12s 9.4g 12g³ 12g* 16.1f 13fg⁴ 14d 12f³ 18f 15g⁴ 16s³) very
big colt; won maiden race at Edinburgh in June narrowly; stays well; unruly on
reappearance and subsequently wore blinkers; fell fifth start; sweating seventh
outing; usually a front runner. *J. Wilson.*

IMPORT LADY 3 ch.f. Import 127–Palfrey Jr (Yrrah Jr) (1980 6s 5d 5f 5d —
5d 5g 1981 12.2s 9d 8g 7g 8s⁴) fair sort; poor form in varied company,
including selling; by no means certain to stay 1½m; sometimes blinkered; sold
600 gns Doncaster June Sales. *Denys Smith.*

I'M VEXED 2 b.c. High Top 131–Sassalya (Sassafras 135) (1981 5g² 5v) Mar **69**
30; 17,000Y; strong, quite useful sort; first foal; dam useful Irish 7f and 1¼m
winner; strong-finishing length second of 11 to Thunderbridge in maiden race at
Newcastle in August; favourite for similar event at Haydock in October but
finished only eleventh to Master-Blow; bred to stay at least 1m; possibly unsuited
by heavy going. *M. W. Easterby.*

INCANDESCE 2 b.c. Wolver Hollow 126–Lavington 64 (Ratification 129) **105**
(1981 6g² 7fg² 8d³ 10g²) Mar 25; strong, rangy, good sort; good mover; half-
brother to 3 winners, including 1976 2-y-o 7f winner Bushy Pieces (by Ribero);
dam, placed twice at 1m, is half-sister to top sprinters So Blessed and Lucasland;
second in 3 good-class races, failing by short head to hold off Solaboy in Champagne Stakes at Salisbury in June, dead-heating with Telephone Man when
beaten 6 lengths by Loyal Toast in Sandwich Stakes at Ascot the following month
and going down by a neck, after trying to make all, in £6,500 event at Newmarket in October won by Paternoster Row; also ran well when 6½ lengths third
of 21 finishers behind Super Sunrise in £4,200 race at Newbury in September;
suited by 1¼m and may get 1½m at 3 yrs; a useful colt who should have a run-
of-the-mill maiden event at his mercy. *P. Cole.*

INCA THIEF (USA) 2 b.c. Chieftain–Native Cindy (Raise A Native) (1981 **78**
6g 6g 7f³ 8d) Apr 18; $70,000Y; strong, useful sort; brother to very useful
American 1980 2-y-o winner Incredible Luck, and half-brother to 2 winners;
dam unraced daughter of smart 1960 2-y-o Little Tumbler; ran on well in closing
stages, despite hanging away from rails, when 1¾ lengths third of 19 in maiden
event won by Wibis Range at Redcar in September; suited by 7f and should
get 1m; possibly needs a firm surface. *S. Norton.*

INCESTUOUS 2 b.g. Mummy's Pet 125–Autumn Breeze (King's Bench 132) —
(1981 6g 6fg) May 2; 20,000Y; fair sort; good walker; brother to fairly useful
sprinters Coded Scrap and Touch of Salt; dam ran only twice; in mid-division
in 20-runner maiden races won by Linda Beard and Anstruther at Newmarket
in August; gelded subsequently. *J. Hindley.*

INCH HIGH 2 ch.f. Starch Reduced 112–Billie Franks (Goldhill 125) (1981 **55**
5fg⁴ 5d⁴ 5s 5f² 5f³ 6f* 6g) Apr 16; small, stocky filly; fifth foal; dam bad plater;
made virtually all when winning by a head from Cautious in poor seller at Ripon
in August (no bid); unlikely to stay 7f; seems to act on any going. *V. Soane.*

IN CONFIDENCE 3 ch.f. Most Secret 119–Isis Rapide (I Say 125) (1980 **39**
NR 1981 7d⁴ 7f³ 8fg) 1,500F, resold 250Y and 600Y; half-sister to a winner
in Austria; dam ran only once; off course 5 months prior to finishing third in
seller at Leicester in August (bandaged in front); stays 7f. *D. Gandolfo.*

INDADO 3 b.g. Manado 130–Indian Beauty 93 (Indiana 129) (1980 6g —
1981 14f 10fg) smallish, well-made gelding; little worthwhile form in maiden
races; blinkered final outing; sold 480 gns Newmarket Autumn Sales. *I.
Walker.*

INDEPENDENTIA 2 br.f. Home Guard 129–Gay Pariso 82 (Sir Gaylord) **68** (1981 6d 6g) Feb 4; first foal; dam, daughter of Musidora winner Jakomima, won over 1m; shaped fairly well for a newcomer when 3½ lengths fifth of 25 to Dev in maiden race at Doncaster in October; moved badly to start when behind in similar event at Newmarket later in month; bred to stay 1m. *B. Hills.*

INDIAN CALL 2 br.f. Warpath 113–Sing High 85 (Sound Track 132) (1981 **72** 6g 6g 6g 8fg 8g*) May 3; 3,000Y; useful sort; good walker; half-sister to several winners, including quite useful 1970 2-y-o 6f and 7f winner Thief Lane (by Mandamus); dam stayed 1m; blinkered and dropped in class, bought in 5,200 gns after leading on line to win 18-runner seller at Newmarket in October by a short head from Sir John Falstaff; runs as though 1¼m will suit her; wore a tongue strap at Newmarket. *J. Fitzgerald.*

INDIAN KING (FR) 2 ch.c. Roi Dagobert 128–Indianapolis (Barbare II **101** p 128) (1981 8v*) Apr 15; half-brother to several winners, notably Prix du Jockey-Club winner Policeman (by Riverman); dam placed over 7f and 1m from only 2 starts at 2 yrs; accounted for more-experienced colts when winning 12-runner maiden race at Longchamp in October by 2 lengths from subsequently-demoted Brazos; will stay 1½m; promising. *C. Milbank, France.*

INDIAN KING (USA) 3 b.c. Raja Baba–Protest (Rash Prince) (1980 **114** 6fg3(dis) 1981 8g* 7fg2 7g* 7s 7g) big, rangy, useful-looking colt; not seen out until quite late in year but did well, winning quite well-contested minor event at Goodwood in August comfortably by 2½ lengths from Rushmoor and Battle of Britain Handicap at Doncaster in September by 5 lengths from Ackermann; made all in latter and was in no danger whatsoever after quickening clear 2f out; also ran well when ½ length second to Belted Earl in another minor event at Goodwood in between (caught in last 50 yards); floundered under pressure in the soft going and ran well below form when fifth of 11 behind stable-companion Home Coming in £8,700 handicap at Ascot later in September and finished only eighth behind Swinging Rebel in another handicap at Newmarket in October (had stiffish task but was rather disappointing again nevertheless); stays 1m but is a free-running sort and isn't certain to stay further; probably needs a sound surface. *G. Harwood.*

Mr J. Levy's "Indian King (USA)"

*Extel Stakes, Goodwood—Indian Trail (nearest camera) lands a gamble,
winning from Golden Flak and Magikin*

INDIAN POOL 5 br.g. Red Alert 127–Black Gnat (Typhoon 125) (1980 —
8fg⁴ 8g⁴ 8g 8fg 1981 8f 10f⁴ 8h) compact, well-made ex-Irish gelding; poor
performer on balance of form; best at around 1m on top-of-the-ground; has
worn blinkers; suitable mount for an inexperienced rider. *M. Pipe.*

INDIAN SONG (CHI) 6 br.g. Silent Song 86–Ivinia (Sun Prince 111) (1980 —
NR 1981 10f) Chilean-bred gelding; winner of 5 races over 5 and 6 furlongs
from 8 outings in his native country; in rear in claiming race at Brighton in
August, first outing on flat in this country; sold 1,025 gns Ascot October Sales.
D. Kent.

INDIAN TRAIL (USA) 3 b.c. Apalachee 137–Majestic Street (Majestic **95**
Prince) (1980 5.8f³ 6s³ 7d⁴ 1981 8d* 8.2fg² 10.4g² 8d⁴ 10fg* 10fg* 10d³
10.2fg⁴ 9g) neat colt; good mover; improved considerably and enjoyed a good
season; landed a third gamble and picked up a valuable prize when beating
Golden Flak a head in Extel Stakes (Handicap) at Goodwood in July, getting
up close home after being held up; had earlier won handicaps at Newbury
(in fine style from Soukab) and Newmarket (quickened up nicely in a slowly-
run race and beat Ardar a shade comfortably by ¾ length); creditable fifth
of 28 behind Braughing in William Hill Cambridgeshire at Newmarket in October;
appears to need further than 1m and stays 1¼m; probably acts on any going;
sweated badly and ran moderately fourth start. *B. Hills.*

INDIGINE (USA) 2 ch.f. Raise A Native–Cajun Princess (Advocator) (1981 **71**
6f 6fg* 6d³) Feb 3; $78,000Y; leggy filly; first foal; dam, granddaughter of
outstanding broodmare Bourtai, won over 6f at 2 yrs; had plenty in hand when
winning 10-runner maiden race at Ayr in July by 1½ lengths from Sanches;
played up in preliminaries when 4¼ lengths third of 6 to Knight Security in
nursery at Haydock following month; bred to stay 7f but is highly strung
and may not do so; sweated up badly when withdrawn at start at Doncaster
in September. *J. W. Watts.*

INDIOLA 3 br.f. Mansingh 120–Gambela 88 (Diplomat Way) (1980 5g 6g
1981 5d 5fg) small filly; plating-class maiden; well beaten in blinkers final
start; sold 460 gns Doncaster May Sales. *J. Winter.*

INDULGENCE 2 ch.f. Prominer 125–Perennial Twinkle (Continuation 120) **76 p**
(1981 8d²) May 18; IR 3,200Y; sister to winning Irish middle-distance stayer
Always Smiling; dam won over 5f at 2 yrs in Ireland; 2/1 favourite, dwelt
but led over 1f out when beaten a length by Sent For You in 14-runner maiden
event at Edinburgh in October; will stay 1¼m+. *Sir Mark Prescott.*

IN FIJAR (USA) 4 b.c. Bold Commander–Apache Queen (Marshal At Arms **121**
114) (1980 8g 8g* 10.5fg³ 9fg⁴ 9.2s³ 10g 10d 1981 8v* 10.5g³ 8fg) big,
rangy colt; good walker; very smart performer; comfortably beat Moorestyle
by a length in Poule d'Essai des Poulains at Longchamp in 1980; had little
difficulty holding Wild Idea's late challenge by 2¼ lengths in Prix Edmond
Blanc at Saint-Cloud in March; 4 lengths third to ready winner Argument in
Prix Ganay at Longchamp in May; outpaced throughout when eighth of 9

413

to Kings Lake in Sussex Stakes at Goodwood in July; stayed 1¼m well; probably acted on any going; genuine and consistent; standing at Haras de La Genevraye, Orne. *M. Saliba, France.*

INKYBOO 5 gr.m. Sayfar 116–Inklet (Never Say Die 137) (1980 8fg 8.3f 10d — 10.1s 8.3f 1981 12d) poor plater; has been tried in blinkers. *Mrs N. Kennedy.*

INNS OF COURT 3 gr.g. Malacate 131–Courting (Quorum 126) (1980 — 5d 5.8g 7g 6f 1981 7fg 12g) compact gelding; poor plater; sometimes blinkered. *M. Haynes.*

IN RHYTHM 4 b.c. Gay Fandango 132–Procession 118 (Sovereign Path 125) ' **66** (1980 7fg 6g 6g⁴ 6g 5.8g 6fg 6d 6d 1981 6s 6s 6d⁴ 6d³ 7fg⁴ 6g* 6fg 6fg 7v 7s 7d) strong colt; won apprentice handicap at Ayr in June; stays .7f; probably acts on any going; good mount for an apprentice; blinkered last 3 starts. *P. Makin.*

INSIDE EDGE 2 br.f. Pongee 106–September Fire (Firestreak 125) (1981 6g) — Jan 15; lengthy filly; sister to 5f to 15f winner Autumn Glow and half-sister to a winner abroad; dam never ran; unquoted when tailed-off last of 14 to Dance In Rome in maiden race at Nottingham in August. *D. Nicholson.*

IN SLIPS 2 b.c. Mount Hagen 127–Get Ready 91 (On Your Mark 125) (1981 **80** 5g² 6s 6f* 6d⁴ 6g⁴ 6fg 5g) Apr 14; 5,000Y; narrow, rather leggy colt; second foal; dam best at 5f; stayed on well when winning 22-runner maiden race at Thirsk in July by a neck from Remodel; put up best subsequent effort on fifth start when 5 lengths fourth of 6 to Houghton Weaver in nursery at Redcar in August; needs further than 5f; apparently needs a sound surface. *Sir Mark Prescott.*

INTEGRITY 3 gr.f. Reform 132–Cry of Truth 129 (Town Crier 119) (1980 **108** 6g* 6d 6fg* 6g⁴ 8fg 1981 6fg² 6f³ 6fg* 6fg 7t³) strong, good-bodied, short legged filly; good mover; second foal; half-sister to 5f winner Truth Will Out (by Blakeney); dam best 2-y-o filly of 1974; ran very well when length second to Runnett in Leisure Stakes at Lingfield and ¾-length third to The Quiet Bidder in Cork and Orrery Stakes at Royal Ascot in June; made all and beat Vocalist in good style by 2½ lengths in well-contested minor event at Newbury the following month; led for nearly 6f but probably didn't last the trip out when 5¾ lengths third of 7 behind Premier Rose in Strensall Stakes at York in September; best at sprint distances; acts well on firm going. *B. Hobbs.*

INTERCONTINENTAL 3 ch.g. Hot Spark 126–Raflex 72 (Skymaster 126) **89** (1980 5f 6fg* 6d 7s⁴ 7d 8fg 1981 7g 8fg* 8fg 7fg 10.2g) quite attractive, useful-looking gelding; has a rounded action; 20/1 and apprentice ridden, held on well by a neck from Countess Olivia in Hong Kong Handicap at Sandown in July, easily best effort; stays 1m; acts on a firm and a soft surface. *E. Eldin.*

INTEREST 3 ch.g. Bold Lad (USA)–Katira 83 (Paveh 126) (1980 5fg 6d 7g **52** 8g 8d 1981 12g 12d 16f⁴ 16fg 16.5f³) strong, close-coupled gelding; poor maiden; stays well; acts on firm going; sometimes sweats up; occasionally blinkered. *M. Francis.*

INTERLUDE 3 gr.f. The Go-Between 129–Sheridans Daughter 75 (Majority — Blue 126) (1980 5g 1981 8fg 5g 6s) small, stocky filly; behind in maiden races and a handicap; dead. *C. Williams.*

INTINTO 4 gr.c. Connaught 130–Cranberry Sauce 119 (Crepello 136) (1980 — 8f³ 10.6fg 10g 10fg 8fg⁴ 8g² 8fg² 10g² 8g³ 8s² 1981 12s³ 10g) good walker; stays 1¼m (gave impression 1½m was beyond him first start); probably acts on any going but goes well on soft; blinkered nowadays; sometimes sweats up; sent to USA. *J. Old.*

INTREPID BOY 4 br.c. Realm 129–Nana's Girl 109 (Tin Whistle 128) (1980 **59** d 5f⁴ 5f³ 5g 5fg 6f 5f 5s 5d 1981 6s³ 5s* 6g⁴ 5d 5g 5g 5f 5fg 5g 5d 5g) strong, useful-looking colt; good mover; sprint handicapper; won at Beverley in April; stays 6f; acts on any going; sold 2,600 gns Newmarket Autumn Sales. *W. Bentley.*

INVESTA 3 br.f. Lombard 126–Idrissa (Tamerlane 128) (1980 6g 6g 7g* 7g* — 7g² 1981 10g 10.2fg 8d) lightly-made filly; useful performer at 2 yrs; didn't recover her form in 1981, best effort on second outing when 8½ lengths fifth of 8 behind Heighten in £3,200 event at Doncaster in September (sweating badly and having first race since May); should be suited by middle distances; sold 16,000 gns Newmarket December Sales. *M. Stoute.*

IONIAN RAJA (USA) 3 b.f. Raja Baba–Ionian Idol (Prince John) (1980 **116** 5.5fg⁴ 5.5d³ 7g* 8g² 8f 8s⁴ 1981 8fg³ 8g³ 8s* 8s 8g 8f 6d 8s³) $75,000Y; leggy filly; second foal; dam, winner at up to 6f in USA, is half-sister to useful 1968 staying Irish 2-y-o Mongolia II; made all and went clear in straight when beating Taduska decisively by 2 lengths in 8-runner Prix de Bagatelle at Longchamp in May; third earlier on same course in Group 3 Prix de la Grotte (about 1½ lengths behind Tropicaro) and Group 1 Poule d'Essai des Pouliches (3 lengths behind Ukraine Girl); ran best subsequent race when 4½ lengths third of 18 behind Princes Gate in Group 3 Prix Perth at Saint-Cloud in November; will probably stay 1¼m; acts well on soft ground. *F. Boutin, France.*

IOWA 2 br.c. So Blessed 130–Montana (Mossborough 126) (1981 6s⁴) May 8; second foal; half-brother to 1980 2-y-o 1¼m seller winner Alabama (by Warpath); dam poor maiden on flat and over hurdles; 16/1, showed he has a fair amount of ability when 9½ lengths fourth of 8 to Mirabeau in £3,500 event at York in October, running on very strongly from halfway after missing break very badly; will stay 7f+; not a particularly taking individual but shouldn't have much difficulty in winning a maiden race in the North if reproducing his York form. *C. Thornton.* — **80 p**

IRENE ADLER 3 br.f. Brigadier Gerard 144–Gingerale (Golden Horus 123) (1980 5.8h⁴ 8fg 1981 8fg 7f 7fg 10.8fg⁴ 10fg² 10f 10.1fg) unimpressive-looking filly; quite a moderate maiden; ran best race fifth start; suited by 1¼m+; slowly into stride third start; sold 2,100 gns Newmarket Autumn Sales. *W. Holden.* — **63**

IRISH COMMANDMENT 4 ch.g. Shiny Tenth 120–Ritruda 95 (Roi Dagobert 128) (1980 6f² 7f* 7.3f 8fg 6g 6s⁴ 6d 7g 1981 6g 7fg 6g⁴ 7g 7.2s 8fg³ 6f⁴ 7.6fg 7fg 6f 7fg 6g 7g) sturdy gelding; good mover; stays 1m; seems to act on any going; sometimes blinkered; has worn bandages in front; inconsistent; sold 400 gns Newmarket Autumn Sales. *F. Durr.* — **61**

IRISH EMPEROR 4 br.c. Realm 129–Empress of Clare 73 (Persian Gulf or Premonition 130) (1980 7f 7g 5g 6g⁴ 6s 6f 6d⁴ 1981 6s 10.4g 10g* 10d⁴ 8fg 10g 8d) useful-looking colt; front-running handicapper; beat Mawal by 8 lengths in apprentice event at Brighton in May; creditable 2¼ lengths fourth to Easter Sun in Daily Mirror Handicap at Epsom in June; evidently suited by 1¼m; suited by some give in the ground; sometimes sweats up; blinkered once in 1980; sold 3,300 gns Newmarket Autumn Sales, probably for export to Italy. *R. Sheather.* — **80**

IRISH FLAX 2 b.g. Connaught 130–Blue Linnet 96 (Habitat 134) (1981 5g 6fg 7.6s 10s) May 11; strong, good-quartered gelding; first foal; dam won 4 times over 5f; in rear in maiden races; off course over 3 months before third outing. *A. Ingham.* — **—**

IRISH GRENADIER 2 b.c. Home Guard 129–Mare D'Erba (Habitat 134) (1981 6f⁴ 6g³ 6f* 7g 7g⁴) Mar 12; IR 22,000F, IR 21,000Y; attractive, rangy colt; first foal; dam unraced granddaughter of smart 1964 2-y-o Unity; led 1f out when winning 9-runner maiden race at Brighton in August by ¾ length from Erotas; ran easily better subsequent race when fourth of 14 to Hello Sunshine in competitive nursery at Doncaster in November; stays 7f and may get 1m at 3 yrs; ran too freely when disappointing favourite on second start. *J. Dunlop.* — **92**

IRISH HEART 3 b.c. Steel Heart 128–Klairlone 116 (Klairon 131) (1980 8g 8g³ 8.2s* 8s* 10.2s* 1981 12fg⁴ 12g including 8.5g 8.5f* 11f² 10f* 13s 8.5f²) good-topped, attractive colt; moderate mover; ran on steadily without quite finding the pace to get on terms and was far from disgraced when 3½ lengths fourth of 7 behind Glint of Gold in Warren Stakes at Epsom in April; remote last of 8 to Riberetto in Ladbrokes Derby Trial at Lingfield following month (faded very quickly and possibly still needed run); subsequently left J. Dunlop's stable to race in North America and did well there, winning handicap at Meadowlands in September and Jockey Club Stakes at Woodbine in October; stays 1½m; acts on any going. *G. Rowntree, Canada.* — **?**

IRISH KEEP 3 b.c. Connaught 130–Golden Keep 77 (Worden II 129) (1980 NR 1981 8g 12g 12s² 14s² 12.3g² 10fg* 12fg² 10d² 10.2fg⁴) strong, sturdy colt; half-brother to very smart but inconsistent miler Buz Kashi (by Bold Lad, Ire) and useful 7f to 19f winner Caporello (by Crepello); dam won from 1¼m to 13f; won 17-runner maiden race at Newmarket in July in good style, leading 1½f out and storming clear up hill to win by 8 lengths from Karadar; runner-up on 5 other occasions, on last 2 beaten a head by On A Cloud (pair clear) in 4-runner minor event at Kempton later in July and 2½ lengths by Say Primula in Andy Capp Handicap at Redcar in August; shade disappointing on final start and gave impression he'd be suited by a return to 1½m; acts on any going. *H. Wragg.* — **96**

IRISH POET 7 ch.h. Allangrange 126–Christina Rosetti 102 (Monet 127) **54**
(1980 12fg 12g 13g 1981 12s³ 16s⁴ 15.8g 12s² 12f 13.8g 13s) poor handicapper;
best form at distances short of 2m, and with some give in the ground; good
mount for an apprentice. *G. Huffer.*

IRISH PRINCE 8 b.g. Irish Ball 127–Miss Jessica 90 (Milesian 125) .(1980 —
11f 1981 16d) lightly-raced plater nowadays; stays 1½m; acts on any going;
sometimes wears blinkers. *J. Doyle.*

IRISH RIFLE 4 b.c. Scottish Rifle 127–Sunsaly 75 (Sallymount 125) (1980 **56**
11.7fg 11.7f³ 12d 10s 1981 18s 12.2fg³ 12v⁴ 12f 14d 12.2fg³ 10.1fg 11.7fg 12f³)
well-made colt; best at around 1¼m (unlikely to stay extreme distances); suited
by firm going; blinkered fifth and final starts; has worn bandages in front.
R. Laing.

IRISH SPARKLE 3 ch.f. Sparkler 130–Limerick Queen (Whistling Wind **72**
123) (1980 5g 5d 6d 1981 6s 6g 6s² 8.2s* 8d³ 8.2s) useful-looking filly;
beat Soffiana 4 lengths after being held up in maiden race at Nottingham in
September, first outing for 4 months; suited by 1m; acts on soft going; ran
moderately final start; sold 1,000 gns Newmarket December Sales. *B. Hills.*

IRRAWADDY 4 b.f. Rapid River 127–Keyvala (Quisling 117) (1980 6f 5h **49**
8f 8s² 10g³ 9.4g 10d² 10f 8g 10s 1981 8g 8g² 8g⁴ 12f³ 8f⁴ 10f* 8.2s²) compact,
lightly-made filly; plater; bought in 1,000 gns after winning at Pontefract in
September; possibly stays 1½m; acts on any going; sweated up badly once at
3 yrs. *J. Carr.*

ISANEMOS (USA) 3 b.c. Mississipian 131–Shiraza (Jaipur) (1980 NR **88**
1981 12fg 11.7g² 16fg* 12d³ 17.1h* 16.5f² 16.1d³ 18.8fg 16s) $17,000Y; com-
pact colt; fourth foal; dam, placed twice from 24 starts, is half-sister to smart
Yorktown; successful in maiden race at York in June (made all and beat Scheming cleverly by a neck) and handicap at Bath in July (beat Cwmyreithin ¼
length); ran respectably most others starts, although disappointed on last
2; suited by 2m; acts on any going, except possibly very soft; sold to D. Barons
12,500 gns Newmarket Autumn Sales. *G. Harwood.*

ISKANNDAROUN 4 b.c. Kalamoun 129–Laparia (St Paddy 133) (1980 —
10fg* 12g* 10d⁴ 12g* 12g⁴ 12g 12fg 1981 12fg 12g 10d 12f 12.3fg 12f) strong,
good-topped colt; good mover; fairly useful performer at his best; didn't find
his form at 4 yrs though wasn't entirely disgraced on third start; stays 1½m;
suited by top-of-the-ground; blinkered third and final outings; sold 3,200 gns
Newmarket Autumn Sales. *M. Stoute.*

ISHKOMANN 2 b.c. Faunus–Irova (Iron Liege) (1981 6f 7fg² 7g² 7d 8.2d) **77**
Mar 25; strong, good-looking colt; excellent mover; brother to Irish middle-
distance winner Ormus, and half-brother to 2 winners in France by Abdos;
dam, French 1m winner, is daughter of high-class Cordova; only quite moderate;
will stay 1½m; sold to BBA 8,400 gns Newmarket Autumn Sales. *M. Stoute.*

ISLA 2 b.f. Reform 132–Krafty Kate 73 (Klairon 131) (1981 6fg) Apr 19; —
well-made filly; third reported foal; half-sister to 2 winning platers; dam won
over 1¼m; 50/1 and distinctly backward, started slowly when tailed-off last of
8 to Cheri Berry in minor event at Epsom in August; sold 400 gns Newmarket
Autumn Sales. *D. Whelan.*

ISLAND WALK 3 b.f. Palm Track 122–Ladyfold 60 (Never Dwell 89) (1980 **62**
5f 1981 7s* 7v 7fg 7g³ 7fg 6g* 6fg* 6d 6g³ 7g*) small filly; did very well
in sellers and won at Catterick, Hamilton, Ayr and Doncaster (fairly valuable
event); attracted no bid first 3 occasions but was bought in 2,500 gns on last
one; stays 7f; probably acts on any going. *W. Haigh.*

ISLES BAY 3 b. or br.f. Manado 130–Gay Baby 101 (Galivanter 131) (1980 **93**
5s 5g* 5fg³ 5g 5g 1981 7s 5d² 5s⁴ 5d³ 6f*) 36,000Y; half-sister to 3 winners,
including useful Irish sprinter Sweet Steal (by Steel Heart); dam beaten 2-y-o;
25/1, showed improved form when beating Pitmarie readily by a length in 18-
runner Carna Fillies Stakes at Naas in November; in frame in handicaps at
Phoenix Park (2) and Leopardstown earlier; by no means sure to stay 7f;
clearly well suited by firm going; reportedly sold privately to race in USA.
P. Norris, Ireland.

ISOM DART (USA) 2 b.c. Bold Forbes–Shellshock 110 (Salvo 129) (1981 **69**
6g 7fg⁴ 7fg 8s) neat, well-made, attractive colt; good walker; fourth foal;
half-brother to 3-y-o 13.4f winner Bell Rammer (by Nijinsky) and 2 other winners,
including midde-distance stayer Sir Billy (by Sir Ivor); dam, half-sister to
top-class Dibidale, was third in 1,000 Guineas and stayed 13f; showed a modicum
of ability in maiden races and a minor event; will be suited by 1¼m. *B. Hills.*

ITAI 2 b.f. Import 127–Even Song (Falcon 131) (1981 6fg 5d⁴ 7d 6g) Jan — 21; 2,000F; strong, compact filly; third living foal; half-sister to 6f to 1½m winner Winter Sunshine (by Crisp and Even); dam showed little sign of ability; plater; not sure to stay 7f; claimed £2,400 final start. *P. Haslam.*

ITALIAN CONNECTION 6 ch.m. Communication 119–Ravenna (Celtic — Ash) (1980 16f 12s 1981 16d) poor maiden; has worn bandages. *M. Eckley.*

ITALIAN MASTER 4 b.g. Workboy 123–Ritratto (Pinturischio 116) (1980 — NR 1981 8.2g 8fg² 8g⁴ 8fg 8.2s) big gelding; plater nowadays; stays 1m; acts on firm going and is possibly unsuited by soft; wears bandages. *D. Garraton.*

ITS-A-TWIST 2 gr.g. Legal Eagle 126–Firmpostie (Goldhill 125) (1981 **69** 6f 7fg 8g 8d) Apr 30; leggy gelding; half-brother to 6f and 7f seller winner Work-shy (by Workboy); dam ran twice; 7 lengths fifth of 15 behind Sagamore in maiden race at Beverley in September, third start and best effort; stays 1m. *H. Wharton.*

IT'S ONLY ME 2 b.f. The Brianstan 128–Toplady 85 (Rockavon 120) (1981 — 5s 6d) Apr 18; unimpressive filly; first reported foal; dam, 2-y-o 7f winner, stayed 1½m; fair seventh of 17 to Colonial Line in modest all-aged maiden race at Nottingham in October; gambled on when well behind in maiden race at Leicester the following month. *Mrs B. Waring.*

IVANO (CAN) 2 ch.c. Snow Knight 125–Smiling Jacqueline (Hilarious) **110 p** (1981 7g*)

The Fasig-Tipton Kentucky Fall Preferred Yearling Sales is an impressive title for a relatively unimportant event on the circuit. Initiated only in 1978, it isn't yet in the big league of American sales and in 1980 its average was only 19,650 dollars compared to 200,425 dollars at Keeneland and 111,159 dollars at Saratoga. In 1981 the average rose only a modest 516 dollars but the sale is likely to receive a considerable boost from the exploits of its top-priced lot of 1980, a 100,000-dollar Snow Knight colt. The colt, now named Ivano, looked a very smart performer in the making when winning his only race at two, the Houghton Stakes at Newmarket in October.

Favourite at Newmarket was Noble Gift, reputedly the best colt in the Stoute stable and a close second to Count Pahlen on his only previous start, while the Mornington Stakes runner-up Father Rooney and Quiet Fling's brother Peacetime were also preferred to Ivano. Noble Gift seemed about to justify favouritism when still on the bridle two furlongs out. Hardly had he taken the lead, though, than he was challenged running out of the Dip by the new-comers Peacetime and Ivano. The stronger challenger proved to be Ivano,

*Houghton Stakes, Newmarket—newcomer Ivano wins from Noble Gift
with another debutant Peacetime in third place*

IVE

whose highly impressive burst of speed took him into the lead close home; so
fast did he finish that he was a length and a half to the good by the line, with
Noble Gift holding off Peacetime by a length. The Houghton Stakes has from
time to time proved an excellent pointer to the classics, numbering Blakeney
and One In A Million among its winners and such as Furioso, Bireme and Posse
among those placed in the race. Ivano may not reach the heights they did
but he looks sure to pick up some good prizes. Peacetime is also a name for
the notebook—he has the makings of a fine three-year-old.

Ivano (Can)
(ch.c. Mar 18, 1979)

	Snow Knight (ch 1971)	Firestreak (br 1956)	Pardal / Hot Spell
		Snow Blossom (br 1957)	Flush Royal / Ariana
	Smiling Jacqueline (b 1969)	Hilarious (b 1950)	Bimelech / Laughter
		Fulfiliole (ch 1960)	Beau Gar / Filiole

Ivano is a strong, good-bodied, attractive colt from Snow Knight's second
crop. Snow Knight will be remembered here as a non-vintage Derby winner
but he went on to win six races in North America at four years, including the
Canadian International Championship and the Man o' War Stakes, and was
voted the champion grass horse. He hasn't yet made much impact at stud
in the States and it's possible his offspring will prove better suited by European
racing conditions. Only time will tell.
    Ivano comes from a European female line. His great-grandam Filiole
won eight times in Italy and was a sister to Filatrice, the top Italian three-
year-old filly of 1952, and a half-sister to Le Filou, a very useful middle-distance
colt who later met with considerable success as a stallion in Australasia. Ivano's
grandam Fulfiliole won a small race at three years in the USA and bred eight
winners, four of them by the Florida-based Hilarious. One of the four, Circus
Flea, was a minor stakes winner and most successful of the others was Ivano's
dam Smiling Jacqueline. Although a daughter of Hilarious, whose twenty
victories were over sprint distances, Smiling Jacqueline stayed well by American
standards, winning nine times at up to a mile and a quarter. Ivano, her first
foal, will stay at least that distance. *H. Cecil.*

IVER 10 b.g. Tacitus 124–Goldella 60 (Golden Cloud) (1980 12f³ 12g² 11.7s —
1981 11.7d 10v) poor middle-distance handicapper nowadays; acts on any
going; good mount for an apprentice; used to wear blinkers; often sweats up.
D. Elsworth.

IVORY WINGS (USA) 3 ch.f. Sir Ivor 135–Kittiwake (Sea-Bird II 145) (1980 112
8g 1981 9s² 10s* 12v* 12g⁴ 10f⁴ 10v³) $335,000Y; small filly; second foal;
half-sister to Irish 1¼m winner Rissa (by Nijinsky); dam high-class winner of 18
races at up to 9f and ranked among best of her sex from 3 yrs to 5 yrs; successful
in a maiden race and in a 110,000 francs event at Longchamp in May, beating
stable-companion River Reef comfortably by ¾ length in latter; in frame subsequently in Oaks (over 20 lengths fourth to Blue Wind), in Prix de
Psyche at Deauville and in Premio Lydia Tesio at Rome; stays 1½m; acts on
any going, but is well suited by plenty of give in the ground. *F. Boutin, France.*

IVY THORNE 2 b.f. Relko 136–Calling The Tune 94 (Tudor Melody 129) —
(1981 7fg 8fg 7g) strong, useful-looking filly; half-sister to winning stayer
Something Special (by Queen's Hussar) and a winner in France; dam ran only at
2 yrs; tailed off at halfway in 16-runner maiden race over 1m at Beverley in
September but ran on to finish 5½ lengths fifth to Gin; will stay well. *F. Durr.*

J

JACINTO TIMES (USA) 2 b.c. Olden Times–Jacinto Rose (Jacinto) (1981 —
7g) Apr 30; $110,000Y; lengthy colt; first foal; dam, half-sister to very suc-
cessful broodmare Peace, won 6f claiming race at 2 yrs; unquoted when tenth
of 23 to Simply Great in maiden race at Newmarket in October; may do better
over further at 3 yrs. *J. Hind'ey.*

JACKALLA 7 b.g. David Jack 125–Candy Girl (Tutankhamen) (1980 14.7f³
11g 1981 12.3d 15.8g) poor handicapper; stays well; seems to act on any

418

going; sometimes sweats up; has worn bandages; probably none too genuine; sold 950 gns Ascot 2nd June Sales. *I. Jordon.*

JACK SPLENDID 6 b.h. John Splendid 116–Grace (Gratitude 130) (1980 5s 5fg 5g 5fg 5fg³ 5d 5f* 5d 1981 5fg 5d 5g 5.3f 5d 5h 5g) big, strong horse; sprint handicapper; acts on any going; has twice been tried in blinkers; sometimes sweats up. *J. Holt.* —

JACOLETTA 2 b.f. Artaius 129–Jarama (Amber Rama 133) (1981 7g 7d 7f³ 7d) Feb 22; 13,500Y; neat, strong filly; third foal; dam unraced half-sister to top-class 1972 2-y-o Jacinth; put up best effort when 4½ lengths third of 16 to Imagination, after leading for 6f, in maiden race at Yarmouth in August; troublesome at start beforehand; will stay 1¼m; possibly needs firm gound. *B. Hobbs.* **74**

JACQUINTA 2 b.f. Habitat 134–Jacinth 133 (Red God 128§) (1981 6fg 6g³) Apr 8; shapely, attractive filly; second live foal; sister to Irish 5f winner Rodolfo; dam best 2-y-o of 1972 and a high-class miler at 3 yrs; looked in need of race after a 3-month absence when favourite for 21-runner maiden race at Newmarket in October and in circumstances ran creditably to finish 1½ lengths third to Not For Show; will stay 7f. *B. Hobbs.* **86**

JACQUI'S FOLLY 3 b.f. Mandamus 120–Archaic 65 (Relic) (1980 5g 5g 5f 5f 6g 7.2d 1981 7f) compact filly; poor mover; in rear in varied company, including selling; blinkered fifth and sixth outings at 2 yrs; sold 300 gns Doncaster November Sales. *A. Smith.* —

JADE AND DIAMOND 3 ch.g. Bold Lad (Ire) 133–Tegleaze 81 (Galivanter 131) (1980 5g 6g⁴ 6s 8.2s² 8d* 1981 10fg⁴ 9s 7f) compact gelding; ran respectably in handicaps at Kempton and York in the spring on first 2 starts; probably needs further than 7f and stays 1¼m; seems to act on any going. *E. Eldin.* **70**

JADE EMPRESS 3 gr.f. Tower Walk 130–Daystar 91 (Major Portion 129) (1980 5fg⁴ 5g² 5f² 5f³ 5g² 5f 5d 1981 5s³ 5d 5v² 5s³ 5d 5fg³ 6f 5fg 5g 6v 5d) close-coupled filly; placed in varied company; runs as though 5f is her trip; has worn bandages; blinkered last 2 starts. *K. Ivory.* **58**

JADE GIRL (USA) 3 b.f. Bold Native–Ma Bloom (Bay Bloom) (1980 6s* 5g² 1981 8d 8g 8f 8s) rather unfurnished filly; behind in handicaps in 1981; should stay 1m; sold 1,000 gns Newmarket December Sales. *P. Calver.* —

JADE RING 2 b.f. Auction Ring 123–Msida (Majority Blue 126) (1981 6g² 6s²) May 26; 7,400Y; neat, attractive filly; half-sister to 3-y-o 9f winner Regal Touch (by Royal Match) and a winner in Belgium; dam, placed over 9f in Ireland, is half-sister to numerous winners; second in 14-runner maiden race at Yarmouth in September and Blue Seal Stakes at Ascot later in month; 16/1, soon in front rank and going pretty well but had no chance with winner when 1½ lengths second to Dancing Rocks on latter course; will be suited by 7f; has the ability to win a race. *J. Toller.* **92**

JAGATEK 5 ch.g. Jimmy Reppin 131–Erisca 88 (Doutelle 128) (1980 10.6s 8d 7d 1981 6s 8s² 8fg 8g⁴) well-made gelding; plater; stays 1m; acts well on soft going; sold 1,350 gns Ascot May Sales. *W. Hastings-Bass.* **45**

JAHODA 4 b.c. Deep Diver 134–Venette (Epaulette 125) (1980 6s 8.2s 6d 7f 6fg 5g 1981 5g) short-running plater; has sweated up; reportedly broke blood vessel once in 1980. *B. Richmond.* —

JALABAD 3 b.c. Kalamoun 129–Wenduyne 113 (Moutiers 127) (1980 7g⁴ 7fg* 7s² 1981 10g 10d 10g) lightly-made colt; good mover; fair performer at 2 yrs; backward when last of 7 behind Shotgun in Heathorn Stakes at Newmarket in April; off course nearly 5 months afterwards and was well beaten in handicaps on his return; should stay 1¼m; seems to act on any going; joined R. Baker after final start. *J. Dunlop.* —

JALAIN 2 b.f. Pitcairn 126–Dutch Bells (The Scoundrel) (1981 7g) Apr 30; 1,600Y; second foal; dam placed in USA; 33/1 and backward when behind in 29-runner maiden race won by Chalon at Newmarket in October. *R. Williams.* —

JALMOOD (USA) 2 b.c. Blushing Groom 131–Fast Ride (Sicambre 135) (1981 7g 7fg 7.2fg* 8g* 8s* 8d³) **126**
John Dunlop must be eager for the start of the 1982 season. Not only does he train a leading Two Thousand Guineas hope in Montekin and a fancied One Thousand Guineas and Oaks candidate in Stratospheric, but also a good

Derby prospect in Jalmood. Jalmood improved considerably after finishing out of the frame on his first two starts and ended his first season with a sterling effort in the William Hill Futurity at Doncaster late in October. When Count Pahlen quickened to take the lead from Norwick entering the final three furlongs Jalmood found himself chopped for speed. Although he still had several lengths to make up at this stage he gamely kept on finding a bit extra and, together with Paradis Terrestre, was closing fast on Count Pahlen in the final stages. At the line he was little more than half a length behind the winner and only a head adrift of the unlucky-in-running Paradis Terrestre.

Jalmood had won his three previous races, starting with a length victory over Cordite Spear in a maiden event at Haydock in September. By the end of the month he had also won twice over a mile at Goodwood. The R J and S Westhampnett Stakes was worth little more than £2,600 to the winner but it attracted quite a strong field with the unbeaten Loyal Toast, a six-length winner of the Sandwich Stakes, starting a short-priced favourite ahead of Jalmood, the dual winner Padalco, the tough and useful Vin St Benet and two newcomers. Jalmood showed he was very much on the upgrade, taking the lead with a quarter of a mile to run and being not at all troubled to score by four lengths and the same from Vin St Benet and Padalco. He was similarly impressive in the Kinrara Stakes, a race won by Bonnie Isle, Master Willie and Kalaglow in the previous three seasons. Again he went on some way from home, after travelling smoothly from the start, and won much more comfortably than his winning margin over Rockfest, a length and a half, suggests. Jalmood acted well on the soft going here; indeed all his best performances have been on easy ground. However the going was fairly firm when he won at Haydock and his subsequent improvement could just as easily be attributed to his needing a mile or simply to his improving with experience. Certainly it's too early to say he needs some give in the ground.

Jalmood (USA) (b.c. Feb 3, 1979)	Blushing Groom (ch 1974)	Red God (ch 1954)	Nasrullah
			Spring Run
		Runaway Bride (b 1962)	Wild Risk
			Aimee
	Fast Ride (br 1966)	Sicambre (br 1948)	Prince Bio
			Sif
		Fast Lady II (b 1948)	Fastnet
			Charbonniere

Jalmood put up his best efforts over a mile at two and distances of a mile and a quarter or more are going to suit him, judging by his relaxed style of racing. His sire Blushing Groom, a top-class miler but he also managed to finish third in the Derby and several members of his first crop have shown a fair amount of stamina: the Irish colt Gold Exchanged and the French filly Kadissya both won over a mile and a quarter; the French colt Nabirpour won over a mile; and his other European winners, Crimson Knight, Rosananti and the useful French filly Embarrassed, all showed they stayed seven furlongs. Most of the dams of these winners were stoutly bred, by such stallions as St Paddy, Sheshoon, Aureole and Tom Rolfe, and Jalmood too has inherited stamina from his dam, the Sicambre mare Fast Ride. Fast Ride was very useful at around seven furlongs at two years and even better over middle distances at three, when she won the Prix Vanteaux prior to finishing fourth in the Prix Saint-Alary and a close third in the Prix de Malleret. She was even considered good enough to take her chance against the colts in the Prix du Jockey-Club. Fast Ride is a half-sister to six winners in France, including the useful mile-and-a-quarter performers Lady Djebel and Goyador, and Jalmood is the fourth of her foals to win. Best of the others is the very useful High Echelon filly Flaunter, a stakes winner at up to a mile and a quarter in the USA, while her Ace of Aces colt Phosphurian is a fairly useful performer at around the same distance in Ireland.

An attractive, well-made colt, Jalmood fetched 120,000 dollars as a foal and 65,000 dollars more as a yearling. According to his trainer he has a very good temperament, with none of the unattractive traits of his grandsire Red God, and certainly races very genuinely. He looks sure to make a very good three-year-old. *J. Dunlop.*

JAMESTINO 3 ch.c. Bustino 136–Miss Wrekin 97 (Pardao 120) (1980 7fg* **91** 7s² 7f² 1981 12.3g 12g⁴ 10.6s 12f* 13g* 14d⁴ 16f⁴ 12g⁴) strong colt; didn't reproduce his 2-y-o form but in July won amateur riders event at Beverley (made virtually all) and small race at Ayr (odds on, beat Ascot Again a length);

creditable fourth to easy winner Valentinian in handicap at Doncaster in September on final outing; well beaten early in year, including in Chester Vase; suited by a test of stamina; evidently acts on any going; blinkered second outing. *M. H. Easterby.*

JAMES WARD 5 b.g. Runnymede 123–Gardenia (Cagire II 122) (1980 NR 1981 16f) has shown no form on flat since 1978 though has won over fences; has worn blinkers. *J. Wilson.* —

JAMOOH (USA) 2 b.c. Pretense–Dixie 118 (Sicambre 135) (1981 6s 6fg 7g 6g 6d) Apr 15; $125,000Y; strong, lengthy colt; has rather a round action; half-brother to several winners, including 8.5f winner Rebellion (by Canonero II), and useful French middle-distance performer Easter Island (by Val de Loir); dam third in Prix de Diane; showed definite ability in 18-runner maiden races on last 2 starts, finishing 7 lengths fifth to Bravado at Newcastle in July and 7½ lengths sixth to Plum Bold at Haydock in August, going on well on latter; had been backward previously; will be suited by 1¼m; always likely to be best served by some give in the ground; a good type who should make a fairly useful 3-y-o. *M. H. Easterby.* 67 p

JAMSHID 4 b.c. Dragonara Palace 115–Never Lonely (Never Say Die 137) (1980 9g 8h 10.6f⁴ 12.3f 9.4fg⁴ 12f 12g⁴ 10.2g³ 10.6d 12f³ 10.4d² 10.6d⁴ 10.2g 10fg⁴ 10d² 10.2v 10f 10.2d 12.5g 11.7d⁴ 12d⁴ 12g² 12fg 12f* 12g 12f² 12f³ 12fg² 12g³ 13f³ 14.7d⁴ 12f³ 12f³ 16.1fg⁴ 16s 13s) compact colt; won handicap at Pontefract in June; stays 2m; suited by top-of-the-ground; suitable mount for a boy; has worn blinkers on 3 occasions; doesn't find a great deal off bridle. *R. Hollinshead.* 64

JAN CAN 3 br.f. Palm Track 122–Ivy Dee 68 (Meldrum 112) (1980 NR 1981 7fg 8.2f 7f 11f) second foal; dam placed over 5f and 1m; in rear in minor and maiden races. *T. Barnes.* —

JANEMAR 6 br.m. Jan Ekels 122–Miramar 78 (Miralgo 130) (1980 NR 1981 8f 12f 12g) poor plater on flat though won over hurdles; dead. *M. Stephens.* —

JANE ROY 4 br.f. Royalty 130–Blackout 98 (Delirium 126) (1980 NR 1981 8v³ 10s⁴) fair sort; poor maiden; beaten in sellers on occasions; stays 1m; acts on heavy going; blinkered once at 2 yrs. *M. W. Easterby.* —

JANE THE JOKER 5 b.m. Busted 134–Kayandjay 93 (Midsummer Night II 117) (1980 NR 1981 10g 12d) poor maiden. *M. Haynes.* —

JANIVY 2 b.f. Legal Eagle 126–Poliwog (Polic 126) (1981 5s 5d* 5g² 5g* 5d³ 6fg) Apr 18; 750f, 290Y; neat filly; good mover; half-sister to 6f winner Tellywog (by Communication); dam a selling hurdler; successful in small races at Newcastle in April and Redcar in May, latter by 2½ lengths from Bright View; just over 3 lengths third of 10 to Singing Sailor in minor event at Pontefract later in May; should be suited by 6f; possibly not at her best on a firm surface; didn't impress in her coat when running moderately final outing (June). *W. Haigh.* 74

JANLARMAR 2 b.f. Habat 127–Princess Caroline 68 (Sovereign Path 125) (1981 5g 5s⁴ 5f 6g 5d 5d 5s⁴ 5g 7d 7g) Feb 4; 1,000Y; plain filly; half-sister to 1½m winner Mischief (by Sassafras); dam from same family as Faberge II and Turbo Jet; only plating class; prominent in nurseries at Ayr and Lingfield in the autumn on fifth and seventh outings; should stay at least 6f; acts on soft ground; sometimes wears blinkers. *A. Bailey.* 69

JANNDAR 2 b. or gr.c. Queen's Hussar 124–Gedera 80 (Palestine 133) (1981 5s³ 5d* 7fg³) Mar 14; small, lightly-built, quite attractive colt; first living foal; dam won at 1m and 1¼m; looked out of race at halfway in £3,400 event at Bath in June but made up a tremendous amount of ground to lead on line, scoring by short head from Street Market; creditable 3½ lengths third of 5 to Padalco in £4,700 event at Newmarket the following month; will stay 1¼m; seems to act on any going; harshly treated in Free Handicap. *F. J. Houghton.* 86

JANUS 3 ro.g. Ragstone 128–January (Fr) (Sigebert 131) (1980 NR 1981 13.3d 10fg³ 12fg 14fg⁴ 12d³ 15.5s³) strong, workmanlike gelding; third foal; half-brother to 1m winner Rifle Green (by Scottish Rifle); dam placed twice at around 11f in France; in frame in maiden races and a gentleman riders event; stays 2m; sold to Mrs N. Smith 2,200 gns Newmarket Autumn Sales. *R. Baker.* 59

JASMINE STAR 5 ch.h. Ridan–Gay Cloud 99 (Golden Cloud) (1980 6fg* 6f* 6f 5fg 5fg² 6fg⁴ 6f² 5g³ 5g 5f 1981 5g 5d* 5s² 5f 6fg³ 5fg* 6g 5fg 5g) tall horse; very useful sprinter; favourite when beating William Ashford a neck in handicap at Leopardstown in May and Boldenthia a head in similar event at 103

421

Phoenix Park in August; beaten a neck by subsequently-disqualified Prince Echo in Ballyogan Stakes at Leopardstown in June but had himself impeded third horse home, Cooleen Jack, and was placed second to latter; 4½ lengths third to Runnett in Matt Gallagher Sprint Stakes at Phoenix Park in July; soundly beaten in Palace House Stakes and King's Stand Stakes over here on first and fourth starts; stays 6f; acts on any going; genuine and consistent. *M. Connolly, Ireland.*

JASON-JOHNS CHOICE 6 br.g. Murrayfield 119–Clares Choice 82 (Petition — 130) (1980 NR 1981 7f) poor performer nowadays; stays 1m; acts on any going. *M. Bradley.*

JASSIM (USA) 3 b.c. Cyane–Lady Bellaston (Tudor Minstrel 144) (1980 66 8g 1981 10d⁴ 11g⁴ 14.6fg² 12d³ 15.5fg*) quite attractive, strong, well-made colt; 15-length winner of poor maiden race at Folkestone in August; in frame in similar races earlier; suited by a test of stamina; seems best on a sound surface. *J. Dunlop.*

JAVA LIGHTS 3 b.c. Manado 130–Sea of Light (Aureole 132) (1980 NR 71 1981 8g 10g 12f² 13g⁴ 14fg 11.7f* 10.1d³) 8,200Y; tall, lengthy, attractive colt; third foal; half-brother to Le Legendaire (by Targowice), a minor winner at up to 13f in France; dam Irish 1¼m winner and daughter of Coronation Stakes winner Ocean; landed the odds by 2 lengths from Cannon Shot in maiden race at Bath in July; good third behind Kings Parade in minor event at Windsor the following month; stays 13f; yet to race on very soft going but acts on any other; sold to Miss S. Morris 5,000 gns Newmarket Autumn Sales. *B. Hills.*

JAVA TIGER 3 gr.c. Saritamer 130–Country Music (Red God 128§) (1980 74 6g 6v³ 1981 6v² 5g² 6g 6fg* 6s 6f* 6f³ 6fg² 6fg* 6f 6g) robust, good sort; good mover; won small maiden race at Hamilton in May and handicaps at Pontefract in June and Catterick in August; stays 6f; seems well suited by firm going; ran moderately in blinkers third start; didn't have best of runs seventh start; needs to be held up; ridden by apprentice N. Connorton on last 2 occasions when successful. *J. W. Watts.*

JAZZ BAND (USA) 2 b.c. Quack–Dixieland Jazz (Royal Serenade 132) 88 (1981 7fg 8g 8d⁴ 8s* 8.2d³ 10g) rangy colt; half-brother to several winners in USA, including Within Hail (by Hail to Reason), a very smart winner at up to 9f; dam once-raced sister to stakes winner Tender Size; favourite when making all to win 15-runner maiden race at Warwick in October by 1½ lengths from Sparkling Sin; should be suited by 1¼m (20/1-shot, had stiffish task and was always well in rear when tried at trip); acts on soft going. *G. Harwood.*

JAZZ FORTESCUE 2 gr.f. Song 132–Porto Novo (Sovereign Lord 120) 55 (1981 5d 5fg 5f 5g) Feb 21; 7,400Y; quite a well-made filly; sister to 2 winners, including 5f to 7f winner Jahil, and half-sister to 2 winners; dam never ran; seems only plating class. *A. Pitt.*

JEALOUS MOOR 3 b. or gr.g. Hotfoot 126–Eleanor Bold 81 (Queen's Hussar 56 124) (1980 NR 1981 7d 9g* 8g 9fg³ 7s² 12d) 1,050F; lightly-made gelding; fourth foal; dam 2-y-o 5f winner; attracted no bid after narrowly winning seller at Ripon in May (apprentice ridden); stays 9f; didn't seem to go through with his effort 2 outings later; wears a bandage on his off-fore. *I. Jordon.*

JEAN DE RESKE (USA) 2 b.c. Sir Ivor 135–Lover's Quarrel (Battle Joined) 92 (1981 7.5f* 8f² 7.5d³ 6g) Mar 14; $120,000Y; half-brother to several winners, 2 of them stakes winners, including Girl in Love (by Lucky Debonair), a very smart winner at up to 9f; dam won California Oaks; won maiden race at Gowran Park in July by ¾ length; clear of remainder when short-head second to What A Demon in small race at Phoenix Park in September and ran well when 1½ lengths third of 13 to Furry Berg in valuable Waterford Glass Nursery at Gowran Park the following month; needed further than 6f at 2 yrs and should stay 1¼m+. *D. O'Brien, Ireland.*

JEAN GREEN 2 ch.f. Porto Bello 118–Saintly Miss 63 (St Paddy 133) (1981 61 6fg 7h 5g² 6s) May 3; lightly-made filly; half-sister to fair 1¼m winner Virgin Soldier (by Queen's Hussar) and a winning sprint plater; dam stayed 1½m; had no chance with very easy winner Bolivar Baby when second of 7 in maiden race at Wolverhampton in September; soundly beaten in valuable seller at Goodwood later in month; should stay 6f. *M. Blanshard.*

JEANJIM 2 b.f. Homeric 133–Dance Mistress (Javelot 124) (1981 6f 6g⁴(dis) 68 7d 8s² 8.2s⁴ 8d) Feb 28; 2,000F, resold 820Y and 5,500Y; lightly-made filly; fourth foal; half-sister to 3-y-o Sunley Builds (by Patch), a fairly useful winner over 7f at 2 yrs; dam from same family as Roan Rocket; dropped in class, ran best race when ¾-length second of 17 to Tarawera in seller at Warwick in October (apprentice ridden); will stay 1½m; acts on soft going. *A. Jarvis.*

JEAN'S DELIGHT 4 b.f. Biskrah 121–Raramie (Be Friendly 130) (1980 —
8fg 1981 5s 6f 10f) neat filly; poor mover; poor form, including in sellers; has been tried in blinkers; has worn bandages; sold 550 gns Ascot August Sales. *M. James.*

JEAN'S GAMBLE 3 b.f. Shoolerville 121–Omnia Opera 83 (Major Portion **42**
129) (1980 6g 6g 6s 6g 7g 7d 8s 1981 12d 12.2s 8g 12.2g³ 13.8g⁴ 12f⁴ 13.8fg) very short-backed filly; in frame in 2 sellers and a handicap; stays 1½m; blinkered fifth outing of 1980. *G. Lockerbie.*

JEAN VARON 2 b.g. Averof 123–Dastina 80 (Derring-Do 131) (1981 5fg **76**
5d 5s 5s 5d 5fg* 6fg³ 7fg* 8f⁴) Mar 26; 7,000Y; compact gelding; first foal; dam, sister to smart 7f performer Tudor Mill, was second over 7f at 2 yrs; made all to land a gamble by 1½ lengths from Wish 'N' Time in nursery at Epsom in August; had previously attracted no bid after winning a seiler at Folkestone in June; suited by 7f and 1m; form only on fast ground; has won both with and without blinkers; gelded towards end of season. *G. Lewis.*

JEBB LANE 4 b.c. The Brianstan 128–Trickster 92 (Major Portion 129) (1980 · **96**
5d 6v 6fg 6f* 5f² 6d 6fg 6g 7fg⁴ 7g² 6g² 5.6g 6fg 1981 7d 7.2d² 8s³ 7g* 7.2s⁴ 8fg 7g 7.6s³) strong, good-bodied colt; useful performer; beat Silly Prices and Africanos all out by a length in £6,400 handicap at Ayr in May; had run creditably earlier when 1½ lengths second of 4 to Dalsaan in Cold Shield Windows Trophy at Haydock, and 2 lengths third to Baronet in valuable handicap at York; stays 1m; acts on any going; sometimes sweats up; blinkered twice in 1980; has run respectably for a boy; consistent. *S. Norton.*

JEBEL ALI 4 b.c. Lord Gayle 124–Itinerant 69 (Sky Gipsy 117) (1980 8f **58**
8fg 10.1fg 10g 8.2s 8g⁴ 8s 8s² 10d³ 1981 10s 10s³ 10d³ 10g⁴ 10s 8g 8.3fg³ 8fg 11.7g³ 10fg 11.7fg³ 10.2g⁴ 12d³) small, robust colt; stays 1½m; seems to act on any going; blinkered eighth start. *J. Benstead.*

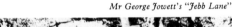

Mr George Jowett's "Jebb Lane"

JECKEL 3 ch.g. High Award 119–Reina Isabel 69 (St Alphage 119) (1980 **66** NR 1981 8s 5fg² 5fg⁴ 6d³ 6d² 6d²) 2,200Y; good-topped gelding; first reported foal; dam placed over 1¼m; in frame in maiden races and handicaps; not certain to stay 1m; apprentice ridden; usually bandaged in front. *E. Eldin.*

JEFFERSON HOUSE 2 ch.c. Supreme Sovereign 119–A Deux 80 (Crepello — 136) (1981 6fg) Apr 14; 2,700Y; leggy colt; good walker; half-brother to 2 winners, including fairly useful 6f to 1½m winner Dasman (by Tower Walk); dam placed from 6f to 1½m; 20/1, never showed when last of 14 to Major Domo in maiden auction event at Newcastle in June. *M. H. Easterby.*

JEMINA REPPINA 2 ch.f. Jimmy Reppin 131–Ranjitara (Right Boy 137) — (1981 5g 5g) Jan 19; 2,700Y; half-sister to a winner in Holland; dam showed only poor form; last in maiden races at Carlisle and Edinburgh in June. *H. Bell.*

JENNYJO 2 b.f. Martinmas 128–Judy O'Grady (Whistler 129) (1981 6g 7v) — Feb 24; IR 2,700F, 6,800Y; rangy, attractive filly; good walker; half-sister to 6f winner Grey Trilby (by Don II); dam never ran; 33/1, showed good speed until lack of fitness and experience told in final 2f when 15 lengths seventh of 17 to Merlin's Charm in maiden race at Newmarket in October; 20/1, in rear in £3,400 event won by My Destiny at York later in month; sold 1,450 gns Newmarket Autumn Sales. *W. Wharton.*

JENNY LOU 3 ch.f. Sunyboy 110–Necora 79 (Royal Record II) (1980 NR — 1981 12.2fg 11f) 550Y, 1,200Y; strong filly; half-sister to 3 winners here and abroad, including 1979 2-y-o 5f winner Buxton Road (by Murrayfield); dam stayed 11f; behind in maiden races at Catterick in July (needed race) and Hamilton in August. *I. Vickers.*

JESTER 2 b.c. Song 132–Trickster 92 (Major Portion 129) (1981 5g* 5g* **119** 6fg⁴ 5d* 5g* 6s*)

Sharpo apart, there's no heir apparent to the title of champion sprinter left vacant by the retirement of Marwell and Moorestyle. Of the other leading older sprinters Crews Hill, Dalsaan, King of Spain, Rabdan and Standaan have either gone to stud or been sent abroad so it's likely that nearly all the pretenders to the sprinting crown are going to come from the rising generation of three-year-olds. As always the picture here will be confused by owners and trainers trying to turn their sprint-bred animals into Guineas candidates but sooner or later the contenders will emerge, one or more certain to be among the following list—Americus, Lucky Hunter, My Lover, Peterhof and Tender King, perhaps even Cajun and Hays, and, possibly the most promising of all, Jester.

Jester has already beaten sprinters from an older generation. In the Coral Bookmakers Champion Sprint at York in October he took on Sweet Monday, Tina's Pet and Poldhu, who had respectively received 8-12, 8-8 and 8-5 in the previous year's Free Handicap, and the filly Martinova who had received 8-3 in the Irish equivalent. Jester had a stiff task, meeting the three colts on terms 5 lb worse than weight-for-age, and it was Tina's Pet, beaten only a head under 9-3 in the Ayr Gold Cup on his latest appearance, who started a short-priced favourite. Jester's task wasn't made easier by the way the race was run. He was held up at the rear as Tina's Pet set a funereal gallop and consequently had a fair bit to do when pulled out to challenge with two furlongs to run. Responding very generously to hard driving, he drew alongside Sweet Monday well inside the final furlong and then proved the stronger by half a length. A gutsy display!

Previously Jester had won four of his five races against his own generation. When he was sent from Yorkshire for the Stuntney Maiden Stakes at Newmarket in April it was obvious from the betting that he'd been showing a lot of ability at home. He started favourite in a twelve-runner field and justified the confidence in style, drawing away up the hill to beat the more-experienced Bold Fort a length and a half. Again he looked something out of the ordinary when accounting for the useful Irish colt The Primate without being extended in the Lily Agnes Stakes at Chester in May but it was nearly three months before he was seen out again. By the time he ran in the New Ham Stakes at Goodwood's main meeting he'd missed his intended target at Royal Ascot and been transferred to Barry Hills's stable from Pat Rohan's, after being sold to Robert Sangster. Jester's effort in the New Ham was a disappointment—he finished only fourth behind El Mansour, Be Be of Kuwait and Plagal after leading for over four of the six furlongs. However, it seems that his connections learnt a valuable lesson since they had him ridden differently afterwards and picked up three good prizes with him.

Before his Coral Bookmakers victory Jester collected two of the most important five-furlong events for two-year-olds, the Prince of Wales's Stakes at York in August and the Harry Rosebery Challenge Trophy at Ayr a month later. Although neither is a pattern event a very smart animal is normally needed to win either of them: among the last ten winners of the York race are Marwell, Abdu, Music Maestro, Haveroid, Paris Review, Sandford Lad and Mansingh, while the Rosebery has fallen to Abdu, He Loves Me, Duke Ellington, Persian Breeze, Melchbourne, Rapid River and Waterloo during the same period. At York Jester started co-favourite with the much-improved Singing Sailor in a field of five, with the prolific winner Chellaston Park best of the others. Chellaston Park had recently carried 9-3 to victory over Lucky Hunter in a nursery at Goodwood and it was she who proved Jester's most serious rival. Just as Jester, who'd been held up, appeared to be coming through strongly to win the race Chellaston Park also quickened splendidly to take a narrow advantage. Jester wouldn't be denied though and he rallied in fine style to catch the weakening filly close home. The winning margin was a head, with Fairy Tern just three quarters of a length away third. A much smoother display followed at Ayr despite Jester's having to give 8 lb to Fairy Tern, 5 lb more than at York. The only one of the other runners not receiving weight was the Convivial Stakes winner Rebollino, trying five furlongs for the first time since May. Jester was again held up, this time after being slightly hampered at the start, and could be seen going well as the ex-Irish filly On Return led for over three furlongs. No sooner was he asked to quicken coming to the last furlong than he'd taken the lead, going on to score by two lengths from Rebollino.

			Sing Sing	Tudor Minstrel
Jester (b.c. Apr 29, 1979)	Song (b 1966)		(b 1957)	Agin the Law
		Intent	Vilmorin
		(gr 1952)	Under Canvas
	Trickster (b 1971)	Major Portion	Court Martial
		(ch 1955)	Better Half
		Lady Jester	Bleep-Bleep
		(b 1964)	Witcracker

Jester isn't the type of sprinter who wins his races with blazing speed from the start; his ability to quicken late in a race may lead his connections to think he'll stay a mile. There's no support in his pedigree for believing that he'll stay. Song was a sprinter pure and simple, as he was bred to be, and only a very small percentage of his progeny has won over a mile. Jester's third dam, Witcracker, did stay well but when mated to that brilliantly speedy horse Bleep-Bleep she produced the two-year-old five-furlong winner First and Jester's

Prince of Wales's Stakes, York—a most forceful ride by Cauthen gets
Jester (right) in front on the line; Chellaston Park is second and
Fairy Tern third

Harry Rosebery Challenge Trophy, Ayr—Jester quickens well to beat Rebollino (far right)

grandam Lady Jester. Lady Jester was an admirable filly who raced with great zest. She was also very useful in the North and by the time she retired at the end of her three-year-old days she'd won seven of her sixteen races, all of which were over five furlongs. The first of Lady Jester's foals to win was Jester's dam Trickster, a fairly useful five-furlong winner at two who later seemed best at distances short of seven furlongs. Two more winners followed, the better of them the five-furlong performer Friendly Jester. Trickster has made an excellent start to her career as a broodmare, producing four foals, all winners, in her first four years at stud. All three prior to Jester were trained by Steve Norton. The first, the Tribal Chief colt Tribal Jester, won over five and six furlongs, the second Jebb Lane, a son of The Brianstan, was a very useful two-year-old over five furlongs and has since won at up to seven; and her third foal, Bretton Park, is by another son of Sing Sing, Mummy's Pet, and therefore closely related to Jester. Interestingly Bretton Park has won three times over six furlongs but has yet to reach the frame in three outings over seven. Ridden the way he is, Jester may stay seven furlongs, but that is likely to be the limit of his stamina.

Hopefully he'll be kept to sprinting and he looks sure to make a name for himself. He's a rangy, attractive colt and a good mover, altogether a grand type of colt, and he races with tremendous enthusiasm. His defeat on his only outing on a firm surface isn't sufficient evidence to say he's unsuited by such ground; what can be said is that he acts well on soft going and that, for what it's worth, both his parents handled all types of ground. *B. Hills.*

JESTER'S BOY 4 b.c. John Splendid 116–Jester's Girl (Will Somers 114§) (1980 6f 6f* 6d 7.2s² 8d³ 7fg 8s³ 1981 7d⁴ 7g⁴ 6f 7g 6g 8f 8d 8v) rather leggy, good sort; fairly useful handicapper on his day; ran well in valuable events first 3 starts but was below form most subsequent outings; stays 1m; acts on any going; has twice worn blinkers but is better without; has run creditably for an apprentice; possibly suited by a sharp track; sold to C. James 5,600 gns Newmarket Autumn Sales. *P. Cole.*   **86** d

JET ROMANCE 3 ch.f. Roan Rocket 128–Romancing 82 (Romulus 129) (1980 5g 6g 8g³ 1981 8d 8g 12fg 12f) neat, lightly-made filly; good mover; showed fair form in useful company on final outing as a 2-y-o; soundly beaten in 1981 in maiden races and an amateur riders handicap; suited by 1m as a 2-y-o; sometimes sweats up. *F. Durr.*   —

JET STAR 4 ch.c. Deep Diver 134–Islay 75 (Parthia 132) (1980 6d 6d 5f 7fg⁴ 7.6f 10.1g 8d 7g 7fg 7fg⁴ 5g 6g 8g 8s 6g 1981 9.4fg 8g 9g 7d) strong colt; plating-class maiden; best at 7f on a firm surface; often blinkered; sometimes sweats up. *I. Jordon.*   —

JILL BUCK (USA) 3 b.f. Buckpasser–Bold Jil (Envoy) (1980 NR 1981 10s 12.2g³ 12f 10fg³ 8fg 12f 10fg*) \$125,000Y; lengthy. quite attractive filly; fourth foal; dam very useful stakes winner at up to 7f; beat Wangle a head in maiden race at Beverley in September; stays 1½m; acts on a firm surface; usually blinkered; sold 40,000 gns Newmarket December Sales. *M. Stoute.*   **68**

JIMJAC 2 b.c. Lochnager 132–Amber Breeze (Arctic Storm 134) (1981 5g 5g) Apr 3; 2,000 2-y-o; small, stocky colt; half-brother to 2 winners, including Irish Sweeps Lincoln winner Quizair (by Quisling); dam ran only at 2 yrs when   —

426

quite useful in Ireland; in rear in 11-runner maiden races at Beverley in July and Newcastle in August; sold 500 gns Doncaster September Sales. *Denys Smith.*

JIMMY BOY 2 b.c. Workboy 123–La Vickstan 72 (El Gallo 122) (1981 5s — 5fg 5d 6f 5.1fg) May 30; 1,450Y; lengthy, workmanlike colt; useless plater; has worn blinkers. *P. Butler.*

JIMMY PERI 2 ch.g. Jimmy Reppin 131–Periplus 85 (Galivanter 131) (1981 — 7f) Apr 24; 5,000Y; leggy, sparely-made gelding; first foal; dam at her best at 2 yrs; unquoted, made little show when eighth of 10 to Major Irish in minor event at Beverley in July. *C. Gray.*

JIMPY 6 b.g. Decoy Boy 129–Stormy Love 77 (Elopement 125) (1980 NR — 1981 12d 10fg) poor handicapper; seems to stay 1½m; probably acts on any going. *J. Bridger.*

JIMS BID 3 ch.g. Communication 119–Bonnie Hellen 80 (Falls of Clyde 126) — (1980 5fg⁴ 5fg² 5g⁴ 1981 8g 8g) leggy, narrow gelding; plater; not certain to stay 1m; blinkered second start. *G. Richards.*

JIM'S TRICKS 4 b.g. Jimsun 121–Floral Palm 69 (Floribunda 136) (1980 **86** 10fg² 10fg* 8g 10g⁴ 10g 10g⁴ 9g* 1981 8fg 10g 8s⁴ 10d 10g 8fg* 8g³ 8fg 9fg⁴ 8.2fg 9g 8s) lengthy, good-looking gelding; good mover; fairly useful handicapper; made all and kept on well to beat I'll See You by ½ length in 4-runner minor event at York in July; stays 1¼m; probably acts on any going; ran creditably in blinkers third outing; bandaged in front first start; suited by front-running tactics. *R. Laing.*

JINJA 3 b.f. St Paddy 133–Feather Duster 80 (Tickler 106) (1980 6g 7d 7f² — 1981 12.2s⁴ 8s) compact filly; didn't run up to her best either outing and wasn't seen out after April; will probably stay 1¼m; possibly needs a firm surface. *K. Ivory.*

JIRETTA 2 b.f. Jimmy Reppin 131–Roblietta (Track Spare 125) (1981 7fg* **72** 7.2fg 7g 8.2s) May 10; well-grown, fair sort; third foal; dam never ran; looked very burly when 33/1-shot for minor event at Doncaster in July but won by short head from Deal On after showing up throughout; ran respectably in 2 nurseries subsequently; stays 1m; seems to act on any going; sweated up third and fourth outings. *G. Toft.*

J. J. CAROLINE 2 b. or br.f. Track Spare 125–Marie Mancini 75 (Roi Soleil **58** 125) (1981 5d⁴ 5g) Mar 30; 3,000Y; compact, workmanlike filly; first foal; dam won over 10.6f; 4½ lengths fourth of 10 to Here's Sue in minor event at Ripon in May, better effort; well-beaten fifth in maiden event at Thirsk later in month, only subsequent start. *M. H. Easterby.*

JOANS PET 3 b.f. Pongee 106–Marphousha (Only for Life 126) (1980 NR — 1981 7f 8g 9g 8f 8.2f 7g 9d) lightly-made filly; half-sister to a winning jumper; dam ran only once; in rear in maiden races and sellers; blinkered last 4 starts; sold 500 gns Doncaster October Sales. *T. Craig.*

JOELLA 3 ch.f. Porto Bello 118–Jolisu 110 (Welsh Abbot 131) (1980 6d 1981 — 8.2s 7d) lightly raced and no worthwhile form in maiden races. *M. Ryan.*

JOE POLES 4 b. or br.c. Sharpen Up 127–Caprice 90 (King's Leap 111) (1980 — 7f 7f 6fg 5s 10f 1981 10v 5f) leggy, attractive colt; headstrong and has shown little worthwhile form. *W. Haigh.*

JOHARA (USA) 2 b.f. Exclusive Native–Never Linger (Never Bend) (1981 **92** 6fg* 7d 6fg) Apr 30; $215,000Y; well-made filly; second foal; dam, winner over 6f and 7.5f in Ireland, is granddaughter of brilliant broodmare Grey Flight; stayed on strongly after taking lead at distance when winning 11-runner Virginia Water Stakes at Ascot in July by 2½ lengths from Triple Tipple; 16/1, not disgraced when last of 6 in £6,100 race won by Sandhurst Prince at Kempton in September, better subsequent effort; should be suited by 7f. *H. T. Jones.*

JOHN BRUSH (USA) 3 b.c. Prince John–Scrub Brush (Bupers) (1980 NR **63** 1981 10d 11.7g² 11.7g 16.5f 12fg) $40,000F; good-looking colt; half-brother to a placed horse in USA; dam won 1m claiming race; caught close home by Gold Ground in maiden race at Bath in May, best effort; looks slow and should stay beyond 1½m. *P. Walwyn.*

JOHN CLARE 3 b.c. Derring-Do 131–Madam Clare 66 (Ennis 128) (1980 — 6d 7d* 7f⁴ 7g 1981 7.3g 7g 8g 10d 7fg) strong, shapely colt; good mover; clear-cut winner of maiden race at Newbury as a 2-y-o; usually had stiffish tasks and was mainly disappointing in 1981; should stay 1m; blinkered final start (finished last). *R. Baker.*

JOHNNIE HUSSAR 3 b.c. Queen's Hussar 124–Corbara II (Marino) (1980 **71**
NR 1981 7d 8g² 7fg² 8fg² 10fg 10f² 10fg* 12s 11d) 16,000Y; workmanlike colt;
half-brother to several winners, including very useful 5f to 9f winner Tickled
Pink and fairly useful 7f performer Red Johnnie (both by Red God); dam won
over 9f in France; second in 4 maiden races before beating Al Khashab by 2
lengths in one at Redcar in September (moved poorly to start and hung left in
straight); stays 1¼m; acts on firm going; sold to W. H. H. Williams 5,000 gns
Newmarket Autumn Sales. *C. Brittain.*

JOHN O'GROATS 4 b.c. Welsh Pageant 132–Romany 87 (King's Bench 132) **91**
(1980 8fg* 10.4f² 10.6fg³ 12g* 12s⁴ 12g² 10.5f 12fg 1981 12fg 10.2g 12g 12f
12f³ 15g 12d³ 14d⁴ 14.6fg⁴ 18g) well-made colt; fairly useful handicapper;
third in valuable events at Haydock and Newmarket in the summer; respectable
7 lengths fourth to Protection Racket in Tote-Ebor at York on eighth outing;
stays 1¾m but isn't certain to get extreme distances; acts on any going with
exception of very soft; best in blinkers; suited by strong handling; sweated up
seventh start. *J. Winter.*

JOHN OLIVER 4 ch.c. Northfields–Pensodoro 71 (Roan Rocket 128) (1980 —
7v 9s* 7g³ 10.4f 7fg² 9f 8.5d⁴ 7s 10s² 8.5v³ 10s² 1981 10.2s 12g) small ex-Irish
colt; narrowly won maiden race at Phoenix Park in 1980; backward both starts
at 4 yrs; stays 1¼m; probably acts on any going; blinkered once in 1980; has run
creditably for a boy; possibly best on a galloping track; sold 4,600 gns Doncaster
August Sales. *M. H. Easterby.*

JOHN'S PRESENT 3 b.g. Gift Card 124–Kirmeen (Charlottesville 135) (1980 **67**
6s 7d 1981 7.6g⁴ 8fg 8fg 8fg 7fg 8fg² 8d³ 10v²) robust, hollow-backed gelding;
placed in maiden races at Salisbury, Goodwood and Kempton in autumn;
seems suited by 1¼m; probably acts on any going; tended to wander under
pressure final outing; sold 3,700 gns Newmarket Autumn Sales *J. Benstead.*

JOHN WILDING 4 ch.g. Roi Soleil 125–Long Hill 91 (Vigo 130) (1980 10fg² —
10fg 1981 10.1fg 10.1fg) neat, strong gelding; poor mover; plating-class
maiden; suited by 1¼m; acts on a firm surface; sold 800 gns Ascot September
Sales. *Mrs D. Oughton.*

JOHN WILLOUGHBY 3 b.c. Run The Gantlet–Sensibility (Hail to Reason) **100**
(1980 7f 7d* 7s* 1981 10d 12g 12fg* 14g² 12fg⁴ 12fg³) rangy, attractive colt;
good mover; took time to come to himself but put up an impressive performance
when odds on for 6-runner handicap at Wolverhampton in July, toying with
his rivals and beating Arnaldo by 1¼ lengths (value nearer 5 lengths); in frame
in minor event at Haydock and handicaps at Newbury and Goodwood the
following month, finishing good third to Valentinian on last-named course on
final outing; possibly finds 1¾m a shade too far; seems to act on any going.
J. Dunlop.

JOINT MERCY 3 gr.g. No Mercy 126–Legal Treasure 46 (Quorum 126) (1980 **51**
5f⁴ 5f² 5f⁴ 6g 6fg 6g 5g³ 6g² 7d³ 6g 7.2s³ 8d 1981 6g 7fg 8g² 8s³ 7g² 8g³ 7g 6fg
6g⁴ 8.2f*) useful-looking gelding; has a round action; plater; sold to
J. Wilson 1,700 gns after winning at Hamilton in September; stays 1m; seems
to act on any going; ran poorly in blinkers once; inconsistent. *G. Richards.*

JOJA ROLY 5 b.g. Souvran 98–River Damsel (Forlorn River 124) (1980 —
8fg 11.7fg⁴ 10fg 11.7fg³ 12fg⁴ 12d 11.7f 12f⁴ 10g² 12f 10f 12f 10fg 12g⁴ 1981 16h
12s) strong, compact gelding; poor handicapper; stays 13f; acts on any going but
goes well on firm; suitable mount for an apprentice; has worn blinkers. *C.
James.*

JO-JO-SAN 3 b.f. Comedy Star 121–Geisha Girl (Soleil Levant 126) (1980 **75**
6fg 6f 7g³ 7g 1981 10s² 10s 12g⁴ 10.2d* 10g³ 11g² 10fg³ 11.5d⁴ 10fg* 10f²
10.1fg⁴ 10d⁴ 11d² 10d³) strong filly; won handicaps at Doncaster in May and
Yarmouth in August; in frame most other starts; appears not to stay 1½m;
seems to act on any going; blinkered nowadays; sold 16,000 gns Newmarket
December Sales. *H. Wragg.*

JOLIETTE 3 ch.f. Jimmy Reppin 131–Colonia (Colonist II 126) (1980 7f³ **84**
1981 9s* 10g⁴ 7fg) strong filly; good walker and mover; stayed on well to beat
Strigida by 2½ lengths in maiden race at Wolverhampton in April; looked sure
to be concerned in finish when making smooth progress on bridle from 3f out
in Playboy Pretty Polly Stakes at Newmarket the following month, but flashed
her tail when coming under pressure and finished over 7 lengths fourth behind
Humming; not disgraced when sixth to Faiz in handicap at Kempton in August
on only subsequent outing; should stay 1¼m; probably acts on any going. *W.
Hastings-Bass.*

JOLLIFFE'S DOUBLE 5 b. or br.g. Pamroy 99–Miss Dunoon 83 (Dunoon **58** Star 110) (1980 NR 1981 9g 12d 12fg 12d² 12s⁴) strong-backed gelding; runner-up in gentleman riders race at Brighton in October; stays 1½m. *A. Bailey.*

JOLLY BURGLAR 2 b.g. Jolly Good 122–Moaning Low 75 (Burglar 128) **62** (1981 5s 5g 6g 6f 6f²) Mar 28; 3,600Y; small, workmanlike gelding; good walker and mover; first foal; dam 6f winner; neck second of 11 to Blandor when favourite for seller at Thirsk in July; will be suited by 7f; wears blinkers. *G. Toft.*

JOLLY GREEN GIANT 6 ch.g. Daring Display 129–Wish 106 (Whistler 129) **59** (1980 8.2d² 12f⁴ 12g 12d 1981 12g 5d 7g³ 7g 7.6g 7fg 7f⁴ 7g* 8f 7fg) compact gelding; poor handicapper; got up close home to win at Catterick in July; best at up to 1m; probably acts on any going; often wears blinkers and has worn a hood as well. *J. Yardley.*

JOLLY LIGHT 2 br.f. Jolly Good 122–Cresset 107 (Henry the Seventh 125) **—** (1981 6d) Apr 24; second foal; half-sister to a winner in USA by Sovereign Path; dam 2-y-o 6f winner; 20/1 when eighth of 15 to Friday Street in minor event at Brighton in October; dead. *B. Hobbs.*

JOLLY MARJIM 4 ch.g. Jolly Me 114–Rose's Leader (Damremont 120) (1980 **—** 8v² 9d⁴ 8h³ 8h³ 9fg³ 8g² 8.2d³ 10fg³ 10s 10.6d 1981 10v 12g² 12g) workmanlike gelding; stays 1½m; acts on any going; has run creditably for an apprentice. *E. Weymes.*

JOLLYMEDE 2 b.f. Jolly Me 114–Berkeley Belle 65 (Runnymede 123) (1981 **—** 5d 6g 5f 7f) Mar 26; small filly; first foal; dam won 1m seller; poor plater; not certain to stay 7f. *D. Gandolfo.*

JOLLY TRIPPER 7 b.g. Tycoon II–Sunday Out 95 (Lord of Verona 120) **—** (1980 16.5g 1981 16g 16fg) poor staying handicapper; acts on any going; has been tried in blinkers; sometimes wears bandages. *D. Jermy.*

JONBEE 3 ch.g. Tickled Pink 114–Thundersquall 109 (Roi de Navarre II 123) **—** (1980 5d 7s 1981 6f 6g 5fg) no worthwhile form, including in a seller. *D. Elsworth.*

JONDALE 4 b.g. Le Johnstan 123–Levandale 102 (Le Levanstell 122) (1980 **82** 8f 10g 10fg⁴ 8d 10s² 10f 8g* 10.2d 8s* 1981 8s 7.2fg 8g 10fg 10.6d⁴ 9d* 8.2fg 8g³ 9g 9s³ 8g) workmanlike gelding; fairly useful handicapper at his best but is inconsistent and unreliable; made all and kept on well to beat Easter Sun by 5 lengths in Falmouth Handicap at York in August; stays 1¼m; seems to act on any going but is ideally suited by some give in the ground; has run creditably for an apprentice; suited by front-running tactics; to be trained by A. Smith. *W. Elsey.*

JONDI 5 b.g. The Parson 119–Miss Sunblest 87 (Whistler 129) (1980 12d **66** 12fg 14fg 12f 10g³ 12g² 12g² 12f³ 12f 14g² 14fg 16fg 1981 18fg 10g³ 13.3g⁴ 12g* 15.5fg³ 10fg³ 12g 15g* 16d³ 16d³) good-looking gelding; unreliable handicapper who doesn't always go through with his effort; won amateur riders race at Salisbury in June and Tennent Trophy at Ayr (beat Halsbury a short head) in July; stays well; acts on any going; sometimes wears blinkers but does just as well without; sometimes sweats up. *P. Mitchell.*

JORDAN 2 b.c. Moulton 128–Jibuti 114 (Djebe) (1981 8g 8g) Feb 5; well- **91** made, attractive colt; half-brother to several winners, including very useful middle-distance winner Cesarea (by Raeburn II); dam very useful from 1m to 1¼m; showed definite ability in large fields for maiden and minor events at Newmarket in October, on second start finishing about 4¼ lengths fifth of 27 to Dudley Wood; not punished unduly on either occasion and should improve enough to win a maiden race over 1¼m+ at 3 yrs. *P. Walwyn.*

JORGE MIGUEL 2 b.c. Welsh Pageant 132–Smeralda 105 (Grey Sovereign **84** 128§) (1981 7d 7fg² 8g²) Mar 21; well-made, good sort; half-brother to 3 winners abroad; dam sprinter; second in maiden races at Yarmouth in August (beaten 2 lengths by Skytrick) and Goodwood in September (2½ lengths behind Queen's Home in 17-runner event); stays 1m. *P. Pritchard-Gordon.*

JOSE COLLINS 4 b.f. Singing Bede 122–Piccadilly Etta 76 (Floribunda 136) **87** (1980 6fg 6fg 5s⁴ 5d² 5fg 5g 5f 5g* 5g 5d³ 5v 1981 5g 5g⁴ 6d 5g* 6g 5g³ 6g 5fg 5.6fg 5.8g⁴ 5s* 5s³ 5s 5g) sturdy filly; not the best of movers; sprint handicapper; won at Ayr in May (amateur riders) and Goodwood in September; beat Royal Diplomat by 2 lengths on latter; best at 5f; best served by an easy surface; suitable mount for an inexperienced rider. *F. Durr.*

JOSELITA 2 b.f. Workboy 123–L'Elita 83 (Porto Bello 118) (1981 5v 5g 5fg 5f) Apr 30; workmanlike filly; third foal; sister to 1980 2-y-o 5f winner Zoilo, and half-sister to a winning plater; dam 2-y-o 5f winner; in rear in varied company, wearing blinkers in valuable seller at York in June on fourth start; sold 320 gns Doncaster August Sales. *M. W. Easterby.* —

JOSEPHINA BIN (USA) 3 b.f. Valid Appeal–Miss Prompt (Mr Randy) (1980 NR 1981 7.6d 6g 6g² 5f² 5f² 5fg* 5.3fg² 5fg) $65,000Y; smallish filly; turns her off-fore out; third foal; half-sister to 2 winners, including high-class 1978 American 2-y-o Jose Binn (by Vertee); dam stakes-placed winner at up to 6f; sire, son of In Reality, was very smart stakes winner at up to 9f; made all and beat Eagle's Quest by 1½ lengths in maiden race at Lingfield in July; second on 4 occasions; speedy and is possibly best at 5f; acts on firm going. *J. Hindley.* **66**

JOSMOLL 4 b.g. Golden Mallard 103–Peach Fair (Lord of Verona 120) (1980 8.2g 10.2g 12g 8f 8f 7g 1981 9g* 8f 10g) big, strong gelding; won amateur riders race at Ripon in May; stays 9f well; sold 3,300 gns Newmarket Autumn Sales. *W. Wharton.* **60 d**

JOSUVY 4 ch.f. Shoolerville 121–Severn Bridge 81 (Hornbeam 130) (1980 6s 6f² 8fg³ 8fg² 8d⁴ 8s* 7s 1981 12d) workmanlike filly; won handicap at Chepstow in 1980; well beaten only start at 4yrs in April; stays 1m; acts on any going. *G. Kindersley.* —

JOTA 5 gr.g. Dragonara Palace 115–Aspiration 53 (Roan Rocket 128) (1980 7fg 8fg 8fg³ 10g 10g⁴ 12f⁴ 10fg³ 10g* 10d 1981 12s³ 12s 9f² 12fg² 10f³ 12g 12d) short-coupled gelding; poor walker; poor handicapper; stays 1½m; acts on any going; good mount for an inexperienced rider; ran as though something was wrong with him final start. *W. Wharton.* **48**

JOUCAS 2 b.c. High Top 131–Alezan Dore 82 (Mountain Call 125) (1981 6fg 6g) Apr 5; strong, lengthy colt; second foal; half-brother to fair 1979 2-y-o 5f performer Deux Etoiles (by Bay Express); dam stayed 7f, and is half-sister to smart middle-distance filly Aloft (by High Top); in rear in minor event at Newmarket in August (moved badly to start) and maiden race at Lingfield in September. *J. Winter.* —

JOULOUVILLE 3 b.c. Reform 132–Queen of Twilight 107 (Off Key 121 or Twilight Alley 133) (1980 7s 1981 8d 12fg 8d⁴ 8s 8d) big, lengthy colt; ran best races in maiden race at Goodwood on third start and handicap at Chepstow on final outing; little other form, including in a gentleman riders event; bred to stay 1½m; has rather a round action and is probably suited by some give in the ground; trained until after first start by P. M. Taylor. *K. Brassey.* —

JOVENITA 2 gr.f. High Top 131–Jovian 88 (Hardicanute 130) (1981 5fg 6g) Apr 5; small filly; fourth foal; dam won twice over 5f at 2yrs; behind in 13-runner minor race at Goodwood in August and 17-runner maiden race at Newmarket in October (didn't impress in paddock). *C. Brittain.* —

JOYFUL AFFAIR (USA) 2 ch.c. One For All–Happy Ending (Groton) (1981 7fg 7fg) Apr 18; $40,000Y; rangy colt; second living foal; half-brother to American 3-y-o Long Live The King (by King's Bishop), a very useful 1m winner at 2 yrs; dam won 6f maiden race; 50/1 and still far from fully wound up when in mid-division in 29-runner maiden race won by Hayakaze at Newmarket in August, second outing. *E. Eldin.* —

JOYSON 2 b.c. Import 127–French Joy (French Beige 127) (1981 5g) Apr 21; neat colt; third foal; half-brother to 1977 2-y-o 5f winner Merency (by Meldrum); dam poor NH performer; unquoted and in need of race when tailed-off last of 11 to Thunderbridge in maiden race at Newcastle in August. *T. Fairhurst.* —

JUBILEE DANCER 5 br.m. Sahib 114–Qalibashi 77 (Master Rocky 106) (1980 10fg 8fg 12d 10g 16.9f 16s³ 12g 16fg 12f 16g³ 17.1d 15s 1981 16s 16fg 16d 18.8fg 12d) plater; stayed well; was suited by some give in the ground; had worn blinkers; collapsed and died at Brighton in October. *K. Bridgwater.* —

JUBILEE EVE 4 b.f. Royalty 130–Little Rapide 90 (Rapace 130) (1980 10s 14.6d 15s 1981 17.1d) lightly-made filly; behind in maiden races and a handicap. *J. Bosley.* —

JUBILEE KING 3 ch.g. Farm Walk 111–Fiametta (High Hat 131) (1980 NR 1981 12.2f⁴ 14.7fg 12.3g 10f 10f) leggy gelding; brother to 2 winners, including fair middle-distance handicapper Hurry Now; dam, half-sister to very good miler Grey Mirage, was placed over 9f in France; well beaten in maiden and minor events, finishing last on first 2 occasions; ran too freely first start; sold to W. Stubbs 3,500 gns Doncaster October Sales. *Miss S. Hall.*

JUBILEE LIGHTS 4 ch.g. Bustino 136–Lovely Light 105 (Henry the Seventh —
125) (1980 10g* 1981 8s 7d 7g 10g 8h) big gelding; made all to win handicap
at Nottingham in 1980; well beaten at 4 yrs; bred to stay 1½m but is a strong
puller and is unlikely to do so; blinkered fourth and fifth starts; sold to J.
Townson 4,200 gns Ascot July Sales. *R. Turnell.*

JUBILEE PRINCE 6 ch.g. Sun Prince 128–Theban Queen (Pindari 124) —
(1980 8f* 10h* 10f* 10.5f* 10fg 10f² 10s 10d³ 10fg⁴ 10g 10fg 8g* 10g 8s 1981
11s 8f 10f 8f 10.2fg 10fg 10fg 10g) moderate handicapper; won 5 times in
1980; below form at 6 yrs; best at up to 10.5f; acts on any going but goes very
well on top-of-the-ground; often starts slowly; good mount for an apprentice.
F. Durr.

JUDD 3 b.c. Sparkler 130–Poppy Day 78 (Soleil II 133) (1980 NR 1981 8f **91**
8f 8g³ 10f* 12f²) 13,000F, 23,000Y; rather lightly-made, useful sort; half-
brother to 3 winners by Tribal Chief, including fairly useful 1978 2-y-o 6f and
7f winner Glashon; dam a sprinter; ran on strongly under pressure when beating
Le Gran Brun by 2½ lengths in maiden race at Yarmouth in August; stayed on
well but couldn't reach winner when 1½ lengths second to Bedford in 4-runner
minor event at York the following month; suited by 1½m and gives impression
he'll stay further; acts on firm going. *C. Brittain.*

JUJU 2 b.f. Dragonara Palace 115–Go Too 78 (Goldhill 125) (1981 5fg* 5g⁴ **78**
6g 6f⁴ 5fg³ 5fg) Mar 9; very leggy filly; third foal; half-sister to Chummy's
Special (by Mummy's Pet), a useful sprinting 2-y-o in 1980; dam sprinter;
quickened well in final furlong to win maiden race at Kempton in April by a
length from Sybolda; creditable third of 9 to Haverhill Lass in nursery at
Warwick in August; probably stays 6f; ran moderately in blinkers final outing.
P. Cole.

JUKEBOX KATIE 2 ch.f. Jukebox 120–Castaway Katie 80 (Never Say Die 137) **63**
(1981 5f 5f⁴ 5fg 6f) Feb 16; lengthy filly; half-sister to 2 winners in Ireland,
including 6f winner Travertine (by Habitat); dam, daughter of Irish 1,000
Guineas winner Ardent Dancer, won over 1½m; 2½ lengths fourth of 13 to Chester
County in minor event at Beverley in July, best effort; had stiffish task in nursery
when tried over 6f (should be well suited by trip). *R. Hollinshead.*

JULARD 5 b.g. Golden Mallard 103–Jury 66 (Lucky Brief 128) (1980 12.5v³ —
12f 12.5s 1981 12.2g) poor maiden; stays 1½m; possibly unsuited by firm
ground. *J. Leigh.*

JULIES HERO 2 b.c. Furry Glen 121–Contourno (Continuation 120) (1981 **55**
5g 6f 7f 7d 7f 8d) Apr 15; IR 1,700Y; sturdy colt; half-brother to fairly useful
1975 2-y-o 5f to 1m winner Shukran (by Illa Laudo); plater; should stay 1m;
sold 740 gns Newmarket Autumn Sales. *P. Rohan.*

JULY THE FOURTH (USA) 4 b.f. Goose Creek 116–Firecracker Love —
(Crackpot) (1980 12d 16.9d⁴ 12f 1981 12.2g) slow maiden on flat but has
won over hurdles. *I. Balding.*

JUMBLE SALE 2 ch.f. Sharpen Up 127–Tabarka (Dicta Drake 126) (1981 5g —
5.8f 5fg) Apr 25; 4,000Y; lightly-made filly; half-sister to 2 winning sprinters,
including fairly useful Last Sale (by Royben); behind in maiden races, one an
auction event; dead. *G. Hunter.*

JUMP JAR 2 b.c. Lochnager 132–Light Jumper 100 (Red God 128§) (1981 **99**
5s* 6s* 5g³ 6g* 6g 6s) Mar 21; 8,000Y; rangy, good sort; good walker and
mover; half-brother to 2 winners by Supreme Sovereign, including fairly useful
miler Bamp; dam won twice over 5f at 2 yrs; successful in minor events at Ripon
and Haydock prior to winning 4-runner Chesters Stakes at Newcastle in June
by 1½ lengths from Apple Blossom; ran below his best on fifth outing in July, and
was then off course until October when well beaten in valuable nursery at
Haydock; suited by 6f; acts well on soft ground. *M. H. Easterby.*

JUNE FAYRE 2 b.f. Sagaro 133–Pasty 122 (Raffingora 130) (1981 7h 8fg) —
June 1; second foal; half-sister to 3-y-o 1m winner Cornish Granite (by Ragstone);
dam best English 2-y-o filly of 1975; second favourite, prominent 5f when over
9 lengths sixth of 13 to Dijla in maiden race at Chepstow in August, first outing
and better effort; should stay 1m. *P. Walwyn.*

JUNGLE JIM 3 b.c. Hotfoot 126–Jungle Queen (Twilight Alley 133) (1980 **99**
6d 7s 8g* 8fg³ 8g 1981 12fg² 12.3g⁴ 14fg) tall, rangy, long-striding colt; ran

well twice in the spring, finishing 1½ lengths second to Sulzano in apprentice handicap at Newmarket and fourth behind 12-length winner Shergar in Chester Vase; eighth of 11 behind Dragon Palace under stiffish weight in handicap at Goodwood in July on only other outing (looked very well but found nothing under pressure); stays 1½m; acts on a firm surface; a very big colt who gave impression at Newmarket that he may be best with a man on his back. *G. Harwood.*

JUNIOR TRUSTEE 2 ch.g. Mr Bigmore 123–Fulfilment (David Jack 125) — (1981 7fg 8g 10s) Jan 28; strong, good-bodied gelding; seems to carry plenty of condition; has a rather round action; half-brother to quite useful middle-distance winners Westminster Abbey (by Royalty) and Stephen's Day (by Bonne Noel); dam ran only twice; well beaten in £4,200 event at Newmarket in July (last of 8) and maiden races in the autumn; likely to need time and long distances. *F. Durr.*

JUNOESQUE 2 b.f. Bustino 136–Laughing Goddess 92 (Green God 128) (1981 | 68 6fg 5fg⁴ 6fg³) Mar 2; lightly-made filly; first foal; dam won from 4f to 6f in France and England; in frame in maiden races at Redcar in July and Nottingham (8 lengths third of 9 to Match Winner) in September; will be suited by 7f. *J. Hindley.*

JUNTA 3 b.c. Brigadier Gerard 144–Siliciana 113 (Silly Season 127) (1980 6g² | 91 7g² 7g* 1981 8fg³ 10.4d² 11d² 11f* 10fg 10.5g³ 9g) strong, good-bodied colt; picked up a valuable prize at Groenendael in June, beating Belloc comfortably by 3 lengths in 5-runner Grand Prix de Bruxelles; ran best subsequent race when third of 4 behind Kings General in Garrowby Stakes (Limited Handicap) at York in September; had run creditably earlier when third to Noalto in Easter Stakes at Kempton, staying-on 6 lengths second to Kirtling in Group 3 Dee Stakes at Chester and head second to Machtvogel (rec 2 lb) in Group 2 Grosser Hertie Preis at Munich; will stay 1½m; acts on firm going and a soft surface; blinkered final start (had stiff task and finished in rear in William Hill Cambridgeshire). *I. Balding.*

JUPITER ISLAND 2 b.c. St Paddy 133–Mrs Moss 81 (Reform 132) (1981 6fg | 74 7f) Feb 23; 10,000Y; well-made, quite attractive colt; good mover; half-brother to several winners, notably very useful 1980 2-y-o 5f winner Pushy (by Sharpen Up); dam 5f 2-y-o winner; 50/1 and still on burly side, put in best work in closing stages when about 11 lengths eighth of 22 to Treboro in 7f maiden race at Newmarket in July; the type to improve with racing and longer distances. *C. Brittain.*

JUPITER'S GEM 3 b.f. Jupiter Pluvius 119–Parry (Pampered King 121) — (1980 NR 1981 14.6fg) 1,000Y; half-sister to several winners here and abroad, including very useful Irish jumper Corrib Chieftain (by Appiani II); dam never ran; dwelt when tailed off in maiden race won by Lara's Song at Doncaster in July. *R. Thompson.*

JURY PALACE 2 b.f. Dragonara Palace 115–Reppeve 45 (Jimmy Reppin 131) | 70 (1981 5fg⁴ 5fg 5g 5d⁴ 6d 7g 5g) Mar 10; 1,450F; useful sort; third produce; dam bad plater; quite moderate form in varied company; should stay 6f but has shown best form at 5f; dwelt first 2 starts. *R. Hollinshead.*

JUSTAFANCY 8 ch.g. Royal Palace 131–Flights Fancy 95 (Worden II 129) — (1980 NR 1981 13v⁴) lightly raced on flat nowadays; stays well; acts on heavy going. *G. Richards.*

JUST A SPARK 2 b.f. Sparkler 130–Pontresina 70 (Ballymoss 136) (1981 7g — 7g) May 31; small filly; second foal; half-sister to 1980 2-y-o 5f seller winner Silver Samantha (by Zeddaan); dam needed a test of stamina; backward when tailed-off last in minor race at Catterick and maiden event at Doncaster in October. *N. Bycroft.*

JUST DAI 4 ch.g. Good Bond 122–Sea Daisy 90 (Mossborough 120) (1980 NR | 35 1981 10g 10.1fg 10fg 8.3g 8fg³ 8fg) rather plain, lightly-built gelding; plater; should stay 1¼m. *I. Dudgeon.*

JUST GAYLE 5 ch.h. Lord Gayle 124–Golden Samantha 88 (Sammy Davis 129) — (1980 6v⁴ 6d 6f 6f 6f 6g 6g 6g 7s 7.2d 8g⁴ 1981 6d 6s 6d 6d) small horse; good walker; mainly disappointing nowadays; best form at 6f; acts on any going but goes well on soft; a difficult ride (tends to hang and sometimes starts slowly); ran moderately in blinkers once; has worn bandages. *E. Weymes.*

JUST GEOFFREY 3 b.g. Comedy Star 121–Solvilium (Vilmorin) (1980 5s 5f — 5fg 7fg 7f 6f 6g 1981 10d) quite attractive, rangy gelding; little worthwhile form; blinkered seventh outing in 1980. *G. Lewis.*

432

JUST GRAYLE 2 gr. or ro.g. Habat 127–Tomboy 95 (Sica Boy 132) (1981 7fg — 7fg 10s) Apr 23; 4,100Y; well-grown, fair sort; bad walker; half-brother to several winners, including very useful middle-distance winner Melantha (by Roan Rocket) and 3-y-o 7f winner Monks Farm (by So Blessed); dam stayed 1½m; ran best race when seventh of 20 to Sunny Look in 1¼m maiden race at Nottingham in October; suited by 1¼m and will probably stay 1½m; possibly needs the mud. *R. Boss.*

JUSTICE PAO 3 b.g. Reform 132–Twill 89 (Crocket 130) (1980 7g 1981 8d **49** 12fg 8g 11.7f 11fg* 12fg² 12fg) sturdy gelding; showed easily best form when dead-heating for first with Target Path in handicap at Edinburgh and when second at Hamilton, both in July; bandaged when behind in a seller only subsequent start; stays 1½m; acts on a firm surface. *P. Haslam.*

JUSTICIA 2 gr.f. Nonoalco 131–Canton Silk 108 (Runnymede 123) (1981 5g* **87** 5g³ 5g* 6d 5f² 6fg 5g 5fg) Apr 2; small, strong, attractive filly; half-sister to useful 3-y-o middle-distance winner Canton Lightning (by Rheingold), very useful 5f to 8.5f winner Royal Pinnacle (by High Top) and a winner in Hong Kong; dam 5f performer; successful in maiden race at Newmarket in April and minor event at Newbury in May, staying on very gamely when scoring by ½ length from Wicked Wave in latter; also ran well in nursery on penultimate outing; form only at 5f; probably acts on any going; sent to California. *G. Harwood.*

JUST IN FUN (USA) 3 b.f. Buffalo Lark–Devilish Queen (Crimson Satan) — (1980 7g 6g 7d 1981 6d 8d 11.7fg) useful-looking, deep-girthed filly; good mover; little worthwhile form in varied company; blinkered final start; sold 3,400 gns Newmarket December Sales. *G. Hunter.*

JUSTINIANI (USA) 3 b.c. Kentuckian–Light Verse (Reverse) (1980 NR **64** 1981 8d 8fg 10d² 12s³ 10fg² 9s 8g) rangy colt; half-brother to 3 winners, including very useful 1976 2-y-o 5f and 6f winner Al Stanza (by Al Hattab); dam unraced half-sister to very useful stakes winner Weekend Fun; sire, son of T.V. Lark, was a very smart winner at up to 1¼m; placed in maiden races at Salisbury, Goodwood and Folkestone in first half of year; off course 4 months afterwards; will stay further than 1½m. *R. Price.*

JUST MARTIN 3 b.c. Martinmas 128–Just Alice (Worden II 129) (1980 **80** 5f 5f 7d 5d* 1981 5s 5d 7fg³ 8d) leggy, lightly-built colt; finished very strongly and ran best race of year when about a length third to Faiz in handicap at Kempton in August; stays 7f; acts on a firm and a soft surface; headstrong and was taken down early to start at Kempton. *R. Price.*

JUST MIST 5 gr.g. Siliconn 121–Firmpostie (Goldhill 125) (1980 8fg 1981 — 8f 8d 8f 7d) sturdy gelding; poor maiden. *W. Wharton.*

JUST WISHING 3 b.f. Wishing Star 117–Lepe 65 (Exbury 138) (1980 6s — 7g 7fg 1981 8.3fg) small, workmanlike filly; fifth of 19 to Scottish Green in seller at Windsor in July, only outing of 1981; likely to need a test of stamina. *J. Winter.*

JYMARIO 3 b.c. Wajima–Meadow Pipit 103 (Worden II 129) (1980 NR 1981 — 12fg 12fg 14f) 180,000Y; lengthy, quite attractive colt; half-brother to several winners, including St Leger and Irish Sweeps Derby second Meadowville (by Charlottesville) and good middle-distance stayer Nuthatch (by Levmoss); dam won both her starts; quite moderate form in maiden and minor races; still didn't look fully fit final start; sold to Miss S. Morris only 540 gns Newmarket Autumn Sales. *M. Jarvis.*

K

KABOUR 3 b.c. Habitat 134–Kermiya (Vienna 127) (1980 NR 1981 8g 6s 5f* **80** 5s) strong, quite attractive colt; has an enlarged off-fore joint; first foal; dam won over 9f and 1¼m in France; showed very good speed when 6¾ lengths fifth of 9 behind King of Spain in Thirsk Sprint Trophy in May; moved badly to start when next seen out in maiden race at Nottingham in July but won fairly impressively by 1½ lengths from Eagle's Quest despite having a far from smooth passage; off course 3 months afterwards; probably stays 6f; acts on any going; sold only 1,800 gns Newmarket Autumn Sales. *F. J. Houghton.*

KADISSYA (USA) 2 b.f. Blushing Groom 131–Kalkeen (Sheshoon 132) (1981 **107** 7d 10v*) Mar 15; first foal; dam very useful over 1¼m in France; won 10-runner maiden race at Saint-Cloud in October in good style by 2½ lengths from

Balada; will stay 1½m; engaged in 1,000 Guineas and Oaks and is evidently well thought of. *F. Mathet, France.*

KAFFIR DANCE (USA) 3 gr.c. One For All–Silvern (Reneged) (1980 **61**
5f³ 6f² 6d⁴ 7fg² 1981 8g 7g 11g 9g 11f³ 13g 12.2fg² 11f 14fg 12g³ 12d) sturdy ex-Irish colt; $28,000F, resold $30,000Y; half-brother to several winners in USA, including stakes-placed Mito Sal (by Mito); dam unplaced in 5 outings; ran best races of 1981 when placed in maiden and minor races at Hamilton, Catterick and Edinburgh; suited by 1½m; blinkered second and final outings; sold 3,200 gns Newmarket Autumn Sales. *G. Richards.*

KAHARA 2 ch.f. Habitat 134–Starina (Crepello 136) (1981 7d*) May 4; **93 p**
first foal; dam, very useful at up to 1¼m in France, is closely related to high-class French middle-distance colt Pevero; a well-bred filly who looked very promising when winning 11-runner newcomers events at Maisons-Laffitte in September by 2 lengths from Olden Damoiselle; will stay at least 1m. *F. Boutin, France.*

KAIMLAW 7 ch.g. Native Prince–Misty Morn 70 (Worden II 129) (1980 **68**
5f* 6g 5s 1981 5g* 5g⁴ 5fg 5fg² 5f² 5g² 5g⁴ 5f 5g* 5f 5f) sprint handicapper; has run tubed; won at Carlisle in June and Redcar in August; ran well when second 3 times in between; best at 5f; acts on firm going; used to wear blinkers; suitable mount for an apprentice; tough. *H. Bell.*

KAIROUAN 3 gr.g. No Mercy 126–Bouboulina (Hornbeam 130) (1980 7f **48**
6d 6d 1981 7d 8d 8g 10d 8fg 9g 10fg) leggy gelding; plater; stays 1¼m. *R. Armstrong.*

KALAGLOW 3 gr.c. Kalamoun 129–Aglow 78 (Crepello 136) (1980 6g* 7g* **112**
7.3fg* 8g* 7.3d* 1981 9fg* 10.5s 12d)
The York spring meeting was one of the most eventful for years. Eighteen out of twenty-one favourites went under, the majority, which included the champion sprinter Moorestyle, the One Thousand Guineas winner Fairy Footsteps and the hitherto-unbeaten Kalaglow, soundly defeated. The results of the Musidora Stakes and the Mecca-Dante Stakes were of special moment, for they threw the betting market on the classics into some confusion: Fairy Footsteps stood a hot favourite for the Oaks, and Kalaglow a strong second favourite behind Shergar for the Derby immediately prior to their respective trials. Kalaglow ran even worse than Fairy Footsteps. He set the pace but was being niggled at four furlongs out and the writing was soon on the wall for him; he was quickly beaten, dropping out to fifth-of-six place behind Beldale Flutter by the end. Excused his performance on account of the soft and somewhat false ground, Kalaglow took his place in the Derby but unfortunately he seemed denied the opportunity of redeeming his reputation when he became involved in bad scrimmaging towards the back of the field after travelling only about three furlongs. He never got into the race subsequently. Kalaglow returned with a leg injury which kept him out for the remainder of the season but he has been fired and the intention is to run him as a four-year-old.
Kalaglow's prospects in 1982 can't be assessed with any precision; let's see him run again, first. At his best he is capable of winning good races, as he showed on the last of his five outings as a two-year-old when he beat Cut Above, without appearing to do more than necessary, in the Horris Hill Stakes at Newbury; and again when on his reappearance in 1981 he ran clean away with the Heath Stakes at Newmarket. Kalaglow couldn't have been more impressive in the Heath Stakes, won two years earlier for his stable by Ela-Mana-Mou. He led from the start, drew well clear from two out and beat Clear Verdict by four lengths after being eased at least two lengths when nothing came to challenge up the hill.

Kalaglow (gr.c. 1978)	Kalamoun (gr 1970)	Zeddaan (gr 1965)	Grey Sovereign / Vareta
		Khairunissa (gr 1960)	Prince Bio / Palariva
	Aglow (ch 1970)	Crepello (ch 1954)	Donatello II / Crepuscule
		Sun Palace (b 1964)	Charlottesville / Sonsa

Kalaglow, as yet unproven beyond nine furlongs, should stay middle distances. His sire stayed a mile and a quarter and has sired good winners over longer distances, Bikala and Castle Keep to name the two most recent; the dam stayed two miles and is herself out of a staying mare. Kalaglow is a rather leggy, useful-looking colt. One of his best points is his smooth, light, flowing action, the type of action often associated with a top-of-the-ground performer. His trainer, we know, regards him as ideally suited by fast ground, and although Kalaglow won the Horris Hill on a softish surface the probability is that the horse will prove his trainer correct provided he returns to the race-course a hundred per cent right. Certainly, after York, we should not entertain backing Kalaglow on really soft going. *G. Harwood.*

KALAMI 3 b.g. Averof 123–Moiety Bird (Falcon 131) (1980 NR 1981 8.2s — 10s 10.1f) 5,000Y; lengthy gelding; third foal; half-brother to 2 winners, including top-class sprinter Sharpo (by Sharpen Up); dam never ran; unplaced in maiden and minor events in first half of year. *M. Jarvis.*

KALASH 5 b.m. Tribal Chief 125–Vital Issue 100 (Immortality) (1980 NR — 1981 8d 7g 6d 7d 7g 6fg 7g) of little account; sold 120 gns Ascot November Sales. *J. O'Donoghue.*

KALKUS 2 b.c. Strongheart 65–Right On (Right Tack 131) (1981 7f 8d 8s⁴ 10g) **65** Jan 31; small colt; second living foal; dam of little account; plater; put up best effort when 2½ lengths fourth of 17 to Tarawera at Warwick in October; should stay 1¼m; acts on soft going. *M. Pipe.*

KALO ASTRO 2 gr.c. Tachypous 128–Miss Rosy (Quorum 126) (1981 7fg) — May 5; 8,000Y; strong, rangy, attractive colt; fifth foal; half-brother to 3 win-ners here and abroad, including 1980 2-y-o 5f winner Alex Flyer (by Hot Spark); dam showed no form; 16/1 and very backward when behind in valuable 19-runner maiden race won by Paperetto at Goodwood in July, only outing. *B. Hobbs.*

KAMAL (USA) 2 b.g. No Robbery–Stampy (Irish Castle) (1981 5g 5fg 6f* **77** 6fg 7fg 6g) Mar 17; $37,000Y; rather lightly-made, useful-looking gelding; good mover; second foal; dam placed in 4 of her 22 starts in USA; won 17-runner maiden event at Yarmouth in June by 2½ lengths from Dragon Fire, easily best effort; hung very badly left next time out and was subsequently gelded; needs at least 6f (off course 2 months before finishing towards rear in 7f nursery); acts well on firm going. *J. Hindley.*

KAMENCHA (CHI) 7 br.m. Kamen–Chanal (Azul Celeste) (1980 7fg 8fg — 8g 9fg 8.3fg 8g⁴ 1981 10d⁴ 10f 11.7fg 11.7g) Chilean-bred mare; winner of 7 of her 8 races (at distances up to 7f) in native country; poor performer over here; suited by 1¼m. *D. Kent.*

KAMENEV 4 b.g. Ribero 126–Welsh Mistress 113 (Abernant 142) (1980 7fg³ — 8g 8d 1981 6v 8s 9g 6g 6fg 10fg 12fg 13.8fg 12.3fg 6d 8s) short-backed gelding; good mover; poor plater nowadays; stays 7f; best form on a firm surface. *D. Chapman.*

KANCHENJUNGA 3 b.f. Hotfoot 126–Climbing Rose 81 (Pirate King 129) **61** (1980 7fg 7fg 7g 1981 7fg 7g 7f² 7.6s 8fg 5f 6d) smallish, well-made, attractive filly; second in maiden race at Thirsk in July; soundly beaten afterwards; should be suited by 1m+; possibly unsuited by soft going; sold 14,000 gns Newmarket Autumn Sales. *F. Durr.*

KANGAROO ISLAND 3 gr.f. Murrayfield 119–Charter Island 88 (Runnymede — 123) (1980 6g 1981 5f 8f 8f 6d) lightly-made filly; soundly beaten in maiden and minor events and a seller; sold 600 gns Doncaster October Sales. *E. Incisa.*

KANSAS 2 b.c. Kalamoun 129–Hello Honey 105 (Crepello 136) (1981 5s² **75** 6s 6s 7d) Jan 26; neat, attractive colt; third foal; half-brother to fairly useful middle-distance winner Concert Hall (by Connaught); dam won 4 times at up to 1½m; ran a bit green when 2 lengths second of 11 to My Dear Fellow in maiden race at Wolverhampton in May; not seen out again until October and was well beaten all starts; should be well suited by 6f+; sold for export to Belgium, 5,100 gns Ascot December Sales. *P. Walwyn.*

KARABERRY 4 b.g. Karabas 132–Holly (Chamossaire) (1980 10f 12f² 12g* — 14g² 14g 12g 13f 1981 13.3s 16.1s 12g 10g³ 11.7fg 11.7fg) workmanlike ex-Irish gelding; stays 1¾m; acts on firm going; suitable mount for an inexperienced rider; blinkered once at 3 yrs. *R. Head.*

KARADAR 3 b.c. Rheingold 137–Shahinaaz (Venture VII 129) (1980 NR **100** 1981 12g 11s² 10s⁴ 10fg² 12fg* 12fg* 12g* 12v* 12g⁴) quite an attractive, well-made colt; half-brother to smart middle-distance winner Karamita (by Shantung) and 4 winners in France; dam won over 1m and 13f in France; improved steadily and had an excellent season; gained his fourth successive win when staying on well to beat Hot Fire 2½ lengths in £3,900 handicap at York in October; had

A.T.S. Trophy (Limited Handicap), Newbury—Karadar catches Capricorn Line (rails) in the last few strides

earlier won maiden event at Brighton, A.T.S. Trophy (Limited Handicap) at Newbury (beat Capricorn Line a head) and £4,700 handicap at Goodwood (won by a neck from Full of Reason); favourite, had every chance when about 5 lengths fourth of 20 behind Lafontaine in William Hill November Handicap at Doncaster; will be suited by 1¾m; acts on any going; sometimes sweats up (did so quite badly at Newbury and York); played up in stalls and was withdrawn under orders first appearance. *M. Stoute.*

KAREEM 3 b.c. Northfields–Red Val 101 (Red God 128§) (1980 5f* 6g 6d* 7d 7.2g* 7g 1981 8d⁴ 8fg 8.2s 8f² 8fg⁴ 8fg) neat, attractive colt; in frame in handicaps, best effort when 1½ lengths second of 18 to impressive winner Olympic Glory in Britannia Stakes at Royal Ascot in June (apprentice ridden); will be suited by 1¼m; probably acts on any going; blinkered last 3 outings and seems of doubtful temperament; racing in USA. *P. Walwyn.* **90**

KAREENA 2 b.f. Riverman 131–Kermiya (Vienna 127) (1981 6fg⁴ 6g³) Mar 18; smallish, attractive filly; second foal; half-sister to 3-y-o 5f winner Kabour (by Habitat); dam won over 9f and 1⅛m in France; short-priced favourite, under pressure most of way but kept on well to be third of 15 to Topaz Too, beaten under a length, in maiden race at Nottingham in August; had finished about 5½ lengths fourth of 11 to Johara in Virginia Water Stakes at Ascot on debut; will be much better suited by 1m and 1¼m. *F. J. Houghton.* **76**

KAREN'S BIRTHDAY 2 br.f. The Brianstan 128–Alexa (Runnymede 123) (1981 5d⁴ 5g⁴ 5fg 5fg 5g 5g 5s³ 5s 5s³ 6d) May 5; 3,500F, 3,500Y; compact filly; half-sister to 3 winners, including fairly useful 1979 2-y-o 5f and 7f winner Millfield Lad (by Jimmy Reppin); in frame in maiden and minor events and a seller; possibly needs some give in the ground; looks a short runner. *S. Matthews.* **62**

KAREN'S GEM 2 b.c. Workboy 123–Colate 59 (Como 120) (1981 5v 5g² 5g 5f 5fg³ 5f 5g³ 5f) May 26; small colt; half-brother to 5f winner Karen's Star (by Aglojo); dam sprint plater; placed in maiden races at Edinburgh and in a seller at Ayr; blinkered sixth outing. *S. Nesbitt.* **54**

KAREN'S STAR 4 b.g. Aglojo 119–Colate 59 (Como 120) (1980 5g 5f* 5f **64**
5g 6g 5fg⁴ 5f 6g³ 1981 6v 6s 5d 5s 5fg⁴ 5g³ 5f 5.1fg² 5g² 5f⁴ 5g⁴ 5f³ 6f 6f² 5g²
5g 5s 5d² 5g) lightly-made gelding; bad mover; sprint handicapper; stays 6f;
suited by top-of-the-ground; has twice been tried in blinkers; ridden by
apprentice A. Nesbitt when successful; has won 3 times at Wolverhampton.
S. Nesbitt.

KARIMA 3 ch.f. Song 132–Impregnable 66 (Never Say Die 137) (1980 5fg⁴ **77**
6g³ 6g⁴ 1981 8d³ 8d* 8f 8.3fg⁴ 8fg 8.5fg⁴ 10g) tall, unfurnished filly; beat
Sea Miss by a neck in 5-runner handicap at Brighton in May; ran creditably
most other outings; stays 1m; yet to race on very soft going, but acts on any other.
N. Gaselee.

KARIPIA 3 ch.f. Sharpen Up 127–Kalopia 80 (Kalydon 122) (1980 5fg 1981 **—**
7fg 8.2s) neat filly; ran promisingly at Newmarket on only outing as a 2-y-o;
well beaten in 1981 in Ladbrokes Nell Gwyn Stakes on same course in April and
poor maiden race at Nottingham in September; should stay 1m; has raced with
her tongue tied down; trained until after first start of 1981 by J. Winter; sold
2,000 gns Newmarket Autumn Sales; *I. Walker.*

KARISSIMA 2 b.f. Kalamoun 129–Kissing 98 (Sing Sing 134) (1981 5f³ 6f² **90**
5fg² 7f³ 8d³ 7g*) Apr 3; rather lightly-made, quite attractive filly; half-sister
to 3 winners, including 3-y-o 1¼m winner Prince Nono and 1¼m winner Bustedaway (by Busted); dam won twice over 5f at 2 yrs; won 12-runner maiden race
at Naas in October easily by 3 lengths from Ulpha; placed in all her previous
races, notably finishing 3½ lengths third of 15 to Prince's Polly in Group 3 Silken
Glider Stakes over 1m at Leopardstown in September; stays 1m well; seems to
act on any going. *D. Weld, Ireland.*

KARKANA 2 b.f. Kouban–Kelty (Venture VII 129) (1981 5fg³ 6g² 6g² 5s) **78**
May 10; small, unfurnished filly; half-sister to 3 winners in France, including
useful 1¼m winner Delsy (by Abdos); dam never ran; sire unraced son of Hauban
and top-class filly Apollonia; runner-up in maiden races at Carlisle in July (½
length behind Meeka Gold) and Nottingham in August (kept on well under pressure when beaten a neck by Dance In Rome); off course 10 weeks subsequently;
almost certainly finds 5f much too sharp and is bred to stay middle distances;
lacks scope; sold 3,100 gns Newmarket Autumn Sales. *M. Stoute.*

KARKOUR (FR) 3 b. or br.c. Relko 136–Koblenza 118 (Hugh Lupus 132) **120**
(1980 NR 1981 10g* 12d 12g* 12s*) half-brother to 3 winners in France,
including useful 1¼m winners Reine de Lenza (by Roi Dagobert) and Korinetta
(by Petingo); dam won French 1,000 Guineas; won 3 of his 4 races and developed
into a smart colt; won newcomers race at Evry in June, minor event on same
course in September (beating Explorer King and Akkad in a close finish) and
Grand Prix de Nantes in November; put up an excellent performance when
beating Proustille by a length in last-named event; gives impression he'll stay
beyond 1½m; acts on soft going; sold out of F. Mathet's stable 440,000 francs
(approx £44,000) Arc de Triomphe Sale in October. *J. Audon, France.*

KARLINSKY (USA) 4 b.c. Rheingold 137–Sea Pay 64 (Sea-Bird II 145) **—**
(1980 12fg 12fg² 16fg 12g⁴ 12d 1981 16fg 16d 14s) well-made, attractive colt;
fair handicapper at his best; showed no form in 1981; stays 1½m but not 2m;
acts on a firm surface and has run badly on soft. *Miss S. Morris.*

KARMINSKI 3 b.f. Pitskelly 122–Autumn Ballad 75 (Tudor Melody 129) **70**
(1980 7d 7g 8fg 1981 12.2s² 10g³ 12d² 12d 12fg² 13g* 13.8fg² 16fg³ 18.1d)
well-grown filly; won small maiden race at Ayr in July; ran moderately final
start and is not certain to get extreme distances; seems to act on any going.
C. Brittain.

KAROL 3 b.c. Kalamoun 129–Le Melody 102 (Levmoss 133) (1980 NR 1981 **?**
8d*) second foal; half-brother to top-class stayer Ardross (by Run The Gantlet);
dam, daughter of Musidora Stakes winner Arctic Melody, won both her starts
over 7f and 1¼m; landed the odds in 12-runner maiden race at Leopardstown
in October on first appearance, leading over 2f out and beating Candle Hill readily
by 1½ lengths; will be suited by middle distances; likely to go on to much better
things. *D. O'Brien, Ireland.*

KARRE 2 b. or gr.c. Pals Passage 115–World's Worse (Frankincense 120) **53**
(1981 5s 6fg⁴ 5g³ 5f² 5d³ 6d) May 30; IR 1,700Y, resold 2,500Y; leggy, rather
unfurnished colt; first foal; dam won over 1½m at 4 yrs in Ireland; in frame
in sellers at Warwick and Hamilton (3); stays 6f; blinkered last 3 outings;
sold 1,500 gns Ascot September Sales. *C. Nelson.*

KARYOBINGA 3 b.f. So Blessed 130–Pine Ridge Gal (Arturo A) (1980 7f —
8d 7g 1981 7g 7g 8.2s 8d 10.2g) rangy, quite attractive filly; poor maiden;
behind in a valuable seller final outing; should stay 1m; wears blinkers. *P.
Makin.*

KASAROSE 2 br.f. Owen Dudley 121–Smokey's Sister (Forlorn River 124) — §
(1981 5fg 6d 6g 6f 5fg) Apr 14; small, lightly-made filly; has little ability and
more than her fair share of temperament. *H. O'Neill.*

KASH-IN 2 b.f. Kashiwa 115–Deviation (Petingo 135) (1981 5fg 5d² 6g² 5d* 81
5s⁴ 5g) Apr 13; IR 1,500Y; useful-looking filly; second foal; dam never ran;
showed improved form, although having first race for 4 months, when winning
16-runner maiden race at Bath in October by 2 lengths from Falaka; not
disgraced in nurseries subsequently; probably stays 6f but best form at 5f;
acts well on a soft surface. *R. Hannon.*

KASHMIR BLUE 4 br.c. Blue Cashmere 129–Gay Donna (Tudor Jinks 121) 62
(1980 6fg 6d⁴ 8.3d 8.2g² 7g³ 8fg* 8fg² 1981 8d 8.5g 8f³ 8f 8f² 8.3g³ 10f) tall,
lightly-made colt; not certain to stay 1¼m; suited by a sound surface; blinkered
final outing; sold 3,800 gns Newmarket Autumn Sales. *M. Stoute.*

KASLAND 4 b.g. Shiny Tenth 120–Smokey's Sister (Forlorn River 124) —
(1980 7fg³ 8.5g 7g³ 10g 10fg 8fg 8.2s 10g 1981 12s) fair sort; plating-class
maiden; stays 7f (well beaten over further); acts on a firm surface. *H. O'Neill.*

KASROY 3 gr.g. Young Emperor 133–Welsh Rhythm (Abernant 142) (1980 NR —
1981 10fg 10f 8g) 4,100Y; rangy, workmanlike gelding; brother to fair 1979
2-y-o 6f winner Welsh Sonata, and half-brother to several winners here and
abroad; dam unraced daughter of Irish 1,000 Guineas winner Sea Symphony;
tailed off in maiden races, twice finishing last. *H. O'Neill.*

KASSAK 5 gr.g. Dragonara Palace 115–Dauphiness 74 (Supreme Sovereign 119) 76
(1980 8g 7f 6g⁴ 5.8g 5v³ 1981 5s³ 6g 5d 6d* 5.3f* 6g* 6fg² 5fg³ 6fg⁴ 6fg⁴ 6fg 6s)
leggy gelding; sprint handicapper; in good form in June, winning at Brighton
(twice) and Lingfield; beat Pagapas Bay a neck on latter; stays 6f; acts on any
going; has worn blinkers but does as well without; sometimes bandaged off-fore;
has run well for an amateur rider. *H. O'Neill.*

KATALIN 2 b.f. Track Spare 125–Bud's Promise 68 (Runnymede 123) (1981 49
5g 5f³ 7.2v) Mar 27; 400F, 500Y; narrow filly; plater; not sure to stay 7f;
sold 290 gns Doncaster October Sales. *C. Spares.*

KATE'S WISH 2 ch.f. Wishing Star 117–Kay's Hour 93 (Bleep-Bleep 134) 65
(1981 5s 5d³ 6f³ 6d⁴ 8.2s) Apr 25; 4,100 2-y-o; leggy, light-framed filly; half-
sister to 2 winners, including fairly useful 1980 2-y-o 5f winner Sandon Buoy
(by Windjammer); dam won twice over 5f; quite moderate form in varied
company; stays 6f but is by no means sure to get 1m; probably acts on any
going. *J. Fitzgerald.*

KATH 3 b.f. Thatch 136–Classical Music 85 (Santa Claus 133) (1980 NR —
1981 8g 6fg 5fg) useful sort; closely related to useful Italian filly Lot of Class
(by Home Guard); dam lightly-raced half-sister to high-class miler Saintly Song;
little worthwhile form in newcomers race at Newmarket (showed good speed)
and maiden races at Newbury (apprentices) and Warwick. *P. Haslam.*

KATHANCO 3 ch.f. Panco 91–Dumb Kathy (Dumbarnie 125) (1980 NR —
1981 16.9fg 12d) half-sister to 3 winners, including fair 1¼m winner Moon
Dance (by Doudance); dam never ran; soundly beaten in maiden race at
Wolverhampton in July and apprentice event (sixth of 16) at Chepstow in
October. *R. Hollinshead.*

KATHRED 3 b.f. Starch Reduced 112–Kathy King (Space King 115) (1980 91
5g 6g³ 5g² 6f* 6d 1981 6g² 6g 6d* 6s* 7f⁴ 6f 6s* 6f³ 6d* 5g 5s⁴ 6g* 6d) very
useful in plating company at 2 yrs; had an excellent campaign in better company
in 1981 and won both handicaps at Windsor, Haydock, Yarmouth, York (beat Katysue
by ¾ length) and Newmarket; beat Chantry Bridge decisively by 1½ lengths
on last-named in October; probably finds 5f on sharp side and stays 7f; acts on any
going but has done most of her winning on an easy surface; suitable mount for
a boy; genuine. *R. Hollinshead.*

KATIE GREY 8 gr.m. Pongee 106–Spotless 89 (Tehran) (1980 8d³ 8fg 1981 —
9g 12g 9g 8s⁴ 16fg 8fg 12fg 8g 16g) poor performer; best run at 1m on soft
going in blinkers; has worn bandages. *W. Atkinson.*

KATOWICE (FR) 5 gr.h. Targowice 130–Kaliopa (Zeddaan 130) (1980 8s 119
8g 8g² 8g³ 7g 8d* 8s* 8g³ 8d⁴ 1981 10d² 10.5g) French horse; smart performer;

put up a good performance in Prix d'Harcourt at Longchamp in April, making running and only being caught close home when head second to Argument (gave 6 lb); injured a leg when beaten a long way behind Argument again in Prix Ganay on same course following month and wasn't seen out again; stayed 1¼m; acted well on soft ground; retired to Haras de Grand Cour, Orne. *P.-L. Biancone, France.*

KATRICK 2 b.f. Sparkler 130–Marbella II 64 (Match III 135) (1981 5d 7f) — Mar 21; 12,500F, 4,600Y; well-made filly; half-sister to 3 winners, including 1980 2-y-o 6f winner Douschkina (by Dubassoff); dam from same family as Miralgo and Parnell; unquoted and apprentice ridden when distant fifth of 8 to Razor Sun in maiden race at Brighton in July, second start. *R. Smyth.*

KATUMBA 5 ch.g. Tower Walk 130–Independence 64 (Runnymede 123) (1980 — 8s 11fg 8f 8.3f³ 7fg 8g 8f 7fg* 7g 8.3f 8fg 1981 8f) plater; stays 1m; probably acts on any going. *B. Richmond.*

KATYANA 4 b.f. Reform 132–Greek Gift (Acropolis 132) (1980 10fg 12fg **51** 10f⁴ 12g 10.1s⁴ 10.1d³ 10.1f 12g 10f 10fg⁴ 8g 14d 1981 18fg 15.5d 10s 12g 10f 10.1fg 12f 10.8fg* 10f² 8g 10.2g) small, quite well-made filly; shows a lot of knee action; plater; bought in 750 gns after winning at Warwick in July; unlikely to stay extreme distances; seems to act on any going; has worn blinkers; claimed out of D. Jermy's stable ninth start. *D. Elsworth.*

KATYSUE 3 gr. or ro.f. King's Leap 111–Sweet Hostess (Candy Cane 125) **94** (1980 5g² 5f² 6fg² 5g* 5g* 5g⁴ 5fg* 5f* 5s* 1981 6f 5f 6f 6g 6d² 5f 7s) strong filly; good walker; had a rather disappointing year, only placing when ¾-length second to Kathred in handicap at York in August; gives impression she's suited by 6f; acts on any going; good mount for an apprentice; sold 6,000 gns Newmarket Autumn Sales. *W. Wharton.*

KAUKAS 2 b.g. So Blessed 130–Balnespick 101 (Charlottown 127) (1981 **73** 5g⁴ 5s 5.8d 5g 6g⁴ 6fg 6fg 8g 6d) Apr 25; 7,600Y; well-made gelding; third foal; dam stayed at least 13f; quite a moderate maiden; didn't run up to his best from a low draw in £4,000 seller at Kempton on sixth outing; will probably stay 1¼m; possibly needs a sound surface. *G. Balding.*

KAYELLA 2 b.f. Fine Blade 121–Peregrine Peach 79 (Falcon 131) (1981 **52** 5s³ 5d 5s 6f 7fg 6d) Feb 20; 1,600F, 4,300Y; quite a useful sort; half-sister to 3 winners abroad; dam stayed 7f; plating-class maiden; will stay at least 1m; blinkered final outing. *W. Wharton.*

KEADEEN 4 b.g. Martinmas 128–Medaea 90 (Darius 129) (1980 8g⁴ 8g 10d — 8.2g 8g 9v* 10s 1981 8fg) sturdy ex-Irish gelding; won maiden race at Hamilton in 1980; behind in seller only start at 4 yrs in August; should stay 1¼m; acts well on heavy going; blinkered once at 3 yrs; sold 1,100 gns Doncaster November Sales. *W. Clay.*

KEARNEY 4 b.c. Sandford Lad 133–Gilded Egg (Faberge II 121) (1980 7s⁴ **109** 6f² 6fg 6g* 6d 1981 6d 6g 6g⁴ 6fg⁴ 6fg 5d) compact, attractive ex-Irish colt; very useful performer; ran creditably on third start when 4 lengths fourth to King of Spain in Duke of York Stakes in May, disputing lead until fading inside final furlong; not disgraced in Ladbrokes Abernant Stakes at Newmarket previous outing; ideally suited by 6f and some give in the ground; blinkered final start; sold 330,000 francs (approx £33,000) Prix de l'Arc de Triomphe Sale in October and has been sent to USA. *M. Smyly.*

KEELBY KAVALIER 3 b.c. Ardoon 124–Elegant Lady 69 (Round Table) **85** (1980 5fg 5s 7g³ 8f* 8fg³ 8fg² 1981 12g* 12d² 11g⁴ 12fg* 13.3g⁴ 14g 13fg² 12fg* 14g²) leggy colt; won handicaps at Doncaster in May, York in July and Leicester in September, beating Oklahoma Star by 1½ lengths in last-named; ran well on other occasions, including when fourth to Taher in Morland Brewery Trophy at Newbury on fifth start and second to Capricorn Line at Newmarket in October on final one; stays 1¾m; acts on firm going and on a soft surface; blinkered final start in 1980. *J. Etherington.*

KEEP BELIEVING 2 ch.f. Sweet Revenge 129–The Star of Sharon 73 (Mid-summer Night II 117) (1981 7.2v) May 5; half-sister to fairly useful 1979 2-y-o 6f winner Wadi Ali (by Red Alert) and a winning plater; dam won over 7f; 10/1, dwelt when behind in 17-runner seller won by Market Rose at Haydock in October. *Miss S. Hall.*

KEEPS GOING RIGHT 4 b.c. Warpath 113–Sindo 91 (Derring-Do 131) — (1980 10v 9g 8f 6f 7.2g 8d⁴ 8d⁴ 8s⁴ 8g* 7fg³ 8fg² 10g 9s 8fg² 9f³ 8g 8.2s 8d² 8d⁴ 10d 1981 8g 8g 8f 8fg) neat colt; plater; stays 9f; probably acts on any going; has worn bandages. *J. Doyle.*

KEEP SILENT 2 b.f. Balidar 133–Thieves Honour (Hook Money 124) (1981 **83**
6f 6fg 6g* 6g² 6d⁴ 7g) May 14; 1,500Y; rather leggy, workmanlike filly; sixth
live foal; dam ran once; cost 3,400 gns to buy in after winning 11-runner seller
at Yarmouth in September, easing up by 5 lengths from Bylon after making
all; 2½ lengths second of 21 to Tickletimes in minor event at Redcar later in
month; not sure to stay 7f; apprentice ridden all outings (at 4-lb overweight
when successful). *A. Jarvis.*

KEEP SMILING 2 b.c. Tumble Wind–Retiro (Pardal 130) (1981 5fg 5fg² **57**
6fg 6fg 6d) Mar 3; IR 7,800Y; quite attractive colt; half-brother to several
winners here and abroad, including 7.5f winner Arboretum (by Celtic Ash);
odds on and apprentice ridden, raced alone from halfway when 4 lengths second
of 7 to Six Legs in maiden race at Edinburgh in July; no worthwhile form subsequently, including when heavily-backed favourite for valuable seller at
Goodwood in July; should be suited by 6f +. *N. Callaghan.*

KEEP YOUR MONEY (USA) 3 ch.c. Hold Your Peace–Financial (Diplomat **94**
Way) (1980 5d 6g⁴ 7g 7d³ 8s² 1981 6v⁴ 6d² 8d* 7f 8fg⁴ 7fg 8.5fg 10f⁴ 9f
7fg⁴ 7.5g) $17,500Y, resold $18,000Y, $82,000 2-y-o; rather lightly-made
colt; poor walker; first foal; dam, half-sister to 3 stakes winners, placed at 3
yrs; made running and held off Santilo by a short head in maiden race at Phoenix
Park in May; ran creditably on next 2 outings when seventh of 20 behind Rasa
Penang in Jersey Stakes at Royal Ascot and fourth of 14 behind Tellurano in
Coolmore Hello Gorgeous Stakes at the Curragh; stays 1m; probably acts on
any going; sent to race in USA. *A. Maxwell, Ireland.*

KELBOMEC (FR) 5 b.g. Direct Flight–Piqueuse (Piqu' arriere) (1980 15.5g³ **119**
15.5g³ 16.5fg 15s* 15g² 13.5g 20d³ 12g* 1981 15.5d* 15.5g³ 12s³ 12d² 15f³
13.5f 20s*) French gelding; smart stayer; touched off Proustille by a short
neck in Prix de Barbeville at Longchamp in April and beat El Badr by 1½
lengths in Prix Gladiateur on same course in September; ran creditably most
starts in between, finishing 1¾ lengths third to Gold River in Prix Jean Prat
at Longchamp, ¾-length third to Lancastrian in Grand Prix d'Evry, 3 lengths
second to decisive winner Vayrann in Prix Jean de Chaudenay at Saint-Cloud
and 3 lengths third to Tipperary Fixer in Prix Kergorlay at Deauville; effective at
1½m and stays very well; acts on any going but goes well in the mud; consistent.
J. C. Cunnington, France.

KELLET LANE 3 ch.f. Sandford Lad 133–Paduia (St Paddy 133) (1980 **—**
6d 8fg 1981 7f 8f 7fg) compact filly; in rear in varied company, including
selling; slowly away when blinkered first start at 2 yrs. *W. Stubbs.*

KELLY'S DAUGHTER 2 b.f. Pitskelly 122–Muraka (Off Key 121) (1981 **—**
6fg) Mar 23; IR 3,300F. IR 3,200Y; useful sort; fourth foal; sister to fairly
useful Irish 9.5f and 1½m winner Whisper Gently, and half-sister to a winner;
dam won bumpers race; unquoted and in need of race when behind in 18-runner
maiden race won by Corsky at Newmarket in July. *P. Haslam.*

KELPIE 3 b.f. Import 127–River Moy (Niagara Falls 104) (1980 6g 1981 7fg **58**
9.4fg³ 8.2fg⁴ 10.6v 12.2g) unfurnished filly; plating-class maiden; stays 9f. *G.
Richards.*

KELTON LASS 4 ch.f. Lord Nelson 107–Mpunga (Guide 118) (1980 NR **—**
1981 16.5g) fourth foal; dam never ran; tailed off in maiden event at Redcar
in August. *J. Jefferson.*

KENNINGHALL (USA) 2 ch.c. Riva Ridge–Reload 119 (Relko 136) (1981 **93**
7f 6d³ 6f 7s 7d⁴) May 14; good sort; half-brother to useful 3-y-o middle-distance
winner Feltwell (by Habitat) and 2 other winners, including useful 1977 2-y-o
1m winner War Whoop (by Moulton); dam won Park Hill Stakes and is half-
sister to 1,000 Guineas winner Full Dress II; outpaced in closing stages when
good fifth to Glancing, beaten 5 lengths, in Champion Two Yrs Old Trophy
at Ripon in August on third outing (ridden by apprentice unable to claim his
5-lb allowance); 7 lengths fourth to Neighboring in nursery at Doncaster in
October, better subsequent effort; will stay 1½m; best run on firm going. *H.
Wragg.*

KENNY O'REILLY 3 b.c. Patch 129–Gracie Square 75 (Nelcius 133) (1980 **68**
5fg 6g 6g 7s 8d 1981 8.3s 12g 12f² 12f* 12g 12d² 12.2g² 12s) neat colt; won
minor event at Hamilton in September by 7 lengths from Fabulous Dunce; had
been gambled on when beating Balda a length in seller at Thirsk earlier in month,
but edged left and hampered runner-up and placings were subsequently reversed;
stays 1½m; probably acts on any going; has run creditably for an apprentice;
trained first 2 starts by M. Blanshard. *W. Bentley.*

440

KENO HILL 6 b.g. Yukon Eric–Rock Me (Rockefella) (1980 NR 1981 16g) —
poor maiden on flat though has won over hurdles. *A. Davison.*

KENSON VENTURE 2 ch.c. Most Secret 119–Flashing Light (Sky Gipsy 117) **76**
(1981 5g 5d² 5fg⁴ 6s² 6fg 5s² 6s 5g²) May 8; 3,000Y; big, strong, hollow-backed
colt; second in maiden and minor events at Windsor, Haydock, Nottingham
and Catterick, coming closest to success at Nottingham in September when
beaten ½ length by Haycombe Barn; only sixth of 15 in a valuable seller seventh
start; stays 6f; acts on soft going; often apprentice ridden; got a little stirred
up when blinkered fifth outing (out of his depth); sold to Newmarket BA 2,500
gns Newmarket Autumn Sales. *A. Jarvis.*

KENT'S PRIDE 3 gr.c. Runnymede 123–Monumental Moment 91 (St Paddy **48**
133) (1980 5h 5fg 5fg 6fg 5f⁴ 5g⁴ 5f 5d* 5s 5s 5s 1981 5d 6g³ 5g 5s 5f 5fg² 5fg
5fg* 6fg 5g 6f 5g 5f) neat colt; apprentice ridden when winning selling handicap
at Catterick in July (no bid); not disgraced at 6f but runs mainly at 5f; probably
acts on any going; often blinkered nowadays. *S. Nesbitt.*

KENTUCKY 3 b.f. Warpath 113–Shenandoah 88 (Mossborough 126) (1980 —
7g 1981 8f 10fg) big, strong filly; good walker; in rear in maiden and minor
events at York (2) and Beverley; will probably need longer distances. *C.
Thornton.*

KENTUCKY LADY 3 b. or br.f. Roman Warrior 132–March Stone 84 (March —
Past 124) (1980 NR 1981 7.6g 8g 10.1fg 10.1fg) strong, lengthy
filly; half-sister to 5 winners, 3 of them successful at 2 yrs; dam 1¼m to 2m
handicapper; behind in maiden and minor races, twice finishing last; has been
tried in blinkers. *B. Swift.*

KENTUCKY RIVER (USA) 3 b.c. Margouillat 133–Riverside (Sheshoon 132) **114**
(1980 9d* 8g⁴ 1981 10d⁴ 11g² 10v³ 11g³ 10g 9g* 10f³ 12g* 12v³ 12g) half-
brother to several winners, notably top-class 1m to 1¼m filly Riverqueen (by
Luthier); dam, a very smart winner at up to 13f, is half-sister to Double-U-Jay;
successful in 7-runner minor events at Clairefontaine in August and at Maisons-
Laffitte the following month; in frame most other starts, including when third
in Group 3 Prix la Force at Longchamp in May (beaten ¾ length by Al Nasr, Fr)
on third outing, in Prix Ridgway at Deauville in August on seventh (beaten
6½ lengths by Detroit) and in Group 2 Prix du Conseil de Paris at Longchamp in
October (just over 8 lengths behind Rahotep); stays 1½m; acts on any going.
J. Cunnington, jnr, France.

KESARINI (USA) 2 ch.f. Singh–Kesar Queen 117 (Nashua) (1981 5g² 5v* **87**
5.8g⁴ 7.2f 7d³) strong filly; first foal; dam won Coronation Stakes and was
third in 1,000 Guineas; landed the odds by a length from African Berry in maiden
race at Windsor in May; also ran well in £2,100 nursery at Doncaster in October,
keeping on to be 5½ lengths third to Neighboring; will be suited by 1m; needs
some give in the ground and acts on heavy going. *G. Hunter.*

KESHCORRAN 5 ch.h. Rarity 129–Cairn Kitty (Reliance II 137) (1980 8g —
7.5s³ 12s* 1981 9v 10s 6g 7.2s) good-bodied, attractive ex-Irish horse; beat
Croghan Hill in Trigo Stakes at Leopardstown in 1980; soundly beaten at 5
yrs, though wasn't entirely disgraced over trip on short side for him in John
of Gaunt Stakes won by Last Fandango at Haydock in June on final start;
needs further than 6f and stays 1½m; acts on soft going; blinkered second outing;
trained part of year by D. Weld. *J. Sutcliffe.*

KESHOON 3 b.f. Sheshoon 132–Matt's Colleen 105 (Epaulette 125) (1980 **60**
8g 8d 1981 6fg 8fg 8.2s 9d* 8s 10d) compact filly; showed a little ability in
maiden races before beating subsequently-disqualified Black Sunset impressively
by 7 lengths in seller at Wolverhampton in October; sold out of D. Kent's stable
2,500 gns afterwards; probably stays 1¼m; acts on a soft surface. *W. Charles.*

KEY SONG 2 ch.f. Crooner 119–The Keys 71 (Major Portion 129) (1981 5.3f **51**
7f 8d 8s⁴ 8.2s) Apr 15; half-sister to fairly useful 1¼m winner Old Knocker (by
Mummy's Pet) but is only a poor plater herself. *M. Hinchliffe.*

KHAIRPOUR 2 gr.c. Arctic Tern 126–Khayra (Zeddaan 130) (1981 8g) —
medium-sized, rather lightly-made, quite attractive colt; good walker; first
foal; dam unraced sister to high-class Kalamoun; 14/1 and fairly forward when
out of first 10 of 29 to Born Hero in maiden race at Newmarket in October;
may do better over 1¼m+ at 3 yrs. *F. J. Houghton.*

KHALEEL 3 br.g. Lochnager 132–Vital Error 105 (Javelot 124) (1980 5d³ **64**
5fg 1981 5d 5d³ 5d 5fg³ 5fg 5f³ 5g³ 6g² 6fg² 5fg 6d 6s) small, compact, good-
topped gelding; runner-up in claiming race at Newmarket and handicap at

Catterick in August; stays 6f; has run creditably for an apprentice; blinkered tenth start; has run moderately on occasions, including in a seller on eleventh start; retained 1,100 gns Newmarket Autumn Sales. *A. Hide.*

KHEDIVE 4 b.c. Habat 127–Klairessa 88 (Klairon 131) (1980 6fg² 6fg 5g*   **83** 6fg 6d² 6s³ 6s 1981 5fg 6s 5.8d*) lengthy, attractive colt; sprint handicapper; blinkered when beating Old Dominion a head at Bath in June; stays 6f; probably acts on any going; sent to USA. *D. Whelan.*

KIFISSIA (FR) 4 b.f. Ortis 127–Hallucination (Sicambre 135) (1980 8g* 8g³   **67** 11g 8d 9.2fg 8d 8s 8.5v* 1981 7d 12d³ 12g 10f² 11.7fg 10g 10.2g⁴ 12d*) rangy ex-French filly; half-sister to 3 winners in France; dam placed over 12.5f in France; beat More Oats by a short head in handicap at Leicester in November; stays 1½m well; acts on any going; blinkered when successful once at 3 yrs. *M. Albina.*

KIKI MOUSE 2 b.f. Song 132–Silesca (Silent Screen) (1981 5s 5fg³ 5d 5s⁴   **66 §** 5d 5.1fg* 5f⁴ 5g 5f) May 3; 3,000Y; quite well-made filly; good mover; second foal; dam won over 7.5f at 2 yrs in France; won 7-runner maiden auction event at Yarmouth in July by 1½ lengths from Libby Jayne; very troublesome at start in all her subsequent races, twice starting slowly, and is one to leave alone; acts well on a firm surface; blinkered fourth and fifth outings; sold to BBA 700 gns Newmarket Autumn Sales. *P. Kelleway.*

KIKKULI 2 b.c. Hittite Glory 125–Siliciana 113 (Silly Season 127) (1981 7g   **80** 7v³) Mar 14; big, well-made colt; half-brother to 3 winners, including useful 3-y-o Junta (by Brigadier Gerard), successful at up to 11f; dam won 1973 Cambridgeshire; 8/1, led to distance when 2 lengths third of 8 to Rocamadour in minor event at Kempton in October; will probably stay 1m. *I. Balding.*

KILCOY CASTLE 3 b.g. On Your Mark 125–Primed (Primera 131) (1980   **—** 5s 5f 5fg 6d 1981 8s 8g 10d) workmanlike gelding; seems of little account; sent to race in Belgium. *P. Rohan.*

KILIAN 3 br.c. Thatch 136–Fortunal (Fortino II 120) (1980 NR 1981 8s* 10f*)   **?** brother to very useful 1978 Irish 2-y-o 6f winner Card Game, and half-brother to 2 winners, including useful 1976 Irish 2-y-o 6f and 7f winner All Serene (by Le Levanstell); dam, placed over 1m at 2 yrs, is half-sister to smart Chamozzle and Richard Grenville; made a most impressive first appearance in 7-runner maiden race at Leopardstown in May, drawing right away in last furlong and beating Voice 8 lengths; not seen out again until September, when landing the odds by 2 lengths from Forelock in 17-runner minor event at Navan; stays 1¼m; acts on any going; should go on to better things. *D. O'Brien, Ireland.*

KILLANIN'S LASS (USA) 2 b.f. Olympiad King–My Violet (Warfare) (1981   **82 p** 6d²) Mar 26; $25,000Y; second foal; half-sister to a winner by Envoy; dam won over 1m; 25/1 and in need of race, never far off pace and kept on well though no match for winner when 5 lengths second of 18 to Wattlefield in maiden race at Newmarket in August; not seen out again; bred to stay 1¼m. *G. Pritchard-Gordon.*

KILLER SHARK 6 b.g. Tyrant–Aquaria (Double-U-Jay 120) (1980 10s 1981   **—** 12s) well-made gelding; lightly raced nowadays; best form at 1¼m on soft ground, although has won once on a firm surface; sometimes blinkered; broke blood vessel only outing of 1980. *G. Pritchard-Gordon.*

KILLINGHOLME CLAY 2 b.c. Targowice 130–Patricia (Sovereign Path 125)   **83** (1981 5g 5g² 6fg²(dis) 7fg*) Apr 9; tall, leggy colt; second foal; dam won twice over 1m in France; pulled hard early on when landing the odds by 1½ lengths from Bombil in 9-runner maiden race at Chester in July; only stays 1m; yet to race on a soft surface; hung very badly third outing. *G. Pritchard-Gordon.*

KILMARK 4 br.c. No Mercy 126–Celebrate 85 (Rockavon 120) (1980 8.2g   **—** 8.2f⁴ 8.2d 8g 7g 8g 1981 7f 8f) narrow colt; poor plater at end of career; stayed 7f; needed a sound surface; sometimes blinkered; pulled up lame final start; dead. *A. Jarvis.*

KILMONA (USA) 3 b.f. Bold Bidder–Shiah Princess (Tulyar 134) (1980   **121** 8g³ 1981 9s* 9.5fg 10.5s⁴ 10.5fg 9d* 10f⁴ 9.2d*) $115,000F; big, rangy filly; closely related to minor American winner Hour Ahead (by Bold Hour) and half-sister to 3 winners, including smart 1973 French 2-y-o Dancer's Prince (by Dancer's Image); dam won at up to 12.5f in France and USA; won maiden race at Evry in March, Group 3 Prix Chloe on same course in July and Group 2 Prix de l'Opera at Longchamp in October; beat Rixe in last 2 races, at Longchamp travelling well throughout in a slowly-run affair and winning by a neck; stays

1¼m; probably acts on any going, but seems suited by some give underfoot; trained until after second start by C. Bartholemew. *G. Sauque, France.*

KILROE'S CALIN 2 ch.f. Be Friendly 130–Miss Soundly (Maelsheachlainn 117) — (1981 8fg 8s 8d) Apr 16; tall, leggy filly; fourth reported foal; dam won over hurdles and fences; unquoted when soundly beaten in maiden and minor events; looks immature at present. *J. Fitzgerald.*

KILRUE 2 b.f. Kinglet 98–Monamolin 109 (Golestan 127§) (1981 5fg 5d 5.8g — 6f 7f 8g) June 1; neat filly; half-sister to 3 winners on flat and several over jumps; dam at her best at 2 yrs; seems of little account. *M. Blanshard.*

KILSYTH 2 b.f. Jolly Good 122–Harmony Thyme 73 (Sing Sing 134) (1981 62 5fg 5g 5f⁴) Apr 2; compact filly; half-sister to 3 winners, including fair 1976 2-y-o 5f winner Tribal King (by Tribal Chief); dam won over 5f at 2 yrs; 2¼ lengths fourth of 16 to Luan Causca in maiden race at Beverley in August, best effort; will be better suited by 6f. *C. Booth.*

KIMACERO 3 b.c. Tycoon II–La Macera (Thunder Road) (1980 NR 1981 — 8f 11d³ 10.2g) fourth living foal; dam never ran; third in seller at Hamilton in October; will stay 1½m. *J. Wilson.*

KIM MARCHELLE 3 ch.g. Jim French–Karonde (Aureole 132) (1980 6d 6s 62 1981 8d 9s 8fg² 8fg 8fg 8h 8s) fair sort; second in maiden race at Warwick in June, best effort; ran moderately in sellers last 2 starts (blinkered final one); will stay 1¼m; sold 600 gns Newmarket Autumn Sales. *R. Laing.*

KINDLY THOUGHT 3 br.f. Record Token 128–Crab Apple (Nelcius 133) — (1980 5d 5fg 1981 6g 6g 7f 5d 5s) strong, compact filly; poor maiden; possibly doesn't stay 7f; blinkered fifth start. *R. Baker.*

KIND MUSIC 2 gr.c. Music Boy 124–La Magna 104 (Runnymede 123) (1981 101 5g* 5s³ 5g² 5f 5f* 6s 5g³) Mar 30; 25,000Y; neat, well-made colt; good walker and excellent mover; second producer; dam won twice over 5f at 2 yrs; winner of minor event at Kempton in May and nursery at Redcar in August, putting up a useful effort under 9-7 when winning latter by ½ length from Epona's Grey; also ran very well in another nursery on final start; best form at 5f but gives us impression he may get 6f as a 3-y-o; action suggests a sound surface suits him best; unruly in stalls when running moderately fourth outing. *M. Stoute.*

KIND OF HUSH 3 b.c. Welsh Pageant 132–Sauceboat 120 (Connaught 130) 118 (1980 6fg⁴ 1981 8g* 8g 12d 10.5g 11.1f* 10g³ 10g)
    Kind of Hush caused one of the sensations of the season when beating the red-hot Guineas favourite To-Agori-Mou in the Ladbrokes Craven Stakes at

September Stakes, Kempton—Kind of Hush wins from Church Parade

Newmarket in April. On form the race looked a virtual formality for To-Agori-Mou and he started at long odds on with Kind of Hush, last of four behind Integrity at Goodwood as a two-year-old on his only previous outing, weak in the market at 25/1. Kind of Hush impressed us no end in the paddock, but we never imagined he'd be capable of winning this particular race. However, after beginning his challenge on the hill he ran on really strongly to lead well inside the last furlong and get home by three quarters of a length.

For a long time Kind of Hush's win seemed a flash in the pan, although there's no denying that on the day he had beaten To-Agori-Mou fair and square. Ridden by Piggott in the Two Thousand Guineas, stable-jockey Cauthen preferring the Free Handicap winner Motavato, Kind of Hush looked short of speed and finished only thirteenth of nineteen, over fifteen lengths behind a noticeably fitter To-Agori-Mou; he didn't fare any better in the Derby either where he was quite badly hampered after only about three furlongs and was always towards the rear. But he redeemed himself in late-summer. His fifth behind Beldale Flutter in the Benson and Hedges Gold Cup at York in August, beaten just over six lengths, was encouraging and he confirmed himself a smart colt with a clear-cut win over the Derby fifth Church Parade in the September Stakes at Kempton. Looking extremely well and muscled up at Kempton—fitter than we had seen him since the Craven Stakes—he was always going well in behind the leaders and quickened very nicely past Church Parade when asked for his effort about a furlong and a half out, soon going clear and winning by three lengths. At Leopardstown later that month he finished a creditable four-length third behind Kings Lake in the Joe McGrath Memorial Stakes, giving us the impression, incidentally, that he would have done even better if he had been more inclined to settle. On his only subsequent outing he finished well down the field behind Vayrann in the Champion Stakes at Newmarket, never having posed any sort of a threat.

		Tudor Melody	Tudor Minstrel
Kind of Hush (b.c. 1978)	Welsh Pageant (b 1966)	(br 1956)	Matelda
		Picture Light (b 1954)	Court Martial
			Queen of Light
	Sauceboat (b 1972)	Connaught (b 1965)	St Paddy
			Nagaika
		Cranberry Sauce (gr 1964)	Crepello
			Queensberry

Kind of Hush is quite an attractive colt who cost 37,000 guineas as a yearling. His sire Welsh Pageant was a top-class miler and his dam Sauceboat was a very smart filly, probably at her very best at around a mile too. Sauceboat was somewhat controversially disqualified after gaining her most important win in the Lockinge Stakes as a four-year-old in 1976. Her win in the Strensall Stakes at York later in the year was one of the last of trainer Sir Noel Murless' illustrious career. Murless trained Welsh Pageant too, and was also associated with many other members of Sauceboat's family, including her dam Cranberry Sauce, the best filly in the country at a mile and a quarter in 1967. Kind of Hush stays better than did either Welsh Pageant or Sauceboat and he promises to get a mile and a half. He has already shown that he acts on firm going and has the type of action which suggests he'll act on soft too; the only time he has encountered a soft surface so far was in the Derby. *B. Hills.*

KINDRED SPIRIT 2 ch.f. Relkino 131–Cavalier's Blush 75 (King's Troop 118) (1981 6s) May 1; big filly; second foal; dam needed a test of stamina; 16/1, made no show when distant seventh of 15 to Ellerene in maiden race at Newbury in October; bred to stay at least 1½m. *W. Wightman.* —

KINETIC 4 b.g. Ridan–Vesper Bell (Larkspur 128) (1980 NR 1981 10f 7g 8d 8g 7g) poor performer nowadays; well beaten in selling handicap final start (taken down early); should stay 1¼m. *J. Fitzgerald.* —

KING BILLY 3 br.g. Sovereign King–Co-Co Mo (Como 120) (1980 NR 1981 12s) tall gelding; fifth living foal; dam well behind in 3 races; needed race when in rear in 20-runner maiden event won by Arios at Redcar in October. *A. Smith.* —

KINGFAST 4 b.g. Hotfoot 126–Tudor Top 104 (Tudor Minstrel 144) (1980 6v 6f 5g 5f 1981 7s 7f) poor plater; sometimes sweats up; sold 600 gns Ascot July Sales. *W. C. Watts.* —

KINGFORD 2 ch.c. Supreme Sovereign 119–Florrie Ford 79 (Kelly 122) (1981 6g) May 8; half-brother to 2 winners, including fairly useful 1m winner —

Rheinford (by Rheingold); dam won over 6f at 2 yrs; 33/1 when last of 18 in maiden race won by Music Lover at Newmarket in October. *R. Williams.*

KING HUSTLER 4 b.g. Supreme Sovereign 119–B. S. R. 68 (March Past 124) — (1980 10.8s* 12.3f 9.6f* 10.1g² 11fg* 12d³ 10g 1981 10.2g) big, workmanlike gelding; won 3 races in 1980; well beaten only start at 4 yrs in September; probably doesn't stay 1½m; acts on any going. *N. Henderson.*

KINGLAKE 3 ch.g. Gulf Pearl 117–Spring Blossom 85 (Queen's Hussar 124) — (1980 NR 1981 5g 8g 8f 8fg) rangy gelding; good walker; brother to poor performer and half-brother to 3 winners, including quite useful 1978 2-y-o 5f winner Mr Minstrel (by Laser Light); dam won over 5f at 2 yrs; showed only glimmer of ability when about 12 lengths sixth of 12 behind Sally Rose in minor event at Salisbury in June on second start. *H. Candy.*

KING NASKRA (USA) 2 b.c. Naskra–Ruddy Jeep (Conestoga) (1981 5fg² 85 6g* 6g³ 7g) June 8; $50,000Y; fair sort; second foal; half-brother to American 3-y-o Bold Ruddy (by Captain Cee Jay), a winner over 6f at 2 yrs; dam won 14 sprint races in USA; won 9-runner maiden race at Yarmouth in July a shade cleverly by a length from Olympic Carnival; subsequently ran creditably in nurseries at Lingfield and Newmarket (4½ lengths fifth of 18 to Straeker in October); will be suited by 1m. *M. Albina.*

KING OF MAN 2 gr.g. Three Legs 128–Auld Rogue (Tarqogan 125) (1981 60 5f 5f 5d) May 1; 5,000Y; neat, quite attractive gelding; third foal; half-brother to very useful Italian 3-y-o All Silk (by Furry Glen); dam, daughter of very smart filly All Saved, won over 7.5f at 2 yrs in Ireland; only plating-class form so far but probably needs further; swerved badly left at start third outing. *C. Thornton.*

KING OF SPAIN 5 br.h. Philip of Spain 126–Sovereign Sails 94 (Sovereign 121 Path 125) (1980 6v 6fg* 6f 6fg² 5f² 6s⁴ 7.3d⁴ 6g³ 6fg² 6s² 1981 6d* 5g* 5g 6d* 6g* 6g* 6fg³ 5fg* 5d 6fg⁴)

After a good two-year-old career when he won four of his seven races, including the Mill Reef Stakes on the disqualification of Main Reef, King of Spain found things tougher in 1979 and 1980, winning just once in seventeen starts. Despite this he maintained his form well, running in good company on occasions, and was probably slightly better at the end of 1980 than at two even though a much rarer visitor to the winner's enclosure. The main cause of this relative lack of success became apparent in the most recent season:

Duke of York Stakes, York—King of Spain (pale blinkers) records his fourth victory of the season with this defeat of Columnist (also blinkered)

Avon Industries Ltd's "King of Spain" (J. Reid)

as he grew older King of Spain developed into a horse for whom waiting tactics were essential. His connections' identification of this requirement made all the difference to King of Spain's record—he enjoyed a splendid year, collecting six races including two pattern events. What's more, he thrived on his racing, impressing us in appearance a number of times.

The season started early for King of Spain and by the time he ran in the Group 3 Duke of York Stakes in May he'd had four outings, winning three of them and ruining his chance by starting very slowly in the Palace House Stakes at Newmarket on the other. His successes in the valuable Cammidge Trophy at Doncaster, where he beat Rabdan by one and a half lengths in spite of idling close home, and the Field Marshal Stakes at Haydock, where he landed the odds from Gypsy Dancer, were both decisive but in the Thirsk Hall Stakes he was forced to pull out all the stops to beat the modest Leader Of The Pack a short head after hitting the front too soon. At York King of Spain was fourth favourite behind Moorestyle, making his seasonal reappearance, Tina's Pet, a good third in the Tote European Free Handicap, and Columnist, the clear-cut winner of the Autobar Victoria Cup under 9-13. Ridden with some confidence, King of Spain won impressively, cruising through to join the leaders entering the final furlong and a half and quickening away in fine style when given the office inside the distance to beat Columnist by two lengths. Moorestyle ran well below form.

There was no immediate rest for King of Spain following this win. Before the end of the month he added the Thirsk Sprint Trophy to his tally and early in June he ran creditably in an £8,000 event won by Runnett at Lingfield. At Thirsk he started at odds on and readily beat Leader Of The Pack by two lengths, hitting the front much later than on their previous encounter and quickly settling matters once shaken up. Seven weeks elapsed before King of Spain ran again, in the Group 3 King George Stakes at Goodwood. Cook,

446

his partner more often than not in 1981, rode a very well-judged race, coming with a perfectly-timed challenge up the centre of the course to lead close home and beat Welshwyn convincingly, albeit narrowly, by a neck with Sayyaf third. King of Spain's last two outings proved that he wasn't up to beating top-class sprinters, though on neither occasion was he disgraced. In the William Hill Sprint Championship at York in August he had every chance a furlong out but could find no more, finishing fifth to Sharpo, and in the Diadem Stakes at Ascot the following month he was never able to get on terms, coming in fourth to Moorestyle.

	Philip of Spain (b 1969)	Tudor Melody (br 1956)	Tudor Minstrel
			Matelda
		Lerida (b 1961)	Matador
King of Spain (br.h. 1976)			Zepherin
	Sovereign Sails (b 1962)	Sovereign Path (gr 1956)	Grey Sovereign
			Mountain Path
		Red Sails (ro 1954)	Vilmorin
			Under Canvas

King of Spain has been retired to the Lockinge Stud, Berkshire, and will stand at £750 + £1,000 (Oct 1st); his owners have retained twenty shares with the other twenty on offer at £6,000 apiece. He is the best runner sired by the runaway 1971 New Stakes winner Philip of Spain who spent just three seasons at stud in England before being exported to Japan at the end of 1975. On the distaff side King of Spain has a good sprinting pedigree. His dam, a sprinter who has also produced the 1975 Irish two-year-old winner Bobanna (by Saintly Song), is a sister out of Red Sails to Sovereign Set, very useful at up to seven furlongs at his best, and a half-sister to Burwell, the best Northern two-year-old of 1973, and the smart sprint handicapper Red Track who, like King of Spain, wore blinkers. Red Sails, a five-furlong performer, was a sister to Song's dam Intent and a half-sister to the Cambridgeshire winner Rexequus and the Royal Hunt Cup winner Spaniards Close.

A strong horse who didn't particularly impress in his slower paces, King of Spain repaid the 8,800 guineas he cost as a yearling many times over. Equally effective at five furlongs and six furlongs, he acted on any going and was consistent. *P. Cundell.*

KING OF SPEED 2 b.c. Blue Cashmere 129–Celeste 83 (Sing Sing 134) (1981 5s⁴ 5f 5g 6g² 6fg⁴ 6g*) May 16; 4,400F, 4,400Y; half-brother to 3 winners, including 5f and 7f winner Sharp Celeste (by Sharpen Up); dam stayed at least 6f; ran best races when apprentice ridden in nurseries last 3 starts, on final one beating Queensbury Star 2 lengths at Lingfield in September; would have gone close to winning on previous start had he not wandered badly throughout final 2f; suited by 6f. *A. Pitt.* **80**

KING OF STRESS 3 ch.g. Galivanter 131–Belmont Girl 74 (Gelert 93) (1980 8.2d 8.2s 8fg 8.2s 1981 12f 12f 13.8f) workmanlike gelding; plater; probably stays 1m; blinkered final start. *K. Stone.* **—**

KING OF THE HILL 3 b.c. Derring-Do 131–Hillsquaw (Hillary) (1980 7f 1981 8d 9s³ 10s 10d) neat colt; third foal: half-brother to 1979 2-y-o 7f winner Nahane (by Porto Bello); dam won over 7f in USA; not disgraced in maiden events at Wolverhampton and Kempton in May on second and third starts; runs as though he'll stay 1½m. *N. Vigors.* **70**

KING RAGAPAN 4 b.g. Ragapan 118–At The Kings Side (Kauai King) (1980 7.5f 12g² 12g* 14g⁴ 12v 11s 12s³ 1981 13.3s 8fg 12g 10fg) big, good sort; ex-Irish gelding; won handicap at Limerick in 1980; well beaten at 4 yrs; stays 1¾m. *D. Elsworth.* **—**

KING RED 3 ch.c. Red God 128§–Saint Agata (Wild Risk) (1980 NR 1981 7d 8d⁴ 8d 8.2f) 41,000Y; medium-sized, quite attractive colt; closely related to French 1¼m winner Never Dare (by Never Bend) and half-brother to a minor winner; dam useful winner at up to 13f in France; plating-class maiden; stays 1m; well beaten in blinkers final outing (June); trained until after second start by G. Harwood. *G. Hunter.* **—**

KING'S BIDDER 3 b.g. Lochnager 132–Ruling Class 92 (King Emperor) (1980 6g 5d 5d 1981 5d 5v) narrow, lightly-made gelding; showed a little ability at 2 yrs; soundly beaten in handicaps at Warwick (last of 14 in apprentice event) and Goodwood (blinkered) in May; should stay 6f. *B. Gubby.* **—**

447

KING'S CHARTER 2 ro.g. Runnymede 123–Apple Queen (Behistoun 131) — (1981 8d) June 12; 640Y, 3,100 2-y-o; half-brother to a winning plater; dam bad plater; 33/1 when last of 23 to Roanoke River in maiden race at Leicester in November. *W. Musson.*

KING'S COLLEGE BOY 3 b.g. Andrea Mantegna–The Guzzler 69 (Behistoun 93 131) (1980 7fg 8d* 1981 12g 12g 12g 13.3g 14fg 16g² 18.8fg* 18.1d⁴ 19s* 16s*) big, rangy gelding; returned to form when blinkers were fitted and won handicaps at Warwick in August, Goodwood in September and Nottingham in October, last 2 events by wide margins; suited by a stiff test of stamina; acts on a firm surface but is well suited by some give in the ground. *N. Vigors.*

KING'S FASHION (AUS) 6 ch.g. Tails–Another Shift (Shifnal) (1980 NR — 1981 9g 8fg) Australian-bred gelding; behind in amateur riders race at Hamilton in June and seller at Edinburgh in July. *Mrs S. Chesmore.*

KING'S FOREST 2 b.g. Realm 129–Pardina 98 (Pardao 120) (1981 6g 6g 70 6fg 6g 5g) Apr 17; 10,000Y; big, well-made, attractive gelding; good mover; half-brother to several winners here and abroad, including fair 1979 2-y-o 5f winner Swinford Rose (by Upper Case); dam won from 6f to 1¼m; put up best effort on third outing when 5¾ lengths fifth of 11 to Captain Henry in maiden race at Yarmouth in August; will be suited by 7f; has scope and may do better at 3 yrs. *H. Wragg.*

KINGS GENERAL 3 b.c. St Paddy 133–Babble On 79 (Acropolis 132) (1980 106 7g* 7fg³ 1981 10fg³ 10.4d 12d 12f⁴ 12f² 10g³ 12d⁴ 10.5f*) strong, quite attractive colt; led over a furlong out and was ridden out to beat Dogberry by ¼ length in 4-runner Garrowby Stakes (Limited Handicap) at York in September; in frame earlier in Guardian Newspaper Classic Trial at Sandown (11½ lengths third to Shergar), King Edward VII Stakes at Royal Ascot, Welsh Derby at Chepstow (length second of 4 to Six Mile Bottom) and good handicaps at Goodwood and Newmarket; stays 1½m; probably best on a sound surface; sent to race in USA. *G. Harwood.*

KING'S GLORY 3 br.c. Royal and Regal–Dazzling Light 116 (Silly Season 94 127) (1980 6d 7g⁴ 7f* 1981 12.3g 10.6s 8f 8fg 10g 12fg 10g*) compact colt; having first outing for new connections and starting at 25/1 when beating Fine Sun by a head in £12,500 Tia Maria Autumn Handicap at Newmarket in October; disappointing earlier in year, although usually faced stiffish tasks; stays 1½m; acts on firm going; sometimes sweats up; blinkered third to fifth outings; sold out of H. Candy's stable 5,200 gns Ascot September Sales. *P. Mitchell.*

KING'S HOLT 2 b.c. Royal Palace 131–Lady Rowley 114 (Royal Levee) 91 (1981 6fg 8g⁴ 8g 7g³) Jan 31; big, rangy colt; third foal; dam very useful 2-y-o sprinter; promising 5 lengths fourth of 30 to Farioffa in maiden race at Newmarket in October; disappointed next time but confirmed he has plenty of ability when 3½ lengths third of 11 to Not For Show in £4,300 race at Doncaster in November; suited by 1m and runs as though he'll get 1¼m; capable of winning in ordinary maiden company. *A. Jarvis.*

KINGS LAKE (USA) 3 b.c. Nijinsky 138–Fish-Bar (Baldric II 131) (1980 133 6g² 6g* 7d* 1981 10s³ 8s* 8fg² 8fg* 8f³ 10g* 12d)
When the patrol camera was introduced there was strong opposition from some traditionalists. We well remember a stipendiary steward telling us what a waste of money it was. 'We've all got eyes and we've all got binoculars. We can see what happens so why do we need a film? Maybe it would be useful at the turn or down the course, but we can all see what happens in the last two furlongs', was his attitude, as though the use of the patrol camera was an affront to his competence. The advantages of having a permanent visual record of a race did not seem to occur to him. Our racereaders are among the best in the business but we know perfectly well that none of them is capable of seeing everything that happens in the last two furlongs of any flat race contested by more than a handful of runners. Nor is anyone else. It's impossible to be looking in two places at once.

Films taken with patrol cameras have been of enormous assistance in the adjudication of objections and stewards inquiries but films are capable of different interpretations and, on occasions, this has led to racecourse stewards themselves being put in the dock. Appeals against the decisions of local stewards occur infrequently and the vast majority result in the decision of the local stewards being upheld. There was a notable exception in the 1981 flat-racing season:

Kings Lake, first past the post in the Airlie/Coolmore Irish Two Thousand Guineas and placed second to To-Agori-Mou after a stewards inquiry, was reinstated after an appeal by his trainer to the Stewards of the Turf Club. Uproar followed the announcement of the result of the appeal. The senior officiating steward at the Curragh on Guineas day, Major Victor McCalmont, a former Senior Steward, resigned from the Turf Club in protest (he later withdrew his resignation) and, almost to a man, the British and Irish racing Press condemned the decision.

Some of the things written in the Press were grossly improper—some might say actionable—and scurrilous rumours were spread on the racecourse by some who should have known better. The Stewards of the Turf Club and the connections of Kings Lake bore the brunt of the adverse comment but we ourselves came in for criticism and disparagement in some quarters as a result of having given evidence at the appeal. Our two racereaders at the Curragh on Guineas day volunteered to act as independent witnesses at the appeal; it was our considered view that Kings Lake should have kept the race. We had no quarrel with anybody, least of all the officiating stewards on Guineas day or the connections of To-Agori-Mou, and for the life of us we couldn't understand why our attendance at the appeal hearing should have caused alarm. We merely expressed our opinion and why anyone should have felt aggrieved because we happened, quite sincerely, to disagree with the decision of the local stewards beat us.

We lay no claim to infallibility but in our view the film of the last two furlongs of the Irish Two Thousand Guineas was misinterpreted. Thirteen went to post, the winner of the Two Thousand Guineas at Newmarket To-Agori-Mou starting at odds on, with Kings Lake and the Two Thousand Guineas runner-up Mattaboy the only others at odds shorter than 12/1. Kings Lake went ahead near the rails with two furlongs to run and To-Agori-Mou, who

Airlie/Coolmore Irish Two Thousand Guineas, the Curragh—the season's most controversial finish: Kings Lake passes the post ahead of To-Agori-Mou but loses the race in the stewards' room. Kings Lake was reinstated after an appeal

Sussex Stakes, Goodwood—the third meeting of Kings Lake and To-Agori-Mou:
Kings Lake bursts through between To-Agori-Mou (No. 10) and Belmont Bay,
with Dalsaan and Noalto close up

had been held up in the early stages, moved up to challenge on the outside of
the field. Both jockeys were soon calling for everything their mounts could
give, To-Agori-Mou having edged over towards Kings Lake, crossing in front
of Dance Bid, who finished fifth, as he did so. About a furlong from home
Kings Lake became unbalanced for a moment as his rider changed his whip
from his left hand to his right. Kings Lake veered towards To-Agori-Mou
who was about half a length behind; the pair came very close together, although
it is our assertion that at this point they did not collide. In the last furlong,
with Kings Lake always just in front, they brushed against each other several
times, To-Agori-Mou in our view returning a Roland for every Oliver. A few
strides before the line To-Agori-Mou's rider stood up in his irons. Kings Lake
got home by a neck with Prince Echo a further three quarters of a length behind
in third and Mattaboy another length and a half away fourth.

Rule 214 of the Irish *Rules of Racing* lays down mandatory disqualification
for any horse whose rider has 'intentionally crossed or jostled another horse
or rider or been guilty of any form of foul riding'. So far as we know no-one
held that the deviation of Kings Lake a furlong from the finish was intentional.
The Curragh stewards took no action against his rider Eddery. In cases of
accidental interference the stewards have the options of altering the placings,
or of allowing the result to stand if in their opinion the interference has not
affected the result of the race. It was the judgement of the Curragh stewards
that 'Kings Lake had interfered with the chances of To-Agori-Mou.' Our view
was that the result had not been affected. The side-on television recording
seemed entirely to bear out the opinion of our racereaders that the momentum
of To-Agori-Mou's challenging run was not lost as a result of the incident a
furlong from home. There was no suggestion of To-Agori-Mou's changing
his legs or putting in a short stride, nor did his rider have to stop riding; Starkey's
standing up in his irons near the finish was flamboyant. No objection was lodged
on behalf of those connected with To-Agori-Mou although we understand there
would probably have been one had the stewards not instigated an inquiry.

Why was there so much bitterness and anger over the decision of the
Stewards of the Turf Club—after a six-hour hearing with lawyers representing
both parties and the Turf Club—to reinstate Kings Lake? Clearly there was
a widespread, genuine opinion that there had been a miscarriage of justice.
But we can't help wondering whether the strained relations at the time between
the Press and the O'Brien stable had anything to do with the vehemence with
which some newspapermen pressed home the point. Only a few weeks before,
O'Brien had placed an embargo on the release of his stable's running plans;
he had apparently been upset by some of the remarks made in the Press after
the announcement that the ante-post favourite Storm Bird would miss the Two

450

Thousand Guineas. One reporter, so the story went, had telephoned Ballydoyle and been told that Storm Bird had worked that day and would run in the Guineas; two or three hours later it was announced that Storm Bird had coughed at exercise and would miss Newmarket. We were unhappy about O'Brien's decision not to co-operate with the Press. Under present conditions the betting public contributes a good deal to racing and it follows, almost as a matter of entitlement, that the public should be kept in the picture about the running plans of horses that are likely to figure in ante-post betting on big races. There are stables whose plans have often been needlessly shrouded in mystery; we hope Ballydoyle will not become another of them. We'd add one more thing before moving on. The Stewards of the Turf Club made no mention in their statement in the Irish Calendar of their reason or reasons for upholding the appeal. Sound public relations surely dictated that some explanation be given, especially bearing in mind the public interest in the case. Leaving everyone in the dark served only to fan the flames of discontent. That said, the opinions of the three Turf Club Stewards were the only ones that counted in the end.

The controversy surrounding the result of the Irish Two Thousand Guineas was one of the season's longest-running talking points and it reached its zenith at Royal Ascot when, on firmish going (it was soft at the Curragh), To-Agori-Mou and Kings Lake met in the St James's Palace Stakes on the first day of the meeting. Neither had been out since the Irish Guineas, although Kings Lake had been spoken of at one time as a possible Derby runner. Understandably perhaps, the St James's Palace Stakes was billed as a showdown and there were many who longed to see To-Agori-Mou come home in front. To-Agori-Mou did come home in front, beating Kings Lake fair and square on the day by a neck after a thrilling battle in the straight. Kings Lake finished six lengths clear of third-placed Bel Bolide and, in conditions ideal for a fast time, the winner was just inside Brigadier Gerard's time record for the course and distance. To-Agori-Mou's trainer had expressed the view beforehand that his horse had improved since the Curragh and it was clear to us, when we saw Kings Lake in the paddock, that he had also come on a lot in the interim. In our view To-Agori-Mou and Kings Lake put up better performances in the St James's Palace Stakes than in the Irish Two Thousand Guineas.

Kings Lake and To-Agori-Mou also met in the Sussex Stakes at Goodwood's July meeting and in the Prix Jacques le Marois at Deauville in August. Kings Lake came out on top at Goodwood but To-Agori-Mou finished in front of Kings Lake at Deauville where the pair were second and third, separated by a nose, five lengths behind France's crack miler Northjet. Northjet was an intended runner for the Sussex Stakes, Britain's most prestigious all-aged race over a mile, and his eleventh-hour withdrawal left the previous year's French Two Thousand Guineas winner In Fijar as the only French-trained representative in the field of nine. There were three other four-year-olds in the field—Dalsaan, Belmont Bay and Kings Lake's stable-companion Last Fandango—but for the second successive year three-year-olds filled the first three places. In conditions similar to those at Royal Ascot, Kings Lake and To-Agori-Mou fought out another thrilling finish. With two furlongs to go Kings Lake seemed hopelessly hemmed in as Last Fandango, To-Agori-Mou and Dalsaan challenged Belmont Bay for the lead. Whether Eddery shouted to Rouse on Last Fandango we don't know but, glancing back and seeing that Kings Lake was trying to squeeze through, Rouse immediately gave way allowing Kings Lake a passage. Showing first-class acceleration and considerable determination Kings Lake went through a very narrow gap between Belmont Bay and To-Agori-Mou inside the final furlong, catching To-Agori-Mou in the last few strides to win by a head. The 50/1-chance Noalto, running the race of his life, also finished very strongly and was only a neck behind To-Agori-Mou in third place with Dalsaan, Belmont Bay and Last Fandango next. Had Kings Lake been beaten he would have been a most unlucky loser.

Since the Sussex Stakes was elevated to the position of a semi-classic in 1963 it has been won by some fine racehorses including Brigadier Gerard, Thatch and Kris. Kings Lake doesn't measure up to any of that trio but he is well up to standard as Sussex Stakes winners go; we have rated him superior to two other recent O'Brien-trained winners of the race, Artaius and Jaazeiro, the latter also a winner of the Irish Two Thousand Guineas. Artaius was an exceptionally versatile performer, among the best of his generation at a mile, a mile and a quarter and a mile and a half, and Kings Lake was also given an opportunity to show what he could do in the best company at longer distances. He had been tried at a mile and a quarter on his seasonal debut, finishing third in the Sean Graham Ballymoss Stakes, a Group 2 pattern race; but he showed much better form when tried again at the trip in September, beating Erins Isle by a length, after encountering trouble on the turn, in the Joe McGrath Memorial Stakes at Leopardstown— Kind of Hush, Blue Wind, Gilded Vanity and Arctique Royale completed the first six. Kings Lake was the fourth successive winner of the Joe McGrath Memorial sent out from Ballydoyle, following Inkerman, Fordham and Gregorian. Kings Lake was impressive, bursting through the field to take the lead a furlong out and having only to be hand ridden to hold the late challenge of Erins Isle. On the strength of this performance Kings Lake was saddled for the Prix de l'Arc de Triomphe; he was always in the middle division and came home eleventh of the twenty-four runners, a little over ten lengths behind the winner Gold River and about the same distance in front of fifteenth-placed Blue Wind as he had been at Leopardstown.

Kings Lake (USA) (b.c. 1978)	Nijinsky (b 1967)	Northern Dancer (b 1961)	Nearctic	Natalma
		Flaming Page (b 1959)	Bull Page	Flaring Top
	Fish-Bar (b 1967)	Baldric II (b 1961)	Round Table	Two Cities
		Fisherman's Wharf (ch 1959)	Alycidon	Herringbone

Kings Lake's sire Nijinsky won the triple crown and has become a stallion of international renown. Most of his runners in Europe have been suited by middle distances and some of them—Quiet Fling, Bright Finish, Caucasus and Niniski for example—have stayed well. The average distance of races won at three years and upwards by Nijinsky's European progeny is eleven furlongs. Kings Lake showed his best form at a mile but on breeding it seemed reasonable to expect him to stay a mile and a half—his dam Fish-Bar, a very useful filly, won at that trip and the grandam Fisherman's Wharf, a daughter of the One Thousand Guineas and St Leger winner Herringbone, was an out-and-out stayer and a half-sister to the Doncaster Cup winner Entente Cordiale and another good-class stayer Dogger Bank. Fish-Bar bred three winners before Kings Lake, two of which raced in Europe and were trained by O'Brien: the Habitat colt Denizen showed smart form at sprint distances and the Sir Ivor filly Cloonlara was one of the fastest two-year-old fillies in our experience. Cloonlara headed the Irish Free Handicap in 1976, 7 lb clear of Godswalk whom she trounced by six lengths on fast ground in the five-furlong Phoenix Stakes, the last of three wide-margin victories from as many starts in her first season. Cloonlara didn't reproduce her sparkling two-year-old form the next season when she became temperamental. Sad to relate, Cloonlara was killed by lightning in the United States during the year; to make matters worse she was in foal to Northern Dancer. Kings Lake was nowhere near so precocious as Cloonlara, showing no more than useful form at two when he won a maiden race at the Curragh in August and a seven-furlong minor event at Naas in October from three starts. In spite of tempting offers for Kings Lake from the United States, his connections decided to retire him to the Coolmore Stud in Ireland, where he should prove a

Joe McGrath Memorial Stakes, Leopardstown—Kings Lake gains his third Group 1 success, beating Erins Isle with Kind of Hush third

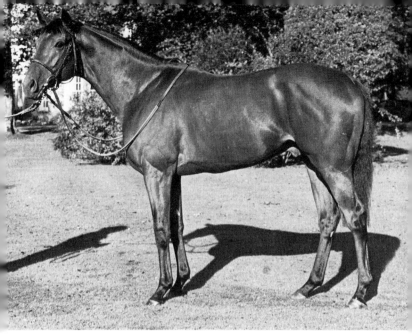

M J. P. Binet's "Kings Lake"

valuable addition to the powerful team of stallions at that stud complex. A neat, very attractive colt who improved in appearance throughout the most recent season, Kings Lake was an extremely genuine and courageous performer who raced with tremendous zest. He probably acted on any going. *V. O'Brien, Ireland.*

KING'S MARCH 2 b.g. Moulton 128–Walk By 113 (Tower Walk 130) (1981 7g 8g 8d) Mar 22; 4,000Y; lengthy gelding; poor walker; second foal; half-brother to a winner in Belgium; dam, very useful sprinter, is half-sister to smart fillies Smarten Up and Solar; behind in sellers at Newmarket (2) and Leicester in the autumn. *W. Musson.* —

KINGS OFFERING 6 b.g. Frankincense 120–Ribble Girl 96 (Trouville 125) (1980 5s 5g 5fg 5f* 5f² 6d 5g 6g² 5fg⁴ 5fg 5d 5f 6g 6d 5d 5d 1981 5d³ 5d⁴ 5d 5fg 5f* 5f⁴ 6fg 5fg 6g 5f 5g 5d 5s 5g 7d) strong, good-topped gelding; sprint handicapper; made all at Wolverhampton in June; best at 5f; acts on any going; good mount for an apprentice; effective with or without blinkers; goes well on a sharp track. *R. Ward.* **63**

KING'S PARADE 3 ch.c. Realm 129–La Lidia 78 (Matador 131) (1980 6g 6g 8g⁴ 8g 8d⁴ 1981 10fg 10g 10g* 10.1d* 10.1g³ 10g) strong, well-made colt; good walker and mover; ran best races when winning handicap at Sandown in July (by 1½ lengths from Show-A-Leg) and minor event at Windsor the following month (made all to beat Norfolk Queen 2 lengths); stays 1¼m well; acts on a soft surface; sold 11,000 gns Newmarket Autumn Sales. *J. Dunlop.* **83**

KING'S QUARRY 2 b.f. Artaius 129–Fawn 105 (Tom Rolfe) (1981 6g) neat filly; first foal; dam won over 6f and 1m, and stayed 1¼m; 6/1 and fit, took some time to get the hang of things but ran on in closing stages to be seventh of 15 to Topaz Too, beaten about 10 lengths, in maiden race at Nottingham in August, only outing. *H. Cecil.* —

453

KING'S RIDE 5 b.h. Rarity 129–Ride 71 (Sovereign Path 125) (1980 8d* **82** 10g 10.2fg³ 8g 10.6d* 10.5g 12f 12fg* 9f 10d 10g 12v⁴ 1981 8d 10fg 12g² 11s 12g 12d² 12g* 16g) tall, attractive horse; fair handicapper at his best but is none too consistent; beat Brigadier Hawk cheekily by ⅓ length in £4,000 race at Lingfield in September; good second earlier in Jockey Club Stakes at Newmarket (15 lengths behind Master Willie) and Newbury Summer Cup (beaten a neck by Morality Stone); better suited by 1½m than shorter distances nowadays (out of depth over 2m); acts on any going, but is very well suited by some give in the ground; has been tried in blinkers. *W. Wightman.*

KINGS SOLDIER 2 b.g. Queen's Hussar 124–Albertina 102 (Great Nephew 126) **66** (1981 6fg 7.6s) Feb 21; lengthy gelding; second live foal; dam, daughter of very smart Victorina, won over 1m; 11/2 when about 6 lengths fifth of 14 to Change Habit in maiden race at Lingfield in October, second outing; gelded subsequently; will stay 1¼m. *P. Walwyn.*

KING'S TOWN (FR) 4 b.g. Sir Ribot–Tatjana (Hornbeam 130) (1980 9fg **66** 12s 11d⁴ 10g 10fg³ 9d 1981 12.5g 16.9s 10.6s* 11.7fg 12d 10fg 10s 8.2s 10s 11s 10.2g*) leggy gelding; plater; won valuable events at Haydock in June (bought in 2,100 gns) and Doncaster in November (no bid); stays 1¼m well; acts on soft going; sometimes blinkered; usually bandaged; sold to M. Tate 1,700 gns Ascot November Sales. *K. Ivory.*

KINNIGGER 3 b.g. Rapid River 127–Princess Gretel 97 (The Phoenix) (1980 **71** 5fg 6g³ 1981 8s* 7g 8fg 8fg 10d 8s) lengthy gelding; had the benefit of the most experienced rider in the race when winning trainers event at Kempton in May by 15 lengths from Graf Traun; usually had stiffish tasks afterwards, but wasn't disgraced final start; stays 1m; acts well on soft going; sometimes sweats up. *M. Francis.*

KIRK MICHAEL 3 ch.g. Duc D'Orleans 76–Silanny (Scintillant or Silver Robert — 111) (1980 NR 1981 14.6f) dipped-backed, rather plain gelding; third foal; dam pulled up on only start over hurdles; 14/1, unruly at start and tailed off a long way out in maiden race won by Shalimar at Ripon in August. *R. Thompson.*

KIROV (USA) 7 b.g. Nijinsky 138–How I Wonder (My Babu 136) (1980 NR — 1981 12fg) successful hurdler; lightly raced and no sign of ability on flat; had worn blinkers; dead. *B. Gubby.*

KIR ROYALE 2 b.c. So Blessed 130–Borana 105 (Aureole 132) (1981 5s 6g **88** 7g 7fg 7.6s³ 8d²) Apr 14; rangy colt; half-brother to 3 winners, including fairly useful 1978 2-y-o 7f winner Solimena (by Welsh Pageant); dam won at 1⅛m; showed improved form when blinkered on last 2 starts, on final one going down by only a short head to Sugar and Mint in 18-runner maiden event at Leicester in November; runs as though he'll stay 1¼m; acts on soft going; made the running last 2 starts. *B. Swift.*

KIRTLING 3 b.c. Grundy 137–Silky 112 (Nijinsky 138) (1980 5f² 6g* 7g⁴ 7s⁴ **129** 1981 8s* 10fg² 10.4d* 12g* 12fg⁴ 10g² 10.5g² 10g)
On reviewing the season a number of its races spring quickly to mind. The Guardian Newspaper Classic Trial run at Sandown in April is just such an event, because of the way Shergar won it and the impact his win had at the time. His was some performance, beating Kirtling, who already had a win in the Rose-berry Stakes at Stockton under his belt, entirely on merit by ten lengths at a mile and a quarter. Kirtling had been a very useful two-year-old, winner of the Chesham Stakes at Royal Ascot, and he developed into one of the better horses of his age at three even though a long way behind Shergar. Kirtling went on from Sandown to win his next two races, the Dee Stakes at Chester (by six lengths) and the Gran Premio d'Italia at Milan; subsequently he finished fourth in the Irish Sweeps Derby and the Prix Eugene Adam, second in the Benson and Hedges Gold Cup and unplaced in the Champion Stakes.
A mile and a quarter was possibly Kirtling's best distance though he was well beaten in the Champion Stakes, dropping out once Master Willie deprived him of the lead with three furlongs to go. He made hacks of Junta, Euclid and company in the Dee Stakes in the spring and put up two very fine performances in defeat, the first of which he didn't receive full credit for, in considerably better races over the same distance in the summer. Kirtling had an extremely stiff task at the weights in the Prix Eugene Adam at Saint-Cloud in July: he was giving weight all round, 4 lb to both the first and second, Bellman and Al Nasr (Fr), and 8 lb to third-placed Church Parade. Yet he finished no more

Dee Stakes, Chester—Kirtling wins easing up

than two lengths down on the winner, and a length and a half down on Church Parade. Piggott, who had been in the saddle at Saint-Cloud, also took the mount in the Benson and Hedges Gold Cup at York in August and gave him a tremendous ride. Piggott dictated things in front, manipulating the pace of the race to the utmost benefit of Kirtling. Two furlongs out Kirtling, Beldale Flutter and Master Willie had quickened to have the race between them; Kirtling soon came under very strong pressure but he managed to hold on in front for a while, and he kept going so well through the last furlong that Beldale Flutter beat him less than a length in the end. Possibly this very punishing finish affected Kirtling's showing in the Champion Stakes; certainly he should have done better at Newmarket than he did.

Kirtling's performances at a mile and a half are not to be sneezed at—they brought him victory in a Group 1 pattern race and a prestigious fourth place in another. But in the Irish Sweeps Derby he ran for all the world like one who would be ideally suited by a return to a shorter trip in the best company. Looking well in himself he chased the leaders, went up to dispute second place entering the straight, was soon hard driven and was beaten two furlongs out; Dance Bid left him five lengths behind in the race for third. Earlier, in the Gran Premio d'Italia run three days before the Epsom Derby, Kirtling succeeded in making all; when challenged by the Derby Italiano sixth Seiorlando he battled on for a short-neck win and prize-money of around £23,000, a sum almost double that for fourth place at Epsom. All told five of Kirtling's six challengers in Milan had run behind Glint of Gold in the Derby Italiano, and they included My Franky, Bold Brigadier and Timur Lang, the second, third and fourth on that occasion. Kirtling started odds on.

Kirtling was sold privately to the owners of the Airdrie Stud in Kentucky between the Gran Premio d'Italia and Irish Sweeps Derby, and he has been syndicated at 100,000 dollars a share. The appeal Kirtling's pedigree will have to American breeders is hard to assess. His dam, by Nijinsky, is from a family known for its exploits on this side of the Atlantic, one known particularly for the outstanding record of its mares at stud. Silky's grandam Horama, a five-furlong

455

sprinter, is the grandam of too many good horses to mention all here. Suffice to pick out a few, of various types—Favoletta, Flashy, Lucky Sovereign, Bright Finish and Shining Finish, and the two best horses out of the very speedy Close Up, the Benson and Hedges Gold Cup winner Moulton and the Derby third Freefoot. Silky is a half-sister to the last-named pair, Moulton being by

		Grundy (ch 1972)	Great Nephew (b 1963)	Honeyway
Kirtling (b.c. 1978				Sybil's Niece
			Word from Lundy (b 1966)	Worden II
				Lundy Princess
		Silky (b 1972)	Nijinsky (b 1967)	Northern Dancer
				Flaming Page
			Close Up (br 1958)	Nearula
				Horama

Pardao and Freefoot by Relko. Silky was more than useful herself on the race-course. She won over five furlongs as a two-year-old, finished second in the Irish One Thousand Guineas and showed more form in good company before losing her zest for the game; she was never raced beyond a mile. Kirtling is Silky's second foal. The most attractive but rather disappointing Abington (by Jukebox) is her first, and the good-looking Crossways (by Habitat) is her third. Kirtling is rather a leggy individual, not so eyecatching as the other two, but he is an excellent mover. He acted on any going and was consistent. *H. Wragg.*

KISS 3 b.f. Habitat 134–Miss Petard 113 (Petingo 135) (1980 NR 1981 5d* 7d 5.8f* 6fg* 6fg* 5.6fg3 6g 6d2) rangy, good sort; good walker; third living foal; sister to Cracking Form, a useful performer at around 1m, and half-sister to very useful middle-distance stayer Meistersinger (by Rheingold); dam, very useful at 2 yrs and 3 yrs, won at up to 1½m; a very well-bred filly who improved steadily and won maiden event at Folkestone and handicaps at Bath, Salisbury and Newmarket, on last-named course in August showing a tremendous turn of speed and beating Effect cleverly by a head; subsequently ran well when placed in Portland Handicap at Doncaster (third to Touch Boy) and Allendale Handicap on same course; bred to stay at least 1m but is evidently regarded as a sprinter; probably acts on any going; goes well for apprentice A. Clark; didn't have best of runs second outing; ran her only moderate race on seventh start. *G. Harwood.* **88**

KISS AND RUN 3 ch.g. Native Bazaar 122–Woodland Promise 76 (Philemon 119) (1980 NR 1981 7fg 8d 8g 8d 8fg) dipped-backed gelding; poor form in varied company, including selling; blinkered fourth start; trained by P. Cole first 4 starts; sold 460 gns Ascot August Sales. *W. Musson.* —

KISSIN KIN 3 br.f. Great Nephew 126–Zelotta 87 (Zeddaan 130) (1980 NR 1981 8s4 10s 8g) 10,000Y; first foal; dam won twice over 1m; 14/1 when 9 lengths fourth of 22 behind Corn Street in minor event at Warwick in October; soundly beaten afterwards; stays 1m; sold 6,200 gns Newmarket December Sales. *F. J. Houghton.* —

KITHAIRON 10 br.h. Klairon 131–Gin-Ginger 82 (Happy Monarch 109) (1980 8d 7v 7s 8f3 7.6f 8fg* 8d3 8d* 8fg3 8fg2 8fg2 8d 8fg2 8s 8.2s* 1981 8.2d 7.6g 8fg 8g3 8g 8fg3 9d 8g 8.2d4 8s4 8.2d 8g) a grand old horse; best at around 1m; acts on any going but is possibly best with some give in the ground; excellent mount for an apprentice; used to wear blinkers; usually gets well behind in early stages. *J. W. Watts.* **69**

KITSON (USA) 3 b.c. Secretariat–Gunite (Crozier USA) (1980 7g 1981 12fg 12g) well-made colt; needed race and ran a bit green when about 10 lengths sixth of 16 behind Taher in maiden event at Kempton in April; chipped a bone when in rear in similar race won by Cornishman at Newmarket the following month. *P. Walwyn.* —

KITTASPEC GAL 4 br.f. Mandamus 120–Dior 80 (Dionisio 126) (1980 8g3 8g 11g4 16f3 18f* 15d* 16.1s 15.8d4 16s2 1981 16s3) unfurnished filly; has a round action; staying handicapper; not disgraced in blinkers only start of 1981 in April; acts on any going; suitable mount for a claimer. *M. H. Easterby.* —

KITTYHAWK 3 b.f. Bustino 136–Sky Fever 108 (Skymaster 126) (1980 6fg4 6g2 6g* 1981 8g 6fg 7.3fg 7fg* 8s2 7g4) **113**
In 1980 the weather and the virus prevented Kittyhawk's campaign from running to plan; nevertheless she still managed to win one of the season's

*Kiveton Park Steel Stakes, Doncaster—favourite Kittyhawk has to be
shaken up to overcome Premier Rose*

most important races for two-year-old fillies, the Lowther Stakes at York.
Her campaign was interrupted again in 1981—she was off the course for three
months at the height of the season, during part of which period her stable was
virtually closed down—but she came right back to her best in the autumn and
confirmed herself a smart filly, one every bit as good as she had been at two.

Kittyhawk started fourth favourite for the One Thousand Guineas and
ran respectably considering she lacked the benefit of a previous race, finishing
a fairly close ninth of fourteen behind Fairy Footsteps. She was subsequently
off the course until late-July, missing such races as the Coronation Stakes at
Royal Ascot and the Child Stakes at Newmarket, and making her return in a
very different type of contest, the Tote Stewards' Cup at Goodwood. She
never showed there. Almost certainly she needed the run, for to our eyes
she looked still a little short of full fitness when fifth behind Dalsaan in the
Hungerford Stakes at Newbury just over a fortnight later. Kittyhawk showed
enough at Newbury to suggest that she was well on the way back to form and
when faced with a simpler task in the Kiveton Park Steel Stakes at Doncaster
in September she made the most of her opportunity. Receiving weight from
all her five opponents she was always going well, so well that she seemed as
if she might win by a wide margin when eased out to challenge Premier Rose
two furlongs out; but Premier Rose has often proved a tough nut to crack
and in the end Kittyhawk had to be ridden out to beat her by half a length.
Kittyhawk met opponents of a different calibre on both of her subsequent
starts and gave a very good account of herself each time. At Ascot later in
September she finished third behind To-Agori-Mou and Cracaval in the Queen
Elizabeth II Stakes, subsequently moved up a place on Cracaval's disqualification. She was beaten only two and a half lengths by the winner and would
have gone closer if she hadn't had to be switched when squeezed between To-
Agori-Mou and the hanging Cracaval about a furlong from home. At Newmarket
in October she faced equally stern opposition in the Bisquit Cognac Challenge
Stakes and finished fourth, five lengths behind the winner Moorestyle. She
showed up for a long way on the outside and moved up to Moorestyle's quarters
briefly about two furlongs out; then she hung slightly when ridden and couldn't
quicken sufficiently to stay with the leaders.

We probably shan't see Kittyhawk racing over here again. She was acquired by Robert Sangster in the summer and has been sent to race in the United States where one of her principal targets in 1982 is said to be the Arlington Million over a mile and a quarter. She'll have to improve a bit to have a chance in such a race; what's more, there's no certainty that she'll get the distance. She hasn't raced beyond a mile, a distance which suits her well, and although her sire the St Leger winner Bustino is an influence for stamina her dam Sky Fever is from a fairly speedy family. Sky Fever, who showed all of her form at five furlongs, winning three times, is a half-sister to the smart sprinter Matinee, winner of the 1974 Portland Handicap. Matinee's first three foals are winners and include the useful fillies Melodrama (by Busted) and Candide (by Bustino). Sky Fever, even with Kittyhawk, hasn't made quite such a good start to her career at stud. Both of her foals before Kittyhawk were disappointing on the flat, although one of them, Sky Rider (by Queen's Hussar), won over hurdles.

Kittyhawk (b.f. 1978)	Bustino (b 1971)	Busted (b 1963)	Crepello
			Sans le Sou
		Ship Yard (ch 1963)	Doutelle
			Paving Stone
	Sky Fever (b 1969)	Skymaster (ch 1958)	Golden Cloud
			Discipliner
		Harlequinade (br 1964)	Klairon
			Columbine

Kittyhawk is plenty good enough to make her presence felt in the States and it will be interesting to see how she fares. A lengthy, quite attractive filly who frequently impressed with her well-being, she probably acts on any going and is a genuine sort. *R. Hern*

KIVA (USA) 2 b.f. Tom Rolfe–Befuddled (Tom Fool) (1981 6fg 6fg* 7fg² 7d) **97**
Mar 22; $140,000Y; neat, attractive filly; good mover; second foal; dam, out of

Miss Caroline R. Alexander's "Kiva"

half-sister to 5 stakes winners, never ran; drew clear from halfway to beat Hithermoor Lass by 6 lengths in 16-runner maiden race at Newbury in August; beaten twice at Goodwood subsequently, running well when 2½ lengths second to all-the-way winner Stratospheric in Waterford Candelabra Stakes later in month but proving a disappointing favourite when distant fifth of 8 to Montekin in £4,800 event in September (didn't take the eye in paddock); will stay 1¼m; acts on a firm surface. *R. Hern.*

KIWI LAD 2 ch.g. Happytown 89–Hampsruth (Sea Hawk II 131) (1981 7g 8s) — Apr 5; 280 2-y-o; first foal; dam never ran; in rear in minor event at Brighton in September and maiden race at Warwick in October. *K. Cunningham-Brown.*

KLAIROVE 2 b.f. Averof 123–Klaire 85 (Klairon 131) (1981 6g 8fg³ 7g) Apr 21; rather lightly-made filly; first foal; dam, half-sister to high-class stayer Proverb, won over 7f at 2 yrs; 33/1 when staying-on 3 lengths third of 17 to Cornish Heroine in maiden race at Leicester in September, best effort; will be suited by middle distances. *R. Akehurst.* — 74

KNAPPING 3 b.f. Busted 134–Peach Stone (Mourne 126) (1980 NR 1981 10.4d 11.5g) lengthy, fair sort; half-sister to 3 winners, including Irish 1½m winner Stony Ground (by Relko); dam won at around 9f in France; soundly beaten in maiden races at Chester in August and Yarmouth in September. *F. Durr.* —

KNAVE OF TRUMPS 2 b.c. Great Nephew 126–Clean Canasta 95 (Silly Season 127) (1981 6d 6fg² 6g* 6g*) Feb 16; neat, good sort; good walker and mover; first foal; dam, out of sister to Charlottown, won over 7f at 2 yrs; quickened clear inside final 2f and was eased a couple of lengths when winning 14-runner maiden race at Yarmouth in September by 2 lengths from Jade Ring; didn't seem to have much in hand when landing the odds in 13-runner minor event at Leicester the following month by 1½ lengths from Claudius Crozet; will be suited by 1m; went to start very freely second outing and was taken down very slowly on fourth. *H. Cecil.* — 95 p

KNIGHTHALL (USA) 3 b.c. King's Bishop–Midnight Hush (Sunrise Flight) (1980 6g 7d 1981 8d 10.1f⁴ 13.1f⁴ 10g 10f³ 9g² 10d⁴ 9s⁴ 10s²) quite a useful sort; quite moderate form in varied company; stays 1¼m (well beaten over 13f); sweated up badly sixth start; sold to A. W. Jones 2,300 gns Newmarket Autumn Sales. *G. Hunter.* — 62

KNIGHTSBRIDGE BOY 2 gr.c. Be Friendly 130–Immaculate (Sovereign Path 125) (1981 6g 7g 7.6s) Apr 15; 500Y; compact colt; half-brother to several winners, including Spanish Oaks winner Delfica (by Hardicanute) and very useful Irish middle-distance filly Slap Up (by Gala Performance); dam lightly raced; little better than plating class on form at 2 yrs. *D. Wilson.* —

KNIGHTSBRIDGE GAME 2 gr. or br.c. Abwah 118–Turnstone 83 (Sea Hawk II 131) (1981 5d 6f 7g 7.6s 8s 8.2s* 8d²) May 31; 300Y; plain colt; second foal; dam 2-y-o winner; plater; beat Spare Wheel all out by ½ length in 12-runner seller at Nottingham in October (bought in 900 gns); ran well next time out; suited by 1m; acts on soft going. *D. Wilson.* — 80

KNIGHT SECURITY 2 b.f. Swing Easy 126–High Destiny 66 (Pall Mall 132) (1981 5g² 5d⁴ 5s 5f* 6f⁴ 6d* 6fg 6fg 6d⁴ 6s*) Apr 27; 3,600F, 4,800Y; leggy filly; third produce; half-sister to a winner in Hungary; dam won 1m seller; won 18-runner maiden event at Pontefract in June and nurseries at Haydock in August and October; seemed to hold an excellent chance with only 7-7 in valuable Buggins Farm Nursery on tenth outing and won well by 2½ lengths from Time To Reflect; may stay 7f; acts on any going; well treated in Northern Free Handicap. *J. Berry.* — 86

KNIGHTS HILL 2 b.g. Auction Ring 123–Alpina 82 (King's Troop 118) (1981 6f 7fg 6f 6fg 6g) Mar 7; 5,000Y; neat, sturdy gelding; good mover; brother to a prolific winner in Italy, and half-brother to 7f winner Markina (by On Your Mark) and a winner in Malaya; dam 1m winner; showed signs of ability, on third outing finishing 5½ lengths fifth of 9 to Irish Grenadier in maiden race at Brighton in August; blinkered final start. *R. Armstrong.* — 65

KNIPTON LADY 3 b.f. Pamroy 99–Robson's Lady 83 (Robson's Choice 105) (1980 NR 1981 8fg 8f) third foal; dam won at around 1m and also over hurdles; in rear in maiden races at Warwick in June (backward) and Pontefract in July. *Miss A. Hill-Wood.* —

KNIPTON PAM 5 b.m. Pamroy 99–Robson's Lady 83 (Robson's Choice 105) (1980 NR 1981 12f⁴) second foal; dam won over 7.6f and 1m and also over hurdles; bandaged in front when tailed-off last in small race at Pontefract in August. *Miss A. Hill-Wood.* —

459

KNOCKIN 2 ch.c. Relkino 131–Knocknagrena (Worden II 129) (1981 8s 8s) — May 1; 11,000Y; lengthy colt; half-brother to numerous winners, including smart 1976 Irish 6f and 7f winner Sovereign Dice (by Supreme Sovereign); dam placed at up to 1¼m in Ireland; unquoted when behind in maiden race at York (very backward) and minor event at Redcar in October. *J. Etherington.*

KNOWN FACT (USA) 4 b.c. In Reality–Tamerett (Tim Tam) (1980 7f⁴ 8fg* — 8d 8g* 7g* 8fg* 1981 7.2d⁴)
It was a bitter disappointment that Known Fact, the top miler of 1980, ran only once as a four-year-old and failed completely to do himself justice in the race concerned. At three he had been awarded the Two Thousand Guineas on Nureyev's disqualification and had won outright the Waterford Crystal Mile, the Kiveton Park Steel Stakes and the Queen Elizabeth II Stakes, getting the better of Kris by a neck in a magnificent race for the last-named. His connections made it plain that in 1981 his campaign would take in top mile-and-a-quarter events as well as those at a mile, and the prospect of seeing him in the Coral Eclipse Stakes and the Champion Stakes was one to savour.

Unfortunately things did not turn out as expected. When we interviewed Jeremy Tree for *Timeform* in mid-June he told us that Known Fact had taken a bit of time to come to hand in the spring, not showing his best form until towards the end of April when he galloped well with Sharpo and Bel Bolide. The four-runner Cold Shield Windows Trophy at Haydock on the first Saturday in May was chosen as Known Fact's preparatory race for the Tote Lockinge Stakes at Newbury but its outcome was far from encouraging. Known Fact hung right in the straight, found little under pressure in the last two furlongs and trailed in a distant last to Dalsaan, beaten by the handicappers Jebb Lane and Davidgalaxy Affair also. Tree admitted 'He ran appallingly. I could in no way account for it. We have had him tested for everything—the vet has looked down his throat, blood tests, everything else—and he's perfectly all right'. Whatever the cause of this bad run, doubts persisted and with Known Fact's failing to satisfy his trainer it was announced before the end of June that he had been retired. He has not been syndicated and will stand at his owner's Juddmonte Farms, Wargrave-on-Thames, Berkshire at a private fee.

		Intentionally	Intent
	In Reality	(bl 1956)	My Recipe
	(b 1964)	My Dear Girl	Rough'n Tumble
Known Fact (USA)		(ch 1957)	Iltis
(b.c. 1977)		Tim Tam	Tom Fool
	Tamerett	(b 1955)	Two Lea
	(b or br 1962)	Mixed Marriage	Tudor Minstrel
		(b 1952)	Persian Maid

European breeders should be clamouring to send their mares to Known Fact. Not only was he a brilliant miler at his best; he is exceptionally well bred, too. His sire, In Reality, earned over three quarters of a million dollars in three season's racing, winning fourteen of his twenty-seven starts at up to nine furlongs. He has been just as successful at stud, for the average annual earnings of his progeny from 1972 to 1981 came to over a million dollars. Known Fact's dam Tamerett, a half-sister to Sharpen Up's sire Atan, won four times at up to one mile and has proved a top-class broodmare. Her four live foals prior to Known Fact were a leading 1970 two-year-old Tamtent and the top-class Tentam (both by In Reality's sire Intentionally), the very good grass horse Terete (by Boldnesian) and a winning sister to Known Fact. Tentam, incidentally, had a highly-promising stud career cut short in February, 1981, when he succumbed to a heart attack at Windfields Farm. In 1978 Tamerett produced the filly Secrettame (by Secretariat), a 400,000-dollar yearling that showed smart form in America at three, and her yearling filly by Chieftain was bought on behalf of Known Fact's owner, Khaled Abdulla, for 670,000 dollars at the Keeneland Selected Sale in July.

Known Fact's looks compliment his performance and breeding, for he is a well-made, good-looking colt of medium size, and was a good mover. A strong puller in his early days, he settled better as he matured, helped in this by his usual jockey Carson, and stayed a mile well. Ideally suited by top-of-the-ground conditions, he was genuine and consistent. *J. Tree.*

KOCHIA 3 b.f. Firestreak 125–Lead Me On (King's Troop 118) (1980 7s 7g **53** 1981 5s 6g⁴ 6fg³ 6d 5f 6g 5d) small, stocky filly; plating-class maiden; stays 6f. *G. Fletcher.*

KOJOSA 3 b.f. Sovereign King–Carmenta (Dumbarnie 125) (1980 NR 1981 — 8f) third foal; dam of little account; bandaged in front when in rear in 20-runner maiden race at Doncaster in July. *W. Stubbs.*

KOMATCH (USA) 2 ch.c. Apalachee 137–Zambezi River (Pretendre 126) **85** (1981 8g 7g) Apr 15; $20,000Y, resold 41,000 gns Y; plain colt; half-brother to a minor winner by Ace of Aces; dam minor French middle-distance winner; made steady, late headway to finish 6½ lengths eighth of 17 to Queen's Home in maiden race at Goodwood in September; again showed ability when 16/1 for Somerville Tattersall Stakes at Newmarket the following month, finishing 9½ lengths eighth of 16 to Wind and Wuthering; will be suited by 1¼m+; could win a race over middle distances at 3 yrs. *J. Hindley.*

KOOKABURRA 2 br.g. Cawston's Clown 113–Lindy Ann (King's Leap 111) **71** (1981 6fg 7f⁴ 8g) May 14; 3,000Y; unfurnished gelding; good mover; second foal; dam unraced twin; 50/1, showed up throughout when 8½ lengths fourth of 18 to Nioulargo in maiden race at Yarmouth in August; hampered on turn and lost place in similar event at Ayr the following month (sweating a little); not sure to stay 1m. *G. Pritchard-Gordon.*

KORYPHEOS 2 b.c. He Loves Me 120–Silly Song (Silly Season 127) (1981 **80** 7fg² 7.6s³) Mar 20; IR 12,500F, IR 11,500Y; leggy, unfurnished colt; third foal; half-brother to Irish 1980 2-y-o 5f winner Keep Chanting (by Auction Ring); dam, half-sister to 3 very useful animals, won over 7f in Ireland; 5 lengths second of 10 to Old Country in minor event at Goodwood in September and finished a remote third to Sabutai in 15-runner maiden race at Lingfield the following month; not sure to stay 1m. *P. Mitchell.*

KRISCHINA 2 ch.f. Music Boy 124–Alchorus 78 (Alcide 136) (1981 6fg⁴) **78 p** Apr 22; 18,500Y; half-sister to top-class 6f and 7f winner Be Tuneful (by Be Friendly); dam won over 9f; well-backed favourite, showed up until lack of experience and fitness told in closing stages when 5 lengths fourth of 15 to Pomegranate in maiden race at Yarmouth in June; looked fairly promising here but wasn't seen out again. *J. Hindley.*

KRISTALLINA 2 b.f. Homeric 133–Go Friendly (Be Friendly 130) (1981 **84** 6g 6d) Mar 24; 6,000F, 3,500Y; lengthy filly; half-sister to 3-y-o Cashmoor (by Ashmore) and 2 winners by Dancer's Image, namely American 7f winner Shady Spring and Garozzo, a useful winner over 1m in Italy; dam poor half-sister to useful stayer Attivo; 50/1, had an extremely stiff task for a newcomer in William Hill Cheveley Park Stakes at Newmarket in September and wasn't disgraced in finishing 11 lengths ninth of 13 to Woodstream; 7/1 when in rear in 16-runner minor event won by Strath of Orchy at Pontefract the following month; likely to need 1¼m+ at 3 yrs. *A. Bailey.*

KRISTEN 2 ch.f. Sheshoon 132–Sweet Boronia 96 (Mandamus 120) (1981 6g 7.6s 10.2g) June 20; small filly; third foal; half-sister to winning sprinter Hunny Bunny (by Streetfighter); dam won from 7f to 1¾m; no worthwhile form in varied company, including selling. *R. Hoad.*

KRISTOS 2 gr.c. No Mercy 126–Jill Somers 76 (Will Somers 114§) (1981 — 5s) Apr 20; first foal; dam second over 5f at 2 yrs; 20/1 when eighth of 9 to Tenth of October in minor event at Windsor in May. *M. Ryan.*

KRUG 3 br.c. Relko 136–Misplanted (Hul a Hul 124) (1980 8g 10g* 1981 **103** 10fg 12g⁴ 12d 16f³ 14d³ 16d³ 12fg² 16fg⁴) compact, attractive colt; in frame most starts, including when 4 lengths third of 13 behind Ore in Queen's Vase at Royal Ascot in June on fourth start, 3 lengths second to Valentinian in handicap at Goodwood in August and 5½ lengths fourth to Crispin in another handicap at Ascot in September; finished well after being given plenty to do in first 2 of those races and in third ran on so well when seeing daylight 1½f out that we gained the impression he would have gone very close to winning had he not lost a good position when seemingly going well ½m out; suited by a test of stamina; sometimes pulls hard; trained by M. Jarvis until after fourth outing; winner over hurdles. *S. Mellor.*

KRUGERAMA 3 br.g. Amber Rama 133–Krugerrand 74 (Goldhill 125) (1980 **51** 5g⁴ 5f² 5fg 5f* 5f 5f 5d 6s 1981 8g 8g⁴ 8g 6f 7f 6d 6f 6fg 6f 8fg 8.2v 12.2g 12d³) sturdy, compact, robust gelding; poor handicapper nowadays; finds 6f too sharp nowadays and seems to stay 1¼m; probably acts on any going; occasionally blinkered. *E. Weymes.*

K-SERA 3 ch.f. Lord Gayle 124–Deirdre (Vimy 132) (1980 5f 5fg 7d² 7g³ **70** 7d* 6s 1981 10g 8.5g² 8f 8.3fg 9f 10fg³ 11fg 10s² 11d 10d) quite a moderate handicapper nowadays; runner-up at Epsom in June (¾ length behind Oh So

Choosy in NMT Ebbisham Stakes) and Lingfield in October; stays 1¼m; acts on a firm surface but is ideally suited by some give in the ground. *C. Brittain.*

KYLE-HELEN 2 b.f. Orange Bay 131–Kyle Keep 73 (Ballymoss 136) (1981 8d) May 19; second foal; dam, winner over 1½m in Ireland, is half-sister to smart miler Skyliner; 33/1 when tailed off in 17-runner seller at Leicester in November. *D. Marks.* —

KYOTO 3 b.g. Averof 123–Klondyke Fire (Klondyke Bill 125) (1980 6d⁴ 7g⁴ 7d² 7fg⁴ 1981 8.2s 6g 8g 10fg⁴ 10.2f 10d 11f 10fg² 10f 9f³ 9g* 8.2d 9s) big, lengthy gelding; won minor event at Wolverhampton in September by 2½ lengths from Knighthall; stays 1¼m; blinkered third outing; inconsistent; retained 11,000 gns Newmarket Autumn Sales. *H. Collingridge.* **67**

L

LA BABOOSHKA 2 b.f. He Loves Me 120–Schull (Yorick II 127) (1981 5g 5s² 5g² 5fg) Apr 3; IR 5,500F; fair sort; half-sister to several winners, including fair 1980 2-y-o 5f filly Bohemian Rhapsody (by On Your Mark) and very useful 6f to 7f performer Step Ahead (by Continuation); dam never ran; second in maiden races at Windsor and Hamilton (odds on, beaten 4 lengths by Mullins Bar) early in season; best run on soft going; blinkered final start (July); sold 2,700 gns Newmarket December Sales. *P. Haslam.* **67**

LA BANDERA 3 ch.f. Morston 125–Patois (I Say 125) (1980 NR 1981 10s) 27,000Y; good-bodied filly; second foal; half-sister to 1½m winner Louise (by Royal Palace); dam twice-raced half-sister to very smart stayer Petty Officer; always behind when ninth of 13 to On Show in maiden race at Nottingham in October. *T. Robson.* —

LA BELLE SOLEIL 2 b.f. Roi Soleil 125–Gracemount 71 (Midsummer Night II 117) (1981 5f 6f 6f) Apr 22; compact, sturdy filly; second foal; dam 1½m winner; only poor form, including in sellers. *W. Wharton.* —

LA BELLE SORCIERE 3 b.f. Sparkler 130–Singing Witch 71 (Sing Sing 134) (1980 5d 5g 5g² 5fg* 6fg³ 5.3g² 1981 5v⁴ 5d 5fg 6fg 5fg 5f) well-made filly; didn't run up to her 2-y-o form in 1981; probably stays 6f; acts on a firm surface; blinkered final start. *J. Sutcliffe.* —

LA BICHE 3 ch.f. Bold Lad (Ire) 133–Tudor Song (Tudor Minstrel 144) (1980 6fg 6s 7d² 6d³ 1981 8.2fg⁴ 7d 10d⁴ 8fg⁴ 8d 8g 8g) strong, useful-looking filly; fourth in small handicap at Nottingham and maiden events at Brighton and Warwick; probably stays 1¼m; doesn't seem much of a battler; blinkered last 3 outings; sold 25,000 gns Newmarket December Sales. *H. T. Jones.* **64**

LA BIRD 2 b.f. Le Johnstan 123–Bird 80 (Firestreak 125) (1981 6fg 7fg 8.2d* 8.2s 8.2s) Apr 10; 880F; lengthy filly; half-sister to 2m winner Alcock (by Alcide); dam 1m winner; plater; showed improved form when winning 13-runner event at Hamilton in September by 1½ lengths from Derwent River; attracted no bid; evidently better at 1m than shorter distances; suited by a soft surface; sometimes bandaged behind. *K. Stone.* **61**

LABISTA 3 br.f. Crowned Prince 128–Balista 86 (Baldric II 131) (1980 5f* 5fg² 5g 5g³ 5f* 5g* 1981 6g 5f 5fg) strong, shapely filly; improved into one of leading 2-y-o fillies of 1980, winning 3 races, including Bexley Stakes at Goodwood (by 10 lengths); didn't recapture her form, and wasn't seen out in second half of season; always likely to be best at minimum trip though is bred to stay 7f; acts well on firm going and has yet to race on soft; blinkered final outing. *B. Hobbs.* —

LABLON 2 ch.c. Laxton 105–Mablon 76 (Majority Blue 126) (1981 5g 5g) Mar 10; compact colt; half-brother to useful 5f performer Mayab (by Maystreak) and a winner in Malaya; dam placed over 5f at 2 yrs; towards rear in maiden and minor events at Ripon and Thirsk in May. *M. H. Easterby.* —

LA BORIE 3 ch.f. Son of Silver 123–Candid Queen 80 (Good Bond 122) (1980 5fg 6s 6g 1981 8.5g 12g 10fg 7f 6f) quite attractive filly; little worthwhile form in maiden races and handicaps. *P. Mitchell.* —

LABURNUM LAD 5 b.g. Bing II–Dollar Fine 64 (Court Harwell 130) (1980 NR 1981 15.8s 12.5g) plater; stays well; seems to act on any going. *J. Calvert.* —

LA CASTELLANA 2 b. or br.f. Sparkler 130–Jeanina (Congolese 109) (1981 5g 7fg 8fg* 7v⁴ 7d*) Apr 28; rangy filly; first foal; dam, bred in Chile, was good winner in Spain; won maiden race at Beverley in September and just came **78**

out best in very tight finish to 16-runner nursery at Leicester in November, beating Neighboring a neck; stays 1m well and will get 1¼m as a 3-y-o; seems to act on any going; genuine; apprentice ridden at Leicester. *F. Durr.*

LA CHAUMIERE 3 gr.f. Thatch 136–Ruby of Iran (Cosmic Bomb) (1980 5g 1981 5f 5f 6f 6d 5fg 5g) leggy filly; poor form in varied company; sometimes blinkered. *H.T. Jones.*

LA COMEDIENNE 2 gr.f. Comedy Star 121–Ruetina 74 (Rugantino 97) (1981 6fg 5.8h 7g) Apr 17; lengthy, lightly-made filly; third foal; sister to 3-y-o 1½m winner Comedian, and half-sister to fairly useful 1978 staying 2-y-o Faringdon Bell (by Mandamus); dam ran 3 times; backed from 10/1 to 7/2 second favourite for 15-runner maiden race at Bath in August on second outing but never got in a blow and finished remote seventh to Cheri Berry; evidently thought capable of better than she's shown so far. *J. Dunlop.*   —

LADY ACQUIESCE 3 br.f. Galivanter 131–Acquire 105 (Burglar 128) (1980 5fg² 5.1g* 5fg⁴ 5.3fg² 6fg 5d 1981 6g 7g 5fg 5fg) neat filly; well beaten in 1981, including in sellers; best form at around 5f; acts on a firm surface; sometimes sweats up; blinkered final start. *C. Williams.*   —

LADY ANTONIA 3 br.f. Owen Anthony 102–Yasmin II 88 (Gilles de Retz 132) (1980 6g 7g 1981 7d² 7.6d) leggy filly; second in maiden race at Leicester in April, first form; never going at Chester the following month, only subsequent outing; will be suited by 1m. *H. Candy.*   66

LADY ARPEGE 3 b. or br.f. Swing Easy 126–Giglet (Frankincense 120) (1980 5g* 6d 5d² 1981 6g 7g⁴ 7g 7f 8.2f 5f 6d) lightly-made filly; didn't run up to her 2-y-o form, but wasn't disgraced in handicaps on occasions; probably stays 7f. *W.H.H. Williams.*   —

LADY ASTIR 3 b.f. Abwah 118–Ma Mitte (Faristan 123) (1980 6g 7f 7g 7fg 7d 1981 9s 6g 7fg 7fg 5fg² 6fg 6fg 6fg 5g) fair sort; missed break when second in selling handicap at Catterick in July, best effort; best at sprint distances; acts on a firm surface; soundly beaten in blinkers third start. *M. McCormack.*   47

LADY AUCTIONEER 2 b.f. Auction Ring 123–Sea Scold (Sea Hawk II 131) (1981 5s 5d 5fg 5fg² 6fg 6g) Apr 21; IR 5,000Y; useful sort; second foal; dam never ran; plater; should be suited by 6f+; blinkered fifth outing (ran creditably). *R. Hannon.*   58

LADY BE MINE (USA) 3 b.f. Sir Ivor 135–My Advantage 89 (Princely Gift 137) (1980 NR 1981 7g⁴ 8d 8fg* 10fg) most attractive filly; half-sister to several winners, including useful 1978 2-y-o 5f and 7f winner Mixed Applause (by Nijinsky) and prolific Italian winner Mycro (by Crocket); dam, a sprinter, is half-sister to dam of Lord Seymour and Marwell; really took the eye when beating Becky Sharp in good style by 2½ lengths in maiden race at Yarmouth in June, cruising into lead 2f out and winning comfortably; appeared not to stay in handicap at Newbury the following month, and wasn't seen out again; stayed 1m; was probably unsuited by soft ground; stud. *H. Cecil.*   76

LADY BLACKFOOT 3 b.f. Prince Tenderfoot 126–Indian Graduate (Chieftain) (1980 5v² 5f² 5fg* 5g³ 5g⁴ 5g² 5d* 5s² 1981 6d² 5s 5f² 6fg² 5fg⁴ 6f) leggy, rather lightly-made filly; a genuine and consistent filly who won twice at Phoenix Park as a 2-y-o; creditable second 3 times on same course in 1981, to Severiano in Castleknock Sprint Stakes, to Clanjolly in Stackallen Stakes and to Runnett in Matt Gallagher Sprint Stakes; also ran creditably when sixth behind subsequently-disqualified Prince Echo in Ballyogan Stakes at Leopardstown and fourth of 19 behind Naomi Joy in Philips Electrical Stakes Handicap at the Curragh; stays 6f; acts on any going. *K. Prendergast, Ireland.*   101

LADY BOUNTY 2 ch.f. Hotfoot 126–Donnarose (Fighting Don) (1981 6fg 6g² 7f³ 7g 7fg⁴ 8g⁴ 8d² 8.2s) Apr 28; lengthy, rather lightly-made filly; sister to modest 1980 2-y-o Quickthorn Lady and half-sister to several winners, including fairly useful 7f to 1m winner Summer Madness (by Silly Season) and useful 7f performer Fighting Lady (by Chebs Lad); dam of little account; in frame in maiden races and two 1m nurseries; put up best efforts in the nurseries, notably going down by ½ length to Pair-of-Deuces at Brighton in October; suited by 1m; yet to prove she acts on extremes of going. *G. Harwood.*   82

LADY CHRISTINA 3 b. or br.f. Welsh Saint 126–Forest Fortune (Fortino II 120) (1980 5.5fg 6.7g⁴ 7g² 6.7g* 10s* 1981 10v 8.2g 10.1s 7s⁴ 8g 7.6fg² 7fg 7g 7g) 3,000F, 5,000Y; tall, narrow, rather lightly-made ex-French filly; fourth foal; half-sister to Lady Pavlova (by Ballymore), a very useful performer at up to   75

14.6f; dam won twice over 1m in Ireland; decisively won minor events at Chateaubriant and Nantes as a 2-y-o; soundly beaten at Saint-Cloud and Nantes early in 1981; tended to hang but nevertheless probably ran best race over here when 2 lengths second to Paulager in handicap at Chester in July; stays 1½m well; probably acts on any going; blinkered last 4 outings in France and final start (ran respectably); didn't move well to start fourth outing; formerly trained by G. Henrot; sold 7,600 gns Newmarket December Sales. *B. Hanbury.*

LADY COX   2 b.f. Sun Prince 128–Lady Rowe 97 (Sir Ivor 135) (1981 6s 6d²) **77** Feb 12; lengthy, attractive filly; third foal; sister to very useful 1980 French 2-y-o 6.5f winner Sun Row; dam, daughter of high-class miler Lucyrowe, won over 6f and 7f; third favourite, confirmed promise of debut when being caught close home and beaten a neck by Dev in 25-runner maiden race at Doncaster in October; will stay 1m; sure to gain compensation in similar company in 1982. *B. Hills.*

LADY CYNARA   3 b.f. Starch Reduced 112–Golden Perch 79 (Sovereign Lord — 120) (1980 5fg 5f 5.8h 6fg 7g 6f 1981 11.7h) small filly; no worthwhile form, including in sellers; has been tried in blinkers. *W. Turner.*

LADY EN DOUCE   2 gr.f. Ballynockan 112–Clare Blue 83 (Blue Streak 106) — (1981 5d) Apr 3; second reported foal; sister to 1980 2-y-o 5f winner Babas Bally; dam won over 5.8f; unquoted and apprentice ridden when last of 8 to Arctic Runner in maiden race at Lingfield in August. *Peter Taylor.*

LADY EVER-SO-SURE   3 ch.f. Malicious–Time of Hope 98 (Matador 131) **66** (1980 5g 5f 5fg 6g* 6d⁴ 6d* 7g² 7s² 7f⁴ 1981 8g 8d 7.2s² 8fg 7fg 10f² 9g² 9f 12f⁴ 12.2g 11g* 12d³) strong, compact filly; fair plater on her day; bought in 1,150 gns after beating Faridella ¾-length at Redcar in September; stays 1½m; acts on any going; wears blinkers. *J. Etherington.*

LADY GREENE   3 br.f. No Mercy 126–Sea Tycoon 80 (Tycoon II) (1980 6fg — 1981 7fg 8g 7v 8.5g 8.3fg 8g) useful sort; soundly beaten in maiden and minor events and handicaps. *A. Pitt.*

LADY JASMINE   3 gr.f. Sun Prince 128–Jasminia 92 (Zeddaan 130) (1980 **64** 6g³ 1981 7g 8d 7.6d⁴ 7f³ 8fg² 7g) strong, good-bodied filly; in frame in maiden races at Chester (blinkered) and Leicester and in minor event at Newmarket; will probably be suited by middle distances; sold 2,200 gns Newmarket December Sales. *R. Hern.*

LADY JENDEAN   2 b.f. Owen Dudley 121–Jendean 68 (Florescence 120) **49** (1981 7g 6f 6f) May 8; 400Y; third foal; dam placed over 5f at 2 yrs; poor plater; sold 310 gns Ascot November Sales. *M. Blanshard.*

LADY JUSTICE   3 ch.f. Status Seeker–Alldyke (Klondyke Bill 125) (1980 — NR 1981 8g) 800F, 3,000Y; sister to a winner in Italy, and half-sister to a winner there; dam closely related to Italian 1,000 Guineas winner Alea II; unquoted when running-on 3½ lengths fifth of 18 behind Same Date in maiden race at Thirsk in May; not seen out again. *R. Boss.*

LADY KAMINA   2 gr.f. Dragonara Palace 115–Miss Carvin (Carvin 127) (1981 — 6g 6fg 7g) Apr 30; workmanlike filly; first foal; dam, half-sister to very useful All Hope, ran 4 times unplaced; little worthwhile form in maiden and minor events. *D. Kent.*

LADY KNIPHOFIA   2 b.f. Sparkler 130–Flora Day 92 (Floribunda 136) (1981 — 5d) Jan 14; 5,400Y; robust, good sort; fifth foal; dam stayed 1m; unquoted and backward when ninth of 15 in maiden race won by Mumruffin at Sandown in June, only outing. *P. Makin.*

LADY LEVLEE   2 br.f. Tarboosh–Soft Drink (Gala Performance) (1981 **58** 5s 5d 5.1fg² 5.1f² 6g) Mar 6; IR 740F, 1,750Y; fair sort; fifth produce; dam ran once; second in sellers at Yarmouth in August; should be suited by 6f+; blinkered fifth outing; sold 1,400 gns Doncaster September Sales. *C. Spares.*

LADY LILY   2 ch.f. Quiet Fling 124–Tambresi 89 (Tamerlane 128) (1981 — 5fg 6f 7fg⁴) May 13; 5,800F, 2,400Y; light-framed filly; fifth foal; half-sister to plating-class 9f and 11f winner Tamingo (by Never Say Die) and to a 2-y-o winner in Belgium; dam won at 7f and 1m; soundly beaten in maiden auction events and a 4-runner minor race. *R. Hollinshead.*

LADY LOAFER (USA)   3 ch.f. Jacinto–The Loafer (Hail To All) (1980 NR — 1981 7d 6g 8f 7fg) $20,000Y; smallish, lightly-made filly; first foal; dam won twice over 6f from 35 starts in USA, and is half-sister to smart 1975 2-y-o Play Boy, successful at up to 1m; seventh in a 17-runner claiming race and a quite valuable seller at Brighton on last 2 starts; sold 860 gns Newmarket July Sales. *R. Simpson.*

LADY LORELEI 3 b.f. Derring-Do 131–Friendly Sound 82 (Be Friendly 130) **105**
(1980 5s² 5g* 6s* 6s⁴ 1981 8s 7d³ 7f 8fg* 7fg* 8f 8g² 8s⁴) neat filly; first foal;
dam won three 7f races; put up useful performances when winning handicaps
at Kempton in July and Newbury in August, on latter course quickening in
good style after being held up and holding on a shade cleverly by ½ length
from Dancing Sally; ran on gamely and finished clear of remainder when ¾-
length second of 5 to Motavato in £3,800 event at Newmarket in September;
didn't have much room when fourth of 6 behind Slaney Maid in Marlborough
House Stakes at Ascot in October; stays 1m; probably acts on any going. *B. Hobbs.*

LADY LORENZA 4 b.f. Lorenzaccio 130–Lady Lowndes 97 (Tamerlane 128) —
(1980 8.3s 9d 8.3g 1981 8g 10.2d) bad plater. *M. Bradley.*

LADY LORRAINE 2 gr.f. Three Legs 128–Happy Evening 89 (Hethersett 134) —
(1981 7fg 8fg 7g) June 1; 1R 1,700F; sturdy filly; half-sister to a winner in
Hong Kong; dam stayed 1½m; behind in maiden races; pulled up first start. *W. Wharton.*

LADY LUAN 2 ch.f. Hot Spark 126–Disa 55 (Dike) (1981 5g 5g 5f) May —
29; 3,000Y; small, short-backed filly; third foal; dam of little account; well
beaten in maiden races at Thirsk, Edinburgh and Wolverhampton; sold 380 gns
Doncaster August Sales. *A. Balding.*

LADY MALA 3 b.f. So Blessed 130–Mala Mala (Crepello 136) (1980 5d 1981 —
8f 5fg) good-topped filly; behind in maiden and minor events. *H. Candy.*

LADY MANETTE 3 ch.f. Manado 130–Suemette (Danseur 134) (1980 NR **64**
1981 7g 10fg 10d³ 12f⁴ 12.3g 10.4d 8fg 15.5s) 19,000Y; rangy filly; half-sister
to 2 Irish winners, including very useful 5f to 1m winner Salette (by Sallust),
and to winners in Belgium and France; dam never ran; in frame in maiden
races at Brighton in May and June; probably stays 1½m; blinkered sixth and
seventh outings; trained most of season by H. Wragg; sold 10,500 gns Newmarket
December Sales. *K. Bailey.*

LADY MANTEGNA 4 b.f. Andrea Mantegna–Grand Central 79 (Grand Roi **62**
118) (1980 11f³ 11.1f⁴ 16f 12d 12d 10.1f 11.7h 12s⁴ 1981 16s* 16fg³) leggy
filly; staying handicapper; trotted up at Nottingham in April; seems to act on
any going but goes well on soft. *R. Laing.*

LADY MENELAUS 3 b.f. Brigadier Gerard 144–Helen of Troy 83 (Grey —
Sovereign 128§) (1980 6g 6fg 1981 7g 7g 12fg 12g) lengthy, fair sort; poor
maiden; blinkered final start; sold 1,050 gns Newmarket December Sales. *P. Makin.*

LADY MURFAX 2 b. or br.f. Ercolano 118–Golden Storm 95 (Golden Cloud) —
(1981 5s 5g 7f 6f) May 28; 1,200F; useful sort; good mover; half-sister to
several winners, including very useful 7f to 1m performer Apple King (by Birdbrook); dam sprinter; unquoted when behind in maiden races. *W. Wightman.*

LADY OF CORNWALL (USA) 3 b.f. Cornish Prince–Molly Ballantine **85**
(Pretense) (1980 NR 1981 8g 7d³ 8g⁴ 10.4fg* 10fg² 10.2g³ 10d* 10g* 10.2g)
strong filly; second foal; dam very smart stakes winner at up to 1m at 2 yrs;
successful in 4-runner maiden race at Chester in July and handicaps at Brighton
and Newmarket in October; led 2f out and ran on strongly to beat Cool Decision
1½ lengths in last-named (apprentices); was suited by 1¼m; didn't race on
extremes of going; stud. *B. Hills.*

LADY OF RENOWN (USA) 2 b.f. His Majesty–Fair Renown (Stage Door **73** p
Johnny) (1981 7g) lightly-made filly; second foal; dam lightly-raced half-
sister to top-class middle-distance colt Little Current; 20/1, chased leaders for
5f and wasn't given a hard time once she started to weaken when 6½ lengths
eighth of 22 to Rocamadour in maiden race at Newmarket in October; bred to
stay middle distances; will be difficult to beat in a run-of-the-mill maiden race
in the North. *J. W. Watts.*

LADY OF SALTASH 3 b.f. High Award 119–Shady 101 (Royal Palm 131) —
(1980 NR 1981 7f) half-sister to very smart 7f and 1m winner Green Girl
(by Petingo); dam won from 6f to 1m; 20/1 when last of 8 behind Seven Seas in
maiden race at Chepstow in July. *C. Williams.*

LADY OSBORNE 3 b.f. Royal Palace 131–Empress of England (Constable 119) —
(1980 9d 1981 12fg 12s 15.5s) rangy filly; in rear in varied company. *G. Balding.*

LADY ROMOHA 4 b.f. Sit In The Corner–Forthcoming 69 (New Brig 120) —
(1980 12.2f 10fg 10d 10f 13.8fg 13.8d 1981 11d 12s) lightly-made filly; poor
plater. *S. Wiles.*

LADY SAXON 2 b.f. Track Spare 125–Il Regalo (Meadow Mint 120) (1981 5s — 7g) May 12; first foal; dam placed over 1m and 1¼m; 33/1 when in rear in maiden races at Folkestone and Newmarket in October. *R. Simpson.*

LADYSHIP 2 b.f. Windjammer (USA)–Just A Dutchess (Knightly Manner) **60** (1981 6g 6fg 6fg 8d 6d) Mar 19; IR 20,000Y; strong, compact filly; closely related to a winner in Norway by On Your Mark and half-sister to very smart sprinter Miami Springs (by Northfields); dam won 7 races at up to 1m; in mid-division in maiden and minor events. *F. Durr.*

LADY SISTER 4 gr.f. Saritamer 130–Soft Chinook (Hitting Away) (1980 7f **67** 6fg* 8fg4 6fg4 6fg 6f4 7g 7d* 6d 1981 7fg 7f2 6f 7f 7g 7fg 6g) sparely-made filly; stays 7f; probably acts on any going; blinkered final start; suitable mount for a boy; sold 2,100 gns Newmarket December Sales. *I. Walker.*

LADY STITTENHAM 2 b.f. Lucky Wednesday 124–Mrs Pankhurst 78 **49** (Reform 132) (1981 5s 5g* 6f 6f) Mar 30; unfurnished filly; poor mover; third foal; dam won over 1¼m; 20/1 and apprentice ridden, stayed on well to score by a length from Arras Girl in 8-runner seller at Stockton in April (retained 580 gns); last in similar events at Stockton and Ripon in June; should be suited by 6f+; possibly needs some give in the ground; sold 520 gns Doncaster August Sales. *M. W. Easterby.*

LADYSWOOD 4 b.f. Great Nephew 126–Expo 80 (Sheshoon 132) (1980 8.2s — 8.2fg 8fg3 7f 8d 8s2 8g3 11.7f 10.6d 12g 11.7h 10fg4 9f 10fg 1981 16g 16g 16s 16.1s 13s) small, lengthy filly; poor plater; often blinkered. *K. Bridgwater.*

LADY TILBURY 2 b.f. African Sky 124–High Gloss (Super Sam 124) (1981 **49** 5v4 5g 5fg 5f 6fg 6f4 7f 5s) Jan 23; IR 3,100Y; lightly-made filly; half-sister to 2 winners, including Irish 5f to 1m winner High Hollow (by Wolver Hollow); dam poor Irish maiden; only poor form, including in sellers last 3 starts, blinkered last 2 outings. *K. Stone.*

LADY TYCOON 2 br.f. No Mercy 126–Sea Tycoon 80 (Tycoon II) (1981 7g) — May 14; half-sister to fairly useful 6f winner Davenport Boy (by Workboy); dam stayed 1¼m; 25/1 when behind in 29-runner maiden race won by Chalon at Newmarket in October. *G. Harwood.*

LADY WESTLEIGH 3 b.f. St Paddy 133–Beetroot 89 (Psidium 130) (1980 — 5d3 5fg 6fg 7d* 7g 7d 1981 12fg 8.5fg 10s) rather lightly-made filly; won maiden race at Brighton at 2 yrs; well beaten in 1981; should be suited by middle distances; possibly needs an easy surface; inconsistent; sold out of R. Smyth's stable 5,000 gns Newmarket July Sales after second outing. *P. Cole.*

LADY WIMPY 3 ch.f. Mansingh 120–High Society 96 (So Blessed 130) (1980 — 5f 1981 8s 6fg 8g) leggy, unfurnished filly; well behind in maiden races and sellers; trained first 2 starts by R. Hannon. *K. Stone.*

LA FEDHALA 3 ch.f. Swing Easy 126–Gay Amanda 75 (Counsel 118) (1980 5f **58** 6g* 6s2 6d4 1981 5fd4 6v3 7f) leggy, light-framed filly; good mover; plater; probably stays 7f; acts on heavy going; sold 1,600 gns Ascot 2nd June Sales. *N. Gaselee.*

LAFONTAINE (USA) 4 b.c. Sham–Valva (Vandale) (1980 8.2g* 8d 10g **94** 10fg3 10fg 10.5f 8s 8g 1981 8d3 8.5d 8d 10fg* 10.2g 10d 10f* 12f2 10g* 12f2 10.5g 14d 10f3 12fg2 12g 9g 12g 12v3 10g 12g*) big, strong colt; fairly useful handicapper; won at Epsom in April (beat One Fleet Street by a neck in City and Suburban Handicap), Yarmouth and Salisbury in June and Doncaster in November; made all to beat On Show 1½ lengths in William Hill November Handicap on last-named; stays 1½m; acts on any going but is very well suited by top-of-the-ground; blinkered third start; possibly needs strong handling and appears suited by forcing tactics; tough and genuine. *C. Brittain.*

LA GAVINA 2 b.f. Sagaro 133–Private Collection 70 (Whistling Wind 123) — (1981 8d) Apr 7; fourth foal; dam stayed 1m; 33/1 when behind in 18-runner maiden race at Leicester in November won by Sugar and Mint. *W. Wightman.*

LA GLINETTE 3 ch.f. Hot Spark 126–Scarlet Woman (Red God 128§) — (1980 5fg 1981 7g 7.2f 6g) fair sort; well beaten including in a claiming race on final start (blinkered, finished last); sold 410 gns Doncaster September Sales. *J. Winter.*

L'AIDA 2 b.f. Import 127–Sunset Song 87 (Song 132) (1981 5fg 5f 5g 5f 5g 5g 5s) — Mar 28; 1,150Y; sturdy filly; bad plater; has worn blinkers and bandages. *J. Doyle.*

William Hill November Handicap, Doncaster—Lafontaine makes all the running to win from fast-finishing On Show. The 1980 winner Path of Peace (centre) is third

LAKENHEATH (USA) 3 ch.c. Northfields–Cheveley Princess 120 (Busted 134) **88**
(1980 NR 1981 12g 12g 12d³ 11.5f* 11d 12g) quite an attractive colt; second foal; dam very smart winner from 7f to 1¼m; blinkered for only time when getting better of Northern Supremo by a short head after ding-dong battle in 14-runner maiden race at Yarmouth in June; off course 4 months afterwards; will probably stay beyond 1½m; probably acts on any going. *H. Wragg.*

LA MANGA 2 ch.f. Sallust 134–Ana de Mendoza (Royal Challenger 129) **—**
(1981 5fg 7h 8s) Mar 3; IR 9,800Y; shapely filly; half-sister to several winners, including useful 1977 Irish 2-y-o 6f winner Don Mendoza (by Lord Gayle); dam placed in Ireland; in rear in maiden races; blinkered third outing; sold 1,050 gns Doncaster November Sales. *G. Hunter.*

LA MASCOTTE 3 b.f. Hotfoot 126–Calling High 88 (Mountain Call 125) **72**
(1980 5f 6f 1981 8.5fg 8.5d* 10g⁴ 8fg 10.1fg) lengthy, quite attractive filly; attracted no bid after beating Ta Morgan ¾ length in seller at Epsom in June; didn't reproduce that form in non-sellers; stays 1m well; acts on a soft surface; blinkered last 2 starts; trained until after fourth start by J. Sutcliffe. *J. Benstead.*

LAMBAY 3 ch.f. Lorenzaccio 130–Treasure Island 80 (Whistling Wind 123) **69**
(1980 5.3d 5g 7fg³ 8g² 7d* 7d⁴ 1981 7fg 8g² 8f 8.2d 8d 10s⁴) close-coupled filly; ran best race of year when second in handicap at Thirsk in May; stays 1m; best form with some give in the ground; trained until after second start by B. Hobbs. *E. Incisa.*

LAMBWATH FLYER 2 b.c. Red Alert 127–Powder Box (Faberge II 121) **—**
(1981 10d) Apr 28; IR 3,000F; closely related to fairly useful 1m to 1½m winner Peppery (by Red God) and half-brother to a winner; dam Irish stayer; 16/1 when behind in 16-runner seller won by Bhaibundi Chewunja at Pontefract in October. *A. Smith.*

LAMLASH 2 gr.c. Habat 127–Iona 92 (Kalydon 122) (1981 6fg 6fg 6fg⁴ 6g **87**
6fg² 7g² 7.6g) Jan 21; 5,200Y; strong colt; good walker; second foal; half-brother to 3-y-o middle-distance winner Mills High (by High Top); dam won twice over 1¾m; prominent in 2 good-class maiden races prior to finishing second in nurseries at Newmarket in August (went down by 1½ lengths to Barooq) and Goodwood in September (beaten ¾ length by Time Charter); possibly better suited by 6f than 7f; has the ability to win an ordinary maiden event. *C. Brittain.*

Grand Prix d'Evry—Lancastrian is a very game winner from Perrault and Kelbomec

LANARKLAND 5 gr.g. Ragstone 128–Kinharvie 63 (Abernant 142) (1980 **83**
NR 1081 10.6s 10.2fg² 9fg 12f³ 12f 12fg 10.2g 8d) tall gelding; fair handicapper; best form at 1¼m; acts on any going but goes particularly well on a
firm surface; ran moderately in blinkers final start. *R. Baker.*

LANA'S SECRET 5 br.m. Most Secret 119–Rosemarkie 75 (Goldhill 125) **65**
(1980 6h 5fg 5fg⁴ 5s³ 5g 5g⁴ 5fg* 5d 5f 5d² 5d 5s 6f 6g⁴ 6fg³ 5d 6d 6s 5v 1981
6d 5d³ 6d 5g 6d) useful-looking mare; sprint handicapper; stays 6f; acts on
any going; often wears blinkers. *G. Lockerbie.*

LANCASHIRE MAID 2 b.f. Goldhill 125–Summer Camp (Varano) (1981 **—**
5d) Apr 20; 400Y; first foal; dam of little account; 10/1, wasn't knocked
about when 10 lengths fifth of 10 to Golden Wilkie in seller at Ripon in May.
M. H. Easterby.

LANCASTRIAN 4 b.c. Reform 132–Rosalie II 66 (Molvedo 137) (1980 10.5d³ **124**
12.5g* 12g* 12.5d⁴ 12.5g* 14.6g 12s² 1981 12fg* 12s* 12f³ 12.5g³ 12g² 12d 12v)
big, strong colt; has a round action; very smart performer; won Prix d'Hedouville at Longchamp in April (beat En Calcat by ¾ length) and Grand Prix d'Evry
in May (battled on gamely to beat Perrault a short head with Kelbomec ¾ length
away third); ran creditably afterwards to be third in Hardwicke Stakes at Royal
Ascot (behind Pelerin) and Grand Prix de Saint-Cloud (behind Akarad) and 2
lengths second to very easy winner Detroit (who rec 8 lb) in 4-runner Prix Foy
at Longchamp; not entirely disgraced when twelfth of 24 to Gold River in Prix
de l'Arc de Triomphe at Longchamp again on sixth start; stays 1½m well; acts
on any going but seems suited by some give in the ground; genuine and consistent.
D. Smaga, France.

LANCE OF ST GEORGE 2 b. or br.c. Warpath 113–Step Softly 81 (St Chad **—**
120) (1981 5f 6f) May 17; 1,900 2-y-o; neat colt; first reported dam;
dam 2-y-o 5f winner; in rear in maiden races at Wolverhampton in June and Haydock
in July. *J. Townson.*

LANDRESSE (FR) 3 ch.f. Go Marching–La Bate (Frontin 122) (1980 7v 10s² **117**
1981 10.5v* 10.5s³ 10.5s² 10.5g³ 10s² 12d² 12g 10.5v³ 10f) third foal; half-
sister to French middle-distance winner Ecault (by Beaugency) and Belgian
winner Seringa (by Matahawk); dam was placed on flat and won over jumps;
won maiden race at Saint-Cloud in March; ran consistently well in pattern races
afterwards and ran placed in Prix Penelope and Prix Cleopatre on same course,
Prix de Royaumont at Chantilly (about a length third to Snow Day), Prix de
Malleret at Longchamp (½-length second to Leandra), Prix de Minerve at Evry
and Prix de Flore at Saint-Cloud again; behind in Yellow Ribbon Stakes at
Santa Anita in November; stays 1½m; acts on heavy going. *H. d'Aillieres,*
France.

LAND WITHOUT STARS 2 b.f. African Sky 124–Jerusalem (Palestine 133) **83**
(1981 5f 6fg³ 6f 6f* 7.3s) Apr 3; IR 6,800Y; neat, attractive filly; half-sister to

468

several winners here and abroad, including fairly useful 1974 2-y-o 5f winner Paul Alison (by Whistling Wind); dam never ran; came from behind to win 14-runner maiden race at Navan in September by 4 lengths from Summer Kiss, best effort; remote sixth of 8 to Last Feather in £6,300 event at Newbury the following month; stays 6f. *A. Redmond, Ireland.*

LANGBAR 3 b.c. Mummy's Pet 125–Grove Hall 66 (Hook Money 124) (1980 —
NR 1981 7g 8.2s 12g) 34,000Y; big, strong colt; half-brother to numerous winners, including smart stayer Hazard (by Sheshoon) and useful miler Hornton Grange (by Hornbeam), herself dam of Swiss Maid; dam won over 1m; behind in minor events at Newmarket and Haydock and in maiden race at Edinburgh in first half of season. *J. Hindley.*

L'ANGELO DI CARLO 2 ch.f. Record Token 128–Emanuela (Lorenzaccio 130) —
(1981 5f 5g 6g) Mar 29; 1,450Y; sturdy filly; second foal; dam twice-raced half-sister to smart French middle-distance stayer El Mina; soundly beaten in auction event at Thirsk in August (needed race) and minor race at Redcar in September; unseated rider leaving stalls when blinkered at Chester in between. *C. Crossley.*

LANGLEY COURT 2 gr.g. Saritamer 130–Marypark 93 (Charlottown 127) **75**
(1981 6g 7d⁴ 7fg 7.6g 8d) May 18; 2,400Y; strong gelding; good walker; half-brother to Norwegian St Leger winner Coulstry (by High Top) and fairly useful stayer Halba (by Habat); dam well suited by long distances; about 5½ lengths fourth of 14 to Loyal Toast in minor event at Lingfield in August; well beaten subsequently, including in nurseries; should stay 1m. *D. Morley.*

LANTIC BAY (USA) 2 b. or br.c. Cornish Prince–Nit Flit (Tom Fool) (1981 **82**
6g³ 7.6s²) May 1; $70,000Y; closely related to high-class 1974 American 2-y-o Ramahorn (by Dewan) and half-brother to 3 winners; dam ran only 3 times; had best well beaten off when 3¾ lengths third of 19 to Zinzara in newcomers race at Goodwood in September; 5/4 favourite for 15-runner maiden race at Lingfield the following month but went down by 2½ lengths to Cordite Spear; will stay 1m. *P. Walwyn.*

LANWADES JENNY 5 b. or br.m. Impecunious–Jenny Junior (Doubtless —
II 111) (1980 NR 1981 15.5f 15.5fg) sixth foal; half-sister to a winning chaser; dam poor hurdler; tailed off in 2 maiden races at Folkestone in August. *H. Sawyer.*

LANWADES JUNIOR 4 b.f. Impecunious–Jenny Junior (Doubtless II 111) —
(1980 NR 1981 9d) seventh foal; half-sister to a winning chaser; dam poor hurdler; tailed off in minor event at Hamilton in September. *H. Sawyer.*

LA PICCOLINA 5 b.m. Tudor Rhythm 112–The Guzzler 69 (Behistoun 131) **61**
(1980 12.2s* 14fg 11.7fg 14g 12.2s³ 12fg 11.7d³ 11.7f 12fg² 12g⁴ 12.2d* 12d 11d*
12d 1981 12.2d² 12.2fg 11s 10.8fg⁴ 13.3g 10.2g 10s³ 12.2s⁴ 11s) small mare; appears not to stay beyond 1½m; acts on any going but seems suited by some give in the ground nowadays; often apprentice ridden; genuine. *P. M. Taylor.*

LA PIROUETTE (USA) 2 ch.f. Kennedy Road–Nedancer (Nearctic) (1981 **73**
5fg 6f² 6fg 6d² 6d) Apr 11; $57,000Y; big, rangy filly; half-sister to 3 winners, including useful 1979 French 2-y-o 7f winner Nebene (by Never Bend); dam unraced granddaughter of Champion filly Parlo; sire high-class winner from 5.5f to 1¼m; second in minor event at Ripon in August and maiden race at Nottingham in September, giving odds-on Dewanadance a good fight before going down by a length in latter; will be suited by 1m; best run on a soft surface; hung and found little off bridle final start. *D. Morley.*

LA POMPADOUR (USA) 3 b.f. Vaguely Noble 140–Good Position (Bold **113**
Ruler) (1980 NR 1981 10g* 10.5s 10s* 10s³ 10f3 10f³ 9.2d) second foal; dam unraced sister to stakes winner Bold and Brave; won newcomers race at Longchamp in April and minor event on same course the following month; third subsequently in 3 fillies' pattern races, namely Prix de Malleret at Longchamp in July (beaten 2½ lengths by Leandra), and Prix de Psyche (2½ lengths behind Sangue) and Prix de la Nonette (promoted after finishing fourth to Leandra) at Deauville in August; suited by 1¼m; acts on any going. *J. Fellows, France.*

LARA'S SONG (USA) 3 b.f. Russian Bank 110–Sweet Seventeen (County **69**
Delight) (1980 NR 1981 11s 12d³ 14fg⁴ 14.6fg* 14g 16.5f* 16s⁴) big, strong filly; sister to winning stayer Cheka, and half-sister to 2 winners in USA; dam never ran; successful in maiden race at Doncaster in July and handicap at Redcar in September, beating Super Spartan a shade comfortably in a slowly-

run race on latter course; short of pace and is suited by a test of stamina; probably acts on any going, but clearly goes well on firm; had stiff task fifth outing. *I. Balding.*

LA REID 3 b. or ro.f. Rarity 129–La Garoupe 87 (Pirate King 129) (1980 NR   —
1981 8d 10d 12g) 6,000F, 12,000Y; half-sister to 2 winners, including useful stayer Chokwaro (by Allangrange); dam stayed 2m; well beaten in minor event at Warwick and maiden races at Brighton and Lingfield in first half of year; sold 1,400 gns Newmarket Autumn Sales. *J. Benstead.*

LARLA 2 b.f. He Loves Me 120–Croque Madame 107 (Crocket 130) (1981 6f 6d   **78**
6g) Apr 2; 200,000 francs Y (approx £20,000); lengthy filly; good mover; fourth foal; half-sister to 3 winners, including very useful French 7.7f and 1¼m winner Ministrel (by Owen Dudley); dam very useful at up to 7f; showed ability all outings, on final start finishing 4¾ lengths sixth of 21 to Not For Show in maiden race at Newmarket in October; will stay 7f. *J. Hindley.*

LARRYR 6 b.g. Capistrano 120–Hill Time (Hill Gail) (1980 NR   1981 12.5s   —
15.8g) poor performer nowadays; stays 1¼m; seems to act on any going; has worn blinkers and bandages. *J. Doyle.*

LARULLAH 6 b.m. Lorenzaccio 130–Gamerullah 85 (Grey Sovereign 128§)   —
(1980 NR   1981 13.8fg) small mare; has shown no sign of ability. *D. Wintle.*

LA SEINE 3 b.f. Blue Cashmere 129–Snap (Snob 130) (1980 6fg 5g 7g 7g   —
6f⁴ 6f   1981 7s 7d 7d 6f 7g 10.1g 8fg 10d 12d 12.2g) workmanlike filly; disappointing maiden; probably stays 7f; blinkered fourth and fifth starts; has worn bandages behind. *S. Matthews.*

LASER LADY 7 b.m. Laser Light 118–Miss Nesta (Conspirator 114) (1980   **83**
6fg 6fg 6d 6g 6f 6d* 7g 6d   1981 7.2fg 7d 7g 6t 6g 6s⁴ 7s³ 0d) fair handicapper on her day; suited by 7f; acts on any going; blinkered twice at 2 yrs; good mount for an apprentice. *W. Haigh.*

LASICION 2 b.c. Laxton 105–Asicion 89 (Above Suspicion 127) (1981 5d   —
6s 6fg⁴ 6f 6d 8f) Mar 5; tall colt; brother to winning sprinter Moor House and half-brother to Maysus (by Maystreak), 3 times a winner over 5f at 2 yrs in 1977; dam won over 5f and 6f at 2 yrs; soundly beaten in varied company. *M. H. Easterby.*

LASKA FLOKO 5 b.h. Thatch 136–Prima 75 (Alcide 136) (1980 7d 10.6fg*   **88**
10fg 10fg* 10.2fg 10fg 10f 12f³ 12g³ 12s 10.5g 12f 1cfg⁴ 14g 12g⁴ 13.3fg⁴ 12s 10g 12v   1981 12fg 10g 12d⁴ 10fg* 10.2g 12g 10.2g 10g) strong, heavy-topped, good sort; useful handicapper on his day; beat Bitte Schon by ¾ length going away at Newmarket (apprentices) in August; probably stays 1¾m; seems to act on any going except very soft; often wears blinkers; suitable mount for an apprentice; inconsistent. *C. Brittain.*

LAST ACT 3 b.f. Gala Performance–Gweedore (Prince Hansel 118) (1980 NR   —
1981 11g 9d 12s 9g 8.5f³ 8.5f² 8s 9s) first foal; dam, Irish 1¼m winner, also won over hurdles; placed in 2 handicaps at Galway in July; stays 1m well; trained by W. Fennin in Ireland until after sixth start. *B. McMahon.*

LAST BUS 6 b.g. Tycoon II–Cloudy Day (Nimbus 130) (1980 6fg 7d 7g⁴   —
8.3g 7g 8fg 7f³ 8f   1981 6s 6g 7.6fg 7f 8d) plater; stays 1m; acts on firm going; has been tried in blinkers; has run well for a boy. *G. Lewis.*

LAST DEVICE 4 b.g. Grey Mirage 128–Gorgeous Device 88 (Falls of Clyde 126)   **56**
(1980 6fg 10.4f 7.2g 7.6g 7f² 7.2d* 7.6d 7g 7d   1981 8g³ 7.6g 8g 7.6fg³ 8f² 8fg² 8f 8f 8.2fg 8f) compact gelding; stays 1m; probably acts on any going; suitable mount for an apprentice; sometimes blinkered. *C. Crossley.*

LAST FANDANGO 4 ch.c. Gay Fandango 132–Welsh Game (Pall Mall 132)   **118**
(1980 8s 7f* 8.5f* 8f² 8d³ 10g   1981 7.2s* 8fg² 10fg 8fg 8fg⁴) lengthy, attractive ex-English colt; very smart performer at his best; won maiden race at Newmarket and Blue Riband Trial at Epsom and finished excellent short-head second to Nikoli in Airlie/Coolmore Irish 2,000 Guineas at the Curragh in 1980; not quite so good at 4 yrs, gaining his only success when making all to beat Milk of the Barley by a short head in John of Gaunt Stakes at Haydock in June; good neck second to Belmont Bay in Queen Anne Stakes at Royal Ascot and wasn't entirely disgraced on final start when 6 lengths fourth to To-Agori-Mou in Waterford Crystal Mile at Goodwood in August; seemed not to stay 1¼m; acted on any going but went well on firm; standing at Castle Hyde Stud at IR £3,000 with 1st October concession. *V. O'Brien, Ireland.*

470

LAST FEATHER (USA) 2 b.f. Vaguely Noble 140–Quill (Princequillo) **111**
(1981 7fg⁴ 7g² 7.3s*)

Few mares have had so long or so spectacular a career as Last Feather's dam Quill. Born back in 1956 she became the champion juvenile filly in the USA, winning six of her eight starts from five and a half to eight and a half furlongs; at three she won two important races, the Acorn Stakes over a mile and the Mother Goose Stakes over nine furlongs, before finishing a close second in the CCA Oaks; and at four she was rated the second-best older filly after winning the valuable Delaware Handicap over a mile and a quarter by nine lengths. After failing to add to her Stakes victories at five she retired the winner of fourteen of her twenty-six starts which, together with four seconds and two thirds, earned 382,041 dollars. Her stud career proved similarly outstanding. Her foal of 1963, First Feather, became the dam of Run The Gantlet, successful in the Washington International and the sire in 1981 of those top winners April Run, Ardross and Providential; her foal of 1966, the champion Canadian grass horse One For All, won thirteen times at up to two miles and has sired one of the handful of mares to win over 1,000,000 dollars, The Very One; her 1970 foal, Shill, bred a champion two-year-old colt in Japan; next came Riboquill, a smart performer in France who finished sixth in the 1974 Prix de l'Arc de Triomphe; then came the 1975 Irish St Leger winner Caucasus who subsequently became one of the best grass performers in the USA. After producing eight foals in ten years Quill's age and exertions finally seemed to be catching up with her—she produced only two foals, both unraced fillies, in the next six seasons—but her final produce, the appropriately-named Last Feather, looks likely to improve Quill's highly impressive record by becoming one of the leading middle-distance fillies in 1982.

Quill's achievement in producing such a good filly at the age of twenty-three is amazing. Of the 1,056 horses listed in that useful reference book *Pedigrees of Leading Winners 1960-1980* only Aggravate, Arctic Storm, Batitu, Chamour, Fighting Charlie, Kauai King, La Bamba, Lagunette and Yellow God were foaled when their dam was aged twenty or more and of those dams only Chamour's was as old as twenty-three. Incidentally the 1980 Oaks winner Bireme was foaled when her dam was eighteen and the 1981 winner Blue Wind was produced by a twenty-one-year-old mare, so if Last Feather improves enough to win the 1982 Oaks, which is by no means out of the question, she'll extend a sequence which will be well-nigh impossible to stretch further.

Last Feather first caught our eye when fourth, beaten less than two lengths by Clare Island, in a maiden race at Sandown in July, one of the earliest seven-furlong events of the season for two-year-olds. It wasn't so much her finishing position that impressed, rather the way she raced on the bridle nearly all the way up the straight without having room to get in a serious challenge. There seemed little doubt that Last Feather would take high rank among the two-year-old staying fillies but she then got loose at home. By the time she was ready to race again over three months later, in the newly-instituted Rockfel Stakes at Newmarket in mid-October, she had missed all three pattern races for fillies of her type. Although a 16/1-shot at Newmarket, she ran very well in a race not run to suit her; the early gallop was slow and she found herself outpaced, possibly through greenness, when the tempo increased with three furlongs to run. Once she met the rising ground it was a different story, and she stayed on very strongly to finish second of eight, two lengths behind Top Hope who was giving her 3 lb. Better was to come a week later in the Rochford Thompson Newbury Stakes at Newbury, formerly known as the Radley Stakes. Last Feather won the race in a style similar to the 1979 winner Shoot A Line, needing to be shown the whip only once to draw right away in the final furlong for a six-length victory over Tikaki.

			Aureole
Last Feather (USA) (b.f. Apr 19, 1979)	Vaguely Noble (b 1965)	Vienna (ch 1957)	Turkish Blood
		Noble Lassie (b 1956)	Nearco
			Belle Sauvage
	Quill (ch 1956)	Princequillo (b 1940)	Prince Rose
			Cosquilla
		Quick Touch (ch 1946)	Count Fleet
			Alms

There's every reason to expect Last Feather to make an excellent three-year-old. None of Quill's previous winners was successful as a two-year-old and, even though Vaguely Noble has sired some good two-year-olds, most of his stock don't reach their best until three or older; his best fillies, Dahlia and

Nobiliary, improved considerably on their juvenile form when given middle distances. Last Feather is also a fine physical specimen—an attractive, rangy filly who both walks and moves well—and her trainer is fortunate to have her and those other potentially smart fillies Current Pattie, Merlin's Charm and Slightly Dangerous to call on in 1982. *B. Hills.*

LAST LIGHT (FR) 3 b.c. Round Table–Lighted Glory 118 (Nijinsky 138) **97** (1980 7g* 1981 8fg² 12fg* 12d) 220,000Y; compact, quite attractive colt; second foal; half-brother to French 1¾m winner Lykon (by Vaguely Noble); dam smart at up to 10.5f; won maiden race at Leopardstown at 2 yrs; ran on well when 1½ lengths second to Tellurano in Coolmore Hello Gorgeous Stakes at the Curragh in June; kept on well and beat Erins Isle (gave 7 lb) by ½ length in 7-runner Group 3 Royal Whip Stakes on same course in July; sweated up and dropped out steadily in straight when over 20 lengths fifth of 6 behind Glint of Gold in Great Voltigeur Stakes at York the following month; stays 1½m; acts on a firm surface and is possibly not at his best on a soft one; sent to race in USA. *V. O'Brien, Ireland.*

LAST LOVE (FR) 3 b.f. Platonic Love–La Sagonaise (Prince Eric) (1980 **115** 7g 8g* 8f 8s 1981 10.5s* 10v³ 10.5fg 12g) strong filly; first foal; dam never ran; put up a good performance when beating Leandra by 1½ lengths in Group 3 Prix Penelope at Saint-Cloud in March; ran creditably when 2¼ lengths third to Tootens in Group 1 Prix Saint-Alary in May next time out but subsequently finished well behind in Prix de Diane and Prix Vermeille; should stay 1½m; acts on any going. *P.-L. Biancone, France.*

LATE HOUR 2 br.f. Reform 132–Midnight Melody 92 (Linacre 133) (1981 **83** 6g 7h⁴ 6d⁴ 6d*) Apr 2; 4,000Y; small filly; second foal; dam 2-y-o 5f winner; backed at long odds, finished strongly to win 22-runner maiden race at Leicester in November by 2 lengths from View Star; will stay 1m. *A. Jarvis.*

LATE MUSIC 2 br.c. Tudor Music 131–Violate (Continuation 120) (1981 **89** 5v² 6s³ 6.3fg² 6fg 7fg³ 7g³ 7g² 8d 9d* 7d⁴) lightly-made colt with a high knee action; second foal; dam never ran; gained a well-deserved success when winning 17-runner maiden race at Gowran Park in October by a length from Graziano; placed in most of his other races in Ireland, running well on sixth start when 1¾ lengths third of 10 to Longleat in Coolmore Try My Best Stakes at Leopardstown in September; outpaced throughout when 6¾ lengths last of 7 to Tender King in Richmond Stakes at Goodwood in July; stays 9f; seems to act on any going; blinkered final outing. *J. Bolger, Ireland.*

LATEST LOVE (FR) 3 b.c. Roi Dagobert 128–Love Lasting (Prince Regent **—** 129) (1980 8fg⁴ 9d 8g² 9g 1981 8fg 8g 8g³ 8g² 9d 9s) ex-French colt; second foal; dam, lightly raced, was placed over 7.5f at 2 yrs; placed twice at Compiegne in July; soundly beaten in maiden event at Wolverhampton in October, on only outing over here; will be suited by 1¼m +; formerly trained by J. Fellows. *A. Jarvis.*

LATIN LIGHT 2 b.f. Roman Warrior 132–Spanish Lantern 92 (Don Carlos) **78** (1981 5d 5g 5f² 5fg³ 6f²) Apr 11; useful sort; first foal; dam stayed well; second in maiden races at Wolverhampton in June and Brighton in August, showing improved form when running Travel Blues to ½ length in latter; better suited by 6f than 5f and will stay further; acts on firm going. *G. Lewis.*

LA TOURELLE 2 b.f. Tower Walk 130–Gallic Law 91 (Galivanter 131) (1981 **89** 5g³ 5g² 5fg² 5fg* 6fg² 6d 5g) Apr 7; strong filly; poor mover; third foal; half-sister to 1980 2-y-o 5f winner Scottish Law (by Scottish Rifle) and fairly useful sprinter Ferriby Hall (by Malicious); dam won twice over 7f at 2 yrs; came through strongly to win 7-runner maiden race at Edinburgh in July by a length from Mayo Moonlight; not disgraced in nurseries at Ayr on next 2 outings, running very well when ½-length second of 6 to Cheap Seats in August; suited by 6f; consistent. *J. W. Watts.*

LAUDERHILL 2 ch.g. Status Seeker–Purple Cuckoo (Continuation 120) (1981 **63** 6fg 7f⁴ 7fg 7f 8f 8g 8.2d 8d) Apr 24; IR 4,000Y; compact gelding; second foal; dam unraced half-sister to very useful miler Rocked and smart stayer Illa Laudo; only plating class; will probably stay 1¼m; blinkered last 2 starts. *K. Stone.*

LAUGH-A-MINUTE 2 b. or br.g. Comedy Star 121–Hat Girl (High Hat 131) **73** (1981 6fg 6fg) Mar 14; 7,200Y; compact, quite attractive gelding; half-brother to several winners here and abroad, including useful sprinter Laldheer (by Swing Easy); dam of little account; shaped well after losing a fair amount of ground at start when 11½ lengths sixth of 16 to Rosier in maiden race at Newmarket in July; 8¼ lengths seventh of 10 to Allocated in £4,500 event at Ascot 2 months later; burst out of stalls when withdrawn at York in between; will be suited by 7f + ; gelded at end of season. *P. Kelleway.*

LAUGHING LEE 2 br.f. Cawston's Clown 113–Lindylee 99 (Grey Sovereign 128§) (1981 5g) May 2; 6,200Y; lengthy, rather lightly-made, quite attractive filly; half-sister to numerous winners, including very useful miler Dalry (by Hethersett); dam useful at 2 yrs; 33/1 but reasonably straight, dwelt and showed very little when last of 12 to Hampton Bay in £3,200 race at Ascot in September, only outing. *G. Hunter.* —

LAUKING 4 ch.g. Lauso–Kingsbay (King's Leap 111) (1980 10s 10s 8fg 11.7g 12g 8.3g 8g 10g 9f 8.2v4 10d4 1981 11d3 10.1d 12s) leggy gelding; plater; stays 11f; acts on heavy going. *D. H. Jones.*

LAURA JENNEY (USA) 2 b.f. Northern Fling–Latonia Thrush (Tudor Minstrel 144) (1981 5s2 5g2 5.3f2 5fg* 5fg2 5d2 5g 5s) tall, lengthy filly; half-sister to very useful French 5f to 1m winner Soyez Brave (by Bold Bidder) and 3 winners in USA; dam won 4 times at up to 6f; sire, smart stakes-winning son of Northern Dancer, won at up to 1¼m; gained a well-deserved victory when winning 18-runner maiden race at Windsor in July by a length from Run Like Mad; beaten less than a length when second in nurseries at Windsor and Newbury in September, being outstayed close home by My Lover after heading him 100 yards out in latter; bred to stay further than 5f but runs as though she's unlikely to do so; possibly unsuited by very soft going; consistent until running poorly last 2 starts, wearing blinkers on seventh outing; exported to Barbados. *I. Balding.* 98

LAURA'S PRIDE 4 ch.g. Midsummer Night II 117–Flashlight 88 (Firestreak 125) (1980 10s4 8fg 10.1fg 8.3f 10.1s 12d 8.3f 10s 1981 12d) bad plater; has worn blinkers; sometimes sweats up. *C. Wildman.* —

LAURENCE MAC 2 gr.g. Grey Ghost 98–Mactavish 90 (St Alphage 119) (1981 6d 7f 5d) Apr 12; compact gelding; first foal; dam won over 6f and 7f at 2 yrs and also won 4 times over hurdles; in rear in maiden and minor events in the North. *T. Barron.* —

LAUREPPA 4 b.f. Jimmy Reppin 131–Lovely Laura (Lauso) (1980 8f4 10g4 12f 1981 12f 16fg* 16d2 16h 16g) tall, lengthy filly; won modest maiden race at Lingfield in July; suited by a test of stamina; acts on a firm and a soft surface; has run creditably for an amateur rider. *N. Gaselee.* 57

LAURIUM 4 b. or br.c. Prince Regent 129–Grecian Palm 78 (Royal Palm 131) (1980 6f2 6f4 6d 6g2 6d 6d 6g 8fg 7g4 6g 8f 1981 10s 8g) compact colt; not certain to stay 1m; best on a sound surface; blinkered twice in 1980; has shown signs on occasions of being none too keen; sold to W. Clay 1,700 gns Doncaster June Sales. *G. Pritchard-Gordon.* —

LAUSANNE 2 b.f. My Swanee 122–Lovely Laura (Lauso) (1981 5fg 5f 7fg 7d 7fg 6g4 7f 8s 8d) May 10; useful sort; half-sister to 1980 2-y-o 5f winner Laughing (by Comedy Star) and 2m winner Laureppa (by Jimmy Reppin); poor plater; probably stays 1m; blinkered fifth, sixth and ninth starts; sold 290 gns Ascot November Sales. *N. Gaselee.* 50

LAUTREC 3 b.c. Wolver Hollow 126–Night Vision 100 (Yellow God 129) (1980 6g 7fg* 1981 10fg3 8g 8fg4 10f 8g3 8s* 8d3) tall, good-looking colt; keen walker and good mover; beat Dr Steve with more in hand than neck margin suggests in 20-runner amateur riders event at Goodwood in September; also in frame in 4 handicaps but ran poorly on his other starts; stays 1¼m; probably acts on any going; sold 10,000 gns Newmarket Autumn Sales. *R. Price.* 81

LAVENDER DANCE 2 gr.f. Dance In Time–Sea Lavender 114 (Never Say Die 137) (1981 5.1f* 6f4 5g2 5fg2 5g* 5f2 5fg4) Feb 16; workmanlike filly; half-sister to winners in France and Belgium; dam, sister to smart miler Casabianca, won at up to 7.3f; odds on when successful in maiden race at Yarmouth in June and in £2,800 event at Windsor in August, beating To The Point cleverly by ½ length in latter; looked to be going very smoothly for much of way when in frame in between in Cherry Hinton Stakes at Newmarket (favourite when fourth of 10 to Travel On), Star Stakes at Sandown (short-headed by My Dad Tom) and St Hugh's Stakes at Newbury (1½ lengths second to On The House); went down by 2 lengths to Fearless Lad when ridden by apprentice unable to claim his 5-lb allowance in £4,000 race at Thirsk in September (favourite); fairly stoutly bred but clearly thought best at 5f; yet to race on a soft surface. *H. Cecil.* 99

LAVENDER GRAY 2 b.f. Bay Express 132–Ma Belle Amie (Never Say Die 72
137) (1981 5g 5d² 7f 6fg 6d⁴) Apr 13; second foal; dam well beaten in maiden
and minor events; only quite moderate; best run at 5f but promises to stay
further. *J Winter.*

LAVENHAM BLUE 3 b.f. Streetfighter 120–Brighton Girl 96 (Right Boy —
137) (1980 NR 1981 12s) big filly; sister to quite moderate 1979 2-y-o
Benny Lynch and 2 poor animals, and half-sister to 3 minor winners; dam
sprinter; needed race and was always behind in 20-runner maiden event won
by Arios at Redcar in October. *J. Wilson.*

LAW BIRD 2 b. or br.c. Legal Eagle 126–Altarnum (Alcide 136) (1981 5s —
5d) Mar 8; 2,800Y; small colt; in rear in maiden race at Wolverhampton in
April and seller at Warwick (blinkered) in May; sold 400 gns Doncaster October
Sales. *W. Marshall.*

LAWERS 2 ch.c. Hot Spark 126–Aspara 58 (Crimson Satan) (1981 5s 5g 69
5fg 5g² 5fg 5d) Apr 3; 17,000Y; compact colt; third foal; closely related to
3-y-o Steel Son (by Steel Heart) and half-brother to 7f winner Varuna (by
Luthier); dam placed over 5f in Ireland and England; quite moderate form
in maiden and minor events; in rear in nurseries subsequently; should stay 6f.
J. Benstead.

LAWNSWOOD MISS 3 b.f. Grey Mirage 128–Lor Darnie 65 (Dumbarnie 50
125) (1980 5g 5f 7g 8fg 9d 7d 1981 8s 10d 10fg 9g 12s* 13fg⁴ 16.9fg 12fg⁴
13.8fg 12g³) narrow filly; attracted no bid after winning selling handicap at
Wolverhampton in May, first form; ran respectably in non-sellers next and last
outings; stays 13f; probably acts on any going; suitable mount for an apprentice.
R. Hollinshead.

LAW OF THE LAND 4 b.g. Tyrant–Coralivia (Le Levanstell 122) (1980 —
10s 10.1g 1981 12.2fg) rangy, good-looking gelding; has a round action;
well beaten all 3 starts on flat. *G. Lockerbie.*

LAWTON'S MEADOW 4 ch.g. Royben 125–Ember Grill 84§ (Indigenous —
121) (1980 8d 6v² 7d 6f 6f* 6fg 6fg 6g 1981 6g 5g³ 6g 6d 7s 6fg 6fg) leggy
gelding; plater; best at sprint distances; acted on any going; sometimes blinkered;
dead. *W. Stubbs.*

LAXMO 3 ch.g. Laxton 105–Mablon 76 (Majority Blue 126) (1980 NR 1981 —
6g) strong gelding; half-brother to useful 5f performer Mayab (by Maystreak);
dam placed over 5f at 2 yrs; needed race and was always in rear when seventh
of 8 to Praetorian Guard in minor event at Thirsk in April; dead. *M. H.
Easterby.*

LAYAL 2 b.c. Blakeney 126–Queen of Twilight 107 (Off Key 121 or Twilight 84
Alley 133) (1981 7fg 7fg 7fg³ 8.2s) Mar 23; 20,000Y; quite well-made colt;
half-brother to several winners, including smart stayer Antler (by Northfields)
and 1m to 2m winner Sunset Ray (by Hotfoot); dam won at up to 1¾m, including
Jockey Club Stakes; 5¼ lengths third of 8 to Triple Axel in minor event at Epsom
in September; had stiff task under top weight in nursery at Nottingham later
in month and wasn't disgraced in finishing sixth of 18 to Dageegah; stoutly
bred and may show improvement when given a thorough test of stamina. *J.
Dunlop.*

LAZEROF 5 b.g. Averof 123–La Liz (Lauso) (1980 NR 1981 10.2s 11s —
6g 10.4s) plater; stayed 1m; appeared suited by some give in the ground;
had worn blinkers; dead. *M. James.*

LEADER OF THE PACK (FR) 5 b.h. Sharpen Up 127–Highland Rocket 81
(Paveh 126) (1980 6d 6f⁴ 6f* 5f 6f² 6fg* 6fg 6fg 6g² 6g 6g 6g 6g 6fg 6d 7s 7g 7d
8s 1981 8s 6g 6fg² 6g* 6g⁴ 6d² 6s 6g³ 6g² 6f⁴ 5fg⁴ 6f⁴ 6g 6f⁴ 6fg⁴ 6g 6f 6f⁴ 6g
6d) good sort; fair handicapper; successful at Thirsk in April; twice ran very
well behind King of Spain on same course afterwards, going down by short
head in £4,900 event and by 2 lengths in Thirsk Sprint Trophy; best at 6f;
acted on any going; needed to be held up; sold 4,000 gns Newmarket Autumn
Sales and is standing at Blakeley Stud, Shropshire. *R. Hollinshead.*

LEAH 3 b.f. Hittite Glory 125–Hannah O'Donoghue 95 (Jimmy Reppin 131) 100
(1980 NR 1981 7d 8d* 10g³ 8s³) 23,000Y; well-made, good sort; second
foal; half-sister to Irish Display (by Daring Display), a useful winner at up to
7f; dam won 3 times at up to 6f at 2 yrs in England and showed form at up to
1¼m at 3 yrs in Ireland; 33/1 but looking very fit and well when beating Pipina
by 1½ lengths in £4,400 event at Ascot in April, getting up inside last furlong

and staying on really well; third twice the following month, behind Strigida in Sir Charles Clore Memorial Stakes at Newbury and behind impressive winner Nasseem in UBM Merchants International Fillies Stakes at Kempton, keeping on gamely both times; will probably stay 1½m; sent to South Africa. *I. Balding.*

LEANDRA (FR) 3 b.f. Luthier 126–Ady Endre (Reliance II 137) (1980 **125**
6g* 7g 7.5g* 1981 8v⁴ 10.5s² 10.5s³ 10.5g² 10s* 10f² 12g² 12d 10f)
Leandra was beaten six times in eight races in France as a three-year-old, but it is very doubtful whether there was a better filly of her age in that country over middle distances apart from April Run. She finished ninth of twenty-four in the Prix de l'Arc de Triomphe, almost level with Tootens whom she had beaten comfortably when second to April Run in the Prix Vermeille. Before that Leandra had won two fillies' pattern races in succession, the Prix de Malleret at Longchamp and the Prix de la Nonette, which used to be run at Longchamp, at Deauville.
Leandra, though twice a winner from three starts as a two-year-old, took time to reveal her true merit and after defeats in a couple of classic trials in the spring she missed the French Oaks in favour of the Prix de Royaumont on French Derby day. She had done creditably in those trials—second to Last´Love in the Prix Penelope and third to April Run in the Prix Cleopatre—and did well in the Royaumont, going down by only a head to Snow Day. A month later Leandra had Snow Day back in fourth place in the Malleret; ridden from behind with fine judgement by Saint-Martin she got up near the finish of a slowly-run race to beat Landresse half a length. Snow Day was clearly below her best on this occasion and she ran much better against Leandra in the Prix de la Nonette, for which the Alec Head-trained Premiere Danseuse started favourite in front of Leandra. The moderate early pace resulting in a sprint finish must have delighted Leandra's connections; at any rate Leandra, this time ridden by Lequeux, once again pounced late on and emerged a narrow winner from Snow Day. Doubly unfortunate for Snow Day, she carried only 8-10 whereas as a Group 3 winner (she had won the Prix Fille de l'Air) she should have carried 8-12; disqualification inevitably followed, leaving second place for Premiere Danseuse. As a Group 2 winner Leandra had carried 9-0.
The pattern of French racing has seen a few changes in the last year or two, mostly revisions in running dates. The Prix Vermeille has been brought forward slightly, and with it the Prix de la Nonette´whose conditions are designed to attract the top fillies returning in preparation for the big middle-distance races of the autumn. In order to put on the Nonette earlier the race has been switched to the final stages of the long Deauville meeting, for Longchamp doesn't reopen after the summer break until September. The first winner of the newly-sited Nonette was Detroit, who went on to finish third in the Vermeille before winning the Arc. Leandra put up a splendid performance in the Vermeille, producing a good run in the straight to pass all except April Run, moving into second place inside the final furlong; she was beaten only a length and a half and accounted for some good animals, including Madam Gay. Snow Day, who finished fifth hampered by a slipping saddle, took her on again in the Arc and finished tenth, a short neck behind, just in front of Kings Lake. Leandra made ground in the straight once again but this time found the opposition too strong; still, she was beaten only about ten lengths. Subsequently Leandra was flown to California to race for Whittingham's stable. She began encouragingly enough in the Yellow Ribbon Stakes at Santa Anita, without managing a place behind the Whittingham-trained, enormously-improved ex-English mare Queen To Conquer.
Leandra's sire Luthier died during the year, a sad loss to a French blood-stock industry which is badly off for good-class stallions at present. Luthier had only once been out of the top four sires of flat winners in France in the

Prix de Malleret, Longchamp—Leandra wins this Group 2 pattern race from Landresse

preceding six seasons and had been number-one in 1976, the year Riverqueen won the Poule d'Essai des Pouliches, the Prix Saint-Alary and the Grand Prix de Saint-Cloud. Leandra's dam Ady Endre never ran. She was sold as a three-year-old for 24,000 francs at the Deauville November Sales and resold for 105,000 francs at the same venue as an eight-year-old. Leandra is her only winner. The next dam Marmara won the Prix Chloe and finished second in the Prix de Royaumont; she was a useful racemare and also a useful broodmare, producing six winners. The third dam Matina raced in Germany, one of ten winners of her dam.

Leandra (Fr) (b.f. 1978)	Luthier (br 1965)	Klairon (b 1952)	Clarion III Kalmia
		Flute Enchantee (b 1950)	Cranach Montagnana
	Ady Endre (b 1971)	Reliance II (b 1962)	Tantieme Relance III
		Marmara (b 1959)	Masetto Matina

Luthier ran his best race when winning the Prix Jacques le Marois over a mile; he stayed eleven furlongs but not, apparently, a mile and a half in the best company. Plenty of his major winners have stayed the trip, and Leandra certainly stays it well. She is a fine middle-distance filly with an excellent turn of foot, well suited by waiting tactics whether racing at a mile and a half or a mile and a quarter. She very clearly acts on any type of ground and is most consistent. *P. Pelat, France.*

LEAP BRIDGE 3 b.c, King's Leap 111–The Tower (High Treason 126) (1980 **43** 6g 6g 7f 6s⁴ 1981 5g 6d 6fg 7g² /s /g) small colt; plater; stays 7f. *Miss L. Siddall.*

LEAP LIVELY (USA) 3 ch.f. Nijinsky 138–Quilloquick (Graustark) (1980 **115** 6f 7g 8g* 8fg* 1981 8.5fg 12g* 12g³ 12f 10g 12g² 12g)
The field that Leap Lively beat in the Johnnie Walker Oaks Trial at Lingfield in May didn't look a particularly strong one beforehand; none of the contestants had won a race in the current season and only Exclusively Raised, a smart two-year-old of 1980 but by no means certain to stay a mile and a half, looked a serious challenger. Subsequent events show it to have been a disappointing field: of the seven runners only Condessa won afterwards, and she certainly didn't show the form at Lingfield that enabled her to win two pattern races at York. Nevertheless Leap Lively, stripping much fitter than when only fifth in the Princess Elizabeth Stakes at Epsom fifteen days earlier, put up a fairly impressive display: making all the running, she was pushed clear three furlongs out and won unchallenged. She had more in hand than her three-length margin over Allegretta, though not quite so much as some observers thought. On the strength of this victory and her smart two-year-old form which included a clear-cut win in the Hoover Fillies Mile at Ascot, Leap Lively started joint-favourite for the Oaks.

Leap Lively (USA) (ch.f. 1978)	Nijinsky (b 1967)	Northern Dancer (b 1961)	Nearctic Natalma
		Flaming Page (b 1959)	Bull Page Flaring Top
	Quilloquick (ch 1969)	Graustark (ch 1963)	Ribot Flower Bowl
		Quillobelle (b 1961)	Princequillo Bellesoeur

In the Oaks Leap Lively finished a tired third behind Blue Wind and Madam Gay after setting a furious pace for a long way—possibly too fast a pace for her own good. Judging by her modest performance in the Lancashire Oaks next time the race took a lot out of her, but she looked nearer her old self in finishing fifth in the Nassau Stakes at Goodwood, and then she came within a neck of a Group 1 success in the Yorkshire Oaks. A particularly game and gritty performance this was in the Yorkshire Oaks, for she battled her way to the front after losing her place when Silken Knot fell, and was thwarted only in the last strides by Condessa's storming run. On her final outing, in the Prix Vermeille at Longchamp, Leap Lively could finish only eighth of ten behind April Run; she wouldn't have been in the first three in that hot race at her best.

476

Johnnie Walker Oaks Trial, Lingfield—Leap Lively leads all the way and is never seriously challenged

Leap Lively should make a valuable broodmare. She is the best of the four winners bred by the minor one-mile winner Quilloquick, the latest being the two-year-old filly Whatabelle (by Honest Pleasure), a winner over six furlongs on her debut at Del Mar in August. Quilloquick comes from a very successful American family: her half-brother Fifth Marine was one of the better three-year-olds of 1976, when his three stakes successes included the nine-furlong American Derby, and her grandam Bellesoeur has proved a very influential broodmare. Bellesoeur's sons included two stakes-winning stayers and the successful stallion Beau Gar, while she is found in the bottom line of the pedigrees of such high-class colts as Hawaiian Sound, Belle's Gold and Mr Leader, the last-named a highly successful stallion in the States. Leap Lively, a grand, big filly, stayed a mile and a half; she raced only on a sound surface. *I. Balding.*

LEATHERSTOCKING 5 ch.g. Levanter 121–Forest Love (Super Sam 124) (1980 NR 1981 12.5s 12g 12d) big gelding; beaten some way in maiden and minor races in the North. *T. Gillam.* —

LEBANONS PRIDE 6 b.g. Windjammer (USA)–Etoile Freda (Florescence 120) (1980 NR 1981 10.1fg 13.4fg 11.7f 7.6s 5s) poor maiden; sold 510 gns Ascot November Sales. *M. Eckley.* —

LE BEAU 3 b.c. Hot Spark 126–La Meme 90 (Pall Mall 132) (1980 7fg 1981 8d 10d⁴ 12d² 12g⁴ 14fg³ 16.9fg*) quite well-made, useful-looking colt; not seen out after beating Olympic Victory a short head in 15-runner maiden race at Wolverhampton in July; suited by a test of stamina; acts on a firm and a soft surface. *P. Cole.* **70**

LE BOURSE 3 b.g. Native Bazaar 122–French Bond (Prince de Galles 125) (1980 5g 6g 1981 8d) smallish, lengthy gelding; soundly beaten, including in sellers; blinkered only outing of 1981. *A. Pitt.* —

LE CHAMP TALOT (FR) 5 b.g. Our Mirage 123–Instantanee (Road House II) (1980 11fg 12.3f 12d 12d 13s 1981 13s 12g 16d 12g) compact gelding; —

inconsistent handicapper; stays 1½m; acts on any going; sold 1,400 gns Ascot July Sales. *R. Hollinshead.*

LE DEBAUCHERY (USA) 2 b.c. King's Bishop–La Cleavage (The Axe **83** 115) (1981 5d 5.8d 7fg* 7fg 7.6g 8g² 8g) Apr 3; $14,000F, $25,000Y; small, quite well-made colt; good mover; first produce; dam won 3 times at up to 1m; wore down stable-companion Nunsruler to win 9-runner maiden race at Brighton in July by 3 lengths; good second to Swift Wing in nursery at Bath in September; will stay 1¼m; form only on a sound surface; inconsistent. *P. Cole.*

LEEKMORE 2 b.c. Welsh Saint 126–Carnmore (Breakspear II) (1981 5d **72** 5fg 6g 5fg³ 5fg 5d 5s 5g³ 5g) May 14; 1,700Y; rather a lightly-made colt; half-brother to a winner here and in Barbados by Jukebox; dam never ran; third in maiden races at Windsor in June and Catterick in October; should stay 6f; probably acts on any going; usually blinkered. *S. Matthews.*

LEE PARK 3 b.c. Impecunious–Urschi (Fort Coulonge) (1980 6s 1981 — 16g) lightly raced and seems of little account. *A. Davison.*

LEFRAK LADY 4 b.f. Starch Reduced 112–Misty Morn 70 (Worden II 129) — (1980 9.6h 8.3s 7g 6fg 6g 6g 1981 8.3s 7fg) bad plater; has been tried in blinkers. *A. Davison.*

LEGAL BEAU 2 ch.c. Legal Tender 94–Sunny Belle (Windsor Sun 116) (1981 — 5fg 6g 6g) Apr 5; compact colt; half-brother to 1m seller winner Captain Cheeko (by Military), and a winning hurdler; dam won selling hurdle; in rear in maiden and minor events; blinkered second outing. *P. Allingham.*

LEGAL EXPERTISE 2 ch.f. Royal and Regal–Firdosa (Relic) (1981 7f **91** 7d* 7d⁴) Mar 28; IR 5,000Y; second reported living produce; half-sister to a winner in Italy, dam closely related to high-class milers Buisson Ardent and Venture VII; won maiden race at Down Royal in September by 3 lengths from Hare Path; not disgraced when 5 lengths fourth of 18 to More Heather in Group 3 Park Stakes at the Curragh the following month; will probably stay 1¼m. *J. Bolger, Ireland.*

LEGAL GAMBOL 3 ch.g. Double-U-Jay 120–Absuleno 78 (Above Suspicion **73** 127) (1980 7f⁴ 7fg 10s 1981 10s* 12g 16f² 16.9fg³) quite attractive, lengthy, lightly-made gelding; won maiden event at Nottingham in April by a short head from Sigir; had stiffish tasks afterwards, best efforts when placed in minor event at Chepstow in June (head second to Halsbury) and handicap at Wolverhampton in July; suited by 2m; acts on any going; sold 3,600 gns Newmarket Autumn Sales. *B. Hills.*

LEGAL LAIRD 7 ch.h. Murrayfield 119–Legal Mistress (Counsel 118) (1980 **48** 10.6fg 8d³ 9g* 10g² 8f 10g 8g 10g 10g 1981 8g 10s* 10g 10f 8g) poor handi-capper; won at Goodwood (apprentices) in May; stays 1½m; suited by some give in the ground; wears blinkers; good mount for an inexperienced rider; sometimes starts slowly. *S. Woodman.*

LEGENDRY KNIGHT 3 br.g. Mansingh 120–Lindy Ann (King's Leap 111) **46** (1980 5fg 5fg 5d 5f 8d 8.2s 8d 1981 8.2s 6fg⁴ 6d³ 6g⁴ 5fg 6f 5f 6fg 6g 6g) compact gelding; plater; ran well in non-sellers on occasions; stays 1m; ran poorly in blinkers final start; sold 560 gns Ascot October Sales. *M. Blanshard.*

LEG GLANCE 2 br.f. Home Guard 129–Boundary 90 (Ballymoss 136) (1981 **87** p 6d² 7g*) Mar 1; IR 14,500Y; fair sort; half-sister to Irish 1½m and 1¾m winner Wee Robin (by Le Levanstell) and a winner in Spain; dam won over 1m; favourite, made all and never looked in any danger when beating Walking Beside You by 2 lengths in 18-runner maiden race at Doncaster in October; creditable length second to Strath of Orchy in minor event at Pontefract earlier in month; will be suited by 1m; a useful filly in the making. *W. Hastings-Bass.*

LEGIOUS 5 ch.g. Malicious–Leganter 79 (Galivanter 131) (1980 12f³ 12f⁴ — 12.3g 12g² 16.1d³ 12f³ 12fg³ 1981 12g² 12g 10g 12s* 11v 12h³ 12g) lengthy gelding; useful at his best; raced in Sweden first 6 starts in 1981, winning at Taby in August; last in handicap at Newmarket in October; possibly doesn't stay 2m; acts on any going; sometimes sweats up; often makes running; changed hands 8,000 gns Doncaster March Sales. *B. Bjorkman, Sweden.*

LEGLESS 2 b.g. Three Legs 128–Raglin (Ragusa 137) (1981 5f 6g 7fg 7f — 8d) Apr 24; 4,400Y; well-grown gelding; half-brother to 2 winners, including 1980 2-y-o 5f winner Donatella (by Arch Sculptor); poor plater; should stay 1m; sold to German International BA 420 gns Newmarket Autumn Sales and reportedly has been exported to Austria. *P. Rohan.*

LE GRAN BRUN (USA) 3 b.g. Our Native–Summary Procedure (Court 71
Martial) (1980 NR 1981 11s 10s 11.5f⁴ 12g 10d² 10fg 10f² 10f* 10g² 10d³)
$18,500F; strong, attractive gelding; half-brother to 2 winners, including minor
Irish 9f winner Supreme Punishment (by King of the Tudors); dam won small
11f race in France; beat Crackaway by a neck in maiden race at Ripon in
September; in frame on several other occasions; stays 11.5f; acts on any going,
except possibly very soft; moved badly to start on first outing. *L. Cumani.*

LEGS AND THINGS 2 gr.f. Three Legs 128–Deirdre (Vimy 132) (1981 92
6v⁴ 5d² 5f 6g* 7d 6g*) Apr 20; 4,600Y; half-sister to numerous winners,
including smart sprinter Royal Captive (by High Treason) and very useful
stayers Melody Rock (by Sayajirao) and Lawrence T (by Tamerlane); dam Irish
2m winner; successful in maiden race at Navan in September and minor event
at Punchestown in October, winning latter by a length from Wolver Maid
(gave 7 lb); not disgraced in between, finishing 6½ lengths eighth of 18 to More
Heather in Group 3 Park Stakes at the Curragh in October; will probably stay
1m; ran badly only outing on firm ground. *N. Meade, Ireland.*

LEGS OF MAN 2 ch.c. Hotfoot 126–Colony 93 (Constable 119) (1981 5f² 70
5f⁴ 6g 7s* 6d 7s) Feb 24; 8,400Y; sturdy colt; has a round action; half-brother
to several winners, including useful French sprint winner Porto (by Klairon);
dam 2-y-o 5f winner; looked to have stiff task when apprentice ridden at 4-lb
overweight in £4,400 nursery at Chester in August but got up to win by a head
from Fair Mount Lad; didn't reproduce that form in 2 more nurseries; needs
7f; evidently best on soft going. *Denys Smith.*

LEIOTRICHOUS 2 b.c. Nonoalco 131–Helmsdale 107 (Habitat 134) (1981 —
6d 8s 8g 6g) Mar 11; 5,200Y; poor walker and mover; half-brother to French
9f winner and 10.5f claiming race winner Straw Hat (by Thatch); dam, closely related
to Derby second Cavo Doro, won over 6f and 7f; soundly beaten in maiden
races at Newmarket (3) and York. *C. Brittain.*

LEISURE GIRL 2 b.f. Native Bazaar 122–Westerlands Prism (Primera 131) 52
(1981 5d 5g 6f³ 5f 5fg 5fg³ 8s) Mar 21; leggy, close-coupled filly; half-sister
to 2 winning platers; 3½ lengths third at Windsor in June and August;
suited by 6f but isn't sure to stay 1m; blinkered fourth outing. *G. Kindersley.*

LEITH GLEAM 3 b.f. Shiny Tenth 120–Jane Escart (Escart III) (1980 —
5g⁴ 5f 6g² 7.2g 7fg 1981 6fg 6fg 8f 8fg 7d) lengthy non-thoroughbred filly;
plater; should be suited by 7f; sometimes blinkered; sold 450 gns Ascot October
Sales. *M. Francis.*

LEITH HILL FLYER 5 b.g. Averof 123–Barlow Fold 99 (Monet 127) (1980 —
NR 1981 12d) slow maiden. *A. Pitt.*

LEITH SPRING 2 b.f. Silly Season 127–Jane Escart (Escart III) (1981 6s 6s 76
6s) Apr 1; rather lightly-made filly; half-sister to 6f winner Leith Lady (by
Joshua); dam poor NH performer; with leaders to distance when 12 lengths sixth
of 11 to Slightly Dangerous in Duke of Edinburgh Stakes at Ascot in October,
second outing and easily best effort; bred to stay 1m. *M. Francis.*

LEIXLIP (USA) 2 gr.f. Drone–Blue Law (Tom Rolfe) (1981 5d² 5g* 5fg³ 87
5d 5d 7s³ 7g) Apr 4; well-made, short-legged filly; second foal; dam unraced
daughter of very smart 1962 American 3-y-o filly Firm Policy; got home by
a neck from unlucky-in-running Falaka when favourite in 19-runner maiden
race at Newbury in June; third subsequently in St Hugh's Stakes at Newbury
in August and 14-runner nursery at Ascot in October, running creditably when
beaten 6 lengths by Be My Native in latter; suited by 7f nowadays; probably
acts on any going but put up best effort in the mud. *J. Tree.*

LELEPO (HUN) 5 b.g. Tacitus 124–Libretto (Imi) (1981 8h) Hungarian- —
bred gelding; has won in Hungary; behind in apprentice race at Bath in August,
first outing in this country. *K. Brassey.*

LE LEVADOR 2 br.c. Levanter 121–Adored (Aggressor 130) (1981 6g) —
May 1; workmanlike colt; second foal; dam showed no worthwhile form;
unquoted and never better than mid-division when seventh of 13 to Lively
Rhythm in maiden event at Salisbury in June. *M. Blanshard.*

LE MAMAMOUCHI (FR) 3 b.c. Tennyson 124–Adele Toumignon (Zeddaan 117
130) (1980 8fg 1981 10v 12fg 12s* 12v 15fg* 15s⁴ 15f) first foal; dam,
half-sister to Preis von Europa winner Acacio D'Aguilar, won over 9f; successful
in handicap at Longchamp in May and 12-runner final 3 Prix Berteux at
Chantilly the following month, in latter beating Choiseul by 5 lengths; subsequently ran creditably when 5 lengths fourth of 11 to Glint of Gold in Group 1

Grand Prix de Paris at Longchamp in July and 6½ lengths sixth of 11 behind Tipperary Fixer in Group 2 Prix Kergorlay at Deauville in August; stays 15f; seems to act on any going. *G. Bridgland, France.*

LEMON GREY 5 gr.g. Dragonara Palace 115–Enlighten (Twilight Alley 133) (1980 NR 1981 8.2f) plating-class maiden; was tried in blinkers; dead. *H. Fleming.* —

LENYGON 6 b.g. Le Levanstell 122–Nanette 100 (Worden II 129) (1980 14f 14f⁴ 12d* 16.1d* 13d² 12g³ 10.6s 14s 1981 18s 8g 12v 12v 18g) fair handicapper at his best; soundly beaten in 1981; one paced and stays well; acts on a firm surface but has done all his winning on a soft one; suitable mount for an inexperienced rider; trained by G. Fletcher first start. *P. Rohan.* —

LEODEGRANCE (USA) 5 b.g. King's Bishop–Reasonably (Hail to Reason) (1980 11.7fg 13.3g 16fg² 16g 12g 16g 14g⁴ 18d 1981 12g 14fg² 14fg* 12s) well-made gelding; made all to win handicap at Salisbury in September; stays 1¾m; ideally suited by firm ground; blinkered once at 3 yrs; trained by G. Balding first start. *D. Elsworth.* **67**

LEONIDAS (USA) 3 ch.c. Exclusive Native–Double Think (Double Jay) (1980 NR 1981 8g 8d 10.ifg 10f 10d* 9f² 10d 10g 10.8s) $100,000Y; workmanlike colt; half-brother to winners by Northern Dancer and Prince John; dam, unplaced 8 times, is half-sister to Cheveley Park winner Gentle Thoughts and Middle Park winner Junius; held up when beating Le Gran Brun by a neck in maiden race at Pontefract in August, first form; didn't battle on quite so well as winner when length second to Fast Trick in minor event at Wolverhampton later in month; stays 1¼m; acts on any going, except possibly very soft; sweated up seventh start; often races with his tongue tied down. *F. J. Houghton.* **72**

LEOPARD BEACH 3 b.c. Wollow 132–Ambuscade 77 (Relko 136) (1980 NR 1981 10d 14fg 18g) 8,800Y; plain colt; half-brother to a winner in Italy and to 1m winner Hornet's Nest (by Realm); dam, winner over 1½m, is half-sister to Smuggler; soundly beaten in maiden and minor races, probably best effort on second start (eighth of 17). *E. Eldin.* —

LEOPARD'S ROCK 7 b.g. Huntercombe 133–Reina Cristina 84 (Tamerlane 128) (1980 10f 12h* 11.1fg⁴ 12d 11.7d 12fg⁴ 12g³ 12fg⁴ 10f⁴ 10fg 10g 1981 12g 12f² 12fg³ 10f 11.7d 10fg³ 10fg⁴ 10g³ 10d) middle-distance handicapper; acts on any going but goes extremely well on top-of-the-ground; suitable mount for an inexperienced rider; not particularly consistent nowadays. *J. Dunlop.* **68**

LE PRETENDANT 7 b.h. Prince de Galles 125–Reine d'Etat 53 (High Hat 131) (1980 NR 1981 13s 15.8g⁴ 17.1g) poor performer; stays 2m; acts on a soft surface and is probably not at his best on very firm going; has worn blinkers; suitable mount for an amateur rider. *D. Hanley.* **41**

LERAZMA 8 b.g. Levanter 121–Razamataz (After Midnight 119) (1980 NR 1981 11g) probably no longer of any account. *W. Barratt.* —

LERINA 2 b.f. Oats 126–Coole Park (Wolver Hollow 126) (1981 5.1f² 5f 5fg) May 15; 5,000Y; small, lightly-made filly; second foal; dam lightly-raced half-sister to smart fillies French Score and Ballet Francais; showed good speed in 12-runner maiden races in June, finishing 6 lengths second to Lavender Dance at Yarmouth but fading steadily from halfway when 8 lengths sixth behind Northern Scene at Wolverhampton next time out; needs further; lacks scope. *B. Hanbury.* **62**

LES DANCER 2 b.c. Northern Flash–Aracara (Prince Tenderfoot 126) (1981 5fg 5d⁴ 5d³ 6g 6fg 7fg 6f 7fg 7.6s 5s 8g) Apr 11; 1,100Y; sturdy colt; second foal; dam placed at up to 1½m in Ireland; in frame in maiden races at Folkestone and Brighton in May but is no better than a plater; stays 7f. *D. Jermy.* **60**

LESLEY ANN 7 b.m. Menelek 114–Royal Rally (Royal Record II) (1980 NR 1981 12s) ex-Irish mare; won bumpers race at Limerick in 1979; has since shown herself a good chaser; tailed off in minor event at Lingfield in October; stays well. *D. Elsworth.* —

LE SOLEIL 7 ch.h. Roi Soleil 125–Mayo Blues 73 (Abernant 142) (1980 10s 12fg² 12fg³ 12f 12g 12g⁴ 12fg⁴ 12fg² 12g² 13.3fg³ 12fg⁴ 14s⁴ 12v 1981 12s⁴ 12fg* 12g³ 12v* 12g 12f³ 12f 12fg 12g² 12fg 12v² 12g) modest handicapper; won at Kempton in April (£6,400 event from Rionore) and Goodwood in May; best at distances short of 1¾m; acts on any going; has been tried in blinkers; good mount for an inexperienced rider. *R. Price.* **81**

LETHE 3 b.f. Birdbrook 110–Enchanted 116 (Song 132) (1980 5d 6s 6d 1981 7f² 7g 7f² 8fg 8fg³ 8g) rangy filly; placed in maiden and minor races in the **69**

summer; possibly best at up to 7f; seems well suited by firm going; sold 13,000 gns Newmarket Autumn Sales. *H. T. Jones.*

LETITGO 5 ch.g. Shoolerville 121–Omnia Opera 83 (Major Portion 129) (1980 9g 8f³ 12d 10s⁴ 10d 1981 8s⁴ 11g 10.1d 12s) plater nowadays; probably stays 1¼m; acts on any going; has been tried in blinkers. *P. Felgate.* **81**

LE TOUQUET 2 b.c. Town Crier 119–Stella Roma (Le Levanstell 122) (1981 5v 6f 6g) Apr 4; 1,200Y, 750Y; leggy colt; brother to a winner in Sweden and half-brother to a winning plater; dam ran 3 times at 2 yrs; probably of little account. *R. Hartop.* **—**

LETSGOMO 2 b.g. Royben 125–Veinarde (Derring-Do 131) (1981 5v 5d 5g³ 5fg* 6f 5fg 5.1d⁴ 6f 5g⁴ 5d) Jan 31; 1,000Y; workmanlike gelding; third foal; dam ran once; sold privately out of P. Rohan's stable after landing the odds by ¾ length from Star Cove in 9-runner seller at Beverley in June; creditable fourth of 8 in nursery at Edinburgh in September, penultimate outing; not certain to stay 6f; suited by a sound surface. *B. Richmond.* **63**

LEUCAS 2 b.c. Blue Cashmere 129–Cherubima (So Blessed 130) (1981 5f 6fg 8g) Apr 8; rangy colt; first foal; dam never ran; behind in varied company, including selling. *A. Dalton.* **—**

LEVEN VALLEY 3 b. or br.f. Ragstone 128–Scottish Lullaby 92 (Aberdeen 109) (1980 NR 1981 10.1d 12fg 12f⁴ 10s) 1,600Y; third foal; half-sister to a winning plater by Gold Rod; dam won at up to 7f; well beaten in maiden races and a seller. *D. Gandolfo.* **—**

LEVOTESSE 3 b.f. Levmoss 133–Kaotesse (Djakao 124) (1980 7g 6fg 7g 8fg 1981 12d 11s 11.7f 11.7fg 18.8fg 16s 16s) neat filly; has shown a little ability in varied company; should stay middle distances. *G. Balding.* **—**

LEWESTON 5 b.g. Levmoss 133–Darrigle (Vilmoray 126) (1980 14.6fg 1981 12s 12d) lengthy gelding; poor maiden; stays well; acts on firm going; ran badly in blinkers once. *J. O'Donoghue.* **—**

LEX (FR) 4 ch.g. Tarbes 125–Toranquine (Right Royal V 135) (1980 12g³ 12g 16f² 18.1g³ 19g² 17.1d 1981 18s 15.8s⁴ 16s⁴) big gelding; staying handicapper; acts on any going; has run creditably for an amateur rider; possibly best on a galloping track. *N. Callaghan.* **66**

LEXHAM VIEW 3 gr.f. Abwah 118–King's Caress 65 (King's Coup 108) (1980 6s 6g 7fg 7g³ 7.2g 7fg 8d 1981 9g³ 9.4g 10d³ 10f 12f 10fg 12fg) leggy filly; poor maiden; behind in sellers last 2 starts; stays 1¼m; blinkered seventh outing as a 2-y-o (dwelt) and on final start. *M. Tompkins.* **51**

LIBBY JAYNE 2 ch.f. Tumble Wind–Ardrose (Pakistan II 84) (1981 5g³ 5d⁴ 5s⁴ 6f 6f³ 5.1fg² 6f 6f 6d) Apr 16; 2,200Y, 3,000Y; fair sort; fourth living foal; half-sister to a 2-y-o winner in New Zealand; dam won twice in New Zealand; in frame in maiden races, on final occasion finishing 1½ lengths second to Kiki Mouse in auction event at Yarmouth in July; best run at 6f; possibly unsuited by really soft going; well beaten last 2 starts (off course over 2 months in between). *G. Huffer.* **67 d**

LIBERATED 5 b.h. Busted 134–Parolee 88 (Sing Sing 134) (1980 8fg 7.2fg 7fg⁴ 7d 8fg 10s* 10fg³ 12fg² 12d⁴ 1981 10fg 8fg* 10f² 10g* 10d* 10.5s 12v⁴ 8.2s) rangy horse; has a high knee action; in good form in August and September and won gentleman riders race at Goodwood and handicaps at Leicester and Goodwood again; beat We'll Meet Again by ½ length for final success; stays 1½m; acts on any going; sometimes blinkered but is better without; game. *R. Baker.* **85**

LIBERTY BOY 2 b.g. Music Boy 124–Cuba Libre (Rum) (1981 6f 6fg) May 5; 2,200Y, 5,200Y; leggy, lightly-made gelding; first foal; dam ran 3 times in Ireland; ran twice in 5 days in August, finishing last in small race at Yarmouth (100/1) and behind in 20-runner maiden race at Newmarket; sold to Susan Piggott BA 540 gns Doncaster November Sales. *R. Armstrong.* **—**

LIBERTY WALK 2 b.c. Free State 125–Path Of Pride (Sovereign Path 125) (1981 7fg 7g) Mar 1; 7,400F, 13,000Y; attractive, well-made colt; very good walker; third foal; half-brother to useful 1m winner Spring with Pride (by Scottish Rifle); dam never ran; 33/1 when behind in large fields of maidens at Newmarket in August (slowly away) and October. *J. Winter.* **—**

LIBRAS SHININGSTAR (USA) 3 b.f. Gleaming–Libra 97 (Hyperion) (1980 6s 6s³ 6f 7g 8d 1981 10d 12s 11.7g 16fg³ 11.7h) small, lightly-made filly; very well bred but is only a modest performer; seems to stay well; blinkered last 2 outings. *F. J. Houghton.* **—**

LICHEN GREEN 3 b.f. Welsh Saint 126–Lichen 93 (Tyrone 130) (1980   **74**
6g³ 6f 6g² 7d³ 1981 8g² 8f* 8g⁴ 10f 8g² 8s) rather unfurnished filly; poor
mover; given a particularly good ride when beating subsequently-disqualified
Sun Blossom by a neck in maiden race at Thirsk in July; also in frame at Ayr,
Newcastle and Leicester; stays 1m (well beaten over 1¼m); acts on firm going.
J. W. Watts.

LIECHTENSTEIN 3 b.c. Sallust 134–Brilliant Gem 83 (Charlottown 127)   —
(1980 6fg 1981 7s 6g 7d) neat colt; showed only a little ability; likely to
have stayed at least 1m; dead. *C. Brittain.*

LIFE OF THE PARTY 2 ch.f. Wolverlife 115–Fun (Jukebox 120) (1981   —
6d) Apr 14; first foal; dam last on only outing; unquoted but showed speed
when out of first 10 of 25 in maiden event won by Dev at Doncaster in October.
J. Hindley.

LIFESTYLE 3 br.f. Jimmy Reppin 131–Cave Girl 67 (Pindari 124) (1980   **80**
5g 5f 6d² 6fg* 7d⁴ 8f² 8s* 1981 8s 8f² 9.4fg⁴ 9f 8g 8.2v) lightly-made filly;
ran on very well in closing stages after losing 6 lengths on bend when neck
second to Solway Winds in handicap at Ripon in June; rather disappointing
afterwards; should stay beyond 1m; acts on any going; blinkered final outing;
often races with her tongue tied down; retained 1,600 gns Newmarket Autumn
Sales. *J. W. Watts.*

LIFT HIGH 2 gr.c. Town Crier 119–Make A Turn (Turn-to) (1981 5s³ 6d)   **74**
Mar 6; 8,400F, 10,500Y; strong, lengthy, useful-looking colt; half-brother to
French 3-y-o Touche d'Or (by Toujours Pret) and 2 minor winners; dam unraced sister to high-class Captain's Gig; 14/1 and ridden by apprentice unable
to claim his 5-lb allowance, ran on well to finish 5¾ lengths third of 9 to Cannon
Shell in minor event at York in October; well beaten in 25-runner maiden
event won by Dev at Doncaster later in month; should stay 6f+. *J. W. Watts.*

LIGHT AND SHADE 2 ch.f. High Line 125–White Light (Amber Light
114) (1981 6fg 5g³ 7g 8s) May 21; fair sort; fifth foal; dam unraced sister to
out-and-out stayer Amberwood; 6½ lengths third of 7 to Bolivar Baby in weakly-
contested maiden race at Wolverhampton in September, easily best effort;
should be suited by a test of stamina. *D. Nicholson.*

LIGHT CAVALRY 4 b.c. Brigadier Gerard 144–Glass Slipper 100 (Relko 136) **124**
(1980 12.3f³ 12f* 12g* 12fg³ 12g² 14.6g* 1981 12s 12f² 12f* 12fg)
    Despite the widely-held view to the contrary, it is nothing new for a large
proportion of top three-year-olds to be retired at the end of their second season,
though the trend towards the premature retirement of good horses may be
increasing. So far as one very important group of three-year-olds is concerned,
an analysis of all the colts that have won English classics since 1920 reveals
no drastic variation from decade to decade in their number running at four,
with there being never less than eleven or more than fourteen. Certainly, to
have three classic-winning colts racing the following season would have been
no more common an event forty years ago than it was in 1981, when Henbit,
Known Fact and Light Cavalry all ran.
    Sadly, Light Cavalry was the only one of the three to show good form, and
even he had his ups and downs in a brief campaign which saw his running solely
over a mile and a half, a trip arguably short of his best. He could hardly have
made a worse start. Favourite for the John Porter Stakes at Newbury in
April, where he looked magnificent, Light Cavalry dropped out of contention
in the last three furlongs and was eased right up, finishing a distant seventh to
Pelerin and beating only his pacemaker Sacrilege and Shoot A Line, who was
all but pulled up. It transpired that he had injured himself, returning with an
enlarged hock and a slightly damaged tendon, and in the days following the race
Cecil was far from hopeful about Light Cavalry's chances of running again.
Fortunately the injuries responded to treatment and two months after Newbury
Light Cavalry went to post for the Hardwicke Stakes at Royal Ascot. He
ran a fine race, setting a strong gallop, having all except one of his opponents
in trouble over two furlongs out and keeping on well once headed by Pelerin
at the distance to go down by three lengths to the latter, with Lancastrian
five lengths back in third.
    Light Cavalry was evidently returning to form, and in the Princess of
Wales's Stakes at Newmarket three weeks later he put up a performance not
far below his best of 1980. Meeting all his seven rivals on unfavourable terms,
Light Cavalry was sent on at a good pace from the start. He lost the lead
to Royal Fountain three furlongs from home, regained it over a furlong out
and then had to face attacks from Castle Keep, who had been switched, and

Mr H. J. Joel's "Light Cavalry"

Centurius. It looked all up with Light Cavalry one hundred yards out as both challengers headed him, but with Piggott riding a fine finish and his mount answering every call in most courageous fashion the race was snatched out of the fire in the dying strides, Light Cavalry winning by a neck and the same from Castle Keep and Centurius. It was obvious that a mile and a half was the minimum trip for Light Cavalry now, and any chance he had of winning the King George VI and Queen Elizabeth Diamond Stakes at Ascot later in July depended upon there being a strong gallop to nullify the pace of his best opponents. With no acknowledged pacemaker in the field, Light Cavalry again went off in front, but the pace was a modest one and it came as no surprise to see him swamped in the straight; he eventually finished last to Shergar. Light Cavalry wore bandages in the pre-parade ring at Ascot. Due to a recurrence of tendon trouble it had been touch and go throughout the preceding week whether he would be able to take part. He didn't run again and in September came the news that he had been sold to stand at Crescent Farm, Kentucky, in 1982 at a fee of 12,500 dollars live foal. His syndication value was nearly two and a half million dollars.

Light Cavalry (b.c. 1977)	Brigadier Gerard (b 1968)	Queen's Hussar (b 1960)	March Past
			Jojo
		La Paiva (ch 1956)	Prince Chevalier
			Brazen Molly
	Glass Slipper (br 1969)	Relko (b 1960)	Tanerko
			Relance III
		Crystal Palace (b 1956)	Solar Slipper
			Queen of Light

Glass Slipper, Light Cavalry's dam, has made an outstanding start at stud. Her first foal, Crystal Coach (by Exbury) was a fairly useful stayer; her second was Light Cavalry; and her third, Fairy Footsteps (by Mill Reef), won the 1981 One Thousand Guineas. Glass Slipper, who stayed well but managed to finish second in the mile-and-a-quarter Musidora Stakes, comes from a good family, being a half-sister to Royal Palace, Prince Consort and Selhurst out of the very smart seven- to ten-furlong performer Crystal Palace. Light Cavalry, a big, rangy colt who carried plenty of condition, showed when

winning the St Leger that he was suited by a mile and three quarters. He
acted well on firm going and was most genuine. *H. Cecil.*

LIGHT HERE 3 ch.c. Touch Paper 113–Belle Josephine (Beau Sabreur 125) **100**
(1980 5v* 5g² 5f* 6d 6s 5d⁴ 7g² 7g* 5g 6.3s³ 7g³ 8s 1981 8d² 7g² 7s⁴ 8s)
lengthy, attractive colt; won at Phoenix Park, Naas and Leopardstown (Mullion
Stakes) as a 2-y-o; ran creditably when 2¼ lengths third to subsequently-
disqualified Wolver Heights in Minstrel Stakes at Leopardstown, head second
to Cooliney Prince (gave 3 lb) in Group 3 McCairns Trial Stakes at Phoenix Park
and 2¼ lengths fourth to Dance Bid in Group 3 Tetrarch Stakes at the Curragh,
all in April; not seen out after finishing seventh of 13 behind Kings Lake in
Airlie/Coolmore Irish 2,000 Guineas at the Curragh in May; stays 1m; acts on
any going; blinkered sixth and seventh outings in 1980; genuine and consistent.
L. Browne, Ireland.

LIGHTNING BOY 3 b.g. Condorcet–Never So Late (Never Say Die 137) —
(1980 5fg³ 6f 7g⁴ 7d³ 6g 7fg³ 7fg 8.2d³ 1981 8.2d 8g 8f 10fg) lightly-made
gelding; plater; will stay 1½m; best form on an easy surface; usually wears
blinkers (ran respectably without on third start); sometimes sweats up. *P.
Kelleway.*

LIGHTNING LABEL 5 br.h. African Sky 124–Soie Sauvage (Shantung 132) **113**
(1980 9f 7fg⁴ 7.2f⁴ 5f 5fg³ 6fg² 6g 7g 6d 5fg 5.3g² 5g⁴ 8g* 5s* 6v* 1981 6g²)
leggy, rather lightly-made horse; smart performer; spent much of 1981 in
USA but didn't run there and was having first outing for 12 months when good
short-head second to Great Eastern in £5,000 race at Doncaster in November;
best at sprint distances though stays 1m; probably acts on any going but has
done all his winning on easy ground; blinkered 3 times in 1980. *P. Kelleway.*

LIGHT SENTENCE 3 bl.g. No Mercy 126–Injudicious 78 (Quorum 126) —
(1980 5.8fg 5.3d 7g 7s 1981 10s 6g) neat gelding; showed a little ability at 2 yrs;
stays 7f; sold 1,650 gns Ascot June Sales. *R. Price.*

LIKEABLE FELLA 4 br.c. Amber Rama 133–Pristina 84 (Petition 130) —
(1980 6d 8v 7fg 8fg 7.6d 7g 8f 7g 8d 1981 7g 8g 7f 7f 10f 7g 10s 8s 8.2s 10s)
strong colt; poor walker and mover; bad plater; has worn blinkers; sold 360 gns
Doncaster November Sales. *B. Richmond.*

LIKI LIKI (USA) 5 b. or br.m. Turn to Mars–Polyandry (Marino) (1980 **113**
10.5g³ 12g 10d* 9.7d 1981 9d⁴ 10.5d 10.5d² 10v³ 10.5g 10.5d 10f³ 10f 10f
9fg* 10.5d* 10g* 9f) French mare; in fine form in the autumn, winning apprentice race and 55,000 francs event at Evry and valuable Grand Prix de Marseille;
beat Green Fire by 5 lengths in last-named; had run well on third start when
nose second to Daeltown in Prix Corrida at Saint-Cloud; best at around 1¼m;
seems to act on any going; tough and genuine; sent to USA. *J. C. Cunningham,
France.*

LILAC LADY 5 b. or br.m. Fair Turn–Reine de Saba (No Argument 107) —
(1980 NR 1981 10f 10s) first foal; dam ran once; beaten a long way in maiden
race at Yarmouth and apprentice event at Nottingham. *R. Thompson.*

LILAC STAR 5 br.m. Hard Man 102–Pink Star (Dunoon Star 110) (1980 **68**
6g 5f 5g* 5.1f* 5s² 5fg³ 5.1g* 5d² 5fg³ 5g² 5d* 5f 5d 5d 5v 1981 5s³ 5fg⁴ 5d
5d⁴ 5g³ 5g 5g²(dis) 5.1f³ 5f 6g 5f 5fg 5g* 5d 5g 5g 5g) tall mare; sprint handicapper; returned to form when beating Lindy Bay convincingly at Redcar in
September; best at 5f; acts on any going; excellent mount for an inexperienced
rider. *D. Leslie.*

LILY THE GREY 4 gr.f. Towern 96–Fag Ash Lil 79 (Dumbarnie 125) (1980 —
12.2fg 12g 1981 12f) compact filly; poor maiden; best run at 7f on firm going.
Mrs M. Rimell.

LINAMAC 6 b.g. Linacre 133–Makura (Pampered King 121) (1980 12d 12h —
12fg 16d 16fg 15.8g 12.5s 1981 12g 12fg 19g⁴) poor staying maiden. *B.
Wilkinson.*

LINDA BEARD 2 b.f. Pitskelly 122–Wavy Navy (Hardicanute 131) (1981 **81**
6fg 6fg 6g*) Jan 30; 4,500Y; strong filly; second foal; half-sister to very
useful Irish middle-distance stayer Red Invader (by Brave Invader); dam
won 3 races at up to 1m in Ireland; 50/1 and apprentice ridden, put up easily
best effort when getting up close home to win 20-runner maiden race at Newmarket in August by a short head from Beldale Ruler; backward first 2 starts;
will be suited by 1m; looked a fair performer in the making but wasn't seen
out subsequently. *R. Armstrong.*

LINDSEY 2 b. or br.f. Mummy's Pet 125–Merchantmen's Girl 58 (Klairon 131) **79**
(1981 5v⁴ 5fg 5d² 5.3f 5fg* 5fg 5fg 5g) Apr 12; small, quite attractive filly; first

foal; dam placed over 6f; made nearly all when winning 13-runner maiden race at Windsor in July by 2½ lengths from King Naskra; not disgraced in better company at Newbury nor in a nursery at Goodwood the following month on next 2 starts; yet to show she acts on extremes of going; dwelt final outing. *D. Elsworth.*

LINDY BAY 4 br.g. Bay Express 132–Lindylee 99 (Grey Sovereign 128§) (1980 6s⁴ 5fg 5f⁴ 8f 8g 5g² 5.6fg* 5s⁴ 5f 6g 5fg 5v 1981 5s³ 5g* 5g 5g 5f 5fg 5fg 5g² 5s⁴ 5g 7g 7s 7g³) strong, good sort; won handicap at Redcar in May; third in fairly valuable selling handicap at Doncaster on final start; stays 7f; acts on any going but goes well on top-of-the-ground; usually blinkered nowadays. *Hbt Jones.* — 67

LINE SLINGER 2 b.f. High Line 125–Snow Tribe 94 (Great Nephew 126) (1981 6g 8d) May 26; fair sort; good walker; second foal; half-sister to modest middle-distance winner Snow Blessed (by So Blessed); dam stayed well and is daughter of St Leger third Cold Storage; soon pushed along when about 10 lengths sixth of 11 to All Risks in 1m. maiden race at Wolverhampton in October; will need long distances. *W. Elsey.* — —

LINGDALE 4 b.g. Crooner 119–Dream (Roan Rocket 128) (1980 7d² 8.2d⁴ 8.5f 9g 10.6d⁴ 10.5g³ 8d 8g 8s² 8g 1981 8d 8s 8d 11g 8g 7d 9s) strong, good sort; carries plenty of condition; not a good mover; ran practically most starts at 4 yrs; stays 1¼m; acts on firm going but is ideally suited by some give in the ground; has worn blinkers. *W. Elsey.* — 82 d

LINGDALE LADY 3 ch.f. Sandford Lad 133–Amore Mare 80 (Varano) (1980 5d 6f 5g³ 5d 1981 6g 6g³ 7d 7.6s 6g 7d 6d 6g) small, strong filly; plating-class maiden; stays 6f. *W. Elsey.* — 60

LINGIA LIL 3 br.f. Mandamus 120–Tecllyn 97 (Technion 96) (1980 5g 5g⁴ 5g 5g⁴ 5f* 6g 5f 1981 5fg 6f 6fg 6fg 6f 5s 6g) strong, workmanlike filly; not disgraced in handicaps second and third starts; probably stays 6f; acts on firm going; inconsistent; blinkered sixth start. *Mrs R. Lomax.* — —

LINGRETA 2 b.f. Pitskelly 122–Sheralanth (Pontifex) (1981 5fg 5s² 5d 6fg 6v² 6s) Apr 3; IR 2,100Y; narrow filly; first foal; dam never ran; put up easily best efforts when length second of 12 to Chellaston Park in maiden race at Nottingham in April and when head second to Bolivar Baby, after making nearly all, in nursery at Kempton in October; stays 6f; evidently needs plenty of give in the ground; good mount for an apprentice. *Peter Taylor.* — 75

LINMILL 3 br.f. Amber Rama 133–Lady Millie 121 (Reneged) (1980 5g⁴ 5fg² 5g³ 6d⁴ 6fg⁴ 5f⁴ 5fg² 5d 1981 7g 6g 7fg⁴ 7fg³ 8f* 8d 8f 8fg) lightly-made filly; in frame in varied races, including a valuable seller, before winning modest maiden race at Pontefract in July; soundly beaten afterwards; stays 1m; best form on a sound surface. *P. Calver.* — 60

LINPAC BELLE 2 ch.f. Steel Heart 128–Prima Bella 76 (High Hat 131) (1981 5s 5g 6g⁴ 7fg 6d 6d 5f 6d 6s) Mar 27; IR 5,000Y; robust filly; second living produce; half-sister to a winner in Italy by On Your Mark; dam stayed well; showed a little ability in several of her races; should stay 7f (well beaten when tried at trip). *W. Elsey.* — 70

LINPAC GOLD 2 b.f. Rheingold 137–Purple Goddess 69 (Red God 128§) (1981 6d 6d 7g) May 13; 8,000Y; sturdy filly; half-sister to several winners, including fairly useful 7f and 1¼m winner Celestial Gem (by Gulf Pearl); dam placed over 5f at 2 yrs; started slowly in maiden race at Hamilton in September but ran on to finish 13 lengths fifth of 13 to Strath of Orchy; behind in similar events subsequently but again missed break on second outing; should be suited by 7f. *W. Elsey.* — —

LINPAC RED 2 ch.g. Red Alert 127–Flotilla 64 (Alcide 136) (1981 6fg 7fg 8.2d 10.2g) Mar 30; 7,800Y; strong gelding; third foal; dam staying half-sister to good 1964 2-y-o Leonardo; in rear in maiden and minor events but made a tardy start on each occasion (hampered on first outing); blinkered third start; probably temperamental and was gelded after final start. *W. Elsey.* — —

LINRO CHARLIE 2 b.c. Happytown 89–Lesley's Fil (Right Boy 137) (1981 5s 7fg 6fg 6f 7f 6s 5g⁴ 5s) Apr 30; 500Y; lengthy colt; poor plater; blinkered last 2 outings. *S. Nesbitt.* — 55

LINUS GINSENG 2 b.g. Song 132–Silleys Maid 100 (Continuation 120) (1981 5g² 5d* 6fg 6fg* 6fg 6g) Mar 12; most attractive gelding; good walker and excellent mover; half-brother to fairly useful 6f to 1m winner Silley's Knight (by Derring-Do); dam sprinter; successful in maiden race at York in May and decisively accounted for 8 other previous winners when winning £2,800 event at — 94

Doncaster the following month by 1½ lengths from Major's Affair; sixth in 2 pattern races, on fifth outing running respectably when 6½ lengths behind End of the Line in Anglia Television July Stakes at Newmarket; suited by 6f; has won on a firm and a soft surface; ran badly final start (bit reluctant to go to start); sold 3,200 gns Newmarket Autumn Sales. *M. Stoute.*

LION CITY 2 b.c. Simbir 130–Fille Sifflante §§ (Whistler 129) (1981 6fg 7f) **81** Apr 30; 2,200Y; workmanlike, well-grown colt; half-brother to 3 winners, including Gulf Ring (by Gulf Pearl), successful at up to 1¼m; dam temperamental half-sister to Queen Mary Stakes winner Grizel; prominent in large fields of maidens at Newmarket in the summer, coming out second best of stand-side group when 8 lengths fifth of 22 to Treboro in 7f race in July; will stay 1m. *E. Eldin.*

LIQUIDATE 5 ch.g. Busted 134–St Pauli Girl 114 (St Paddy 133) (1980 12fg — 10fg⁴ 9g⁴ 10.2g⁴ 10g* 8.2g² 8f 8g 8g 1981 14fg) big, rangy gelding; well beaten only start at 5 yrs in August; bred to stay well; acts on a firm surface; sold 3,100 gns Ascot June Sales. *L. Kennard.*

LIQUID SILVER 3 gr.f. On Your Mark 125–Madlin 102 (Sovereign Path 125) **54** (1980 NR 1981 6g³ 7g³ 6fg³ 6d) 8,600Y; lengthy filly; half-sister to 3 winners, including 1978 Irish 2-y-o 7.5f winner Sassalin (by Sassafras); dam won over 6f at 2 yrs; third in maiden and minor events; well beaten in a seller when blinkered final start; stays 7f. *P. Calver.*

LIQUIFACTION (USA) 2 b.c. Cyane–Fenway (Bolinas Boy) (1981 6f* 7fg* **92** 7d) Mar 4; $77,000Y; half-brother to 4 winners in USA; dam, winner at up to 7f, is sister to smart filly Faneuil Hall and very useful Faneuil Boy; successful twice at Naas in July, beating Shir Khan a head in 17-runner maiden race and Duncor 2½ lengths in minor event; 14/1 when about 9 lengths seventh of 11 to Day Is Done in National Stakes at the Curragh in September; will stay at least 1m. *D. O'Brien, Ireland.*

LIR 4 b. or br.c. Lord Gayle 124–Mag (Noble Jay) (1980 7g 9f 12g² 12f⁴ 10fg² — 12f 6g 12g 1981 12g⁴) small ex-Irish colt; stays 1½m; probably acts on any going; usually blinkered. *A. Moore.*

LISA GREENE (USA) 2 br.f. Shecky Greene–Hail Lisa (Hail to Reason) **70** (1981 6g 6g) May 11; $55,000Y; small filly; fourth foal; half-sister to 2 winners by Spanish Riddle, including minor stakes winner Scaramouche; dam 1m winner; wasn't knocked about once her chance had gone when about 10 lengths seventh of 17 to I'm Hot in maiden race at Newmarket in October, first outing and better effort. *L. Cumani.*

LISARDA 2 b.c. Moulton 128–Alisarda (Aureole 132) (1981 7f 6g 6g) Apr 23; — 820Y; rangy colt; fifth living foal; dam never ran; well beaten in minor and maiden races (not fully fit first 2 starts). *N. Guest.*

LISTEN TO ME 2 b.f. He Loves Me 120–Karen Chase 82 (Will Somers 114§) — (1981 5d 5fg 8d 5s) Feb 26; 27,000Y; well-made filly; half-sister to numerous winners, including useful middle-distance handicapper Mr Fordette (by Gulf Pearl); dam maiden sprinter; soundly beaten in maiden races, including one at Catterick. *L. Kennard.*

LITTLE ATOM 4 gr. or ro.c. The Go-Between 129–Native Nymph 97 (Indi- **61** genous 121) (1980 5fg 5fg² 5fg 5h* 5fg² 5s 5s 5f² 5f* 5d 5d 1981 5s 5g⁴ 5g² 5fg 5g 5fg³ 5f 5fg⁴ 5.8f 6f* 5f 6f 6f 6g) robust colt; sprint handicapper; won at Ripon in August; stays 6f; needs top-of-the-ground; blinkered twelfth start; sold 800 gns Doncaster November Sales. *D. Leslie.*

LITTLE BALLERINA 2 b.f. Britanny–Donna Pavlova (Don II 123) (1981 **76** 5fg 5g* 5d³ 6fg 5fg³ 5g*) May 7; 2,500F; neat filly; second live produce; dam poor maiden; always prominent when successful twice at Edinburgh, winning maiden race in June and nursery in September; form only at 5f; slowly away first outing (seller) and dwelt on sixth; sold to Mrs G. Forbes, probably for export, 2,100 gns Newmarket Autumn Sales. *T. Craig.*

LITTLE BIRDIE 3 gr.f. Town Crier 119–Sunningdale Sandy 53 (Sea Hawk — II 131) (1980 6g 6fg 6d 1981 7d 8d 10f 10g 8h 10h) well-grown filly; poor form, including in sellers; blinkered last 2 starts. *D. Hanley.*

LITTLE DARLING 3 ch.f. Paddy's Progress 113–Flying in Space (Bleep- — Bleep 134) (1980 7d 7fg 1981 10s 8f 7f 10.8fg) lightly-made filly; behind in maiden races and sellers; sold 400 gns Ascot September Sales. *M. Ryan.*

LITTLE DEEP 3 ch.g. Galivanter 131–Skerne Springs 79 (Canadel II 126) **49** (1980 5f 6g 5d 7fg 7d 7fg³ 7g 8.2d 8fg³ 8d 1981 11v⁴ 10s 8g 9d⁴ 12g 12g 8.2fg²) plain gelding; plater; stays 1m; acts on a firm and a soft surface. *H. Bell.*

LITTLE GINGER 2 ch.f. Cawston's Clown 113–Henrietta Georgina 72 (Rustam   —
127) (1981 5fg 6fg 6fg) Apr 9; tall, leggy filly; bad plater; tailed off final
start (reluctant to go to post). *M. H. Easterby.*

LITTLE LONDON 2 br.g. Pieces of Eight 128–Whistler's Princess (King   **50**
Emperor) (1981 6g 6f 6f³ 6f 6g 8g) Apr 2; 2,000Y; neat gelding; plater;
2¾ lengths third of 8 to Chantilly Girl at Leicester in July, best effort; should
stay further than 6f; blinkered fifth outing. *T. M. Jones.*

LITTLE MAY 2 b.f. Soldier Rose 98–Tunic (Muckle John 115) (1981 6f   —
5g) May 29; neat filly; of no account. *W. Charles.*

LITTLE MERCY 3 gr.f. No Mercy 126–Petite Rock (Goldhill 125) (1980   **56**
NR 1981 8.2s³ 9s 10g) big, lengthy filly; third foal; half-sister to winning
hurdler Demi Rock (by Double-U-Jay); dam 9f winner; plating-class maiden;
not disgraced over 1¼m. *J. Winter.*

LITTLE NEWMARKET 6 b.g. Gold Rod 129–Sage Warbler (Le Sage 128)   —
(1980 12d 12d* 16.1d² 13g 14d³ 12d⁴ 15d³ 10.6s⁴ 1981 15.8s 12g) poor staying
handicapper; seems to act on any going, except firm; suitable mount for an
inexperienced rider. *Mrs A. Cousins.*

LITTLE PADDY 2 b.g. St Paddy 133–Annie 65 (Damremont 121) (1981   —
8g) Apr 15; 580Y; 260 2-y-o; half-brother to modest 5f and 1m winner Huntley
Wood (by Spanish Gold); dam sister to smart middle-distance handicapper
Damredub; unquoted when last of 13 to Brigado in maiden race at Edinburgh in
October. *G. Richards.*

LITTLE ROBERT 2 br.c. Wolver Hollow 126–La Lola (Le Levanstell 122)   **90**
(1981 5fg² 5g³ 6d² 6g² 6fg* 6fg³ 6fg 7d³ 6fg 5fg 5g 6s) Feb 26; 4,600F, 7,600Y;
well-made, attractive colt; brother to 1980 2-y-o 7f winner Hollow Laughter;
dam won over 6f at 2 yrs in Ireland; won 17-runner maiden race at Folkestone
in June by ½ length from Puff of Smoke; not disgraced when 6½ lengths sixth of 7
to Tender King in Richmond Stakes at Goodwood the following month on seventh
start; usually shows plenty of pace but nevertheless finds 5f on sharp side nowadays and stays 7f; acts on a firm and a soft surface; consistent. *A. Ingham.*

LITTLE SMASHER 2 b.f. Jimsun 121–Metis 55 (Be Friendly 130) (1981   **74**
5s 5fg³ 6g 6fg 6f 6f* 6g² 6fg) Mar 27; 320Y; neat filly; sister to 2 poor animals;
dam a plater; won 8-runner nursery at Folkestone in August under 7-7, beating
Sussex Queen ½ length; good 2½ lengths second to Walter Mitty under a penalty
in similar race at Windsor later in month; will probably stay 7f; acts on firm
going. *M. Haynes.*

LITTLE STARCHY 3 b.c. Starch Reduced 112–Misty Morn 70 (Worden   **82**
II 129) (1980 5s 5f 5fg 5h 5fg² 5fg 5d⁴ 5d² 5fg 5fg 5g² 5f 5fg² 5fg² 5d* 1981
5d² 5fg*(dis) 6d 6s 5d) fair sort; made all and held on well by 1½ lengths from
Sandon Buoy in handicap at Sandown in April but was subsequently disqualified
when traces of theobromine were found in his system; best at 5f; acts on a firm
and a soft surface; off course almost 4 months before final start. *J. O'Donoghue.*

LITTLE STEEL 2 ch.c. Steel Heart 128–Nagin 120 (Pretense) (1981 5v   —
5v 5fg) May 12; 2,900Y; neat, dipped-backed colt; second foal; dam, best
at 6f, won in Ireland, England and France; well beaten in varied company,
including selling, but still needed run final start. *B. Gubby.*

LITTLETON SONG 3 ch.f. Song 132–L'Aventura 65 (Elopement 125) (1980   —
5fg⁴ 5fg 5g 6s 7d³ 6fg* 6g⁴ 6fg 7d 6s⁴ 1981 7d 6f 6fg 6f) neat filly; made all
in nursery at Folkestone as a 2-y-o; no form in 1981; stays 7f; probably acts
on any going; usually wears blinkers nowadays. *P. Cundell.*

LITTLE TYRANT 4 br.g. Tyrant–Tadorna 81 (Sea-Bird II 145) (1980   —
8.2fg 6f 6fg 8g 8d 1981 8s 11g 8g⁴) neat gelding; poor plater nowadays;
has worn blinkers. *B. Richmond.*

LITTLE VEE 2 ch.g. Roi Soleil 125–Lynella (Clear Run 109) (1981 5v⁴   —
5s 5fg 5f) Mar 14; lengthy gelding; fifth foal; dam of no account; no worthwhile
form, including in sellers; headstrong. *J. Berry.*

LITTLE WOLF 3 ch.c. Grundy 137–Hiding Place 109 (Doutelle 128) (1980 **117**
6d* 1981 10g³ 10g³ 11g* 12d² 12fg³ 12s*)
    Almost certainly we have yet to see the best of Little Wolf. Winner of his
only race at two years, he had his three-year-old career restricted to five races,
largely as a result of contracting a virus in early summer. In those five races
he managed to win the Group 3 St Simon Stakes at Newbury in October and
the Mecca Bookmakers' Scottish Derby at Ayr in July; he was placed in the

other three, two of them pattern events. Little Wolf's victory in the Mecca Bookmakers' Scottish Derby was a smart effort, made the more meritorious as he was having his first outing since contesting the Heathorn Stakes at Newmarket two and a half months previously. At Newmarket he had looked burly; he had been the first to come under the whip, having looked to be getting nowhere three furlongs out, and had stayed on very strongly in the closing stages to finish third to Shotgun. At Ayr Little Wolf was clearly suited by the extra distance and, having made most of the running, he battled on really gamely to hold Six Mile Bottom by a neck with Flighting two lengths away in third and Shotgun back in fourth.

Thereafter Little Wolf was campaigned in pattern races over a mile and a half. He ran well to finish second to Glint of Gold in the Great Voltigeur Stakes at York in August and third behind Critique and Fingal's Cave in the Cumberland Lodge Stakes at Ascot the following month. In both races he kept on dourly and most gamely, giving the impression that he would be very well suited by further. On the strength of these performances Little Wolf was made favourite for the St Simon Stakes, and he confirmed the progress he had made through the year. Settled in the middle of the field as Riberetto made the running, Little Wolf took rather a long time to get going after the field of seven had turned into the straight. Only in the last quarter-mile did he really begin to make ground and get into the race, and from then on he had a tremendous tussle with his stable-companion Baffin, the verdict in the balance until the last few strides. Little Wolf finally got the better of Baffin by a neck, with Shaftesbury a further five lengths back in third. Both the winner and the runner-up look to have a bright future at four years.

Little Wolf is the tenth foal of his dam and the ninth winner. He is a full brother to Major Gundry, a useful middle-distance winner, and a half-brother to, among others, Royal Hunt Cup winner Camouflage (by March Past), Horris Hill Stakes winner Disguise (by Klairon) and the best of them all, the high class

*St Simon Stakes, Newbury—a stirring finish between stable-companions
Little Wolf (hooped cap) and Baffin*

Lord Porchester's "Little Wolf"

top-of-the-ground horse Smuggler (by Exbury). The dam Hiding Place won four races at three years, including the Nell Gwyn Stakes. Hiding Place's dam Jojo was also a most successful broodmare, producing twelve winners on the flat from fourteen foals, including Brigadier Gerard's sire Queen's Hussar. Like Little Wolf, Smuggler raced in Lord Porchester's colours and showed himself a very genuine and consistent performer at three years; he won three races, all at a mile and a half, including the Princess of Wales's Stakes and the Gordon Stakes. Smuggler often looked as though he'd be well suited by further. In fact he raced only at a mile and a half at four and just twice beyond that distance at five, at the latter age winning the Yorkshire Cup over a mile and three quarters and the Henry II Stakes over two miles; in six outings at a mile and a half after his three-year-old days he was unable to win, although he did twice finish third in the Coronation Cup.

		Grundy (ch 1972)	Great Nephew (b 1963)	Honeyway
				Sybil's Niece
Little Wolf			Word from Lundy (b 1966)	Worden II
(ch.c. 1978)				Lundy Princess
		Hiding Place (ch 1963)	Doutelle (ch 1954)	Prince Chevalier
				Above Board
			Jojo (gr 1950)	Vilmorin
				Fairy Jane

Little Wolf, a close-coupled, quite attractive colt, is well suited by a mile and a half and he too gives the impression that he'll be suited by further. It seems that he'll get an opportunity of racing at longer distances quite early in his four-year-old career, for his first major objective in 1982 is reported to be the Yorkshire Cup, the distance of which should suit him very well. It will be interesting to see what sort of campaign will be planned for him after that, for at present he isn't up to beating the best at a mile and a half. Little Wolf has yet to race on really firm going but acts on any other; it is worth noting, however, that his absence from the racecourse between April and July was ascribed partly to the virus and partly to the firm ground. *R. Hern.*

LIVELY RHYTHM 2 b.c. Sharpen Up 127–French Music (French Beige 127) **89**
(1981 5.8d 6g* 7fg* 7g 7g⁴ 7d) Mar 1; 10,500F, IR 20,000Y; good-bodied, quite attractive colt; extremely good mover; half-brother to 2 minor winners; dam ran only once; won maiden race at Salisbury in June and small race at Leicester the following month, beating Optimistic Dreamer by 3 lengths without being extended in latter; stayed on well when creditable 4¼ lengths fourth of 18 to Straeker in nursery at Newmarket in October; below form in another nursery at Doncaster later in month; will be suited by 1m; possibly needs a sound surface; sold to German International BA 19,000 gns Newmarket Autumn Sales. *G. Harwood.*

LIVELY ROSE 2 ch.f. Wolverlife 115–Baby Rose (Our Babu 131) (1981 **85**
5fg 5d* 5g 6fg 6fg² 6g* 6fg 5d) Apr 24; leggy filly; half-sister to 2 winners abroad; dam never ran; winner of maiden race at Wolverhampton in May and nursery at Windsor in August, making all to score by 1½ lengths from Suggestive in latter; suited by 6f; acts on a firm and a soft surface; goes well for apprentice S. Dawson. *N. Vigors.*

LIZMOR 2 gr.c. Morston 125–Elizabeth Wales 95 (Abernant 142) (1981 8g) **—**
Mar 29; half-brother to useful middle-distance performer Proven (by Tudor Melody); dam sprinter; 20/1 and backward, soon chased along when out of first 10 of 29 to Born Hero in maiden race at Newmarket in October. *I. Balding.*

LOAN CHARGE 5 b.g. Lombard 126–Something Else 68 (Paveh 126) (1980 **45**
10s³ 8fg 9fg 12f* 10g³ 10g 10.2g 1981 10d 10v³ 10.8fg 7f) poor handicapper; stays 1½m; acts on any going; suitable mount for an apprentice. *R. Turnell.*

LOBKOWIEZ 2 b.c. Radetzky 123–Fulcrum Miss (Fulcrum) (1981 6fg 6g **117**
7fg 7fg³ 8f* 8fg* 8s³)
When Lobkowiez finished third, just over three lengths behind Norwick, in the Royal Lodge Stakes at Ascot in September he accomplished a most unusual feat—reaching the frame in a pattern race just two years after his sire last did the same. Radetzky will be remembered as a very smart but headstrong performer who was twice returned to training after spells at stud. He clearly increased his appeal to breeders by winning the Queen Anne Stakes and finishing second to Jaazeiro in the Sussex Stakes after his first season at stud; whereas the 1979 *Return of Mares* shows only three foals from seven mares, he had eighteen foals from twenty-nine mares in 1980 and seventeen foals from twenty-four mares in 1981. Lobkowiez is Radetzky's only runner so far; if he's typical of his sire's stock, Radetzky deserves more support.

		Huntercombe	Derring-Do
	Radetzky	(b 1967)	Ergina
	(br 1973)	Selina Fair	Hugh Lupus
Lobkowiez		(b 1964)	Raggoty Ann
(b.c. Apr 30, 1979)		Fulcrum	Spy Song
	Fulcrum Miss	(ch 1955)	Fulmar
	(b 1967)	Unicrose	Bey
		(br 1953)	Rose of Bengal

Lobkowiez's performance in the Royal Lodge was his best—he chased Norwick hard all the way up the straight until losing second place only close home to Silver Hawk—but he'd earlier shown rapidly improving form and had won two good-class nurseries. It wasn't until his fourth outing that he managed to gain a place, in a Brighton maiden race, and when he made his first appearance in a nursery, at York early in September, only two of his eight opponents carried less weight. Lobkowiez won like a progressive colt, racing with the leaders throughout and scoring a shade comfortably by half a length from Lucky Choice; and an 8-lb penalty didn't stop his winning again at Doncaster eight days later in the competitive Prince of Wales's Nursery. Once Lobkowiez hit the front three furlongs out only Final Strike of the other fifteen runners was able to get in a challenge and Final Strike was still a neck behind at the line. How much Lobkowiez improved in the space of little more than three weeks can fairly be gauged from his form against Santella Man—at York he beat him a length, receiving 18 lb, whereas in the Royal Lodge he beat him four lengths at level weights.

Mrs C. M. Elliot-Lemoine's "Lobkowiez"

Lobkowiez is a neat colt; what he lacks in size he more than makes up for with courage, showing the same determination Radetzky used to in his prime. Radetzky stayed a mile and a quarter and Lobkowiez, who was so well suited by a mile at two, will probably stay that distance—his close relative, the fairly useful Von Erlach, stays at least nine furlongs although by the sprinter Huntercombe. Lobkowiez's family's record is unimpressive in recent generations. Lobkowiez and Von Erlach are the only winners from Fulcrum Miss's first six foals but her tally should improve when her yearling and foal, full brothers to Lobkowiez, reach the races. Fulcrum Miss gained her four successes in sprint claiming races in the USA, running for a claiming price of only 2,000 dollars; the grandam Unicrose won only a small nine-furlong race at Longchamp and none of her winners in the States managed even to gain a place in a stakes race; and the third dam Rose of Bengal failed to win, as did four of her eight foals.

Is Lobkowiez likely to raise the family fortunes at three? We think not although he's a smart, game performer and acts on any going. His connections aim very high—indeed the race chosen for Lobkowiez's debut was no less than the Coventry Stakes—so Lobkowiez, who doesn't appear to have much scope, will probably spend most of the season fighting a losing battle against the best of his generation. *C. Brittain.*

LOCHADOO 3 b.f. Lochnager 132–Quick Draw 70 (Kalydon 122) (1980 NR 1981 9s 10s) second foal; dam, 1¼m winner, is closely related to very smart Ksar; tailed off in maiden event at York and seller at Nottingham in October. *K. Stone.* —

LOCH ARD 2 b.c. Music Boy 124–Caesar's Love 85 (Above Suspicion 127) (1981 6g) Mar 24; 9,800Y; rangy colt; half-brother to very useful 1974 2-y-o 1m winner Caesar's Flame (by Hotfoot); dam placed over 1¼m on only start; 25/1 and in need of run, always chasing leaders when seventh of 22 to Ash Ridge in maiden race at Newmarket in October; likely to do better in 1982. *B. Hobbs.* — p

LOC

LOCH BOYLE 3 b.g. Lochnager 132–Rise 68 (Fury Royal 108) (1980 5h⁴ —
5f* 6fg⁴ 5fg 7g 7g 5d 5fg 7d 1981 7s 9.4g 11fg 13.8fg 6s 5fg 7f 10.4s 12f 10s)
small gelding; no worthwhile form over a variety of distances in 1981, including
in sellers; blinkered sixth start; pulls hard; trained part of season by C. Gray;
sold 340 gns Doncaster November Sales. *T. Fairhurst.*

LOCH GATE 3 br.f. Lochnager 132–Nimble Gate 64 (Nimbus 130) (1980 5f —
5f 5g 5fg 1981 6g 7fg 5f 5f 5fg 6fg 8fg 10.6v 13.8g) compact, good-bodied filly;
poor form in varied company, including selling; has been tried in blinkers;
sold 540 gns Doncaster October Sales. *P. Asquith.*

LOCHLINNHE 2 b.c. Lochnager 132–Sunbird II (River Chanter 121) (1981 6g) **72 p**
Mar 24; IR 6,800F, resold 7,200Y; half-brother to 4 winners in Italy; dam won 4
times at 2 yrs and 3 yrs in Italy; 33/1 when about 6 lengths seventh of 26 to
Perang Tejam in maiden race at Doncaster in November, staying on well over final
2f; may improve. *Miss S. Hall.*

LOCHNESS LASS 7 br.m. Track Spare 125–Mascarade 58 (Pirate King 129) —
(1980 NR 1981 17.1d) lightly raced and no sign of ability; has been to stud and
produced foals by Roi Soleil and Dragonara Palace. *J. Thorne.*

LOCHRANZA 10 br.g. Highland Melody 112–Earall (Khalkis 127) (1980 12d³ —
13v* 13f* 12g³ 13d* 12g³ 11fg⁴ 14.7g⁴ 14d 12g² 14f³ 13s³ 12g³ 12.5s 1981 12s
12.5s 12s 13g 12fg 14.6f 13fg⁴ 12fg 12v 12s) fairly useful and very genuine
front-running handicapper at his best but has deteriorated; best at up to 13f;
ideally suited by some give in the ground nowadays; acts on any track; has
worn blinkers; suitable mount for an inexperienced rider; occasionally sweats up.
J. Carr.

LOCHTILLUM 2 b.c. Song 132–Spring Storm 74 (March Past 124) (1981 6d —
6g 7g) Apr 6; 4,000F, 3,200Y; good-quartered colt; first produce; dam, half-
sister to very smart miler General Vole, won over 1m and 1¼m; unquoted when
behind in large fields of maidens; moved badly to start final outing. *J. Douglas-Home.*

LOCKER TARN 3 b.f. Hittite Glory 125–Miss Fenton 98 (Palestine 133) —
(1980 5d 5g 5f 5g 1981 5g 6g 7fg 9s 7fg 7.2f 6f) compact filly; behind in
maiden and minor events; blinkered final outing as a 2-y-o. *T. Fairhurst.*

LOCKETTS LANE 6 gr.m. Mandamus 120–Moselle Mist 64 (Sovereign Path —
125) (1980 NR 1981 10g) half-sister to 3 winning jumpers; dam sprint plater;
soundly beaten in minor event at Pontefract in May, first outing on flat. *H.
Wharton.*

LOCKINGTON LAD 3 ch.c. Song 132–Twin-Set (Double Jump 131) (1980 —
5fg⁴ 6g 6g 1981 8f 7f) fair sort; plating-class maiden; probably stays 1m;
started slowly second outing as a 2-y-o and wore blinkers on third; sold 460 gns
Doncaster October Sales. *M. H. Easterby.*

LOCKWOOD GIRL 2 b.f. Prince Tenderfoot 126–Malmsey (Jukebox 120) **81**
(1981 5s* 5d* 5g* 5d² 6d 6fg³ 5g) Apr 21; 2,500Y; lengthy filly; first foal; dam
won over 1¼m and 1¾m in Ireland; successful in auction race at Leicester and
in minor event at Folkestone (beat Paul's Ivory 2 lengths) in first weeks of
season, and was awarded a small race at Thirsk late in April because 3-length
winner Witch's Point carried 4 lb too little; creditable third of 11 to Mummy's
Game in minor race at Windsor in July; better suited by 6f than 5f; seems to
act on any going; not raced after early August; sold 16,000 gns Newmarket
December Sales. *G. Hunter.*

LOGAN 4 b.g. Biskrah 121–Amber Star (Amber Rama 133) (1980 10fg 7h³ —
7s 8g* 10.1fg 10f 1981 8fg 10d⁴ 10f 7f) rather lightly-made gelding; won
maiden race at Sandown in 1980; well beaten at 4 yrs; possibly stays 1¼m;
blinkered nowadays. *M. Masson.*

LOHENGRIN 5 b.g. Rheingold 137–Goosie 112 (Sea-Bird II 145) (1980 12fg³ **95**
16g 1981 12d 12g 14g* 12f²) rangy gelding; useful handicapper on his day;
beat Tudor Wynk by 2 lengths at Sandown in July; ran well only subsequent
start on Brighton in August; stays well; seems to act on any going but goes well
on a sound surface; inconsistent. *J. Dunlop.*

LOMBARDI (USA) 3 b.c. Northern Dancer–Julia B (Herbager 136) (1980 **83**
6fg³ 1981 8s² 10fg 8d² 8v² 12g) big, useful sort; showed signs of inexperience
and wasn't given an unnecessarily hard time when ¾-length second of 4 to Kirtling
in Roseberry Stakes at Stockton in April; disappointing last of 8 behind Shergar
in Guardian Newspaper Classic Trial at Sandown later in month; off course
afterwards until autumn, when second in maiden event won by Organdy at
Goodwood and 4-runner £3,000 race won by Cracking Form at York; promises
to stay middle distances. *B. Hills.*

492

L'OMETTO 3 gr.g. Zeddaan 130–Rucellina (Clouet II 113) (1980 5fg 5f 6f **64**
6s³ 6s³ 6g 6g 6f 6g 6s 1981 6g 7d 5.3f 6g⁴ 6d 6g 10d³) quite attractive, close-
coupled gelding; stayed on and showed improved form when about 1½ lengths
third to Morice in minor event at Leicester in November, first outing for new
connections; had run in sellers on occasions earlier; suited by 1¼m; form only
on soft ground; blinkered fourth outing; sold out of G. Lewis' stable 875 gns
Ascot August Sales. *B. Palling.*

LONE BIDDER 3 b.f. Auction Ring 123–Seul 69 (Faberge II 121) (1980 6d⁴ **91**
6fg* 6s 7fg* 1981 8g³ 8v 8f 10f⁴ 8.5f 8fg 8g⁴) Irish filly; in frame 3 times,
on first 2 occasions in Edenderry Stakes at Phoenix Park in May (3½ lengths
third to Blue Wind) and handicap on same course in July; behind in Goffs
Irish 1,000 Guineas at the Curragh (ninth of 15) and Coronation Stakes at Royal
Ascot (last of 10) in between; stays 1¼m; acts on firm going; sometimes blinkered.
M. Kauntze, Ireland.

LONELY DAWN (USA) 2 b.f. Plenty Old–Dueling Time (Duel) (1981 6g) **—**
Mar 29; 9,400Y; lengthy filly; sister to American 4-y-o Mr John L; dam won
claiming races at up to 7f; 6/1 but pretty backward when well down the field in
19-runner maiden race won by One Degree at Newmarket in October. *B. Hills.*

LONGCLIFFE 6 br.g. Mandamus 120–Pepin (Midsummer Night II 117) **59**
(1980 NR 1981 10s 10s² 10g 12.2s) big gelding; middle-distance handicapper;
acts on any going. *P. Felgate.*

LONGGOE 3 ch.f. Lorenzaccio 130–Mey 78 (Canisbay 120) (1980 7fg 7d **—**
1981 7f 8f 8fg 7g) lightly-made filly; plater; will be suited by 1¼m. *W. Hastings-
Bass.*

LONGLANDS LADY 3 ro.f. Grey Mirage 128–Ursula 78 (Songedor 116) (1980 **59**
5fg 5d* 5g³ 1981 5d* 6g³ 5g 5fg 5fg* 5g 5g 6fg 6f 5f) sturdy filly; plater at
2 yrs; successful in 1981 in handicaps at Hamilton in April and Carlisle in July;
seems best at 5f; acts on a firm and a soft surface. *J. Berry.*

LONGLEAT (USA) 2 ch.c. The Minstrel 135–Fair Arrow (Turn-to) (1981 **104**
6fg* 7g* 8d²) May 21; $250,000Y; smallish, strong, attractive colt; half-brother

M J. P. Binet's "Longleat"

to 2 winners, one a stakes winner, and to dam of high-class filly Alma North (by Northern Dancer); dam, placed at 2 yrs, is out of half-sister to champion 2-y-o filly Diableretta; impressed us when landing the odds by ¾ length from Hay Habit in Coolmore Try My Best Stakes at Leopardstown in September, cruising through into lead 1f out despite having been stopped in his tracks when moving up from last place after halfway; had previously won maiden race at the Curragh when 4/1 on; 7/4 on for 10-runner Beresford Stakes at the Curragh in October but went down by 4 lengths to Assert; will probably stay 1¼m. *V. O'Brien, Ireland.*

LONG LEGEND (USA) 3 ch.f. Reviewer–Lianga 133 (Dancer's Image) **106** (1980 6f* 1981 6fg* 6g 6fg* 6f 5d*) well-made, attractive filly of quality; second foal; sister to very useful 1979 2-y-o 5f and 6f winner La Legende; dam top-class winner from 4.5f to 1m; successful in handicaps at Newmarket in April and Yarmouth in July and in minor event at Newbury in September, in last-named event quickening very nicely when switched, after being held up, and beating Pontin Lad a shade cleverly by a length; rather disappointing on both her other starts; bred to stay 1m but is apparently regarded as a sprinter; yet to race on very soft going, but acts on any other. *H. Cecil.*

LONGRIDGE 5 b.g. Derring-Do 131–Charlotteen 95 (Charlottown 127) (1980 **45** 8d 10v 10fg 8f 8f 10h⁴ 12fg 8fg⁴ 10f 8g² 9g³ 8fg² 10g³ 8f² 10f³ 12.2d 1981 8g* 10fg³ 8fg) plater; attracted no bid after winning at Carlisle in June; effective at 1m and stays 1¾m; seems to act on any going; often blinkered but is effective without. *S. Nesbitt.*

LONGTOFT 2 gr.c. Tachypous 128–Donrae 106 (Don II 123) (1981 5g³) **68** p June 5; second foal; dam at her best at 2 yrs when winner twice over 5f; 14/1, made steady headway in last 2f after running green when 1¼ lengths equal third of 11 to Thunderbridge in modest maiden race at Newcastle in August, only outing; will stay 6f. *M. H. Easterby.*

LORDAVILLE 2 b.g. Lord Nelson 107–Vaudaville 77 (Vigo 130) (1981 5s) — Feb 15; lengthy gelding; good walker; half-brother to 2 winning sprinters by Most Secret, including fairly useful Broon's Secret; dam ran only at 2 yrs; 12/1 8th and in need of race, made little show when eighth of 9 to Haycombe Barn in maiden race at Nottingham in September. *A. Bailey.*

LORD CHARLES 2 b.g. Malicious–Port-le-Dor (Le Dieu d'Or 119) (1981 — 8g 8.2d 10g) May 5; half-brother to 1977 2-y-o 5f winner Larry Oren (by Galivanter); poor form in sellers. *G. Toft.*

LORD CLEWES 3 ch.c. Status Seeker–Calcine 75 (Roan Rocket 128) (1980 **67** 6g 7g* 7g³ 7fg⁴ 8f³ 8s² 8fg 1981 10s³ 10.6d 12.3d) workmanlike colt; quite a moderate handicapper; had stiffish tasks in 1981, best effort on reappearance; not raced after May; stays 1¼m; acts on any going but is possibly best on soft. *K. Stone.*

LORD DRIFT 2 ch.c. Touch Paper 113–Driftwood 85 (Epaulette 125) (1981 — 6fg 6f) May 26; IR 300F, IR 2,200Y; short-backed colt; always well behind in maiden auction event and a seller in July; sold 330 gns Ascot October Sales. *Peter Taylor.*

LORD FITZROY 10 ch.g. pedigree unknown (1980 NR 1981 16f 12fg) of — little account. *T. Kersey.*

LORD JACK (FR) 4 ch.c. Sir Tor–Vacance (Vandale) (1980 8.5d² 12fg **119** 8.5d 8s 10.5d 12.5g³ 11g* 10.5v² 1981 12d 12s 12d* 12fg 12g* 12s 12g* 12.5d 12g* 13.5f 12g⁴ 10s⁴ 12s) smart French colt; won 80,000 francs races at Saint-Cloud and Chantilly, handicap at Longchamp and Grand Prix de Vichy; held on by short neck from strong-finishing Cracaval in last-named in August; ran respectably most subsequent starts, including when sixth to Perrault in Grand Prix de Deauville, fourth to Detroit in Prix Foy at Longchamp and fourth to Glenorum in La Coupe de Maisons-Laffitte; stays 13.5f; acts on any going. *H. Gleizes, France.*

LORD LAFF 3 b.c. Tumble Wind–You Never Can Tell (Never Say Die 137) — (1980 6g 7fg 1981 6s 6fg 6g 5.3fg 6f 10fg 10fg) strong, very attractive colt; poor form in varied company, including selling; seemed to be running on over 1¼m on sixth start; blinkered fifth outing. *G. Lewis.*

LORD MELBOURNE 7 br.g. Meldrum 112–Aberdevine 92 (Abernant 142) — (1980 NR 1981 7f 13g⁴ 12f³ 8.2d) strong gelding; poor performer nowadays; wears bandages. *J. S. Wilson.*

LORD NORTH 4 gr.g. Zeddaan 130–Laria (Silver Shark 129) (1980 12g 68
9fg 8g 8f 12g 7g 12s 1981 13fg*) ex-Irish gelding; beat Desert Star 1½ lengths
in amateur riders race at Nottingham in April; stays 13f; acts on a firm surface.
A. Pitt.

LORD OF MISRULE 7 gr.h. Supreme Sovereign 119–Mirth (Tamerlane 128) —
(1980 12fg 11.7fg 10fg⁴ 12f 10fg⁴ 10s² 11.7s² 10g 8g 11.7f² 8g 10fg³ 10g 1981
12d) poor handicapper; stays 1½m: acts on any going; usually wears blinkers;
suitable mount for an inexperienced rider. *M. Haynes.*

LORD OF THE REALM 3 ch.c. Realm 129–Suir-Delight (Precipitant 113) 73 d
(1980 5s 5s 7d 6g 1981 7s 7fg² 7.6d³ 7g 6s* 5.8d 6fg 7fg 6fg 7g 6s) small colt;
beat Singwara by a neck in handicap at Kempton in May; placed at Epsom
and Chester (had stiff task) earlier; stays 7f; probably acts on any going;
soundly beaten last 6 starts. *G. Beeson.*

LORDS (USA) 2 b.c. Hoist the Flag–Princessnesian (Princequillo) (1981 93 p
8d*) Apr 14; $1,050,000Y; ninth foal; half-brother to 4 winners, including
1972 Irish 2-y-o 6f winner Bold Enchantress (by Bold Ruler), herself dam of
smart Fordham; dam high-class winner of 11 races at up to 1½m; comfortably
accounted for more experienced colts when 2/1 on for 20-runner maiden race
at Leopardstown in October, scoring by 2½ lengths from Condell; will stay 1½m;
a very well-related colt who should make a good 3-y-o. *V. O'Brien, Ireland.*

LORD SAUL 2 br.c. Saulingo 122–Winkle 74 (Whistler 129) (1981 6g 6s —
5d) Mar 23; 1,400Y; strong, useful-looking colt; half-brother to a winner in
Barbados; dam granddaughter of champion 1956 2-y-o Sarcelle; no worthwhile
form, including when favourite for valuable seller on second start; sold 320 gns
Ascot November Sales. *D. Kent.*

LORD SCRAP 5 ch.g. Tower Walk 130–La Concha (Le Levanstell 122) (1980 58
5s 5g 6fg³ 6g 6g² 6d⁴ 5.8f* 5f 6fg 6d 1981 6s 6fg 5g 6d 6g 6fg³ 6f 5.8f² 6fg 5h⁴
6fg) good-looking gelding; sprint handicapper; stays 6f; probably acts on
any going; usually blinkered at 2 yrs and wore them again final start; excellent
mount for a boy. *B. Swift.*

LORD WESSCAM 3 b.c. Sassafras 135–Coral Lee (Le Levanstell 122) (1980 —
6fg 7g 8g 1981 8.5fg 10s 10d 12fg 10d 10d 8.5d 8.3fg 16fg) small, compact
colt; plater; should stay at least 1½m; has been tried in blinkers. *S. Matthews.*

LORD WIMPY 3 gr.g. Dragonara Palace 115–My Worry 72 (March Past 70
124) (1980 5s³ 5fg³ 6f⁴ 6d 7d 7d³ 6g 7f³ 7g 7d 1981 8s² 7s² 7fg*(dis) 7g²
7d² 7d 7d 8f 7f 7f* 7fg 8g 6g) useful sort; won handicap at Epsom in April
(beat Faiz a length but drifted badly in last furlong and was disqualified) and
maiden race at Folkestone in August (made all); inconsistent however, and was
unplaced in a seller and a claiming race on last 2 starts; best at 7f; acts on any
going; blinkered once in 1980 (had stiff task); apprentice ridden third and fourth
starts, but tends to hang and is by no means an easy ride. *R. Hannon.*

LORENETTE 4 ch.f. Lorenzaccio 130–Crepinette 64 (Saint Crespin III 132) —
(1980 8d 12g* 12g³ 11d³ 13g 12d 12d 1981 16fg) won poor 4-runner event
at Leicester at 3 yrs; well beaten in handicap, only outing in 1981; stayed 1½m;
acted on a soft surface; dead. *D. Gandolfo.*

LORENTINO 4 b.g. Lorenzaccio 130–Timur's Daughter 103 (Tamerlane 128) —
(1980 8f 10.4f 10.8s* 10s² 10d⁴ 12g* 10g² 1981 12.3d 12g 13g) well-made
gelding; has a long stride; had stiffish tasks in 1981; suited by 1½m; acts on soft
going. *D. Francis.*

LORENZAN 5 b.m. Lorenzaccio 130–Habituee (Habitat 134) (1980 NR —
1981 10d) poor plater; has worn blinkers. *C. Dingwall.*

LORIOT 4 ch.g. Lord Gayle 124–Golden Moss 91 (Sheshoon 132) (1980 8g* —
10g 12fg³ 11.5g⁴ 11fg³ 12s 10g² 11s² 10s³ 1981 10s 16d 12f 13g) leggy
ex-Irish gelding; won maiden race at the Curragh at 3 yrs; well beaten in varied
company in 1981; stays 1½m; probably acts on any going; trained part of
season by J. M. Oxx. *H. Collingridge.*

LORN GODDESS 2 b.f. Red God 128§–Heavenly Decision (Decidedly) 90
(1981 5s 5g 5d 5f⁴ 5fg² 5fg⁴ 5fg² 5f* 5fg⁴ 6g* 6d) May 2; IR 12,500Y; fourth
foal; dam second over 5.5f and 8.5f in France; winner of maiden race at Mallow
and nursery at Phoenix Park in August by a length from top-weighted
Ormsary; also in frame in races won by Achieved at Phoenix Park on seventh
and ninth outings, finishing 2½ lengths second in maiden race and 4 lengths

Miss Angela Eastwood's "Lorn Goddess"

fourth of 7 after being hampered in Gallaghouse Phoenix Stakes; stays 6f; acts on firm going; blinkered fifth and ninth outings. *L. Browne, Ireland.*

LOST FOR WORDS 4 b.f. Firestreak 125–Sombrilla (Big Game) (1980 **56** d
8.2d 7f² 8fg 6fg* 6fg 7g 6g 6g 6d 6g 1981 12s² 13s⁴ 12g 10g 10f 12g) leggy, light-bodied filly; poor handicapper; evidently stays 1½m; acts on any going; sometimes sweats up; sold 700 gns Newmarket December Sales. *R. Boss.*

LOST VALLEY 4 b.f. Perdu 121–Long Valley 71 (Ribero 126) (1980 8g 1981 —
5s) lightly-raced plater; should stay 1m. *J. Hill.*

LOTUS DANCER 2 b.f. Midsummer Night II 117–Kushbehar 80 (Behistoun —
131) (1981 6f 6f) Apr 14; small, lightly-made filly; first foal; dam at her best at 2 yrs when 6f winner; in rear in sellers at Doncaster in June and Ripon in July. *S. Wiles.*

LOUDMOUTH 2 b. or br.g. Mummy's Pet 125–Fortissimaid 75 (Fortissimo —
111) (1981 8g 8s 6s) Apr 4; first foal; dam won sellers over 13.8f and 15.8f; in rear in maiden races in the autumn. *W. C. Watts.*

LOUP DE MER 2 b.f. Wolver Hollow 126–Milveagh 92 (Milesian 125) (1981 **83**
6f² 7fg³ 6d³ 7g*) Apr 2; IR 19,000Y; rather leggy filly; half-sister to several winners here and abroad, including fair 1975 2-y-o 6f winner Eagle Hill (by Tudor Music); dam won at up to 1m; blinkered when keeping on well to beat Czar's Bride by 2 lengths in 17-runner maiden event at Leicester in October; placed in good-sized fields earlier; will be suited by 1m. *M. Stoute.*

LOU PIGUET (FR) 3 b.c. Habitat 134–Tuneria (Tanerko 134) (1980 5.5d* **126**
7d² 8s* 9fg⁴ 7.5g³ 1981 8d 11fg 8s* 9g 10g 8g⁴ 8s⁴ 7v²) brother to successful
Italian colt Hagg Hagg, subsequently a winner in USA, and half-brother to a
winner by Thatch; dam French middle-distance winner; won 7-runner Group 3
Prix de la Jonchere at Longchamp in May by ½ length from Redoutable; ran
race of his life when 4 lengths second to Moorestyle in Group 1 Prix de la Foret
on same course in October on final outing, finishing very well having been only
sixth with 2f to run and beating such high-class performers as Belmont Bay,
Sharpo and Hilal; beaten about 2 lengths when fourth in between in Prix Messidor
at Maisons-Laffitte (behind Ya Zaman) and Prix du Rond-Point at Longchamp
(behind Daeltown); best form at up to 1m; very well suited by the mud; usually
blinkered; a high-class colt judged on his running in the Foret. *J. C. Cunnington,
France.*

L'OUVERTURE 3 gr.f. Bustino 136–Key of the Kingdom 111 (Grey Sovereign **49**
128§) (1980 7fg 7g 1981 7fg 7v 12g 16fg⁴ 12d³ 12fg³) leggy, useful sort; in
frame in varied company, including selling at Newmarket; stays 2m; blinkered
fourth outing. *J. Sutcliffe.*

LOUVIERS 3 br.g. Vitiges 132–Vive la Reine (Vienna 127) (1980 NR 1981 **75**
10.1d⁴ 10s* 10fg 11g⁴) compact, good-bodied gelding; half-brother to 2 winners,
notably very smart 1978 2-y-o 6f and 7f winner R. B. Chesne (by Brigadier
Gerard); dam, winner at 1½m in France, is sister to Vaguely Noble; won 18-runner
maiden event at Leicester in May a shade cleverly by ½ length from Carved Opal;
not seen out after finishing fourth of 7 to Rodeo in handicap at Ayr in July
(blinkered); promises to stay 1½m; acts on soft going (didn't run particularly well
on a firm surface third start). *M. Stoute.*

LOVEGROVE 2 b.f. Floriana 116–Come On Darling 66 (Darling Boy 124) —
(1981 5fg 6f 6f 8g) Mar 15; strong filly; bad plater; sold 450 gns Doncaster
October Sales. *Miss A. Hill-Wood.*

LOVELY NADA 2 br.f. Supreme Sovereign 119–Dame Fortune 84 (Kashmir II —
125) (1981 6f) Mar 24; 3,000F; half-sister to fair 1978 2-y-o 7f winner Avanti
Carlo (by Lorenzaccio); dam won over 9f; 20/1 and apprentice ridden when
behind in 17-runner maiden race won by Gayonara at Stockton in June. *W.
Wharton.*

LOVE ME DO 2 b.f. He Loves Me 120–Gang Plank 84 (Tower Walk 130) **60**
(1981 6fg 7d 7g⁴) Feb 12; IR 6,200F, resold IR 7,000Y; lengthy, deep-girthed
filly; second produce; dam showed a little ability at 2 yrs; quite a moderate
maiden; will probably stay 1m. *M. Smyly.*

LOVE ME LADY 2 b.f. He Loves Me 120–Lady Relka (Relko 136) (1981 7g) —
Apr 19; IR 4,000F, 3,600Y; first foal; dam, half-sister to top French hurdler
Hardatit, won small 9f race at 2 yrs in France; unquoted and rather backward
when behind in 22-runner maiden race won by Count Pahlen at Newmarket in
October. *J. Sutcliffe.*

LOVE ME TRUE 2 b.f. He Loves Me 120–Lady Lambourn 82 (Habitat 134) —
(1981 5g) June 1; neat filly; good walker; first foal; dam won over 7f and 1½m;
33/1, looked fit and well but never got into race at any stage when eleventh of
12 behind Hampton Bay in £3,200 event at Ascot in September. *B. Hills.*

LOVE PATROL 6 b.m. Green God 128–Alcmena 81 (Alcide 136) (1980 NR —
1981 12f 12f) sturdy mare; of no account; has worn blinkers. *K. Bridgwater.*

LOVE TANGLE 2 gr.f. Wollow 132–Pearl Grey (Gulf Pearl 117) (1981 6g⁴) **77** p
Apr 8; 40,000Y; third living foal; half-sister to a winner in USA by Realm; dam,
Irish 1½m winner, is half-sister to Belmont Stakes winner Celtic Ash; backed
from 33/1 to 10/1, ran on strongly to finish about 5 lengths fourth of 18 to Music
Lover in maiden race at Newmarket in October; will stay 1¼m; likely to improve
M. Smyly.

LOVE TRYST 3 b.f. Wolver Hollow 126–Cupid's Delight 84 (St Paddy 133) —
(1980 NR 1981 14g 16.9fg 16g) fourth foal; half-sister to Norfolk Arrow (by
Blakeney), successful over 2m and a useful hurdler; dam, half-sister to good
stayer Rangong, won twice over 1½m from 3 starts; beaten some way in maiden
races; sold 650 gns Ascot December Sales. *G. Balding.*

LOW MILEAGE 4 b.g. Royben 125–Ritz Bar 99 (Royal Palm 131) (1980 6f —
6fg 6fg 7f 5fg 7g 6g 1981 8f 6g 6fg 7f) leggy gelding; sprint plater; has worn
blinkers; sold 775 gns Ascot September Sales. *N. Callaghan.*

LOW

LOWNDES COURT 3 b.g. High Top 131–Queen's Cove 98 (Sing Sing 134) — (1980 6g 7fg 7s 1981 8fg 10.1d 7s 16fg 7f 10d) rather lightly-made gelding; poor form, including in sellers; probably stays 7f; sold out of D. Sasse's stable 470 gns Ascot 2nd June Sales after third start. *M. Chapman.*

LOWTHER STREET 3 gr.f. Grey Mirage 128–Sherbet (Zarathustra 131) — (1980 6fg 7g 1981 8s 8fg 12d 14s⁴ 16g⁴) strong filly; has shown a little ability in maiden events and a handicap. *D. Ancil.*

LOYAL TOAST (USA) 2 b.c. Raise A Cup–Queen Ribot (Sir Ribot) (1981 **101** 7fg* 7d* 8g⁴) May 5 $65,000Y; strong, rangy, attractive colt; second foal; dam, stakes winner over 1m, won 13 times at up to 6 yrs; momentarily ran green when asked to quicken at distance in 8-runner Sandwich Stakes at Ascot in July but then lengthened his stride in excellent style to win by 6 lengths from dead-heaters Incandesce and Telephone Man; didn't reproduce that form when short-priced favourite for minor events at Lingfield in August (got home by only a neck from High Pitched) and Goodwood the following month (8¾ lengths fourth of 6 to Jalmood after having every chance at distance); subsequently suffered a haemorrhage and died; would have stayed 1m; possibly needed a firm surface. *G. Harwood.*

LUAN CAUSCA 2 b.f. Pampapaul 127–Tintale (Tin Whistle 128) (1981 5f 5f* **70** 5g 5g 5g) Apr 17; small, workmanlike filly; half-sister to 2 winning platers and a winner in Belgium; dam ran 4 times; made all when winning 16-runner maiden race at Beverley in August by 1¼ lengths from Cawston Star; will stay 6f. *W. Wharton.*

LUCAYAN LADY 2 br.f. Swing Easy 126–Mary Mullen 88 (Lorenzaccio 130) **81** (1981 5g 5s³ 6d* 6g) Apr 15; sturdy filly, third foal; half-sister to 1979 2-y-o 1m seller winner Mannerism (by Saritamer); dam won over 5f at 2 yrs; stayed on well to beat Gentle Star by 1½ lengths in 15-runner minor event at Pontefract in October; suited by 6f; yet to race on a firm surface. *R. Sheather.*

LUCINSKI 2 b.f. Malinowski 123–Lucindale (Ballyciptic 122) (1981 7g) Apr — 16; IR 3,400F, 4,000Y; lightly-made filly; half-sister to 1977 2-y-o 5f winner Sterling Lucy (by Sterling Bay) and a winner abroad; dam never ran; 33/1 when behind in 29-runner maiden race won by Chalon at Newmarket in October. *R. Hollinshead.*

LUCKY CHOICE 2 br.c. Lucky Wednesday 124–Pams Choice 87 (Mandamus **84** 120) (1981 5s 6g 7g⁴ 7fg⁴ 8f² 8g 8s³ 7d⁴) Apr 8; strong, good-bodied colt; third reported produce; dam won over 1m; ran best races when forcefully ridden over 1m at York in September and October, finishing ¾-length second to Lobkowiez in nursery and 4½ lengths third to Florida Son in maiden race; will stay 1¼m; acts on any going; one paced and needs to lie up with leaders; blinkered last 2 outings (hampered at start on final appearance). *M. H. Easterby.*

LUCKY DEVIL 8 b.g. Great Nephew 126–Good Fortune 65 (Native Prince) — (1980 NR 1981 12.3d 14g) probably of little account nowadays; has worn blinkers and bandages; sold 320 gns Ascot December Sales. *M. James.*

LUCKY DUTCH 2 b.c. Lucky Wednesday 124–Dutch May 109 (Maystreak 118) **80** (1981 5g 5fg* 6f 6s 7g) May 29; fair sort; second foal; dam won 7 sprint races at 2 yrs and 3 yrs; stayed on well when winning 16-runner maiden race at Redcar in May by 2 lengths from Drago; off course most of summer and finished towards rear on return (not disgraced in £3,500 event at York on fourth start); should stay 7f. *M. W. Easterby.*

LUCKY FIDDLER 2 b.g. Old Lucky 113–Semi-Quaver (Seminole II) (1981 **69** 5.8f 5fg 5fg) June 3; lengthy gelding; second foal; dam never ran; unquoted and still backward when about 4½ lengths fifth of 13 to Nawab in maiden race at Salisbury in August, second start and only sign of ability. *R. Turnell.*

LUCKY FORTUNE 2 ch.g. Gulf Pearl 117–Queen's Pet (Pall Mall 132) (1981 **90** 5g 5g⁴ 5d* 6f² 5f² 6g³) Apr 12; IR 6,600Y; neat, strong gelding; half-brother to fairly useful sprinter Hedge School (by Swinging Junior); dam never ran; showed improved form to win 15-runner maiden race at Leicester in May by ¾ length from Plagal; second twice the following month, coming up against a useful newcomer when beaten 3 lengths by Custer at Leicester and going down by short head to Never So Lucky in 18-runner event at Windsor; effective at 5f and will stay 7f; seems to act on any going; exported to Hong Kong. *B. Hanbury.*

498

Great Surrey Stakes, Epsom—Lucky Hunter is driven out to beat My Dear Fellow (centre) and Fly Baby

LUCKY HUNTER   2 b.c. Huntercombe 133–Lucky Omen 99 (Queen's Hussar **118** 124)   (1981 5g⁴ 5g* 5d* 5f 5g 5g² 6d⁴ 5g 6g²)

Nothing that Lucky Hunter had done before the William Hill Middle Park Stakes at Newmarket in October indicated that he was capable of finishing second in that race, and it was no great surprise when he was returned at 66/1. Not even his appearance in the paddock—he looked particularly well in himself and impressed us, whereas earlier in the year he had had a tendency to get a little worked up in the preliminaries—could shake the evidence of the form-book, which seemed to show him to be just useful and not particularly consistent. However, having made the running Lucky Hunter looked for a moment or two as though he was going to hold on before going down by only three quarters of a length to Cajun.   Although it wasn't a particularly strongly-run race there is nothing to suggest that Lucky Hunter was flattered by the outcome.

Lucky Hunter had shown ability on his first two outings, picking up a maiden race at Lingfield on the second of them.   He ran six times subsequently before the Middle Park Stakes, putting up his best performances in winning the Great Surrey Stakes at Epsom, and finishing a head second to Chellaston Park under top weight in a nursery at Goodwood and fourth, beaten under four lengths by Full Extent, in the Gimcrack Stakes at York.   He didn't run within a stone of those performances in his other races, the Norfolk Stakes at Royal Ascot, the Star Stakes at Sandown and the Flying Childers Stakes at Doncaster. In the last of these, just three weeks before the Middle Park Stakes, he put up an abysmal performance to finish last of seven.

Lucky Hunter (b.c. May 7, 1979)	Huntercombe (b 1967)	Derring-Do (br 1961)	Darius / Sipsey Bridge
		Ergina (br 1957)	Fair Trial / Ballechin
	Lucky Omen (b 1974)	Queen's Hussar (b 1960)	March Past / Jojo
		Brass (gr 1964)	Sovereign Path / Dancing Hill

Lucky Omen, whose first foal Lucky Hunter is, was also in Lucky Hunter's stable in her racing days; she won over five and six furlongs as a two-year-old. Her form at three wasn't so good, and she was only once in the frame in five outings from seven furlongs to a mile and a half.   The second dam, Brass, showed no worthwhile form in two starts at two years but has fared better at stud with four winners, Lucky Omen being probably the best of them.   Lucky Hunter's sire, Huntercombe, was a top-class sprinter, numbering the Middle Park Stakes, July Cup and Nunthorpe Stakes among his six victories.   Not all his offspring have been sprinters—Pyjama Hunt, who finished fourth in the Derby, and Radetzky, a very smart performer at up to a mile and a quarter, are examples of those who stayed further—but Lucky Hunter's dam showed her best form

Mr R. N. Khan's "Lucky Hunter"

at sprint distances and Lucky Hunter's style of racing suggests that he too will be best served by five and six furlongs. A strong, compact, good sort of colt, Lucky Hunter has shown his best form on an easy surface. On the evidence of his final outing and his physical appearance that day he has the makings of a very smart sprinter. *C. Brittain.*

LUCKY IVOR (USA) 2 b.c. Sir Ivor 135–Carnival Queen (Amerigo 116§) **70 p** (1981 7d⁴) half-brother to numerous winners, notably Italian Oaks winner Carnauba (by Noholme II), very useful miler Hey Rube (by Intentionally) and smart Pink Tights (by Vertex), successful at up to 1m; dam, half-sister to $297,000 earner Three Rings, won 5 times at up to 1m; 20/1 and ridden by 7-lb claimer, made late headway to finish 5 lengths fourth of 22 to Starbells in minor event at Chepstow in October; should improve a fair bit when tackling middle distances at 3 yrs. *J. Dunlop.*

LUCKY JOKER 2 br.f. Cawston's Clown 113–Charlie's Double (Fighting **67** Charlie 127) (1981 5g 5s⁴ 6s² 6f 7fg* 6fg 7s 7g) Mar 25; 1,050F; lengthy filly; half-sister to winning 3-y-o stayer Shooting Butts (by Tycoon II) and 6f and 1m winner Robolin (by Master Sing); dam never ran; proved well suited to 7f when leading close home to win 10-runner maiden race at Wolverhampton in July by a neck from Wollotteen; last all subsequent outings; finds 6f too sharp and will stay 1m; seems to act on any going. *R. Hollinshead.*

LUCKY LOVE 3 b.f. Mummy's Pet 125–Gay Jennie 69 (Lord Gayle 124) **58** (1980 5g 5g 5d 1981 6fg 6d 5fg 6f 6fg 6fg* 6g) small filly; bought in 1,250 gns after beating Mount Eliza readily by 4 lengths in selling handicap at Windsor in September; will probably stay 7f; acts on a firm surface. *W. Wightman.*

LUCKY LUCY 2 gr.f. Comedy Star 121–Lovely Beak (Counsel 118) (1981 6s **63** 6fg 6f 7fg) Feb 12; 6,200Y; fair sort; sister to useful 1m to 1¼m winner Starfen, also a smart winner over hurdles, and is half-sister to a winner; dam ran only

500

once; showed speed when sixth in maiden races at Haydock and Redcar on first 2 starts, on latter course finishing about 8 lengths behind Full Extent in 18-runner event; well beaten next 2 outings; should stay 7f; wears bandages. *C. Gray.*

LUCKY MAN 5 b.g. Manacle 123–Quite Sweet 100 (Super Sam 124) (1980 8f **92** 7fg* 8f³ 7f⁴ 7g* 7d² 8g³ 7g 6g 7.3fg⁴ 7fg² 6d³ 1981 8s 7d 7d³ 7g 7fg 7fg 7g 7fg² 7fg² 7fg³ 7s² 6s* 7d) workmanlike gelding; fairly useful handicapper; beat subsequently-disqualified Royal Diplomat by 4 lengths at Newbury in October; had run well in valuable race at Ascot previous start; stays 1m; acts on any going; good mount for a boy; tough and genuine. *P. M. Taylor.*

LUCKY MISTAKE 4 gr.f. Averof 123–Kingdom Come 77 (Klondyke Bill 125) **34** (1980 8s 8s 6f 6h³ 6g 6s 6fg 6fg 6d 5d 7g* 8fg 8d 7s 1981 10.2s 7d 8g 7d 8d 7d 8g³ 8f 7f 8f 10g 8f) strong filly; plater; possibly stays 1m; acts on hard going; blinkered twice in 1980; has worn bandages. *W. Marshall.*

LUCKY MUM 2 gr.f. Lucky Wednesday 124–Mum's Song 76 (Saintly Song 128) — (1981 5f 7g 6g 6g 6s) Apr 28; rather leggy filly; first foal; dam 2-y-o 5f winner; only poor form; has worn bandages behind; blinkered fifth outing; formerly trained by G. Lockerbie; sold 500 gns Doncaster November Sales. *K. Stone.*

LUCKY OXTON 2 b.g. Lucky Wednesday 124–Oxton Lady 81 (Chebs Lad 120) **59** (1981 5g 5g 5g 5f 7fg) Mar 1; leggy, narrow non-thoroughbred gelding; third foal; dam useful sprint plater; staying-on seventh of 12 to Rapid Knot in maiden race at Catterick in August, only glimmer of ability; evidently suited by 7f. *M. W. Easterby.*

LUCKY SEASON 2 br.f. Lucky Wednesday 124–Honey Season 66 (Silly **52** Season 127) (1981 5g⁴ 5d⁴ 5g* 6f²) May 15; rather leggy filly; first foal; dam plating class at 2 yrs; didn't have much to beat when favourite for 7-runner seller at Carlisle in May and made all to win by 2½ lengths from Next Decade; 2 lengths second of 5 to odds-on Saga's Humour in similar race at Stockton the following month, only subsequent appearance; bred to stay 1¼m. *M. W. Easterby.*

LUCKY SEVENTEEN 9 b.h. So Blessed 130–Alcina (Alycidon 138) (1980 NR — 1981 10d 10d 12d 12s) no longer seems of any account; changed hands 900 gns Ascot August Sales. *D. Weeden.*

LUCKY TINA 3 br.f. Workboy 123–March Poulet (March Past 124) (1980 6d — 6g 1981 6s 6g 7g 6g) leggy, short-backed filly; no sign of ability, including in a seller; blinkered third outing. *J. Berry.*

LUCKY TUESDAY 2 ch.f. Lucky Wednesday 124–Lady Phoenix (Lorenzaccio **50** 130) (1981 5g² 5g 6g 7f 7.2v 5g) Mar 8; lightly-made filly; second foal; dam unraced half-sister to very speedy Lady Rowley; placed in small race at Doncaster in May but subsequently descended to sellers without success; should stay beyond 5f; sold 320 gns Doncaster October Sales. *M. W. Easterby.*

LUCKY WEDDING 2 b.f. Lucky Wednesday 124–Lilmi Love 82 (Miralgo 130) **70** (1981 5s 6fg 5g 5d 5s⁴) May 24; 1,450Y (privately); half-sister to 6f and 7f winner Love Me Two (by Double Jump); dam won at 1¼m; prominent in maiden races at Lingfield and Folkestone in the autumn on third and fifth outings; not bred for sprinting; blinkered last 2 outings. *V. Soane.*

LUCY BROTHERTON 2 br.f. Pieces of Eight 128–Sterling Kate (Sterling Bay) — (1981 5s 6f) Mar 9; lengthy filly with poor hind legs; first foal; dam poor Irish maiden; unquoted when behind in maiden race in April and minor event in July, both at Nottingham. *W. Holden.*

LUIGI'S GIRL 3 b.f. The Brianstan 128–Malton Hope 92 (High Treason 126) — (1980 5g 5f 1981 5fg 8fg 6f) small, lightly-made filly; poor maiden; has been tried in blinkers. *B. Hills.*

LULAV 3 br.g. Prince Regent 129–Scarletta 103 (Red God 128**§**) (1980 5fg 6f **93** 7d 1981 12s 12d* 10f 12fg³ 14g⁴ 12fg* 10fg³ 10fg 11.1fg³ 10g² 9g³ 12g) well-made gelding; won maiden race at Folkestone in June and quite well-contested minor event at Newmarket in July, showing improved form when beating Ma Femme a head in latter; placed in handicaps subsequently, running particularly well when 4 lengths third of 28 behind Braughing in William Hill Cambridgeshire at Newmarket in October (raced on apparently disadvantageous far side for most of way); stays 1½m; acts on a firm and a soft surface; trained first 4 starts by R. Smyth. *R. Hannon.*

LULWORTH COVE 2 b.f. Averof 123–Princess Zena 96 (Habitat 134) (1981 **114** 4.5g 6g 6g* 7s 5v) Mar 13; 6,400F; first foal; dam won over 5f at 2 yrs, her only season to race; won small race at Clairefontaine in August by a neck; put up surprisingly good effort when 21/1 for all-aged Prix du Petit Couvert at Longchamp in October on fifth outing, being beaten only 2½ lengths into fifth-of-seven place behind Park Romeo; evidently suited by 5f. *J. C. Cunnington, France.*

LUMEN 6 br.g. Prince Tenderfoot 126–Bright Match 73 (Match III 135) (1980 16s 12g 12fg² 13.3fg 1981 16d 12fg 18g) compact, deep-girthed gelding; useful hurdler; lightly raced on flat nowadays; best form at up to 1½m although ran respectably over 18f final start; seems to act on any going but goes well on a sound surface; used to wear blinkers; suitable mount for an inexperienced rider. *J. Gifford.* **77**

LUNARIA (USA) 2 ch.f. Twist The Axe–Flame Tamer (Court Martial) (1981 5g 5f 6g) Apr 7; 27,000Y; smallish, lengthy filly; good walker; half-sister to 3 winners, notably smart 1979 2-y-o sprinter Abeer (by Dewan); dam 6f winner; beaten some way in maiden races at Salisbury, Kempton and Nottingham (blinkered) in the summer and looks very moderate. *J. Tree.* **—**

LUNAR WIND 5 ch.g. Windjammer (USA)–Lunar Star (Star Gazer 123) (1980 7d 8.2fg 8f 8f² 8f⁴ 9fg* 8fg³ 9g³ 11g 8.2g⁴ 8.2g⁴ 8fg 8d 1981 9f* 8fg* 8fg 8f* 9d 8.2f² 7g³ 8fg*) leggy, narrow gelding; quite a modest handicapper; successful at Ripon (apprentices), Edinburgh (made all), Thirsk (apprentices) and Beverley; best at up to 9f on top-of-the-ground; has worn blinkers; good mount for an apprentice. *D. Yeoman.* **76**

LUSITANICA 4 b.f. Pieces of Eight 128–Auspice 84 (Aureole 132) (1980 10g 10.1fg 10s 10g 1981 10g 8d⁴ 10g* 10fg 10.2fg 10d² 10g* 10fg* 10fg³ 11g⁴ 12g 12g* 12s 12g² 10.2d⁴) lengthy filly; showed much improved form in handicaps in 1981, winning at Ripon, Nottingham (trotted up), Yarmouth and Newmarket; beat End of War and Capricorn Line by ¾ length on last-named in October; suited by 1½m or more; has won on a firm surface but is ideally suited by some give in the ground; suitable mount for an apprentice; usually held up; tough and consistent. *M. Tompkins.* **80**

LUTANIST 4 ch.g. Luthier 126–Escorial 110 (Royal Palace 131) (1980 13s² 14g⁴ 1981 16fg 13s⁴) lengthy gelding; modest maiden at his best; should stay 1¾m; suited by soft going; moved badly to post second start. *P. Makin.* **—**

LUXEMBOURG 3 b.g. Royal Palace 131–Karen 106 (Primera 131) (1980 7fg 8g 7d 1981 8s 11v² 12.5s 10v⁴ 12s² 12g 12g³ 12.3d 12g 12fg 14fg) workmanlike gelding; placed in maiden and minor events early in year; should have stayed at least 1¾m; acted on soft going; often blinkered and occasionally looked none too keen; dead. *W. Stubbs.* **—**

LUXULAM 3 b.c. Tower Walk 130–Immaculate (Sovereign Path 125) (1980 5fg 6g 8d³ 7d³ 7d 1981 7d 8g 8f³ 7f 7fg² 7fg³) big, strong, good-looking colt; placed in varied company, and looked a shade unlucky when second in handicap at Warwick in June; stays 1m; ran freely in blinkers final start in 1980. *R. Armstrong.* **68**

LUXURIATE (USA) 4 b.g. Tom Rolfe–Dee Dee Luxe (Cavan) (1980 10.8s 16f 16f² 14g³ 14g 16fg 1981 14fg) lightly-made gelding; staying maiden; acts on firm going; usually blinkered in 1980. *I. Wardle.* **—**

LUXURY 2 b.f. Ragapan 118–Vanessa's Queen (Faberge II 121) (1981 5g³ 5d 6g³ 7fg² 7f 7fg² 8fg 8g³ 8fg² 8s⁴ 10s* 10.2g³) May 7; lightly-made filly; fifth reported foal; dam never ran; prominent on most of her outings and won 22-runner maiden race at Nottingham in October by 1¼ lengths from Hawaiian Heir; will be suited by 1½m; probably acts on any going; sometimes sweats up and rarely impresses in paddock but is consistent. *J. Carr.* **88**

LUZ BAY 6 b.h. Mountain Call 125–Palmaressa 80 (Royal Palm 131) (1980 11.7fg* 10h² 11.1fg* 12f⁴ 1981 12d 12fg 12d 10f 10f³ 11.7fg 12f³ 12f² 10f⁴ 12d* 12fg³ 12fg) strong, well-made horse; won claiming race at Newmarket in August; in frame in varied company, including selling, on several other occasions; stays 1½m; probably acts on any going; often blinkered; sold 1,500 gns Ascot December Sales. *T. Gosling.* **53**

LYDIAN (FR) 3 ch.c. Lyphard 132–Miss Manon (Bon Mot III 132) (1980 8.5fg 8s³ 8g* 1981 10d² 11fg* 12g* 12s* 12f³)
Lydian's controversial refusal to enter the stalls probably cost him a place behind Shergar in the Derby. His record is better than that of Scintillating Air and Shotgun if not of Glint of Gold; he was clearly a high-class horse even though he gained his major victories in Germany and Italy. We, like everyone else, saw all too little of him but we were impressed with his performance under **120**

Ecurie Aland's "Lydian"

difficulties in the Prix Niel at Longchamp in September on what turned out to be his final racecourse appearance: after slipping at the start, losing a lot of ground and injuring himself in the process, he finished third of seven behind Akarad, reaching a challenging position early in the straight and eventually going down by only four and a half lengths despite being eased a length and a half or so when clearly held by the winner and Rahotep. In the circumstances it wouldn't have been a surprise had he turned the tables in the Prix de l'Arc de Triomphe.

Lydian (Fr) (ch.c. 1978)	Lyphard (b 1969)	Northern Dancer (b 1961)	Nearctic
			Natalma
		Goofed (ch 1960)	Court Martial
			Barra II
	Miss Manon (b 1970)	Bon Mot III (ch 1963)	Worden II
			Djebel Idra
		Miss Molly (br 1965)	Molvedo
			Miss Glasso

His injury cost Lydian a run in the Arc. By the end of October he was being advertised as a stallion by Alchemy Farm in Kentucky at 30,000 dollars, live foal; advertised, too, as a 1981 group winner in three countries, 'a handy winner of the Prix Noailles at Longchamp over Singing Boy'. Well, that blurb is a shade misleading since Lydian only 'won' the Noailles on the disqualification of Explorer King for having traces of nandrolone in his system; Explorer King passed the post first ahead of Lydian, then came Arc d'Or not Singing Boy, who was actually fourth in the original result. The distances were a length; a length and a half; a length and a half. Subsequently the placed horses were moved up in order. No doubts attended Lydian's pattern-race victories elsewhere. There was another disqualification in the Gran Premio di Milano in June but that concerned the runner-up Navarino who after being trounced four lengths by Lydian was relegated to third for leaning on third-placed Ladislao di Oppelm. Both second and third are older horses, not quite in the top international bracket. Lydian also accounted for some older horses, as well as the French three-year-old Tow, in the Grosser Preis von Berlin at Dusseldorf in July. He beat the

LYD

top-class German five-year-old Konigsstuhl by a length and a half, the pair well clear of Tow and five others who included the out-of-form Shoot A Line.

Lydian is the third important winner from the first three foals of his dam, the 1973 Prix de Diane fourth Miss Manon; Sharpman (by Sharpen Up) and Mot D'Or (by Rheingold) were his predecessors. Sharpman split a pastern while running third to Top Ville in the Prix du Jockey-Club of 1979 and had to be retired; earlier he had finished second in the Prix Lupin and the Poule d'Essai des Poulains. Mot D'Or beat the latest Washington International winner Providential in the Prix Hocquart and finished third in the Grand Prix de Paris in 1980. The dam won three races at around a mile and a quarter. She is out of a half-sister to the high-class miler Prudent Miss; the third dam Miss Glasso is out of a half-sister to another well-known mile winner, the One Thousand Guineas winner Happy Laughter.

Lydian has fine looks and a good temperament besides an outstanding pedigree, and he is by no means overpriced by today's American standards as a stallion. His withdrawal from the Derby which so upset his connections, who deemed he hadn't been given a fair chance by the handlers, should not be held against him: he was a bit stubborn but never gave trouble on any other occasion. Lydian was well suited by a mile and a half. He seemed to act on any going. *Mme C. Head, France.*

LYDIA ROSE 4 b.f. Mummy's Pet 125–Sprightly Sprite 80 (Babur 126) (1980 **55** 8g² 9d⁴ 8g 8g 10s⁴ 10s 1981 10d 10d³ 10f 10fg⁴ 10fg 10g 10g 10g³ 12d) middle-distance handicapper; seems to act on any going; trained by D. Weeden part of season; sold 2,800 gns Ascot November Sales. *W. Musson.*

LYMOND 2 b.c. Rapid River 127–Gill Breeze (Farm Walk 111) (1981 5s 5g⁴ **65** 6t⁴ 6f 6fg 0fg 5s) Mar 29; 2,200Y; quite a useful sort; half-brother to 5 winners, including 7f winner Secret Gill (by Most Secret); dam never ran; fourth in maiden races at Thirsk in May and Haydock in July; will probably stay 7f; blinkered last 2 outings; will be more at home in sellers. *J. Calvert.*

LYN AFFAIR 4 b.f. Royal Palace 131–True Dresden 58 (Vilmoray 126) — (1980 8s⁴ 10g⁴ 11.7fg 10.6f 12.2fg² 16g 12g⁴ 14.6fg 11d 1981 10.2d 12d) work-manlike filly; plating-class maiden; stays 1½m; acts on a firm surface; wears blinkers; has had her tongue tied down. *N. Kernick.*

LYNCONWISE 3 br.g. Tudor Music 131–Shopping Wise (Floribunda 136) **78** (1980 6g 6fg 7d 5d 5d 6s³ 1981 7g 8d⁴ 8g⁴ 8s* 8d* 10f⁴ 8d 9fg) leggy, lightly-made gelding; won handicaps on successive days at Leicester in May, beating Cornish Granite by 10 lengths on first occasion (apprentice ridden) and Wise Man by 1½ lengths on second (apprentice event); best form at up to 1m; revels in the mud; genuine. *J. Bolger, Ireland.*

LYNESS DETECTIVE 2 b.c. Most Secret 119–Whistlewych 40 (Whistler 129) — (1981 5g 5g 7f) Feb 16; 520Y; workmanlike colt; half-brother to 3 winners, including useful 1976 sprinting 2-y-o Feuda¹ Wytch (by Tribal Chief); dam of little account; unquoted when in rear in maiden races at Thirsk in May, Catterick in June and Redcar (last of 18) in September. *S. Nesbitt.*

LYNN LIGHTFOOT 2 b.f. St Paddy 133–Quick Half 60 (Quorum 126) (1981 — 5g 7.2v) May 19; first foal; dam won over hurdles; well beaten both outings, one of them in a seller. *D. McCain.*

LYPHARD'S PRIDE (USA) 2 b. or br.c. Lyphard 132–Maidsmorton (Bold **98** Ruler) (1981 7fg² 8g) Mar 12; $260,000Y; neat, attractive colt; second foal; dam once-raced daughter of very smart filly Firm Policy; took some time to warm to his task in 8-runner Fitzroy House Stakes at Newmarket in August but began to make relentless progress 2f out and failed by only a neck to overhaul Chulia Street; never looked like winning 30-runner maiden race when second favourite at Newmarket in October but kept on fairly well to finish 5½ lengths fifth to Farioffa; will stay 1¼m; sure to win a race in 1982. *M. Stoute.*

LYPHMAS (USA) 2 b.c. Lyphard 132–Christmas Belle (Santa Claus 133) **100** p (1981 7g*) Apr 16; attractive colt; half-brother to 11f and 1¾m winner Tom Noel (by Tom Rolfe); dam, Irish middle-distance winner, is half-sister to smart Royal Sword; 7/2, made virtually all and stayed on well to win 9-runner minor event at Newmarket in August by ½ length from Be My Native; quite a taking individual who should improve over middle distances at 3 yrs. *H. Cecil.*

LYUBIANKA 3 br.g. Town Crier 119–Aberdevine 92 (Abernant 142) (1980 — NR 1981 6s 6v 10f 8d) 5,400Y; smallish, useful sort; half-brother to 2 minor winners; dam won at 5f and 7f; behind all outings, including in sellers; trained first 2 starts by A. Pitt. *A. Moore.*

M

MACAROY (FR) 2 ch.c. Tyrant–Voile (Baldric II 131) (1981 5fg*) May 7: **108** p
60,000 francsY (approx. £6,000); first foal; dam, second over 10.5f in France, is
half-sister to numerous winners, including Pram, herself dam of Prix de Diane
winner Dunette; looked sure to make a smart 2-y-o when winning Prix Yacowlef
at Deauville in August by 3 lengths from Baltimore Bullet but didn't race again;
will stay 1m; blinkered at Deauville. *N. Pelat, France.*

MACMILLION 2 br.c. So Blessed 130–Salsafy 81 (Tudor Melody 129) (1981 **110**
6d 6g² 6fg 7fg* 6f² 6d² 7s) Jan 21; 24,000Y; workmanlike colt; second foal;
closely related to useful 3-y-o Baz Bombati (by Sun Prince), a winner at up to
1¼m; dam won over 12.2f; disputed lead throughout when winning 18-runner
maiden race at Newbury by ¾ length from newcomer General Anders; bettered
that effort on next 2 starts, finishing 2½ lengths second to Prima Voce in nursery
at Kempton in September and excelling himself when 3 lengths second of 8 to
Hays in Mill Reef Stakes at Newbury later same month; will be suited by 1m;
ran badly on only outing on very soft going. *Mrs B. Waring.*

MAC'S DELIGHT 4 ch.g. Scottish Rifle 127–Halkissimo 61 (Khalkis 127) **69**
(1980 12.5g⁴ 10.4f⁴ 10.5f 10fg³ 9g* 8g² 8d 8s 9fg³ 10.4d* 10.2g⁴ 10d 10s 1981
12.3d³ 12s⁴ 12g² 10g² 11g² 10.2fg³ 12.3fg* 10f³ 12f² 15.8g) strong gelding;
won handicap at Chester in July; fine short-head second to Shaftesbury in quite
valuable race at Thirsk in August; stays 1½m; acts on any going but goes well
on top-of-the-ground; often blinkered but is effective without; suitable mount
for a boy; doesn't always find much off bridle; sold 10,500 gns Newmarket
Autumn Sales. *Denys Smith.*

MADAM DIX PER CENT 2 b.f. Import 127–Yolancar 65 (Kibenka 119) —
(1981 7fg 8fg) Apr 27; 1,000Y; plain, leggy filly; half-sister to 1½m winner
Yolanso (by Lauso); dam poor maiden; in rear in maiden races at Catterick in
August and Beverley in September. *S. Nesbitt.*

MADAME BLEU 2 gr.f. Bruni 132–La Sinope (Thatch 136) (1981 6f 6f) —
May 24; first foal; dam unraced half-sister to smart Gale Bridge; behind in
maiden races at Stockton and Doncaster in June. *K. Stone.*

MADAM GAY 3 b.f. Star Appeal 133–Saucy Flirt 102 (King's Troop 118) **125**
(1980 6g 6d 7g² 1981 8.5fg² 8g 10.5s² 12g² 10.5fg* 10fg⁴ 12fg² 10s³ 12g³ 10g)
     The Prix de Diane de Revlon at Chantilly in June fell easily to Madam Gay,
a remarkable filly who hadn't previously won a race of any description. Very
few classics (the Diane is the French equivalent of the Oaks run over a slightly
shorter distance) are won by maidens, still fewer by those making as many as
their eighth appearance on the racecourse; Douve, the last maiden before
Madam Gay to win the event back in 1955, had run four times previously.
But Madam Gay was no ordinary maiden. She'd been campaigned all along
with a vigour and aggression typical of her connections, from the Chesham Stakes
to the Oaks before being sent to France, rewarding them with second place in
the Waterford Candelabra Stakes at Goodwood in 1980 and, in 1981, with third
place in the Princess Elizabeth Stakes at Epsom and second in the Musidora
Stakes at York and the Oaks; on another occasion she missed fourth in the One
Thousand Guineas by the narrowest of margins. Like Douve, Madam Gay
failed to win again. That this could happen was due entirely to her being
repeatedly called upon to tackle the best. There was, in fact, little that smacked
of anticlimax about Madam Gay's subsequent running. She beat all except

*Prix de Diane de Revlon, Chantilly—Madam Gay follows up her Epsom Oaks
second with a fine win from Val d'Erica (far side), April Run
(No. 5) and Ukraine Girl*

Shergar in the King George VI and Queen Elizabeth Diamond Stakes and went on to add substantially to her earnings with another two fine performances abroad, third place in the Arlington Million in the United States and Prix Vermeille in France. By the end of the season she had amassed an enormous amount of prize money—£236,916, win and place at exchange rates prevailing at the relevant time—which put her second to Shergar in the season's list, well ahead of the other fillies Marwell, Blue Wind, Fairy Footsteps and Condessa.

Madam Gay was beaten by the last four in the first half of the year—a length by Fairy Footsteps and a short head by Marwell in the Guineas, four lengths by Condessa in the Musidora and seven by Blue Wind in the Oaks. She had been running well, consistently well, only to find at least one too good for her; she had no excuses for her defeats except when a slight lack of condition just told behind Petroleuse and Applemint first time out in the Princess Elizabeth. Her record suggested there might also be at least one too good for her in the Prix de Diane, although some held that the return to a shorter distance would suit her and also that she had come up against one of the best Oaks winners for years in Blue Wind. Madam Gay had finished ten lengths clear of third-placed Leap Lively at Epsom; off the bridle early in the straight, she had battled along to overhaul Leap Lively at about the same point as the winner, then had been left standing over the last two furlongs. The field for the Diane contained among its fourteen starters the top two three-year-old fillies in France on current form, the Prix Saint-Alary winner Tootens and the Poule d'Essai des Pouliches winner Ukraine Girl, plus the easy Prix Cleopatre winner April Run and Val d'Erica, the Italian Guineas and Oaks winner. Tootens started favourite at 7/2; Madam Gay started at 9/1 along with Val d'Erica and the Saint-Alary third Last Love. Madam Gay produced a sparkling display, only eight days after her gruelling race at Epsom. She came from behind in a fast-run contest (El Dancerina, pacemaker for the Prix Vanteaux runner-up Derly, saw there was no hanging about) and sprinted past Val d'Erica to win easing up by four lengths in a record time after the Italian runner had looked set for victory two furlongs out. April Run, a different proposition over longer trips in the autumn, ran on to touch off Ukraine Girl for third. According to Madam Gay's jockey Piggott, winning his second successive Diane, they would have won by at least six lengths but for being driven wide by Tootens. This was doubtful.

Winning by four lengths wasn't enough, in our opinion, to give Madam Gay a good chance against the colts in her next race, the Coral Eclipse Stakes, yet in defeat she ran well below the form we, and apparently most other observers, anticipated. She never got in a blow in finishing fifth of seven behind Master Willie (subsequently she was awarded fourth place upon the disqualification of Hard Fought). In the parade she appeared hard trained. After such a strenuous season Madam Gay had ample grounds for one below-par, jaded performance; plenty of fillies in her shoes would have been well over the top already. If Madam Gay was feeling the effects of her races by then she pretty soon recovered, for three weeks after the Eclipse she earned a run in the newly-instituted Arlington Million by a magnificent four-length second to Shergar in the King George VI and Queen Elizabeth Diamond Stakes at Ascot, late in July. On that occasion she turned the Eclipse tables on Master Willie and Fingal's Cave, beating Fingal's Cave by a short head for second place. She played such a prominent part in England's premier middle-distance event for three-year-olds and upwards that she was right there on the outside on the turn, with Master Willie and Light Cavalry only marginally ahead and Shergar virtually level on the rails. She quickly took the measure of the two older colts and, as in the Oaks, battled on to the very last stride even though finding the winner going away from her. In the thirty-one years of the King George only four fillies have come out on top and only Almeria, Gladness, Petite Etoile, Highclere, Mrs Penny and Madam Gay have been second.

The Arlington Million, run on turf at Arlington Park, Chicago, on August 30th attracted a field worthy of the occasion of its inauguration despite the failure of half the original 14 selected horses to get to post. As the name suggests a million-dollar purse was offered, split five ways: 600,000 dollars to the winner, 200,000 dollars to the second, 110,000 dollars to the third, 60,000 dollars to the fourth and 30,000 dollars to the fifth. The world-wide entry initially comprised 274 horses at 1,000 dollars, whittled down to 87 at the first forfeit stage (an extra 2,500 dollars) and 52 at the second forfeit stage (a further 2,500 dollars); 5 supplementary entries then came in at 35,000 dollars, at which point a selection panel picked their first 14 plus 10 reserves. Madam Gay, a supplementary entry, was on the panel's preferred list as, naturally, was America's best grass horse, the six-year-old John Henry. In the end Madam

Gay and Fingal's Cave represented England, Argument represented France; there was never much chance that any of the top European middle-distance three-year-old colts would be present, nor, we think, will there be in the future since the race cuts too much across the pattern of European racing. Madam Gay fully justified a typically bold venture. Carrying 4-lb overweight at Piggott's near-minimum 8-5, she was beaten only a nose by John Henry and another American horse The Bart, beaten only a nose and two and a half lengths after being in strong contention from some way out. Incidentally the weight-for-sex allowance in the Arlington Million is an imaginative 5 lb, the same as in the Derby.

When in the States Madam Gay was, according to report, up for sale to the Americans at an asking price of two million dollars. If so, there were no takers, and two weeks later she appeared at Longchamp for the Prix Vermeille, against Val d'Erica, April Run and company. To her great credit she looked perky when she walked round the paddock there, still bright in her coat. Judging by her connections' post-race comments—that she didn't quite get the mile and a half!—connections were a shade disappointed that she couldn't win. For our money Madam Gay thoroughly distinguished herself once again. Having been held up in the last three of ten, with plenty to do on the turn into the fairly short straight, she went after the leaders heading for home; by then April Run was in front, and Madam Gay never managed to reach her, coming under the whip approaching the last furlong and losing second place to Leandra in the last furlong. Still, Madam Gay was beaten only one and a half lengths and a head behind fillies who went on to finish third and ninth respectively in the Prix de l'Arc de Triomphe. Madam Gay *was* sold, privately to M Wildenstein, after the Prix Vermeille and has been sent to the USA. Before she departed she ran in the Champion Stakes, finishing ninth of sixteen to Vayrann, never really in the race. Fillies have done well over the years in the Champion Stakes but very few who have been raced as hard as Madam Gay. She was beaten by under ten lengths.

Madam Gay's sire won the Prix de l'Arc de Triomphe, her dam was a sprinter.

M D. Wildenstein's "Madam Gay"

Star Appeal has made a pleasing start to his stud career and had the distinction of two prominent runners in the One Thousand Guineas, with Go Leasing finishing two places ahead of Madam Gay. The dam Saucy Flirt won over six furlongs at York and Leicester; she was a useful handicapper though not the best of her dam Picnic Party's numerous winners. That honour went either to her sister, the speedy two-year-old of 1967, Canteen, or to the very useful sprint handicapper Staincross; another half-brother, the stayer Mount Irvine, was quite useful at his best. Picnic Party was a sprint handicapper out of a winning daughter of the well-known mare Babylon, the dam of Espresso. Madam Gay cost 8,000 guineas as a yearling at the Newmarket October Sales. Saucy Flirt had bred two minor winners at that time—Four Jets (by Jolly Jet), the winner of a two-mile seller at Catterick, and Flirt's River (by Forlorn River), successful in Brazil. Four Jets was bought out of his seller, and subsequently won on the flat and over jumps in Belgium.

Madam Gay (b.f. 1978)	Star Appeal (b 1970)	Appiani II (b 1963)	Herbager / Angela Rucellai
		Sterna (br 1960)	Neckar / Stammesart
	Saucy Flirt (br 1968)	King's Troop (b 1957)	Princely Gift / Equiria
		Picnic Party (b 1959)	Honeyway / Garden City

Madam Gay is a tall, lengthy, quite attractive filly, and a really good mover who seems to act on any going. She is a top-class middle-distance performer, very tough and genuine, and she should do well in the United States. *P. Kelleway.*

MADELINE 3 b.f. Cavo Doro 124–Recce (Donore 119) (1980 NR 1981 10s 8fg 10f) small filly; half-sister to fair 1976 2-y-o 5.9f winner Heath Wood (by Murrayfield); dam never ran; behind in 2 maiden races and an apprentice event; still looked in need of race and moved badly final start. *M. Ryan.* —

MADIGAN MILL 4 ch.f. Mill Reef 141–La Speroana 68 (Roan Rocket 128) (1980 10f 8d 1981 10f 12f 11.5fg* 10fg³ 11.1f) lengthy, light-framed filly; good mover; floored odds laid on On A Cloud by 4 lengths in small race at Yarmouth in August; will stay 1¾m; acts on a firm surface. *J. Winter.* 66

MADISON STYLE 3 b.g. Crowned Prince 128–Monte Rosa (Crepello 136) (1980 5fg² 5.8fg³ 6g² 7f² 1981 8g 7g 7f 7g³ 6f 8fg² 7.2g 9f 8f 8g) leggy, lightly-made gelding; ran creditably on several occasions, notably when very close third behind Dancing Sally in handicap at Salisbury in June and 1½ lengths second to Cracking Form in ladies race at Ascot in July, but appeared to lose his form and ran poorly in blinkers on final start; well suited by 1m and will probably stay 1¼m; often bandaged. *F. J. Houghton.* 74

MAD MOMENTS 3 gr.g. Saritamer 130–Argent Soleil 68 (Silver Shark 129) (1980 5d 5f³ 5fg 5s 6fg 5f 6g 1981 5s 6g 7g 7fg 6g) sprint plater; blinkered third start; retained 560 gns Newmarket Autumn Sales. *G. Blum.* —

MAD MONEY 3 br.g. Silly Season 127–Generous Thought 81 (Compensation 127) (1980 NR 1981 8fg 12g 10fg 10d 12fg) 550Y; big gelding; second foal; brother to smart French filly Wild Idea, winner at up to 9f; dam placed at up to 7f at 2 yrs; ran best race in maiden event at Newmarket in August on fourth start; sold 780 gns Doncaster November Sales. *W. Musson.* —

MADONA 2 ch.f. Manado 130–Light Diamond (Florescence 120) (1981 5s 5.3f 5fg³ 5g 5d) Feb 17; IR 9,400F, 16,000Y; small, rather lightly-made filly; fourth foal; half-sister to 3 winners, including fairly useful 3-y-o miler Paterno (by Young Emperor); only poor form; hasn't a great deal of scope. *P. Haslam.* 53

MAD TYCOON 3 b.g. Tycoon II–Polly Mead (Rasputin 83) (1980 5f 5s 5d 5d 1981 10s) strong gelding; poor form, including in a seller. *A. Jarvis.* —

MAELSTROM LAKE 2 b.c. Auction Ring 123–Skyway 76 (Skymaster 126) (1981 4s² 5g* 5s* 5.5d* 6f²) 118
Something of a scandal hit the British turf back in 1970 when the running of a two-year-old filly making her first appearance was reported to the Stewards of the Jockey Club: the filly in question, Skyway, was owned by the Duke of Norfolk, a member of the Jockey Club, former vice-chairman of the Turf Board

Prix Robert Papin, Maisons-Laffitte—Maelstrom Lake takes the first two-year-old pattern race of the French season; Green Forest finishes strongly to snatch second place from the filly Grease (No. 8)

and the Queen's Representative at Ascot. The Stewards, finding there was a case to answer, fined Skyway's trainer John Dunlop £500 and suspended her rider Ron Hutchinson for fourteen days. That was the only time Skyway hit the headlines as a racehorse. She failed to win at two, even though tried in selling company, and was sold at the end of the season for 1,900 guineas. After scrambling home in a mile-and-a-quarter maiden race at Hamilton on her only outing at three Skyway drifted into obscurity until cropping up ten years later as the dam of one of the best French two-year-olds, Maelstrom Lake.

Maelstrom Lake's clashes with Green Forest were one of the features of the summer two-year-old racing in France, the pair meeting three more times after Green Forest got the verdict by a neck on their debut, in a four-furlong dash at Maisons-Laffitte in May. By the time they met again two months later in the Prix du Bois at Longchamp Maelstrom Lake had also got off the mark, leading throughout in a Maisons-Laffitte maiden race, and he comfortably levelled the score with Green Forest at Longchamp; after disputing the lead from the start he drew away from two furlongs out to score by a length and a half from Shayina, with his old rival only fourth.

Their next meeting was in a much more important event, the Group 1 Prix Robert Papin at Maisons-Laffitte towards the end of July which also attracted the unbeaten Italian filly Grease. Maelstrom Lake was soon well placed as Grease disputed the lead with the smooth Evry winner Colman and the Prix du Bois third Pampabird, and was clearly the main danger to the Italian filly as Grease took a narrow advantage two furlongs out. By the distance he had taken her measure and then held off the fast-finishing Green Forest, who seemed to have been given plenty to do, by half a length. Green Forest was backed to take his revenge in the Prix Morny over the slightly longer trip of six furlongs at Deauville a month later, starting second favourite to the filly River Lady, a highly impressive winner of both her starts. Gain his revenge he did but in unsatisfactory circumstances: Maelstrom Lake was given a poor ride by his regular partner Doleuze. First of all Maelstrom Lake hampered the English colt Tender King in crossing to the rails in the early stages; then he managed to get into all sorts of trouble in a five-horse field, twice failing to obtain a run and finding an opening only inside the final furlong, by which time it was too late. In the end he failed by three quarters of a length to catch Green Forest. As a result of the incident with Tender King Doleuze received an eight-day suspension.

Hopes that the Prix de la Salamandre would shed more light on which was the better disappeared when Maelstrom Lake was withdrawn shortly before the race. The ground was considered too soft for him, even though he had previously won in similar conditions; perhaps what his trainer really feared was that seven furlongs on soft ground would prove too stiff a test of stamina. Unfortunately the Prix Morny proved to be Maelstrom Lake's last race in France. He had

M Jacques Feuillard's "Maelstrom Lake"

been sold to Walter Haefner, owner of the Moyglare Stud, before the Salamandre and towards the end of October it was announced that he had been sent to the USA.

Maelstrom Lake's exportation is regrettable. We have outlined in our notes on Glancing the shortage of high-class sprinters in France, and Maelstrom Lake, even though he will probably stay seven furlongs given the chance, could well have developed into a champion sprinter there. Maelstrom Lake has the make and shape of a sprinter—he's a strong-quartered, good sort—and the pedigree of one. He's a son of the successful young sire Auction Ring, whose temperament prevented his staying anything like so far as one would have

Maelstrom Lake (b.c. Mar 31, 1979)	Auction Ring (b 1972)	Bold Bidder (b 1962)	Bold Ruler / High Bid
		Hooplah (b 1965)	Hillary / Beadah
	Skyway (b 1968)	Skymaster (ch 1958)	Golden Cloud / Discipliner
		Emerald Isle (b 1961)	Kelly / Bridle Way

expected, out of Skyway who, despite her modest form, was bred to be a fast filly. Skyway's sire was that tough, high-class sprinter Skymaster and her dam, the five-furlong winner Emerald Isle, was a three-parts sister to the top-class Sound Track, winner of the King's Stand Stakes and beaten only once in eight races. Skyway is one of Emerald Isle's seven winners in Britain and Ireland; in contrast her own record as a broodmare had been very ordinary until Maelstrom Lake came along. From six previous foals she had bred only a winner in Cyprus by Realm, the winning hurdler Level Flight (by Pitcairn) and Flying Bid, a sister to Maelstrom Lake who eventually won a race over a mile and a quarter at Listowel as a four-year-old after eighteen unsuccessful starts in England. To another mating with Auction Ring Skyway foaled the plating-class filly Miss Cyprus, so it isn't altogether surprising that Maelstrom Lake fetched only 3,000 guineas when sold at the Houghton Sales. *E. Bartholomew, France.*

510

Galtres Stakes, York—Ma Femme wears down Rollrights (checks)

MAESGLAS 5 b.g. King Log 115–Fairy First 54§ (Fairey Fulmar 124) (1980 —
8v 8fg 8.2d 9g 8g 9fg 13s 1981 8g) poor plater; stays 9f; best form on a sound
surface; sometimes blinkered. *H. Bell.*

MA FEMME 3 b.f. Bustino 136–Habituee (Habitat 134) (1980 NR 1981 **107**
12g² 12d* 12fg² 10g² 12d* 14.6g³ 12s) strong, good-bodied filly; good walker;
third foal; half-sister to a poor animal by Lorenzaccio; dam French 1m winner;
neck winner of minor event at Lingfield in June (from Rosetta Stone) and Galtres
Stakes at York in August (from Rollrights); improved steadily up straight and
stayed on to wear down her rival close home on latter course, pair finishing 7
lengths clear; didn't seem to find a great deal off the bridle when 1¼ lengths third
to Alma Ata in Park Hill Stakes at Doncaster in September and was never seen
with a chance when seventh of 11 to Flighting in Princess Royal Stakes at Ascot
in October; second on all her other starts, in maiden race at Lingfield, in quite
well-contested minor event at Newmarket (went down by a head to Lulav) and
in handicap at Nottingham (beaten 10 lengths by Lusitanica under a big weight);
stays 1¾m; acts on a firm and a soft surface. *B. Hobbs.*

MAGELKA 2 ch.f. Relkino 131–Magical 95 (Aggressor 130) (1981 7g 7f⁴ 8fg) **77**
Apr 21; good-topped filly; closely related to useful 1978 2-y-o 1m winner Atataho
(by Royalty) and half-sister to 3 winners, including useful 1¼m winner Easter
Sun and fair 3-y-o 1m and 1¼m winner Magikin (both by Bustino); dam won
twice over 5f at 2 yrs; ran best race over 1m, finishing 5¾ lengths fifth of 15 to
Rockfest after making much of running in £3,600 event at Goodwood in
September; will be suited by 1¼m. *M. Jarvis.*

MAGESTERIAL (USA) 4 b.c. Northern Dancer–Courting Days (Bold Lad, **116**
USA) (1980 7g⁴ 1981 10s² 12s 10fg³ 10fg* 12fg* 9f*) $250,000Y; big,
attractive colt; good mover; second foal; dam, winner over 1¼m in Ireland, is
half-sister to very smart 9f and 1¼m stakes winner Glowing Tribute and comes
from family of Allez France; smart performer who won four of his eight career
starts; gained three of those successes in 1981 when he stayed on well to beat
Bonol a length in 4-runner Land of Burns Stakes at Ayr in July, gamely held off
Old Oak Tree by a head in driving finish to Blandford Stakes at the Curragh in
August and made all to beat Dance Bid by 1½ lengths in Whitehall Stakes at
Phoenix Park in September (odds on); placed in two important races earlier,
going down by 2½ lengths to Erins Isle in Sean Graham Ballymoss Stakes at
the Curragh and coming home 1½ lengths third to Hard Fought (gave 7 lb) in

511

Mr R. E. Sangster's "Magesterial"

Prince of Wales's Stakes at Royal Ascot; stayed 1½m; acted on any going; syndicated at 125,000 dollars per share and is to stand at Spendthrift Farm, Kentucky, at $30,000 live foal. *V. O'Brien, Ireland.*

MAGGIEKNOCKATER 4 b.f. Sharpen Up 127–Jemimaville 80 (Royal Palace 131) (1980 NR 1981 8d 7g³ 8f 7g) rangy filly; has been hobdayed; first foal; dam stayed very well; seems only plating class; should stay 1m; sweated up and pulled hard third start; sold 4,000 gns Newmarket December Sales. *B. Hobbs.* **60**

MAGIC EARS 2 ch.f. Mandrake Major 122–Burning Ears 87 (Firestreak 125) (1981 6f 7g 7fg 7g) Apr 20; smallish, workmanlike filly; third foal; dam won over 1m and 1¼m, and is half-sister to smart 1977 2-y-o Fire Angel; behind in maiden races. *E. Weymes.* **—**

MAGIC FORMULA 3 b.f. St Paddy 133–La Leventina (Le Levanstell 122) (1980 6fg 6g³ 7fg 10s 1981 16g⁴ 12s 12fg 8f 10fg 13.8g) small filly; plating maiden; possibly doesn't stay 2m; blinkered final start (claimed by G. Toft). *P. Rohan.* **36**

MAGICIAN 2 br.g. Blue Cashmere 129–Our Circe (Burglar 128) (1981 6f 5fg 6fg 5v 6s 7g⁴) Apr 21; 5,200Y; compact gelding; first foal; dam ran once at 2 yrs; blinkered, ran far and away his best race when 7½ lengths fourth of 13 to Final Strike in £2,900 race at Newmarket in October; evidently suited by 7f. *M. Jarvis.* **75**

MAGIKIN 3 b.c. Bustino 136–Magical 95 (Aggressor 130) (1980 NR 1981 8g* 10.4g* 10fg³ 10fg³ 12fg 14.6g) neat, attractive colt; brother to useful 1¼m winner Easter Sun, and half-brother to useful 1978 2-y-o 1m winner Atataho (by Royalty) and fair middle-distance winner Hurakan (by Seaepic); dam won twice over 5f at 2 yrs; won Wood Ditton Stakes at Newmarket in April (in quite good **88**

512

style by 1½ lengths from Grand Unit) and slowly-run minor event at Chester in May (beat unlucky-in-running Indian Trail a neck); about 2 lengths third in handicaps won by Indian Trail at Newmarket and Goodwood (Extel Stakes) in July; didn't respond particularly well to pressure in handicap at Newbury in August and was used as a pacemaker in St Leger at Doncaster on his only subsequent outing; should stay 1½m; sent to Hong Kong. *R. Hern.*

MAGJOY 2 b.f. Le Johnstan 123–Rockfire 65 (Epaulette 125) (1981 5g 5f) Mar 21; 900F; leggy, lightly-made filly; half-sister to 2 winning platers and a winner in Belgium; dam won 6f seller at 2 yrs; well beaten in maiden events at Thirsk in May and Pontefract in June. *H. Wharton.* —

MAGNAMALA 2 ro.g. Runnymede 123–Mala Mala (Crepello 136) (1981 5g 5s 5fg³ 6fg 6f 5f³ 5fg 5g) May 2; 1,500Y; lengthy, quite useful sort; good walker; third foal; dam unraced sister to Derby fourth Great Wall; plating-class maiden; not disgraced first outing over 6f; wears blinkers nowadays; sold 900 gns Doncaster October Sales. *J. Etherington.* 65

MAGNETO 4 b.f. John Splendid 116–Magibbillibyte 77 (Constable 119) (1980 7d² 7g 8fg⁴ 7g 7g⁴ 6g 8g⁴ 1981 6v* 6s 6g 6d 7s² 6fg² 6g² 6fg³ 6fg 5f 6d 6g 7g) strong filly; plater; attracted no bid after winning comfortably at Ayr in March; stays 1m; well suited by some give in the ground; has twice worn blinkers; trained part of season by N. Callaghan (claimed after fifth start). *D. Garraton.* 61

MAGNOLIA LAD 8 b.h. Mummy's Pet 125–Julita 87 (Rockavon 120) (1980 6s 6d² 5g 6g 6h² 5g 6d 6fg 5d 6g 5d³ 5s 6f 5d 5d³ 6d³ 6d 6v⁴ 1981 6s 6g² 6g 6d⁴ 6g 6g² 6fg 6f³ 6f 6f* 6f 6fg² 6f² 5f 6fg³ 6f 7d) sprint handicapper; won at Pontefract in July; runner-up in seller on second start; stays 7f; acts on any going; suitable mount for an apprentice; has worn blinkers; has sweated up; inconsistent; sold 1,000 gns Newmarket Autumn Sales. *R. Hollinshead.* 66

MAGNUM BONUM (USA) 2 b.g. Full Pocket–June Wedding (Stevward) (1981 6f 6fg 7g) Mar 16; $23,000Y, resold $30,000Y; strong, compact, good sort; second foal; dam won 9 sprint races, including claiming events; showed a little ability first start; had stiffish task when tried over 7f; gelded subsequently. *M. Jarvis.* 66

MAGONIS 2 b.f. Blakeney 126–Ribaria (Ribero 126) (1981 8d⁴) May 25; first foal; dam ran only twice; 20/1, ran pleasingly when about 5 lengths fourth of 18 to Sugar and Mint in maiden race at Leicester in November; very stoutly bred and should improve when given a test of stamina in 1982. *P. Cole.* 74 p

MAHABBA (USA) 2 ch.f. Elocutionist–Amphora 110 (Ragusa 137) (1981 6fg 7g⁴ 6d³) May 23; 44,000Y; well-made filly; half-sister to 2 winners, including 1979 2-y-o stakes winner Icy Lassie (by Iccapade); dam won Lancashire Oaks and is half-sister to good fillies Example and Expansive; in frame in end-of-season maiden races at Leicester, on second occasion running as though 6f was far too short for her when 3½ lengths third to Late Hour; bred to stay 1½m; could well improve if given the chance to tackle a distance more in keeping with her pedigree. *H. T. Jones.* 74

MAHER 3 b.f. Simbir 130–High Dice 93 (High Hat 131) (1980 7g 9d 1981 12.2g⁴ 12.2g⁴ 16fg 12f 13.8g) unfurnished filly; poor fourth in sellers at Catterick in April and May; bandaged final outing. *T. Kersey.* —

MAIDA VALE 2 br.f. Furry Glen 121–Gifted Samanta (Divine Gift 127) (1981 5.3fg³ 7f³ 6s) Apr 8; lightly-made filly; first foal; dam never ran; plater; will probably stay 1m. *S. Woodman.* 56

MAIDIGA (USA) 2 ro.c. Tumiga–Mobile Maiden (Prince John) (1981 7g 8g) Apr 9; $12,500Y; useful sort; half-brother to 2 winners, including smart 1978 American 2-y-o sprinter Wind Factor (by Francis S); dam placed at 2 yrs and 3 yrs; unquoted when behind in large fields of maidens at Newmarket in October (showed speed 5f on second outing). *J. Hindley.* —

MAIGUESIDE 3 br.c. Guillaume Tell 121–Evening Blaze (Soderini 123) (1980 NR 1981 10d 14s 16f³ 16fg) 11,000F, 11,500Y; neat colt; half-brother to fairly useful 1978 Irish 2-y-o 5f and 6f winner Windy Sunset (by Tumble Wind); dam placed over 1½m in Ireland; showed only form when 7 lengths third behind Halsbury in minor event at Chepstow in June; stays 2m; sold 6,800 gns Newmarket Autumn Sales. *C. Nelson.* —

MAILMAN 2 ch.c. Malacate 131–Sallail (Sallust 134) (1981 6d 7f³ 7f 8d²) Mar 20; IR 8,600Y; big, useful-looking colt; good mover; first foal; dam Irish 7f winner; placed in large fields of maidens at Newmarket in July (2¾ lengths 92

third to Treboro) and Bath in October (clear of remainder when ½-length second to newcomer Suez); will be suited by 1¼m; seems to act on any going. *I. Balding.*

MAIN ROYAL 4 b.g. Averof 123–Sovereign Sails 94 (Sovereign Path 125) (1980 — 7v 8fg 8fg² 8fg 8d 7g 7g 8d³ 7d 1981 6g 8fg 8fg 7.3d) big, strong gelding; stays 1m; acts on a firm and a soft surface; blinkered once in 1980; sold 2,200 gns Newmarket Autumn Sales. *W. Wightman.*

MAINTOP 4 b.g. High Top 131–Jujube 103 (Ribero 126) (1980 8f 8f* 10.6s **88** 1981 10fg 10g 10d³ 10g 10f* 10g 10d 10fg* 10f 10g) strong, shapely gelding; fair handicapper; won at Ripon in July and Newcastle in August; gives impression he'll be suited by 1½m; possibly unsuited by very soft ground but acts on any other; blinkered last 4 starts; sold 8,600 gns Newmarket Autumn Sales. *P. Walwyn.*

MAISON D'OR 4 br.f. Goldhill 125–Open House 91 (Road House II) (1980 — 6v⁴ 6d⁴ 6f 1981 7g 5fg) poor performer nowadays; stays 6f. *W. H. H. Williams.*

MAJESTIC GUARD 2 ch.c. Home Guard 129–Paros 63 (Pardao 120) (1981 **107** 7.5f* 8g² 9d⁴ 7v) Mar 14; 50,000Y; big, rangy colt; third produce; half-brother to quite useful 1977 2-y-o 7f winner Lady Abernant (by Abwah), subsequently a winner over 1½m, and to a winner in France; dam won over 1½m; ran on newcomers race at Deauville in August by 3 lengths from Mr Badger; ran in pattern events afterwards, failing by only a short neck to catch Persepolis in Prix La Rochette at Longchamp, finishing 1½ lengths fourth of 9 to Trigonome in Prix Saint-Roman on same course and modest fifth of 10 to Zino in Criterium de Maisons-Laffitte; one paced and will be suited by 1¼m +; possibly not at his best on heavy going. *M. Saliba, France.*

MAJESTIC MAHARAJ 6 br.h. Taj Dewan 128–Canaan (Santa Claus 133) **99** (1980 12.3d³ 12f* 18.4f⁴ 12fg* 16d 18.4g* 12g 14g 18g⁴ 15s² 14s³ 1981 16.1s 12f 16g 12f⁴ 18.4fg³ 14d 15g* 14s*) strong, useful-looking horse; good mover; fairly useful handicapper; won amateur riders race at Ayr in September and handicap at York in October; made all and was clear in straight when beating Star Burst by 5 lengths in latter; stayed well; acted on any going; good mount for an amateur; ran very freely when tried in blinkers; sold 8,200 gns Newmarket Autumn Sales and is standing at Hart Hill Stud, Dorset. *J. Hanson.*

MAJESTIC NURSE 6 br.m. On Your Mark 125–Bristol Milk 88 (Raise You Ten **80** 125) (1980 8d 8g 8.5fg³ 10d* 6fg 8g 8s 1981 8s 8f³ 8.5fg 8.5fg 8d* 10s 8s³ 8d 10d³ 12g) rather lightly-made mare; beat Old Oak Tree by 3 lengths in 18-runner Irish Cambridgeshire at the Curragh in September; not entirely disgraced 2 outings later when third to Princes Gate in handicap at Ascot (didn't impress in paddock); stayed 1¼m; acted on any going; suitable mount for an apprentice; sold, covered by Wolver Hollow, 24,000 gns Goffs November Sales. *M. Cunningham, Ireland.*

MAJESTIC TOWER 2 ch.c. Tower Walk 130–Tzu-Hsi 66 (Songedor 116) (1981 — 5v) Apr 13; 6,800Y; sturdy colt; third foal; half-brother to winning 3-y-o sprinter Dragonist (by Dragonara Palace); dam 6f winner; unquoted but fit when well behind in 13-runner £2,500 event won by Royal Revenge at Beverley in April, only outing. *C. Gray.*

MAJIEDA 3 ch.f. Kashmir II 125–Manushka (Sheshoon 132) (1980 6f³ 5g 1981 **67** 8f² 10.2f² 10.1fg⁴ 10g 8fg 7g) tall, quite attractive filly; second in maiden races at York and Doncaster in June, but seemed to go the wrong way temperamentally and is one to treat with caution; stays 1¼m; acts on firm going; blinkered nowadays; acted as pacemaker for Nasseem on fourth start. *F. J. Houghton.*

MAJOR DAY 4 br.g. Singing Bede 122–Penny Model (Pendragon) (1980 10f — 12fg 11g 8.2g 1981 13d 7fg 5d) non-thoroughbred gelding; poor plater; has worn blinkers; sold 520 gns Ascot December Sales. *J. S. Wilson.*

MAJOR DOMO 2 br.c. Mandrake Major 122–Queezy 86 (Lear Jet 123) (1981 **84** p 6fg*) Apr 2; 3,900Y; strong, good sort; first foal; dam, half-sister to Cesarewitch winner Assured, won over 5f at 2 yrs; co-favourite, quickened away in good style in last furlong and was eased close home when beating Hot Anna 3 lengths in 14-runner maiden auction event at Newcastle in June; has plenty of scope and looked capable of holding his own in better company but wasn't seen out again. *Denys Smith.*

MAJOR DRAKE 2 ch.c. Mandrake Major 122–Lametta 94 (Alycidon 138) (1981 —
7g 8s) Apr 14; 6,000F, 6,000Y; well-grown colt; half-brother to several winners,
including fairly useful stayer Lampardal (by Pardal); dam stayer; 20/1 when
behind in maiden races at Leicester in September and Warwick (dwelt) in October.
J. Hardy.

MAJOR GUNDRY 4 ch.c. Grundy 137–Hiding Place 109 (Doutelle 128) (1980   **86**
10.6d* 12g² 12f4 12g⁴ 13.3d 10.5g 10.2g 12d⁴ 1981 12fg⁴ 14d⁴ 14s 12f 11.7fg⁴
12d²) strong, compact colt; stays 1¾m; acts on a firm and a soft surface; often
blinkered; sold 19,000 gns Newmarket December Sales. *I. Balding.*

MAJOR HONOUR (USA) 2 b.g. Envoy–Our Own Hit (Bold Hitter) (1981 6fg —
7g 7f) Apr 9; $8,200F, $30,000Y; workmanlike gelding; first foal; dam, placed
at 2 yrs, is daughter of Irish 1,000 Guineas second Owenello; well behind in
maiden and minor events. *E. Eldin.*

MAJORIAN 3 b.c. Majority Blue 126–Tinker Lass (Tin Whistle 128) (1980 5s   **81**
7fg 7d 8d* 1981 8s² 8g 10.1f* 10f 10fg 10g 11s⁴) quite a useful-looking colt;
won handicap at Windsor in June by 2½ lengths from Northern Prince, making
all; inconsistent however, and possibly needs things his own way; stays 1¼m;
evidently acts on any going; sold to W. H. H. Williams 6,000 gns Newmarket
Autumn Sales. *R. Price.*

MAJOR IRISH 2 ch.g. Malinowski 123–Irish Blade (Track Spare 125) (1981 **90**
5g 5s* 6f³ 7f* 6f² 6f³ 7fg² 7fg³) Apr 24; 3,200Y; sparely-made gelding; second
foal; half-brother to winning Irish miler Cut The Cake (by Fine Blade); dam never
ran; narrow winner of maiden race at Wolverhampton in May and minor event
at Beverley in July, making all to score by a head from Steelstock in latter; head
second to Sanches in 7f nursery at Yarmouth in August; will stay 1m; acts on
any going; consistent; gelded after eighth outing and sent to Hong Kong. *E.
Eldin.*

MAJOR ROCK 2 ch.c. Mandrake Major 122–Rock Snake 76 (Rockefella) (1981 —
6s 6s) May 31; 2,500Y; big colt; half-brother to numerous winners, including
useful stayers Frog and Ophite (both by French Beige); dam disappointing; in
rear in £2,100 seller at Goodwood in September and 15-runner maiden race at
Newbury in October. *S. Matthews.*

MAJOR'S AFFAIR 2 br.g. Mandrake Major 122–Fair Jacqueline 79 (Fortino II **98**
120) (1981 5s* 5v 5g* 5g⁴ 6fg² 6g³) Apr 28; close-coupled gelding; half-brother
to 2 winners, including fairly useful Irish 6f winner Pagensand (by Sandford Lad);
dam won over 6f; won maiden race at Stockton in April and 10-runner minor
event at Ripon in June, staying on well to beat Martini Time 3 lengths in latter;
placed in well-contested events at Doncaster and Ayr subsequently, at Ayr
finishing just over 3 lengths third of 7 to Take The Floor in £4,600 event in July;
suited by 6f and may stay further; has won on soft going but has shown best
form on a sound surface; sent to Hong Kong. *E. Weymes.*

MAJOR SETBACK 2 b.c. Brigadier Gerard 144–Bedfellow 104 (Crepello 136) **84**
(1981 6g³ 6fg) May 4; strong, good-bodied colt; good mover; second foal; dam,
half-sister to Oaks winner Polygamy and Cheshire Oaks winner One Over Parr,
stayed at least 1½m; came out best of 8 newcomers when promising length third
of 11 to Master Cawston in Ribero Stakes at Doncaster in September; second
favourite for Clarence House Stakes at Ascot later in month but couldn't quicken
after disputing lead for 4f, coming home 8 lengths sixth of 10 to Allocated; bred
to stay middle distances; looks the type to do better at 3 yrs. *P. Walwyn.*

MAJOR SINCLAIR 2 b.g. Mandrake Major 122–Stroppy Lou (Shantung 132) **69**
(1981 5d 5s 6f 5f 7fg³ 7g⁴ 7.2fg) May 13; 3,700Y; rangy gelding; half-brother to
5f to 10.6f winner Bright Charlie (by Saintly Song); dam never ran; beaten 5½
lengths when in frame in maiden races won by Pamparino at Catterick and by
Rockfest at Chester, both in August; ran badly in nursery at Haydock the
following month; suited by 7f and will stay 1m. *M. H. Easterby.*

MAKBUBA'S GIRL 3 gr.f. Tycoon II–Makbuba 86 (Dumbarnie 125) (1980 —
7g 5g 5g 5g 1981 7d 7s 8s 10f⁴ 12f 10g 13.8fg) small filly; plater; stays 1¼m;
suited by a sound surface; sold 1,250 gns Ascot August Sales and resold 410 gns
Ascot October Sales. *S. Mellor.*

MAKINARIA 2 b.f. Song 132–Makinlau 88 (Lauso) (1981 5f 6fg 6f) May 18; —
small filly; second foal; dam won from 1m to 1½m; poor maiden; sold 400 gns
Newmarket Autumn Sales. *B. Hanbury.*

MAKIN MUSIC 3 b.f. Song 132–Makinlau 88 (Lauso) (1980 5fg 6s 6g 5g 5.1fg —
1981 5d 5d 7fg 7f 8.2f 8.2g 10f 10fg 8.2s 8d) small filly; plating-class maiden;
not certain to stay 1¼m. *F. Dever.*

MALADHU 2 b.c. Malacate 131–Mhairi Dhu 88 (Great Nephew 126) (1981 5v 6s) —
Mar 15; fair sort; first foal; dam won over 9.4f; distant seventh of 15 to Risk
Taker in maiden race at Newbury in October, second outing; needs further and
will stay 1¼m. *T. Robson.*

MALAYSIAN KING 2 b. or br.c. Saulingo 122–Orestia (Orestes) (1981 5.3f 6fg —
5.8h 7d) June 1; 3,500 2-y-o; half-brother to several winners here and in USA,
including very useful Irish 6f and 7f winner Dempsey (by My Swanee); dam
minor winner in USA; poor form, including in a seller; blinkered third and fourth
starts. *R. Hannon.*

MALIA 3 b.f. Malacate 131–Lady Beck 104 (Sir Gaylord) (1980 5fg* 5f³ 6g 7s —
1981 8d 6g 10f 10.1fg) compact filly; no form since winning maiden race at
Haydock early in 1980; should stay at least 1m; sweated up second start; off
course almost 3 months before final outing. *F. J. Houghton.*

MALICIOUS LOVE 4 b.f. Malicious–Larkspur's Love (Larkspur 128) (1980 **59**
12f 16d 16.9d 14g 14g³ 14fg³ 14g 16.1s³ 15s* 15d* 1981 13s 14g 16d³ 16.1s 15.5d⁴
15.5d) quite attractive filly; staying handicapper; acts on soft going; suitable
mount for an inexperienced rider. *H. Collingridge.*

MALICIOUS RED 5 br.g. Malicious–Elected 74 (Red God 128§) (1980 NR —
1981 11d) poor performer; stays well. *J. Leigh.*

MALICOURT 4 ch.c. Malicious–Sweet Councillor (Privy Councillor 125) (1980 **47**
11v* 12fg 12d 15s 16g 16.1s 1981 12.5s⁴ 11s 10d² 10s 10fg 8fg³ 8.2g 8fg³ 10fg³
7g³) small, robust colt; plater; stays 1¼m; seems to act on any going; blinkered
nowadays; looked none too enthusiastic once at 3 yrs. *A. Balding.*

MALITEVKA 3 b.f. Lombard 126–Faridina 100 (Sky Gipsy 117) (1980 5f —
1981 10.2g 10.6v) leggy, sparely-made filly; lightly raced and little worthwhile
form (last on both outings in 1981); trained first outing by K. Stone. *R. Williams.*

MALLARD SONG 7 b.g. Tudor Melody 129–Romping (Sir Gaylord) (1980 NR **50**
1981 16g 16.9s 13.1g 10f 16fg 16h² 12f 19s⁴ 18g) staying handicapper; goes well
on top-of-the-ground; has worn bandages; has run respectably for an amateur
rider. *Dr A. Jones.*

MALMAISON 6 b.m. Royal Palace 131–Samanda (Alycidon 138) (1980 14.7f⁴ —
12g 16.1d 14g 1981 13fg) poor staying maiden. *H. Wharton.*

MALMAR 2 ch.f. Palm Track 122–Wicker (Pinza 137) (1981 5g 6s 5d 6d) Jan —
28; 700 2-y-o; light-framed filly; half-sister to a winning plater; dam never ran;
well beaten, including in a valuable seller. *J. Mulhall.*

MALORS 2 ch.f. Malicious–Orseniga 97 (Privy Councillor 125) (1981 5fg 5d 7fg **50**
10d 10d 8g 8d) May 15; 500Y; big, rangy filly; fifth foal; dam stayed at least 13f;
poor plater; blinkered final outing. *D. Dale.*

MALPASO 5 ch.h. Sun Prince 128–Tapia (Tanerko 134) (1980 16s 16f⁴ 17.1f³ —
16fg* 16g* 16g4 19f* 16s 16g 16.1s 1981 10f 19g) lightly-made horse; has been
hobdayed; stays well; acts well on firm going; usually blinkered nowadays;
genuine; sometimes sweats up; bandaged in front at 5 yrs; has won only at
Beverley. *A. Smith.*

MALSEEDY 3 ch.f. Malicious–Ballyseedy 73 (Dicta Drake 126) (1980 5fg 5fg **57**
6fg 6g 7g 6fg 6fg 7f³ 8.2d* 8fg⁴ 8.2s⁴ 8fg 10d² 8d 8d 1981 12s³ 12s² 12.3d 12g 12d³
12.5f 12fg 12fg⁴ 13fg 10fg 11g 10d⁴ 10.2g) small filly; plater; placed in non-
sellers in the spring; stays 1½m well; acts on any going; occasionally blinkered;
sometimes bandaged behind; suitable mount for an apprentice. *W. Stubbs.*

MALVAN 5 b. or br.g. Decoy Boy 129–Khanum 81 (Soueida 111) (1980 8fg **68**
8.2s* 8f 8f 10g4 7f 8fg 8fg 8d⁴ 8d² 8.2s* 8s² 1981 8s² 9d* 8d* 11s⁴ 10s 10d⁴
10g 8f 10g 8s² 11s³) quite a moderate handicapper; won at Wolverhampton in
April and Salisbury in May; also first past post in London Gold Cup at Newbury
later in May but was demoted to fourth for impeding another runner; evidently
stays 11f; acts on any going, but is well suited by soft; has worn blinkers but is
better without; good mount for a boy. *R. Turnell.*

MALZA 4 b.g. Malicious–Zagapu 72 (Supreme Sovereign 119) (1980 10s 10.8s⁴ —
12f⁴ 11.7fg⁴ 13s 11.7s 13.1g 12d³ 12g 12fg² 14fg³ 12g* 12f 1981 12.2d 12.2fg
14g 15.5d 12g) neat gelding; stays 1¾m; probably acts on any going; often
wears blinkers; suitable mount for an inexperienced rider. *R. Hannon.*

MA MERE L'OIE (FR) 2 b.f. Lightning 129–Pollenka 122 (Reliance II 137) **104** p
(1981 8v*) Apr 25; first foal; dam very smart from 1m to 10.5f in France;
6/4 favourite, looked very promising when winning 8-runner maiden race at
Longchamp in October by 2 lengths from Miss Mat; will stay 1¼m; will make a
good 3-y-o; engaged in 1,000 Guineas and Oaks. *F. Mathet, France.*

MANAL (FR) 2 b.f. Luthier 126–Top Twig (High Perch 126) (1981 7g) Feb **74 p**
17; $525,000Y; good sort; sister to French Derby second Twig Moss and very
smart middle-distance winner Tip Moss, and half-sister to several winners,
including very smart 1m to 1½m performer Twig (by Hul a Hul); dam last on
both starts; 20/1 but looking fit, prominent throughout and stayed on reasonably
well when about 7 lengths sixth of 29 to Chalon in maiden race at Newmarket in
October; will do better over middle distances. *H. T. Jones.*

MANCHESTERSKYTRAIN 2 b.c. Home Guard 129–Aswellas 93 (Le Levans- **92**
tell 122) (1981 7fg 6fg² 6fg*) Feb 11; 21,000F; strong, well-made colt; good
mover; half-brother to 2 winners, including 7f winner Albany Victor (by Mount
Hagen); dam won 3 times over 7f at 2 yrs; made most of running when winning
9-runner maiden race at Epsom in August by ¾ length from Polar Star, the pair
clear; had previously finished 5 lengths second of 11 to easy winner Foam Bath
in £3,300 event at Salisbury; a free-running sort but should stay 7f; improving
type. *R. Smyth.*

MANDALEA 3 b.f. Son of Silver 123–Manila II 74 (Mourne 126) (1980 NR **—**
1981 10s) 1,400F, 575 3-y-o; half-sister to 2 winners, including fair miler Roman
Fantasy (by Calpurnius); dam showed a little ability at 2 yrs; unquoted when no
tailed-off last of 13 behind Dovetail in maiden race at Nottingham in October.
D. Weeden.

MANDALIA 4 b.f. Mansingh 120–Hay-Hay 62 (Hook Money 124) (1980 5fg **—**
5d 5g 6fg 1981 6s 6g 7.6g 8g 6fg 6fg 7fg 10f) neat filly; poor sprint handicapper; behind in seller final start; has run respectably over 6f and 7f but is best
at 5f; acts on firm going; blinkered fifth start; has shown signs of temperament
on occasions. *L. Barratt.*

MANDAV 3 ch.c. Sallust 134–Robusta (Saint Crespin III 132) (1980 5f⁴ 5f **—**
6fg³ 6fg³ 7fg² 7f* 7f* 7s 7d 1981 7g 7fg 7d 7f) smallish colt; ridden by apprentice M. Hills when successful in nurseries at Redcar and Lingfield as a
2-y-o; disappointing in 1981, but ran well until badly hampered second start;
gives impression he needs further than 7f nowadays; acts well on firm going and
is unsuited by soft. *J. Hindley.*

MANDECK MAJOR 2 b.c. Mandrake Major 122–Deck (Le Dieu d'Or 119) **—**
(1981 5s 5s 5g 6f 6f 5f 8.2d 7.2v) May 27; 2,200Y; workmanlike colt; third foal;
dam ran twice; no sign of ability, including in sellers; blinkered seventh outing;
sold 300 gns Doncaster November Sales. *S. Nesbitt.*

MANDRAKE BELLE 2 ch.c. Mandrake Major 122–Janabelle 101 (Gentle Art **75**
121) (1981 5d 5v³ 5f⁴ 5f) Apr 19; 4,000Y; half-brother to 2 winners, including
sprinter Kelso Belle (by Town Crier); dam won at up to 7f; quite moderate form
in minor events; may stay 6f; acts on any going. *B. Gubby.*

MANDRIANO 2 ch.g. Manado 130–Indian Runner (Sallust 134) (1981 5g⁴ **74**
6fg⁴) Mar 12; IR 14,500Y; first foal; dam never ran; fourth at Lingfield and
Folkestone in June, on latter running on to finish 3¾ lengths behind Little
Robert in 17-runner maiden race; will stay 7f. *G. Pritchard-Gordon.*

MANDY'S TIME 5 b.m. High Time 96–Mandy's Melody (Highland Melody **43**
112) (1980 10fg 1981 10.2s² 11.5fg) poor performer; will be suited by 1½m;
acts well on soft going; has run respectably for an amateur rider. *J. Harris.*

MAN EN CO 3 b. or br.g. Shantung 132–J'Accuse (I Say 125) (1980 5f 5fg **—**
6g 1981 12g 12.2g³ 8g 12g) lengthy gelding; plater; will stay beyond 1½m;
has worn blinkers. *G. Richards.*

MANICOU'S GEM 2 b.g. Tack On 114–Manicou's Dream (Manicou) (1981 **—**
7fg 7d) Mar 22; third reported foal; dam fair hurdler; unquoted when in rear
in maiden race at Salisbury (backward) and minor event at Brighton in September. *R. Smyth.*

MANILLA BAY 3 ch.c. Weavers' Hall 122–Pale Ivory 108 (Silver Shark 129) **97**
(1980 6fg 9.7f 7fg 8.5s³ 7.9v² 1981 12d³ 10s 14g⁴ 10g* 8s 13s* 12f 11.5f⁴)
4,000Y; leggy colt; second foal; half-brother to fair 1979 2-y-o 6f winner
Brigadier James (by Brigadier Gerard); dam useful from 5f to 1m at 2 yrs;
successful in maiden event at Navan in May and handicap at Leopardstown in
June; ran well over trip on sharp side for him when about 10 lengths sixth of 13
behind Kings Lake in Airlie/Coolmore Irish 2,000 Guineas at the Curragh in
between and wasn't disgraced when about 8 lengths sixth of 10 behind Bustomi
in King Edward VII Stakes at Royal Ascot; stayed 13f; not disgraced on firm
going but was well suited by some give in the ground; dead. *M. Cunningham,
Ireland.*

MANILOW 4 ch.c. Singing Bede 122–Lease Lend 96 (Cash and Courage 116) **81**
(1980 5d 5v 5fg 5fg 5f³ 1981 6g 5g 5.3f² 5g 5g* 5g* 5fg) strong, good sort;
sprint handicapper; won at Leicester and Sandown in July; best form on a
sound surface; has run well for an apprentice; ran badly final start. *B. Swift.*

MAN IN THE MIDDLE 5 ch.g. Good Bond 122–Sharp Work 110 (Beau **68**
Sabreur 125) (1980 8d 10s 10f 10d 8.2g 8fg 8fg 9g³ 8.2s 1981 10.2d 8d 10s 8.5g
8fg 8d² 8.2d* 8.2s*) big gelding; unreliable handicapper; decisively won at
Hamilton and Nottingham in October; stays 9f; acts well in the mud; effective
with and without blinkers; sometimes starts slowly. *D. Sasse.*

MANITA 3 ch.f. Manacle 123–Conchita 113 (Matador 131) (1980 5h³ 5fg 5s*
5fg* 6g 5f 5g 5g 6s 1981 6s 6s) lengthy filly; fair performer at 2 yrs; last in
handicaps at Lingfield and Folkestone in October, wearing blinkers on latter
course; stays 6f; seems to act on any going. *R. Hoad.*

MANITOBA 4 ch.f. Mansingh 120–Dauphiness 74 (Supreme Sovereign 119) —
(1980 7g 8g⁴ 7g* 10fg 8.2s 1981 8.3fg 8fg 7g) small filly; plater; stays 7f;
has been tried in blinkers. *J. Gilbert.*

MANNA GREEN 3 ch.f. Bustino 136–Marcela 107 (Reform 132) (1980 8d —
1981 8g) workmanlike filly; in rear in maiden races at Redcar in 1980 and at
Thirsk in May. *Hbt Jones.*

MANNS BITTER 4 ch.f. Shiny Tenth 120–Candy Girl (Tutankhamen) (1980 **47**
8.2s 8fg 7f 8d* 6d² 8d³ 8fg 8fg² 8.2d² 9f* 9s² 11d² 1981 8.2fg³ 10fg 9d 10fg⁴
10s 8.2s 10.2g) unfurnished, leggy filly; plater; stays 11f; acts on any going;
sometimes wears blinkers; suitable mount for an apprentice; often fails to
impress in paddock, changed hands 2,000 gns Doncaster August Sales. *A.
Balding.*

MANNS BROWN 2 b. or br.f. No Mercy 126–Nettleton 64 (Shiny Tenth 120) **56**
(1981 5s 5d 5d 5fg 5fg³ 5fg² 5.3f⁴ 6f²) May 5; 1,050Y; small filly; first foal;
dam once in frame over 5f; second in maiden auction event at Warwick in June
and seller at Leicester in July, being claimed after going down by 2½ lengths to
Chantilly Girl in latter; gives impression 5f suits her better than 6f. *D. Marks.*

MANNTIKA 2 gr.f. Kalamoun 129–Manushka (Sheshoon 132) (1981 6g⁴) **71** p
Apr 9; third foal; half-sister to 1978 French 2-y-o 7.5f and 9f winner Grey
Amber (by Amber Rama); dam, minor 11f winner, is sister to very useful French
long-distance horse Croque Monsieur; 10/1, put up a creditable first effort when
6¾ lengths fourth of 19 to Zinzara in newcomers race at Goodwood in September;
will be well suited by 1m+; should improve. *F. J. Houghton.*

MAN OF SONG 3 br.g. Mansingh 120–Lindiana 84 (Indiana 129) (1980 5fg —
5s 5d⁴ 5fg³ 5fg 6g 6d* 6g 1981 6fg 8g 10f 11g 8.2f 6g 6g) neat gelding; won
nursery at Newbury in 1980 but didn't appear to train on; yet to show he stays
beyond 6f; has run respectably on a firm surface but seems well suited by some
give in the ground; best form in blinkers; trained most of season by S. Mellor.
R. Hollinshead.

MAN OF SPIRIT 2 b.g. Vitiges 132–Dauphine 102 (Pampered King 121) —
(1981 7g 7fg 7fg) Apr 27; attractive, well-made gelding; half-brother to 3
winners, including Free Handicap winner Man of Harlech (by Welsh Pageant)
and fairly useful stayer Man of France (by Crepello); dam genuine stayer;
prominent over 3f when seventh of 18 to Tulsa Flyer in £2,600 race at Salisbury
in August, second start; eased from 10/1 to 20/1 when behind in maiden race on
same course the following month (wasn't knocked about unnecessarily); will
stay 1¼m+; gelded after third outing. *J. Dunlop.*

MAN O'LAW 3 br.c. Manado 130–Rising Lark (Ballymoss 136) (1980 NR —
1981 9s) 13,000F, 13,000Y; half-brother to fairly useful stayer Francesco (by
Royal and Regal); dam unraced half-sister to St Leger and Irish Sweeps Derby
second Meadowville; 25/1 and in need of race when last of 17 behind Blakenor in
maiden race at Wolverhampton in May; sold to R. Walsh 600 gns Goffs August
Sales. *Mrs R. Lomax.*

MAN ON THE RUN 6 b.g. Mandamus 120–Cathy Jane 86 (Lauso) (1980 —
12g 16g 17.1d 1981 18fg) staying handicapper; acts on any going; usually
ridden up with leaders. *J. Baker.*

MANOR FARM LAD 2 ch.c. Free State 125–Ranjita 84 (Ballylinan 118) **64**
(1981 7fg 6g) May 28; 4,200Y; half-brother to 3 winners, including consistent

sprinter Bien Etonne (by Jimmy Reppin); dam sprinter; having first race for
more than 2 months when $7\frac{1}{2}$ lengths sixth of 19 to One Degree in maiden event
at Newmarket in October; not certain to stay 7f (faded closing stages when tried
at trip). *W. O'Gorman.*

MAN OVERBOARD 2 b.c. Auction Ring 123–Storm Lass 65 (Typhoon 125)   **90**
(1981 5f³ 6fg² 6g³ 6fg 7.3d² 8s)   Apr 10; 11,500Y; compact colt; fourth foal;
half-brother to a winning hurdler; dam placed at up to 9f in Ireland; placed in
maiden races prior to finishing creditable 4 lengths second of 11 to Candide in
nursery at Newbury in September; remote sixth of 9 to Grease in Gran Criterium
at San Siro, Milan, in October; best run over 7f on a soft surface. *L. Cumani.*

MANSTONE 4 ch.g. Ragstone 128–Roman Nose 95 (Nosca) (1980 12g 16d   **49**
16s⁴ 12f 14.6d³ 16f⁴ 15s 16g⁴ 16d   1981 16s 12g 15.8g 12d 12g³ 16g³ 12s³ 12fg
12f)   small gelding; plater; stays well; best form on soft ground; wears blinkers.
T. Fairhurst.

MANSTON MARAUDER 5 b.g. Dubassoff–Smokey's Sister (Forlorn River   **52**
124) (1980 13.1fg⁴ 16f³ 12fg   1981 11s 12d 14d² 11.7v² 13.1g⁴ 17.1d⁴ 12g 14fg)
well-made gelding; seems to stay 2m; acts on any going; ran poorly in blinkers
once; has run well for an apprentice. *R. Hannon.*

MA PIERRETTE 2 b.f. Cawston's Clown 113–Wigeon 80 (Divine Gift 127)   **65**
(1981 6f 6g 5.1fg* 6f⁴ 5g)   Apr 4; IR 1,000F, 1,500Y (privately), 520 2-y-o;
leggy, unfurnished filly; first produce; dam won 5 times at up to $1\frac{1}{4}$m; had her
4 opponents well strung out when winning seller at Yarmouth in August by $2\frac{1}{2}$
lengths from Lady Levlee; bought in 1,300 gns afterwards; appeared to show
improved form in much better company at Ripon the following month, keeping
on strongly to finish $4\frac{3}{4}$ lengths fourth of 8 to Pomegranate, but ran poorly next
outing; better at 6f than 5f, and may well stay 1m at 3 yrs. *D. Dale.*

MAPLE QUEEN 5 br.m. Warpath 113–Queen Mab (Twilight Alley 133)   **48**
(1980 NR   1981 10g 14.6f² 16.1f)   poor handicapper; would have stayed well;
broke a shoulder final start and was destroyed. *C. Thornton.*

MAPUTO PRINCE 2 ch.c. Red Regent 123–Spring Blossom 85 (Queen's   **70**
Hussar 124) (1981 5f 6f* 7g²)   Apr 18; IR 2,000Y (privately); neat colt;
good mover; half-brother to 3 winners, including fairly useful sprinter Mr
Minstrel (by Laser Light); dam won over 5f at 2 yrs; apprentice ridden at overweight, won 11-runner seller at Doncaster in June by a neck from Bye-Law
despite being badly hampered at distance; bought in 2,100 gns; went down by
only a short head to Starter's Image, after edging left in closing stages, in valuable
19-runner seller at Newmarket the following month; suited by 7f; acts on firm
going; claimed £7,555 at Newmarket and is now racing in Italy. *P. Rohan.*

MARACAS BAY 2 b.g. Simbir 130–Valiretta (Go Marching) (1981 7fg 8d)   **—**
Apr 2; IR 4,000F, resold 4,000Y; big gelding; first foal; dam won 5 times over
middle distances in France; in rear in maiden races at Newbury in July and
Bath (last of 16) in October; sold 2,000 gns Newmarket Autumn Sales. *J.
Bethell.*

MARASALI (FR) 3 b.c. Tennyson 124–Monique (Tanerko 134) (1980 10s⁴   **116**
10d* 1981 12s³ 12d² 12s* 15s² 12.5d 15s² 12v)   strong, deep-girthed, good-
bodied colt; half-brother to numerous winners in France, including very useful
1m to $1\frac{1}{4}$m filly Gayka (by Kalamoun), smart 1968 2-y-o Marrakech (by Le Haar)
and French 1,000 Guineas fourth Ortanique (by Relic); dam won from 9f to 13f,
including Prix de Royallieu; beat Two Step by $1\frac{1}{2}$ lengths in Prix Nimbus at
Saint-Cloud in May; ran easily best subsequent races when second to Tipperary
Fixer in two Group 3 races at Longchamp, going down by $\frac{3}{4}$ length in Prix de
l'Esperance in May and by a neck after making running in Prix de Lutece in
September; one paced and needs a test of stamina; acts on soft going and has
yet to race on a sound surface. *F. Mathet, France.*

MARCAO (FR) 2 br.c. Djakao 124–Brave Marinette (Dancing Lad) (1981   **114**
9d* 8s² 10s²)   Feb 15; third foal; half-brother to Princesse Bea (by Misti IV), a
winner at up to 13f in France; dam, poor maiden, is half-sister to very useful
French middle-distance filly Brave Ketty and French 2,000 Guineas runner-up
Pen Mane; improved with racing, winning small race at Fontainebleau by a neck
in October, going down by a nose to Nabirpour in minor event at Maisons-
Laffitte the following month and putting up a smart effort when $1\frac{1}{2}$ lengths
second of 14 to Bon Sang (gave 4 lb) in Criterium de Saint-Cloud later in November; will stay $1\frac{1}{2}$m. *G. Bridgland, France.*

MARCELLO (FR) 4 b.c. Sir Gaylord–Marlia (Crepello 136) (1980 12f 12fg³ **73**
12f 10f³ 10g 9g² 14s 12s 1981 10fg* 10s⁴ 10s* 12s 11s³ 10.6g⁴ 10g² 11.7d² 10s²
10d 10f⁴ 12g 10g² 12.3s³ 11.7g² 12f* 10fg⁴ 10g 12s² 10.5s* 11s 12d) quite
attractive colt; won 2 small races at Cagnes-sur-Mer early in year and handicaps
at Kempton in September and York in October; stays 1½m; acts on any going;
blinkered once in 1980; often bandaged behind, usually thereabouts but doesn't
always look that genuine and isn't one to trust implicitly; sold out of C. Brittain's
stable 10,000 gns Newmarket Autumn Sales towards the end of his busy season.
A. Bates, France.

MARCHING ON 7 b.h. Tudor Melody 129–Procession 118 (Sovereign Path 125) **87**
(1980 6v 5g 6g² 5f 6fg 5g³ 5fg⁴ 5d 5d² 5fg 5f² 5d* 1981 5g⁴ 5f 5fg 7f* 6fg 5h³
5g 5d³ 5s) fairly useful handicapper at his best; won apprentice race at
Catterick in July; stayed 7f but was better at sprint distances; acted on any
going; had worn blinkers; standing at Lindrick Stud, Malton, at £250 + £250
live foal or £500 n.f.n.f. *Sir Mark Prescott.*

MARCH SPARK 5 b.g. Sparkler 130–March Malona 88 (Derring-Do 131) **75**
(1980 10g 9.5g 10g 9s 9g 1981 8g 8g²) quite useful (rated 97) in 1979; well
beaten in varied company in France at 4 yrs; well backed when going down by
1¼ lengths to Silly Prices in Zetland Gold Cup (Handicap) at Redcar in May;
not seen out again; stays 11f; acts on a firm surface but is well suited by soft
ground; reportedly difficult to train. *C. Thornton.*

MARCOM BOY 3 b.g. Mummy's Pet 125–Evening Shoe 111 (Panaslipper 130)
(1980 NR 1981 11s 10.1fg 12f 12d) 3,000F, 725Y; quite a well-made gelding;
good walker; half-brother to 5 winners, including Dime A Dance, successful over
6f and 7f, and 1m winner Disco Beat (both by No Mercy); dam third in Irish
1,000 Guineas; in rear in maiden and minor events and a handicap. *P. Mitchell.*

MARDI GRAS 2 gr.c. Martinmas 128–Miss Pimm 88 (Gentle Art 121) (1981 **76**
5fg⁴ 5d 5d³ 5f³ 5fg³ 6fg³ 6fg²) Feb 25; IR 6,600F, 6,600Y; neat, strong colt who
carries plenty of condition; half-brother to several winners here and abroad,
including 1976 2-y-o 6f winner Sir Lord (by Lord Gayle); dam won over 5f at
2 yrs; in frame in maiden races, on final occasion finishing 6 lengths second of 9
to Match Winner at Nottingham in September when having first race for 2
months; stays 6f; seems to act on any going; has shown a tendency to hang;
blinkered fifth and sixth starts. *B. Hobbs.*

MARDY 3 b.g. Mummy's Pet 125–Tackard 87 (Hard Tack 111§) (1980 5f 5f —
6g 5d 1981 9s) fair sort; quite a moderate maiden; not sure to stay beyond
sprint distances. *W. C. Watts.*

MARECHAL (FR) 4 b.c. Bolkonski 134–Miss Univers (Le Fabuleux 133) (1980 **57**
10s² 12s³ 12fg* 12fg⁴ 12g 13.1g² 13.3d 14fg² 16.5fg 12fg 16fg 16s 12g⁴ 1981 12d⁴
12d⁴ 14g 12v 13.3g 12f 12fg³ 16g 12s³) workmanlike colt; stays 1¾m; probably
acts on any going; sold out of S. Woodman's stable 1,950 gns Ascot July Sales
after seventh start. *V. Soane.*

MARGO'S STAR 2 ch.g. Fleece 114–Miss Starch 64 (Lucky Sovereign) (1981 —
5fg 5g 5s) May 2; sturdy gelding; third foal; half-brother to winning plater
Fiesta Girl (by Deadly Nightshade); dam plater; behind in maiden and minor
events but showed speed 3f on second start. *J. O'Donoghue.*

MARGUERITE GERARD 4 b.f. Rheingold 137–God Sent 75 (Red God 128§) **63**
(1980 7f 8fg 12fg⁴ 12d⁴ 12d⁴ 12f² 11fg 12f 10fg* 10f² 10g 10d 1981 10.2s 13fg³
12g³ 12f 12f⁴) workmanlike filly; stays 13f; probably acts on any going;
suitable mount for an inexperienced rider. *W. Elsey.*

MARIACHO 3 b.c. Mariacci 133–Sea Queen (Le Fabuleux 133) (1980 9g* **112**
9fg* 1981 10.5fg³ 12s³ 12g) half-brother to fair 1979 2-y-o King Hagen
(by Mount Hagen); dam French maiden; won minor race at Evry and
Prix Saint-Roman at Longchamp on his only starts at 2 yrs, and looked a good
colt in the making; ran only 3 times in 1981 however and wasn't seen out after
finishing in rear behind Bikala in Prix du Jockey-Club at Chantilly in June;
had earlier finished in frame in two Group 2 races at Longchamp, finishing 3½
lengths fourth of 6 behind subsequently-disqualified No Lute in Prix Greffulhe
and 2¼ lengths third to Rahotep in Prix Hocquart; stays 1½m; probably acts on
any going; trained until before final outing by F. Palmer. *M. Zilber, France.*

MARIBAN 2 b.f. Mummy's Pet 125–Gay Ribbon (Ribero 126) (1981 6s 6fg) —
May 8; well-grown filly; third foal; dam never ran; lost ground at start in maiden

events on both outings, but ran on to finish 6¾ lengths fifth of 13 to Westonbirt at Haydock in June on first start; always seemed to have difficulty in going pace when ninth of 18 to Full Extent at Redcar. *W. Elsey.*

MARILENA   2 b.f. Rolfe 77–Nevilles Cross 67 (Nodouble)   (1981 5s² 5g 5g² 6f   **65**
6g* 5f⁴ 7s⁴ 7g)   Mar 31; 220Y; lightly-made filly; third foal; dam stayed 1m; won 12-runner auction event at Newcastle in July by a length from Allten Unlimited; beaten only a length when excellent fourth to stable-companion Legs of Man in 7f nursery at Chester in August; will stay 1¼m; best form with some give in the ground. *Denys Smith.*

MARINE·   3 b.g. Hittite Glory 125–Seaside (Mossborough 126)   (1980 6d 6g 8d   **62**
8d   1981 8.2s² 8g 8g 8g³ 9s³)   well-made, quite attractive gelding; placed in maiden races at Nottingham and Wolverhampton and minor race at Salisbury in between; off course 4 months before final outing; will be suited by 1¼m; blinkered last 2 starts; sold 7,400 gns Newmarket Autumn Sales. *I. Balding.*

MARIS BARD   3 b.g. Bold Lad (Ire) 133–Lady Gaston 76 (Pall Mall 132)   (1980   —
5d 5d   1981 5g 7d 5d 6f 5f)   rangy gelding; poor sprint maiden; sold 900 gns Ascot August Sales. *R. Hollinshead.*

MARKENFIELD   2 b.c. Oats 126–Belleek (Never Say Die 137)   (1981 8s)   Feb   —
17; IR 10,000Y; half-brother to 3 winners, including useful 1972 Irish 2-y-o 5f and 6f winner Sancerre (by Golden Horus); dam placed at up to 1m; 12/1, eased once chance had gone when never-dangerous ninth of 15 to Twist Home in maiden race at York in October, only outing. *J. W. Watts.*

MARKET MELODY   4 b.f. Highland Melody 112–Sandalshoon 103 (Red God   —
128§)   (1980 7g³ 8g² 8f⁴ 8f 8g 7s   1981 8g⁴ 8g⁴ 10.2f 8f 8s 9s 8s)   lengthy filly; good walker; plating-class maiden; stays 1m; possibly needs some give in the ground; doesn't always impress in paddock. *J. Carr.*

MARKET ROSE   2 b.f. Most Secret 119–Rosemarkie 75 (Goldhill 125)   (1981   **72**
5d 5fg⁴ 5g 5fg⁴ 6g⁴ 5f 6f⁴ 6d 7.2v*)   Apr 20; neat filly; sister to 5f-winner Lana's Secret and half-sister to a winner; dam won over 13f; showed improved form when tried over 7f, winning by 4 lengths from Milanion in 17-runner seller at Haydock in October (no bid); runs as though she'll stay 1m; acts well on heavy going. *C. Gray.*

MARKIE   5 br.g. On Your Mark 125–Jeannette (Whistler 129)   (1980 7f 7f 8d   **52**
7.2d 8.2s 7d 8.2s 7s   1981 8fg 7.6fg 10f 8fg 10g 10f³ 8g 10g² 13.8g³ 12g 12d)   well-made, attractive gelding; good walker; fairly useful at his best but has deteriorated; well beaten in valuable seller seventh start; stays 1½m; acts well on firm going; sometimes blinkered; usually wears bandages. *R. E. Peacock.*

MARKING TIME   3 b.c. On Your Mark 125–Cariole 84 (Pardao 120)   (1980 5d³   **93**
5d³ 5s* 6d*   1981 7d* 8d 6g* 6g 7d 6f* 5fg⁴ 6g 6fg³ 6g)   big, strong colt; led entering last furlong and held on gamely by ½ length from Ponchielli in William Hill Trophy (Handicap) at York in June; successful earlier in quite valuable

William Hill Trophy, York—the most valuable event on Timeform Charity Day which raised £57,231 for cancer charities.   Marking Time wins from Ponchielli (right) and Chantry Bridge

handicaps at Doncaster (beat Welham Green by 2½ lengths after making nearly all) and Lingfield (beat Archimboldo a length); stays 7f; evidently acts on any going; successful twice for apprentice B. Crossley; often bandaged behind; has sometimes shown a tendency to hang. *B. Hanbury.*

MARKS DREAM 2 b.f. On Your Mark 125–Dream World (Quadrangle) (1981 — 5s 5s 5g 5f 7fg) Mar 10; IR 550F, 1,800Y; strong filly; first produce; dam won 1½m maiden race in Ireland but was disqualified; no sign of ability, including in a seller (last of 13); has worn blinkers. *T. Fairhurst.*

MARLEYCOMBE HILL 2 b.c. Sagaro 133–L'Anguissola 102 (Soderini 123) — (1981 8g 8s 10s) Apr 13; smallish colt; half-brother to smart sprinter Smarten Up (by Sharpen Up) and very useful fillies Solar (by Hotfoot) and Walk By (by Tower Walk); dam won three 6f races at 2 yrs; in rear in minor and maiden races in the autumn (sweated up third start); immature and weak at 2 yrs. *W. Wightman.*

MARMAGOA 3 br.c. Saritamer 130–Miss Argyle 92 (Mountain Call 125) (1980 **80** 5d 5d2 1981 6fg 6d 5s2 5d* 6d2 5fg* 5d3 5g 5s 5d 5s) fair sort; ran creditably most starts and won handicaps at Brighton in May and Warwick in June; stays 6f; probably acts on any going; lost his chance at start seventh outing; retained 5,400 gns Doncaster March Sales; sold 2,800 gns Newmarket Autumn Sales. *N. Vigors.*

MARNET 2 ch.g. Sweet Revenge 129–Tra-La-La (Penhurst) (1981 7g) Apr 3; — IR 2,900F, 4,600Y; sturdy gelding; half-brother to several winners, including sprinter Heavenly Choir (by St Alphage); dam never ran; unquoted and very backward when last of 18 behind General Anders in £4,100 race at Ascot in September. *K. Ivory.*

MAROUKIIY 2 b.f. Queen's Hussar 124–Maroukh (Kashmir II 125) (1981 6f — 7g) Mar 29; well-grown filly; second foal; dam ran only twice; unquoted when behind in maiden race at Nottingham in July and minor event at Catterick in October. *C. Brittain.*

MARQUESSA D'HOWFEN 2 br.f. Pitcairn 126–Fire-Screen 92 (Roan Rocket **93** 128) (1981 6d4 7f*) Apr 23; 10,000F; small, lightly-made filly; first foal; dam won over 10.2f; outsider of party and overshadowed in paddock, led approaching

Gilbey Champion Racehorse Futurity, York—the outsider of the party Marquessa d'Howfen wins from stable-companion Realms Reason

final furlong and ran out a worthy ½-length winner from stable-companion Realms Reason in 6-runner Gilbey Champion Racehorse Futurity at York in September; will stay 1¼m; fairly useful but lacks scope. *W. Hastings-Bass.*

MARSHALL BOLDELLA 3 b.g. Jimsun 121–Maella (Traffic) (1980 8d 1981 — 10d 9f 16f 14fg) rangy gelding; showed signs of a little ability in maiden race at Beverley on third start; has shown a little temperament too however. *R. Hollinshead.*

MARSHAL OSTHOFF 2 ch.c. Royal Match 117–Compliment (Tudor Music 131) 83 (1981 6fg 7f 7g⁴ 7d) Feb 5; IR 5,000Y; medium-sized, useful sort; second foal; half-brother to winner of a seller at 1m in France; dam unraced half-sister to top-class filly Humble Duty; looked unlucky when gambled on in 16-runner nursery at Leicester in November, finishing less than a length behind La Castellana in fifth place after not enjoying the best of runs (ridden by an apprentice unable to claim his 5lb allowance); will stay 1m; best form with some give in the ground. *I. Walker.*

MARSHGATE 3 b.g. Shiny Tenth 120–Tweetie Pie (Falcon 131) (1980 6fg 7g 50 d 6f 1981 8d* 7f 8f 10fg 10d) lengthy gelding; plater; bought in 2,200 gns after winning at Brighton in May; stays 1m. *D. Marks.*

MARSH REED 5 ch.h. Thatch 136–Austria 93 (Henry the Seventh 125) (1980 — NR 1981 12f³ 13g²) big, strong ex-Irish horse; seemed only plating class; stayed 13f; bandaged in 1981; dead. *J. Wilson.*

MARSTAIN 4 ch.g. Porto Bello 118–Florecilla 90 (Matador 131) (1980 6d 5v* — 6s 7fg 6fg² 6g 5fg 5.3fg 7d 5f 7fg³ 7fg 7g³ 5d 6s⁴ 6d 1981 8d 6d⁴ 5.8g⁴ 6f 6fg 6f 7fg 7fg 7h 6f 10s⁴) quite attractive, lengthy gelding; poor handicapper; suited by 7f or more; probably acts on any going; sometimes blinkered but does at least as well without; trained most of season by W. Wightman. *R. Hoad.*

MARTELLI 3 b.f. Pitskelly 122–Martita 99 (Tacitus 124) (1980 6s 6fg 7g 7g — 8fg* 8d⁴ 1981 8.3fg 8f 8.3g) useful sort; little form in 1981 and possibly didn't train on; will stay 1¼m; sometimes blinkered. *H. T. Jones.*

MARTIAL ARTS 5 ch.g. Gulf Pearl 117–Martial Air 113 (Court Martial) (1980 70 10g 8fg 10d 8g³ 8.3f² 8fg 1981 7d 8d 8h 8fg) good-bodied gelding; modest handicapper nowadays; gives impression he'll be suited by a return to a longer distance than 1m and stays 1¼m; acts on firm going; blinkered second start; has run moderately when sweating up. *J. Tree.*

MARTIALIS 2 b.c. Martinmas 128–Adamay (Florescence 120) (1981 5f 5.8f* 79 6g² 7g³ 7f* 6g⁴) Apr 24; IR 2,600F, 4,000Y; compact colt; third foal; dam won juvenile hurdle; successful in maiden auction event at Bath and nursery at Thirsk in July, scoring by 2 lengths from Mercia Sound in latter despite tending to put head in air; will stay 1m; acts on firm going; not raced after August. *S. Mellor.*

MARTIES BOY 4 b.g. Caliban 123–La Martinella (Mandamus 120) (1980 10s 47 8s⁴ 8fg 6d³ 8g 6g 1981 7d 6fg³ 8g 6d) lightly-made gelding; poor handicapper; best at 6f though is bred to stay further; acts on a firm and a soft surface. *M. Haynes.*

MARTINEAU 2 br.c. Martinmas 128–Romardia 75 (Romulus 129) (1981 7g) 78 p Mar 7; 5,200F, 22,000Y; strong colt; half-brother to minor winners here and in France; dam won over 7f; unquoted and backward (moved bit short to start) when tenth in 16-runner Somerville Tattersall Stakes won by Wind and Wuthering at Newmarket in October; will probably stay 1m; looks the type to make a useful horse in time. *B. Hobbs.*

MARTINI TIME 2 bl.f. Ardoon 124–Swinging Time (High Treason 126) (1981 90 5s² 5s² 5fg* 5d² 5g 5g² 5fg² 5f* 5f³) Jan 21; IR 2,000Y; small, compact filly; good mover; fourth foal; half-sister to a winner over hurdles; dam Irish 6f and 7f winner; made all to win maiden auction event at Epsom in April and nursery at Folkestone in July, putting up an excellent effort to beat Sylvan Barbarosa ¾ length in latter; also second in 5 of her other races; speedy but will probably stay 6f; seems to act on any going; tough and genuine. *D. Morley.*

MARTINOVA 3 b.f. Martinmas 128–Pavlova (Fidalgo 129) (1980 6d 6f* 5s* 111 d 1981 7s³ 7s* 8v³ 8f 12fg 8d 6f³ 6s) rather a lightly-built filly; half-sister to several winners, notably high-class 1¼m performer Lucky Wednesday (by Roi Soleil); dam, winner over 1½m in Ireland, is half-sister to good stayer Random Shot; led final furlong and ran on well when beating Overplay (rec 4lb) by ½

Athasi Stakes, the Curragh—Martinova holds on well from Overplay (left) and Castlemaine

length in Group 3 Athasi Stakes at the Curragh in April; started favourite for Goffs Irish 1,000 Guineas on same course in May and finished good third, a length behind Arctique Royale and Blue Wind; ran best subsequent race when about a length third to Isles Bay in Carna Fillies Stakes at Naas in September; soundly beaten in Coronation Stakes at Royal Ascot, Irish Guinness Oaks and Gilltown Stud Stakes at the Curragh, and Coral Bookmakers Champion Sprint at York on her other starts; best form at up to 1m and is not certain to stay $1\frac{1}{2}$m; has won on firm going but is ideally suited by plenty of give underfoot; has twice won for an apprentice. *C. Collins, Ireland.*

MARTIN PHILIP 3 br.c. Saulingo 122–Feenion (Technion 96) (1980 5.3d* 6fg 6g 5d 1981 5s 5fg 6d² 5d 6fg³ 6f 5fg 7d) compact colt; placed in handicap at Brighton in April and minor event at Naas in July; stays 6f; blinkered fourth outing; formerly trained by R. Price. *Mrs B. McKeever, Ireland.* **71**

MARTINTIDE 2 ch.f. Bustino 136–Marcela 107 (Reform 132) (1981 5s³ 5g* 5d 6d³ 7f 8f) Mar 24; small, lightly-made filly; third foal; half-sister to 1979 2-y-o 6f claiming race winner Martinholme (by Saritamer); dam won three 6f races at 2 yrs; won 9-runner maiden race at Pontefract in April by 2½ lengths from Hello Cuddles; having first race for over 2 months when running on to finish good third of 6 to Royal First in nursery on same course in August; best form at up to 6f but is bred to stay $1\frac{1}{2}$m; possibly unsuited by firm ground; lacks scope; sold 5,600 gns Newmarket December Sales. *W. Hastings-Bass.* **75**

MARTON BOY 3 br.c. Tycoon II–Marton Lady 103 (March Past 124) (1980 5fg* 5g* 6g⁴ 6g³ 6d⁴ 5f 1981 6g 5g 6d⁴ 6g 6f 5s 5g) robust colt; quite a moderate sprint handicapper; ran best race on third start; acts on a firm and a soft surface; has run moderately in blinkers; trained part of season by M. H. Easterby. *S. Wiles.* **—**

MARULA 2 ch.f. Be My Guest 126–Galana (Reform 132) (1981 6g) Mar 27; lightly-made filly; second foal; half-sister to 3-y-o Habella (by Habitat), a winner at up to 7f; dam, half-sister to Derby runner-up Cavo Doro, won over $1\frac{1}{4}$m and $1\frac{1}{2}$m in Ireland; unquoted when behind in 22-runner maiden race won by Ash Ridge at Newmarket in October. *L. Cumani.* **—**

MARWELL   3 b.f. Habitat 134–Lady Seymour 109 (Tudor Melody 129)   (1980 **133**
5d* 5fg* 5g* 5g* 6fg*   1981 7.3s* 8g⁴ 6s* 5f* 6g* 5d² 6fg² 5d*)

Marwell set the seal on a brilliant career with victory in the Prix de l'Abbaye
de Longchamp in October, in which race she had behind the only two horses ever
to beat her in a sprint, Sharpo and Runnett. In the course of two seasons she won
ten races from thirteen starts, including four of Group 1 status, was never out of
the frame, and was beaten out of the first two places only when tried over a mile
in the One Thousand Guineas. Top-class sprinting fillies, not counting two-year-
olds, have been scarce in the last twenty years or so.   Over that period we would
place only Matatina, Secret Step, Gay Mairi, La Tendresse, Abergwaun, Be
Tuneful, Lianga and Marwell in the top flight; and none except the sprinter/miler
Lianga had a record to compare with Marwell's.

At the start of the season the big question was whether Marwell would stay
the Guineas distance. She'd been the leading two-year-old filly of 1980, rivalled
only by Tolmi who'd unfortunately not been able to race after July; the pair had
never met. Marwell ran in five races at two and won the lot, never going further
than six furlongs, the distance of the William Hill Cheveley Park Stakes. She won
the first four in effortless fashion, picking up pattern races at Goodwood (the
Molecomb Stakes) and Doncaster (the Flying Childers Stakes) along the way,
and showing the rare ability to quicken virtually in a stride. When she tackled
six furlongs at Newmarket she proved less impressive in beating the consistent
Welshwyn and Pushy, though she gave no real clue in running to her prospects
of staying further. Very much in her favour, she obviously had a good temperament—an unusually placid one for a filly. Against her was her sire Habitat's
record, in so far as only one of his twelve previous two-year-old pattern-race
winners had gone on to win over as great a distance as a mile at three. On top of
this, her brother and stable-companion Lord Seymour had been raced only at up
to seven furlongs in his second season after showing high-class form over six
furlongs as a two-year-old. Marwell's display on her reappearance in the Fred
Darling Stakes over seven furlongs and sixty yards at Newbury in April held out
every encouragement. After settling beautifully in a truly-run, four-horse affair,
she quickened into the lead over a furlong out and came away smoothly from the
runner-up Star Pastures. However, the race for the Guineas left little room for
doubt that a mile in such company was a shade too far. Held up to get the trip,
she moved to within a length of Fairy Footsteps in the final furlong but never
threatened to close the gap entirely; in the last hundred yards it was Tolmi, Go
Leasing and Madam Gay who were making ground on the leader. Marwell
managed to hold on to fourth place from Madam Gay by only the skin of her
teeth.

If Fairy Footsteps was the best filly on the day in the One Thousand Guineas
she can't be given credit for being the best in the race. Marwell went straight back
to sprinting and soon began to leave her Guineas form behind. As a preliminary
to a shot at the first of the very small number of Group 1 sprints run during the
season, the King's Stand Stakes at Royal Ascot, she was sent for the Gus Demmy
Memorial Stakes over six furlongs at Haydock and won it sufficiently convincingly from Age Quod Agis and Noalto to start 5/4 favourite for the King's
Stand, last won by a filly in 1973 by Abergwaun. The current sprint champion
Moorestyle didn't oppose her at Ascot nor did the previous year's winner African
Song—the former was waiting for the William Hill July Cup because of the firm
ground, the latter had been retired—but the 1980 King's Stand second Runnett
took her on, along with the 1980 William Hill Sprint Championship winner

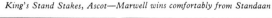

King's Stand Stakes, Ascot—Marwell wins comfortably from Standaan

William Hill July Cup, Newmarket—Marwell is an impressive winner from the 1980 winner Moorestyle

Sharpo, Standaan, who had beaten Sharpo in the Palace House Stakes in the spring, and eight others. Marwell had been improving physically during her second season, which was more than Lord Seymour had done, and took the eye in the paddock at Royal Ascot—with her elegance as much as anything else. Surprisingly, with Standaan in the field, Marwell was able to go the pace virtually all the way in extremely fast conditions; she had to be ridden to make her challenge approaching the final furlong but always looked like getting there, and in the end she won comfortably by two lengths from Standaan. Runnett finished third while Sharpo ran badly, unable to beat handicappers.

The July Cup at Newmarket was the occasion of the first of two meetings between Marwell and Moorestyle. As on their second meeting she came out the better. To be fair to Moorestyle he would probably have given her a tougher time in the autumn, but the authority of Marwell's victory in the July Cup was so complete that to conceive his ever beating her at weight-for-sex over five or six furlongs is very difficult. Marwell won by three lengths; Moorestyle readily accounted for the rest of the field which included two French challengers, Sonoma and Ancient Regime, the Danish-trained Music Streak, Standaan and the quite well-fancied English three-year-olds Cut Throat and Anoner Realm. With Standaan present there was once again no hanging about. Marwell was always travelling quite smoothly behind him, she delivered her challenge at virtually the same time as Moorestyle two furlongs out, soon gained the upper hand and quickened clear. As Moorestyle stayed on Marwell gamely maintained her advantage, ridden out with hands and heels.   Marwell was the first filly to win the July Cup since Lianga in 1975; Secret Step won it in 1963.

Prix de l'Abbaye de Longchamp—Marwell gains her fifth victory of the season as British runners dominate this event again; Sharpo is second and Rabdan third

Nothing could serve better to illustrate the impact Marwell made at Newmarket than the fact she started an odds-on favourite for the William Hill Sprint Championship at York the following month, 11/10 on to be precise. The race, which is still absurdly under-rated in the European Pattern at Group 2 (who could possibly defend such a state of affairs with reasoned argument?), attracted the best English sprinters except for Runnett and Rabdan, neither of whom would have been seriously considered a danger to Marwell at that time. Perhaps we should have said the best older English sprinters, for the two-year-olds, who had been known to win the race occasionally when it was renowned as the Nunthorpe Stakes, are no longer eligible to compete. Marwell beat Moorestyle by a length and a half this time, outpacing him again. Inexplicably though, she was herself beaten, on merit, to the tune of two and a half lengths by Sharpo. She couldn't be faulted in the paddock but definitely failed to run up to her best. Sharpo came past Moorestyle and Marwell around the furlong pole and was well in command from that point. The possibility now existed that Marwell was going over the top. Possibility drew nearer probability two weeks later when she lost by a neck to Runnett at 13/8 on in the Vernons Sprint Cup at Haydock. The race has seen a hot favourite overturned occasionally, and this occurrence was usually put down to the lateness of the season, and the attendant conditions, at which it used to be run. On this occasion, as at York, the only reason for Marwell's defeat seemed to be that she wasn't good enough on the day. She chased the leader Sayyaf and struggled for a long time to catch him, eventually succeeding as she really surged into her stride entering the final furlong. She remained in front until the fast-finishing Runnett caught her, by no means unawares, in the last few strides. Sayyaf finished only two and a half lengths behind, so clearly Marwell once again hadn't quite shown top form.

By now we were prepared for the worst when Marwell went for the Prix de l'Abbaye de Longchamp, especially as Runnett and Sharpo, who hadn't run since York, were in the ten-strong field. Furthermore Sonoma, third in the July Cup, and Ancient Regime, might be more difficult to beat there now they were back on their home ground. Marwell in the paddock scarcely looked like a filly who was past her best: she seemed on excellent terms with herself, but then she had seemed on equally good terms at Haydock and York. She and Moorestyle's 'stand-in', the admirable Rabdan, a much travelled, much improved and still improving four-year-old, were the pick of the paddock. Sharpo, who started at even money, was very much on his toes, while Cooleen Jack and Naomi Joy looked outclassed. Kearney, sold for approximately £33,000 in Paris the day before, and Music Streak completed the number. The only significant absentee from the race was Moorestyle, though a top-class two-year-old would have added spice to the contest. In days gone by two-year-olds had managed to win the Abbaye, just as they had the Nunthorpe. In the race the fastest starter proved to be Music Streak. He led at a tremendous pace, taking Sharpo and one or two of the others off their legs; Runnett, for all that he is best when coming from behind, put himself at a grave disadvantage by dwelling in the stalls. Marwell, fast away, couldn't overtake Music Streak until two lengths from home. Once in front she had to fight all the way and was very strongly pressed through the final furlong by Sharpo. Under hard driving from Swinburn she hung on exceptionally gamely for a neck win. Rabdan finished third, Ancient Regime fourth, Runnett fifth and Sonoma sixth, slightly less than six lengths covering them. Marwell became the first older filly to win the Prix de l'Abbaye de Longchamp since Lianga; the brilliant French two-year-old filly Sigy won in 1978.

Although Marwell's record is one that would be difficult for any filly or colt to surpass she fell a long way short of a place among the top five money earners, win only, in the country during 1981. Her four wins in England brought in a total of £88,973, which is less than Master Willie drew in the Coral Eclipse Stakes. Add her £29,014 for the Prix de l'Abbaye de Longchamp and she is still behind Shergar's pick-up in the King George VI and Queen Elizabeth Diamond Stakes; add further her £30,114 place money and, sadly, the total still comes to less than first prize for the Derby. It's a crazy world we live in. The sooner the authorities redress the balance in the distribution of prize money at the top between all groups of racehorses—be they sprinters, milers, middle-distance horses or stayers—the better. The injustice is glaring at present. All told, by the way, Marwell won £210,653 in her career, £31,518 of that sum in the Cheveley Park.

At today's prices broodmares aren't literally worth their weight in gold, but on her retirement Marwell is closer to it than most. She has all the qualities one could hope for unless, perhaps, one were in business to produce a Gold Cup winner under either set of Rules. Her breeding is impeccable. Her sire Habitat is so successful that his three-generation pedigree is surely engraved on the memory

Mr E. J. Loder's "Marwell"

of a fair proportion of those concerned with the raising and racing of the thoroughbred in Europe and even further afield. His portrait and list of principal winners
can be found in the Airlie Stud's feature in the stallion section of this Annual.
On that list, it will be seen, are two winners of the Prix de l'Abbaye de Longchamp
besides Marwell in Double Form and Sigy; Double Form also won the King's
Stand Stakes and the Vernons Cup, while two other Habitats, Hot Spark and

Marwell (b.f. 1978)	Habitat (b 1966)	Sir Gaylord (b 1959)	Turn-to	
			Somethingroyal	
		Little Hut (b 1952)	Occupy	
			Savage Beauty	
	Lady Seymour (b 1972)	Tudor Melody (br 1956)	Tudor Minstrel	
			Matelda	
		My Game (br 1957)	My Babu	
			Flirting	

Hittite Glory, won the Flying Childers in the days before it was demoted to
Group 2. Habitat is also the sire of Marwell's erstwhile adversaries Sonoma and
Sayyaf. Marwell's brother Lord Seymour, a very good-looking individual, was one
of two two-year-old pattern-race winners in Great Britain and Ireland in 1979
for Habitat, the other being Smokey Lady, the winner of the Gallaghouse Phoenix
Stakes in Ireland. Lord Seymour won the Mill Reef Stakes at Newbury. The
following season he didn't grow much and failed to add to his wins from four
starts, on one occasion finishing third to Sayyaf in the Gus Demmy and on
another seventh to Kearney in the Cork and Orrery Stakes. He is now at stud in
Australia. Marwell's dam Lady Seymour also won the Phoenix Stakes. Injury cut
short her career and she was retired the unbeaten winner of two five-furlong races.
Lord Seymour is her first foal, Marwell her second and there is a two-year-old
colt by Nonoalco coming along in 1982. Lady Seymour's breeding compliments
her daughter's. Tudor Melody was almost as successful a sire as Habitat in his

528

time; and My Game is a half-sister to the Eclipse winner Arctic Explorer and the very useful middle-distance performer Ferneley, and a granddaughter of The Cobbler's dam Overture. My Game, unraced, produced five winners at up to a mile besides Lady Seymour.

On looks Marwell yields nothing to Lord Seymour at his best. Most attractive, well-made, medium-sized; elegant, as we said, and an excellent mover. She is every inch a top-class filly in action and repose. At this point we should not let the opportunity pass of mentioning what superb condition she was kept in throughout her very busy season. Marwell, a notably genuine individual, showed her form whatever the state of the ground and was equally effective at five furlongs and six furlongs. Sprinting will be fortunate to see her like among the so-called weaker sex inside another few seasons. She begins her new career with a visit to Great Nephew. *M. Stoute.*

MARYAM 4 gr. or ro.f. Rarity 129–Lost Angel 99 (Parthia 132) (1980 8v 8fg³ 8fg* 8s 10.2g 8.2s 8.2s* 7d 1981 8fg 10.8d 8g 7g 8d) well-made, quite attractive filly; won twice in 1980; well beaten at 4 yrs; should stay 1¼m; probably acts on any going. *D. Marks.* —

MARY BROWNING 3 br.f. Grisaille 115–Virtuosity (Reliance II 137) (1980 5f 5g 6g 7g 1981 11.7fg 10fg) lightly-made filly; poor maiden; sold 360 gns Ascot September Sales. *D. Elsworth.* —

MARY BURNS (USA) 2 b. or br.f. Advocator–Burns' Babe (Fleet Nasrullah) (1981 6g 6f² 6d) May 2; $42,000Y; leggy, rather narrow filly; half-sister to 3 winners, including useful miler Anglepoise (by Angle Light) and Dorwil's Babe (by Promised Land), a very useful stakes winner at up to 6f; dam won twice at up to 5f at 2 yrs; kept on strongly under pressure when ½-length second of 10 to Tropical Blaze in minor event at Ripon in August; rather disappointing sixth of 15 behind Lucayan Lady in similar event at Pontefract in October, only subsequent start; will be suited by 7f; possibly not at her best on a soft surface. *S. Norton.* 76

MARYLAND COOKIE (USA) 3 b.f. Bold Hour–Efficiency (Dondeen 123) (1980 5f⁴ 5d⁴ 5.8fg* 5fg 6g* 6s² 6s² 1981 7s³ 7fg⁴ 7g 6s 5d 5.8fg² 5h* 5fg⁴ 5f² 5fg² 6s³ 5s* 6v) compact, good-bodied filly; good mover; successful in handicaps at Bath (made virtually all) and Ascot, on latter course in October getting up on line under very strong pressure to beat Ferryman in Bovis Stakes; ½-length second to Tinjar in valuable handicap at York (caught close home) and to Mummy's Game in minor event at Beverley in between; ran creditably earlier against stiffer opposition, including when third of 14 behind Go Leasing in Salisbury 1,000 Guineas Trial; stays 7f, but seems better at shorter distances; acts on any going; genuine and consistent; sweated up second start; best in blinkers nowadays; sold 88,000 gns Newmarket December Sales. *J. Bethell.* 101

MARY LE BOW 4 b.f. Levmoss 133–Great Paul 117 (Great Nephew 126) (1980 12.2fg⁴ 12d² 12.2f³ 16fg³ 14.7g² 16f 14d 14.7d⁴ 1981 16g 14.6f³ 16.1f 13.8fg⁴) lengthy filly; appears to stay 2m; probably acts on any going; blinkered final start; probably none too enthusiastic. *M. H. Easterby.* 46

Bovis Handicap, Ascot—Piggott excels to get Maryland Cookie (blinkers) home by a short head from Ferryman

MARY MAGUIRE 4 b.f. Rapid River 127–Flicka (Balidar 133) (1980 5f 6f³ 5h 5d⁴ 6g³ 6g 7g 8f 7g 5f 5s 1981 5s⁴ 5s 5g 6g 6fg 6fg² 6g² 6f* 5f* 5fg 6s 6v 6s) **58** unfurnished filly; plater; successful in better company at Pontefract and Hamilton in September; best at sprint distances; acts on any going but is suited by firm; usually blinkered at 3 yrs; sometimes sweats up; suitable mount for a claimer. *S. Nesbitt.*

MARY MITSU 2 br.f. Tarboosh–Misty Hill (Hill Clown) (1981 5g* 5f2) Feb **96** 10; IR 9,400Y; workmanlike filly; second foal; half-sister to a winner in USA by Prince Tenderfoot; dam won over 13f and 1¾m in France; favourite, always front rank when winning 17-runner maiden race at Phoenix Park in May by 2 lengths from Miss Lilian; favourite again, showed good speed and had every chance when 3 lengths second of 6 to Tender King in Windsor Castle Stakes at Royal Ascot the following month; bred to stay at least 1m; transferred to J. Dunlop's stable after Royal Ascot but didn't race again. *M. Kauntze, Ireland.*

MARZIE 2 b.f. Silly Season 127–Terran Royal (Right Royal V 135) (1981 6fg — 7f 8d 8d) Apr 12; small, lightly-made filly; second foal; dam well beaten in 3 races; no worthwhile form in sellers. *P. Asquith.*

MASCARENHAS 6 b.g. Windjammer (USA)–Harvest Child 79 (Tamerlane 128) — (1980 14g 12fg 1981 12g 12fg) poor maiden; stays well; acts on firm going; usually wears blinkers; sold 720 gns Ascot August Sales. *T. Gosling.*

MASHIN TIME 2 b.f. Palm Track 122–Baggin Time 91 (Pinsun 108) (1981 6f **68** 6f² 6fg* 7f⁴) Jan 27; narrow, leggy filly; lacks scope; not the best of movers; second foal; dam won from 5f to 1½m; showed improved form when winning easily by 8 lengths from Spotty Jane in seller at Carlisle in July (bought in 1,800 gns); creditable fourth of 11 after running bit wide into straight in nursery won by Martialis at Thirsk later in month; will stay 1m. *M. H. Easterby.*

MASQUERADER 3 gr.c. Dancer's Image–Dash On 93 (Klairon 131) (1980 6g⁴ **65** 6g 1981 7fg 7g 11d 10f 8fg 9s² 7d 8g) strong, attractive colt; quite a moderate maiden; stays 9f; wears blinkers; sent to France. *P. Makin.*

MASSENA 5 ch.g. Our Mirage 123–Barlassina (Taine 131) (1980 10.2g 12d — 10.5s 12d 1981 12d 12.2s) lengthy gelding; poor performer nowadays; stays 13f well; acts on any going. *D. Sasse.*

MASSIMO 2 b.c. Blakeney 126–Never a Fear 121 (Never Say Die 137) (1981 — 8g 10g) Apr 25; 16,000Y; stocky, strong, attractive colt; brother to Bird Reserve, placed from 5f to 1m, and half-brother to 2 minor winners; dam a smart staying 2-y-o who disappointed at 3 yrs; 25/1 and backward (moved short to post), showed up for quite a long way when out of first 10 of 29 behind Born Hero in 1m maiden race at Newmarket in October; always struggling and finished well beaten in well-contested £6,500 event won by Paternoster Row on same course later in month; bred to stay well. *L. Cumani.*

MASTER AT ARMS 3 br.g. Scottish Rifle 127–Bella Lisa (River Chanter 121) — (1980 NR 1981 11s 13.3d) 2,500F, 4,700Y; fair sort; half-brother to 3 winners, including fairly useful sprinter Kingsfold Lad (by King's Troop); dam ran only 3 times; in rear in maiden races at Newbury in May and June, finishing last on latter occasion. *Mrs R. Lomax.*

MASTER-BLOW 2 ch.g. Roi Soleil 125–Surfacing (Worden II 129) (1981 6d³ **83** 6s² 7f 6d 5v* 6s) May 6; leggy gelding; half-brother to 1¼m winner Rough-Cast (by Blast) and a winner abroad; won 5f maiden race at Haydock in October, running on to beat Chart Topper 1½ lengths; will stay 1m; acts on any going. *W. Elsey.*

MASTER BOATMAN 2 ch.c. Riverman 131–Ya Ya 84 (Primera 131) (1981 **83** 6d 7f⁴ 7g³) Apr 6; quite a useful sort; good walker; brother to 3-y-o 7f and 11f winner Seven Seas and half-brother to smart 7f to 10.6f winner Fluellen (by Welsh Pageant); dam, half-sister to Park Hill Stakes winner African Dancer, stayed well; stayed on without looking dangerous when 5½ lengths fourth of 8 to Busaco in £3,800 race at York in September and when 5½ lengths third of 23 to Simply Great in maiden race at Newmarket the following month; will stay 1¼m+. *H. Wragg.*

MASTER BUNBURY 2 b.c. Song 132–Fleur d'Amour 85 (Murrayfield 119) **51** (1981 5g 5fg⁴ 6f 6fg 6g 6g 6s) Mar 24; first foal; dam won over 6f and 7f; poor plater; dead. *P. Cundell.*

MASTER CARL 2 b.c. Pitskelly 122–Lepello (Le Levanstell 122) (1981 5d² 5g³ **95** 6f 7f⁴ 7d³ 7.3d 7f) Feb 5; IR 3,000Y; big, strong colt who carries a lot of condition; third foal; half-brother to 1980 Irish 2-y-o 7.5f winner Le Boosh (by

Tarboosh); dam never ran; put up best efforts when length second to Linus Ginseng in maiden race at York in May and 2¼ lengths third to Brookline under top weight in 7f nursery at Newmarket in August; evidently needs at least 7f; seems to act on any going but goes well on a soft surface; ran poorly last 2 starts. *P. Rohan.*

MASTER CAWSTON 2 ch.c. Cawston's Clown 113–Teresa Way 66 (Great **95** White Way) (1981 6fg³ 6g* 6s 6g) Apr 18; tall, useful sort; good mover; second foal; dam placed over 5f at 2 years; ridden by apprentice unable to claim his 5-lb allowance in 11-runner Ribero Stakes at Doncaster in September but ran on strongly to win by a head from Bali Dancer; easy in market, ran on steadily without being knocked about when creditable 3½ lengths seventh of 17 to Bold Fort in nursery at Newmarket the following month on fourth outing; will stay 7f; ran poorly on soft ground third start; fairly useful and will win more races in 1982. *H. Wragg.*

MASTER DAVENPORT 9 b.g. Hot Brandy 119–Acacallis 80 (Red God 128§) — (1980 NR 1981 16f) poor maiden on flat but is a fairly useful chaser. *J. Webber.*

MASTER GOLFER 3 ch.g. Swing Easy 126–Wimosa 92 (Mossborough 126) **92** (1980 5d³ 5d 5g⁴ 7d 7fg³ 7.6f³ 7fg* 7s² 1981 7g 8fg 7d* 8g* 8fg 8fg* 8f³) well-made, good sort; easy winner of seller at Newmarket in 1980; did well in better company in 1981 and won handicaps at Epsom in June, Newmarket in July (beat Golden Flak a shade cleverly in £8,200 Addison Tools Handicap) and Kempton in August; held on very gamely from Paterno in a driving finish when apprentice ridden on last-named course; stays 1m; acts on any going; usually blinkered in 1980. *J. Sutcliffe.*

MASTER MARTIN 3 b.c. Martinmas 128–Princess Irmgard 83 (Delirium 126) **66** (1980 5fg 5f 5f² 6d⁴ 7g³ 7d 8d 8.2s 7v 1981 8g³ 10.4g 8fg* 7.6g 8f 8g³ 10.4s 10f 10d) neat colt; won slowly-run handicap at Beverley in June in quite good style by 1½ lengths from Sincerely Mills; probably stays 1¼m; suited by a sound surface; ran poorly fourth and fifth starts; sold 2,000 gns Ascot November Sales. *R. Hollinshead.*

MASTER OAKLEA 3 br.g. Panama Canal 105–Quick Return (The Bo'sun 114) — (1980 7f 7g 6fg 7fg 1981 10g 12g 16d 14fg) strong, compact gelding; has shown a little ability in maiden and minor races; probably stays 1½m; blinkered final start. *P. Mitchell.*

MASTER SCORCHIN 10 b.g. Goldhill 125–Miss Scorchin 67 (Firestreak 125) — (1980 NR 1981 9g) poor maiden on flat though has won over hurdles and fences; has worn blinkers. *R. Carter.*

MASTER'S VOICE 3 b.c. Record Token 128–Hascombe Lady 70 (Galivanter — 131) (1980 6d 7g 8d 8d 8s 8d 1981 8d 11.7g 10.1fg 8.3fg 8fg 8g 9g) strong, workmanlike colt; plater; stays 1m; acts on soft going; blinkered fifth start. *J. Douglas-Home.*

MASTER THIEF 10 ch.g. Pieces of Eight 128–Tudor Song (Tudor Minstrel 144) **40** (1980 14fg 16g 1981 15.5d² 16d⁴ 15.5d 16.9s) poor stayer; acts on any going; suitable mount for an apprentice; used to wear blinkers. *P. Makin.*

MASTER TONY 3 ch.c. Galivanter 131–Andromache 112 (Delirium 126) (1980 — 5f 5f 6g 6g 7fg 7g 5fg 7.2d 1981 7fg 7g 7f 6fg 5fg 7f) compact colt; poor plater; occasionally blinkered; sometimes ridden by lad in paddock. *W. Haigh.*

MASTER WILLIE 4 ch.c. High Line 125–Fair Winter 111 (Set Fair 129) (1980 **129** 8s* 10f4 10.5f² 12f² 12s 10.5d* 10d² 10d² 1981 12g* 12d* 10fg* 12fg4 10.5g³ 10g)
The final words on Master Willie in *Racehorses of 1980*—'as genuine and dependable as any in training . . . altogether an excellent horse to go to the big meetings with'—were borne out by his four-year-old career, or at least by the first part of it. Having won the Benson and Hedges Gold Cup and finished second in the Derby and the Champion Stakes in 1980, he confirmed his status in the most recent season by winning two of Britain's oldest and most prestigious races, the Coronation Cup and the Coral Eclipse Stakes. Master Willie became only the sixth to complete the double in the same year: King Salmon, runner-up in Hyperion's Derby, and the Derby winner Windsor Lad did so in the 'thirties; and the French-trained Tropique won both races in 1956, an achievement matched since by Ballymoss and Royal Palace, both of whom went on to win Britain's most important open-aged event the King George VI and Queen Elizabeth Stakes. Master Willie managed only fourth place in the King George and his career ended in anti-climax with below-par performances in the Benson and Hedges Gold Cup and in

the Champion Stakes. Nevertheless, he was an admirable racehorse, a never-say-die competitor of a type that so often endears itself to the racing public. He was sold in the autumn for a sum believed to be around 7,000,000 dollars (£3.8m at prevailing exchange rates) and is to take up stud duties alongside Northern Dancer, The Minstrel and company at Windfields Farm, Maryland, United States in 1982.

We cannot recall the last time that the first three in a Derby met in a race the next season. The appearance of Henbit, Master Willie and Rankin in the Jockey Club Stakes must have delighted Newmarket's management; it certainly provided the highlight of Friday's programme at the spring meeting. Henbit, making his comeback after a serious leg injury sustained in the Derby, was made favourite at 7/4, with Master Willie at 2/1; Rankin, beaten three quarters of a length and a length and a half at Epsom but with the benefit of two outings in the current season, came next at 4/1. The Jockey Club Stakes was no contest: Master Willie turned the race into a procession, pouncing on the front-running Henbit and Rankin with more than two furlongs to go and galloping on with obvious relish to win by fifteen lengths, a staggering margin for any race on the flat, let alone a pattern race contested by three horses good enough to be placed in a Derby! Impressive though it was, Master Willie's performance was not all that it seemed: the 100/1-shot King's Ride finished second with Rankin only fourth and Henbit last in a field of six.

Henbit and Rankin were each seen out only once after their crushing defeat in the Jockey Club Stakes, Rankin being one of four opponents for Master Willie in the Coronation Cup at Epsom's summer meeting. The Coronation Cup, run over the Derby course, is open to three-year-olds but no horse of that age has contested the race since Effervescence finished fifth to Persian Gulf in 1944 when it was run at Newmarket; the event is the second-most valuable in Britain open to horses above the age of three before the King George VI and Queen Elizabeth Diamond Stakes in July. Also in the field in 1981 were the Irish Sweeps Derby runner-up Prince Bee, having his first race of the season, and the fillies Mrs Penny and Vielle. Master Willie started at 2/1 on and won by two lengths and two and a half lengths from Prince Bee and Vielle. After setting only a modest gallop in the first half mile, Master Willie was seen at his most impressive as he stretched the field with a sustained burst down the hill and round Tattenham Corner; Master Willie straightened out for home with an advantage of four or five lengths and, although his lead was being reduced gradually in the final furlong, he was never seriously threatened.

Master Willie earned £43,770 for his owner at Epsom but he picked up more than twice that sum a month later in the Coral Eclipse Stakes over Sandown's testing mile-and-quarter course. With a first prize of £90,650, the Coral Eclipse ranked third in value behind the Derby and the King George in the British Calendar. The Coral Eclipse has more than doubled in value in three years and in 1981 its first prize was on a par with that offered for the Irish Sweeps Derby, a race which is a strong counter-attraction for the best middle-distance three-year-olds. The recent efforts of the sponsors and the Sandown racecourse executive are to be applauded: the Eclipse provides one of the first major opportunities to test the relative strength of the classic three-year-olds and the best of the older generation that have remained in training and, as such, it is potentially a much more significant contest than the Sweeps Derby which is run seven days earlier. The Sweeps Derby has become something of an automatic target for the Epsom

Coronation Cup, Epsom—Master Willie never looks likely to be caught by Prince Bee or Vielle

Coral Eclipse Stakes, Sandown—Master Willie again makes all. Hard Fought is subsequently disqualified and Vielle (right) promoted to second place

Derby winner in recent years—Mill Reef was the last Derby winner to contest the Eclipse and seven of the ten subsequent winners have gone on to the Curragh. Whether the Coral Eclipse will succeed in attracting a greater number of outstanding representatives from the current classic crop than it has of late remains to be seen but the injection of prize money can only increase its chances of doing so. In any case, the race now provides another much-needed worthwhile opportunity for the older generation, and any move that helps to encourage owners of good horses to keep them in training as four-year-olds is warmly welcomed in this quarter.

The field for the Coral Eclipse Stakes numbered seven, one more than the previous year when it was won by Britain's top middle-distance four-year-old Ela Mana-Mou who went on to win the King George. The only representative of the classic generation in 1981 was the Prix de Diane de Revlon winner Madam Gay who had finished second in the Oaks. Master Willie's main rival appeared to be Hard Fought who had won successively the Earl of Sefton Stakes at Newmarket, the Westbury Stakes over the Eclipse course and distance, and the Prince of Wales's Stakes at Royal Ascot; Vielle, who had run with credit against Hard Fought in the latter's two previous races, was also in the field. Master Willie dictated the pace throughout, stepping up the gallop before the home turn and striding out in typically determined style when hard driven in the straight; he had to pull out everything to hold off the subsequently-disqualified Hard Fought by three quarters of a length with Vielle another half a length away third. Fourth-placed Fingal's Cave, who finished two and a half lengths behind Vielle, was promoted to third. Our impression after Sandown was that Master Willie might prove better suited by a mile and a half than by shorter distances as a four-year-old and we gave him a much better chance than most did against the Derby winner Shergar in the King George VI and Queen Elizabeth Diamond Stakes at Ascot. Front-running tactics had seemed to suit Master Willie well enough at Epsom and Sandown but his connections remained convinced that he was a better horse ridden from behind when tackling a mile and a half and Waldron was instructed to ride a waiting race at Ascot. Master Willie finished a disappointing fourth of seven after expending valuable energy fighting his jockey in the early stages in his attempt to take up a front-running role; he might have done better allowed to stride along, although he wouldn't have beaten Shergar however he had been ridden. Master Willie's two remaining races were over a mile and a quarter and on the first occasion he seemed to confirm the impression that the trip had become a shade too sharp for him. In the Benson and Hedges Gold Cup at York's August meeting, he was beaten three quarters of a length and the same by the front-running three-year-olds Beldale Flutter and Kirtling, coming under the whip and seeming to be a little outpaced two furlongs out but gamely pulling them back towards the finish. He ran one of his few poor races in the Champion Stakes at Newmarket in October, fading to finish tenth of sixteen after showing in the lead with three furlongs to go.

Master Willie (ch.c. 1977)	High Line (ch 1966)	High Hat (ch 1957)	Hyperion
			Madonna
		Time Call (b 1955)	Chanteur II
			Aleria
	Fair Winter (ch 1964)	Set Fair (ch 1949)	Denturius
			Ria Geno
		Winter Gleam (ch 1959)	Aureole
			Red Winter

Master Willie was largely responsible for putting High Line near the top of the sires' list for the second successive year; Master Willie's first-prize earnings in 1981 were £149,424 which accounted for slightly more than two thirds of High Line's total. The average distance of races won at three years and upwards by High Line's progeny is thirteen furlongs and most of his good-class winners have needed a mile and a half or more; none has been so effective at a mile and a quarter as Master Willie, though Crimson Bean was very smart. Master Willie's dam Fair Winter was not much to look at, and she failed to make a very low reserve when offered in the sale-ring before she had seen a racecourse; she won seven races, making remarkable progress as a three-year-old when she graduated from minor handicap company to running against the best of her age and sex,

Mr R. Barnett's "Master Willie"

winning the Nassau Stakes at Goodwood and finishing fourth, after getting
boxed in, in the Sun Chariot Stakes at Newmarket, for which she started favourite. Fair Winter, by the sprinter Set Fair out of a mare who stayed two miles,
never raced at further than a mile and a quarter. Fair Winter produced five
minor winners before Master Willie. Like his dam, Master Willie is somewhat
unimpressive in appearance, being a rather plain, lengthy colt; he is, however, a
good walker. He acted on any going. *H. Candy.*

MA TANTE 2 b.f. Manado 130–Great Aunt II (Mourne 126) (1981 5fg 5d* 5g* **82**
6fg 5d⁴ 6d) Feb 16; IR 5,400F; leggy, useful-looking filly; good walker; has a
rather round action; sixth foal; dam won in USA; justified favouritism in maiden
race at Salisbury in May and 12-runner minor event at Lingfield in June (held off
Rublink by ⅛ length); returned to form after being off course 3 months, finishing
4 lengths fourth of 14 to My Lover when apprentice ridden in valuable nursery at
Newbury in September; ran poorly fourth and sixth starts (sweating on latter);
should be well suited by 6f; possibly needs some give in the ground; sold 7,000
gns Newmarket December Sales. *H. Candy.*

MATCHLESS DANCER 5 ch.h. Bold Lad (Ire) 133–Blue Butterfly 105 **58**
(Majority Blue 126) (1980 8fg 8fg 7h 10g 10.1g 10.1g 8g* 7f 8g³ 1981 10d² 9g⁴
10d 12d 8f* 7g 8.3d²) strong, good sort; plater; bought in 1,300 gns after winning at Yarmouth in June; stays 1¼m; acts on any going; often hooded and
sometimes wears blinkers as well; bandaged nowadays; suitable mount for an
inexperienced rider. *J. Jenkins.*

MATCH MASTER 2 ch.c. Roman Warrior 132–Giglet (Frankincense 120) **105**
(1981 5fg 6f² 6fg⁴ 6d³ 6g) Apr 15; 12,000Y; quite well-made, good sort; good
walker and mover; third foal; half-brother to 1980 2-y-o 5f winner Lady Arpege
(by Swing Easy); dam showed no form; still a maiden but is a pretty useful colt
nonetheless and went down only by a short head to Sangalkan in £5,600 maiden
race at York in June; prominent in pattern races subsequently, running on
strongly when 2¼ lengths fourth of 11 to End of the Line in Anglia Television
July Stakes at Newmarket, having first race for 2 months when 5½ lengths third
of 8 to Hays in Mill Reef Stakes at Newbury and being beaten only 5½ lengths
when eleventh of 13 to Cajun in William Hill Middle Park Stakes at Newmarket
in October; suited by 6f and may stay further; seems to act on any going. *C.
Nelson.*

MATCH WINNER (FR) 2 br.c. Dancer's Image–Mosstown (Mossborough 126) **113**
(1981 6g³ 6fg* 7g* 7.3s³) good-topped, useful sort; fifth foal; half-brother to
smart middle-distance performer Masked Marvel (by Hard to Beat); dam won at
up to 9f in France; landed the odds in facile style in maiden race at Nottingham
in September, scoring by 6 lengths from Mardi Gras, and had plenty in hand when
winning minor event at Yarmouth later in month by a length from Saysaban; led
soon after halfway when co-favourite for 8-runner Horris Hill Stakes at Newbury
in October but was outpaced in closing stages and was beaten 1¾ lengths into third
place behind easy winner Montekin; will stay 1¼m; improved with every race as a
2-y-o and could well continue on the upgrade at 3 yrs. *H. Cecil.*

MATILDA CAVE 3 b.f. King's Leap 111–Camilla Mary (Molvedo 137) (1980 —
5f⁴ 5g² 6s 6g* 6fg² 7fg* 1981 8s 7d 7fg 6fg) narrow, lightly-made filly; none
too good away from front; poor form in handicaps in 1981; should stay 1m; acts on a firm
surface; went down very freely indeed when tailed off final start; sold 700 gns
Newmarket December Sales. *M. Tompkins.*

MATISON 3 br.c. Workboy 123–Miss Mattie 71 (Hill Clown) (1980 NR 1981 —
10.2g) second foal; dam, who won over 1½m, comes from same family as Altesse
Royale; 12/1 when in rear in valuable 23-runner seller won by King's Town at
Doncaster in November. *M. H. Easterby.*

MATTABOY 3 ch.c. Music Boy 124–Green Chartreuse 91 (French Beige 127) **124**
(1980 5g* 6fg² 5g³ 6fg² 6f* 1981 7g 8g 8g² 8s⁴ 8fg 9g)
Mattaboy performed the most unusual feat of contesting the Two Thousand
Guineas and its French and Irish equivalents, the Poule d'Essai des Poulains
which is run first of the three and the Airlie/Coolmore Two Thousand Guineas
which is run last. The races follow in quick succession and inevitably present a
most demanding schedule for both trainer and horse. In 1981 Longchamp was
followed within six days by Newmarket after which there was a break of only a
fortnight before the Curragh. Mattaboy, one of the leading two-year-olds of 1980,
put up differing performances in the three races, easily his best being at Newmarket. He was never going well at Longchamp and trailed home eighth of ten
behind Recitation; consequently he was a virtually-unconsidered 50/1-chance
when arguably an unlucky loser at Newmarket. Mattaboy was crossed and

hampered soon after leaving the stalls in the Two Thousand Guineas and then
pulled very hard at the back of the field for the first three furlongs. It wasn't until
halfway that he got any sort of run, but once he did he came through the field
very quickly and was in a challenging position two furlongs out. He got the better
of a tremendous duel with Bel Bolide, whom he had beaten narrowly in the
Middle Park Stakes as a two-year-old, and failed only in the last few strides to
repel the challenge of To-Agori-Mou. He was beaten a neck. To-Agori-Mou again
came out the better at the Curragh where Mattaboy, probably unsuited by the soft
going, never really threatened to be concerned in the finish but stayed on under
pressure into fourth, about two and a half lengths behind the winner Kings Lake.

Mattaboy missed his next objective through running a temperature on the
morning of the St James's Palace Stakes at Royal Ascot, and he came out only
twice more. He made little show when taking on Kings Lake and To-Agori-Mou
again in the Sussex Stakes at Goodwood and was subsequently sent to be trained
by P. Howe in the United States. Reportedly he failed to acclimatise there and
after finishing unplaced at Saratoga in August was returned to his old stable at
Newmarket in the autumn.

		Jukebox	Sing Sing
	Music Boy	(b 1966)	Bibi Mah
	(ch 1973)	Veronique	Matador
Mattaboy		(b 1966)	Narcisse
(ch.c. 1978)		French Beige	Bois Roussel
	Green Chartreuse	(b 1953)	Nivea
	(b 1970)	Green Velvet	Epaulette
		(ch 1965)	Greenheart

Mattaboy's sire Music Boy has made a good start to his career at stud. Music
Boy was a very smart sprinter and he is, not surprisingly, proving a strong influence for speed; he was also represented in 1981 by the Ayr Gold Cup winner
First Movement and the good Scandinavian sprinter Music Streak. Mattaboy,
out of the French Beige mare Green Chartreuse, stays as well as any of his sire's
offspring. He is the fourth foal of Green Chartreuse, a mare who won at up to
seven furlongs as a two-year-old and is a half-sister to the good Italian middle-
distance colt Stateff. Green Chartreuse has produced one other winner, the
modest sprinter Glen Gorse (by Forlorn River).

If Mattaboy can reproduce his Two Thousand Guineas running, and he may
well reproduce it given the right conditions, he will be very much a force to
reckon with in good mile races such as the Lockinge Stakes and the Queen Anne
Stakes. A strong, compact colt who is well suited by a sound surface, he tends to
pull hard in the early stages and seems to do best when he can be covered up. It
is possibly significant that he has run his best races on the Rowley Mile, a straight
course. *R. Armstrong.*

MATURE 2 b.f. Welsh Pageant 132–Material 107 (Song 132) (1981 5g 5fg 6g — 7g) Feb 20; leggy, lightly-made filly; not a particularly good mover; second foal; half-sister to Immaterial (by Habat), second in 3 sprint races at 2 yrs; dam won five 5f races at 2 yrs; only plating-class form in maiden races; best run over 7f; retained 620 gns Newmarket Autumn Sales. *E. Weymes.*

MAURICE'S TIP 3 b.g. Jolly Me 114–Spaniard's Darling (Darling Boy 124) **42** (1980 6s 6g 6g 7fg 1981 8s² 7v² 8.2s 8g 8g³ 7f 8f² 8f 8.3fg² 8.2s 7s 8.2s) compact gelding; plater; stays 1m; acts on any going; usually blinkered nowadays. *M. Tompkins.*

MAURITZFONTEIN 2 b.c. Habitat 134–Reine Dagobert 76 (Roi Dagobert 128) **91** (1981 7g 7g⁴) Apr 6; 160,000Y; neat, attractive colt; third foal; half-brother to Irish 3-y-o 1¼m winner Buoyant (by Lyphard); dam, half-sister to Grand Prix de Paris winner Matahawk, won over 1½m; ran on well when 7½ lengths sixth of 21 finishers when beating Count Pahlen in maiden race at Newmarket in October; again showed promise when 4 lengths fourth of 15 to Ivano, after leading for a long way, in Houghton Stakes on same course later in month; will stay 1m. *H. Candy.*

MAVOURNEEN (USA) 2 ch.f. Hail The Pirates 126–Blaheen (Beekeeper) — (1981 6g 6g 7g) tall, rather narrow filly; half-sister to 3 minor American winners; dam won claiming races at up to 1m; behind in end-of-season maiden races at Newmarket. *R. Armstrong.*

MAWAL 4 b.c. Tudor Melody 129–Rebus 97 (Busted 134) (1980 7.5s 7s 9g 8g — 1981 10v³ 8g³ 10g² 10f 10f 10f) attractive ex-French colt; only plating class; stays 1¼m; probably not at his best on firm ground; occasionally wears blinkers. *M. Albina.*

MAWJ 2 b.f. Sharpen Up 127–Village 91 (Charlottesville 135) (1981 6fg 5g 6d³   **67**
5d) Apr 8; 43,000Y; lightly-made filly; half-sister to 2 winners, notably useful
miler Yamadori (by Mountain Call); dam, half-sister to Parthia, best at up to
1¼m; apprentice ridden when 6½ lengths third of 13 to Strath of Orchy in maiden
race at Hamilton in September; will stay 1m. *F. Durr.*

MAXINE'S HERE 3 b.f. Copte–Consequently 101 (Con Brio 121) (1980 5d 5s*   **52**
5g 5g 6s² 6g 7f 6g   1981 8s 10s² 8f 10f 10f 8f 7s 8s) small filly; poor plater; stays
1¼m; appears to act on any going. *W. Wharton.*

MAYBEHANDY 3 b.f. Some Hand 119–Unpredictable 103 (Pardal 130) (1980   **65**
5g 5fg³ 6d² 6g² 6fg 8.2g² 1981 7s⁴ 8s⁴ 8g* 8g³ 8fg 9fg 7g² 8g 7fg* 7s³) leggy
filly; successful in sellers at Thirsk in April (bought in 3,300 gns) and Newmarket
in August (no bid), on latter course quickening up pretty well and winning by 5
lengths from Venja; suited by 7f and 1m; probably acts on any going; ran a
bit too freely when apprentice ridden sixth start. *M. Camacho.*

MAY DO 3 b.f. Foggy Bell 108–Rags and Tatters (Rugantino 97) (1980 5.8fg   **—**
7d 7g 1981 11.7g 16fg 8fg) lightly-made filly; behind in varied company,
including in Jersey. *K. Lewis.*

MAYGATE 3 gr.f. Malicious–Sovereign Gate 81 (Sovereign Path 125) (1980 7g   **47**
1981 10fg 12d 16.9s 14f 10fg 12fg 12g 10s 10d²) strong filly; temperamental plater;
stays 1¼m; ran through rails when apprentice ridden sixth outing and started
slowly all subsequent outings; usually blinkered. *A. Hide.*

MAYHEM 8 b.g. Maystreak 118–Amaconda 83 (Dignitary 121) (1980 NR   **—**
1981 10.2fg) poor handicapper; stays 1¼m; seems to act on any going; best in
blinkers; tailed off (heavily bandaged in front) only outing in 1981. *W. A.
Stephenson.*

MAYO MOONLIGHT 2 ch.f. Mansingh 120–Sky Miss (Skymaster 126) (1981   **75**
5f³ 5fg² 6g 6fg³ 5h*) May 8; 9,200Y; third foal; half-sister to 1980 Irish 2-y-o 5f
winner Azurette (by Owen Anthony); dam poor half-sister to very smart Sexton
Blake; favourite when beating Shared Moment by 1½ lengths in 10-runner nursery
at Chepstow in August; best form at 5f, but stays 6f; acts on hard going; has run
well for an apprentice. *Sir Mark Prescott.*

MAYSINA 3 ch.f. Sheshoon 132–Mirtala (Hauban 132) (1980 7fg² 8f³ 1981   **—**
10g 11.5g) lengthy filly; rather a disappointing maiden; should stay 1¼m; sold
6,600 gns Newmarket December Sales. *M. Stoute.*

MAZERAT 2 b.f. Ballynockan 112–Cissac (Indian Ruler 89) (1981 6f 7fg)   **—**
May 13; sister to poor animal, and half-sister to 5f winner Tou Fou (by Royben);
dam of little account; well behind in maiden race at Nottingham in July (last of
23) and minor event at Warwick in August. *D. Ancil.*

MBAIKI (FR) 3 b.c. Saint Roch–Seidnaya (Santon 114) (1980 7.5g 9g 8g* 8d*   **113**
10d⁴ 1981 10.5v³ 12s* 11fg 12s² 12g 15s 12f 15s³ 12v 12v² 12s⁴ 10.5v) half-
brother to Seidnayon (by Dark Star), successful at around 1¼m and also a winner
over jumps; dam never ran; gained one of his 2 wins as a 2-y-o in a seller but is
very much better than a plater; beat Choiseul by 3 lengths in minor event at
Saint-Cloud in April; placed on several other occasions, notably in Group 2 Prix
Hocquart at Longchamp in May (1½ lengths second to Rahotep) and in Group 3
Prix de Lutece on same course in September (about 2 lengths third to Tipperary
Fixer); also ran creditably on other occasions, including when about 10 lengths
sixth behind Bikala in Prix du Jockey-Club at Chantilly; stays well; acts on
heavy going; blinkered seventh outing. *E. Lellouche, France.*

MCCARTHY 3 b.c. Steel Heart 128–Chevy Chase (Raise You Ten 125) (1980   **—**
5fg³ 6g² 6d³ 6d 7g 7g* 7s³ 7g⁴ 7g 1981 8.5fg 8g 6fg 6g 8d 10.2fg 10.8s⁴) strong,
quite attractive colt; very useful performer at 2 yrs; disappointing in varied
company in 1981; probably stays 11f (running on over trip final start); probably
needs some give in the ground; trained by A. Bailey until after second start;
blinkered fifth start. *W. O'Gorman.*

MEAN FRANCINE 2 b.f. African Sky 124–Levrosa (Levmoss 133) (1981 6s)   **— p**
Mar 1; IR 2,200F, 4,000Y; tall, good-topped filly; first produce; dam never ran;
unquoted, showed up quite well until 2f out when 10½ lengths sixth of 12 to
Dancing Rocks in Blue Seal Stakes at Ascot in September; will stay 1m; will
probably do better. *P. Kelleway.*

MEDICO (USA) 3 b.c. Cougar–Remedia (Dr Fager) (1980 NR 1981 8g 11g   **—**
14fg) $77,000Y; strong, good-bodied colt; first foal; dam, winner at up to 7f, is
daughter of Oaks and Prix Vermeille winner Monade; well beaten after finishing
ninth of 18 behind Magikin in newcomers race at Newmarket in April; sold 600
gns Newmarket Autumn Sales. *P. Walwyn.*

MEDINA PALACE 5 br.g. Amber Rama 133–Palace of Medina 94 (Royal Palace —
131) (1980 NR 1981 10g) strong gelding; behind in maiden and minor races.
J. Carr.

MEEKA GOLD (USA) 2 b.c. Ward McAllister–Locklear (First Landing) (1981 **98**
6g* 6g² 7f* 8g*) May 8; $8,000Y; strong, good sort; first foal; dam, winner
twice over 6f, is daughter of sprint stakes winner Coppahaunk; developed into a
useful colt; successful in maiden race at Carlisle in July and in nurseries at Beverley in August (odds on) and Ayr in September (struggling early in straight but
ran on to win by ½ length from Big Trouble); suited by 1m; yet to race on a soft
surface. *S. Norton.*

MEGILLA 3 b.g. Auction Ring 123–Miss Christine 103 (Pall Mall 132) (1980 —
NR 1981 8fg 10f) 11,500Y; big, lengthy gelding; half-brother to two 2-y-o
winners, including fair 5f performer Crystal Miss (by Frigid Aire); dam at her
best at 2 yrs; behind in maiden races at Kempton in July (needed race) and
Yarmouth in August (moved badly to start); sold 400 gns Ascot October Sales.
D. Thom.

MEGS GIRL 3 b.f. Wabash 99–Donbrilla (Donore 119) (1980 7fg 7g 1981 12s) —
compact, leggy filly; tailed off in maiden races. *A. W. Jones.*

MELADON 8 br.g. Astec 128–Celadon (Milesian 125) (1980 9v 10v 13g 13g —
16g² 1981 16.1s 12g⁴ 10g 15g⁴) small, strong ex-Irish gelding; quite useful at
his best on flat but is better known as a hurdler nowadays; stays well; finished
lame final start. *S. Mellor.*

MELANIE'S PET 2 br.f. Saulingo 122–Messua 97 (Abernant 142) (1981 5f 5f) —
Mar 24; 1,700Y; compact filly; half-sister to fairly useful miler Burning Bright
(by Buisson Ardent); dam daughter of French Oaks and Grand Prix de Paris
winner Bagheera; towards rear in sellers at Ripon in August; has worn bandages;
sold 460 gns Doncaster September Sales. *B. Lunness.*

Mr C. K. G. Rowe's "Meeka Gold"

MELATINA 3 br.f. Nero's Charger–Tina's Whistle 51 (Whistling Wind 123) — (1980 5fg 7.2d 6s 1981 6d 6g 5fg 8fg 6fg 7f) of little account; has been tried in blinkers; sold 470 gns Doncaster September Sales. *W. Clay.*

MELBA TOAST 7 br.g. Meldrum 112–Ivory Coast 90 (Poaching 115) (1980 **61** 5fg* 5fg 5fg 5g⁴ 5fg 5fg 6g² 5d 5d 5f 1981 7g 6g* 5s 6s 5g² 5g* 6fg 5fg* 5fg² 5d⁴ 5f 5fg 6f³ 5f² 6d³ 5g 5g) strong gelding; plater; attracted no bid when winning at Pontefract in April and Edinburgh in June; successful in better company at Edinburgh in July; stays 6f; acts on hard going; suitable mount for an inexperienced rider; often wears blinkers; withdrawn after breaking out of stalls once during year. *T. Taylor.*

MELCAIRN 2 br.g. Pitcairn 126–Karatha (Mossborough 126 or Tamerlane 128) **75** (1981 7f 8s 8s) Apr 1; 6,200Y; leggy gelding; half-brother to several winners here and abroad; dam half-sister to very smart Caterina and Scottish Rifle; noted running on in maiden races on first 2 starts at Redcar in September and York the following month, on latter course staying on strongly to finish 8 lengths seventh of 15 to Twist Home after being virtually tailed off at halfway; will stay middle distances. *K. Stone.*

MELDON JOKER 4 b.g. Sweet Story 122–Meldon Lass (Fedor II 107) (1980 — NR 1981 9fg) tailed-off last in minor event at Hamilton in May. *Mrs A. Bell.*

MELINDRA 2 b.f. Gold Form 108–Welsh Spear (Welsh Saint 126) (1981 5fg 5g) — Apr 28; 400F, 500Y; second foal; dam unraced; in rear in maiden races at Lingfield in July and September. *J. Davies.*

MELINGO 3 b.c. Saulingo 122–White Legs (Preciptic 122) (1980 5g² 5f 6g⁴ 5d* **76** 5g² 5f³ 5g 7fg 6s 1981 5s 6g* 7d² 6s⁴ 7g 7f 6f 7g 7g 6d) strong, robust colt; made all and beat Dragonist a length in handicap at Pontefract in April; second in similar race at Thirsk in May, best subsequent effort; stays 7f; possibly not at his best on very soft going but acts on any other; occasionally blinkered, but seems better without; sweating ninth outing. *J. Etherington.*

MELISSA JANE 3 gr.f. No Mercy 126–Rich Harvest (Bounteous 125) (1980 **94** 7g 6f³ 7d⁴ 1981 8d³ 8f* 8.2f* 8g² 8.5fg* 8g³ 8g⁴) lengthy filly; good mover; improved and won handicaps at Doncaster and Nottingham in July (decisively) and at Epsom in August, on last-named course needing to be ridden right out to hold on by ¾ length from Ring Bidder after moving very smoothly into lead at distance; looked likely to win £3,200 event at Doncaster in September by a wide margin when leading on bridle 3f out but weakened inside last furlong and finished about a length third to Salamina (short-priced favourite, but facing stiffish task); will stay 1¼m; seems to act on any going; sold 11,000 gns Newmarket December Sales. *J. Dunlop.*

MELLOW MOOD 2 b.f. Badedas 81–June Clare (Fairwell) (1981 5.8f 7fg 8d) — May 29; sister to 1m and 1½m winner Sadedab; dam of little account; emulating her dam. *J. Edmunds.*

MELODRAMA 3 b.f. Busted 134–Matinee 119 (Zeddaan 130) (1980 7g⁴ 1981 **102** 6fg* 7fg³ 7.2fg⁴ 8d* 8g² 12s) tall, lengthy, rather lightly-made filly; won 23-runner apprentice maiden race at Newbury in August (made just about all) and 6-runner £3,000 event on same course in September (held up), showing far more resolution than runner-up when beating Ganimede by 2 lengths in latter; in frame in minor event at Goodwood and handicap at Haydock in between and in £5,100 handicap at Ascot afterwards, in last-named event later in September being caught on line by Hindi after going clear 2f out; probably didn't get trip when in rear behind Flighting in Princess Royal Stakes at Ascot in October; promises to stay beyond 1m; acts on a firm surface, but seems suited by some give underfoot. *R. Hern.*

MELON PATCH 3 b.g. Thatch 136–Melon Flower (Relko 136) (1980 5g³ 5f² **75** 6g² 6fg² 6g* 6g 1981 6fg 7g 7d² 7d) compact, well-grown ex-Irish gelding; quite a useful performer as a 2-y-o; made much of running when 2½ lengths second behind easy winner Beeleigh in £4,000 handicap at Chester in May; ran too freely in blinkers only subsequent outing over here; stays 7f; probably acts on any going; exported to Hong Kong. *M. Stoute.*

MEL'S CHOICE 3 b. or br.g. Birdbrook 110–Port Meadow 83 (Runnymede 123) **54** (1980 5fg 5fg³ 5d* 5f 1981 5g 5f 5f 6d⁴ 5d⁴ 6f⁴ 5f 5g 7g 7v) good-topped gelding; fourth in handicaps at Hamilton (2) and Pontefract in the summer, best efforts; stays 6f; probably acts on any going; well beaten in blinkers final start. *J. Etherington.*

MELTING POT 2 b.g. Manado 130–Blendwell (Typhoon 125) (1981 6fg) Apr — 16; IR 6,400F, IR 5,500Y; tall, leggy gelding; fourth produce; dam won over 7f and 9f in Ireland; 25/1 and in need of run, missed break when always behind in 16-runner maiden race won by Rosier at Newmarket in July. *B. Hanbury.*

MELTING SNOWS 2 b.f. High Top 131–Midsummertime (Midsummer Night II 117) (1981 7d* 7g) Feb 18; well-made filly; fifth foal; half-sister to Park Hill winner Idle Waters (by Mill Reef); dam never ran; stayed on really well when winning 18-runner maiden race at Newbury in September by ¾ length from Believer; 12/1, gave weight all round when never-dangerous 6¾ lengths eighth of 15 to Ivano in Houghton Stakes at Newmarket the following month; will stay middle distances. *F. J. Houghton.* **88**

MELYNO 2 b.c. Nonoalco 131–Comely (Boran) (1981 5.5g 6f³ 6.5f* 6.5s 7.5s*) Mar 31; half-brother to several winners in France, notably top-class 7f to 10.5f winner Pharly (by Lyphard) and Irish 2,000 Guineas runner-up Comeram (by Amber Rama); dam very useful middle-distance filly; won maiden race at Deauville in August and Group 3 Prix Thomas Bryon at Saint-Cloud in October, holding on by a short neck from odds-on Tampero after making running in latter; only eighth of 10 to Pas de Seul when favourite for Prix Eclipse at Saint-Cloud in between (hampered); will be suited by 1m. *F. Mathet, France.* **111**

MEMENTA MIA 3 ch.f. Music Boy 124–Young Mementa (Young Christopher 119) (1980 5s* 5f⁴ 5f² 5fg⁴ 5g⁴ 5fg² 6fg* 6g³ 6s³ 5g* 1981 5s 5fg³) neat, strong-quartered filly; a useful and consistent filly at 2 yrs; ran only twice in 1981 and wasn't seen out after finishing 4½ lengths fourth to subsequently-disqualified Little Starchy in handicap at Sandown in April; stays 6f; acts on any going. *C. Nelson.* **—**

MENDELITA 5 ch.m. King's Company 124–Ermine Beauty (Young Emperor 133) (1980 15.8fg² 12d³ 15fg⁴ 16.1s 1981 12d 12g 15.8g) staying maiden; acts on any going. *W. Stubbs.* **—**

MEND IT 3 ch.g. Patch 129–Startop 72 (Divine Gift 127) (1980 7g 7fg 10s 1981 10g 9f 11.5g⁴ 14s 12.2g 10d) leggy, close-coupled gelding; poor form in varied company; trained by D. Dale first outing. *V. Mitchell.* **—**

MENJOU 2 b.g. He Loves Me 120–Goldwyn Princess 72 (Native Prince) (1981 6g) Apr 26; 28,000Y; workmanlike gelding; half-brother to very smart sprinter African Song (by African Sky); dam twice-raced half-sister to very useful filly Broadway Melody; unquoted and apprentice ridden when behind in 21-runner maiden race won by Not For Show at Newmarket in October. *R. Sheather.* **—**

MENT MORE 6 br.m. Sahib 114–Rural Poem (Zarathustra 131) (1980 14fg 17.1f 1981 12fg) bad maiden. *R. Akehurst.* **—**

MERCHANDISER 3 b.g. Sit In The Corner–Salambos (Doon 124) (1980 NR 1981 10.1g 8d) 900F; leggy gelding; first foal; dam behind in seller on only start; showed a little ability in maiden races at Windsor in August and Goodwood in September; looks rather weak at present. *N. Gaselee.* **—**

MERCHANT PRINCE 9 b.g. Hopeful Venture 125–Milonia (Tambourine II 133) (1980 NR 1981 8f) poor performer; behind in seller only start in 1981; stays 1¼m; acts on firm going; used to race with tongue tied down. *B. Richmond.* **—**

MERCHANT TUBBS 7 b.g. Great Nephew 126–Buff Beauty 92 (Mossborough 126) (1980 NR 1981 11.5d) poor performer; stays 1m; acts on any going. *M. Ryan.* **—**

MERCIA SOUND 2 b.g. Wishing Star 117–Audition (Tower Walk 130) (1981 5d 5s 5fg² 5f³ 6g³ 7f² 8f 7fg 8d 8s) May 4; IR 2,700F, IR 1,200Y (privately), 2,100 2-y-o; useful second produce; dam never ran; quite moderate form in varied company; stays 1m; acts on firm going. *R. Hollinshead.* **63**

MERCIFUL SUN 3 gr.f. No Mercy 126–Follow the Sun (Kythnos 126 or Saint Crespin III 132) (1980 6fg 7g 1981 7fg 7g 8fg 10fg 10f⁴) compact filly; fourth in a seller at Folkestone in September, best effort; stays 1¼m; blinkered fourth start. *M. Haynes.* **—**

MERCREDI 2 b.g. Mount Hagen 127–Amorce 81 (Le Levanstell 122) (1981 6s 6g) Apr 6; half-brother to 1978 2-y-o 5f winner Calamorce (by Caliban); dam placed from 5f to 1½m; 33/1 when well behind in maiden races at Newbury and Newmarket (ridden by 7-lb claimer) late in season. *J. Holt.* **—**

MERCURIAL 3 ch.f. Hotfoot 126–Mary Mars (Red God 128§) (1980 5f 5fg 5g 6d 6fg 1981 7v 12g⁴ 9.4g 12.2g 12.5f 12fg 13.8g) lengthy filly; only poor form, including in sellers; stays 1½m. *B. Wilkinson.* **—**

MERCY CURE 5 gr.m. No Mercy 126–Sinecure (Parthia 132) (1980 5.1fg 5.3d 5fg 5fg³ 5f 5g 1981 5fg 5d 5.1fg³ 5fg² 5f² 5fg* 5.6f* 5g 5f* 5fg⁴ 5g 5g) sprint **65**

540

handicapper; won at Warwick and Doncaster (made all) in July and at Ripon in September; stays 6f; acts on firm going; blinkered once at 3 yrs; sometimes sweats up; suitable mount for an apprentice; genuine and consistent. *D. Dale.*

MERIDA STAR 2 b.c. Comedy Star 121–Miss Merida 64 (Midsummer Night II 117) (1981 7d 5h 5.1d) Apr 23; 2,000F, 1,950Y; compact colt; of little account. *C. Mackenzie.* —

MERITOUS 6 b.g. Decoy Boy 129–Welsh Huntress 106 (Big Game) (1980 5d 6v 6d 5g 6d 6g⁴ 6fg² 6g* 6fg 6g 5f³ 6g* 6g 6s³ 6d 6d 6s* 5v 1981 6d 6g 6fg³ 6f 6f 6fg 6g 5fg 6d 5d 6s) big, lengthy gelding; sprint handicapper; best at 6f; acts on any going but is suited by some give in the ground; has worn blinkers and bandages; trained by W. Stubbs part of season. *T. Taylor.* 76 d

MERLANE 6 b.g. Tamerlane 128–Harry's Daughter (Will Somers 114§) (1980 12f 14g² 16f 14s 10s 8g 7d³ 12s 10v 1981 9g 12s 12s² 12.8s⁴ 12g² 10fg 11.5d 12g) sturdy ex-Irish gelding; second in maiden races at Clonmel and Thurles in June; well beaten in amateur riders events at Newmarket (2) and Yarmouth over here; stays 1¾m; acts on soft going. *G. Balding.* —

MERLIN'S CHARM (USA) 2 b.f. Bold Bidder–Lucky Spell (Lucky Mel) (1981 6f⁴ 7d 6g*) May 4; $130,000Y; leggy, quite attractive filly; second foal; dam very smart winner of 12 races at up to 9f; left her previous form well behind when storming clear up final hill to win 17-runner maiden race at Newmarket in October by 3 lengths from Vadrouille, the pair 6 lengths clear; disappointed when tried over 7f but should stay at least 1m; possibly needs a sound surface; a very useful filly in the making judged on her last performance. *B. Hills.* 102

MERRY MEADOW 7 b.g. Meadow Mint 120–Glad Tidings 90 (Palestine 133) (1980 NR 1981 15.5f) plating-class maiden on flat though has won over hurdles. *A. Moore.* —

MERSING 2 b. or br.c. Ardoon 124–Ashling's Lass 89 (Levmoss 133) (1981 6fg 7g) Apr 12; IR 5,000Y (privately); second foal; half-brother to 1¼m winner Wonderful Surprise (by Run The Gantlet); dam 11f winner; well beaten in large fields of maidens; sold 500 gns Doncaster November Sales. *R. Armstrong.* —

MESSENGER OF PEACE 5 ch.g. Simbir 130–Pipeline 85 (Gulf Pearl 117) (1980 12f 18.4f 14f 16fg 16d 1981 18fg) lengthy gelding; fairly useful performer at his best but appears to be on downgrade; stays 1¾m; acts on firm going and has yet to race on really soft; has run respectably in blinkers; broke blood vessel once in 1980; sold out of R. Boss's stable only 600 gns Doncaster January (81) Sales. *W. R. Williams.* —

METALLIC 2 b.f. Saulingo 122–Aurelie (Aureole 132) (1981 5g 5d 6g 5g* 6f⁴ 6fg⁴ 6fg³ 7d* 8.2d) Mar 20; 1,700Y; neat filly; half-sister to several winners, including fair 3-y-o 1m winner Sha'lan (by Arch Sculptor); dam won over 7f at 2 yrs in Ireland; attracted no bid when successful in sellers at Hamilton in June and Redcar in August; beat Towngate Cross by 7 lengths in 12-runner event on latter; suited by 7f but has yet to show she stays 1m; best form on an easy surface; best in blinkers and didn't wear them when running moderately final start. *G. Richards.* 66

METRO MAID 2 ch.f. Connaught 130–Relza 91 (Relko 136) (1981 7g) Mar 23; lengthy filly; half-sister to fairly useful middle-distance winner Toussaint (by So Blessed) and a winner in France by Welsh Pageant; dam stayer; 20/1 and backward when behind in 16-runner maiden race won by Tants at Leicester in October. *Sir Mark Prescott.* —

MEXICAN LINK 3 gr.c. The Go-Between 129–Tijuana 91 (Floribunda 136) (1980 5s 5fg 6g 5d* 6fg² 6g 1981 6s 7s 5fg* 6fg⁴ 5d² 5f 5s 6g) strong colt; winning plater at 2 yrs; 25/1 when winning non-selling handicap at Windsor in July by 2 lengths from Heavy Weapon; stays 6f well; acts on a firm and a soft surface; sold 3,100 gns Newmarket Autumn Sales. *J. Holt.* 59

MIANACH OIR 3 b.f. Wolver Hollow 126–Regency Gold (Prince Regent 129) (1980 5f 6fg 7.3d³ 1981 8d 10fg 8fg 8fg* 8f* 8g⁴) lengthy, lightly-built filly; won maiden race at Salisbury and minor event at Thirsk, beating Morias 2 lengths when blinkered on latter course in September; should be suited by 1¼m (having first race for more than 2 months when tried at trip); acts on firm going; has shown signs of being not entirely genuine and wore blinkers last 2 starts. *F. J. Houghton.* 72

MIANALCO 2 br.g. Nonoalco 131–La Mia Raggazza 76 (Alcide 136) (1981 6f) Mar 1; 2,000Y; compact gelding; has an enlarged off-fore knee; half-brother to French 9f winner Fils en Vert (by St Paddy); dam, half-sister to high-class miler

Lucyrowe, won over 7f at 3 yrs; unquoted when tailed off in 12-runner maiden race won by Woodcutter at Haydock in July. *M. Naughton.*

MICHAEL'S EMPEROR 2 b.c. Young Emperor 133–Strolling Sweetly (Le Levanstell 122) (1981 5g) May 21; 2,300Y; fifth living foal; dam never ran; unquoted and in need of race, didn't move well to start and was slowly away when last of 15 to Red Sunset in maiden race at Newmarket in May. *A. Goodwill.* —

MICHAEL'S REVENGE 2 ch.c. Garda's Revenge 119–Diamonds Galore 95 (Luminary 132) (1981 7fg) Apr 11; 6,600Y; quite well-made colt; half-brother to several winners here and abroad, including useful 1967 2-y-o 5f winner Stop Thief (by Red God); dam fairly useful over 5f in Ireland at 2 yrs; 33/1 but very fit, sweated up badly and was very coltish prior to finishing behind in 29-runner maiden race won by Hayakaze at Newmarket in August. *A. Goodwill.* —

MICKEY TIM 4 br.c. Gay Fandango 132–Amicable 73 (Bold Ruler) (1980 7f 8.2g3 7g* 8g 10f2 10fg2 11.1g3 10f 1981 10fg 10g 12fg 10fg3) tall, attractive colt; fair handicapper at his best but isn't particularly reliable; suited by middle distances; acts on firm going; has twice worn blinkers; doesn't always look too keen; sold 2,000 gns Newmarket Autumn Sales. *J. Dunlop.* **60 §**

MICK'S RITUAL 2 ch.g. Malacate 131–Aurabella 113 (Aureole 132) (1981 6fg4 6fg 6g4 8fg 8.2d) Mar 26; 5,200Y; rather leggy, quite useful sort; half-brother to minor French 9f and 1¼m winner Lisabella and to Queen's Vase winner Royal Aura (both by Right Royal V); dam won Irish Guinness Oaks; fourth in minor events at Newcastle in June and August; bred to stay 1½m; blinkered fifth outing. *M. W. Easterby.* **63**

MICK THE KNIFE (USA) 2 b.c. Blade–What a Gal (Personality) (1981 6fg 7f 7g 10s) Apr 24; $32,000Y; good-bodied colt; first foal; dam won over 1m at 4 yrs; 33/1 when behind in sizeable fields of maidens, moving badly to start on third occasion and pulling up seemingly distressed on final start (blinkered). *G. Pritchard-Gordon.* —

MICK THE LARK (USA) 4 b.c. Mickey McGuire–Chance Gauge (Degage) (1980 NR 1981 13d 12g 12d 12g 16fg4 16.1f4 20.4fg3 15.8g4 16.5g 15.8g) workmanlike colt; poor walker; slow maiden; stays well; acts on a firm surface; has twice worn blinkers; retained 600 gns Newmarket Autumn Sales. *G. Richards.* **46**

MIDDLEHAM 5 ch.g. Amber Rama 133–Mathilde 84 (Whistler 129) (1980 7.2fg 6fg 7g 7f3 7f 10fg3 7g3 7f* 8fg 7fg 8fg3 7.2d 1981 8v* 7.2fg3 7.6g 8d 7g 8g) tall, useful-looking gelding; won handicap at Beverley in April; stays 1¼m; acts on any going; blinkered once at 3 yrs; suitable mount for a boy. *E. Weymes.* **69**

MIDDLETON SUE 2 ch.f. Rugantino 97–Twyford Ridge (Schapiro 99) (1981 6d4 6fg3 5d 8g4) Feb 28; plain filly; half-sister to 5f and 1½m winner Comedy Croft (by Comedy Star); dam ran 3 times; in frame in maiden races and a £2,500 seller, in latter beaten little more than a length by Indian Call at Newmarket in October; will be suited by longer distances. *R. Hannon.* **69**

MIDDLIN THRANG 3 b.c. Farm Walk 111–Darling Do (Derring-Do 131) (1980 6g2 8g3 1981 9s 8g* 8.2s4 10.6s 12.3g 8f3 8.2f2 8g4 8d 8.2d) neat colt; finished length second to Norton Cross in handicap at Redcar in May, but was awarded race when traces of illegal substance were found in winner's system; in frame in several handicaps afterwards but was disappointing nevertheless; should stay middle distances but seemed to find 1½m too far fifth start (ran freely early on); acts on any going; seems none too genuine. *Miss S. Hall.* **70**

MIDNIGHT ROUND 2 gr.f. Royal Palace 131–Failing Light 70 (Ballymoss 136) (1981 5fg 6f) Apr 4; 2,000Y; leggy, light-framed filly; half-sister to 3-y-o middle-distance winner Great Light (by Great Nephew) and a winner in France; dam half-sister to dam of 1,000 Guineas winner Nocturnal Spree and Prix St Alary winner Tootens; in rear in maiden auction events. *N. Gaselee.* —

MIDRIDGE DRIFT 3 ch.f. Most Secret 119–Lyn's Pride 85 (Star Moss 122) (1980 5d 5s 5f 5fg4 6g 6fg 6fg 1981 5g 5g 6g) sturdy filly; poor plater; sometimes blinkered; sold 420 gns Doncaster May Sales. *W. Stubbs.* —

MIDSUMMER BOY 4 b.g. Midsummer Night II 117–Rosie Crucian (Polkemmet 91) (1980 10f 13s 10s4 10s 12d 13g3 15.5g4 16s 1981 12fg) strong, shapely gelding; plating-class maiden; stays well; has run respectably for an apprentice. *D. Gandolfo.* —

MIGELITTO (FR) 9 ch.g. Lorenzaccio 130–Vivien 66 (Nearco) (1980 18d 16.1d4 16fg4 15f4 18fg3 22.2fg 16.1d 20.4g* 19f4 20g3 16g2 17.4s3 18d 1981 18s —

16g) out-and-out staying handicapper; acts on any going but is suited by firm; has worn blinkers; suitable mount for an apprentice; retained 1,100 gns Ascot May Sales. *M. Naughton.*

MIGHTY FLY 2 b.f. Comedy Star 121–Lettuce 60 (So Blessed 130) (1981 5fg **73** 5d 5f³ 5.8h⁴) May 13; strong filly; second foal; dam, half-sister to Grand National winner Rubstic, was placed over 1¼m; 2½ lengths third of 9 to Super Natalie in small race at Chepstow in July, best effort; should be suited by 6f. *D. Elsworth.*

MIGHTY MARINER (USA) 2 ch.c. Majestic Prince–Ta Neil (Fiddle Isle) **—** (1981 8s) May 14; $15,000Y; first foal; dam won 6f claiming race at 3 yrs; 12/1 when behind in 17-runner maiden race won by Barfoot at Warwick in October. *G. Hunter.*

MIGOLETTY 2 b.f. Oats 126–Loch Leven 87 (Le Levanstell 122) (1981 8g 8fg **—** 8d) Mar 10; 7,600F, 13,000Y; lightly-made filly; fourth produce; dam disqualified 2-y-o 6f winner; ran best race when 7¾ lengths seventh of 16 to Gin in maiden event at Beverley in September, second outing; stays 1m. *P. Haslam.*

MIGRATEUR (FR) 9 gr.g. Tiffauges 124–Mistoufle (Marino) (1980 12g 1981 **—** 6g 8d 16d 10.6s 10f 12f 15g) lightly-made gelding; no longer seems of any account; has worn blinkers. *W. Marshall.*

MIGRATOR 5 b.g. My Swallow 134–Houbichka (Swoon's Son) (1980 NR **80+** 1981 12f*) ex-Irish gelding; well backed when beating Aberfield by 2 lengths in ladies race at Chepstow in September; stays 1½m; acts on any going; smart hurdler. *L. Kennard.*

MIGUEL CLEMENT (USA) 2 ch.c. Avatar–Harvest Girl (Herbager 136) **92 p** (1981 7f³ 7g³) Apr 2; $50,000Y; rangy colt; first foal; dam, very useful stakes winner at 2 yrs and 3 yrs, won at up to 1m; third twice at Yarmouth, finishing 5½ lengths behind Nioulargo in 18-runner maiden race in August and 1½ lengths behind easy winner Match Winner, after starting very slowly, in minor event in September; an immature colt who gives the impression he'll do much better over middle distances at 3 yrs. *M. Stoute.*

MIGUELINI 2 b.c. Prince Regent 129–Jenny 99 (Red God 128§) (1981 6fg 7d **83** 6fg 6f* 7g 6g) Mar 30; IR 3,200F, 15,500Y; neat, strong colt; half-brother to 2 winners, including fairly useful middle-distance performer Inishlacken (by Connaught); dam won at up to 7f in England and France; won 12-runner maiden race at Hamilton in September in good style when blinkered, making all to score by 5 lengths from Gaiters; not disgraced when again blinkered in Somerville Tattersall Stakes at Newmarket the following month (sweated up); 14/1 and not wearing blinkers when never placed to challenge in nursery on final start; will stay 1m; acts on firm going. *P. Haslam.*

MIKADORA 4 b.f. Cavo Doro 124–Mimika 85 (Lorenzaccio 130) (1980 10h 12d **—** 1981 15.8s 8g 10fg⁴ 8f 10f⁴ 12f 10fg 10s 10s) strong, compact filly; plater; stays 1¼m; sometimes sweats up; has worn bandages. *T. Kersey.*

MIKE CHANNON 5 b.g. Rheingold 137–Miss Match (Match III 135) (1980 **—** 10f³ 10d 11.7f 16fg 16f* 16fg 1981 15.8s 18fg 16h) quite well-made gelding; staying handicapper; acts on any going; has won for an amateur rider. *P. Makin.*

MILANION 2 ro.c. Roman Warrior 132–Fleora 61 (Fleece 114) (1981 5s 5fg 6g⁴ **76** 5f 5g 6d 7.2v² 6d 8g 8f* 7g³) May 5; 300Y; compact colt; first foal; dam middle-distance maiden; 33/1, stayed on well to win 17-runner seller at Leicester in November by ½ length from Knightsbridge Game (retained 1,100 gns); good third of 14 to Hello Sunshine in nursery at Doncaster later in month; stays 1m well; needs some give in the ground and acts on heavy going. *J. Wilson.*

MILITARY BAND (FR) 3 b.c. Sassafras 135–Melody Hour 105 (Sing Sing 134) **92** (1980 NR 1981 14fg* 12f³ 14fg* 16f* 14g* 18g³) tall, rather narrow, fair sort; second foal; half-brother to 1979 2-y-o 5f winner Bandsman (by So Blessed); dam useful 5f winner at 2 yrs; has reportedly been difficult to train and didn't make his first appearance until June; successful in 4 of his 6 races however, at Yarmouth (3, making all each time) and at Thirsk (beat Chemin de Guerre in good style in £3,300 handicap); beat Sunset Ray by 7 lengths in 3-runner handicap on former course in September when gaining his last success; started favourite for 30-runner Tote Cesarewitch at Newmarket in October and looked likely winner when bursting into lead going into the Dip but faltered slightly up hill and didn't see trip out so well at around 2m; acts on firm going; ridden by apprentice N. Day twice when successful; will win more races. *H. Cecil.*

MILK FRUIT BEER 2 ch.f. Roman Warrior 132–Czar's Diamond 66 (Queen's Hussar 124) (1981 5s 5g 5g 7f 7.2v 8g) Apr 4; 1,900Y; leggy filly; half-sister to 3 winners, but is a bad plater herself; blinkered last 2 outings; sold out of J. Berry's stable 480 gns Doncaster May Sales after second outing. *J. Tierney.* —

MILK HEART 2 ch.c. Steel Heart 128–Cafe au Lait 98 (Espresso 122) (1981 5s⁴ 5s 5g⁴ 6fg 6d 8.2d 6d²) Apr 24; 16,000Y; compact colt; half-brother to several winners, including fairly useful stayer Brando (by Busted); dam stayed 1½m; ran easily best race when ¼-length second of 11 to Virgi in nursery at Hamilton in October; best form at 6f; wears blinkers. *P. Haslam.* **80**

MILK OF THE BARLEY 4 b.c. Mummy's Pet 125–Tots (Dual 117) (1980 7g⁴ 6f 6.3s 5fg⁴ 6.3d 6fg³ 8d³ 6s⁴ 1981 6d³ 9d² 7.2s² 6g 7g* 7.3fg⁴ 5d 8fg 8s 6g³) tall, short-backed ex-Irish colt; smart performer; held on by short head from Premier Rose in 6-runner Beeswing Stakes at Newcastle in July; in frame several other starts, putting up good efforts on third and sixth when finishing strongly to be short-head second to Last Fandango in John of Gaunt Stakes at Haydock in June and just over 4½ lengths fourth to Dalsaan in Hungerford Stakes at Newbury in August; needs further than 6f and stays 9f; seems to act on any going but is well suited by soft; sweated up fourth start; gives impression he needs to be held up; trained by A. Jarvis seventh to ninth starts. *W. O'Gorman.* **115**

MILLADENE 4 ch.f. Duc D'Orleans 76–Strudel (Vimadee 120) (1980 NR 1981 10.6d 9f) first foal; dam won a selling hurdle; backward when behind in maiden race at Haydock and apprentice event at Ripon in August. *R. Whitaker.* —

MILLFIELD REP 2 ch.g. Jimmy Reppin 131–Polly Darling 80 (Darling Boy 124) (1981 5v 5d 5g 5f 7f 10d³) May 5; 3,200F, 4,000Y; lightly-made gelding; closely related to Of seller winner Darling June (by Midsummer Night II); dam won at up to 6f and was placed at up to 1½m; plater; stayed on well to be 2¼ lengths third of 16 to Bhaibundi Chewunja at Pontefract in October; suited by 1¼m and some give in the ground; unseated rider when refusing to race on second start and wore blinkers when well beaten on fourth; sold to G. Blum 1,850 gns Newmarket Autumn Sales and has, reportedly, been sent to Belgium. *P. Rohan.* **63**

MILLFIELD ROYAL 4 b.f. Royalty 130–Most Precious (Matador 131) (1980 10f 8fg 8.2d* 9s³ 8.2v* 1981 9fg 8g 8fg 8g 8fg 8s 8.2s) leggy filly; plater; stays 9f; needs some give in the ground; has worn blinkers. *M. Naughton.* **48**

MILL PLANTATION 2 b.c. Northfields–Fairly Hot 109 (Sir Ivor 135) (1981 7g) May 12; neat, attractive colt; first foal; dam, daughter of 1,000 Guineas winner Full Dress II, was useful but temperamental performer at up to 1¼m; unquoted and in need of run, always towards rear in 18-runner £4,100 event won by General Anders at Ascot in September; looks capable of better in time. *H. Wragg.* — p

MILLS AHEAD 4 b.c. Sallust 134–Tackaway 77 (Hard Tack 111§) (1980 8d³ 7fg 1981 6.5fg 6.5s 6s* 6g 6g) strong, compact colt; won handicap at Catterick in April; ran moderately afterwards; stays 1m; acts on soft going; usually blinkered; sold 2,000 gns Ascot August Sales. *D. Ringer.* **62**

MILLS HIGH 3 b.f. High Top 131–Iona 92 (Kalydon 122) (1980 6f 6fg³ 7g 1981 9s³ 10fg⁴ 8s 10fg* 10.6v² 12.2g* 10.2d) small, fair sort; won maiden race at Beverley (first outing for 4 months) and minor event at Catterick; beat Only A Shanty a shade comfortably by a head on latter course in October; stays 1½m; probably acts on any going. *C. Brittain.* **73**

MILLY MONROE 2 b.f. Lochnager 132–Polly Peachum 123 (Singing Strand) (1981 5fg 5f 5f³ 6g 7g 6d) Jan 30; useful sort; good walker; second foal; dam very genuine and consistent sprinter; showed a little ability in varied company; unlikely to stay 7f; has plenty of size and scope and could improve enough to win in the North in 1982. *J. Fitzgerald.* **64**

MINAGE 2 gr.f. Prince de Galles 125–Mellormoor (Forlorn River 124) (1981 5d 5fg³ 5g 6fg 6g 6g 5g 8s) leggy, lightly-made filly; bad plater; has worn blinkers. *R. Hoad.* **42**

MINDBLOWING 4 gr.f. Pongee 106–Forlorn Leap (Forlorn River 124) (1980 5s³ 5f 5fg 5f⁴ 6fg 7fg⁴ 7d³ 7f 7.3fg 1981 6v* 7s 6f 6fg 7f) leggy, light-framed filly; plater; bought in 1,150 gns after winning at Windsor in May; stays 7f; acts on any going; has worn blinkers. *R. Boss.* **63**

MINIBANK 3 b.c. Saritamer 130–Tilt Guard 75 (Crepello 136) (1980 5.1f 5g 6d² 6s 6g 1981 6fg 7s 7f² 7fg* 8f³ 8fg³ 8.3fg 8f⁴ 8.2fg* 8g⁴ 8g) good-topped, **73**

workmanlike colt; won handicaps at Warwick in June and Nottingham in September, latter by 2 lengths from Praiselien; stays 1m; acts on firm going; successful with blinkers and without; sold to M. Bradley 4,600 gns Newmarket Autumn Sales. *C. Brittain.*

MINIGOLD 11 br.g. Goldhill 125–Minette 90 (Flush Royal 127) (1980 9.6fg 10g³ 8fg² 7g⁴ 1981 10d 10d 8f³ 10fg) plater; stays 1¼m; acts on any going; often wears bandages; has worn blinkers. *A. Davison.* **30**

MINIMICRO 2 b.f. Decoy Boy 129–Miniwonder (Henry the Seventh 125) (1981 5g 5fg 6g 7g) Apr 28; small filly; bad plater. *P. Rohan.* **—**

MINK COAT 2 gr.f. Young Emperor 133–Clear Whistle 80 (Tin Whistle 128) (1981 5d² 5s* 5d³ 5g 6fg³ 6g⁴ 5f 6g) Apr 27; 1,000F, 5,400Y; rather leggy, useful sort; half-sister to fairly useful 1977 2-y-o performer Whisting Jenny (by Swing Easy) and a winning plater; dam in frame on both outings; landed the odds easily in maiden race at Stockton in April; bettered that effort when third to Paul's Ivory in minor event at Windsor in June on fifth start and when fourth to Atossa in £4,300 event at York in July; better suited by 6f than 5f; acts on any going with possible exception of really firm; ran badly in blinkers fourth outing; off course 3 months before final start; sold 2,500 gns Newmarket December Sales. *P. Haslam.* **77**

MINMAX 3 b.c. Record Run 127–Paddy's Tickle (Shooting Chant) (1980 5fg 5f⁴ 5fg 6g⁴ 7fg² 7f² 7.6f² 7d⁴ 7d² 1981 7fg³ 8g² 7g* 7d* 7g* 8fg 7.6g²) leggy, good-topped colt; in very good form in first half of season and won maiden event at Lingfield and minor events at Leicester and Epsom, staying on strongly and putting up a particularly good performance when beating Singwara by 4 lengths on last-named course in June; had very stiff task and ran another fine race when about 5 lengths fifth of 10 behind Belmont Bay in Queen Anne Stakes at Royal Ascot and was beaten only short head by Noble Philip in handicap at Lingfield; not seen out after June; stays 1m; probably acts on any going; consistent; suitable mount for an apprentice; wears blinkers nowadays. *P. K. Mitchell.* **91**

MINNEHOWHOW (USA) 2 b. or br.f. Apalachee 137–Just Perturbed (Jesterson) (1981 6g 7f) Apr 19; small, quite attractive filly; first foal; dam won 3 small sprint races in USA; unquoted when towards rear in maiden races at Nottingham and Brighton in August; sent to France. *R. Sheather.* **—**

MINNE LOVE 2 ch.f. Homeric 133–Late Love 107 (Great White Way) (1981 5fg 5.8h 5g 6g* 6fg³ 5d⁴ 6g) Feb 18; IR 6,000Y; small filly; half-sister to French 3-y-o 1¼m winner Bitter Rice (by Sassafras) and useful 1979 French 2-y-o 5f winner Coeur d'Acier (by Steel Heart); dam second in Gimcrack Stakes; plater; bought in 2,000 gns after making all to win 15-runner race at Windsor in August by 2 lengths from Parabems; in frame in valuable seller and 15-runner nursery (sweated up) afterwards; bred to stay at least 1m. *C. Nelson.* **67**

MINNIE BROWN 3 b. or br.f. Autre Prince 125–Charmarose 89 (Hard Ridden 131) (1980 NR 1981 5g 8g 12fg 8g) 550 2-y-o; half-sister to 2 winners, including fair stayer Demon Flush (by Eudaemon); dam won over 5f at 2 yrs; soundly beaten in varied company, including selling; sold 280 gns Ascot December Sales. *J. S. Wilson.* **—**

MINSDEN 2 ch.c. Habitat 134–Moon Min (First Landing) (1981 6g) Apr 9; 58,000F; strong, compact, good sort; good walker; third foal; brother to 1¼m winner Moon Pad; dam unraced half-sister to very smart American 1963 2-y-o Traffic; second favourite for 11-runner Ribero Stakes at Doncaster in September but was beaten fully 2f out and finished only ninth to Master Cawston; clearly well thought of and is probably capable of better. *J. W. Watts.* **— p**

MINSDEN'S IMAGE 3 gr.f. Dancer's Image–Ellida (Crepello 136) (1980 7g⁴ 7s² 8d³ 1981 12g 12.5f⁴ 16fg* 16.9fg 16f) good-bodied filly; in frame in varied company before winning poor maiden race at Newcastle in June; stays 2m; acts on any going; occasionally blinkered (not at Newcastle); looks ungenuine. *J. W. Watts.* **63 §**

MINSHAANSHU AMAD (USA) 2 br.c. Northern Dancer–Tappahannock (Chieftain) (1981 8s 7.3s) May 21; $700,000Y; strong, compact colt; second foal; half-brother to a winner by Al Hattab; dam, sister to champion handicap mare Cascapedia, was a very useful stakes winner at up to 1m; in need of race, by no means disgraced in 9-runner Royal Lodge Stakes at Ascot in September, keeping in touch for some way before finishing over 15 lengths seventh of 9 to Norwick; still looked to be carrying a lot of condition when 12/1 for Horris Hill Stakes at Newbury the following month and dropped out in final 2f to finish over 15 lengths sixth to Montekin; a nice colt who should do better over middle distances at 3 yrs. *F. J. Houghton.* **91 p**

MINSTREL BIRD 2 br.f. Tudor Music 131–Friendly Polly (Be Friendly 130) —
(1981 5d 5fg 5fg 8fg 7.2v) Mar 14; IR 700F, 2,600Y; rather leggy filly; second
foal; dam third twice over 5f at 3 yrs in Ireland; only poor form, including when
blinkered in seller on final outing. *J. Etherington.*

MINSTREL'S LODGE 4 gr.g. Habat 127–Forever 68 (Never Say Die 137) —
(1980 10s 10fg 8g 1981 10.2f 8f) deep-girthed gelding; probably of little
account; has worn blinkers. *J. Edmunds.*

MINTESSA 3 ch.f. Politico 124–Bovick 75 (Compensation 127) (1980 5f 5d 8fg —
1981 8fg 8f 13.8f 11g) fair sort; seems of little account; should stay 1½m. *M. W.
Easterby.*

MINUETTO 2 ch.f. Roan Rocket 128–Parlais 101 (Pardao 120) (1981 5d² 5s³ **59**
5g⁴ 5g 5g 5fg 5fg 6s 6d) Feb 5; small filly; half-sister to useful 5f winner Mi
Favorita (by Mummy's Pet); dam sprinter; in frame in modest maiden company,
wearing blinkers when 5½ lengths fourth of 8 to Miss Trilli at Ayr in May; off
course over 2 months before fourth start and was soundly beaten on return.
D. Sasse.

MINUS MAN 3 br.g. Firestreak 125–Cheb's Honour 70 (Chebs Lad 120) (1980 **47**
6s 6g 6s 1981 7d 6g 8f* 8fg⁴) lengthy gelding; showed improved form when
winning selling handicap at Brighton in August (no bid); gives impression he'll
stay beyond 1m; acts on firm going. *W. Holden.*

MIO MEMENTA 2 b.f. Streak 119–Young Mementa (Young Christopher 119) **61**
(1981 6g 5d⁴) half-sister to several winners, including useful 1980 2-y-o 5f and
6f winner Mementa Mia (by Music Boy); dam never ran; favourite when 5½ lengths
fourth of 9 to Spanish Fury in maiden race at Hamilton in October, better effort.
C. Nelson.

MIPURDU 4 br.g. Perdu 121–Mim-Joa 56 (Welsh Abbot 131) (1980 3g 0s 5s 5g
8g 8fg 8s 1981 6fg 6f 6f 6f 5d) fair sort; poor handicapper; stays 6f; probably
acts on any going; blinkered nowadays; trained part of season by Mrs J. Pitman;
sold 850 gns Doncaster November Sales. *Miss S. Hall.*

MIRABEAU 2 ch.c. Sharpen Up 127–La Mirabelle 92 (Princely Gift 137) (1981 **115**
6g 6g² 6g* 6s*)
    Mirabeau was given an easy first season, away from the best youngsters, and
performed with sufficient promise to suggest he is going to make a name for himself as a three-year-old. A good sort of colt, he impressed us favourably as an
individual when he made his debut in the Fulbourn Stakes at Newmarket in
July, and although he cut no ice in the race—merely progressed steadily after
stumbling badly and losing ground out of the stalls—he was going about his work
in pleasing style at the end. Next time out saw him second at a length and a half,
after being badly outpaced around halfway, to Rebollino in the Convivial Stakes
at York; following which race he was sent to Doncaster, where he made all the
running in the Mining Supplies Stakes, holding on gamely in a driving finish to
beat Rose Du Soir by a short head.
    All three of Mirabeau's races so far had been at six furlongs, and he would
clearly have been much better suited had they been over seven. His last race, the
Marston Moor Stakes at York in October, was at six furlongs also, but this time
on soft ground. Revelling in the conditions underfoot, Mirabeau went right
away in the last furlong to win in tremendous style by five lengths. One would
think that this was easily his best performance and a smart performance too, yet,
strangely, the handicapper seems to have ignored it. Come On The Blues, for
instance, five lengths behind in second place, has been set to meet Mirabeau on a
pound *worse* terms in the Free Handicap. Come On The Blues may be weighted
fairly in relation to all the other two-year-olds in the Free Handicap, but on the
evidence of the Marston Moor Stakes he is most certainly not weighted fairly in
relation to Mirabeau.

		Atan	Native Dancer
	Sharpen Up	(ch 1961)	Mixed Marriage
	(ch 1969)	Rocchetta	Rockefella
Mirabeau		(ch 1961)	Chambiges
(ch.c. Apr 20, 1979)		Princely Gift	Nasrullah
	La Mirabelle	(b 1951)	Blue Gem
	(ch 1966)	La Bastille	Nearco
		(b 1957)	La Baille

    Interestingly, Mirabeau is a full brother to Jeroboam, who ran second to
Lyric Dance in the Free Handicap in 1979. But whereas Jeroboam was a speedy

sort who raced only once beyond seven furlongs, Mirabeau gives the impression that there is a fair bit of stamina in his make-up. It is true that La Mirabelle, his dam, was a sprinter, but no less than seven of La Mirabelle's eight winning half-brothers and half-sisters won over a mile and three quarters or more, and La Mirabelle's grandam, the high-class La Baille, won the Park Hill Stakes. We expect Mirabeau to get at least a mile. Whether or not he will need soft ground to be seen to advantage when racing at around that distance remains to be seen. All that can be said at the moment is that he acts well on soft going and has yet to race on firm ground. *H. Wragg.*

MIRACLE BABY 3 b.f. Workboy 123–Ma's Baby 90 (Ashford Lea 95) (1980 — 5fg⁴ 5g* 6fg 1981 5f 6f 5f 6f) leggy, lightly-made filly; mainly disappointing in 1981; form only at 5f. *M. H. Easterby.*

MIRAMAR REEF 2 b.c. Mill Reef 141–Thalassa 94 (Appiani II 128) (1981 7fg **81 p** 7f) May 20; strong, good sort; good mover; second foal; dam won over middle distances in England and France; very reluctant to go to start at Newmarket in August and made little show in race, coming home 7½ lengths sixth of 8 finishers behind Chulia Street in Fitzroy House Stakes; 50/1; with leaders to straight when remote seventh of 8 to Silver Hawk in Intercraft Solario Stakes at Kempton the following month; should do better over middle distances in 1982. *C. Brittain.*

MIREA (USA) 2 ch.f. The Minstrel 135–Mlle Vitesse (Tom Rolfe) (1981 6f² 7s*) **104** Mar 20; $110,000Y; first foal; dam unraced half-sister to high-class American filly White Star Line and good French 1972 2-y-o Filiberto; went down by a head to Exclusive Order after leading 2f out in 8-runner newcomers event at Deauville in August; made virtually all when favourite for 12-runner maiden race at Maisons-Laffitte in October, winning by 1½ lengths from Mistretta; will be suited by 1¼m; could go on to better things; engaged in 1,000 Guineas and Oaks. *F. Boutin, France.*

MIRROR BOY 4 ch.c. Pieces of Eight 128–Knocknashee 70 (Astec 128) (1980 **95 d** 8v 7f 10.2fg* 10g* 10g² 12s* 13.3d² 12g² 13.3fg 12d² 12v 1981 12fg³ 12d 13.3s² 10d 10g 10g) well-made colt; fairly useful handicapper at his best; went down by a length to Derring Rose in Aston Park Stakes at Newbury in May; well beaten afterwards; stays 13f; probably acts on any going but is suited by some give in the ground; ran poorly in blinkers once at 2 yrs; usually held up and is suited by a strongly-run race. *R. Price.*

MIRTHFUL 4 b. or br.f. Will Somers 114§–French Line 98 (Set Fair 129) (1980 **58** 8g 10fg⁴ 9fg 10.6d 7.6d 7.2g³ 7g 6fg 8.2s 7s² 6d 1981 8.2d⁴ 8g³ 9fg³ 9.4g* 11g² 10.6f* 10f 10g⁴ 10g³ 10f*) sturdy filly; made all to win handicaps at Carlisle in June, Haydock in July and Chepstow in September; gives impression she'll stay 1½m; acts on any going; sometimes wears blinkers but is better without; suitable mount for a boy. *W. Elsey.*

MISHOU L'AMOUR 3 b.c. Royal Palace 131–First Watch (Primera 131) (1980 — 8d 8d 1981 8d 8fg⁴ 8d 10.1d 7s 10s) workmanlike colt; plater; should be suited by middle distances; trained part of season by P. M. Taylor. *R. Baker.*

MISLOP (USA) 2 b.f. Our Hero–Belle De Jour (Speak John) (1981 7fg 7fg 5g) — Apr 17; $35,000Y; smallish, lightly-made filly; second foal; dam won 6f claiming race; behind in maiden and minor events, including one at Catterick (16/1). *J. Hindley.*

MISNEAGH 3 b.f. Midsummer Night II 117–Florica 80 (Floriana 106) (1980 — NR 1981 8d 8fg 11.7g) second foal; dam won sellers over 1m and 1¼m; behind in maiden races at Warwick (2) and Bath in spring; sold 1,500 gns Doncaster June Sales and resold 410 gns Ascot November Sales. *A. Bailey.*

MISS ABWAH 2 b.f. Abwah 118–Ladies Night 65 (Midsummer Night II 117) **53** (1981 7fg 6f 6f 6s 5d) Mar 19; fair sort; has a round action; third living foal; dam won over 1m; plater; ran best race on fourth outing; will stay 7f; gives impression soft ground suits her better than firm. *Miss S. Hall.*

MISS ACROW 2 b.f. Comedy Star 121–Queen's Penny (Queen's Hussar 124) — (1981 7.6s) Feb 28; half-sister to several winners, including smart 5f to 7f winner Hillandale (by Crossing The T) and fairly useful sprinter Queen's Pride (by Royben); dam never ran; unquoted when last of 13 behind Sandwalker in maiden race at Lingfield in October. *G. Balding.*

MISS ADMINGTON 5 br.m. Double Jump 131–Solly Graham 82 (Romulus 129) **39** (1980 7fg 10s⁴ 10.2g 10g 10g 11g² 9d 12fg 12f 10fg⁴ 12d⁴ 12.5s 1981 10.8d 10g 9.4g 12fg² 12f 12.2fg 12f 10f) neat mare; poor handicapper; stays 1¼m. *R. Hollinshead.*

Mr W. P. Clarke's "Miss Behaving"

MISS ANONYMOUS 3 b.f. Pamroy 99–Umbriferous 93 (Quorum 126) (1980   —
NR 1981 12d) 700F, resold 340Y and 470 2-y-o; half-sister to 2 winning
jumpers; dam won over 5f at 2 yrs; unquoted, apprentice ridden and blinkered
when last of 13 behind Alma Ata in minor event at Folkestone in May. *B.
Hanbury.*

MISS BEAMISH 3 ch.f. Hornet 116–My Sheroka (pedigree unknown) (1980   —
5g 5g 1981 10g) neat non-thoroughbred filly; in rear in maiden races in the
Midlands. *E. Eldin.*

MISS BEHAVING 2 ch.f. Steel Heart 128–Miss Knightsbridge 90 (Sovereign   **94**
Path 125) (1981 5s 5d⁴ 5d* 6g* 6d) Mar 17; first foal; dam won from 5f to 7f; a
useful filly who won 13-runner maiden race at Phoenix Park in June (kept on
strongly to beat Peterhof 2½ lengths) and well-contested race on same course in
August (by 2 lengths from odds-on Rose Red); second favourite for Moyglare
Stud Stakes at the Curragh in September but dropped out soon after halfway to
finish only tenth of 14 to subsequently-disqualified Sweet Side; suited by 6f; yet
to race on a firm surface. *S. Murless, Ireland.*

MISS BISHOP 3 ch.f. Elvis 96–Bishop's Marigold (Bishop's Move 92) (1980   —
NR 1981 7d) small, compact filly; first known foal; dam never ran; tailed
off in maiden race at Ayr and sellers at Redcar and Hamilton in September. *T.
Fairhurst.*

MISS BUSHBY 5 b.m. King's Leap 111–Tommie (Final Score 113) (1980 5g   —
5f* 5fg⁴ 6g 5f 1981 5g 6fg 5g) leggy, fair sort; plater; best form at 5f; acts on
hard going; has been tried in blinkers. *J. Fitzgerald.*

MISS CHESSY 3 ch.f. Swing Easy 126–Tassel (Ragusa 137) (1980 5v² 5g³ 5g²   **50**
5f² 5f² 6g³ 6d 5d³ 5fg 6s⁴ 1981 6v⁴ 5g³ 5g³ 6fg² 6g 6f 5fg 6d 7fg 6fg³ 6d 7s)
lightly-made filly; placed in maiden and minor events and a seller; runs as though
7f will suit her (has had stiffish tasks when tried at trip); acts on any going;
blinkered eighth start. *J. Berry.*

MISS CHEYNE 2 br.f. Mansingh 120–Cheyne Walk 58 (St Paddy 133) (1981 **57**
5f 6fg 8.2d³ 8d 8.2s 8d) Apr 28; 1,500F, 1,050Y; neat filly; poor mover; first
produce; dam ran only 3 times; plater; suited by 1m; form only on a soft surface;
wears blinkers; sold 360 gns Doncaster November Sales. *J. Etherington.*

MISS CINDY 6 br.m. Mansingh 120–Iridium 78 (Linacre 133) (1980 6f 7g 7g **64**
7fg 7f² 7f 7fg⁴ 1981 7d 7.6g 7g 7f 7fg* 7g) useful-looking mare; showed only
form in 1981 when beating odds-on Steeple Bell by a neck in handicap at Redcar
in June; stayed 1m; needed a firm surface; had worn blinkers; covered by
Sonnen Gold. *J. Etherington.*

MISS COMMUNE 3 b.f. Communication 119–Yes Miss (Entanglement 119) **—**
(1980 NR 1981 12.2fg 16fg 12.2fg) 600Y; small filly; sixth foal; dam winning
hurdler; apprentice ridden when behind in maiden races at Catterick (2) and
Beverley. *D. Yeoman.*

MISS COUTURE 4 br.f. Tamerlane 128–Tragara (Buisson Ardent 129) (1980 **—**
7f 8fg 8fg 10.2g 16fg 16s 13.8fg* 13.8d 1981 15.8g 18g) wide-margin winner of
seller at Catterick in 1980; well beaten in non-sellers at 4 yrs; stays 1¾m; acts on
a firm surface; blinkered once in 1980. *J. W. Watts.*

MISS DIAWARD 4 br.f. Supreme Sovereign 119–Gay Pretendre (Pretendre 126) **75**
(1980 8g 8g³ 10g⁴ 8.2g² 9s³ 9d³ 12d* 1981 10.8d 12fg³ 11d* 12d*) quite attractive, lengthy filly; good walker; won handicaps at Hamilton in September and
Edinburgh in October (trotted up); stays 1½m; acts on any going; has
run creditably for an apprentice; trained by Mrs J. Pitman first start. *Miss
S. Hall.*

MISSELLY 3 gr. or ro.f. Linacre 133–Paddys Choice (Runnymede 123) (1980 **—**
7fg 5g 5f 7d 5d 1981 7g 10d 10f 5fg) small, lengthy filly; of no account. *T.
Kersey.*

MISS FALCON 5 br.m. King's Company 124–Grannie Boyd 67 (Linacre 133) **—**
(1980 7v 6h 7f 6g 6f 1981 11d 8fg) poor plater; has worn blinkers. *R.
Cambidge.*

MISS FANDANGO 2 ch.f. Gay Fandango 132–Nana's Girl 109 (Tin Whistle 128) **—**
(1981 5fg 5f 5fg 5g) Feb 28; strong, good sort; good walker; half-sister to several
winners, including Royal Boy (by Realm), a smart performer at up to 7f, and good
1977 2-y-o Aythorpe (by Ridan); dam useful at up to 1m and sister to very smart
Tin King; only poor form so far in maiden and minor events; probably needs
further; blinkered fourth outing. *G. Pritchard-Gordon.*

MISS FRESHNESS 3 gr.f. Grey Mirage 128–Valiant Victress (Nulli Secundus **—**
89) (1980 6f 1981 8s 10g 12g) soundly beaten in maiden and minor races and
a seller; sold 660 gns Doncaster June Sales. *E. Carter.*

MISS GALLANT 2 ch.f. Gallo Gallante 96–Miss Me (Pinturischio 116) (1981 **57**
5d 5g 7fg 7fg 7fg) Apr 30; leggy, rather unfurnished filly; second foal; dam poor
novice hurdler/chaser; showed a little ability in maiden races and a minor event
on her last 3 starts; runs as though she'll stay 1m. *T. Barnes.*

MISS GAYLORD 4 b.f. Cavo Doro 124–Sea Pearl 75 (Sea Hawk II 131) (1980 **43**
10g 11.7s 10.1d³ 16.9f 1981 8s 11d 10g* 15.8g 12s 10.6s 12g 10fg³ 10.1fg⁴ 12f)
light-framed, narrow filly; plater; bought in 960 gns after winning at Pontefract
in April; suited by 1¼m (isn't certain to stay 2m); acts on a firm and a soft surface;
has worn blinkers; often bandaged nowadays. *K. Ivory.*

MISS GENEROUS 4 b.f. Bronze Hill 96–Generous Device 69 (Bounteous 125) **—**
(1980 10fg 10g 12f² 1981 12g 15.8g) strong filly; plating-class maiden; best run
at 1½m on firm going. *M. Camacho.*

MISS GLANCY 3 gr. or ro.f. Wollow 132–Silecia (Sky Gipsy 117) (1980 6g 5g **61**
5f 5g 6g 1981 8s 7fg 6fg⁴ 8fg 6g 6g* 6fg) small filly; plater; made all and beat
Winner Takes All by 6 lengths in 21-runner apprentice selling handicap at
Windsor in August; bought in 1,350 gns afterwards; stays at 6f; has been
tried in blinkers; unruly at start fifth outing; sold 5,400 gns Newmarket December Sales. *P. Haslam.*

MISS HAGEN 3 ch.f. Mount Hagen 127–Laikipia 89 (St Paddy 133) (1980 5g **—**
6g 7d 6f 5d 1981 9g 6g 12g 7g) short-backed filly; plater; has worn blinkers;
sold 480 gns Doncaster June Sales. *B. Richmond.*

MISS HASTY 2 b.f. Hasty Word 84–Ol Arabel (Relic) (1981 5fg 8g 8s) Mar 24; **—**
small, workmanlike filly; no sign of ability in maiden race and sellers. *J. Peacock.*

MISS HIBERNIAN 2 br.f. Ascendant 96–Ladyrullah (Bluerullah 115) (1981 **—**
5fg 5d 5v 7g 8.2s 8d) Feb 1; small, lightly-made filly; of no account. *P. Butler.*

MISSILE MISS 3 ch.f. Firestreak 125–Flora Leigh 94 (Floribunda 136) (1980 —
NR 1981 7f 7fg 7fg 12g 12d) lengthy filly; half-sister to a winner in Brazil;
dam, half-sister to smart fillies Weeber and Amicable, stayed 1¼m; behind in
varied company, including selling. *W. Holden.*

MISS IMPORT 3 ch.f. Import 127–Chinese Falcon 81 (Skymaster 126) (1980 **71**
5g 5f 1981 5g* 5g 5d 5fg* 5g 5fg 5.6f 5d* 5fg 5f 5g* 5d) workmanlike filly;
made all in maiden event at Pontefract in April and handicaps at Catterick in
June, Pontefract in August and Wolverhampton in September, coming home 4
lengths ahead of Mustika on last-named course; speedy and is likely to prove best
at 5f; acts on a firm and a soft surface; sometimes sweats up badly; sometimes
slowly away; none too consistent; successful with blinkers and without. *T.
Barron.*

MISSIVE (FR) 4 ch.f. Bold Lad (USA)–Miss Monde (Cadmus 124) (1980 8f³ —
1981 8f 8f 10fg) fair sort; poor form, including in a seller; stays 1m; sold 400 gns
Newmarket Autumn Sales. *J. Fitzgerald.*

MISS KATIE 2 b.f. Porto Bello 118–Serein (Prince Chevalier) (1981 5d 5d 6fg) —
Apr 3; 1,500Y; lightly-made filly; half-sister to several minor winners here and
in Belgium; dam lightly-raced half-sister to Hotfoot; no worthwhile form,
including in auction events; blinkered third outing. *Mrs J. Reavey.*

MISS KENTUCKY 2 b.f. Wolver Hollow 126–Kentucky Robin 73 (Falcon 131) —
(1981 6d 8fg) Apr 23; sister to moderate 1¼m winner Red Wolver, and half-
sister to 2 winners; dam won at up to 11f; modest seventh in sizeable fields of
maidens at Windsor in August and Leicester in September; sold to BBA 3,500 gns
Newmarket Autumn Sales. *H. Cecil.*

MISS LAUSIENNE 5 b.m. Lauso–Tackienne (Hard Tack 111§) (1980 12.5v —
10fg 10h² 12.3d 13.8f* 13g³ 15.8g 1981 15.8s 12g) plater; well beaten in better
company in 1981; suited by a test of stamina; acts on hard going and is probably
unsuited by soft. *G. Lockerbie.*

MISS LILIAN 2 b.f. Sandford Lad 133–Bustina (Busted 134) (1981 5s 5g² 6s² **97**
5s² 5fg³ 6fg² 6f* 7.9f* 6d⁴ 5g³ 7d 6g) Apr 17; IR 3,200F, IR 5,800Y; second foal;
half-sister to Irish 3-y-o 6f winner Wintina (by Tumble Wind); dam fourth of 16
on only start at 2 yrs in France; finally got off the mark when winning maiden
race at Phoenix Park in August by 5 lengths and landed the odds by a short head
from Lady Hart in minor event at Dundalk later in month; in frame subsequently in Moyglare Stud Stakes at the Curragh (1¼ lengths fourth of 14 to
subsequently-disqualified Sweet Sind) and Goffs Stakes on same course (5 lengths
third of 11 to Americus); has won over 1m but is possibly better at shorter
distances; acts on any going; consistent. *P. Norris, Ireland.*

MISS LONGCHAMP 2 ch.f. Northfields–Miss Paris 111 (Sovereign Path 125) — p
(1981 6g) May 31; neat, attractive filly; third foal; half-sister to 1978 2-y-o 6f
winner Miss St Cyr (by Brigadier Gerard); dam, third in Cheveley Park, stayed
1m; 20/1, ran on to some purpose, after getting behind, when 15 lengths eighth
of 17 to Merlin's Charm in maiden race at Newmarket in October; sure to leave
this form behind at 3 yrs, probably over 7f and 1m. *M. Stoute.*

MISS LOUISE 4 b.f. Virginia Boy 106–Chetim (Arctic Time 127) (1980 8fg 8s —
10.2g 9.4fg 13.8d⁴ 11s 1981 11d 10g) big, strong filly; poor plater; has been
tried in blinkers; sold 400 gns Doncaster June Sales. *R. E. Peacock.*

MISS LYPTOSOL 3 b.f. Grisaille 115–Miss Season (Silly Season 127) (1980 —
NR 1981 8g 8f 7.6s) 620F, resold 580F; lightly-made filly; third produce; dam
never ran; behind in maiden races. *J. Berry.*

MISS MACAULEY 2 b.f. Rarity 129–Red Coral 80 (Red God 128§) (1981 6f) . —
Feb 7; 6,800F, 550Y; fourth foal; dam 2-y-o 5f winner; unquoted when behind
in moderate minor event at Nottingham in July. *J. Harris.*

MISS MAREMMA 2 b.f. Ashmore 125–Mismaloya 116 (Emerson) (1981 6fg⁴ **66**
6fg⁴ 7fg 8fg 7d) Mar 9; 10,000Y; lightly-made filly; half-sister to French 1m
winner Mescalero (by Stupendous) and useful miler Mystificateur (by Nonoalco);
dam fourth in 1,000 Guineas; poor maiden; should be suited by 7f+ (tailed off
only outing over 1m). *R. Hollinshead.*

MISS MARKEY 3 b.f. Gay Fandango 132–Buffy (French Beige 127) (1980 NR **98** d
1981 7fg³ 10.5s 10.6v³ 9s³ 10.2d 10g³) 30,000Y; good-bodied, attractive filly;
half-sister to 2 winners, including fairly useful 1976 2-y-o 5f winner Royal Hand
(by Realm); dam, Irish 6f winner, is half-sister to very smart filly El Mina; looked
very promising when staying-on 2½ lengths third to Fairy Footsteps in Ladbrokes

Nell Gwyn Stakes at Newmarket in April; didn't fulfil that promise but was third in minor and maiden events at Haydock, York and Newmarket in the autumn, best effort on last-named course when blinkered first time; stayed 1¼m; needed a sound surface; retired to stud. *B. Hills.*

MISS MARSTAIN 2 ch.f. Song 132–Insurance 106 (Yellow God 129) (1981 5g 5fg 6fg 5g 5s⁴ 5s) May 23; useful sort; third foal; sister to 6f winner Cover Note; dam won twice over 6f at 2 yrs; only quite moderate; best run on soft going; blinkered third and fifth outings. *W. Wightman.* **67**

MISS MENTON 3 b.f. Brigadier Gerard 144–Miss Monaco 107 (Crepello 136) (1980 6g 6s* 1981 6fg) leggy filly; won minor event at Stockton at 2 yrs; needed race and finished in rear on only outing of 1981 (June); will stay 1m; sold 3,000 gns Newmarket December Sales. *W. Hastings-Bass.* **—**

MISS METRO 4 b.f. Upper Case–Pilgrim Soul 89 (Tudor Melody 129) (1980 5f 7f 8.5f⁴ 10.1g 8g⁴ 10fg 9s 1981 10fg) big, well-made filly; poor maiden; well beaten in seller only start at 4 yrs in July; should stay 1¼m. *G. Harman.* **—**

MISS MIRABELLE 5 br.m. Miracle 116–La Belle 118 (Vilmorin) (1980 7f 7g 7f 7g 7fg 1981 8s 7s* 7d* 7.6g² 7.2s² 7g² 7fg* 7g 7.6s 7.2v) sturdy mare; returned to form in 1981, winning handicaps at Stockton and Wolverhampton in April and at Sandown in July; stays 1m; acts on any going. *M. Jarvis.* **75**

MISS NELSKI 4 ch.f. Most Secret 119–Nelski 83 (Skymaster 126) (1980 5s 5d 5d³ 5v 1981 6g 5d 5fg 5f 6f 7f² 5g* 8f 6f 5f 5fg³ 5g³ 5g⁴ 5d* 5g 5g) small, strong filly; won handicaps at Carlisle in July and Pontefract in October; effective at 5f on a stiff track and stays 7f; seems to act on any going; usually blinkered. *J. Etherington.* **70**

MISS NINIAN 3 gr.f. The Go-Between 129–Sevantha 80 (Henry the Seventh 125) (1980 5fg 6fg³ 1981 6g 6d 7f 8fg 11g 13.8g) lightly-made, unfurnished filly; poor plater. *W. Bentley.* **—**

MISS PERFECT 2 ch.f. Beau of Paree–Perfect Harmony (Darling Boy 124) (1981 5g 6fg 8fg 8.2d 8s) May 14; good-bodied individual; useless plater; has worn blinkers. *S. Matthews.* **—**

MISS POINCIANA 4 b. or br.f. Averof 123–Miss Twomey (Will Somers 114§) (1980 7fg 7g 6g³ 5fg³ 6d² 5fg 5f³ 5d 1981 5s* 5g³ 5g 5f 5fg* 5g⁴ 5fg² 5f⁴ 5f 5fg 5f² 5g*) strong filly; sprint handicapper; won at Stockton in April (apprentices), Edinburgh in July (amateur riders) and Edinburgh again in October; stays 6f; acts on any going; often sweats up; suitable mount for an inexperienced rider. *M. Camacho.* **69**

MISS POSY 2 b.f. Pitskelly 122–Pushpa Ji Rao (Sayajirao 132) (1981 6fg* 6fg 5d 7f 8g 7g) Apr 4; workmanlike filly; half-sister to numerous winners here and abroad, including fairly useful 5f performer Golden Dukat (by Golden Horus); dam fifth in Irish Oaks; 2½-length winner from Fine Touch in 17-runner seller at Warwick in June (bought in 2,600 gns); well beaten in nurseries and a valuable seller on last 3 starts (most unimpressive in appearance on final appearance, when blinkered); should stay at least 7f. *J. Douglas-Home.* **56**

MISS PRUDENT 2 b.f. Jolly Me 114–Acca Larentia (Romulus 129) (1981 5s* 5d⁴ 5d² 5fg² 5fg* 6g* 7f 6d 7s² 7d) May 25; 260Y; leggy, light-framed filly; good mover; half-sister to 2 winners in France; dam won twice over 1¼m in Ireland; successful in maiden auction event at Redcar in June; also awarded 2 other races by stewards, a seller at Beverley in April after winner failed its dope test and valuable 18-runner seller at York in July after being crossed by neck winner Four For Music; attracted no bid at York; excellent length second of 13 to French Gent in nursery at York in October; will stay 1m; has won on a firm surface but seems well suited by some give in the ground; has run respectably for a 7-lb claimer. *C. Gray.* **79**

MISS PUCCI 3 br.f. So Blessed 130–Italian Idol (Sheshoon 132) (1980 5fg 7g 7g 7d 1981 8s 8g³ 9.4g 12.2g 8f³ 8f) strong, useful sort; made running when in frame in maiden races at Carlisle in May and Thirsk in July, best efforts; stays 1m but is a strong puller and gives impression she's worth trying over a shorter trip; sometimes sweats up. *M. W. Easterby.* **56**

MISS QUAVER 3 b.f. Averof 123–Quick Burn 94 (Carnival Dancer 113) (1980 5s² 5d* 5fg* 1981 7fg 6s 6g 5g⁴ 5fg) close-coupled, sharp sort; good mover; usually had stiff tasks in 1981, best efforts when in frame in handicaps at Lingfield and Chester in summer; appeared not to stay beyond 5f; seemed to act on any going; sometimes sweated up; dead. *R. Hannon.* **81**

MISS REDMARSHALL   4 ch.f. Most Secret 119–Miss Marvel 59 (Palestine 133)   **77**
(1980 5s⁴ 6d² 5g³ 5g² 5g*(dis) 5d* 6g² 5f⁴ 5d 5fg*   1981 5g⁴ 5g* 5fg² 5fg 6f 5g 5g³
5f* 5f 5fg 5g³ 5s)   plater at 2 yrs; modest handicapper nowadays; beat Covergirls
Choice by 2 lengths in £6,300 race at Doncaster in May and accounted for Shy
Talk by a neck at Beverley in August; best at 5f; probably acts on any going;
usually blinkered; suitable mount for a claimer; bandaged off-hind fourth start;
suited by front-running tactics; game; sold 15,000 gns Newmarket December
Sales. *J. Mason.*

MISS SABRINA   3 b.f. Simbir 130–Mistrust (Rustam 127)   (1980 7f 7g 7fg   —
1981 10s 7d 7g 7f 6fg)   neat, strong, quite attractive filly; well behind in varied
company, including selling; blinkered last 3 starts; sold 680 gns Ascot July Sales.
B. Swift.

MISS SOMERSAULT (USA)   2 b.f. Ali Oop–Little Jen (Time Tested)   (1981   —
6fg 7fg 8g 10g)   Mar 26; $55,000Y; well-grown filly; third foal; half-sister to 2
winners, including useful 1980 2-y-o 5f winner Tax Haven (by No Robbery); dam
won at up to 1m; sire at his best at 2 yrs when high-class winner at up to 6f;
seems of little account; sold 440 gns Doncaster November Sales. *J. Hindley.*

MISS STARCHY   2 b.f. Starch Reduced 112–Antheia 76 (Acropolis 132)   (1981   —
5fg 5f)   Apr 11; 450F; light-framed filly; sister to 6f winner Fairmile Lad, and
half-sister to a winning plater; dam ran twice; unquoted when in mid-division in
maiden races at Nottingham and Wolverhampton in June. *B. Gubby.*

MISS ST JAMES'S   3 b.f. Sovereign Path 125–Miss London 95 (Pall Mall 132)   —
(1980 6s 6g² 6fg* 6d³ 7d*   1981 7f)   well-grown filly; quite useful at 2 yrs, when
winning at Carlisle and Doncaster; not disgraced when 2 lengths fifth of 17 to
Singwara in handicap at Leicester in June, only outing of 1981; may well stay
1m; acts on a firm and a soft surface. *M. Stoute.*

MISS ST MAWES   3 b.f. Derring-Do 131 Terre Promise (Soderini 123)   (1980   **90**
6g² 6g⁴ 6g* 6d³   1981 7g⁴ 10.6d⁴ 9s² 10f⁴ 10f² 9d⁴ 10d)   leggy filly; fairly useful
handicapper; in frame most starts, best efforts when second to Regal Steel at
York in May and to Palatinate at Nottingham in June; stays 1¼m; acts on any
going; didn't run up to her best fourth and last outings; sold 14,000 gns Newmarket Autumn Sales, reportedly for export to South Africa. *B. Hobbs.*

MISS STOLEN   2 b.f. Steel Heart 128–Sumintra 82 (El Gallo 122)   (1981 5d 5d   —
5g 5g 6g)   Feb 1; 2,700Y; sturdy filly; half-sister to 2 winners, including quite
useful Irish sprinter Concordia (by Realm); dam sprint maiden; only plating class;
sold to W. Turner 340 gns Doncaster October Sales. *W. Marshall.*

MISS STREAKY   3 b.f. Saulingo 122–Sweet Miss (Silver Cloud 121)   (1980 NR   —
1981 9d 6d 7d 8fg 8fg)   5,000Y; lengthy, lightly-made filly; third foal; dam,
placed at up to 1¼m in Ireland, is half-sister to Sweet Solera; soundly beaten in
varied company, including selling on final start (blinkered); sold 360 gns Ascot
October Sales. *F. J. Houghton.*

MISS SUKI   4 b.f. Upper Case–La Garoupe 87 (Pirate King 129)   (1980 11fg 12f   —
12g   1981 12g 12f 16f⁴)   strong filly; poor maiden; blinkered once in 1980.
W. Clay.

MISS TAYMORE (USA)   4 b. or br.f. Sham–Bend an Oar (Never Bend)   (1980   **76**
8d³ 8f⁴ 10.5f 10g 8g 7f⁴ 7s 6d 6fg* 6d*   1981 6s 7.2fg 6g 6d 7g 8s³ 7d 7f 6d 7d³ 6d⁴
7s)   lengthy filly; stays 1m though is better at shorter distances; acts on any
going; suitable mount for an apprentice; used to take a good hold; sold 20,000
gns Newmarket December Sales. *S. Norton.*

MISS TOURIST (USA)   2 ch.f. Unconscious–I'm A Dame (Bold Hour)   (1981   —
5fg 7g)   May 20; $20,000Y; strong, lengthy filly; second foal; half-sister to a
winner by West Coast Scout; dam won claiming races over sprint distances; sire,
son of Arc winner Prince Royal II, was high-class winner at up to 1¼m; blinkered,
apprentice ridden and on backward side when in rear in £3,100 event at Goodwood
in September and 22-runner maiden race at Newmarket in October. *F. Durr.*

MISS TRILLI   2 ch.f. Ardoon 124–Grecian Palm 78 (Royal Palm 131)   (1981 5g   **89**
5s² 5g* 5fg² 5g² 5f³ 5g³ 5g)   smallish, attractive filly; half-sister to several winners, including useful sprinter Trillium (by Psidium); dam temperamental 5f
sprinter; made all to win by 3 lengths from Morcal when favourite for 8-runner
maiden race at Ayr in May; ran well in most of her subsequent races, notably
when second to Vaigly Star in Hilary Needler Trophy at Beverley the following
month on next outing and when third to Bright View in £7,600 nursery at Redcar
in September; speedy and may not stay beyond 5f; off course nearly 3 months
before sixth start (sweated up) *G. Pritchard-Gordon.*

MISS TWIGGY   3 gr.f. Tycoon II–Golden Herb 80 (Goldhill 125)   (1980 5fg 5fg   **61**
5fg³ 5fg* 5g² 5d 5g⁴ 5f 5f   1981 5s 5fg 5g 5fg⁴ 5.1fg 6f³ 7f)   compact filly; ran

best races of year when in frame in handicaps at Catterick (apprentice ridden) and Nottingham in summer; stays 6f (well beaten over 7f on final start); ran badly in blinkers second outing. *J. Harris.*

MISS WATERLOO 4 ch.f. Brigadier Gerard 144–Miss Bali 95 (Crepello 136) — (1980 including 11s 10g 9g* 10g* 1981 including 8.5g² 10g 12g 12.2s 8g) ex-Italian filly; won 2 races in Italy at 3 yrs, including 1¼m Premio Giovanni Falck at Milan; runner-up 3 times from 6 starts in Italy in 1981; has shown only a little ability in this country; stays 1¼m. *M. Jarvis.*

MISS WORTH 3 ch.f. Streak 119–Bodicea (King's Troop 118) (1980 5fg 5fg* 68 5fg 5d³ 5g 5.3fg* 5fg⁴ 6g 1981 6f 5.3f* 5fg 6f 6fg) small, narrow filly; plater in 1980; beat Arch Melody 2 lengths in handicap at Brighton in July; ran moderately afterwards; probably stays 6f; well suited by firm going; good mount for an apprentice. *C. James.*

MISS ZOLLY 2 b. or br.f. Realm 129–Dolly-Longlegs 74 (Majority Blue 126) — (1981 5fg 6fg) May 16; IR 9,400Y; half-sister to fairly useful 1980 2-y-o sprinter Arndean (by Auction Ring) and a winner in Italy; dam won 6f claiming race at 2 yrs; no sign of ability in maiden races, finishing last of 12 at Folkestone on second outing; sold 370 gns Ascot September Sales. *B. Swift.*

MISTER CHAS 2 ch.g. Dragonara Palace 115–Dauphiness 74 (Supreme — Sovereign 119) (1981 5f 6g) Mar 25; 5,600Y; brother to moderate sprinter Kassak, and half-brother to a winning plater; dam 2-y-o 5f winner; 20/1 when behind in 18-runner minor event won by Never So Lucky at Windsor in June; withdrawn under orders from similar event at Salisbury the following month (went lame after false start) *J. Holt.*

MISTEREFF 4 b.g. Track Spare 125–Ring True 80 (Gulf Pearl 117) (1980 7f 8g — 8fg 8d⁴ 7fg 8g 1981 6fg 7f 8.3fg 8g 8fg) very small gelding; poor plater; seems to stay 1m; sold 300 gns Doncaster October Sales. *R. Mason.*

MISTER LUCKY 4 br.g. Royalty 130–Fair Songstress 100 (Compensation 127) 69 d (1980 8.2s² 7f 10f 12f* 10.1g 11g² 12g 10.2g⁴ 10fg² 11.7d⁴ 10d 12s* 12g 1981 10s³ 12d 11.7fg 12f 13.3d 12d 12g 12d) useful sort; stays 1½m; acts on any going; suitable mount for a boy; sold 2,900 gns Newmarket Autumn Sales. *R. Hannon.*

MISTER PITT 2 b.c. Pitskelly 122–High Command (High Hat 131) (1981 5f 71 6fg 7fg⁴ 7s 8s²) Mar 29; IR 8,000Y, 7,600Y; compact, quite attractive colt; half-brother to 2 winners in Ireland, including stayer High Simbir (by Simbir); dam placed over 6f at 2 yrs in Ireland; blinkered, ran best race in nursery at Wolverhampton in October, finishing clear of 6 others when head second to Change Habit; will probably stay 1¼m; best run on soft going. *G. Hunter.*

MISTIGORA 2 ch.f. Algora 110–Pink Slip (Indigenous 121) (1981 6f 5f) May 65 13; sixth foal; dam well beaten in 2 races at 2 yrs; beaten about 5 lengths by Super Natalie when fifth in minor event at Chepstow in July, second outing and better effort; not sure to stay 6f. *B. Palling.*

MISTRA (FR) 3 b.f. Huntercombe 133–Marenla (Duc de Gueldre 129) (1980 8g 119 7.5g 1981 10.5g* 9s* 8s³ 7s² 6.5fg 8f 8fg 8s 7s² 8s*) 90,000 francs Y (approx. £9,400); half-sister to 2 minor winners; dam won at up to 13f; won maiden race at Saint-Cloud in March, minor event at Evry in May and quite well-contested Prix Coronation at Saint-Cloud again in November; beat stable-companion Jark by ¾ length in last-named event; ran consistently well on her other starts (mainly in better company) and was placed 3 times, including when about a length third to Alik in Group 3 Prix de Sandringham at Chantilly in June and short-neck second to Gosport in Group 3 Prix de la Porte Maillot at Longchamp in July; stays 10.5f, but is effective at much shorter distances; acts on any going; genuine. *J. Cunnington, jnr, France.*

MISTRAL MAN 2 ch.c. Sweet Revenge 129–What a Breeze (Whistling Wind 99 123) (1981 5s³ 6d 7fg 7fg⁴ 6d* 8d⁴) Apr 22; IR 3,500F, IR 10,000Y; second reported living foal; dam in rear in maiden and minor events; put up best effort when making much of running to win 16-runner maiden race at the Curragh in September by 5 lengths from Raconteur; third favourite when never-dangerous 12½ lengths fourth of 10 to Assert in Beresford Stakes on same course the following month; not certain to stay 1m; acts well on a soft surface; blinkered last 3 outings. *M. O'Toole, Ireland.*

MISTRESS GAY 3 ch.f. Lord Gayle 124–Such Moor 77 (Santa Claus 133) (1980 76 NR 1981 9d* 10g* 10g² 10g 13.8fg 10g 10s 8.2d³) 5,600F, 15,500Y; fifth produce; half-sister to 4 winners, including fairly useful 2-y-o 6f winners Tarenure (by Targowice) and En Avant (by Sallust); dam won over 1½m; won maiden race

MIS

at Wolverhampton in May (in good style) and minor event at Ripon in June; placed in ladies race at Lingfield and handicap at Hamilton afterwards; had stiffish tasks in between; will stay 1½m; acts on a soft surface; genuine. *Sir Mark Prescott.*

MISTRESS KIPLING 2 b.f. Nonoalco 131–Miller's Lass 103 (Mill Reef 141) **75**
(1981 6fg 5fg⁴ 6fg³ 5.8h³ 8s) Apr 5; tall, rangy, quite attractive filly with a long stride; first foal; dam, out of half-sister to Hethersett, won at up to 11.5f in Ireland; in frame in maiden races at Goodwood, Newbury and Bath in the summer, running best race when ¾-length fourth of 8 to Ibtihaj at Goodwood; ran poorly when tried over 1m but should be well suited by trip; possibly unsuited by soft going. *B. Hills.*

MISTRESS ROSEMARY 2 b.f. Cawston's Clown 113–Canty Day 87 (Canadel —
II 126) (1981 5f 5fg 6d) Apr 20; strong filly; second reported foal; dam 2-y-o 5f winner; plating-class maiden. *W. Haigh.*

MISTY GLEN 5 b.m. Leander 119–Tudor Style 98 (Owen Tudor) (1980 NR **45**
1981 12f 17.1d² 16f² 16.1f) strong, lengthy mare; suited by a test of stamina; probably acts on any going; has run creditably for an apprentice. *M. Bradley.*

MISTY HALO 2 b.f. High Top 131–Ringed Aureole 77 (Aureole 132) (1981 8fg **93**
8d* 8.2d* 8s) Mar 1; well-grown, good sort; first foal; dam won from 1½m to 2m; won maiden race at Wolverhampton and minor event at Hamilton in October, latter by 2 lengths from Napa Valley; didn't have best of runs when fifth of 29 to Arrowood Dream in minor event at Redcar later in month; will stay 1½m. *Sir Mark Prescott.*

MITIGATOR 5 br.g. Brigadier Gerard 144–Mitigation 91 (Milesian 125) (1980 **57**
10g 10d 10fg² 9g 8d 1981 8f⁴ 10f⁴ 10d² 9f 8g³ 10g⁴) useful-looking gelding; modest at his best but has deteriorated; blinkered when third in valuable seller at Doncaster in September (didn't look entirely genuine), runs as though 1¼m is his limit; possibly unsuited by very soft ground; sold to S. Holland 2,400 gns Doncaster October Sales. *W. Hastings-Bass.*

MIYSAM 2 b.f. Supreme Sovereign 119–Enniscrone 73 (Royal Palm 131) (1981 **60**
5g* 5g 5f) Apr 25; 4,200Y; neat, lightly-made filly; good mover; first foal; dam won over 5f and 6f and stayed 1m; made all to win 6-runner maiden race at Haydock in April by ¾ length from Knight Security; in rear in minor event at Pontefract and valuable seller at York subsequently; should be suited by 6f. *W. O'Gorman.*

MIZEN 3 b.f. Ampney Prince 96–Summer Princess (Wynkell 88) (1980 NR —
1981 10.6v 10s) sixth foal; dam of little account; well beaten in minor event at Haydock and seller at Nottingham in October. *A. W. Jones.*

MIZZENHEAD (USA) 6 br.g. Mill Reef 141–Black Satin 114 (Linacre 133) **48**
(1980 12.5v 13g² 12.5s 1981 12s* 12s) strong, lengthy gelding; won poor maiden race at Beverley in April; will stay beyond 13f; acts on soft going. *M. W. Easterby.*

MOAT HOUSE 2 ch.g. Sun Prince 128–Stickpin 74 (Gulf Pearl 117) (1981 5s **74**
7fg 7fg 7g³ 7.6s 6d³ 8.2s 6g) Jan 20; 3,000Y; strong, compact, good-bodied gelding; fourth foal; half-brother to fair 1980 2-y-o 6f winner African Pearl (by African Sky); dam placed over 5f and 7f at 2 yrs; third in maiden race at Leicester and in nursery at Hamilton in the autumn; should stay 1m (ran badly when tried at trip but was having second race in 2 days). *D. Thom.*

MOCK AUCTION 2 b.f. Auction Ring 123–Magden 77 (Major Portion 129) **55**
(1981 6g⁴ 6g 5fg³ 5fg 5f³ 5g) Apr 13; fair sort; half-sister to several winners, including useful Italian colts Henghel (by Young Emperor) and Ipparco (by African Sky); dam half-sister to good stayer New Brig; modest third in 6-runner maiden race and 4-runner nursery in Scotland; should stay 6f. *Denys Smith.*

MOCK SUN 5 ch.g. Sharpen Up 127–Parhelia 84§ (Dante) (1980 8fg 10.6fg 10g —
1981 10f) poor plater; stays 1m; has worn bandages. *J. Mulhall.*

MODESTINE 3 b.f. Welsh Pageant 132–Dauphine 102 (Pampered King 121) **73**
(1980 6g 6fg 1981 7g 7f 10d 10fg² 10s² 10g⁴) small, lightly-made filly; poor walker; quite a moderate maiden; suited by 1¼m; sold 9,600 gns Newmarket December Sales. *J. Dunlop.*

MOLON LAVE 4 b.g. Welsh Pageant 132–Another Princess 83 (King Emperor) **78**
(1980 8f 8fg 8fg 7fg 7g² 8d⁴ 7g 1981 7.6g* 6g 7fg 7g⁴ 7fg² 6fg³ 8fg* 8g³ 7.6s 8fg* 8fg²) big, strong gelding; modest handicapper; won at Chester in May (made all), Ascot in July (apprentices) and Newmarket in August; finds 6f too sharp and stays 1m; suited by top-of-the-ground; sweated up badly when blinkered once in 1980. *C. Brittain.*

554

MOMBASA 2 b.f. Furry Glen 121–Ardrums (Native Prince) (1981 6fg 7g 8s) **65**
Jan 29; IR 2,200Y; big, lengthy filly; fourth foal; sister to Irish 7f winner
Glenardina and half-sister to 2 winners, including 1980 Irish 2-y-o 5f winner
Singari (by Jukebox); dam won over 5f at 2 yrs in Ireland from only 2 starts;
seventh of 29 to Arrowood Dream in minor event at Redcar in October, best
effort; ninth of 16 in valuable seller at Doncaster on debut; evidently suited by
1m on soft ground. *G. Toft.*

MONACO DANCER 2 b.g. Ampney Prince 96–Molly Cockell (Wynkell 88) —
(1981 5fg 6d 5fg) Apr 14; brother to 1m and 1¼m winner Ampney Duke but is
a bad plater himself. *D. Elsworth.*

MONARCHY 4 b.g. Royalty 130–Cama 85 (Pardao 120) (1980 11fg 16d 1981 —
18.8fg 17.1d 11.7fg 11.7f) strong, workmanlike gelding; poor maiden; has worn
blinkers. *J. Bosley.*

MON BEAUX 7 ch.g. Continuation 120–Affectionately 82 (Mark-Ye-Well) —
(1980 12s 1981 10.6s) lightly raced nowadays and is probably of little account.
J. Yardley.

MONCLARE TROPHY 2 ch.c. Sandford Lad 133–Blue Warbler (Worden II **70**
129) (1981 5g 6fg 5fg³ 6g) May 8; lightly-made colt; half-brother to 1977 2-y-o
5f winner Bronze Princess (by Hul a Hul) and a winner in Italy; dam unraced
half-sister to Dewhurst Stakes winner King's Lane; quite moderate form in varied
company; will probably stay 1m. *P. Cole.*

MONDAY NIGHT 5 b.m. Jukebox 120–Fair Halo (Nimbus 130) (1980 7fg 8.3f⁴ —
9.6f 8g 1981 10.1fg 12f 6fg 5.8f) small mare; poor plater; stays 1m; sometimes
wears blinkers. *N. Mitchell.*

MONEVETTE 3 ch.f. Sweet Revenge 129–Nom de Plume 70 (Aureole 132) **61**
(1980 5f 5fg 6fg* 7f 7g* 1981 8g 8g 12g² 8s* 8.2f) light-framed filly; bought in
1,050 gns after winning seller at Carlisle in June; possibly doesn't quite stay 1½m;
acts on soft going; seems best in blinkers; apprentice ridden last 3 outings; sold
4,000 gns Newmarket December Sales. *G. Toft.*

MONEY IN 7 b.g. Jukebox 120–Lev Star (Le Levanstell 122) (1980 NR 1981 —
10fg) poor performer nowadays; beaten in seller only start at 7 yrs in July;
stays 1¾m; best on a sound surface. *W. Marshall.*

MONKS FARM 3 b.g. So Blessed 130–Tomboy 95 (Sica Boy 132) (1980 7g 7fg² **86**
7d² 1981 7g 7.6g³ 8g⁴ 7g*) lengthy gelding; kept on well to beat Hit Record
a length in handicap at Sandown in July; may well stay 1¼m; acts on a firm and
a soft surface; exported to Hong Kong. *J. Dunlop.*

MONMOUTH (FR) 3 ch.c. Welsh Pageant 132–Cockade 104 (Derring-Do 131) —
(1980 8g 1981 8.2s 10.1f 12.3g) workmanlike colt; sixth of 14 to Danlifar in
minor event at Windsor in June on second start; not certain to stay 1½m. *T.
Robson.*

MONNOW MILL 2 b. or br.c. Kambalda 108–Well of Dreams (Military 112) —
(1981 5.8g 5f 7fg) May 5; first foal; dam never ran; well beaten in maiden races
and a minor event. *O. O'Neill.*

MON'S BEAU 6 b.g. Mon Plaisir 121–Beauatire 86 (Beau Sabreur 125) (1980 **87** d
16s* 18.4f 20d 16d* 19g⁴ 18d 18s 1981 16fg 16.1s* 16s 16g 21fg 16d 16fg 18g)
out-and-out staying handicapper; got home by a short head from Nimble Dove
at Haydock in May; suited by some give in the ground; suitable mount for a boy;
occasionally sweats up; game. *G. Beeson.*

MONT-A-L'ABBE 4 b.f. Military 112–Miss Monet 80 (Monet 127) (1980 NR —
1981 10v 12g 12d 8fg 12f 12g) 750Y; big filly; half-sister to 3 minor winners; dam
5f 2-y-o winner; little sign of ability in varied company. *W. Elsey.*

MONTAZEM 4 ch.g. Sharpen Up 127–Sundream (Petingo 135) (1980 5f 5f⁴ 7f — §
6fg² 5g 6g² 6d 8d 1981 6v³ 6g 5g 5g⁴ 6g 5g 7f) inconsistent and unreliable
plater; stays 6f; acts on any going; usually wears blinkers. *J. Berry.*

MONTCLAIR 3 b.c. Habitat 134–Artist and Model (Ribot 142) (1980 6fg³ 6g² **86**
6d² 1981 7fg 8g² 8g* 7d* 8f² 7g) good sort; won handicaps at Doncaster in
May (couldn't have been much more impressive) and Sandown in June, on latter
course quickening smoothly and beating Rollin Hand by a length; didn't handle
track particularly well when second to Ardoony in another handicap at Beverley
in July; stays 1m; acts on any going but is possibly best with some give in the
ground; blinkered second and fifth starts; needs holding up and is probably best
on a turning track. *M. Stoute.*

MONTE ACUTO 7 ch.g. Mountain Call 125–Island Woman 76 (King's Troop **57** 118) (1980 8fg³ 8fg 8fg³ 8g³ 8d* 9f 8f² 8.3fg 8fg² 8g⁴ 8g² 1981 8s 7fg 8g 7g 8d 8f 8fg³ 8f² 8g³ 8d³ 8s⁴) strong, well-made, attractive gelding; mile handicapper; acts on any going; has twice run below form in blinkers; good mount for an apprentice; doesn't always impress in paddock nowadays; sold to G. Cottrell 2,200 gns Ascot October Sales. *G. Harwood.*

MONTEKIN 2 b.c. Mount Hagen 127–Sweet Relations (Skymaster 126) (1981 **120** 6fg² 7fg* 7f² 7d* 7.3s*)

Physically no two-year-old impressed us more throughout 1981 than the strong, very attractive Montekin. He continually drew favourable comments from our paddock critics—comments such as 'looked in really great shape', 'couldn't have looked better', 'pick of paddock', 'continues to do well', 'really took the eye'; and he also impressed us with his extremely good action. There was a great deal to like about his form too—he won three of his five starts and ended his first season with a particularly smart display in the Horris Hill Stakes at Newbury in October.

The Horris Hill possibly suffered in 1981 from its proximity to the William Hill Futurity at Doncaster which carried nearly three times the first prize of £19,977 offered at Newbury. At any rate the field wasn't a particularly strong one: three of the eight runners were maidens and none of the eight had even been placed previously in a pattern event. Montekin's form was as good as anything else's—he'd gone down by only a neck to Codrington in the Granville Stakes at Ascot, won a £3,100 event at Kempton in good style in August, finished a five-length second to Silver Hawk when a short-priced favourite for the Intercraft Solario Stakes and finally won a good-class event with ease at Goodwood in September and he started co-favourite for the Horris Hill with the promising Nottingham and Yarmouth winner Match Winner. Montekin's supporters must have been counting their winnings some way out at Newbury: he won in exceptionally smooth style, with Eddery riding at his most confident. After moving into second place behind Match Winner with a quarter of a mile to run, Eddery bided his time and could be seen looking round for dangers before the furlong pole had been reached. Montekin clearly already had the measure of the leader and the third-placed Wongchoi but it wasn't until the final hundred yards that he was eventually given a little rein, then going on to win very comfortably by a length and a half from the strong-finishing Busaco.

How much Montekin had in hand is anyone's guess. Eddery rode the cheekiest of races and afterwards said in a television interview that Montekin could have won by six or seven lengths had he let him go. We're not for a moment suggesting that Eddery should have given Montekin a hard race but if the colt could have won by six or seven lengths why didn't he let him do so? Why risk being caught on the very soft ground? Ridden out with hands and heels, Montekin could also have gained experience which would have stood him in good stead in his intended spring objectives, the Greenham Stakes and the Two Thousand Guineas, neither of which he's likely to win without coming off the bridle. And what of the colt's reputation? Surely a six- or seven-length winner of the Horris Hill would have received a much higher weight in the Free Handicap than the 8-11 allotted to Montekin, consequently increasing the colt's value and stallion potential considerably. Perhaps Eddery was simply trying to boost Montekin's confidence. It was noticeable in the Solario Stakes that Montekin hung badly under pressure and, while it's far too early to be dogmatic about it, there's a possibility that like those other good sons of Mount Hagen, Dickens Hill and Cracaval, he needs tender handling to show his best.

		Bold Bidder	Bold Ruler
	Mount Hagen	(b 1962)	High Bid
	(ch 1971)	Moonmadness	Tom Fool
Montekin		(ch 1963)	Sunset
(b.c. Apr 21, 1979)		Skymaster	Golden Cloud
	Sweet Relations	(ch 1958)	Discipliner
	(b 1973)	Night Off	Narrator
		(b 1962)	Persuader

As well as exceptional looks and smart form, Montekin also has a sound pedigree to his name, coming from a family that produced several good winners in the past for the Holliday family. Although his third dam Persuader was at her best at two, winning all her four races including the Horris Hill, she also finished third in the Stewards' Cup over six furlongs at three and won over a mile and a quarter at four. Persuader bred numerous winners, including the useful sprinter No

Horris Hill Stakes, Newbury—Eddery wins very cheekily indeed on Montekin.
Others in the picture are Wongchoi who finished fourth and Match
Winner (light cap) who finished third

Argument, later to become a successful sire of jumpers, and his sister Night Off, winner of both the Cheveley Park Stakes and the One Thousand Guineas. Unfortunately Night Off wasn't particularly fertile, producing only five living foals in her first twelve years at stud, but she was a success as a broodmare. Her first foal, Madame's Share, won four races including the Group 3 Prix d'Astarte over a mile; her second foal to live, Baldur, was third to Grundy in the William Hill Dewhurst Stakes; her third, Sweet Relations, is the dam of Montekin; and her fifth, Waffles, won over nine furlongs in Ireland in 1981.

Sweet Relations made no show in either of her races and was sold, carrying a foal to Lochnager, her first, for 15,000 guineas in 1977. Her purchaser got a wonderful bargain. The resultant Lochnager colt, Night Relations, fetched 15,500 guineas as a foal and later won in Italy; Montekin, her second produce, sold for 29,000 guineas as a foal in Ireland; and her third foal, a filly by Sallust, fetched 62,000 guineas when sold as a yearling at Goffs in 1981. There is also a filly foal by Be My Guest out of Sweet Relations which will surely be much sought after if sent to the sales. By way of contrast Montekin's purchasers as a foal must regret having bought him—they received only 14,500 guineas when they re-submitted him as a yearling at the Newmarket December Sales.

Montekin has been entered in both the Two Thousand Guineas and the Derby. The distance of the latter is likely to be beyond him even though Mount Hagen stayed a mile and a half, but he should develop into one of the leading home-trained Guineas candidates. Montekin never stopped improving at two and he's such a grand stamp of colt that he could well make more progress over the winter than some of his contemporaries. *J. Dunlop.*

MONTROAN 2 ch.g. Roan Rocket 128–Montana Girl 110 (Ballymoss 136) **78**
(1981 6g 7d 6s²) Apr 29; 10,500Y; half-brother to several winners here and abroad, and to very useful but disappointing Mayo Girl (by Connaught); dam, a miler, is daughter of sister to top-class sprinter Abelia; 2½ lengths second of 13 to Puesdown in maiden race at Hamilton in October, best effort; should be suited by 7f; sold 3,300 gns Newmarket Autumn Sales. *G. Harwood.*

MONZA 3 b.f. Hotfoot 126–Romella (Romulus 129) (1980 NR 1981 13f 14g⁴ 12fg 8.2s⁴) lengthy, sparely-made filly; half-sister to 2 winners, including 1m winner Pulcinella (by Shantung); dam never ran; has shown a little ability in maiden races; sweating third start. *P. Cundell.* —

MONZA LADY 3 b.f. Balliol 125–Acceleration (On Your Mark 125) (1980 5fg 5fg 5fg⁴ 5fg* 5d² 5g⁴ 6d* 6g⁴ 7fg 6s² 6s* 1981 7v* 7d³ 6g 7d 8f² 7f² 7.2g³ 7.2fg 6g 7g³ 7s³) lengthy, rather leggy filly; beat Dawn Redwood 1½ lengths in 4-runner handicap at Ayr in March; placed on 6 other occasions; finds 1m just beyond her; acts on any going; sold 4,800 gns Newmarket December Sales. *E. Weymes.* 80

MOONBAT 2 gr.g. Habat 127–Lady Of The Moon 89 (Crepello 136) (1981 6s) Apr 15; big, robust gelding; first foal; dam, sister to Derby fourth Great Wall, won 3 times over 1¼m; unquoted and on backward side, unseated rider at start prior to finishing 16 lengths fifth of 15 to Ellerene in maiden race at Newbury in October (showed speed for long way). *M. Smyly.* —

MOON CRYSTAL 3 b.f. The Brianstan 128–Moon's Last 95 (Ballylinan 118) (1980 5f 5.3d 5f 5g 1981 5d) lightly-made filly; plating-class maiden. *G. Beeson.* —

MOONDUSTER 2 b.f. Sparkler 130–Go Gracefully 85 (Jolly Jet 111) (1981 7g) Apr 16; 3,000Y; second foal; dam stayed extremely well; unquoted and backward, dwelt and was always struggling when in rear in 15-runner maiden race won by Awaasif at Ayr in September. *C. Thornton.* —

MOONLIGHT SERENADE 3 b.f. Crooner 119–March Moonlight 86 (March Past 124) (1980 5d 5f⁴ 5.0h 5g 5fg 7d 1981 5g³ 5f 6fg 8fg 8f 8s³ 8d 10d) neat filly; third in maiden event at Bath and seller at Warwick; stays 1m; sometimes blinkered. *M. Hinchliffe.* 52

MOONLIGHT SONATA 3 br.f. So Blessed 130–Midsummer Madness 66 (Silly Season 127) (1980 6d 6v* 1981 7d 8s 6d) lightly-made, useful-looking filly; didn't recover her 2-y-o form; burly on reappearance and sweating and unimpressive in paddock on next start; should stay 1m; yet to race on a sound surface; sold 4,000 gns Newmarket December Sales. *C. Thornton.* —

MOONLIT KNIGHT 4 ch.g. Silly Season 127–Thieves Honour (Hook Money 124) (1980 12fg 1981 10fg 12f³) tall gelding; well beaten in maiden and minor races. *A. Jarvis.* —

MOONVEIN 4 ch.f. New Member 119–Idyll-Liquor (Narrator 127) (1980 10g 8.5f⁴ 10s 10.8fg 8fg³ 1981 11.7d 15.5f 18g) leggy, unfurnished filly; poor plater; stays 1m; acts on firm going. *G. Fletcher.* —

MOORES MIRACLE 3 ch.c. Manacle 123–Treasure Flower 67 (Donore 119) (1980 6d* 6g 1981 6g 6g 7g 6g) robust, good sort; good mover; won maiden race at York in good style as a 2-y-o; had stiffish tasks in handicaps in 1981 and finished in rear at Newmarket, York, Sandown and Nottingham; should stay 7f. *R. Armstrong.* —

MOORESTYLE 4 b.c. Manacle 123–Guiding Star 70 (Reliance II 137) (1980 7f* 8g² 7f* 6d* 6.5d² 6g* 5f* 7g* 7v* 1981 6g 6g² 6.5fg* 5d³ 8fg² 6fg* 7g* 7v*) 132
   If the old maxim 'Nature abhors a vacuum' possesses more than a grain of truth it is possible that 1982 will reveal a colt capable of filling adequately the gap left by the departure of Moorestyle, whose magnificent career has now ended with his retirement to the National Stud. Possible but not certain, for while each season has its stars few shine as brightly as Moorestyle who had a rare combination of qualities. Raced in an adventurous fashion that did great credit to his connections, he matched toughness with brilliance, courage with consistency and showed a versatility which came as a breath of fresh air in a period when the top horses tend to be campaigned at specialised distances after their two-year-old seasons. Would that there were more like him.
   It took Moorestyle some time to come to himself in 1981 and early on he and his admirers had to endure a bit of buffeting. Twice replated before the Duke of York Stakes in May, he looked fit but didn't particularly impress in the paddock and was in trouble by halfway, finally finishing a modest sixth to King of Spain after losing two shoes during the race as well. Less than a month later he was involved in the sort of freak accident which a fatalist could see as proving Evelyn Waugh's assertion 'Fortune is the least capricious of deities, and arranges things on the just and rigid system that no one shall be very happy for very long.' The

Prix Maurice de Gheest, Deauville—Moorestyle gains his first victory of the season, bettering the course record in the process

Mecca-Dante Stakes winner Beldale Flutter, second favourite for the Derby, got loose on Newmarket Heath and careered into Moorestyle, knocking him down. We have no idea how many horses were exercising there that morning but it was a singular piece of ill-luck that the two concerned in the collision should have been top-class colts. As it was, Moorestyle, unlike Beldale Flutter, was not seriously injured though towards the end of the year his trainer reflected that it almost certainly took him much longer to recover fully from this mishap than was thought at the time. Nonetheless on his next start, in the William Hill July Cup at Newmarket, a race he had decisively won in 1980, Moorestyle looked better beforehand than at York and showed a little more sparkle, having every chance two furlongs out before being outpaced by Marwell who beat him three lengths.

No sprinter of Marwell's calibre opposed Moorestyle in the Group 2 Prix Maurice de Gheest at Deauville three weeks after the July Cup and he won in cracking style. With penalties, allowances or both in their conditions, a number of Group 2 and Group 3 races in the European pattern of racing can have a weight range not far removed from limited handicaps. In the 1980 running of the Maurice de Gheest Moorestyle, penalised for his July Cup win, had had to hump 9-3 and give weight all round when touched off by the four-year-old Boitron whereas in 1981, not having done enough during the current season to earn a penalty, he was able to meet his nine opponents on level or favourable terms— the Cork and Orrery Stakes winner The Quiet Bidder, for instance, received only 1 lb from him. The French, to whom Moorestyle was no stranger, understandably made him an odds-on chance. After lying close up as Spoleto and Ancient Regime took them along he burst clear when asked to quicken in the last two furlongs and beat Diamond Prospect readily by a length, breaking the course record.

Moorestyle tasted defeat twice more before ending the year in a blaze of glory. Though a sparkling winner of the five-furlong Prix de l'Abbaye de Longchamp at three he seemed to find that trip too sharp at four in the William Hill Sprint Championship at York in August. Always prominent, he had no answer to Sharpo's acceleration in the last furlong and a half and came home a four-length third with Marwell also beating him. At the behest of the Horserace Betting Levy Board which had, on the recommendation of its Stallion Advisory Committee, bought twenty-five shares in him at a total cost of £1,375,000 in March, Moorestyle stepped up in distance for his next run, in the Waterford Crystal Mile at Goodwood later in the month. It was his first outing over a mile since In Fijar had beaten him a length in the previous year's Poule d'Essai des Poulains and the Board must have been delighted with his performance. Up against a miler of the highest class in To-Agori-Mou, Moorestyle was taken straight into the lead and maintained this position until the Guineas winner cruised past him a couple of furlongs from the finish and quickly went three lengths clear. It looked as if Moorestyle would be soundly beaten but with To-Agori-Mou tending to take things easy and Moorestyle rallying in fine fashion the gap between the two diminished rapidly inside the distance and was closed to half a length at the line. Moorestyle was going on so strongly that he would undoubtedly have won given a little bit further to travel and it is a testimony to his effectiveness at a mile that the

559

Diadem Stakes, Ascot—Piggott and Moorestyle always have matters under control

Greenham Stakes winner Another Realm was five lengths away third with Last Fandango, a close second to Belmont Bay in the Queen Anne Stakes, fourth.

Moorestyle wasn't headed in any of his remaining races. Paddock inspection prior to the Diadem Stakes at Ascot in September revealed his looking tremendous, scarcely recognisable as the colt that had slightly disappointed us in appearance before the Duke of York Stakes. He treated spectators to a vintage display of sprinting, putting up one of the best timefigures we have computed for a sprinter, 1.56 fast. Quickly into his stride, he never looked likely to be caught and the most anxious moment for his supporters occurred about two furlongs out when a large dog suddenly appeared on the track ahead of the field. Moorestyle, momentarily perplexed by this manifestation, propped a little but with the dog's beating a hasty sideways retreat Moorestyle was able to continue with no further distractions, winning easily by a length and a half from Crews Hill. The remainder, headed by the Hungerford Stakes winner Dalsaan and including King of Spain and Sayyaf, were well strung out. There was no unexpected excitement in the Bisquit Cognac Challenge Stakes at Newmarket the following month and Moorestyle gained his second convincing win in the event. Setting a reasonable gallop from the word go, he quickened at the foot of the hill and had the race in safe keeping from there on; hard as Dalsaan, Motavato and Kittyhawk tried they were unable to reach him and he passed the post one and a half lengths to the good.

On the final day of the Longchamp season Moorestyle in the Prix de la Foret and Ardross in the Prix Royal-Oak brought the total of French Group 1 races won by English-trained horses in 1981 to six, the other successes being Recitation's in the Poule d'Essai des Poulains, Madam Gay's in the Prix de Diane, Glint of Gold's in the Grand Prix de Paris and Marwell's in the Prix de l'Abbaye. In addition to this high tally of wins, second places were achieved in the Poule d'Essai des Pouliches, the Prix Jacques le Marois, the Prix de l'Abbaye and the Grand Criterium and only four of the twenty-three French Group 1 races lacked participants from this side of the Channel. Interestingly the scale of the assault on these events has increased from an annual average of nineteen runs in the mid-'seventies to one of thirty-three during the past three years. This is not the result of a sudden improvement in the quality of horses trained here, or of a dramatic deterioration of those in France which might make the races easy to win—the number of high-class performers in each country doesn't vary by a great amount from year to year. The cause is the renewed and large-scale enterprise displayed by English-based trainers, nineteen of whom sent runners in 1981. Paradoxically this development has occurred at a time when the prize money for many of the twenty-three races has been in the doldrums—since 1976 two have fallen in value and nine have risen by 20 per cent or less. The Prix de la Foret has done better than most, being worth 40 per cent more in 1981 than it was five years previously, but it is still one of the least well-endowed of the forty-two Group 1 events in England and France. Be that as it may, the 1981 running of the race exemplified

560

the current trend. There were two English challengers besides Moorestyle, namely Belmont Bay and Sharpo, while a third, Dalsaan, was withdrawn on the day because of the very heavy ground. The remaining six runners included the Prix Jean Prat winner Cresta Rider, the Tote Lockinge Stakes and Prix du Moulin runner-up Hilal, the Prix de la Jonchere winner Lou Piguet and the consistent but luckless Diamond Prospect. Drawn on the outside, Moorestyle pinged out of the stalls and within the space of a furlong and a half Piggott crossed him over to the far rail and let him bowl along in front. Entering the straight he was travelling strongly on the bridle ahead of Belmont Bay, who was finding the pace a bit hot, Hilal and Diamond Prospect; Sharpo had made up ground after a slow start and was beginning a run up the centre of the course. As the rest struggled to keep up with him Moorestyle drew further clear and with Piggott's giving him a couple of reminders in the last furlong and riding him right out he won convincingly by four lengths from Lou Piguet, who made up a considerable amount of leeway in the closing stages. Diamond Prospect was a neck back in third, Belmont Bay fourth and Sharpo, who ran out of stamina, fifth. Moorestyle became the third horse to win the Foret two years running, following Fine Top and Sanedtki; it was a glorious finale to his career and quite an emotional one, for the crowd gave him a rousing reception and even Piggott, not noted for displays of emotion, appeared visibly moved. Interviewed by a member of the French Press Piggott remarked that Moorestyle was the best sprinter/miler he had ridden; coming from the man who rode Thatch that is praise indeed.

Moorestyle (b.c. 1977)	Manacle (b 1964)	Sing Sing (b 1957)	Tudor Minstrel
			Agin the Law
		Hard and Fast (b 1957)	Hard Sauce
			Boodley
	Guiding Star (ch 1969)	Reliance II (b 1962)	Tantieme
			Reliance III
		Star of Bethlehem (b 1959)	Arctic Star
			Merry Xmas

It would be difficult to improve on Moorestyle's record of thirteen wins from twenty-one starts, mostly in the best company and on all types of going, but despite this his scheduled syndication at £55,000 a share had to be scrapped due to lack of interest by potential shareholders. Instead, twenty-nine nominations were put on offer at 8,000 guineas each, half payable on the arrival of a live foal, and because of oversubscription a ballot for these was held early in November. The relative absence of enthusiasm for the shares is presumably explained not only by the fact that Moorestyle didn't hit form until late in the year but also by the commercially unfashionable nature of his pedigree. By the good five-furlong

Bisquit Cognac Challenge Stakes, Newmarket—another easy win for Moorestyle; Dalsaan is second

Prix de la Foret, Longchamp—a fine finale to a glorious racing career

sprinter Manacle, now in Australia, out of a Reliance II mare that won over fifteen and a half furlongs at Folkestone as a four-year-old, Moorestyle may not be bred in the purple compared with a number of stallions but that won't stop his siring winners even if they fail to fetch vast sums at the sales. He only needs to impart half his qualities to his offspring to do well. It is not as though his pedigree is devoid of attractive elements. The Sing Sing sire line has enjoyed great success in recent times with such as African Sky, Jukebox, Music Boy, Mummy's Pet, Song and Manacle himself all getting plenty of winners; nor is Moorestyle the only good horse to have come from his dam's family. Whilst Guiding Star has produced just one winner besides Moorestyle—the Huntercombe colt Hunter Star who scored in Trinidad—her dam, Star of Bethlehem, developed into a useful staying handicapper in Ireland after winning over six furlongs at two and was a half-sister to a number of winners here and abroad, notably Khalkis, successful in the Eclipse Stakes. The third dam, Merry Xmas, finished second in the Irish Cambridgeshire and was a half-sister to the dam of the smart stayer Prince Hansel.

Moorestyle cost 4,000 guineas as a yearling and became one of the biggest assets of his owners, Moores International Furnishings Ltd., as well as a great asset to British racing. A tall, lengthy, quite attractive colt and an excellent mover, he sweated up on occasions in his final season. Sweating or not, Moorestyle always ran his heart out; 1982 will be the poorer for his absence and we wish him well in his new career. *R. Armstrong.*

Moores International Furnishings Limited's "Moorestyle" (L. Piggott)

MOOR HOUSE 4 b.g. Laxton 105–Asicion 89 (Above Suspicion 127) (1980 5h   **74**
5d* 6fg* 6s   1981 6s 7d 6g 6g⁴ 6g 6f)   strong gelding; sprint handicapper; stays
6f; acts on a firm and a soft surface; often blinkered; sold 1,500 gns Doncaster
September Sales. *M. H. Easterby.*

MOOR OF STREETS 4 b.f. Spanish Gold 101–Pensong 84 (Pendragon) (1980   —
NR 1981 6d 8g 8f) bad plater; has worn blinkers. *J. Wilson.*

MOORVIEW 2 b.c. Mansingh 120–Sicalaine 52 (Sica Boy 132) (1981 5v 5s 5d)   **62**
May 6; rangy colt; half-brother to Precious View (by Sit In The Corner), winner
of sellers over 6f and 7f; dam placed at up to 1m; showed a little ability on second
and third outings, on third beaten 5 lengths by Hazim when fifth of 13 in maiden
race at Redcar in October; not sure to stay beyond 5f. *J. Etherington.*

MOQUETTE 2 b.f. Moulton 128–Miss Tweedie 114 (Aberdeen 109) (1981 6g 8g)
Apr 4; 3,900F; lengthy filly; half-sister to quite useful 1977 2-y-o 5f winner
Knight (by Realm); dam very useful at 6f and 7f; behind in maiden races at
Newmarket in October. *R. Hollinshead.*

MORALITY STONE 4 b.c. Ragstone 128–Miss Casanova 84 (Galivanter 131)   **85**
(1980 8fg 12f 12s* 12s³ 13.3d 10f 12g³ 11.1g* 12g² 12g   1981 12fg 12g 11s* 12d*
12fg* 12fg³ 12.5fg² 14d 10d² 12g 12v) robust, well-made colt; fair handicapper;
successful at Newbury (twice) and Carlisle; awarded London Gold Cup on disqualification of Malvan for first Newbury win and beat King's Ride a neck in
Summer Cup for second; should stay 1¾m; has won on a firm surface but is ideally
suited by some give in the ground; has run creditably for an amateur rider. *P.
Mitchell.*

MORAYSHIRE 4 b.c. Royal Palace 131–Outward Bound 79 (Sing Sing 134)   **97**
(1980 8fg³ 10.2g 8fg* 1981 9g² 8fg 10fg⁴ 8fg 10.2g 9g) lengthy colt; good mover;
useful performer; excellent ½-length second of 9 to Hard Fought (gave 3 lb) in
Earl of Sefton Stakes at Newmarket in April, pair finishing 8 lengths clear; well
beaten in varied company afterwards; stays 9f; acts well on firm ground; sold to
W. Musson 4,000 gns Newmarket Autumn Sales. *B. Hobbs.*

MORCAL 2 ch.f. Dragonara Palace 115–Evening Shoe 111 (Panaslipper 130)   **56**
(1981 5fg³ 5d 5g² 5g³ 5f 6f³ 7g 5g) May 24; 5,000Y; leggy filly; half-sister to
several winners, including useful sprinter Grey Shoes (by Grey Sovereign); dam
third in Irish 1,000 Guineas; placed in varied company, including selling on final
occasion; blinkered sixth outing and looks ungenuine. *N. Callaghan.*

MORE HARMONY 3 br.c. Morston 125–Melody Maid (Tudor Melody 129)   **84**
(1980 6d 7f³ 7f² 7v 1981 12fg 11.7g³ 10fg* 12g⁴ 13.3g 12fg* 11f² 12fg 11.7d)
quite attractive colt; won minor event at Nottingham in June (shade cleverly by
a neck from Dragon Steed) and handicap at Ascot in July (got up close home and
beat Hunston by ½ length); stays 1½m; very well suited by a firm surface; ran
moderately fifth start and was rather disappointing in blinkers eighth outing;
didn't handle track well at Bath on second outing. *J. Bethell.*

MORE HASTE 2 ch.f. Morston 125–Fly For Home 78 (Habitat 134) (1981 7g)   —
Apr 17; 8,000Y; well-grown filly; third foal; half-sister to useful 3-y-o Belloc (by
Wollow), successful at up to 1m; dam, 1½m winner, is half-sister to very smart
out-and-out stayer Biskrah; 25/1 when in rear in 16-runner maiden race won by
Clymene at Leicester in October; bred to stay 1½m+. *J. Bethell.*

MORE HEATHER 2 b.f. Ballymore 123–Lady Tyrrel (Pall Mall 132) (1981 6d   **97**
7f² 6g⁴ 7d*) Apr 13; 10,000Y; second foal; dam Irish 11f winner and daughter
of prolific winner-producer Northern Beauty; 25/1-winner of 18-runner Park
Stakes at the Curragh in October, leading 2f out and keeping on to score by 2½
lengths from Santa Roseanna (gave 5 lb); in frame previously in maiden races at
Naas (length second to Tinktura) and Navan (2 lengths fourth to Legs and
Things); will be very well suited by 1¼m+. *L. Browne, Ireland.*

MORE LAVENDER 4 b.c. Reliance II 137–Lavender Girl 92 (Petition 130)   **65**
(1980 8v 12s² 13g 12d² 1981 12g 10f* 10g 11.7f) tall ex-Irish colt; won handicap at Leicester in June; stays 1½m; acts on any going; sold 5,200 gns Ascot
October Sales. *J. Dodd.*

MORE OATS 3 b.c. Morston 125–Dashing Diana (Silver Shark 129) (1980 8fg   **85**
8g 1981 12g² 12g⁴ 12fg² 11fg² 11.7h² 12g* 12g² 12s³ 12s* 12d²) quite attractive,
well-made colt; good mover; won maiden race at Goodwood in September and
handicap at Folkestone in October, latter cleverly by ½ length from Oklahoma
Star; runner-up on 6 other occasions; will stay beyond 1½m; acts on any going;
tended to hang third start; sold 21,000 gns Newmarket Autumn Sales before final
start and will be trained in 1982 by A. Klimscha in France. *G. Harwood.*

MORGAN'S CHOICE   4 ch.c. Reliance II 137–Piave (Alcide 136)   (1980 8f   **68**
10.2fg 11f 12g 10.1g³ 11.7s* 13.1f³ 13.3d   1981 12.2fg 11.7d 11.1s 12.2fg 13.1f
14fg* 13.1h* 14fg)   small, well-made colt; got up in last strides to win handicaps
at Salisbury and Bath in August; stays 1¾m; acts on any going; usually wears
blinkers; sold 8,100 gns Ascot October Sales.   *J. Dodd.*

MORGAN'S PEARL   4 ch.c. Gulf Pearl 117–Morganette (Tudor Music 131)   **—§**
(1980 10.2d³ 10s 12.5h³ 11.7f 12fg² 11fg² 14d* 14g² 16fg³ 14g* 18d 14g²   1981
14g⁴ 16g)   useful sort; not a good mover in his slower paces; fair handicapper at
his best; started slowly both starts early in 1981, on second occasion being left
100 yds and appearing not to be too willing to race; stays well; acts on any going
with possible exception of very soft.   *W. O'Gorman.*

MORIAS   3 ch.c. Sallust 134–Purple Goddess 69 (Red God 128§)   (1980 6fg 6s   **71**
1981 8d 8d 8s⁴ 8fg* 8f² 7.2v 7g 8s)   short-coupled colt; showed improved form
when beating Naif by 3 lengths in maiden race at Salisbury in August and when
2 lengths second to Mianach Oir in minor event at Thirsk in September; will stay
1¼m; suited by a firm surface; sold 3,500 gns Newmarket Autumn Sales.   *C.
Brittain.*

MORICE   3 b.c. Morston 125–Ardice 91 (Hard Tack 111§)   (1980 NR   1981 8d³   **81**
10d* 12s⁴ 10d*)   8,600Y; well-made colt; half-brother to fairly useful stayer
High Dice (by High Hat); dam 6f to 1m performer; landed the odds in maiden
race at Salisbury in May and minor event at Leicester in November, on latter
course beating Cavalier Servente by 1¼ lengths when having first race for 5
months; will stay beyond 1¼m; has raced only on a soft surface.   *R. Price.*

MORKULLA (SWE)   6 ch.m. Royal Park 114–Canary Bird 79 (Bleep-Bleep 134)   **39**
(1980 10.1fg³ 8f 10g² 10s⁴ 10g* 10fg 10fg 12.5s³   1981 10.2s 8d 12s³ 10.8fg 8fg⁴
10fg 10f 10g 10.6s 10s³)   leggy mare; inconsistent plater; stays 1½m; seems to act
on any going; often wears blinkers; good mount for an inexperienced rider.
G. Fletcher.

MORNING AFTER   2 gr.c. Busted 134–Flying Nelly 107 (Nelcius 133)   (1981   **81** p
7g 8g)   Mar 30; 62,000Y; strong, well-made, quite attractive colt; third foal;
closely related to 3-y-o 1¼m winner Neltino (by Bustino) and half-brother to 1979
2-y-o 5.8f winner Nelly Do-Da (by Derring-Do); dam stayed 13f but was best at
1m to 1¼m; put up a pleasing first effort when 25/1 for maiden race at Newmarket
in October, finishing just over 6 lengths fifth of 21 to Count Pahlen; favourite for
another Newmarket maiden race later same month but was hidden along some
way from home and never looked dangerous, eventually coming home tenth of 30
to Farioffa after being eased; bred to stay middle distances; worth another chance.
G. Harwood.

MORNING ENQUIRY   4 ro.f. Perhapsburg 112–Dawn Reign 82 (Perfect   **—**
Sovereign)   (1980 8g 10.1g 6g 12g   1981 10g 10f 16d 10f 15.5f 12g 10s)   of little
account.   *P. K. Mitchell.*

MORNING LEE   7 br.g. Arctic Judge 94–Stacy Lee 95 (French Beige 127)   **—**
(1980 NR   1981 14fg 14fg 19s)   poor performer nowadays; stays well; acts on
any going; sold to D. Wintle 1,800 gns Ascot November Sales.   *P. Cundell.*

MOROCCO BOUND   2 gr.c. Roan Rocket 128–Hoppity 72 (Negotiation)   (1981   **—**
7d)   May 1; 3,200Y; brother to 11f winner Space Dancer; dam half-sister to
smart sprinter Hopiana; unquoted when out of first 10 in 22-runner minor event
won by Starbells at Chepstow in October.   *S. Woodman.*

MORSE PIP   2 b.c. Bay Express 132–Code of Love 99 (Bleep-Bleep 134)   (1981   **76**
5g 5s³)   May 6; fourth foal; brother to 3-y-o 5f winner Telegraph Boy, and half-
brother to a winner in Austria; dam sprinter; 3 lengths third of 20 to Illicit in
maiden race at Warwick in October; may stay 6f.   *S. Woodman.*

MORSTONS MAID   2 ch.f. Morston 125–Dairy Queen 76 (Queen's Hussar 124)   **—**
(1981 5fg 6fg 7fg 6d)   Mar 27; 6,600F; lightly-made filly; half-sister to 2 winners
by Birdbrook, including very useful Parlour Game, successful at up to 8.5f; dam
placed from 6f to 1¾m; well behind in maiden and minor races.   *W. Bentley.*

MORTON THE HATTER   5 b.g. Galivanter 131–Andromache 112 (Delirium   **57**
126)   (1980 NR   1981 15.5d² 16g⁴ 16g² 15.5f³ 16d*)   staying handicapper; won
amateur riders race at Lingfield in August; acts on a soft surface.   *M. Masson.*

MOSES SAMPSON   3 b.g. Bold Lad (Ire) 133–Countess Decima (Sir Gaylord)   **64**
(1980 NR   1981 5fg 8g 6fg 6f 7f* 7fg³ 6g 5s⁴ 5s)   11,000Y; stocky gelding; half-
brother to 3 winners, including French sprinter Miliar (by Thatch) and fairly
useful 1m to 1¼m winner Countess Lor (by Lorenzaccio); dam never ran; beat
Tara's Chieftain by ¾ length in maiden race at Folkestone in August; in frame in

handicaps afterwards; stays 7f; acts on any going; blinkered nowadays; trained by R. Smyth first 2 starts. *R. Hannon.*

MOSHI-MOSHI 2 ch.c. Cawston's Clown 113–Copthorne Polly (Double-U-Jay 120) (1981 7g) Apr 12; good-topped colt; second foal; dam showed no worthwhile form; unquoted, in need of race and very green when last of 17 to Northleigh in maiden race at Leicester in September. *M. Bradley.* —

MOSSAT 4 gr.g. Busted 134–Abettor 103 (Abernant 142) (1980 10fg 12g2 10g* 10f3 1981 12g 10d) strong gelding; won maiden race at Newmarket in 1980; well beaten both starts at 4 yrs; will stay 1¾m; has run respectably for an apprentice. *B. Palling.* —

MOSSDRUM 3 br.f. Meldrum 112–Mosscombe (Mossborough 126) (1980 NR 1981 12f 15.5g 16.5g 12d*) half-sister to quite useful 1969 2-y-o 6f winner Sly Look (by Derring-Do) and to another winning 2-y-o; dam, poor maiden, is sister to top-class stayer Morecambe; beat Cybrandian by 2½ lengths in maiden race at Hamilton in October; best run at 1½m on a soft surface; blinkered first outing. *E. Weymes.* **64**

MOSSMORRAN 2 b.g. Kinglet 98–Black Print (Compensation 127) (1981 5d3 5g 5g4 6f 6fg 7f) bad plater. *J. Berry.* **43**

MOSSO 2 b.f. Ercolano 118–Mossy 95 (Mossborough 126) (1981 5.8g* 6d* 7.3s) Feb 3; 5,600Y; well-made filly; good walker; half-sister to 5f and 7f winner McMartim (by Decoy Boy) and to a winner in Norway; dam won at up to 1½m; got up close home to win maiden race at Bath and 8-runner Kingsclere Stakes at Newbury in June, running on under very strong pressure to beat Broadway Lodge a short head in latter; not seen out again until October, when remote fifth of 8 to Last Feather in £6,300 event also at Newbury; bred to stay middle distances. *J. Toller.* **81**

MOSSWERN 2 ch.f. Towern 96–Mossy's Delight 44 (Mossy Face 98) (1981 5s2 5s*(dis) 5g2 5s 6g 6f* 7fg2 7g2 7f2 5f 7g 8d) May 7; leggy, lightly-made filly; third foal; dam poor plater; successful in sellers at Beverley in April (no bid) and Ripon in June but was disqualified in July from her Beverley win after failing dope test; bought in 2,800 gns after outclassing her 13 rivals at Ripon; subsequently ran very well when second in minor event at Catterick and in nurseries at Beverley, excelling herself when running Meeka Gold to a head in August on ninth outing; will stay 1¼m; acts on any going; thoroughly genuine. *G. Toft.* **80**

MOTAVATO (USA) 3 br.c. Apalachee 137–Lovelight 112 (Bleep-Bleep 134) (1980 5f2 5f* 6d2 6f* 6g4 1981 7g* 8g 8.5d3 8g* 7g3) **122**
Few horses impressed more with their physical progress from two to three than did Motavato before the Tote European Free Handicap at Newmarket in

Tote European Free Handicap, Newmarket—an authoritative performance by Motavato who beats The Quiet Bidder (rails) and Tina's Pet (centre)

April. He had altered considerably over the winter and developed into a big, powerful, most attractive individual; really commanding. He impressed with his powerful, long stride going to post, too, and he ran a race in keeping with his improved appearance. After being held up towards the rear of the field he was switched to the outside and produced a terrific run up the hill that always looked like carrying him to the front. He won with great authority from The Quiet Bidder, Tina's Pet and Bel Bolide, and in doing so came right into the reckoning for the Two Thousand Guineas in which his stable also had Kind of Hush, winner of the previous day's Ladbrokes Craven Stakes. Motavato was a disappointment in the Guineas, in which he was stable-jockey Cauthen's choice and started second favourite. He looked to have lost quite a lot of condition and he never promised to get into the contest, finishing tenth of nineteen behind To-Agori-Mou. He also looked a bit light before the Diomed Stakes at Epsom in June but considering he's not an ideal type for the course he didn't do too badly to finish third to Saher.

Motavato was plagued with all sorts of troubles after the Diomed, including a pulled muscle in his quarters and two bouts of ringworm, and he was off the course for nearly four months. He made a full recovery, returning to run two more excellent races at Newmarket. He looked tremendously well again when reappearing in the Petition Stakes in September—a mile race confined to three-year-olds who hadn't won a pattern race in 1981—and he won by three quarters of a length from Lady Lorelei; we gained the impression that at seven furlongs he would have won with much more authority. The opposition was a good deal stiffer in the Bisquit Cognac Challenge Stakes over that distance the following month and in finishing third behind Moorestyle and Dalsaan, Motavato put up his best-ever performance. Looking perhaps even better than he had in the Petition Stakes, he was held up and had plenty to do when the leaders quickened but so well did he buckle down to his task when pulled to the outside passing the Bushes that he was beaten only three lengths by Moorestyle.

We haven't seen many of Apalachee's offspring over here yet, and Motavato is easily the best of them. We wrote up Apalachee as the most promising horse for

Mr R. E. Sangster's "Motavato"

years after his very comfortable win over Mississipian in the 1973 Observer Gold
Cup but he ran only twice at three and wasn't seen out after finishing third to
Nonoalco in the Two Thousand Guineas, starting the shortest-priced favourite in
forty years. Apalachee has taken time to establish himself as a stallion but is
doing quite well now. He was also represented in Britain in 1981 by the useful
mile-and-a-quarter handicapper Indian Trail and in his native country his winners include the high-class 1980 two-year-old High Counsel and Apalachee Honey,
one of the leading two-year-old fillies of 1981. Motavato's dam Lovelight was an
extremely game sprinter who won the Northumberland Sprint Trophy and was
second to Red Alert in the Stewards Cup. Motavato is her third foal and first
winner. She has since produced the Empery filly Flicker to a Flame who ran with
considerable promise when third in a maiden race at Newmarket in October and
looks sure to win races.

Motavato (USA) (br.c. 1978)	Apalachee (b 1971)	Round Table (b 1954)	Princequillo
			Knight's Daughter
		Moccasin (ch 1963)	Nantallah
			Rough Shod
	Lovelight (gr 1971)	Bleep-Bleep (b 1956)	Hard Sauce
			Curtsey
		Lovely Beam (gr 1956)	Infatuation
			Port Beam

Motavato stays in training, and should pick up another decent race or two if
he gets conditions in his favour. His optimum distance is probably seven furlongs
and he's well suited by a strongly-run race in which he can be held up and produced with a late run. He has such a long stride that he will always be seen to
best advantage on a galloping track but he doesn't appear to be beholden to the
state of the going; he seems to act on any. In view of the problems he has had and
his relative inexperience it is quite likely that the best of him is yet to come. He
won't have to improve much to win a pattern race of some description, and he
must be kept on the right side. *B. Hills.*

MOTHER OF THE WIND 3 b.f. Tumble Wind–Navy Colors (Bupers) (1980 —
5f 5.8g 6d⁴ 7d 7fg* 7d 8.2g⁴ 7g 1981 8s 7fg 8g 7f 10fg 8d) quite attractive,
well-made filly; plater nowadays; not disgraced over 1¼m; possibly needs a sound
surface. *C. Nelson.*

MOTIVATE 4 b.c. Run The Gantlet–Motionless 109 (Midsummer Night II 117) —
(1980 11d⁴ 13d² 13s⁴ 11d 14.6d 1981 12.5g 15g 18.1d 12s) big, useful sort; has
shown no form for some time; stays 13f; yet to race on a firm surface; has worn
blinkers; trained by W. H. H. Williams part of season. *G. Kindersley.*

MOTORCENTRE 3 b.g. Abwah 118–Arctic Dream 75 (Arctic Slave 116) (1980 —
5s 5d 7d 1981 5d 6g) of little account. *S. Holland.*

MOTOR-PLAN SUPREME 3 b.c. Tudor Rhythm 112–Lady Amber Hope —
(Golden Surprise 65) (1980 5.1g 5d 1981 7g 7fg 6fg 6g 9d) useless; has worn
blinkers. *D. Thom.*

MOTT THE HOOPLE 3 gr.g. Goldhill 125–Belligerent 74 (Roan Rocket 128) 66
(1980 5s 5s³ 5s 7fg 6g 6g* 5f 6g 6f 1981 5s 5d² 7d² 7g* 7.2s³ 6g² 8.2f² 7.6fg 6d
8.2f³ 7g² 6d* 8.2d) neat gelding; won seller at Doncaster in May (bought in
2,500 gns) and handicap at Hamilton in September; stays 1m; acts on any going,
except possibly very soft; best in blinkers. *P. Haslam.*

MOU-FERNI-TYCHI 2 br.c. Royal and Regal–Vesper Bell (Larkspur 128) 93
(1981 6fg² 7fg³ 6fg 6g) Mar 25; IR 26,000Y; handsome colt; brother to French
3-y-o Glittertind, a very useful 7f winner in 1980, and half-brother to fairly useful
7f to 1½m winner Carnlea House (by Reindeer); dam ran once; looked very
promising when 1½ lengths second of 12 to Torrey in maiden event at Goodwood
in July; failed to win in 3 subsequent starts; had very stiff task in valuable nursery at Newmarket in October on fourth outing and in circumstances ran very
well to finish 5½ lengths eleventh behind Vaigly Star; will stay 1m; sure to win
a race in 1982. *G. Harwood.*

MOUFIDE 2 b.c. African Sky 124–Supreme Punishment (King of the Tudors 129) —
(1981 5s) Apr 9; fair sort; first foal; dam Irish 9f winner; 25/1 and in need of
race when ninth of 18 to Town Flier in maiden race at Nottingham in September.
A. Hide.

MOUHANNED 3 b.c. Ashmore 125–French Bird (Guersant 129) (1980 7fg 7g 72 d
8g 1981 8.2s* 10d 9s 8g 8f 8.2f) compact, good sort; made nearly all and
showed much improved form when winning maiden event at Nottingham in April

MOU

in good style by 7 lengths from Marine; about 7 lengths sixth of 9 to Cut Above
in White Rose Stakes at Ascot later in month, best subsequent effort; stays 1¼m;
evidently acts well on soft going; usually a front runner; ran wide on bend final
start; sold to R. E. Peacock 3,900 gns Newmarket Autumn Sales. *C. Brittain.*

MOUNTAINEER 2 br.g. Legal Eagle 126–Madzoro (Combat 123) (1981 5v³ 5s **50**
5g 8g 8.2d 7d) Mar 24; 2,750Y (privately); lightly-made gelding; half-brother to
1978 2-y-o 5f winner Solidor (by Songedor); dam never ran; poor maiden; has
worn a tongue strap; blinkered final start. *H. Bell.*

MOUNTAIN HIGH 3 b.f. Mount Hagen 127–Deep Brook (Wolver Hollow 126) **79**
(1980 NR 1981 10.5s² 10fg 12.3g³ 10.4d² 10fg⁴ 9f* 8d² 7g) 46,000Y; rangy
filly; second foal; half-sister to fair 1978 2-y-o 5f winner Honiara (by Pitcairn);
dam, unraced, comes from same family as Hanu and Tin King; ran very
promisingly when ¾-length second of 4 to Pipina in £4,000 event at York in May;
didn't really fulfil that promise, but on same course in September beat Dollymixture Boy by 5 lengths in maiden race; not certain to have stayed 1¼m; acted
on any going; wore blinkers in her later races; didn't impress in paddock on
occasions; retired to stud. *B. Hills.*

MOUNTAIN LODGE 2 b. or br.f. Blakeney 126–Fiddlededdee 94 (Acropolis 132) **– p**
(1981 6g) Mar 15; compact filly; sister to moderate 12.5f winner Governor's
Camp, and half-sister to 1¼m and 2m winner Fiddle-Faddle (by Silly Season);
dam third in Park Hill Stakes; 13/2, made no show when behind in 17-runner
maiden race won by Merlin's Charm at Newmarket in October; evidently quite
well thought of but will need a good test of stamina to show to advantage. *J.
Dunlop.*

MOUNTAIN MONARCH 4 b.g. Royal and Regal–Sally of the Hills 80 **73**
(Sallymount 125) (1980 10.8v* 12fg 16f³ 17.1fg³ 16fg* 19g³ 16g³ 18.1g²
19g³ 16d 1981 15.5d⁴ 18fg⁴ 16g² 16g³ 16s 16f² 16g 19fg 16d 19s) quite attractive, strong gelding; staying handicapper; acts on any going; suitable mount for
a boy; wears blinkers; inconsistent. *S. Woodman.*

MOUNTAIN RECORD 3 ch.c. Jukebox 120–Grindlewald 76 (Le Levanstell 122) **60**
(1980 5f 5fg⁴ 6s 5f² 1981 6s⁴ 6fg* 5fg) workmanlike colt; attracted no bid after
winning seller at Haydock in April (made all); seems to find 5f on sharp side and
stays 6f; seems to act on any going. *J. Hardy.*

MOUNTAIN THYME 3 b.f. Lochnager 132–Elspeth Ann 68 (Pardao 120) **–**
(1980 5f 5g⁴ 5g 1981 6g 8g 7fg 5fg) lengthy filly; only poor form, including in a
seller on final start (blinkered); sold 500 gns Doncaster August Sales. *M. W.
Easterby.*

MOUNTCOUT 2 ch.f. Manado 130–Beaume (Faraway Son 130) (1981 5v 6f **–**
8d) Mar 25; 1,700Y; leggy, lightly-built filly; first foal; dam unraced granddaughter of 1,000 Guineas and Oaks winner Sweet Solera; bad plater. *P. Butler.*

MOUNT EATON 8 b.g. Florescence 120–Golden Pumpkin 86 (Monet 127) **–**
(1980 6v 6f 7f³ 7g 9.5f 1981 13fg 9g 13f 12f 12f 10.5s) strong ex-Irish gelding;
has been fired; poor performer nowadays; stays 7f; acts on any going; usually
wears blinkers; has won for an apprentice. *J. Leigh.*

MOUNT ELIZA 3 b.f. Welsh Saint 126–Shantung Lassie (Shantung 132) (1980 **41**
5s⁴ 5s 6fg⁴ 5.1fg² 5.1fg² 6g 6f 1981 6s 6fg⁴ 6g⁴ 6g⁴ 7fg 6fg² 7g) compact filly;
plater; stays 6f; acts on a firm surface. *G. Blum.*

MOUNT-GLOW 5 br.g. Aglojo 119–Mountain Queen 58 (Sovereign Path 125) **–**
(1980 NR 1981 12s 12g) lightly-made gelding; tailed off in maiden race at
Beverley and minor event at Carlisle in first part of season. *R. Whitaker.*

MOUNT IRVINE BAY 3 b.c. Targowice 130–L'Eaulne (Busted 134) (1980 **–**
5.8fg 1981 8.2s 12s) well-made colt; behind in maiden races; sold 520 gns
Newmarket Autumn Sales. *J. Bethell.*

MOUNT MAGIC 5 ch.g. Mount Hagen 127–Magical Music (Sing Sing 134) **44**
(1980 12fg³ 12f 12h 12.2fg 12f 8.2d 15d 9s 1981 11g* 12s 8g 10fg* 11g³ 10f 12fg⁴
9g 12.2fg 11d 12d 12g) leggy gelding; plater; won at Edinburgh in April (bought
in 950 gns) and Beverley in June (attracted no bid after trotting up in apprentice
race); stays 1½m; suited by top-of-the-ground. *R. Allan.*

MOUNT PARNASSUS 4 b.g. Mountain Call 125–Greek Serenade (Grey
Sovereign 128§) (1980 8.2s 8fg 10.1s 10fg 8f 8g 7g 1981 10.1fg⁴ 12f) workmanlike gelding; plater; probably stays 1¼m; suited by a sound surface; often
blinkered. *M. Pipe.*

568

MOURNDYKE 9 ch.g. Klondyke Bill 125–Moura (Mourne 126) (1980 14fg 14fg —
16fg 11d 1981 16s) poor staying handicapper; bandaged nowadays. *R.
Atkins.*

MOUSEHOLD 5 ch.h. Silly Season 127–Sedulous 96 (Restless Wind) (1980 8f* **54**
8f* 8f 8fg³ 7fg⁴ 8g 1981 8g 8.2f³ 8f³ 8fg) strong, lengthy horse; poor handicapper; suited by 1m; acts on firm going; good mount for a boy; often makes the
running; sold 640 gns Newmarket Autumn Sales. *I. Walker.*

MOYBROOK 5 br.h. The Brianstan 128–River Moy (Niagara Falls 104) (1980 **74**
5d 6v² 6g³ 7f² 6f² 6f* 6d³ 6fg² 6fg² 6d² 6d 6fg² 6s 7.2d 6fg⁴ 1981 6v³ 6s 6g 6d³
6g² 8fg 6f*) strong horse; quite a modest handicapper; won at Nottingham in
July; stayed 1m; acted on any going; sometimes blinkered; gave trouble at start
on occasions and was destroyed after fracturing skull in stalls at Redcar in July.
G. Richards.

MOYSPRUIT 2 br.g. Import 127–River Moy (Niagara Falls 104) (1981 6d 5v³) **72**
Apr 17; strong gelding; half-brother to 3 winners, including fair 6f winner Moybrook (by The Brianstan); dam chaser; 20/1 when strong-finishing 3 lengths third
to Master-Blow in 21-runner maiden race at Haydock in October; refused to enter
stalls when withdrawn at Redcar later in month; should stay 6f. *G. Richards.*

MR FLUOROCARBON 2 ch.c. Morston 125–Western Air 101 (Sound Track 132) **81 p**
(1981 6s) Apr 18; 58,000Y; well-made, quite attractive colt; half-brother to
3-y-o 1¼m winner Western Knight (by Grundy) and 3 other winners, including
very smart 1975 2-y-o 5f performer Western Jewel (by Tower Walk); dam best
at 5f; 14/1, showed up well to distance and was eased once he started to weaken
when 9½ lengths fifth of 11 to Slightly Dangerous in Duke of Edinburgh Stakes at
Ascot in October; will stay at least 1m; should improve. *R. Laing.*

MR FOODBROKER (NZ) 6 b.g. Grey William 61–Sweet Delight (Ribotlight **?**
100) (1980 NR 1981 15.5f²) New Zealand-bred gelding; easily won NH Flat
races at Hereford and Market Rasen in 1980; second favourite when 2½ lengths
second to easy winner Centreline in minor event at Folkestone in July; stays
well; acts on firm going. *D. Kent.*

MR FRESHNESS 3 ch.g. Tumble Wind–Beba Saint (Welsh Saint 126) (1980 **71**
6g 6s⁴ 5f 7g 7.2g 6s 6fg³ 7d³ 6d 1981 8f 8f⁴ 8.2fg³ 10f*) workmanlike gelding;
showed improved form when beating Crackaway by ½ length in maiden race at
Ripon in August; suited by 1¼m; probably acts on any going; blinkered final
outing at 2 yrs. *E. Carter.*

MR GOLD SPUR 2 ch.c. Windjammer (USA)–Everlasting Rose (Continuation **64**
120) (1981 5s 6fg² 6f³ 5f 6fg 5d) Apr 22; 2,400Y; third reported foal;
placed over 5f at 2 yrs in Ireland; placed in maiden auction events at Warwick
in June (neck second to Warm Order) and Folkestone in July (2 lengths third of
15 to Panatella); towards rear in nurseries last 2 starts; suited by 6f and will
probably stay further. *R. Akehurst.*

MR GUS 3 b.g. Tower Walk 130–Chapeau Bleue (High Hat 131) (1980 5s 5f² —
5fg² 5h⁴ 5fg² 6fg* 7g* 7f² 1981 7d 8f 8g) compact, good-bodied gelding; carries
plenty of condition; quite useful at 2 yrs; little worthwhile form in 1981, including
in a valuable seller; well suited by 7f and should stay 1m; sweated up badly but
ran well final outing in 1980. *W. O'Gorman.*

MR KEEPS 2 b.c. Orange Bay 131–Keeps (Roan Rocket 128) (1981 8s 10.2g) —
May 16; 5,200Y; second foal; half-brother to fairly useful 1980 2-y-o 5f winner
I'll See You (by Averof); dam twice-raced half-sister to very smart miler Buz
Kashi; unquoted when in rear in maiden race at Warwick in October and minor
event at Doncaster the following month. *D. Marks.*

MR MALLORY (USA) 3 b.g. Bold Hour–West Bramble (Krakatao 130) (1980 **63**
7fg 7d 7d² 8d 1981 7d 7g⁴ 8g 7.2s⁴ 7f³ 7fg 7g² 7fg 7.6s 6f) lengthy, lightly-made
gelding; in frame in varied company, including selling; not sure to stay 1m; has
run well in blinkers; sweated badly and was well beaten eighth start. *J.
Fitzgerald.*

MR MARSHALL 3 b.c. Swing Easy 126–Insurance 106 (Yellow God 129) (1980 **80**
NR 1981 7d² 8.2d² 7fg) 11,500Y; strong, useful sort; second foal; half-brother
to 6f winner Cover Note (by Song); dam won twice over 6f at 2 yrs; showed
promise in first 2 races, when second to Praetorian Guard in maiden race at Newcastle in April (ran green and went down by a neck) and to Chief Admiral in
amateur riders event at Haydock in May (heavily-backed favourite but facing a
stiffish task); ran poorly in blinkers when odds on for maiden event at Redcar

later in May, and wasn't seen out again; stays 1m; possibly needs some give in the ground. *M. H. Easterby.*

MR MISCHIEF 3 ch.g. Sharp Edge 123–Talarea 76 (Takawalk II 125) (1980 — 6fg 5fg 5d 1981 6d 7.6g 5.3fg) lightly-made gelding; behind in varied company; sometimes blinkered. *M. Masson.*

MR MONEY BAGS 3 b.g. Pieces of Eight 128–My Sweet Afton 73 (Javelot 124) — (1980 6g 7d 8.2s 1981 10s 10s 11d 10g 16.9fg) compact gelding; poor plater. *R. Morris.*

MR MOONRAKER 4 b.g. Idiot's Delight 115–Burlington Belle (Galivanter 131) — (1980 8f 10.1fg 8fg* 8g⁴ 8.3d² 8g 13.3d 10.2v 1981 12s 13.1g 17.1d) tall, narrow, unfurnished gelding; not certain to stay 13f; acts on a firm and a soft surface. *Miss S. Morris.*

MR PERFECT 2 b.g. Mummy's Pet 125–River Palace (Royal Palace 131) (1981 — 7fg) Mar 12; 2,700F; leggy gelding; third live foal; half-brother to 1½m winner Bazz's Boy (by Dragonara Palace); dam ran only twice; unquoted, looked green going down and was soon behind in race when tailed-off last of 15 to Super Sunrise in minor event at Newcastle in August. *E. Weymes.*

MR PERUSER (USA) 2 b.c. Mr Prospector–Speak Softly (The Pruner) (1981 94 5.1f* 6fg 6fg⁴ 7fg 6f³ 6fg) Mar 8; $65,000Y; small colt; excellent mover; first foal; dam never ran; beat Come On The Blues by ¾ length in 12-runner maiden event at Yarmouth in June; not disgraced in most of his subsequent races and would have finished closer with a trouble-free run when 1¾ lengths third of 8 to Pomegranate in small race at Ripon in September; should stay 7f (had stiffish task under top weight in nursery when tried at trip); sweated up sixth outing but ran well. *L. Cumani.*

MR PETIT 4 gr. or ro.g. Zeddaan 130–Balholm 61 (Le Levanstell 122) (1980 45 10s* 8f 9f⁴ 10h 10g 13.8g³ 12fg⁴ 10fg* 13.8fg² 1981 13s 11s³ 12g 10d 10g 12f 12.2fg² 12f) narrow, lightly-made gelding; plater; stays 1½m; probably acts on any going; has been tried in blinkers; has worn bandages; races with head held high. *P. Asquith.*

MRS CURRIE 2 b.f. He Loves Me 120–Nanno (Busted 134) (1981 7fg 6d 8d³ 74 8s*) Mar 23; 10,500Y; lengthy filly; third live foal; half-sister to fair 1½m winner Instant Prime (by Simbir); dam unraced half-sister to Gulf Pearl; got home by a short head from Broken Rail when winning 17-runner maiden race at Warwick in October; will stay 1¼m; acts on soft going. *W. Hastings-Bass.*

MRS HONG KONG 2 b.f. Town Crier 119–Perfect Lady 85 (Sovereign Lord 120) 61 (1981 5fg 5d* 5g³ 6fg 6g⁴ 6d 5f⁴) May 13; 1,000Y; leggy, lightly-made filly; turns front feet in; half-sister to 3-y-o 6f seller winner Wembley Market (by Malicious); dam won over 5f at 2 yrs; plater; retained for 1,800 gns after justifying favouritism by 7 lengths from Fine Touch in 6-runner event at Warwick in April; modest fourth at Lingfield and Wolverhampton subsequently; stays 6f; acts on a soft surface. *M. Blanshard.*

MRS HUBBARD 3 ch.f. Silly Season 127–Mrs Paddy 69 (Acropolis 132) (1980 63 7g 10.2s 1981 8d* 8d³ 10d³ 8s 10.2s 11.7fg 10d 12g³ 10s⁴ 12d) strong filly; dead-heated with Affair in Paris in minor event at Cagnes-sur-Mer in February; in frame in claiming handicap and seller much later on; stays 1½m; acts well on a soft surface; sold to M. Tompkins 925 gns Ascot December Sales. *W. Hastings-Bass.*

MR SINCLAIR 3 b.g. Lochnager 132–Lively Lassie (Never Say Die 137) (1980 — 5d² 5f³ 5fg 6s 6d 1981 8g 5d⁴ 6s 8f 8f 8d) rather unfurnished gelding; good walker; ran best race on second outing; best form at 5f; possibly unsuited by very soft ground; sold 1,200 gns Doncaster September Sales. *M. H. Easterby.*

MRS LEADBETTER 3 b.f. Birdbrook 110–Cricket Bat 87 (Indigenous 121) 66 (1980 5fg 5fg² 5fg 5g 5s² 1981 7g 6g 6f 6f* 6f² 6f 6f 6g) workmanlike filly; won maiden race at Nottingham in July by 5 lengths from Henrietta Maria; ran well in handicap next time; will possibly stay 7f (needed race and wasn't entirely disgraced over trip); has run creditably on soft going but seems ideally suited by firm; often apprentice ridden; sold 800 gns Newmarket Autumn Sales. *G. Pritchard-Gordon.*

MRS LOVE IT 2 b.f. Rapid River 127–Fibeel 72 (Most Secret 119) (1981 5s 5d² 70 5g³ 5fg 5fg 6d⁴ 6g 6d) Mar 18; lightly-made filly; first foal; dam won three 5f races; in frame in maiden and minor events and is capable of winning if dropped to selling company; stays 6f; possibly needs some give in the ground; blinkered final start. *G. Lockerbie.*

MR SNUGFIT 4 b.g. Jukebox 120–Sinzinbra 112 (Royal Palace 131) (1980 — NR 1981 12d) has a round action; poor maiden on flat though has won over hurdles. *M. W. Easterby.*

MRS PALMER 3 b.f. Martinmas 128–Harford Belle 97 (Track Spare 125) (1980 **75** 5g 5fg² 5.8g* 5fg* 6fg³ 7.3fg⁴ 6d* 1981 6g 7d 8f 8g³ 7.3d 8d⁴ 6g⁴ 6s³ 6d³) lengthy, lightly-made filly; ran best races on last 3 starts when in frame in handi-caps at Leicester (2) and Nottingham in the autumn; stays 1m, but is better at shorter distances; acts on a firm and soft surface; blinkered eighth start. *R. Hannon.*

MR SPENCER 4 b.c. Charlottown 127–Monk's Mistress (Rasputin 83) (1980 — 13s 12s 14g 14g 1981 12.5s 8fg 7g 10s) light-framed colt; poor plater; has worn blinkers. *Miss A. Hill-Wood.*

MRS PENNY (USA) 4 ch.f. Great Nephew 126–Tananarive (Le Fabuleux 133) **?** (1980 7.3fg² 8fg³ 8fg³ 10.5g* 12g² 10.5d⁴ 12f* 12f 1981 12d⁴ 12f 10s 10s² 11f 11f* 12f 10f) lengthy filly; excellent mover; third foal; dam useful winner at up to 1¾m; a very game, genuine and admirably consistent filly in 1980 when she won Prix de Diane de Revlon at Chantilly and Prix Vermeille at Longchamp and was placed in several important races; didn't run to form first 2 starts in 1981 in England, finishing a long way behind Master Willie in Coronation Cup at Epsom and Pelerin in Hardwicke Stakes at Royal Ascot; subsequently sent to USA and won Queen Charlotte Handicap at Meadowlands in October by ¾ length from Office Wife; also ran well when 3 lengths second to Match The Hatch in Man-hattan Handicap at Belmont Park in September; suited by 1½m; acted on any going; trained by I. Balding first 2 starts; visits Northjet. *T. Skiffington, USA.*

MR SUGAR (USA) 2 b.g. Sadair–Bird Guide (Sunrise County) (1981 6fg 6fg — 6d) Feb 27; $3,700F, $63,000Y; well-made gelding; third foal; half-brother to 2 minor winners; dam, winner of claiming races over 6f and 1m, is half-sister to Irish Sweeps Derby winner Malacate; showed ability in maiden races at Epsom in September and Doncaster the following month on last 2 starts; will stay at least 1m. *J. Sutcliffe.*

MRS WILLIE 2 b.f. St Paddy 133–Theodolinda 63 (Lombard 126) (1981 5f 5.3f — 6g 7fg 8s 7.6s) Mar 20; workmanlike filly; first foal; dam lightly-raced half-sister to smart 1967 2-y-o Lowna; unquoted when behind in maiden and minor events. *M. Masson.*

MUBHEDJ (USA) 2 b.c. Key To The Mint–Colombade 89 (Boldnesian) (1981 **87** 6f³ 6fg 6fg² 6g* 6fg⁴ 5.3d) Apr 15; $100,000Y; compact, fair sort; second foal; dam won 3 times at up to 1m; justified favouritism in good style in small race at Windsor in August, scoring by 4 lengths from Dance In Rome after making much of running; also in frame in Chesham Stakes at Royal Ascot (1¼ lengths third of 9 to Cajun) and in 2 more minor events at Windsor, on final occasion finishing 3 lengths fourth of 11 to Epithet in September; almost certainly finds 5f too sharp and is bred to stay at least 1m; ran badly after becoming upset in stalls on second outing. *H. T. Jones.*

MUDSLINGER 3 gr.g. Roan Rocket 128–Galosh 86 (Pandofell 132) (1980 NR — 1981 16.9s⁴) big, rangy gelding; half-brother to 3 winners, including good 1979 Northern 2-y-o Silly Prices (by Silly Season), successful at up to 1m; dam needed long distances; needed race and wasn't disgraced when 20 lengths fourth of 12 to Shooting Butts in maiden event at Wolverhampton in May, only outing. *Sir Mark Prescott.*

MUD WALK 2 gr.f. Godswalk 130–Mudela (Sir Gaylord) (1981 5g⁴ 5g 5f) Apr **77** 25; IR 7,200F; quite a useful sort; half-sister to a number of winners here and abroad, including useful but inconsistent middle-distance performer King for a Day (by Crowned Prince); dam useful winner in Italy and half-sister to Gyr; showed enough speed on first 2 outings to suggest she would win a race but un-fortunately had to be destroyed after breaking down at Leicester in June. *E. Eldin.*

MUFFET'S GOLD 3 b. or br.f. Cavo Doro 124–Little Miss Muffet 102 (Tourment — 132) (1980 NR 1981 10d 11.7g 12f 13f) lightly-made filly; half-sister to several winners here and abroad, including very useful middle-distance filly Seventh Bride (by Royal Record II), herself dam of Oaks winner Polygamy; dam best at 1½m; poor form in maiden and minor events. *H. Candy.*

MUJIB (USA) 2 b.c. L'Enjoleur–Native Street (Native Dancer) (1981 7g) **83 p** Mar 30; $850,000Y; strong, useful-looking colt; good walker and mover; closely related to a stakes-placed winner by Buckpasser, and half-brother to numerous winners, notably smart stakes winners Royal and Regal and Regal and Royal (both by Vaguely Noble), successful at up to 9f and 1m respectively; dam, good winner at 2 yrs and 3 yrs, won at up to 8.5f; third favourite, never far behind and looked to be running on really well towards finish when 7½ lengths fifth of 18 behind General Anders in £4,100 event at Ascot in September; will stay 1¼m; clearly has ability and should improve and win races next year. *J. Tree.*

MULATA 2 gr.g. Mandrake Major 122–Raffinata (Raffingora 130) (1981 6g) May 2; 1,900F, 1,900Y, 8,400 2-y-o, resold 1,000 2-y-o; second produce; half-brother to fair 1980 2-y-o 6f winner Foresters Lad (by Porto Bello); dam never ran; 33/1, finished well beaten in 26-runner maiden race at Doncaster in November won by Perang Tejam. *G. Lockerbie.* —

MULLENAN 6 br.g. Master Buck–Midgy (Polyfoto 124) (1980 14g 1981 12.2fg 16f 12.3g 15.8g 16f) strong gelding; staying maiden on flat though has won over hurdles; sold 3,000 gns Ascot October Sales. *T. Barron.* —

MULLINS BAR 2 ch.g. Cawston's Clown 113–Hyperion Rose 54 (Cash and Courage 116) (1981 5fg4(dis) 5d4 5g* 6fg 7g 7fg 7.3d 7d) Mar 14; 3,000F, 4,600Y; compact, good quartered gelding; half-brother to a winning plater; dam half-sister to Lucky Brief; started on terms for first time when showing improved form to win 7-runner maiden race at Hamilton in June easing up by 4 lengths from La Babooshka; again lost a lot of ground at start in £4,200 nursery at York in August on fifth outing, but soon recovered and kept on to finish creditable fifth, 3¾ lengths behind Shining Start; evidently stays 7f; always behind when blinkered sixth start. *G. Hunter.* 75

MULL OF KINTYRE 3 ch.c. Murrayfield 119–Geordie Lass 58 (Bleep Bleep 131) (1980 5d3 5fg 5d* 6s 5g 5fg3 5s4 5d 5d 6g2 6s 5d4 1981 5s 6fg 7g 5s 6d4 5g2 8f2 10fg 7fg4 8f 7d 6g) smallish, good-bodied colt; plater; stays 1m but not 1¼m; seems to act on any going; sold 2,300 gns Newmarket Autumn Sales. *P. Haslam.* 54

MUMMY'S ANGEL 2 br.f. Mummy's Pet 125–Charonne 87 (Charlottown 127) (1981 5d 5s 5fg 5.8f3 6g 7f) Mar 25; 2,300Y; a useful-looking filly but is only a poor plater. *T. Marshall.* 53

MUMMY'S DELIGHT 2 b.f. Mummy's Pet 125–Damsel 86 (Pampered King 121) (1981 5g 5g 6fg4 5g2 5.1fg* 6d* 6fg 5f2) Apr 6; 3,800Y; lightly-made filly; fifth foal; dam 2-y-o 1m winner; sold out of P. Haslam's stable 3,000 gns after getting up close home to win 6-runner seller at Yarmouth in June; bought in 2,600 gns after winning easing up in another Yarmouth seller the following month; not disgraced when second of 4 to Cedrella in nursery at Hamilton in September; suited by 6f; has won on a firm and a soft surface. *H. Collingridge.* 60

MUMMY'S GAME 2 b.c. Mummy's Pet 125–Final Game 83 (Pardao 120) (1981 6fg3 6fg* 6fg* 7fg4 6fg3 5fg* 6g 6g2 6s4) Apr 12; workmanlike colt; second foal; closely related to 3-y-o 5f winner Boldwin (by Song); dam won over 1¼m; successful in minor events at Windsor and Redcar in July and in 5-runner all-aged race at Beverley in September; put up best effort at Beverley, producing a good turn of foot to win by ¾ length from Maryland Cookie after having a fair bit to do at halfway; ran well next 2 outings in nurseries at Newmarket, particularly when ½-length second of 17 to Bold Fort under top weight in October; best at 5f and 6f; didn't run up to best on soft going (though may have been feeling his hard season); usually held up; a tough, genuine and useful colt. *W. O'Gorman.* 103

MUMMY'S PLEASURE 2 b.c. Mummy's Pet 125–Par Bloom (Pardal 130) (1981 7g4 6g2) May 8; 6,200Y; tall, lengthy colt; half-brother to 3 minor winners and successful jumper Alick (by Abwah); dam placed at up to 11f in France; in frame in big fields of maidens at Newmarket in October, finishing 7 lengths fourth to Simply Great and 1½ lengths second to Not For Show; stays 7f; should win a maiden race at one of the minor meetings. *P. Haslam.* 89

MUMMY'S PRIDE 3 b.f. Mummy's Pet 125–Wontell 80 (Buisson Ardent 129) (1980 5d 6g 6fg4 6d 5g 1981 8.2g 7f 5fg 6fg 10s 9d 8s) compact filly; plater; not without ability but is temperamental and untrustworthy; often blinkered. *J. Edmunds.* —

MUMMY'S STAR 7 br.g. Mummy's Pet 125–Dycord 81 (Royal Record II) (1980 22.2fg 16.1d 1981 12s2 12f 10fg 12fg4 12f 16d 16f3 16h3) poor handicapper nowadays; stays 2m; best form on a sound surface; suitable mount for an amateur rider; usually wears blinkers. *S. Mellor.* 46

MUMMY'S TREASURE 3 b.c. Mummy's Pet 125–Gold Bloom 72 (Klondyke **79** d
Bill 125) (1980 6g 5fg* 5d 6s 5g 1981 5fg 5fg 5fg* 5fg* 6fg 5g 5fg 5g 5d)
compact colt; ran best races when making all in handicaps at Chester and
Wolverhampton in July; speedy and probably best suited by an easy 5f; acts on
a firm surface; trained until after sixth outing by P. Haslam. *Mrs J. Reavey.*

MUMRUFFIN 2 b.f. Mummy's Pet 125–Java Sparrow 96 (Mossborough 126) **96**
(1981 5d* 5g* 5fg⁴ 5fg³ 5g 5s) May 2; small, useful-looking filly; half-sister to
several winners, including very useful 1972 2-y-o Claudius (by Romulus) and
fairly useful 7f and 1m performer Amadina (by Great Nephew); dam won from
1m to 1¼m; a speedy filly who won both her starts in June, 15-runner race at
Sandown (unchallenged by 5 lengths from Lindsey) and 5-runner minor event
at Lingfield (made all to win by 2½ lengths from Silojoka, who received 8 lb);
sweated up badly when third favourite for 6-runner Molecomb Stakes at Goodwood in July and went off too fast for her own good, fading to finish 3 lengths
third to Prowess Prince after holding substantial lead to below distance; barely
stays 5f; on toes in paddock when soundly beaten last 2 starts; lacks scope and
may not train on. *F. J. Houghton.*

MUMTAZ WAY 3 gr.f. Sovereign Path 125–Thaya (St Paddy 133) (1980 NR —
1981 8g 8f 8fg) 7,400Y; small, short-backed filly; second foal in this country;
dam, half-sister to top-class sprinter Green God, won twice in Italy; behind in
maiden and minor races at Thirsk, Bath and Kempton. *T. Robson.*

MURCOT 2 br.f. Royal and Regal–Relic Spirit (Relic) (1981 6d* 6fg 6f³ 6.3fg **93**
8d 7.6d⁴) Mar 30; IR 6,400Y; leggy, close-coupled filly; third foal; half-sister to
useful 1980 Irish 2-y-o 5f performer Heart n' Soul (by Bold Lad, Ire) and a winner
in Austria; dam second 4 times over sprint distances in Ireland; 25/1 when
winning 20-runner maiden race at Navan in June by a length from Valentia;
length third of 7 to Okavango in Irish Chorus Stakes on same course in July and
was beaten only 2 lengths when fourth of 13 to Furry Berg in valuable nursery at
Gowran Park in October; will stay 1m. *J. Bolger, Ireland.*

MURILLO 5 b.g. Windjammer (USA)–Fuiseog (Eudaemon 129) (1980 7d* 7.2d2 **99**
8g³ 7fg 8g 7f² 6s² 7s² 6d² 7s² 1981 6v* 7d* 7d³ 6s* 6f 6fg 6fg 6d) neat gelding;
useful handicapper; enjoyed a good season and won at Ayr, Newcastle and
Kempton; beat Celtic Halo comfortably by 3 lengths in Victor Wild Stakes on
last-named in May; ran creditably in good handicaps on several other occasions;
best at up to 7f; acts on any going but is very well suited by some give in the
ground; wears blinkers, and a small bandage on his off-fore. *J. W. Watts.*

MURMANSK (USA) 3 b.f. Nijinsky 138–Mohmond (Jaipur) (1980 6g 7fg² 7g² **67**
8fg⁴ 7d² 7g² 1981 9s⁴ 10d 8f³) compact filly; good mover; in frame on most
outings, but doesn't find much under pressure and is one to be wary of; should
stay 1¼m; probably acts on any going. *H. Cecil.*

MUSANDAM 2 ch.c. Mount Hagen 127–Trekker 86 (Grey Sovereign 128§) —
(1981 8g) June 2; 6,200Y; third living foal; half-brother to useful 5f winner
Jameson (by Huntercombe); dam won twice over 1¼m; unquoted and backward
when always behind in 27-runner minor event won by Dudley Wood at Newmarket in October. *M. Masson.*

MUSHREF (USA) 3 b.c. Key To The Mint–Forever Amber (Bold Lad, Ire 133) **106**
(1980 6fg² 7g* 6f³ 1981 8g 7.6d* 8g² 7f 8fg⁴ 7f³ 8s) compact, quite attractive
colt; good mover; beat Goodbye Starter by 6 lengths in £2,900 event at Chester
in May, going well throughout and being ridden clear in straight; in frame afterwards in Balmoral Castle Stakes at Ayr (½-length second to Buffavento), Group 3
Oettingen-Rennen at Baden-Baden (fourth behind Aspros) and £6,400 event at
Goodwood (4 lengths third of 5 behind Belmont Bay), seeming to show improved
form in last-named race in September; fifth of 12 to Esclavo in Group 2 Premio
Vittorio di Capua at Milan in October; stays 1m; probably acts on any going;
sent to race in USA. *H. T. Jones.*

MUSICAL BRIDGE 3 ch.g. Thatch 136–Sweet Sound 74 (Sound Track 132) —
(1980 6fg 6s 6d 1981 8g) strong gelding; little worthwhile form in maiden and
minor events and a handicap. *M. Chapman.*

MUSICAL LADY 2 ch.f. Music Boy 124–Pritillor 93 (Privy Councillor 125) —
(1981 5d 5fg 6g 8.2s) Mar 8; 2,000F, 3,400Y; fourth produce; half-sister to 1m
and 1½m winner Robert Adam (by Mansingh); dam best at up to 1¼m; little

worthwhile form in varied company, including selling; sweated up badly fourth outing; trained part of season by M. Blanshard; sold 360 gns Ascot November Sales. *C. Nelson.*

MUSICAL MELODY 3 ch.f. Cornuto 111–Musical Ayre (Raoul 87) (1980 NR 1981 7.6g 7g) lightly-made filly; first known foal; dam maiden hurdler; last in maiden races at Lingfield and Salisbury (sweating) in June. *B. Swift.* —

MUSICAL MINX 3 b.f. Jukebox 120–Battling Bessie (Typhoon 125) (1980 6g* 7fg 7fg³ 6fg 1981 5s³ 5d⁴ 6d³ 5.8g 5s³ 5d⁴ 6f² 7f⁴ 7f² 6d 6g² 6f² 6f² 6d) useful sort; quite a moderate handicapper; in frame most outings; stays 7f; acts on any going; sometimes blinkered; ran moderately fourth start. *C. Nelson.* **70**

MUSICAL PRINCE 8 br.g. Prince Consort 121–Toccata (Kythnos 126) (1980 NR 1981 10d 12g 12f 10d 12d²) strong gelding; poor handicapper nowadays; stays 1¼m; acts on any going; has been tried in blinkers; sold 1,300 gns Ascot September Sales. *W. Musson.* —

MUSICAL PRINCESS 4 b. or br.f. Cavo Doro 124–Toccata (Kythnos 126) (1980 10f⁴ 10.6d 10.6s 12s 1981 12g 12g 12g 10.2f 10f³ 10g 12.3fg⁴ 10fg³ 12f) compact filly; plating-class maiden; stays 1¼m; seems to act on any going. *E. Weymes.* **54**

MUSICAL SCORE 2 ch.c. Music Boy 124–Acknowledgement (Fleet Nasrullah) (1981 7g² 7g) Apr 19; 6,800Y; attractive colt; half-brother to a winner in Italy by My Swallow; dam unraced daughter of $122,000 earner Tinkalero; led 1f out in 22-runner maiden race at Newmarket in October but couldn't hold Rocamadour's challenge and went down by 1½ lengths; not disgraced when 5½ lengths sixth of 15 to Ivano in Houghton Stakes on same course later in month; stays 7f; can win in ordinary maiden company in 1982. *G. Pritchard-Gordon.* **87**

MUSIC CITY 3 gr.c. Town Crier 119–Floating Melody 101 (Tudor Melody 129) (1980 7d² 1981 6g³ 7d² 6fg⁴ 7.6s* 7fg 7.3d³ 7s⁴ 6g* 6s) well-made colt; won maiden race at Chester in August (by 12 lengths) and handicap at Leicester in October (beat Perdiccas a short head); in frame most other outings; stays 7f; not disgraced on a firm surface, but clearly acts well on soft going; sold to M. Bradley 7,400 gns Newmarket Autumn Sales. *P. Walwyn.* **77**

MUSIC LOVER 2 b.c. Gay Fandango 132–In The Clover (Meadow Mint 120) (1981 6fg⁴ 6g*) Apr 17; 7,000Y; quite attractive colt; first foal; dam won over 7f at 2 yrs in Ireland; having first run for 3 months, confirmed promise shown on debut when winning 18-runner maiden race at Newmarket in October by ¾ length from Beldale Lustre, showing considerably more resolution up hill than runner-up; will stay 1m; should win again. *P. Walwyn.* **92**

MUSIC NIGHT 4 ch.c. Jukebox 120–Directrice (Zank)′ (1980 6v⁴ 5g 5fg 6fg 6fg* 5g³ 5g 6s³ 5g⁴ 6d 1981 6g⁴ 6fg² 6f 6f² 5g³ 5g 6f* 7fg 5f 6f 5g* 5fg 6s 6d 5g) sturdy colt; former plater; won handicaps at Pontefract in August (made all) and Ayr in September; stays 6f; acts on any going; best in blinkers; has run respectably for an apprentice; suited by enterprising riding tactics. *D. Chapman.* **63**

MUSIC STREAK (DEN) 3 b.c. Music Boy 124–Dawn Streak 65 (Derring-Do 131) (1980 5.5g* 7g* 8d 1981 8g* 8g² 6g 6g* 6g* 5d) strong, medium-sized, useful sort; third known foal; half-brother to fair 5f winner Night Owl (by Burglar), subsequently a good winner in Hong Kong; dam showed only poor form; won £5,000 event in Denmark and £6,400 event in Sweden before finishing in rear in Grand Criterium at Longchamp as a 2-y-o; successful in 1981 at Klampenborg in May and August and at Taby in September, beating Buster Brown by ½ length after making all in valuable Taby International Sprinter Stakes on latter course; finished towards rear behind Marwell in William Hill July Cup at Newmarket and Prix de l'Abbaye de Longchamp, but showed tremendous speed to lead for 3f in latter in October; speedy, but evidently stays 1m. *S. Jensen, Denmark.* **116**

MUSKOKA 2 b.f. Hotfoot 126–Miss Dallas 89 (March Past 124) (1981 6d) Mar 8; lightly-made, smallish filly; first foal; dam won from 1¼m to 1½m; 10/1 and fit, never really on terms when ninth of 23 to Dalmally in maiden race at Leicester in November; lacks scope. *G. Harwood.* —

MUSKY 2 ch.f. Owen Dudley 121–Camusky 77 (Charlottown 127) (1981 8d 7g) Mar 20; robust filly; third foal; half-sister to Lonely Signorita (by Hotfoot), winner over 7.5f and 10.6f, and to a winner abroad; dam placed over 1½m; in rear in maiden races at Wolverhampton and Leicester in October. *W. Wharton.* —

MUSLAB (USA) 2 ch.c. Stage Door Johnny–Forever Amber (Bold Lad, Ire 133) — (1981 8d) May 13; 92,000Y; second living foal; half-brother to 3-y-o Mushref (by Key To The Mint), a winner at up to 7.6f; dam, winner over 7.1f in Ireland, is daughter of Irish Oaks winner Ambergris; 14/1 when well behind in 23-runner maiden race at Leicester in November won by Roanoke River. *P. Walwyn.*

MUSODO 2 b.f. African Sky 124–Ginkgo (Green God 128) (1981 5d 6f 6f 5g) — Apr 23; IR 3,800F, IR 5,200Y; fair sort; half-sister to winning 3-y-o sprint plater Veeya (by Deep Diver); no worthwhile form, including in sellers; exported to Barbados. *P. Rohan.*

MUSTAPHA 3 ch.g. Warpath 113–Piccalilli 78 (Klairon 131) (1980 NR 1981 71 10.2g 12g⁴ 16fg* 16.5g 16s) tall gelding; poor walker; fourth foal; brother to 1¾m winner Mortadella and to a winning plater; dam seemed to stay 1¾m; got up under strong riding to beat Tallishire Homes a neck in maiden race at Beverley in June; suited by a test of stamina; acts on a firm surface; sold out of C. Thornton's stable 6,400 gns Doncaster August Sales after third outing and didn't run well afterwards (needed race fourth start). *M. Camacho.*

MUSTIKA (USA) 3 b.c. Torsion–Bosuns Strike (Bosun) (1980 5f* 5g 5d 5g 61 1981 6fg 5g 8f 6fg 5g² 5s) neat colt; well beaten in 1981, except when 4 lengths second to Miss Import in handicap at Wolverhampton in September; failed to negotiate bend properly at Catterick on fourth start; should stay 6f if ridden with restraint but seems best at 5f; best run on firm ground; wore bandages final start as a 2-y-o; sold 1,550 gns Newmarket Autumn Sales, probably for export to Scandinavia. *E. Eldin.*

MY ADRIANA 2 ch.f. Roman Warrior 132–La Melodie 77 (Silly Season 127) (1981 6g 6g) Mar 17; 5,600F; big, strong filly; second produce; half-sister to a winning plater; dam stayed 1m; unquoted when in rear in maiden races at Yarmouth in September (backward and decidedly green) and Newmarket in October. *G. Pritchard-Gordon.*

MY ANNASSAR 3 b.f. Queen's Hussar 124–My Polyanna 81 (Polyfoto 124) 62 (1980 NR 1981 11.5f 12fg⁴ 14g³ 14fg² 14fg² 15.5g 10s³ 10g) very lightly-made filly; first foal; dam, thoroughly genuine and consistent performer, stayed 1½m; placed in maiden races at Sandown, Yarmouth (2) and Nottingham; stays 1¾m; ran moderately in blinkers sixth start; trained most of season by J. Hindley. *M. Ryan.*

MY BALLY-ANNA 6 b.m. Another River 89–Balidium 69 (Psidium 130) (1980 — 12fg 1981 8fg 7fg) bad maiden; has been tried in blinkers. *N. Guest.*

MY BLUE HEAVEN 2 br.f. Blue Cashmere 129–Christmas Pageant (March Past — 124) (1981 5d 5g) Apr 23; 2,000F, 2,200Y; half-sister to useful middle-distance handicapper Christmas Post (by Tycoon II); dam showed no form; in rear in minor events at Brighton in May (slowly away) and Lingfield in June. *S. Matthews.*

MY BLUETTE 3 b.f. My Swallow 134–Bluets 74 (Hitting Away) (1980 8fg 8d 58 1981 12.2g 8fg* 9g² 10.8s 10d 10.2g) lengthy, unfurnished filly; first past post in sellers at Warwick in August (bought in 1,400 gns) and Wolverhampton in September; beat Bourienne a shade comfortably on latter course but was placed second for interference 2½f out (claimed out of J. Etherington's stable £2,500); behind in better company afterwards; stays 9f; acts on a firm surface; wears blinkers. *W. Charles.*

MYCENAEN 2 ch.g. Be My Guest 126–Street Light 120 (St Chad 120) (1981 6g 80 5fg 7fg⁴ 7g 8s²) Mar 13; IR 154,000Y; strong, full-quartered gelding; second living foal; half-brother to useful 5f and 6f winner Highland Light (by Home Guard); dam smart sprinter; in frame in maiden races at Salisbury and Warwick, wearing blinkers when 4 lengths second of 17 to Fort Garry on latter course in October; suited by 1m and soft going; gelded at end of season. *J. Tree.*

MY CHALLENGE 3 b.g. Copte–Wolfsburg (Neckar) (1980 5fg 5s 7g 5d 7fg 8fg — 8.2g 8d 8.2s 1981 7d 8d 10s 13fg 16.9fg 16fg) narrow, light-framed gelding; poor form in varied company, including selling; ran best race over 1¼m; blinkered last 3 starts in 1980. *K. Bridgwater.*

MY CONNOISSEUR 2 b.c. Connaught 130–Honerone 85 (Sammy Davis 129) — p (1981 6s⁴) Apr 10; 13,000Y; quite attractive, good sort; brother to 2,000 Guineas runner-up and Derby third Remainder Man, and half-brother to a winner; dam stayed at least 1m; unquoted, wasn't disgraced when never-dangerous 13 lengths fourth of 15 to Ellerene in maiden race at Newbury in October; will do better over further in 1982. *J. Holt.*

Star Stakes, Sandown—My Dad Tom (right) gets up in the last strides to beat Lavender Dance

MY DAD TOM (USA) 2 b.c. My Dad George–His Lady Fair (Tom Fool) (1981 **109**
5d 5d* 5d 6g* 5f* 6f* 5f* 6fg 5g* 7fg³ 7s 6g) Feb 26; $15,000F, 7,000 gns Y;
smallish, useful sort; good mover; half-brother to 2 minor winners in USA; dam
unraced half-sister to Kentucky Oaks winner Hidden Talent and high-class 1959
American 2-y-o Heavenly Body; a very tough individual who gained his most
important success when winning for sixth time, coming through to win 8-runner
Star Stakes at Sandown in July by a short head from Lavender Dance after taking
a long time to get into top gear; had previously won at Chester, Catterick, Beverley, Pontefract (beat Algardi 5 lengths) and Bath (by 8 lengths from Justicia);
far from disgraced when length third of 5 to Treboro in Lanson Champagne
Stakes at Goodwood at end of July and ran very well when just over 4 lengths
seventh of 13 to Cajun in William Hill Middle Park Stakes at Newmarket in
October (looked tremendously well despite his hard season); only fourteenth of
15 to Let's Don't Fight in Arlington-Washington Futurity at Arlington Park in
August (eleventh start); gave impression 7f was just too far for him at 2 yrs;
seems to act on any going but is well suited by top-of-the-ground conditions; has
won 4 times for apprentice K. Willey; tough, genuine and consistent. *B. Hills.*

MY DANNY BOY 4 ch.g. Malicious–Sinecure (Parthia 132) (1980 12s 10s 16f³ —
13.8fg 14fg 13s 13g 1981 11g 12s 12.2fg 16fg 20.4fg⁴ 13.8fg) strong, compact
gelding; plater; suited by a test of stamina; acts on firm going. *B. Richmond.*

MY DEAR FELLOW 2 ch.c. Tower Walk 130–Righteous Girl 93 (Right Boy 137) **99**
(1981 5s* 5d² 5g 5f³ 5s 5g⁴) May 1; 17,000 Y; smallish, strong, useful sort; doesn't
always impress in slower paces; half-brother to numerous winners, including 1980
2-y-o 5f winner Goody Goody (by Mummy's Pet); dam 2-y-o 5f and 6f winner;
driven right out to win maiden race at Wolverhampton in May by 2 lengths from
Kansas; ran well in most of his subsequent races, including when very good 2¼
lengths third of 8 to Day Is Done in Group 3 Norfolk Stakes at Royal Ascot; runs
as if he will be suited by 6f; acts on any going. *N. Vigors.*

576

Mr M. C. Talbot-Ponsonby's "My Dear Fellow"

MY DECREE 3 b.f. Noble Decree 127–My Sunny 76 (Grey Dawn II 132) (1980 —
NR 1981 8fg 8fg⁴ 8.2s 10d) 5,600Y; sturdy filly; first foal; dam won over 5f
and 13.8f; only poor form, and was unplaced in a selling handicap on final start;
should stay 1¼m; sold 700 gns Newmarket December Sales. *R. Sheather.*

MY DESTINY (USA) 2 b.f. L'Enjoleur–Carlese (Proud Clarion) (1981 5d 6fg 97
6f⁴ 6g² 7d* 7v*) Mar 17; $48,000Y; well-made, quite attractive filly; third foal;
half-sister to a minor winner; dam unraced sister to Salesian, a stakes winner at
up to 1m; improved with every race and led inside last 2f to beat Dame De Fer
a length in 19-runner maiden race at Yarmouth in September; easily bettered
that effort in 15-runner Malton Stakes at York the following month, revelling in
the very testing conditions and winning in good style by 3 lengths from Tants;
will be suited by 1¼m; best form on soft ground. *M. Albina.*

MY DOUBLETTE (HOL) 3 gr.f. Pentathlon–Darling Caroline (Ilix) (1980 NR ?
1981 7d 9d⁴ 14f 12f 12fg 9fg² 9d 9s*) tall, sparely-made filly; third foal; half-
sister to Dutch Derby winner Corral's Bond (by Good Bond), a fair middle-
distance handicapper in this country; dam third in Dutch Oaks; fourth to Sarah
Bernhardt in maiden event at Wolverhampton in May, best effort over here; sent
to Holland afterwards and won minor event at Duindigt on final outing; stays 9f;
probably acts on any going; trained by G. Huffer first 5 starts. *H. van der Kraats,
Holland.*

MYDRONE 2 b.c. Mummy's Pet 125–Wordrone (Worden II 129) (1981 5d*(dis) 105
5g* 6f* 6d³ 6f³ 6g 6s² 7g⁴) Apr 29; workmanlike colt; half-brother to smart
Lady Mere (by Decoy Boy), a winner from 5f to 1m; dam ran once; won at Thirsk
in May and August and at Beverley in June; beat 3 fairly useful animals when
gaining his third success, staying on well to beat Bright View ½ length; disqualified
in July from his first win at Thirsk, having failed his dope test; also put up 4
useful efforts in defeat, notably finishing 3 lengths third of 8 to Full Extent in

577

Mr C. Atkinson's "Mydrone"

Gimcrack Stakes at York in August and length second of 8 to Risk Taker in minor event at Redcar in October; will stay 1m; acts on any going; tough and genuine. *M. H. Easterby.*

MY EMPRESS 2 b.f. Young Emperor 133–Coral Isle (Mill Reef 141) (1981 6fg²) **60** Feb 27; 2,500F; leggy filly; first produce; dam never ran; 16/1 but fairly straight, stayed on from 2f out when ½-length second of 13 to Royal Carnival in seller at Newcastle in August, only outing. *C. Booth.*

MY EVA 2 b.f. Auction Ring 123–Ballinacurra (King's Troop 118) (1981 6d) — Mar 12; 7,000Y; second foal; dam ran once; unquoted when eleventh of 15 in maiden race won by Welsh Partner at Windsor in August. *B. Swift.*

MY FAIR ORCHID 2 ch.f. Roan Rocket 128–Cama 85 (Pardao 120) (1981 5fg⁴ **71** 5g³ 6fg 7g 5fg 5g⁴ 6fg 5fg 5d 5g 5d⁴ 5s³ 6d) Mar 22; 3,000Y; small, lightly-made filly; half-sister to winners in Holland and Hong Kong by Sharpen Up; dam won over 6f at 2 yrs; quite a moderate maiden; should stay beyond 5f; probably acts on any going; has worn a tongue strap; blinkered penultimate start. *S. Matthews.*

MY FANCY 2 ch.f. Roi Soleil 125–Pat's Fancy 82 (Falcon 131) (1981 6d 5g² 5v **72** 5d* 5g) May 10; second foal; dam stayed 7f; made virtually all to beat Central Carpets 4 lengths in 8-runner minor event at Edinburgh in October; in rear in nursery on same course later in month; should be suited by 6f; yet to race on a firm surface. *J. Berry.*

MY GODDESS 2 ch.f. Palm Track 122–Captain Frances (Captain's Gig) (1981 **63** 5g 5g 6g⁴ 6f 6g 7g) Feb 19; plain filly; second foal; sister to 3-y-o Scottish Dream, a winner at up to 15f; dam last on only start; plating-class maiden; put in best work in final 2f when 4½ lengths fourth of 17 to Saddlers Creek in minor event at Carlisle in June; needs at least 6f and will stay 1¼m (had plenty to do at weights and dwelt when tried over 7f). *J. Calvert.*

MY HABAT 2 gr.g. Habat 127–Wake Island 101 (Relic) (1981 6f 6fg 6d 7f 7g **62** 6s⁴ 8g) Apr 22; 4,600Y; strong gelding; poor mover; half-brother to several winners, including fairly useful Wide Awake (by Major Portion); dam unreliable sprinter; not disgraced in sellers fourth and sixth starts, staying on to be 5 lengths fourth of 15 to Purnima at York in October on latter; soon tailed off when last of 18 over 1m; blinkered third outing; sold 1,350 gns Newmarket Autumn Sales. *C. Brittain.*

MY JEM 3 b.f. My Swallow 134–Senna (Sica Boy 132) (1980 5fg³ 5fg* 5g* 6fg³ **73** 6g² 5fg* 5s³ 6s 1981 5d³ 6s 5.8g 5d⁴ 5fg 5fg⁴ 5f⁴ 6g* 6g 7g 6s) quite well-made filly; in frame in several handicaps and at Chester in August when blinkered first time was awarded one after finishing third behind Effect and Cudgel, first 2 having hampered her; ran moderately in blinkers twice afterwards; possibly finds 5f on sharp side and stays 6f; seems to act on any going; sold 4,300 gns Newmarket Autumn Sales. *S. Mellor.*

MY LADY BLUE 2 gr.f. Import 127–Supremelos (Supreme Sovereign 119) **—** (1981 6f) Mar 1; £1,000F (privately); first foal; dam never ran; unquoted, missed break when last of 15 to Custer in minor event at Leicester in June. *D. Ancil.*

MY LOUISE 3 ch.f. Manado 130–Molly Malone (Bold Lad, Ire 133) (1980 NR **54** 1981 7.2f² 7f 8fg 9g³ 10d 12d) 26,000Y; lightly-made filly; half-sister to 2 winners, including fairly useful 1979 2-y-o 6f winner Live Ammo (by Home Guard); dam half-sister to Hot Spark and Bitty Girl; placed in maiden race at Haydock in July (dwelt) and minor event at Wolverhampton in September; seems to stay 9f. *G. Huffer.*

MY LOVER 2 br.c. Pitskelly 122–Miss Wittington (Red God 128§) (1981 5f 5f² **111** 5fg* 5d* 5g* 5s*)

It's expecting a lot of My Lover to do as well at three as his trainer's star sprinters So Blessed, Tudor Music and Green God, yet he was certainly one of the most progressive youngsters around in 1981 and has only to maintain his rate of improvement to develop into one of the best second-season sprinters. He has already won a pattern race, the Cornwallis Stakes at Ascot in October, in good style. The field wasn't a strong one, consisting only of the maiden Golden Green and My Dear Fellow, both having their first race since June, My Lover and four fillies, the mercurial Hello Cuddles, the consistent Corley Moor, the nippy Mumruffin and the Irish challenger Sweet Side, the disqualified 50/1-winner of the Moyglare Stud Stakes on her latest start. Sweet Side had the soft ground she requires at Ascot but was never able to go the pace set by My Lover who led throughout, quickened below the distance and won by two and a half lengths from Sweet Side, receiving only one slap of the whip in the process. My Lover showed here that he's very well suited by soft going; he had won on a firm surface in the early stages of his career.

	Pitskelly (br 1970)	Petingo (b 1965)	Petition
My Lover (br.c. Feb 16, 1979)			Alcazar
		French Bird (b 1959)	Guersant
			Golden Pheasant
	Miss Wittington (b 1966)	Red God (ch 1954)	Nasrullah
			Spring Run
		Sun Cycle (b 1961)	Crepello
			Persian Wheel

My Lover had previously made a lot of progress in a relatively short time. He ran twice at Wolverhampton in August; the first time he looked backward after a two-month absence and was beaten six lengths by Run Like Mad in a minor event; then he scrambled home by a short head from Blue Emmanuelle in a £690 maiden race. He never looked back afterwards and picked up a couple of valuable nurseries prior to the Cornwallis. In the Champagne Louis Roederer Trophy at Newbury in September he seemed sure to be beaten when headed in the final furlong by Laura Jenney, who was giving him 7 lb. He showed plenty of courage though, fighting back under strong riding to win by three quarters of a length. A 7-lb penalty didn't prevent his making all in the Bloodstock and General Insurance Nursery at Newmarket nearly two weeks later. It was here he first

Cornwallis Stakes, Ascot—My Lover makes all to win from Sweet Side (not in picture)

showed he might be up to pattern-race company; he had most of his rivals, several of them speedy animals, in trouble by halfway and won impressively by three lengths from Four For Music after being clear throughout the final quarter mile.

A lengthy, quite attractive colt, My Lover was well bought as a yearling for 5,200 guineas in Ireland, only 400 guineas more than he'd fetched when sold there as a foal. He has already won over £24,000 and looks sure to win plenty more. His trainer was no doubt attracted to him as a son of Pitskelly, a very smart horse Jarvis trained to win the Free Handicap, the Jersey Stakes and Bunbury Cup, all over seven furlongs. My Lover's races have been confined to five furlongs but he should manage to stay six: his dam Miss Wittington, a poor maiden in Ireland, is a half-sister to two winning Irish stayers and a daughter of the Irish nine-furlong winner Sun Cycle. Before My Lover Miss Wittington had bred only three minor winners abroad plus a winning hurdler but she is a well-bred mare, by Red God out of a daughter of the One Thousand Guineas fourth Persian Wheel. Persian Wheel was also placed in several top fillies races, including the Coronation Stakes, and was herself a daughter of the brilliant Sun Chariot, winner of the One Thousand Guineas, Oaks and St Leger. *M. Jarvis.*

MY MARAVILLA (USA)   2 b. or br.f. Blushing Groom 131–Monade 129 **68 p** (Klairon 131) (1981 5g⁴ 6fg) Mar 28; $253,000Y; compact filly; half-sister to numerous winners in USA, notably very smart Pressing Date (by Never Bend), a stakes winner at up to 1m; dam won Oaks; took a long time to get the hang of things when 9 lengths fourth of 19 to Bahamas Princess in maiden event at Salisbury in June; never-dangerous 8 lengths sixth of 12 to Bless The Match in St Catherine's Stakes at Newbury the following month, only subsequent start; will be suited by 1¼m. *R. Hern.*

MY MONRO   2 b.f. Ancient Monro 89–Mi Lu 80 (Gilles de Retz 132) (1981 6f **46** 6f 5d⁴ 6f 5fg 8fg 8d 8s) fair sort but is only a poor plater. *S. Nesbitt.*

MY MY MARIE   2 b.f. Artaius 129–Raffmarie 78 (Raffingora 130) (1981 7g) **—** Mar 27; 34,000Y; compact, attractive filly; second living foal; half-sister to 6f and 1¼m winner No-U-Turn (by Nonoalco); dam, sister to Cheveley Park winner Pasty, stayed 6f; 33/1 and very backward when well behind in 29-runner maiden race at Newmarket in October won by Chalon. *B. Swift.*

MY POLSTAR 2 b.c. Tickled Pink 114–Polita 86 (Constable 119) (1981 5.8d —
5fg) Apr 4; fourth living foal; dam best at 5f; unquoted when in rear in maiden
races at Bath in June and Windsor in July. *M. McCormack.*

MY RAJAH 4 b.g. Martinmas 128–Gala Belle (Galivanter 131) (1980 6d 8g 10f² —
8g² 8g 12g³ 12s* 1981 12f 12f 12d) leggy gelding; won maiden race at Doncaster in 1980; well beaten at 4 yrs; stays 1½m; needs some give in the ground;
sold out of R. Price's stable 3,900 gns Doncaster March Sales. *Denys Smith.*

MYRA'S PET 3 b.f. Auction Ring 123–Blue Saree (Sayajirao 132) (1980 5s⁴ 5g **71**
5d⁴ 6g 1981 8.5fg 12d 7fg 7f* 7f⁴ 7fg* 7fg 7fg* 7f³ 7fg² 7g 7fg 7d) small, narrow
filly; won maiden race at Chepstow in July and 2 handicaps at Yarmouth in
August; beat Steeple Bell by 1½ lengths when apprentice ridden on last occasion;
stays 7f; acts on firm going; ran erroneously as Sister Kitty for R. Smyth first 2
outings; retained 4,300 gns Newmarket December Sales. *R. Williams.*

MY ROYALTY 2 b.f. Royalty 130–Sky Lustre 101 (Skymaster 126) (1981 5.1f —
6fg 5g 5h⁴) May 28; 1,000Y; lightly-made filly; half-sister to 3 winners, including
useful sprinter Moneymaster (by Hook Money); dam useful over 5f at 2 yrs;
beaten a long way in varied company. *C. Mackenzie.*

MY SISTER 3 b.f. Nonoalco 131–Santa's Sister 104 (Middle Brother) (1980 NR **101**
1981 7g* 12fg⁴ 8d 10g 8g) 60,000Y; quite an attractive filly; third foal; half-
sister to winners in USA and Italy by Upper Case; dam, useful winner at up to
1m, is half-sister to Yorkshire Cup winner Noble Saint; 33/1-winner of 11-runner
Mulcahy Stakes at Phoenix Park in April, leading over 1½f out and beating Lady
Tiffany comfortably by 1½ lengths; had stiff tasks afterwards but ran creditably
when about 7 lengths fourth of 10 to Blue Wind in Irish Guinness Oaks at the
Curragh 3 months later and was by no means disgraced when about 2 lengths
sixth to Tumblein in Gilltown Stud Stakes at the Curragh again on next outing
in September; stays 1½m. *T. Curtin, Ireland.*

MYSTERY MISS 2 b.f. Mummy's Pet 125–Sewing Maid 68 (So Blessed 130) **50**
(1981 5fg 6g 5fg⁴ 5.1f⁴ 5g) Mar 27; 2,000F; leggy filly; poor plater; sold out of
P. Haslam's stable 660 gns Doncaster September Sales after fourth outing. *H.
Fleming.*

MYSTIC MARGARET 2 b.f. Realm 129–Primed (Primera 131) (1981 6fg 7f) **61**
May 3; 1,450Y; strong filly; half-sister to 2 winners, including 1½m and 1¾m
winner Georgian Girl (by Prince Tenderfoot); dam well bred but of little account;
didn't look fully fit when fifth in maiden auction events at Kempton and Doncaster in July, in latter beaten 6½ lengths by Garfunkel; probably stays 7f. *A.
Hide.*

MYSTIC PRINCESS 2 ch.f. English Prince 129–Ornella (Princely Gift 137) —
(1981 6d) May 2; 2,600F, 1,000Y; lightly-made filly; fifth foal; dam won over 7f
at 2 yrs in France; 33/1 but fit when well beaten in maiden race at Leicester in
November won by Late Hour. *W. Musson.*

MYSTIFIED 2 b.f. Jimsun 121–Andrew's Girl 84 (Quorum 126) (1981 5g 6d —
5.8h 8g) Mar 19; well-made filly; half-sister to a winner in Malaya by Polyfoto;
dam 2-y-o 6f winner; remote fifth of 15 to Cheri Berry in maiden race at Bath in
August, third outing and only glimmer of ability; should stay beyond 6f; blinkered
last 2 outings. *I. Balding.*

MY STORY 10 br.g. Sweet Story 122–Langton Girl 90 (Langton Abbot) (1980 —
NR 1981 8s) of little account; has been tried in blinkers. *D. Chapman.*

MY SUSIE GIRL 2 ro.f. Roi Soleil 125–Oram Belle (Quorum 126) (1980 6fg 6f ---
9f 1981 8.3g 10fg 10s 10d) quite attractive, lightly-made filly; plating-class
maiden. *R. Baker.*

MY TIMMY 4 b.g. Lauso–Yanoula 79 (Nosca) (1980 10fg 1981 13v³ 15.8fg* **61**
12s) big, rangy gelding; stayed on strongly to win handicap at Catterick in April;
suited by a test of stamina; seems to act on any going. *M. W. Easterby.*

MY UNCLE SAM 5 b.g. Charlottown 127–My Audrey 100 (Pall Mall 132) (1980 —
13g 12f 16.1s 1981 15.8g 13g³ 12f 13fg) lengthy, good sort; poor handicapper;
stays well. *C. Thornton.*

MY WELLIE 8 b.g. Marcus Brutus 108–Snow Boots 62 (Marshal Pil 108) (1980 —
13g 12fg 12f 12.2fg* 12d 13.8f 1981 10f 12f 12f 13.8fg 15.8fg) poor middle-
distance handicapper; acts on any going; has been tried in blinkers; has worn
bandages; usually held up; often apprentice ridden. *W. C. Watts.*

N

NABILA (USA) 3 b.f. Foolish Pleasure–Opec (Bagdad) (1980 6fg 7g 1981 7g **58**
8fg 7f 6f³ 6fg 6fg 8.2s*) lengthy, slightly hollow-backed filly; good mover;
beat Pale Moon by a head in poor maiden race at Nottingham in September;
stays 1m; acts on any going; sent to USA. *L. Cumani.*

NABIRPOUR (USA) 2 b.c. Blushing Groom 131–Alama (Aureole 132) (1981 **?**
8fg 8d³ 8s*) Apr 14; half-brother to French 2,000 Guineas winner Nishapour
(by Zeddaan); dam won over 13f in France and is closely related to good French
stayer Misyaaf; always well placed when winning minor event at Maisons-
Laffitte in November by a nose from Marcao; will stay at least 1¼m; entered in
Derby. *F. Mathet, France.*

NAE HASSLE 2 ro.f. Swing Easy 126–Observation 81 (Coronation Year 124) —
(1981 5d) Apr 18; 900Y; well-grown, leggy filly; half-sister to fairly useful
1979 2-y-o 5f winner Ayoub (by The Go-Between), subsequently successful in
Denmark, and to a winner in Trinidad; dam stayed 1m; 16/1 when last of 9 to
Ten-Traco in seller at Wolverhampton in May. *J. Berry.*

NAGALIA 2 br.f. Lochnager 132–La Gallia 70 (Welsh Saint 126) (1981 5s³ **80**
5d⁴ 5g³ 5g² 5f² 5fg 6d³ 5f³ 6fg* 5g* 6d* 6d) Apr 21; 1,050Y; lightly-made filly;
first live foal; dam won 3 times over 1½m and also won over hurdles; in splendid
form in September, winning 21-runner maiden auction event at Redcar and
nurseries under low weights at Beverley and Hamilton, gaining final success by
1½ lengths from High Port; placed several times previously, including in selling
company; stays 6f; probably acts on any going; ran moderately in blinkers
sixth outing. *K. Stone.*

NAHANE 4 b.f. Porto Bello 118 Hilloquaw (Hillary) (1980 10 ?fg² 10f⁴ 10g⁴ —
8fg 9g 1981 10f 10f 16.1f 12g³) compact, quite attractive filly; quite a moderate
handicapper at her best but has shown no form for a long time; stays 1¼m;
suited by a sound surface. *P. Bevan.*

NAIF 3 b.c. Nonoalco 131–Ashavan 114 (Persian Gulf) (1980 NR 1981 7g **64**
7g 8f 10fg 8g² 8fg² 11fg 12g 10fg 9s) 12,500Y; big, good-topped colt; has a
round action; half-brother to several winners, including Frassino (by Kalamoun),
a useful winner from 7f to 11.2f here and in Italy; dam, half-sister to Belmont
Stakes winner Celtic Ash, stayed 2m; put up easily best efforts when second in
maiden races at Sandown in July and Salisbury in August; should stay 1¼m;
often bandaged; sold to G. Lockerbie 920 gns Newmarket Autumn Sales. *F.
Durr.*

NAMIB (FR) 3 ch.g. Kashmir II 125–Noble Maid (Vaguely Noble 140) (1980 —
NR 1981 7f 10g 11s) 480 2-y-o; dipped-backed gelding; third foal; dam
won over 1m and 9f in French Provinces; bad plater; blinkered first outing.
N. Hall.

NANCYS BOY 2 b.g. Crooner 119–Never So Late (Never Say Die 137) (1981 —
5s) May 14; tall, robust gelding; third foal; dam Irish 1½m winner; last of 11 to
Fool's Dance in £2,700 event at Kempton in May; sold 420 gns Doncaster
September Sales. *P. Kelleway.*

NANNINA 6 b.m. Martinmas 128–Auriann (Aureole 132) (1980 7d 6g 5.1g **51**
6g 6g 6g 7fg 8f 8.2s⁴ 8s 1981 12.3d² 12d 12g 12.3fg 10fg) lengthy, light-framed
mare; poor handicapper; suited by 1½m; acts on any going. *I. Walker.*

NANUSHKA 2 b.f. Lochnager 132–Monashka 73 (Sica Boy 132) (1981 6fg —
7fg 6d 7v) Apr 6; lengthy filly; half-sister to several winners, including stayer
Thorganby Balashka (by Ballymoss); dam half-sister to Altesse Royale, Yaroslav
and Imperial Prince; in rear in maiden races and a £3,400 event. *R. Hobson.*

NAOMI JOY 4 b.f. Sun Prince 128–Red Dot 100 (Red God 128§) (1980 **86**
5g² 6g³ 5g³ 6fg³ 6d 6d 12s 1981 9d 10d 9s 6.3fg* 6fg* 8d 5d) 5,400Y; half-
sister to 2 winners, including Tardot (by Targowice), a useful performer at up to
1m; dam sprinter; ridden by 5-lb claimer when winning valuable handicaps at
the Curragh in June (well backed, beat Nazwa by 2 lengths in Midsummer Scurry
Handicap) and August (favourite, scored by a length from Real Torque in Philips
Electrical Stakes); showed little on her other starts, on final one finishing last to
Marwell in Prix de l'Abbaye de Longchamp in October; evidently best at sprint
distances; goes well on top-of-the-ground; sold 36,000 gns Newmarket December
Sales. *J. Hassett, Ireland.*

NAPA VALLEY 2 b.f. Wolver Hollow 126–Frondia 76 (Parthia 132) (1981 **89**
7d 8fg* 8.2d²) Mar 16; half-sister to good continental stayer Duky (by Mid-

summer Night II), useful French 5f and 1¼m winner Prince Dias (by So Blessed) and a winner in Belgium; dam, half-sister to Gold Cup winner Shangamuzo, won over 1½m; won 17-runner maiden race at Leicester in September by a neck from Fallen Angel; creditable 2 lengths second of 9 to Misty Halo in minor event at Hamilton the following month; will be suited by 1½m. *F. Durr.*

NAP HAND 2 ch.c. Some Hand 119–Coconut 75 (Tesco Boy 121) (1981 5v 5d 5g 7g 7g³ 7d 8fg 8.2d) Mar 26; 1,800F, 2,500Y; workmanlike colt; half-brother to 2 minor middle-distance winners; dam stayed 1m; plater; suited by 7f but has yet to show he stays 1m; blinkered fifth, sixth and eighth starts; exported to Singapore. *P. Rohan.* **59**

NARRIBINNI (NZ) 9 br.g. Dusky Hunter–Superform (Clarification 110) (1980 NR 1981 13.3s³ 16f 12g) New Zealand-bred gelding; very useful hurdler at his best and successful chaser; 9 lengths third to Derring Rose in Aston Park Stakes at Newbury in May, easily best effort on flat in this country; should stay well; acts on soft going; wears blinkers. *N. Mitchell.* **—**

NARSINH (USA) 2 b.c. Avatar–Fizz (Idle Hour 121) (1981 7fg) neat colt; fourth foal; dam won 7 times from 3 yrs to 6 yrs in Argentina, including 17.5f Gran Premio de Honor and 15f Premio Chacabuco, and is sister to very good Argentinian mares Farm and Factory; 33/1, showed distinct signs of greenness but got hang of things in closing stages when staying-on eighth of 18 to Tulsa Flyer in £2,600 race at Salisbury in August; should stay well. *J. Dunlop.* **— p**

NASHITA (USA) 8 b.m. Nashua–Flor del Viento (Gulf Stream 120) (1980 NR 1981 6f 8f 5fg 7.6s 7g 8fg) only plating class; stays 1m; acts on any going; has worn blinkers. *J. Mulhall.* **—**

NASH ROLLER (USA) 3 ch.g. Nashua–Gray Lawn Rabbit (Native Charger) (1980 7d 7fg 7fg 1981 9.4g 12g 13g³ 11f⁴ 15fg² 16.9fg⁴) strong gelding; plating-class maiden; looks slow. *T. Robson.* **56**

NASRUDIN (FR) 3 b.c. Filiberto 123–Niamara 110 (Emerson) (1980 6fg 7fg 7g 1981 8fg 8f 12.2fg 9.4g) big colt; poor form, including in a seller at 2 yrs; stays 1m. *B. Wilkinson.* **50**

NASSEEM (FR) 3 gr.f. Zeddaan 130–Noureen (Astec 128) (1980 5g* 5g³ 6d* 6fg³ 6fg 1981 10g 8s* 8f³ 10g 7g³ 8s 8s⁴) lengthy, quite attractive filly; **118**

UBM Merchants International Fillies Stakes, Kempton—Nasseem revels in the soft ground

excellent walker and good mover; first foal; dam unraced half-sister to Tajubena,
a very smart winner at up to 1½m; revelled in the soft going when beating
Salamina by 7 lengths in UBM Merchants International Fillies Stakes at Kempton
in May, travelling strongly throughout and storming clear in last furlong; third
afterwards in Coronation Stakes at Royal Ascot in June (2½ lengths behind
Tolmi) and well-contested £3,800 race at Goodwood in September (made running
and stuck on well to be beaten 2 lengths by Star Pastures); not disgraced when
about 1¼ lengths fourth of 10 to Mistra in Prix Coronation at Saint-Cloud in
November; best form at up to 1m (well beaten in Nassau Stakes at Goodwood
when tried at 1¼m); has run respectably on fast ground but needs some give to
show her best form; tends to get rather stirred up in preliminaries nowadays;
trained most of season by F. J. Houghton. *F. Mathet, France.*

NATHACHA 3 b.f. Thatch 136–Solar Echo (Solar Slipper 131) (1980 NR
1981 10fg 10.2h 10s) 74,000Y; lengthy filly; half-sister to several winners,
notably high-class 6f to 1m gelding Boldboy (by Bold Lad, Ire) and smart 1966
Irish 2-y-o Sovereign Slipper (by Fortino II); dam ran only once; in rear in
maiden events; started slowly first outing; backward final start (first race for
over 3 months). *T. Robson.* —

NATHANIEL 4 b.g. Shantung 132–Pink Standard 81 (Tudor Melody 129) 57
(1980 10s³ 8f 8fg 8g 11d⁴ 10.6d 8fg 10s 1981 7s 8g 8g 10f⁴ 10f³ 10g* 12f² 12fg)
sturdy gelding; poor handicapper; well-backed favourite when winning at
Redcar in August; appears to stay 1½m; acts on any going. *M. W. Easterby.*

NATIONAL IMAGE 4 b.g. Sassafras 135–Pepi Image 111 (National) (1980 —
10s⁴ 10g* 11g* 12d 1981 13.4d 13.3s) ex-Irish gelding; successful in maiden
race at Limerick and handicap at Galway at 3yrs; had stiff tasks both starts
in 1981; stays 11f. *M. Tate.*

NATION WIDE 8 b.g. Irish Ball 127–Misylda 100 (Faubourg II 127) (1980 81
14.6fg 16.1fg⁴ 16g⁴ 16.1s³ 16.1s* 14g⁴ 15d³ 1981 16s² 14fg 18.4d²
18d 16g 16fg 16.1d* 15.8g*) modest handicapper; won at Newmarket and
Chester in August; went down by 5 lengths to Donegal Prince in Ladbroke
Chester Cup on third start; suited by a strong gallop and stays really well;
acts on any going but seems suited by some give in the ground; has been tried
in blinkers; often gets himself well behind in early stages and is not the most
genuine of animals. *H. Wragg.*

NATIVE BREAK (USA) 4 b. or br.g. Native Charger–Commercial Break —
(Stevward) (1980 8d 10v⁴ 12fg* 12.5fg⁴ 13.8fg* 12d 13.8f² 15.8f⁴ 14.7f 16.1s
15.8d 1981 16fg) compact gelding; has a round action; stays 1¾m; acts on
firm going and isn't at his best on soft; sometimes sweats up. *S. Holland.*

NATIVE GUEST 2 b.f. Be My Guest 126–Native Soil 71 (Herbager 136) 76
(1981 6g 6f 7f 7g 6d³ 7g) May 19; 3,000Y; compact filly; second foal; dam
won over 1¾m; 1¾ lengths third of 15 to Lucayan Lady in minor event at
Pontefract in October; will stay 1¼m; moved badly to start fourth outing.
F. Durr.

NATIVE SON (FR) 2 b.c. Faraway Son 130–Noble Native 98 (Indigenous 121) 78
(1981 6g 7fg³ 6fg 8s 8g⁴) Apr 28; fair sort; poor walker; half-brother to 3
winners at up to 1m; dam stayed 1m; stayed on when in frame in minor event
at Goodwood in September (6 lengths third of 10 to Old Country) and maiden
race at Edinburgh in October (5¾ lengths fourth of 13 to Brigado); also ran
creditably third start; suited by 7f and 1m; sweated up at Goodwood. *C. Austin.*

NATURE'S WAY 3 b.f. Zamindar–Free and Easy (Liberator III) (1980 5.8fg* —
6g 1981 8.5g 7fg 7g) light-framed filly; won maiden race at Bath as a 2-y-o;
weak in market when in rear in handicaps at Epsom and Doncaster in June
and at Lingfield in September; should stay beyond 6f. *N. Vigors.*

NAUGHTY TWINKLE 2 b.f. Red Alert 127–Sapphire Lady (Majority Blue 126) 47
(1981 5fg 5fg⁴ 5g 5f) Feb 2; 1,000Y; stocky filly; half-sister to fairly useful
1977 2-y-o 5f performer Supergas (by Realm); dam quite useful 2-y-o 5f winner
in Ireland; only poor form, including in an auction event; will stay 6f. *W. H. H.
Williams.*

NAUTEOUS 2 b.c. Nonoalco 131–Sassabunda 108 (Sassafras 135) (1981 6g 79
7g 7f) Feb 18; $82,000Y; quite attractive colt; first foal; dam short-head
second in Irish Guinness Oaks; showed ability on first 2 outings, notably when
5 lengths fifth of 26 to Tin Boy at Newmarket on his debut, but finished remote
eighth of 14 to Cadi Ha when blinkered in small race at Leicester in August
on third (bumped after halfway); should be suited by 7f+. *P. Walwyn.*

NAUTIC STAR 3 b.c. Connaught 130–Starbright (Petingo 135) (1980 7d —
1981 12g) behind in minor event at Doncaster as a 2-y-o and maiden race at
Newmarket in April. *C. Brittain.*

NAUTIQUE 3 ch.f. Windjammer (USA)–Porthole (Major Portion 129) (1980 —
5s 5f 6s³ 6d 6fg⁴ 8fg 7d 1981 8s 9s 8g⁴ 8f 12f 10fg 7fg 10fg 10s) leggy filly;
plater; not disgraced over 9f; has been tried in blinkers. *W. Wharton.*

NAVAJO BRAVE (USA) 3 br.c. Navajo–Rosy Lark (T. V. Lark) (1980 7f 8d **65**
1981 12s² 12g 16s³ 12d² 16.9fg⁴ 15.5f²) tall colt; placed in varied company;
stays 2m; acts on any going. *G. Hunter.*

NAVIGATIONAL AID 4 b.g. Blind Harbour 96–Tiny Clanger 73 (Sky Gipsy **84 d**
117) (1980 10v* 12g* 10f³ 12g 16g² 16fg³ 18d 18s 1981 12s 12g 14.6f* 16f*
15g 14d 15g) big, rangy gelding; fair handicapper; won at Doncaster in June
and Beverley in July; stays 2m but not 2¼m; acts on any going; blinkered once in
1980; suited by strong handling; sold to W. Holden 4,700 gns Newmarket
Autumn Sales. *J. W. Watts.*

NAWAB 2 b.c. Young Emperor 133–Tokara (Hard Tack 111§) (1981 5g 6g **92**
5fg* 5fg⁴ 6s⁴) Apr 26; 13,000Y; leggy, rather lightly-made, quite attractive
colt; second foal; half-brother to very useful 3-y-o Spark of Life (by Home Guard),
a winner at up to 7f; dam unraced sister to top-class miler Sparkler; favourite,
always going pretty well when beating Pacific Sparkler decisively by 2 lengths
in 13-runner maiden race at Salisbury in August; prominent on his other starts,
on final outing finishing creditable fourth of 14 to Better Portion in nursery at
Newbury in October (first outing for nearly 2 months); stays 6f. *I. Balding.*

NAZARETH 2 ch.f. Roi Soleil 125–Suku 80 (Light Thrust 114) (1981 5g 5g 5g) —
1,600F, resold 1,100Y; plain filly; half-sister to sprint winner Tricia's Treasure
and a winner in Malta (both by My Swanee); dam won over 1m; only poor
form in sellers. *T. Fairhurst.*

NEAT 3 ch.g. Wollow 132–Brilliantine 109 (Stage Door Johnny) (1980 7v **101 ?**
1981 8d* 8fg³ 10.1s³) tall, lengthy gelding; didn't look fully fit when reappearing
in 26-runner maiden race at Newbury in April but won virtually unchallenged by
3 lengths from On Show; seemed reluctant to struggle when 1½ lengths third of 13
behind Home Coming in minor event at Sandown later in month and was tried in
blinkers when 6 lengths third of 6 behind Splendidly Gay in minor event at
Windsor in May (sweated up and weakened quickly in last 1½f); should stay
at least 1¼m; possibly not at his best on a firm surface; gelded after final outing.
J. Tree.

NEEDLE POINT 5 ch.m. Duneed 84–Primlia (Reverse Charge 115) (1980 —
NR 1981 16f) third foal; dam staying chaser; behind in poor maiden race
at Beverley in June. *P. Haslam.*

NEEDS SUPPORTING 3 b.f. Home Guard 129–Miss Robust (Busted 134) **79**
(1980 NR 1981 8.5g⁴ 7d 8fg* 8fg⁴ 12fg² 11g² 12f* 11.7g* 12f⁴ 12fg²) 14,000Y;
strong, attractive filly; good walker; second foal; half-sister to quite moderate
1m winner Mistress Medina (by Averof); dam never ran; won maiden race at
Warwick in June and handicaps at Brighton (in good style) and Windsor in
August; ran better subsequent race when second to Telsmoss in apprentice
handicap at Epsom in September; suited by 1¼m; acts on firm going; struck into
and unseated rider at Sandown on second start. *B. Hills.*

NEEDWOOD NAP 3 b.f. Some Hand 119–Suku 80 (Light Thrust 114) (1980 —
5f 5fg 5fg 1981 9s 8d 6g 7fg 8f 8fg) compact, well-made filly; poor plater.
B. McMahon.

NEERAN 3 ch.f. Wollow 132–Ship Yard 107 (Doutelle 128) (1980 NR 1981 —
13.3d) 35,000Y; tall, lengthy filly; half-sister to several winners, including top-
class middle-distance stayer Bustino (by Busted) and very smart French stayer
Oarsman (by Aureole); dam won over 7f and 1m at 2 yrs; 20/1 when ninth of
12 behind Centrinole in maiden race at Newbury in June, only outing. *C. Nelson.*

NEIGHBORING (USA) 2 b. or br.c. Herculean–Friendly Neighbour (Deck **89**
Hand) (1981 5d 7g 7fg 7g 7fg 7fg⁴ 7g 7d* 7d²) Mar 21; $25,000Y; close-
coupled, useful-looking colt; first foal; dam won 2 sprint races; sire stakes-placed
son of Bold Ruler; showed much-improved form in 15-runner £2,100 nursery at
Doncaster in October, having won a long way out and beating Garfunkel
unchallenged by 4 lengths; ran extremely well under a penalty next time out;
will stay 1m; acts well on soft ground; possibly needs a galloping track; ran
moderately when blinkered in valuable seller on seventh outing; sold for export
to Austria, 10,000 gns Doncaster November Sales. *G. Balding.*

NEILAH (CAN) 2 b.c. Knightly Dawn–Main Saggy (Saggy) (1981 5g 5fg 5f 5g   — 8s) May 27; $21,000Y, $30,000 2-y-o; good sort; half-brother to 3 winners, including Main Pan (by Pan Dancer), a smart winner of 22 races at up to 1m; dam won 15 times; sire, son of Sir Gaylord, won Jersey Derby; plating-class maiden; should stay 1m; blinkered fourth outing. *R. Hannon.*

NELLO (USA) 3 b.f. Charles Elliott–Color Me Blonde (Craigwood) (1980 6fg³   — 5f⁴ 6d 6d* 1981 7d 7.3g 7f 7g 7f⁴ 7f 8g 7d 7g) plain filly; ran creditably in a handicap fourth start but was mainly disappointing, including in sellers when blinkered on last 2 outings; should stay 1m; often fails to impress in paddock; sold 1,000 gns Ascot December Sales. *G. Balding.*

NELTINO 3 gr.c. Bustino 136–Flying Nelly 107 (Nelcius 133) (1980 7g² 8fg   **97** 7g³ 1981 12s* 12f) small, robust colt; second foal; half-brother to 1979 2-y-o 5.8f winner Nelly Do Da (by Derring-Do); dam stayed 13f but was best at 1m to 1¼m; made an impressive reappearance when beating Show-A-Leg by 4 lengths in handicap at Kempton in May, taking up running 2f out and soon going clear; hard driven from halfway when disappointing eighth of 14 behind Feltwell in King George V Stakes (Handicap) at Royal Ascot the following month; reportedly had a training accident afterwards and didn't race again; was suited by 1½m; acted well on soft going and was probably unsuited by firm; standing at Elms Stud, Denton, Northants, at no charge to approved mares. *R. Hern.*

NEMORINO (USA) 2 b.c. Sir Ivor 135–Sans Moi (Herbager 136) (1981 6d 7g⁴)   **81** Feb 27; $80,000Y; fourth foal; half-brother to a winner by Bold Reasoning; dam, placed at 3 yrs, is sister to Del Mar Oaks winner Snap Apple and half-sister to very smart Balzac; odds on when 1¼ lengths fourth of 15 to Chronicle in minor event at Naas in October; withdrawn at start when brought over for William Hill Futurity Stakes at Doncaster later in month; will be suited by middle distances; should win races. *D. O'Brien, Ireland.*

NEMR 4 ch.c. Thatch 136–Grecian Craft 90 (Acropolis 132) (1980 9s* 9.2fg 8d²   **122** 10fg* 9d 10s³ 10d 8d 8v* 1981 10s 8d⁴ 8s 8d⁴ 9d* 10f* 11v* 12g) smart performer; in good form in second half of season, winning Prix Ramus at Maisons-Laffitte, Prix Gontaut-Biron at Deauville (beat Vielle by 1½ lengths) and Premio Federico Tesio at Milan; accounted for Dance Bid by 4 lengths in last-named in September; not disgraced earlier in year when fourth in Prix de Ris-Orangis at Evry (behind Hilal) and Prix du Chemin de Fer du Nord at Chantilly (to Gosport); suited by middle distances; acts on any going; blinkered once at 2 yrs. *M. Saliba, France.*

NEOTERIC 2 ch.f. Some Hand 119–Neophyte II (Never Say Die 137) (1981 5f   — 8d 7g) Mar 13; strong filly; half-sister to a winner in Jamaica; dam never ran; backward when soundly beaten in minor event and 2 maiden races. *D. Elsworth.*

NEPCOTE 3 b.c. Sparkler 130–Babuette 93 (Our Babu 131) (1980 NR 1981   — 8fg 10g 12d⁴ 12g³ 16f) 10,000Y; compact, quite useful soft; half-brother to 2 winners, including fairly useful 1973 2-y-o 5f winner Burglar's Moll (by Burglar); dam disappointing maiden at up to 1½m; in frame in maiden races at Folkestone and Lingfield in June; stays 1½m; probably unsuited by firm going. *R. Price.*

NEPENTHA 3 br.f. Great Nephew 126–Opium 97 (Espresso 122) (1980 8f 8g²   **72** 1981 8g³ 11s 10s² 10fg⁴ 10f³ 11f³) leggy, quite useful sort; placed in maiden races, including when 4 lengths second of 24 to impressive winner Bettyknowes at Kempton in May; rather disappointing however and may have her own ideas about the game; probably stays 11f; sold 3,500 gns Newmarket December Sales. *B. Hobbs.*

NEPOTISM 4 b.c. Great Nephew 126–Lantana 74 (St Paddy 133) (1980 8fg   **90** 12g* 12g 12d² 13.3d 11d 12g 11.1g 10g 8d 1981 7d 11.1s⁴ 10.8fg³ 10g 12.2fg* 12fg² 12f³ 14fg³ 12fg* 12h* 12.5g) big, strong colt; fair handicapper; successful at Warwick in June and Kempton and Chepstow (odds on) in August; also first past post at Leicester in July but was moved down a place for hampering runner-up; stays 1¾m; probably acts on any going; blinkered twice in 1980. *G. Balding.*

NEPOTIST (USA) 6 ch.g. Executioner–Lemos (Sea-Bird II 145) (1980 NR   — 1981 6d 10f 12f) poor maiden. *D. Jermy.*

NERVE 3 b.f. Daring Display 129–Bordelaise 96 (Above Suspicion 127) (1980   — 6g 6g 6g 5d 1981 8g 12g) of no account. *J. Doyle.*

NESITA BELL 2 b. or br.f. Keren 100–Whinthorpe Belle (Pongee 106) (1981   — 8fg) May 15; first foal; dam of no account; slowly away when tailed-off last of 17 to Cornish Heroine in maiden race at Leicester in September. *M. Ryan.*

NETHER REGIONS 2 ch.c. Netherkelly 112–Polly Jinks (Ron 103) (1981 8g **55**
8.2d 10g) May 16; rather leggy colt; fourth foal; dam left at start on only outing;
plater; about 5 lengths fifth of 17 to Princely Dancer in September, second start and best effort; probably stays 1¼m. *D. Ringer.*

NETTLEFOLD 3 b.f. Netherkelly 112–Barlow Fold 99 (Monet 127) (1980 7fg —
1981 8f 7f 10.1d 8h) good-topped filly; in rear in maiden and minor events and
a seller (last of 14); blinkered third start; sold 500 gns Ascot September Sales.
R. Baker.

NEVER ENOUGH 3 b.f. Sandford Lad 133–Suffice 84 (Faberge II 121) (1980 —
6g 6d 1981 10fg 10d 10d 8.3fg) strong, well-made filly; good walker; has
shown a little ability in varied company; possibly doesn't quite stay 1¼m; sold
to A. Ingham 2,700 gns Ascot September Sales. *M. Smyly.*

NEVER SAY WHEN 3 ch.f. Roman Warrior 132–Cordon Rouge 99 (Never Say —
Die 137) (1980 6g 5f 5.3g 6fg 7d 1981 6s 7fg 5v 5v 5f) strong filly; not
entirely disgraced in a seller on fourth start; sold 1,250 gns Ascot 2nd June Sales.
D. Whelan.

NEVER SO LUCKY 2 b.c. So Blessed 130–Lucky Janie 87 (Dual 117) (1981 **106**
5f* 5f⁴ 6fg² 6g 6fg³ 7g⁴ 6g 6s* 7g) Mar 19; 9,800F; attractive, well-made colt;
particularly good mover; half-brother to several winners, including fair middle-
distance winner Lucky Mickmooch (by Blakeney); dam won from 5f to 1m;
favourite when winning 18-runner minor event at Windsor in June and 18-
runner nursery at Nottingham in October, putting up best performance to beat
Worlingworth in good style by 1½ lengths in latter; stays 7f; acts on any going
but best effort on soft; consistent until running moderately final start. *G.
Harwood.*

NEVER TALK 2 br.c. Most Secret 119–To Rome (Romulus 129) (1981 5fg* **103**
5g* 5d³ 5g² 5fg³ 6f 5g³ 5g) Apr 6; 3,600Y; workmanlike colt; good walker and
mover; third reported foal; dam unraced half-sister to smart Pals Passage;
successful twice in April, winning maiden race at Epsom by 2½ lengths and minor
event at Stockton pretty comfortably by 3 lengths; placed at York, Thirsk,
Kempton (good third to Childown Blue in nursery when having first race for
nearly 3 months) and Doncaster (1¼ lengths third to Fearless Lad) subsequently;
not sure to stay beyond 5f; gives impression a sound surface suits him best;
ridden by apprentice S. Jarvis first 6 outings, including in 2 races when he
couldn't claim his 5-lb allowance, and by 7-lb claimer T. Jarvis on final start. *A.
Jarvis.*

NEWARK 6 br.g. Folkestone–Street Hawker 74 (Ben Hawke 94) (1980 8s 8fg —
12g² 14.6fg 16.5fg 12g 12s) rangy gelding; poor handicapper; stays 1½m;
acts on any going. *H. O'Neill.*

NEW CONTINENT (USA) 3 ch.g. Son Ange–Clover Blossom (Green Ticket) **63**
(1980 6fg 8fg 10s 1981 10s 10fg 11.7s 10f³ 13.1f³ 8fg 12g* 12g² 12d³ 12d⁴)
rangy gelding; made virtually all when winning apprentice handicap at Wolverhampton in September by 5 lengths from Northern Prince; stays 1½m; acts on
any going, except possibly very soft. *E. Eldin.*

NEW EMBASSY (USA) 4 b.g. Dynastic (USA)–Joys Will (Yes You Will) **84**
(1980 6s 6fg⁴ 6d 5fg 5g 8g⁴ 8d 1981 6f 5s 6d 5g²) strong, well-made, good-
quartered gelding; sprint handicapper; acts on any going. *G. Balding.*

NEW EXPRESS 2 br.c Bay Express 132–Natasha 87 (Native Prince) (1981 —
6g) Feb 19; 9,200F, 5,000Y; strong colt; good walker; half-brother to two
2-y-o winners, including fair 1980 5f performer Be Sharp (by Sharpen Up);
dam won 3 times over 5f at 2 yrs; backed from 33/1 to 10/1 but definitely
needed race when remote ninth of 14 to Knave of Trumps in maiden race at
Yarmouth in September. *G. Huffer.*

NEWGATE 8 b.g. Blakeney 126–Set Free 90 (Worden II 129) (1980 12.2g **45**
12d 12fg⁴ 12fg 12g 12fg⁴ 15d 1981 12.3d 12d 15g* 16g 16g 12fg 13.8fg³ 14.7fg³
16fg⁴ 17.4g 13d) staying handicapper; won at Ayr in May; acts on any going;
has been tried in blinkers. *A. Scott.*

NEW JERUSALEM 4 b. or br.g. Reform 132–Desertville 92 (Charlottesville 135) —
(1980 11fg³ 11.7fg 12g 14d* 12g² 21fg³ 14g² 17.4s⁴ 1981 13.3s) lengthy
gelding; has a round action; developed into a useful stayer at 3 yrs; bandaged
in front and moved badly to post when behind in Aston Park Stakes at Newbury
in May on only start in 1981; well suited by a test of stamina; possibly not at
his best on very soft ground; best in blinkers (didn't wear them at Newbury).
A. Smith.

NEW LEGEND 3 b.c. Empery 128–Ethiopia (Will Somers 114§) (1980 NR 1981 10s 10d) 70,000Y; short-backed, fair sort; third foal; dam, French 1m winner, is sister to Balidar and Balliol; kept on fairly well when eighth of 24 to Betty-knowes in maiden event at Kempton in May, first and better effort. *J. Winter*. —

NEWLIFE CONNECTION 2 b.c. Rapid River 127–Weirdi 76 (Yrrah Jr) (1981 6fg 6g 6fg⁴ 7f 8d 7d) June 5; leggy, narrow colt; fourth foal; dam placed over 1m at 2 yrs; only plating class; beaten over 13 lengths when making late headway to finish fourth of 8 to Rosananti in maiden race at Newcastle in August; should stay 7f. *W. A. Stephenson*. —

NEW MODEL 3 b.g. Reform 132–Fashion Model 100 (Road House II) (1980 8g 1981 8fg 8g 7.6g 12f) strong, workmanlike gelding; soundly beaten in maiden and minor events; sold 440 gns Ascot July Sales. *B. Swift*. —

NEW MORNING 2 b.f. Wolverlife 115–Carol Barnett (Frigid Aire) (1981 5d) Mar 19; leggy filly; first foal; dam won several times at around 1m in Ireland; unquoted and in need of race when last of 9 finishers behind Lively Rose in maiden race at Wolverhampton in May. *G. Richards*. —

NEWS BARON 2 ch.c. Be My Guest 126–Misty Cat (Misty Flight) (1981 6g 7f 8g⁴ 7g 7g 8.2s⁴) Mar 27; 9,000Y; strong colt; good walker and mover; half-brother to a winning plater; dam, half-sister to high-class sprinter Caerphilly, won 1m claiming race in USA; fourth in a maiden race and a nursery but finished only eleventh of 29 when third favourite for valuable seller at Newmarket on fourth outing; will probably stay 1¼m; sold to Susan Piggott B.A. 4,100 gns Newmarket Autumn Sales and sent to France. *P. Haslam*. 65

NEW STRIKE (USA) 3 br.c. Dynastic (USA)–Latin Wave (Roman Line) (1980 5f⁴ 5fg 5.8fg 6d³ 7g³ 7d⁴ 7h 8.2g 8d 1981 7s 7fg⁴ 7g² 6d 6v² 7s) small, quite useful sort; plater; runner-up at Doncaster and Windsor in May; stays 7f; best form with some give in the ground; has run creditably for an apprentice, has worn blinkers; sold to race in Australia. *G. Balding*. 55

NEW THATCH 3 b.g. Thatch 136–Tinkling Sound 93 (Sound Track 132) (1980 5fg 5fg 1981 8d) good-bodied gelding; very lightly raced in maiden races, but has shown a little ability; sold 760 gns Newmarket Autumn Sales. *B. Hills*. —

NEW YEARS DAY (USA) 3 ch.c. Personality–Super Legend (Lucky Debonair) (1980 6g* 6fg² 6f 7.3d 1981 6d) strong, lengthy colt; won Granville Stakes at Ascot at 2 yrs; about 7 lengths sixth of 8 behind Swan Princess in minor event at Folkestone in April on only outing of 1981; should be suited by 7f; bolted once at 2 yrs and had to be withdrawn. *P. Cole*. —

NEXT DECADE 2 gr.g. Shiny Tenth 120–Follow The Brave 68 (Owen Anthony 102) (1981 5g² 6f² 6fg* 6fg 7f 6s³ 6f 5g) May 1; small gelding; first foal; dam plating class at 2 yrs; sold out of Sir Mark Prescott's stable 4,000 gns after winning seller at Warwick in June; appeared to show improved form when 4¼ lengths third of 7 to Balanchine in small race at Chester in August but didn't confirm that improvement; probably needs further than 5f; has won on a firm surface but seems better on soft going. *A. Balding*. 69

NICE N'EASY 7 ch.g. Crooner 119–Young Mementa (Young Christopher 119) (1980 NR 1981 12f 16g) seems of little account nowadays; has worn blinkers. *V. Soane*. —

NICE VALUE 7 ch.g. Goldhill 125–Sinecure (Parthia 132) (1980 5d³ 6s 7.2d 5.8fg 6d⁴ 6d* 6g 6g 6g* 6fg 5.8fg 7.2d 6s 7d 7s 1981 6v 6s 5g 6d⁴ 5.8g 6f 6f 6fg⁴ 5fg* 6g 5.8g 6d 7d) sprint handicapper; won trainers race at Catterick in August; stays 6f; acts on any going but is well suited by some give in the ground; blinkered once in 1979. *R. Hollinshead*. 69

NICHOLAS BILL 6 ch.h. High Line 125–Centro 86 (Vienna 127) (1980 12d* 13.3d* 12g⁴ 12f 12d² 1981 12s 16d* 14d² 12f 15f² 13.5f) 120

Nicholas Bill has been retired to the Hunsley House Stud at Little Weighton in Yorkshire. His record in four seasons of racing was one of a good, honest horse, and included wins in the Princess of Wales's Stakes, the Geoffrey Freer Stakes, the Jockey Club Cup and the Sagaro Stakes twice. Nicholas Bill also ran a number of fine races in defeat, none finer than his sixth, only four lengths or so behind Detroit, in the Prix de l'Arc de Triomphe in 1980. He had a highly respectable turn of foot for one who stayed two miles and he acted on any going, but was probably suited by some give in the ground in the latter part of his career.

Nicholas Bill gave well below-par performances on two occasions in 1981, both at a mile and a half. For both there were valid excuses: in the John Porter

Mr R. Barnett's "Nicholas Bill"

Stakes at Newbury first time out in the spring he looked in need of the run, and in the Hardwicke Stakes at Royal Ascot the firm ground, especially over that distance, was probably his undoing. Otherwise he ran consistently well, although not quite attaining the standard he reached in 1980. He looked to have a clear chance on his best form in the Sagaro Stakes at Ascot in April and he duly won with little fuss by two and a half lengths from Son Fils; thereupon he started favourite for the Yorkshire Cup. Unfortunately for Nicholas Bill, assumptions that Ardross would need the race and would find the mile and three quarters too sharp proved unfounded, and Nicholas Bill had no chance with the best stayer in Europe; nevertheless he battled on for second place, beaten three lengths. After Royal Ascot Nicholas Bill was sent to Deauville in August for his last two races—opportunities for his type are extremely limited in England around this time. In the Prix Kergorlay he looked all over the winner a furlong out but started to change his legs on the firm ground and was caught close home by the three-year-old Tipperary Fixer; in the Grand Prix de Deauville he finished seventh under top weight, less than five lengths behind the improving Perrault.

		High Line (ch 1966)	High Hat (ch 1957)	Hyperion
Nicholas Bill (ch.h. 1975)				Madonna
			Time Call (b 1955)	Chanteur II
				Aleria
		Centro (b 1966)	Vienna (ch 1957)	Aureole
				Turkish Blood
			Ocean Sailing (br 1950)	Big Game
				Kyanos

In Master Willie, Crimson Beau and Nicholas Bill, High Line has three high-class sons to represent him at stud. Nicholas Bill's fee of 750 guineas plus 750 guineas (live foal) is the lowest of the three, which perhaps is partly a reflection of the fact that he stayed the furthest. However, although Nicholas

Bill stayed two miles he had the speed to win at a mile and a half, and it is probably in his favour in this topsy-turvy racing world that he failed to stay on his only venture beyond two miles. His dam, who won over seven furlongs at two but failed to train on, is a half-sister to a speedy filly in Sea Music, a winner of eight races at five and six furlongs as a two-year-old. Centro's first four foals, all by High Line, have won, the other three being the Lancashire Oaks winner Centrocon, the one-paced stayer Athford and the good stayer Centroline. The second dam possessed a very good turn of foot and won six races at up to a mile and a half. It is to be hoped that Nicholas Bill, an admirable racehorse, enjoys a successful stud career. *H. Candy.*

NICKADVENTURE 5 ch.g. On Your Mark 125–High Gloss (Super Sam 124) **48**
(1980 8s 7fg 8fg 8h* 7h⁴ 8fg³ 8fg 8d³ 6d 8fg 8fg³ 1981 7g³ 8.2g 10.4s 10f² 12.3fg
10.6s) workmanlike gelding; poor handicapper; beaten in a seller second start;
stays 1m; acts on any going; suitable mount for an inexperienced rider; doesn't
look too enthusiastic; bandaged nowadays. *N. Tinkler.*

NIGHT CLOWN 2 b.c. Cawston's Clown 123–Night On (Narrator 127) (1981 **—**
6d) May 27; 2,400F, 10,500Y, 4,200 2-y-o; half-brother to a minor winner
and to winners over hurdles here and in Italy; dam, a twin, is sister to 1,000
Guineas winner Night Off; 25/1 when out of first 10 in 25-runner maiden event
won by Dev at Doncaster in October. *A. Bailey.*

NIGHT WATCH (USA) 7 br.g. Stage Door Johnny–Lucretia Bori (Bold **64**
Ruler) (1980 14fg 1981 12g 12s³ 14g⁴) strong, good-looking gelding; fairly
useful staying handicapper at his best but is on the downgrade; appears to act
on any going; genuine; good mount for an inexperienced rider. *I. Balding.*

NIGREL 3 b.f. Sovereign Path 125–Cappelle (Relko 136) (1980 NR 1981 8.2fg **—**
8.2d) 3,000Y; second foal; half-sister to a winner in Norway; dam never ran;
in rear in maiden event and small race at Hamilton in July. *P. Haslam.*

NIKIFOROS 2 ch.c. Music Boy 124–Contadina (Memling) (1981 6g 7g) May **— p**
18; 45,000Y; well-made, quite attractive colt; brother to fairly useful 1980
2-y-o 6f winner Composer, and half-brother to 3 winners, including very useful
colts Manor Farm Boy (by Mansingh) and Conbrian (by The Brianstan); dam
never ran; backward when 6½ lengths seventh of 11 to Master Cawston in £6,000
event at Doncaster in September; unquoted when ninth of 23 in maiden race won
by Simply Great at Newmarket the following month; not sure to stay 7f. *C.
Brittain.*

NIMBLE DOVE 5 b.m. Starch Reduced 112–Red Dove (All Red 110) (1980 **62**
8d 12s 1981 12.2d 16d* 16.1s² 16.9s* 16s 18.8fg 20fg) smallish, lightly-made
mare; staying handicapper; won at Warwick in April and Wolverhampton in
May; ran well in between; seems to need some give in the ground; game. *G.
Price.*

NIMBO 3 b.g. Mummy's Pet 125–Maureens Honey 93 (Taste of Honey 92) **—**
(1980 7g 7g 7fg 1981 10s 12d 8f 7fg⁴ 8s) leggy gelding; fourth in seller at
Catterick in June; should stay 1m; sold to N. Waggott 1,050 gns Newmarket
July Sales. *N. Callaghan.*

NINE OF DIAMONDS 3 b.g. Dragonara Palace 115–Shari (Rustam 127) **§§**
(1980 6s 1981 8d 6g 7f 7d 6g) compact gelding; showed a good deal of temperament on only start as a 2-y-o and showed no form in 1981, including in a seller;
left at start final outing (blinkered); one to leave alone; sold 370 gns Ascot
November Sales. *R. Akehurst.*

NINEVEH 3 ch.f. Import 127–Catamaran 82 (Lauso) (1980 5f 5.8fg 6fg 7g **51**
7f 7fg 1981 8fg 10d 8g³ 11g 8f⁴ 8fg 12g³ 10s* 12.2g 10s 10d 10.2g) neat, strong
filly; sold out of W. Wightman's stable 1,150 gns after winning selling handicap
at Nottingham in September; stays 1½m; acts on any going, but seems suited by
soft; ran moderately in blinkers sixth start. *A. Balding.*

NIOULARGO 2 b.c. Pitskelly 122–Morzine (On Your Mark 125) (1981 6fg **107**
7d² 7f* 7g* 8g*) Apr 15; IR 3,000F, 3,500Y; quite attractive colt; good mover;
first produce; dam plating-class Irish maiden; put up a useful effort when winning
13-runner Rowley Mile Nursery at Newmarket in September but needed to be
given a very hard race to hold on by a short head from Skytrick; had previously
won 2 races in good style at Yarmouth, beating Old Country 3 lengths in 18-
runner maiden race in August and Sandwalker cleverly by ½ length under 9-7 in
nursery in September; suited by 7f and 1m; genuine; could make a very good
handicapper. *R. Armstrong.*

*Rowley Mile Nursery Handicap, Newmarket—Two fine jockeys in full
flight: Piggott and Nioulargo (nearer camera) hold on from
Eddery and Skytrick*

NIWIN'S PRESENT 2 gr.g. Free State 125–Faridetta 107 (Good Bond 122) —
(1981 6g 7f) May 20; 5,200Y; small, strong gelding; first foal; dam won four 5f
races at 2 yrs; 66/1 and badly in need of race when in rear in 15-runner maiden
event won by Celestial Dancer at Yarmouth in September; behind in similar race
at Redcar later in month. *G. Pritchard-Gordon.*

NOALTO 3 ch.c. Nonoalco 131–Lyrical 110 (Gratitude 130) (1980 6g 6g⁴ **116**
6g* 7s⁴ 6f* 7g² 7.3d⁴ 1981 8fg* 8g 6s³ 7f³ 7f 8fg³ 7.3fg³ 8fg⁴ 10g² 8s⁴ 10g)
   As in the previous season Noalto showed his best form at the height of
summer when the rattle of hooves could be plainly heard.   He ran the race of his
life in the Sussex Stakes at the end of July, finishing very strongly and being
beaten a head and a neck by Kings Lake and To-Agori-Mou; in a few more
strides Noalto would have won.   In none of his other races did Noalto show form
within a stone of that at Goodwood and we have rated him on the best of his
other form.   His only win from eleven starts came in the Easter Stakes at
Kempton in April but the pick of his other performances were undoubtedly his
third in the Hungerford Stakes at Newbury in August to Dalsaan and Star
Pastures and his very close fourth to Phydilla later the same month in the Prix
Quincey at Deauville in which he looked an unlucky loser, finishing very strongly
after encountering difficulty finding an opening.

Noalto (ch.c. 1978)	Nonoalco (b 1971)	Nearctic (br 1954)	Nearco Lady Angela
		Seximee (ch 1956)	Hasty Road Jambo
	Lyrical (ch 1966)	Gratitude (ch 1953)	Golden Cloud Verdura
		Sweet Sonnet (b 1958)	Honeyway Verse

   Noalto's conformation—he is a big, robust colt—is of the type more likely to
be suited by a galloping track than a sharp one, but he is a fine mover and his

591

Easter Stakes, Kempton—Noalto gains his only win of the season;
Star Fleet (hoops on cap) finishes second

record suggests that he is very well suited by a sharp track: he gave his most impressive performance as a two-year-old at Ripon. The Diomed Stakes at Epsom's summer meeting, and the Sussex Stakes and the Waterford Crystal Mile, both at Goodwood, would be targets for him as a four-year-old if he were ours. A hot, dry summer would enhance Noalto's chance of gaining a pattern-race victory; he acts on any going but is unquestionably best on firm. He is better suited by a mile than a mile and a quarter.

Nonoalco, the sire of Noalto, was a top-class two-year-old and a good Guineas winner, with good looks and a fine pedigree, but he failed to make the grade as a stallion in Europe and was sold to the Japanese in 1981. Noalto's dam was a tough and most consistent animal, a winner five times at six furlongs as a three-year-old. She has bred three other winners, notably the smart middle-distance performer Rhyme Royal (by Crepello). We shouldn't leave Noalto without recording that he was tried in blinkers on his fifth outing in the most recent season. *F. Durr.*

NOB 3 b.g. Mansingh 120–Fatherless 63 (Ragusa 137) (1980 6d 6g 1981 9s 8s 8f 9f 8fg 8fg² 9d*) strong, compact gelding; plater; sold to Denys Smith 2,600 gns after beating Corbie Lynn by 12 lengths at Hamilton in September; stays 9f; acts on a firm and a soft surface. *M. Jarvis.*   **52**

NOBELLION 2 gr.f. No Mercy 126–Tabellion 79 (Tabbas 99) (1981 5fg 6g 6f 5fg) Mar 20; 1,000F, 2,000Y; leggy filly; first foal; dam showed ability at 2 yrs; plating-class maiden. *J. Mason.*   **—**

NOBLANNA (USA) 3 b.f. Vaguely Noble 140–Anne la Douce 123 (Silnet 131) (1980 NR 1981 11s³ 12d² 12fg* 12fg³ 11.2d³ 10fg* 12fg³ 10d³ 10g) 70,000Y; good-bodied, attractive filly; half-sister to numerous winners, notably very smart middle-distance horse Anne's Pretender (by Pretense); dam dead-heated in Prix Vermeille; successful in apprentice races at Newmarket in June (maiden event, made nearly all) and Goodwood in August (handicap), on latter course staying on well and beating Pick A Straw a length; stays 1½m well; probably acts on any going; moved badly to post and was never going particularly well seventh start; below form final outing. *G. Harwood.*   **85**

NOBLE BLOOM (USA) 2 b.c. Vaguely Noble 140–April Bloom 108 (Bold Lad, Ire 133) (1981 8v 8v*) Apr 5; $200,000Y; half-brother to 2 winners by The Axe, including April Axe, a smart stakes winner at up to 1m; dam won twice over 5f at 2 yrs and was in frame in good races at up to 1m; always in first 2 when winning 15-runner maiden race at Maisons-Laffitte in November by 2½ lengths from Beaufais; will stay 1¼m; a well-bred colt who should win good races. *M. Saliba, France.*   **102 p**

592

NOBLE EMBLEM 2 b.c. Swing Easy 126–La Jumelle (Aureole 132) (1981 5d — 5g 5d 7g 6fg) Mar 15; 980F, 900Y; rangy colt; third produce; dam never ran; no sign of ability, including in a valuable seller; blinkered fifth outing. *C. Wildman.*

NOBLE GIFT (USA) 2 br.c. Vaguely Noble 140–Queenly Gift (Princely Gift 96 p 137) (1981 7g2 7g2) Mar 30; $130,000Y; attractive colt; good walker and very good mover; half-brother to several winners in USA, including stakes winners Princely Axe (by The Axe) and Linda Summers (by Crozier); dam unraced sister to 2,000 Guineas fourth Fidelio; short-priced favourite, kept on very well when ¾-length second to Count Pahlen in 22-runner maiden race at Newmarket in October, giving strong impression he would have won with more experience; again found one too good for him when favourite for 15-runner Houghton Stakes on same course later in month but was far from disgraced in finishing 1½ lengths second to Ivano; runs as though he needs a stiffer test of stamina and will make a good middle-distance 3-y-o. *M. Stoute.*

NOBLE LEGEND 3 b.g. Noble Decree 127–Novelista 101 (El Gallo 122) 79 (1980 7g 8.2s 8s 10.2s3 1981 9s 12g 10.6d 8g 9s*) lengthy, dipped-backed geld-ing; good walker; rather disappointing until beating Hit The Road a neck in maiden race at Carlisle in June (short-priced favourite, made all); should be suited by middle distances; acts on soft going. *M. H. Easterby.*

NOBLE PERRY 3 b.f. Perdu 121–Noble Nugget (Klondyke Bill 125) (1980 5f 42 5fg 6g2 7g4 6g 6d 5d 1981 6s4 6fg3 6g 6g) leggy filly; in frame in maiden races at Hamilton in the spring; will stay 1m. *Mrs A. Bell.*

NOBLE PHILIP (USA) 4 b.c. Noble Decree 127–Quezette (Test Case 125) 63 (1980 7f 8.2fg 7f 10d 8g 8.2s 8fg 8d 7g 8g 7d2 7s 1981 7d 7fg 8d 8f4 7.6g* 8f 7fg 7fg 7fg 7h4 7fg) compact colt; won handicap at Lingfield in June; stays 1m; probably acts on any going; blinkered once in 1980, sometimes bandaged. *M. McCourt.*

NOBLEU 4 ch.g. Blue Cashmere 129–Palanna 87 (Pall Mall 132) (1980 8f 57 8fg 8f 8fg* 8d 8g3 8s 8f* 8.2d 1981 10.5d 10f3 10f4 8f 8fg 8f 9d 10fg 8g 8g2 8s* 11d 8g) compact gelding; won handicap at Newcastle in October; blinkered when behind in valuable seller ninth start; stays 1¼m; acts on any going; suitable mount for an apprentice. *P. Asquith.*

NOBLE WHIN 3 ch.g. Flatbush 95–Noble Device (El Cid 109) (1980 5d4 — § 5f 5h4 5f2 5fg 5f 6g4 5g 5d* 5d4 5s 1981 6s4 5d 5g3 5d2 5d 5g 5g 6fg 5fg 8f 7g 7fg 9f 5d) neat, strong gelding; unreliable handicapper; ran moderately in a seller seventh start; stays 6f; acts on any going but seems particularly well suited by a soft surface; occasionally blinkered as a 2-y-o; bolted with inex-perienced claimer once in 1980. *H. Bell.*

NO BOMBS 6 b.g. St Paddy 133–Land of Fire 99 (Buisson Ardent 129) (1980 104 12f* 13fg* 14d* 14.7g 14.7g3 12fg* 1981 12fg* 12g) big, useful sort; useful per-former; cracked a cannon bone at 5 yrs and was having first outing for 12

Moet and Chandon Silver Magnum, Epsom—Mr Thomson Jones and No Bombs (checks) win for the second year in succession. Gay George is a close second with the ill-fated Get Stoned third

months when gaining second success in Moet and Chandon Silver Magnum (gentlemen riders) at Epsom in August, leading close home to beat Gay George by a neck; in rear under top weight in William Hill November Handicap at Doncaster on only other start; effective at 1¾m and stays 2m; evidently acts on any going; tough and genuine and has a good turn of foot; used to give trouble at start on occasions; goes well for apprentice K. Hodgson. *M. H. Easterby.*

NO CLOWN 2 b.g. Cawston's Clown 113–Sweet Hortense 71 (King's Troop 118) **76**
(1981 5g⁴ 6f⁴ 6fg 6f⁴ 5fg* 6fg 6d) Feb 10; 5,600Y; strong, sprint type; third foal; half-brother to a winner in Malaya; dam stayed 1m; put up best effort when strongly ridden in 9-runner nursery at Newcastle in August, winning by a length from Cedrella; best form at 5f; acts on firm going and wasn't disgraced on only outing on a soft surface; hung when blinkered sixth outing. *M. H. Easterby.*

NO CONTEST 2 ch.c. Nonoalco 131–Never So Lovely 87 (Realm 129) (1981 **79**
5g 5g⁴ 6f 6g 7d 7g⁴ 6g⁴ 6s* 6s) Apr 8; IR 3,000Y; workmanlike colt; good mover; first foal; dam 6f winner; kept on well when winning 10-runner maiden race at Hamilton in October by 2 lengths from Shileen; creditable fourth of 17 to Bold Fort in £4,500 nursery at Newmarket the previous week; stays 7f; acts on soft going; poorly drawn and didn't run up to his best on final start. *F. Durr.*

NOCTURNAL BOY 5 ch.h. Realm 129–Night Attire 77 (Shantung 132) **?**
(1980 6v 6fg⁴ 6f 6fg 6g² 6g 6g⁴ 6g 6g 5d⁴ 6fg 6d* 1981 6v) fair handicapper; behind only outing at 5 yrs in this country at Ayr in March; subsequently sent to USA and won 7f claiming race at Calder in September; seems to stay 1m; probably not at his best on very soft ground. *N. Callaghan.*

NO DEFECT 2 ro.g. No Mercy 126–Ruby's Chance 71 (Charlottesville 135) **70**
(1981 6g 6f 6fg 6fg 7.2v 8g) Mar 20; 3,100Y; rather unfurnished gelding; fourth foal; half-brother to 2 winners abroad; dam won over 1½m but was disqualified; beaten in sellers on second, third and sixth outings but ran well under a biggish weight in 21-runner maiden auction event at Redcar in September on fourth, finishing 4½ lengths eighth to Nagalia; left jockey in stalls on next appearance; should be suited by 7f. *Hbt Jones.*

NO HACK 2 ch.c. High Line 125–Cut and Thrust 78 (Pardal 130) (1981 7fg 8d) —
Apr 13; tall, lightly-made colt; half-brother to middle-distance winner Abielle (by Abwah) and a winner in Holland; dam won over 8.5f; behind at Newbury in large fields for maiden race in August (33/1) and £4,200 event in September (16/1). *H. Candy.*

NO ILLUSION 4 ch.f. Grey Mirage 128–Leitha (Vienna 127) (1980 NR **48**
1981 10s* 10f 12f 12d 10s³ 10s⁴) plater; won at Leicester in May (bought in 2,000 gns); stays 1½m; acts well on soft going; often bandaged. *D. Wintle.*

NO INK 2 b.f. No Mercy 126–Inklet (Never Say Die 137) (1981 5g 6fg 5g) —
Apr 3; half-sister to fairly useful 2-y-o winners by Sayfar and Caerdeon; dam, a twin, is daughter of smart sprinter Ink Spot; unquoted when behind in maiden races, including one at Folkestone. *D. Grissell.*

NOIRIO 2 b.c. Blakeney 126–Noirima 110 (Right Tack 131) (1981 5g 6f 7g) —
Jan 27; neat, strong, good-quartered, attractive colt; first foal; dam very useful at up to 1m; second favourite for 6f event at Leicester in June but couldn't quicken after looking dangerous 2f out and finished only sixth of 15, 15 lengths behind Custer; off course subsequently till September (well beaten in good-class event); bred to stay middle distances. *B. Hobbs.*

NO LUTE (FR) 3 b.c. Luthier 126–Prudent Miss 120 (Prudent II 133) (1980 **129**
8.5f⁴ 8s² 1981 10v* 10.5g*(dis) 10.5s* 12g 10g⁴)
No Lute, who joined Cecil from France in the summer, will probably be his stable's chief hope in the top middle-distance races for older horses in 1982 until Ardross is brought back to a mile and a half in the second half of the year. He'll be a worthy representative, too, if he can recover the form which saw him

Prix Lupin, Longchamp—No Lute wins from The Wonder, Dunphy and Bikala

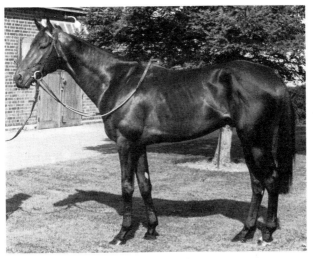

Mr R. E. Sangster's "No Lute"

an impressive winner from a strong field in the Prix Lupin at Longchamp in May.
He looked a high-class colt there—at that stage the best of the French classic
three-year-olds—and reproduction of that form would make him a formidable
challenger in such races as the John Porter Stakes and the Coronation Cup.
No Lute was given an enterprising ride in the Lupin and dominated the race.
His rider Eddery had him in the lead on settling down and proceeded to set a
very steady pace until quickening clear in good style in the straight. No Lute
never looked likely to be caught and passed the post three lengths clear of The
Wonder, with Dunphy third and the subsequent Prix du Jockey-Club winner
Bikala fourth. He clearly wasn't in the least inconvenienced by the heavy
rain or very soft going. Curiously No Lute was down on the race card as trained
by Robert Sangster, one of his part-owners. No Lute had been trained by
the Norwegian Paus when winning the Prix Santoi at Saint-Cloud in March
narrowly from Bikala and the Prix Greffulhe at Longchamp in April by a length
from The Wonder. But after a post-Greffulhe test revealed traces of the anabolic
steroid nandrolone in No Lute's system, the horse was disqualified, and Paus
was fined 100,000 francs and had his trainer's licence taken away indefinitely
only the day before the Lupin. Apparently the drug had been administered to
No Lute in February as a conditioner after a bout of coughing, but the drug's
effects should have worn off long before the Greffulhe. Reportedly tests on
No Lute a few days before the Lupin were negative, so he was allowed to run.

No Lute (Fr) (b.c. 1978)	Luthier (b 1965)	Klairon (b 1952)		Clarion III Kalmia
		Flute Enchantee (b 1950)		Cranach Montagnana
	Prudent Miss (b 1967)	Prudent II (ch 1959)		My Babu Providence
		Miss Glasso (br 1961)		Ratification Tulip

No Lute came under the care of Albert Klimscha, junior, after the Lupin,
racing once in his name. He dead-heated for seventh place behind Bikala in
the Prix du Jockey-Club at Chantilly in June, his only race over a mile and a

595

half, a distance which he should stay. He started favourite but ran poorly and was beaten almost twenty lengths. X-rays on No Lute showed pulled ligaments behind and above the off-fore knee, which probably accounts for his poor showing. No Lute subsequently joined Cecil at Newmarket and had his first race for him in the Valdoe Stakes at Goodwood in September. He finished last of the four runners, about six lengths behind Prince Bee, and didn't do himself justice. Apparently he was taking time to acclimatise and didn't fulfil his engagement in the following month's Prix de l'Arc de Triomphe, but we understand that he was working better at home towards the end of the season. We fancy that English racegoers will see a different No Lute from the one at Goodwood in due course.

No Lute is a big, attractive colt who cost 640,000 francs (around £68,000) when bought at Deauville as a yearling. His sire Luthier, who also won the Lupin, sadly died in 1981 after a heart attack. The dam Prudent Miss was a very smart miler who won the Prix d'Astarte and was second to Pampered Miss in the Poule d'Essai des Pouliches. She's a half-sister to two winners, including the very useful middle-distance stayer Miss Molly, grandam of Lydian, Mot D'Or and Sharpman. Prudent Miss has also produced two winners by Riverman, namely Provider, a modest winner at up to a mile and a quarter, and River Lady, a top-class two-year-old filly in France in 1981. *H. Cecil.*

NOMADIC PLEASURE 3 ch.f. Habitat 134–Petite Marmite 110 (Babur 126)   **91** (1980 5s² 5g² 6d 1981 7s 9s* 8d²) strong, good sort; half-sister to 3 winners, including Prix Vermeille winner Paulista (by Sea Hawk II); won maiden event at Wolverhampton in April by ¾ length from For The Flag; not seen out after finishing 2 lengths second to Oh So Choosy in minor event at Warwick later in month; stayed 9f; acted on soft going; retired to stud. *J. Tree.*

NONCHALANT 6 b.h. Wolver Hollow 126–Aspasie (Milesian 125) (1980   **52** 8fg 7g³ 7g 8d 10.5g 10fg 8g 1981 8v³ 8g) rangy horse; good walker; third in seller at Ayr in March; best form at up to 1¼m; acts on a firm and a soft surface; has worn a tongue strap; has twice worn blinkers; sometimes wears bandages. *A. Smith.*

NON-CONFERENCE 2 ch.f. My Swanee 122–Chinook Maiden (Siliconn 121)   **—** (1981 5f) lengthy, unfurnished filly; first foal; dam never ran; unquoted, finished out of first 11 of 18 behind Knight Security in maiden event at Pontefract in June. *J. Berry.*

NONOARTICA 3 b.f. Nonoalco 131–Limuru 83 (Alcide 136) (1980 6 starts,   **?** including 6v* 6d² 8d³ 1981 including 7fg) 75,000Y: half-sister to 5 winners, including Derby runner-up Cavo Doro (by Sir Ivor); dam, 1m and 1¼m handicapper, is half-sister to good miler Saintly Song; successful once from 6 starts in Norway as a 2-y-o; about 10 lengths sixth of 9 to Fairy Footsteps in Ladbrokes Nell Gwyn Stakes at Newmarket in April; successful 4 times in Norway afterwards, including in 1¼m Peugeot Cup at Övrevoll in August; acts on heavy going. *T. Dahl.*

NO NO BLUETTE 2 ch.f. Nonoalco 131–Blue Rid (Ridan) (1981 6fg 6fg)   **—** Feb 20; 30,000,000 lire Y (approx £14,000); good-bodied filly; first foal; dam, half-sister to Dewhurst winner King's Lane, won 4 times in Italy, including once over 1m; behind in maiden races at Newbury in August (12/1) and Salisbury in September (50/1, disputed lead for 3½f). *I. Balding.*

NO NO HOLDINGS 5 b.g. Nonoalco 131–Marie Curie 96 (Exbury 138) (1980   **37** 8s⁴ 8s* 9.6fg 7fg 8h 8f⁴ 10d 9d² 8fg 8fg⁴ 8d 10d 1981 11d* 8g 10fg 10f 9fg 11.5fg 12d) lightly-made gelding; plater; won apprentice seller at Wolverhampton in April (bought in 850 gns); stays 11f; acts on soft going; has been tried in blinkers. *P. Feilden.*

NONSTOP 2 ch.c. Nonoalco 131–Fast Motion 86 (Midsummer Night II 117)   **72** (1981 7g 8g 8s) Mar 15; tall, rangy colt; third foal; half-brother to 1½m winner Alanood (by Northfields); dam won over 6f at 2 yrs; showed speed in maiden and minor races, finishing eighth in big fields on first and third outings; may be suited by a return to distances short of 1m; didn't move well to start second outing. *W. O'Gorman.*

NOOKIE BEAR 4 ch.g. Be Friendly 130–Marla (Hul a Hul 124) (1980 10fg   **—** 10g 8g 11d 11.7g 1981 11.7d) tall, narrow gelding; plating-class maiden; best run at 7f on a firm surface; blinkered only start in 1981. *P. Mitchell.*

NO PARTING 7 b.m. Baldric II 131–Heidi II (Venture VII 129) (1980   **—** NR 1981 15.5fg) poor maiden. *J. Bridger.*

NORDAN ENTERPRISE 3 br.f. Rapid River 127–C'Est Bien (Gaily Mill 86)   —
(1980 5g 6g 6f³ 6f 6d 5d 1981 7g⁴ 7fg 6fg 5fg) lightly-made filly; fourth in
seller at Doncaster in May; possibly stays 7f; blinkered third start; sold 380 gns
Doncaster August Sales. *M. Camacho.*

NORD HINDER 3 gr.g. Spitsbergen 103–Tipulidae (Game Rights 91) (1980   —
8d 1981 14g 11.7f) no worthwhile form in maiden races. *L. Kennard.*

NOREENA 2 b.f. Nonoalco 131–Vela 123 (Sheshoon 132) (1981 6fg 7g) Apr 30;   —
half-sister to 3 winners, including Irish 1¼m winner Nikitina (by Nijinsky); dam
won Criterium des Pouliches; in rear in maiden race at Salisbury and minor event
at Brighton in September. *R. Smyth.*

NORFOLK FLIGHT 4 br.g. Blakeney 126–First Light 82 (Primera 131) (1980   93
10.2d⁴ 10s 8s 8f* 10f* 11.7s 12g² 10fg⁴ 10f* 8g 11fg* 12g 10.2v² 1981 8g³ 11s
10.6s³ 10f² 10f* 10.2fg⁴ 10f³ 10d* 11f⁴ 10fg 10fg* 10g* 9g 10g) strong gelding;
front-running handicapper; successful at Brighton in June (trotted up), Yarmouth in July and Goodwood and Brighton again in September; beat Lulav
by 2½ lengths for final success; suited by middle distances; acts on any going but is
ideally suited by top-of-the-ground; suitable mount for an inexperienced rider;
genuine. *W. Hastings-Bass.*

NORFOLK GOLD 4 b.f. Gilded Leader 75–Norfolk House (Cantab 94) (1980   47
12g 11d 10g 12f 10fg 8d⁴ 10.8d 10s³ 1981 8g* 10.6s* 10f 10fg 8f⁴ 8h 10d) lightly-
built filly; poor mover; plater; successful at Pontefract (bought in 1,350 gns)
and Haydock (bought in 1,550 gns) in May; stays 1¼m well; acts on any going.
B. McMahon.

NORFOLK QUEEN 3 b.f. Blakeney 126–Eringa 101 (Saint Crespin III 132)   63
(1980 6fg² 7f² 7g³ 1981 10g³ 10.1d² 12d 10fg⁴ 10s²) neat, attractive filly;
stayed on when second in minor race at Windsor in July and maiden event at
Nottingham in October; should be suited by 1½m (had stiff task, sweated up
and was never going well when tried at trip). *J. Bethell.*

NORFOLK REALM 3 b.c. Realm 129–Norfolk Light 86 (Blakeney 126)   81 d
(1980 5fg 7fg 7d* 1981 7d 8.2fg 8g* 10g³ 8fg² 8fg 8fg⁴ 8g 8g 8.2v² 8v⁴) rangy
colt; beat Ardoony by a length in Thirsk Hunt Cup (Handicap) in May; second
in handicaps at Redcar (to Atlantic Boy in Ronaldshay Cup) and Haydock afterwards; ran moderately in between; stays 1¼m; probably acts on any going;
blinkered seventh outing; sold to P. Makin 6,200 gns Newmarket Autumn
Sales. *C. Brittain.*

NORFOLK STORM 3 b.c. Blakeney 126–Crystal Palace 121 (Solar Slipper   —
131) (1980 7d 1981 10d 13f 13.1g⁴ 15.5s⁴) quite an attractive, well-made
colt; rather a disappointing maiden; looks slow; sold out of H. Cecil's stable
3,600 gns Ascot August Sales after second outing. *M. McCormack.*

NORMAN'S BOY 3 ch.g. Tarboosh–Flattery (Atan) (1980 5f 6fg 6d 7g²   —
7fg² 1981 8d) fair sort; second in sellers as a 2-y-o; should stay 1m; wears
blinkers. *D. Hanley.*

NORMAN STYLE 3 b.c. Malacate 131–Autocratic (Tyrant) (1980 6g* 8d   107
1981 8.2fg⁴ 10.4d 7g⁴ 6f 6fg 7g* 7g 7g² 7g) lengthy, workmanlike colt; won
Harry Peacock Challenge Cup (Handicap) at Newcastle in July, leading in last
furlong and keeping on to beat Piperhill by ½ length; ran creditably in varied
company on several other occasions, on last 2 finishing 1½ lengths second to
Swinging Rebel in £3,500 handicap and 6½ lengths fifth of 7 behind Moorestyle in
Bisquit Cognac Challenge Stakes, both at Newmarket in October (ran particularly well in latter); not disgraced at 1¼m but seems best at around 7f; ridden
by a lad in paddock; sold to BBA 25,000 gns Newmarket December Sales.
J. W. Watts.

NORROY 4 ch.g. Northfields–Tzaritsa 113 (Young Emperor 133) (1980 8g   68
8g² 8fg³ 8d² 7fg* 8g 10s 8d 8d 1981 7g* 7.6fg 8fg* 8f³ 7fg⁴ 10g 8s) well-made
gelding; successful in handicaps at Lingfield in June (heavily backed in apprentice event) and at Doncaster in July; ran badly in between (reportedly finished
lame); suited by 1m; seems to act on any going; blinkered once in 1980. *R.
Baker.*

NORTHAMPTON 3 ch.f. Northfields–Cobble (Major Portion 129) (1980 NR   —
1981 10g) 12,000Y; small, useful-looking filly; half-sister to a winner in Italy;
dam won over 7.5f in Ireland; weak in market when last of 8 behind Strigida in
Sir Charles Clore Memorial Stakes at Newbury in May (dwelt, but was much
close up); retained 7,000 gns Newmarket December Sales. *B. Hills.*

NORTH ASTRA (USA) 2 br.f. Far North 120–Princeton Pride (Cornish   93
Prince) (1981 6s* 8g 7g* 8d) Mar 8; $180,000Y; third foal; half-sister to

smart Murrtheblurr (by Torsion), a stakes winner at up to 1m; dam stakes-placed winner at up to 6f; winner twice at Naas, beating Miss Lilian a neck in maiden race in May and Shoubad Melody 4 lengths in minor event in October; favourite despite a 5-lb penalty when modest fifth of 15 to Tumble Belle in nursery at Leopardstown later in October; should stay 1m; yet to race on a firm surface; blinkered last 2 outings. *D. Weld, Ireland.*

NORTH BRITON 2 b.c. Northfields–Juliette Marny 123 (Blakeney 126) — p (1981 6d 8g) Apr 14; neat, attractive colt; third living foal; dam won Oaks and Irish Guinness Oaks; behind in large fields of maidens at Newbury in June (20/1) and Newmarket in October (33/1, showed up to past halfway); should do better over further in 1982. *J. Tree.*

NORTHERN CHANCE 3 b.f. Northfields–Good Opportunity (Hail to Reason) 78 (1980 NR 1981 7g² 8d³ 7d 7g² 7f 7f 7f² 8fg* 7g) useful-looking, good sort; third living foal; half-sister to 1977 French 1¼m 2-y-o winner Better Opportunity (by Prince Regent) and a winner in Italy; dam twice-raced half-sister to Bold and Brave, a very smart winner at up to 1m; beat Refreshment by 1½ lengths in maiden race at Goodwood in August, cruising through almost on a tight rein when an opening appeared and winning very smoothly indeed; stays 1m; yet to race on very soft going, but seems to act on any other; blinkered last 2 outings; has occasionally started slowly; looked as if she was past her best final outing. *J. Winter.*

NORTHERN ECLIPSE 4 b.c. Derring-Do 131–Haunting Melody 96 (Sing 74 Sing 134) (1980 6fg 6d 6g⁴ 5d 5d 1981 5g² 5g 5f⁴ 6g 5g*) leggy, fair sort; sprint handicapper; awarded race at Doncaster in November; acts well on firm going; has run respectably for an apprentice; trained by G. Fletcher first 2 starts. *P. Haslam.*

NORTHERN INTEREST 2 gr.c. My Swanee 122–Frisky Molly 64 (Dumbarnie — 125) (1981 7fg) Mar 14; 920F, 1,800Y; poor mover; half-brother to fair 5f winner Fingora (by Raffingora); dam won at up to 1m; 8/1, dwelt when tailed-off last of 12 behind Rapid Knot in maiden race at Catterick in August. *M. Tompkins.*

NORTHERN KING 4 gr.c. Northfields–Kathinka 79 (Sovereign Path 125) §§ (1980 7f 10g 12g 8g 10.4g 8fg 8f 1981 15.8s) compact colt; has shown a little ability but is thoroughly unreliable nowadays and is best left alone. *T. Kersey.*

NORTHERN MINSTREL (USA) 3 ch.g. Orbit Dancer–Old Tinker (Old 58 Glendale) (1980 6d 8fg 8g⁴ 1981 10.6s 8.2f² 8f⁴ 8f 7d 7s 7g) dipped-backed gelding; quite moderate form, including in sellers; stays 1m; looked none too genuine third start; retained 1,700 gns Newmarket Autumn Sales. *J. Fitzgerald.*

NORTHERN PRINCE 3 b.c. Northfields–Cecilia Q.C. 89 (Counsel 118) (1980 74 7d 1981 8.2s³ 10d² 10.2d* 10.1f² 10g³ 10f³ 12f³ 11.7g⁴ 12g² 12g) small colt; beat Green Memory by 5 lengths in apprentice handicap at Bath in June; placed on most other starts; best form at 1¼m; acts on any going; sold 7,000 gns Newmarket Autumn Sales. *P. Walwyn.*

NORTHERN RELISH 2 br.g. Relko 136–Northern Lady 95 (The Brianstan — 128) (1981 7f) May 20; first foal; dam won 3 sprint races at 2 yrs; needed race and was always struggling when in rear in maiden race won by Connaught River at Redcar in September. *P. Calver.*

NORTHERN SCENE 2 ch.f. Habitat 134–Algonkin (Tom Rolfe) (1981 5g⁴ 78 5g* 5f 6fg 5g 6g) Apr 17; small, quite attractive filly; fourth foal; dam, winner over 1m and 9f at 6 yrs in Ireland, is half-sister to very successful American broodmare Durga; landed the odds decisively by 3 lengths from Latin Light in maiden race at Wolverhampton in June; should be suited by 6f (had stiffish tasks when tried at trip); blinkered fifth appearance. *F. J. Houghton.*

NORTHERN SUPREMO (USA) 3 ch.c. Northern Dancer–Roussalka 123 88 (Habitat 134) (1980 6g 1981 8fg⁴ 11s*(dis) 11.5f² 12f 12g²) small, strong, deep-girthed colt; first foal; dam won 7 races at up to 4 yrs, including Nassau Stakes twice; seemed to beat Ardar on merit by ½ length in maiden race at Newbury in May but was subsequently disqualified and his rider fined £400 for improper riding; odds on when second in similar races won by Lakenheath at Yarmouth in June and Amal Naji at York in July, sticking on well on former course but looking none too genuine on latter; beaten less than 3 lengths when sixth to Feltwell in King George V Stakes (Handicap) at Royal Ascot in between; stayed 1½m; didn't stride out particularly well to post at

Yarmouth and was possibly ideally suited by some give in the ground; blinkered last 2 outings; syndicated to stand at Owens Farms, Washington. *H. Cecil.*

NORTHGATE LODGE 3 b.g. Warpath 113–Pall Nan 86 (Pall Mall 132) **60**
(1980 7g 8d 1981 16.5fg* 15.8fg 18f) leggy gelding; showed improved form when beating Triple Secret 2 lengths in maiden event at Redcar in July; had stiff tasks when behind in handicaps afterwards; stays well; acts on a firm surface. *M. H. Easterby.*

NORTH HUT 3 ch.f. Northfields–Whispering II 111 (Whistler 129) (1980 NR **—**
1981 6g 5fg) lightly-made, unimpressive filly; half-sister to 3 winners, including useful 1974 2-y-o 6f winner Quietness (by Ribero); dam won twice over 5f from 3 starts at 2 yrs; well behind in apprentice event at Nottingham (needed race) and maiden race at Warwick in August. *D. H. Jones.*

NORTHJET 4 ch.c. Northfields–Jellatina (Fortino II 120) (1980 7s* 6d* 5g* **136**
6g* 6g 6.5d 6d² 6s³ 5f 1981 8d 8s* 7s³ 9.2s² 8f* 8f*)
During the past four years the outright or partial purchase of good horses halfway through their careers has been a speciality of Serge Fradkoff, and on balance he appears to have had the Midas touch. While one side of the coin reveals the occasional failure like Try To Smile, who has repaid little of the sizeable amount spent on him following his good run in the 1979 Prix Robert Papin, the other shows several major successes. Sanedtki proved herself a top-class performer, annexing among other races the Prix de la Foret (twice), the Prix du Moulin and the Santa Margarita Handicap; Kilijaro also won a number of important events in Europe and America, notably the Prix du Moulin and the Yellow Ribbon Stakes; Providential gained successes in the Prix Greffulhe and the Washington International; and Protection Racket won the 1981 Tote-Ebor Handicap, Doncaster Cup and Irish St Leger after Fradkoff purchased a half-share in him from the part-owner of Kilijaro. Each of the four was undoubtedly a fair investment—Sanedtki cost approximately £116,500 and Kilijaro about £200,000—but none can compare in this respect with Northjet who developed into the best miler in Europe only a few months after Fradkoff, outbidding a

Prix Jacques le Marois, Deauville—Northjet puts up an exceptional performance to win from To-Agori-Mou (No. 10) and Kings Lake (dark colours) with Hilal fourth

group of breeders from New Zealand, had bought him for a sum reported to be in the region of 400,000 dollars.

The general reaction to Northjet's rise to the top can be best summed up by borrowing Sir Walter Scott's phrase 'respect was mingled with surprise', for the colt's brilliantly impressive win in the Prix Jacques le Marois came as something of a shock. Talk before the race largely concerned Kings Lake and To-Agori-Mou who between them had collected many of the best mile races in England and Ireland and had fought out a pulsating series of finishes in the Airlie/Coolmore Irish Two Thousand Guineas, the St James's Palace Stakes and the Sussex Stakes. Given that the three-year-old milers in France did not appear outstanding—To-Agori-Mou's stable-companion Recitation had decisively outpointed most of them in the Poule d'Essai des Poulains—and that the older French milers looked fully exposed as short of the absolute top class, it was generally anticipated that Kings Lake and To-Agori-Mou would be more than capable of accounting for the home defence at Deauville. The mainstays of that defence seemed to be the Prix d'Ispahan winner The Wonder, the Poule d'Essai des Pouliches winner Ukraine Girl, and Cresta Rider, Gosport, Hilal and Northjet, each of whom had won at least one pattern race in the current season.

Northjet's previous career had not been without interest. After winning the second of his three starts in Italy at two he had proved the best Italian sprinter early in 1980, winning four times, and had been transferred from Brogi to Douieb following a course-record breaking win in the Premio Melton at Rome, where he beat the English challenger Marching On by a length and a half. Well beaten behind Kearney in the Cork and Orrery Stakes at Royal Ascot on his next start, Northjet subsequently ran creditably in some good six-furlong races in France, gaining places behind Kilijaro in the Prix de Meautry and the Prix de Seine-et-Oise. Even so, at the end of the year Northjet was the best part of a stone below the top class, and his first four starts in 1981, though they showed he was suited by further than six furlongs, still left him with quite a bit to find to stand a chance of beating tip-top opponents. After finishing fifth to Hilal in the Prix de Ris-Orangis at Evry Northjet had won the Prix du Muguet at Saint-Cloud by a neck from Joberan and had gone on to run creditably in two races at Longchamp, giving weight all round when a two-and-a-half-length third to Prince Mab in the Prix du Palais Royal and keeping on well without really threatening the winner when a two-length second to The Wonder in the Prix d'Ispahan. It had also been intended to run him in the Sussex Stakes, but the appearance of a small abscess on a fetlock-joint on the eve of the race prevented his participation.

On the evidence of the Jacques le Marois it was very fortunate for Kings Lake that Northjet didn't run at Goodwood. Sea's Valley, acting as Northjet's pacemaker, went on immediately the stalls opened and set a cracking gallop until Cresta Rider, on whom front-running tactics had paid off in the Prix Jean Prat, took over at halfway and maintained the pace for another two furlongs. At this point challengers loomed up in the shape of Kings Lake, To-Agori-Mou, Hilal and Northjet, the last of whom had never been far behind the leaders and was obviously travelling smoothly. Three hundred yards out there were, on the face of it, several in with a chance; a few moments later Northjet pulled his way to the front on the bridle and then produced a spectacular surge which saw his sprinting away from his toiling rivals with every stride. Pushed out with hands and heels only, he passed the post in splendid isolation, an effortless five lengths clear of To-Agori-Mou who got the better of Kings Lake by a nose in a desperate struggle for second with Hilal and The Wonder very close up in fourth and fifth. The time was the second fastest recorded over the course.

Northjet hadn't just won, he had trounced a top-class field in a manner which brooked no argument. The result emphatically was not, as some had it, a fluke. We have pointed out before that pure chance provides a poor explanation for unexpected outcomes to races—there are invariably more logical reasons to hand. In this instance one might have been that all Northjet's best opponents ran a long way below form, but this takes some swallowing. The trip was almost certainly a bit sharp for The Wonder, the ground perhaps firmer than ideally suited To-Agori-Mou and Kings Lake (whose jockey Eddery also finished the race without his whip), but none of these excuses was put forward with great conviction and Starkey, the rider of the second, expressed the opinion that his mount would not have beaten Northjet even if underfoot conditions had been easier. Allowing for this, the inescapable conclusion is that it was primarily Northjet's remarkable improvement which enabled him to win as he did, and that improvement was probably due to the track, the tactics employed and the ground. Credence can be given to Douieb's claim that Northjet was very well

Prix du Moulin de Longchamp—Northjet breaks the course record;
Hilal (No. 4), The Wonder (far side) and Phydilla
cross the line next

suited by the straight mile, a new experience for him, since some horses go particularly well on this type of course where they are able to stride along without meeting any turns to interrupt their momentum or disturb their balance. Allied to this, the presence of a pacemaker to ensure a strong gallop throughout was evidently exactly what Northjet needed—in none of his previous starts had these tactics been tried.   Above all, Northjet encountered firm going for the first time in 1981 at Deauville and benefited considerably from this.   He had run well enough on soft in the past but the Jacques le Marois showed that on firm he was capable of producing the exceptional.

Fortunately for Northjet his next run, in the Prix du Moulin de Longchamp, again saw the ground in his favour.   He had two pacemakers, Sea's Valley being joined by Try To Smile; the nine other runners included four beaten pointless at Deauville, namely Gosport, Hilal, The Wonder and Ukraine Girl, the English challengers Belmont Bay and Another Realm, and Phydilla (also trained by Douieb) and Ya Zaman, successful respectively in the Prix Quincey and Prix Messidor.   Northjet, who had started at a shade over 7/1 at Deauville, was odds on this time, coupled with his stable companions.   He duly won, but did so less authoritatively.   As his pacemakers set the necessary fast pace, Northjet pulled very hard for his head in third or fourth place.   Moving through to lead as they swung for home, he looked to be going well more than a furlong out but failed to burst clear as at Deauville and Head was forced to ride him right out in the closing stages to win by a length and a half, a nose and the same from Hilal, The Wonder and Phydilla, all of whom were gaining on him at the finish.   The pace was so strong that Northjet broke the course record set by Homing in the 1978 Prix du Rond-Point.   Afterwards Douieb blamed the turning track as the cause of Northjet's performance not fully coming up to expectations.   There is probably something in this, but it is equally significant that Northjet, by pulling hard, must have weakened his reserves of strength faster than at Deauville, thereby lessening his chances of quickening so dramatically.   Nonetheless, it was still a fine display, well in advance of his pre-Deauville form.

Though Northjet had stayed nine furlongs in the Prix d'Ispahan, the way he pulled at Longchamp made us far from confident about his prospects of staying the mile-and-a-quarter trip of his last intended engagement, the Champion Stakes. As it was, his stamina wasn't put to the test for he contracted a chill the week before the race and was packed off to stud.   He will stand alongside such as Accipiter, Elocutionist, Far North, Nikoli and Kirtling at the Airdrie Stud, Kentucky, his owner retaining twenty shares and the other twenty being sold at 375,000 dollars apiece, placing a total valuation of fifteen million dollars on him.   If all goes according to plan his first book of mares will include Kilijaro and Mrs Penny.

Northjet's sire Northfields ran thirty times in two seasons' racing in America, gaining his biggest win in the nine-furlong Louisiana Derby.   He has sired a number of very good performers besides Northjet, notably Northern Treasure, Oats, North Stoke and Star Pastures.   The dam, Jellatina, won a nine-furlong apprentice handicap at Gowran Park at three and was sent to Sweden the following year after fetching 4,400 guineas at the Newmarket December Sales. She was returned to Ireland after being resold at the same venue as a five-year-old for 10,500 guineas.   Before Northjet she produced three winners on the flat and

601

Mr S. Fradkoff's "Northjet"

one over the jumps, by far the best of them the good Italian sprinter Madang (by Habitat), a three-parts brother to Northjet, who won the Premio Melton twice and the Prix du Gros Chene and went down by four lengths to Gentil-hombre in the 1977 Prix de l'Abbaye. In 1979 Jellatina had a filly by Oats and in 1980 a colt by Solinus. Her dam, Queenpot, won the One Thousand

		Northern Dancer (b 1961)	Nearctic
Northjet (ch.c. 1977)	Northfields (ch 1968)		Natalma
		Little Hut (b 1952)	Occupy
			Savage Beauty
	Jellatina (b 1966)	Fortino II (gr 1959)	Grey Sovereign
			Ranavalo
		Queenpot (br 1945)	Big Game
			Poker Chip

Guineas but foaled nothing approaching her own ability, while the third dam, a useful Irish two-year-old, also produced the Champagne Stakes winner Wat Tyler and Quarterdeck, the dam of the Irish Oaks winner Ambergris and grandam of Petingo. Northjet cost his original owner 24,000 guineas as a foal at the Newmarket December Sales. A nice colt with a flaxen mane and tail, he was, given the right conditions, a brilliant miler whose win at Deauville will remain long in the memory of those who saw it. *O. Douieb, France.*

NORTHLEIGH 2 ch.c. Reform 132–Sarsgrove 70 (Hornbeam 130) (1981 6fg 6fg³ 7g* 7d² 7d 7d²) Jan 31; quite attractive, well-made colt; half-brother to 3 winners, including fairly useful 6f and 7f winner Pay Roll (by Burglar); dam won at up to 1½m; justified favouritism in workmanlike style in **17**-runner maiden race at Leicester in September, winning by 1¼ lengths from Beldale

Dynasty; ran well in his subsequent races, including on final start when length second to Don Giovanni in minor event at Leicester in November; will stay middle distances. *J. Dunlop.*

NORTH LIGHT 2 b.c. Northern Flash–Shortigal (Galivanter 131) (1981   — p
7g) May 6; 3,000F, 11,000Y; strong colt; third foal; half-brother to a winner abroad; dam unraced half-sister to smart middle-distance handicapper Royal Match; 20/1 and not fully fit when behind in 16-runner Somerville Tattersall Stakes at Newmarket in October. *P. Walwyn.*

NORTHORPE 2 b.g. Mummy's Pet 125–Jaragua (Flaneur 109§) (1981 6f2   **78**
6f 6g) Apr 30; 3,000F, 8,200Y; big, rangy gelding; fifth living foal; dam won over 10.5f in France and also over hurdles; failed by a length to wear down all-the-way winner Bustello in 23-runner minor event at Nottingham in July, best effort. *G. Huffer.*

NORTH WEST 6 ch.g. Welsh Pageant 132–Heather Grove (Hethersett 134)   **46**
(1980 12f 10fg 10fg 1981 15.5d* 16g2 15.5d3 13.3g2 12f 15.5fg* 16fg2 16.5f* 16fg) tall, short-backed gelding; staying handicapper; goes well at Folkestone and won 3 times there; seems to act on any going; used to wear bandages. *M. Masson.*

NORTH YARD 5 b.g. Realm 129–Campitello (Hornbeam 130) (1980 10d   —
1981 10.2s 7d) ex-Irish gelding; winner of 2 handicaps at Phoenix Park in 1979; lightly raced on flat since though has won over hurdles; appears not to stay 1¼m; acts on firm going. *Mrs M. Rimell.*

NORTON CROSS 3 gr.g. Realm 129–Zameen (Armistice 131) (1980 5f4   **83**
5f4 6g* 6s 6f4 8g4 1981 5s 7d4 8g*(dis) 8g* 10d4 8f 8s) sturdy gelding; good mover; won handicaps at Redcar in May (subsequently disqualified when traces of an illegal substance were found in his system) and Ayr in July; showed improved form to beat Africanos a neck in latter; probably stays 1¼m; possibly needs some give in the ground; does best when ridden up with pace; ran poorly last 2 starts. *M. H. Easterby.*

NORWICH BOY 4 b.g. Averof 123–Teresa-Hernandez (Queen's Hussar 124)   — §
(1980 6d 5fg 5g 6g 6g4 5g 6g 1981 6d 8f 8.3fg) leggy gelding; plater; stays 6f; suited by some give in the ground; has worn blinkers; usually sweats up; looks ungenuine; sold 500 gns Ascot August Sales. *D. Weeden.*

NORWICK (USA) 2 b.c. Far North 120–Shay Sheery (A Dragon Killer) (1981   **125**
5g4 5.8g* 6fg* 6f* 7.2f* 7fg2 8s* 8s2 8g4)
In November an unbelievable bid of 40,000,000 dollars for Northern Dancer was rejected. An offer of this size for a stallion rising twenty-one illustrates as well as anything can how bloodstock prices have risen in recent years. There are plenty of other examples, as American breeders fall over themselves to obtain sons and grandsons of this most fashionable stallion. In 1980 a single share in Lyphard was sold at auction for 950,000 dollars; Storm Bird's shares were priced at 750,000 dollars, placing a total valuation on him of 30,000,000 dollars; two separate shares in Nijinsky were sold for 500,000 dollars at auction back in 1979; Northjet's syndication value is 15,000,000 dollars; Nureyev, after one season in France, has been syndicated at 355,000 dollars a share; Cresta Rider's 250,000 dollars a share works out at a total of 10,000,000 dollars; Northern Baby, after one season in Ireland, was sold to the United States for 12,000,000 dollars; Magesterial's share price is 125,000 dollars while Euclid's is 45,000 dollars; and nominations to both Lydian and Dance Bid cost 30,000 dollars. Turning to the yearling market—three colts by Northern Dancer were sold in 1981 for 3,500,000 dollars, 3,300,000 dollars and 2,950,000 dollars respectively.

Although one is driven by such statistics to wonder where it will all end, events in 1981 go some way towards explaining this amazing demand for Northern Dancer bloodstock. He himself sired the William Hill Cheveley Park Stakes winner Woodstream and several of his sons also sired top two-year-olds. The Minstrel and Be My Guest both made a big impact with their first runners, each siring two pattern-race winners; the unraced Staff Writer sired one of the best American two-year-olds, Timely Writer; the 6,215-dollar earner Vice Regent sired Deputy Minister, possibly the best North American two-year-old; and Far North, another son having his first runners, sired one of the best staying two-year-olds in Europe, Norwick.

How good Norwick was didn't become apparent until he ran in the Royal Lodge Stakes at Ascot in September, on his first appearance for eleven weeks. He'd shown himself a tough and useful colt, winning a maiden race at Bath, a £4,000 event at York under top weight, the Fenwolf Stakes at Ascot and the two-runner Cock of the North Stakes at Haydock, all in the space of little more than a month. He'd also run well when second, giving 8 lb, to the comfortable winner Padalco at Newmarket in July, but his form wasn't nearly so impressive as that of some of the other Royal Lodge runners. Silver Hawk, the favourite, had trounced Montekin, Red Sunset and Wind and Wuthering in the Intercraft Solario Stakes on his latest appearance; Zilos had won the Seaton Delaval Stakes; and Telephone Man had recently finished a good fourth in a big race in the States. Even Norwick's stable-companion Santella Man, who'd been running in nurseries, started at a shorter price. However, Norwick proved well suited by the distance of a mile and the soft ground he was meeting for the first time. In the race he set a fast pace. The chasing group, headed by Lobkowiez, narrowed his lead to a length and a half approaching the final turn but they got no closer; Norwick quickened the tempo, fought off Lobkowiez's persistent challenge halfway up the straight and then galloped on strongly to hold Silver Hawk's late run by three lengths.

In 1980 Norwick's stable sent out the second in the Royal Lodge Stakes, Recitation, who went on to win France's most important two-year-old race, the Grand Criterium, before finishing fourth in the William Hill Futurity. Norwick ran in the same races. He failed to win either but confirmed his improvement with an excellent effort in the Grand Criterium. Once again forcing tactics were employed on him. He took over from Persepolis' pace-maker Pushkin a furlong before the turn into the straight and galloped on most resolutely all the way home but this time he was up against a top-class colt in Green Forest. He was mastered at the distance and eventually went down by two and a half lengths. Norwick had no difficulty holding on to second place, four lengths ahead of Rollins and seven ahead of the previously-unbeaten Irish colt Anfield.

Like Recitation before him, Norwick finished fourth in the Futurity at

Royal Lodge Stakes, Ascot—Norwick stays on extremely well to beat Silver Hawk and Lobkowiez

Mr A. E. Bodie's "Norwick"

Doncaster. However, whereas Recitation indisputably ran well below form, Norwick, having his third hard race in a month, appeared to run within a few pounds of his best. After going on at halfway Norwick was quickly challenged by Count Pahlen and narrowly lost his lead. Although he hung on grimly until inside the final furlong he was always coming off worse and in the end he was passed also by Paradis Terrestre and Jalmood. At the line he was beaten little more than two lengths.

Norwick (USA) (b.c. Jan. 24, 1979)	Far North (b 1973)	Northern Dancer (b 1961)	Nearctic
			Natalma
		Fleur (b 1964)	Victoria Park
			Flaming Page
	Shay Sheery (b or br 1969)	A Dragon Killer (b 1955)	Roman Sandal
			Lutza
		Annie K. (b 1963)	Jester
			Sic Sic

Norwick, a 75,000-dollar yearling, is a well-made, impressive-looking individual, all in all a fine advertisement for his sire. Far North was a very smart racehorse in France, winning the Prix Saint-Roman over nine furlongs at two and the Prix Omnium over a mile at three when he also finished fifth in the Irish Sweeps Derby; what's more he is a full brother to The Minstrel. Norwick became Shay Sheery's third winner from her first three foals, following Irish Amy (by O'Hara) and On The Phone (by Selari), successful respectively in claiming races at up to nine furlongs and six furlongs. Shay Sheery too gained her four victories, all over sprint distances, in claiming company and her dam Annie K.'s sole success in thirty-nine starts came in a six-furlong claiming event. Annie K. fared much better at stud than she'd done on the racecourse. To Bosun she produced the very useful stakes performers Tico's Donna and

Cisk, winners respectively at up to nine furlongs and a mile, while her son by Damascus, Royal Damascus, won a good race in Puerto Rico. In addition to Shay Sheery she bred two other winners by the very smart miler A Dragon Killer, one of whom, Eric's Champ, was a very useful sprinter at three. Norwick has no doubt increased the appeal of the family a good deal; his yearling brother sold for 120,000 dollars at the Keeneland September Sale and Shay Sheery fetched 340,000 dollars when sold in November.

None of the relatives mentioned in the preceding paragraph won at distances longer than nine furlongs but Norwick ran at two as though he will eventually be suited by a mile and a quarter, possibly further. A tough and courageous colt, he looks sure to figure prominently in more of the top races, especially if he encounters soft going. *G. Harwood.*

NO SALE 2 b.c. Nonoalco 131–Salote 109 (Forli) (1981 7fg 8d) Mar 28; neat, well-made, attractive colt; first foal; dam suited by 1¼m; 12/1 and very much in need of race when never-dangerous 11 lengths sixth of 19 to Dageegah in maiden race at Salisbury in September; eighth of 15 to The Nub in similar race at Bath in October. *R. Hern.* —

NOSEY'S DAUGHTER 2 b.f. Song 132–Roman Nose 95 (Nosca) (1981 5d 6fg) Apr 23; half-sister to numerous winners; dam 2-y-o 6f winner; unquoted when in rear in maiden races at Lingfield and Folkestone in August. *P. Mitchell.* —

NOT AT HOME 2 gr.f. Homeric 133–Desert Nymph (Silver Shark 129) (1981 7d 7g⁴) Feb 8; small, lengthy filly; second living foal; dam third in Irish 1,000 Guineas; 14/1, never far off pace and kept on quite well when 4¼ lengths fourth of 29 to Chalon in maiden race at Newmarket in October, easily better effort; will stay 1¼m. *R. Hern.* **80**

NOT FOR SHOW 2 b.c. Mummy's Pet 125–Emperor Star (King Emperor) (1981 6g* 7g*) Mar 25; 7,400Y; good-looking colt; good walker; second foal; brother to 3-y-o Azaam, successful at up to 7f; dam of little account; unbeaten in end-of-season races at Newmarket and Doncaster; pushed out vigorously with hands and heels to take 21-runner maiden race by 1½ lengths from Mummy's Pleasure on first-named and beat Voyant in similar style by 2½ lengths in 11-runner £4,300 race at Doncaster; impressed us at Doncaster and could develop into a very useful horse at up to 1m in 1982. *G. Harwood.* **106 p**

NOTRE PLAISIR (HOL) 4 ch.c. Mon Plaisir 121–Crowd Pleaser 47 (Don II 123) (1980 6fg 7.6f 8f* 9g 12g* 10g 14.5g2 1981 12d 12g³ 12.5s 12fg⁴ 10s) smallish, lengthy ex-English colt; successful in Dutch 2,000 Guineas (awarded race) and Dutch Derby at Duindigt in 1980; apprentice ridden when third in handicap at Thirsk in April, only worthwhile form in this country; stays 1¾m; appears to act on any going; blinkered final outing; often bandaged; trained by N. Guest first 4 starts. *H. Wolffers, Holland.* **53**

NOUMAYR 2 b.c. Mount Hagen 127–Noureen (Astec 128) (1981 5fg 7fg 7d* 7g 8d) Mar 14; compact, quite attractive colt; second foal; half-brother to very useful 3-y-o Nasseem (by Zeddaan), a winner at up to 1m; dam unraced half-sister to Tajubena, a very smart winner at up to 1¼m; 33/1 when showing improved form to beat Nioulargo ¾ length in 18-runner maiden race at Newmarket in August; not disgraced in nurseries subsequently; will be suited by 1¼m; needs some give in the ground. *F. J. Houghton.* **86**

NO-U-TURN 3 b.c. Nonoalco 131–Raffmarie 78 (Raffingora 130) (1980 7fg⁴ 6g³ 6fg* 6d² 7v 1981 7g 8f³ 8f 10f 10fg 10f² 10.4s 10fg² 10d 11d 12g 10s*) attractive, well-made colt; made virtually all and beat Knighthall easily by 8 lengths in apprentice event at Nottingham in October; placed earlier in handicaps at Pontefract, Leicester and Epsom; stays 1¼m but probably not 1½m; acts on any going; didn't handle track at Beverley on third start; not particularly consistent; sold to S. Mellor 11,000 gns Newmarket Autumn Sales. *F. Durr.* **82**

NUGGETS DAUGHTER 2 b.f. Nugget 90–Lady Keeper (Worden II 129) (1981 5fg) May 21; small filly; fourth foal; dam poor maiden; unquoted and in need of race, swerved right leaving stalls and was always behind in 16-runner maiden race won by African Berry at Catterick in August. *K. Stapleton.* —

NUN'S PRIDE 3 ch.c. Manacle 123–Casona (Upper Case) (1980 5f 6f² 7d 1981 7d 5v 7s) neat colt; plater; no form in 1981; acts on firm going; blinkered second outing; sold 520 gns Newmarket July Sales. *P. Cole.* —

NUNSRULER (USA) 2 b.c. Jacinto–Take Your Mark (Round Table) (1981 5d² 5fg 5d² 7f² 7fg² 7fg* 7fg*) Jan 24; $25,000Y; small, sharp sort; good **97**

walker; first foal; dam lightly-raced daughter of stakes winner Society Column, successful at up to 1¼m; well suited by forcing tactics as he showed when making all to win twice in August, beating Saenredam 2 lengths after racing alone in maiden race at Brighton and Hla Tun 1½ lengths in 16-runner minor event at Warwick; will be suited by 1¼m; seems to act on any going. *P. Cole.*

NUNSWALK   4 ch.f. The Parson 119–Vital Error 105 (Javelot 124)   (1980   — 7f 8fg 7fg 10g 12g 14g 13.1f 12fg² 10fg⁴ 12fg⁴ 10f   1981 10.2d)   short-coupled filly; plater; stays 1¾m; acts on a firm surface; has worn blinkers and is possibly ungenuine. *M. Bradley.*

NUREDDIN   3 b.c. Brigadier Gerard 144–Conning Tower 98 (Connaught 130)   **98** (1980 NR   1981 7d* 10.6fg* 8d³ 8.2s 8fg 7f* 8.2fg)   16,000Y; strong, lengthy colt; first foal; dam best at up to 1m; won newcomers race at Doncaster in March and handicap at Yarmouth in August, on latter course beating Train of Thought by 1½ lengths going away when having first race for over 6 weeks; beaten ¾ length by Video Tape in £2,900 event at Haydock in between but was hampered by him and by third-placed Uppety and was subsequently awarded race; gave impression on final start that he would be suited by a return to longer distances than 1m and stays 1¼m well; acts on any going; racing in USA. *W. O'Gorman.*

NUROSE   6 ch.g. Tobrouk–Gondolina (Aggressor 130)   (1980 12fg⁴ 12fg 12fg³   — 10fg 12d² 12g⁴ 12fg 12d 12d 12d   1981 12s)   poor middle-distance handicapper; seems to act on any going; has worn bandages; usually blinkered. *A. Hide.*

NUTTY SLACK   3 gr.g. Saritamer 130–Mary Mullen 88 (Lorenzaccio 130)   **57** (1980 5fg 5fg 5s 5.8g 7fg 7g 7fg 8d 7fg 7d   1981 8g 8f³ 8fg 8fg 8h² 8fg 8d)   useful sort; placed in minor event at Bath and maiden race at Chepstow in summer; stays 1m; blinkered occasionally at 2 yrs. *R. Turnell.*

O

OAKEN LAD   5 b.g. Frankincense 120–Charlies Double (Fighting Charlie 127)   — (1980 NR   1981 12g 8h 8f)   no sign of ability in varied company. *M. Tate.*

OATLANDS   2 br.f. Ampney Prince 96–Sing Saucey (Hard Sauce 131)   (1981   — 5s)   Apr 6; fifth foal; dam of little account; unquoted when last of 17 to Fast Lad in maiden race at Warwick in October. *J. Czerpak.*

OBADIAH   2 b. or br.c. Joshua 129–Ripatip 68 (Indigenous 121)   (1981 6f 6fg   — 7f 7g 7g)   big, rangy colt; bad mover; plating-class maiden. *A. Dalton.*

OBERGURGL   3 br.f. Warpath 113–Snow Goose (Santa Claus 133)   (1980 8d   **69** 8d   1981 8g 12fg* 12g³ 13.8fg² 13fg* 13g⁴ 13d 16.5f⁴ 14g³ 12d² 13s² 18g⁴)   fair sort; decisively won maiden race at Hamilton in May and handicap at Nottingham in June; also placed in several handicaps, including in a valuable seller at Doncaster; stays well; probably acts on any going; has raced with her tongue tied down; sold 6,200 gns Doncaster November Sales. *C. Thornton.*

OBROVAC (USA)   3 ch.c. Time Tested–Counterpart (Prince John)   (1980 6g²   — 8d*   1981 8g 10fg)   neat, attractive colt; good mover; second in Duke of Edinburgh Stakes at Ascot before winning maiden race at Sandown as a 2-y-o; looked extremely well when reappearing in £3,100 event won by Tugoflove at Newbury in June but possibly just needed race and weakened into fifth after being a fairly close third approaching the distance; pulled hard when last of 12 behind Regal Steel in fairly valuable handicap at Newmarket later in month, and wasn't seen out again; should stay 1¼m; sold 5,600 gns Newmarket Autumn Sales. *R. Price.*

OCEAN DREAM   2 ch.g. Meldrum 112–Bon Feu 75 (Blason 109)   (1981 7g 8d)   — Feb 16; fourth foal; brother to a winning plater; dam, plater, stayed 1m; unquoted when in rear in end-of-season sellers. *Mrs A. Cousins.*

OCEAN KING (FR)   3 b.c. Dubassoff–Tartarbee 72 (Charlottesville 135)   — (1980 NR   1981 14.7fg 12.2fg)   500Y; sparely-made colt; half-brother to 7f to 1¼m winner Made My Day (by Double Jump); dam placed over 1m; slipped up after 3f in maiden race at Redcar in July; tailed off in similar event at Catterick in August. *J. Doyle.*

OCH AYE   3 br.f. Lochnager 132–Daisy Knot 81 (Acer 123)   (1980 7g⁴   1981   **64** 7d 9d 8.5fg 7d² 7g³ 7d 8d)   big filly; placed in maiden races at Sandown and Salisbury in June; stays 7f and wasn't disgraced over 9f. *J. Bethell.*

OCHIL HILLS STAR   8 b.g. Chebs Lad 120–Turkish Maid 58 (Menelek   **41** 114)   (1980 8.2g 7f² 9fg² 7g* 9f 8fg 8.2g 8d 8d 8.2s   1981 8v 7g 8.2d 8g* 9fg) plater; bought in 2,200 gns after winning at Edinburgh in April; stays 1¼m; acts on any going; has been tried in blinkers; good mount for an inexperienced rider. *Mrs A. Bell.*

ODIN'S RAVEN 3 br.c. Jukebox 120–Bare Costs (Petition 130) (1980 6g³ 6g⁴ 6d* 6s* 7d 7d² 1981 8.2fg 7g 6g 7.6s) strong, good sort; none too good a mover; mainly disappointing in 1981; stays 7f; acts well on soft ground; pulled up after saddle slipped third outing; sold 2,000 gns Newmarket Autumn Sales. *J. Hindley.*

OFFA'S MEAD 12 ch.g. Rathlin–Eridantini (Indigenous 121) (1980 5s 5g 5.8fg 5d 5g 5fg 5d 6g 1981 5d 5s 5f) sprint handicapper; has shown little form since 1979; acts on any going; sometimes wears bandages; suitable mount for an amateur rider; does best when brought wide to race alone. *M. Bradley.*

OFFERING 3 b.f. Dubassoff–Ready and Willing 82 (Reliance II 137) (1980 7g 1981 12.2g⁴ 12g³ 12fg⁴ 15.5g⁴) rangy filly; in frame in maiden races; stays 1½m. *Sir Mark Prescott.*   **52**

OFF THE HOOK (USA) 2 b.c. Full Out–Incommunicado (Double Jay) (1981 6g²) Apr 11; $57,000Y; rangy, good-looking colt; half-brother to several winners in USA, notably very smart 1979 staying 2-y-o Koluctoo Bay (by Creme dela Creme); dam ran only at 4 yrs when stakes-placed winner of 3 of her 6 starts; co-favourite and pretty fit, found lack of previous experience telling in closing stages and went down by a short head to Perang Tejam in 26-runner maiden race at Doncaster in November; will be suited by 1m; looks the type to train on and should win a race in 1982. *G. Harwood.*   **88** p

OFF THE REEL (USA) 2 b.f. Silent Screen–Harbour Queen (Young Emperor 133) (1981 6g 6g) Apr 3; $50,000Y; big filly; second foal; half-sister to fairly useful 3-y-o 7f and 1m winner Ice Harbour (by Icecapade); dam, half-sister to very useful 1976 French staying 2-y-o El Criollo, won over 1m; finished in splendid style when about 12 lengths fifth of 17 to Merlin's Charm in maiden race at Newmarket in October; 9/1, faded after being pushed along some way from home when out of first 9 of 22 to Ash Ridge in another Newmarket maiden event later in month; will stay 1¼m. *J. Hindley.*   **72**

O'GARA 4 ch.c. Lord Gayle 124–Moygara (Red God 128§) (1980 12s³ 10s 1981 12s 8fg 12g 10f⁴ 10fg 8h 10h³) ex-Irish colt; poor plater; stayed 1½m; acted on hard going; dead. *G. Balding.*

NMT Ebbisham Stakes (Handicap), Epsom—Oh So Choosy (rails) is all out to win from K-Sera

OH SO CHOOSY (USA) 3 ch.f. Top Command–Snobishness (Forli) (1980   **89**
second twice from 4 starts in USA 1981 8d* 8.5g* 8f* 8fg 8g) leggy, quite
attractive filly; third foal; dam smart French middle-distance performer;
second twice in USA in 1980; won her first 3 races over here, namely 16-runner
minor event at Warwick, NMT Ebbisham Stakes (Handicap) at Epsom and
Fern Hill Stakes (Handicap) at Ascot; disputed lead from start and held on
well by ¾ length from Susanna (USA) after quickening clear inside final furlong
on last-named course in June; behind in valuable handicaps at Newmarket
and Ascot on last 2 starts; will stay 1¼m; acts on firm going and a soft surface;
ridden by apprentice S. Payne. *I. Balding.*

OILEANN CARRIG 2 b.f. Pitcairn 126–Dreamy Idea 68 (Double Jump 131)   **80 p**
(1981 6v*) May 2; IR 5,200Y; half-sister to several winners, including sprinter
Yoohoo (by Mountain Call); dam ran only twice at 2 yrs; caught Ormsary
close home when winning 10-runner minor event at the Curragh in May by a
neck; looked promising but wasn't seen out again; will stay 1m. *J. M. Oxx,
Ireland.*

O. I. OYSTON 5 b.g. Martinmas 128–Last Lap 75 (Immortality) (1980   **73**
7d² 7v* 7f 7.6f 8fg 8d² 7g 7.6g³ 7f⁴ 7.6d* 6fg* 7fg² 7s⁴ 6d 1981 6v 7s 7.2s
7g 10.6g 7.6fg 8f⁴ 9g³ 8f 7.6s* 7d 7.2v⁴ 7v³ 7g) leggy gelding; trotted up in
handicap at Chester in August; stays 9f but not 1¼m; acts on any going; has
worn blinkers but is better without; has run creditably for an apprentice;
suited by front-running tactics and a turning track. *J. Berry.*

OKAVAMBA 3 ch.f. Wollow 132–Orapa 88 (Aureole 132) (1980 6s 6fg*   **70**
6g 1981 7g 8s 10fg) neat filly; last in handicaps on all outings in 1981, but
wasn't far behind in race won by Bettyknowes at Kempton in July on final start;
will stay 1¼m; sweated up second start. *H. Wragg.*

OKAVANGO 2 b.f. Homeric 133–Airy Queen (Sadair) (1981 6f*) Mar 26;   **90 p**
second foal; half-sister to 3-y-o French 1½m winner Don Alfredo (by Simbir);
dam won at 2 yrs and 3 yrs in Italy; second favourite, with leaders throughout
when winning 7-runner Irish Chorus Stakes at Navan in July by a head from
Karissima, only outing; should make a useful filly over middle distances. *K.
Prendergast, Ireland.*

OKLAHOMA STAR 3 gr.f. Hotfoot 126–America 112 (Buisson Ardent 129)   **82**
(1980 6s 7fg 7fg* 7d 7d 1981 8.2fg² 8g³ 10d* 10.1f 10.8fg³ 11f⁴ 12fg² 12s²
11d) neat filly; won handicap at Folkestone in June readily by 4 lengths from
Hiz; placed most other outings; stays 1½m; acts on any going. *M. Jarvis.*

OLD ARTHUR 3 ch.c. Record Run 127–Owey (Sovereign Gleam 117) (1980   **—**
NR 1981 10d 9d⁴) 8,000Y; plain colt; second foal; half-brother to Planet
Queen (by Red Alert), winner 3 times over 5f at 2 yrs in Ireland; dam unraced
half-sister to Quisling; remote fourth in seller at Hamilton in September;
sold 560 gns Doncaster October Sales. *W. H. H. Williams.*

OLD BIRD 4 gr.g. Birdbrook 110–Elfin Smile (Be Friendly 130) (1980 6f   **—**
8h 6fg² 6g⁴ 1981 6s 5g 5g) fair sort; plating-class maiden; should stay
beyond 6f; has worn bandages; sold 940 gns Newmarket July Sales. *W.
Stubbs.*

OLD COUNTRY 2 b.c. Quiet Fling 124–Little Miss 92 (Aggressor 130) (1981   **99 p**
7f² 7fg* 7d³) Apr 14; 13,500F; tall, rather lightly-made colt; good walker
and mover; half-brother to several winners, including late 1980 2-y-o 5f winner
Sheba's Glory (by Averof); dam, half-sister to Favoletta and Furioso, won
over middle distances; probably didn't have a great deal to beat in £3,100 event
at Goodwood in September but couldn't have been more impressive, scoring
hard held by 5 lengths from Korypheos; pushed along throughout when second
favourite for £4,800 race on same course later in month and was eased when
well held in final furlong, coming home 5 lengths third of 8 to Montekin; will
stay 1¼m; the type to make a better 3-y-o. *L. Cumani.*

OLD DOMINION (USA) 4 b.g. In Reality–Virginia Green 83 (Nashua)   **96**
(1980 5s⁴ 6s³ 5fg³ 6f* 6f³ 6f* 6fg 6g⁴ 6g² 6g 6s 6g 6s* 5g 6d 1981 6s 6fg⁴ 6g⁴
6s⁴ 6g* 5.8d² 6f³ 6fg 6fg 5.6fg 6g 6v) strong, good sort; good mover; fairly
useful handicapper; beat Corn Street by ¾ length at Epsom in June; in frame in
valuable races on several other occasions; suited by 6f and may stay further;
acts on any going; genuine. *I. Balding.*

OLDERFLEET 3 ch.f. Steel Heart 128–Cafe au Lait 97 (Espresso 122) (1980   **59**
NR 1981 9d⁴ 8g 8g² 8d² 8g 8g² 8.2s 8g) 32,000Y; well-made filly; half-sister

to quite useful stayer Brando (by Busted) and 3 other winners, including fairly useful 1977 2-y-o sprint winner Milk and Honey (by So Blessed); dam stayed 1¼m; second in maiden races at Thirsk, Bath and Yarmouth; ran poorly last 2 starts; stays at least 1m. *W. Hastings-Bass.*

OLD HOLLOW 3 b.g. Wolver Hollow 126–Red Madonna 84 (Red God 128§)   — (1980 6s 7fg 7s 1981 7d 7f 8.3fg 6fg 10fg⁴ 10s 10s) poor plater; suited by 1¼m; sold to A. Bailey 500 gns Newmarket Autumn Sales. *J. Bethell.*

OLD JOCUS 2 b. or br.c. Comedy Star 121–Archaic 65 (Relic) (1981 7.6s⁴ 7d) **72** Feb 22; half-brother to very smart 1978 2-y-o 5f winner Schweppeshire Lad (by Decoy Boy); dam ran only 5 times; 6½ lengths fourth of 15 to Cordite Spear in maiden race at Lingfield in October; tenth of 22 behind Starbells in minor event at Chepstow later in month; will stay 1¼m. *I. Balding.*

OLD KNOCKER 5 b.h. Mummy's Pet 125–The Keys 71 (Major Portion 129) **77** (1980 7v 7fg 8fg 10f* 10.1g 11.7s 9f 8g 10fg 10g* 12d³ 12s 12d 1981 11s 10fg² 10f 11.7g² 10fg 11.7g³ 12d) attractive horse; quite a moderate handicapper; suited by middle distances nowadays; acts on any going, except perhaps very soft; usually wears blinkers; often sweats up; suitable mount for a boy; has worn bandages; inconsistent. *R. Laing.*

OLD MASTER 2 br.g. Auction Ring 123–Pagan Times 72 (Native Prince) — (1981 6fg) Apr 27; 10,500Y; second living foal; dam lightly raced: 50/1 and on backward side, moved down badly prior to finishing in rear in 14-runner minor event won by Aegean Beauty at Newmarket in August; dead. *J. Winter.*

OLD OAK TREE 3 b.c. Ardoon 124–Roanoke (Charlottesville 135) (1980 5f **101** 1981 8v 10d 8g* 10s* 8s³ 10d 9fg* 8fg* 12fg² 11.1f⁴ 8d² 8g) 11,500Y; rather lightly-made, workmanlike colt; half-brother to 3 winners, including useful middle-distance performer Rathdowney (by Ballymore); dam unraced half-sister to Waterloo; had a good year and won maiden race and handicap at the Curragh, valuable Hennessy Handicap at Leopardstown (beat The Shaker by 1½ lengths) and Coolmore Gay Fandango Stakes at the Curragh again; beat odds-on Worldwatch decisively by 4 lengths in last-named in July; also ran well at the Curragh when second in Blandford Stakes (head behind Magesterial) and Irish Cambridgeshire Handicap (beaten 3 lengths by Majestic Nurse); rather disappointing when 11 lengths fourth to Kind of Hush in September Stakes at Kempton; stays 1½m; has a slightly round action and is possibly not at his best on very firm going, but acts on any other; sold to race in USA. *K. Prendergast, Ireland.*

OLD ROWLEY 3 b.c. Copte–Cennen-Olive (Wolver Hollow 126) (1980 NR — 1981 7g 8g) narrow colt; second foal; dam of no account; behind in end-of-season minor events at Newmarket and Doncaster. *Mrs J. Pitman.*

OLD STAGER (USA) 3 ch.c. Forli–Queen of the Stage (Bold Ruler) (1980 8g — 1981 8fg) tall, narrow colt; ran pleasingly in maiden race at Newmarket at 2 yrs; looked and moved well in minor event won by Critique at Kempton in August on only outing of 1981, but dropped out completely in straight to finish last of 6; sold to D. Grissell 3,100 gns Newmarket Autumn Sales. *J. Dunlop.*

OLE FAITHFUL 2 bl.g. Warpath 113–Truly Yours 93 (So Blessed 130) — (1981 6g 7f) May 10; second foal; half-brother to 1980 2-y-o 6f seller winner Consent (by Connaught); dam, winner twice over 5f at 2 yrs, appeared to stay 1¼m; behind in maiden races at Doncaster and Redcar in September. *C. Thornton.*

OLRO'S FOLLY 5 br.g. African Sky 124–Shlanta 85 (St Paddy 133) (1980 **46** 10fg⁴ 8f 7g 6fg³ 7fg 6fg 1981 8fg 7f² 10f 7f⁴ 8fg) fair sort; poor handicapper;

Britannia Stakes (Handicap) Ascot—Olympic Glory wins easing up from Kareem

evidently effective at 6f and hasn't been disgraced over 1¼m; suited by fast ground. *J. Harris.*

OLYMPIC CARNIVAL (USA) 2 b.c. Greek Answer–Streamer (Jet Jewel) **82**
(1981 6g 6g² 6fg) $10,000F, $19,000Y; quite well-made colt; half-brother to 2 minor winners in USA; dam, half-sister to top-class Gun Bow, won 7 times at up to 7f in USA; in front rank throughout when length second of 9 to King Naskra in maiden race at Yarmouth in July, easily best effort; taken down early at Newmarket on third outing; will stay 1m. *J. Winter.*

OLYMPIC GLORY 3 ch.c. Hittite Glory 125–Nalindele 78 (Miralgo 130) **106**
(1980 5d 5g* 6g* 6fg² 6s³ 5f 6g⁴ 1981 7g² 7g⁴ 8f* 8g⁴) strong, lengthy, useful sort; good mover; put up an impressive performance in 18-runner Britannia Stakes (Handicap) at Royal Ascot in June, bursting through inside final furlong and winning easing up by 1½ lengths from Kareem; also in frame in 3 handicaps at Newmarket, appearing to be given a lot to do in a rather slowly-run race when 1½ lengths fourth to Master Golfer under a penalty in July; stays 1m; very well suited by a sound surface; sent to race in USA. *G. Harwood.*

OLYMPIC VICTORY (USA) 3 b.c. Nijinsky 138–Shama (Bold Ruler) **70**
(1980 7g 8g 1981 11s 11.7g⁴ 11.7g⁴ 10f 14g² 16.9fg²) smallish, strong, quite well-made colt; good mover; quite a modest maiden; suited by a test of stamina; blinkered third start. *I. Balding.*

OMAR KHAYYAMS SON 4 b.g. Furry Glen 121–Sara Tal (Cagire II 122) **—**
(1980 12s⁴ 16f 13g 16fg³ 14fg 15.5g² 16f³ 14d 16fg 16d 14.6d⁴ 12s 1981 15.8g 12fg 12fg 19g) robust gelding; staying maiden; probably acted on any going; dead. *D. Morley.*

ON A CLOUD (USA) 3 b.c. Val de l'Orne 130–Pleasant Flight (Bold Ruler) **89**
(1980 8d 8g² 1981 10d³ 12fg* 11.5fg² 12fg* 14fg² 13fg) well-made colt; successful in quite well-contested 4-runner minor event at Kempton in July (beat Irish Keep gamely by a head) and in 7-runner minor event at Salisbury in August (made virtually all and stayed on to win by a length from Charlie Dan); second in minor event at Yarmouth in between and in 3-runner March Stakes at Goodwood later in August, on latter course keeping on quite well under pressure but making no impression on 8-length winner Capstan; stays 1¾m; acts on a firm and a soft surface; genuine. *J. Dunlop.*

ONE DEGREE 2 b.f. Crooner 119–Rhythm 64 (Bleep-Bleep 134) (1981 6fg **80**
6fg 5g² 5d³ 5d 6s 6g*) Apr 22; strong, sturdy non-thoroughbred filly; sister to very useful 3-y-o Vocalist, successful at up to 1m, and half-sister to useful 1979 2-y-o 5f and 6f winner Pink Blues (by Tickled Pink); dam seemed to stay 1½m; led 1f out and ran on strongly when beating Whichcombe ½ length in 19-runner maiden race at Newmarket in October; will stay 1m; form only on an easy surface; has run well for an apprentice. *F. Durr.*

ON EDGE 6 gr.g. Sharp Edge 123–The Country Lane 90 (Red God 128§) **89**
(1980 8s³ 8fg² 9fg* 8fg² 9fg* 9g² 8d⁴ 9f⁴ 8d⁴ 9fg² 8g 9g 1981 9d 8fg* 8g* 8d² 8g* 8f* 9fg* 8f* 8f* 8fg 9fg* 8.2fg 8v⁴ 9s) smallish gelding; former plater; has made tremendous strides and is now a fair handicapper; enjoyed a remarkable season, winning at Warwick, Kempton (apprentices), Thirsk (trotted up), Stockton (twice), York (beat Black Mike 1½ lengths in £4,000 race), Brighton (beat Braughing a head in Brighton Mile) and Wolverhampton; stays 9f; suited by top-of-the-ground; blinkered once at 2 yrs; suitable mount for a claimer; does best when held up; most consistent. *J. Spearing.*

ONE FLEET STREET 4 b.c. Habitat 134–The Creditor 127 (Crepello 136) **87**
(1980 8f 8fg* 10f* 10.2fg³ 8fg 8g² 10g⁴ 10f* 10g* 9f 1981 8s 10fg² 10.2g⁴ 10d² 10fg 10fg* 10fg 10.2g) strong, well-made, good-looking colt; good mover; fairly useful handicapper; held off Camacho by a neck at Salisbury in August; had previously been narrowly beaten in 2 valuable races at Epsom, by Lafontaine in City and Suburban Handicap and by Easter Sun in Daily Mirror Handicap; suited by 1¼m and may stay further; seems to act on any going but goes well on firm ground; blinkered when successful once at 3 yrs; suited by front-running tactics; suited by strong handling; genuine; sold 20,000 gns Newmarket December Sales. *P. Walwyn.*

ON HER OWN 3 b.f. Busted 134–Turiana (Citation) (1980 7g 9d² 1981 12g **80**
12fg² 12f² 12f* 16.5f* 15.8g⁴ 16h* 14fg 18g 14g) rather an unfurnished filly; gained her third win when beating Mallard Song by 4 lengths in amateur riders handicap at Chepstow in September; successful earlier in maiden event and handicap at Folkestone, scoring by 12 lengths in latter; suited by a test of

stamina; has run respectably on dead ground but is very well suited by top-of-the-ground; ran poorly eighth start. *G. Harwood.*

ON LEAVE 4 br.g. Queen's Hussar 124–Bound Over (Taj Dewan 128) (1980 6h² 7.6f 10f² 10g* 12d 1981 11g) workmanlike gelding; plater; stays 1½m; probably acts on any going. *S. Leadbetter.* —

ONLY A SHANTY 3 ch.g. Busted 134–The Bungalow 81 (Habitat 134) (1980 8g 1981 10d² 12.2g² 12s*) useful sort; beat Charlie Dan very easily by 6 lengths in moderately-contested maiden race at Newbury in October; second at Nottingham and Catterick earlier; will stay 1¾m; acts on soft going; sold to L. Kennard 11,000 gns Newmarket Autumn Sales. *B. Hills.* **79**

ON RECORD 3 ch.c. Record Token 128–Whitestake 74 (Compensation 127) (1980 5f 5fg 1981 6fg 9g 5f) strong colt; poor walker and mover; behind in maiden and minor races; blinkered final start; trained by F. Durr first outing. *D. Leslie.* —

ON RETURN 2 gr.f. On Your Mark 125–Magnificent Return 94 (My Swanee 122) (1981 6fg 6g³ 5f* 5g) Mar 10; lengthy, useful-looking ex-Irish filly; first foal; dam, Irish 2-y-o 5f winner, is daughter of smart 2-y-o What's-A-Name; disputed lead throughout when winning maiden race at Phoenix Park in September by 2 lengths from Papsies Pet; led 3f and wasn't disgraced when 6¼ lengths last of 5 to stable-companion Jester in Harry Rosebery Stakes at Ayr later in month; stays 6f; trained by J. Harrington in Ireland first 3 outings. *B. Hills.* **89**

ON SHOW 3 br.f. Welsh Pageant 132–African Dancer 116 (Nijinsky 138) (1980 5g 1981 8d² 11g³ 12d 14.6g 10s* 12g²) rather a lightly-made filly; first foal; dam won Cheshire Oaks and Park Hill Stakes; showed ability in varied company before beating Modestine by ¾ length with fair bit in hand in maiden race at Nottingham in October (looked particularly well and was ridden with great confidence); didn't get going until too late but stayed on very strongly when 1½ lengths second of 20 behind Lafontaine in William Hill November Handicap at Doncaster; stays 1½m; well suited by some give in the ground; bandaged near-fore last 4 starts. *H. Wragg.* **92**

ON SONG 3 b.f. Ardoon 124–Champion Jay (Double-U-Jay 120) (1980 5g 5f 6d³ 1981 8s² 9s⁴ 8.5fg 10.2g⁴ 10d 10d*) sturdy filly; won maiden race at Leicester in March on merit by 1½ lengths from Daring Dame, but was judged to have hampered runner-up and placings were reversed; sold 3,100 gns after winning seller at Folkestone in June comfortably; raced in Belgium afterwards, and won there; stays 1¼m; acts on soft going. *R. Price.* **69**

ON THE BEACH 3 ch.c. Sandford Lad 133–Curragha (Le Levanstell 122) (1980 6fg 7fg 7s 1981 8d 8fg 8d 12.2g⁴ 12d) robust, good sort; good mover; fourth in apprentice race at Catterick in October (first outing for 4 months); behind in a valuable seller only subsequent start; stays 1½m; sold 900 gns Newmarket Autumn Sales. *G. Hunter.* —

ON THE HOUSE (FR) 2 b.f. Be My Guest 126–Lora (Lorenzaccio 130) (1981 6fg 5fg* 6f* 6g²) **109**

The Coolmore group of studs' policy of allowing its stallions much larger than average books of mares pays dividends in more ways than one. Income from stallion fees is of course substantially boosted, but perhaps more important in the long run is the statistically greater chance their stallions have of reaching the leading sires list. Once upon a time a full book was regarded as 44 mares but in 1978 some of the Coolmore stallions covered considerably more: according to *The Statistical Record* Deep Run covered 167, Gay Fandango 57, Mount Hagen 72 and Red Alert 78, while the first-season sires Be My Guest and Godswalk, who in the past would almost certainly have been limited to fewer than 40 mares, respectively covered 54 and 64 mares. Coolmore is now in the happy position of being able to advertise Godswalk as 'the leading first crop sire—individual winners and races won' and Be My Guest as 'a leading sire of two-year olds'. Both did extremely well: Godswalk sired no fewer than thirteen winners of seventeen races from thirty-two runners in Britain and Ireland, while Be My Guest's ten winners from twenty-one runners in the same countries collected sixteen races, with two more scoring in France and Italy. Neither's success was purely numerical—Godswalk numbered the fast animals The Primate, Celestial Path and Celestial City among his winners; and Be My Guest, in addition to the leading Irish colts Anfield and Assert, sired one of the best sprinting two-year-old fillies in England, On The House.

When On The House first appeared on the racecourse it was clear from her starting price that she was highly regarded—she was a clear favourite in a field of eleven well-bred newcomers at Ascot in July. She finished only sixth of eleven to Johara but showed in her next two races that her trainer's confidence in her hadn't been misplaced, winning good-class events at Newbury in August and York in September. In the St Hugh's Stakes at Newbury she proved far too strong in the last furlong for the favourite Lavender Dance, beating her a length and a half. This was a good effort—the six other runners, all previous winners, were at least four lengths further behind—and On The House started favourite for the Crathorne Stakes at York despite having to give weight to all her seven rivals. Again she produced a good turn of foot to win, this time by half a length from the Princess Margaret Stakes runner-up Apples of Gold, and she would have scored by further with a clearer run.

On The House ended her first season with a fine effort in the William Hill Cheveley Park Stakes at Newmarket on the last day of September. In Circus Ring's absence On The House was the most strongly fancied of the home-trained runners, starting co-favourite in a field of thirteen with the Irish challenger Woodstream. In the race there was nothing to choose between the two fillies as they moved through to dispute the lead with Bless The Match and Admiral's Princess at the distance but On The House was soon fighting a losing battle against Woodstream; edging to her left under hard riding, she went down by a length and a half.

	Be My Guest (ch 1974)	Northern Dancer (b 1961)	Nearctic
On The House (Fr) (b.f. Mar 20, 1979)			Natalma
		What a Treat (b 1962)	Tudor Minstrel
			Rare Treat
	Lora (b 1972)	Lorenzaccio (ch 1965)	Klairon
			Phoenissa
		Courtessa (b 1955)	Supreme Court
			Tessa Gillian

Surprisingly On The House, a lengthy filly from an excellent family, failed to reach her modest reserve at the Houghton Sales. During the year her sire's yearlings were generally in great demand—twenty-three by him averaged over

Sir Philip Oppenheimer's "On The House"

38,000 guineas—and it's hard to imagine that On The House's female line failed to find favour with potential purchasers. Her third dam Tessa Gillian, a full sister to that highly-influential stallion Royal Charger, had a splendid career both on the racecourse and at stud. She won the Molecomb Stakes, finished second in both the Cheveley Park and the One Thousand Guineas and became the dam of both the Gimcrack winner Test Case and the very smart two-year-old Gentle Art. Although Tessa Gillian's daughter Courtessa was a twin and didn't race, she too bred a first-rate performer, the King's Stand Stakes winner D'Urberville. Lora, a three-parts sister to D'Urberville, didn't repay any of her 28,000-guinea purchase price on the racecourse but she is more than making amends at stud, producing the seven-furlong winner Loralane (by Habitat) as her first foal and On The House as her second. Watch out for her yearling filly by Riverman and her colt foal by Busted when they reach the races.

On The House went into winter quarters as third favourite at 16/1 for the One Thousand Guineas. She needs to improve if she's to stand a chance of winning that race and there must be some doubt whether she'll be suited by a mile. She wasn't finding much up the final hill at the end of six furlongs in the Cheveley Park, and it's interesting that her dam Lora, as well as being a close relative of the very fast D'Urberville, is a sister to the six-furlong winner Klairessa and a half-sister to three other winners, none of which won over further than seven furlongs. *H. Wragg.*

ON THE SPOT 2 gr.c. Town Crier 119–Creolina 72 (Quorum 126) (1981 6f 6fg 6g 6f 6fg 7f 6g 6d) Mar 1; 4,000F, 8,400Y; quite attractive colt; half-brother to a minor winner; dam placed over 6f at 2 yrs; little better than plating class; stays 7f; blinkered fourth outing; sold 2,600 gns Newmarket Autumn Sales. *C. Brittain.* **62**

ON THE WARPATH 2 ro.c. Bustino 136–Cheyenne 83 (Sovereign Path 125) (1981 7.2fg 8g 10s) Apr 19; rangy, useful-looking colt; first foal; dam, 6f winner at 2 yrs, is sister to very useful Warpath and half-sister to very smart Dakota; behind in maiden races in the autumn; the type to do better with time and long distances. *C. Thornton.* **—**

ON YOUR BRIDGE 2 b.f. Scottish Rifle 127–Off The Mark (On Your Mark 125) (1981 5fg 6fg 8g² 8.2d 10d) Mar 31; 400Y; lightly-made filly; second foal; half-sister to a winning plater by Red God; dam won over 1m in France; plater; 33/1, showed only worthwhile form when 2½ lengths second of 22 to Preston Manor at Leicester in September; should stay 1¼m. *Miss L. Siddall.* **55**

OOPS-A-DAISY 2 br.f. Warpath 113–Sunflower 96 (Paveh 126) (1981 7g 10.2g) May 11; useful-looking filly; good walker; half-sister to 2 winners, including quite useful sprinter Flower (by So Blessed); dam a miler; well behind in maiden race at Leicester in October (dwelt) and minor event at Doncaster in November. *C. Thornton.* **—**

OPAL LADY 3 b.f. Averof 123–Hum 69 (Crooner 119) (1980 5fg 1981 6g² 6g 6d 5fg 6f³ 6f⁴ 6f* 7h 7g) quite a well-made filly; won maiden race at Brighton in August; should be suited by 7f; acts on firm going; blinkered nowadays. *G. Lewis.* **64**

OPEN DAY 2 ch.c. Northfields–Knighton House 113 (Pall Mall 132) (1981 8g) Apr 15; quite an attractive, well-made colt; half-brother to several winners, including smart 1977 French 2-y-o 6f and 1m winner River Knight (by Riverman); dam, sister to Reform, very useful at up to 1¼m; 25/1 and far from fully wound up, made a pleasing first appearance when just over 4 lengths sixth of 27 to Dudley Wood in minor event at Newmarket in October, racing in behind the leaders for much of way and not being knocked about when starting to struggle in Dip; a good sort who is sure to do a lot better over middle distances at 3 yrs. *R. Hern.* **91 p**

OPEN THE BOX (USA) 2 b.c. Key To The Kingdom–T.V. Miss (T.V. Lark) (1981 5g³ 5.8g² 6fg 6f 6s²) Apr 9; $28,000Y; workmanlike, good sort; fifth foal; half-brother to 3 winners, including minor stakes winner T.V. Pruner (by The Pruner); dam, half-sister to $269,000-earner Twin Time, won over 6f; placed in minor event at Newbury in May, 15-runner maiden race at Bath in July and 14-runner nursery at Newbury in October, running well in blinkers to finish 4 lengths second to Better Portion on last-named course; beaten favourite other starts; will stay 1m; needs some give in the ground and acts on soft going. *G. Balding.* **84**

OPERATION CYRIL 3 ch.g. Jimmy Reppin 131–Western Vale (Milesian 125) **62**
(1980 6g 6g⁴ 7f 1981 7s 8s 9d² 9.4g² 8g) fair sort; placed in maiden event
at Hamilton and handicap at Carlisle in spring; stays 9f. *N. Guest.*

OPTIMATE 4 b.c. Great Nephew 126–Queen of Arisai 73 (Persian Gulf) (1980 **78**
6d² 6d* 6fg 6g 8g 6s 6d 5s 1981 10.2d 7.2fg² 7d 7d 6f 7f 6fg 6g 5g 6s 6d*)
strong, good-bodied, quite attractive colt; fair handicapper at his best; beat
Song Minstrel by 2 lengths at Redcar in October; stays 7f; seems to act on any
going but is ideally suited by some give in the ground; sometimes blinkered;
inconsistent; racing in California. *C. Brittain.*

OPTIMISTIC DREAMER 2 b.c. Full of Hope 125–La Crima (Runnymede **66**
123) (1981 7fg 7fg² 7g) Apr 26; 6,600Y; leggy, lightly-made colt; third foal;
half-brother to 3-y-o 1½m winner Voice of Progress (by Matahawk) and a winner
in Belgium; dam won over 7.6f in French Provinces; went down by 3 lengths
to easy winner Lively Rhythm in minor event at Leicester in July; will be suited
by 1¼m+. *I. Walker.*

ORANGE SILK 2 ch.f. Moulton 128–Orange Sensation 69 (Floribunda 136) **68**
(1981 5s 5d² 6fg 5d 6fg 7g 6s² 6g) Feb 17; 2,300Y; small filly; half-sister to
numerous winners here and abroad, including 3-y-o 6f and 7f winner Paltango
(by Royal Palace) and useful 1976 2-y-o Swift Sensation (by My Swallow);
dam placed at up to 7f at 2 yrs; runner-up in maiden auction event at Haydock
in May and seller at York in October; blinkered when beaten 1½ lengths by
Purnima in latter; again blinkered when under 3 lengths fifth of 21 to Commissar
in valuable seller at Newmarket later in month; should be suited by 7f; best
form with some give in the ground. *J. W. Watts.*

ORANGE SORBET 2 b.f. Orange Bay 131–Sandfly (French Beige 127) **71**
(1981 7g 7.2d⁴ 7fg 8g² 8.2d 10s) Apr 3; 4,000Y; leggy filly; half-sister to useful
5f to 1¼m winner Ippolyti (by Derring-Do); dam French 1¼m winner; ran
best race when 1½ lengths second of 14 to Outlaw in maiden race at Ayr in
September; disappointing subsequently; bred to stay at least 1¼m. *M. H.
Easterby.*

ORANGE TIP 2 b.f. Orange Bay 131–Blessed Beauty 97 (Rustam 127) (1981 **77 p**
8g) Mar 31; 3,600Y, 5,400Y; rangy filly; half-sister to 2 winners, including
1979 2-y-o 5f winner Burnside (by Roan Rocket); dam won at up to 7f; unquoted
and backward, wasn't knocked about when 8 lengths ninth of 29 to Born Hero
in maiden race at Newmarket in October; will probably stay 1¼m; should do
better in 1982. *G. Pritchard-Gordon.*

ORANGE VALLEY 3 br.f. Alto Volante 109–Noaxe To Grind (The Axe **61**
115) (1980 7f 10s 1981 10s 9d⁴ 12d 10.1fg³ 10fg 8f⁴ 8d² 8fg 7fg 8.2s) quite
a moderate maiden; in frame in varied company, including selling; should
stay at least 1½m; trained most of season by G. Pritchard-Gordon. *J. Scallan.*

ORASTON 3 ch.f. Morston 125–Orange Cap (Red God 128§) (1980 6d* **115**
6g⁴ 8g⁴ 1981 12.2fg 10g* 10fg 10fg 10f³ 10v*) lengthy filly; half-sister to
smart French 1m and 1¼m performer The Abbot (by Sea Hawk II) and prolific
Italian winner Opera Italiana (by Connaught); dam useful winner at up to 1m
in France; stayed on well to beat odds-on Cracking Form by 2½ lengths in
4-runner minor event at Newbury in July; gained a far more valuable and
prestigious prize in Group 1 Premio Lydia Tesio at Rome in October, beating
Rattling Wind a short head; 4½ lengths last of 3 behind very comfortable winner
Home On The Range in Sean Graham Fillies Stakes at Kempton, best effort
in between; should stay 1½m; evidently well suited by plenty of give in the
ground. *F. J. Houghton.*

ORATAVO 3 br.g. The Brianstan 128–Nimble Star (Space King 115) (1980 **80**
5fg 5f 6d 5.8f 7fg 7d 8.2g² 8d* 1981 10d 10.2d³ 10.2f* 10f* 10.8fg² 10g* 10d*
10fg 10d⁴ 10s* 10.2g) lightly-made gelding; plater at 2 yrs; did very well in
1981 and won handicaps at Bath (apprentice event), Brighton, Newmarket and
Lingfield (two); beat K-Sera a length for second success at Lingfield in October;
stays 11f; has won on firm going but has produced best form with give in the
ground; apprentice ridden nowadays. *J. Sutcliffe.*

ORCHARD COTTAGE 2 b.g. Scottish Rifle 127–Stately Gala (Gala Per- **54**
formance) (1981 6g 7f⁴ 7g 7g 8.2fg 8f 8fg 8.2d) Apr 13; 1,450Y; neat gelding;
good mover; half-brother to a winner in Barbados; dam never ran; only poor
form, including in sellers; stays 1m; often blinkered nowadays. *M. Naughton.*

ORCHESTRATE (USA) 3 ch.c. Northern Dancer–Directoire (Gun Bow) **—**
(1980 NR 1981 10g 8d) $335,000Y; small, strong, stocky colt; brother to

smart French middle-distance filly La Dorga, closely related to 2· winners by Nijinsky, including very useful 1976 French 2-y-o Borodine, and half-brother to 2 more winners; dam won over 6f at 2 yrs in USA and is out of sister to champion 2-y-o's Bold Lad (USA) and Successor; fading out of contention when brought down in minor event at Goodwood in September; never going particularly well when remote seventh of 15 behind Organdy in maiden race on same course later in month. *G. Harwood.*

ORE 3 ch.c. Ballymore 123–Minatonka (Linacre 133) (1980 8s* 1981 7g³ 8g⁴ 8s 12v³ 16f* 12fg 14d⁴) big, strong, workmanlike colt; third foal; half-brother to bumpers race winner Karatonka (by Karabas); dam Irish 1m winner; in frame in very useful company before winning Queen's Vase at Royal Ascot in June by 2½ lengths from Protection Racket, leading 2f out and striding away in great style in last furlong; far from disgraced when about 11 lengths fifth behind easy winner Shergar in Irish Sweeps Derby at the Curragh later in June; having first subsequent race when 9 lengths fourth of 7 to Protection Racket in Irish St Leger on same course in October, and didn't run up to his best; suited by a test of stamina; acts on any going but is well suited by firm; blinkered third start (towards rear in Airlie/Coolmore Irish 2,000 Guineas). *K. Prendergast, Ireland.* **108**

ORGANDY 3 b.f. Blakeney 126–Silk Stocking 109 (Pardao 120) (1980 NR 1981 7d 12.3d 8d* 8s³ 10.2d³) strong, robust filly; second foal; half-sister to 7f and 1m winner Blue Patrol (by Queen's Hussar); dam, half-sister to good sprinter Shiny Tenth, stayed 1¼m; having first outing for nearly 5 months and looking as if she might need race when beating Lombardi decisively by 1½ lengths (pair clear) in maiden race at Goodwood in September; stayed on extremely well under quite strong driving when close third behind Slaney Maid in Marlborough House Stakes at Ascot in October but was a shade disappointing when 6 lengths third to all-the-way winner Rollrights in £6,400 event at Doncaster later in month; should stay beyond 1m; yet to race on a sound surface; sold 70,000 gns Newmarket December Sales. *R. Hern.* **84**

Queen's Vase, Ascot—Ore strides out in style to win from Protection Racket and Krug (mostly hidden by winner)

ORGANIST 3 b.f. Jupiter Pluvius 119–Hurdy-Gurdy 90 (Espresso 122) **69** (1980 NR 1981 7g 10.4g³ 12s⁴ 12f) useful sort; half-sister to Oaks second Vielle (by Ribero) and useful 1¼m winner Sideshow (by Welsh Pageant); dam won at up to 1¼m; in frame in slowly-run minor event at Chester and maiden event at Goodwood in May, giving impression on latter course that she was possibly unsuited by soft going; should stay 1½m; pulled up after being struck into on final start (July). *B. Hobbs.*

ORIANNA FALLACI 4 b.f. Petrone 124–New Horizon (Alcimedes 113) **69** (1980 12fg³ 12f² 12g² 11s³ 14s* 14v* 16s³ 1981 16d 16.1s⁴ 12f 12f 16g²) lengthy ex-Irish filly; staying handicapper; runner-up to Beechwood Seeker at Newcastle in August; appears to act on any going but is evidently suited by soft; has worn a tongue strap; gave trouble on way to post and started slowly third outing and refused to enter stalls before intended final start; trained part of season by S. Murless; sold 1,000 gns Newmarket December Sales. *M. H. Easterby.*

ORIENTAL PRINCE 7 br.g. Le Prince 98–Asia (Milesian 125) (1980 won **63 d** once in Holland 1981 7d⁴ 9g² 12g 8fg 12g² 10fg 10fg 10fg 11.7fg 12d 11d) compact ex-Dutch gelding; a winner 9 times in Holland, including once in 1980; runner-up in amateur riders and ladies races at Ripon in first part of season; stays 1½m. *M. Ryan.*

ORILLA 2 gr.f. My Swanee 122–Hora Royale 82 (Kibenka 119) (1981 6fg 5g 5f⁴ **47** 9g) Apr 27; first foal; dam won over 1m in this country and also won in Spain; 3¾ lengths fourth of 6 to Revida Girl at Folkestone in July, first outing in a seller; subsequently exported to Holland and ran at least once there. *T. Marshall.*

ORIXA 2 b.f. Owen Dudley 121–Couloir 114 (Court Martial) (1981 5.8h² 5.8f **79** 7f³ 7fg² 7g) May 11; half-sister to several winners, including useful 5f to 1m winner Collapse (by Busted) and useful miler Coulomb (by Crepello); dam at her best at 2 yrs when very useful over 5f; placed in maiden races and a 20-runner nursery, running very well when short-headed by Towering in latter at Leicester in September; failed to run up to her best next start (didn't move well to post); will stay 1m; yet to race on a soft surface; sold to Mrs G. Forbes 7,000 gns Newmarket Autumn Sales. *H. Candy.*

ORLANDOLAND 2 br.c. Reliance II 137–Bombshell 76 (Le Levanstell 122) **—** (1981 6g) Apr 22; strong, good-bodied colt; fourth foal; half-brother to poor 1¼m winner Miss Minefield (by Northfields); dam won over 8.5f; 50/1, on toes in paddock and missed break when always in rear in 11-runner Ribero Stakes won by Master Cawston at Doncaster in September; a backward sort who will need time and longer distances. *J. Hanson.*

ORLEY FARM 6 br.h. Lorenzaccio 130–L'Envoi (Ossian II) (1980 NR **47** 1981 8s 8v 8f 10f² 10f 10f 8f 8g 13.8g⁴) plater; stays 1¾m; acts on firm going; sometimes wears blinkers; looks a difficult ride; sold 1,000 gns Doncaster October Sales. *J. Hardy.*

ORMOLU (USA) 2 b.c. Val de l'Orne 120–Donna Chere (Conestoga) (1981 8d) **— p** Mar 10; $135,000Y; fourth foal; half-brother to a winner by Bold Reason; dam won 7 small races at up to 1m from 9 starts at 2 yrs and was placed in 3 stakes events at 3 yrs; easy in market when remote sixth of 18 to Sugar and Mint in maiden race at Leicester in November. *J. Tree.*

ORMSARY 2 b. or br.c. Jukebox 120–Fire Bell 93 (Firestreak 125) (1981 5d² **92** 5d* 6v² 5d* 6fg 5fg 5fg² 6g²) May 3; IR 2,300Y; compact colt; half-brother to several winners, including 5f sprinter Dafydd (by Welsh Saint); dam half-sister to very useful stayers Khalekan and Aegean Blue; proved a good buy, winning maiden auction event in May and 4-runner Emily Persse Cup in June, both at Phoenix Park; beat Red Jersey 1½ lengths when gaining second success; also second 4 times, carrying top weight in nurseries on last 2 occasions; stays 6f; seems to act on any going. *S. Murless, Ireland.*

ORMUS (FR) 4 b.g. Faunus–Irova (Iron Liege) (1980 7d 10v² 11.5g* 12v* 11s **—** 14v 16v 1981 8s 13d 8fg 9g 12g 12fg 12f) workmanlike ex-Irish gelding; won maiden race at Down Royal and minor event at Listowel in 1980; not disgraced in handicaps at the Curragh and Leopardstown in April on first 2 starts at 4 yrs but was well beaten in amateur riders races and a handicap afterwards; suited by middle distances; suited by some give in the ground; trained part of year by J. Bolger. *W. Bentley.*

O-ROSE FORTUNATA 2 b.f. Hot Spark 126–Pandomyne 71 (Pandofell 132) **84** (1981 5d* 7.2f³ 6g³ 8f 6fg 6g) Apr 8; 9,000F, 9,600Y; rather light-framed filly;

half-sister to 3 winners, including 1979 2-y-o 6f winner Inzera (by Decoy Boy); dam 1¾m winner; stayed on in good style to win 15-runner maiden race at York in May by ½ length from Venetian Joy; not disgraced in several of her subsequent races, on sixth outing finishing 11 lengths tenth of 13 to Woodstream in William Hill Cheveley Park Stakes at Newmarket; stays 7f but finished only eighth of 9 in nursery when tried over 1m. *R. Hollinshead.*

ORP BALTIC 2 ch.g. Some Hand 119–Cedez Cela (Bleep-Bleep 134) (1981 **58** 5g 5g 5d 5fg 6d² 5f 6s 6d) Apr 26; well-grown, leggy gelding; head second of 12 to Bowscar in seller at Haydock in August; suited by 6f; best form on an easy surface; last of 11 in nursery when blinkered final outing. *J. Berry.*

ORRIN 2 ch.c. Bustino 136–Never Can Tell (Tambourine II 133) (1981 7f **80** 7fg² 8g) May 17; 8,200Y; quite a useful sort; fourth foal; dam from same family as Never Too Late II; going on strongly when head second of 17 to Return To Power in minor race at Warwick in August, best effort; will stay 1½m. *F. J. Houghton.*

O SOLO MIO 2 b.f. Porto Bello 118–Correct Approach 77 (Right Tack 131) **71** (1981 6fg 5f* 6g² 6s³ 5d³ 6g) Apr 2; fair sort; good walker; first foal; dam at her best at 2 yrs; plater; bought in 1,750 gns after getting up close home to win by a head from Will George at Wolverhampton in August; placed in big fields on next 2 outings and did very well to go down by only a head and a short head to Will George when ridden by apprentice at 8-lb overweight in non-selling nursery at Wolverhampton in October (would have won had she kept a straight course); stays 6f well; has won on firm going but has shown better form on soft; sold 1,150 gns Ascot December Sales. *P. Cole.*

OSWIN 4 b.c. Silly Season 127–Angello 87 (Crepello 136) (1980 9fg 10d 8f⁴ **—** 8g 8.2s 1981 12f 12f) big, good-bodied colt; only plating class; should stay middle distances; possibly needs a galloping track. *D. Francis.*

OUI MONSIEUR 7 b.g. Levanter 121–Melody Call 55 (Tudor Melody 129) **59** (1980 12fg² 12f⁴ 12fg* 12f⁴ 13.3g 12d 12g 16.5fg 12g 1981 15.5d 12d³ 12g* 12v³ 12g⁴ 16f 12fg 16d 12fg) poor handicapper; won at Lingfield in May; stays 2m; acts on any going; suitable mount for an inexperienced rider. *M. Haynes.*

OUR BARA BOY 4 b.g. Baragoi 115–Primeapple (Primera 131) (1980 10s **71** 10s 12fg 12fg³ 10fg⁴ 12f 13s⁴ 14d² 16.9d* 14fg* 16f 16s² 14g 17.1d 16s 1981 16fg 16.1s³ 18d 18.1d³ 16s* 18g) narrow, light-framed gelding; beat Al Kuwait a length in £4,000 handicap at Ascot in October; suited by a test of stamina; acts on any going with possible exception of very firm; effective with or without blinkers; suitable mount for a boy. *M. Ryan.*

OUR BIRTHDAY 5 b.h. Great Nephew 126–Renoir Picture 90 (Relko 136) **49** (1980 10s 9s 8fg 8fg⁴ 8fg* 8fg 9g 9fg 8g² 8g* 9g² 8d 8s 1981 9d⁴ 8fg⁴ 8d 8d⁴ 8v 8.3g 8.3g⁴ 10f 8s) neat horse; good mover; poor handicapper; probably stays 1¼m; acts on any going; wears blinkers; sometimes starts slowly. *J. Benstead.*

OUR FOXBAR 6 ch.m. Swinging Junior 118–Shepherd's Crook 81 (Current **66** Coin 118) (1980 5v 6g⁴ 6d⁴ 6f 6h 6fg 5g* 6g³ 5s 5g² 5g³ 6g 5d* 5s 6s 5d 6d⁴ 7d 1981 6v⁴ 6g² 5g 5g 5fg 6g 6g 6fg² 5d 5g 6fg³ 5fg⁴ 7f 6f 6d⁴ 6d* 6d 6d) lengthy mare; former plater; won handicap at Redcar in October; best at sprint distances; has won on a firm surface but is very well suited by some give in the ground; sold 1,650 gns Newmarket Autumn Sales. *M. Naughton.*

OUR LAL 5 b.m. Levmoss 133–Oola Rose (Breakspear II) (1980 16d 16s **§§** 12s⁴ 12d 1981 17.1g 16.9s) leggy mare; poor performer; appears to have gone the wrong way temperamentally (refused to race both starts in 1981); best left alone. *S. Harris.*

OUR LUCKY JIM 3 b.c. Jimsun 121–Ruby's Chance 71 (Charlottesville 135) **47** (1980 7fg 7f 8s 10.2s 1981 10v 12.2fg³ 16f 12.2fg 12f 13.8fg² 13.8g 11g) fair sort; placed in a minor event and a seller at Catterick; suited by 1½m and more; blinkered last 3 outings. *Hbt Jones.*

OUTLAW 2 ch.c. Morston 125–Heathfield 99 (Hethersett 134) (1981 7g 7fg³ **77** 8.2fg² 8g* 8g) May 19; quite a well-made colt; good walker and mover; half-brother to 5 winners, most at least useful, including very useful 1976 2-y-o 6f winner Fife and Drum (by Queen's Hussar); dam won from 6f to 1m; got on top inside last furlong when beating Orange Sorbet 1½ lengths in 14-runner maiden race at Ayr in September; had very stiff task under 9-10 in valuable nursery at Newmarket later in month and finished in rear behind Nioulargo; will be suited by 1¼m. *R. Hern.*

618

OUT OF HAND 2 ch.c. Some Hand 119–Crusheen (Typhoon 125) (1981 6g **70** 7f 7.2fg³ 7g 7g) Mar 24; 1,100Y; strong, lengthy colt; half-brother to 3 winners, including 3-y-o sprinter H. R. Micro (by High Award); dam ran twice at 2 yrs in Ireland; ran creditably when ¾-length third of 13 to Scoutsmistake in maiden race at Haydock in September (kept on under vigorous riding); well beaten subsequently; stays 7f well; wears a bandage on near-hind. *D. Dale.*

OVER AND EASY (USA) 2 ch.c. Explodent–Determined Route (Determined **64** Man) (1981 5v 5g 5g 5fg 5g 6g⁴ 6fg) Apr 10; $50,000 2-y-o; lengthy colt; fourth foal; brother to 3 winners, including stakes-placed Smooth Journey; dam won 6f claiming race; stayed on when 9 lengths fourth of 26 to Al Hasa in maiden race at Nottingham in August; in rear in valuable seller at Kempton the following month but had worst of the draw and was eased right up once chance had gone; will stay 1m; ran poorly in blinkers on fourth outing. *J. Sutcliffe.*

OVER AND OVER 2 b.g. Tumble Wind–Olvera (Molvedo 137) (1981 5fg **70** 5f³ 6g⁴ 5d) Feb 7; IR 24,000Y; lightly-made gelding; good walker; half-brother to several winners in Italy and to 1979 French 2-y-o 5f winner Fast Foot (by Prince Tenderfoot); dam, placed in Italy, is half-sister to several good Italian winners; beaten just over 5 lengths when in frame in maiden race won by Drago at Catterick in July and in minor event won by Mubhedj at Windsor in August; almost certainly finds 5f much too sharp and will be suited by 7f and 1m. *J. Hindley.*

OVER HERE (USA) 2 b. or br.f. Tisab–Way To Go (Olympia) (1981 5g 5g **51** 5f) Mar 29; $40,000Y; half-sister to numerous winners, including stakes winners Toward (by Bagdad) and Transportation (by Sir Gaylord); dam, winner at 2 yrs, is half-sister to champion filly Doubledogdare; poor form in maiden and minor events; sweated up when tried in blinkers third outing; dead. *J. W. Watts.*

OVERPLAY 3 b.f. Bustino 136–Melodramatic 112 (Tudor Melody 129) (1980 **107** 8.5d* 8g² 1981 7s² 8v⁴ 12fg³ 12fg⁴ 11.5fg* 12g 12fg⁴ 14d 12d² 10g2) 62,000Y; lengthy, quite attractive filly; walks well; half-sister to fairly useful miler Crown Witness (by Crowned Prince) and successful Irish stayer Public Opinion (by Run The Gantlet); dam very useful winner at 7f and 9f at 3 yrs; landed the odds in great style by 10 lengths from Lagolette in minor event at Galway in July; stayed on well after being one of several runners hampered on home turn when 3 lengths fifth behind Condessa in Yorkshire Oaks at York the following month; had run creditably on occasions earlier, including when ½-length second behind Martinova in Group 3 Athasi Stakes at the Curragh, about 2½ lengths fourth to Arctique Royale in Goffs Irish 1,000 Guineas on same course and 1¾ lengths third behind Strigida in Ribblesdale Stakes at Royal Ascot; second in Trigo Stakes (beaten 5 lengths by The Neurologist) and minor event at Leopardstown in the autumn; stays 1½m; probably acts on any going; blinkered last 4 outings. *D. Weld, Ireland.*

OVERSHOE 3 ch.g. Import 127–Snow Boots 62 (Marshal Pil 108) (1980 5g — 5f 7g 1981 8s 7fg 5f) leggy gelding; plating-class maiden; should stay 7f. *W. C. Watts.*

OVER THE PEAK 3 br.f. High Top 131–Self Satisfied 100 (Great Nephew 126) — (1980 6g 5f 1981 8fg 7f 7g 10.2h 8fg 8.2s) small filly; well beaten in varied company; lacks scope. *W. Wightman.*

OVER THE RAINBOW 4 b.g. Song 132–Lady Matador 108 (Matador 131) **85** (1980 5d 5f² 5fg³ 5s⁴ 5g 6fg 5f 1981 5fg³ 5d⁴ 5fg 5.1f⁴ 6f⁴ 5fg 6f 6fg 5.6fg 5g) strong, compact, sprint type; has an enlarged near-fore; fair handicapper; ran really well when fourth to Great Eastern, beaten 3 short heads, in Wokingham Stakes at Royal Ascot in June on fifth start; stays 6f; acts on any going; blinkered once in 1980; sometimes sweats up. *J. Winter.*

OVER THE TOP 3 b.g. Upper Case–Shelby (Pall Mall 132) (1980 8g³ 8s **68** d 8d³ 1981 12fg 10.6s² 12f 11.5d 12d2) lightly-made gelding; close second in valuable selling handicap at Haydock in June and claiming race at Newmarket in August (blinkered); stays 1½m. *W. O'Gorman.*

OVERTRICK 6 b.h. Great Nephew 126–Jackyda 71 (Royal Palm 131) (1980 **103** 7d⁴ 7s⁴ 7fg 6fg 6d² 6fg 6s² 6g 6d 1981 5g 6.5fg³ 6.5s* 5s³ 6d³ 6s 6fg 6g² 6fg³ 6d 6s 6d* 6g) useful handicapper; landed odds in race at Cagnes-sur-Mer early in year and beat Kiss by 1½ lengths in Allendale Handicap at Doncaster in October; ran well on several other occasions; stays 7f; suited by some give in the ground and revels in the mud; usually held up; sold 20,000 gns Newmarket December Sales. *J. Dunlop.*

OVERULE 4 b. or br.c. Dawn Review 105–Miss Counsel (Counsel 118) (1980 NR — 1981 10.1fg 10.1fg⁴) behind in maiden and minor events. *D. Marks.*

OWEN ROCK 2 ch.c. Owen Dudley 121–Gillycan (Rockavon 120) (1981 6fg — 6g 7fg 8g) May 5; 3,500Y; compact colt; fourth foal; dam of little account; in rear in maiden and minor events. *I. Jordon.*

OWNIA STAR 2 br.f. Wishing Star 117–Paulownia (Palestine 133) (1981 5s) — Apr 10; IR 1,350F, 960Y; neat, lightly-made filly; half-sister to winners by King's Company and Lord David; dam never ran; 16/1 and in need of race when in rear in 18-runner auction event awarded to Epona's Grey at Ripon in April. *E. Eldin.*

OXSLIP 2 b.f. Owen Dudley 121–Opencast 97 (Mossborough 126) (1981 6fg **73 p** 7fg*) Apr 23; strong, good sort; excellent mover; half-sister to a number of winners, including very useful stayer Kambalda (by Right Royal V); dam 1¼m winner and half-sister to good winners Shaft and Bunker; 20/1, led from halfway and held on well to win 22-runner maiden race at Newmarket in July by a short head from Beldale Fleet; none too well away on debut; almost certainly far better than we are able to rate her and should make a useful 3-y-o when tackling 1¼m+. *G. Pritchard-Gordon.*

OYSTON ESTATES 5 gr.g. Goldhill 125–Port Relic 90 (Relic) (1980 6v³ — 6d³ 6fg 7h 6f³ 6g⁴ 6d 6d⁴ 5g 7g⁴ 7fg 6s* 6d 6s 1981 6g 6s 8.2d) strong gelding; seems to stay 7f; probably acts on any going; effective with and without blinkers; good mount for an apprentice; goes well at Hamilton. *T. Robson.*

OYSTON IDOL 5 b.m. Continuation 120–Lissome Lisa (Sir Ribot) (1980 5f — 5f 5f 1981 12.2fg 12.2g 8g) poor plater; sometimes wears blinkers. *J. Charlton.*

OYSTONS WINDMILL 2 b.c. Silly Season 127–Westmorland Jane 76 (Vimy — 132) (1981 7g 7.2v 7g) Apr 16; tall, leggy colt; half-brother to several winners, including good Brazilian winner Bac (by Sharpen Up); dam placed at up to 17f when named Ciboulette; soundly beaten in sellers; sold 720 gns Doncaster November Sales. *J. Berry.*

P

PABLEU 2 b.c. Blue Cashmere 129–Palanna 87 (Pall Mall 132) (1981 7f⁴ **76+** 7g) May 3; rather lightly-made colt; third foal; brother to 1m winner Nobleu and half-brother to a minor winner; dam stayed at least 1m; 2½ lengths fourth of 19 to Wibis Range in maiden event at Redcar in September; not disgraced when seventh of 18 to Leg Glance in similar event at Doncaster in October; will stay 1m. *P. Asquith.*

PACIFIC SPARKLER 2 ch.c. Sparkler 130–Shanghai Lady 87 (Crocket 130) **86** (1981 6d 6g³ 7fg² 5fg² 5fg³ 7s 7d² 7d) Mar 9; 11,000F, 15,000Y; neat colt; second foal; dam sprinter; placed in maiden and minor races, on final occasion running particularly well when going down by ½ length to Starbells at Chepstow in October; stays 7f; acts on a firm and a soft surface; ran moderately in a nursery final start. *P. Cole.*

PACIFIC SPENDOUR 2 gr. or ro.c. Roan Rocket 128–Fir Tree 90 (Santa — Claus 117) (1981 7fg 7fg) Feb 1; 1,200Y; plain colt; fourth foal; half-brother to a winner in Malaya; dam, half-sister to smart stayer Celtic Cone, stayed 1¾m; behind in August in 18-runner maiden race won by Crellistovi at Ayr (dwelt) and 15-runner minor event won by Super Sunrise at Newcastle. *H. Bell.*

PADALCO 2 ch.c. Nonoalco 131–Paddy's Princess (St Paddy 133) (1981 **95** 6d³ 6fg* 7fg* 7fg 8g³) Mar 2; 14,000Y; lengthy, quite attractive colt; very good mover; second foal; dam good French middle-distance stayer; made all when landing the odds comfortably in 26-runner maiden race at Doncaster in June (beat Barooq 2½ lengths) and in Bernard van Cutsem Stakes at Newmarket the following month (very confidently ridden when scoring by ½ length from Norwick who gave 8 lb); not seen out again until September when distant last of 8 to Achieved in Laurent Perrier Champagne Stakes at Doncaster; ran much better on final start to finish 8 lengths third of 6 to Jalmood in minor event at Goodwood; will be suited by 1¼m. *H. Cecil.*

PADANG 3 ch.g. Patch 129–Tragara (Buisson Ardent 129) (1980 NR 1981 — 12.5s) 3,000F, 4,400Y; tall, short-backed gelding; half-brother to 3 winners, including 5f and 6f winner Elton Abbess (by Tamerlane); dam, winner in Italy, is daughter of very smart filly Romantica; always behind in maiden event won by Pomposity at Stockton in April; had refused to enter stalls on intended first appearance. *T. Fairhurst.*

PADDLE WHEEL 5 b.m. Huntercombe 133–Paddle Boat 98 (St Paddy 133) **37** (1980 6g 8fg 7g 6g² 6d 7.6g² 5fg 6g³ 6g 6s 1981 7d 6fg 7.6g 5s 6f 7.6fg 6fg³ 7f⁴ 6g 8fg) smallish mare; plater; best form at distances short of 1m; acts on firm going; suitable mount for a boy; bandaged near-fore nowadays. *D. H. Jones.*

PADDOCK BAR 2 ch.f. Roman Warrior 132–Motionless 109 (Midsummer — Night II 117) (1981 5g 5g 7g) Mar 21; fair sort; half-sister to 1m winner Speedy Tack (by Right Tack); dam third in English and Irish 1,000 Guineas; little worthwhile form in maiden races; changed hands 500 gns Ascot October Sales after third start. *G. Kindersley.*

PADDY'S GUIDE 11 ch.g. Guide 118–Bellisle 108 (King's Bench 132) (1980 — NR 1981 16.5g) of little account. *Mrs A. Bell.*

PADINGO 2 b.c. Saulingo 122–Paduia (St Paddy 133) (1981 5g 5s² 5g 5g **54** 5s) Feb 13; IR 2,700F, 1,400Y; well-grown colt; second foal; dam ran once in Italy; carried 1 lb overweight when short-headed by Steel Stockholder in 9-runner maiden auction event at Haydock in June; ran respectably in a seller on final outing; will be suited by 6f; acts well on soft going; twice sweated up. *D. Garraton.*

PADRELO 2 b.c. Relkino 131–Expadeo 82 (St Paddy 133) (1981 7g 7fg **80** 7fg 7g⁴ 7d) Apr 24; small, quite well-made colt; good mover; first foal; dam won over 1½m; only quite moderate; will be suited by middle distances; sold to A. Pitt 1,800 gns Ascot November Sales. *R. Hern.*

PADSKI 8 ch.g. St Paddy 133–No Relation 94 (Klairon 131) (1980 18d⁴ **47** 16s⁴ 16fg 16.1s⁴ 18s² 1981 18s 16s³ 16.1fg³ 16.1s 16.9s 18d⁴ 18.8fg 22.2f 16fg² 16.1f³ 16fg 16g 18f 16.5g² 16.1s⁴ 18g⁴) poor handicapper; stays well; acts on any going; has run respectably for a claimer; none too enthusiastic. *R. Hollinshead.*

PADUCAH 5 b.g. Swing Easy 126–Hunting Bee (Honeyway 125) (1980 7f **68** 6f 6h 6s³ 6g 6d 6g² 5fg³ 6fg⁴ 5d⁴ 6s³ 6g 5f³ 6s 1981 7s 6s³ 7g 6g 6d 7g⁴ 8fg* 12fg 11g 9f⁴ 8fg 7.6fg⁴ 8g³ 7g) strong, rangy gelding; won amateur riders race at Redcar in May; suited by 7f and 1m but doesn't stay 1½m; seems to act on any going; usually wears blinkers; suitable mount for an inexperienced rider; sold 3,000 gns Newmarket Autumn Sales. *T. Fairhurst.*

PAGAN DEITY 2 ch.f. Brigadier Gerard 144–Criminelle (Crepello 136) (1981 **71 p** 6fg²) Feb 21; 9,400F; fourth produce; dam lightly-raced sister to 2 winners; did extremely well to finish 1½ lengths second of 11 to Mummy's Game, after starting slowly, when second favourite for minor event at Windsor in July; will stay 1¼m; looked reasonably promising here but wasn't seen out again. *J. Dunlop.*

PAGAPAS BAY 4 br.c. Welsh Saint 126–Cherry Plum (Primera 131) (1980 **72** 6fg 5fg 5d 5s 6g 5g* 5d³ 6s³ 1981 6s* 6s* 6g* 6d² 6g² 5.1fg* 6g) lengthy colt; not a good mover in his slower paces; plater at 3 yrs; showed improved form in 1981, winning handicaps at Nottingham (made virtually all), Hamilton, Ripon and Yarmouth; stays 6f; seems to act on any going but goes well on soft; blinkered once in 1980; sometimes sweats up; suitable mount for a boy. *A. Jarvis.*

PAINTHORPE HOUSE 2 br.g. Tycoon II–Marton Lady 103 (March Past — 124) (1981 6f 7d) Mar 19; quite attractive gelding; brother to very smart sprinter Haveroid and fair 1980 2-y-o 5f winner Marton Boy, and half-brother to 2 winners; dam sprinter; tailed off at halfway in minor event at Ripon in July but then ran on to finish 14 lengths fifth of 6 to Steel Stockholder; close up 5f when last of 6 to Cassley River in £3,100 race at Redcar following month; not certain to stay 7f; sold to D. Chapman 580 gns Doncaster October Sales. *M. H. Easterby.*

PAINT MY WAY 3 ro.c. The Go-Between 129–Warmheart (Arctic Storm — 134) (1980 5.8fg 5d 5s 5.8fg 5d 5fg 1981 5h 5f) robust colt; seems of little account. *M. Bradley.*

PAIR-OF-DEUCES 2 b.f. Some Hand 119–Lost in Silence (Silent Spring **73** 102) (1981 5fg 5d⁴ 6fg 6s* 8d* 8s) Mar 13; 1,000Y; fair sort; second living foal; dam never ran; surprisingly attracted no bid after winning valuable 20-runner seller at Goodwood in September by 2½ lengths from Purnima and quickly gained another success, leading from halfway to win £3,200 nursery at Brighton in October by ½ length from Lady Bounty; stays 1m but best form at 6f in the mud; genuine. *R. Hannon.*

PAIS DE GALES 3 b. or br.g. Mummy's Pet 125–Regal Artist 72 (Breakspear — II) (1980 5f 5fg 7d 7d 8fg 1981 8fg 7fg 7f) lightly-made gelding; no worth-while form in maiden and minor events. *W. A. Stephenson.*

PALACE GENIE 3 br.g. Royal Palace 131–My Ginny 83 (Palestine 133) — (1980 NR 1981 10.2f) lengthy gelding; second foal; half-brother to 1979 2-y-o 5f winner Aunty Bessie (by No Mercy); dam 2-y-o 6f winner; always behind in 22-runner maiden race won by Habus at Doncaster in June. *Miss S. Hall.*

PALACE STREAM 2 ch.g. Dragonara Palace 115–Magic Maiden 97 (Magic **66** Red) (1981 5g 5g³) May 7; 11,000F, 14,000Y; rather lightly-made gelding; half-brother to several winners, including fairly useful 2-y-o's Hey Presto, Petulengra and Sunny Smile (all by Mummy's Pet); dam 7f winner; second favourite when 3½ lengths third of 13 to Pia Fort in maiden race at Thirsk in May; will stay 6f. *E. Eldin.*

PALACE TRAVEL 2 b.f. High Top 131–Palava (Pall Mall 132) (1981 6g) — Feb 28; IR 36,000Y; lengthy, good sort; second live foal; dam unraced half-sister to very useful performers Command Freddy and Ridaness; 20/1, seemed rather green when always behind in 17-runner maiden race won by Merlin's Charm at Newmarket in October; will stay at least 1m; has scope. *G. Hunter.*

PALATARA 3 gr.f. Dragonara Palace 115–La Sarmate (Hard Sauce 131) **52** (1980 NR 1981 8.5d³ 7fg⁴ 8h) 2,200F, 3,000Y; compact, rather lightly-made filly; half-sister to useful French and American winner General Order (by Home Guard) and a winner in Italy; dam unraced granddaughter of Prix de l'Arc de Triomphe winner La Sorellina; in frame in sellers at Epsom and Brighton in summer; will stay 1¼m; ran moderately in blinkers final start. *B. Hills.*

PALATINATE 3 b.c. Rheingold 137–Cloudbreaker 95 (Nimbus 130) (1980 7f **82** 1981 12fg⁴ 12s 10d 12f² 10f* 12fg* 12.3g² 10fg⁴ 12fg⁴) attractive, well-made colt; won handicaps at Nottingham in June (beat Miss St Mawes ½ length, despite tending to hang left) and at Hamilton the following month (smoothly); in frame in similar events afterwards; stays 1½m; gives impression he's well suited by top-of-the-ground conditions; doesn't find much off the bridle. *M. Stoute.*

PALE DANCER (FR) 2 br.f. Dancer's Image–Nopala (Yelapa 130) (1981 6fg*) **95 p** Mar 25; 41,000 francs Y (approx £4,410); first foal; dam, 2-y-o 6f winner, is half-sister to very useful middle-distance performer Captain Nemo; won valuable newcomers race at Chantilly in September by short head from Parannda; will stay at least 1m; now trained by D. Becquemin; entered in 1,000 Guineas. *M. Blackshaw, France.*

PALE MOON 3 ch.f. Jukebox 120–Rose of Tralee 114 (Buisson Ardent 129) **58** (1980 7g 1981 8fg³ 7f 8.2s² 7g 6d 8g) lengthy filly; placed in maiden races at Warwick in June and Nottingham in September, best efforts; stays 1m; blinkered and sweating fifth start. *B. Hills.*

PALESTINES GOLD 4 gr.c. Gold Form 108–Palmural 111 (Palestine 133) — (1980 8d 9.4g 12g 12.3d 1981 12g) neat colt; no sign of ability in maiden and minor races. *I. Jordon.*

PALETTE KNIFE 3 b.g. Bay Express 132–My Bushbaby 100 (Hul a Hul 124) — (1980 5d 1981 10s 10.1d 10s 8s 8s 10d 8g) compact gelding; in rear in varied company. *Peter Taylor.*

PALLOMERE 2 b.f. Blue Cashmere 129–Pallona 62 (Royal Palm 131) (1981 **85** 6s 7g³) Mar 28; lengthy, lightly-made filly; third foal; half-sister to 2 winners abroad; dam stayed 1½m; unquoted, prominent most of way when 8 lengths fifth of 12 to Dancing Rocks in Blue Seal Stakes at Ascot in September; 25/1 for 29-runner maiden race at Newmarket the following month but finished 2¼ lengths third to Chalon, running on steadily under hand riding only; likely to stay 1m; taken down very quietly at Newmarket. *E. Eldin.*

PALMABELLA 4 ch.f. Palm Track 122–Lady Amabel (I Say 125) (1980 — 7.2fg 6d 7fg 8fg³ 8d³ 7g 7f 8d 1981 7s 6g) leggy, unfurnished filly; plater; stays 1m; acts on a firm and a soft surface; sometimes sweats up. *A. Potts.*

PALMERO 4 b.g. Palm Track 122–Duresme 76 (Starry Halo 122) (1980 NR **66** 1981 12s*(dis) 16.1s⁴ 14s³) big, workmanlike gelding; trotted up in poor maiden race at Beverley in April (subsequently disqualified for having traces of theobromine in system); stays 1¾m but not 2m; acts well on soft going. *K. Stone.*

PALMERSTON 8 ch.g. Aureole 132–Hunting Bee (Honeyway 125) (1980 NR —
1981 16fg 16g 16g) moderate stayer in 1978; well beaten in 1981; acted on
any going; sometimes blinkered; dead. *J. Dunlop.*

PALM THE ACE 3 b.g. Palm Track 122–Aces High 62 (Acer 123) (1980 5f **33**
5d 5.1g⁴ 7g 5d 1981 6s 10s 8fg 7d⁴ 8g 5v³ 5fg 6fg 8s 6g) small gelding; plater;
probably stays 1m. *R. Hoad.*

PALOS HEIGHTS 2 b.f. Lochnager 132–Ruling Class 92 (King Emperor) **51**
(1981 6g 6g⁴ 6f 6d 7fg 6f² 8fg 8d 7g) May 4; 1,150Y; lightly-made filly; third
foal; dam raced 1½m; plater; in frame at York and Hamilton in the summer;
yet to prove she stays 1m. *J. Fitzgerald.*

PALTANGO 3 ch.g. Royal Palace 131–Orange Sensation 69 (Floribunda 136) **65**
(1980 6d³ 7g² 7.2d 5d 7d⁴ 7d 1981 8fg 7f 7g 7f³ 7fg 7f 6f⁴ 6f* 7g) useful sort;
blinkered when winning handicap at Thirsk in September; soundly beaten when
blinkered again only subsequent start; stays 7f; probably acts on any going; has
given the impression of being none too genuine and swerved start seventh
outing. *M. W. Easterby.*

PALUMBA 3 b.f. Derring-Do 131–Dove 92 (Sea Hawk II 131) (1980 5g³ 5g* **89**
6g³ 5fg 6f⁴ 1981 8.5g 10fg 10g⁴ 10d³ 8fg⁴ 8g 8g³) neat filly; didn't run up to her
best although was in frame in handicaps, best effort when strong-finishing
third to Silca Star Key at Newmarket in October on final start; will be suited
by a return to 1¼m. *H. Candy.*

PAMIREE 2 b.f. Hittite Glory 125–Royal Princess 81 (Meadow Mint 120) —
(1981 5d 5fg 5d 5d 5.3f 5f⁴) Mar 30; 2,500Y; sharp sort; first foal; dam 2-y-o
5f winner; no worthwhile form, including in a seller. *A. Ingham.*

PAMPABIRD 2 b.c. Pampapaul 121–Wood Grouse 56 (Celtic Ash) (1981 **110**
5g* 5s³ 5.5d⁴) Mar 23; IR 29,000F, 25,000Y; half-brother to 2 winners,
including Great Sound (by Meadow Mint), successful at up to 7f at 2 yrs in Ireland
and subsequently a very useful stakes winner in USA; dam, half-sister to
Pitskelly, stayed 13f; showed very useful form in first half of season, winning
newcomers event at Maisons-Laffitte and finishing in frame behind Maelstrom
Lake in Prix du Bois at Longchamp (2¼ lengths third of 6) and Prix Robert
Papin at Maisons-Laffitte (3 lengths fourth of 10); not seen out again; will
stay 1m; entered in 2,000 Guineas and Derby. *J. Cunnington, jnr, France.*

PAMPALAD (USA) 2 b.c. Naskra–Retirement (Royal Gem) (1981 5g 5d 8s⁴) —
June 3; $270,000Y; neat, attractive colt; half-brother to several winners, 3
of them stakes winners, including Secret Retreat (by Clandestine), a smart
winner at up to 1m; dam won 6 times at 2 yrs and 3 yrs; beaten 13 lengths
when fourth of 17 to Barfoot in maiden race at Warwick in October and seems
only a poor maiden; will stay 1¼m. *J. Tree.*

PAMPARINO 2 b.c. Pampapaul 121–Annacloy (Majority Blue 126) (1981 **78**
5g 6fg 7fg 7fg*) Apr 22; IR 30,000Y; sturdy colt; second foal; dam speedy
early-season 2-y-o in Ireland; in no danger from 2f out when beating Sporting
Painting by 5 lengths in 12-runner maiden race at Catterick in August; stays
7f; pulled hard third start; sold 2,900 gns Newmarket Autumn Sales. *B. Hills.*

PAMPERDALE 2 br.c. Hotfoot 126–Angello 87 (Crepello 136) (1981 6fg*) **85** p
Feb 20; useful-looking colt; half-brother to several winners, including Royal
Lodge winner Adios (by Silly Season); dam won at 1m; not seen out after
winning 20-runner maiden race at Newmarket in June by ½ length from Big
Trouble; will be well suited by 1m or more. *W. Hastings-Bass.*

PAMPERED GIPSY 2 b.g. Pampapaul 121–Gipsy Heart (Skymaster 126) **80**
(1981 7f 6fg 8s 6g 7d 6g) Apr 20; 1,100Y; rangy, good sort; poor walker and
mover; fourth living foal; dam unraced sister to smart Sky Gipsy; quite moderate
form in end-of-season maiden races; stays 7f; blinkered last 2 starts. *A. Bailey.*

PAMPERED ISLE 3 b.f. Mummy's Pet 125–Barnie's Isle (Dumbarnie 125) —
(1980 5v⁴ 5f 5fg 5fg 5d³ 5f⁴ 5d 5s 1981 7fg 8f 8.2s) unfurnished filly; no form
in 1981; off course 4 months prior to being well beaten in a seller on final start;
blinkered fourth outing in 1980. *W. C. Watts.*

PANATELLA 2 br.f. Firestreak 125–Chebs Lass 84 (Chebs Lad 120) (1981 5fg **77**
6f* 7d³ 6g⁴) Apr 12; 2,700Y; compact filly; sister to 3-y-o 1¼m winner Ridgefield and 1979 2-y-o 6f winner Awahnee Lady; dam won twice over 7f at 2 yrs;
won 15-runner maiden auction event at Folkestone in July by 1½ lengths from
Garfunkel; beaten less than 4 lengths when third of 6 to Cassley River in £3,100
race at Redcar following month and when fourth of 16 to King of Speed in
nursery at Lingfield in September; will be suited by 1m. *V. Soane.*

PANAVISE 4 b.g. Silly Season 127–Field Daisy (White Fire III) (1980 8g 8g³ — 1981 10.2s⁴ 8fg) short-backed gelding; quite moderate at his best; stayed 1¼m; acted on soft going; dead. *P. Cundell.*

PANAY 3 b.f. Arch Sculptor 123–Sundalgo 82 (Fidalgo 129) (1980 5v³ 5s* 5fg³ 5f³ 5f³ 5g³ 5f 1981 6g 6g⁴ 5g 6s 5f 5fg 5fg 5fg 5g 5f 6fg 6g 6d 7s) compact filly; plater; stays 6f; acts on any going; blinkered eighth start; sold 680 gns Newmarket Autumn Sales. *T. Fairhurst.*

PANCHAO 2 b.c. Mummy's Pet 125–Love Always (Be Friendly 130) (1981 5s **54** 5s 5s 5d 5g 6g³ 5f 6g 7g 7g 6fg³ 7d 5f) Apr 21; 5,400Y; lightly-made, sharp sort; plater; stays 6f; best form on a sound surface; sometimes wears blinkers; sold to Newmarket BA 1,400 gns Newmarket Autumn Sales. *T. Fairhurst.*

PANDORAS GOLD 2 b. or br.f. Wishing Star 117–Moss Girl 59 (Star Moss 122) **68** (1981 5fg⁴ 6fg 5d 5s 5g* 5g) Apr 17; IR 2,000Y; narrow, unfurnished filly; fourth foal; dam poor half-sister to The Go-Between; dropped in class, stayed on to win 14-runner seller at Catterick in October a shade cleverly by ½ length from Singularity; attracted no bid; should be suited by 6f+. *Peter Taylor.*

PANTO ISLAND 3 ch.g. Silly Season 127–Wrekinianne 96 (Reform 132) (1980 **42** 5d 5f³ 5f 6fg 6d 8.2g 6g 1981 8v 10s 9d 7g 6d 6d³ 7g 7f⁴ 7g⁴ 9fg 8fg 13.8g 7g) leggy, quite useful-looking gelding; plater; not certain to stay 1¾m; often wears a hood nowadays; sold 620 gns Doncaster September Sales. *T. Fairhurst.*

PANTOMIME KING 3 b.g. Moulton 128–Miss Jessica 90 (Milesian 125) (1980 6g 7f 1981 12s 10g) rangy gelding; in rear in varied company. *Peter Taylor.*

PAPAFINGO 4 ch.g. Simbir 130–Asail (Atan) (1980 12d 16.9d³ 14.7g 11.5g⁴ — 1981 10.2s) tall, narrow gelding; poor maiden; stays well. *Mrs J. Pitman.*

PAPERACER 2 ch.g. Jukebox 120–Almanac 89 (London Gazette 117) (1981 **69** 5d 5s 5s 6g 6fg 5d 5s⁴ 5s 6s) Feb 10; 11,500F; robust, close-coupled gelding; first produce; dam won over 7.5f at 2 yrs, and also won over hurdles; quite a moderate maiden; stays 6f; appears to act on any going; ran poorly in blinkers eighth start. *D. Elsworth.*

PAPERETTO 2 br.c. Godswalk 130–Goosie-Gantlet 63 (Run The Gantlet) **91** (1981 6g 6fg² 7fg*) useful-looking colt; first foal; dam, daughter of very useful Goosie, stayed well; finished very strongly to win valuable 19-runner maiden race at Goodwood in July by 1½ lengths from Escapism; will stay 1m; fairly useful. *B. Hills.*

PAPER LAD 4 b.g. Touch Paper 118–Church Bay 76 (Reliance II 137) (1980 **36** 5f 5h² 5fg 5fg 6g 6s 6s 5f 1981 5s 6g 6fg³ 6fg⁴ 6g 5fg) neat gelding; plater; stays 6f; needs a sound surface; sometimes sweats up; sometimes blinkered; sold 540 gns Newmarket Autumn Sales. *R. D. Peacock.*

PARABEMS 2 b.f. Swing Easy 126–Lunar Queen 96 (Queen's Hussar 124) **72** (1981 6f 6f 5fg² 7f 6d² 6g² 5s 5s*) Feb 11; 3,200Y; lengthy filly; poor mover; third living foal; half-sister to 3-y-o Royal Duty (by Import), a winner at up to 7f; dam won three 5f races at 2 yrs; plater; bought in 900 gns after beating Sallwah comfortably by 3 lengths at Redcar in October; not disgraced in nursery seventh start; stays 6f; seems suited by some give in the ground. *C. Williams.*

PARADISE (FR) 2 br.f. Brigadier Gerard 144–Orsa Maggiore 117 (Ruysdael II **99** p 122) (1981 9d³ 10v 8s*) Mar 31; second foal; dam outstanding filly in Italy, winner of Oaks d'Italia, Gran Premio di Milano and Premio Roma; left her previous form well behind when winning 12-runner maiden race at Maisons-Laffitte in November hard held by 2½ lengths and 4 lengths; a well-bred filly who could go on to much better things at 3 yrs; entered in 1,000 Guineas and Oaks. *G. Bonnaventure, France.*

PARADISE BIRD 3 ch.f. Sallust 134–Fair Darling 93 (Darling Boy 124) (1980 — 5g 6d 6d* 6g³ 6s* 1981 7d 7g 6fg 6g 6d 6d) small filly; fairly useful at 2 yrs; disappointing in 1981; bred to stay 1m; acts on soft going; blinkered fifth start; sold 10,500 gns Newmarket December Sales. *P. Calver.*

PARADIS TERRESTRE (USA) 2 b.c. Empery 128–Pixie Tower 116 (Songedor **126**+ 116) (1981 7s* 8d²)
　　To breed and own colts so promising that they start favourite for the season's last three big two-year-old events, the William Hill Dewhurst Stakes, the Horris Hill Stakes and the William Hill Futurity, would be many an owner/breeder's idea of heaven on earth. Daniel Wildenstein was in this seemingly happy position in 1981 but by the end of the season he, like Adam before him, found paradise lost: Simply Great trailed in seventh of nine in the Dewhurst,

Match Winner came home third behind the easy winner Montekin in the Horris Hill, and, perhaps most frustrating of all, Paradis Terrestre was beaten in the Futurity at Doncaster through misfortune.

It was a little surprising to find Paradis Terrestre as short as 6/4 to beat the likes of the Royal Lodge winner Norwick and the four-length Beresford Stakes winner Assert in the Futurity but there was no denying the outstanding promise of his sole racecourse performance, a scintillating effort in the Hyperion Stakes at Ascot a fortnight earlier. There, when favourite in an eleven-strong field which included Sans Blague, a four-length winner of an eighteen-runner maiden race at Newbury, and Alvor, an impressive five-length winner on his debut, Paradis Terrestre had looked a champion in the making; from well over a quarter of a mile out he could be seen travelling very easily indeed and he needed to be given only a little rein to quicken right away in the final furlong, putting seven lengths between himself and Alvor by the line. He never even came off the bridle. Few animals put up so smart a display on their debut, and an even better one followed in defeat at Doncaster—he failed by only half a length to overhaul Count Pahlen after a most unlucky run. As End of the Line, Norwick, General Anders and Count Pahlen disputed the lead in the early stages Paradis Terrestre was well placed and travelling smoothly. Then, as he jockeyed for position with Assert, Super Sunrise and Ashenden after covering little more than two furlongs, he stumbled twice and in no time at all was only twelfth of the thirteen runners. He was still at the rear as the field swung into the straight. His cause wasn't helped at this stage by his having to be switched outside to see daylight and by the time he'd completed his manoeuvres Paradis Terrestre was several lengths off the leaders, Count Pahlen and Norwick. He didn't quicken instantly but once into his stride he battled his way up to the leaders, keeping on gamely and strongly under pressure to snatch second place close home by a head from Jalmood. His rider, Piggott, tended to play down ill fortune, saying: 'In the straight, I always had him where I wanted him—except at the finish. Had he been able to quicken as I had hoped, he would have won. Had he been more experienced, I dare say he might have won. But on the day he was definitely second best'. Much as

Hyperion Stakes, Ascot—Paradis Terrestre is out on his own at the finish

we admire Piggott's judgement we have to disagree with him here—had Paradis Terrestre not lost his good early position we feel sure he would have won. And while we're disagreeing with people, we'd like to take Paradis Terrestre's owner to task for his assertion after the Futurity that Simply Great 'is three or four lengths in front of this one'. Maybe Simply Great is the freer, more impressive worker at home but there's nothing in either of Simply Great's racecourse performances to suggest that he's anywhere near as good as, let alone markedly superior to, Paradis Terrestre.

Paradis Terrestre (USA) (b.c. Mar 22, 1979)	Empery (b 1973)	Vaguely Noble (b 1965)	Vienna	
			Noble Lassie	
		Pamplona II (b 1956)	Postin	
			Society's Way	
	Pixie Tower (gr 1970)	Songedor (ch 1959)	Matador	
			Fazeley	
		Cawston Tower (gr 1956)	Maharaj Kumar	
			Silver Ribbon	

Paradis Terrestre is easily the best winner so far by the 1976 Derby winner Empery. Although Empery stands at the Gainesway Farm in Kentucky he hasn't yet met with much success in the States, siring only two stakes winners (neither the winner of a Graded event) and just four American two-year-old winners from his first two crops. His fee of 20,000 dollars suggests that he's not particularly highly regarded there—Gainesway has no fewer than twenty-nine stallions standing at higher fees—and he'd probably be more popular standing in Europe where he was also represented in 1981 by the Prix Saint-Roman second Empery Card, the Prix Yacowlef runner-up Baltimore Bullet and the promising Flicker to a Flame.

We described Empery as 'essentially a stayer' but Paradis Terrestre's dam Pixie Tower was a very different type of animal. She won over five furlongs at Wolverhampton as a two-year-old before being sold and sent to France; at three she won over six furlongs at Fontainebleau prior to returning to England where she became Wildenstein's first British winner, scoring twice over five furlongs and showing smart form. She was a genuine and consistent filly. Pixie Tower's dam Cawston Tower was also a thoroughly dependable sprinter; she won five races over five furlongs and another over six, while her full brother Silver Kumar was a very successful stayer who gained all his five wins over the minimum trip. Good filly though she was, Pixie Tower wasn't the best of Cawston Tower's six winners, that accolade falling to Cawston's Pride; an exceptional two-year-old, Cawston's Pride was behind only My Swallow, Mill Reef and Brigadier Gerard in the 1970 Free Handicap after winning all her eight starts, each over five furlongs. Before her death at the age of eight Cawston's Pride bred the Coventry Stakes winner Cawston's Clown and the champion sprinter Solinus. None of the animals in the family already mentioned won over a distance longer than a mile but it's interesting that Cawston's Pride, to a mating with Never Say Die, produced a smart performer at up to a mile and a half, Man of Vision; and Pixie Tower's only previous runner Premier Ministre, by the Kentucky Derby winner Cannonade, was a very smart winner in the USA, successful in four Grade 3 stakes events from nine to eleven furlongs. There must be a fair chance, therefore, that Paradis Terrestre will stay a mile and a quarter, and he may stay a mile and a half.

Besides the question of Paradis Terrestre's distance there's the question of his training on. While we greatly admired his performances at two, and his nice, easy action, we can't say the same about his physical appearance. He's a lightly-made, narrow colt who runs up very light behind the saddle, so much so that at first glance we took him for a filly at Ascot. However, he's not the first good animal of unimpressive appearance from his family: Pixie Tower was a lightly-made, sharp sort as a juvenile and Cawston's Pride was an angular filly who carried little surplus flesh. Pixie Tower's apparent lack of physical scope didn't stop her improving about a stone from two to three and if her son can improve even a fraction of that amount he's sure to take high rank among his age-group. As yet he has raced only on a soft surface but his action suggests he'll handle fast ground too. *H. Cecil.*

PARASHA 2 ch.f. Bold Lad (Ire) 133–Mirtala (Hauban 132) (1981 5f 5g) Apr 7; neat, quite attractive filly; poor mover; fifth foal; half-sister to 3 winners, including Maysapour (by Huntercombe), a winner at up to 9f in England and France; dam half-sister to a high-class sprinter Moubariz; made little show in maiden races at Kempton and Beverley (seventh of 11) in July. *M. Stoute.*

PARC DE PRINCESSE 4 br.f. Murrayfield 119–Moss Princess (Star Moss — 122) (1980 NR 1981 11.7f 9f 8g) compact filly; third foal; dam won at up to 9f in France; poor maiden. *M. Tate.*

PARENT 8 br.g. Great Nephew 126–Piragua 85 (Petition 130) (1980 NR — 1981 8.2d) has been pin-fired; fair handicapper at his best; lightly raced nowadays; stays 1¼m well; acts on any going; has been bandaged in front. *E. Weymes.*

PARISCENE 3 gr.f. Dragonara Palace 115–Rennet 109 (King's Bench 132) **71** (1980 5g 5g⁴ 5f² 5fg* 5fg 6f 5d 1981 6fg 5fg² 6g² 5d 5fg 5fg 5f) leggy filly; ran creditably in handicaps at Sandown and Newmarket in spring on first 2 starts; only just stays 6f; acts on firm going; blinkered final start. *N. Callaghan.*

PARISH PRIEST 3 b. or br.g. Realm 129–St Padina 91 (St Paddy 133) (1980 — NR 1981 12g 14d 12fg 12g 10s) 500 3-y-o; fair sort; poor form, including in a seller. *J. O'Donoghue.*

PARISIO (USA) 2 b.c. Sham–Miralla 120 (Allangrange 126) (1981 7g) Mar **75 p** 18; $45,000Y; rather narrow, lengthy colt; first foal; dam won Irish 1,000 Guineas and is half-sister to smart sprinter Wolverlife; 12/1 when never-dangerous 6¾ lengths ninth of 22 to Rocamadour in maiden race at Newmarket in October; will stay 1¼m+; should improve. *J. Hindley.*

PARK BRIDGE 4 ch.g. Park Lawn 111–Asa-Bridge 77 (Como 120) (1980 **59** 10.8v 6f* 7f 5h² 8g* 7d 7g³ 8g 8g² 8g 1981 6fg 8d 7s 8g 8f³ 8.3fg³ 8.3fg³ 8.2g² 8h* 7h 8g2) compact gelding; plater; won at Bath in August (no bid); stays 1m well; suited by top-of-the-ground and acts on hard going; has worn bandages *D. H. Jones.*

PARKDALE 4 ch.c. Swing Easy 126–Miss McWorden 75 (Worden II 129) **86** (1980 5d 5f* 5fg² 6d² 6fg* 6g² 7g 6f 1981 7g 8g 5d 6g 10.2g 8g⁴) big, strong, well-made colt; excellent mover; won at York and Newcastle as a 2-y-o and ran well in top company too; didn't run up to his best in 1981, but wasn't disgraced on occasions, including when 4¾ lengths fifth of 12 behind Long Legend in minor event at Newbury in September on third start (well-backed third favourite despite having first race for almost 4 months); stays 1m (made no show over 1¼m); seems to act on any going; ran respectably in blinkers final outing; sweated up on reappearance; sometimes ridden by a lad in paddock; to be trained in 1982 by J. Fitzgerald. *P. Rohan.*

PARK JET 5 b.g. Lear Jet 123–Parallelogram 63 (Pardal 130) (1980 10f **34** 10g 10f 1981 10.6s 8f 14.6fg⁴ 10f 16.5g) poor plater; stays 9f; acts on a firm and a soft surface; sometimes blinkered; has sweated up. *L. Barratt.*

PARK PLACE 3 b.f. Royal and Regal–Tanndara (Venture VII 129) (1980 **89** 7g* 7g 1981 8.5fg 8s² 8f⁴ 10fg³ 10g³ 9f⁴ 10fg 8.2v⁴ 8d* 8d* 8g*) neat filly; ran consistently well and in the autumn won handicaps at Redcar and Chepstow and a minor event at Doncaster, all in good style; beat Frogtown by 2 lengths on last-named course; stays 1¼m; acts on any going; sometimes sweats up; genuine; sold 48,000 gns Newmarket December Sales. *H. T. Jones.*

PARK ROMEO 5 b.h. Irish Love 117–Trinacria (Relic) (1980 including 7g³ **121** 6g³ 6g⁴ 7g³ 8g² 8v* 1981 including 8.5d³ 5s* 8d 7g* 8g³ 7g* 8g* 6fg 6d⁴ 8v 5v*) smart performer; much travelled this year, winning at Cagnes-sur-Mer, 4 times in Germany, including 1m Spreti Memorial at Munich, and at Longchamp; put up an excellent effort in Prix du Petit Couvert on last-named in October, beating Sonoma by 1½ lengths; not disgraced when fourth to Rabdan in Prix de Seine-et-Oise at Maisons-Laffitte; effective at 5f and stays 1m; acts on heavy going; tough. *H. Cohn, Germany.*

PARLOUR GAME 4 gr.f. Birdbrook 110–Dairy Queen 76 (Queen's Hussar 124) — (1980 7f* 7.3f* 8.5f* 10g⁴ 7d* 8d² 7fg* 8fg 8fg⁴ 8s 1981 8d) rangy, useful-looking ex-English filly; useful handicapper in 1980; soundly beaten in William Hill Lincoln Handicap at Doncaster in March; subsequently sent to USA and won an 8.5f allowance race at Saratoga in August; best at up to 8.5f; possibly unsuited by very soft going but acts on any other; genuine and consistent. *R. Smyth.*

PAR PAK 2 b.c. Maystreak 118–Rugby Princess 82 (El Gallo 122) (1981 **62** 6fg 5f 6f² 6g 6f 6d 5f² 5.1f* 5f⁴ 5g) tall, rather leggy colt; second known foal; dam won 1¼m seller; second in sellers at Haydock and Ripon prior to winning by 1½ lengths from Lady Levlee when odds on for 7-runner event at Yarmouth in August (bought in 1,100 gns); will stay 1m; best form on firm ground; has worn bandages; ran poorly final start. *J. Czerpak.*

PARRE TRIA 2 b.g. Sparkler 130–Flotsam 67 (Rustam 127) (1981 6g 7fg **65**
7d 8.2fg² 7f² 7g) May 2; 5,400F, 2,500Y; well-made gelding; half-brother to 3
winners here and abroad, including 1½m winner Fledge (by Sharp Edge); dam
half-sister to numerous winners; placed in 18-runner sellers at Haydock and
Chepstow in September, going down by ½ length to Zostera Marina when favourite
for latter; will stay 1¼m; has worn bandages; sold to T. Marshall 3,000 gns
Ascot November Sales. *D. Sasse.*

PART-EX 8 b.g. Star Moss 122–Eilan Aigas 93 (Counsel 118) (1980 NR 1981 **44**
12g³ 12g³ 12g* 15g²) former plater; won 5-runner handicap at Hamilton in
June (apprentice ridden); stays 1½m; acts on a soft surface. *R. Allan.*

PARTHIA'S PICTURE 2 b.c. He Loves Me 120–Parthia's Image 92 (Parthia **93**
132) (1981 5s 5g 6f³ 6fg³ 8g³ 7d* 7g²) Mar 20; 41,000Y; shapely, attractive
colt; fifth foal; half-brother to Irish 1½m winner Audmore (by Connaught); dam,
who stayed well, is half-sister to dam of Kilijaro; well-backed favourite when
beating Change Habit 2½ lengths in 13-runner minor event at Chepstow in
October; third in good-class events at Kempton (to Hays) and Goodwood (to
Torrey) and £4,600 nursery at Newmarket (behind Nioulargo, having been given
plenty to do and having none too clear a run) on previous 3 starts; runs as
though 1¼m will suit him; probably acts on any going. *G. Lewis.*

PARTHOLLOW 3 b.g. Wolver Hollow 126–Princess Parthia (Parthia 132) **—**
(1980 NR 1981 8d 7fg) 38,000Y; strong, good-looking gelding; brother to
French Hollow, a very useful winner at up to 1¼m in France, and half-brother
to several other winners, including fair 1979 2-y-o 5f winner Gay Parthia (by
Gay Fandango); dam ran only once; on backward side and green when in rear in
maiden races at Newbury and Newmarket in April; gelded afterwards. *B. Hills.*

PARTICULAR MISS 2 b.f. Luthier 126–One Over Parr 114 (Reform 132) **70**
(1981 6g 6fg⁴) Feb 11; smallish, quite attractive filly; second foal; dam, sister
to Polygamy, won Cheshire Oaks and Lancashire Oaks; stayed on strongly without
finding any extra pace when 7 lengths fourth of 19 to Dawn Ditty in maiden race
at Salisbury in September; will stay 1½m. *P. Walwyn.*

PARTNERPLAN 6 b.g. Green God 128–Pladda (Reliance II 137) (1980 9.6fg **—**
12d 10g 10f 1981 12d 12f 15.5f 15.5f³) plater; stays 2m; acts on firm going;
often sweats up. *P. K. Mitchell.*

PARTNERPLAN TOO 3 b.g. Young Emperor 133–Hi Jay (Double-U-Jay 120) **—**
(1980 6s 6f 1981 7d 10.1f 6f) little worthwhile form in maiden and minor
events; blinkered final start. *M. Masson.*

PARTON GEORGE 2 b.c. Streetfighter 120–Larullah (Lorenzaccio 130) **—**
(1981 5d 5s 5.8g 6d 5.8f 6g 7d) Apr 28; 350F; sturdy colt; useless plater; has
worn blinkers. *D. Wintle.*

PARTON GOLD 3 ch.f. The Go-Between 129–Golden April 71 (Sovereign **—**
Lord 120) (1980 5f² 5g 5fg 5d³ 5d 5d 1981 7f) close-coupled, fair sort;
showed some form at 2 yrs but is temperamental and one to be wary of. *D.
Wintle.*

PARTON PRINCE 3 b.c. Andrea Mantegna–Greek Bazaar 49 (Philemon 119) **—**
(1980 6g 6fg 6g 7f 1981 10.8fg) compact colt; bad plater. *D. Wintle.*

PARTY DANCER 2 ch.f. Be My Guest 126–Blue Saree (Sayajirao 132) (1981 **—**
5g 5g) May 10; 3,000Y; sparely-made filly; half-sister to winners here and
abroad, including fairly useful 6f to 1m winner The Frummer (by Prince Tenderfoot); dam ran twice; in rear in minor event at Pontefract in April and maiden
race at Carlisle (blinkered) in June; sold 400 gns Doncaster August Sales.
M. H. Easterby.

PARTY TRICK 2 br.f. Streak 119–Belle Mere (Tacitus 124) (1981 5d 5g **49**
5f² 7f 8s) Feb 10; well-grown, fair sort; poor plater; form only at 5f; blinkered
final outing. *C. James.*

PASADINA LAD 3 ch.g. Sandford Lad 133–Damsel II (Chamier 128) (1980 **69**
NR 1981 6g 7d 8fg³ 10f) 7,600F, 7,400Y; neat gelding; half-brother to a winner
in Italy by Pentotal; dam won 7 races in Italy; ran creditably in maiden races
at Newmarket in April and Redcar in June on first and third outings; doesn't
stay 1¼m; sold 2,400 gns Newmarket Autumn Sales. *G. Huffer.*

PAS DE CHAT 2 b.f. Relko 136–Kitten 102 (Pardal 130) (1981 6fg 7fg) **—**
May 26; light-framed filly; half-sister to useful middle-distance stayer Grand
Chat (by Grand Roi) and fairly useful middle-distance winner Mon Chat (by
Great Nephew); dam best at up to 7f; in rear in minor events at Windsor in
July and Epsom in September; needs further. *N. Callaghan.*

*Prix Eclipse, Saint-Cloud—Irish-trained Pas de Seul holds
on well from Rollins and Dear Patrick*

PAS DE SEUL 2 b.c. Mill Reef 141–Thereby 99 (Star Moss 122) (1981 6f² **117**
6.3fg* 6.5s*)
The Prix Eclipse run at Saint-Cloud at the end of September isn't particularly
well known outside France.   Perhaps because of its proximity, both in distance
and time of year, to the Middle Park Stakes and Cheveley Park Stakes the
race rarely attracts an overseas runner but frequently features some of the
best French juveniles.   Since raised in distance from six to six and a half
furlongs in 1966 the Prix Eclipse has fallen to two colts, Cabhurst and Targowice,
which later headed the French Free Handicap and to three, Cabhurst, Stratege
and Roan Star, which went on to beat the older horses in the Prix de la Foret.
The 1979 Grand Criterium winner Dragon had previously finished only third
in the Eclipse and the top-class miler Bellypha and the subsequent classic
winners Caro, Sassafras and Moulines were all beaten.   1981 did see a foreign
challenger—the lightly-raced Mill Reef colt Pas de Seul from Ireland who came
away with the first prize of 160,000 francs (about £16,000) and his value considerably boosted by a win in a pattern race.
Both Pas de Seul's previous outings had been in maiden races in Ireland in
July—after going down by three quarters of a length to Royal Rendevouz at
Phoenix Park he'd landed the odds at the Curragh ten days later, disputing
the lead throughout to win by two and a half lengths from Late Music—and
his starting price of just over 4/1 at Saint-Cloud seemed a fair reflection of his
chance.   By the time the field reached halfway his chance looked much brighter;
whereas Pas de Seul was well placed behind the pacemaker My Best Man the
favourite Melyno, a half-brother to Pharly and Comeram, had lost all chance
through being hampered.   Once Pas de Seul took the lead entering the three-furlong straight only Rollins of his nine rivals was able to mount a serious challenge;
the Irish colt ran on too strongly even for him, getting home by half a length.
The merit of Pas de Seul's performance was highlighted by the subsequent
efforts of the other horses in the frame: Rollins finished third of ten to Green
Forest in the Grand Criterium on his next outing; Dear Patrick, beaten two
and a half lengths, went down by only a length in the battle to Beau Pretender in the Prix
de Conde three weeks later; and Coussika, a five-length fourth, later won the
Prix des Reservoirs and finished a creditable third in the Criterium of Saint-
Cloud.   Incidentally Melyno made amends for his display here by winning the
Prix Thomas Bryon.

Pas de Seul (b.c. May 8, 1979)	Mill Reef (b 1968)	Never Bend (b 1960)	Nasrullah Lalun
		Milan Mill (b 1962)	Princequillo Virginia Water
	Thereby (br 1965)	Star Moss (ch 1960)	Mossborough Star of France
		Besides (b 1952)	Naucide Bees Knees

Pas de Seul's yearling price of 80,000 guineas compares favourably with
several other Mill Reef colts' at the equivalent sale in 1981; sons of Arkadina,

629

Parsimony and Hayloft sold respectively for 640,000, 460,000 and 300,000 guineas. Unlike those three mares Pas de Seul's dam Thereby wasn't a pattern-race winner, but she was quite a useful winner, she comes from a good winner-producing family and has a respectable record at stud. A daughter of the St Leger second Star Moss, Thereby was best at up to nine furlongs, gaining her three wins over six, seven and eight furlongs; no doubt she inherited some speed from her dam, the useful five-furlong winner Besides and from her grandam, the sprinter Bees Knees. The best of Thereby's previous six winners here and abroad was a sprinter, the very useful 1972 two-year-old Captive Dream (by Sing Sing), but interestingly she is a half-sister to the remarkable Grey Sovereign mare Costmary, ten of whose fourteen wins were gained over middle distances, and to Okeover, the dam of the Goodwood Cup winner Girandole. Even though Pas de Seul showed plenty of pace in all his races at two we expect him to stay a mile and a quarter at three, or even a mile and a half if he learns to conserve his energy. A lightly-raced, good-looking colt, Pas de Seul has plenty of scope for further improvement and his young trainer is a lucky man to have him and those other smart colts Anfield and Assert to represent him in 1982. *D. O'Brien, Ireland.*

PASQUIER 2 b.g. Shiny Tenth 120–Tweetie Pie (Falcon 131) (1981 5s 5g) — May 19; 940Y; fourth foal; brother to 7f winner My Sylvia and 3-y-o 1m seller winner Marshgate; dam never ran; no sign of ability in minor event at Folkestone in March and maiden auction race at Kempton in May. *H. O'Neill.*

PASSERINE 7 b.m. My Swallow 134–Marie Denise 68 (Dual 117) (1980 16f — 15.8fg 15g³ 1981 16s 16g) poor staying handicapper; acts on any going but is well suited by some give in the ground; suited by forcing tactics; has run respectably for an apprentice. *C. Spares.*

PASSING MOMENT (USA) 2 ch.c. Parade of Stars–Thelma Dear (Bally-   70 donnell) (1981 5.1f 6fg 7g⁴ 6g 6f³ 5fg 7g) May 13; $30,000Y; lightly-built colt; good walker; brother to 3-y-o Carob Star, a winner of claiming races at up to 6f at 2 yrs, and half-brother to several minor winners; dam won over 6f, including a claiming race; sire, son of T.V. Lark, won small races at up to 9f; quite moderate form in maiden and minor races; will stay 1m. *G. Pritchard-Gordon.*

PASSIONATE 4 br.f. Dragonara Palace 115–Old Scandal 72 (Elopement 125)   54 (1980 6fg 7f 8g 7.2g 8d 9d 1981 8.2g 5s³) poor maiden; well beaten in seller first start; best run at 5f on soft going; often blinkered. *B. McMahon.*

PASSIONATE DANCER 2 b.c. Gay Fandango 132–Kiss Me 82 (Tamerlane — 128) (1981 5g 6fg) Mar 23; IR 11,000F, IR 15,600Y; well-made, quite attractive colt; closely related to modest 6f and 1¼m winner Saucy Sergent (by Home Guard) and half-brother to 3 winners here and abroad; dam won over 5f at 2 yrs; in rear in maiden races at Windsor in August and Epsom in September; sold 1,000 gns Newmarket Autumn Sales. *B. Swift.*

PASS NO REMARKS 2 b.f. Wolverlife 115–Place To Place (No Robbery)   78 (1981 5s⁴ 5g* 5fg⁴ 6f 5f² 5g* 5d³ 5h) Apr 6; IR 1,500Y; unfurnished filly; half-sister to Sosue Me (by Judgable), winner over 7f at 2 yrs in 1976 and subsequently successful in USA, and to a winner abroad; dam won at up to 6f in USA; made all to win 12-runner maiden race at Carlisle in June by ¾ length from Nagalia and ran on gamely to beat Antilla by 2 lengths in 9-runner nursery at Nottingham in August; should be suited by 6f (had stiffish task when tried at trip); probably acts on any going though ran below her best on hard final start; genuine. *B. McMahon.*

PASTO 2 b.c. Vitiges 132–Palmas (Neckar) (1981 6f 6fg³ 7fg⁴ 6g) Feb 12; big, rather leggy colt; first reported foal; dam German-bred daughter of useful 6f to 1m performer Princess Corviglia; soundly beaten when in frame in small races at Carlisle and Leicester in July; had stiffish task in nursery fourth outing; will stay 1m. *W. Hastings-Bass.*

PATAS BLANCAS 3 br.f. Tumble Wind–Vivungi (Exbury 138) (1980 5g   61 1981 6d 6g 6d⁴ 6f⁴ 6fg⁴ 8f³ 8fg 8fg⁴ 6fg* 7g 7g) rangy filly; ran creditably in varied company before beating Community Star a shade comfortably by a length in maiden event at Epsom in August; ran poorly afterwards; stays 1m; acts on firm going; blinkered final start; sold 1,100 gns Newmarket Autumn Sales. *G. Lewis.*

PATCHINIA 3 b.f. Patch 129–Tapia (Tanerko 134) (1980 6s 7d* 7f 8d   1981 10v³ 12s 12g 10.5s⁴ 13.8fg 11d 12d 10d) tall, leggy filly; well beaten after running respectably on reappearance, but had very stiff task on fourth start and was off course nearly 4 months before sixth outing; bred to stay 1½m, but pulls hard; acts on heavy going; taken down early to start as a 2-y-o. *S. Norton.*

PATCHIT 2 b.f. Patch 129–Milonia (Tambourine II 133) (1981 6s 5fg³ 7f 7f 8d) **49**
IR 1,800F, IR 1,800Y; light-framed filly; only poor form in sellers; will stay 1¼m; sold 2,000 gns Newmarket Autumn Sales. *P. Rohan.*

PATERNO 3 ch.c. Young Emperor 133–Light Diamond (Florescence 120) (1980 **98**
7fg 7.9g⁴ 9.5s 7.9v* 1981 8.2s 8d 6g 10fg 8.3fg* 8g² 8.3g* 8f* 8fg² 8f* 8.2fg* 9g 8g) 5,000F; close-coupled, good sort; ex-Irish colt; third foal; half-brother to 2 winners, including 1978 2-y-o 6f winner Noble Mistress (by Lord Gayle); dam won over 5f at 4 yrs in Ireland; had a good season and won handicaps at Windsor (two), Ripon (also two) and Haydock; put up an excellent effort under an 8-lb penalty in £5,900 event on last-named course in September, getting home by ½ length from Docklands after idling in front; eleventh of 28 behind Braughing in William Hill Cambridgeshire at Newmarket the following month; stays 1¼m, but races mainly at 1m; acts on any going; successful 3 times for apprentice M. Banner (wandered quite badly in front first 2 occasions). *R. Armstrong.*

PATERNOSTER ROW 2 b.c. Godswalk 130–Abergara (Abernant 142) (1981 **106**
7g 7g 10g*) June 3; 10,000Y; big, strong colt; good mover; half-brother to 3 winners, including Irish 9f to 1½m winner Edmund Tudor (by Lord Gayle); dam last on only start; well-backed second favourite, showed vastly improved form when staying on resolutely up final hill to peg back Incandesce close home and win 13-runner Jennings the Bookmakers Zetland Stakes at Newmarket in October; had previously shown signs of ability, although green and backward (attracted little market support); runs as though he'll be suited by 1½m; the type to make a good 3-y-o. *B. Hobbs.*

PATHIAN 3 b.f. Abwah 118–Pilamenon 90 (Parthia 132) (1980 7s 1981 8g) —
towards rear in maiden races at Ayr as a 2-y-o and at Doncaster in May. *J. W. Watts.*

PATH OF PEACE 5 br.g. Warpath 113–Turtle Dove (Gyr 131) (1980 12d² **100**
13v² 12.3d* 12f⁴ 12f 12f 13fg² 13g 12g 13s* 14s² 14s² 12v* 1981 12s 12d* 16d* 12g² 12f 14f 13d⁴ 14s 12g³) small gelding; useful performer; won handicap at Haydock and small race at Thirsk in May, getting home by a neck from Blakes Beacon in latter; ran well final start when 2¼ lengths third to Lafontaine in William Hill November Handicap at Doncaster; stays 2m; well suited by plenty of give in the ground. *C. Thornton.*

PATH TO GLORY 2 ch.c. Habitat 134–Garvey Girl (Princely Gift 137) (1981 **105**
5fg² 5d* 5g² 5s²) May 29; 35,000Y; neat, attractive colt; brother to 4 winners, including joint-top 2-y-o filly of 1973 Bitty Girl and high-class sprinter Hot Spark, and half-brother to 4 other winners; dam Irish 2-y-o 5f winner; won 20-runner maiden race at Newbury in September, keeping on really well to score by a length from Ellerene; second on both subsequent starts, running well when beaten a head by Hampton Bay in minor event at Ascot but proving no match for 5-length winner Cannon Shell when disappointing favourite for £3,300 event at York; may stay 6f; has rather a high knee action but didn't run well on only outing on very soft ground; hasn't much scope. *M. Jarvis.*

PATOUCHE 3 ro.f. Shiny Tenth 120–Shallot (Sheshoon 132) (1980 8d 1981 **37**
8g 12fg 10f 13.8f⁴ 10f 12g³) plater; probably stays 1¾m; sometimes blinkered; sold 960 gns Doncaster August Sales. *J. Etherington.*

PAT PONG 2 b.f. Mummy's Pet 125–Caught-At-It 77 (Poaching 115) (1981 **62**
5g⁴ 5g 5g³ 5f 5f 5g 6g) Apr 28; strong filly; bad mover; sister to a winner in Belgium and half-sister to several winners, including fairly useful 5f performer Panglima (by Tribal Chief); dam best at 7f to 1m; 5 lengths third of 11 to Russeting in maiden race at Beverley in July, first outing for 3 months; dwelt next time out (had stiffish task); should be suited by 6f. *T. Fairhurst.*

PAULAGER 3 b.g. Lochnager 132–Hopeful Subject 82 (Mandamus 120) (1980 **93**
5h⁴ 5fg* 6d³ 7.2d* 1981 8g 7g 7.2s* 7.6fg* 8fg 7.2g 7g 7d 7g) strong gelding; put up good performances when winning handicaps at Haydock in June (by 2½ lengths from Barwin) and Chester in July (by 2 lengths from Lady Christina), making virtually all both times; didn't run up to his best afterwards (looked bit light eighth outing); seems to find 1m too far; probably acts on any going. *M. H. Easterby.*

PAU

PAUL'S IVORY 2 b.c. Pampapaul 121–Pale Ivory 108 (Silver Shark 129) **85** (1981 5s⁴ 5d² 5fg* 5d* 5g² 6d³ 6fg* 6g 6g) May 13; IR 8,000Y; neat colt; third foal; half-brother to fair 1979 2-y-o 6f winner Brigadier James (by Brigadier Gerard), subsequently successful in Trinidad, and to Irish 3-y-o 1¼m and 13f winner Manilla Bay (by Weavers' Hall); dam useful from 5f to 1m at 2 yrs; a genuine colt who won maiden race at Nottingham and minor event at Brighton in April and quite well-contested race at Windsor in June; got home by a short head from B. A. Poundstretcher at Windsor; well beaten in nurseries afterwards; bred to stay 1m; seems to act on any going; reportedly exported to West Indies. *J. Sutcliffe.*

PAULY DIAMOND 8 b.g. Polyfoto 124–Gratel 95 (Gratitude 130) (1980 NR — 1981 9g) ex-Irish gelding; useful (rated 104) at 2 yrs; lightly raced on flat since. *J. Charlton.*

PAUSE FOR THOUGHT 4 ch.g. Jukebox 120–Madlin 102 (Sovereign Path **69** 125) (1980 7d 8h² 8fg⁴ 1981 8f 8f 7g³ 9fg³ 9fg* 8g⁴ 8f⁴ 8.2f³ 8f⁴ 8g 8.2d² 8s² 8.2d 7s) tall, useful-looking gelding; landed the odds in handicap at Hamilton in July; ran creditably on several other occasions; stays 9f; acts on any going; has twice worn blinkers; sometimes sweats up; possibly best on a galloping track; suitable mount for an apprentice; none too genuine. *Denys Smith.*

PAVARICO 3 gr.g. Record Token 128–Dark Dolores 83 (I Say 125) (1980 5f⁴ — 1981 6g) lengthy gelding; last in minor events at Newmarket as a 2-y-o and at Folkestone in June; blinkered in latter; sold 280 gns Ascot 2nd June Sales. *K. Ivory.*

PAVILION 3 gr.c. Habitat 134–Game All 109 (Alcide 136) (1980 6g² 7d 5d⁴ **86** 1981 6g* 6g 6g 6fg 6f* 6f 7g 6d) attractive colt; good mover; well-backed favourite when winning maiden race at Redcar in May (made all, apprentice ridden) and handicap at Nottingham in July, beating Russian Romance a head when blinkered in latter; didn't run up to his best in blinkers afterwards; should stay 7f; probably acts on any going. *H. T. Jones.*

PAWNBROKER 3 ch.g. Lombard 126–Italian Sky 94 (Skymaster 126) (1980 — 8g 10s 1981 9g 10d) tall, rangy, narrow gelding; well beaten in maiden races; looks a plater. *G. Harman.*

PAWS AND JAWS 3 b.g. Dubassoff–Margareta II (Tabriz 111) (1980 NR — 1981 8g 10.1fg) 520Y; fair sort; a twin; half-brother to fair middle-distance performer Midsummer Lad (by Midsummer Night II) and a winner in Italy; dam won at up to 9f in France; tailed off in minor event at Salisbury and seller at Windsor in June. *J. Douglas-Home.*

PEACE CALL 4 b.f. Martinmas 128–Awaken (Narrator 127) (1980 10.8s 8g — 1981 9f 11.7fg) lightly-made filly; behind in varied company; sold 800 gns Ascot October Sales. *M. Blanshard.*

PEACEFUL LIGHT 2 ch.f. Red God 128§–Enchanted Evening II (Sailor) — (1981 5g 5g 5g) May 9; 6,000Y; neat filly; half-sister to two 2-y-o winners, including French 7.5f winner Hit It Off (by Hardicanute); dam lightly-raced half-sister to very smart middle-distance filly Yasmin; no worthwhile form in maiden and minor events; trained by D. Whelan first 2 outings. *F. Durr.*

PEACETIME (USA) 2 b.c. Nijinsky 138–Peace 113 (Klairon 131) (1981 7g³) **94** P lengthy, attractive colt; brother to very smart middle-distance performer Quiet Fling, and half-brother to several winners, including Cambridgeshire winner Intermission (by Stage Door Johnny) and very useful middle-distance stayers Peaceful (by Crepello) and Armistice Day (by Rheingold); dam won Blue Seal Stakes; acquitted himself extremely well when 2½ lengths third of 15 to Ivano in Houghton Stakes at Newmarket in October, travelling strongly for much of race and being sympathetically handled once first 2 had his measure; has plenty of improvement in him, looks certain to win races when tackling middle distances at 3 yrs and is one to follow. *J. Tree.*

PEACOCK CHARM 5 ch.g. Crisp and Even 116–Besselsleigh Lass (Quorum **44** 126) (1980 12.2f 1981 15.8s³ 15.8g² 16g 12s²) staying handicapper; acts on soft going. *J. Mason.*

PEADAR PIPER 2 ch.c. Red Alert 127–Cayenne (Hornbeam 130) (1981 7fg* **104** 7fg* 6.3fg⁴) Feb 21; half-brother to 3 winners, including 6f to 1m winner Royal Estate (by Realm); dam, winner over 7f in Ireland, is half-sister to top-class Caro; successful at Leopardstown in June and July, picking up quite a valuable prize when winning 12-runner Hennessy V.S.O.P. Stakes by ¾ length from Vana

Vichi on second outing; gave at least 3 lb all round when just over 1½ lengths fourth of 6 to Dara Monarch in Ballsbridge-Tattersalls Anglesey Stakes at the Curragh in August (reportedly split a pastern); will stay 1m. *T. Curtin, Ireland.*

PEARLAWAY 3 b.c. Derring-Do 131–Pearlesque 88 (Gulf Pearl 117) (1980 — 6g⁴ 5.8f 7fg* 7d² 7g 1981 7g 7g 7.3g 7f 8g 7fg 6fg) small, strong colt; disappointing after finishing creditable eighth of 25 behind Button Top in handicap at Newmarket in April on reappearance; should stay 1m; acts on a firm and a soft surface; blinkered final start; sold 3,900 gns Newmarket Autumn Sales. *P. Walwyn.*

PEARL OF WISDOM 3 b.f. Ballymore 123–French Oyster (Gulf Pearl 117) — (1980 NR 1981 7v 7g 8fg 10.8fg 10f) 3,700F, 12,500Y; attractive, good-bodied filly; second living foal; dam second over 7f and 9f from 3 starts in Ireland; in rear in maiden races and 2 sellers. *B Swift.*

PEARLS DISPLAY 5 b.g. Daring Display 129–Caesar's Love 85 (Above — Suspicion 127) (1980 NR 1981 7d 10g 11.7d 17.1d 12f) poor handicapper; behind in seller final start; has worn blinkers. *K. Cunningham-Brown.*

PEAR SUNDAE 2 b.f. Shiny Tenth 120–Alice Perrers (Twilight Alley 133) — (1981 7d 7g) May 20; well-grown, leggy filly; second foal; dam never ran; beaten some way in maiden races at Chester in August (seventh of 14) and Leicester in October; retained 440 gns Newmarket Autumn Sales. *W. Elsey.*

PEDDAR'S WAY 2 b.f. So Blessed 130–Palmitin 88 (Crepello 136) (1981 6d — 6f 7d) Mar 3; 3,000Y; workmanlike filly; sister to useful 1977 2-y-o 7f winner So Gifted but finished last in 2 of her 3 races (maiden and minor events); has worn bandages; sweated up second start; sold 410 gns Doncaster October Sales. *B. Lunness.*

PEDOMETER 2 b.c. Great Nephew 126–Shebeen 124 (Saint Crespin III 132) **96 p** (1981 8g²) Feb 14; 100,000Y; attractive colt; first live foal; dam very smart middle-distance performer; third favourite, finished about 7 lengths clear of far-side group when promising ¾-length second of 29 to Born Hero in maiden race at Newmarket in October; a well-bred colt who looks a certain winner over 1¼m+ in 1982. *J. Tree.*

PEEK-A-BOO 4 b.f. Bustino 136–True Love 89 (Princely Gift 137) (1980 **82** 7.2d* 8g² 8.2g² 9g 7.2g 7s* 7d* 7s 7s 1981 7.2s 8fg⁴ 7s 7g 7s* 7s² 7d³ 8g³) lengthy, rather dipped-backed filly; good walker; returned to form when beating Gusty's Gift by 1½ lengths in handicap at Wolverhampton in October; ran creditably afterwards; best at up to 1m; acts well on soft going; sold 9,800 gns Newmarket December Sales. *C. Thornton.*

PEGASSE 3 ch.f. Arts and Letters–Walk In The Sun (Walker's) (1980 6fg **61** 1981 12d 13.4fg² 16fg 12fg³ 12f 12s 10g) attractive filly; placed in maiden races at Chester in July and Wolverhampton in August but is inconsistent; suited by 13f; blinkered final outing; sold to M. Ryan 27,000 gns Newmarket December Sales. *G. Hunter.*

PELERIN (FR) 4 b. or br.c. Sir Gaylord–Padrona 103 (St Paddy 133) (1980 9f **125** 10fg 10.5f* 12f⁴ 12s 12g 12g⁴ 1981 12s* 13.4d* 12f* 12fg 12f* 12d) Those who believe that the appetite for work can be sharpened by inactivity would have been heartened by Pelerin's comeback as a four-year-old. An excellent staying-on fourth to Henbit in the 1980 Derby, he had run below that form afterwards in the Irish Sweeps Derby, the King George VI and Queen Elizabeth Diamond Stakes and the Great Voltigeur Stakes, looking increasingly like a colt that had gone to the pack. There consequently appeared to be little reason for optimism about his prospects in 1981, but the eight-month break he had after the Voltigeur evidently worked wonders. Without the blinkers he had worn on his last five starts at three Pelerin returned to his best, racing genuinely and consistently and picking up over £85,000 from four important successes.
In the John Porter Stakes at Newbury in April Pelerin received weight from half his opponents—the St Leger winner Light Cavalry, Nicholas Bill, Shining Finish and Shoot A Line—but considering his record it was no surprise that he started at 16/1. His performance belied these odds as he won in a style reminiscent of another Wragg-trained winner of the race, Freefoot. Slightly lucky to get a run up the rails as Son Fils weakened, he showed a good turn of foot to lead close home and beat Cravacal and Shining Finish by a head and the same; Light Cavalry and Shoot A Line, both injured, were a long way back. Next on the agenda was the Ormonde Stakes at Chester in May. With Sea Chimes running poorly Pelerin didn't have much to beat but in the event he only pegged

633

back Billbroker in the last hundred yards to win by a length and a half after being hampered when beginning his run approaching the home turn.

Pelerin's achievement in adding the Hardwicke Stakes at Royal Ascot to his tally was unparalleled, for while Aggressor, Soderini and Rheingold had won the John Porter as well as the Hardwicke none of them had run in the Ormonde. The Hardwicke was contested by a representative field. From France came the Grand Prix d'Evry winner Lancastrian; from Ireland the Clive Graham Stakes winner Triomphe; and the English challengers besides Pelerin were Light Cavalry, the 1980 Prix de Diane and Prix Vermeille winner Mrs Penny, Castle Keep, Nicholas Bill, Shaftesbury and Shining Finish. Held up, as was becoming the usual practice with him, Pelerin came after the front-running Light Cavalry in the straight, made rapid progress to reach him and quickly asserted his superiority, winning in fine style by three lengths with Lancastrian five lengths back in third.

Pelerin won one of his remaining races, the Grosser Preis von Baden at Baden-Baden in September. There were numerous inconsistencies in the Pattern of Racing when it was introduced a decade ago; while some have been ironed out others remain. The best German races were included in the Pattern at an early stage but even now more than a third of them, notably the Deutsches Derby and Aral-Pokal, are confined to indigenous horses. More oddly, the three Group 1 races open to horses of all countries do not have uniform conditions. The Grosser Preis von Berlin sees runners meeting on strict weight-for-age and-sex terms, as in all the Group 1 events in England, France, Ireland and Italy, but the Preis von Europa has an allowance for horses that haven't won a Group 1 race whilst the Grosser Preis von Baden has a similar allowance plus an additional one for horses that haven't won a Group 2 race or finished second in a Group 1 race. Since Group 1 races are supposed to be 'championship' events it seems extraordinary that a differential scale of weights should persist in the Preis von Europa and the Grosser Preis von Baden, and it would be helpful if the European Pattern Committee were to eliminate this anomaly. To show the peculiarities of the current position: Pelerin, a high-class colt even though he hadn't been placed in a Group 1 race, received weight from three of his seven opponents at Baden-Baden, namely Czubaryk, the 1980 German Derby winner Navarino and Strong Gale; he also met the 1981 German Two Thousand Guineas and Derby winner Orofino on favourable terms. A short-priced favourite as he was entitled to be, Pelerin didn't need the allowance for he made mincemeat of his rivals, storming ahead two furlongs out and winning by a couple of lengths from Hohritt. Though eased down in the final furlong he still broke the course record.

John Porter Stakes, Newbury—a driving finish with Pelerin (rails) just getting the better of Cracaval (left): Shining Finish is third

Hardwicke Stakes, Ascot—Pelerin comes home clear from Light Cavalry

In both the King George VI and Queen Elizabeth Diamond Stakes and the Prix de l'Arc de Triomphe Pelerin's limitations were exposed. At Ascot he never reached a challenging position when fifth to Shergar, though in mitigation his jockey claimed he lost all chance when pushed against the rails half a mile out; at Longchamp he was close up early on but soon dropped back to finish seventeenth to Gold River.

Pelerin (Fr) (b. or br.c. 1977)	Sir Gaylord (b 1959)	Turn-to (b 1951)	Royal Charger
			Source Sucree
		Somethingroyal (b 1952)	Princequillo
			Imperatrice
	Padrona (gr 1969)	St Paddy (b 1957)	Aureole
			Edie Kelly
		Donna (gr 1956)	Donore
			Bashful

Towards the end of the season Pelerin was sent to America where he will race before being retired to The Stallion Station, Kentucky. Whatever he does on the track in the States he should be a good proposition at stud. His sire, Sir Gaylord, died in 1981 but certainly left his mark with more than fifty stakes winners. Several of his best colts have gone on to make a name for themselves as stallions, notably Habitat, Lord Gayle and Sir Ivor, whilst another of his progeny, Lord Gaylord, sired the best American two-year-old of 1980, Lord Avie. The dam, Padrona, was bought on behalf of Pelerin's owner for 40,000 guineas on the dispersal of the late Lord Rosebery's bloodstock in 1975. She has produced two other winners, Fair Melys (by Welsh Pageant), successful over seven furlongs and a mile, and the three-year-old mile-and-three-quarter winner Al Nasr (by Green Dancer). Padrona, a lightly-raced filly who won over sprint distances at two and stayed a mile and a quarter the following year, was a half-sister to numerous winners out of the speedy Donna, the best of them the One Thousand Guineas second Gwen.

Pelerin, a strong, attractive colt and a good walker and mover, is highly effective at a mile and a half but should have no trouble staying a mile and three quarters. Though he has won on soft going he is ideally suited by firm, a surface he may well encounter regularly in the States. *H. Wragg.*

635

PELLEGRINI (USA) 3 ch.c. Snow Knight 125–Solometeor (Victoria Park) — (1980 6fg² 6fg* 6d² 8.2g* 7g 1981 12fg 10g⁴) well-made colt; successful in Fenwolf Stakes at Ascot and £4,100 event at Haydock as a 2-y-o; didn't make much show in either race in 1981 but wasn't disgraced when 11 lengths fourth to Fee in handicap at Newmarket in October; should stay 1½m; acts on a firm and a soft surface; sent to race in USA. *R. Price.*

PENANG HILL 2 b.c. Saulingo 122–Divine Heights (Divine Gift 127) (1981   **75** 6g 6f⁴ 6f⁴ 5f³ 6v³ 6g²) Mar 13; IR 4,300F, 9,000Y; neat colt; second reported produce; dam never ran; in frame in minor events and nurseries, final occasion when 4 lengths second to Hello Sunshine in nursery at Newmarket in November; gives impression he'll be suited by 7f; probably acts on any going; sold 4,000 gns Doncaster November Sales. *R. Armstrong.*

PENCIL OF LIGHT 3 b. or br.f. Flashback 102–Royal Halo (Will Somers 114§) — (1980 NR 1981 7fg 10.1fg 8.3fg 10s) first foal; dam of little account on flat and over hurdles; poor plater. *M. Bolton.*

PENCIL POINT 3 ch.c. Sharpen Up 127–Miss Carefree 99 (Hill Clown) (1980   **100** 6d 6g³ 5d² 5fg³ 5d 5g² 6g² 1981 5g² 6fg² 5fg* 5fg* 6f* 5.6fg² 6d³ 5g*) leggy colt; good mover; had a very fine season and was gaining his fourth success when winning William Hill Handicap at Ascot in September by ¾ length from Piencourt under 9-7 (in command around halfway and kept on gamely); earlier won handicaps at Newmarket (by 6 lengths), Goodwood and Yarmouth; also ran excellent races in defeat when placed in Portland Handicap at Doncaster (¾-length second to Touch Boy) and Ladbrokes (Ayr) Gold Cup (about ½-length third to First Movement, finishing first on far side) on sixth and seventh starts; stays 6f, but best at 5f; yet to race on very soft going but acts on any other; genuine and consistent; possibly has further improvement in him and will win more races. *P. Haslam.*

PENDLE'S SECRET 5 ch.m. Le Johnstan 123–Secret Folly 83 (Infatuation   **36** 129) (1980 9fg 10d 12fg 10fg³ 1981 8s 11g² 12g³ 10.6s 10f) plater; seems not to stay 1½m; possibly unsuited by very soft going; has worn bandages. *B. Wilkinson.*

Mr J. Duffel's "Pencil Point"

PENDULINA 3 br.f. Prince Tenderfoot 126–Rosemarin (Mossborough 126) **102**
(1980 NR 1981 8d 10s⁴ 8f* 7.9f* 8fg*) half-sister to 3 winners, including
useful 7f performer Oldstock (by Sovereign Path); dam, useful Irish handicapper,
won from 9.4f to 1½m; improved and won her last 3 races, namely maiden race
at Phoenix Park and minor event at Dundalk, both in July, and Cornelscourt
Fillies Stakes at Leopardstown in August; got up again close home to beat odds-
on Ranking Beauty a head in last-named; best form at around 1m on fast ground;
blinkered last 2 starts. *K. Prendergast, Ireland.*

PENMARRIC (USA) 3 b.c. Cornish Prince–Hello Teddy Bear (Court Martial) **110**
(1980 5fg* 5g* 5.5g 6g 1981 7s⁴ 6g 6f 5fg⁴ 5d) lightly-made, leggy colt;
impressive winner of Erroll Stakes at Ascot and National Stakes at Sandown on
first 2 starts as a 2-y-o but was disappointing in high-class company afterwards;
ran best race of 1981 when about 2 lengths fourth of 8 behind King of Spain in
King George Stakes at Goodwood in July on fourth start; best form at 5f but
should stay further. *G. Hunter.*

PENNARD ROSE 2 ch.f. White Prince 73–Pennard Bell (Caballero 91) (1981 —
5.8h 6fg) May 19; first foal; dam never ran; last in maiden and minor events,
starting slowly on first outing. *A. Andrews.*

PENNY FOREVER 2 b.f. Forlorn River 124–Penny Levy 69 (Levmoss 133) —
(1981 5g 5f 6f 5fg 5g 7g) Feb 18; 3,400Y; first foal; dam won over 1m; behind in
maiden and minor events; sold 400 gns Doncaster November Sales. *R. Whitaker.*

PENNY'S DREAM 2 b.c. Dawn Review 105–Orabella II 111 (Set Fair 129) **68**
(1981 5d 5g 5d 6g 6f 8g³ 8.2d 8g 8g* 7d) Apr 5; 2,300Y; well-grown, leggy
non-thoroughbred colt; closely related to a winner in France and a winning
hurdler (both by March Past) and half-brother to 2 winners; dam very useful
winner at up to 1½m; plater; awarded race after finishing length second to Pure
Lust in nursery at Doncaster in October (no bid); will stay 1¼m. *P. K. Mitchell.*

PENNY SNOW 4 b.f. Jukebox 120–Efficiency (Pardao 120) (1980 6s 1981 —
10.2s 8d 7g 8f) leggy filly; of little account; trained part of year by G. Fletcher.
W. Musson.

PENSCYNOR 5 br.g. Lord Gayle 124–I Will (I Say 125) (1980 12f² 9g² 10g —
8g 14g 1981 8s⁴ 12g 9d 9fg 9fg) lengthy ex-Irish gelding; useful performer at
his best but has deteriorated; stays 1½m; acts on any going; sometimes blinkered
and has worn a hood as well; trained by J. Bingham first start. *W. Stubbs.*

PENSEUR (FR) 2 br.g. Luthier 126–Sweet and Lovely (Tanerko 134) (1981 —
6f 6g 7fg) May 16; half-brother to numerous winners, including American 3-y-o
Syndar (by Lyphard), 1978 2-y-o 6f winner Gay France (by Sir Gaylord) and
Grand Prix de Toulouse winner Super Dan (by Dapper Dan); dam miler; poor
form in maiden races at Yarmouth and Newcastle in June and Ayr in July; will
stay 1¼m+. *B. Hanbury.*

PENTAGRAM 2 b.f. Wishing Star 117–Olivia Staypleton 88 (Road House II) **64**
(1981 5d 7f³ 7fg 7g 7fg 7g 8.2s) May 27; IR 1,050F, 920Y; neat, strong filly;
fourth foal; half-sister to fair 1m and 10.4f winner Chaplins Nightclub (by St
Chad); dam best at up to 1¼m; fairly prominent in sizeable fields of maidens on
second, third and fourth outings; should be suited by 1m. *W. Elsey.*

PENTAX 2 bl.c. Tickled Pink 114–Friendly Gift (Be Friendly 130) (1981 5g **75**
5.8g 5f 5f 5f 5fg 5g) Mar 23; small colt; good walker; second foal; dam unraced
sister to successful sprinter Friendly Fun; showed some ability in first half of
season but ran moderately last 3 starts, twice wearing blinkers. *D. Elsworth.*

PENWITH 5 b.h. Welsh Saint 126–Sweet Meadow 67 (Meadow Court 129) —
(1980 16fg 1981 12g 11.7d 14s) tall, slightly hollow-backed horse; poor handicapper nowadays; stays 2m; acts on any going but goes well in the mud; has worn
a bandage on near-fore. *P. Cole.*

PENWOOD 6 b.m. Precipice Wood 123–Penview 73 (Pendragon) (1980 16s* **63**
16s* 16g⁴ 12d 13s 1981 13s 18g²) staying handicapper; revels in the mud;
suitable mount for an apprentice. *N. Hall.*

PEPERINO 3 b.f. Relko 136–Pepin (Midsummer Night II 117) (1980 NR —
1981 11.7g 13.3d 14fg 12g 13.1g 16s 13.3s 12d) tall, lengthy filly; third foal;
half-sister to useful sprinter Shayboob (by The Go-Between) and to 1m and 9f
winner Longcliffe (by Mandamus); dam poor maiden; little worthwhile form in
varied races, including a claiming handicap; slipped up fifth start. *P. Cundell.*

PEPINA 5 ch.m. Shoolerville 121–Pepstep 88 (Polic 126) (1980 6f⁴ 7.2fg 7f —
7fg 7fg 7f* 7fg 1981 7f 7f 8.2d) small, stocky mare; in rear all starts in 1981,

being reluctant to go to post on second; best at 7f; acts on firm going and is possibly not at her best on a soft surface. *T. Taylor.*

PEPPER WINE   4 b.g. Tudor Harmony 104–Melba Sauce (Sing Sing 134)   —
(1980 8f 8f   1981 8g 7d 5g⁴ 6g)   compact gelding; well beaten in varied company.
Denys Smith.

PEPPERY   4 b.c. Red God 128§–Powder Box (Faberge II 121)   (1980 8fg 10.1g*   **95**
10d* 10d* 10g* 12fg² 10.5f⁴   1981 10.2d 10.6g³ 12d⁴ 12s² 12g* 12f 12v 12g)
neat, attractive colt; good mover; fairly useful handicapper; comfortably beat
Mac's Delight by 2 lengths at Thirsk in May; stays 1½m; probably acts on any
going but seems suited by some give in the ground; suitable mount for a claimer.
P. Rohan.

PERANG TEJAM   2 b.f. Sharpen Up 127–Carcosa 103 (Sovereign Lord 120)   **85**
(1981 6g⁴ 6g*)   Mar 4; big, useful-looking filly; half-sister to French 5f winner
Flash Connection (by Hot Spark); dam won over 6f and 7f at 2 yrs; joint-
favourite, made virtually all and just held off newcomer Off the Hook in 26-runner
maiden race at Doncaster in November; may stay 7f. *W. Hastings-Bass.*

PERCA   2 ch.g. Royalty 130–The Perch 109 (King's Bench 132)   (1981 5d 6g 7fg   —
7fg 8s)   Apr 10; 1,800Y; rather leggy, lengthy gelding; half-brother to 2m
winner Charlotte Mary (by Lauso); dam stayed 7f and is half-sister to Joshua;
poor maiden; blinkered fifth outing. *M. Masson.*

PERCASE   2 b.g. Tachypous 128–Pertinacity 106 (Aggressor 130)   (1981 5fg 5g   **74**
6g)   Feb 18; neat gelding; half-brother to 3 winners, including useful performers Persevering (by Blakeney) and Sailcloth (by Shantung); dam middle-
distance performer and half-sister to very smart Petty Officer; 4½ lengths fifth
of 13 to Lively Rhythm in maiden race at Salisbury in June, third outing and
first indication of merit; likely to do better when given the opportunity of
tackling 1¼m+. *I. Balding.*

PERCHANCE   2 ch.f. Connaught 130–Mey 78 (Canisbay 120)   (1981 7d 7g*   **72**
8.2s³)   Mar 5; smallish, fair sort; sister to quite a moderate filly and half-sister
to 2 winners, including 1¼m winner Restful (by Ribero); dam, best at 1¼m, is
half-sister to smart Albany and Magna Carta; successful in valuable 29-runner
seller at Newmarket in September by 1½ lengths from Rootless (changed hands
for a record 19,000 gns); 4½ lengths third of 13 to Bluethroat in nursery at
Nottingham the following month; will be suited by 1¼m; yet to race on a firm
surface. *W. Hastings-Bass.*

PERCOL   2 b.f. Silly Season 127–Sea-Hit 85 (Bleep-Bleep 134)   (1981 5g 6g 6d)   —
May 1; 4,300 2-y-o; leggy, rather lightly-made filly; half-sister to several minor
winners here and abroad but seems of no account herself. *T. Taylor.*

PERCY PERFECT   2 b.c. Kinglet 98–Legal Gift (Arctic Judge 94)   (1981 5v   —
6g)   June 13; first foal; dam won selling hurdle; unquoted when last in 9-runner
minor event at Windsor in May and 13-runner seller at Nottingham in August.
G. Thorner.

PERDICCAS   3 br.g. Perdu 121–Requisition 101 (Petition 130)   (1980 5fg 5f   **64**
6fg 6g 7fg 6s 7d³   1981 7s 7fg 7d³ 6d² 7.6g 8.3fg 6f 7f 8f² 8fg 7g 7d² 6g² 6g)
compact gelding; poor mover; placed in varied company, including selling;
stays 1m; has often worn blinkers but seems better without; often bandaged
behind. *C. Austin.*

PERFECT CHOICE   3 b. or br.f. Bold Lad (Ire) 133–Elite Princess 105 (Prince   **64**
Regent 129)   (1980 NR   1981 7d 8fg⁴ 9d 7fg* 8fg⁴ 7f 7g 7g)   good sort; first
foal; dam useful Irish 2-y-o sprinter; apprentice ridden, swerved right across field
when beating Rikasso Beauty by 1½ lengths in handicap at Doncaster in June;
mainly disappointing otherwise; possibly best at 7f; acts on a firm surface;
sweated up badly sixth start; blinkered final outing. *P. Walwyn.*

PERGODA   3 b.g. High Top 131–Saint Joan 63 (Grey Sovereign 128§)   (1980 5f   **69**
5f² 5fg 6g 5f* 5fg 5d³ 5d 5f 5s   1981 5f 5fg³)   useful-looking gelding; claimed
after finishing third in selling handicap at Catterick in July (edged left); should
stay 6f; seems to act on any going, except perhaps very soft; doesn't find much
off bridle. *M. W. Easterby.*

PERGOLA (USA)   3 b.f. Thatch 136–Regent Queen (Buckpasser)   (1980 7d²   **110**
6v*   1981 7g 7f* 8g³ 8d⁴)   second foal; dam, out of a sister to top American
stallion What A Pleasure, won over 6f in USA; beat Polisteppin by ¾ length in
minor event at Phoenix Park in July; in frame subsequently in Prix d'Astarte
at Deauville in August (4 lengths third to Epsiba) and Gilltown Stud Stakes at

the Curragh in September (length fourth to Tumblella); stays 1m; acts on any going. *V. O'Brien, Ireland.*

PERICULO LUDUS (FR) 5 ch.g. Timmy My Boy 125–La Beuvriere (Right **52** d
Royal V 135) (1980 8fg 13.4f 9fg³ 12f 9g 10d² 10g 11.5g⁴ 7g 10s 9g 1981 11s²
10.4g 11.7d 8f 10f 10f 10f) workmanlike gelding; not a good mover; poor
handicapper; stays 11f; seems to act on any going; sometimes wears blinkers;
looked none too keen once in 1980. *J. Harris.*

PERLEE (FR) 2 b.f. Margouillat 133–Zirconia 105 (Charlottesville 135) (1981 **109** p
8g* 8d³) Mar 31; 130,000 francs Y (approx £13,000); rangy, quite useful-looking
filly; second foal; half-sister to a 2-y-o winner by Roi Lear; dam useful at up to
1m in France; played up at start prior to winning 7-runner Prix de Toutevoie
at Longchamp in September by ¾ length from Summer Review; ran on stoutly
after being held up when just over 3 lengths third of 8 to Play It Safe in Group 1
Prix Marcel Boussac on same course the following month; will stay at least 1¼m;
has the makings of a smart 3-y-o. *C. Milbank, France.*

PERLESSE 3 gr.f. Bold Lad (USA)–Perle Grise (Zeddaan 130) (1980 6g² 6f **81**
6d* 6s² 1981 7.3g³ 8f 7d⁴ 6g²) 6,000F; quite well-made, good-quartered filly;
in frame in handicaps at Newbury, Redcar and Ayr; probably best at sprint
distances; acts on soft going and is unsuited by firm; blinkered final start. *M.
Stoute.*

PERMABOS 2 b.g. Dubassoff–Blue Ann 60 (Road House II) (1981 6fg) May **—**
4; 750F, 6,000Y; rangy gelding; half-brother to 2 winners, including tough and
useful 1980 staying 2-y-o Sula Bula (by Midsummer Night II); dam plater; 25/1,
always struggling when out of first 10 in 26-runner maiden race won by Padalco
at Doncaster in June. *K. Stone.*

PERMA FINA 2 b.f. Nonoalco 131–Ginger 90 (Red God 128§) (1980 6f 7d **—**
1981 10d 11.7fg 12.2g) neat, attractive filly; good mover; showed a little ability
at 2 yrs; behind all starts in 1981, wearing blinkers on last one; best run at 7f
on a soft surface. *M. Stoute.*

PERPLEX 2 ch.c. Be My Guest 126–Catherine Linton (High Echelon) (1981 **75**
6g 5g 7fg 7g 7fg² 7g 8g 8.2d² 8d) Apr 4; 4,000Y; rather leggy colt; poor mover;
first foal; dam, who never ran, comes from same family as Malinowski, Gielgud
and Try My Best; quite a moderate maiden; failed by only a short head to catch
Blandor when apprentice ridden in slowly-run 1m nursery at Hamilton in
September; will stay 1¼m; best run on a soft surface; wears blinkers. *Denys
Smith.*

PERRAULT 4 ch.c. Djakao 124–Innocent Air 75 (Court Martial) (1980 **130**
10.5g* 12g* 12.5s³ 12g² 13.5g² 12s 1981 10s² 12fg³ 12s* 12s² 12.5d* 13.5f*
12d⁴ 12f)
Perrault's development into a top-class performer was in some ways appropriate for a colt bearing the name of the man of letters Charles Perrault, since
among the celebrated collection of fairy-tales the latter served up to the French
public in 1697 was *Cinderella*, with its treatment of a dramatic rise in status.
Perrault the horse might not have made as big a leap as Cinderella but his
progress was nonetheless impressive. More than a stone inferior to the leaders
of his generation at three, he improved throughout 1981 and his performance
in the Prix de l'Arc de Triomphe proved conclusively that over a mile and a
half he had become one of the best of his age in Europe.
   Until he ran moderately in America on his final start Perrault was a model
of consistency, winning three times and finishing in the frame on his four other
appearances. Only one of his successes came easily and he became a regular
participant in tight finishes. Placed early on in the Prix Exbury at Saint-
Cloud (second to Armistice Day) and the Prix d'Hedouville at Longchamp
(third to Lancastrian after twice being hit in the face by a whip in a driving
finish), Perrault gained his first win of the year in La Coupe at Longchamp
in May, making up ground hand over fist in the last two furlongs to lead close
home and beat the 1979 St Leger winner Son Of Love by a head. Later in
the month he had a magnificent tussle with Lancastrian in the Grand Prix
d'Evry, eventually giving best by a short head, and in July he wasn't extended
to land the odds by two and a half lengths from Roi Guillaume in the Prix
Maurice de Nieuil at Saint-Cloud.
   The Grand Prix de Deauville is rarely won by a tip-top horse nowadays
and Perrault was the best winner since Val de Loir in 1963. Unlike Val de
Loir, who won with some ease, Perrault had to pull out all the stops. His
ten opponents included two from England, Castle Keep and the top weight

*Grand Prix de Deauville—the blinkered Perrault holds on gamely from
British challenger Castle Keep with Glenorum third*

Nicholas Bill, the 1979 and 1980 winners of the race First Prayer and Glenorum,
plus Lord Jack and Kelbomec, successful respectively in the Grand Prix de
Vichy and Prix de Barbeville.   The gallop was not a strong one and after having
trouble getting a run as the field bunched early in the straight, Perrault made
strong headway to lead a hundred and fifty yards out; battling on manfully
to the line he held off Castle Keep, who was receiving 5 lb, by a short head with
Glenorum three quarters of a length away third.   On the eve of the Prix de
l'Arc de Triomphe at Longchamp Perrault was available at 66/1 in some English
lists; he started at 27/1, coupled with the good filly Leandra.   Never far off the
pace, he was brought through to challenge soon after they turned for home,
went past the weakening Detroit and Ardross without difficulty and came
upsides Bikala about one and a half furlongs out.   Bikala proved a much
tougher nut to crack and hard as Perrault tried he couldn't seize the advantage;
halfway through the last furlong he had given his all and with Bikala drawing
away from him he also failed to hold off Gold River and April Run, finally
finishing less than three lengths fourth to Gold River.   Though well held at
the end Perrault had run the race of his life—he beat the fifth horse, Ardross,
by two lengths and most of the best middle-distance performers in Europe
were further back.

After the Arc Serge Fradkoff purchased a share in Perrault and the colt
was sent to California to race with Charlie Whittingham.   His first run out there
suggested that his exertions at Longchamp and earlier in the year had taken
their toll, for he was never going well in the Oak Tree Invitational at Santa
Anita and ended up in last-of-seven spot behind John Henry.   It is to be hoped
that if Perrault runs again he succeeds in reproducing his best form.

	Djakao		Tanerko		Tantieme
	(b 1966)		(br 1953)		La Divine
Perrault			Diagonale		Ribot
(ch.c. 1977)			(ch 1959)		Barley Corn
	Innocent Air		Court Martial		Fair Trial
	(ch 1962)		(ch 1942)		Instantaneous
			Aldousa		Vatellor
			(br 1949)		Aurora

Perrault's sire, Djakao, won the Grand Prix de Deauville himself and
sired two other top-class colts, Mariacci and Frere Basile, before dying at the
age of twelve.   Frere Basile, who died in 1981 after just two seasons at stud,
gained a fourth place in the Arc in similar fashion to Perrault.   On the dam's
side Perrault comes from a family which has provided the last two Earls of
Derby with several good performers.   The dam, Innocent Air, won three times
at up to ten and a half furlongs in the French Provinces as a four-year-old
and has produced three winners besides Perrault, notably the fairly useful

seven-furlong to one-mile handicapper Black Minstrel (by Luthier) and the three-year-old mile-and-a-quarter winner Marinko (by Rheingold) whose promising career was cut short when he fractured a bone in a leg in the Prix du Lys in June. Innocent Air is a sister to a winner and half-sister to three winners out of Aldousa, a filly who was best in blinkers and won over six furlongs and a mile. Aldousa was extremely well bred, for her dam, the One Thousand Guineas second Aurora, foaled numerous winners including Borealis, Alycidon and Acropolis.

   Perrault, who cost 14,500 guineas as a foal and 260,000 francs as a yearling, is suited by a mile and a half or more and acts on any going. Like his grandam he is best in blinkers but it would be difficult to find a more genuine or consistent sort. *P. Pelat, France.*

PERSEPOLIS (FR) 2 gr.c. Kalamoun 129–Perlita (Baldric II 131) (1981 **108** 6fg³ 7.5f* 8g* 8s) Mar 16; 1,600,000 francs Y (approx £160,000); attractive colt; second foal; half-brother to French 1979 2-y-o 9f winner Perliere (by Rheingold); dam, placed at up to 1m in France, is daughter of French 1,000 Guineas winner Pola Bella; won maiden race at Deauville in August in good style by 3 lengths and picked up a valuable prize in Prix La Rochette at Longchamp the following month; opened up a big lead early in straight in latter and held on to win by a short neck from Majestic Guard; disappointed when only seventh of 10 to Green Forest, beaten over 11 lengths, in Grand Criterium at Longchamp in October; should stay 1¼m; possibly unsuited by very soft going. *F. Boutin, France.*

PERSIAN PACT 3 br.c. Persian Breeze 121–Bridge of Stories 80 (Appian **65** Bridge 111) (1980 6s 5fg 6s 5fg⁴ 5g² 5d 1981 5s 5g² 5t² 5f³ 6f² 5.8f 6f 5fg 6fg⁴ 5f³ 5fg³ 6v³ 6g) compact, good-quartered colt; placed most starts, including in 2 apprentice events; stays 6f; seems best on a sound surface. *W. Wharton.*

PERSIAN PRINCESS 4 ch.f. Palm Track 122–Persian Silver 61 (Cash and **67** Courage 116) (1980 8f 8.2f² 8.2d² 8.2g* 8g⁴ 8.2d* 7.2g 8.2s³ 10s³ 1981 10g 8s 10.6f⁴ 9fg² 8.2d² 8.2f 8.2d*) robust filly; won handicap at Hamilton in September; stays 1¼m; acts on any going; has run creditably for an apprentice; ran poorly second start. *C. Crossley.*

PERSONAL CALL 8 b.g. Personality–Damaring (Saidam) (1980 NR 1981 **—** 12g 8s 16fg 12d) no longer of any account. *R. Atkins.*

PETE AND DUD 2 ch.g. Owen Dudley 121–Athena Royale 80 (Athens Wood **66** 126) (1981 5d² 5s⁴ 6f 7d 8.2fg 8fg⁴ 10d² 10g) Mar 22; compact gelding; first foal; dam 1¼m winner; plater; will be suited by 1½m; said to be unsuited by really soft ground. *W. Musson.*

PETERHOF (USA) 2 b.c. The Minstrel 135–Millicent (Cornish Prince) (1981 **116** 5d² 5fg* 6d 5g* 6g)
   Mate one Derby winner, The Minstrel, with a half-sister to another, Mill Reef, and what do you get? The answer, unlikely though it seems, is Peterhof, winner of the Curragh Stakes, one of Ireland's best five-furlong events for juveniles, and the Flying Childers Stakes which, as a Group 2 event, is England's

Flying Childers Stakes, Doncaster—Peterhof draws clear from Prowess Prince to gain his second pattern-race victory

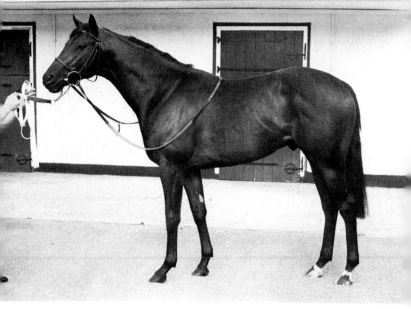

Mr R. E. Sangster's "Peterhof"

most important five-furlong race open to two-year-old colts. Peterhof started favourite for both races. Although comfortably beaten by Miss Behaving on his debut at Phoenix Park a month earlier, Peterhof was made an odds-on chance to beat the Tyros Stakes winner Watties Rock and seven others in the Curragh Stakes in July. He produced the anticipated improvement in rather unexpected fashion; he raced wide of the others near the stand rails, came through to cut down the leader The Primate in the closing stages and won by half a length. This was a good effort—The Primate later failed by only a short head to beat Achieved in the Gallaghouse Phoenix Stakes, and the third horse, Watties Rock, was all of six lengths behind the runner-up. Better was to follow in the Flying Childers at Doncaster on St Leger day. Here Peterhof met the winners of two of England's three previous five-furlong pattern races—Fly Baby, winner of a substandard Queen Mary Stakes, and Prowess Prince, successful in the Molecomb Stakes and a close second in the Norfolk Stakes, the other of the three pattern events. From the off Peterhof had no difficulty in keeping up with that very fast starter Mumruffin and had her struggling soon after halfway. Fly Baby, who had also shown speed throughout towards the outside, hung on to him for another furlong but by the distance the only possible source of danger to Peterhof was Prowess Prince. He couldn't raise a serious challenge though and Peterhof ran on strongly to beat him four lengths, with Fly Baby hanging on to third place a further five lengths behind.

Although Peterhof showed no signs of stopping at the end of his five-furlong races he failed to produce his form when tried over six. At 6/5 on for the Gimcrack Stakes at York in August he finished only fifth of eight, four and a half lengths behind Full Extent, fading in the final hundred yards after coming under the whip fully two furlongs out. And when a 7/2-shot for the William Hill Middle Park Stakes at Newmarket in October he began to challenge Lucky Hunter strongly for the lead with over a quarter of a mile to run, only to weaken markedly on meeting the rising ground inside the final furlong. Cajun, Wattlefield and Tender King all passed him and at the line he was beaten over three lengths.

642

There are some speedy elements close up in Peterhof's pedigree which could go some way towards explaining his lack of stamina. For example Nearctic, The Minstrel's grandsire, was capable of winning over five furlongs in 58.2 seconds as a four-year-old in 1958, the season when he also won at up to nine furlongs and become Canadian Horse of the Year; and Cornish Prince, Peterhof's maternal grandsire, covered six furlongs in 69.8 seconds when gaining the last of his stakes victories towards the end of his three-year-old days, having earlier won over a mile. There's hardly any racecourse evidence available regarding the staying powers of the mares in Peterhof's female line—his dam Millicent, third dam Virginia Water and fourth dam Red Ray never ran, while his grandam Milan Mill was unplaced on her one appearance. However, many of their offspring stayed a mile or more: Virginia Water bred the Royal Lodge second Goose Greek and Berkeley Springs, runner-up in both the One Thousand Guineas and Oaks; Milan Mill, in addition to Mill Reef, produced the Princess Elizabeth Stakes winner Memory Lane and the useful miler Mille Fleurs; and of Millicent's previous three winners one, the In Reality filly Marston's Mill, was a stakes-placed winner at up to a mile, and another, the Tom Rolfe horse Beverly Mill, scored up to nine furlongs in modest company.

Peterhof (USA) (b.c. Apr 9, 1979)	The Minstrel (ch 1974)	Northern Dancer (b 1961)	Nearctic
			Natalma
		Fleur (b 1964)	Victoria Park
			Flaming Page
	Millicent (b 1969)	Cornish Prince (br 1962)	Bold Ruler
			Teleran
		Milan Mill (b 1962)	Princequillo
			Virginia Water

Whatever you make of Peterhof's pedigree, the racecourse evidence is overwhelming that he's best at five furlongs. In some ways he had the look of a speedy two-year-old about him; although a strong, shapely colt he was very small, with a short, sharp action, and he had to make a lot of use of himself against his bigger, longer-striding opponents. His lack of size is likely to tell against him at three but at his best he's a smart colt and should win another race or two if he trains on. He seems to need a sound surface. *V. O'Brien, Ireland.*

PETER HUTT 3 b.g. Streak 119–Jamuna (Canisbay 120) (1980 5s 5g 5fg 5f 5d 6f 7fg 1981 8.5fg 10g) lightly-made gelding; poor maiden; ran best race in a seller at 2 yrs; should stay further than 5f; acts on a soft surface. *D. Jermy.* —

PETE ROCKET 2 ch.g. Roan Rocket 128–Devadara 73 (Royal Levee or Hill Clown) (1981 5s 5fg² 5fg* 6g 6fg 7fg 7g⁴ 8.2d 7g) Mar 6; 2,800F, 3,400Y; sturdy gelding; third foal; half-brother to Irish 3-y-o 9f winner Goldspear (by Pieces of Eight) and 1m and 1¼m seller winner Stewart's Rise (by Good Bond); dam showed some ability at 2 yrs; won 7-runner maiden race at Hamilton in May by ½ length from Fast Lad; prominent in several nurseries subsequently; will probably stay 1¼m; yet to show he acts on extremes of going. *P. Haslam.* **74**

PETER THE BUTCHER 4 br.g. Autre Prince 125–Circumstance 72 (Bleep-Bleep 134) (1980 8d 8.2d 10f³ 12fg 12fg⁴ 11fg 9g³ 8fg 8g⁴ 9g³ 8d³ 9g 8.2d⁴ 8f 1981 8g 10f* 10f 10f 11fg) poor handicapper; won at Pontefract in June; well beaten afterwards; stays 1¼m but not 1½m; acts on any going; blinkered once in 1980. *S. Nesbitt.* **60 d**

PETHAM BELLE 3 ch.f. Red Alert 127–Glen Devon (Klairon 131) (1980 5f 5g 5.3d³ 6fg 7g 1981 7fg 7fg 12fg⁴ 12.2g³ 14fg³ 12.2fg 12f⁴ 14g) neat filly; in frame in maiden races and a handicap; probably stays 1¾m; soundly beaten in blinkers final start; sold 1,050 gns Newmarket Autumn Sales. *J. Winter.* **61**

PETHI MOU 2 b.c. Bold Lad (Ire) 133–Seamstress (Sea Hawk II 131) (1981 6f 5f 7g 7fg 7d 7fg 7g 8.2s) May 28; IR 6,000F, 8,200Y; strong, lengthy colt; half-brother to fairly useful 6f performer Classy Dame (by Jukebox); dam ran only twice; poor form, including in a seller; blinkered last 2 starts; sold to National Horse BA 1,100 gns Newmarket Autumn Sales. *S. Mellor.* —

PETITE HESTER 3 b.f. Wollow 132–Lady Hester (Native Prince) (1980 7g 7d³ 1981 8.2s 7d 7s 7fg² 7g 7f² 7f* 7.2fg³ 7g³ 7g*) small, lengthy, quite attractive filly; relegated to second after beating Huppel ½ length in minor event at Catterick in June on fourth start (apprentice ridden); subsequently won handicaps at Doncaster in July and Catterick in October (readily); should stay 1m; needs a sound surface and acts on firm going. *I. Balding.* **85**

PETITE JOIE (ITY) 2 b.f. Canisbay 120–Melancolie (Petingo 135) (1981 5fg 7g 6g 6d 6d) well-made filly; half-sister to a winner on flat and over jumps in Italy by Reform; dam, winner 4 times at 3 yrs in Italy, is daughter of Italian Oaks winner Macrina d'Alba; showed a little ability, although soundly beaten, in end-of-season maiden races; will stay 1¼m; blinkered final outing. *R. Armstrong.*

PETITE KATHY 2 br.f. Goldhill 125–Kathy King (Space King 115) (1981 5f 5f 7.2v 10d) May 21; 500 2-y-o; small, close-coupled filly; both looks and runs as though she's useless. *J. Wilson.* —

PETITE MIELLE 2 b.f. Hot Spark 126–Mrs Bee 74 (Sallust 134) (1981 6fg 6g) Apr 5; 4,200Y; leggy filly; excellent mover; first foal; dam 1¼m winner; 2 lengths fifth of 14 to Aegean Beauty in minor event at Newmarket in August; again ran well in 11-runner Ribero Stakes at Doncaster the following month, finishing 4¾ lengths fifth behind Master Cawston after chasing leaders for 4⅛f; will probably stay 7f. *R. Williams.* 75

PETITE REALM 2 b.f. Realm 129–Deep Brook (Wolver Hollow 126) (1981 5fg³ 5fg* 5d* 5g 6fg² 6fg³ 5fg⁴ 6g) Jan 30; IR 25,000Y; neat filly; half-sister to fair 1978 2-y-o 5f winner Honiara (by Pitcairn) and 3-y-o 9f winner Mountain High (by Mount Hagen); dam, unraced, comes from same family as Tin King and Hanu; successful twice in the spring, beating Fimi comfortably in maiden event at Sandown and having little trouble accounting for 2 rivals in £2,300 event at Folkestone; in frame afterwards in small race at Chester and in 2 good races at Newbury, on latter course finishing 2½ lengths third to Bless The Match in July and 5¾ lengths fourth to On The House in August; also ran well in valuable nursery on final start; gives impression 6f is her limit; acts on a firm and a soft surface; consistent; sold 38,000 gns Newmarket December Sales and is to be trained by J. Bolger in Ireland. *R. Simpson.* 95

PET MILER 3 b.g. Mummy's Pet 125–Mile by Mile 92 (Milesian 125) (1980 6fg 5g 1981 7d 6fg 7f 8fg) rather lightly-made gelding; little worthwhile form, including in sellers; sold 460 gns Ascot September Sales, resold 340 gns same venue in December. *P. Cole.* —

PETONA 3 b. or br.f. Mummy's Pet 125–Princess of Verona 95 (King's Leap 111) (1980 6g 1981 7f 7fg 8g) neat, short-backed filly; little worthwhile form. *M. Jarvis.* —

PETRA'S SEAL 3 ch.f. Privy Seal 108–Alison's My Girl 77 (Appiani II 128) (1980 NR 1981 9d 12d 8fg) 2,500Y; neat, lightly-made filly; first foal; dam won 1¼m seller at 2 yrs; towards rear in varied company. *R. Hollinshead.* —

PETROCELLI 3 b.g. Ragstone 128–Veracious 86 (Astec 128) (1980 NR 1981 12d 14g³ 16.9fg³ 16.5g² 16f) workmanlike gelding; first foal; dam effective from 1¼m to 2m; placed in maiden races at Salisbury, Wolverhampton and Redcar but is ungenuine; stays well; blinkered final start. *J. Dunlop.* 62

PETROLEUSE 3 b.f. Habitat 134–Plencia (Le Haar 126) (1980 6fg* 1981 8.5fg* 10v) lengthy, very attractive filly; good mover; fourth foal; half-sister to outstanding middle-distance filly Pawneese (by Carvin), smart French 1¼m winner Patia (by Don II) and fair middle-distance performer Pathfinder (by Bold Lad, Ire); dam useful winner at around 1½m in France; landed the odds by ½ length from Shark Song in Blue Seal Stakes at Ascot as a 2-y-o; looked to have done quite a lot of work when reappearing in Princess Elizabeth Stakes at Epsom in April and turned in a good performance, producing a most impressive turn of foot inside last furlong to win by ½ length and a short head from Applemint and Madam Gay after tending to hang and looking in trouble halfway up straight (seemed unsuited by course and changed her legs several times); had no chance in straight and was unable to act on heavy ground when eighth of 10 behind Tootens in Prix Saint-Alary at Longchamp later in month on only subsequent outing; should stay 1¼m; acts on a firm surface; sent to USA. *H. Cecil.* 104

PETROLIC (USA) 3 b. or br.g. Dynastic–Maryland Queen (Piave) (1980 NR 1981 8s 8g 12d) 25,000Y; ex-French gelding; second foal; half-brother to Queens Doctor (by Plenty Old), a minor winner at up to 1m in USA; dam won 18 small races at up to 1m; in rear in maiden race won by Mossdrum at Hamilton in October; also in rear on both outings in France when trained by A. Klimscha, jnr. *A. Jarvis.* —

PETRUS 3 b.g. Mummy's Pet 125–Super Nova 86 (Raise You Ten 125) (1980 6s 6g 1981 10.5s 12f 11.5fg³ 12.2fg 12g 12g) lightly-made gelding; has been hobdayed; little worthwhile form in varied company, including selling; twice had stiff tasks; blinkered final start; sold 400 gns Newmarket Autumn Sales. *D. Morley.* —

M D. Wildenstein's "Petroleuse"

PETTISTREE 3 ch.c. Sallust 134–Kokuwa (Klairon 131) (1980 6d 6g 5s* 5d² 1981 5s 6g 6g 5d² 5g 6f 5g 5s 6g 6d) fair sort; improved and showed useful form on his last 2 outings as a 2-y-o; disputed lead and stayed on really well under strong pressure when neck second to Welshwyn in £4,500 event at Sandown in June (quite well backed), only worthwhile form in 1981; should stay 6f; acts well on soft going; blinkered eighth start. *N. Callaghan.* **92** d

PETWORTH PARK 2 br.f. Mummy's Pet 125–Lancashire Lass 73 (King's Troop 118) (1981 6g³ 6f 5fg*) Mar 12; 3,000F, 6,400Y; lightly-made filly; good walker; half-sister to a winning plater; dam sprinter; had 3 races from flag start and showed plenty of ability on 2 occasions (ruined her chance by a slow start on second outing); beat Godstruth 1½ lengths in good style in maiden race at Wolverhampton on final start; clearly temperamental though and had to be mounted on course and then refused to enter stalls before being withdrawn on intended third outing: stays 6f. *S. Woodman.* **79**

PEYTON PLACE 4 b.c. Pitcairn 126–Modern Millie 95 (Milesian 125) (1980 5fg⁴ 6g 5g 1981 6fg 6g 6v) full-quartered, good sort; sprint handicapper; well beaten in seller final start; best run at 5f on a firm surface. *C. Williams.* **—**

PHANTOM FLYER 2 gr.c. Dragonara Palace 115–La Balconne 75 (Taj Dewan 128) (1981 5f 6g 6fg 6s 6g⁴) Mar 27; 1,750Y, 2,000 2-y-o; leggy, lightly-made colt; first foal; dam won over 1¼m and over hurdles; blinkered and dropped in class, ran creditably in sellers on last 2 starts, on second occasion staying on well to be 1½ lengths fourth to Commissar in valuable event at Newmarket in October; will probably stay 1m; sold 750 gns Ascot November Sales. *W. Musson.* **74**

PHAROS RAAPHORST (HOL) 2 br.c. Tyrant–Selina Fair 94 (Hugh Lupus 132) (1981 5d⁴ 5fg 5g⁴ 6.5fg 6.5v*) May 19; lengthy, useful-looking colt; half-brother to several winners, including Radetzky (by Huntercombe), a very smart performer at up to 1¼m, and useful stayer Party Time (by Parthia); **?**

dam won over 1¼m; fourth in minor event at Sandown in June (6 lengths behind Plagal) and Van Brienens Memoriaal in Holland the following month (5½ lengths behind Boxberger Speed); subsequently won 12-runner event at Duindigt in October; will stay 1m; acts on heavy going. *H. Wolffers, Holland.*

PHILIP MARTIN 2 b.c. Tumble Wind–Supreme Song (Supreme Sovereign **109** 119) (1981 7f⁴ 7d³ 6g) lengthy colt; second foal; dam ran once; 66/1 and having first race for 2 months, ran very well for a maiden when 1¼ lengths third of 11 to Day Is Done in Group 2 National Stakes at the Curragh in September; again far from disgraced when 4½ lengths eighth of 13 behind Cajun in William Hill Middle Park Stakes at Newmarket the following month; stays 7f; very useful and should win races. *J. Roe, Ireland.*

PHILLIP HENRY 2 b.g. Scottish Rifle 127–Galoprise 88 (Tudor Music 131) **49** (1981 6s 7f 6f 7g³ 6f) Feb 19; 4,000Y; small gelding; fourth foal; brother to fair 1979 2-y-o 7f winner Highland Bear; dam won over 6f; blinkered when 5½ lengths third of 8 to Golden Lisle in seller at Beverley in July; will stay 1m. *N. Tinkler.*

PHOENIX PRINCE 4 b.g. Ampney Prince 96–Lady Bashful (Don't Look — 107) (1980 NR 1981 13d 12g) soundly beaten in maiden race at Hamilton in April and minor event at Carlisle in May. *J. Fitzgerald.*

PHOTO 2 b.f. Blakeney 126–Photo Flash 119 (Match III 135) (1981 6fg 7fg²) **79 p** Mar 31; half-sister to very useful stayer Golden River (by Rheingold) and fairly useful Lucky Shot (by Reform), winner at up to 1¾m; dam second in 1,000 Guineas and half-sister to Welsh Pageant; had every chance when 5 lengths second of 16 to Top Hope in maiden race at Yarmouth in August, first outing for over 2 months; likely to show better form when given a test of stamina in 1982. *H. Cecil.*

PHRED 8 ch.g. Continuation 120–Phrygia (Mossborough 126) (1980 8g 1981 — 12f) poor plater; stays 11f; acts on any going; has worn blinkers. *Dr A. Jones.*

PHRYNE 3 ch.f. Jimmy Reppin 131–Phaedima 76 (Darius 129) (1980 5g — 6g 7g 6d 1981 8d 12.2g 10fg) compact, good-bodied filly; little worthwhile form in varied company; blinkered in 1981; sold 500 gns Ascot July Sales. *W. Elsey.*

PHYDILLA (FR) 3 b.f. Lyphard 132–Godzilla 106 (Gyr 131) (1980 6g* 7g² **126** 7d* 6.5s* 1981 8fg 7s 8g² 8fg* 8f⁴)
According to the International Classification Phydilla was the joint fourth-best three-year-old filly to run in France, Great Britain or Ireland in 1981: she is to be found on the same mark as Condessa, behind only Marwell, April Run and Blue Wind. Presumably she gets her rating from her performance in the Prix du Moulin de Longchamp in the autumn. On that occasion she finished fourth of twelve in a very strong field, comfortably ahead of Belmont Bay and Another Realm, going down by only a length and a half and two noses behind the colts Northjet, Hilal and The Wonder. She had every chance, still holding second place to Northjet about a furlong from home, in a race which produced a new course record for a mile.

		Northern Dancer	Nearctic
	Lyphard	(b 1961)	Natalma
	(b 1969)	Goofed	Court Martial
Phydilla (Fr)		(ch 1960)	Barra II
(b.f. 1978)		Gyr	Sea-Bird II
	Godzilla	(ch 1967)	Feria
	(ch 1972)	Gently	Grey Sovereign
		(gr 1962)	Be Careful

The Prix du Moulin was the last of Phydilla's five-race season, and her high-class performance in it was certainly her best by far. She had seemed to have the makings of a leading filly when winning on three of her four starts as a two-year-old, including in the Prix Eclipse at Saint-Cloud, but she was backward when we saw her a well-beaten favourite in the Prix de la Grotte at Longchamp in April on her reappearance and she ran only another once, unplaced in the Prix de la Porte Maillot in July, before the start of Deauville month. Phydilla made a welcome return to form at Deauville, following up a good second to the ex-Belgian four-year-old Epsiba in the Prix d'Astarte (she finished strongly after getting boxed in) with a win in the Prix Quincey, another Group 3 event, this one not confined to fillies. On their best form the colts Diamond Prospect and Noalto seemed to have the Prix Quincey between them— fairly recently Diamond Prospect had been second to Moorestyle in the Prix

Prix Quincey, Deauville—Phydilla wins from Diamond Prospect (No. 7), Tellurano (No. 4), Noalto (No. 8) and Mistra

Maurice de Gheest and Noalto third to Kings Lake in the Sussex Stakes and to Dalsaan in the Hungerford Stakes. Phydilla was conceding both a pound. In a very tight race Phydilla managed to squeeze into the lead at the distance and hold on by a neck from Diamond Prospect; the Irish three-year-old Tellurano, conceding a head behind the second and a short neck in front of the unlucky-in-running Noalto. Epsiba was only sixth.

Phydilla is the second foal of her dam, and a half-sister to the French four-year-old Aristarque (by Rheingold) who won a seller at around a mile and a half at Deauville. The dam Godzilla is an interesting mare. She was bred in England, raced in Italy as a two-year-old after being sold for 10,000 guineas at the Newmarket Yearling Sales, then was brought back to race in England by Robert Sangster, the owner-breeder of Phydilla. She showed useful form. In Italy she won five times at distances up to around a mile and was rated third-best of her sex behind Carnauba and Sinthesis. She tackled good sprinters over here, on one occasion finishing a creditable fourth to Steel Heart in the Duke of York Stakes, and gave the impression she needed further than five furlongs—which perhaps wasn't too surprising for a daughter of the Derby second Gyr. However, there's not much stamina on the dam's side. Godzilla's dam Gently is a daughter of the Gimcrack Stakes and Champagne Stakes winner Be Careful; Gently herself won over six furlongs and seven furlongs, appearing also to need further than five. Gently, incidentally, is grandam of the very smart Italian two-year-old Grease.

Phydilla would probably not have stayed much further than a mile, for she was difficult to settle. She acted on any going. Plans to run her in the Yellow Ribbon Stakes at Santa Anita late in the autumn had to be abandoned because she was struck into in the Moulin, and she'll be at stud in 1982. *O. Douieb, France.*

PHYLJAN 2 ch.f. Flashback 102–Headliner (Pampered King 121) (1981 5f 6g 5.3d) Mar 27; sixth foal; sister to a plater; dam ran only once; last in maiden and minor races. *M. Bolton.* —

PHYLLIRA (FR) 3 b.f. Sea Break 129–Armoricana (Bel Baraka 120) (1980 7g 8fg 1981 12.2s³ 12d³ 10.2d⁴ 16fg³ 12f 16f 16fg* 16f 16s 18g²) smallish, 66 rather lightly-made filly; stayed on well when winning maiden race at Warwick in July; had stiffish tasks afterwards, but ran well when 5 lengths second to Chemin de Guerre in minor event at Doncaster in October; suited by a test of stamina; probably acts on any going; blinkered ninth outing; sold 14,000 gns Newmarket December Sales. *P. Kelleway.*

PIA FORT 2 b.c. He Loves Me 120–Gammon (Pia Star) (1981 5g* 6d) May **76** 22; IR 4,300F, IR 3,000Y, resold 8,200Y; tall, lengthy colt; half-brother to a winner in Spain; dam won claiming races at up to 6f in USA; 16/1, finished strongly to win 13-runner maiden race at Thirsk in May by ½ length from Venetian Joy; always struggling when remote seventh of 8 to Full Extent in Gimcrack Stakes at York in August (25/1); should be suited by 6f; gave trouble at start when withdrawn from Coventry Stakes at Royal Ascot and from Middle Park Stakes at Newmarket on other appearances. *R. Hollinshead.*

PIANOLA 2 b. or br.f. Welsh Pageant 132–Hurdy-Gurdy 90 (Espresso 122) **76 p** (1981 8g) Feb 24; robust, good-quartered, short-legged filly; sister to useful 1¼m winner Sideshow, and half-sister to very smart middle-distance filly Vielle (by Ribero); dam won at up to 1¼m; third favourite, wasn't disgraced when 10¼ lengths ninth of 30 to Farioffa in maiden race at Newmarket in October, making up a lot of ground to have a chance 2f out and then not being punished once she began to tire; will stay 1¼m; evidently thought capable of a good deal better, and should leave this form behind in 1982. *B. Hobbs.*

PIASTRE 2 b.f. Royal Palace 131–Astoria 92 (Derring-Do 131) (1981 6fg 7d) — Apr 3; strong, good sort; half-sister to several winners, including 1980 2-y-o 7f winner More Stones (by Morston) and useful 7f to 1⅛m winner Shortbread (by Crisp and Even); dam stayed 1¼m and is sister to 2,000 Guineas third Dominion; always niggled at to go pace when 9 lengths eleventh of 19 to Enthralment in maiden race at Salisbury in September; 20/1 when ninth of 18 to Sans Blague in similar race at Newbury later in month; bred to stay 1¼m+; looks capable of better. *I. Balding.*

PIBROCH LASS 4 br.f. Highland Melody 112–Quite Safe 74 (Quorum 126) — (1980 6fg 5.8f⁴ 5g 5.3d⁴ 5.3d² 5fg 5.3fg 5d 1981 5.3f 5.3f) compact, attractive filly; poor sprint handicapper; not certain to stay 6f; seems to act on any going; suitable mount for a claimer; sold 530 gns Ascot December Sales. *B. Wise.*

PICK A STRAW 3 b.c. Thatch 136–Piccadilly Lil 92 (Pall Mall 132) (1980 **69** NR 1981 7s 7d³ 7.6f 11f² 10f⁴ 10fg* 8.3fg 10fg²) 42,000Y; lengthy, rather lightly-made colt; sixth foal; half-brother to a winner in Malaysia by Upper Case; dam 2-y-o 6f winner; won bad maiden race at Ayr in August and was in frame in varied company, but is none too genuine; stays 11f; behind in blinkers seventh start; sold to Miss S. Morris 4,000 gns Newmarket Autumn Sales. *B. Hills.*

PICKLED TINK 4 b.f. Tickled Pink 114–Brown Jockeen 75 (Jock Scot 121) — (1980 8f 8fg 12d 10.8s 1981 12f 10.1fg) small filly; behind in varied company. *M. Scudamore.*

PICKS PINTA 2 ch.g. Broxted 120–Wispy Vision 70 (Gulf Pearl 117) (1981 — 6g 7.2d 8.2d) June 4; workmanlike gelding; poor mover; second foal; brother to a poor plater; dam won over 1m; beaten some way in maiden races, finishing last of 20 on final start. *D. Francis.*

PICOTEE 3 br.f. Pieces of Eight 128–Gail Time (Arctic Time 127) (1980 — NR 1981 8d) half-sister to smart staying hurdler Town Ship (by Behistoun); dam won from 9f to 1⅛m in Ireland; always behind and was pulled up over 2f out in maiden race at Bath in June. *C. James.*

PIECE OF THE REALM 3 ch.f. Realm 129–Fall to Pieces 101 (Forli) (1980 — 6fg* 6f³ 7g 1981 8d) moderate performer at 2 yrs; well beaten only outing in 1981 (May); stays 6f (has had stiffish tasks over further). *H. Candy.*

PIECES OF GOLD 4 b.f. Pieces of Eight 128–Reproach Me Not (Connaught — 130) (1980 8v² 8fg 12f 12d 12s⁴ 10fg 10fg 8g 1981 8.5d 10s 10.4g 10g 10g 11d) fair, lightly-made sort; ex-English; quite a useful filly at her best but is frequently run out of her depth; soundly beaten at 4 yrs; stays 1½m; acts on any going; blinkered final outing; trained by G. Beeson first 3 starts. *P. Russell, Ireland.*

PIEL CANELA (SPA) 4 b.f. Sallust 134–Padella (St Paddy 133) (1980 — 7d³ 7.6f⁴ 8g⁴ 10fg 8fg 1981 9g 8g 8f 7fg 8f 8s 6fg 6f 7g) strong filly; only plating class; should stay beyond 1m; blinkered sixth to eighth starts. *A. Jarvis.*

Mr R. E. Sangster's "Pilgrim"

PIENCOURT 3 br.c. Averof 123–French Bugle 71 (Bleep-Bleep 134) (1980 **73**
5d 5d³ 6s 1981 6g 7fg* 7g³ 7d⁴ 6f 6f 7fg 7f 5d 5g² 6g 6g) compact, quite
attractive colt; 25/1 when winning maiden event at Epsom in April; in frame
at Newmarket, Epsom and Ascot subsequently, on last-named course in September finishing ¾-length second of 20 behind Pencil Point in £5,100 handicap
after being outpaced; stays 7f; best form on a sound surface; had stiff task when
blinkered ninth outing. *C. Austin.*

PIEROTH 3 b.g. Averof 123–Terex (Khalkis 127) (1980 NR 1981 10s 7fg **62**
8fg³ 8g⁴ 8fg⁴ 8g³ 8d) fair sort; half-brother to 2 winners, including fairly
useful stayer Ventrex (by Henry the Seventh); dam half-sister to 2 good
animals; in frame in maiden races; will be suited by a return to 1¼m; wears
blinkers. *J. Winter.*

PILGRIM (USA) 2 b.c. Northern Dancer–Fleur (Victoria Park) (1981 6d*) **94** p
May 11; $1,250,000Y; brother to Derby winner The Minstrel and smart French
1m and 9f winner Far North, and half-brother to 2 winners; dam, stakes-placed
winner at up to 1m, is half-sister to Nijinsky (by Northern Dancer); didn't
appear until October (reportedly kept off course by a number of minor setbacks)
when drawing clear in final furlong to win 11-runner maiden race at the Curragh
comfortably by 3 lengths from Tony Tan; sure to leave this form well behind
when tried over 1m or more. *V. O'Brien, Ireland.*

PILLAR TO POST 3 b.f. Decoy Boy 129–Rose Red 95 (Ballymoss 136) —
(1980 5fg 5fg 5.8fg 5g* 1981 6f 6fg 6s 5s 6d) small filly; plater at 2 yrs; no
form in 1981; should stay 6f. *D. Wilson.*

PILOT FLYER 2 br.f. Saulingo 122–Terina (Bold Lad, Ire 133) (1981 6fg **74**
6fg³ 6d) Mar 15; 3,400Y; half-sister to 1977 2-y-o 5f winner Oakenash (by

Realm); dam ran only 3 times; looked likely winner when joining leaders 1½f out in maiden race at Salisbury in September but couldn't find any extra and finished third of 19, 1¼ lengths behind Enthralment; ran poorly in maiden race at Hamilton later in month; not sure to stay beyond 6f; possibly unsuited by a soft surface. *C. Nelson.*

PILTON 3 ch.g. Record Token 128–Wordless 74 (Worden II 129) (1980 8g 1981 10v) big, strong gelding; needed race when behind in minor event at Newmarket at 2 yrs and maiden race at Kempton in October. *T. Robson.*

PIMPERNELS TUNE 4 br.c. Blakeney 126–Melody Maid (Tudor Melody 129) (1980 9fg² 12f 1981 12s 14d 12d 10f 11.7f 12d) neat colt; only plating class; will be suited by long distances. *J. Bethell.*

PINCENTS 7 ch.g. Queen's Hussar 124–Piave (Alcide 136) (1980 11.7fg 14fg² 13.1fg 17.1fg 14g 13.1h 14fg² 1981 14d 13.1g) middle-distance handicapper; burly both starts in 1981; well suited by top-of-the-ground; wears blinkers; has won 5 times at Bath; sold 2,100 gns Ascot October Sales. *J. Dodd.*

PINDEN 3 b. or ro.g. Golden Tack 102–Pink Slip (Indigenous 121) (1980 NR 1981 7s 8.2s 8fg) workmanlike gelding; fifth foal; dam well beaten in 2 races at 2 yrs; behind in maiden races at Leicester (needed run), Nottingham and Warwick; dead. *B. Palling.*

PINE 3 ch.f. Supreme Sovereign 119–Ash 102 (Hornbeam 130) (1980 NR 1981 8fg 10s) quite a well-made filly; half-sister to several winners here and abroad, including Irish middle-distance winner Rhodante (by Busted); dam stayed 2m; behind in maiden races at Goodwood in August (on backward side) and Nottingham in October. *R. Hern.*

PINE GYPSY 3 b.f. Workboy 123–Gypsy Refrain 86 (Romany Air 118) (1980 NR 1981 10.1fg 13f) 660F, 1,250Y; plain filly; sister to winning stayer Happy Worker, and half-sister to a winner; dam out-and-out stayer; in rear in minor event at Windsor and in maiden event (last of 10) at Nottingham in summer. *D. Gandolfo.*

PINK BLUES 4 b.f. Tickled Pink 114–Rhythm 64 (Bleep-Bleep 134) (1980 7v 7f 6f² 6g 6fg 6s 6d 6s 6v 1981 5g) lightly-made non-thoroughbred filly; sprint handicapper; had stiffish task when well beaten only start at 4 yrs in July; suited by 6f; appears to act on any going; has run well for a boy. *F. Durr.*

PINK CHAMPAGNE 2 b.f. Sparkler 130–In The Purple (Tudor Melody 129) (1981 6s 8s) Apr 17; leggy, lightly-made filly; second foal; dam ran only once; in rear in large fields of platers at Goodwood and Warwick; sold 280 gns Ascot November Sales. *J. Douglas-Home.*

PINKERSUN 4 br.g. Tickled Pink 114–Sun Queen 76 (Lucky Sovereign) (1980 10.1s 6fg 6g 5g 6f⁴ 5d 6d 5s 1981 6g) light-framed, dipped-backed gelding; little worthwhile form, including in a seller; best run at 6f on firm going; blinkered twice in 1980. *L. Barratt.*

PINKERTON'S MAN 5 br. or bl.h. Will Hays–Miss Pinkerton (Above Suspicion 127) (1980 8d³ 7v 8f³ 8fg² 8d* 8d² 8d² 8g 8.2g³ 8d² 8g 8d 7f 1981 8.2d 8s 8.2d 7s) neat, well-made horse; stays 1m; acts on any going; has worn blinkers. *G. Richards.*

PINK PATH 2 b.g. Warpath 113–Darwin Tulip (Campaign 106 or Pirate King 129) (1981 7g) Mar 21; lightly-made gelding; half-brother to 2 winners, including 1½m and 13f winner High Rainbow (by High Line); dam never ran; 20/1 and in need of race, made some late headway to be ninth of 18 to Leg Glance in maiden race at Doncaster in October; may improve over further at 3 yrs. *J. Etherington.*

PINK TANK 8 b.h. Wolver Hollow 126–Pinks (Pink Flower) (1980 13s 12f 12fg 12fg 14f³ 12g 14g 12fg² 14fg² 12.5g 12d 10.8d 1981 12s 11.7d) modest middle-distance handicapper; acts on any going but seems well suited by a sound surface; has twice been blinkered; suitable mount for apprentice; acts on any track; usually held up; sometimes wears bandages. *M. Ryan.*

PINNOKE 3 ch.c. Habat 127–Pearlesque 88 (Gulf Pearl 117) (1980 NR 1981 5f 5fg 12d) premature foal (Dec 13); half-brother to 3 winners, including 3-y-o Pearlaway (by Derring-Do), a winner over 7f in 1980, and Pearlescent (by My Swallow), a smart winner at up to 1m; dam won over 5f and is sister to numerous winners; ran best race on second start when about 5 lengths sixth of

650

12 behind Biting Wit in maiden race at Warwick in August (dwelt); not certain to stay 1½m. *Mrs M. Rimell.*

PINOLA 2 b.c. Sallust 134–Pavlova (Fidalgo 129) (1981 6fg 7g 8d 7d) May **74** 22; 30,000Y; compact, quite attractive colt; half-brother to numerous winners, notably high-class 1¼m performer Lucky Wednesday (by Roi Soleil) and Irish 1,000 Guineas third Martinova (by Martinmas); dam winner over 1¼m in Ireland, is half-sister to good stayer Random Shot; showed only sign of ability in 1m maiden race at Bath in October, staying on to finish seventh of 17 to Suez; runs as though he needs a thorough test of stamina; blinkered last 2 outings. *J. Bethell.*

PINXTON 2 b.c. Free State 125–Belinda Pocket 84 (Pampered King 121) **78** (1981 5fg 6f³ 7g 7fg* 7fg⁴ 7fg² 8f) May 20; 2,500Y; narrow colt; moves well; half-brother to two 2-y-o winners; dam won over 5f at 2 yrs; ran best race when making nearly all to win 5-runner minor event at Wolverhampton in July by a head from Grey Mercy; 2 lengths second to Cassley River in nursery on same course the following month; should stay 1m. *R. Armstrong.*

PIPERHILL 3 ch.c. Red God 128§–Parthian Song (Parthia 132) (1980 5d* **111** 6d* 6g* 1981 8fg 7s³ 7.2f* 7g² 6g* 6d) lightly-made colt; returned to form when beating Rollin Hand by a length in Sporting Chronicle Handicap at Haydock in July, leading entering last furlong and being ridden right out; beat Overtrick decisively by a length after having a little difficulty going early pace in Nottingham Stewards Cup (Handicap) the following month; creditable ½-length second to Norman Style in handicap at Newcastle in between; should stay 1m (didn't have best of runs when tried at trip); has a smooth action and is well suited by firm going (beaten at halfway on easy ground when favourite for Ladbrokes (Ayr) Gold Cup on final start); went particularly well for apprentice N. Day; usually bandaged in front; sold privately and sent to USA. *H. Cecil.*

Mr C. d'Alessio's "Piperhill" (N. Day)

PIPINA (USA) 3 b.f. Sir Gaylord–Favoletta 115 (Baldric II 131) (1980 NR **81** 1981 7d² 8d² 10.5s* 10.5g 12d) lightly-made, active filly; half-sister to 3 winners, including fair middle-distance winner Audley End (by Nijinsky) and smart 5f performer Amaranda (by Bold Lad, Ire); dam won Irish 1,000 Guineas; always going well when beating Mountain High by ¾ length in £4,000 minor event at York in May; last afterwards in Prix de Royaumont at Longchamp in June and Galtres Stakes at York in August (seemed to be carrying plenty of condition and possibly needed race); had earlier been second in newcomers race at Newbury and £4,400 event at Ascot (beaten 1½ lengths by Leah); stays 1¼m well; acts on soft going. *H. Wragg.*

PIPING QUEEN 3 b.f. Tudor Music 131–Harambee 64 (Doutelle 128) (1980 **—** 5s 6g 6g 6g 8fg³ 7.2d² 8s² 8d* 10.2s 1981 12d 12g 11.7f 12fg 12fg 13d 12d 8s 10d) compact filly; second in sellers prior to winning a nursery at 2 yrs; disappointing in 1981; stays 1m well (wasn't entirely disgraced over 1½m on reappearance); seems to act on any going; blinkered fourth outing as a 2-y-o. *D. Morley.*

PIPINIA 2 b.f. No Mercy 126–Pepperita 79 (Nelcius 133) (1981 7g) May 9; **—** strong, fair sort; third foal; half-sister to 2 winners, including 3-y-o 7f and 1m winner Young Daniel (by Dragonara Palace); dam won over 7.6f at 2 yrs; 20/1 and in need of race when last of 15 to Awaasif in maiden event at Ayr in September; sold 480 gns Newmarket Autumn Sales. *T. Craig.*

PIPP 'N' STREAK 2 b.c. Streak 119–Pibroch III (Specific 103) (1981 7fg **55** 8g⁴ 8.2d) Apr 20; fair sort; brother to 1980 2-y-o 5f winner Flash Gordon; dam never ran; plater; stays 1m. *T. Marshall.*

PIPUL 4 b.f. Pitskelly 122–Kay's Hour 93 (Bleep-Bleep 134) (1980 10s⁴ 10g **—** 0f 10.6fg 0g 0d 10.1d 10fg 10d 1081 12f 13.8fg 9g 11d³ 12.2fg 10 4s 12 3fg) plater nowadays; best at around 1m; sometimes blinkered; seldom impresses in paddock. *T. Fairhurst.*

PITLOCHRY 4 b.g. Pitcairn 126–Nicias 94 (Acropolis 132) (1980 10.8s 7fg **—** 7s³ 8.3d 7f 12d⁴ 12d⁴ 1981 12s) lengthy gelding; poor maiden; should stay middle distances; acts on soft going; has run moderately in blinkers; sold out of S. Woodman's stable 3,500 gns Ascot January (81) Sales. *J. Jenkins.*

PITORA 5 b.g. Pitcairn 126–Orenda (Cranach) (1980 6f 8fg 8fg 6g 7fg 7g 8fg **—** 7v 7d 7s² 1981 9d 8fg 9g) compact ex-Irish gelding; poor performer nowadays; stays 1m; appears to act on any going; suitable mount for an apprentice. *G. Lockerbie.*

PITRASI 2 br.c. Pitskelly 122–Princess Ru (Princely Gift 137) (1981 6g 7f³ **70** 7g 6f* 6g) Apr 26; IR 11,000Y; smallish, fair sort; half-brother to several winners, including National Stakes winner Trasi Girl (by Le Levanstell); dam poor maiden; cost 4,400 gns to buy in after battling on gamely to win 17-runner selling nursery at Ripon in August by a head from Chicanery; ran moderately when apprentice ridden in selling nursery at Brighton the following month; stays 7f; yet to race on a soft surface; sold 5,600 gns Newmarket Autumn Sales. *Sir Mark Prescott.*

PITREAVIE 2 b.c. Pitskelly 122–Catchatartar 82 (Tamerlane 128) (1981 **65** 6fg 6g 7f 7g 7fg 8g 8g 10g 10s) Mar 28; IR 6,000Y; small colt; half-brother to numerous winners, including Premier Harde (by Hardicanute), a smart winner at up to 11f in France; dam 2-y-o 5f winner; ran best races in maiden races at Ayr in July and Beverley in September on fourth and sixth starts; beaten at sixth in sellers subsequently; stays 1m but probably not 1¼m; often blinkered nowadays; sold 1,150 gns Newmarket Autumn Sales. *C. Brittain.*

PITSBIRD 3 br.g. Pitskelly 122–Reelin Bridge (New Day) (1980 6fg 5g 6g **—** 7f 6fg⁴ 7fg 1981 7d 7g 7f 5fg 6f 7d) lightly-made gelding; plater; stays 7f. *T. Gosling.*

PIT STOP 5 b.g. Pitskelly 122–Mrs Moss 81 (Reform 132) (1980 5g 5d 5g 5fg **64** 5fg 5fg 5g 1981 5s 5s² 5d 5f 5fg⁴ 5f 5.1fg 5fg 5g 5f 5f 5g 5s 5d 5s³ 5g) narrow, leggy gelding; poor mover; inconsistent sprint handicapper; best form at 5f but probably stays 6f; acts on any going, but is particularly well suited by soft; effective with or without blinkers; has worn bandages; suitable mount for an apprentice. *W. Stubbs.*

PITSYCATO 2 b.c. Pitskelly 122–Movement 79 (Daring Display 129) (1981 **—** 6fg 7g) Apr 3; 10,000Y; quite attractive colt; good mover; first foal; dam won over 6f and 7f; second favourite for 16-runner maiden race at Leicester in September on second outing but never got into race, finishing seventh to Airwair. *R. Price.*

PITSYLVAN 3 b.f. Pitskelly 122–Hill Time (Hill Gail) (1980 7g 8.2s 8d 1981 **52** 8d⁴ 9g² 9.4fg 10fg* 11.7g 8.2f 10s) plater; trotted up by 4 lengths from Silly Moo at Newmarket in July (bought in 5,200 gns); stays 1¼m; ran poorly third start; blinkered nowadays. *Sir Mark Prescott.*

PITTENCRIEFF 6 ch.g. Manacle 123–Anatevka (Privy Councillor 125) (1980 **77** 11fg² 12f⁴ 10s² 11d² 11fg 10s³ 12g 10d 12d⁴ 12.2fg* 12g² 12.2d² 13.8d* 12d 1981 12g 12g 12d⁴ 13fg 11g⁴ 12f³ 12.2fg⁴ 12.2g* 12v⁴ 13.8g*) workmanlike gelding; poor mover nowadays; modest handicapper; goes well at Catterick and won there in September and October; stays 1¾m; acts on any going; ran moderately when tried in blinkers; sometimes bandaged in front; suited by a strong gallop. *E. Weymes.*

PITTER PAT 2 b.f. Pitskelly 122–Tudor Saint (Tudor Music 131) (1981 **77 §** 5d 5s³ 5g* 5g⁴ 5g⁴ 5s² 5f* 5f 5d⁴ 5g 5g⁴ 5d 5f 5fg* 5fg 5g) May 3; IR 500F, 2,500Y; small, lightly-made filly; second foal; dam never ran; successful in maiden race at Edinburgh in April, valuable 20-runner seller at York in June (bought in 3,800 gns) and nursery at Windsor in September, making all for last 2 wins; ran best race for some time when scoring by ½ length from Laura Jenney at Windsor; speedy and is clearly regarded as a 5f performer; said by trainer to be unsuited by soft ground but ran well on it on sixth outing (2½ lengths second to Tender King); inconsistent. *T. Fairhurst.*

PITTI DONNA 3 ch.f. Hot Spark 126–Juvenescence 87 (Golden Horus 123) **62** (1980 5f 6g 8d 1981 8s³ 7.6d 8fg 7f³ 7f² 8fg 7d) rather leggy filly; second in maiden races at Thirsk and Folkestone in summer; stays 1m; acts on any going; sweating second start; dwelt final outing; sold 4,000 gns Newmarket Autumn Sales. *C. Brittain.*

PIT YOUR WITS 5 b.h. Pitskelly 122–Sweet Chupatti (Rustam 127) (1980 **64** NR 1981 9d 10.4g 8d* 8v² 10s 8d³ 7.6s² 8.3g 7.3d 12d* 12.2s* 10.2g) well-made, useful-looking horse; quite a modest handicapper; won at Wolverhampton (twice) and Warwick; stays 1½m; acts on any going except perhaps very firm; has worn blinkers; bandaged nowadays; suitable mount for an apprentice. *D. H. Jones.*

PIXIE 2 b.f. Pitcairn 126–Rixensart 77 (Credo 123) (1981 7.5f* 8d) Feb 14; **88** 16,000Y; lengthy filly; half-sister to 2 winners, including 1979 2-y-o 5f winner Aurora's Harbinger (by Sallust); dam, half-sister to Irish 2,000 Guineas winner Furry Glen, won over 6f at 2 yrs; beat Present Arms by 2 lengths (pair 5 lengths clear) in 14-runner maiden race at Gowran Park in August; favourite for 15-runner Silken Glider Stakes at Leopardstown the following month but dwelt after becoming very worked up at start and finished last behind Prince's Polly; should be suited by 1m; clearly highly regarded but seems temperamental. *K. Prendergast, Ireland.*

PIZARRO (USA) 3 ch.c. Sadair–Melinda A (Port Wine) (1980 NR 1981 8g⁴ **88** 8g 7d³ 8f* 8fg⁴ 8f* 8fg⁴ 7g⁴ 8v²) $45,000F, 150,000 gns Y; tall, attractive colt; first foal; dam, minor winner at up to 6f, is half-sister to smart animals Air Peruvian and Miss Arellano (both by Sadair) and comes from same family as Empery; won maiden race at Thirsk in July and handicap at Pontefract (in quite good style, despite edging left) in September; also in frame in Wood Ditton Stakes at Newmarket, minor events at Brighton and Kempton and handicaps at Ascot (apprentices), Newmarket (didn't have best of runs) and Kempton (creditable 7 lengths second to Princes Gate); suited by 1m; acts on any going. *P. Walwyn.*

PLACE CONCORDE 3 b.c. Habitat 134–Guillotina 118 (Busted 134) (1980 **69 d** NR 1981 8fg 8g⁴ 7.6g² 8d² 7fg² 10f 7g 8d 5d 6d) good-looking colt; brother to useful 1977 2-y-o 7f winner Shorthouse, and half-brother to another dam smart middle-distance stayer; second in maiden races at Lingfield and Bath and in minor event at Folkestone, all in June; ran moderately afterwards, wearing blinkers on ninth outing; needs at least 7f; trained by P. Walwyn first 5 starts. *W. A. Stephenson.*

PLACER QUEEN 2 ch.f. Habitat 134–Santa's Sister 104 (Middle Brother) **– p** (1981 7v) Apr 28; IR 68,000Y; fourth foal; half-sister to Irish 3-y-o My Sister (by Nonoalco), winner of 7f Mulcahy Stakes, and 2 winners abroad by Upper Case; dam useful winner at up to 1m; 8/1 and on backward side, dwelt when always in rear in 15-runner £3,400 event won by My Destiny at York in October; looks capable of better. *B. Hills.*

PLAGAL 2 ch.c. Music Boy 124–Saucy Councillor 64 (Privy Councillor 125) **96**
(1981 5d 5d² 5g⁴ 5d* 6fg⁴ 6f 6fg³ 7s 7s 6s) Apr 8; 5,500F, 5,000Y; strong, sturdy
colt; half-brother to 1977 2-y-o 5f seller winner Saucy Gypsy (by Sky Gipsy)
and a winner abroad; dam placed over 1¼m; kept on very gamely to win 6-runner
minor event at Sandown in June by ½ length from odds-on Cavallerizzo; ran
well only once afterwards (when blinkered first time), being beaten only a short
head and a head by El Mansour in New Ham Stakes at Goodwood late in July;
suited by 6f, but isn't sure to stay 7f; yet to show he acts on extremes of going;
blinkered seventh to ninth outings; sent to race in USA and is now trained by
H. Palma. *C. Brittain.*

PLANTAGENET 5 b.g. English Prince 129–Paddyflower 88 (St Paddy 133) —
(1980 10fg 12d³ 12.3d⁴ 12.2f⁴ 12fg 1981 12.2g) poor maiden; stays 1½m;
suited by some give in the ground; has been tried in blinkers. *J. Mason.*

PLASH (CAN) 5 b.g. Herbager 136–Flame d'Or (Champlain) (1980 NR —
1981 10fg 16d 11.7fg⁴) sturdy ex-French gelding; showed ability in useful
company in France at 2 yrs and 3 yrs but was well beaten over here in 1981;
stays 1½m; has worn blinkers. *G. Balding.*

PLATINUM RING 3 b.f. Auction Ring 123–Palaska (Mountain Call 125) —
(1980 NR 1981 7d 7g 8g 8.2s) 6,200Y; fair sort; first foal; dam unraced
half-sister to smart stayer Pragmatic; towards rear in maiden races; blinkered
final start; tends to sweat up. *J. Douglas-Home.*

PLAYBOY BUNNY 3 b.f. African Sky 124–Spa Track (Track Spare 125) —
(1980 5f 6fg 6s 6f 1981 8f 8fg 8f) leggy filly; soundly beaten in maiden races;
badly hampered final start; sold 460 gns Newmarket Autumn Sales. *F. Durr.*

PLAYBOY JUBILEE 4 b.c. Connaught 130–Paphos 99 (Vilmorin) (1980 **99**
10fg³ 10 4f* 10 6fg² 10d 10 5d 1981 9g³ 8s 8fg 7fg³ 7f 7f⁴ 8fg 9g 7g³) good-
looking, rangy colt; good mover; very useful at his best; creditable third at
Newmarket in Earl of Sefton Stakes in April (8½ lengths behind Hard Fought),
valuable Van Geest Stakes in June (3 lengths behind Dalsaan) and handicap in
October (hung right); seems to need further than 7f and stays 1¼m well; acts well
on firm ground and is possibly unsuited by soft; possibly has his own ideas about
the game. *F. Durr.*

PLAYFUL PADDY 5 br.g. St Paddy 133–Toccata (Kythnos 126) (1980 10fg* **58**
11.7fg² 10g 10g 10g* 8fg 10f* 10g⁴ 10.2d 1981 10.5d² 10g³ 8fg 10g⁴ 10f² 10f
10g 10.2g) middle-distance handicapper; probably acts on any going; may be
best held up till late. *J. Bethell.*

PLAY IT SAFE 2 ch.f. Red Alert 127–Prudent Girl 92 (Primera 131) (1981 **117**
5fg³ 7s* 7f² 8d* 8d*)

Mrs Bert Firestone had the pleasure in 1981 of campaigning not only April
Run and Blue Wind, the top three-year-old fillies in the eleven-furlong-plus
section of the International Classification, but also Play It Safe who, together
with Circus Ring and Height of Fashion, was rated the best filly in the two-year-
old classification. We haven't rated Play It Safe so highly as Circus Ring but
her record entitles her to be regarded the best of the French fillies—she won two
of the four French pattern events confined to her sex and finished a close second
in one of the other two.

Play It Safe's first pattern-race success came in the Group 3 Prix d'Aumale
at Chantilly in mid-September. By then she'd already run out an easy winner
of a maiden race on the same course and gone down by only half a length to the
strong-finishing Exclusive Order in the Group 3 Prix du Calvados at Deauville,
performances good enough to make her favourite at Chantilly. However, her
run at Deauville suggested she wouldn't have much to spare over three of her
d'Aumale rivals—she'd finished only half a length in front of Embarrassed, a
length in front of Bouillonnante and two and a half lengths ahead of Albala.
Over an extra furlong and on changed going it was a very different story. Play
It Safe won impressively, putting up a splendid exhibition of front running, and
came home four lengths and a short head clear of Bouillonnante and Albala, with
Embarrassed a soundly-beaten fourth on the softish ground.

Play It Safe's regular partner Paquet deserted her in the Group 1 Prix
Marcel Boussac on Arc day; he rode her stable-companion River Lady, an odds-
on shot rumoured to be markedly superior at home. Play It Safe instead received a superb ride from Piggott. He jumped her off in front, stole a couple of
lengths rounding the home turn and then drove her out for all he was worth up
the straight. For her part Play It Safe answered all her rider's demands most
generously, hanging on to her fast-diminishing advantage by a head from River

*Prix Marcel Boussac, Longchamp—Play It Safe battles on gamely under
very strong driving to hold off fast-finishing River
Lady (No. 9); Perlee is third*

Lady, the recipient of nothing like so good a ride from Paquet. Incidentally
Play It Safe again easily accounted for Bouillonnante who later finished a good
second to Coussika in the Prix des Reservoirs, the last of the four juvenile fillies'
pattern events.

	┌ Red Alert	┌ Red God	┌ Nasrullah
	│ (ch 1971)	│ (ch 1954)	└ Spring Run
Play It Safe	┤	└ Ashton Jane	┌ Gratitude
(ch.f. Feb 25, 1979)	│	(ch 1960)	└ Rye Girl
	│	┌ Primera	┌ My Babu
	└ Prudent Girl	│ (b 1954)	└ Pirette
	(b 1968)	└ Bride Elect	┌ Big Game
		(b 1952)	└ Netherton Maid

    Whereas April Run was purchased as a yearling and Blue Wind as a
two-year-old, Play It Safe is home bred; the Firestones also owned Red Alert in
his racing days. Play It Safe is easily the most important winner from Red
Alert's first four crops—he has sired only one other pattern-race winner, Crimson
Heather, despite having covered at least two hundred and seventy mares in
his first four seasons in Ireland. His exportation to Japan in 1981 therefore
came as no surprise. Play It Safe's sire might not have been a success at stud
but her dam Prudent Girl has an impressive record in her relatively short time at
stud. Prudent Girl's second foal, the Mill Reef filly Miller's Lass, was a useful
filly in Ireland, winning from seven and a half to eleven and a half furlongs;
her third, the Run The Gantlet colt Providential, won the Criterium de Saint-
Cloud at two, finished third in the Prix du Jockey-Club at three and won the
Washington International at four; and her fourth is Play It Safe. The next in
order is a yearling filly by Ballymore called Practical. Although Prudent Girl
was no more than a fairly useful mile-and-a-quarter winner herself, her success at
stud might have been anticipated: her dam Bride Elect won the Queen Mary
Stakes before becoming an outstanding broodmare and her grandam, the Oaks
second Netherton Maid, was a sister to the Oaks winner Neasham Belle. All
eleven of Bride Elect's runners won at least once, with the St Leger winner
Hethersett and those very smart horses Proud Chieftain and Royal Prerogative
the best of them. Another of Bride Elect's sons Never Beat became the leading
sire in Japan while a daughter, Ambrosia, bred that good horse Hard Fought.
    Eight of Bride Elect's winners were successful over a mile and a quarter or
more, including Play It Safe's dam; there must be a good chance therefore that
Play It Safe too will stay a mile and a quarter, even though she's by a six- and
seven-furlong performer. Both Play It Safe and River Lady are entered in the
One Thousand Guineas and Oaks so it's on the cards that one will come over for
an English classic. Should anything go wrong with Circus Ring the game and
consistent Play It Safe must stand an excellent chance in the Guineas. She
isn't the most taking of fillies, being rather leggy and close-coupled, but she has
plenty of size about her and should train on. Although she has run well on
firm going her best efforts so far have been on a soft surface. *F. Boutin, France.*

PLAY ME 3 b. or br.f. Murrayfield 119–Dinamarsh (Nelcius 133) (1980 5s 5fg
5g 5f 5d 1981 5d 6g 8f) only poor form, including in sellers; unseated her
apprentice rider twice on second start; blinkered on reappearance; sold 400 gns
Doncaster November Sales. *D. Leslie.* —

PLAYTOI 2 ch.f. Mansingh 120–Recce (Donore 119) (1981 6f) Feb 26;
half-sister to fair 1976 2-y-o 5.9f winner Heath Wood (by Murrayfield); dam
never ran; unquoted and on backward side, moved badly to start when behind
in 15-runner maiden race won by Swift Wing at Nottingham in July. *M. Ryan.* —

PLAZA TORO 2 ch.g. Ashmore 125–Duke Street (Lorenzaccio 130) (1981
7g 7fg 8s³ 10s⁴) Apr 19; 6,000Y; lengthy gelding; second foal; half-brother to
useful 3-y-o Buffavento (by Connaught), successful at up to 1m; dam won
small races over 7f and 1m in France; quite a moderate maiden; will probably
stay 1¼m. *Sir Mark Prescott.* 77

PLEASANT DREAM 2 b.f. Sharpen Up 127–Enchanted 116 (Song 132)
(1981 5fg⁴ 5g² 5f² 5fg* 5g⁴ 5d 5fg) Apr 14; leggy, rather lightly-made filly;
second foal; dam smart sprinting 2-y-o; ran on strongly to win 13-runner maiden
race at Wolverhampton in July by 4 lengths from Hawk's Nest after being clear,
racing alone on far side, from halfway; hung quite badly right in final 2f when
apprentice ridden in nursery at Goodwood the following month, but wasn't
disgraced in finishing 2 lengths fourth of 12 to Chellaston Park; unlikely to stay
6f; blinkered last 4 outings. *H. T. Jones.* 89

PLEASURE BID 6 br.m. Mon Plaisir 121–Irish Biddy (Devonian) (1980 NR
1981 10f) half-sister to top-class chaser Charlie Potheen (by Spiritus); dam
point-to-pointer; behind in maiden race at Yarmouth in August. *W. Musson.* —

PLEDGE 8 br.g. Rarity 129–Boucle 86 (Princely Gift 137) (1980 12.2v 12.2s
8fg 10s 11.7s 8g² 11.7g 10s⁴ 13.1h 12f 10.2g 1981 11.7d 10s 12s 13.1g² 8d
12.2fg 11.7g 10fg 10.2d) poor handicapper nowadays; seems to stay 1¾m;
appears to act on any going; below his best when tried in blinkers; good mount
for an apprentice; often makes the running. *H. Candy.* 55 d

PLUM BOLD 2 b.f. Be My Guest 126–Plum Fool (Silly Season 127) (1981
6d* 6g) Apr 22; attractive, rather lightly-made filly; good mover; third foal;
half-sister to 1980 2-y-o 5.8f winner Plum Lane (by Thatch); dam half-sister to
top-class French 1969 2-y-o Breton; led over 3f out, quickened nicely when
shaken up inside distance and drew 4 lengths clear of Shadows Lengthen to
win 18-runner maiden race at Haydock in August; 9/1 when only twelfth of 13
to Woodstream in William Hill Cheveley Park Stakes at Newmarket the following
month; will be suited by 1m. *F. J. Houghton.* 83

PLUM LANE 3 br.c. Thatch 136–Plum Fool (Silly Season 127) (1980 5fg³
5.8fg* 6d 6g 1981 7g³ 7g 6g³ 6fg 8g 7fg 7fg⁴ 7h 7g) big, workmanlike colt; good
mover; third in handicaps at Newmarket in May and Newbury in June, making
very good late progress in latter; disappointing however; bred to stay 1m; acts
on a firm surface; sometimes slowly away; blinkered seventh and eighth outings;
sold 2,000 gns Newmarket Autumn Sales. *I. Balding.* 85 d

POETIC SMILE 5 ch.m. Calpurnius 122–Teersaway 74 (Weepers Boy 124)
(1980 10fg 7fg³ 8g 7.6g 7fg 8.3fg 8g 8.2s 8d 6s 6g 1981 6s 7g 6fg² 6fg 6g 6fg 7g)
small mare; plater; stays 1m; acts on a firm surface; wears bandages nowadays;
suitable mount for an apprentice. *W. Turner.* 32

POINT NORTH 3 b. or br.c. Lorenzaccio 130–Off Scent 92 (Faberge II 121)
(1980 7g 7d 8.2g 8.2s 7v 1981 8g⁴ 11fg 10fg² 13g³ 11d⁴ 12.3g 10.6fg 10d)
strong colt; quite moderate form in varied company; stays 13f. *W. H. H.
Williams.* 59

POKERFAYES (USA) 2 b.c. Poker–Faye's Delight (Barbs Delight) (1981 5fg
5s⁴ 6s 6g³ 7g 8g³ 8d) Apr 13; $25,000Y; neat colt; first foal; dam unraced half-
sister to Poking (by Poker), a stakes winner at up to 9f; quite moderate form in
maiden races in the North; will stay 1¼m; blinkered fourth, fifth and seventh
outings, running badly on fifth. *S. Norton.* 74

POLAR STAR 2 b.c. Rarity 129–Arctic Chimes (Arctic Slave 116) (1981 6g³
6fg² 7g) May 13; 16,500Y; leggy colt; excellent mover; half-brother to several
winners, including Irish 6f to 1m winner Little Bitty Tear (by Sterling Bay); dam
sister to very useful filly Arctic Melody; beaten 2 short heads by Linda Beard
in maiden race at Newmarket in August; didn't have clearest of runs and looked
a bit unlucky when failing by ¾ length to catch Manchesterskytrain in similar
race at Epsom the following month; ran moderately third start but should be
well suited by 7f+. *H. T. Jones.* 90

POLDHU   3 b.c. Manado 130–First Bleep (Bleep-Bleep 134)   (1980 5fg² 6f* 6g³ 6d* **106**
6g³ 6fg³ 6f³   1981 7s 6g³ 6f 7fg⁴ 6fg 5fg* 6fg⁴ 6g⁴ 6s³ 6d)   lengthy, sparsely-made
colt; gained only success of year when beating Captains Treasure by 4 lengths
in 4-runner minor event at Ostend in August (blinkered first time); in frame
subsequently in Goldene Peitsche at Baden-Baden, handicap at Newmarket and
Coral Bookmakers Champion Sprint at York, looking exceptionally well in himself when 2½ lengths third to Jester on last-named course in October; put up
easily best previous effort when 3 lengths fourth of 8 to Dalsaan in Van Geest
Stakes at Newmarket and had run moderately on third (sweated up) and fifth
outings; probably stays 7f; seems to act on any going; usually held up and
doesn't find much off bridle; sold 15,000 gns Newmarket December Sales. *M.
Jarvis.*

POLIPUTER   3 br.f. Politico 124–Computer 69 (Chanteur II 135)   (1980 NR   —
1981 8f 7fg 12.2fg 8g)   compact filly; half-sister to a winner abroad; dam won
over 13f; behind in varied company, including selling. *D. Chapman.*

POLISTEPPIN   3 ch.f. Jimmy Reppin 131–Polistina 106 (Acropolis 132)   (1980 **92**
6g 5.8h 6d   1981 8d* 8.5fg² 7f² 8f* 11.5f³ 11.5fg³)   smallish filly; useful sort;
won maiden race at Warwick and finished good second to Harp Strings in
handicap at Epsom in April; ran well in Ireland afterwards, beating Voice by
2½ lengths in minor event at Navan in July and being placed on all her other
starts, including in Ulster Harp Derby at Down Royal later in month (2¾ lengths
third to Dance Bid); stays 11.5f; probably acts on any going; trained by G.
Beeson until after second outing; sold 8,000 gns Newmarket December Sales.
P. Russell, Ireland.

POLLARDSTOWN   6 b.g. Lord Gayle 124–Mear-Aille (Hard Ridden 131)   (1980 **86**
18.4f² 20d 16d 12fg 14g   1981 18.4d 12s 16s³)   high-class performer over
hurdles and a fair stayer on flat; not disgraced in 1981; acts on any going;
suitable mount for an apprentice; tough and genuine; often wears blinkers. *S.
Mellor.*

POLLIFORM   4 b.g. Reform 132–Pollinella 108 (Charlottown 127)   (1980 7fg⁴ **50**
8f 8.2f 6f 12h 11fg⁴ 11g² 9f 12g 12d 11fg² 12fg³ 11g³ 13d 11d³ 12.3s² 10g³ 12.3g
11d³ 12d³   1981 13v 12.5s⁴ 12g⁴ 11g³ 10.6s 8g 11g 10g² 11d* 12f 12.2fg³ 10.4s⁴
12f²)   neat, attractive gelding; plater; won non-selling handicap at Hamilton
in July; stays 1½m; acts on any going; has run creditably for a claimer;
doesn't always impress in paddock; blinkered nowadays. *H. Bell.*

POLLY PERKINS   7 ch.m. Souvran 98–Sabbath (Twilight Alley 133)   (1980   —
NR   1981 10.1fg)   second foal; dam never ran; behind in minor event at
Windsor in June, first outing on flat. *G. Price.*

POLLY ROYAL   3 ch.f. Music Boy 124–Royal Tactic 62 (Right Tack 131)   **69**
(1980 5d² 5.8h³ 5fg 5g³ 5d   1981 6s 5g 5fg 6f* 6f 7g* 7g 7d⁴ 7s 8g)   neat filly;
won maiden race at Folkestone in July and handicap at Lingfield in September,
latter by ¾ length from Sharp Celeste; stays 7f; probably acts on any going.
G. Hunter.

POLLY'S BROTHER   3 ch.c. Roi Soleil 125–Polairia 66 (Polic 126)   (1980 6g **90**
6s   1981 7s³ 8d⁴ 11.7g 7fg² 8f³ 7g* 7g* 6g* 7g* 7s)   smallish, fair sort; bought
out of B. Hills's stable 3,900 gns after winning selling handicap at Newcastle in
July and proved a shrewd purchase; improved and won handicaps at Doncaster (apprentice event by 5 lengths), Ayr and Redcar (£4,200 event), all in
September, on last-named course quickening well and beating Christmas Cottage
by a length; also ran creditably final start; best form at up to 7f; has run
creditably on a firm surface but seems suited by some give in the ground;
sometimes tends to hang. *M. H. Easterby.*

POLLY SOLEIL   4 br.f. Roi Soleil 125–Polairia 66 (Polic 126)   (1980 8g 8.2g **59**
8.2s³ 8s 10g² 10d*   1981 10.2s³ 10s² 12.3d⁴ 13.1g 10.8s 10s³)   lengthy filly;
probably stayed 1½m; acted well on soft ground; suitable mount for an inexperienced rider; sold, covered by Kala Shikari, 7,000 gns Newmarket December Sales.
B. Hills.

POLLY WOLLY DOODLE   4 br.f. Warpath 113–Bolton Girl 87 (Blue Light-   —
ning 114)   (1980 10.2g 10g   1981 12.3g 16g)   tall, leggy filly; poor maiden;
sold 900 gns Doncaster November Sales. *C. Thornton.*

POLWICK   4 b.g. Red Alert 127–Gay Sylvia (Sayajirao 132)   (1980 9g 7fg⁴ 6fg **61**
6fg 7g* 7f⁴ 7g 7g 8g   1981 9d² 10d² 8g³ 11.7d* 11.7g 10f⁴ 12f 12.2g)   well-
made gelding; won handicap at Windsor in May; stays 11.7f; acts on a soft surface; sometimes blinkered; has run creditably for an apprentice; has been
bandaged in front. *M. Ryan.*

Mrs John W. Hanes's "Pomegranate"

POMEGRANATE (USA) 2 b.f. Damascus–Caspian 122 (Bold Bidder) (1981 **96**
6fg* 6g 6f*) short-coupled, rather lightly-made filly; half-sister to a winner
in USA by Bagdad; dam, daughter of Cheveley Park winner Crimea II, showed
very smart form at up to 1m; ridden by apprentice N. Day when successful in
maiden race at Yarmouth in June (beat slow-starting stable-companion Baltimore Belle a length) and in minor event at Ripon in September (ran on to beat
odds-on Rosier a neck); very much on her toes in paddock, was bit reluctant to
go down to post when favourite for John Courage Stakes at York in between and
wasn't persevered with after losing a lot of ground at start, coming home last of
7 to Atossa; will be suited by 1m; clearly has plenty of ability but is possibly
rather highly-strung. *H. Cecil.*

POMME D'EBENE 2 b.f. Kalamoun 129–Pomme Rose (Carvin 127) (1981 **103** p
7.5f* 8g3) Apr 10; sharp sort; half-sister to three winners in France, including
very smart middle-distance performer Noir et Or (by Rheingold) and very
useful 3-y-o 9f winner Buisson Rose (by High Top); dam smart at up to 1¼m;
won 11-runner maiden race at Deauville in August by 6 lengths from Malakya
without coming off bit; last into straight in Group 3 Prix La Rochette at Longchamp the following month but ran on under pressure to finish just over ½-length
third of 7 to Persepolis; likely to improve further and should win good races at
up to 1¼m. *J. Cunnington, jnr, France.*

POMPOSITY 4 ch.g. Pompous 118–Brave Heart 90 (Never Give In 97) (1980 **57**
10s 10g 10fg 1981 12.5s*) tall, leggy gelding; won poor maiden race at
Stockton in April; stays 1½m; suited by some give in the ground; sold 1,350 gns
Newmarket Autumn Sales. *J. Hardy.*

PONCHIELLI 3 b.c. Pitskelly 122–Pennycress 99 (Florescence 120) (1980 6g **107**
6d4 6g 6d* 6s2 6d4 6s 1981 7g 6s 6s 6f2 5fg* 5fg3 6fg 5d3 5fg* 5f4 5.6fg)
smallish, strong, good sort; usually a very good mover; improved and won
handicaps at Sandown in July (dead-heated with Crews Hill) and Newbury in

Happy Valley Handicap, Sandown—Ponchielli (nearest camera) gets up to force a dead-heat with Crews Hill

August (beat Steel Charger in very good style by 3 lengths); also in frame at York (twice), Newmarket and Haydock; stays 6f, but is probably best at 5f; acts on any going, but is probably best on firm. *R. Armstrong.*

PONTET 3 b.f. Ballynockan 112–Cissac (Indian Ruler 89) (1980 5s 5s 5g 6s 7g 6g 8fg 1981 8s 11d² 8fg 12s⁴ 10s 10f 12f⁴ 9g 10s³ 9d³ 13.8g) neat filly; plater; suited by 1¼m; acts on any going; has been tried in blinkers; often apprentice ridden. *D. Ancil.* **45**

PONTIN LAD 3 br.g. Mansingh 120–Mildura 98 (Vilmorin) (1980 5f* 5f* 5g³ 5.1g² 1981 5g⁴ 5g 5fg 5.3f* 5fg³ 5d² 5s) neat, strong, attractive gelding; good mover; returned to form when beating fast-finishing Epsom Imp by ½ length in minor event at Brighton in August; put up good efforts when placed in handicap at Epsom and minor event at Newbury (length second to Long Legend) in September; unlikely to stay 6f; acts on any going, except possibly very soft; looked a most unsuitable ride for an apprentice on third start. *H. T. Jones.* **97**

PONTIN LASS 2 gr.f. Manado 130–Grey Symphony (Track Spare 125) (1981 6fg 6f 6fg 6g⁴ 7g) Apr 25; IR 23,000Y; lightly-made filly; first foal; dam won over 6.5f at 2 yrs in France; quite a moderate maiden; will stay 1m; sold to BBA 2,000 gns Newmarket Autumn Sales. *H. T. Jones.* **72**

PONTOON 3 b.g. Grey Mirage 128–Penview 73 (Pendragon) (1980 6g 7.2d 1981 16f 10g) compact gelding; well beaten in maiden and minor races. *N. Hall.* **—**

PONTOS 2 b.c. Averof 123–Filandria 90 (French Beige 127) (1981 6f² 6fg² 6fg 8.2s⁴ 8g⁴) Feb 12; leggy colt; half-brother to 9f winner Refifi (by Reform); dam, winner at up to 1¾m, is half-sister to top-class sprinters So Blessed and Lucasland; in frame in maiden races and a nursery, running particularly well on final outing when staying on strongly to be over 5 lengths fourth of 29 to Born Hero in maiden event at Newmarket in October; will stay middle distances; acts on any going. *C. Brittain.* **87**

POODLEFAKER 2 ch.c. Galivanter 131–Gigi 85 (Acropolis 132) (1981 6g) Apr 22; 3,000F; neat colt; half-brother to 2 winners, including useful 1¼m winner Spring Frolic (by Silly Season); dam, sister to smart 1m filly Fiji, stayed 1¼m; 14/1, faded after 4f when about 12 lengths sixth of 9 to King Naskra in maiden race at Yarmouth in July, only outing; sold 1,300 gns Newmarket Autumn Sales. *H. Cecil.* **—**

659

POP A LONG (USA) 7 b.h. Baldric II 131–Popkins 120 (Romulus 129) —
(1980 8fg 6g 8s 1981 7.6fg) poor handicapper; stays 1¼m; often wears bandages; has worn blinkers; usually apprentice ridden. *H. Wragg.*

POPSI'S HOPE 3 b.g. Mandamus 120–Popsie's Pride (Border Legend 119) —
(1980 NR 1981 12g 10v) small gelding; half-brother to 2 winners by Hill
Clown, including very useful stayer Popsi's Joy; dam never ran; unquoted
when in rear in maiden races at Lingfield in June and Kempton (sweating)
in October. *M. Haynes.*

POPSI'S JOY 6 b.g. Hill Clown–Popsie's Pride (Border Legend 119) (1980 **102**
14f 14fg* 16fg 16f* 16fg* 16g* 16g³ 14g* 16.1fg² 14g³ 14g* 18d* 14g* 1981
18s⁴ 16fg³ 16g* 16f⁴ 16g 21fg⁴ 16d⁴ 14d 14.6fg 16fg) useful handicapper;
beat Mountain Monarch very cheekily by a neck under 10-0 at Newmarket in
April; not disgraced several subsequent starts, including when fourth in Queen's
Vase at Royal Ascot (to Ore) and Goodwood Cup (behind Ardross); stays well;
acts on any going but may be suited by some give in the ground nowadays;
invariably held up and has a useful turn of foot; goes well for L. Piggott; genuine.
M. Haynes.

POPSI'S MANDATE 7 br.g. Mandamus 120–Popsie's Pride (Border Legend —
119) (1980 NR 1981 16.9s³ 18.8fg) poor staying handicapper; acts on soft
going. *J. Yardley.*

PORTER 2 b.g. Mummy's Pet 125–Morelia 76 (Murrayfield 119) (1981 5f **58**
5f⁴ 6g 7f 8s) May 14; 1,100Y, 4,200 2-y-o; leggy gelding; poor mover and has
a round action; first foal; dam 2-y-o 7f winner; plater; not sure to stay 7f.
E. Carter.

PORTERHOUSE 4 ch.c. Red Alert 127–Yatagirl (Yatasto) (1980 6g 5g —
1981 8f 6g 5h² 6f) workmanlike colt; beaten at 5f on hard going; blinkered
last 2 starts; often bandaged in front. *D. H. Jones.*

PORTETTE 2 gr.f. Wolver Hollow 126–Portden (Worden II 129) (1981 **79**
6fg 8fg³ 8d* 8s) Apr 10; 3,000Y; rather lightly-made filly; sister to a poor
animal and half-sister to 3 winners, including fairly useful 3-y-o Redden (by
Red God), successful at up to 7.3f; dam Irish 9f winner; co-favourite when
winning 16-runner maiden race at Bath in October by 2½ lengths from Haystack;
will stay 1¼m; acts on a firm and a soft surface. *C. Spares.*

PORT MOULTON 2 ch.f. Moulton 128–Safe Port (Above Suspicion 127) —
(1981 5s) May 6; third foal; dam never ran; 33/1, started none too well when
in rear in 20-runner maiden race won by Illicit at Warwick in October. *P.
Duggins.*

PORTOGON 3 gr.c. Porto Bello 118–Helgonet (Soueida 111) (1980 5fg **78**
5f² 5g* 1981 5s 6fg² 5fg 7.3g⁴ 7f 6f* 6fg³ 7f* 7fg 7fg² 7fg² 7g 7s³) big, strong,
workmanlike colt; won handicaps at Chepstow in June and Thirsk in July,
latter by a length from Monza Lady; ran creditably several other starts; stays
7f; acts on any going. *T. Marshall.*

PORTO LOUISE 2 ch.f. Porto Bello 118–Irene Louise 65 (Match III 135) —
(1981 6fg 7h 8fg 8s) Apr 30; half-sister to 2 minor winners; dam poor half-
sister to high-class sprinter Import (by Porto Bello); no worthwhile form in
maiden races and a seller. *W. Turner.*

PORTULACA 3 ch.f. Porto Bello 118–Sea Daisy 90 (Mossborough 126) (1980 —
5g⁴ 5d 5.8g³ 7g 6fg 7g⁴ 1981 7d 8fg 10.2h 10.4d 10.1g⁴ 10fg 10fg) lightly-
made, useful-looking filly; good walker; quite a moderate maiden; unplaced
in a seller on final start; probably stays 1¼m; blinkered sixth outing. *I. Balding.*

POSHTEEN 6 ch.m. Royal Smoke 113–Camlet 60 (Fleece 114) (1980 NR **54**
1981 7d 5.8g³) strong mare; fair sprinter at her best; has been to stud and
produced a colt by New Member in 1980; stays 6f; acts well on firm going;
has worn blinkers. *O. O'Neill.*

POSITRON 2 br.f. Free State 125–Naiche (Tribal Chief 125) (1981 5d 5f **80 ?**
5fg 8fg³ 7g* 8.2s) Feb 27; small filly; first foal; dam 4 times unplaced at 3 yrs;
won 16-runner maiden race at Leicester in October by a short head from Angelus
Chimes; last of 13 under a 10-lb penalty in nursery at Nottingham later in
month; best run at 7f but wasn't disgraced over 1m on fourth outing; possibly
unsuited by soft ground. *W. Wharton.*

POSTERITY 2 b.f. Continuation 120–Hillset (Hill Clown) (1981 5s⁴ 5s* **62**
6f 6g) Apr 9; lightly-made filly; half-sister to two 2-y-o winners, including
fair 5f winner Pompously (by Pompous); dam of no account; plater; bought

in 1,750 gns after winning 3-runner race at Nottingham in April by 5 lengths from Chrisdee; well beaten afterwards; should stay 6f; possibly needs some give in the ground; sold 700 gns Newmarket Autumn Sales. *J. Hardy.*

POT PLANT 3 b.f. Busted 134–Honey Pot 111 (Hotfoot 126) (1980 NR 1981 9s) big filly; second foal; half-sister to 1979 2-y-o 5f winner Concession (by Connaught); dam very useful sprinting 2-y-o; 16/1, never went pace when ninth of 13 behind Joliette in maiden race at Wolverhampton in April; sold 1,700 gns Newmarket July Sales and resold $16,000 at Florida Breeders Sales at Ocala in October. *P. Walwyn.* —

POUNENTES 4 b.g. Tumble Wind–La Chanteuse 81 (Hethersett 134) (1980 7v 7fg 8f* 8f² 11f² 1981 12g² 13fg 11g⁴ 12d 11fg 12g) workmanlike gelding; stays 1½m; seems to act on any going; best in blinkers; has run well for an apprentice; ran poorly fourth outing. *G. Richards.* 62

POWDER HORN 4 b.f. Scottish Rifle 127–Ticking Hill 93 (Hillary) (1980 10g³ 12fg⁴ 12g 12d 10fg 10g⁴ 10s 1981 8s⁴ 11g⁴ 11.7fg 10fg 12g) leggy filly; middle-distance plater; sometimes blinkered; doesn't always impress in paddock; sold out of W. Elsey's stable 1,000 gns Ascot May Sales after second start. *W. Musson.* —

POWERSCOURT (USA) 4 b.g. Buckpasser–Irish Manor (Bold Ruler) (1980 7f 8f 8h 1981 8d) most attractive gelding; showed ability in Southern maiden and minor races at 2 yrs; didn't find his form in 1980 and ran abysmally only start at 4 yrs in May; will be suited by middle distances; sold 950 gns Ascot December Sales. *J. Dunlop.* —

POYLE CRUSHER 4 ch.c. Sweet Revenge 129–Swan Ann 84 (My Swanee 122) (1980 7v* 8s² 7f 7g 8g 8d⁴ 8fg⁴ 8g 1981 8d 10g) rangy colt; useful performer in 1980; soundly beaten both starts at 4 yrs; stays 1m; suited by some give in the ground; sold 8,000 gns Ascot October Sales and is to race in Italy. *J. Gifford.* —

PRADERA 2 br.c. Jukebox 120–Garonne (Majetta 115) (1981 6g) Feb 27; IR 8,000Y; first foal; dam fairly useful winner over 7.5f at 2 yrs in Ireland; ran considerably better than finishing position suggests when tailed-off last behind One Degree in 19-runner maiden race at Newmarket in October, breaking very smartly and disputing lead for 4f (20/1). *H. Candy.* —

PRAED STREET 4 gr.c. Habitat 134–West Two 104 (Connaught 130) (1980 8g 8g 8fg² 13g 8g 10f 1981 8g 8g³ 10d 14d 10f 8.3fg 10.1fg) small, strong colt; plater; best run at 1m on a firm surface; often blinkered; sold 1,600 gns Ascot September Sales. *R. Atkins.* 46

PRAETORIAN 4 gr.g. Home Guard 129–Song In The Air 83 (Tudor Melody 129) (1980 7fg 10.1f 1981 8.3fg) behind in varied company, including selling; has worn blinkers and bandages. *G. Thorner.* —

PRAETORIAN GUARD 3 b.c. Home Guard 129–Prinia 77 (On Your Mark 125) (1980 6fg⁴ 1981 7d* 6g* 6g 7g* 8g³ 6f⁴ 8g 7g³ 8g* 8fg 8f² 7g 8d 8v³) compact, quite useful sort; gaining his fourth win when beating Melissa Jane a neck in handicap at Newcastle in August, showing a good turn of foot to get up close home after having to overcome all sorts of problems; had earlier won maiden event on same course, minor event at Thirsk and handicap at Redcar; also in frame in good company on several other occasions, including when ridden by 7-lb claimer, but runs badly from time to time; finds 6f on fast ground too sharp for him and stays 1m; acts on any going; has plenty of ability but tends to hang and isn't the most genuine of animals. *Denys Smith.* 93

PRAGMATIC 6 gr.h. Relko 136–Paracelle (Vimy 132) (1980 16fg* 14f 16f 1981 20f⁴) big, rangy horse; smart stayer at his best; bandaged in front when remote last of 4 to Ardross in Gold Cup at Royal Ascot in June on only start in 1981; acted on a firm surface but was better suited by some give in the ground; stud in Ireland. *F. J. Houghton.* —

PRAIRIE DUNES 2 ch.c. Red Alert 127–Peggy Dell (Sovereign Gleam 117) (1981 5d* 5fg* 5d 6d 5g³ 5fg* 6fg³ 6f) Apr 12; 7,200Y; fair sort; good mover; first foal; dam won over 7f at 2 yrs in Ireland; successful in maiden race at Newbury, minor event at Epsom and well-contested race at Windsor, putting up quite a useful effort when beating Burnbeck 2 lengths after dwelling at start at Windsor in July; yet to prove he stays 6f; best form on a sound surface although has won on a soft one; sent to Hong Kong. *G. Hunter.* 91

PRAIRIE QUEEN 3 ro.f. Roan Rocket 128–Pirogue 99 (Reliance II 137) (1980 NR 1981 10.2h⁴ 11.7f² 12d⁴ 12f²) 6,200Y; lightly-made filly; third foal; half-sister to winning stayer Admirals Barge (by Brigadier Gerard); dam, closely 65 related to good stayer Torpid, won over 1m; in frame in maiden races; will stay beyond 1½m; possibly not at her best on easy ground; looked irresolute final start; sold 25,000 gns Newmarket December Sales. *B. Hills.*

PRAISELIEN 3 b.g. So Blessed 130–Collateral 99 (Compensation 127) (1980   **77**
5fg 5fg 6g* 6g* 6d* 6g² 6g 6d² 6g 1981 10fg 12g 7g* 8g 8.2g² 8fg* 8f 8.2fg² 8g)
lightly-made gelding; successful in handicaps at Catterick in June (gambled on)
and Redcar in July, beating Sheer Delight by ½ length in 4-runner event on
latter course; by no means certain to stay middle distances; acts on a firm and
a soft surface; sent to Hong Kong. *T. Marshall.*

PRAJAI 2 b.c. Sun Prince 128–Anice (Crepello 136) (1981 5s³ 5v³ 5fg 6s 8.2s)   —
May 28; 1,400F, 4,600Y; leggy colt; half-brother to 3-y-o 1m and 9f winner
Chief Speaker (by Nonoalco) and a winner in Italy; remote third in minor events
in March; should be suited by 1m (had very stiff task in nursery when tried at
trip); blinkered third outing. *T. Fairhurst.*

PRANCING LADY 2 ch.f. Owen Dudley 121–Gay City 99 (Forlorn River 124)   —
(1981 6f) May 23; 800Y; half-sister to 1978 2-y-o 5f winner Blessingtonia
(by So Blessed); dam sprinter; 25/1, backward and bandaged behind when
always in rear in 15-runner maiden race won by Atossa at Doncaster in June.
B. Hanbury.

PREACHER MAN 4 b.c. Gulf Pearl 117–Miss Etta (King's Troop 118) (1980   —
10.5d 12g² 10.2g 15s⁴ 12.2d 12d 15s⁴ 1981 10s 12s 13fg 10.6s 11d 12d 12d)
poor form, including in a valuable selling handicap; has been tried in blinkers.
B. Lunness.

PREAUX (FR) 3 b.g. Cavan–Jolie Follette (Penhurst) (1980 NR 1981 14.6f)   —
sturdy gelding; first reported foal; dam placed over jumps in France; unquoted
and in need of race when tailed off in maiden event won by Shalimar at Ripon
in August. *D. Morley.*

PRECEDENT 2 ch.c. Continuation 120–Majestic Gift (Majetta 115) (1981 5g   —
6f) Mar 27; strong colt; in rear in maiden and minor events at Ripon and
Pontefract in the summer; sold 360 gns Doncaster October Sales. *J. Hardy.*

PRECIOUS EGG 2 ch.f. Home Guard 129–Gilded Egg (Faberge II 121) (1981   —
6fg 6g) Apr 17; small filly; fourth foal; half-sister to 2 winners, including Cork
and Orrery Stakes winner Kearney (by Sandford Lad); dam won over 6f and 7f
in Ireland; seventh of 16 to Kiva in maiden race at Newbury in August; 33/1
when making no show in similar 17-runner race won by Merlin's Charm at
Newmarket in October. *M. Smyly.*

PRECIOUS JADE 4 ch.f. Northfields–Love Letter 91 (Gratitude 130) (1980   **57**
7s 7fg 7.2d² 8g³ 8g² 7d³ 8.2s 1981 8d 7g³ 7g* 8fg² 7fg 8g⁴ 7f⁴ 7g) compact filly;
narrowly won handicap at Edinburgh in June; stays 1m; seems to act on any
going; suitable mount for an inexperienced rider. *W. Hastings-Bass.*

PRECIOUS MOMENTS 3 b.c. Furry Glen 121–Contourno (Continuation   —
120) (1980 5f³ 5f³ 6d 1981 7d 7.6g 6fg 8g 10d) attractive, rangy colt; very
good mover; has shown a little ability in maiden and minor events and a handicap but was tailed off final start; sold 2,600 gns Doncaster November Sales.
R. Price.

PRE-EMINENCE 5 b.g. Kadir Cup 97§–Predora (Premonition 130) (1980   —
NR 1981 16.5g) big gelding; winner over hurdles; tailed off in modest minor
event at Redcar in September, first outing on flat. *D. Garraton.*

PRELKO 6 br.g. Relko 136–Pretty Cage 110 (Cagire II 122) (1980 16f* 15.8fg   —
16s³ 16d⁴ 1981 16s) strong, compact gelding; has been fired; stays well; acts on
any going; wears bandages. *J. Fitzgerald.*

PREMIERE DANSEUSE (FR) 3 ch.f. Green Dancer 132–Opalia (Cambremont   **116**
121) (1980 NR 1981 10d 9s* 10s³ 8fg² 8d* 8f* 10f² 9.2d 10.5v 8s) half-sister
to 2 winners; dam won at 5f and 1m in France; successful in maiden race at
Evry in April, minor event at Chantilly in July and Prix de la Calonne at
Deauville in August, beating Rixe by 1½ lengths on last-named course; subsequently ran well in 3 fillies pattern races, including when third (subsequently
awarded second) to Leandra in Prix de la Nonette at Deauville; well beaten final
outing; stays 1¼m; acts on any going. *A Head, France.*

PREMIER LASS 2 b.f. Lochnager 132–Obedience (Reliance II 137) (1981 5d   **74**
6fg 5f² 7fg 6fg 6fg 5s³ 6v⁴ 6d⁴) Mar 30; 2,000F; small, active filly; half-sister to
a winning plater; dam ran only 3 times; in frame in maiden races and a nursery;
promises to stay 7f; acts on any going. *P. Mitchell.*

PREMIER ROSE 4 b.f. Sharp Edge 123–Florintina 104 (Floribunda 136) **117**
(1980 7.3fg 6f² 6d⁴ 7g² 7d² 7fg² 7g² 7g* 8g² 1981 10fg 8fg 7g² 7f* 7fg² 8v)
   The conditions of the Strensall Stakes at York in September favoured
Premier Rose. While she had regularly shown herself a very useful performer
she had never succeeded in picking up a prize worth £3,000 and accordingly was
allowed 4 lb. Two of her rivals, Star Pastures and Vocalist, were penalised 6 lb
as winners since their two-year-old days of a race worth £4,000; as a result Star
Pastures, odds on following wins from Tolmi at Newmarket and Goodwood and a
good second in the Hungerford Stakes at Newbury, actually had to concede the
year-older Premier Rose 2 lb. Star Pastures' task proved just beyond her.
Premier Rose, having taken up the running two furlongs from home, stayed on
courageously to hold Star Pastures by three quarters of a length. Premier
Rose was ex-jockey Eldin's second important success as a trainer, following
Prowess Prince's victory in the Molecomb Stakes.

			Silver Shark (gr 1963)	Buisson Ardent
		Sharp Edge (gr 1970)		Palsaka
			Cutle (ch 1963)	Saint Crespin III
Premier Rose (b.f. 1977)				Cutter
			Floribunda (b 1958)	Princely Gift
		Florintina (b 1968)		Astrentia
			B.S.R. (br 1957)	March Past
				Grand Fun

   As in 1980, Premier Rose won only once. She ran very well in defeat in her
race on each side of the Strensall Stakes—listed races over seven furlongs at
Newcastle (the Beeswing Stakes) and Doncaster (the Kiveton Park Steel Stakes).
In the former she failed by a head to catch Milk of the Barley, staying on well, and
in the latter went down by half a length to Kittyhawk, to whom she was conceding several pounds more than weight-for-age. On her other three starts, all at
longer distances, Premier Rose was well beaten. She was moved from Cole's
stable after her reappearance in the mile-and-a-quarter Prince of Wales's Stakes
at Royal Ascot, where she had set a scorching gallop with Sea Chimes before
dropping out quickly soon after the home turn. Premier Rose also showed in the
front rank until the last quarter mile in the Child Stakes at Newmarket. She
can be excused her final run on account of the desperate ground when seventh of
thirteen behind Aspros in the Grosser Kaufhof Preis at Cologne in October.
   Premier Rose's dam Florintina died in January, 1981. She was a useful

*Strensall Stakes, York—Premier Rose stays on strongly under
pressure to beat Star Pastures (rails)*

handicapper, a winner three times at seven furlongs and once over a mile. She was rather more able than her dam, a poor plater, and her grandam, who won three five-furlong sellers at two years. Of Florintina's five foals, three have won, the best being the sisters Shapina and Premier Rose. Shapina won three races up to a mile, including the Fred Darling Stakes. Premier Rose, a rangy filly who did well physically from three to four, also stays a mile, but has shown her best form at seven furlongs. She appears to act on any going and is a very tough and genuine filly. *E. Eldin.*

PREPARATION 2 ch.f. On Your Mark 125–Reddish Radish (Red God 128§) **82**
(1981 5g 5g³ 5fg 6f³ 6fg* 5fg 6g 5s* 5g*) May 9; IR 2,800F, IR 5,000Y; has a nice, smooth action; closely related to Irish 9f winner Murphy's Law (by Windjammer); dam ran once; winner of maiden race at Folkestone in August and nurseries at Lingfield and Newmarket late in season; beat Spanish Fury and 19 others on last-named; stays 6f; probably acts on any going. *R. Smyth.*

PRESENT COMPANY 3 b.g. Morston 125–Crisalgo 83 (Miralgo 130) (1980 —
7g 7g 8fg 8d 1981 15.5d 10d) little worthwhile form, including in a seller; should stay well. *A. Ingham.*

PRESS BARON 2 b.c. Touch Paper 113–Miss Dorothy 87 (Major Portion 129) **75**
(1981 6fg 5.8f³ 6g 6fg) Apr 14; IR 6,800F, 10,500Y; half-brother to 3 winning sprinters, including modest 1977 2-y-o 5f winner Mrs Bacon (by Balliol); dam won over 5f at 2 yrs; kept on when 1¼ lengths third of 12 to Dance of Life in maiden race at Bath in July, best effort; ran freely final start. *J. Dunlop.*

PRESS GANG 6 gr.g. Precipice Wood 123–Beige Etoile 54 (French Beige 127) —
(1980 NR 1981 9s) successful handicap hurdler; behind in maiden event at Hamilton in October, first outing on flat. *J. S. Wilson.*

PRESTON MANOR 2 b.c. Riboboy 124–Amatitlan (Amber Rama 133) **63**
(1981 7.2d 7fg 8g* 8d) Apr 5; 4,700F, 1,000Y; neat, lightly-made colt; first produce; dam second 3 times at up to 10.5f in France; third favourite and ridden by 5-lb claimer, made all and was clear from halfway when beating On Your Bridge by 2½ lengths in 22-runner seller at Leicester in September (bought in 1,900 gns); tailed off in similar event next time out; bred to stay 1¼m+. *A. Jarvis.*

PRESUMPTUOUS 3 b.f. Gay Fandango 132–Paracelle (Vimy 132) (1980 —
8.2s 1981 9d 12d 13f) big filly; half-sister to smart stayer Pragmatic (by Relko) and 2 winners in France; behind in maiden races; pulled hard when blinkered final start. *F. J. Houghton.*

PRETENCIOSA (FR) 2 ch.f. Anne's Pretender 124–Denosa 109 (Worden II 129) —
(1981 6d) June 8; 5,000F; half-sister to French middle-distance winner Zeddenosa (by Zeddaan); dam stayed at least 1m; 25/1 when eighth of 23 to Dalmally in maiden race at Leicester in November; sold 1,100 gns Doncaster November Sales. *G. Pritchard-Gordon.*

PRETTY GOOD 6 ch.g. Pretty Form 97–Jolie 64 (Jolly Jet 111) (1980 7.6f —
6h 7.2fg 5fg³ 6g 6g 5g⁴ 6g 8d 6fg 6f⁴ 1981 7.6g 6d 8fg 6g 7f) poor handicapper; best at sprint distances; seems to act on any going but goes well on firm; good mount for an inexperienced rider; has worn blinkers. *A. W. Jones.*

PRETTY LASS 4 br.f. Workboy 123–Pretty Cage 110 (Cagire II 122) (1980 —
12.2fg 12g 12.2f 12fg 12d 1981 16g) poor maiden; has worn blinkers. *R. Woodhouse.*

PRETTY MUSIC 3 ch.f. Music Boy 124–Pritillor 93 (Privy Councillor 125) —
(1980 5d 5fg³ 6g⁴ 5s 1981 7d 5fg 5f 5f 5.3fg) workmanlike filly; soundly beaten in 1981; stays 6f; possibly not at her best on soft ground; started slowly third start; sold 600 gns Doncaster September Sales. *D. Weeden.*

PRETTY PICTURE 2 ch.f. Grundy 137–Miss Pinkie 121 (Connaught 130) — p
(1981 6d) Mar 31; first foal; dam, good staying 2-y-o who stayed 1¼m at 3, is half-sister to Welsh Pageant and several smart performers; easy in market for 22-runner maiden race at Leicester in November and finished ninth to Late Hour; looked green and backward here and should do better over middle distances. *H. Cecil.*

PRETTY POTENT 2 br.f. Potent Councillor 98–Pretty Story 89 (Premonition —
130) (1981 7fg 10d) May 6; 360Y; small, lightly-made filly; half-sister to 1m winner Lucy Walter (by Galivanter) and a winner abroad; dam won 4 races at 1¼m; in rear in minor event at Warwick in August and seller at Pontefract in October; sold 370 gns Doncaster October Sales. *J. Tierney.*

PRETTY TOUGH 3 b.c. Firestreak 125–Idyll-Liquor (Narrator 127) (1980 —
5d 5v 5f 5.8fg 1981 8f 12d 12f 8f) rangy colt; only plating class; should stay
middle distances; blinkered last 2 starts. *N. Tinkler.*

PREVAIL 2 b.c. Steel Heart 128–Lavendula Rose 108 (Le Levanstell 122) 87
(1981 5g 5fg³ 7g⁴ 6fg⁴ 6d² 6g³) Feb 28; 47,000Y; neat, strong, attractive colt;
good mover; brother to useful 1980 2-y-o 5f and 7f winner Stats Emmar, and
half-brother to 4 winners, including Miss Mars (by Red God), a very useful
stakes winner at up to 9f in USA; dam, third in Irish Guinness Oaks, is half-
sister to Wrekin Rambler; in frame in varied company, coming closest to
success when neck second of 9 to Wink after making much of running in £4,200
nursery at Ayr in September; gives impression 6f is his optimum trip; acts on
a firm and a soft surface; blinkered final outing; withdrawn after giving a lot
of trouble at start on intended sixth appearance. *J. Tree.*

PRICE OF PEACE 3 gr.g. Averof 123–Kingdom Come 77 (Klondyke Bill 68
125) (1980 5.8fg⁴ 5fg 7g* 7d 6fg 6d 1981 8s⁴ 7fg* 6s⁴ 8f 7f³ 7g³ 7.2g 8f⁴ 8f
7g 9d² 8d² 11d³) big gelding; beat subsequently-disqualified Hissing Sid
3 lengths in handicap at Warwick in April; also in frame in varied company,
including selling; stays 11f; seems to act on any going; sometimes hangs under
pressure and isn't an easy ride; has run creditably in blinkers; has worn bandages
in front; trained part of season by J. Hill. *J. Doyle.*

PRICKLES 5 b.g. Reform 132–Flashy 107 (Sir Ivor 135) (1980 NR 1981 —
8g) lightly raced nowadays; stays 1m; needs a firm surface; has worn blinkers;
sold 340 gns Doncaster October Sales. *B. Richmond.*

PRIDDY BLUE 4 b.f. Blue Cashmere 129–Priddy Fair 108 (Preciptic 122) —
(1980 8f 7fg 8g 9fg⁴ 8f 10g 15.8fg 10.6d 12.2d 10s 1981 8.2g⁴ 10.6s 10.6s 9f
8g) leggy filly; plater; stays 9f; acts on a firm surface; has worn blinkers.
P. Asquith.

PRIDE AND FAITH (USA) 4 ch.c. Blood Royal 129 or Angle Light–Tomboy —
Tamele (Verbatim) (1980 7f 7fg 7fg 1981 7fg 8fg 7f 8fg 7fg 6fg) lengthy
colt; has been hobdayed; fairly useful (rated 97) at 2 yrs; has shown little form
in handicaps since; should be suited by 1m; acts on any going; blinkered final
start; often wears a bandage or boot on near-hind. *E. Eldin.*

PRIDE OF FAIRFIELD 2 b.f. Evanavitch 87–Lingala (Pinturischio 116) 50
(1981 5d 6g 6f 6f 7g² 7fg² 8fg 8.2d) Mar 16; small filly; bad mover; half-sister
to a winner in Malaya; dam lightly raced on flat and over hurdles; plater;
suited by 7f but ran badly over 1m; suitable mount for an apprentice. *P.
Rohan.*

PRIESTCROFT BOY 8 b.g. Chebs Lad 120–Alfreda 78 (Fidalgo 129) (1980 62
8fg⁴ 10.6g³ 8d 8d² 8d⁴ 8fg² 8fg⁴ 8g⁴ 8f 8fg 1981 8g 10.6s 8fg 8f 9g² 8f 10g²
10f² 11fg 8g 10.6s² 11d) one-time quite moderate handicapper; stays 1¼m; acts
on any going; sometimes wears blinkers; good mount for an inexperienced rider.
M. H. Easterby.

PRILE OF QUEENS 2 b.f. Three Legs 128–Queen's Bazaar (Queen's Hussar —
124) (1981 5g 5g 6f 6f⁴ 7fg 7d 6f) May 29; IR 1,100F; plain filly; bad plater;
not certain to stay 7f. *I. Vickers.*

PRIMA VOCE (USA) 2 b.c. Elocutionist–Que Mona (Ribot 142) (1981 5g* 105
6f* 6g) May 14; $25,000Y; well-made colt; good mover; half-brother to 2
winners in USA; dam, daughter of Oaks winner Monade, won over 6f at 4 yrs;
came with a strong late run to win maiden race at Sandown in July (by ½
length from Tap On The Head) and nursery at Kempton in September (looked
very well indeed when comfortable 2½-length winner from Macmillion); favourite
when top weight for valuable nursery at Newmarket in October but faded in
final 2f and finished in rear behind Vaigly Star; should be suited by 1m. *R.
Armstrong.*

PRIMSIDE 5 b.g. Connaught 130–Never Alone 86 (Never Say Die 137) (1980 —
16g 16g 16s 16fg 13g 16fg 17.1d³ 1981 19s 17.1d) small gelding; poor performer nowadays; suited by a test of stamina; probably acts on any going;
sometimes blinkered. *C. Wildman.*

PRIMULA BOY 6 ch.g. Sallust 134–Catriona 96 (Sing Sing 134) (1980 6f 96
6f² 6fg² 5g⁴ 6fg* 6fg 6g 6d 6s⁴ 6f² 6d 6d⁴ 6v 1981 6g 6g 6g 6f 6f* 6fg 6fg 6g⁴
6f³ 6fg 5.6fg 6d) useful handicapper; won Home Ales Gold Tankard at Nottingham in June by ½ length from Gamblers Dream; twice ran creditably afterwards;
best form at sprint distances; acts on any going; has worn blinkers but is better
without; goes well for W. Higgins. *W. Bentley.*

PRINCE 7 br.g. Prince de Galles 125–Regal Artist 72 (Breakspear II) (1980 **52**
8f 8f 8f³ 8fg 8fg⁴ 10.2g³ 9g³ 10fg 10fg² 11d* 12.2g 12.3d 8fg* 8f³ 9g 8.2s   1981 8fg
8f 8g 10f 8f² 8f 8fg 8f³)   poor handicapper; stayed 11f; was possibly unsuited
by very soft ground; successful with blinkers and without; tended to get behind
early on; dead.   *K. Stone.*

PRINCE ABWAH 2 gr.c. Abwah 118–Jeldi 58 (Tribal Chief 125) (1981 —
5s 5.1f 5f 6g 6d 7g) Feb 6; 2,000Y; 5,400Y; small colt; in rear in maiden and
minor events and a valuable seller (last of 29). *W. Marshall.*

PRINCE ALLEGRO (USA) 2 b.c. Full Out–La Franzette (Hitting Away) **75**
(1981 6d 6g⁴ 7d) Feb 21; $51,000Y; quite attractive colt; sixth foal; half-
brother to 3 winners in USA and Puerto Rico; dam, 6f winner, is half-sister
to smart Determined Man; favourite, didn't have best of runs when 3½ lengths
fourth of 22 to Tardous in maiden race at Lingfield in September; should
stay 7f; sold to National Horse BA 7,200 gns Doncaster November Sales. *J. Dunlop.*

PRINCE BEE 4 b.c. Sun Prince 128–Honerko 112 (Tanerko 134) (1980 8f² **128**
10fg 10.4f² 12fg* 12s² 12fg* 12g* 12f* 1981 12d² 12.5g 10g* 12d 10g⁴)
West Ilsley stables started the season with a powerful fleet of high-class
four-year-olds, headed by the Derby winner Henbit, the Irish Guinness Oaks and
Yorkshire Oaks winner Shoot A Line and Prince Bee, a colt who suffered only
one defeat—in the Irish Sweeps Derby—in his last five races as a three-year-old.
It would have been understandable had the owners of Henbit and Prince Bee
in particular succumbed to the financial pressure to retire such high-class colts
at the end of their three-year-old days; as things turned out neither Henbit nor
Prince Bee succeeded in enhancing his reputation, Henbit being retired after
only two races. Shoot A Line also had an undistinguished season except for
finishing second in the Gold Cup. Prince Bee won only once from five starts
but he is to soldier on as a five-year-old and it would be most unwise for anyone
to write him off: the bare facts of his record as a four-year-old do not tell the
whole story.

Prince Bee (b.c. 1977)	Sun Prince (ch 1969)	Princely Gift (b 1951)	Nasrullah
			Blue Gem
		Costa Sola (ch 1963)	Worden II
			Sunny Cove
	Honerko (b 1968)	Tanerko (br 1953)	Tantieme
			La Divine
		Be a Honey (b 1959)	Honeys Alibi
			Neola

Prince Bee wasn't seen out as a two-year-old and took some time to get the
hang of things in his first season. He didn't strike winning form until his fourth
outing when he battled on well in the Predominate Stakes at Kempton to beat
the subsequent Derby third Rankin, who conceded 5 lb. Five weeks or so later
Prince Bee beat all except Tyrnavos at the Curragh and then took successively
the Gordon Stakes, the Great Voltigeur Stakes and the Prix Niel, ending the
season only a little behind the best at a mile and a half and with the prospect
of making a shade more than normal improvement from three to four. Prince
Bee had given the impression that a mile and three quarters would suit him—
he had shown no great powers of acceleration and had needed to be rousted along
from some way out in most of his races. The lack of balance in the present
pattern of racing meant, almost inevitably, that Prince Bee would be aimed at
the big mile-and-a-half races as a four-year-old and he reappeared at the Epsom
summer meeting in the Coronation Cup. He looked in fine shape, clearly having
progressed well over the winter, and although he drifted in the market he
finished a creditable second to Master Willie, beaten two lengths; in a slowly-run
race Prince Bee couldn't quicken with Master Willie as the latter sharpened the
pace down the hill and round Tattenham Corner, but he kept on gamely and
was steadily cutting into Master Willie's lead as the post was reached. Judged
on this performance, Prince Bee looked set for a good season but little went right
for him afterwards. He came back without his front shoes, reportedly having
suffered some interference, when sixth of ten to Akarad in the Grand Prix de
Saint-Cloud in July and wasn't seen out again for ten weeks, missing the King
George VI and Queen Elizabeth Diamond Stakes which had been spoken of as
his main objective. He gave a good performance on his return to win the
Valdoe Stakes over a mile and a quarter at Goodwood, being driven out to beat
the three-year-old Noalto, who received 8 lb more than weight-for-age, by three

Sir Michael Sobell's "Prince Bee"

lengths. After a poor effort in the Prix de l'Arc de Triomphe, in which he seemed more strongly fancied than Hern's other runner, the St Leger winner Cut Above, Prince Bee ended his season with fourth place in the Champion Stakes, looking in tremendous condition and running very well although showing unmistakeable signs that the trip was too sharp for him in the best company.

Prince Bee's sire did most of his racing at a mile and didn't stay beyond a mile and a quarter; the dam stayed at least a mile and a half and her only foal before Prince Bee was the smart staying two-year-old Balteus who later showed fairly useful form at a mile and a half and won over hurdles. Prince Bee, a strong, attractive colt and a good mover, acts on any going and is genuine. There are more good races to be won with him. *R. Hern.*

PRINCE BEOWULF 3 gr.c. Young Emperor 133–Aibrean (Amber Light 114) **44** (1980 5fg³ 5fg⁴ 5fg 6fg 6d 5d 6d 1981 8s 7d 6g 7.2s 6d² 6g⁴ 7f 6f 6fg* 7g 6fg 5g⁴ 6g) fair sort; bought in 980 gns after winning seller at Carlisle in July; ran moderately afterwards; stays 6f; seems best in blinkers; sold 1,000 gns Ascot November Sales. *R. Hollinshead.*

PRINCE BLESS 3 b.c. So Blessed 130–Pearl Star 110 (Gulf Pearl 117) (1980 **78** NR 1981 8g⁴ 8fg³ 9g* 11.7g* 11.1fg² 16g⁴ 14g) 25,000Y; strong, attractive colt; good mover; fifth foal; half-brother to Startingo (by Petingo), successful at up to 13f, and to middle-distance winner Star Burst (by Busted); dam game performer at up to 7f; won maiden race at Newcastle in July and 6-runner handicap at Windsor in August, latter in good style by 5 lengths from Aldenham; ran on very well under pressure when 1½ lengths second to Blare in handicap at Kempton in September, best subsequent effort; suited by middle distances (never really going but was nearest finish when tried at 2m); acts on a firm surface; sold to Mrs N. Smith 11,000 gns Doncaster November Sales. *J. Dunlop.*

667

PRINCE COPPER 3 ch.c. Ampney Prince 96–Rose of Ennis 78 (Ennis 128) —
(1980 5s 5fg 5d 5f 5g² 6f 6s 6s 1981 6s 8f 7fg 6fg 10.1fg 8.3fg) small, close-coupled colt; plater; best run at 5f; sometimes blinkered. *R. Hoad.*

PRINCE DIAMOND 3 b.c. Prince Tenderfoot 126–Spare Filly 95 (Beau Sab- 81
reur 125) (1980 5fg² 5fg 6d 6g 1981 7s* 7s² 9d² 9s⁴ 10g² 11.7fg³ 10g) strong,
quite attractive colt; 5-length winner of maiden race at Doncaster in March;
narrowly beaten when placed at Stockton, Newcastle, Epsom and Windsor
afterwards, seeming to idle in front when going down by a head to Diwali in a
handicap at Epsom in June; stays 1½m; seems to act on any going but is well
suited by soft; ran moderately final start. *B. Hills.*

PRINCE DILIGENCE 4 b.c. Prince Tenderfoot 126–Cariole 84 (Pardao 120) 62
(1980 7fg² 8g² 8g 8fg* 8.2s³ 8fg 8d² 8fg* 1981 8fg 8fg² 8f² 8f 8.2fg 8fg 7.2v)
leggy, sparely-made colt; ran tubed; stayed 1m; acted on any going; sometimes
sweated up; occasionally wore a tongue strap; dead. *T. Barron.*

PRINCE ECHO 3 ch.c. Crowned Prince 128–Dawn Echo (Don II 123) (1980 **119**
6g 6s* 6.3s² 7g² 1981 7s* 8g 8s³ 5s*(dis) 8fg 6g⁴ 6fg⁴ 6fg 6fg 7g)
Vincent O'Brien has won the race named after his 1958 Gold Cup winner with
several of his potential stars in recent years: Nijinsky, Minsky, Apalachee and
Night Alert all started their three-year-old careers on a successful note in the
Gladness Stakes at the Curragh. So it was not surprising to learn that he
intended to run Storm Bird in the latest race prior to sending him for the Two
Thousand Guineas. In the event Storm Bird had to be withdrawn on the eve
of the race and Prince Echo, rated the third-best Irish two-year-old of 1980,
started favourite in a field of six. Prince Echo duly won, but by only a short
head from Cimon, to whom he was conceding 8 lb.
What the outcome would have been with Storm Bird present is difficult
to say. Prince Echo is a pretty good horse for all that the Gladness turned out
the only race he won. He did pass the post first, a neck in front of Jasmine Star,
in the Ballyogan Stakes over five furlongs at Leopardstown in June, but was

Mrs J. O'Brien's "Prince Echo"

subsequently placed last, having ducked both to right and left in the closing
stages, the race being awarded to the third horse home, Cooleen Jack. By and
large it was Prince Echo's fate to be campaigned in top-class races which he
simply lacked the ability to win. He made the frame three times in such events
—finishing third, at a length, to Kings Lake in the Irish Two Thousand Guineas,
fourth behind Marwell, Moorestyle and Sonoma in the William Hill July Cup,
and fourth behind Runnett in the Matt Gallagher Sprint Stakes at Phoenix
Park. Outings in the Two Thousand Guineas, the St James's Palace Stakes,
the Vernons Sprint Cup, the Diadem Stakes and the Bisquit Cognac Challenge
Stakes brought him nothing. He disappointed us in the last-named, with his
sudden collapse after going well to two furlongs out.

		Raise A Native	Native Dancer
	Crowned Prince	(ch 1961)	Raise You
	(ch 1969)	Gay Hostess	Royal Charger
Prince Echo		(ch 1957)	Your Hostess
(ch.c. 1978)		Don II	Grey Sovereign
	Dawn Echo	(gr 1966)	Diviana II
	(gr 1973)	Solar Echo	Solar Slipper
		(b 1957)	Eastern Echo

Prince Echo, a strong, good-quartered colt, cost 7,000 guineas as a yearling.
He's the only pattern-race winner from the last Irish crop sired by Crowned
Prince, who now stands in Japan. The dam Dawn Echo, who showed no sign
of ability in three races in England and Ireland, is a sister to the very useful
Seminar, winner of three five-furlong races at two years and fourth in the Queen
Mary and the Lowther Stakes, and a three-parts sister to the 1966 Beresford
Stakes winner Sovereign Slipper. Even better than these was one of Dawn
Echo's half-brothers, that wonderful gelding Boldboy. Dawn Echo's second
produce, a yearling filly by Be My Guest, fetched 42,000 guineas at the Newmarket Premier Sales in October. Prince Echo's third dam was the versatile
Eastern Echo, second in the Park Hill Stakes in between winning two good races
over a mile; the next dam was a sister to the St Leger winner Singapore.
Prince Echo is hard to weigh up so far as his distance is concerned. He
obviously stays a mile but has a lot of speed, and judging by the way he was
run in the second half of the season, connections regarded him as essentially
a sprinter. Perhaps he would benefit from a return to a mile. Prince Echo
acts well on soft going and hasn't run up to his best on firmish ground; he has
yet to race on really firm. He was blinkered in the July Cup and the Challenge
Stakes. He will be trained by Cecil in 1982. *L. Browne, Ireland.*

PRINCE ELO (USA) 2 b.c. Elocutionist–Family Planning (Cyane) (1981 **82 p**
7g 7g) Apr 10; $50,000Y; attractive, lengthy colt; brother to American 3-y-o
Financial Genius, a very useful 1m winner at 2 yrs, and half-brother to 3 winners;
dam, sister to minor stakes winner, won at up to 1m; unquoted and ridden by
apprentice unable to claim, noted making very nice progress without being hard
ridden when seventh of 18 to General Anders in £4,100 race at Ascot in September; 20/1 when behind in 15-runner Houghton Stakes won by Ivano at Newmarket the following month; will stay 1¼m; the type to do better at 3 yrs.
J. Dunlop.

PRINCE FANDANGO 3 ch.c.. Gay Fandango 132–Procession 118 (Sovereign **—**
Path 125) (1980 NR 1981 8fg) 39,000Y; quite well-made colt; brother to
6f winner In Rhythm and half-brother to 2 winners, including useful sprinter
Marching On (by Tudor Melody); dam 5f sprinter; easy in market and slightly
mulish in paddock, never got into race when seventh of 16 to Icen in maiden
race at Salisbury in September; sold 625 gns Ascot December Sales. *J. Dunlop.*

PRINCE GLEAM (USA) 2 ch.g. Son Ange–Romance First (Ambernash) **80**
(1981 5g 5.1f 6fg 6f 6g2) Apr 14; $20,000Y; rather lightly-made, useful sort;
good mover; first foal; dam, half-sister to $308,000-earner Crack Ruler, ran
4 times unplaced; showed improved form in 26-runner maiden race at Nottingham in August, going down by 3 lengths to all-the-way winner Al Hasa; gelded
subsequently; will be suited by 1m. *E. Eldin.*

PRINCE GUARD 2 ch.c. Home Guard 129–Crassula (Canisbay 120) (1981 **—**
8d 8s) Apr 9; 6,000Y; big, fair sort; half-brother to 3 winners, including out-
and-out-stayer Colway Boy (by Faraway Son); dam, winner at around 1m in
France, is closely related to smart filly Amicable; distant seventh of 17 to Barfoot
in maiden race at Warwick in October, second outing. *S. Matthews.*

PRINCE HESTER 2 ch.g. Sun Prince 128–Lady Hester (Native Prince) **66**
(1981 5s² 5fg⁴ 5g*) May 10; 8,000Y; small, lengthy gelding; second foal; half-
brother to 3-y-o 7f winner Petite Hester (by Wollow); dam, granddaughter of
Zanzara, won over 5f and 6f in Ireland; favourite on all starts, finally getting off
mark when beating Mosswern a shade comfortably by ½ length in 8-runner
minor event at Catterick in April; sent to Hong Kong. *A. Bailey.*

PRINCE LIGHTNING 3 ch.c. Royal Match 117–Up In Arms (Breakspear II) **62**
(1980 6g 7d 1981 10d 11.7g³ 12d 12g² 12d³ 12fg 13f²) plating-class maiden;
stays 13f; lacks pace. *R. Price.*

PRINCE LORENZO (FR) 5 b.h. Lorenzaccio 130–Check Royale (Meadow —
Court 129) (1980 NR 1981 12g) ex-French horse; won minor event at
Saint-Cloud and Grand Prix de Compiegne as a 3-y-o and also ran creditably
in smart company; last of 6 to King's Ride in £4,000 event at Lingfield in September, only subsequent start; stays 1½m; acts on a soft surface. *M. Ryan.*

PRINCELY CHIEF (USA) 9 br.g. Chieftain–Corner Garth 102 (Solonaway **47**
128) (1980 11fg 13g⁴ 12f 1981 13s 12g² 12.5g⁴ 12g 11g⁴ 12f 11.7fg) strong,
well-made gelding; poor handicapper; stays 13f; suited by top-of-the-ground.
D. Ringer.

PRINCELY DANCER 4 ch.g. Connaught 130–Italian Idol (Sheshoon 132) **§§**
(1980 8g 8.5g² 12f 10f 1981 8.2f 12g 12g) strong, fair sort; thoroughly temperamental and has been banned from racing by Stewards of Jockey Club; has
worn blinkers; sold out of J. Etherington's stable 850 gns Ascot May Sales.
R. Hoad.

PRINCELY GEM 2 ch.c. Sun Prince 128–Rockeater 94 (Roan Rocket 128) **70**
(1981 7fg 7f 8g 8.2d*) Mar 4; 5,400Y; small, compact colt; first foal; dam
stayed 11f; gambled on and dropped in class when staying on under hard driving
to beat Firemaster 3 lengths in 17-runner seller at Nottingham in September
(bought in 1,550 gns); will stay 1¼m. *J. Etherington.*

PRINCELY LAD 3 ch.g. Sun Prince 128–Edissa 66 (Honeyway 125) (1980 **41**
8d 8d² 8s 1981 10fg 8d 8g 8g 9d² 10s⁴ 11s) small, unimpressive gelding;
plater; stays 1¼m; sometimes blinkered; tends to sweat up. *R. Baker.*

PRINCELY WARRIOR 2 ch.g. Roman Warrior 132–Longwings 75 (Vimy 132) —
(1981 5g 5.8g 5d 6d) May 15; compact gelding; half-brother to a winning hurdler;
dam winning stayer on flat and quite a useful hurdler; seems of little account.
J. Holt.

PRINCE MAB (FR) 3 ch.c. Targowice 130–Princess Mab (Turn-to) (1980 **119**
5d³ 5.5fg³ 5.5d* 6g* 6s* 6fg³ 7g² 1981 8d 8g 7s* 7s 6d³ 7s) neat, shapely colt;
second foal; brother to winning sprinter Princesse Margo; dam won at 9f and is
out of half-sister to Sir Ivor; very smart at 2 yrs; won Group 3 Prix du Palais
Royal at Longchamp in May by 2 lengths from Diamond Prospect; off course 2
months before best subsequent race, when 5½ lengths third of 9 to Rabdan in
Group 3 Prix de Seine-et-Oise at Maisons-Laffitte in September; best form at up
to 7f, but wasn't disgraced over 1m, including when just over 6 lengths fifth of
10 behind Recitation in Poule d'Essai des Poulains at Longchamp in April;
didn't race on really firm going, but seemed to act on any other; usually blinkered;
retired to Haras du Petit Tellier, Argentan. *A. Head, France.*

PRINCE MAJ (USA) 3 b.c. His Majesty–Lady Rosse (Hail to Reason) (1980 **97**
6g 1981 11s⁴ 10d⁴ 10d³ 12.3g* 12.2f* 12.3g* 14f³) \$160,000Y; well-made,
attractive colt; in good form in summer and was gaining his third win in succession when beating Dark Proposal by 5 lengths in minor event at Newcastle;
had earlier won maiden event on same course (beat Irish Keep 6 lengths) and 4-
runner minor event at Catterick (made virtually all and beat Super Service a
short head); suited by 1½m; seems to act on any going; wears blinkers; finished
lame final start. *M. Stoute.*

PRINCE NONO 3 br.c. Nonoalco 131–Kissing 98 (Sing Sing 134) (1980 7f **74**
1981 10d 11.5d³ 12d² 12f* 12fg⁴ 12d) rangy colt; beat Cons Pal by 4 lengths in
maiden race at Beverley in August; gives impression he'll be very well suited by
further than 1½m; probably acts on any going; blinkered fourth and fifth outings;
sold to R. Hartop 11,500 gns Newmarket Autumn Sales. *M. Stoute.*

PRINCE NORTHFIELDS 4 b.c. Northfields–The Game 80 (Petition 130) —
(1980 10d⁴ 10g 1981 10fg 10g) attractive, lengthy colt; easily won minor event
at Lingfield at 2 yrs; lightly raced and little worthwhile form since; will stay
1½m; acts on a firm surface; sold to Mrs N. Smith 2,200 gns Ascot July Sales.
J. Dunlop.

PRINCE OF CAPRI (USA) 2 br.c. Cornish Prince–Queen of Capri (Forli) **91** p
(1981 6s³) Apr 17; $175,000Y; quite a well-made colt; closely inbred to Bold
Ruler; half-brother to 2 winners in USA; dam unraced daughter of stakes winner
Bold Consort, a sister to top American 2-y-o's Bold Lad (USA) and Successor;
20/1 and on backward side, acquitted himself very well when 3½ lengths third of
15 to Risk Taker in maiden race at Newbury in October, showing up throughout
and finishing 15 lengths clear of fourth; will stay 1m; should make a useful
3-y-o. *M. Jarvis.*

PRINCE OF KASHMIR 2 ch.c. Blue Cashmere 129–Matala 65 (Misti IV 132) **65**
(1981 6h³ 6s) May 20; good-bodied colt; fourth foal; dam winning hurdler;
apprentice ridden at 7-lb overweight when 9 lengths third of 7 to Charbonnel in
newcomers race at Chepstow in September; well behind in maiden event won by
Ellerene at Newbury the following month. *P. M. Taylor.*

PRINCE OF LIGHT 9 b.g. Laser Light 118–Royal Escape 94 (King's Bench **54**
132) (1980 10v 8f 10.6fg* 8fg⁴ 8fg 9g 8d 8fg* 8f 8s 1981 8g 8g 10.6s 10g* 9f
8fg⁴ 12fg* 10fg³ 10g 10f 12.2g 12fg) plater; successful in better company at
Beverley in June and Edinburgh in July; stays 1½m; acts on any going except
heavy; good mount for an apprentice; suited by an uphill finish and has won 5
times at Carlisle. *Denys Smith.*

PRINCE OF PRINCES 2 br.c. Bustino 136–Princess Runnymede 108 **76**
(Runnymede 123) (1981 7g⁴ 7d³ 8g) rangy, attractive colt; third foal; dam
stayed 6f; only quite moderate form in minor events and a maiden race; runs as
though 1¼m will suit him. *J. Dunlop.*

PRINCE OF SHEBA (USA) 5 b.g. Raja Baba–Miss Glamour Gal (Ambiorix —
130) (1980 5s 6g 6h 7fg 5.1g² 5g* 1981 5g 5.8g 5f 5d⁴) lightly-made gelding;
good mover; poor handicapper; stays 7f; probably acts on any going; sometimes
wears blinkers; sold 1,750 gns Ascot September Sales. *J. Sutcliffe.*

PRINCE OF SPAIN 6 b.h. Philip of Spain 126–Miss Meryl 80 (River Chanter **68**
121) (1980 7v³ 7fg⁴ 7g 8fg² 7h² 7fg⁴ 7h* 8d⁴ 8fg 7d³ 7fg 7f⁴ 7fg⁴ 7s⁴ 1981 7d⁴
8fg 8d² 7g 7v² 8d² 7f 8f 7.6fg⁴ 8fg⁴ 8h³ 8h 8fg⁴) quite a modest handicapper;
stays 1m; acts on any going; suitable mount for an apprentice; blinkered once
in 1980. *P. M. Taylor.*

PRINCE REVIEWER (USA) 3 b.g. Reviewer–Belle Sorella 99 (Ribot 142) **68**
(1980 NR 1981 8g 8fg 10.1fg³ 8s² 8s 8.2s 8d⁴) 47,000Y; attractive gelding;
closely related to French 1m and 1¼m winner Babbitt (by Bold Lad, USA) and
half-brother to Bel Sorel (by Lyphard), successful at up to 1¾m in France;
dam, middle-distance stayer, is sister to Ribofilio; placed in minor event at
Windsor and maiden race at Yarmouth in July; stays 1¼m; sold out of J. Dunlop's stable 6,600 gns Ascot July Sales after fourth start. *A. W. Jones.*

PRINCE RUNNYMEDE 4 br.c. Great Nephew 126–Princess Runnymede 108 —
(Runnymede 123) (1980 9f 10.2d 12s 10s 1981 7d 7g 7s 7f 6fg) neat, quite
attractive colt; poor plater; sometimes wore blinkers; broke a leg in July and
was destroyed. *J. Douglas-Home.*

PRINCE SANDRO 4 br.g. Hotfoot 126–Otra 88 (Sayajirao 132) (1980 8fg⁴ **95** d
10g⁴ 8fg* 8g 10.1d² 11d* 10fg⁴ 12g 13s² 12d 1981 12s 11s* 12g* 12d* 11s³
12g 12d 14fg) big, well-made gelding; fairly useful handicapper at his best; in
fine form in the spring, winning under big weights at Wolverhampton, Kempton
and Thirsk; stays 13f; suited by some give in the ground; has a good turn of
foot; sold privately out of F. J. Houghton's stable after fifth start and ran badly
for his new connections, looking none too keen on one occasion. *P. Cundell.*

PRINCE SANTIAGO (USA) 2 b.c. Cougar II–Hasty Aysha (Hasty Road) —
(1981 8g) May 25; $65,000Y; fourth foal; half-brother to 3 minor winners;
dam unraced daughter of Chilean Derby winner Aysha; unquoted and very
much in need of race when behind in 30-runner maiden event won by Farioffa at
Newmarket in October; has scope for improvement and may do better over
middle distances in 1982. *J. Dunlop.*

PRINCE'S DRIVE 3 b.g. Sovereign Path 125–Fille de Fizz (Ragusa 137) —
(1980 5fg 6g 7g 7fg 8g 1981 10s 10d 8.5d) poor maiden; well beaten in a seller
final start; blinkered fifth outing of 1980. *S. Woodman.*

PRINCES GATE 4 br.c. Realm 129–Consensus (Majority Blue 126) (1980 6f **124**
8fg 8d* 10d* 8g* 8d⁴ 8g* 9f 8s 1981 8s 8.5g³ 8f³ 8g 8fg* 8fg³ 8fg 8fg 8g 8s* 8v*
8s*)
    In recent times the Prix Perth at Saint-Cloud in November has been a happy
hunting ground for English horses with Lord Gayle, Sparkler, Dominion and
Jellaby all winning the race and Sparkler again and Gold Rod coming in second

*Prix Perth, Saint-Cloud—Princes Gate and Diamond Prospect dominate
the finish*

during the 'seventies. In 1981 there were two challengers from England, Cracking Form and Princes Gate, and it was a comment on how much the latter had improved that he was allowed to start at only 11/1. In mid-August Princes Gate had carried 8-1 in a valuable handicap at Newbury, receiving weight from nearly half of his opponents, and finished seventh to Commodore Blake. At that stage he looked fully exposed as no more than a fairly useful performer. He had run solely in handicaps, beating Teamwork at Sandown in July and running well to be third to the same colt in the Royal Hunt Cup at Royal Ascot on his third start, but the handicapper seemed to have his measure and his prospects of catching the judge's eye again before the end of the year appeared no better than average.

Princes Gate's devastating win in a £4,000 handicap at Ascot in October consequently came as something of a revelation. Looking very well he showed a fine turn of foot to storm away in the straight and won ridden out by eight lengths from Buzzards Bay, who had run creditably in the William Hill Cambridgeshire on his previous start. Another facile success followed at Sandown later in the month when Princes Gate cantered home in what had promised to be a competitive handicap, beating Pizarro by seven lengths. Princes Gate was obviously improving but even so he looked to have his work cut out in the Prix Perth. The race often attracts a large field and in 1981 eighteen took part, including the consistent Diamond Prospect, recently third to Moorestyle in the Prix de la Foret; the Prix Corrida and Prix du Rond-Point winner Daeltown; the Poule d'Essai des Pouliches third Ionian Raja and the Prix de la Nonette runner-up Premiere Danseuse. Confidently ridden, Princes Gate led a furlong out and always looked like holding Diamond Prospect as they drew clear of the remainder, eventually scoring by half a length with Ionian Raja four lengths further back. Diamond Prospect had admittedly had a hard season but the distance between him and the third suggests he ran to within a pound or two of his best and Princes Gate's performance was certainly a very smart one, well in advance of anything he had achieved before.

Princes Gate (br.c. 1977)	Realm (b 1967)	Princely Gift (b 1951)	Nasrullah
			Blue Gem
		Quita II (b 1962)	Lavandin
			Eos
	Consensus (br 1967)	Majority Blue (ch 1961)	Major Portion
			Gorm Abu
		Mutual Consent (b 1950)	Fairwell
			Sans Reproche

There cannot be many runners on the Flat at present like Princes Gate with a third dam foaled in the same year as Hyperion and a fourth dam who was a contemporary of the triple crown winner Gainsborough. His dam Consensus won over six furlongs at two in Ireland and has produced two previous winners, the good Italian horse Mispy and the French middle-distance winner Happy Bunny (both by Pall Mall). The next two dams both had long innings at stud. Mutual Consent won from one and a half miles to two and a half miles and foaled numerous winners, notably the very smart miler Pally and the game middle-distance handicapper Pally's Double, while the progeny of Sans Reproche won all over the globe.

Princes Gate, a 16,000-guinea yearling, is a strong, workmanlike colt who is ideally suited by a mile on soft going though he has won over a mile and a quarter and on a firm surface. To judge by his mark in the William Hill Lincoln (10-9) Princes Gate is unlikely to be spending his time in handicaps in 1982; it remains to be seen whether he will be up to beating the sort of opponents he will probably meet in alternative engagements like the Tote Lockinge Stakes and the Queen Anne Stakes. *H. T. Jones.*

PRINCE SOL 2 b.g. Roi Soleil 125–Princess Story 64 (Prince de Galles 125) — (1981 7.2v) Mar 20; 1,600F, 480Y; first foal; dam won two 8.3f sellers and is daughter of sister to Compensation; 20/1, dwelt when behind in 17-runner seller won by Market Rose at Haydock in October; sold 360 gns Doncaster November Sales. *A. W. Jones.*

PRINCE'S POLLY 2 b.f. English Prince 129–Suspicious Polly (Above Suspicion **103** 127) (1981 7fg* 7fg2 7fg2 8d* 7d3) Apr 3; lengthy, deep-girthed filly; third foal; dam won 3 times at up to 1¼m in Ireland; one of the best staying 2-y-o fillies in Ireland, the winner of a maiden race at Leopardstown in June and of Group 3 Silken Glider Stakes on same course in September; led early in straight in latter and kept on gamely to win by 2½ lengths from Realms Reason (rec 6 lb); ran well on her other appearances, finishing ¾-length second to Fly Start in Ardenode Stud Stakes, going down by only a neck to clever winner Woodstream in minor event, both also at Leopardstown, and putting up a particularly good effort when giving at least 4 lb to her 17 rivals in Group 3 Park Stakes at the Curragh in October, finishing 2½ lengths third to More Heather (rec 12 lb); will be suited by 1¼m+; acts on a firm and a soft surface; has run well for an apprentice; game and consistent. *T. Nicholson, Ireland.*

PRINCESS ARABELLA 3 b.f. Crowned Prince 128–Fair Arabella (Chateaugay) **73** (1980 NR 1981 7d 8d 7fg* 7f3 7fg 7f2 7f) tall, lengthy filly; half-sister to 3 winners, notably Oaks winner Fair Salinia (by Petingo); dam won at up to 1m in USA and is half-sister to top-class French miler Faraway Son; stepped up on previous efforts when quickening away to beat Johnnie Hussar by 4 lengths in maiden race at Redcar in May; placed subsequently in minor event at Leicester and handicap at Redcar; stays 7f; acts on firm going; ran moderately in blinkers final start. *M. Jarvis.*

PRINCESS BALLYMOSS 3 ch.f. Ballymoss 136–Wigmore Street 80§ (Aureole — 132) (1980 NR 1981 9s 11f) half-sister to a winning plater by Negotiation; dam sister to very useful Hotroy; tailed-off last in maiden races at Carlisle in June and Hamilton (blinkered) in August. *T. Craig.*

PRINCESS COSTER 6 b.m. Prince Regent 129–Costerini 70 (Soderini 123) — (1980 12s 12f 7f 7.9g 6g 5g 9g 8.5g 5g4 8.5d 5g 1981 12s 14g 9.5f 16f 12d) ex-Irish mare; fairly useful (rated 90) at 2 yrs; poor handicapper nowadays; stays 9f; often blinkered; trained by M. McCausland first 4 starts. *D. Elsworth.*

PRINCESS CURRENT (USA) 2 ch.f. Little Current–Captain's Mate (Turn-to) **75** (1981 7g4(dis) 7f4) Apr 9; $130,000Y; close-coupled filly; half-sister to 3 winners, including smart 6f to 9f winner Huguenot (by Forli); dam unraced sister to high-class Captain's Gig; failed to keep a straight course when tiring in final furlong and was disqualified after finishing 3¾ lengths fourth of 16 to Hula Ruler in maiden event at Sandown in July; beaten 5½ lengths into fourth place behind Hostess when co-favourite for 16-runner maiden race at Brighton the following month; will be much better suited by 1¼m. *M. Stoute.*

PRINCESS DINA 3 b.f. Huntercombe 133–Russian Princess 99 (Henry **69** the Seventh 125) (1980 7g 7fg 6f2 6d2 1981 8fg 8fg 8fg4 8fg3 9f4 9s) goodbodied, useful-looking, rangy filly; good walker and mover; in frame in maiden races at Salisbury and Goodwood in August and York in September; below form when blinkered final outing. *J. Dunlop.*

PRINCESS GALICIA 3 b.f. Welsh Pageant 132–Galicia 105 (Great Nephew **69** 126) (1980 6g 6g4 7g 6d4 6d2 1981 6g4 7d 7fg 8fg2 8d) well-made filly; in frame in minor event at Kempton in May and maiden race at Warwick in August; bred to stay 1¼m; sold 14,000 gns Newmarket December Sales. *J. Dunlop.*

PRINCESS GAYLE 3 b.f. Lord Gayle 124–Ermyn Lass 64 (Ennis 128) (1980 **107**
5s* 5g* 5s³ 5g 1981 6g* 6g 6f 6fg 6g² 6f 7s) lightly-made filly; poor mover;
half-sister to 3 winners by Carnival Dancer, notably smart sprinter Ubedizzy,
and to Middle Park winner Cajun (by Red Regent); showed improved form
when beating Pariscene comfortably by 2½ lengths in £3,400 handicap at Newmarket in May; finished clear of remainder and ran another good race when
neck second to Ackermann in Northumberland Sprint Trophy (Handicap) at
Newcastle in August; ran creditably twice in between, when fairly close-up
eighth of 16 behind The Quiet Bidder in Cork and Orrery Stakes at Royal
Ascot on third start (had no sort of run) and when sixth of 30 behind Crews
Hill in Tote Stewards' Cup at Goodwood; suited by 6f; probably acts on any
going; sometimes sweats up; didn't run up to her best last 2 starts. *M. Stoute.*

PRINCESS IMPERIAL (USA) 2 b.f. Blood Royal 129–Perfect Setting **60**
(Bold Lad, USA) (1981 5d 6s 6f 6f 7d* 8f 8.2s) small, quite well-made filly;
good mover; second foal; half-sister to a minor winner by Marshuas Dancer;
dam won over 6f at 3 yrs; favourite and dropped in class, hit the front
100 yds out and beat Storming going away by a length in 14-runner seller at
Newmarket in August (bought in 2,800 gns); will be suited by 1¼m+; possibly
needs some give in the ground; blinkered fourth start. *G. Pritchard-Gordon.*

PRINCESS KINI 2 ch.f. Sun Prince 128–Scarcroft 66 (King's Bench 132) **58**
(1981 5d 5g 5d) May 12; IR 24,000Y; leggy filly; half-sister to several winners,
including useful 1976 2-y-o King Croesus (by Green God) and useful sprinter
Last Tango (by Be Friendly); dam won at 7f; very reluctant to go to post at
Epsom in June on second outing but ran respectably to finish 7½ lengths sixth
of 12 to Cavallerizzo; again gave trouble before going down final start (well
beaten); will be better suited by 6f. *R. Simpson.*

PRINCESS KOFIYAH 4 b.f. High Line 125–Kofiyah 95 (Petition 130) (1980 —
8.2g 8g² 8g 9.4fg² 8f* 1981 7d 9fg 7f 7.6fg 8f) leggy, light-framed filly;
didn't find her form in 1981; will stay 1¼m+; acts well on firm going. *N.
Guest.*

PRINCESS MONA 2 br.f. Prince Regent 129–Monaspear (Breakspear II) —
(1981 6g 6s 7g) Apr 28; second foal; sister to Irish 6f to 1m winner Kaksi;
dam won three 1¼m races; in rear in minor event at Windsor in August and
maiden races at Newbury (last) and Newmarket (sweating) in October. *J.
Benstead.*

PRINCESS MOURN 3 b.f. Royal and Regal–Bella Fino (Major Portion 129) —
(1980 7.2d 8.2g 7g 10s 1981 12d 12d 12f 15.5g 10s) fair sort; little worthwhile
form in varied company. *R. Hollinshead.*

PRINCESS SALUKI 2 gr.f. Broxted 120–Misplanted (Hul a Hul 124) (1981 —
5g 6g 5g 6f 8fg 6g 7v 6s) Mar 30; 3,300Y; compact, sturdy filly; second foal;
half-sister to useful staying 3-y-o Krug (by Relko); dam placed at around 1½m
in Ireland; of little account. *R. Whitaker.*

PRINCESS SCARLETT 3 b.f. Prince Regent 129—White Goddess 65 (Red —
God 128§) (1980 NR 1981 10.6v 11d) sister to a winner in Austria, and half-
sister to 6f and 11f winner China God (by Cumshaw); dam only plating class; well
beaten in minor event and seller in October. *D. Francis.*

PRINCESS SCYLLA 4 ch.f. Ballymoss 136–Treasury (Henry the Seventh —
125) (1980 7d 7fg 10.2fg 1981 11.7fg 12f 11.7g 10fg 8s 6g) small filly; poor
maiden. *G. Balding.*

PRINCESS SEAL 2 b.f. Prince Tenderfoot 126–Finesse 87 (Miralgo 130) **94**
(1981 5g 5s* 5d* 5f² 7d) Feb 15; IR 6,400Y; quite attractive filly; half-sister
to 2 winners, including fair 6f to 1¼m winner Zarzaitine (by Murrayfield); dam
won over 1½m; 12/1, failed by only a short head to overhaul Fly Baby when
second of 11 in substandard Queen Mary Stakes at Royal Ascot in June; had
previously won maiden race at Navan and minor event at Phoenix Park, latter
by ½ length from Legs and Things; should stay 1m; acts on any going; looked
to have the makings of a useful filly at Royal Ascot but was off course subsequently until October, when remote fifth of 10 to Sharp Singer in Group 3
Larkspur Stakes at Leopardstown. *M. Cunningham, Ireland.*

PRINCESS VIRGINIA 2 br.f. Connaught 130–Virginia Wade 116 (Virginia **69** p
Boy 106) (1981 8d³ 7g⁴) Mar 2; rangy non-thoroughbred filly; good walker;
second foal; half-sister to 1980 5f winner Court Queen (by Hotfoot); dam
won five times over 5f; beaten 6 lengths when in frame in maiden races
at Wolverhampton (third of 11 to Misty Halo) and Leicester (ran very green

when fourth of 17 to Loup de Mer) in October; may prove best at distances short of 1m; looks the type to train on. *P. Cole.*

PRINCESS VRONSKI 3 b.f. The Brianstan 128–Vron 91 (Anwar 120) (1980 5fg 5f 6f 5g 5s 1981 5g 5d) workmanlike filly; little worthwhile form, including in sellers. *J. Toller.* —

PRINCE STRASSE 2 b.c. Dragonara Palace 115–Catherine Street (Pall Mall 132) (1981 5s 5s 5fg) Apr 11; 2,000Y; compact colt; useless plater; blinkered third start; sold 440 gns Newmarket July Sales. *P. Haslam.* —

PRINCE TEMPO (USA) 2 b.c. Timeless Moment–Se Anda (Tudor Grey 119) (1981 6h⁴ 6d) Mar 31; $45,000Y; sixth foal; half-brother to 3 winners, including Spanish Fake (by Sham), a very useful stakes winner at up to 1m; dam sister to a stakes winner; faded after coming under pressure 2f out when about 9 lengths fourth of 7 to Charbonnel in newcomers race at Chepstow in September; weak in market when in rear in minor event at Brighton the following month; sold to German International BA 1,100 gns Newmarket Autumn Sales. *J. Dunlop.* **58**

PRINCE VALENTINE 7 b.g. Crowned Prince 128–Feeval 96 (Alcide 136) (1980 NR 1981 10.6s 8f 10f 10f³ 8fg² 8d 12d) strong gelding; plater; suited by middle distances; acts on any going; often blinkered and has worn bandages. *D. H. Jones.* **44**

PRINCE VANDEZEE 2 ch.c. Some Hand 119–Casona (Upper Case) (1981 6s 8.2s⁴ 8d) neat colt; second foal; dam pulled up on one of her 3 outings; plater; 3¾ lengths fourth of 12 to Knightsbridge Game at Nottingham in October; stays 1m; bandaged first start; sold 310 gns Ascot December Sales. *P. Cole.* **63**

PRINCE WARREN 4 b.g. Pieces of Eight 128–Bobelle 62 (Pirate King 129) (1980 8.2d 8.5f 8fg 10g² 8g⁴ 12s² 10g 12g⁴ 1981 10v 10s 11s 10g 9d 8d 10f 10f 10fg 12v) small gelding; good mover; fair handicapper at his best but ran poorly most starts at 4 yrs; suited by middle distances; acts on any going but is particularly well suited by soft; sometimes sweats up; has twice worn blinkers; has been bandaged in front. *W. Stubbs.* —

PRIONSAA 3 ch.c. Crowned Prince 128–Frame Up 66 (Alycidon 138) (1980 6g² 1981 9fg 8g² 8fg 6fg² 6fg* 6f 6g⁴ 8d) well-grown colt; poor mover; won handicap at Ayr in August all out by ¾ length from Java Tiger; has run respectably at 1m, but best form at 6f; acts on a firm surface; has raced with his tongue tied down. *W. H. H. Williams.* **61**

PRIORS PADDY 2 b.g. Jukebox 120–Kix 71 (King Emperor) (1981 5s 5s 5g) Apr 8; IR 5,600Y; rather leggy gelding; of no account; blinkered when last in seller on third start. *P. Haslam.* —

PRIORY LANE 3 b.c. Martinmas 128–Jane Shaw (Galivanter 131) (1980 7fg 6s² 6fg* 7fg⁴ 6g 1981 8.2fg 8.2d³ 8d 10d⁴ 10fg 10g 7fg* 7g 8g 8v 8g⁴) tall, lightly-built colt; apprentice ridden when beating Rikasso Beauty by 3 lengths in handicap at Newmarket in August; also in frame in amateur riders event and 2 other handicaps; effective at 7f and seemed to stay 1¼m; seemed to act on any going, except possibly heavy; trained by S. Mellor until after fifth start; dead. *R. Hollinshead.* **88**

PRISON PAYMENT 3 ch.g. Song 132–Miss Filbert 95 (Compensation 127) (1980 5fg 5d⁴ 5g² 5g³ 5.8fg 5g 6g 6g³ 6g 5d³ 1981 5s* 5d 7d 6d 6d² 6s³ 6d 5.8g 6f 7fg 7d⁴ 6d) neat, strong gelding; ridden by a claimer when narrowly winning handicap at Salisbury in April; in frame 3 times afterwards, on last occasion in a seller; stays 7f; acts on soft going; none too consistent; sold 340 gns Ascot November Sales. *R. Hannon.* **68**

PRIVATE AUDIENCE 5 b.h. So Blessed 130–Private View 74 (Derring-Do 131) (1980 10g 14.6g⁴ 16g 11.5g 1981 14fg 14d 11.5³ 12g 12fg 12f 10f²) rather narrow horse; middle-distance handicapper; acts on any going. *G. Beeson.* **54**

PRIVATE BENJAMIN 2 br.f. Queen's Hussar 124–Beguiling 66 (Tower Walk 130) (1981 6s 6g) third foal; half-sister to 1979 2-y-o 5f seller winner Enchante (by Manacle); dam ran 4 times; in rear in sellers at York (didn't impress in paddock) and Newmarket (showed a little speed) in October. *C. Nelson.* —

PRIVATE CRAFT 4 b. or br.g. Private Walk 108–River Craft (Reliance II 137) (1980 10f 10g 7f 10s 9v 1981 8s 10s 12s 8fg 9d² 12f) ex-Irish gelding; plater; should stay 1½m; acts on a soft surface; blinkered when successful at 2 yrs but hasn't worn them since; trained part of season by E. Harty. *W. H. H. Williams.* **46**

PRIVATE LIVES 3 b.f. So Blessed 130–Private View 74 (Derring-Do 131)   **70**
(1980 5fg 1981 8fg* 8d 7d 7fg 10f 8.2g) leggy, lightly-made filly; having first
race for nearly a year when beating Fair of Face a neck in maiden race at Warwick in April, getting up on line; soundly beaten afterwards, but had stiff tasks
several times; stays 1m; sold 4,100 gns Newmarket Autumn Sales. *J. Winter*.

PRIVY CONSORT 7 b.g. Prince Consort 121–Sweet Councillor (Privy Coun- —
cillor 125) (1980 NR 1981 14.6f 16g 16f 13d) one-time useful performer;
lightly raced nowadays; suited by a test of stamina; acts on any going; suited by
a strong gallop; has worn bandages. *A. Balding*.

PROBABILIST 2 gr.g. Mount Hagen 127–Tiara III (Persian Gulf) (1981 5.8g —
7fg) Mar 15; useful sort; half-brother to several winners, notably smart Another
Realm (by Realm), successful from 5f to 7f; dam ran only once; 25/1, beginning
to make progress when badly hampered 1f out in maiden race at Bath in June,
eventually coming home eighth of 15 to Mosso; not seen out again until September
when well beaten in similar event won by Tender Venture at Salisbury; should be
suited by 7f+. *B. Hills*.

PROCLAIMER 3 gr.f. Town Crier 119–Deck (Le Dieu d'Or 119) (1980 5fg 5d³ —
6fg⁴ 7f 5d 6d 6g 1981 5fg 7f) lightly-made filly; plater; stays 6f; usually
blinkered at 2 yrs; missed break on reappearance and ran wide on bend only
other start. *Miss L. Siddall*.

PRODIGIOUS GIRL 2 ch.f. Windjammer (USA)–Scarletta 103 (Red God 128§) **60**
(1981 5g³ 5g⁴ 5f) Apr 24; 8,200Y; narrow filly; has a high knee action; half-
sister to 3 winners, including 3-y-o 1½m winner Lulav (by Prince Regent) and
fairly useful 5f to 7f winner Gerfalcon (by Falcon): dam at her best at 2 yrs;
fourth in minor events at Doncaster in May and Ripon in June, but was moved
up to third in Doncaster race after winner failed dope test; off course nearly 3
months before final outing; will be suited by further. *J. Etherington*.

PROFESSOR'S CHOICE 2 b.f. Mount Hagen 127–Nishat (Sayajirao 132) **86**
(1981 6g² 7d* 7d⁴) Apr 9; IR 6,400Y; leggy, rather narrow filly; good mover;
half-sister to several winners, including useful 1971 2-y-o 6f winner Jakim and
useful French 1m winner Spanish Fort (both by Fortino II); dam stayed at least
1¼m; favourite when winning 7-runner maiden race at Redcar in October by ½
length from Escapism, the pair a long way clear; again stayed on when creditable
fourth to Don Giovanni in minor event at Leicester in November; will stay 1¼m.
H. T. Jones.

PROFIT WARRANT 2 b.c. Ashmore 125–Stipa (Silver Shark 129) (1981 6fg **62**
6fg 6f 6d* 6f 6s 6g 6v) Mar 28; 1,300Y; tall, leggy colt; fifth foal; half-brother
to 2 winners; dam won at up to 6.5f in France; plater; apprentice ridden, beat
Parabems a short head at Lingfield in August (no bid); sweated up but wasn't
disgraced when fifth of 20 to Pair-of-Deuces in £2,100 seller at Goodwood the
following month on sixth outing; will stay 1m; acts on soft going; inconsistent.
P. K. Mitchell.

PROGRESSIVE 2 b.c. Hot Spark 126–Fair Path (Javelot 124) (1981 5fg 5fg —
6g) June 1; 7,500F; rather lightly-made, close-coupled colt; poor walker; half-
brother to 3 winners, including useful 1975 2-y-o 5f performer Trample (by
Tyrant); soundly beaten in maiden races; sold 330 gns Ascot October Sales. *J.
Sutcliffe*.

PROMENADE CONCERT 3 b.f. Tower Walk 130–Music Mistress 83 (Guide —
118) (1980 5f 5fg 7f 5g 1981 8fg 7f 8g 8s) leggy, rather sparely-made filly;
good mover; only poor form, including when blinkered in seller as a 2-y-o. *C.
Spares*.

PROPER GENTLEMAN 3 b.c. Manacle 123–Molly Morgan 91 (Pirate King —
129) (1980 5fg³ 5h 6g 6d³ 7fg 7d 1981 8g 10s 11.7g 8d 6g) leggy colt; quite
moderate form at 2 yrs; yet to prove he stays beyond 6f; sold 575 gns Ascot
September Sales. *J. Douglas-Home*.

PROPUS 7 b.g. Never Say Die 137–Amante 121§ (Tehran) (1980 NR 1981 8fg —
7f 9d 12.2fg) strong, compact ex-Irish gelding; won over 1½m in Ireland in 1977
and 1978; beaten in varied company over here, including selling; should stay well.
G. Richards.

PROSERPINE 4 ch.f. Proverb 127–Aucuba 98 (Hornbeam 130) (1980 10g⁴ **49**
12s 12d 1981 11.1s 12f 14fg 16fg 17.1h⁴ 16g 14fg 16g²) rangy filly; staying
maiden; acts on hard going. *P. M. Taylor*.

Tote-Ebor Handicap, York—Protection Racket stays on really well to win from Another Sam and long-time leader Shaftesbury

PROTECTION RACKET (USA) 3 b.c. Graustark–Protectora (Prologo) **122**
(1980 7fg 7d 8g³ 1981 12g² 12.3d³ 14g* 16f² 14fg* 14d* 18fg* 14d*)
    Few horses made more improvement in 1981 than Protection Racket, whose season began with a defeat in a Newmarket maiden race and ended with a clear-cut win in the Irish St Leger. He won four more races on the way, including two major ones, and impressed as a splendidly tough and genuine staying colt and a great credit to his trainer.

Doncaster Cup—Protection Racket sets a course record as he lands the odds from Heighlin

*Irish St Leger, the Curragh—Protection Racket adds a classic success
to his tally with this victory over Erins Isle*

Protection Rocket was well thought of as a two-year-old and started
favourite for the Houghton Stakes on one occasion, but he was something of
an overgrown baby and was handicapped by his lack of pace; the best he managed
was third in a maiden race at Newmarket on his final outing.   An inability to
quicken continued a short-coming in his early races as a three-year-old but
once his stamina was brought into play he really came into his own.   He won
a quite well-contested maiden event at Newmarket in May and a small handicap
at Yarmouth in June and in between ran an excellent race in defeat when a two-
and-a-half length second to Ore in the Queen's Vase at Royal Ascot, the season's
first long-distance pattern race open to three-year-olds.

Protection Racket was clearly improving fast and he became one of the
best-backed horses ante-post for the Tote-Ebor Handicap at York in August,
his next target.   Reportedly trainer Hindley felt that Protection Racket was
basically a two-mile plus horse and originally had reservations about going for
the Ebor, but the new part-owner Fradkoff, who had bought a half-share from
breeder Seltzer after Yarmouth, was keen to have a shot at the St Leger and
saw the Ebor as an ideal test for him; if Protection Racket was to have any
chance in the Leger he would have to win the Ebor off his mark (he had only 7-7
in the original handicap, and carried 8-1 after the weights had risen).   Protection
Racket duly won the Ebor, and in quite good style too.   He was settled in the
middle of the field as Shaftesbury attempted to make all the running and he
wasn't asked to improve his position until the field straightened up for home.
Protection Racket is a long-striding individual, and reportedly he had a little
trouble coming round the bend, yet once into the straight and ridden along he
began to make good headway.   At the two-furlong marker Shaftesbury was
still about five lengths clear and looking as if he could well win the race for the
second successive year; then Protection Racket began to peg him back
relentlessly, and got on top about a furlong out.   After that he wasn't seriously
troubled by the strong finish of Another Sam who followed him home in second,

a length and a half behind at the end.

The plan to run Protection Racket in the Leger was dropped when Shergar was announced a definite starter; in its stead he was aimed for the traditionally less well-contested Irish St Leger at the Curragh with a run in the Doncaster Cup on the way. The Doncaster Cup is rarely strongly contested nowadays and with Ardross withdrawn on race-day because of the firmish ground Protection Racket started odds on to beat the handicappers Donegal Prince, Heighlin and Prow. He accomplished his task without a great deal of fuss, beating Heighlin by a length and a half after travelling well throughout, and in doing so he broke the course record set by that great stayer Alycidon in 1949. He also became the race's first three-year-old winner since the gelding Piaco won in 1966. The Irish St Leger promised to provide a far more exacting test than the Doncaster Cup: Protection Racket was expected to have a fight on his hands against the likes of Erins Isle, who last time out had divided Kings Lake and Kind of Hush in the Joe McGrath Memorial Stakes at Leopardstown, and Ore who admittedly hadn't raced for well over three months. In the event Erins Isle proved Protection Racket's toughest opponent, without causing him too much trouble. Protection Racket was once again always going well and after taking over from the front-running Bedford two furlongs out he was in complete command. He stayed on splendidly under hands-and-heels riding to come home three lengths clear of Erins Isle, the remaining five runners well strung out. His win provided the trainer with a first classic win and gave stable-jockey Taylor, who had won on M-Lolshan in 1978, compensation for having missed the ride at both York and Doncaster through being unable to do the weight. Talk of running Protection Racket in the Washington International, not at all a suitable race, came to nothing and he wasn't seen out again.

Protection Racket's sire Graustark appears quite often nowadays in the pedigrees of European racehorses—he's the sire of Caracolero, Gregorian and Monseigneur among others—but the distaff side of the pedigree is a good deal less familiar. The dam Protectora is Chilean-bred and one has to go back to her great grandam Far Horizon to find an ancestor of hers who raced over here;

Mr S. Fradkoff's "Protection Racket"

Far Horizon won at Pontefract and Newcastle in 1946 and bred a minor winner over here before being sent to Chile. Protectora, by the Chilean triple-crown winner Prologo out of the maiden Dauka, was an outstanding racemare in Chile where she won nine times from six furlongs to a mile and a half. Her wins there include those in the Chilean One Thousand Guineas, El Ensayo (reportedly regarded as the first leg of the triple crown) and the Chilean Oaks, which she won by twenty lengths; she was also second in the Chilean Derby, apparently running well below expectations. Chilean standards no doubt fall some way short of those we are accustomed to but Protectora also went on to do well in North America. She won four races there and almost 95,000 dollars, gaining her most important wins in the Nettie Handicap and the Orchid Handicap, and she proved herself a smart filly by any yardstick. Protection Racket is her first foal. She has since had a colt by Exclusive Native called Protective who raced as a two-year-old in the States in 1981.

			Tenerani
		Ribot	Romanella
	Graustark	(b 1952)	Alibhai
	(ch 1963)	Flower Bowl	Flower Bed
Protection Racket (USA)		(b 1952)	Paresa
(b.c. 1978)		Prologo	Despejada
	Protectora	(b 1962)	Prince d'Orange
	(b 1969)	Dauka	Darika
		(br 1962)	

We look forward to seeing more of Protection Racket in 1982. A strong, rangy, late-developing type, he has improved virtually with every race so far and it's quite likely that we've still to see the best of him. A race such as the Gold Cup would suit him well—he's a relentless galloper who will keep pulling out more—but we understand his owners intend to race him over middle distances in France (he has been transferred to O. Douieb's stable). We would have thought him sure to win more good races when stamina is at a premium. He's an admirable sort, seemingly indifferent to the state of the ground, and he should be kept on the right side. *J. Hindley.*

PROTOS 2 b.c. Tumble Wind–Naughty Lass 82 (Run The Gantlet) (1981 **80** 7fg 7fg 7g 10s³) Apr 26; 9,000Y; strong, close-coupled, quite attractive colt; good mover; first foal; dam won over 1¼m and 1½m in Ireland; 2¼ lengths third of 20 to Sunny Look in maiden event at Nottingham in October, easily best effort; will stay 1½m; acts on soft going. *B. Hobbs.*

PROUD BREED 3 b.f. Nonoalco 131–Ruta (Ratification 129) (1980 6d — 1981 10d) smallish, rather lightly-made filly; behind in maiden event at Salisbury in May (apprentice ridden and in need of race); subsequently sent to Canada. *J. Dunlop.*

PROUD LUCY 2 b.f. Dubassoff–Dissipation 83 (Disciplinarian) (1981 6fg **58** 7f 5fg 5g 5s) Feb 5; 1,450F; fair sort; sister to 6f and 7f winner Winged Beauty, and half-sister to 2 winners, including fair 1980 2-y-o Dissipated Dollar (by My Swallow); dam won over 5f at 2 yrs; only plating class; probably needs further than 5f. *H. Collingridge.*

PROUD SUE 2 b.f. Owen Anthony 102–Primmy 56 (Primera 131) (1981 — 7fg 7f) Apr 22; 3,400Y; sister to fairly useful 7f to 9f winner Cannon King and winning sprinter Copper Beeches; dam stayed 1½m; behind in maiden races at Warwick in July and Yarmouth in August; sold 520 gns Doncaster September Sales. *P. Kelleway.*

PROUSTILLE (FR) 4 b.f. Armos–Chinoise (Kurun 127) (1980 8v⁴ 10.5v² **117** 9.5g 10fg 12g* 10.5g 12.5s² 12d² 13.5g 13.5g 12f 12.5d⁴ 12s 12g⁴ 1981 10s 15.5d² 15.5g² 20v⁴ 12.5d 15f 12fg³ 20s³ 15.5v² 12s² 12v*) smart performer; hacked up from Tarsiere in a minor event at Maisons-Laffitte in November; ran creditably on a number of other occasions, notably when second in Prix de Barbeville (short neck behind Kelbomec), Prix Jean Prat (beaten neck by Gold River) and Prix Royal-Oak (4 lengths behind Ardross), all at Longchamp, and Grand Prix de Nantes (went down by a length to Karkour); effective at 1½m and stays very well; needs some give in the ground; sometimes bandaged; has had her tongue tied down; tough and genuine. *P. Biancone, France.*

PROW 4 ch.c. Hotfoot 126–Bedeni 100 (Parthia 132) (1980 11fg 12g 10s 11.7g* **85** 13.3d 1981 12.5s* 12v² 12.3d² 16g* 16d⁴ 15.8g* 16g 15g 14.7d³ 14d 18fg⁴ 16g⁴ 16.1s) good-topped, good-looking colt; staying handicapper; successful at

Stockton in April (awarded race on disqualification of dead-heaters Syncopate and Ski's Double who both had illegal substances in system), Ripon in May (trotted up) and Catterick in June; acts on heavy going; blinkered twice in 1980; game. *S. Nesbitt.*

PROWESS PRINCE (USA) 2 b.c. Cornish Prince–Irish Reel (Irish Lancer) **104** (1981 5g² 5d 5g* 5f² 6fg³ 5fg* 6d 5g²) May 7; $67,000Y; quite attractive, rather leggy colt; excellent mover; fourth foal; closely related to a winner by Reviewer; dam stakes-placed winner of 11 races at up to 7f; came through strongly in final furlong to win Group 3 Molecomb Stakes at Goodwood in July by 1½ lengths from Hazim; had previously won maiden race at Doncaster in May; also placed in 3 pattern races, failing by only a neck to hold off Day Is Done after hanging badly left in Norfolk Stakes at Royal Ascot, finishing 2 lengths third of 11 to End of the Line, after looking very dangerous, in Anglia Television July Stakes at Newmarket and coming out clear second when beaten 4 lengths by Peterhof in 7-runner Flying Childers Stakes at Doncaster's St Leger meeting (sweated up quite badly); ran badly in Gimcrack Stakes at York in August; gives impression he barely stays 6f; needs a sound surface; evidently not the easiest of rides; sent to race in USA. *E. Eldin.*

P'TITE TETE (FR) 5 b.h. Tombeur–Socquette (Silnet 131) (1980 10g 10.6g² **120** 9.2d 9.7d⁴ 11g 10d* 10g 13.5g 10g* 10f³ 10g² 12s² 1981 10.5v* 11.5d 12fg 9.2s* 9.7s* 8.5f 8.5d² 10s 12g⁴) sixth living foal; brother to 2 winners in France, including smart middle-distance filly Rosy Ride; dam won 4 times at up to 11f in France; showed improved form in 1981, winning handicap at Saint-Cloud and 70,000 francs event and Prix Dollar at Longchamp; beat Falamoun by ¾ length in last-named in May; subsequently sent to USA and finished second to Rossi Gold in Swoon's Son Handicap at Arlington Park in August; best at up to 1¼m; suited by some give in the ground; trained by G. Delloye first 5 starts. *R. Frankel, USA.*

Mr S. L. Liem's "Prowess Prince"

PTS PONTOON 3 ch.g. Roi Soleil 125–Miss Cervinia 72 (Memling) (1980 —
NR 1981 12s 12fg 16fg 12d) lightly-built gelding; third foal; brother to a
winner in Sweden; dam stayed 1½m; no sign of ability in maiden races and a
claimer; sold 1,400 gns Ascot September Sales. *G. Harwood.*

PUBLIC OPINION 4 b.g. Run The Gantlet–Melodramatic 112 (Tudor Melody —
129) (1980 14f⁴ 12f⁴ 14g* 14g² 16.5g* 14fg² 16g⁴ 14s* 16g 16v* 16s 1981 16d
16.1s 22.2f) small, rather lightly-made gelding; staying handicapper; successful
at Bellewstown, Killarney, Galway and Listowel in 1980; soundly beaten in 1981,
including in Queen Alexandra Stakes at Royal Ascot on final start; stays well;
acts on any going. *M. Kauntze, Ireland.*

PUESDOWN 2 ch.f. Gay Fandango 132–Pewsey 96 (Appiani II 128) (1981 **82**
.5g 5fg 6f 7g 6d⁴ 6s*) Mar 31; IR 9,000F, 10,000Y; small, workmanlike filly;
good walker; third produce; dam won twice over 5f at 2 yrs; improved when
raced on soft ground in the autumn and won 13-runner maiden event at Hamilton
by 2½ lengths from Montroan; promises to stay 7f. *N. Guest.*

PUFF OF SMOKE 2 b.g. Godswalk 130–Bay Tree (Relko 136) (1981 5.8g **83**
5.8d 6fg² 7g* 7d 7fg) Apr 17; IR 13,000F, IR 10,000Y; rather lightly-made
gelding; half-brother to 1976 2-y-o 6f winner Realm Tree (by Realm), subsequently
successful abroad, and to 2 other winners; dam Irish 1½m winner; won 18-runner
maiden race at Salisbury in July by a length from Tidworth Tattoo with rest well
strung out; suited by 7f and may well stay 1m; best form on a sound surface.
J. Sutcliffe.

PULHAM VENTURE 4 b.g. Tudor Music 131–Mille Fleurs (Floribunda 136) —
(1980 10s⁴ 10g³ 8.2g 8fg 8.2g⁴ 8g 8fg 10fg⁴ 8.2s 1981 9s 7g 6fg) small gelding;
plater; stays 1¼m; has worn blinkers; sold to K. Morgan 420 gns Ascot August
Sales. *D. Weeden.*

PULLMAN EXPRESS 2 b.g. Bay Express 132–La Presidente 69 (Primera 131) —
(1981 5f 7f 10d) Mar 22; 5,000Y (privately); fair sort; half-brother to fairly
useful 1979 2-y-o 7f winner Black Earl (by So Blessed); dam won over 1½m;
unquoted when well beaten in sellers; sold to BBA 740 gns Newmarket Autumn
Sales and has been exported to Belgium. *P. Rohan.*

PULSE RATE 5 b.g. Prince Tenderfoot 126–Florence Nightingale 78 (Above —
Suspicion 127) (1980 10d 8g 11s* 9f³ 1981 12g) quite an attractive gelding;
useful performer in 1980; ran just once at 5 yrs when behind in William Hill
November Handicap at Doncaster won by Lafontaine; probably stays 1½m;
acts on any going; genuine. *M. H. Easterby.*

PULVERATOR (USA) 3 b.g. Annihilate 'Em–Fabric (Loom) (1980 NR —
1981 10d 12fg) $35,000Y; lengthy gelding; third foal; half-brother to a minor
winner by Dynastic; dam won 4f claiming race at 3 yrs; in rear at Sandown in
June and Brighton (led 7f) in July; sold 1,200 gns Ascot Sales later in July.
B. Swift.

PUNCTILIO (USA) 2 b.c. Forli–Minstrelete (Round Table) (1981 7g*) **88 p**
Mar 11; $185,000Y; second foal; half-brother to a winner in USA; dam, winner
over 1m, is half-sister to top-class Gay Fandango (by Forli); co-favourite when
impressively beating Charity Bid by 4 lengths in 16-runner maiden race at the
Curragh in September; will stay 1m; a very useful colt in the making. *V.
O'Brien, Ireland.*

PURE LUST 2 ch.c. Sallust 134–St Rosalie (Aureole 132) (1981 5g 5f 6g **77**
7f 7g 8g³ 8g²) May 21; IR 6,000Y; compact colt; half-brother to 3 winners,
including 1m and 1½m winner Mount Grace (by Mountain Call); plater; attracted
virtually no market support on his first 6 starts but, following his performance
on sixth outing (made up a deal of ground and looked a most unfortunate loser
when close third at Newmarket) was heavily gambled on in selling nursery at
Doncaster in October and (sent Penny's Dream a length; relegated to second
here for hampering runner-up; will be suited by 1¼m; well capable of gaining
compensation in 1982 and is one very much to keep an eye on in plating company.
P. Rohan.

PURNIMA 2 b.g. Prince Tenderfoot 126–Chandravati (Hard Tack 111§) **75**
(1981 6g 5g⁴ 5fg⁴ 6s² 6s*) Mar 24; IR 13,000F, 19,000Y; strong, good-bodied,
attractive gelding; half-brother to several winners here and abroad, including
prolific Italian winner American Graffiti (by Saintly Song); dam placed in France;
well backed when beating Orange Silk 1¼ lengths in valuable 15-runner seller at
York in October (bought in 8,600 gns); rather unfortunate second to Pair-of-
Deuces in similar event at Goodwood the previous month; suited by 6f, and will
stay 7f; seems to act on any going. *J. Sutcliffe.*

Mr Denis McCarthy's "Punctilio"

PURRRFECT MOVER 3 ch.g. Snow Warning 64–Peral Five 72 (Will Somers —
114§) (1980 NR 1981 15.5s) third foal; half-brother to very useful 9f to
14.7f winner Try Sandicliffe (by Star Appeal); dam stayed 1½m; last of 20 behind
Tree Mallow in maiden race at Folkestone in October. *M. Bolton.*

PUSEY STREET 4 ch.f. Native Bazaar 122–Diamond Talk (Counsel 118) **80**
(1980 5fg³ 6f 6f⁴ 5f 5.8fg³ 5d² 5fg³ 5f³ 6s 8h 5f 5.8g 6fg⁴ 6fg³ 6d 1981 6s 6s
5.8g 5.8d³ 6f 6g 6f⁴ 5.8f* 5d* 5fg 5h 5fg 5.8g 5d 5s) leggy, light-framed filly;
sprint handicapper; won at Bath and Windsor in the summer; acts on any
going; suitable mount for a boy. *J. Bosley.*

PUTRA TINJAR 2 b.c. Owen Anthony 102–Anwyl 104 (Welsh Abbot 131) **53**
(1981 5d 6f 5fg³ 5f 5f) Mar 26; small colt; brother to 6f winner Payin Anthony
and a winner in Malaya; dam won over 6f at 2 yrs; poor plater; should stay 6f;
sold to W. Stubbs 360 gns Ascot August Sales. *J. Holt.*

PUTT WOOD 2 ch.f. Record Token 128–Orma (Double Jump 131) (1981 6fg **62**
5fg 6fg⁴ 7.6g) Apr 1; leggy filly; first foal; dam plating-class half-sister to Tudor
Music; seemed to have very stiff task, even with bottom weight, in 7.6f nursery
at Lingfield in September and in circumstances ran well to finish 7½ lengths
fifth to Santella Man; evidently needs 7f+. *J. Winter.*

PUY-DE-VENT 4 b.c. Tumble Wind–Puya (Psidium 130) (1980 7f 6f 5fg³ **51**
5d 5g 5g 5fg 5g 6f² 1981 7d 7fg⁴ 8d 5fg) strong, attractive colt; stays 7f;
acts on firm going; best in blinkers; has shown signs of temperament. *M. Tate.*

PYKESTAFF 4 b.c. Giacometti 130–Miss Melanie (Hard Ridden 131) (1980 **48**
7s⁴ 6f⁴ 8h 7fg 6f² 7g 8g 10f 6g³ 6g 7g 7g 6d 6d 1981 10s 10s 6fg 12d 7g⁴ 7s 7g
6fg 6f² 6fg 7f² 6f⁴ 6g 8d 6g 8g) leggy colt; plater; best at up to 7f; acts on
firm going; often wears blinkers; sometimes sweats up. *C. Austin.*

PYMOOR PET 3 b.f. Mummy's Pet 125–Gold Ribbon 106 (Blast 125) (1980 5d **78**
1981 5d 5fg* 6g) neat filly; made virtually all on advantageous far side and went
clear from distance when beating Charlie's Song by 5 lengths in 17-runner
maiden race at Sandown in April (25/1 and apprentice ridden); best at 5f;
possibly needs a sound surface. *P. Cole.*

Q

QUACK SHOT (USA) 4 b.f. Quack–Bombycid (Shantung 132) (1980 8g 10fg —
1981 10.1fg) narrow filly; poor form, including in a seller; has worn blinkers.
D. Wintle.

QUAESTOR 3 b.g. Track Spare 125–Syltung (Shantung 132) (1980 5d 5s **78**
7g⁴ 7g 1981 9d 8f 10.2f 12f* 12f* 12fg) fair sort; dropped in class when
making most of running and beating Hego's Hero by 6 lengths in seller at
Thirsk in August (no bid); showed better form when beating Green Memory by
1¼ lengths in 4-runner non-seller at Leicester later in month; stays 1½m; probably
acts on any going; often sweats up; had stiffish task final start; sent to France.
J. Hardy.

QUAE SUPRA 4 ch.f. On Your Mark 125–Lunar Star (Star Gazer 123) **57**
(1980 6f 5fg 5d⁴ 5d* 5g⁴ 5fg⁴ 5fg 1981 6s 5f² 5f 5f³ 5h 5fg² 5g 5d) sprint
handicapper; best at 5f; probably acts on any going; usually wears blinkers.
P. Cundell.

QUAGLINO 3 ch.g. Sandford Lad 133–Esprit d'Or 86 (Jolly Jet 111) (1980 —
NR 1981 8f 8h) 9,800Y; first foal; dam, half-sister to high-class miler Gold
Rod, won 1m amateur riders race; in rear in maiden races at Pontefract in June
(moved poorly to start) and Chepstow in August; sold out of W. O'Gorman's
stable 460 gns Newmarket July Sales. *J. Bosley.*

QUAINT 3 b.f. St Paddy 133–Quine 91 (Counsel 118) (1980 5d 7d 7g⁴ 7fg 9d —
1981 6f 12d 10.4d 8fg) quite an attractive filly; disappointing maiden; stays
7f (well beaten over further); lacks scope. *N. Henderson.*

QUAKER STAR 5 b.g. Blast 125–Star of Bethlehem 77 (Arctic Star) (1980 8f —
8fg² 9g 9g² 8fg³ 10s³ 8t 8fg⁴ 8fg 8g 8s³ 1981 8v 8fg 8.2t 8t 8g 10g 8s 8.2d)
neat gelding; poor handicapper; soundly beaten in valuable seller fifth start;
seems to stay 1¼m; acts on any going; ran poorly in blinkers once; has shown
a tendency to hang. *B. Lunness.*

QUALITAIR PRINCE 2 b.c. Saulingo 122–Sabra's Star 65 (Midsummer **66**
Night II 117) (1981 5g 5g 6g 7f 6g⁴ 7g 8d*) Mar 28; IR 2,400Y; rangy colt;
half-brother to Irish 1978 2-y-o 5f and 7.9f winner Highest Regards (by Pitcairn),
subsequently successful abroad; dam placed over 1m; improved in the autumn
and was always going well when winning 7-runner selling nursery at Redcar
in October by 2½ lengths from Idle Warrior; attracted no bid; suited by 7f and
1m; acts on a soft surface. *P. Rohan.*

QUALITY OF MERCY 3 b.f. Sovereign Path 125–Taking Silk (Shantung 132) **74**
(1980 NR 1981 7v² 7.6g* 8g² 10.1fg⁴ 12g 12fg) 44,000Y; strong, deep-
girthed filly; sister to Romantic Love, disqualified winner of 1978 Italian
1,000 Guineas, and half-sister to 3 winners; dam never ran; won maiden race
at Lingfield in June; second in similar event at Goodwood and in minor event
at Salisbury; best form at up 1m; possibly needs some give in the ground;
game; slowly away final start. *G. Harwood.*

QUALITY ROAD 3 b.g. Roman Warrior 132–Llynian 81 (Ballylinan 118) **61**
(1980 5v 5g⁴ 5f² 5h² 5f³ 6d 5d³ 6g 5f 5g* 5fg 6d 5d 5f² 5f 5d 1981 6s 5d 6g*
6g³ 5d² 6g² 5s* 6s 5fg 6fg 8f 6d) neat, strong gelding; won seller at Pontefract
in April (bought in 1,800 gns) and apprentice handicap at Haydock in June;
stays 6f; acts on any going; usually wears blinkers (didn't at Haydock);
didn't run up to his best last 5 starts, including in sellers; trained most of season
by G. Richards. *N. Tinkler.*

QUALITY SUPREME 6 gr.g. No Mercy 126–Stolen Love 85 (Alcide 136) —
(1980 NR 1981 10s 12g 9d 8fg³ 10.6s 9g 8fg 9g³ 8g⁴ 10.4s 8g) poor maiden;
probably stays 10.6f; well suited by top-of-the-ground; has worn blinkers;
suitable mount for an inexperienced rider. *Denys Smith.*

QUAM CELERRIME 3 gr.f. Hasty Word 84–Hasty Decision 85 (Elopement —
125) (1980 5g 5f 6g 6fg 7fg 6d⁴ 7g 8.2d 8fg 8fg 1981 12f 13.8fg 16f 13.8g 13.8g)
workmanlike filly; of little account; usually blinkered at 2 yrs. *W. Bentley.*

QUARRY BANK 6 b.g. Be Friendly 130–Farafa (Sing Sing 134) (1980 5d **50**
6g⁴ 6z 7fg 5g 8.2d* 6s 6s 7s 1981 8s 8.2g 6z² 7v* 6d 7s) plater; won non-
selling apprentice handicap at York in October; stays 1m; acts well on soft
going; has been tried in blinkers. *S. Nesbitt.*

QUAY BOY 3 b.c. Sandford Lad 133–Princess Quay (Babur 126) (1980 **80**
5fg 5f* 5f* 6g 6g 1981 5.8g 5v* 5.8g² 5.1f* 5g⁴ 5fg 5fg 5.8g 5s) good-quartered,

quite attractive colt; successful in handicaps at Goodwood in May (made all and beat Jade Empress by 5 lengths) and Yarmouth in June (ridden along most of the way and beat Delta's Pride by 1½ lengths); ran well in between; should stay 6f; acts on any going; best in blinkers nowadays; sent to Hong Kong. *R. Laing.*

QUAY MAN 6 ch.g. Quayside 124–Hannah Mary 80 (Faberge II 121) (1980 NR 1981 13d 16fg 20.4fg) quite moderate at his best; lightly raced on flat nowadays; stays 1½m; has worn blinkers and bandages. *J. S. Wilson.* —

QUDESA 2 ch.c. Swing Easy 126–Gambit (King's Troop 118) (1981 5d 8g) Mar 6; 7,400Y; rangy colt; has scope; half-brother to 6f winner Migrant (by My Swallow); dam closely related to outstanding sprinter Floribunda; unquoted when in rear in 14-runner maiden races at York in May and Ayr in September (last behind Outlaw, probably needing race). *K. Stone.* —

QUEEN BERENGARIA (CYP) 3 ch.f. Esperos–Turnbeam (Hornbeam 130) (1980 7d 1981 12g 12f 10.1g) tall, useful-looking filly; ran best race when never-dangerous fifth of 16 behind Downbeat in maiden event at Windsor in August on final start. *J. Dunlop.* —

QUEEN OF MACEDON (USA) 2 b.f. An Act–Little Corrie (Exclusive Nashua) (1981 5fg) Apr 6; $19,000Y, $110,000 2-y-o; fifth foal; dam won 6 times at up to 6f in USA, including claiming events; sire high-class winner at up to 9f; 15/2 when 9 lengths fifth of 18 to Laura Jenney in maiden race at Windsor in July, only outing; may do better when tackling 1m+. *M. Albina.* —

QUEEN OF THE BLUES 2 b.f. Steel Heart 128–Social Smash (Social Climber) (1981 5d⁴ 5g 5fg* 6f 5fg 5f⁴ 5g³) Feb 7; 18,000Y; lengthy, quite useful sort; half-sister to Irish 1979 2-y-o 7f and 8.5f winner Moving in Sound (by Targowice) and a winner in USA by Captain's Gig; dam, placed at 3 yrs in USA, is half-sister to Belmont Stakes winner Sherluck; held on to win 13-runner maiden race at Redcar in July by ¾ length from Favoured Lady after being clear 2f out; had stiff tasks subsequently, wearing blinkers when in frame in £4,000 race at Thirsk and nursery at Edinburgh (top weight) in September; gives impression 5f is her trip. *M. W. Easterby.* **79**

QUEEN OF THE KOP 3 b.f. Queen's Hussar 124–Bound Over (Taj Dewan 128) (1980 6g 8f 8fg 1981 12g 12d⁴ 12f³ 16fg 14fg³ 16f 14g⁴ 16.5g⁴ 10s³) small filly; in frame in varied races, including in an amateur riders race; seems not to stay 2m; sold 1,600 gns Newmarket Autumn Sales. *F. Durr.* **60**

QUEEN'S AGLO 4 gr.f. Aglojo 119–Mountain Queen 58 (Sovereign Path 125) (1980 7fg 8g 10g 10g 10g 8f 7g 1981 8g 10d) useless plater; has worn blinkers. *S. Wiles.* —

QUEEN'S BIDDER 4 br.f. Auction Ring 123–Stormy Queen 64 (Typhoon 125) (1980 5g 5.8f* 5f⁴ 5fg 5fg 6s 5.8g 1981 5fg 5fg 5fg 5.8g) small, full-quartered filly; sprint handicapper; stays 6f; acts on firm going and is possibly unsuited by soft. *B. Gubby.* —

QUEENSBURY BOY 3 ch.g. Manacle 123–Lynn Regis (Ballymoss 136) (1980 5d⁴ 5s 5.1f³ 6d 7d³ 6d 6g 6g 6d⁴ 6g 6g 6g 8.2s 1981 7g 7d) leggy gelding; quite a moderate maiden; stays 7f; acts on firm going and a soft surface; sold 690 gns Doncaster June Sales. *C. Spares.* —

QUEENSBURY BUBBLES 2 ch.f. Kashiwa 115–Crossboyne (Polyfoto 124) (1981 5d 5.1f 6fg 5g) Mar 29; stocky filly; yet to show any ability but started favourite for all-aged seller at Beverley in September on fourth outing (tenth of 16). *D. Dale.* —

QUEENSBURY GIRL 3 b.f. Whiffenpoof 97§–Samataj (Taj Dewan 128) (1980 5d 5h 5fg 6f 1981 8fg 6f 6fg 7g) leggy, very lightly-made filly; well beaten, including in sellers; sold 320 gns Doncaster September Sales. *C. Spares.* —

QUEENSBURY LADY 4 b.f. Undulate–Dream Shared (Majority Blue 126) (1980 10s² 12f 12h 12g 14g 1981 12s 10d 10g) plain, light-framed filly; poor walker; poor maiden; best run at 1¼m on soft going. *D. Dale.* —

QUEENSBURY SAM 2 b.c. Cavo Doro 124–Dream Shared (Majority Blue 126) (1981 7g 8g) May 6; compact, good sort; third reported foal; dam never ran; last in large fields of maidens at Newmarket in October (soon tailed off second occasion). *D. Dale.* —

QUEENSBURY STAR 2 b.f. Wishing Star 117–Silent Mover (Burglar 128) (1981 5s 5s 5g³ 5d⁴ 5.1fg 6f* 6g* 6fg 5fg³ 6g² 6d 5g) Mar 4; 420Y; neat filly; first foal; dam never ran; won 17-runner seller at Doncaster in July (no bid) and nursery at Windsor the following month, latter by 1½ lengths from King of Speed; effective at 5f and 6f; acts on firm going. *D. Dale.* **76**

QUEEN'S CHAMPION 2 ch.c. Run The Gantlet–Royal Saint 117 (Saint — Crespin III 132) (1981 6g 7s) Apr 17; rangy, quite attractive colt; brother to Irish Sweeps Derby and Doncaster St Leger third Classic Example and half-brother to several winners, including smart middle-distance performer Illustrious Prince (by Le Levanstell) and very useful As You Desire Me (by Kalamoun), successful at around 1m in France; dam smart miler and sister to Altesse Royale; beaten over 10 lengths when seventh of 22 to Tardous in maiden race at Ling-field in September; dropped out after halfway when tenth of 11 to Paradis Terrestre in Hyperion Stakes at Ascot the following month; bred to stay at least 1½m; the type to better at 3 yrs. *P. Walwyn.*

QUEEN'S COUP 3 ch.f. Dragonara Palace 115–Kumon Lass 92 (King's Coup — 108) (1980 5fg 5fg 5fg 5fg 5g 7d 5f 7g 5g 8d 8.2s 1981 9g 6d 8f) narrow, leggy filly; only poor form, including in sellers. *K. Bridgwater.*

QUEEN'S EQUERRY 4 b.g. Hotfoot 126–Queendom 109 (Quorum 126) (1980 **63** 7.6f⁴ 8g 8g 8.3g⁴ 10f* 10.6d² 8d³ 10d 1981 10fg 10d² 12fg⁴ 12f 10fg* 10fg 10f 10s 10d) small, useful-looking gelding; good mover; won handicap at Brighton in August; well beaten afterwards; best at 1¼m; probably acts on any going; sold to A. Ingham 3,000 gns Newmarket Autumn Sales. *W. Wightman.*

QUEEN'S HOME 2 b.c. Royal Palace 131–Come On Honey 94 (Never Say **89** Die 137) (1981 7d 7fg³ 8g* 10g) May 14; deep-girthed, attractive colt; brother to very useful stayer Royal Hive and half-brother to high-class middle-distance stayer Attica Meli (by Primera) and very useful 5f to 1½m filly Be Sweet (by Reform); dam daughter of 1,000 Guineas winner Honeylight; beaten less than 2 lengths in big fields of maidens at Newmarket prior to winning 17-runner maiden race at Goodwood in September in workmanlike style by 2½ lengths from Jorge Miguel; probably past his best for season when running moderately on final start; will stay well; could make a useful handicapper at 3 yrs. *H. Cecil.*

QUEEN'S PATTERN 4 ro.c. Perhapsburg 112–Annamanda (Tycoon II) — (1980 8fg³ 10f 12.2fg 9.4d 12g 12g³ 10d⁴ 12d 12.5s 1981 10v 12g 8s) fair sort; only plating class; will stay beyond 1½m; often wears blinkers. *P. Asquith.*

QUEEN'S PRIDE 5 b.g. Royben 125–Queen's Penny (Queen's Hussar 124) **91** d (1980 6v* 7f⁴ 6f 6fg* 6fg 6s 6s 5s 1981 6s² 6g 6s 6d 6f² 6fg) compact, useful sort; poor mover; fair handicapper; stays 7f; acts on any going; suitable mount for an apprentice; blinkered last 2 starts. *P. Cole.*

QUEENS ROAD 3 br.f. Ballymore 123–Hailing Distance 94 (Hail to Reason) — (1980 7fg 8fg 8.2s 1981 10.4d 16f 12d) workmanlike filly; behind in maiden and minor races; blinkered final start. *Mrs C. Lloyd-Jones.*

QUEEN'S ROYALE 6 b.m. Tobrouk–Fibula (King's Bench 132) (1980 9.6fg **46** 7g 6s⁴ 7g* 8.3g* 10g² 8.3fg² 12f 1981 10d⁴ 10d² 7fg 11.7fg 11.7fg³ 12d⁴ 8.3g⁴ 8.3g 10s) plater; stays 1½m; seems to act on any going; has worn blinkers. *M. Bolton.*

QUEEN'S SPRITE 2 ch.f. Queen's Hussar 124–Sprightly Sprite 80 (Babur — 126) (1981 7d) Apr 8; 3,000Y; fair sort; half-sister to 3 winners, including middle-distance winner Darcy (by Crooner); dam middle-distance performer; unquoted and very backward when last of 18 to Sans Blague in maiden race at Newbury in September. *J. Davies.*

QUEENSWAY ROSE 3 b.f. Crooner 119–Maizenrose 89 (Rustam 127) (1980 **67** NR 1981 8f 8f* 8fg 10f 8.2f) neat filly; sister to very useful 5f performer Minstrel, and half-sister to 2 winners; dam stayed 1m; ran on after showing greenness to dead-heat with Quite Ducky in 14-runner minor event at Stockton in June; ran creditably on her other starts; probably stays 1¼m; acts on firm going. *F. Durr.*

QUEEN TAHMOOR (USA) 2 br.f. Our Hero–Spurwink Mommy (Dancer's **74** Image) (1981 6g 6fg³) Apr 26; $53,000F; neat filly; second produce; dam stakes-placed sprint winner; 33/1, ran on steadily without being knocked about when 5½ lengths third of 19 to Dawn Ditty in maiden race at Salisbury in September; will be suited by 7f. *G. Balding.*

QUELLINEY 2 ch.f. High Line 125–Quelle Pas (Kelling 122) (1981 6g 6f 6fg⁴ **70** 8d³ 8s³ 8d) Apr 13; 2,000Y; leggy, lengthy filly; half-sister to 2 winning platers; dam poor selling hurdler; third in 15-runner maiden race at Bath (beaten 3¼ lengths by The Nub) and 11-runner nursery at Newbury (7 lengths behind subsequently-disqualified Rajhaan) in October; will be suited by 1¼m+; best form with give in the ground. *D. Gandolfo.*

QUENLYN 2 b.f. Welsh Pageant 132–Lynwood Sovereign 102 (Connaught — 130) (1981 6f 7g 7fg) Apr 16; second foal; half-sister to fairly useful 1980 2-y-o 5f winner Chumwar (by So Blessed); dam stayed well; blinkered when seventh of 17 to Return To Power in minor event at Warwick in August, third outing and first sign of ability; will stay 1¼m; sold 750 gns Ascot November Sales. *P. Cundell.*

QUEST (USA) 2 ch.f. The Minstrel 135–Belle Pensee (Ribot 142) (1981 **90 §** 5f³ 6f 6fg 8fg³ 7d³ 7g²) Feb 18; $200,000F; neat, attractive filly; good walker; second foal; dam, French 1¼m winner, is half-sister to Cheveley Park winner Gentle Thoughts and Middle Park winner Junius; a beautifully-bred filly who has plenty of ability, as she showed when 1½ lengths third of 11 to Fly Baby after having little room in Queen Mary Stakes at Royal Ascot on her debut, but isn't always inclined to use it; looked sure to win 18-runner maiden race at Newbury in September on fifth outing when cruising up to leaders at distance but her head went up and she flashed her tail under pressure, eventually finishing 2¼ lengths third to Melting Snows; stays 1m; had none too clear a run on third and sixth outings, latter in a small race at Catterick (beaten a head by Spring Lane). *G. Harwood.*

QUETIVEL 2 b.f. Supreme Sovereign 119–Mossy Girl (Ballymoss 136) (1981 — 6fg 7d 6d) Feb 12; rangy filly; second foal; half-sister to 1m seller winner Poporinio (by Porto Bello); dam of little account; unquoted when behind in large fields of maidens at Salisbury and Newbury (speed 4f) in September and Leicester in November. *P. M. Taylor.*

QUICKBEAM 3 ch.f. Roan Rocket 128–Ostrya 116 (Hornbeam 130) (1980 **54** 8d 1981 9d² 9.4g 12.2g* 12f⁴) narrow, very lightly-made filly; finished very fast when beating All Summer a head in maiden race at Catterick in June (apprentice ridden); had stiffer task only subsequent start; suited by 1½m. *E. Weymes.*

QUICK OFF THE MARK 2 ch.f. On Your Mark 125–Skimmer 86 (Skymaster **54** 126) (1981 5g 5d 5f 6f³ 6f⁴ 5f 6f 5g 5s) Mar 7; IR 1,600F, 1,600Y; small, strong filly; second foal; dam won over 6f at 2 yrs; poor plater; stays 6f; blinkered final start; sold out of M. Camacho's stable 620 gns Doncaster October Sales after eighth outing. *D. Chapman.*

QUIEN SABE 3 b.g. Sapsford 95–Kouli Dokhtar (Nordlys 94) (1980 NR — 1981 8d 10v) strong gelding; sixth foal; half-brother to 1½m winner Magic Ruler (by Torullo); dam never ran; well beaten in maiden races at Goodwood in September and Kempton (still needed race) in October. *C. Read.*

QUIET CANNON 4 b.g. Connaught 130–Green Chiffon 83 (Crepello 136) — (1980 12g* 12s* 11.7s* 12g 12g* 12fg 1981 10.6g 12d 13fg 13g 12f 15fg 12v) good-bodied gelding; useful handicapper at 3 yrs; didn't run up to his best in 1981; stays 1½m; needs some give in the ground; blinkered final start. *J. Berry.*

QUIET COVE 3 ch.c. Import 127–Corcyra Beach 60 (Behistoun 131) (1980 — 5g 6g³ 6g 6g 1981 8s 9g 12g 12g 8s) rangy colt; good mover; well beaten all starts, including in sellers; has been tried in blinkers; sold 500 gns Doncaster August Sales. *P. Asquith.*

QUIET JUSTICE (USA) 2 b.g. Stop the Music–Around The Court (Illustri- — ous) (1981 7fg 7.2fg 7d) Feb 26; $26,000Y; first foal; dam, from same family as Cesarewitch winner Grey of Falloden, won 6 times at up to 6f including claiming races; plating-class maiden. *G. Hunter.*

QUILPEE MAI 4 b.f. Pee Mai 107–Boyden Memory 80 (Combat 123) (1980 7f — 7fg 8f 10f♂ 10f³ 14d 13.4g 14g⁴ 10g 12g 12.2g² 11.5f♂* 8fg 10g 10f♂ 13g 11.7d 1981 12g 11.7d 12g 12g 14f³ 15g³ 14.6f 14d 14.6f 8d 11.5fg 10f) well-made filly; poor handicapper; stays 1¾m; suited by fast ground; blinkered twice at 2 yrs; suitable mount for an inexperienced rider. *D. Thom.*

QUISTADOR 5 ch.h. Le Johnstan 123–Little Bo Bleep 71 (Bleep-Bleep 134) **46** (1980 6h 5.1f 5.1g 6fg 6fg 5f 5fg⁴ 1981 16s 10f³) strong horse; poor performer nowadays; possibly stays 1¼m; acts on a firm and a soft surface; blinkered once in 1980; changed hands 3,100 gns Newmarket July Sales. *M. Chapman.*

QUITE DUCKY (USA) 3 b.f. Majestic Prince–Hillhouse High (Quadrangle) **72** (1980 NR 1981 7fg 8f* 8f* 9f² 12d 8g 8s) $25,000Y; lengthy, plain, rather angular filly; third foal; half-sister to a winner by Reviewer; dam unraced half-sister to dam of top American horses Fort Marcy and Key To The Mint; made virtually all to win maiden race by 5 lengths from Sultano and to dead-heat with Queensway Rose in minor event, both at Stockton in June; close

QUI

second in apprentice event at Ripon in August; will stay 1¼m; acts on firm going; had stiffish tasks last 3 starts (blinkered last one); sent to race in USA. *S. Norton.*

QUITE HOT 2 ch.g. Hotfoot 126–Quite Sweet 100 (Super Sam 124) (1981 5d 5g 7fg) Apr 25; strong, rangy gelding; half-brother to fairly useful 5f to 7f winner Lucky Man (by Manacle); dam best at up to 1¼m; only fifth when short-priced favourite for maiden races in May on first 2 starts; should be suited by 7f; seemed unsuited by Chester track on third appearance; clearly thought to have more ability than he's shown so far; gelded after third outing. *P. Rohan.* **60**

QUITE LUCKY 4 ch.f. Precipice Wood 123–Quite Sweet 100 (Super Sam 124) (1980 10fg 10g 12g 10.2fg 10.1fg 11.7h² 12f 16fg² 1981 14d⁴ 14fg 10.2d 12s) strong filly; staying maiden; acts on hard going; has run creditably for an amateur rider. *P. M. Taylor.* **—**

QUITE RIGHT 5 b.g. Ribero 126–Sheer Bliss 76 (St Paddy 133) (1980 14fg 16fg 16g 16fg 14fg 16g 17.1d 16.1s 1981 16f) robust, good-bodied gelding; poor performer nowadays; stays very well; acts on any going; blinkered once at 3 yrs. *W. Clay.* **—**

R

RABDAN 4 b.c. Bold Lad (Ire) 133–Bualim (Khalkis 127) (1980 6.5g³ 6.5g* 8g² 7.6f 8g² 8g³ 7g* 7g³ 6g² 7g* 6s⁴ 7s² 7g² 6d³ 1981 6.5g* 8d² 8.5d* 6d² 6g* 7d² 7.6g² 7d* 6f 6fg 6fg* 6fg* 6d* 5d³) **129**
The annual early-season invasion of Cagnes-sur-Mer by horses from Britain has increased considerably in dimensions since it started in the 'sixties. At that time a handful of trainers sent horses across with limited success, whereas in 1981 fourteen trainers sent thirty-one horses who won ten and were placed in twenty-five of their eighty-nine races. In retrospect Rabdan, successful twice at Cagnes, was easily the best of the group. During a strenuous campaign in which he ran fourteen times on courses ranging from Lingfield to Baden-Baden he improved by leaps and bounds into a top-class sprinter, winning three pattern races and putting up the performance of his life in one of the premier five-furlong events of the season, the Prix de l'Abbaye on his final appearance.

Between his second success at Cagnes and his win in the Prix de Meautry at Deauville Rabdan was only twice out of the first two in seven starts, when behind in the Cork and Orrery Stakes at Royal Ascot and the Tote Stewards' Cup at Goodwood. He showed he was on the upgrade with a three-quarters-of-a-length win from Runnett in the Ladbrokes Abernant Stakes at Newmarket, gave lumps of weight away when scoring in a handicap at Epsom and came in second in the Cammidge Trophy at Doncaster (to King of Spain), the Autobar Victoria Cup at Ascot (behind Columnist) and a handicap at Lingfield. Facing considerable tasks in handicaps—he was burdened with 10-0 in the Stewards' Cup—Rabdan was kept to pattern races from August onwards and did himself and his new owner Robert Sangster, who had bought him before Goodwood, proud.

The betting for the eight-runner Prix Meautry scarcely reflected Rabdan's chance in the race for he was the outsider of the party at 23/1 even though his form was as good as that of several at shorter odds, notably the 9/2-shot Enchantment. Favourite was the King George Stakes runner-up Welshwyn; the Cork and Orrery Stakes third Integrity was another English challenger and Ancient Regime looked the best of the French. Rabdan made a mockery of the betting, leading a furlong out and readily accounting for Enchantment by two lengths with Welshwyn third. A fortnight later Rabdan started favourite for Germany's principal sprint, the Goldene Peitsche at Baden-Baden. He confirmed his improvement, quickly putting paid to Esclavo after heading him at the distance and winning effortlessly by a length, breaking the course record. Later in September Rabdan was returned to France to try for a hat-trick in the Prix de Seine-et-Oise at Maisons-Laffitte. Kilijaro had won both the Meautry and the Seine-et-Oise in 1980 and Rabdan duly followed her example. A short-priced favourite, he faced eight rivals including Ancient Regime again, the Prix du Palais Royal winner Prince Mab and the smart German horse Park Romeo who was later to win the Prix du Petit Couvert. None of them got a look in as Rabdan made all the running after starting fast and quickened away in the closing stages to beat Ancient Regime and Prince Mab by three lengths and two and a half.

Rabdan's great run came to an end in the Prix de l'Abbaye de Longchamp

Prix de Meautry, Deauville—a British 1, 2, 3 as Rabdan wins from Enchantment and Welshwyn

but in defeat he revealed how good he had become. Once more quickly away, he was always up with the leaders and though outpaced by Marwell and Sharpo in the last furlong and a half he kept on extremely well to be beaten just over a length. Piggott lodged an objection against Marwell, claiming she had impeded Rabdan when crossing over to the rails in the last hundred yards, but the stewards overruled it; as we saw things Piggott did momentarily have to stop riding but this had no effect on the result. The Prix de l'Abbaye was Rabdan's last race; a half-share in him was purchased by Stavros Niarchos and he is to be syndicated for a total of 750,000 dollars to replace Nureyev at the Haras de Fresnay-le-Buffard, Orne.

<table>
<tr><td rowspan="8">Rabdan
(b.c. 1977)</td><td rowspan="4">Bold Lad (Ire)
(b 1964)</td><td rowspan="2">Bold Ruler
(b 1954)</td><td>Nasrullah</td></tr>
<tr><td>Miss Disco</td></tr>
<tr><td rowspan="2">Barn Pride
(ch 1957)</td><td>Democratic</td></tr>
<tr><td>Miss Alycia</td></tr>
<tr><td rowspan="4">Bualim
(b 1967)</td><td rowspan="2">Khalkis
(b 1960)</td><td>Vimy</td></tr>
<tr><td>Merry Xmas</td></tr>
<tr><td rowspan="2">Cannon Ball
(b 1959)</td><td>By Thunder!</td></tr>
<tr><td>Bebe Grande</td></tr>
</table>

A neat, attractive colt, Rabdan cost only 3,800 guineas as a yearling and proved among the best runners sired to date by the top two-year-old of 1966, Bold Lad, whose other progeny has included such very good performers as Ballad Rock, Boldboy, Daring Display, Persian Bold and Waterloo, most of whom had speed in excess of stamina. Neither the dam, Bualim, nor grandam, Cannon Ball, managed to win though both were placed, the former at up to ten and a half furlongs in France and the latter over sprint distances in England at two. Bualim has produced two winners besides Rabdan, notably the useful French

Prix de Seine-et-Oise, Maisons-Laffitte—another pattern-race victory for Rabdan

sprinter Baradaan (by Habitat), while Cannon Ball foaled seven winners, among them the smart French middle-distance stayer A Chara. The third dam, Bebe Grande, more than makes up for the failure of Bualim and Cannon Ball to score on the track since she won eight of her nine starts as a two-year-old, including the Gimcrack, Champagne and Cheveley Park Stakes, and was placed in both the One Thousand and Two Thousand Guineas the following year. One of the five winners she produced was Baby Doll, dam of Pieces of Eight.

Rabdan stayed a mile but was unquestionably best at sprint distances, and acted on any going with the exception of very firm. Genuine, consistent and very tough, he was altogether an admirable colt and a credit to his trainer. *R. Armstrong.*

RABINSKI 6 br.g. Balliol 125–Sens Unique 79 (Faubourg II 127) (1980 NR 1981 9g 12fg 13.4fg) poor maiden; has worn blinkers. *Mrs C. Lloyd-Jones.* —

RACEAWAY 3 b.c. Lauso–Kingsbay (King's Leap 111) (1980 7fg 1981 10s 12d 16d 16.9fg2 16g) workmanlike colt; showed only form in handicap at Wolverhampton in July, when 8 lengths second to Castelnau; pulled up at Nottingham the following month; suited by a test of stamina. *C. James.* **54**

RACONTEUR 4 b.c. Rarity 129–Festival Diplomat (Diplomat Way) (1980 8.2s* 10g4 8fg 8d3 8g* 8.3g2 1981 8d 8g 8d) smallish colt; well beaten in handicaps in 1981; best at around 1m; probably acts on any going. *A. Gillam.* —

RACONTEUR (USA) 2 ch.c. The Minstrel 135–Bubbling (Stage Door Johnny) **104**
(1981 6d2 7g* 7g)
'It ain't what you do, it's the way that you do it'. There are times when the majority of the betting public seem to stick to the principle of the old song-line with the result, often, that they lose their way. It is remarkable what ridiculous odds will be accepted in an important race about a horse on the strength of an easy victory in minor company, particularly if he is from a fashionable stable. The latest running of the William Hill Dewhurst Stakes

Mr R. E. Sangster's "Raconteur (USA)"

provided two striking examples: the betting was dominated by Simply Great (6/4) and Raconteur (15/8), neither of whom had raced outside maiden company. Raconteur was given experience in a couple of races in Ireland before being sent to Newmarket. Beaten at 9/4 on at the Curragh in mid-September, he landed the odds at the same course a fortnight later, trotting up by eight lengths—but against opposition that no-one should have pretended was strong enough to test a prospective classic colt. When it came to a real test Raconteur failed to make the grade, finishing eighth of nine to Wind and Wuthering after going to the start rather too freely. Raconteur may turn out to be a good deal better than his Dewhurst running suggests, but he won't be carrying any of our cash until he has shown himself to be so.

Raconteur (USA) (ch.c. Mar 27, 1979)	The Minstrel (ch 1974)	Northern Dancer (b 1961)	Nearctic
			Natalma
		Fleur (b 1964)	Victoria Park
			Flaming Page
	Bubbling (ch 1972)	Stage Door Johnny (ch 1965)	Prince John
			Peroxide Blonde
		Sparkling (ch 1967)	Bold Ruler
			Striking

A handsome colt and a grand mover, Raconteur cost 285,000 dollars as a yearling. He is the first living foal of Bubbling, a smart stakes winner at a mile and a half-sister to Effervescing, a high-class winner at up to a mile and a half. Raconteur will stay a mile and a half. *V. O'Brien, Ireland.*

RADICAL RETHINK 3 b.g. Owen Anthony 102–Press Button 58 (Precipice Wood 123) (1980 5f³ 5fg³ 5g 5d 5g 6d³ 7fg⁴ 8d² 1981 10s³ 12d 8g 8.3fg 8.3g) leggy, light-framed gelding; plater; stays 1¼m; seems to act on any going; well beaten in blinkers final start; sold 1,650 gns Ascot September Sales. *W. Musson.* **54 d**

RAFAEL MOLINA (USA) 5 b.g. Ace of Aces 126–Rainbow Rose (Ambiorix 130) (1980 12.3d² 12f³ 12fg² 12f² 12fg³ 13d³ 10.6d 11fg* 10d² 11d 10.5g⁴ 10d 1981 13v* 12d) big, strong gelding; won handicap at Ayr in March; stays 13f; acts on any going. *Denys Smith.* **75**

RAFFIA SET 8 b.g. Raffingora 130–Sue Set 99 (Set Fair 129) (1980 6g⁴ 6fg 6fg 5s³ 5g 5g 6g 5d 6s 1981 6s 5.3f 6fg) sprint handicapper; acts on any going; usually wears blinkers and bandages. *J. Bethell.* **—**

RAFFLE PRIZE 2 b. or br.f. So Blessed 130–Queen Anne's Lace 103 (Mossborough 126) (1981 5fg 5g 5f⁴ 5f* 6d²) May 3; 5,000Y; half-sister to 2 winners, including useful 5f and 7f winner Lacewing (by Double Jump); dam, winner over 7f and 1m at 2 yrs in France, finished fourth in 1965 Oaks; put up best effort when winning 9-runner maiden race at Hamilton in June by a neck from Legs of Man; went down by 12 lengths to odds-on Fimi in 3-runner event on same course in July; should stay 6f+. *P. Haslam.* **63**

RAGAFAN 4 ch.g. Ragstone 128–Hi-Baby 102 (High Treason 126) (1980 11.7fg 16g 1981 8fg 10fg⁴ 11.5d 12g³ 12fg) compact gelding; stays 1½m; has worn blinkers; has run respectably for an amateur rider. *R. Smyth.* **—**

RAG DANCER 4 br.c. Ragstone 128–May Day Follies 80 (Bleep-Bleep 134) (1980 10s* 9g² 12.3f 10.6fg 10.6d 10fg 10s² 12g 9f 10.6s² 8.2s* 8.2s 10.2v 1981 10s⁴ 11g* 12d 12g* 12fg 13g 12f 11fg 11d³ 12d³ 12g³) lightly-made colt; won handicaps at Edinburgh in April and Carlisle in May; stays 1½m; needs some give in the ground. *W. Elsey.* **64**

RAGE GLEN 4 gr.f. Grey Mirage 128–Septieme Ciel (Welsh Abbot 131) (1980 8.2g 9s 10.2d² 1981 8v 8g 7d³ 7g 7g 7g 8g 10.2f 10fg 7g 7d³ 7v 7g 7g 7s 7g) compact filly; inconsistent handicapper; beaten in valuable seller final start; probably best at around 7f nowadays; suited by some give in the ground; blinkered sixth start; headstrong; one to be wary of. *W. Stubbs.* **45**

RAGFLINT 2 b.g. Ragstone 128–Graceful Scot (Aberdeen 109) (1981 6f 10s) fifth foal; half-brother to a winning sprinter Isthatchew (by Burglar); dam never ran; unquoted and needed race when in rear in maiden events at Yarmouth (last) in June and Nottingham in October. *P. Feilden.* **—**

RAG-ON-FIRE 2 gr.f. Dragonara Palace 115–Farida Jinks 106 (Tudor Jinks 121) (1981 5.1fg³ 5fg³ 5fg 5d) Apr 18; 1,900Y; small, lightly-made filly; half-sister to several winners, including useful 5f performers Faridina (by Sky Gypsy) and Faridetta (by Good Bond); dam 5f sprinter; showed a little ability all 4 starts, final outing in a nursery; not sure to stay 6f. *W. Musson.* **62**

RAGSTONE GIRL 2 b.f. Ragstone 128–Right Prospect 77 (Right Boy 137) —
(1981 7g 8d 7g) May 23; leggy, unfurnished filly; half-sister to 2 winners,
including prolific 5f to 7.6f winner Calibina (by Caliban); dam won 5f seller at
2 yrs; well beaten in maiden races. *D. H. Jones.*

RAGTIME ROSE 2 b.f. Ragstone 128–Miss Venus (Comedy Star 121) (1981 —
6g 7g) Mar 11; quite attractive, lightly-made filly; second foal; half-sister to
fairly useful 3-y-o sprinter Sharp Venita (by Sharp Edge); dam never ran; 20/1
when never-dangerous seventh of 21 to Not For Show in maiden race at Newmarket in October; well beaten in similar event on same course later in month;
should be suited by 7f+. *G. Hunter.*

RAGUSA IMP 7 ch.g. Caliban 123–Palvee 79 (Queen's Hussar 124) (1980 NR —
1981 12f) plater; stays 1½m; acts on firm going; has worn blinkers. *R. Sturdy.*

RAHOTEP (FR) 3 b.c. Matahawk 127–La Masure (Net 116) (1980 7.5g* 127
8d⁴ 10s 1981 10.5d* 12s* 12g⁴ 12f² 12d 12v*) .

Rahotep, for reasons that we are unable to make out, failed to do himself justice in the Prix de l'Arc de Triomphe: he was never in the hunt and
finished among the back six. His record otherwise bears close inspection.
Subsequently he trotted up in a Group 2 pattern race, the Prix du Conseil de
Paris, and prior to the Arc he also showed ability of a high order, winning one of
the classic trials at Longchamp, the Prix Hocquart, and finishing in the frame
in the French Derby and Prix Niel. He could have another good season as
a four-year-old provided he stands training better than his sire and grandsire did;
he has been only lightly raced and may have more than normal improvement in
him.

The Prix Hocquart, which Rahotep won after making an encouraging start
at two years and beginning 1981 with a victory in a minor event at Saint-Cloud,
wasn't the strongest-contested of the French trials by a long chalk. He beat
Mbaiki, who had run nowhere in the Prix Noailles, by a length and a half. He
showed better form in the French Derby, the Prix du Jockey-Club at Chantilly
in June—fourth of twelve to Bikala, beaten approximately seven lengths—and
better still in the Prix Niel at Longchamp in October. In the Prix Niel Rahotep
went down by only half a length, receiving 2 lb, to Akarad who next time out
started favourite for the Arc. He ran a brave race, tracking Akarad in mid-
field and hanging on to him when the tempo quickened. The Prix du Conseil
de Paris, worth £32,039 to the winner, attracted two runners besides Rahotep
who had taken part in the Arc two weeks previously, Lancastrian (twelfth)
and Gap of Dunloe (sixteenth); Lancastrian had been a close second in the Prix
du Conseil de Paris of 1980, Gap of Dunloe had been third in the 1981 Prix du
Jockey-Club. These two at their best represented the chief threat to Rahotep,
a strong threat, but Rahotep had things all his own way, chased home by the
second-division three-year-olds Two Step and Kentucky River. Rahotep
inflicted a crushing defeat on his nine rivals, storming in eight lengths clear;
the way he quickened in the heavy ground after taking the lead with under
two furlongs to go was very impressive indeed.

	Matahawk	Sea Hawk II	Herbager
	(br 1972)	(gr 1963)	Sea Nymph
Rahotep (Fr)		Carromata	St Paddy
(b.c. 1978)		(b 1965)	Carrozza
	La Masure	Net	Clarion III
	(b 1965)	(ch 1957)	Sans Tares
		Miss Pink	Black Devil
		(b 1943)	Hello II

Rahotep's sire Matahawk was himself a wide-margin winner over the course,
in the Grand Prix de Paris in 1975; that was his only success and he never raced
again, breaking down during his preparation for the Arc. Judging by the way
Rahotep finished in two of his last three races, especially the final one, he has
inherited a fair amount of his sire's stamina and will stay further than a mile
and a half in the somewhat-unlikely event of his being called upon to do so.
The dam, by the miler Net (a half-brother to the Washington International
winners Worden II and Mahan), won over distances between six furlongs
and a mile and a quarter in the French Provinces. In all, she won seven of her
twenty-seven races and was placed in another nine, keeping her form through
to her four-year-old days. She had the useful miler Bois Mineau (by Franc
Luron) among four previous foals by none-too-fashionable stallions, and had
another runner by a Grand Prix de Paris winner, the two-year-old Drole de
Dame (by Funny Hobby), showing form in France in the latest season. La

Prix Hocquart, Longchamp—a comfortable win for Rahotep in this French Derby trial

Masure, the dam, is a sister to a winner and a half-sister to several more, including the useful sprinter Miss Klaire II, dam of the smart miler Miracle. The second dam Miss Pink, hardy soul, won seventeen races and was placed a further twenty times between the ages of two and five. Some of this information was available in the catalogue for the Goffs Special Sale at Deauville in 1979, where Rahotep realized the highest public price of that year for a Matahawk yearling—115,000 francs or approximately £12,100. If paying that much for one of his breeding was an unusual risk it has turned out a risk well worth taking. Rahotep acts on any going but is particularly well suited by soft. *B. Secly, France.*

RAILWAY MATCH   2 ch.c. Royal Match 117–African Dusk (African Sky 124)   **42** (1981 6f 6f 7f 6d³ 7d)   Mar 6; 1,700Y; sturdy colt; bad plater; dead. *P. Feilden.*

RAINBOW HILL   3 ch.g. Royalty 130–Hill Cloud 60 (El Gallo 122) (1980   — 6fg 7fg 7s   1981 11s 10fg 8fg 8h)   big, strong gelding; has shown a little ability in maiden and minor races; probably stays 1¼m; sweated up quite badly third start. *P. M. Taylor*

RAIN DANCER   2 gr.c. Dancer's Image–Marala (Sir Khalito)   (1981 5g 6d 6fg)   **68** Apr 30; 5,200Y; strong, good-bodied colt; half-brother to 1979 French 2-y-o 6.5f winner Massalia (by Targowice); dam won over 1¼m in France; 8/1, put in best work in closing stages when 3½ lengths fifth of 14 to Sweet Ecstasy in £4,000 seller at Kempton in August, third outing; will be well suited by 7f+. *W. O'Gorman.*

RAISE A HAND   3 b.c. Auction Ring 123–My Fawn 67 (Hugh Lupus 132)   **61** (1980 NR   1981 10.5f 13.4fg 13f³ 16.5f³ 16f² 15.5s)   13,500Y; tall, good sort; half-brother to 6 winners, including smart French stayer Chawn (by St Chad) and quite useful middle-distance winner Border Dawn (by Pitcairn); dam once-raced half-sister to Knotty Pine; placed in maiden races at Nottingham, Redcar and Beverley in the summer; stays well; sold to P. Makin 5,000 gns Newmarket Autumn Sales. *J. Hindley.*

RAISE THE OFFER   2 b.f. Auction Ring 123–Raise the Roof (Raise You   — Ten 125)   (1981 5fg 7f 8d)   Feb 21; 9,400Y; strong, compact filly; half-sister to 6f and 1m winner Roi-Des-Toits (by Roi Soleil) and to winners in Belgium and Italy; dam won at up to 17f in Ireland; little worthwhile form in maiden races but finished seventh of 16 on final outing; probably stays 1m. *F. Durr.*

RAISINGSHA (FR)   2 gr. or ro.c. Raisingelle–Shamsha (Bold Lad, USA)   **67** (1981 6f 7fg³ 7fg 7d 8d)   stocky colt; first foal; dam unraced half-sister to very smart French stayer Shafaraz; ran on steadily when 6½ lengths third of 9 to Killingholme Clay in maiden race at Chester in July; tailed off in nurseries last 2 starts; should be suited by 1m. *N. Guest.*

RAJA MUDA (USA)   2 br.c. Raja Baba–Aurilla (Winged T)   (1981 5g 5s)   **65** May 11; $38,000Y; strong, well-made colt; half-brother half-sister to 2 stakes winners; never in hunt when seventh of 12 behind Hampton Bay in £3,200 event at Ascot in September; favourite for 17-runner maiden race at Warwick the following month but finished only eighth to Fast Lad. *F. J. Houghton.*

RAJHAAN   2 br.c. English Prince 129–Amana (Relko 136)   (1981 6g 7fg* 8d 8s²)   **102** Apr 2; IR 11,000F, 14,000Y; smallish, robust, well-made colt; half-brother to French middle-distance winner Akabar (by Taj Dewan) and winning French stayer Azfazar (by Exbury); dam won 4 middle-distance races in French

693

RAM

Provinces; won maiden race at Salisbury in September, storming through to
beat Rocamadour 2½ lengths after having had difficulty finding an opening;
bettered that effort when length winner of nursery at Newbury the following
month, but was moved down a place for hanging very badly right and hampering
runner-up Even Banker inside last (would probably have won fairly comfortably
if keeping straight); will be suited by 1½m+; probably acts on any going but
acts well in the mud. *F. J. Houghton.*

RAMADA 4 ch.g. St Alphage 119–Strathclair (Klairon 131) (1980 8d 10s 5f⁴ —
6f* 6fg 5g 6g⁴ 6g⁴ 6s⁴ 7g 1981 5g 10f 6fg 6g) strong, compact gelding; plater;
stays 6f; acts on any going; often wears blinkers. *B. Richmond.*

RAMANNOLIE (FR) 3 b.c. Caro 133–Manoline (Vieux Manoir 132) (1980 93
7f³ 7g 1981 8d² 9s² 8.2s* 8g* 8f* 8fg³ 8fg³) tall, lightly-made colt; has a
round action; won maiden race at Haydock in June and quite well-contested
minor event at Bath in July, in latter beating Arrowhead gamely by a head;
beaten 2 lengths on merit by Fandango Time in minor event at Salisbury in
between but received a hefty bump a furlong out and placings were reversed;
third in ladies race won by Cracking Form at Ascot later in July and in minor
event won by Critique at Kempton in August; will stay 1½m; acts on any
going; genuine; sent to USA. *H. T. Jones.*

RAMAS SILK 3 gr.f. Amber Rama 133–Guiletta 63 (Runnymede 123) (1980 —
5fg 5g 5g 1981 6d 6f 7f 8.3fg 10d 10.1g 10fg) seems of little account; blinkered
final start. *P. Ashworth.*

RAMBLING RIVER 4 b.c. Forlorn River 124–Who-Done-It 98 (Lucero 124) 73
(1980 5f 6fg 6fg⁴ 6d 5g 6d 5.6g 6f 6d 5v 1981 5g 5g 5f 5f 5fg³ 6f² 5g⁴ 5f* 5g³ 6f⁴
5f⁴ 5fg² 5fg³ 5fg 5d³ 5g 5g) strong, useful sort; sprint handicapper; made
virtually all to beat Think Ahead by 4 lengths at Thirsk in August (hung badly
left in last 2f); best form at 5f; has won on a soft surface but is better on a sound
one; blinkered nowadays; has worn a bandage on his near-fore. *W. A.
Stephenson.*

RAMBORO AGAIN 4 gr.c. Runnymede 123–Balisland's Queen 93 (Abernant 72
142) (1980 6d 6s² 6v² 6d* 5f* 6f 5f* 5s 5fg⁴ 5g 5.3fg⁴ 5d 5d 1981 5s 5d² 5fg*
5g 5fg² 5fg) compact colt; sprint handicapper; won at Hamilton in May; stays
6f; acts on any going; suitable mount for an inexperienced rider; sent to USA.
P. Haslam.

RAMETTA 3 ch.f. Amber Rama 133–Nevetta 108 (Never Say Die 137) (1980 —
5g 5f³ 6fg 7d 7g 7s 6f 7g 1981 8g 9.4g 12g 12.5f⁴ 9.4fg 7f⁴ 7fg 7f 6fg 8fg) fair
sort; plater; probably stays 1½m; form only on a sound surface; occasionally
blinkered. *T. Fairhurst.*

RAMIANA (USA) 2 ch.f. Blushing Groom 131–Irish Meadow (St Paddy 133) 68
(1981 7fg 7fg 7d) Mar 28; $75,000Y, resold 420,000 francs Y (approx £42,000);
lengthy, rather narrow filly; half-sister to French 1½m winner Frontage (by
Never Bend); dam, half-sister to Irish Sweeps Derby winner Meadow Court, won
over 7f in Ireland; showed ability in maiden company on first 2 starts, finishing
4¾ lengths fifth of 12 to Clare Island at Sandown in July and ninth of 22 to
Oxslip from a poor draw at Newmarket later in month; dwelt when soundly
beaten in similar company at Yarmouth final start; will be suited by 1m+. *J.
Hindley.*

RAMJAK 2 b.g. Mandrake Major 122–Melanesia (South Pacific 87) (1981 5g —
5fg 6f) Mar 18; leggy, workmanlike gelding; has a round action; soundly
beaten in varied company, including selling. *J. Etherington.*

RAMO'S LADY 2 ch.f. Malinowski 123–Romp 67 (Romulus 129) (1981 6fg —
7fg 8fg 7g) Apr 10; 5,000 2-y-o; fair sort; half-sister to smart 1972 Irish
2-y-o North Wall (by King's Troop) and good German chaser Romping to Work
(by Be Friendly); dam of little account; dropped in class when over 10 lengths
fifth of 13 to Anatolia in seller at Edinburgh in October, fourth start and only
sign of ability; should be suited by 1m. *H. Collingridge.*

RAMPRIDES STAR 2 b.c. Rambah 67–Mistress Pride (Orbit 106) (1981 6fg) —
May 8; non-thoroughbred colt; third known foal; dam won 3 times over hurdles;
unquoted when tailed-off last of 26 to Padalco in maiden race at Doncaster in
June and is probably useless. *H. Fleming.*

RAMSHACKLE 3 b.f. Manacle 123–Private Collection 70 (Whistling Wind 123) —
(1980 7g 6fg 7g 1981 6g 7f 6fg) rangy filly; little worthwhile form in maiden
and minor events. *W. Wightman.*

RANCHO 2 gr.g. Warpath 113–Poncho 80 (Ragusa 137) (1981 6s⁴) Apr 25;
fourth foal; brother to 1978 2-y-o 1m winner Sombrero; dam stayed 1½m;

694

put in best work in closing stages when 7½ lengths fourth of 10 to No Contest in maiden race at Hamilton in October, only outing; dead. *C. Thornton.*

RANJI 2 br.c. Mansingh 120–Princely Maid 71 (King's Troop 118) (1981 5fg 5d 5s 6fg 5f 5.1d 5g) Feb 8; compact colt; good mover; half-brother to several winners, including Lady Constance (by Connaught), very useful at up to 7f; plater; best run at 5f on firm ground; blinkered final start; sold to German International BA 940 gns Newmarket Autumn Sales. *M. Jarvis.* **64**

RANKIN (FR) 4 ch.c. Owen Dudley 121–Cup Cake (Dan Cupid 132) (1980 8s 12fg² 12f³ 12s 12fg⁴ 10d⁴ 1981 9g⁴ 10fg² 12g⁴ 12d) quite attractive colt; good mover; high-class performer at 3 yrs when excellent third to Henbit in Derby and fourth to Cairn Rouge in Champion Stakes; didn't run up to his best in 1981 though wasn't disgraced on first 2 starts in April when in frame behind Hard Fought in Earl of Sefton Stakes at Newmarket (9 lengths fourth) and Westbury Stakes at Sandown (1½ lengths second); ran moderately when remote fourth of 6 to Master Willie in Jockey Club Stakes at Newmarket in May and deplorably when tailed-off last of 5 to same horse in Coronation Cup at Epsom in June; subsequently sent to race in America; needs further than 9f and stays 1½m; goes well on top-of-the-ground and is possibly unsuited by very soft going; suited by a strongly-run race. *G. Harwood.* **118**

RA NOVA 2 b.c. Ragstone 128–Miss Casanova 84 (Galivanter 131) (1981 7d) June 12; fourth live foal; brother to fair middle-distance winner Morality Stone and half-brother to another winner; dam 2-y-o 6f winner; unquoted when ninth of 13 behind Parthia's Picture in minor event at Chepstow in October; may improve over middle distances as a 3-y-o. *P. Mitchell.* **—**

RANSOM (FR) 2 ch.c. Rose Laurel 125–Cup Cake (Dan Cupid 132) (1981 7fg 7fg 8d) Apr 25; 23,000Y; well-made colt; half-brother to Derby third Rankin (by Owen Dudley); dam won over 1m and 11f in France and also over hurdles; fifth in maiden races at Salisbury in September and Bath in October on last 2 starts, on latter course finishing 5½ lengths behind The Nub in 15-runner event; will be suited by 1½m. *P. Walwyn.* **68**

RAPERON 3 b.f. Rapid River 127–Reignon 74 (Lucky Brief 128) (1980 5g* 5g⁴ 7g⁴ 1981 8f 7f 10.2g) workmanlike filly; behind in handicaps in 1981; trained by M. H. Easterby first 2 starts. *T. Kersey.* **—**

RAPID KNOT 2 b.g. Rapid River 127–Love-Knot (No Mercy 126) (1981 6f 6fg² 7fg* 7.2fg* 8g 7s) May 10; strong, plain gelding who carries plenty of condition; poor walker and has a round action; first foal; dam ran only twice; winner of maiden race at Catterick in August and £4,400 nursery at Haydock the following month, holding on well under quite strong driving to beat Short and Sharp by ¾ length in latter; suited by 7f but isn't sure to stay 1m; acts on a firm surface. *Miss S. Hall.* **85**

RAPID LAD 3 b.c. Rapid River 127–Seacona (Espresso 122) (1980 5fg 5d 5d 6g 6g 7.2s 5s* 1981 5f 5g⁴ 6fg 6f 6f 7g 7g 5g⁴) compact colt; plater at 2 yrs; not disgraced in non-selling handicaps on occasions in 1981; yet to prove he stays 7f; acts well on soft going; blinkered fifth outing; sold to J. Spearing 2,500 gns Doncaster November Sales. *A. Gillam.* **55**

RARE GIFT 2 b.c. Rarity 129–Awash (Busted 134) (1981 7fg 7fg² 7.6g⁴) Apr 13; 12,500Y; tall, lengthy, useful-looking colt; first living foal; dam modest daughter of smart 5f to 7f winner Fluke, a half-sister to Buoy and Bireme; looked sure to win 29-runner maiden race at Newmarket in August when clear 1f out but was caught on line by Hayakaze; favourite when 2 lengths fourth of 7 to Triple Axel in £7,100 event at Lingfield the following month; will stay middle distances; shouldn't be hard pressed to win a maiden event. *J. Sutcliffe.* **91**

RARE MUSIC 7 b.g. Rarity 129–Meadow Music (Tom Fool) (1980 NR 1981 8s 12d) workmanlike ex-Irish gelding; lightly raced on flat nowadays and is probably no longer of any account. *W. Musson.* **—**

RARE SCOTCH 3 ch.g. Rarity 129–Melody Ryde 90 (Shooting Chant) (1980 NR 1981 8.2s 8fg 10d 12s 14fg 12f) 6,400Y; workmanlike gelding; first foal; dam won over 7f and 1½m here, and also won over hurdles in Ireland; poor form in maiden races, best effort on third start; should be suited by 1½m; blinkered last 2 starts. *N. Vigors.* **—**

RARFY JAMES 2 ch.c. Gay Fandango 132–Gold Court 79 (Gentle Art 121) (1981 8g 6g) Apr 28; 2,100Y; strong colt; half-brother to 1976 2-y-o 5f winner Royal Princess (by Meadow Mint); dam, closely related to good sprinter Monet, won over 5f at 2 yrs; behind in October in maiden race at Newmarket (33/1) and minor event at Leicester (25/1). *G. Huffer.* **—**

Mr Upali Wijewardene's "Rasa Penang"

RASA PENANG 3 ch.c. Gay Fandango 132–Lancette (Double Jump 131) **118**
(1980 7g* 7g³ 1981 8.5fg² 10s⁴ 7d³ 8.5fg³ 8g 7g 7f* 7g⁴ 7.3fg 6fg) well-made,
attractive colt; second foal; half-brother to fairly useful 1979 Irish 2-y-o 7f
winner Lagolette (by Green God); dam, half-sister to Gimcrack winner Golden
Horus, placed at up to 1½m in France; returned to form after a miserable effort
in handicap company when winning 20-runner Jersey Stakes at Royal Ascot in
June in fine style by 3 lengths from Star Pastures, being clear of stand-side group
throughout and never looking in much danger; had run well most previous starts,
finishing in frame at Cagnes-sur-Mer (twice), Doncaster and Epsom (Ladbroke
Blue Riband Trial) and about 5½ lengths seventh of 19 behind To-Agori-Mou in
2,000 Guineas at Newmarket; stays 8.5f; particularly well suited by top-of-the-
ground conditions; had stiff task final outing; sent to race in USA. *R.
Armstrong.*

RASHANA 2 ch.f. Sharpen Up 127–Hunter's Melody 70 (Off Key 121) (1981 **74**
5fg⁴ 5g³ 5g³ 6f* 5g 6g 6v) Mar 24; 21,000F; quite a useful sort; half-sister to
Irish 1¼m winner Hunting Call (by Averof) and 2 winners in France; dam
staying half-sister to numerous winners; in frame in maiden races prior to winning
7-runner all-aged minor event at Folkestone in September by 1½ lengths from
Steel Son; will stay 1m; acts on firm going; blinkered fifth outing. *W. O'Gorman.*

RASHERCAP 3 br.g. Home Guard 129–Ciotog (Varano) (1980 10g 1981 12s) —
big, rangy gelding; showed promise on only outing at 2 yrs; sweating a bit but
fairly fit when soundly beaten in minor event at Wolverhampton in May; likely
to need time and long distances. *B. Hobbs.*

RASPBERRY RUFFLE 3 gr.f. Town Crier 119–Leisure Bay 71 (Jock Scot 121) —
(1980 NR 1981 8fg 8.2s) first foal; dam, staying maiden on flat, won once
over hurdles; tailed-off last in maiden races at Salisbury and Nottingham.
Mrs J. Reavey.

RAY

RATAMATAZ 7 b.g. Shiny Tenth 120–Water Rat 83 (Hard Tack 111§) (1980 —
5d 6s* 6d³ 6g 6d 6fg 6g 5fg 6fg 5d³ 5d 6g 6g 7d 1981 5d 5fg 7g 5f 5fg 7s 5s) poor
sprint handicapper; behind in seller on sixth start; acts on any going;
blinkered twice in 1980; goes well for a boy. *D. Marks.*

RATAN BOY 5 br.g. Workboy 123–Rubbish (Major Portion 129) (1980 6g **41**
5fg 5f 6fg 6d 5.8f² 7fg³ 1981 7g 6d 7fg 6f² 7fg⁴) useful sort; poor handicapper;
stays 7f; acts on hard going and has yet to race on really soft; best in blinkers.
G. Lewis.

RA TAPU 4 ch.c. Sun Prince 128–Bracey Bridge 115 (Chanteur II 135) (1980 **75**
8d 10s⁴ 12s³ 15s² 12d* 1981 12d³ 14fg⁴ 18.4d 15.5d² 14fg) tall colt; staying
handicapper; probably acts on any going; has run respectably for an apprentice;
has worn bandages. *P. Mitchell.*

RATHMOY'S SPARKLE 3 b.g. Sparkler 130–Trigamy 112 (Tribal Chief 125) **66 d**
(1980 5v³ 5v³ 5fg* 6fg³ 6g⁴ 6g² 6d² 7fg² 6fg³ 7d 1981 7g 7fg 7d⁴ 8s 8g 7f 7f
8g 7g 8d 8.2s) compact gelding; close fourth in handicap at Warwick in May
(apprentice ridden); ran respectably in valuable seller on eighth start; stays 1m;
possibly not at his best on heavy going. *N. Callaghan.*

RATHVINDON 2 ch.f. Realm 129–Alice Kyteler (Crepello 136) (1981 5s* **93**
5f 6.3fg⁴ 6d 6g²) Mar 25; rather unfurnished filly; fourth foal; half-sister to Irish
6f to 1¼m winner Coven (by Sassafras) and very useful French 1¼m winner
Interdit (by English Prince); dam winner over 9f; put up a pleasing first effort
when wearing down Miss Lilian to win 15-runner maiden race at Leopardstown in
May by 1½ lengths; last of 11 to Fly Baby in Queen Mary Stakes at Royal
Ascot the following month; wasn't disgraced when 5¾ lengths fourth of 9 to
Anfield in Group 3 Railway Stakes at the Curragh at the end of August nor
when ½-length second of 16 to Afghan in Birdcatcher Nursery at Naas in
October; will probably stay 7f. *M. Kauntze, Ireland.*

RATTLE (FR) 2 br.f. Riverman 131–Kassa (Kashmir II 125) (1981 8s*) **?**
Mar 28; 310,000 francs Y (approx £31,000); third reported foal; dam won small
races over 1m and 9f in France; second favourite, came through strongly in
closing stages to win 10-runner newcomers event at Maisons-Laffitte in November
by ¾ length from Flying Machine; will stay 1¼m. *C. Milbank, France.*

RAVENSBOURNE 8 br.h. Siliconn 121–Suzy Wong II 71 (Mincio 127) (1980 —
10s 8s 10d* 8fg 10g* 8g 1981 12.2fg) plater; has been fired; stays 1¼m; acts
on heavy going; has worn blinkers; wears bandages. *R. Akehurst.*

RAVENS TOWER 4 gr.c. Tower Walk 130–Grey Mink 86 (Double Jump 131) —
(1980 7v² 7s³ 7f 8h⁴ 8fg 8g³ 7g 8.2s⁴ 8.3g 8fg³ 8.2d³ 8f 11s³ 9g 10d 1981 8d 8d 8f)
lengthy colt; quite a moderate handicapper at his best; well beaten in seller
final start; not certain to stay middle distances; suited by some give in the
ground. *M. Pipe.*

RAWALPINDI 3 b.g. Hotfoot 126–Rotisserie 106 (Tesco Boy 121) (1980 7f³ **81**
7d 1981 10s 10d* 12g 10g* 12d) strong, medium-sized, quite attractive
gelding; ran easily best races when 2-length winner of minor events at Brighton in
April (from Halsbury) and May; should stay 1½m (beaten a long way out and ran
badly both times when tried at trip); possibly not at his best on very soft going;
exported to Hong Kong. *G. Harwood.*

RAWLINSON END 3 b.c. Song 132–Wong Way Girl 99 (Kibenka 119) (1980 **76**
6g 5d² 5d 5d⁴ 1981 6s 6fg⁴ 7s² 7d* 7.2s 7g³ 7g 7g 8d 7d⁴) neat, strong colt; good
walker; won 16-runner minor event by a head from Gay Georgia at Brighton in
May; in frame in handicaps at Newbury and Leicester afterwards; suited by 7f;
has run respectably on a firm surface but best form with some give in the ground;
ran very badly in blinkers fifth start. *R. Laing.*

RAY CHARLES 3 gr.c. Sun Prince 128–Ivory Gull 70 (Sea Hawk II 131) **96**
(1980 7g 7s 1981 10s* 11.7f* 11.7fg² 11.7fg² 12fg³ 10fg 10d³ 10.6s³ 11d) tall,
narrow colt; none too good a walker or mover; successful in poor maiden race at
Folkestone in March and handicap at Windsor in June; ran well in handicaps most
other outings, though when third in quite valuable races at Goodwood (to
Grain Race) on fifth start and Newbury (to Atlantic Boy) on seventh; suited by
1½m and will possibly stay further; acts on any going; genuine and consistent;
sold to D. Nicholson 14,000 gns Newmarket Autumn Sales. *G. Harwood.*

RAY'S BELLE 3 gr.f. Fleece 114–Sovereign Comment (Sovereign Path 125) —
(1980 5f 6fg 6d 1981 8fg 8g) leggy, narrow, unfurnished filly; behind in maiden
auction and maiden events. *J. Berry.*

RAZ

RAZOR SUN (USA) 2 b.f. Blade–Summer Hill (Sir Gaylord) (1981 5g² **83**
5fg⁴ 6s³ 6fg³ 7f* 7d² 7.2fg 8.2s) Mar 11; $47,000Y; neat, good-quartered filly;
good walker and mover; closely related to a winner at up to 1m by Vitriolic and
half-sister to several minor winners; dam never ran; beat Chaste Lady by a
head in 8-runner maiden race at Brighton in July; ¾-length second to Tenth of
October in nursery at Lingfield following month; should stay 1m; seems to act
on any going. *B. Hills.*

READING 2 ch.c. Vitiges 132–Shortbread 104 (Crisp and Even 116) (1981 **70**
5g 6f⁴ 7fg³ 7d 6fg) May 7; 20,000Y; short-backed, quite attractive colt; good
mover; first foal; dam, winner over 7f here and 1½m in Norway, is daughter of
sister to Dominion; didn't find a lot under pressure when in frame in 8-runner
Fenwick Stakes at Ascot in June (5½ lengths fourth to Norwick) and slowly-run
minor event at Kempton in July (3 lengths third of 5 to Santella Man); ran
moderately in £4,000 seller at Kempton in August on final start; should be
suited by 1m but has shown signs of being headstrong; wears blinkers; sold
2,600 gns Ascot September Sales. *J. Tree.*

REALERT 5 ch.g. Red Alert 127–Persian Mourne (Mourne 126) (1980 7fg —
1981 11.7v 13.1g 10f) attractive gelding; has shown no form since 1979; stays
1m; acts on firm going and is probably unsuited by soft; usually wears blinkers.
N. Mitchell.

REALES 3 ch.g. Gay Fandango 132–Ameliorate (Reform 132) (1980 NR 1981 —
8d 8fg 7.6s 6fg) 10,000Y; quite an attractive, well-made gelding; third foal;
dam ran twice; not disgraced when sixth of 9 behind Noalto in Easter Stakes
at Kempton in April on second outing; off course afterwards until August and
was well beaten on his return; stays 1m; blinkered last 3 outings; one to be wary
of; sold 1,800 gns Newmarket Autumn Sales. *B. Hills.*

REALLY LUCKY (USA) 3 ch.f. Northern Dancer–Realty 126 (Sir Ivor 135) **114**
(1980 8.5g 6.5d⁴ 7v 1981 10fg* 9s² 10.5g⁴ 9d 8v* 8s) French filly; blind in one
eye; first foal; dam high-class sprinter, winner of both Prix du Gros-Chene
and Prix du Petit Couvert; first past post 3 times at Longchamp, in maiden
race in April, minor event in May (relegated to second) and in Prix de Saint-Cyr
in October; put up a good performance when having first race for 3 months
in last-named, winning in fine style by 3 lengths from Nostalgic Memory; also
ran well when fourth of 8 behind Snow Day in Group 3 Prix de Royaumont
at Chantilly in June (beaten only just over a length); stays 10.5f; probably
acts on any going, but goes well on heavy. *Mme C. Head, France.*

REALLY PROUD 7 b.g. Silly Season 127–Pollster 101 (Majority Blue 126) —
(1980 NR 1981 10fg 16d) lightly raced and probably of little account nowadays. *M. Bolton.*

REALMS REASON 2 ch.f. Realm 129–Countess Eileen 111 (Sassafras 135) **92**
(1981 6fg 7fg² 7f² 8d² 7g⁴) May 4; 16,500Y; big, rangy filly; first foal; dam
won over 1m and 1½m and was third in Irish St Leger; second in 3 good races,
going down by a neck to Full Extent in Heronslea Stakes at Ayr in August, by
½ length to stable-companion Marquessa d'Howfen in Gilbey Champion Racehorse Futurity at York the following month and by 2½ lengths to Prince's Polly
in Silken Glider Stakes at Leopardstown later in September; short-priced
favourite for 16-runner Somerville Tattersall Stakes at Newmarket in October
but faded from the Dip and was beaten just over 5 lengths into fourth place
behind Wind and Wuthering (gave 15 lb); will be suited by a return to 1m;
sure to win in maiden company. *W. Hastings-Bass.*

REAY'S SONG 7 ch.g. Songedor 116–Lady Reay (Queen's Hussar 124) (1980 —
NR 1981 12.5s 12s⁴ 12s) lightly raced and of little account on flat though
has won over hurdles. *M. Naughton.*

REBEL STAR 3 b.g. Rebel Prince 110–Star of Relic (Relic) (1980 NR 1981 —
16d 15.5f³ 15.5f 15.5fg² 12fg) 1,600Y; half-brother to 3 winners, including
prolific Swedish winner Samuel Whiskers and 1979 2-y-o 5f seller winner Stellar
Link (both by The Go-Between); dam never ran; has shown a little ability in
maiden and minor races; seems to stay 2m. *B. Wise.*

REBOLLINO 2 b.c. Nebbiolo 125–Cloe (Shantung 132) (1981 5g² 6g* 7f² 5g²) **110**
Apr 9; 8,200Y; big, rangy colt; none too good a mover; half-brother to winning
3-y-o sprinter Bold Scuffle (by Bold Lad, Ire) and 2 winners in Italy; dam won
at 2 yrs and 3 yrs in Italy; put up a useful effort to win 12-runner Convivial
Maiden Stakes at York in August when having first race for over 3 months,
scoring by 1½ lengths from Mirabeau; far from disgraced when second twice the
following month, just failing to see trip out so well as Busaco when beaten 1¼

698

Convivial Maiden Stakes, York—Rebollino puts up a useful effort to defeat Mirabeau (not in picture) and Beldale Lustre

lengths in Sancton Stakes on same course and putting up a very useful effort when beaten 2 lengths by Jester in 5-runner Harry Rosebery Challenge Trophy at Ayr; seems best at 5f and 6f; looks the type to train on. *T. Fairhurst.*

RECITATION (USA) 3 b.c. Elocutionist–Irish Party (Irish Lancer) (1980 **124** 5f³ 5f* 6d* 6s² 8g² 8fg² 8d* 8d⁴ 1981 7s* 8g* 12g 9.2s 7s²)

Recitation spent most of his career in the shadow of To-Agori-Mou and a fair amount of his second season out of the public eye; he left the racing scene virtually unnoticed in the autumn, for stud duties in the United States. He was never rated more than second best in the yard and lacked his stable-companion's consistency, but great care must be taken to avoid the injustice of under-estimating him. He did, after all, win the most important two-year-old race at Royal Ascot, the Coventry Stakes, and France's most important two-year-old race, the Grand Criterium; and at three he was a very convincing winner of the Poule d'Essai des Poulains, the French Two Thousand Guineas.

Recitation received 9-1 in the Tote European Free Handicap, 5 lb less than To-Agori-Mou and 6 lb less than top-weight Storm Bird who between them had fought out the finish of England's most important two-year-old race of 1980, the William Hill Dewhurst Stakes. His consistency left something to be desired but he hadn't been out of the frame in eight starts and was obviously a top-class horse at his best. He ran away with the Coventry Stakes, striding powerfully clear for a five-length success: Motavato, Bel Bolide and Another Realm chased him home. Much later in the year, following a close second to Robellino in the Royal Lodge Stakes, he became only the third foreign-trained horse to win the Grand Criterium since the war—Sir Ivor in 1967 and My Swallow in 1970 were the others—beating Critique in a very tight, punishing finish. Shortly after—too soon after, probably—he was sent for the William Hill Futurity at Doncaster and was beaten into fourth place behind Beldale Flutter, Shergar and Sheer Grit.

Recitation began to work extremely well in the spring, and was trained

Poule d'Essai des Poulains, Longchamp—Recitation wins in good style from Redoutable and Cresta Rider

for the Poule d'Essai des Poulains run at Longchamp in April on the Sunday before the Two Thousand Guineas. To-Agori-Mou was the stable's selected for the Guineas, which is usually the more strongly-contested affair. Recitation did everything required of him in his preliminary in the Salisbury Two Thousand Guineas Trial Stakes at the beginning of April, so in that respect he outpointed To-Agori-Mou. He won by two lengths and a neck from Tahoe and Dalby Mustang, the latter of whom went on to run third to Kind of Hush and To-Agori-Mou in the Ladbrokes Craven Stakes. He looked very well indeed in the paddock, with plenty left to work on. In the race he was a shade slow out but had sufficient speed to get through quickly onto the stand rail; thereafter he was always going easily, in control throughout, and long after halfway he still had his head on one side. Had the Poule d'Essai des Poulains been run in England there isn't much doubt he would have started favourite.

In fact Cresta Rider, coupled with the pacemaker Steel Age, started 5/4 favourite for the Poulains; Recitation started second favourite at 24/10 in the field of ten. Cresta Rider, an imposing individual by Northern Dancer, had won three races including the Criterium de Maisons-Laffitte from four starts; his defeat, entirely on merit, occurred in the Grand Criterium when he finished fourth, beaten just over a length. Connections anticipated he would be much better served by the faster ground. The field also included two French horses who had been highly rated in the Free Handicap, Prince Mab (8-12) and Big John (8-10), and an English horse, Mattaboy, who had finished a creditable sixth to Motavato under a big weight in the race for the Free Handicap; but it's clear that the Poulains once again took less winning than its English counterpart. Recitation, beautifully turned out and enterprisingly ridden, readily confirmed his superiority over those French contemporaries who had so far been put up against him. He was dashed through on the inside on the home turn after racing in third place behind a strong pace set by Steel Age, and very quickly had the race in his pocket. As for Cresta Rider, it was virtually the Grand Criterium all over again: he looked as though he could win, but Recitation's powerful, raking gallop cracked him easily and he was beaten three and a half lengths into third place. Recitation was striding out with great resolution towards the end, giving the strong-finishing Redoutable, who had been second to Cresta Rider three weeks earlier in the Prix de Fontainebleau, no chance; he won by two and a half lengths. Mattaboy ran poorly and beat only two home, one of them the pacemaker.

Nothing looked more logical than to go next for the Prix du Jockey-Club, the French Derby, with Recitation. The course would suit him better than Epsom; travelling to France obviously held no terrors for him; there were no doubts about his staying a mile and a half, on the contrary everything pointed to his being suited by that sort of trip; and though he would be meeting a largely different set of French horses there was no telling they were significantly better than those he had already beaten. That's how we saw it, anyway. However, when Recitation went to Chantilly he was a sore disappointment: he never promised to take a hand, found nothing when asked for an effort in the straight and trailed in alongside No Lute, joint-seventh and almost twenty lengths behind the winner. His performance is difficult to explain except in terms of his failing to stay or having one of his 'off days'. Given the fact that Bikala and Akarad were significantly better than the French milers, Recitation should still have been in with a chance of a place at his best. Recitation ran only twice more. His trainer evidently thought he didn't stay, for he brought him back to nine furlongs in the Prix d'Ispahan at Longchamp in July and then to seven in the Harroways Stakes at Goodwood in September. The Prix d'Ispahan

700

was one of the races on a Longchamp card postponed a week because of a Pari-Mutuel strike. Recitation had been away from his home stable for ten days when he ran, which might account for his finishing over eight lengths down on The Wonder, in sixth place; he was beaten by Cracaval and by Cresta Rider, the latter of whom he couldn't pass in the straight. In the Harroways Stakes he ran well, particularly for a horse having his first outing for twelve weeks. On terms slightly worse than weight-for-age, he finished a two-length second of five to the powerful front-running Belmont Bay, fighting back from last place after being outpaced at halfway.

		Gallant Romeo (b 1961)	Gallant Man
Recitation (USA) (b.c. 1978)	Elocutionist (b 1973)		Juliets Nurse
		Strictly Speaking (b 1967)	Fleet Nasrullah
			Believe Me
	Irish Party (br 1968)	Irish Lancer (b 1957)	Royal Charger
			Tige O'Myheart
		Party Favor (b 1960)	Tim Tam
			Beaukiss

Perhaps we should not have been so dogmatic about Recitation's prospects of staying a mile and a half. Not a lot is known about Elocutionist's characteristics as a sire, for Recitation is one of his first crop; furthermore the pedigree is American, and American pedigrees can be difficult to interpret, since American racing concentrates so heavily on distances up to a mile and a quarter. Elocutionist won at up to nine and a half furlongs—the distance of the Preakness Stakes, his best win; he was third in the Kentucky Derby over a mile and a quarter. His sire was a stakes winner at up to eight and a half furlongs. Irish Party, the dam, by a Royal Charger horse who also won at up to eight and a half furlongs, won two stakes races at around the same distance. She bred three previous winners, easily the best of them the colt Irish Icecapade (by Icecapade), now retired to stud the winner of minor stakes races at up to a mile. The next

Mr Hilary J. Boone's "Recitation"

two dams were minor winners, Party Favor being quite stoutly bred seeing she is by Tim Tam, who won over a mile and a half, out of a Mahmoud mare.

Recitation has been retired to the same stud as Storm Bird, the Ashford Stud in Kentucky, and will stand at 40,000 dollars, live foal, as compared with 175,000 dollars, live foal, for Storm Bird's services. A big, well-made, long-striding colt, apparently best at up to a mile (even now we aren't convinced he wouldn't have been equally effective at a mile and a quarter), he acted on any going. *G. Harwood.*

RECLINE 2 b. or br.f. Wollow 132–Balista 86 (Baldric II 131) (1981 5d² 5s² 5f **70** 5s²) Apr 5; small, very lightly-made filly; half-sister to 2 winners, including very speedy 1980 2-y-o Labista (by Crowned Prince); dam stayed 7f; second in maiden races at Chester, Haydock and Lingfield; having first race for nearly 4 months when beaten 2 lengths by Sound of the Sea on last-named course in October; should be suited by 6f +; ran poorly only outing on firm going; has very little scope; sold 2,500 gns to K. Ivory Newmarket Autumn Sales. *B. Hobbs.*

RECONQUEST 3 ch.c. Red Alert 127–La Concha (Le Levanstell 122) (1980 **77** 5f* 5g 6fg⁴ 6g 6fg 6d 6s* 6g 1981 6g 6fg 6fg 6g 6s⁴ 6g³ 6d 5g) small colt; quite a moderate handicapper; will stay 7f; acts on any going; sold to J. Harris 2,100 gns Newmarket Autumn Sales. *D. Kent.*

RECORD ANSWER 2 b.f. Record Token 128–Tender Answer (Prince Tender- **80** foot 126) (1981 5.1f 7fg⁴ 8fg⁴ 8fg 7g) May 15; leggy, lightly-made filly; first foal; dam useful winner over 7f at 2 yrs in Ireland; finished in good style when 1½ lengths fourth of 29 to Hayakaze in maiden race at Newmarket in August and was again going on at finish when 4½ lengths fourth of 15 to Rockfest in £3,600 event at Goodwood the following month; better suited by 1m than shorter distances. *R. Williams.*

RECORD BREAKER 5 b.h. Jukebox 120–Bare Costs (Petition 130) (1980 **53** 7v 7g 5f 5f 6f 6fg 1981 7d 7d 7d³ 10g 8d 8g⁴ 8f 8f 7fg⁴ 7.6s 7h2 6d 6g) lengthy horse; stays 1m; seems to act on any going; blinkered once in 1980; has run respectably for an apprentice. *B. McMahon.*

RECORD CHOICE 6 b.m. Jukebox 120–Debatable 84 (Counsel 118) (1980 — 11fg 10h 10f 12f³ 10f 10s 1981 12g 10g 8.2fg) poor plater; usually acts on any going; usually wears blinkers and has also worn a hood; none too generous in a finish. *W. Stubbs.*

RECORD CLEAN 2 ch.g. Record Run 127–Maryfield (Hul a Hul 124) (1981 — 5s 5g 5g 5g 5fg 7g) Mar 21; 2,900Y; compact gelding; bad plater; blinkered last 2 outings. *J. Mason.*

RECORD REVIEW 2 b.f. Record Token 128–Right View 75 (Right Tack 131) **67** (1981 5s* 5g² 6d 8d) Mar 24; well-made filly; good walker; second foal; dam won over 5f early at 2 yrs; won 9-runner event at Catterick in April by 7 lengths from Grey Gem; off course over 4 months after going down by 2½ lengths to odds-on Benfen in small race at Redcar the following month and was well beaten in nurseries on return; not sure to stay 1m. *W. Wharton.*

RECORD ROYALE 3 br.g. Record Token 128–Mahal 101 (Tutankhamen) — (1980 5s 5s 6s 6fg 7fg 6g 1981 7fg 10.1d 8.3s 8f) small, rather narrow gelding; only poor form, including in sellers; sold 420 gns Newmarket July Sales. *G. Balding.*

RECORD STAR 3 ch.g. Jukebox 120–St Rosalie (Aureole 132) (1980 5f 5f **60** 5.3d 7g 5fg 6g 6g 1981 7fg 6d 6v 7f³ 9d* 10f³ 10f* 10fg* 8f³ 8fg) compact gelding; did well in sellers and was bought in each time after winning at Hamilton in July and Folkestone (twice) in August; cost 1,300 gns to buy in on last occasion; ran creditably in a non-seller penultimate start; stays 1¼m; probably acts on any going; successful with blinkers and without. *G. Lewis.*

RECORD SURPRISE 3 b.f. Record Run 127–Bonne Surprise 105 (Grey — Sovereign 128§) (1980 6d 6s 8d 8d 6d⁴ 6s² 1981 6v 5d 5g 5g) lengthy filly; well beaten in 1981; ran best races of 1980 at 6f; often wears blinkers nowadays. *N. Callaghan.*

RECORD TREASURE 2 ch.f. Record Token 128–Legal Treasure 46 (Quorum — 126) (1981 6s 6d) May 8; half-sister to 4 winners, 3 of them fairly useful, including sprinter Single Gal (by Mansingh); dam poor plater; 33/1 and needing race when about 10 lengths fifth to Risk Taker in very slowly-run 8-runner minor event at Redcar in October; soundly beaten in maiden event at Leicester the following month. *J. W. Watts.*

702

RED AND GOLD 2 b.g. Red Alert 127–Aucuparia (Celtic Ash) (1981 7fg⁴)   — p
Jan 22; half-brother to 2 winners, including useful stayer Toondra (by Northfields); dam poor daughter of Park Hill Stakes winner Vertencia; with leaders
much of way when 10 lengths fourth of 15 to Skytrick in maiden race at
Yarmouth in August; gelded subsequently; will probably stay 1m. *M. Jarvis.*

RED ARTIST 5 ch.g. Red Alert 127–Lane House 68 (Bounteous 125) (1980   **49**
12.5h 10fg 10f 10d 12d 1981 10.2s 13fg 10d³ 10.8fg 12d 10fg 11.5d 10f³ 12fg)
neat, fair sort; third in seller at Folkestone in May and claiming race at Brighton
in August; stays 1¼m; probably acts on any going; blinkered sixth start.
J. Perrett.

RED BERET 2 ch.f. Air Trooper 115–Berostina 88 (Ribero 126) (1981 5f 5fg)   —
May 18; 2,000Y; lightly-made filly; second foal; half-sister to 1980 2-y-o 6f
winner Holdall (by Manacle); dam, winner over hurdles, was at her best at
2 yrs on flat; in rear in maiden races at Pontefract and Catterick in July; dead.
P. Asquith.

RED CARD 2 b.g. Red Alert 127–The Game 80 (Petition 130) (1981 7g)   —
Mar 18; 2,200Y; closely related to fairly useful 5f to 1¼m performer Lefki
(by Red God) and half-brother to several winners, including smart miler Whistling
Glory (by Whistling Wind) and very useful 6f and 7f winner Penny Post (by
Balidar); dam won at 1¼m; 20/1 and in need of race when behind in 18-runner
maiden event won by Leg Glance at Doncaster in October. *J. Etherington.*

RED CLIP 7 b.g. Double Red 122–Barnstables 72 (Pay Up) (1980 9fg 1981 8g   —
10g 8f) poor maiden; stays 1m; has sweated up. *J. Gilbert.*

RED CREST 4 ch.f. Red God 128§–Crested Egret (Great Heron 127) (1980   —
5d 6f³ 8f³ 8g⁴ 8f 8f 8d 1981 8g 12d 10.8fg 11g 12f 8f 9f⁴ 10.1g) neat, strong
filly; plating-class maiden; stays 9f; acts on firm going; blinkered once at 3 yrs.
G. Huffer.

REDDEN 3 ch.g. Red God 128§–Portden (Worden II 129) (1980 5s 5fg² 6f*   **87**
1981 7s 7g 7.3g* 7.6g 7f 7g⁴ 8.3g 10fg² 10fg) attractive, well-made gelding;
injured himself after winning Woodcote Stakes at Epsom as a 2-y-o; returned
to form despite hanging violently left when beating Rowania ¾ length in handicap
at Newbury in May (well backed); put up best subsequent efforts when in
frame in similar events at Sandown in July and Kempton in August; evidently
stays 1¼m; acts on firm going; blinkered fifth start; wore tongue-strap at
Newbury. *B. Swift.*

RED ELLETTE 2 ch.f. Red Alert 127–Ellette 105 (Le Levanstell 122) (1981   **72**
5s³ 5d 5s 6fg² 6fg² 5f* 5fg⁴ 6fg 5fg 6g 5d) Apr 15; IR 1,300Y; fair sort; good
mover; fourth living foal; dam won over 5f and 1m at 2 yrs in Ireland; beat
Another Way a length in 9-runner maiden auction event at Folkestone in August;
out of first 6 in nurseries last 4 starts; will stay 7f; best form on a firm surface;
dwelt ninth outing. *S. Mellor.*

REDENHAM 5 b.g. Brigadier Gerard 144–Secret Ray 114 (Privy Councillor 125)   **50**
(1980 7f 8f 8fg 11d* 12.3g⁴ 8d 10s 10d 8fg* 12.2fg² 8g² 10.2d 1981 8fg 8f
9g 10g 10f 11fg 12.2g³) big gelding; poor handicapper; stays 1½m; acts on a
firm and a soft surface; often blinkered; has looked ungenuine on occasions;
has worn a bandage on near-hind. *W. A. Stephenson.*

REDESIGN 3 ch.g. Red Alert 127–Miss Remont 89 (Damremont 120) (1980 6fg   **48**
6fg 6fg 1981 8fg 11.7g 12s 7.6g 7f² 7fg 8fg³ 8.3d⁴) quite well-made gelding;
plater; gives impression he'll stay 1¼m; probably acts on any going; often
blinkered. *T. Marshall.*

RED FANTASTIC 2 b.c. Red God 128§–Amablai (Levmoss 133) (1981 7g 7fg   **86**
8g 7g 10g) June 3; 12,500Y; sturdy, quite attractive colt; third foal; half-
brother to Balu (by Ballymore), a useful winner at up to 1¾m in Ireland and
France; dam, half-sister to Derby third Oats, won at up to 2m in Ireland; put
up a fair effort when staying on to finish 9¼ lengths seventh of 16 to Wind and
Wuthering in Somerville Tattersall Stakes at Newmarket in October on fourth
outing; not entirely disgraced next time out and probably stays 1¼m. *P. Mitchell.*

RED FIELD 3 b.c. Tudor Rhythm 112–Glebe 83 (Tacitus 124) (1980 7g³ 7d   **54**
7fg 7fg 7g 6g 6d 1981 8.2s⁴ 12d² 12d³ 12g 12d³ 16f 12f 13d 16s) strong, lengthy
colt; plating-class maiden; suited by 1½m; had a very poor run seventh start;
trained most of season by H. Westbrook. *W. Holden.*

RED FLASH (FR) 3 b.c. Red Lord 124–Bunting Grace (Hodell 120) (1980 5.5g   **106**
8g³ 1981 6.5g* 8d* 10s³ 8d 7g* 7d⁴ 7f 8g² 8g 6d 8d) 105,000 francs Y (approx
£11,100); half-brother to 2 winners, including useful 1978 2-y-o Thalie Dancer (by

Dancing Lad); dam never ran; successful in maiden event and small race at Cagnes-sur-Mer early in year and minor event at Le Croise-Laroche in May; in rear in Jersey Stakes at Royal Ascot on seventh start; seems to stay 1¼m; possibly not at his best on firm going. *C. Milbank, France.*

REDFOOT 2 gr.c. Abwah 118–Redhead 66 (Hotfoot 126) (1981 5g 5g 5f 5s 5g) 48
Apr 7; 5,200Y; small colt; bad walker; first foal; dam won 9f seller; only poor form in maiden races and a seller; probably needs further. *C. Spares.*

REDFORD 3 ch.c. Red God 128§–Ashton Jane 86 (Gratitude 130) (1980 5fg³ 68
5fg³ 5d⁴ 6d 6fg 1981 7v⁴ 8s 12d³ 9g* 10d 12s² 9s² 12s 12f 7f 7fg 9f 12f⁴ 9f* 7f)
strong, quite attractive, good sort; successful in maiden race at Mallow in April
(made all) and handicap at Tramore in August; last of 14 behind Feltwell in King
George V Stakes (Handicap) at Royal Ascot on ninth start; seems to stay 1½m;
acts on any going; often blinkered. *H. de Bromhead, Ireland.*

RED FORT 2 ch.g. Mansingh 120–Ixia (Le Fabuleux 133) (1981 5.8g 6f 6d 6g) —
May 1; 8,000Y; strong, good sort; good mover; half-brother to 3-y-o middle-
distance winner Tajonski (by Bolkonski) and 2 winners in France; dam French
1¼m winner and also won over jumps; well beaten in maiden races; unseated rider
leaving stalls second outing; blinkered last 2 starts. *R. Hollinshead.*

RED GOLD 3 ch.c. Red Alert 127–Golden Samantha 88 (Sammy Davis 129) 86 d
(1980 5fg³ 6fg 6d 6d 5fg² 5g* 5g³ 5d* 5g² 1981 6g 5f 5fg² 6fg 5fg 6g⁴ 5g⁴ 6d)
well-made, quite attractive colt; rather disappointing in 1981, best effort when
2¼ lengths second to Pencil Point in handicap at Goodwood in July; best form at
5f; yet to show he acts on extremes of going (may well have found ground too
firm on second start); sold to B. Hanbury 8,400 gns Newmarket Autumn Sales.
P. Cundell.

REDGRAVE GRAPHICS 2 b.g. Welsh Saint 126–Born Friendly (Takawalk II —
125) (1981 6g 8g 5s 8s) Mar 30; IR 2,800F, IR 3,800Y, 5,600 2-y-o; big,
strong gelding; brother to Irish 7f and 1m winner Matagouri and half-brother to
two 2-y-o 5f winners; in rear in maiden races; pulled very hard final start; has
worn bandages. *R. Whitaker.*

RED INJUN 2 b.c. Mill Reef 141–Ardneasken 84 (Right Royal V 135) (1981 70 p
7.2fg² 8g) May 9; medium-sized, quite attractive colt; half-brother to several
winners, including high-class stayer Dakota (by Stupendous) and very useful
middle-distance performer Warpath (by Sovereign Path); dam out-and-out
stayer; second favourite and pretty fit, failed by only ¾ length to catch Scoutsmistake in 13-runner maiden race at Haydock in September and would almost
certainly have won had he handled the turns better; again lost his pitch on the
turn when disappointing favourite for similar event at Ayr later in month:
will be well suited by 1½m; worth another chance. *C. Thornton.*

RED JAY 5 ch.m. Redundant 120–Jayberne § (Double-U-Jay 120) (1980 54
8s 10fg 11.7f* 10g 10s 12g* 11.7d* 12fg 11.7fg³ 13.1h³ 12fg 14g 12.2d 1981
12fg 10s 12d 12g 11.1s 12f 11.7fg³ 12g 11.7fg* 11.7fg 11.7g 11.7g 12g) fair
sort; poor handicapper; won at Windsor in July; stays 1½m; acts on any going
except soft; sometimes sweats up badly. *S. Matthews.*

*Coventry Stakes, Ascot—Red Sunset has to battle hard to withstand the
last-furlong challenge of Chris's Lad; Bronowski finishes third*

RED JERSEY 2 ch.g. Red Alert 127–Dunstells (Saint Crespin III 132) (1981 **88**
5v⁴ 5d³ 5g* 5s² 5d² 5f) Feb 23; IR 9,000F, 13,000Y; quite attractive gelding;
half-brother to 2 winners, including French stayer Dunskelly (by Pitskelly);
dam ran only twice; favourite when beating Epiphron and Reelin Elly narrowly
in minor event at Navan in May; 2½ lengths second of 8 to Day Is Done in
Marble Hill Stakes at the Curragh later in month and wasn't disgraced when
1½ lengths second to Ormsary in 4-runner Emily Persse Cup at Phoenix Park in
June; should stay 1m; ran poorly on firm going in Windsor Castle Stakes at
Royal Ascot and possibly needs some give in the ground; got very much above
himself in paddock when blinkered at Ascot and was subsequently gelded.
P. Prendergast, Ireland.

RED LADY 3 gr.f. Warpath 113–Whisky Lima 82 (Midsummer Night II 117) **62**
(1980 7g³ 8d² 1981 8g 13g* 15.8g 16f) narrow, lightly-made filly; stayed on
when beating subsequently-disqualified Java Lights a length in maiden race at
Ayr in June; suited by 13f (well beaten over 2m); sold 5,200 gns Doncaster
November Sales. *C. Thornton.*

RED LANCE 2 ch.g. Red Alert 127–Shonna (Carlemont 132) (1981 6g 7g 7fg   —
7fg 7fg 10s) Apr 5; IR 4,500F, 3,800Y; lengthy gelding; third produce; half-
brother to Irish 3-y-o middle-distance winner Regal Show (by Royal and Regal);
dam, placed over 7f in French Provinces, daughter of smart sprinter Empress
Sissi; only plating class; blinkered final outing. *Mrs J. Reavey.*

REDOUTABLE (FR) 3 b.c. Tyrant–Alvina (Snob 130) (1980 7.5g 7.5d* **117**
8g* 1981 8d² 8g² 8s² 12g 10fg² 8fg 8s³) strong, sturdy French colt; 145,000
francs Y (approx £15,300); half-brother to 3 minor French winners; dam French
1¼m winner; didn't win in 1981 but put up several very good efforts; finished well
when 2½ lengths second to Recitation in Poule d'Essai des Poulains at Longchamp
in April; placed in 3 other pattern races on same course, in Prix de Fontainebleau
earlier in month (½-length second to Cresta Rider), Prix de la Jonchere in May
(beaten ½ length by Lou Piguet) and Prix du Rond-Point in September (2 lengths
third to Daeltown); best form at 1m, although stays 1¼m; has run respectably
on a firm surface but seems better on soft. *F. Palmer, France.*

RED PETAL 3 ch.f. Red Alert 127–Petal (Whistler 129) (1980 6f 7f 7d 7fg **53**
6g 6d 6v⁴ 6s 1981 7s 6s 6g⁴ 6g 7g² 7s 8g³ 8fg 7fg 10fg³ 8d 11.5fg 10s²) compact
filly; placed in varied company, including selling; stays 1¼m; blinkered seventh
to ninth starts; suitable mount for an inexperienced rider. *W. Marshall.*

RED RAGUSA 5 ch.m. Homeric 133–Gay Crocket 88 (Crocket 130) (1980   —
NR 1981 8.2g) neat, lightly-made mare; plater; stays 9f. *C. Crossley.*

RED REPORT 3 ch.g. Red Alert 127–No Fooling 83 (Narrator 127) (1980 6g   —
6g 1981 9s 10fg 10fg 10f 16g³ 15.5g 10.6s 12d) strong, useful sort; good walker;
poor form in varied company; seems to stay 2m. *F. Durr.*

RED ROSIE 2 ch.f. Red Alert 127–Benita 94 (Roan Rocket 128) (1981 5d 5g⁴ **91**
5.3f* 6fg³ 6fg⁴ 6fg³ 5fg²) Apr 13; IR 3,400F, 7,000Y; neat filly; half-sister to
1m winner Hell Bent (by Busted); dam sprinter; led inside distance to beat
Laura Jenney ½ length in 12-runner maiden race at Brighton in June; in frame in
nurseries afterwards, on final occasion going down by ¾ length to Childown Blue
at Kempton in August; effective at 5f and 6f; acts on firm going; has run well for
an apprentice. *R. Smyth.*

RED SEAM 2 ch.c. Red Alert 127–Court Time (Arctic Time 127) (1981 5d 5s³ **67**
5.8g 6g 7d) Apr 15; IR 3,000Y; strong, shapely colt; walks well; half-brother to
3 winners, including useful stayer Cicero's Court (by Lauso); dam winning Irish
stayer; prominent in maiden auction events on second and fourth outings,
staying on to finish 1½ lengths fifth of 15 to Sylvan Barbarosa at Epsom in June
on fourth; should stay 7f. *N. Vigors.*

RED SEED 7 ch.h. Red God 128§–Alcina (Alycidon 138) (1980 including **80**
4.5v* 9g* 1981 10fg³ 10g 8f 8fg 8f 8f 7fg 8fg) compact horse; fair performer
here in 1976; subsequently sent abroad and won 10 races from 4.5f to 11f in
Scandinavia; creditable 1¾ lengths third to Lafontaine in City and Suburban
Handicap at Epsom in April; well beaten most subsequent starts and didn't
find much off bridle second outing; stays 11f; probably acts on any going;
trained by T. Dahl first 3 outings. *P. Haslam.*

RED SUNSET 2 b.c. Red God 128§–Centre Piece 73 (Tompion) (1981 5g 5g* **111**
5s² 6fg* 6fg 7fg² 7f³ 7fg⁴) Mar 31; attractive, well-made colt; good walker and
has an excellent, smooth action; brother to very smart sprinter Greenland Park,
and half-brother to a winner; dam ran 4 times at 2 yrs; won 16-runner Coventry
Stakes at Royal Ascot in June, leading inside final furlong and running on under

Mr Patrick Burns's "Red Sunset"

pressure to score by ¾ length from Chris's Lad; had previously made all to win maiden race at Newmarket; in frame in 3 other valuable races within the space of 12 days in August and September, going down by a length to Beldale Bid in 5-runner Grand Criterium International d'Ostende, finishing 6 lengths third of 8 to Silver Hawk in Intercraft Solario Stakes at Kempton and running very well when 5½ lengths fourth of 8 behind Achieved in Laurent Perrier Champagne Stakes at Doncaster; stays 7f; has run respectably on soft going but action suggests he's a different proposition on a sound surface. *G. Harwood.*

RED TAPE (FR) 2 b.c. Yours 125–Papoose (Powhatan II) (1981 5fg 5fg⁴ 6f **72** 6g⁴ 5g) Feb 13; 4,400Y; fourth live foal; dam won twice over 4.5f in France; fourth in maiden race and a nursery at Windsor in the summer; possibly better at 5f than 6f; dwelt third and final outings, wearing blinkers on latter. *W. O'Gorman.*

RED TOFF 4 b.g. Red God 128§–Hit It Off (Hardicanute 130) (1980 6f **54** d 7.3f 10f 8fg 10.8s 10.1f 10fg 16f* 1981 12d 16g 12v 16g² 16g 16fg 16fg 14g 10f 12f 14g 10.2g) strong, good-looking gelding; good mover; staying handicapper; well beaten in valuable seller final start; suited by top-of-the-ground; sometimes blinkered but is better without; trained most of season by C. Brittain. *C. Austin.*

RED TREASURE 3 ch.f. Red Alert 127–Persian Mourne (Mourne 126) (1980 **61** 5d 6fg 6d³ 5f 6d 6g⁴ 7fg 1981 8s²) small, lengthy filly; plater; close second to Hissing Sid at Doncaster in March; stays 1m; sent to Switzerland. *P. Rohan.*

RED TUESDAY 2 ch.c. Lucky Wednesday 124–Cordon Rouge 99 (Never Say **66** Die 137) (1981 6f 7f 7fg 7g 7.6s) May 8; 5,800Y; rangy colt; fourth living foal; dam suited by 1½m; remote fifth in maiden and minor races on last 2 starts, one a 15-runner event; bred to stay 1¼m+. *H. Collingridge.*

REDWOOD LODGE 3 b. or br.f. On Your Mark 125–Lost Horizon (Narrator **—** 127) (1980 5s 5fg 5s 5d 5.8g 5g 5.8f 5fg⁴ 6fg 7.2d 8d³ 8d 1981 8g 12g⁴ 10d 15fg) compact filly who carried plenty of condition; plater; seemed to stay 1½m; acted on a firm and a soft surface; had worn blinkers and had also raced with her tongue tied down; dwelt first outing; dead. *T. Craig.*

REDWYN 3 b.c. Hipster 101–Diana Carlos 64 (Don Carlos) (1980 NR 1981 10fg 8.2s 8s 10s) second foal; dam placed over 5f at 2 yrs but was of little account; little sign of ability in varied company; blinkered last 2 starts (slowly away first occasion); apprentice ridden. *P. Brookshaw.* —

REEDMACE 3 b.c. Thatch 136–Pampas Flower 80 (Pampered King 121) (1980 NR 1981 8fg3 8f* 10f3 8d3 8g) big, rangy colt; half-brother to 4 winners, including useful 6f and 7f winner Evita (by Reform); dam, half-sister to top-class performers Gratitude and Highest Hopes, won at 1m; stuck on really well when beating Icen by a neck in 20-runner maiden race at Doncaster in July; third in 2 minor events and a handicap; possibly doesn't stay 1¼m; probably acts on any going. *E. Weymes.* **77**

REEM 3 b.f. Mummy's Pet 125–Autumn Breeze (King's Bench 132) (1980 NR 1981 7f3 7f4 7f3 7.2fg) 11,000Y; rangy, useful sort; good walker; sister to fairly useful sprinter Coded Scrap and fairly useful 1977 2-y-o sprinter Touch of Salt; dam ran only twice; in frame in maiden races at Chepstow, Leicester and Folkestone (blinkered) in summer; stays 7f; sold 1,000 gns Newmarket December Sales. *Sir Mark Prescott.* **60**

REEMAN 3 b.g. Star Appeal 133–Mary Morison (Ragusa 137) (1980 NR 1981 10fg 10fg) 15,000F, 28,000Y; small gelding; half-brother to a winner in Belgium; dam, daughter of 1963 Princess Royal Stakes winner Vhairi, won over 11f in France; showed some ability in maiden races at Leicester (eighth of 15) and Ascot (7 lengths sixth of 8 to Crimson Royale) in July; will stay 1½m; sold to J. Hardy 2,100 gns Newmarket Autumn Sales. *P. Walwyn.* —

REFINED LAD 4 br.g. Master Sing 109–Polite 79 (Polic 126) (1980 12fg 7f 6d 1981 10s) tall gelding; plater; unlikely to stay 1½m; has worn blinkers; sold 2,000 gns Ascot 2nd June Sales. *P. Cundell.* —

REFRESH 3 b.g. Reform 132–Jujube 102 (Ribero 126) (1980 7g 7fg4 8g4 1981 13.3d 14fg 15.5f 16g) good-bodied gelding; good mover; didn't run up to his best in 1981 and is evidently ungenuine; probably stays 2m; wears blinkers; sold 2,900 gns Doncaster August Sales. *P. Walwyn.* —

REFRESHMENT 3 br.f. Nonoalco 131–Intermission 117 (Stage Door Johnny) (1980 NR 1981 8fg 8fg2) quite attractive, well-made filly; first foal; dam, half-sister to Quiet Fling, won Cambridgeshire; couldn't match winner's pace but ran creditably when 1½ lengths second to Northern Chance in maiden race at Goodwood in August; not seen out again; stays 1m. *J. Tree.* **75**

REGAIN 3 b.f. Relko 136–Defy (Alcide 136) (1980 NR 1981 12g3 12fg2 12fg2 12s* 12g) 8,600F; second foal; dam, second over 1¼m in France, is half-sister to very smart performers Double-U-Jay and Riverside (the dam of Riverqueen); landed odds by 7 lengths from Dutch Princess in 10-runner £2,000 race at Lingfield in October; placed in maiden races earlier; will probably stay beyond 1½m; seems to act on any going. *J. Dunlop.* **86**

REGAL GOD 6 ch.m. Green God 128–Regal Foam 51 (Primera 131) (1980 NR 1981 6g 5s) lightly-raced plater. *M. James.* —

REGAL HEIRESS 3 b.f. English Prince 129–Hardiemma 81 (Hardicanute 130) (1980 NR 1981 10fg 12d* 10fg 14g 13d* 13.3s2) strong, well-made filly; poor mover; half-sister to Derby winner Shirley Heights (by Mill Reef) and a winning plater; dam won at up to 11f; successful in maiden race at Doncaster in May (steadily drew clear to beat Beaux Arts (Fr) smoothly by 3 lengths) and handicap at Nottingham in September (stayed on well to beat Tree Mallow by 2 lengths despite losing ground at each bend); beaten 15 lengths when second to Bodham in handicap at Newbury in October; ran poorly third start; stays 1¾m; almost certainly needs some give in the ground; sold 70,000 gns Newmarket December Sales. *M. Stoute.* **81**

REGAL MAN 2 ch.c. Manado 130–Naiad Queen (Pampered King 121) (1981 6fg 7f 8g) Mar 20; 29,000Y; quite a good sort; fourth foal; half-brother to 2 winners in Ireland, including useful 1980 2-y-o 5f winner Rising Tide (by Red Alert); dam fairly useful at up to 7f in Ireland; prominent in large fields of maidens at Doncaster and Newmarket on first 2 outings (off course 3 months before third); quite a nice type of colt who could improve and make a fair handicapper in 1982. *M. Jarvis.* **74**

REGAL MINNIE 2 ch.f. Royal Match 117–Hillberry Corner 70 (Atan) (1981 5fg) Mar 16; IR 10,500Y; half-sister to 3 winners, including very useful 1978 —

French 2-y-o 5f and 7f winner Chrisfranol (by African Sky); dam 2-y-o 5f winner; unquoted when behind in 20-runner maiden race won by Travel On at Warwick in June. *C. Nelson.*

REGAL STEEL 3 ch.c. Welsh Pageant 132–All Souls 96 (Saint Crespin III 132)   **88**
(1980 7g³ 7.2d⁴ 8.2s⁴ 7v 1981 7d 12g 9s* 10d³ 10.6s 11d* 12f³ 10fg* 10fg 10d 14g³ 12fg³ 12g³ 12v 12g) compact colt; successful in handicaps at York in May and Newbury and Newmarket in June, battling on gamely to beat Show-A-Leg and Full of Reason by ½ length and the same in British Bloodstock Agency Stakes on last-named course; ran creditably on other occasions too, but also ran the odd bad race; stays 1¾m; acts on any going; suited by strong handling. *R. Hollinshead.*

REGAL TOUCH 3 b.c. Royal Match 117–Msida (Majority Blue 126) (1980   **81**
7f 6g⁴ 1981 8,*(dis) 7g⁴ 8d² 10g 8f 10.2fg 9d* 8v² 10.2g² 8s²) big, strong colt; good walker; has a round action; decisively won maiden race at Beverley in April and minor event at Hamilton in September, but was disqualified on first occasion when traces of an illegal substance were found in his system; second in handicaps at York (missed break), Doncaster and Redcar in October; stays 1¼m; suited by give in the ground; has run creditably in blinkers. *M. H. Easterby.*

REGALUS 7 br.g. Dike–March The First 90 (Martial 131) (1980 12d 13v⁴   —
12d 14f 12fg 12f 12fg³ 12.3g³ 12g⁴ 12fg 16.1fg³ 1981 12fg 14g 12f 14.6f⁴ 14d 16g) poor performer nowadays; seems to stay 1¾m; acts on any going; has worn blinkers. *H. Westbrook.*

REGAL VILLAGE 5 b.g. Royal and Regal–Chitterne (Ommeyad 120) (1980   —
8fg 8g 1981 13.4fg 9d 14d) of little account; has worn bandages and blinkers. *M. James.*

REGENCY BRIGHTON 3 ch.f. Royal Palace 131–Gay City 99 (Forlorn River   —
124) (1981 7d 6d 1981 9d 12f 8f 7f 10.2h 9g) plain filly; behind in maiden and minor races and a handicap; dwelt second and last starts. *M. Tate.*

REGENCY ELITE 6 br.g. Prince Regent 129–Leit Motif 95 (Fortino II 120)   **55**
(1980 7f* 7g⁴ 8d 7g 6d² 8fg* 8.2g² 8fg* 8f² 8fg 7.2d 8s 1981 6v 7g 8g 8g 9f 8fg³ 8fg² 10g² 8f⁴ 12f 11fg⁴ 10g³ 13d 12s) robust gelding; stays 1¼m; acts on any going except very soft; has twice been tried in blinkers; suitable mount for an apprentice; sold 1,600 gns Newmarket Autumn Sales. *Denys Smith.*

REGENCY PRINCE 3 b. or br.c. Furry Glen 121–Lyonata (Atan) (1980 5d*   **68**
5v²(dis) 5h 5g 6d² 7d 6s 1981 7g 8g 8g⁴ 10g 7g³ 8g⁴ 7f* 7g) leggy, narrow sort; good walker; bought in 2,600 gns after winning seller at Beverley in August; seems best at 7f; seems to act on any going; sometimes hangs under pressure; bandaged in front sixth outing; sent to Singapore. *P. Rohan.*

REGENT GIRL 2 b.f. Ardoon 124–Lady Gregory (Manacle 123) (1981 5g   —
5f 6f 6f 5g 6d 5s) Mar 27; 675Y (privately), 1,600 2-y-o; strong, compact filly; bad mover; third foal; dam ran twice; poor plater. *J. Doyle.*

REGENT LEISURE 2 b.c. Undulate–Happy Families 64 (Swaps) (1981 7f)   —
Apr 19; well-made colt; second foal; dam ran only 4 times; 50/1 and very backward, soon out of contention when last of 8 to Silver Hawk in Intercraft Solario Stakes at Sandown in September. *R. Simpson.*

REHOBOAM 3 b.c. Mummy's Pet 125–La Mirabelle 92 (Princely Gift 137)   **54§**
(1980 5f² 5fg 5fg² 5fg³ 5.1g³ 5g² 1981 5d⁴ 5g⁴ 6g 9fg 8g 5g 8g 7fg⁴ 7f⁴ 6f³ 6fg² 6d⁴ 6d) lengthy, narrow colt; good mover; has been hobdayed; disappointing maiden; second in seller at Newcastle in August; stays 7f; ungenuine and is one to be wary of. *T. Craig.*

REIDOR 3 br.g. Roi Soleil 125–Bella Musica (Sing Sing 134) (1980 5f 5fg*   —
1981 6s 6g 6g 7f⁴ 8.2s) compact gelding; fourth in seller at Beverley in August, best effort of 1981; probably stays 7f; has raced with his tongue tied down. *W. Haigh.*

REINFORCE 3 gr.c. Runnymede 123–Dibby's Cousin (Be Friendly 130)   **38**
(1981 5fg 5d³ 5d³ 5fg³ 5f⁴ 5.1fg⁴ 8s) May 18; 3,100F, 1,500Y; neat, short-backed colt; plater; unlikely to stay 1m; blinkered third to sixth outings; sold to National Horse Belgium 1,100 gns Newmarket Autumn Sales. *J. Hardy.*

REJUVENATOR 5 bl. or br.g. Reliance II 137–Juvenescence 87 (Golden Horus   —
123) (1980 8f 12.3f 12f 1981 15.8g) strong gelding; poor maiden; has worn blinkers. *T. Barron.*

REKAL 3 gr.c. Busted 134–Idover 95 (Fortino II 120) (1980 6fg 6g 6g 8s⁴   **78**
1981 12d⁴ 10d 10f* 12f 10fg² 10g 11.1fg 10.2fg² 10g) quite well-made colt; led

close home and beat Crackaway a short head in handicap at Leicester in June; ran best subsequent races when second in similar events at Kempton in July and Doncaster in September; stays 1½m; seems best on a firm surface. *C. Brittain.*

RELATIVE EASE 10 ch.g. Great Nephew 126–Glider 83 (Buisson Ardent 129) (1980 5fg 5f⁴ 5fg⁴ 5d² 5g* 5f² 5f 6g² 5s⁴ 6f 6g 5v 1981 6g² 6g 5g² 6g 5f 6f 5fg 5f 5f* 5fg 5fg 5g 5d 5g 5g 5g) sprint handicapper; won at Wolverhampton (amateur riders) in August; best at 5f nowadays; acts on any going but is particularly well suited by top-of-the-ground; has worn blinkers; splendid mount for an inexperienced rider; sometimes sweats up; has worn a tongue strap; best on an easy course. *D. Chapman.*   **59**

RELATIVITY 3 br.c. Welsh Pageant 132–Relza 91 (Relko 136) (1980 NR 1981 12d 16g) lightly-made colt; blind in his off-eye; soon struggling when tailed off in maiden races at Doncaster and Thirsk in spring. *R. Williams.*   **—**

RELIANCE NEWS 3 b.f. English Prince 129–Mink Fur (Victoria Park) (1980 7g 7g 7g 8fg 10d* 8s 1981 10s 10.1d² 10d* 10f 12f 10f 10fg) maiden; bought in 1,900 gns after winning at Pontefract in May; not disgraced over 1¼m; ideally suited by some give in the ground; pulled up and died at Newmarket in July. *N. Callaghan.*   **47**

RELINKA 2 b.f. Reliance II 137–Darlingka 77 (Darling Boy 124) (1981 5fg 5fg 6f 8fg 8d) Apr 13; 400Y; leggy, lightly-made, narrow filly; fourth foal; dam won twice over 1¼m; poor maiden. *G. Lockerbie.*   **55**

RELKILIA 2 ch.f. Relkino 131–Russellia (Red God 128§) (1981 6fg 6g 6g 6g 6s² 5s) Mar 9; 5,000Y; tall, useful-looking filly; half-sister to 2 winners, including 3-y-o 7f and 1m winner Gallea (by Prince de Galles); dam placed at up to 10.5f in France; improved late in season, notably when staying on strongly to finish 1½ lengths second to Hello Sunshine in valuable seller at York in October; finds 5f totally inadequate and is bred to stay 1¼m; acts on soft going. *N. Callaghan.*   **74**

RELKINA (FR) 2 b.f. Relkino 131–Grizel 113 (Grey Sovereign 128§) (1981 6fg⁴ 6g 6g⁴) Mar 17; 160,000 francs Y (approx £16,000); quite attractive filly; half-sister to 7f winner Song in the Air (by Tudor Melody) and 1978 2-y-o 5f winner Young Barnaby (by Crowned Prince); dam won Queen Mary Stakes; prominent in large fields of maidens at Newbury, Doncaster and Newmarket, on last-named course beaten nearly 10 lengths when fourth of 17 to Merlin's Charm in October; will stay 1m. *R. Hern.*   **81**

RELKOTINA 2 b.f. Relko 136–Tartown 89 (Gratitude 130) (1981 6fg 7g) Apr 16; well-made filly; fourth foal; half-sister to fair 1979 2-y-o 5f winner Lady Tartown (by Supreme Sovereign); dam sprinter; soundly beaten in maiden race at Epsom and minor event at Brighton (last of 13) in September. *R. Simpson.*   **—**

RELUCTANT HERO 2 br.g. Home Guard 129–Mia Cosa 78 (Ragusa 137) (1981 5g 5g³ 6f 7.2fg) Apr 24; 2,500Y; leggy, quite useful sort; half-brother to a winner in Italy by Sovereign Path; dam, half-sister to smart Irish 1971 2-y-o Open Season, won 3 times in Italy; 1¼ lengths third of 13 to She's My Girl in maiden auction event at Redcar in May; missed break next time out and was then off course over 2 months; should be well suited by 6f+. *J. Etherington.*   **55**

REMA 6 b.m. Will Hays–Miss Wolff 91 (Vilmorin) (1980 9.6f⁴ 9.6h³ 7fg 7d 7g³ 8.3g 7fg² 8.3f² 7f² 8fg 8g 8g 1981 10d 8s 7fg 7f) plater; stays 9.6f; seems to act on any going; has worn blinkers. *J. O'Donoghue.*   **—**

REMAINDER IMP 4 ch.g. Jimmy Reppin 131–Romany Girl 103 (Worden II 129) (1980 7d* 10d 7fg 8d 7.6d² 8.3d³ 8g 7d 8s⁴ 1981 8v⁴ 8g⁴ 8f 8f 8f⁴ 8s 7d) close-coupled, useful-looking gelding; stays 1m; acts on any going but is suited by some give in the ground; sometimes gives trouble at start; occasionally wears blinkers; has worn bandages; has run creditably for an apprentice. *R. Turnell.*   **57**

REMODEL 2 b.f. Continuation 120–Touch It Up (Trojan Monarch) (1981 5f 6g² 6fg² 7g 7g³ 6s) Apr 7; lightly-made filly; half-sister to useful sprinter Renovate (by The Go-Between); dam won 4 small races in USA; neck second to In Slips in 22-runner maiden race at Thirsk in July; placed afterwards in valuable sellers at Goodwood and Newmarket; stays 7f; suited by a sound surface and ran badly on soft ground final start. *J. Hardy.*   **66**

REMOULEUR 3 ch.c. Sharpen Up 127–Coulter Belle 80 (Quorum 126) (1980 5f² 5fg 6g 6fg 7.3fg³ 7f² 7g* 1981 8fg² 8.2s 8fg 10g 8d) good-bodied colt;   **91 d**

good walker and excellent mover; 3 lengths second to Beeleigh in £4,900 handicap at Sandown in April; no subsequent form; stays 1m (pulled hard when tried at 1¼m); possibly needs a sound surface; sometimes takes a long time to find his stride; sold 5,800 gns Newmarket Autumn Sales. *R. Price.*

RENDSLEY GIRL   2 ch.f. Hot Spark 126–Singing Girl 96 (Sing Sing 134)   (1981   **56**
5fg 6g⁴ 6fg 5s)   Mar 19; 6,600Y; useful-looking filly; half-sister to very useful
sprinter Tingo and smart French colt Tin Band, a winner at up to 1m (both by
Petingo); dam a sprinter; only poor form in maiden races. *J. Winter.*

RENOVATE   4 ro.c. The Go-Between 129–Touch It Up (Trojan Monarch)   **86** d
(1980 5d* 6fg 6fg 6f* 5fg 5fg 5g 6g⁴ 6g 5.6g 6d   1981 8d 7.2fg⁴ 7d 6g² 6d² 6g*
6f 6f 6f 6g 5d 6d⁴ 6s 5g)   sturdy colt; poor mover in his slower paces; fair
handicapper; beat Celtic Halo a length at Redcar in May (apprentice ridden);
best at 6f though seems to stay 1m; acts on any going; blinkered once in 1980.
J. Hardy.

RENREBO   4 b.g. Ribero 126–Tikki Tavi 92 (Honeyway 125)   (1980 NR   1981   —
10g 12.3g 12.2g⁴)   tall, lean gelding; plating-class maiden. *M. Naughton.*

RENT A NATIVE (USA)   2 b.f. Be A Native–Borrow It (Dependability)   —
(1981 6fg 7d)   Apr 13; $4,500F, 12,500 gns Y; well-made filly; first produce;
dam won claiming races at up to 1m; sire, son of Exclusive Native, won from
4.5f to 1m; unquoted when behind in large fields of maidens at Salisbury and
Newbury in September. *H. Candy.*

RENUMBER (USA)   2 b.f. Soy Numero Uno–Recall (Reneged)   (1981 5d)   —
May 4; $100,000Y; closely related to a minor winner by Damascus, and half-
sister to Irish 3-y-o Roll of Drums (by Hoist the Flag) and several winners;
dam smart stakes winner at up to 1m; 10/1 when behind in 16-runner maiden
race won by Kash-In at Bath in October. *H. Candy.*

REPAID   3 ch.c. Sandford Lad 133–High Ransom 88 (High Treason 126)   (1980   —
NR   1981 7d)   5,000Y; neat, quite attractive colt; half-brother to several
winners, notably very useful 2-y-o sprinters Durandal (by Bay Express) and
Sanders Lad (by Amber Rama); dam won over 7f; made much of running when
ninth of 10 behind Nureddin in newcomers race at Doncaster in March (looked
burly). *Mrs J. Reavey.*

RESIDE   5 ch.h. Quayside 124–Resurgence (Runnymede 123)   (1980 8d 10fg⁴   **88**
8d³ 12fg⁴ 8g 8f   1981 10.6g 10g 9fg 8fg² 8fg* 9fg* 8g 10.6d 9d 8f² 7g⁴ 9g 8v)
strong horse; fairly useful handicapper; successful at Carlisle (from Top O'
Th' Lane) and York (beat Honest Record by 1½ lengths) in July; has won over 1½m
but is better at shorter distances; best served by a sound surface; has run respectably when sweating up; suitable mount for an apprentice; sometimes starts slowly
nowadays. *E. Carter.*

RESIGNING   2 br.c. Continuation 120–Final Girl (Dadda Bert 95)   (1981 5d   —
5g 5g⁴ 7f 8.2d)   Mar 30; neat, lightly-made colt; poor walker and mover; poor
plater; sold to A. Neaves 400 gns Newmarket Autumn Sales. *J. Hardy.*

RESTLESS CAPTAIN   3 ch.g. Sandford Lad 133–Kirkwall 74 (Sheshoon 132)   —
(1980 6g 6g³ 7d² 8.2g⁴   1981 9d 7d 8fg 8d 7g 9s⁴)   workmanlike gelding; good
mover; rather disappointing in 1981, although often had stiff tasks; may stay
1¼m; acts on a soft surface. *G. Richards.*

RESTLESS LADY   4 ch.f. Sandford Lad 133–Super Restless (Restless Wind)   —
(1980 6fg 8.5f 10s 10g   1981 9d 10f 10f)   rangy filly; little worthwhile form in
maiden races and handicaps; stays 1¼m; sold 2,100 gns Doncaster August Sales.
R. Price.

RETAINER   7 ch.g. Gay Pilot 92–Most Precious (Matador 131)   (1980 16g   —
12.3d 1981 10.4s)   poor maiden; has worn blinkers. *J. Leigh.*

RETHINK   9 br.h. Hauban 132–White Flame (Venture VII 129)   (1980 NR   —
1981 12s 8f)   probably no longer of any account; has worn blinkers and bandages.
A. Dalton.

RETSEL   2 ch.c. Scottish Rifle 127–Once For All (Quorum 126)   (1981 6d³   —
6fg 8d 8.2s)   Feb 21; small colt; half-brother to 4 winners; dam never ran; stayed
on when seventh of 15 to The Nub in maiden race at Bath in October, third start
and only worthwhile effort; will stay 1¼m. *R. Baker.*

RETURN TO ME   2 b.c. Music Boy 124–Perkasa 74 (Huntercombe 133)   —
(1981 6g 6g)   Apr 2; stocky colt; first foal; dam won two 5f sellers; behind in
maiden races and handicaps. *J. Toller.*

RETURN TO POWER   2 b.g. Relko 136–Resurgence (Runnymede 123)   **80**
(1981 7fg* 7fg)   Mar 13; 11,000Y; tall, sparely-made gelding; half-brother to

710

2 winners, including very useful Reside (by Quayside), successful at up to 1½m; dam lightly raced and showed no ability; looked quite a useful colt in the making when getting up in closing stages to win 17-runner minor race at Warwick in August by a head from Orrin; favourite for £3,200 race at Goodwood the following month but pulled hard early on and could finish only sixth of 10, 9½ lengths behind Old Country; will stay middle distances; sold to P. Makin 5,400 gns Newmarket Autumn Sales. *G. Harwood.*

RETZA 6 ch.g. Richboy 117–Shari (Rustam 127) (1980 6s 7d 1981 6s 10d 8g 10g 10s 8f⁴ 10fg) plater nowadays; stays 1m; probably acts on any going; often blinkered; has worn bandages; good mount for an apprentice. *A. Davison.* —

REVELS END 2 br.f. Welsh Pageant 132–Curfew 76 (Midsummer Night II 117) (1981 6fg 8d³) Feb 16; quite attractive filly; third reported foal; closely related to 3-y-o Goodbye Starter (by Owen Dudley), a useful winner over 5f at 2 yrs; dam placed over 6f at 2 yrs; kept on gamely under pressure when 2½ lengths third of 11 to All Risks in maiden race at Wolverhampton in October (moved short to post); will stay 1¼m. *P. Walwyn.* **79**

REVES CELESTES (USA) 2 b.f. Lyphard 132–Tobira Celeste (Ribot 142) (1981 7g) small, lightly-made filly; third foal; half-sister to French 3-y-o Le Vague A L'Ame (by Vaguely Noble) and French middle-distance winner Tender Night (by Sir Gaylord); dam won at up to 9f and is half-sister to A Thousand Stars, a smart performer at up to 1¼m in France and USA; 25/1 and very fit, stayed on well in later stages to finish fairly close-up tenth of 29 to Chalon in maiden race at Newmarket in October; lacks scope but may improve over further in 1982. *B. Hills.* — p

REVIDA GIRL 2 b.f. Habat 127–Lady Anne Neville 92 (Right Boy 137) (1981 5fg 5f 5f* 5f 5h³ 5fg) Apr 9; 2,100Y; workmanlike filly; has a rather round action; half-sister to a winning plater; dam won all her 4 starts, each at 5f; heavily backed and dropped in class, made all in 6-runner seller at Folkestone in July (bought in 1,100 gns); respectable 4 lengths third to Mayo Moonlight in nursery at Chepstow following month; yet to race on an easy surface; blinkered last 2 outings. *C. Williams.* **63**

REVOCATION (USA) 4 ch.c. Reviewer–Recall (Reneged) (1980 10.1fg* 12f³ 10.1g⁴ 8d* 8fg 8g³ 8g³ 1981 8fg* 7.6g⁴ 8fg²) good sort; fair handicapper; stayed on strongly to beat Teamwork by 2 lengths at Kempton in April; best at up to 1¼m; acts on a firm and a soft surface; sent to USA. *P. Walwyn.* **87**

REXRIBO 2 b.c. Riboboy 124–Expresso 76 (Roan Rocket 128) (1981 8d 8g) Mar 28; rangy colt; half-brother to 1½m winner Expadeo (by St Paddy) and a winner in Belgium; dam ran twice; in mid-division in £4,200 event at Newbury in September and in 30-runner maiden race at Newmarket in October (stayed on). *M. Jarvis.* — p

RHADI BOY 3 b.g. New Model 129–Nagaradhi (Pardal 130) (1980 NR 1981 5fg 7g 6g⁴ 6f 8fg 8s 8d) big, rangy gelding; half-brother to winners in Italy by Fleece, Porto Bello and Traditionalist; dam half-sister to speedy 1965 Irish 2-y-o Lady Matador; plating-class maiden; ran best race when apprentice ridden on third start; sold to J. Tierney 1,700 gns Newmarket Autumn Sales. *R. Armstrong.* —

RHEEDIA (FR) 3 b.f. Riverman 131–Severinia (Shantung 132) (1980 NR 1981 8f 10fg) half-sister to smart 1977 2-y-o Bolak (by Bold Lad USA) and fair 7f winner Sandforinia (by Sandford Lad); dam French 1½m winner; in rear in maiden races at Pontefract in June and Ayr in July; sold 18,000 gns Newmarket December Sales. *J. W. Watts.* —

RHEIN BRIDGE 3 b.f. Rheingold 137–Fishermans Bridge 113 (Crepello 136) (1980 7d⁴ 8s* 1981 12.3d³ 12g* 12g 12f* 12g 14.6g 12s) **107**

Rhein Bridge didn't turn out so good as her half-sister, the 1979 Yorkshire Oaks winner Connaught Bridge, but she won the Lancashire Oaks and a useful acquisition to her owner Robert Sangster's impressive collection of broodmares. The leading British-trained three-year-old staying fillies of 1981 were a humdrum collection and such races as the Cheshire Oaks, the Lancashire Oaks, the Yorkshire Oaks, the Park Hill Stakes and the Princess Royal Stakes, all of which Rhein Bridge contested, each went to a different filly. Rhein Bridge won the Lancashire Oaks by a short head in a driving finish from Royal Realm with the maiden Sextant two and a half lengths away third, ahead of the

Timeform Derby Special Offer Stakes, Thirsk—Rhein Bridge is a decisive winner from Golden Brigadier

Cheshire Oaks winner Hunston and the Oaks third Leap Lively; Rhein Bridge responded very gamely to strong riding in the straight after Hunston and Leap Lively had appeared to have the race between them three furlongs out. Rhein Bridge had finished third to Hunston at Chester on her reappearance and had followed up by winning the Timeform Derby Special Offer Stakes at Thirsk

Rhein Bridge (b.f. 1978)	Rheingold (b 1969)	Faberge II (b 1961)	Princely Gift
			Spring Offensive
		Athene (b 1960)	Supreme Court
			Necelia
	Fishermans Bridge (ch 1970)	Crepello (ch 1954)	Donatello II
			Crepuscule
		Riva (b 1964)	Relic
			Canvas

in May in good style from three colts who had taken on Shergar in the Chester Vase. The Timeform Derby Special Offer Stakes was staged because Thirsk's traditional April fixture, which features the Timeform Race Card Stakes, was lost in 1981; the Timeform Race Card Stakes, conceived as a preparatory race for the Newmarket classics and won in 1979 by the subsequent Two Thousand Guineas winner Tap On Wood, will be resumed in 1982. Rhein Bridge's connections decided to let her take her chance in the Oaks on the strength of her performance at Thirsk; she started at 25/1 and came home a distant seventh to Blue Wind.

Lancashire Oaks, Haydock—Rhein Bridge holds on in a driving finish from Royal Realm

712

Rhein Bridge is a good sort in appearance, much more impressive as an individual than the leggy Connaught Bridge. Their dam Fishermans Bridge has produced four foals in seven years at stud. Her first foal was Rhein Bridge's sister Freia, a moderate winner at a mile; her 1980 foal, a colt by Shirley Heights, died and she was barren to Shirley Heights in 1981. Fishermans Bridge was a determined front-runner and put up very useful performances when winning the Ebbisham Handicap by five lengths and when second in the Nassau Stakes; she wasn't raced beyond a mile and a quarter. Fishermans Bridge acted well on firm going, as did Rhein Bridge who had a win on soft ground to her credit as a two-year-old. Rhein Bridge's grandam Riva won over six furlongs and stayed a mile and her great grandam Canvas, a half-sister to the St Leger winner and Oaks runner-up Cantelo, won at eleven furlongs and a mile and a half. Rhein Bridge was tried in blinkers on her final outing but she was a genuine filly. *J. W. Watts.*

RHEINGOLD'S GIFT 3 b.c. Rheingold 137–Love Story 79 (Aureole 132) **73** (1980 7fg 8fg 10s 1981 10s² 12s* 12s* 12g³ 12g³ 13.8fg 11.5d³ 13.8fg² 14fg 12fg 13d 16s) small, narrow colt; won poor maiden race at Hamilton in April (by 7 lengths) and minor event at Carlisle in May; suited by 1¾m; probably acts on any going; ridden by claimer when successful; ran moderately last 4 starts; sold 5,200 gns Newmarket Autumn Sales. *C. Brittain.*

RHEINIEKEN 4 b.g. Rheingold 137–Priddy Maid 111 (Acropolis 132) (1980 — NR 1981 10g) strong gelding; in need of run when well-beaten eighth of 17 to Commodore Riva in modest maiden race at Stockton in April. *E. Weymes.*

RHEINSTEEL 4 b.c. Rheingold 137–Latona (Royal Record II) (1980 won 4 **99** times in Norway 1981 10fg⁴ 10.5g 8s⁴ 9.7s 11fg⁴ 12d* 11.7g 11.1f 12g) strong, good sort; first reported foal; dam, half-sister to useful sprinter Trillium, was unplaced once here but won in Norway at 3 yrs and 4 yrs; leading 3-y-o in Norway in 1980 when successful four times, including in 2,000 Guineas and Derby; beat Beggar's Bridge a head in 5-runner minor event at Lingfield in August; fourth earlier in Westbury Stakes at Sandown (to Hard Fought), Tote Lockinge Stakes at Newbury (to Belmont Bay) and Grand Prix Prince Rose at Ostend (behind Strong Gale), giving weight all round on first 2 courses; stays 1½m; trained by T. Dahl first 4 starts. *I. Balding.*

RHESUS (USA) 2 b.c. Raja Baba–Gorgon (Herbager 136) (1981 6f) Apr 2; $155,000Y; lengthy, workmanlike colt; second foal; dam, placed at 3 yrs, is half-sister to smart American middle-distance winner Star Envoy; 15/2 and ridden by apprentice unable to claim his allowance, showed only a bit of early speed when last of 13 to Sangalkan in £5,600 event at York in June. *H. Cecil.*

RHIANNON 3 b.f. Welsh Pageant 132–Lady Lowndes 97 (Tamerlane 128) **56** (1980 8d³ 8d 1981 7fg 10.2g 9g 8.2s²) neat filly; poor maiden; towards rear in seller on reappearance; should stay 1¼m+; sold out of P. Cundell's stable 2,100 gns Newmarket July Sales after second start. *R. Hollinshead.*

RHINESTONE COWBOY 2 br.c. On Your Mark 125–Jeannette (Whistler 129) — (1981 5fg 5s 5g) Feb 2; 6,600Y; strong, rangy, good sort; good walker; brother to fairly useful 7f and 1m winner Markie, and half-brother to several winners; dam once-raced half-sister to Irish 1,000 Guineas winner Shandon Belle; showed only sign of ability when 8½ lengths sixth of 12 to Ma Tante in minor event at Lingfield in June, third outing; will be suited by 6f. *P. K. Mitchell.*

RHODADE 2 b.f. Cavo Doro 124–Bravade 81 (Blast 125) (1981 5fg 6g 5g — 6f 8fg 7g 8d 7g) Mar 3; 4,400F; rangy filly; second produce; dam, sister to very useful Rhodomantade, won 1m seller; only poor form, including in sellers; blinkered last 2 outings. *T. Fairhurst.*

RHODEO FANFARE 2 br.c. Rhodomantade 110–Oriental Slipper 62 (Tycoon — II) (1981 8s) Feb 9; first foal; dam won 3 sellers at up to 1m; unquoted when tailed-off last of 17 to Fort Garry in maiden race at Warwick in October. *P. Makin.*

RHUS (USA) 4 b.c. Riva Ridge–Bold Pink (Bold Bidder) (1980 10v* 10g* **102** 9d² 11s 1981 10fg 9d 12g³ 10fg 12d) attractive, well-made ex-French colt; smart at 3 yrs when he won newcomers race at Evry and Premio Lazio at Rome and finished good ¾-length second to Huguenot in Prix Daphnis at Evry; ran easily best race over here when creditable ¾-length third to Baz Bombati in well-contested minor event at Beverley in June; stays 1½m; possibly needs some give in the ground; tailed off and looked sour in blinkers final start; sold only 3,600 gns Newmarket Autumn Sales. *M. Stoute.*

713

RHYME ROYAL 6 ch.g. Crepello 136–Lyrical 110 (Gratitude 130) (1980 **104**
12g³ 11s⁴ 12v² 1981 10fg² 10.2g³ 12f 10.4s* 11g⁴ 9s 12g) rangy gelding, who
carries a lot of condition; useful handicapper; had easy task when winning
apprentice race at Chester in August by 25 lengths; had run creditably earlier
when 7 lengths second to Galveston in Rosebery Stakes at Kempton and 3½
lengths third to Bonol in £9,300 race at Doncaster; needs further than 9f and
stays 1½m; appears to act on any going but goes very well in the mud; usually
ridden up with the leaders; genuine; ran moderately third and final starts.
R. Hern.

RHY-YAN TUDOR 2 b. or br.c. Tudor Rhythm 112–Tudor Yan 72 (Tudor Bar —
91) (1981 5g 5g 5f 7fg 7fg 7.2fg 6s) May 14; neat colt; second living foal; dam
won 6f seller at 2 yrs; only plating class. *T. Fairhurst.*

RIANA 5 b.m. Royal and Regal–Sea Holly 93 (Larkspur 128) (1980 NR 1981 —
10.8d 16f) staying maiden; acts on firm going; has worn blinkers. *Mrs J.
Pitman.*

RIBBLE ROUSER 8 ch.g. Marcus Brutus 108–Ribble Reed 75 (Bullrush 106) **52**
(1980 18d 16f² 15f* 18fg⁴ 15.8fg* 16fg 15.8f* 15.8g 15.8d 1981 15.8g 15g⁴
15.8g 16f³ 16f³ 18f) staying handicapper; acts on any going; has worn blinkers;
suitable mount for an apprentice; often makes the running; inconsistent. *W. C.
Watts.*

RIBBLE WAY 2 b.f. Forlorn River 124–Ribbleston 75 (The Brianstan 128) —
(1981 5s 5fg) May 7; leggy, fair sort; first foal; dam best at 5f; very backward
when soundly beaten in maiden race at Stockton in April and seller at Beverley
in June; refused to enter stalls on intended third appearance. *W. C. Watts.*

RIBERETTO 3 b.c. Ribero 126–Love Resolved (Dan Cupid 132) (1980 7f **107**
8g* 7.3d 1981 12g* 12d 12f 13.3fg⁴ 14.6g 16g 12s⁴) big, rangy colt; good
mover; half-brother to 1½m and 15f winner Lone Raider (by Shantung) and
useful 5f to 7f winner Tribal Warrior (by Tribal Chief); dam placed over 13f in
France; 66/1, improved vastly on his 2-y-o form in 8-runner Ladbrokes Derby
Trial at Lingfield in May, making running at good gallop and staying on strongly
to beat Sheer Grit by 1½ lengths; raced mainly in top company afterwards,
probably best efforts when eighth of 18 to runaway winner Shergar in Derby
on next start (disputed lead much of way), last of 4 behind Ardross in Geoffrey
Freer Stakes at Newbury in August and fourth of 7 to Little Wolf in St Simon

*Ladbrokes Derby Trial Lingfield—66/1-shot Riberetto makes all to beat
Sheer Grit*

Stakes on same course in October; should stay 2m (not entirely disgraced when fifth of 9 to Centroline in Jockey Club Cup at Newmarket over the trip). *R. Boss.*

RIBMIS   3 b.f. Simbir 130–Miss Parsons (Welsh Abbot 131) (1980 NR 1981 — 14fg 10s) 920F, resold 500Y; half-sister to Irish 9f winner Roccadonna (by Don II); dam Irish 5f winner; fifth of 13 behind easy winner Dovetail in 1¼m maiden race at Nottingham in October, easily better effort. *G. Harman.*

RIBO CHARTER   4 b.g. Ribero 126–Grecian Charter (Runnymede 123) (1980 **76** d 8s 10f 12f² 12f 10.5d³ 12fg³ 12g 12d 16fg* 12g³ 14d² 1981 10fg 16g 16g²(dis) 16g 20fg 16.1g⁴ 16d⁴) lengthy gelding; useful at his best but is none too consistent or genuine; stays well; seems to act on any going; sometimes sweats up; has won for an amateur rider; sold to M. Chapman 1,600 gns Newmarket Autumn Sales. *P. Kelleway.*

RIBODEN   3 b.g. Ribero 126–True Dresden 58 (Vilmoray 126) (1980 5f 6f 6g **46** 7fg 1981 10s³ 12g 7g* 7f 7fg 8d 8s) plain gelding; attracted no bid after winning seller at Newmarket in May; probably stays 1¼m (ran respectably in non-seller over trip); in rear when blinkered final start. *G. Fletcher.*

RIBONNY (FR)   5 b.m. Fast Hilarious–Ribbon Candy (Ribot 142) (1980 **33** 10v³ 12.3s³ 15g 13s⁴ 12g 12.5s 1981 15.8s² 13d³ 15.8g) small mare; poor handicapper; stays well; revels in the mud. *W. Elsey.*

RIBOT FAIR   4 b.f. Andrea Mantegna–Fair Exchange (Port Frere 108) (1980 — 11fg 10fg 12fg 8d² 10.1s* 11d 1981 11.7d 10g) workmanlike filly; plater; stays 1¼m; suited by some give in the ground; virtually refused to race once in 1980. *D. Gandolfo.*

RIBOT STAR   2 b.c. Star Appeal 133–Ribo Pride 77 (Ribero 126) (1981 7fg — 7fg 7fg 10s 10.2g) May 2; neat colt; good walker; second foal; dam won over 1½m; in rear in varied company. *J. Fox.*

RICARDO   2 b.c. Sallust 134–Keep Going 113 (Hard Sauce 131) (1981 7fg) **68** p Apr 15; 64,000Y; tall, attractive colt; half-brother to 4 winners, including smart 6f and 7.3f winner Skyliner (by African Sky) and useful filly Slip the Ferret (by Klairon); dam won 6 times over 5f at 2 yrs; third favourite, took time to get the hang of things in maiden race at Newmarket in August but made steady, late headway to finish 7½ lengths eighth of 29 to Hayakaze; may stay 1m; a taking individual who will almost certainly improve considerably with the benefit of this experience. *G. Harwood.*

RICCA-DONNA   2 b.f. Dance In Time–Pop Music (Val de Loir 133) (1981 **70** 6g 8fg 7g) Mar 15; 14,000F; fourth foal; half-sister to a minor French winner by Crowned Prince; dam unraced daughter of smart 2-y-o Runnello; in middivision in maiden race at Beverley and minor event at Catterick in the autumn on last 2 outings; will stay 1¼m. *C. Brittain.*

RICHARD G.   8 b.g. Double Jump 131–Tevere 104 (Romulus 129) (1980 NR — 1981 8fg 10fg) lightly raced nowadays and is probably no longer of any account. *S. Kernick.*

RICH LANDING   3 b.g. Communication 119–Cabarita 88 (First Landing) — (1980 NR 1981 7d) unfurnished gelding; second foal; dam 6f winner; pulled up lame at Leicester in May on only outing. *R. Cambidge.*

RICHMEDE   8 gr.g. Runnymede 123–Scilly Isles 54 (Silly Season 127) (1980 — NR 1981 13.3d) probably no longer of any account on flat. *M. Stephens.*

RICH POETESS   5 ch.m. Richboy 117–One Poem (La Varende 125) (1980 NR — 1981 14.6fg) third live foal; half-sister to a winner in France by Canisbay; dam placed at up to 1¼m in France; well beaten in maiden race at Doncaster in July. *R. Baker.*

RICH RETURN   3 b.f. High Line 125–Lost Riches 75 (Forlorn River 124) — (1980 NR 1981 7g 8fg 12d) big, rangy filly; fourth foal; sister to a poor animal; dam stayed 6f; in rear in maiden and minor races. *D. Wilson.*

RICH VIRGINIA   5 b.g. Tycoon II–Smokey Joe (My Smokey 125) (1980 — NR 1981 12g) tailed off in minor event at Pontefract in April. *J. Tierney.*

RIDAN FLIGHT   5 b.g. Ridan–Irish Flight (Ballymoss 136) (1980 10s 8.3f — 1981 13s) wiry gelding; poor plater; sold 420 gns Ascot 2nd June Sales. *H. O'Neill.*

RIDARRAGH   7 b.g. Ridan–Relegere (Relic) (1980 NR 1981 12g 12.2g) — poor maiden. *J. Yardley.*

RIDGEFIELD   3 br.g. Firestreak 125–Chebs Lass 84 (Chebs Lad 120) (1980 8g **79** 1981 10s* 10fg² 10d² 12g 10g 12f 10fg²) useful-looking gelding; landed odds hard held from Cavendish in maiden event at Leicester in March; runner-up in handicap at Kempton (given quite a lot to do), in White Rose Stakes at Ascot (beaten 3 lengths by Cut Above after none too clear a run) and in apprentice event at Leicester (first race for 2½ months); didn't run well fourth to sixth starts, but had stiff task on first occasion; should stay 1½m; possibly better suited by a soft surface than a firm one; trained most of season by G. Harwood. *D. Thom.*

RIFLE SHOT 2 bl.c. Scottish Rifle 127–West Shaw 101 (Grey Sovereign 128§)   —
(1981 5g 5f) Mar 8; 9,200Y; heavy-topped colt; half-brother to several winners here and abroad, including 1,000 Guineas second Marisela (by Sheshoon); dam at her best at 2 yrs; backward when soundly beaten in minor events at Beverley in June. *A. Smith.*

RIGBY LANE (USA) 2 ch.c. Transworld 121–Sea Grey 91 (Sea Hawk II 131)   67
(1981 5s 6d 6fg 7d) May 4; $15,000Y; quite well-made colt; half-brother to a winner in France by Ragusa; dam won twice over 7f; beaten less than 7 lengths when sixth of 7 to Algardi at Epsom in June, second outing and only sign of ability; off course 3 months before final start; will be well suited by middle distances. *G. Lewis.*

RIG FORCE 5 b.g. Club House 110–Secondhand Rose 102 (Hethersett 134)   —
(1980 NR 1981 16s) strong gelding; lightly raced nowadays; stays 1¾m; acts on any going; has worn blinkers. *B. Richmond.*

RIGHT DIAMOND 4 b.g. Right Tack 131–Garzoni (Ribot 142) (1980 10s*   85
12g² 12fg³ 13s* 12g* 12.2s* 13.3d³ 14g² 1981 12.2d 16fg 14d 12v² 12d) good-bodied gelding; fair handicapper; stays 1¾m; suited by some give in the ground; ran poorly final start in June. *G. Balding.*

RIGHT OF LIGHT 7 ch.h Tyrant–Daisy June (Epaulette 125) (1980 6fg   97
6f² 7.2fg³ 6fg 7d³ 7fg⁴ 6fg³ 7f³ 7fg² 6fg² 7g 1981 7g 7fg* 8fg³ 7fg⁴ 7g*) neat horse; won handicaps at York in June and Newbury in July, subsequently sent to USA and won 7.5f claiming race at Bay Meadows in September; stays 1m; probably acts on any going; usually held up; needs strong handling; finds little off bridle. *P. Makin.*

RIGHT REGENT 3 ch.c. Kambalda 108–Vetsera (Hopeful Venture 125)   83
(1980 6fg 8d 8d 1981 12d² 13.3d² 16d* 13.3g 16fg³ 16g 16s 18g) compact colt; beat Castelnau a neck in maiden race at Lingfield in June (pair 15 lengths clear); good third to Ayyabaan in handicap at Ascot the following month; off course 2 months afterwards; suited by a test of stamina; acts on a firm and a soft surface. *D. Elsworth.*

RIGHTS OF MAN 3 ch.g. Morston 125–Proper True (Right Tack 131) (1980   81
7fg 7g³ 1981 10v* 10.5s) lengthy gelding; looked backward when beating Feltwell ¾ length in maiden race at Beverley in April; not seen out after finishing behind in £4,000 event at York the following month (bandaged in front and didn't move well to start); stays 1¼m; acts on heavy going; sent to France. *G. Pritchard-Gordon.*

RIKA MIA 2 ch.f. Cavo Doro 124–Mimika 85 (Lorenzaccio 130) (1981 8d⁴)   78 p
Feb 18; strong, lengthy filly; second foal; dam won over 5f at 2 yrs; not fully fit when 2¾ lengths fourth of 11 to All Risks in maiden race at Wolverhampton in October; will be suited by 1¼m; may do better. *C. Brittain.*

RIKASSO BEAUTY 3 ch.f. Double-U-Jay 120–Mary Bold (Hard Ridden 131)   75
(1980 5s 5s 5g⁴ 5fg² 5h 5fg* 6fg³ 7g* 6d 7g 7fg 6g 6fg² 6s 5f 1981 7s 8g 8fg 7fg² 7f³ 8.2g 7f 7fg² 7fg) leggy, light-framed filly; quite a moderate handicapper; lost her place at halfway but finished well, despite tending to hang, when second to Priory Lane at Newmarket in August on eighth start; stays 7f; probably acts on any going; sometimes sweats up. *D. Thom.*

RINGAL 3 br.g. Auction Ring 123–Jeannette (Whistler 129) (1980 5fg² 6fg   —
6fg² 5fg³ 5.3g³ 5fg 1981 7fg 5g 5g) strong, well-made gelding; disappointing maiden; didn't look particularly enthusiastic final outing; stays 6f; yet to race on a soft surface; blinkered once as a 2-y-o; sold 500 gns Ballsbridge December Sales. *F. Durr.*

RING BIDDER 3 b.c. Auction Ring 123–Miss Holborn (Pall Mall 132) (1980 6g   84
6g² 8s² 7d* 1981 8.5fg³ 8d⁴ 10s 8s 8.2fg* 8g³ 7g 7d² 8f 8fg² 8fg 8f 8.5fg² 8g² 8d 9s) useful sort; ran on gamely to beat Oklahoma Star 1½ lengths in 5-runner handicap at Nottingham in April; second on 4 other occasions; suited by 1m; acts on any going; well beaten when blinkered fourth outing; sold to R. Hollinshead 7,000 gns Newmarket Autumn Sales. *C. Brittain.*

RING FINGER 3 b.f. Auction Ring 123–Fianna 99 (Royal Palm 131) (1980 5f   —
5g 1981 6fg 8d⁴) compact filly; soundly beaten in varied company; sold 4,000 gns Newmarket December Sales. *B. Hills.*

RINGMORE LAD   2 br.g. Roi Soleil 125–Pippy Greene 72 (Yellow God 129)   —
(1981 5d 5fg 5fg 6f 6g)   Apr 30; lightly-made gelding; third foal; dam stayed 7f;
in rear in maiden races and sellers.   *J. Holt.*

RING MOYLAN   3 b.f. Auction Ring 123–Moneycashen 72 (Hook Money 124)   **79**
(1980 5fg³ 5f³ 5g² 6g² 6s³ 7g* 7s   1981 7g 7d 6d* 7.2s 6f 8fg⁴ 7f³ 7.2fg* 7g³ 7g 7s)
neat, well-made filly; good mover; won handicaps at Folkestone in June (apprentice event, made all) and Haydock in September, on latter course holding on
bravely by ½ length from Shademah; probably stays 1m; acts on any going; sold
7,000 gns Newmarket December Sales.   *M. Jarvis.*

RING OF QUALITY   3 b.c. Auction Ring 123–Metrovision (Golden Vision 105)   **76**
(1980 6d³ 6g* 6g² 7fg³ 6fg   1981 8g² 8g*)   strong, good-topped colt; beat
Essam by ½ length in handicap at Carlisle in May; subsequently sold privately
to race in Belgium and won twice there, including over 9f.   *Sir Mark Prescott.*

RING OUT   3 b.g. Auction Ring 123–Miss Etta (King's Troop 118)   (1980 6g⁴
7f³   1981 6g)   rangy gelding; good mover; in frame in maiden races as a 2-y-o;
behind at Newmarket in April; won twice in Holland afterwards.   *W. O'Gorman.*

RING THE BELL (NZ)   4 b.c. Rangong 123–Witchcraft (Mystery 125)   **115**
(1979/80 won 3 out of 9 starts in New Zealand 1980/1 won 8 out of 15 starts from
7f to 1½m in Australasia   1981 8fg³ 10s 12d)   NZ $3,000Y (approx £1,600);
big, strong colt; third foal; dam won over 1m in New Zealand; has proved a rare
bargain and was the top 3-y-o in New Zealand in 1980/1 when he earned a record
NZ $217,725; won New Zealand Derby (beat Amyl by a length), Alison Stakes,
Avondale Champion Stakes and Avondale Guineas, and finished second in Great
Northern Guineas and close third in Air New Zealand Stakes; also ran very well in
Australia, winning Canterbury Guineas in March and going down by ½ length to
Our Paddy Boy in AJC Derby at Randwick in April; had stiffish task when 7½
lengths third of 4 finishers to Boathouse in £3,100 race at Goodwood in September;
beaten under 6 lengths when respectable sixth of 9 to Vayrann in Prix du Prince
d'Orange at Longchamp later in month but finished remote nineteenth of 24 to
Gold River in Prix de l'Arc de Triomphe on same course in October; stays 1½m
well; trained in Australasia by N. Atkins.   *H. Westbrook.*

RING THE CHANGES   3 b.f. Auction Ring 123–Whispering Star 78 (Sound   **72**
Track 132)   (1980 6g 6.5d   1981 5g² 6.5g 6.5s 5g 6d 5fg 5fg* 6g⁴)   small ex-
French filly; 15,000Y; half-sister to numerous winners, including very useful
performers Seadiver, Pearl Star and Portese (all by Gulf Pearl), last-named
successful at up to 1m, and smart sprinter Blue Star (by Majority Blue); dam
won over 5f on only start; sweated up when finishing strongly to beat Steel Son
by ½ length in 16-runner maiden race at Kempton in September; creditable fourth
in handicap at Newmarket in October; stays 6f; best form on a sound surface;
formerly trained by C. Bartholomew; sold 41,000 gns Newmarket December
Sales.   *M. Smyly.*

RINGTINGO   2 b.c. Rustingo 94–Ringers Girl (Varano)   (1981 8d)   Mar 22;   —
first foal; dam never ran; unquoted when last of 17 to Suez in maiden race at
Bath in October.   *K. Bridgwater.*

RINY REEF   3 b.f. Mill Reef 141–Harriny 94 (Floribunda 136)   (1980 NR   —
1981 8s 11.5fg⁴ 10.4d)   26,000F, 45,000Y; neat filly; second produce; dam
stayed 7f; behind in maiden and minor races; dead.   *C. Brittain.*

RIO DEVA   3 b.c. Spanish Gold 101–Deva Rose 80 (Chestergate 111)   (1980   **62**
7fg 6g 8fg⁴ 8s 8g   1981 7d⁴ 8g 8g³ 8.2s 9g⁴ 8f² 10fg 10f 11.5d 9g² 10f³ 10f³ 10.4s
10f 10d⁴ 8.2s 11d 10d⁴)   smallish, useful sort; poor maiden; beaten in seller once
at 2 yrs; stays at least 1¼m; probably acts on any going, except possibly very
soft; doesn't find a great deal off the bridle and is rather inconsistent.   *R.
Hollinshead.*

RIONORE   6 b.h. Ribero 126–True Course 124 (Hill Gail)   (1980 8f 12h 12fg*   **73**
12g⁴ 15g² 11g* 10.4d² 12.5g⁴ 12s 12v   1981 11s 12fg² 12.5s* 10.5g³ 12fg⁴ 12f
12.5g⁴ 10.7g)   well-made ex-Irish horse; awarded handicap at Duindigt in
May; stayed well; probably acted on any going; wasn't particularly reliable;
broke a leg at Duindigt in July and was destroyed.   *M. Ryan.*

RIPCORN (USA)   4 b.c. Cornish Prince–Ripit (Relko 136)   (1980 10.1s² 12s*   **81**
12g² 14d⁴   1981 10g 11.1s 12fg* 12f² 12f* 12fg² 11.7g⁴ 12s)   most attractive
colt; good mover; won handicaps at Folkestone in June and August; suited by
1½m and should stay further; acts on any going; sweated up fourth start; sold
to N. Tinkler 6,400 gns Newmarket Autumn Sales.   *P. Walwyn.*

RISING FAST   4 b.g. High Line 125–Sunny Sovereign 85 (Lucky Sovereign)   **60**
(1980 10.8v³ 10.8s 10.1fg 12.3g 11.1g 12d   1981 11s 14d 16.9s 18.8fg* 17.1d*

16g⁴ 16fg 19fg³ 19s² 17.1d² 18g) lengthy, good sort; staying handicapper; won at Warwick and Bath in June; ran creditably several times afterwards; probably acts on any going; usually blinkered nowadays; has sweated up. *D. Elsworth.*

RISING TIDE 3 ch.f. Red Alert 127–Naiad Queen (Pampered King 121) (1980 5fg 5f² 5g 5g* 5g 5g* 5g⁴ 1981 5g 5s 5f 5fg 5fg) strong, rangy filly; useful performer at 2 yrs; in rear all outings in 1981, including Palace House Stakes at Newmarket in May and James Lane Handicap at Ascot in June; should stay 6f; blinkered fourth start; sold 15,000 gns Newmarket December Sales. *M. Kauntze, Ireland.* —

RISK 2 b.c. Reform 132–Doubly Sure 59 (Reliance II 137) (1981 6g 7g³ 8g³) May 5; elegant colt; half-brother to outstanding miler Kris (by Sharpen Up); dam, placed over 1¼m, is daughter of high-class staying 2-y-o Soft Angels; third in big fields of maidens at Newmarket in October, staying on well when beaten a length by Count Pahlen and when beaten 2½ lengths by Born Hero; will probably stay 1½m; certain to win a maiden race at 3 yrs. *P. Walwyn.* **93**

RISK TAKER 2 b.c. Auction Ring 123–Dance Away (Red God 128§) (1981 6g² 7.6s² 6s* 6s* 7d³) Mar 4; IR 7,600F, IR 17,500Y; quite attractive, short-backed colt; brother to 3-y-o 7f winner Round Dance, and half-brother to 3 winners, including Irish 7f to 1¼m winner Maculata (by Right Tack); dam fairly useful 2-y-o 5f winner; beat Mydrone very comfortably by a length in very slowly run 8-runner minor event at Redcar in October; had previously landed the odds in 15-runner maiden race at Newbury by a length from Famous Star; didn't produce anything like that form on his 2 attempts over further; hung fire when jockey drew whip on third outing but ran on extremely well once he put whip down; useful. *G. Harwood.* **106 ?**

RITARIUS 2 ch.g. Wollow 132–Mellifont (Hook Money 124) (1981 6g) Apr 27; IR 1,000Y; brother to useful French 1½m winner Bartolo Campo and half-brother to 1979 2-y-o 5f and 6f winner Mephisto Waltz (by Dancer's Image) and to Red Prince (by Red God), a winner over 5f at 2 yrs and 6 times in Scandinavia; dam useful winner over 5f at 2 yrs in Ireland; unquoted and in need of race, showed up 4f and ran better than finishing position suggests when out of first 9 of 15 to Annesley in maiden event at Salisbury in June. *C. James.* —

RITSON 2 ch.c. Record Token 128–Florabette (Floribunda 136) (1981 5fg 5d 7f 7g 8.2d) Apr 8; 1,100Y; smallish, workmanlike colt; half-brother to 3 winners, including 3-y-o 9f and 11f winner Target Path (by Scottish Rifle); dam never ran; showed signs of ability in non-sellers, but was soundly beaten in a seller final start (sweating). *H. Westbrook.* —

RITUAL DANCE 2 gr.f. Godswalk 130–Faith Lift (Nearctic) (1981 5g 5d 5s* 5g) Apr 23; 4,000Y; neat filly; good mover; second foal; half-sister to winning Irish 3-y-o sprinter Singing My Song (by Mr Leader); dam won 6f claiming race at 3 yrs in USA; having first race for 4 months when leading inside final furlong to win 15-runner maiden race at Folkestone in October by 2 lengths from Spanish Fury; not disgraced when fifth of 9 to Fearless Lad in £2,600 race at Doncaster later in month; will stay 6f; yet to race on a firm surface. *B. Hanbury.* **84**

RIVA BE GOOD (USA) 4 ch.g. Riva Ridge–Best Go (Mongo) (1980 12fg³ 16f⁴ 13.8fg³ 16g 10d³ 16f 1981 13.1h 12f) leggy, narrow gelding; in frame in varied company, including selling; stays well; ran moderately in blinkers once. *O. O'Neill.* —

RIVADON (USA) 5 b.g. Riva Ridge–Sarah Bernhardt (Buckpasser) (1980 10.2d 1981 10.6s) moderate maiden at his best; behind in valuable selling handicap only start at 5 yrs in June; should stay at least 1¼m; possibly unsuited by soft ground. *W. Clay.* —

RIVAL 3 b.g. Forlorn River 124–La Magna 104 (Runnymede 123) (1980 5f 5d 6g 6fg 8d 8.2s 8d³ 1981 10.1d⁴ 10.1fg 10.8fg 10g) compact gelding; plater; stays 1¼m. *T. Marshall.* —

RIVER BREEZE 3 b.f. Rapid River 127–Groovy 86 (Sound Track 132) (1980 5f 5g* 5g 5f³ 5s 1981 5fg) rather leggy filly; quite a moderate performer at 2 yrs; always struggling only outing of 1981 (bandaged); may stay 6f; probably unsuited by soft ground. *J. Doyle.* —

RIVER BRI 2 br.g. Rapid River 127–Briana 64 (The Brianstan 128) (1981 5g 5fg 6fg 8g 7g) May 3; strong gelding; good mover; first foal; dam placed over 5f at 2 yrs; in rear in minor and maiden races. *G. Toft.* —

RIVER HILL (FR) 2 b.c. Riverman 131–La Marelle (Dike) (1981 8.5d* 8v²) **107**
big, rangy, good sort; excellent walker; second foal; dam useful French middle-
distance performer; didn't look fully wound up when winning 11-runner newcomers event at Longchamp in October by ½ length from Brazos, rallying splendidly, without being hard ridden, after making virtually all; odds on for 4-runner
race at Maisons-Laffitte later in month but went down by a neck to Bel Emir;
will be suited by 1¼m+; the type to do much better at 3 yrs. *Mme C. Head,
France.*

RIVERHILL BOY 3 b.g. Manacle 123–My Grace (Sahib 114) (1980 NR 1981 —
8fg 12g 10.1f 8f 8.3fg 8.3g 8.3fg 8.3g 8fg³ 7d) 1,400Y; first foal; dam won in
Norway; plater; ran best race on ninth start, despite putting head in air; stays
1m; pulled up seventh start; has worn blinkers. *C. Wildman.*

RIVERHILL LAD 3 ch.g. Streak 119–Fleur de Sol 64 (Vilmorin) (1980 5f —
5f 5d 5d 5s 1981 7.6g 8.3fg 10fg 8d) useful-looking gelding; plater; possibly
stays 1m (not entirely disgraced second start); has been tried in blinkers. *C.
Wildman.*

RIVER LADY 2 ch.f. Riverman 131–Prudent Miss 120 (Prudent II 133) **116**
(1981 6fg* 6g* 6f³ 8d²)
It's an indication of River Lady's reputation that she started odds on for two
Group 1 races, the Prix Morny and the Prix Marcel Boussac, and perhaps an
indication of her merit that she didn't win either. She ran by no means badly
in either race, though, and is without doubt a smart filly if not yet the champion
she's clearly thought to be.
River Lady had won both her races before the Morny in fine style, trotting
up by six lengths in an eleven-runner newcomers race at Chantilly in June
before disposing of five opponents, all colts, with ease in an 80,000-franc event,
the Prix de Cabourg, at Deauville. So impressive was she that the Deauville
punters preferred her in the Morny to the Richmond Stakes winner Tender King
and the first two in the Robert Papin, Maelstrom Lake and Green Forest.
Entering the final quarter mile she looked about to justify the support, looming
up outside Green Forest with her jockey sitting still, but she couldn't find the
pace to pass him and in the end lost second place close home to Maelstrom Lake,
about a length behind the winner.
It was rumoured that in a gallop shortly before the Marcel Boussac River
Lady had slaughtered her stable-companion Play It Safe and, with stable-jockey
Paquet aboard at Longchamp in October, River Lady started at 7/10. Paquet,
of all the jockeys in the race, should have been fully aware of the second favourite
Play It Safe's formidable front-running capabilities—he'd ridden her in all her
previous races, in the latest of them making all to win a Group 3 event by four
lengths. However, he held River Lady up as Play It Safe set the pace and his
filly was still only fifth of eight into the straight. Her position worsened
when Piggott on Play It Safe stole a couple of lengths by pushing on round the
turn and from then on River Lady was struggling. Under very strong driving
she steadily whittled down Play It Safe's advantage but was still a head behind
at the line. Paquet's efforts were rewarded with booing from the favourite's
supporters, and it has to be said that with a little more enterprise on his behalf
the result might have gone the other way.

		⎧ Never Bend	⎧ Nasrullah
	⎧ Riverman	{ (b 1960)	⎨ Lalun
	{ (b 1969)	⎩ River Lady (USA)	⎧ Prince John
River Lady	{	{ (b 1963)	⎨ Nile Lily
(ch.f. Mar 29, 1979)	{	⎧ Prudent II	⎧ My Babu
	⎩ Prudent Miss	{ (ch 1959)	⎨ Providence
	(b 1967)	⎩ Miss Glasso	⎧ Ratification
		(br 1961)	⎨ Tulip II

By the time of the Deauville Yearling Sales in August 1980 Riverman was
already the height of fashion; the exploits of one son, the top-class miler Irish
River, were still fresh in the mind; another son, Policeman, had recently won the
Prix du Jockey-Club; and two daughters, the three-year-old fillies Detroit and
Gold River, were already showing signs of developing into outstanding performers.
At Deauville the competition for Riverman's daughter out of the very smart miler
Prudent Miss was intense, so much so that the filly, later named River Lady, set
a new French record price for a yearling of 1,800,000 francs, or approximately
£180,000. At the time of the sale the only other winner out of Prudent Miss
was River Lady's brother Provider, successful in several small races at up to a mile

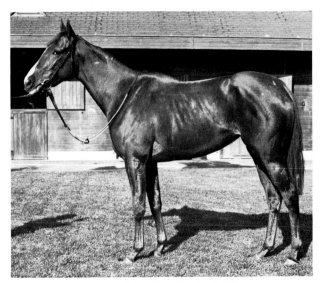

Mr S. S. Niarchos' "River Lady"

and a quarter, so River Lady must now be worth considerably more following the win of her three-year-old half-brother No Lute (by Luthier) in the 1981 Prix Lupin. Prudent Miss's dam, the unraced Miss Glasso, also bred the very useful mile-and-a-quarter filly Miss Molly, the grandam of those very smart French colts Sharpman, Mot D'Or and Lydian.

River Lady should stay a mile and a quarter. She's an attractive filly, with a little more scope than Play It Safe, and looks sure to make a big name for herself at three. She appears to act on any going but has yet to encounter really soft. *F. Boutin, France.*

RIVER PRINCE (USA) 3 br. or bl.c. Forli–Intrepid Lady (Bold Ruler) (1980 **113** NR 1981 7g² 6d³ 5f² 6g* 5fg) third foal; half-brother to very useful 1m and 1¼m filly Calandra (by Sir Ivor) and Irish 1m winner Fonthill Abbey (by Habitat); dam, winner over 1½m in France, is sister to very smart 1968 American 2-y-o filly Big Advance; beat Castlemaine a head in maiden race at Phoenix Park in April but edged right and placings were reversed after a stewards inquiry; won Herbertstown Stakes on same course in August by ¾ length from Tellurano (pair clear); placed twice at Phoenix Park in between, on second occasion dead-heating with Lady Blackfoot 2½ lengths behind Clanjolly in Stackallen Stakes; bred to stay 1m; sent to race in USA. *V. O'Brien, Ireland.*

RIVERS EDGE 3 b.g. Sharpen Up 127–Ebb and Flo 82 (Forlorn River 124) **59** (1980 5.1f 6g² 6g² 6g 6s 1981 6s 6fg² 7g* 7d) neat gelding; runner-up in a seller prior to gaining narrow win in maiden race at Edinburgh in April; suited by 7f; sometimes wears a muzzle; has been tried in blinkers; apprentice ridden nowadays. *W. Stubbs.*

RIVERS LAD 3 ch.c. Rarity 129–Takette (Takawalk II 125) (1980 NR **61** 1981 12fg 12g 12s⁴ 12s 12d) 7,000Y; rangy colt; brother to very useful middle-distance performer Decent Fellow, also a very smart hurdler, and to 1979

2-y-o 7f winner Rivers Maid, and half-brother to another winner; modest fourth
to Regain in 10-runner £2,000 race at Lingfield in October. *G. Balding.*

RIVER WARRIOR   3 b.g. Forlorn River 124–Wounded Knee 78 (Busted 134)   **48**
(1980 6g 6g 6d   1981 10s 11.7g 10.1f 10g 10.1fg²)   small, narrow gelding;
second in seller at Windsor in July; stays 1¼m; blinkered last 2 starts; sold
675 gns Ascot December Sales. *C. James.*

RI-WINE   2 b. or br.f. Free State 125–My Cousins 54 (My Swallow 134)   (1981   **62**
5d 5fg 6fg 5.8f* 6d 6g)   Apr 2; small, close-coupled filly; first foal; dam slow
maiden; attracted no bid after showing improved form to win seller at Bath
in July by 4 lengths from Anniversary Waltz; didn't reproduce that form;
will be suited by 1m; suited by a sound surface. *P. Feilden.*

RIXE (FR)   3 ch.f. Brigadier Gerard 144–Rapid Item 68 (Northern Dancer)   **118**
(1980 8v³ 10s³ 10s⁴   1981 11.5s² 12d³ 11d* 10s² 12g³ 9d² 8f² 8s² 9.2d² 10.5v² 8s³)
second foal; half-sister to French 10.5f winner Gnullia (by Margouillat); dam
won up to 11f in French Provinces; won maiden race at Longchamp in May by
2¼ lengths from Plainsong; placed all other starts, notably when runner-up
to Kilmona in Group 3 Prix Chloe at Evry in July (beaten ¾ length) and Group 2
Prix de l'Opera at Longchamp in October (beaten a neck) on sixth and ninth
starts, and when length second to Votre Altesse in Group 3 Prix de Flore at
Saint-Cloud in October on penultimate outing; stays 1½m but best form at
shorter distances, acts on any going; genuine. *F. Boutin, France.*

RIYAHI   2 b.c. Red God 128§–Ravela II (Tanerko 134)   (1981 5g⁴ 6fg* 8g*)   **112**
Apr 5; half-brother to several winners in France; dam, half-sister to high-class
sprinter Fortino II, won at up to 13f; won twice at Deauville in good style,
beating Georgios 3 lengths in maiden race and The Sun God 4 lengths in valuable
Prix des Foals; suited by 1m, and will probably stay 1¼m; entered in Derby.
F. Mathet, France.

RIZLA RED   2 b.f. Mansingh 120–Erminia 61 (Gulf Pearl 117)   (1981 5s 6d 5g 7f   **66**
7d 10g²)   Mar 28; 5,000Y; rangy, useful sort; first foal; dam won 6f seller
and also a selling hurdle; dropped in class when going down by 2½ lengths to
Getting Plenty in seller at Leicester in October; stays 1½m; blinkered fourth
outing; sold 500 gns Newmarket Autumn Sales. *R.Hannon.*

R. J. WALLIS   6 b.g. David Jack 125–Josuelind 78 (Nimbus 130)   (1980 8s   **59**
8fg 7g* 8fg* 7fg 7d 8fg³ 7fg 7f⁴   1981 7fg² 7g 6g³ 7f 7.6fg)   poor handicapper
nowadays; best at up to 1m; probably acts on any going; good mount for a boy;
sold to Mrs E. Kennard 3,500 gns Ascot October Sales. *A. Pitt.*

ROAN MIST   3 b.g. Roan Rocket 128–Barchessa 67 (Prince Chevalier)   (1980   **—**
6fg 7d⁴   1981 8g)   big, strong gelding; good mover; prominent in 2 maiden
races at Newbury as a 2-y-o; ran as if needing race when sixth of 16 behind St
Pedro in similar event at Newmarket in April; should be suited by 1m. *D. Kent.*

ROANOKE RIVER   2 ch.f. Roan Rocket 128–Warrior Queen 95 (King's Bench   **79**
132)   (1981 7g 8d*)   Mar 10; IR 8,600F, IR 5,600Y; big filly; half-sister to
several winners, including fairly useful Rama Tibodi (by Amber Rama), successful
at up to 7.6f; dam middle-distance performer; 20/1, beat Haven's Pride ½ length
in 23-runner maiden race at Leicester in November; will stay 1¼m; the type
to improve further at 3 yrs. *Sir Mark Prescott.*

ROAN RENAGADE   2 ro.c. Grey Mirage 128–Bontet (Bounteous 125)   (1981   **53**
5s 5f 5fg 7fg 6g 5f)   Mar 30; 300F; small colt; poor plater; blinkered sixth
outing. *J. Spearing.*

ROBARD   3 ch.c. Brigadier Gerard 144–Kentucky Robin 73 (Falcon 131)   (1980   **—**
6g 7g 7f⁴ 7s   1981 10s 8s)   big colt; showed some ability at 2 yrs; well beaten
in 1981, but had stiff task on final outing and possibly isn't at his best on soft
going; should stay 1¼m. *G. Lewis.*

ROBELLINO (USA)   3 b.c. Roberto 131–Isobelline (Pronto)   (1980 6fg* 6g²   **113**
7d* 7s* 8fg* 8d   1981 8.5fg² 10.5s⁴ 12d 8fg⁴ 9s 8g* 10.5g² 8fg)   deep-girthed,
good sort; second foal; dam won over 7f at 2 yrs in Ireland; high-class colt as
a 2-y-o, successful 4 times, including in Royal Lodge Stakes at Ascot (quickened
nicely to beat Recitation ½ length) and Seaton Delaval Stakes at Newcastle;
gained sole success of 1981 when beating moderate Dunham Park by 3 lengths
in minor event at Newcastle in August; had stayed on strongly and made winner
pull out all the stops when neck second to Centurius (rec 5 lb) in Ladbroke Blue
Riband Trial at Epsom on reappearance in April but was rather disappointing in
between, finishing fourth of 6 behind Beldale Flutter in Mecca-Dante Stakes at

721

York, fourteenth of 18 behind runaway winner Shergar in Derby (always behind), fourth to To-Agori-Mou in St James's Palace Stakes at Royal Ascot and eighth of 10 to Dunphy in Prix Daphnis at Longchamp; didn't show any sparkle when 1½ lengths second of 3 behind Church Parade in High Line Stakes at York later in August and on his only other outing broke down in £3,100 event won by Boathouse at Goodwood in September, suffering a hairline fracture to his off-fore cannon bone; should have stayed 1½m; didn't race on really firm ground, but seemed to act on any going; syndicated to stand at Derry Meeting Farm, Pennsylvania, at a fee of $15,000 (live foal). *I. Balding.*

ROBERT ADAM 6 ch.g. Mansingh 120–Pritillor 93 (Privy Councillor 125) (1980 12s 13d 12fg* 12fg⁴ 12fg 12f 12fg⁴ 10fg 1981 10f) poor handicapper; stays 1½m; acts on any going; sometimes wears blinkers; suitable mount for an inexperienced rider; sold 660 gns Doncaster January (81) Sales. *M. McCormack.* —

ROBERTA STAR (USA) 3 b.f. Roberto 131–Starmount Belle 110 (Nantallah) (1980 6fg 7g 7g³ 8fg⁴ 1981 12d 10fg⁴ 12fg⁴ 15.5s) leggy, fair sort; in frame in varied company; best form at up to 1¼m. *R. Akehurst.* —

ROBERT LOUIS (USA) 2 ch.c. Forceten–Three Black Spots (Viceregal) (1981 10s) third foal; dam stakes-placed winner at up to 1m; 20/1 and backward when not in first 10 of 22 behind Luxury in maiden event at Nottingham in October; sent to France. *R. Sheather.* —

ROBIN HOOD 6 br.g. Tudor Melody 129–Hirondelle 86 (Falcon 131) (1980 16f² 17.1f 1981 18.8fg 17.1d) poor handicapper nowadays; stays well; acts on any going; has worn blinkers. *A. Andrews.* —

ROBOUT (USA) 2 b.c. Full Out–Robustious (Rambunctious) (1981 5g 5.1f 6g 7f⁴ 7fg 7f² 7s 7fg 7g* 8d 7g) Apr 29; $50,000Y; smallish, compact colt; first foal; dam stakes-placed winner at up to 11f from 3 yrs to 7 yrs; put up best effort when making virtually all to win 16-runner nursery at Catterick in September by a head from Glossy Ibis; suited by 7f and forcing tactics (not disgraced when tried over 1m); possibly not at his best on very soft going; goes well for an apprentice; blinkered fifth to eighth starts; sold 10,500 gns Newmarket Autumn Sales. *N. Callaghan.* **73**

ROCAMADOUR 2 b.c. Royal Match 117–Blakeney Belle (Blakeney 126) (1981 7fg² 7g* 7v*) May 4; 7,000Y; quite attractive, full-quartered colt; second foal; half-brother to Irish 3-y-o 7f winner Doon Belle (by Ardoon); dam poor half-sister to smart Daring Boy and Daring March; quickened to lead in final furlong when winning 22-runner maiden race at Newmarket in October by 1½ lengths from Musical Score and 8-runner minor event at Kempton later in month by ½ length from Honriette; will stay 1¼m; ridden by apprentice M. Saunders all outings. *A. Pitt.* **91**

ROCK BALLET (USA) 2 b.c. Riva Ridge–Tally Round (Round Table) (1981 8g) Jan 23; $105,000Y; lengthy, quite attractive colt; third foal; brother to a minor winner; dam, sister to smart middle-distance winner Knight in Armor, won 4 times at up to 9f; unquoted and green when out of first 10 of 29 to Born Hero in maiden race at Newmarket in October; may do better when tackling 1¼m+. *P. Walwyn.* —

ROCKBARTON 6 b.g. Lord Gayle 124–June's Slipper (No Argument 107) (1980 NR 1981 16d) ex-Irish gelding; won maiden race at Ballinrobe in 1979; well beaten in amateur riders race at Lingfield in July; stays well. *A. Moore.* —

ROCK CONCERT 4 br.f. Star Appeal 133–Plumtree Plain (Primera 131) (1980 11.7f 11fg* 12fg⁴ 1981 12s 12.2fg 12s 12.2fg 12d 12d 12.2g 10s) neat filly; poor handicapper nowadays; well beaten in seller final start; will stay beyond 1¼m; one paced; sold 1,500 gns Ascot December Sales. *R. Whitaker.* —

ROCKER 3 ch.c. Habitat 134–Treacle 85 (Hornbeam 130) (1980 6fg 6d 7s 8d 1981 7d 7g) small, hollow-backed colt; soundly beaten in maiden and minor races and a handicap; blinkered in 1981. *J. Douglas-Home.* —

ROCKETONE 3 gr.c. Roan Rocket 128–Sweetstone (Honeyway 125) (1980 6d 1981 8d 10.1d 10.1v⁴ 10.1f 10g 10.1fg 11g 8fg 10.1g³ 10.1fg³) robust colt; quite a moderate maiden; stays 1¼m. *J. Benstead.* **57**

ROCKET ROLL 2 b.c. Touch Paper 113–Fig Roll (Hard Tack 111§) (1981 5g 5d 5f 6f 6f 5s) Mar 12; IR 1,200F, IR 5,200Y; compact colt; bad mover, half-brother to 1973 2-y-o 5f winner Fair Gazelle (by Star Gazer) and a winner in Czechoslovakia; dam won over 9f in Ireland; only plating class; sold 540 gns Doncaster November Sales. *R. Armstrong.* **64**

ROCKET SONG 3 gr.g. Roan Rocket 128–Our Song 70 (Song 132) (1980 6g* 6fg⁴ 8d² 7d⁴ 1981 9.4g* 11fg* 8g² 10d³ 10fg 10.6fg* 12f³ 11d* 10.2d* 11d) **87**

strong gelding; good walker and mover; had a most successful time and won handicaps at Carlisle, Hamilton and Haydock, minor event at Hamilton and apprentice race at Bath; beat Burleigh decisively by 4 lengths in last-named event in October; needs further than 1m and seems to stay 1½m; acts on a firm and a soft surface; genuine and consistent. *Sir Mark Prescott.*

ROCKFEST (USA) 2 ch.f. Stage Door Johnny–Rock Garden 86 (Roan Rocket **104** 128) (1981 6d³ 7fg³ 7g² 7g* 8fg* 8s²) strong, well-made, attractive filly; half-sister to a winner in Scandinavia; dam 1m winner and half-sister to very smart Glen Strae; led inside final furlong to win maiden race at Chester in August by a neck from Barooq and £3,600 event at Goodwood the following month by ½ length from Dreaming Away, putting up a particularly gritty display in latter; excellent 1½ lengths second of 12 to Jalmood in £3,300 race at Goodwood later in September; will stay 1½m; seems to act on any going; very genuine and improved all the time. *J. Tree.*

ROCK TELL 2 ch.g. Guillaume Tell 121–North Rock (Northfields) (1981 **53** 5fg 6f 7f 7g⁴ 8fg³ 8.2d 8d) Apr 23; IR 3,200F; leggy gelding; plater; will stay 1¼m; blinkered last 3 outings; formerly trained by K. Stone; sold 500 gns Ascot November Sales. *G. Lockerbie.*

ROCKY GREEN (USA) 2 b.c. Shecky Greene–Flower O'Kings (Day Court) — (1981 6d 5v) Apr 19; $16,000Y, $40,000 2-y-o; strong, compact colt; half-brother to a minor winner; dam out of half-sister to top-class English performers Royal Palm and Royal Serenade; 11/1 when seventh of 20 finishers behind Master-Blow in maiden race at Haydock in October, second outing; should stay 6f. *P. Haslam.*

RODDY 2 b.g. Gold Rod 129–Miss Dike (Dike) (1981 6d) June 4; sturdy — gelding; first foal; dam won at 1½m in Ireland and also won over hurdles; unquoted and in need of race when last of 16 to Rosananti in minor event at Ayr in September. *A. W. Jones.*

RODEO 3 ch.c. Bustino 136–Hitesca 110 (Tesco Boy 121) (1980 6g 6g 8.2s **91** 1981 8d⁴ 11g* 12g² 11g* 11d* 12d* 13d²) compact, sturdy colt; had a fine

Great Yorkshire Handicap, York—Rodeo has to survive a stewards inquiry after beating Crested Lark (rails) and Fascadale. At an inquiry instituted some time later by the Disciplinary Committee of the Jockey Club, E. Johnson, the rider of Rodeo, was found guilty of careless riding and suspended for ten days

season and was gaining his fourth win when beating Crested Lark by a short head in handicap at York in August, just getting up after having none too clear a run; outstayed by Salora Lady and beaten ½ length in Bogside Cup (Handicap) at Ayr the following month, after looking to have race sewn up when going clear over 2f out; successful earlier in maiden race and a handicap at Ayr, and in another handicap at Redcar; stays 1½m; yet to race on a firm surface; has a good turn of foot and is one to keep on the right side. *C. Thornton.*

RODSHOT 6 gr.g. Abwah 118–Warning Shot (Premonition 130) (1980 7g 8fg⁴ — 8.2g³ 12g³ 12.2g⁴ 10g⁴ 12.3d 12f 12.2fg 1981 8s 15.5f³) poor handicapper; stays well; acts on any going; has run creditably in blinkers; has run well for an amateur rider. *D. Grissell.*

ROESSA 2 b.f. Relkino 131–Rose Red 95 (Ballymoss 136) (1981 6fg 8s 7g) — Apr 12; neat, quite attractive filly; half-sister to a winning plater by Decoy Boy and a winner abroad; dam won over 7f at 2 yrs and stayed well; behind in maiden races; will be suited by 1½m+. *F. J. Houghton.*

ROGER BACON 6 gr.g. Comedy Star 121–Tinsel 95 (Right Boy 137) (1980 5s 79 5fg 5fg 5d 5.6g 5fg 5g 5g 5s 5s 1981 5g 6.5fg 6.5s³ 7.5g⁴ 5s² 5g² 5s² 6s 6fg 6g³ 6s 5.8d 6f 6f 6g 5fg 6fg 5fg 5.8g² 5g 5s) strong, compact gelding; carries plenty of condition; poor mover; sprint handicapper; stays 6f; acts on any going; usually wears blinkers. *R. Baker.*

ROGER NICHOLAS 2 b.g. Immortal Knight 103–Lovesome Hill 57 (Murray-field 119) (1981 8g 7g) Apr 24; 230Y; leggy, lightly-made gelding; first foal; dam, plater, stayed 1¼m; last but one in 15-runner maiden event at Beverley in September and in 9-runner minor event at Catterick in October; has very little scope. *J. Calvert.*

ROI GUILLAUME (FR) 3 b.c. Busted 134–Rescousse 130 (Emerson) (1980 **119** 7.5g 7.5d² 1981 12fg² 12s² 12s* 12.5d² 12.5f*) French colt; half-brother to smart French 1m winner Reine Imperiale (by King Emperor) and very useful French middle-distance performer En Calcat (by Margouillat); dam won Prix de Diane and was second in Prix de l'Arc de Triomphe in 1972; won minor event at Evry in May and Prix de Menneval at Deauville in August, latter in good style by 1½ lengths from Top Dancer; second on all his other starts, in maiden event at Longchamp, minor event at Evry and Group 2 Prix Maurice de Nieuil at Saint-Cloud, putting up a smart performance when beaten 2½ lengths by Perrault on last-named course; stays 1½m well; acts on any going. *J. Cunnington, jnr, France.*

ROLLAHEAD 4 ch.c. Tower Walk 130–First Round 97 (Primera 131) (1980 **94** 6fg⁴ 5f⁴ 5fg 1981 6fg³ 6g 6d 5.3f⁴ 5g) strong, compact colt; fairly useful handicapper; creditable third to Denmore under 10-0 at Epsom in April; possibly needs a sound surface. *R. Price.*

ROLLESTON 7 ch.g. Communication 119–Chamolive 56 (Poaching 115) — (1980 NR 1981 8f) poor performer; well beaten in seller only start at 7 yrs in June; stays 11f; suited by some give in the ground. *W. Wharton.*

ROLLING RIVER 5 b.m. Warpath 113–Shenandoah 88 (Mossborough 126) — (1980 12.3s 12fg 12f* 12fg* 12d⁴ 13.8f⁴ 13g 12fg⁴ 12fg 10g 1981 14.6f 15fg 16f 13fg 12g) lightly-made mare; plater; should stay 1¾m; acts on firm going; gave trouble at stalls when blinkered once in 1980. *K. Morgan.*

ROLLIN HAND 3 b.c. Some Hand 119–Josilu (Caliban 123) (1980 5s* 5f² **77** 5fg⁴ 5f³ 6d² 6g 6g⁴ 7d 1981 6fg 7d⁴ 8s³ 7d² 7f³ 7.?f² 7g 7g 8s² 7d) useful-looking colt; good walker; placed in handicaps at Goodwood, Sandown, Wolverhampton, Haydock and in minor event at Warwick; length second to Piperhill in Sporting Chronicle Handicap at Havdock; stays 1m; acts on any going; has run well for an apprentice; sweated up fifth start; ran badly final outing. *P. Cole.*

ROLLINS (FR) 2 b.c. Hul a Hul 124–Pomposa (Bewitched) (1981 6fg² 4.5g⁴ **116** 5.5d 6f* 6.5s² 8s³ 7v⁴) fourth foal; half-brother to French 1m to 1¼m winner Mag Meld (by Staunch Eagle); dam second in a 1½m claiming race; ran well in good races after winning maiden race at Deauville in August, finishing ½-length second to Pas de Seul in Prix Eclipse at Saint-Cloud, running on strongly to be 6½ lengths third of 10 to Green Forest in Grand Criterium at Longchamp and 6 lengths fourth of 10 to Zino when second favourite for Criterium de Maisons-Laffitte; well suited by 1m and will probably stay further; seems to act on any going; blinkered first 3 outings. *J. Fellows, France.*

ROLL OF DRUMS (USA) 3 b.c. Hoist the Flag–Recall (Reneged) (1980 **94** 7s² 1981 7s³ 7d) $375,000Y; tall, lengthy, quite attractive colt; sixth foal; half-brother to 1m and 1¼m winner Revocation (by Reviewer) and 4 minor winners; dam smart stakes winner at up to 1m; veered right across course over 2f out and went down by 3 lengths to Lord Never in maiden race at the Curragh as a 2-y-o (subsequently found to have fractured a cannon bone); favourite when 1½ lengths third of 9 to Dance Bid in Group 3 Tetrarch Stakes at the Curragh on reappearance in April; found little under pressure and was most disappointing when about 7 lengths fifth of 6 behind Cragador in City of York Stakes at York when next seen out in August (odds on); will be suited by further than 7f and is likely to stay middle distances; sent to race in USA. *V. O'Brien, Ireland.*

ROLLRIGHTS 3 ch.f. Ragstone 128–Skiboule (Boulou) (1980 7s³ 8d* 1981 **106** 10g² 12fg² 12f 12d² 14.6g 12s* 10.2d*) lightly-made filly; has a round action; first foal in this country; dam won in Belgium; second in 3 good fillies races, namely Playboy Pretty Polly Stakes won by Humming at Newmarket in May, Ribblesdale Stakes won by Strigida at Royal Ascot in June and Galtres Stakes won by Ma Femme at York in August; ran on bravely and went down by only a neck on last 2 courses; made all when gaining well-deserved wins in minor event at Lingfield (completely outclassed opposition) and Huddersfield and Bradford Building Society Stakes at Doncaster, both in October, in latter event beating Cons Pal in good style by 3 lengths; rather disappointing on her other 2 starts, but didn't handle bend in Lancashire Oaks at Haydock on first occasion; stays 1½m; possibly not at her best on very firm going, but seems to act on any other; genuine; sold to race in USA. *J. Dunlop.*

ROLOSCOPE 3 b.f. Barolo 94–Border Scope (Border Chief 101) (1980 NR — 1981 12d) non-thoroughbred filly; second foal; dam fair point-to-pointer; last of 16 behind Mossdrum in maiden race at Hamilton in October. *Mrs C. Lloyd-Jones.*

ROMANETTE 4 ch.f. Copper Man–Young Rowette 99 (Delirium 126) (1980 — 9fg 8f 1981 6g 8f 8f 8fg) poor plater; has worn blinkers. *D. Leslie.*

ROMAN HYACINTH 2 ch.f. Roman Warrior 132–Sea Fern (Klondyke Bill 125) — (1981 5g 5g) Apr 6; tall, close-coupled filly; third foal; half-sister to fairly useful 5f to 1m winner Fernaro (by Sharpen Up); dam won over hurdles; showed good speed and ran better than finishing position suggests when out of first 10 of 19 behind Bahamas Princess in maiden event at Salisbury in June, second start; dead. *R. Hannon.*

Huddersfield and Bradford Building Society Stakes, Doncaster—an enterprising ride by Piggott on Rollrights

ROMAN QUEST 2 b.c. Roman Warrior 132–Miss Richton 80 (Lauso) (1981 **78**
5v[4] 5fg[3] 5g* 5f 6f* 5fg 6fg[2] 6fg) Apr 21; 5,100Y; big, useful sort; second foal;
half-brother to a winner abroad by Forlorn River; dam won at up to 7f at 2 yrs;
successful in maiden race at Catterick in June and in 5-runner nursery at
Leicester in August, beating Straeker decisively by 2 lengths in latter; better at 6f
than 5f; acts on firm going; good mount for an apprentice; seemed to run too
freely when blinkered final outing. T. Fairhurst.

ROMAN STONE 3 ch.f. Roman Warrior 132–Riotous 97 (Silver Cloud 121) —
(1980 NR 1981 6g 8g 7f 8f 10f 8f 6d 7s) 4,600Y, 3,000 2-y-o; lengthy filly;
fourth foal; dam won over 5f at 2 yrs; soundly beaten in varied company,
including in selling; has been tried in blinkers. W. Bentley.

ROMANTIC AFFAIR 3 ch.f. Weepers Boy 124–Dawn Affair 77 (Entanglement —
118) (1980 5v 1981 10s 12fg 7d) useless; sold 520 gns Ascot May Sales.
P. K. Mitchell.

ROMANTIC TANGO 2 ch.f. Gay Fandango 132–Romantic Cruise (Nice —
Guy 123) (1981 5.8g 5f 7fg 8s) Apr 14; neat, sturdy filly; poor mover; half-
sister to Irish 9f winner Miss Ballyclough (by Double-U-Jay) and a winner
in Malaya; well beaten in maiden races and sellers; blinkered final outing. D.
Wintle.

ROMAN TREASURE 3 ch.g. Roman Warrior 132–Most Precious (Matador —
131) (1980 5d 6d 6d 6g 6fg 6f 7g 6f 7f 1981 8g 7f) bad plater; has worn
blinkers. Miss L. Siddall.

ROMOSS 3 ch.g. Royal Match 117–Pamela Rose 107 (Vilmorin) (1980 5f **77**
5f[3] 6fg[3] 5fg 6g[2] 5f[4] 5s 5d[4] 1981 8g[2] 8d[3] 10.2f[4] 10fg* 10fg 9f 10.5f[4] 10fg[2] 11fg
10d) strong, rangy gelding; in frame in varied company before beating Point
North by 8 lengths in maiden race at Ayr in July; had stiffish tasks and ran
creditably most subsequent outings; stays 1¼m; probably acts on any going;
trained until after fifth start by P. Rohan. R. Whitaker.

ROMSAL 2 ch.g. Roman Warrior 132–Salambos (Doon 124) (1981 7g) Mar —
15; 2,300F, 1,300Y; well-grown, useful sort; second foal; dam behind in seller
on only start; weak in market and green when always behind in 11-runner
maiden race won by Big Trouble at Yarmouth in July. A. Jarvis.

RONDAROSA 3 b.f. Mummy's Pet 125–Stockingful (Santa Claus 133) (1980 **72**
6d 6d 1981 6s* 7g* 7g[3] 6s[4] 7fg 6fg 7.2v 6s) neat filly; won poor maiden race
at Stockton and minor event at Catterick in April, beating Sincerely Mills
by 1½ lengths in latter; ran moderately most subsequent outings, looking ungenuine on second occasion and wearing blinkers on third; will probably stay
1m; acts on soft going; apprentice ridden second and third starts; sold 14,000
gns Newmarket December Sales. J. W. Watts.

RONTINO 4 b.c. Bustino 136–Tudoron 108 (Tudor Melody 129) (1980 9f[3] **102**
12f[3] 12g 12d 1981 10fg 10g* 8.5d 10fg[3] 12fg) attractive, robust colt; fairly
useful performer; beat Wise Owl by 1½ lengths in minor event at Pontefract
in May (pair 10 lengths clear); far from disgraced when 3½ lengths third of
4 to Magesterial in Land of Burns Stakes at Ayr in July; appeared 1½m; appeared
to act on any going; blinkered once at 3 yrs; stud in Wales. M. Jarvis.

ROOFER 3 gr.g. Brittany–Piccadilly Rose 63 (Reform 132) (1980 5fg 6fg **63**
7d 7fg 7fg 8d 7d 6s[4] 1981 6s[4] 6g 7d[3] 6s[3] 7fg[4] 8g 9s 10d) robust gelding; not
a good mover; third in maiden races at Leicester and Haydock in spring;
runs as if 6f is on sharp side and should stay 1m; usually blinkered; trained by
M. Ryan first 6 starts and was off course 5 months before seventh. R. Boss.

ROOKERY HILL 2 b. or br.c. Dance In Time–Lyndy Sue 70 (Major Portion —
129) (1981 6fg 6fg) Mar 4; fair sort; half-brother to several winners here
and abroad, including quite useful 1m to 1½m handicapper Kildoon (by Kalydon);
dam disappointing; backward when in rear in 14-runner minor event at Windsor
in July and 11-runner £3,300 race at Salisbury in August; sold to German
International BA 1,150 gns Newmarket Autumn Sales. D. Whelan.

ROOT GINGER (CAN) 3 b.f. Val de l'Orne 130–Fallen Tear (Manacle 123) **75**
(1980 NR 1981 11.7g* 12.2fg 12fg[4] 14.6fg[2] 17.1d[4] 16s) strong, lengthy filly;
half-sister to a winner in North America by Tentam; dam, winner 3 times at
up to 1m, is half-sister to smart animals Big Bead and Red Berry; looked as
if race was needed when beating Takeafence in quite nice style by 1½ lengths
in maiden race at Bath in June; probably ran best subsequent races in handicaps
at Doncaster and Bath on fourth and fifth starts; stays well; ran badly final
start. B. Hills.

ROOTLESS 2 gr.f. Mandrake Major 122–Counter Coup (Busted 134) (1981 **68**
7f 7g² 8d 6g) Apr 8; 2,300Y; smallish, fair sort; has been tubed; half-sister
to fair 6f to 1m winner Greyburn (by Saintly Song); dam lightly-raced daughter
of smart filly Alborada; always prominent when 1½ lengths second of 29 to
Perchance in valuable seller at Newmarket in September; weakened very
quickly in closing stages when odds on for similar event at Leicester next time
out; stays 7f; possibly unsuited by a soft surface. *B. Hobbs.*

RORY O'MORE 2 ch.c. Gay Fandango 132–Skippon 93 (Supreme Court   —
135) (1981 5g 6s) May 7; 12,000Y; strong, useful sort; half-brother to 3
winners, including fairly useful 1971 2-y-o 5f and 5.8f winner Facade (by Double
Jump); dam 5f and 6f winner at 2 yrs but disappointed afterwards; moved
most unimpressively to start when last of 17 in maiden race at Thirsk in May;
not seen out again until end of season when eighth of 13 to Puesdown in similar
race at Hamilton. *W. H. H. Williams.*

ROSACEAE 2 b.f. Sagaro 133–Floradora Do 85 (Derring-Do 131) (1981 **75**
5d 6fg²) Apr 27; compact filly; half-sister to useful 3-y-o 1¼m and 1¾m winner
Capricorn Line (by High Line); dam won at up to 7f; 33/1, put in best work
in closing stages when dead-heating for second place, 2 lengths behind Bless
The Match, in 22-runner maiden race at Lingfield in June; bred to stay 1½m+.
I. Balding.

ROSANANTI 2 ch.f. Blushing Groom 131–Clarina (Klairon 131) (1981 6fg **104**
6fg² 6fg* 6d* 7s²) well-made filly; half-sister to 2 winners, including good
English and German performer Claddagh (by Bold Lad, Ire); dam won twice
over 1¼m in Ireland; won maiden race at Newcastle in August very cheekily
by a head from Dageegah and again won comfortably when beating Fearless
Lad 2 lengths in minor event at Ayr the following month; creditable 2 lengths
second of 11 to Spanish Pool in valuable nursery at Lingfield in October (well-
backed favourite); will stay 1¼m; probably acts on any going. *J. Dunlop.*

ROSE CHARTER 4 gr.c. Runnymede 123–Tavel (Tabriz 111) (1980 5d   **59**
5v³ 6f 5fg² 5d 5d 1981 5s 5s 7d 6g 12f* 10f²) strong colt; won handicap
at Hamilton in June; suited by middle distances; acts on any going; ran
moderately in blinkers once at 3 yrs; trained by R. Price first 2 outings.
W. Bentley.

ROSE DU SOIR (USA) 2 ch.f. Dewan–Pembroke Lane (Olden Times)   **91**
(1981 7f⁴ 6g² 6g²) Mar 31; $44,000Y; well-made filly; fourth foal; half-sister
to a winner by Prove It; dam 2-y-o 5f winner; runner-up in sizeable fields of
maidens at Doncaster in September (failed by short head to overhaul Mirabeau)
and Newmarket in October (favourite, went down by 2½ lengths to I'm Hot); runs
as though she will be very well suited by a return to 7f and will stay further;
should win a race. *J. Hindley.*

ROSEFOX 4 ch.f. Owen Anthony 102–Sovereign Bracelet (Manacle 123) (1980
8f 7fg 8fg 7f 7f 8f 1981 7f 10f 8f 8.3fg 8.3d) small, quite well-made filly;
poor plater; has worn blinkers. *M. Bradley.*

ROSE IGNITION 3 ch.f. Hot Spark 126–Rodi (Le Dieu d'Or 119) (1980 5d   —
1981 6g 7.6d) small filly; little worthwhile form in maiden races. *H. Wragg.*

ROSELINGO 3 b.f. Saulingo 122–Rose Marullah 109 (Valerullah 113) (1980 **59**
5s⁴ 1981 7f 5f³) neat filly; third behind fairly impressive winner Kabour in
maiden race at Nottingham in July; best form at 5f. *D. H. Jones.*

ROSE MUSIC 3 ch.f. Luthier 126–Rambling Rose 118 (Silly Season 127) **86**
(1980 6s 7g⁴ 1981 7g 7f* 7fg 7f* 7f* 7fg 8d*) leggy filly; had a good season
and won minor event at Leicester and 3 handicaps at Brighton; beat Seven
Hearts by ½ length on latter course in September when gaining her last success;
stays 1m; probably acts on any going. *R. Armstrong.*

ROSE OF DAVEEN 4 ch.f. Proverb 127–Cayton Rose (Aggressor 130) (1980 —
14f 16d 16.9d⁴ 1981 16f) tall filly; slow maiden; stays well; has been bandaged.
D. Morley.

ROSE OF IRELAND 3 b. or br.f. Bold Lad (Ire) 133–Rosalie II 66 (Molvedo **76 §**
137) (1980 NR 1981 8fg 10.2h 10.1g 10fg 9s) quite an attractive, good-
bodied filly; half-sister to 4 winners, notably good filly Cistus (by Sun Prince),
a winner at up to 1¼m, and very smart middle-distance performer Lancastrian
(by Reform); pushed along almost from start when 3 lengths sixth of 10 behind
Fabulous Salt in Masaka Stakes at Kempton in April; very disappointing
afterwards (blinkered twice) and is probably temperamental; should stay 1¼m;
sold to F. Boutin 33,000 gns Newmarket December Sales. *R. Hern.*

ROSE OF MONTREAUX 2 ch.f. Habat 127–Gliding 94 (Tudor Melody 129) **85** p
(1981 6d³) Apr 15; 15,000Y; rangy, robust filly; second foal; half-sister to
useful 7f and 8.5f winner Bay Street (by Grundy); dam, winning sprinter, is
half-sister to very smart 1973 2-y-o Splashing; easy in market but looking reasonably fit, shaped quite promisingly when 1¼ lengths third of 23 to Dalmally
in maiden race at Leicester in November, running on well over final 2f without
being knocked about unnecessarily; should improve and win a race at 3 yrs. *P.
Cole.*

ROSE OF RABY 3 b.f. Averof 123–Softly Glowing 90 (Tutankhamen) (1980 **69**
5fg 5.1f* 5g² 7g 7g² 7fg² 1981 6g 7g 6fg 6fg⁴ 7fg⁴ 6g 6fg⁴ 6s³ 6s) leggy, narrow
filly; good mover; in frame in handicaps, running on after a slow start when
close third of 20 behind Royal Diplomat at Lingfield in October; acts on any
going; blinkered sixth start; sold 2,000 gns Newmarket December Sales. *W.
Wightman.*

ROSE OF SHENFIELD 5 b.m. Upper Case–Singing Witch 71 (Sing Sing 134) **—**
(1980 8f 8fg 8d 8g 7fg 1981 6f 6s⁴) small mare; poor handicapper nowadays;
best form at 6f; acts on any going; suitable mount for a boy. *R. Boss.*

ROSE RED (USA) 2 ch.f. Northern Dancer–Cambrienne 95 (Sicambre 135) **92**
(1981 6fg* 6g²) closely related to a winner in Holland by Nijinsky, and half-
sister to high-class 1m to 1½m winner Critique (by Roberto) and 2 other winners;
dam, half-sister to top-class miler Carlemont, won over 7f at 2 yrs; impressive all-
the-way winner of minor event at Phoenix Park in August, scoring by 5 lengths
from Truculent Scholar; unruly at start when 5/2 on for 10-runner race on
same course later in month and went down by 2 lengths to Miss Behaving;
will be suited by 1m+. *V. O'Brien, Ireland.*

ROSE STANDISH 5 b. or br.m. Gulf Pearl 117–Wild Bee (Hill Gail) (1980 **—**
14f 16.1f² 18.8g⁴ 16fg 14.6fg 16s 1981 12f 16g 18g) strong mare; good mover;
poor staying handicapper; acts on firm going. *R. Cambidge.*

ROSE TRACK 9 b.g. Track Spare 125–Camp Follower 90 (Darius 129) (1980 **53**
10s 1981 8fg³ 10fg) strong, sturdy gelding; very lightly raced nowadays; stays
1¼m; seems to act on any going; has worn blinkers; suitable mount for an
inexperienced rider. *J. Toller.*

ROSETTA STONE 3 ch.f. Guillaume Tell 121–Lady Clodagh 113 (Tyrone **89**
130) (1980 7g 7g 8fg 1981 11s⁴ 14s* 12d² 13g³ 16.1d² 14.6g 16g) lengthy
filly; has a rather round action; made all and was in little danger after quickening
the pace turning for home in maiden race at Haydock in June, coming home
5 lengths clear of Irish Keep; second in minor event at Lingfield and handicap
at Newmarket afterwards; had stiffish tasks in Park Hill Stakes at Doncaster
and Jockey Club Cup at Newmarket on last 2 starts; suited by a test of stamina;
acts on soft going. *G. Pritchard-Gordon.*

ROSIE BLACK 3 gr.f. Roan Rocket 128–Maltese Cat 58 (Pall Mall 132) **—**
(1980 5f⁴ 7g 7fg⁴ 7g³ 8d* 8d⁴ 1981 11.7s 10.2d 10h² 10g) lengthy filly;
outclassed by sole opponent Flighting in minor event at Chepstow in September;
didn't run up to her best in handicaps on her other starts; should stay middle
distances; blinkered final outing; sold 25,000 gns Newmarket December Sales.
P. Cole.

ROSIER 2 br.f. Hotfoot 126–Pink Sky 86 (Midsummer Night II 117) (1981 **99**
6fg* 6g 6fg* 6f² 6g) Mar 31; lengthy, good-quartered, attractive filly; half-sister
to useful 1½m winner Night Sky (by Star Moss) and useful Town Sky (by Town
Crier), winner at up to 1m; dam won over 6f at 2 yrs; showed a useful turn of
foot when winning 16-runner maiden race at Newmarket in July by ½ length
from Paperetto and 15-runner minor event at Windsor the following month by
4 lengths from Mubhedj; went down by a neck to Pomegranate when odds
on for minor event at Ripon in September and ran well when 4½ lengths tenth of 17
to Vaigly Star in valuable nursery at Newmarket the following month; will be
suited by 1m; yet to race on a soft surface. *B. Hobbs.*

ROSINA COPPER 4 ch.f. Song 132–Jane Somers 64 (Will Somers 114§) **—**
(1980 8fg 5g 6g 5f³ 5d 6d 1981 5h 8d) leggy, lightly-made filly; best run at
5f on firm going. *J. Old.*

ROSNI 2 b. or br.f. Blakeney 126–Dash On 93 (Klairon 131) (1981 7fg) **—** p
May 8; 53,000Y; half-sister to 4 winners, including good Italian horse Le Michel
(by Le Levanstell) and smart miler Alert (by Red Alert); dam won at 1½m; 20/1,
never got in a blow when remote sixth of 16 to Top Hope in maiden race at
Yarmouth in August; bred to stay well and may do better when tackling further.
H. Cecil.

ROSOVAIR 2 ch.f. Sallust 134–Rose Amber (Amber Rama 133) (1981 5f —
6fg 5fg 6g 5fg) May 21; 2,500Y; strong filly; useless; sold 410 gns Doncaster
October Sales. *W. H. H. Williams.*

ROSSETT 2 ch.c. Jukebox 120–Flo Kelly (Florescence 120) (1981 6g) Mar 2; —
IR 6,200Y; second reported foal; half-brother to 5f and 7f winner Kellord (by
Lord Gayle); dam fairly useful Irish sprinter; unquoted and ridden by 7-lb
claimer when ninth of 19 to One Degree in maiden race at Newmarket in October.
J. Toller.

ROSTON 3 ch.c. Morston 125–Rose Mullion 82 (Tudor Melody 129) (1980 7f **58**
8.2s 1981 12.3g 14fg 16.5g) leggy, close-coupled colt; has shown a little
ability in maiden and minor races; sold 330 gns Doncaster November Sales.
M. Camacho.

ROSTRA 2 b.f. Legal Eagle 126–Oca (O'Grady) (1981 5fg) Apr 26; half-sister —
to a winning plater and a winner in Trinidad; dam moderate plater; 20/1 when
remote seventh of 18 to Laura Jenney in maiden race at Windsor in July.
M. Smyly.

ROSY COTTAGE 3 b.f. Thatch 136–Rose Noir (Floribunda 136) (1980 5fg² —
5f² 5fg* 5g² 6g²) 1981 7g 5.8g) leggy, lightly-made filly; fair performer
at 2 yrs; had stiff tasks in handicaps in 1981 and was hampered final start;
stays 6f; yet to race on a soft surface; sent to USA. *B. Hills.*

ROSY FUTURE (FR) 5 gr.m. Shiny Tenth 120–Future Chance 86 (Hopeful —
Venture 125) (1980 NR 1981 8g) well beaten, including in sellers. *G.
Fletcher.*

ROTINGO 6 b.h. Petingo 135–Sea Lichen 106 (Ballymoss 135) (1980 12s 8fg —
7fg 7f⁴ 1981 14d 8f 7.6fg 7f) poor handicapper; well beaten in seller final
start; stays 1¼m; acts on any going; sometimes wears blinkers. *Mrs D. Oughton.*

ROUAULT 3 b.c. Wollow 132–Rossellina (Tenerani 135) (1980 NR 1981 —
10s 10d 10v) tall, lightly-made colt; has a badly enlarged off-fore knee; half-
brother to several winners, including Italian Derby winner and Doncaster St
Leger third Ruysdael II (by Right Royal V); dam won Italian 1,000 Guineas
and is sister to Ribot; behind in maiden races, finishing last at Kempton in
October on final outing (bandaged, off course 4 months beforehand). *F. J.
Houghton.*

ROUGH PATH 2 ch.f. Warpath 113–Groovy 86 (Sound Track 132) (1981 —
6g 5.8h 5fg 7g) May 7; well-grown filly; half-sister to 2 minor winners and a
winning hurdler; dam 2-y-o 5f winner; apprentice ridden when in rear in maiden
races. *D. Nicholson.*

ROUGH SKETCH 3 gr.f. Runnymede 123–Doodle 87 (Doudance 99) (1980 —
NR 1981 7fg 8f) 3,100Y; lengthy filly; third foal; dam won from 9f to 11.7f;
in rear in maiden races at Lingfield in May and Thirsk (tailed-off last) in July;
trained by I. Balding first outing. *E. Incisa.*

ROUND DANCE 3 b.f. Auction Ring 123–Dance Away (Red God 128§) (1980 **73**
5f 1981 8g² 8.2s² 8.5g 7d* 8.2v) rangy filly; overcame a slow start when
winning modest maiden race at Ayr in September in good style; second at
Doncaster and Haydock earlier; sweated up and lost her action coming down
hill when running moderately at Epsom on third start and was subsequently off
course over 3 months; stays 1m; acts on soft going. *J. Winter.*

ROUND TOWER 2 b.f. High Top 131–Circlet 97 (Baldric II 131) (1981 6fg **76**
8fg 7g) Mar 6; quite attractive, lengthy filly; first foal; dam, half-sister to
1,000 Guineas and French Oaks winner Highclere, stayed 1½m; beaten less than
7 lengths on all outings, on final one finishing 4 lengths fifth of 16 when co-
favourite for maiden race won by Clymene at Leicester in October; will be
suited by middle distances. *R. Hern.*

ROUNSTAN 2 b.c. The Brianstan 128–Rounceval 79 (Ridan) (1981 5f 5fg **65**
6f 5f⁴ 5f* 5f⁴) May 17; 5,200Y; sturdy colt; first foal; dam won twice at around
1m; plater; won 16-runner event at Ripon in September by 1½ lengths from
Will George (bought in 4,000 gns); should be suited by 6f; sold 2,600 gns Newmarket Autumn Sales. *P. Haslam.*

ROUT ORDER (USA) 2 ch.c. Final Retreat 85–Plain Maggie (Greatest) **111**
(1981 6.5fg* 6g 7f³ 7.5s*) half-brother to winners in USA by Plenty Old and
Charles Elliott; dam minor stakes winner over 6f at 2 yrs; sire won over 5f and
6f at 2 yrs in England and subsequently won 3 times at up to 11f on flat and
a 15f hurdle race in Germany, racing until he was 9; put up a very useful effort
in Prix Belfonds at Maisons-Laffitte in September, winning comfortably by

729

1½ lengths from Mir Bal with subsequent good winners Trigonome and Sau-monee third and fourth; had earlier won newcomers race at Evry in July; will stay 1¼m; acts on firm going but is probably better on soft; entered in Derby. *J. Cunnington, jnr, France.*

ROWANIA 3 br.f. Workboy 123–Ruritania (Pampered King 121) (1980 5s 5fg 5fg 1981 6d⁴ 5.8g³ 7.3g² 8s⁴ 5g 5.8g) strong filly; in frame in handicaps, finishing ¾-length second to Redden after a slow start at Newbury in May; needs further than 5f but possibly doesn't quite stay 1m, at least when conditions are testing; has run well for an apprentice; off course almost 3 months before finishing last on final outing. *J. Hill.* **64**

ROWANNA LADY 2 ch.f. Goldhill 125–Brighton Jet 69 (Jolly Jet 111) (1981 6f⁴ 5f 6fg⁴ 6g 5.3fg² 5f) Apr 18; 2,000Y; fair sort; second foal; dam won sellers over 6f and 7f; prominent in modest maiden company, including when 1½ lengths second of 5 to Sweet For Days in claiming race at Brighton in August; stays 6f; blinkered third and fourth starts. *W. O'Gorman.* **64**

ROWLANDSON 5 b.h. Blakeney 126–Rotisserie 106 (Tesco Boy 121) (1980 12d 16s 14f* 16fg³ 1981 10g 12g 12fg* 12fg⁴ 12d⁴ 14fg 12fg⁴ 12g 12v) most attractive horse; good mover; fairly useful handicapper; made most and held off Hymnos by a neck at Kempton in July; stays 1¾m but apparently not 2m; very well suited by top-of-the-ground; ran poorly last 2 starts, sweating up badly on first occasion; sold only 850 gns Ascot December Sales. *D. Elsworth.* **92**

ROWLEY'S MISTRESS 2 b.f. Free State 125–Kirmidian (Bold Bidder) (1981 6s) May 31; 2,500Y; smallish, good-topped filly; half-sister to 3 winners, including useful middle-distance stayer Russian George (by Hard to Beat); dam, half-sister to French Derby third Gunter and smart Bold Pirate, won over 4.5f at 2 yrs in France; 33/1 and backward when distant last of 15 to Risk Taker in maiden race at Newbury in October. *G. Hunter.* **—**

ROYABER 5 ch.g. Sandford Lad 133–Honeymoon II (Ballymoss 136) (1980 8d 7g 8fg 7d 8d 8g³ 8g² 8g² 8.3fg 8h 8g 8d² 8g⁴ 7d 1981 8fg 7g* 7fg⁴ 7f³ 7fg³ 7g² 7fg 7fg³ 8fg⁴ 8fg³ 7g³ 7s 8s⁴ 7d) big, strong gelding; won handicap at New-market in May; stays 1m; acts on any going. *J. Benstead.* **75**

ROYAL ABERNANT 4 ch.g. Royal Palace 131–Achnanellan 85 (Abernant 142) (1980 NR 1981 8.2g 10.6s 12g 14.6f 16.5fg⁴ 16.5g⁴ 16f) poor plater; dead. *P. Rohan.* **—**

ROYAL AFFAIR 2 b.f. Royal Palace 131–Maddelena (Tudor Melody 129) (1981 6fg 7g 7d) Apr 21; small filly; third foal; dam plating-class half-sister to high-class middle-distance stayer Relay Race; soundly beaten in sizeable fields of maidens at Newmarket (2) and Catterick (didn't move well) in the summer; sold 400 gns Newmarket Autumn Sales. *W. Hastings-Bass.* **66**

ROYAL AGAMEMNON 2 gr. or ro.c. Royal Palace 131–Abergrove 103 (Abernant 142) (1981 6g 6g) Apr 5; 5,400Y; robust colt; half-brother to 2 winners, including fairly useful stayer Marzook (by Blakeney); dam best at 6f; well beaten in end-of-season maiden races at Newmarket and Doncaster (early speed). *A. Pitt.* **—**

ROYAL AGNES 2 ch.f. Royal Palace 131–Omnia 80 (Hill Clown) (1981 6fg⁴ 7.2d³ 7fg⁴ 6d) Feb 6; sturdy filly; second foal; sister to a winner in Italy; dam, who won over 12.3f, comes from same family as Royal Hive (by Royal Palace); in frame in maiden and minor events, on final occasion finishing about 3 lengths fourth of 17 to Return To Power at Warwick in August; needs much further than 6f and is bred to stay well. *G. Pritchard-Gordon.* **71**

ROYAL AND LOYAL 3 ch.g. Queen's Hussar 124–Lake of the Woods (Never Say Die 137) (1980 NR 1981 7g 8f 8fg 11.5d 14g² 16.5g* 16.1s² 16s) 5,000Y; compact gelding; half-brother to winning middle-distance plater Lake Superior (by Right Tack); dam poor half-sister to numerous winners; won modest minor event at Redcar in September in good style by 6 lengths from Padski; creditable second to Wild Rosie in apprentice handicap at Haydock the following month; suited by a test of stamina; acts on soft going; tended to hang fifth start and was subsequently blinkered. *E. Eldin.* **68**

ROYAL BAIZE 3 b.g. Supreme Sovereign 119–Green Velvet (Epaulette 125) (1980 NR 1981 8.2s⁴ 10fg* 12g³ 12g 12.3fg⁴ 13.8g* 16f 13.8fg* 12fg 12fg* 13s⁴) 18,000Y; lightly-made, quite attractive gelding; good walker; half-brother to several winners, notably very smart Italian middle-distance performer Stateff (by Pieces of Eight); dam won over 5f and 9f in France; successful in minor race at Nottingham and handicaps at Catterick (2) and Salisbury (apprentices); made nearly all and beat Coupole by 2½ lengths in last-named event in September; **79**

stays 1¾m; best form on a sound surface; showed a turn of foot each time when winning at Catterick; sold to J. Baker 15,000 gns Newmarket Autumn Sales. *J. Hindley.*

ROYAL BAT   5 gr.m. Crowned Prince 128–Die Fledermaus (Palestine 133)   **49** (1980 7d 7.2d⁴ 6s⁴ 6g 6g 6d 5s³ 1981 5s 5s³ 6s* 5d³ 5fg 6s 6d) useful-looking mare; sprint handicapper; narrowly won at Nottingham in April; stays 6f; acts on soft going; suitable mount for an apprentice; blinkered and wore a hood twice at 4 yrs; sold 675 gns Ascot November Sales. *I. Walker.*

ROYAL BEACON   4 b.g. Manacle 123–Vicomtesse 97 (Relko 136) (1980 8fg 10fg 8fg 12s 12d 1981 12g 17.1g) big, well-made gelding; has shown no form on flat since 1979; best run at 1m on a firm surface; usually blinkered; changed hands privately 8,000 gns Ascot August Sales. *J. Cann.*

ROYAL BLOOD   3 gr.c. Bay Express 132–Porsanger (Zeddaan 130) (1980   **82** d 5fg² 5fg³ 5.3d³ 5s* 5fg³ 5fg² 5g 5g 1981 5d² 5s 5fg 5fg 5.3fg 5h³ 5g) compact colt; sprint handicapper; inconsistent; blinkered final start; sold 1,650 gns Newmarket Autumn Sales. *C. Nelson.*

ROYAL BOUNTY   3 b. or br.g. English Prince 129–Royal Levi (Levmoss 133)   **—** (1980 7fg 7f 8d 10s 1981 10s 12fg 12d) strong, lengthy gelding; little worth-while form in maiden races and a handicap; sometimes blinkered. *N. Vigors.*

ROYAL BROXTED   2 ch.g. Broxted 120–Smokey Princess 83 (My Smokey 125) (1981 6s 6g) Apr 15; lengthy non-thoroughbred gelding; fifth reported foal; dam stayed 1¼m well; well beaten in maiden races at Hamilton in October and Newmarket the following month. *A. W. Jones.*

ROYAL CARNIVAL   2 b.f. Carnival Dancer 113–Royal Escapade 87 (Galivanter   **61** 131) (1981 5f 6fg* 7f 8d) May 30; lightly-made filly; third foal; dam placed at up to 10.8f; 25/1, attracted no bid after winning 13-runner seller at Newcastle in August by ½ length from My Express; not sure to stay beyond 6f. *W. A. Stephenson.*

ROYAL CHARMER   2 b.f. Wolver Hollow 126–Pale Ale (Shantung 132) (1981   **99** p 8d*) Apr 20; third foal; half-sister to 2 winners, including smart French stayer Stout Fellow (by Sir Gaylord); dam very useful middle-distance performer in France; accounted for some well-bred fillies when finishing strongly to win 16-runner newcomers event at Maisons-Laffitte in September by 1½ lengths from Marie d'Irlande; will stay 1½m; should develop into a very useful middle-distance filly. *B. Secly, France.*

ROYAL COACHMAN   7 br.h. Supreme Sovereign 119–Swinging Nun (Tudor   **—** Melody 129) (1980 18f³ 10d 14g 1981 16s 18fg 17.1g) good sort; poor staying handicapper; acts on any going; sometimes bandaged. *R. Hannon.*

ROYAL CONNECTION   5 b.g. Royalty 130–Jamuna (Canisbay 120) (1980   **—** 7fg 9fg⁴ 12g 10g 1981 7v 7d) lengthy gelding; poor handicapper nowadays; has worn bandages; sold 420 gns Ascot 2nd June Sales. *M. Bradley.*

ROYAL DIPLOMAT   4 ch.g. The Go-Between 129–Grace (Gratitude 130)   **63** (1980 7s 6f 6g 6g* 6g⁴ 6g³ 5.8g⁴ 1981 6fg 6s 6d 5.8g* 6fg 5s² 6s* 6s² 6s²(dis)) attractive gelding; sprint handicapper; won at Bath in June and Lingfield in October; stays 6f; acts on any going; suitable mount for an apprentice. *J. Holt.*

ROYAL DRAGOON   3 gr. or ro.c. Dragonara Palace 115–Royal Line 51   **—** (Henry the Seventh 125) (1980 7g 1981 12d 10s 8fg) no worthwhile form in maiden races (twice last); sold 480 gns Ascot September Sales. *M. Ryan.*

ROYAL DUTY   3 b.g. Import 127–Lunar Queen 96 (Queen's Hussar 124)   **74** (1980 6fg 5g³ 5g* 5d² 5d 6d 6g 5d² 1981 5g 6f⁴ 5f 8f⁴ 7fg² 7f* 7d 7f 7f 7g) lengthy, useful sort; good mover; made all and beat Princess Arabella easily in handicap at Redcar in August; stays 7f (finds 1m beyond him); probably acts on any going, but is well suited by firm; sometimes blinkered; ridden by apprentice P. Eddery when successful; disappointed last 3 starts and gives impression he's not entirely genuine. *E. Weymes.*

ROYAL FIRST   2 b.f. Royal Match 117–January 68 (Aggressor 130) (1981 5s   **74** 5s 5g³ 5d 7g² 6d* 7f) Jan 20; IR 500F, 1,700Y; small filly; half-sister to 1975 2-y-o 5f winner Gala Season (by Gala Performance); dam, a plater, won at up to 1m; put up best effort when favourite for 6-runner nursery at Pontefract in August, staying on strongly under pressure to win by 2 lengths from Burn Up; will be suited by 1m; possibly not at her best on firm going. *C. Spares.*

ROYAL FLING   2 ch.c. Quiet Fling 124–Observer Royal (King's Troop 118)   **—** (1981 7fg 7g) May 26; 1,550Y, resold 5,600Y; lengthy, rather unfurnished colt; first produce; dam poor maiden; soundly beaten in maiden races at Yarmouth in August (started none too well) and Leicester in September (very troublesome in preliminaries). *A. Goodwill.*

ROYAL FOUNTAIN   4 br.c. Royalty 130–Fountain 90 (Reform 132)   (1980   **113**
8f* 10fg* 10.5f³ 10.5d   1981 9g 10s² 12f 11fg³ 11.7fg*) strong, good sort; has rather a pounding action; smart performer at his best; long odds on, made all and beat Gay George easily by 5 lengths in 6-runner minor event at Windsor in August; placed earlier in Clive Graham Stakes at Goodwood in May (length second to Triomphe who rec 3 lb) and Grand Prix Prince Rose at Ostend in July (11 lengths third to Strong Gale); soundly-beaten fifth in Earl of Sefton Stakes and Princess of Wales's Stakes, both at Newmarket, on his other starts; stayed 1½m; acted on any going; game; standing at Kirkley West Thorn Stud, Newcastle. *P. Walwyn.*

ROYAL GALA   3 b.f. Royal Palace 131–Sweet Alyssum (Gala Performance)   —
(1980 5d   1981 5d 7f) neat filly; lightly raced and no sign of ability; blinkered final start. *L. Barratt.*

ROYAL GLOW   2 ch.c. Royal Match 117–Morning Glow (Grey Dawn II 132)   —
(1981 5s 7fg) May 7; IR 3,600F, 4,000Y; plain colt; half-brother to fairly useful 1979 2-y-o 6f winner Hurtwood Lad (by Realm); dam placed in USA; in rear in small race at Windsor in May and 20-runner maiden event at Salisbury in September (needed run). *M. Blanshard.*

ROYAL GRANT   2 b.f. Royalty 130–Gold Pension 76 (Compensation 127)   **59**
(1981 5s² 5g² 6f 6d) May 1; 800Y; third foal; half-sister to 6f winner Phil Bennett (by Mountain Call); dam best at 5f; runner-up to Bonne Baiser in maiden auction race at Hamilton and minor race at Edinburgh (went down by ¾ length) in April; not seen out again until September when soundly beaten in small races at Hamilton; should be suited by 6f. *W. H. H. Williams.*

ROYAL HERITAGE (FR)   3 b.g. Welsh Pageant 132–Escorial 110 (Royal   —
Palace 131)   (1980 7d 7f² 8d* 7s*   1981 8d 8f) lengthy gelding; quite a useful performer at 2 yrs; soundly beaten in 1981; possibly finds 1m too sharp and will be suited by middle distances; acts on any going; joined E. Incisa after final outing. *I. Balding.*

ROYAL HOME   2 ch.f. Royal Palace 131–Home Fire 99 (Firestreak 125)   —
(1981 7g 6g) Mar 24; useful-looking, good sort; first foal; dam fairly useful sprinter; behind in large fields of maidens at Newmarket in October, starting at 16/1 and 33/1. *J. Dunlop.*

ROYAL IDOL   7 b.g. Royal Captive 116–Lesanne (Faberge II 121)   (1980   —
10.1g 16g 14fg   1981 14fg) quite a moderate hurdler; of little account on flat; has worn bandages. *R. Atkins.*

ROYAL INSIGHT (USA)   2 ch.c. Majestic Prince–Foresight (Forli)   (1981 8z)   — p
Apr 3; $100,000Y; attractive colt; second foal; dam once-raced daughter of Marchandeuse, a stakes winner at up to 9f; 25/1 and in need of race, prominent early on but finished out of first 13 in 27-runner minor event won by Dudley Wood at Newmarket in October; will stay 1¼m; likely to do better. *M. Stoute.*

ROYAL INVITATION   2 ch.f. Be My Guest 126–Supremely Royal (Crowned   **73**
Prince 128)   (1981 5fg 5f 5f³ 6fg* 6d⁴ 6g) Apr 1; fair sort; first foal; dam, poor maiden, comes from top American family; won 12-runner nursery at Salisbury in September under bottom weight, scoring impressively by 1½ lengths from Ten-Traco; 9 lengths fourth to Hollywood Party in similar event at Nottingham later in month but would have been considerably closer had she got a run earlier; will stay 1m; ridden by 7-lb claimer last 3 starts. *L. Cumani.*

ROYAL ISABEL   5 br.m. Royalty 130–Copious (River Chanter 121)   (1980 NR   —
1981 8f 8s 5f) of little account. *K. Bridgwater.*

ROYAL KINGDOM   4 b.c. Saritamer 130–Derring May (Derring-Do 131)   **67**
(1980 6fg 5fg⁴ 5.8g* 5g 6g⁴ 6g³ 6g² 5.8g*   1981 6s 6fg 6g 6fg 5.8f 6d* 6g³ 6g 6s) small, strong colt; sprint handicapper; beat Danny Park ¾ length at Newmarket in August; stays 6f; seems suited by some give in the ground. *M. Smyly.*

ROYAL MERLIN   2 gr.c. Young Emperor 133–Magic Lady (Gala Performance)   —
(1981 5d 7d 6g) Apr 27; 4,200Y; close-coupled colt; fourth foal; dam placed over 1⅓m in Ireland; unquoted when behind in maiden and minor races late in season. *D. Hanley.*

ROYAL NECKLACE 2 b.f. Royal and Regal–Daisy Chain 103 (Darius 129) —
(1981 6g) Feb 28; 10,000Y; half-sister to several winners, including smart
6f to 1½m winner Duke of Normandy (by Roberto); dam won at 1m; unquoted
when distant ninth of 12 to Mubhedj in small race at Windsor in August. *G. Lewis.*

ROYAL ORLEANS 3 br.c. Crowned Prince 128–Hispanica 85 (Whistling —
Wind 123) (1980 7g⁴ 7d 1981 8g 12s 8fg 8f 8d) strong, lengthy colt; quite
moderate form in varied company; unlikely to be suited by 1½m; blinkered
last 2 starts. *J. Carr.*

ROYAL POWER 4 b.c. Runnymede 123–Alangia 101 (Shantung 132) (1980 —
7f 8fg 8fg 10fg 8.3d 1981 12g 9s 12d) neat colt; little worthwhile form in
varied company, including selling; trained by G. Pritchard-Gordon first start.
B. Richmond.

ROYAL QUESTION 2 ch.f. Grey Ghost 99–Royal Raintree (Royal Duet) **50**
(1981 6f* 6f 6fg 5f) Apr 25; neat non-thoroughbred filly; fifth foal; dam winning
point-to-pointer; edged left and then right in last 2f, appearing to take second's
ground, when winning 9-runner seller at Pontefract in July by a neck from
Bye-Law; in rear subsequently; will be suited by a return to 6f+. *T. Barron.*

ROYAL RASCAL 3 gr.g. Scallywag 127–Sea Queen (Ribomar 108) (1980 **54**
6fg 8d 1981 10d 12s 11.7g 13f⁴ 14.7fg³ 14g 15.5s 10d) tall, useful-looking
gelding; has a high knee action; plating-class maiden; looks very one paced;
behind in blinkers last 2 outings; trained by D. Elsworth until after third start.
C. Spares.

ROYAL REALM (USA) 3 ch.f. Blood Royal 129–Tomboy Tamele (Verbatim) **107**
(1980 7fg² 7g³ 7g* 8s³ 1981 10.6s³ 12fg³ 12f* 12f² 12f² 12f* 12g 12f* 14.6g⁴) strong,
fair sort; won handicap at Pontefract in June (by ½ length from Palatinate)
and weakly-contested minor events on same course in August and September,

Mr Catesby W. Clay's "Royal Realm"

winning last 2 with plenty in hand; ran a very fine race when short-head second to Rhein Bridge in Lancashire Oaks at Haydock (stayed on strongly after having a little difficulty going early pace) and also ran very well when 2 lengths fourth to Alma Ata in Park Hill Stakes at Doncaster in September (finished very well after appearing to be given plenty to do and having none too clear a run); wasn't disgraced when sixth to Condessa in Yorkshire Oaks at York; stays well; acts on any going but is very well suited by firm; genuine. *S. Norton.*

ROYAL RENDEVOUZ 2 b.c. Artaius 129–Ruta (Ratification 129) (1981   **94 ?**
6f* 7fg⁴) May 11; IR 77,000Y; half-brother to several winners, notably French Derby and Prix de l'Arc de Triomphe winner Sassafras (by Sheshoon) and smart French 1m to 1¼m winner Sorbi (by Stupendous); dam won at 2 yrs in Ireland; favourite when winning 12-runner maiden race at Phoenix Park in July by ¾ length from Pas de Seul, the pair clear; beaten below distance when odds on for Ardenode Stud Stakes at Leopardstown the following month, coming home 5¼ lengths fourth of 7 to Fly Start; will stay 1¼m. *T. Curtin, Ireland.*

ROYAL REVENGE 2 ch.c. Sweet Revenge 129–Charley's Aunt 80 (Will Somers   **93**
114§) (1981 5v* 5d² 5d² 5f³ 7fg 6s) May 4; IR 1,500Y (privately); rangy, good sort; excellent mover; half-brother to several winners, including 1980 2-y-o 6f winner Royal Aunt (by Martinmas); dam won from 1m to 1¼m; drew right away to win 13-runner £2,500 event at Beverley in April by 10 lengths from Benfen; giving weight to winner when second in 2 good-class races subsequently, going down by a length to Crimson Court (rec 7 lb) in Garter Stakes at Ascot and finishing well clear of 6 other previous winners when beaten a length by French Gent (rec 11 lb) in Tattersalls' Yorkshire Stakes at York; below form subsequently; should stay 7f; acts on heavy going and seems unsuited by a firm surface. *P. Rohan.*

ROYAL REX 5 b.h. Royal Prerogative 119–Ballynulta 91 (Djebel) (1080   **65**
10.2d⁴ 10s 9fg² 10g* 9g² 10g³ 10d² 10g² 10g³ 9g 10.2d⁴ 10s 1981 10d* 10.4g⁴ 10v⁴ 10f 9fg 10g 10.2g 12d) small horse; won handicap at Leicester in April; best at around 1¼m; seems to act on any going; blinkered once at 3 yrs. *J. Tierney.*

ROYAL RHAPSODY 2 b.f. Royal Palace 131–Lady Rhapsody 101 (Northern   **—**
Dancer) (1981 7fg 8g) Apr 11; small filly; first foal; dam won over 1m and 1¼m; in mid-division in maiden races at Ayr in August and Edinburgh in October; will be suited by middle distances. *J. W. Watts.*

ROYAL ROAN 2 gr. or ro.c. Roan Rocket 128–Dearest Alice (Alcide 136)   **—**
(1981 5fg 5d 7.6s 8s) Apr 19; IR 2,400Y; strong, compact colt; behind in maiden races and a seller; blinkered final outing. *M. McCourt.*

ROYAL SMILE 3 ch.c. Royal Palace 131–Pollster 101 (Majority Blue 126)   **—**
(1980 5.8fg 6d 1981 11s 12f) well beaten in maiden and minor events; trained by P. M. Taylor first start. *N. Callaghan.*

ROYAL SWAN 3 b.c. Souvran 98–May Britt 62 (Sammy Davis 129) (1980   **—**
8d 1981 12g 16f 14g 15.5s) rangy colt; little worthwhile form; probably ran best race on second start. *M. Haynes.*

ROYAL TALK 2 b. or br.f Royal Smoke 113–Diamond Talk (Counsel 118)   **—**
(1981 5f 5.8h 5g 7g) May 2; half-sister to 3 winners, including fair sprinter Pusey Street (by Native Bazaar) and 3-y-o winner Corn Street (by Decoy Boy), successful at up to 1m; dam never ran; behind in maiden races, finishing tailed off final start. *J. Bosley.*

ROYAL TROUPER 2 b.g. Comedy Star 121–Dancing Class 75 (Compensation   **80**
127) (1981 5s 6g⁴ 6g) May 27; big, rangy gelding; third foal; dam poor maiden; 3¾ lengths fourth of 13 to Knave of Trumps in minor event at Leicester in October, best effort; stays 6f. *A. Hide.*

ROYALTY MISS 2 b. or br.f. Royalty 130–Blue Delphinium 75 (Quorum   **—**
126) (1981 5fg 5f) May 6; 600F, 300Y; second foal; dam fourth twice at 2 yrs; last in 18-runner maiden race at Windsor in July and 9-runner maiden auction event at Folkestone in August. *A. Neaves.*

ROYAL VULCAN 3 ch.c. Royal Match 117–Acropolita Mia 75 (Acropolis   **83**
132) (1980 7fg 7.2d 1981 10s* 9fg³ 12d² 11d³ 12f 10d² 10g 10.5s 12s⁴) beat Green Memory by 4 lengths in maiden race at Nottingham in April; placed several times afterwards, but didn't run up to his best last 3 starts; suited by middle distances; needs some give in the ground; useful young hurdler. *N. Callaghan.*

ROYAL WRITER 2 b.g. Lochnager 132–Pronuba (Sica Boy 132) (1981 5fg   **—**
5fg 6fg 7g 5s) Feb 21; 5,000Y; lengthy gelding; half-brother to a winning plater

and 2 winners abroad; dam placed over 1¼m in Ireland; of little account. *A. Pitt.*

ROYBIRDIE 4 gr.f. Mansingh 120–Donna Julia 79 (Don II 123) (1980 6f⁴ 7f **52**
7fg 7.6f 6g 6s⁴ 6f 7g² 8s 6d 1981 8s* 8fg 7d 8g² 8.3s² 10.6s 10.1fg 8.3fg) leggy
filly; plater; won at Leicester in March (no bid); stays 1m well; acts on any
going; often blinkered; sent to Jersey and has won there. *G. Balding.*

ROYLBID 2 ch.f. Royalty 130–Rosebid 92 (Whistling Wind 123) (1981 8d) —
Mar 21; 1,100Y; tall, lengthy, lightly-made filly; fourth foal; half-sister to
quite useful 1972 2-y-o 5f winner Magical (by Aggressor); dam won first time
out at 2 yrs and raced only at 5f; 25/1 but fit, never in hunt when eighth of 11 to
Misty Halo in maiden event at Wolverhampton in October; sold 400 gns
Newmarket Autumn Sales. *A. Jarvis.*

ROYSIA 4 b.c. Tumble Wind–Beautician (Barron's Court) (1980 7fg 7fg 7g **69**
8d 10g⁴ 10g² 10g* 10.6d 10g* 10fg 1981 10d 10g³ 10f 10.2fg) small, sturdy
colt; suited by 1¼m and may stay further; best form on a sound surface; has had
his tongue tied down; sold 3,000 gns Doncaster November Sales. *G. Pritchard-
Gordon.*

RUBBINO 2 b.c. Red Alert 127–Lucasta (High Hat 131) (1981 6f 8.2d 10.2g) —
June 3; 8,000Y; half-brother to 2 winners by Martinmas, including Cambridge-
shire winner Braughing; dam never ran; behind in maiden races at Hamilton in
September and minor event at Doncaster (blinkered, prominent 6f) in November.
S. Norton.

RUBINA PARK 3 b.f. Ashmore 125–Keep Going 113 (Hard Sauce 131) (1980 **64**
7d 1981 10s⁴ 10s³ 10fg 10g⁴ 12fg* 13.1g) rangy filly; in frame in 3 maiden
races before beating Ginosa by a length in one at Wolverhampton in August;
had stiff task final start; suited by 1½m; probably acts on any going. *M. Ryan.*

RUBLINK 2 ch.c. Swing Easy 126–Femme Fatale 67 (King's Leap 111) (1981 **80**
5fg 5g²) May 21; 5,200Y; second living foal; dam, placed over 5f at 2 yrs,
is half-sister to Middle Park Stakes winner Spanish Express; went down by
only ½ length to odds-on Ma Tante in 12-runner minor event at Lingfield in
June; will probably stay 6f. *C. Nelson.*

RUBY AND SAPPHIRE 2 b.c. Manado 130–Festal 72 (Alcide 136) (1981 **77**
7f 8s⁴) Feb 10; IR 16,500Y; unfurnished colt; first living produce; dam 1¼m
winner; having first race for 3 months when 6½ lengths fourth of 29 to Arrowood
Dream in minor event at Redcar in October; will be suited by 1¼m. *E. Eldin.*

RUBYLINE 2 b.f. Silly Season 127–Jewel Tower 91 (Double-U-Jay 120) (1981 —
5d 5s 5d 6d) Mar 23; 1,300Y; leggy, unfurnished filly; half-sister to 1980 2-y-o
6f winner Sospirae (by Sandford Lad) and a winning plater; dam won over 6f
at 2 yrs; no worthwhile form, including in a seller. *W. Stubbs.*

RUBY RAY 3 ch.f. Laser Light 118–Witty (Will Somers 114§) (1980 5d 5.8h —
6fg 5d 6s 1981 8m 6g 6g 5g 8f) sturdy filly; behind in varied company, including
selling; sweated up third outing in 1980; sold 440 gns Ascot 2nd June Sales.
W. Wightman.

RUBY RED DRESS 4 b.f. Sparkler 130–Red Cape 84 (Matador 131) (1980 **54**
8s 10fg 12.3d 10.6d 10s³ 10g 10.2v 1981 12s³ 12g* 13g² 12g² 11fg⁴ 13fg² 12.3s
11fg 12d² 12g²) big, well-made filly; made all to win slowly-run handicap at
Thirsk in April; runner-up 5 times afterwards; may stay 1¾m; best form with
some give in the ground; suitable mount for an apprentice. *M. Camacho.*

RUDIN 2 ch.c. Red God 128§–Ashton Jane 86 (Gratitude 130) (1981 5g) —
June 4; 6,400Y; strong colt; brother to 3 winners, including Irish 3-y-o 9f winner
Redford and high-class Red Alert, successful at up to 7f; dam 2-y-o 5f winner;
20/1 when 9½ lengths sixth of 8 to Kind Music in minor race at Kempton in May;
looked the type to improve but wasn't seen out again. *I. Balding.*

RUDRA 3 b.g. Busted 134–Land of Song 82 (Sing Sing 134) (1980 NR 1981 **59**
14f²) 66,000Y; strong, lengthy gelding; brother to 1¼m winners Bustilly and
Downbeat and half-brother to 2 winners by High Top; dam, half-sister to out-
and-out stayer Celtic Cone, won over 5f; co-favourite when short-head second
of 15 finishers behind Bay of Mist in maiden race at Yarmouth in June, just
getting worse of a dour struggle; not seen out again; stays well. *J. Hindley.*

RUDRY GRANGE 3 br.c. Stype Grange 92–Pearl Bailey (Sing Sing 134) **53**
(1980 5g 5d 8d 1981 8d 8d 10.1d 5v⁴ 7f⁴ 8f⁴ 8fg) small colt; poor walker;
bought in 1,700 gns after winning selling handicap at Leicester in June narrowly;
stays 1m; acts on any going, but is probably well suited by a sound surface.
D. H. Jones.

RUDRY PARK 2 gr.f. Blue Cashmere 129–Lenana (Never Say Die 137) (1981 **55**
5s 5s 6f 6f⁴ 6d 6fg 8g) May 9; lengthy filly; fifth foal; half-sister to a winning
plater by Hill Clown; dam unraced daughter of Coronation Stakes winner
Aiming High; plater; probably stays 1m. *D. H. Jones.*

RUEFUL LADY 2 b.f. Streetfighter 120–Chinese Princess (Sunny Way 120) —
(1981 5s 5s) closely inbred; half-sister to 1978 2-y-o 1m seller winner Magic Kit
(by Namnan); dam unraced half-sister to very smart Streetfighter; in rear in
maiden races at Warwick and Wolverhampton (distant last of 11) in October.
D. Marks.

RUFFO (USA) 2 b.c. Riva Ridge–Brave Lady (Herbager 136) (1981 7fg³ 8d) **84**
Apr 22; $55,000Y; lengthy colt; has a capped hock; none too good a walker
or mover; half-brother to 3 winners, including good American chaser Popular
Hero (by Nijinsky); dam, stakes-placed winner over 5f at 2 yrs, is half-sister to
high-class Intrepid Hero and smart Predictable; ran well when staying on
strongly to finish 2¼ lengths third of 24 to Busaco in maiden race at Newbury
in August and wasn't disgraced from a poor draw when favourite for £4,200
event on same course the following month (showed up for 6f and was eased once
chance had gone); should stay middle distances. *R. Price.*

RUFFORD LINE 2 b.c. High Line 125–Thorganby Bella (Porto Bello 118) **61**
(1981 7fg 7g⁴ 7fg 6fg 6fg 7fg 8d 10.2g) Mar 30; lightly-made colt; half-brother
to 1980 2-y-o 5f winner Bella Travaille (by Workboy); poor maiden; ran well in
valuable seller on fifth start; stays 7f; blinkered fifth and sixth starts. *R.
Hobson.*

RUGBY EXCAVATION 3 b.f. Lord Nelson 107–Misty Belle (Foggy Bell 108) —
(1980 8fg 1981 10s) plain filly; seems useless. *J. Czerpak.*

RUMMELD 2 br.f. Meldrum 112–Ivory Coast 90 (Poaching 115) (1981 5fg⁴) **64 p**
June 4; compact, fair sort; sister to sprint winner Melba Toast; dam fairly
useful at 2 yrs; 20/1 and looking as though run would do her good, shaped well
when running on to finish 3¼ lengths fourth of 15 to Chere Jane in maiden race
at Catterick in July; not seen out again; will stay 6f. *M. W. Easterby.*

RUMPOLE 2 b.g. Mandamus 120–Thunder Bay 64 (Canisbay 120) (1981 6fg **—**
7fg) Feb 24; big, good-topped individual; third foal; dam stayed 1½m; behind
in 14-runner minor event at Windsor in July and 18-runner £2,600 race at
Salisbury in August. *M. Blanshard.*

RUM PUNCH 5 gr.g. Warpath 113–Brandy (Busted 134) (1980 10.2g 12.2f **—**
12g 12.2g³ 12f³ 12d² 1981 10g) workmanlike gelding; poor handicapper;
will be suited by 1¾m+; has worn bandages. *C. Thornton.*

RUNAROUND SUE 2 b.f. Porto Bello 118–Fair Camilla 81 (Tiger 125) (1981 **66**
6f 5.3f² 6fg* 6g) Mar 23; workmanlike filly; second foal; dam won over 1m and
1¼m; cost 4,600 gns to buy in after holding on under strong pressure to win
valuable seller at Goodwood in July by a head from Remodel; moved badly to
post when well beaten in similar race at Newmarket in October; stays 6f well.
P. Cole.

RUN DEEP 5 b.g. Deep Run 119–Tilly 64 (Le Levanstell 122) (1980 NR **43**
1981 12g 12s² 17.1d 14.6f 16g⁴ 18.8fg) smallish gelding; second in seller at
Wolverhampton in May; stays well; acts on soft going; retained 3,100 gns
Ascot October Sales. *D. Gandolfo.*

RUN FOR HER LIFE 3 b.f. Runnymede 123–Gallows Gal 107 (High Treason **57**
126) (1980 5g 5g³ 6d 1981 5fg 5d 6g 8d 7fg 10f* 10fg²) neat filly; won seller
at Folkestone in September; suited by 1¼m; acts on firm going. *J. Winter.*

RUN HARD 6 b.g. Run The Gantlet–Isola D'Asti 106 (Court Harwell 130) **79**
(1980 18f 1981 18.4d⁴ 16.9s² 16s³ 16fg) modest handicapper on flat but is
better known as a jumper nowadays; stays well; acts on any going; has been
bandaged in front. *R. Turnell.*

RUN LIKE MAD 2 b.f. Silly Season 127–Powderhall 81 (Murrayfield 119) **90**
(1981 5g² 5fg² 5f* 5fg³ 5.3d² 6g) May 18; small filly; second foal; half-sister to
3-y-o 7f seller winner Bila Shaka (by No Mercy); dam won 4 races at up to 10.6f;
made all when winning 14-runner minor event at Wolverhampton in August
easing up by 6 lengths from My Lover; placed in minor events at Salisbury
(2 lengths third of 7 to Fairy Tern) and Brighton (well-backed favourite, beaten
a short head by Bolivar Baby) the following month; form only at 5f; probably
acts on any going. *W. Hastings-Bass.*

736

RUNNELA 3 gr.f. Runnymede 123–River Palace (Royal Palace 131) (1980 5f —
6fg 7g 1981 8fg 10.6v 8s 10v) light-framed, narrow filly; little worthwhile
form; trained by J. O'Donoghue first start; sold 480 gns Doncaster November
Sales. *C. Williams.*

RUNNETT 4 b.c. Mummy's Pet 125–Rennet 109 (King's Bench 132) (1980 **125**
6fg* 6fg2 5fg2 6d 5g 5fg3 5fg* 6s* 1981 6g2 5g 6fg* 5f3 6fg* 6fg* 5d)
    Scarcely a year goes by without at least one foreign pattern race falling to an
English sprinter aged three or more, and in 1981 the haul was a large one—Marwell, Moorestyle and Sharpo won in France, Rabdan in France (twice) and
Germany and Runnett in Ireland. None of these successes was more deserved
than Runnett's in the Matt Gallagher Sprint at Phoenix Park in July since it
provided him with a first pattern-race win in three seasons of consistent endeavour
that had seen his knocking on the door in several of the best races.
    The Matt Gallagher is Ireland's most valuable sprint and nearly all the
leading home sprinters took part, notably the Greenlands Stakes winner Drama,
Cooleen Jack, who had been awarded the Ballyogan Stakes, Gods Mark, Jasmine
Star and the disqualified Ballyogan winner Prince Echo. Runnett, with a
length win over Integrity in an £8,000 race at Lingfield and places in the
Ladbrokes Abernant Stakes at Newmarket (three parts of a length second to
Rabdan) and the King's Stand Stakes at Royal Ascot (three and a half lengths
third to Marwell) behind him, started favourite. He justified the support in style,
quickening impressively at the furlong pole and rapidly putting daylight between
himself and his nearest rivals, eventually winning without being asked a serious
question by two and a half lengths and two lengths from Lady Blackfoot and
Jasmine Star.
    With one good race to his name Runnett lost little time in adding another,
the Vernons Sprint Cup at Haydock in September. The reputation this race has
for producing surprise results is not really based in fact since the majority of its
runnings have been won by market leaders and only one winner, Absalom in 1978,
has started at more than 10/1. Even so, no-one could say Runnett's defeat of
the odds-on Marwell was anticipated. Over sprint distances Marwell had lost
just once, in the William Hill Sprint Championship, and her brilliant wins in the
King's Stand Stakes and William Hill July Cup suggested she would have little
difficulty coping with Runnett, Crews Hill, Sayyaf, Prince Echo and Sanu at
Haydock. Few of the season's best races changed so dramatically in the closing
stages as the Vernons Cup. Sayyaf made the running from Marwell and a
furlong out he still held a decisive advantage; Runnett, who had been held up in
last place, was moving through between Prince Echo and Crews Hill to launch a
challenge. As Sayyaf began to run out of steam, the strongly-ridden Marwell
made up the leeway and led less than a hundred yards from home. She looked

*Vernons Sprint Cup, Haydock—Runnett (left) comes with a storming run to catch
Marwell close home*

set to land the odds, but Runnett and his jockey Raymond had other ideas. Coming with a tremendous rattle on the outside Runnett went past Sayyaf as though the latter was standing still and then passed Marwell in the shadow of the post to score by a neck. Sayyaf was two and a half lengths further away. We don't think Marwell ran to top form but this was still a high-class effort by Runnett, the best of his career.

The Vernons Cup confirmed that in first-rate company six furlongs was Runnett's ideal distance but he was returned to the minimum trip for his final race, the Prix de l'Abbaye de Longchamp. Whatever chance he had wasn't increased by his starting slowly after rearing as the stalls opened; though scrubbed along into fourth at the distance he never looked like troubling the principals and finished fifth to Marwell.

Runnett (br.c. 1977)	Mummy's Pet (b 1968)	Sing Sing (b 1957)	Tudor Minstrel Agin the Law
		Money for Nothing (br 1962)	Grey Sovereign Sweet Nothings
	Rennet (b 1963)	King's Bench (b 1949)	Court Martial King's Cross
		Emulsion (b 1949)	Nepenthe Olein

Rennet, Runnett's dam, whose name appeared incorrectly as Rennett in Volume 38 of the *General Stud Book* and in several previous editions of this annual, has become a regular partner of Mummy's Pet at stud. By him she has foaled three other winners, namely Placid Pet, successful over a mile, the very useful 1977 two-year-old five-furlong performer Cala-Vadella and the 1981 two-year-old five-furlong winner Russeting. Her yearling colt, also by Mummy's Pet, fetched 23,000 guineas at the Newmarket Premier Sales. Rennet has produced three winners by other stallions, notably the speedy Tribal Feast (by Tribal Chief). On the track she won seven times from five furlongs to a mile and a quarter and was one of five winners out of the useful sprinter Emulsion whose dam Olein won the Coronation Stakes, Nassau Stakes and Sussex Stakes.

In 1982 Runnett will stand alongside Orchestra at the Cleaboy Stud in Ireland at a fee of IR £3,000 (October 1st no foal no fee). A big, lengthy colt and a good mover, Runnett was suited by six furlongs and waiting tactics. He acted on any going and wore blinkers once in 1980. *J. Dunlop.*

RUNNING BACK (FR) 3 b.c. Great Nephew 126–Robinie (Fortino II 120) **109** d (1980 6d² 6d⁴ 8v³ 7.5g* 8.5v³ 1981 7.5d 10s* 12d 12.5d 10fg 9.5d 6g) neat ex-French colt; good sort; dam, who has been in Germany, is unraced half-sister to Blushing Groom and Bayraan; made all and beat Akkad by 2 lengths in 70,000 francs event at Longchamp in May; probably ran best subsequent race when sixth of 9 behind Vayrann in Prix Jean de Chaudenay at Saint-Cloud in June on next start; last of 15 behind Great Eastern in £5,000 6f event at Doncaster in November on only outing over here; probably stays 1½m; acts on soft going; trained most of season by J. Cunnington, jnr. *R. Armstrong.*

RUNNING BOLD 2 b. or br.c. Runnymede 123–Miss Lovely (Mansingh 120) — (1981 5fg 5f 6g) Apr 14; no worthwhile form, including in a seller; sold 460 gns Ascot October Sales. *A. Ingham.*

RUNNING ROCKET 4 gr.c. Runnymede 123–Rosy Morn (Roan Rocket 128) **77** (1980 6v² 7f 7h⁴ 6f 8.2d* 8g³ 10s* 9g³ 8.2d 8.2g 10s³ 8d 1981 8.2d 8d 10.2g² 8g 10g 9fg 9fg³ 11d³ 10g 11d² 12d 10fg⁴ 11g³ 8.2d³ 9s 8.2d) light-framed colt; fair handicapper at his best but is inconsistent and unreliable; suited by 1¼m or more; appears to act on any going; sold 5,800 gns Newmarket Autumn Sales. *T. Craig.*

RUNNY HONEY 2 b.f. Runnymede 123–Irma Flintstone 110 (Compensation **56** 127) (1981 5d⁴ 5s 7f 6d) Apr 9; 5,400Y; third foal; sister to a poor plater; dam 5f performer; only plating class; unlikely to stay 7f; blinkered fourth outing; sold 400 gns Doncaster October Sales, probably for export to Scandinavia. *G. Hunter.*

RUN RABBIT RUN 4 b.g. Caliban 123–Flapperette 92 (Hardicanute 130) — (1980 10s 8s 11fg 6d 1981 8s) small, light-framed gelding; poor plater; should stay at least 1¼m; acts on a soft surface; sold 725 gns Ascot May Sales. *D. McCain.*

RUN RECORD RUN 3 ch.f. Record Run 127–Firecrest 58 (Firestreak 125) — (1980 6f 7fg 7g² 7g 7d 1981 8f 8g 10s) lengthy filly; well beaten in 1981

*Stockholm Cup, Taby, Sweden—Russian George wins from ex-English Lindoro (No. 2)
and another British challenger Spin of a Coin*

(needed race on reappearance in September and was bandaged in front final
start); should stay 1m; blinkered final outing of 1980. *V. Mitchell.*

RUSCELLI (FR) 4 b.c. Val de l'Orne 130–Coy Maid (Habitat 134) (1980 **120**
8g 8g³(dis) 8fg* 9fg² 10s 12f³ 12f 1981 7g⁴ 8g² 8g* 10.5g⁴ 9.7s⁴ 8g 10f 10f² 10s⁴ 10v⁴)
neat colt; very smart performer at his best but has won only 2 of his 18 starts;
ran creditably when in frame in Prix Ganay (4½ lengths fourth to Argument),
Prix Dollar (about 2 lengths fourth to P'tite Tete) and Prix du Prince d'Orange
(1¼ lengths fourth to Vayrann), all at Longchamp, and Prix Ridgway at Deauville
(1½ lengths second to Detroit); stays 1½m; acts on any going. *F. Palmer, France.*

RUSHMENOTTE 6 b.m. Tycoon II–Post-Op (Even Money 121) (1980 NR —
1981 12g) first foal; dam won over hurdles and fences; tailed off in maiden race
at Haydock in April, first outing on flat. *M. Tate.*

RUSHMOOR 3 br.g. Queen's Hussar 124–Heathfield 99 (Hethersett 134) **96**
(1980 6fg 6g² 6d³ 1981 7g⁴ 8g² 8g² 8fg* 10.5s² 10.2g*) strong, useful-looking
gelding; first past post in handicap at Salisbury in July (subsequently relegated
to second), maiden race on same course in August and handicap at Doncaster
in October; beat Regal Touch 1½ lengths in last-named; second on 2 other
occasions, putting little heart into finish once; stays 1¼m; probably acts on any
going; blinkered last 2 outings; sold to G. Richards 22,000 gns Newmarket
Autumn Sales. *R. Hern.*

RUSSELL UP 2 b.g. Reliance II 137–My Dearest Sarah 79 (Anwar 120) (1981 —
8d) Apr 3; 3,000F; half-brother to several minor winners; dam sprint plater;
33/1 when tailed-off last in end-of-season maiden race at Leicester. *G. Balding.*

RUSSETING 2 b.f. Mummy's Pet 125–Rennet 109 (King's Bench 132) (1981 **76** p
6fg 5g*) Mar 3; 28,000Y; strong filly; sister to 3 winners, including high-class
sprinter Runnett and very useful 1977 2-y-o 5f performer Cala-Vadella, and
half-sister to 3 winners; dam stayed 1¼m; stayed on well when making 11-runner
maiden race at Beverley in July by 3 lengths from Witch's Point, giving impression she'll eventually be better suited by 6f than 5f. *W. Hastings-Bass.*

RUSSIAN GEORGE (FR) 5 ch.h. Hard to Beat 132–Kirmidian (Bold Bidder) **106**
(1980 13d* 12f* 11f² 12fg* 12fg* 16d² 15g² 12.5d 16f⁴ 12v³ 1981 18s³ 16fg*
16d³ 14d 16.1s² 12f* 12fg⁴ 16d² 11.1f³ 12g*) lengthy horse; useful handicapper; beat Dawn Johnny a length in Queen's Prize at Kempton in April,
Lafontaine by 2 lengths in Bessborough Stakes at Royal Ascot and Lindoro by
1½ lengths in valuable Stockholm Cup at Taby, Sweden, in September; subsequently sent to USA and ran respectably in 11f Knickerbocker Handicap at

Aqueduct in November; stays 2m; acts on any going but goes well on fast ground; has won for an amateur rider; genuine. *G. Hunter.*

RUSSIAN ROMANCE 3 ch.g. Red Alert 127–Wild Romance 96 (Pirate King **72** d
129) (1980 5f³ 5fg 5fg 6g² 6s⁴ 6fg 1981 6s³ 6g³ 5fg 6g 6g 6f² 6fg² 7f 7.6s² 7fg
7g² 7s⁴) well-made, good-looking gelding; in frame in varied company; stays
7.6f; blinkered third start in 1980; sold 5,200 gns Newmarket Autumn Sales.
C. Brittain.

RUSSIAN SALAD 2 ch.g. Malinowski 123–Bordelaise 96 (Above Suspicion **65**
127) (1981 6g 7.2fg 8g 8g) May 9; 6,200Y; good-topped gelding; half-brother
to 2 winners, including 6f and 1m winner Love Supreme (by Sallust); dam won
over 5f at 2 yrs and is sister to Irish 1,000 Guineas second and Irish Guinness
Oaks third Loyalty; quite a moderate maiden; only eighth of 18 to Indian Call
in £2,500 seller at Newmarket in October on final start; will be well suited by
1¼m. *Sir Mark Prescott.*

RUSSIAN WINTER 6 b.h. King Emperor–Am Stretchin (Ambiorix 130) **72**
(1980 6d 6d* 7f 6f⁴ 5fg* 5fg* 6f² 6d* 6d* 5s³ 5g* 6fg² 5d² 6g 5d* 6s 5d 1981
6s 5d* 5fg* 5g² 5f 6f 5fg 5d 5fg 5f 5fg 5fg⁴ 5g 6d) lengthy horse; sprint handicapper; successful at Haydock and Redcar in May; beat Miss Redmarshall 2
lengths in Northern Sprint Handicap on latter; probably unsuited by soft going;
usually wears blinkers; excellent mount for an inexperienced rider; possibly best
on a galloping track; genuine. *A. W. Jones.*

RUST FREE 2 gr.f. Free State 125–Iridium 78 (Linacre 133) (1981 6g 5g 5s 6g) —
Mar 25; 3,000Y; workmanlike filly; half-sister to 3 winners, including 5f and 7f
winner Miss Cindy (by Mansingh); dam stayed 1¼m; plating-class maiden;
eighth of 22 in maiden event won by Ash Ridge at Newmarket in October, fourth
outing; will be suited by 1m. *G. Beeson.*

RUSTICARA 2 b.f. Tachypous 128–Ranikhet (Tanerko 134) (1981 5fg 6fg 8fg) —
Apr 24; 7,200F; workmanlike filly; half-sister to French 1½m and 1¾m winner
Nanital (by Exbury); dam placed over 1¼m in France; bandaged when in rear
in maiden races and a seller. *M. W. Easterby.*

RUSTIC CHARM 3 br.g. Palm Track 122–Polly-Ann Tanja (Cletus) (1980 **59**
6g 1981 8s 8g 7fg 7g* 8fg* 10fg⁴ 9g 8s 7g) smallish, workmanlike gelding;
attracted no bid after winning sellers at Ayr in June and July; stays 1m; acts on
a firm surface; blinkered nowadays; fell seventh start. *J. Carr.*

RUSTLE OF SPRING 2 ch.f. Leander 119–Geraghty Girl 54 (Frankincense —
120) (1981 5s 6d) first foal; dam poor plater; probably no better than her dam.
G. Price.

RUSWARP 3 b.g. Gold Form 108–Lady Cortina 80 (Cortachy 107) (1980 **79**
5f* 5fg³ 5fg 6fg 1981 7d 5d 5f⁴ 5f² 5f⁴ 5f² 6g 5f 5fg 5f) quite a moderate
handicapper; probably ran best races when second twice at Beverley in summer;
form only at 5f on firm ground. *D. Garraton.*

RUTH POP 2 b.f. Wishing Star 117–Gardinella (Tanavar 118) (1981 5f 7f 7f) —
May 1; IR 500F, 950 2-y-o; small, compact filly; poor mover; of no account;
blinkered third start. *J. Doyle.*

RYECROFT 3 b.c. Condorcet–Moonlight Story (Narrator 127) (1980 7g 7fg —
1981 12s⁴ 12g 16s) useful-looking colt; little sign of ability in varied company;
sold out of R. Armstrong's stable 1,200 gns Doncaster January Sales and resold
2,600 gns Ascot July Sales. *D. Dale.*

RYTHMIQUE (USA) 2 ch.f. The Minstrel 135–Georgica (Raise A Native) **98**
(1981 8s* 8v) Feb 13; $435,000Y; second foal; dam, half-sister to Kentucky
Derby winner Cannonade, won 3 sprint races; won 4-runner Prix de la Cascade
(fairly valuable newcomers event) at Longchamp in September by 1½ lengths
from Springtown; swerved at start when 3/1 for Group 3 Prix des Reservoirs
on same course the following month and came home only eighth of 9 behind
20/1 stable-companion Coussika; will stay 1¼m+; blinkered on debut; engaged
in 1,000 Guineas and Oaks. *F. Boutin, France.*

S

SABA NEJD 3 b.c. Malacate 131–Padova (Forli) (1980 6g³ 6g* 8fg 1981 **83**
10fg 12g³ 12d 12g 12d* 12g⁴ 13d) neat, strong, attractive colt; good walker
and mover; ran best races on second and fifth outings, in latter getting up in
last strides to beat Eastern Air a head in handicap at Lingfield in August
(apprentice ridden); stays 1½m; acts on a soft surface; sweated up and ran

poorly in blinkers third start; sold to T. Marshall 6,800 gns Newmarket Autumn Sales. *P. Walwyn.*

SABEK 3 ch.c. Virginia Boy 106–Diamonds For Ever (Ionian 128) (1980 — 5.1g 5g 7d 1981 10fg 8fg) strong, compact colt; little worthwhile form in maiden and minor races. *F. Durr.*

SABRE DANCE 2 b.c. Dance In Time–Sarissa 105 (Reform 132) (1981 7d) — May 25; first foal; dam won over 5f and 6f at 2 yrs; 20/1, dwelt and was always behind in 11-runner minor event won by stable-companion Don Giovanni at Leicester in November. *H. Cecil.*

SABUTAI (USA) 2 b.c. Mr Leader–Osprey (Beau Gar) (1981 8d⁴ 7.6s* 97 7.3s) Jan 26; $30,000F, $97,000Y; tall, quite attractive, close-coupled colt; half-brother to 2 winners in USA; dam, winner of 6f claiming race, is half-sister to high-class Atoll; had field well strung out when winning 15-runner maiden race at Lingfield in October by 3 lengths from Risk Taker; no danger in final ¼m when about 14 lengths fifth of 8 to Montekin in Horris Hill Stakes at Newbury later in month; may stay 1¼m; yet to race on a sound surface. *I. Balding.*

SACERDOTOPHRENIA 2 b.f. Welsh Saint 126–Poquito (Major Portion — 129) (1981 6fg) Apr 1; 9,000Y; half-sister to very useful 6f and 1¼m winner Senorita Poquito (by Connaught) and to a winner in Corsica; dam won from 5f to 1½m in Ireland; unquoted when behind in 18-runner maiden race won by Circus Ring at Newmarket in July; sold 2,600 gns Newmarket December Sales. *C. Brittain.*

SACHA'S SONG 3 ch.g. Crooner 119–Bouleversee (Napoleon Bonaparte 63 114) (1980 7fg 7fg 6fg 8d 7fg 1981 12g 11.7g⁴ 11.7s*) big gelding; not seen out after beating Wally Wombat a length in handicap at Windsor in May; suited by 1½m; acts on soft going. *R. Hannon.*

SACRILEGE 5 b.h. St Paddy 133–Rebuke (Princely Gift 137) (1980 10v* 86 9g* 8f 10g* 10.5g⁴ 10fg 10f² 9f 10g 1981 12s 16g*(w.o.) 10.4g* 10s) attractive horse; fair handicapper; beat China Royal by a head in driving finish at Chester in May; had earlier made pace for stable-companion Light Cavalry in John Porter Stakes at Newbury and walked over at Newmarket; stays 1¼m well; acts on any going but seems suited by some give in the ground; genuine; broke a bone in a leg in June. *H. Cecil.*

SADDLE ROCK ROAD (USA) 3 b.g. Elocutionist–Lay In (Turn-to) (1980 59 NR 1981 8g 8g² 8g² 8g 7fg* 8.3fg 10fg 8f³ 8d⁴ 7fg) lengthy, lightly-made, unimpressive-looking gelding; plater; stayed on well under strong pressure when beating Polly's Brother ½ length in 19-runner seller at Newmarket in June (subsequently sold for 3,600 gns); stays 1m; probably acts on any going; wears blinkers; ran poorly fourth and last starts; sold to D. Jermy 1,600 gns Ascot September Sales. *J. Hindley.*

SADDLERS CREEK 2 b.c. Connaught 130–Coral Beach 118 (Relko 136) 86 (1981 5d³ 6g* 6fg² 7fg³ 7f 8fg 8g⁴) Mar 18; neat, strong colt; fifth foal; half-brother to useful staying hurdler Shell Burst (by Busted); dam smart middle-distance filly; won 17-runner minor event at Carlisle in June by 1½ lengths from Bright View; ran best subsequent races in 1m nurseries in September, wearing blinkers when 2½ lengths fourth of 8 to Meeka Gold at Ayr; needs a test of stamina; seemed unsuited by Catterick track on fourth outing; sold to BBA 6,000 gns Doncaster November Sales. *J. W. Watts.*

SADEDAB 8 br.h. Badedas 81–June Clare (Fairwell) (1980 10.2d 13s 12fg 32 12fg 12f 16g 17.1fg 13g 17.1d 18s 1981 12s 10.6s 10f³) plater; stays 2m; acts on any going; sometimes wears blinkers; suitable mount for an apprentice. *J. Edmunds.*

SAENREDAM 2 b.c. Malacate 131–Exmoor Lass 86 (Exbury 138) (1981 81 7f 7fg⁴ 7fg² 7d² 7fg³ 8.2fg² 8d) Feb 25; IR 16,500Y; neat, well-made colt; good walker and mover; third foal; half-brother to a winner in South Africa; dam 2-y-o 7f winner; second in maiden races and a nursery, in latter going down by 2½ lengths to Sir John Falstaff at Nottingham in September (found little after looking dangerous); will be suited by middle distances; below form final start. *J. Dunlop.*

SAFE HOUSE 2 b.f. Lyphard 132–Manor (Round Table) (1981 6g 6g) 79 Mar 27; small, lengthy, deep-girthed filly; good mover; half-sister to a winner by Bold Reasoning; dam unraced daughter of high-class 1954 2-y-o Our Betters; fifth in sizeable fields of maidens at Newmarket in October, beaten 7½ lengths by I'm Hot and 4¼ lengths behind Not For Show; will be seen to better advantage over longer distances. *H. Wragg.*

SAFFAR 2 ch.c. Sassafras 135–Night Vision 100 (Yellow God 129) (1981 — 5d 8d) Apr 15; 6,200Y; second foal; half-brother to 3-y-o Lautrec (by Wolver Hollow), a winner at up to 1m; dam, half-sister to high-class Take a Reef, won over 6f at 2 yrs; behind in maiden races at Salisbury in May and Bath in October (showed speed to halfway). *R. Smyth.*

SAGAMORE 2 b.c. Sagaro 133–Veruschka (Turn-to) (1981 5d 6g³ 6fg 8g* **86** 7s⁴ 10g) Feb 28; quite attractive colt; closely related to French 1½m winner Marlena (by Sheshoon), also successful in Switzerland; dam French 2-y-o 6f winner; won 15-runner maiden race at Beverley in September by 2 lengths from Forward when having first race for 3 months; not disgraced under a 7-lb penalty at York the following month, staying on to finish 5½ lengths fourth of 13 to French Gent after having to be switched; should be suited by 1¼m (always behind when tried over trip). *F. Durr.*

SAGA'S HUMOUR 2 ch.f. Bustino 136–Summer Day 117 (Golden Cloud) **61** (1981 5fg³ 6f* 6fg⁴ 6f³ 5d⁴) May 1; small filly; half-sister to several winners, including useful 7f performer Heave To (by Pirate King); dam won six 5f races at 2 yrs; sold out of Sir Mark Prescott's stable after running on strongly to win 5-runner seller at Stockton in June by 2 lengths from Lucky Season; apprentice ridden when in frame in nurseries afterwards (one a selling nursery); will be suited by a return to 6f+; probably acts on any going. *Denys Smith.*

SAGE KING 3 b.c. Shantung 132–Lady Gaylord (Double Jump 131) (1980 **86** 8d² 8.2s* 8.2s² 1981 10.6d 10.6s 12.3fg* 13fg* 14g 13d) lengthy, quite attractive colt; looked really well when returning to form in handicap at Newcastle in June, winning in great style by 4 lengths from Way of the Wold; comfortably landed the odds by 2½ lengths from Salora Lady in similar race at Ayr the following month; suited by 1½m+; seems to act on any going; ran poorly fifth start, *J. W. Watts.*

SAGITTARIO 2 br.c. Windjammer (USA)–Light House (Primera 131) (1981 — 5d 5v 5.8h 7fg 7fg) Mar 24; 4,800Y; neat colt; brother to Irish 5f winner Sea Maiden and a winning hurdler; dam half-sister to top German horse Luciano; no sign of ability in maiden and minor events. *M. Blanshard.*

SAGITTA ROCKET 4 b.f. Roan Rocket 128–Salonica II (Ocarina 131) — (1980 10g⁴ 12h³ 12.2fg³ 12g 1981 14g 15.5d) well-made, deep-girthed filly; one-paced maiden; stays 1½m; best form on fast ground. *J. Winter.*

SAHER 5 b.h. Great Nephew 126–Another Chance 75 (Romulus 129) (1980 **115** 8d⁴ 10s 7fg 7.6f* 7.2fg 7g* 8d⁴ 8g³ 8g* 8d* 8f 7g⁴ 8g² 8d³ 1981 8d* 8s² 7d 10s³ 8.5d* 8fg)

With the exception of the war years, the field of nineteen that contested the William Hill Lincoln Handicap at Doncaster was the second-smallest since 1919, King's Ride having defeated only seventeen rivals in 1980. This recent reduction in the size of Lincoln fields was an inevitable consequence of a tightening up of the conditions of entry. Now the conditions are being relaxed again. The 1981 Lincoln, which attracted forty-seven entries, was open only to four-year-olds and upwards officially rated at least forty; the qualifying standard was dropped to thirty for the 1982 running, for which there are fifty-nine entries.

The latest Lincoln winner was the best since Frankincense in 1968. Saher improved about a stone from four to five and was a shrewd acquisition by his owner, who bought Saher privately during the winter from another patron of the stable. It is interesting to note that Teamwork, whom Saher's owner

William Hill Lincoln Handicap, Doncaster—Saher just holds off Herons Hollow (rails) with Hurricane Hill (sheepskin noseband) third and Bonol (centre) fourth

Mr J. C. Smith's "Saher"

bought out of Harwood's stable at the back-end of 1981, is among the entries for 1982. Saher's victory in the Lincoln, in which he beat Herons Hollow by half a length after bursting clear about two furlongs out, gave some indication of his improvement but it was in his next race, the Playboy Bookmakers' Newbury Spring Cup, that he really showed his merit. There, on considerably worse terms, he left Herons Hollow five lengths behind and failed by only half a length to cope with another improved horse, Belmont Bay. Following a disappointing fifth to Columnist when favourite for the Autobar Victoria Cup at Ascot and a rather better third to Triomphe in the Clive Graham Stakes at Goodwood, Saher gained a deserved pattern-race success in the Diomed Stakes at Epsom on Derby Day. He didn't have to cope with a particularly strong field there; nevertheless Saher, with his apprentice jockey unable to claim his allowance, put up a smart performance, leading over a furlong from home and holding Shasavaan by a length. This was Saher's trainer's first success at Epsom, a course on which he never won as a jockey. On his final appearance, in the Queen Anne Stakes at Royal Ascot, Saher didn't run up to his best on the firm surface but would have been pushed to trouble Belmont Bay and Last Fandango anyway.

Saher (b.h. 1976)	Great Nephew (b 1963)	Honeyway (br 1941)	Fairway Honey Buzzard
		Sybil's Niece (ch 1951)	Admiral's Walk Sybil's Sister
	Another Chance (b 1967)	Romulus (b 1959)	Ribot Arietta
		Recount (gr 1961)	Narrator Moonstone

Saher has been retired to the Ongar Stud at Clonsilla in Co. Dublin at a fee of 1,750 Irish guineas with the special live foal concession. He is yet another pattern-race winner sired by Great Nephew. Saher's dam Another Chance didn't win but has produced three winners, including Saher's sister School Road, a winner at six and seven furlongs. Another Chance comes from a good family. Her second dam Moonstone produced eleven winners, among them Saher's grandam Recount, the dams of Greengage (Coronation Stakes) and Even Star (Irish One Thousand Guineas), and Twilight Hour, the grandam of Nocturnal Spree (One Thousand Guineas) and Tootens (Prix Saint-Alary). Saher, a strong, attractive horse, stayed a mile and a quarter and acted on any going, but was particularly well suited by some give in the ground in the later stages of his career. Genuine and consistent, he was best when held up, possessing a good turn of foot. He was blinkered once at three years. Saher invariably looked well in 1981. *R. Sheather.*

SAHIBSON 5 br.h. Sahib 114–Consula 88 (Privy Councillor 125) (1980 NR 1981 10.2s 8fg) useful sort; quite moderate in 1979; no form at 5 yrs; seems to stay 1m; apparently acts on any going but is particularly well suited by soft; has been blinkered. *J. Calvert.* —

SAILORD 5 b.g. Gold Rod 129–Sailanna 97 (Sailing Light 119) (1980 9.6fg 9fg 7g 7g² 8fg* 7fg* 8.3fg 8.3f 8fg 8fg³ 8d 8d 1981 8.2g³ 8g 8.2fg 8s 7fg 9fg* 8fg³ 8.2g 8fg 8s) plater; bought in 950 gns after winning at Wolverhampton (apprentices) in July; stays 9f; acts on a firm surface; often wears blinkers; often sweats up; suitable mount for an apprentice; usually bandaged. *J. Berry.* 42

SAILOR'S HAZE (USA) 3 b.f. Pat McGroder–Grand Ma Julia (Prince Taj 123) (1980 8g 1981 9.4g) little sign of ability in maiden races. *G. Richards.* —

SAILOR'S PRAYER 3 gr.c. Martinmas 128–Coral Mermaid (Silver Shark 129) (1980 5s² 5fg* 5f 5f³ 5f 1981 6s 8.2g 7fg 6f 6f 5fg* 6s* 6d 5s⁴ 5s⁴) leggy colt; poor walker; successful in apprentice handicaps at Beverley in September (gambled on) and Newcastle in October (beat Twixt' Tween in good style); didn't have best of runs in either of his last 2 races; stays 6f; acts on any going. *R. Thompson.* 76

SAILORS REVENGE 3 ch.g. Sweet Revenge 129–Admiral's Bird 61 (Sea Hawk II 131) (1980 7d 7g 8g 1981 10s 12fg 12g 15.5d) tall gelding; has shown a little ability in varied company; blinkered final start. *G. Beeson.* —

SAINERA (USA) 3 b.f. Stop the Music–Summer Hill (Sir Gaylord) (1980 6g³ 7fg* 8g 1981 7s 6g 6s³ 6fg 7fg 10g) leggy, lightly-made filly; often had stiff tasks in 1981, best effort when 3 lengths third of 5 behind Kathred in handicap at Haydock in June; promises to stay 1m; blinkered third and fourth outings; sometimes unimpressive in paddock. *L. Cumani.* 86

SAINT CRESPIN BAY 2 ch.c. Bay Express 132–Crisp Piece 90 (Saint Crespin III 132) (1981 5s 5g³ 5g 5fg 5g 5.3d 5g*) Mar 20; 2,500Y; workmanlike colt; half-brother to 2 winners, including 1971 Irish 2-y-o 1m winner Rusty River (by Forlorn River); dam placed over 6f and 7f; made all to win maiden race at Catterick late in season by 1½ lengths from Kenson Venture; clearly thought to be a 5f performer. *S. Matthews.* 75

SAINT DUBASSOFF 2 b.c. Dubassoff–Saint Shari 81 (Saint Crespin III 132) (1981 7fg 7fg 7g 8s) Feb 2; 850F; in rear in maiden and minor events; blinkered fourth outing. *J. Spearing.* —

SAINTINGO 4 b.f. Saulingo 122–Saint Veronica (Saint Crespin III 132) (1980 8f⁴ 8fg 7g 8g² 8.3f 12s 1981 8f 8h 6g) plater; stays 1m; has worn blinkers. *S. Kernick.* —

SAINT JONATHON 4 b.c. Welsh Saint 126–Climbing Rose 81 (Pirate King 129) (1980 8v* 8f* 8fg 10.5f⁴ 12f 12g³ 12d 8g³ 1981 8d⁴ 10s² 12s 10d 8s) strong, attractive colt; good mover; smart performer at 3 yrs; didn't run up to his best in 1981 though wasn't disgraced when 2¼ lengths second to Gilded Vanity at Cagnes-sur-Mer in February; ran poorly fourth start and was off course 4 months afterwards; needs further than 1m and stays 1½m; acts on any going. *B. Hills.* —

SAINTLY BLESSING 2 ch.f. Manado 130–Sainthill (St Alphage 119) (1981 5s) Mar 15; 25,000Y; first foal; dam twice-raced sister to Sandford Lad; eased from 7/4 to 4/1 at Windsor in May and faded from below distance to finish remote sixth of 17 in maiden race won by Silojoka, only outing; sold 10,000 gns Goffs November Sales. *H. Cecil.* —

SAINT MIA 3 ch.f. Arch Sculptor 123–Blue Bleep (Bleep-Bleep 134) (1980 5s³ 5f 5fg³ 5fg⁴ 5f 1981 5s 5v 5h³ 5fg) well-made filly; poor maiden; well beaten in seller second outing; runs as though she'll stay 6f; blinkered fourth and fifth outings in 1980. *J. Hill.*

SAINT MOTUNDE 8 ch.m. Tyrant–Saint Veronica (Saint Crespin III 132) **69** (1980 8fg 8g 7g* 6g 6fg³(dis) 7fg 6g 7g 7f⁴ 6f² 8fg⁴ 1981 8v 8g⁴ 6d 8.4g³ 8g 7f⁴ 8f² 10f 8f³ 8f* 7g* 7fg* 7f* 8.2fg³ 7fg 7.2v) quite a modest handicapper; in excellent form in August, winning at Pontefract, Newcastle, Folkestone and Beverley; best at up to 1m; appears to act on any going but is suited by top-of-the-ground; sometimes blinkered in 1979. *B. McMahon.*

SAINT ROSE 3 b.f. Welsh Saint 126–Bawn Rose (Menelek 114) (1980 5f 5fg — 6s 7fg 7g 1981 8s 8s 9.4fg 12.2g 13fg 10fg) lightly-made filly; poor plater; trained until after second outing by P. Rohan. *I. Jordon.*

SAINTS 'N' SCHOLARS 2 br.c. Welsh Saint 126–Lovely Linan (Ballylinan **84** 118) (1981 6s 7fg 7g 8g 7g² 6s) Mar 20; IR 11,000Y; workmanlike colt; half-brother to several winners, including fairly useful 3-y-o middle-distance winner Spin of a Coin (by Boreen) and fairly useful 1m and 1¼m winner Sweet Accord (by Balidar); dam never ran; ¾-length second of 15 to newcomer Chronicle in minor event at Naas in June; ran in good-class races on 3 of his previous starts, on third outing finishing 10 lengths fifth of 8 to Height of Fashion in Acomb Stakes at York in August; stays 7f. *J. Bolger, Ireland.*

SAIRIYA 2 b.f. Huntercombe 133–Sayraf (Ragusa 137) (1981 5f³ 5fg⁴) Mar **71** 3; second living foal; half-sister to 1¼m winner Sashka (by Levmoss); dam won over 1m at 2 yrs in France; in frame in maiden races at Folkestone (2½ lengths third of 10 to Ghawar) and Wolverhampton (4½ lengths fourth of 9 to Petworth Park) in August; will be well suited by 6f; sold 2,200 gns Newmarket Autumn Sales. *M. Stoute.*

SAJAMA (USA) 3 b.f. Mississipian 131–Poundcake (Hail to Reason) (1980 **108** NR 1981 10g² 12.5f* 12g 12s² 10f³ 12f⁴ 10f 9f) $70,000Y; tall, rather leggy filly; first foal; dam lightly-raced French middle-distance winner; beat Friluck 2½ lengths in maiden event at Deauville in August; close second to Golden Moony in similar race on same course earlier, and to Samata in Prix Joubert at Evry in October; didn't particularly impress in paddock and was never going well when last of 10 finishers behind Condessa in Yorkshire Oaks at York on third outing; sent to race in North America after fourth start and ran creditably there, including when third to De La Rose in E. P. Taylor Stakes at Woodbine and fourth to Euphrosyne in Long Island Handicap at Aqueduct, both in October; stays 1½m well; acts on any going. *M. Zilber, France.*

SALAMINA 3 ch.f. Welsh Pageant 132–Femme Elite (Young Emperor 133) **93** (1980 5fg 5f* 6g* 6fg 1981 8s² 8f 8fg 8g* 8s) leggy filly; kept on strongly, although having no chance with winner, when 7 lengths second to Nasseem in UBM Merchants International Fillies Stakes at Kempton in May; ran best subsequent race when beating Susanna (USA) by ¾ length in £3,200 event at Doncaster in September, getting up close home after being held up; had stiff tasks in between; will probably stay beyond 1m; acts on any going; sweated up third and fourth outings. *G. Pritchard-Gordon.*

SALDATORE 4 ch.g. Sallust 134–Chaduaille (St Chad 120) (1980 10d 8fg 8fg — 7.6f³ 8fg⁴ 8g 1981 10.2s 13fg) tall, useful-looking gelding; plating class; stays 1m; acts on firm going; has sweated up; often blinkered in 1980. *D. Morley.*

SALDORO 2 ch.c. Cavo Doro 124–Salonica II (Ocarina 131) (1981 6g 7g 8g) — neat, good-bodied colt; half-brother to 1972 French 2-y-o 8.5f winner Straight Away (by Emerson) and 2 winners on the Continent; dam won over 5f at 2 yrs in France; unquoted when in rear in maiden races. *J. Winter.*

SALFORD RENTAL 3 br.c. Connaught 130–Luciennes 108 (Grey Sovereign — 128§) (1980 NR 1981 11.7g 16fg⁴ 8f) 18,000Y; good sort; half-brother to 3 winners, notably very smart sprinter Broxted (by Busted); dam won her first 2 races at 2 yrs; beaten quite some way in maiden races at Bath (needed race), York (fourth to Isanemos) and Pontefract, all in June; broke out of stalls and was withdrawn on intended debut. *R. Hollinshead.*

SALFORD SUPREME 4 ch.c. On Your Mark 125–Lady Midge 120 (Nearco) **32** (1980 8d 6fg 6h⁴ 6fg 6s 8d 6g 1981 10.1d³ 8.3g⁴ 7f 8d 10f⁴ 10f 11.7fg) small colt; plater; stayed 1¼m; seemed to act on any going; usually apprentice ridden; dead. *D. Nicholson.*

SALLAMETTI (USA) 3 b.f. Giacometti 130–Gay Sally (Sir Gaylord) (1980 6s — 7fg 8d⁴ 8.2v⁴ 1981 12d⁴ 12.5f 13.8f 12f 16s 12d) lengthy, lightly-made filly; poor maiden; blinkered when running moderately in a seller third start (claimed out of J. Hindley's stable £1,800); probably stays 2m. *M. Naughton.*

745

Bogside Cup (Handicap), Ayr—Salora Lady gets up close home to beat Rodeo

SALLWAH 2 b.f. Balidar 133–Welsh Jewel 72 (Welsh Pageant 132) (1981 5g **63**
5g² 5f³ 5f 5g⁴ 6s 5s²) Mar 16; IR 1,000Y; sparely-made filly; first foal; dam in
frame in 5f maiden events at 2 yrs; only a plater, but ran very well in a nursery
fifth outing; should stay 6f. *C. Booth.*

SALLY JON JEAN 3 ch.f. Lord Gayle 124–Mecara 90 (Gulf Pearl 117) (1980 **60**
6fg³ 1981 7fg 7d 10.2h³ 10d³ 10f) plating-class maiden; stays 1¼m; sold
6,200 gns Goffs November Sales. *C. Nelson.*

SALLY ROSE 3 b.f. Sallust 134–Desert Flower 93 (Ballymoss 136) (1980 6f³ **92**
1981 8g* 10fg* 10.6d² 10.2fg* 10d) neat filly; good walker; successful in minor
event at Salisbury in June and handicaps at Newbury in July (won by a neck
from Fee) and Doncaster in September (beat Rekal by 1½ lengths); no match
for Fee in handicap at Haydock on third outing, finishing 6 lengths second;
would probably have stayed beyond 1¼m; was evidently better on a firm surface
than a soft one; game and genuine; retired to stud. *R. Hern.*

SALLY'S SILVER 5 gr.m. No Mercy 126–Pin Worker (Pindari 124) (1980 5fg **44**
6h 6fg 6g 6g 5.8f 5f 6g⁴ 6g³ 1981 5s⁴ 6s⁴ 6s⁴ 6d 5.8g 6f 5.3f³ 6f 5fg) light-
framed mare; poor sprint handicapper; acts on any going. *J. Benstead.*

SALLY'S SYMPHONY 2 b.f. Song 132–My Sweet Afton 73 (Javelot 124) **44**
(1981 5s³ 5d³ 5s³ 6fg 5f 8.2fg) May 14; 1,000Y; small filly; bad plater; slowly
away fourth and fifth outings. *E. Weymes.*

SALORA LADY 3 b.f. Sassafras 135–Rocaserena 104 (Jimmy Reppin 131) **109**
(1980 7g 8d 10.2s 1981 12.2s* 10s 12g² 12d³ 13fg² 14.6g² 13d* 12s³ 14s) neat
filly; won poor maiden race at Catterick in April; vastly improved later on and
ran well in 2 good fillies' races, finishing ¾-length second to Alma Ata when
50/1-chance in Park Hill Stakes at Doncaster in September and 5½ lengths third
to easy winner Flighting in Princess Royal Stakes at Ascot in October, staying
on well both times; very leniently treated in Bogside Cup (Handicap) at Ayr in
between and got up close home to beat Rodeo by ½ length; suited by a test of
stamina (likely to show further improvement when tackling 2m or more);
probably acts on any going, but is well suited by soft. *E. Weymes.*

SALSA ROSA 2 br.f. African Sky 124–Rosemarin (Mossborough 126) (1981 **84**
5fg³ 6d³ 6g*) Apr 6; 22,000Y; half-sister to several winners, including useful 6f
and 7f performer Oldstock (by Sovereign Path) and useful 3-y-o Irish miler

Pendulina (by Prince Tenderfoot); dam, useful Irish handicapper, won from 9.4f to 1½m; favourite when winning 13-runner maiden race at Navan in September by a length from Toast of the Town; will be suited by 7f and 1m. *P. Prendergast, Ireland.*

SALT 3 ch.f. Sallust 134–Albercaro 88 (Hard Tack 111§) (1980 5g2 5d* 5fg2 6fg* 5d2 5fg 1981 5s 5fg 6f 6f 5s) light-framed filly; ran respectably in handicaps in 1981; gives impression 6f suits her better than 5f; acts on a firm and a soft surface; sold 12,000 gns Newmarket December Sales. *H. T. Jones.* **71**

SALTHOUSE 4 b.g. Blakeney 126–Grisle Run 94 (Stupendous) (1980 10fg 10.8s4 10.1d 10d2 9d 1981 12s 13s2 14g 12g2 12s 14g2 13fg3 14f 12fg 12d) attractive, neat, strong gelding; moved down to second after beating Al Kuwait on merit by 1½ lengths in handicap at Nottingham in April; stays 1¾m; needs some give in the ground; apprentice ridden at Nottingham. *N. Callaghan.* **61**

SALUBRE 4 ch.g. Sallust 134–Orange Grove 81 (Aggressor 130) (1980 10.1g3 10.2g* 10.1s* 12g3 10.5g 1981 10fg3 10.4g3 10s 10d 8g 10.4s2 10d) sturdy gelding; fairly useful handicapper; creditable third at Kempton in April (7½ lengths behind Galveston in Rosebery Stakes) and Chester in May; stays 1½m; probably acts on any going; blinkered and pulled hard once in 1980; has run respectably for a lady rider. *F. J. Houghton.* **96**

SALUD (GER) 3 br.c. Lombard 126–Shantou (Charlottown 127) (1980 8g 1981 10fg* 12g 12d3 12g3 14fg2 14d2 14fg3 12fg4) good-topped, quite attractive colt who did well physically; showed signs of inexperience when winning minor event at Nottingham in April by 2 lengths from Haresceugh; placed in handicaps afterwards, appearing unlucky at Yarmouth in July on sixth start when length second to Alma Ata (looked to be holding eventual winner when he shied at a piece of paper and lost his action inside distance); stays 1¾m; yet to race on extremes of going; coltish in paddock when running moderately second outing; sold to BBA (Italia) 16,500 gns Newmarket Autumn Sales. *M. Stoute.* **86**

SALUE (GER) 3 br.f. Lord Udo–Santayana 96 (Tamerlane 128) (1980 7g 7v* 1981 10g4 12.2fg) big, strong ex-German filly; dam, winner 3 times at up to 7f in Ireland, is daughter of top-class German filly Santa Cruz III and from family of Star Appeal; won maiden race at Dortmund as a 2-y-o; best behind Home On The Range in 4-runner minor event at Newbury and 7-runner Warwick Oaks, both in June; should stay middle distances; shows a lot of knee action in her slower paces and is always likely to need plenty of give in the ground. *B. Swift.* **—**

SALUTIUS 2 ch.c. Sallust 134–La Grisette (Fortino II 120) (1981 5f 5g3 6fg 6fg3 6d 5s4) Feb 11; small, stocky colt; half-brother to fairly useful 1979 2-y-o 6f winner Viva L'Armour (by Gay Fandango) and a winner in Malaya; dam won at up to 1¾m in Ireland; in frame 3 times, including in a nursery; will stay 1m; sometimes sweats up badly; blinkered final outing (ran respectably). *M. Jarvis.* **72**

SAMASHA 3 gr.f. Sharp Edge 123–Yofi (Articulate 121) (1980 5fg 5s 6fg 1981 8fg 10.1d 10d 8fg) little worthwhile form, including in sellers; dead. *S. Harris.* **—**

SAM-BAM 2 b.f. Shiny Tenth 120–Flight Feathers (Ribocco 129) (1981 5d* 5f4 6g 5h4 6g 6g) May 24; 440Y; neat filly; dam poor half-sister to champion American mare Old Hat; ridden by 7-lb claimer to win 8-runner maiden auction event at Brighton in May; fourth in nurseries at Folkestone and Chepstow subsequently but was beaten in selling company last 2 starts; stays 6f; sold 2,000 gns Newmarket Autumn Sales. *R. Smyth.* **71**

SAMBA SCHOOL 3 ch.f. Roi Soleil 125–Legal Fiddle 81 (Canisbay 120) (1980 NR 1981 10d 10fg 11.7h) lengthy, lightly-made filly; second reported foal; dam won at 1½m; in rear in maiden and minor races. *R. Laing.* **—**

SAM CARMEDY 4 b.g. My Swallow 134–Watch Em Go (Hidden Treasure) (1980 9d2 8fg 8d 9.4g 8.2g3 7g 10f 11d 1981 12g 8f 9.4fg 8g4) robust gelding; plating-class maiden; seemed to stay 9f; acted on a soft surface; ran a bit freely in blinkers once; dead. *Denys Smith.* **—**

SAME DATE 3 b.f. Mandamus 120–Catherine Rose 59 (Floribunda 136) (1980 6g 6fg 6fg 7g2 8fg2 6d 7d 6d 1981 9s 8s 8g* 7fg3 12f 10.1fg 12fg 12d) workmanlike filly; ran best race for some time when beating Olderfleet by 1½ lengths in 18-runner maiden race at Thirsk in May; should stay 1¼m; evidently **66**

needs a sound surface; a very difficult ride who seems to go well for apprentice J. Rowe (has often carried overweight when ridden by him); pulled up, believed to be lame, on seventh start; not one to rely on. *S. Mellor.*

SAMI 3 b. or br.c. So Blessed 130–Slipperty 99 (Hardicanute 130) (1980 5f³ 1981 5g⁴ 5f³ 5f* 5fg* 5fg 5fg³ 5fg² 6fg* 6f*) good sort; gaining his fourth win within a month when beating Mrs Leadbetter by ½ length under 10-lb penalty in handicap at Ripon in August; successful earlier in maiden event at Nottingham, apprentice race at Edinburgh and handicap at Redcar; suited by 6f; acts on firm going; tough and genuine; trained by P. M. Taylor first outing; sent to race in USA. *G. Huffer.* **78**

SAM JOHN 2 b.c. Malinowski 123–Star of Sierra (Quisling 117) (1981 6g) Feb 16; third foal; half-brother to 3-y-o Sierra Wind (by Windjammer) and Irish 7f winner Sierra Boy (by African Sky); dam Irish stayer; 8/1, made late progress without looking dangerous when about 11 lengths fifth of 19 to Zinzara in newcomers race at Goodwood in September; will stay 1¼m; may do better. *R. Price.* **— p**

SAMMY BEAR 3 gr.f. Rupert Bear 105–Samba 69 (Sammy Davis 129) (1980 5fg 5d 6fg 1981 5g² 5g 5g* 5d* 5f* 5g* 6g³ 5d 5g) compact filly; much improved and was gaining her fourth successive win when making all and beating El-Pez-Espada in tremendous style by 7 lengths in handicap at Hamilton in June; had earlier won maiden race at Thirsk, handicap at Pontefract and minor race at Stockton; off course nearly 4 months and facing stiffish tasks when well beaten in handicaps last 2 starts; had been placed in apprentice seller at Carlisle on reappearance; speedy and seems best at 5f; probably acts on any going; sweated up eighth outing. *W. Bentley.* **69**

SAMMY WATERS 2 b.c. Rapid River 127–Sambell 71 (Sammy Davis 129) (1981 5f* 5d 5f 5f*) May 11; 800Y; compact colt; third live foal; dam won 1m seller; won 10-runner maiden auction event at Pontefract in June and came with a strong late run to win by ¾ length from Typecast in valuable seller at York in September (bought in 4,200 gns); will stay 6f; acts on firm going. *C. Booth.* **69**

SANAD 2 ch.g. Sandford Lad 133–Asail (Atan) (1981 7fg) Mar 18; 9,200F; workmanlike gelding; half-brother to 5f winner Land of Point (by Pontifex); dam sister to prolific 1971 2-y-o winner Sea Music; behind in 19-runner maiden event won by Wibis Range at Redcar in September; sold 920 gns Newmarket Autumn Sales. *W. O'Gorman.* **—**

SAN BENITO 4 ch.g. Spitsbergen 103–Pollytooky (Polic 126) (1980 8fg 16g 8g 1981 11.7f) plain gelding; poor plater; has worn blinkers. *W. R. Williams.* **—**

SANCHES 2 b.f. Sandford Lad 133–Cobble (Major Portion 129) (1981 5d 5fg 6fg² 7g 7fg* 7fg⁴ 8f 8d² 8g 7d) May 8; IR 3,600Y; lightly-made filly; half-sister to a winner in Italy; dam Irish 7.5f winner; outsider of party when finishing strongly to win 4-runner nursery at Yarmouth in August by a head from Major Irish; creditable second of 5 to Bancario in another nursery at Yarmouth the following month; stays 1m; has won on a firm surface but put up best effort on a soft one; sold 6,600 gns Newmarket December Sales. *R. Williams.* **72**

SANCTA 2 b.f. So Blessed 130–Soft Angels 124 (Crepello 136) (1981 6g³ 7g³) May 25; well-made, quite attractive filly; fourth living foal; half-sister to very useful 5f and 7f winner Dulcet (by Tudor Melody) and to Doubly Sure (by Reliance II), dam of Kris; dam best 2-y-o filly of 1965 but disappointed afterwards; third in maiden races in October at Newmarket (9 lengths behind Merlin's Charm) and Leicester (stuck on very well when beaten ¾ length by Positron); will be suited by 1m. *P. Walwyn.* **79**

SANDAAN 2 b.c. Zeddaan 130–St Louisan 109 (St Chad 120) (1981 6s⁴ 5s) Apr 17; tall, slightly narrow colt; fourth foal; half-brother to French 11f winner Vale of Tears (by Val de l'Orne) and a winner in Morocco; dam useful winner over 5f at 2 yrs; shaped very well when 5½ lengths fourth of 11 to Slightly Dangerous in Duke of Edinburgh Stakes at Ascot in October; odds on for moderate all-aged maiden race at Nottingham later in month, but gave trouble at start and was never going well, finishing eighth of 17 behind Colonial Line; stays 6f. *G. Harwood.* **90 ?**

SANDALAY 3 ch.c. Sandford Lad 133–No Delay 72 (Never Say Die 137) (1980 5f 6d 7g² 7d 8fg 10s 1981 10g³ 12g 12d 11g⁴ 12.3fg 12d* 12fg 14s³) big, rangy **68**

colt; beat Sorochinsky Fair by 5 lengths in maiden race at Hamilton in July; stays 1¾m (staying on strongly over trip on final start); best form with some give in the ground; usually makes the running. *P. Rohan.*

SANDHAVEN   4 ch.g. Sandford Lad 133–Phobos 65 (Relko 136)   (1980 7d   — 7fg 6g 6g 6fg 6d³ 6s   1981 6s)   smallish gelding; sprint handicapper; stays 6f; acts on a firm and a soft surface; usually blinkered nowadays. *D. Grissell.*

SANDHURST PRINCE   2 ch.c. Pampapaul 121–Blue Shark (Silver Shark 129)   **123 p** (1981 6fg* 6fg*)
'A top horse—I've nothing but good to say about him' is how Guy Harwood summed up Sandhurst Prince for us towards the end of the season. Harwood has trained such high-class animals as Ela-Mana-Mou, Young Generation, To-Agori-Mou and Recitation in the last few seasons so he, more than most, should know what he's talking about, and his opinion is reflected in the betting for the Two Thousand Guineas. Sandhurst Prince didn't even race in a pattern event at two yet early in December the Tote had him favourite at 7/1 for the Guineas ahead of the seven-length Dewhurst winner Wind and Wuthering and the unlucky Futurity loser Paradis Terrestre at 12/1, the Laurent Perrier Champagne Stakes winner Achieved at 14/1 and the impressive Horris Hill winner Montekin at 16/1, with the Futurity and Middle Park winners, Count Pahlen and Cajun, at 25/1 and 33/1 respectively. 7/1 doesn't look particularly good value at this stage—all six colts on the same or higher marks in the International Classification are fellow Guineas entrants—but there's no denying Sandhurst Prince's tremendous promise.

Sandhurst Prince won the Chertsey Lock Stakes in August and the Sirenia Stakes in September, both at Kempton, in the style of a top-class colt. Although the Chertsey Lock Stakes was instituted only in 1974, already horses of the quality of Roland Gardens, More Light, Two of Diamonds, Cracaval, Saint Jonathon and Rasa Penang have made their debut in it. For some reason its distance was shortened from seven to six furlongs in 1981 and the race conditions remained unchanged and the 1981 field was the usual mixture of unraced and lightly-raced colts, with the only winner among the thirteen runners the Yarmouth winner Silver Hawk. The betting suggested that Sandhurst Prince and Silver Hawk had the race between them, with the more-experienced colt narrowly starting favourite, and so it turned out. Sandhurst Prince was soon up disputing the lead against the far rails, clearly going exceptionally well for Raymond who took the mount in place of the injured Starkey. Given a little rein at halfway Sandhurst Prince lengthened his stride and began to pull away. With a quarter of a mile to run Silver Hawk moved into second place and gave chase for the next furlong but Sandhurst Prince, receiving 6 lb, was always going much the better; in the closing stages Sandhurst Prince left Silver Hawk behind and won very comfortably by four lengths. The third horse, Northleigh, was another five lengths back.

This was a tremendous first effort, one which suggested strongly that Sandhurst Prince would make his mark in top company, yet his trainer said afterwards that he had no ambitious plans for the colt in the immediate future. Possibly he wished to bring Sandhurst Prince along steadily, but his options were limited anyway. Sandhurst Prince had been so backward early in the summer that when the autumn pattern events closed on July 1st he wasn't among the stable's fifteen entries for the Champagne Stakes, its eleven for the Mill Reef, twenty-two for the Royal Lodge, seventeen for the Middle Park or twenty-nine for the Dewhurst. The present entry system is much more sensible than it used to be—the closing date for the Mill Reef, Middle Park and Dewhurst was advanced to July from February in 1978—but it's obviously still far from perfect. A later closing date, with a much higher entrance fee to mitigate the fall in stake money, would arguably be a fairer system all round; the late-developers like Sandhurst Prince would at least have a chance of running.

With no race of major importance for him Sandhurst Prince came out in the Sirenia Stakes at Kempton just a fortnight later. Since being switched to September, in 1979, the Sirenia Stakes has drawn remarkably good fields for a race that doesn't even rank as a listed race, the next best thing to a pattern event; Pace Jean, Hard Fought and Braughing took the first three places in 1979 and in 1980 Cut Throat accounted for Pushy, Nasseem and Sweet Monday. In 1981 the field of six consisted of the unbeaten Custer, who numbered a victory over Codrington in the Washington Singer Stakes among his five wins; Foam Bath, the winner of both his starts including a £3,300 race at Salisbury by five lengths; Admiral's Princess, winner of the Erroll Stakes at Ascot; Johara, successful in Ascot's Virginia Water Stakes; Childown Blue, a fairly useful

Sirenia Stakes, Kempton—Sandhurst Prince quickens in the style of a very good colt and wins easily

winner of three races; plus Sandhurst Prince who shared favouritism with Foam Bath at 7/4. Sandhurst Prince was just as impressive against this class of opposition as he'd been on his debut. This time he disputed the lead from the start, went clear below the distance and had so much in hand that Starkey was able to ease him up in the final fifty yards. At the line he had three lengths and the same to spare over Foam Bath and the subsequent Cheveley Park third Admiral's Princess, both of whom received 3 lb.

Although Sandhurst Prince was among the stable's thirty-seven entries in the Horris Hill and its thirty in the Futurity, these races were all of seven

Mr J. C. Thompson's "Sandhurst Prince" (G. Starkey)

weeks away and a more immediate engagement was found for him in the Prix de la Salamandre at Longchamp. The Salamandre is, like the Futurity, a Group 1 event but it has a much more realistic closing date, just eighteen days before the race. Unfortunately Sandhurst Prince missed a clash with Green Forest in the Salamandre, having in his trainer's words 'shown a certain amount of muscle tissue breakdown' and in mid-October it was announced that he wouldn't race again at two. We've therefore had to assess him on his performances in just two races, neither of which saw him fully extended, and it's anyone's guess as to exactly how good he is. Unlike his trainer we aren't yet in a position to say he's a top horse, but we can certainly say he gives every indication that he will be one day.

		Pampapaul (b 1974)	Yellow God (ch 1967)	Red God
Sandhurst Prince (ch.c. Mar 16, 1979)				Sally Deans
			Pampalina (br 1964)	Bairam II
				Padus
		Blue Shark (b 1970)	Silver Shark (gr 1963)	Buisson Ardent
				Palsaka
			Well Armed (ch 1961)	Persian Gulf
				Armentieres

Guy Harwood and his associate James Delahooke are proving amongst the shrewdest judges of a yearling around today. Sandhurst Prince, whom they picked up for 16,000 guineas in Ireland, is typical of the type they go for: he's a big, rangy, good-actioned colt of similar build to his sire Pampapaul. Pampapaul's racing career proved very much an anticlimax after his defeat of The Minstrel and Nebbiolo in the Irish Two Thousand Guineas but he made a bright start as a stallion in 1981, siring eight winners from nineteen runners in Britain and Ireland as well as the very useful French colt Pampabird. Sadly Pampapaul died in August, 1979, after only two seasons at stud, and to make matters worse the Irish also lost that other high-class son of Yellow God, Nebbiolo, in 1980.

The owners of Sandhurst Prince's dam Blue Shark are great supporters of the Red God sire line. In her five years at stud before foaling Sandhurst Prince Blue Shark produced a colt by Green God which died, was barren to Yellow God's brother St Alphage, foaled a colt, Saint Geran, by Red Alert and was then barren to Red Alert again two years later. Saint Geran was a fair winner over a mile and a quarter and Blue Shark's only other previous foal, the Gay Fandango colt Snake Hips, is a winner over a mile in the States. Blue Shark herself showed so little ability in her four races at two that she was sold for only 1,700 guineas at the end of the season. None of her three winning half-brothers and -sisters was out of the ordinary but her dam, the fair mile-and-a-half winner Well Armed, was a half-sister to the good 1962 two-year-old Forearmed and to Parlez-vous, the dam of those smart colts High Game, Estaminet and Amboise. Blue Shark would probably have stayed middle distances given the chance and Sandhurst Prince will have no difficulty staying a mile, even though he races quite freely. As yet he's raced only on a firm surface. *G. Harwood.*

SANDICLIFFE AGAIN (FR) 2 b.c. So Blessed 130–Never A Lady 112 (Ponti- **87** fex) (1981 5s 6s³ 7.3s) Feb 5; IR 21,000Y; lengthy, fair sort; first foal; dam won over 5f and 1m; made steady headway from halfway when 8 lengths third of 8 to Mirabeau in £3,500 event at York in October, easily best effort; had stiff task when in rear in Horris Hill Stakes won by Montekin at Newbury later in month; stays 6f and may get 7f in 1982. *B. Hills.*

SANDIFOOT 2 ch.c. Hotfoot 126–Sandray's Palace (Royal Palace 131) (1981 **80** 8s 7g) Apr 9; rangy, attractive colt; first foal; dam showed no ability; second favourite when sixth in maiden race at York and Doncaster in October, on latter being beaten 4½ lengths by Leg Glance (18 ran); may do better over middle distances. *J. W. Watts.*

SANDIWOOD 3 b.f. Saritamer 130–Tamergene 100 (Tamerlane 128) (1980 **—** 5fg 5g 6f 1981 5d 6f 5fg 5fg) small filly; in rear in varied company, including selling. *D. Marks.*

SANDMOOR COURT 3 b.g. Moulton 128–Queen Anne 88 (Faraway Son 130) **—** (1980 NR 1981 12f 16.5fg 10fg) 2,100 2-y-o; big gelding; dam 2-y-o 6f winner; behind in amateur riders event and 2 maiden races. *N. Tinkler.*

SANDOLI 3 gr.f. Sandford Lad 133–Greytino 91 (Fortino II 120) (1980 5.1g **—** 1981 6g) small filly; last in maiden race at Yarmouth as a 2-y-o and in well-contested minor event at Lingfield in June. *J. Winter.*

SANDON BUOY 3 b.g. Windjammer (USA)–Kay's Hour 93 (Bleep-Bleep 134)   **93**
(1980 5s 5g* 5fg 6g³ 6g⁴ 1981 5fg* 6g 5f² 5fg³ 5fg⁴ 5d 6g 6g) lightly-made
gelding who doesn't usually impress in paddock; useful handicapper; beaten
1½ lengths by Little Starchy at Sandown in April but was awarded race when
winner was disqualified for having theobromine in his system; placed in 2 good
handicaps in June, going down by a neck to Sanu in James Lane Handicap at
Ascot and finishing about 3 lengths third of 15 behind Ferriby Hall and Sanu
in Gosforth Park Cup at Newcastle, better effort on former course; stays 6f;
acts on firm going; had stiff task when blinkered fifth start; sent to Hong Kong.
R. Armstrong.

SANDRA BELLA 6 br.m. Crooner 119–Bella Sandra 88 (Botticelli 129) (1980   **48**
NR 1981 12g² 12.2fg⁴ 12f 16fg³ 19fg 16g³ 14fg) poor handicapper; stays 2m;
acts on hard going; often bandaged. *I. Wardle.*

SANDRA'S SECRET 4 b.f. Most Secret 119–Grovenka (Kibenka 119) (1980   **87**
6f 6f³ 6f 5fg* 5fg² 5s* 5g* 5g 5g 5fg 5d* 5f 5.6g 5g² 5d* 5v 1981 5g⁴ 5g 5d⁴ 5fg
5g² 5f² 5fg 5g 5s³ 5g² 5g) leggy, narrow filly; moderate plater at 2 yrs; fair
handicapper nowadays; runner-up at Epsom and Stockton in June and Edinburgh in October; best at 5f; acts on any going; blinkered twice at 2 yrs; ridden
for 4 successes by apprentice N. Connorton; trained by R. Whitaker first 6 starts.
D. Garraton.

SANDRA'S SOVEREIGN 2 b.f. Workboy 123–Ruritania (Pampered King 121)   **—**
(1981 5g 6g) Apr 18; 1,500Y (privately); workmanlike filly; half-sister to 3
winners; dam unraced half-sister to high-class 1964 staying 2-y-o Leonardo;
little sign of ability in minor events at Catterick and Redcar in September. *D.
Garraton.*

SANDWALKER 2 b.c. Pampapaul 121–Kazama (Relko 136) (1981 5g² 6d⁴   **94**
6fg² 7g² 7.6s*) Feb 11; IR 9,800F, 13,000Y; sturdy colt; half-brother to a
winner in France by Exbury; dam ran only once; led inside last to beat Escapism
by 2 lengths in 13-runner maiden race at Lingfield in October; will be suited by
1¼m and more; seems well suited by soft ground. *G. Pritchard-Gordon.*

SANDY MOON 2 b.f. Moulton 128–Windy Sea 105 (Sea Hawk II 131) (1981   **—**
5g 6g 6fg) Mar 21; 4,200Y; leggy, lightly-made filly; first foal; dam won over
7f and 1¼m; in rear all outings, final start a valuable seller; needs further. *T.
Fairhurst.*

SANDY SEA 7 b.m. Be Friendly 130–Vivid Blue 74 (Aegean Blue 110) (1980   **—**
NR 1981 8fg 13.8fg 12f) poor plater; has worn blinkers and bandages. *R. E.
Peacock.*

SANGALKAN 2 gr.c. Godswalk 130–Wilhelmina (Proud Chieftain 122) (1981   **94**
5s 6f* 7g² 7fg⁴ 6s) Mar 7; 41,000F, 40,000Y; big, strong, good-bodied colt;
good mover; half-brother to several winners, including very useful sprinter
Burlington Boy (by Whistling Wind) and useful 5f to 7f winner Dunmurry Boy
(by Tudor Music); dam stayed 9f; rallied well to lead on line when winning 13-
runner Duchess of Kent Stakes at York in June by a short head from Match
Master; put up best subsequent effort when giving at least 10 lb to all his 9
opponents in minor event on same course the following month, finishing 5 lengths
second to Confession; stays 7f but gives impression he may prove better at 6f;
acts on firm ground and was always struggling on soft final appearance. *B.
Hobbs.*

SANGUE 3 b.f. Lyphard 132–Prodice 122 (Prominer 125) (1980 NR 1981   **115**
10.5d* 10f* 12g 9.2d 10f² 12f) 228,000Y; strong, compact, good-bodied filly;
third reported foal; sister to French 1¼m winner Bubble Company; dam won
Prix Saint-Alary on a disqualification and finished second in Prix de Diane; won
minor event at Evry in July and Group 3 Prix de Psyche at Deauville in August,
finishing strongly to beat Kounboula by a length in latter; soundly beaten in
Prix Vermeille (virtually tailed off) and in Prix de l'Opera at Longchamp afterwards; subsequently sent to race in North America and ran creditably there,
notably when 2½ lengths second to De La Rose in E. P. Taylor Stakes at Woodbine in October; should stay 1½m; seems to act on any going. *M. Zilber, France.*

SANHEDRIN (FR) 4 ch.g. Satingo 129–India (Hautain 128) (1980 10.1d 12d³   **59**
12s 1981 11.7fg⁴ 11.7fg⁴ 11.7g⁴) fair sort; stays 1½m; probably acts on any
going. *G. Balding.*

SAN ISIDRO 2 ch.c. Sallust 134–Ladys View 109 (Tin Whistle 128) (1981 5f   **68**
7fg 7g 7.6s 7d) May 21; IR 27,000Y; quite well-made colt; half-brother to
winning 3-y-o miler Al-Allam (by Sun Prince) and a winner in Denmark; dam
speedy 2-y-o; only plating class; stays 7f. *R. Smyth.*

*Duchess of Kent Stakes, York—Sangalkan (No. 17) rallies well to
catch Match Master*

SANJARIDA 3 b.g. Sandford Lad 133–Caught In The Rye 97 (Manacle 123)   **87**
(1980 NR 1981 6g² 5g* 5g* 6fg 6d 5fg) 2,600F, 6,800Y; leggy, lightly-made
gelding; first produce; dam won 3 times at up to 6f at 2 yrs; won maiden race at
Bath (comfortably) and handicap at Salisbury, both in June, latter gamely by
½ length from Pencil Point; in rear all subsequent starts, on last one looking
most unco-operative in blinkers; stays 6f. *M. Smyly.*

SANNA'S POST 2 ch.c. Pieces of Eight 128–Santa Laura 64 (Canisbay 120)   **—**
(1981 6g 7.6s) Apr 25; first reported foal; dam won over 5f at 2 yrs; in rear in
maiden races at Lingfield in September and October. *M. Masson.*

SANS BLAGUE (USA) 2 ch.f. The Minstrel 135–Joking Apart 120 (Jimmy   **91**
Reppin 131) (1981 6fg 7d* 7s) Mar 28; attractive, rangy filly; good mover;
third foal; half-sister to very useful middle-distance filly Deadly Serious (by
Queen's Hussar); dam very smart at up to 1m; disputed lead throughout and
stayed on really well to win 18-runner maiden race at Newbury in September by
4 lengths from Dish Dash; couldn't quicken when creditable fifth of 11 to most
impressive winner Paradis Terrestre in Hyperion Stakes at Ascot the following
month; will be suited by 1m; a very taking individual who should make a useful
3-y-o. *R. Hern.*

SANS DOT 3 b.f. Busted 134–Juliette Marny 123 (Blakeney 126) (1980 NR   **92**
1981 10g⁴ 12fg) tall, rather unfurnished filly; said to be a whistler; second
living foal; dam won Oaks and Irish Guinness Oaks and is sister to St Leger
winner Julio Mariner and half-sister to Oaks winner Scintillate; ran with considerable promise when about 3½ lengths fourth of 8 behind Strigida in Sir
Charles Clore Memorial Stakes at Newbury in May, running in close touch
throughout and running on really well without her rider resorting to the whip;
rather disappointing when about 8 lengths sixth of 9 behind Strigida in Ribblesdale Stakes at Royal Ascot the following month and wasn't seen out again;
should stay at least 1½m; possibly not at her best on a firm surface; sold 74,000
gns Newmarket December Sales. *J. Tree.*

Mr Roy Taiano's "Santella Man"

SANTA ROSEANNA 2 br.f. Caracol–Santa Vittoria 100 (Ragusa 137) (1981 **97**
7.5f* 6d² 7d²) Apr 16; sister to German 3-y-o Santa Elena, second in Group 3
Grosser Preis der International Harvester over 10.5f, and half-sister to winners
in Germany, including San Vicente (by Priamos), winner of Group 2 Grosser
Hansa-Preis over 11f and Group 3 Bayerisches-Zuchtrennen over 1¼m; dam,
half-sister to smart animals Dominion Day, Sir Penfro and Padroug, finished
fourth in Irish 1,000 Guineas but failed to win in 9 outings; acquitted herself
well in good company at the Curragh after winning maiden race at Gowran Park
in July by 5 lengths, finishing 1½ lengths third of 14 to Sweet Side in Moyglare
Stud Stakes (promoted to second on winner's disqualification) and 2½ lengths
second of 18 to More Heather (rec 5 lb) in Park Stakes; will stay 1½m (sire won
Grosser Preis von Baden at that distance); will make a very useful 3-y-o. *J.
Bolger, Ireland.*

SANTA ROYALE 4 br.f. Royal and Regal–Galloping Santa (Santa Claus 133)   **?**
(1980 NR 1981 16d 22.2f 8fg 16d 14d² 16g) second foal; dam won over 9f and
1¼m in Ireland; won bumpers races at Naas in March and Tramore in June;
soundly beaten most other starts, including when last to Donegal Prince in
Queen Alexandra Stakes at Royal Ascot in June on second start; stays well.
H. de Bromhead, Ireland.

SANTA'S BELLE 3 ch.f. Bonne Noel 115–Lavender Belle (Le Levanstell 122)   **—**
(1980 NR 1981 11.7f 8fg) 400Y, 650 3-y-o; half-sister to 2 winners by Ragusa,
including Irish 9f winner La Sona; dam won over 1m and 1¼m in Ireland; tailed
off in maiden races at Bath in July and Salisbury (still on backward side) in
August. *L. Kennard.*

SANTELLA MAN 2 ch.c. Nebbiolo 125–Belle Bretonne 90 (Celtic Ash) (1981 **109**
7fg* 7fg* 7g 8f³ 7.6g* 8s⁴) Feb 23; 12,000Y; well-made colt; good mover;
second foal; dam, who needed at least 2m, is half-sister to very useful Shaftesbury; successful in 6-runner maiden race at Sandown (beat Beldale Bid a neck)
and slowly-run £2,900 event at Kempton (made all to account for Voyant
comfortably by 2 lengths), both in July, and £4,100 nursery at Lingfield in
September; scored by 2½ lengths from Brookline in last-named; also ran well

754

when in frame in nursery at York and 9-runner Royal Lodge Stakes at Ascot, staying on nicely to be about 7 lengths fourth to stable-companion Norwick in latter later in September; will stay 1½m; acts on any going; very useful and looks the sort to train on. *G. Harwood.*

SANTELLAS 3 b.c. Arch Sculptor 123–Stop Thinking (Divine Gift 127)   (1980   **88**
7g⁴ 1981 7s³ 8d* 8.5fg* 8d* 10.1d 8g 8.3fg 8fg 8fg² 8.2v 8d)   good-topped, attractive colt; won maiden event at Warwick (easily), minor event at Epsom and handicap at Salisbury (made all) in the spring; flashed his tail under pressure but nevertheless ran best race for a while when second in handicap at Salisbury in September; best form at around 1m; probably acts on any going; blinkered eighth start; inconsistent; sold 4,400 gns Newmarket Autumn Sales. *G. Harwood.*

SANU 3 b.c. Steel Heart 128–Light Link 99 (Tudor Music 131)   (1980 5d 5g 5d   **111**
6g² 5g* 5g* 5g* 6fg⁴ 5fg 1981 6g 6g³ 6f 5g* 5fg² 6fg² 5fg³ 5d 5d 6fg 6fg) neat colt; returned to form in 12-runner James Lane Handicap at Ascot in June, leading a furlong out and holding on by a neck from Sandon Buoy (pair clear) despite hanging very badly right; very good second under penalties in Gosforth Park Cup (Handicap) won by Ferriby Hall at Newcastle later in month and in Tote Sprint Trophy (Handicap) won by Enchantment at Ayr in July; also ran very well when third to Pencil Point in handicap at Goodwood later in July; stays 6f; acts well on firm going (far from disgraced on dead however when facing stiff task ninth start). *F. Durr.*

SAOUD 2 b.c. Habitat 134–Narcotic (Narrator 127)   (1981 6g 6g)   Apr 13;   **— p**
26,000Y; big, strong colt; closely related to modest 1m winner Hypodermic (by Steel Heart) and half-brother to 2 winners, including useful sprinter Fine Silver (by Silver Shark); dam, middle-distance winner in Ireland, is daughter of 1,000 Guineas winner Hypericum; second favourite, disputed lead until 1½f out when eighth of 19 to One Degree in maiden race at Newmarket in October; distinctly backward on debut. *H. T. Jones.*

Mr R. N. Tikkoo's "Sanu"

SAPPHIRE 2 b.f. Warpath 113–So Precious 100 (Tamerlane 128) (1981 6g) —
Apr 14; neat filly; good walker; third live foal; half-sister to 1½m winner Midsummer Madness (by Silly Season); dam won at up to 1¼m and stayed 1½m;
unquoted, ridden along most of way when not in first 10 of 21 behind Tickletimes
in minor event at Redcar in September; will need 1¼m+. *C. Thornton.*

SARAH BERNHARDT 3 ch.f. Ballymore 123–Song of Westmeath (Golden   **75**
Horus 123) (1980 7g 1981 9d* 10g 10fg 12fg 13fg 15d² 16s* 16s² 16s) leggy,
lightly-made filly; won maiden race at Wolverhampton in May and handicap
at Newcastle in October, latter in very good style by 20 lengths from Canoodle
after being enterprisingly ridden; second to Halsbury in 3-runner £4,300 event
at Ayr in between and to Aniece in handicap at Warwick afterwards; suited
by a test of stamina; acts well on soft going; sold 8,600 gns Newmarket December
Sales. *W. Elsey.*

SARAH'S VENTURE 2 br.f. Averof 123–Railway Hill (Guersant 129) (1981   **63**
5s 5d⁴ 5f³ 6g 5f 5h 5s 7d) May 21; half-sister to several winners, including
fairly useful 1976 2-y-o 7f winner Sleeper (by Track Spare); dam won over 5f
in Ireland; in frame in minor event at Brighton in May and maiden race at
Leicester (3¾ lengths third to Starlust) in June; should stay 6f; blinkered sixth
start; trained by C. James first 6 outings. *P. Mitchell.*

SARAJILL 2 b.f. High Line 125–Centro 86 (Vienna 127) (1981 7d) May 25;   — p
lengthy, quite attractive filly; sister to 4 winners, including very smart 3-y-o
stayer Centroline, high-class middle-distance stayer Nicholas Bill and very
useful 1¼m to 2m filly Centrocon; dam 2-y-o 7f winner; 25/1, made little show
when behind in 18-runner maiden race won by Sans Blague at Newbury in
September; will stay 1½m+; looks capable of much better in time. *H. Candy.*

SARAK 2 br.g. Jolly Good 122–Sarasingh 93 (Mansingh 120) (1981 5s 5v   **49**
6f 6g 7f³ 6f 6f 8.2fg) Apr 29; 2,100Y; leggy gelding; first foal; dam won over
6f at 2 yrs; plater; showed improved form in blinkers when 1¾ lengths third
of 14 to Hittite Prince at Thirsk in July; well beaten subsequently, twice
wearing blinkers; suited by 7f but ran poorly over 1m; formerly trained by
R. Whitaker. *E. Carter.*

SARASARA (USA) 2 b.f. London Company–Swoon's Flower (Swoon's Son)   —
(1981 5d) leggy, lightly-made filly; good mover; half-sister to a minor winner
by What A Pleasure; dam smart stakes winner at up to 9f; 14/1, made no show
in 20-runner maiden race won by Path To Glory at Newbury in September;
needs much further. *I. Balding.*

SARATOGA CHIP (USA) 3 b.f. Plenty Old–Saratoga Gal (Royal Orbit)   **59**
(1980 7g 1981 7.6d 9f 7f 7f 7f 6fg⁴ 7s* 7g 7g) lightly-made filly; ridden by
7-lb claimer when beating Jealous Moor 3 lengths in selling handicap at Newcastle in October, best effort; bought in 2,000 gns afterwards; seems suited by
7f and soft ground; sold 940 gns Newmarket Autumn Sales. *R. Sheather.*

SARATOGA JIM (USA) 2 b.c. Accipiter–Billiken (Herbager 136) (1981   —
7fg 7d) Feb 28; $30,000Y; good-topped, useful sort; fifth foal; half-brother
to a winner by Francis S; dam won 3 times at up to 1m; behind in big fields
of maidens at Newmarket in July and August (last). *E. Eldin.*

SARDANA 2 b.c. Gay Fandango 132–Blajina (Bold Lad, Ire 133) (1981 7g)   —
Mar 16; IR 9,600Y; neat colt; first foal; dam ran twice at 2 yrs; 20/1 and in
need of race, dropped out at halfway and finished seventeenth of 18 to Leg
Glance in maiden race at Doncaster in October; sold 680 gns Doncaster November
Sales. *J. W. Watts.*

SARDINE 3 b.f. Saritamer 130–Rose Arbour 106 (Pall Mall 132) (1980 5g²   —
5f 6f 6s 6g 7g 6fg 5g⁴ 6g 1981 6g 6d 5.3fg⁴ 5g) lengthy filly; not a good
mover in her slower paces; quite moderate form in varied company; probably
stays 6f; sometimes troublesome at start as a 2-y-o; occasionally blinkered
(has run well in them); sold 430 gns Ascot October Sales. *A. Ingham.*

SARITAMER CITY 2 b.f. Saritamer 130–Carmine City 104 (Charlottesville   —
135) (1981 6g) May 15; 3,000Y; well-grown filly; half-sister to 3 winners,
including good Japanese filly Inter-Smash (by Derring-Do); dam stayed at
least 2m; unquoted, chased leaders and wasn't knocked about once her chance
had gone when over 9 lengths sixth of 15 to Topaz Too in maiden race at
Nottingham in August. *M. Smyly.*

SAROAN MEED 2 ch.f. Midsummer Night II 117–Glistening 84 (Aureole   —
132) (1981 7g 6d) Apr 3; half-sister to 11f winner Glitter (by Reliance II)

756

and a winner in Italy; dam winning stayer and half-sister to high-class long-distance horse Proverb; well behind in sizeable fields of maidens at Salisbury in July and Windsor in August. *D. Gandolfo.*

SARSFIELD 3 br.g. Lord Gayle 124–Sayann (Sayajirao 132) (1980 8.5s⁴ **65** 7s 9.5s³ 1981 10g 12f³ 13f² 16.9fg) ex-Irish gelding; brother to Irish 13f winner Yksi and half-brother to several winners, including fairly useful Irish middle-distance stayer Whistle For Gold (by Whistling Wind); dam lightly raced; placed in minor event at Leicester and maiden race at Nottingham, finishing 6 lengths second to Tomaschek on latter course in July; stays 13f; formerly trained by J. Oxx. *Mrs M. Rimell.*

SASHAMEL 2 ch.c. Tower Walk 130–Misty Echo 58 (Mountain Call 125) **66** (1981 7fg 6g⁴ 6g 7fg 8.2s 8s 7g⁴) May 2; 3,500F; useful sort; second foal; dam ran only at 2 yrs; only plating class; gives impression 1m is too far for him; blinkered last 2 outings. *M. Ryan.*

SASOL 2 ch.f. Bustino 136–Wrekinianne 96 (Reform 132) (1981 7.2f²) Mar **78 p** 2; 9,200Y; big, rangy filly; has plenty of scope; sister to fair stayer Sir Gordon and half-sister to fair miler Staffordshire Knot (by Welsh Pageant) and a bumpers winner; dam stayed 1m; 8/1, behind turning into straight but ran on to finish 2½ lengths second of 6 to Swiftfoot in Rose of Lancaster Stakes at Haydock in July; hung badly on firm ground here; bred to stay 1¼m+; looked a useful Northern 2-y-o in the making but didn't race again. *M. H. Easterby.*

SASS 3 ch.c. Sassafras 135–Sister Agnes 90 (St Paddy 133) (1980 7g 8fg **100** 1981 12fg 10g² 12g 12d 13.3d² 14fg² 15g 12g* 14d) rangy colt; stayed on well under pressure despite edging to his right when beating Cool Decision by 4 lengths in amateur riders maiden race at Newmarket in August; had run creditably in varied company earlier and had been second in Heathorn Stakes at Newmarket (beaten ¾ length by Shotgun when 100/1-chance) and maiden races at Newbury (to Centroline) and Sandown (to Brigadier Hawk); had particularly stiff tasks third and fourth starts, latter race the Derby (eleventh of 18); stays well; yet to race on extremes of going; reportedly sent to Italy. *P. Kelleway.*

SASSALA 2 gr.f. Sassafras 135–Key of the Kingdom 111 (Grey Sovereign 128§) **—** (1981 8d) Feb 8; 3,100Y; leggy, unfurnished filly; second foal; dam speedy 2-y-o; unquoted and somewhat backward, always behind when eighth of 11 to All Risks in maiden race at Wolverhampton in October. *R. Boss.*

SASS-GO 3 br.f. Sassafras 135–Dame Margot 96 (Le Levanstell 122) (1980 **105** NR 1981 12fg³ 12g² 14g³ 12g* 12f* 12d³ 12d4) 4,100F; leggy, lightly-made filly; half-sister to Bustam (by Busted), successful from 1¼m to 2½m in France; dam won over 1m in Ireland; evens favourite when winning maiden race at Lingfield and minor event at Wolverhampton in June, on latter course getting on top entering final furlong and going away to win by 2 lengths from Bay of Mist; in frame subsequently in Group 3 Prix de Minerve at Evry in July (excellent 1¼ lengths third to Anitra's Dance) and Galtres Stakes at York in August (never really in race but stayed on to finish about 10 lengths fourth behind stable-companion Ma Femme); possibly doesn't stay 1¾m; probably acts on any going. *B. Hobbs.*

SASSY BELLE 2 ch.f. Sassafras 135–Bright Bird 101 (Laser Light 118) **—** (1981 7d 6g) Feb 7; stocky filly; second foal; dam won four 5f races; in rear in sizeable fields of maidens at Yarmouth in September and Newmarket in October (last of 17); looks headstrong; sold 620 gns Doncaster November Sales. *M. Jarvis.*

SATIN GRANGE 3 br.g. Satingo 129–Court Circular (Ambiorix 130) (1980 **70 d** 5fg 5d³ 6d² 6g³ 6g³ 6d 6d 1981 8d 10d 8d³ 8d 10fg 9f 10g⁴) quite attractive gelding who carries plenty of condition; in frame in apprentice handicaps at Leicester in May and Newmarket in October; probably stays 1¼m; blinkered sixth outing at 2 yrs; sold 4,900 gns Newmarket Autumn Sales. *B. Hobbs.*

SAUCY FLUSH 2 br.g. Meldrum 112–Lady Loveliness (Flush Royal 127) **—** (1981 7g 7fg 8g 10.2g) Apr 13; leggy gelding; half-brother to minor 1½m winner Sounds Lovely (by Naval Sound); dam hurdler; showed only glimmer of ability when about 9 lengths sixth of 14 to Arrowood Dream in 1m maiden race at Beverley in September; not sure to stay 1¼m. *E. Weymes.*

SAUCY LASS 2 b.f. Bold Lad (Ire) 133–Morwena (Masetto) (1981 6fg 6g 5fg⁴ **64** 6fg 5g) May 4; 4,500Y; compact, quite attractive filly; half-sister to 2 winners in France; dam won twice over middle distances; only plating class; should stay at least 6f; blinkered fifth outing; sold 800 gns Newmarket Autumn Sales. *H. Candy.*

SAUCY SERGENT 4 b.g. Home Guard 129–Miss Me 82 (Tamerlane 128) **53** (1980 6s 6f 7fg 8fg 6fg* 8f 8d 7.6g 9g 10g 10fg* 8f³ 10g³ 8.2d 8fg³ 10d⁴ 10.2v³ 1981 9g 10g⁴ 10.5d 10g 10fg 10f 10g 12f 10.5s⁴ 11d 10d2) compact gelding; middle-distance handicapper; seems to act on any going; sometimes blinkered but is effective without; sweated up third start; has won for an apprentice. *R. Hollinshead.*

SAUCY'S SISTER 2 ch.f. Malicious–Beryl's Song 86 (Sing Sing 134) (1981 — 5d 5s 5s) Mar 1; sister to moderate 1978 2-y-o 6f winner Saucy Melody; dam fair 2-y-o; of little account; slowly away first outing. *W. Wightman.*

SAUCY TWINKLE 2 b.f. Comedy Star 121–Ebnalblue (Prince de Galles 125) **49** (1981 5d 5s 5s* 5fg* 5g 5f 6fg) Feb 21; neat filly; third foal; dam never ran; bought in after winning early-season sellers at Wolverhampton (1,050 gns) and Warwick (950 gns after scoring by 1½ lengths from Britannia Trailer); ran poorly subsequently; seems to act on any going; wears blinkers. *P. Haslam.*

SAUCY VENTURE 2 b.g. Young Emperor 133–Reina Isabel 69 (St Alphage — 119) (1981 5d 5g 7fg) Apr 15; 1,000Y; small gelding; second reported foal; dam placed over 1¼m; last in minor and maiden events. *G. Richards.*

SAULANN 3 b. or br.c. Saulingo 122–Lucerne 76 (Gun Shot) (1980 5d⁴ 5fg⁴ **61** 5f² 5g* 5g² 5d² 6g⁴ 6s⁴ 6s 6s 1981 5d 6g 6g 6f 7g 7g 7g⁴) compact colt; ran respectably in handicaps on occasions; possibly finds 7f a shade too far; suited by some give in the ground; started slowly when blinkered sixth outing. *W. H. Williams.*

SAULINGDALE 3 b.c. Saulingo 122–Hibernia III 120 (Masetto) (1980 6f 7f **67** 8g 7d 7v³ 1981 7s² 7s* 7g³ 7d 8g) small colt; beat Prince Diamond ½ length in handicap at Stockton in April; not sure to stay 1m; well suited by the mud; apprentice ridden last 4 starts; exported to Hong Kong. *W. Elsey.*

SAULINGO SONG 2 b. or br.c. Saulingo 122–Comino Song (Tudor Music 131) **54** (1981 5s 5g 5g 5fg 5.3f³ 5.3fg⁴ 5fg 6g) May 20; 1,600Y; fair sort; second foal; dam ran only 4 times; in frame in claiming races at Brighton in July and August; didn't run up to his best over 6f; sold 290 gns Ascot October Sales. *J. Benstead.*

SAUL SERVICE 2 b.f. Saulingo 122–Good Service 88 (Espresso 122) (1981 **45** 5s 5s 5g³ 5g⁴ 5fg) Apr 18; IR 2,400F, 500Y; neat filly; closely related to useful miler Mandate (by Manacle); dam won over 5f and 6f at 2 yrs; plater; in frame at Stockton in April and Redcar in May; blinkered last 3 starts. *I. Vickers.*

SAUNTERING 3 b.g. Farm Walk 111–Leila (Grey Sovereign 128§) (1980 — NR 1981 14.7fg 10.6d 10fg) strong gelding; brother to a poor animal and half-brother to 2 winners; dam of little account; ran best race on second outing, when sixth of 12 behind Habitor in maiden race at Haydock in August (still backward). *Miss S. Hall.*

SAUSOLITO 3 br.g. Relko 136–Rosia Steps 98 (Red Pins 114) (1980 5f 6d⁴ — 6d² 7fg* 7s³ 8g 7d 1981 12fg 7f 8f) rangy gelding; fair performer at 2 yrs; soundly beaten in 1981, but had stiff tasks; should stay middle distances; seems to act on any going. *M. H. Easterby.*

SAUVAGE 3 b.c. Wolver Hollow 126–Belle Affaire 96 (Elopement 125) (1980 **94** 7fg² 7f³ 7g 19fi 8g* 8.2s³ 8f 7.2f³ 8fg 9f* 10.2fg 10g) strong, good-bodied colt; good walker and mover; won maiden race at Pontefract in April (very easily) and handicap at Ripon in August, latter in good style by 3 lengths from Angle Fire after being held up; third in Cecil Frail Handicap won by Silver Season and Sporting Chronicle Handicap won by Piperhill, both at Haydock, in between; stays 9f; acts on any going. *M. Stoute.*

SAVAHRA 2 b.f. Free State 125–Avahra 108 (Sahib 114) (1981 5g 7fg 6d 8s **75** 10s) May 25; neat filly; second foal; half-sister to fairly useful 5f and 6f winner Pavahra (by Mummy's Pet); dam stayed 6f; 5¼ lengths fifth of 14 to Florida Son in 1m maiden event at York, easily best effort; not sure to stay 1¼m. *P. Rohan.*

SA-VEGAS 2 b.f. Star Appeal 133–Rotondo (Royal Buck) (1981 8fg 8fg 8d2) **81 p** Mar 11; 22,000F; strong, deep-girthed, attractive filly; fifth foal; half-sister to 4 winners here and abroad, including stayer Hardirondo (by Hardicanute); dam won over 1½m in Ireland; joint-favourite but still in need of race, stayed on stoutly under vigorous hand riding to finish neck second of 11 to Misty Halo in maiden event at Wolverhampton in October; will be suited by 1½m; a grand stamp of filly who will do better at 3 yrs. *J. Dunlop.*

Andy Capp Handicap, Redcar—Say Primula beats Irish Keep to gain his fifth win of the season

SAVILE PARK 3 b.g. Reformed Character 107–Angel's Halo (Aureole 132)   **60**
(1980 6fg 8d* 1981 8g 12fg 10fg* 9g 11s) neat gelding; dropped in class when
beating Alfred Milner by 2½ lengths in selling handicap at Pontefract in August;
bought in 1,150 gns afterwards; ran moderately in sellers last 2 outings; should
stay 1½m; probably acts on any going; burst a blood vessel fourth outing; sold
out of M. H. Easterby's stable 1,100 gns Ascot August Sales after fourth outing
and resold to D. Burchell 1,100 gns Ascot December Sales. *M. James.*

SAWLEY SAM 3 ch.g. Sunotra 86–Marwood Queen 57 (Maystreak 118) (1980   **—**
NR 1981 12g) 680 3-y-o; first live foal; dam plater; tailed-off last of 7 behind
Elizabeth Howard in minor event at Edinburgh in September. *H. Bell.*

SAXON FARM 2 ch.c. Hittite Glory 125–Kemoening 78 (Falcon 131) (1981   **71**
5s 5s 5s 6fg 7fg⁴ 7g 8g³ 8d) Mar 26; 2,500Y; good-topped colt; fourth foal;
half-brother to a winner over hurdles; dam placed from 1m to 1¼m; quite a
moderate maiden; stays 1m; sweated up sixth outing. *S. Mellor.*

SAYFARI 3 b.g. Sayfar 116–Flying Nun 66 (Welsh Abbot 131) (1980 7g 7fg   **51**
7fg 1981 12fg 12.5f³ 16f 16g 14.6f⁴ 16f 16.5f) leggy gelding; seems a very
slow maiden. *Sir Mark Prescott.*

SAYFAR'S GREY 3 gr. or ro.c. Sayfar 116–Antigua III (Worden II 129) (1980   **—**
5fg 1981 5d) small colt; lightly raced and no form; dead. *D. Leslie.*

SAY PRIMULA 3 ch.c. Hotfoot 126–Renoir Picture 90 (Relko 136) (1980   **99**
8s² 1981 8v* 9s* 9d³ 10g* 12f 10fg 10g* 10d* 10.2g⁴ 10d³ 12v³) lengthy
colt; improved and had an excellent season; gaining his fifth win when beating
Irish Keep by 2½ lengths in Andy Capp Handicap at Redcar in August, quickening
into lead in last 2f and running on strongly; had earlier won minor events at
Ayr and Ripon, Holsten Export Lager Handicap at Newmarket (beat Show-
A-Leg by 1½ lengths) and another handicap at Newcastle; best form at up to
1¼m; best form with some give in the ground; didn't have best of runs on third
and tenth starts; has a useful turn of foot, but tends to hang and isn't the
easiest of rides. *J. W. Watts.*

SAYSABAN 2 ch.c. Sassafras 135–Side Step (Double Jump 131) (1981 7g²   **93**
10s) Mar 24; 11,500F; third foal; dam placed at up to 1½m in Ireland; 12/1
and in need of race, shaped well when length second to easy winner Match
Winner in minor event at Yarmouth in September, making headway from halfway without rider resorting to whip; acted as pacemaker for stable-companion
Bon Sang in Criterium de Saint-Cloud in November, only subsequent start;
will stay 1½m; trained until after first start by W. O'Gorman. *M. Saliba,
France.*

SAYYAF 4 b.c. Habitat 134–Pavello 94 (Crepello 136) (1980 7d 5fg⁴ 5fg²   **117**
6f* 6fg² 6fg² 6d 5fg⁴ 6g⁴ 5g* 6fg⁴ 1981 6fg 5fg³ 5g 6fg³ 5fg² 6fg)
small, quite attractive colt; smart sprinter; always going well when beating
Durandal quite comfortably by 1½ lengths in 4-runner Rous Memorial Stakes

759

(Handicap) at Ascot in July; creditable third afterwards in King George Stakes at Goodwood (blinkered when beaten 2¼ lengths behind King of Spain) and Vernons Sprint Cup at Haydock (led until inside last furlong when 2¾ lengths behind Runnett); odds on when 2 lengths second to Hello Cuddles in 4-runner Scarbrough Stakes at Doncaster in September; stays 6f; acts well on firm ground; genuine and consistent. *W. O'Gorman.*

SAZERAC 7 ch.h. Tarbes 125–Kirmidian (Bold Bidder) (1980 NR 1981 10f) middle-distance plater; has worn blinkers. *M. Bradley.* —

SCARLET SAGA 2 gr.f. No Mercy 126–Leading Rose (Scarlet Ruler 93) (1981 5f 7d) Apr 5; first foal; dam showed no worthwhile form; in rear in minor event at Wolverhampton in August (backward) and maiden race at Yarmouth the following month. *D. Ringer.* —

SCARLET TOWN 3 b.c. Town Crier 119–Sindo 91 (Derring-Do 131) (1980 5d*(dis) 5f 5fg⁴ 6s² 6g³ 5g 6d 5s⁴ 6g 6d 1981 6v 6s³ 8g 6g 6g³ 8g³ 8.2s 9g⁴ 8f² 10.4fg⁴ 8.2fg* 8d³ 8f 8g 8.2v 8d⁴ 8g) small, lightly-made, quite attractive colt; good mover; won maiden event at Hamilton in July; none too genuine however; stays 1m; acts on any going. *R. Hollinshead.* **61**

SCARROWMANWICK 3 b.c. Tickled Pink 114–Almadena 73 (Dairialatan 111) (1980 5.8f 5g³ 6g⁴ 6fg² 6f* 6f* 6d 1981 7g 7fg² 7g* 7.6g 8f 7.2f 6g* 6g⁴ 6fg 6g* 6d 6s) quite a useful sort; good walker; successful in handicaps at York in May (valuable Norwest Holst Trophy, from Ganimede) and July and at Newmarket in September (beat Think Ahead by 1½ lengths in £4,600 event); reportedly very slowly away when sixth of 14 behind Super Sky in Group 3 Premio Umbria at Rome in November on final outing; best form at up to 7f (always behind when tried over 1m); acts on firm going but ran best races of 1981 on good; blinkered after sixth outing. *N. Vigors.* **107**

SCHEMING 3 ch.g. Great Nephew 126–Look Out 84 (Vimy 132) (1980 NR 1981 8g 12g⁴ 14g⁴ 16fg² 16f³ 14fg² 16g* 16s) 20,000Y; smallish, deep-girthed gelding; half-brother to several winners, including 7f and 1m winner Beechwood Con (by Siliconn) and French out-and-out stayer Second Watch (by Paveh); dam half-sister to very smart stayer Raise You Ten; placed in maiden races prior to landing the odds by 6 lengths from Abo Ace in minor event at Lingfield in September; stays well. *P. Cole.* **69**

SCHOLAR'S RING 5 b.g. Continuation 120–Schull (Yorick II 127) (1980 8d 7v 12h 14.7f* 9f 12g 10f 8d 1981 14.6f 10f 8g 8.2d) strong gelding; poor performer; behind in valuable seller third start; seems to stay well; probably acts on any going except heavy; has worn blinkers; sometimes bandaged. *P. Haslam.* —

Norwest Holst Trophy, York—a good finish with Scarrowmanwick (right) winning from Ganimede, Spindrifter (stripes) and Norman Style (left)

Mrs Archie Kidd's "Scarrowmanwick"

SCINTILLATING AIR 3 b.c. Sparkler 130–Chantal 74 (Charlottesville 135) **120**
(1980 5f 5fg³ 6f⁴ 6fg 7d* 7fg³ 7d* 1981 8g 8g 10.5g³ 12d³ 12f)

With the notable exception of the winner, the Derby field in 1981 was not
a particularly high-class one by the standards of the race. The Derby third
Scintillating Air has won only two of his twelve races, a maiden event at Newmarket and a nursery at York. Following Freefoot and Rankin, Scintillating
Air became only the third horse in over twenty years to be placed in the Derby
and go through his three-year-old career without a win. There were extenuating
circumstances though. Scintillating Air missed the second part of the season
after injuring a leg in the Princess of Wales's Stakes at Newmarket's July
meeting on his only outing after Epsom.

Stepping up considerably on his two-year-old form, Scintillating Air had
three good-class performances to his name by the time the Princess of Wales's
Stakes came round. He finished sixth of nineteen in the Two Thousand
Guineas, beaten about five lengths by the winner To-Agori-Mou after showing
prominently most of the way. Then, at York's May meeting, he came third
to Beldale Flutter and Shotgun, beaten three quarters of a length and three
lengths, in Britain's most valuable Derby trial, the Mecca-Dante Stakes run
over ten and a half furlongs. On these performances Scintillating Air was
worth his place in the Derby field, though his stamina for the job had to be
taken on trust, as for that matter did the stamina of others in the field at far
shorter odds—he started at 50/1. Scintillating Air gave a typically game
performance at Epsom, running on under strong pressure in vain pursuit of
Shergar in the straight, after being close up from the start, and looking likely
to be second until collared by Glint of Gold well inside the final furlong.

A strong, burly sort, Scintillating Air is a stuffy type, likely to need a race
after a lay-off, a point that should be borne in mind when he reappears as a
four-year-old. We pointed out in our essay on Rankin in *Racehorses of 1980*
that the conditions of the John Porter Stakes and the Jockey Club Stakes
favour horses that haven't won pattern events and we expect Scintillating Air

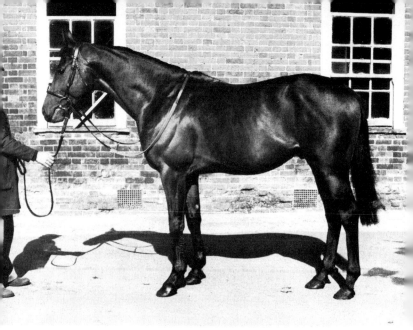

Mr K. C. Dodson's "Scintillating Air"

to have one or both of these events as an early target, provided he recovers fully from injury. Scintillating Air stayed on so well in the Derby that we should be a little surprised to see his racing at shorter distances again, particularly as his stable also houses the Champion-Stakes placed Amyndas. Both Scintillating Air and Amyndas are by Sparkler, a top-class performer who was never raced beyond a mile but stayed in training until he was five and remained thoroughly

Scintillating Air (b.c. 1978)	Sparkler (b 1968)	Hard Tack (b 1955)	Hard Sauce Cowes
		Diamond Spur (ch 1961)	Preciptic Diamond Princess
	Chantal (ch 1971)	Charlottesville (b 1957)	Prince Chevalier Noorani
		Miss Mary (b 1965)	Bounteous Mary Tavy

genuine and consistent to the end; he has had an Oaks winner (Scintillate) and a One Thousand Guineas winner (Enstone Spark) from five crops to race. Scintillating Air's dam Chantal was placed in mile-and-a-quarter maiden events at Ayr and Warwick as a three-year-old; she ran disappointingly when tried at a mile and a half but should have stayed at least that distance on breeding. She produced two foals before Scintillating Air, the plating-class maidens Aconbury (by Realm) and Chalk Down (by Saritamer), and her two-year-old of 1981 Filabeg (by Swing Easy) was in training with Fitzgerald at Malton. Scintillating Air has run creditably on a firm surface but has shown his best form with some give in the ground. *B. Hobbs.*

SCIROCCO 3 b.c. Welsh Saint 126–Till 85 (Hook Money 124) (1980 5fg 5f⁴(dis) **56**
6fg 5fg⁴ 1981 7fg⁴ 6s 7s 7f* 8fg⁴ 10f 8.2g 7f) tall, useful-looking colt; plater; sold out of R. Price's stable 1,700 gns after beating Redesign 6 lengths at Leicester in June; ran moderately afterwards; stays 7f; acts well on firm ground; sold

480 gns Doncaster September Sales and resold for same amount at same venue in November. *W. Clay.*

SCOT BENNETT 3 b.g. Tarboosh–Hell's Mistress (Skymaster 126) (1980 6s 7fg 1981 12fg 10fg 10.8fg 12fg³ 12fg* 12.2g² 12d 10.2g) fair sort; attracted no bid after beating Balda a head in selling handicap at Newmarket in August; blinkered, looked ungenuine and swerved under pressure when ¾-length second to Pittencrieff in non-selling handicap at Catterick the following month; will probably stay beyond 1½m; acts on a firm surface. *C. Brittain.* **59**

SCOTCH MUSKET 2 ch.f. Scottish Rifle 127–Press Button 58 (Precipice Wood 123) (1981 6d 7fg) Mar 6; 3,300Y; third foal; half-sister to 3-y-o Radical Rethink (by Owen Anthony); dam ran only at 2 yrs; soundly beaten in maiden races at Windsor and Brighton in August. *G. Beeson.* **—**

SCOTTISH AGENT 5 gr.g. Porto Bello 118–Alys Grey 91 (Grey Sovereign 128§) (1980 won in Belgium and Holland 1981 6g* 6g* 6fg² 6f 6fg* 6g 6.5f² 7g* 6fg 6fg 6s 6s 6d 6s⁴) tall gelding; won handicaps at Carlisle, Hamilton, Newcastle and Ostend; stays 7f; acts on firm going; blinkered twice in 1979; sometimes bandaged behind; retained 2,500 gns Newmarket Autumn Sales. *M. Ryan.* **56**

SCOTTISH BELLE 4 br.f. Scottish Rifle 127–Persian Belle 77 (Darius 129) (1980 7f 12g 10fg 14d 1981 12s 12f 10fg 16d) leggy filly; poor performer nowadays; often blinkered and has worn a hood as well. *A. Moore.* **—**

SCOTTISH BOY 2 b.g. Music Boy 124–Klontina (Klondyke Bill 125) (1981 5s 5g⁴ 5g⁴ 5g 5g⁴ 6fg 5g* 5g 6d⁴ 7d² 6d 7d) Mar 23; 3,500Y; well-grown gelding; second foal; dam in rear in maiden races; favourite, attracted no bid after winning 6-runner seller at Ayr in July; showed improved form when going down by a short head to Danish Express in 14-runner nursery at Edinburgh in October; evidently better suited by 7f than shorter distances; acts on a soft surface; best in blinkers. *J. Berry.* **73**

SCOTTISH DREAM 3 ch.c. Palm Track 122–Captain Frances (Captain's Gig) (1980 6f 6f 8s³ 8g* 8d 8s 6d 1981 13.8fg 12.3fg 13fg³ 16g 15g* 13d²) lengthy colt; stayed on strongly when beating Silly Twist by 1½ lengths in handicap at Edinburgh in September; suited by a test of stamina; acts on a firm and a soft surface. *G.Lockerbie.* **74**

SCOTTISH GREEN 3 ch.g. Scottish Rifle 127–Nuque (Suceso) (1980 5.8fg 7fg 7g 8.2g 8d⁴ 8.2s 1981 6fg 6g 8f* 8.3fg* 8g³ 9d 7g) neat gelding; won sellers at Wolverhampton (bought in 1,650 gns) and Windsor (no bid) in summer; will stay 1¼m; acts on firm going; wears blinkers; sometimes sweats up. *P. Makin.* **56**

SCOTT'S ENTERPRISE 2 b.c. Prince Regent 129–Zulu Queen (Sovereign Path 125) (1981 6g 6fg 6fg⁴ 7.2d) Mar 9; IR 5,600Y; stocky colt; third foal; brother to useful French 3-y-o sprinter Zulu Prince and a winner in Malaya; dam won at up to 7f in Ireland; only quite moderate; should be suited by 7f. *R. Williams.* **64**

SCOUTSMISTAKE 2 b. or br.g. Prince Tenderfoot 126–Summer Serenade 96 (Petingo 135) (1981 6fg 7.2fg* 7g) May 24; neat, quite attractive gelding; third reported live foal; half-brother to fairly useful 1977 2-y-o 6f and 1m winner Kadsai (by Lorenzaccio); dam stayed at least 9f; held on well under pressure when winning 13-runner maiden race at Haydock in September by ¾ length from fast-finishing Red Injun; 16/1, prominent 5f when behind in nursery at Newmarket the following month; stays 7f well and may get 1m. *P. Walwyn.* **72**

SCRAPPIT 3 b.g. Laser Light 118–Ballydell (Pall Mall 132) (1980 6fg 6d 8s 8.2s⁴ 8d 1981 7s 8s 10v 8.2fg* 8g) big, plain gelding; made all in selling handicap at Hamilton in May; stayed 1m; probably acted on any going; bandaged last 2 starts; dead. *S. Norton.* **67**

SCRUMPTIOUS (USA) 2 b.f. Nijinsky 138–Queen Pot (Buckpasser) (1981 7g) May 13; big, rangy, attractive filly; sister to French 1½m winner Gallantsky, and half-sister to 2 winners in USA and 3-y-o Potiphar's Wife (by Sir Ivor); dam, daughter of champion 1966 American 3-y-o filly Lady Pitt, won 3 times over sprint distances; drifted from 8/1 to 16/1 for 29-runner maiden race at Newmarket in October and faded out of contention in closing stages to finish twelfth of 29 to Chalon; took the eye in paddock and on way to start here, and should do better over middle distances at 3 yrs. *I. Balding.* **— p**

SCRUTTON 2 b. or br.c. Decoy Boy 129–Fastina 59 (Goldhill 125) (1981 5s) May 22; small colt; first foal; dam winning hurdler; 7/1 and bit backward, **—**

763

moved poorly to start and was tailed off from halfway in seller won by subsequently-disqualified Mosswern at Beverley in April. *N. Callaghan.*

S. D. DEMO 3 b.c. Mansingh 120–Blickling 64 (Blakeney 126) (1980 5fg² **64**
6d³ 5.8fg² 6g³ 6fg³ 6s 6g³ 1981 7d 6g 7s⁴ 7s* 7f 8.3fg) compact colt; bought
in 4,200 gns after beating Magneto by 2 lengths in seller at Kempton in May
(made nearly all); ran moderately afterwards; should stay 1m; acts on any
going; wears blinkers. *Mrs J. Reavey.*

SDENKA PRINCESS 3 b.f. Prince de Galles 125–Sdenka 79 (Habitat 134) —
(1980 6d 6fg 1981 11s 10s) strong, workmanlike filly; first foal; dam placed
over 7f; unquoted when in rear in maiden races. *Mrs R. Lomax.*

SDENKA ROYAL 2 b. or br.f. Queen's Hussar 124–Sdenka 79 (Habitat 134) —
(1981 5g 5g 7g) Mar 28; fair sort; second foal; dam placed over 7f; equal ninth
of 19 to Bahamas Princess in maiden event at Salisbury in June, second outing;
not seen out again until late in season and needed run when remote sixth of
16 to Tants in similar race at Leicester; formerly trained by Mrs R. Lomax.
A. Hide.

SEA AURA 3 b.f. Roi Soleil 125–Sinkit (Sing Sing 134) (1980 6fg⁴ 6fg* 1981 **89**
7g 8s³ 7g² 7g⁴ 8g 7g) sturdy, good sort; fourth foal; dam never ran; placed in
handicaps at York and Doncaster in May, finishing 4 lengths second to Havoc
in quite valuable event on latter course after being off the bridle from the start;
having first subsequent outing and in need of race when creditable 8 lengths
fourth of 6 to Star Pastures in well-contested £3,800 race at Goodwood in September (moved badly to post); may well prove best at 7f; probably acts on any going.
G. Pritchard-Gordon.

SEABATTLE (USA) 2 b.c. Cannonade–Smooth Siren (Sea-Bird II 145) (1981 —
7g 8g) Apr 3; 24,000Y; rangy colt; half-brother to very useful 1¼m filly Sirenivo
(by Sir Ivor); dam won over 6f at 3 yrs in USA; behind in big fields of maidens
at Newmarket in October, starting at 16/1 and 33/1. *P. Walwyn.*

SEA CHIMES 5 ch.h. Gulf Pearl 117–Canterbury Belle (St Alphage 119) ?
(1980 10g* 10.2fg* 10fg* 12f* 10g⁴ 1981 including 13.4d⁴ 10fg 8.5f 12f³ 11f
12f) tall, lengthy ex-English horse; good mover; developed into a very smart
performer at 4 yrs, winning Coronation Cup at Epsom on fourth start; didn't
run anywhere near his best first 2 starts in 1981, when remote fourth of 5 to
Pelerin in Ormonde Stakes at Chester in May and last of 10 to Hard Fought
in Prince of Wales's Stakes at Royal Ascot; subsequently sent to USA and put
up easily best effort over there when less than a length third to Spruce Needles
in Arlington Handicap at Arlington Park in September; stays 1½m; acts on
any going but is well suited by top-of-the-ground; sometimes sweats up; often
makes the running and has a good turn of foot as well; trained by J. Dunlop
until after second outing. *F. Alexander, USA.*

SEA CLAIRE 2 b.f. Seapic 100–Act The Creep (Gala Performance) (1981 —
6g) Apr 28; first foal; dam runner-up in 2 Irish bumpers events; unquoted
when last of 26 to Al Hasa in maiden race at Nottingham in August.
K. Bridgwater.

SEAGAS JETS 2 br.c. Balidar 133–Rudella 95 (Raffingora 130) (1981 6f —
8.2s) Apr 14; 4,200F; strong colt; has a roundish action; first foal; dam won
over 5f at 2 yrs; in rear in small race at Ripon in September and seller at
Nottingham in October; bandaged in front on latter. *W. Wharton.*

SEA HARRIER 2 ch.f. Grundy 137–Anchor 106 (Major Portion 129) (1981 — p
7g) Mar 29; twin sister to Didimo and half-sister to several winners, notably
high-class stayer Sea Anchor (by Alcide); dam, useful winner over 6f and 7f,
is half-sister to Oaks winner Bireme (by Grundy); 33/1-shot for 29-runner
maiden race at Newmarket in October but showed some promise, staying on
nicely in latter stages, and not being knocked about, to finish eighth to Chalon;
will stay 1¼m+; sure to do better. *R. Hern.*

SEA HAVOC 2 ch.f. Busted 134–Sea Lichen 106 (Ballymoss 136) (1981 **72**
6f 5d² 6d⁴) Mar 22; sparely-made filly; half-sister to several winners here and
abroad, including quite useful 1¼m and 11f winner Rockeater (by Roan Rocket);
dam fourth in 1,000 Guineas; ran creditably in maiden races at Wolverhampton
(first outing for 3 months) and Doncaster in October; 3 lengths second of 15
to Avonmore Wind on former course and about 2¼ lengths fourth to Dev on
latter (would have been a bit closer but didn't have best of runs inside last);
will be suited by middle distances. *H. Wragg.*

SEAJAN 5 gr.m. Mandamus 120–Sea Empress (Perhapsburg 112) (1980 12d —
13d 13.8fg 12fg³ 16g 16.1d⁴ 14g* 12.3g² 12g 1981 14f⁴ 12fg 16s) poor performer;
stays well; acts on a firm and a soft surface; has won for an amateur rider.
K. Ivory.

SEAMAB 2 b.f. Sallust 134–Some Dame 72 (Will Somers 114§) (1981 5g **66**
5d³ 5f³ 5fg³ 6d⁴) Apr 23; neat filly; third foal; half-sister to a winning plater
in France by Tower Walk; dam half-sister to Espresso, won at up to 11f; third in
maiden races at Folkestone, Nottingham and Redcar; should be suited by 6f+;
sold 4,300 gns Newmarket Autumn Sales. *H. T. Jones.*

SEAMAN'S LOVE 2 ch.f. Royben 125–Snotch (Current Coin 118) (1981 —
7g) Mar 12; 1,100Y; second foal; dam unraced half-sister to dam of Juliette
Marny, Julio Mariner and Scintillate; 20/1 and in need of race when tailed off
in 16-runner maiden event won by Positron at Leicester in October. *C.
Brittain.*

SEAMARTIN 2 b.c. Martinmas 128–Paphos 99 (Vilmorin) (1981 7fg 8d) —
Feb 9; big, strong, quite attractive colt; closely related to 1m winner Buffoon
(by Silly Season) and half-brother to several winners, including useful 1974
2 y-o Uncle Remus (by Great Nephew) and useful 1980 3-y-o 10.4f winner
Playboy Jubilee (by Connaught); dam sprinter; decidedly burly, could off after
2f when in rear in 19-runner maiden race won by Dageegah at Salisbury in
September; blinkered when pulled up at Newbury later in month. *I. Balding.*

SEA MINSTREL 7 b.g. Seaepic 100–Lunar Hornpipe 75 (Mossborough 126) —
(1980 12d 6g³ 8f 8fg 10.6g 7.6g 1981 10.6s 10f 8.2d) plater; stays 1¼m;
acts on a firm surface; has worn a hood and blinkers. *M. James.*

SEA MISS 3 b.f. Matahawk 127–Lillima 73 (Crooner 119) (1980 7fg³ 8g **73**
9d³ 1981 7s 10fg 8d⁴ 7g 8d² 8.5g* 10f² 10f 10fg⁴ 9f 8g 8g 8d) leggy filly;
made all and beat subsequently-disqualified Sister Kitty ¾ length in maiden
event at Epsom in June; creditable second to Fiesta Fun in minor event at
Brighton later in month; stays 1¼m; got loose before start third outing; moved
very short to post and was well beaten tenth start; often had stiff tasks in her
later races; sold 1,800 gns Newmarket December Sales. *P. Kelleway.*

SEA OF ECHOES 3 b.c. Wolver Hollow 126–Sea of Moyle 111 (Skymaster **91**
126) (1980 5f² 6fg* 6f³ 6s⁴ 7g* 7f² 7g 7g 8s 1981 7fg 9f 8g 11.5d*) Irish
colt; not seen out until August but showed he retained his form and on final
start beat Ladoucette in good style by 4 lengths in 16-runner Ulster Champion
Stakes at Down Royal in October; suited by middle distances; seems to act on
any going; usually apprentice ridden. *S. McGrath, Ireland.*

SEA PIGEON (USA) 11 br.g. Sea-Bird II 145–Around The Roses (Round —
Table) (1980 18.4f 9f* 16d⁴ 12g² 15g³ 14.7g* 14f² 11s* 12fg³ 14s 1981 18.4d)
good-looking gelding; top-class performer over hurdles and tip-top handicapper
on Flat from 1977 to 1980, winning 15 races, notably Ladbroke Chester Cup
(twice), Tote-Ebor Handicap and Doonside Cup; never on terms and eased
in straight when behind in Ladbroke Chester Cup only start of 1981 in May;
stays 2¼m but best form at up to 15f; acts on any going but well suited by some
give in the ground nowadays; best held up for late burst. *M. H. Easterby.*

SEAQUIN 3 b.f. Shiny Tenth 120–Sea Magic (Hardicanute 130) (1980 5fg⁴ —
5f 6g 6fg 7d 8fg* 9d³ 8d 1981 10.2d 7fg 10f 8fg 8fg 10fg 8d) neat filly; plater;
stays 9f; acts on a firm and a soft surface; tailed off in blinkers last 2 starts.
R. Baker.

SEA ROCKET 3 b.f. Saucy Kit 76–Another Wave (Haris II 93) (1980 7.2d —
8d 1981 12.2s 13.8f 12g) smallish filly; behind in varied company, including
selling; blinkered final start; sold 400 gns Newmarket Autumn Sales. *S. Norton.*

SEASON'S DELIGHT 2 b.f. Idiot's Delight 115–Jo (Jock Scot 121) (1981 —
5f 7fg) Jan 25; half-sister to useful hurdler Celtic Isle (by Celtic Cone); dam,
poor staying chaser, won 3 point-to-points; in rear in minor events at Wolverhampton and Warwick in August. *G. Price.*

SEASURF 3 b.f. Seaepic 100–On Demand 80 (Mandamus 120) (1980 7g* **106**
7g 7.3d² 1981 8g³ 8f 8fg³ 10g 8fg² 7f) lengthy, useful-looking filly; stayed on
well and put up an extremely good effort when 3¾ lengths third to Star Pastures
in Child Stakes at Newmarket in July on third outing; disappointing afterwards,
easily best effort when ¾-length second of 3 behind Vocalist in Atalanta Stakes
at Kempton the following month; should be suited by 1⅛m; acts on firm going
and a soft surface. *M. Jarvis.*

SECOND EVENT 4 b.f. Fine Blade 121–Gala Tess (El Gallo 122) (1980   **77**
8fg³ 10.8g³ 8.3fg 8.3f 8.3fg* 1981 10fg 11.7d 10fg 12s⁴ 12g* 10d) rangy
filly; fair handicapper; beat Silcakey in fine style by 2½ lengths at Leicester in
October; stays 1½m; acts on any going. *D. Kent.*

SECOND TIME LUCKY 6 ch.g. Shiny Tenth 120–Luscious Bit 87 (Ennis   **—**
128) (1980 NR 1981 7f) quite moderate at his best; lightly raced nowadays;
stays 1½m; acts on any going; sometimes blinkered; has worn bandages. *T.
Fairhurst.*

SECRET ARMY 3 b.g. Record Run 127–Gatecrasher (Will Somers 114§)   **58**
(1980 5f 5f 7f 6g 1981 7s 8g* 8g 8g² 8fg⁴ 8f 7fg 9f) compact gelding; ran best
races in handicaps at Ripon, when beating Dawn Redwood 2½ lengths in May
and when second to Hissing Sid in June (sweated up); suited by 1m; possibly
not at his best on firm ground; takes a strong hold and needs strong handling;
blinkered final outing at 2 yrs; sold 3,600 gns Doncaster November Sales,
reportedly to race in Sweden. *Miss S. Hall.*

SECRET EXPRESS 5 gr.h. Most Secret 119–Empress Donna 48 (Don II   **48**
123) (1980 6.5g 5g 5v 6v³ 6g* 6f² 6h 6f 6fg 6fg² 6d² 6fg 6fg 5f 6g 5d 6g⁴ 6v
1981 6s 6s³ 6fg 6g 5fg 6g⁴ 5g⁴ 6g 6f 6g³ 6f⁴ 5d 6s 6s) lightly-made horse; poor
sprint handicapper; best form at 6f; acts on any going; wears blinkers and sometimes bandages; has been ridden in spurs. *W. Stubbs.*

SECRET GILL 4 gr.f. Most Secret 119–Gill Breeze (Farm Walk 111) (1980   **86**
8s² 8g 8f³ 8g² 7s 8d³ 7d³ 7s* 1981 7d* 7.2s* 7g* 8g² 8g 7fg² 7g² 7f² 7d³ 7s²
7d² 7g*) lengthy, rather unfurnished filly; fair handicapper; successful at
Thirsk (twice) and Haydock in May and Doncaster in October; stays 1m;
acts on any going but is well suited by an easy surface; ridden by apprentice
B. Jones when gaining all her successes; consistent. *Miss S. Hall.*

SECRET HARBOUR 3 ch.c. Home Guard 129–Summer Day 117 (Golden   **64**
Cloud) (1980 5g⁴ 6g 7f 6d 1981 8.2s 7fg 8g 8g 7.6g³ 8fg³ 8fg 10fg 6g) strong,
well-made colt; third in maiden races at Lingfield and Salisbury; stays 1m;
sometimes sweats up; looked sour in blinkers fourth start; sold 4,000 gns Newmarket Autumn Sales. *C. Brittain.*

SECRET KNIGHT 2 b.g. Cavo Doro 124–Treasure Boat 54 (Hook Money 124)   **68**
(1981 6g 7f⁴ 7g 8f 8f 8.2s 8d) Mar 4; IR 3,700F, 6,000Y; strong, good sort;
good walker and mover; brother to 2 minor winners; dam poor maiden; ran
best race in nursery at Pontefract in September on fifth start, finishing 2¾ lengths
fifth of 12 to A.T.S. Prince after leading for 7f; suited by 1m; blinkered fifth
and sixth outings; dwelt seventh; sold 2,500 gns Doncaster October Sales.
M. H. Easterby.

SECRET PURSUIT 2 b.g. Ardoon 124–Shangara (Credo 123) (1981 6fg)   **71**
Mar 21; 5,600Y; small gelding; half-brother to useful middle-distance stayer
Pal's Bambino (by Pals Passage) and 2 winners over hurdles; dam won twice
over 5f at 2 yrs in Ireland; unquoted and burly when never-dangerous 5 lengths
sixth of 9 to Mummy's Game in minor event at Redcar in July; subsequently
gelded; will stay 1m+. *M. H. Easterby.*

SECRET SLAVE 2 b.g. Most Secret 119–May Slave (Arctic Slave 116) (1981   **—**
7fg) May 1; workmanlike gelding; third foal; dam behind in 3 novice hurdles;
unquoted and in need of race when tailed off in 15-runner minor event won by
Jiretta at Doncaster in July. *J. Blundell.*

SEGESTA 2 b.c. Blue Cashmere 129–Ann's Beam (Bold and Free 118) (1981   **—**
6fg 5g) Mar 19; 400Y; lightly-made colt; first foal; dam well behind both
starts; in rear in sellers at Doncaster and Beverley (all-aged event) in September.
J. Tierney.

SELBORNE LASS 5 b.m. Deep Run 119–Kilkis (Khalkis 127) (1980 NR   **—**
1981 11g) apparently of little account on flat though has won a selling hurdle;
sold 800 gns Ascot May Sales; resold same venue 875 gns in August. *W. Barrett.*

SELBORNE RECORD 3 ch.g. Record Run 127–Flatter Me (Palestine 133)   **63**
(1980 7g 8s 8s 1981 12.3g³ 12.3g 12d 12s³ 12d 10.2g2) rather leggy gelding;
placed in varied races, on final occasion in valuable seller at Doncaster in
November; gives impression he'll stay well; looked a bit light second start.
J. Etherington.

SENANG HATI 2 b. or br.c. Nonoalco 131–Sweet Sound 74 (Sound Track 132)   **—**
(1981 6fg 8s) Feb 18; 4,000Y; big, strong colt; half-brother to several winners,
including high-class 1973 2-y-o sprinter The Blues (by Majority Blue); dam ran

only at 2 yrs; behind in large fields in maiden race at Doncaster in June and minor event at Redcar in October (last of 29). *Denys Smith.*

SENORITA QUERIDA 2 b.f. Steel Heart 128–Senorita Rugby 86 (Forward **82** Pass) (1981 5g* 6f⁴ 5f) Jan 29; 5,000Y; attractive filly; second foal; sister to useful 3-y-o sprinter Steel Pass; dam won twice over 7f; came from well off the pace to win 13-runner minor event at Newmarket in May by ¾ length from Idle Days; 50/1, wasn't disgraced when 7 lengths eighth of 11 to Fly Baby in Queen Mary Stakes at Royal Ascot on third start; runs as though 7f will suit her; ridden by apprentice J. Finlayson first 2 outings. *N. Guest.*

SENTA'S GIRL 3 br.f. Averof 123–Senta 103 (Chanteur II 135) (1980 5f — 1981 8fg 8fg 10fg⁴ 12d 12fg 10fg⁴) rather a leggy filly; fourth in maiden races at Ascot and Beverley; mainly disappointing, although twice had stiff tasks; should stay 1½m; sold 8,000 gns Newmarket December Sales. *G. Huffer.*

SENT FOR YOU 2 b.c. Moulton 128–Questa Notte 104 (Midsummer Night II **81** 117) (1981 8g 8.2d³ 8d*) Apr 21; 24,000Y; second foal; half-brother to a winner in Italy by Sharpen Up; dam useful 6f performer; apprentice ridden, beat Indulgence a length in 14-runner maiden event at Edinburgh in October; stays 1m well and will probably get 1¼m; acts on a soft surface. *F. Durr.*

SEPARATE BID 3 b.c. Auction Ring 123–Fellow's Eyot (Roan Rocket 128) — (1980 6g³ 7fg 1981 8fg 6f) lightly-raced maiden; showed some ability at 2 yrs; possibly better suited by 6f than 7f; retained 1,050 gns Newmarket Autumn Sales. *I. Walker.*

SEPTAGON 3 b. or br.g. Condorcet–Septima 82 (Primera 131) (1980 NR — 1981 12g) 300F, 8,500Y; lengthy gelding; half-brother to 3 winners here and abroad; dam, half-sister to good 1964 2-y-o Leonardo, won over 1¼m; soundly-beaten seventh of 14 behind Brave Hussar in minor race at Kempton in May, only outing. *J. Hindley.*

SEPT ETOILE 3 b.c. Auction Ring 123–Musical Watch (Tudor Melody 129) **92** (1980 6d 6g 6g 8.5s* 8s⁴ 1981 10s³ 9d² 10g² 7.6d2 8d* 8fg³ 8f² 8.5fg³ 10f* 8g) strong, useful sort; favourite when winning apprentice race at Phoenix Park in June and handicap on same course in August, in latter beating Prom comfortably by 1½ lengths; placed in varied company on most other starts, including when 2 lengths third to Tellurano in Coolmore Hello Gorgeous Stakes at the Curragh on sixth outing; stays 1¼m; acts on any going. *D. Weld, Ireland.*

SERIOUSLY FOLKS (CAN) 2 b.c. Kamaraan 129–Hyacinth (O'Calaway) — (1981 8s 7d) June 18; $11,000Y; brother to a winner, and half-brother to another; dam winner of claiming races at up to 9f; soundly beaten in maiden race at Warwick (ninth of 17 to Mrs Currie) and minor event at Chepstow (eighth of 13 to Parthia's Picture) in October. *H. Candy.*

SERPICO 3 br.g. Drumbeg 94–Porringer (Vigo 130) (1980 5v² 5s⁴ 5fg⁴ 5f — 1981 8v 8.2s) leggy, narrow gelding; poor plater; blinkered final outing. *J. Berry.*

SERPINA 3 b.f. Saritamer 130–A Deux 80 (Crepello 136) (1980 6fg² 5g 1981 — 7s 6fg 6g) neat filly; good walker and mover; disappointing maiden; should stay at least 7f; blinkered final start; sold 720 gns Newmarket July Sales. *F. J. Houghton.*

SERVUS 2 b.f. Sandford Lad 133–Game Laura (Relic) (1981 6fg 7f 7g 7g **62** 8.2s) Mar 17; IR 4,000F, 2,300Y; small, rather lightly-made filly; good mover; half-sister to 2 winners, including Caven Mill (by Clever Fella), successful here and in Belgium; dam half-sister to The Go-Between; plater; stays 7f; blinkered last 3 outings. *A. Hide.*

SETKATDEU (FR) 2 ch.c. Viceregal–Galiote (Hauban 132) (1981 4s 5.5d* **114** 7g* 5.5d 7.5fg⁴ 9d 10v) Feb 8; 62,000 francs Y (approx £6,200); second foal; half-brother to French middle-distance winner Sheshoon's Son (by Sheshoon); dam 2-y-o 6f and 7f winner; won minor event in June and 80,000-franc Prix la Fleche in July, both at Evry; prominent in 3 valuable races afterwards, receiving 4-lb beating when fourth to Natagai in Prix des Yearlings at Deauville, 6-lb beating when fifth to Trigonome in Prix Saint-Roman at Longchamp and 1-lb beating when fifth behind Beau Pretender in Prix de Conde, again at Longchamp; stays 1¼m; probably acts on any going but goes well on heavy; blinkered first outing. *R. Touflan, France.*

SET N' MATCH 2 ch.f. Music Boy 124–Tennis Ball 61 (Charlottown 127) **64** (1981 5d⁴ 5d 6f 7fg 6d) Mar 19; 4,000Y; good-bodied filly; first foal; dam second in 5.8f seller at 2 yrs; no better than plating class; sold 400 gns Newmarket Autumn Sales. *B. Hobbs.*

SET

SET SAIL 2 b.f. Alpenkonig–Sayonara (Birkhahn) (1981 6g 6f 8fg 8d 7g) **64**
Mar 13; small filly; half-sister to 2 good winners in Germany, including German
2,000 Guineas winner Swazi (by Herero); dam, winner of 5 races in Germany
and second in German Oaks, is half-sister to German Derby winner Stuyvesant;
poor maiden; sold 1,600 gns Doncaster October Sales. *E. Weymes.*

SETTA SPRATT 3 b.f. Firestreak 125–Meg Swerie (Whistler 129) (1980 5g —
1981 6g 7s 7fg 6g 5fg 6fg) small, plain filly; poor form in varied company,
including selling; unseated rider third start; sold 300 gns Ascot November
Sales. *S. Matthews.*

SETTIMINO (USA) 3 b.c. Exclusive Native–Lucretia Bori (Bold Ruler) **62§**
(1980 7g 8fg 1981 10d 8f² 8fg³ 7.6fg³ 6f 6fg 8fg) strong, short-legged colt;
placed in maiden races and a handicap but has his own ideas about the game;
stays 1m (had stiff task and needed race when tried at 1¼m); wears blinkers
and has worn a hood as well. *F. J. Houghton.*

SETTLED 2 b.f. Blue Cashmere 129–Fair Helen (Hopeful Venture 125) (1981 **61**
5s* 5g* 5g* 5g) Mar 23; 1,000Y; lengthy, rather leggy filly; fourth foal; dam
never ran; bought in after justifying favouritism in sellers at Nottingham in
April (1,150 gns) and Bath in May (1,050 gns); claimed out of Mrs J. Reavey's
stable when winning 9-runner claiming race at Brighton later in May by 1½
lengths from Sweet For Days, but ran last of 6 in £3,800 race at Ayr in June
(bandaged near-hind); will stay 6f. *W. Stubbs.*

SEVEN BRIDGES ROAD 2 ch.f. Malinowski 123–Welshpool 75 (Henry the **71**
Seventh 125) (1981 7d⁴ 7g) Apr 30; 9,000Y; half-sister to 3 winners here and
abroad, including 7f and 1m winner Africano (by African Sky); dam ran in
England and Ireland; 5½ lengths fourth of 19 behind My Destiny in maiden
event at Yarmouth in September; didn't have clear run when second favourite
for small race at Catterick the following month, finishing about 4 lengths sixth
of 15 to Spring Lane; will stay at least 1m. *H. Cecil.*

SEVEN HEARTS 5 ch.h. Some Hand 119–Vienna Love 68 (Vienna 127) **93**
(1980 8f 8d² 8d³ 8g² 8g⁴ 8g* 8fg² 10fg³ 8s² 1981 8g³ 8s² 8f 8fg⁴ 8fg 8fg² 8f
10d 8d² 9s* 8.2s³) strong horse; good mover; fairly useful handicapper; went
down by 1½ lengths to Fine Sun in valuable apprentice handicap at York in
October but was hampered by winner and awarded race; had run well several
previous starts; stays 9f; seems to act on any going; wears blinkers nowadays;
often sweats up; suitable mount for an apprentice; sometimes wears a boot on
off-fore; consistent; sold privately and will be trained by K. Brassey. *W.
Hastings-Bass.*

SEVEN SEAS (FR) 3 b.f. Riverman 131–Ya Ya 84 (Primera 131) (1980 NR **76**
1981 7g 7g² 7f* 9f³ 11.1fg⁴ 10d² 10s⁴ 11s* 10d⁴) leggy filly; half-sister to 7f to
10.6f winner Fluellen (by Welsh Pageant); dam, half-sister to Park Hill Stakes
winner African Dancer, stayed well; successful in weakly-contested maiden
race at Chepstow in July (made all) and handicap at Newbury in October; gave
trouble at start and seemed reluctant to take hold of her bit in latter, but cruised
into lead 2f out and won by 8 lengths from Commonty; stays 11f; acts on any
going, but clearly goes well on soft; has plenty of ability but evidently has
more than her share of temperament too. *H. Wragg.*

SEVERIANO (USA) 3 ro. or gr.c. Native Royalty–Erin O'Connell (Dondeen **103**
123) (1980 5f 5g* 5g* 5g⁴ 5d³ 6.3s 5g³ 1981 5d 6d* 6s 5s 6.3fg 7.9f³) lengthy,
quite attractive colt; about 4 lengths fifth to smooth winner King of Spain
in £3,700 event at Haydock in April on reappearance; beat Lady Blackfoot
by 2½ lengths in 16-runner Castleknock Sprint Stakes at Phoenix Park the
following month, best subsequent effort; best form at 6f, but not disgraced
at 1m on final start (July); probably acts on any going. *M. Kauntze, Ireland.*

SEVERN SOVEREIGN 2 b.c. Fischio–Nimble Star (Space King 115) (1981 —
5s 8d) Mar 24; second foal; half-brother to 3-y-o middle-distance winner
Oratavo (by The Brianstan); dam never ran; unquoted when distant sixth of
11 to Sonseri in maiden race at Wolverhampton in October; tailed off in similar
event over 1m at Leicester next time out. *D. Wintle.*

SEW NICE 2 br.f. Tower Walk 130–Sew and Sew 96 (Hard Tack 111§) (1981 **57**
5v 5v 5g) May 30; fair sort; second living foal; dam won twice over 5f at
2 yrs; only poor form in maiden and minor events. *E. Weymes.*

SEXTANT 3 b.f. Star Appeal 133–Fluke 117 (Grey Sovereign 128§) (1980 NR **98**
1981 10g² 12f³ 10.1fg* 12d 10f² 10d*) small, well-made filly; fifth foal; dam
won from 5f to 7f, and is half-sister to high-class 1½m to 1¾m performer Buoy
and Oaks winner Bireme; easy winner of minor events at Windsor in July

768

(by 5 lengths from Fair of Face) and Nottingham in September (by 8 lengths from Only A Shanty); ran in better company on her other starts, finishing second behind Home On The Range in minor event at Newbury and Sean Graham Fillies Stakes at Kempton, 2½ lengths third of 7 behind Rhein Bridge in Lancashire Oaks at Haydock, and about 11 lengths sixth to Ma Femme in Galtres Stakes at York; stayed 1½m; probably acted on any going; blinkered last 2 starts; retired to stud. *R. Hern.*

SEYMOUR LADY 3 b.f. Malicious–Asheldham Lady (Typhoon 125) (1980 5s 5s² 5s³ 5fg 6g² 6fg 6g⁴ 7f 6s² 6fg 6g 8d 8.2s⁴ 1981 8g 11.7fg 10.2h) leggy filly; plater at 2 yrs; no form in non-sellers in 1981; should stay 1m; best form with some give in the ground; sold out of G. Kindersley's stable 650 gns Ascot May Sales. *N. Mitchell.* —

SHAAB 6 b.h. Busted 134–Chieftain Girl (Chieftain) (1980 16s 16fg³ 14fg⁴ 16f* 16fg² 16fg 16fg³ 16g⁴ 16g 16.9f* 16f* 16g 17.1d 18d 1981 16s 16fg* 18.4d 16.9s 16g 16f⁴ 16g 16fg⁴ 16fg⁴) fair staying handicapper; won at Warwick in April; acts on any going but is particularly well suited by firm; one paced and is suited by a strong gallop. *J. Benstead.* 81

SHAADY 2 b.c. Habitat 134–L'Eaulne (Busted 134) (1981 5fg* 5f³) Feb 5; 30,000Y; strong, compact, deep-bodied colt; fourth reported foal; dam, useful performer in France, won over 1¼m; looked a very useful colt in the making when justifying favouritism in 19-runner maiden race at Nottingham in June, drawing clear in final 1½f to win by 4 lengths from Cheap Seats; didn't move well to start when 13/8-on for 5-runner Chesterfield Stakes at Newmarket the following month and finished only third, 5 lengths behind Custer, after dwelling at start; will be better suited by 6f+; gives strong impression he's not at his best on really firm ground. *M. Stoute.* 93+

SHACKIN BRIG 4 b.g. New Brig 120–Tillside (Lucky Brief 128) (1980 NR 1981 12s) soon tailed off when last in maiden race at Beverley in April. *R. Ward.* —

SHADEMAH 3 b.f. Thatch 136–Shamim (Le Haar 126) (1980 NR 1981 7g² 8.5g² 7f* 8g 7.2fg² 8.2v* 8s* 8g) sturdy filly; third foal; half-sister to 2 French winners, including high-class middle-distance colt Shakapour (by Kalamoun); dam, half-sister to high-class 1¼m to 2m performer Kamaraan, won over 1m at 2 yrs; successful in maiden race at Thirsk in July and handicaps at Haydock and Newbury in October; gained first 2 wins with great ease and was never in much danger when beating Corn Street by 2½ lengths on last-named course; may stay 1¼m; acts on any going; hung quite badly under pressure fourth start. *M. Stoute.* 88

SHADEY DOVE 7 b.m. Deadly Nightshade 107–Red Dove (All Red 110) (1980 NR 1981 12g⁴ 13.3s⁴ 16.1s* 22.2f 12.2fg 12.3fg 16fg 16h 16s) winner several times over hurdles; stayed on well to beat Russian George decisively by 1½ lengths in Lymm Stakes at Haydock in May; had run respectably previous 2 starts; suited by a test of stamina; probably needs some give in the ground; game. *G. Price.* 81 d

SHADOWS LENGTHEN 2 b. or br.f. Star Appeal 133–Sweet Hour 91 (Primera 131) (1981 6d² 6f³ 8fg⁴) Apr 11; neat, strong filly; half-sister to 2 winners, including useful middle-distance performer Lake Naivasha (by Blakeney); dam 2-y-o 5f and 6f winner; in frame in maiden and minor events at Haydock, Ripon and Leicester; will stay 1¼m. *R. Hern.* 73

SHADY DRIVE 3 b.f. Warpath 113–Counter Coup (Busted 134) (1980 7g 1981 8d 8fg 10.2g) no worthwhile form in maiden events and a handicap. *J. Hill.* —

SHADY NOOK 6 b.g. Green God 128–Pilica's Melody (Tudor Melody 129) (1980 11f* 12fg³ 12s* 12f⁴ 14g⁴ 11.7f³ 13.3fg² 1981 11s 12f 11.7fg³) useful handicapper at his best; modest third of 6 to Royal Fountain in minor event at Windsor in August, his best effort in 1981; stays 13f; acts on any going; often sweats up; has a good turn of foot; sold to S. Pattemore 19,000 gns Ascot October Sales. *J. Dodd.* 93

SHAFTESBURY 5 b.h. Prince de Galles 125–Belle-Dame 92 (Primera 131) (1980 14f³ 16fg 14d⁴ 12f² 12fg* 14.7g² 14g* 14f* 14.6g⁴ 1981 12s 13.4d³ 14f* 12f 12f* 14d³ 14.6fg 16g⁴ 12s³ 12s) well-made, useful sort; has an enlarged off-hind hock; not the best of movers in his slower paces; smart handicapper; successful in quite valuable events at York in June (made all in 2-runner race) and Thirsk in August (made most and rallied very gamely when headed to beat Mac's Delight a short head); also ran creditably on several occasions, notably 114

769

Michael Sobell Handicap, York—Shaftesbury beats sole opponent Flying Officer very comfortably

when excellent 4 lengths third to Protection Racket in Tote-Ebor Handicap at York in August on sixth start; stays 1¾m; acts on any going but is well suited by top-of-the-ground; genuine and consistent; suited by a strong gallop and often makes the running; sold 28,000 gns Newmarket December Sales. *M. Stoute.*

SHA'LAN 3 b.c. Arch Sculptor 123–Aurelie (Aureole 132) (1980 6fg 7fg 7s 8d* 1981 8s⁴ 10fg 8.2d⁴ 8s 8g* 8.2g 7fg 8d) well-made colt; beaten a neck by Rushmoor in handicap at Salisbury in July, but was bumped inside last furlong and placings were subsequently reversed; suited by 1m (not entirely disgraced over further); blinkered last 3 starts, running respectably on first occasion; sold 4,500 gns Ascot November Sales, reportedly to race in Italy. *G. Hunter.*   **77**

SHALIMAR 3 ch.g. Amber Rama 133–Enchanting 83 (Behistoun 131) (1980 NR 1981 10.2f 13fg² 14.6f*) big, lengthy gelding; second foal; dam won over 10.6f; won modest maiden event by neck from Graf Traun at Ripon in August; suited by 1¾m. *C. Thornton.*   **68**

SHALLAAL (USA) 2 ch.c. Honest Pleasure–Grass Court (Herbager 136) (1981 7fg⁴) Apr 17; $175,000Y; strong, well-made, deep-girthed colt; second foal; dam, unplaced 7 times, is sister to smart American stayer Outdoors; 14/1, made a highly promising debut when 5 lengths fourth of 5 to Padalco in £4,700 event at Newmarket in July, getting behind early on but then running on in excellent style, without jockey ever resorting to his whip, until lack of fitness told in final furlong; looked a good colt in the making but unfortunately pulled a muscle and was lame afterwards. *J. Dunlop.*   **76 p**

SHALL WE TELL 3 b.g. Guillaume Tell 121–Muraka (Off Key 121) (1980 7g 1981 7g 9s) well-made, quite attractive gelding; lightly raced and no form in maiden and minor events; sold 925 gns Ascot November Sales. *D. Kent.*   **—**

SHALOTRA 5 gr.g. Redundant 120–Long Hill 91 (Vigo 130) (1980 NR 1981 13d) poor maiden on flat though has won over hurdles; probably stays 1m; acts on a firm surface. *T. Craig.*   **—**

770

Mr J. A. McCaughey's "Shaftesbury"

SHALWA 3 b.f. Broxted 120–Hopeful Gift 95 (Bounteous 125) (1980 5g² 5.8f² — 5.8h* 7fg³ 8fg 6d 1981 6s 6s 6fg) quite well-made filly; had stiffish tasks and didn't recover her 2-y-o form; suited by 7f at 2 yrs; acts on hard going; trained by P. M. Taylor until after second outing; sent to USA. *G. Huffer.*

SHAMBALA 2 gr.c. Sandford Lad 133–Hialeah (Snob 130) (1981 5g 6fg) Feb — 17; IR 5,000F, 11,000Y; half-brother to minor winners in Ireland and Belgium; dam placed in Ireland; in rear in minor event at Lingfield in June (dwelt) and 11-runner maiden race at Yarmouth in August. *F. Durr.*

SHAMROCK GIRL 3 b.f. Workboy 123–Whistlewych 40 (Whistler 129) (1980 — NR 1981 7fg 8f 7.2f 7f 6g 6d) strong filly; half-sister to 3 winners, including useful 1976 sprinting 2-y-o Feudal Wytch (by Tribal Chief); dam of little account; little worthwhile form; needs further than 6f; ran wide entering straight when ridden by 7-lb claimer on second outing. *J. Carr.*

SHAMROCK NAIL 2 b.c. He Loves Me 120–Come Aboard 82 (Whistler 129) **76** (1981 5d 6d 6fg 6d 5fg 5d 5v 5d²) Apr 27; 20,000Y; compact, quite attractive colt; half-brother to several winners, including useful 1976 French 2-y-o 5.5f winner Deep Deep (by Gulf Pearl); dam sprinter; ran best race when neck second of 13 to Hazim in maiden race at Redcar in October; should stay 6f; raced alone when blinkered seventh outing. *R. Hollinshead.*

SHANGARRY 3 br.g. Pitskelly 122–Jean Armour 88 (Delirium 126) (1980 5s **86** 7d² 7g⁴ 7g* 7f² 8g 1981 8s* 8s³ 10d) well-made gelding; did well physically from 2 yrs to 3 yrs and made a successful reappearance in handicap at Doncaster in March, quickening clear under strong riding in last furlong to beat Lord Wimpy by 3 lengths; ran better subsequent race on next start; stays 1m; acts on any going; exported to Hong Kong. *R. Price.*

SHARAVOGUE 4 gr.f. Silly Season 127–Charter Island 88 (Runnymede 123) — (1980 7g 6g 7fg 6g 7d 6g 1981 7f 8f) useful sort; well beaten in varied company, including claiming; has worn blinkers. *C. Williams.*

SHA

SHARED MOMENT 2 br.f. Bay Express 132–Saintly Angel 87 (So Blessed 130) **94**
(1981 5d⁴ 5g³ 5f 5fg* 5g 5d 5h²) Mar 16; IR 4,000Y; neat filly; first foal; dam
lightly-raced 2-y-o 5f winner; 11/10-favourite when making all to win 15-runner
maiden race at Windsor in June; had run well on previous outing when 5½ lengths
sixth of 11 to Fly Baby in Queen Mary Stakes at Royal Ascot; creditable 1½
lengths second of 10 to Mayo Moonlight under top weight in nursery at Chepstow
in August; unlikely to stay beyond 5f; suited by fast ground. *B. Swift.*

SHARED SECRET 2 ch.g. Most Secret 119–Mountain Child 70 (Mountain Call —
125) (1981 6f) June 6; workmanlike gelding; first reported foal; dam quite
moderate at 2 yrs; 10/1 and in need of race, pushed along throughout when ninth
of 16 to Queensbury Star in seller at Doncaster in July. *C. Booth.*

SHARELLE 3 b.f. Relko 136–Damiana 84 (Mourne 126) (1980 8g 8d 10s 1981 —
12d 10d 8s 12g 10.1fg) big, well-made filly; has shown a little ability in varied
company, although was well beaten in a seller on final start; probably not at her
best on a sharp track; claimed £2,400 last outing. *P. Cundell.*

SHARK SONG 3 gr.f. Song 132–Sylvanecte 70 (Silver Shark 129) (1980 6g⁴ **98**
6fg² 6d* 5d* 1981 7fg² 8g 6g² 6f 6fg³ 6fg including 6f 8g* 8.5f⁴ 8.5g* 9g*)
strong, attractive, good sort; second in Ladbrokes Nell Gwyn Stakes at Newmarket in April (beaten 2½ lengths by impressive winner Fairy Footsteps) and
in £7,900 handicap on same course in May (went down by ¾ length to Sharp
Venita); not disgraced on her other starts over here, including when eighth of
14 behind Fairy Footsteps in 1,000 Guineas, also at Newmarket, seventh of 16
behind The Quiet Bidder in Cork and Orrery Stakes at Royal Ascot and 2½
lengths third to Integrity in minor event at Newbury in July; subsequently sent
to race in USA and won allowance races there at Belmont (two) in September
and Aqueduct in November; effective at 6f and evidently stays 9f; seems to act
on any going. *J. Hindley.*

SHARLIE'S WIMPY 2 ch.c. Tumble Wind–Sweet Sharlie 77 (Fighting Charlie **98**
127) (1981 5.8g³ 5g* 6fg² 5g³ 5fg 6fg³ 7fg 6d 6g) May 6; IR 11,500Y; strong,
most attractive colt; good mover; third foal; half-brother to 5f to 7f winner
Effect (by Martinmas); dam won over 1m at 3 yrs; ran on very gamely to beat
Tender King a neck in £3,100 Berkshire Stakes at Newbury in June; subsequently
ran very well in several good races, finishing third to My Dad Tom in Star
Stakes at Sandown in July, third to Custer in Washington Singer Stakes at
Newbury in August and sixth to Hays in Mill Reef Stakes, again at Newbury, in
September on eighth outing; stays 6f but didn't run up to his best when tried
over 7f (became upset in stalls after a long delay at start); yet to tackle really
firm or soft ground. *P. Cole.*

SHAROKEE (USA) 2 ch.f. Key To The Kingdom–Sharomar (To Market) **75**
(1981 5fg⁴ 5f³ 5s*) Feb 7; $58,000Y; well-made, attractive filly; half-sister to
2 winners, including sprint stakes winner Mr Exclusive (by Iron Ruler); dam
stakes-placed sister to stakes winners Coppahaunk and Sharon Market; having
first race for over 2 months when winning modest maiden event at Lingfield in
October by a neck from Churra; will stay 6f; hung badly on very firm going on
second outing. *M. Stoute.*

SHARP CELESTE 4 ch.f. Sharpen Up 127–Celeste 83 (Sing Sing 134) (1980 **81**
6fg 6fg 6d 7g³ 5.8g⁴ 7fg² 6fg⁴ 8g³ 5g* 8g 7g* 7g* 1981 7fg³ 7.6g⁴ 8.5g 8fg 7g²
8d 7g*) small filly; ridden by 5-lb claimer unable to draw his allowance when
gamely beating Azaam by ½ length in £4,300 handicap at Newmarket in October;
stays 1m; acts on a firm surface; suitable mount for a boy. *A. Pitt.*

SHARP DANCER 3 ch.f. Sharpen Up 127–Georgia (Hopeful Venture 125) —
(1980 5g 5.1fg 5g 5f 1981 8fg 7f 8.2s 6g) compact filly; plating-class maiden;
should be suited by 7f+; sold 400 gns Newmarket Autumn Sales. *E. Eldin.*

SHARP END 3 b.c. Sharpen Up 127–Death Ray 100 (Tamerlane 128) (1980 **79**
6d² 7f 1981 8d 6g⁴ 6f 8fg* 8g³ 8d²) big, well-made colt; beat Aventura by
2 lengths in maiden race at Salisbury in September, first outing for 2 months;
also in frame in handicaps; suited by 1m and will probably stay further; acts
on a firm and a soft surface (possibly not at his best on very firm); best in blinkers;
sold 7,200 gns Newmarket Autumn Sales. *R. Hern.*

SHARP MELODY 2 b.f. Hot Spark 126–Tulchan 95 (Tudor Melody 129) **57**
(1981 5s² 5d 5fg² 5d⁴ 5d 6f 7f) Feb 19; third foal; dam won over 6f and 1¼m;
second twice, going down by 3 lengths to Windy Lad in minor event at Folkestone in March and by 4 lengths to Here's Sue in 12-runner maiden race at
Warwick in April; soundly beaten in seller on sixth outing; form only at 5f;
blinkered final start. *R. Hoad.*

772

SHARPO 4 ch.c. Sharpen Up 127–Moiety Bird (Falcon 131) (1980 5f* **132**
6g² 6d³ 5g* 5g² 5f² 1981 5g³ 5s* 5f 5d* 5d² 7v)

At the time, the withdrawal of lot 320 from the 1979 Newmarket Autumn Sales didn't cause much of a stir since the colt concerned, Sharpo, had run just once, finishing well beaten in a maiden race at Newbury in September. In the event his connections have every right to feel relieved that they took him out of the sale. Though Sharpo fractured a bone in a hind leg after leaving the stalls awkwardly at Newbury, the injury healed over the winter and during the past two seasons he has developed into a tip-top sprinter, becoming the first horse to annex the William Hill Sprint Championship in successive years since Right Boy won it as the Nunthorpe Stakes in 1958 and 1959.

Both the races Sharpo won in 1981 he took in smashing style. Following a slightly disappointing run behind the tremendously speedy Standaan in the Palace House Stakes at Newmarket in May, in which he never threatened to get to the winner at any stage and finished third, Sharpo started at odds on eight days later in the Prix de Saint-Georges at Longchamp. The Saint-Georges has been something of a graveyard for favourites in recent years but Sharpo made no mistake, catching and passing Standaan by halfway and striding clear to beat Wicked Lady easily by two and a half lengths. Standaan came in third with the 1980 Prix d'Arenberg and Prix du Petit Couvert winner Greenway, having her only run of the year, fourth. This success was the fourth in the race for Sharpo's owner and trainer—Constans became almost a standing dish for them in the early 'seventies, winning from 1972 to 1974—but it didn't tell us anything new about Sharpo. Wicked Lady wasn't one of the best European sprinters by any means, for she subsequently finished unplaced in the Prix du Gros Chene, Prix de Meautry and Prix de Seine-et-Oise, while the other runners subsequently managed to pick up only one race between them.

A seller up until 1921, the Nunthorpe Stakes was radically elevated in status the following season since when such great sprinters as Mumtaz Mahal, Gold Bridge, The Bug, Abernant, Right Boy, Floribunda and Deep Diver have appeared on its roll of honour. Under the sponsorship of the William Hill Organisation who took it over in 1976, its added money has increased considerably with the result that it is now the most valuable five-furlong event in Europe. The 1981 race was worth over £5,000 more than the King's Stand Stakes and it was arguably contested by a better field. The King's Stand winner Marwell was odds on; Moorestyle, reverting to the minimum trip for the first time since winning the 1980 Prix de l'Abbaye from Sharpo, started second favourite; the seven other runners included the Tote Stewards' Cup winner Crews Hill, the King George Stakes winner King of Spain, Standaan and Sharpo himself. The last-named was freely available at 14/1, largely because he had run poorly in the King's Stand on his previous appearance, being one of the first beaten and dropping back rapidly in the last two furlongs to finish last but one. This lamentable display was explained by the fact that Sharpo had been badly jarred up by the firm going and apparently his participation at York was in some doubt until his trainer knew there would be some give in the ground. Sharpo put up a majestic performance. Always going well as his jockey Eddery elected to track Moorestyle while Standaan set his customary blistering gallop, he was switched outside a furlong and a half from home and showed a scintillating burst of speed to sweep into the lead from Marwell. Nudged along with hands and heels, he went on to win by two and a half lengths from the filly with Moorestyle a length and a half away third, Crews Hill fourth and King of Spain fifth. Moorestyle almost certainly found five furlongs too sharp for him at four, but even leaving him out of account Sharpo had dealt with nearly all the best English sprinters in a cavalier manner and it was difficult to envisage his losing his next engagement, the Prix de l'Abbaye de Longchamp.

The Prix de l'Abbaye once again revealed the paucity of good French sprinters. Of the original thirty entries, only ten were trained in France, the remainder coming from England (thirteen), Ireland (six) and Denmark (one). The final ten runners included only two French, and the first four in the betting were all English—Sharpo a short-priced favourite then Marwell, Rabdan and Runnett. The ground was ideal for Sharpo, on the soft side of good, but not for the first time in his career he lost a race he was widely expected to win. Astonishingly for one who had travelled smoothly throughout at York he seemed unable to go the pace in the early stages as the Danish colt Music Streak took them along. Left with plenty to do from halfway, he ran on strongly under strenuous riding from Eddery but the post came too soon and he failed by a neck to reach Marwell, a length ahead of Rabdan. On his final start Sharpo

Prix de Saint-Georges, Longchamp—odds-on Sharpo strides clear to beat Wicked Lady with the other British challenger Standaan third

was given the chance of running over seven furlongs for the first time in the Prix de la Foret at Longchamp again. None too well away, he quickly made ground approaching the home turn and looked sure to gain a place halfway up the straight until his stamina failed completely in the last hundred and fifty yards; he eventually finished fifth to Moorestyle.

Sharpo (ch.c. 1977)	Sharpen Up (ch 1969)	Atan (ch 1961)	Native Dancer / Mixed Marriage
		Rocchetta (ch 1961)	Rockefella / Chambiges
	Moiety Bird (ch 1971)	Falcon (b 1964)	Milesian / Pretty Swift
		Gaska (ch 1961)	Gilles de Retz / Sally Deans

Sharpen Up sired a number of good winners besides Sharpo, notably Kris and Sharpman, before being exported to America in 1980. He is standing at Gainesway Farm where his 1982 fee of 50,000 dollars will be the same as that for the first-season stallion Cresta Rider. This is an interesting illustration of the extent to which a fashionable pedigree can seemingly make an entirely-unproven stallion as attractive a proposition as a tried and tested one. Sharpo's dam, Moiety Bird, is an unraced daughter of Gaska, a very useful two-year-old who has spent most of her stud career in the States where she has produced several minor winners. Moiety Bird's other runners to date haven't shown anything like Sharpo's ability—Demi Feu (by Firestreak) won at up to a mile and a quarter but is now thoroughly temperamental while the three-year-old Kalami (by Averof) finished well beaten on all his three starts in 1981. The third dam, Sally Deans, had a good record as a broodmare after winning twice at a mile, foaling seven winners, four of them by Red God. Three of her Red God foals have left their mark, Yellow God and St Alphage at stud as well as on the track (though the former is now in Japan and the latter died in 1976)

William Hill Sprint Championship, York—Sharpo returns to his best to win Europe's most valuable sprint; Marwell is second and Moorestyle third

and Redowa by becoming the dam of the very smart Red Regent whose first crop contained the 1981 Middle Park winner Cajun.

With a good pedigree and top-class form Sharpo has the right credentials to put his name on the map when retired to stud; that will be not just yet however for he stays in training. An attractive, close-coupled colt and a good mover, he did well physically from three to four. If he is able to reproduce his York running the three-year-olds will find him a very tough nut to crack over five or six furlongs provided the ground is easy—though he ran two fine races on firm at three we doubt whether he will be risked on such a surface again. A very relaxed individual, he goes well for Eddery. *J. Tree.*

SHARP SINGER (USA)   2 b.c. The Minstrel 135–Cutty (Smart)   (1981 8s* **117** p 7d*)

In 1976 the Larkspur Stakes at Leopardstown fell to The Minstrel, who went on to win the William Hill Dewhurst Stakes, the Derby, Irish Sweeps Derby and the King George VI and Queen Elizabeth Diamond Stakes before retiring to stand alongside his sire, the famed Northern Dancer, at the Windfields Farm, Maryland. The Minstrel's first runners reached the races in 1981, performing so splendidly that The Minstrel now more than ever looks a ready-made replacement for his ageing sire. From only twenty-nine foals he sired four winners in North America, All In Mist, Devastating Lady, Espy and Le Point de Mire; two winners in France, the Boutin-trained fillies Mirea and Rythmique; and no fewer than eight winners in Britain and Ireland, namely Afghan, winner of the valuable Birdcatcher Nursery under 9-7; Crusoe, successful on his only start; Longleat, winner of a valuable non-pattern race in Ireland; Peterhof, winner of both the Curragh and Flying Childers Stakes; the eight-length Curragh winner Raconteur; the Newbury winner Sans Blague; Solaboy, winner of the Champagne Stakes at Salisbury; and the unbeaten Sharp Singer. Appropriately enough the highest weighted of his three representatives in the Tote European Free Handicap is Sharp Singer, winner of the 1981 Larkspur Stakes.

Like The Minstrel before him Sharp Singer came to the Larkspur Stakes the winner of his only previous start. The Larkspur, which used to be run towards the end of September on the same day as the Joe McGrath Memorial Stakes, was moved back a month in 1981 to October 24th. Coincidentally Sharp Singer made his debut on the day of the Joe McGrath in the Oldbawn Maiden Stakes, the race Critique won the previous year before going on to finish second in the Grand Criterium. The 1981 Oldbawn was split into two thirteen-runner divisions. The first produced such an impressive display from Golden Fleece that he was subsequently rated inferior only to Achieved in the Irish Classification, and there was also plenty to like about Sharp Singer's performance in his division. The fast early pace had many off the bit by halfway but Sharp Singer never had difficulty lying up close behind the leaders, took over in front early in the straight and needed pushing out only with hands and heels to win by three lengths from Lennoxbrook. Promising though Sharp Singer's effort was he started only third favourite in a ten-strong field for the

Larkspur Stakes, Leopardstown—a comfortable win for Sharp Singer; Sun Worship finishes second well clear of the rest

Mr R. E. Sangster's "Sharp Singer"

Larkspur behind Sun Worship, a close fourth in the National Stakes and a short-head second in the Ashford Castle Stakes, and the filly Princess Seal. Princess Seal hadn't been out since finishing a short-head second in the Queen Mary Stakes in June and was done with early in the straight. Sun Worship proved a tougher rival, going to the front soon after the start, but he had no answer when Sharp Singer came to challenge turning into the straight. Sharp Singer soon left him toiling, and ran home four lengths clear with the rest, headed by Remanded who'd won a nursery on his last outing, at least eight lengths further behind.

Sharp Singer (USA) (b.c. May 26, 1979)	The Minstrel (ch 1974)	Northern Dancer (b 1961)	Nearctic
			Natalma
		Fleur (b 1964)	Victoria Park
			Flaming Page
	Cutty (b 1969)	Smart (ch 1959)	Thinking Cap
			Enchanted Eve
		Real Sincere (b 1955)	Brookfield
			Blue Charmer

The top half of Sharp Singer's pedigree is as fashionable as any in the world, while the other half is contrastingly obscure. Looking at the bottom line, the third dam Blue Charmer failed to reach the first three in any of her four races and her seven winners, none of them placed in a stakes race, collectively earned only 77,807 dollars. Real Sincere's contribution to that total was 14,180 dollars from four wins, a second and a third, and of her eight winners only Sharp Singer's dam Cutty was of stakes class. Unraced at two, Cutty won three times in each of the next three seasons and at four won a division of the Osunitas Stakes over eight and a half furlongs on turf at Del Mar. Although a stakes winner—one of only four by her sire—Cutty was no more than useful. There must therefore be a good story behind how and why she came to be mated with The Minstrel—her other foals are by stallions who wouldn't be mentioned in the same breath.

Her first, the seven-furlong and a mile claiming-race winner Whisky Galore, was by Cavamore whose fee at the time was a mere 750 dollars; her second foal Ashendene, a son of the once-raced, once-unplaced Stoic, was sold for only 8,500 dollars as a yearling before going on to win in claiming company; her third reported produce is Sharp Singer; and her next, a yearling colt by the little-known Good Behaving, fetched only 15,000 dollars when sold at Keeneland in 1981. It was a shrewd move to consign Sharp Singer to the Goffs Premier Yearling Sales in Ireland where, as the only representative of his sire, he sold for 100,000 guineas.

Sharp Singer has already shown himself a smart colt so the relative mediocrity of his female line needn't worry us when assessing his prospects. He's had only two races so far, neither of them arduous, and promises to make an even better horse at three. Middle distances should suit him very well—his maternal grandsire Smart won over thirteen furlongs—and he should win good races for his new owners, McNall and Hunt, who have sent him to be trained by Douieb in France. *A. Maxwell, Ireland.*

SHARP STAR 3 ch.g. Sharpen Up 127–Sara's Star 70 (Sheshoon 132) (1980 5f 5f³ 6f⁴ 6g⁴ 6g 6fg 6g 8.2g 6g⁴ 7d 1981 8d³ 7d⁴ 8g* 7g² 7fg⁴ 8fg 8fg) leggy gelding; won maiden event at Edinburgh in June; suited by 1m; suited by some give in the ground; blinkered sixth to eighth outings in 1980. *G. Blum.* **64**

SHARP VENITA 3 b.f. Sharp Edge 123–Miss Venus (Comedy Star 121) (1980 5f* 5f² 6fg 5g 5fg² 5f³ 5fg 5f 6g 1981 6g 6g* 7d 6f 6f 6g² 7g) lengthy, rather unfurnished filly; walks and moves well; produced a strong burst to beat Shark Song ¾ length in Holsten Diat Pils Handicap at Newmarket in May; ¾-length second to Spanish Hind in similar event at Goodwood in September; ran moderately in between (unimpressive in paddock first 2 occasions and off course 2½ months before third); stays 6f; acts on firm going; often apprentice ridden. *W. Musson.* **81**

SHARSHA (FR) 3 b. or br.f. Labus–Semnica (Bon Mot III 132) (1980 7fg 7g³ 8fg³ 8.2s* 1981 12s³ 10g⁴ 12d 11.7f) lightly-made filly; good mover; rather disappointing in 1981, although in frame in handicaps at Ripon and Pontefract in April; suited by 1½m; evidently well suited by soft going; blinkered last 2 starts. *M. Stoute.* **73**

SHASAVAAN 3 b.c. Red God 128§–Shaara (Sanctus II 132) (1980 5g* 6g* 7.3d³ 1981 7g 8d* 8.5d² 8fg 8fg⁴) attractive, round-barrelled, quality-looking colt; good mover; returned to form in £2,600 event at York in May after running very disappointingly indeed on reappearance, travelling well throughout and beating Fandango Time by 3 lengths; ran easily best subsequent race when length second of 6 behind Saher in Diomed Stakes at Epsom the following month; last in St James's Palace Stakes at Royal Ascot in June and 4-runner minor event at York in July, in latter looking short of speed in a slowly-run race; stays 1m; best form with some give in the ground. *M. Stoute.* **111 d**

SHAYBOOB 4 ch.g. The Go-Between 129–Pepin (Midsummer Night II 117) (1980 6s* 6fg⁴ 6d³ 6g* 6g* 6fg 6d 6s⁴ 6d⁴ 1981 6d⁴ 7fg 7f 6fg 6g³ 6fg⁴ 6d 6g³) big gelding; fairly useful handicapper; ran respectably most starts in 1981 but didn't manage to win; stays 7f; acts on any going but is suited by some give in the ground; sometimes wears blinkers; genuine. *W. O'Gorman.* **95**

SHAYINA 2 gr.f. Run The Gantlet–Safaya (Zeddaan 130) (1981 5g* 5s² 5g* 5g*) May 30; third foal; half-sister to smart French 7f to 1¼m performer Safita (by Habitat); dam won twice over 5f at 2 yrs in France; a speedy filly who won newcomers event at Maisons-Laffitte in June and good prizes at Vichy in July and August, beating Tybern 4 lengths in Prix des Jouvencelles and Saumonee 1½ lengths in Prix des Reves d'Or; met her only defeat at the hands of Maelstrom Lake, going down by 1½ lengths in Prix du Bois at Longchamp; should stay beyond 5f. *F. Mathet, France.* **109**

SHEBA'S GLORY 3 br.g. Averof 123–Little Miss 92 (Aggressor 130) (1980 5g 5fg² 5f* 5g³ 6g² 6fg 6d 6g 6g 1981 12fg³ 12d 12d 12d 12.5f 12g 12g) small, compact gelding; burly and sweating when strong-finishing third to Sulzano in apprentice handicap at Newmarket in April; ran moderately afterwards, but had stiff task sixth start and was subsequently off course over 4 months; evidently well suited by 1½m; well beaten when blinkered once as a 2-y-o; sold 4,600 gns Newmarket Autumn Sales. *F. Durr.* **83**

SHECKLES 3 ch.f. English Prince 129–Shek-O 92 (Forward Pass) (1980 NR 1981 12f 14g 14.6fg) 12,500Y; lengthy filly; first living produce; dam 2-y-o 6f winner; well behind in minor event at Wolverhampton in June and maiden races at Salisbury and Doncaster (blinkered) in July. *F. J. Houghton.* **—**

SHEDAR 3 b.f. Owen Anthony 102–Saratoga Maid (Saratoga Skiddy 113) — (1980 5.3fg 5g 6fg 5f 5g 1981 5d 7d 7d 5v 6g) only poor form, including in sellers; blinkered last 2 starts. *R. Hoad.*

SHEER DELIGHT 3 ch.f. Gay Fandango 132–Sheer Joy (Major Portion 129) **92** (1980 5g 6s³ 6d 7g⁴ 1981 8s 8f* 7fg* 8f⁴ 8fg² 8f) well-made, robust filly; improved and in June won maiden race at York (ran on well under pressure and beat Majieda by ½ length) and minor event at Folkestone (by 7 lengths); gave impression she would have been suited by 1¼m; was well suited by firm ground; given plenty to do by her apprentice rider fourth start; retired to stud. *B. Hills.*

SHEER GRIT 3 b.c. Busted 134–Abettor 103 (Abernant 142) (1980 6g 7g* 8g* **104** 8d³ 1981 7d 10fg⁴ 12g² 12d 12f² 14fg³ 11.1f) rangy, attractive colt; has rather a round action; smart and genuine as a 2-y-o, winning at Kempton and Doncaster and finishing excellent third behind Beldale Flutter and Shergar in William Hill Futurity, also at Doncaster; disappointing in 1981, although was second in Ladbrokes Derby Trial at Lingfield in May (held up, looked a difficult ride when going down by 1½ lengths to Riberetto) and 3-runner Churchill Stakes at Ascot in June (made running but couldn't quicken at all when challenged by Six Mile Bottom and was beaten ¾ length); never really on terms when about 20 lengths sixth of 18 behind runaway winner Shergar in Derby on fourth start, best of his other efforts; stays 1½m; best form with some give in the ground; probably suited by forcing tactics; said to have jarred a shoulder at Ascot. *C. Brittain.*

SHELL TOP 3 ch.f. Spitsbergen 103–Mis Tor (Little Cloud 113) (1980 NR — 1981 10.1fg 10.1g) third foal; dam placed over jumps; bought 850 gns Ascot March Sales; behind in minor event at Windsor in July and maiden race (last of 16) on same course in August; sold 675 gns Ascot November Sales. *J. Davies.*

SHENOULA 3 ch.f. Sheshoon 132–Yanoula 79 (Nosca) (1980 5d 5s 6d 1981 — 12g 12.2g 12f 13.8f) lengthy filly; soundly beaten in varied company, including selling; blinkered final start. *W. Haigh.*

SHERE BEAUTY 4 b.f. Mummy's Pet 125–Mossgo 106 (Vigo 130) (1980 **§§** 7.2fg 8fg 1981 6d 6s) tall, sparely-made filly; moderate (rated 83) at 2 yrs but has gone the wrong way temperamentally and is best left severely alone; has worn blinkers. *W. Stubbs.*

SHERELCO 3 ro.c. Relko 136–Mary D 99 (Vigo 130) (1980 5g 6g 6fg 6g 1981 — 10d) leggy, lengthy, lightly-made colt; little worthwhile form in maiden and minor events; blinkered fourth outing in 1980; dead. *S. Matthews.*

SHERGAR 3 b.c. Great Nephew 126–Sharmeen (Val de Loir 133) (1980 8fg* **140** 8d² 1981 10fg* 12.3g* 12d* 12fg* 12fg* 14.6g⁴)

Who but Shergar could be Europe's 'Horse of the Year' in 1981? There wasn't a middle-distance performer to stand comparison with him and he built up an imposing record in some of the most important events for a horse of his type. Shergar's Derby win was one of the most prodigious in the long history of the race: he demolished the field by ten lengths, the widest margin of victory officially recorded in an Epsom Derby. Shergar won the Derby in the manner of a great racehorse and his exhibition will remain an abiding memory of the racing year. Until his unexpected defeat in the St Leger, Shergar was unbeaten as a three-year-old. He won the Guardian Newspaper Classic Trial and the Chester Vase before Epsom and then took the Irish Sweeps Derby and the King George VI and Queen Elizabeth Diamond Stakes; in none of these events did he win by less than four lengths. Alas, Shergar did not contest Europe's most prestigious and most competitive mile-and-a-half race, the Prix de l'Arc de Triomphe in October. Although he reportedly worked well at home after the St Leger—and tests carried out in the interim showed him to be in excellent health—his connections apparently felt there was too much at stake to risk a repeat of his below-par run at Doncaster. There was never much hope that the racing public would have the chance to see Shergar as a four-year-old. Such was the clamour for his services as a stallion that thirty-four shares in him offered before the King George were quickly taken up at £250,000 each, representing a valuation of £10,000,000, a record syndication for a stallion to stand in Europe. Shergar has been retired to his owner's Ballymany Stud in the Irish Republic.

Shergar was lightly raced as a two-year-old, having only two outings, in the Kris Plate at Newbury in September—when he won impressively—and in the William Hill Futurity at Doncaster in October. He was well fancied for

Guardian Newspaper Classic Trial, Sandown—Shergar comes home alone

the Futurity and ran extremely well for one so inexperienced to beat all except
Beldale Flutter. The general reaction to the result of the Futurity seemed
unduly critical—we said so in our essay on Beldale Flutter in *Racehorses of 1980*—
and Shergar's performance earned him only joint thirty-first place in the Tote
European Free Handicap which was published on December 4th. We held
a higher opinion of Shergar's form than did the official handicapper and went
on record as saying that Shergar had the makings of a very good colt over
middle distances. Before the 1981 flat season got under way Shergar stood
at 33/1 in the ante-post market on the Derby (he wasn't entered for the Two
Thousand Guineas) but it didn't take long for him to become a leading Epsom
fancy. Reappearing in the Guardian Newspaper Classic Trial over a mile and
a quarter at Sandown's April meeting, Shergar very much took the eye beforehand, clearly having done well over the winter, and he won in devastating style,
by ten lengths ridden through to the end after taking the lead three furlongs
from home. Coincidentally, each of the three previous Derby winners, Shirley
Heights, Troy and Henbit, had made his seasonal reappearance in the Sandown
Trial, Shirley Heights being beaten ten lengths by Whitstead, and Troy and
Henbit winning narrowly. Shergar followed the path to Epsom taken by
Henbit, appearing next in the Chester Vase at the beginning of May. It has
been said that racing at Chester is the turf's equivalent of greyhound racing,
for the circuit is only just over a mile round and is on the turn almost throughout.
Yet Chester has often proved a reliable testing ground for Derby horses. The
nature of the Chester course means that if a horse is to have any chance of
success he must be able to adapt to the unusual conditions; Epsom, with its
uphill, right- and left-handed bends in the first half mile and its downhill swing
round Tattenham Corner into the straight, demands a similar degree of adaptability. Shergar went to the head of the Derby ante-post lists after another
impressive display. When he moved smoothly past the leader Sunley Builds
with more than three furlongs left the Chester Vase was over barring some
accident. In the straight there was only one horse in it: Shergar stormed

Chester Vase—another sparkling victory for Shergar

clear to win by twelve lengths from Sunley Builds. Two days later Shergar's Derby prospects received another boost when Kirtling, second in the Guardian Newspaper Classic Trial, won the Dee Stakes at Chester by six lengths; Kirtling also won the Gran Premio d'Italia, a Group 1 race, on the Sunday before the Derby.

By Derby Day Shergar's performances at Sandown and Chester looked outstandingly the best of the Derby trials and he started the shortest-priced Derby favourite—at 11/10 on—since Sir Ivor in 1968 and became only the third horse in the now-extensive post-war era to start at odds on for the race. Defeat for the favourite would have been the biggest upset in the Derby since Tudor Minstrel failed through lack of stamina in 1947. Shergar looked a virtual certainty. What was there to stand in his way? He had shown much the best form of any of the Derby runners; his ability to stay a mile and a half was proven; he seemed sure to handle the Epsom course; and his equable temperament made the prospect of his being upset by the preliminaries at Epsom seem very remote. The possibility that he might not be so effective on the prevailing dead ground (his performances at Sandown and Chester were returned on a sound surface) or that his nineteen-year-old rider Swinburn might lack the experience for the occasion seemed slender reeds for the connections of his opponents to clutch at. What was the opposition? As usual, the best of the French stayed at home for the Prix du Jockey-Club, run on the Sunday after the Derby: the unbeaten Al Nasr and Lydian (who refused to enter the stalls) comprised the foreign challenge, the Irish being without a representative for the first time since 1959. The overseas form that seemed to have most bearing on the Derby was that shown by Glint of Gold who had won the Derby Italiano after being successful over the Epsom Derby course in the Warren Stakes in April. The challenge to Shergar would have been stronger had Beldale Flutter, winner of Britain's most valuable Derby trial, the Mecca-Dante Stakes at York, not met with a bad accident the week before Epsom. The second, third, fourth and fifth in the Mecca-Dante, Shotgun, Scintillating Air, Robellino and Kalaglow, all ran in the Derby, Shotgun, on whom Piggott took the ride, starting second favourite. The Hern stable which had sent out the two previous Derby winners was represented by Church Parade, fourteenth in the Two Thousand Guineas, in which Scintillating Air finished sixth and another Derby runner

Kind of Hush thirteenth. Lydian's withdrawal reduced the size of the Derby field to eighteen which included several who had no chance of winning any Derby, let alone one with Shergar in the field.

So the stage was set for arguably the most one-sided Derby of modern times. The favourite's backers never had a moment's anxiety. Shergar got away well and took up a position among the leaders, perfectly placed to avoid being cut off or squeezed out in the early stages. At halfway the Ladbrokes Derby Trial winner Riberetto and the 100/1-shot Silver Season were at the head of affairs; Shergar was third, within easy striking distance of the first two and two or three lengths clear of the main body of the field, many of whom were already struggling to keep up. Not for a long time had we seen so many of the runners in a Derby under pressure so far from home. As the field descended Tattenham Hill the question was not so much whether Shergar would win but by how far! Just look at the photograph of the field rounding Tattenham Corner. Swinburn is standing up in his irons; Shergar is cantering. At this point Shergar was the only horse in the race still firmly on the bridle. He was pulling over the leaders and once into the straight Swinburn let him go to the front. Moving past Riberetto and Silver Season on the bit, Shergar stretched out magnificently when pushed along, quickly setting up an unassailable lead. He received three or four cracks with the whip in the closing stages by which time he had the race well and truly in his pocket. Not until well inside the final furlong did Swinburn glance behind—'I couldn't believe how far clear we were'—and he then began to ease Shergar but for which the winning distance would have been nearer twelve lengths than the official ten.

Just how good a horse was Shergar on Derby Day? We have already stated that he won the Derby in the manner of a great horse. The phrase 'a great horse' means to us one of such superlative merit as to make him far superior to the general run of classic winners. In our view Shergar was such a horse. It can be said with justification that, the runner-up Glint of Gold

Derby Stakes, Epsom—rounding Tattenham Corner Shergar is poised on the outside of Silver Season and Riberetto. Scintillating Air (checked cap) is fourth closely followed by Church Parade and the grey Shotgun. Next come Glint of Gold (noseband), Kings General, Sheer Grit, Robellino and Sunley Builds (far right)

excepted, a mediocre Derby field faced Shergar. The field looked under strength at the time and by the end of the season the records of those behind Shergar and Glint of Gold did not make impressive reading. The third, Scintillating Air, beaten two lengths by Glint of Gold, didn't win a race in five outings during the season and fourth-placed Shotgun was beaten often enough to show that, as a three-year-old at any rate, he could not be regarded as good opposition when judged by normal Derby standards. The same could be said of the next six home, Church Parade, Sheer Grit, Silver Season, Riberetto, Sunley Builds and Kings General. It would be unwise to use Glint of Gold as a yardstick: he met ill-luck in running and did remarkably well to get second place. That said, only five members of the Derby field finished within twenty lengths of Shergar and it is not often that any race, let alone a classic, is won in such style. Shergar's victory stands out among Derby triumphs: his Derby-winning performance was, in our view, the best in the post-war era.

None of those that had taken on Shergar at Epsom opposed him in the Irish Sweeps Derby at the Curragh a little over three weeks later. Kirtling and Hern's representative Cut Above were the only ones among Shergar's ten opponents to start at odds shorter than 20/1. Twelve days after Epsom Shergar got loose while being prepared for a gallop at home and remained free until caught by a van driver outside Henry Cecil's stables. To the relief of his trainer Shergar came to no harm—'There wasn't a scratch on him when we got him back'—and he went to post at the Curragh as hot a favourite, at 3/1 on, as Sir Ivor was when beaten by Ribero. With Swinburn under suspension the mount went to Piggott, who had ridden Shergar in his races as a two-year-old. The going was on the firm side (Shergar never encountered extremes of going in his career) and Piggott's instructions were not to let the horse down unless it became really necessary. He followed the instructions to the letter, riding Shergar very cheekily after passing the leaders, as if they were a row of trees, on the home turn. Shergar and Piggott toyed with the opposition in the last three furlongs, coming home unchallenged four lengths ahead of Cut Above with Dance Bid a further length and a half away third and Kirtling another five lengths behind in fourth. As at Epsom, Shergar looked a class apart from the rest.

Shergar's victory in the Irish Sweeps Derby maintained the excellent recent record of Epsom Derby winners in the race. Henbit did not run as a three-year-old after Epsom but Shergar was the fourth Epsom Derby winner in five years to take the Sweeps Derby. The overall record since the Sweeps Derby was inaugurated in 1962 confirms, however, that the race is by no means a formality for a horse that has won the Epsom Derby. Thirteen Epsom Derby winners have contested the Irish Sweeps Derby: Santa Claus, Nijinsky, Grundy, The Minstrel, Shirley Heights, Troy and Shergar were successful; Larkspur, Charlottown, Sir Ivor, Blakeney, Roberto and Empery went away defeated, as did the only Prix du Jockey-Club winner to contest the race Caracolero. Incidentally, Shergar's victory margin in the Sweeps Derby hasn't been bettered in twenty runnings of the race; Santa Claus and Troy also won by four lengths.

With the Derby and the Irish Sweeps Derby safely in the bag, it was announced that Shergar would be aimed for what has become Britain's most important middle-distance event, the King George VI and Queen Elizabeth Diamond Stakes at Ascot. The King George is Britain's Prix de l'Arc. No event in Europe, bar the Arc itself, has its list of winners over the last thirty years studded with more illustrious names—Pinza, Ribot, Ballymoss, Alcide, Ragusa, Nijinsky, Mill Reef, Brigadier Gerard, Grundy, Troy and the only dual winner Dahlia. Winners of the race have sired the winners of over thirty European classics. Since the King George was instituted as the King George VI and Queen Elizabeth Festival of Britain Stakes in 1951, it has overwhelmingly succeeded in its main purpose, that of bringing together in competition top-class horses from different generations and different countries. The King George usually provides evidence of how the best of the current year's crop of European three-year-olds measure up, over a mile and a half, to each other and to their immediate predecessors. Counting Shergar's victory, sixteen three-year-olds, thirteen four-year-olds and two five-year-olds have won the King George. One hundred and forty-six foreign-trained horses have run in the race, eighty-five from France, thirty-eight from Ireland, fifteen from Italy, three from Germany, two from Belgium, and one from Japan, Norway and the United States. The King George is an invaluable part of the European programme of major events and the end of the third week in July, by which point the top few three-year-olds at a mile and a half have been pretty well revealed, is precisely the right time for it.

Derby Stakes, Epsom—a moment of Derby history: Shergar is a record ten lengths clear at the line. He is chased home by Glint of Gold, Scintillating Air and Shotgun

Shergar and the Prix de Diane de Revlon (French Oaks) winner Madam Gay were the only representatives of their generation in the 1981 King George field. The five older horses taking part, among them the previous year's St Leger winner Light Cavalry and the second and fourth in the 1980 Epsom Derby, Master Willie and Pelerin, were certainly among the best available in this country; but the absence of a foreign challenge, for the first time in the history of the King George, was disappointing. Such was Shergar's reputation that he started at 5/2 on in spite of the fact that Master Willie and Pelerin had carried all before them as four-year-olds, winning between them the Jockey Club Stakes, the Coronation Cup, the Coral Eclipse Stakes, the John Porter Stakes, the Ormonde Stakes and the Hardwicke Stakes. Shergar won with the authority almost everyone expected, although the race itself did not turn out to be the hell-for-leather affair so widely anticipated, and circumstances dictated that Shergar wasn't able to deliver his challenge as early as had become his wont. One might well have thought that with a horse of Shergar's turn of foot in the race a slow pace would have been avoided at all costs; but Piggott on Light Cavalry only dawdled along in the lead at first. Master Willie, disputing second place with Shergar, expended valuable energy fighting his jockey in the early stages in his attempt to take up a front-running role. The pace picked up after half a mile and was sharpened again when Master Willie was at last given his head approaching the five-furlong marker. Rounding the final turn Shergar, in third place on the rails, was boxed in by Madam Gay who had been brought up on his outside some time before. Fortunately for Shergar's rider, Light Cavalry came off the rails as the runners straightened out for home, leaving Shergar a gap through which he quickened in style. Swinburn set him going in earnest with two furlongs to go and the race was decided in a few moments. Striding up to Master Willie, Shergar went to the front more than a furlong from home with the race won. Madam Gay and Fingal's Cave, who surpassed himself on this occasion, proved too strong in the closing stages for Master Willie but were unable to make any impression on Shergar who drew away to win most decisively by four lengths, an official margin of victory bettered in the race only by Ribot, Mill Reef and Dahlia. A short head separated Madam Gay and Fingal's Cave who finished four lengths ahead of Master Willie with Pelerin, who never got in a blow after being squeezed against the rails before the home turn, back in fifth.

With the £119,206 earned in the King George, Shergar lifted his first-prize earnings to £388,970 which put him into fourth place in the list of leading European-based money winners, behind only the fillies Dahlia (£497,741) and Allez France (£493,100), and Troy (£415,735). For readers interested in such statistics, seven others have passed the £300,000 mark: Youth (£366,624), Alleged (£327,315), Exceller (£324,694), Three Troikas (£316,676), The Minstrel (£315,212), Grundy (£312,122) and Mill Reef (£300,422). The totals for Dahlia and Exceller do not include money earned after their permanent transfer to the United States. The statistics provide evidence, if any were needed, of the disproportionate support given in Europe to the top middle-distance races: no specialist sprinter, miler or stayer figures anywhere near the top of the prize-money league. Regular readers will know that we consider this discrimination, which is particularly harsh against sprinters and stayers, to be unfair. Merit of any kind deserves its reward and high-class races with substantial stakes should be provided for horses of all types, whatever their best distance. At present, it is the top-class mile-and-a-half horse that earns most of the prestige and prize money. The Derby winners, the King George and Prix de l'Arc winners are regarded as the elite and racing people are often slow to acknowledge outstanding merit among racehorses in other categories.

Shergar's victory in the King George placed him in the company of a select band—Nijinsky, Grundy, The Minstrel and Troy—who have won the Derby, Sweeps Derby and King George. The Minstrel didn't race after Ascot but both Grundy and Troy went on to contest the Benson and Hedges Gold Cup at York in August. The Benson and Hedges would, in our view, have been an ideal race for Shergar. Unlike Troy, who fairly early in his three-year-old career gave the impression of being a true mile-and-a-half horse, Shergar had shown the type of speed that would have made him equally effective at the Benson and Hedges trip of ten and a half furlongs. Troy could sustain a magnificent burst at the end of his races but he wasn't able to lie up with the strong early pace in the Derby as Shergar was. Shergar was a horse with almost instant acceleration, one who could be jumped into top gear in a few strides; Troy needed some time to get opened out. We were convinced that Shergar could have equalled Troy's feat of winning a Benson and Hedges. However, with the Prix de l'Arc reportedly his major objective, Shergar was let down after Ascot and his connections announced that he would have a preliminary race before Longchamp. Most observers assumed that the September Stakes at Kempton would be that race and the announcement, made on Benson and Hedges day, that Shergar would run in the St Leger came as a major surprise and led to hasty revision of the ante-post market. Bustomi and Glint of Gold, who had headed the betting at 2/1 and 11/4, were pushed out to 8/1 and 10/1 as Shergar was installed at 5/2 on.

Shergar was the first Derby winner to contest the St Leger since Nijinsky; the latter, too, wasn't seen out between the King George and the Leger. Four other winners of the King George had gone on to contest the St Leger, all of them, like Nijinsky, starting at odds on: Tulyar (1952), Ragusa (1963), Meadow Court (1965) and Ile de Bourbon (1978). The memories of the defeats of Meadow Court and Ile de Bourbon, and also of Alleged at 7/4 on in 1977,

...ved as a reminder that the St Leger is rarely as cut-and-dried as it sometimes looks. Shergar had far and away the best form of any horse in the race in 1981 but could he produce at one mile six and a half furlongs something approaching the outstanding form he had shown at a mile and a half, bearing in mind that his trainer was timing his preparation to have him at his peak three weeks later for the Prix de l'Arc?

Various stories to Shergar's detriment circulated in the period leading up to the St Leger: how he hadn't been showing his usual sparkle on the gallops; how he had become mulish at home; how his trainer had booked the round gallop at Newmarket ten days before the Leger but Shergar hadn't worked as planned; and so on and so forth. In the week before the race the bookmakers began to field against him—at one time 6/4 on was freely available—but on the day, after both trainer and jockey had declared that Shergar had been working exceptionally well and had never been better, he started at 9/4 on. Hardly anyone doubted, as the runners went to post, that Shergar would win the St Leger. He looked in the pink of condition beforehand—we don't agree with those who asserted *after his defeat* that he appeared to have lost condition since Ascot—and he seemed his usual calm and collected self in the preliminaries and on the way to post. He did show one or two signs of edginess, particularly down at the start, but no more so than on an earlier occasion, before the Sweeps Derby. Had it been almost any other horse but Shergar we are pretty sure most people would have put his St Leger defeat down to lack of stamina. As the field turned into the straight Shergar seemed to be travelling smoothly close behind the leaders, poised to take over as soon as his rider gave him the office. But, three and a half furlongs from home Swinburn began to look uneasy and from the three-furlong pole the pictured changed quickly: Shergar faltered, giving the sort of impression you would get if you saw a car travelling at speed and it suddenly ran out of petrol. Swinburn took his whip to Shergar, but to no avail. In the final quarter of a mile Cut Above, Glint of Gold and Bustomi went further and further away from him; eleven and a half lengths separated Shergar from Cut Above at the line, a turn round of fifteen and a half lengths on the Sweeps Derby running of the two horses. Few of the other excuses or explanations

Irish Sweeps Derby, the Curragh—Shergar again outclasses his opponents

King George VI and Queen Elizabeth Diamond Stakes, Ascot—Swinburn gives Shergar a grateful slap down the neck as he wins from Madam Gay and Fingal's Cave

that have been put forward to account for Shergar's disappointing run seem to us convincing enough for repetition, let alone acceptance. Shergar is a quick-actioned horse, the antithesis of the typical, long-striding, staying type. If he didn't fail through lack of stamina—and we find it astonishing that anyone could be adamant after his St Leger performance that he was capable of staying a mile and three quarters—then the only other explanation we could contemplate is that Shergar was over the top for the year. Yet those who worked closest with him said before and after the Leger that he was working well at home. Nevertheless, it has to be admitted that it wouldn't be the first time that the sensitive nose of the bookmaking fraternity had detected sooty particles in the atmosphere when others couldn't. Whatever the reason for Shergar's failure in the St Leger, his defeat should not be used—as some correspondents used it—to belittle the horse. His status surely stands or falls on his performances in the Derby, the Sweeps Derby and the King George.

That Shergar did not contest the Prix de l'Arc de Triomphe was a great disappointment. Everyone agrees that an owner has a perfect right to do as he likes with his property so long as it does not infringe the rules of racing or the law of the land. But, that said—and accepting that all was well with Shergar— it was difficult not to sympathise with an article by Tony Morris which appeared in *The Sporting Life* on October 7th. The best of journalism is generally like Beaujolais—enjoyable if consumed straight away, but not worth keeping. Morris' piece was a notable exception. Expressing amazement that Shergar's retirement should be announced in the course of a statement which affirmed that, to all appearances, the horse was perfectly well, Morris slammed the decision to miss the Arc as 'flagrantly unsporting, contrary to the true spirit of horse racing'. He went on: 'There is no earthly point in our staging championship races when the supposed champions, though admittedly fit and well, do not contest them. It makes a mockery of a universally approved system'. The world is what it is, more's the pity, and no amount of such propaganda is likely to change the highly-commercialised attitudes of some of the present generation of leading owners on the flat. There are many less adventurous owners than the Aga Khan—no-one could accuse him of shirking a challenge with Shergar in the first part of the season and he did run Shergar in the somewhat-unfashionable St Leger, something that others we could name probably wouldn't have done. We quote from Morris' article, not to use it as a stick with which to beat Shergar's connections, but because we too are unhappy that commercial expediency should apparently be a dominant factor when it comes to deciding whether a horse keeps his appointment in a championship field. No doubt it will be said, perhaps with some justification, that it is easy for us to talk. After all, we didn't have a quarter of a million pounds or more invested in Shergar. But we'd point out that the majority of leading owners in North America are, by and large, much bolder than their European counterparts. Look at the racing record of Secretariat, for example, who was syndicated long before the end of his racing career and continued racing after unexpected defeats. As Morris put it: 'Nobody knocked Secretariat because he suffered the occasional reverse. Nobody looked for excuses. Everybody accepted that, once in a while, the very best runners get beaten'.

Thanks principally to Shergar, the Aga Khan ended the British season as leading owner in only the third season since he began patronizing English stables again after a break of thirteen years. Having acquired in recent seasons some of Madame Francois Dupre's bloodstock and also much of Marcel Boussac's when the latter's studs and stables were dispersed, the Aga Khan's is the largest racing and breeding operation in Europe. He has more than one hundred and seventy broodmares and started 1981 with one hundred and forty-seven horses in training. With yearlings, foals, fillies out of training and stallions, his bloodstock empire numbers more than five hundred. Shergar comes from a family developed by the Aga Khan's grandfather between the wars. Shergar's seventh dam is the legendary Mumtaz Mahal, bought on the Aga Khan's behalf by George Lambton for 9,100 guineas, a very large sum in those days, at the Doncaster Yearling Sales in 1922. Lambton, who first bought

H. H. Aga Khan's "Shergar"

yearlings for the Aga Khan in 1921, was told to concentrate on fillies that he thought suitable to form the nucleus for a stud and only to buy a colt if really keen on him. The success of the Aga Khan's yearling purchases at the sales at which Mumtaz Mahal was bought probably exceeds that of any market venture made by an owner in a single year before or since: for 4,000 guineas Lambton secured Diophon, who won the Two Thousand Guineas, and for 3,000 guineas he got Salmon Trout, who won the St Leger; the Aga Khan's first trainer Dick Dawson bought, for 250 guineas, Friar's Daughter who became the dam of the Aga Khan's unbeaten triple crown winner Bahram and also of Dastur, runner-up in the Two Thousand Guineas, Derby and St Leger. Renowned as 'the fastest filly in the annals of the turf', Mumtaz Mahal won five of her six races and topped the Free Handicap as a two-year-old; she won two of her four starts as a three-year-old including the King George Stakes at Goodwood and the Nunthorpe at York, before being retired to stud, her prize-money winnings repaying with interest her purchase price. Mumtaz Mahal had nine foals: seven of them were winners, five in Britain or Ireland, one in France and one in India, and three of her daughters became distinguished broodmares—Mah Mahal (the dam of Mahmoud), Mumtaz Begum (the dam of Nasrullah) and the unraced Rustom Mahal (the dam of Abernant).

Shergar (b.c. 1978)	Great Nephew (b 1963)	Honeyway (br 1941)	Fairway / Honey Buzzard
		Sybil's Niece (ch 1951)	Admiral's Walk / Sybil's Sister
	Sharmeen (b 1972)	Val de Loir (b 1959)	Vieux Manoir / Vali
		Nasreen (b 1964)	Charlottesville / Ginetta

Shergar's dam Sharmeen, whose fifth dam is Mumtaz Begum, was a fairly useful performer, a winner at ten and a half furlongs and placed at up to a mile and a half. Shergar is her second foal, the first being Shaiyneen (by Kalamoun), a minor winner at up to nine furlongs in France. Sharmeen is by the French Derby winner Val de Loir, who had plenty of stamina in his pedigree, out of Nasreen who gained her only win over an extended mile and a half. Sent to Sassafras, Nasreen bred the very smart Naasiri who stayed well. Speed is very much in evidence further back on the dam's side of Shergar's pedigree. The third dam Ginetta won the French One Thousand Guineas and the Prix du Moulin and was second in the Prix de l'Abbaye as a two-year-old; the fourth dam Diableretta, who went wrong temperamentally at three, was an outstanding two-year-old, winner of the Queen Mary, July, Cherry Hinton and Molecomb Stakes, and second in the Cheveley Park. Shergar's sire Great Nephew was a mile- to mile-and-a-quarter horse and the average distance of races won at three years and upwards by his progeny is nine furlongs. Great Nephew has sired only a handful of horses that have won beyond a mile and a half.

In appearance Shergar is a deep-girthed, good sort. He has a most distinctive style of galloping; a good-actioned colt in his slower paces, he has a short, scurrying action at his top pace, not the most graceful we have seen in a top racehorse but certainly one of the most effective. Before his races he always had an alertness about him that we like to see in a horse and he usually gave the impression of being of most placid temperament; he was collected and sensible in the preliminaries and a most amenable customer when racing, wasting no energy and doing as he was bid without any fuss. As an individual we liked him immensely. As a performer we consider him one of the best horses in our experience, inferior only to Sea-Bird (rated at 145), Ribot (142) and Mill Reef (141) in the specialist middle-distance category. *M. Stoute.*

SHERRYMAN 3 b.g. Manacle 123–Sherry Girl 81 (Appiani II 128) (1980 5d 6g 7g 10d 1981 12g 7f) neat gelding; bad plater; blinkered third outing at 2 yrs; sold 380 gns Doncaster September Sales. *I. Vickers.* —

SHE'S INCREDIBLE (USA) 2 ch.f. Le Fabuleux 133–Her Prerogative (Buckpasser) (1981 6fg³) Apr 22; sister to Fabulous Time, a smart stakes winner at up to 1¼m as a 4-y-o, and half-sister to a stakes-placed winner; dam, daughter of champion 2-y-o filly Queen of the Stage, won over 5f at 2 yrs; 14/1, put up a particularly promising first effort in 11-runner minor event at Windsor in September, coming with a very strong run which failed by only a neck and the same to take her past previous winners Epithet and Cajun; will stay middle distances; a well-bred filly who looks sure to make a very useful performer. *J. Dunlop.* **83 p**

SHE'S MY GIRL 2 b. or br.f. Mandamus 120–Boston Flyer 57 (Mansingh **69**
120) (1981 5s³ 5s² 5fg³ 5g⁴ 5g* 5fg 5.3f* 5fg 5f³ 6fg⁴ 5f⁴ 5g⁴ 5d* 5s* 5g) Mar
12; 1,700Y; lightly-made filly; first foal; dam won over 5f at 2 yrs; disqualified
after winning auction event at Ripon in April; stood up very well to a hard
season, gaining further victories in auction race at Redcar, claiming event at
Brighton and nurseries at Ayr and Folkestone, running on under hard riding
to win by a length from Bold Saracen at Folkestone in October; stays 6f; acts
on any going; has worn bandages; has won twice for apprentice P. Howard;
tough and genuine. *K. Ivory.*

SHIFTER 2 b. or br.f. Red Alert 127–Move Over (Galivanter 131) (1981 —
5g 6g 5v) May 26; sturdy filly; third foal; dam won over 7f at 2 yrs in Ireland;
in rear in maiden and minor events. *W. Elsey.*

SHILEEN 2 b.f. Kalamoun 129–Silver Spring (Match III 135) (1981 7d 6s²) **71**
May 18; neat filly; closely related to a winner at around 1m in Belgium by
Zeddaan, and half-sister to useful French 5.5f to 1m winner Silver Do (by
Derring-Do); dam, daughter of high-class French filly Solitude, won twice
at around 1m; clear of rest when 2 lengths second of 10 to No Contest in maiden
race at Hamilton in October; should be suited by 7f; sold 6,000 gns Newmarket
Autumn Sales. *M. Stoute.*

SHIMAAL (USA) 2 ch.f. Foolish Pleasure–Chalk Face (Nearctic) (1981 **68** p
6g) Mar 14; $240,000Y; neat filly; good walker; second foal; dam stakes
winner over 9f at 4 yrs; 14/1, showed speed for long way when about 13 lengths
sixth of 17 to Merlin's Charm in maiden race at Newmarket in October; should
improve over 1m+. *H. T. Jones.*

SHINE FORTH 3 ch.g. Shiny Tenth 120 Furlcy 91 (Decoy Buy 129) (1980 **64**
NR 1981 5g 6g 7g* 7f⁴ 7fg 7f² 8fg) lengthy, plain gelding; dam
2-y-o 5f winner; apprentice ridden when winning seller at Catterick in June
(no bid); gave impression he'd probably have won if his saddle hadn't slipped
when fourth to Portogon in handicap at Thirsk in July; disappointed fifth
and last starts; stays 7f; sold 1,100 gns Doncaster October Sales. *M. H.
Easterby.*

SHINERSEA 2 b.f. Shiny Tenth 120–Sea Magic (Hardicanute 130) (1981 —
8fg 8g) Apr 8; narrow filly; sister to 1980 2-y-o 1m winner Seaquin and half-
sister to a winner; dam never ran; in rear in maiden races at Leicester in
September and Newmarket (last of 30) in October. *M. Ryan.*

SHINING FINISH 4 b.c. Nijinsky 138–Lacquer 118 (Shantung 132) (1980 **119**
12fg* 16g 13.3d 12d* 12g* 12d* 12d* 1981 12s³ 14d³ 12f) very attractive
colt; good mover; very smart performer at 3 yrs when he won 5 races, notably
St Simon Stakes at Newbury; ran very well first start in 1981, going down by
2 heads to Pelerin (rec 3 lb) in John Porter Stakes at Newbury in April; respectable 5 lengths third to Ardross in Yorkshire Cup at York in May but ran
poorly in Hardwicke Stakes at Royal Ascot on final appearance; seemed to
stay 1¾m; ideally suited by some give in the ground; stud in Australia. *J.
Tree.*

SHINING START 2 b.f. Lord Gayle 124–Scintillation 55 (Ballyciptic 122) **79**
(1981 5d 5d 5fg⁴ 6g² 7g* 7.2fg³ 7d) May 22; 9,800Y; rather lightly-made filly;
good mover; sister to a poor maiden in France and half-sister to 3 winners,
including fairly useful 1977 2-y-o 5f to 6f winner Edgar Hunt (by Polyfoto);
dam stayed 1m; looked to have an excellent chance with bottom weight in
£4,200 nursery at York in August and got up close home to win by a neck from
Brown Gold after being repeatedly denied a run (still last of 8 with 150 yards
to run); creditable third of 9 to Rapid Knot in similar event at Haydock in
September; will stay 1¼m; acts on a firm surface. *C. Booth.*

SHINING TOR 4 b.c. High Top 131–Wolverene 114 (Relko 136) (1980 **100**
10fg² 11f* 12g⁴ 11d⁴ 1981 10.2fg³ 12g³) strong colt; good mover; very useful
at 3 yrs; lightly raced in 1981, finishing respectable 3¼ lengths third to Heighten
in £3,000 race at Doncaster in September, but disappointing in 3-runner minor
event at Beverley later in month; suited by 1½m; acts on firm going and is
possibly unsuited by a soft surface; sold to Denys Smith 6,700 gns Doncaster
November Sales. *J. W. Watts.*

SHINY FUTURE 4 ch.f. Shiny Tenth 120–Pemba (Sodium 128) (1980 —
8fg 10.2fg 8d 12s 1981 8h) no worthwhile form in varied company, including
selling. *M. Pipe.*

SHINY HOUR 2 ch.c. Shiny Tenth 120–Lizzylyn 84 (Tower Walk 130) (1981 **73**
5s⁴ 5d* 6g 5f³ 5f 6g 5g) Apr 21; 2,500Y; well-grown colt; first foal; dam won

over 5f at 2 yrs; won 12-runner maiden auction event at Haydock in May going away by 1½ lengths from Orange Silk; ran well on 3 occasions afterwards, including in 2 nurseries; should stay 6f. *M. McCormack.*

SHINY STAR 2 b.c. Shiny Tenth 120–High Drama 90 (Hill Clown) (1981 — 7g 8s) Apr 10; 1,600Y; fair sort; first foal; dam, half-sister to Cambridgeshire winner Negus, stayed well; unquoted when behind in maiden races at Leicester (coltish in paddock and moved very badly to start) and Warwick; sold 360 gns Doncaster October Sales. *J. Hardy.*

SHISA 2 b.f. Hot Spark 126- Distinctiveness (Distinctive) (1981 6g 6f) **70** Feb 5; 5,200Y; third foal; closely related to useful 1980 2-y-o 5.1f and 6f winner Steelinctive (by Steel Heart), subsequently successful in maiden races in USA; dam lightly-raced half-sister to American Derby winner Determined King; showed good speed 5f when 4½ lengths fifth of 23 to Baltimore Belle in maiden race at Nottingham in July, unquoted outing. *B. Hanbury.*

SHMAIN 2 ch.c. Sheshoon 132–Maiden d'Or 87 (Songedor 116) (1981 7g) — Apr 30; third foal; dam won at up to 1m; unquoted and very backward when always behind in 18-runner maiden race won by Leg Glance at Doncaster in October. *A. Balding.*

SHOCK TREATMENT 2 ch.f. Hot Spark 126–Parez 67 (Pardao 120) (1981 **76** 5fg³ 5fg) Feb 21; 10,000Y; leggy, useful-looking filly; fourth foal; half-sister to Irish 3-y-o 6f winner Peoria (by Sweet Revenge) and two 2-y-o winners; dam, disappointing sister to 2 useful winners, seemed not to stay 1m; ran very well for a newcomer when close-up third of 8 to Ibtihaj in maiden race at Goodwood in July, pressing winner throughout; favourite for £3,100 event on same course in September but faded in final 2f to finish 6 lengths fifth of 8 to Dancing Rocks. *P. Walwyn.*

SHOEBUTTON 2 ch.f. Habat 127–Forgotten Dreams 82 (Shoemaker 121) **60** (1981 6g 6g 6g 8fg⁴) Apr 26; leggy filly; second foal; half-sister to 1980 2-y-o 1m winner Flying Dreamer (by My Swallow); dam won 3 times over 2m; only plating class; ran best race over 1m. *P. Calver.*

SHOE FREAK 2 b.f. Huntercombe 133–Judy Gee (Will Somers 114§) (1981 — 5fg 5fg 5f) Apr 17; IR 820F, 1,200Y; small, light-framed filly; of no account; destroyed after breaking leg in seller at Ripon in August. *J. Calvert.*

SHOONBEAM 2 ch.g. Sheshoon 132–Dust Sheet (Silly Season 127) (1981 — 5s 6g 6fg 5f 7g 6s 7.6s) May 6; smallish, fair sort; half-brother to 6f winner Chicken Again (by Royalty); dam ran twice; in rear all outings, including in sellers. *P. K. Mitchell.*

SHOOT A LINE 4 b.f. High Line 125–Death Ray 100 (Tamerlane 128) (1980 **112** 12.3f* 12f 12d* 12d* 12d* 14.6g* 1981 12s 20f² 12s 11g²)

Shoot A Line's record in 1981 did something to confirm our comments in *Racehorses of 1980* concerning the lack of incentives the European racing programme provides for owners to keep high-class three-year-old fillies in training. To highlight the unsatisfactory nature of the present position it is instructive to compare European pattern events with their North American equivalents, graded stakes. While in Great Britain, France and Ireland only a quarter of such races for fillies over the age of two are open to four-year-olds, in North America the fraction is three quarters. It goes without saying that every year in North America there is a healthy number of smart four-year-old fillies in training and they undoubtedly add much to the good of the season. Not so in Europe, where generally only a handful of these run at four. Some progress has been made in the past decade, but the Pattern of Racing is still loaded against four-year-old fillies and is loaded particularly heavily against those needing at least a mile and a half to be seen to best advantage. The Brownstown Stakes, Princess Royal Stakes, Prix de Pomone and Prix de Royallieu are the only options available to a trainer if he wishes to give a filly like Shoot A Line a break from running against the colts and the Princess Royal is the only one of the four in England. Moreover, since the Brownstown Stakes and the Prix de Pomone take place within a week of each other, and the other two within a day, the opportunities are even more limited than they appear at first sight.

All things considered it came as no great surprise that Shoot A Line had to take on colts on each of her four starts in 1981. Each time she lost, twice running poorly and twice respectably. Her poor efforts were in the John Porter Stakes at Newbury, in which she injured herself in the stalls, lost her action after three quarters of a mile and was pulled up behind Pelerin, and the Grosser Preis von Berlin at Dusseldorf, in which she was beaten before the first turn and

Mr R. A. Budgett's "Shoot A Line"

trailed in seventh of eight to Lydian. The Gold Cup at Royal Ascot and the Doonside Cup at Ayr, both four-runner events, saw a different Shoot A Line but still not the one who at three had won five pattern races including the Irish Guinness Oaks and Yorkshire Oaks. At Royal Ascot Ardross and Shoot A Line had the race to themselves in the last two furlongs but despite trying her utmost to get on terms the filly couldn't match Ardross, an outstanding stayer, and was flattered by her length's proximity to him at the end. At Ayr the trip was short of Shoot A Line's best; she made the running at a fair gallop but had no chance with Castle Keep in the last quarter of a mile and went down by a length, a margin which again didn't give a true indication of the winner's superiority on the day.

Shoot A Line (b.f. 1977)	High Line (ch 1966)	High Hat (ch 1957)	Hyperion
			Madonna
		Time Call (b 1955)	Chanteur II
			Aleria
	Death Ray (b 1959)	Tamerlane (br 1952)	Persian Gulf
			Eastern Empress
		Luminant (b 1951)	Nimbus
			Bardia

Death Ray, successful five times at around a mile, has produced several winners in addition to Shoot A Line, the best of them the very smart More Light (by Morston) who won the Gordon Stakes and ran second in the William Hill Dewhurst Stakes and Jockey Club Cup. The grandam Luminant also threw the July Cup winner Daylight Robbery. A good walker Shoot A Line was not an impressive filly in appearance, being lengthy and lightly made. She was essentially a stayer, and to compensate for this it should pay to mate her with stallions that showed reasonable speed. Very genuine, she acted on any going but was ideally suited by some give in the ground. *R. Hern.*

791

SHOOTING BUTTS 3 b.g. Tycoon II–Charlies Double (Fighting Charlie 127) **81**
(1980 NR 1981 10fg⁴ 16s 16.9s* 16g⁴ 16f 16.9fg 16.1s) 2,600Y; workmanlike
gelding; half-brother to 6f and 1m winner Robolin (by Master Sing); dam never
ran; beat Covent Garden 8 lengths in maiden event at Wolverhampton in May;
didn't have full use made of his stamina next 3 starts and was off course 3 months
before his last; suited by a test of stamina; acts well on soft going. *R. Hollinshead.*

SHOOTING HIGH 2 b.f. Busted 134–Regal Miss 90 (Sovereign Path 125) **81**
(1981 7d 6g⁴) Apr 25; well-made filly; third foal; half-sister to winning sprinter
Regal Jim (by Jimmy Reppin); dam ran only at 2 yrs when winner at up to 6f;
20/1, prominent throughout and stuck on well when 5½ lengths fourth of 17 to
I'm Hot in maiden race at Newmarket in October; will be suited by a return to 7f.
P. Walwyn.

SHOOTING MATCH 3 gr.g. Home Guard 129–Bundling (Petingo 135) (1980 **41**
5d 5s³ 5f 5f 5s 5s 7f 7fg 1981 6fg³ 7g³ 6g³ 8g³ 6d 8s 8fg³ 8fg² 8fg* 9g 11g 9d)
workmanlike gelding; sold out of R. Williams' stable 2,100 gns after beating
Donallan a head in seller at Edinburgh in July; well beaten afterwards; stays
1m; probably acts on any going but seems best on a sound surface; sometimes
blinkered (wore them at Edinburgh); has run creditably for a boy. *Mrs A. Bell.*

SHORT AND SHARP 2 ch.f. Sharpen Up 127–Brevity 76 (Pindari 124) (1981 **88**
6fg³ 5fg 6g³ 7.2fg² 7g) Mar 23; lengthy, rather lightly-made filly; half-sister to
several winners, including prolific 1975 2-y-o sprint winner Short Reign (by
Tribal Chief); dam won over 7f at 2 yrs; third in maiden races at Newmarket and
Nottingham prior to finishing excellent ¾-length second of 9 to Rapid Knot in
£4,400 nursery at Haydock in September (had plenty to do turning into straight
but ran on very strongly); better at 7f than shorter distances and will stay 1m;
ran poorly second and fifth outings and is none too consistent. *W. Hastings-Bass.*

SHOTGUN 3 gr.c. Warpath 113–Brief Flight 108 (Counsel 118) (1980 6g³ **116**
7d* 8f* 1981 10g* 10.5s² 12d⁴ 11g⁴ 10.5g 11g³)
For the first time in twenty-three years the North provided a leading fancy
for the Derby. The majority of the twenty-eight Northern challengers between
Guersillus, who started at 9/1 in 1958, and Shotgun, who started 7/1 second
favourite in 1981, have been rank outsiders. Neither Guersillus nor Shotgun
proved good enough to gain a place: Guersillus missed third to Hard Ridden
by a short head and a head, and Shotgun came fourth, beaten ten lengths, two
lengths and the same by Shergar, Glint of Gold and Scintillating Air. Remainder Man, third at 40/1 to Shirley Heights, is the only Northern-trained horse to
gain a place in the Derby since Dante. Dante won a war-time substitute at

*Heathorn Stakes, Newmarket—the grey Shotgun battles on gamely to beat Sass
(not in picture) with Little Wolf (left) third and Buffavento fourth*

Newmarket but no Northern-trained horse has won the Epsom Derby since Pretender in 1869.

A progressive sort as a two-year-old, Shotgun won the Heathorn Stakes on his reappearance at Newmarket in April, when reportedly short of work, and finished second in the Mecca-Dante; but he owed his market position at Epsom partly to the fact that Piggott was on board, having asked Shotgun's connections for the ride. No jockey knows better than Piggott where to be in the Derby field and he had Shotgun well placed at the top of Tattenham Hill. However, as some had feared, the strong, rangy Shotgun didn't stride out to full advantage on the downhill gradient and he had lost a little ground on the leaders as they straightened up for home. Piggott subjected him to a very forceful ride in the final three furlongs, persevering almost to the line. Somewhat surprisingly, Piggott reported that Shotgun found the Derby trip a little too far, and his later races were at shorter distances. His form deteriorated, however, possibly as a direct result of his very hard race at Epsom. Below-par performances in the Mecca Bookmakers Scottish Derby, the Benson and Hedges Gold Cup and the Doonside Cup obviously undermine confidence in Shotgun's future but a winter's rest may refresh him, as it did the 1980 Derby fourth Pelerin.

Shotgun stays a mile and a half but if he is to enhance his reputation we think it could be at around a mile and a quarter. Before the Derby hardly anyone entertained doubts about his being suited by a mile and a half. We certainly didn't. At the time, his second to Beldale Flutter in the Mecca-Dante Stakes at York in May over ten and a half furlongs was seen as a highly-promising performance by a horse sure to be suited by further. In fact, it was probably his best performance of the season: he was beaten three quarters of a length by Beldale Flutter and finished three lengths ahead of third-placed Scintillating Air. What's more, Shotgun's second place in the Mecca-Dante owed more to finishing pace than to stamina: he came from behind in a slowly-run race. It is also significant that he was able to lie up, without difficulty, with the strong early pace in the Derby. His connections tell us that Shotgun could start his four-year-old campaign in the Doncaster Mile at the March meeting; the Earl of Sefton Stakes at Newmarket's Craven meeting and the Westbury Stakes at Sandown, pattern races at nine furlongs and a mile and a quarter respectively, would also be on his programme if he were ours.

Shotgun (gr.c. 1978)	Warpath (gr 1969)	Sovereign Path (gr 1956)	Grey Sovereign / Mountain Path
		Ardneasken (br 1964)	Right Royal V / Alice Delysia
	Brief Flight (b 1960)	Counsel (b 1952)	Court Martial / Wheedler
		Par Avion (b 1948)	Phideas / Acid Flight

Shotgun's sire Warpath and his dam Brief Flight were both trained, like Shotgun, at Spigot Lodge, Middleham, Brief Flight by Lyde and Warpath by trainer Thornton's predecessor Sam Hall. Warpath, a genuine and consistent animal, stayed a mile and a half but did most of his racing at around a mile and a quarter; as a sire he gets plenty of horses who stay well. Brief Flight, who had a deformed off-hind leg and cost only 210 guineas as a yearling, won the Northern Free Handicap and was probably best at six or seven furlongs. She has bred several winners including Shotgun's brother Arrow, a winner at nine furlongs and a mile and a half in Britain and subsequently winner of the Spanish St Leger; the smart mile- to mile-and-a-quarter performer Aviator (by Frankincense) was Brief Flight's best offspring before Shotgun. Warpath was best on a sound surface but Brief Flight acted well on soft going; although Shotgun won on firm as a two-year-old, his two best performances at three were on a soft surface. *C. Thornton.*

SHOW-A-LEG 3 b.c. Tumble Wind–Lovely Woman 81 (Primera 131) (1980 **107** 5fg³ 5f 6f² 7g* 7d* 8g³ 8.2g* 7s 1981 10fg 10g² 12s² 11d⁴ 10fg² 10fg 10g² 10g* 10.8s* 10.2g) shapely colt; gained a well-deserved success when staying on strongly to beat Super Service by ¾ length in £4,900 handicap at Ascot in September; always going well when beating Beggar's Bridge by 3 lengths in minor event at Warwick the following month; in frame most previous starts, although didn't move well to post and ran below form on seventh; stays 1½m; acts on any going; genuine and consistent; sold 34,000 gns Newmarket Autumn Sales, and is reportedly to act as a pacemaker for Glint of Gold in 1982. *B. Hobbs.*

SHOW OF HANDS 5 b.g. Royal Prerogative 119–Lindylee 99 (Grey Sovereign   **74**
128§) (1980 8f* 8fg 7fg³ 7f* 7f 7g 1981 7g* 8g² 7g² 7g* 6fg³ 8.2g³ 8g³ 7g³ 7f³
7d 7v) tall gelding; quite a moderate handicapper; won at Edinburgh in April
and June; stays 1m; acts well on firm going; blinkered once in 1979; suitable
mount for a boy; usually ridden up with pace; suited by an easy track. *J. W.
Watts*.

SHOWPIECE 7 b.g. Daring Display 129–Magic Thrust 102 (Zarathustra 131)   —
(1980 7d 6g* 1981 6s 7fg 6d 7f 7g⁴ 6fg 7f 7f 6fg 7g) dipped-backed gelding;
plater; stays 7f; acts on any going; excellent mount for a boy; has worn blinkers.
D. Wilson.

SHOW TENT 2 ch.f. Abwah 118–Carmel Valley (Real Good Deal) (1981   —
6fg 6g 6d) Apr 26; 2,600Y; quite an attractive filly; third foal; dam well
behind outings; plating-class maiden. *G. Lewis*.

SHUFFLING 10 ch.g. St Chad 120–Shoofly 83 (Skymaster 126) (1980 6fg 7f   **73**
6fg 6fg 7g 6fg² 6f 1981 6fg³ 6fg 6d⁴ 5f 6fg) useful handicapper at his best;
stayed 7f; acted on any going; was tried in blinkers; sometimes wore bandages;
collapsed and died at Newmarket in August. *W. Hastings-Bass*.

SHURLAND 5 br.g. Mandamus 120–Prattler 68 (Narrator 127) (1980 10.6s   —
12.5s 10d 1981 9s 10g 8g⁴ 10f 9f 8.2g) strong, good sort; poor handicapper;
soundly beaten in seller final start; seems to stay 1¼m; sold 1,050 gns Ascot
September Sales. *M. W. Easterby*.

SHUTTLE D'OR 3 ch.g. Goldhill 125–Northern Flight (Borealis) (1980   —
6g 1981 8g 8fg 10.1fg) rangy gelding; little worthwhile form in maiden and
minor events; sold 875 gns Ascot December Sales. *D. Elsworth*.

SHY TALK 5 ch.m. Sharpen Up 127–Skymistress 91 (Skymaster 126) (1980   **60**
6h 6fg 5g 5s⁴ 6fg³ 5f 6g 6d 6f 6fg 6d 1981 6s 5s 5f³ 5fg 5g² 6fg* 5d 5f² 5f²
5f³ 6f* 6fg 5g) leggy, unfurnished mare; sprint handicapper; attracted no
bid after winning seller at Redcar in July and beat Gin Game a head at Chepstow
in September; suited by 6f; seems to act on any going; ran moderately when
blinkered once; sometimes bandaged off-hind; suitable mount for an inexperienced
rider. *A. W. Jones*.

SICASANTA 9 ch.g. Sica Dan 116–Christmas Rush (Klondyke Bill 125)   **45**
(1980 6f 5fg 5fg 5g 5fg 7g 5g 5g 5d 1981 5s 5s 5h 6fg) poor sprint plater; acts
on any going; has worn blinkers. *P. Cundell*.

SICONDA 2 ch.f. Record Token 128–Quickmatch 89 (Match III 135) (1981   **66**
5s² 5h³ 5g 5d 5g 8fg 8d³ 8.2s 8d⁴) Mar 26; 7,600F; workmanlike filly; half-
sister to 2 winners abroad; dam best at 1m; in frame in early-season maiden
events and sellers at the back end; stays 1m. *R. Hollinshead*.

SIDE HILL STAR 3 b.f. Comedy Star 121–Outcry (Alcide 136) (1980   —
7fg 7fg 6g 1981 12.2fg 16fg 12f 12.2g) smallish, compact filly; well beaten in
maiden and minor events; blinkered final start; sold 1,400 gns Newmarket
Autumn Sales. *D. Morley*.

SIDELINE 3 b.f. Ardoon 124–Royal Train (Aureole 132) (1980 5fg 6g 7d²   **52**
7fg* 8.2g 8g 7fg* 7f 7d 7d 1981 7fg 8g⁴ 7g 7f 12fg⁴ 8d 10f² 9g 11g) lightly-
made, leggy filly; none too good a mover; plater; doesn't appear quite to stay
1½m; probably acts on any going, but seems suited by firm; blinkered sixth
start; retained 400 gns Newmarket Autumn Sales. *K. Ivory*.

SIDE TRACK 5 br.h. Track Spare 125–Bench Game (King's Bench 132)   **86**
(1980 10.6fg 10fg² 10.4f³ 11f 10f* 10fg* 10fg 10.6d* 10.2g³ 11s⁴ 10.5s² 1981
10.2d⁴ 10.6g² 12fg* 12d² 12s* 13g* 14d 12fg³ 12g) well-made horse; not a
good mover nowadays; fair handicapper; successful at Epsom, York and Ayr;
suited by 1½m or more; acts on any going; usually held up; genuine; goes well
for G. Duffield; sold 6,200 gns Doncaster November Sales. *G. Pritchard-
Gordon.*

SIERRA MORENA (GER) 2 b.f. Experte–Sonett (Priamos 123) (1981   **48**
6fg⁴ 5f 7f² 7fg 7fg³) unfurnished filly; dam won twice in Germany; sire top
German 2-y-o of 1971 and second in German Derby and St Leger; plater; will
stay middle distances; sold 500 gns Newmarket Autumn Sales. *Sir Mark Prescott.*

SIGH 4 gr.f. Highland Melody 112–Sioux 95 (Nimbus 130) (1980 8fg 9f 8f*   —
8f 8d² 8fg 10g 8f 1981 12g 8fg 8g 8fg 7.6fg 10f 8d) workmanlike filly;
quite modest at her best; well beaten at 4 yrs; best at 1m; seems to act on any
going; often bandaged behind; has won for an apprentice. *A. Smith.*

SIGIR 3 ch.g. Simbir 130–La Girouette (Double Jump 131) (1980 8g 8g 1981 **70**
10s² 12d³ 11.5f 10v) tall, useful-looking gelding; placed in maiden races at
Nottingham and Haydock in spring; soundly beaten in similar races subsequently
but was off course 4 months before last start; suited by 1½m and will stay
further; possibly needs some give in the ground; sold to P. Mitchell 9,200 gns
Newmarket Autumn Sales. *L. Cumani.*

SIGNA 3 b.f. On Your Mark 125–Tumblova (Karabas 132) (1980 5.1f 5g —
1981 10s 10d) small filly; no sign of ability, including in sellers. *J. Scallan.*

SIGN DANCER (USA) 2 ch.c. Fifth Marine–Queen Magi (T.V. Commercial) **76**
(1981 6f 6f³ 6g* 6fg 6fg 8g) Apr 22; $65,000Y; well-made colt; second foal;
dam unraced half-sister to champion Canadian handicap mare Victorian Queen;
won 9-runner maiden race at Ayr in July by a neck from Glazepta Again; creditable sixth of 13 to Nioulargo in 1m nursery at Newmarket in September; will
stay 1¼m; yet to race on a soft surface; blinkered fourth outing. *G. Hunter.*

SILARI 7 gr.g. Birdbrook 110–Ciao Ciao Bambina (Welsh Abbot 131) (1980 **53**
8s³ 8.2fg 9.6h 7fg⁴ 8g 8f⁴ 8g 8fg 7.6d 7g 8fg³ 8g 1981 8fg 7f³ 8f 7g 7.6fg* 7fg
7f² 7fg² 7.6s 7h³ 8f 7g 8d 6s) plater; won apprentice handicap at Chester in
July; stays 1m; acts on any going but is suited by a sound surface; good mount
for an apprentice; sold to J. Harris 1,000 gns Newmarket Autumn Sales. *C.
Wildman.*

SILCAKEY 4 b.f. High Line 125–Resurgence (Runnymede 123) (1980 10g **55**
12g 10.1f 10f³ 10fg³ 8g² 10f³ 9s 10g 1981 12s⁴ 11.7d 11.7v⁴ 9.4g 10f 12.2s
12g²) lengthy, light-framed filly; stays 1½m; suited by top-of-the-ground;
blinkered third and fourth starts, running poorly on latter; didn't look too
genuine fifth outing. *M. Ryan.*

SILCA STAR KEY (USA) 3 b.c. Majestic Prince–Who's to Know (Fleet **98**
Nasrullah) (1980 6d 1981 8g 10s 7.6g* 8fg⁴ 7.3d* 8fg* 8d* 8v 8s) strong,
well-made, attractive colt; had a fine year and won maiden race at Lingfield
and handicaps at Newbury, Ascot (apprentices), Goodwood and Newmarket;
beat Singwara a head in last-named in October; stays 1m; probably unsuited
by very soft going; sold to H. Westbrook 25,000 gns Newmarket Autumn
Sales. *G. Harwood.*

SILENCER 4 br.g. Pinsun 108–Roychateau (Royal Record II) (1980 9g —
12h 13.8fg⁴ 10g 12g⁴ 13.8f² 11d³ 10g 12d 15s 1981 8g 11g 8g 8g⁴ 10f) neat
gelding; plater; stays 1¾m; acts on firm going; has worn blinkers; sometimes
sweats up. *R. Allan.*

SILENCE RULES (USA) 2 b.f. Secretariat–Love of Learning (Hail to Reason) **82**
(1981 6fg 6fg³ 8g⁴) Mar 18; lengthy, attractive filly; half-sister to winners
in USA by Forli and Arts and Letters; dam, 6f winner, is sister to very smart
middle-distance horse Halo and half-sister to top-class filly Tosmah; beaten
only 2 necks when third of 17 to Cricket Field in maiden race at Newbury in
August; beaten some way out when remote last of 4 to Height of Fashion in
May Hill Stakes at Doncaster in September; should be well suited by 1m. *I.
Balding.*

SILENT STREAM 2 b.f. Simbir 130–Regal Fountain 84 (Grey Sovereign 128§) **109 p**
(1981 6d*) Mar 3; half-sister to several winners, notably high-class French
sprinter King of Macedon (by Diatome); dam stayed 7f; looked promising on
her only start, winning newcomers event at Chantilly in July by a length from
Arrabida; will probably stay 1m; engaged in 1,000 Guineas and Oaks. *J.
Cunnington, jnr, France.*

SILENT TEARS 4 br.f. Weepers Boy 124–Skilla (Mexico III) (1980 6v **45**
6d 7fg 7f 6fg 6fg 6g 6g³ 6d* 6d 6fg 1981 5s 5fg 5d 5g 5fg³ 5fg* 5f) small
filly; won handicap at Warwick in June; had run in sellers earlier; stays 6f;
acts on a firm and a soft surface; blinkered nowadays. *M. Cousins.*

SILK EMPRESS 2 gr.f. Young Emperor 133–Taking Silk (Shantung 132) —
(1981 7f 5s) Apr 20; 28,000Y; smallish, rather leggy filly; good walker;
closely related to 3-y-o 7.6f winner Quality of Mercy and disqualified 1978
Italian 1,000 Guineas winner Romantic Love (both by Sovereign Path), and
half-sister to 3 winners; dam never ran; little sign of ability in maiden races
at Yarmouth in August (50/1) and Lingfield in October (4/1). *F. Durr.*

SILKEN EASE 3 br.f. Swing Easy 126–Twice Shy (Lord of Verona 120) —
(1980 5f² 6g 5fg³ 6g⁴ 1981 6g 7fg³ 8fg 8f 10fg 8d) rather leggy filly; plating-
class maiden; suited by 7f. *W. Haigh.*

SILKEN KNOT 3 ch.f. Nonoalco 131–Silken Way 103 (Shantung 132) (1980 **101**
6f* 7g³ 8g² 1981 8fg 10g 12g) lengthy filly; excellent mover; won Virginia
Water Stakes at Ascot and was placed in Waterford Candelabra Stakes at Goodwood and May Hill Stakes at Doncaster as a 2-y-o; destroyed after falling and
breaking both forelegs in Yorkshire Oaks won by Condessa at York in August;
had run promisingly when sixth to Star Pastures in Child Stakes at Newmarket
the previous month but was rather disappointing in between; should have been
suited by longer distances than 1m; blinkered final start. *R. Hern.*

SILK FASHION 7 b.m. Breeders Dream 116–Maud 87 (Vilmorin) (1980 12s **47**
12fg 10fg 10g* 12d² 12f 1981 10d* 13fg 10d⁴ 10s 10fg* 10f 11.5fg⁴) plater;
won at Folkestone in April (bought in 720 gns) and Yarmouth in July (bought
in 850 gns); stays 1½m; seems to act on any going; suitable mount for an
apprentice; has been tried in blinkers. *D. Wilson.*

SILK SCREEN 2 ch.c. Relkino 131–Silken Way 103 (Shantung 132) (1981 8g **84**
7g) Mar 26; rangy colt; second foal; half-brother to very useful staying 1980
2-y-o Silken Knot (by Nonoalco); dam, daughter of smart Boulevard, won over
1¼m from 3 starts at 3 yrs; ran well for long way when just over 9 lengths fifth
of 6 to Jalmood in minor event at Goodwood in September; favourite for 22-
runner maiden race at Newmarket the following month but faded after disputing
lead for over 5f, finishing about 8 lengths tenth to Rocamadour; bred to stay
1¼m+. *R. Hern.*

SILKY BABY (USA) 3 b.c. What A Pleasure–Gazala 124 (Dark Star) (1980 **115 d**
7d² 7.5d* 1981 9.7fg* 10.5s 9g 9s) half-brother to 4 winners, notably Irish
St Leger winner Gonzales and top-class Mississipian (both by Vaguely Noble)
and tip-top 1976 3-y-o Youth (by Ack Ack); dam won French 1,000 Guineas
and Oaks; got up near finish after being held up when beating Dunphy by a
short head in Group 3 Prix de Guiche at Longchamp in April; unplaced subsequently in Prix Lupin and Prix Daphnis on same course and in Prix Jean Prat
at Chantilly in between, probably best effort on latter course when 8 lengths
fifth of 9 to Cresta Rider; stayed 1½m; acted on a firm and a soft surface;
standing at Pillar Stud, Lexington, Kentucky, $10,000 live foal. *J. Cunnington,
jnr, France.*

SILLEY'S KNIGHT 5 b.g. Derring-Do 131–Silley's Maid 100 (Continuation 120) **86**
(1980 8d 7.6f 7f* 7.6f 8d 7g 8g 8g 8g* 1981 8g³ 7g 7d 8f 7g 8d 7s 8g) strong,
good-bodied, attractive gelding; fairly useful handicapper at his best but is
inconsistent and unreliable; suited by 1m; acts on any going; usually blinkered
nowadays. *J. Hanson.*

SILLY MOO 3 b.f. Silly Season 127–Rikis (Town Crier 119) (1980 7fg 7fg 5d **54**
1981 10g 10fg 10fg² 12fg 10f⁴ 10fg 10fg³ 10s) narrow, compact filly; plater;
stays 1¼m; sold to T. Hallett 660 gns Newmarket Autumn Sales. *D. Morley.*

SILLY PRICES 4 b.c. Silly Season 127–Galosh 86 (Pandofell 132) (1980 8.2fg **79**
8g 8g 8s 8f 1981 8g⁴ 8g*(dis) 10.5d 8g* 7g²) strong, compact, good-bodied
colt; very useful at 2 yrs; well beaten in 1980 but ran much better in 1981, winning 2 handicaps at Redcar in May; disqualified for having an illegal substance
in his system on first occasion but stayed on well to beat March Spark 1½ lengths
in Zetland Gold Cup on second; stayed 1m; probably acted on any going;
blinkered once in 1980; suitable mount for an apprentice; standing at Acrum
Lodge Stud, West Auckland at £250 n.f.n.f. *M. H. Easterby.*

SILLY STEVEN 2 b.c. Silly Season 127–Super Anna (Super Sam 124) (1981 **82**
7g 6g³) May 4; 2,100Y; lengthy colt; third foal; half-brother to Irish 3-y-o 1m
winner Darby Creek (by Jukebox); dam won at up to 1¼m in Ireland and also
won over hurdles; stayed on when 3 lengths third of 13 to Knave of Trumps in
minor event at Leicester in October; bred to stay 1¼m. *R. Hannon.*

SILLY TWIST 4 b.c. Silly Season 127–Twist of Lemon 80 (Northfields) (1980 **54**
10s 8g 12g 9f⁴ 9f⁴ 9f* 9g 10g⁴ 8d 10g 12g 12.2d* 1981 8d³ 8d 10.6s 10f 12f³ 12f³
15.8g² 13.8fg² 14.6f* 16g 15.8g 13fg⁴ 15g² 13d) good sort; ex-Irish; poor
handicapper; well ridden when scoring at Doncaster in July; stays well; probably
acts on any going; possibly none too genuine. *J. Fitzgerald.*

SILMIRA 4 gr.f. Grey Mirage 128–Silent Post 70 (Dumbarnie 125) (1980 8f **62**
8fg² 10.1s² 10.1d 11.7f 10fg⁴ 10fg² 10g 10s 1981 10s 10g⁴ 10v 8fg* 12d* 8fg⁴ 8h)
plain filly; bought in 1,500 gns after winning seller at Leicester in July; won
match at Lingfield the following month; stays 1½m; probably acts on any going;
has run respectably for an apprentice. *Mrs R. Lomax.*

SILOJOKA 2 br.f. Home Guard 129–Pereliance (Reliance II 137) (1981 5g 5s* **89**
5g³ 5f⁴ 5g² 6fg² 6fg⁴ 7d⁴ 7fg⁴ 6g) Mar 14; 11,000Y; strong, useful sort; half-

sister to 1¾m winner Chryso Mou (by Moulton) and to 2 winners in France; dam, half-sister to very smart Golden Horus, showed useful form at around 1½m in France; got up close home to win 17-runner maiden race at Windsor in May by ¾ length from La Babooshka; ran creditably in several good races afterwards, including Group 2 Queen Mary Stakes at Royal Ascot on fourth outing (beaten 2½ lengths into fourth place by Fly Baby) and Group 3 Waterford Candelabra Stakes at Goodwood in August on ninth (6¼ lengths fourth of 6 to Stratospheric); will probably stay 1¼m; acts on any going but has shown best form on a sound surface. *J. Benstead.*

SILVER CREEK 3 b.c. English Prince 129–Corbalton 103 (Milesian 125) (1980 — 7g 7fg⁴ 7g³ 8g³ 1981 12s⁴) quite attractive colt; twice third to very good colts as a 2-y-o when trained in Ireland by C. Collins; stayed on at one pace when 9 lengths fourth of 14 to St Malo in maiden race at Haydock in May, only outing of 1981; will stay further than 1½m. *I. Walker.*

SILVER DANCER 3 b.g. Tarboosh–Dark Dam (Linacre 133) (1980 7d 7fg 7fg⁴ — 8g 1981 8g 10.1d 12f⁴ 16f⁴ 16s 12d⁴) lightly-made gelding; quite a moderate maiden; possibly doesn't quite stay 2m; blinkered last 4 outings; sold 1,500 gns Ascot November Sales. *N. Gaselee.*

SILVER GATES 3 ch.f. Pieces of Eight 128–Seven Gates 77 (Henry the — Seventh 125) (1980 5fg 5fg 6g 7g 8s 1981 8s 10g 8d 12g 10f) lightly-made filly; poor walker; plater; stays 1m. *G. Lockerbie.*

SILVER HAWK (USA) 2 b.c. Roberto 131–Gris Vitesse (Amerigo 116§) (1981 **118** 6fg* 6fg² 7f* 8s²)

With Egypt very much one of racing's backwaters it seems strange that just as one ex-Egyptian trainer, Maurice Zilber, retires after an outstanding career in Europe, another, Michael Albina, looks about to join the ranks of England's leading trainers. Albina has already enjoyed great success training Arabian horses in the Middle East, sending out over eight hundred winners in Jordan, Egypt and Lebanon, and in 1981 he made a very promising start to his career training thoroughbreds in England. With the greater part of his small string well-bred two-year-olds it wasn't to be expected that he'd be quickly off the mark. Indeed it wasn't until July that he sent out his first winner, King Naskra, but in the second half of the season he produced several promising juveniles, including Cannon Shell, I'm Hot and My Destiny, as well as one of the best two-year-old colts, Silver Hawk.

Silver Hawk's first effort of real note came in his third race, the Intercraft Solario Stakes at Kempton in September. He'd made his debut only a month before, upsetting the odds laid on Balanchine in a maiden event at Yarmouth, and had then lost little caste in defeat in the Chertsey Lock Stakes at Kempton. There, giving 6 lb all round, he'd had the rest well strung out when beaten four lengths by the newcomer Sandhurst Prince, an effort which received a considerable boost from Sandhurst Prince's excellent Sirenia Stakes win just a day before the Solario. Even so Silver Hawk started only third favourite at Kempton behind Montekin and Corked, both impressive when first and second in a small race on the same course in August. Making up the field were Red Sunset, winner of the Coventry Stakes; Vin St Benet, a close fourth in the Lanson Champagne Stakes on his latest start; Wind and Wuthering, not yet the colt who won the Dewhurst; and two 50/1 shots. After one of the 50/1 shots Miramar Reef had led in the early stages, Red Sunset soon passed him and was still in front turning into the three-furlong straight where Silver Hawk was already at his quarters. Before long Silver Hawk took a narrow advantage

Intercraft Solario Stakes, Kempton—Silver Hawk strides clear in excellent style to beat Montekin

SIL

and then made the others look very ordinary with the burst of speed he produced at the distance, sprinting away to win by five lengths. Montekin managed to beat Red Sunset for second place by a length despite hanging under pressure. Silver Hawk ended his first season in the Royal Lodge Stakes at Ascot three weeks later, for which he was favourite ahead of the Seaton Delaval Stakes winner Zilos. He put up another smart performance to finish second of nine to the all-the-way-winner Norwick. However he had looked a bit dull in his coat beforehand and in the race never appeared to be going so smoothly on the soft ground at Ascot as he had on firm at Kempton. After racing in fifth or sixth place he dropped back to last coming to the turn into the straight and then lost more impetus when carried a bit wide by Zilos. From then on Silver Hawk was struggling to peg back Norwick's advantage. With a furlong and a half left to run he'd moved into third place but he was never going to reach the leader and it took him all his time to deprive Lobkowiez of second place by a neck.

Silver Hawk (USA) (b.c. Apr 19, 1979)

Roberto (b 1969) — Hail to Reason (br 1958) — Turn-to / Nothirdchance; Bramalea (b 1959) — Nashua / Rarelea

Gris Vitesse (gr 1966) — Amerigo (ch 1955) — Nearco / Sanlinea; Matchiche II (gr 1956) — Mat de Cocagne / Chimere Fabuleuse

Silver Hawk has an excellent pedigree—he's by the very successful Roberto out of Gris Vitesse, the winner of one of France's top mile races, the Prix Jacques le Marois—so he surely can't have been an impressive-looking yearling. His price of 77,000 dollars at the Fasig-Tipton Selected Summer Yearling Sale compares poorly with the average price of 177,688 dollars paid for sixteen Roberto yearlings in 1980. Indeed only two were knocked down for less and his price was just 27,000 dollars more than Roberto's fee in 1981. Silver Hawk doesn't particularly take the eye nowadays, being workmanlike and compact.

Silver Hawk comes from a family that has met with plenty of success in all spheres in France. His great-grandam Chimere Fabuleuse was a half-sister to the Grand Steeplechase de Paris winner Nagara and bred a good hurdles winner, the Grand Course de Haies d'Enghien winner Le Courtillet, and a very useful winner on the flat, Matchiche II, winner of the mile-and-a-half Prix de la Nonette. Chimere Fabuleuse had also won the Prix de la Nonette in the days when it was over eleven furlongs. Matchiche bred winners in Italy, France and the States, five altogether, with the French-raced Clem's Match and Gris Vitesse the best of them. The useful Clem's Match won at up to a mile and a quarter but Gris Vitesse showed surprising speed for a filly whose sire and dam won at up to a mile and three quarters and a mile and a half respectively; she won the Prix Yacowlef over five furlongs at two and never raced beyond a mile, winning the Prix Jacques le Marois on the last of her six outings. Easily the best of Gris Vitesse's three previous winners is the Graustark colt Blast Off, a very useful winner from a mile to eleven furlongs in France who finished in the rear when a 66/1-shot for the 1980 Derby. If Silver Hawk meets his engagement in the Derby he's unlikely to start at anything like so long a price—he has the makings of a very smart performer over a mile or more and looks sure to help put his trainer's name more firmly on the map in 1982. *M. Albina.*

SILVER KETTLE 3 gr.g. Habat 127–The Maid (Milesian 125) (1980 6g 1981 5g 7.6g 6g 6g) useful-looking gelding; good mover; no sign of ability, including in a seller; bandaged in front only start at 2 yrs. *G. Balding.* —

SILVER LEO 3 br.g. Dubassoff–Fingerofortune 100 (Fortino II 120) (1980 6d 6d 7g 7g* 8g² 7fg 8g 8d 8.2s 1981 12s 8.2fg 9.4g 13.8fg 13fg 7f 8fg) strong, useful sort; disappointing handicapper; suited by 7f and 1m as a 2-y-o; possibly needs a sound surface; blinkered final start of 1980. *J. Harris.* —

SILVER MANTLE 2 b.f. Bustino 136–Moonlight Night 112 (Levmoss 133) (1981 7g 8g) Apr 1; lengthy, useful-looking filly; second foal; dam, third in Oaks, is half-sister to high-class Main Reef; in mid-division in maiden and minor events at Doncaster and Newmarket at the back end; may do better when given a test of stamina in 1982. *H. Cecil.* —

SILVER MELODY 4 b.f. Highland Melody 112–Silver Cherry 69 (Silver Cloud 121) (1980 7fg 8s 7g 8fg 7fg 7f² 8f 8.2v 1981 8s 10d⁴ 10s 10fg 10f) unfurnished filly; plater; stays 1¼m; probably acts on any going; often blinkered; has run respectably for an apprentice. *J. Doyle.* —

798

Cecil Frail Handicap, Haydock—Silver Season makes virtually all the running to win from Von Erlach (far right) and Sauvage (far left)

SILVER RULER 3 b.c. Sovereign Path 125–Argentessa 80 (Sing Sing 134) **75** (1980 7d 1981 7fg 7g* 7d 7d⁴ 7g 7f* 7f 8.3fg 8g) strong, attractive colt; won minor event at Brighton in May and handicap at Bath in July, latter by ¾ length from Violino Fandango after being held up; should stay 1m; probably acts on any going; sometimes starts slowly; sold to M. Banks 5,200 gns Newmarket Autumn Sales. *P. Walwyn.*

SILVER SEASON 3 b.c. Martinmas 128–Silver Ray 70 (Skymaster 126) **110** (1980 5fg 6g 7f 7fg 7s⁴ 1981 8g⁴ 8g*(dis) 10g* 8.2s* 12d 8f 10d 8d* 8fg² 8fg 9g 10g) lengthy colt; has a rather round action; hung left under pressure and was disqualified after beating Bunter a length in 20-runner maiden race at

Mr M. Hassan's "Silver Season"

Kempton in May; made virtually all in £3,400 event at Lingfield and Cecil Frail Handicap at Haydock later in month, in latter event sticking on really well and beating Von Erlach by 2½ lengths; returned to form when beating Captain Nick by 1½ lengths in Rose of York Handicap at York in August and ran another game race when 3 lengths second to Bunter in Northern Goldsmiths Handicap at Newcastle later in month, but was rather disappointing afterwards; effective at 1m and ran well over 1½m in Derby (disputed lead until turning for home and finished seventh of 18 behind Shergar); acts on a firm surface but is ideally suited by some give in the ground (reportedly jarred himself on firm on sixth start); front runner. *C. Brittain.*

SILVERSMITH 8 gr.g. Silver Shark 129–La Connaisseuse 78 (King's Bench 132) (1980 NR 1981 16fg) lightly raced and of little account on flat nowadays but is a fairly useful chaser. *L. Kennard.* —

SILVER SNOW 3 gr.f. Abwah 118–Silver Yarn (Peter's Yarn 106) (1980 6fg 8fg² 8d⁴ 1981 8g 8f 8f⁴ 8.2f* 8fg³ 8.2d* 8f⁴ 10.6fg 8g) well-grown, rather leggy filly; won apprentice maiden race and minor event at Hamilton in summer; didn't have best of runs and wasn't disgraced in between; stays 1m well; seems to act on any going; had stiff task final outing. *P. Rohan.* 64

SILVER STRIKER 2 b.c. Furry Glen 121–Grannie's Slipper (Allangrange 126) (1981 6f 6g 7.2fg 8g) May 5; IR 840F, IR 3,800Y; useful sort; first foal; dam, who never ran, is closely related to Irish 1,000 Guineas runner-up Lovely Kate; no worthwhile form in maiden and minor events. *E. Eldin.* —

SILVER SURPRISE 3 br.f. Son of Silver 123–Bunny Club 66 (Astec 128) (1980 NR 1981 8f 8fg 10fg* 10.6v) rangy filly; third foal; closely related to hurdles winner Teal Eye (by Mon Fils); dam ran only 3 times; apprentice ridden, showed improved form when beating Modestine in quite good style by 2½ lengths in maiden race at Salisbury in September; stays 1¼m; acts on a firm surface. *M. Pipe.* 78

SILVERY MOON 4 ch.f. Lorenzaccio 130–Aunt Jobiska 71 (Grey Sovereign 128§ or Aureole 132) (1980 6f 1981 8g⁴ 8g 8fg) lengthy, unfurnished filly; only plating class; stays 1m. *W. Hastings-Bass.* —

SIMBAD 5 b.g. Simbir 130–Amsterdam Lassie (Arctic Storm 134) (1980 NR 1981 18g) won over 7f in Ostend at 2 yrs; lightly raced on flat since, though has won over hurdles; should stay well. *R. Fisher.* —

SIMBEAU 4 b.g. Simbir 130–Serendip (Sing Sing 134) (1980 NR 1981 10f) 860 3-y-o; eighth of 12 in ladies race at Brighton in August. *H. O'Neill.* —

SIMBIRICA 3 ch.f. Simbir 130–Erica (Ballyciptic 122) (1980 NR 1981 10s) 3,100Y; third foal; half-sister to 1978 Irish 2-y-o 5f and 6f winner Gomera (by Young Emperor); dam, lightly raced, showed a little ability; tailed off in maiden race won by Dovetail at Nottingham in October. *P. Felgate.* —

SIMBOL EQUATION 3 b.c. Simbir 130–Golda 81 (Red God 128§) (1980 NR 1981 12fg 10.1g 13.1g 14s⁴) 2,100F; half-brother to fairly useful 1975 Irish 2-y-o 5f winner Harford Belle (by Track Spare); dam moderate half-sister to Oaks winner Ginevra; slow maiden. *D. Ancil.* —

SIMBULA 2 b. or br.g. Simbir 130–Lavarna (Le Levanstell 122) (1981 5g⁴ 6f) Mar 2; 7,800Y; big, useful sort; good walker; half-brother to useful miler Brian's Venture (by Sallust), and to useful jumper Tip the Wink and bumpers winner Tip the Tide (both by Tiepolo II); dam Irish 1¼m winner; found 6f too sharp when creditable 5 lengths fifth of 13 to Sangalkan in £5,600 event at York in June; gelded subsequently; likely to need at least 1¼m at 3 yrs. *M. H. Easterby.* 70

SIMETTE 4 ch.g. Simbir 130–Machete (Macherio) (1980 10s* 10d³ 12fg² 16g³ 12d⁴ 12s 17.4s 16.1s 14g³ 13s 1981 12fg 12g⁴ 14s 13.1g 13.3g³ 16g 16fg² 14g 16g³ 17.1d³ 12g³) quite well-made, useful-looking gelding; staying handicapper; appears to act on any going; blinkered nowadays; sold to C. James 6,200 gns Newmarket Autumn Sales. *J. Bethell.* 72

SIMINGIA 3 ch.f. Simbir 130–Notonia 73 (Never Say Die 137) (1980 NR 1981 12s³ 16fg 16f 15fg 12f 13.8fg) smallish, fair sort; poor maiden; behind in sellers last 2 outings; best run at 1½m; blinkered fourth start; sold 2,100 gns Ascot August Sales. *J. W. Watts.* —

SIMLA 5 ch.h. Simbir 130–Persian Gal 68 (Persian Gulf) (1980 12d 12fg⁴ 14f² 12f 12g* 12fg³ 12g³ 12f² 12g 12fg² 12g 1981 13s³ 12fg² 12g* 13.1g* 16f 12f 79

13.1h⁴ 14fg 12g) lightly-built horse; modest handicapper; won at Brighton in May and Bath in June; effective at 1½m and stays well; acts on any going; ran moderately in blinkers once; suitable mount for a boy; sold to D. Wintle 1,450 gns Newmarket Autumn Sales. *P. Walwyn.*

SIMMIES LOVE 2 ch.f. Record Token 128–Love Is Blind 90 (Hasty Road) —
(1981 5g 5g 5d 6f 6d) Mar 8; 4,800Y; quite a well-made filly; fourth living foal; dam 2-y-o 6f winner; in rear in maiden and minor events. *R. Hollinshead.*

SIMPLICITY 4 b.g. The Brianstan 128–Sovereign Help 98 (Sovereign Lord 120) —
(1980 5h 5f 5g 6s 1981 8g 6g) lightly-made gelding; plater; stays 6f; probably acts on any going; sometimes sweats up; often blinkered. *T. Fairhurst.*

SIMPLY GREAT (FR) 2 b.c. Mill Reef 141–Seneca (Chaparral 128) (1981 **96 p**
7g* 7g)
Those who listened to the tall stories in the autumn about this supposed champion must have been disillusioned by his performance in the William Hill Dewhurst Stakes at Newmarket in October. Starting 6/4 favourite, he was one of the first beaten and came home seventh of nine, a long way behind the winner Wind and Wuthering. Simply Great's starting price was a measure of his home reputation, not of his public form which consisted of a smooth three-length win from twenty-two others in a division of the Westley Maiden Stakes over the Dewhurst course and distance earlier in the month. The difference between the level of performance required to win a maiden race and that required to win a race of the importance of the Dewhurst is much greater than the majority of the betting public seem to appreciate: 6/4 about Simply Great in the Dewhurst was preposterous to anyone with a sense of proportion in betting matters. Simply Great made headlines before he set foot on a racecourse: a number of hefty ante-post bets were struck for the 1982 Two Thousand Guineas some time before he made his debut. His halo has slipped a little but he is still among the ante-post favourites for the Guineas as we write. He has a lot of improvement to make before we can seriously consider him for the classics but he was broken in his coat when he ran in the Dewhurst and may well be capable of much better than he showed in that race. Nevertheless, we strongly advise readers against falling over themselves to bet on him for the classics at this stage. Far better to see first how he performs in his first race as a three-year-old.

		Mill Reef	Never Bend	Nasrullah
Simply Great (Fr) b.c. May 23, 1979)		(b 1968)	(b 1960)	Lalun
			Milan Mill	Princequillo
			(b 1962)	Virginia Water
		Seneca	Chaparral	Val de Loir
		(b 1973)	(b 1966)	Niccolina
			Schonbrunn	Pantheon
			(b 1966)	Scheherezade III

Simply Great is a well-made, deep-girthed colt but, in a string of horses, we should not pick him out as a classic winner on looks; he hasn't a lot of scope. He is, however, a most impressive mover. He should stay at least a mile and a half. His sire and dam won at the trip; and Seneca's sire Chaparral was the best staying three-year-old of his generation in France and was beaten a short head in the Prix du Cadran the next year, while Seneca's dam won the German One Thousand Guineas and Oaks and showed very smart form at up to thirteen furlongs in France. Simply Great is Seneca's second foal—her first was the modest Prince Tenderfoot three-year-old Spook, runner-up in minor events in France at a mile and at ten and a half furlongs early in 1981. *H. Cecil.*

Westley Maiden Stakes, Newmarket—an impressive debut by much-vaunted Simply Great

SIMPSON JERSEY 7 br.h. Highland Melody 112–Leisure Hour (Persian **55** Gulf) (1980 12f³ 13.3g* 12d² 14.6g 11.7f* 10s³ 12g 1981 12s 12s⁴ 12v 12g* 12g) middle-distance handicapper; won at Pontefract in April; acts on any going; has worn blinkers; suited by a strongly-run race. *B. McMahon.*

SINCERELY MILLS 3 ch.f. Ardoon 124–Coastal Rocket 74 (Roan Rocket 128) **66** (1980 5fg⁴ 5f 6g³ 6s 7fg³ 8g³ 8fg 1981 7g 7d* 7g² 8s 8fg² 8g 8fg³ 8f) quite well-made filly; won maiden event at Leicester in April; placed in minor event and 2 handicaps afterwards; stays 1m; acts on a firm and a soft surface; sold 4,000 gns Newmarket Autumn Sales. *C. Brittain.*

SINGALONG JOE 3 ch.c. Sharpen Up 127–Captive Flower 99 (Manacle 123) **52** (1980 6d 6g⁴ 5.1g 7s³ 7v 1981 8.2s 7f 8g⁴) leggy, light-framed colt; plating-class maiden; stays 1m; acts on soft going; sold 1,700 gns Newmarket Autumn Sales. *I. Walker.*

SING BABY SING 3 b.f. Caruso 112–Triarder 43 (Hard Ridden 131) (1980 **—** 5d 5d⁴ 5f 5f 6g² 5g⁴ 6f 1981 8g 8.2g 12f) leggy filly; bad plater; occasionally blinkered. *Mrs C. Lloyd-Jones.*

SINGING BOY (FR) 3 b.c. Fort Coulonge–Messine II (Boree 113) (1980 **113** 5.5g² 5.5g² 5.5d² 5.5g³ 5.5g* 6.5s 10d² 1981 10.5v⁴ 9.2fg² 11fg³ 10v 12fg³ 10g 12.5f³ 12f 10.5g 12v) French colt; half-brother to a minor winner; dam won at up to 1m; dead-heated for first in minor event at Evry at 2 yrs; didn't manage to win in 1981, but was in frame on several occasions, including when close second to Bikala in handicap at Longchamp in April, 4 lengths fourth to subsequently-disqualified Explorer King in Group 2 Prix Noailles on same course later in month, third to Bellman in Group 3 Prix du Lys at Chantilly in June (beaten neck and same) and 1¾ lengths third to Roi Guillaume in Prix de Menneval at Deauville in August; stays 1½m; probably acts on any going. *J. Daubin, France.*

SINGING DANDY 2 ch.g. Dynastic 105–Nottingham Belle 78 (Chanteur II **61** 135) (1981 6g 5fg² 6g 6g 5f 6fg⁴) Apr 18; 750Y; compact, plain gelding; half-brother to several winners here and in South Africa, notably useful 5f to 7f winner Janabelle (by Gentle Art); dam a miler; plater; will stay 7f; had tongue tied down last 2 outings. *H. Bell.*

SINGING FOOL 5 gr.g. Singing Bede 122–Dilwyn 84 (Immortality) (1980 **31** 12s 10g 1981 7g 8.5g 8f 12fg 10f² 8f) poor maiden; stays 1¼m; acts on firm going; blinkered once in 1980. *D. Jermy.*

SINGING JOHNNY 2 b.g. Record Run 127–Seasoning 74 (Silly Season 127) **—** (1981 5g 6s) Apr 30; IR 2,000F, 1,200Y; third foal; dam won over 7f at 2 yrs; unquoted when in rear in maiden races at Redcar in May (auction event) and Carlisle in June. *J. Fitzgerald.*

SINGING SAILOR 2 br.c. Mansingh 120–Sealady (Seaepic 100) (1981 5s **98** 5v³ 5d* 5d* 6s 5g² 5f* 6fg⁴ 6g² 5d) Apr 2; 1,300Y; small, quite well-made colt; second foal; dam never ran; steadily developed into a useful colt, winning maiden auction event at Salisbury and small races at Pontefract and Beverley by early-July; quickened in excellent style when beating Chellaston Park by 3 lengths at Beverley; prominent in quite valuable races on ninth and tenth outings, going down by 3 lengths to Take The Floor in Strathclyde Stakes at Ayr in July (after looking to have race in his pocket when clear at halfway) and being beaten only 2½ lengths when last of 5 to Jester in Prince of Wales's

Pontins Holiday Stakes, Newmarket—Sing Softly quickens well to beat Travel On (braces), Bless The Match (hooped cap) and Blakesware County

Stakes at York the following month; best at 5f; yet to prove he acts on really soft going; tough and genuine. *C. Spares.*

SING SOFTLY 2 br.f. Luthier 126–Melody Hour 105 (Sing Sing 134) (1981 **92 p** 6fg*) Jan 22; tall, lengthy, attractive filly; good mover; third foal; half-sister to fairly useful 3-y-o stayer Military Band (by Sassafras) and 1979 2-y-o 5f winner Bandsman (by So Blessed); dam useful 5f winner at 2 yrs; didn't realise what was required of her until given a crack 2f out when favourite for £4,200 event at Newmarket in June, but then lengthened her stride most impressively to win going away by a length from Travel On; will stay 1¼m; reportedly had a setback after Newmarket but should make a very useful filly at 3 yrs if making a full recovery. *H. Cecil.*

SINGULARITY 2 ch.f. Mansingh 120–Standoffish (Be Friendly 130) (1981 **67** 5g 5f 5fg 5g 5g³ 6s 5g² 5s) Mar 5; 3,000Y; leggy filly; fourth foal; dam never ran; plater; unseated rider at halfway on only outing over 6f; sold 600 gns Doncaster November Sales. *J. Etherington.*

SINGWARA 3 br.f. Blue Cashmere 129–Exeat (Quartette 106) (1980 5g 5f⁴ **92** 5g 6d 1981 6g 6g² 7v* 6s² 7g² 7f* 7g 6fg 7fg³ 8g³ 8g²) big, well-made filly; improved and gained narrow wins in maiden event at Goodwood and handicaps at Leicester and Newmarket; quickened up impressively and had something in hand when beating Hindi and Canaille in close finish in Duchess of Montrose Handicap on last-named course in July (apprentice ridden); ran creditably several other starts; stays 1m; acts on any going, but is possibly best with some give underfoot; lost chance by dwelling eighth start. *J. Benstead.*

SIN NO MORE 4 b.g. So Blessed 130–Moghari 78 (Djebe) (1980 8g 1981 **—** 16fg 12.3g) seems of little account; has worn blinkers. *M. Reddan.*

SIR BADSWORTH 3 b.g. Tarboosh–High Reserve (Young Emperor 133) **—** (1980 NR 1981 10f 10d) big, rangy gelding; second foal; dam never ran; behind in a maiden and a minor event at Nottingham; blinkered in latter. *H. Wharton.*

SIR BLESSED 2 b.c. So Blessed 130–Morinda 87 (Matador 130) (1981 6d 6fg **88** 7g² 7g³ 8d³) May 2; 7,000Y; useful-looking colt; half-brother to 3 winners, including 6f and 1m winner Zaharoff (by Wolver Hollow); dam won at 7f and 1m; placed in maiden races in the autumn, final occasion when very close third of 18 to Sugar and Mint at Leicester in November; stays 1m; has the ability to win in modest maiden company. *R. Williams.*

SIR DOMINO 3 ch.g. Morston 125–Dominant 86 (Behistoun 131) (1980 7g **69** 8g 7g 1981 11s 12d 10.5f 10fg 11f⁴ 10f³ 12g 12f² 10.6s⁴) leggy, unfurnished gelding; ran best races when placed in maiden events at Ripon and Redcar in September (ridden by 7-lb claimer both times); stays 1½m. *F. Durr.*

SIR DORO 4 b.c. Cavo Doro 124–Privas (Preciptic 122) (1980 10.2d² 12fg³ **64** 10.5f 13.3fg 12g 14g² 12d² 14.7d* 17.4s 1981 13.3g 12g 12s) strong, good-bodied colt; well beaten at 4 yrs; stays well; acts on a firm and a soft surface; blinkered twice in 1980. *G. Balding.*

SIRENA 4 ch.f. Red Alert 127–Buenaventura II (Celtic Ash) (1980 7f 8fg **60** 10f² 10s³ 12s⁴ 11.5g* 12g³ 10.1g* 10fg* 10g³ 1981 9g³ 12f 12fg⁴ 12f⁴ 14f²) rangy, good-bodied filly; stays 1¾m; acts on any going; best in blinkers; suitable mount for an inexperienced rider; genuine; sold 4,000 gns Newmarket December Sales. *Sir Mark Prescott.*

SIR GERALD 2 ch.c. Roan Rocket 128–Sucu Sucu 73 (Tudor Jinks 121) **—** (1981 5g 6fg 7fg 6fg 6g) May 22; 6,800F; workmanlike colt; carries plenty of condition; half-brother to numerous winners in this country and abroad, notably very smart miler Redundant (by Busted); dam sprinter; no worthwhile form in maiden and minor events. *J. Benstead.*

SIR GIVENCHY 3 ch.c. High Line 125–Topolass 79 (Acropolis 132) (1980 **—** NR 1981 12d 15fg 16.5fg 12fg 10g) 650Y; leggy, sparely-made colt; half-brother to a winner in Brazil; dam, sister to very useful performer Atopolis, won over 1¼m; poor form in varied company, including selling. *W. Musson.*

SIR GORDON 4 ch.g. Bustino 136–Wrekinianne 96 (Reform 132) (1980 10f **—** 10g 8g 14fg 14d² 15.5g* 14d* 1981 16s) big, strong gelding; fair performer at 3 yrs; ran deplorably only start in 1981 in April; suited by a test of stamina; acts on a soft surface; one paced. *D. Nicholson.*

SIR JESTER 3 br.g. Bronze Hill 96–Jet Maiden (Star Gazer 123) (1980 5fg 51
5fg 5d 5g* 6g³ 8.2d⁴ 8fg 8.2s 1981 13.8fg 8f 7fg 6g 8g⁴) small gelding; not a
good mover; plater; stays 1m; has been tried in blinkers. *R. Johnson.*

SIR JOHN FALSTAFF (USA) 2 br.c. True Knight–Laughing Allegra (His 80
Majesty) (1981 5g 6fg 7g⁴ 7f⁴ 8.2fg* 8d 8.2s 8g² 8d²) Apr 2; $25,000Y; neat,
rather lightly-made, quite attractive colt; first foal; dam, closely related to
smart 1¼m winner Prince Dantan, ran only 3 times; ran out a comfortable 2½-
length winner from Saenredam in nursery at Nottingham in September; disappointing afterwards until blinkered in sellers at Newmarket and Leicester on
last 2 starts (tried to make all both times and was caught close home); will stay
middle distances; acts on a firm and a soft surface. *P. Cole.*

SIR KEVITA 2 b.c. Regal George–Ellie Mae IV (pedigree unknown) (1981 —
7fg 8.2d 8s) non-thoroughbred colt; sire unraced son of Floriana; probably of
little account. *A. Bailey.*

SIR LUCKY 2 ch.g. Bonne Noel 115–Mount Gay (Divine Gift 127) (1981 6d 54
8.2d 8d) May 9; IR 1,450Y (privately); lightly-made gelding; fourth foal; dam
never ran; blinkered when behind in sellers in second half of season. *C. Crossley.*

SIR PLUS (FR) 3 b.g. Pampered King 121–Nephopolis (Acropolis 132) (1980 —
NR 1981 12s 12s) big, rangy gelding; fourth reported foal; dam showed
only poor form; soundly beaten in £2,000 race at Lingfield and maiden race at
Newbury, both in October; looks more of a jumper. *D. Morley.*

SIR PRIZE SING 2 br.c. Master Sing 109–Anagola 64 (Queen's Hussar 124) 44
(1981 5s 5fg³ 6f 5f 5f 5s) May 3; 400F; well-grown colt; poor mover; closely
related to a winner in Belgium by Manacle; bad plater; form only at 5f; not
disgraced when blinkered fifth outing. *P. Felgate.*

SIR ROB 2 ch.c. Gulf Pearl 117–Maria's Bisca 74 (Hook Money 124) (1981 6fg 59
6g 7fg⁴ 7d 6f 8fg 8.2d³ 8d) May 30; 2,200Y; compact colt; half-brother to 2
winners; dam won at 1⅛m; plater; in frame at Redcar in July and Nottingham in
September; will stay 1¼m+; lost chance by running wide into straight sixth
outing. *Hbt Jones.*

SIR SAMUEL (USA) 4 ch.c. L'Enjoleur–Amber Fields (Ambiorix 130) 75
(1980 5fg 5fg 5fg 8h 6f 5g 5fg 5g 5.3fg 5fg* 5f 5g 1981 6s 5fg 5g 8.5g 5g² 5fg³
6g⁴ 5h 5fg 5g* 5g 5s² 5g) big, well-made, good sort; inconsistent sprint handicapper; won at Goodwood in September; has form over 6f but is better at 5f;
acts on any going; blinkered last 3 starts in 1980. *W. Wightman.*

SIR SHOSTAKOVICH 2 br.c. Rheingold 137–Sinful 72 (Grey Sovereign 128§) 88
(1981 7fg³ 7fg² 8.5g* 7d) Apr 17; IR 3,800Y; half-brother to numerous winners
here and abroad, including very useful sprinter Adams Pet (by Super Sam);
dam ran only at 2 yrs; placed in 13-runner maiden races at Leopardstown in
August, finishing 2 lengths third to Anfield and length second to Sun Worship,
prior to winning 11-runner maiden event at Galway in September by 2½ lengths
from Rijoto; 12/1 when ninth of 11 to Day Is Done in National Stakes at the
Curragh later in September; will probably stay 1¼m. *L. Browne, Ireland.*

SIR TRISTAN 4 br.c. Brigadier Gerard 144–Ysolda 100 (Elopement 125) 88
(1980 8g⁴ 8fg 10s 11d³ 10fg⁴ 1981 8g* 10.2g 10f³ 8fg 10fg 8s* 8v⁴ 8g) compact
colt; fairly useful handicapper; won at Pontefract in April and trotted up in
apprentice race at Ascot in October; appears to stay 11f; acts on any going
but goes well on soft; started very slowly penultimate outing. *R. Sheather.*

SISTER KITTY 3 b.f. Lochnager 132–Anneiv (Vienna 127) (1980 5g 6s² 69
8d⁴ 7d 1981 5d² 7fg 7d 8.5g²(dis) 8d* 8g 9.4fg 8fg³ 8.3g² 8f² 8d³ 8.2v 8d)
small, lightly-made filly; ran erroneously as Myra's Pet first 3 starts when
trained by R. Smyth, best effort when second to Kiss in maiden race at Folkestone in April; ran well in varied company afterwards, and beat Beggar's Bush
by 7 lengths in maiden race at Bath in June; stays 1m; acts on any going.
R. Williams.

SISTER RESISTA 2 b.f. Record Token 128–Silk Willoughby (Pirate King 129) —
(1981 7.2f⁴ 6fg) Apr 11; 5,400Y; sister to 3-y-o 7f winner Hit Record and
half-sister to fair 7f performer Marston (by Tribal Chief); dam unraced sister to
smart stayer Avast; chased along throughout when 4½ lengths fourth of 6 to
Swiftfoot in £3,000 event at Haydock in July; 20/1 when making little show in 19-
runner maiden race won by Dawn Ditty at Salisbury 2 months later. *B. Hills.*

SISTER SASSAFRAS 2 b.f. Sassafras 135–The Nun 99 (Saint Crespin III 132) —
(1981 7d) Mar 14; well-made filly; half-sister to winners here and in France,

including fair 1974 2-y-o 5f winner Pilgrim Soul (by Tudor Melody); dam 1½m winner; 14/1, made no show when behind in 18-runner maiden race won by Sans Blague at Newbury in September. *M. Stoute.*

SITEX 3 b.c. Record Run 127–Glorious Light 53 (Alcide 136) (1980 5f 5fg **60** 5.3d² 6s² 6g² 6g³ 6fg 1981 5s 6d² 6fg 8fg 7g 6g³ 6d⁴ 5d² 6g 6fg 6fg 6s 6s) useful-looking colt; poor walker; plating-class maiden; best form at sprint distances but is bred to stay 1m+; suited by some give in the ground. *M. Bolton.*

SITICA 4 b.g. Siliconn 121–Time Call (Chanteur II 135) (1980 7d⁴ 6fg 7f 6fg — 1981 5s⁴ 5d 6g 6g 6f) narrow, fair sort; better suited by 6f than 5f and should stay 7f; goes well on a soft surface and is unsuited by really firm going; sometimes sweats up. *G. Toft.*

SIT THI DEAWN 2 ch.g. Jimmy Reppin 131–Sky Flight (Roan Rocket 128) — (1981 5fg 5d) May 8; 780Y; small gelding; first foal; dam never ran; only poor form in sellers at Warwick and Wolverhampton in the spring. *J. Berry.*

SIX CLUBS (USA) 2 ch.c. Charles Elliott–Augusta J. (Lenso) (1981 6g⁴ 7d) — Mar 26; strong, good sort; third foal; brother to useful 1980 2-y-o 7f performer Blackfoot and half-brother to a minor winner in USA; dam won 3 times at up to 1m at 4 yrs; started at 13/8 for 4-runner Chesters Stakes at Newcastle in June but faded very quickly soon after halfway and finished 9 lengths last to Jump Jar; didn't move well to start and was never going when in rear in 18-runner maiden event won by Noumayr at Newmarket in August. *R. Sheather.*

SIX LEGS 2 gr.g. Three Legs 128–Alta Moda (Snob 130) (1981 5s 5g 5g³ 5g³ **71** 5fg* 5g) Apr 16; IR 6,000F, IR 13,500Y; strong gelding; none too good a mover in his slower paces; ran best race when winning 7-runner maiden event at Edinburgh in July by 4 lengths from Keep Smiling after being clear from halfway; should stay 6f; possibly needs a firm surface; blinkered last 2 outings; sent to Hong Kong. *Denys Smith.*

SIX MILE BOTTOM 3 b.c. Brigadier Gerard 144–Bamba 76 (Busted 134) **111** (1980 6g³ 6fg 7fg 7fg* 7d* 1981 9fg 12g³ 12g³ 10v 12f* 12f* 11g² 12d⁴ 11.1f 8g 10g) neat, strong, attractive colt; first foal; dam, second 3 times at around 1m, is daughter of high-class Sovereign; accounted for small fields in Churchill Stakes at Ascot in June (beat Sheer Grit very smoothly by ¾ length) and Welsh Derby at Chepstow in July (quickened up best in a slowly-run race and beat Kings General by a length); went down by a neck to Little Wolf (rec 3 lb) in Mecca Bookmakers Scottish Derby at Ayr later in July; finds 1½m too short and stays 1½m well; has won on a soft surface, but is suited by firm going; ran disappointingly ninth start and subsequently had stiff tasks in handicaps. *H. Wragg.*

SKATEBOARD 5 b.g. Tower Walk 130–Palgal (Le Prince 98) (1980 10s 8s — 11.7f 8fg 12fg 8g² 8d 12d 1981 10d) lengthy, good sort; plater; best at up to 1m; sold to D. Wilson 800 gns Ascot June Sales. *R. Carter.*

SKELBROOKE 4 b.f. Mummy's Pet 125–Deep Freeze 75 (Varano) (1980 — 7.2d 7g 9.4fg* 10s³ 9g³ 10s² 10d 1981 9g 9fg) unfurnished filly; quite modest at her best but isn't too consistent; stays 1¼m; seems to act on any going; didn't look too genuine once in 1980. *E. Weymes.*

SKERRY DANCE 4 br.f. Ragstone 128–Sea Tune (Klairon 131) (1980 8fg **68** 7.6f 8g² 10fg² 10f 1981 12d⁴ 12g 12d* 12f² 12f⁴ 14fg) quite attractive, lightly-made filly; good mover; won handicap at Lingfield in August; stays 1½m; seems to act on any going. *R. Price.*

SKEWSBY 5 b.h. Andrea Mantegna–Rogali 80 (Royal Avenue 123) (1980 — 16s 16g 12g 12fg 15.8d 18s 1981 18g) big, useful sort; good walker; staying handicapper; has shown no form for a long time; probably acts on any going. *M. W. Easterby.*

SKILFUL SPARK 5 br.g. Lightning Trial 103–Clever Pixie 69 (Goldhill 125) — (1980 NR 1981 13.4fg) fair sort; sweated up when behind in maiden race at Chester in July. *Mrs M. Rimell.*

SKIN DEEP 8 b.m. Prevailing–Vanity Case 77 (Counsel 118) (1980 5d 6v **65** 7f³ 7.6f 7fg* 8g 7g 7d 6g 7s 7d 1981 6s⁴ 6s* 6s 8g 7g 8f 6f² 6f⁴ 6d 6g 6fg 6s) compact mare; fair handicapper at her best but has deteriorated; won at Ripon in April (apprentices); probably stays 1m; acts on any going; blinkered once in 1979; suitable mount for an apprentice; sweated up very badly fifth start; sold to N. Mitchell 1,550 gns Ascot November Sales. *W. Musson.*

SKINFLICK 6 b.g. Polyfoto 124–Bag of Bones (Relic) (1980 NR 1981 8fg) — plater; stayed 1m; acted on firm going; often wore bandages; dead. *G. Blum.*

SKI RUN 6 b.g. Workboy 123–Snow Rum (Quorum 126) (1980 7v 8.2fg² 10f **75**
8s² 10g³ 8fg² 10fg² 10fg* 11g* 10s* 1981 12s 10f 10g³ 12f⁴ 10fg² 12g² 11fg²
10g* 11d² 10.5s³ 11d* 10.2g³ 8g) former plater; middle-distance handicapper
nowadays; won at Beverley in September and Redcar in October; acts on any
going; usually races with tongue tied down; has worn bandages in front; suitable
mount for a claimer; genuine and consistent. *P. Wigham.*

SKI'S DOUBLE 5 br.g. Double-U-Jay 120–Some Poser (Will Somers 114§) **71**
(1980 12d 13d 11fg³ 12.3f 12f 10.6g 12d 12d 12.3g 12g³ 15.8d³ 12fg² 12.2fg³ 12d³
12d* 12s²(dis) 10.2d² 12d² 1981 12s* 12s* 12.5s*(dis) 12v 12.3d 12.3d⁴ 12g⁴
12f² 12f² 12.3fg³ 12.3s⁴ 13fg 11fg³ 12fg² 12v* 12d⁴ 12.2s³ 12g 12d) middle-
distance handicapper; successful at Doncaster (awarded race) and Leicester in
March and Haydock in October; also dead-heated at Stockton in April but was
disqualified for having traces of theobromine in system; stays 1½m; acts on any
going; often apprentice ridden though finds little off the bridle and has shown
tendency to hang; ran poorly fourth start. *R. Hollinshead.*

SKY BLUE PINK 4 gr.f. Singing Bede 122–Farida Jinks 106 (Tudor Jinks 121) —
(1980 5f 5d² 5d 5d 5g 5f 5g 5fg 5d 5d* 1981 5s 5s) sturdy filly; inconsistent
sprint handicapper; suited by some give in the ground; usually wears blinkers.
G. Fletcher.

SKYBOOT 2 b.c. African Sky 124–Sans Sabots (Whistler 129) (1981 6g 5s 6g) —
Feb 6; 12,500Y; close-coupled, useful sort; half-brother to numerous winners,
including fair miler L'Eveque (by St Chad); dam never ran; seventh of 19 to One
Degree in maiden race at Newmarket in October, third outing and probably
best effort; bolted on way to start second outing. *A. Pitt.*

SKYBRIGHT 3 b.f. The Brianstan 128–Sky Hostess 72 (Skymaster 126) (1980 —
5fg 5.1fg 6fg 9d 8d 7d 6d 1981 8s 8d 8g 10s 8fg 8d 12fg⁴ 10d 12d) leggy filly;
plater; stays 1½m; sweated up third start. *G. Blum.*

SKY HIGH GUY (USA) 2 b.c. Son Ange–Gay Minette (Sir Gaylord) (1981 —
7.6s) Apr 12; $14,000Y; half-brother to winners in USA and Puerto Rico by
Bold and Brave; dam, winner over 1m and 9f, is daughter of Manotick, a very
smart winner at up to 1½m; 50/1 when tenth of 15 to Cordite Spear in maiden
race at Lingfield in October. *J. Bethell.*

SKY JUMP 7 ch.g. Double Jump 131–Damascus Sky (Skymaster 126) (1980 **67 d**
7d 7v⁴ 7g 6s 6d 7g* 6g* 7fg* 7f 7d 1981 6s 7d² 7d 7fg* 7d⁴ 7g 5.8f 7f 7fg 7fg 6s)
narrowly won apprentice handicap at Epsom in April; stays 7f well; appears to
act on any going; has been tried in blinkers; good mount for a boy. *B. Swift.*

SKYLANDER 2 b.c. African Sky 124–Lagosta (Ragusa 137) (1981 7g 6s) —
Mar 30; IR 5,000Y; quite attractive, well-made colt; fourth foal; dam, closely
related to Racquette and half-sister to Arctique Royale and Le Melody, won
over 7f and 1m in Ireland; behind in October in maiden races at Newmarket
(very slowly away) and Newbury (20/1, showed up well 4½f); bandaged near-
fore both starts. *J. Dunlop.*

SKYLINE DRIVE 7 ch.g. High Line 125–Picture Palace 83 (Princely Gift 137) **68**
(1980 16fg 14fg 18.8g³ 17.1fg* 1981 12g 16.9s 11.7v* 16s 14s* 17.1d 12s 12v 16s)
quite a modest handicapper; won at Windsor in May and Haydock in June;
stays well; acts on a firm surface, but is ideally suited by plenty of give in the
ground; has twice been tried in blinkers. *C. James.*

SKYRAM 2 b.g. Sagaro 133–Molly Fay 69 (Faberge II 121) (1981 8g 8s 8g) —
May 26; strong, compact gelding; third foal; half-brother to a winner in Denmark
by Reliance II; dam, winner over 1½m and useful hurdler in this country, also
successful on flat and over jumps abroad; backward when behind in maiden
and minor events; will need a thorough test of stamina. *D. Morley.*

SKYSTREAK 3 br.g. Workboy 123–Skymistress 91 (Skymaster 126) (1980 NR —
1981 5g) big, strong gelding; half-brother to quite useful sprinter Shy Talk
(by Sharpen Up); dam best at sprint distances; unquoted, apprentice ridden and
in need of race when behind in 18-runner minor event at Thirsk in May (dwelt
and was outpaced early on). *M. W. Easterby.*

SKYTRAIN HOSTESS 3 ch.f. Roan Rocket 128–Djenarelle (Djefou) (1980 —
5d 7g 6g 7g* 7g 1981 8s 10.2g) lengthy filly; won maiden race at Salisbury
at 2 yrs; should have stayed at least 1m; dead. *R. Smyth.*

SKYTRAIN JETSET 2 b.c. Rheingold 137–Caramel 93 (Crepello 136) (1981 **80**
7fg 7d 7fg 8s) May 28; 21,000F; lengthy colt; half-brother to numerous
winners, including very useful middle-distance performer Northern Princess
(by Sir Ivor); dam won at 1½m; improved as he became fitter and wasn't
disgraced when 10½ lengths sixth of 12 to Jalmood in £3,300 event over 1m at
Goodwood in September; will stay 1½m. *R. Smyth.*

SKYTRICK 2 b.c. African Sky 124–Fascinating Trick (Buckpasser) (1981 7fg* **105** 8g²) Apr 22; $45,000Y; big, rangy, attractive colt; good mover with a long raking stride; fourth foal; half-brother to 3-y-o 1m and 9f winner Fast Trick (by Northfields); dam twice-raced sister to best 1971 American 2-y-o filly Numbered Account and smart middle-distance colt Cunning Trick; put up a good effort for a newcomer when winning 15-runner maiden race at Yarmouth in August by 2 lengths from Jorge Miguel; went down by a short head to Nioulargo in 13-runner nursery at Newmarket the following month but would certainly have won if he hadn't wandered badly when in lead over 1f out; stays 1m well; useful and will win more races at 3 yrs. *L. Cumani.*

SKYVANN PRINCE 3 b. or br.c. Beechwood 56–Skyvale 68 (Skymaster 126) — (1980 NR 1981 7g 7g) small, strong colt; sixth foal; dam poor performer; unquoted and backward when behind in minor event and seller at Catterick in first half of season. *T. Kersey.*

SKY WALK 4 b. or br.f. Tower Walk 130–Nuageuse (Prince Regent 129) — (1980 6d 6h³ 6fg² 6d⁴ 6fg 6s 6g 1981 8s 6fg 5d 6d³ 5.3f 5.1fg⁴ 6fg 6fg 5d) small, strong filly; good walker; plater; stays 6f; seems to act on any going; sold 500 gns Newmarket Autumn Sales. *N. Guest.*

SLADELANDS 3 b.g. Owen Anthony 102–Lavant 101 (Le Lavandou 111) — (1980 6g 6d 1981 7.6g⁴ 8g 10fg 6fg 9s) useful-looking gelding; plating-class maiden; should stay 1m; sold 740 gns Newmarket Autumn Sales, probably to race in Belgium. *W. Wightman.*

SLANE SPARKLER 2 ch.f. Sparkler 130–Petingalyn (Petingo 135) (1981 5s **58** 5s 5fg³ 5f⁴ 5fg⁴ 6f) Mar 31; 3,200F, 1,600Y; leggy filly; has a round action; second foal; sister to 1979 2-y-o 6f winner Sponsorship; dam of no account; in frame in maiden auction events at Redcar, Pontefract and Carlisle prior to running poorly in seller at Doncaster in July; should be suited by 6f. *W. Wharton.*

SLANEY MAID 3 br.f. Furry Glen 121–Pastina 92 (March Past 124) (1980 **110** 5fg 7.9f 7g* 7fg* 7fg 1981 10g 9g 10s 10d⁴ 9d 8f 8f⁴ 7f* 7fg* 8fg² 8.5fg* 8g³ 8s* 8d* 10d) small, quite attractive filly; half-sister to several winners, including smart Irish 7f to 2m winner Slaney Idol (by Simbir) and useful middle-distance performer Evermore (by Charlottown); dam sprinter; had a very good year and won handicaps at Phoenix Park, the Curragh, Galway and Leopardstown and 6-runner Marlborough House Stakes at Ascot; produced with a really strong run to lead close home when beating Countess Olivia and Organdy a neck and the same in last-named race in October on thirteenth start; 6 lengths third of 18 behind Belted Earl in Desmond Stakes at the Curragh on previous start; probably stays 1¼m; acts on any going; successful with blinkers and without; whipped round at start second outing at 2 yrs; slipped up sixth start. *L. Browne, Ireland.*

SLEDGEHAMMER 5 ch.g. Double Jump 131–Naval Patrol 105 (Blue Peter) — (1980 NR 1981 13g⁴ 12f) strong gelding; little worthwhile form in maiden and minor races; has worn bandages. *G. Richards.*

SLEEPLINE GOLD 4 br.f. Goldhill 125–Camerons Counsel (Jolly Jet 111) — (1980 8fg 7g 7f 8fg 7.2g 5d 6g 1981 6s⁴) workmanlike filly; modest fourth in seller at Folkestone in March; stays 6f; acts on a firm surface; has been blinkered; has worn bandages. *P. Cundell.*

SLEEPLINE PRINCESS 3 ch.f. Royal Palace 131–Tin Mary 96 (Tin King 126) **73** (1980 5fg 5g 5g³ 5fg 6g* 7d⁴(dis) 7fg 6g³ 1981 8fg 8s 8fg 7f 6fg² 6fg 6f 6fg 7f 7fg 8f 7.3d 10g 11.7d) leggy, close-coupled filly; ran best race of year when length second to Gabitat in handicap at Lingfield in July; not disgraced next time; best form at 6f; sometimes blinkered; sweated up tenth outing; trained part of season by R. Armstrong. *S. Matthews.*

SLEEPLINE PROMISE 2 b.f. Record Token 128–Herods Palace 95 (Palestine **63** 133) (1981 5s 5s³ 5fg 5g 5d) Apr 21; 10,500Y; useful sort; good walker; half-sister to several winners, including fairly useful 6f winner Viking Skipper (by Manacle); dam a miler; showed only a modicum of ability; bred to stay 1m; trained by R. Armstrong first 2 starts. *P. Cundell.*

SLEEPY HOLLOW 2 br.f. Wolver Hollow 126–Perfect Aim 97 (Busted 134) **77** (1981 6d 7h 6d) May 20; fourth foal; half-sister to 6f winner Winning Shot (by Thatch); dam 2-y-o 6f winner and half-sister to good fillies Aiming High and Tender Annie; fifth of 15 on first and third outings, on latter wearing blinkers when beaten 2¾ lengths by Friday Street in minor event at Brighton in October; should by suited by 7f or more. *I. Balding.*

SLEIGH QUEEN 3 b. or br.f. Comedy Star 121–Snow Rum (Quorum 126) — (1980 5d 7g 1981 9s 6f⁴ 6f 6f 5g 5s 5s) compact filly; plating-class sprint maiden; fell third outing. *R. Akehurst.*

SLENDERHAGEN (GER) 5 b.h. Alpenkonig–Saxifraga (Alizier 131) (1980 **108** including 8g³ 7g* 8g 8v³ 1981 7.2s 8fg³ 7g 8g³ 7fg) good-quartered, attractive ex-German horse; successful 8 times in his native country, notably in Oettingen-Rennen at Baden-Baden in 1979; creditable third to Belmont Bay in Queen Anne Stakes at Royal Ascot on second start; not disgraced next start but ran moderately afterwards; stays 9f; probably acts on any going; may need strong handling; sold privately and will be trained by K. Brassey. *M. Stoute.*

SLICK WILLIE 2 b.c. Red Alert 127–Kilcurley Lass (Huntercombe 133) **68** (1981 6d 6g) Apr 20; IR 2,000F, IR 3,000Y; first foal; dam unraced half-sister to high-class 1969 2-y-o Divine Gift; 7 lengths fifth of 19 to One Degree in maiden race at Newmarket in October, second outing and better effort. *M. Jarvis.*

SLIGHTLY DANGEROUS (USA) 2 b.f. Roberto 131–Where You Lead 120 **101** P (Raise A Native) (1981 6s*)

Unbroken in June and a five-length winner of the Duke of Edinburgh Stakes at Ascot by early-October is the unusual record so far of Slightly Dangerous. Her display at Ascot was so full of promise that she was immediately quoted at prices from 20/1 to 25/1 for the 1982 One Thousand Guineas and Oaks and we shouldn't care to contradict her trainer's assertion that she'll make a very high-class filly. Slightly Dangerous won by five lengths despite being palpably green; her rider had to shake her up vigorously to make her race in earnest soon after halfway but once into her stride she moved up quickly, joined the front rank coming to the final furlong and needed only one slap of the whip to quicken right away from Snow Forecast, Vallancy and Gandaan. A splendid first effort and surely there's much better still to come.

Slightly Dangerous is certainly bred well enough to win a classic: her sire Roberto was second in the Two Thousand Guineas before winning the Derby; her dam Where You Lead was second to Mysterious in the 1973 Oaks; and her grandam Noblesse put up one of the most devastating displays ever seen in the Oaks when trotting up by ten lengths in 1963. The popularity of the family was shown at the Fasig-Tipton Sales in November when Where You Lead, in foal to Foolish Pleasure, was sold for 1,000,000 dollars and her daughter by Herbager, I Will Follow, for 510,000 dollars carrying to Tromos. I Will Follow

Duke of Edinburgh Stakes, Ascot—a very easy win for Slightly Dangerous on her only appearance

was a smart filly, winner of the Group 3 Prix de Minerve over a mile and a half, and Where You Lead's other runner, the Damascus filly La Nobleza, also won in France, scoring over seven and a half furlongs.

Slightly Dangerous (USA) (b.f. Apr 8, 1979)	Roberto (b 1969)	Hail to Reason (br 1958)	Turn-to / Nothirdchance
		Bramalea (b 1959)	Nashua / Rarelea
	Where You Lead (ch 1970)	Raise A Native (ch 1961)	Native Dancer / Raise You
		Noblesse (ch 1960)	Mossborough / Duke's Delight

Slightly Dangerous is a rangy, quite attractive filly, physically just the type to make a lot of improvement from two to three. She could well prove effective enough over a mile in the early stages of her three-year-old career to put up a bold show in the Guineas but it's over longer distances that we expect her really to make her mark. Perhaps like Where You Lead and Noblesse she'll win the Musidora Stakes on her way to the Oaks. *B. Hills.*

SLIMPIN 2 br.f. Starch Reduced 112–Pin 90 (Pindari 124) (1981 7fg 7f) — lengthy filly; half-sister to 4 minor winners; dam stayed at least 1¼m; last in maiden races and looks of no account. *J. Czerpak.*

SLITHERUM 6 ch.h. Frankincense 120–Scorton Green 84 (Above Suspicion 127) (1980 12.2v* 12fg 12fg 13.3g 12d 1981 12s) poor handicapper; stays 1½m; acts on any going but revels in the mud; has worn blinkers; sold 500 gns Ascot May Sales. *R. Hannon.*

SLOANE STREET 4 b.g. Pitcairn 126–Pleaseme 100 (Javelot 124) (1980 **51** 10g 10.1fg⁴ 10fg 12g 12d 12s 1981 12g 12g 12fg³ 12f⁴ 12d⁴ 12d) workmanlike gelding; poor handicapper; fifth in valuable selling handicap at Doncaster on final start; stays 1½m; suited by fast ground; often blinkered. *J. Fitzgerald.*

SMACKOVER 6 ch.h. Pontifex (USA)–Atanya (Atan) (1980 7fg³ 8f 7fg 8g⁴ **76** d 8fg 8d 7d 8s 1981 8fg² 10fg 7.6g 7.6s 8d³ 7s) strong, good-bodied horse; useful handicapper at his best but is on the downgrade; best at around 1m; acts on any going but is suited by top-of-the-ground; sometimes blinkered; usually held up and is not the easiest of rides; doesn't always look too keen; sold 1,300 gns Ascot November Sales. *I. Walker.*

SMART AMBITION 3 ch.c. Amber Rama 133–Ember Grill 84§ (Indigenous — 121) (1980 NR 1981 8g 10.1fg 10.1fg) 1,800F, 3,000Y; half-brother to 3 winners, including quite useful 6f to 1¼m winner Twickenham (by Martinmas); dam won over 5f at 2 yrs but then disappointed badly; in rear in minor events at Salisbury and Windsor (2) in summer. *C. Wildman.*

SMART GUARD 4 b.g. Shiny Tenth 120–Smartie Pants 69 (Galivanter 131) — (1980 6d 6d² 7fg 6g 7d 7fg 7g 8f 8fg 7d 1981 7s 8g² 8g 7d⁴ 7g 7f 8f 11.5d) big, rangy gelding; poor maiden; stays 1m; acts on a soft surface; sweated up badly twice at 3 yrs; has twice been blinkered; has been bandaged in front. *B. Richmond.*

SMART MART 2 ch.g. Jimmy Reppin 131–Fochetta (Fortino II 120) (1981 **60** 6f 6f³ 7fg³ 7f 7fg*) May 28; 600Y; 1,000 2-y-o; workmanlike, sturdy gelding; fourth live foal; dam ran only 3 times; plater; bought in 1,050 gns after beating Pride of Fairfield by 3 lengths at Catterick in August; suited by 7f on a sound surface. *N. Tinkler.*

SMILAX 2 b.f. Free State 125–Smiling 62 (Silly Season 127) (1981 6g) Mar — 30; 5,400F; second foal; dam, placed at up to 13.8f, won over hurdles; 16/1, never got in a blow when 10 lengths fifth of 12 to Mubhedj in small race at Windsor in August. *J. Dunlop.*

SMILE FOR ME 3 br.c. Song 132–Teersaway 74 (Weepers Boy 124) (1980 — 5d 5fg 5d⁴ 1981 5s 5g 5g 5fg 7fg 8g 7s 10d) small, quite attractive colt; good mover; disappointing maiden; behind in a seller final start; not sure to stay beyond 5f; blinkered third start; trained first 3 outings by F. J. Houghton. *W. Turner.*

SMILING PRINCESS 3 b.f. Prince de Galles 125–Golden Giggle (Golden — Dipper 119) (1980 7d 8g 1981 10.1fg 10.1d 12fg⁴ 12fg) plain filly; well beaten in maiden and minor races and a gentleman riders event; tends to sweat up. *I. Dudgeon.*

SMITH SEAL 6 b.h. Royal Palace 131–Dilly 89 (Princely Gift 137) (1980   **52**
8fg* 8fg 8fg* 8fg 8fg 8fg* 8fg²(dis) 9f 8.3fg 8fg 8.2s   1981 7d 8fg 7g 7g* 8f 8fg⁴
8fg 8f 7fg⁴ 8h 10fg 8d)   poor handicapper; won at Brighton in June; best at
around 1m; seems to act on any going but goes very well on top-of-the-ground;
usually wears blinkers; sometimes sweats up. *R. Baker.*

SMITHY LANE 3 b.g. Pitskelly 122–Seamstress (Sea Hawk II 131) (1980   –
5fg 5d 7s   1981 10d 11.7s 10g 10fg 11.5d 12g 8d 5f 10.4s 15.5f 10.6s)   strong
gelding; little worthwhile form in varied company; has been tried in blinkers;
trained part of season by Mrs A. Finch. *C. Wildman.*

SMOKE SCREEN 5 b.h. Blakeney 126–Cigarette Case 89 (Faberge II 121)   –
(1980 11fg 12fg 14f*   1981 13s 18g)   good sort; moves well; suited by 1¾m
when conditions aren't testing; acts on any going; blinkered twice at 3 yrs. *R.
Hollinshead.*

SMOKE SINGER 6 b.h. Crooner 119–Smokey Dawn 78 (March Past 124)   **89**
(1980 6v² 5fg 5f 6fg³ 5fg 5s 6d 5g 6fg 7g 11.1fg³ 10d 9f 10g 7s   1981 6f* 5.6fg
6d 6g 7g 6v⁴ 6d 6g)   neat, strong horse; fairly useful performer; won minor
event at Brighton in August; creditable fifth on next outing to Touch Boy in
Portland Handicap at Doncaster in September; effective at 5f and 6f and stays
11f; acts on any going; blinkered once at 5 yrs. *A. Bailey.*

SMOKEY BEAR 6 b.h. Gulf Pearl 117–Seul 69 (Faberge II 121) (1980 10fg²   **89**
12f⁴ 10.5f² 10fg* 12g* 12.3g* 12g 15g* 12fg 13s² 18d   1981 12g⁴ 20fg)   fairly
useful handicapper at his best; lightly raced in 1981; doesn't always impress in
his slower paces; stays well; acts on any going; has run creditably for an
amateur. *J. Hanson.*

SMOKEY SHADOW 4 gr.g. Dragonara Palace 115–Camdamus 83 (Mandamus   **67**
120) (1980 8fg 8fg* 8.2g⁴ 8f 8f² 10.8d³   1981 8s 8d⁴ 8g 8g)   fair sort; stays 1m
well; acts on firm ground; blinkered last 2 starts. *E. Eldin.*

SNAP TIN 3 ch.f. Jimmy Reppin 131–Hunu (Hul a Hul 124) (1980 5v 5d 5g   **41**
5f 5f⁴ 6s 5f 5fg 8fg 6d 5s   1981 7g 8f⁴ 8fg² 7f 6g 8fg 10f 11g 8s 6s)   leggy filly;
plater; stays 1m; sometimes wears blinkers. *R. Ward.*

SNIFFY 2 b.c. Saulingo 122–Alizarina (Ragusa 137) (1981 5d 5s 6f² 5fg 5fg)   **63**
Feb 14; IR 5,600Y; good sort; half-brother to quite useful 1978 2-y-o 5f winner
Blue For You (by Habitat) and 2 winners abroad; dam, unraced, is closely
related to leading Italian stallion Andrea Mantegna and half-sister to Italian
Derby winner Appiani II; 1½ lengths second of 17 to Queensbury Star in seller at
Doncaster in July, first race for over 2 months and best effort; evidently better at
6f than 5f; acts on firm going; blinkered second and fourth outings. *W.
O'Gorman.*

SNOOZE 3 b.f. Cavo Doro 124–Lazy Time (Linacre 133) (1980 NR   1981 8fg   **50**
10d 10.4d 15.5g² 15.5s)   3,800Y; workmanlike filly; third living foal; half-sister
to 2 winners by Philip of Spain, notably useful 5f performer Go Total; dam
lightly-raced half-sister to smart 1976 2-y-o Forty Winks; second in maiden
event at Catterick in September; suited by a test of stamina; wears bandages.
J. Toller.

SNOOZY TIME 3 b.f. Cavo Doro 124–Noddy Time 97 (Gratitude 130) (1980   –
5fg 5fg 5f* 5f 6g 6d⁴ 8g 6d   1981 8g 6d)   strong, good sort; well beaten in 1981
(not seen out until September); should be suited by 7f+; blinkered fourth
outing as a 2-y-o; sold 1,000 gns Newmarket Autumn Sales. *D. Thom.*

SNOW BLESSED 4 br.g. So Blessed 130–Snow Tribe 94 (Great Nephew 126)   –
(1980 8d⁴ 10g 10f⁴ 8fg 12g* 12d 12.2f* 12.3fg³ 12.2g 10d⁴ 10.2g² 10s* 10g 10.5s
10s   1981 16g 12f 16fg)   big, strong gelding; successful in varied company in
1980; well beaten at 4 yrs (bandaged first start); stays 1½m well; acts on any
going; blinkered nowadays. *R. Johnson.*

SNOW DAY (FR) 3 b.f. Reliance II 137–Vindaria (Roi Dagobert 128) (1980   **123**
NR   1981 10.5s* 10.5g* 10.5g* 10s⁴ 10f²(dis) 12g 12d 10g)
   For the second year running we saw a very unlucky filly in the Prix Vermeille: in 1980 Detroit got out all too late to catch Mrs Penny and Little Bonny, in
1981 Snow Day finished fifth of ten to April Run after her saddle slipped.
Undoubtedly Detroit was the unluckier. Victory would have been a moral
certainty had she enjoyed a clear run, whereas Snow Day finished around five
lengths down on a winner whose form is manifestly superior. Subsequently
April Run beat Snow Day again in the Prix de l'Arc de Tromphe; later still

Prix Fille de l'Air, Saint-Cloud—Snow Day wins from Barb's Bold and Daeltown (rails)

Madam Gay also beat her again in the Champion Stakes, a race in which neither was ever in the hunt. If Snow Day didn't measure up to the best three-year-old middle-distance fillies she wasn't too far behind them and she had a pretty impressive record, easily one of the best of her sex sired by Reliance II. She finished tenth in the Arc, virtually level with Leandra and Tootens, in front of all the British and Irish runners except Ardross. Of her five races before the Vermeille she won the first three—the Prix de la Celle-Saint-Cloud at Longchamp, the Prix de Royaumont at Chantilly and the Prix Fille de l'Air at Saint-Cloud—and made the frame behind Leandra in the other two—the Prix de Malleret at Longchamp and the Prix de la Nonette at Deauville. Snow Day had evidently been on the point of exhausting her supply of good fortune before the Vermeille, for she was disqualified from a very close second place in the Nonette on account of carrying 2 lb too little. That second was obviously a better effort than her fourth in the Malleret, too little weight or not. The pick of her victories was the one in the Prix de Royaumont, a Group 3 race as is the Prix Fille de l'Air. It was the pick despite being the hardest earned of the three, since she accounted for Leandra and Landresse at level weights, by a head and a length; the Fille de l'Air, in which she beat Nobiliary's half-sister Barb's Bold, took less winning; the Prix de la Celle-Saint-Cloud was merely an event for fillies that hadn't previously run.

	Snow Day (Fr) (b.f. 1978)	Reliance II (b 1962)	Tantieme (b 1947)	Deux pour Cent
				Terka
			Relance III (ch 1952)	Relic
				Polaire
		Vindaria (b 1974)	Roi Dagobert (b 1964)	Sicambre
				Dame d'Atour
			Heavenly Body (br 1957)	Dark Star
				Dangerous Dame

Snow Day is the first foal of an unraced American-bred mare imported to France as a yearling. Vindaria, by the exported French horse Roi Dagobert (fourth in the Arc in 1967), is a half-sister to several winners, easily the best of them the one-mile to middle-distance filly A Thousand Stars (by Hoist the Flag). A Thousand Stars broke a hind leg in the Yellow Ribbon Stakes in 1980 and had to be put down. She had shown high-class form in the United States that year and in France earlier; she won the Prix Perth and finished third in the French One Thousand Guineas in 1978. The next dam Heavenly Body was a high-class performer, too. She was rated joint second-best two-year-old filly of 1959 in the States, and she won three stakes races, notably the Matron Stakes. Her sister Hidden Talent won the Kentucky Oaks.

Snow Day has been retired to stud. A medium-sized filly, she stayed a mile and a half and acted on any going. *F. Boutin, France.*

SNOWFLAKE 4 b.f. Warpath 113–Snow Goose (Santa Claus 133) (1980 NR 1981 16f) small, lightly-made filly; sister to Wild Goose Chase, successful at up to 2m, and half-sister to a winner; dam never ran; behind in poor maiden race at Beverley in June; sold to S. Cole 1,050 gns Doncaster August Sales. *C. Thornton.* —

SNOWFLAME 3 b. or br.f. Sassafras 135–Snow Damsel (Mandamus 120) (1980 8.2s 1981 12.2g 12g 12fg) soundly beaten in maiden events. *C. Nelson.* —

811

SNOW FORECAST (USA) 2 ch.c. Far North 120–Promise You (Promised **96**
Land) (1981 6fg² 6s²) Apr 20; $80,000Y; attractive, lengthy colt; half-brother
to 2 minor stakes winners by Blade and to 2 stakes-placed winners; dam won 8
sprint races, including claiming events; showed plenty of ability when second
twice at Ascot in the autumn, keeping on very well when beaten ¾ length by
Allocated in Clarence House Stakes but being completely outgunned by 5-length
winner Slightly Dangerous when favourite for Duke of Edinburgh Stakes; will
stay 1m; won't have much difficulty winning in maiden company. *G. Hunter.*

SNOW MAID 3 gr.f. High Top 131–Snow Habit (Habitat 134) (1980 NR **90**
1981 7g*) second foal; half-sister to a winner in Scandinavia by Upper Case;
dam half-sister to dam of Count Pahlen; backed at long odds and looked to have
done plenty of work when winning 18-runner maiden race at Salisbury in June,
taking decisive advantage ½m out and storming home 5 lengths clear of Northern
Chance; looked a useful performer in the making, but wasn't seen out again;
will stay 1m. *P. Cole.*

SNOW TREASURE (USA) 3 ch.c. Northern Dancer–Impetuous Lady (Hasty **92**
Road) (1980 NR 1981 9g³ 10d* 12v 10.5f³ 10f²) $530,000Y; big, well-made
colt; brother to stakes winners Northern Fling, a very useful winner at up to
1¼m, and Countess North, winner of 7f Comely Stakes, and closely related to
several winners, notably Regal Gal (by Viceregal), a smart winner at up to 1¼m,
and smart stakes winner Impetuous Gal (by Briartic); dam ran once; odds on when
beating Grand Felice by 2¼ lengths in maiden event at Phoenix Park in May;
blinkered when placed afterwards in £4,900 event at York (about 5 lengths third
to Dogberry) and minor event at Phoenix Park in August (length second to
What a Riot), looking a shade reluctant on former course; should stay 1½m;
possibly unsuited by heavy going; sent to race in USA. *V. O'Brien, Ireland.*

SOBA 2 ch.f. Most Secret 119–Mild Wind (Porto Bello 118) (1981 5g 6g 6f 6fg **66**
7fg 7fg 6d 6d 5g³) Mar 10; fair sort; only plating class; not sure to stay 7f;
blinkered last 2 outings. *D. Chapman.*

SOCIAL OCCASION 2 ch.f. Balidar 133–Formula 72 (Reform 132) (1981 6g —
5s) May 18; 520Y; compact filly; second foal; half-sister to 3-y-o 5f seller
winner Chilston (by Tower Walk); dam 1m winner; well beaten in sellers in
October. *R. Akehurst.*

SOCKS UP 4 ch.g. Sharpen Up 127–Mrs Moss 81 (Reform 132) (1980 6s 7f 7d **85**
7s 7.2d³ 7d 6g* 6fg 5s 1981 6s* 6g 6f 6fg 6g 7.3d 7s³ 7g⁴ 6s) leggy, somewhat
lightly-made gelding; good mover; beat Winter Wind a head in £4,400 handicap at
Newbury in May; not disgraced several subsequent starts; stays 7f; ideally suited
by some give in the ground; blinkered twice in 1980; hung badly on occasions in
1980 and didn't look an easy ride but did little wrong at 4 yrs. *F. J. Houghton.*

SOFFIANA 3 b.f. Realm 129–Welsh Game (Pall Mall 132) (1980 NR 1981 8g **55**
7fg 7g 7f 6f 8.2s² 6d) 17,000Y; smallish, quite attractive filly; second foal; half-
sister to high-class miler Last Fandango (by Gay Fandango); dam very useful
French performer at around 1m; tried to make all when 4 lengths second to Irish
Sparkle in maiden race at Nottingham in September; stays 1m; blinkered fifth
start; has worn a tongue strap; sold 1,650 gns Newmarket December Sales. *C.
Brittain.*

SOFT TOP 2 b.g. High Top 131–Softly Glowing 90 (Tutankhamen) (1981 5s) —
May 11; half-brother to 1980 2-y-o 5.1f winner Rose of Raby (by Averof) and
1½m winner King Ashoka (by Relko); dam won over 6f at 2 yrs; 10/1 when well
behind in 11-runner maiden race won by Sonseri at Wolverhampton in October.
C. James.

SOFT VOICE 4 b.f. Simbir 130–Tuscan Tune 75 (Tudor Melody 129) (1980 **66**
8f³ 13s 13g² 15.5g⁴ 11fg 14fg⁴ 1981 12g* 12d) lengthy filly; won 7-runner
maiden race at Brighton in September; stays well; possibly needs a sound surface.
M. Stoute.

SOHEIR 4 ch.f. Track Spare 125–My Dearest Sarah 79 (Anwar 120) (1980 7f —
7fg 8fg 11.1f² 10.2fg* 9.6f³ 10.5d 9g² 10.1g 11.7d 10g 10.2d 10.2v 1981 10f)
small filly; middle-distance handicapper; acts on firm going and is unsuited by
soft; blinkered once in 1980. *M. Ryan.*

SOLABOY (USA) 2 ch.c. The Minstrel 135–Seminar 113 (Don II 123) (1981 **110**
6g* 6fg 7g) Mar 19; $220,000Y; strong, well-made, full-quartered, attractive
colt; third foal; half-brother to fairly useful 1m winner Rapid Class (by Cannonade); dam, half-sister to Boldboy, was very useful over 5f at 2 yrs and won over
1m in USA at 3 yrs; one of first off bridle in 9-runner Champagne Stakes at
Salisbury in June but stayed on so well he got up to win by short head from

Incandesce; beaten afterwards in Anglia Television July Stakes and William Hill Dewhurst Stakes at Newmarket, running well considering he'd been off the course for over 3 months when about 9 lengths fifth of 9 to Wind and Wuthering in latter; will stay 1¼m; very useful. *R. Hern.*

SOLAIRE PRINCE 3 b.c. Jimsun 121–Demta (Astec 128) (1980 5fg 8d 7s —
1981 8s 7fg 7d³ 7g 10.2f 10fg 10fg) plater; should stay middle distances; sold 500 gns Ascot October Sales. *T. M. Jones.*

SOLAR GRASS 6 b.g. Veiled Wonder–Fair Marilyn (Macherio) (1980 8f 8f **63**
5fg 8g 5d 5d 5fg² 5fg* 5d⁴ 6d* 5d² 6fg* 6s² 6d⁴ 6v³ 1981 6d 6s 5s 6g 5d² 5s⁴ 5g³ 5fg 6g 6f 6g 5fg 6fg) strong, fair sort; sprint handicapper; stays 6f; probably acts on any going; suitable mount for an inexperienced rider. *W. Charles.*

SOLARIUM 3 br.g. Scottish Rifle 127–Daydreamer 78 (Star Gazer 123) (1980 **39**
6d 7d 6g 7fg⁴ 8.2g 8fg 1981 12g 12fg 12g² 13.8fg⁴) compact gelding; poor plater; suited by 1½m; sometimes wears blinkers. *W. Musson.*

SOLAR WIND (USA) 2 ch.c. Northern Dancer–Courting Days (Bold Lad, **82 p**
USA) (1981 6d2) Mar 9; $410,000Y; brother to smart Irish middle-distance winner Magesterial; dam, winner over 1¼m in Ireland, is half-sister to very smart 9f and 1¼m stakes winner Glowing Tribute; started none too well when odds on for 17-runner maiden race at the Curragh in October and failed by a short head to catch Classical Dancer; sure to do much better over 1m or more. *V. O'Brien, Ireland.*

SOLDIER 4 ch.c. Sun Prince 128–Militello 71 (Habitat 134) (1980 7f 8d* 8g³ —
8fg 10g 11fg 1981 10.6s) lengthy colt; good mover; should stay beyond 1m; possibly needs some give in the ground. *W. Clay.*

SOLDIER BIRD 2 ch.f. Shiny Tenth 120–Ibis 96 (Tamerlane 128) (1981 5d —
6g 6fg 7.2v) May 15; useful sort; sister to fair 1976 2-y-o 1m winner Slick Chick; dam won over 6f at 2 yrs; well beaten in varied company, including selling. *R. Hannon.*

SOLDIER ON 2 b.g. Queen's Hussar 124–Tegleaze 81 (Galivanter 131) (1981 —
7g 7fg) May 26; strong, short-legged, attractive gelding; fourth foal; half-brother to 1980 2-y-o 1m winner Jade and Diamond (by Bold Lad, Ire); dam 2-y-o 5f winner; backward when behind in large fields of maidens at Salisbury and Goodwood (last of 19) in July. *B. Swift.*

SOLE BIDDER 3 b. or br.g. Touch Paper 113–Mariola 93 (Royal Hamlet 115) —
(1980 6d 5g 6g 6s 1981 8g 8d 8f 12f) leggy gelding; well behind in varied company, including selling; sometimes blinkered. *E. Carter.*

SOLE INVESTMENT 7 b.g. Prince de Galles 125–Cantella (Never Say Die —
137) (1980 NR 1981 13d) novice hurdler; lightly raced and no sign of ability on flat. *T. Craig.*

SOLEROF 3 b.c. Averof 123–Solhoon 74 (Tycoon II) (1980 7fg 6g 7fg² 7fg **64**
1981 7d 7f³ 8f⁴ 7f 8fg) lengthy colt; plating-class maiden; ran moderately last 2 starts (sweated up on final one); stays 1m. *P. Cole.*

SOLOMON'S LAMP 4 ch.g. Pall Mall 132–Spring Blossom 85 (Queen's Hussar —
124) (1980 9d 8g* 8d 1981 8g 10f 8fg³ 10g 8f 8f 10g 12.2g 12d) lengthy gelding; has rather a round action; poor handicapper nowadays; well beaten in valuable selling handicap final start; best form at 1m on a sound surface; sold 2,500 gns Newmarket Autumn Sales. *I. Walker.*

SOLTARA 3 b.f. The Go-Between 129–Dear Sol (Dear Gazelle 113) (1980 6s —
5d 1981 8s 8.2s) lightly-made filly; well behind in minor events and sellers; sold 380 gns Doncaster May Sales. *W. Stubbs.*

SOLWAY WINDS 3 b.g. Windjammer (USA)–Maggie Mine 85 (Native Prince) **89**
(1980 5f 5fg³ 6d³ 6d* 6fg* 6d 6d 1981 8g 8d⁴ 7g 8f* 7g 7d² 7f 7g³ 7d 7g) leggy gelding; stayed on well when beating Lifestyle a neck in handicap at Ripon in June; ran creditably when placed in similar events at Redcar and Doncaster (apprentices) afterwards; stays 1m; seems to act on any going. *N. Crump.*

SO LYRICAL 2 br.f. So Blessed 130–Land of Song 82 (Sing Sing 134) (1981 **68 p**
6fg⁴) Mar 21; 16,000Y; half-sister to several winners, including fair 1976 2-y-o 5f winner Top Soprano (by High Top); dam, half-sister to out-and-out stayer Celtic Cone, won over 5f; 16/1, made late headway when 7 lengths fourth of 16 to Kiva in maiden race at Newbury in August; will stay 7f. *P. Cundell.*

SOME CHERRY 5 br.m. Some Hand 119–Cherry Brandy (Tenerani 135) **41**
(1980 8s 8.2d* 10g 8.2fg 8g³ 7fg² 8d 8fg 8.2s 1981 11g 8fg 8g² 7fg³ 8fg⁴ 8fg 8.2d) unfurnished mare; plater; seems best at around 1m; acts on a firm and a soft surface. *T. Taylor.*

SOME GRANGE 2 b.f. Some Hand 119–Grange Park 73 (Derring-Do 131) —
(1981 5f 6f) May 13; compact filly; fifth foal; dam poor maiden; unquoted
when behind in maiden races at Nottingham in June and July. *W. Wharton.*

SOME HOPE 3 ch.f. Gallo Gallante 96–Negara (Niagara Falls 104) (1980
NR 1981 11f) half-sister to smart chaser Bishop's Pawn (by Bishop's Move);
dam never ran; 25/1 when last of 10 in maiden race won by Tofique at Hamilton
in June. *G. Richards.*

SOME JET 3 ch.c. Some Hand 119–Jetador 73 (Queen's Hussar 124) (1980
5d 6s 1981 7.2s 8f 6g 7.6s2(dis) 6d 7s) neat colt; disqualified after finishing
12 lengths second to Music City in maiden race at Chester in August (ridden
by 7-lb claimer); unplaced in sellers on other occasions; stays 7.6f. *C. Crossley.*

SOMEL 3 b.g. Averof 123–Sygnome 53 (Precipice Wood 123) (1980 NR 1981 —
9d 10fg 9s 10f 10g 14fg 14g 18g) big gelding; first foal; dam poor staying
maiden; has shown a little ability in varied company; blinkered fourth start;
trained most of season by C. Brittain. *J. S. Wilson.*

SOME LOVE 2 b.f. Some Hand 119–Love Triangle (Daring Display 129) **55**
(1981 5fg3 5d 5d 5.3f 5fg 7fg 6fg 8s) Apr 23; first foal; dam ran twice at 2 yrs;
only poor form, including when blinkered in claiming race on fourth start;
sold 320 gns Doncaster November Sales. *H. Westbrook.*

SOMERFOLDS 2 ch.f. Some Hand 119–Florica 80 (Floriana 106) (1981 —
8g 7d 7g 7.6s) Apr 30; good-topped filly; third foal; dam won sellers over 1m
and 1¼m; in rear in sizeable fields of maidens and selling platers. *A. Davison.*

SOMERFORD GLORY 3 b.f. Hittite Glory 125–Peregrine Peach 79 (Falcon —
131) (1980 NR 1981 7g 7f) 720F; small, workmanlike filly; half-sister to
2 winners abroad; dam won over 5f at 2 yrs in Ireland; in rear in maiden races
at Salisbury and Leicester in summer. *R. Baker.*

SOMERSDAY 2 b.f. Some Hand 119–Spring Day (Vic Day 126) (1981 7d —
7.6s 10s) May 24; workmanlike filly; second reported foal; dam won over
hurdles and fences; soundly beaten in maiden races at Newbury in September
and Lingfield (seventh of 15) and Nottingham in October. *M. Francis.*

SOMERS HEIR 6 b.g. Will Somers 114§–Treatisan 67 (Milesian 125) (1980 **57**
7d3 7v 7fg 7d 1981 7g 7v 8f 8f 8.2s4 7d) poor handicapper nowadays; stays
1m; goes well in the mud; occasionally wears blinkers; best form on a round
course; suitable mount for a boy. *D. Wintle.*

SOMETHING SPECIAL 4 b.c. Queen's Hussar 124–Calling The Tune 84 **66**
(Tudor Melody 129) (1980 11.7fg4 12fg* 12f2 12f 12g 11.7s 12.3fg 1981 8g
12s 12g 12f 12g 15fg* 13.8fg 15.8f 18f2 18.1d 17.1d 18g) well-made, good-looking
colt; won handicap at Edinburgh in July; suited by a test of stamina; ideally
suited by fast ground; blinkered once in 1980; suited by front-running tactics;
sold 2,300 gns Newmarket Autumn Sales. *F. Durr.*

SOMETIME SOON 3 gr.f. No Mercy 126–Cansanta 96 (Canisbay 120) (1980 —
5fg 5g3 6g 6g 8.2g 8g 7d3 1981 8fg 7d 7g 7g) compact filly; poor maiden; tailed
off in sellers last 2 starts; stays 1m; acts on a soft surface. *H. Collingridge.*

SONANT 4 ch.g. Master Sing 109–Mutchkin 65 (Espresso 122) (1980 6d4 6d —
6f2 6f 1981 10.2g 8s 8.2s) leggy gelding; plating-class maiden; stays 6f;
acts on firm going. *R. Turnell.*

SON FILS 6 ch.h. Mon Fils 124–Crespinall 100 (Saint Crespin III 132) (1980 **104**
10s2 12g* 13.4f3 12fg 12d2 12fg 13.3d3 1981 8s 12s4 16d2 12f) tall, narrow
horse; really good mover; useful performer; creditable 2¾ lengths fourth to
Pelerin in John Porter Stakes at Newbury in April and 2½ lengths second
to Nicholas Bill in 5-runner Sagaro Stakes at Ascot later in month; effective
from 1¼m to 2m; acts on any going but is best with some give in the ground;
game and genuine; not seen out after July. *M. Pipe.*

SONG BOY 2 ch.c. Music Boy 124–Sorceress 72 (On Your Mark 125) (1981 **60**
5v 5g 5g4 5g) June 4; 3,700Y; workmanlike colt; first foal; dam stayed 1¼m;
put up easily best effort when 1¾ lengths fourth of 13 to She's My Girl in maiden
auction event at Redcar in May (sweated up quite badly); runs as though 6f
will suit him; sold 340 gns Doncaster October Sales. *J. Hardy.*

SONG MINSTREL 3 b.g. Song 132–Tribal Festival 65 (Tribal Chief 125) **75**
(1980 5fg 5s 5s 1981 5g 8f 7f 6fg* 6g* 6d2 6fg3 6f 6d2 6d2 6d*) compact gelding;
won minor event and handicap at Ayr in July and apprentice handicap at
Leicester in November; by no means certain to stay 1m; acts on a firm and a
soft surface; blinkered nowadays. *M. Camacho.*

SONG MYDAD 2 b.c. Song 132–Sheinter (Sheshoon 132) (1981 5fg 5fg 7.2v) — May 15; 300Y; compact colt; half-brother to a winning plater and a winner abroad; dam ran only at 2 yrs; in rear in maiden races and a seller. *J. Townson.*

SONGS PRIDE 2 b.c. Song 132–Sun Star (Watteau) (1981 5.8g 5f 5fg 7d 73 9g 6.5v) Feb 17; fair sort; second reported foal; half-brother to a modest handicapper in Holland; dam poor Dutch maiden; fairly prominent in maiden and minor events at Windsor in June and July on second and third outings; not sure to stay 7f; sent to Holland; trained by J. Bethell first 4 starts. *A. Pije, Holland.*

SON OF SHAKA 5 b.h. Tribal Chief 125–Pink Garter (Henry the Seventh 98 125) (1980 6f² 6f 6g 5g 5s⁴ 1981 6s² 5g* 6s 5g³ 5g 5g 6fg 6fg³ 5fg⁴ 5.6fg) big, strong, sprint type; fairly useful handicapper; beat Covergirls Choice by ¾ length at Lingfield in May (odds on); better suited by 6f than 5f; acted on any going but went particularly well on top-of-the-ground; suited by front-running tactics; blinkered twice in 1980; game; sold 10,000 gns Newmarket Autumn Sales; retired to stud at a fee of £200, live foal. *R. Price.*

SONOMA (FR) 3 ch.f. Habitat 134–Satu (Primera 131) (1980 5d 6d 5s* 6.5g* 121 1981 6.5s² 6s* 5fg* 6g³ 5d 5v² 5v)
Good three-year-old sprinters were unusually thin on the ground in 1981 — only two names appear in the five to six-furlong category for that age group in the International Classification, which has a weight range of 20 lb. Marwell is out on her own; then comes the French filly Sonoma. There were only sixteen, including Marwell and Sonoma, in the whole 40-lb span of the British Handicap. Sonoma, lacking the brilliance of her sister Sigy and not up to beating several of the leading English older horses never mind Marwell, was still probably the best sprinter trained in France on her day. She won races at Maisons-Laffitte and Chantilly, the Prix du Gros Chene on the latter course smoothly from Ancient Regime, and ran creditably in defeat in two of the championship deciders. She finished third of fourteen in the William Hill July Cup, beaten three lengths and a length and a half behind Marwell and Moorestyle; and sixth of ten in the Prix de l'Abbaye de Longchamp, almost six lengths down on Marwell. After the Abbaye she was beaten twice, once on her home ground and once in Italy, starting favourite both times and odds on the second time. The German horse Park Romeo, fourth to Rabdan in the Prix de Seine-et-Oise, beat her a length and a half in the Prix du Petit Couvert at Longchamp, with Ancient Regime third and Sparkling Boy fourth; on similarly heavy going at Milan she was unplaced behind another German horse, Mister Rock's, in the Premio Omenoni.

Sonoma (Fr) (ch.f. 1978)	Habitat (b 1966)	Sir Gaylord (b 1959)	Turn-to Somethingroyal
		Little Hut (b 1952)	Occupy Savage Beauty
	Satu (b 1965)	Primera (b 1954)	My Babu Pirette
		Creation (ch 1960)	Crepello Cyclorama

Sigy's brilliance waned after her two-year-old days. At two she won the Prix de l'Abbaye on her final appearance, showing a clean pair of heels to Solinus, Double Form and the rest of a top-class field. She won four of her six races that season but only one of her four—the Prix du Gros Chene—the next. Sigy and Sonoma are the winners among their dam's five runners; the filly foal of 1979, Sephira (by Luthier), has shown promise in France. Satu, the dam, won the Prix Fille de l'Air (now classified Group 3) over a distance of approximately eleven furlongs; she is out of a Crepello mare, Creation, who won a poor one-mile

Prix du Gros Chene, Chantilly—a smooth win for Sonoma from Ancient Regime

maiden race at Newmarket in 1963 and subsequently bred winners in Japan. Some of the mares from this family used to belong to the Sassoon Studs, possibly the best-known of them the 1957 Imperial Produce Stakes winner Pin-wheel, a half-sister by Pinza to Creation, out of the useful sprinter Cyclorama. Sonoma is a rangy filly who seems to act on any going. Like Sigy she may safely be taken to be a sprinter though her pedigree isn't obviously that of one. *Mme C. Head, France.*

SONSERI 2 b.f. Prince Tenderfoot 126–Domani 106 (Mourne 126) (1981 5s*)   **77** p
Apr 3; third foal; half-sister to 2 winners, including very useful 6f to 1m winner Apres Demain (by King Emperor); dam, winner over 6f and 7f, is half-sister to very smart Duke Ellington (by Prince Tenderfoot), Matatina and Showdown; 6/4 favourite, didn't have much to beat when winning 11-runner maiden race at Wolverhampton in October easily by 2½ lengths from Escape Clause; a well-bred filly who should do a good deal better over 6f+ at 3 yrs. *R. Price.*

SOPHIA WESTERN 3 ch.f. Steel Heart 128–La Grisette (Fortino II 120)   —
(1980 5d 1981 7f 8fg 6g 6f 6v) sturdy filly; soundly beaten all outings, but seemed to take a while to get fit; started slowly fourth outing. *A. Gillam.*

SOPHRETTO 2 ch.c. Hot Spark 126–Permutation 79 (Pinza 137) (1981   —
5s 6g 6g 8g 8s) May 14; 4,400Y; strong colt; half-brother to 6f and 7f winner Helexian (by Song); no worthwhile form in maiden and minor events; sold 600 gns Doncaster October Sales. *J. Hardy.*

SOROCHINSKY FAIR 3 b.g. Legal Eagle 126–Sarasail 58 (Hitting Away)   **53**
(1980 7f 7d 1981 8g 8g 7fg 8g3 8s2 12f 12d2) workmanlike gelding; plater; placed in non-seller at Hamilton final start; stays 1½m; acts on soft going; trained part of season by W. Bentley (claimed £2,400 fifth start). *R. Johnson.*

SORROW 2 b.f. Wolver Hollow 126–Penitent 85 (Sing Sing 134) (1981 5s)   —
Feb 28; sister to fairly useful sprinter Penumbra and half-sister to 2 other winners; dam closely related to top sprinter Song; very weak in market when in rear in 15-runner maiden race won by Ritual Dance at Folkestone in October. *G. Harwood.*

SOSPIRAE 3 ch.f. Sandford Lad 133–Jewel Tower 91 (Double-U-Jay 120)   **74**
(1980 5fg 6g 6d2 7g 6d* 7fg3 7s 7d 1981 7d 6s3 5d3 6g) smallish filly; quite a useful performer at 2 yrs; didn't run up to her best when third in minor event at Nottingham and handicap at Hamilton in April; stays 7f; seems to act on any going. *N. Guest.*

SO SPLENDID 4 b.f. John Splendid 116–Lady Maggie (Distinctive 118)   —
(1980 8fg 9f 8g 8f 6fg 8fg 6g 8g 6d 1981 8g 6g 8fg4) compact filly; poor plater; stays 1m. *Mrs B. Waring.*

SO SWIFTLY 3 br.f. So Blessed 130–Hirondelle 86 (Falcon 131) (1980 5g   **75**
6d 1981 7.2f3 8g3 10f 8.2f 8.2s4 9s* 8d) smallish, lengthy, useful sort; made all and was never in much danger when beating Clarista 4 lengths in maiden race at York in October; quite moderate form otherwise; stays 9f; acts well on soft going; sold 8,500 gns Newmarket December Sales. *C. Thornton.*

SOUKAB 3 ch.c. Good Counsel–Colonial Cousin (Tom Rolfe) (1980 7g 7.6g4   **75**
7fg 8d2 7d 1981 8s 8s2 8d2 10g2 10.1d 10f 10fg3 10f4 12d 10fg4 10f* 11.7fg2) strong, well-made, attractive colt; second several times before beating Playful Paddy by ¾ length in handicap at Beverley in August; stays 1½m; acts on any going; usually wears blinkers; front runner; winner in USA. *G. Lewis.*

SOUL SINGER 6 b. or br.h. Saulingo 122–Ribocana (Molvedo 137) (1980 6s   —
6d 6g3 7fg 6fg3 7f 6d 7d 6fg 6fg* 7g 7.3fg 6fg 7g 1981 6fg) quite a useful handicapper on his day; not disgraced only start at 6 yrs in April; stays 7f well and has run respectably over 1m; appears to act on any going but is well suited by a sound surface; acts on any track. *B. Swift.*

SOUMARK 3 b.f. Weatherbird 112–Sousocks (Soueida 111) (1980 NR 1981   **37**
9s 16g3 16f 13.8g 16g 14fg 16s) strong filly; first foal; dam seemed of no account over hurdles; poor staying maiden. *W. Musson.*

SOUND MONEY 2 gr.c. Supreme Sovereign 119–Corsley Bell 96 (Owen Tudor)   **60**
(1981 5d 5d3 5s 6g 5fg 5f) Mar 5; 2,000Y; small, lightly-made colt; closely related to smart miler Town Crier (by Sovereign Path); 3 lengths third of 20 to Fair Mount Lad in maiden race at Salisbury in May; ran badly afterwards, including in sellers; should stay 6f; blinkered sixth outing; one to leave alone; sold 280 gns Ascot November Sales. *G. Beeson.*

SOUND OF THE SEA 2 b.f. Windjammer (USA)–Running Cedar (Bryan   **72**
G.) (1981 5g 5f 5s* 6s) Apr 19; 4,400Y; lightly-made, fair sort; half-sister to

a winning plater by Realm and a winner abroad; dam won at up to 1m in USA; having first race for over 2 months, put up easily best effort when winning modest maiden race at Lingfield in October by 2 lengths from Recline; should stay 6f (badly drawn when tried at trip); suited by soft going. *W. Wightman.*

SOUSTRA 4 b.f. Souvran 98–Moonstream 62 (Forlorn River 124) (1980 8fg 10g 7fg 7g 6g² 6d 1981 6f 6g 5.3f) tall, lightly-made filly; plater; best run at 6f. *P. Ashworth.* —

SOUTHERN DANCER 2 b.c. Connaught 130–Polyandrist 92 (Polic 126) (1981 8g⁴ 8s 7s) May 8; tall, fair sort; fifth living foal; half-brother to 3 winners, including very useful 5f performer Trigamy (by Tribal Chief); dam best at up to 1¼m; showed promise in 2 races at Goodwood in September, finishing 5¾ lengths fourth of 17 to Queen's Home in maiden race and 9½ lengths fifth of 12 to Jalmood in £3,300 event; again showed plenty of ability when 13 lengths seventh of 11 to Paradis Terrestre in Hyperion Stakes at Ascot the following month; stays 1m; sure to win in ordinary maiden company. *R. Price.* **82**

SOUTHERN FRONTIER 3 b.g. Derring-Do 131–Sage Willow 69 (Mossborough 126) (1980 5d* 5s* 6d³ 6fg 1981 8fg 7.6d 12g 12g 16s) compact, good-quartered gelding; useful performer at 2 yrs; disappointing in 1981 (last on 3 occasions) and seemed not to train on; should stay at least 1m; seems to act on any going; blinkered second outing; sold 400 gns Newmarket Autumn Sales. *F. J. Houghton.* —

SOUTHERN SWANEE 3 ch.f. My Swanee 122–Buggles 66 (Kelly 122) (1980 6f³ 6g* 5g* 5g² 5fg² 5d* 6s³ 6fg 7.3d 1981 7d⁴ 7s 6fg 6g 6g 7f 6fg 6fg 7.2v 7v) rangy filly; fair performer at 2 yrs; disappointing in 1981; stays 7f; seems to act on any going; blinkered ninth outing; changed hands 7,800 gns Newmarket July Sales. *D. Dale.* —

SOUTHFORK STAR 2 b.c. Malacate 131–Beatrice Frost 78 (Princely Gift 137) (1981 5f) Feb 13; 6,400Y; strong colt; half-brother to 2 winners in Italy; dam winning stayer; 25/1 and backward when in rear in 16-runner maiden event won by Changatu at Leicester in June; likely to need further; sold 620 gns Ascot December Sales. *R. Boss.* —

SOUTHOE BELL 3 gr.f. Saritamer 130–Nylon Pirate (Derring-Do 131) (1980 5d 5f 5g³ 5h⁴ 5d 5s³ 5g³ 5g 5g³ 5s* 5d 1981 5s 8.2g) neat filly; won nursery at Nottingham in 1980; well beaten in 1981 but was burly both starts and off course 4 months between them; should stay 6f; acts well on soft going; usually blinkered at 2 yrs. *D. Thom.* —

SOUVENT 6 ch.g. Souvran 98–Vengeance (Preciptic 122) (1980 NR 1981 12g) poor maiden. *W. Musson.* —

SOVEREIGN CASTLE 3 ch.f. Habat 127–Track Music 74 (Track Spare 125) (1980 6g 6fg 5fg³ 5.1fg 5.1fg⁴ 1981 5d 5g 5s 5f 5fg 5fg⁴ 5fg⁴) big, strong filly; has shown some ability in varied company, including selling; seems better suited by 5f than 6f; blinkered last 2 starts; sometimes bandaged; sold 1,500 gns Newmarket July Sales. *K. Ivory.* **49**

SOVEREIGN CELLAR 3 gr.g. Sovereign Path 125–Kessella (Le Levanstell 122) (1980 7f 1981 8f 10g 11f 9g 9d) useful-looking gelding; plater; not disgraced over 9f on fourth start. *Miss L. Siddall.* —

SOVEREIGN FLAME 3 ch.f. Supreme Sovereign 119–Flaming Peace 104 (Queen's Hussar 124) (1980 6f 6s* 1981 7s 6g 6g⁴ 6fg 5.3fg 6f 8d) useful-looking filly; ridden by claimer when winning maiden race at Ayr at 2 yrs; mainly disappointing in 1981; should stay 7f; acts on soft going; blinkered sixth start. *M. McCormack.* —

SOVEREIGN ISLAND 2 gr.c. Supreme Sovereign 119–Practicality (Weavers' Hall 122) (1981 7f 7g 6g) May 28; tall, leggy colt; first foal; dam, half-sister to very smart miler Poacher's Moon, ran once at 3 yrs; in rear in maiden races at Yarmouth, Newmarket and Doncaster (sweating). *N. Guest.* —

SOVEREIGN LANDING 3 gr.c. Sovereign Path 125–Pearl Harbour 83 (Martial 131) (1980 5d² 5fg³ 5f² 6g³ 6fg³ 7f³ 7fg⁴ 6s* 8s 1981 7s³ 7d² 8g 8g 7fg 7d³ 7g 7.2v) leggy, narrow colt; below his best in 1981 although was placed on occasions, including when 2½ lengths second to Ardoony in Northern Free Handicap at Newcastle in April; stays 7f; seems to act on any going but goes particularly well on soft; blinkered last 2 outings in 1980 and seventh start. *M. H. Easterby.* **69**

SOVEREIGN MUSTAPHA 3 b.g. Track Spare 125–Sovereign Game 60 (Sovereign Path 125) (1980 5s 5f 5f 6g² 7d 6fg³ 6f⁴ 8g 1981 8g 7d 10f 12g 11.5fg) neat gelding; mainly poor form, including in sellers; probably stays 1½m; acts on a firm surface; usually blinkered; often amateur ridden. *M. Haynes.* —

SOVEREIGN NOTION 2 b.c. He Loves Me 120–Notonia 73 (Never Say Die   **91**
137) (1981 5d 6s* 6fg 7fg³ 7fg² 8g³) Mar 14; IR 15,500Y; rangy colt; good
mover; half-brother to 2 winners in France; dam, half-sister to Psidium, won
over 1½m; won maiden race at Phoenix Park in May by 2 lengths from Truculent
Scholar; made no show when in rear in 16-runner Coventry Stakes at Royal
Ascot the following month but ran well when 2¼ lengths third of 12 to Peadar
Piper in Hennessy V.S.O.P. Stakes at Leopardstown, length second of 13 to
Burrendale in nursery at Galway and 8 lengths third of 11 to Anfield in Ashford
Castle Stakes at the Curragh, last-named in September; stays 1m; seems to act
on any going. *M. Kauntze, Ireland.*

SOVEREIGN PAUL 2 gr.g. Supreme Sovereign 119–Joshua's Daughter 61   —
(Joshua 129) (1981 5fg) June 5; sparely-made gelding; first foal; dam stayed
1½m; 14/1 when last of 13 to Lindsey in maiden race at Windsor in July; withdrawn at start at Wolverhampton the following month. *D. Elsworth.*

SOVEREIGN RING 2 b.f. Welsh Saint 126–Zulu Lady (Proud Chieftain 122)   —
(1981 5d 5d 5f) Feb 25; IR 5,000F; leggy filly; half-sister to Zulu Queen (by
Sovereign Path), a useful winner at up 7f in Ireland, and a winning hurdler;
dam won from 5f to 7f in Ireland; in rear in maiden and minor events; blinkered
third outing. *A. Bailey.*

SOVEREIGN ROYAL 2 b.c. Sovereign King–Carmenta (Dumbarnie 125)   —
(1981 6fg 6f 7.2v 8d) Mar 21; fourth foal; dam of no account; well behind in
maiden races and sellers. *H. Fleming.*

SOVEREIGN SAGE 3 b.f. Sovereign Path 125–Hot Spot (Vienna 127) (1980   —
7d 9d 1981 8d 7g) well behind in maiden and minor events. *R. Akehurst.*

SOVEREIGN'S ESCORT 7 gr.h. Supreme Sovereign 119–Jean Amour 88   —
(Delirium 126) (1980 NR 1981 16.9s 12d) poor handicapper; stays 1¼m;
acts on any going. *P. Felgate.*

SOVEREIGN SHOT 3 ch.f. Supreme Sovereign 119–Shot (I Say 125) (1980   —
7g 8fg 7d 1981 12g 10.1fg 8fg 8h 10f) lengthy filly; plater; should stay 1¼m.
M. Blanshard.

SOVEREIGNS IMAGE 2 gr.c. Grey Mirage 128–Sovereign Help 98 (Sovereign   **70**
Lord 120) (1981 5g 6g 6fg⁴ 7f 7g⁴ 8d* 8g 8g³ 8.2s* 7d) May 12; small, strong
colt; good walker and mover; half-brother to 1979 2-y-o 5f winner Simplicity (by
The Brianstan); dam won five 5f races; quite a useful plater; bought in 1,550 gns
after winning at Redcar in October (wandered about under pressure) and attracted
no bid when decisively accounting for Dromoland Castle by ¾ length at Nottingham later in month; suited by 7f and 1m; acts well on soft ground; effective with
or without blinkers; has twice given trouble in preliminaries; gives us impression
he's well suited by strong handling. *R. Hollinshead.*

SOVEREIGN'S QUILL 2 gr. or ro.c. Young Emperor 133–Blissful Hour   —
(Hardicanute 130) (1981 7.2d 7g) Apr 19; IR 5,000Y; leggy colt; first foal;
dam won over 7f at 2 yrs in Ireland and also 4 hurdle races; in rear in maiden
races at Haydock and Chester in August. *C. Crossley.*

SOVEREIGN STEED 3 gr.c. Royalty 130–Green Sovereign (Sovereign Path   **65**
125) (1980 7d 1981 8g 9s 10v³ 12d) compact colt; 2 lengths third to Taj El
Moulouk in maiden event at Kempton in October, first race since May; stays
1¼m (not disgraced over 1½m, but possibly didn't quite get trip); bandaged
only outing at 2 yrs. *E. Eldin.*

SOVEREIGN TOWER 4 b.g. Tower Walk 130–Field Mouse 108 (Grey Sovereign   —
128§) (1980 8s 8fg 8f 1981 11d 6g 7g 6fg 8.3fg) lengthy gelding; poor plater.
W. Charles.

SPACE ACE 4 br.g. Space King 115–This and That (Fedor II 107) (1980 NR   —
1981 15.8g 8f 10f 19g 8f) poor maiden; sold 1,050 gns Ascot September Sales.
R. Woodhouse.

SPACED 2 gr.c. Godswalk 130–Jaidlamour (Jaipur) (1981 5fg 6fg 6fg) May   —
14; IR 2,400Y; good sort; first living foal; dam won small 9f race in France and
also twice over jumps; having first race for over 2 months when 7 lengths sixth
of 10 to Paul's Ivory in minor event at Windsor in June; dwelt and always behind
when apprentice ridden at Newmarket the following month. *R. Armstrong.*

SPACE LEADER (USA) 9 ch.g. Mr Leader–She's in Orbit (Arctic Prince 135)   —
(1980 NR 1981 17.1g 12s 15.5d) probably no longer of any account. *B. Palling.*

SPAGHETTI SAUCE 7 ch.g. Sallust 134–Gayness (Merry Boy) (1980 NR   —
1981 10.4s) hunter chaser; probably no longer of any account on flat; has worn
bandages. *D. Ancil.*

SPANISH BAY 3 b.g. Roan Rocket 128–Spanish Sail 113 (Matador 131) **77**
(1980 6g³ 7f³ 7g² 1981 8fg* 10g⁴ 8f 7fg 7g) attractive gelding; ran a bit green
when landing odds by a neck from Aventura in 24-runner maiden event at
Warwick in April; seemed to find trip too far when fourth to Silver Season in
£3,400 race at Lingfield in May; stays 1m; moved badly to post second and
third starts and ran moderately in blinkers final outing; sold to M. Masson
6,800 gns Ascot August Sales. *G. Pritchard-Gordon.*

SPANISH FASNET (USA) 3 b.c. Master Derby–Glen Cova (Hill Rise 127) **52**
(1980 6fg³ 7g 6fg³ 6g 1981 6fg 6g 8.2g⁴ 8.2f 6fg³) quite attractive, well-made
colt; excellent mover; rather disappointing in 1981, although wasn't disgraced
when third in maiden event at Epsom in August; should be suited by 7f+;
wears blinkers nowadays. *G. Hunter.*

SPANISH FURY 2 ch.f. Double Jump 131–Tweezer (Songedor 116) (1981 5s **87**
5g 5fg³ 5fg⁴ 5fg³ 6d³ 5s² 5d* 5g²) May 11; lightly-made filly; first foal; dam
behind in maiden race and seller; finally got her head in front when winning 9-
runner maiden race at Hamilton in October by 3 lengths from Swinging Baby;
good ½-length second to Preparation in 21-runner nursery at Newmarket later in
month; best form at 5f, and with some give in the ground. *M. Ryan.*

SPANISH HANDFUL 6 br.g. Philip of Spain 126 Double Handful 96 (Major **48**
Portion 129) (1980 10v³ 10v⁴ 8f 8f 8.2d 8fg 7g³ 6fg 8s 1981 8v* 10v² 8.2d
8.2d 9g 8d 10.6s) plater; won at Ayr in March (bought in 1,900 gns); stays 1¼m;
revels in the mud; sometimes blinkered; has worn bandages; suitable mount for
an apprentice. *W. Stubbs.*

SPANISH HAT 3 gr.f. Gay Fandango 132–Dancing Hat 73 (High Hat 131) **—**
(1980 5g 5d 1981 10s³) tall, lengthy filly; lightly-raced maiden; only plating
class; runs as though she'll stay 1½m. *B. Hills.*

SPANISH HIND 3 ch.c. On Your Mark 125–Desist 92 (Supreme Court 135) **80**
(1980 5fg 5fg⁴ 5f³ 5s* 5g* 5g 6g 1981 6d 6s 6s 5.8f 6fg² 5fg 6g* 6g) neat colt;
well-backed favourite when beating Sharp Venita by ¾ length in handicap at
Goodwood in September; appears suited by 6f; seems to act on any going;
sometimes taken down early to start. *G. Lewis.*

SPANISH POINT 2 ch.c. Malacate 131–Bracken Girl (Skymaster 126) (1981 **63**
7fg 7fg 7g 6s 6g) Apr 12; IR 3,000Y; big, heavy-bodied colt; fourth foal; dam,
placed in Ireland, is half-sister to useful milers Golden Mean and Owen Anthony;
poor maiden; ran best race when 6 lengths sixth of 16 to Airwair, after leading
for 6f, at Leicester in September on third outing. *D. Sasse.*

SPANISH POOL 2 b.c. Gay Fandango 132–Watermark 83 (Henry the Seventh **100**
125) (1981 5g⁴ 5g* 6fg³ 8fg³ 7s*) Apr 1; IR 8,600Y; neat, quite attractive
colt; good walker; half-brother to fair sprinter Gin Game (by Red Alert) and a
winner in Trinidad; dam won over 1m at 2 yrs and is closely related to smart

*John Sutcliffe Trophy (nursery), Lingfield—Spanish Pool wins the season's
most valuable nursery from Rosananti*

performer Entanglement; won maiden race at Ayr in May and valuable John Sutcliffe Trophy (nursery) at Lingfield in October, running on to beat Rosananti 2 lengths in latter; has run well over 1m but gave us impression 7f was his optimum trip at 2 yrs; seems to act on any going; should make a useful handicapper at 3 yrs. *J. Hindley.*

SPANNERLEE 3 b.g. Swing Easy 126–Volley (Ratification 129) (1980 5fg **51** 5.8fg 6s 6s 6f 7fg 1981 6fg 7g⁴ 7.6g 8f 10fg 7f⁴ 8fg 7g² 8d) tall, leggy gelding; plater; suited by 7f; blinkered nowadays; sold 1,000 gns Ascot December Sales. *G. Balding.*

SPARE PIECE 3 ch.f. Track Spare 125–Word Perfect (Worden II 129) (1980 — NR 1981 8f 12.2fg 12d 8g) lengthy filly; half-sister to several winners, including very useful English and French 5f to 7f winner Giriama (by Tribal Chief); dam never ran; little worthwhile form, including in valuable seller final start; fell third outing; sold 520 gns Newmarket Autumn Sales. *J. Hindley.*

SPARE THE ROD 3 gr.f. Sweet Revenge 129–Grilse Run 94 (Stupendous) **62** (1980 6d³ 6d 1981 8d² 8d 10.2g 12g 11.7fg³ 12fg 10s 10s²) narrow filly; placed in varied company, on last occasion in selling; evidently stays 1½m; seems to act on any going. *T. Marshall.*

SPARE WHEEL 2 ch.f. Track Spare 125–Lady Councillor (Privy Councillor 125) **67** (1981 8d 8s 8.2s²) Apr 6; 680Y; fourth foal; dam ran only 3 times; plater; kept on well to be ½-length second of 12 to Knightsbridge Game at Nottingham in October; will stay 1¼m; yet to race on a sound surface. *P. Cundell.*

SPARKLER BRIGHT 3 b.f. Dubassoff–Hotazur 52 (Hotfoot 126) (1980 5d — 6fg 6fg 7fg 1981 8f) workmanlike filly; in rear in maiden races and a handicap; has been tried in blinkers; sold 270 gns Ascot November Sales. *J. O'Donoghue.*

SPARKLER CLEAR 3 b.g. Double Jump 131–Fiery Flo 78 (Firestreak 125) — (1980 5s 5f 6f 6s 7g 6f 7f³ 6fg 7.6f 7fg 10s 1981 10fg 10g 10fg 10.1fg 15.5f 15.5fg³ 12fg) plating-class maiden; probably stays 2m; has worn blinkers. *T. Gosling.*

SPARKLER'S STAR 3 b.f. Sparkler 130–Miss Poker Face (Raise You Ten 125) — (1980 5f 6g³ 5g² 5d² 7fg 5g² 1981 10s 7f 5fg) very small filly; plater; should be suited by 7f and more; sometimes blinkered. *P. Haslam.*

SPARKLING BARRON 4 b.g. Sparkler 130–Little Miss Muffet 102 (Tourment — 132) (1980 12s 11fg 10fg 1981 12g) strong, good-bodied gelding; poor maiden; probably stays 1½m; sold 775 gns Ascot 2nd June Sales; resold 780 gns Doncaster November Sales. *B. Swift.*

SPARKLING BOY 4 br.c. Comedy Star 121–Tinsel 95 (Right Boy 137) (1980 **109** 6f* 6f² 7f 5f* 6fg* 6d 5fg 6d 6fg⁴ 6g 6g 5.6g² 6s* 6fg 6d 1981 7d 7.6g 6g 6s³ 7.6g 5f 5fg 6g 6fg³ 6f⁴ 5.6fg 6g 5v⁴ 6s²) useful sort; good mover; very useful performer; put up particularly good efforts when just under 5 lengths fifth of 12 behind Marwell in King's Stand Stakes at Royal Ascot in June on sixth start, under a length third behind Crews Hill in Tote Stewards' Cup at Goodwood in July, 2¼ lengths fourth to Park Romeo in 5f Prix du Petit Couvert at Longchamp in October and short-neck second to Super Sky in Premio Umbria at Rome in November; best at sprint distances; acts on any going; sometimes wears blinkers but is effective without. *P. Kelleway.*

SPARKLING EARS 4 ch.f. Sparkler 130–Burning Ears 87 (Firestreak 125) **42** (1980 8f 9.4d³ 9.4g 8.2g³ 10g 10fg 9g 1981 9.4fg 8fg 9f³ 8.2f 9d⁴ 8g) small filly; only plating class; stays 1¼m; seems to act on any going; has run creditably for an apprentice. *E. Weymes.*

SPARKLING FORM 2 ch.c. Gold Form 108–Light Spark 73 (Twilight Alley — 133) (1981 7fg 6fg 6s) Mar 21; fifth foal; half-brother to a good winner in Hong Kong by Philip of Spain; dam placed over 5f at 2 yrs; well there 5f when ninth of 16 behind Super Sunset in seller at Doncaster in September, second outing. *R. Whitaker.*

SPARKLING GIRL 2 ch.f. Hot Spark 126–Lady Gaston 76 (Pall Mall 132) — (1981 5g 6fg 5.8h) May 4; 24,000Y; half-sister to fairly useful 1976 2-y-o 5f winner Sunny Spring (by Realm); dam, 2-y-o 5f winner, is half-sister to smart animals Cyrus and Right of the Line; little worthwhile form in maiden and minor events. *B. Swift.*

SPARKLING GRACE 6 b.h. No Mercy 126–Sparkle 82 (Alycidon 138) (1980 — NR 1981 6d 12.3fg) poor handicapper; was tried in blinkers; dead. *M. Reddan.*

SPARKLING LADY 3 ch.f. Hot Spark 126–Eilan Aigas 93 (Counsel 118) — (1980 5fg³ 5fg² 5f⁴ 5g³ 5g 5fg 1981 5f 6f 5g 5fg) neat filly; showed some ability at 2 yrs; speedy and isn't certain to stay beyond 5f; blinkered final start; sold 2,500 gns Doncaster November Sales. *C. Thornton.*

SPARKLING MISS 2 b.f. Sparkler 130–Miss Poker Face (Raise You Ten 125) — (1981 8.2d) Mar 24; 1,700Y; second foal; sister to a poor plater; dam fairly useful hurdler; unquoted when in rear in 20-runner maiden race won by Trickshot at Hamilton in September. *W. H. H. Williams.*

SPARKLING REFAIN 2 b.f. Song 132–Sparkling Jewel (Faberge II 121) **46** (1981 5s⁴ 5s³) Feb 9; 1,900Y; lengthy, plain sort; half-sister to 3-y-o Rumasa (by Lochnager), useful 6f to 9f winner Champagne Willie (by The Brianstan) and a winner over hurdles; dam of little account; showed only a little ability behind subsequently-disqualified winners El Pato and Mosswern in maiden race at Doncaster and seller at Beverley (favourite) early in season. *A. Smith.*

SPARKLING SIN 2 b. or br.c. Sparkler 130–Sinkit (Sing Sing 134) (1981 **79** 5v 5g² 6fg⁴ 7g 5d 8s² 8d⁴) May 3; 5,000Y; tall, good-bodied colt; half-brother to 1980 2-y-o 6f winner Sea Aura (by Roi Soleil); dam never ran; second in minor event at Kempton in May and maiden race at Warwick in October, running best race for some time when beaten 1½ lengths by Jazz Band in latter; evidently suited by 1m; acts on soft going. *R. Boss.*

SPARK OF LIFE 3 br.c. Home Guard 129–Tokara (Hard Tack 111§) (1980 **108** 6g* 6s* 7g* 1981 7g 7s* 7f 8fg² 8fg 10d) lightly-made colt; unbeaten in 3 races at 2 yrs; landed the odds in good style by 4 lengths from Star Fleet in 5-runner Heron Stakes at Kempton in May, quickening smoothly after being held up; did best work in closing stages when 2 lengths second to Golden Flak in Food Brokers Trophy (Handicap) at Newmarket in July, best subsequent effort; stays 1m (found little under pressure in blinkers when tried at 1¼m); probably not at his best on very firm going, and acts well on soft. *M. Stoute.*

SPECIAL MISSION 5 ch.g. Royal Trip–Treaty 86 (Ratification 129) (1980 — NR 1981 9g) beaten some way in amateur riders race won by Spindrifter at Hamilton in June. *J. S. Wilson.*

SPECIAL PLEASURE 2 b.f. Saulingo 122–Ordinary Fare (What A Pleasure) **97** (1981 5d⁴ 6fg⁴ 5f* 5fg 5fg 5g⁴ 5g² 5g) Apr 8; 5,000F; tall, lightly-built filly; good mover; third produce; half-sister to a winner in Norway by Run The Gantlet; dam unraced half-sister to a minor stakes winner; always going well when favourite for 10-runner maiden race at Kempton in July and won quite comfortably by 3 lengths from Welsh Partner, the pair clear; also ran well when ½-length second of 9 to Fearless Lad in £2,600 race at Doncaster in October; evidently thought best at 5f; acts on firm going; sweated up fourth outing; a free-running filly who finds little off bridle. *R. Armstrong.*

SPECTACULAR SKY 3 b.c. African Sky 124–Orient Queen (King's Troop 118) — (1980 6g⁴ 1981 6fg 5fg) quite attractive, robust, well-made colt; ran with a great deal of promise when close fourth of 10 behind Shasavaan in Duke of Edinburgh Stakes at Ascot as a 2-y-o; needed run when remote sixth of 8 to Integrity in minor event at Newbury in July; looked very fit and well but never got into race when last of 8 behind King of Spain in King George Stakes at Goodwood in July on only other start. *R. Armstrong.*

SPECTINA 5 ch.m. White Speck 88–Tacitina (Tacitus 124) (1980 9d 1981 — 9.4fg 12.2fg 15.8fg) poor maiden. *R. Johnson.*

SPEED OF LIGHT 6 ch.g. Laser Light 118–Herality (Immortality) (1980 **45** 16fg 1981 12.2fg² 16g² 15g* 12f³) staying handicapper; easily won 3-runner event at Edinburgh in June; had run respectably previous 2 starts; acts on any going; suitable mount for an apprentice. *G. Lockerbie.*

SPEED THE PLOUGH 3 b.f. Grundy 137–Southwark Star 97 (Midsummer — Night II 117) (1980 NR 1981 8d 8.5fg 8fg 8.2s) first foal; dam won Lincoln; behind in £4,400 event at Ascot and maiden races at Epsom, Warwick and Nottingham, twice finishing last; blinkered last 2 starts; sold 1,850 gns Newmarket December Sales. *P. Makin.*

SPEKES VALLEY 5 ch.m. Green God 128–Winbeam (Hornbeam 130) (1980 — 7fg 10.1fg 1981 10.2s) poor plater; not certain to stay 1¼m; sometimes wears blinkers; has run creditably for an apprentice; sold 620 gns Ascot August Sales. *S. Kernick.*

SPIDERWOOD 2 b.g. Tudor Rhythm 112–Calibre (Caliban 123) (1981 6g⁴ **69** 7g 7fg 6fg) May 1; rather leggy gelding; first foal; dam won selling hurdles; under 5 lengths fourth of 13 to Tulsa Flyer in maiden event at Salisbury in June; no worthwhile form in similar events and a nursery subsequently; should be suited by 7f; apprentice ridden all outings. *P. M. Taylor.*

SPIKEY BILL   4 ch.c. Souvran 98–Whitton Lane (Narrator 127) (1980 8f **52**
10.1s 8.3g 8g 8s 10s² 10d   1981 10.1d* 8d 12s² 10d)   tall colt; plater; won at
Windsor in May (bought in 2,000 gns); possibly stays 1½m; acts on soft going.
P. Mitchell.

SPINDRIFTER   3 ch.c. Sandford Lad 133–Late Spring 101 (Silly Season 127) **108**
(1980 5d* 5fg² 5f* 5h* 5fg* 6fg* 6g* 6g* 7f* 6g* 6g* 6f² 6f² 7g* 8d² 7d*
5s² 7v   1981 7g³ 9g*)   neat, robust colt; good walker; an exceptionally tough
and genuine colt who enjoyed prolific success at 2 yrs, scoring 13 times, gaining
nearly all his wins in the North; needed race and in circumstances ran very well
when 2½ lengths third of 13 behind Scarrowmanwick in valuable handicap at
York in May on reappearance; landed the odds by 1½ lengths from Tesoro Mio
in amateur riders event at Hamilton the following month; had to be put down
after fracturing a leg on the gallops in July; stayed 9f; acted on any going and
on any track; an admirable racehorse who was a credit to his trainer. *Sir
Mark Prescott.*

SPINNER   2 b.f. Blue Cashmere 129–Penny Pincher 95 (Constable 119) (1981 —
6g 5s)   May 4; sturdy non-thoroughbred filly; second foal; half-sister to fairly
useful sprinter Tobermory Boy (by Mummy's Pet); dam 5f sprinter; tenth of
20 to Illicit in maiden race at Warwick in October, second outing. *J. Hardy.*

SPIN OF A COIN   3 bl.c. Boreen (Fr) 123–Lovely Linan (Ballylinan 118) **88**
(1980 6g 7g⁴ 10s* 10.2s*   1981 12.3d* 10g³ 12d 14fg⁴ 11f* 12fg³ 12.5g* 12g³)
strong, attractive colt; won handicaps at Chester in May (decisively by 1½
lengths from St Mawes) and Ostend in August (beat Weavers' Pin by 2 lengths
in valuable race) and Grote Prijs der Nederlanden at Duindigt in September
(accounted for King by 3 lengths); finds 1¼m on sharp side and stays 1¾m;
probably acts on any going. *R. Price.*

SPINOLA   3 gr.f. Sweet Revenge 129–Manche 82 (Palestine 133) (1980 7g 5g —
1981 5g 7d 7f)   plain filly; well beaten in varied company, including selling.
K. Morgan.

SPLENDID AGAIN   6 b.g. John Splendid 116–Maella (Traffic) (1980 8fg **46**
1981 16f 12fg* 15fg² 20.4fg²)   former plater; won amateur riders handicap at
Carlisle in July; stays well; acts on any going; good mount for an inexperienced
rider; has worn bandages; trained by G. Lockerbie first start. *N. Tinkler.*

SPLENDIDLY GAY   3 b.f. Lord Gayle 124–Splendidly (Luminary 132) (1980 **80**
6g⁴ 9.5s   1981 10s 10.1s* 12f 16.5f 16.1d 14.6fg 12g 14s* 13s)   4,200Y; smallish,
workmanlike ex-Irish filly; half-sister to several winners, including very useful
milers Tack On (by Hard Tack) and Sotto Il Vulcano (by Right Tack); dam
half-sister to very useful middle-distance stayer Shackleton; 50/1 and apprentice
ridden when beating Admiral's Heir comfortably by a length in 6-runner minor
race at Windsor in May; stayed on gamely and ran easily best subsequent race
when head second to Al Nasr in £3,200 event at York in October, and was
subsequently awarded race; stays 1¾m; needs some give in the ground; trained
by P. Norris first start. *G. Huffer.*

SPLENDID SURPRISE   4 b.f. Status Seeker–Gig (Dionisio 126) (1980 6v —
5g³ 5fg² 5fg⁴ 5f 6d 6d⁴ 5d 6s   1981 6s 6fg 6g 6fg⁴ 8g 6d 8.2s)   small filly; plater;
stays 6f; acts on a firm and a soft surface; has run respectably for a boy; has
worn blinkers. *W. H. H. Williams.*

SPLIT THE BREEZE   2 gr.g. Roan Rocket 128–First Flight 78 (Pirate King —
129) (1981 5g 6d)   Jan 28; useful-looking gelding; brother to useful 1977
Irish 2-y-o 7f winner Jetsetter; dam stayed 1½m; unquoted when behind in maiden
and minor events at Newbury, showing up to 2f out on second outing in June.
Mrs R. Lomax.

SPOILT FOR CHOICE   3 b.g. The Brianstan 128–Song of May 79 (Sing **54**
Sing 134)   (1980 5fg 5fg⁴ 6g 5fg 7d 6g 6d 5g⁴ 5d⁴ 6s   1981 6f 7fg 6fg 5fg 7g³ 8s
7g² 7s)   neat gelding; placed in handicaps at Yarmouth in September (seller)
and Catterick in October; stays 1m; possibly unsuited by really soft going;
blinkered last 2 outings; trained until after third start by J. Mulhall. *C. Spares.*

SPOLETO   3 b.c. Nonoalco 131–Antrona 126 (Royal Palace 131) (1980 6g* **119**
6.5s   1981 7d² 8g 7s 7s 8g³ 6.5fg 8f*)   rangy, attractive colt; first foal; dam,
one of best of her sex at 2 yrs and 3 yrs, won at 6f to 1¼m; won valuable handicap
at Deauville in August in fine style by 6 lengths from Roll of Power, but unfortunately injured himself; had been placed in far better company earlier,
going down by only ½ length to Diamond Prospect in 6-runner Prix Djebel at
Maisons-Laffitte in April and finishing 2 lengths third to Ya Zaman in Group 3

822

Prix Messidor at Maisons-Laffitte in July; far from disgraced when about 7 lengths ninth of 19 behind To-Agori-Mou in 2,000 Guineas at Newmarket on second start and just over 3½ lengths fifth to easy winner Moorestyle in Group 2 Prix Maurice de Gheest at Deauville on sixth outing; suited by 1m and will probably stay 1¼m; probably acts on any going. *F. Boutin, France.*

SPORTING COVERGIRL 4 b. or br.f. Luthier 126–Dance All Night 106 (Double-U-Jay 120) (1980 8v³ 8s³ 9.4fg* 9g 10g 8.5fg 10g 1981 8s 10s* 9d³ 10g 10s 8fg 10d 8g² 7d 7.5g⁴ 10d 12s⁴) quite useful sort; ex-English; won handicap at Nottingham in April (apprentice ridden); second in similar event at Navan in September; stays 1½m; probably acts on any going; trained by N. Callaghan first 7 starts. *D. Weld, Ireland.* **58**

SPORTING PAINTING 2 ch.c. Red Alert 127–Golden Ash (Skymaster 126) (1981 5fg 7g 7fg² 8f 7g 7g 8d) Feb 20; 6,800Y; lengthy colt; first foal; dam never ran; showed up in a variety of races, on sixth outing finishing ninth of 29 to Perchance in valuable seller at Newmarket in September; stays 1m; blinkered third to fifth outings; sold to Newmarket BA 1,600 gns Newmarket Autumn Sales. *E. Eldin.* **66**

SPOTSYLVANIA 3 b.c. Empery 128–First Draft (Tom Rolfe) (1980 NR 1981 10s 8g 10d 8.5d 10fg 10fg³ 10fg³ 9g³ 10fg 7g²) 24,000Y; neat colt; second foal; dam placed 5 times in USA; plater; stays 1¼m; blinkered sixth and seventh starts; sold out of J. Bethell's stable 1,000 gns Ascot August Sales after seventh start. *D. H. Jones.* **56**

SPOTTY JANE 2 gr.f. Jimmy Reppin 131–Spotty 97 (Vigo 130) (1981 5d⁴ 5s² 6f³ 6f 6f* 6fg²) Apr 3; 500Y; small filly; half-sister to a winning plater; dam won three 5f races at 2 yrs; held up, won 9-runner auction seller (no bid) at Pontefract in June by 4 lengths from Cawstonella; not certain to stay beyond 6f; acts on any going; sold 2,100 gns Newmarket July Sales, probably for export to Italy. *G. Blum.* **58**

SPREADING SUNSET 3 ch.f. Amber Rama 133–Lantana 74 (St Paddy 133) (1980 5f 5fg 5f² 6fg⁴ 1981 6d 6d) tall, useful sort; in frame in maiden races as a 2-y-o; had stiff tasks when last in handicaps in 1981; usually blinkered. *J. Douglas-Home.* —

SPRIGHTLY WILLOW 2 b.f. Native Bazaar 122–Woodland Promise (Philemon 119) (1981 5fg) Feb 17; third foal; sister to fair 5f to 7f winner Crofthall; dam unplaced on flat and over hurdles; 16/1 when in rear in 13-runner maiden race won by Lindsey at Windsor in July. *P. Cole.* —

SPRING AIR 2 br.c. Frigid Aire–Spring Fever 110 (Botticelli 129) (1981 7g) May 25; IR 3,200F, 2,500Y; half-brother to several winners, including very smart middle-distance stayer Fool's Mate (by Busted); dam, very useful 2-y-o, stayed at least 13f; 20/1, prominent ½m out when seventh of 13 to Balanchine in minor event at Brighton in September; should improve when tackling middle distances at 3 yrs. *R. Price.* — p

SPRING BIRD 4 b. or br.f. Workboy 123–March Poulet (March Past 124) (1980 8d 6d 8f 6g 6g³ 6g 6f 7d 6s 1981 10.2g 8s) leggy filly; plater; best at 6f; acts on soft going; has worn blinkers. *D. Elsworth.* —

SPRING ENDEAVOUR 2 b.c. Jimsun 121–Alice-Emma (Kolper 107) (1981 7fg) May 14; second reported foal; dam placed over hurdles; 20/1 and ridden by 7-lb claimer, started slowly when last of 11 behind Nunsruler in maiden event at Brighton in August. *J. Jenkins.* —

SPRING LANE 2 br.f. Forlorn River 124–Merry Cindy 63 (Sea Hawk II 131) (1981 7h² 8g* 7g*) Mar 1; 2,500F; first produce; dam won over 15f; did well to win 15-runner maiden race at Edinburgh in September by 2½ lengths from Blue Do, after being hampered at halfway, and ran on gamely to win small race at Catterick the following month by a head from Quest; stays 1m and may get further (seems to have inherited a fair measure of her dam's stamina). *Sir Mark Prescott.* **85**

SPRINGS ETERNAL 2 ch.f. Sagaro 133–Oudalia 107 (Gala Performance) (1981 6fg) May 1; second foal; half-sister to 1980 2-y-o 5f winner Boganach (by Town Crier); dam best at sprint distances; unquoted, struggled to go pace early on but ran on well to finish 5½ lengths sixth of 19 to Enthralment in maiden race at Salisbury in September; should do better over further. *M. Smyly.* — p

SPRINGSTEEN 2 ch.f. Sunyboy 110–Sleepy (Hereward the Wake 75) (1981 10.2g) May 2; small filly; fourth foal; dam poor hurdler; 33/1 when tailed off in 26-runner minor event at Doncaster in November won by Yard Bird. *H. O'Neill.*

SPRINGWELL LANE (USA) 2 ch.f. Singh–Funny Comedienne (Bolinas Boy) — (1981 7.6s 6g) Mar 7; $35,000 2-y-o; quite attractive filly; second foal; dam, winner over 1¾m at 4 yrs in Ireland, is sister to $230,000-earner Famed Comedian; behind in 15-runner maiden race won by Sabutai at Lingfield in October and in 26-runner maiden event won by Perang Tejam at Doncaster the following month. *R. Price.*

SPURSTOW 3 b.g. Saulingo 122–Dian (Dike) (1980 5d 5f 5f² 5d³ 6fg 6fg³ 6d⁴ 5d² 8fg 6f 1981 6g 6d 6g 8fg* 8f 8g) lightly-made, compact gelding; apprentice ridden when winning selling handicap at Warwick in June; sold out of J. Hardy's stable 900 gns afterwards; stays 1m; probably acts on any going; sometimes blinkered; swerved leaving stalls third start; carried a good deal of overweight on fifth start. *R. Ward.* **45**

SPYLAW 2 br.g. No Mercy 126–La Dolce Vita 78 (Sallymount 125) (1981 6fg 7g 7f 8g 8s) Apr 22; 3,400F, 2,300Y; half-brother to a winning plater and a winner in Norway; dam won over 5f at 2 yrs; poor plater; started slowly third outing and ran badly in blinkers on final appearance. *J. Douglas-Home.* —

STAFFORDSHIRE KNOT 6 ch.g. Welsh Pageant 132–Wrekinianne 96 (Reform 132) (1980 8fg 8f 7.6f² 7.2fg 9g 7g 8d 7.6g 8f³ 1981 8g) poor handicapper nowadays; stays 1m well; acts on any going; used to wear blinkers; often ridden up with the pace; suitable mount for a boy; inconsistent. *R. Hollinshead.* —

STAG'S HORN 2 b. or br.g. Blue Cashmere 129–Falling Gold 77 (High Echelon) (1981 6f 5g 7.2d 6fg 6f 6s 6s⁴) June 7; small gelding; second living foal; dam won over 1m and 1½m; twice out of first 7 in valuable sellers but has the ability to win in ordinary plating company, as he showed when 3¾ lengths fourth of 13 to Puesdown in maiden race at Hamilton in October; should stay 7f; wears blinkers; sold 1,700 gns Doncaster November Sales. *E. Weymes.* **76**

STALSUNO 4 b.f. Bay Express 132–Lancashire Lass 73 (King's Troop 118) (1980 12g 13.8f 10g 8f 10f 13.8fg 1981 8.2g 10g) small, lightly-made filly; poor plater; suited by 1¼m. *J. Townson.* —

STALY'S PET 2 b.f. Mummy's Pet 125–Stalybridge 88 (The Brianstan 128) (1981 5fg 5fg 5f 7v 7g 6d 6g) big, strong filly who carries plenty of condition; second foal; dam won twice over 7f at 2 yrs and stayed 1¼m; poor maiden. *Hbt Jones.* —

STANDAAN (FR) 5 gr.h. Zeddaan 130–Castania (Orsini 124) (1980 5fg⁴ 6f⁴ 5f 5f³ 5fg 6d 6fg 6d³ 6g 5.6g 5fg 1981 6d 6g 5g* 5s³ 5fg 5f² 6g 5fg 5d) **118** Standaan's tally of five victories in thirty-seven outings over four seasons doesn't read like the record of an outstanding horse, but Standaan was a horse

Palace House Stakes, Newmarket—outsider Standaan makes all to beat a good field

with one outstanding quality—his pace. Time and again he showed in the highest class that nothing was capable of living with him over three furlongs. With such exceptional early pace Standaan had threatened for a long time to pick up a pattern race, but his three-length victory over Gypsy Dancer in the Palace House Stakes at Newmarket in May caused something of a shock. Standaan hadn't won since his all-the-way success in the Spillers Stewards' Cup at Goodwood in 1979, seventeen outings back, and there was nothing to inspire confidence in his chance at Newmarket other than the fact that he was returning to five furlongs. The field was a strong one including, as it did, Sharpo, Valeriga (these two making their seasonal reappearance), Runnett, Crews Hill and King of Spain; and Standaan's previous outings of the year, on which he had been soundly beaten at Doncaster and Newmarket, had been disappointing. In the event Standaan went off in front as usual, was soon clear, and won unchallenged.

The rest of Standaan's year followed a familiar pattern: campaigned exclusively in good company, by and large he performed creditably. He was placed twice, finishing third to Sharpo in the Prix de Saint-Georges at Longchamp and running a fine race to be second, at two lengths, to Marwell in the King's Stand Stakes at Royal Ascot. Also worthy of mention is Standaan's sixth place, some seven lengths behind Sharpo, in the hotly-contested William Hill Sprint Championship at York on his final outing.

		(Grey Sovereign	(Nasrullah
	(Zeddaan	(gr 1948)	(Kong
	((gr 1965)	(Vareta	(Vilmorin
Standaan (Fr)	{	(gr 1953)	(Veronique II
(gr.h. 1976)		(Orsini	(Ticino
	(Castania	(br 1954)	(Oranien
	((b 1969)	(Chios	(Nearco
		(b 1956)	(Chione

In *Racehorses of 1967* we wrote that 'if ever a horse was made for racing at the French distance of 900 metres (about four and a half furlongs) it was Zeddaan . . .' We weren't the only ones taken by surprise when Zeddaan won the French Two Thousand Guineas and the Prix d'Ispahan as a three-year-old, the latter by eight lengths over a distance of about nine furlongs. Zeddaan was sent to Japan in 1978 but in the past couple of years he has had two exceptionally speedy sons representing him in Europe, Standaan and Adraan, the latter a winner of three five-furlong pattern races. Standaan's dam is an unraced daughter of the versatile German Derby winner Orsini and a mare who won over seven and a half furlongs in Ireland. The third dam Chione, closely related to Meld, won the Galtres Stakes. Besides Standaan Castania has bred one winner, that being Stanaure (by Aureole), successful over middle distances in the French Provinces. Standaan, a strong, quite useful sort, stayed six furlongs but was better at five in the later stages of his career. He seemed to act on any going, although he was ideally suited by a sound surface. He was tried once in blinkers in 1979, running below his best. Standaan has been purchased by Tim Rogers of the Airlie Stud and has been sent to the Grangewilliam Stud in New Zealand. *C. Austin.*

STAND EASY 4 b.g. Connaught 130–Paresseuse 114 (Relko 136) (1980 10g* 10g² 6fg 11.7g⁴ 10s 1981 10g⁴ 10fg³ 10s² 10s 10.4g 11.1s) big, strong gelding; placed twice at Cagnes-sur-Mer early in year; will stay beyond 1½m; seems to act on any going; sweated up final start; sold to I. Wardle 7,200 gns Newmarket July Sales. *W. Hastings-Bass.* —

STANDLAKE (FR) 5 b. or br.m. Fireside Chat 122–Flight Feathers (Ribocco 129) (1980 NR 1981 15.5f) poor plater. *A. Neaves.* —

STANDON ROCK 3 ch.g. Mansingh 120–Teenager 71 (Never Say Die 137) (1980 5d 5g³ 6fg² 6g 6fg 7f² 7g 7d² 1981 7s 7s 8.2fg 8fg 8s 10d* 9d 12g⁴ 12v⁴ 12g⁴ 12g) shapely gelding; returned to form in 17-runner maiden event at Newmarket in August, battling on well under pressure from rear of field and getting up close home to beat The Disco Dago by a head; fourth in handicaps at Newmarket (twice) and York in October; needs 1¼m+; seems to act on any going; blinkered once in 1980. *P. Kelleway.* **69**

STAR ALLIANCE 3 b.f. Big Morton 85–Wet and Windy (Babu 117) (1980 NR 1981 8.2g 8g 7.2f 8fg 8d) first foal; dam never ran; in rear in maiden and minor races and a handicap. *R. Morris.* —

STARAWAK 2 b.f. Star Appeal 133–Arawak 109 (Seminole II) (1981 7fg 7g **66**
7d) Mar 27; 21,000Y; close-coupled filly; half-sister to several winners, notably
Spring In Deepsea (by Captain's Gig), a smart winner at up to 9f here and in
USA; dam third in Yorkshire Oaks and Irish Guinness Oaks; ran best race on
introduction when 5½ lengths sixth of 12 to Clare Island in £3,800 maiden race
at Sandown in July, weakening only at distance (25/1); well beaten in maiden
events on same course later in month and at Yarmouth in September; bred
to stay middle distances. *C. Brittain.*

STAR BELLA 2 b.f. Star Appeal 133–Dobella (Sovereign Lord 120) (1981 —
5fg 6fg 6g) May 5; compact filly; half-sister to 1977 2-y-o 6f seller winner
Belle-et-Vite (by Le Johnstan); dam placed over hurdles; little worthwhile
form in maiden and minor events; probably needs further. *G. Beeson.*

STARBELLS 2 b.c. Star Appeal 133–Haybells (Klairon 131) (1981 7d*) **83**
Apr 28; 6,000Y; half-brother to winning stayer Haywire (by Galivanter) and
a winning hurdler; dam lightly-raced half-sister to smart Haymaking; 25/1,
didn't have best of runs inside last 2f but quickened to beat Pacific Sparkler
by ½ length in 22-runner minor event at Chepstow in October; quite stoutly
bred, and will stay at least 1½m; reportedly sent to Hong Kong. *R. Price.*

STARBLOOM 4 b.f. Lorenzaccio 130–Star of Bagdad 95 (Bagdad) (1980 —
11fg² 11.7fg 12.3f 1981 12s) unfurnished filly; poor maiden; stayed 11f;
acted on a firm surface; blinkered once in 1980; sold, consigned by Brigadier
Gerard, 36,000 gns Newmarket December Sales. *Miss A. Sinclair.*

STAR BURST 4 b.g. Busted 134–Pearl Star 110 (Gulf Pearl 117) (1980 **80**
8.2g 11d* 11g² 10.6d 1981 12s 15g 14s² 12f² 12.3fg² 12g* 13d* 14.7fg² 15.8g
12g³ 13d* 14s² 12s* 12g² 16g) modest handicapper; goes very well at Hamilton
and won 4 times there in 1981; also runner-up 6 times, on final occasion when
beaten 1¼ lengths by Istimewa in Naas November Handicap; stays 1¾m; acts
on any going but goes well on soft; good mount for a boy; sweated up badly
fifth start; game and consistent. *D. Francis.*

STAR COVE 2 ch.f. Porto Bello 118–Your Star (On Your Mark 125) (1981 **58**
5s² 5g² 5fg² 5f² 6f* 5d*) Apr 22; 600Y (privately); workmanlike filly; third
live foal; half-sister to a winning 2-y-o plater; dam ran only once; ran well
in sellers and won at Haydock and Hamilton in July, being sold for 2,600 gns
after beating Flighty Francis a length on latter; stays 6f well; seems to act on
any going; trained by W. Haigh first 4 outings. *D. Garraton.*

STARFINDER 4 b.c. Comedy Star 121–Delfina (Salvo 129) (1980 8v 10g **59**
10fg* 8.2fg⁴ 10fg 8f² 8fg 9g* 8f 9g 1981 10.5d 10g 9fg 10fg³ 10f² 11fg³ 10d 10g
10.5s 8.2d²) compact colt; stays 11f; seems to act on any going but is suited
by a sound surface; sweated up badly once in 1980; blinkered seventh to ninth
starts; sold to M. Camacho 2,700 gns Newmarket Autumn Sales. *E. Weymes.*

STAR FLEET 3 ch.g. Record Token 128–New Way 103 (Klairon 131) (1980 6f **80**
7g 8fg 1981 8fg² 8g 6d 7s² 7g⁴ 5f 10fg² 10fg 8d 11.5fg² 12.3fg³ 16g² 14g) compact, lightly-made gelding; raced over a very wide range of distances and was
runner-up in Easter Stakes and Heron Stakes at Kempton, in amateur riders
races at Newmarket and Yarmouth and in a handicap at Newmarket; ran
moderately on several other starts; evidently stays 2m; seems to act on any
going; inconsistent; front runner. *P. Kelleway.*

STAR FORGE 2 b.c. Reform 132–Mathilde 84 (Whistler 129) (1981 5d 7d 7fg —
7.2fg) Mar 31; 2,800Y; small colt; half-brother to numerous winners, including speedy 1974 2-y-o Material (by Song); in rear in maiden and minor events and
looks of little account. *J. Tierney.*

STAR HEADING 3 ch.f. Upper Case–Star Dell (Red God 128§) (1980 5fg⁴ —
5fg³ 5g² 6d³ 7g² 6s² 6d 8s 5s³ 1981 6v 6s³ 8g 6fg 6g⁴ 6d 6f 7d) poor maiden;
stays 7f; best form with some give in the ground; sometimes blinkered. *W. H. H.
Williams.*

STAR ISSUE 3 br.f. Comedy Star 121–Top Secret 90 (Manacle 123) (1980 **58**
5f 5.1f² 5.1g² 6g 5.1fg⁴ 5f 6g 1981 7g 6f 7fg 5fg 8f² 8f* 8fg³ 9g 9s³ 6s 10g²)
neat filly; bought in 1,100 gns after beating Black Sunset decisively by 4 lengths
in selling handicap at Yarmouth in August; left J. Winter's stable to race in
Holland after next start, and was placed twice there; evidently stays 1½m;
acts on firm going; blinkered second outing. *H. van der Kraats, Holland.*

STAR KID 6 ch.g. Stardao 83–Babulass (Babu 117) (1980 5f 5f 5fg 5g* 5fg **49**
5f 5d 5d 5d² 1981 5s 5d 5g 5g³ 5g 5f 5g 5fg 6d 6s) sprint handicapper; best

form at 5f; acts on soft going; goes well on tracks with an uphill finish. *V. Mitchell.*

STARLUST 2 b.f. Sallust 134–Welsh Star 102 (Welsh Abbot 131) (1981 **79**
5g 5f* 5f² 6g 6fg) May 23; 16,000Y; neat filly; half-sister to several winners, including Welsh Pearl (by Gulf Pearl), very useful winner at up to 1m here and in USA, and fairly useful miler Star Prince (by Realm), subsequently highly successful in Malaysia and a winner in USA; dam won 3 times over 6f at 2 yrs and is half-sister to very smart 6f and 7f filly Star Bird; 3-length winner from Hartnell's In Love in 12-runner maiden race at Leicester in June; had every chance in £5,000 nursery at Newmarket in August, but finished only 6 lengths fifth of 11 to Tin Boy; probably stays 6f; swerved after being reluctant to leave stalls on final outing and virtually took no part. *R. Armstrong.*

STAR OF ANDROS (FR) 3 ch.f. Habitat 134–Star of Bagdad 95 (Bagdad) —
(1980 NR 1981 8fg 7fg 7f) 170,000Y; tall, lengthy, quite attractive filly; second foal; dam won over 1m and is half-sister to Malinowski and Gielgud; never dangerous in Masaka Stakes at Kempton in April and maiden races at Salisbury in June and Chepstow in July. *F. J. Houghton.*

STAR OF ENZO 3 b.c. Comedy Star 121–Cry Help 94 (Martial 131) (1980 **80**
5fg 5fg 5f⁴ 5f 6g 5fg* 5d 5d 5d 1981 5g 5f 5fg² 5f 5fg 5g* 5fg* 5f 5s 5s³) small, fair sort; successful in handicaps at Nottingham and Wolverhampton in August, beating Brassy ½ length on latter course; probably acts on any going; blinkered fifth outing as a 2-y-o. *T. Marshall.*

STAR PASTURES 3 b.f. Northfields—Spirit in the Sky 106 (Tudor Melody 129) **124**
(1980 7g² 7g³ 7g³ 6f* 6s* 1981 7.3s² 8g² 8v 7f² 8fg* 7fg* 7.3fg² 7f² 7g* 10g² 10f²)
Most racehorses who run up as high a percentage of second places as Star Pastures did would be in danger of attracting adverse criticism; but not, for one minute, was she. What a grand, supremely honest filly! She was a credit to her trainer, improving with virtually every race during a very busy season as a three-year-old and only once failing to make the first two in top-class or high-class company—that when beaten by underfoot conditions. By the end of the year

Mr R. E. Sangster's "Star Pastures"

she had few superiors among her age and sex at distances between seven furlongs and a mile and a quarter.

The state of the going is important to Star Pastures. To be seen at her best, for her fine turn of foot to be seen at its best, she needs a sound surface. She isn't so ineffective on soft going that she couldn't win decisively on it as a two-year-old or run creditably against Marwell in the Fred Darling Stakes first time out at three, but she is so much more to be reckoned with on top-of-the-ground and she was unable to do herself justice on very heavy going in the Goffs Irish One Thousand Guineas. Star Pastures faded right out to seventh at the Curragh—a disappointment after her second to Ukraine Girl in the Poule d'Essai des Pouliches at Longchamp three weeks earlier (she had been beaten only one and a half lengths there, after none too clear a run). In all probability Star Pastures was the best miler in the Irish One Thousand field. She had easily the best subsequent record at around that distance: raced only on a sound surface she won three good prizes for fillies and narrowly missed winning three others, and gave an excellent account of herself against the colts on the two other occasions.

The races Star Pastures won were the Group 3 Child Stakes at Newmarket in July, the American Express Royal Wedding Day Stakes at Goodwood later in the month and the Heathorns Stakes at Goodwood in September. Each time she accounted principally for the One Thousand Guineas second Tolmi, showing that very bright finishing speed of hers: the respective winning distances were three lengths (a very easy three), a length, then two lengths, with Tolmi at a disadvantage of 6 lb the first time and 3 lb the second. Their third meeting, at level weights, clinched the argument. In the nature of things, no matter how much thought goes into framing the conditions for events such as the Child Stakes a thoroughly equitable distribution of weights seldom results. Star Pastures herself was faced with a clear disadvantage in the Jersey Stakes at Royal Ascot, the Hungerford Stakes at Newbury in August and the Strensall Stakes at York in September. In the first instance she had to concede 3 lb to the colts Rasa Penang and Noalto, whom she divided; in the second she was at weight-for-age but not weight-for-sex with Dalsaan and carried the same weight as Noalto when dividing them; and in the third she had to concede 2 lb to the year-older filly Premier Rose when the pair had the finish to themselves. Star Pastures went down by three lengths to Rasa Penang from a modest draw, by two and a half to Dalsaan, and by three quarters to Premier Rose.

Star Pastures didn't exactly get off lightly either in the Sun Chariot Stakes at Newmarket in October, her last race in this country and her first at a mile and a quarter. The conditions treated her better than Go Leasing, though, who had to carry 4 lb more, and her task was made easier by Piggott's putting up overweight on the favourite Home On The Range, bringing the latter up to within a pound of Star Pastures. Very woolly in her coat by now (she hadn't been too impressive in the paddock on any recent appearance) Star Pastures turned in her customary gritty performance and stayed the trip well. She was always going smoothly, came to challenge Home On The Range running into the Dip and made the winner fight all the way for her neck victory. Star Pastures' autumn campaign had been geared to an attempt at winning the Yellow Ribbon Stakes, an invitation race for fillies and mares with 300,000 dollars guaranteed run over a mile and a quarter on turf at Santa Anita, California, on November 1st. She eventually made the long journey, fortunate to find the going firm when she arrived, and ran the race of her life for second place to Queen To Conquer in a hot field. Virtually just off the aeroplane, she went down by only a neck to the older ex-English mare, caught near the finish after taking the lead inside the last furlong; Kilijaro was fourth, Mrs Penny and the good French fillies Leandra and Landresse among those down the back. Star Pastures' 60,000 dollars prize money shouldn't be her last over there by any means. She remains in training in the United States.

Star Pastures (b.f. 1978)	Northfields (ch 1968)	Northern Dancer (b 1961)	Nearctic	Natalma
		Little Hut (b 1952)	Occupy	Savage Beauty
	Spirit in the Sky (b 1969)	Tudor Melody (br 1956)	Tudor Minstrel	Matelda
		Flight (b 1962)	Court Harwell	Torch Bearer

Star Pastures cost 24,000 guineas as a yearling. Evidently the scar of a recent facial injury detracted from her appearance then, and even now she's not an imposing filly, being on the small side; what there is of her is quite attractive, though, when she's at her best. Star Pastures' dam easily won a small race over a mile and a half at Pontefract and is out of a dour stayer, but showed better form over shorter distances. She won a handicap over ten furlongs at Epsom and was placed in the Fred Darling Stakes, Nassau Stakes and Prix de Royaumont. Flight, the grandam, won five times at distances of two miles or more and ran in the 1966 Cesarewitch; she was a half-sister to the useful stayer Marechal Drake and a granddaughter of that good broodmare Camp Fire, an unlucky One Thousand Guineas fourth. Star Pastures' dam has some way to go to rival Camp Fire's record at stud, for the latter bred nine winners including General Gordon, Bivouac, Campaign and Creole. So far she has produced five runners, four of whom have won. The winners were minor ones apart from Star Pastures—Fine Wine (by Petingo), Riviere Bleue (by Riverman) and Spirit of Crow (by Crowned Prince), the last two abroad. Fine Wine won over seven furlongs at Edinburgh as a two-year-old in 1977 for Star Pastures' stable. *J. Hindley.*

STARPOSE 4 b.f. Prince Ippi–Sternwacht (Waldcanter) (1980 including 8s[2] 11s 8s[4] 8g[3] 8s[2] 1981 10s 8g 8h 8d) big ex-German filly; half-sister to 2 winners in Germany; dam, half-sister to Star Appeal, won 9 races in Germany and Italy; won a race in Germany at 2 yrs and finished equal second in German 1,000 Guineas at Dusseldorf in 1980; well beaten in varied company all starts in this country; should stay middle distances; acts on soft going; broke out of stalls and was withdrawn third outing. *B. Swift.*   —

STAR PRINCESS (FR) 2 b.f. Sun Prince 128–Baracoa (Dark Star) (1981 4s[4] 5.5s* 6g* 7f 7s[3] 8s 8v) small, rather lightly-made filly; fifth foal; half-sister to a winner over jumps in France; dam never ran; won twice at Maisons-Laffitte, gaining second success by ¾ length from Keep In Step in minor event in July; had stiff tasks afterwards but was far from disgraced when 3 lengths third of 5 to Green Forest in Prix de la Salamandre at Longchamp in September and when about 10 lengths fifth of 10 to same horse in Grand Criterium on same course next time out; stays 1m; acts on soft going. *P. Biancone, France.*   **109**

STARPROOF 2 b. or br.f. Comedy Star 121–Whiffenretz 75 (Whiffenpoof 97§) (1981 5g 5d[4] 6f 6f 6fg[2] 7fg 6f 8.2d 10d) Mar 3; 680Y; leggy filly; second foal; dam best at 5f; plater; seems to stay 7f. *G. Richards.*   **46**

STARRY ANGEL 3 b.f. Comedy Star 121–Wayward Angel (Starry Halo 122) (1980 NR 1981 16g) first foal; dam never ran; 33/1 when tailed off in maiden race won by Farsound at Nottingham in August. *M. Smyly.*   —

STARTERS IMAGE 2 ch.f. On Your Mark 125–Dame's Delight (Ballymoss 136) (1981 5s 5d 5f[4] 6f[2] 7g* 7fg* 7s 8d) Apr 18; quite a well-made filly; first foal; dam never ran; changed hands for 6,200 gns after winning valuable 19-runner seller at Newmarket in July; made all when outsider of 6 in nursery the following month, scoring by 2 lengths from odds-on Bancario; better suited by 7f than shorter distances but has yet to show she stays 1m; acts on firm going and ran moderately on a soft surface last 2 starts; suited by forcing tactics. *W. Hastings-Bass.*   **78**

STARTINGO 7 ch.g. Petingo 135–Pearl Star 110 (Gulf Pearl 117) (1980 NR 1981 12.5g 10fg 12.3fg 15.8g) poor handicapper nowadays; behind in seller second start; stays 13f; acts on soft going; wears blinkers; has twice sweated up and run very badly; reportedly suffers from back trouble; bandaged nowadays. *N. Chamberlain.*   —

STAR VENTURE 5 br.g. Swing Easy 126–Street Vendor 60 (High Perch 126) (1980 7v[2] 6d[4] 7fg[3] 7f[3] 7f[3] 7f 7g 10d 7fg[4] 7fg[4] 7fg 6fg[2] 6s[4] 1981 7fg[4] 6f 7f[3] 6f[2] 7f 6fg[3] 6f 6d 6s) strong gelding; doesn't impress in his slower paces; suited by 7f and may stay 1m; acts on any going; has worn blinkers but is better without; suitable mount for an apprentice; has had tongue tied down. *G. Huffer.*   **60**

STATE COUNCELLOR 5 b.g. Royal and Regal–Sensibility (Hail to Reason) (1980 8f* 12f 8f* 8f[2] 8fg[2] 9g* 8g 9g[3] 9fg[3] 8s[3] 8.2d* 8f* 9g[4] 1981 8s) ex-Irish gelding; won 5 times in 1980; well beaten only start at 5 yrs in March; best form at up to 9f; acts on any going; has worn blinkers but is better without; good mount for an inexperienced rider. *Denys Smith.*   —

STATE HOUSE (USA) 2 ch.c. Full Pocket–Star Empress (Young Emperor 133) (1981 6fg 6f) Apr 9; $23,000Y; lengthy, rather sparely-made colt; third foal; dam minor stakes winner at up to 7f; in rear in July in maiden races at York (moved very poorly to start) and Thirsk (16/1). *J. W. Watts.*   —

STATELY ROCKET 3 ch.f. Roan Rocket 128–Noble Duty (Reliance II 137) (1980 NR 1981 12g) 8,000Y; big, rangy filly; second foal; half-sister to useful stayer Sentry Duty (by Sparkler); dam won over 13f in France; 33/1 and backward when last of 15 behind Cornishman in minor race at Newmarket in May. *B. Hobbs.*

STATE ROMANCE 2 b. or br.f. Free State 125–Eastern Romance 73 (Sahib 114) (1981 5.8g 5f 5fg 5f⁴ 5h 7d) Apr 5; lightly-made filly; first foal; dam won 6f seller at 2 yrs; plating-class maiden. *R. Laing.* — **60**

STATES GENERAL 2 b.c. Swing Easy 126–Without Reproach 102 (Above Suspicion 127) (1981 8s⁴ 7g) Feb 10; 10,500Y; workmanlike, lengthy colt; half-brother to several winners, including useful stayer Hikari (by Petingo); dam won Lancashire Oaks; backward both starts but showed signs of ability in small race at Newcastle (12 lengths fourth of 6 to easy winner Bancario) and 18-runner maiden event at Doncaster (eighth behind Leg Glance), in October; probably stays 1m. *Denys Smith.* — **— p**

STATESIDE 2 ch.f. Free State 125–Bashi 73 (Zarathustra 131) (1981 7.2fg 7g 8fg 8d) Feb 27; small filly; half-sister to several winners, including quite useful sprinter Attymon Place (by Mummy's Pet); dam ran only at 2 yrs; towards rear in maiden races in September and October; bandaged off-hind final start. *K. Stone.* — **—**

STATE TROOPER 4 ch.c. Status Seeker–Sarah Pipellini (French Beige 127) (1980 8.2d³ 7f 8fg² 7.2g* 8f⁴ 8d³ 8fg⁴ 9g* 7fg² 7f 8.2d³ 8s³ 8d⁴ 1981 10.2d² 10s 8g² 10g* 10.5d³ 8.5g 8d* 8g* 10g) strong colt; fairly useful handicapper; successful at Lingfield, Sandown and York; made all on last 2, staying on strongly at York in July to beat Dunham Park by 2 lengths; stays 1¼m; acts on any going; has run well for an apprentice; suited by front-running tactics; genuine and consistent. *B. Hanbury.* — **96**

ST ATHAN'S BOY 3 ch.c. Imperial Crown 96–Moneywise (Hook Money 124) (1980 7g 1981 12fg 10d 14d 16fg) compact colt; poor form in maiden and minor events. *M. Haynes.* — **—**

STATS EMMAR 3 br.f. Steel Heart 128–Lavendula Rose 108 (Le Levanstell 122) (1980 5fg* 5g 7.2s* 6g* 7g 1981 8fg⁴ 12g 8s) rangy, attractive filly; good mover with a long stride; won at Kempton, Haydock and Newbury as a 2-y-o; always prominent and kept on when about a length fourth of 10 behind Fabulous Salt in Masaka Stakes at Kempton in April; well beaten in good company at Lingfield and Kempton the following month, probably setting too strong a gallop for her own good on latter course; not certain to stay 1½m; rather excitable nowadays; sent to USA. *R. Price.* — **86**

STAYING ALIVE (USA) 4 ch.c. Vitriolic–Back in Paris (Carry Back) (1980 8fg³ 8g* 8fg² 7g 8g² 8g 1981 6s 8g 10f⁴ 10.2fg* 10.5g 10d 10.6d 10fg⁴ 10fg) tall, strong colt; has a round action; stayed on well to win handicap at Doncaster in June; ran atrociously most subsequent starts and is best left alone; well suited by 1¼m; acts on a firm surface; blinkered fifth start (pulled hard); sold 3,200 gns Newmarket Autumn Sales. *L. Cumani.* — **74 §**

STAY SECRET 4 b.g. Most Secret 119–Sayvanter (Galivanter 131) (1980 5h 5fg 5f 5g 5f* 5g 5.6fg 6g 6d³ 6d 5s³ 6s* 6s 1981 6g 5g 6g² 5g 6g 5g 5f 5f 5g 6d 8.2d) poor mover; plater; stays 6f; acts on any going; best in blinkers. *W. Bentley.* — **54 d**

ST BENEDICT 4 br.c. So Blessed 130–Catalonia 97 (Abernant 142) (1980 5f 5fg 5f 5g 5s 5d 1981 6v⁴ 5s 6g³ 6g 6g² 6g 8fg 6fg 7f³ 7g) strong, good sort; plater; stays 7f; acts on firm going. *A. Smith.* — **54**

ST BRIDE 3 b.f. St Paddy 133–Season Ticket (Silly Season 127) (1980 6fg 8d 1981 8d 11.7fg) little worthwhile form in varied company; sold 340 gns Ascot October Sales. *G. Hunter.* — **—**

ST CONAL 2 ch.c. Status Seeker–Irish Picture (Dual 117) (1981 5s 7g 8s 10s) Apr 25; IR 2,000F; useful-looking colt; half-brother to a winner in Brazil; dam fourth twice in Ireland; little worthwhile form in minor and maiden races; blinkered fourth start. *G. Beeson.* — **—**

ST CORDELIA (FR) 4 ch.f. Roi Lear 126–St Isabel (Saint Crespin III 132) (1980 NR 1981 9s⁴ 10g² 8g³ 10g 13g² 9.5g* 10.5g 10.5g 11v* 12v³ 12s) ex-English filly; third foal; half-sister to winners in France by Roan Rocket and Mon Fils; dam won over 1m and 1¼m in France; won 3-runner gentleman riders race at Lisieux in August and handicap at Longchamp in October; runner-up in maiden race at Stockton on second start; stays 13f; acts on heavy going; often wears bandages; good mount for an inexperienced rider; trained by R. Sheather first 3 starts; sold 29,000 gns Newmarket December Sales. *J. R. Lyon, France.* — **66**

ST DAVID'S DAY 3 b.g. Welsh Pageant 132–Whipped Cream 77 (Alycidon 138) — (1980 NR 1981 8g 12g) big, deep-girthed gelding; brother to Royal Plume, a very useful winner at up to 1½m, and half-brother to 2 other winners; dam disappointing half-sister to Connaught; in rear in newcomers race won by Magikin at Newmarket in April (backward) and minor race won by Cornishman on same course in May. *H. Cecil.*

STEADY THE BUFFS 2 b.f. Balidar 133–Dinant 114 (Abernant 142) (1981 — 6fg 7g 7g) May 13; IR 3,100Y; big filly; poor walker; sister to a winner in Italy and half-sister to several winners; dam winning sister to 1,000 Guineas winner Abermaid; backward when in rear in 17-runner maiden races at Newbury and Leicester (2). *M. McCourt.*

STEEL BAY 2 b.c. Red Alert 127–Spadilla 59 (Javelot 124) (1981 7.2d² 7d²) **98** Mar 26; IR 6,400F, IR 10,500Y; compact, quite attractive colt; closely related to Wyn-Bank (by Green God), successful at up to 1¼m, and half-brother to a winner; dam Irish 1½m winner; ran well when length second in maiden race won by Candide at Haydock in August and in £4,800 race won by Montekin at Goodwood in September, leading for over 5f in latter and finishing clear of 6 others; will be suited by 1m, and may get further; a sure winner in maiden company. *P. Cole.*

STEEL CHARGER 4 b.c. Steel Heart 128–Belaying Pin (Iron Peg §§) (1980 **79** 8f 7fg 5g⁴ 5s 5fg 5g* 5.3fg² 1981 5s² 5fg* 5g 5g* 5g 5f 5fg 5fg 5fg² 5fg* 5g 5g) strong, compact, good sort; sprint handicapper; successful at Epsom in April, Newmarket in May and Epsom again in September; beat Daffyd by 2 lengths for final success; best at around 5f; probably acts on any going; blinkered once in 1980. *R. Boss.*

STEEL CHOICE 2 b.c. Comedy Star 121–Port Meadow 83 (Runnymede 123) **82** (1981 5v 5d² 5s 6g 6g* 7g³ 7f⁴ 8f 8g 8d) Mar 27; 4,100Y; strong colt; sixth foal; half-brother to 1980 2-y-o 5f winner Mel's Choice (by Birdbrook) and a winning plater; dam probably stayed 1m; won by a head from Fort Garry in 9-runner minor event at Ayr in June (20/1); ran creditably in nurseries afterwards; stays 1m; acts on any going with possible exception of really soft; blinkered last 2 outings; consistent. *J. Etherington.*

STEEL CITY 7 ch.h. Sharpen Up 127–Tantau's Delight 77 (Tantieme 136) **57** (1980 8f³ 8fg 8d² 8g⁴ 8fg³ 8d 8g³ 1981 9d 8f 8f⁴ 8h* 8fg² 8h 8h) poor 1m handicapper nowadays; won apprentice race at Bath in July; acts well on firm going and is not at his best on soft; suited by waiting tactics; suitable mount for an inexperienced rider; has been tried in blinkers; none too genuine. *G. Cottrell.*

STEEL COMMANDER 3 b.c. Steel Heart 128–Commander Ali (Bold Com- **91 d** mander) (1980 7d 1981 10d 6d* 7d² 6d² 7f 6.3fg 6.3fg 7.5g 9d 8s) first foal; dam, half-sister to several winners, won twice at up to 10.7f in France; beat Clanjolly by ¾ length in maiden event at the Curragh in April; second twice at Phoenix Park afterwards, beaten a head by Singing My Song in a handicap in June on second occasion; had stiff task when in rear in 7f Jersey Stakes won by Rasa Penang at Royal Ascot; stays 7f; blinkered seventh start. *D. Weld, Ireland.*

STEEL EASY 2 b.g. Swing Easy 126–Netley (Major Portion 129) (1981 5f — 6f 5g 7d) Mar 24; 5,600Y; workmanlike gelding; good mover; half-brother to fairly useful 1979 2-y-o 7f winner Harvester Solar (by Porto Bello) and 3 winners abroad; dam won over 1½m in France; beat only 3 horses home in 4 starts, final appearance in a seller; blinkered third and fourth starts. *M. W. Easterby.*

STEEL GARRISON 3 br.c. Steel Heart 128–Party Tricks (Tom Fool) (1980 **72 d** 5d 5d* 5fg³ 5fg* 5g² 5fg 5g² 6d 5f 5g 5g 1981 5s⁴ 5d³ 5g 5s 5fg 5fg 6g 6fg) neat, strong colt; in frame in handicaps in the spring but became disappointing and was unplaced in a claiming race and a seller on last 2 starts; should stay 6f; probably acts on any going; sometimes blinkered; sold 2,300 gns Ascot September Sales. *G. Hunter.*

STEEL GLOW 2 b.c. Steel Heart 128–Lucybird (Sea-Bird II 145) (1981 6g **87** 7d⁴ 6g³) Apr 27; IR 24,000Y; strong, good sort; half-brother to a winning hurdler; dam unraced daughter to Sun Chariot Stakes winner Lucaya; always prominent when 1¾ lengths third of 22 to Ash Ridge in maiden race at Newmarket in October, best effort; promises to stay 7f+; has plenty of scope and will win races at 3 yrs. *B. Hills.*

STEEL KID (USA) 2 b.c. Caro 133–Gallant Trial (Gallant Man) (1981 7g **81** 8g 7fg 7g) Apr 29; $400,000Y; stocky colt; third foal; half-brother to a winner by Vaguely Noble; dam very useful winner at up to 1m; chased leaders for over 5f when 4 lengths fifth of 18 to Leg Glance in maiden race at Doncaster in October, third start and best effort; should stay 1m. *R. Armstrong.*

STEEL LINK 4 gr.f. The Go-Between 129–Copper Cold (Democratic 124) —
(1980 6g 1981 6s) sturdy filly; temperamental plater; has been tried in blinkers. *R. Hoad.*

STEEL PART 3 ch.g. Steel Heart 128–Dalriada (Ribot 142) (1980 5s 5f³ **44**
5fg 1981 8s 6g 5v 7f 5fg 6fg² 6g) very small gelding; plater; close second at Carlisle in July; should stay 1m; slowly away final start. *D. Gandolfo.*

STEEL PASS 3 b.c. Steel Heart 128–Senorita Rugby 86 (Forward Pass) **106**
(1980 5fg² 6fg⁴ 6d² 6s² 5.8f* 6fg 6fg 6d 6g* 1981 7d 6g⁴ 6g 6d* 6g² 6fg² 6f*
6fg 6d 6fg) good-bodied colt; successful in handicaps at Brighton in May and Newmarket in July, on latter course producing a powerful run to win by 2 lengths from Bold Scuffle; narrowly beaten in similar races at Newbury (by Dawn's Delight) and Newmarket (by Bold Scuffle) in between; rather disappointing last 3 starts, on first occasion when well-backed favourite for Tote Stewards' Cup at Goodwood; best at around 6f; acts on any going; often used to be blinkered; well suited by waiting tactics; benefits from strong handling and goes particularly well for L. Piggott. *G. Hunter.*

STEEL PRINCE 4 b.g. Ampney Prince 96–Cofimvaba (Verrieres 131) (1980 —
NR 1981 12g 8f) no sign of ability in maiden races. *D. H. Jones.*

STEEL PROFILE 3 ch.c. Manado 130–Moon Cake (Red God 128§) (1980 —
NR 1981 6fg⁴) 7,200Y; fifth foal; dam twice-raced half-sister to unbeaten Hardicanute; outsider of party, showed speed early on when last of 4 to Java Tiger in maiden race at Hamilton in May (apprentice ridden). *W. H. H. Williams.*

STEEL SON 3 ch.c. Steel Heart 128–Aspara 58 (Crimson Satan) (1980 6f **70**
6fg 6g 6s 1981 6g 6g³ 5f 5f² 5fg³ 6f 5fg² 5fg² 6f² 5g⁴ 5fg) strong, well-made colt; placed in varied company; stays 6f; acts on firm going; blinkered last 4 starts; sold 2,000 gns Newmarket Autumn Sales. *F. Durr.*

STEELSTOCK 2 br.g. Tamerlane 128–Lady Talisman (Continuation 120) **81**
(1981 5d 6g³ 6fg³ 7f² 7g 7f³ 7fg² 8fg 8g 8s) Mar 20; IR 4,600F, 3,500Y; useful sort; good walker; sixth produce; dam poor Irish maiden; failed by only a head to catch Major Irish in minor event at Beverley in July but couldn't get Chase The Wind off the bit in 2-runner event at Newcastle the following month; well behind subsequently in nurseries and a maiden event; should stay 1m; acts well on firm going. *K. Stone.*

STEEL STOCKHOLDER 2 gr.c. Habat 127–Caitlin 78 (Abernant 142) (1981 **95**
5v 5g 5d² 5s* 5f² 5f* 6f* 7fg² 6f⁴ 6d) Feb 3; 3,500Y; strong colt; fifth foal; dam, sister to high-class Port Merion, won over 1m; improved considerably after winning maiden auction event at Haydock in June, and put up fairly useful performances to win minor events at Ripon in July by 1½ lengths from Fimi and by 2 lengths from Vaigly Star; created a favourable impression when gaining third success, having race sewn up 1f out and winning on bridle (could have trebled his winning margin); gave 9 lb to winner when 3 lengths second of 10 to Chulia Street in minor race at Redcar later in July; probably better suited by 6f than 7f; best form on firm going; looks the sort to train on. *M. W. Easterby.*

STEEL VENTURE 2 b.c. Full of Hope 125–Grove Star (Upper Case) (1981 8s) —
Mar 31; rather lightly-made, lengthy colt; first foal; dam once-raced half-sister to smart Uncle Pokey; 10/1, wasn't knocked about when behind in 15-runner maiden race won by Twist Home at York in October; immature at 2 yrs. *B. Hills.*

STEELWORKS 3 ch.c. Steel Heart 128–Hariota 73 (Hook Money 124) (1980 **75**
6g 5g 1981 8fg⁴ 8fg* 8g 8fg* 8.5fg 8fg) compact, sturdy colt; won maiden race and handicap at Warwick in summer; ran moderately in between and on last 2 outings; stays 1m; acts on a firm surface; blinkered first 3 starts. *B. Hills.*

STEEPLE BELL 5 b.g. Tower Walk 130–Nine Lessons 101 (Santa Claus 133) **97**
(1980 8fg 8d 7g² 7d* 7fg² 7g* 7fg 7g* 1981 6g 7g 7.6g² 7fg² 7f 8g⁴ 7fg² 7g³ 7s⁴ 9s) lengthy, quite attractive gelding; good walker; fairly useful handicapper; creditable 2 lengths second to Cajolery in Queen Elizabeth Stakes at Lingfield in June on third outing; stays 1m; seems to act on any going; does best when ridden up with pace; genuine. *M. Stoute.*

STEERS 2 b.c. He Loves Me 120–Mile Cross 88 (Milesian 125) (1981 5g 5fg —
6fg 8s 6s) Apr 10; IR 3,200Y; smallish, quite attractive colt; good walker;

half-brother to useful sprinter Puza (by Realm); dam best at up to 1m; only plating class; sweated up third outing. *Peter Taylor.*

STELLA'S PET   9 ch.g. Elvis 96–Fairworth 74§ (Fair Seller 126)   (1980 NR   **35** 1981 8s 8g²)   plater; stays 1¼m; appears to act on any going, but is particularly well suited by firm; suitable mount for an apprentice. *W. Storey.*

STEP DANCE (USA)   2 ch.c. Dance Spell–Sealand (Luthier 126)   (1981 8g)   **— p** Feb 1; 125,000Y; rather lightly-made colt; second living foal; half-brother to very useful French middle-distance filly Sealy (by Filiberto); dam won 3 times at up to 7.5f in France; unquoted but reasonably straight, made steady progress to join leaders going into Dip but then started to struggle and wasn't persevered with when twelfth of 27 to Dudley Wood in minor event at Newmarket in October; will benefit from this experience and may do better over middle distances at 3 yrs. *J. Tree.*

STEPOUT   2 b.f. Sagaro 133–Pepstep 66 (Polic 126)   (1981 7d 7.6s⁴)   Apr 2;   **65** half-sister to several winners, including 7f winner Pepina (by Shoolerville); dam won over 5f and seemed to stay 1m; made late progress to finish 5 lengths fourth of 14 to Change Habit in maiden race at Lingfield in October; likely to need 1¼m or more at 3 yrs. *M. Smyly.*

STERLONIA   5 b. or br.m. Sterling Bay–Milonia (Tambourine II 133)   (1980 8s   **61** 8f 8fg² 9g 7g⁴ 8fg 8f 8fg 10g 8.2d² 8g 8.2s   1981 8.2f* 10f² 10f² 8g)   compact mare; won handicap at Nottingham in July; looked unlucky next start; stays 1¼m; seems to act on any going. *E. Eldin.*

STERN   5 br.g. No Mercy 126–Rudder (Reliance II 137)   (1980 7g³ 7f 7f* 8.3fg   **68** 8g⁴ 7d   1981 7g 6g 6f* 5.6f³ 6d 6f³ 6fg)   quite a moderate handicapper; won at Thirsk in July; needs at least 6f and stays 1m; acts on firm going; blinkered once at 3 yrs. *I. Walker.*

STERRIDGE VALLEY   3 gr.f. Dragonara Palace 115–Standoffish (Be Friendly   **—** 130)   (1980 5f 5f 6fg 5g 5.8g⁴ 5s 5g 5g   1981 5v 5g 5fg 6g)   strong, compact filly; plater; ran out soon after start on second outing in 1980 and wore blinkers on seventh. *J. Hill.*

STEWART'S RISE   4 ch.f. Good Bond 122–Devadara 74 (Royal Levee or   **46** Hill Clown)   (1980 6fg 7s² 6g 7g 10g² 10f 10fg² 10g² 8d*   1981 10.8d² 8d 10.8fg 10fg 10f* 10f⁴ 10f 10g² 10fg⁴ 10fg)   leggy, light-framed filly; doesn't always impress in paddock; plater; bought in 1,100 gns after winning at Nottingham in June; stays 11f; acts on any going; sometimes sweats up; suitable mount for an apprentice. *B. McMahon.*

STICK IN THE MUD   2 ch.f. Wollow 132–Albercaro 88 (Hard Tack 111§)   (1981 6fg 6f 6g)   Apr 7; useful sort; half-sister to several winners, including 3-y-o Salt (by Sallust), a fairly useful winner over 5f and 6f at 2 yrs, and very useful sprinter Bold Tack (by Bold Lad, Ire); dam 5f sprinter; soundly beaten all starts but was backward on first 2 occasions and showed early speed in maiden race at Newmarket in October on third. *H. T. Jones.*

STICKY HABIT   3 b.f. Habitat 134–Honey Portion 107 (Major Portion 129)   **79** (1980 NR   1981 8fg² 8fg* 8fg³ 10fg* 10g 10g)   quite an attractive, well-made filly; closely related to 2 winners by Sir Ivor, notably Irish Guinness Oaks third I've a Bee, and half-sister to several other winners, including smart French stayer Honeyville (by Charlottesville); dam miler; successful in maiden race at Kempton in July and handicap on same course in August, in latter quickening clear about 2f out and holding on by 3 lengths from Redden; didn't run well last 2 starts, on first occasion wearing blinkers; was suited by 1¼m; acted on a firm surface; sold 135,000 gns Newmarket December Sales and is reportedly to be covered by Robellino   *M. Stoute.*

STILL FREE   3 ch.g. Manacle 123–Shilly Shally 89 (Sallymount 125)   (1980   **60** 6fg² 6fg   1981 8d 7d 8d⁴ 5f 8fg⁴ 6fg 8h⁴ 8fg)   lightly-made gelding; plating-class maiden; stays 1m. *R. Turnell.*

STILL HOPE   5 gr.g. No Mercy 126–Shilly Shally 89 (Sallymount 125)   (1980   **54** 8fg³ 10fg² 10h⁴ 8d 8fg³ 8fg⁴ 8g 8g 8fg* 8h 8g²   1981 10s 8fg² 8g³ 8f³ 7fg 8h² 8f)   workmanlike gelding; stays 1¼m; acts on hard going; sometimes wears blinkers; good mount for an inexperienced rider. *R. Turnell.*

STIMLER   4 b.c. Charlottown 127–Pardalina 69 (Pardal 130)   (1980 7d 7fg   **47** 8fg² 8d 7fg* 7.6d⁴ 7s 10g 7g 8fg* 8g⁴ 7f   1981 7fg 8g⁴ 11.7fg 8g 7f 7fg 8fg 12g)   lightly-made colt; plater; should stay beyond 1m; acts on a firm and a soft surface; often blinkered; suitable mount for a boy. *M. Bolton.*

STINGO 2 b.c. Mansingh 120–Quita II 105 (Lavandin 128) (1981 5s⁴) May 1; — p
half-brother to several winners here and abroad, notably top-class sprinter
Realm (by Princely Gift); dam won Lingfield Oaks Trial and is half-sister to
Prix de l'Arc de Triomphe winner Oroso; second favourite when 7 lengths
fourth of 11 to stable-companion Sonseri in maiden race at Wolverhampton
in October; should do better. *R. Price.*

ST JOLES 8 b.g. Welsh Saint 126–Gleniffer Braes (Hard Tack 111§) (1980 NR —
1981 8f 12fg) useful at up to 1½m in 1976; lightly raced on flat since though
has won over hurdles; very well suited by top-of-the-ground; has worn bandages.
P. Ashworth.

ST MALO 3 b.g. Martinmas 128–Tomelilla (High Hat 131) (1980 8d⁴ 79
1981 10fg³ 12g⁴ 12s* 13.8fg³ 12fg³ 14fg 13d⁴ 12s³ 12d*) lightly-made gelding;
has been hobdayed; got the better of a desperate finish when beating Irish Keep
a head in maiden event at Haydock in May; sold to H. Blackshaw 5,000 gns
after beating Obergurgl by a neck in £4,500 selling handicap at Doncaster in
October; stays 1¾m; probably acts on any going. *J. Hindley.*

ST MAWES 3 b.c. Relko 136–Asturia 104 (The Phoenix) (1980 7g 8fg 10s* 105
10.2s² 1981 12fg 12.3d² 12g* 12g⁴ 12fg² 14fg) big, rangy colt; went clear
turning for home and soon had his race won when beating Feltwell by 3 lengths
in handicap at Thirsk in May; also in frame in handicaps at Chester and
York and in minor event at Beverley (close fourth to Baz Bombati and
would probably have won if his apprentice rider had made more use of him);
broke down badly at Goodwood in July and wasn't seen out again; would have
been suited by further than 1½m; probably acted on any going but was suited
by some give in the ground; dead. *B. Hobbs.*

ST MAWES BAY 2 ch.f. Jimmy Reppin 131–Terre Promise (Soderini 123) 76
1981 6f 7d 6d⁴) May 13; good-topped, useful sort; half-sister to fair 1980
2-y-o 6f winner Miss St Mawes (by Derring-Do) and minor winners in France
and USA; dam ran once; showed some ability in maiden and minor races and
at Pontefract in October finished less than 2 lengths fourth of 15 behind Lucayan
Lady; will stay 1m. *B. Hobbs.*

STOIC 2 b.c. Oats 126–Gentle Way 74 (Gentle Art 121) (1981 7fg 8s 7.6s) May —
23; IR 11,000Y; medium-sized, quite attractive colt; half-brother to 3 winners,
including fair 1980 2-y-o 5f winner Directorate (by Gay Fandango) and good
Belgian winner Arpad (by Connaught); showed a little ability in minor races
at Goodwood on first 2 outings; swerved badly halfway final appearance;
probably stays 1m; sold to A. Moore 440 gns Ascot October Sales. *J. Dunlop.*

STOKE CITY 4 ch.g. Habat 127–Wind Break 91 (Borealis) (1980 12fg³ —
10.4f 10fg 10fg 12g 16d 1981 15.8s 12g) strong gelding; poor maiden; stays
1½m; sold to E. Jones 1,200 gns Doncaster May Sales. *R. Hollinshead.*

STOKE ST MARY 6 ch.g. Jukebox 120–All Royal 98 (Primera 131) (1980 —
NR 1981 12g 16g) big, strong gelding; probably no longer of any account.
W. Elsey.

ST OONA 3 ch.f. Ardoon 124–I'm No Saint (St Chad 120) (1980 5d 5.8f 5d —
1981 5g 5f) poor form in maiden races; probably needs further; whipped
round at start and took no part on final outing; sold 420 gns Newmarket July
Sales. *G. Hunter.*

STOPOVER 2 b.f. Bruni 132–Cannon Ball 91 (By Thunder! 122) (1981 7fg⁴ 7fg) 65
May 28; 17,500Y; lightly-made, quite attractive filly; good walker; half-sister
to numerous winners, including good French stayer A Chara (by Worden II);
dam daughter of Bebe Grande; 2¼ lengths fourth of 10 to Lucky Joker in maiden
race at Wolverhampton in July; not disgraced against stiffer opposition next
time out; will stay at least 1¼m. *B. Hills.*

STORM BIRD (CAN) 3 b.c. Northern Dancer–South Ocean (New Providence) —
(1980 6d* 6.3s* 7g* 7g* 7s* 1981 10s)
　　Two things, the saying goes, are certain: death and taxes. It seems racing
men may soon have to add a third to the list, so regular is becoming the failure
of the top colt in the Free Handicap to make his mark on the classic scene!
The 1981 flat-racing season was not long under way before the Two Thousand
Guineas picture ominously began to resemble that of the three previous seasons.
Then, as most readers will hardly need reminding, the winter favourite—Try
My Best in 1978, Tromos in 1979 and Monteverdi in 1980—proved an expensive
failure. In fact, Try My Best was the only one to take his place in the Guineas
field; and he started at evens and trailed in last of nineteen. Like Try My Best,

Tromos and Monteverdi, Storm Bird topped the Two-Year-Old Free Handicap after winning the William Hill Dewhurst Stakes which is widely regarded nowadays as Britain's most important race for two-year-olds. The Dewhurst was Storm Bird's fifth successive win—he beat To-Agori-Mou by half a length—and, in our view, he showed better form as a two-year-old than any of his trainer's previous winners of the race which included Nijinsky and The Minstrel. Storm Bird seemed a very worthy ante-post favourite to emulate the victories of Nijinsky in the Two Thousand Guineas and of Nijinsky and The Minstrel in the Derby.

Misfortune struck Storm Bird even before the new season opened: one night his box was broken into and he had his mane and tail hacked by an ex-stable lad in an attack which received enormous publicity. Much worse followed. After being declared for his planned preparatory race, the Gladness Stakes at the Curragh at the beginning of April, Storm Bird was found to be slightly lame in a hind leg and, on veterinary advice, was withdrawn. The injury wasn't severe and Storm Bird was soon sound again, but Guineas hopes were dashed when, in mid-April, he reportedly started coughing. He remained one of the Derby favourites, however, until it was learned that he would also have to miss the Irish Two Thousand Guineas.

Storm Bird next made the headlines when it was announced at the Goodwood July meeting that a group of North American breeders had bought him for the enormous sum of 30,000,000 dollars (around £16m at prevailing exchange rates), Mr Sangster and his associates reportedly retaining a quarter share. Thoroughbreds, like any other commodity, are worth what can be got for them—otherwise we should have to describe this particular purchase as preposterous. To be worth that sum Storm Bird will have to turn out to be almost as good a stallion as his sire Northern Dancer whose fee in 1981 was set at 225,000 dollars, and it must be long odds against that. Storm Bird's fee in 1982 was set at 175,000 dollars, live foal. Shortly after Storm Bird had changed hands came the news that he could be regarded as a definite runner for the Prix de l'Arc de Triomphe. On the strength of reports that he had worked brilliantly with Kings Lake in a gallop, Storm Bird was the subject of some hefty ante-post wagering on the Arc; his odds tumbled from 16/1 to 6/1 in two days. Not for the first time backers of Storm Bird got their fingers burned. He ran most disappointingly in the Prix du Prince d'Orange at Longchamp in September, finishing seventh of nine behind Vayrann, and wasn't seen out again.

			Nearctic	Nearco
			(br 1954)	Lady Angela
	Northern Dancer		Natalma	Native Dancer
	(b 1961)		(b 1957)	Almahmoud
Storm Bird (Can)			New Providence	Bull Page
(b.c. 1978)			(b 1956)	Fair Colleen
	South Ocean		Shining Sun	Chop Chop
	(b 1967)		(b 1962)	Solar Display

Storm Bird's pedigree was dealt with thoroughly in *Racehorses of 1980*. Northern Dancer is one of the world's most sought-after stallions and Storm Bird's dam South Ocean, who won the nine-furlong Canadian Oaks, has a good record at stud and is also the dam of Northernette, a very good full sister to Storm Bird. Storm Bird fetched 1,000,000 dollars when sent up to the sales as a yearling and Mr Sangster and his associates went to 3,500,000 dollars to secure his yearling full brother at Keeneland's July Selected Sale in 1981. Storm Bird raced only on an easy surface but he was a good-actioned colt who would probably have acted on firm. He won at up to seven furlongs as a two-year-old and should have stayed middle distances at three. A tall, quite attractive colt when we visited Ballydoyle in the spring, he looked to have grown and thickened out over the summer when we saw him at Longchamp. *V. O'Brien, Ireland.*

STORMING 2 ch.g. Red Alert 127–Winbeam (Hornbeam 130) (1981 5fg 5g **59** 7fg 7d² 8.2fg 8g 7g) Feb 9; 2,200Y; strong gelding; closely related to quite a moderate sprint plater and half-brother to a winner abroad; moderate plater; stays 1m; usually blinkered nowadays. *D. Dale.*

STORM LADY 3 b.f. Realm 129–Storm Lass 65 (Typhoon 125) (1980 5g **—** 5s 5s 8d 6d 1981 6s 5d) quite an attractive, neat filly; evidently of little account. *P. Kelleway.*

STORMY JIM 3 ch.c. Jimmy Reppin 131–Stormy Gal 71 (Rockavon 120) **74** d (1980 5f³ 5f 5f⁴ 6g 7f* 8g³ 7fg* 8g* 7d 7v² 1981 8g⁴ 7g 7g² 8f 8f⁴ 8g 7g 7g 7.2v

8v 7g[4] 8s 8g) strong colt; ran best race of year when 3 lengths second to Praetorian Guard in handicap at Redcar in May; mainly disappointing; suited by
7f and 1m; acts on any going; started very slowly fourth appearance. *Hbt
Jones.*

STORTON 2 b.c. Morston 125–Love Story 79 (Aureole 132) (1981 7fg 7g 7fg[4] **88**
7fg 8g[3] 8d[4] 8d[2]) Mar 26; 10,000Y; quite attractive colt; second foal; half-
brother to 3-y-o 1½m winner Rheingold's Gift (by Rheingold); dam won twice
over 1m; placed in nurseries at Bath and Pontefract, staying on really well when
neck second to A.T.S. Prince in 20-runner event on latter in October; will be
suited by 1½m; best form with some give in the ground. *B. Hills.*

STOTFIELD MAJOR 3 ch.g. Queen's Hussar 124–Guiding Light 78 (Crepello **—**
136) (1980 7g 8.2s 1981 9d) well-grown gelding; little sign of ability, including
in a seller; sold 380 gns Doncaster May Sales. *J. Berry.*

STOWMARKET 3 b.c. Realm 129–Sovereign 129 (Pardao 120) (1980 6g **60**
6d 6fg 6g[2] 1981 7s 5s 7d 6s 6f 6f 6f[3] 6fg 6g 6v) smallish, quite attractive colt;
disappointing in 1981, best effort when close third to Sami in handicap at Ripon
in August (apprentice ridden); stays 7f; sometimes has his tongue tied down;
has worn blinkers; sold 800 gns Newmarket Autumn Sales. *H. Wragg.*

ST PADDY'S BABY 2 ch.g. St Paddy 133–Isomer 60 (Runnymede 123) (1981 **69**
5d 5d 5.3f[4] 7f 6f 5d 5.3d 5s) Mar 1; leggy, lightly-made gelding; second foal;
dam won sellers over 6f and 7f; just over 5 lengths fourth of 9 to Childown Blue
in maiden event at Brighton in June, probably best effort; should stay 7f (had
stiff task and looked very lean and light when tried at trip); blinkered final
outing. *O. Jorgensen.*

ST PEDRO 3 b.c. St Paddy 133–Jinkin (King's Troop 118) (1980 8g 1981 **78**
8g* 10.2g 8s[4] 7d) lightly-made colt; kept going under very strong riding when
beating Habitor by 1½ lengths in maiden event at Newmarket in April on reappearance; off course 5 months before finishing fourth to Bronzamer in handicap
at Redcar in October; stays 1m. *E. Eldin.*

STRACOMER QUEEN 3 br.f. Prince Tenderfoot 126–Si (Ragusa 137) **106**
(1980 6f 7.9f 6fg 7s* 7g[3] 7fg 8g[4] 7d[4] 7d[4] 1981 9d[4] 7s 7g* 8d* 10d[2] 8v 10fg[3]
12fg[3] 8d 8g) Irish filly; fifth foal; sister to fairly useful 6f and 7f winner Tender
Answer and half-sister to a winner over hurdles; dam unraced daughter of
smart 5f winner Acquiesced; won handicaps at Phoenix Park and Leopardstown
in May, beating Jasmine Prince both times; ran in better company afterwards,
running particularly well when third to Happy Bride in Pretty Polly Stakes at
the Curragh in June and to Blue Wind in Irish Guinness Oaks on same course in
July (beaten just over 3 lengths both times); off course over 2 months after latter
race and ran moderately on her return (blinkered final start); suited by middle
distances; probably acts on any going. *P. Russell, Ireland.*

STRAEKER 2 ch.c. Sharpen Up 127–Princess Tavi (Sea Hawk II 131) (1981 **98**
6fg[3] 6f* 6d* 6f[2] 7g* 7g) Apr 12; compact, fair sort; first foal; dam well beaten all
starts; showed improved form when winning £4,500 nursery at Newmarket in
October, taking command 2f out and striding up the hill in grand style to win a
shade cleverly by 3 lengths from Imagination; successful earlier in small races at
Pontefract and Hamilton in July; well suited by 7f and will stay 1m; seems to
act on any going; looked decidedly wintry and ran below his best final start;
looks the type to make useful handicapper at 3 yrs. *J. W. Watts.*

STRAIT LAKE 2 b.f. Sallust 134–Broad River 75 (Chieftain) (1981 5fg 6fg **—**
7.6s) Apr 7; 8,000Y; sister to fairly useful 1978 2-y-o Ballacorey and half-sister
to 4 winners, including useful 1976 Irish 2-y-o Laughing River (by Dike); dam
placed over 5f at 2 yrs; distant sixth of 12 to Preparation in maiden race at
Folkestone in August, second outing; sold to Curragh BA 4,200 gns Newmarket
Autumn Sales. *R. Smyth.*

STRAPLESS 2 b.f. Bustino 136–Dame Foolish 121 (Silly Season 127) (1981 **84**
6fg 6fg* 7d 7.2fg) Mar 17; small, strong, well-made filly; good walker and mover;
second foal; dam at her best at 2 yrs when second in Cheveley Park Stakes;
never going so well as Westonbirt when length second of 13 in minor event at
Windsor in July but was crossed by winner and was awarded race by stewards;
creditable sixth of 9 to Rapid Knot in £4,400 nursery at Haydock in September
on fourth start; should stay at least 1¼m; sold 21,000 gns Newmarket Autumn
Sales. *P. Walwyn.*

STRASS CHANDERLIER 2 b.g. Roi Soleil 125–Lochness Lass (Track Spare **66**
125) (1981 6g 7fg 7fg 7g) Mar 19; 900Y, resold 3,200Y; compact gelding; poor
mover; first produce; dam well beaten in 3 outings at 2 yrs; 50/1 for maiden

race at Newmarket in July on second start but wasn't disgraced, finishing seventh of 22 to Oxslip; out of first 11 of 29 to Perchance in seller, again at Newmarket, 2 outings later; will stay 1m. *C. Williams.*

STRATH OF ORCHY 2 br.f. Lochnager 132–Silver Teal 79 (Meldrum 112) **96**
(1981 5fg 5fg⁴ 5fg³ 6d³ 6d* 6s³ 6d*) May 10; compact filly; good walker; third foal; dam won over 5f and 1½m; off course 3 months after third outing and showed improved form on return, notably when winning maiden race at Hamilton in September easily by 6 lengths from Late Hour and 16-runner minor event at Pontefract in October by a length from Leg Glance; suited by 6f; best form with some give in the ground; game and genuine. *K. Stone.*

STRATOSPHERIC (USA) 2 b.f. Majestic Light–Clear Ceiling (Bold Ruler) **114**
(1981 7d 7fg* 8fg²)
   In *Racehorses of 1979* we remarked that were Quick As Lightning to be put up for sale the sky would be the limit. She went on to win the following year's One Thousand Guineas and eventually to race with limited success in Florida, but tragedy struck in the spring of 1981 when, having been retired, Quick As Lightning was found dead in her box shortly before she was due to be covered, having ruptured her aorta and bled to death internally. To lose such an able, beautifully-bred filly before she'd had even one foal must have been a bitter blow for her owner, Ogden Mills Phipps, but at least by the end of the year he had the consoling knowledge that in Stratospheric, Quick As Lightning's two-year-old half-sister, he has an excellent replacement, one which could even emulate Quick As Lightning's Guineas success.
   Stratospheric's career has so far run on very similar lines to Quick As Lightning's; each made the first of her three appearances at two at Newmarket early in August before running in both the Waterford Candelabra Stakes and the Hoover Fillies Mile. However, whereas Quick As Lightning lost only the Waterford Candelabra Stratospheric's single success came in that race. Only six turned out for the Candelabra at Goodwood in August, a race elevated to pattern-race status for the first time in 1981: they included the Cherry Hinton Stakes winner Travel On, recently an excellent second when giving weight to Circus Ring at York; Kiva, a Hern-trained filly who'd trotted up by six lengths at

Mr Ogden Mills Phipps' "Stratospheric" (P. Eddery)

Newbury a fortnight earlier; and the Cecil filly Baltimore Belle who'd accounted for a useful field in the Sweet Solera Stakes at Newmarket. Stratospheric's chance didn't look very bright; she too had run in the Sweet Solera, trailing home in last place, as the betting suggested she would, without ever looking likely to get into the race. In an interview John Dunlop gave *Timeform* shortly before Stratospheric's debut he said of her 'She doesn't show a great deal but, in fact, neither did Quick As Lightning until we ran her. She's one of those animals that work well enough without really impressing, but give the impression they could do more if they really wanted to'. Stratospheric must have begun to work a good deal better after her Newmarket experience—she was backed from 50/1 to 16/1 at Goodwood. A well-made, attractive filly, she impressed greatly in the paddock, looking the clear pick on the day and the filly with most scope for further improvement. She proved outstanding in the race. She went into the lead straight away and the race was hers from the moment she quickened away early in the straight. Nothing ever looked likely to catch her and she eventually won easing down by two and a half lengths from Kiva. Perhaps the other jockeys allowed Stratospheric a little too much rope but they were trying to peg her back from a long way out without making any impression.

Eddery, after giving Stratospheric such a splendidly enterprising ride at Goodwood, employed different tactics when she started second favourite to Height of Fashion for the Hoover Fillies Mile at Ascot a month later: he dropped her back to last of eight as the favourite went off in front at a fast pace. No doubt with an eye to the filly's future he was trying to teach her to settle. Unfortunately Stratospheric was to have trouble finding her way through the field. Turning into the straight Eddery chose to keep Stratospheric on the rails, then looked for a while as though he would challenge to Height of Fashion's left before finally switching back to the rails below the distance. Even then she looked likely to run into trouble as Height of Fashion began to drift right, but in the end she had room enough and battled on to get within half a length. With a clearer passage for Stratospheric it would have been a very close thing.

		Majestic Prince	Raise A Native
	Majestic Light	(ch 1966)	Gay Hostess
	(b 1973)	Irradiate	Ribot
Stratospheric (USA)		(gr 1966)	High Voltage
(b.f. Apr 23, 1979)	Clear Ceiling	Bold Ruler	Nasrullah
	(b 1968)	(b 1954)	Miss Disco
		Grey Flight	Mahmoud
		(gr 1945)	Planetoid

Back in May, 1952 two fillies belonging to Mrs Henry Carnegie Phipps, High Voltage and Misty Morn, were born thirteen days apart at the Claiborne Farm. High Voltage was to become the top two-year-old filly in the States while at three, after winning the eleven-furlong CCA Oaks for Mrs Phipps' Wheatley Stable, she was ranked second only to Misty Morn, the winner of nine of her twenty-two races that season including one over thirteen furlongs. High Voltage had forty-five races in all and Misty Morn forty-two but neither filly's stud prospects suffered from her very strenuous racing career: High Voltage produced three stakes winners, one of them the champion sprinter Impressive, while Misty Morn became the dam of the champion American two-year-olds Successor and Bold Lad. Both mares are related to Stratospheric. Stratospheric's sire is High Voltage's grandson Majestic Light, a very good winner of eleven races from a mile to a mile and a half in the USA; he topped the *Daily Racing Form* Free Handicap for grass horses in 1977 ahead of Caucasus, Exceller and King Pellinore. For a horse who needed time and middle distances Majestic Light has made a most encouraging start to his stud career at Claiborne. In addition to Stratospheric his first runners include Laser Light, one of the best juveniles in the States. Misty Morn's connection with Stratospheric is that she's a half-sister to Clear Ceiling, Stratospheric's dam. Clear Ceiling, although a winner of five races at up to six furlongs, was nowhere near as successful as four of her five winning brothers and sisters; Bold Princess, Bold Queen and Great Era were all smart fillies and her brother What A Pleasure, a leading two-year-old in 1967, headed the list of leading American stallions in both 1975 and 1976. Stratospheric is Clear Ceiling's second winner from her first four foals.

Will Stratospheric prove that lightning can strike twice in the same place by winning the One Thousand Guineas? We shouldn't be surprised if she did. She needs to improve if she's to beat Circus Ring but as we said earlier she has plenty of scope; of the other top fillies Height of Fashion hasn't been entered for the Guineas while Woodstream may not even be trained for the race. And will Stratospheric, unlike Quick As Lightning, stay the Oaks distance? No-one can say for sure but with Ribot, Nasrullah and Mahmoud among her great-grandsires she must have reasonable prospects of doing so. Whatever her trip, she's sure to make an excellent three-year-old. *J. Dunlop.*

STRAWBERRY SPECIAL 2 b.c. Bay Express 132–Square Acre (Palestine 133) **65**
(1981 5s 5g 7g) Mar 26; small colt; half-brother to winners here and abroad; dam half-sister to Doutelle and Above Suspicion; just over 7 lengths fifth of 18 to Town Flier in maiden race at Nottingham in September; well beaten in 2 sellers subsequently. *A. Hide.*

STRAWMAN 4 ch.c. Thatch 136–Purple Goddess 69 (Red God 128§) (1980 —
5fg* 6f 5d 5g 1981 6s 10d 7d 10g 11.7v 10d³ 12g 12f 8.3fg 8.3d 10s) strong, good-bodied colt; plater; stays 1¼m; acts on a firm and a soft surface; has been tried in blinkers. *A. Davison.*

STREAKWOOD SUE 2 br.f. Workboy 123–Pickwood Sue 74 (Right Boy 137) —
(1981 5g 5s) Apr 16; 800Y; first foal; dam 5f winner; behind in minor event at Catterick and maiden race at Warwick in the autumn. *W. Wharton.*

STREAMON 2 b.f. Rapid River 127–Reignon 74 (Lucky Brief 128) (1981 6f 7f) —
Apr 17; lengthy, lightly-made filly; fourth foal; sister to 1980 2-y-o 5f winner Raperon: dam, useful hurdler, stayed 1½m; well beaten in minor event at Pontefract and seller at Redcar in September. *M. H. Easterby.*

STREET CRIER 3 ch.c. Town Crier 119–Decatullus (Catullus) (1980 6d 5d —
1981 8d 8g 8g 7d 7g 6s 8.3fg 8g) strong, workmanlike colt; good mover; poor performer; has worn blinkers; sold 420 gns Newmarket Autumn Sales. *S. Matthews.*

STREET MARKET 2 ch.c. Porto Bello 118–Balgreggan (Hallez 131) (1981 **100**
5.8g³ 5d² 5f* 5f² 5d³ 5d* 5g⁴ 5g) Mar 17; workmanlike colt; first foal; dam twice-raced half-sister to smart stayer Golden Love; always front rank when

Mr G. S. Tuck's "Street Market"

winning maiden race at Wolverhampton in June and nursery at Chester in August, latter by ¾ length from High Authority; ran fast for 4f, despite swerving at start, when good fourth of 5 to Jester in Harry Rosebery Challenge Trophy at Ayr in September; promises to stay 6f; probably acts on any going; useful. *N. Vigors.*

STREGGA 3 b.f. Roman Warrior 132–Mehir 59 (King's Company 124) (1980 5g 5g³ 5fg 5g 5f 5g 1981 7g 6g 6d 5.3f 5g) small filly; poor maiden; should stay 6f; blinkered last 3 outings. *M. Masson.* —

STRETCHEES 2 b.f. Full of Hope 125–Shy Meld 65 (Meldrum 112) (1981 8fg 8s) May 15; plain sort; second foal; dam winning sprint plater; in rear in maiden race at Beverley in September (missed break) and minor event at Newcastle in October (100/1). *I. Jordon.* —

STRIDER BROWN 5 b. or br.g. Menelek 114–Vulcacity (Vulgan 123) (1980 NR 1981 13d 16f) non-thoroughbred gelding; well beaten in varied company, but is a winning hurdler. *H. Bell.* —

STRIGIDA 3 b.f. Habitat 134–Catalpa 115 (Reform 132) (1980 7g 1981 9s² 10g* 12fg* 10g³) **120**

    Strigida continued a remarkable family tradition when winning the Ribblesdale Stakes at Royal Ascot. Her dam Catalpa had won the race in 1976 and her grandam Ostrya in 1963. The Ribblesdale has been an exceptionally lucky race for Lord Howard de Walden, who owned all three plus the 1970 winner Parmelia, unrelated to the others. Ostrya's dam Malcolmia also ran in the race in 1955 and started second favourite, but reportedly was upset by the thundery conditions, dwelt at the start, and trailed in last of eleven behind Ark Royal. Strigida was given a brilliant ride by Piggott in the Ribblesdale. He held her up in last place for most of the way to conserve her stamina and still had her a long way behind the leaders on the turn where front-running Rollrights was making the best of her way home. Strigida looked to have a near-impossible task but Piggott brought her with a strong challenge up the centre of the course and got her up under hard riding in the last strides to beat Rollrights by a neck; the pair finished a length and a half clear of the Irish-trained Overplay with the remainder well strung out. Piggott

Ribblesdale Stakes, Ascot—Strigida beats Rollrights (left) and Irish challenger Overplay

had employed similar tactics on Strigida in the Sir Charles Clore Memorial Stakes at Newbury in May on Strigida's previous outing, producing her to lead on the line under hard riding and beat Viendra by a head after looking to be in a pocket with plenty to do a furlong and a half out.

Strigida had only two other races as a three-year-old and was placed in both. At Wolverhampton in April on her reappearance she chased home Joliette in a maiden event, and at Goodwood in August on her final outing she finished third behind Go Leasing in the mile-and-a-quarter Nassau Stakes. She faced a stiff task in the latter, conceding weight to all her opponents except the four-year-old Vielle, and she put up an excellent performance, better even than that at Royal Ascot considering the strength of the opposition. She was held up again and produced with a steady run on the outside of the field which just about took her upsides the leaders at the distance. From there she could find no extra and she was beaten a length and three quarters by the winner, with Vielle dividing the pair.

Strigida (b.f. 1978)	Habitat (b 1966)	Sir Gaylord (b 1959)	Turn-to
			Somethingroyal
		Little Hut (b 1952)	Occupy
			Savage Beauty
	Catalpa (b 1973)	Reform (b 1964)	Pall Mall
			Country House
		Ostrya (b 1960)	Hornbeam
			Malcolmia

Strigida's win in the Ribblesdale Stakes marked a significant point in the illustrious stud career of her sire Habitat: she became his first pattern-race winner over further than a mile and a quarter. Habitat is regarded as an influence more for speed than stamina, and he had Marwell, Sonoma and Dalsaan representing him in 1981. But Strigida was by no means Habitat's only important middle-distance winner of the year—he also had Strigida's stable-companion Home On The Range, and the colt Hard Fought. Strigida is Catalpa's first foal. She slipped twins to High Top in 1979 and has since produced a filly by Grundy named Shawnee and another by Dance In Time that is unnamed as yet. Catalpa is easily the best winner produced by Ostrya, a half-sister to Oncidium, the Coronation Cup and Jockey Club Cup winner subsequently a leading sire in Australasia.

Strigida has been retired to stud and visits Stratospheric's sire Majestic Light in 1982. A lengthy filly who stayed a mile and a half when ridden with restraint, she seemed to act on any going and was very game. *H. Cecil.*

STRIKE ACTION 4 b.g. Tyrant–Corte (Alcide 136) (1980 8d³ 9.4g 10g 8g 8.2s 1981 12f) poor walker; little worthwhile form in varied company; has worn blinkers. *R. Allan.* —

STRIKE AGAIN 3 ch.g. Redundant 120–Kimolina (Ki Myth 96) (1980 5g 5f 5d³ 7fg⁴ 6fg 7d 1981 8fg 8f) big, strong gelding; in frame in maiden events as a 2-y-o; had stiff tasks when well beaten in handicaps in July; stays 7f. *G. Lockerbie.* —

STRING OF STARS 3 ch.f. Jukebox 120–Lunar Star (Star Gazer 123) (1980 NR 1981 6s 5g 5g) 2,000Y; fair sort; half-sister to 3 winners, including fairly useful 1978 2-y-o 5f winner Moving Star (by Windjammer); dam won over 9.5f in Ireland; well beaten in maiden events in spring; still but backward second outing and was sweating third start. *A. Gillam.* —

STRIP FAST 8 ch.m. Virginia Boy 106–Light Gail (Hill Gail) (1980 8g 8fg² 8fg 11.7g³ 10fg 10.4d⁴ 8.3fg 10.2d³ 1981 10f⁴ 8f 8f* 8h⁴ 8f 8.3g 7h) neat mare; won handicap at Chepstow in July; stays 1¼m; probably needs a sound surface; game; excellent mount for a boy. *D. H. Jones.* 55

STROMBOLI 2 b.g. The Brianstan 128–Authorise 95 (Ribot 142) (1981 5g 6fg 7fg 7g 7d) May 6; 4,200Y; brother to a winner in Malaya and half-brother to winners here and in France; dam won at 1¼m; little worthwhile form in maiden and minor events. *T. Marshall.* 59

ST TERRAMAR 6 b.h. St Alphage 119–Terramar Lass (Tom Rolfe) (1980 5g 5f² 5f 5f 5f⁴ 5g* 5g³ 5g 5d 5d 5f 5.6g⁴ 5fg 5g 5g⁴ 5s 1981 6fg 5g 5d 5g 6f 5g³ 5d 6f 5fg 5.8g 5g 5s 5s) sprint handicapper; appears to act on any going but is particularly well suited by a sound surface; acts on any track; suitable mount for a boy; best in blinkers; sometimes bandaged on off-fore; often starts slowly; trained part of season by N. Guest. *C. James.* —

STUART KING 4 ch.g. Sassafras 135–Miss Scotland 111 (Henry the Seventh 125) (1980 10fg* 12g² 12d⁴ 12g 1981 12.2d 9g² 8d 8fg 9g 11fg⁴) neat gelding; stays 1¼m; acts well on firm ground; has worn blinkers; inconsistent and has shown sign of temperament; racing in Belgium. *R. Hollinshead.* —

STUBBINGTON GREEN 4 br.g. Swing Easy 126–Lake Victoria 94 (Stupendous) (1980 6s 7fg 6g 6g 6g 7g³ 8d 1981 10g 10d 8g 10fg 7f² 8f² 10f² 8fg 10f⁴ 10f) leggy gelding; plater; stays 1¼m; acts on any going; wears blinkers. *D. Yeoman.* **43**

STUCK FOR WORDS 4 ch.f. Some Hand 119–Clear Speech (Articulate 121) (1980 7h 6fg 10f 10.1s 10s 10fg* 8fg² 11.7fg 10f 1981 10s⁴ 7g 8fg 8fg) quite well-made filly; plater; stays 1¼m; probably acts on any going; suitable mount for a boy. *A. Moore.* **41**

STUDIO COPY (FR) 4 b.c. Habitat 134–Artists Proof (Ribot 142) (1980 8.2g 8d³ 8g 8g 1981 12d) big, rangy colt; plating-class maiden; stayed 1m; blinkered on only start at 4 yrs in April; dead. *K. Bailey.* —

STUNT PILOT 2 ch.c. Northfields–Gwendolyn (Bagdad) (1981 7fg 7g) Apr 4; 17,000Y; attractive colt; half-brother to 3-y-o 7f winner Copt Hall Princess (by Crowned Prince) and a winner in Belgium; dam, placed 3 times in USA, comes from a good family; in rear in 16-runner maiden race won by Rajhaan at Salisbury in September; destroyed after breaking a leg in similar event at Newmarket the following month. *B. Hills.* —

STYLISH MOVER 2 b.c. Martinmas 128–Fuiseog (Eudaemon 129) (1981 5fg 5d 5g) May 16; IR 7,600F, 2,000Y; narrow, lightly-made colt; half-brother to numerous winners, including smart French and Irish middle distance performer former Star Lark (by Le Levanstell) and fairly useful 6f and 7f winner Murillo (by Windjammer); dam won over 7.9f in Ireland; only poor form in maiden races; off course 4 months before final start. *D. Jermy.* —

SUAVITY (USA) 4 b.c. Personality–Smooth 114 (Sound Track 132) (1980 6fg 7g 7g⁴ 8d³ 1981 7d 7.6g 6g 7fg 7g 8d) strong, well-made, attractive colt; good mover; useful performer at his best; well beaten in 1981; stays 7f but not 1m; best form on an easy surface and has run poorly on really firm going; sometimes sweats up. *D. Whelan.* —

SUBRIQUETTE 3 b.f. English Prince 129–Lady Mickey (Swaps) (1980 6f 6f 1981 12d 11.7g 10d 12g⁴ 12d 12d³ 12fg⁴ 14g³ 12f) big, workmanlike filly; has shown some ability in maiden races and an amateur riders event; stays 1¾m; blinkered last 4 outings, looking decidedly unwilling on last 2 occasions; gave trouble at start once; sometimes sweats up; sold 2,400 gns Newmarket Autumn Sales. *M. Smyly.* **62**

SUBURBAN SUE 3 ch.f. Native Bazaar 122–Susanella 83 (Eborneezer 105) (1980 5fg 5f² 5.8fg 6g³ 6g 5.8h³ 1981 8d 8h 8h 8fg) leggy filly; plater; stays 6f; acts on hard going; sold 500 gns Ascot November Sales. *G. Cottrell.* —

SUCCESSOR 12 ch.g. Great Nephew 126–Loidien 95 (Ribot 142) (1980 12f² 10g 12fg³ 13g 12fg 13.1h* 10g 1981 10f 12f) middle-distance handicapper; acts on any going; has worn blinkers; good mount for an inexperienced rider; has won 7 times at Chepstow. *R. Turnell.* **45**

SUCHONG 3 b.f. No Mercy 126–Tea Leaf (Cracksman NZ) (1980 7f 7g 1981 6g 7fg) big, strong, quite attractive filly; behind in varied company, including selling; tends to sweat up; sold 800 gns Ascot July Sales. *P. Makin.* —

SUDDEN STAR 2 b.f. Grundy 137–Sudden Glory 98 (Luthier 126) (1981 7d 8d) Apr 13; neat filly; second foal; half-sister to 3-y-o Craigour (by Mill Reef), a fairly useful winner over 7f in 1980; dam won over 6.5f and 1m in France; soundly beaten in maiden races at Newbury in September and Wolverhampton the following month. *P. Walwyn.* —

SUE ELLEN 3 b.f. High Line 125–Gracemount 71 (Midsummer Night II 117) (1980 NR 1981 11.5f 14fg⁴ 14s) workmanlike filly; first foal; dam 1¾m winner; remote fourth of 5 behind Military Band in minor event at Yarmouth in July. *R. Boss.* —

SUE LARK 6 ch.m. Sir Lark 101–Susanella 83 (Eborneezer 105) (1980 NR 1981 11.7f³ 12d³) poor maiden; stays 1½m. *R. Keenor.* **53**

SUE'S PRINCE 3 b.c. King Log 115–Fairy First 54§ (Fairey Fulmar 124) (1980 5d 6g 7d 6g³ 7f 8d 8d 1981 12d⁴ 10fg⁴) plater; should be suited by middle distances. *W. H. H. Williams.* —

SUEZ 2 br.g. Scottish Rifle 127–Somalia 96 (Alcide 136) (1981 8d* 7v 7g) **93**
Feb 23; 5,000Y; good-looking gelding; fourth living foal; dam stayed well;
put up a pleasing first effort in 17-runner maiden race at Bath in October,
coming through strongly to win by ½ length from Mailman with rest well beaten
off; 5¼ lengths sixth of 8 to Rocamadour in minor event at Kempton later in
month, better subsequent effort (looked wintry and was probably past his best
for season when well beaten in nursery at Doncaster on third outing); will be
suited by 1¼m; gelded at end of season. *R. Hern.*

SUFFIELD PARK 3 b.f. Wolver Hollow 126–Jungle Princess (Native Prince) —
(1980 6fg 8d 8d 1981 8fg 10g 10fg) well-made, attractive filly; has shown
a little ability in maiden races; should stay 1¼m; sold 780 gns Newmarket July
Sales. *F. J. Houghton.*

SUGARAN 3 b.f. Hardiran–Sugar Bowl (King of the Castle) (1980 NR —
1981 8d 9d 7f 8d) second foal; dam never ran; tailed off all outings, twice
starting slowly; has been tried in blinkers. *D. Wintle.*

SUGAR AND MINT (USA) 2 ch.f. Key To The Mint–Acidulee (Vitriolic) **85**
(1981 8g 8d*) May 6; $85,000Y; quite attractive filly; first living foal; dam
unraced half-sister to Yes Dear Maggy, a smart stakes winner at up to 9f;
got up close home to beat Kir Royale a short head in 18-runner maiden race
at Leicester in November; had finished last when second favourite for similar
event at Newmarket on debut; will be suited by 1¼m. *M. Albina.*

SUGAR COATED 3 b.f. Track Spare 125–Star Abbess 86 (Welsh Abbot 131) —
(1980 5d⁴ 5fg 6fg 1981 7g 6g 6f 6f 7f 8fg⁴ 8fg 7g 10s 10d) leggy, light-framed
filly; poor form in varied company, including selling; stays 1m; blinkered sixth
and seventh starts, sweating up on first occasion. *M. Masson.*

SUGAR TENDER (USA) 2 b.c. Blade–Dance Guest (Uppercut) (1981 5g 6g) —
Mar 2; $55,000Y; strong, good sort; good mover; closely related to a winner
by Bold and Brave and half-brother to 2 winners, including minor 1980 2-y-o
sprint stakes winner Sasume (by Shecky Greene); dam, from same family as
Habitat, won twice at up to 7f at 2 yrs; not fully wound up when behind in
maiden races at Newmarket in May (14/1) and July (33/1). *J. Sutcliffe.*

SUGGESTIVE 2 b.f. Bold Lad (Ire) 133–Nighty Night (Sassafras 135) (1981 **76**
5fg 5g² 6f⁴ 6g² 7g) May 9; 9,200Y; quite attractive, lightly-made filly; second
foal; dam unraced half-sister to 1969 Criterium des Pouliches winner Vela;
second in maiden race at Newbury in July (failed by 1½ lengths to hold off
Fairy Tern) and 9-runner nursery at Windsor the following month (went
down by same margin to Lively Rose); will stay 1m; possibly needs some give
in the ground. *J. Dunlop.*

SUJONO 3 b.f. Grey Mirage 128–Bird of Honour 63 (Dark Heron 106) (1980 NR **58**
1981 9d 10d 9d² 11.7fg 13.1g) big filly; fifth foal; dam won over 1½m and was also
a successful staying hurdler; ran on when 5 lengths second of 11 behind Mistress
Gay in maiden race at Wolverhampton in May; should be suited by 1¼m+
(had stiffish tasks last 2 outings); slowly away on first outing. *M. Scudamore.*

SULA BULA 3 b.c. Midsummer Night II 117–Blue Ann 60 (Road House II) **100**
(1980 5g² 5f³ 6d* 7g² 7g** 7s² 7d² 7f* 8g* 7v* 1981 10.4d 9d 8g⁴ 8f³ 7g 8fg)
quite a useful-looking colt; developed into one of the best 2-y-o's in the North
in 1980 and won 5 races, notably Gilbey Champion Racehorse Futurity at York
and Steel Plate Autumn Stakes at Doncaster; disappointing in 1981, running
by far his best race when 3 lengths third of 6 behind Ardoony in £4,600 handicap
at Beverley in July (made running and kept on); a free-running sort who may
prove best at up to 1m; acts on any going; one to be wary of until showing signs
of a return to form. *M. H. Easterby.*

SULLOM VOE 4 b.f. Cumshaw 111–Lady Cortina 80 (Cortachy 107) (1980 NR —
1981 12.3fg³ 12g 9d) workmanlike filly; half-sister to winning sprinter Queensway (by Typhoon); dam won at up to 1m; poor maiden. *R. Allan.*

SULPHUR 3 ch.c. Simbir 130–Dazzling Hue (Double Jump 131) (1980 8g —
1981 10d 10fg) quite an attractive, small, well-made colt; good walker and
mover; showed up well for a long way when 15 lengths sixth of 17 behind
Western Knight in maiden race at Sandown in June; very disappointing at
Folkestone later in month on only subsequent outing; possibly unsuited by firm
going. *P. Walwyn.*

SULTANO 3 b.c. Kashmir II 125–Saltana 101 (Darius 129) (1980 NR 1981 **69**
8f² 8fg) 5,000F, 11,500Y; lengthy, quite attractive colt; half-brother to a

winner in France; dam won over 6f and 7f at 2 yrs and stayed 1½m; 5 lengths second of 19 behind Quite Ducky in maiden race at Stockton in June; still not fully wound up when making no show at Redcar later in month, only subsequent outing; will be suited by 1¼m. *L. Cumani.*

SULZANO 3 b.c. Rheingold 137–Ribasha (Ribot 142) (1980 7g 6g 7g 1981 **90** 10g² 10d² 10s² 10s⁴ 12s* 12fg* 12.3d 10fg 10fg⁴ 12fg³ 12g) well-made colt; runner-up 3 times at Cagnes-sur-Mer in February; successful in handicaps at Ripon and Newmarket (apprentice event) in April on his return, beating Jungle Jim by 1½ lengths in latter despite drifting badly; ran creditably on occasions afterwards, although was tailed-off last final outing; will stay further than 1½m; probably acts on any going; blinkered fifth to seventh starts and again on final outing. *W. Hastings-Bass.*

SUMMARY 4 b.g. Mandamus 120–Abstract 73 (French Beige 127) (1980 — 10d³ 8f⁴ 10f⁴ 9.6f² 10s 10s³ 10fg 10fg³ 10.1g 10fg 1981 9d 10f) well-made gelding; good walker; fair handicapper; needed run both starts at 4 yrs; stays 1¼m; acts on any going; blinkered twice in 1980. *M. H. Easterby.*

SUMMERCOVE 5 br.g. My Swallow 134–Honey Bend 101 (Never Bend) — (1980 NR 1981 8d) ex-Irish gelding; lightly raced on flat nowadays; stays 1m; seems to act on any going. *A. Moore.*

SUMMER HOUSE 2 gr.f. Habat 127–Autumn Double 72 (Double Jump 131) **59** (1981 5f 6f 6fg² 7g) May 14; big, lengthy filly; third foal; half-sister to winning 3-y-o sprinter Heavy Weapon (by Bay Express); dam won over 9f; close third of 10 to Super Sunset in seller at Doncaster in September; fair seventh in 16-runner maiden race at Leicester later in month; may stay 1m; capable of winning a modest seller. *J. Hardy.*

SUMMER PATH 4 gr.f. Warpath 113–Summersoon 89 (Sheshoon 132) **54** (1980 8f 7fg 16g 10g² 9s* 10.6d 14.7f³ 12fg² 15d 1981 12g 12g³ 15.8g³ 12s* 12.3fg⁴ 11d 12v 11d 12d⁴) compact filly; plater; won non-selling handicap at Carlisle in June; stays well; acts on any going. *M. Camacho.*

SUMMER SILKS 2 ch.f. Shantung 132–Summer Love 60 (Silver Cloud 121) — (1981 8g) Mar 9; half-sister to 3 winners, including fairly useful 1973 2-y-o winner Hayloft (by Bold Lad, Ire); dam won over 1¼m; unquoted, showed speed for some way when tenth of 13 to Brigado in maiden race at Edinburgh in October. *G. Fletcher.*

SUM STAR 6 br.m. Comedy Star 121–Quotient 91 (Quorum 126) (1980 8fg* 6h² 6fg* 6f* 7g* 6g² 5fg 5g* 6d³ 6f 1981 6g 6g 6g) rangy mare; poor handicapper nowadays; effective from 5f to 1m; acts on hard going; blinkered once at 4 yrs. *J. Berry.*

SUN BLOSSOM 3 b.f. Blakeney 126–Penumbra 99 (Wolver Hollow 126) **65** (1980 6fg³ 6d 1981 8fg 8f²(dis) 7f 10fg 8d) neat, attractive filly; disqualified for hampering another runner after going down by a neck to Lichen Green in maiden race at Thirsk in July (would probably have won with a clear run); didn't reproduce that form; suited by 1m. *M. Smyly.*

SUNBURST (FR) 5 b.g. Sassafras 135–Miss Sunshine (Mourne 126) (1980 — 6f 8fg 13.4f 12g* 10f³ 10s 12g⁴ 12g 12d 13g 10s² 16fg 10g 13s 1981 15.5d) big ex-French gelding; stays 1½m; probably acts on any going but seems well suited by some give in the ground; has been tried in blinkers; sold to J. Tierney 5,400 gns Doncaster May Sales. *A. Jarvis.*

SUNCHARMER 8 ch.g. Roi Soleil 125–Indian Beauty 93 (Indiana 129) — (1980 NR 1981 8f) poor maiden; wears blinkers. *B. Wise.*

SUNDANCE KID 2 b.g. Star Appeal 133–Shady Side 82 (Pall Mall 132) (1981 **71** 8s 7d 7g) May 18; small, strong, lengthy gelding; half-brother to a winner by Gulf Pearl; dam won over 5f at 3 yrs; 7 lengths sixth of 22 in 7f minor event won by Starbells at Chepstow in October on second outing; should stay 1m. *W. Hastings-Bass.*

SUNDHOPE LYNN 2 bl.g. Rapid River 127–Read Aloud 57 (Town Crier 119) **54** (1981 8.2d 8d) Mar 1; 700 2-y-o (privately); third foal; dam of little account; 25/1, showed up most of way when 4¾ lengths fifth of 13 to La Bird in seller at Hamilton in September; in rear in maiden race at Edinburgh the following month (had tongue tied down). *H. Bell.*

SUN DIVER 3 ch.g. Sun Prince 128–Sea Swallow 90 (Dan Cupid 132) (1980 — 5f 6g 7g 7d 7fg 7f² 7d³ 7d⁴ 1981 7s 8g 7g 8g 8fg³ 7.6fg 7g 8d 6fg) neat, strong gelding; mainly poor form in 1981, including in a seller on final outing; will stay 1¼m; best in blinkers; sold 780 gns Doncaster September Sales. *Denys Smith.*

SUNITI 3 b.f. Derring-Do 131–Sounion 69 (Vimy 132) (1980 5g 7g 1981 **68** 12fg² 12.5f* 12f³ 12.2fg² 12.3g* 12f 13fg) rather lean, lightly-made filly; often unimpressive in paddock; 1½-length winner of handicaps at Stockton in June (beat Canoodle) and at Newcastle in July (from Palatinate); stays 1½m well; acts on firm going. *J. W. Watts.*

SUNLEY BUILDS 3 ch.c. Patch 129–Dance Mistress (Javelot 124) (1980 **102** 7fg 7g* 7d* 10g 1981 8g⁴ 12.3g² 12d 12f 10.8s) quite attractive, rangy colt; made all in Hyperion Stakes at Ascot and Houghton Stakes at Newmarket as a 2-y-o; kept on well when in frame in Ladbrokes Craven Stakes at Newmarket in April (5 lengths fourth to Kind of Hush) and in Chester Vase in May (12 lengths second to Shergar), having several very useful colts behind him and running a particularly fine race in latter event; 200/1 when ninth of 18 behind runaway winner Shergar in Derby in June, best subsequent effort; well backed when running poorly in minor event at Warwick in October on final start, first outing for 4 months; well suited by 1½m and will stay further; acts on a soft surface; blinkered fourth start (went too fast for his own good). *G. Hunter.*

SUNLEY SPECIAL (USA) 3 b.f. Proud Clarion or Triple Bend–Ancora — (Ribot 142) (1980 6g 7d 1981 10s 10.2g 12g⁴ 10s⁴) quite a well-made American-bred filly; plating-class maiden; stays 1¼m. *G. Hunter.*

SUNLIT RIVER 4 br.f. Roi Soleil 125–River Moy (Niagara Falls 104) (1980 — 8f 10fg 9.4fg 9.4d² 8g³ 12d 9.4g 10f 9.4fg 9s 9v 1981 12.5s) well-made filly; poor maiden; stays 9f well; suited by some give in the ground; blinkered once in 1980. *W. Haigh.*

SUNNINGDALE QUEEN 3 ch.f. Gay Fandango 132–Lisabella (Right Royal **74** V 135) (1980 5g 7d³ 7.2d 7fg 1981 12f² 12fg* 12.2f³ 14fg 12fg⁴ 10.6fg⁴) lengthy, quite attractive filly; in frame on most outings, and at Brighton in July beat On Her Own by ½ length in a maiden race; stays 1½m; probably acts on any going; sold 22,000 gns Newmarket December Sales. *B. Hills.*

SUNNY ISLAND (USA) 2 ch.c. Our Native–Gwinn Island (Groton) (1981 — 6g 6fg) Mar 28; $45,000Y; robust colt; fourth foal; brother to 2 American winners; dam won twice at up to 5f at 3 yrs; tracked leaders most of way and wasn't given a hard time when seventh of 20 to Linda Beard in maiden race at Newmarket in August; came home only tenth of 11 to Captain Henry, after having every chance 2f out, when second favourite for similar event at Yarmouth later in month. *E. Eldin.*

SUNNY LOOK 2 ch.f. Lombard 126–Sooner or Later (Sheshoon 132) (1981 8d² **81 p** 10s*) May 10; fair sort; sister to a winner in Holland and half-sister to middle-distance winners Solatia (by Kalydon) and Salian (by Salvo); dam lightly-raced half-sister to Oaks third Suni; favourite after a promising debut, won 20-runner maiden race at Nottingham in October comfortably by 1½ lengths from Bullring; a fairly useful staying 3-y-o filly in the making. *J. Hindley.*

SUNNY SOUTH 2 ch.c. Be My Guest 126–Flaring Angel (Nentego 119) (1981 **80 p** 6d 6d*) May 8; IR 51,000Y; third living produce; dam won twice at up to 6f, including a claiming event, at 2 yrs in North America; favourite when winning 12-runner maiden race at Naas in November by 2½ lengths from Brown Ford; will stay at least 1m. *V. O'Brien, Ireland.*

SUN OF SCHWEPPES 4 b.c. Roi Soleil 125–March Malona 88 (Derring-Do **93** 131) (1980 7v 7f 6f 7g² 6g³ 6s 6g³ 6s 1981 10fg³ 8d 7fg⁴ 8d²(dis) 7fg* 7.6s⁴ 7g* 8s) small, strong colt; poor mover; fairly useful handicapper; won twice at Catterick in the summer; stays 1m; suited by top-of-the-ground; effective with or without blinkers; has run creditably for a lady rider. *W. O'Gorman.*

SUNSET RAY 5 br.m. Hotfoot 126–Queen of Twilight 107 (Off Key 121 or **72** Twilight Alley 133) (1980 11f 14f² 12g 12s³ 8g* 10g² 8s 1981 14g* 10g 14g* 14f* 16g 16.1g* 14.7fg* 14g² 12g) well-made mare; had a good season and won handicaps at Newmarket (three), Yarmouth and Redcar; stays well; acts on any going but is suited by top-of-the-ground; genuine. *J. Winter.*

SUNSET WONDER 5 ch.g. Tickled Pink 114–Rainbow Wonder (Runnymede **59** 123) (1980 17.1fg⁴ 11.7f² 12fg* 13.1h⁴ 10.2g 1981 10f 12f³ 12g) lightly-made gelding; former plater; stays well; acts on firm going. *L. Kennard.*

SUN

SUNSHINE GAL 3 br.f. Alto Volante 109–Chinese Princess (Sunny Way 120) **53**
(1980 8fg 8d 7d 1981 8g 12fg 8fg 8fg 9fg 10s² 10d³) neat filly; plater; should
stay beyond 1¼m. *N. Guest.*

SUNSHINE LIE 7 b.g. Shiny Tenth 120–Liebeslust (Mangon) (1980 10.2d
11fg* 10h² 12.3f⁴ 12.2fg⁴ 10.6g 10.2g 10fg 1981 8g) middle-distance handicapper; acts on any going; has been tried in blinkers; suitable mount for an
apprentice. *M. Camacho.*

SUNSPEED 3 b.g. Warpath 113–Croisette 95 (Sunny Way 120) (1980 7f —
1981 10.6d 11f 15.5g 11g) neat gelding; beaten some way in maiden races
and a seller. *C. Thornton.*

SUN MARTIAL 2 b. or br.c. Nonoalco 131–Turkish Treasure 111 (Sir Ivor 135) **108**
(1981 5fg 7fg* 7d⁴ 8g² 7d²) Feb 20; first foal; dam ran only at 2 yrs when very
useful winner over 6f and 7f; odds on when winning 13-runner maiden race at
Leopardstown in August by a length from Sir Shostakovich; in frame afterwards
in much better races, finishing 1¾ lengths fourth of 11 to Day Is Done when
favourite for National Stakes at the Curragh, short-head second to Anfield
(who gave 7 lb) in Ashford Castle Stakes on same course and 4 lengths second of
10 to Sharp Singer when odds on for Larkspur Stakes at Leopardstown; suited
by 1m; blinkered final 2 starts. *V. O'Brien, Ireland.*

SUPER ACT (USA) 2 b.f. Native Royalty–Air Maid (Fleet Nasrullah) (1981 **71**
5g² 5s⁴) Feb 18; $75,000Y; tall, narrow filly; sister to Chatta, a very useful
stakes winner at up to 7f, closely related to a minor stakes winner by Marshua's
Dancer and half-sister to useful French filly Gamina (by Gallant Man); dam,
daughter of top Argentinian filly Donna, won over 5f at 3 yrs; did well
to finish ¾-length second of 14 to Celestial City after being hampered in maiden
race at Newmarket in May, but had a very hard race in the process; favourite
for 5-runner minor event at Newbury later in month but finished only fourth to
Justicia after disputing lead at distance (reportedly lost a shoe and punctured
her hoof on a nail). *M. Albina.*

SUPER BEE JAY 2 gr.g. Mummy's Pet 125–Gold Ribbon 106 (Blast 125) **66**
(1981 5v* 5v* 5v⁴ 5g⁴ 6f) May 20; 6,000F, 11,000Y; compact, well-made gelding; half-brother to 2 winners, including fairly useful 1976 2-y-o 6f winner
Sarasingh (by Mansingh); dam won over 7f and 1m at 2 yrs; comfortably justified
favouritism in maiden and minor events on consecutive days at Ayr in March; runs
as though 6f should suit him; probably needs some give in the ground; sent to
Hong Kong. *N. Callaghan.*

SUPER BRAT 2 b.g. Shiny Tenth 120–Mishabo (Royalty 130) (1981 6g) —
May 5; workmanlike gelding; first foal; dam never ran; 50/1 when last of 9 to
King Naskra in maiden race at Yarmouth in July. *R. Carter.*

SUPERB SINGER 2 ch.f. Music Boy 124–Sinzinbra 112 (Royal Palace 131) **47**
(1981 5s 5s⁴ 5s² 5g 5d 6f⁴ 6f 5f) May 28; 2,100F, 660Y; tall, leggy filly; third
foal; half-sister to a winning hurdler; dam won at up to 1¼m; only poor form in
sellers and auction events; stays 6f; usually bandaged on all legs. *K. Ivory.*

SUPERDELLA 4 ch.f. Pelso Lad 87–April Love (Spiritus 88) (1980 NR 1981 —
10f) second foal; dam temperamental point-to-pointer; in rear in minor event
at Ripon in August. *J. Leigh.*

SUPER EAGLE 3 b.g. Legal Eagle 126–Superbum 69 (Super Sam 124) (1980 —
5v 5d 5f³ 6g 7g 5s 8.2g 8s 5s 1981 8s 6g 6g 7g 6v) small, strong gelding; bad
plater; should stay 1m; has worn blinkers; sold 620 gns Ascot July Sales. *W.
Marshall.*

SUPER GRASS 2 b.c. Thatch 136–Pepi Image 111 (National) (1981 6.3fg 6fg) **81**
May 20; ex-Irish colt; fourth foal; half-brother to Irish 6f winner President Elect
(by Prince Regent) and Irish middle-distance winner National Image (by
Sassafras); dam third in Irish 1,000 Guineas; faced a stiff task for a newcomer
when 33/1 for Ballsbridge-Tattersalls Anglesey Stakes at the Curragh in August
and came home remote last of 6 to Dara Monarch after missing break; beaten
only 2½ lengths when fifth to Chivalry in 17-runner maiden race on same course
later in month; subsequently transferred to M. Stoute's stable. *N. Meade,
Ireland.*

SUPERIOR SAINT 3 b.c. Welsh Saint 126–Superina 62 (Super Sam 124) **73** d
(1980 5f 5fg 6g 6g³ 7d 7d 8g 7s 7s⁴ 1981 8s 7fg³ 7g² 7d⁴ 8d³ 7g 8.3fg² 8fg 6fg⁴
8fg 8s 8s 8d) strong, compact, short-legged individual; in frame in varied
company; stays 1m well; blinkered occasionally; bandaged near-fore eighth start
(ran moderately); unseated his amateur rider on way to start eleventh outing,
but ran creditably. *R. Hannon.*

846

SUPERNACULUM 7 gr.g. Supreme Sovereign 119–Perpelia (Red God 128**§**) — (1980 8g 12d 10d 10g 16f 1981 10.2s) one-time useful performer but was no longer of any account; dead. *M. Tate.*

SUPER NATALIE 2 ch.f. On Your Mark 125–Super Amber (Yellow God 129) **80** (1981 5d 5.1f³ 5.1fg⁴ 5f* 5fg² 5g² 5h 5g 5f) Apr 18; 850Y; fair sort; none too good a mover; second foal; half-sister to 3-y-o 1¼m seller winner Elite Petite (by Welsh Saint); dam never ran; showed improved form when making all to win 9-runner minor event at Chepstow in July by a length from Street Market; behind in nurseries on last 3 outings; not sure to stay beyond 5f; swerved start final appearance; sold to Newmarket BA 920 gns Newmarket Autumn Sales. *A. Jarvis.*

SUPER SEASON 3 ch.g. Silly Season 127–Floral Gift 84 (Princely Gift 137) — (1980 6g 7fg 1981 8fg 8g 8d) strong, good sort; little worthwhile form, but wasn't entirely disgraced considering his slow starts on last 2 outings; sold to T. Hallett 850 gns Ascot August Sales. *R. Hollinshead.*

SUPER SERVICE 3 b.g. Rheingold 137–Ensnarer (Bold Ruler) (1980 6d **85** 7f² 8d 8d 1981 8s³ 8g⁴ 10g² 11.7fg* 12.2f² 12fg 10g² 11.7d³ 11s) lengthy, attractive gelding; good mover; beat Ray Charles a short head in handicap at Windsor in June; runner-up afterwards in minor event at Catterick and £4,900 handicap at Ascot, spoiling his chance by hanging when beaten ¾ length by Show-A-Leg in latter in September (apprentice ridden); stays 1½m; acts on any going; disappointed sixth and last starts; sold to BBA (Italia) 12,000 gns Newmarket Autumn Sales. *P. Walwyn.*

SUPER SMILE 3 b. or br.c. High Top 131–Hedge Warbler 89 (Sing Sing 134) **53** (1980 5f 6d³ 6g 5f³ 5g* 5f 6g 5d 1981 5d 5d 5fg 6fg 5g 6fg³ 6fg 6d³ 5s 6g) small, compact colt; stays 6f; acts on firm going and a soft surface; has run creditably for an apprentice; wouldn't run on when blinkered seventh start. *N. Callaghan.*

SUPER SPARTAN 3 ch.g. Roi Soleil 125–Last Summer 66 (Will Somers 114**§**) **55** (1980 5fg 6d 7fg 6f* 6g 8f³ 7f 8.2s 8d⁴ 1981 10s² 10s³ 12d⁴ 11fg⁴ 13.8fg⁴ 13.8g³ 16f 13.8fg 15g³ 16.5f² 16s⁴ 13.8g 16s) strong, lengthy gelding; won seller at Thirsk as a 2-y-o; in frame in handicaps in 1981; stays well; seems to act on any going; sometimes blinkered but does as well without; often held up but is better ridden up with pace. *J. Etherington.*

SUPER SUNRISE 2 b.c. Sagaro 133–Lay Aboard (Sing Sing 134) (1981 7fg⁴ **117** 7fg* 8d* 8d)
Sagaro, the outstanding stayer of the mid-'seventies, made a successful if unspectacular start to his stud career. Of eighteen two-year-olds to race two were winners and one of them, Super Sunrise, proved a smart performer. This is as good a start as could reasonably be expected since Sagaro's stock will presumably need time and distance to show their best. Super Sunrise didn't race until July and won over seven furlongs and a mile; Sagamore, Sagaro's other winner, was also successful over a mile.

Super Sunrise made his debut in the Sandwich Maiden Stakes at Ascot. He looked rather in need of the outing and raced towards the rear of the eight-runner field for much of the way. However, his finishing effort put him automatically in many note-books: once switched from an unpromising position on the rails he made excellent late progress to finish fourth, half a length behind the dead-heaters Incandesce and Telephone Man and a further six lengths behind Loyal Toast. Super Sunrise confirmed the good impression he made, and improved with each race. He was easy in the market but still started joint-favourite for a fifteen-runner minor event at Newcastle in August and duly won by half a length, quickening nicely to master Two Minutes despite running a little green. Super Sunrise's jockey gave his mount as easy a race as possible and had only to push him out. Super Sunrise's next race, the Haynes, Hanson and Clark Stakes at Newbury in August, was the same event which (known as the Kris Plate) provided Henbit and Shergar with their first victories. Super Sunrise confirmed himself an improving colt well suited by a mile with a convincing success from twenty-one rivals. The field split into two groups, with Super Sunrise on the occasionally-advantageous stand side. Always nicely placed and going well, Super Sunrise took the lead soon after the two-furlong marker and galloped on to beat Gouverno by two and a half lengths. Neither Henbit nor Shergar won his race after the Kris Plate, each running in Group 1 races. Super Sunrise followed that pattern in the William Hill Futurity Stakes at Doncaster, without showing as good form as his two predecessors. He put up easily his best performance, keeping on to finish fifth, under five lengths behind Count Pahlen, after being prominent from the start.

Super Sunrise is the fourth produce and first winner of Lay Aboard, who never raced due to an injury as a foal. None of the first four mares on the bottom line of the pedigree won a race although the third dam, All Aboard, finished third in the Cherry Hinton Stakes. That's not to say that Super Sunrise's family is a poor one: his dam is a sister to a winner and half-sister to four more including Mahler, a very useful miler. All Aboard, sister to Derby and Gold Cup winner Ocean Swell and half-sister to Oaks runner-up Iona, numbered winners of the National Breeders' Produce Stakes, the Blue Riband Trial and the

Super Sunrise (b.c. Mar 23, 1979)	Sagaro (ch 1971)	Espresso (ch 1958)	Acropolis
			Babylon
		Zambara (b 1966)	Mossborough
			Grischuna
	Lay Aboard (b 1970)	Sing Sing (b 1957)	Tudor Minstrel
			Agin the Law
		Golden Hind (b 1961)	Aureole
			All Aboard

Galtres Stakes among her eleven successful produce, as well as Copenhagen, several times champion sire in New Zealand. Super Sunrise, a rangy colt, is clearly expected by connections to take after his sire as he has been entered for the Derby but not the Two Thousand Guineas. Super Sunrise cost 4,600 guineas as a foal and must be considered a bargain, for he wasn't far behind the best at two years. He acts on a firm and a soft surface, having yet to race on extremes. *G. Hunter.*

SUPER SUNSET 2 b.c. Owen Dudley 121–Kissin' Cousin 74 (Be Friendly 130) **63** (1981 5s 5g³ 5g⁴ 5f⁴ 6fg*) Apr 19; 1,400F, 6,000Y; neat colt; first foal; dam twice-raced sister to very useful sprinter As Friendly; in frame in maiden races prior to winning valuable seller at Doncaster in September by a neck from Harris Tweed in a blanket finish; sold to H. Blackshaw 4,300 gns afterwards; stayed 6f; dead. *G. Hunter.*

SUPERTRAMP 3 b.g. Mummy's Pet 125–Babanina (Bleep-Bleep 134) (1980 **58** 5fg⁴ 5g* 5g 5g 5d 6f 5s 1981 5d 5g² 5f 5f 5g² 6g 6g 5f⁴ 5d) useful sort; second in handicaps at Beverley in June and July, best efforts; not sure to stay 6f; blinkered last 2 outings, running respectably on first occasion but dwelling and finishing tailed off on second; sold 2,600 gns Doncaster October Sales. *J. Fitzgerald.*

SUPPER'S READY (USA) 3 br.g. Nalees Man–Irish Wedding (Advocator) **91** (1980 5d 6g³ 5d* 6g² 7d* 1981 8s 10fg 8g³ 8fg 10fg) lightly-made, quite attractive gelding; well beaten after finishing 2½ lengths third to Von Erlach in handicap at Brighton in May; stays 1m; form only with some give in the ground; has run well for an apprentice; blinkered last 3 starts. *H. Candy.*

SUPREME BROWN 2 b.f. Most Secret 119–Lush Gold 91 (Goldhill 125) (1981 **—** 5g) Mar 6; second foal; sister to a poor plater; dam won over 5f and 1m, and is sister to very useful sprinter Lush Park; 3/1, beaten soon after halfway when remote fifth of 6 to Miysam in maiden race at Haydock in April. *M. H. Easterby.*

SUPREME FJORD 3 ch.f. Targowice 130–Macaw 85 (Narrator 127) (1980 **—** 6fg 7g³ 8fg 7d* 7d² 7v* 1981 7g 8.2s 7.2g 8g 8d 8d 8g) small, lightly-made filly; won small race at Catterick and well-contested nursery at Doncaster as a 2-y-o; didn't recover her form, although wasn't entirely disgraced fifth and sixth starts; better at 7f than 1m; very well suited by some give in the ground; good mount for an apprentice; retained by trainer 17,000 gns Newmarket December Sales. *M. Jarvis.*

SUPREME VISTA 8 b.g. Supreme Sovereign 119–Alta-Vista (Skymaster 126) **—** (1980 NR 1981 13s 13s 13s 13s) does little racing on flat nowadays; has been tried in blinkers; bandaged in 1981. *B. Richmond.*

SURFER 4 ch.g. Gulf Pearl 117–Land Ho (Primera 131) (1980 8g 10.1g² **70** 1981 12g*) attractive gelding; not seen out after winning 16-runner maiden race at Haydock in April by a head from Cornishman; stays 1½m. *J. Tree.*

SURRUPTITIOUS 2 ch.f. Northfields–Nanette 100 (Worden II 129) (1981 **—** 5fg 6f 8fg 8fg 6d) May 8; IR 60,000Y; small, short-legged filly; sister to 3 winners, including smart middle-distance filly Nanticous and Spillers Stewards' Cup winner Repetitious, closely related to useful sprinter Tanella (by Habitat) and half-sister to another winner; dam stayed 1¼m; well related but seems little better than plating class; trained by G. Harwood first 2 outings. *R. Armstrong.*

SUSANNA 3 b.f. Warpath 113–Susan McIntyre 67 (Double Jump 131) (1980 **64** NR 1981 9f 10d* 9d³ 12d* 10.2g) tall, lengthy, lightly-made filly; third foal; sister to quite useful 1977 2-y-o 6f winner Siouxsie, and to Sweet Sioux, a winner several times in Trinidad; dam stayed 1½m; successful in minor event at Ayr in September (made all) and claiming handicap at Leicester in November (claimed out of C. Thornton's stable); ran moderately in a valuable seller final start; stays 1½m; acts on a soft surface; sold to T. Craig 6,200 gns Doncaster November Sales. *M. Camacho.*

SUSANNA (USA) 3 b.f. Nijinsky 138–Full Dress II 115 (Shantung 132) (1980 **81 §** 6f 7g 1981 7s 8s² 12v⁴ 8f³ 8f² 8fg⁴ 8fg⁴ 8fg³ 9f 8g² 10.6v⁴ 12s) big, strong, attractive filly; ran best races when close second in Fern Hill Stakes (Handicap) won by Oh So Choosy at Ascot in June and in £3,200 event won by Salamina at Doncaster in September; in frame on most other starts but was very disappointing and has her own ideas about the game; should be suited by middle distances; acts well on firm going; sometimes blinkered; temperamental and is one to leave alone. *H. Wragg.*

SUSANS SONG 2 b.f. True Song 95–Ships Cat (The Bo'sun 114) (1981 5d **—** 5fg 5s 7g 10.2g) May 15; small, lightly-made non-thoroughbred filly; in rear in sellers, maiden and minor races and is probably of little account. *D. Dale.*

SUSAN'S SUNSET 3 br.f. Welsh Saint 126–Honi Soit (Above Suspicion 127) **60** (1980 5fg 5fg 5g 6g 7g 8d 1981 7d 7g 7f 8.3d* 7f* 8h⁴ 8.2fg³ 8f 8d) neat filly; won selling handicaps at Windsor (no bid) and Brighton (changed hands 1,850 gns) in August; stays 1m; probably acts on any going. *S. Woodman.*

SUSIE REEVES 2 ch.f. Tumble Wind–Stormy Queen 64 (Typhoon 125) (1981 **76** 6fg⁴ 8fg³ 6d) May 11; 28,000Y; small, rather lightly-made filly; fourth foal; half-sister to modest sprinter Queen's Bidder (by Auction Ring); dam, Irish 2m winner, is half-sister to Sandford Lad; in frame in minor event at Windsor in August and maiden race at Leicester in September; suited by 1m and will stay 1½m; sent to race in USA. *H. Cecil.*

SUSSEX QUEEN 2 ch.f. Music Boy 124–Counsel's Opinion 83 (Counsel 118) **82** (1981 5fg² 6fg* 6f²) Mar 13; 4,100F, 4,400Y; half-sister to several winners, including fairly useful stayer Panco (by Panaslipper); dam effective at 6f to 1m; dead-heated with Town Special in 11-runner maiden race at Lingfield in July; excellent ½-length second of 8 to Little Smasher in nursery at Folkestone the following month; suited by 6f. *W. Musson.*

SUTHEON (HOL) 3 ch.c. Pantheon–Susy A (Aldis Lamp) (1980 6.5g 1981 **—** 8g 12d 10.7d⁴ 9.5d* 10d* 9v* 10.7fg 9g⁴ 9d² 10g² 9.5v) sturdy Dutch-bred colt; first foal; dam won 3 races over 6.5f at 5 yrs; behind in maiden events at Stockton (needed race) and Folkestone when trained by M. Ryan; subsequently raced in Holland and won minor events at Duindigt (2) and Schaesberg; stays 1¼m; acts on heavy going. *P. van Bloemen Waanders, Holland.*

SUZY MANDEL 6 ch.g. Our Mirage 123–Sparkling Jewel (Faberge II 121) **40** (1980 NR 1981 13d⁴ 15g³ 15g) strong gelding; staying maiden. *R. Allan.*

SUZY'S PAL 3 b. or br.g. Mummy's Pet 125–Deep Freeze 75 (Varano) (1980 **58** NR 1981 7g 10.1v² 10fg 10fg 16.9fg 12g 16s) 4,000F, 4,000Y; strong gelding; brother to 9f winner Skelbrooke and half-brother to a minor winner; dam won over 1¼m; poor form, including in a claiming handicap; unlikely to stay 2m; possibly needs plenty of give in the ground; sold 2,600 gns Ascot October Sales. *S. Mellor.*

SVALBARD (USA) 4 b.g. Rheingold 137–Brent's Queen (Crozier USA) (1980 **—** 10s 12d³ 10d 10.5fg 12d 1981 12f 12s 10d 10.5g 10.5d⁴ 12g² 12.2g) ex-French gelding; middle-distance handicapper; in frame at Saint-Cloud and Maisons-Laffitte in July; modest fifth in apprentice race at Catterick in October on final start; stays 1½m; best form on an easy surface; blinkered once in 1980; trained part of season by A. Paus, A. Klimscha and M. Blackshaw. *A. Jarvis.*

SWAFFHAM 3 b.g. Moulton 128–Joey 110 (Salvo 129) (1980 NR 1981 **54** 8g 8g 8fg 8s³ 7d 8f 8g) workmanlike gelding; third foal; brother to fairly useful 1m and 1¼m winner Chevington; dam, winner over 5f and 7.6f, stayed 1¼m; showed only form when third of 18 to Becky Sharp in maiden race at Yarmouth in

July; bred to stay middle distances; blinkered fifth and ninth starts; not one to rely on; sold to S. Leadbetter 2,600 gns Newmarket Autumn Sales. *H. Wragg.*

SWALLANGA 3 ch.c. My Swallow 134–Vanga (Rockavon 120) (1980 6d² **98** 1981 8s 7g² 7s² 10d³ 8s 8fg* 12fg 9f) quite an attractive colt; brother to very useful Command Freddy, successful at up to 1m in France, and half-brother to 2 winners, including very useful 6f to 1¼m performer Ridaness (by Ridan); dam won at up to 1½m in France; beat Zillionairess by 4 lengths in 5-runner maiden race at Phoenix Park in July; placed earlier in maiden race on same course, Tetrarch Stakes at the Curragh (beaten short head by Dance Bid), and Nijinsky Stakes at Leopardstown (1¾ lengths third to Young Kildare); in rear in Airlie/Coolmore Irish 2,000 Guineas at the Curragh on fifth start; stays 1¼m (not entirely disgraced over 1½m); probably acts on any going. *D. Hughes, Ireland.*

SWALLOW HILL 7 b.g. My Swallow 134–Hillowton (Mister Gus) (1980 **—** NR 1981 17.1h 13.1f) lightly raced on flat nowadays; stays 1½m; best form on a sound surface. *L. Kennard.*

SWANEE-ROCK 2 ch.g. My Swanee 122–Rock Dandy (Master Rocky 106) **—** (1981 6fg 7g 8g) Apr 20; narrow non-thoroughbred gelding; half-brother to two 2-y-o winners; dam ran twice over hurdles; behind in a variety of races, including a valuable seller. *J. Bethell.*

SWAN PRINCESS 3 br.f. So Blessed 130–Swan Ann 84 (My Swanee 122) **94** (1980 5d* 5f3 5h* 5f² 5fg⁴ 5fg² 5fg² 5g* 5g 1981 6d* 6fg 5f 5fg³) good sort; a useful performer as a 2-y-o, and an exceptionally speedy one too, winner of 4 races including Group 1 Phoenix Stakes; made all and held on by 1½ lengths from 100/1-chance Sitex in minor event at Folkestone in April; disappointing afterwards, although had much stiffer tasks; evidently stays 6f; seems to act on any going; headstrong and is usually taken down early. *B. Swift.*

SWAN RIVER 3 ch.f. Roan Rocket 128–Parmelia 118 (Ballymoss 136) (1980 **61** 6s⁴ 6g 1981 8fg 9g 10f³ 11f) compact filly; quite a moderate maiden; taken down early when third at Ripon in August, best effort of 1981; suited by 1¼m; ran poorly second and final starts; sold 12,500 gns Newmarket Autumn Sales. *E. Weymes.*

SWANSEA BAY 2 b.c. Moulton 128–Calling High 88 (Mountain Call 125) (1981 **81** 5g⁴ 5s² 5s* 6f³ 6fg 7fg 7fg³ 7f 10f²) Apr 4; 7,800Y; big, lengthy colt; third foal; half-brother to 3-y-o 8.5f seller winner La Mascotte (by Hotfoot) and 1m winner My Natalie (by Rheingold); dam 2-y-o 6f winner; landed the odds by a length from Heads You Win in maiden race at Leopardstown in May; third afterwards in Fenwolf Stakes at Ascot in June (3½ lengths behind Norwick), Ardenode Stud Stakes at Leopardstown in August (beaten 2¾ lengths by Fly Start after making much of running) and minor event at Tralee in September (moved up to second by stewards after finishing 4½ lengths third to Gold Exchanged); evidently stays 1¼m; acts on any going. *M. Kauntze, Ireland.*

SWASHBUCKLING 6 b.g. Prince de Galles 125–Galosh 96 (Pandofell 132) **73** (1980 NR 1981 15.5d* 16s* 20fg⁴ 16g) really big gelding; won handicaps at Folkestone and Kempton in May; stays well; acts on any going; genuine; goes well for B. Crossley. *R. Simpson.*

SWAYING TREE 4 ch.g. Swing Easy 126–My Bushbaby 100 (Hul a Hul 124) **55** (1980 7g 6fg² 6g* 7g* 6f 1981 6g 7.2s 7g² 7fg⁴ 8fg 8g 7g 6f 7d 8.2d 7v⁴ 7g) strong gelding; carries plenty of condition; stays 1m; acts on a firm surface; usually blinkered nowadays; has worn bandages; sold 780 gns Newmarket Autumn Sales. *R. D. Peacock.*

SWEDISH RHAPSODY 3 br.f. Targowice 130–Tuola (High Flown 117) **74** (1980 5f⁴ 5g* 6d⁴ 7g² 7fg⁴ 1981 7g³ 8g 8s² 8f 8g⁴ 10g² 10f⁴ 8fg 10s) useful-looking filly; good mover; in frame in handicaps at Newbury (2), Wolverhampton, York and Leicester; stays 1¼m; blinkered ninth outing; sweated up badly eighth start; has given impression she has a mind of her own; sold 6,000 gns Newmarket December Sales. *G. Pritchard-Gordon.*

SWEET ANDY 2 br.c. Ardoon 124–Black Honey 91 (March Past 124) (1981 **64** 5g⁴ 5s 5s⁴ 6g⁴ 6fg 7f 6fg 7g 8f 8.2fg 6fg 5s) May 4; IR 2,100F, 1,600Y; neat colt; half-brother to a winner in Italy; dam won over 9f and 1½m in Ireland; plating-class maiden; yet to show he stays 1m; blinkered final outing; has run well for an apprentice. *J. Gilbert.*

SWEET AS A NUT 5 b.m. Birdbrook 110–Roman Dawn 87 (Neron 121) —
(1980 6fg 6g 6g 6s² 7d 1981 12fg) tall, lengthy mare; poor handicapper;
stays 7f; best form with some give in the ground; suitable mount for an apprentice
W. Wightman.

SWEET AS SUGAR 2 ch.c. The Minstrel 135–Cappella 98 (Crepello 136) **89**
(1981 6fg³ 7f⁴) May 21; 72,000Y; neat colt; half-brother to Silk Hat II (by
Shantung), a very useful stakes winner at up to 1m, and smart Fiesta Libre (by
Damascus), successful at up to 9f; dam middle-distance performer; kept on well
when 2¼ lengths third of 14 to Codrington in Granville Stakes at Ascot in July;
could never find the pace to get on terms when favourite for £6,300 event at York
in September, coming home 3 lengths fourth of 6 to Marquessa d'Howfen;
will be suited by middle distances. *P. Kelleway.*

SWEET ECSTASY 2 ch.f. Rarity 129–Acrasia 74 (Bold Lad, Ire 133) (1981 **74**
5g⁴ 6fg⁴ 6f 6fg* 6d) Apr 15; IR 6,600Y; neat, quite attractive filly; good
walker; first foal; dam lightly-raced daughter of very useful 7f and 9f winner
Melodramatic; dropped in class, cost 6,000 gns to buy in after leading close
home to win £4,000 seller at Kempton in August by a neck from Brockley Belle;
had run well in better company on first 2 outings; will be suited by 7f+; didn't
seem at ease on really firm ground when disappointing favourite on third start;
sold 5,800 gns Newmarket December Sales. *W. Hastings-Bass.*

SWEET FOR DAYS 2 b. or br.f. Red Alert 127–Brother John (Will Somers **74**
114§) (1981 5s 5d 5fg⁴ 5g² 6f² 6f³ 5fg⁴ 5.3fg* 5fg 5s³) Apr 26; 2,000Y;
lightly-made filly; sister to 1979 2-y-o 5f winner Red Jane and half-sister to
another winner; dam placed over 7f in Ireland; beat Rowanna Lady 1½ lengths
in 5-runner claiming race at Brighton in June; in frame most of her other starts,
including in sellers and a nursery, putting up her best effort of a busy season
in latter at Lingfield on final outing when third to Preparation; stays 6f; acts
on any going but evidently goes particularly well in the mud. *R. Hannon.*

SWEET HIGHNESS 3 ch.f. Sweet Revenge 129–Her Worship 61 (Privy **58**
Councillor 125) (1980 5fg 1981 8g 8d 12.2g 15.5g 12d³) lengthy filly; plating-
class maiden; suited by 1½m; apprentice ridden, unseated rider, bolted and was
withdrawn on one occasion as a 2-y-o. *R. Williams.*

SWEETHILL 3 gr.f. Runnymede 123–Clouded Lamp 99 (Nimbus 130) (1980 —
5f 5fg 5.8fg 5.8fg 7d⁴ 7f 6g 7g 1981 7g 5.8f 8f 10fg 10f 10fg 10d) small filly;
only poor form, including in a seller; stays 7f; sometimes blinkered; sold to
G. Ripley 600 gns Ascot November Sales. *M. McCormack.*

SWEET JAPONICA 2 b.f. Native Bazaar 122–Edlin (Monet 127) (1981 5fg **49**
6fg³ 6g 7g 6f 6f⁴ 6f³ 6f 6s 8g 7g) lightly-made filly; half-sister to 2 winning
platers; in frame in sellers at Nottingham, Ripon and Hamilton; not sure to
stay 7f; blinkered sixth appearance; claimed out of J. Douglas-Home's stable
£2,400 on second outing. *W. Stubbs.*

SWEET MARK BOY 5 ch.h. Decoy Boy 129–Sweet Reason (Elopement 125) —
(1980 7v 8fg 7g 7d 8d 1981 6s 8fg 10.1d) strong horse; plater; best form
at 7f; seemed to act on any going; ran poorly when tried in blinkers; dead.
J. Jenkins.

SWEET MONDAY 3 b.c. Sweet Revenge 129–Solly Graham 82 (Romulus 129) **111**
(1980 5f 5.8fg² 6fg* 6fg⁴ 6fg* 1981 6g² 6f 7s⁴ 6s² 6g) lengthy colt; developed
into a very smart 2-y-o in 1980; only lightly raced in 1981, easily best efforts
when second in minor event at Lingfield in June (beaten a length by Chemin)
and Coral Bookmakers Champion Sprint at York in October (led below distance
but couldn't hold Jester's strong late challenge and went down by ½ length);
suited by 6f and will probably stay 7f (had stiff task and was having first race
for over 3 months when tried at trip); probably acts on any going; usually sweats
up. *J. Holt.*

SWEET OPIUM 4 b.f. Bigivor–Poppy-Jill (Normandy 103) (1980 NR 1981 —
10fg 12d) first foal; dam of little account; tailed off in apprentice races at
Leicester and Chepstow in the autumn. *M. Tate.*

SWEET PLEASURE 3 b.f. Sweet Revenge 129–Arrangement 72 (Floribunda **88** d
136) (1980 7g 6g* 6s 6fg 1981 8fg³ 7g 8fg 7fg 8d) strong, good sort; won
Convivial Stakes at York as a 2-y-o; disappointing in 1981, best effort when
6 lengths third to Beeleigh in £4,900 handicap at Sandown in April; stays
1m; inconsistent. *C. Nelson.*

SWEET SALINITY (USA) 2 b.f. Blushing Groom 131–Woozem (Hail to — p
Reason) (1981 6fg) Feb 3; $75,000Y; sixth foal; half-sister to 3 minor
winners in USA; dam, smart stakes winner at up to 1m, is half-sister to good
winners Run For Nurse and Gallant Romeo; 50/1 and ridden by 7-lb claimer,
showed up 4f when 8½ lengths sixth of 9 to Silver Hawk in maiden race at
Yarmouth in August, only outing; will be suited by 1m; may do better. *M.
Stoute.*

SWEET SATISFACTION 2 ch.f. Sweet Revenge 129–Pendula 76 (Tamerlane **71**
128) (1981 5g 5g 6f 6g 6g³ 7.6s) Apr 17; 1,400Y; small filly; fifth foal; dam won
at up to 1¾m; 5 lengths third of 21 to Tickletimes in minor event at Redcar in
September; also ran creditably second outing; suited by 6f; form only on good
ground so far. *C. Spares.*

SWEET SIDE 2 b.f. Quayside 124–Sweet Delight (Klairon 131) (1981 5d* **101**
5s 6v³ 5fg 5fg 5f 6d³ 5s²) Mar 29; IR 560F; small, lightly-made filly; second
foal; dam never ran; 50/1-winner of Group 2 Moyglare Stud Stakes at the Curragh
in September but wandered about, hampering Woodstream and Santa Roseanna
in final furlong, and was moved down to third by stewards; had previously won a
minor event at Naas in April but had been beaten in nurseries on her 3 outings
immediately before her Curragh win, finishing fifth of 7 twice and last of 5;
ran well on only outing in England, putting in best work in closing stages to be
2½ lengths second of 7 to My Lover in Cornwallis Stakes at Ascot in October;
stays 6f well and should get 1m; needs some give in the ground. *M. Quaid,
Ireland.*

SWEET SOLICITOR 2 ch.g. Legal Eagle 126–Sharp and Sweet (Javelot 124) —
(1981 5g 5.8f 7g 8d 8s 6g) Apr 24; smallish, workmanlike gelding; good mover;
half-brother to 3 winners, notably very useful Sweet Reclaim (by Compensation);
dam half-sister to Sweet Revenge; behind in maiden races. *W. Wightman.*

SWEET SPARK 3 b.f. Hot Spark 126–Sweet Serenade 93 (High Perch 126) —
(1980 5f* 6g 6d³ 1981 8.5g 6f) strong filly; won maiden race at Wolverhampton
in 1980; had stiff tasks when last in handicaps at Epsom in June (probably
needed race) and Nottingham in July; stays 6f; seems to act on any going. *B.
Hills.*

SWEET TANGO 3 b.f. Gay Fandango 132–Rogan Honey (Abernant 142) —
(1980 5f 1981 8f 8f 8fg) fair sort; towards rear in maiden races at Pontefract
and Thirsk (still needed race) in July and in apprentice event at Yarmouth in
August. *F. Durr.*

SWEET VENGEANCE 3 b.f. Reliance II 137–Maddelena (Tudor Melody 129) —
(1980 NR 1981 8s 10s) second foal; dam plating-class half-sister to high-class
middle-distance performer Relay Race; in rear in minor event at Warwick and
maiden race at Nottingham in October. *C. James.*

SWELL HILL (USA) 2 b.c. Val de l'Orne 130–Dancing Sadie (Dancer's Image) —
(1981 8d) Mar 26; $20,000F, 17,000 gns Y; first produce; dam won 5 small
races at up to 1m; 14/1 when tenth of 23 to Roanoke River in maiden race at
Leicester in November; sold 800 gns at Ascot Sales later in month. *J. Tree.*

SWELTER 5 br.m. Tickled Pink 114–Sun Queen 76 (Lucky Sovereign) (1980 **91**
5d* 5d* 5d* 5.6g* 5g 1981 5fg⁴ 5f 5fg⁴) strong, slightly hollow-backed mare;
sprint handicapper; won 4 races in 1980, notably William Hill Portland Handicap;
ran creditably first start at 5 yrs but was well beaten afterwards; best at around
5f; seemed to act on any going but was suited by some give in the ground; game;
covered by Exdirectory. *F. Durr.*

SWIFTBLADE 2 br.f. Tachypous 128–Swordblade 84 (Pall Mall 132) (1981 —
5.1f 5fg 7g 7h 7d 6g) Apr 17; 3,600Y; compact filly; half-sister to numerous
winners, including useful 5f to 7f winner Don Quixote (by Galivanter); dam
2-y-o 5f winner and half-sister to very smart 1¼m horse Tacitus; in rear in varied
company, including selling. *C. Mackenzie.*

SWIFT DECISION 2 b.c. Streak 119–Judiciary 74 (Above Suspicion 127) —
(1981 5g⁴ 5.1f 5.8d 7d 8s 8g) May 13; tall, lengthy colt; half-brother to very
smart miler Legal Eagle (by Manacle) but is a poor plater himself; sold to Newmarket BA 1,000 gns Newmarket Autumn Sales. *W. Marshall.*

SWIFT ENCOUNTER 2 b.c. Owen Dudley 121–Pop Gun 85 (King's Troop 118) **75**
(1981 5g 7fg 7g 7fg 7g 8d⁴ 8d) Feb 11; 5,800Y; small colt; fourth produce;
half-brother to 1979 2-y-o 5f winner Hot Gun (by Hotfoot); dam best at 5f;
3 lengths fourth of 16 to Portette in maiden race at Bath in October, best effort;
stays 1m. *R. Williams.*

SWIFTFOOT   2 b.f. Run The Gantlet–Whitefoot 108 (Relko 136)   (1981 7.2f*   **92**
8s⁴)   Feb 5; well-made, attractive filly; half-sister to several winners, including
useful 1979 2-y-o 6f winner Neenah (by Bold Lad, Ire); dam stayed at least 1½m;
looked in need of race when evens favourite for 6-runner Rose of Lancaster
Stakes at Haydock in July but outclassed her rivals to win by 2½ lengths from
Sasol; not seen out again until late-September but looked fit prior to finishing
3½ lengths fourth of 12 to Jalmood in £3,300 race at Goodwood; will stay well.
R. Hern.

SWIFT KISS   4 b.c. Sparkler 130–Fiery Kiss 82 (Floribunda 136)   (1980 8f   **64**
8fg 10fg³ 10s 10fg 11.7d 10.8d 12.5s   1981 8s⁴ 8s 8g 8g 8f³ 10f² 10f²(dis) 11.7fg
10f 10h* 10fg* 10f)   neat colt; plater nowadays; successful at Chepstow (bought
in 2,400 gns) and Nottingham (bought in 2,600 gns) in September; stays 1½m;
suited by a sound surface; has run creditably for an apprentice; below form in
blinkers once; sold 1,000 gns Newmarket Autumn Sales.   *R. Williams.*

SWIFT PALM   4 b.g. Some Hand 119–March Stone 84 (March Past 124)   **80**
(1980 8d 8.2d² 10.6f* 12fg   1981 8s 8d 8d* 10g⁴ 8g* 10fg 8fg³ 10s³ 12.2s 8s³ 8g*)
lengthy gelding; decisively won apprentice handicaps at Newbury in June and
Sandown in July and beat Twickenham a short head in handicap at Doncaster in
November; stays 1¼m; has won on firm going but seems to need some give in the
ground nowadays; suitable mount for a boy.   *P. Cundell.*

SWIFT STEP (USA)   3 b.g. Shecky Greene–Fur Boots 94 (Northern Dancer)   **—**
(1980 5f 6d 7g 7g 7g   1981 10.1fg 12fg 10f)   robust, good sort; poor form in
maiden and minor races; not certain to stay 1½m.   *G. Balding.*

SWIFT WING   2 b.f. Malinowski 123–Mear-Aille (Hard Ridden 131)   (1981 6g   **102**
6f* 7h* 7.2fg⁴ 8g*)   Feb 12; IR 38,000Y; quite attractive filly; good mover; half-
sister to 7f to 1¾m winner Pollardstown (by Lord Gayle), also a high-class winner
over hurdles, and to 3 winners abroad; dam half-sister to dam of Vaguely Noble;
had a good season, winning maiden race at Nottingham in July and nurseries
at Bath in August and September; put up a useful effort under 9-7 when
gaining final success by 1½ lengths from Le Debauchery; will be suited by
1¼m; yet to race on a soft surface; game and consistent.   *J. Dunlop.*

SWING BACK   4 br.f. Great Nephew 126–Well Rowed (Delta Judge)   (1980 8g   **—**
8g 7s 6d   1981 10fg 8f 5fg)   lengthy filly; behind in varied company; blinkered
nowadays.   *R. Hollinshead.*

SWING FIRE   2 b.c. Swing Easy 126–Quick Burn 94 (Carnival Dancer 113)   **77**
(1981 5s* 5d⁴ 5g⁴ 5v⁴ 5s)   Apr 27; 5,800Y; robust, short-legged colt; fifth foal;
half-brother to fair 1980 2-y-o 5f winner Miss Quaver (by Averof); dam winning
sister to smart sprinter Ubedizzy and half-sister to Cajun; well-backed favourite
when winning 14-runner maiden race at Leicester in March in good style; moderate fourth on next 3 outings and was well beaten when blinkered and poorly
drawn on final start; yet to race on a firm surface.   *Mrs J. Reavey.*

SWING GENTLY   4 br.f. Swing Easy 126–Native Soil 71 (Herbager 136)   **—**
(1980 10fg³ 8h 10fg 10.4g⁴ 10g 10fg 10.4d   1981 7g 12d 7fg)   lengthy filly;
poor maiden; not certain to stay 1¼m; often blinkered.   *A. Moore.*

SWINGING BABY   2 br.f. Swing Easy 126–Hi-Baby 102 (High Treason 126)   **73**
(1981 5s⁴ 5d 5fg³ 5g² 5d 5d² 6d)   Mar 21; well-grown, useful sort; sister to 5f and
7f winner Easy Boy and half-sister to several winners, including good Italian
winners Travolta (by Porto Bello) and Hoche (by Celtic Ash); dam 5f and 6f winner at 2 yrs; off course most of summer but subsequently finished second in nursery
at Beverley (beaten head by Nagalia) and maiden race at Hamilton (went down
by 3 lengths to Spanish Fury); should stay 6f (weakened closing stages when
tried at trip).   *J. Fitzgerald.*

SWINGING MOON   2 ch.c. Swing Easy 126–Moon Gem (Moontrip)   (1981 5d   **82**
5fg 7.6s 7d³)   Apr 24; third foal; dam, well beaten on all outings, is half-sister to 3
American stakes winners; 4½ lengths third to Parthia's Picture in minor event at
Chepstow in October; will stay 1m.   *P. Cole.*

SWINGING REBEL   3 br.c. Swing Easy 126–Rebecca (Quorum 126)   (1980 6d   **87**
1981 10d 10.1v³ 8.2s 8d⁴ 10fg 8.3fg* 7fg* 7g⁴ 7g* 7g* 7s 8s)   lengthy colt;
improved and won handicaps at Windsor in August, at Kempton and Lingfield
in September and at Newmarket in October, ridden by apprentice S. Dawson
each time; ran on well to beat Norman Style by 1½ lengths in £3,500 race on
last-named course; possibly stays 1¼m, but best form at shorter distances;

Mrs V. M. Duery's "Swinging Rebel"

has run creditably on soft going, but seems suited by a sound surface; bandaged near-hind on reappearance. *N. Vigors.*

SWINGING RHYTHM 3 ch.g. Swing Easy 126–Soft Chinook (Hitting Away) **81**
(1980 5fg 6g 5g² 5fg* 1981 6fg 6d³ 6s 5d 7fg 8fg 7fg 6fg² 6s 6g) lengthy gelding; good mover; placed in handicaps at Windsor in May and Salisbury in August, on latter course finishing good second to Kiss despite looking light and unimpressive in paddock; stays 6f (not disgraced over 7f seventh start); acts on a firm and a soft surface; sometimes sweats up and did so badly final start. *J. Holt.*

SWINGING SWANEE 3 gr.g. My Swanee 122–Spin Out 97 (Pall Mall 132) **41**
(1980 5d 5s 6fg 6f 7d 8fg 10d 10d 1981 16g² 14f 17.1d 16f 16.9fg) leggy gelding with poor forelegs; poor maiden; has run in sellers; stays well. *W. Marshall.*

SWINGING TRIO 5 ch.g. Swing Easy 126–Algarve 94 (Alcide 136) (1980 —
6f 6fg 6fg 6g 6fg 6fg 8d 1981 8d 8d 7g 8fg) well-made gelding; good mover; fairly useful handicapper at his best but has shown no form for a long time; stays 7f; acts on any going; blinkered once. *R. Atkins.*

SWING THE AXE 4 gr.f. No Mercy 126–Beech Tree 67 (Fighting Ship 121) **52**
(1980 8.2d 10.6f 9.4g 8g 8.3d⁴ 7fg 7g² 8g 7fg* 7d 7s 1981 7d² 8d 7g 7g 8f 8f 10fg 12g²) workmanlike filly; poor handicapper; second in seller on final appearance; stays 1½m; probably acts on any going; blinkered seventh and eighth starts; sold 2,300 gns Doncaster September Sales. *D. Weeden.*

SWORD EDGE 4 ch.g. Sharpen Up 127–Coulter Belle 80 (Quorum 126) —
(1980 8d 8v⁴ 10g 12fg 1981 12s 8f) workmanlike gelding; poor form, including in a seller; has worn bandages. *W. C. Watts.*

854

SWORD PRINCE 4 ch.g. Sun Prince 128–Cutlass Bay 68 (King's Bench 132) — (1980 12.3d 16f 14d 1981 10.1fg 12f) poor plater. *Dr A. Jones.*

SWYNFORD'S PASSION 2 ch.f. Jimmy Reppin 131–Fleet Messenger **71 p** (Hotfoot 126) (1981 5f*) June 6; lengthy filly; first foal; dam never ran; 25/1, always well there when winning 11-runner maiden race at Nottingham in June by 1½ lengths from Glossy Ibis; transferred to I. Balding's stable afterwards; will stay 6f+. *W. O'Gorman.*

SYBOLDA 2 b.f. Malacate 131–Covey 114 (Rustam 127) (1981 5fg² 5g 5d **82** 7fg 8g³ 6g 6d) Mar 14; IR 7,000F, resold 8,200Y; neat, quite attractive filly; good mover; half-sister to 3 winners here and abroad; dam very useful over 5f at 2 yrs; not entirely disgraced behind smart fillies on fourth, fifth and sixth outings, on fifth finishing 12¾ lengths third of 4 to Height of Fashion in May Hill Stakes at Doncaster in September; stays 1m; best form on a sound surface. *P. Kelleway.*

SYLLOGIZER 2 gr.g. Godswalk 130–French Bird (Guersant 129) (1981 6g — 6fg 6f 5.1d 5v) June 10; 12,000Y; leggy, close-coupled colt; half-brother to several winners, including 3-y-o 1m winner Mouhanned (by Ashmore) and very smart 7f performer Pitskelly (by Petingo); dam sprinter; little worthwhile form in maiden races but showed up for 4f in sizeable fields on second and third outings; well beaten in blinkers final outing. *F. Durr.*

SYLVAN BARBAROSA 2 ch.c. Native Bazaar 122–The Silver Darling 75 **92** (John Splendid 116) (1981 5fg³ 5g⁴ 5s⁴ 6g* 6f⁴ 5fg² 6fg* 5f² 5d 5g 6g) May 2; 1,800Y; 2,600 2-y-o; quite well-made colt; second foal; dam second in this country before winning at 2 yrs in Belgium; successful in maiden auction event at Epsom in June and in £5,000 nursery at Lingfield the following month, making all to win by ½ length from Vin St Benet in latter; excellent length second to Hays in minor race at Sandown in between; effective at 5f and 6f; best form on a sound surface. *P. Mitchell.*

SYLVER SAGE 2 gr.g. Pals Passage 115–Sylvarna (Seminole II) (1981 6g 7g) — Mar 31; IR 4,700F, IR 7,000Y; fourth foal; half-brother to Scroll (by Roll of Honour), winner from 9f to 1¾m in Ireland and successful over hurdles; dam won over 5f and 7f at 2 yrs in Ireland; soundly beaten in September in newcomers race at Goodwood (8/1) and maiden event at Leicester (distant eighth of 17); sold, probably for export, 800 gns Newmarket Autumn Sales. *H. Candy.*

SYLVIA'S SECRET 3 b.f. Most Secret 119–Princess Chesnut (King Chesnut 120) **41** (1980 NR 1981 8g 7f 7f³ 8fg 5g) 500Y; small filly; third foal; dam never ran; plater; suited by 7f; has a round action and gives impression she'll be suited by some give in the ground. *A. Smith.*

SYMPATIQUE 3 b.c. Simbir 130–Fun of the Fair (Skymaster 126) (1980 6d **69** 7g³ 7fg⁴ 8.2g³ 7d 7f 1981 10d² 8s 10.1fg³ 8f⁴ 10f⁴ 11.5d² 12f 11.5g² 10d*) strong, good sort; moves well; led 3f out and came right away to beat Chief Speaker by 15 lengths in minor event at Brighton in September; in frame in varied races earlier, including an amateur riders race; stays 11.5f; seems to act on any going but is evidently well suited by some give underfoot; tends to hang and is not the most genuine of animals; sold to N. Gaselee 12,500 gns Newmarket Autumn Sales. *C. Brittain.*

SYNCOPATE 5 br.m. Highland Melody 112–Manipulation 90 (Appiani II 128) **65** (1980 10.2d 10v* 10s* 12fg² 12f 12f³ 12fg² 12d 11g³ 13d² 12.3g² 13g² 16.9f⁴ 12g 12.2fg 12fg 13s³ 12d 12s 1981 10.2d 10v* 12.5s*(dis) 12v³ 12.3d 12.5g* 12d³ 12d² 12s* 12g⁴ 13g⁴ 12.2g 15g 12v) neat mare; had a good season, winning handicaps at Ayr, Stockton and York, two of them apprentice events; also dead-heated at Stockton but was disqualified for having theobromine in system; stays 13f; acts on any going; good mount for an apprentice; very tough and genuine; trained by G. Lockerbie first 11 starts. *N. Tinkler.*

SY OUI 2 b.g. The Brianstan 128–Mystic Halo (Aureole 132) (1981 5g² 5s* 5fg) **79** Apr 4; 4,400Y; good sort; third foal; dam of no account; made all to win 7-runner auction event at Goodwood in May by ½ length from The Cairnwell; not seen out again for 3 months when modest fifth of 6 to Childown Blue in nursery at Kempton; will stay 6f; gelded at end of season and sent to Hong Kong. *R. Price.*

SYSTEMS ANALYSIS 5 b.h. Rheingold 137–Maragay 65 (Match III 135) **42** (1980 18d 16s 16f 12.3f 16fg² 16g* 16g 16f² 16s 18f⁴ 16g 16g² 17.1d 1981 12g 15.8g 19g² 16g 16g 16.1s) leggy, light-framed horse; has a round action; staying handicapper; suited by top-of-the-ground; suitable mount for an apprentice; often makes the running; sometimes bandaged in front. *A. Smith.*

SZIKH (HUN) 4 b.c. Peleid 128–Song Time (Song 132) (1980 ? 1981 7fg — 6f 10fg 6g) Hungarian-bred colt; soundly beaten in varied company, including selling, in this country. *M. Blanshard.*

SZYMANOWSKI 2 ch.c. Malinowski 123–Ismene II (Silnet 131) (1981 7g⁴) **75 p** May 14; IR 25,000Y; half-brother to numerous winners in France, including very useful 7f to 1¼m winner Insulaire (by Aureole); dam won over 7f and 1m in France; 16/1, going on steadily when 8½ lengths fourth of 9 to Match Winner in minor event at Yarmouth in September; will stay at least 1m; will probably do better. *J. Hindley.*

T

TABERNACLE 8 b.g. Manacle 123–Tabarka (Dicta Drake 126) (1980 12d — 8s 10g 10fg 1981 10.2s 13fg 9g 8fg) poor plater; stays 1¼m; seems to act on any going. *K. Bridgwater.*

TABLOID 2 ch.c. Touch Paper 113–Last Fairy (Bold Lad, Ire 133) (1981 5s **94** 5g* 6d⁴ 6fg 5fg* 5fg*) Apr 9; IR 3,900Y; first foal; dam half-sister to St Leger runner-up Patti; a useful colt over 5f, winner of maiden race at Phoenix Park in May and of nurseries at Leopardstown in July and August; gave at least 8lb all round when gaining first nursery success and carried second-top weight when scoring by 3 lengths from Ormsary in second; best form on a sound surface; sent to USA. *M. Connolly, Ireland.*

TACHYWAUN 2 b.g. Tachypous 128–Merency 75 (Meldrum 112) (1981 5s² **96** 5d³ 5g³ 6f³ 6fg* 6fg² 6g⁴ 7g 6f⁴ 6fg) Feb 2; 9,500Y; neat, strong gelding; first foal; dam won over 5f at 2 yrs; favourite, gained a well-deserved success when beating Saddlers Creek by 3 lengths in minor event at Newcastle in June; subsequently acquitted himself well in useful company, including when 1½ lengths second of 4 to Full Extent in Black Duck Stakes at York in July and when 4½ lengths fourth of 8 to Glancing in Champion Two Yrs Old Trophy at Ripon the following month; stays 7f well; seems to act on any going; game and consistent; gelded late in season and sent to Hong Kong. *J. Etherington.*

TAFFY JONES 2 br.c. Welsh Pageant 132–Shallow Stream 100 (Reliance II — 137) (1981 7d) May 1; 1,700 2-y-o; second foal; dam, 1¼m 2-y-o winner, is daughter of half-sister to Cantelo; unquoted when out of first 10 in 22-runner minor event won by Starbells at Chepstow in October. *M. McCormack.*

TAHER (FR) 3 b.c. Weavers' Hall 122–Lotties Charm (Charlottesville 135) **112** (1980 7g 8g 1981 12fg* 12g 16g 12g* 13.1f* 13.3g* 12fg³ 14d 16g) big, long-striding colt; improved considerably and developed into a very useful colt; put up an excellent display under top weight in Morland Brewery Trophy (Handicap) at Newbury in July, leading 2f out and winning very cheekily by ½ length from Capricorn Line; successful earlier in maiden race at Kempton and handicaps at Salisbury and Bath (odds on), winning in very good style on last 2 courses; had his limitations exposed however when 7½ lengths third of 5 to Bustomi in Gordon Stakes at Goodwood later in July, and never really promised to take a hand when 12 lengths fifth of 22 behind Protection Racket in Tote-Ebor (Handicap) at York in August or when seventh of 9 behind Centroline in Jockey Club Cup at Newmarket in October; suited by 1½m and more; acts on firm going and is possibly not at his best on a soft surface; sold privately before final start and has been sent to race in Australia. *G. Harwood.*

TAHOE (FR) 3 br.c. Dancer's Image–Darada (Relko 136) (1980 6v* 6s* 6g* **106** 6v² 8d² 1981 7s² 8g 7s) 35,000Y; small, fair sort; half-brother to 2 winners, including useful 6f to 1m winner Carelko (by Caro); dam won twice over 9f at 3 yrs; won 3 times from 5 starts in Norway as a 2-y-o; 50/1, ran on well under pressure and just held off shorter-priced stable-companion Dalby Mustang for second when beaten 2 lengths by convincing winner Recitation in Salisbury 2,000 Guineas Trial in April; sixth of 9 behind Kind of Hush in Ladbrokes Craven Stakes at Newmarket later in month; last of 12 to Prince Mab in Group 3 Prix du Palais Royal at Longchamp in May; stays 1m; acts on heavy going and has yet to race on a firm surface; sent to USA. *T. Dahl.*

TAI FU KWAI 2 gr.g. Sagaro 133–Rebecca (Quorum 126) (1981 6fg 7f⁴ 7fg **70** 6g³ 7g 7.2v² 8g) May 24; 1,100Y; compact gelding; half-brother to 3-y-o 7f and 1m winner Swinging Rebel (by Swing Easy) and a winner in Barbados; dam poor half-sister to Irish Sweeps Derby winner Steel Pulse; in frame in varied company, including selling; will be suited by 1¼m+ (blinkered when running moderately over 1m); acts on any going. *C. Williams.*

Mr R. E. Sangster's "Taher"

TAIKA CHANCERY 4 b.g. Andrea Mantegna–Greek Bazaar 49 (Philemon 119) — (1980 10.8s 10g 12f 12h 10.8fg* 10fg² 10f 1981 14.6f 16.1f 19g) lightly-made gelding; plater; best form at around 1¼m; acts on a firm surface. *A. Potts.*

TAI LEE 2 gr g. No Mercy 126–Cansanta 96 (Canisbay 120) (1981 5d⁴ 5fg⁴ — 75 6g² 6g 6fg 7fg 5g 6s) May 7; 5,000Y; quite well-made gelding; brother to fair 1978 2-y-o 6f winner Santaclaire and a winner abroad, and half-brother to winning miler Sharpener (by Sharpen Up); dam won twice over 5f at 2 yrs; put up best effort when 4 lengths second of 18 to Bravado in maiden race at Newcastle in July, first outing for over 3 months; stays 6f well; blinkered fifth and sixth outings; slowly into stride on seventh. *R. Williams.*

TAIWANESE (USA) 3 ch.f. Giacometti 130–Miss Toshiba 113 (Sir Ivor 135) 60 (1980 NR 1981 7d 10fg 10f 12d 14fg³ 15.8g³ 16.5g 8g) big, well-made filly; first foal; dam won from 7f to 1½m in Scotland and Ireland prior to showing very smart form over 9f in USA; third in maiden races at Haydock and Catterick in September; stayed at least 1¾m; front runner; gave impression she wasn't entirely genuine; retired to stud. *B. Hills.*

TAJ EL MOULOUK (FR) 3 ch.c. Green Dancer 132–Barbentane (Prudent II 69 133) (1980 6d³ 8g³ 8.5g 10d 1981 8fg⁴ 10fg³ 10fg² 10fg³ 10v*) leggy, lightly-made ex-French colt; half-brother to several winners in France and Ireland, including very smart 6f to 1m winner Boitron (by Faraway Son) and very useful Benthose (by Dapper Dan), a winner at up to 1m; dam won twice over 5f at 2 yrs in France; in frame in 3 maiden races prior to winning one at Kempton in October by a length from Johns Present; will stay 1½m; probably acts on any going; blinkered final outing in 1980. *M. Albina.*

TAJONSKI 3 ch.g. Bolkonski 134–Ixia (Le Fabuleux 133) (1980 NR 1981 74 7g 10s³ 10d 8fg 10fg 11.5d* 16f 10f) 10,000F, 16,500Y; leggy, quite useful sort; half-brother to 2 winners in France, including Intrigue (by Tyrant), successful at up to 1½m; dam French 1¼m winner and also won over jumps; stayed

857

on well to beat Sympatique a head in amateur riders maiden race at Yarmouth in July; doesn't seem to stay 2m; seems to need some give in the ground. *R. Armstrong.*

TAKACHIHO 9 b.h. Don II 123–Face Lift (Herbager 136) (1980 8fg 11g 8.2d 8fg 8d 8.2s 12g 11fg 10.2d 1981 8s 10v⁴ 12g* 12g³ 12g 8fg 8fg 10f) poor handicapper; won at Edinburgh in April; effective at 1m to 1¼m; well suited by top-of-the-ground conditions; used to wear blinkers; suitable mount for an apprentice. *T. Craig.* **42**

TAKE A CARD 2 ch.c. Tachypous 128–Cigarette Case 89 (Faberge II 121) (1981 6g⁴ 7d) Apr 17; quite a useful sort; half-brother to 3 winners, including 1½m and 1¾m winner Smoke Screen (by Blakeney) and 1¼m winner Latakia (by Morston); dam won from 1m to 11f; weak 10/1-shot but pretty fit, nearest at finish when 2¾ lengths fourth of 15 to Celestial Dancer in maiden race at Yarmouth in September; seventh of 22 behind Starbells in minor event at Chepstow the following month; will stay 1¼m. *M. Stoute.* **80**

TAKE-A-CHOICE 3 ch.f. Take a Reef 127–Quandary 80 (Aureole 132) (1980 5g 5g 5f 6d 6fg 1981 10s) neat filly; no sign of ability, including in a seller on only outing of 1981 (sweating and burly); sold 400 gns Doncaster November Sales. *R. Whitaker.* **—**

TAKEAFENCE 3 ch.g. My Swallow 134–Set Piece 69 (Firestreak 125) (1980 5f 5f 6fg 1981 10s⁴ 10d 12g³ 11.7g² 14f 16f 14g 12fg) workmanlike gelding; placed in a handicap and a maiden race in first half of season, but became disappointing; stays 1½m. *R. Hannon.* **69 d**

TAKE AIM 8 ch.g. Firestreak 125 Take a Chance 107 (Rockefella) (1980 8fg⁴ 13.8f 9g⁴ 10g 1981 9f) poor plater; effective from 1m to 13f; probably acted on any going; often wore blinkers; inconsistent; dead. *W. Storey.* **—**

TAKE A ROSE 2 b.f. Take a Reef 127–Lavender Rose (Beau Lavender 96) (1981 5d) Apr 30; 800Y; second foal; half-sister to Irish 3-y-o Tumbling (by Tumble Wind); dam never ran; unquoted and very green when last of 10 in seller won by Golden Wilkie at Ripon in May. *H. Wharton.* **—**

Go Racing in Yorkshire Trainers' Trophy Stakes, Thirsk—a driving finish with Take The Floor (nearer camera) getting up to beat Never Talk

TAKEN FOR GRANTED   3 b.c. Martinmas 128–Romanee Conti (Will Somers   **89**
114§)   (1980 7f 7fg³   1981 10g³ 10s 8fg* 8g³ 8v* 8s)   tall, lengthy colt; made
virtually all when winning maiden race at Newbury in July and £3,800 handicap
at York in October, on latter course beating Regal Touch in great style by 8
lengths; almost 10 lengths third behind Indian King in quite well-contested
minor event at Goodwood in between; stays 1¼m; acts on a firm surface but
clearly revels in the mud; sold to R. Carter 9,400 gns Newmarket Autumn
Sales. *P. Walwyn.*

TAKE THE FLOOR (USA)   2 b.c. Cornish Prince–That's Show Biz (Promised   **109**
Land)   (1981 5s* 5g* 6fg 6g* 6d² 6d 6g)   Mar 23; $70,000Y; well-made,
attractive colt; fourth foal; dam very useful stakes winner over 9f at 5 yrs;
successful in maiden race at Haydock, minor event at Thirsk and 7-runner
Strathclyde Stakes at Ayr before end of July; outpaced at halfway at Ayr
but stayed on strongly to win by 3 lengths from Singing Sailor; met his defeats
in pattern races, putting up his best efforts when 2½ lengths second of 8 to
Full Extent in Gimcrack Stakes at York in August and when 4½ lengths ninth of
13 to Cajun in William Hill Middle Park Stakes at Newmarket in October on
seventh start (sweated up badly and didn't move well to post); usually has
difficulty going the pace and will be well suited by 7f+; seems to act on any
going; suited by a galloping track. *G. Hunter.*

TAKHOS   2 b.c. Tachypous 128–Riboﬂeur 74 (Ribero 126)   (1981 6fg 6g⁴ 7g   **67**
5g 5fg⁴)   well-grown, useful sort; good mover; first foal; dam placed
from 7f to 1¾m; showed enough ability in maiden races and a nursery to suggest
he can win a seller; bred to stay at least 1½m. *Denys Smith.*

TALAJA (FR)   2 b.f. Kalamoun 129–Tremogia (Silver Shark 129)   (1981 5d*   **110**
7g 7s* 8v)   May 6; third foal; sister to Tassmoun, a smart winner at up to
1¼m in France; dam unraced half-sister to very smart middle-distance stayer
Sauvage and daughter of Prix Saint-Alary winner Tonnera; won newcomers
race at Longchamp in May by a length from Ypsilon and 80,000-franc Prix
de l'Obelisque on same course in September by 2 lengths from Absolute; favourite
for Group 3 Prix des Reservoirs, again at Longchamp, in October but could
finish only fifth, 3¼ lengths behind Coussika (rec 4 lb); will stay 1¼m; yet to race
on a firm surface. *F. Mathet, France.*

TALK IT OVER (FR)   4 ch.g. Lyphard 132–Town Talk (Charlottesville 135)   **62**
(1980 9.2fg 11g 10.5fg 9.2fg² 10s 10d 12g   1981 12fg³ 12d⁴)   small, close-
coupled ex-French gelding; in frame in two gentleman riders races in the autumn;
stays 1½m; seems to act on any going; wore blinkers in 1980; sold 850 gns Ascot
November Sales. *F. Winter.*

TALLINGTON   2 b.c. Wollow 132–Quality Blake 91 (Blakeney 126)   (1981   **—**
6fg 7g)   Apr 21; lightly-built colt; first foal; dam won at up to 15f; unquoted
when behind in large fields of maidens at Newmarket in August and October;
dead. *R. Williams.*

TALLISHIRE ABODE   3 b.g. Crooner 119–Tudor Cream 73§ (Tudor Melody   **—**
129)   (1980 5s* 5f 5f 5d 6s³   1981 5d 6g 8f 7g)   lengthy gelding; good walker
but doesn't move well in his slower paces; won maiden race at Nottingham
early in 1980; no form in 1981; acts on soft going; retained by trainer
420 gns Newmarket Autumn Sales. *F. Durr.*

TALLISHIRE HOMES   3 b.c. Lombard 126–Maladie d'Amour 98 (Fidalgo   **70**
129)   (1980 6fg 7g³ 7fg³ 7d⁴ 8d 10s³   1981 12s 16fg² 15fg* 16f⁴ 16.5f⁴ 16f)
quite well-made, attractive colt; apprentice ridden when beating Nash Roller
by 5 lengths in maiden race at Edinburgh in July; stayed well by a test of stamina;
acted on any going; pulled up lame final start; dead. *F. Durr.*

TAMANGO   3 gr.f. Murrayfield 119–Relax 73 (Seminole II)   (1980 7fg 8fg 7g   **—**
1981 8d 12f 7g)   lightly-made filly; little worthwhile form in maiden and minor
events and a seller; sometimes sweats up. *K. Stone.*

TAMARIND GEM   4 ch.f. Salvo 129–Twisette (Alcide 136)   (1980 12fg   1981   **—**
15.8s)   poor maiden; has been tried in blinkers. *R. Johnson.*

TAMDOWN FLYER   3 b.c. Hotfoot 126–Swing The Cat (Swing Easy 126)   **72**
(1980 5f 7g² 7fg 8g⁴ 8d   1981 6fg* 6s³ 6fg* 6f⁴ 6f 7g)   leggy, light-framed colt;
beat large fields in handicaps at Windsor in June (beat Pencil Point ½ length)
and July (short-headed Spanish Hind); also in frame twice at Yarmouth; stayed
1m as a 2-y-o but raced only over 6f and 7f in 1981; acts on any going. *W.
O'Gorman.*

TAMERCO   4 b. or br.g. Saritamer 130–Congola (Bold Lad, Ire 133)   (1980 8fg   **—**
12fg 14f   1981 10g)   narrow gelding; poor maiden on balance of form; unlikely
to stay 1½m. *K. Cunningham-Brown.*

TAMER GRANGE 2 gr.f. Saritamer 130–Hornton Grange 101 (Hornbeam — 130) (1981 6s) Mar 24; quite attractive, well-made filly; sister to 1½m winner Birch Grove, and half-sister to several winners, including Champion Stakes winner Swiss Maid (by Welsh Pageant); dam won at up to 1m; 12/1 and on backward side, prominent for 4f when in rear in 15-runner maiden race won by Ellerene at Newbury in October. *H. Candy.*

TA MORGAN 3 b.g. Targowice 130–Sericana (Petingo 135) (1980 7fg 7s² **82** 1981 8s³ 7d 8.5d² 7fg* 7f* 8.2g 7g 8.3fg² 8.3g* 8.3g* 8d² 8g) tall, lengthy gelding; enjoyed a good summer and won minor event at Folkestone and handicaps at Brighton and Windsor (two), making all on 3 occasions; had been placed in sellers early in season; stays 1m well; acts on any going; successful with blinkers and without. *G. Lewis.*

TAMPA BAY 5 b.h. Ickford 101–Tide and Time (Easter Island 101) (1980 — 8fg 10g 10g 8g 10fg 6g 1981 6g 6g 5f 7g 6fg) tall horse; poor handicapper; last in seller on final start; best form at sprint distances; seems to act on any going; blinkered once at 2 yrs. *D. Leslie.*

TAMPERO (FR) 2 br.c. Pharly 130–Bienvenida (Tom Rolfe) (1981 7d³ 6f **110** 8fg* 8s² 7.5s²) Feb 9; first foal; dam won over 9f at 2 yrs and 1¼m at 3 yrs in France; second in two Group 3 pattern races after winning at Clairefontaine-Deauville in August, going down by 2 lengths to Bon Sang in Prix des Chenes at Longchamp and by short neck to Melyno in Prix Thomas Bryon at Saint-Cloud; will stay 1¼m. *J. Cunnington, jnr, France.*

TANCRED WALK 2 b.c. Farm Walk 111–Darling Do (Derring-Do 131) (1981 **78** 7g 7.2fg⁴ 8g² 7d) June 1; smallish, fair sort; brother to 3 winners, notably very useful 1m to 1¾m winner Move Off; dam unraced half-sister to high class miler Quorum; sweating, led below distance when 3½ lengths fourth of 14 to Jalmood in maiden race at Haydock in September; went down by 6 lengths to Arrowood Dream when favourite for 14-runner event at Beverley later in month but had a broken noseband flapping about his head for much of race; ran respectably in nursery on final start; will be suited by 1¼m; takes a good hold. *Miss S. Hall.*

TANGAROA 4 b.f. Lord Gayle 124–Yavana (Milesian 125) (1980 8fg 10fg — 8fg 8g 8g 1981 12f 16fg 16g 19s 17.1d 18g) lengthy filly; poor maiden on flat but has won over hurdles. *D. Elsworth.*

TANT PIS 3 b.f. Silly Season 127–Westmorland Jane 76 (Vimy 132) (1980 — NR 1981 10s) lightly-made, quite attractive filly; half-sister to several winners, including 1979 2-y-o 6f winner Blue Jane (by Blue Cashmere) and good Brazilian winner Bac (by Sharpen Up); dam placed at up to 17f when named Ciboulette; remote seventh of 11 behind Great Light in maiden race at Nottingham in April; sold 675 gns Ascot July Sales. *J. W. Watts.*

TANTS 2 ch.f. Vitiges 132–Hants 111 (Exbury 138) (1981 7v² 7g*) Apr 7; **88 p** tall, useful-looking filly; half-sister to 2 winners, including very useful 1978 2-y-o 6f to 1m winner Potemkin (by Sir Gaylord), subsequently a stakes winner in USA; dam won 4 times at around 1¼m; landed the odds a shade comfortably by 4 lengths from Brandon Creek in maiden race at Leicester in October; had previously run a fine first race in £3,400 event at York, finishing clear of 13 others when 3 lengths second to My Destiny; will be suited by 1¼m; the type to make a useful 3-y-o. *H. Cecil.*

TAPDANCER 3 b.g. Hotfoot 126–Giselle 104 (Pall Mall 132) (1980 5fg 5d — 1981 6fg 5.8g 6f 6fg 8fg) quite well-made gelding; disappointing maiden; found little under pressure when dropped to selling company final start; bred to stay at least 1m; blinkered last 3 starts; sold to W. Clay 410 gns Ascot September Sales. *M. Smyly.*

TAP ON THE HEAD (USA) 2 b.c. Inverness Drive–La Femme Fatal **77** (Burd Alane) (1981 5f 6f 5g² 6g 5fg) Mar 13; $47,000Y; strong, well-made colt; second foal; dam twice-raced half-sister to 2 stakes winners; sire won from 6f to 8.5f; went down by only ½ length to Prima Voce in maiden race at Sandown in July; ran poorly next outing and wore blinkers when modest seventh of 15 to Pitter Pat in nursery at Windsor in September on final start; should stay beyond 5f. *J. Tree.*

TAP YOUR FEET 2 br.f. Hotfoot 126–Musical Piece 91 (Song 132) (1981 — 5f) Apr 23; small filly; first foal; dam best at sprint distances; 16/1, moved poorly to start prior to finishing seventh of 11 to Swynford's Passion in maiden race at Nottingham in June, only outing; has no scope. *B. Hanbury.*

TARA'S CHIEFTAIN 3 b.g. African Sky 124–Hillberry Corner 70 (Atan) (1980   **72**
6g   1981 8d 8d 8s 7f² 8f 8f* 8g 8.2d⁴ 8s)   compact gelding; won handicap at
Chepstow in September by 3 lengths from Carry Over; stays 1m; often blinkered;
sweated up fifth outing. *G. Huffer.*

TARAWERA 2 b.f. Royben 125–Targa (Stani) (1981 5s 8fg 8s*) May 1;   **67**
rather lightly-made filly; half-sister to winning Irish stayer Tintoretto (by
Dschingis Khan); dam German; dropped in class, bought in 1,250 gns after
showing improved form to win 17-runner seller at Warwick in October by
¾ length from Jeanjim; suited by 1m and will probably stay further; acts on
soft going; sold 720 gns Newmarket Autumn Sales. *P. Walwyn.*

TARDOUS 2 ch.g. Take a Reef 127–Dousabel (Doutelle 128) (1981 6g*)   **80 p**
Apr 6; IR 5,600F, 5,800Y; half-brother to minor winners here and in Norway
and to dam of useful 1979 2-y-o Schwepperusschian (by Take a Reef); dam
never ran; backed from 12/1 to 7/1, made all when winning 22-runner maiden
race at Lingfield in September by a short head from Bernard Sunley; will stay
1¼m; probably has improvement in him; gelded at end of season and sent to
Hong Kong. *R. Price.*

TARGET PATH 3 b.c. Scottish Rifle 127–Florabette (Floribunda 136) (1980   **73**
NR   1981 8d 9d* 8.2d 10g⁴ 11.7s 11g* 10f⁴ 11fg* 12g⁴ 12f 11d) strong colt;
half-brother to 6f winners Workshop (by Workboy) and Doublette (by Double
Jump), both subsequently successful abroad; dam never ran; successful in
maiden race and handicap at Hamilton and another handicap at Edinburgh,
dead-heating with Justice Pao on latter course in July; stays 11f; probably
acts on any going; blinkered fifth start; ran moderately last 2 outings, but had
stiff task on first occasion. *C. Nelson.*

TARLETON 4 b. or br.g. Workboy 123–Lady Jester 108 (Bleep-Bleep 134)   **40**
(1980 8g 8g⁴ 6g⁴ 7.6d 8g   1981 8.2g 6g 6d 6g 7f³ 6fg 6fg³ 6g 6fg 7g⁴ 7v) plater;
stays 1m but is probably better at shorter distances (has good early pace);
acts on firm going; finds little off the bridle. *P. Rohan.*

TARROPEKE 7 gr.g. Good Bond 122–Pen Friend 90 (Vigo 130) (1980 10.2d   **—**
8.2g 1981 10.2s) poor performer nowadays. *D. McCain.*

TARRYSTONE 2 br.f. So Blessed 130–Bajour 89 (Forlorn River 124) (1981   **—**
6g)   May 3; 16,500Y; rather lightly-made filly; second reported live foal;
dam, half-sister to smart Pugnacity, won from 5f to 7f; unquoted, missed
break and was always struggling when tenth of 12 to Rebollino in £5,400 maiden
race at York in August. *C. Nelson.*

TARSUS (FR) 2 ch.c. Hotfoot 126–Yole Tartare (Captain's Gig) (1981 6g   **—**
7g 6g) Feb 26; 11,500F, 22,000Y; good-looking colt; first produce; dam,
minor 9f winner at 2 yrs in France, is half-sister to smart French filly Premiere
Harde; in mid-division in 19-runner newcomers race at Goodwood in September and in 21-runner maiden event at Newmarket in October (third outing);
bred to stay at least 1m. *B. Swift.*

TARTAN BOY 4 gr.g. Sovereign Path 125–Tantara (Pakistan II 84) (1980   **—**
8g 8s 5s 1981 8d 5.8g 6f 6g) rangy gelding; poor maiden. *R. Turnell.*

TARTAN VELVET 3 br.f. Meldrum 112–Yettina (Tycoon II) (1980 NR   **49**
1981 5fg 6fg⁴ 8f 7d) strong filly; second reported foal; dam behind in maiden
races both starts; has shown a little ability in varied company, including selling.
E. Weymes.

TARVIE 4 ch.f. Swing Easy 126–Tamergene 100 (Tamerlane 128) (1980 6fg³   **—**
6g² 6d 6d³ 6g* 6g 6s 6g* 6d⁴ 1981 6g) neat, attractive filly; useful sprinter
at 3 yrs; backward when last only start in 1981 in September; stays 6f; best
form on a sound surface; game. *P. Walwyn.*

TASHI 2 b.f. Swing Easy 126–My Conkers 70 (Aggressor 130) (1981 5g 5g   **—**
6f) Feb 24; fourth foal; dam 6f winner; in rear in maiden and minor events,
finishing last of 23 on third outing; sold 400 gns Newmarket Autumn Sales. *K.
Ivory.*

TASOMUDU 2 ch.c. Tachypous 128–High Ransom 88 (High Treason 126)   **69**
(1981 5f⁴ 6fg 6fg 6s) Mar 10; 6,400Y; strong, compact colt; half-brother to
several winners, including very useful 2-y-o sprinters Sanders Lad (by Amber
Rama) and Durandal (by Bay Express); dam won over 7f; showed ability
behind useful animals; will stay 7f. *W. Musson.*

TAUFAN (USA) 4 b.c. Stop the Music–Stolen Date (Sadair) (1980 7f² 8fg 6fg*   **—**
6g   1981 5g) strong, attractive colt; excellent mover with a long stride;
lightly raced but was smart at his best; won Asda Sprint Trophy at Thirsk
and finished good second to Moorestyle in Tote Free Handicap at Newmarket

in 1980; outpaced throughou when seventh of 13 to Standaan in Palace House Stakes at Newmarket on only start of 1981 in May; gave impression 7f was his optimum trip; probably acted on any going; possibly needed a galloping track; blinkered and had tongue tied down final start in 1980; standing at Rathbarry Stud, Co. Cork. *F. J. Houghton.*

TAWFIQ (USA) 2 ch.c. Blushing Groom 131–Manta (Ben Lomond 111) (1981 7g 8s³) Apr 2; $190,000Y; good-looking colt; good mover; fourth foal; half-brother to a minor winner by Hoist the Flag; dam high-class winner of 18 races at up to 11f; showed ability on both outings, finishing 4 lengths third of 29 to Arrowood Dream in minor event at Redcar on second (spoilt effort by hanging right in closing stages); will stay 1¼m; capable of winning in ordinary maiden company. *H. T. Jones.* **80**

T. BELLE 2 br.f. Foggy Bell 108–Susan 88 (Hard Tack 111§) (1981 8g 8d) Mar 13; half-sister to 3 winners, including quite useful 1977 2-y-o 7f and 1m winner Suetown (by Charlottown); dam 5f sprinter; unquoted when behind in end-of-season maiden races at Newmarket and Leicester. *C. Spares.* **—**

TEAGARDEN 4 b. or br.g. Home Guard 129–Rose Princess (Princely Gift 137) (1980 7fg 8fg 12.3d 10g 11.7fg 16fg 1981 7d 7d 12d 7f 8f 8fg) work-manlike gelding; plater; stays 7f; has worn blinkers; sometimes bandaged. *D. Sasse.* **—**

TEAMWORK 4 br.c. Workboy 123–Affirmative 96 (Derring-Do 131) (1980 6s 8g 8g* 8fg 8fg* 8fg³ 1981 8s 8fg² 8d² 8v³ 8f* 8fg² 8g* 8fg² 9g) strong, good-bodied colt; fairly useful handicapper; quickened well when beating Greenwood Star a neck in 20-runner Royal Hunt Cup at Royal Ascot in June and Paterno a short head at Sandown in July; runs as if he'll stay 1¼m; acts on any going but seems suited by top-of-the-ground; consistent; trained until after eighth outing by G. Harwood. *R. Sheather.* **95**

TEA-POT 5 ch.m. Ragstone 128–Desert Ash (Celtic Ash) (1980 16fg 15.5g 16f⁴ 15.5f³ 17.1d 1981 14s* 16s² 16g 15.5fg² 16fg 14fg 16g* 17.1d 18g 14g*) workmanlike mare; staying handicapper; won at Goodwood in May, Lingfield in September and Newmarket in October); seems to act on any going but is well suited by soft; genuine. *M. Blanshard.* **71**

TEARS OF GOLD 3 ch.f. Grisaille 115–Jenhill (Continuation 120) (1980 5fg 5f 5d⁴ 6f 6g 8d 1981 6s) small filly; well beaten, including in a seller. *P. K. Mitchell.* **—**

TEBRO TEDDY 2 gr.c. Bronze Hill 96–Tippity Top 56 (High Top 131) (1981 6g 7f 7d 10d 8.2s) May 20; 2,700Y; small, lengthy colt; no sign of ability in minor events and sellers in the North; blinkered fourth and fifth starts. *J. Doyle.* **—**

TEDARI 2 b.g. Native Bazaar 122–Form (Reform 132) (1981 5d 5g⁴) May 6; 550F, 3,000 2-y-o; lightly-made gelding; third living foal; dam unraced; showed early speed when just over 7 lengths ninth of 20 to Fair Mount Lad in maiden race at Salisbury in May; modest fourth of 7 to Tenth of October in minor event at Bath 3 days later. *R. Hannon.* **—**

Royal Hunt Cup Handicap, Ascot—Teamwork wins Royal Ascot's most valuable handicap from Greenwood Star (hidden on rails) and Princes Gate (left)

TEDHAM MOSS 4 b.g. Ballymore 123–Madelon 112 (Saint Crespin III 132)   **77**
(1980 9.4g³ 12g³ 12fg* 13s* 12.3d³ 15s³ 16.1s² 15d² 1981 12v 12.3d* 18.4d
15.8g 16s 14s 14g 18g) fair sort; had a round action; won handicap at Newcastle
in April; ran poorly towards end of season; stayed well; acted well on soft going;
seldom impressed in paddock; possibly needed a galloping track; bandaged
behind once; dead. *W. Elsey.*

TEEJAY 2 b.c. Jimmy Reppin 131–Billingsgate 82 (High Perch 126) (1981   **63**
6f 6g 6g 7f 6s³) Apr 20; 6,200F, 14,500Y; compact colt; brother to Jinnylyn,
quite a useful performer at up to 7f, and half-brother to 2 winners; dam won
over 1¼m; 6 lengths third of 10 to No Contest in maiden race at Hamilton in
October, best effort; should stay 7f; acts on soft going. *B. Lunness.*

TEESPORT BOY 4 b.g. Huntercombe 133–Zaza 85 (Pinza 137) (1980 6v   —
7d² 6d 6f⁴ 7g 5fg 6s 1981 7s 8.2g 8g 10d 8f 6fg) robust, good-bodied gelding;
plater; suited by 7f; seems to act on any going; often blinkered; trained part
of season by E. Carter. *G. Harman.*

TE KENAWA (USA) 4 b.g. Wajima–Karmana (Abernant 142) (1980 7f²   —
8fg* 8f* 8fg⁴ 10fg² 10.2g⁴ 1981 9g 8d) tall, rather leggy gelding; not a good
mover in his slower paces; useful performer at 3 yrs; not disgraced when sixth
to Hard Fought in Earl of Sefton Stakes at Newmarket in April but could
finish only seventh of 8 to Shasavaan in £2,600 race at York in May; not seen
out again; stays 1½m; form only on a sound surface. *H. Cecil.*

TEK RIBA 3 b.f. Palm Track 122–Kindling 80 (Psidium 130) (1980 5f 5g   **53**
8fg 8.2s 7d 8d 1981 8s 8g 12.5f 12fg³ 15fg³ 16.5g³ 16f⁴) strong filly; has rather
a round action; poor form in maiden races and a handicap; evidently stays 2m;
front runner; sold 1,700 gns Doncaster September Sales. *E. Weymes.*

TELEGRAMS AGAIN (HOL) 4 br.f. Pentathlon–Darling Caroline (Ilix)   **?**
(1980 including 10g² 12g 12g 1981 10.2s 13fg⁴ 12.5s 10g* 15.5f⁴ 10.7d² 18s³)
ex-Dutch filly; second foal; half-sister to Dutch Derby winner Corral's Bond
(by Good Bond); dam third in Dutch Oaks; won ladies race at Duindigt in
August; fourth in amateur riders race at Nottingham in April, best effort in this
country; stays well. *M. Ryan.*

TELEGRAPH BOY 3 b.c. Bay Express 132–Code of Love 99 (Bleep-Bleep 134)   **65**
(1980 NR 1981 6fg 7fg 5fg 5d 5s 5s* 6s) strong, close-coupled colt; third foal;
half-brother to a winner in Austria by Rheingold; dam sprinter; showed only
worthwhile form when beating Touch My Heart by a length in handicap at
Wolverhampton in October; evidently suited by 5f and soft going; moved
moderately to post third start. *W. Wightman.*

TELEPATHY 2 b.c. He Loves Me 120–Clear Belle (Klairon 131) (1981 6g)   —
May 10; 15,000Y; half-brother to 2 winners, including useful Italian winner
Laser Belle (by Laser Light), and to a bumpers winner; dam poor maiden; 14/1
when out of first 10 in 19-runner maiden race won by One Degree at Newmarket
in October. *R. Williams.*

TELEPHONE MAN 2 b. or br.c Record Token 128–Needless 81 (Petingo 135)   **114**
(1981 5s² 6fg⁴ 7fg² 7fg² 7g² 7s⁴ 8s 7g 7v²)
    Generally speaking a colt would be considered both moderate and costly if he
failed to win any of his nine starts in his first season, as did Telephone Man.
However, neither description is applicable to Telephone Man. He was good
enough to reach the frame in important races in three countries and he has
already repaid his yearling purchase price of 11,500 guineas several times over.

		Jukebox	Sing Sing
	Record Token	(b 1966)	Bibi Mah
	(ch 1972)	Bare Costs	Petition
Telephone Man		(b 1965)	Bootless
(b. or br.c. Apr 1, 1979)		Petingo	Petition
	Needless	(b 1965)	Alcazar
	(b 1974)	Never In Need	Never Say Die
		(b 1957)	Patroness

By the time he made the first of his trips abroad, to America for the Arlington-
Washington Futurity late in August, Telephone Man had finished fourth to
Red Sunset in the Coventry Stakes at Royal Ascot and a close second to Treboro
in the Lanson Champagne Stakes at Goodwood and to Zilos in the Seaton
Delaval Stakes at Newcastle from five starts. Even so he started at over 30/1 at
Arlington. The other English challenger, My Dad Tom, seemed to hold a much
better chance but it was Telephone Man who proved much more at home on the

rain-sodden dirt course: he came from a long way back to finish fourth, just over three lengths behind the American Lets Dont Fight. Telephone Man's best subsequent effort came in blinkers in the Criterium de Maisons-Laffitte in October. As in several of his previous races he couldn't accelerate when challenged but to his credit he plugged on to finish second, two lengths behind the top weight Zino.

Telephone Man is the first foal of Needless, a winner twice at a mile and a half. Needless is a granddaughter of the smart sprinter Patroness and a great granddaughter of that magnificent broodmare Verdura, whose eleven winners from twelve foals also included Highest Hopes, Pharsalia and Gratitude. A big, rangy colt, Telephone Man seems sure to go on and win the race he deserves at three, though in good company his lack of pace will handicap him, especially at a mile or less. Round-actioned but a good walker, he seems to act on any going. *P. Kelleway.*

TELEPRITY 3 b.f. Welsh Pageant 132–Ankole 85 (Crepello 136) (1980 5d 6fg³ 8.2d 1981 7g) lengthy filly; good mover; showed ability in useful company at 2 yrs; backward and unimpressive in paddock when well beaten on only outing of 1981 (April); bred to stay middle distances; possibly unsuited by a soft surface; winner in USA. *F. Durr.* —

TELLINGO 3 gr.f. Rustingo 94–Teller 64 (Quorum 126) (1980 5d 6g 1981 12d) plater; lightly raced and no worthwhile form. *G. Price.* —

TELL ME A STORY 4 ro.f. Roan Rocket 128–Novelista 101 (El Gallo 122) (1980 5d 5fg² 6g 5g 5g 5f 1981 5d) small, sturdy filly; poor handicapper; should stay 6f; suited by fast ground; ran badly in blinkers once. *R. Baker.* —

TELL TALE LASS 2 b. or br.f. Guillaume Tell 121–Shantung Lassie (Shantung 132) (1981 5s 5g 5s 7fg 7d 7fg 10d⁴ 10g 8d) Mar 31; 650Y; small filly; third foal; dam won at up to 1½m in France; plater; bred to stay 1½m; blinkered final outing. *W. Marshall.* **48**

Mr Max Fine's "Telephone Man"

Coral Autumn Cup, Newbury—Telsmoss (left) is one of forty-five winning rides during the season for champion apprentice Crossley

TELLURANO 3 ch.c. Guillaume Tell 121–Uranus (Manacle 123) (1980 8g 7d² 1981 7g* 10d 7f 8fg* 7fg* 8fg⁴ 6g² 8fg³) big, rangy colt; brother to Belgian winner Beldale Guillaume, and half-brother to 5f winner Tralee Falcon (by Falcon); dam won twice over 5f at 2 yrs in Ireland; successful in maiden race at Phoenix Park, Coolmore Hello Gorgeous Stakes at the Curragh and Ballycorus Stakes at Leopardstown, putting up a good performance when beating Gods Mark by 2 lengths in last-named event in July; placed in Herbertstown Stakes at Phoenix Park (¾-length second to River Prince) and Group 3 Prix Quincey at Deauville (very close third behind Phydilla and Diamond Prospect) the following month; about 9 lengths sixth of 20 behind Rasa Penang in Jersey Stakes at Royal Ascot on third start; not certain to stay 1¼m; probably acts on any going, but evidently acts well on a firm surface; sweated up on fourth start; a very smart colt judged on his Deauville running; sent to race in USA. *K. Prendergast, Ireland.* **121**

TELSMOSS 5 b.h. Levmoss 133–Elakonee Wind 110 (Restless Wind) (1980 8d 10g⁴ 8fg 10d⁴ 8g 10fg* 11fg³ 11.7fg² 11.7f* 12f* 12g³ 12f² 10fg² 10.5s* 10g 1981 10fg 11s 10fg 11.7fg 11.7fg 12g 11.7g* 12fg* 14fg² 13.3d*) small horse; poor walker; fairly useful handicapper; returned to form in second half of season, winning £4,000 race at Windsor, apprentice handicap at Epsom and Coral Autumn Cup (Handicap) at Newbury; stayed on extremely well to account for Glasgow Central by ¾ length on last-named; stays 1¾m; acts on any going; suitable mount for an inexperienced rider; does best when ridden up with pace. *P. Mitchell.* **91**

TENDER ANGUS (USA) 3 ch.c. Grey Dawn II 132–Colfax Miss (Raise A Native) (1980 7g 7d 1981 12d* 12g 12g² 10fg 10.2fg³ 10g 10g³ 10.5s) heavy-topped colt; has a grand, long stride; short-priced favourite when winning maiden race at Doncaster in March in good style by 5 lengths from Dogberry (made all); in frame subsequently in handicaps at Newbury, Doncaster and Newmarket; iron broke sixth start and effort must be ignored; didn't seem to handle track at Epsom on second start; runs as if he'll stay further than 1¼m; acts on a firm and a soft surface (always behind on very soft going final start). *G. Harwood.* **82**

TENDER HEART 5 br.g. Prince Tenderfoot 126–Pirana (High Hat 131)   ?
(1980 8d 8f 8f³ 8g* 10.5g² 8fg² 9f 1981 7.6g 8d 8f) good-looking gelding;
good mover; very useful handicapper in 1980 when he won Royal Hunt Cup;
backward when in rear first 3 starts in England at 5 yrs; subsequently sent to
USA and won 8.5f allowance race at Belmont Park in September; ran well to
be nose second to Goldiko in 11f Louisiana Downs Handicap following month;
stays 11f; acts on any going; blinkered twice at 2 yrs. *J. Sutcliffe.*

TENDER KING 2 b.c. Prince Tenderfoot 126–Cider Princess (Alcide 136) **115**
(1981 5g² 5s* 5d 5g² 5f* 6fg² 6fg* 6f⁴ 6g⁴ 7g³)
In view of the fact that his trainer hadn't sent out a two-year-old to win
first time out in more than five years and considering that the horse didn't
appear fully wound up, it was rather surprising to find Tender King a very
well-backed favourite on his debut in a minor event at Lingfield in May. He
finished second, beaten half a length by the more experienced Better Portion.
On that occasion only Tender King's relative inexperience proved his downfall,
and his subsequent performances showed that the confidence of his connections
in his ability was not at all misplaced.
By the end of July Tender King had proved himself a very useful two-
year-old. His victory in the Richmond Stakes at Goodwood followed excellent
efforts in winning the Windsor Castle Stakes at Royal Ascot by three lengths
from Mary Mitsu and in finishing second, beaten a short head by End of the
Line, in the Anglia Television July Stakes at Newmarket. He had also won
a minor event at Leicester, ran disappointingly in blinkers in the Great Surrey
Stakes at Epsom, and finished a close second to Sharlie's Wimpy in the Berkshire
Stakes at Newbury. Tender King's victory at Goodwood was gained in fairly
good style: held up, he came with a good challenge from the distance and
sprinted to the front in the last fifty yards under hand riding to beat Cajun
by a neck with End of the Line a length and a half away in third.

	Prince Tenderfoot (b 1967)	Blue Prince (b 1951)	Princequillo
Tender King			Blue Denim
(b.c. Mar 25, 1979)		La Tendresse (b 1959)	Grey Sovereign
			Isetta
	Cider Princess (ch 1971)	Alcide (b 1955)	Alycidon
			Chenille
		Paris Princess (br 1958)	Prince Chevalier
			Viviparus

Tender King was given every opportunity after Goodwood to prove himself
in the top flight, for he was the only English-trained two-year-old to contest
three Group 1 pattern races in 1981. Well though he ran in all three, he
showed himself a few pounds behind the best. In the Prix Morny at Deauville
Tender King started second favourite in a small but select field of five. He
was the chief sufferer from the early bumping that brought Maelstrom Lake's

Windsor Castle Stakes, Ascot—Tender King is clear of Irish challenger Mary Mitsu

Richmond Stakes, Goodwood—Tender King quickens well to win from Cajun (right), End of the Line (dark cap) and Hays (almost hidden)

jockey an eight-day suspension, and did very well to finish fourth, under two lengths behind Green Forest. In the William Hill Middle Park Stakes and the William Hill Dewhurst Stakes at Newmarket Tender King again finished in the frame: in the former he went down by less than two lengths to Cajun, making steady progress into fourth in the closing stages, and in the latter he was third to wide-margin winner Wind and Wuthering, losing second place to Be My Native well inside the final furlong.

Tender King's sire Prince Tenderfoot was best at sprint distances but the majority of his progeny stay a mile or further; they include Tender Heart, with whom the stable won the Royal Hunt Cup in 1980. Tender King is the third foal of his dam, who won over nine furlongs in Ireland. The third dam, out of an unraced half-sister to Musidora, won at up to a mile and produced three winners of note, Paris Princess and Viviptic, both winners of the Beresford Stakes, and Vivi Tarquin, winner of the Gold Vase at Ascot. Paris Princess, Tender King's second dam, was a smart staying two-year-old, winning the National Stakes at the Curragh. Tender King should stay a mile, held up to do so; his best performances in 1981 were produced with waiting tactics. Tender King has shown his best form on a sound surface. He is a tough, consistent, quite attractive colt, well worth the 8,200 guineas he cost as a yearling. *J. Sutcliffe.*

TENDER NIECE 2 b. or br.f. Prince Tenderfoot 126–Nasty Niece (Great **69** Nephew 126) (1981 5fg 8fg 5s 6d 6d) Feb 27; 12,000Y; first foal; dam won over 7f at 2 yrs in Canada; fifth in large fields for maiden races at Warwick and Leicester at the back end (third and fifth starts); stays 6f; blinkered at Leicester. *J. Spearing.*

TENDER TRADER (USA) 2 ch.g. Our Michael–My Roue (Hilarious) **71** (1981 5fg 5d² 5s 5.8d³ 5g 5d 6fg 6fg²) Feb 12; $7,700Y; resold $20,000Y; strong, useful-looking gelding; good mover; half-brother to several winners, including useful 7f to 1m winner Frisky Ruler (by Golden Ruler); dam won twice up to 7f in USA; quite a moderate maiden; returned to form when heavily-backed favourite for valuable 16-runner seller at Doncaster in September, staying on to finish 3 lengths second to Countach; will be suited by 7f; acts on a firm and a soft surface; sometimes wears bandages or boots in front. *G. Lewis.*

TENDER VENTURE 2 br.g. Prince Tenderfoot 126–Hopeful Maid (Hopeful **88** Venture 125) (1981 5s 6fg⁴ 7fg 7fg 7fg* 7fg) Apr 22; IR 13,000Y; neat gelding; second foal; dam poor half-sister to Irish Sweeps Derby winner Weavers'

TEN

Hall; blinkered, made virtually all and held on under vigorous driving to win 17-runner maiden race at Salisbury in September by a short head from subsequently-disqualified Escapism, easily best effort; didn't wear blinkers next time (well-backed second favourite) and ran poorly; may stay beyond 7f; acts on a firm surface. *G. Pritchard-Gordon.*

TENEA 2 b.f. Reform 132–Stilvi 126 (Derring-Do 131) (1981 6g) Apr 9: — p useful-looking filly; sixth foal; half-sister to 5 winners, all at least smart, notably 1,000 Guineas second Tolmi (by Great Nephew), Middle Park winner and 2,000 Guineas second Tachypous (by Hotfoot), top 1978 2-y-o Tromos (by Busted) and Irish Sweeps Derby winner Tyrnavos (by Blakeney); dam extremely speedy and game performer; third favourite, never threatened leaders but was beaten less than 6 lengths when sixth of 11 to Master Cawston in Ribero Stakes at Doncaster in September; will stay 1m; sure to do better at 3 yrs. *B. Hobbs.*

TENNIS TRACK 3 br.f. Track Spare 125–Get Set 65 (Stupendous) (1980 6s 47 7s 7d 6s 6g 7d 8d 1981 7g 8g 8f 13g 10g 10g³ 9g⁴ 11s*) lightly-made filly; plater; sold 3,500 gns after beating Decoy Lad a length at Wolverhampton; stays 11f; trained first 7 starts by R. Mason. *R. Hollinshead.*

TENNYSON COUNTRY 2 b.c. Sandford Lad 133–En Famille (Alcide 136) — (1981 6fg 7fg) May 14; neat, attractive colt; good walker and mover; half-brother to winners in France and Italy, including 1981 3-y-o Rilo (by Sassafras); dam once-raced half-sister to Great Nephew; behind in sizeable fields of maidens at Newmarket in June (16/1) and Yarmouth in August (20/1); sold 500 gns Ascot September Sales. *M. Stoute.*

TENORIA 4 ch.f. Mansingh 120–Ibozia 73 (Mossborough 126) (1980 8h 54 8fg 11.7s⁴ 11.7s² 11.7g 11d² 10.6d* 12fg³ 1981 12fg 12s 12d³ 12.5s³ 12g⁴ 16.9s 15.5d³ 14f⁴ 15.5fg) small filly; stays well; suited by some give in the ground; blinkered final start; twice hasn't looked too enthusiastic; sold 2,500 gns Newmarket July Sales. *M. Jarvis.*

TENTH HUSSAR 3 ch.f. Shiny Tenth 120–Floral Palm 69 (Floribunda 136) — (1980 5fg 6s 5fg 6f 5fg⁴ 5g 1981 6f 8f 6g 5g 10.8s) big, lengthy filly; quite a moderate maiden on the balance of her form; blinkered last 2 starts. *Peter Taylor.*

TENTH OF OCTOBER 2 b.c. Shiny Tenth 120–Seam 100 (Nearula 132) 96 (1981 5d³ 5d* 5g* 5s* 5g 6s⁴ 6fg 7d* 8fg 8s 7s) Mar 23; 2,700Y; useful sort; half-brother to several winners, including smart 1966 staying 2-y-o Slip Stitch (by Parthia); dam a miler; ridden by 5-lb claimer when running on strongly to win maiden race at Warwick in April, minor events at Bath and Windsor in May and nursery at Lingfield in August; top weight, held off Razor Sun by ¾ length in last-named; stays 7f (had stiff tasks both outings over 1m); best form with some give in the ground; blinkered final outing (didn't move well to start and ran moderately). *S. Mellor.*

TEN-TRACO 2 b.f. Forlorn River 124–Cithern 91 (Canisbay 120) (1981 87 5d*(dis) 5d* 5fg³ 6fg* 6d 7s 6fg² 6s* 7s⁴ 6s) Jan 30; 700F; workmanlike filly; third living produce; dam, half-sister to smart 1¼m to 13f winner Zimbalon, won over 7f at 2 yrs; retained for 1,700 gns and 1,200 gns respectively after winning sellers at Leicester and Wolverhampton in the spring; disqualified in August from her Leicester win after traces of caffeine and theobromine were found in her system; proved better than a plater, winning nurseries at Windsor in July (by a neck from Red Ellette) and Ascot in September (valuable Golden Gates Nursery, beat El Mansour by ¾ length); best form at 6f; seems to act on any going; consistent and very genuine. *D. H. Jones.*

TENTWORT 4 ch.f. Shiny Tenth 120–Pinguicula (Pinza 137) (1980 8h 13s 76 d 12g² 14.6d* 1981 12s⁴ 15g² 16g 16f² 15g³ 14.7fg⁴ 14d 17f 16s⁴ 18g³ 18g³) lengthy filly; stays well; acts on any going but seems suited by some give in the ground. *W. Elsey.*

TEQUILLA SUNRISE (FR) 2 b.f. Nonoalco 131–Treacle 85 (Hornbeam 130) 79 p (1981 7g²) rather leggy, useful-looking filly; half-sister to several winners, including useful Ivory Girl (by Sir Ivor), a winner at up to 1½m; dam, half-sister to Darling Boy, won twice at 1¼m; 20/1, kept on well when 2½ lengths second of 16 to Clymene in maiden race at Leicester in October; will stay 1¼m; has the scope to improve. *P. Walwyn.*

TERESILLA (FR) 4 gr.f. High Echelon–Tarakanova (Bold Lad USA) (1980 — 12f 12.3f 12h² 12f² 12.2fg⁴ 12d⁴ 12g 12.3d³ 11.7fg* 12.2fg 13g* 10d² 16s 1981

10.5d 12g 13.1f 12fg 16h 12g)   lightly-made filly; fair handicapper at her best; not disgraced first start but ran moderately afterwards; stays 13f; seems to act on any going; trained part of season by R. Sheather. *M. Blanshard.*

TESORO MIO   6 b.h. Cavo Doro 124–Captive Flower 99 (Manacle 123)   (1980   **94** 10.6fg² 10f⁴ 12g 10.5g 10fg³ 10fg 10.6d³ 10d   1981 9g² 10fg 10.5g 10g³ 10fg 12d* 10fg 13d 12g 12g³)   fair sort; fairly useful at his best; won going away by 1½ lengths from Canton Lightning in £9,000 handicap at Newmarket in August; suited by 1¼m; seems to act on any going but goes well on top-of-the-ground; suited by a strong gallop; usually held up; blinkered nowadays. *J. Etherington.*

TESTING TIMES (USA)   3 br.g. Olden Times–Fierce Ruffian (What A   **§§** Pleasure)   (1980 6g⁴ 6d 5g⁴ 6fg 6g⁴ 5g   1981 7fg 10.1v 6d)   strong, compact gelding; ran a good first race at Royal Ascot as a 2-y-o but hasn't fulfilled his promise; has been tried in blinkers; one to leave severely alone. *A. Pitt.*

TESTON LAD   4 b.g. Blast 125–Right On Time 78 (Right Boy 137)   (1980   **—** 9f 6d⁴ 6s² 7g 6fg 6f³ 7f³ 8s 6d   1981 6d 6d 7fg 7fg)   lengthy, fair sort; plating-class maiden; best at 6f or 7f; acts on any going. *P. K. Mitchell.*

TEXAS GOLD   2 ch.g. Dragonara Palace 115–Concisely (Connaught 130)   **—** (1981 5fg 6d)   Apr 4; 4,500Y; big gelding; first foal; dam unraced half-sister to very useful Giriama; behind in maiden race at Warwick in April and seller at Lingfield (blinkered) in August. *P. Cole.*

THAHUL (USA)   4 b.c. Nijinsky 138–Queen City Miss (Royal Union)   (1980   **67** 13.3fg 12s 14g² 16f³ 13g⁴ 12s   1981 15.5d 13.1g 14d* 16.1f* 16fg³ 16.1d 14fg) deep-girthed, rangy colt; good walker; won maiden race at Sandown in June and handicap at Haydock in July; needs a test of stamina; probably acts on any going; often blinkered; suited by a galloping track; genuine; ran poorly sixth start. *F. J. Houghton.*

THAI ANNA   3 b.f. Amber Rama 133–Brevity 76 (Pindari 124)   (1980 5h   **—** 5d 5f*   1981 5fg 5f)   plater; well beaten in 1981; none too well away twice as a 2-y-o; sold 1,600 gns Newmarket July Sales. *I. Vickers.*

THAI KING   3 b.c. Tower Walk 130–Miss Bangkok (Sovereign Path 125)   **66** (1980 NR   1981 6s² 6g² 6s* 6fg 7f 6fg⁴ 6s 6d 6d)   quite a useful sort; not a particularly good mover; second foal; half-brother to very useful sprinter Great Eastern (by Jukebox); dam never ran; apprentice ridden when beating Dewberry by ¾ length in maiden event at Haydock in May (won comfortably despite tending to wander in front); also in frame at Leicester (dwelt), Pontefract and Ayr; will probably stay 7f; acts on a firm surface but is well suited by some give in the ground; behind when blinkered eighth start; sold 4,500 gns Newmarket Autumn Sales. *W. Hastings-Bass.*

Owens Group of New Zealand Handicap, Newmarket—Northern challenger Tesoro Mio wins this valuable event from Canton Lightning (grey) and John O'Groats

THARSUS GIRL 2 br.f. Blakeney 126–Just Larking (Sea-Bird II 145) (1981   **66**
6f 6g 7fg 8fg 10s) Mar 18; IR 6,000Y; lightly-made filly; third living foal; dam
won at up to 1m in USA and is daughter of very useful Just Kidding; showed
a little ability in maiden races in the North; will be very well suited by 1¼m and
more. *P. Rohan.*

THATCHCOMBE 3 b.c. Thatch 136–Coulomb 108 (Crepello 136) (1980 NR   **—**
1981 7fg 8g 9s 10s) 16,000Y; strong, compact colt; good walker; half-brother
to 9.4f winner Concern (by Brigadier Gerard) and a winner in Belgium; dam
miler; unquoted and still in need of race when about 8 lengths fifth of 16 behind
St Pedro in maiden race at Newmarket in April on second start; should stay
1¼m; possibly needs a sound surface; sold 775 gns Ascot 2nd June Sales. *P.
Walwyn.*

THATCHING TIME 4 b.c. Thatch 136–Boscage 104 (Queen's Hussar 124)   **—**
(1980 8f 7fg 8g 7d4 7d* 7g 7d 1981 8g 7f4 7fg 7g 7fg 8fg 8fg 10f) strong, well-
made colt; poor performer nowadays; beaten in a seller on seventh outing; best
at 7f; seems to act on any going; often blinkered at 3 yrs; highly-strung; sold
1,050 gns Newmarket Autumn Sales. *P. Cole.*

THAT'S MAGIC 3 ch.f. Bay Express 132–Alumina 86 (Fortino II 120) (1980   **73**
5fg2 5g 5fg 5s2 5d 5d3 6g2 6s2 5d2 1981 6g 6g 7f* 7f 7f 7.2fg 7g 7g 6g 7g) neat
filly; beat Kanchenjunga in tremendous style by 5 lengths in maiden race at
Thirsk in July; didn't reproduce that form, being tried twice in blinkers; suited
by 7f; acts on any going; sold to J. Parkes only 400 gns Doncaster November Sales.
J. Etherington.

THAT'S MY SON 2 b.c. Busted 134–Take a Chance (Baldric II 131) (1981   **97**
6f 7fg 7fg 6g 7g3 8d) Apr 6; 06,000Y; big, strong, attractive colt; good walker;
half-brother to 3 minor winners; dam won Prix Yacowlef and is sister to outstanding Australian sire Without Fear; showed much improved form when ridden
from behind on last 2 starts, running on well to finish 4½ lengths third of 16 to
Wind and Wuthering in Somerville Tattersall Stakes at Newmarket and finishing
ninth of 13 to Count Pahlen in William Hill Futurity at Doncaster, both in
October; bred to stay middle distances; a grand individual with plenty of scope
who is capable of winning races in his own class. *C Brittain.*

THAUMATURGE 3 b.c. Thatch 136–Grecian Craft 90 (Acropolis 132) (1980   **66**
7f 8fg 1981 12g 10f 16d3 12f4 12f3 15.5f* 13.1h3 14fg4 16g 13.3s) strong colt;
won maiden race at Folkestone in August; needs a test of stamina; probably
acts on any going; usually wears blinkers nowadays. *R. Smyth.*

THE ADRIANSTAN 6 ch.g. Sparkler 130–Riberta 89 (Ribot 142) (1980   **—**
8d 8d 8d 1981 10s 11s) useful handicapper at his best but is completely
unreliable; stays 1¼m; acts on any going; has been tried in blinkers; sometimes
starts slowly; not an easy ride. *D. Hanley.*

THE AZADSTAN 3 gr.g. Saritamer 130–The Dupecat 75 (Javelot 124) (1980   **55**
NR 1981 8g 10g 8g 7g2 8f2 7fg4 8d) quite attractive gelding; close second in
seller at Catterick and claimer at Brighton in June; worth trying at 1¼m again;
wears blinkers nowadays; sold 2,200 gns Ascot October Sales. *J. Sutcliffe.*

THE BAKER 11 ch.g. Super Sam 124–Azizah (Zarathustra 131) (1980 NR   **—**
1981 16.1s) probably of little account on flat nowadays. *J. Yardley.*

THE BARONS LODGE 3 b.g. The Brianstan 128–Villa Vera (Gilles de Retz   **68**
132) (1980 6g 5fg* 5.1fg 6f 6g 1981 7d 6s3 7fg2 6g) compact gelding; plater;
stays 7f; probably acts on any going; blinkered last 2 starts; exported to Hong
Kong. *P. Haslam.*

THE BEGINNING 3 ro.f. Goldhill 125–Histoun (Behistoun 131) (1980 NR   **46**
1981 6g 5f 7.2f 8g3 9g 8f 8fg3 8.2s3 9s) 500F; fair sort; sister to a poor plater who
later won in Isle of Man; dam poor maiden; placed in sellers; suited by 1m.
C. Booth.

THE BYSTANDER 2 b.c. Owen Anthony 102–Pearl River (Bourbon Prince)   **—**
(1981 5d) May 13; smallish, lengthy colt; third reported foal; half-brother
to a winning plater by Grisaille; dam winning sprinter in Australia; unquoted
but looking well, showed signs of greenness on way to start when eighth of 15
behind Avonmore Wind in maiden event at Wolverhampton in October. *J. Holt.*

THE CAIRNWELL 2 b.f. Mount Hagen 127–Deep Company 94 (Carnival   **76**
Dancer 113) (1981 5s2 5g 5fg3 5.8h2 5g4 5s2) Mar 19; 4,800F, resold 4,700Y;
rangy filly; fourth foal; sister to Salona, placed at up to 7f as a 2-y-o in 1978;
dam won over 5f and 6f at 2yrs and comes from same family as King's Company,
Deep Diver and Baby Brew; in frame in auction event and maiden races; stays
6f; acts on any going. *H. T. Jones.*

THE CEIRIOG 6 ch.m. Deep Diver 134–La Foire II 90 (Arabian) (1980 12fg 13.4g³ 1981 15.8g) fair sort; staying maiden; acts on any going; has worn blinkers and bandages. *J. Yardley.* —

THE CLEAVER 5 br.g. Status Seeker–Sayann (Sayajirao 132) (1980 NR 1981 17.1d) lightly raced on flat nowadays; stays 1½m; best with some give in the ground. *K. Lewis.* —

THE CLIFTONIAN 3 b.c. Firestreak 125–Ile de France 84 (French Beige 127) (1980 5.8fg³ 6s² 6s 6g 8.2g³ 8g 1981 10.1d* 10.1v* 10g 10.1f 10f⁴ 10g) lengthy, useful-looking colt; won 2 minor events at Windsor in May, beating Danlifar by 2 lengths on first occasion and Suzy's Pal very easily by 3 lengths on second; had stiffish tasks in handicaps most subsequent starts; will stay 1½m; acts on heavy going; none too consistent. *R. Hannon.* **84 d**

THE DICE MAN (USA) 2 ch.c. Key To The Mint–Bases Loaded (Northern Dancer) (1981 7g⁴) Mar 11; $110,000Y; shapely colt; fifth foal; half-brother to 3-y-o Silent Basis (by Silent Screen), a stakes-placed winner at up to 6f at 2 yrs; dam won over 7f in USA; easy third favourite and in need of race, ran on again close home after losing place 2f out to be 4 lengths fourth of 18 to Leg Glance in maiden event at Doncaster in October; will be suited by 1m or more; wasn't given a hard time of it here and should do better in 1982. *H. Cecil.* **81 p**

THE DINMONT 2 b.c. Mummy's Pet 125–Veronique 96 (Matador 131) (1981 6fg⁴ 6g* 6fg) Mar 27; robust, good sort; brother to smart sprinter The Pug, closely related to very smart sprinter Music Boy (by Jukebox) and half-brother to 2 winners; dam sprinter; won 5-runner Rous Memorial Stakes at Goodwood in August in style of a very useful colt, leading throughout and quickening in really good style to win by 2½ lengths from General Anders; odds on, eased after sustaining a suspected fracture of his off-fore 2f out when 9 lengths fifth of 11 to Foam Bath in £3,300 race at Salisbury later in month; reportedly will be back in training in 1982. *J. Dunlop.* **98**

THE DISCO DAGO 3 ch.g. Record Token 128–Repel (Hardicanute 130) (1980 NR 1981 10d² 10fg⁴ 12.2g³ 12s⁴) small, workmanlike gelding; fourth living foal; dam never ran; in frame in maiden and minor races in second half of season; gives impression he'll stay further than 1½m. *G. Pritchard-Gordon.* **67**

THE DISSIDENT 3 b.c. Lyphard 132–Siraf 85 (Alcide 136) (1980 7g² 1981 8d) attractive, useful-looking colt; second in maiden race at Newmarket as a 2-y-o; favourite, showed good speed before finishing out of first 9 of 26 behind Neat in similar race at Newbury in April; will stay 1¼m; sold 3,000 gns Newmarket Autumn Sales. *H. Cecil.* —

THE DOWNS 5 b.g. Blast 125–Princess Lorna 63 (Royal Palm 131) (1980 9.5f 7g 8g² 9g² 8d² 8g 8g* 1981 8g 8d 10f 8.3d 8.3g 7g) ex-Irish gelding; plater; stays 9f; acts on soft going; blinkered twice in 1980; has sweated up. *H. O'Neill.* **43**

THE ESCAPER (USA) 5 b.g. Ack Ack–Psychedelic Dream (Carry Back) (1980 8s 10s 1981 13f⁴) big, rangy gelding; poor maiden on balance of form; suited by 13f; sold 825 gns Ascot October Sales. *D. Kent.* —

THE FLOORLAYER 3 b.g. Import 127–Lonely Nymph 60 (Forlorn River 124) (1980 5g 5d 7s 1981 5f 10.1fg 8fg 11.7h) little worthwhile form over a wide range of distances. *D. Elsworth.* —

THE FRIEND 3 ch.c. Run The Gantlet–Loose Cover 106 (Venture VII 129) (1980 8g 1981 8d* 8.2s³ 10f 12fg 12fg 12g³ 13d 16s⁴) lightly-made, quite attractive colt; poor walker; 20/1 when beating stable-companion Ramannolie a neck in 24-runner maiden event at Warwick in May; third behind easy winner Herbie Quayle in minor event at Haydock and behind Karadar in £4,700 handicap at Goodwood afterwards; seems to stay 2m; possibly unsuited by very firm going; blinkered nowadays *H. T. Jones.* **77**

THE GANGER MAN 2 b.g. Crash Course 128–Black Gnat (Typhoon 125) (1981 7fg 8s 6s) Feb 26; IR 6,800Y; lengthy, heavy-topped gelding; half-brother to 4 winners here and abroad, including 1977 2-y-o 5f winner The Gate (by On Your Mark); dam won 7 times from 5f to 9f in Ireland; no worthwhile form in maiden races in the autumn. *R. Hannon.* —

THE GOLDSTONE 9 ch.g. Murrayfield 119–Delph 89 (Final Score 113) (1980 10.2d 8s⁴ 8fg 11d⁴ 1981 10s* 12.2d 8fg 8d 10s² 10v 10f) poor handicapper nowadays; won at Leicester in March; stays 11f; acts on any going; has been tried in blinkers; suitable mount for an inexperienced rider. *W. Wightman.* **52**

THE GOVERNOR (FR) 2 ch.c. Grundy 137–Cley 85 (Exbury 138) (1981 7d) —
big colt; fourth foal; half-brother to 3 winners, including 3-y-o 1½m and 13f winner
Bodham (by Bustino) and French 12.5f winner Habey (by Habat); dam, 1½m
winner, is half-sister to Blakeney and Morston; 33/1, always struggling when
distant seventh of 8 to Montekin in £4,800 event at Goodwood in September;
will need a stiff test of stamina. *J. Dunlop.*

THE GRADER 3 ch.f. Master Sing 109–Full Swing 71 (Ballyciptic 122) —
(1980 NR 1981 5fg 6f 5g) second reported living foal; dam, half-sister to
smart Lord Helpus, won over 5f at 2 yrs; last in maiden races at Lingfield (2)
and Folkestone. *J. Long.*

THE GROCKALL 3 ch.f. Balidar 133–Laarne (Le Haar 126) (1980 7g 8d 8d —
1981 10.1fg 10.2h 12g 16s³ 15s) quite well-made filly; about 16 lengths third
of 15 behind Aniece in handicap at Warwick in October, only form of year;
evidently stays 2m. *R. Laing.*

THE HERTFORD 10 b.g. Supreme Sovereign 119–Emerald Velvet 7b —
(Sheshoon 132) (1980 10.2d 10s 10fg 12s 11.7d 1981 10s) unreliable and
of little account nowadays; sold 560 gns Doncaster October Sales. *N. Gaselee.*

THE HOOLEE 3 ch.f. Four Burrow 91–Primasilia 76 (Romulus 129) (1980 —
6fg 7g 1981 14.6fg 10.6d 10.4d 10fg) leggy filly; in rear in maiden races and
seems of little account. *R. Hollinshead.*

THE HUYTON GIRLS 3 ch.f. Master Sing 109–Artway 82 (Articulate 121) **67**
(1980 5d 5d 5d 5s 5s 6d 1981 6v³ 5d* 5g³ 5s* 5d* 6f 5fg 5fg 5d 5s 5s 5s) fair
sort; improved and won maiden event and handicap at Wolverhampton and
another handicap at Sandown in first half of year; well beaten afterwards (out
of her depth sixth start and off course 2 months before tenth), best form at
5f but not disgraced over 6f; acts on soft going; often apprentice ridden. *M.
James.*

THE IMMIGRANT 4 b.g. Martinmas 128–Seul 69 (Faberge II 121) (1980 —
8d 10.1f 10fg 12g 8d 11d 1981 6s 7g 10fg 8f⁴ 8fg) leggy, narrow gelding; poor
plater; stays 1m; seems to act on any going; has been tried in blinkers; has
worn bandages. *K. Ivory.*

THE KNIFE 3 b.g. Fine Blade 121–Mary Kanga 67 (Charlottesville 135) (1980 **60**
5.8fg 5f 7s 7d 7fg 8fg 7fg 1981 8fg 11.7g 11.7g 8f³ 8f² 8fg² 8.3fg) small, lightly-
made gelding; plater; placed at Wolverhampton, Bath and Leicester in summer;
should stay further than 1m; occasionally blinkered. *J. Bosley.*

THE LONDONER 2 b.g. Hittite Glory 125–Foxhorn (Hornbeam 130) (1981 —
7g) May 3; 3,900F, 7,400Y; half-brother to 2 winners, including fair 1980 2-y-o
5f to 7f performer Horncastle (by Hornbeam); dam never ran; 33/1 when well
behind in 18-runner maiden race won by Puff of Smoke at Salisbury in July.
G. Balding.

THE MIXER 4 b.c. Biskrah 121–Full Swing 71 (Ballyciptic 122) (1980 16s —
12g 10.1f 10fg 15.5g 8s 1981 10d 8.3s 7s 7fg 15.5f) strong, good sort; poor
plater; often blinkered. *J. Long.*

THE MUTINEER 3 b.c. Pitcairn 126–Pallet (Pall Mall 132) (1980 NR —
1981 8g 10g 12d) 6,200Y; workmanlike colt; third foal; half-brother to useful
1979 2-y-o sprinter Art Bidder (by Auction Ring); dam won over 1½m in Ireland;
well beaten in maiden races; sold 400 gns Newmarket Autumn Sales. *R.
Hollinshead.*

THE NEUROLOGIST 3 ch.f. Ragstone 128–Flower Centre 98 (Jaipur) (1980 **114**
5f 5fg³ 6fg* 6f 7g⁴ 10v* 8g 1981 9d 14g³ 12s* 14f³ 12fg² 12fg 12d* 16d* 12d*)
1,800Y; second foal; closely related to 5f and 8.3f winner Stamen (by Ballymore);
dam won twice over 1m at 2 yrs; improved and developed into a
very useful filly, on final start beating Overplay by 5 lengths in Trigo Stakes
at Leopardstown in October; had beaten Potato Merchant by 2½ lengths in
30-runner Irish Cesarewitch on the Curragh earlier in month and had previously
won handicaps at Mallow and Listowel; stays well; acts on any going. *E.
O'Grady, Ireland.*

THE NIDD 2 b.f. Rapid River 127–Molly Mayfield (Clear River 114) (1981 —
5g) May 16; third foal; unquoted when behind in 21-runner minor event won
by Begham Bay at Catterick in September. *C. Thornton.*

THE NUB 2 br.c. Mr Bigmore 123–Sun Queen 76 (Lucky Sovereign) (1981 **97**
7fg 7fg⁴ 8s³ 8d*) Apr 1; strong, workmanlike colt; has a round action; fourth
foal; half-brother to successful sprinter Swelter (by Tickled Pink); dam sprinter;

left his previous form behind when tried over 1m, staying on well to finish 2½ lengths third of 12 to Jalmood in £3,300 event at Goodwood in September and beating Boukayr by 3 lengths in 15-runner maiden race at Bath in October (favourite); will be suited by 1½m; acts well on soft going. *F. Durr.*

THE OLD FELLER 5 gr.g. Starch Reduced 112–Spanish Gal (El Gallo 122) **49 d**
(1980 8s 8g 7fg 7f* 6s* 6g 6g 7g 6g 7fg 6s 6s 1981 6s 6s² 7fg 6s 8fg 7f 6f 7fg 6fg 8.3d 8f 6g) plater; best at 6f and 7f (doesn't stay 1m); acts on any going; usually wears blinkers; has run creditably for an apprentice; sold 1,150 gns Ascot August Sales. *K. Ivory.*

THEO'S BABY 3 ch.f. Lombard 126–Anatevka (Privy Councillor 125) (1980 —
5s 5g⁴ 5fg 8.2g 1981 12g 12f 12g 10.6s) narrow, leggy filly; poor maiden; pulled very hard when behind in a seller third start. *F. Durr.*

THE OWLS 2 b. or br.g. Pieces of Eight 128–Keino (Kautokeino) (1981 **72**
6fg 6g 7fg⁴ 7.6fg⁴ 8.2s 8g 8d) Mar 27; narrow, workmanlike gelding; second foal; dam never ran; fourth in maiden race at Catterick and nursery at Lingfield prior to finishing close-up fifth of 18 to Indian Call in £2,500 seller at Newmarket in October on sixth start; will stay 1¼m+ ; probably acts on any going; ran badly in blinkers final outing; sold 410 gns Ascot November Sales. *M. Tompkins.*

THE PAIN BARRIER 2 b.c. Blakeney 126–Vilswitch 93 (Vilmorin) (1981 **77 p**
7fg⁴) Mar 21; good-bodied, quite attractive colt; half-brother to smart sprinter Vilgora (by Raffingora) and useful 1978 2-y-o Ghazal (by Averof); dam sprinter; 25/1, wasn't given a hard time when staying-on 6½ lengths fourth of 10 to Old Country in £3,100 event at Goodwood in September; will stay middle distances; will do better. *J. Sutcliffe.*

THE PARROT 2 b.g. Pampapaul 121–Puka (Parthia 132) (1981 6d 7fg 7fg³ **77**
7d³) Apr 14; 26,000Y; rangy, quite attractive gelding; closely related to fair Irish stayer Nitucket (by Yellow God), and half-brother to 3-y-o 1½m winner Fitzgayle (by Lord Gayle) and a good winner in Japan by Northfields; dam never ran; blinkered when third twice in August, beaten 4 lengths by Tulsa Flyer in £2,600 event at Salisbury and 6½ lengths by Crimson Knight in maiden race at Chester; gelded subsequently; will be suited by middle distances. *J. Tree.*

THE POLCHAR 3 b.g. Tudor Rhythm 112–Mary Newall 69 (Coronation Year —
124) (1980 6g⁴ 6g 1981 8.2s 9g 8g 6d 8.3fg 8d) lengthy, fair sort; plater; gives impression he may be suited by 1½m+ ; wore bandages at 2 yrs; blinkered final start; sold 420 gns Ascot August Sales and won over hurdles after being tubed. *R. Carter.*

THE PRIMATE 2 gr.c. Godswalk 130–Silver Bullion (Silver Shark 129) (1981 **105**
5v* 5g² 5s³ 5fg² 5fg² 5g²)
We didn't see The Primate at his best in the Lily Agnes Stakes at Chester in May on his only visit to England. His form in that race, two and a half lengths behind the easy winner Jester who was giving him 6 lb, bears no resemblance to his useful form in Ireland.

			Dancer's Image		Native Dancer
	Godswalk		(gr 1965)		Noors Image
	(gr 1974)		Kate's Intent		Intentionally
The Primate			(b 1964)		Julie Kate
(gr.c. Apr 17, 1979)			Silver Shark		Buisson Ardent
	Silver Bullion		(gr 1963)		Palsaka
	(b 1969)		Bullen		King of the Tudors
			(ch 1956)		Ratho

The Primate turned out on the very first day of the Irish season in the Castrol Maiden Stakes at Phoenix Park, becoming the first Northern Hemisphere runner by Godswalk, a stallion who had himself made his debut in the race five years earlier. Whereas Godswalk finished only third his son, a short-priced favourite, made all in the heavy ground and won by three quarters of a length from Wolverbee. The Primate looked sure to win more races, but in fact he went through the rest of the season without a further success. Another decisive defeat followed soon after Chester when he finished only third to Day Is Done in the Marble Hill Stakes and he was then given a nine-week break. He came back a much better colt. Indeed only three good youngsters from Vincent O'Brien's stable prevented his winning two pattern races, the Group 3 Curragh Stakes and the Group 1 Gallaghouse Phoenix Stakes, and a listed race at the Curragh, the Goffs Two-Year-Old Stakes. He ran the same race on each of the three occasions, coming to the distance in the lead only to be cut down in the closing stages—by Peterhof, Achieved and Americus respectively, by half a length, a short head and a length; on each occasion he easily accounted for the other runners. Perhaps one of the reasons for his improved displays was the faster ground; he acts on heavy going, but he seems to stay better on good to firm.

The Primate isn't much to look at, being both small and rather lightly made, and he fetched only 4,000 guineas as a yearling in Ireland, 6,000 guineas less than he'd been sold for there the previous year. He's the second winner from Silver Bullion's first six foals, following the fairly useful St Alphage sprinter The Sign Centre who is now racing with success in Malaya. Silver Bullion is an unraced half-sister to the very useful sprinter Smooth, winner of the Molecomb Stakes, as well as the fairly useful miler Tracker and three other winners. His grandam Bullen failed to win but her dam Ratho won five races, four of them over sprint distances. It would be a major surprise if The Primate were to turn out anything other than a sprinter himself; indeed it's doubtful whether he'll be fully effective over six furlongs. The Primate is now trained by Weld, having been sold out of Connolly's stable after the Phoenix Stakes. Weld has met with a lot of success in the past with such sprinters as Hot Spark, Steel Heart and Red Alert but he faces an uphill task with The Primate; good colt though he is, The Primate found it difficult enough to win races at two and the opportunities for a five-furlong sprinter in Ireland are distinctly limited outside handicap company. *D. Weld, Ireland.*

THE PROFESSOR 4 br.g. Welsh Pageant 132–Pulchra 107 (Celtic Ash) — (1980 9g³ 10fg² 10fg² 10d³ 12g 12.3s³ 12f²(dis) 15.8fg² 14.7f* 1981 13.8fg 14.6f⁴ 15.8fg 16.1fg) tall gelding; stays well; probably acts on any going, blinkered final start; gives impression he needs strong handling; sold 2,800 gns Newmarket Autumn Sales. *J. W. Watts.*

THE QUIET BIDDER 3 b.c. Auction Ring 123–Capule (Middleground) **115** (1980 6g* 6fg* 6s³ 5f³ 5g² 1981 7g² 8g 6s 7.2s³ 6f* 6.5fg 7.3fg) quite useful sort; half-brother to 3 winners, including fairly useful 1975 2-y-o 6f and 7f winner El Capitan (by Captain's Gig), subsequently successful in Belgium and France; dam minor 2-y-o 5f winner in USA; gained a well-deserved success in 16-runner Cork and Orrery Stakes at Royal Ascot in June, getting up close home to beat Crews Hill by ½ length; in frame earlier in Tote European Free Handicap at Newmarket (1½ lengths second to Motavato) and John of Gaunt Stakes at Haydock (1½ lengths third to Last Fandango); also ran well in between, including when about 7 lengths eighth of 19 behind To-Agori-Mou in 2,000 Guineas at Newmarket; didn't run up to his best in Prix Maurice de Gheest at

Cork and Orrery Stakes, Ascot—The Quiet Bidder (No. 15) gets the better of Crews Hill with Integrity and Welshwyn (neither shown) close behind

Deauville or Hungerford Stakes at Newbury, both in August, on last 2 starts; effective at 6f and stays 1m; acts on any going; genuine; to be trained by M. Stoute. *R. Hollinshead.*

THE RECESSION 3 ch.f. Redundant 120–Grandaire 65 (Grand Roi 118) — (1980 NR 1981 6g) third foal; dam won 6f seller at 2 yrs; looked fit when tailed-off last of 14 behind Bracadale in apprentice event at Nottingham in August. *B. McMahon.*

THE RED DUKE 2 ch.c. Red Alert 127–Dutchess of Man (Petingo 135) 81 ? (1981 6g 8g⁴ 8s²) Feb 20; 4,600F, 3,200Y; big, strong colt; first produce; dam well beaten on all 3 outings; made up a fair bit of ground in straight when 7 lengths fourth of 15 behind Sagamore in maiden race at Beverley in September; again put in best work in closing stages when 4 lengths second to easy winner Bancario in 6-runner minor event at Newcastle the following month; runs as though 1¼m will suit him; has scope and should win a race in the North at 3 yrs. *R. D. Peacock.*

THE RIPLEYITE 2 ch.c. Northfields–Red Ruby 113 (Tudor Melody 129) 73 (1981 5g 6g 6g 7fg³ 6fg 6fg⁴ 6f⁴ 7g³ 7d) Feb 15; IR 20,000Y; quite attractive colt; first foal; dam, half-sister to smart sprinter Laser Light, was very useful miler; quite moderate form in varied company; probably finds 6f on sharp side nowadays and will stay 1m; probably acts on any going. *G. Balding.*

THE RUGBY CLUB (USA) 4 ch.g. Giacometti 130–Blabla 118 (Lavandin 128) 88 (1980 5g 9f* 9g 8d 7g 1981 10g* 10d 9g⁴ 8.5f 8.5f* 10fg⁴ 10fg* 10g) robust, short-legged, useful-looking ex-Irish gelding; won apprentice races at Navan in May, Galway in July (both handicaps) and Leicester in September; will stay 1¼m; suited by top-of-the-ground; trained by D. Hughes part of season. *D. Morley.*

THE SCREENING 2 ch.c. Touch Paper 113–Bermuda 81 (Doutelle 128) 78 (1981 5d 5f³ 5fg 6d 6v) May 19; 8,000Y; compact colt; good walker; half-brother to Irish 3-y-o 5f winner Moorebay (by Manado) and winners in USA and Sweden, including Swedish 1,000 Guineas winner Kreta (by Acropolis); dam won over 1m and 1¼m; 2 lengths third of 18 to Never So Lucky in minor event at Windsor in June, best effort; should be suited by 6f; pulled up fifth outing. *R. Price.*

THE SERGEANT 9 br.g. King's Troop 118–Sincerity 91 (Soderini 123) — (1980 8g 1981 8g) rangy gelding; of little account nowadays. *J. Carr.*

THE SMALL MIRACLE 3 gr.c. Most Secret 119–Grey Aglow 89 (Aglojo 119) 77 (1980 5f 5fg 7f 6g 8.2v* 8s* 7v 1981 10.7d³ 12d⁴ 10d² 12fg² 11g 10g 10g² 9s² 12s³ 12g² 12d) workmanlike colt; in frame in handicaps most outings and was second at Leicester (twice), Beverley, York and Newmarket; stays 1½m; has run respectably on a firm surface, but revels in the mud; trained by W. Elsey first 6 outings; has run creditably in blinkers. *J. Etherington.*

THE SOLENT 5 ch.g. Exbury 138–West Side Story 127 (Rockefella) (1980 §§ 14s⁴ 1981 12g 12f 20.4fg 15.8g 19g 16f 8g 8g 12d 11d) workmanlike gelding; very useful stayer as a 3-y-o; temperamental nowadays and is best left alone. *D. Chapman.*

THE SURVEYOR 5 br.g. Goldhill 125–Shortino 71 (Fortino II 120) (1980 — 10s 8f 8f⁴ 8g 7g 9d 12d 1981 8.2g) plater; stays 1m; acts on firm going. *R. Hollinshead.*

THETCHU 3 b.g. Averof 123–Cavalier's Blush 75 (King's Troop 118) (1980 — 7d 8d 1981 8d 10.2f 9.4fg) fair sort; behind in maiden and minor events. *T. Robson.*

THE THATCHER 3 b.c. Thatch 136–Jolie Fleur 111 (Exbury 138) (1980 — 7fg* 7fg² 1981 8f 10fg) big, strong, good sort; has a good long stride; won minor event at Yarmouth as a 2-y-o; had stiff task, possibly needed race and had difficulty getting a run when promising eighth of 18 behind Olympic Glory in Britannia Stakes (Handicap) at Royal Ascot in June; had another stiff task when sixth of 9 behind Indian Trail in Extel Stakes (Handicap) at Goodwood in July, only other outing; joined R. Turnell's stable afterwards; will stay 1¼m; withdrawn after unseating his amateur rider at start and galloping loose at Goodwood in September. *H. Cecil.*

THE TURNED REVENGE 4 ch.g. Sweet Revenge 129–Turnstone 83 (Sea — Hawk II 131) (1980 6h 6fg 8d 10fg 1981 10f 10.1g 12fg) poor plater; best run at 6f on a firm surface; has worn bandages in front. *J. Bridger.*

THE VAGRANT 3 ch.c. Sandford Lad 133–Battlemaid (Captain's Gig) **46**
(1980 5fg 5d   1981 6s 6g³ 6s 6s 7.6g 6f 6f 7f³ 7f² 7f² 8g)   lengthy colt; placed in
3 sellers in August; stays 7f; blinkered nowadays and is not particularly genuine;
sold 400 gns Ascot October Sales.   *G. Lewis.*

THE VIC 5 gr.g. Saritamer 130–Blue Sash 107 (Djebe) (1980 8.2s 12.5s —
1981 10.6s)   poor performer; behind in seller only start in 1981; stayed 9.4f but
not 1¼m; dead.   *S. Nesbitt.*

THE WONDER (FR) 3 br.c. Wittgenstein 123–The Lark (Lanark 123) (1980 **129**
5.5d⁴ 7d* 8g* 9fg³ 10s* 10v*   1981 10.5s* 10.5s² 12g 9.2s* 8f 8f³ 10g)
The Wonder ran respectably, although below his best, for sixth-of-sixteen
placing behind Vayrann in the Champion Stakes at Newmarket in October, lying
handily positioned until outpaced from the Dip.   He finished seven lengths
down on his compatriot.   Beforehand fears had been expressed that he mightn't
be in sufficiently good form to do himself justice: he hadn't been working well,
apparently.   The Wonder was one of the leading French three-year-olds at a
mile to a mile and a quarter, a good, honest horse though not so able that he would
be expected generally to have an outstanding chance of winning the Champion
Stakes in a normal year.   He had been defeated on five of his six starts during the
season, having gained one of his two wins on the disqualification of No Lute in
the Prix Greffulhe; No Lute had beaten him again next time out in the Prix
Lupin.   The Wonder's best runs in defeat had come behind Northjet in two
of the races that decide the mile championship of Europe, the Prix Jacques le
Marois at Deauville in August and the Prix du Moulin de Longchamp in
September.   The month prior to Deauville The Wonder had staked an early claim
on his own behalf to that mile championship with a cracking performance in
the Group 1 Prix d'Ispahan at Longchamp, winning by two lengths from Northjet,
with Cresta Rider, Cracaval, Hilal, Recitation, Aryenne and four others behind.
But Northjet soon proved beyond reasonable doubt who was the better.   In the
Marois Northjet won by five lengths; The Wonder finished fifth, beaten only a
nose, a head and a nose To-Agori-Mou, Kings Lake and Hilal.   In the
Moulin Northjet broke the track record as he won by a length and a half from
Hilal; The Wonder missed second place by only a nose, running on extremely
gamely under pressure and making up a remarkable amount of ground after
being outpaced.
We have seen most of The Wonder's races and for long enough held the
impression he was essentially a stayer.   We wrote him up as one as a two-year-old
after he'd won two good ten-furlong races in the mud, the Prix de Conde and the
Criterium de Saint-Cloud.   But looking back on his record now it's obvious he's
just as effective at a mile as nine furlongs or ten furlongs, even though he seems
more comfortable racing at the longer distances.   And whether he stays further
than ten is in doubt after his modest showing in the French Derby, in which he
faded two furlongs from home and was eased up to tenth of twelve behind
Bikala.   Significantly he was put straight back to nine furlongs after that.

		Wittgenstein (br 1971)	Roi Dagobert (b 1964)	Sicambre
The Wonder (Fr) (br.c. 1978)				Dame d'Atour
			Stavroula (b 1956)	Nasrullah
				Segula
		The Lark (gr 1972)	Lanark (gr 1963)	Grey Sovereign
				Vermilion O'Toole
			Norman Lass (b 1968)	Timmy Lad
				Golden Glory

The Wonder is by the little-used stallion Wittgenstein, whom one would
expect to sire horses that stay a mile and a half given the right material, out of
a mare by the Gimcrack runner-up Lanark, a horse whom one wouldn't anticipate
being an influence for stamina.   Nevertheless The Lark did stay: she ran thirty

Prix d'Ispahan, Longchamp—The Wonder gains a Group 1 victory over Northjet,
Cresta Rider, Cracaval and Hilal

Mme A. du Breil's "The Wonder"

times on the flat and gained one of her three wins over a mile and three quarters in the French Provinces. The Wonder is her first foal. The second dam, a half-sister to the French Two Thousand Guineas winner Moulines, was a plating-class daughter of the English one-mile winner Golden Glory, a mare by Never Say Die. The Wonder is a tall, lengthy colt, an attractive one who often impresses in the paddock. He acts on any going. *J. de Chevigny, France.*

THIJSSEN 2 ch.c. Habat 127–Kirisana 82 (Darius 129 or Kribi 110) (1981 7g 5s 6s) May 29; 18,500F, 13,000Y; attractive, shapely colt; half-brother to 2 winners, notably top-class sprinter Gentilhombre (by No Mercy); dam won over 13f; finished in good style when 5¾ lengths sixth of 20 to Illicit in 5f maiden race at Warwick in October, second outing and best effort; should be suited by 6f+. *W. O'Gorman.*   **68**

THINK AHEAD 3 b.f. Sharpen Up 127–Regal Splendour 76 (Sovereign Path 125) (1980 5fg* 5h* 5g 6d² 5f² 5f* 5fg* 5s 1981 5v³ 5f 5fg⁴ 5f² 6fg* 6f² 6g* 6g² 6g³) leggy filly; won handicaps at Yarmouth in August and September, beating Casa Esquillina readily by 2 lengths after being held up on second occasion; second in similar races at Ripon in between (started very slowly) and at Newmarket afterwards, staying on very strongly indeed after having difficulty getting a run when going down by 1½ lengths to Scarrowmanwick in 20-runner event on latter course; suited by 6f; acts well on firm going; genuine and consistent. *H. T. Jones.*   **104**

THIRD GENERATION 3 b.f. Decoy Boy 129–Once Removed (Great Nephew 126) (1980 5fg 5.1f 5d 1981 5s³ 5g⁴ 5s 5f 5f 7f 5fg 5g⁴ 5fg 6g) big, leggy filly; plating-class sprint maiden; blinkered fifth outing; started slowly sixth appearance. *H. Collingridge.*   **54**

THIRD REALM 2 b.g. Realm 129–Such Moor 77 (Santa Claus 133) (1981 6fg 5d 6g 6g) Mar 24; IR 13,000Y; compact gelding; sixth foal; half-brother to 4 winners, including fairly useful 6f winners Tarenure (by Targowice) and En Avant (by Sallust); dam won over 1½m; in mid-division in large fields of maidens at Newmarket on first, third and fourth outings; will stay 7f. *F. Durr.*   **—**

THIS ONES FOR YOU 2 b.c. Malacate 131–Spoiled Wine (Pampered King 121) (1981 5s² 5v 6fg 5fg 6f⁴ 7f 6g 6f) Apr 11; IR 1,800Y; lengthy, fair sort; half-brother to several winners; dam won at up to 1½m in Ireland; poor maiden; only eighth of 17 in selling nursery at Ripon on eighth outing; bred to stay 1½m but is headstrong and unlikely to do so. *G. Toft.* **68**

THOMAS NEALE 4 b.c. Manacle 123–Albatross (Petros 118) (1980 NR 1981 8g 8fg 7fg 8s 7f) neat colt; well beaten in varied company; has worn blinkers; sold 280 gns Ascot October Sales. *G. Huffer.* **—**

THORNTON 2 ch.c. Gay Fandango 132–Moorland Song (Mossborough 126) (1981 6g 6f) Apr 11; 8,600Y; rangy colt; half-brother to 3 winners in France and Belgium; dam won over 2m in France at 4 yrs; missed break and was always in rear in maiden races at Newcastle in June and Thirsk (last of 21 finishers) in July. *M. H. Easterby.* **—**

THOUGHTFUL 2 ch.f. Northfields–Wishful Thinking 104 (Petition 130) (1981 6s⁴) Apr 29; well-made, robust filly; half-sister to several winners, including Princess Royal Stakes winner Heavenly Thought (by St Paddy), herself dam of Homing and Water Mill; dam won at 1⅛m and 1½m; 6/1, showed up quite well throughout and wasn't knocked about when 4 lengths fourth of 12 to Dancing Rocks in Blue Seal Stakes at Ascot in September; will be suited by 7f+; a promising debut from a filly who is sure to do better at 3 yrs. *R. Hern.* **81 p**

THREE BARS 6 ch.g. Mountain Call 125–Syncopation (Infatuation 129) (1980 NR 1981 12g 16f) poor maiden. *J. Harris.* **—**

THREE CROWNS 3 b.f. Connaught 130–Soverena 98 (Sovereign Lord 120) (1980 NR 1981 7d* 12f 11s) 29,000Y; strong, well-made filly; half-sister to 3 winners, including very useful middle-distance performer So Royal (by Tudor Melody) and very smart 1975 French staying 2-y-o Luna Real (by Roan Rocket), subsequently successful at up to 1¾m; dam, a sprinter, is half-sister to top-class sprinter Set Fair; 50/1, apprentice ridden at overweight and backward when beating Och Aye by a length in 16-runner maiden race at Sandown in June, coming from a long way back and finding a good turn of speed; had stiff tasks afterwards when tailed off in Lancashire Oaks at Haydock in July and handicap at Newbury in October; will stay at least 1m; acts on a soft surface. *P. Makin.* **69**

THREE DEALERS 2 gr.g. Realm 129–Magna 107 (Runnymede 123) (1981 5s 5s 5d⁴ 5d² 5s* 5g² 5g* 6f 5fg) May 11; IR 3,200Y; neat, rather lightly-made gelding; half-brother to 2 fairly useful winners by Gulf Pearl, namely Burma Pink and Charta Pearl; dam 2-y-o 5f winner; speedy in plating company and made all to win at Wolverhampton and Thirsk in May, attracting no bid after scoring by 5 lengths from Star Cove on latter; form only at 5f with some give in the ground; blinkered third and fourth starts, running well on fourth. *R. Hollinshead.* **68**

THREE DEEP 2 ch.g. Royal Match 117–Tinterne (Tin King 126) (1981 5fg 5.8f 6fg 5f³ 6fg 5g 8.2s) May 22; IR 2,000Y; half-brother to 2 winners, including 1979 2-y-o 5f winner Lupaka (by Red Alert); dam poor maiden; little better than his dam; stays 6f (well beaten in seller over 1m). *W. Wharton.* **61**

THREE JOKERS 2 ch.g. Some Hand 119–Doubtful Request (Cheveley Lad 105) (1981 5g 5fg 6d 5v 5d 5g 5d) May 10; 3,500Y; well-grown, fair sort; brother to 5f winner Five Aces and half-brother to a winner; ran far and away his best race on heavy going, finishing 6 lengths sixth of 21 to Master-Blow in maiden race at Haydock in October; ran poorly in a Catterick seller sixth outing and wore blinkers on seventh. *J. Berry.* **64**

THRICE NIGHTLY 2 ch.f. Gallant Romeo–Zest (Crepello 136) (1981 6s 6s) lengthy, attractive, full-quartered filly; half-sister to several winners, including Oaks winner Ginevra (by Shantung); dam of little account; always behind in Blue Seal Stakes at Ascot and in 15-runner maiden race at Newbury in the autumn; will stay 1¼m; looks capable of better. *B. Hills.* **—**

THRILLING 5 b.m. So Blessed 130–Loop the Loop 81 (Hopeful Venture 125) (1980 10v² 12fg 12fg 8fg 8s 10g 9fg 10fg 10s⁴ 8.2s⁴ 8s 10d 1981 8g 8f² 8f² 8f 8.2d³ 8s 8.2d) workmanlike mare; poor handicapper; stays 1¼m; acts on any going; has worn blinkers. *C. Thornton.* **48**

THRYLOS 2 b.c. Moulton 128–Grenadiere 111 (Right Royal V 135) (1981 8d) Apr 4; 2,000Y; big colt; half-brother to smart middle-distance stayer Stetchworth (by Nijinsky) and to very useful Battlecry (by Bold Lad, Ire), a winner at up to 15f; dam, very useful stayer, is half-sister to good winners Full Dress II, Reload and Boulette; unquoted, very backward and bandaged in front when badly tailed off in £4,200 event at Newbury in September. *D. Sasse.* **—**

THUJA 2 b.c. Mummy's Pet 125–Blakey (Blakeney 126) (1981 5fg **6f** 6d 8d) —
Apr 25; compact colt; second foal; dam slow maiden; poor maiden; should
stay 1m; sweated up second outing; sold 1,200 gns Doncaster November Sales.
M. Camacho.

THUMPS 5 gr.g. Town Crier 119–Galosh 86 (Pandofell 132) (1980 NR 1981 —
10fg 10g) rangy gelding; backward both starts in 1981; stays 13f; acts on any
going; blinkered once at 3 yrs. *M. H. Easterby.*

THUNDERBRIDGE 2 br.c. Rapid River 127–Sayvanter (Galivanter 131) **82**
(1981 5g* 6s) June 5; 2,400Y; smallish, strong colt; half-brother to 5f and
6f winner Stay Secret (by Most Secret); dam ran twice; beat I'm Vexed by a
length (value 1½ lengths) in 11-runner maiden race at Newcastle in August; had
much stiffer task in £3,500 event at York in October and was far from disgraced
in finishing 11½ lengths sixth of 8 to Mirabeau; stays 6f. *S. Norton.*

THUNDER WONDER 3 b.g. Winden 109–Saffron Princess (Thriller 77) **45**
(1980 6fg 6fg 7d 7fg 7fg 1981 16f 14g 10.8fg4 8fg 8.3g2 10h 8g4 10s2) small,
lightly-made gelding; plater; stays 1¼m well; has shown a tendency to hang;
fell sixth start; sometimes sweats up. *D. Elsworth.*

TIBOUCHINA 2 br. or gr.f. Runnymede 123–Reproach Me Not (Connaught 130) **75**
(1981 6g 6g) Mar 20; lengthy filly; second foal; half-sister to fairly useful
1979 2-y-o 5f and 1m winner Pieces of Gold (by Pieces of Eight); dam French
plater; unquoted, had every chance until weakening in last furlong when 7¾
lengths sixth of 17 to I'm Hot in maiden race at Newmarket in October, second
start and better effort; probably stays 6f. *M. Smyly.*

TIBULLUS 3 b.g. Tack On 114–Fibula (King's Bench 132) (1980 NR 1981 —
7.6g 12d 10.1fg 10fg 10.1fg) a twin; half-brother to several minor winners;
dam never ran; in rear in varied company, including selling. *M. Bolton.*

TICKLETIMES 2 b. or br.f. Home Guard 129–Lucerne 76 (Gun Shot) (1981 **94**
5fg 6fg 6f3 7g 7d2 6g4 7f4 6g*) Mar 30; IR 9,000F, 7,200Y; rather lightly-made
filly; half-sister to several winners, including 1980 2-y-o 5f winner Saulann
(by Saulingo); dam won at up to 11f; in frame in 3 good-class fillies races,
finishing 2¼ lengths third of 10 to Travel On in Cherry Hinton Stakes at Newmarket in July, ½-length second of 8 to Baltimore Belle in Sweet Solera Stakes
on same course later in month and 6¼ lengths fourth of 8 behind very easy
winner Circus Ring in Lowther Stakes at York in August; didn't run up to
that form on several occasions in lesser company, but beat Keep Silent by
2½ lengths when blinkered in minor event at Redcar in September; bred to stay
at least 1m; seems to act on any going; bandaged near-fore last 3 outings;
inconsistent and isn't to be trusted. *W. O'Gorman.*

TIDDLEY 3 ch.f. Filiberto 123–Neater (Double Jump 131) (1980 5.8h 7d **66**
10d 11fg3) sparely-made filly; ran on fairly well from back of field when 8
lengths third of 6 behind Bedford in maiden race at Kempton in August; will
stay 1½m. *J. Dunlop.*

TIDMARSH 3 gr.c. Direct Flight–Alips De Mons (Zeddaan 130) (1980 NR —
1981 7.6g 8g 10s) 2,200F, 2,000Y; tall colt; first foal; dam unraced half-sister
to smart 1967 French 3-y-o Ancyre; in rear in varied company, including selling.
S. Matthews.

TIDWORTH TATTOO (USA) 2 ch.c. Native Charger–Beautiful World **81**
(Dr Fager) (1981 5d 6d3 6fg 7g2 7fg 7fg) Feb 9; $51,000Y; tall, long-striding
colt; third foal; half-brother to 2 winners, one of them stakes placed; dam won
2 sprint races at 2 yrs; ran well most starts, on fourth and fifth finishing length
second of 18 to Puff of Smoke in maiden race at Salisbury in July and about
4 lengths fifth of 19 to Paperetto in £5,000 maiden event at Goodwood later in
month; will stay 1m; has worn bandages. *D. Elsworth.*

TIDY WORK 6 b.g. Workboy 123–Roxanne (Sheshoon 132) (1980 NR **47**
1981 12s2 12g 12d 10fg 12f) sturdy gelding; stays 1½m; acts on soft going;
has worn blinkers. *K. Stone.*

TIGER TOWN 2 br.c. Town Crier 119–Another Clare (Blason 109) (1981 5d **62**
5f 5f* 6f* 6g 7fg3 6g) Apr 21; 3,000F, 4,200Y; neat colt; half-brother to a
winning 2-y-o plater and a winner in Malaya; dam of no account; showed
himself a useful plater when winning at Beverley (bought in 6,000 gns) and
Brighton (beat Starter's Image 2½ lengths, retained 2,700 gns); beaten in
nurseries subsequently, finishing 2¾ lengths third of 4 to Sanches at Yarmouth
in August; promises to stay 7f; acts well on firm going; wears blinkers; has
run respectably for an apprentice. *P. Haslam.*

TIG

TIGER TRAP (USA) 2 gr.f. Al Hattab–Polynesian Charm (What A Pleasure) 80
(1981 6fg 6fg³) Mar 11; $100,000Y; lengthy, useful-looking filly; a grand
mover; third foal; sister to a winner in USA; dam half-sister to numerous
winners, including smart 1969 American 2-y-o Clover Lane; didn't get a clear run
when strong-finishing 8½ lengths fifth of 16 to Kiva in maiden race at Newbury
in August; again finished very well, after getting a bit unbalanced round
Tattenham Corner, when just over a length third of 8 to Cheri Berry in minor
event at Epsom later in month; likely to stay 1m. *I. Balding.*

TIGGI'S 2 b.f. Owen Dudley 121–Princess Nefertiti (Tutankhamen) (1981 6s) —
Mar 29; small, lengthy filly; half-sister to 3 winners; last of 13 to Westonbirt
in maiden race at Haydock in June; sold 280 gns Doncaster September Sales.
J. Wilson.

TIGRANES (USA) 2 b.c. Decidedly-Hill Whisper (Hillary) (1981 7.6s 8g 8g) — p
Apr 10; $24,000F; rangy colt; good mover; brother to a winner in USA and half-
brother to Madera Sun (by Montparnasse II), a very useful stakes winner at up to
1m; dam, 1m winner, comes from same family as J. O. Tobin; behind in maiden
and minor events at Lingfield and Newmarket (2) in October; has lots of scope
and will do better over further at 3 yrs. *J. Dunlop.*

TIJUCA 2 ch.c. Roi Soleil 125–Royal Message 57 (Town Crier 119) (1981 5g —
7fg 8g 8s) Mar 14; 7,200Y, 2,500Y; good-bodied colt; well beaten in varied
company, including selling; sold 850 gns Ascot November Sales. *D. Sasse.*

TIKAKI (USA) 2 b.f. Hawaii–Kushka (First Landing) (1981 7g 7g⁴ 7.3s²) 95
well-made, quite attractive filly; half-sister to 2 winners, including Lefty (by
Prince John), a smart stakes winner at up to 1m; dam stakes-placed winner of
4 sprint races; put up an improved performance in blinkers when 6 lengths
second to Last Feather in 8-runner £6,300 event at Newbury in October, having
no chance with winner but finishing 4 lengths clear of third horse; will stay 1¼m;
acts on soft going; sure to win a race or 2 at 3 yrs if reproducing her Newbury
form. *R. Hern.*

TILLMAN 2 b.g. Swing Easy 126–Spytra 64 (Spy Well 125) (1981 6g 6f⁴ 7fg 7f) 72
Feb 6; half-brother to fair sprinter Spy Chief (by Tribal Chief); dam, poor
performer on flat, won over hurdles; prominent in maiden races at Carlisle in
July and Brighton (3 lengths fourth of 9 to Irish Grenadier) in August; not sure
to stay 7f. *F. Durr.*

TILLYMORGAN 3 b.f. Lochnager 132–Hodhard 101 (Hard Sauce 131) —
(1980 5f 5fg 1981 8fg 8.2s) seems useless; sold 410 gns Doncaster November
Sales. *M. W. Easterby.*

TILLY SCOTT 2 b.f. Roi Soleil 125–Scottish Double (Dual 117) (1981 6fg 7d —
6d) Apr 22; half-sister to 2 winners; dam once-raced sister to useful middle-
distance stayer Double Quick; unquoted when in rear in maiden and minor events
M. Masson.

TIMBER TRACK 4 b.g. Palm Track 122–Kindling 80 (Psidium 130) (1980 85
12fg⁴ 10g² 10f* 12d* 13.3d* 1981 12fg 13g³ 12g* 12d 14d 13g* 14s) big
gelding; has a round action; fair performer; landed the odds in small races at
Beverley in July and Ayr in September; didn't particularly impress on latter;
should stay 1¾m; unsuited by very soft going but acts on any other. *E. Weymes.*

TIME CHARTER 2 b.f. Saritamer 130–Centrocon 112 (High Line 125) 103
(1981 5d³ 6fg* 6fg 7g* 7s) Apr 6; strong, well-made filly; excellent walker; first
foal; dam, very useful winner from 1m to 2m, is sister to Nicholas Bill and
Centroline; successful in £2,800 event at Leicester in July and 9-runner nursery at
Goodwood in September, putting up a useful effort to win by ¾ length from Lamlash under 9-7 in latter; seventh of 11 to Spanish Pool under top weight in
valuable nursery at Lingfield in October; better suited by 7f than shorter
distances and will stay 1m; possibly not at her best on soft going. *H. Candy.*

TIME GENTS 6 b.g. Polyfoto 124–Blue Mistress (Skymaster 126) (1980 12g² —
12d 5g 10g³ 12.5s 1981 10.2s 7g⁴ 8f) fair sort; ex-Irish gelding; seems only
plating class; stays 1½m; changed hands 1,500 gns Ascot January (81) Sales.
D. H. Jones.

TIME-TABLE 3 b.f. Mansingh 120–Queen of Time (Roi Dagobert 128) 65
(1980 6f 6v² 1981 6s* 6f³ 7g 8f) won maiden race at Hamilton in April; ran
creditably in a handicap next time; gives impression she'll stay 1m; acts on any
going; well beaten in blinkers final start. *J. W. Watts.*

880

TIME TO REFLECT 2 ro.g. Roan Rocket 128–Game Girl 85 (Abernant **77**
142) (1981 5g⁴ 6g² 6g 6f 6s² 6s³) Apr 24; 5,200F, resold 4,300Y; rather
leggy gelding; half-brother to numerous winners here and abroad, including
brilliantly speedy 1972 2-y-o The Go-Between (by Runnymede); dam ran only
at 2 yrs; placed in maiden race and 2 nurseries, running best race when 2½
lengths second of 8 to Knight Security in valuable nursery at Haydock on
fifth outing; will probably stay 7f; gives impression he will always need some
give in the ground. *M. Camacho.*

TIME WIND 2 b.f. Dance In Time–Schoolhouse Dale 72 (Reform 132) (1981 **72**
5d 5g 6s⁴ 6fg⁴ 7f 8f 8fg² 8d 8.2s² 8g) Feb 11; compact filly; first foal; dam won
over 1¼m; second in maiden race at Beverley in September and nursery at
Hamilton in October; will be suited by 1¼m; possibly not at her best on very
firm going but acts on any other; wears blinkers. *W. Elsey.*

TIMONIER (FR) 4 b. or br.g. Satingo 129–Trelex (Exbury 138) (1980 11.7fg **56**
14g 12fg⁴ 10.1g⁴ 1981 10g³ 12g⁴ 12.2fg 12f 15.8g) tall gelding; plating-class
maiden; stays 1½m; has run respectably for an apprentice. *Denys Smith.*

TIM WHISKY 3 br.g. Home Guard 129–Song God 96 (Red God 128§) (1980 **—**
6d 1981 7.6g 8d) strong, deep-girthed gelding; lightly-raced maiden; has
shown some ability; apprentice ridden; sold 680 gns Newmarket July Sales.
P. Cole.

TINA'S PET 3 b.c. Mummy's Pet 125–Merry Weather 69 (Will Somers 114§) **119**
(1980 6fg 6s² 6fg* 6f* 5s* 1981 7g³ 6g 5f 6g 5.6fg 6d² 6s⁴) well-made, attractive
sprint type; not the best of movers; second foal; half-brother to 7f seller
winner Indian Spring (by Mansing); dam won over 9.4f; very smart performer
on his day; looked to have done well physically when reappearing in Tote
European Free Handicap at Newmarket in April and ran well too, finishing
about 1½ lengths third to Motavato after being prominent throughout; disappointing in top company next 3 starts but looked tremendously well and put
up a splendid performance under a stiff weight when going down by a head
to stable-companion First Movement in Ladbrokes (Ayr) Gold Cup in September,
being caught close home after going clear on stand side 2f out; very disappointing fourth of 5 behind Jester in Coral Bookmakers Champion Sprint at York in
October; stays 7f; acts on any going; blinkered fourth start; sold privately
before final outing. *G. Huffer.*

TIN BOY 2 br.c. Welsh Pageant 132–Tin Mary 96 (Tin King 126) (1981 **97**
5g 6g* 6g*) May 8; 10,000Y; quite a useful sort; brother to useful 1m to 1¾m
winner Gallant Welsh, and half-brother to 2 winners, including 1980 2-y-o
6f winner Sleepline Princess (by Royal Palace); dam stayed 1m; successful
twice at Newmarket in the summer, beating Forest Ride ¾ length in 26-runner
maiden race and Westonbirt 1½ lengths in £5,000 nursery; will stay at least 1m.
W. Hastings-Bass.

TINDERELLA 2 ch.f. Hot Spark 126–Flying Fancy (King of the Tudors 129) **59**
(1981 5d⁴ 6f 5d 6d) Feb 4; half-sister to 3 winners here and in USA, including
1978 2-y-o 5f winner Fancy Work (by Sparkler) and very useful Flight to Glory
(by Native Charger), a stakes winner at up to 7f in USA; dam, winner in USA,
is daughter of very speedy Krakenwake; only plating class herself; blinkered
third outing. *M. Hinchliffe.*

TINJAR 3 ch.c. Brittany–Sweet Minuet (Setay 105) (1980 6s 6d 6g* 6g² **93**
6fg 5g³ 1981 6g 6s 6s 6g 5fg 6fg⁴ 6fg 6g³ 5f* 5g) strong colt; hampered at
start and in circumstances did particularly well to get up close home and beat
Maryland Cookie ½ length in Playboy Bookmakers' Sprint (Handicap) at York
in September; in frame earlier in handicaps at Lingfield and Newcastle (third
to Ackermann in Northumberland Sprint Trophy); stays 6f, but probably
best at 5f; suited by a sound surface; blinkered nowadays. *J. Holt.*

TINKTURA 2 ch.f. Pampapaul 121–Tigerin (Prodomo) (1981 6fg⁴ 7fg³ **92 p**
7f*) Apr 15; half-sister to 2 winners, including fairly useful Irish middle-
distance stayer Grey Tiger (by Willowick); dam top-rated 3-y-o filly in Germany
in 1965; improved steadily and put up a fairly useful effort when winning
11-runner maiden race at Naas in September by a length from More Heather;
will stay 1¼m; probably still has improvement in her. *S. Murless, Ireland.*

TINNYCROSS 2 ch.f. Sallust 134–Modern Millie 95 (Milesian 125) (1981 5d³ **95**
6d 6g² 5d⁴ 5g* 6d*) Mar 5; IR 6,600F, IR 6,200Y; half-sister to 2 winners
by Deep Diver; dam won twice over 5f at 2 yrs; won twice in October, beating
Fenacapan a length in 18-runner maiden race at Mallow and Red Realm 4 lengths

when giving upwards of 7 lb to her 14 rivals in minor event at Fairyhouse; 8 lengths fourth of 9 to Americus in Waterford Testimonial Stakes at the Curragh earlier in month; will stay 7f; yet to race on a firm surface. *J. Bolger, Ireland.*

TINTERELLO 2 ch.c. Continuation 120–Polly Bellino 56 (Dadda Bert 95) — (1981 5d 5fg 8g 8s) Mar 22; compact colt; fifth living foal; half-brother to successful plater and hurdler Archetto (by Arcticeelagh); dam won at 1¼m; of little account. *J. Hardy.*

TIN TESSA 3 b.f. Martinmas 128–Gala Tess (El Gallo 122) (1980 5fg³ 5.8h* 60 5g² 6f⁴ 1981 6g 6d 7g 5.8f³ 6f³ 5fg 5.8g) rangy, somewhat unfurnished filly; good walker and mover; ran best races when third in handicaps at Bath and Folkestone in summer; should stay 7f; form only on a sound surface and acts on hard ground. *I. Balding.*

TIPO 4 gr.g. Silly Season 127–Gay Life 72 (Zeus Boy 121) (1980 10.8s 11f³ — 12f³ 10g² 10s 1981 11.7v 11.1s 8fg 8fg 12g⁴ 12f⁴ 11.5d 12f) strong, compact gelding; excellent mover; needs further than 1m and stays 1½m; suited by top-of-the-ground; often blinkered and is possibly none too genuine. *S. Mellor.*

TIPPERARY FIXER 3 b.c. Targowice 130–Rabisina (Alcide 136) (1980 8d 125 8v 1981 12fg⁴ 12d 12s² 15s* 15s² 15f* 15s* 15.5v) Tipperary Fixer was the best French-trained three-year-old regularly to race over long distances in 1981. He was the only one of his type to appear in the International Classification, in which he was allotted a rating 8 lb below Cut Above, 7 lb below Glint of Gold and 4 lb below Bustomi; indeed, he was the only one to contest the Prix Royal-Oak at Longchamp in October, a race confined to three-year-olds until 1979. In short, quality French staying three-year-olds were thin on the ground. Tipperary Fixer improved greatly with distance, and with the removal of the blinkers he had worn on four of his first five starts. He opened his account in a pattern race, the Prix de l'Esperance at Longchamp in May, but that was less of a feat than it might seem: none of the seven runners had run in a pattern race in 1981. Tipperary Fixer picked up two better races before the year was out, the Prix Kergorlay at Deauville in August, in which he beat Nicholas Bill by half a length, and the Prix de Lutece at Longchamp the following month by a neck from Marasali. He all but threw the latter away by swerving under the whip when challenging. All three victories were over fifteen furlongs and in all three Tipperary Fixer put in a powerful finish, as he also did when a three-length second to Glint of Gold in the Grand Prix de Paris at Longchamp in July. Tipperary Fixer's last run, in the Prix Royal-Oak, was a disappointment; although he had little chance on the book with his elders Ardross and Gold River, he ought to have fared better than a remote sixth of seven.

Tipperary Fixer (b.c. 1978)	Targowice (b 1970)	Round Table (b 1954)	Princequillo
			Knight's Daughter
		Matriarch (b 1964)	Bold Ruler
			Lyceum
	Rabisina (b 1966)	Alcide (b 1955)	Alycidon
			Chenille
		Rosellina (b 1957)	Tenerani
			Romanella

Tipperary Fixer cost only 2,600 guineas in Ireland as a yearling, having changed hands for 2,900 guineas a year earlier. That he was picked up so cheaply is not particularly surprising. His sire Targowice wasn't then very popular and his dam, Rabisina, was raced unsuccessfully at two in Italy; before Tipperary

Prix Kergorlay, Deauville—Tipperary Fixer beats British challenger Nicholas Bill

Fixer the latter had bred one winner from three foals to race—Ball of Fire (by Luthier), a winner at two years in France and also successful over jumps. Rabisina does belong to a most successful Italian family: she is a half-sister to St Leger third and Italian Derby winner Ruysdael II out of an Italian One Thousand Guineas winner, herself a sister to Ribot. Tipperary Fixer, a big, grand type of colt, is suited by fifteen furlongs and races as though he will stay further. He has had his limitations exposed and we are unlikely to see him in the Gold Cup, but he should be good enough to pay his way in France as a four-year-old. *J. Fellows, France.*

TIPPI 2 br.c. Saritamer 130–Trigamy 112 (Tribal Chief 125) (1981 5fg⁴ 5fg **54** 5.1d 5s 6s 5g 5s) May 11; workmanlike colt; sold out of N. Callaghan's stable 950 gns Doncaster August Sales after showing a little ability in 2 races in the spring; soundly beaten subsequently, including in sellers; blinkered sixth outing. *W. Stubbs.*

TIP TOOL 4 ch.g. Redundant 120–Liliberto (Umberto 118) (1980 10g 10s — 10.8s 10d 1981 12g) big, good-looking gelding; poor maiden; has worn blinkers and bandages. *W. Marshall.*

TIRAWA (USA) 2 b.c. Majestic Prince–Imalulu (Black Beard) (1981 6g) — p Apr 2; $90,000Y; good-looking, lengthy colt; good mover; half-brother to a winner in USA; dam, sister to stakes winner Miss Imorullah, won 3 times at up to 6f in USA; 20/1, ran on quite well without being unnecessarily hard ridden when eighth of 21 to Not For Show in maiden race at Newmarket in October; will be suited by 1m; the type to do better at 3 yrs. *M. Jarvis.*

TIR NA OG 2 ch.c. Condorcet–Trinacria (Relic) (1981 6g 6f³ 8g) May 7; **75** compact, quite attractive colt; has a round action; half-brother to several winners, including very useful sprinter Rundontwalk (by Takawalk II) and good Continental sprinter Park Romeo (by Irish Love); dam never ran; ran best race when third to Wattlefield in minor race at Yarmouth in the summer; should have been suited by 1m; dead. *B. Hobbs.*

TIT FOR TAT 2 b.g. Warpath 113–Yours and Mine 83 (Tin Whistle 128) — (1981 6d 6g) Feb 14; fourth foal; brother to Sioux and Sioux, winner 4 times over 7f and once over 1m at 2 yrs in 1977; dam stayed 9f; well behind in maiden races won by Dev and Perang Tejam at Doncaster late in season; needs further. *C. Thornton.*

TIVOLI (FR) 3 gr.c. Caro 133–Take Off (Nasram II 125) (1980 7f 1981 — 10fg⁴) rangy, good sort; seventh of 19 to King's Glory in maiden race at Newmarket as a 2-y-o; favourite and looking fit when about 7 lengths fourth to Salud in minor event at Nottingham in April on only running of 1981 (didn't get going until winner had gone clear); will stay 1½m. *H. Cecil.*

T. J. CUNNIFFE 3 ch.g. Communication 119–Miss Helen (Only For Life — 126) (1980 5d³ 5fg 5fg³ 5f² 5f⁴ 5f² 6s 5f 5fg 8d 1981 5d 5g 5d 5g 5g 11d) big gelding; plater; barely stays 5f. *A. W. Jones.*

TO-AGORI-MOU 3 br.c. Tudor Music 131–Sarah Van Fleet (Cracksman 111) **133** (1980 6d² 7g* 7f* 7g* 7s² 1981 8g² 8g* 8s² 8fg* 8fg² 8f² 8fg* 8s* 10g)
To-Agori-Mou was a good Two Thousand Guineas winner, better than any since Brigadier Gerard apart from the promoted Known Fact and, perhaps, Bolkonski who beat Grundy. He contributed much more to the year than some of his recent predecessors and until his defeat in the Champion Stakes in his last race he was never out of the first two. After the Guineas he won another three pattern races over the distance, in one of them beating the leading English four-year-old Moorestyle, in another the Airlie/Coolmore Irish Two Thousand Guineas winner Kings Lake. He and Kings Lake stood out from the rest of the three-year-old milers in Europe; their rivalry was one of the highlights of the season.
To-Agori-Mou isn't the sort to hit top form right away: he carries a tremendous amount of condition and is a big, rangy, hefty individual—a grand type of colt but one who needs a lot of work. He wasn't ready on his first outing, and for our money he didn't reach his peak until Royal Ascot when he won the St James's Palace Stakes on his fourth appearance of the season in a great race with Kings Lake. By then there seemed some possibility that he'd been over-rated while, in contrast, the true merit of his stable-companion Recitation had been overlooked. First time up To-Agori-Mou had been beaten by Kind of Hush in the Ladbrokes Craven Stakes; next he had squeezed home from Mattaboy in the

Guineas; then he had been beaten by Kings Lake in the Irish Guineas. To-Agori-Mou's continuing high standing with the public owed a lot to his performances as a two-year-old and to his trainer's unshakeable confidence in To-Agori-Mou's ability; he had lost the Irish Guineas in controversial circumstances but not so controversial that they provided an excuse for his falling short of his reputation. As a two-year-old the horse had won three successive races in style, one of them the Intercraft Solario Stakes, before finishing a close second to Storm Bird, well in front of the Prix de la Salamandre winner Miswaki and the Laurent Perrier Champagne Stakes fourth Kirtling, in the William Hill Dewhurst Stakes. Only Storm Bird had been rated his superior in the Tote European Free Handicap of 1980. All through the spring, right up to Royal Ascot, his trainer had praised him to the skies; eventually his trainer proved correct.

Despite his three-quarter-length defeat by Kind of Hush at levels, a lack-lustre, relatively modest performance on his part, To-Agori-Mou started favourite at 5/2 ahead of the Free Handicap winner Motavato (5/1) and Kind of Hush (9/1) in a Guineas field of nineteen from which Storm Bird was an absentee. The fact of his starting a clear favourite reveals something about the strength of the field as well as the loyalty of his support: although To-Agori-Mou turned out to be a good Guineas winner he didn't face outstanding opposition by any means. Apart from Motavato and Kind of Hush, the former of whom had carried 8-13 in the Free Handicap following the raising of the weights 12 lb, the better-fancied horses were the 1980 William Hill Futurity winner Beldale Flutter, third to Another Realm in the Clerical, Medical Greenham Stakes on his reappearance; Another Realm himself; the Free Handicap fourth Bel Bolide; and Church Parade, Prince Echo and Noalto; the rest started at 33/1, or longer. In the race easily the strongest threat materialized from Mattaboy, sixth under 9-7 in the Free Handicap and in the rear behind Recitation on different going in the Poule d'Essai des Poulains. Mattaboy nearly won after encountering bad luck in the first half of the race; he improved rapidly into a challenging position two furlongs out, got the better of a long battle with the front-running Bel Bolide by a length and a half and failed by only a neck to hold off To-Agori-Mou. The favourite, drawn one, which is considered by some to be a disadvantage when the stalls are placed on the far side, ran, misleadingly, like a horse who would be much better suited by another two furlongs. Held up in an admittedly slowly-run affair, he came to the Bushes moving strongly on the bridle in a good position still on the outside. At this stage he threatened to win as easily as we should have expected him on the promise of his Dewhurst running, but in the end he had to struggle; halfway through the last furlong he even looked beaten, and he managed to snatch the lead only in the last few strides. To-Agori-Mou's victory gave his trainer his

Two Thousand Guineas Stakes, Newmarket—a close finish with To-Agori-Mou prevailing from Mattaboy (centre) and Bel Bolide (left)

St James's Palace Stakes, Ascot—To-Agori-Mou gets the better of Kings Lake in their second encounter

first English classic win and jockey Starkey his fourth; Starkey had had to work very hard, though mainly with hands and heels, and on reflection he had to apply more pressure to get Shirley Heights and Fair Salinia home at Epsom.

Although the finish of the Irish Two Thousand Guineas, run two weeks later, concerned principally Kings Lake and To-Agori-Mou in what was to become a familiarly even match, there are grounds for believing that neither showed his best form. Prince Echo was less then a length behind, and Mattaboy less than two and a half on unsuitably soft going. The controversial race, described in detail in Kings Lake's commentary, went in the first instance to Kings Lake by a neck; To-Agori-Mou was subsequently promoted by the local stewards, then demoted by higher authority. Whatever the merits of the final decision it has to be said that neither principal was particularly impressive, and To-Agori-Mou once more managed somehow to create the illusion that he was short of speed for racing at a mile.

However, plans were to keep To-Agori-Mou at a mile for the present. Kala-glow was stable-choice for the Derby, Recitation for the Prix du Jockey-Club, and To-Agori-Mou took on Kings Lake again in the St James's Palace Stakes. Interestingly, Starkey abandoned his earlier riding tactics in favour of lying up with the pace in third-of-eight place at Royal Ascot, and he was able to slip through on the rails into the straight, past Robellino and Bel Bolide, early in the straight. Soon To-Agori-Mou went a length clear. Kings Lake steadily reduced the advantage running to the line but in a thrilling battle never got his nose in front. Although the margin between first and second was the same as in To-Agori-Mou's two previous races, a neck, here at last came the sparkling perfor-mance expected from him. Here also came a demonstrably improved per-formance from both him and Kings Lake: Bel Bolide finished six lengths adrift of Kings Lake in undisputed third place. Both To-Agori-Mou and Kings Lake had now earned the right to be regarded as top-class horses, well up to the standard of classic winners over the years; very likely with nothing between them, unless Starkey's magnificently enterprising and determined jockeyship had led to To-Agori-Mou's being flattered.

In fact, there turned out to be nothing between this outstanding pair of three-year-olds; they ran virtually to the ounce in their two subsequent meetings, in the Sussex Stakes at Goodwood in July and the Prix Jacques le Marois at Deauville in August, races which for them followed straight on from Royal Ascot. What's more it transpired that To-Agori-Mou could, after all, run his race from behind. He was held up in the Sussex Stakes and showed a lot of pace when asked to join the leaders in the straight. He came there very easily, distinctly a cut above his elders Last Fandango, Dalsaan and Belmont Bay as he took the lead at the distance, but Kings Lake managed to catch him near the finish and win by a head. At Deauville as little as a nose separated them, To-Agori-Mou in front. They were, however, left with only second and third places to fight over as the French four-year-old Northjet unbelievably ran right away for a five-length win—unbelievably because by August there seemed no doubt whatever that either To-Agori-Mou or Kings Lake was the best miler in Europe; deciding between them, if and when the choice had to be made, was apparently the only problem. If Northjet hadn't been compelled to miss the Sussex Stakes because of an abscess on a foot we should probably have known already that good as To-Agori-Mou and Kings Lake could be seen to be, there was one better around. To-Agori-Mou, not so burly as at Goodwood, ran a very courageous race for his second place; two furlongs from home he disputed the lead but he soon came under strong pressure, rolling about, and only his determination kept Kings Lake, Hilal and The Wonder at bay.

To-Agori-Mou had the benefit of tackling Northjet at weight-for-age in the Marois, it being a Group 1 pattern race. In the Group 2 Waterford Crystal Mile at Goodwood later in August, his third big race in five weeks, he met Moore-style at a 2 lb disadvantage compared with weight-for-age, Last Fandango and Milk of the Barley at a 7 lb disadvantage, and he gave Another Realm 5 lb; the only other runner was his pacemaker Bonnie Charlie, who became redundant through missing the break. The race marked Moorestyle's return to something approaching his old form, but the Two Thousand Guineas winner beat him by half a length. What was most impressive about To-Agori-Mou was the way in which he picked up the tip-top older horse a couple of furlongs from the finish after tracking him most of the journey—he cruised past and quickly went three lengths clear, crossing over to the far rail. Having gone clear To-Agori-Mou tended to idle; his stride began to shorten in the last furlong, too, and a rally by Moorestyle had the winner hanging on at the post. The others finished decisively beaten. A subsequent objection for crossing by Moorestyle's jockey Piggott was overruled, the objector forfeiting his deposit.

Waterford Crystal Mile, Goodwood—Starkey and To-Agori-Mou hold the renewed challenge of Piggott and Moorestyle

Queen Elizabeth II Stakes, Ascot—Piggott stands in for the suspended Starkey as To-Agori-Mou defeats subsequently-disqualified Cracaval. Kittyhawk (left) was promoted to second place

Tough customer that he is, To-Agori-Mou could not in all fairness be asked to cross swords once again with Northjet in the last Group 1 of the season for the milers, the Prix du Moulin de Longchamp, only eight days after the Waterford Crystal Mile. Northjet won, incidentally, by a length and a half and a nose from Hilal and The Wonder. Instead To-Agori-Mou was held back for the Queen Elizabeth II Stakes at Ascot run towards the end of September, in which he met Hilal, Milk of the Barley and another older horse Cracaval at level weights, Noalto at 7 lb and the three-year-old filly Kittyhawk at 10 lb: yet again facing a theoretical disadvantage. In the paddock he couldn't have looked in better shape to tackle the task in hand—in magnificent condition, as well as at any time during the season, which is saying a great deal. In the race, a roughish affair which resulted in second-placed Cracaval's relegation to third for interfering with To-Agori-Mou and Kittyhawk in the last furlong or so, he prevailed by a length. Piggott, deputising for Starkey, brought him through steadily from last place to lead just inside the last furlong, and the horse kept on well.

Right at the end of the season To-Agori-Mou was given the opportunity of showing his paces at a mile and a quarter, in the Champion Stakes. In finishing fifth of sixteen at Newmarket, beaten just over six lengths by the French challenger Vayrann, he obviously didn't show his form though he had behind him several top-class horses as well as Noalto and Kind of Hush. He improved on the bridle from the rear as though he was going to get into the race over two furlongs out, but he still had plenty to do and in the end couldn't do it; he simply kept on steadily up the hill, ever just out of striking range. To judge a horse on his performance at this stage of his long season, especially on one in the Champion Stakes, is fraught with risks: the lesson taught by experience is to exercise extra caution. With this lesson in mind we should not go so far as to assert that To-Agori-Mou didn't stay the trip, only to rest for the time being on the incontrovertible evidence that his form at a mile is much better. As he is to race on in the United States there is an outside chance that he'll be given another shot at the distance.

To-Agori-Mou (br.c. 1978)	Tudor Music (br 1966)	Tudor Melody (br 1956)	Tudor Minstrel
			Matelda
		Fran (ch 1959)	Acropolis
			Madrilene
	Sarah Van Fleet (b 1966)	Cracksman (ch 1958)	Chamossaire
			Nearly
		La Rage (br 1954)	Mieuxce
			Hell's Fury

There is little new to add to the details of To-Agori-Mou's breeding. It's common knowledge that his trainer has invested extremely shrewdly in the yearling market over the years, generally putting conformation above pedigree, steering well clear of fashion; as a result he picked up, for the same owner,

Mrs Andry Muinos' "To-Agori-Mou"

racehorses of the calibre of Ela-Mana-Mou and To-Agori-Mou for the respective sums of 4,500 guineas and 20,000 guineas. To-Agori-Mou has amassed £206,794 in prize money so far. One difficulty that can easily arise from putting conformation above pedigree is, of course, a difficulty in realising a price commensurate with racing ability when the time arrives to sell as a stallion. Apparently, no acceptable offer came for To-Agori-Mou by the end of the season, therefore he has been sent to race in the USA where he'll be in the American breeders' shop window, so to speak.

Tudor Music, To-Agori-Mou's sire, did less than well in his ten years at stud, for all that he was a top-class sprinter and as handsome as any to be seen. Orchestra and Lady Segrave are his only other pattern winners. The dam Sarah Van Fleet is a winning mare by the stayer Cracksman, a sire perhaps best known as the sire of the good two-mile chaser Stopped. Sarah Van Fleet won five times over hurdles and twice in bumpers events. She had two previous foals one of whom, the quite useful five-furlong handicapper Van Laser (by Laser Light), won. The other, Flying Clipper (by Tepukei), fetched 42,000 guineas covered by Rusticaro at the latest December Sales; she ran last of eleven in a two-year-old maiden at Limerick on her only outing. The foal of 1979, a filly by Royal Match called Play It Safe, is in training at Pulborough. Whoever eventually does stand To-Agori-Mou will be relatively short of worthwhile facts to advertise concerning the pedigree unless they dig as far back as the fourth dam Sister Sarah (foaled in 1930). A great granddaughter of Pretty Polly, Sister Sarah was a highly influential broodmare and her name is kept regularly before us nowadays through the efforts of her daughters Lady Angela (a grandam of Northern Dancer) and Sybil's Sister (a grandam of Great Nephew); another daughter Caerlissa is a grandam of St Paddy.

To sell To-Agori-Mou on performance and looks alone would be child's play. His record is there for all to see, the record of a top-class, outstandingly tough, determined miler who gives his running on any type of ground; if he has a fault it's that he tends to run lazily once he's done enough to reach the front. And anyone with the slightest eye for a horse will not be slow to appreciate that his conformation does full credit to his record: he's a magnificent specimen. *G. Harwood.*

TOBERJOVIC 3 b.g. Tudor Rhythm 112–Decked Out 77 (Doutelle 128) — (1980 6f 10d 1981 10s 15.5d) useless. *A. Davison.*

TOBERMORY BOY 4 b.g. Mummy's Pet 125–Penny Pincher 95 (Constable **85** 119) (1980 6s² 6f 5fg* 5fg 5g* 5fg⁴ 5s 5fg⁴ 5g 1981 5g 5d 5fg 5g⁴ 5f³ 6f² 5.6f² 5g² 5.6fg 5g 5s) neat gelding; fair handicapper; stays 6f; acts on any going; suitable mount for a boy. *J. Hardy.*

TOCCATA (USA) 3 ch.f. Mr Leader–Thespianess (Parthia 132) (1980 NR **64** 1981 7d 5f³ 6f³ 7f 6v² 6d) small filly; half-sister to 2 winners by Bold Favorite; dam, winner at up to 1m in USA, is half-sister to very successful broodmare Money for Nothing; placed in maiden and minor events, staying on very strongly when 3 lengths second to easy winner Habella at York in October (sweated up badly); stays 6f; sold 20,000 gns Newmarket December Sales. *M. Jarvis.*

TOCHARA 4 b.g. Spanish Gold 101–Toccatina 79 (Bleep-Bleep 134) (1980 NR — 1981 10g) behind in varied company, including selling. *D. Wilson.*

TOE TAPPER 3 ch.f. Record Run 127–Cobblers Daughter 84 (Right Boy 137) **67** (1980 6g 7fg 7g² 7fg* 1981 10s 10.2g 10g 7fg 7f² 8.3fg³ 7f 7g) rather a short-backed filly; placed in handicaps at Doncaster and Windsor in summer; should stay 1¼m; sold 3,400 gns Newmarket Autumn Sales. *G. Pritchard-Gordon.*

TOFIQUE 3 ch.c. Patch 129–Tra-La-La (Penhurst) (1980 8d 1981 10s² **65** 10d 11f* 11g² 13d³) rangy colt; won maiden event at Hamilton in June by ¾ length from Pick A Straw; ¾-length second to Hit The Road in small race on same course following month; should be suited by further than 11f but was beaten a long way over 13f (blinkered); acts on any going; sold 3,600 gns Newmarket Autumn Sales. *C. Nelson.*

TOGG (FR) 3 ch.g. Carvin 127–Pachuca (Pan II 130) (1980 6fg² 6s⁴ 7d 8.2s **77** 1981 10d 12d³ 14g 14s² 11.5fg 12f* 14g³ 12f* 12d 11g² 12g³ 12s) neat ex-English gelding; won maiden race at Clonmel in August and handicap at Limerick in September; placed on several other occasions, including in handicap at Leicester in April (third to Cima); stays 1¾m; acts on any going; blinkered fifth start; often apprentice ridden. *J. Murphy, Ireland.*

TO KAMARI MOU 2 ch.c. Moulton 128–Scala di Seta 85 (Shantung 132) — (1981 7fg) Mar 7; 64,000Y; smallish, chunky colt; brother to high-class Italian 5f to 1½m winner Stone and half-brother to good Italian 1978 2-y-o Stouci (by Upper Case); dam won over 1½m; 16/1, pushed along a long way from home when last of 10 to Old Country in £3,100 event at Goodwood in September. *G. Harwood.*

TOLMI 3 b.f. Great Nephew 126–Stilvi 126 (Derring-Do 131) (1980 6s* 6g* **120** 1981 8g² 8s⁴ 8f* 8fg² 7fg² 7g²)

Tolmi didn't turn out quite the world-beater that her two good two-year-old wins and her impeccable pedigree suggested she might, but there weren't many better fillies around and she might have won the One Thousand Guineas if her preparation hadn't been interrupted by a pulled muscle in her quarters. For a while it looked as if Tolmi wouldn't even be able to run in the Guineas: her injury prevented her from having a preparatory race and reportedly for five days she was able only to walk out. She responded very well to treatment though and worked well the week before the race, but by Guineas day she had still to get her coat and she looked as if she could be made fitter. In the race Tolmi went well from the start, tracking the leaders as Fairy Footsteps set off to make all; and going into the Dip she looked to be moving better than the eventual winner. She couldn't quicken up the hill though and was beaten a neck by Fairy Footsteps in a thrilling finish, the pair being very closely followed over the line by Go Leasing, Marwell and Madam Gay. Trainer Hobbs preferred to praise the skill of his vet for enabling Tolmi to run at all rather than to blame her defeat on her interrupted preparation, but when drawn on the subject of her injury he commented fairly 'I'm not saying that it made the difference, but it can't have helped'.

Tolmi gained some compensation for her Guineas defeat in the Coronation Stakes at Royal Ascot, as her stable's 1973 Guineas runner-up Jacinth had

Coronation Stakes, Ascot—a smooth win for Tolmi from Irish challenger Happy Bride

also done, but only after a most disappointing effort in the UBM Merchants Fillies Stakes at Kempton in May which had some critics claiming that she wasn't training on. Although she never looked like winning at Kempton, and trailed in a remote fourth of six behind the seven-length winner Nasseem, her defeat is not hard to explain. In our opinion she was completely unsuited by the rain-softened ground, and in being brought up the centre of the course she was in all probability racing on the worst of it. True, she had won on ground recorded as soft at Newmarket as a two-year-old, but on that occasion she was one of only two fillies in a field of twenty-one who raced up the stand side where the ground was quite possibly not so bad. In addition her trainer feels that Tolmi may have resented being restrained. Hobbs, who is better qualified to judge than any, is convinced that Hide, who rode her in all except her final race, disappointed Tolmi in the early stages—'None of Stilvi's family is amenable to restraint and you've got to let them run the races they want to do'. At Royal Ascot different tactics were employed, and with the ground riding firm we saw a different filly. Tolmi was always up with the pace, travelling well behind the leader Nasseem, and the only time she looked in any trouble was when getting slightly boxed early in the straight. Once switched to the outside for a run at the distance she always looked like winning. She got up well inside the last furlong and won rather cleverly by half a length from the Irish filly Happy Bride.

The second half of Tolmi's season saw her runner-up to Star Pastures, whom she hadn't previously met, on three consecutive occasions. When Star Pastures beat her by three lengths in the Child Stakes at Newmarket in July on the first occasion there were those who said Tolmi had run moderately and was inconsistent. But subsequent events showed she faced a very stiff task indeed, conceding 6 lb to Star Pastures. In the American Express Royal Wedding Stakes at Goodwood later in the month she went down by a length to Star Pastures, conceding 3 lb, and in the Heathorns Stakes on the same course in September Star Pastures unequivocally resolved doubts which was the better filly; Star Pastures beat Tolmi by two lengths at levels. Each time it was Star Pastures' superior finishing speed that settled the issue; we know of no valid excuses for Tolmi, although we did get the impression in the Goodwood races that Tolmi perhaps found the distance of seven furlongs on the sharp side. The Sussex Stakes at Goodwood and the Queen Elizabeth II Stakes at Ascot were mentioned at one time or another as targets for Tolmi but she was retired after the Heathorns Stakes without ever meeting the colts; judging from the way in which Dalsaan dealt with Star Pastures in the Hungerford Stakes Tolmi wouldn't have stood much chance against them.

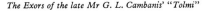

Tolmi (b.f. 1978)	Great Nephew (b 1963)	Honeyway (br 1941)	Fairway / Honey Buzzard
		Sybil's Niece (ch 1951)	Admiral's Walk / Sybil's Sister
	Stilvi (b 1969)	Derring-Do (br 1961)	Darius / Sipsey Bridge
		Djerella (ch 1960)	Guersant / Djeretta

Tolmi is to be covered by the miler Posse in her first season at stud. A strong, compact, well-made, attractive sort, she is the first filly produced by Stilvi and so her career at stud will be watched with particular interest. It would be asking a great deal of her to do as well as Stilvi, for Stilvi's record is an exceptional one. Stilvi's record has been repeated often in previous volumes of *Racehorses* but it is well worth outlining again. Tolmi is Stilvi's fifth foal and all five have been good racehorses. The first, Tachypous (by Hotfoot), won the Middle Park Stakes and was second in the Two Thousand Guineas; he is now at stud, and his first crop includes the Cherry Hinton Stakes winner Travel On. Stilvi's second foal was Taxiarchos (by Brigadier Gerard); he won the Land of Burns Stakes and is now at stud in South Africa. Thirdly came Tromos (by Busted) who won the Dewhurst Stakes unchallenged and was the outstanding two-year-old of 1978; he is now at stud in the United States. Stilvi's fourth foal, Tyrnavos (by Blakeney), provided her with her first classic winner in the 1980 Irish Sweeps Derby; he too is now at stud. Stilvi has since produced a filly by

The Exors of the late Mr G. L. Cambanis' "Tolmi"

Reform named Tenea and an unnamed colt by Mill Reef, the former of which has raced once so far and is engaged in the 1982 One Thousand Guineas. The mare was barren to Bustino in between.

Sadly Tolmi's owner, who bought Stilvi as a yearling and has bred so successfully from her, died in July. Stilvi was his first good winner over here with the National Stakes, the Duke of York Stakes and the King George Stakes amongst her five wins, but his success as an owner has by no means been limited to Stilvi and her offspring. In 1981, for example, there was also the high-class middle-distance colt Amyndas and the useful two-year-old Zilos. Mr Cambanis was also a leading owner in Greece. He had six home-bred Derby winners there, three of whom were out of the English mare Golden Chance whom he bought for 400 guineas. The Cambanis racing interests are to be continued by the widow. Had the horses been dispersed and sold at public auction Tolmi and her Mill Reef half-brother, to pick two of the plums, would surely have realised astronomical prices. *B. Hobbs.*

TOLSTOY 5 b.h. Reform 132–Stardom 75 (Hornbeam 130) (1980 10fg 10f **88** 10g* 12g 10.6d³ 10d* 10.5g² 10.2g² 10g² 10g 1981 10fg 10d² 12s 10.2d* 10fg 11.1s² 10f³ 11.7fg² 10f² 11.7d² 11fg* 10g³) lightly-made, attractive horse; fair handicapper; won at Doncaster in March and Ostend in August; beat Fo by ½ length in valuable Grand Handicap International on latter; stays 11.7f; acts on any going but seems suited by some give in the ground nowadays; blinkered twice in 1980; doesn't always find much off bridle; sold 15,000 gns Newmarket December Sales. *M. Jarvis.*

TOMASCHEK (USA) 3 ch.c. Secretariat–Gems and Roses (Stage Door Johnny) **106** (1980 NR 1981 12g 14g² 13f* 16f* 14f*(w.o.) 14f* 14f² 18.1d* 18g) $340,000Y; good-topped colt; good mover; poor walker; second foal; half-brother to a minor winner by Graustark; dam smart stakes winner at up to 1¼m; developed into a useful young stayer, winning maiden race at Nottingham and minor event at Thirsk in July and handicaps at Yarmouth in August and September; also walked over at Yarmouth; put up good performances when beating Castelnau by 1½ lengths (pair well clear) at Thirsk and when winning comfortably by 2 lengths from Hill of Slane at Yarmouth in September; second favourite for Tote Cesarewitch at Newmarket in October, but never looked likely to take a hand and was allowed to coast in well behind; finds 1¾m on short side and is well suited by 2m or more; yet to race on very soft going but acts on any other. *H. Cecil.*

TOM DOWDESWELL 5 br.g. Balidar 133–Georgian Princess 75 (Tamerlane **67** 128) (1980 5.8fg 5fg* 5d 5d 1981 5s 5d 5fg³ 5g 5f* 5f² 6fg 5.8f 5d 5f) strong, good sort; sprint handicapper; won at Beverley in June; stays 6f; best form on top-of-the-ground; usually blinkered. *J. Bethell.*

TOM HORN 4 br.g. Warpath 113–Creek Alley 91 (Klairon 131) (1980 9.4g 10fg 1981 11s) big gelding; poor form, including in a seller; blinkered once at 2 yrs. *J. Berry.*

TOMMY'S CHOICE 2 ch.c. Some Hand 119–Nikali 89 (Siliconn 121) (1981 — 5fg 5d 6fg) Mar 18; sturdy, compact colt; bad mover; second foal; dam second twice over sprint distances at 2 yrs; in rear in maiden race and sellers at Warwick; bandaged final start (June). *M. Bradley.*

TOMMY'S GOLD 3 b.f. Goldhill 125–Golden Palermo 70 (Dumbarnie 125) — (1980 5f 5fg 5fg 6g 5d² 5fg 5fg 5s 1981 5s 5d 5g 6g 8f) small filly; plater; speedy and is better at 5f than 6f; has been tried in blinkers; sold 400 gns Ascot 2nd June Sales. *M. Tompkins.*

TOMPION 7 b.g. Crozier 117–Valeria (Vulgan 123) (1980 NR 1981 12fg) — fairly useful hurdler at his best; lightly raced and no form on flat. *Mrs D. Oughton.*

TOM'S STAR 3 bl. or br.f. Comedy Star 121–Fleet Street Fifty 51 (I Say 125) — (1980 5g 5g 1981 8f 5.8f) compact filly; seems of no account, although has yet to run in a seller; has been tried in blinkers. *W. R. Williams.*

TOM STRAUSS 6 ch.g. Tompion–Ortica (Alcaeus 127) (1980 5d 6s 6g — 6f³ 8g 8d 6g 7f 7f 1981 8d 7g 10.6s) useful sort; has been fired; poor handi-capper nowadays; evidently best at sprint distances; acts on any going; often wears blinkers. *M. Blanshard.*

TONGSUNIAN 4 gr.g. Moulton 128–Queen's Message 93 (Town Crier 119) **60** (1980 7f³ 8.2g 8fg² 8fg 10f 1981 7fg 10fg³ 10f4) lightly-made gelding; stays 1¼m; acts on firm going; spoilt chance by hanging second outing; taken to post early last 2 starts. *W. Hastings-Bass.*

Prix Saint-Alary, Longchamp—Tootens records a comfortable win over Tropicaro and Last Love in this Group 1 event

TOOLRANGER 4 gr.g. Owen Anthony 102–Pen Friend 90 (Vigo 130) (1980 NR 1981 8d) poor maiden; sold 680 gns Ascot August Sales. *S. Harris.* —

TOO OFTEN 2 b.c. Cawston's Clown 113–Wolfsburg (Neckar) (1981 6g 6fg 7fg) evidently useless. *W. Charles.* —

TOOTENS 3 ch.f. Northfields–Night Attire 77 (Shantung 132) (1980 8g 7.5g* 1981 9.5fg⁴ 10v* 10.5fg 12g 12d) attractive filly; half-sister to several winners, notably 1,000 Guineas winner Nocturnal Spree (by Supreme Sovereign); dam sister to smart 1972 staying 2-y-o filly Setsu; close fourth to Bernica in Prix Vanteaux at Longchamp in April on reappearance; won Group 1 Prix Saint-Alary on same course the following month in good style, challenging entering last furlong and going clear to beat Tropicaro comfortably by 2 lengths; unplaced afterwards in Prix de Diane de Revlon at Chantilly in June (fifth to Madam Gay), Prix Vermeille at Longchamp in September and Prix de l'Arc de Triomphe on same course in October, but ran on well in straight and was far from disgraced when about 10 lengths eighth of 24 behind Gold River in last-named race; probably stays 1½m; well suited by plenty of give in the ground. *E. Bartholomew. France.* **124**

TOPAMAR 2 gr.f. High Top 131–Amaryllis 92 (Tudor Melody 129) (1981 6g) Apr 4; 760Y; sturdy filly; half-sister to minor winners here and in Belgium; dam won over 5f at 2 yrs; in need of race when behind in 17-runner maiden event won by Glossy Ibis at Redcar in August; sold 300 gns Doncaster October Sales. *M. H. Easterby.* —

TOPAZ TOO 2 ch.f. Sun Prince 128–Brilliant Gem 83 (Charlottown 127) (1981 5fg 6g* 6f 6g 6v) Apr 16; 26,000Y; well-made, attractive filly; second foal; dam lightly-raced half-sister to smart staying filly Pink Gem; ran on strongly to beat My Destiny by ½ length in 15-runner maiden race at Nottingham in August; soundly beaten afterwards, including in 2 nurseries (tailed off at halfway final start); will stay 1¼m. *G. Harwood.* **78**

TOP CREATOR 2 b.c. High Line 125–Corneater (Skymaster 126) (1981 8g) Apr 12; 17,000Y; strong, rangy colt; second foal; dam ran once; 16/1, showed signs of inexperience on way to start but ran promisingly when about 8 lengths eighth of 29 to Born Hero in maiden race at Newmarket in October; wasn't knocked about here and is sure to do better over 1¼m+ at 3 yrs. *B. Hills.* **80 p**

TOP GOLD 2 b.f. Supreme Sovereign 119–Dyna Bell 62 (Double Jump 131) (1981 5g) May 3; fifth foal; sister to a winner in Malaya; dam won 1¼m seller; 20/1 when behind in 20-runner maiden race won by Welwyn at Lingfield in September. *J. Holt.* —

TOPHOLE (FR) 3 b.f. High Top 131–Tuck In (Princequillo) (1980 NR 1981 8fg) lengthy filly; half-sister to Bolide (by Bold Lad, Ire), a smart winner at up to 1¼m, and 2 winners in USA; dam never ran; unquoted when behind in 21-runner race won by Taken For Granted at Newbury in July; sold 4,800 gns Newmarket December Sales. *R. Hern.* —

TOP HOPE 2 b.f. High Top 131–Port Ahoy 93 (Petingo 135) (1981 7fg* 7f² 7g*) **115**
In July 1937 a filly out of Rockliffe made a pretty inauspicious start to her racecourse career, finishing eighth of eleven in a seller at Sandown having been a backmarker the whole way. Fortunately the filly, subsequently named Rockfel,

Rockfel Stakes, Newmarket—Top Hope keeps on strongly to beat the fast-finishing Last Feather (far right) who is only fourth at this point

turned out a good deal better than her debut suggested she would, resembling in this respect that great stayer Son-in-Law who also commenced his racing life in a seller. Given 7-10 in the Free Handicap after winning a maiden race on the last of her four starts at two, Rockfel blossomed the following season into one of the best fillies seen in England between the wars, adding six races to her tally including the One Thousand Guineas, the Oaks and the Champion Stakes and sharing top weight with Bois Roussel in the Free Handicap. Over forty years on the 1981 Newmarket Houghton meeting saw a race deservedly, if belatedly, instituted in her honour, and to judge by the quality of the field that contested it the Rockfel Stakes has a bright future.

The result was a bit of a turn-up, the 12/1-shot Top Hope beating the 16/1-maiden Last Feather. Top Hope's price seemed a fair reflection of her prospects. She had won a Yarmouth maiden race in August by five lengths from Photo and finished equal second of four, half a length behind Tropical Blaze, when odds on for a slowly-run £4,600 event at Chepstow in September, but her seven opponents included several with demonstrably better form. A highly promising Cecil-trained filly Vadrouille, second at Newmarket earlier in October, was favourite; next in the betting came Zinzara, a good third to Height of Fashion in the Hoover Fillies Mile; the unbeaten Candide who had looked a smart filly in the making when winning a nursery at Newbury under top weight four weeks previously; and the consistent Admiral's Princess, successful in the Erroll Stakes and third to Woodstream in the Cheveley Park. Top Hope put up a much-improved performance to take the prize. Held up as Candide set a modest gallop, she was still just about last with two and a half furlongs to travel but this seemed not to bother her jockey Swinburn in the least. His confidence was justified; immediately he asked Top Hope to improve on the far side she produced a fine turn of foot that left her rivals floundering as she led outside the distance and kept on well to beat the strong-finishing Last Feather by two lengths. While Candide evidently ran well below her best and Zinzara, a filly with proven stamina, wasn't suited by being waited with in a relatively slowly-run affair, we see no reason to doubt the winner's merit. Last Feather went on to win a £6,300 event at Newbury a week later by six lengths and four, and the obvious conclusion is that Top Hope is a smart filly.

Top Hope (b.f. Feb 10, 1979)	High Top (br 1969)	Derring-Do (br 1961)	Darius
			Sipsey Bridge
		Camenae (b 1961)	Vimy
			Madrilene
	Port Ahoy (ch 1974)	Petingo (b 1965)	Petition
			Alcazar
		Guiding Light (ch 1965)	Crepello
			Arbitrate

High Top gets plenty of winners over middle distances or further—the St Leger winner Cut Above is by him—and we anticipate Top Hope's staying at least a mile and a quarter for her dam's family is a fairly stout one. Top Hope is the first foal of Port Ahoy, who won over six and seven furlongs at two and stayed a mile and a half the following year; the second, a Star Appeal colt, fetched 17,000 guineas at the Newmarket October Open Sales. The grandam Guiding Light, a lightly-raced half-sister to the dual Brown Jack Stakes winner Valuation, has produced three other winners, notably the useful La Dolce who stayed one and a half miles. Guiding Light was bred by the Royal Studs; her dam Arbitrate ran third in the Lingfield Oaks Trial and was a half-sister to Above Suspicion and Doutelle out of the Yorkshire Oaks and Cesarewitch winner Above Board.

Top Hope didn't take the eye in the paddock or on the way down at Newmarket—she's small, lengthy and rather lacking in scope—and we cannot be entirely confident about her making normal improvement over the winter. If she does, her turn of foot is likely to stand her in good stead though whether it will enable her to emulate Rockfel is another matter. *M. Stoute.*

TOP LAD 2 gr.c. Town Crier 119–Pinnacle 70 (High Perch 126) (1981 6d 5.3f 6s²) May 25; 7,200Y; small, quite attractive colt; good walker and mover; half-brother to 2 winners, including Senator Sam (by Meldrum), a winner 9 times from 6f to 1½m (including 6 victories at 2 yrs); dam best at up to 1½m; second favourite although having first race for 4 months, made much of running when 2 lengths second of 15 to Ellerene in maiden race at Newbury in October; will be suited by 1m; disappointed on only outing on firm going. *R. Price.* **78**

TOP MATCH 2 ch.c. Royal Match 117–Hilltop Chimes (Mountain Call 125) (1981 7fg 7g 7fg³ 7fg 7fg) Mar 21; IR 2,700F, 3,500Y; leggy colt; third foal; dam poor Irish maiden; only seventh of 11 in maiden race in July on second outing but left that form well behind in maiden race at Ayr in August, finishing 2¼ lengths third of 18 to Crellistovi after showing up throughout; will stay 1m; had tongue tied down third and fourth starts; ran moderately last 2 outings. *H. Bell.* **68**

TOP OF THE MARK 3 ch.g. On Your Mark 125–None-So-Pretty (Never Say Die 137) (1980 5f 5s⁴ 5d³ 6g 6s⁴ 6f* 6fg 5g 1981 5s 6f 5f 6f⁴ 6s 6f 7fg² 7fg⁴ 6f) strong gelding; often had stiffish tasks, but ran well when length second to Saint Motunde in handicap at Folkestone in August; suited by 7f; acts on any going but goes well on firm; blinkered sixth outing; possibly not the most genuine of animals; sold 3,200 gns Newmarket Autumn Sales. *C. Brittain.* **73**

TOP OF THE TABLE 5 b.h. Royal Prerogative 119–Fenland Queen (King's Troop 118) (1980 10f 8fg 12f 16g 1981 10g 12f) fairly useful at his best but has deteriorated markedly; has been tried in blinkers; not one to trust. *D. Marks.* **— §**

TOPOLINO SAURO 2 ch.f. El-Birillo–Souris Francais (Decoy Boy 129) (1981 6s 6d) May 4; leggy, close-coupled filly; first foal; dam unraced; in rear in 15-runner maiden race won by Risk Taker at Newbury in October and in 23-runner event at Leicester the following month. *Mrs R. Lomax.* **—**

TOPORI 2 br.g. High Top 131–Lady Oriana 91 (Tudor Melody 129) (1981 6g) Feb 17; good mover; first foal; dam, daughter of very smart sprinter Merry Madcap, won over 7f at 2 yrs; unquoted, going on well at finish when ninth of 26 to Tin Boy in maiden race at Newmarket in July; looked fairly promising here but was gelded in September. *B. Hills.* **—**

TOP O'TH' LANE 4 b.g. Palm Track 122–Poachings Folly (Poaching 115) (1980 8f* 8h² 10g 8g⁴ 7fg³ 9g⁴ 8d 7s 1981 7d 7.2s 9fg⁴ 8fg 8fg² 8g 8g⁴ 7f² 7f* 7d 7v) lengthy gelding; beat Secret Gill by 1½ lengths in handicap at York **72**

in September; stays 9f; ideally suited by top-of-the-ground; blinkered tenth outing. *W. Haigh.*

TOP REEF 3 br.c. Take a Reef 127–Bienvenida 75 (Sheshoon 132) (1980 6g 6fg 6s 5.1fg 8.2d⁴ 7.2s 8d 8d 10.2s 1981 12s 10s* 10s² 12g² 12d² 12d³ 11fg³ 13.8fg 11.7f⁴ 12fg 16.9fg 10.8fg 12g 13d) small, lengthy colt; attracted no bid after beating Campton a short head in selling handicap at Nottingham in April; placed in non-sellers afterwards, but ran poorly later in season; suited by 1½m; has run creditably on firm going, but is ideally suited by soft; slipped up eleventh start; suitable mount for an apprentice. *D. Leslie.* **50** d

TOPSIN (FR) 6 ch.h. Dictus 126–Top Twig (High Perch 126) (1980 12fg 11.7fg³ 10f⁴ 12fg 10g 12fg 10d 8fg 10fg² 11.7f 10g 13.1h 10.2g 12g 10d 1981 8s 7fg 7g 10d 14d 8d) good-looking horse; poor handicapper; best form at distances short of 1¾m; acts on firm going; has run moderately in blinkers; sometimes starts slowly. *O. Jorgensen.* —

TOPTOOL 3 b.g. The Brianstan 128–Grecian Cloud 76 (Galivanter 131) (1980 5.8fg 6fg 6d 5.8g³ 6g 1981 8d 7fg* 7d 8g 8g 7g⁴ 8.3g 7fg 8g 7d³) close-coupled, useful-looking gelding; bought in 2,250 gns after beating The Barons Lodge by 4 lengths in seller at Kempton in April; ran creditably on occasions afterwards, including in better company; stays 7f; usually blinkered, but has run creditably without; sold 3,600 gns Ascot November Sales. *P. Cundell.* **65**

TOP TRAVELLER 6 ch.h. Galivanter 131–Apex 72 (Donore 119) (1980 NR 1981 8h 8h) poor handicapper; suitable mount for a boy. *M. Bradley.* —

TORBAY EXPRESS 5 b.g. Owen Anthony 102–Luckhurst (Busted 134) (1980 5s 5g 6f 5f 5.8fg 5s 5g 5.8f 5fg 5d 5f 1981 5d* 5d) sturdy gelding; made all to win apprentice handicap at Warwick in May; best at 5f; acted on any going; blinkered once; dead. *M. Blanshard.* **57**

TORREMODO 3 gr.g. Grey Mirage 128–Smiling 62 (Silly Season 127) (1980 6g 7.2d 8fg 1981 8s³ 9d 9.4g 10.8s 12d) lightly-made gelding; third in maiden race at Stockton in April; stays 1m; off course over 5 months after third start. *A. W. Jones.* **56** d

TORREY (USA) 2 ch.c. Torsion–Deltaville (Delta Judge) (1981 5f² 6fg* 6d⁴) Feb 22; $77,000Y; quite an attractive, rather leggy colt; good walker and mover; second foal; half-brother to a winner in USA; dam, half-sister to 3 minor stakes winners, won twice at up to 5f; always going smoothly when odds on for 12-runner maiden race at Goodwood in July and stayed on strongly to win fairly comfortably by 1½ lengths from Mou-Ferni-Tychi; left behind in final furlong when 8 lengths fourth of 8 to Hays in Mill Reef Stakes at Newbury in September; suited by 6f. *R. Hern.* **96**

TORSION PRINCE (USA) 2 b.c. Torsion–Lucky Flirt (Lucky Debonair) (1981 5g² 7g² 7fg⁴ 7d⁴ 7fg) May 4; $35,000Y; lengthy, attractive colt; good mover; second foal; dam, half-sister to good filly Copano, won at up to 1m; in frame at Thirsk, Yarmouth, Goodwood and Newmarket, beaten only about 1½ lengths when fourth of 18 behind Noumayr in maiden event on last-named course in August; stays 7f; has given trouble at start on several occasions; ran badly final appearance. *N. Callaghan.* **82**

TORY JAYNE 3 b.f. Sovereign Bill 105–Whiffenretz 75 (Whiffenpoof 97§) (1980 NR 1981 12d 8.5g 12g 12fg 15.5f⁴ 12fg 12f) lightly-made filly; first living foal; dam won 3 times at around 5f; poor form in maiden and minor races and a handicap. *M. Haynes.* —

TO THE POINT 2 ch.f. Sharpen Up 127–Right as Rain 96 (King's Bench 132) (1981 5d* 5g² 7g² 7fg⁴ 5g² 5d* 5g) Jan 18; 25,000Y; leggy, light-framed filly; half-sister to several winners, including 1980 2-y-o 5f winner Barnet Heir (by Great Nephew) and very useful sprinter As Friendly (by Be Friendly); dam 2-y-o 5f winner; winner of maiden race at Chester in May and 4-runner event at Goodwood in September, latter by 3 lengths from Balcanoona; in frame in 2 good races in between, finishing 2½ lengths second of 8 to Celestial City in Uplands Park Acorn Stakes at Epsom and 3¾ lengths fourth of 6 to Prowess Prince in Molecomb Stakes at Goodwood; will be suited by 6f; best form with some give in the ground; sweated up a bit and ran moderately seventh outing. *G. Hunter.* **96**

TOTTERIDGE 4 b.f. Huntercombe 133–Catherine's Plea 95 (Petition 130) (1980 8fg 7g 8g 1981 8g 9fg) fair sort; poor plater; sold to M. Tate 540 gns Ascot August Sales. *R. Hannon.* —

Portland Handicap, Doncaster—fourth win of the season for Touch Boy as he beats Pencil Point

TOUCH BOY 5 b.h. Touch Paper 113–Hello Amy 70 (Forlorn River 124) **100**
(1980 6fg 6fg 6d 5g 5fg 6s 6g 5.6g³ 6s 6d 1981 5s 5g 6g⁴ 7.6g 5fg² 6g⁴ 5fg
5f* 5fg 6f 5g* 5d³ 5fg* 5.6fg* 6d 5s 6d) compact, robust horse; fairly useful
handicapper; had a good year, winning at Haydock (twice) Newcastle and
Doncaster; beat Pencil Point by ¾ length in Portland Handicap on last-named
in September; best form at sprint distances; acts on any going; effective with or
without blinkers. *J. Berry.*

TOUCHING WOOD (USA) 2 b.c. Roberto 131–Mandera 112 (Vaguely Noble **91** p
140) (1981 7s³) May 11; \$200,000Y; small, strong colt; second foal; half-
brother to Irish 1½m winner Mansky (by Nijinsky), also successful over hurdles;
dam won Princess Royal Stakes over 1½m; 33/1 and distinctly burly, ran an
excellent first race when 8½ lengths third of 11 behind impressive winner Paradis
Terrestre in Hyperion Stakes at Ascot in October, keeping on very well; will
stay 1½m; sure to improve. *H. T. Jones.*

TOUCH MY HEART 3 b.f. Steel Heart 128–Kiyofuji 98 (Grey Sovereign 128§) **61**
(1980 5g 1981 7g 5g³ 5f² 5g 5g 5f 5s⁴ 5s² 6g) 1,000 2-y-o; strong filly; third foal;
dam won twice over 5f at 2 yrs; placed in maiden and minor events and a
handicap; acts on any going; suitable mount for an apprentice; trained by
J. Scott in Ireland until after fourth outing. *D. Gandolfo.*

TOUCH OF CLASS (FR) 4 ch.f. Luthier 126–La Theve (Red God 128§) **47**
(1980 10.1s 10.2fg 14g 17.1d 10g 1981 8s 8s 8f 10.1fg* 10fg 10f⁴ 12g⁴) leggy,
sparely-made filly; dropped in class when hacking up in seller at Windsor in
July (sold out of R. Simpson's stable 3,500 gns); stays 1½m; acts on a firm
surface; sometimes blinkered (wasn't when successful); sweated up badly
final start (ran respectably). *W. Hastings-Bass.*

TOUGH AN ROUGH 3 b.g. Saulingo 122–Frensham 67 (Floribunda 136) **—**
(1980 5d³ 5f³ 5h² 5fg² 5g* 5g 5fg³ 1981 5d 5d 5fg 5d) small, sharp sort;
well beaten in 1981 and didn't appear to train on; unlikely to stay 6f; probably
acts on any going; blinkered second start (finished last); trained until after second
outing by M. Tate; sold 500 gns Doncaster September Sales. *W. Wharton.*

TOUGH BABU 3 br.g. No Mercy 126–Lily Elsie 74 (Our Babu 131) (1980 **—**
8fg 8.2s 1981 8.2d 12fg 15.5f 8s 12d 15.5s) useful-looking gelding; in rear
in varied races, including in amateur riders events; wears blinkers; trained
by A. Hide first outing. *A. Bailey.*

TOUGH CRITIC (USA) 2 b.c. Grey Dawn II 132–In Devotion (Boldnesian) **90**
(1981 5f 6g* 6f³ 6fg* 7fg 6d² 6g⁴ 7g) Apr 21; \$20,000Y; big, lengthy colt;
third foal; brother to a minor winner; dam placed once from 9 starts; won
maiden race at Hamilton in June; showed improved form in nurseries, winning
one at Windsor in August and finishing in frame at Nottingham and Newmarket
(2½ lengths fourth of 17 to Vaigly Star); runs as though he should be suited by 7f;
probably acts on any going. *G. Huffer.*

TOUJOURS VERT 2 ch.f. Northfields–Gently 95 (Grey Sovereign 128§)   **71** p
(1981 6g) Mar 18; 175,000Y; half-sister to numerous winners, including good
Italian 1974 2-y-o Godzilla (by Gyr); dam, daughter of Gimcrack Stakes and
Champagne Stakes winner Be Careful, won at 6f and 7f; 13/2, came out best of
newcomers when 6¼ lengths sixth of 21 to Mirabeau in maiden race at Doncaster
in September; will stay 7f; bound to improve. *M. Stoute.*

TOUSAN 2 b.f. Mandrake Major 122–Lochville 83 (Charlottesville 135) (1981   **50**
5f 5fg 5fg) Mar 31; 1,500Y; smallish, dipped-backed filly; half-sister to 3
winners here and abroad, including 1971 2-y-o 5f winner Renard Rouge (by
Kashmir II), subsequently a useful winner at up to 1½m in France; dam won
over 8.7f; poor maiden; sold 290 gns Doncaster October Sales. *Denys Smith.*

TOWERING 2 br.c. Tower Walk 130–Up And At It 72 (Tamerlane 128)   **88**
(1981 5fg 6g 6g² 6g² 8f³ 7fg* 8d³ 8.2s*) Apr 17; 9,000F, 6,000Y; tall, leggy colt;
half-brother to 2 winners, including 2m winner Conation (by Connaught); dam
2-y-o 7f winner; a genuine and consistent colt who won nurseries at Leicester
and Hamilton in the autumn, latter by 2 lengths from Time Wind; stays 1m
well; acts on any going but is particularly well suited by soft. *Sir Mark
Prescott.*

TOWER JOY 7 b.h. Tower Walk 130–Great Joy (Kythnos 126) (1980 7fg*   **93**
8fg² 7f⁴ 8fg² 7g* 7d 7fg² 7fg* 7.3fg² 7fg* 7g 1981 6g 8g 7g³ 7f* 8f⁴ 7f² 7fg 8fg³
7fg³ 8fg) strong, good-looking horse; fairly useful handicapper; decisively beat
Lady Sister by 3 lengths at Yarmouth (apprentices) in June; ran well most
subsequent starts, notably when 3¼ lengths fourth to Teamwork in Royal Hunt
Cup at Royal Ascot and 1½ lengths second to Captain Nick in Ward Hill Dunbury
Cup at Newmarket; stays 1m; acts on any going; excellent mount for an
apprentice; consistent. *L. Cumani.*

TOWER LADY 2 b.f. Tower Walk 130–Marie Denise 68 (Dual 117) (1981   **48**
5s 5s⁴ 5fg² 5g 5d 5.1fg 5f 6d² 6g) Apr 29; small, short-backed filly; half-sister to
2 winners, including stayer Passerine (by My Swallow); dam a stayer and quite
useful hurdler; plater; probably needs at least 6f nowadays; sweated up badly
when blinkered sixth outing. *G. Blum.*

TOWER WIN 4 ch.c. Tower Walk 130–Takawin 109 (Takawalk II 125) (1980   **53**
5v⁴ 5fg 5.8f³ 6f 6fg 7g 7f 6g 8s³ 6d 1981 7d⁴ 8fg⁴ 8d³ 10v 8f⁴ 8f² 10f 8fg 8.3g³
8f³ 8d* 10d) quite attractive colt; won minor event at Brighton in October;
stays 1m; acts on any going; blinkered 3 times in 1980; sometimes sweats up;
changed hands 4,000 gns Ascot 2nd June Sales. *J. Benstead.*

TOWN FLIER 2 b.g. Town Crier 119–Go Baby Go 81 (Takawalk II 125)   **90**
(1981 5fg 5s* 6d² 6s) Feb 22; compact gelding; good walker; second foal; dam
won 19f hurdle race; led well inside final furlong when winning 18-runner maiden
race at Nottingham in September by a length from Illicit, the pair 5 lengths clear;
good ½-length second of 15 to Friday Street in minor event at Brighton the
following month; will stay 1m; acts well on soft ground. *N. Vigors.*

TOWNGATE CROSS 2 b.f. Royal Match 117–Blue Bleep (Bleep-Bleep 134)   **54**
(1981 6g 7f³ 7f⁴ 7g⁴ 7d² 8.2fg⁴) Feb 7; narrow filly; poor mover; fourth foal;
dam won over 5f at 2 yrs in Ireland; plater; in frame most starts, on final one
being moved up to fourth after finishing fifth to Helshaw Grange at Haydock in
September (held every chance when nearly put over rails in final furlong); will
stay 1m. *M. H. Easterby.*

TOWN JENNY 3 b.f. Town Crier 119–Just Jenny 88 (Ennis 128) (1980 5d   **56**
6s 1981 8d 7fg 7f 5fg³ 5fg 7f 6fg 6f 5d 5s) quite a well-made filly; plating-class
maiden; not disgraced over 7f on third start. *R. Hollinshead.*

TOWNLEY STONE 2 b.g Legal Tender 94–Dream Isle (Indian Ruler 89)   **66**
(1981 7d 10.2g) June 20; rangy gelding; second foal; half-brother to NH Flat
race winner Sister Brown (by Murrayfield); dam prolific winner over hurdles and
fences; backed from 33/1 to 10/1, stayed on very strongly in straight to finish
about 14 lengths fifth of 26 to Yard Bird in minor event at Doncaster in November
on second outing; will stay well. *J. Webber.*

TOWN MASTER 3 b.c. Town Crier 119–Anjonic 56 (Le Levanstell 122)   **—**
(1980 8fg 6d 1981 10fg 8d 6g) leggy colt; about 11 lengths fifth of 8 behind
Critique in minor event at Nottingham in September on reappearance, best
effort; sold 1,750 gns Newmarket Autumn Sales. *B. Hanbury.*

TOWN SKY 5 gr.h. Town Crier 119–Pink Sky 86 (Midsummer Night II 117)   **70**
(1980 8g 8s⁴ 8d 7.6d 6f 6g 5d³ 6d² 7s⁴ 1981 7g² 8d* 8g² 8d 8s² 8fg³ 8fg 8fg 10.4s²)
strong horse; good mover; has been hobdayed and has had a soft palate operation;

quite a modest handicapper; won at Newcastle in April; stays 1m; acts on any going, except very firm; has shown a tendency to hang; often blinkered but is effective without; sold 1,400 gns Newmarket Autumn Sales. *S. Norton.*

TOWN SPECIAL 2 ch.g. Town Crier 119–Come On Girl (Sheshoon 132) (1981 **85**
5s 5d 5fg⁴ 5fg² 5fg* 5g 6fg 5.3d) Mar 22; quite attractive gelding; half-brother to fairly useful 2-y-o sprint winners City Link Lass and Daikoku (both by Double Jump); dam never ran; prominent in sizeable fields of maidens prior to dead-heating with Sussex Queen in 11-runner maiden race at Lingfield in July; should stay 6f (wore blinkers when last of 11 in nursery on first attempt at trip); suited by a firm surface; gelded late in season. *P. Ashworth.*

TRACK LIGHTING (USA) 2 ch.c. Le Fabuleux 133–Celestial Lights (Bold — p
Ruler) (1981 7fg) good-bodied, attractive colt; third foal; dam, winner at up to 7f, was one of best American 2-y-o fillies in 1973, and is half-sister to high-class colts Majestic Light and Fluorescent Light; unquoted, decidedly burly and very green, showed promise when coming through from rear to finish remote ninth of 19 to Dageegah in maiden race at Salisbury in September; will stay middle distances; has plenty of scope and is sure to do much better. *J. Dunlop.*

TRACK SET 2 b.f. Track Spare 125–Get Set 65 (Stupendous) (1981 6fg 6f 5g —
6g) Mar 28; leggy filly; sister to 3-y-o 11f seller winner Tennis Track; dam won over 1¼m; soundly beaten in sellers in the Midlands; brought down 1½f out on third start; sold 300 gns Doncaster October Sales. *R. Mason.*

TRACY'S SPECIAL 4 b.g. High Top 131–Devastating 103 (Honeyway 125) —
(1980 12s 12g 13.3fg 14g 15.5g 1981 14fg) big, strong gelding; poor maiden; blinkered once in 1980; retained 550 gns Ascot May Sales. *R. Hannon.*

TRADE HIGH 2 b.g. Tower Walk 130–Lucky Deal 93 (Floribunda 136) (1981 **80**
5s⁴ 5g² 5g³ 5d⁴ 5g² 5g³ 6fg 7d 7g³) May 3; 8,400Y; lightly-made gelding; half-brother to 3 minor winners; dam 2-y-o 5f winner; in frame in maiden and minor events; stays 7f; dwelt sixth outing. *G. Richards.*

TRADING 8 b.m. Forlorn River 124–Part Exchange 78 (Faubourg II 127) **62**
(1980 NR 1981 15.5d 12f* 13.8fg*) staying handicapper; won at Brighton (seller, no bid) and Catterick in July; suited by top-of-the-ground; suitable mount for an inexperienced rider. *W. Holden.*

TRADITIONAL MISS 6 ch.m. Traditionalist–Starboard Miss 81 (Right Boy **87**
137) (1980 10.8f 10g³ 8.2s 8fg* 9f³ 8.3fg⁴ 8g* 8h* 1981 8d 7g* 7v³ 8g⁴ 8f* 8fg* 8f³ 8h² 8fg 8h* 8h* 7fg²) fair handicapper; had a fine year and won at Newbury (apprentices), Chepstow, Brighton, Bath and Chepstow (apprentices) again; stays 1¼m; seems to act on any going but goes well on firm; good mount for an apprentice. *J. Hill.*

TRAILING ROSE 2 ch.f. Undulate–Ixia 91 (I Say 125) (1981 7g) Apr 24; —
good walker; half-sister to useful 1m and 1¼m winner Cardinal Flower (by Sharpen Up); dam very game winner at up to 1½m; 33/1 for 29-runner maiden race at Newmarket in October and finished tailed-off last behind Chalon; sold 400 gns Ascot December Sales. *G. Pritchard-Gordon.*

TRAIN OF THOUGHT 3 b.f. Bay Express 132–Kirkby 85 (Midsummer **79**
Night II 117) (1980 6g² 6g² 7fg² 7g 1981 7f 7f* 8g² 7.2g² 7f² 7fg 7g) lightly-made, lengthy filly; raced alone when beating Petite Hester by 4 lengths in 22-runner maiden race at Leicester in July; second in 3 handicaps the following month; possibly doesn't quite stay 1m; acts on firm going; dwelt when blinkered sixth start. *R. Armstrong.*

TRALEE FALCON 5 ch.m. Falcon 131–Uranus (Manacle 123) (1980 5f³ **67**
5g⁴ 6d 5fg² 6g 5g 5d 5f 5fg² 6g² 6fg² 6s² 5v 1981 6g⁴ 6g 7fg 7g² 7f³ 6f³ 7fg 7g 7.6s) small mare; stays 7f; acts on any going; blinkered several times in 1980; suitable mount for a boy; doesn't find much off bridle. *J. Fitzgerald.*

TRAMPLER 4 br.c. Bustino 136–Chieftain Girl (Chieftain) (1980 12fg⁴ 12fg⁴ **61**
12g³ 16d* 12g* 13.8g² 18f 12g 1981 16g⁴ 14g 16g³ 16f 16fg 12s⁴ 18g) neat, well-made colt; suited by a test of stamina; acts on a firm and a soft surface; ran poorly when sweating up badly once at 3 yrs. *J. Scallan.*

TRANSFLASH 2 br.c. Auction Ring 123–Gwen Somers (Will Somers 114§) —
(1981 6fg 6d) May 11; IR 6,800Y; leggy, useful-looking colt; third foal; dam unraced half-sister to smart animals Cyrus and Right of the Line; beaten some way in 11-runner minor event at Doncaster in June (started slowly) and 18-runner maiden race at Newmarket in August. *I. Walker.*

TRANSIENT (USA) 2 gr.c. For The Moment—Cutalong (The Axe 115) **75** p
(1981 7v) Apr 14; $57,000Y; lengthy, useful-looking colt; second foal; half-

brother to a minor winner; dam, winner at up to 6f, is half-sister to very useful sprinter Delice (by What A Pleasure); sire, son of What A Pleasure, was high-class winner at up to 9f: 10/1, always about same place and wasn't knocked about when 4¼ lengths fifth of 8 to Rocamadour in minor event at Kempton in October; looked a bit weak here and will do better at 3 yrs. *J. Tree.*

TRANSIT 2 b.f. Thatch 136–Bella Carlotta (Charlottesville 135) (1981 7d) — p
May 26; strong, good-bodied, short-legged, quite attractive filly; sister to 3-y-o 1m winner Herbie Quayle and half-sister to 3 other winners, notably very useful middle-distance colt Beauvallon (by Val de Loir); dam very useful sister to Sussex Stakes winner Carlemont; eased from 6/1 to 14/1 and made no show when behind in 18-runner maiden race won by Sans Blague at Newbury in September; will stay at least 1m; needed this race and looks capable of better. *B. Hills.*

TRANSONIC 2 br.f. Continuation 120–Sassanian Queen 71 (Baragoi 115) **60**
(1981 5s 5f* 5f 5g) June 12; lengthy filly; first foal; dam won 5f seller at 2 yrs; attracted no bid after winning 20-runner seller at Ripon in August, first outing for over 4 months; second favourite when seventh of 13 to Sammy Waters in valuable seller at York on next outing; will be well suited by 6f; dwelt final start. *J. Hardy.*

TRAPEZEY 3 ch.g. Red Alert 127–Floatingonair (Whistling Wind 123) (1980 **41**
5d 8d 1981 6s 5g 5v² 5g² 7g 6fg) light-framed gelding; placed in a seller and an apprentice handicap; usually blinkered nowadays (ran badly without final start); dwelt second outing. *R. Morris.*

TRAQUAIR 12 b.g. Klairon 131–Brandina (Never Say Die 137) (1980 8fg —
7f⁴ 10fg* 10d² 9g³ 8g 10fg 10g* 12g 12fg 10g 10d* 1981 8d⁴ 10f) grand old gelding; best at 1¼m nowadays; acts on any going; excellent mount for a boy. *J. Dunlop.*

TRAVEL BLUES 2 b.f. Hittite Glory 125–Blue Rag 70 (Ragusa 137) (1981 **79**
6g³ 7g⁴ 6f* 6f 6fg 6g) Mar 10; 7,400Y; neat, quite attractive filly; good mover; second foal; half-sister to fairly useful 1980 staying 2-y-o plater Blue Garter (by Targowice); dam 9f winner; won 10-runner maiden race at Brighton in August by ½ length from Latin Light after dwelling at start; hampered on only attempt over 7f and probably stays trip; ran moderately last 3 outings; sold to B. Hanbury 7,400 gns Newmarket Autumn Sales. *P. Walwyn.*

TRAVEL ON 2 b f. Tachypous 128–Chiltern Red (Red God 128§) (1981 5d² **111**
5d² 5fg* 6fg² 6f* 6g² 7fg 8d)

In *Racehorses of 1980* we wrote that it would be fascinating to see whether Stilvi, the dam of Tachypous, Taxiarchos, Tromos, Tyrnavos and Tolmi, could extend her influence even further through her grandchildren from Tachypous' first crop. Tachypous made a successful beginning to his stud career with four winners from eighteen starters, including the fairly useful performers Fimi (winner of four races) and Tachywaun, and Travel On became his first important winner when taking the Group 3 Cherry Hinton Stakes at Newmarket in July.

Travel On's form prior to the Cherry Hinton Stakes fell some way below what one would expect of a potential pattern-race winner. She had won once, picking up £690 for a victory in a maiden race at Warwick, and had been runner-up on her three other outings; she had failed through greenness on her debut but been beaten on merit by Admiral's Princess in a minor event at Brighton and Sing Softly in a £4,200 race at Newmarket. The betting on the Cherry Hinton Stakes suggested that the race lay between two fillies that had created quite an impression on their debuts, Lavender Dance (in winning a maiden race at Yarmouth by six lengths) and Quest (in finishing fast into third in the Queen Mary Stakes at Royal Ascot). In the event neither was able to make the first three as 25/1-shot Travel On, dripping with sweat beforehand, ran out a decisive winner. Having been held up, Travel On moved through smoothly to take up the running about a furlong out and win going away by a length and a half from Bright View.

Travel On was raced only in pattern races after Newmarket. She ran her best race in the Lowther Stakes at York, in which she had to concede 5 lb to all seven rivals, including Circus Ring. As widely anticipated, Travel On proved no match for Circus Ring; she ran a very brave race however, keeping on under pressure to the end and coming four lengths clear of third-placed Corley Moor. In her remaining two races Travel On failed over longer distances to reproduce anything like that form. She finished fifth of six behind Stratospheric when the favourite for the Waterford Candelabra Stakes at Goodwood and last of

Mr R. A. Patrick's "Travel On"

eight to Play It Safe in the Prix Marcel Boussac at Longchamp in October. It is difficult to draw any conclusions from these performances other than that Travel On was probably past her best for the season. In neither race was she ever on terms; at Goodwood she was off the bit at halfway and at Longchamp for most of the race.

Travel On (b.f. Mar 13, 1979)	Tachypous (b 1974)	Hotfoot (br 1966)	Firestreak
			Pitter Patter
		Stilvi (b 1969)	Derring-Do
			Djerella
	Chiltern Red (ch 1973)	Red God (ch 1954)	Nasrullah
			Spring Run
		Ashton Jane (ch 1960)	Gratitude
			Rye Girl

Travel On is the second foal of Chiltern Red, a poor sister to three winners including Red Alert. She is closely related to Chiltern Red's first produce Chilblains (by Hotfoot), a winner at six furlongs and a mile here at two before winning several races in Italy. Both Travel On's second dam, who failed to train on, and third dam won at two years. Rye Girl, the third dam, was a plating half-sister to Crimson, winner of the 1953 Lowther Stakes. Interestingly, she is the grandam of Cajun. Travel On, a neat, strong, good-quartered filly and a good mover, cost 9,400 guineas as a yearling. She showed steady physical improvement throughout the year. Her best form is on a sound surface. *P. Walwyn.*

TREAD A MEASURE 3 b.g. Tudor Rhythm 112–Lady Jewel (Kibenka 119) **48**
(1980 6g 6d 1981 8d 8fg 8d⁴ 8d 10g 7fg 7fg 8fg² 8.2fg 8.2d⁴ 8d) quite an attractive, useful-looking gelding; has shown a little ability, including in sellers; stays 1m; blinkered sixth (started slowly) and tenth outings. *J. Douglas-Home.*

Mr A. P. Ward's "Treboro"

TREBORO (USA) 2 b.c. Roberto 131–Costly Dream (Cohoes) (1981 5fg **112** p
5s 6f² 7f* 7g* 7fg*)

In these days when many an expensive yearling receives kid-glove treatment
it was refreshing to witness the no-nonsense handling of Treboro in 1981. At
240,000 dollars Treboro was the most expensive horse trainer Harwood had ever
bought and so just the type one would have expected to be brought along slowly,
especially since he has the Derby winner Roberto as his sire and Costly Dream, a
filly who didn't reach her peak until four, as his dam. However, when it became
clear in the spring that Treboro wasn't learning as much as he should in his home
gallops he was dispatched forthwith to the races, becoming the first of the stable's
forty-odd two-year-old colts to make his debut. Like Recitation the year before,
he ran in the Sandown Park Maiden Stakes late in April; he came home sixth of
twelve to Wind and Wuthering and showed exactly why he was being given early
racecourse experience. He showed distinct signs of greenness, failed to stretch
out on the way to the start and then was caught flat-footed as the stalls opened.
Two more races were needed to teach him what was required, the Rivermead
Maiden Stakes at Kempton where he clearly found the five furlongs too sharp,
and the Chesham Stakes at Royal Ascot. His effort in finishing second to
Cajun in the Chesham was a marked advance on his previous form but even here
Treboro seemed not to know what was required of him: after running into trouble
in the early stages and receiving some hefty cracks from Starkey he took a long,
long time to find his stride. Once in full flight though, he showed to good effect,
finishing so well that Cajun, who'd looked home and dry a furlong out, held him
off by only three quarters of a length.

The Chesham Stakes also showed that six furlongs was a little short for Treboro; given an extra furlong he never looked back and he won three races in July

902

beginning with the Plantation Maiden Stakes at Newmarket. He started at 6/4 on in a field of twenty-two at Newmarket and was always in command, comfortably holding off the fast-finishing newcomer Ashenden by two lengths. He also started favourite when gaining his other successes in the Donnington Castle Stakes at Newbury and the Lanson Champagne Stakes at Goodwood. The opposition at Newbury wasn't anything out of the ordinary and Treboro, giving upwards of 5 lb all round, never looked likely to be beaten once he hit the front two furlongs out, accounting for Diamond Shoal by a length ridden out only with hands and heels. Treboro's task at Goodwood looked a good deal stiffer; only My Dad Tom, the winner of six of his nine previous starts, carried the same weight as Treboro and the pair had to give 3 lb to Vin St Benet, a good third to Ashenden under a big weight at Newmarket on his latest start, and 8 lb to both the promising Blue Emmanuelle and the Coventry Stakes fourth Telephone Man. Treboro proved well up to his task, taking the lead passing the three-furlong marker and staying on strongly to keep the others at bay. The length by which he beat Telephone Man, who had rallied in remarkable style to pip My Dad Tom and Vin St Benet for second place, didn't give a true indication of his superiority: not for the first time Treboro tended to race lazily, rather like a previous winner of the Lanson Champagne Stakes, Troy. The latter went on to run in the Royal Lodge Stakes, a race that was also said to be Treboro's target. Unfortunately Treboro had to miss the race, having chipped a sesamoid, leaving his stable-companion Norwick to deputise successfully.

Treboro's season, therefore, came to an end before he'd had a chance to race in the top events over seven furlongs and a mile. This, together with his disinclination to do anything more than is necessary in his races, has led, almost inevitably, to his appearing on a mark some way behind the likes of Wind and Wuthering and Green Forest. However we're sure there was still plenty of improvement in Treboro and it's very interesting that his trainer said of him 'Make no mistake about this colt: I think he's top class and could well be my main Derby hope'.

Treboro (USA) (b.c. Apr 10, 1979)	Roberto (b 1969)	Hail to Reason (br 1958)	Turn-to / Nothirdchance
		Bramalea (b 1959)	Nashua / Rarelea
	Costly Dream (b 1971)	Cohoes (b 1954)	Mahmoud / Belle of Troy
		Dan's Dream (ch 1961)	Your Host / Rosella

Treboro is a well-made, good sort of colt and a good walker. He also has an attractive pedigree. Roberto continues to do well at stud and in 1981 sired the winners of well over a million dollars in the States as well as the good British winners Critique, Robellino, Silver Hawk and Slightly Dangerous. Treboro's grandam Dan's Dream never ran but she's a full sister to Miss Todd, one of the best American two-year-old fillies of 1955, and at stud has produced numerous winners. Eight of them, of which six won stakes races, were foaled consecutively from 1967 to 1974. If some of Dan's Dream's stakes winners weren't anything special they were certainly tough with Royal Knightmare having fifty-seven races, Jesta Dream Away fifty and Go On Dreaming fifty-one, while the very useful 1976 two-year-old Once Upon A Star had fifty-three in all. Treboro's dam Costly Dream was the best of them, winning fifteen races in all at up to a mile, including four small stakes at three and the 50,000-dollar Berlo Handicap at four when she was rated only 10 lb behind the top older filly Susan's Girl, one of few mares ever to have won over a million dollars. Treboro is Costly Dream's second foal. He's said to have made a complete recovery from his injury so we should see him making up for lost time in 1982. He acts well on firm ground and races as though middle distances will suit him admirably. *G. Harwood.*

TREELINE 3 b.f. High Top 131–Crepe Myrtle 80 (Crepello 136) (1980 NR **59** 1981 6g³ 7d 7f⁴ 5f⁴ 6fg² 5fg 8.2s) small, quite attractive filly; closely related to useful 1976 2-y-o 5f winner Ground Cover (by Huntercombe), subsequently a stakes winner in North America; dam won over 1m; in frame several times, coming out easily best of those racing on far side with 2½ lengths second of 23 behind Melodrama in apprentice maiden event at Newbury in August; best form at up to 6f, but should stay further. *J. Tree.*

TREE MALLOW 3 b.f. Malicious–Potentilla 89 (Nearula 132) (1980 7fg 7d **71** 1981 10d 12f 12fg³ 12d² 12g⁴ 13d² 15.5s* 14g³) lightly-made filly; won 20-

runner maiden race at Folkestone in October; good third to Tea-Pot in handicap at Newmarket later in month; suited by a test of stamina; has run creditably on a firm surface, but is well suited by some give in the ground; sometimes sweats up. *M. Smyly.*

TRE FONTANE 3 b.c. Windjammer (USA)–St Tropez 99 (Princely Gift 137) **93** (1980 5f 5fg* 5fg² 5d* 5g⁴ 6d⁴ 5g⁴ 5g⁴ 5g³ 5s² 5g 1981 6g 6g 6g 5f 6g* 6s 6g) good sort; useful performer at 2 yrs when trained by J. Etherington; raced in USA in the spring and was last in allowance races at Santa Anita and Hollywood Park (two); ran best race on his return when beating Go Total ½ length in minor event at Brighton in September; stays 6f; seems to act on any going; sold 8,000 gns Newmarket December Sales. *M. Jarvis.*

TRENDBUCKER (USA) 2 b.c. Far North 120–Sentimental Girl (Antonio **61** Canale) (1981 7d⁴ 8g) May 30; $50,000Y; useful sort; half-brother to a winner in USA and good Puerto Rican filly Just A Memory (by Olden Times); dam 6f winner in USA; 10/1 and in need of race when 11¼ lengths fourth of 14 to Crimson Knight in maiden race at Chester in August; still not fully wound up when in rear in similar event won by Outlaw at Ayr the following month. *S. Norton.*

TRESTLE 2 gr.f. Three Legs 128–Abbie West 112 (Abernant 142) (1981 5d 7d) **— p** Mar 24; IR 6,800F, 33,000Y; leggy, quite attractive filly; excellent mover; half-sister to very useful 1975 2-y-o 5f winner Grey Home (by Habitat) and useful 1974 2-y-o 6f winner West Two (by Connaught); dam very useful at up to 7f; unquoted and having first race for 4 months, showed up most of way when about 12 lengths fifth of 18 to Sans Blague in maiden race at Newbury in September; stays 7f; still has improvement in her. *L. Cumani.*

TRIBAL EYE 6 b.m. Tribal Chief 125–Nocturnal (Combat 123) (1980 6fg **—** 6g 6fg 6fg 6fg³ 6g 6d³ 6fg⁴ 8d 1981 6g 5.8g) rangy mare; blind in one eye; sprint handicapper; best at 6f; acts on any going, but goes well on firm; usually held up; has run well for an apprentice; has won 3 times at Brighton. *P. Cole.*

TRIBAL GIRL 2 b.f. Hittite Glory 125–Lagoon Girl (First Landing) (1981 **36** 5g³ 6f 6fg) bad plater; sold 380 gns Doncaster August Sales. *R. Fisher.*

TRIBAL WARLORD 5 ch.g. Scottish Rifle 127–Callidice 77 (Worden II 129) **—** (1980 13g 1981 12s⁴) strong, compact gelding; plater; probably stays 1¾m. *M. Naughton.*

TRICHORIA 3 b.f. Saritamer 130–Thermopylae 91 (Firestreak 125) (1980 5f **62** 5fg 5g 7g 5g 5d² 6g⁴ 8s 1981 8s 5d³ 5.8g² 6s 5f 6f³ 5.3fg 6f) quite attractive filly; in frame in varied races, including in a valuable seller as a 2-y-o; best form at up to 6f, but not disgraced over 1m. *R. Smyth.*

TRICKSHOT 2 br.g. Workboy 123–Lemoncilla (Philemon 119) (1981 7g 7fg 7f **88** 7fg³ 8g 8.2d* 7s³ 8.2d⁴ 8.2s²) Apr 13; useful sort; third foal; dam never ran; won 20-runner maiden race at Hamilton in September by 2 lengths from Crackhill; twice ran creditably in nurseries afterwards, on final start finishing 4 lengths second to Bluethroat at Nottingham in October; suited by 1m; best form on soft ground but has run respectably on a firm surface; bridle slipped on fifth outing. *K. Stone.*

TRIFLING 2 b.f. Tower Walk 130–Whiffle 105 (King's Troop 118) (1981 6f⁴) **66 p** Apr 18; fifth living foal; half-sister to 3-y-o 1m and 1¼m winner Windpipe (by Leander); dam stayed 1m; 14/1, had every chance at distance when promising 4 lengths fourth of 10 to Tropical Blaze in minor event at Ripon in August; sympathetically handled here; will stay 7f+. *J. W. Watts.*

TRIGONOME (FR) 2 b.c. Trio–Gondolys (Hœdell 120) (1981 5g 5.5g² 7d* **110** 6g⁴ 7f 8g² 8fg⁴ 7.5s⁴ 9d*) third reported foal; brother to minor winners over 1½m and 7f in France; dam won over jumps at 3 yrs; beaten in a small race at Bernay in June on second outing but later won minor event at Evry in July and Group 3 Prix Saint-Roman at Longchamp in October, getting home by short neck from Empery Card after being held up for late run at Longchamp; suited by 9f and will probably stay further; suited by a soft surface; sold 610,000 francs at Arc de Triomphe Sale a few hours after his Saint-Roman win. *R. Collet, France.*

TRIGOWEN 3 ch.g. Owen Anthony 102–Salvo of Conkers 79 (Salvo 129) **—** (1980 6g 5s 5.8fg 6s 5g³ 5g 1981 7d 6d⁴ 8d 5f) plating-class maiden; ran well on second start; probably stays 7f. *B. Palling.*

Clive Graham Stakes, Goodwood—lightly-raced Triomphe beats Royal Fountain

TRIMA KASEH 4 gr.f. Warpath 113–Silver Swell (Silver Cloud 121) (1980 NR —
1981 10f) poor form, including in a seller; has sweated up. *W. Barrett.*

TRIOLOGY 3 b.g. Hot Spark 126–Playtime (Primera 131) (1980 5s 5d 6s 7g³ 8d —
1981 10g 8f 10.1fg 12fg) smallish gelding; well beaten in 1981; should stay 1m.
D. Weeden.

TRIOMPHE (USA) 4 br.c. Hoist the Flag–Dinner Partner (Tom Fool) **114**
(1980 10s* 1981 10d² 9d* 10s* 12f) $600,000Y; medium-sized, quite attractive
colt; doesn't impress in his slower paces; half-brother to numerous winners,
including Jim French (by Graustark), winner of Santa Anita Derby and second
in Kentucky Derby and Belmont Stakes, and 3-y-o Don't Sulk (also by Graustark)
successful in Prix de Royallieu; dam very useful stakes winner over 6f and 1m;
only lightly raced but is a smart performer; landed odds in £1,000 race at
Leopardstown in May and ran on well to beat Royal Fountain by a length in
Clive Graham Stakes at Goodwood later in month; well beaten when favourite
for Hardwicke Stakes at Royal Ascot in June, only subsequent start; should
stay 1½m; acts on soft going. *V. O'Brien, Ireland.*

TRIPLE ALLIANCE 2 b.c. Shantung 132–Rhodie Blake 101 (Blakeney 126) — p
(1981 7g) May 25; 11,000Y; compact, attractive colt; second foal; half-brother
to useful 1980 2-y-o 6f and 7f winner Rahway (by Sovereign Path), subsequently
a winner in USA; dam ran only twice, winning over 7f at 2 yrs, and is sister to very
smart Roscoe Blake; weak in market when behind in 15-runner Houghton Stakes
won by Ivano at Newmarket in October; will need 1½m+ at 3 yrs; should do
better. *G. Harwood.*

TRIPLE AXEL (USA) 2 b.c. Dance Spell–Shivering (Etonian) (1981 7fg **102+**
7fg* 7.6g* 8s) Mar 21; $200,000Y; sturdy, good-looking colt; excellent mover;
first foal; dam, winner over 6f at 3 yrs in USA, is half-sister to very smart
It's Freezing, successful from 6f to 9.5f in Ireland and in USA; still had a lot to do
at distance when favourite for 8-runner minor event at Epsom in September
but ran on extremely well to catch Fol Hardi close home, winning by a neck;
wore down Wind and Wuthering (gave 4 lb) to win valuable Burr Stakes at
Lingfield later in month by ¾ length; beaten early in straight and finished

905

Burr Stakes, Lingfield—Triple Axel wins from Wind and Wuthering and Busaco

13½ lengths eighth of 10 to Green Forest in Grand Criterium at Longchamp in October; will stay 1¼m and may well get 1½m; possibly better than we are able to rate him. *I. Balding.*

TRIPLE DANCER 2 b.c. Dance In Time–Triple First 117 (High Top 131) **?**
(1981 9d*) Mar 15; 40,000Y; first foal; dam thoroughly game winner of 7 races from 5f to 1¼m, including Musidora, Nassau and Sun Chariot Stakes; favourite, led at distance when winning 10-runner newcomers event at Evry in October by ¾ length from Strong Blake; will stay at least 1¼m; should make a very useful colt; entered in Derby. *J. Cunnington, jnr, France.*

Mr E. N. Kronfeld's "Triple Axel"

TRIPLE SECRET 3 b.c. Relko 136–Secret Isle (Voluntario III) (1980 7d 7f 8s **60**
1981 12g⁴ 12d⁴ 11g³ 15fg⁴ 16.5fg² 16.5fg⁴ 16g 16f³ 18f⁴ 16g 16s) lengthy colt;
plating-class maiden; stays very well; ran too freely when blinkered tenth start;
sold 2,600 gns Newmarket Autumn Sales. *Denys Smith.*

TRIPLE TIPPLE (USA) 2 b.f. Raise a Cup–Ameridouble (Nodouble) (1981 **86**
6fg² 6g) Mar 9; $34,000Y; lengthy filly; third foal; half-sister to French 1½m
winner Ranan (by Ace of Aces); dam unraced half-sister to very useful middle-
distance filly Trillionaire; sire, son of Raise A Native, ran only at 2 yrs when
a leading sprinter; seemed to be going very easily indeed approaching distance
in Virginia Water Stakes at Ascot in July but then had difficulty finding an
opening and in circumstances did well to finish 2½ lengths second of 11 to Johara;
third favourite for Lowther Stakes at York the following month, but finished
only seventh of 8 to Circus Ring after being beaten some way out (said to have
pulled a muscle); will stay at least 1m; must be given another chance to confirm
the favourable impression she created at Ascot. *L. Cumani.*

TRISKELION 2 b.c. Three Legs 128–Maynooth Belle (Busted 134) (1981 5f **—**
7fg 5s 6g) Mar 19; IR 3,100F, 3,000Y; small, strong colt; first produce; dam,
out of half-sister to Psidium and Thymus, never ran; in rear in maiden races,
one an auction event; blinkered fourth outing. *S. Woodman.*

TRISTAM 3 b.c. Continuation 120–Stevie 79 (The Phoenix) (1980 NR **—**
1981 6g 8fg 7f 12g) leggy, unfurnished colt; half-brother to several winners;
dam sprinting half-sister to Deep Diver; poor form in maiden races, a seller
and a claiming race; sold 460 gns Newmarket Autumn Sales. *J. Hardy.*

TROCADERO 2 b.c. Sagaro 133–True Love 89 (Princely Gift 137) (1981 6d) **—**
Apr 10; neat colt; half-brother to several winners, including quite useful 7f winner
Peek-A-Boo (by Bustino) and 3-y-o 1m and 9f winner Battalion (by Bustino);
dam 2-y-o 5f winner; unquoted and in need of race, always struggling when behind
in 16-runner minor event won by Rosananti at Ayr in September. *C. Thornton.*

TROJAN KING 2 b.c. Free State 125–Shari (Rustam 127) (1981 6g) Apr 30; **—**
8,200Y, 6,000 2-y-o; half-brother to 4 winners, including very smart 5f filly
Harem (by Tribal Chief); dam, sister to Double Jump, won at 2 yrs in Italy on
only start; 25/1 when in rear in 19-runner newcomers event won by Zinzara at
Goodwood in September. *B. Swift.*

TROJAN SECRET 3 br.c. Averof 123–Camina Bay 109 (Whistling Wind 123) **62**
(1980 NR 1981 8f³ 10d) sparely-made colt; brother to Foveros, a smart
winner at up to 8.5f, and half-brother to 2 winners; dam useful sprinting 2-y-o;
raced in touch from start and stayed on reasonably well when 3½ lengths third
to Essam in maiden race at Beverley in August, easily better effort; stays 1m.
C. Brittain.

TROLL LADY 4 b.f. Crisp and Even 116–Fire Hawk 70 (Firestreak 125) **46**
(1980 8s² 8fg 8g 9f 1981 10g 10.1d 10s⁴ 12d 15.5fg⁴ 12g⁴ 12g* 12.2g 12d) leggy
filly; plater; won claiming handicap at Leicester in September; stays 1½m;
probably needs some give in the ground; sometimes sweats up. *P. Feilden.*

TROOPER SERGEANT 2 b.g. Queen's Hussar 124–Grass Widow (Thatch 136) **77**
(1981 6d 7g 7fg³ 6g 6fg³ 7g) Apr 11; lightly-made gelding; first foal; dam unraced
half-sister to high-class 1973 2-y-o The Blues; third in maiden race at Warwick in
July and nursery at Salisbury in September; stayed on very strongly when
beaten 1½ lengths by Royal Invitation in latter; stays 7f; sold 2,000 gns Newmarket Autumn Sales. *H. Candy.*

TROPICAL BLAZE (USA) 2 b.f. Chieftain–Ribot's Gold (Ribot 142) (1981 **100**
6fg* 6f* 7f*) Mar 18; $40,000Y; small filly; sixth foal; half-sister to a winner in
USA by Fleet Nasrullah; dam never ran; ridden by apprentice N. Day when
successful in maiden race at Doncaster in July, minor event at Ripon in August
and £4,600 race at Chepstow in September; put up a useful effort when rider
couldn't claim his 5-lb allowance at Chepstow, winning by ½ length from dead-
heaters Top Hope and Blakesware County in slowly-run 4-runner affair; will
stay 1¼m; has raced only on fast ground; genuine. *H. Cecil.*

TROPICAL LOVE 3 ch.g. Red Alert 127–Luluna (Pinza 137) (1980 5fg 7g **69**
8fg 8d 6s 8d 1981 12d 8f⁴ 8.2g* 7g* 9g 8fg) neat, strong gelding; ran easily best
races when winning maiden race at Hamilton (by 6 lengths) and minor race at
Edinburgh in June; should stay beyond 1m; apprentice ridden nowadays.
B. Hanbury.

TROPICAL PARK 6 b.m. My Swallow 134–Hialeah (Snob II 130) (1980 12g **—**
16fg 1981 12s³) lengthy mare; poor maiden. *J. Mason.*

TROPICARO (FR) 3 b.f. Caro 133–Tropical Cream (Creme dela Creme) **116**
(1980 8g* 8f* 7v 1981 10.5s 8fg* 8g 10v² 12g 10s) leggy, lightly-built filly;
second foal; half-sister to useful French 1¼m winner Tropical Lightning (by
Lyphard); dam smart performer at 2 and 3, winner of 10½f Prix Cleopatre;
won 2 races at Longchamp as a 2-y-o, including Prix Marcel Boussac; beat
Marie Noelle by a nose in Group 3 Prix de la Grotte at Longchamp in April,
setting a good pace and fighting back gamely when headed; led before turn and
kept on battling on when 2 lengths second of 10 behind Tootens in Prix Saint-
Alary on same course the following month; not disgraced when fifth to Ukraine
Girl in Poule d'Essai des Pouliches at Longchamp on third start but ran well
below her best in Oaks at Epsom in June (lost her place completely after 6f
and finished tailed-off last of 12) and Prix de Malleret at Longchamp in July;
should stay 1½m; acts on any going; very game. *M. Zilber, France.*

TROUVAILLE 7 b.h. Tratteggio 123–Helen Allingham (Busted 134) (1980 7fg —
10f* 9g 12d² 12fg 8.2d 1981 12fg 12fg 16g 16f 10.6s) plater; seems to stay
1⅛m; appears to act on any going; has worn blinkers; usually wears bandages;
good mount for an inexperienced rider. *R. E. Peacock.*

TRUDY'S BOY 5 ch.g. Doeskin 105–Cash Deal 71 (Hook Money 124) (1980 —
8fg⁴ 8.3fg 10.1f 16f 12g² 12d 1981 8s⁴ 12d) big gelding; plating-class maiden;
stays 1½m; acts on soft going; suitable mount for an amateur rider. *R. Akehurst.*

TRUESIGN 3 b.g. Upper Case–Corneater (Skymaster 126) (1980 5f 6g 5d 6v³ —
6s 1981 6s 6fg) plater; bandaged on off-fore in 1981; sold out of R. Hollinshead's stable 1,650 gns Doncaster January Sales and resold 500 gns same venue
in September. *B. Lunness.*

TRU MAR 5 ch.h. Northfields–High Corinda 85 (High Treason 126) (1980 14f —
14fg² 16f³ 18fg 12d 14g⁴ 16g² 14g³ 12g² 1981 18.4d) big, rangy horse; has
won over 2m but gives impression shorter distances suit him better; possibly
needs a sound surface. *Mrs M. Rimell.*

TRUPER GEE 3 b.g. Rheingold 137–Cappuccilli 111 (Lorenzaccio 130) (1980 **56**
7d 1981 8fg 10s 16s 12g 8fg 10f 7g 12fg* 9g 12fg 12f 12g⁴ 11d² 12d 12d²) small
gelding; plater; showed much improved form when beating Bloak Moss a neck at
Newmarket in July (bought in 1,000 gns); suited by 1½m; acts on a firm and a
soft surface; sweated up and ran freely when well beaten in blinkers sixth start.
R. Whitaker.

TRUST SALLY 2 b.f. Sallust 134–Trust Sylvia (Linacre 133) (1981 5s 5g **65**
5fg 5f 5f* 5g 5f 5g³) Feb 23; 2,200Y; neat, sturdy filly; half-sister to a winner in
Belgium by Green God; dam unplaced 4 times; beat Blue Rain 1½ lengths in seller
at Ripon in August (no bid); evidently thought best at 5f; acts on firm going.
W. Wharton.

TRUSTY CATCHER (USA) 3 ch.g. Pass Catcher–In Trust (Buckpasser) **63**
(1980 7d 1981 8g 10f² 11fg⁴ 8fg) rangy gelding; in frame in maiden races at
Yarmouth and Kempton; suited by middle distances; sweating final start.
H. T. Jones.

TRYTON LINES 4 b.c. Wolver Hollow 126–Djenarelle (Djefou) (1980 7d² —
7d 8f² 8h* 8fg⁴ 10d⁴ 10fg* 8f³ 1981 8g 8fg 8g 8f 10f) good sort; successful in
maiden race and slowly-run handicap at Pontefract at 3 yrs; well beaten in 1981
(had stiffish tasks first 3 starts); stays 1¼m· suited by fast ground; blinkered
final start; sold 1,400 gns Doncaster October Sales. *M. H. Easterby.*

TRYTRAVELSCENE 3 gr.f. Dragonara Palace 115–Ash Fell 83 (Bleep-Bleep **63**
134) (1980 5g² 5d* 5g² 5f 1981 5d 5fg 5d 5f³ 5s 5g) strong filly; didn't
recover her 2-y-o form, although ran respectably on occasions; may stay 6f;
blinkered final outing. *P. Makin.*

TSAR'S BRIDE 3 b.f. Song 132–Empress of Russia 79 (Royal Palace 131) —
(1980 6s⁴ 5g 6f 1981 8fg) big, rangy filly; showed a little ability at 2 yrs; last on
only appearance of 1981; sold, covered by Persian Bold, 8,000 gns Newmarket
December Sales. *A. Ingham.*

TUBES CARE 2 b.f. Moulton 128–Drury Lane 83 (Gala Performance) (1981 —
8fg 8s 8s 10.2g) May 1; 500Y; big, strong filly; third foal; half-sister to 1980
2-y-o 6f seller winner Supreme Show (by Supreme Sovereign); dam won over 1m;
on backward side when towards rear in maiden and minor events in the North in
the autumn; moved badly to start second outing. *Hbt Jones.*

TUDOR BELL STAR 2 b.c. Wishing Star 117–Affectionately 82 (Mark-Ye- —
Well) (1981 6h 7f 8s) May 28; IR 1,300Y; half-brother to 3 winners here and
abroad, including useful 5f and 1m winner King Oedipus (by Gala Performance),

subsequently a winner in USA; well beaten in newcomers race and sellers. *D. Wintle.*

TUDOR BOB 3 b.g. Tudor Rhythm 112–La Belle 118 (Vilmorin) (1980 5s **68** 6d 7fg 7f⁴ 8d³ 1981 8s* 10s* 12d 10f⁴ 10d 10fg 10d) tall gelding; won maiden race at Stockton and handicap at Nottingham in April; stays 1¼m (never got into race when tried at 1½m); acts on any going. *M. Jarvis.*

TUDOR CLAIRE 4 b.f. Tudor Music 131–Traffic Offence 61 (Traffic Judge) — (1980 11fg⁴ 8fg² 8g³ 8g 10g 10.6d 10g 12.5s 12s 1981 8.2g 8g 8g) fair sort; plater; best form at 1m; probably acts on any going; doesn't always impress in paddock. *H. Collingridge.*

TUDOR DREAM 3 b. or br.f. Averof 123–So Smooth (Pall Mall 132) (1980 — 5g⁴ 5d* 6fg³ 5f 5d 6s⁴ 1981 7v⁴ 6g 6f 5g 8.2f 6d) leggy, lengthy filly; well beaten in handicaps and sellers in 1981; finds 5f on sharp side nowadays and should stay 7f; usually apprentice ridden; sold 420 gns Doncaster October Sales. *W. H. H. Williams.*

TUDOR FANTASY 2 b.f. Welsh Pageant 132–Tadorna 82 (Sea-Bird II 145) — p (1981 6g) Apr 27; third foal; half-sister to a winning plater and to Stifelius (by Thatch), winner of Group 3 Premio d'Estate in Italy; dam suited by 1½m+ and closely related to Gyr; second favourite when about 12 lengths sixth of 19 to Zinzara in newcomers event at Goodwood in September; likely to do better when tackling middle distances at 3 yrs. *J. Dunlop.*

TUDOR IMP 3 b.g. Tudor Rhythm 112–Palvee 73 (Queen's Hussar 124) — (1980 NR 1981 7g 8d 10d) 380 2-y-o; narrow gelding; half-brother to a minor winner; dam won at up to 7f; no form, including in sellers; blinkered final start; sold 280 gns Ascot November Sales. *P. Butler.*

TUDOR'S DILEMMA 4 b.f. Tudor Rhythm 112–Horn's Dilemma (Quadriga — 97) (1980 8s 8f 10.8s⁴ 10s 9.4g* 8.2s 10f 8fg 1981 11.7v 10.8fg 10f 12f 8.3d) lengthy filly; plater nowadays; stays 9f well; suited by some give in the ground; sold 500 gns Ascot August Sales. *D. Jermy.*

TUDOR SECRETARY 2 b.f. Balidar 133–Cockleshell (Stephen George 102) — (1981 5d 5fg 5s 6g) Apr 28; first foal; dam of little account; in rear in maiden races and a seller. *J. Holt.*

TUDORVILLE 3 br.c. Shoolerville 121–Razia 97 (Martial 131) (1980 5fg **51** 5f 6fg 6fg 6fg 7g² 8.2d* 8s⁴ 8.2s* 8s³ 7v 1981 10v² 12d 12g 12d 12.3g 10g 10g 12f 12fg 13d 12s² 12d) rangy colt; good walker; has rather a round action; second in handicaps at Ayr in March and Hamilton in October, going down by short head to Star Burst on latter course; not disgraced in a valuable seller final start; stays 1½m; acts very well on soft going; occasionally blinkered (better without). *K. Stone.*

TUDOR WYDDIAL 4 b.g. Tudor Rhythm 112–Chung May (Blarney Stone — 121) (1980 10s⁴ 12fg 13s 16s³ 14g² 14.6fg⁴ 14fg² 14g⁴ 16fg⁴ 15s 1981 12g 12d) leggy, narrow gelding; one paced and needs a test of stamina; probably acts on any going; suitable mount for an inexperienced rider. *A. Hide.*

TUDOR WYNK 8 br.g. Wynkell 88–Wandering Rose (Tudor Minstrel 144) **56** (1980 13.3g⁴ 1981 13.1g³ 12.2fg 12g³ 14g²) consistent handicapper; stays 1¾m but possibly not 2m; acts on any going; was tried in blinkers once at 2 yrs; good mount for an apprentice. *D. Elsworth.*

TUFTY LASS 3 b.f. Forlorn River 124–Teresa-Hernandez (Queen's Hussar — 124) (1980 NR 1981 10fg 8.2s 5s) workmanlike filly; half-sister to winning sprinter Vaquero (by Burglar); dam never ran; last in 3 maiden races. *B. Richmond.*

TUGBOAT 2 ch.c. Grundy 137–Pirate Queen 77 (Pirate King 129) (1981 — 6fg 7d 7fg 8g) Apr 7; rangy, quite attractive colt; good mover; half-brother to 3 winners, notably Goodwood Cup winner Tug of War (by Reliance II); dam placed over 7f at 2 yrs; no worthwhile form in varied company but has plenty of scope and may improve when given a thorough test of stamina. *D. Whelan.*

TUGOFLOVE 5 b.h. Tudor Rhythm 112–Speyside 84 (Live Spirit 121) (1980 **95** 6f³ 6fg³ 8g 7g⁴ 7d 7g* 7g² 7g² 6d 7s 1981 8s⁴ 8g⁴ 7g 8g* 8fg³ 8fg² 8fg* 9g) quite well-made horse; fairly useful performer; won Hermitage Stakes at Newbury in June (beat Herbie Quayle by ½ length) and £6,100 handicap at Doncaster in September (scored by ¾ length from Hillsdown Gold); suited by 7f and 1m; probably acts on any going; does best when held up. *R. Laing.*

TULSA FLYER 2 b.c. He Loves Me 120–Happy Thought 57 (Kauai King)   **97**
(1981 6d 6g* 7g* 7fg* 8s 7.3s)   Feb 28; IR 29,000Y; compact, strong-quartered
colt; first foal; dam slow half-sister to smart stayer Stetchworth; successful
in 13-runner race at Salisbury in June, 9-runner minor event at Sandown in July
(made all and stayed on strongly to account for Annesley by 8 lengths) and
18-runner £2,600 race at Salisbury again in August; battled on gamely to beat
Devon Air a head in last-named; last subsequently in Royal Lodge Stakes at
Ascot and Horris Hill Stakes at Newbury; should stay 1m; probably needs a
sound surface. *P. Cole.*

TUMBLE BAY 2 b.g. Tumble Wind–Mia Culpa (Le Levanstell 122) (1981   —
6d 7f 8s)   Mar 20; fair sort; half-brother to a poor winning plater; dam never
ran; behind in minor and maiden events. *M. Naughton.*

TUMBLEDOWNHILL 3 ch.c. Tumble Wind–Little Hills (Candy Cane 125)   **52 §**
(1980 5f³ 5f³ 5f⁴ 6g* 7.2d³ 6fg² 6d³ 7d 7.2g 7fg   1981 8.2fg 10.6d 8g 8.2s 7f
7.2f 6g³ 7g² 7.2g 7g 7g)   workmanlike colt; placed in 2 handicaps at Ayr in July;
best at up to 7f; occasionally blinkered; often starts slowly. *C. Crossley.*

TUMBLE HOME 3 b.f. Tumble Wind–Rudder (Reliance II 137) (1980   —
6f⁴ 6d⁴   1981 5f 5g)   narrow, very lightly-made filly; fourth in maiden races
at Newmarket as a 2-y-o; well beaten in similar race and a handicap (last) in
1981. *I. Walker.*

TUMBLE JIM 2 b.g. Tumble Wind–Little Rastro (Above Suspicion 127)   **58**
(1981 5g 5.8g⁴ 6g 7d 7g)   Feb 9; 4,200Y; rangy, quite attractive gelding; good
mover; second living foal; dam unraced half-sister to high-class French miler
Fl Rastro; only poor form, including in a valuable seller; sold 500 gns Newmarket
Autumn Sales. *G. Harwood.*

TUMBLE WHIRL 3 b.g. Tumble Wind–Mary Money (Hook Money 124)
(1980 5fg 5fg 6fg 6g 6fg* 7f 6g 6g   1981 7g 7fg⁴)   compact gelding; plater;
stays 7f; yet to race on a soft surface. *P. Rohan.*

TUNE UP 4 ch.f. On Your Mark 125–Sing Along (Nasram II 125) (1980   **47**
5fg 5s 6g³ 8.3g 7fg³ 8.2g⁴ 7g² 7g 7d 7s   1981 8.2g 8fg⁴ 7d³ 7.6d 10.6s⁴ 8f³ 10.1fg³
10f* 10f² 8.3d 10g⁴)   lightly-made filly; plater nowadays; attracted no bid
after winning at Nottingham in July; suited by 1¼m on a sound surface; sometimes blinkered. *D. H. Jones.*

TUNGUSKA 2 b.f. Busted 134–Sunblast 108 (Roan Rocket 128) (1981 7v⁴   **76**
7g)   May 19; rather narrow filly; third foal; closely related to Irish 1¼m and
1¾m winner Ladoucette (by Bustino) and half-sister to quite useful 7f performer
Carlyle (by Wolver Hollow); dam won at up to 1m; 14/1, showed up well for
long way when creditable 7½ lengths fourth of 15 to My Destiny in £3,400 event
at York in October; 6/4 favourite for maiden race at Leicester later in month
but weakened over 1f out and finished only seventh of 16 to Positron; bred to
stay 1½m+. *H. Cecil.*

TUNKU (USA) 2 b.c. Jacinto–Avanti Girl (Royal Levee) (1981 5.1f 6fg 6g)   —
Apr 11; $42,000Y; neat colt; half-brother to several winners, including a good
winner in Puerto Rico; dam, winner of 5f claiming race, is half-sister to very smart
Twist The Axe; only plating-class form so far. *R. Armstrong.*

TUNSTALL 2 ch.c. Palm Track 122–Goldwis 94 (Golden Cloud) (1981 6d)   —
Apr 11; half-brother to 2 winners by Sit In The Corner, including dual 1977
2-y-o 5f winner Dollar-A-Corner; dam won from 5f to 7f; 20/1 when out of first
10 of 25 in maiden race won by Dev at Doncaster in October. *Mrs A. Cousins.*

TURBO 6 gr.g. Song 132–Field Mouse 108 (Grey Sovereign 128§) (1980 6g*   **51**
5fg 6f³ 6f⁴ 6fg² 5fg² 6g⁴ 5fg³ 7g² 7fg³ 6f 6s 6d   1981 6s² 6s 7d 6g² 6g³ 6g 7g² 6f³ 6fg
7.6fg 7.6s 8f⁴ 8f 8fg)   strong gelding; poor handicapper; stays 7f; acts on any
going; has worn blinkers; has had tongue tied down; good mount for an inexperienced rider. *A. W. Jones.*

TURI 2 b. or br.c. Welsh Pageant 132–Turiana (Citation) (1981 5g 6fg 7f 7fg)   —
Apr 11; 14,000Y; compact colt; third living foal; half-brother to successful
3-y-o stayer On Her Own (by Busted); dam, winner at up to 7f, is half-sister to
Kentucky Derby and Preakness Stakes winner Forward Pass; no worthwhile
form in maiden and minor events; blinkered fourth outing. *B. Swift.*

TURKOMAN 2 b.g. Patch 129–Arctrullah (Great Captain) (1981 5g 5.8g⁴ 6f   **79**
7fg 7.2fg 7s⁴ 8s 8s)   May 19; IR 9,000Y; strong, compact gelding; half-brother to
numerous winners, including good Italian middle-distance colt Art Style (by Le
Levanstell); dam won twice at 2 yrs; quite a moderate maiden; 4½ lengths
fourth of 11 to Spanish Pool in valuable 7f nursery at Lingfield in October;
should stay 1m; blinkered sixth and seventh outings; inconsistent. *D. Sasse.*

TURN BACK THE TIME (USA) 3 b.c. Youth 135–Topolly (Turn-to) **87**
(1980 7g⁴ 8fg⁴ 1981 9fg³ 8.2s* 12s) tall, lengthy, attractive colt; good mover;
looked very well indeed and ran most promisingly when less than 5 lengths
third behind impressive winner Kalaglow in Heath Stakes at Newmarket in
April on reappearance, making good headway over last 2f and going on really
well to finish; reportedly jarred his off-fore knee afterwards and was having first
subsequent race when beating Frogtown by 1½ lengths in maiden event at
Haydock in October (weak favourite and apprentice ridden); not knocked
about when his chance had gone when about 20 lengths fifth to Little Wolf in St
Simon Stakes at Newbury later in month; should be suited by middle distances;
probably acts on any going. *B. Hills.*

TURNBERRY 2 b.c. Sallust 134–Cherry Bird 68 (Abernant 142) (1981 5d **61**
5fg 6fg 5fg 5.1d⁴ 5s) Mar 11; 9,200Y; brother to fairly useful 1978 2-y-o 7f
winner Master Piper, and half-brother to several winners, including Francesca
Bionda (by Majority Blue), the best Italian 2-y-o filly of 1971; dam ran only at
2 yrs; beaten over 11 lengths when fourth of 9 to Worlingworth in maiden event
at Yarmouth in September; blinkered final outing. *D. Ringer.*

TURNBERRY ISLE 2 ch.c. Realm 129–Sailing Along 104 (Crooner 119) **67**
(1981 5g 5fg 5f⁴ 5.1d³ 6fg⁴ 5f 7g) Mar 9; 10,500Y; neat, well-made colt; good
mover; first foal; dam won over 6f and 7f at 2 yrs; plater; ran best race in valuable
event at Newmarket in September on seventh outing, running on in good style to
finish 3½ lengths fifth of 29 to Perchance; better suited by 7f than shorter
distances. *F. Durr.*

TURTLE HILL 2 b.f. Home Guard 129–Bantam 64 (Combat 123) (1981 **67**
5fg³ 6g 6g 7g) Mar 15; 15,000Y; strong filly; half-sister to several winners,
including high-class 1m to 1¼m performer Gold Rod (by Songedor); dam won 5f
seller at 2 yrs; only quite a moderate filly; seems to stay 7f. *C. Thornton.*

TUTHILL BELLO 3 ch.f. Porto Bello 118–Grill Room 79 (Connaught 130) **64**
(1980 5h 5g 6g³ 6g 6d 8g 1981 6g² 6s² 7fg⁴ 6d 6f 6f) strong filly; poor form,
including in a seller as a 2-y-o; second in non-sellers in first 2 races of 1981;
possibly doesn't quite stay 7f; ran moderately in blinkers fifth start; usually
apprentice ridden; sold to W. Stubbs 1,100 gns Doncaster September Sales.
A. Jarvis.

TUTHILL BOND 4 ch.g. Good Bond 122–Whirlibird 78 (The Pelican) (1980 **—**
8.2d* 8fg² 8.2fg 10g 8g 8fg 8g 1981 10s) leggy, narrow gelding; fairly useful at
his best but has shown no form for some time; stays 1m; acts on any going; has
sweated up; none too consistent. *N. Callaghan.*

TUTHILL WARRIOR 3 ch.g. Roman Warrior 132–Tiny Tot 80 (Counsel 118) **—**
(1980 6g 6f 5s 1981 7g 8fg 6g) good-topped individual; little worthwhile
form in varied company, including selling; sometimes bandaged in front; sold
out of N. Callaghan's stable 800 gns Doncaster January Sales and resold for
350 gns same venue in October. *B. Lunness.*

TUYENU 5 ch.m. Welsh Pageant 132–Attuned (Faberge II 121) (1980 10s **60**
8f⁴ 10fg 7.2d 9g 7d 1981 8s 7s 8v 8g⁴ 9f 7.6fg² 8f* 8fg* 8f 7g) big mare; in
good form in July and won handicaps at Thirsk and Redcar (apprentices);
best at around 1m and appeared not to stay 1¼m; probably acted on any going;
blinkered third start; suitable mount for an apprentice; covered by Hotfoot.
M. Camacho.

T. V. STAR 4 ch.f. St Columbus 98–Bloomsbury Girl 63 (Weepers Boy 124) **—**
(1980 6d 6s⁴ 5f⁴ 6f 7f² 7g 7g 8f³ 8fg 7.6d² 8g* 8d 8f 1981 7f 9f 8f 8fg 10f 10f 8s)
sparely-made filly; well beaten at 4 yrs; stays 1m; probably acts on any going.
B. Lunness.

TWEEL 5 b.m. Owen Dudley 121–Miss Tweedie 114 (Aberdeen 109) (1980 14fg **49**
12fg 15f 16f 14g 12d 12.2d 12d 1981 16s³ 18fg² 17.1g² 16s 18.8fg⁴ 22.2f 16fg)
staying handicapper; probably acted on any going; used to wear blinkers;
dead. *D. Elsworth.*

TWICE AS FRESH 2 ch.c. Free State 125–Rose Mullion 82 (Tudor Melody 129) **—**
(1981 7d 7d) Apr 25; fair sort; fourth foal; half-brother to 1978 2-y-o 5f winner
Regina Magna (by Blakeney); dam won over 5f at 2 yrs; well beaten in £4,800
race at Goodwood in September (needed race) and minor event at Chepstow
the following month. *J. Bethell.*

TWICE LUCKY 2 b.f. Condorcet–Fortuity (Fortino II 120) (1981 5fg 7d³ **66**
8s 7g 8d) May 10; 440Y; leggy, narrow filly; half-sister to 2 winners, including
1979 Irish 2-y-o 6f winner Cutarue (by English Prince); dam winning hurdler;

2 lengths third of 14 to Princess Imperial in seller at Newmarket in August; also showed a little ability in sizeable fields of maidens in the Midlands at the backend; stays 1m. *N. Guest.*

TWICE NICE 4 b.f. Double Jump 131–Marie Denise 68 (Dual 117) (1980 12g 12.2f⁴ 13.8g² 16f⁴ 14d³ 15.8fg 14.6d 1981 15.8g 15.5d 16g 17.1d) leggy filly; in frame in varied company, including selling; stays well; probably acts on any going. *V. Soane.* —

TWICKENHAM 5 b.g. Martinmas 128–Ember Grill 84§ (Indigenous 121) (1980 7g 7fg 10g⁴ 10s* 10d 8g* 8g³ 9fg 10d³ 1981 8d 8g* 8.3fg 8fg 8f* 9fg² 8fg 8g²) leggy gelding; poor walker; won handicaps at Salisbury in June and Wolverhampton in August; stays 1¼m; acts on any going; suitable mount for a boy; genuine. *I. Balding.* 82

TWIDALE 8 ch.g. Twilight Alley 133–Leadendale Lady 90 (Damremont 120) (1980 16f 1981 13.8g) fairly useful jumper; poor staying maiden on flat. *J. Wilson.* —

TWISS-N-DOE 3 br.f. Downstream 105–Babulass (Babu 117) (1980 NR 1981 6fg) small filly; half-sister to several minor winners; dam ran twice; backward when last of 14 behind Cherry Corner in seller at Newcastle in August. *T. Barnes.* —

TWIST HOME (FR) 2 b.c. Homeric 133–Doctor's Choice 116 (Petingo 135) (1981 6d 8g 8s* 8s² 10.2g²) well-made, attractive colt; good walker; first foal; dam smart French 2-y-o 1m winner; won 15-runner maiden race at York in October by ½ length from Favoloso despite edging left when challenging; runner-up in large fields for minor events won by Arrowood Dream and Yard Bird at Redcar and Doncaster subsequently; will be suited by 1½m; yet to race on a firm surface; badly hampered leaving stalls on second outing; the type to make a useful handicapper at 3 yrs. *G. Harwood.* 96

TWIXT' TWEEN 4 ch.f. The Go-Between 129–Che Bella (Beau Sabreur 125) (1980 6d 8f⁴ 8f⁴ 8d³ 8.2d 7d 7fg 6f* 5d 5s 6f 5d* 1981 7d 6g 5fg⁴ 5g 5.6f⁴ 5fg 5f⁴ 7d 6d² 6s² 5g²) small, lightly-made filly; won apprentice handicap at Hamilton in July; best at sprint distances; acts on any going; suitable mount for a boy; got very upset at start fifth outing; sold 6,200 gns Newmarket Autumn Sales. *W. H. H. Williams.* 71

TWO MINUTES 2 ch.c. High Line 125–Elm Park (Aberdeen 109) (1981 7f 7f² 7fg² 8s) Apr 12; 6,600F; lightly-made, useful sort; half-brother to 2 winners, including fairly useful 1980 2-y-o 5f and 6f winner Cleat (by Take a Reef); dam never ran; beaten a shade comfortably when runner-up in minor events at Yarmouth and Newcastle in August, going down by ¾ length to Hula Ruler on former and finishing 6 lengths clear of third horse when beaten ½ length by Super Sunrise in 15-runner event on latter (dwelt); should be suited by 1m; never going well on only outing on soft going and evidently can't handle it. *G. Pritchard-Gordon.* 89

TWO STROKE 4 ch.f. Malicious–Palouci 59 (Palestine 133) (1980 6f 7d 8g 1981 8g 8d 8f 10f) small, lightly-made filly; poor form, including in a seller; sometimes bandaged behind. *W. Wharton.* —

TYEJEST 3 b. or br.f. Tycoon II–Fair Jest 79 (Dumbarnie 125) (1980 5d 6fg 7fg 5fg 1981 6g⁴ 8g* 7fg 8fg 7fg 6fg 8fg 6d 6d) compact filly; plater; showed improvement when beating Saddle Rock Road 1½ lengths at Newmarket in May (bought in 2,600 gns); well beaten afterwards, including in non-sellers; appears suited by 1m; tends to sweat up; blinkered last 2 outings; hung very badly and gave impression she's no longer genuine eighth start; sold 750 gns Doncaster October Sales. *G. Harman.* 62

TYPECAST 2 br.g. Tachypous 128–Ile de France 94 (French Beige 127) (1981 5fg 5g 5d⁴ 5s 6g 6f 6f 5f² 5g³ 6g* 6g 5g) Apr 14; 6,200F, 4,000Y; workmanlike gelding; good mover; closely related to 3-y-o 1¼m winner The Cliftonian (by Firestreak) and half-brother to 1¼m winner Village Idol (by Blakeney); dam won at up to 7f; ran well 3 times in September and made all to win 16-runner selling nursery at Brighton by a length from O Solo Mio (bought in 2,500 gns); usually shows plenty of pace and isn't sure to stay beyond 6f; blinkered fifth and seventh outings. *Mrs J. Reavey.* 72

TYPHOON POLLY 2 ch.f. Lord Gayle 124–Polinesia (Takawalk II 125) (1981 6f 6fg 8s*) Apr 18; third foal; half-sister to Polly Pearl (by Gulf Pearl), a winner from 6f to 1m in France; dam useful winner at up to 1m in France; rallied strongly under pressure to win maiden race at Longchamp in October 107 by ¼ length from Valse Noble, the pair 5 lengths clear; will stay 1¼m; entered in Oaks. *C. Milbank, France.*

TYRANNOS 8 ch.h. Tyrant–Orange Sash (Sica Boy 132) (1980 NR 1981 7g 8h³) lightly raced and apparently difficult to train though has won several times at up to 1¼m; seems to act on any going. *J. Baker.* —

TYRANT PRINCE 2 b.g. English Prince 129–Little Trilby 107 (Tyrant) (1981 8g 8g 8d) May 6; 5,200Y; second foal; dam best at 6f and 7f; well beaten in maiden races. *J. Fitzgerald.* —

TYTHERINGTON CHANT 2 ch.f. Tachypous 128–Gold Cypher 76 (Pardao 120) (1981 6g⁴ 6d) Apr 21; half-sister to useful 1980 2-y-o Cardie Girl (by Sharpen Up) and several winners; dam ran only at 2 yrs; 33/1 and in need of race, always prominent and kept on well when length fourth of 20 to Linda Beard in maiden race at Newmarket in August; subsequently off course till November when fair fifth of 22 to Late Hour in similar race at Leicester; will stay 1m. *W. Hastings-Bass.* 78

TY-WITH-BELLE 2 b.f. Pamroy 99–Saucy Walk (Saucy Kit 76) (1981 5d 5d 5f 7g 8d 7g 6d) Apr 18; small filly; first foal; dam ran once over hurdles; fifth 3 times in 16-runner maiden races, running well on fourth outing when beaten 3 lengths by Airwair at Leicester in September; should be suited by 1m; blinkered sixth outing. *B. Palling.* 67

U

UKRAINE GIRL 3 ch.f. Targowice 130–Paddy's Flair (Alcide 136) (1980 6g 7.5d* 8g* 8f 1981 7d² 8g* 10.5fg⁴ 8f 8f 9.2d) 121

Ukraine Girl's win in the Poule d'Essai des Pouliches at Longchamp in May was a surprise to most, and the manner of its achievement even more of one. The best-fancied runners were Tropicaro and Marie Noelle, first and second in the Prix de la Grotte on the same course in April, Ancient Regime and Star Pastures, while Ukraine Girl was amongst the outsiders at odds of over 20/1 on the Pari-Mutuel. Ukraine Girl had looked a good filly in the making when winning two races as a two-year-old, including the Prix d'Aumale at Chantilly, but on her final outing had finished last behind Tropicaro in the Prix Marcel Boussac. Her second to Layalina in the slowly-run Prix Imprudence at Maisons-Laffitte in April on her reappearance hadn't done much to redeem her reputation; on top of that her regular jockey Saint-Martin was claimed to ride another outsider, Joberine. Saint-Martin and trainer Collet had been working hard on the gallops to teach Ukraine Girl to settle, for it was felt that her tendency to pull hard in slowly-run races was hindering her development. Fortunately connections managed to acquire so able a deputy as Eddery who carried out his instructions to perfection. Ukraine Girl settled nicely at the back of the field as Tropicaro's pacemaker Fair Contessa made the running, and she wasn't asked to improve until after the field had straightened up for home. When given the office she accelerated to such effect that she went from last to first in what seemed like no time at all. Once in front over a furlong out she was in no danger whatever and she needed only to be pushed out with hands and heels to win by a length and a half and the same from Star Pastures and Ionian Raja.

Ukraine Girl proved difficult to place afterwards, so much so that she failed to reach the first three in any of her four subsequent races. She didn't run badly—far from it. The following month she seemed not to get the trip as well as the ones in front in the Prix de Diane de Revlon at Chantilly, but nevertheless she finished a creditable fourth to Madam Gay. Ridden to conserve her stamina, she made up a deal of ground from the rear of the field in the straight and flattered for a moment before finishing over four lengths behind Madam

Poule d'Essai des Pouliches, Longchamp—Ukraine Girl shows a good turn of foot to beat British-trained Star Pastures and Ionian Raja

Gay, just edged out of the placings by Val d'Erica and April Run. On her next two outings Ukraine Girl met most of Europe's best milers in the Prix Jacques le Marois at Deauville in August and the Prix du Moulin de Longchamp in September, both won by Northjet, and ran creditably to finish in sixth and seventh places respectively. Ukraine Girl was the only filly in the former event, when beaten about seven lengths altogether and only about two lengths behind the placed horses To-Agori-Mou and Kings Lake. On her final outing Ukraine Girl finished towards the rear behind Kilmona in the Prix de l'Opera at Longchamp on Arc day; she was given plenty to do in a slowly-run race and never really looked like getting on terms.

Ukraine Girl (ch.f. 1978)	Targowice (b 1970)	Round Table (b 1954)	Princequillo / Knight's Daughter
		Matriarch (b 1964)	Bold Ruler / Lyceum
	Paddy's Flair (b 1964)	Alcide (b 1955)	Alycidon / Chenille
		Paddy's Sister (b 1957)	Ballyogan / Birthday Wood

Targowice is proving his worth as a stallion all too late. Since being exported to Japan he has been represented in France by such good performers as Greenway, Prince Mab and Tipperary Fixer, besides Ukraine Girl, and in Ireland by the sprinter Cooleen Jack. Ukraine Girl's dam Paddy's Flair, prevented from racing by injury, has produced two other winners, Flair Path (by Ragusa), third in both the Irish Two Thousand Guineas and the Prix du Jockey-Club in 1979, and Irish Reel (by Dancer's Image), a winner on the flat and over jumps in France. The grandam Paddy's Sister was a top-class two-year-old in 1959 when unbeaten in five races, including the Queen Mary Stakes, the Gimcrack and the Champagne Stakes; then injury intervened with her, too. Easily the most successful of her offspring was the Ragusa colt Ballymore, winner on his racecourse debut of the Irish Two Thousand Guineas in which Flair Path was third.

Ukraine Girl was sent to the Houghton Sales as a yearling in accordance with the current policy of the Mullions of putting all the yearlings under the hammer on alternate years. A modest reserve of 8,000 guineas was placed on her but she coughed so badly in the sale-ring that she failed to raise a bid. The decision to send Ukraine Girl to be trained in France when she recovered can have given the Mullions little cause for regret; she's clearly going to be a valuable addition to their Ardenode Stud. Ukraine Girl will visit Shergar, in whom her owners have acquired a share, in 1982. The courtship began after the Derby with the following telegram—'Ukraine Girl sends her congratulations to Shergar, and hopes that one day she may be one of his blushing brides'. The Aga Khan replied 'Shergar is a village in Kashmir where they have a keen appreciation of Ukraine Girls'. Ukraine Girl, a small, close-coupled filly who was probably at her best at a mile, never raced on very soft going but showed she acted on any other. She had an excellent turn of foot. Her occasional tail-flashing seemed not to reflect any lack of generosity. *R. Collet, France.*

ULTRASONIC 2 br.c. Prince Tenderfoot 126–Native Charm (Red God 128§) — (1981 5fg 6fg 6fg 5g⁴ 6g 5g 5g 6g) May 16; IR 8,000Y; workmanlike colt; third foal; half-brother to Irish 1m and 1¼m winner Beaunatif (by Royal Buck); dam, who never ran, is closely related to Greenland Park; plating-class maiden; best at 5f. *R. Hollinshead.*

UNBIASED (USA) 3 b.f. Foolish Pleasure–Unfurled (Hoist the Flag) (1980 6s 1981 7f* 8s 8f³ 8g⁴ 7g) lengthy, useful sort; showed a good turn of foot when beating Northern Chance a shade cleverly by 1½ lengths in maiden race at Newmarket in April; moved up a place after finishing fairly close fourth behind Oh So Choosy in Fern Hill Stakes (Handicap) at Ascot in June; off course almost 3 months afterwards and didn't really recover her form; stays 1m; ran creditably on soft going as a 2-y-o but seems well suited by firm. *L. Cumani.* 75

UNCLE DAI 2 ch.c. Import 127–Silver Cherry 69 (Silver Cloud 121) (1981 5.8fg³ 6fg 5.8f 7g 6s 6g³) Mar 17; 4,000Y; tall, strong, slightly hollow-backed colt; fourth foal; dam 1m winner; third in maiden auction event at Bath in July and valuable seller at Newmarket in October, staying on well to be 1¼ lengths behind Commissaar on latter; not disgraced in valuable seller at Newmarket on fourth start; runs as though he'll be suited by 1m; blinkered last 3 outings; sold 5,600 gns Newmarket Autumn Sales. *B. Hills.* 74

UNCLE DICK   4 b.c. Right Tack 131–Golly Green (Super Sam 124)   (1980 10fg⁴   **70**
11.7fg* 14f³ 12d 13.1f⁴ 12d   1981 12.2d⁴ 12.3d 12f³ 12fg² 12f* 13f² 12f⁴ 12.2g)
strong, useful sort; won handicap at Folkestone in July; stays 13f; acts well on
firm ground; blinkered seventh outing; ran poorly second start; sold 5,200 gns
Newmarket Autumn Sales. *B. Hills.*

UNCLE SALTY (USA)   3 ch.c. Nodouble–So Vain (Drone)   (1980 6g⁴ 7s   —
1981 7fg 10s⁴ 10f 10d 10g) lengthy, useful sort; plating-class maiden; stays
1¼m. *L. Cumani.*

UNDER-RATED   3 b.g. Undulate–Ruffino 99 (Como 120)   (1980 7fg 7g 7g   —
1981 8fg 10.2f 12f 12.3g 10fg) workmanlike gelding; little worthwhile form in
maiden and minor events. *M. W. Easterby.*

UNDISMAYED   3 ch.g. Supreme Sovereign 119–Intrusion 101 (Aggressor 130)   —
(1980 6s   1981 10s 10fg 16g 15.8g) lengthy gelding; poor form in varied company and looks very slow; blinkered fourth start. *W. Holden.*

UNIQUE LADY   3 br.f. Lord David 121–Westerlands Prism (Primera 131)   **69**
(1980 7g 7fg 7fg   1981 10d 8.3s* 10d² 8g³ 9fg² 11fg³ 10f³ 9g*) leggy filly;
attracted no bid after winning sellers at Windsor in May and Newcastle (in good
style) in August; placed all outings in between, including in non sellers; stays
11f; probably acts on any going; claimed out of D. Elsworth's stable £2,125
after third outing, and trained next by G. Lockerbie. *N. Tinkler.*

UNITED   8 b.g. Merger–Destiny Day 109 (Tim Tam)   (1980 NR   1981 14d   —
12fg 12f) poor middle-distance handicapper; behind in seller final start; acts
on any going; has worn blinkers. *R. Hannon.*

UNIT TENT   3 bl.g. Double-U-Jay 120–Signal Melody 70 (Bleep-Bleep 134)   **61**
(1980 5f 5s 6g³ 6g² 5g 7.6f 7f   1981 6g 6d 7fg 10.1fg 8g 10.1fg 10s* 10d*) neat,
quite attractive gelding; plater; in good form in autumn and was bought in
after winning at Nottingham (2,600 gns) and Leicester (2,100 gns); stays 1¼m;
acts well on soft going. *G. Lewis.*

UNIVERSAL PENNY   3 ch.f. Royal Match 117–Rose of Damascus (Ommeyad   —
120)   (1980 5v 5s 5f 6s 7d 6f² 5d* 6g   1981 10f 10.1f 12f) fair sort; made all
in valuable seller at Sandown at 2 yrs; had stiffish tasks in handicaps in 1981;
yet to show she stays middle distances; acts on any going; blinkered last 3
outings as a 2-y-o. *W. Marshall.*

UNLIMITED   2 b.c. Crooner 119–Eridantini (Indigenous 121)   (1981 5s 5fg)   —
Apr 28; leggy, lightly-made colt; half-brother to prolific sprint winner Offa's Mead
(by Rathlin); dam never ran; towards rear in maiden races at Leicester in
March and Warwick in April. *P. Cole.*

UP COUNTRY   3 br.g. Upper Case–The Country Lane 90 (Red God 128§)   **66**
(1980 6s 7fg 7.6g   1981 12fg 13fg 13.1f² 12fg³ 10g 8h* 8f 8d⁴) useful-looking
gelding; beat Nutty Slack by 4 lengths in maiden race at Chepstow in August;
had stiffish tasks afterwards; effective at 1m and stays 13f; acts on hard going.
H. Candy.

UPLANDS PARK   2 b.c. Rheingold 137–God Sent 75 (Red God 128§)   (1981   —
7f 7fg) Mar 14; rangy colt; third foal; brother to 1¼m winner Marguerite
Gerard; dam placed over 5f at 2 yrs; prominent 2f out when behind in large fields
of maidens at Newmarket and Goodwood in July; bit coltish in paddock at
Goodwood. *C. Brittain.*

UPPETY   3 b.c. Rouser 118–Pavillon 88 (French Beige 127)   (1980 8g* 1981   **90**
10.6fg³ 12g² 12d 14fg³ 13f* 12f² 13fg 12g) useful sort; overcame a slipped saddle
when beating Uncle Dick very gamely by 1½ lengths in handicap at Nottingham
in July; also placed in minor events at Haydock and Thirsk (second to Halsbury)
and in handicaps at Yarmouth and Ripon (possibly didn't handle course well);
suited by 1¾m and will stay further; acts on firm going; badly hampered at
Epsom on third start; tailed off final outing. *B. Hobbs.*

UP TEMPO   2 b.g. Dance In Time–Graceful 83 (Grey Sovereign 128§)   (1981 6g)   —
May 9; half-brother to fair sprinter Sandia (by Saritamer) and a winner in
Holland; dam 2-y-o 7f winner; unquoted and very burly, missed break and
always struggling when in rear in 14-runner maiden race won by Knave of
Trumps at Yarmouth in September. *A. Hide.*

U-TURN   2 ch.f. Red Alert 127–Hy Carol (High Hat 131)   (1981 5s 5d 5d)   —
May 13; 3,400Y; half-sister to 9f and 1¼m winner Caralist (by Traditionalist);
dam of little account; in rear in maiden and minor events at Folkestone in the
spring; slowly away first outing. *R. Smyth.*

V

VACANI 2 b.f. Dance In Time–Italian Sky 94 (Skymaster 126) (1981 6d 7fg 6d) —
May 18; well-grown filly; half-sister to 2 winners, including 7f winner Procella
(by Derring-Do); dam 2-y-o 5f winner; towards rear in large fields of maidens
at Newmarket (2) and Pontefract. *W. Hastings-Bass.*

VADROUILLE (USA) 2 b.f. Foolish Pleasure–Vincennes 111 (Vieux Manoir **107**
132) (1981 6g² 7g³) rangy, attractive filly; fourth live foal; dam second in
Irish Guinness Oaks and daughter of Irish 1,000 Guineas and Epsom Oaks winner Valoris; went down by 3 lengths to more-experienced Merlin's Charm when
favourite for maiden race at Newmarket in October but easily accounted for 15
others; again favourite for 8-runner Rockfel Stakes on same course later in month
but wasn't able to quicken in a slowly-run race and was beaten 2 lengths into
third place behind Top Hope; will be suited by middle distances; a useful filly
who is sure to win races. *H. Cecil.*

VAGABOND VICTOR 5 b.g. Levmoss 133–Tanndara (Venture VII 129) —
(1980 NR 1981 16d) of little account on flat though has won over hurdles.
P. Allingham.

VAGUELY DIVINE (USA) 3 b.f. Master Derby–Louisianan (Vaguely Noble —
140) (1980 5f 5d 6d 1981 5d 6s 5g) quite well-made filly; lightly raced and
rather disappointing; bred to stay at least 1m; sold 1,400 gns Newmarket July
Sales. *G. Hunter.*

VAGUELY FAIR 3 b.f. Royal and Regal–Fairama (Amber Rama 133) (1980 —
NR 1981 7f 8f 8f 9s 8g) 420Y; compact filly; poor mover; first foal; dam
showed no form in 3 races; tailed off in maiden and minor races. *V. Mitchell.*

VAGUELY JAMES 7 ch.g. Jimmy Reppin 131–Vaguely Hopeful 65 (Fortino —
II 120) (1980 16fg 15f 16.5fg⁴ 14g 16g 17.1d⁴ 18d 1981 15.5d) poor stayer;
needs some give in the ground; sometimes blinkered. *G. Beeson.*

VAIGLY STAR 2 b.f. Star Appeal 133–Dervaig 90 (Derring-Do 131) (1981 **108**
5s² 5fg* 6f 6f² 6d 6g*) Apr 30; compact, good-quartered filly; good walker;
third foal; half-sister to 2 winners, including high-class sprinter Vaigly Great
(by Great Nephew); dam won over 5f at 2 yrs and became a leading sprinter in
Trinidad; winner of £4,000 Hilary Needler Trophy at Beverley in June and
£9,200 Martini Trophy (Nursery) at Newmarket in October, putting up a very
useful effort when staying on well to beat Blue Emmanuelle 1½ lengths in latter;
will stay 7f and may get 1m. *M. Stoute.*

VAIN DEB 2 b.f. Gay Fandango 132–Saint Mildred 89 (Saint Crespin III 132) —
(1981 6g 6fg 7fg) May 2; IR 2,000F, 9,400Y; fair sort; half-sister to 2 winners,
including modest miler Miss Raffles (by Green God); dam stayed 1¾m; in rear
in maiden races and a valuable seller. *P. Haslam.*

*Martini Trophy Nursery Handicap, Newmarket—Vaigly Star stays on well
to beat Blue Emmanuelle and Wicked Wave (rails) in this very
valuable nursery*

VAL DE MOUGINS (FR) 4 b.c. Val de l'Orne 130–Goodbye 73 (Linacre 133) **114**
(1980 10g 10.5d³ 10.5g* 10.5g 10g³ 10v* 10.5d   1981 10.5d³ 9.7fg 12d 9.7s 12g
12.5f 12fg 10g³ 10s² 10g 10.5s²) attractive French colt; second to smooth
winner Glenorum in I.a Coupe de Maisons-Laffitte in September and to Jeune
Prince in 70,000 francs race at Saint-Cloud in November; not entirely disgraced on
third and fourth starts, when eighth of 12 to Lancastrian in Grand Prix d'Evry
and equal fifth of 11 to P'tite Tete in Prix Dollar at Longchamp; in rear behind
Vayrann in Champion Stakes at Newmarket on penultimate outing; possibly
stays 1½m; suited by some give in the ground; blinkered seventh start; trained
part of year by A. Paus, A. Klimscha and M. Blackshaw. *D. Becquemin, France.*

VAL D'ERICA 3 ch.f. Ashmore 125–Laconia 58 (Great Nephew 126) (1980 **119**
including 8g² 8v* 1981 8g* 8v* 11d* 10.5fg² 10g* 12g⁴ 11g* 12s) 5,000F,
4,000Y; half-sister to 6f and 7f winner Spartan Call (by Realm); dam half-
sister to numerous winners, including very useful stayer Tudor Tale; the leading
filly in Italy as a 2-y-o when successful twice, including in Premio Dormello
at Milan; outstanding among her sex in Italy in 1981 and won 5 more races
at Milan, namely Premio Seregno, Premio Regina Elena, Oaks d'Italia, Premio
Bellotta and Premio Sergio Cumani; made all and beat Rattling Wind by 2
lengths in Oaks d'Italia in May; ran well in France on 2 other occasions, when
4 lengths second to Madam Gay in Prix de Diane at Chantilly and about 4¼
lengths fourth to April Run in Prix Vermeille at Longchamp; probably over
the top when fifth of 7 behind Konigsstuhl in Gran Premio del Jockey Club
at Milan in October; stayed 1½m; seemed to act on any going; visits Mill Reef
in 1982. *A. Botti, Italy.*

VALENTINIAN 3 ch.c. Morston 125–Appian Way 89 (Romulus 129) (1980 **105**
8g⁴ 1981 12g 13.3d⁴ 14g* 14g* 14g⁴ 12fg* 12g* 13.3d⁴) strong colt; developed
into a useful colt and won maiden race at Salisbury, minor event at Haydock
(both in good style) and handicaps at Goodwood and Doncaster; led 3f out and
strode clear when beating Ski Run 6 lengths (value at least 8) on last-named
course in September; rather disappointing when fourth in Melrose Handicap
won by Centroline at York on fifth start (got rather upset in stalls) and in Coral
Autumn Cup (Handicap) won by Telsmoss at Newbury on final start (unsuited
by the softish ground); will probably stay 2m; evidently needs a sound surface.
R. Hern.

VALE OF BELVOIR 2 b.f. Steel Heart 128–Gables End (Roi Soleil 125) —
(1981 6fg 5d³ 5d 5d) Apr 1; 3,000Y; strong filly; carries plenty of condition;
second foal; dam won over 5f at 2 yrs in Ireland; 4¾ lengths third of 8 behind
My Fancy in minor event at Edinburgh in October, best effort; should stay
6f; acts on a soft surface and didn't move well to start on a firm one. *Denys
Smith.*

VALERIGA 5 b.h. Polyfoto 124–Bag of Bones (Relic) (1980 5fg* 6f 6g³ 6g⁴ **110**
5fg* 5g² 6fg 5f³ 5v* 7s² 6v 1981 5g* 5f) strong, full-quartered, muscular
horse; good mover; high-class sprinter who won 6 races in his career, including
Palace House Stakes at Newmarket and King George Stakes at Goodwood in
1980; ran only twice at 5 yrs, when 4 lengths fourth to Standaan in Palace
House Stakes at Newmarket and 5 lengths sixth to Marwell in King's Stand
Stakes at Royal Ascot; stayed 7f but was better at shorter distances; acted
on any going; usually sweated up and often gave trouble going to post but was
genuine and consistent; standing at Cheltenham Stud, New South Wales,
Australia. *L. Cumani.*

VALEUR (USA) 3 b.f. Vaguely Noble 140–Brown Berry (Mount Marcy) (1980 —
NR 1981 10fg) lightly-built filly; half-sister to numerous winners, notably
high-class French middle-distance colt Monseigneur, top-class American colt
Avatar (both by Graustark) and very good American middle-distance performer
Unconscious (by Prince Royal II); dam won 6f stakes race; looked backward
and made little show when thirteenth of 16 behind Home On The Range in
maiden event at Sandown in April, only outing. *F. J. Houghton.*

VALIANCY 2 b.f. Grundy 137–Val's Girl 113 (Sir Ivor 135) (1981 6s³ 7.3s⁴) **87** p
Apr 13; 82,000F; small, robust, deep-girthed filly; third produce; half-sister
to fairly useful 1979 2-y-o maiden Val's Mill (by Mill Reef); dam second in Oaks
and daughter of Irish 1,000 Guineas and Epsom Oaks winner Valoris; showed
up very well throughout when 5½ lengths third of 11 to Slightly Dangerous in
Duke of Edinburgh Stakes at Ascot in October; kept on without looking likely
to get on terms when over 10 lengths fourth of 8 to Last Feather in £6,300
event at Newbury later in month; sure to make a useful filly over middle distances
in 1982. *F. J. Houghton.*

VALLEY-ANN 3 ro.f. Runnymede 123–Right Abella 74 (Right Boy 137) (1980 —
5g 5fg 1981 8fg 6fg) small filly; well beaten, including in sellers; bandaged
in 1981. *J. Hill.*

VALOIS 3 b.f. Lyphard 132–Camenae 72 (Vimy 132) (1980 NR 1981 7d —
7.2f 10f) quite an attractive, neat filly; half-sister to several winners, notably
2,000 Guineas winner High Top and very smart miler Camden Town (both
by Derring-Do); dam won at 1¾m, and is half-sister to dams of Paulista and
Tudor Music); didn't stride out well to start but ran quite promisingly when
3 lengths fifth of 15 finishers behind Three Crowns in maiden race at Sandown
in June; disappointing at Haydock and Yarmouth afterwards; bred to stay
1¼m but pulls hard; sent to USA. *M. Stoute.*

VAN HAGEN 5 b.g. Mount Hagen 127–Lesanne (Faberge II 121) (1980 —
NR 1981 16f 12g) poor middle-distance performer. *S. Woodman.*

VANITY FAIR 2 b.c. Cawston's Clown 113–Summer Sales 94 (Tropique 128) **80**
(1981 5.8g 5.8d 5f⁴ 5fg* 6g 6s) Mar 31; useful sort; half-brother to a winner
over hurdles; dam won over 6f at 2 yrs; fully fit for first time when justifying
favouritism by ¾ length from Sussex Queen in 13-runner maiden race at Warwick
in June; not seen out again until end of season when in rear in minor event and
nursery; should stay 6f; sold 3,200 gns Newmarket Autumn Sales. *D. Elsworth.*

VANRENOS 3 b.f. Gold Rod 129–Supafrag 55 (Track Spare 125) (1980 6s —
5d 6d 5d 7f* 8.2d 1981 7f 8f 8s 11s 10s) small filly; plater; no worthwhile
form in 1981; suited by 7f and should stay 1m; form only on firm going. *W.
Clay.*

VARTKEZ (FR) 4 b.g. A Tempo 127–Caecilia 76 (Skymaster 126) (1980 —
10.1s 13g 10s* 10.1g² 12f⁴ 10fg⁴ 1981 10s 12d 11.7v 12fg) strong, sturdy
gelding; won maiden race at Nottingham in 1980; ran poorly at 4 yrs; should
stay 1½m; acts on soft going and is possibly unsuited by firm; sold 1,300 gns
Newmarket Autumn Sales. *D. Morley.*

VASCAR 6 ch.g. Roi Soleil 125–Kindling 80 (Psidium 130) (1980 10.6s 1981 —
12.5s² 15.8g) strong gelding; poor handicapper on flat but is a useful hurdler;
stays 1½m; acts well on soft going; has worn bandages in front. *J. Berry.*

VASLAV (USA) 3 ch.c. Nijinsky 138–Waterloo 120 (Bold Lad, Ire 133) (1980 **97**
NR 1981 7d² 8g*) big, strong, rangy colt; half-brother to fairly useful 1m
to 9f winner Water Frolic (by Sir Ivor) and useful 1978 French 2-y-o 6f winner
Water Woo (by Tom Rolfe); dam won Cheveley Park Stakes and 1,000 Guineas;
never far away and stayed on really well when most promising ¾-length second
of 6 to Cragador in City of York Stakes at York in August; looked much fitter
when landing the odds by 4 lengths from Olderfleet in 18-runner maiden event
at Yarmouth the following month; stays 1m; looks the type to have further
improvement in him and should win more races. *H. Cecil.*

VAYRANN 3 br.c. Brigadier Gerard 144–Val Divine (Val de Loir 133) (1980 NR **133**
1981 10s* 12d² 12d* 15s³ 10s* 10g*)
 Vayrann put up one of the finest performances witnessed in England during
the season when, in October, he won a really well-contested Champion Stakes in
clear-cut fashion by two lengths from the previous year's winner Cairn Rouge.
He was never out of the first four of sixteen. When he took over the lead at the
Bushes from the Benson and Hedges runner-up Kirtling and the 1980 Champion
Stakes runner-up Master Willie he took over moving very strongly on the bridle;
once he'd hit the front he never looked like being caught, responding all too
powerfully for the chasing group as Saint-Martin rode him out up the hill. The
Champion Stakes has produced its share of turn-ups; in comparison with some

*Prix Jean de Chaudenay, Saint-Cloud—Vayrann is clear from Kelbomec and
subsequently-disqualified Argument (rails)*

Champion Stakes, Newmarket—Vayrann passes the post in front of Cairn Rouge and Amyndas

past results the latest one seemed positively straightforward, the chief surprise provided by the 66/1-shot Amyndas' taking third place. Vayrann had started second favourite on the strength of an impressive record in France, two and a half points behind To-Agori-Mou who had never attempted a longer distance than a mile in public before and who in the event ran below his best; Cairn Rouge, specially prepared for her second attempt on the race, had started joint-third favourite with Master Willie. However, at the time of writing the result evidently isn't so clear-cut as first seemed. Reportedly an analysis of Vayrann's post-race sample proved positive and a Jockey-Club inquiry is pending which could affect the placings in the race. Should the inquiry go against the first past the post then the value of his performance may be called into question in some quarters. Whatever the outcome, connections at least have the option of carrying on with Vayrann in the hope that he will continue to show outstanding form. When Relko was under a cloud after winning the Derby Mathet set about erasing the doubts raised by the doping inquiry in the grand manner, and had the last laugh when Relko gave the complete answer to his critics by winning the French St Leger.

Vayrann's record in France, a country which also operates an efficient testing system and disqualified several of its big-race winners on the flat and over the sticks in 1981, notably the Greffulhe winner No Lute, is an impressive one indeed. He won three of his five races and might easily have had even better to show if he hadn't been called upon to deputise for his stable-companion Akarad in the Grand Prix de Paris in July. Vayrann is no more a long-distance horse than Akarad; if anything he's less, and his finishing third to Glint of Gold in that race, beaten only four and a half lengths, was an extraordinary performance for one whose best distance is probably five furlongs shorter. Tipperary Fixer, the best French-trained three-year-old to race regularly over the long trips, beat him only a length and a half for second place. Before the Grand Prix de Paris Vayrann had won a newcomers event at Saint-Cloud by five lengths and the Prix Jean de Chaudenay (formerly run as the Grand Prix du Printemps) on the same course most decisively by three lengths from the smart, older staying horse Kelbomec. In his only race in between he had been beaten a length and a half by Akarad at level weights in the twelve-furlong Prix de l'Avre at Longchamp, a race which attracted much more important horses, in those two, than its standing in the Calendar warranted. Vayrann's running on his only outing subsequent to the Grand Prix de Paris put him right in the Champion Stakes picture. Storm Bird captured most of the headlines before and, indeed, after

the Prix du Prince d'Orange at Longchamp in September but Vayrann finished well ahead of him. Vayrann won this ten-furlong event by half a length from Bikala, who was giving him 2 lb. He produced a good run from the middle of the field in the straight which took him to the front inside the last furlong and he got home in a driving finish; Diamond Prospect was third and the four-year-old Ruscelli fourth. Before Vayrann was sent to Newmarket Bikala had finished second in the Prix de l'Arc de Triomphe. The Prix du Prince d'Orange is always one of the strongest-contested of the autumn trials in France, and had been won the previous year by Dunette from Three Troikas and Northern Baby.

		Queen's Hussar	March Past
	Brigadier Gerard	(b 1960)	Jojo
	(b 1968)	La Paiva	Prince Chevalier
Vayrann		(ch 1956)	Brazen Molly
(br.c. 1978)		Val de Loir	Vieux Manoir
	Val Divine	(b 1959)	Vali
	(b 1971)	Pola Bella	Darius
		(br 1965)	Bella Paola

Vayrann's great-grandam Bella Paola won the Champion Stakes in 1958. She was one of the best racemares of the last thirty years, no doubt about that; the same season she also won the One Thousand Guineas, Oaks and Prix Vermeille for trainer Mathet. Her record as a broodmare is a first-rate one; she produced several worthy of herself on the racecourse, notably Vayrann's grandam Pola Bella who was in the top class at middle distances in France and won two good races at a mile—the Prix du Moulin de Longchamp and the Poule d'Essai des Pouliches and finished second in the Prix de Diane (the French Oaks) and Prix Vermeille. Vayrann's dam Val Divine was possibly the pick of Pola Bella's runners, a fair winner at around a mile and a quarter at Maisons-Laffitte and placed four times in six starts. Her only previous foals, Niece Divine (by Great Nephew) and Flocon D'Avoine (by Habitat) have been minor winners in

H.H. Aga Khan's "Vayrann"

France, each scoring on more than one occasion. The foal of 1979 is a colt by Red God, one of the last by the long-lived stallion, called Valiyar.

Vayrann is an attractive colt, one of the nicest of Brigadier Gerard's off-spring yet seen out and by far one of the best. For a horse of his exceptional racing ability Brigadier Gerard has made a slow start as a sire, but has now had Light Cavalry to represent him as well as this undoubtedly top-class horse. Vayrann is not so stout a stayer as Light Cavalry: Light Cavalry would have beaten him at fourteen furlongs-plus any day of the week but probably hardly ever at a mile and a half and never at less. Vayrann, as many French horses of considerable greater experience, has yet to encounter a firm surface; he obviously handles soft ground well. Before we leave him we should mention that the 1982 Champion Stakes, in which he will take all the beating in the world if he is sent over, will have a guaranteed value of £100,000 and will be known as the Dubai Champion Stakes, the Al Maktoum family having guaranteed sponsorship for the next five years. Sponsorship should doubly secure the future of a race which has not, in recent times, had any difficulty in attracting foreign competition. In fact, to name a race in England in the last twenty years which has received better support from foreign owners and trainers apart from the King George VI and Queen Elizabeth Stakes would be difficult, if not impossible. If the sponsors' money can attract even better fields, what races we should see! *F. Mathet, France.*

VEEYA 3 gr.g. Deep Diver 134–Ginkgo (Green God 128) (1980 5f 5fg² 5fg* 5d 5fg 5d 1981 6s 6g⁴ 5g* 5fg 5.1fg 6fg 5g 6d) fairly useful-looking gelding; good walker; plater; head second to Brians Star in apprentice seller at Carlisle in May (subsequently awarded race on disqualification of winner for having illegal substances in system); best form at 5f on a sound surface; occasionally blinkered, but seems better without; retained 800 gns Newmarket May Sales. *A. Bailey.* **62** d

VELESO 3 b.g. Jimsun 121–Dracaena 62 (Double Jump 131) (1980 5f 6d 6d* 7g⁴ 6g⁴ 1981 8s 7.3g 7.6fg 8fg 10.1fg 8s 10d) useful sort; quite useful at 2 yrs; didn't recover his form in 1981; probably stays 7f; acts on a soft surface; sometimes sweats up; slipped up fifth start. *R. Hannon.* —

VELOUR STREAK 2 ch.f. Firestreak 125–Ballyvelour 68 (Ballyciptic 122) (1981 6g 8d³ 8.2s) Mar 16; 4,000F; small filly; first produce by a thoroughbred stallion; dam, winner of 1¼m seller, is half-sister to smart Lord Helpus; plater; 4¾ lengths third of 16 to Sovereign Help at Redcar in October; will stay 1¼m. *E. Eldin.* **57**

VELVET HABIT 3 ch.f. Habitat 134–Red Velvet 114 (Red God 128§) (1980 7d⁴ 6d* 1981 6fg² 6g* 6g³ 6s 7g 7.2g⁴ 6g³ 6s) strong filly; good walker; overcame a poor draw when beating Corn Street very gamely by a neck in handicap at Kempton in May; in frame in similar races, being well backed on last 2 occasions; best form at 6f; acts on a firm and a soft surface; blinkered last 3 outings. *P. Walwyn.* **84**

VENDACE 3 br.g. Secret Ace 97–Springtime (Bleep 108) (1980 NR 1981 12g 12g) fourth foal; dam won over hurdles; behind in minor event at Carlisle and maiden race at Edinburgh in June. *J. Fitzgerald.* —

VENDIBILITY 3 b.c. Auction Ring 123–Wiener City (Chief III 130) (1980 5f 5f 6g 5d⁴ 5s 6s 1981 8s 7v*(dis) 8g³ 7g³ 8g 7s) lightly-made colt; poor mover; plater; apprentice ridden, attracted no bid after making most of running to win at Beverley in April by 7 lengths from Wyton Bar; later disqualified when traces of an illegal substance were found in his system; stays 1m; acts on heavy going; sold 470 gns Doncaster November Sales. *G. Toft.* **61**

VENETIAN JOY 2 br.f. Windjammer (USA)–Veneziana 91 (Tiger 125) (1981 5g⁴ 5d² 5fg³ 5g⁴ 5d⁴ 5d³ 5g) Apr 17; 6,200Y; fair sort; sister to useful 1977 2-y-o 6f to 1m winner Sicalu, subsequently a good winner in Norway, and half-sister to a winner in Holland; dam stayed 1¼m; in frame on most starts but isn't so consistent as form-figures suggest; looked to be cruising 1½f out in £4,000 race at Beverley in June but found little under pressure, eventually finishing 1½ lengths third to Vaigly Star; off course over 3 months afterwards; not bred to be a 5f performer; blinkered fourth and sixth outings; gives strong impression she's not genuine and isn't to be trusted. *M. W. Easterby.* **80** §

VENJA 3 ch.c. Native Bazaar 122–Avengeress 73 (Aggressor 130) (1980 8fg² 8s 1981 7fg² 6d 7s* 7fg⁴ 7fg² 7f 7fg² 7d*) leggy, light-framed, lengthy colt, **67**

successful in sellers at Kempton in May (bought in 3,100 gns) and Brighton in October (sold to A. Moore 4,000 gns); stays 1m; probably acts on any going. *P. Cole.*

VENTURION 7 b.h. Hopeful Venture 125–Snow Rum (Quorum 126) (1980 NR 1981 10d 16g 15.5fg) poor handicapper; beaten in seller first start; probably stays 1¼m. *J. Davies.* —

VENUS STAR (USA) 2 b.f. Barachois–Final Word (Final Ruling) (1981 6g 6g 6d²) rather lightly-made filly; half-sister to 2 winners in USA; dam, half-sister to Derby third Hunza Dancer, won twice at 5f in USA; 2 lengths second of 22 to Late Hour in maiden race at Leicester in November, easily best effort; will stay 7f. *M. Albina.* **78**

VERAMENTE 6 b.g. Sassafras 135–Quelle Blague (Red God 128§) (1980 NR 1981 10s) lightly raced on flat nowadays; best form over middle distances; seems to act on any going; has been tried in blinkers; suitable mount for an inexperienced rider. *S. Mellor.* —

VERDA 3 gr.f. The Go-Between 129–Fiffa 59 (Town Crier 119) (1980 NR 1981 7f 8g 8fg⁴ 8fg 8.2s 8s 6g 7g) stocky filly; first foal; dam, plating-class middle-distance maiden on flat, won over hurdles; poor maiden; behind in a seller final outing; stays 1m; blinkered sixth start. *R. Hannon.* **57**

VERNHAM STREET 3 b.g. Streetfighter 120–Bois Le Duc (Kalydon 122 or March Past 124) (1980 NR 1981 8d 9s 11.7g 8fg* 7f 8fg 6fg* 6g* 7g⁴) 700F; strong, lengthy gelding; first foal; dam poor maiden; won handicaps at Leicester in July and Windsor and Goodwood in September (apprentices), beating Alpine Rocket decisively by 2 lengths on last-named course; behind in similar races in between first 2 wins; effective at 6f and stays 1m; acts on a firm surface; apprentice ridden. *H. Candy.* **66**

VEROWEN 3 ch.g. Owen Anthony 102–Sovereign Bracelet (Manacle 123) (1980 5f 5h³ 5fg⁴ 5fg 6fg⁴ 5s 1981 5g 5f 6f 6fg 6f 5d) lightly-made gelding; plater; better suited by 6f than 5f and should stay further; sometimes blinkered. *W. Stubbs.* —

VERSAILLES PALACE 2 b.g. Royal Palace 131–Bravour II (Birkhahn) (1981 6g 7g³ 7fg) Apr 26; quite attractive gelding; half-brother to winners here and in France, including very useful 1976 2-y-o 5f and 6f winner Brave Lass (by Ridan); dam best 2-y-o filly of her year in Germany and won German 1,000 Guineas; 33/1, showed up throughout when 6 lengths third of 18 to Puff of Smoke in maiden race at Salisbury in July, best effort; will be suited by 1m. *H. Candy.* **69**

VERY FRIENDLY 5 b.g. Be Friendly 130–Little Hexa (Exar 130) (1980 8s 8s 8fg 8.2d² 8fg 10.4d 8d 1981 10f) poor plater; stays 1¼m; acts on any going. *P. Bevan.* —

VESTAL TELEGRAPH 2 b.g. Sayfar 116–Flying Nun 66 (Welsh Abbot 131) (1981 5d⁴ 5d 6fg 6g 8.2d) half-brother to 6f and 1m winner Welch Soldier (by Easter Island); dam won over 5f at 2 yrs; poor plater; should stay 1m. *D. Leslie.* **43**

VICOLS LAD 3 ch.g. Sandford Lad 133–Lady Exbury 111 (Exbury 138) (1980 5fg 6s 6fg 6g 1981 8d 8d 7f 8fg 8g 8d) smallish, fair sort; poor form, including in sellers; probably stays 1m; blinkered last 2 starts; sold 775 gns Ascot October Sales. *G. Balding.* —

VICTOR HUGO 4 b. or br.c. Vaguely Noble 140–Anna Karenina (Princely Gift 137) (1980 8s 8f 6h 5fg 1981 10d 8fg) compact colt; poor form, including in a seller; has worn blinkers; sold 1,600 gns Ascot 2nd June Sales. *V. Soane.* —

VICTORIAN PAINTING 2 ch.g. Hot Spark 126–Linden Lea 91§ (Hornbeam 130) (1981) (1981 5s 5fg 5d) Feb 24; 2,600F, resold 4,000Y; lengthy gelding; half-brother to 2 winning platers; dam at her best at 2 yrs; in rear in maiden and minor events; off course 5 months before final outing; sold to National Horse Belgium 400 gns Newmarket Autumn Sales. *W. Wightman.* —

VICTORIA PALACE 2 br.f. Prince Tenderfoot 126–Gull (Fleet Nasrullah) (1981 6fg 6g) Jan 28; 6,000Y; good sort; half-sister to winners in Ireland and USA; dam won 1m claiming race in USA; in rear in maiden races at Newmarket in July (started very slowly and finished last) and October (showed up to halfway). *N. Guest.* —

VICTORIA SPIRIT 4 ch.f. Henry the Seventh 125–Golf Ball (Persian Gulf) (1980 10s 1981 15.8s 15.8g 16d 10.6s 12.3fg) neat filly; poor plater; wore blinkers; sometimes bandaged; broke a leg in June and was destroyed. *M. Reddan.*   —

VICTOR'S BOAST (USA) 3 ch.g. Roberto 131–Noble Mark 120 (On Your Mark 125) (1980 5s³ 5fg³ 5f³ 5f⁴ 7fg³ 7.2g³ 1981 10fg* 12.3d) small, compact gelding; made all when beating Golden Brigadier by 1½ lengths in handicap at Epsom in April; probably unsuited by going when tailed off at Chester the following month; suited by 1¼m; acts well on firm ground; exported to Hong Kong. *B. Hills.*   **83**

VICTORY HOUSE 2 ch.c. Habitat 134–Star Court 102 (Aureole 132) (1981 5g³) Mar 24; neat colt; second foal; half-brother to useful 1978 2-y-o 7f winner Etoile des Indes (by Kashmir II); dam won over 7f at 3 yrs and is half-sister to Owen Dudley and Abwah; 5/1, showed speed throughout and wasn't unduly hard ridden when 3 lengths third of 17 to Chris's Lad in maiden race at Newmarket in April; looked reasonably promising here but wasn't seen out again. *H. Cecil.*   **79 p**

VICTORY HYMN 5 gr.g. Seaepic 100–Decorators Ditty (Sing Sing 134) (1980 10fg 8fg 1981 12g 16.9s 10f 10f* 10fg 10fg⁴) quite well made gelding; easily won modest minor event at Brighton in July (apprentice ridden); stays 1¼m; probably acts on any going; trained by N. Henderson first start. *P. Cole.*   **47**

VICTORY PRIZE 3 b.g. Quayside 124–Prize (Le Prince 98) (1980 NR 1981 12g 12.2g) 2,000Y; first foal; dam, who never ran, comes from same family as a top 1955 Irish 2-y-o Sarissa; probably of little account; bandaged first start. *J. Doyle.*   —

VIDEO KING 2 b.c. Blue Cashmere 129–Florintina 104 (Floribunda 136) (1981 6fg³ 5fg 7fg 7f 7s) Apr 2; 16,000Y; rangy colt; half-brother to 3 winners, including useful 5f to 1m winner Shapina and smart 6f to 1m performer Premier Rose (both by Sharp Edge); dam won at 7f and 1m; quite a moderate colt; gives impression he doesn't stay 7f; sold 3,600 gns Newmarket Autumn Sales. *C. Brittain.*   **72**

VIDEO TAPE (USA) 3 br.c. Cannonade–Virunga 115 (Sodium 128) (1980 7d 8g* 1981 10.6fg² 10d 10g) tall, rangy colt; appeared to beat Nureddin on merit by ¾ length in £2,900 event at Haydock in April, but hung left and bumped Nureddin and placings were subsequently reversed; subsequently ran moderately in Heathorn Stakes and quite valuable handicap, both at Newmarket; will stay 1½m; usually ridden by apprentice N. Day; hurdling in France and has won there. *H. Cecil.*   **84**

VIDOR (USA) 2 br.f. Vaguely Noble 140–Prestissimo (Bold Reasoning) (1981 8v*) Mar 15; $150,000Y; first foal; dam, stakes-placed winner at up to 6f, is half-sister to high-class 1981 2-y-o Jalmood; third favourite when winning 14-runner newcomers event at Maisons-Laffitte in October in tight finish with Goosalley and Pasvaria; will stay 1½m; well bred and looks certain to improve a good deal; engaged in 1,000 Guineas and Oaks. *M. Zilber, France.*   **?**

VIELLE 4 b.f. Ribero 126–Hurdy-Gurdy 90 (Espresso 122) (1980 7f 10fg* 12f² 12s* 10fg* 12d² 10f 1981 10fg³ 10s⁴ 12d³ 10fg² 10fg² 10g² 10f² 10fg* 10g)   **121**

    More often the understudy than the star would be an apt summary of Vielle's career now that she has been retired to the paddocks to visit Posse. Admittedly she did win six races, notably the 1980 Lancashire Oaks and Nassau Stakes, but she was runner-up on no fewer than ten occasions in events worth almost £275,000. Second in the Oaks and Yorkshire Oaks at three, she filled the same position four times in 1981 and until her success in the Virginia Stakes at Newcastle she was in some danger of ending the season as one of its most talented losers.

    Vielle's first three starts saw her finishing third to Hard Fought when palpably unfit in the Westbury Stakes at Sandown, a moderate fifth, promoted to fourth, behind Triomphe in the Clive Graham Stakes at Goodwood, after which her trainer expressed doubts about her enthusiasm, and third to Master Willie, beaten over four lengths, in the Coronation Cup at Epsom. At this stage there was no guarantee that she had trained on fully, but the Prince of Wales's Stakes at Royal Ascot dispelled any doubts on this score. Though outpaced by Hard Fought she kept on fairly well up the centre of the course to go down by only three parts of a length to him with several smart performers behind her. Because no filly has won the Eclipse Stakes and not many have been placed in it the claim has been made that it is a jinx race for them. There is, of course,

Mr T. F. Blackwell's "Vielle"

no such thing as a jinx race, and one of the chief reasons for this mediocre record in simple enough. Fillies seldom contest the Eclipse and from 1960 to 1980 only nine ran in it whereas forty-four ran in the Champion Stakes, for instance. Two, Vielle and Madam Gay, took part in the 1981 Coral Eclipse at Sandown and while Madam Gay ran below form Vielle surpassed herself, being awarded second place after Hard Fought became involved in a barging match with her inside the distance. Vielle didn't help matters by hanging in towards the rails halfway up the straight but she was undoubtedly hampered by the colt and was justifiably promoted after ending up in the centre of the course, just over a length behind the all-the-way winner Master Willie.

		Ribero (b 1965)	Ribot (b 1952)	Tenerani
Vielle (b.f. 1977)				Romanella
			Libra (ch 1956)	Hyperion
				Weighbridge
		Hurdy-Gurdy (b 1970)	Espresso (ch 1958)	Acropolis
				Babylon
			Street Singer (br 1954)	Kingsway
				Record Serenade

In both the Nassau Stakes at Goodwood and the Prix Gontaut-Biron at Deauville Vielle again found one to beat her. At Goodwood she was unlucky to come up against Go Leasing on one of her good days and went down by a length; in France she was held up and made steady progress in the straight to finish a length and a half behind Nemr. Some criticised Piggott for his performance here but since Vielle was never an easy ride, showing a tendency to hang and, in 1981, finding little under pressure, such criticism was probably unfair. Success at last came Vielle's way in the four-runner Virginia Stakes at Newcastle, her third race in August. On the face of it she had an easy task; starting at 9/4 on she was always going well, led three furlongs out and only had to be pushed out to account for Viendra by three lengths. On her final start Vielle ran moderately in the Sun Chariot Stakes at Newmarket, as she had in 1980.

Vielle is the third foal of the mile to mile-and-a-quarter winner Hurdy-Gurdy; the first, Sideshow (by Welsh Pageant), showed useful form over one and a quarter miles and her two-year-old Pianola (also by Welsh Pageant) displayed distinct signs of ability when well backed on her only outing in 1981. Hurdy-Gurdy is a half-sister to numerous winners, including the Irish St Leger third Torano, out of the high-class sprinter Street Singer, one of whose half-sisters produced the admirable Raffingora. Vielle is a robust, round-barrelled, attractive filly who carries a lot of condition and is a good walker and mover. She stayed a mile and a half and acted on any going. *B. Hobbs.*

VIENDRA (USA) 3 ch.f. Raise A Native–Friendly Relations (Nearctic) (1980 **113** NR 1981 7.6d* 10g² 10v 8fg⁴ 10g⁴ 12g 10fg² 10f) $275,000 2-y-o; tall, attractive, deep-girthed filly; sister to Americanized, successful 3 times at up to 6f, closely related to minor winner Kindhcartedness (by Exclusive Native), and half-sister to 2 other winners; dam won once over 6f from 12 starts and is half-sister to dam of Nijinsky; beat What Heaven by 2½ lengths in maiden race at Chester in May on first outing; in frame in Sir Charles Clore Memorial Stakes at Newbury later in month (caught close home and beaten head by Strigida), Child Stakes at Newmarket in July (stuck on well and finished fourth to Star Pastures), Nassau Stakes at Goodwood in August (fourth again, behind Go Leasing) and Virginia Stakes at Newcastle later in August (3 lengths second to Vielle); sixth of 9 behind De La Rose in E. P. Taylor Stakes at Woodbine, Canada, in October; suited by 1¼m and will probably stay 1½m (started slowly and was hampered on home turn when behind in Yorkshire Oaks over 1½m); acts on a firm and a soft surface; very useful. *B. Hills.*

VILASA 3 ch.f. Grundy 137–Nagin 120 (Pretense) (1980 NR 1981 10s 7f 7d — 8fg 8g) lengthy, lightly-made filly; first foal; dam, best at 6f, won in Ireland, England and France; seventh of 20 behind stable-companion Rose Music in minor event at Leicester in June, second and best effort. *R. Armstrong.*

VILLACANA 2 b.f. Lord Gayle 124–Etoile Freda (Florescence 120) (1981 — 7d 7f) May 7; IR 4,800Y; close-coupled filly; half-sister to Irish 6f winner Superb (by Roi Soleil), also successful in Belgium; dam never ran; unquoted when soundly beaten in sizeable fields of maidens at Newmarket and Yarmouth in August. *I. Walker.*

VILLAGE SHERIFF (USA) 3 b.c. Apalachee 137–Musical Chimes (Our — Michael) (1980 NR 1981 8fg 10d) $30,000Y; small, quite well-made colt; first foal; dam unraced half-sister to 2 minor stakes winners; behind in maiden races at Newbury in July and Newmarket (last of 17) in August. *E. Eldin.*

VINCENT'S PRIDE 2 ch.c. Guillaume Tell 121–Chi-Chi (Sing Sing 134) (1981 **86 p** 9d*) Apr 24; IR 11,500Y; first foal; dam lightly-raced daughter of very smart French filly Tawny Owl; won easily by 4 lengths from Derby Dilly in 14-runner maiden race at Gowran Park in October; will stay 1¼m; impressive here and could make a smart 3-y-o. *K. Prendergast, Ireland.*

VIN ST BENET 2 b.c. The Brianstan 128–Hopeful Gift 95 (Bounteous 125) **104** (1981 5g 5g 5fg* 7fg* 6fg² 7fg³ 7fg⁴ 7f 8g²) Apr 10; 2,600Y; useful-looking colt; half-brother to 1980 2-y-o 5.8f winner Shalwa (by Broxted) and 2 winning jumpers; dam won over 9f; won maiden auction race at Warwick in June and minor event at Yarmouth in July; ran well in £5,000 nursery at Lingfield, £4,200 race at Newmarket (gave away a lot of weight all round when 5 lengths third of 8 to Ashenden), Lanson Champagne Stakes at Goodwood (ran on strongly to finish length fourth of 5 to Treboro) and minor event at Goodwood (4 lengths second to Jalmood) afterwards; may well stay 1¼m; acts on a firm surface; tough, genuine and consistent. *M. Tompkins.*

VIOLINO FANDANGO 3 b.c. Gay Fandango 132–Parkhurst (Sing Sing 134) **72** (1980 5s 5.8fg² 7s² 7f* 7h* 8f 1981 10fg 6s 7g 7f 7f² 7fg 8f) tall colt; ran well when ¾-length second to Silver Ruler in handicap at Bath in July; didn't have best of runs next time; stays 7f well; acts on any going; sold to P. Feilden 3,000 gns Newmarket Autumn Sales. *B. Hills.*

925

VIPPON (HUN) 8 b.g. Pomade Kiraly–Veritas (Imi) (1981 10fg) Hungarian-bred gelding; has won 9 times in Hungary from 1m to 11f; behind in amateur riders race at Lingfield in July, first outing in this country. *K. Brassey.* —

VIRGI 2 b.f. Tudor Rhythm 112–Golden Linnet 96 (Sing Sing 134) (1981 5s 6f 6f 6fg 6g 6d*) May 11; 2,700Y; fair sort; half-sister to 3 winners, including fairly useful 5f performer Blue Linnet (by Habitat); dam won over 5f and 6f and is half-sister to good sprinter Monet; finished strongly to win 11-runner nursery at Hamilton in October under 7-7; beaten in 2 sellers previously; will stay 7f; suited by a soft surface; reportedly racing in Florida. *P. Rohan.* **69**

VIRGINIA DRIVE 9 ch.g. Virginia Boy 106–Wood Grouse 56 (Celtic Ash) (1980 NR 1981 17.1h) lightly raced on flat nowadays and is probably no longer of any account. *O. O'Neill.* —

VIRGINIA HEIGHTS 4 ch.f. Virginia Boy 106–Weirdi 76 (Yrrah Jr) (1980 8fg 8f 9.4fg 8f 7g 1981 7f 6fg 7fg) narrow, sparely-made filly; poor plater; sometimes sweats up; sold 420 gns Ascot October Sales. *W. A. Stephenson.* —

VIRGIN SOLDIER 5 b.g. Queen's Hussar 124–Saintly Miss 63 (St Paddy 133) (1980 10fg* 10g 12g2 12fg2 10d 1981 11s 12d2 12s) leggy gelding; stays 1¼m; acts on a firm and a soft surface; suitable mount for an inexperienced rider; retained 6,000 gns Newmarket Autumn Sales. *J. Old.* **66**

VIRIBUS (FR) 5 b.g. Sir Gaylord–Vasveliya (Saint Crespin III 132) (1980 10.6fg 12f 10.6s3 10s2 1981 11s 10d 10.4g 12g4 12f4) good mover; stays 1¼m well; acts on any going; has worn blinkers; has run creditably for a boy; sold to Earl Jones 2,800 gns Ascot July Sales. *R. Hollinshead.* —

VISCONTI 5 b.g. Lord Gayle 124–Jane Shaw (Galivanter 131) (1980 8g 12fg3 10s* 1981 12g 13g* 15.8g 16f2 14d) close-coupled gelding; has had a soft palate operation; does more racing over hurdles than on flat; heavily backed when winning 6-runner handicap at Ayr in June; stays well; acts on any going; suitable mount for an inexperienced rider. *M. Dickinson.* **71**

VITAL SPIRIT 2 b.f. Tachypous 128–Vital Error 105 (Javelot 124) (1981 5fg 6f3 5fg4 6fg 5d) Mar 3; leggy filly; half-sister to numerous winners, including useful French middle-distance performer Major Busted (by Busted); dam best at up to 7f; ¾-length third to In Slips in 22-runner maiden race at Thirsk in July, best effort; bred to stay at least 1m; blinkered final start. *J. Etherington.* **65**

VITINGO 2 ch.c. Vitiges 132–Petlady 81 (Petingo 135) (1981 7fg 8d) May 27; 16,500Y; fair sort; first foal; dam won over 6f at 2 yrs; behind in 15-runner races at Doncaster in July and Bath in October; blinkered on latter; sold 3,600 gns Newmarket Autumn Sales. *C. Brittain.* —

VIVA SINGAPURA 3 b.g. Town Crier 119–Magibbillibyte 77 (Constable 119) (1980 5f 6fg 6d 1981 6f 6g 7f) rangy gelding; in rear in varied company, including selling, but didn't look fully fit and gave impression he's not without ability; blinkered final start. *M. W. Easterby.* —

VIVIDUS 6 b.g. Vivify–Blue Grace (Darling Boy 124) (1980 NR 1981 10g4) novice hurdler; not disgraced in ladies race at Lingfield in June, first outing on flat. *D. Ringer.* —

VOCALIST 3 b.f. Crooner 119–Rhythm 64 (Bleep-Bleep 134) (1980 6g 5s* 5g* 6g2 1981 7g 8g 8v 8f 8fg3 6fg2 7fg 8fg* 7f4 7g 8g4 8s 7g) compact non-thoroughbred filly; beat Seasurf rather cheekily by ¾ length in 3-runner Atalanta Stakes at Kempton in August; had finished 2½ lengths second to Integrity in well-contested minor event at Newbury the previous month and also ran creditably in top-class company on other occasions, including in 1,000 Guineas at Newmarket (close sixth of 14 to Fairy Footsteps), Goffs Irish 1,000 Guineas at the Curragh (sixth of 15 to Arctique Royale) and Coronation Stakes at Royal Ascot (fifth of 10 to Tolmi); stays 1m; probably acts on any going but is well suited by soft. *F. Durr.* **109**

VOCIFEROUS 2 ch.f. Vitiges 132–Too Much 100 (Major Portion 129) (1981 7f) May 24; 6,400Y; rangy, good sort; half-sister to several winners here and in France, including fairly useful 7f to 1¼m winner Princess Pageant (by Welsh Pageant); dam won at up to 1m; unquoted and in need of race, chased leaders for 5f when behind in 16-runner maiden race at Yarmouth in August; will stay 1¼m; has scope for improvement. *I. Walker.* —

VOICE OF PROGRESS 3 b.g. Matahawk 127–La Crima 63 (Runnymede 123) (1980 NR 1981 12d 12fg4 12f4 12g2 12g*) 800Y; second foal; half- **73**

brother to a winner in Belgium; dam won over 7.6f in French Provinces; in frame in maiden races before beating More Oats by 1½ lengths in apprentice handicap at Ascot in September (made virtually all and stayed on very well); will stay beyond 1½m. *J. Dunlop.*

VON ERLACH   3 b. or br.c. Huntercombe 133–Fulcrum Miss (Fulcrum)   (1980   **95** 6fg* 6fg 6f 7.3d   1981 7g 8g* 8.2s² 8f 8fg³ 8fg³ 10g 10d 9g 8g 10.2g 10g)   well-made, quite attractive colt; good mover; beat Montclair by ½ length in handicap at Brighton in May; placed subsequently in handicaps at Haydock (staying-on second to Silver Season in Cecil Frail), Sandown and Newmarket (strong- finishing third to Golden Flak in Food Brokers Trophy); creditable sixth of 28 behind Braughing in William Hill Cambridgeshire at Newmarket in October on ninth start; stays 9f (not entirely disgraced over 1¼m); probably acts on any going. *F. Durr.*

VOORTREKKER   3 b.g. Prince Regent 129–Trekker 86 (Grey Sovereign 128§)   — (1980 NR   1981 8s 9.4g 12.2fg 13g 10fg)   second living foal; half-brother to useful 5f winner Jameson (by Huntercombe); dam won twice over 1¼m; tailed off in maiden and minor races; trained by J. Leigh first outing. *W. Elsey.*

VORACITY   2 ch.c. Vitiges 132–Wolverene 114 (Relko 136)   (1981 7g)   Apr 15;   — p half-brother to 3-y-o 1m winner Wiveton (by Blakeney) and 2 other winners, in- cluding useful 11f winner Shining Tor (by High Top); dam game stayer; unquoted, nearest at finish when out of first 9 of 22 to Count Pahlen in maiden race at Newmarket in October; will do better over middle distances. *J. Winter.*

VORVADOS   4 br.c. The Go-Between 129–Keravnos 64 (Ionian 128)   (1980   **80** 5fg 6f³ 6f² 6f³ 6g⁴ 6fg² 6g 6g 5f 7fg   1981 5s⁴ 6s 6fg 5g⁴ 6d² 6g 5.3f 6fg* 6g* 6fg 6fg 6g 6s³ 6d)   lightly-built colt; fair handicapper; won at Brighton and Salisbury in July; best form at 6f; acts on any going; blinkered fifth and sixth starts; has run creditably for an apprentice. *M. Haynes.*

VOTE BAROLO   2 b.f. Nebbiolo 125–Polling Station 91 (Polly's Jet)   (1981   — 5s 6s)   Mar 19; IR 7,400F, IR 6,400Y; half-sister to several winners, including fairly useful 1975 2-y-o 7f winner Lord Elect (by Lord Gayle); dam sprinter; well beaten in end-of-season maiden races in the Midlands. *T. Robson.*

VOTING DAY   3 b.f. Swing Easy 126–Miss Wolff 91 (Vilmorin)   (1980 5fg   — 5f 5.8h 6fg 5d*   1981 5s²(dis) 7d 5.8g 5g 5.8f 6fg)   rangy filly; ¾-length second to Heavy Weapon in handicap at Doncaster in March; later disqualified when traces of an illegal substance were found in her system; best form at 5f on soft going but runs as if she should stay a bit further; bandaged near-hind fourth start; blinkered final outing. *J. Hill.*

VOTRE ALTESSE (FR)   3 b.f. Riverman 131–Vahinee (Mourne 126)   (1980   **122** 7d* 8s*   1981 10f 8s* 9.2d³ 10.5v*)   half-sister to several winners in France, including very smart but short-lived Dragoon (by Le Fabuleux) and very useful 5f to 9f winner Virgin (by Zeddaan); dam won at 2 yrs; not seen out until late in August but showed smart form; won 90,000 francs event at Longchamp in September and Group 3 Prix de Flore at Longchamp in October; beat Rixe both times, by 1½ lengths and a length respectively; ran on steadily when dead-heating for third, just over a length behind Kilmona, in Group 2 Prix de l'Opera at Longchamp in between; stays 1¼m well; acts on heavy going. *M. Saliba, France.*

VOYANT   2 ch.c. Star Appeal 133–Vernier 94 (High Hat 131)   (1981 7fg²   **93** 7.6g 7g²)   Mar 12; quite well-made colt; second live foal; dam won over 1½m and 13f; improved steadily and showed himself a fairly useful animal when staying on well to finish 2½ lengths second of 11 to Not For Show in £4,300 race at Doncaster in November; will be suited by middle distances; could make a decent 3-y-o handicapper. *B. Hobbs.*

VRONSKY   5 gr.g. Warpath 113–Janabelle 101 (Gentle Art 121)   (1980 5g   — 7f 5f³ 6h 7g² 7g 7f 6s 5fg   1981 12.5s 12s 9fg 10.6s 8g 14.6f)   strong, compact gelding; plater; not certain to stay middle distances; seems to act on any going; sometimes wears blinkers. *C. Gray.*

VUILLARD (USA)   3 ch.c. Raise A Native–Swift Syrian (Tom Rolfe)   (1980   **57** NR   1981 7d³ 8fg 10g 10.1f⁴ 10f⁴ 10fg) $80,000Y; small, quite attractive colt; first foal; dam twice-raced daughter of smart Syrian Sea, a sister to Secretariat; in frame in newcomers race (tended to hang under pressure) and minor events; stays 1¼m; bit coltish in paddock second outing; ran poorly final start; sold 700 gns Goffs October Sales. *R. Price.*

W

WAFFLES 3 b.f. Wollow 132–Night Off 124 (Narrator 127) (1980 NR 1981 **100**
10s² 10fg⁴ 12fg 12d 9d*) big, rangy filly; half-sister to smart 2-y-o's Madame's
Share (by Major Portion) and Baldur (by Breton); dam won Cheveley Park
Stakes and 1,000 Guineas; landed the odds by 6 lengths from Maryville Bick
in 17-runner maiden race at Gowran Park in October; had earlier finished in
frame in minor event and Pretty Polly Stakes at the Curragh in June, finishing
about 5 lengths fourth behind Happy Bride in latter; over 10 lengths fifth of 10
behind Blue Wind in Irish Guinness Oaks at the Curragh and never-dangerous
eighth of 12 behind Ma Femme in Galtres Stakes at York on her other starts;
stays 1¼m; gave a little trouble at start at York. *V. O'Brien, Ireland.*

WAHED 6 gr.g. Red God 128§–Welsh Crest 86 (Abernant 142) (1980 8f⁴ 8f **62**
9fg⁴ 8fg 8s 6d 7f* 5g 7g 8f* 8d 1981 7f* 7f 8g 8f³ 7g 8f² 7g⁴ 8fg²) won handicap
at Beverley in June; stays 1m but not 1¼m; probably unsuited by soft ground;
has worn blinkers; good mount for an inexperienced rider; does best when
brought wide to race alone; sold 900 gns Newmarket Autumn Sales. *Denys
Smith.*

WAIT AND SEE 6 b.g. Biskrah 121–Cool Spirit (Hot Brandy 119) (1980 **—**
NR 1981 18fg) staying handicapper; lightly raced on flat nowadays; acts
on any going; wears blinkers. *Mrs M. Rimell.*

WAKKAD 5 ch.h. Northfields–Gold Pollen 110 (Klondyke Bill 125) (1980 **—**
8f 8f² 8f 8fg 8fg 1981 8g 7fg 7f 8f 8fg) compact, useful sort; poor handicapper; stays 1m; acts on firm going and is possibly unsuited by soft. *W.
Haigh.*

WALDUCK 4 ch.g. Native Bazaar 122–Avengeress 73 (Aggressor 130) (1980 **—**
NR 1981 10.8fg) 4,300Y, 460 2-y-o; behind in seller at Warwick in July.
M. Chapman.

WALEED 6 br.h. Tudor Melody 129–Toast Record 91 (El Gallo 122) (1980 **—**
NR 1981 12s 11s) showed no form in 1981; stayed 1½m; acted well on firm
going; dead. *W. Musson.*

WALK ALONG 2 ch.g. Farm Walk 111–Leger Bar 63 (French Beige 127) **69**
(1981 7d⁴ 7f) Feb 12; lightly-made gelding; brother to middle-distance winner
Walk Around, and half-brother to fair 5f and 7f winner Water of Life (by Mummy's Pet); dam moderate plater; never in hunt when over 8 lengths fourth of
6 to Cassley River in £3,100 race at Redcar in August; 12 lengths last of 8 after
swerving at start in £3,800 race won by Busaco at York the following month;
will need at least 1¼m at 3 yrs. *W. Haigh.*

WALKIES 2 b.c. Tower Walk 130–Jamar 81 (Kashmir II 125) (1981 5d⁴ 6g³ **76**
6g³ 6fg 7fg 7.6s³ 7d 8d) Mar 29; second reported foal; dam, 5f winner at 4
yrs and 5 yrs, is half-sister to smart Lightning Label; 25/1 when about a length
third of 14 to Change Habit in maiden race at Lingfield in October, easily best
effort; beaten in 3 sellers and under a low weight in a nursery previously; will
stay 1m; best run on soft going. *N. Guest.*

WALKING BESIDE YOU (USA) 2 br.c. Gleaming–Roses for the Star 114 **85**
(Stage Door Johnny) (1981 7g²) leggy American-bred colt; dam, half-sister
to Ribocco and Ribero, was second in Oaks; 15/2 and one of the fittest of newcomers, stayed on well to finish 2 lengths second of 18 to Leg Glance in maiden
race at Doncaster in October; dead. *F. J. Houghton.*

WALK MARCH 3 b.c. Sharpen Up 127–Walk By 113 (Tower Walk 130) (1980 **—**
6fg 5fg 5d 1981 6s 8fg 8d) strong, lengthy, useful sort; good walker and
mover; behind in maiden and minor races over here; ran as if finding 1m too far
second start; sold 500 gns Ascot July Sales and subsequently won in Belgium.
W. Wightman.

WALLYFRED 3 ch.f. Manado 130–Javatina 87 (Javelot 124) (1980 5g 5g **41**
8.2d³ 7f 1981 10v 8g 12g 12.2g² 9fg 10f³ 13.8f 10g³ 10f 9g 10d 9d 11d 10s)
light-framed filly; plater; stays 1½m; acts on any going; blinkered nowadays;
none too genuine; sometimes starts slowly; sold 700 gns Newmarket December
Sales. *J. Fitzgerald.*

WALLY WOMBAT 3 b.c. Abwah 118–Enlighten (Twilight Alley 133) (1980 **60**
5fg 7fg 7fg 8g 7fg 1981 12d 11.7s² 11.7g³ 11.7f 11.7fg 10f 8s 12.2s) quite a
well-made, burly sort; plating-class maiden; suited by 1½m; probably needs
some give in the ground. *J. Holt.*

David Dixon Sprint Trophy, York—Walter Osborne is clear of his rivals

WALNUT WONDER 6 b.g. Crozier 117–Gretna Wonder 46 (Elopement 125) **42**
(1980 NR 1981 17.1g³) useful hurdler; lightly raced on flat nowadays; stays
well. *L. Kennard.*

WALTER MITTY 2 b.g. Perdu 121–Buttonback 73 (Fleece 114) (1981 **82**
5fg 6f³ 6fg* 6g³ 6g* 6f) Mar 14; 1,900Y; neat gelding; fourth foal; dam won
7.2f seller at 2 yrs; won 20-runner maiden auction event at Kempton in July
and 7-runner nursery at Windsor in August; favourite, ran on well to beat
Little Smasher 2½ lengths in latter; will be suited by 7f; yet to race on a soft
surface; sent to Hong Kong. *G. Pritchard-Gordon.*

WALTER OSBORNE 4 ch.c. Welsh Pageant 132–Island Princess (Raise A **101**
Native) (1980 8d⁴ 5g² 6fg² 5f² 7fg 6d³ 5g² 5g* 5s* 5d 5s* 5g* 1981 5s 5d²
5d³ 5d* 5fg³ 5fg 5fg* 6fg 5g 5.6fg 5g*) lengthy, attractive ex-Irish colt; useful
handicapper; successful twice at York, in David Dixon Sprint Trophy in May
(beat Escovitch by 3 lengths) and in £3,200 race in July (accounted for Kaimlaw
by a short head), and in minor event at Edinburgh in September; best at 5f;
acts on any going; has won for a 5-lb claimer; ran dismally in blinkers penultimate start; racing in USA. *M. W. Easterby.*

WALTHAM TERRACE 2 b.f. Auction Ring 123–Dandy Brush 82 (Will **—**
Somers 114§) (1981 5s 5d 5fg 5f 6fg) May 4; 3,700Y; compact filly; half-
sister to several minor winners; dam showed form only at 2 yrs; soundly beaten
in maiden races in the North, one an auction event; sweated up very badly
second start. *W. Haigh.*

WALTZ 2 ch.f. Jimmy Reppin 131–Strip The Willow 79 (Native Dancer) (1981 **— p**
6s³) Feb 18; lightly-made, useful-looking filly; sister to very smart 7f and 1m
filly Joking Apart and useful 6f to 1m winner Strathspey, and half-sister to
a winner; dam unplaced 5 times; third favourite, ran on really well in final
2f and finished clear of remainder when 5 lengths third of 15 to Ellerene in maiden
race at Newbury in October; will be suited by 7f and 1m; will probably do a
fair bit better at 3 yrs. *I. Balding.*

WANCHAI LASS 4 b.f. Balliol 125–Fairy Goddess (Yellow God 129) (1980 **—**
6v 6d⁴ 5h 6fg 5g² 5f² 6g 6s 5fg* 1981 6fg 7g 5g) neat filly; plater; stays 6f;
isn't at her best on very soft going; sometimes blinkered but is effective without;
sold 500 Doncaster November Sales. *G. Toft.*

WANDERING ABOUT 3 b.c. Farm Walk 111–Wandering On (Klairon 131) **44**
(1980 5g 8d 7f 7d³ 6s 10.2s 1981 10s 8s 10g 12.5f 9s 9fg⁴ 10f² 13.8f 9d 10f
13.8fg) workmanlike colt; plater; tended to wander when ¾-length second to
Goldliner Abbey at Beverley in July; stays 1½m; often apprentice ridden;
often bandaged; has worn blinkers; virtually pulled up final start. *J. Calvert.*

WANGAROO (USA) 2 b.c. Charles Elliott–Saratoga Gal (Royal Orbit) (1981 **61**
5s 6g 6g 6d³ 7fg 8.2fg⁴ 10s) sturdy colt; second foal; half-brother to 3-y-o
7f seller winner Saratoga Chip (by Plenty Old); dam won claiming races over
6f and 1m in USA; in frame in a minor event and a nursery but is little better
than a plater; stays 1m; blinkered third outing. *G. Pritchard-Gordon.*

WANGLE 3 ch.f. Great Nephew 126–Criminelle (Crepello 136) (1980 6g **68**
1981 7f 8fg 10.1g⁴ 10fg² 10d) stocky, plain filly; just failed to get up when head
second to Jill Buck in maiden race at Beverley in September, giving us strong
impression she would have won if her jockey had begun his effort sooner; well
beaten next time; suited by 1¼m; possibly needs a sound surface; sold to T.
Hallett 3,000 gns Newmarket December Sales. *J. Dunlop.*

WARBURY DELL 2 br.f. Warpath 113–Slightly Saucy 74 (Galivanter 131) **81**
(1981 6f4 7d³ 7fg 8g 8g) Apr 30; 1,600Y; leggy, lightly-made filly; third living
foal; dam stayed well; stayed on very well in closing stages to be just under
a length third of 18 behind Noumayr in maiden race at Newmarket in August;
looked very lean and was bandaged near-hind when running respectably next
time out; finished in rear on both subsequent starts; bred to stay 1¼m+; best
run on a soft surface. *M. Tompkins.*

WARESLEY 3 gr.c. Town Crier 119–Nasca 81 (King's Bench 132) (1980 6g **69**
6g 5f 5f 6f 1981 6d 6g 5f 5fg³ 5fg 5f² 5f* 5g²(dis)) neat, strong colt; won
19-runner £2,800 event at Redcar in September; disqualified after finishing
head second of 21 to Doubtwash Girl in handicap at Catterick the following
month; stays 6f; acts well on firm going; blinkered last 5 starts. *G. Huffer.*

WARFLIGHT 2 b.c. Warpath 113–Brief Flight 108 (Counsel 118) (1981 6d **76**
8.2d) Mar 8; big, useful-looking colt; brother to Derby fourth Shotgun and
to Arrow, successful at up to 1½m here and subsequently a good winner in
Spain, and half-brother to several winners, including smart Aviator (by Frankincense); dam won Northern Free Handicap; put up a promising effort over a
trip all too short for him when about 12 lengths sixth of 16 to Rosananti in minor
event at Ayr in September, making up a considerable amount of ground after
being unable to go early pace; co-favourite for similar event at Hamilton the
following month but never got in a blow and finished modest sixth of 9 to Misty
Halo; likely to stay 1½m; impressed us at Ayr and is worth another chance at 3
yrs. *C. Thornton.*

WARILY 3 ro.c. Balidar 133–Admonish 101 (Palestine 133) (1980 6g 7s* **74**
1981 8d 8fg 10g 11.7fg 8.2g 8g 8d* 16s 8d) quite a well-made colt; good
walker; beat Sharp End by a head in handicap at Bath in October; had stiffer
tasks in similar events earlier; stays 1m (unlikely to get 2m); suited by some
give in the ground and acts on soft going; blinkered fifth start; trained much
of season by J. Tree. *R. Smyth.*

WARM GLOW 2 ch.f. Hot Spark 126–Golden Mullet (Star Moss 122) (1981 **—**
5fg 6f) Apr 2; half-sister to a winner in Austria; dam of little account; soundly
beaten in sellers at Lingfield in June and Haydock in July. *J. Bethell.*

WARM HEARTED 2 b. or br.f. Steel Heart 128–Tamarisk Way 92 (Tamerlane **103+**
128) (1981 5fg* 6g* 6g* 6fg* 6d*) Mar 30; 27,000Y; neat filly; half-sister
to several winners, notably Nagwa (by Tower Walk), a smart winner of 13
races at up to 7f at 2 yrs in 1975; dam sprinter; unbeaten in five races, gaining
easily most important success in fifth of them when beating Apples of Gold
by 1¼ lengths, with the minimum of fuss, in 6-runner Firth of Clyde Stakes
at Ayr in September; had previously won maiden race at Windsor, minor events
at Newcastle and Ripon and nursery at Goodwood; impressive at Goodwood,
coming through very smoothly when asked to quicken 1½f out and staying on

*Firth of Clyde Stakes, Ayr—Warm Hearted gains her fifth successive win;
Apples of Gold (not in picture) finishes second and Dawn Ditty third*

well to score by a length from Wink; settles very well and will probably stay
7f but is far from certain to get 1m; probably acts on any going; seems to do no
more than is necessary; a grand filly who should acquit herself well in pattern-
race company. *F. Durr.*

WARM ORDER 2 b.c. Hot Spark 126–Canaan (Santa Claus 133) (1981   **77**
5s 5.1f⁴ 5fg³ 6fg* 7g 8d) June 4; 5,000Y; strong, compact colt; half-brother
to Irish 3-y-o 13.5f winner Diamond Land (by Sparkler) and 2 other winners,
including useful 1½m to 2¼m winner Majestic Maharaj (by Taj Dewan); dam
unraced half-sister to St Leger winner Cantelo; won 9-runner maiden auction
event at Warwick in June by a neck from Mr Gold Spur; subsequently ran
poorly in nurseries; should stay beyond 6f; acts on firm going. *P. Feilden.*

WARMSPUN PROOF 5 ch.m. Proof Positive 117–Warmspun 86 (Specific   —
103) (1980 NR 1981 10g) probably no longer of any account. *G. Lockerbie.*

WARM WIND 2 b.f. Tumble Wind–Unsuspected 95 (Above Suspicion 127)   **77**
(1981 6fg 7fg* 7fg 8d⁴) May 15; neat filly; first foal; dam won 8 times from 1m
to 1¾m; favourite when winning 16-runner maiden race at Catterick in July
by 1½ lengths from Royal First; not disgraced in nursery at Epsom on next
outing; should be suited by 1m (had stiff task when tried at trip). *M. Stoute.*

WAR OF CLOWNS 2 ch.c. Cawston's Clown 113–Piece or War (Martial   **44**
131) (1981 5s 5g 5g³ 6f⁴) May 4; 2,500F, 3,000Y; fair sort; half-brother to
several winners here and abroad, including fair 1974 2-y-o winner Musical
Piece (by Song); in frame in sellers, wearing blinkers when 5 lengths fourth
of 5 to Saga's Humour at Stockton; very coltish and unseated rider
on way to start on second outing. *G. Toft.*

WAROOKA 4 gr.g. Veiled Wonder–Grey Parrot (Abernant 142) (1980 8g   **56**
6s 6g 6d³ 1981 6d 6v⁴ 5.8g 5g* 5g³ 5d* 5h 5s 6d 6g) leggy gelding; has a
round action; won 2 handicaps at Hamilton in July; best at sprint distances;
suited by some give in the ground; trained part of season by R. Smyth. *G.
Lewis.*

WARRENICE LAD 2 gr.g. Abwah 118–Broadway Lass 70 (March Past 124)   **62**
(1981 5g 5g⁴ 6g⁴ 6f 7fg* 7d⁴ 8f 8fg 8.2d⁴ 8d⁴ 8d⁴ 8d⁴) Mar 22; 1,050F; narrow,
plain gelding; bad mover; fourth produce; dam ran only at 2 yrs; attracted no
bid after staying on to win 13-runner seller at Redcar in July by ½ length from
Garthland Arms; stays 1m; acts on a firm and a soft surface; wears blinkers;
bandaged eighth outing. *K. Stone.*

WARREN LASS 2 ch.f. Brittany–Whiphand 83 (Supreme Court 135) (1981   —
5d 5d 5g 6d 6g) Apr 27; 1,500F; small, lightly-made filly; soundly beaten in
sellers; blinkered fifth outing; trained part of season by R. Hobson. *M.
Hinchliffe.*

WARRI 2 b.c. Rolfe 77–Lotto 83 (Derring-Do 131) (1981 5.8d 7g* 7fg 8g   **77**
8.2s) Feb 26; strong, neat colt; first foal; dam 7f winner; seemed to catch
jockey on second unawares when getting up close home to win 18-runner maiden
race at Salisbury in July by ½ length from Arrowood Dream; not disgraced
next 2 starts; will be suited by 1¼m. *F. J. Houghton.*

WARSAW CONCERTO 2 b.g. Import 127–Lonely Nymph 60 (Forlorn River   —
124) (1981 5d 5fg 5s) Apr 28; 3,700Y; big, strong gelding; behind in maiden
races, wearing bandages on hind legs when last of 25 on third outing; dead.
R. Hannon.

WAR SHIP 2 b.f. Brigadier Gerard 144–Helm 81 (Royal Palace 131) (1981 6s)   — p
Mar 27; small, lightly-made filly; first foal; dam, lightly-raced winner over 1¼m,
is half-sister to Bireme, Buoy and Fluke; 10/1, didn't stride out on way to start
when remote eighth of 15 to Ellerene in maiden race at Newbury in October;
will be better suited by longer distances. *R. Hern.*

WAR TRACK 2 b.c. Warpath 113–Miss O'Brien 67 (Gulf Pearl 117) (1981   **64**
5g 7fg 7fg 7fg 7.2v 8s 10g⁴ 8.2s) Apr 28; neat colt; third foal; dam won 7f
claiming race at 2 yrs; plater; ran best race when 5¼ lengths fourth of 14 to
Getting Plenty at Leicester in July; will be suited by 1½m; blinkered sixth
and seventh starts; sold 500 gns Newmarket Autumn Sales. *R. Hannon.*

WARWICK TRAILER 3 ro.c. Sharp Edge 123–Grace (Gratitude 130) (1980   **51**
5v³ 5s⁴ 5f³ 5g 5f³ 5fg 6d⁴ 6g² 1981 5v 5g 7f 5fg 5fg 6fg 6g² 6g 6g³ 6fg) compact
colt; plater nowadays; should stay 7f; probably acts on any going; has worn a
bandage on his off-fore; has run creditably in blinkers. *J. Holt.*

Mrs C. Collins' "Watties Rock"

WATER OF LIFE 3 b.g. Mummy's Pet 125–Leger Bar 63 (French Beige 127) **75**
(1980 5f 5fg 6g 6fg⁴ 6g² 5g* 5f* 5fg⁴ 5s² 5g 1981 5g⁴ 5f 5fg 6g 7fg³ 7d* 8f 7g 7s)
workmanlike gelding; led over a furlong out and sprinted clear to beat Solway
Winds by 6 lengths in handicap at Redcar in August; stays 7f (never going well
when behind over 1m); acts on any going, but seems suited by some give in
the ground; sold 6,000 gns Doncaster November Sales. *W. Haigh.*

WATET KHET (FR) 2 b.f. Wittgenstein 123–Abamira (Abdos 134) (1981 **73 p**
7g) sister to poor French 3-y-o Wentorf, and half-sister to French middle-
distance winner Along and Dance (by Sword Dancer); dam, winner over 7f and
1¼m, was fourth in Prix de Diane; 25/1, shaped very well indeed when 6½ lengths
seventh of 22 to Rocamadour in maiden race at Newmarket in October, making
good progress from halfway after dwelling at start and being last early on; will be
suited by middle distances; sure to be all the better for this run. *B. Hills.*

WATTIES ROCK 2 ch.c Record Token 128–Camerons Counsel (Jolly Jet **97**
111) (1981 5v 5g³ 5s* 6fg* 5fg³ 5fg³ 5fg*) May 3; 5,600Y; fourth foal; dam
never ran; a winner 3 times at the Curragh, gaining last 2 successes in Tyros
Stakes in June (by short head from Sheelin Rose) and in nursery in August (ridden
by 5-lb claimer when scoring by ¾ length from Sougoli); third in between in
9-runner Curragh Stakes in July (6½ lengths behind Peterhof) and 7-runner
Gallaghoue Phoenix Stakes at Phoenix Park in August (2½ lengths behind
Achieved); stays 6f; seems to act on any going. *C. Collins, Ireland.*

WATTLEFIELD 2 b.c. Red God 128§–Short Commons 109 (Hard Tack 111§) **117**
(1981 6fg 6d* 6f* 6d 6g³)
'Provided the ground isn't too fast, I shall run him in the Mill Reef Stakes
at Newbury and it will be interesting to see how he gets on. He's a progressive
colt and I couldn't be more pleased with him at the moment.' So said Wattlefield's trainer when asked about his two-year-olds in late-summer. Wattlefield
did indeed contest the Mill Reef Stakes, starting favourite in a field of eight,
but his performance was very disappointing: held up, he almost got to the
leaders approaching the distance but weakened quickly to finish only seventh

behind Hays. This was by no means a true reflection of Wattlefield's merit, for at his best he was a smart two-year-old.

Wattlefield had gone to Newbury with a high reputation, founded on runaway victories in his last two races. His potential had been clear on his debut in the Granville Stakes at Ascot in July, in which he finished seventh of fourteen behind Codrington. Wattlefield, a grand sort of colt and a good walker, really caught our eye in the paddock that day and ran a much better race than his finishing position suggests, showing good speed for about four furlongs before lack of fitness started to tell. He confirmed this promise in style at Newmarket a fortnight later when, looking fitter but still with a bit to work on, he ran out a five-length winner from seventeen rivals in a maiden race. Particularly impressive was the speed Wattlefield produced when shaken up, which carried him some seven lengths clear before he was eased up. Wattlefield won his next race, a minor event at Yarmouth, just as easily, beating Al Hasa by six lengths. Despite his changing legs a couple of times on the firm ground we were impressed once again by another of Wattlefield's qualities—an extravagant, light, long-striding action.

Possibly Wattlefield's action proved his downfall at Newbury; although he had won at Newmarket on similar going and moved attractively to the start, the good to soft ground may well have been against him in such good company, especially since he appeared to encounter the worst of the going by racing down the middle of the course. Wattlefield left that form far behind on a sound surface in the William Hill Middle Park Stakes at Newmarket twelve days later. He went to post really well and, having broken fast, was travelling strongly on the bridle at halfway; for a while after that he seemed as though he would drop out but he kept on well to the end, although appearing to hang slightly, to finish a length third to Cajun.

Wattlefield (b.c. Feb 15, 1979)	Red God (ch 1954)	Nasrullah (b 1940)	Nearco
			Mumtaz Begum
		Spring Run (b 1948)	Menow
			Boola Brook
	Short Commons (b 1962)	Hard Tack (b 1955)	Hard Sauce
			Cowes
		Padus (br 1955)	Anwar
			Cherry Way

Neither of Wattlefield's parents is still alive, Red God having died in 1979 and Short Commons in October, 1980. He is the last foal of Short Commons, a useful racemare who ran away with the 1965 Free Handicap and finished a close fourth to Ardent Dancer in the Irish One Thousand Guineas. Short Commons was a pretty good broodmare too; her seven winners here and abroad include the very smart performers Common Land (by Klairon) and He Loves Me (by Sovereign Path). The grandam Padus won three middle-distance races and has the distinction of having produced the Irish Guinness Oaks winner Pampalina, herself the dam of the Irish Two Thousand Guineas winner Pampapaul. Wattlefield stays six furlongs well and will probably get a mile at three years. With his pedigree, looks and action Wattlefield will be quite a valuable property if he goes on to pick up a decent prize or two. *M. Stoute.*

WAVERLEY HALL 3 br.g. Great Nephew 126–Haunting Melody 96 (Sing Sing 134) (1980 NR 1981 8g 12d) strong, robust gelding; half-brother to 4 winners, including 2 very useful performers by Derring-Do, namely Daring Song, who stayed 7f, and speedy 1979 2-y-o Northern Eclipse; dam miler; twelfth of 18 in newcomers race won by Magikin at Newmarket in April; last throughout in Derby in June; sold 1,500 gns Newmarket Autumn Sales. *R. Simpson.*   —

WAY OF THE WOLD 3 b.c. Sandford Lad 133–Tatty Kay (Tarqogan 125) (1980 5g 5d 6fg⁴ 6fg² 7g 8d³ 8fg 1981 11v* 10s 12g* 12g 13fg² 12fg⁴ 12.3fg² 12fg³ 12g² 12.3fg 13fg 15g 13d) small colt; won maiden race at Ayr in March and minor event at Edinburgh in April (apprentice ridden); placed in handicaps afterwards, including an amateur riders event, but was soundly beaten last 4 starts; stays 13f; probably acts on any going; tried in blinkers as a 2-y-o; retained 5,300 gns Doncaster January (81) Sales. *S. Norton.*   **70**

WEARMOUTH 5 b.g. Pitcairn 126–Pyracantha 68 (Firestreak 125) (1980 10fg⁴ 11f 10d* 10g 12g 10fg 10g² 12s 1981 10fg² 10g 10d 10d 12f² 13.1f4 10fg⁴ 10fg³) well-made gelding; middle-distance handicapper; acts on any going. *W. Wightman.*   **74**

WEAVERS' PIN 4 b.c. Weavers' Hall 122–Priceless Pin (Saint Crespin III 132)   **91**
(1980 9f² 10f* 10f⁴ 16g* 12d 12s 10v⁴ 16s   1981 8s 12g³ 9g 12f² 10fg* 12.5fg
11f² 12d 16f* 8fg 14.6fg 15g³ 11s 11d 15.8g² 14g)   neat ex-Irish colt; successful
in amateur riders races at Lingfield (well backed) and Beverley in the summer;
stays well; needs top-of-the-ground; trained by S. McGrath first 2 starts. *W.
Bentley.*

WEBBS JEWEL 2 b.f. Shiny Tenth 120–Prompt Delivery (Catullus) (1981   **72**
5fg 5.3f 5d 5s 8d³)   Apr 30; sister to 3-y-o Hanham Road, and half-sister to a
winner in USA; dam won over 5f and 6f in USA; 33/1, showed improved form
when close-up third of 17 to Comtec Princess in 17-runner seller at Leicester in
November, staying on strongly; evidently suited by 1m and some give in the
ground. *D. Marks.*

WEDDED BLISS 5 b.m. Relko 136–True Love 89 (Princely Gift 137) (1980   **60**
9fg 8fg 7s 8g 12.2g 10f 12fg 13.8d 12d   1981 16s* 15.8g³ 16g 12g 16g 15.8g*
12fg* 16g⁴ 15.8fg 16fg* 12.2g 16g² 13d 12d 18g)   sturdy mare; poor plater in
1980; showed improved form at 5 yrs, winning handicaps at Beverley, Catterick,
Doncaster (amateur riders) and Newcastle; stays well; seems to act on any
going; suited by waiting tactics and has a good turn of foot; has given trouble
on way to post. *D. Chapman.*

WEDDING VOWS 5 b.m. Traditionalist–Sealed Contract 76 (Runnymede 123)   —
(1980 5f² 5f² 5fg² 6g 5fg 5fg² 5d³ 5f² 5d 5fg 5d⁴   1981 5g)   useful sort; sprint
handicapper; best form at 5f; probably acted on any going but was well suited
by firm; ran creditably in blinkers once; dead. *W. Haigh.*

WEDNESDAY DOY 2 ch.c. Lucky Wednesday 124–Hutton Barns 92 (Saintly   **60**
Song 128)   (1981 5d 5s 6g 6f 7f⁴ 7.2v 6s)   May 3; 3,600Y; leggy, lengthy colt;
first foal; dam at her best at 2 yrs when 5f winner; plater; fourth of 27 to Welsh
Cloud at Redcar in September; stays 7f; acts on any going. *G. Toft.*

WEDNESDAY'S CHASE 2 ch.g. Lucky Wednesday 124–Royal Huntress   **63**
(Royal Avenue 123)   (1981 6fg 7f⁴ 7g 7d)   Apr 12; tall, narrow gelding; first
foal; dam winning hurdler; running-on 2¾ lengths fourth of 18 behind Connaught River in maiden race at Redcar in September, best effort; will be suited
by 1¼m; acts on firm going. *W. Elsey.*

WEE FRED 2 b.c. Swing Easy 126–Roseanne 68 (St Paddy 133)   (1981 5g 5g   **54**
5g 5fg² 5f 5f³ 5f)   May 16; small colt; second foal; dam won over 1½m and is half-
sister to Derby third Mount Athos and smart sprinter John Splendid; placed
twice in selling company, running second to Cool Wind at Newcastle in June
and third to Trust Sally at Ripon in August; had stiff task in nursery in between;
should stay 6f+. *P. Calver.*

WEE GEEFAYE 3 b.f. Crooner 119–Wee Geenova 78 (Gallup Poll or Blast 125)   —
(1980 5f 5fg 7g 8fg 8d   1981 8.3fg 9fg)   lengthy filly; behind in maiden races
and sellers. *Mrs R. Lomax.*

WELCIANA 2 b.f. Welsh Pageant 132–Damiana 84 (Mourne 126)   (1981 7g)   —
Apr 2; 8,000Y; third live foal; dam 1m winner; 50/1 when well behind in 18-
runner maiden race won by Puff of Smoke at Salisbury in July; sold 750 gns
Ascot November Sales. *P. Cundell.*

WELCOMBE 4 b.c. Mountain Call 125–Angel Row 96 (Prince Regent 129)   —
(1980 7f 6d 6g 7g 8f   1981 8s 6s 7d 6g 10g 8fg 6f 6fg 8g 8.2g 7v 7g)   strong,
well-made colt; good mover; fair handicapper at his best; plater nowadays;
stays 7f; seems to act on any going; blinkered seventh and final starts (also
wore a hood on latter); sometimes bandaged; sold 920 gns Doncaster November
Sales. *R. Hobson.*

WELD MAIN 2 b.c. Mansingh 120–Sarong 97 (Taj Dewan 128)   (1981 8g)   —
May 6; 8,000Y; second foal; half-brother to 3-y-o Hindi (by Mummy's Pet),
successful at up to 1m; dam 1m winner; 33/1 when out of first 13 in 27-runner
minor event won by Dudley Wood at Newmarket in October. *M. Jarvis.*

WELHAM GREEN (USA) 3 b.c. Tom Rolfe–Near Lyn (Nearctic) (1980   **93**
6fg* 7.6g² 7f⁴ 7d   1981 7d² 6s* 6d⁴)   well-made, quite attractive colt; put up a
useful performance when beating Ganimede by 1½ lengths (pair 10 lengths clear)
in minor event at Nottingham in April; also in frame in handicap at Doncaster
and minor event at Folkestone; bred to stay at least 1m but best form at 6f;
acts on any going; sent to race in USA. *G. Harwood.*

WELL APPRAISED 3 br.f. Wolver Hollow 126–Emma Canute 93 (Hardicanute   **74**
130)   (1980 6s 6g 8fg   1981 10fg³ 10.2g* 10s 8d)   tall filly; odds on when

beating Eastern Air comfortably by 2 lengths in handicap at Bath in May;
not seen out again until October and was well beaten under stiff weights on her
return; will stay 1½m. *P. Cole.*

WELL BLEST 3 b.f. Well Meant 65–Liebeslust (Mangon) (1980 NR 1981 —
16.9fg) half-sister to several winners here and in Germany, including useful
stayer Vishvamitra (by Mossborough) and Sunshine Lie (by Shiny Tenth),
successful from 1m to 11f; dam won twice at 2 yrs in Germany; unquoted when
behind in 15-runner maiden race won by Le Beau at Wolverhampton in July.
D. Ancil.

WELLESLEY 3 br.g. Noble Decree 127–Las Ventas (Breton 130) (1980 NR —
1981 8fg 10.1d⁴ 8g 9s 7g) strong, workmanlike gelding; second produce; dam
poor plater; soundly beaten in maiden and minor races; blinkered fourth start.
R. Sheather.

WELL GREASED 4 b.or br.f. Workboy 123–Jolly Smooth 84 (Jolly Jet 111) **43**
(1980 7f 7f² 7f² 7fg* 6fg⁴ 7g³ 7g 8.2g* 8d 1981 10.8d 10g 8f 8.3g 8fg³ 8s) lengthy
filly; poor handicapper; stays 1m well and wasn't entirely disgraced over 1¼m
on second start; acts well on firm going; good mount for a boy. *W. Holden.*

WE'LL MEET AGAIN 4 b.c. Song 132–Coaster 61 (Right Tack 131) (1980 6s **81**
5f 6f 6fg² 7fg⁴ 7g 6fg 7d 6d² 1981 7d³ 8fg² 8d* 8v* 10s⁴ 10d* 10f* 10d 10fg 10d²
10s*) workmanlike colt; fair handicapper; had a good year, winning at Warwick,
Goodwood, Sandown, Leicester and Ascot; beat Big Pal comfortably by 2½
lengths in £4,100 event on last-named in October; stays 1¼m; acts on any going
but goes well on soft; has run creditably for a boy; consistent. *J. Benstead.*

WELLSWAY 3 br.f. Tycoon II–Lartway 81 (Lauso) (1980 NR 1981 8fg) —
half-sister to a winning hurdler; dam won at up to 1¾m; unquoted when tailed-
off last of 16 to Icen in maiden race at Salisbury in September. *B. Forsey.*

WELSH BALLET 4 b.f. Owen Anthony 102–Graceful Scot (Aberdeen 109) —
(1980 8f 12g 12g 11.5fg⁴ 8g 1981 10s) sturdy, compact filly; plating-class
maiden; possibly stays 1¼m; wears blinkers. *P. Feilden.*

WELSH BLOSSOM 6 b.m. Welsh Saint 126–Riding High (Hard Ridden **79**
131) (1980 5f 6fg⁴ 6fg² 5g 6g 6g* 6s 6fg* 5.6g 6fg* 7g 6d 6v 1981 6g 6s
6f* 6f 6f 6f 6fg 6d 6f 6fg 6fg 5g) leggy mare; fair handicapper at her best;
won at Leicester in June; disappointed most subsequent starts; best at 6f;
not at her best on soft ground; blinkered on 2 of her last 3 outings; suitable
mount for an apprentice; goes well at Newmarket; game. *W. Wharton.*

WELSH CHANTER 5 b.h. Welsh Pageant 132–Miss Ryvita 75 (St Paddy —
133) (1980 9f⁴ 8d 10d* 1981 16g*(w.o.)) big, attractive horse; cracked
a cannon bone at 2 yrs; only lightly raced but was a very smart performer;
put up a fine performance in Valdoe Stakes at Goodwood in 1980, running on
strongly to beat Master Willie by 1½ lengths; walked over at Newmarket only
appearance at 5 yrs in October; suited by 1¼m; not at his best on very soft
ground but acted on any other; genuine; standing at Bachelor's Lodge Stud, Co.
Meath, fee IR £1,000 (1st Oct). *H. Cecil.*

WELSH CLOUD 2 b.f. Welsh Saint 126–Treble Cloud (Capistrano 120) (1981 **71**
5g* 5g 6fg⁴ 6d 6fg 6f 7f*) Mar 9; IR 2,600F, 800Y; well-made filly; first produce;
dam ran twice in Ireland; successful in maiden auction event at Catterick
in April and 27-runner seller at Redcar in September (20/1 and ridden by 7-lb
claimer); beat Angus Sprite in latter (no bid); well beaten in between; suited
by 7f; acts on firm ground; blinkered last 4 starts. *A. Jarvis.*

WELSH DIAMOND 3 b.f. High Top 131–Camarina 62 (Aureole 132) (1980 —
5g 6g² 7f 6d 8.2g³ 8.2s 8s 1981 12.5f 12fg 10f 8g) bad mover; plater; one
paced and should stay 1½m; probably unsuited by soft going; has worn blinkers.
P. Calver.

WELSH FOLLY 3 b.f. Welsh Saint 126–By Mistake 64 (Miralgo 130) (1980 —
6d* 6d 1981 8fg 7f 7d) sparely-made filly; behind in sellers in 1981; should be
suited by 7f and 1m; sold 560 gns at Ascot November Sales. *P. Makin.*

WELSH KERNEL 2 ch.g. Kernel Rose–Tenby Lady (Kadir Cup 97§) 1981 —
5fg 5f 6g) Apr 17; small gelding; first foal; dam bad plater and poor point-
to-pointer; looks useless. *A. Potts.*

WELSH NOBLE 3 b.c. Welsh Saint 126–Just A Glimmer 75 (Dumbarnie **67**
125) (1980 5d⁴ 5d³ 5f⁴ 5d* 6g 6d 6g 5f 5d 6s² 1981 6s² 8s⁴ 6f 6fg² 6d³ 7fg
7f³ 6f 6f 6d* 7g) good-topped colt; attracted no bid after winning seller at

935

Ayr in September; probably stays 1m; possibly not at his best on very firm going but acts on any other; suitable mount for an apprentice; trained part of season by W. Wharton. *A. Balding.*

WELSH PARTNER 2 b.f. Welsh Saint 126–King's Mate 91 (King's Bench 132) (1981 5f² 6d* 6f³) Mar 28; lengthy filly; good walker; sister to useful 5f to 7f performer Welsh Mate and half-sister to 3 winners; dam a sprinter; won 15-runner maiden race at Windsor in August by 1½ lengths from Bolivar Baby; made much of running when good 2 lengths third of 8 to On The House in Crathorne Stakes at York the following month; stays 6f well; seems to act on any going; very reluctant to go down and was withdrawn at start at Ayr on intended fourth outing. *H. T. Jones.* **91**

WELSH REEL 3 br.g. Tudor Music 131–Particella (Parthia 132) (1980 5f² 6s 7g 6g 6f 6s 7.5d 1981 6v* 10fg 7d* 7v* 7f 8g 6d) 2,200Y; workmanlike gelding; half-brother to fair Irish middle-distance winner Prancing Prince (by Simbir) and Irish 5f to 1m winner My My (by My Swanee); dam French plater; apprentice ridden when winning maiden race at Naas in March and minor event at Phoenix Park and handicap at the Curragh in May; usually had stiff tasks on his other starts, including when in rear in Guardian Newspaper Classic Trial at Sandown and Jersey Stakes at Royal Ascot; best form at up to 7f but should stay further; acts on any going but goes well in the mud; blinkered fifth outing in 1980. *J. Murphy, Ireland.* **98**

WELSHWYN 3 b.f. Welsh Saint 126–Takawin 109 (Takawalk II 125) (1980 5fg* 5fg* 5g² 5g² 5fg² 1981 5fg 5d* 6f⁴ 6g 5fg² 6fg³ 5fg³) lengthy, useful-looking filly; half-sister to 3 winners, including sprinter Careless Princess (by Prince Regent); dam sprinter; waited with when beating Pettistree a neck in £4,500 event at Sandown in June; in frame most other starts, including in Salisbury 1,000 Guineas Trial (4 lengths second to Go Leasing), Cork and Orrery Stakes at Royal Ascot (about 1½ lengths fourth to The Quiet Bidder), King George Stakes at Goodwood (neck second to King of Spain) and Prix de Meautry (3½ lengths third to Rabdan); best at sprint distances (didn't stay 1m in 1,000 Guineas on second start); probably acts on any going; has often given trouble at stalls but races most genuinely; looked and ran as though she had had enough for time being on final start. *J. Benstead.* **108**

WELTHI 8 b.g. probably Welsh Abbot 131–Thisbe (Midsummer Night II 117) (1980 NR 1981 15g) poor stayer; acts on hard going; used to wear blinkers; good mount for an inexperienced rider. *M. Francis.* **—**

WELWYN 2 b.f. Welsh Saint 126–Takawin 109 (Takawalk II 125) (1981 5g 5fg 6fg⁴ 5fg⁴ 5g* 5g) Feb 23; robust, quite attractive filly; sister to very useful 3-y-o sprinter Welshwyn and half-sister to 3 winners; dam sprinter; made all to win 20-runner maiden race at Lingfield in September by ½ length from One Degree; stays 6f. *J. Benstead.* **79**

WEMBLEY MARKET 3 ch.g. Malicious–Perfect Lady 85 (Sovereign Lord 120) (1980 5fg² 5g³ 5.8g 5f 6fg 6g 1981 5s 5d⁴ 5d³ 5f³ 6g* 5fg 6f 7d 6d 6f 7s 7g) narrow, leggy gelding; sold out of K. Ivory's stable 2,000 gns after beating Quality Road a neck in seller at Ripon in June; in frame in better company earlier; stays 6f; used to wear blinkers; ran too freely seventh start; sold 270 gns Doncaster October Sales. *T. Craig.* **51**

WENSLEYDALE 3 b.g. Upper Case–Wether Fell (Klairon 131) (1980 NR 1981 8s 8g 12.2fg) tall gelding; half-brother to several winners, including French 1m winner La Rouquine (by Silly Season); dam once-raced half-sister to 1,000 Guineas second Marisela; behind in maiden and minor races. *R. D. Peacock.* **—**

WENSUM GIRL 4 ch.f. Ballymoss 136–Lady Colonist 67 (Colonist II 126) (1980 12.2fg 1981 12.2fg) seems of little account. *B. Richmond.* **—**

WESSCAM 5 ch.m. Scottish Rifle 127–Decatullus (Catullus) (1980 11fg 10.8f² 8fg 10d 11.7s⁴ 11.7s³ 11.7f⁴ 14g 10g 12fg 1981 8d 8d 10s 12d 10d 8fg³ 10.1d 10d 12f) small, close-coupled mare; plater; stays 11.7f; probably acts on any going; has worn blinkers; weak finisher; trained by S. Matthews first 8 starts. *T. M. Jones.* **38**

WESSTIMES 2 ch.g. Record Token 128–Reigning Grace 108 (Roan Rocket 128) (1981 7g 7f 7g 7.2fg 6g 6d 6g) Mar 9; 5,400Y; lengthy, plain sort; fourth foal; dam won at up to 1¼m; ran respectably when fifth in maiden races at Haydock and Yarmouth in September on fourth and fifth outings, in latter beaten 3½ lengths by Celestial Dancer; bred to stay at least 1m; sold to German International BA 2,900 gns Newmarket Autumn Sales. *W. O'Gorman.* **78**

WESTACOMBE 4 br.f. Huntercombe 133–Ambient 68 (Amber Rama 133)   **99**
(1980 6d2 5fg* 6f* 6f2 6d2 6fg2 5g* 5fg* 6s2 5f* 5fg3 5g   1981 5g 5d 6g3 5fg4
5fg 5fg3 5g 5g 5h* 5.6fg4 6d 5s2 6d)   rangy, full-quartered filly; useful performer;
long odds on when easily winning all-aged race at Chepstow in August; ran
creditably on several other occasions, notably when 3½ lengths fourth to Touch
Boy in Portland Handicap at Doncaster in September and 3 lengths second to
Effect in £5,100 race at York in October; stays 6f; acts on any going; genuine
and consistent. *M. Camacho.*

WESTAMIST 2 ch.f. Malacate 131–Clearing Mist 62 (Double Jump 131)   (1981   **75**
6f 7v 8s)   Apr 6; IR 5,600F, resold 5,000Y; strong, short-coupled filly; half-
sister to 3 winning sprinters, including fair Wyddial Park (by Tarboosh); dam
lightly-raced half-sister to high-class sprinter Mountain Call; 7¾ lengths fifth of
15 to My Destiny in £3,400 event at York in October on second start, best effort;
gave impression further would suit her here but ran moderately over 1m. *M.
Camacho.*

WEST END BOY 3 ch.g. Tarboosh–Smiling Diplomat (Dual 117)   (1980 5fg   **—**
5f 7fg 8fg 8d   1981 10.1d 6v)   of little account; has been tried in blinkers.
Dr A. Jones.

WESTERING BREEZE 3 gr.c. Windjammer (USA)–Inishanier (Prevailing)   **—**
(1980 5g4 1981 6g 5g 5g 5g 6f 5fg 5f 5d4 5d4 7g)   3,400Y; leggy, lightly-made
ex-Irish colt; first foal; dam Irish 5f winner; fourth in selling handicap at Edinburgh and maiden race at Redcar in October, only form over here; blinkered
last 3 starts; trained by G. Lockerbie until after sixth outing. *W. Bentley.*

WESTERING HOME 7 b.g. Continuation 120–Rose of the West (Royal Buck)   **—**
(1980 NR 1981 16d)   poor performer nowadays; stays 1¼m; acts on firm
going. *S. Mellor.*

WESTERN HERO 2 ch.g. Scottish Rifle 127–Cheyenne Queen 87 (Yellow   **61**
God 129)   (1981 6f 6g 7f 7d)   May 22; 2,400Y; rangy, workmanlike gelding;
first foal; dam 2-y-o 5f winner; 7¾ lengths seventh of 14 to Garfunkel in maiden
auction event at Doncaster in July, third outing and best effort; will be suited
by 1m. *M. Naughton.*

WESTERN KELLY 4 b.f. Netherkelly 112–Mandy's Melody (Highland Melody   **—**
112)   (1980 NR 1981 12f 10.2f 7f)   seems of little account. *J. Harris.*

WESTERN KNIGHT 3 ch.c. Grundy 137–Western Air 101 (Sound Track 132)   **91** d
(1980 7f 7g2 1981 9fg 10d* 12fg 10fg 10d 10g 10g)   big, strong, rangy colt;
made virtually all and beat Amina impressively by 4 lengths in 17-runner maiden
race at Sandown in June; looked shade one paced in closing stages when creditable 2½ lengths fifth of 14 behind Feltwell in King George V Stakes (Handicap)
at Royal Ascot later in month, next outing and best subsequent effort; had
shown a fair amount of promise earlier when trained by P. Walwyn; stays
1½m; probably acts on any going; ran freely in blinkers final outing. *R. Laing.*

WESTERN RIVER 8 b.g. Yellow River 114–Westerlands Rosebud (Combat   **—**
123)   (1980 14g 1981 12d)   probably of no account; has worn blinkers. *K.
Ivory.*

WESTERPAYNE 3 b.g. Mummy's Pet 125–Hay-Hay 62 (Hook Money 124)   **—**
(1980 5v4 5f 5g3 1981 5d 5fg)   sprint maiden; ran best race in a seller on final
outing as a 2-y-o. *J. Hill.*

WEST FAILTE (USA) 2 b.g. West Coast Scout–Rubye Brooks (Bold Hour)   **70**
(1981 7fg 7fg4 7f 7fg)   May 12; 5,400Y; well-made, quite attractive gelding;
excellent mover; brother to 2 minor winners in USA; dam won over 1m; sire
high-class winner at up to 1¼m in USA; only quite moderate; put up best efforts
on first 2 outings; gelded after fourth; will stay 1¼m. *B. Hills.*

WESTGATE STAR 2 b.g. He Loves Me 120–Sea Swallow 90 (Dan Cupid 132)   **66**
(1981 6g 6g 6d)   May 16; 5,800Y; rangy gelding; half-brother to 3 winners,
including 2-y-o 7f winner Good Companions (by Lorenzaccio); dam won over
1¼m; wasn't disgraced when about 7 lengths sixth of 18 to Bravado in maiden
race at Newcastle in July nor when eighth of 12 to Rebollino in £5,400 maiden
event at York the following month, first 2 starts; off course 2 months subsequently; will stay 1m. *C. Booth.*

WESTON BAY 4 b.g. Mon Fils 124–Mineral 67 (Tarqogan 125)   (1980 8.2fg   **—**
8fg* 8h2 8d   1981 8f 8.3fg4 8g)   compact gelding; plater; will stay 1¼m; acts
on any going; wears blinkers nowadays. *M. Pipe.*

WESTONBIRT 2 ch.f. Queen's Hussar 124–Mountain Greenery 83 (Chamossaire)   **93**
(1981 5s 6s* 6fg3 6fg2 6g2 7g4 7s)   Apr 3; strong, sturdy filly; good mover;

937

sister to 2 winners, including useful miler Boscage, and half-sister to 2 other winners; dam won at 7f and 1m; successful in maiden race at Haydock in June and minor event at Windsor in July but was moved down to second by stewards after beating Strapless a length in latter (crossed Strapless entering final furlong but was clear at time and won on merit); subsequently ran well in 2 valuable nurseries, particularly when 1½ lengths second of 11 to Tin Boy at Newmarket in August; will be suited by 1m; seems to act on any going; below her best final appearance. *B. Hobbs.*

WESTWOOD DANCER 2 b.f. Home Guard 129–Great Beauty (Tarqogan 125) (1981 5s 5d* 7g 7f 6fg 7s 7g 8.2d 7d) Mar 20; 2,500Y; strong, quite well-made filly; half-sister to 1976 Irish 2-y-o 7f winner Evening Primrose (by Varano); dam ran once; had only 2 to beat when winning maiden race at Hamilton in April by ¾ length from Flying Mail; beaten in nurseries afterwards; should stay at least 7f. *T. Fairhurst.* **60**

WET BOB 3 ch.c. Run The Gantlet–River Craft (Reliance II 137) (1980 7d 7s 6v² 1981 8d⁴ 10.1fg 11.7f⁴) small, stocky ex-Irish colt; second foal; half-brother to 1979 Irish 2-y-o 5f winner Private Craft (by Private Walk); dam, sister to very smart 1m and 1¼m winner Rymer, was last on only start; second in maiden event at the Curragh as a 2-y-o; fourth in similar races at Bath in June and July; stays 1½m; seems to act on any going; blinkered final start; sold 4,400 gns Ascot October Sales. *J. Dodd.* **61**

WHANGAREI 3 b.f. Gold Rod 129–Vilmainder 78 (Remainder 106) (1980 7g 7fg 7f 6fg³ 7g⁴ 1981 7s 6d* 7f 8.2f 8.2g³ 8f³ 8fg* 8g* 8.2s*) plain filly; did extremely well in selling company and won at Leicester in May (no bid), Wolverhampton in August (bought in 950 gns), Bath in September (bought in 3,100 gns) and Haydock in October (no bid); stays 1m well; acts on any going; genuine. *B. McMahon.* **59**

WHAT-A-CASE 4 b. or br.f. Upper Case–Off Scent 92 (Faberge II 121) (1980 8f 8fg 9.4g 8.2d 8.2d 6d 1981 8v 6g 10g 12f 7g) leggy, narrow filly; poor plater nowadays; should stay at least 1m; has worn blinkers. *W. H. H. Williams.* **—**

WHAT A LIFE 2 b.g. Wolverlife 115–More The Perrier (Rarity 129) (1981 5f) Apr 19; IR 1,750F, IR 960Y, 3,100 2-y-o; first produce; dam never ran; unquoted when last of 7 to Begham Bay in maiden race at Hamilton in August. *Denys Smith.* **—**

WHAT A RIOT 3 b.g. Sun Prince 128–Mill's Girl (Le Levanstell 122) (1980 7.5fg² 7fg* 7fg* 10v 8s 1981 9d 10g³ 10d 13s 12d 12fg 12f* 14f* 14f² 10f* 12fg* 11.5fg) 8,000Y; fourth foal; dam Irish 1⅜m winner; had a good season and was gaining his fourth win when beating The Neurologist by 2½ lengths in quite valuable handicap at Phoenix Park in August; had beaten Snow Treasure a length in minor event on same course earlier in week and had previously won handicaps at Naas (by 12 lengths) and Gowran Park; may well stay 2m (stoutly bred on dam's side); acts well on firm ground; apprentice ridden 3 times when successful. *L. Browne, Ireland.* **115**

WHATATIPOFF 4 b.c. Jimmy Reppin 131–Stately Gala (Gala Performance) (1980 7f 8fg² 7f 8g⁴ 8g 1981 10.2s 13fg 9g 8fg 12fg 10fg) compact, good-topped colt; plating-class maiden; best run at 1m on a firm surface; sold 1,100 gns Ascot August Sales. *W. Charles.* **—**

WHAT HEAVEN 3 b.f. So Blessed 130–Stolen Love 85 (Alcide 136) (1980 6s⁴ 5fg 6g³ 5s⁴ 1981 7g 8g 7.6d² 6g* 8.5g³ 7g) lightly-made, quite attractive filly; won 15-runner minor event at Newbury in May driven out by 3 lengths from Singwara; ran well in better company, including when close-up seventh of 14 behind Fairy Footsteps in 1,000 Guineas at Newmarket in April and 2¾ lengths third to Oh So Choosy in NMT Ebbisham Stakes (Handicap) at Epsom in June (kept on well, though no match for first 2 who raced on opposite side); stays 1m well; possibly best on a sound surface; ran moderately sixth start; sold privately to race in California. *P. Kelleway.* **97**

WHEEL SPIN (USA) 2 b. or br.c. Northerly–Hot Wheels (Tulyar 134) (1981 5f) May 9; $32,000 2-y-o; half-brother to winners in USA by Diplomat Way and Dike; dam prolific winner of claiming races at up to 1m in USA; very weak in market when remote seventh of 10 to Ghawar in maiden race at Folkestone in August; likely to need at least 1m (sire gained most of his wins at 1m to 1¼m). *M. Albina.* **—**

WHENYOURTRAINSGONE 2 b. or br.c. Free State 125–Great Blue White 73 (Great Nephew 126) (1981 7g 8s*) May 21; 3,000 2-y-o; fair sort; fourth foal; half-brother to winning 3-y-o sprinter Blue Singh (by Mansingh); dam **85**

938

closely related to Cheveley Park winner Lalibela; well-backed favourite, surprisingly attracted no bid after winning 17-runner seller at Warwick in October by 10 lengths from Getting Plenty; stays 1m well; evidently much better than the average plater and could pay his way in handicap company at 3 yrs. *R. Boss.*

WHERE'S HENRY 6 ch.g. Hotfoot 126–Long Days 92 (Bleep-Bleep 134) **42**
(1980 9.6fg³ 10.1fg 7f 8g 1981 8f 7g 8.3g³) plater; best form at up to 9.6f; acts on a firm and a soft surface. *A. Neaves.*

WHEY 2 b.f. Sallust 134–Melka (Relko 136) (1981 5s* 5g 5fg 6s 6s) Mar 16; **85**
IR 5,200Y; compact filly; third foal; half-sister to French 9f winner Double Fisted (by Tyrant); dam won over 1½m in Ireland; 20/1, came through strongly from distance to win 25-runner maiden race at Kempton in May going away by 2½ lengths from Telephone Man; in rear in quite valuable events subsequently, finishing last in nurseries at Haydock and Newbury (blinkered) in October on last 2 starts; not bred to be a sprinter and should stay at least 1m; acts on soft going. *H. T. Jones.*

WHICHCOMBE 2 br.f. Huntercombe 133–Debatable 84 (Counsel 118) (1981 **79** p
6g²) May 4; half-sister to smart 7f to 1½m winner Brandon Hill (by Wolver Hollow); dam stayed 1¾m; 20/1, stayed on well over final 3f when ½-length second of 19 to One Degree in maiden race at Newmarket in October; will probably do better over 7f+. *M. Smyly.*

WHISKEY SKID 3 ch.g. Northfields–Shot Silk 110 (High Treason 126) (1980 —
5v 5f² 5f* 5fg 5fg⁴ 6fg⁴ 6f 7g 6f 8g 1981 12d 8fg 12fg 12.2fg) small ex-Irish gelding; awarded a race at Naas as a 2-y-o after winner failed a dope test; no form in 1981 but wasn't sure to stay beyond 6f; dead. *M. Reddan.*

WHISKY GO GO 5 ch.g. Grey Mirage 128–My Nan (Pampered King 121) (1980 **41**
11d² 12s 1981 12s 12g³ 12g* 12g 13g 12fg 12.2g) compact gelding; well backed when winning handicap at Edinburgh in June; stays 1½m. *R. Morris.*

WHISPER GENTLY 4 b.f. Pitskelly 122–Muraka (Off Key 121) (1980 9f⁴ —
10f 12f² 12g* 12g 10s 8g 12d* 12d* 12g 12g 12d 16g 1981 12g 12f 12fg) lightly-made ex-Irish filly; won handicaps at the Curragh, Killarney and Galway in 1980; behind in amateur riders races at 4 yrs; stays 1½m; probably acts on any going; has worn blinkers. *W. Bentley.*

WHISPER TO ME 3 br.f. Cavo Doro 124–Myna Tyna 85 (Blast 125) (1980 —
5g 5d 5d 5d 1981 7f 7f 7f 8.2g 7.2fg 9g) little worthwhile form in varied company, including selling. *R. Hollinshead.*

WHISTLER'S IMAGE 5 br.g. Dancer's Image–Spring Azure 98 (Mountain **40**
Call 125) (1980 9g 1981 7s 8s³ 8g 7g² 8g 7f 10g 8s) neat, strong, good sort; poor handicapper; stays 1m; acts on any going; wears blinkers; suitable mount for an apprentice. *J. Hardy.*

WHISTLING JIM 3 b.g. Jimsun 121–Metis 55 (Be Friendly 130) (1980 6g —
7g 6fg 7f 1981 12fg 8fg 12f 10f 16f 12f 13.8g) of little account; bolted going to start on fourth appearance and unseated rider on sixth; has been tried in blinkers. *Hbt Jones.*

WHISTLING TOWER 3 b.c. Tower Walk 130–Whistling Gold (Whistling Wind **73**
123) (1980 7s 8fg³ 8d² 8d² 1981 10.2d 10d⁴ 8fg⁴ 10.1fg* 10d 10.6g 10g³ 12g) short-backed colt; beat Carved Opal decisively by 1½ lengths in minor event at Windsor in July; ran best subsequent race on seventh outing; stays 1¼m well; acts on a firm and a soft surface; blinkered last 2 starts; sold 3,700 gns Newmarket Autumn Sales. *C. Brittain.*

WHITBY HIGH LIGHT 2 ro.f. Roan Rocket 128–Alive Alivo 77 (Never **62**
Say Die 137) (1981 5fg 5fg 5f⁴ 5d 8f 7g 7d⁴) Mar 13; 6,800Y, 3,000Y; sturdy filly; poor mover; half-sister to several winners here and in Italy, including Phoenix Stakes winner Areola (by Kythnos); dam showed ability at 2 yrs; only plating class; prominent under low weights in nurseries last 3 starts; will stay 1¼m+. *J. Calvert.*

WHITE MORNING 2 ch.f. Swing Easy 126–Carina Janie 88 (Silver Cloud 121) **66**
(1981 5fg 5.8h 6fg 5g⁴ 5d) May 2; seventh foal; dam 1¼m winner; put up easily best effort when 2¼ lengths fourth of 15 to Bold Saracen in maiden race at Bath in September; should stay 6f. *J. Cann.*

WHITE SAINT 3 b.f. Welsh Saint 126–Whitewood 74 (Worden II 129) **83**
(1980 5fg 5d 1981 10g² 11f* 13.1g² 12d² 13.3s) neat filly; beat Elizabeth Howard by 4 lengths in maiden race at Hamilton in August; second on 3 other

starts; stays 13f; acts on firm ground and a soft surface but didn't run up to her best on very soft ground final start (pulled hard); sold 7,000 gns Newmarket December Sales. *B. Hills.*

WHITE'S UMBRELLA 4 ch.g. Siliconn 121–Lurex (Golden Cloud) (1980 10g —
8.5g 10g 8f⁴ 7.2fg 1981 8.3s 10s 7g) sturdy, compact gelding; plater; not certain to stay 1¼m; sometimes sweats up badly. *P. Bevan.*

WHITMARSH 3 br.f. Hessonite 88–Miss Warwick (Stupendous) (1980 NR **56**
1981 7f³ 8f³ 8fg⁴) small filly; second reported living foal; dam never ran; in frame in 2 maiden races at Thirsk in July and a seller at Redcar in September; stays 1m. *W. Haigh.*

WHITTINGTON (USA) 3 b.g. Best Turn–Novee (Judgable) (1980 5f 6fg **57**
7g 8g 7s² 7d 1981 12g 10.1f 10.1fg 10f 8.2f³ 8f 9g) workmanlike gelding; ran respectably on occasions in 1981, including in an amateur riders event; stays 1¼m; acts on any going. *G. Balding.*

WHITTON 2 b.g. Kemal 120–Star Clipper (Polly's Jet) (1981 5s 5s⁴ 5g³ 5g 6g) **54**
May 4; IR 320F, resold IR 1,800Y; light-framed gelding; half-brother to a winning hurdler by Woodville II; dam won 5 times over 5f in Ireland; in frame in small races at Catterick in April and Redcar (4 lengths third of 4 to Benfen) in May; should be well suited by further than 5f; sweated up fourth outing; had tongue tied down final start. *J. Mason.*

WHITWORTH 3 ch.g. Hot Spark 126–Clarity 98 (Panaslipper 130) (1980 7f **70**
8d⁴ 10s⁴ 1981 14g 12f 13.8fg* 13fg² 12.3fg³ 13.8g² 16f⁴ 13.8fg⁴ 13fg* 16g) rangy gelding; has been hobdayed; successful in handicaps at Catterick in June and Nottingham in September, on latter course beating Keelby Kavalier ½ length in an 18-runner event; stays 2m; probably acts on any going but is evidently well suited by firm; possibly requires a strong gallop; pulled up lame final start. *D. Morley.*

WHOBEYOU 3 b.f. Le Johnstan 123–The Rose Royale (Takawalk II 125) —
(1980 NR 1981 7d 7s) 2,200Y; second foal; sister to modest 1978 2-y-o 5f winner Bart; dam once-raced half-sister to smart miler My Drifter; well beaten in minor event at Leicester (backward) and seller at Kempton in May. *J. Sutcliffe.*

WHO'S FREE 6 b.m. Sit In The Corner–Forthcoming 69 (New Brig 120) —
(1980 NR 1981 15.8fg) staying handicapper; seems to act on any going; has worn blinkers. *T. Cuthbert.*

WIBIS RANGE 2 b.c. Wolver Hollow 126–Polonaise (Takawalk II 125) (1981 **82**
6g 7.2d 6fg² 7f*) May 28; 3,000Y; tall, leggy colt; brother to fairly useful middle-distance winner Prince of Padua, and half-brother to fairly useful 7f and 1m winner Huppel (by Huntercombe); dam won over 9f at 2 yrs in Ireland; showed improved form last 2 starts, and led close home when beating Exclusive Air a neck in 19-runner maiden event at Redcar in September (edged slightly left); will stay 1¼m; acts on firm going. *M. Naughton.*

WICKED WAVE (USA) 2 b.f. North Sea–Simply Furious (Delta Judge) **90**
(1981 5s² 5.8g* 6d 6fg 6fg 6fg³ 6g³ 7.3s) sturdy filly; good walker; half-sister to a minor winner in USA; dam, 6f winner, is half-sister to top-class Cox's Ridge; sire won at up to 8.5f; made all to win 7-runner minor event at Bath in June by ½ length from odds-on End of the Line; easily bettered that effort when 2¼ lengths third of 10 to Allocated, after leading for a long way, in Clarence House Stakes at Ascot in September and when 1¾ lengths third of 17 to Vaigly Star in valuable nursery at Newmarket in October; stays 6f well (had stiffish task and was well beaten over further); seems to act on any going. *M. Francis.*

WICKWELL 8 b.g. Wolver Hollow 126–Wise Counsel (Counsel 118) (1980 **51**
10v 11fg 9fg 12h³ 10.6g² 12.3g 11.5g 12fg 11.5fg³ 12.3g 10g 10.6s 11g 1981 12g⁴ 10.6s* 9g 10f 12fg³ 10.6s) poor handicapper; won at Haydock in June (amateur riders); stays 1½m; acts on any going; good mount for an inexperienced rider; inconsistent and doesn't find much off bridle. *A. W. Jones.*

WIDD 4 b.g. Derring-Do 131–Tin Mary 96 (Tin King 126) (1980 7f 8fg 7g 7s* **76**
6fg⁴ 6fg 6g⁴ 6fg⁴ 8fg 1981 6g 7.6g³ 7g* 8.5g 7f 8f) workmanlike gelding; won handicap at Brighton in May; well suited by 7f and should stay 1m; seems to act on any going; blinkered once at 3 yrs; retained 2,600 gns Doncaster October Sales. *M. Masson.*

WILD CALL 4 ch.g. Communication 119–So Wild 64 (Lauso) (1980 NR —
1981 7s 6d 10f 7fg 6f) soundly beaten in varied company, including selling; has twice worn blinkers. *J. Bridger.*

WILDERNESS 3 b.f. Martinmas 128–Gala Belle (Galivanter 131) (1980 NR **88**
1981 7d* 8fg² 10g 7g 7d) 500F, 8,000Y; lengthy filly; sister to 1½m winner My
Rajah and half-sister to useful 1977 Irish 2-y-o sprinter Galant Prince (by
Prince Tenderfoot) and a winner in Italy; dam showed only poor form; 33/1
though one of fittest in field when winning 11-runner newcomers race at Newbury
in April, bursting clear well over a furlong out and winning by 3 lengths from
Pipina despite wandering and swishing her tail under pressure; neck second to
Fabulous Salt in Masaka Stakes at Kempton later in month, easily best subsequent effort (had very stiff task in a handicap fourth start and was subsequently
off course over 3 months); stays 1m; sweating and was bandaged near-hind
final start. *R. Williams.*

WILD FEET 2 ch.c. Hotfoot 126–Generous Thought 81 (Compensation 127) —
(1981 6g 6g) May 16; 8,400F, IR 15,000Y; third foal; half-brother to smart
French 7f to 9f winner Wild Idea (by Silly Season); dam at her best at 2 yrs;
in mid-division in large fields for maiden races at Newmarket and Doncaster
late in season. *M. Albina.*

WILD PRINCESS 2 b.f. Free State 125–Marita (Right Royal V 135) (1981 6fg —
6g) Apr 16; 12,000Y; smallish filly; half-sister to several winners in France,
notably very useful 1979 French 5.5f to 7f winner Koboko (by Balidar); dam
won over 9f and 10.5f; soundly beaten in maiden races at Newmarket (ninth
of 18) and Ayr in July. *B. Hills.*

WILD PUMPKIN 4 b.f. Auction Ring 123–Wild Thyme 63 (Galivanter 131) —
(1980 12d 12s 8.2g 7g 12d 1981 8f 10f 16fg⁴ 16.5f 12g³ 16fg) lengthy, narrow
filly; plating-class maiden; stays well; trained for part of season by Peter Taylor.
P. Ashworth.

WILD ROSIE 5 gr.m. Warpath 113–Rosie Wings 102 (Telegram II 130) (1980 **66**
13s 15f 15.8g 15g² 14.6g² 15.8f² 16f* 16s² 16fg* 16fg³ 16.1s* 16.1s³ 15.8d 1981
12s 15.8g² 16f 15fg³ 16g 16fg² 17.4g* 16.1s* 18g 18g*) staying handicapper;
awarded Eglinton and Winton Memorial Handicap at Ayr in September after
being hampered by length winner Beechwood Seeker; successful afterwards at
Haydock (apprentices) and Doncaster; acted on any going; suitable mount
for a boy; game and genuine; stud. *C. Thornton.*

WILD RUN (FR) 2 b.f. Luthier 126–Wow 106 (Baldric II 131) (1981 6f 6g)
neat, lightly-made filly; lacks scope; a half-sister to useful 1979 2-y-o 5f and 6f
winner Why Not (by Dancer's Image) and a winner in Trinidad; dam won over
1¼m; 25/1 when eighth of 15 to Atossa in maiden race at Doncaster in June;
never landed a blow when behind in similar event won by Glossy Ibis at Redcar
in August; bred to stay middle distances. *H. Cecil.*

WILD RUPERT 3 ch.c. Rupert Bear 105–So Wild 64 (Lauso) (1980 NR —
1981 10.1v 10s 8f 6f 6fg) workmanlike colt; third foal; dam won 5f seller at 2
yrs; behind in varied races, including a claimer and a seller (last 4 times);
blinkered last 2 starts; sold 420 gns Ascot July Sales. *R. Atkins.*

WILDRUSH 2 b.g. Free State 125–Ribble Reed 75 (Bullrush 106) (1981 5fg **71**
6fg 7g³ 7fg) Feb 22; big gelding; half-brother to Ribble Rouser (by Marcus
Brutus), successful from 7f to 2m; dam sprint plater; ran best race when 4
lengths third of 16 to Warm Wind in maiden race at Catterick in July; needs at
least 7f. *W. C. Watts.*

WILLAWAY 3 b.f. Willipeg 112–Pontesbury (Falls of Clyde 126) (1980 6g —
1981 6fg 5fg 5g 5s 5s) rather plain, big filly; soundly beaten in maiden races
and a handicap; usually bandaged in front, and didn't stride out at all well
second start. *D. Ancil.*

WILLERBY 4 b.g. Great Nephew 126–Sera Sera 88 (Hill Clown) (1980 8g 8g³ —
8.2d 1981 10.2fg 10f 10f 11d 8g) neat gelding; poor maiden; suited by 1¼m;
sold out of J. Fitzgerald's stable 4,000 gns Doncaster August Sales after third
start. *T. Craig.*

WILL GEORGE 2 br.g. Abwah 118–Grey Miss 72 (Grey Sovereign 128§) **68**
(1981 5v 5g³ 5g 5fg 5fg 5f 6g⁴ 5f² 5f 5f² 5fg⁴ 5f* 5d* 5g) May 6; 1,600Y; small
gelding; third foal; half-brother to a winner in Switzerland; dam stayed 7f;
second in sellers at Wolverhampton and Ripon before making all under low weights
to win nurseries at Redcar in September and Wolverhampton in October;
clearly thought best at 5f; has won on firm and dead ground; usually blinkered
nowadays; below his best final start. *K. Stone.*

WILL GULF 4 ch.g. Gulf Pearl 117–Gwen Somers (Will Somers 114§) (1980 —
10.8v 10g 7f 8.5f² 7d 8f 8g 1981 10d 12s) strong gelding; plater; stays 1m
well; acts on firm going; often blinkered. *W. Stubbs.*

WILLIAM'S PET 3 b.g. Elvis 96–Sallyanda 65 (Marcus Superbus 100) (1980 —
NR 1981 12g 8s 8fg 6fg 6fg 10f⁴ 7g 8.2s) small gelding; second reported foal;
dam won 6f seller at 2 yrs; poor form in varied company, including selling;
blinkered final outing. *W. Storey.*

WILLIAM THE FIRST (USA) 6 b.g. Fleet Nasrullah–Minorstone (Ribot —
142) (1980 11fg³ 12.5s 1981 16s 16.9s) plater nowadays; stays middle
distances; probably best on a sound surface; has been tried in blinkers. *A.
W. Jones.*

WILLIE GAN 3 ch.g. McIndoe 97–Queen's Bay 73 (King's Troop 118) (1980 **66**
5d 6d 5fg³ 5fg³ 6s 5d 5d⁴ 5s 1981 6s² 5g* 5f 5f 5fg⁴ 5g 5g² 5fg* 6s 8d)
quite a useful sort; won minor event at Edinburgh in April (made all) and
apprentice handicap at Catterick in August; stays 6f; probably acts on any going.
Denys Smith.

WILL OF VICTORY 3 gr.f. Dancer's Image–Warsaw (Bon Mot III 132) **86**
(1980 6f² 6s* 1981 8fg³) strong, well-made filly; second foal; dam, smart
winner over 11f and 13f on only starts, is half-sister to top American mare
Waya; ran very promisingly when second to Silken Knot in Virginia Water
Stakes at Ascot and trotted up in maiden race at Nottingham as a 2-y-o; disputed lead most of way when about a length third of 10 behind Fabulous Salt
in Masaka Stakes at Kempton in April on only outing in England in 1981
(favourite); stays 1m; sent to USA. *H .Cecil.*

WILLOW BOY 4 br.g. Virginia Boy 106–Brave Eliza (Brave Invader) (1980 —
10s 9f² 7f 12f* 8g 9.5f 14s 9.5g 1981 12g 8fg 8fg 12.2fg 12fg 8f 12d 12.2g)
big ex-Irish gelding; won maiden race at Clonmel in 1980; soundly beaten
at 4 yrs; stays 1m; acts on firm going; sometimes wears blinkers. *W. Wharton.*

WILLOWBROOK WORLD 2 ch.g. Free State 125–Jantu 81 (Deep Diver —
134\ (1981 5fg 7g 8s) Apr 8; 1,700F, 8,000Y (privately); small, good-bodied
gelding; first foal; dam 6f winner; in rear in maiden races in the Midlands.
W. Wharton.

WILLOW HERB 3 gr.f. Habat 127–Windflower 77 (Crepello 136) (1980 **63**
8g 7s 6g 1981 5g³ 6s² 6g² 7s 5fg⁴ 6g 6f* 6g) neat filly; apprentice ridden
when beat'ng Habella a head in handicap at Hamilton in August; seems best
at sprint distances; acts on any going; ran a bit freely in blinkers sixth start
(claiming race). *W. Hastings-Bass.*

WILLSPAL 3 ch.c. Firestreak 125–Beauklarion (Klairon 131) (1980 7f 8g **62**
1981 10s* 12g⁴ 12.5f³ 10g³ 10f 12.3g³ 10g 10d 11d⁴ 10s) sturdy colt; beat
High Circles 1½ lengths in maiden race at Newcastle in April; in frame in varied
races afterwards, including in a seller; stays 1½m; seems to act on any going;
occasionally blinkered; sold 880 gns Doncaster November Sales. *J. Etherington.*

WILL WISP (USA) 2 b. or br.c. Charles Elliott–Thundering Streak (Craig- —
wood) (1981 7fg 6g 7g) lengthy, useful sort; brother to 1980 2-y-o 6f winner
Flash 'N' Fire and to a stakes-placed winner in USA, and half-brother to very
useful sprinter Flash N Thunder (by Key To The Kingdom); dam won over
4f at 2 yrs; unquoted when soundly beaten in maiden races; sent to France at
end of season. *R. Sheather.*

WILLYBOY 9 b.g. Willipeg 112–Northern Democracy 56 (Democratic 124) —
(1980 NR 1981 12fg) poor plater; stays 1¼m; probably acts on any going;
suitable mount for an apprentice; wears bandages. *A. Potts.*

WILLY WITEFOOT ESQ 2 ch.c. Hotfoot 126–Mountain of Mourne 87 —
(Mountain Call 125) (1981 7g 7d) May 25; rather lightly-made colt; second
foal; dam stayed 1m; beaten about 9 lengths when sixth of 11 to Don Giovanni
in minor event at Leicester in November, second outing and better effort;
will stay 1m. *M. Jarvis*

WIMBLEDON'S PET 2 b.f. Mummy's Pet 125–Wimbledon 105 (Abernant —
142) (1981 5d⁴ 5f 6f 6d 5s) Mar 11; compact filly; half-sister to several
winners, including fairly useful sprinter Young and Foolish (by Crocket); dam
won over 5f at 2 yrs; plating-class sprint maiden. *Miss A. Hill-Wood.*

WIMSEY 4 b.g. Run The Gantlet–Bell Song 101 (Tudor Melody 129) (1980 —
12g 12d 16fg 15.5g³ 1981 15.5d 15.5d 16d) tall, lengthy gelding; staying
handicapper; won private sweepstakes at Plumpton in May; blinkered second
start. *R. Hoad.*

WINART 3 br.c. Scottish Rifle 127–Alice (Parthia 132) (1980 6f 6g³ 7g³ **80**
7f 6g⁴ 6fg 8d 1981 8.2s* 10s² 10.4g⁴ 9s³ 8d³ 8d* 10d³) neat colt; has a round

action; in frame on all starts and won maiden race at Nottingham in April and handicap at Pontefract in October; bred to stay beyond 1¼m; form only on an easy surface. *G. Pritchard-Gordon.*

WIND AND REIGN 3 b.f. Tumble Wind–Tyrant Gleam (Tyrant) (1980 **41** 5fg 5f 5f 5fg 5f 5d⁴(dis) 6fg 5d 5s 1981 6s 5g 5fg 5g 5fg⁴ 6fg 5fg 8f 13.8g 5d³) small filly; plater; has run respectably over 1m; sometimes blinkered. *D. Chapman.*

WIND AND WUTHERING (USA) 2 br.c. No Robbery–J.A's Joy (Johns **132** Joy) (1981 5fg* 5g* 6fg 6fg⁴ 7f⁴ 7.6g² 7g* 7g*)
    In a popularity poll, a horse whose four wins from six starts included three victories in Group 1 events is virtually certain to have the edge on one with a single Group 1 success among his four wins from eight races. Our investigation of the weights leads us to think that when the handicappers compiled the Tote European Free Handicap they chose their top horse on that basis—the greater number of important wins from fewer outings—otherwise how could they have awarded top position to Green Forest, the winner of the Prix Morny, Prix de la Salamandre and the Grand Criterium, 3 lb ahead of the tremendously impressive William Hill Dewhurst Stakes winner Wind and Wuthering? The Free Handicap isn't, or shouldn't be, a popularity poll: it should be a representation in weight of the value of a horse's achievements on the racecourse; no more, no less. Green Forest has been given credit for slightly more than he achieved: he's been rated 7 lb better than Norwick who received only a 5-lb beating in the Grand Criterium; 5 lb better than Zino who received a 4-lb beating in the Salamandre; and respectively 7 lb and 10 lb better than Maelstrom Lake and Tender King who received beatings of 2 lb and 5 lb in the Morny. Wind and Wuthering on the other hand has been given a great deal less credit for his Dewhurst performance than it deserves. The handicappers appear to believe that the Dewhurst result reflects the respective merits of the five colts who chased Wind and Wuthering home at Newmarket: Be My Native and Tender King, who were separated by a neck in second and third places, both received 8-11; Codrington, one and a half lengths further behind in fourth, has been given 8-8; Solaboy, a neck back in fifth place, received 8-7; and Telephone Man, another length and a half behind, received 8-6. Fair enough. And yet they have given Wind and Wuthering, who won the race by seven lengths, only 9-4, just 7 lb more than Be My Native. They seem to be saying Wind and Wuthering's performance wasn't worth its full value. Let's take a look at it.
    Although Wind and Wuthering made all the running there was no suggestion that his rivals allowed him to give them the slip; for the first couple of furlongs he led by no more than two lengths from Diamond Cutter, Telephone Man and Raconteur, beginning to increase his advantage only when pushed along at halfway. His rivals were simply unable to do anything about him as he steadily forged clear. Of the market leaders Raconteur put up a bolder show than Simply Great but he was back-pedalling fully two furlongs out, leaving Tender King, the winner of the Richmond Stakes and a close fourth in the Middle Park, as Wind and Wuthering's main pursuer. Even Tender King, with his good turn of foot, could make no impression and Wind and Wuthering galloped on with tremendous enthusiasm to come home unchallenged. Be My Native, who'd had his field well strung out in an Ascot nursery on his latest outing, came through strongly to snatch second place off Tender King. The timefigure for the race was the second-fastest of the season by a two-year-old, which gives independent confirmation of the reliability of the form. In our opinion Wind and Wuthering is value for every one of the seven lengths, and deserved to be recognised as number-one among the European two-year-olds.
    Wind and Wuthering had earlier started favourite for the only other pattern race he's contested, the Coventry Stakes at Royal Ascot, having looked a very promising youngster on his previous appearances. After battling on gamely to win the Sandown Park Maiden Stakes in April by a length and a half from Ghawar, he'd beaten Better Portion very comfortably by four lengths in the Kris Stakes at Newbury in May. It was, therefore, disappointing to see him trail home only tenth behind Red Sunset in the Coventry. His trainer was at a loss to explain his poor display on the day of the race but the explanation became only too obvious the following morning—Wind and Wuthering couldn't put his near-hind to the ground because of a pulled muscle. Two months passed before he could race again. He looked just in need of the race on his reappearance at Newbury, running creditably in the circumstances to finish fourth to Custer in the Washington Singer Stakes, beaten about two and a half lengths. Two defeats followed in September, in the Intercraft Solario Stakes at Kempton and

Kris Plate, Newbury—an early-season success for Wind and Wuthering who wins from Better Portion

the Burr Stakes at Lingfield. In the Solario he started at 14/1 and came home only fourth, eight lengths behind Silver Hawk. Wind and Wuthering clearly didn't take kindly to restraint in the early stages here, and a return to more forceful tactics at Lingfield later in the month produced better results: after making the running for nearly six furlongs he battled on so well he went down by only three parts of a length to the promising Triple Axel, who received 4 lb.

Wind and Wuthering's last three defeats seemed to establish him as a useful colt, nothing more. Only nine days later, though, Wind and Wuthering left his previous form well behind in the Somerville Tattersall Stakes, a listed race worth nearly £9,000, at Newmarket on the first day of October. He appeared to have a stiff task under 9-4, conceding at least 7 lb to his fifteen rivals, including 15 lb to Realms Reason, a creditable second in the Group 3 Silken Glider Stakes on her latest start, and 10 lb to Imagination who'd won her only start in pleasing style. Wind and Wuthering had made the running or disputed the lead in

Somerville Tattersall Stakes, Newmarket—Wind and Wuthering returns to winning form

most of his previous races but often not at a pace fast enough to offset his lack of instant acceleration. This time he set a stronger gallop and had the measure of his opponents when he lengthened his stride with a quarter of a mile to run. Showing no sign of stopping he came home two and a half lengths clear of the newcomer Wongchoi who received 12 lb. Clearly Wind and Wuthering is a truly formidable opponent ridden this way, as his fellow Dewhurst runners were to discover just fifteen days later.

Wind and Wuthering (USA) (br.c. Mar 4, 1979)	No Robbery (b 1960)	Swaps (ch 1952)	Khaled
			Iron Reward
		Bimlette (b 1944)	Bimelech
			Bloodroot
	J.A's Joy (b or br 1965)	Johns Joy (br 1946)	Bull Dog
			My Auntie
		Belle Rebelle (br 1950)	Count Fleet
			Gala Belle

Wind and Wuthering followed in the footsteps of Ribofilio, Nijinsky, Mill Reef, Crowned Prince, Cellini, The Minstrel, Try My Best and Storm Bird, to become the ninth North American-bred winner of the Dewhurst in the last fourteen years. All his predecessors were blue-blooded individuals and, with the exception of the owner-bred Mill Reef, all were expensive yearlings. There's nothing blue-blooded or expensive about Wind and Wuthering. He was sold for 22,000 dollars as a foal at Keeneland and for only 10,500 guineas as a yearling at the Houghton Sales; and his sire No Robbery's fee was 4,000 dollars at the time he covered J.A's Joy. No Robbery isn't a particularly well-known stallion over here. He was a very smart racehorse in the early 'sixties but clearly had a lot of training troubles: he ran only twice at two, winning over six and seven furlongs; his second season was limited to only five races, of which he won minor events over six furlongs and a mile and the Wood Memorial Stakes over nine furlongs; and after winning a small six-furlong race on his only appearance at four he was retired to stud. He's met with plenty of success, siring the winners of around 8,000,000 dollars and numerous stakes winners, including the very smart animals Replant, Safe and Track Robbery, and the very good 1981 two-year-old Out Of Hock. His best previous winner over here is Bold Pirate, winner of the nine-furlong Prix Saint-Roman at two and the John Smith's Magnet Cup over a mile and a quarter at four.

J.A's Joy failed to win, achieving just two second places from six races; nevertheless Wind and Wuthering is the sixth of her first nine foals to win. Best

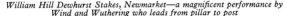

William Hill Dewhurst Stakes, Newmarket—a magnificent performance by Wind and Wuthering who leads from pillar to post

Mr R. M. Cyzer's "Wind and Wuthering"

of the others was Mitos Joy (by Mito), a smart sprinter in 1975, while Ne de Gagner (by Bupers) has won over 100,000 dollars. J.A's Joy is herself a half-sister to a stakes winner by No Robbery in Strike A Bargain, the winner of a six-and-a-half-furlong stakes event at four who was still winning races as a ten-year-old. Strike A Bargain was the only stakes performer among Belle Rebelle's six winners but Belle Rebelle, who was placed in the Falls City Handicap, a stakes race over a mile, was a half-sister to no fewer than four stakes winners; one of the four, Revoked, was among the best American two-year-olds of 1945 and later became a very successful sire.

Wind and Wuthering has been entered for both the Two Thousand Guineas and the Derby. We doubt whether he'll have the necessary stamina for the Derby but regard him as extremely good value at his current odds of 12/1 for the Guineas. He has already shown that the Rowley Mile course suits his powerful, front-running style of racing down to the ground and, with the exception of Green Forest, his opponents will have to improve several pounds if they're to prevent his becoming the third all-the-way Guineas winner in the last eleven years, following High Top and Mon Fils. He's tall, lengthy and quite attractive, with plenty of scope, so should make at least normal improvement; incidentally he's also a particularly good walker. He hasn't yet raced on a soft surface but his best performances have come when there has been a little give in the ground. His trainer is a lucky man to have such a fine replacement for retired stable stars Master Willie and Nicholas Bill. *H. Candy.*

WINDBREAKER 3 b.c. Windjammer (USA)–Miss Pinkerton (Above Suspicion — 127) (1980 NR 1981 7d 8g 14g) 25,000Y: compact colt; closely related to Tumbledownwind (by Tumble Wind), a smart performer at up to 1m, and half-brother to Pinkerton's Man (by Will Hays), successful at up to 1m, and to a winner in Mexico; dam won over 1½m in Ireland; in rear in maiden events at Leicester in April, Doncaster in May (dwelt) and Yarmouth in September; sold 800 gns Newmarket Autumn Sales. *I. Walker.*

WIND CATCHER (FR) 4 b.c. Busted 134–Wadi (Snob 130) (1980 10g* —
12f* 1981 12g) useful sort; won maiden race at Nottingham and minor event
at Wolverhampton in 1980; had stiffish task only start at 4 yrs in May; will stay
1¾m. *H. Cecil.*

WINDE UP 5 b.h. Vilmoray 126–Sibilant 106 (Whistler 129) (1980 8fg 7fg   45
6fg 6g⁴ 5g 6g³ 6d 6g 5.8f 8.3f⁴ 6g   1981 6s² 7g 6d 6fg* 6g 5g³ 6g) small, lengthy
horse; plater; won at Catterick in June (sold out of S. Matthews's stable 2,700
gns); best at 6f; probably acted on any going; sometimes blinkered; broke a leg
at Ostend in August and was destroyed. *D. Garraton.*

WINDIER 2 b.f. Luthier 126–Winden (Worden II 129) (1981 6fg 7d) Mar 24;   —
tall, rather narrow filly; half-sister to winners in Italy by Great Nephew and
Ribero and to Gran Premio d'Italia winner Wale (by Ardale); dam never ran;
33/1 and very green, began to get the hang of things in closing stages when 11
lengths equal-sixth of 19 to Dawn Ditty in maiden race at Salisbury in September;
made no show in similar race won by Melting Snows at Newbury later in month;
bred to stay middle distances. *P. Walwyn.*

WINDMILLS 2 ch.c. Red Alert 127–Nice Tack 106 (Hard Tack 111§) (1981   89
5g⁴ 5d 5g* 6d 6fg 5fg⁴ 5.1d² 5d 6fg 5g 6s) Feb 7; 7,800Y; smallish, sturdy colt;
brother to fair 1978 2-y-o 7f winner Broads Master, subsequently successful
in Scandinavia; dam stayed 7f; made virtually all when comfortably winning
10-runner maiden race at Doncaster in May by 1½ lengths from Harris Tweed;
in frame in nursery at Leicester (didn't have best of runs) and 4-runner race at
Yarmouth (went down by 3 lengths to long odds-on Custer) afterwards; form
only at 5f; sold to S. Matthews 5,000 gns Newmarket Autumn Sales. *C. Brittain.*

WINDOW BOX 2 ch.f. Swing Easy 126–Rose Arbour 106 (Pall Mall 132)   —
(1981 7f 6fg 8d 7g) May 9; 5,000F; small filly; good walker; half-sister to 3
winners, including fairly useful 1979 staying 2-y-o Ben Elid (by Upper Case),
subsequently winner of Austrian St Leger; dam stayed 1m; no worthwhile form in
maiden races; blinkered fourth outing. *H. Candy.*

WINDPIPE 3 ch.g. Leander 119–Whiffle 105 (King's Troop 118) (1980 5g 7d   72
1981 8g* 8g* 8g³ 10g* 11g³ 10fg 10f 8g*) workmanlike gelding; had a good
season and won maiden event at Edinburgh and handicaps at Thirsk, Newcastle
and Redcar (apprentices); beat subsequently-disqualified Celtic Halo 1½ lengths
in last-named race in September (blinkered first time); effective from 1m to 1¼m
(probably doesn't stay 11f); pulled up when stirrup iron broke sixth start.
J. W. Watts.

WINDS OF MARCH 4 br.f. Tyrant–March Brown 90 (March Past 124)   —
(1980 8fg 9f 14f 11.7fg 16f⁴ 12.2fg 12.2f³ 11.7h   1981 16fg 14g) rangy, good
sort; plating-class maiden; possibly stays 1⅛m; acts on firm going; usually wears
blinkers; trained part of season by P. Mitchell; sold 1,200 gns Newmarket
Autumn Sales. *M. McCormack.*

WINDSOR BRIDGE 2 b.f. Swing Easy 126–Grecian Bridge 90 (Acropolis 132)   75
(1981 6fg 6fg 6fg³ 6g 6d 7d) Feb 17; attractive, good-bodied filly; good walker;
half-sister to 3 winners, including good-class 1m to 1¼m performer Roy Bridge
(by March Past); dam from same family as Ribocco and Ribero; quite moderate
form in maiden and minor events; probably stays 7f; blinkered last 2 starts.
H. T. Jones.

WINDSOR BROOK 4 ch.f. Deep Diver 134–Cherry Pie 81 (Rockavon 120)   —
(1980 6f 5h 5s   1981 6g 8.3s 6v 7f) lightly-made filly; poor sprint plater;
has been tried in blinkers; sold 510 gns Ascot July Sales. *V. Soane.*

WINDSOR TOKEN 3 ch.f. Record Token 128–Windsor Walk (Sovereign Path   —
125) (1980 NR   1981 6g) 1,000F, 6,000Y; big, robust filly; good mover;
fourth foal; dam unraced half-sister to speedy Song of Songs; unquoted and
ridden by 7-lb claimer when in rear in 16-runner minor event won by Hot Ember
at Kempton in May (never seen with a chance). *P. Kelleway.*

WINDSOR WARRIOR 4 gr.g. Supreme Sovereign 119–Coleen's Peep (Don't   —
Look 107) (1980 10.1g 12g 12fg³ 14fg 12fg 11s   1981 12g 10f 12g 11.7g)
lengthy gelding; poor maiden; best run at 1½m on a firm surface; blinkered
once in 1980. *Peter Taylor.*

WINDY LAD 2 ch.c. Tumble Wind–Bold Bird (Bold Lad, Ire 133) (1981 5s*   83
5d⁴ 5fg 5g 5v* 5s⁴ 6f 5fg⁴ 5d 5d 5s) Apr 22; IR 900F, 4,000Y; compact colt;
third produce; dam unraced sister to useful sprinter Bold and Fast; made all
to win minor events at Folkestone in March and Windsor in May, latter by a

length from odds-on B. A. Poundstretcher; fourth afterwards in fairly useful company at Kempton and Windsor; revels in the mud; blinkered final outing. *S. Matthews.*

WINDY SPOT 7 br.g. Silly Season 127–Lonely Leopardess 80 (Pardal 130) — (1980 11.7f 1981 11.7f) poor maiden. *G. Cottrell.*

WINDY WILLOW 3 ch.c. Windjammer (USA)–Morning Glow (Grey Dawn II 132) (1980 5fg 1981 8d) compact colt; lightly raced and little worthwhile form (last on only outing of 1981). *B. Hills.* —

WINGED DAGGER 12 b.g. Falcon 131–Gay Natasha 105 (Prince Chevalier) (1980 12fg* 11.7fg² 12f³ 12fg² 12g³ 12g⁴ 12f³ 12g³ 1981 12d 12g³ 12d) middle-distance handicapper; acts on any going but is suited by a sound surface; has worn blinkers; suitable mount for an apprentice. *J. Old.* —

WINGED KESTREL 3 br.g. Reliance II 137–Feather Top 85 (Falcon 131) (1980 NR 1981 12fg 10.1fg 10.1g) first foal; dam fair middle-distance winner; behind in maiden race at Lingfield and minor events at Windsor. *D. Underwood.* —

WING VELVET 3 b.c. Sayfar 116–Tide and Time (Easter Island 101) (1980 6g 5d 1981 6s 7fg 10s³ 10d 8.5d 10f 8.2g 8fg 8.2s 7g) poor form, including in sellers; suited by 1¼m; spoilt his chance by hanging seventh start. *D. Leslie.* **52**

WINK (USA) 2 b.f. Forli–Glisk (Buckpasser) (1981 6g* 7d 6fg² 6f³ 6d*) Apr 3; medium-sized, attractive filly; third foal; dam, half-sister to $1,000,000-earner Royal Glint, won 3 times at up to 6f; successful in maiden race at Lingfield in June (ridden by 7-lb claimer) and £4,200 nursery at Ayr in September (wore down Provail to win by a neck); should stay 7f; seems to act on any going, possibly needs holding up; useful. *J. Dunlop.* **101**

WINKING FIELDS 5 ch.g. Northfields–Winky Joe (Eudaemon 129) (1980 8s 11fg 12f⁴ 11.5fg 12g 1981 11d) poor plater; has worn blinkers; wears a tongue strap. *D. Weeden.* —

WINMARIE 3 b.g. Windjammer (USA)–Mary's Dream (Midsummer Night II 117) (1980 5f 6g 1981 8d 11.7g) no worthwhile form in maiden events. *J. Hill.* —

WINNER TAKES ALL 4 b.c. Singing Bede 122–Julita 87 (Rockavon 120) (1980 7f 6fg 6f 5fg 5s³ 6g 5.6fg⁴ 6g 6d 6d⁴ 1981 6s 6s 6d³ 5s² 6d 7s⁴ 5fg 6f 7f 6f 6g² 6f 6g* 7g) compact colt; poor handicapper; won claiming race at Newmarket in October despite hanging right; fifth in fairly valuable selling handicap final start; stays 7f; suited by some give in the ground; blinkered nowadays; has run respectably for a boy. *D. Marks.* **56**

WINNIE'S PET 2 ch.f. Crooner 119–Princess of Verona 95 (King's Leap 111) (1981 5s 5.1fg 5fg 5f 6g 5g) May 31; 2,500Y; neat filly; second foal; dam, half-sister to Music Boy, was best at 5f; bad plater; blinkered final start. *K. Ivory.* —

WINNINGS THE GAME 3 b.f. Workboy 123–Pams Choice 87 (Mandamus 120) (1980 5.1f³ 5g 5d 7d 1981 5g 8.2d 7g 8g 8f 8.2f) workmanlike filly; poor maiden; behind in sellers last 3 starts; not sure to stay 7f. *T. Taylor.* —

WINSOR BOY 5 br.g. Comedy Star 121–Spatula (Epaulette 125) (1980 5fg* 5fg* 6h 5.8fg 5.8fg² 5g² 5fg* 5d² 5fg2 5g³ 5g⁴ 5d⁴ 1981 5fg) close-coupled gelding; modest handicapper; trotted up 3 times in 1980; burst out of stalls at Epsom in April and subsequently broke his neck after jumping a rail; best at 5f; probably acted on any going; blinkered once at 2 yrs; dead. *R. Turnell.* —

WINTERGRACE (USA) 2 ch.f. Northern Dancer–Stylish Pattern (My Babu 136) (1981 6fg² 6d³) lengthy, unfurnished filly; half-sister to several winners, including top-class 1m to 1½m performer Artaius (by Round Table) and American stakes winner Stylish Genie (by Bagdad); dam half-sister to smart middle-distance colt Arthurian and $438,000-earner Spring Double; proved no match for 7-length winner Circus Ring when favourite for 18-runner maiden race at Newmarket in July; odds on for maiden event at Windsor the following month but could finish only 1¾ lengths third of 15 to Welsh Partner after leading to below distance; will be suited by 1m. *H. Cecil.* **80**

WINTERLUDE 3 b.f. Wollow 132–Won't Linger (Worden II 129) (1980 NR 1981 8fg 10fg) 16,000Y; half-sister to numerous winners, including smart stayer Hazy Idea (by Hethersett); dam unraced half-sister to several good winners, including very smart Heath Rose; in rear in maiden races at Warwick in August and Redcar in September. *M. Jarvis.* —

WINTERREISE 3 b.g. Fine Blade 121–Pouilly Fuse (Tudor Music 131) (1980 **65**
6d 1981 8g 8g 10.2g 9s 13g 12.3g 10fg 9s³) strong gelding; 1½ lengths third
to Battalion in maiden event at Hamilton in October, best effort. *W. Bentley.*

WINTER SUNSHINE 5 b.m. Crisp and Even 116–Even Song (Falcon 131) **57**
(1980 10v² 16s² 12f 16fg 12fg 11.7s 11g 12g³ 12.2fg 13s² 1981 11s* 12.2fg*
12.5g² 13fg⁴ 12g³ 12f³ 15fg⁴ 12g³) neat mare; won handicaps at Hamilton
(apprentice event) and Warwick in April; effective at 1½m and stays well;
acts on any going; sometimes wears blinkers but is effective without; suitable
mount for a boy. *P. Haslam.*

WINTERTIME 4 br.g. Keren 100–Cuddly Toy (Sovereign Lord 120) (1980 **—**
NR 1981 10g) in rear in varied company, including selling. *G. Richards.*

WINTER WIND 5 b.h. Tumble Wind–Northern Beauty (Borealis) (1980 **89**
5d 5g³ 5f³ 6fg* 6g³ 6g 5d* 6g 5g 6s³ 6d* 7d 1981 5s³ 6s* 6g 6g* 6s² 6s 6fg⁴
6fg 6v 6g) very attractive horse; good mover with a nice, easy action; fair
handicapper; beat Queen's Pride a neck in Unicheq Sprint at Salisbury and Son
of Shaka by ¾ length in £4,000 race at Newmarket, both in April; best at sprint
distances; acts on any going but seems suited by some give in the ground
nowadays; blinkered once at 3 yrs; needs to be held up and goes well for B.
Raymond. *D. Kent.*

WINTER WORDS 2 b.c. Wollow 132–Prinia 77 (On Your Mark 125) (1981 **97**
5f⁴ 5f² 6fg* 6fg⁴ 6g² 6g 7g) May 21; 7,400Y; close-coupled, quite useful sort;
none too good a mover in his slower paces; second foal; half-brother to 3-y-o
6f to 1m winner Praetorian Guard (by Home Guard); dam, 1¼m winner, is
closely related to Mandrake Major; decisive 4-length winner from Man Overboard in 10-runner maiden race at York in July; subsequently acquitted himself well in Richmond Stakes at Goodwood (4¾ lengths fourth of 7 to Tender
King) and nurseries at Redcar and Newmarket (just over 3 lengths sixth of 17
to Vaigly Star in £9,200 event on sixth outing); should be well suited by 7f
(never dangerous when tried at trip but had none too clear a run); yet to race
on a soft surface. *G. Pritchard-Gordon.*

WIPPIN CRUST (USA) 2 ch.c. Balompie 122–Song of Life (Personality) **—**
(1981 7f 7fg 8g) Mar 11; $11,000Y; strong colt; second foal; half-brother to
a minor winner in USA; dam never ran; 4 lengths seventh of 15 to Jiretta in
minor event at Doncaster in July, second outing; not seen out again until
October when on burly side; should stay 1¼m+. *I. Walker.*

WISE CHOICE 2 b.f. Sagaro 133–Light Duty 113 (Queen's Hussar 124) **—**
(1981 7g) Feb 18; well-grown, leggy, rather plain filly; second foal; half-sister
to Paradise Bay (by Mill Reef), a very useful performer at up to 1½m; dam, very
useful middle-distance filly, is sister to 1,000 Guineas and Prix de Diane winner
Highclere; 14/1, didn't impress in paddock prior to finishing tailed-off last of
16 to Positron in maiden race at Leicester in October. *R. Hern.*

WISE MAN 5 ch.g. Frankincense 120–Sans Gene 77 (Songedor 116) (1980 **50**
7fg² 9g 10g⁴ 9fg 9fg 8g² 10.6s² 8.2s² 8.2s⁴ 1981 8.2g 12g 8d² 8g² 10g 8g 8s)
workmanlike gelding; plater; stays 1¼m; acts on any going but seems well
suited by some give in the ground; suitable mount for an inexperienced rider;
sold 1,250 gns Doncaster October Sales. *J. Fitzgerald.*

WISE OWL 4 ch.c. Crowned Prince 128–Tawny Owl 123 (Faberge II 121) **62**
(1980 NR 1981 10g² 10g⁴ 10.1fg² 10.6d² 10d⁴) good-looking colt; promises
to stay 1½m; acts on a firm and a soft surface. *H. Wragg.*

WISE SOLUTION 2 ch.c. Solution–Miss Worden 40 (Worden II 129) (1981 **—**
5d 6f) May 1; first foal; dam winning hurdler; tailed off in minor and maiden
events at Brighton in April and August. *B. Wise.*

WISHING ROSE 2 b.f. Wishing Star 117–Rag Flowers (Tarqogan 125) **58**
(1981 5g 5d 6f⁴ 6fg 7f* 7g 7d⁴ 7f 7f 8fg) Apr 15; 1,600Y; small, lightly-made
filly; sister to 3-y-o 1¼m winner Creative Star and half-sister to 2 winners in
Ireland, including 1976 2-y-o 7.5f winner Flower Grange (by Allangrange);
plater; bought in 2,100 gns after showing improved form to win 8-runner seller
at Beverley in July; not disgraced in 2 of her subsequent races; suited by 7f
and should stay 1m; wears blinkers nowadays; sold 620 gns Newmarket Autumn
Sales. *M. Tompkins.*

WISH 'N' TIME 2 b.f. Broxted 120–Something To Hide 66 (Double-U-Jay **85**
120) (1981 5d 5d³ 5g³ 5.8h* 7s 7fg² 8fg⁴) sturdy, workmanlike filly; second
foal; dam fair staying hurdler; made all to win 7-runner maiden race at Bath
in July by 7 lengths from slow-starting Orixa; afterwards ran creditably in

nurseries at Epsom and Doncaster (came from long way behind); will stay 1¼m; seems to need a firm surface. *B. Hills.*

WITCHINGHAM LASS 4 ch.f. Sweet Revenge 129–Callidice 77 (Worden **48** II 129) (1980 7f 6fg³ 7fg 7g 6fg³ 6fg³ 6fg 6fg 7g* 6fg 6fg 6s 6d 1981 7f⁴ 7g 6fg⁴ 6f³ 8g 6d) strong filly; poor handicapper; stays 7f; seems to act on any going; often blinkered; suitable mount for an apprentice. *R. Hannon.*

WITCH'S POINT 2 br.c. Lochnager 132–Vacation 102 (Remainder 106) **77** (1981 5v³ 5g*(dis) 5g² 5g³ 6f⁴ 5g² 6g 5fg² 5g 6s³) Apr 17; 8,200F, 8,000Y; useful sort; half-brother to 1977 2-y-o 5f winner Cosmic Dancer (by Communication); dam 2-y-o 5f winner; won minor event at Thirsk in April but carried 4 lb less than he should have done and was disqualified; second in another minor race at Thirsk, maiden event at Beverley and nursery at Redcar, and wasn't entirely disgraced when 4½ lengths third of 16 to Hello Sunshine in valuable seller at York in October; best form at 5f; blinkered eighth and ninth outings, looking none too genuine on second occasion. *M. H. Easterby.*

WITHY COPSE 4 b.c. Blakeney 126–Chiltern Lass 100 (High Hat 131) (1980 **—** 10.1fg 11.5f 13d* 16s 14.6fg* 14fg³ 14fg² 14g⁴ 13s* 1981 12fg) neat colt; won maiden race at Ayr and handicaps at Doncaster and Nottingham in 1980; virtually tailed off only start at 4 yrs in August; stays well; probably acts on any going. *M. Stoute.*

WIVETON 3 br.g. Blakeney 126–Wolverene 114 (Relko 136) (1980 7fg³ **89** 1981 8fg* 13.3g³ 14d² 14g 10d³ 10d³) useful-looking gelding; beat Sticky Habit impressively by 2 lengths in minor event at Doncaster in June; placed in handicaps most subsequent outings, including when about ½-length third to very cheeky winner Taher in Morland Brewery Trophy at Newbury following month, 6 lengths second to Courchevel at Haydock in August (amateur riders) and 2½ lengths third to Carved Opal at Newbury in September on fifth outing; needs further than 1¼m and stays 1¾m; acts on a firm and a soft surface; ran disappointingly fourth start and was given a great deal to do on final one; gelded after last outing. *W. Hastings-Bass.*

WODONGA (USA) 2 ch.f. Shecky Greene–La Duena (Jacinto) (1981 5d³ **81** 5s* 5f 7g³ 6fg) Mar 23; $57,000Y; strong, lengthy, workmanlike filly; has an excellent long stride; third foal; dam minor stakes winner at up to 1m; 4/7, made all when winning 4-runner maiden race at Haydock in May; beaten only about 5½ lengths when creditable seventh of 11 to Fly Baby in Queen Mary Stakes at Royal Ascot the following month and again ran well when 2¼ lengths third of 8 to Shining Start in £4,200 nursery at York in August; stays 7f; action suggests she needs a sound surface; ran badly final start. *J. W. Watts.*

WOLF CUB (USA) 4 b.c. Apalachee 137–Wolverida (Wolver Hollow 126) **44** d (1980 6f 5d 5d 5d 1981 6s 5d⁴ 5g 5fg 8g 8.3fg) neat colt; sprint handicapper; well beaten in seller final start; best at 5f on a soft surface; sold 260 gns Ascot November Sales. *C. Austin.*

WOLFE TONE 4 b.c. Ballymore 123–Djidda II (Free Man) (1980 9s² 1981 **—** 11f) ex-Irish colt; quite a modest maiden at his best; stayed 9f; dead. *Sir Mark Prescott.*

WOLLINGO 3 b.f. Wollow 132–Sabrewing 105 (Petingo 135) (1980 5fg² **—** 5f 6g 1981 7fg 7f 8d) neat, unfurnished filly; plating-class maiden; should stay 1m; blinkered final start. *A. Hide.*

WOLLISA 2 br.f. Wollow 132–Gallissa (El Gallo 122) (1981 5g 6g³ 5f⁴ 5fg 6d⁴) **67** Apr 12; 31,000Y; quite attractive, light-framed filly; good mover; half-sister to 3 winners, including Phoenix Stakes winner Perla (by Young Emperor); dam fairly useful over 5f at 2 yrs in Ireland and is half-sister to Lorenzaccio; in frame in maiden races; probably better suited by 6f than 5f; not disgraced in blinkers fourth outing; sold 19,000 gns Newmarket December Sales. *R. Price.*

WOLLOTTEEN 2 ch.f. Wollow 132–Charlotteen 96 (Charlottown 127) (1981 **66** 5d 7fg² 7g 6d) Apr 28; 10,000Y; lightly-built filly; half-sister to 1m seller winner Longridge (by Derring-Do); dam, middle-distance performer, is half-sister to dam of Homing and Water Mill; went down by a neck to Lucky Joker in tight finish to 10-runner maiden race at Wolverhampton in July; not seen out again until late in season when tailed off in 2 similar races at Leicester; will stay 1¼m. *G. Hunter.*

WOLLOW WILL 2 b.c. Wollow 132–Ready and Willing 82 (Reliance II 137) **78** (1981 7g 8g) May 14; 29,000Y; tall, narrow colt; fourth foal; half-brother to a winner in Italy; dam won over 12.2f and comes from good family; tenth of 16 in Somerville Tattersall Stakes won by Wind and Wuthering at Newmarket in October; last in 27-runner minor event on same course later in month; will be suited by 1¼m; immature at 2 yrs. *B. Hills.*

WOLVER BAY 3 b.c. Bay Express 132–Wolver Valley 72 (Wolver Hollow 126) — (1980 5.1g 7d 7d 1981 8s 10s 12.3g 10f) neat colt; little worthwhile form, but still needed race on third start; sold to W. Clay 860 gns Doncaster October Sales. *M. Camacho.*

WOLVER DEER 2 b.f. Wolverlife 115–Petite Gazelle (Star Gazer 123) (1981 — 5g 5f 6fg 6fg 6s) May 7; lengthy, useful-looking filly; half-sister to 2 winners, including useful sprinter Deer Leap (by Deep Diver); dam Irish 2-y-o 6f winner; stayed on steadily when sixth of 19 to Bahamas Princess in maiden race at Salisbury in June and when fifth of 10 to Special Pleasure in similar race at Kempton in July, first 2 outings; ran badly subsequently, including in a seller; should stay beyond 5f; blinkered final outing; sometimes bandaged near-hind. *N. Vigors.*

WOLVER HEIGHTS 3 b.c. Wolver Hollow 126–Mariska (Tanerko 134) **99** (1980 7s 8s* 1981 8d*(dis)10s 12fg 10g 8g) tall, rangy, attractive colt; second living foal; dam twice-raced sister to Relko; enterprisingly ridden when 20/1-winner of 9-runner Minstrel Stakes at Leopardstown in April, quickening into clear lead after 3f and holding on by 2½ lengths from Lord Trendy; disqualified some time afterwards when theobromine was found in his system; well behind subsequently in 3 races at the Curragh (including Irish Sweeps Derby) and in Joe McGrath Memorial Stakes at Leopardstown; should stay middle distances; acts on soft going. *M. O'Toole, Ireland.*

WOLVER MAID 2 b.f. Wolverlife 115–Fale Maid 93 (Rise 'N Shine II) (1981 **96** 5d* 5g 6g2) Apr 24; 3,200Y; half-sister to 3-y-o 1¼m winner Carved Opal (by Arch Sculptor) and a winner in Belgium; dam won over 6f at 2 yrs and stayed 1¼m; apprentice ridden, had her opponents well strung out when winning 11-runner minor event at Leopardstown in May by 8 lengths from Be A Dancer; not seen out again until the autumn when seventh of 11 to Americus in Goffs Stakes at the Curragh and length second of 14 to Legs and Things under top weight in minor event at Punchestown (favourite); will be suited by 7f and 1m; trained by L. Browne first outing. *D. Weld, Ireland.*

WONDER DREAM 2 ch.c. Free State 125–Arctic Dream 75 (Arctic Slave 116) — (1981 6g 5g 5f) Feb 1; 6,600F, 4,300Y; useful-looking non-thoroughbred colt; fourth reported foal; dam best at sprint distances; behind in maiden races at Newmarket and Sandown in July, showing up to past halfway in latter; reluctant to go to post and refused to start third outing. *E. Eldin.*

WONDERFUL STAR 2 ch.c. Wishing Star 117–Concurrence (Majority Blue **76** 126) (1981 6g 7fg 6fg 6g 7g3) Apr 29; IR 5,000F (privately), 5,600Y; big, lengthy colt; half-brother to 7f and 1m winner Farmers Choice (by St Chad); dam Irish 7f winner; improved with racing, on fifth outing finishing 5½ lengths third of 16 to Adonis Rex in maiden race at Leicester in September; will be suited by 1m. *J. Holt.*

WONDERFUL SURPRISE 4 b.c. Run The Gantlet–Ashling's Lass 89 (Lev- — moss 133) (1980 12fg 10fg4 11s2 12s* 12d* 1981 12f 13.3s 12s 12v 14s) compact, quite attractive colt; should stay beyond 1½m; acts well on soft going; blinkered once at 3 yrs; bandaged in front nowadays. *E. Eldin.*

WONDER WOOD 2 ch.c. High Line 125–Alice (Parthia 132) (1981 8g 8s) — Apr 27; 4,100F; strong, lengthy colt; half-brother to several winners, including fairly useful 1979 Irish 2-y-o 6f winner Surface Heat (by Hot Spark); dam never ran; behind in large fields for maiden race at Newmarket and minor event at Redcar in October; the type to do better over longer distances. *Sir Mark Prescott.*

WONGCHOI 2 b.c. Bustino 136–Lady of Chalon (Young Emperor 133) (1981 **108** 7g2 7s4 7.3s4) Mar 7; 9,600Y; strong, attractive colt; closely related to winning miler Royal Obligation (by Busted) and half-brother to smart sprinter Enchantment (by Habitat); dam minor winner at up to 6f in USA; in frame behind very good colts in 3 races in October, finishing 2½ lengths second of 16 to Wind and Wuthering in Somerville Tattersall Stakes at Newmarket, 11 lengths fourth of 11 to Paradis Terrestre in Hyperion Stakes at Ascot and 1¾ lengths fourth of 8 to Montekin in Horris Hill Stakes at Newbury; will stay 1m; yet to race on a firm surface; certain to win races if not tried too highly at 3 yrs. *E. Eldin.*

WOODCUTTER 2 ch.g. Wollow 132–Conciliation 98 (St Paddy 133) (1981 **83**
5f 6f*) Mar 30; smallish, workmanlike gelding; good mover; second foal;
half-brother to 1980 2-y-o 7f winner Briar (by Brigadier Gerard); dam, half-
sister to smart middle-distance horse Colum, won over 6f and 7f at 2 yrs; ran
on strongly to justify favouritism by 2¼ lengths from Harris Tweed in 12-runner
maiden race at Haydock in July; will be suited by 7f+; gelded and exported to
Hong Kong. *R. Hern.*

WOODRUSH 4 b.f. Mummy's Pet 125–Regal Silk (Henry the Seventh 125) **—**
(1980 5fg 5d 5g 5f 5.6fg 7d 5fg⁴ 5g 1981 6s 5s 5s 6g 6g 6fg 5g 6fg 6g) poor
sprint plater; acts on soft going; has worn blinkers. *D. Chapman.*

WOODSTREAM (USA) 2 ch.f. Northern Dancer–Rule Formi (Forli) (1981 **113**
6fg* 7fg* 6d* 6g*)
If it requires 2,150,000 dollars to buy Ivanjica, 730,000 guineas to buy
Greenland Park and 900,000 Irish guineas to buy Arkadina, how much would
it require to buy a very taking two-year-old whose sire is the world's most
fashionable stallion; whose half-brother is a classic winner; whose record includes
a win in Britain's only Group 1 race for two-year-old fillies, the William Hill
Cheveley Park Stakes; and who was officially rated the best of her age and sex
in Ireland by no less than 8 lb? We'll probably never know the answer since
the filly in question, Woodstream, is most unlikely to come up for sale; there
can be no doubt that her price would be astronomical should she do so. Having
listed Woodstream's numerous selling points we must qualify them: she's not,
at least not yet, the exceptional filly she might sound. She may be easily the
best filly in Ireland but she has been rated the same as Glancing and Top Hope
in the International Classification, a pound superior to Travel On and inferior to
Circus Ring, Height of Fashion, Play It Safe, River Lady and Stratospheric.
And although her form reads 1111 she has in fact been beaten once, gaining her
success in the Group 2 Moyglare Stud Stakes on a disqualification.
Let's begin with Woodstream's performance in the Moyglare at the Curragh
in September. She started favourite in a field of fourteen on the strength of
two cleverly-gained victories: in a maiden race at Phoenix Park in July she'd
beaten Miss Lilian comfortably by a length, and in a small race at Leopardstown
the following month she'd been ridden with great tenderness by Eddery to

*Moyglare Stud Stakes, the Curragh—Sweet Side (second from right) is first home
but is placed third after a stewards inquiry, the race being awarded to
Woodstream (centre) with Santa Roseanna (far right) placed second*

hold the challenge of Prince's Polly by a neck. Woodstream therefore came to the Moyglare without having experienced pressure, and this seemed to tell against her in a competitive race. With two furlongs to run Woodstream appeared to be travelling very smoothly, in the front rank, but when she came under pressure below the distance she didn't find nearly so much as expected and she was soon hotly challenged by the 50/1-shot Sweet Side. Unfortunately Sweet Side veered right inside the final furlong, first of all hampering another challenger, Santa Roseanna, and then colliding with Woodstream. Although Sweet Side didn't exactly help her own cause Woodstream was unable to hold her and went down by a neck, with Santa Roseanna a length back in third place. There was little doubt that Sweet Side would be disqualified and the stewards eventually moved her down to third, awarding the first prize of 16,680 punts to Woodstream.

Woodstream then paid her first visit to England for the Cheveley Park at Newmarket on the last day of September. With Circus Ring side-lined through lameness and the Prix d'Arenberg winner Glancing a late withdrawal, Woodstream was left the only pattern-race winner among thirteen runners. Even so punters found it hard to decide between her and On The House, the winner of the St Hugh's Stakes at Newbury and the Crathorne Stakes at York; eventually the pair started co-favourites. There was little to choose between Woodstream and On The House for much of the race. They raced side by side in the middle of the pack until moving past the third favourite Hollow Heart to challenge entering the final quarter mile. For a while they battled line-abreast with Bless The Match and Admiral's Princess for the lead, and only running out of the Dip did they begin to draw away. Once on the rising ground it was Woodstream who proved the stronger, staying on in fine style under pressure to beat On The House a length and a half. A very useful effort but we can't rate it any higher than that: Admiral's Princess, beaten three lengths into third place, had previously been beaten twice as far by Sandhurst Prince at Kempton and was later beaten nearly three lengths by Top Hope in the Rockfel Stakes; Corley Moor, beaten six lengths into sixth place, had earlier finished over ten lengths behind Peterhof at Doncaster and six lengths behind the very easy York winner Circus Ring; and back in ninth and tenth places, each beaten about eleven lengths, were the newcomer Kristallina, who subsequently finished in the rear in a small race at Pontefract, and O-Rose Fortunata, a modest eighth in a nursery at Doncaster last time out.

In our opinion the latest Cheveley Park took less winning than most; we have rated Woodstream lower than any other Cheveley Park winner in over thirty years. Perhaps this isn't too surprising in view of the change of emphasis in the programme of races for the better juvenile fillies gradually being encouraged by the authorities. Not so very long ago there were no valuable races for two-year-old fillies over seven furlongs and a mile but, no doubt prompted by the introduction of the Criterium des Pouliches (now the Prix Marcel Boussac) in 1969, the British authorities sanctioned a new mile race at Ascot in 1973, one over seven furlongs at Goodwood in 1974 and another mile race at Doncaster in 1975. All three have since been made Group 3 pattern events, known respectively now as the Hoover Fillies Mile, the Waterford Candelabra Stakes and the May Hill Stakes. Also, the seven-furlong Rochford Thompson Newbury Stakes, formerly the Radley Stakes, has been promoted to listed race status and 1981 saw the first running of the Rockfel Stakes, an £8,000 event over seven furlongs. On the other hand one of the best five-furlong events for first-season fillies, the Molecomb Stakes, was opened to colts in 1981 for the first time in fifty years—with colts taking the first two places—while another long-established five-furlong fillies race, the Lowther Stakes, was switched to a distance of six furlongs in 1976. In other words, there's more catering for stamina than a decade ago. Interestingly no Cheveley Park winner has gone on to success in the One Thousand Guineas since Waterloo in 1972 became the fourth to do so in a period of eight years; in fact only three of the twenty-seven fillies placed in the Cheveley Park since then have managed even to gain a place in the Guineas. Where are the Guineas winners coming from nowadays? The 1981 winner Fairy Footsteps had won the Waterford Candelabra Stakes, the 1980 winner Quick As Lightning the Hoover Fillies Mile.

Don't think our comparatively low opinion of Woodstream's two-year-old form means we have little regard for her prospects as a three-year-old. That's not the position at all. With the exception of Circus Ring there was little to choose between the other leading fillies and Woodstream is as promising as any of them. What of Woodstream's appearance?—we said she was very taking. Well, John Oaksey resurrected a highly colourful description for her which would do, saying she had 'a head like a lady and a farewell like a cook'. She is

William Hill Cheveley Park Stakes, Newmarket—Woodstream is a decisive winner from On The House

in fact a very attractive, strongly-made filly; she's also a good walker and a good mover, although her action is so smooth it may not be well served by very soft ground. As also touched on, her pedigree is first rate, too. The first three dams never ran a single race between them but each has made her mark at stud. Rule Formi's four previous foals include the useful Irish six- and seven-furlong winner Indian Lore (by Apalachee) and the top miler Jaazeiro (by Sham), winner of the Irish Two Thousand Guineas, St James's Palace Stakes and the Sussex Stakes; Miss Nasrullah's six foals to race all won, and Not Afraid, in

			Nearctic		Nearco
	Northern Dancer		(br 1954)		Lady Angela
	(b 1961)		Natalma		Native Dancer
Woodstream (USA)			(b 1957)		Almahmoud
(ch.f. May 14, 1979)			Forli		Aristophanes
	Rule Formi		(ch 1963)		Trevisa
	(ch 1969)		Miss Nasrullah		Nasrullah
			(ch 1958)		Not Afraid

addition to the smart American stayer Brave Lad, bred the high-class staying two-year-old Prince John who went on to become one of America's leading sires. As with many American breds it's hard to estimate what distance Woodstream will stay. Her trainer, who has handled more of Northern Dancer's offspring than most and handled both the headstrong Indian Lore and Jaazeiro, the latter of whom never won beyond a mile, is said to regard her primarily as an Oaks filly. O'Brien is also said to regard the Goffs Irish One Thousand Guineas as a more suitable spring target for her, because of its later place in the Calendar, than the Guineas at Newmarket. The only O'Brien-trained winner of the One Thousand Guineas was Glad Rags back in 1966, whereas he's won the Irish equivalent with Valoris in 1966, and for Woodstream's owner Robert Sangster with Lady Capulet in 1977 and with Godetia in 1979. Woodstream must have excellent prospects of giving him a fourth success at the Curragh but should anything go wrong with Circus Ring over the winter it would be no surprise to see Woodstream meet her engagement at Newmarket. *V. O'Brien, Ireland.*

WOOLAW 2 b.f. Golden Mallard 103–Calaburn 71 (Caliban 123) (1981 6f³ 7f 5g) Apr 15; neat filly; first foal; dam won five times from 6f to 1¼m; wasn't disgraced considering she dwelt at start when 4½ lengths third of 5 to Saga's Humour in seller at Stockton in June; not seen out again until the autumn when well beaten in similar events. *Hbt Jones.* **42**

WOOLCANA 4 ch.f. Some Hand 119–Golden Mary 71 (Bounteous 125) (1980 5fg 6fg 6f 6fg 5d* 5s 5.8g 6d⁴ 5fg 5.3fg 6g 5f 5g 5d 6d 1981 5h 5fg) neat filly; sprint handicapper; best at 5f; acts on a firm and a soft surface; occasionally blinkered. *J. Bosley.* **—**

WOOLY WONG 3 gr.f. Lorenzaccio 130–Wimbledon 105 (Abernant 142) (1980 5g⁴ 6fg³ 6g 1981 6g⁴ 6g³ 6s 6f 6g) workmanlike filly; in frame in maiden races; runs as though 7f will suit her. *Miss A. Hill-Wood.* **—**

WORD OF MOUTH 2 ch.c. Town Crier 119–Valdesta 106 (Persian Gulf) (1981 6d 7g 6g) May 3; 7,800Y; neat colt; brother to French 9f winner Valiant Cry and half-brother to French 3-y-o 6.5f winner Vantage (by Bay Express) and 1¼m winner Ben Donachan (by Reform); dam, closely related to Rustam and **—**

954

Zabara, won 3 times over 7f; behind in maiden and minor events, 2 of them at Leicester; sold 1,300 gns Ascot November Sales. *P. Walwyn.*

WORKACHOLIC 3 b.f. Workboy 123–Silver Teal 79 (Meldrum 112) (1980 NR 1981 8fg 7.2f) 2,600Y; second foal; dam won over 5f and 1½m and also over hurdles; in rear in maiden races at Warwick (slowly away) and Haydock (last) in summer; still needed race in latter. *S. Wiles.* —

WORK MATE (USA) 2 ch.c. Secretariat–Wedding (Noholme II) (1981 7g 8g) Mar 29; 66,000Y; big, strong, heavy-bodied colt; second foal; half-brother to French 3-y-o White King (by Vaguely Noble); dam, 1¼m winner in France on only start, is half-sister to brilliant filly Dahlia; 14/1 and still far from fully fit, disputed lead for 6f on far side when out of first 10 of 29 to Born Hero in maiden race at Newmarket in October, second outing; will stay middle distances; the type to improve with racing. *R. Hern.* **73 p**

WORKRIGHT 3 br.c. Workboy 123–Right Beauty 66 (Right Boy 137) (1980 5fg 5f⁴ 5d³ 5d⁴ 6g³ 5f 5s 8g 8g 1981 5f 8.2fg² 8g 8fg) strong colt; plating-class maiden; seemed to stay 1m; blinkered twice in 1980; appeared to have a mind of his own; dead. *A. Jarvis.* **57**

WORLD LEADER (FR) 4 ch.c. Bolkonski 134–Worlica (Bon Mot III 132) (1980 8f³ 8fg 10.5f 10.6fg⁴ 10g* 10.5d 14.6g³ 1981 12f 12fg³ 11.1f 10g³ 12fg) strong, rangy colt; very smart at 3 yrs; not so good in 1981 though finished respectable third in Alycidon Stakes at Goodwood in July (behind Capstan) and Valdoe Stakes on same course in September (to Prince Bee); effective at 1¼m and stays 1¾m; seems to act on any going; sometimes sweats up; often pulls hard, isn't an easy ride and goes well for R. Guest. *L. Cumani.* **108**

WORLD RECORD (USA) 2 b.c. Lt Stevens–Dreamy Hill (Hill Prince) (1981 6f 6fg 6fg 7g² 6v) May 6; $34,000F, 12,500 gns Y; workmanlike colt; good walker and mover; half-brother to winners in USA and Puerto Rico; dam half-sister to dam of Kentucky Derby and Belmont Stakes runner-up Run Dusty Run; ran best race when tried over 7f, going down by 2 lengths to Airspin after making much of running in 16-runner maiden race at Leicester in September; will probably stay 1m; badly drawn final outing. *H. Candy.* **88**

WORLINGWORTH 2 ch.c. Jimmy Reppin 131–Derring Maid (Derring-Do 131) (1981 5d 5f 5fg 5.1d* 6d 6g 6s²) Apr 20; short-backed colt; third foal; dam of little account; off course 2½ months prior to winning 9-runner maiden race at Yarmouth in September; showed only worthwhile form afterwards when 1½ lengths second to Never So Lucky in nursery at Nottingham in October; will stay 7f+; best form with give in the ground. *M. Ryan.* **93**

WORLINGWORTH WAY 2 b.c. Porto Bello 118–Taormina (Windjammer) (1981 6g 7g) Mar 24; first foal; dam never ran; in rear in maiden races at Yarmouth and Leicester (tailed off) in September. *M. Ryan.* —

WORTH AVENUE 5 ch.h. Busted 134–Lavenham Rose 85 (Floribunda 136) (1980 12f⁴ 15h⁴ 12d³ 1981 13s* 16g* 13fg* 14s⁴ 16d* 15.8g) staying handicapper; enjoyed a fine season, winning at Nottingham, Lingfield (twice) and Hamilton; acts on any going. *I. Walker.* **70**

WOT THE DICKINS 3 gr.g. Runnymede 123–Gardenia (Cagire II 122) (1980 7s⁴ 7g³ 1981 8d 7d 10.8fg 12fg) tall gelding; quite a moderate maiden; not disgraced over 1¼m in amateur riders handicap on final start. *S. Mellor.* —

WRIGHTWAY BLUES 3 b.f. Majority Blue 126–Kitty Wake (Milesian 125) (1980 6fg³ 6s³ 5d* 6d 5s 1981 5s 5d 5f 6s) sturdy filly; rather disappointing in 1981; off course 4 months before final start (blinkered); stays 6f; probably acts on any going. *B. Hanbury.* —

WRONG PAGE (USA) 3 br.c. Sir Ivor 135–Kateri (Pretense) (1980 6g 7g 7d² 8g 1981 11.7g 13.3d 12g² 10fg⁴ 11g* 11f* 10fg³ 12d* 14g 12g) fair sort; made most of running when winning maiden race at Newbury in July and small handicaps at Wolverhampton in August and Goodwood in September; battled on really well and held off White Saint by a head in last-named; stays 1½m (beaten a long way out over 1¾m); yet to race on very soft going, but acts on any other; has run creditably for an apprentice. *P. Cole.* **87**

WULTALK (USA) 2 gr.c. Quadrangle–Angkor Vat (Le Fabuleux 133) (1981 7g⁴ 7fg³ 8g³) Mar 16; $16,000F, 30,000 gns Y; neat, well-made colt; first produce; dam never ran; in frame in maiden races at Yarmouth (2) and Beverley, coming from a long way back on the turn when 5 lengths third of 15 behind Sagamore on latter course in September on third occasion; will be suited by middle distances. *H. Cecil.* **84**

WURLI 3 b.f. Wolver Hollow 126–Tanella 103 (Habitat 134) (1980 6g² 5g 7g 7g 6s³ 1981 7f 8f³ 8f⁴ 8.2f 7g) small, lightly-made filly; in frame in maiden and minor events at Thirsk; will stay 1¼m; sweating third start. *E. Weymes.* —

WYKE 3 b.g. No Mercy 126–Harvest Melody 103 (Tudor Minstrel 144) (1980 6g 1981 8g 8d 8s) workmanlike gelding; little worthwhile form in maiden and minor races; sold 1,200 gns Ascot November Sales. *R. Baker.* —

WYNBURRY 4 br.f. No Mercy 126–Lucinda Anne (Abernant 142) (1980 5f² 5f⁴ 5fg² 6f⁴ 5g² 5g 7g⁴ 6g 6g³ 6g⁴ 6f³ 6g 5f³ 5fg 5d² 5d 1981 5f 5g 5g) sprint handicapper; stays 6f; acts on any going; often blinkered; has sweated up; suitable mount for a boy. *E. Weymes.* —

WYNFIELD GILL 2 b.f. Maystreak 118–Rantzesther 66 (Bally Russe 113) (1981 8d) May 30; first foal; dam poor maiden; unquoted and in need of race when tenth of 11 to Misty Halo in maiden race at Wolverhampton in October. *D. McCain.* —

WYN MILUV 3 gr.f. Young Emperor 133–Bargy Music (Tudor Music 131) (1980 6d 6g 6fg* 7fg 6d* 6g 5d 6s 1981 5s 6g 7d 6v 5.3f 6fg 6fg 6g) neat filly; poor form in 1981, best effort in a seller on seventh start (blinkered first time); suited by 6f but probably doesn't get 7f; acts on a firm surface but put up best effort as a 2-y-o on a soft one; nearly unseated her rider when stumbling fifth outing. *R. Hannon.* 39

WYNNWITH RULER (USA) 2 b.g. Cannonade–Maui Maid (Kauai King) (1981 6g 7d) Mar 21; $26,000F, $50,000Y; good-bodied gelding; half-brother to 2 minor winners in USA; dam, from same family as Mrs Penny, won over 6t at 4 yrs; unquoted when last behind Solaboy in 9-runner Champagne Stakes at Salisbury in June and behind Loyal Toast in 14-runner minor event at Lingfield in August, on each occasion swerving violently 3f out; gelded subsequently. *N. Vigors.* —

WYNNWITH SOVEREIGN 3 br.g. Sovereign Path 125–Sheer Bliss 76 (St Paddy 133) (1980 6d 1981 7d 7.6g 8fg 10.1fg³ 10.1g⁴ 10f⁴ 11.1fg 12f) disappointing maiden; stays 1¼m; swerved badly leaving stalls second outing; sold to M. Hinchliffe 1,800 gns Ascot December Sales. *N. Vigors.* —

WYNNWITH STAR (USA) 2 b.c. Silent Screen–Finest Star (Pia Star) (1981 6g 7d) Apr 29; $40,000Y; first foal; dam twice-raced half-sister to stakes winner Kate's Intent, the dam of Godswalk; unquoted when well beaten in newcomers race at Goodwood in September and minor event (last) at Chepstow the following month. *N. Vigors.* —

WYTON BAR 3 b.g. Royal Palace 131–Swordblade 84 (Pall Mall 132) (1980 5d 5v 5g 5f³ 5g 6g 7g 5d 5f 8fg 1981 8s 8s* 10s 7v* 8g 6d 6g) unfurnished gelding; plater; won at Stockton (no bid) and Beverley in April, being awarded latter after finishing 7 lengths second to Vendibility as traces of an illegal substance were found in winner's system; stays 1m; acts on heavy going; has worn blinkers. *A. Smith.* 46

X

XANTHOS 3 b.g. Welsh Saint 126–Treat (High Treason 126) (1980 NR 1981 7s 8.2s 8.2d³ 10.6d 10.4s 8f 8.2f) 4,600F, 6,000Y; strong, sturdy gelding; poor mover; half-brother to French 7f and 1m winner Darling Dale (by Tyrant); dam Irish 6f winner; poor maiden; stays 1m; seems suited by give in the ground; sold out of B. Hills's stable 1,200 gns Newmarket May Sales. *D. Francis.* 52

XARFINA 4 b.f. High Line 125–Zugela 90 (Zucchero 133§) (1980 12fg 11f 13.3fg 12g* 13.1g³ 13.3d⁴ 14d* 1981 14fg 14d) strong, good-topped filly; fair performer at 3 yrs; needed run both starts in 1981; will stay beyond 1¾m; suited by some give in the ground; has run well for an apprentice; game; sold 2,400 gns Newmarket December Sales. *W. Wightman.* —

XENIA 3 b.f. High Line 125–Zugela 90 (Zucchero 133§) (1980 6d 7g 7g 8g 1981 12g 12s 12f³ 12d³ 12fg 12g 13.1g) lengthy filly; third in maiden races at Brighton in July and Lingfield in August; will be suited by 1¾m; slipped up sixth start. *W. Wightman.* 63

Y

YAMALCO 2 b.g. Nonoalco 131–Madina 119 (Beau Prince II 131) (1981 5g 5g 5d 5f 6fg 5f² 5fg 8.2d) May 9; compact gelding; good mover; brother to 69 very smart French miler Nonoalca, and half-brother to 2 winners, including very useful 1980 French 2-y-o 1m winner Riverdina (by Riverman); dam won Prix Morny; cost approximately £173,000 as a foal in France but is little better than a plater; probably stays 1m; weakened in final furlong on 4 of his last 5 outings; sold to BBA (probably for export to Italy) 2,300 gns Newmarket Autumn Sales. *F. Durr.*

YAMAMOTO 3 b.g. Deep Diver 134–Amber Goddess 50 (Yellow God 129) **56** (1980 NR 1981 7s 7fg 8g² 8g 8g* 10s 8d 7g) 1,500Y; quite a well-made gelding; first foal; dam ran 4 times; bought in 3,000 gns after beating Irrawaddy by 1½ lengths in seller at Ayr in May; stays 1m (not sure to stay 1¼m); blinkered last 4 outings; trained by P. Rohan first 5 starts (off course 4 months afterwards). *R. Hoad.*

YANKEE BALLAD 5 br.m. Mansingh 120–Dawn Songster (Primera 131) — (1980 NR 1981 12s) of little account; changed hands 1,050 gns Doncaster June Sales. *R. Hobson.*

YANKEE DOODLE DANDY 3 ch.g. Amber Rama 133–Virginia (Pirate King — 129) (1980 NR 1981 9.4fg 10fg 12d 14fg) brother to 1m and 9.4f winner Nun, and half-brother to a minor winner; dam lightly-raced sister to very useful stayer Avast; well beaten in minor and maiden events; sold 1,350 gns Doncaster November Sales. *C. Thornton.*

YARD BIRD 2 ch.c. Busted 134–Final Orders (Prince John) (1981 7g³ 10.2g*) **92 p** Apr 13; half-brother to several winners, including very useful middle-distance filly Tutu (by Ballymoss) and very useful stayer Hans Brinker (by Dike); dam ran only twice; favourite, following a promising debut, was always going well when winning 26-runner minor event at Doncaster in November by 2½ lengths from Twist Home; looks sure to make a useful stayer at 3 yrs. *B. Hobbs.*

YAT DING YAN 3 gr.f. Birdbrook 110–Edict 51 (Privy Councillor 125) — (1980 5fg 5f 5d 7f 5d 6s 1981 7g 8g 7f 10f 7f 6s) of no account. *R. Ward.*

YA ZAMAN (USA) 4 b.c. Gallant Man–Irish Exchange (Swaps) (1980 8s* **120** 8s 6.5s* 7g* 7s*(dis) 7d 7v⁴ 1981 10.5v* 10d 8g* 8f 12v⁴ 12s⁴) big colt; smart performer; won 70,000 francs event at Maisons-Laffitte in March and beat Daeltown readily by 2 lengths in Prix Messidor on same course in July; not disgraced most other starts, on penultimate occasion finishing fourth to easy winner Rahotep in Prix du Conseil de Paris at Longchamp in October; stays 1½m; acts well on soft going. *M. Saliba, France.*

YELED 3 br.g. Youth 135–Lalibela 123 (Honeyway 125) (1980 7f⁴ 7g 1981 8g **78** 10fg 10g 12s² 12d 12f⁴) big, lengthy gelding; in frame in minor event at Goodwood in May (wandered under pressure and finished 4 lengths second to Dogberry) and in King George V Stakes (Handicap) at Royal Ascot in June, having stiff task when about 2¼ lengths fourth of 14 behind Feltwell in latter; ran very badly at Epsom in between; stays 1½m; broke out of stalls and was unable to compete on second outing (under orders at time). *P. Kelleway.*

YELLOW ASH 2 ch.f. Roman Warrior 132–Hepash 81 (Henry the Seventh 125) — (1981 6f 6g) May 17; fifth foal; half-sister to 3-y-o 1m winner Zaccio (by Lorenzaccio); dam best at 1m; unquoted and burly when behind in sizeable fields of maidens; sold 340 gns Doncaster November Sales. *M. Camacho.*

YELLOW JERSEY 5 ch.g. Levmoss 133–Merta (Jaipur) (1980 16s³ 14fg³ **68** 16fg 14g* 16fg 16g² 14g 14s* 14g 1981 12fg 14d 14g³ 16s 14d⁴ 14g³ 16.1d⁴) lengthy gelding; not a particularly good mover; staying handicapper; very well suited by some give in the ground; suitable mount for an apprentice; blinkered last 2 starts; game; sold 1,900 gns Doncaster August Sales. *P. Cole.*

YIORGAKIS 4 ch.g. Amber Rama 133–Malpractice (Pall Mall 132) (1980 6d — 5v² 8s 5fg 5h 6fg 5fg 5s 1981 6s 7g 5fg) fair sort; poor handicapper; not certain to stay 1m; acts on heavy going; often blinkered; has run respectably for an apprentice. *G. Fletcher.*

YO-HO 2 b.g. Mansingh 120–Unclaimed Treasure 81 (Nice Guy 123) (1981 5s **64** 5fg 5f 6fg 5fg 7fg³ 7fg 8.2fg) Apr 25; 4,000Y; workmanlike gelding; brother to successful 7f to 1½m performer Manstrove and half-brother to 2 winners in Spain; plating-class maiden; suited by 7f (dwelt when tried over 1m); acts on firm going; blinkered nowadays. *J. Hardy.*

YOLANSO 5 ch.g. Lauso–Yolancar 65 (Kibenka 119) (1980 NR 1981 15.8g — 12g 14.6f 12f⁴ 13.8fg 12d 18g) plain gelding; poor performer; stays 1½m; acts on soft going. *P. Asquith.*

YOOHOO 7 ch.g. Mountain Call 125–Dreamy Idea 68 (Double Jump 131) **57**
(1980 6fg 5fg 5fg 5d⁴ 7g 5f* 6g⁴ 5s² 6f 6fg 1981 5s 6g 6d 6g 7g 5f 6f 5fg) sprint
handicapper; stays 6f; acts on any going; usually wears blinkers. *C. Booth.*

YORK COTTAGE 4 b.c. Royal Palace 131–Misnomer 85 (Milesian 125) —
(1980 12f* 12fg³ 12d* 12g² 14.6fg⁴ 12g* 14g 12f⁴ 12fg² 11s² 12g* 12v² 12.5s*
1981 12g³) quite attractive colt; won 5 times in varied company at 3 yrs;
not disgraced only start of 1981 in September; stays 1¾m; acts on any going;
usually blinkered; consistent; sold privately 10,000 gns Ascot December Sales.
N. Gaselee.

YORKSHIRE DANCER (USA) 4 b.c. Northern Fling–Spiral On (On-And-On) **71**
(1980 7d 6v³ 7d 6fg 6fg 6g 8fg² 8.2g² 8f 8fg³ 8d 8d 7s 7s 1981 7d 7g 7g 7fg
8.2f* 8f*(dis) 8fg* 8g 8.2d) small, robust colt; made all when first past post
in handicaps at Hamilton in August (trotted up) and Ripon (disqualified for
causing interference in first furlong) and Salisbury in September; stays 1m well;
probably acts on any going but goes well on fast ground; blinkered twice in
1980; suited by front-running tactics; sold 7,600 gns Newmarket Autumn Sales.
F. Durr.

YORKSHIRE SONG 2 b.c. Song 132–Audela 76 (Sovereign Path 125) (1981 **65**
5v 5g 5g⁴ 7f 5fg 5g 5v) Apr 26; 4,000Y; strong, compact colt; only plating
class; broke leg and was destroyed at Haydock in October. *Hbt Jones.*

YORK TERRACE 4 b.c. Derring-Do 131–Slipperty 99 (Hardicanute 130) —
(1980 8g⁴ 8fg⁴ 10.8s² 10.1f* 10f* 10.1g 10f 1981 12g 14g 11.7g) small, good
sort; won maiden event at Windsor and small race at Ripon in 1980; well beaten
all starts at 4 yrs; should stay 1⅜m; acts on any going. *D. Elsworth.*

YOUNG ATHENA 3 br.f. Young Emperor 133–Alea-Yacta (Javelot 124) —
(1980 6d 6d 6f 7g 1981 8d 12.2g 13g 12f 10fg 10f 9g⁴) small filly; plater;
stays 1¼m; wears blinkers; slowly away sixth start. *C. Booth.*

YOUNG COUSIN 3 ro.c. Streetfighter 120–Happiness (Right Boy 137) —
(1980 5.8fg 5s 5.8fg 5fg 6fg 5g⁴ 5d 1981 5s 7fg 6f 5.8f 7f) workmanlike colt; no
worthwhile form in 1981; best at 5f at 2 yrs. *M. Bradley.*

YOUNG CROFTIE 4 b.g. Sit In The Corner–Open Arms 77 (Dignitary 121) **49**
(1980 7s 7f 8f 7f³ 6fg⁴ 7fg 7.6g⁴ 6g² 6g 6f⁴ 7.6d 1981 6s 7d 8g 6g 6g 6g 6g² 8.2g
7h 6f) compact gelding; stays 7f; acts on firm going; effective with or without
blinkers. *R. Morris.*

YOUNG DAI 4 b.g. Streetfighter 120–Happiness (Right Boy 137) (1980 5s —
5fg 5fg 5g 5s 5fg² 5g 1981 5fg 5.8d 5fg 7g 11.7f) small gelding; sprint handicapper; acts on a firm surface; often blinkered. *M. Bradley.*

YOUNG DANIEL 3 b.c. Dragonara Palace 115–Pepperita 79 (Nelcius 133) **88**
(1980 6s 1981 7fg 8fg 10d 7fg* 7fg* 7fg* 7fg³ 8fg² 8f* 7f) well-made colt;
improved in summer, winning handicaps at Kempton (apprentices), Doncaster,
Newmarket and Yarmouth; beat Sister Kitty by a neck on last-named course;
suited by 1m; acts on firm going; genuine and consistent. *R. Armstrong.*

YOUNG IMPORT 3 ch.c. Import 127–Bishop's Song 67 (Bishop's Move 92) —
(1980 5g 7f 7d 1981 8s 8g 8g 8d 13.8g 12s) sturdy colt; little worthwhile
form, but didn't run in a seller; not certain to stay 1m; left at start third outing.
G. Lockerbie.

YOUNG INCA 3 gr.g. Young Emperor 133–Sunny Eyes (Reliance II 137) **65**
(1980 5d 1981 7fg 6g 7d 7g 6f 5.3f³ 6f² 6f 7f* 10.1fg 7g) leggy gelding; won
maiden race at Folkestone in August; stays 7f; acts on firm going; blinkered
nowadays; sold 2,400 gns Newmarket Autumn Sales. *R. Smyth.*

YOUNG KILDARE 3 b.c. Hotfoot 126–Vahine 72 (Umberto 118) (1980 **102**
6.3d² 7g 6.3g 1981 10d 10s 10d* 12v² 12fg) 13,000Y; quite an attractive
colt; half-brother to numerous winners, including very useful 1978 2-y-o 5f
to 7f winner Kingsbere (by Dragonara Palace) and smart Irish middle-distance
stayer Mr Kildare (by Hill Clown); dam won at up to 1¼m; 33/1, beat Erins Isle
(gave 9 lb) a neck in 14-runner Nijinsky Stakes at Leopardstown in May, getting
up in last 50 yards; went down by a length to same horse at levels in Gallinule
Stakes at the Curragh later in month; not seen out after finishing seventh of 12
behind Shergar in Irish Sweeps Derby at the Curragh again in June; stays
1½m; ran respectably in blinkers second outing. *L. Browne, Ireland.*

YOUNG OFFICER 2 br.g. Mandrake Major 122–Only Child 68 (Foggy Bell 108) **50**
(1981 5s 5g 5fg⁴ 5g⁴ 5fg 6f) Apr 19; compact gelding; second foal; dam 6f
winner; only poor form, including in sellers; ran badly in blinkers when tried
over 6f. *Denys Smith.*

YOUNG ROBIN 4 ch.g. High Line 125–Goldilocks II (Pinza 137) (1980 7f **51**
8fg 12g⁴ 12.2f 12g 1981 15.8s 16s 16g⁴ 15.8g⁴ 16f 17.4g 16.5g* 16.1s) leggy
non-thoroughbred gelding; won poor minor race at Redcar in September; stays
well; possibly suited by some give in the ground. *N. Crump.*

YOUNG ROYALIST (USA) 3 br.c. Youth 135–My Great Aunt (Bold Ruler) **56**
(1980 8d 1981 8s 8fg 11.7g 13fg 7f³ 7f⁴ 8fg) leggy, lightly-made colt; plating-
class maiden; should stay middle distances; sold to G. Lockerbie 1,600 gns
Newmarket Autumn Sales. *P. Cole.*

YOUR MAN 2 ch.c. Vitiges 132–Mary Connor 99 (Royal Avenue 123) (1981 6g —
5f) Apr 26; 7,200F; half-brother to 3-y-o 9f winner Blakenor (by Blakeney)
and a winner in Trinidad; dam won 4 times over 1m; remote eighth in maiden
races at Windsor in August and Folkestone in September; needs further than 5f;
sold to BBA 1,000 gns Newmarket Autumn Sales. *F. Durr.*

YULE LOG 9 b.g. Firestreak 125–Christmas 86 (Santa Claus 133) (1980 NR —
1981 16s 16d) staying handicapper; has worn blinkers; bandaged nowadays.
D. Wintle.

YUM YUM PRINCE 4 b.g. English Prince 129–Yum Yum Girl (Sailor) —
(1980 10f⁴ 12f 12f 10g³ 11g² 14g 13g 13d 1981 12.5s 12s 10g 8f 11f 10f 12.2fg)
workmanlike ex-Irish gelding; plating-class maiden; stays 11f; has run respectably for an apprentice; blinkered nowadays. *G. Lockerbie.*

Z

ZACCIO 3 ch.c. Lorenzaccio 130–Hepash 81 (Henry the Seventh 125) (1980 **63**
5.8g 7fg⁴ 7g⁴ 8d³ 10.2s 1981 10s 12fg 7g 8g⁴ 8f* 10f² 10f² 8.3fg 8h 8fg 8f)
quite an attractive colt; won claimer at Brighton in June by ½ length from
The Azadstan, leading close home; unplaced in sellers twice; stays 1¼m; has run
creditably on a soft surface but seems well suited by firm going; blinkered
third start; sold to D. Grissell 5,000 gns Newmarket Autumn Sales. *J. Bethell.*

ZAHAROFF 6 b.h. Wolver Hollow 126–Morinda 87 (Matador 131) (1980 —
6g 5fg 6fg³ 6h³ 6g 5.8f³ 6fg 5f 7fg 8g 5fg 1981 5fg 5f 5fg) strong, useful
sort; poor handicapper nowadays; stays 1m; acts on hard going; occasionally
wears blinkers; inconsistent; sold 250 gns Ascot November Sales. *M. Bradley.*

ZAKUSHKI 4 br.f. Royal Palace 131–Kushi 65 (Paridel 112) (1980 12d —
1981 12f) small, lightly-made filly; tailed-off last in 2 maiden races. *J. Jenkins.*

ZAMANDRA 6 b.m. Foggy Bell 108–Zamanda (Amber X 133) (1980 NR **39**
1981 16fg 16.5fg³) poor maiden on flat though has won over hurdles. *J.
Fitzgerald.*

ZANUBIA 2 ch.f. Nonoalco 131–Russian Princess 99 (Henry the Seventh 125) — p
(1981 6s) Mar 21; 25,000Y; rangy filly; half-sister to numerous winners,
including good French middle-distance stayer Paddy's Princess (by St Paddy);
dam, half-sister to Connaught, won over 6f at 2 yrs; unquoted, showed up quite
well until 2f out when eighth of 12 to Dancing Rocks in Blue Seal Stakes at Ascot
in September; will be suited by 1m; will probably do better. *J. Winter.*

ZARATUNE 3 b.f. Badedas 81–Petune (Cheetah Peter 87) (1980 NR 1981 —
9d 8fg 16.9s) neat filly; second known foal; dam never ran; slow maiden.
J. Edmunds.

ZAYNALA 2 gr.f. Habat 127–Zaheen (Silver Shark 129) (1981 6d²) May 5; **88** p
second foal; dam, half-sister to top-class Zeddaan, won over 5f at 2 yrs in France;
second favourite, went down by ½ length to Dalmally in 23-runner maiden race
at Leicester in November, having made a lot of the running; may stay 7f; a
pleasing first effort. *M. Stoute.*

ZEBRA CROSSING 6 br.g. Pals Passage 115–Jungle Law 67 (Martial 131) —
(1980 9f 1981 20.4fg 12f 15g) useless and probably temperamental; has
worn blinkers and a hood; has worn bandages; trained by J. S. Wilson part of
season. *W. H. H. Williams.*

ZEDATIVE (FR) 4 gr.f. Zeddaan 130–Noble Native 88 (Indigenous 121) (1980 **60**
5fg³ 5fg* 5g³ 5s³ 5fg 5d 5d 1981 5s 5fg 5g³ 5g 5g) useful-looking filly; sprint
handicapper; only just stays 5f; probably acts on any going. *C. Austin.*

ZELDABEC 4 b.f. Saulingo 122–African Dawn 72 (Chanteur II 135) (1980 —
7f 8fg 7fg 8g 1981 10d 10fg 7g 6fg) neat filly; bad plater; has worn blinkers.
Hbt Jones.

ZEPHYROS 4 b.c. Auction Ring 123–Miss Stephen (Stephen Paul 131) (1980 — 5f² 6f* 6fg² 5g² 6g 7g 1981 6d 6g 6d 5fg 5fg 6fg) small, quite well-made colt; fair sprinter at his best but became thoroughly unreliable; wore blinkers; sold out of G. Pritchard-Gordon's stable 5,000 gns Doncaster January (81) Sales; dead. *H. Bell.*

ZEPHYR'S PRIDE 2 br.c. Runnymede 123–Sea Daisy 90 (Mossborough 126) **64** (1981 5s³ 5s³ 5v* 5g³ 5g 7fg 6fg 6fg 6s 6s) May 2; 2,400F, 3,000Y; fair sort; good mover; third foal; dam won over 10.4f; had field well strung out when winning 16-runner maiden auction event at Beverley in April; didn't show much worthwhile form subsequently, including in selling company; should stay beyond 5f; evidently needs plenty of give in the ground; ran too freely when blinkered ninth outing; sold to BBA 460 gns Newmarket Autumn Sales. *K. Ivory.*

ZERO READER 2 ch.f. Track Spare 125–Harvest Reap (Majority Blue 126) — (1981 5s 7g) Mar 13; first foal; dam of little account; backward when last in maiden races at Lingfield and Leicester in October. *R. Akehurst.*

ZERXES 3 b.g. Targowice 130–High Command (High Hat 131) (1980 5f 5fg — 6g⁴ 6f³ 7g 1981 6fg 8g 8f 6fg 6g 7fg 7g) neat gelding; quite a moderate maiden on the balance of his form; sweated quite badly when unplaced in a seller final start; probably stays 7f; has been tried in blinkers and also in a hood. *R. Armstrong.*

ZHUKOV 2 br.c. Malinowski 123–Star Set (Sunny Way 120) (1981 5g 5fg 7.6s) — Apr 7; IR 4,500Y; small colt; half-brother to 3 winners, including 1979 2-y-o sprinter Rosette (by Red Alert); dam never ran; unquoted when in rear in maiden races; blinkered third outing. *C. James.*

ZILOS 2 b.c. Grundy 137–Sandarey 94 (Darius 129) (1981 6d* 6fg 7g* 8s) **108** Apr 3; 15,000Y; big, well-made colt; half-brother to numerous winners, in-

The Exors of the late Mr G. L. Cambanis' "Zilos"

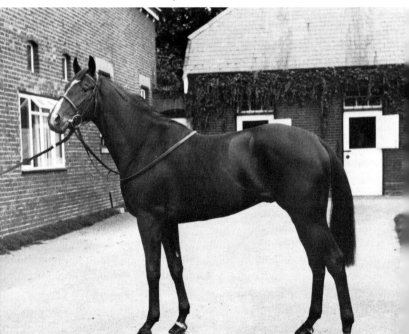

cluding quite useful 7f to 1¼m winner Sousa (by March Past); dam won at 1m and 11f; won 24-runner maiden race at Newbury in June by a neck from strong-finishing Busaco and stayed on well to beat Telephone Man by ½ length in 7-runner Seaton Delaval Stakes at Newcastle in August; stayed on in straight without threatening principals when about 10 lengths fifth of 9 to Norwick in Royal Lodge Stakes at Ascot in September; last of 11 to End of the Line in Anglia Television July Stakes at Newmarket on only other start (didn't stride out on firmish ground); will stay 1½m; suited by some give in the ground. *B. Hobbs.*

ZINO 2 b.c. Welsh Pageant 132–Cyriana (Salvo 129) (1981 5.5g² 7s* 7f* 7s² 7v*) **123**

There was a time when the Criterium de Maisons-Laffitte was as prolific a source of future classic winners as almost any race in France. In a ten-year period from 1962 to 1971 it featured two Derby winners, Relko and Sea-Bird II, a St Leger winner Athens Wood, an Irish Sweeps Derby winner Steel Pulse, three Poule d'Essai des Pouliches winners, Gazala, Pola Bella and Mata Hari, two Prix de Diane winners, Blabla and Gazala, a Prix du Jockey-Club winner Astec, a Grand Prix de Paris winner Danseur, a Poule d'Essai des Poulains winner Riverman and a disqualified Poulains winner, Faraway Son. A most impressive list. However, in more recent years, since the introduction of graded pattern races, the Group 2 Maisons-Laffitte race seems to have lost ground to the Prix de la Salamandre, a Group 1 event run over the same distance earlier in September. Because of its earlier place in the Calendar the Salamandre provided a more suitable stepping stone to the Grand Criterium but in 1981 the French authorities made a move which may restore the Criterium de Maisons-Laffitte to its former competitiveness: they switched it from late-September to the end of October, in effect giving it the place in the Calendar previously held by the Prix Thomas Bryon, a race which has also frequently proved an excellent guide in the past. In 1981 the Thomas Bryon seemed to suffer because of its new position in the Calendar, just a day after the Grand Criterium, drawing only six runners, whereas the Criterium de Maisons-Laffitte attracted a promising field of ten. Among the ten were the Grand Criterium third Rollins; Majestic Guard, close up when in the frame in two previous pattern races; Honeyland, an improving Alec Head-trained colt; the English challenger Telephone Man; and the well-bred, once-raced winners Kastiliya and Oral Agreement. Favourite though was Zino, an odds-on shot on the strength of his excellent second to Green Forest in the Prix de la Salamandre, and he proved much too good for the others. Telephone Man, wearing blinkers for the first time, raced freely in the lead for much of the way, chased by Honeyland and Zino, but once Zino challenged below the distance the race was as good as over: he forged steadily clear in the heavy ground to beat the English colt two lengths, providing his trainer with his fourth successive win in the race (Boutin also trained the disqualified 1977 winner Cosmopolitan). Honeyland, who'd also headed Telephone Man at one stage, faded again to finish a length behind in third place. Neither Rollins nor Majestic Guard managed to land a blow, receiving beatings of six lengths and seven lengths respectively. Considering that Zino was conceding upwards of 4 lb all round this was a very smart display.

Zino had also started an odds-on favourite for the Prix de la Salamandre at Longchamp in September even though opposed by the Prix Morny winner Green Forest. The support for him stemmed from very impressive displays in the summer in a maiden race at Chantilly, where he'd sprinted clear to win by five lengths from Ypsilon, and in the fairly valuable Criterium de Bernay at Deauville, where those useful colts Academic, Rout Order and Trigonome had been unable to prevent his landing the odds by the same margin. Early in the straight at Longchamp Zino looked likely to win again. After making the running he still seemed to be coasting on the bridle but he couldn't quicken when Green Forest challenged coming to the distance and was worn down inside the final furlong, eventually crossing the line a length and a half behind.

Although Mr Oldham's Citadel Stud now numbers fewer than a dozen broodmares, scarcely a season goes by without its producing at least one major winner: Stintino, Ormindo, Sagaro, Antrona, Pevero, Tarona, Scorpio and Corvaro all won important races in the 'seventies. Zino, also home bred, is related to two of these: his dam Cyriana, who was third over a mile and a quarter in France, is a half-sister to Stintino, winner of the Prix Lupin and third in the Derby, and to Ormindo, winner of both the Chester Vase and Ormonde Stakes. Cyriana is also a full sister to Tempio, a smart colt who finished a close fifth in the 1973 Prix du Jockey-Club. Zino is her third winner from her first three foals, following the 1979 French two-year-old nine-furlong winner Sargo (by

Criterium de Maisons-Laffitte—the blinkered Telephone Man stays on past Honeyland for second place to Zino

Caracolero) and Livorno (by Satingo), a winner over seven furlongs at two in Ireland in 1980.   Cyriana's parents, the top-class middle-distance horse Salvo and the very smart five-furlong performer Cynara, also raced in the Oldham colours and, keeping it a family concern, Cyriana's next foal, Leventina, is a yearling filly by Sagaro; she was covered in 1981 by Scorpio.

		⎰Tudor Melody	⎰Tudor Minstrel
	⎰Welsh Pageant	(br 1956)	⎱Matelda
	(b 1966)	⎱Picture Light	⎰Court Martial
Zino	⎱	(b 1954)	⎱Queen of Light
(b.c. Apr 26, 1979)	⎰	⎰Salvo	⎰Right Royal V
	⎱Cyriana	(ch 1963)	⎱Manera
	(gr 1972)	⎱Cynara	⎰Grey Sovereign
		(gr 1958)	⎱Ladycroft

Zino is a tall, good-looking colt who walks well.   His trainer said at the time of his Maisons-Laffitte victory that Zino was still growing a lot and that he believed he hadn't finished improving.   Zino's form at two was good enough to earn him second place in the French Free Handicap, 5 lb behind Green Forest, so he needs only to make slightly more than normal improvement to put himself bang in the classic picture.   He'll stay a mile and a quarter, possibly a mile and a half, and has already shown he acts on any going.   *F. Boutin, France.*

ZINZARA (USA) 2 b.f. Stage Door Johnny–Old Gypsy (Olden Times) (1981 **109** 6g* 8fg³ 7g)   Mar 24; $46,000F; very attractive filly; good mover; fourth produce; half-sister to 2 minor winners; dam minor stakes winner at up to 1m; showed excellent speed for a filly of her breeding when favourite for 19-runner newcomers event at Goodwood in September, making all to win by 3 lengths from Risk Taker; good length third of 8 to Height of Fashion in Hoover Fillies

962

Mile at Ascot later in month (received 4 lb from first 2) but seemed to find 7f too sharp in a slowly-run race when 4½ lengths fifth of 8 to Top Hope in Rockfel Stakes at Newmarket in October; bred to stay middle distances; useful. *H. Wragg.*

ZIPARIB 3 ch.c. Ribston 104–Zaraspar 70 (Zarathustra 131) (1980 5v³ 5f² 5f* 6fg² 6g 7g 7g 1981 9.4g⁴ 9s 12g 10f 13.8fg 12f 13fg 8d) strong colt; disqualified after finishing second in handicap at Carlisle in May; well beaten afterwards; stays 9f; sold to O. Brennan 2,400 gns Doncaster November Sales. *W. Elsey.*   67 d

ZIRCON'S SUN 2 b.c. Roi Soleil 125–Zircon (Pall Mall 132) (1981 6fg 7fg 7f 8d) Apr 27; lightly-made colt; third living foal; dam ran once; unquoted when behind in minor and maiden events. *R. Laing.*   —

ZOBO 4 ch.c. Welsh Pageant 132–Babanina (Bleep-Bleep 134) (1980 7s 7fg 7fg 12fg 8g³ 8d 9.4fg 8.2s 1981 8v 11d 5g 6g 10.1d 10d) workmanlike colt; plater; best run at 1m; sold 510 gns Doncaster May Sales. *R. Hollinshead.*   —

ZOILO 3 b.c. Workboy 123–L'Elita 83 (Porto Bello 118) (1980 5f 5g 5f⁴ 5g* 5s 1981 5s 5f 5f 5fg 5fg 6f 5fg² 5fg 5g³ 5g) big, strong colt; not disgraced in handicaps on occasions and was placed at Redcar in September and Catterick in October; unlikely to stay 6f; probably not at his best on soft going; usually bandaged in front nowadays; sometimes blinkered. *M. W. Easterby.*   72

ZORO 6 ch.g. Cavo Doro 124–Camina Bay 109 (Whistling Wind 123) (1980 12fg 11.1fg 10f⁴ 10s 10g* 10g² 11.7g* 12fg 10g 12fg 12g 1981 12.2d 10fg 12d² 12g 10v 12d⁴ 10d 10f 10fg² 12f² 16.5g 11.7fg 12f 16d 12f 12fg) moody and unreliable middle-distance handicapper; twice second in sellers in July; acts on any going; sometimes blinkered and refused to race in them on eleventh outing; inclined to put head in air under pressure and is not an easy ride. *A. Ingham.*   59 §

Sir Philip Oppenheimer's "Zinzara"

ZOS

ZOSTERA MARINA 2 b.f. Tudor Rhythm 112–Swannery 94 (My Swanee 122) **63**
(1981 6f 6d 6g 7f*) Feb 17; smallish, plain filly; third foal; sister to useful 1979
2-y-o 6f winner Atlantic City; dam 2-y-o 5f winner; ran best race when winning
by ½ length from Parre Tria in 18-runner seller at Chepstow in September (sold
to D. Wintle 1,250 gns at subsequent auction); suited by 7f; badly hampered third
outing. *P. Walwyn.*

ZUHUR 3 b. or br.f. Reform 132–Vivante 87 (Bold Lad, Ire 133) (1980 5g **63**
1981 5g² 6g 6f⁴ 7f³ 6f* 6f) neat filly; good walker; made all in handicap at
Folkestone in August; bred to stay 1m; acts on firm going; sometimes sweats
up. *A. Hide.*

ZULAIKA HOPWOOD 3 b.f. Royalty 130–Zulaika 75 (Worden II 129) **72**
(1980 NR 1981 8g 10.2g⁴ 12f* 14g 12g 12d) tall, leggy, rather unfurnished filly;
half-sister to 2 winners, including quite useful 1971 2-y-o 7f and 1m winner
Crawter (by Track Spare); dam won at 1½m; readily beat Java Lights by 2 lengths
(pair clear) in 15-runner minor event at Leicester in June; ran moderately
afterwards; suited by 1½m (had stiffish task and was always behind over 1¾m).
W. Holden.

ZULU WARRIOR 2 ch.g. Cawston's Clown 113–Miss Taurus 79 (Bullrush 106) —
(1981 5d⁴ 6fg 6d 7.2v) Feb 14; workmanlike gelding; fifth foal; closely related
to 4 poor animals; dam sprinter; 33/1 when about 4½ lengths fourth of 8 to
Balcanoona in maiden race at Leicester in April; not seen out again until
September and was soundly beaten in varied company, including selling.
A. W. Jones.

TIMEFORM
CHAMPIONS OF 1981

HORSE OF THE YEAR (RATED AT 140)
SHERGAR
3 b.c. Great Nephew–Sharmeen (Val de Loir)
Owner H. H. Aga Khan   *Trainer* M. Stoute

BEST TWO-YEAR-OLD COLT (RATED AT 132)
WIND and WUTHERING (USA)
2 br.c. No Robbery–J. A's Joy (Johns Joy)
Owner Mr R. M. Cyzer   *Trainer* H. Candy

BEST TWO-YEAR-OLD FILLY (RATED AT 122)
CIRCUS RING
2 b.f. High Top–Bell Song (Tudor Melody)
Owner Snailwell Stud Company   *Trainer* M. Stoute

BEST SPRINTER (RATED AT 133)
MARWELL
3 b.f. Habitat–Lady Seymour (Tudor Melody)
Owner Mr E. J. Loder   *Trainer* M. Stoute

BEST MILER (RATED AT 136)
NORTHJET
4 ch.c Northfields–Jellatina (Fortino II)
Owner Mr S. Fradkoff   *Trainer* O. Douieb

BEST MIDDLE-DISTANCE HORSE (RATED AT 140)
SHERGAR
3 b.c Great Nephew–Sharmeen (Val de Loir)
Owner H. H. Aga Khan   *Trainer* M. Stoute

BEST STAYER (RATED AT 131)
ARDROSS
5 b.h. Run The Gantlet–Le Melody (Levmoss)
Owner Mr C. A. B. St George   *Trainer* H. Cecil

1981 STATISTICS

The following tables show the leading owners, trainers, breeders, jockeys, horses and the sires of winners during the 1981 season. Except for the list of sires, which relates to racing in both Great Britain and Ireland, the statistics refer only to racing under Jockey Club Rules. Some of the tables are reproduced by permission of *The Sporting Life*.

OWNERS

	Horses	Races Won	Stakes £
1. H. H. Aga Khan	12	22	441,655
2. R. Sangster	38	60	313,403
3. R. Barnett	4	11	199,175
4. C. A. B. St George	10	21	157,413
5. Mrs A. Muinos	2	7	141,326
6. A. Kelly	2	4	133,617
7. H. J. Joel	7	13	105,302
8. Sir P. Oppenheimer	8	14	96,259
9. D. Wildenstein	11	20	94,161
10. E. Loder	2	5	89,824
11. Mrs B. Firestone	3	3	89,282
12. Sir J. Astor	2	3	87,747

TRAINERS

	Horses	Races Won	Stakes £
1. M. Stoute	53	95	723,785
2. H. Cecil	52	107	588,358
3. G. Harwood	50	97	489,551
4. R. Hern	41	64	342,924
5. H. Candy	13	30	289,754
6. J. Dunlop	39	67	254,817
7. B. Hills	51	82	253,134
8. B. Hobbs	28	50	242,079
9. M. Jarvis	22	35	227,358
10. H. Wragg	21	37	182,805
11. C. Brittain	37	54	167,720
12. V. O'Brien	8	8	166,992

BREEDERS

	Horses	Races Won	Stakes £
1. H. H. Aga Khan	13	23	445,368
2. W. and R. Barnett	4	11	199,175
3. W. L. Jones, Jnr	3	8	140,903
4. Rathduff Stud	4	7	131,308
5. The late P. J. Prendergast	2	5	117,639
6. H. J. Joel	6	11	113,737
7. E. J. Loder	5	12	112,472
8. Swettenham Stud	11	13	89,111
9. Sir J. Astor	2	3	87,747
10. P. Mellon	11	18	78,859
11. Hascombe and Valiant Studs	9	14	77,415
12. Miss E. B. C. Laidlaw	2	2	76,284

		JOCKEYS				Total	Per
		1st	2nd	3rd	Unpl	Mts	Cent
1.	L. Piggott.. ..	179	113	87	324	703	25·46
2.	W. Carson ..	114	82	75	305	576	19·79
3.	P. Eddery.. ..	108	96	69	373	646	16·71
4.	E. Hide	105	85	85	410	685	15·32
5.	G. Duffield ..	94	78	78	443	693	13·56
6.	G. Starkey ..	90	85	61	292	528	17·04
7.	S. Cauthen ..	87	85	75	369	616	14·12
8.	P. Cook	83	66	66	335	550	15·09
9.	B. Raymond ..	73	60	69	432	634	11·51
10.	J. Lowe	69	49	58	473	649	10·63
11.	W. R. Swinburn ..	65	50	58	310	483	13·45
12.	B. Rouse	65	83	74	443	665	9·77

	HORSES	Races	Stakes
		Won	£
1.	Shergar (3 yrs) b.c. Great Nephew—Sharmeen	4	295,644
2.	Master Willie (4 yrs) ch.c. High Line—Fair Winter	3	149,424
3.	Beldale Flutter (3 yrs) b.c. Accipiter—Flitter Flutter	2	129,052
4.	To-Agori-Mou (3 yrs) b.c. Tudor Music—Sarah Van Fleet	4	127,949
5.	Ardross (5 yrs) b.h. Run The Gantlet—Le Melody	4	103,974
6.	Marwell (3 yrs) b.f. Habitat—Lady Seymour	4	88,973
7.	Cut Above (3 yrs) b.c. High Top—Cutle ..	2	86,483
8.	Blue Wind (3 yrs) ch.f. Lord Gayle— Azurine	1	74,568
9.	Vayrann (3 yrs) br.c Brigadier Gerrard—Val Divine	1	66,732
10.	Condessa (3 yrs) ch.f. Condorcet—Varinessa	2	66,126
11.	Wind And Wuthering (2 yrs) b.c. No Robbery—J.A.'s Joy	4	65,247
12.	Fairy Footsteps (3 yrs) b.f. Mill Reef—Glass Slipper	2	61,818

	SIRES OF WINNERS		Races	Stakes
		Horses	Won	£
1.	Great Nephew (1963), by Honeyway	12	23	468,253
2.	Habitat (1966), by Sir Gaylord ..	35	64	369,711
3.	High Line (1966), by High Hat ..	9	21	222,086
4.	Bustino (1971), by Busted ..	29	54	208,559
5.	High Top (1969), by Derring-Do..	18	37	202,312
6.	Hotfoot (1966), by Firestreak ..	24	45	163,352
7.	Lord Gayle (1965), by Sir Gaylord	17	27	161,997
8.	Nijinsky (1967), by Northern Dancer	9	15	148,899
9.	Tudor Music (1966), by Tudor Melody	11	18	147,750
10.	Brigadier Gerrard (1968), by Queen's Hussar	14	20	132,613
11.	Accipiter (1971), by Damascus ..	1	2	129,052
12.	Mummy's Pet (1968), by Sing Sing	24	38	124,387

AN INTERNATIONAL CLASSIFICATION 1981

The following ratings for horses which ran in France, Great Britain or Ireland were allotted jointly by the official Handicappers concerned and published on 3rd December. The rating given to each horse represents the official assessment of its merit against a norm of 100.

TWO-YEAR-OLDS, 1981

Green Forest ..	88	Hays	79	Full Extent ..	76
Wind And Wuthering ..	85	Height Of Fashion ..	79	Silver Hawk ..	76
Count Pahlen ..	84	Lucky Hunter ..	79	Travel On ..	76
Jalmood ..	83	Play It Safe ..	79	Assert	75
Paradis Terrestre ..	83	Wattlefield ..	79	Bright View ..	75
Sandhurst Prince ..	83	Be My Native ..	78	Chellaston Park	75
Zino	83	Montekin ..	78	Codrington ..	75
Achieved ..	82	River Lady ..	78	Coussika ..	75
Cajun	81	Stratospheric ..	78	Dom Donizetti	75
Maelstrom Lake	81	Tender King ..	78	End Of The Line	75
Norwick	81	Glancing ..	77	Fearless Lad ..	75
Bon Sang	80	Peterhof (USA)	77	Jester	75
Sharp Singer ..	80	Top Hope ..	77	Melyno.. ..	75
Anfield..	79	Woodstream ..	77	Pas de Seul ..	75
Circus Ring ..	79	Americus ..	76	Persepolis ..	75
		Custer	76	Super Sunrise ..	75
		Day Is Done ..	76	Treboro ..	75

THREE-YEAR-OLDS, 1981

Shergar ..	100	Kirtling ..	86	Amyndas ..	81
Bikala	91	Bustomi ..	84	Cresta Rider ..	81
Cut Above ..	90	Condessa ..	84	Fairy Footsteps	81
Marwell ..	90	Critique ..	84	Home On The Range ..	81
Akarad ..	88	Phydilla ..	84	Star Pastures ..	81
April Run ..	88	Rahotep ..	84	Ukraine Girl ..	81
Beldale Flutter	88	Recitation ..	84	Belted Earl ..	80
Kings Lake ..	88	Bellman ..	83	Go Leasing ..	80
To-Agori-Mou	88	Leandra ..	83	Sonoma ..	80
Vayrann ..	88	Madam Gay ..	83	Tolmi	80
Glint Of Gold..	87	Al Nasr (Fr) ..	82	Votre Altesse ..	80
The Wonder ..	87	Erins Isle ..	82		
Blue Wind ..	86	Tipperary Fixer	82		

FOUR-YEAR-OLDS AND UPWARDS, 1981

Northjet ..	92	Rabdan.. ..	86	Last Fandango	81
Moorestyle ..	91	Hard Fought ..	85	Nicholas Bill ..	81
Ardross ..	90	Pelerin	85	Vielle	81
Gold River ..	90	Belmont Bay ..	84	Armistice Day..	80
Sharpo	90	Dalsaan ..	84	Fingal's Cave ..	80
Light Cavalry ..	89	Detroit	83	Glenorum ..	80
Hilal	87	Runnett ..	83	Katowice ..	80
Perrault ..	87	Crews Hill ..	82	Kelbomec ..	80
Argument ..	86	Lancastrian ..	82	Nemr	80
Master Willie ..	86	Cairn Rouge ..	81		

THE FREE HANDICAPS

TWO-YEAR-OLDS OF 1981

The following are the weights allotted in the Tote European Free Handicap published on 3rd December. The race is to be run over seven furlongs at Newmarket on 14th April, 1982.

Horse	st	lb
Green Forest ..	9	7
Wind and Wuthering ..	9	4
Count Pahlen ..	9	3
Jalmood ..	9	2
Paradis Terrestre	9	2
Sandhurst Prince	9	2
Zino ..	9	2
Achieved ..	9	1
Cajun ..	9	0
Maelstrom Lake	9	0
Norwick ..	8	13
Bon Sang ..	8	13
Sharp Singer ..	8	13
Anfield ..	8	12
Circus Ring ..	8	12
Hays ..	8	12
Height of Fashion	8	12
Lucky Hunter ..	8	12
Play It Safe ..	8	12
Wattlefield ..	8	12
Be My Native ..	8	11
Montekin ..	8	11
River Lady ..	8	11
Stratospheric ..	8	11
Tender King ..	8	11
Glancing ..	8	10
Peterhof (USA) ..	8	10
Top Hope ..	8	10
Woodstream ..	8	10
Americus ..	8	9
Custer ..	8	9
Day Is Done ..	8	9
Full Extent ..	8	9
Silver Hawk ..	8	9
Travel On ..	8	9
Assert ..	8	8
Bright View ..	8	8
Chellaston Park	8	8
Codrington ..	8	8
Coussika ..	8	8
Dom Donizetti	8	8
End of the Line	8	8
Fearless Lad ..	8	8
Jester ..	8	8
Melyno..	8	8
Pas de Seul ..	8	8
Persepolis ..	8	8
Super Sunrise ..	8	8
Treboro ..	8	8
Ashenden ..	8	7
Beldale Bid ..	8	7
Chulia Street ..	8	7
Clare Island ..	8	7
Ivano ..	8	7
Last Feather ..	8	7
Lobkowicz ..	8	7
On The House..	8	7
Prima Voce ..	8	7
Red Sunset ..	8	7
Simply Great ..	8	7
Solaboy ..	8	7
Warm Hearted	8	7
Born Hero ..	8	6
Macmillion ..	8	6
Merlins Charm	8	6
My Dad Tom ..	8	6
Not For Show ..	8	6
Telephone Man	8	6
Zilos ..	8	6
Zinzara ..	8	6
Busaco ..	8	5
Chris's Lad ..	8	5
Lyphmas ..	8	5
My Lover ..	8	5
Paternoster Row	8	5
Rebollino ..	8	5
Admiral's Princess ..	8	4
Dancing Rocks	8	4
Foam Bath ..	8	4
Incandesce ..	8	4
Janndar ..	8	4
Match Winner	8	4
Nioulargo ..	8	4
Prowess Prince	8	4
Slightly Dangerous ..	8	4
Take The Floor	8	4
The Dinmont ..	8	4
Triple Axel ..	8	4
Vaigly Star ..	8	4
Alvor ..	8	3
Farioffa	8	3
Gouverno ..	8	3
Mirabeau ..	8	3
Mydrone ..	8	3
Bancario ..	8	2
El Mansour ..	8	2
Padalco..	8	2
Skytrick ..	8	2
Vin St. Benet ..	8	2
Baltimore Belle	8	1
Bless The Match	8	1
Dawn Ditty ..	8	1
Fol Hardi ..	8	1
Kiva ..	8	1
Mummy's Game	8	1
Old Country ..	8	1
Risk ..	8	1
Rosananti ..	8	1
Santella Man ..	8	1
Awaasif ..	8	0
Be Be of Kuwait	8	0
Candide ..	8	0
Come On The Blues ..	8	0
Dageegah ..	8	0
Fimi ..	8	0
Fly Baby ..	8	0
French Gent ..	8	0
Hollywood Party	8	0
Lavender Dance	8	0
Marquessa D'Howfen ..	8	0
Match Master ..	8	0
Never Talk ..	8	0
Rockfest ..	8	0
Swift Wing ..	8	0
Torrey ..	8	0
Tropical Blaze ..	8	0
Welsh Partner ..	8	0
Apples of Gold	7	13
General Anders	7	13
Knave of Trumps ..	7	13
Realms Reason	7	13
Sharlie's Wimpy	7	13
Silojoka ..	7	13
Steel Stockholder ..	7	13
Wink ..	7	13
Allocated ..	7	12
Bold Fort ..	7	12
Corley Moor ..	7	12
Devon Air ..	7	12
Hampton Bay ..	7	12
I'm Hot ..	7	12
Jump Jar ..	7	12
My Dear Fellow	7	12
Risk Taker ..	7	12
Sabutai ..	7	12
Singing Sailor ..	7	12

THREE-YEAR-OLDS OF 1981

The following handicap, published on 3rd December, is for information only. The figures shown against each horse represent the official assessment of its merit against a norm of 100.

Horse	Rating	st	lb
Shergar	100	10	0
Cut Above	90	9	4
Marwell	90	9	4
Beldale Flutter	88	9	2
Kings Lake	88	9	2
To-Agori-Mou	88	9	2
Vayrann	88	9	2

Glint of Gold	87	9	1	Church				Rhein Bridge	66	7	8
Blue Wind	86	9	0	Parade	75	8	3	Salora Lady	66	7	8
Kirtling	86	9	0	Shotgun	75	8	3	Six Mile			
Bustomi	84	8	12	Boathouse	74	8	2	Bottom	66	7	8
Condessa	84	8	12	Dalby				Spindrifter	66	7	8
Critique	84	8	12	Mustang	74	8	2	Ackermann	65	7	7
Recitation	84	8	12	Fabulous Salt	74	8	2	Bedford	65	7	7
Madam Gay	83	8	11	Leah	74	8	2	Full of Reason	65	7	7
Amyndas	81	8	9	Leap Lively	74	8	2	Indian King	65	7	7
Fairy Foot-				Fiesta Fun	73	8	1	Petroleuse	65	7	7
steps	81	8	9	Cut Throat	72	8	0	Rollrights	65	7	7
Home On The				Kittyhawk	72	8	0	Royal Realm	65	7	7
Range	81	8	9	Robellino	72	8	0	Sweet			
Star Pastures	81	8	9	The Quiet				Monday	65	7	7
Belted Earl	80	8	8	Bidder	72	8	0	Fee	64	7	6
Go Leasing	80	8	8	Viendra	72	8	0	Ore	64	7	6
Sonoma	80	8	8	Centroline	71	7	13	Piperhill	64	7	6
Tolmi	80	8	8	Kalaglow	71	7	13	Sheer Grit	64	7	6
Happy Bride	79	8	7	Rasa Penang	71	7	13	Taher	64	7	6
Motavato	79	8	7	Another				Admiral's			
Nasseem	79	8	7	Realm	70	7	12	Heir	63	7	5
Scintillating				Flighting	70	7	12	Faiz	63	7	5
Air	79	8	7	Countess				Overplay	63	7	5
Centurius	78	8	6	Tully	69	7	11	Poldhu	63	7	5
Mattaboy	78	8	6	Ghadeer	69	7	11	Scarrowmanwick			
Noalto	78	8	6	Harp Strings	69	7	11		63	7	5
Strigida	78	8	6	Tahoe	69	7	11	Silver Season	63	7	5
Kind of Hush	77	8	5	Alma Ata	68	7	10	Spark of Life	63	7	5
Age Quod				Capstan	68	7	10	Kings			
Agis	76	8	4	Humming	68	7	10	General	62	7	4
Little Wolf	76	8	4	Ganimede	67	7	9	Pencil Point	62	7	4
Protection				Grecian Sea	67	7	9	Shasavaan	62	7	4
Racket	76	8	4	Mushref	67	7	9	Applemint	61	7	3
Tina's Pet	76	8	4	Sanu	67	7	9	Baz Bombati	61	7	3
Baffin	75	8	3	Welshwyn	67	7	9	Home			
Bel Bolide	75	8	3	Chemin	66	7	8	Coming	61	7	3
				Integrity	66	7	8	Shark Song	60	7	2
				Ma Femme	66	7	8				

FOUR-YEAR-OLDS AND UPWARDS, 1981

The following handicap, published on 3rd December, is for information only. The figures shown against each horse represent the official assessment of its merit against a norm of 100.

Moorestyle	91	10	0	King of Spain	79	9	2	Shaftesbury	68	8	6
Ardross	90	9	13	Prince Bee	79	9	2	Great Eastern	67	8	4
Sharpo	90	9	13	Rankin	78	9	1	Saher	67	8	4
Light Cavalry	89	9	12	Castle Keep	76	8	13	Son Fils	67	8	4
Hilal	87	9	10	Columnist	76	8	13	Triomphe	67	8	4
Master Willie	86	9	9	Magesterial	76	8	13	Captain Nick	65	8	2
Rabdan	86	9	9	Princes Gate	76	8	13	Galveston	65	8	2
Hard Fought	85	9	8	Ring The Bell	76	8	13	Heighlin	65	8	2
Pelerin	85	9	8	Standaan	76	8	13	Donegal			
Belmont Bay	84	9	7	Milk of the				Prince	64	8	1
Dalsaan	84	9	7	Barley	74	8	11	Lightning			
Runnett	83	9	6	Slenderhagen	74	8	11	Label	64	8	1
Crews Hill	82	9	5	Sayyaf	73	8	10	Billbroker	62	7	13
Lancastrian	82	9	5	Bonol	70	8	7	Escovitch	62	7	13
Cairn Rouge	81	9	4	Premier Rose	70	8	7	Sparkling Boy	62	7	13
Last				Shining				Overtrick	61	7	12
Fandango	81	9	4	Finish	69	8	6	Enchantment	60	7	11
Nicholas Bill	81	9	4	Gypsy Dancer	68	8	5	Rontino	60	7	11
Vielle	81	9	4	Royal				Russian			
Fingal's Cave	80	9	3	Fountain	68	8	5	George	60	7	11
Cracaval	79	9	2								

AN IRISH CLASSIFICATION 1981

THE TWO-YEAR-OLDS

Published on 3rd December, for information only.

Achieved	9	7	Watties Rock	8	3	Condell	7	8
Golden Fleece	9	6	Miss Lilian	8	2	Furry Berg	7	8
Sharp Singer	9	5	More Heather	8	2	Future Spa	7	8
Anfield	9	4	Rose Red	8	2	Karissima	7	8
Peterhof (USA)	9	2	Santa			Los Christianos	7	8
Woodstream	9	2	Roseanna	8	2	Murcot	7	8
Americus	9	1	Mistral Man	8	1	Noras Mark	7	8
Day Is Done	9	1	Ormsary	8	0	Pixie	7	8
Raconteur			Conversion	7	13	Present Arms	7	8
(USA)	9	1	Hay Habit	7	13	Sheelin Rose	7	8
Assert	9	0	Mary Mitsu	7	13	Shir Khan	7	8
Codrington	9	0	Tinnycross	7	13	Sir Shostakovich	7	8
Pas de Seul	9	0	Wolver Maid	7	13	Sovereign		
Dara Monarch	8	13	Chronicle	7	11	Notion	7	8
Philip Martin	8	12	Liquifaction	7	11	Time Goes		
Sun Worship	8	11	Lorn Goddess	7	11	Quickly	7	8
The Primate	8	11	Miss Behaving	7	11	Vincents Pride	7	8
Peadar Piper	8	10	Remanded	7	11	Barbender	7	7
Longleat	8	9	Tinktura	7	11	Berlin	7	7
Lords	8	9	Vana Vichi	7	11	Crusoe	7	7
Punctilio	8	9	Chivalry	7	10	Dubjo	7	7
Fly Start	8	8	Cooliney			Ifsowhynot	7	7
Prince's Polly	8	8	Princess	7	10	Jean De Reske	7	7
Afghan	8	7	Oileann Carrig	7	10	Land Without		
Princess Seal	8	5	Swansea Bay	7	10	Stars	7	7
Royal			Duke of Dollis	7	9	Late Music	7	7
Rendevouz	8	5	Legal Expertise	7	9	North Astra	7	7
Aloe	8	4	Legs And			Salmette	7	7
Tabloid	8	4	Things	7	9	Salsa Rosa	7	7
Celestial Path	8	3	Okavango	7	9	Squinch	7	7
Pilgrim	8	3	Red Jersey	7	9	What A Demon	7	7
Sweet Side	8	3						

THREE-YEAR-OLDS OF 1981

The following ratings were published on 3rd December for information only. The rating given to each horse represents the official assessment of its merit against a norm of 100.

Shergar	100	Belted Earl	80	What A Riot	74
Cut Above	90	Happy Bride	80	Dance Bid	73
Kings Lake	88	Prince Echo	78	Martinova	72
To-Agori-Mou	88	Tellurano	78	Slaney Maid	71
Blue Wind	86	Kind of Hush	77	Countess Tully	69
Kirtling	86	Protection		Pergola	67
Condessa	84	Racket	76	Clanjolly	66
Critique	84	Arctique Royale	75	Cooliney Prince	65
Erins Isle	82	Cooleen Jack	74	Overplay	65

FOUR-YEAR-OLDS AND UPWARDS, 1981

The following ratings were published on 3rd December for information only. The rating given to each horse represents the official assessment of its merit against a norm of 100.

Runnett	83	Magesterial	76	Gilded Vanity	70
Cairn Rouge	80	Triomphe	72	Jasmine Star	67

972

THE FRENCH FREE HANDICAPS

TWO-YEAR-OLDS, 1981

The following are the weights allotted in the Handicap Libre, published on 10th December.

Green Forest ..	10	0	Alfred's Choice	8	13	Flayosc	8 10
Zino	9	10	Beau Pretender	8	13	Harbour ..	8 10
Maelstrom Lake	9	7	Honeyland ..	8	13	Riverhill ..	8 10
Norwick ..	9	7	Marcao ..	8	13	Setkatdeu ..	8 10
Bon Sang ..	9	6	Talaja	8	13	Shayina ..	8 10
Play It Safe ..	9	5	Trigonome ..	8	13	Arrabida ..	8 9
River Lady ..	9	4	Dear Patrick ..	8	11	Bell Tempo ..	8 9
Tender King ..	9	4	Discoureur ..	8	11	Big Shot ..	8 9
Glancing ..	9	3	Embarrassed ..	8	11	Bois de Grace ..	8 9
Chellaston Park	9	1	Empery Card ..	8	11	Famoso ..	8 9
Coussika ..	9	1	Lulworth Cove	8	11	First Water ..	8 9
Dom Donizetti	9	1	Mirea	8	11	Imyar	8 9
Melyno.. ..	9	1	Pampabird ..	8	11	Keep In Step ..	8 9
Pas de Seul ..	9	1	Perlee	8	11	Lisfort	8 9
Persepolis ..	9	1	Pomme d'Ebene	8	11	Meandre ..	8 9
Exclusive Order	9	0	Star Princess ..	8	11	Morse Code (Fr)	8 9
Majestic Guard	9	0	Academic ..	8	10	Or Epi	8 9
Riyahi	9	0	African Joy ..	8	10	Premier Concert	8 9
Rollins	9	0	Albala	8	10	Saronic.. ..	8 9
Tampero ..	9	0	Bel Emir ..	8	10	Shango.. ..	8 9
Telephone Man	9	0	Bouillonnante ..	8	10	Typhoon Polly..	8 9
Akiyda	8	13					

THREE-YEAR-OLDS, 1981

The following are the weights allotted in the Handicap Libre, published on 10th December.

Bikala	10	3	Big John ..	9	3	Really Lucky ..	9 0
Marwell ..	10	2	Brustolon ..	9	3	Roi Guillaume..	9 0
Akarad	10	0	Prince Mab ..	9	3	Sass-Go ..	9 0
April Run ..	10	0	Sangue	9	3	Two Step ..	9 0
Kings Lake ..	10	0	Tootens ..	9	3	Vanann.. ..	9 0
To-Agori-Mou	10	0	Val d'Erica ..	9	3	Asania	8 13
Glint of Gold ..	9	13	Anitra's Dance	9	2	Buisson Rose ..	8 13
The Wonder ..	9	13	Another Realm	9	2	Libergold ..	8 13
Phydilla ..	9	11	Kounboula ..	9	2	Mistra	8 13
Rahotep ..	9	11	Landresse ..	9	2	Mourtazam ..	8 13
Recitation ..	9	11	Le Mamamouchi	9	2	Palace Gold ..	8 13
Vayrann ..	9	11	Paillardise ..	9	2	Premiere	
Bellman ..	9	10	Silky Baby ..	9	2	Danseuse (Fr)	8 13
Kirtling ..	9	10	Tropicaro ..	9	2	Alik	8 11
Leandra ..	9	10	Bardenac ..	9	1	Arad	8 11
Madam Gay ..	9	10	Don't Sulk ..	9	1	Ardash	8 11
Al Nasr (Fr) ..	9	8	La Pompadour	9	1	Barbotte ..	8 11
Tipperary Fixer	9	8	Last Love ..	9	1	Derly	8 11
Cresta Rider ..	9	7	Marasali ..	9	1	Greenway ..	8 11
Ukraine Girl ..	9	7	Mariacho ..	9	1	Hatra	8 11
Sonoma ..	9	6	Noalto	9	1	Hayel	8 11
Votre Altesse ..	9	6	Ranapour ..	9	1	In Tissar ..	8 11
Spoleto.. ..	9	5	Redoutable ..	9	1	Ionian Raja ..	8 11
Tellurano ..	9	5	Rixe	9	1	Kentucky River	8 11
Church Parade	9	4	Tow	9	1	Layalina ..	8 11
Diamond Prospect	9	4	Ancient Regime	9	0	Lord Never ..	8 11
Dunphy ..	9	4	Arc d'Or ..	9	0	Mbaiki	8 11
Gap of Dunloe..	9	4	Assita	9	0	Nyono	8 11
Kilmona ..	9	4	Ecube	9	0	Singing Boy ..	8 11
Lou Piguet ..	9	4	Fin Gourmet ..	9	0	Taduska ..	8 11
Lydian	9	4	Ivory Wings ..	9	0	Tonar	8 11
Snow Day ..	9	4	Karkour ..	9	0	Top Dancer ..	8 11
Star Pastures ..	9	4	Nijinsky's Secret	9	0	Vorias	8 11
Bernica.. ..	9	3	Princely Ruler ..	9	0		

FOUR-YEAR-OLDS AND UPWARDS, 1981

The following are the weights allotted in the Handicap Libre, published on 10th December.

Northjet	..	10	4	In Fijar	..	9	4	Moon Ingraver	9	0
Moorestyle	..	10	3	King James	..	9	4	Prince Melchior	9	0
Ardross	..	10	2	Daeltown	..	9	3	Proustille	..	9	0
Gold River	..	10	2	Castle Keep	..	9	2	Aryenne	..	8	13
Sharpo	..	10	2	En Calcat	..	9	2	Bobiffic..	..	8	13
Hilal	..	9	13	Epsiba ..	..	9	2	Confetti	..	8	13
Perrault	..	9	13	Falamoun	..	9	2	Esclavo..	..	8	13
Argument	..	9	12	Lord Jack	..	9	2	Gresham	..	8	13
Rabdan..	..	9	12	Manjam	..	9	2	Joberan	..	8	13
Belmont Bay	..	9	11	Park Romeo	..	9	2	New Grandame	8	13
Detroit ..	..	9	10	Prince Bee	..	9	2	Noalcoholic	..	8	13
Runnett	..	9	10	Princes Gate	...	9	2	Red Rocket	..	8	13
Lancastrian	..	9	8	Ruscelli	..	9	2	Standaan	..	8	13
Nicholas Bill	..	9	7	Ya Zaman	..	9	2	Astonished	..	8	11
Vielle ..	..	9	7	Daniri ..	..	9	1	Dhaubix	..	8	11
Armistice Day..		9	6	Dom Menotti	..	9	1	El Badr	..	8	11
Glenorum	..	9	6	First Prayer	..	9	1	Enchantment	..	8	11
Katowice	..	9	6	Marson..	..	9	1	Give Off	..	8	11
Kelbomec	..	9	6	Bylly the Kid	..	9	0	Goldiko	..	8	11
Nemr ..	..	9	6	Cherubin	..	9	0	Perouges	..	8	11
Cracaval	..	9	5	Hereas ..	..	9	0	Ring The Bell ..	8	11
P'tite Tete	..	9	5	Liki Liki	..	9	0	Sea's Valley	..	8	11
Good to Beat	..	9	4	Monsieur				Son of Love	..	8	11
Gosport	..	9	4	Dagobert	..	9	0	Sparkling Boy ..	8	11

ERRATA & ADDENDA

"RACEHORSES OF 1980"

Alangrove Sound (Can)	
Another Realm	12,500Y
Blue Singh	is a filly
Camisite	won over 6f
Chantry Bridge	beat Angle Fire
Corinne's Gold	dam is Beaute Royale
Dancing Sally	6th at Newbury
Indado	1975 2-y-o 6f winner Suncharmer
In Fijar	did not have his tongue tied down
Middlin Thrang	dam half-sister to Quorum
Palatinate	trainer M. Stoute
Redoubtable (Fr)	is Redoutable (Fr)
Runnett	final form figure 6s*
Saucey Devil	wasn't dead
Shree	dam's sire Floribunda
Southern Swanee	Redcar in June

"RACEHORSES OF 1981"

Green Forest (USA)	M. Fustok was 2nd in French Owner's List in 1981

EUROPEAN GROUP 1 PATTERN RACES 1981

1   PREMIO PARIOLI (3y) 1m
£17,021   Rome   20 April
Timur Lang 9-2 OPessi....1
Helenio 9-2 LBietolini..nk.2
Roman Top 9-2
   LFicuciello 3.3
Belviale 9-2 RFestinesi..ns.4
Semipalatinsk 9-2
   GDettori ns.5
Stifelius 9-2 PPerlanti.....3.6
El Balista 9-2
   ADi Nardo 2.7
Bihar 9-2 BJovine.......1¼.8
Panjandrum 9-2
   GPucciatti ½.9
Pizzocorno 9-2 GFois.....3.10
Jessamine 9-2
   GSorrentino 6.11
Erodoto 9-2 CFelace.... 4.12

3/5 Semipalatinsk, Panjandrum,
Erodoto (grouped), 2/1 TIMUR
LANG and Helenio, 5/1 Stifelius,
11/2 El Balista, 8/1 Belviale, 10/1
Pizzocorno, 20/1 Bihar, 30/1 Roman
Top, 45/1 Jessamine.
   Razza Spineta (L. Brogi) 12ran
1m 40.9 (Soft).

2   PREMIO REGINA ELENA
            (3y f)   1m
£17,021   Rome   25 April
Val d'Erica 8-11 PPerlanti..1
Holga 8-11 LBietolini...2½.2
Scrocca 8-11 SAtzori....3½.3
Altobella 8-11 OPessi....1.4
Yang Tze 8-11 GDettori 2½.5
Savaii 8-11 LFicuciello...4.6
Safari Girl 8-11 GPucciatti.3.7
Neve di Federici 8-11
   AManzi 3.8
Spring Lady 8-11
   EBietolini 6.9
Solda 8-11 GSorrentino...3.10

4/6 VAL D'ERICA, 2/1 Scrocca,
4/1 Holga, 5/1 Yang Tze, 6/1
Altobella, 18/1 Savaii, 33/1 Spring
Lady, 45/1 Safari Girl, 50/1 Neve
di Federici, 66/1 Solda.
   Scuderia dell'Abete Blu (A.
Botti) 10ran 1m 44.5 (Heavy).

3   POULE D'ESSAI DES
     POULAINS (3y c)   1m
£40,250   Longchamp   26 April
Recitation 9-2 GStarkey...1
Redoutable 9-2
   YSaint-Martin 2½.2
Cresta Rider 9-2 PPaquet.1.3
Kisty 9-2 ALequeux 2.4
Prince Mab 9-2 FHead....¾.5

Big John 9-2 GDoleuze..ns.6
Princely Ruler 9-2
   MPhilipperon ½.7
Mattaboy 9-2 PEddery.....4.8
Hayel 9-2 AGibert........8.9
Steel Age 9-2 PLagoutte..5.10

5/4 Cresta Rider and Steel Age,
24/10 RECITATION, 6/1 Re-
doutable, 33/4 Prince Mab, 12/1
Hayel, 13/1 Big John, 17/1 Mattaboy, 29/1 Princely Ruler, 50/1
Kisty.
   A. Bodie (G. Harwood) 10ran
1m 40.7 (Good).

4   ONE THOUSAND
     GUINEAS (3y f)   1m
£52,180   Newmarket   30 April
Fairy Footsteps 9-0
   LPiggott 1
Tolmi 9-0 EHide.......nk.2
Go Leasing 9-0 GStarkey.nk.3
Marwell 9-0 WRSwinburn.½.4
Madam Gay 9-0
   A Murray s.hd.5
Vocalist 9-0 P Robinson...½.6
What Heaven 9-0 PYoung..1.7
Shark Song 9-0 BTaylor.1½.8
Kittyhawk 9-0 WCarson...½.9
Grecian Sea 9-0 JMercer.¾.10
Swedish Rhapsody 9-0
   GDuffield 1½.11
Welshwyn 9-0 BRouse....2.12
Auction Bridge 9-0
   SCauthen 5.13
Belleair Dream 9-0
   PEddery 8.14

6/4 FAIRY FOOTSTEPS, 7/2
Marwell, 11/2 Tolmi, 10/1 Kitty-
hawk, 13/1 Go Leasing, 33/1
Auction Bridge, 50/1 Grecian Sea,
Madam Gay, Shark Song, Welsh-
wyn, 100/1 Belleair Dream, Vocalist,
What Heaven, 200/1 Swedish
Rhapsody.
   H. Joel (H. Cecil) 14ran 1m 40.43
(Good).

5   TWO THOUSAND
     GUINEAS (3y)   1m
£64,136   Newmarket   2 May
To-Agori-Mou 9-0
   GStarkey 1
3   **Mattaboy** 9-0 JReid....nk.2
Bel Bolide 9-0 PEddery.1½.3
Cut Throat 9-0 PWaldron.2½.4
Another Realm 9-0
   JMercer ¾.5
Scintillating Air 9-0
   GBaxter s.hd.6

976

Rasa Penang 9-0 PTulk....¼.7
The Quiet Bidder 9-0
    SPerks 2.8
Spoleto 9-0 PPaquet.....hd.9
Motavato 9-0 SCauthen..½.10
Prince Echo 9-0 PCook...3.11
Dalby Mustang 9-0
    BTaylor ½.12
Kind of Hush 9-0
    LPiggott 5.13
Church Parade 9-0
    WCarson ½.14
Beldale Flutter 9-0
    YSaint-Martin s.hd.15
Star Fleet 9-0 MMiller...½.16
Cooliney Prince 9-0
    GMcGrath hd.17
Accession 9-0 BRaymond.¾.18
Noalto 9-0 PRobinson....¾.19
5/2 TO-AGORI-MOU, 5/1 Mot-
avato, 9/1 Kind of Hush, 10/1
Beldale Flutter, 13/1 Another
Realm, 14/1 Bel Bolide, 15/1
Church Parade, 20/1 Prince Echo,
22/1 Noalto, 33/1 Cut Throat, 40/1
Spoleto, 50/1 Cooliney Prince,
Mattaboy, 60/1 Dalby Mustang,
66/1 Accession, 100/1 Rasa Penang,
Scintillating Air, Star Fleet, The
Quiet Bidder.
    Mrs A. Muinos (G. Harwood)
19ran 1m 41.43 (Good).

6   POULE D'ESSAI DES
    POULICHES (3y f)   1m
£39,405   Longchamp   3 May
    Ukraine Girl 9-2 PEddery..1
    Star Pastures 9-2 BTaylor1½.2
    Ionian Raja 9-2 PPaquet.1½.3
    Ancient Regime 9-2
        MPhilliperon 2.4
    Tropicaro 9-2 ALequeux..½.5
    Marie Noelle 9-2 LPiggott.nk.6
    Joberine 9-2
        YSaint-Martin 3.7
    Salmana 9-2 FHead.......½.8
    Aliberta 9-2 JHeloury.....5.9
    Fair Contessa 9-2
        J-PLefevre 10.10
6/4 Fair Contessa and Tropicaro,
Marie Noelle, 29/4 Ancient Regime,
Star Pastures, 13/1 Ionian Raja,
18/1 Joberine, 21/1 UKRAINE
GIRL, 38/1 Salmana, 42/1 Aliberta.
    Mrs. J. Mullion (R. Collet)
10ran 1m 41.0 (Good).

7   PRIX GANAY   1m 2½f
£39,405   Longchamp   3 May
    Argument 4-9-2 ALequeux.1
    Armistice Day 5-9-2
        YSaint-Martin 3.2
    In Fijar 4-9-2 AGibert....1.3
    Ruscelli 4-9-2 HSamani....½.4
    Detroit 4-8-13 PEddery.s.hd.5
    Rheinsteel 4-9-2 LPiggott.15.6

Sabzawar 4-9-2 PPaquet.s.nk.7
Katowice 4-9-2 SGorli.....4.8
Highway 4-9-2 ABadel.....10.9
Evens ARGUMENT, 7/4 Detroit
and Highway, 31/4 In Fijar, 9/1
Katowice, 11/1 Armistice Day,
14/1 Rheinsteel, 31/1 Ruscelli,
43/1 Sabzawar.
    B. McNall (M. Zilber) 9ran
2m 12.2 (Good).

8   DERBY ITALIANO (3y) 1½m
£37,768   Rome   10 May
    Glint of Gold 9-2 JMatthias.1
    My Franky 9-2 GStarkey..2.2
    Bold Brigadier 9-2
        WCarson 5.3
1* Timur Lang 9-2 OPessi..nk.4
    Troubetzkoy 9-2 PPaquet.hd.5
    Seiorlando 9-2 PPerlanti...1.6
1² Helenio 9-2 LBietolini ½.7
    Metaponto 9-2 SFancera..6.8
    Giant 9-2 EHide..........4.9
    Devil's Ditch 9-2
        GDettori 4.10
1³ Roman Top 9-2
        LFicuciello 6.11
    Pope Eugenio 9-2
        RFestinesi 12
    Vassillo 9-2 RSannino......13
4/5 GLINT OF GOLD, 3/1
Troubetzkoy, 4/1 My Franky,
5/1 Timur Lang and Helenio,
9/1 Bold Brigadier, 16/1 Devil's
Ditch, 18/1 Seiorlando, 25/1 Giant,
33/1 Metaponto, 50/1 Roman Top,
100/1 Pope Eugenio, 200/1 Vassillo.
    P. Mellon (I. Balding) 13ran
2m 30.9 (Good).

9   AIRLIE/COOLMORE
    IRISH TWO THOUSAND
    GUINEAS (3y)   1m
£50,427   The Curragh   16 May
    Kings Lake 9-0 PEddery....1
5* To-Agori-Mou 9-0
        GStarkey nk.2
5   Prince Echo 9-0 SCraine..¾.3
5² Mattaboy 9-0 AMurray...1½.4
    Dance Bid 9-0
        WSwinburn 1.5
    Manilla Bay 9-0 TMurphy.7.6
    Light Here 9-0 CRoche...3.7
    Boundary Bay 9-0
        GMcGrath s.hd.8
    Ore 9-0 GCurran......s.hd.9
    Lord Trendy 9-0
        PVGilson 3.10
    Swallanga 9-0 DGillespie...11
    Noble Monk 9-0
        PShanahan 12
    Sierra Wind 9-0 MJKinane.13
9/10 To-Agori-Mou, 5/1 KINGS
LAKE, 15/2 Mattaboy, 12/1 Light
Here, 16/1 Dance Bid, Prince
Echo, Swallanga, 25/1 Noble Monk,

33/1 Lord Trendy, Ore, 66/1 Boundary Bay, Manilla Bay, Sierra Wind.

Kings Lake finished first, in front of To-Agori-Mou, but was disqualified and placed second after an inquiry by the local stewards. Kings Lake was later reinstated as the winner on appeal.

J. P. Binet (V. O'Brien) 13 ran 1m 47.7 (Soft).

10 PRIX LUPIN (3y) 1m 2½f
£43,141 Longchamp 17 May

No Lute 9-2 PEddery	**1**
The Wonder 9-2 LPiggott	3.**2**
Dunphy 9-2 FHead	1½.**3**
Bikala 9-2 SGorli	nk.4
Ardash 9-2 YSaint-Martin	4.5
Great Substence 9-2 AGibert	3.6
Explorer King 9-2 HSamani	1.7
Silky Baby 9-2 MPhilipperon	6.8
Vorias 9-2 ABadel	20.9

7/4 Dunphy, 3/1 The Wonder, 13/4 Ardash, 11/2 Great Substence, NO LUTE, 27/4 Silky Baby, 18/1 Bikala, 22/1 Explorer King, 48/1 Vorias.

R. Sangster (R. Sangster) 9ran 2m 18.9 (Soft).

11 OAKS D'ITALIA (3y f) 1m 3f
£23,022 Milan 17 May

2* **Val d'Erica** 8-11 PPerlanti	**1**
Rattling Wind 8-11 GDettori	2.**2**
2³ **Scrocca** 8-11 WCarson	2.**3**
Tiniwas 8-11 SFancera	4.4
Antruiles 8-11 PAgus	½.5
Sainte Nitouche 8-11 SDettori	dist.6

4/6 VAL D'ERICA and Tiniwas, Evens Rattling Wind, 11/2 Scrocca, 20/1 Sainte Nitouche, 33/1 Antruiles.

Scuderia dell'Abete Blu (A. Botti) 6ran 2m 22 (Soft).

12 GOFFS IRISH ONE
THOUSAND GUINEAS
(3y f) 1m
£28,902 The Curragh 23 May

Arctique Royale 9-0 GCurran	**1**
Blue Wind 9-0 WSwinburn	s.hd.**2**
Martinova 9-0 PEddery	1.**3**
Overplay 9-0 JDeegan	1½.4
Happy Bride 9-0 DGillespie	2.5
4 Vocalist 9-0 GStarkey	hd.6

6² Star Pastures 9-0 BTaylor..5.7
Castlemaine 9-0 AMurray.2½.8
Lone Bidder 9-0 MJKinane 1½.9
Stracomer Queen 9-0 SMartinez............1.10
Citissima 9-0 PVGilson.....11
Callixena 9-0 RCarroll.....12
Speedy Rose 9-0 SCraine...13
Rhein Honey 9-0 GMcGrath 14
Drama 9-0 CRoche........15

5/2 Martinova, 6/1 Blue Wind, 7/1 ARCTIQUE ROYALE, Star Pastures, 9/1 Happy Bride, 10/1 Vocalist, 12/1 Drama, 20/1 Overplay, 25/1 Castlemaine, Lone Bidder, 33/1 Stracomer Queen, 66/1 Callixena, Citissima, Rhein Honey, Speedy Rose.

J. P. Binet (K. Prendergast) 15ran 1m 49.3 (Heavy).

13 PRIX SAINT-ALARY (3y f)
1½m
£39,267 Longchamp 24 May

Tootens 9-2 GDoleuze	**1**
6 **Tropicaro** 9-2 YSaint-Martin	2.**2**
Last Love 9-2 J-LKessas.½.**3**
Assita 9-2 ALequeux	1.4
Asania 9-2 MPhilipperon..¾.5
Bernica 9-2 PPaquet	½.6
Viendra 9-2 SCauthen	10.7
Petroleuse 9-2 LPiggott...¾.8
Maiden's Blush 9-2 OMongelluzzo	dist.9
6 Fair Contessa 9-2 J-PLefevre	10.10

5/2 Petroleuse, 3/1 Bernica and Maiden's Blush, 15/4 Assita, 19/4 Asania, 11/2 Tropicaro and Fair Contessa, 10/1 Viendra, 21/2 TOOTENS, 12/1 Last Love.

Mlle C. Lynch (E. Bartholomew) 10ran 2m 15.1 (Heavy).

14 PRIX DU CADRAN 2½m
£30,541 Longchamp 24 May

Gold River 4-8-13 FHead..**1**
Hereas 4-9-2 YSaint-Martin	3.**2**
Chicbury 4-9-2 GDoleuze	2½.**3**
Proustille 4-8-13 MPhilipperon	¾.4
El Badr 6-9-2 AGibert	4.5
Son of Love 5-9-2 ALequeux	10.6

6/10 GOLD RIVER, 17/4 Son of Love, 5/1 Proustille, 25/4 El Badr, 15/2 Hereas, 26/1 Chicbury.

J. Wertheimer (A. Head) 6ran 4m 38.0 (Heavy).

15 PREMIO PRESIDENTE
DELLA REPUBBLICA 1½m
£17,760   Rome   24 May
Ladislao di Oppelm
5-9-7 SFancera..........1
Pian del Lupo 4-9-7
VPanici 1.2
Marmolada 4-9-3
GDettori 3.3
Ganimede (ITY) 5-9-7
RSannino ¾.4
Haul Knight 5-9-7 OPessi..4.5
Schweppervescence 5-9-7
LFicuciello 6.6

3/5 Marmolada, 5/2 Pian del
Lupo, Ganimede, 7/2 Haul Knight,
4/1 LADISLAO DI OPPELM,
20/1 Schweppervescence.

Scuderia S. Bartholomeo (P.
Miliani) 6ran 2m 2.15 (Good).

16 GRAN PREMIO D'ITALIA
(3y)   1½m
£23,061   Milan   31 May
Kirtling 9-2 LPiggott......1
8 **Seiorlando** 9-2
GDettori s.nk.2
8 **Timur Lang** 9-2
LBietolini 2.3
8³ Bold Brigadier 9-2
WCarson ¾.4
8 Giant 9-2 PPerlanti.......5.5
8² My Franky 9-2 GStarkey..3.6
Baldog 9-2 SAtzori 10.7

3/5 KIRTLING, 5/2 My Franky,
8/1 Bold Brigadier, 9/1 Seiorlando,
20/1 Timur Lang, 25/1 Giant, 60/1
Baldog.

E. Moller (H. Wragg) 7ran
2m 30.1 (Good).

17 DERBY STAKES (3y) 1½m
£149,900   Epsom   3 June
Shergar 9-0 WRSwinburn..1
8* Glint of Gold 9-0
JMatthias 10.2
5 **Scintillating Air** 9-0
GBaxter 2.3
Shotgun 9-0 LPiggott.....2.4
5 Church Parade 9-0
WCarson 4.5
Sheer Grit 9-0 JMercer...1¾.6
Silver Season 9-0
EJohnson 1.7
Riberetto 9-0 PEddery...hd.8
Sunley Builds 9-0
PWaldron 4.9
Kings General 9-0
BTaylor 3.10
Sass 9-0 JReid........s.hd.11
Krug 9-0 BRaymond.....4.12
Kalaglow 9-0 GStarkey...3.13
Robellino 9-0 PCook....2.14
Golden Brigadier 9-0
PBradwell 6.15

5 Kind of Hush 9-0
SCauthen ¼.16
Al Nasr (Fr) 9-0 AGibert.20.17
Waverley Hall 9-0
BCrossley ¾.18

10/11 SHERGAR, 7/1 Shotgun,
11/1 Kalaglow, 13/1 Glint of Gold,
16/1 Al Nasr, 22/1 Riberetto, 25/1
Church Parade, Kind of Hush,
28/1 Robellino, Sheer Grit, 50/1
Scintillating Air, 66/1 Krug, 100/1
Silver Season, 150/1 Golden Brig-
adier, Kings General, 200/1 Sunley
Builds, 500/1 Sass, 1,000/1 Waverley
Hall.

H. H. Aga Khan (M. Stoute)
18ran 2m 44.21 (Dead).

18 CORONATION CUP 1½m
£43,770   Epsom   4 June
Master Willie 4-9-0
PWaldron 1
Prince Bee 4-9-0
WCarson 2.2
Vielle 4-8-11 LPiggott...2½.3
Mrs Penny 4-8-11
JMatthias 5.4
Rankin 4-9-0 GStarkey..bad.5

1/2 MASTER WILLIE, 11/2
Prince Bee, 6/1 Mrs. Penny, 11/1
Vielle, 33/1 Rankin.
R. Barnett (H. Candy) 5ran
2m 44.49 (Dead).

19 OAKS STAKES (3y f) 1½m
£74,568   Epsom   6 June
12² **Blue Wind** 9-0 LPiggott....1
4 **Madam Gay** 9-0 JReid....7.2
Leap Lively 9-0
JMatthias 10.3
Ivory Wings 9-0 PPaquet..5.4
4³ Go Leasing 9-0
GStarkey 7.5
Fruition 9-0 PRobinson....3.6
Rhein Bridge 9-0 EHide..¾.7
Fiesta Fun 9-0 PCook.....4.8
Canton Lightning 9-0
SCauthen 1.9
Humming 9-0 WCarson..8.10
Allegretta 9-0
WRSwinburn 12.11
13² Tropicaro 9-0
ALequeux dist.12

3/1 BLUE WIND, Leap Lively,
11/2 Go Leasing, 6/1 Tropicaro,
10/1 Madam Gay, 16/1 Humming,
25/1 Ivory Wings, Rhein Bridge,
33/1 Allegretta, Canton Lightning,
100/1 Fiesta Fun, Fruition.
Mrs. B. Firestone (D. Weld,
Ireland) 12ran 2m 40.93 (Good).

20 PRIX DU JOCKEY-CLUB
(3y)   1½m
£90,827   Chantilly   7 June
10 **Bikala** 9-2 SGorli.........1

979

Akarad 9-2
YSaint-Martin 4.2
Gap of Dunloe 9-2
GWMoore 2¼.3
Rahotep 9-2 J-LKessas. . .¾.4
Nijinsky's Secret 9-2
MPhilipperon s.nk.5
Mbaiki 9-2 MPlanard. . . .2½.6
10* No Lute 9-2 PEddery. . . .8.7
3* Recitation 9-2
GStarkey d-ht.7
3² Redoutable 9-2 HSamani. . .8.9
10² The Wonder 9-2 LPiggott.½.10
Mariacho 9-2 ALequeux.15.11
Magnum 9-2 JHeloury. 12
7/4 No Lute and Magnum, 7/2
Akarad, 11/2 Rahotep, 23/4 Recita-
tion, 9/1 The Wonder, 14/1 Maria-
cho, 17/1 BIKALA, 18/1 Redout-
able, 20/1 Nijinsky's Secret, 38/1
Gap of Dunloe, 44/1 Mbaiki.
J. Ouaki (P.-L. Biancone) 12ran
2m 29.5 (Good).

21 PREMIO EMILIO
TURATI 1m
£21,368 Milan 7 June
Peloponnes 6-9-3
DRichardson 1
15³ **Marmolada** 4-9-0
GDettori 1.2
Vargas Llosa 5-9-3
MDepalmas ½.3
Norwegian 4-9-3 APerrotta.¾.4
Sea's Valley 4-9-3
LBietolini 3.5
15² Pian del Lupo 4-9-3
PPerlanti 1½.6
All Silk 3-8-4 SDettori. . . .½.7
Arturo Franco 4-9-3
VPanici 3.8
Esclavo 5-9-3 ADiNardo. . .2.9
15 Ganimede (ITY) 5-9-3
PAgus 6.10
18/10 Marmolada, 5/2 Pian del
Lupo, Ganimede, 4/1 Esclavo,
9/2 PELOPONNES, 10/1 All
Silk, 14/1 Norwegian, 25/1 Sea's
Valley, 33/1 Vargas Llosa, 50/1
Arturo Franco.
Stall Mazel-Tov (H. Degner)
10ran 1m 37.2 (Good).

22 GRAN PREMIO
DI MILANO 1½m
£38,363 Milan 14 June
Lydian 3-8-6 MDepalmas. . .1
15* **Ladislao di Oppelm**
5-9-6 SFancera. 4.2
Navarino 4-9-6 TPotters. . . .3
Van der Linden 5-9-6
CForte 3.4
Lotar 4-9-6 GDettori. . .s.hd.5
Prince Spruce 4-9-6
CWigham 6.6
Scouting Miller 4-9-6
LFicuciello 1½.7

Barbaccio 4-9-6 ADiNardo.1.8
Champoluc 3-8-6 VPanici. . .5.9
Evens LYDIAN, 5/2 Lotar, 5/1
Navarino, 7/1 Ladislao di Oppelm,
17/1 Prince Spruce, 20/1 Champoluc, 25/1 Van der Linden, 33/1
Barbaccio, 60/1 Scouting Miller.
Navarino finished second, a short
head in front of Ladislao di Oppelm,
but was adjudged to have leaned
heavily upon him in the last furlong
and was disqualified and placed
third.
Ecurie Aland (Mme C. Head,
France) 9ran 2m 28.1 (Good).

23 PRIX DE DIANE
DE REVLON (3y f) 1m 2½f
£71,365 Chantilly 14 June
19² **Madam Gay** 9-2 LPiggott. . .1
11* **Val d'Erica** 9-2 PPerlanti. .4.2
April Run 9-2
GStarkey s.nk.3
6* Ukraine Girl 9-2
PEddery s.lnd.4
13* Tootens 9-2 GDoleuze. . . .¾.5
13 Bernica 9-2 PPaquet. . .s.nk.6
Kilmona 9-2 AGibert. 1½.7
13 Assita 9-2 ALequeux. ½.8
Libergold 9-2
YSaint-Martin 6.9
13 Asania 9-2 MPhilipperon.2½.10
River Reef 9-2 J-CDesaint. . .0
Derly 9-2 FHead. 0
El Dancerina 9-2 FPBruneau. .0
13³ Last Love 9-2 SGorli. 0
7/2 Tootens, 19/4 April Run, 13/2
Derly and El Dancerina, 33/4
Ukraine Girl, Libergold, 9/1
MADAM GAY, Val d'Erica, Last
Love, 16/1 Bernica, 17/1 Asania,
23/1 Assita, 37/1 River Reef, 40/1
Kilmona.
G. Kaye (P. Kelleway) 14ran
2m 6.5 (Good to Firm).

24 GOLD CUP 2½m
£39,013 Ascot 18 June
Ardross 5-9-0 LPiggott. 1
Shoot A Line 4-8-11
WCarson 1.2
Ayyabaan 4-9-0 PEddery.10.3
Pragmatic 6-9-0 JReid. . . .10.4
30/100 ARDROSS, 7/2 Shoot A
Line, 20/1 Pragmatic, 50/1 Ayya-
baan.
C. St. George (H. Cecil) 4m 51.23
(Firm).

25 KING'S STAND STAKES
5f
£33,750 Ascot 19 June
4 **Marwell** 3-8-6
WRSwinburn 1
Standaan 5-9-3 BRouse. . .2.2

980

Runnett 4-9-3 WCarson..1½.**3**
Cooleen Jack 3-8-9
 GStarkey nk.4
Sparkling Boy 4-9-3
 BTaylor 1.5
Valeriga 5-9-3 JReid......½.6
Jasmine Star 5-9-3
 WSwinburn 3.7
Tina's Pet 3-8-9
 BRaymond nk.8
Durandal 4-9-3 PCook....2.9
Steel Charger 4-9-3
 GBaxter s.hd.10
Sharpo 4-9-3 PEddery...hd.11
Swan Princess 3-8-6
 MLThomas 8.12

5/4 MARWELL, 11/4 Sharpo,
8/1 Runnett, 12/1 Tina's Pet, 14/1
Valeriga, 15/1 Standaan, 20/1
Cooleen Jack, 25/1 Jasmine Star,
33/1 Sparkling Boy, Steel Charger,
Swan Princess, 66/1 Durandal.
 E. Loder (M. Stoute) 12ran
1m 0.44 (Firm).

26 IRISH SWEEPS DERBY
         (3y)   1½m
£90,756   The Curragh   27 June
17* **Shergar** 9-0 LPiggott......1
     Cut Above 9-0 WCarson..4.**2**
9   **Dance Bid** 9-0
     WSwinburn 1½.3
16* Kirtling 9-0 PEddery......5.4
9   Ore 9-0 GCurran........¾.5
20³ Gap of Dunloe 9-0
     SGorli s.hd.6
     Young Kildare 9-0
     MJKinane 2½.7
     Baz Bombati 9-0 CRoche..1.8
     Jolly Heir 9-0 TMurphy...7.9
     Crowned Hare 9-0
     DJMurphy ¾.10
     Wolver Heights 9-0
     AMurray ¾.11
     Bustineto 9-0
     GMcGrath ½.12

1/3 SHERGAR, 12/1 Kirtling, 14/1
Cut Above, 20/1 Young Kildare,
25/1 Ore, 33/1 Dance Bid, Gap of
Dunloe, 40/1 Wolver Heights,
100/1 Baz Bombati, Jolly Heir,
500/1 Crowned Hare, Bustineto.
 H. H. Aga Khan (M. Stoute)
12ran 2m 32.7 (Good to Firm).

27 CORAL ECLIPSE STAKES
              1¼m
£90,650   Sandown   4 July
18* **Master Willie** 4-9-7
     PWaldron 1
18³ Vielle 4-9-4 GBaxter......2
     Fingal's Cave 4-9-7
     JMercer 2½.3
23* Madam Gay 3-8-6
     LPiggott 3.4

Last Fandango 4-9-7
 PEddery 2½.6
Czubaryk 5-9-7
 PRobinson 12.7
Hard Fought 4-9-7
 WRSwinburn........ disq.

6/4 MASTER WILLIE, 100/30
Hard Fought, 4/1 Last Fandango,
Madam Gay, 18/1 Vielle, 25/1
Fingal's Cave, 100/1 Czubaryk.
 Hard Fought finished second,
three quarters of a length behind
Master Willie with Vielle half a
length away third, but after a
stewards' inquiry was disqualified
and placed last.
 R. Barnett (H. Candy) 7ran
2m 7.44 (Good to Firm).

28 GRAND PRIX DE PARIS
         (3y)   1m 7f
£40,614   Longchamp   4 July
17² **Glint of Gold** 8-11
     JMatthias 1
     Tipperary Fixer 8-11
     GDoleuze 3.2
     Vayrann 8-11
     YSaint-Martin 1½.3
     Le Mamamouchi 8-11
     HSamani ½.4
20   Nijinsky's Secret 8-11
     MPhilipperon 5.5
     Yellow Marmalade 8-11
     ALequeux 2½.6
20   Mbaiki 8-11 MPlanard.....2.7
     Lizard Danieli 8-11
     PPaquet ns.8
     Tow 8-11 SGorli........ns.9
     Mont Pelion 8-11
     AGibert 1½.10
     Choiseul 8-11 FHead......11

6/4 Vayrann, 16/10 GLINT OF
GOLD, 17/2 Nijinsky's Secret, 9/1
Le Mamamouchi, 12/1 Tow, 15/1
Mbaiki, 17/1 Tipperary Fixer,
20/1 Choiseul, 37/1 Mont Pelion,
56/1 Yellow Marmalade, 70/1
Lizard Danieli.
 P. Mellon (I. Balding) 11ran
3m 25.5 (Soft).

29 PRIX D'ISPAHAN   1m 1¼f
£40,614   Longchamp   4 July
20   **The Wonder** 3-8-9
     ALequeux 1
     Northjet 4-9-6 FHead....2.2
3³   **Cresta Rider** 3-8-9
     PPaquet ¾.3
     Cracaval 5-9-6 SCauthen...½.4
     Hilal 5-9-6 AGibert.......2.5
20   Recitation 3-8-9
     BRaymond 3.6
     Aryenne 4-9-3
     YSaint-Martin 1.7
3   Princely Ruler 3-8-9
     MPhilipperon ¾.8

981

Wild Idea 4-9-3
J-PLefevre 4.9
Confetti 4-9-6 SGorli...1½.10
21 Norwegian 4-9-6
APerrotta 11

11/4 Recitation, 7/2 Aryenne, 15/4
Cresta Rider, 15/2 Hilal, 9/1
Cracaval, 10/1 Northjet, 13/1
Confetti, THE WONDER, 28/1
Princely Ruler, 49/1 Wild Idea,
53/1 Norwegian.
Mme A. Du Breil (J. de Chevigny)
11ran 1m 57.7 (Soft).

30 GRAND PRIX DE
    SAINT-CLOUD   1m 4½f
£72,595   Saint-Cloud   5 July
20² **Akarad** 3-8-9 YSaint Martin.1
20* **Bikala** 3-8-9 SGorli......2.2
    Lancastrian 4-9-8
    MPhilipperon ½.3
23³ April Run 3-8-6
    PPaquet nk.4
14* Gold River 4-9-5
    FHead 2½.5
18² Prince Bee 4-9-8
    WCarson ¾.6
7* Argument 4-9-8 LPiggott..1.7
    Ecube 3-8-9 ALequeux...15.8
    Sir Raleigh 4-9-8
    PBruneau 2½.9
    Choucri 4-9-8
    J-PLefevre dist.10

27/10 AKARAD, 3/1 Argument and
Choucri, 7/2 Bikala, 17/4 Gold
River and Sir Raleigh, 9/2 Lan-
castrian and Prince Bee, 13/1
April Run, 18/1 Ecube.
H. H. Aga Khan (F. Mathet)
10ran 2m 38.9 (Good).

31 WILLIAM HILL
    JULY CUP   6f
£37,098   Newmarket   9 July
25* **Marwell** 3-8-8
    WRSwinburn 1
    Moorestyle 4-9-6
    LPiggott 3.2
    Sonoma 3-8-8 FHead....1½.3
9³ Prince Echo 3-8-11
    PEddery ½.4
5   Cut Throat 3-8-11
    PWaldron 4.5
5   Another Realm 3-8-11
    JMercer 4.6
    Milk of the Barley 4-9-6
    TIves hd.7
4   Welshwyn 3-8-8 BRouse.d-ht.7
25 Sparkling Boy 4-9-6
    BTaylor 2.9
    Leader of the Pack 5-9-6
    SPerks ½.10
25² Standaan 5-9-6 WCarson..4.11
25 Tina's Pet 3-8-11 EHide.nk.12
    Music Streak 3-8-11
    RGuest ¾.13

6   Ancient Regime 3-8-8
    GWMoore 14

13/8 MARWELL, 7/4 Moorestyle,
9/1 Sonoma, 14/1 Another Realm,
16/1 Cut Throat, 20/1 Prince Echo,
25/1 Ancient Regime, Standaan,
40/1 Tina's Pet, Welshwyn, 50/1
Milk of the Barley, Sparkling Boy,
100/1 Leader of the Pack, Music
Streak.
E. Loder (M. Stoute) 14ran
1m 14.10 (Good).

32 IRISH GUINNESS OAKS
            (3y f)   1½m
£34,975   The Curragh   18 July
19* **Blue Wind** 9-0 WSwinburn.1
    Condessa 9-0 DGillespie.2½.2
12 **Stracomer Queen** 9-0
    WCarson ¾.3
    My Sister 9-0 DHogan....4.4
    Waffles 9-0 PEddery.......3.5
12* Arctique Royale 9-0
    GCurran 3.6
12' Martinova 9-0 PShanahan.2½.7
    Hailebury 9-0 TMurphy...½.8
12 Citissima 9-0 JDeegan....1½.9
    Dietician 9-0 TCarberry.15.10

4/6 BLUE WIND, 7/2 Arctique
Royale, 10/1 Waffles, 16/1 Condessa,
My Sister, 20/1 Stracomer Queen,
22/1 Martinova, 50/1 Hailebury,
250/1 Citissima, Dietician.
Mrs B. Firestone (D. Weld)
10ran 2m 35.9 (Good to Firm).

33 KING GEORGE VI AND
    QUEEN ELIZABETH
    DIAMOND STAKES   1½m
£119,206   Ascot   25 July
26* **Shergar** 3-8-8
    WRSwinburn 1
27 **Madam Gay** 3-8-6
    GStarkey 4.2
27³ **Fingal's Cave** 4-9-7
    PEddery s.hd.3
27* Master Willie 4-9-7
    PWaldron 4.4
    Pelerin 4-9-7 BTaylor...2½.5
29 Cracaval 5-9-7
    SCauthen s.hd.6
    Light Cavalry 4-9-7
    LPiggott ½.7

2/5 SHERGAR, 7/1 Master Willie,
15/2 Pelerin, 12/1 Light Cavalry,
40/1 Fingal's Cave, Madam Gay,
80/1 Cracaval.
H. H. Aga Khan (M. Stoute)
7ran 2m 35.40 (Good to Firm).

34 PRIX ROBERT PAPIN
            (2y)   5½f
£27,829 Maisons-Laffitte 26 July
    Maelstrom Lake 8-11
    GDoleuze 1

982

Green Forest 8-11
  AGibert ½.2
Grease 8-9 ADiNardo. . . . ½.3
Pampabird 8-11
  MPhilipperon 2.4
Princely Penny 8-9
  YSaint-Martin 2.5
Top Nice 8-9 JDupin. . . . nk.6
Rollins 8-11 PPaquet. 3.7
Setkatdeu 8-11 HSamani. . . 2.8
Colman 8-11 ALequeux. . . 4.9
Saxham 8-11 JTaillard. . . . 3.10
23/10 MAELSTROM LAKE, 3/1
Grease, 7/2 Pampabird, 9/2 Colman,
10/1 Princely Penny, 12/1 Green
Forest, 15/1 Setkatdeu, 26/1 Rollins,
46/1 Top Nice, 84/1 Saxham.
  J. Feuillard (E. Bartholomew)
10ran 1m 5.6 (Dead).

35 GROSSER PREIS
    VON BERLIN   1½m
£26,667   Dusseldorf   26 July
22★ **Lydian** 3-8-6 FHead. 1
    Konigsstuhl 5-9-7 PAlafi.1½.2
28 **Tow** 3-8-5 SGorli. 7.3
    Wauthi 4-9-6 PRemmert. . . 4.4
27 Czubaryk 5-9-7 LMader. . 10.5
    Miltown Eagle 3-8-5
      MHofer 1.6
24² Shoot A Line 4-9-2 WCarson. 7
    Ishama 3-8-5 RGuest. 8
Ecurie Aland (Mme C. Head,
France) 8ran 2m 36.5 (Soft).

36 SUSSEX STAKES   1m
£49,350   Goodwood   29 July
9★ **Kings Lake** 3-8-10
      PEddery 1
9² **To-Agori-Mou** 3-8-10
      GStarkey hd.2
5   **Noalto** 3-8-10 JMercer. . nk.3
    Dalsaan 4-9-2
      WRSwinburn 1½.4
    Belmont Bay 4-9-7
      LPiggott s.hd.5
27 Last Fandango 4-9-7
      BRouse 3.6
9   Mattaboy 3-8-10 WCarson. 8.7
7³ In Fijar 4-9-7 AGibert . . . 7.8
    I'll See You 3-8-10
      GDuffield 9
11/8 To-Agori-Mou, 5/2 Kings
Lake, 11/2 Belmont Bay, 7/1
Mattaboy, 20/1 Last Fandango,
28/1 Dalsaan, In Fijar, 50/1 Noalto,
100/1 I'll See You.
  J. P. Binet (V. O'Brien, Ireland)
9ran 1m 39.38 (Good to Firm).

37 GALLAGHOUSE
    PHOENIX STAKES (2y) 5f
£12,242   Phoenix Park 8 August
    Achieved 9-0 PEddery. 1
    The Primate 9-0
      CRoche s.hd.2

Watties Rock 9-0
  PShanahan 2½.3
Lorn Goddess 8-11
  SCraine 1½.4
Zanskar 8-11 JMorgan. . . 3½.5
Shir Khan 9-0 TMurphy. . . 1.6
Dance Empress 8-11
  DHogan 1½.7
4/6 ACHIEVED, 3/1 The Primate,
9/1 Shir Khan, 10/1 Dance Empress,
16/1 Watties Rock, 33/1 Lorn
Goddess, Zanskar.
  R. Sangster (V. O'Brien) 7ran
57.7secs (Good to Firm).

38 PRIX JACQUES LE
    MAROIS   1m
£32,110   Deauville   16 August
29² **Northjet** 4-9-2 FHead. 1
36² **To-Agori-Mou** 3-8-9
      GStarkey 5.2
36★ **Kings Lake** 3-8-9
      PEddery ns.3
29 Hilal 5-9-2 AGibert. hd.4
29★ The Wonder 3-8-9
      ALequeux ns.5
23 Ukraine Girl 3-8-6
      YSaint-Martin 1½.6
29³ Cresta Rider 3-8-9
      PPaquet 1.7
21 Esclavo 5-9-2 RSuerland. . . 3.8
3   Big John 3-8-9 GDoleuze. 2½.9
    Gosport 5-9-2 J-CDesaint. 2.10
21 Sea's Valley 4-9-2
      ABadel t.o.11
5/2 To-Agori-Mou, 3/1 Kings
Lake, 7/1 Cresta Rider, 73/10
NORTHJET and Sea's Valley,
31/4 Ukraine Girl, 17/2 The
Wonder, 10/1 Gosport, 12/1 Hilal,
16/1 Big John, 34/1 Esclavo.
  S. Fradkoff (O. Douieb) 11ran
1m 34.5 (Firm).

39 BENSON AND HEDGES
    GOLD CUP   1m 2½f
£85,880   York   18 August
5   **Beldale Flutter** 3-8-10
      PEddery 1
26 **Kirtling** 3-8-10 LPiggott. . ¾.2
33 **Master Willie** 4-9-6
      PWaldron ¾.3
    Centurius 3-8-10 GStarkey. 4.4
17 Kind of Hush 3-8-10
      SCauthen ¾.5
17 Shotgun 3-8-10 EHide. . . 2½.6
27²(dis) Hard Fought 4-9-6
      WRSwinburn 3.7
33³ Fingal's Cave 4-9-6
      WCarson 5.8
30 Ecube 3-8-10 ALequeux. . . 6.9
5/2 Master Willie, 7/2 Hard Fought,
5/1 Fingal's Cave, 6/1 Centurius,
9/1 BELDALE FLUTTER, 11/1

Kirtling, 14/1 Kind of Hush, 30/1
Shotgun, 33/1 Ecube.
A. Kelly (M. Jarvis) 9ran 2m
13.28 (Good).

40 YORKSHIRE OAKS
              (3y f)   1½m
£41,356   York   18 August
32² **Condessa** 9-0 DGillespie....**1**
19 **Leap Lively** 9-0
              JMatthias nk.**2**
19 **Fiesta Fun** 9-0 PEddery...½.**3**
     Home On The Range 9-0
              LPiggott ¾.4
12 Overplay 9-0 WSwinburn.1½.5
     Royal Realm 9-0 JLowe..hd.6
19 Rhein Bridge 9-0 EHide...4.7
13 Viendra 9-0 SCauthen.....3.8
19 Go Leasing, Home On The
     Range 9-0 GStarkey..6.9
     Sajama 9-0 ALequeux...t.o.10
     Silken Knot 9-0 WCarson...f
4/1 Go Leasing, Home On The
Range, 5/1 CONDESSA, Overplay,
7/1 Leap Lively, 8/1 Rhein Bridge,
11/1 Viendra, 12/1 Royal Realm,
16/1 Silken Knot, 20/1 Sajama,
25/1 Fiesta Fun.
     C. Singer (J. Bolger, Ireland)
11ran 2m 35.32 (Good).

41 PRIX MORNY (2y)   6f
£27,273   Deauville   23 August
34² **Green Forest** 8-11 AGibert.**1**
34★ **Maelstrom Lake** 8-11
              GDoleuze ¾.**2**
     River Lady 8-8 PPaquet.hd.**3**
     Tender King 8-11
              PWaldron 1.4
     Gavo 8-11 WRSwinburn...5.5
9/10 River Lady, 5/2 Tender King,
21/4 Maelstrom Lake, 66/10
GREEN FOREST, 25/1 Gavo.
     M. Fustok (M. Saliba) 5 ran 1m
11.9 (Firm)

42 GROSSER PREIS
     VON BADEN   1½m
£38,889   Baden-Baden   6 Sept.
33 **Pelerin** 4-9-4 GStarkey.....**1**
     Hohritt 7-9-4 MHofer....2.**2**
     Maivogel 3-9-4
              HHorwart 1½.**3**
     Orofino 3-8-9 PAlafi.......½.4
35 Czubaryk 5-9-6 LMader..3½.5
     Dhausli 4-9-4 JDupin.....½.6
     Strong Gale 6-9-6
              PRemmert 7
22 Navarino 4-9-6
              DRichardson 8
     Sir P. Oppenheimer (H. Wragg)
8ran 2m 27.6 (Firm).

43 PRIX DU MOULIN
     DE LONGCHAMP   1m
£37,915   Longchamp   6 Sept.
38★ **Northjet** 4-9-2 FHead......**1**

38 **Hilal** 5-9-2
              YSaint-Martin 1½.**2**
38 **The Wonder** 3-8-12
              ALequeux ns.**3**
     Phydilla 3-8-9 Eddery....ns.4
36 Belmont Bay 4-9-2
              LPiggott 2.5
31 Another Realm 3-8-12
              PCook 2.6
38 Ukraine Girl 3-8-9
              GDubroeucq 2.7
     Ya Zaman 4-9-2 AGibert...¾.8
38 Gosport 5-9-2 J-CDesaint.1½.9
6³ Ionian Raja 3-8-9
              PPaquet 3.10
38 Sea's Valley 4-9-2
              ABadel 0
     Try To Smile 4-9-2
              RJallu 0
6/10 NORTHJET, Phydilla, Sea's
Valley and Try To Smile, 7/2
Hilal and Ya Zaman, 23/4 The
Wonder, 8/1 Belmont Bay, 18/1
Ukraine Girl, 20/1 Gosport, 42/1
Another Realm, 54/1 Ionian Raja.
     S. Fradkoff (O. Douieb) 12ran
1m 35.2 (Firm).

44 ST LEGER STAKES
              (3y)   1¾m 127y
£76,190   Doncaster   12 Sept.
26² **Cut Above** 9-0 JMercer.....**1**
28★ **Glint of Gold** 9-0
              JMatthias 2½.**2**
     Bustomi 9-0 LPiggott....4.**3**
33★ Shergar 9-0 WRSwinburn..5.4
     Brigadier Hawk 9-0
              JSeagrave 25.5
17 Riberetto 9-0 EHide....dist.6
     Magikin 9-0 BRaymond.....7
4/9 Shergar, 4/1 Glint of Gold,
13/2 Bustomi, 28/1 CUT ABOVE,
66/1 Riberetto, 250/1 Magikin,
Brigadier Hawk.
     Sir J. Astor (R. Hern) 7ran
3m 11.60 (Good).

45 PRIX VERMEILLE
              (3y f)   1½m
£68,426   Longchamp   13 Sept.
30 **April Run** 9-2 PPaquet.....**1**
     Leandra 9-2 FHead.....1½.**2**
33² **Madam Gay** 9-2
              LPiggott hd.**3**
23² Val d'Erica 9-2
              YSaint-Martin 3.4
     Snow Day 9-2 PEddery...½.5
     Landresse 9-2 SCauthen.s.nk.6
23 Tootens 9-2 GDoleuze.....2.7
40² Leap Lively 9-2
              JMatthias 6.8
     Sangue 9-2 ALequeux.....¾.9
23 Last Love 9-2 SGorli....20.10
7/4 Madam Gay, 7/2 Val d'Erica,
48/10 APRIL RUN, 8/1 Sangue,

984

10/1 Landresse, 12/1 Leandra, 16/1 Tootens, 19/1 Leap Lively, 22/1 Snow Day, 26/1 Last Love.

Mrs B. Firestone (F. Boutin) 10ran 2m 32.9 (Good).

46 JOE MCGRATH MEMORIAL STAKES 1¼m
£18,359 Leopardstown 19 Sept.

38³	Kings Lake 3-8-11 PEddery	1
	Erins Isle 3-8-11 DGillespie	1.2
39	Kind of Hush 3-8-11 SCauthen	3.3
32★	Blue Wind 3-8-8 WSwinburn	2½.4
	Gilded Vanity 4-9-2 SMartinez	hd.5
32	Arctique Royale 3-8-8 GCurran	4.6
	Countess Tully 3-8-8 SCraine	2.7
32	My Sister 3-8-8 CRoche	2.8
	Pieces of Gold 4-9-2 JVSmith	¾.9
26	Wolver Heights 3-8-11 AMurray	nk.10
	Red Nanda 3-8-8 TMurphy	12.11
	Run of Diamonds 4-9-5 JDeegan	12

2/1 Blue Wind, 9/4 KINGS LAKE, 4/1 Kind of Hush, 10/1 Gilded Vanity, 16/1 Arctique Royale, Erins Isle, 20/1 My Sister, 25/1 Countess Tully, 50/1 Pieces of Gold, Red Nanda, Run of Diamonds, Wolver Heights.

J. P. Binet (V. O'Brien) 12ran 2m 6.3 (Good).

47 PRIX DE LA SALAMANDRE (2y) 7f
£30,581 Longchamp 20 Sept.

41★	Green Forest 8-11 AGibert	1
	Zino 8-11 PPaquet	1½.2
	Star Princess 8-8 SGorli	1½.3
	Exclusive Order 8-8 MPhilipperon	2.4
	Beldale Bid 8-11 PEddery	6.5

9/10 Zino, 2/1 GREEN FOREST, 7/2 Exclusive Order, 8/1 Beldale Bid, 19/1 Star Princess.

M. Fustok (M. Saliba) 5ran 1m 24.3 (Soft).

48 WILLIAM HILL CHEVELEY PARK STAKES (2y f) 6f
£45,238 Newmarket 30 Sept.

	Woodstream 8-11 PEddery	1
	On The House 8-11 LPiggott	1½.2

	Admiral's Princess 8-11 JMercer	1½.3
	Current Pattie 8-11 SCauthen	¾.4
	BlessThe Match 8-11 GDuffield	nk.5
	Corley Moor 8-11 BRaymond	1½.6
	Silojoka 8-11 EHide	3.7
	Aegean Beauty 8-11 MBirch	hd.8
	Kristallina 8-11 RGuest	2.9
	O-Rose Fortunata 8-11 SPerks	nk.10
	Sybolda 8-11 PRobinson	½.11
	Plum Bold 8-11 JReid	4.12
	Hollow Heart 8-11 PWaldron	3.13

5/2 On The House, WOODSTREAM, 9/2 Hollow Heart, 9/1 Plum Bold, 10/1 Admiral's Princess, 20/1 Bless The Match, 25/1 Aegean Beauty, Corley Moor, Current Pattie, 50/1 Kristallina, 66/1 O-Rose Fortunata, Silojoka, Sybolda.

R. Sangster (V. O'Brien, Ireland) 13ran 1m 14.12 (Good).

49 WILLIAM HILL MIDDLE PARK STAKES (2y) 6f
£42,862 Newmarket 1 October

	Cajun 9-0 LPiggott	1
	Lucky Hunter 9-0 BRouse	¾.2
	Wattlefield 9-0 WRSwinburn	nk.3
41	Tender King 9-0 PWaldron	¾.4
	Peterhof (USA) 9-0 PEddery	1½.5
	End of the Line 9-0 SCauthen	¾.6
	My Dad Tom 9-0 GBaxter	s.hd.7
	Philip Martin 9-0 AGibert	hd.8
	Take The Floor 9-0 EHide	hd.9
	Chris's Lad 9-0 JReid	1.10
	Match Master 9-0 JMercer	nk.11
	Hays 9-0 BRaymond	s.hd.12
	Mydrone 9-0 MBirch	1½.13

15/8 Hays, 7/2 Peterhof, Tender King, 10/1 Wattlefield, 11/1 End of the Line, 20/1 CAJUN, 25/1 Philip Martin, 33/1 Match Master, My Dad Tom, Mydrone, Take The Floor, 50/1 Chris's Lad, 66/1 Lucky Hunter.

J. Stone (H. Cecil) 13ran 1m 16.49 (Good).

50 PREMIO LYDIA TESIO (3y + 4y f) 1¼m
£18,921 Rome 3 October

	Oraston 3-8-9 JReid	1

985

11² **Rattling Wind** 3-8-9
GDettori s.hd.**2**
19 **Ivory Wings** 3-8-9
MDepalmas 2½.**3**
Idelka 3-8-9 EBietolini 6.4
11³ Scrocca 3-8-9 PPerlanti . . 1½.5
2 Altobella 3-8-9 OPessi 2.6
Bee Imperial 3-8-9
SFancera 3.7
Mary Gloria 4-9-0
GPucciatti 10.8
5/6 Ivory Wings, 6/5 Rattling
Wind and Mary Gloria, 7/1 Idelka,
12/1 ORASTON, 14/1 Scrocca,
16/1 Altobella, 33/1 Bee Imperial.
Oceanic Ltd (F. J. Houghton)
8ran 2m 10.5 (Heavy).

51 PRIX MARCEL BOUSSAC
(2y f)   1m
£29,014   Longchamp   4 October
Play It Safe 8-9
LPiggott 1
41³ **River Lady** 8-9
PPaquet hd.**2**
Perlee 8-9 GDoleuze 3.3
First Water 8-9
APerrotta 2.4
Tudorville 8-9
YSaint-Martin ¾.5
Bouillonnante 8-9
FPegurri s.hd.6
Albala 8-9 GWMoore 2½.7
Travel On 8-9 JMercer 6.8
7/10 River Lady, 22/10 PLAY
IT SAFE, 37/4 Tudorville, 11/1
Travel On, 15/1 Perlee, 23/1
Albala, 25/1 Bouillonnante, 53/1
First Water.
Mrs B. Firestone (F. Boutin)
8ran 1m 46.9 (Dead).

52 PRIX DE L'ABBAYE
DE LONGCHAMP   5f
£29,014   Longchamp   4 October
31★ **Marwell** 3-9-8
WRSwinburn 1
25 **Sharpo** 4-9-11
PEddery nk.**2**
Rabdan 4-9-11 LPiggott . . 1.3
31 Ancient Regime 3-9-8
MPhilipperon 2.4
25³ Runnett 4-9-11 BRaymond . ½.5
31³ Sonoma 3-9-8 FHead 2.6
31 Music Streak 3-9-11
RGuest ns.7
25 Cooleen Jack 3-9-11
AMurray 1½.8
Kearney 4-9-11
WSwinburn 1½.9
Naomi Joy 4-9-8
JMercer 1½.10
Evens Sharpo, 42/10 MARWELL,
17/4 Rabdan, 23/4 Runnett, 9/1
Sonoma, 20/1 Ancient Regime,
45/1 Naomi Joy, 48/1 Music Streak,
59/1 Cooleen Jack, 61/1 Kearney.

E. Loder (M. Stoute) 10ran
58.7 secs (Dead).

53 PRIX DE L'ARC
DE TRIOMPHE   1½m
£193,424   Longchamp   4 October
30 **Gold River** 4-9-1
GWMoore 1
30² **Bikala** 3-8-11 SGorli ¾.**2**
45★ **April Run** 3-8-8
PPaquet ns.**3**
Perrault 4-9-4 HSamani 2.4
24★ Ardross 5-9-4 LPiggott 2.5
30 Argument 4-9-4
ALequeux 1½.6
30★ Akarad 3-8-11
YSaint-Martin ¾.7
45 Tootens 3-8-8 GDoleuze . . .3.8
45² Leandra 3-8-8
GDubroeucq hd.9
45 Snow Day 3-8-8
AGibert s.nk.10
46★ Kings Lake 3-8-11
PEddery s.nk.11
30³ Lancastrian 4-9-4
MPhilipperon 5.12
30 Prince Bee 4-9-4
JMercer 1½.13
44★ Cut Above 3-8-11
BTaylor hd.14
46 Blue Wind 3-8-8
WSwinburn nk.15
26 Gap of Dunloe 3-8-11
WRSwinburn 2.16
42★ Pelerin 4-9-4 EHide 1½.17
40★ Condessa 3-8-8
DGillespie 2½.18
20 Rahotep 3-8-11
J-LKessas s.hd.19
7 Detroit 4-9-1 FHead 3.20
Ring The Bell 4-9-3
NTiley 21
46 Gilded Vanity 4-9-1
GCurran 22
39★ Beldale Flutter 3-8-11
AMurray 23
Action Man 6-9-4 OLarsen.24
2/1 Akarad, 7/2 Detroit, Kings Lake
and Snow Day, 11/2 Ardross, 13/2
April Run and Blue Wind, 12/1
Beldale Flutter, 14/1 Lancastrian
and Prince Bee, Bikala, 25/1
Rahotep, 27/1 Perrault and Leandra,
32/1 Argument, 33/1 Pelerin, 38/1
Cut Above, 53/1 GOLD RIVER,
99/1 Action Man, Ring The Bell,
Gilded Vanity, Gap of Dunloe,
Tootens, Condessa.
J. Wertheimer (A. Head) 24ran
2m 35.2 (Dead).

54 IRISH ST LEGER
(3y)   1¾m
£19,045   The Curragh   10 October
Protection Racket 9-0
BTaylor 1

986

46² **Erins Isle** 9-0
DGillespie 3.**2**
Bedford 9-0 JMatthias...5.**3**
26 Ore 9-0 GCurran.........1.4
40 Overplay 8-11 WSwinburn.4.5
Sailor King 9-0 CRoche....3.6
Ashpin 9-0 TMurphy....25.7
6/4 PROTECTION RACKET, 2/1
Erins Isle, 3/1 Ore, 14/1 Bedford,
Overplay, 16/1 Sailor King, 50/1
Ashpin.
S. Fradkoff (J. Hindley) 7ran
3m 12.4 (Dead).

55 GRAND CRITERIUM
(2y) 1m
£48,828 Longchamp 11 October
47* **Green Forest** 8-11 AGibert.**1**
Norwick 8-11 GStarkey..2½.**2**
34 **Rollins** 8-11
YSaint-Martin 4.**3**
Anfield 8-11 CRoche......3.4
47³ Star Princess 8-8 SGorli....¾.5
Morse Code 8-11
J-CDesaint nk.6
Persepolis 8-11 PPaquet....1.7
Triple Axel 8-11 LPiggott..2.8
Bosto 8-11 ALequeux.....8.9
Pushkin 8-11 PLagoutte.hd.10
14/10 GREEN FOREST, 13/4
Norwick, 11/2 Persepolis and
Pushkin, 15/2 Triple Axel, 33/4
Rollins, 9/1 Anfield, 18/1 Star
Princess, 27/1 Bosto, 28/1 Morse
Code.
M. Fustok (M. Saliba) 10ran
1m 46.2 (Soft).

56 PREIS VON EUROPA 1⅛m
£73,170 Cologne 11 October
44² **Glint of Gold** 3-8-11
JMatthias **1**
42 **Czubaryk** 5-9-2 LMader.3½.**2**
Struna 3-8-7 VJakovlev...2.**3**
Dom Menotti 4-9-2
ABadel 4.4
Solaris 3-8-7 PAlafi......nk.5
Surdut 3-8-11 JOchocki...4.6
Jarabub 4-9-6 MMelnicki....7
35 Wauthi 3-8-11
Damas 3-8-11
ATschugujewez 9
Amarkson 3-8-7 GBocskai..10
P. Mellon (I. Balding) 10ran
2m 43.8 (Heavy).

57 GRAN CRITERIUM
(2y) 1m
£18,921 Milan 11 October
34³ **Grease** 8-8 ADiNardo......**1**
Dark Angel 8-8
GPucciatti 3.**2**
How To Go 8-11
VPanici 5.**3**
Ormeggio 8-11 CForte....2.4

Pardolero 8-11 GDettori...2.5
Man Overboard 8-11
SDettori ½.6
Pointe de Mire 8-11
MDepalmas 1.7
Laffitte 8-11 PAgus.......2.8
Nijinsky Model 8-11
APerrotta 6.9
2/5 GREASE, 5/2 Pardolero and
How To Go, 9/2 Nijinsky Model,
10/1 Pointe de Mire, 20/1 Dark
Angel, 25/1 Laffitte, 33/1 Man
Overboard, 40/1 Ormeggio.
A. Boesso (G. Benetti) 9ran
1m 44.8 (Heavy).

58 WILLIAM HILL
DEWHURST STAKES
(2y) 7f
£51,358 Newmarket 16 October
Wind and Wuthering
9-0 PWaldron............**1**
Be My Native 9-0
BRaymond 7.**2**
49 **Tender King** 9-0
GBaxter nk.**3**
Codrington 9-0
SCauthen 1½.4
Solaboy 9-0 JMercer.....nk.5
Telephone Man 9-0
PRobinson 1½.6
Simply Great 9-0
LPiggott 4.7
Raconteur (USA) 9-0
PEddery 3.8
Diamond Cutter 9-0
EJohnson 2½.9
6/4 Simply Great, 15/8 Raconteur,
8/1 Tender King, 11/1 WIND
AND WUTHERING, 12/1 Cod-
rington, 50/1 Be My Native,
Solaboy, Telephone Man 100/1
Diamond Cutter.
R. Cyzer (H. Candy) 9ran
1m 26.81 (Good).

59 CHAMPION STAKES 1¼m
£66,732 Newmarket 17 October
28³ **Vayrann** 3-8-10
YSaint-Martin **1**
Cairn Rouge 4-9-0
AMurray..............2.**2**
Amyndas 3-8-10 GBaxter.2.**3**
53 Prince Bee 4-9-3
JMercer 1½.4
38² To-Agori-Mou 3-8-10
GStarkey ¾.5
43³ The Wonder 3-8-10
AGibert ¾.6
Critique 3-8-10 LPiggott...½.7
Castle Keep 4-9-3
PEddery nk.8
45³ Madam Gay 3-8-7 JReid...2.9
39³ Master Willie 4-9-3
PWaldron nk.10

987

40   Go Leasing 3-8-7
     WRSwinburn ¾.11
53   Snow Day 3-8-7
     PPaquet ¾.12
36³ Noalto 3-8-10 GDuffield.12.13
46³ Kind of Hush 3-8-10
     SCauthen nk.14
     Val de Mougins 4-9-3
     HSamani 4.15
39² Kirtling 3-8-10
     BRaymond ½.16

5/1 To-Agori-Mou, 15/2 VAY-RANN, 8/1 Cairn Rouge, Master Willie, 9/1 Critique, The Wonder, 14/1 Kirtling, Madam Gay, 18/1 Prince Bee, Snow Day, 20/1 Castle Keep, 33/1 Go Leasing, Kind of Hush, 50/1 Noalto, 66/1 Amyndas, 100/1 Val de Mougir.s.
   H. H. Aga Khan (F. Mathet) 16ran 2m 8.05 (Good).

60   WILLIAM HILL
     FUTURITY STAKES
         (2y)   1m
£55,786 Doncaster   24 October

    Count Pahlen 9-0 GBaxter . . 1
    Paradis Terrestre 9-0
     LPiggott ½.2
    Jalmood 9-0 GDuffield. . hd.3
55² Norwick 9-0 GStarkey . . . 1½.4
    Super Sunrise 9-0
     WRSwinburn 2½.5
    Ashenden 9-0 SCauthen . . 1½.6
    Gouverno 9-0 JBleasdale . . 1.7
    Assert 9-0 CRoche s.hd.8
    That's My Son 9-0 EHide . . 7.9
    General Anders 9-0
     BRaymond 1½.10
    Exclusive Air 9-0 TIves . . 1½.11
    Favoloso 9-0 JMatthias . . . 3.12
49   End of the Line 9-0
     EJohnson 13

6/4 Paradis Terrestre, 4/1 Norwick, 5/1 Assert, 10/1 Jalmood, 12/1 Super Sunrise, 16/1 Ashenden, 18/1 That's My Son, 20/1 General Anders, 22/1 End of the Line, 25/1 COUNT PAHLEN, 50/1 Exclusive Air, Favoloso, Gouverno.
   Mrs A. Villar (B. Hobbs) 13ran 1m 42.40 (Dead).

61   PRIX DE LA FORET   7f
£33,461 Longchamp 25 October
31² Moorestyle 4-9-12
     LPiggott 1
    Lou Piguet 3-9-11
     J-CDesaint 4.2
    Diamond Prospect 3-9-11
     YSaint-Martin nk.3
43   Belmont Bay 4-9-12
     JMercer ¾.4
52² Sharpo 4-9-12
     PEddery ½.5

43² Hilal 5-9-12 AGibert 1½.6
29   Princely Ruler 3-9-11
     MPhilipperon 10.7
38   Cresta Rider 3-9-11
     PPaquet ¾.8
5   Dalby Mustang 3-9-11
     JTandari 15.9

8/10 MOORESTYLE, 3/1 Diamond Prospect and Hilal, 13/2 Sharpo, 10/1 Princely Ruler, 11/1 Belmont Bay, 13/1 Cresta Rider, 18/1 Lou Piguet, 79/1 Dalby Mustang.
   Moores International Furnishings Limited (R. Armstrong) 9ran 1m 30.4 (Heavy).

62   PRIX ROYAL-OAK 1m 7½f
£33,461 Longchamp 25 October
53   Ardross 5-9-3 LPiggott 1
14   Proustille 4-9-0 SGorli . . . 4.2
53★ Gold River 4-9-0 FHead.2½.3
14   El Badr 6-9-3 AGibert 3.4
    Alma Ata 3-8-9 TIves ½.5
28² Tipperary Fixer 3-8-12
     MPhilipperon 10.6
14³ Chicbury 4-9-3 GDoleuze.15.7

8/10 Gold River, 23/10 ARDROSS, 13/2 Tipperary Fixer, 13/1 Proustille, 15/1 El Badr, 16/1 Alma Ata, 24/1 Chicbury.
   C. St. George (H. Cecil) 7ran 3m 56.7 (Heavy).

63   GRAN PREMIO DEL
     JOCKEY CLUB (Gr 1) 1½m
£40,798   Milan   25 October
35² Konigsstuhl 5-9-3 PAlafi . . . 1
    Solero 3-8-11 SDettori 5.2
    Bellman 3-8-11
     GDettori 2½.3
43   Ya Zaman 4-9-3 BTaylor . . ½.4
45   Val d'Erica 3-8-8 PPerlanti.8.5
50   Idelka 3-8-8 LBietolini 10.6
    Giannino Umbro 4-9-3
     CForte 4.7

6/5 KONIGSSTUHL, 6/4 Bellman, 5/2 Val d'Erica, 6/1 Ya Zaman, 10/1 Solero, 33/1 Giannino Umbro, 50/1 Idelka.
   Gestut Zoppenbroich (S. von Mitzlaff, Germany). 7ran 2m 37.3 (Soft).

64   PREMIO ROMA (Gr 1) 1½m
£26,247   Rome   15 November
    Dentz 3-8-9 VPanici 1
22   Scouting Miller 4-9-0
     GDettori 3.2
56² Czubaryk 5-9-0 LMader.hd.3
    Don't Sulk 3-8-6
     PPaquet 4.4

Enoc 4-9-0 GPisa ½.5
Salora Lady 3-8-6 JReid ...3.6
15 Haul Knight 5-9-0
 SFancera 2.7
63 Giannino Umbro 4-9-0
 CForte 1½.8
54³ Bedford 3-8-9 JMatthias ..1½.9
 Shaftesbury 5-9-0 GStarkey2.10
 Jabo 5-9-0 Miss FPflunger .3.11
63² Solero 3-8-9 SDettori 2.12

Efidanville 3-8-9 LPiggott.4.13
5/2 Don't Sulk, 9/2 Shaftesbury,
5/1 Bedford, 6/1 Czubaryk, 7/1
Solero, 10/1 Salora Lady, 22/1
Scouting Miller, 25/1 Efidanville,
30/1 Jabo, 33/1 Haul Knight, 40/1
Giannino Umbro, 66/1 Enoc,
85/1 DENTZ.
Razza di Vedano (F. Regoli)
13ran 3m 4.5 (Soft).

INDEX

990

991

TRAINERS

The figures in brackets are the number of winners each trainer has had over the past five seasons, from 1977 to 1981 inclusive. Quarters and telephone numbers are given after the trainer's name.

Akehurst, R. P. J.   (13:15:14:9:1)
Lambourn
       Lambourn (0488) 71850
Albina, M. H.   (—:—:—:0:10)
Newmarket
       Newmarket (0638) 61998
Allan, A. R.   (—:0:1:0:3)
St Boswells
       St Boswells (083 52) 2403
Allingham, P. B.   (3:0:0:0:0)
Luton   Offley (046 276) 337
Ancil, D. I.   (3:2:2:2:0:)
Banbury   Banbury (0295) 711006
Andrews, A. M.   (—:—:—:—:0)
Taunton
   Bishops Lydeard (0823) 432 632
Armstrong, R. W.   (19:30:38:29:45)
Newmarket
       Newmarket (0638) 3333/4
Armytage, R. C.   (0:0:0:0:0)
East Ilsley
       East Ilsley (063 528) 203
Arnold, A. T.   (—:0:0:0:0)
Bridgnorth
       Quatt (0746) 780400
Ashworth, P. H.   (6:6:0:1:3)
Epsom   Epsom (037 27) 20336
Asquith, P.   (—:12:9:6:5)
Wetherby   Wetherby (0937) 62122
Atkins, R. A. L.   (0:1:2:0:0)
Elstead   Elstead (0252) 702028
Atkinson, W.   (0:0:0:0:0)
Carlisle   Carlisle (0228) 25649
Austin, C. A.   (—:2:2:4:2)
Wokingham
       Wokingham (0734) 786 425

Bailey, A.   (—:—:—:6:4)
Newmarket
       Newmarket (0638) 750 847
Bailey, K. C.   (—:0:0:0:0)
East Ilsley
       East Ilsley (063 528) 253
Bailey, P. G.   (0:0:0:0:0)
Wantage
       Amesbury (098 02) 22138
Bain, Mrs P. A.   (—:—:—:—:0)
Baydon
       Marlborough (0672) 40708
Baker, J. H.   (—:0:1:0:0)
Tiverton
       Tiverton (088 42) 56618
Baker, R. J.   (—:—:—:—:6)
Manton
       Lockeridge (067 286) 298
Balding, A.   (0:2:5:4:8)
Doncaster
       Doncaster (0302) 710221
Balding, G. B.   (22:16:17:26:14)
Weyhill   Weyhill (026 477) 2278

Balding, I. A.   (33:39:39:49:39)
Kingsclere
       Kingsclere (0635) 298210
Barnes, T. A.   (0:5:3:1:0)
Ousby
       Langwathby (076 881) 379
Barons, D. H.   (0:0:0:0:0)
Kingsbridge
       Loddiswell (054 855) 326
Barratt, L. J.   (2:3:2:1:0)
Oswestry
       Queens Head (069 188) 209
Barrett, W. A.   (—:—:—:—:0)
Lincoln
   Fenton Claypole (063684) 413
Barron, T. D.   (—:—:0:0:5)
Thirsk   Thirsk (0845) 587 435
Beeson, E. E. G.   (0:2:8:6:5)
Lewes
       Lewes (079 16) 4581 and 5654
Bell, Mrs A. M.   (—:—:—:—:1)
Biggar   Skirling (089 96) 273
Bell, C. H.   (0:0:0:6:6)
Hawick   Denholme (045 087) 278
Benstead, C. J.   (16:18:17:17:19)
Epsom   Ashtead (037 22) 73152
Bentley, W.   (—:—:—:7:6:11)
Middleham
       Wensleydale (0969) 22289
Berry, J.   (6:20:11:15:19)
Lancaster   Forton (0524) 791179
Bethell, J. D. W.   (25:14:15:19:14)
Fordingbridge
       Rockbourne (072 53) 220
Bevan, P. J.   (0:0:0:0:0)
Kingstone
   Dapple Heath (088 921) 647 or 670
Blakeney, R. E.   (0:0:0:0:0)
Devizes   Cannings (038 086) 254
Blanshard, M. T. W.   (—:—:0:4:5)
Lambourn
       Lambourn (0488) 71091
Blum, G.   (9:5:7:6:5)
Newmarket
       Newmarket (0638) 2734
Blundell, J. W.   (—:—:—:—:0)
Grimsby
   North Thoresby (047 287) 256
Bolton, M. J.   (2:2:1:5:0)
East Grinstead
   Dormans Park (034 287) 403
Booth, C. B. B.   (2:1:5:1:6)
Flaxton
   Whitwell-on-the-Hill (065 381) 586
Bosley, J. R.   (—:—:2:1:4)
Bampton
   Bampton Castle (0993) 850 212
Boss, R.   (15:18:14:21:9)
Newmarket
       Newmarket (0638) 61335

Bradley, J. M. (8:7:4:2:0)
Chepstow
Chepstow (029 12) 2486
Brassey, K. M. (—:—:—:—:0)
Lambourn
Lambourn (0488) 71508
Brennan, O. (0:0:0:0:0)
Newark   Caunton (063 686) 332
Bridger, J. J. (—:—:—:—:0)
Chichester
Eastergate (024368) 3525
Bridgwater, K. S. (0:4:2:1:0)
Solihull   Knowle (056 45) 77026
Brittain, C. E. (31:52:34:25:54)
Newmarket
Newmarket (0638) 3739 and 4347
Brookshaw, P. T. (—:—:—:—:0)
Melton Mowbray
Melton Mowbray (0664) 813161
Butler, P. (0:0:0:0:0)
Lewes   Plumpton (0273) 890124
Bycroft, N. (—:—:—:—:0)
Brandsby, Yorkshire
Brandsby (034 75) 641

Callaghan, N. A. (24:40:34:14:29)
Newmarket
Newmarket (0638) 4040
Calver, P. (0:2:7:2:2)
Ripon   Ripon (0765) 700313
Calvert, J. B. (9:3:0:5:3)
Hambleton
Thirsk (0845) 597373
Camacho, M. J. C. (20:17:13:7:16)
Tadcaster
Tadcaster (0937) 833294
Cambidge, B. R. (0:0:0:0:0)
Shifnal
Weston-under-Lizard (095 276) 249
Candy, H. D. N. B. (32:35:39:28:30)
Wantage   Uffington (036 782) 276
Cann, J. F. (0:1:0:0:0)
Cullompton, Devon
Kentisbeare (088 46) 356
Carr, E. J. (13:11:4:3:4)
Hambleton
Thirsk (0845) 597 288
Carter, E. (2:2:2:0:3)
Malton   Malton (0653) 3522
Carter, R. (3:0;0:2:0)
Swaffham
Gooderstone (036 621) 226
Cecil, H. R. A. (74:108:128:84:107)
Newmarket
Newmarket (0638) 2192
or 2387 (home)
Chamberlain, N. (—:—:—:0:0)
West Auckland
Bishop Auckland (0388) 832 465
Chapman, D. W. (2:2:2:5:11)
Stillington, York
Easingwold (0347) 21683
Chapman, M. C. (0:0:0:0:0)
Market Harborough
Clipston (085 886) 255
Charles, W. (0:0:1:3:0)
Warwick
Warwick (0926) 43878

Charlton, J. I. A. (—:—:—:—:0)
Stocksfield
Stocksfield (06615) 3247
Clay, W. (0:0:0:2:0)
Uttoxeter
Uttoxeter (088 93) 2068
Cole, P. F. I. (47:56:61:48:50)
Lambourn
Lambourn (0488) 71632
Cole, S. N. (0:0:0:0:0)
Newport Pagnell
Northampton (0604) 870330
Collingridge, H. J. (1:3:9:3:7)
Newmarket
Newmarket (0638) 5454
Cottrell, L. G. (0:0:2:2:2)
Cullompton, Devon
Kentisbeare (088 46) 320
Cousins, M. A. (—:1:0:1:1)
Tarporley
Little Budworth (082 921)
260/316
Cousins, Mrs S. A. (—:—:—:1:0)
Carnforth
Carnforth (052 473) 3058
Craig, T. (24:16:10:5:5)
Dunbar   Dunbar (0368) 62583
Cross, R. F. (0:0:0:0:0)
Alnwick   Chattan (066 85) 247
Crossley, C. C. (6:8:7:12:4)
Wirral   (051 648) 1546
Crump, N. F. (0:4:3:2:3)
Middleham
Wensleydale (0969) 23269
Cumani, L. M. (30:53:19:26:30)
Newmarket
Newmarket (0638) 61569 and 5432
Cundell, P. D. (12:10:10:10:10)
Compton
Compton (063 522) 267/8
Cunningham-Brown, K. O.
(—:—:—:—:0)
Stockbridge   Wallop (026 478) 611
Cuthbert, T. A. (—:—:—:0:0)
Carlisle   Carlisle (0228) 60822
Czerpak, J. D. (—:—:—:0:1)
Kenilworth
Coventry (0203) 304 724

Dale, D. (0:0:4:4:7)
Newmarket
Newmarket (0638) 61586
Dalton, A. (5:2:2:3:0)
Newmarket
Newmarket (0638) 3741
Davies, J. D. J. (—:—:—:0:0)
Billinghurst
Billinghurst (040372) 2678
Davison, A. R. (0:2:6:0:0)
Caterham
Caterham (0883) 43857
Delahooke, M. C. (0:0:0:0:0)
Cheltenham
Bishops Cleeve (024 267) 2162
Dever, F. (2:1:0:0:0)
Newark
Mansfield (0623) 870276

Dickinson, M. W.   (—:—:—:1:1)
Harewood
  Office: Harewood (0532) 886536
  Home: Harewood (0532) 886346
Dingwall, C. B. J.   (3:0:1:0:0)
East Ilsley
      East Ilsley (063 528) 253
Dodd, J. E.   (—:—:—:—:3)
Beckhampton
      Avebury (067 23) 345
Dodds, J. P.   (0:0:0:0:0)
Alnwick   Chatton (066 85) 216
Douglas-Home, J. T. A.
              (—:—:0:0:1)
Wantage
     East Hendred (023588) 247
Doyle, J. C. M.   (—:—:—:5:0)
Wetherby
   Wetherby (0937) 63855 (home)
      or 65051 (stable)
Dudgeon, I. M.   (0:1:0:0:0)
Warminster
   Codford St Mary (09855) 477
Duggins, P. H.   (—:—:—:—:0)
Shepton Mallet, Somerset
    Upton Noble (074 985) 527
Dunlop, J. L.   (42:73:96:91:67)
Arundel   Arundel (0903) 882194
  Home: Arundel (0903) 882106
Durr, F.   (—:—:38:51:42)
Newmarket
     Newmarket (0638) 2090
Easterby, M. H.   (46:50:74:63:38)
Malton
   Kirby Misperton (065 386) 600
Easterby, M. W.   (24:12:31:17:25)
Sheriff Hutton
    Sheriff Hutton (03477) 368
Eckley, M. W.   (—:—:—:0:0)
Ludlow   Brimfield (058 472) 372
Edmunds, J.   (2:1:0:0:0)
Birmingham
     Wythall (0564) 822334
Edwards, J. A. C.   (1:0:0:0:0)
Ross-on-Wye
   Harewood End (098987) 259
Eldin, E.   (—:—:0:11:11)
Newmarket
  Newmarket (0638) 2036 or 3217
Elsey, C. W. C.   (21:18:12:26:11)
Malton   Malton (0653) 3149
Elsworth, D. R. C. (—:—:10:12:10)
Chippenham   Box (0225) 742 471
Etherington, J.   (29:22:24:20:20)
Malton   Malton (0653) 2842
Fairbairn, G. B.   (—:—:0:0:0)
Hallington
  Great Whittington (043 472) 215
Fairhurst, T.   (18:34:20:11:13)
Middleham
   Wensleydale (0969) 23362
Feilden, P. J.   (—:—:3:3:4)
Newmarket
     Exning (063877) 637
Felgate, P. S.   (0:0:0:1:0)
Nottingham
    Whatton (0949) 50335

Finch, Mrs A.   (0:0:0:0:0)
Shaftesbury
   East Knoyle (074 783) 305
Fisher, A. L.   (0:0:0:0:0)
Melton Mowbray
     Leicester (0533) 605907
Fisher, R. F.   (—:—:—:—:0)
Ulverston
    Ulverston (0229) 55664
Fisher, W. E.   (0:0:0:0:0)
Chewton Mendip
   Chewton Mendip (076121) 283
Fitzgerald, J. G.   (15:9:15:13:14)
Malton   Malton (0653) 2718
Fleming, H.   (0:0:0:1:2)
Cleethorpes
    Cleethorpes (0472) 65215
Fletcher, G. G.   (—:—:2:3:4)
Newmarket
    Newmarket (0638) 68826
Forsey, B.   (—:—:—:—:0)
Warminster
   Codford St Mary (09855) 491
Forster, T. A.   (0:0:0:0:0)
Letcombe Bassett
    Wantage (023 57) 3092
Fox, C. J.   (—:—:—:—:0)
Amesbury
    Shrewton (0980) 620 861
Francis, M. E. D.   (7:2:3:3:3)
Lambourn
    Lambourn (0488) 71700
Francis, W. D.   (0:2:4:2:4)
Malpas   Tilston (082 98) 208
Gandolfo, D. R.   (6:3:4:2:3)
Wantage   Wantage (023 57) 3242
Garraton, D. T.   (—:—:—:1:3)
Malton   Rillington (094 42) 506
Gaselee, N.A.D.C.   (0:3:2:5:6)
Lambourn
    Lambourn (0488) 71503
Gifford, J. T.   (1:0:3:1:0)
Findon   Findon (090 671) 2226
Gilbert, J. A.   (—:—:—:1:1)
Oakham   Somerby (066 477) 614
Gillam, T. A.   (0:0:0:1:0)
Boroughbridge
   Boroughbridge (09012) 2592
Goodwill, A. W.   (6:5:2:7:5)
Newmarket
    Newmarket (0638) 61831
Gosling, T.   (6:4:2:4:1)
Epsom   Epsom (037 27) 22080
Graham, N. R. H.   (—:—:—:—:0)
Gray, C. W.   (—:—:—:1:4)
Beverley   Beverley (0482) 882490
Grissell, D. M.   (—:—:—:—:0)
Heathfield, E. Sussex
    Brightling (042 482) 241
Gubby, B.   (—:—:2:4:2)
Bagshot   Bagshot (0273) 63282
Guest, W. N.   (6:5:14:11:4)
Newmarket
    Newmarket (0638) 61680

Haigh, W. W.   (8:10:6:9:13)
Malton   Malton (0653) 4428

Haldane, J. S.   (—:—:—:—:0)
St Boswells
St Boswells (083 52) 2342
Hall, N.   (0:0:0:2:0)
Burton-on-Trent
Barton-under-Needwood (028 371)
2279
Hall, Miss S. E.   (9:7:15:7:12)
Middleham
Wensleydale (0969) 40223
Hallett, T. B.   (—:0:0:0:0)
Saltash   Saltash (075 55) 2064
Hanbury, B.   (21:18:8:25:21)
Newmarket
Newmarket (0638) 3193
Home: Wickhambrook (044 082)
396
Hanley, D. L.   (5:2:0:0:2)
Lambourn
Lambourn (0488) 72169
and 72219
Hannon, R. M.   (37:47:30:37:29)
Marlborough
Collingbourne Ducis (026 485) 254
Hanson, J.   (9:12:8:13:5)
Wetherby   Wetherby (0937) 62841
Hardy, J.   (22:31:14:17:10)
Staunton
Long Bennington (0400) 81212
Harman, G. R.   (—:—:—:—:2)
Helmsley   Helmsley (0439) 70838
Harris, J. L.   (2:0:2:1:0)
Melton Mowbray
Harby (0949) 60671
Harris, S. T.   (—:—:0:1:0)
Amersham
Amersham (02403) 21718
Hartop, R. W.   (—:—:—:0:0)
Cheltenham
Andoversford (024 282) 448
Harwood, G.   (50:59:48:69:97)
Pulborough
Pulborough (079 82) 2335
Haslam, P. C.   (7:10:25:38:35)
Newmarket
Newmarket (0638) 4525
and 4523
Hastings-Bass, W. E. R. H.
(26:27:27:26:44)
Newmarket
Newmarket (0638) 2024
Haynes, M. J.   (6:12:16:12:9)
Epsom
Burgh Heath (073 73) 51140
Head, R. A.   (0:0:0:0:0)
Lambourn
Lambourn (0488) 71411
Henderson, N. J.   (—:0:0:0:0)
Lambourn
Lambourn (0488) 72259
Hern, W. R.   (74:74:61:65:64)
West Ilsley
East Ilsley (063 528) 219 and 251
Hide, A. G.   (2:4:5:4:8)
Newmarket
Newmarket (0638) 2063
Hill, C. J.   (13:12:13:7:6)
Barnstaple   Barnstaple (0271) 2048

Hills, B. W.   (76:86:56:61:82)
Lambourn
Lambourn (0488) 71548
Hill-Wood, Miss A. K.
(—:—:—:0:0)
Grantham   Knipton (047 682) 226
Hinchliffe, M. J.   (—:—:—:0:0)
Lambourn
Marlborough (0672) 40755
and Chaddleworth (04882) 586
Hindley, J. J.   (41:42:41:46:32)
Newmarket
Newmarket (0638) 4141/2
Hoad, R. P. C.   (—:—:—:2:1)
Lewes   Lewes (07916) 77124
Hobbs, B. R.   (65:43:42:60:50)
Newmarket
Newmarket (0638) 2129
Hobson, R.   (—:13:5:4:0)
Worksop
Home: Mansfield (0623) 822 835
Stable: Worksop (0909) 475 962
or 475 425
Holden, W.   (11:15:8:4:5)
Newmarket   Exning (063 877) 384
Holland, S. F.   (1:6:2:0:0)
Shrewsbury
Upton Magna (074 377) 228
Hollinshead, R.   (49:50:25:26:57)
Upper Longdon
Armitage (0543) 490298
Holt, L. J.   (6:6:12:9:10)
Tunworth
Long Sutton (025 681) 376
Houghton, R. F. J.   (54:47:39:42:29)
Blewbury   Blewbury (0235) 850480
Huffer, G. A.   (—:—:23:11:18)
Newmarket
Newmarket (0638) 730391
and 730118
Hunter, G. H.   (25:24:22:30:29)
East Ilsley
East Ilsley (063 528) 250

Incisa, D. E.   (—:—:—:—:0)
Leyburn
Ingham, A. P.   (19:16:9:3:3)
Headley   Ashtead (037 22) 72859
Ivory, K. T.   (11:11:15:9:19)
Radlett   Radlett (092 76) 6081

James, C. J.   (3:5:3:10:3)
Newbury
Great Shefford (048 839) 280
James, M. B. C.   (—:—:—:0:3)
Whitchurch
Whitchurch (0948) 3155 or 4067
James, S. S.   (0:0:0:0:0)
East Ilsley
East Ilsley (063 528) 248
Jarvis, A. P.   (3:13:5:6:24)
Royston
Royston, Herts (0763) 46611
Jarvis, M. A.   (27:31:39:30:35)
Newmarket
Newmarket (0638) 61702
and 2519
Jefferson, J. M.   (—:—:—:—:0)
Malton   Malton (0653) 7225

Jenkins, J. R. (—:—:—:1:2)
Horsham
Lower Beeding (040 376) 606
Jermy, D. C. (2:2:0:0:1)
Carshalton
(01-668) 3765 or 8814
Johnson, R. (—:—:0:1:2)
Bishop Auckland
Bishop Auckland (0388) 762113
Jones, A. W. (2:5:3:8:5)
Oswestry   Oswestry (0691) 59720
Jones, Dr A. (2:0:0:0:0)
Swansea   Clydach (0792) 3504
Jones, D. H. (2:0:3:4:14)
Pontypridd
Newtown Llantwit (044 362) 2515
Jones, Hbt (7:2:5:9:1)
Malton   Malton (0653) 2630
Jones, H. T. (15:20:13:40:40)
Newmarket
Newmarket (0638) 4884
Jones, T. M. (0:0:1:0:1)
Guildford   Shere (048 641) 2604
Jordon, I. D. (1:2:2:0:1)
Newcastle-on-Tyne
Newcastle-on-Tyne (0632) 869143
Jorgensen, O. (—:—:—:0:0)
Heathfield, Sussex
Heathfield (043 52) 2551

Kearney, P. J. (—:—:—:0:0)
Cheltenham
Withington (024 289) 253
Keenor, R. F. (0:0:0:0:0)
Chulmleigh
Chulmleigh (076 98) 432
Kelleway, P. A. (6:26:21:23:11)
Newmarket
Newmarket (0638) 61461
Kennard, L. G. (1:0:0:2:1)
Bishops Lydeard
Bishops Lydeard (0823) 432550
Kennedy, Mrs K. A. A.
(—:—:0:0:0)
Lambourn
Lambourn (0488) 71636
Kent, D. W. J. (8:17:5:10:7)
Chichester
West Ashling (024 358) 231
Kernick, S. G. (0:0:0:0:1)
Kingsteignton
Newton Abbot (0626) 5899
Kersey, T. (0:2:0:2:0)
West Melton
Rotherham (0709) 873166
Kindersley, G. (1:0:0:0:1)
Newbury
Great Shefford (048 839) 301

Laing, D. R. (—:—:8:7:17:12)
Lambourn
Lambourn (0488) 71825
Lamb, C. R. (0:0:0:0:0)
Seahouses
Seahouses (0665) 720260
Leadbetter, S. J. (—:1:0:0:0)
Denholm
Denholm (045 087) 260

Leigh, J. P. (0:0:0:1:0)
Willoughton, Lincs.
Hemswell (042 773) 210
Leslie, D. M. (—:1:7:7:5)
Leicester   Tugby (053756) 257/357
Lewis, E. R. K. (—:—:—:0:0)
Carmarthen
St Clears (0994) 230383
Lewis, G. (—:—:0:5:26)
Epsom
Ashtead (037 22) 77662 or 77366
Lloyd-Jones, Mrs C. F.
(—:—:—:—:0)
Abergele
Abergele (0745) 824 730
Lockerbie, G. (—:—:—:1:5)
Middleham
Wensleydale (0969) 22736
Lomax, Mrs R. A. (3:3:5:2:2)
Marlborough
Marlborough (0672) 40288
Long, J. E. (0:0:0:0:0)
Canterbury
Elham (030 384) 229
Lunness, B. W. (22:8:—:—:0)
Pocklington, Yorkshire
Market Weighton (0696) 60460
MacKenzie, C. (—:—:—:0:0)
Boxford, Suffolk
Boxford (0787) 210 756
Makin, P. J. (12:6:10:7:8)
Ogbourne Maisey
Marlborough (0672) 52973
Marks, D. (4:13:8:4:2)
Lambourn
Lambourn (0488) 71767
Marshall, T. C. (10:6:12:6:7)
Lambourn
Lambourn (0488) 71025
Marshall, W. C. (35:26:16:6:1)
Newmarket
Newmarket (0638) 61574
Mason, J. (—:—:—:4:3)
Stockton   Stockton (0642) 580561
Mason, R. E. G. (9:5:3:2:0)
Guilsborough
Guilsborough (060 122) 381
Masson, M. J. (15:4:3:3:11)
Lewes   Lewes (079 16) 4984
Matthews, S. G. (1:0:2:7:6)
Winchester
Winchester (0962) 880808
McCain, D. (1:0:0:0:0)
Birkdale
Southport (0704) 66007 and 69677
McCormack, M. (—:—:—:3:3)
Wantage   Childrey (023 559) 433
McCourt, M. (6:4:2:3:7)
Letcombe Regis
Wantage (023 57) 4456
McDonald, R. (—:—:—:0:0)
Duns, Berwickshire
Chirnside (089 081) 218 or 446
McLean, D. B. (—:0:0:0:0)
Morpeth   Felton (067087) 478
McMahon, B. A. (0:1:2:6:17)
Tamworth
Tamworth (0827) 62901

Mellor, S. T. E. (8:4:4:10:18)
Lambourn
Lambourn (0488) 71485
Miller, C. J. V. (2:0:0:0:0)
Stratford-on-Avon
Alderminster (078 987) 296
and 232
Mitchell, N. R. (—:—:—:—:0)
Sherborne, Dorset
Buckland Newton (030 05) 272
Mitchell, P. (3:6:7:12:14)
Epsom Ashtead (037 22) 73729
Mitchell, P. K. (—:0:0:0:6)
Folkington Polegate (032 12) 2437
Mitchell, V. J. (4:2:2:1:0)
Bishopsthorpe
York (0904) 36099
Moore, A. (0:0:0:1:0)
Woodingdean
Brighton (0273) 681679
Morgan, K. A. (—:—:—:0:0)
Grantham Knipton (047 682) 738
Morley, M. F. D. (1:3:0:5:12)
Bury St Edmunds
Culford (028 484) 278
Morris, R. W. (—:—:1:1:1)
Welshpool
Trewern (093874) 355
Morris, Miss S. O. (0:0:0:0:0)
Chard
Chard (046 06) 3187 and 3379
Mulhall, J. (4:4:0:0:0)
York York (0904) 706321
Musson, W. J. (0:1:2:4:3)
Newmarket
Newmarket (0638) 2380

Naughton, M. P. (8:3:0:5:3)
Richmond
Richmond (0748) 2803
Neaves, A. S. (1:3:1:0:0)
Faversham Eastling (079 589) 274
Nelson, C. R. (4:16:16:31:9)
Lambourn
Lambourn (0488) 71391
Nesbitt, S. (7:11:16:3:9)
Middleham
Wensleydale (0969) 23645
Nicholson, D. (2:0:0:3:1)
Stow-on-the-Wold
Stow-on-the-Wold (0451) 30417
Norton, S. G. (2:5:14:14:29)
Barnsley Bretton (092 485) 450

O'Donoghue, J. (0:0:1:1:0)
Reigate Reigate (073 72) 45241
O'Gorman, W. A. (16:32:25:30:25)
Newmarket
Newmarket (0638) 3330
Old, J. A. B. (2:2:3:3:5)
Salisbury
Fontwell Magna (0747) 811648
Oliver, J. K. M. (0:0:0:0:0)
Hawick Denholm (045 087) 216
O'Neill, H. (0:0:2:5:4)
Coldharbour
Dorking (0306) 6223

O'Neill, O. (1:0:0:0:0)
Cheltenham
Bishops Cleeve (024 267) 3257
Oughton, Mrs D. R. (0:0:0:0:0)
Findon
Findon (090 671) 2113 or 9871
Owen, E. H. (0:0:0:0:0)
Denbigh
Llandyrnog (082 44) 264

Page, W. R. (—:—:1:0:0)
Billinghay Billinghay (05266) 365
Palling, B. (—:0:0:0:2)
Cowbridge
Cowbridge (04463) 2089
Pattemore, S. P. (0:0:0:0:0)
Somerton Somerton (0458) 73112
Payne, H. W. (0:0:0:—:0)
Peacock, J. H. (0:0:0:0:0)
Ludlow Seifton (058 473) 217
Peacock, R. D. (8:9:3:3:6)
Middleham
Wensleydale (0969) 23291
Peacock, R. E. (0:0:2:1:0)
Tarporley
Tarporley (082 93) 2716
Perrett, A. C. J. (0:0:0:0:0)
Cheltenham
Andoversford (024 282) 244
Pipe, M. C. (0:0:3:4:2)
Wellington, Somerset
Craddock (0884) 40715
Pitman, Mrs J. S. (1:1:1:1:1)
Lambourn
Lambourn (0488) 71714
Pitt, A. J. (7:9:9:9:5)
Epsom Epsom (037 27) 25034
Potts, A. W. (1:0:0:0:0)
Barton-on-Humber
Saxby All Saints (065 261) 750
Prescott, Sir Mark
(26:28:30:34:36)
Newmarket
Newmarket (0638) 2117
Price, G. H. (—:—:0:0:3)
Leominster
Steens Bridge (056 882) 235
Price, H. R. (73:61:60:48:31)
Findon Findon (090 671) 2388
Priday, J. (—:—:0:0:0)
Kington Lyonshall (054 48) 230
Pritchard-Gordon, G. A.
(41:39:58:47:36)
Newmarket
Newmarket (0638) 2824

Ransom, P. B. (0:0:0:0:0)
Leominster
Wigmore (056 886) 253
Read, C. P. (—:—:—:1:0)
Pulborough
West Chiltington (079 83) 3489
Reavey, Mrs C. J. (—:—:—:—:7)
East Hendred
East Hendred (023 588) 297
Reddan, M. T. (—:—:0:0:0)
Houghton-le-Spring
Houghton-le-Spring (0783) 844639

Richards, G. W. (11:10:14:19:12)
Greystoke
Greystoke (085 33) 392
Richmond, B. A. (6:3:1:1:0)
Wellingore
Lincoln (0522) 810578
Rimell, Mrs M. (—:—:—:—:0)
Kinnersley
Severn Stoke (090 567) 233
Ringer, D. S. (3:5:5:3:3)
Newmarket
Newmarket (0638) 2653
Robson, T. W. (—:—:—:—:0)
Upper Lambourn
Lambourn (0488) 71368
Rohan, H. P. (19:18:28:28:23)
Malton Malton (0653) 2337/8
Ryan, M. J. (5:6:23:11:14)
Newmarket
Newmarket (0638) 4172

Sasse, D. J. G. (6:11:14:2:3)
Lambourn
Lambourn (0488) 71902
Sawyer, H. (—:—:—:—:0)
Scallan, J. J. (—:—:0:0.0)
Colchester
Nayland (0206) 262613
Scott, A. (—:0:2:1:1)
Alnwick
Wooperton (066 87) 252 or 288
Scudamore, M. J. (0:0:0:0:0)
Hoarwithy, Herefordshire
Carey (043 270) 253
Shaw, B. (—:0:0:0:0)
Cheltenham
Cheltenham (0242) 25705
Sheather, R. (—:6:10:15:13)
Newmarket
Newmarket (0638) 4687 and 2468
Siddall, Miss L. C. (—:—:—:—:0)
Leeds
Appleton Roebuck (090 484) 291
Simpson, R. (—:—:5:3:5)
Epsom Epsom (037 27) 22846
Sinclair, Miss A. V. (3:3:1:0:0)
Lewes
Lewes (079 16) 6619 and 3851
Smith, A. (5:8:1:4:5)
Beverley Hull (0482) 882520
Smith, Denys (30:28:53:35:29)
Bishop Auckland
Bishop Auckland (0388) 603317
Smyly, R. M. (9:8:5:12:11)
Lambourn
Lambourn (0488) 71408
Smyth, R. V. (19:12:9:17:20)
Epsom Epsom (037 27) 20053
Soane, V. St John (—:—:—:0:2)
Didcot
Blewbury (0235) 850 338
or 850 845
Spares, C. W. (—:—:—:—:7)
Newmarket
Newmarket (0638) 4674
Spearing, J. L. (1:0:4:3:11)
Alcester
Bidford-on-Avon (078 988) 2639

Stapleton, K. G. (0:0:0:0:0)
Skipton Skipton (0756) 2703
Stephens, M. (—:—:—:—:0)
Taunton
North Curry (082 349) 656 or 335
Stephenson, W. A. (6:5:9:3:2)
Bishop Auckland
Rushyford (0388) 720213
Stone, K. (—:0:9:17:14)
Malton
Malton (0653) 4597 (stable)
and 3586 (home)
Storey, W. L. (—:—:—:—:0)
Consett
Edmundbyers (0207) 55259
Stoute, M. R. (62:69:80:101:95)
Newmarket
Newmarket (0638) 3801
Stubbs, R. W. (0:2:7:4:4)
Northallerton
Haxey (0427) 53086
Sturdy, R. C. (4:1:—:1:0)
Shrewton, Wilts.
Shrewton (098 062) 472
Sutcliffe, J. R. E. (18:24:21:19:24)
Epsom Ashtead (037 22) 72025
Swift, B. C. (23:22:24:22:8)
Headley
Leatherhead (037 23) 77209
and 77308
Tate, F. M. (3:1:1:2:0)
Kidderminster
Chaddesley Corbett (056 283) 243
Taylor, Peter (0:0:0:3:1)
Churt
Frensham (025125) 3529
Taylor, P. M. (3:8:8:12:2)
Upper Lambourn
Lambourn (0488) 71667.
Taylor, T. (0:0:0:2:3)
Ashbourne
Rocester (0889) 590334
Thom, D. T. (3:4:5:7:0)
Newmarket Exning (063 877) 288
Thompson, R. (—:—:—:—:2)
Bourne, Lincolnshire
Bourne (077 82) 2974
Thompson, V. (0:0:0:0:0)
Alnwick
Embleton (066 576) 272
Thorne, J. (0:0:0:0:0)
Bridgwater Holford (027 874) 216
Thorner, G. E. (—:—:—:—:0)
Letcombe Regis
Wantage (023 57) 3003
Thornton, C. W. (34:35:33:32:26)
Middleham
Wensleydale (0969) 23350
Tierney, J. (4:1:1:1)
Stafford
Wheaton Ashton (0785) 840833
Tinkler, N. D. (—:—:—:0:3)
Thirsk Thirsk (0845) 537336
Toft, G. (10:9:11:8:6)
Malton Malton (0653) 5039
Toller, J. R. (—:—:—:0:3)
Newmarket
Newmarket (0638) 68503

Tompkins, M. H. (—:—:—:4:9)
Newmarket
Newmarket (0638) 61434
Townson, J. (—:—:—:—:0)
Blackburn
Whalley (025 482) 3412
Tree, A. J. (17:24:30:30:23)
Beckhampton
Avebury (067 23) 204 and 244
Tuer, K. H. (—:0:0:0:0)
Penrith
Pooley Bridge (085 36) 238
Turnell, A. R. (4:1:4:9:2)
Ogbourne Maisey
Marlborough (0672) 52542
Turner, W. G. M. (—:0:1:0:0)
Tavistock
Mary Tavy (082281) 237
Underhill, S. (0:—:—:0:0)
Worcester
Upton Snodsbury (090 560) 622
Underwood, D. B. (0:0:1:0:0)
Bramley
Guildford (0483) 893147
Vergette, G. M. (0:0:0:0:0)
Peterborough
Market Deeping (0778) 342226
Vickers, I. (—:—:2:1:0)
Darlington
Dinsdale (032573) 2450
Vigors, N. A. C. (12:15:13:13:21)
Lambourn
Lambourn (0488) 71657
Walker, I. S. (15:17:14:16:13)
Newmarket
Exning (063 877) 291 and
Newmarket (0638) 2457
Walwyn, F. T. T. (0:1:1:0:0)
Lambourn
Lambourn (0488) 71555
Walwyn, P. T. (110:70:44:78:53)
Lambourn
Lambourn (0488) 71347
Ward, R. C. (2:1:2:2:2)
Doncaster
Doncaster (0302) 700574
Wardle, I. P. (0:0:0:0:0)
East Horrington
Wells (0749) 73167
Waring, Mrs B. H. (—:—:0:0:1)
Wellington
Wellington (082 347) 3418
Watson, A. (0:0:0:0:0)
Skipton Earby (028 284) 2228
Watts, J. W. (57:50:46:47:51)
Richmond
Richmond (0748) 2287
Watts, W. C. (12:8:3:7:0)
Bridlington
Bridlington (0262) 73719
Webber, J. H. (0:1:2:0:0)
Banbury Cropredy (029 575) 226
Weeden, D. E. (8:16:5:4:0)
Newmarket
Newmarket (0638) 730 587
Westbrook, H. C. (1:3:3:2:1)
Newmarket
Newmarket (0638) 67689

Weymes, E. (17:24:9:19:16)
Leyburn
Wensleydale (0969) 40229
Wharton, H. (0:0:0:1:1)
Wetherby Wetherby (0937) 65002
Wharton, W. (12:15:15:24:10)
Melton Mowbray
Waltham-on-the-Wolds (066 478)
258 and
Melton Mowbray (0664) 65225
Whelan, D. (8:6:3:1:1)
Epsom
Epsom (037 27) 22763 and 21482
Whiston, W. R. (0:0:0:0:0)
Market Drayton
Hodnet (063 084) 203
Whitaker, R. M. (—:0:0:5:4)
Leeds Leeds (0532) 892265
Whittle, J. R. F. (—:—:—:—:0)
Uppingham
Morcott (057 287) 278
Wigham, P. (7:2:1:4:2)
Malton Rillington (094 42) 332
Wightman, W. G. R. (29:27:17:14:14)
Upham, Hants.
Bishop's Waltham (048 93) 2565
Wildman, C. P. (—:—:—:2:3)
Salisbury
Durrington Walls (0980) 52226
Wiles, S. J. (—:—:0:0:0)
Flockton
Flockton (0924) 848468 (stable)
and 84897 (home)
Wilkinson, B. E. (0:0:0:0:1)
Middleham
Wensleydale (0969) 23385
Williams, C. N. (—:—:—:0:2)
Reading Bradfield (0734) 744 309
Williams, R. J. R. (—:—:—:—:12)
Newmarket
Newmarket (0638) 3218
Williams, W. H. H. (—:26:19:15:2)
Ayr Ayr (0292) 266232
Williams, W. R. (0:0:0:0:0)
Exeter Rennford (0392) 832 834
Willis, H. (—:—:0:0:0)
Winchester
Twyford (0962) 713483
Wilson, J. H. (—:—:1:2:5)
Preston
Hesketh Bank (077 473) 2780
Wilson, D. A. (—:—:—:0:5)
Epsom
Ashtead (037 22) 77645
and 73839
Wilson, J. S. (—:—:—:0:1)
Motherwell
Motherwell (0698) 62653
Winter, F. T. (1:0:5:0:0)
Lambourn
Lambourn (0488) 71438
Winter, J. R. (22:23:31:13:19)
Newmarket
Newmarket (0638) 3898

999

Wintle, D. J. (1:1:0:0:1)
Westbury-on-Severn
Westbury-on-Severn (045 276) 459
Wise, B. J. (5:1:1:0:0)
Polegate
Polegate (032 12) 3331 and 2505
Woodman, S. (8:10:4:4:4)
Chichester
Chichester (0243) 527136
Woodhouse, R. D. E.
(—:—:—:—:0)
York
Whitwell-on-the-Hill
(065 381) 637
Wragg, H. (39:34:30:33:37)
Newmarket
Newmarket (0638) 2328

Yardley, J. (1:0:2:1:2)
Droitwich
Worcester (0905) 620477
Yeoman, D. (0:1:0:0:4)
Richmond
Richmond (0784) 811756

The following also held a licence for part of the year:

Bingham, J. D.

Blagrave, H. H. G., The late

Brookshaw, S. J., The late

Chesmore, Mrs S. M. P.

Rimell, F. T., The late

JOCKEYS

The figures in brackets show the number of winners each jockey has ridden in this country during the past five seasons, from 1977 to 1981 inclusive. The telephone numbers and riding weights are added, where known.

Appleton, D. N. (—:—:0:0:0) 8 4
Dinsdale (032573) 2450
Apter, E. R. (20:29:20:6:0)...
c/o Beverley (0482) 885041
Armstrong, J. (0:0:—:0:0)... 8 7
Tockwith (09015) 493
Astbury, C. F. (—:—:—:0:0). 8 11
Rugeley (088 94) 77038
Atkinson, D. J. (1:0:5:3:0).... 8 0
Wantage (023 57) 3164

Balding, J. (0:0:0:1:0)....... 8 9
Doncaster (0302) 710096
Ballantine, H. (19:—:—:1:1). 7 10
Balmer, W. N. (0:—:—:0:0).. 8 7
c/o Wensleydale (0969) 22736
Banner, M. A. (—:2:4:5:7)... 8 4
c/o Newmarket (0638) 3333/4
Barker, R. S. (2:2:0:0:0)..... 8 4
c/o Malton (0653) 2842
Barnes, M. A. (0:—:—:0:0).. 9 0
Langwathby (076881) 257
Baxter, G. E. (62:63:64:52:57) 7 13
Lambourn (0488) 71320
Bentley, W. (0:0:0:0:0)...... 7 10
Wensleydale (0969) 22289
Birch, M. (62:65:77:71:56)... 8 0
Malton (0653) 3885
Black, J. (1:0:0:3:1)......... 7 12
c/o Newmarket (0638) 730391
or 730118
Bleasdale, J. (67:90:41:41:18). 8 0
Bedale (0677) 22222 and
Wensleydale (0969) 23350
Blossier, P. R. B.
(—:—:—:—:1)............ 7 7
Newmarket (0638) 2380
Bond, A. M. (25:19:16:16:12). 7 12
Stetchworth (063 876) 681
Bray, M. J. (0:—:—:—:0).... 7 12

Butler, K. R. (0:0:0:0:0:1)..... 7 7
Winchester (0962) 880310

Cadwaladr, G. E. (0:—:0:0:0) 8 6
Chester (0244) 07898
Carmody, T. M. (—:0:0:0:0). 9 7
Carroll, D. (—:0:—:0:0)..... 7 9
Carson, W. F. H.
(160:182:142:166:114)...... 7 9
Newmarket (0638) 3623 and
East Ilsley (063 528) 348
Cauthen, S. M.
(—:—:52:61:87)........... 8 3
Lambourn (0488) 71381
Charlton, S. F. (0:0:0:1:0)... 8 12
Bishop Auckland
(0388) 833 584
Charnock, L. (25:15:25:15:23) 7 7
Malton (0653) 5703
Cheese, P. (0:1:2:0:0)........ 7 12
Clotworthy, B. J. (2:0:0:0:0). 7 13
Wensleydale (0969) 22289
Cochrane, Mrs Anne
(—:—:0:0:0)............. 7 9
Cochrane, R. (0:0:6:21:22)... 8 3
Newmarket (0638) 5807 or
4687
Colquhoun, P. R.
(3:7:12:7:10)............. 7 13
Exning (063877) 219
Cook, P. A. (72:90:80:90:83).. 8 0
Wanborough (079 379) 552
Cousins, A. M. (—:5:1:0:0).. 8 4
Cheltenham (0242) 23393
Coyle, M. (—:—:—:—:0).... 8 5
c/o Weyhill (026 477) 3225
Cressy, A. (1:—:—:0:0)...... 8 8
Crook, A. (2:—:—:1:0)...... 7 12
c/o Boroughbridge
(09012) 2592

Crowther, N. (9:13:15:15:1).. 8 4
Newmarket (0638) 68896
Curant, R. D. (15:25:31:18:21) 7 13
Hungerford (048 86) 3216
and Boxford (048 838) 433
D'Arcy, P. W. (0:9:11:3:1)... 7 12
Newmarket (0638) 3974
Darley, K. P. (11:70:14:19:14) 7 7
Wolverhampton (0902)
337195 and 724541
Davies, N. (—:—:0:0:0)...... 8 4
Newmarket (0638) 4524
Dineley, D. D. (0:0:2:4:3).... 8 0
Harwell (023 586) 7832
Douthwaite, G. (1:—:—:—:0) 7 10
Duffield, G. P.
(60:75:76:78:94)........... 7 11
Stetchworth (063 876) 544
Dwyer, C. A. (9:16:20:23:11). 8 3
Malton (0653) 3471
Eccles, S. (9:25:23:12:0)..... 8 1
Hungerford (04886) 3096
Eccleston, C. H. (19:29:4:2:0) 7 10
York (0904) 21374
Eddery, P. J. J.
(176:148:123:130:108)..... 8 3
Cheltenham (0242) 28763
Elder, B. (—:—:—:0:0)...... 7 8
01-642 2123
Elliott, R. S. (1:1:0:0:0)...... 8 0
Avebury (06723) 204 and 244
Ellison, B. (—:—:0:0:0)..... 8 11
Emes, I. M. (0:—:0:0:0)..... 8 5
East Ilsley (063 528) 253
Enright, G. P. (—:—:—:0:0). 9 5
Worthing (0903) 61117
Errington, J. A. (1:—:—:—:0) 8 7
Ulverston (0229) 63120
Ferguson, R. J. (8:1:2:2:0)... 7 9
Newmarket (0638) 2004
Flint, A. W. (0:0:—:0:0)..... 8 7
c/o Malton (0653) 3149
Fox, R. D. S. (29:14:17:26:16) 7 9
Seagry (0249) 720103
Francois, C. G. A. (0:0:0:0:2) 8 0
c/o Winchester (0962) 880808
Gibson, Dominic J.
(1:0:0:0:1)............... 7 10
Newmarket (0638) 7506531
Giles, M. S. (1:2:0:0:1)...... 8 4
c/o Newmarket (0638) 3801
Gosney, G. (7:7:5:1:2)....... 8 0
c/o Tadcaster (0937) 833294
Gray, O. J. (9:11:10:8:10).... 8 0
Coverdale (0969) 22403
Guest, R. (—:—:1:7:7)...... 8 5
Newmarket (0638) 61508
Gunn, G. P. (12:2:2:1:6)..... 8 2
Home: Newmarket
(0638) 68724
Office: Newmarket
(0638) 4674
Gwilliam, C. K. (—:—:—:0:0) 8 2
c/o Findon (090 671) 2388
Hedley, B. F. (0:0:0:0:0)..... 8 3
Malton (0653) 3749 or 2511
Henry, B. (2:11:0:0:0)....... 8 2
Hull (0482) 882520

Hide, E. W. G.
(111:88:53:106:105)........ 8 3
Malton (0653) 2132 and
Newmarket (0638) 750155
Higgins, J. J. (1:0:10:9:3)..... 8 2
Newmarket (0638) 750123
Higgins, W. F. (6:2:11:13:2).. 7 8
Compton (063 522) 438
Hood, B. (5:0:0:0:0)......... 7 12
Malton (0653) 2842
Horrocks, A. (—:—:—:—:0). 8 1
Hunt, Mrs L. I. (—:—:—:0:0) 8 7
Hutchinson, Richard
(11:0:3:5:0).............. 7 12
Ayr (0292) 66232
Ives, T. A. (41:29:38:53:42)... 8 2
Newmarket (0638) 4605
Jago, B. (9:11:16:30:18)...... 8 0
Epsom (037 27) 21025
Jenkinson, I. P. (4:2:4:1:0)... 7 7
Epsom (037 27) 24484
Jesse, W. A. (—:—:—:—:0).. 7 0
Jobar, R. S. (—:—:—:—:0) 9 4
Lambourn (0488) 38242
Johnson, E. (72:86:61:49:30).. 7 10
Newmarket (0638) 4674
Johnson, I. E. (13:0:3:19:8)... 8 3
Kintbury (04885) 749 or
Boxford (048838) 433
Johnston, Miss V.
(—:—:—:—:0)............ 7 12
Kahtani, M. K. R.
(—:—:—:—:0)............ 8 8
Kelleher, P. (—:4:2:3:6)..... 8 0
c/o Carlisle (0228) 25649
Kettle, M. (10:5:1:4:7)....... 8 0
Newmarket (0638) 712428
Kimberley, A. A.
(39:44:27:15:8)............ 8 3
Newmarket (0638) 3267
Knight, S. G. (—:—:—:0:0).. 9 0
Kentisbeare (08846) 375
Launchbury, A. T.
(—:—:—:0:0)............. 7 12
Lawes, S. D. (2:2:8:0:0)...... 7 11
Leason, K. M.
(24:20:14:10:11)........... 7 9
Rotherham (0709) 548170
Leonard, C. S. (3:5:3:2:5).... 7 0
Newmarket (0638) 751048
Logie, J. (—:1:0:1:0)......... 8 0
c/o East Hendred
(023 588) 247
Lowe, J. J. (86:57:49:54:69)... 7 7
York (0904) 489040
Madden, P. J. (10:26:8:8:8)... 8 5
Newmarket (0638) 750603
Maitland, D. (6:4:3:0:1)..... 7 7
Newmarket (0638) 61615
Marshall, E. T. (0:—:—:0:0). 7 7
Marshall, R. C. (30:10:9:1:0). 8 2
Newmarket (0638) 61751
Matthias, J. J. (21:25:23:41:37) 8 3
c/o Kingsclere (0625) 298210
and 297205
McGhin, R. (—:0:0:2:0)..... 8 0
c/o Ashtead (03722) 73729

McGregor, J. P. (—:—:—:0:0) 8 2
McGuffie, Miss E. M.
(—:—:2:0:0)............... 8 0
Newmarket (0638) 4485
McIntosh, N. (0:1:0:0:0)..... 7 0
c/o Dunbar (0368) 62583
McKay, D. J. (24:17:23:11:26) 7 7
Lambourn (0488) 71735 and
Box (022 121) 2777
McNamee, C. J. (0:0:0:0:0)... 8 0
Lambourn (0488) 71956
Mercer, J.
(102:115:164:103:64)....... 8 4
Hermitage (0635) 200 306
Middleton, S. R.
(1:—:—:—:0)............. 8 2
Miller, M. M. (5:0:19:14:19).. 7 10
Newmarket (0638) 730374
Mills, A. E. (—:—:—:0:0).... 8 0
Wensleydale (0969) 23350
Moore, G. M. (0:0:0:0:0)..... 8 4
Boroughbridge (090 12) 2037
Morris, F. N. (—:—:—:—:0). 8 10
Trewern (093 874) 288 or 355
Moss, C. J. T. (15:14:9:2:0)... 8 2
Daventry (032 72) 5906
Muddle, R. J. (4:24:17:9:1)... 7 12
Passfield (042877) 316
Murphy, P. A. (—:—:—:—:0) 9 0
c/o Houghton-le-Spring
(0783) 844 639
Naughton, Mrs A. M.
(0:—:0:1:0)............... 8 4
Richmond (0748) 2803
Nicholls, D. (22:8:0:4:7)..... 8 0
Wetherby (0937) 61291
Nicholson, W. J. C.
(—:0:2:0:0)............... 7 12
Nutter, C. (11:8:6:0:6)....... 7 9
Newmarket (0638) 68153
O'Hagan, A. T.
(—:—:—:—:0)............. 8 7
Tenbury Wells (0584) 810 627
Oldham, D. W.
(—:—:—:—:0)............. 8 7
Leeds (0532) 865 295
Oldroyd, G. R. (11:4:7:4:3).. 8 3
Malton (0653) 5991
O'Leary P. (0:1:1:1:0)....... 7 9
01-979 6046
O'Neill, J. J. (0:0:7:3:0)...... 9 0
Skelton (085 34) 275
Oxland, R. (0:0:0:0:0)....... 8 0
c/o Newmarket (0638) 3286
Parkes, L. C. (6:4:0:0:0)..... 7 5
Malton (0653) 2845
Peckham, M. A. (—:0:1:0:0). 7 7
Ely (0353) 720895
Perkins, P. (0:7:0:1:1)....... 8 0
Perks, S. A. (14:15:8:5:41).... 8 3
Hednesford (054 38) 4836
Piggott, L.
(103:97:77:156:179).......... 8 6
Newmarket (0638) 2584
Procter, B. T. (0:1:3:3:1).... 8 3
East Ilsley (063 528) 376 and
219

Ramshaw, G. (15:5:6:4:3).... 8 3
Burgh Heath (073 73) 53611
Rawlinson, A. C.
(—:—:—:3:4)............. 8 4
Newbury (0635) 31218
Raymond, B. H.
(56:48:58:62:73)........... 8 4
Newmarket (0638) 730387
Raymont, S. J. (5:15:26:4:5) . 7 12
c/o Avebury (06723) 204
and 244
Reid, J. A. (33:54:72:79:54)... 8 2
Boxford (048 838) 433 and
Chieveley (063521) 8801
Reilly, B. A. (3:0:—:0:0)..... 9 0
Kintbury (04885) 644
Robinson, C. E. (—:—:—:0:0) 8 3
Robinson, P. P.
(—:7:51:59:31)............ 7 12
c/o Newmarket (0638) 2090
Rodrigues, C. (10:8:0:0:0)... 7 3
Newmarket (0638) 61443
Rogers, T. (3:11:16:39:18).... 8 2
Thatcham (0635) 63047
Rouse, B. A. (48:60:42:43:65). 7 11
Epsom (037 27) 22140
Salmon, S. E. W.
(12:10:2:8:14)............. 7 8
Newbury (0635) 66589
Seagrave, J. (43:15:25:24:23). 8 4
Malton (0653) 2692
Sexton, G. C. (16:11:16:9:23). 8 0
Newmarket (0638) 4367
Shrimpton, P. R. E.
(1:2:0:0:0)............... 7 8
Shrive, A. H. (—:—:—:—:0). 8 5
Skeats, G. H. (0:0:2:—:1).... 8 6
Malton (0653) 5278
Skilling, J. F. (—:—:—:1:1).. 8 2
Smith, Dennis (—:—:—:0:0). 8 5
c/o Ashtead (03722) 73152
Sozzi, Miss T. L.
(—:—:—:0:0)............. 8 3
Starkey, G. M. W.
(76:107:98:82:90).......... 8 5
Mildenhall (0638) 714672
Still, R. W. (15:4:11:—:2).... 7 6
Newmarket (0638) 750755
Street, R. (25:17:13:3:8)..... 7 7
Lambourn (0488) 71412 and
71548
Stevens, J. W. (—:—:—:—:0) 8 0
Stroud, M. R. H. (—:0:0:1:0). 8 0
Sturrock, T. T. (—:0:2:0:0).. 8 4
Abingdon (0235) 831730
Swinburn, W. R. J.
(—:12:47:49:65)........... 8 0
Booking: Cheltenham (0242)
28763
Home: Newmarket (0638)
3371
c/o Newmarket (0638) 3801
Taylor, B. (83:59:56:32:48)... 8 4
Newmarket (0638) 4605
Taylor, K. (—:—:—:0:0)..... 7 7
Thomas, M. L.
(98:52:48:27:15)........... 7 9
Newmarket (0638) 3960

Tinkler, C. H. (0:0:0:0:0).... 9   4
Malton (0653) 5981
Treanor, A. (—:—:—:1:0)... 7   9
c/o Cannings (038 086) 245
Tucker, K. J. (—:0:1:0:0).... 8   0
Newmarket (0638) 3209
Tulk, P. F. (10:2:14:10:8).... 8   2
Newmarket (0638) 3209
Waldron, P. (44:42 53:53:49). 8   1
Inkpen (04884) 263
Weaver, R. I. (10:11:13:10:10) 8   3
Chieveley (063531) 519 or
Weyhill (026477) 2278
Webster, S. G.
(18:23:10:13:12)........... 7   11
Wensleydale (0969) 23576
Welsh, G. (0:—:0:0:1)....... 7   10
Wensleydale (0969) 23350
Wernham, R. A.
(9:—:—:—:0)............. 8   0
Carlton (0933) 843 858
Wharton, W. J.
(18:25:18:15:4)........... 8   2
Somerby (066 477) 614
Wigham, M. (32:56:25:37:19). 8   2
Rillington (09442) 332
Wigham, R. (—:—:—:—:0).. 8   0
c/o Tamworth (0827) 62901

Wilkins, L. F. (0:0:0:0:0)..... 8   0
Bagshot (0276) 71030
Wilkinson, W. P. (—:—:0:1:0) 8   1
Epsom (037 27) 28788
Williams, C. N. (3:1:0:0:0)... 8   4
Bradfield (0734) 744 309
Williams, J. A. N. (0:0:0:0:0). 8   6
Clydach (044 15) 3407
Winter, P. D. (3:5:12:1:2)... 7   12
East Ilsley (063 528) 342
Wood, M. (4:4:12:16:10)..... 7   10
c/o Greystoke (08533) 392
Woolley, S. J. (4:5:1:3:1)..... 8   3
Yates, D. I. (1:3:5:2:0)....... 8   0
Hungerford (04886) 3475
Yeoman, Mrs M. M.
(0:0:0:0:0)............... 8   7
York (0904) 28693
Young, P. J. (26:13:15:22:33). 8   4
Newmarket (0638) 730371
and 5050

The following relinquished his
licence during the season:

Lucas, T. G. (—:—::10:14:26)

APPRENTICES

The following list shows the employer and riding weight of every apprentice who holds a current licence to ride on the Flat, and the number of winners he or she has ridden, wins in apprentice races being recorded separately.

Apprentices may claim 7 lb until they have won 10 races, 5 lb until they have won 50 races and 3 lb until they have won 75 races. Apprentice races are excepted in all these cases. The allowance each apprentice is entitled to claim is shown in brackets. The claim may be exercised in all handicaps and selling races, and in all other races with guaranteed prize money of not more than £3,500.

Adams, J. A. (7) 1 ap........ 7   0
(G. Lewis)
Adams, N. M. (7) 1......... 7   2
(J. Sutcliffe)
Alcock, G. (7).............. 8   10
(H. T. Jones)
Alderman, A. A. (7) 1 ap.... 8   2
(J. Jenkins)
Alford, P. G. (7)............ 7   0
(R. Price)
Allen, C. N. (7)............. 7   7
(P. Brookshaw)
Anderson, P. J. O. (7)....... 7   7
(R. Hollinshead)
Atkinson, C. B. (7).......... 7   8
(J. Etherington)
Austin, G. P. (7)............ 6   10
(G. Toft)
Beecroft, M. C. (7) 6+4 ap.. 7   12
(T. Fairhurst)
Belcher, N. (7).............. 7   2
(R. Smyth)
Bell, K. (7) 1 ap............ 7   7
(R. Hollinshead)

Bell, P. (7)................. 7   9
(J. Etherington)
Bennett, R. A. (7).......... 8   7
(C. Crossley)
Berry, M. (7) 1 ap.......... 7   12
(J. Berry)
Billingham, M. A. (7)....... 8   0
(M. Tate)
Blake, J. W. (7) 2+2 ap...... 7   3
(H. Wragg)
Blakiston, N. A. (7)......... 8   4
(B. Hobbs)
Bloomfield, P. S. (7) 3+11 ap 7   13
(G. Harwood)
Bourton, D. D. (7).......... 7   7
(R. Atkins)
Bowmer, S. J. (7)........... 7   7
(M. Jarvis)
Bradshaw, K. (7) 1.......... 7   0
(M. Stoute)
Bradwell, P. (5) 30+9 ap.... 7   7
(C. Brittain)
Bree, I. J. (7)............... 7   4
(S. Matthews)

Brockbank, D. (7) 1+1 ap... 7 6
(G. Pritchard-Gordon)
Brough, J. H. (7)............ 8 6
(J. Wilson)
Brown, D. (7) 2 ap......... 7 0
(M. Masson)
Brown, G. (7) 2 ap......... 7 7
(J. Fitzgerald)
Brown, J. H. (7) 1 ap....... 7 8
(I. Balding)
Brown, W. J. (7)............ 8 0
(M. Ryan)
Buckton, S. A. (7) 1........ 7 7
(J. Calvert)
Burnham, M. J. (7) 1 ap..... 7 0
(G. Balding)
Butler, P. S. (7)............ 7 0
(D. Marks)
Cameron, P. (7)............ 7 12
(F. Durr)
Campbell, C. R. (7) 2+1 ap.. 7 7
(K. Ivory)
Campbell, R. (7) 9+6 ap.... 8 0
(C. Thornton)
Caplen, K. (7)............. 8 3
(D. Wilson)
Carcary, D. R. (7) 1 ap...... 8 3
(R. Hollinshead)
Carlisle, N. A. (5) 34+3 ap... 7 0
(R. Hollinshead)
Carroll, J. (7) 1 ap.......... 7 0
(G. Richards)
Carter, C. A. (7)............ 7 0
(P. Cundell)
Carter, R. P. (7)............ 7 0
(J. Winter)
Carter, Miss W. J. (7)....... 7 0
(E. Carter)
Chilton, M. J. (7) 1+2 ap.... 9 7
(G. Balding)
Clark, A. S. (5) 47+3 ap..... 7 7
(G. Harwood)
Clements, B. E. (7).......... 7 8
(R. Hern)
Coates, C. (7) 1 ap.......... 6 7
(T. Fairhurst)
Collinson, A. (7)............ 5 10
(G. Harwood)
Collinson, T. (7)............ 5 8
(G. Harwood)
Connorton, N. B. (5) 46+7 ap 7 11
(J. W. Watts)
Cooney, P. J. (7)........... 7 9
(A. Pitt)
Cooper, Miss S. J. (7)....... 7 0
(F. J. Houghton)
Coughlan, C. M. (7)......... 7 9
(S. Mellor)
Cox, C. G. (7) 1............. 7 0
(P. Cundell)
Cox, J. D. (7)............... 7 0
(J. Tree)
Crossley, B. G. (3) 67+5 ap.. 7 6
(G. Huffer)
Cullen, E. M. (7)............ 8 0
(J. Dunlop)
Cullen, S. T. (7) 2+2 ap..... 7 0
(L. Cumani)

Dawe, N. J. (7) 2+10 ap..... 7 4
(J. Dunlop)
Dawson, S. (7) 9+1 ap....... 7 0
(N. Vigors)
Day, N. P. (5) 42+7 ap...... 8 0
(H. Cecil)
Dennison, S. E. J. (7) 4 ap... 8 2
(R. Armstrong)
Dickie, G. (7) 1+1 ap........ 7 2
(R. Smyth)
Dicks, A. C. (7)............. 6 10
(M. Bradley)
Dixon, I. (7)................ 7 0
(C. Thornton)
Dodd, D. (7) 4 ap............ 8 4
(G. Richards)
Donkin, S. (7)............. 7 5
(M. H. Easterby)
Doughty, P. A. (7).......... 7 7
(C. Crossley)
Driver, S. A. (7)............ 8 2
(J. Winter)
Eddery, P. A. (5) 32+6 ap.... 7 6
(R. Hollinshead)
Feilden, Miss J. I., (7) 1 ap... 7 7
(P. Feilden)
Ford, D. A. P. (7) 1 ap....... 7 4
(M. Jarvis)
Ford, D. K. (7) 1 ap......... 7 9
(C. Nelson)
Ford, T. J. (7).............. 7 0
(R. Hannon)
Fortune, J. H. (7) 2+1 ap.... 7 6
(I. Walker)
Fotheringham, R. (7)....... 7 0
(J. W. Watts)
Fowler-Wright, D. J. (7)..... 6 4
(R. Smyth)
Fox, D. (7) 1 ap............. 7 2
(A. Hide)
Fozzard, M. G. (7) 1 ap...... 7 2
(F. Durr)
Freer, S. (7)............... 7 10
(R. Hollinshead)
Fretwell, K. (7) 7+5 ap...... 7 7
(B. Hanbury)
Fry, M. J. (7) 9+4 ap........ 7 4
(D. Smith)
Geran, A. J. (7)............. 6 10
(G. Huffer)
Geran, M. P. (7)............ 7 12
(G. Huffer)
Gibson, A. (7)............... 7 9
(D. Weeden)
Gilbert, Miss S. P. (7)....... 8 0
(J. Gilbert)
Gilchrist, M. F. (7).......... 7 7
(J. Dunlop)
Gilmour, S. H. (7).......... 7 7
(G. Balding)
Glozier, A. D. (7)........... 7 0
(J. Toller)
Goldie, N. A. (7)............ 7 0
(A. Jarvis)
Goswell, P. W. (7).......... 7 13
(R. Simpson)
Graham, B. A. (7).......... 7 7
(T. Craig)

1004

Green, M. S. (7) 2 . . . . 7 12
(R. Simpson)
Gregg, J. (7) 1 . . . . 7 5
(N. Vigors)
Griffin, D. A. (7) 7 7
(P. M. Taylor)
Griffiths, S. P. (7) 2 ap 6 0
(S. Nesbitt)
Guest, E. J. (7) 3 + 1 ap 7 12
(E. Eldin)
Guest, Miss Sally (7) 7 10
(N. Guest)

Hadley, S. R. (7) 1 + 3 ap 7 8
(R. Hern)
Hamey, A. (7) 7 12
(S. Mellor)
Hamm, M. A. (7) 8 7
(B. Wise)
Harding, T. J. (7) 7 10
(M. Haynes)
Harris, J. A. (7) 8 10
(J. Harris)
Harrison, M. J. (7) 7 7
(A. Ingham)
Harrison, P. (7) 7 0
(C. Brittain)
Hastie, R. M. (7) 8 2
(C. Nelson)
Hayes, B. E. (7) 7 0
(R. Hollinshead)
Hayes, W. J. (7) 3 ap 6 5
(D. Nicholson)
Heard, C. (7) 8 0
(R. Hern)
Hill, P. D. (7) 1 ap 6 7
(W. Wharton)
Hills, M. P. (5) 20 + 7 ap 7 0
(J. Hindley)
Hills, R. J. (5) 17 + 4 ap 6 10
(H. T. Jones)
Hindley, M. G. (7) 1 + 1 ap . . . 8 4
(P. Rohan)
Hodgson, K. (5) 45 + 10 ap 7 10
(M. H. Easterby)
Hodgson, R. A. (7) 2 ap 7 4
(W. Stubbs)
Holgate, C. S. (7) 1 ap 7 12
(W. Musson)
Homewood, S. M. (7) 7 12
(N. Callaghan)
Honeywill, B. G. (7) 8 7
(B. Hobbs)
Hopkinson, P. (7) 7 7
(D. Gandolfo)
Horsfall, S. S. (7) 5 11
(J. Berry)
Houlker, T. D. (7) 7 7
(R. Hollinshead)
Howard, P. T. (7) 7 + 7 ap 7 1
(P. Haslam)
Newmarket (0638) 4525
Howe, N. J. (5) 42 + 12 ap 7 9
(P. Walwyn)
Hughes, G. (7) 2 ap 7 10
(P. Rohan)
Humphries, G. M. (7) 8 3
(I. Walker)

Hurd, P. A. (7) 1 ap 8 0
(S. Norton)
Imrie, S. T. (7) 7 10
(W. Bentley)
Jarvis, S. J. (5) 37 + 3 ap 8 2
(A. Jarvis)
Jarvis, T. O. (7) 3 + 1 ap 8 6
(A. Jarvis)
Jenkins, C. V. (7) 7 11
(F. Durr)
Jenkins, J. P. (7) 7 11
(L. Cumani)
Jewell, S. (7) 1 + 2 ap 7 9
(R. Sheather)
Johnson, C. A. (7) 8 3
(Sir Mark Prescott)
Jones, B. (5) 20 + 5 ap 7 0
(R. Hollinshead)
Jones, K. (7) 8 7
(W. A. Stephenson)
Jones, L. (7) 7 0
(R. Hannon)
Kaye, J. A. (7) 1 . . . . 6 10
(P. Kelleway)
Keightley, S. L. (7) 2 ap 9 0
(P. M. Taylor)
Kennedy, J. B. (7) 1 ap 7 4
(H. Candy)
Kerr, R. (7) 7 5
(N. Tompkins)
King, G. N. (7) 6 10
(B. Hobbs)
King, P. L. (7) 6 7
(R. Hern)
Knight, Miss D. J. (7) 7 0
(G. Beeson)
Lawes, S. D. (5) 15 + 1 ap 7 13
(J. Etherington)
Lawson, R. (7) 7 10
(P. Taylor)
Leader, A. B. (7) 7 7
(Sir Mark Prescott)
Leeming, Miss V. M. (7) 8 0
(J. Wilson)
Lloyd, M. D. (7) 7 4
(W. Holden)
Loftus, J. (7) 6 7
(J. Carr)
Lomax, G. (7) 7 4
H. T. Jones)
Longair, C. (7) 7 7
(W. Williams)
Mackay, A. (5) 27 + 9 ap 7 3
(E. Eldin)
Newmarket (0638) 67780
Malham, M. S. T. (5) 12 + 8 ap 7 10
(P. Cole)
Mann, C. J. (7) 9 0
(N. Henderson)
Martin, J. S. (7) 7 4
(D. Wilson)
Mason, K. J. (7) 7 0
(D. Smith)
Mason, P. F. (7) 7 2
(P. Cole)
Matthews, B. (7) 1 . . . . 8 7
(H. T. Jones)

McAndrew, M. A. (7)....... 7 7
(J. Fitzgerald)
McCready, C. (7)........... 7 8
(P. Makin)
McCrystal, S. (7) 1 ap...... 7 2
(R. Armstrong)
McDermott, G. S. (7)....... 8 0
(K. Stone)
McGilligan, A. N. (7)....... 8 0
(I. Jordon)
McGlone, A. D. (5) 19+7 ap   7 0
(R. Hannon)
McKeon, W. A. P. (7) 8+2 ap 8 3
(F. Durr)
McKeown, D. R. (5) 25+7 ap. 7 9
(W. Hastings-Bass)
McIlfatrick, C. (7) 1+7 ap... 9 0
(J. Old)
McLean, J. A. (7) 1.......... 6 8
(H. Candy)
McNamee, V. (7)............ 7 0
(R. Akehurst)
Melhuish, Miss L. A. (7)..... 7 0
(W. Musson)
Membury, L. M. (7)......... 7 7
(D. Elsworth)
Mercer, A. 67+7 ap......... 7 7
(J. W. Watts)
Mitchell, S. (7)............. 8 4
(W. A. Stephenson)
Montgomery, D. J. (7)...... 6 11
(G. Blum)
Morrell, Miss A. M. (7)..... 7 12
(J. Holt)
Morris, D. (7).............. 8 3
(J. Jenkins)
Morris, W. A. F. F. (7)..... 8 7
(F. Yardley)
Mose, P. (7)................ 7 0
(G. Harwood)
Moseley, M. F. (7) 2........ 7 8
(R. Laing)
Myers, Miss N. (7).......... 6 7
(J. Berry)

Nesbitt, H. A. (5) 39+4 ap... 6 10
(S. Nesbitt)
Newnes, W. A. P. 82+5 ap... 7 4
(H. Candy)
Nolan, P. M. (7)............ 8 0
(K. Bridgwater)

O'Brien, G. J. (7)........... 7 2
(P. Walwyn)
Oliver, M. A. (7)............ 7 5
(G. Lewis)
Ollivier, C. G. (5) 12+3 ap... 7 11
(B. Lunness)
Market Weighton (0696) 60488
Osborne, S. (7)............. 7 7
(S. Matthews)
O'Sullivan, P. (7).......... 7 7
(H. Wragg)
Park, A. (7)................ 7 7
(G. Lewis)
Parker, G. (7).............. 7 2
(C. Brittain)
Panes, O. J. (7)............ 7 9
(C. Mackenzie)

Parr, S. (5) 19+10 ap........ 8 0
(H. Wragg)
Payne, S. M. (5) 20+7 ap.... 7 7
(I. Balding)
Pearson, B. (7)............. 7 7
(D. Jermy)
Peat, Miss C. (7)........... 7 3
(G. Blum)
Peerless, C. B. (7) 1 ap...... 8 4
(C. Wildman)
Pinto, L. (7)................ 7 11
(F. Durr)
Plumb, V. (7)............... 7 12
(G. Huffer)
Pope, M. J. (7)............. 7 7
(J. Benstead)
Potel, S. A. (7)............. 8 0
(R. Hoad)
Powdrell, K. M. (7) 1 ap..... 7 2
(P. Cole)
Preece, G. A. (7)........... 7 7
(R. Baker)
Price, D. J. (7) 2........... 7 7
(F. J. Houghton)
Price, N. M. (7)............ 8 7
(C. Booth)
Proctor, T. (7)............. 8 2
(M. Stoute)
Proud, A. (5) 18+2 ap....... 7 8
(J. Hardy)
Purchase, J. E. (7).......... 7 12
(I. Balding)

Quinn, T. R. (7) 1 ap........ 7 2
(P. Cole)

Radcliffe, K. (7) 1 ap....... 7 0
(H. Candy)
Rawlinson, A. (7) 1 ap....... 7 5
(F. Durr)
Newbury (0635) 31218
Raymont, K. N. (7) 3+7 ap.. 7 10
(J. Tree)
Reid, M. (7)................ 7 7
(M. Stoute)
Rimmer, M. E. (3) 54+9 ap.. 7 11
(G. Pritchard-Gordon)
Rimmer, M. T. (7).......... 9 0
(G. Pritchard-Gordon)
Roberts, J. (7)............. 7 12
(B. Swift)
Robinson, S. (7) 1........... 7 7
(C. Gray)
Ross, K. R. (7) 2+2 ap....... 7 2
(M. Smyly)
Rowe, J. (5) 21+7 ap........ 8 11
(S. Mellor)
Ryan, S. L. (7)............. 6 8
(Mrs C. Reavey)
Ryan, W. (7)............... 7 0
(R. Hollinshead)

Salmon, I. P. A. (7) 1 ap..... 7 7
(R. Price)
Sanderson, Miss H. L. (7)... 7 7
(M. McCourt)
Saunders, M. G. (7) 4+3 ap.. 7 7
(A. Pitt)
Scarfe, M. F. (7)............ 8 0
(D. Jermy)

Shelton, R. L. (7) 1 ap....... 7 11
  (J. Benstead)
Sherren, Miss Y. S. (7) 1 ap.. 8 7
  (D. Morley)
Shipley, P. A. (7)........... 8 2
  (R. Hollinshead)
Shoesmith, C. W. (7)........ 8 0
  (J. W. Watts)
Silkstone, J. (7)............. 7 0
  (P. Walwyn)
Simmons, Miss S. M. (7).... 8 8
  (N. Callaghan)
Simms, D. A. (7)............. 7 7
  (I. Walker)
Sims, D. J. (7) 3 + 3 ap....... 8 7
  (P. Cundell)
Skuse, S. R. (7).............. 8 5
  (M. Blanshard)
Smith, D. R. (7)............. 6 8
  (C. Elsey)
Spink, Miss K. A. (7)........ 7 4
  (R. Ward)
Steers, C. (7)................ 6 7
  (A. Jarvis)
Stevens, J. S. (7)............ 7 7
  (W. Marshall)
Stockton, J. (7)............. 8 0
  (J. Doyle)
Storey, C. V. (7) 5 + 2 ap..... 7 7
  (M. W. Easterby)
Storrie, G. (7)............... 7 10
  (B. Gubby)
Sweetapple, I. R. (7)........ 7 3
  (C. Austin)
Sykes, A. D. (7) 1 ap........ 7 12
  (S. Norton)
Tanner, W. G. (7) 2 ap...... 7 3
  (W. Hastings-Bass)
Taylor, Miss J. (7).......... 8 7
  (H. T. Jones)
Taylor, T. (7)................ 5 7
  (J. Bethell)
Thompson, D. W. (7)........ 8 0
  (D. Smith)
Thompson, Miss J. S. (7).... 8 0
  (R. Ward)
Thorpe, Miss G. M. M. (7).. 7 0
  (R. Hollinshead)
Tootell, J. D. (7)............ 7 0
  (C. Thornton)
Tudor, P. (7)................ 7 10
  (E. Weymes)

Varnham, R. (7) 1........... 7 13
  C. James)
Vaughan, N. J. (7) 9 + 5 ap... 7 13
  (D. Francis)
Walker, D. R. (7)........... 7 10
  (J. Holt)
Waller, I. M. (7)............ 7 2
  (J. Mason)
Ward, G. I. (7).............. 8 0
  (N. Bycroft)
Wardrope, B. (7)........... 7 7
  (J. Tree)
Warner, J. A. (7) 1 ap....... 7 12
  (N. Guest)
Webb, Miss S. J. (7)......... 8 0
  (P. K. Mitchell)
Weiss, A. L. (7)............. 7 2
  (F. Durr)
West, S. J. (7).............. 9 0
  (T. Hallett)
Willey, K. M. (5) 10 + 2 ap... 7 11
  (B. Hills)
Williams, Miss J. H. (7)..... 7 7
  (J. W. Watts)
Williams, K. E. J. (7) 1 + 4 ap 7 4
  (Sir Mark Prescott)
Williams, S. J. (7)........... 8 0
  (G. Lewis)
Wood, M. A. (7).............. 7 0
  (J. Wilson)
Woods, W. E. (7)............ 7 0
  (G. Harwood)
Woolnough, K. L. (7)........ 7 5
  (M. Haynes)
Young, D. (7)................ 8 0
  (W. Hastings-Bass)
Young, P. W. (7) 1 ap........ 7 10
  (P. Asquith)
Young, S. (7) 8 + 10 ap....... 8 0
  (M. Tompkins)

The following winning apprentices
of 1981 relinquished their licences
during the season:
Barnes, R. (7) 1 ap
Dunne, J. (7) 1 ap
Finlayson, J. (7) 3 + 1 ap
Gillingham, W. (7) 1 ap
McFeeters, D. M. (7) 2 ap
Morris, S. (5) 28
Sidebottom, R. (5) 37 + 9 ap

AYR

Scotland's Premier Racecourse

FLAT MEETINGS 1982

Monday and Tuesday   March 29 and 30

Friday (Evening) and Saturday   May 28 and 29
    The Tia Maria Handicap 7f (£9,000)
    The P.G. Tips Tea Cup (Amateur Riders) 5f
    The Philip Cornes Nickel Alloys Stakes (Qualifier) 5f
    The Balmoral Castle Stakes, 3-y-o, 1m (£6,000)

Friday and Saturday   June 18 and 19
    The Belleisle Stakes, 2-y-o only, 5f (£5,000)
    The Long John Scotch Whisky Handicap.
    1m, 3-y-o and up (£6,000)

Friday (Evening) and Saturday   July 9 and 10
    The Tote Sprint Trophy, 6f (£15,000)
    The Land of Burns Stakes, 1m 2f (£15,000)

Saturday, Monday and Tuesday   July 17, 19 and 20
    Mecca Bookmakers Scottish Derby, 1m 5f, 3-y-o only
      (£20,000)
    The Johnnie Walker Black Label Handicap
    The John Barr Scotch Whisky Stakes
    The Tennent Trophy (Handicap) 1m 7f (£15,000)
    The Strathclyde Stakes, 2-y-o only, 6f (£7,000)

Tuesday and Wednesday   August 3 and 4
    The Heronslea Stakes, 2-y-o, 7f (£7,000)

THE WESTERN MEETING

Wednesday, Thursday, Friday and Saturday—September 15, 16, 17 & 18
    The Eglinton & Winton Memorial Handicap, 2m 1f (£7,000)
    The Kyle & Carrick Handicap, 1m (£6,000)
    The Doonside Cup, 1m 3f (£16,000)
    The Ladbrokes Ayrshire Handicap, 1m 3f (£10,000)
    The Harry Rosebery Challenge Trophy, 2-y-o, 5f (£16,000)
    The Ladbrokes (Ayr) Gold Cup, 6f (£25,000)
    The Weir Memorial Trophy (Handicap), 1m 2f (£7,000)
    The Ladbrokes Leisure Nursery Handicap, 6f (£5,000)
    The Sam Hall Stakes, 1m 7f (£4,000)
    The Bogside Cup, 1m 5f (£7,000)
    The Firth of Clyde Stakes, 2-y-o fillies, 6f (£12,000)
    The Ladbroke Strathclyde Handicap, 1m (£5,000)
    The Crown Plus Two Apprentice Championship (Handicap),
      5f (£3,000)
    The Holsten Diat Pils Handicap, 7f (£7,000)

Total Amount of Added Prize Money
for 1982 Flat £385,000

Ayr is one of Britain's best equipped and leading racecourses.
Free Stabling and Accommodation for Lads and Girls.
Landing facilities for Helicopters in Centre of Course.

Further Particulars from

W. W. McHarg   Racecourse Office.
General Manager and Secretary   2 Whitletts Road,
and Joint Clerk of the Course.   Ayr.
    Telephone: Ayr (0292) 264179

CHARACTERISTICS OF RACECOURSES

ASCOT.—The Ascot round course is a right-handed, triangular circuit of 1m 6f 34yds, with a run-in of 2½f. There is a straight mile course, over which the Royal Hunt Cup is run, and the Old mile course which joins the round course in Swinley Bottom. All races shorter than a mile are decided on the straight course. From the 1½-mile starting gate the round course runs downhill to the bend in Swinley Bottom, where it is level, then rises steadily to the turn into the straight, from where it is uphill until less than a furlong from the winning post, the last hundred yards being more or less level. The straight mile is slightly downhill from the start and then rises to the 5f gate, after which there is a slight fall before the junction with the round course. Despite the downhill run into Swinley Bottom and the relatively short run-in from the final turn, the Ascot course is galloping in character; the turns are easy, there are no minor surface undulations to throw a long-striding horse off balance, and all races are very much against the collar over the last half-mile. The course is, in fact, quite a testing one, and very much so in soft going, when there is a heavy premium on stamina. In such circumstances races over 2 miles to 2¾ miles are very severe tests.
DRAW: The draw seems of little consequence nowadays.

AYR.—The Ayr round course is a left-handed, oval track, about twelve furlongs in extent, with a run-in of half a mile. Eleven-furlong races start on a chute which joins the round course after about a furlong. There is a straight six-furlong course of considerable width. The course is relatively flat, but there are gentle undulations throughout, perhaps more marked in the straight. It has a good surface and well-graded turns, and is a fine and very fair track, on the whole galloping in character.
DRAW: In races over seven furlongs and a mile a low number is desirable. On the straight course the draw is ordinarily of little consequence.

BATH.—The Bath round course is a left-handed, oval track, just over a mile and a half in extent, with a run-in of nearly half a mile. There is an extension for races over five furlongs and five furlongs and 167 yards. The run-in bends to the left, and is on the rise all the way. The mile and the mile-and-a-quarter courses have been designed to give over a quarter of a mile straight at the start, and the track generally is galloping rather than sharp. The course consists of old downland turf.
DRAW: The draw seems of little consequence nowadays.

BEVERLEY.—The Beverley round course is a right-handed, oval track, just over a mile and three furlongs in extent, with a run-in of two and a half furlongs. The five-furlong track bends right at halfway. The general galloping nature of the track is modified by the downhill turn into the straight and the relatively short run-in. The five-furlong course is on the rise throughout, and so is rather testing even in normal conditions; in soft going it takes some getting, particularly for two-year-olds early in the season.
DRAW: High numbers have an advantage over the five-furlong course.

BRIGHTON.—The Brighton course takes the shape of an extended 'U' and is 1½ miles in length. The first three furlongs are uphill, after which there is a slight descent followed by a slight rise to about four furlongs from home; the track then runs more sharply downhill until a quarter of a mile out, from where it rises to the last hundred yards, the finish being level. The run-in is about 3½ furlongs, and there is no straight course. This is essentially a sharp track. While the turns are easy enough, the pronounced gradients make Brighton an unsuitable course for big, long-striding horses, resolute gallopers or round-actioned horses. Handy, medium-sized, fluent-movers, and quick-actioned horses are much more at home on the course. There are no opportunities for long-distance plodders at Brighton.
DRAW: In sprint races a low number is advantageous, and speed out of the gate even more so.

CHESTER RACES

1982

MAY MEETING

Tuesday, May 4th	CHESTER VASE
Wednesday, May 5th	THE LADBROKE CHESTER CUP
Thursday, May 6th	169th DEE STAKES

SUMMER MEETING

Friday (Evening), July 9th
(probable time of first race 6.30 p.m.)
Saturday, July 10th

AUGUST MEETING

Friday, August 20th
Saturday, August 21st

For further particulars please apply to
Secretaries, Chester Race Company Ltd.,
2, George Street, Chester (Tel. 48976).

CARLISLE.—Carlisle is a right-handed, pear-shaped course, just over a mile and a half in extent, with a run-in of a little more than three furlongs. The six-furlong course, of which the five-furlong course is a part, the mile course, and the mile and a half course start on three separate off-shoot extensions. For the first three furlongs or so the course runs downhill, then rises for a short distance, levelling out just beyond the mile post. From there until the turn into the straight the course is flat, apart from minor undulations. The six-furlong course, which bears right soon after the start, and again at the turn into the straight, is level for two furlongs, then rises fairly steeply until the distance, from which point it is practically level. The track is galloping in character, and the six-furlong course is a stiff test of stamina for a two-year-old.
DRAW: High numbers have an advantage which is more marked in the shorter races.

CATTERICK.—The Catterick round course is a left-handed, oval track, measuring one mile and 180 yards, with a run-in of three furlongs. The five-furlong course bears left before and at the junction with the round course. From the seven-furlong starting gate the round course is downhill almost all the way, and there is a sharp turn on the falling gradient into the straight. The five-furlong course is downhill throughout, quite steeply to start with, and less so thereafter. Catterick is an exceedingly sharp track with pronounced undulations of surface, and it is therefore an impossible course for a big, long-striding animal. Experience of the track counts for a great deal, and jockeyship is of the utmost importance.
DRAW: A low number gives a slight advantage over five furlongs, and a much more definite one in the six and seven-furlong course but a quick start is essential whatever the draw. A slow beginner on the inside is almost certain to be cut off.

CHEPSTOW.—The Chepstow round course is a left-handed, oval track, about two miles in extent, with a run-in of five furlongs. There is a straight mile course, over which all races up to a mile are run. The round course has well-marked undulations, and the straight course is generally downhill and level alternately as far as the run-in, thereafter rising sharply for over two furlongs, and then gradually levelling out to the winning post. Notwithstanding the long run-in and general rise over the last five furlongs, this is not an ideal galloping track because of the changing gradients.
DRAW: High numbers have a slight advantage on the straight course.

CHESTER.—Chester is a left-handed, circular course, only a few yards over a mile round, the smallest circuit of any flat-race course in Great Britain. It is quite flat and on the turn almost throughout, and although the run-in is nearly straight, it is less than two furlongs in length. The Chester Cup which is invariably run at a very strong gallop all the way, is a testing race demanding exceptional stamina and is always won by an out-and-out stayer. Apart from extreme distance events, such as the Cup and other 2½m races, the course is against the long-striding, resolute galloper and greatly favours the handy, medium-sized, sharp-actioned horse.
DRAW: A low number is of great importance in races at up to seven and a half furlongs and a quick beginning is essential. It is virtually impossible to overcome a slow start over sprint distances.

DONCASTER.—Doncaster is a left-handed, pear-shaped course, over 15 furlongs round and quite flat, except for a slight hill about 1¼ miles from the finish. There is a perfectly straight mile, and a round mile starting on an off-shoot of the round course. The run-in from the turn is about 4½ furlongs. This is one of the fairest courses in the country, but its flat surface and great width, its sweeping turn into the straight, and long run-in, make it galloping in character, and ideal for the big, long-striding stayer.
DRAW: The draw is of no importance on the round course. On the straight course high numbers used to have a considerable advantage, but nowadays low numbers are usually favoured.

EDINBURGH.—The Edinburgh round course is a right-handed oval track nearly a mile and a quarter in extent, with a run-in of half a mile. There is a straight five-furlong course. The track is flat, with slight undulations and a gentle rise from the distance to the winning post. The turns at the top end of the course and into the straight are very sharp, and handiness and adaptability to negotiate the bends is of the utmost importance. The big, long-striding, cumbersome horse is at a distinct disadvantage on the round track, especially in races at up to a mile and three furlongs, but to a lesser extent in races over longer distances.

DRAW: High numbers have an advantage in seven-furlong and mile races.

EPSOM.—Epsom is a left-handed, U-shaped course, 1½ miles in extent, with an interior unfenced track, known as the Metropolitan course, used only in 2¼-mile races. In these races the horses start at the winning post and proceed the reverse way of the course, branching off to the right just before reaching Tattenham Corner and rejoining the course proper just over 8½ furlongs from the winning post. The Derby course is decidedly uphill for the first half-mile, level for nearly two furlongs and then quite sharply downhill round the bend to Tattenham Corner and all the way up the straight until approaching the final furlong, from where there is a fairish rise to the winning post. The run-in is less than four furlongs. The 7f and 6f courses start on tangential extensions. The 5f course is quite straight and sharply downhill to the junction with the round course. Races over 2¼ miles are, of course, true tests of stamina, and races over 1½ miles can also be testing if the pace over the first uphill four furlongs is strong, as it frequently is in the Derby. Otherwise the track is not really testing in itself, and races up to 8½ furlongs are very sharp indeed, the sprint courses being the fastest in the world. Owing to its bends and pronounced downhill gradients, Epsom favours the handy, fluent-actioned, medium-sized horse: big horses sometimes handle the course well enough, but cumbersome horses, long-striding gallopers, or those with pronounced 'knee-action' are not suited by it and are frequently quite unable to act upon it, especially when the going is firm or hard. Any hesitation at the start or slowness into stride results in considerable loss of ground over the first furlong in sprint races. For this reason Epsom is no course for a green and inexperienced two-year-old, slow to realise what is required.

DRAW: In races up to eight and a half furlongs a low number is advantageous, but quickness out of the gate is of far greater importance, particularly in five-furlong, six-furlong and seven-furlong races.

FOLKESTONE.—The Folkestone round course is a right-handed, pear-shaped track, about ten and a half furlongs in extent, with a run-in of two and a half furlongs. There is a straight six-furlong course. The course is undulating, with the last part slightly on the rise, but notwithstanding its width, the easy turns and the uphill finish, it is by no means a galloping track.

DRAW: Low numbers have a slight advantage on the straight course.

GOODWOOD.—The Goodwood track consists of a nearly straight 6f course, with a triangular right-handed loop circuit. The Goodwood Cup, about 2m 5f, is started by flag in front of the stands: the horses run the reverse way of the straight, branch left at the first or lower bend, go right-handed round the loop and return to the straight course via the top bend. Races over 2m 3f, 1¾m, 1½m and 1¼m are also run on this course, but 1m races rejoin the straight course via the lower bend. Although there is a 5f run-in for races of 1¼m and upwards, the turns and, more specially, the pronounced downhill gradients from the turn make Goodwood essentially a sharp track, favouring the active, handy, fluent mover rather than the big, long-striding horse. This is of lesser importance in 2m 3f and 2m 5f races, where the emphasis is on sound stamina, and of greater importance in the shorter distance races, particularly in sprints and especially when the going is on top. The 5f course is one of the fastest in the country.

DRAW: A high number is regarded as advantageous in sprint races, but the advantage is not great. Alacrity out of the gate is certainly of importance in five-furlong races.

1012

HAMILTON.—The Hamilton track is a perfectly straight six-furlong course, with a pear-shaped, right-handed loop, the whole being a mile and five furlongs in extent from a start in front of the stands, round the loop and back to the winning post. The run-in is five furlongs. The turns are very easy, and the course is undulating for the most part, but just over three furlongs from the winning post there are steep gradients into and out of a pronounced hollow, followed by a severe hill to the finish.
DRAW: Middle to high numbers are thought to have a slight advantage in races over the straight course.

HAYDOCK.—Haydock is a left-handed, oval-shaped course, about 13 furlongs round, with a run-in of 4½ furlongs, and a straight 5-furlong course. Races of 6 furlongs and 1½ miles start on tangential extensions to the round course. This course is rather galloping in character, with a rise of twenty-one feet throughout the straight.
DRAW: Horses drawn in the low numbers are regarded as having an advantage in races of six, seven and eight furlongs. On the straight course the draw is of no consequence when the going is sound, but when it is soft, horses racing under the stand rails (high numbers) seem to be favoured.

KEMPTON.—Kempton is a right-handed, triangular course, just over 13 furlongs round. The ten-furlong Jubilee course starts on an extension to the round course. Sprint races are run over a separate diagonal course. The Kempton track is perfectly flat with normal characteristics, being neither a sharp track nor a galloping one.
DRAW: On the sprint course a draw near the rails is advantageous when the ground is soft.

LEICESTER.—The Leicester round course is a right-handed, oval track, about a mile and three quarters in extent, with a run-in of four and a half furlongs. The straight mile course, on which all races of up to a mile are run, is mainly downhill to halfway, then rises gradually for over two furlongs, finishing on the level. The course is well-drained, the bends into the straight and beyond the winning post have been eased and cambered, and the track is galloping. For two-year-olds early in the season it poses quite a test of stamina.
DRAW: High numbers have an advantage in races at up to a mile and the advantage seems to be more marked when the going is on the soft side.

LINGFIELD.—The Lingfield round course is a left-handed loop, which intersects the straight course of seven furlongs and 140 yards nearly half a mile out and again less than two furlongs from the winning post. The run-in is not much more than three furlongs. For nearly half its length the round course is quite flat, then rises with easy gradients to the summit of a slight hill, after which there is a downhill turn to the straight. The straight course has a considerable downhill gradient to halfway, and is slightly downhill for the rest of the way. The straight course is very easy, and the track as a whole is sharp, putting a premium on speed and adaptability, and making relatively small demands upon stamina, though this does not, of course, apply to races over two miles. The mile and a half course, over which the Derby Trial is run, bears quite close resemblance to the Epsom Derby course.
DRAW: On the straight course high numbers have a slight advantage in normal conditions but when the going is heavy low numbers are favoured.

NEWBURY.—The Newbury round course is a left-handed, oval track, about a mile and seven furlongs in extent, with a run-in of nearly five furlongs. There is a straight mile course, which is slightly undulating throughout. Races on the round mile and over the extended seven furlongs start on an extension from the round course. Notwithstanding the undulations this is a good galloping track, and excellent arrangements have been made for watering the course.
DRAW: A high number used to be a fairly considerable advantage over the straight course, but since the narrowing of the track the advantage seems to have disappeared

RACING FIXTURES 1982
HAYDOCK PARK

JANUARY
8th & 9th Fri. & Sat.*
Gamekeepers' Chase (£3,500); Vaux Breweries Novice Chase (Qualifier) (£1,500) (Friday); Tote Northern Hurdle (£10,000); Haydock Park National Trial Chase (£5,000); Timeform Chase Novices Trial (£4,000); Philip Cornes Hurdle (Qualifier) (£1,500) (Saturday).
23rd Sat.*
Peter Marsh Chase (£16,000); Premier Long Distance Hurdle (£6,000); Haydock Park Champion Hurdle Trial (£8,000); Haig Novice Hurdle (Qualifier) (£1,500).

MARCH
5th & 6th Fri. & Sat.*
White Rabbit Chase (£3,500); Hattons Hunters' Chase (£1,000) (Friday); Greenall Whitley Breweries Chase (£14,000); Timeform Chase (£14,000); Victor Ludorum Hurdle (£10,000) (Saturday).

APRIL
7th Wed.
Field Marshal Stakes (£5,000); Freddy Fox Handicap (£4,000).
10th Sat.
Valspar Paints Handicap (£10,000); Philip Cornes Nickel Alloys (Qualifier) (£2,000); Danny Maher Handicap (£5,000).

MAY
1st & 3rd Sat. & Mon.
Cold Shield Windows Trophy (£15,000); Ordsall Lane Handicap (£5,000); Cold Shield Windows Handicap (£3,000); Cold Shield Windows 4,000 Guineas (£4,200) (Saturday); Royal Doulton Handicap Hurdle (£38,500); Minton Chase (£3,850); Royal Crown Derby Stakes (£2,200) (Monday).
28th & 29th Fri. & Sat.
John Davies Handicap (£3,500) (Friday); Gus Demmy Stakes (£11,000); Cecil Frail Handicap (£20,000); Lymm Stakes (£5,000) (Saturday).

JUNE
4th & 5th Fri. (Evening) & Sat.
Blackburn Handicap (£3,500); Burtonwood Brewery Handicap (£4,000) (Friday); Stones Best Bitter Handicap (£12,000); John of Gaunt Stakes (£20,000) (Saturday).

JULY
2nd & 3rd Fri. & Sat.
Great Central Handicap (£3,500) (Friday); Lancashire Oaks (£25,000); Old Newton Cup (£20,000); Sporting Chronicle Handicap (£8,000) (Saturday).

AUGUST
6th & 7th Fri. (Evening) & Sat.
Matthew Peacock Handicap (£3,500) (Friday); Tia Maria Handicap (£10,000); Better Bet Coral Handicap (£8,000); Harvey Jones Handicap (£7,500) (Saturday).

SEPTEMBER
3rd & 4th Fri. & Sat.
Claude Harrison Trophy (£4,000); Lytham Stakes (£4,000) (Friday); Vernon's Sprint Cup (£50,000); Morecambe Handicap (£7,500); Liverpool Handicap (£4,000); Fleetwood Nursery (£5,000) (Saturday).

OCTOBER
1st & 2nd Fri. & Sat.
Outland Handicap (£3,500) (Friday); Otis Handicap (£10,000); Brooke Bond Oxo Final (£4,000); Crown Plus Two Apprentice Handicap (£2,500); Buggins Farm Nursery Handicap (£7,000) (Saturday).
13th & 14th Wed. & Thurs.
Oak Handicap (£3,500) (Wednesday) Beech Handicap (£3,500) (Thursday).

NOVEMBER
24th & 25th Wed. & Thurs.*
Edward Hanmer Memorial Chase (£10,000); Sporting Chronicle Handicap Book Northern Hurdle (£4,000) (Wednesday); Garswood Pattern Hurdle (£3,000); Parker Rosser Handicap Chase (£5,000); Vaux Breweries Novice Chase (Qualifier) (£1,500) (Thursday).

DECEMBER
15th & 16th Wed. & Thurs.*
Boston Pit Handicap Chase (£3,000) (Wednesday); Burnley Handicap Chase (£3,000) (Thursday).

All enquiries to:
**HAYDOCK PARK RACECOURSE
NEWTON-LE-WILLOWS WA12 0HQ
MERSEYSIDE
Phone: Ashton-in-Makerfield 727345**

N.B. The details given above are correct at time of going to press, but factors outside the control of the Haydock Park Executive may result in alterations having to be made.

* National Hunt

NEWCASTLE.—Newcastle is a left-handed, oval-shaped course of 1m 6f in circumference. There is also a straight course, over which all races of seven furlongs or less are run. The course is decidedly galloping in character, and a steady climb from the turn into the straight makes Newcastle a testing track, particularly for two-year-olds early in the season. Ability to see the journey out thoroughly is most important.
DRAW: The draw is of no particular consequence.

NEWMARKET ROWLEY MILE COURSE.—The Cesarewitch course is two and a quarter miles in extent, with a right-handed bend after a mile, the last mile and a quarter being the straight Across the Flat. From the Cesarewitch start the course runs generally downhill to a sharp rise just before the turn. There are undulations throughout the first mile of the straight, then the course runs downhill for a furlong to the Dip, and uphill for the last furlong to the winning post. This is an exceedingly wide, galloping track, without minor irregularities of surfaces, so it is ideal for the big, long-striding horse, except for the descent into the Dip, which is more than counterbalanced by the final hill. Ability to see the trip out thoroughly is essential.
DRAW: There is no material advantage.

NEWMARKET SUMMER COURSE.—The Newmarket Summer course is two miles and twenty-four yards in extent, with a right-handed bend at halfway, the first mile being part of the Cesarewitch course, and the last the straight Bunbury Mile. The course runs generally downhill to a sharp rise just before the turn. There are undulations for the first three-quarters of a mile of the straight, then the course runs downhill for a furlong to a dip, and uphill for the last furlong to the winning post. This is an exceedingly wide, galloping track, ideal for the big, long-striding horse, except for the descent into the dip which is more than counterbalanced by the final hill. Ability to see the trip out thoroughly is essential.
DRAW: The draw confers little advantage.

NOTTINGHAM.—The Nottingham round course is a left-handed, oval track, about a mile and a half in extent, with a run-in of four and a half furlongs. There is a straight 6f course but no longer a straight mile. The course is flat and the turns are easy.
DRAW: High numbers are slightly preferred over the straight course.

PONTEFRACT.—Pontefract is a left-handed track, a mile and a half in extent occupying three-parts of an oval. There is no straight course, and the run-in is only just over two furlongs. There are considerable gradients and a testing hill over the last three furlongs. The undulations, the sharp bend into the straight, and the short run-in disqualify it from being described as a galloping track, but there is a premium on stamina.
DRAW: A low number is advantageous particularly over five furlongs but it becomes a decided disadvantage if a horse fails to jump off well.

REDCAR.—Redcar is a narrow, left-handed, oval track, about a mile and threequarters in extent, with a run-in of five furlongs, which is part of the straight mile course. The course is perfectly flat with normal characteristics, and provides an excellent gallop.
DRAW: The draw confers no advantage.

RIPON.—The Ripon course is a right-handed, oval circuit of 13 furlongs, with a run-in of 5f, and a straight 6f course. Owing to the rather cramped bends and the surface undulations in the straight, the Ripon track is rather sharp in character.
DRAW: On the straight course the draw is of no importance but in races on the mile course, horses drawn in the high numbers seem to have an advantage.

SALISBURY.—The Salisbury track is a right-handed loop course, with a run-in of seven furlongs, which, however, is not straight, for the mile course, of which it is a part, has a right-handed elbow after three furlongs. For races over a mile and threequarters horses start opposite the Club Enclosure, and running away from the stands, bear to the left, and go round the loop. The course, which is uphill throughout the last half-mile is galloping and rather testing.
DRAW: Low numbers are favoured in sprints when the going is soft.

1017

SANDOWN.—Sandown is a right-handed, oval-shaped course of 13 furlongs, with a straight run-in of 4f. There is a separate straight course which runs across the main circuit and over which all 5f races are decided. From the 1¼m starting gate, the Eclipse Stakes course, the track is level to the turn into the straight, from where it is uphill until less than a furlong from the winning post, the last hundred yards being more or less level. The 5f track is perfectly straight and rises steadily throughout. Apart from the minor gradients between the main winning post and the 1¼m starting gate, there are no undulations to throw a long-striding horse off balance, and all races over the round course are very much against the collar from the turn into the straight. The course is, in fact, a testing one, and over all distances the ability to see the trip out well is of the utmost importance.

DRAW: On the five-furlong course high numbers have a considerable advantage in big fields when the ground is soft.

STOCKTON.—The Stockton track is a left-handed course, nearly a mile and three quarters in extent, with a run-in of half a mile. The five- and six-furlong courses start on separate tangential extensions, the five-furlong track joining the round course on a left incline after a furlong, and the six-furlong track being so laid out as to give a straight start of two furlongs before the bend to the run-in. The turns are sweeping and easy, and the course is perfectly flat, but it is rather a sharp track, and for a flat course it is very fast indeed when the going is firm. The premium is always upon speed.

DRAW: A low number is a fairly considerable advantage in five- and six-furlong races, and is also advantageous in seven-furlong and mile races.

THIRSK.—The Thirsk round course is a left-handed, oval track, just over a mile and a quarter in extent, with a run-in of half a mile. There is a straight six-furlong course, which is slightly undulating throughout. The round course itself is almost perfectly flat, but though the turns are relatively easy and the ground well levelled all round, the track is on the sharp side, and by no means ideal for a horse that requires time to settle down, and time and space to get down to work in the straight.

DRAW: High numbers have an advantage on the straight course.

WARWICK.—Warwick is a broad, left-handed, oval track, just over a mile and threequarters in extent, with a run-in of about three and a half furlongs. There is no straight course, the five-furlong course having a left-hand elbow at the junction with the round course. Mile races start on an extension from the round course, the first four and a half furlongs being perfectly straight. This is a sharp track, with the emphasis on speed and adaptability rather than stamina. The laboured galloper is at a disadvantage, especially in races at up to a mile.

DRAW: A high number is advantageous in races up to a mile when the ground is soft, but a quick beginning is also important.

WINDSOR.—Windsor racecourse, laid out in the form of a figure eight, is 12½ furlongs in extent. In races of around 1½ miles both left-handed and right-handed turns are encountered, but in races over 1m 70 yds only right-handed turns are met. The last five furlongs of the course are straight, except for a slight bend to the right three furlongs from the finish. The six-furlong start is now on an extension of this straight. Although perfectly flat throughout, the bends make this track rather sharp in character. However, as there is a nearly straight 5f run-in the relative sharpness of the track is of no consequence in the longer races. Big, long-striding horses which normally require a more galloping course are at little or no disadvantage over these trips. The course gives spectators a very good view of the racing, since the runners are broadside on to the stands for all but about 20 yards of the circuit, and all starts are in sight of the stands.

DRAW: In five- and six-furlong races horses drawn in the high numbers have an advantage provided they start well enough to be able to avoid being squeezed out or impeded at the slight right-hand elbow in the straight.

PRINCIPAL RACES 1982

Date	Race	Value
11th May	DAVID DIXON SPRINT TROPHY (H)	£10000
	MUSIDORA STAKES (GROUP 3)	£26000
12th May	MECCA-DANTE STAKES (GROUP 2)	£45000
	HAMBLETON STAKES (H)	£15000
	TATTERSALLS YORKSHIRE STAKES	£5000
13th May	YORKSHIRE CUP (GROUP 2)	£35000
	DUKE OF YORK STAKES (GROUP 3)	£25000
	NORWEST HOLST TROPHY (H)	£15000
	FRESHFIELDS HOLIDAYS SPRINT	£5000
11th June	EAGLE DEVELOPMENT STAKES	£5000
12th June	WILLIAM HILL TROPHY (H)	£15000
9th July	LIN PAC STAKES	£6000
10th July	JOHN SMITH'S MAGNET CUP (H)	£25000
17th August	BENSON & HEDGES GOLD CUP (GROUP 1)	£100000
	YORKSHIRE OAKS (GROUP 1)	£50000
	HIGH LINE STAKES	£8000
18th August	GREAT VOLTIGEUR STAKES (GROUP 2)	£40000
	LOWTHER STAKES (GROUP 2)	£24000
	TOTE-EBOR (H)	£30000
	ALLIED BAKERIES TROPHY	£10000
19th August	WILLIAM HILL SPRINT CHAMPIONSHIP (GROUP 2)	£50000
	GIMCRACK STAKES (GROUP 2)	£30000
1st September	GARROWBY STAKES (H)	£15000
	GILBEY CHAMPION RACEHORSE FUTURITY	£10000
	UK WISEMAN OPTICAL SPECTACULAR	£5000
2nd September	STRENSALL STAKES	£7000
6th October	CHESTERFIELD HANDICAP	£6000
7th October	GREEN HOWARDS CUP	£4000
9th October	CORAL BOOKMAKERS CHAMPION SPRINT	£12000
	CROWN PLUS 2 APPRENTICE CHAMPIONSHIP (FINAL)	£7000
	CARLING BLACK LABEL LAGER STAKES	£5000

(Subject to confirmation)

Contact **John Sanderson ● Manager**
York Race Committee ● The Racecourse
York ● Telephone (0904) **22260/23148**

YORK
Great Races Great Racing

WOLVERHAMPTON.—The Wolverhampton round course is a left-handed, pear-shaped or triangular track, just over a mile and a half in extent, with a run-in of five furlongs. There is a straight course of five furlongs. The course is level throughout, with normal characteristics.
DRAW: The draw confers no advantage.

YARMOUTH.—The Yarmouth round course is a narrow, left-handed, oval track, about thirteen furlongs in extent, with a run-in of five furlongs. There is a straight mile course. Apart from a slight fall just before the run-in, the track is perfectly flat, with normal characteristics.
DRAW: High numbers have a slight advantage on the straight course.

YORK.—York is a left-handed, U-shaped course, 2 miles in extent, and quite flat throughout. There is also a perfectly flat straight course, over which all 5f and 6f races are run. 7f races start on a spur which joins the round course after about two furlongs. The run-in from the turn is nearly 5 furlongs. This is one of the best courses in the country, of great width throughout and with a sweeping turn into the long straight. The entire absence of surface undulations makes it ideal for a long-striding, resolute galloper, but it is really a splendid track, bestowing no great favour on any type of horse.
DRAW: The draw used to be of no consequence, but recently low numbers have had a marked advantage, particularly when the ground has been on the soft side.

Stallion
Section

Timeform Ratings quoted in the Stallion Section are those which appeared in the 'Racehorses' annuals except where otherwise stated.

Standing at the Sandley Stud, Gillingham, Dorset

AIR TROOPER

ch 1973 King's Troop - Aries (Acropolis)

Air Trooper won 7 races (8-10½f), £29,959 including Rosebery Handicap (by 4 lengths), Newbury Spring Cup (by 3 lengths), Sandown Cup (by 6 lengths), Hong Kong Handicap (by 4 lengths) and John Smith's Magnet Cup (carried 9-6). He was second (**beaten head**) in **Group 2 Queen Elizabeth II Stakes** (beating **Radetzky, Don, Duke Ellington**, etc.).

Racehorses of 1977: 'On each occasion when successful Air Trooper was held up and produced a fine turn of foot in the closing stages . . . a strong colt . . . thoroughly dependable.'

Sire KING'S TROOP is sire of the winners of 255 races, £286,530, in the British Isles including **King's Company** and **Majetta**, both successful sires.

Dam ARIES is half-sister to 6 winners including the dam of leading sire **Double-U-Jay** and grandam of **Riverqueen** (French 1,000 Guineas Gr 1 etc.).

AIR TROOPER's first runners included **Cheri Berry** (Sherwood Stakes, Epsom and Tog Hill Stks, Bath, record time) and others of promise.

All enquiries: Sandley Stud, Gillingham, Dorset.
Tel: (074-76) 2696 or (093-581) 3182

CONDORCET

Bay, 1972 by LUTHIER-PAN AMERICAN, by Pan II

GROUP I SIRE WITH HIS FIRST CROP

In 1981, sire of **CONDESSA** (Gr. I Yorkshire Oaks, Gr. III Musidora Stakes (beating classic winners **MADAM GAY** and **FAIRY FOOTSTEPS,** see below), etc.; 2nd Gr. I Irish Guinness Oaks; reportedly sold for over $500,000), **FORELOCK** (also 3rd Gr. III Mulcahy Stakes), and the winners of more than £100,000 with just 2 crops of racing age.

Group Winner and Classic Placed

Winner of 5 races and £114,750, from 2-4 years, including Prix Maurice de Nieuil (Gp II). PLACED in 8 other GROUP RACES, including 2nd Poule d'Essai des Poulains (Gp. I), beaten 1 length by GREEN DANCER (European Champion 1st Season Sire 1979).

His sire, **LUTHIER,** Prix Lupin, Prix Jacques Le Marois, etc., and Fr. 953,285, is also sire of RIVERQUEEN, ASHMORE, TWIG MOSS, MONTCONTOUR, GUADANINI, GALIANI, RIVERTON, NO LUTE, etc.

His dam, **PAN AMERICAN,** has bred four winners from her first four runners and is closely related to FULL OF HOPE. His fourth dam is own sister to the dam of PRINCE ROSE, an influential stallion sire. CONDORCET is an exceptional cross for most mares.

All Enquiries to:
JOSEPH McGRATH, Brownstown Stud, Curragh, Co. Kildare. *Tel: Curragh 41303.*

CHAMPION CANADIAN THREE-YEAR-OLD

DANCE IN TIME

Bay 1974, 16 h., by NORTHERN DANCER, out of ALLEGRO, by CHOP CHOP
WINNER OF SEVEN RACES $122,100 AT 2 AND 3 YEARS INCLUDING
TWO LEGS OF THE CANADIAN TRIPLE CROWN

TWO races at 2 years over 6 furlongs. **FIVE** races at 3 years. Stakes Winner at 6½f. to 1½m., including: Prince of Wales Stakes, Fort Erie, 1½m. (Gr 1 Can.) Breeders Stakes, Woodbine, 1½m. (Gr 1 Can.) beating his three parts brother GIBOULEE on both occasions, and Friar Rock Stakes, Woodbine 6½f. (beating Champion 2-year-old and Queens Plate winner SOUND REASON).

SUCCESSFUL 1st SEASON SIRE
Total stakes won by produce £32,545 in 1981
Winners include

KEEP IN STEP
Stakes winner of Prix de la Vallee d'Auge, Deauville, Prix de Saint-Arnoult, Deauville.

LAVENDER DANCE
Stakes placed winner of 2 races, 2nd St. Hugh's Stakes and 4th Cherry Hinton Stakes (Gr. 3).

TRIPLE DANCER
Winner of Prix de Saint-Pierre-Azif, Evry, his only start.

DON GIOVANNI

DANCE IN ROME

FULL 1978-1982
Approved mares. (Dance In Time will cover no more than 50 mares in 1982)

All enquiries to: Leslie Harrison, Plantation Stud, Exning, Newmarket. Tel: Exning (063877) 341 *or* the Secretaries to the Syndicate: London Thoroughbred Services Ltd., 21 Embankment Gardens, Chelsea SW3. Tel: (01-351 2181). Telex: 916950.

At Aston Park Stud, Aston Rowant, Oxfordshire

The HIGHEST STAKES WINNER
sired by DERRING-DO
DOMINION

Bay 1972 by DERRING-DO out of PICTURE PALACE (PRINCELY GIFT)

Dominion won 14 races (8-9f) and over £145,289 including Prix Perth, St-Cloud, Gr 3 and Bernard Baruch H'cap, Saratoga, Gr 3; also placed in eight other pattern races including 2,000 Guineas (third to **Bolkonski** and **Grundy**). Retired to stud perfectly sound after 46 races. He holds the 8½f record at Gulfstream Park.

Derring-Do; Sire of sires, **HIGH TOP, ROLAND GARDENS, PELEID,** (Classic winners) also **HUNTERCOMBE, CAMDEN TOWN, DERRYLIN, JAN EKELS** etc. and sire of **HIMAWARI, VARISHKINA, STILVI** (dam of **TACHYPOUS, TAXIARCHOS, TYRNAVOS** and **TOLMI**).

Picture Palace won 2 races and bred nine winners including PROMINENT, 19 races, Prix Foy Gr 3, etc.; she is also a half-sister to 5 other winners.

First Season 1979: FULL in 1979, 1980 and 1981
First crop foals averaged 15,987 gns. First yearling sold in 1981 made 36,000 gns.
The property of a syndicate

Syndicate Chairman: **R. J. McCreery,** Stowell Hill, Templecombe, Somerset. Tel: (0963) 70212. Syndicate Secretary: **Penny Willder,** Aston Park House, Aston Rowant, Oxford. Tel: (0844) 51433. Stud Manager: **Mrs. A. J. Cuthbert,** Tel: Tetsworth 417. Office: (0844) 51492.

FINAL STRAW

A LEADING MILER

Ch. 1977, 15h. 3 in. by THATCH, out of LAST CALL, by KLAIRON

Winner of FIVE races and placed SIX times at 2 and 3 years (5-8f); total earnings £116,708.
At 2 years won 4 races including: Gr 2, Laurent Perrier Champagne Stakes (7 furlongs), Gr 3, Seaton Delaval Stakes (7 furlongs), Gr 3, July Stakes (6 furlongs); also 3rd Gr 2, Coventry Stakes (6 furlongs).
At 3 years won Gr 3, Clerical Medical Greenham Stakes (7 furlongs); also 2nd Gr 1, Sussex Stakes (1 mile), beaten a head, 2nd Gr 1, Prix Jacques le Marois (1 mile), beaten a neck, 2nd Gr 2, St. James's Palace Stakes (1 mile), 3rd Airlie/Coolmore Irish 2,000 Guineas (1 mile), beaten ½ length.
Dam: Last Call - winner at 3 years; dam of 6 winners including:
FINAL CHORD, 3 races, including Britannia Stakes, Royal Ascot, L.R., also second in Extel Handicap, Goodwood, L.R.
Curtains, 3 races, also placed second in Galtres Stakes, York, L.R., dam of 2 winners including Heighten, 5 races, £8,187, at 3 years 1981.
TOP CALL, 2 races, £3,572.
FINAL STRAW, see above.
ACHIEVED, full brother to FINAL STRAW, 3 races. £43,090, at 2 years, 1981, including Gallaghouse Phoenix Stakes, Phoenix Park, Gr 1, and Laurent Perrier Champagne Stakes, Doncaster, Gr 2. Unbeaten at 2 years.
Grandam: Stage Fright—Winner at 3 years, dam of 4 winners, including HARDIESSE (4 races, at 2 and 3 years, including Gr 3 Cheshire Oaks, and Gr 3, Prix de Malleret, Longchamp, also 3rd in Gr 1, Yorkshire Oaks and 4th in Gr 1, Epsom Oaks); also Opening Chorus (placed at 3 years, herself dam of 8 winners, including Italian Stakes winner TERRY). Half-sister to 7 winners, including Stakes winner DIFFIDENCE and Donna, herself the dam of 11 winners, including GWEN, PADRONA (dam of Pelerin), and DON COMISO. Family of HERBAGER, LAUSO, DURTAL, DETROIT, etc.

FULL 1981-1982 FEE: On application

All enquiries to: The Director, National Stud, Newmarket. Tel: Newmarket (0638) 3464. *or:* the Secretaries to the Syndicate: London Thoroughbred Services Ltd., 21 Embankment Gardens, Chelsea SW3. Tel: (01) 351 2181. Telex: 916950.

IMPERIAL FLING

Bay, 1976, by NORTHERN DANCER out of ROYAL DILEMMA by BUCKPASSER

THE ONLY GROUP WINNING SON OF NORTHERN DANCER AT STUD IN ENGLAND

Winner of two races and £31,097 at two and three years:

At Two Years

WON Erroll Stakes, Ascot, 5f, by three lengths

3rd Champagne Stakes, Doncaster, Group II, 7f

3rd Champion Two Year Old Trophy, Ripon (Stakes race), 6f

At Three Years

WON Bayerisches Zuchtrennen, Munich, Group III, 12f

2nd Grosser Hertie-Preis, Munich, Group II, 11f

4th Classic Trial, Sandown, Group III, 10f, to TROY

First foal of a winning daughter of the champion U.S.A. Two Year Old QUEEN EMPRESS (15 races and $431,428) herself a full sister to KING EMPEROR (13 races and $453,918).

NORTHERN DANCER has sired LYPHARD, NIJINSKY, THE MINSTREL, NORTH-FIELDS, TRY MY BEST, NORTHERN BABY, NUREYEV, STORM BIRD, GIBOU-LEE, NORTHERNETTE, FANFRELUCHE, WOODSTREAM. He is the most influential living sire of sires with his sons and grandsons responsible for the Group I winners GREEN DANCER, ILE DE BOURBON, NINISKI, THREE TROIKAS, MONTEVERDI, PRINCESSE LIDA and ARYENNE.

Fee: £1,000 + £1,000 (1st October terms) approved mares only
Enquiries to: Miss F. VITTADINI
Beech House Stud, Newmarket (0638) 730335

Excellent fertility in 1981 with 40 of his 44 mares tested in foal—

JULIO MARINER

Bay 1975 BLAKENEY-SET FREE (WORDEN II)

Won St. Leger Stakes (quickened well to beat Le Moss, Ile de Bourbon, etc. in record time). Racehorses of 1978: **127.**

Sire

BLAKENEY won Derby; 2nd King George VI and Queen Elizabeth Stakes. A leading stakes sire incl. **JULIETTE MARNY** (Oaks, Irish Oaks), **JULIO MARINER, SEXTON BLAKE, ROSCOE BLAKE, TYRNAVOS** (Irish Sweeps Derby), etc. **CHAMPION SIRE OF 2-Y-O's 1977.**

Dam

SET FREE won at 3 years; dam of Classic winners **JULIETTE MARNY** (dual Oaks winner), **SCINTILLATE** (Oaks), and **JULIO MARINER.** Half-sister to **SPREE** (Nassau Stakes; 2nd 1,000 Guineas and Oaks). Family of **SHOWDOWN** (leading sire in Australia).

JULIO MARINER retired to stud in 1979. **FULL 1979-1981.** JULIO MARINER will have his first runners in 1982. His 12 first crop yearlings averaged **19,011 gns.** in 1981.

Enquiries for JULIO MARINER to: British Bloodstock Agency, 11a Albemarle Street, London W1X 4DB. 01-493 9402. Telex: 27403 or Alton House, Newmarket (5021). Telex: 817157 or R. E. Waugh, Ashley Heath Stud, Newmarket (730102).

KAMPALA

Bay, 1976, by KALAMOUN out of STATE PENSION

Group winner of eight races and £66,424 from 6f to 1m.

"A worthy son of a horse who would have scaled the heights as a stallion if he had not died early . . . he (Kampala) has an impressive pedigree and promises to be more than just a commercial success. I shall be disappointed if he fails to sire runners of distinction."
(Tony Morris writing in Owners' Magazine Feb. 1981)

"Kampala has a pedigree to match his racing ability"
(Racehorses of 1980)

Full First 2 Seasons 1981-82—Excellent Fertility.

Stands at: Rathbarry Stud, Fermoy, Co. Cork.
Apply: Liam Cashman, Tel Fermoy (025) 36362

CHAMPION EUROPEAN MILER

KRIS

Chesnut 1976, 16h. 0½ in. by SHARPEN UP, out of DOUBLY SURE, by RELIANCE II
CURRENT HOLDER OF THREE COURSE RECORDS

WINNER OF 14 OF HIS 16 STARTS INCLUDING 8 PATTERN RACES: Sussex
Stakes, Lockinge Stakes, Queen Elizabeth II Stakes, St. James's Palace Stakes,
Waterford Crystal Mile, Clerical Medical Greenham Stakes, Bisquit Cognac Challenge
Stakes, Horris Hill Stakes and 2nd The 2,000 Guineas, Queen Elizabeth II Stakes.

KRIS has covered 40 mares in his first season with an expected fertility of 90%—included
amongst those mares tested in foal are the following:
BIREME, CALAHORRA, CONNAUGHT BRIDGE, GIFT WRAPPED, GREENLAND
PARK, HORNTON GRANGE (dam of SWISS MAID), ISTEIA, KOBLENZA, MAKE-
ACURTSEY (dam of PINEY RIDGE), OH SO FAIR (dam of ROUSSALKA), ONE
IN A MILLION, PAMPERED DANCER (dam of MOOMBA MASQUERADE),
POPAWAY (half-sister to CHEVELEY PRINCESS), SINGE (dam of ONE IN A
MILLION), SLEAT (half-sister to ATHENS WOOD), TOUR DES DAMES (half-sister
to OAK HILL), VIVE LA LIBERTE (half-sister to VAL DE LOIR and VALORIS).

FULL FIRST SEASON 1981   FEE: ON APPLICATION

All enquiries to: J. F. Day (Manager), Thornton Stud, Thornton-le-Street, Thirsk.
Tel: Thirsk (0845) 22522. *or:* the Secretaries to the Syndicate:
London Thoroughbred Services Ltd., 21 Embankment Gardens, Chelsea SW3.
Tel: (01-351 2181). Telex: 916950.

LE MOSS

Ch 1975, LE LEVANSTELL—FEEMOSS (BALLYMOSS)

Own brother to LEVMOSS (European Champion 1969: Prix de l'Arc de Triomphe, Gold Cup and Prix du Cadran) and SWEET MIMOSA (French Oaks, 1970)

Gold Cup, Gr I — Le Moss inflicts the first of his three defeats on Ardross.

Le Moss won 11 of his 15 races, £173,519, including Gold Cup Gr I (twice), Goodwood Cup Gr 2 (twice), Doncaster Cup Gr 3 (twice) and Queens Vase Gr 3. Also 2nd St Leger Gr I. *Racehorses of 1980* said: 'Le Moss is a phenomenon . . . a top-class racehorse . . . we rate Le Moss slightly higher than his famous brother Levmoss . . . an extremely tough and genuine racehorse, as brave and willing as they come'. **Rated 135.**

His sire **Le Levanstell** was an outstanding miler (Sussex Stakes Gr I) and is sire of Levmoss, My Swallow, Allangrange, Sweet Mimosa etc. His dam **Feemoss** won Beresford Stakes Gr 2 and is dam of 6 winners from 6 foals incl Le Moss, Levmoss, Sweet Mimosa etc and is half-sister to the dam of Nikoli, Captain James and Sutton Place.

Enquiries to: **Joseph McGrath (as above).   Tel.: Curragh 41303**
or: **BBA (Ireland) Ltd, 51 Lansdowne Road, Ballsbridge, Dublin 4**
(Tel.: Dublin 686222.   Telex: 25599)

Standing at Beech House Stud, Cheveley, Newmarket

ORANGE BAY

Bay 1972, by CANISBAY out of ORANGE TRIUMPH by MOLVEDO

Arguably the best older horse in training in 1977, **ORANGE BAY**
won 9 races from two to five years including:

Italian Derby, Rome, Group I
Hardwicke Stakes, Royal Ascot, Group II
Premio Emanuele Filiberto, Milan, Group II
Cumberland Lodge Stakes, Ascot, Group III
Jockey Club Stakes, Newmarket, Group III

Also placed in six Group I races including *twice* in King George VI
and Queen Elizabeth Diamond Stakes, Ascot.

"*. . . a tremendous effort to run The Minstrel to a short head . . .
rallied splendidly after looking likely to be beaten comfortably . . .*"
TIMEFORM Annual Rating 131

TOTAL EARNINGS approx £135,500

Some shareholders nominations available at £1,000 +
£1,000 (1st October terms) Approved mares only
Excellent fertility in 1981.

Apply: Miss F. Vittadini, Beech House Stud, Newmarket.
Telephone: (0638) 730335
or Rustons & Lloyd, 136 High Street, Newmarket.
Telephone: (0638) 61221

POSSE

Ch. 1977 **FORLI**—IN HOT PURSUIT (**BOLD RULER**)

St James's Palace Stakes 1980: Posse easily beats Final Straw

At 2 years: placed 2nd Houghton Stakes, Newmarket (to Night Alert, with Bireme (Oaks) 3rd) on his only start.

At 3 years: won Sussex Stakes, Gr 1, St James's Palace Stakes, Gr 2; 2nd 2,000 Guineas, Gr 1; 3rd Clerical Medical Greenham Stakes, Gr 3; 4th Airlie/Coolmore Irish 2,000 Guineas, Gr 1, all his starts. Total earnings £96,652.

His sire FORLI was undefeated classic winner in Argentine. Horse of the Year at 3, Argentine Triple Crown, also a good winner in the United States. Sire of over 30 stakes winners including FOREGO, THATCH, INTREPID HERO, HOME GUARD, BOONE'S CABIN, FORMIDABLE, GAY FANDANGO. Also a leading broodmare sire (sire of the dams of NUREYEV and JAAZEIRO).

His dam IN HOT PURSUIT was only raced at 2 and won 3 races from 5 starts including Fashion Stakes Gr 3. Full sister to FULL OF HOPE, DISCIPLINARIAN, BOLD SULTAN, etc., and half-sister to DISCIPLINE.

The Property of a Syndicate.
Standing at Derisley Wood Stud Farm, Woodditton Road, Newmarket, Suffolk CB8 9HF.
Apply to A. W. Johnson, The Manager, as above. Tel: Newmarket (0638) 730055 or 730100. Telex: 817886.
or: Secretaries to the Syndicate, Rustons and Lloyd, High Street, Newmarket. Tel: Newmarket (0638) 61221. Telex: 817970.

SHERGAR

(Bay colt 1978)
by GREAT NEPHEW out of SHARMEEN
Bred by H.H. the Aga Khan

At 3 years

At 2 years

Won Kris Plate
Newbury
1 mile, in record time

2nd William Hill Futurity Stakes **Gr I**
Doncaster   1 mile

Won Guardian Newspaper Classic
Trial **Gr III** Sandown 1 1/4 miles

Won Chester Vase **Gr III**
Chester 1 1/2 miles

Won **Derby Stakes** Gr I
Epsom 1 1/2 miles

Won **Irish Derby** Gr I
The Curragh 1 1/2 miles

Won King George VI and Queen
Elizabeth Diamond Stakes **Gr I**
Ascot 1 1/2 miles

All enquiries and applications for nominations : Ghislain Drion, Manager,
His Highness the Aga Khan's Irish Studs, Ballymany Stud, The Curragh, Co Kildare.
Tél. (45) 41510

TAUFAN (USA)

Bay, 1977, by STOP THE MUSIC out of STOLEN DATE

Ranked above **Moorestyle, Final Straw, Posse, Dalsaan, Hard Fought, Runnett, Henbit, Night Alert, Belmont Bay, Master Willie** in "Racehorses of 1979". Winner of £17,916 at 2 and 3 in a brief career curtailed by a racing injury. 4th fastest timefigure of the season by a two-year-old.

"Taufan came out the same horse at the weights as Known Fact and 8 lb better than Mrs Penny". (*Racehorses of 1979 discussing the Mill Reef Stakes*).

From the first crop of brilliant young sire **STOP THE MUSIC** (ranked second only to **SECRETARIAT** as a 2-y-o, leading second crop sire in U.S.A., and level with **NORTHERN DANCER** in Average-Earnings Index)—3rd foal of **STOLEN DATE**, won 3 races at 2 and 3, already dam of stakes winners **BUBINKA** and **STOSHKA** and half-sister to Comely Stakes winner **BEST IN SHOW** (herself dam and grandam of champion two-year-olds **MALINOWSKI** and **TRY MY BEST**).

First season 1982—Full.

Stands at: Rathbarry Stud, Fermoy, Co. Cork.
Apply: Liam Cashman. Tel. Fermoy (025) 36362.

Young Generation wins Prix Jean Prat beating Pitasia and Boitron

AT WHITSBURY MANOR STUD, NR. FORDINGBRIDGE, HAMPSHIRE

YOUNG GENERATION

AN OUTSTANDING EUROPEAN MILER

Bay 1976, 16h 2ins, by BALIDAR out of BRIG O'DOON by SHANTUNG

Winner of 4 races, £110,880, at 2 and 3 years (5-9f).

WON	Lockinge Stakes,Gr II, Newbury, beating Skyliner, Formidable, Spence Bay.
WON	Prix Jean Prat, Gr II, Chantilly, beating Pitasia, Boitron.
WON	Richmond Stakes, Gr II, Goodwood, by 3 lengths.
2nd	Middle Park Stakes, Gr I, Newmarket, beaten 1 length in course record time.
2nd	St. James's Palace Stakes, Gr II, Royal Ascot, to Kris.
2nd	Greenham Stakes, Gr III, Newbury, to Kris.
3rd	2,000 Guineas, Gr I, Newmarket, beaten ½ length, short head, beating Lyphard's Wish, Boitron.
3rd	Prix Morny, Gr I, Deauville.
4th	Mill Reef Stakes, Gr II, Newbury.

FULL 1981 with 49 mares (fertility over 90%)   FEE: £3,500 straight

All enquiries to: London Thoroughbred Services Ltd., 21 Embankment Gardens, Chelsea SW3. Tel: (01) 351 2181. Telex: 916950. *or:* C. J. Harper, Whitsbury Manor Stud, Nr. Fordingbridge, Hants. Tel: Rockbourne (07253) 283.

AIRLIE STALLIONS 1982

1981: Champion Sire (Individual Winners and Races Won)   (HABITAT)

1980: Champion Sire   (PITCAIRN)
Champion Broodmare Sire   (HIGH HAT)

1979: Champion Sire   (PETINGO)
Champion Sire of 2-Y-O's   (HABITAT)

1978: Champion Sire (Races Won) (PETINGO)

For the stallions listed in
the following pages apply to:

Captain A. D. D. Rogers,
Airlie Stud,
Lucan,
County Dublin,
Irish Republic.
Tel: Dublin 280267 or 281548
Telex: 31049 TROG E.1

ARTAIUS

CHAMPION OF EUROPE AT A MILE & A MILE AND A QUARTER IN 1977 when winner of Sussex Stakes, Gr 1 (beating Relkino, Nebbiolo, Mrs McArdy, etc.), Eclipse Stakes Gr 1 (in course record time) and Classic Trial Stakes Gr 3. Also 2nd in Prix du Jockey Club, Gr 1, Benson & Hedges Gold Cup, Gr 1, and Beresford Stakes, Gr 2 (only start at 2). **Timeform 129.**
Stud Record: Full since retiring to stud in 1978. 24 yearlings sold in 1980 averaged 31,792 gns; 1981 yearlings averaged 57,246 gns (20 sold). First crop winners (8 winners of 14 races, £54,843) included Day Is Done (National Stakes Gr 2, Norfolk Stakes Gr 3), Delices, Atossa etc.

	Round Table (b 1954)	Princequillo	Prince Rose Cosquilla
ARTAIUS (bay 1974)		Knight's Daughter	Sir Cosmo Feola
	Stylish Pattern (b 1961)	My Babu	Djebel Perfume II
		Sunset Gun II	Hyperion Ace of Spades

By ROUND TABLE, winner of 43 races, $1,749,869, Champion North American Sire 1972. Sire of over 70 stakes winners incl. ARTAIUS, TARGOWICE (a leading sire), BALDRIC, KING PELLINORE, APALACHEE, FLIRTING AROUND etc.
Out of STYLISH PATTERN, dam of 7 winners, including ARTAIUS, EMBROIDERY (Ascot 1,000 Guineas Trial Gr III), STYLISH GENIE (Fairway Fun Stakes and $49,195) Her dam won at 3 years in England and bred 5 winners including SPRING DOUBLE (22 wins, $438,317, Pimlico Futurity, etc.; stakes sire in USA) and ARTHURIAN (Churchill Stakes, Ascot). Traces to PRETTY POLLY.

Stands at: Airlie Stud, Lucan, Co. Dublin.
Apply: Capt A. D. D. Rogers, Airlie Stud, Lucan, Co. Dublin (tel: Dublin 280267; telex 31049 TROG E. I.)

CUT ABOVE

Cut Above won the Gr. 1 St Leger (beating Shergar, Glint of Gold, Bustomi), the Gr. 3 White Rose Stakes (by 3 lengths) and £124,066. He was also 2nd Gr. 1 Irish Sweeps Derby (to Shergar, beating Kirtling, Dance Bid etc) and Gr. 3 Horris Hill Stakes (btn ¾l); and 3rd Gr. 2 Geoffrey Stakes. **Timeform 130.**

See pages 239-242 of this volume.

Stud Record

Cut Above retires to stud in 1982.

CUT ABOVE (b. 1978)	High Top (br. 1969)	Derring-Do	Darius Sipsey Bridge
		Camenae	Vimy Madrilene
	Cutle (ch. 1963)	Saint Crespin III	Aureole Neocracy
		Cutter	Donatello II Felucca

By **HIGH TOP**, 5 races, £61,322, including Gr. 1 2,000 Guineas, Gr. 1 Observer Gold Cup. A leading European sire, including Top Ville (Gr. 1 French Derby), Cut Above, Circus Ring (unbeaten, Gr. 2 Lowther Stakes), Triple First, etc.

Out of **CUTLE**, 2 races, at 3 years. Dam of 5 winners, including Sharp Edge (Gr. 1 Irish 2,000 Guineas, sire of group and stakes winners in England and a leading sire of 2-y-o's in Australia with his first crop in 1981). She is half-sister to the sires Torpid, Sloop and Tepukei. Her dam won Gr. 1 Yorkshire Oaks and is half-sister to the dams of Hermes (outstanding sire in New Zealand), Eagle (classic sire in Japan), Mariner (a leading sire in Australia), etc. Family of Bireme, Buoy, Sea Anchor, Shoot A Line, etc.

DOUBLE FORM

Europe's record-breaking sprinter 1979. The first horse ever to win the King's Stand Stakes, Gr. 1, and the Prix de l'Abbaye, Gr. 1, in the same year; and winner of £94,000 in first-place money, record earnings for a sprinter trained in England or Ireland. Also won Vernons Sprint Cup, Gr. 2, Temple Stakes, Gr. 3, Great Eastern Handicap (top-weight), Thirsk Hall Stakes and £127,154.

Racehorses of 1979: 'He defeated every leading contender on both sides of the Channel . . . Double Form's record as a four-year-old is that of a top-class racehorse, and for consistency he beats Thatching'. **Timeform 130.**

Stud Record
Full since retiring to stud in 1980. First yearlings 1982.

DOUBLE FORM (b. 1975)	Habitat (b. 1966)	Sir Gaylord	Turn-to Somethingroyal
		Little Hut	Occupy Savage Beauty
	Fanghorn (ch. 1966)	Crocket	King of the Tudors Chandelier
		Honeymoon House	Honeyway Primavera

By **HABITAT**, 5 races, £40,751, European Champion Miler, Gr. 1 Prix du Moulin, etc. Champion sire of 2-y-o's four times. Leading sire of individual winners and races won 1981. A leading sire of Group-winners, including Flying Water, Rose Bowl, Habat, Homing, Sigy, Steel Heart, Hittite Glory, Marwell, etc.
Out of **FANGHORN**, winner of 2 races at 2 years; 3rd Gr. 1 French 1,000 Guineas, Her grandam Primavera won Gr. 2 Queen Mary Stakes, and traces to Pretty Polly, ancestress of Great Nephew, Nearctic, Don, Donatello II, St. Paddy, Brigadier Gerard, etc.

Stands at: Airlie Stud, Lucan, Co. Dublin
Appy: Capt. A. D. D. Rogers, Airlie Stud, Lucan,
Co. Dublin (tel. Dublin 280267; telex 31049 TROG E.I.)

Airlie..

ELA-MANA-MOU

Europe's record-breaking middle-distance champion 1980. In 1980 Ela-Mana-Mou won the King George VI and Queen Elizabeth Diamond Stakes, Gr 1, Coral Eclipse Stakes, Gr 1, Prince of Wales's Stakes, Gr 2, and Earl of Sefton Stakes, Gr 3, earning £236,332 in first-prize money, a record for a 4-y-o trained in England. In a splendid career he also won Royal Lodge Stakes, Gr 2 (allotted 9-2 2-y-o Free Handicap, ahead of Troy), King Edward VII Stakes, Gr 2, and was also 2nd Grand Prix de Saint-Cloud, Gr 1, 3rd Prix de l'Arc de Triomphe, Gr 1, 3rd King George VI and Queen Elizabeth Diamond Stakes, Gr 1, 4th Derby, Gr 1. **Timeform 132.**

Stud Record
Ela-Mana-Mou retired to stud in 1981; his first crop will be foals in 1982.

ELA-MANA-MOU (b.c. 1976)	Pitcairn (b 1971)	Petingo	Petition
			Alcazar
		Border Bounty	Bounteous
			B Flat
	Rose Bertin (ch 1970)	High Hat	Hyperion
			Madonna
		Wide Awake	Major Portion
			Wake Island

By **PITCAIRN**, Champion Sire 1980—also sire of CAIRN ROUGE (Champion Stakes, Gr 1, Goffs Irish 1,000 Guineas, Gr 1) Flighting (Princess Royal Stakes, Gr 3) and pattern-placed KAHAILA, PETRINGO and BONNIE ISLE.
Out of **ROSE BERTIN**, winner at 3 years. Her dam WIDE AWAKE won the Ebbisham Stakes and was 3rd Nell Gwyn Stakes, Gr 3, traces to BELLE OF ALL, champion filly of 1950 and 1951, 1,000 Guineas, Gr 1, Cheveley Park Stakes, Gr 1, etc.

Stands at: Simmonstown Stud, Celbridge, Co. Kildare, Ireland.
Apply to Captain A. D. D. Rogers, Airlie Stud, Lucan, Co. Dublin, Ireland. Tel: Dublin 280267 or 281548. Telex: 31049. Trog E.l.

HABITAT

CHAMPION EUROPEAN MILER OF 1969 when winner of Prix du Moulin de Long-champ, Gr 1, Lockinge S, Gr 2 Prix Quincey, Gr 3 and Wills Mile, Gr 3. **Timeform 134**
Stud Record   First Runners 1973.   Sire of winners of 594 races, £2,634,561
Champion sire of 2-y-o's 4 times and Leading Sire (individ. winners and races won) 1981.
Principal winners: FLYING WATER (1,000 Guineas, Gr 1, Champion Stakes, Gr 1, Prix Jacques le Marois, Gr 1), ROSE BOWL (Champion Stakes, Gr 1), DOUBLE FORM (King's Stand Gr 1, Prix de l'Abbaye Gr 1, Vernons Sprint Gr 2), MARWELL (King's Stand Gr 1, July Cup Gr 1, Prix de l'Abbaye Gr 1, Cheveley Park Gr 1), HOMING (Queen Elizabeth II Stakes, Gr 2), SIGY (Prix de l'Abbaye de Longchamp Gr 1), HABITONY (Santa Anita Derby, Gr 1), HABAT (Middle Park Stakes, Gr 1), STEEL HEART (Middle Park Stakes, Gr 1), HITTITE GLORY (Middle Park Stakes, Gr 1, Flying Childers Stakes, Gr 1), HOT SPARK (Flying Childers Stakes, Gr 1), DALSAAN, STRIGIDA, HARD FOUGHT etc. Fertility 93%.   Yearlings have made up to 350,000 gns and in 1981 17 yearlings averaged 102,567 gns.

HABITAT (bay 1966)	Sir Gaylord (b 1959)	Turn-to	Royal Charger Source Sucree
		Somethingroyal	Princequillo Imperatrice
	Little Hut (b 1952)	Occupy	Bull Dog Miss Bunting
		Savage Beauty	Challenger II Khara

By SIR GAYLORD winner of 10 races, Sire of SIR IVOR (Champion at 2 and 3 years, winning Epsom Derby, Washington International, etc., a leading sire).   Out of LITTLE HUT also dam of NORTHFIELDS (Louisiana Derby, classic sire with his first crop) and GUEST ROOM (SW of $172,954).

Stands at: Grangewilliam Stud, Maynooth, Co. Kildare.
Apply: Capt. A. D. D. Rogers, Airlie Stud, Lucan,
Co. Dublin. (tel. Dublin 280267; telex 31049 TROG E.I.)

Airlie..

1042

HENBIT

Britain's champion middle-distance three-year-old 1980. Henbit won the Gr. 1 Derby (beating Master Willie, Pelerin, Hello Gorgeous, Nikoli, Water Mill, Tyrnavos, Monteverdi), the Gr. 3 Chester Vase (beating Light Cava¹ry) and the Gr. 3 Classic Trial Stakes (beating Master Willie, Huguenot etc). He was also 4th in the Gr. 1 Dewhurst Stakes (beating Final Straw). **Henbit cracked his off-fore cannon bone when winning the Derby.**

Racehorses of 1980: 'Held onto his lead (in the Derby) extremely gamely. . . . There is little doubt that Henbit sustained his injury at the point he hung right; how much it affected his performance is impossible to say. . . . He must have been hampered to some extent'. **Timeform 130.**

Stud Record
Henbit retires to stud in 1982.

HENBIT (b. 1977)	Hawaii (b. 1964)	Utrillo	Toulouse Lautrec
			Urbinella
		Ethane	Mehrali
			Ethyl
	Chateaucreek (ch. 1970)	Chateaugay	Swaps
			Banquet Bell
		Mooncreek	Sailor
			Ouija

By **HAWAII**, won 21 races in South Africa and USA, $326,963, Gr. 1 Man O'War S., Gr. 1 United Nations H., etc. Champion Grass Horse. Also Champion at 2, 3 & 4 in S. Africa. Also sire of Hunza Dancer, Hawaiian Sound, Sun and Snow (Kentucky Oaks), Triple Crown, etc.
Out of **CHATEAUCREEK** won 6 races, $24,203 at 2 & 3 years, including Delta Queen H.; Henbit is her second foal. His grandam bred 5 winners and his third dam was a stakes winner and dam of Ouija Board (National Stallion S., etc. at 2: sire); grandam of Limit to Reason (Gr. 1 Champagne S.; sire of stakes winners).

Stands at: Airlie Stud, Lucan, Co. Dublin
Apply: Capt. A. D. D. Rogers, Airlie Stud, Lucan,
Co. Dublin (tel. Dublin 280267; telex 31049 TROG E.1.)

Airlie..

KALA SHIKARI

Top European Sprinter by Huntercombe. Winner of 6 races and £36,814 including Prix du Gros-Chene, Chantilly, Gr 3 (beating Arch Sculptor, Polly Peachum and Mendip Man), Prix de Seine-et-Oise, Maisons Laffitte, Gr 3 (beating Raga Navarro, Mendip Man, Vitiges, Girl Friend, Polyponder, Hittite Glory, etc.), 2nd Prix du Petit Couvert, Longchamp, Gr 3, 3rd Palace House Stakes, Newmarket, Gr 3, 3rd Duke of York Stakes, Gr 3. **Timeform 125.**
Stud Record: First crop are runners in 1982. Estimated fertility 86.5% for 1981 covering season. His yearling average in 1981 (to end of Nmkt open sale) was five times his nomination fee.

		Derring-Do	Darius
	Huntercombe		Sipsey Bridge
	(b 1967)		Fair Trial
KALA SHIKARI		Ergina	Ballechin
(b/br 1973)			Gold Bridge
	Vigour	Vilmorin	Queen of the Meadows
	(gr 1961)		Eble
		Pompeienne	Pomelane

By HUNTERCOMBE, won 6 races and £39,415 incl. Middle Park Stakes, Gr I, July Cup, Gr 2, Nunthorpe Stakes, Gr 2, etc., sire of winners of £739,493 incl. PYJAMA HUNT, RADETZKY, KALA SHIKARI, GROUND COVER, ABBEYDALE—all stakes winners. Out of VIGOUR, won at 2 yrs: dam of 5 winners and out of own sister to Pomare (winner of Poule d'Essai des Pouliches).

Stands at: Blackmore Vale Stud, Sandley, Gillingham, Dorset (07476) 3396.
Apply: C. R. C. Watkins at the stud or Capt. A. D. D. Rogers, Airlie Stud, Lucan, Co. Dublin (tel: Dublin 280267 or 281548; telex 31049 TROG E.I.).

1044

TUMBLE WIND

Winner of 9 races (5½f-12f), $249,175 including Haggin S and Westchester S, 2 (at 2 years), Hollywood Derby, Gr 1, Argonaut S, Gr 2, San Vincente S, Gr 3, etc. Second Hollywood Juvenile Championship, Gr 2 and Santa Anita Derby, Gr 1. Course record breaker for 1½m at Santa Anita.

Stud Record

Tumble Wind has sired the winners of more than 300 races and over £700,000 including MILLINGDALE LILLIE (Fred Darling Stakes, Gr 3, 2nd Goffs Irish 1,000 Guineas, Gr 1, 4th 1,000 Guineas, Gr 1), TUMBLEDOWNWIND (Gimcrack Stakes, Gr 2, Rous Memorial Stakes, 4th 2,000 Guineas, Gr 1), COOLINEY PRINCE (McCairns Trial Gr 3 1981) PEPPONE (Criterium di Roma, Gr 3), WINDY CHEYENNE (Hollywood Nursery), DRIFTIN' ALONG (La Habra Stakes), LYON BAY (Grand Prix du Chasse de Princes), TARZAN, WINDY SUNSET, ISONDA, MOULIN ROUGE, DOGS BAY, WINTER WIND, TUMBLELLA (Gilltown Stud Stakes 1981) and TUMBLER.

		Windy City II	Wyndham
	Restless Wind		Staunton
	(ch 1956)	Lump Sugar	Bull Lea
TUMBLE WIND			Sugar Run
(bay 1964)			British Empire
	Easy Stages	Endeavour II	Himalaya
	(b 1953)		Kiev
		Saturday Off	Mexican Tea

His sire RESTLESS WIND has sired the winners of over $6,000,000 including PROCESS SHOT (Champion 2-y-o filly, $463,200), WINDJAMMER (Keeneland Breeders Futurity, Kentucky Jockey Club S) and ON YOUR MARK (a noted sire of fast 2-y-o's). This is a male line renowned for speed and precocity.

His dam EASY STAGES is own-sister to the dam of HUL A HUL, sire of record breaking 2-y-o Chamozzle. Third dam Mexican Tea is also third dam of classic filly FLYING RYTHM (Hollywood Oaks) and grandam of FLYING LILL (Kentucky Oaks).

Stands at: Grangewilliam Stud, Maynooth
Apply: Capt. A. D. D. Rogers, Airlie Stud, Lucan,
Co. Dublin (tel. Dublin 280267; telex 31049 TROG E.I.)

BBA (IRELAND) LTD
Stallions for 1982

At Corbally Stud, Celbridge, Co Kildare
(Dublin 288081/2)

Junius (USA)
b 1976 by **Raja Baba**
—Solid Thought (Solidarity)

Pitskelly
br 1970 by **Petingo**
—French Bird (Guersant)

Persian Bold
br 1975 by **Bold Lad**
—Relkarunner (Relko)

At Ballygoran Stud, Maynooth, Co Kildare,
(Dublin 286204/286264/286373)

Octavo (USA)
ch 1975 by **Roberto**
—Countess Albie (Pet Bully)

At Milford Stud, Milford, Co Carlow
(Carlow 46133)

On Your Mark
(USA)
ch 1964 by **Restless Wind**
—Super Scope (Swaps)

At Brownstown Stud, Curragh, Co Kildare
(Curragh 41303)

Le Moss
ch 1975 by **Le Levanstell**
—Feemoss (Ballymoss)

At Tara Stud, Tara, Co Meath
(Navan 25203)

Wolverlife
b 1973 by **Wolver Hollow**
—Miralife (Miralgo)

**BBA (Ireland) Ltd., 51 Lansdowne Road, Dublin 4.
Tel: Dublin 686222. Telex: 25599.**

1046

COOLMORE STALLIONS 1982

BE MY GUEST
CAPTAIN JAMES
CROFTER
DALSAAN
GAY FANDANGO
GODSWALK
HELLO GORGEOUS
HOME GUARD
KINGS LAKE
LAST FANDANGO
LONDON BELLS
NORTHFIELDS
THATCH
THATCHING
TRY MY BEST

BE MY GUEST

Ch. 1974 by Northern Dancer ex What a Treat by Tudor Minstrel

Won 4 races and £28,814 at two and three years. His wins included Waterford Crystal Mile (Gr 2), Blue Riband Trial Stakes (Gr 3), Epsom. ("... *a scintillating performance.*" *Timeform*), and Desmond Stakes (Gr 3). Also placed second in Nijinsky Stakes (Gr 2). Timeform 126. Dam won 11 races and $321,608 including Alabama Stakes (Gr 1) A leading sire of 2-y-o's with 10 winners of 16 races, £71,190, including ANFIELD (Ashford Castle Stakes, Gr 3, Railway Stakes, Gr 3), ASSERT (Beresford Stakes, Gr 2), ON THE HOUSE (St. Hugh's Stakes, 2nd, Cheveley Park, Gr 1) etc. 1981 yearlings made up to IR 239,400 gns.

BE MY GUEST (USA)	Northern Dancer	Nearctic	Nearco
			Lady Angela
		Natalma	Native Dancer
			Almahmoud
	What a Treat	Tudor Minstrel	Owen Tudor
			Sansonnet
		Rare Treat	Stymie
			Rare Perfume

COOLMORE

Stands at COOLMORE-Bob Lanigan
Tel: Clonmel (052) 31298
Telex: 80695

CAPTAIN JAMES

Bay 1974 by Captain's Gig ex Aliceva by Alcide

Won 3 races and £31,346 at
two, three and four years.
His wins included 1978
Waterford Crystal Mile (Gr 2),
*defeating Group 1 winners Formidable
and Jaazeiro.*
Timeform 123.
Half-brother to Nikoli (Irish
2,000 Guineas Gr 1) and Sutton
Place (Coronation Stakes Gr 2).
His dam is half-sister to
Feemoss, dam of Levmoss,
Le Moss and Sweet Mimosa.
A half-brother to Captain James
realised a record 300,000 gns
at Goffs 1980.
His first crop yearlings made
up to IR 34,020 gns.

	Turn-to	Royal Charger
Captain's Gig		Source Sucree
	Make Sail	Ambiorix
CAPTAIN JAMES		Anchors Aweigh
	Alcide	Alycidon
Aliceva		Chenille
	Feevagh	Solar Slipper
		Astrid Wood

COOLMORE

**Stands at GRANGE STUD
David Magnier or Robert Hall
Tel: Fermoy (025) 31966 (office) or
31465 (home).   Telex: 28470**

CROFTER

Ch. 1977 by Habitat ex Marie Curie by Exbury

Winner of 3 consecutive races and second twice from 5 starts. He was second in the Prix de la Foret (**Gr. 1**), *beaten 1 length by Horse of the Year Moorestyle and beating triple champion Kilijaro* and the Prix Perth (**Gr. 3**). By Champion Miler Habitat, one of Europe's outstanding sires, his winners including Marwell, Flying Water, Rose Bowl, Hard Fought, Steel Heart, Hot Spark, Dalsaan, etc. Marie Curie, a winner and group-placed, has produced 3 winners from her first 3 foals. She is half-sister to Mariel (**Gr. 2**, Pretty Polly Stakes, second **Gr. 1** Irish 1,000 Guineas; dam of Sarah Siddons, **Gr. 1** Irish 1,000 Guineas). Her dam won **Gr. 3** Fred Darling Stakes, **Gr. 3** Musidora Stakes and is half-sister to Ragusa (**Gr. 1** Irish Derby, **Gr. 1** St. Leger, outstanding sire).

Habitat	Sir Gaylord	Turn-To
		Somethingroyal
CROFTER (USA)	Little Hut	Occupy
		Savage Beauty
	Exbury	Le Haar
Marie Curie		Greensward
	Ela Marita	Red God
		Fantan II

COOLMORE

Stands at GRANGE STUD
David Magnier or Robert Hall
Tel: Fermoy (025) 31966 (office) or
31465 (home). Telex: 28470

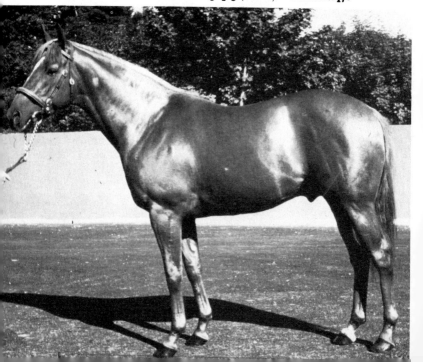

DALSAAN

Bay 1977, by Habitat ex Dumka by Kashmir II

Won 5 races and £63,189 from two to four years. His wins included Hungerford Stakes, Gr. 3, *(by 2½ lengths, beating Star Pastures, Bel Bolide, Kittyhawk)*, **Cold Shield Windows Trophy** *(beating Known Fact)*, **Van Geest Stakes, Heron Stakes** *(by 20 lengths)*, **Marston Moor Stakes** *(by 5 lengths, at 2 years)*. Also second in Challenge Stakes, Gr. 3, fourth in Sussex Stakes, Gr. 1, St. James's Palace Stakes, Gr. 2, and Queen Anne Stakes, Gr. 3. Never out of the first four. Timeform 125.

By Champion miler HABITAT, the leading sire of group winners in Europe and four times Leading Sire of 2-year-olds. Out of a winner of the French 1,000 Guineas, Gr. 1. Grandam, a half-sister to FLOSSY (Champion Stakes, Gr. 1), is from the family of DERRING-DO, NEVER BEAT (Champion Sire in Japan four times), HETHERSETT, ROYAL PREROGATIVE (classic sire in South Africa, 1981), HARD FOUGHT, PROVIDENTIAL, etc.

Habitat	Sir Gaylord	Turn-to
		Somethingroyal
	Little Hut	Occupy
DALSAAN		Savage Beauty
	Kashmir II	Tudor Melody
		Queen of Speed
Dumka		Prince Taj
	Faizebad	Floralie

COOLMORE

**Stands at CASTLE HYDE STUD
—Tom Gaffney or Gay O'Callaghan
Tel: Fermoy (025) 31689/31966
Telex: 28470**

GAY FANDANGO

Ch. 1972, by Forli ex Gay Violin by Sir Gaylord

Won 2 races and £15,443 at three years, his only season to race. Won Waterford Crystal Mile **(Gr 2)** (*beating Rose Bowl, Roussalka, Mark Anthony etc*), **and Jersey Stakes, (Gr 3), Royal Ascot.** Also second in Queen Elizabeth II Stakes (Gr 2), Ascot (*to Rose Bowl and beating Anne's Pretender, Bolkonski, etc.*). Timeform 132. Sire of the winners of 74 races, £307,310, including Last Fandango (Blue Riband Trial, Gr 3, 2nd Irish 2,000 Guineas Gr 1, *(btn sh. hd)*, Rasa Penang (Jersey Stakes, Gr 3), Adolfina (stakes winner, placed Italian Oaks and 1,000 Guineas), Moomba Masquerade (Land of Burns Stakes), Spanish Dancer (Irish Sweeps Autumn Handicap) etc.

	Forli	Aristophanes	Hyperion
			Commotion
GAY FANDANGO		Trevisa	Advocate
(USA)			Veneta
	Sir Gaylord	Turn-To	
Gay Violin		Somethingroyal	
	Blue Violin	First Fiddle	
		Blue Lu	

COOLMORE

**Stands at GRANGE STUD
David Magnier or Robert Hall
Tel: Fermoy (025) 31966 (office) or
31465 (home). Telex: 28470**

GODSWALK

Grey 1974 by Dancer's Image ex Kate's Intent by Intentionally

Won 8 races and £56,321 over
5 and 6 furlongs.
His wins included King's
Stand Stakes (Gr 1) and Norfolk
Stakes (Gr 3), Royal Ascot,
Ballyogan Stakes, Leopardstown
(Gr 3), Airlie Coolmore Castle
Hyde Stakes, Waterford
Testimonial Stakes and Marble
Hill Stakes, Curragh.
Top 2-y-o colt on 1976 Irish
Free Handicap rated superior
to The Minstrel, Pampapaul,
Nebbiolo and Captain James.
Timeform 130.
Dam stakes winner of 8 races.
The leading first crop sire
(individual winners and races
won). Sire of 15 winners of
20 races incl. The Primate,
Assembler, Celestial City,
Celestial Path, Sangalkan,
Paternoster Row, etc. One of his
yearlings fetched Fr 1,650,00 at
Deauville Select Sales 1981.

GODSWALK	Dancer's Image	Native Dancer	Polynesian
			Geisha
		Noors Image	Noor
			Little Sphinx
	Kate's Intent	Intentionally	Intent
			My Recipe
		Julie Kate	Hill Prince
			Doggin It

COOLMORE

Stands at CASTLE HYDE STUD
Tom Gaffney or Gay O'Callaghan
Tel: Fermoy (025) 31689/31966
Telex: 28470

HELLO GORGEOUS

Ch. 1977 by Mr. Prospector—Bonny Jet by Jet Jewel

Won 4 races, £129,647 at 2 and 3 years, (6-10½f), including **William Hill Futurity, (Gr 1)**, (*beating In Fijar, Choucri*); **Royal Lodge Stakes, (Gr 2)**, (*beating Star Way*); **Mecca-Dante Stakes (Gr 2)**, (*beating Master Willie, Water Mill, Tyrnavos*) **and Ballymore Stakes**, (*beating Millingdale Lillie*). **Also placed second in the Eclipse Stakes, (Gr 1)**, (*beaten ¾ length by Ela Mana Mou, beating Gregorian, Sea Chimes*), **and Heathorn Stakes.** Rated 9—4 on Free Handicap, above Henbit, Shoot A Line, Quick as Lightning, Tyrnavos Master Willie, Night Alert, Moorestyle, etc. Rated 9-9 on Free Handicap at 3 years, above Hard Fought, Final Straw, etc. Timeform 128.

MR. PROSPECTOR, Champion in U.S.A. Champion first crop sire in 1978. Champion sire of 2-year-olds in 1979. Sire of It's In The Air (Champion 2 and 3-year-old filly), Hello Gorgeous, Fappiano (Metropolitan H'cap, Gr 1, 1981), Antique Gold, Gold Stage, Miswaki, etc. Re-syndicated 1980 for $24,000,000.

HELLO GORGEOUS (USA)	Mr. Prospector	Raise a Native	Native Dancer
			Raise You
		Gold Digger	Nashua
			Sequence
	Bonny Jet	Jet Jewel	Jet Pilot
			Crepe Myrtle
		Bonny Bush	Mr. Busher
			San Bonita

COOLMORE

Stands at COOLMORE-Bob Lanigan
Tel: Clonmel (052) 31298
Telex: 80695

HOME GUARD

Brown 1969 by Forli ex Stay at Home by Bold Ruler

Won 7 races and £30,357. His wins included Tetrarch Stakes (Gr 3) (7 f), Diadem Stakes (Gr 3) (6 f) and Philips Electrical Rockingham Stakes (5 f). Also second in Prix de L'Abbaye (Gr 1) and third in Eclipse Stakes (*to Brigadier Gerard*). Timeform 129. From his first 5 crops, sire of the winners of 148 races, £550,793, including MARQUEE UNIVERSAL (Dixie Handicap Gr 2, Edgemere Handicap Gr 3, 1980), SONNEN GOLD (7 races, including Gimcrack Gr 2), MANJAM (3 races, including Prix du Petit Couvert Gr 3), HOUSE GUARD, WATCHDOG, WARMINGTON, SPARK OF LIFE, SILOJOKA, etc.

Forli	Aristophanes	Hyperion
		Commotion
	Trevisa	Advocate
HOME GUARD		Veneta
(USA)	Bold Ruler	Nasrullah
		Miss Disco
Stay at Home		
	Alanesian	Polynesian
		Alablue

COOLMORE

**Stands at Haras de Victot
Victot Pontfol, 14430 Dozule, France
Enquiries to Tommy Stack, Longfield
Stud.   Tel: Thurles (0504) 42234
Telex: 33003**

KINGS LAKE

Bay 1978 by Nijinsky ex Fish Bar by Baldric II

Won 5 races, £147,847 at two and three years (6-10f), including Irish 2,000 Guineas, Gr. 1, (*beating To-Agori-Mou, Mattaboy, Dance Bid*), **Sussex Stakes, Gr. 1,** (*beating .To-Agori-Mou, Belmont Bay, Mattaboy, In Fijar*), **and Joe McGrath Memorial Stakes, Gr. 1,** (*beating Blue Wind, Arctique Royale, Kind of Hush*); **also second in St. James's Palace Stakes, Gr. 2,** and third in **Prix Jacques le Marois, Gr. 1,** and **Ballymoss Stakes, Gr. 2.** Timeform 133. His sire, triple crown winner and Horse of the Year NIJINSKY, is already responsible for 49 stakes winners, including European Champion ILE DE BOURBON, Leading European First Crop Sire GREEN DANCER, PRINCESSE LIDA, NINISKI, CZARAVICH, DE LA ROSE, LEAP LIVELY, etc. Stakes winner FISH BAR is also dam of Champion 2-year-old CLOONLARA.

		Northern Dancer	Nearctic
	Nijinsky		Natalma
		Flaming Page	Bull Page
KINGS LAKE			Flaring Top
(USA)		Baldric II	Round Table
	Fish Bar		Two Cities
		Fisherman's	Alycidon
		Wharf	Herringbone

LAST FANDANGO

Ch. 1977 by Gay Fandango ex Welsh Game by Pall Mall

Won 3 races, £62,985, at 3 and 4 years, over 7 and 8½ furlongs, including **Ladbroke Blue Riband Trial Stakes, Gr. 3**, (*beating Marathon Gold and Johnny O'Day*) **and John of Gaunt Stakes.** Second (*beaten a short head by Nikoli*) **in Airlie Coolmore Irish 2,000 Guineas, Gr. 1**, (*beating Final Straw, Posse, Monteverdi, Huguenot, etc*), **Queen Anne Stakes, Gr. 3**, (*beaten a neck*). Third **in St. James's Palace Stakes, Gr. 2**, (*behind Posse and Final Straw, beating Dalsaan*). Fourth **Waterford Crystal Mile, Gr. 2.** Timeform 125. "... well made colt ... races with tremendous enthusiasm".
By **GAY FANDANGO**, won **Waterford Crystal Mile, Gr. 2**, **Jersey Stakes, Gr. 3**, out of **WELSH GAME**, winner of 5 races £27,000, and group-placed in France. From the family of **Mount Hagen, Amerigo, Hornbeam.**

	Gay Fandango	Forli	Aristophanes
			Trevisa
		Gay Violin	Sir Gaylord
LAST FANDANGO			Blue Violin
	Welsh Game	Pall Mall	Palestine
			Malapert
		Nantgarw	Abernant
			Lynsted

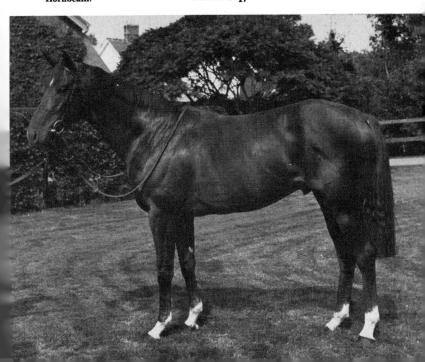

LONDON BELLS

Bay 1977 by Nijinsky—Shake A Leg by Raise A Native

Won 4 races in Ireland and U.S.A., £35,749 at 2 and 3 years, including Erne Plate, the Curragh, by 8 lengths in course record time previously held by Nijinsky and The Minstrel; second in Coventry Stakes, Royal Ascot (Gr 2), *beating Final Straw by 3 lengths* **and Rochester Cup; fourth in Lanson Champagne Stakes. Rated 8—11 on Irish Free Handicap, above Smokey Lady, Night Alert, Nikoli, etc.**

Timeform *"big, strong, good-bodied, attractive colt."*

NIJINSKY, Champion at 2 and 3 years, sire of 49 Stakes winners, including dual European Champion Ile de Bourbon, Green Dancer, *(leading European First Crop Sire. 1979)* **Kings Lake, Czaravich, Upper Nile, Terpsichorist, Princesse Lida, Night Alert, Leap Lively, etc.**

SHAKE A LEG, a Group winner of 9 races and also dam of Vaguely Modest (Selene Stakes, (Gr 3)), is by RAISE A NATIVE, sire and grandsire of champions Exclusive Native, Affirmed, Alydar, Genuine Risk, Mr Prospector, etc.

	Northern Dancer	Nearctic
Nijinsky		Natalma
	Flaming Page	Bull Page
LONDON BELLS		Flaring Top
(USA)	Raise A Native	Native Dancer
		Raise You
Shake A Leg		Fleet Nasrullah
	Fleeting Doll	Chinese Doll

COOLMORE

Stands at CASTLE HYDE STUD
Tom Gaffney or Gay O'Callaghan
Tel: Fermoy (025) 31689/31966
Telex: 28470

NORTHFIELDS

Ch. 1968 by Northern Dancer ex Little Hut by Occupy

Won 7 races and $195,071 at two and three years. His wins included Louisiana Derby (Gr 2), Hawthorne Derby (Gr 3), and Kent Stakes (Gr 3). Sire of the winners of 388 races, £1,316,745 from his first seven crops, including NORTHJET (Prix Jacques le Marois, Gr 1, Prix du Moulin, Gr 1) NORTHERN TREASURE (Irish 2,000 Guineas, Gr 1, Blandford Stakes, Gr 2), TOOTENS (Prix St. Alary, Gr 1), OATS (Blue Riband Trial, Gr 3, Jockey Club Stakes, Gr 3, Ormonde Stakes, Gr 3), NANTICIOUS (Ribblesdale Stakes, Gr 2, Silken Glider Stakes, Gr 3), NORTH STOKE (Joe McGrath Memorial Stakes Gr 1), BAPTISM, STAR PASTURES, NORTHERN VIEW, MIAMI SPRINGS, VAN HOUTEN, etc. NORTHFIELDS is half-brother to HABITAT.

		Nearctic	Nearco
NORTHFIELDS (USA)	Northern Dancer		Lady Angela
		Natalma	Native Dancer
			Almahmoud
	Little Hut	Occupy	Bull Dog
			Miss Bunting
		Savage Beauty	Challenger II
			Khara

COOLMORE

Stands at COOLMORE-Bob Lanigan
Tel: Clonmel (052) 31298
Telex: 80695

THATCH

Bay 1970 by Forli ex Thong by Nantallah

Champion two-and-three-year-old. Won 7 races and £40,277 at two and three years. His wins included July Cup (Gr 1), Sussex Stakes (Gr 1) *(by 3 lengths from Jacinth)*, and St James' Palace Stakes (Gr 2) *(by 15 lengths)*. Also placed fourth in Prix Morny (Gr 1) and 2,000 Guineas (Gr 1). Timeform 136. From his first 5 crops, sire of the winners of 162 races, £734,118, incl. ACHIEVED (Gallaghouse Phoenix Stakes, Gr 1, Laurent Perrier Champagne Stakes, Gr 2), FINAL STRAW (Laurent Perrier Champagne Gr 2, July Stakes Gr 3, Greenham Stakes Gr 3, Seaton Delaval Stakes Gr 3), THATCHING (Wm Hill July Cup, Gr 1, European Sprint Champion), GOLDEN THATCH, NEMR, DENTZ (Premio Roma, Gr 1), TRES GATE, etc. His yearlings averaged IR 36,051 gns and made up to IR 132,300 gns in 1981.

	Forli	Aristophanes	Hyperion
			Commotion
		Trevisa	Advocate
THATCH (USA)			Veneta
	Thong	Nantallah	Nasrullah
			Shimmer
		Rough Shod	Gold Bridge
			Dalmary

COOLMORE

Stands at LONGFIELD STUD
Tommy Stack - Tel: Thurles (0504)
42234. Telex: 33003

THATCHING

Bay 1975 by Thatch ex Abella by Abernant

Won 4 races and £50,606 at three and four years.
His wins included **William Hill July Cup (Gr 1)**, by 5 lengths, *(beating Vaigly Great, Greenland Park, Devon Ditty, King of Troy, Absalom, One in a Million, Sigy, etc)*, **Cork and Orrery Stakes (Gr 3)** by 4 lengths, and **Duke of York Stakes (Gr 3).** Also won **William Hill Sprint Championship (Gr 2)** by 2½ lengths *(beating Ahoonora, Double Form, etc. but disqualified).* **Champion European Sprinter on International Classification.** Timeform 131.
Dam won three races and placed second Challenge Stakes (Gr 3). (Timeform 121.) Full brother to **Golden Thatch** (Greenlands Stakes (Gr 3), Ballyogan Stakes (Gr 3). Half brother to **Ashford Castle** (won over $100,000 in U.S.A.). Family of **Reform, Val de Loir, Ridan, Apalachee, King Pellinore, Thatch, Nureyev,** etc.

	Forli	Aristophanes
Thatch		Trevisa
	Thong	Nantallah
THATCHING		Rough Shod
	Abernant	Owen Tudor
Abella		Rustom Mahal
	Darrica	Darius
		Erica Fragrans

COOLMORE

Stands at LONGFIELD STUD
Tommy Stack - Tel: Thurles (0504)
42234. Telex: 33003

TRY MY BEST

Bay 1975 by Northern Dancer ex Sex Appeal by Buckpasser

Champion European two-year-old. Won 4 races and £48,239 at two and three years from 5 starts. His wins included the William Hill Dewhurst Stakes (Gr 1), Larkspur Stakes (Gr 3) and Vauxhall Trial Stakes (Gr 3). Timeform 130p.

Try My Best cost $185,000 as a yearling and is half-brother to the unbeaten Group winner, Solar. His dam is half-sister to champion two-year-old Malinowski, (a leading first crop sire 1981) Gielgud (Laurent Perrier Champagne Stakes, Gr 2) and Monroe (Ballyogan Stakes, Gr 3).

1981 yearlings averaged IR 76,615 gns. 33 mares in foal in 1981 (80% fertility).

		Nearctic	Nearco
	Northern Dancer		Lady Angela
		Natalma	Native Dancer
TRY MY BEST			Almahmoud
(USA)		Buckpasser	Tom Fool
	Sex Appeal		Busanda
		Best In Show	Traffic Judge
			Stolen Hour

Fee private and nominations available from shareholders only.

COOLMORE

Stands at COOLMORE-Bob Lanigan
Tel: Clonmel (052) 31298
Telex: 80695

CONNAUGHT

Bay 1965
By ST. PADDY out of NAGAIKA by GOYAMA

Sire of the winners of over £859,951, including CONNAUGHT BRIDGE (Yorkshire Oaks Gr. 1, Nassau Stakes Gr. 2), SAUCEBOAT (Child Stakes, Gr. 3), ASTERINA (Seaton Delaval Stakes Gr. 3), MISS PINKIE (Argos Star Fillies' Mile, Gr. 3), REMAINDER MAN (Ormonde Stakes Gr. 3, Tote Free Handicap, 2nd 2,000 Guineas, Gr. 1, 3rd Derby Stakes, Gr. 1), SENORITA POQUITO (Nettie Stakes, Gr. 3, Canada), DUKEDOM (White Rose Stakes, Gr. 3), PLAYBOY JUBILEE (Dee Stakes, Gr. 3), CLARE ISLAND, etc.

Syndicated

WELSH PAGEANT

Bay 1966
By TUDOR MELODY out of PICTURE LIGHT by COURT MARTIAL

Sire of the winners of over £895,095, including GWENT (Jersey Stakes, Gr. 3), ORCHESTRATION (Coronation Stakes, Gr. 2, Athasi Stakes, Gr. 3), ROYAL PLUME (Dee Stakes, Gr. 3), SWISS MAID (Champion Stakes, Gr. 1, Sun Chariot Stakes, Gr. 2), KIND OF HUSH (Craven Stakes, Gr. 3), ZINO (Criterium de Maisons-Laffitte, Gr. 2, 2nd Prix de la Salamandre, Gr. 1), FLUELLEN, MAY BECK, GALLANT WELSH, AVGERINOS, WELSH CHANTER, CANIO, FIESTA FUN, etc.

Syndicated

1063

B. B. A. STALLIONS 1982

BALIDAR
MEDDLER STUD,
NEWMARKET, SUFFOLK.

BELDALE FLUTTER
BANSTEAD MANOR STUD,
NEWMARKET, SUFFOLK.

BUSTINO
WOLFERTON STUD,
SANDRINGHAM, NORFOLK.

DRAGONARA PALACE
BARLEYTHORPE STUD,
OAKHAM, LEICESTER.

FAIR SEASON
LITTLETON STUD,
WINCHESTER, HAMPSHIRE.

FREE STATE
BARLEYTHORPE STUD,
OAKHAM, LEICESTER.

GREAT NEPHEW
DALHAM HALL STUD,
NEWMARKET, SUFFOLK.

GUNNER B
LIMESTONE STUD,
WILLOUGHTON,
GAINSBOROUGH, LINCOLNSHIRE.

HIGH TOP
WOODLAND STUD,
NEWMARKET, SUFFOLK.

HITTITE GLORY
NEW ENGLAND STUD,
NEWMARKET, SUFFOLK.

ILE DE BOURBON
BANSTEAD MANOR STUD,
NEWMARKET, SUFFOLK.

JULIO MARINER
ASHLEY HEATH STUD,
NEWMARKET, SUFFOLK.

KING OF SPAIN
LOCKINGE STUD,
WANTAGE, OXON.

LUCKY WEDNESDAY
HARNESS GROVE STUD,
WORKSOP, NOTTS.

MANSINGH
RED HOUSE STUD, EXNING
NEWMARKET, SUFFOLK.

MILL REEF
NATIONAL STUD,
NEWMARKET, SUFFOLK.

MUMMYS PET
BARLEYTHORPE STUD,
OAKHAM, LEICESTER.

MUSIC MAESTRO
BEECHGROVE STUD,
BRIGG, LINCS.

NINISKI
LANWADES STUD,
NEWMARKET, SUFFOLK.

PORTO BELLO
HERRIDGE STUD,
COLLINGBOURNE
DUCIS, WILTS.

B. B. A. STALLIONS 1982

PYJAMA HUNT
SHADWELL STUD,
THETFORD, NORFOLK.

RABDAN
HARAS FRESNAY-LE-BUFFARD,
NORMANDY, FRANCE.

RADETZKY
LONGHOLES STUD,
CHEVELEY, NEWMARKET.

RECORD TOKEN
LIMESTONE STUD,
WILLOUGHTON,
GAINSBOROUGH, LINCS.

REFORM
SHADWELL STUD, THETFORD,
NORFOLK.

RELKINO
BARTON STUD, BURY ST.
EDMUNDS, SUFFOLK.

ROYALTY
BARTON STUD, BURY ST.
EDMUNDS, SUFFOLK.

SARITAMER
SOUTHCOURT STUD,
LEIGHTON BUZZARD, BEDS.

SCORPIO
BALLYLINCH STUD,
THOMASTOWN,
CO. KILKENNY, IRELAND.

SHIRLEY HEIGHTS
SANDRINGHAM STUD,
KINGS LYNN, NORFOLK.

STAR APPEAL
NATIONAL STUD, NEWMARKET,
SUFFOLK.

SWING EASY
BUTTERSTOCKS STUD,
HORSHAM, SUSSEX.

TOWER WALK
LIMESTONE STUD,
WILLOUGHTON,
GAINSBOROUGH, LINCS.

TOWN CRIER
SOUTHCOURT STUD, LEIGHTON
BUZZARD, BEDS.

WHITSTEAD
SIDE HILL STUD,
NEWMARKET, SUFFOLK.

WINDJAMMER
BUTTERSTOCKS STUD,
HORSHAM, SUSSEX.

British Bloodstock Agency
11A ALBEMARLE STREET, LONDON W1X 4JB
Telephone: 01-493 9402   Telex: 27403

or ALTON HOUSE, NEWMARKET CB8 9AF
Telephone: Newmarket (0638) 5021   Telex: 817157

STALLIONS FOR 1982

Tully, Kildare

MALINOWSKI (B. 1973)
(U.S.A.)
Sir Ivor   Sir Gaylord
Attica
Best in Show   Traffic Judge
Stolen Hour

Winner of Dunmurry Maiden
Stakes and placed second in
William Hill Dewhurst Stakes
(Gr. I) from only two starts at 2
years. Allocated Top Weight in
Irish 2 y.o. Free Handicap.
Winner of Ladbroke Craven
Stakes (Gr. III) - his only race
at 3 years.
Total Stakes: £12,161.
Fee: IR£4,000 - Special Live Foal.

AHONOORA (Ch. 1975)
Lorenzaccio   Klairon
Phoenissa
Helen Nichols   Martial
Quaker Girl

Winner of 7 races including
Stewards' Cup Goodwood,
King George Stakes (Gr. III),
Willam Hill Sprint Championship
York (Gr. II), 2nd King's Stand
Stakes (Gr. I), Ascot.
Total Stakes: £86,589.
Fee: IR£2,750 - Special Live Foal.

SALLUST (Ch. 1969)
Pall Mall   Palestine
Malapert
Bandarilla   Matador
Interval

Winner of Richmond Stakes,
Diomed Stakes, Prix de la
Porte Maillot, Goodwood Mile,
Sussex Stakes, Prix du Moulin
de Longchamp. Track record
holder for I mile Goodwood.
Total Stakes: £57,925.
Fee: IR£6,500 - Special Live Foal.

ROYAL MATCH (Ch. 1971)
Sovereign Path   Grey Sovereign
Mountain Path
Shortwood   Skymaster
Go Honey

Winner of 13 races and placed
14 times out of 37 starts,
including Liverpool Spring Cup,
Sandown Cup, Bessborough
Stakes, London Gold Cup.
Ultramar Jubilee Stakes, Great
Yorkshire Handicap and
Quortina Challenge Cup.
Total Stakes: £45,109.
Fee: IR£750 - Special Live Foal.

AFRICAN SKY (B. 1970)
Sing Sing   Tudor Minstrel
Agin The Law
Sweet Caroline   Nimbus
Lackaday

Winner of his only starts at 2
years. Winner at 3 years of
Prix Fontainebleau Longchamp
(Gr. III) beating KALAMOUN,
Prix Palais Royal Longchamp
(Gr. III), Prix Quincey Deauville
(Gr. III) beating SPARKLER,
Prix de la Foret Longchamp,
(Gr. I) Total Stakes: £63,000.
Fee: IR£4,500 - Special Live Foal.

LORD GAYLE (B. 1965)
Sir Gaylord   Turn-To
Somethingroyal
Sticky Case   Court Martial
Run Honey

Winner of 8 races, once
unplaced, including William Hill
Gold Cup, Mitre Stakes,
Ripon Rowels, Prix Perth
(Gr. III), and two races at
Saratoga.
Total Stakes: £23,482.
Fee: IR£4,500 - Special Live Foal.

SWEET REVENGE (Ch. 1967)
Compensation   Gratitude
Shillelagh
Too Much Honey   Honeyway
Honey Hill

Winner of ten races from 2 to
5 including King's Stand
Stakes, Prix de l'Abbaye de
Longchamp, Prix Maurice de
Gheest, Champion 2 y.o.
Trophy etc. and placed nine times.
Total Stakes: £40,424.

Fee: IR£700 - Special Live Foal.

CRASH COURSE (B. 1971)
Busted   Crepello
Sans le Sou
Lucky Stream   Persian Gulf
Kypris

Winner of five races including
March Stakes, Ascot Stakes, Top
Rank Club H. and Doncaster
Cup (Gr. III) Slipped up when
favourite for Goodwood Cup
(Gr. III) Total stakes £29,470.

Fee: IR£1,000 - Special Live Foal.

TUG OF WAR (Ch. 1973)
Reliance II   Tantieme
Relance III
Pirate Queen   Pirate King
Cantus

Winner of 10 races including
Heyshott Handicap, Gordon
Carter Handicap (Twice),
Northumberland Plate (twice)
Goodwood Cup (Gr. III).
Total Stakes £57,155.

Fee: IR£500 - Special Live Foal.

TEPUKEI (B. 1970)
Major Portion   Court Martial
Better Half
Cutter   Donatello II
Felucca

Winner of 3 races, including
White Rose Stakes, St. George's
Stakes, and placed Second
King Edward VII stakes.
Total Stakes £6,236.

Free range Fee: IR£300
Special Live Foal.

Terms and Conditions
The terms for all stallions include
a special live foal concession.
The service fee becomes payable
on 15th October 1982 unless a
veterinary certificate of barren-
ness is produced on or before that
date.

 írish NATÍONAL STUD

τully, kilδare

For further information and application forms apply:
The Manager, Irish National Stud Co Ltd, Tully, Kildare.
Telephone 045/21251/21301/21377 Telex 31770.

1068